Civil Procedure

Civil Procedure

Fifth Edition

Larry L. Teply
Professor of Law
Creighton University

Ralph U. Whitten
Senator Allen A. Sekt Professor of Law
Creighton University

Carolina Academic Press
Durham, North Carolina

ISBN 978-1-61163-074-9
LCCN 2012952601

Carolina Academic Press
700 Kent Street
Durham, NC 27701
Telephone (919) 489-7486
Fax (919) 493-5668
www.cap-press.com

Printed in the United States of America

PREFACE

Since the publication of the fourth edition of this book, significant developments have occurred in many areas of civil procedure, especially with regard to personal jurisdiction, venue, pleading, and the *Erie* Doctrine. These developments have necessitated a fifth edition to assure that practitioners, students, and others using the text have available the most up-to-date description and evaluation of procedural topics that is possible in a single-volume, "hornbook" treatment of the subject.

Our principal aims are twofold. First, it is our aim that practitioners can use this book to (1) enhance their awareness of recent developments in the field of Civil Procedure, (2) identify procedural issues that they might not otherwise recognize, (3) provide research leads to cases and the relevant periodical literature through the extensive footnotes accompanying the textual discussion, and (4) provide persuasive authority in support of positions in making procedural arguments to courts on behalf of clients. Throughout, we have attempted to provide critical analysis of the procedures discussed, whether they be derived from court decisions, statutes, or court-made rules, such as the Federal Rules of Civil Procedure.

Second, it is our aim that students can use this book as an aid to obtain general background information *or* to assimilate the detail necessary to prepare for the examination that they will encounter at the end of the standard Civil Procedure course. We have tried to avoid excessive detail that is inherent in multi-volume treatises, which would overwhelm students of basic civil procedure. Yet we do not avoid discussion of the most conceptually difficult matters of state and federal practice because that discussion is essential to a full understanding of the subject. We have also retained extensive historical material explaining the evolution of the modern procedural rules and systems that are the main focus of the book. This historical material is essential to provide a complete understanding of current procedural systems—it is hard to know "where you are" when you don't understand "where you have come from." Furthermore, to assist students and others visualize how the textual explanations of specific procedural issues apply, we continue to provide numerous illustrations of the operation of procedural rules or doctrines throughout this edition.

Two areas of coverage deserve special note. First, this edition retains the extensive treatment of federal practice in prior editions. We continue to believe this coverage is justified both because of the ever-increasing importance of the federal courts in the United States and because of the influence of federal practice on the states, particularly through the vehicle of the Federal Rules of Civil Procedure. The extensive treatment of federal materials also makes this book useful to students in courses in Federal Courts and Federal Practice and Procedure. Even though we extensively discuss federal practice, this edition also preserves the thorough exploration of code and other state procedural practices contained in the prior editions. Some state procedural systems still contain significant features of code practice, while being influenced in other respects by the Federal Rules of Civil Procedure. We also treat non-code procedure when relevant.

Second, increasing activity in the lower federal courts within the topic known as the "*Erie* doctrine" (which is the main focus of Chapter 5) is reflected in all chapters dealing with the Rules of Decision Act and Rules Enabling Act problems that are occupying those courts. The descriptive and analytical help in these subsections is, we believe, unique among civil procedure texts. This material enhances the value of the text not only to students of Civil Procedure, but also to students of other courses in which the *Erie* doctrine is pertinent, such as Federal Courts and Conflict of Laws.

We owe a sizeable debt to the persons who supported and encouraged us in the preparation of this edition, as well as those who helped with the original work. Particular mention should be made of the research support supplied to us by Creighton University Law School. Thanks are also due to our librarian, Kay Andrus and his extraordinary staff. Throughout the preparation of all editions, they have solved our research problems with alacrity.

We especially want to recognize our research assistants for their excellent review and editing of this edition: Grant Engrav, Amy Garreans, Meredith Rogers, William Osborne, Rachael Timm, and William Wray. In addition, Cara Horn, Kelli Huser, Jen Jacobsen, Laurel Johnson, Laura Nigro, T.J. O'Neil, and Jenny Wehrman proofread this edition. We also want to recognize contributions made to the prior editions by Frederick L. Abboud, Jr., Rickee Arntz, William Beck, Jen Bries, Mark Curran, Mary Jo Donahue, Robin Green, Beth Hanson, Laurie Heer-Clark, Sharon A. Hansen, Sandy Henderson, Lisa Henkel, Karen Kassebaum, Michael Matukewicz, Shannon O'Connor, Patricia O'Leary, Angela Smith, Robert Teply, and Debra Zorn. We also appreciate the efficient and cheerful secretarial assistance provided by Pat Andersen and Pam Flint as well as the excellent copying service provided by Colleen Kelly-Firmature.

We want to note the prior four editions of this book were published by Foundation Press (now part of Thomson Reuters) as part of their University Textbook Series. We express our appreciation to the publisher and staff of Foundation Press for their past efforts in helping shape this book. We also express our appreciation to Foundation Press for relinquishing the copyright to allow us to shift the publication of this edition of this book to Carolina Academic Press, which is our current publisher of our casebook on the subject: *Civil Procedure: Cases, Text, Notes, and Problems* (also coauthored by Denis F. McLaughlin of Seton Hall University School of Law). We also thank the able staff of Carolina Academic Press for their assistance in producing this edition.

Finally, we want to express our appreciation to respective spouses, Frances Gayle and Jean for their continuing support, understanding, and encouragement.

Larry L. Teply & Ralph U. Whitten
January 2013

SUMMARY OF CONTENTS

TABLE OF CONTENTS

Page

Page

Page

Page

Page

TABLE OF CASES

References are to Pages. Bold page numbers indicate the beginning of significant textual discussion of a case.

‡

Civil Procedure

Chapter 1

INTRODUCTION TO CIVIL PROCEDURE AND PRACTICE

Civil Procedure is the body of rules that prescribes the manner of conducting "civil actions." Section A of this chapter discusses the role of civil actions in the administration of justice. Section B examines the important distinction between "substantive" and "procedural" rules. This distinction permeates the entire subject of Civil Procedure. Section C discusses the role of the "adversary process" in Anglo-American systems of civil procedure. It also considers various procedural and ethical constraints on the adversary process. Section D examines the historical evolution of the Anglo-American procedural systems. This historical background will be essential to understanding many aspects of modern civil procedure. Section E examines methods of "alternative dispute resolution" that are becoming increasingly important in the American system of justice.

SECTION A. THE ROLE OF CIVIL ACTIONS IN THE ADMINISTRATION OF JUSTICE

1. The Relationship Between Civil, Criminal, and Administrative Actions

In the Anglo-American legal system, three basic types of proceedings are used to resolve disputes, enforce rights, or punish wrongs: civil actions, criminal actions, and administrative actions. Civil actions are governed by noncriminal substantive law and are conducted according to the applicable rules of civil procedure. Criminal and administrative actions are conducted, respectively, according to rules of criminal procedure and administrative procedure.[1] Although civil, criminal, and administrative actions reflect different choices about how substantive legal norms should be enforced, significant overlap and interplay exist among these types of proceedings.

Illustration 1-1. Assume that a police officer issues a traffic citation to a motorist. The citation initiates a minor criminal proceeding under a substantive

---

1. *See, e.g.*, Jack B. Weinstein, *Compensation for Mass Private Delicts: Evolving Roles of Administrative, Criminal, and Tort Law*, 2001 U. ILL. L. REV. 947 (providing an excellent discussion of the overlap and interplay of administrative, criminal, and civil actions in the context of compensating victims of mass torts). *But cf.* Issachar Rosen-Zvi & Talia Fisher, *Overcoming Procedural Boundaries*, 94 VA. L. REV. 79 (2008) (proposing to replace the civil-criminal regime with (1) different rules for "symmetrical litigation"—when individuals or institutions are on both sides—and "asymmetrical litigation"—when individuals are on one side and institutions are on the other; and (2) increasing procedural protections as the remedy or sanction on the defendant becomes more severe).

criminal ordinance or statute. If the motorist pleads guilty or if a court finds the motorist guilty after a hearing, the ordinance or statute will usually provide for a fine. In this situation, society has chosen the criminal law and a criminal proceeding as the exclusive means of assuring compliance with speed limits.

Illustration 1-2. More serious traffic violations may result in both criminal and civil proceedings. For example, killing a pedestrian while driving under the influence of alcohol may result in a charge of motor vehicular homicide. This crime is usually a felony punishable by imprisonment. The deceased pedestrian's estate may also bring a civil wrongful death action against the motorist to recover damages that result from the pedestrian's death. Because a single act can violate both criminal and civil substantive rules, corresponding criminal and civil proceedings may be brought to enforce those rules. The criminal proceeding vindicates the public's interest in deterring drunk driving. The civil proceeding compensates the deceased's survivors for losses they have suffered because of the death. In this way, the dual set of criminal and civil laws and proceedings serves both public and private interests.

* * * * *

Criminal and civil proceedings can interact in complicated ways. For example, in many jurisdictions, a party in a civil action can use a criminal judgment to establish facts that are common to both the criminal and civil proceeding.

Illustration 1-3. The criminal conviction for motor vehicle homicide described in *Illustration 1-2* may be used in a civil proceeding to establish that the defendant was driving while intoxicated. If the defendant has had a full and fair opportunity to litigate the issue in the criminal proceeding, the civil plaintiff will not have to offer evidence on this issue in the civil action. Instead, the plaintiff will be able to show by an appropriate procedure that the issue has been adjudicated in the criminal proceeding. The civil court will then accept the criminal finding as conclusive.[2] This procedure is valuable to the civil plaintiff for at least two reasons. First, it is usually easy for the plaintiff to prove that an issue has been fully and fairly adjudicated in the criminal action. Second, it is less expensive than reproducing all the evidence of the defendant's culpable behavior in the civil proceeding.[3]

* * * * *

Another way in which civil and criminal actions can interact involves the habeas corpus remedy. A person convicted of a criminal offense can sometimes seek a writ of habeas corpus to challenge the validity of the criminal judgment. A habeas corpus proceeding is a civil action in which a person in the custody of another (such as the warden of a prison) seeks to have the custodian justify the

---

2. In legal terms, the criminal judgment is "res judicata" and has an "issue preclusion" effect in the civil action. Res judicata and issue preclusion are described more fully in Chapter 13 *infra* ("Finality in Litigation").

3. Because of special protections afforded to the defendants in criminal cases, it would be impossible to reverse this example and use a finding in the civil proceeding in a later criminal action. The defendant in a criminal case is constitutionally entitled to have the facts of guilt proved beyond a reasonable doubt by the government. In a civil action, however, the plaintiff will usually not have such a stringent burden of proof. Thus, to allow the government to use a civil judgment to establish facts in a criminal action would deprive the criminal defendant of the benefit of the higher burden of proof required in criminal actions. *See* Chapter 13(C)(2)*(d)* *infra* ("Differences in the Burden of Proof").

confinement. If the justification is an invalid criminal judgment, the confined person can obtain a release or retrial, whichever is appropriate.

Illustration 1-4. Assume that *P* is convicted in a state court and then imprisoned for violating a state criminal statute. Assume further that *P* believes that the state criminal statute violates the U.S. Constitution. After exhausting the remedies available in the state courts—*i.e.*, first presenting the merits of the constitutional claim to the state courts—*P* may petition an appropriate U.S. District Court for a writ of habeas corpus. In the habeas corpus proceeding in federal court, the court will determine the validity of *P's* constitutional claim. If the claim is meritorious, the court will order *P's* release.[4]

* * * * *

The functions of the criminal law can sometimes be achieved by a civil proceeding. Likewise, criminal proceedings can indirectly support the objectives of civil proceedings.

Illustration 1-5. Assume *D* violated a substantive civil rule of law (*e.g.*, committed an intentional tort) and consequently harmed *P*. In some circumstances, *P* can seek not only compensatory damages, but also punitive damages, in a civil action. Like criminal fines, punitive damages are designed to deter and punish the defendant. In the civil proceeding, *P*, the aggrieved plaintiff, keeps both the compensatory and the punitive damages that the court awards. In contrast, a criminal defendant ordinarily pays a fine to the governmental authority that brought the criminal action. By awarding punitive damages, civil proceedings can fulfill some of the purposes of the criminal law.

Illustration 1-6. In some civil proceedings, courts issue orders to a party that, if disobeyed, can result in both civil and criminal contempt proceedings. Civil contempt proceedings perform the function of assuring future compliance with court orders. Alternatively, a civil contempt fine can be tailored to compensate a party for losses that the party has suffered as a result of a violation of a court order. For example, the court may order a defendant who disobeys a court order to pay a civil contempt fine each time the defendant disobeys the order in the future. Criminal contempt proceedings are designed to punish a party for a past violation of a court order. The court may impose a fixed fine or term of imprisonment on a party who disobeys a court order even once. Thus, criminal contempt proceedings also help assure general compliance with civil court orders through the deterrent operation of the criminal law.[5]

* * * * *

Administrative proceedings also interact with civil and criminal proceedings in important ways. In their simplest form, administrative proceedings occur

---

4. *See* 28 U.S.C. §§ 2241-2254. The federal habeas corpus action described in this illustration is by no means the criminal defendant's only method of challenging the constitutional validity of the state statute. The state trial court in which the criminal action is pending may invalidate the statute, or a state appellate court may do so after the defendant is convicted. The U.S. Supreme Court has appellate jurisdiction to review the decisions of the state courts when an issue of federal law is involved in the case, such as the constitutional issue in this illustration. *See* 28 U.S.C. § 1257. Thus, a refusal of the state courts to rule favorably on the criminal defendant's constitutional claim could result in reversal by the U.S. Supreme Court. All of these possibilities, and perhaps others, may avoid the need for a federal habeas corpus proceeding.

5. Criminal and civil contempt are discussed further in Chapter 6(G) *infra* ("Provisional Remedies").

when governmental officials, performing their duties, make preliminary determinations of fact or law. For example, tax assessors value property and set tax rates. Government pension administrators determine the level of benefits that potential beneficiaries are entitled to receive. Police officers make preliminary determinations that motorists have violated the traffic laws and issue traffic citations. In these examples as well as countless others, an administrative determination may later be the subject of a civil or criminal judicial proceeding.

Administrative agencies conduct all administrative proceedings. Several kinds of administrative agencies exist. Some agencies are simply departments of the executive branch headed by cabinet officers. These agencies help the chief executive officer—for example, the President at the national level—carry out the various constitutional responsibilities of the executive branch.[6] Other administrative agencies also exist within the executive branch, although they do not have "cabinet rank."[7] Finally, some agencies are designated as "independent" of the executive branch for political reasons. Technically, these agencies are arms of the legislative branch of government and usually have complicated regulatory responsibilities.[8]

Agencies charged with the enforcement of a regulatory scheme perform a variety of functions. Typically, the legislature enacts a statute that directs an agency to accomplish socially desirable objectives in a certain area of concern. The agency then formulates regulations designed to carry out the legislature's directive.[9] The agency may then enforce the regulations in various ways, depending upon the authorizing legislation and other statutes. The legislature may simply authorize the agency to bring civil or criminal court proceedings to enforce the regulatory scheme. Often, however, the legislature may authorize the agency to enforce a regulatory scheme in a specific type of administrative proceeding. In this case, the determination made in the agency proceeding will be subject to judicial review in a civil court proceeding. Usually, a party aggrieved by an agency's action must exhaust administrative remedies before seeking judicial review of the agency's action.[10]

Illustration 1-7. Congress has authorized the National Labor Relations Board (NLRB) to prohibit unfair labor practices by employers engaged in interstate or foreign commerce. To this end, the NLRB may hold administrative hearings to determine whether an employer is engaged in such practices. If the NLRB finds that the employer has engaged in unfair labor practices, the employer may obtain judicial review of the agency's determination in the federal courts. However, prior

---

6. The Defense, Justice, and State Departments are examples of such agencies. *See* RICHARD J. PIERCE, JR. ET AL., ADMINISTRATIVE LAW AND PROCESS § 4.4.1 (4th ed. 2004).

7. The Environmental Protection Agency is an example of such an agency. *See id.*

8. Examples of such agencies at the national level are the Federal Trade Commission and the Securities and Exchange Commission. *Id.* Independent agencies are often referred to as "regulatory agencies." *See id.* This terminology is somewhat misleading, as it suggests that other kinds of agencies do not perform regulatory functions. However, agencies like the Environmental Protection Agency, an agency attached to the executive branch, also perform complicated regulatory functions.

9. *See id.* §§ 1.4.1-1.4.2 (discussing the National Traffic and Motor Vehicle Safety Act).

10. *See id.* § 5.7.2.

to seeking judicial review, the employer must exhaust its remedies before the NLRB.[11]

* * * * *

In addition to agency-initiated proceedings, private parties may initiate appropriate proceedings before an agency or a court. In such a proceeding, the private party may seek to prevent a threatened enforcement of an administrative regulation or order.[12] Likewise, in some schemes of administrative adjudication, private parties are both plaintiffs and defendants.

Illustration 1-8. In a typical workers' compensation scheme, workers who are disabled while engaged in job-related activities may institute proceedings before a workers' compensation tribunal. This proceeding determines the facts, the extent of the worker's disability, and the level of appropriate compensation for that disability. In such a proceeding, the defendant will usually be either the worker's employer or the employer's insurer. The losing party may obtain review of the tribunal's determination in an appropriate court proceeding. Typically, the courts will review whether the tribunal's determinations of law were correct and whether the evidence supported the tribunal's findings of fact.[13]

* * * * *

Although distinct procedures exist for civil, criminal, and administrative actions, all three share many common themes. Most importantly, the state and federal constitutions contain due process clauses. Before life, liberty, or property may be taken from individuals, due process clauses require that individuals receive adequate notice of the proceedings and an opportunity to be heard in defense. Due process requirements apply to all civil, criminal, and administrative proceedings.[14] Likewise, many of the same rules of evidence govern civil and criminal proceedings,[15] although special rules apply to criminal proceedings due to constitutional requirements.[16] Ordinary rules of evidence do not usually apply in administrative proceedings. However, some standards in administrative procedural rules are analogous to those in civil and criminal rules of evidence.[17]

---

11. *See id.* § 5.7.2, at 195-96 (discussing Myers v. Bethlehem Shipbuilding Corp., 303 U.S. 41, 58 S. Ct. 459, 82 L. Ed. 638 (1938)).

12. The appropriate kind of proceeding depends on the statutory scheme. *See generally id.* § 5.3.

13. *See, e.g.*, Crowell v. Benson, 285 U.S. 22, 52 S. Ct. 285, 76 L. Ed. 598 (1932) (providing an example and discussion of judicial review in a workers' compensation proceeding).

14. The basic requirements of due process in civil proceedings are discussed in Chapter 3 *infra* ("Personal Jurisdiction and Service of Process") and Chapter 6(G) *infra* ("Provisional Remedies"). Due process issues are also discussed in Chapter 8(D)(4) ("Class actions") and Chapter 13(C)(3)*(a) infra* ("The Mutuality of Estoppel Rule and Traditional Exceptions to the Rule").

15. *See, e.g.*, FED. R. EVID. 101, 1101(b).

16. *See, e.g.*, Miranda v. Arizona, 384 U.S. 436, 86 S. Ct. 1602, 16 L. Ed. 2d 694 (1966) (statements from defendants during incommunicado interrogation in police-dominated atmosphere, without full warning of constitutional rights, were inadmissible because they were obtained in violation of constitutional privilege against self-incrimination); Mapp v. Ohio, 367 U.S. 643, 81 S. Ct. 1684, 6 L. Ed. 2d 1081 (1961) (evidence obtained in search violating the Fourth and Fourteenth Amendments inadmissible and vitiated conviction); *cf.* United States v. Leon, 468 U.S. 897, 104 S. Ct. 3405, 82 L. Ed. 2d 677 (1984) (Fourth Amendment did not require exclusion of evidence used in the prosecution's case in chief that had been obtained by officers acting in reasonable reliance on a search warrant issued by a detached and neutral magistrate but ultimately found to be invalid).

17. *Compare* FED. R. EVID. 402 (inadmissibility of irrelevant evidence) *with* 5 U.S.C. § 556(d) (while an agency may receive any oral or documentary evidence, "the agency as a matter of policy shall provide for the exclusion of irrelevant, immaterial, or unduly repetitious evidence").

2. Limits of Civil Actions in Resolving Disputes

As discussed in the preceding subsection, civil actions provide a means of resolving disputes. However, not all disputes will be deemed to be appropriate for adjudication. For example, courts will ordinarily not adjudicate "political questions" involving matters within the responsibility of other governmental authorities, such as foreign relations and national security.[18] Some refusals to adjudicate are attributed to constitutional limits on the judicial power.[19] In addition, some disputes may be clearly within a court's power to resolve, but a court may decline to do so as a matter of sound application of policy considerations and the wise use of judicial power.[20] When a court concludes that an adjudication of a civil action would be inappropriate, the court will rule that the case is not "*justiciable*."[21]

SECTION B. THE SUBSTANCE-PROCEDURE DISTINCTION

Procedural rules are said to define the form and method by which legal rights are enforced. Substantive rules are said to define the legal rights themselves. Thus, procedure is often referred to as "adjective law" because procedural rules function to secure the objectives of the substantive law.

Illustration 1-9. Assume that *D* is driving too fast and hits *P*, a pedestrian. The substantive law of torts contains, *inter alia*, rules that make one person liable to another for negligence. This liability exists when (a) the substantive tort law imposes on a person a duty to exercise due care; (b) that person fails to conform to the duty; (c) a direct causal connection exists between the breach of duty and an injury inflicted on another person; and (d) the injured person actually suffers some damage. Substantive tort rules provide that under these circumstances *D* must pay damages to *P*. These rules also govern how *P's* damages should be measured. In contrast, the law of procedure establishes, *inter alia*, (a) the method by which the injured party *P* may begin a lawsuit against the tortfeasor, *D*; (b) the degree of detail with which the injured party must describe the "claim"; and (c) the rules governing

---

18. *See* JOHN E. NOWAK & RONALD D. ROTUNDA, CONSTITUTIONAL LAW § 2.15 (8th ed. 2010) (discussing political questions).

19. *See* 13 CHARLES A. WRIGHT ET AL., FEDERAL PRACTICE AND PROCEDURE: JURISDICTION AND RELATED MATTERS § 3529, at 611-12 (3d ed. 2008) (noting that in a federal context, such refusals are often attributed to limits on the judicial power created by Article III of the U.S. Constitution).

20. *See id.* at 612 (noting that in a federal context, "a refusal to exercise the judicial power even in cases within the reach of Article III [reflects] prudential principles for wise administration of power"); *see also, e.g.*, McDonald v. John P. Scripps Newspaper, 210 Cal. App. 3d 100, 257 Cal. Rptr. 473 (1989) (error committed by national spelling bee contest officials not justiciable); Cudahy Junior Chamber of Commerce v. Quick, 41 Wis. 2d 698, 165 N.W.2d 116 (1969) (effects of fluoridation in the context of a "bet" during the course of public debate in a campaign not justiciable); Georgia High Sch. Ass'n v. Waddell, 248 Ga. 542, 285 S.E.2d 7 (1981) (error made by officials in a football game not justiciable); Evans v. Evans, 161 Eng. Rep. 466, 467 (Consistory Ct. 1790) ("Courts of Justice do not pretend to furnish cures for all the miseries of human life. They redress or punish gross violations of duty, but they go no farther; they cannot make [people] virtuous; and, as the happiness of the world depends upon its virtue, there may be much unhappiness in it which human laws cannot undertake to remove.").

21. *See* 13 CHARLES A. WRIGHT ET AL., FEDERAL PRACTICE AND PROCEDURE: JURISDICTION AND RELATED MATTERS § 3529, at 612 (3d ed. 2008) (noting that the central concepts of justiciability are often elaborated by more specific categories, including standing, ripeness, mootness, advisory opinions, feigned and collusive cases, administrative questions, and political questions).

how the injured party must prove the facts constituting the breach of the duty, the injury, and the other elements of the tort.

* * * * *

Although "pure" substantive rules and "pure" procedural rules exist, many rules are a mixture of both substance and procedure. Some rules that seem to be procedural are adopted for substantive reasons. Likewise, some rules that seem to be substantive are adopted for procedural reasons.

Illustration 1-10. *P* and *D* collide in their automobiles. The accident occurred in State *X* where both *P* and *D* live. *P* sues *D* in State *X* to recover damages for personal injuries received in the accident. The law of State *X* establishes the following "burden-of-proof" rule: the plaintiff must bear the burden of proving (a) that *D* was negligent; (b) that *D's* negligence directly caused *P's* injuries; and (c) the extent to which *P* was injured. Lawmakers often establish such rules purely for reasons of procedural policy. The plaintiff normally has the burden of proving these elements simply because the plaintiff is the party requesting relief. Thus, it is both convenient and fair that the plaintiff be required to produce evidence of a particular quality on certain basic elements of the "claim for relief."[22]

Illustration 1-11. In *Illustration 1-10*, suppose that the substantive law of State *X* provides that a plaintiff in a negligence action cannot recover if (a) the plaintiff was contributorily negligent and (b) that negligence contributed to the plaintiff's injuries. Assume that State *X* requires that the defendant prove that the plaintiff was contributorily negligent. Lawmakers sometimes allocate the burden of proof in this fashion because they disfavor the defense of contributory negligence.[23] Under such circumstances, lawmakers have arguably adopted the burden-of-proof rule for a substantive reason—even though the rule regulates an aspect of trial procedure. Procedural policies generally involve *efficiency* considerations, which include, but are not limited to, the orderly, speedy, and inexpensive administration of judicial proceedings. Lawmakers are not aiming at efficiency considerations when they create a burden-of-proof rule designed to make it harder for one side to win. Rather, the lawmakers are aiming at achieving a substantive social objective that transcends efficiency in judicial proceedings.

Illustration 1-12. Statutes of frauds require that certain kinds of contracts be in writing to be enforceable. Oral contracts falling within the scope of a statute of frauds are, therefore, unenforceable. Statutes of frauds are designed, in part, to regulate the out-of-court behavior of parties contemplating the formation of contracts. They are often designed to avoid the difficulties of proof inherent in a civil action in which one party asserts the existence of an oral contract and the other party denies its existence. This requirement is arguably a procedural one because it focuses on the fallibility of the evidentiary process employed in a judicial proceeding.[24] However, statutes of frauds are sometimes supported by an "admoni-

---

22. *See generally* MCCORMICK ON EVIDENCE § 337 (Kenneth S. Broun ed., 6th student ed. 2006).

23. *Cf. id.* at 564; *see also* RESTATEMENT (SECOND) OF CONFLICT OF LAWS § 133 illus. 2 (1971).

24. *See* D. Michael Risinger, *"Substance" and "Procedure" Revisited, with Some Afterthoughts on the Constitutional Problems of Irrebuttable Presumptions*, 30 UCLA L. REV. 189, 206-07 (1982); *cf.* RESTATEMENT (SECOND) OF CONFLICT OF LAWS § 141 cmt. b (1971) (discussing whether statutes of frauds should be classified as substantive or procedural for conflict-of-laws purposes).

tory" or "cautionary" policy instead of, or in addition to, this procedural policy. For example, the legislature may want the parties in certain kinds of contracts to stop and think carefully before entering into the contracts in order to prevent "ill-considered and impulsive promises."[25] A written document is thought to assure that promises will be carefully considered before being made. This policy is a "substantive" one because it focuses on behavior outside the context of litigation rather than the problems that oral contracts would cause in the litigation process.

* * * * *

Identifying the policy reasons behind various rules provides insight into the extent to which particular rules should be considered "substantive" or "procedural." Legal disputes, however, are not abstract inquiries. In resolving concrete disputes, the policy reasons behind a rule are often not the most significant factors in categorizing a rule as substantive or procedural. Unless one knows why it is important to categorize a rule in the first place, the policies supporting the rule will give little guidance about whether a particular rule should be considered substantive or procedural.

Illustration 1-13. Assume that a legislature delegates the power to make rules of civil practice and procedure to one or more courts within a jurisdiction. Assume further, however, that the legislature limits this rulemaking power to rules of practice and procedure that do not "abridge, enlarge, or modify any substantive right."[26] Before one can determine whether a particular rule of practice or procedure is valid or invalid under such a standard, one must know the purpose of this legislative limitation. Assume that the legislative history of such a statute reveals that the legislature did not want the courts to create rules that would affect parties' behavior at the primary stages of activity—*i.e.,* when they are driving automobiles, entering into contracts, etc. Otherwise, the courts are free to create any rules that regulate the judicial process. Once the purpose of this limitation is understood, it is easy to see that the courts could not create a statute of frauds such as the one described in *Illustration 1-12*, even if the exclusive reasons for doing so concerned the fallibility of the evidentiary processes in the adjudication of contract cases. Statutes of frauds affect a party's behavior at the primary stages of the contract-formation process. Therefore, *within the meaning of the legislative qualification*, the statute of frauds would be substantive even if a court created it purely for procedural reasons. On the other hand, the courts could create a burden-of-proof rule such as the one described in *Illustration 1-11*. Even if a court created the rule to disfavor the defense of contributory negligence, the rule does not affect the decisions of persons at the primary stages of activity (in driving automobiles, etc.). Thus, the rule does not abridge, enlarge, or modify substantive rights *within the meaning of the statutory qualification.*[27]

---

25. *See* 2 E. ALLAN FARNSWORTH, FARNSWORTH ON CONTRACTS § 6.1, at 356 (4th ed. 2004) (discussing the "cautionary" function of statutes of frauds).

26. *See, e.g.*, 28 U.S.C. § 2072(b).

27. When examining whether federal courts are obligated to apply state law in certain federal civil actions, it will be possible to see that application of federal, rather than state, burden-of-proof rules can be considered a substantive act. However, this is because the reasons for classifying rules as substantive or procedural in that context are different than the reasons for the statutory qualification in this illustration. *See generally* Lawrence B. Solum, *Procedural Justice,* 78 S. CAL. L. REV. 181 (2004); Chapter 5 *infra* ("Sources of Law").

SECTION C. THE ADVERSARY SYSTEM

1. The Adversary Process

The Anglo-American legal system relies primarily on the "adversary process" to resolve civil disputes. This process requires the parties to (a) begin the lawsuit, (b) define the issues, (c) develop proof in support of their respective positions, and (d) present that proof to a court. The rules and principles of civil procedure establish the framework for this development and presentation.

Certain assumptions about the best path to justice and efficiency underlie the "adversary system." These assumptions may or may not be true. For example, many substantive rules of law are designed to serve broader interests than those of private parties. Often, substantive rules reflect social goals. By placing the primary responsibility on private parties to initiate and develop litigation within the adversary process, the adversary system forces the parties to choose whether and to what extent substantive rules of law should be enforced. The system thus assumes that the policies underlying the substantive rules of law will be adequately fulfilled by relying upon the decisions of private parties.

Under the adversary system, the parties try to present their own evidence in the best possible light and the opponent's evidence in the worst possible light. The adversary system assumes that party presentation provides the best chance of finding the truth. The system also assumes that parties will develop and present cases affecting their private interests more efficiently than, for example, a public agency with no direct interest in the outcome. Thus, the system assumes that the parties are in the best position to decide whether a case is worth pursuing. Furthermore, party presentation places the expense of developing and presenting cases on the persons most directly affected rather than on the taxpayers at large.

Under the adversary system, lawyers ordinarily act as advocates for the parties. The idea is that skilled advocates operating on opposite sides of a case will develop and present all aspects of the case completely. Of course, this approach assumes that the lawyers for each side are of relatively equal competence. It also assumes that the financial resources available to each side are relatively equal.

Traditionally, the judge's role in the adversary system is reactive. For example, whether by design or through inadvertence, the parties may fail to present genuine factual or legal issues for decision. Ordinarily, if the parties do not raise such issues, the judge will not raise them. Even under the traditional adversary model, however, exceptions to this reactive role exist. The most notable exception relates to a court's institutional power to act. Even in the absence of the parties raising the issue, a court will raise a lack of subject-matter jurisdiction "on its own motion."[28] Nevertheless, on most matters, the parties are the masters of the case. The judge plays a relatively limited, nonintrusive role in the investigation and presentation of the litigation.

---

28. *See* Chapter 2 *infra* ("Subject-Matter Jurisdiction").

Of course, flaws may exist in the assumptions supporting the use of the adversary system.[29] A party presenting a case may seek to mislead rather than to establish the truth. The plaintiff, who initiates the case, may have every incentive to move it forward efficiently. On the other hand, the defendant may stand to lose a great deal upon completion of the lawsuit. Thus, the defendant may have the incentive to delay. Another inherent problem involves the lawyers' varying levels of competence. Different lawyers are no more of equal competence than different doctors, engineers, plumbers, or members of any other profession. The financial resources available to the parties may, more often than not, be significantly different. Furthermore, judges are subject to the biases and prejudices of other human beings and differ widely in their intelligence and temperament.

2. Procedural Constraints

Given these potential flaws, one would expect procedural rules to attempt to mitigate the rigors of a pure adversary system. Indeed, modern civil procedure aims to secure the just, speedy, and inexpensive determination of civil actions.[30] Thus, modern rules of procedure attempt to enhance the strengths of the adversary process and to guard against its weaknesses.[31]

Illustration 1-14. For instance, Rule 11 of the Federal Rules of Civil Procedure prohibits, *inter alia*, presentation of pleadings, motions, or other papers to the court "for any improper purpose, such as to harass or to cause unnecessary delay, or needless increase in the cost of litigation."[32]

3. Ethical Constraints

In addition to the attempt by modern procedural rules to mitigate the rigors of a pure adversary system, professional disciplinary rules and ethical considerations place limits on the pursuit of pure party interests in litigation.

Illustration 1-15. Under the Model Rules adopted by the American Bar Association in 1983,[33] lawyers have a duty to use the procedures provided by law

---

29. *Cf.* JOHN P. FRANK, AMERICAN LAW: THE CASE FOR RADICAL REFORM 126-27 (1969) ("[N]o one else pursuing truth would proceed as do lawyers and judges. The [adversary system] may or may not be a sure way of determining truth, but it is surely the most awkward method ever devised.").

30. *See* FED. R. CIV. P. 1 (requiring that the Federal Rules of Civil Procedure be construed and administered to secure these goals).

31. For an argument that attorney excesses on behalf of clients have been partially caused by changes in civil procedure, see Jonathan T. Molot, *How Changes in the Legal Profession Reflect Changes in Civil Procedure*, 84 VA. L. REV. 955 (1998).

32. FED. R. CIV. P. 11(b)(1); *see* Chapter 6(F) *infra* ("Good Faith Pleading"), in which Rule 11 sanctions are discussed fully.

33. The American Bar Association (ABA) has adopted three different sets of ethical rules during the past century. In 1908, the ABA adopted Canons of Professional Ethics, which contained 32 hortatory statements. In 1969, the ABA replaced the Canons with a much more extensive Code of Professional Responsibility, which consisted of nine Canons (axiomatic norms expressing in general terms the standard of professional conduct expected of lawyers), 138 Ethical Considerations (aspirational objectives toward which every member of the profession should strive), and 41 Disciplinary Rules (the minimum level of conduct below which no lawyer may fall without being subject to disciplinary action such as censure or disbarment). The Code of Professional Responsibility was adopted (with some modifications or omissions) as the basis for professional discipline in every state but California. In 1983, the ABA again revised its standards governing professional conduct in the form of

"for the fullest benefit of the client's cause." At the same time, lawyers also have an ethical "duty not to abuse legal procedure."[34] Several Model Rules directly apply to civil litigation.

First, the Rules provide that "[a] lawyer shall not bring or defend a proceeding, or assert or controvert an issue therein, unless there is a basis for doing so that is not frivolous, which includes a good faith argument for an extension, modification or reversal of existing law."[35]

Second, the Rules require lawyers to "make reasonable efforts to expedite litigation consistent with the interests of the client."[36]

Third, the Rules prohibit lawyers from knowingly making false statements of material facts or offering false evidence. Lawyers must also disclose any legal authority in the controlling jurisdiction known to be directly adverse to their client's position when opposing counsel has not disclosed that legal authority to the tribunal. Furthermore, lawyers must disclose material facts to the tribunal to prevent assisting a client's criminal or fraudulent act.[37]

Fourth, the Rules prohibit a variety of unfair conduct. Lawyers may not conceal, falsify, or destroy evidence. Nor may they allude in trial to matters that they do not reasonably believe to be relevant.[38]

Fifth, the Rules provide that lawyers shall not improperly seek to influence judges, jurors, or other officials. Nor shall lawyers engage in conduct intended to disrupt a tribunal.[39]

Sixth, the Rules prohibit lawyers from knowingly making false statements of law or material fact to third persons in the course of representing their clients. The Rules also require lawyers to disclose material facts to third persons when that disclosure is necessary to avoid assisting their clients in fraudulent or criminal acts (unless lawyer-client confidentiality limits that disclosure).[40]

Seventh, the Rules prohibit lawyers from directly communicating about the subject of the litigation with a party when they know another lawyer represents that party in the matter (unless the other lawyer has consented or the law otherwise permits the communication).[41]

Eighth, the Rules prohibit lawyers from stating or implying that they are disinterested when dealing on behalf of their clients with persons not represented by counsel.[42]

Model Rules of Professional Conduct (consisting of a Terminology section, 52 Model Rules, and explanatory Comments). *See* CHARLES W. WOLFRAM, MODERN LEGAL ETHICS § 2.6 (1986). A large majority of the states have now adopted the Model Rules as the basis for professional discipline. *See* 2 GEOFFREY C. HAZARD ET AL., THE LAW OF LAWYERING: A HANDBOOK ON THE MODEL RULES OF PROFESSIONAL CONDUCT app. B (3d ed. 2010) (listing adopting jurisdictions). In May 1998, the American Law Institute approved a comprehensive RESTATEMENT (THIRD) OF THE LAW GOVERNING LAWYERS (2000).

34. MODEL RULES OF PROFESSIONAL CONDUCT Rule 3.1 cmt. (1983).

35. *Id.* Rule 3.1.

36. *Id.* Rule 3.2.

37. *Id.* Rule 3.3(a).

38. *Id.* Rule 3.4.

39. *Id.* Rule 3.5.

40. *Id.* Rule 4.1.

41. *Id.* Rule 4.2.

42. *Id.* Rule 4.3.

Ninth, the Rules state that lawyers "shall not use means that have no substantial purpose other than to embarrass, delay, or burden a third person, or use methods of obtaining evidence that violate the legal rights of such a person."[43]

4. Litigation Costs

(a) Allocating the Direct Costs of Litigation

Litigation in an adversary system is expensive.[44] Some of the "direct" costs of litigation are the salaries of court employees; janitorial services; the time of the litigants, jurors, and witnesses; investigation expenses; expert witness fees; and the legal fees of the litigants' lawyers.[45] The litigants bear some of these direct costs through filing fees and other expenditures. The taxpayers also bear some of the costs through expenditures of public funds to maintain the court system. How a legal system divides these costs between the litigants and the public affects access to the courts.[46] That division reflects fundamental judgments about the functions of a government.[47]

Furthermore, how a judicial system allocates the costs *among the litigants themselves* may influence the litigants' conduct and even the decision to use the judicial process at all.[48] A judgment in a lawsuit will ordinarily award "costs" to the prevailing party.[49] The law in each jurisdiction defines "taxable" (recoverable) costs. Taxable costs usually are small in comparison to the overall expenses of litigation. Examples of taxable costs in the federal courts include fees of the clerk and marshall, fees of court reporters for the printed or electronically recorded transcripts obtained for use in the case, and fees for witnesses.[50] Shifts in the liability for costs can be designed to encourage specific policies or actions.

Illustration 1-16. Federal Rule 68 shifts costs to encourage settlement. If the plaintiff rejects an "offer of judgment" and then fails to obtain a more favorable

---

43. *Id.* Rule 4.4.

44. Litigation "costs" have been described in various ways. *See, e.g.*, FLEMING JAMES, JR. ET AL., CIVIL PROCEDURE § 13.3, at 585-86 (6th ed. 2011) (cost of litigation includes (1) "opportunity," "uncertainty," and "illiquidity" costs; (2) "information processing" costs; and (3) "psychological" costs (or losses) arising from "worry, loss of sleep, tension, and spasms of rage"); Richard A. Posner, *An Economic Approach to Legal Procedure and Judicial Administration*, 2 J. LEGAL STUD. 399, 400 (1973) ("direct" costs and "error" costs).

45. *See* Richard A. Posner, *An Economic Approach to Legal Procedure and Judicial Administration*, 2 J. LEGAL STUD. 399, 401 (1973).

46. *See generally* Frank I. Michelman, *The Supreme Court and Litigation Access Fees: The Right to Protect One's Rights*, 1973 DUKE L.J. 1153; John F. Vargo, *The American Rule on Attorney Fee Allocation: The Injured Person's Access to Justice*, 42 AM. U. L. REV. 1567 (1993). Congress has provided for the waiver of filing fees in the federal district courts. *See* 28 U.S.C. § 1915(a) (in forma pauperis); *cf.* Boddie v. Connecticut, 401 U.S. 371, 91 S. Ct. 780, 28 L. Ed. 2d 113 (1971) (due process prevents a state from imposing filing, service, and publication fees on welfare recipients seeking divorces).

47. *See generally* Rex E. Lee, *The American Courts as Public Goods: Who Should Pay the Costs of Litigation?*, 34 CATH. U. L. REV. 267 (1985); Phillip L. Spector, *Financing the Courts Through Fees: Incentives and Equity in Civil Litigation*, 58 JUDICATURE 330 (1975).

48. *See generally* Thomas D. Rowe, Jr., *The Legal Theory of Attorney Fee Shifting: A Critical Overview*, 1982 DUKE L.J. 651; Thomas D. Rowe, Jr., *Predicting the Effects of Attorney Fee Shifting*, 47 LAW & CONTEMP. PROBS. 139 (1984); Steven Shavell, *Suit, Settlement and Trial: A Theoretical Analysis Under Alternative Methods for the Allocation of Legal Costs*, 11 J. LEGAL STUD. 55, 58-69 (1982); Note, *Use of Taxable Costs to Regulate the Conduct of Litigants*, 53 COLUM. L. REV. 78 (1953).

49. *See, e.g.*, FED. R. CIV. P. 54(d) ("Costs; Attorney's Fees").

50. *See* 28 U.S.C. § 1920.

judgment, the plaintiff must pay the "costs" (as defined by law) incurred after the offer was made.[51]

* * * * *

A significant litigation expense is the attorney's fee. However, under the "American Rule," the attorney's fee of the winning party is ordinarily *not* a recoverable cost.[52] Judicially created exceptions to the American Rule include the "common fund" rule,[53] the "substantial benefit" rule,[54] and the "private attorney general" theory.[55] Statutes likewise establish exceptions to the American Rule.

Illustration 1-17. Examples of federal statutes creating exceptions to the American Rule include the Freedom of Information Act;[56] Securities Act of 1933;[57] Packers and Stockyards Act;[58] Truth in Lending Act;[59] Water Pollution Control Act;[60] Clayton Act;[61] and federal civil proceedings vindicating civil rights.[62]

Illustration 1-18. The Equal Access to Justice Act (EAJA)[63] provides that a court, unless prohibited by statute, has the *discretion* to award reasonable attorney's fees and expenses to the prevailing party in any civil action brought by or against the U.S. Government.[64] The EAJA also *requires* a court to award attorneys' fees, unless prohibited by statute, to an otherwise eligible prevailing party in such an action "unless the court finds that the position of the United States was substantially justified or that special circumstances make such an award unjust."[65]

* * * * *

Additionally, procedural rules sometimes provide exceptions.

---

51. *See* FED. R. CIV. P. 68 ("Offer of Judgment"); *see also* Chapter 10(F) *infra* ("Miscellaneous Methods of Disposing of an Action Without Trial"), in which Rule 68 is more fully discussed.

52. *See* Alyeska Pipeline Serv. Co. v. Wilderness Soc'y, 421 U.S. 240, 247, 95 S. Ct. 1612, 1616, 44 L. Ed. 2d 141, 147 (1975) ("In the United States, the prevailing litigant is ordinarily not entitled to collect a reasonable attorney's fee from the loser."); *see also* DAN B. DOBBS, LAW OF REMEDIES § 3.10(1), at 276-77 (2d student ed. 1993) (describing this rule, its development, and its rationales).

53. Persons who share in a fund produced or preserved by a prevailing plaintiff's litigation are responsible for a proportionate part of the costs of the litigation, including the attorney's fee. *See* DAN B. DOBBS, LAW OF REMEDIES § 3.10(2), at 279-81 (2d student ed. 1993).

54. This "substantial benefit" rule extends the "common fund" rule to cases involving non-cash benefits in the context of institutional defendants. *Id.* § 3.10(2), at 281-83 (discussing this extension and critiquing the restitutionary argument made in such cases); *see* Hall v. Cole, 412 U.S. 1, 93 S. Ct. 1943, 36 L. Ed. 2d 702 (1973) (union defendant liable for plaintiff union member's attorney's fees after establishing free speech rights for the union membership generally); Mills v. Electric Auto-Lite Co., 396 U.S. 375, 90 S. Ct. 616, 24 L. Ed. 2d 593 (1970) (corporate defendant liable for plaintiff shareholder's attorney's fees after plaintiff established intangible rights on behalf of all shareholders).

55. The "private attorney general" theory supports the recovery of attorney's fees from the defendant when substantial public benefits have resulted from litigation that otherwise might not be brought. DAN B. DOBBS, LAW OF REMEDIES § 3.10(2), at 283 (2d student ed. 1993).

56. 5 U.S.C. § 552(a)(4)(E).

57. 15 U.S.C. § 77k(e).

58. 7 U.S.C. § 210(f).

59. 15 U.S.C. § 1640(a)(3).

60. 33 U.S.C. §§ 1365(d), 1369(b)(3).

61. 15 U.S.C. § 15(a).

62. *See* Civil Rights Attorney's Fee Awards Act, 42 U.S.C. § 1988(b).

63. 28 U.S.C. § 2412.

64. *Id.* § 2412(b) (including U.S. agencies and U.S. officials acting in their official capacity).

65. *Id.* § 2412(d)(1)(A).

Illustration 1-19. Federal Rule 56(g) allows courts to assess reasonable expenses, including attorney's fees, against a party who presents affidavits in bad faith in the context of a summary judgment motion.[66]

(b) "Error" Costs

From an economic viewpoint, legal procedures should attempt to minimize the sum of the (1) "direct" and (2) "error" costs of litigation. Sometimes, the judicial system fails to perform the "allocative or other social functions assigned to it" by mistakenly imposing, or failing to impose, liability.[67] This failure creates error costs. Such costs are just as real as direct costs and cause an inefficient allocation of resources.[68]

Illustration 1-20. Assume that *D's* product causes occasional injuries. Assume also that *D* can buy relatively inexpensive safety devices that could reduce the accident rate significantly. If the substantive (tort) law imposes liability for these accidents and if the law is flawlessly enforced, *D* will be induced to purchase the optimum quantity of safety devices. However, if the law is not perfectly enforced—for example, because of inaccurate determinations in civil proceedings brought to impose liability—*D* will procure a suboptimum quantity of safety devices. This suboptimal procurement will result in a social loss.[69]

SECTION D. THE HISTORICAL EVOLUTION OF CIVIL PROCEDURE

Modern American procedural systems are the products of a long evolutionary process. Some parts of these systems are entirely the result of historical accident and can only be understood as such. Other parts represent the cumulative efforts of modern procedural reform aimed at updating older procedures to fit modern conditions. Even when the reform process has resulted in a modern rule that has largely replaced an older rule, knowing the purpose of the reform is essential to interpreting and applying the modern rule properly.

This section discusses the origins of modern systems of civil procedure in English and early American practice. This history is complex, but the material presented here is limited to what is necessary to understand the reforms that have produced modern procedural rules. It also provides an essential background for an understanding of modern remedies and the modern right to a jury trial.

---

66. *See* FED. R. CIV. P. 56(h) ("Affidavit or Declaration Submitted in Bad Faith"); *see also* Chapter 10(C) *infra* ("Summary Judgment"), in which summary judgment practice is more fully discussed; *cf.* 28 U.S.C. § 1447(c) (order remanding a removed case from federal court to state court "may require payment of just costs and any actual expenses, including attorney fees," caused by improper removal); FED. R. CIV. P. 11 (sanctions for instituting or conducting litigation in bad faith or engaging in dilatory or abusive tactics); DAN B. DOBBS, LAW OF REMEDIES § 3.10(3), at 290-91 (2d student ed. 1993) (litigation misconduct and contempt of court).

67. Richard A. Posner, *An Economic Approach to Legal Procedure and Judicial Administration*, 2 J. LEGAL STUD. 399, 400-01 (1973).

68. *See id.*

69. *Id.* at 402-06 (analyzing in detail error costs in accident cases). One would not, however, "want to increase the direct cost [of litigation] by one dollar in order to [produce more accurate determinations that would] reduce error costs by 50 (or [even] 99) cents." *Id.* at 401.

1. Origins of the Common-Law Courts

The English common law originated in the new procedures and judicial machinery brought to England after the Norman Conquest in 1066. Before the Conquest, local courts—the Hundred, Shire, and County courts—administered justice based on local customs.[70] After the Conquest, a system of central royal courts—the King's Bench, Exchequer, and Common Pleas—was established.[71] These royal courts did not replace the local courts. Instead, the royal courts heard litigants who were dissatisfied with the quality of justice in the local courts.[72]

2. Issuance of Writs by the Chancellor

In the system of Norman administration, the chancellor was the king's secretary. The office of chancellor was strictly a "household" office.[73] The king conducted the administration of the realm by having the chancellor write out and dispatch orders.[74] As each of the three royal common-law courts formed, each court was limited to the business delegated to it by one of these administrative orders. These orders came to be known as *original writs*.[75]

In effect, the original writs were the means by which litigants obtained permission to sue in the royal courts. Litigants purchased these writs from the chancellor. The litigants had to choose the proper writ to recover. If the facts that were ultimately proved fell outside the selected writ ("*form of action*"), the plaintiff lost—even if the facts proved would have been sufficient to support a recovery under another writ. Thus, the forms of actions embodied in the writs were "pigeon-holes" into which plaintiffs had to fit their cases. If the plaintiffs failed, they could start over—provided a proper form of action covered the situation and they had the wherewithal to do so.[76]

At first, the chancellor awarded these writs "according to the apparent justice and need of the case."[77] Eventually, several types of writs came to be granted routinely (called "*writs of course*").[78]

3. The Initial Development of the Forms of Action

Writs routinely granted by the Chancellor fell into three basic categories: (1) *real actions* (involving the ownership and possession of land), (2) *ex contractu personal actions* (based on a contract, express or implied), and (3) *ex delicto*

---

70. *See* JOSEPH H. KOFFLER & ALISON REPPY, HANDBOOK OF COMMON LAW PLEADING § 8, at 32-33 (1969).

71. *See id.* at 33.

72. *See id.*; *see also* Daniel Klerman, *Jurisdictional Competition and the Evolution of the Common Law*, 74 U. CHI. L. REV. 1179 (2007).

73. *See* THEODORE F.T. PLUCKNETT, A CONCISE HISTORY OF THE COMMON LAW 695 (5th ed. 1956).

74. *See* JOSEPH H. KOFFLER & ALISON REPPY, HANDBOOK OF COMMON LAW PLEADING § 8, at 33 (1969).

75. *See id.* at 34.

76. FREDERIC W. MAITLAND, THE FORMS OF ACTION AT COMMON LAW 3-4 (1936).

77. BENJAMIN J. SHIPMAN, HANDBOOK OF COMMON-LAW PLEADING § 29, at 59 (3d ed. 1923).

78. *See* JOSEPH H. KOFFLER & ALISON REPPY, HANDBOOK OF COMMON LAW PLEADING § 9 (1969).

personal actions (arising out of or founded upon a wrong or a tort).[79] Each writ represented a particular *form of action*.

(a) Real Actions

Real actions focused on property rights. They were primarily used for the specific recovery of seisin—the possession of a freehold estate in real property.[80]

Illustration 1-21. Assume that *D* ousted *P* from possession of land on which *P* was living and that *P* wanted to regain possession. *P* would use one of the real actions, most likely one based on a writ of entry. Such a writ came to "lie" (be available) against a person whose possession had been derived from a disseisin.

(b) Ex Contractu *Personal Actions*

Ex contractu personal actions focused on contract rights. Debt, covenant, detinue, and account were the principal forms of *ex contractu* actions. Each was used in slightly different circumstances.

A writ of *debt* was used when services had been rendered, goods had been sold and delivered, or money lent, but the defendant refused to pay the agreed-upon amount due.[81]

Illustration 1-22. *D* orally promised to buy *P's* horse for $100. *P* gave *D* the horse, but *D* then refused to pay. *P* could use a writ of debt because the transaction was half-completed and the sum due was fixed ($100).

* * * * *

Several specific variants of debt existed. *Debt on a specialty* was used when a promise to pay a fixed sum was acknowledged in a sealed instrument—one in which the parties to be bound affixed their name and seal. Such an instrument could be a deed or a bond. The promise was often subject to a "condition subsequent": a fixed sum would become due if the obligor failed to observe a covenant, failed to pay rent, or failed to repay money borrowed.[82] *Debt on a statute* would lie when a statute permitted an injured private party to recover a definite sum as a penalty or forfeiture.[83] *Debt on a record* was also another important variant. If the plaintiff had won an action and the defendant had refused to pay, the plaintiff would ordinarily obtain a writ of execution from the court. This writ would direct the sheriff to seize

---

79. *See id.*

80. Real actions included the writ of right, the assize of novel disseisin, and the assize of mort d'ancestor. *See id.* § 10, at 47-53; *see also* Joseph Biancalana, *The Origin and Early History of the Writs of Entry*, 25 L. & HIST. REV. 513 (2007).

81. Thus, debt (also called "debt on a simple contract") would only lie to force the defendant to carry out the *half-completed* transaction if the sum due was *fixed*. The theory was that the debtor was holding back something which had been granted and which, therefore, actually belonged to the creditor—not that the debtor was merely under an obligation to pay. *See* BENJAMIN J. SHIPMAN, HANDBOOK OF COMMON-LAW PLEADING §§ 52-53, at 132-35 (3d ed. 1923).

82. *See id.* at 135.

83. For example, assume that a statute provides a monetary penalty for engaging in unauthorized fishing or hunting. *D* was caught fishing on *P's* land. Assuming that the statute provided that the landholder was entitled to the penalty, debt on a statute would be the proper form of action for *P* to recover the penalty. The underlying theory was that, by force of the statute, *D* "owed a debt" to *P*. *See* JOSEPH H. KOFFLER & ALISON REPPY, HANDBOOK OF COMMON LAW PLEADING § 141, at 295-97 (1969); EDMUND M. MORGAN & FRANCIS X. DWYER, INTRODUCTION TO THE STUDY OF LAW 94 (2d ed. 1948).

and sell the defendant's property to satisfy the judgment. After a year and a day from the date of the recovery of a judgment, the courts would no longer issue a writ of execution because the judgment would be presumed to have been satisfied. Thereafter, an action of debt on a record was the only means to enforce the judgment. In such an action, the plaintiff did not have to prove the elements of the original claim. Instead, to obtain a new judgment, the plaintiff had to prove the prior judgment was still in force, but still unsatisfied.[84]

Covenant was used to recover "unliquidated" (unascertained in amount) damages when the promise was under seal.[85]

Illustration 1-23. *D* promised in writing under seal to buy *P's* horse by paying *P* its "reasonable value." *P* then delivered the horse, but *D* refused to pay. Covenant would be the proper form of action because (1) the promise was under seal and (2) the amount was unliquidated. Debt on a specialty would not lie because the amount was not a specific, fixed amount (but instead the "reasonable value" of the horse).

* * * * *

Detinue was used to recover unlawfully detained chattels.[86]

Illustration 1-24. *P* loaned a horse to *D*. *D* liked it so much that *D* refused to give it back. *P* could sue *D* in detinue when *D*, the bailee, refused to return a specific ascertained chattel (the horse).

* * * * *

Account was used to force fiduciaries to provide an accounting.[87]

(c) Ex Delicto *Personal Actions*

In addition to real and *ex contractu* actions, the chancellor also issued writs to redress wrongs and to recover personal property. The most important type of writ used to redress wrongs was the writ of trespass.

(i) Trespass

A writ of trespass covered injuries committed with actual or implied force. Courts would imply force when the injury was immediate and direct—for example,

---

84. *See* BENJAMIN J. SHIPMAN, HANDBOOK OF COMMON-LAW PLEADING §§ 52-53, at 136 (3d ed. 1923).

85. Later, covenant could also be used when the amount under seal was liquidated; in that instance, debt on a specialty and covenant were concurrent, provided there was an express covenant (promise) to pay the debt or there were words that could be so construed. *See id.* § 55, at 141-43.

86. At first, detinue and debt were identical actions; as detinue slowly "branched off" from debt, detinue came to lie for the recovery of specific ascertained chattels (such as a specific horse), while debt would lie for a fixed amount of money or for a fixed amount of unascertained chattels (such as fifty bushels of grain). Detinue was initially available to a bailor when the bailee wrongfully detained the bailed goods ("chattels"). It was also available to recover goods lost by the plaintiff when the finder refused to surrender them after a proper demand had been made. In detinue actions, the defendant had the option of returning the chattel or paying its value to the plaintiff. The plaintiff also received damages for wrongful detention of the chattel. *See* EDMUND M. MORGAN & FRANCIS X. DWYER, INTRODUCTION TO THE STUDY OF LAW 97-98 (2d ed. 1948).

87. When a person received property for the use and benefit of other persons (*e.g.*, collected rents or sold goods on their behalf), the law imposed an obligation to account for the proceeds or the property. Account would lie when such a *fiduciary relationship* existed between the parties (one founded upon a trust or confidence) and when the amount due was *uncertain and unliquidated*. If the sum was certain, however, debt would be the proper form. *See* JOSEPH H. KOFFLER & ALISON REPPY, HANDBOOK OF COMMON LAW PLEADING § 154, at 310-11 (1969).

when the defendant peacefully but wrongfully came onto the plaintiff's land. When an injury to property was involved, the plaintiff had to be in actual or constructive possession of the property at the time of the injury.[88] One writ of trespass in its various forms could cover several wrongs, including:

(1) assault and battery;

(2) injury to personal property;

(3) carrying away of personal property (trespass de bonis asportatis);

(4) trespass to real property (trespass quare clausum fregit);

(5) false imprisonment; and

(6) trespass for a loss of services, as in an action by a husband, father, or master for enticing away, seducing, or debauching his wife, daughter, or servant (trespass per quod servitium amisit).[89]

Illustration 1-25. Assume that *D* sneaked onto *P's* land and stole *P's* horse from *P's* barn. In this situation, a trespass to real property (trespass quare clausum fregit) and a carrying away of personal property (trespass de bonis asportatis) have occurred. *P* could use one writ of trespass to recover damages for these harms.

(ii) Replevin

Replevin originated as a form of action to keep "distress" within bounds. A feudal lord could "distrain" (seize) a vassal's chattels when the vassal failed to render feudal services or to pay rent that was due. Distress was also permitted when trespassing animals were causing damage. In these situations, the distressed chattels could be held until the services were rendered, the amount in arrears was paid, the proper compensation was offered, or security was given if the matter was to be taken to court.

When a wrongful distraint or an improper refusal to return the distrained chattels had occurred, a replevin action could be brought. If the plaintiff won, the plaintiff not only had the chattels returned, but also recovered damages for their wrongful detention.[90] The theory of replevin was broad enough to cover any case of *wrongful taking*, not merely wrongful distress.[91]

Illustration 1-26. Assume *D* stole *P's* horse. *P* wanted its return, with damages for its wrongful detention. Replevin came to lie for any wrongful taking from the plaintiff's possession. If *P* posted security, *P* could have the horse returned at the outset of the replevin action. If *P* won the lawsuit, *P* could recover damages arising from *D's* wrongful detention of the horse. Detinue would not have been the

---

88. *Id.* § 77, at 152.

89. *See* BENJAMIN J. SHIPMAN, HANDBOOK OF COMMON-LAW PLEADING § 35, at 66 (3d ed. 1923).

90. EDMUND M. MORGAN & FRANCIS X. DWYER, INTRODUCTION TO THE STUDY OF LAW 90 (2d ed. 1948); *see also* JOSEPH H. KOFFLER & ALISON REPPY, HANDBOOK OF COMMON LAW PLEADING § 127, at 254-55 (1969). The writ directed the sheriff to return the distrained chattels to the plaintiff after pledges were furnished to assure that the action would be prosecuted. To prevent the defendant from being deprived of distress remedy if the plaintiff disposed of the chattels before trial and became insolvent, the Statute of Westminster II, 13 Edw. I, ch. 2 (1285), required the plaintiff to give security for the return of the chattels if the defendant won the suit. EDMUND M. MORGAN & FRANCIS X. DWYER, INTRODUCTION TO THE STUDY OF LAW 89-90 (2d ed. 1948).

91. JOSEPH H. KOFFLER & ALISON REPPY, HANDBOOK OF COMMON LAW PLEADING § 127, at 255 (1969). Late in the fifteenth century, replevin was extended by judicial decision to apply to any wrongful taking. EDMUND H. MORGAN & FRANCIS X. DWYER, INTRODUCTION TO THE STUDY OF LAW 91 (2d ed. 1948).

proper form of action under these circumstances because detinue was available only when the defendant acquired possession *lawfully*—for example, when the plaintiff loaned a chattel to the defendant who later refused to return it. In contrast, replevin would be proper because the defendant *unlawfully* obtained possession (by a trespass). *P* would not want to use trespass de bonis asportatis because *P* wanted the horse returned. In trespass, the plaintiff would receive damages (the value of the horse), not the return of the horse.

4. Subsequent Development of the Forms of Action

At first, the king was interested in only certain types of cases, such as breaches of the king's peace. The standardized forms of the original writs were limited accordingly.[92] Inevitably, as the king's interests expanded, the power of the king's courts clashed with the interests of the feudal lords who controlled the local courts. In 1258, the Barons extracted the Provisions of Oxford from Henry III, which forbade the chancellor from framing new writs without permission from the king and the king's council.[93]

In 1285, the Statute of Westminster II authorized the chancery clerks to issue new writs in cases similar to (*in consimili casu*), but not quite identical with, those in which writs had been previously granted.[94] Subsequent developments focused on the gradual expansion of the trespass action rather than the issuance of new writs creating entirely new forms of action.[95] The principal "offshoots" from

---

92. The following is an example of a writ of trespass:

> The King to the Sheriff, &c. If [*P*] shall make you secure, &c. then put by gages and safe pledges [*D*] that [*D*] be before us on the morrow of All Souls, wheresoever we shall then be in England, to show wherefore [*ostensurous quare*] with force and arms [*vi et armis*] [*D*] made an assault upon [*P*] at [a specified location] and beat, wounded and ill treated [*P*], so that [*P's*] life was despaired of, and other enormous things to [*P*] did, to the great damage of [*P*] and against our peace [*contra pacem nostram*]: and have there the names of the pledges and this writ. Witness, &c.

1 ANTHONY FITZ-HERBERT, NATURA BREVIUM 86 I (9th ed. 1794), *reprinted in* RICHARD H. FIELD ET AL., MATERIALS FOR A BASIC COURSE IN CIVIL PROCEDURE 1050 (10th ed. 2010). This writ reflected the concept of the "king's peace" as the original basis of the royal court's jurisdiction. First, this writ used the term "*vi et armis*" to indicate that an application of force had occurred. Second, it stated not only that *P* was damaged, but also that *D's* actions were "against our peace." *See* FREDERIC W. MAITLAND, THE FORMS OF ACTION AT COMMON LAW 39-40 (1936). The writ directed the sheriff to assure the appearance of the defendant "by gages and safe pledges" if the plaintiff gave security to prosecute ("if [*P*] shall make you secure"). This stringent process against defendants made the action very popular with plaintiffs. *See id.*

93. FREDERIC W. MAITLAND, THE FORMS OF ACTION AT COMMON LAW 8 (1936). The Provisions to which Henry III (1216-1272) agreed imposed an oath upon the chancellor that no writs should be granted "excepting Writs of Course without the Commandment of the King and of his Council who shall be present." JOSEPH H. KOFFLER & ALISON REPPY, HANDBOOK OF COMMON LAW PLEADING § 8, at 43 (1969). "Writs of course" referred to writs for which precedent might be found in the form book (Register of Writs) kept in the Chancery. The Provisions of Oxford were annulled five years later, but the chancellor's former power to issue writs appears not to have been restored. ROBERT W. MILLAR, CIVIL PROCEDURE OF THE TRIAL COURT IN HISTORICAL PERSPECTIVE 18 (1952).

94. *See* Statute of Westminster II, 13 Edw. I, ch. 24 (1285).

95. *See* FREDERIC W. MAITLAND, THE FORMS OF ACTION AT COMMON LAW 44 (1936); WILLIAM F. WALSH, A HISTORY OF ANGLO-AMERICAN LAW 70 (2d ed. 1932). Legal scholars differ on the extent of the impact of the Statute of Westminster II on the subsequent development of the forms of action. *See* JOSEPH H. KOFFLER & ALISON REPPY, HANDBOOK OF COMMON LAW PLEADING § 45 (1969) (summarizing the varying views). For example, Millar maintains that this statute had a substantial effect on the subsequent development of the writ system.

> Whatever might have been the case had it been given a more liberal construction, this statute mark[ed] a definite check upon the writ-issuing power. Except for the later development under [this] statutory authority which gave us the action of trespass on the case and its derivatives, the tally of writs was complete, the area of common-law justice determined.

ROBERT W. MILLAR, CIVIL PROCEDURE OF THE TRIAL COURT IN HISTORICAL PERSPECTIVE 19 (1952). Although

the writ of trespass were the following: (1) trespass on the case, (2) assumpsit, (3) trover, and (4) ejectment. The development of these writs spawned much of England's substantive common law. As discussed below, this development also reflected the plaintiffs' efforts to avoid problems of proof in certain circumstances and to avoid certain modes of trial. It also reflected the plaintiffs' efforts to secure different measures of damages and to secure better remedies.

(a) Trespass on the Case

Trespass covered immediate and direct injuries committed with actual or implied force. When injury to property was involved, the plaintiff must have been in actual or constructive possession of the property at the time of the injury.[96] In contrast, *trespass on the case* (or simply "*case*") covered situations in which the action of trespass did not apply—*i.e.*, indirect or consequential injuries to persons, goods, or land resulting from the defendant's negligence or wrongful acts.[97]

Illustration 1-27. Assume that a log was thrown onto a highway and hit someone standing in the highway. Trespass would be the proper form of action because the wrong was "immediate." On the other hand, if a log was wrongfully left on a highway and someone later stumbled over it in the dark, trespass on the case would be the proper form because the injury was "consequential."[98]

* * * * *

Over a long period, the courts worked out the distinctions between trespass and trespass on the case. Case is the source of the modern law of negligence and nuisance. It was also the proper form of action to recover for injuries to incorporeal (intangible) rights, such as libel, slander, deceit, malicious prosecution, or improper use of an easement.[99] Furthermore, case was the form of action used to recover for injuries to reversionary interests. Such interests included that of a bailor of a chattel lent for a specific term and that of a landowner whose land was in the possession of a tenant for a term of years.[100]

* * * * *

Like some other forms of action, trespass and case were concurrent in certain situations.[101]

---

it is debated whether trespass on the case really originated under the Statute of Westminster II, there is no question that subsequent developments of the forms of action focused on the gradual expansion of the trespass action (into trespass on the case, etc.) rather than on the issuance of entirely new writs creating entirely new forms of action.

96. *See* section D(3)*(c) supra* ("*Ex Delicto* Personal Actions").

97. For a discussion of the development of trespass on the case from trespass, see JOSEPH H. KOFFLER & ALISON REPPY, HANDBOOK OF COMMON LAW PLEADING § 84, at 175-76 (1969).

98. *See* Reynolds v. Clarke, 93 Eng. Rep. 747, 748 (K.B. 1726).

99. JOSEPH H. KOFFLER & ALISON REPPY, HANDBOOK OF COMMON LAW PLEADING § 84, at 174-75 (1969).

100. Assume that *D* wrongfully damaged a dwelling house on land owned by *P*. However, the house was leased for a term of years to *L* when it was injured. *P* could not sue in trespass because *P* was not in possession of the land at the time of the injury. Case was the proper form of action to recover for the injury to *P's* reversionary interest. *L* could sue in trespass and recover damages for the injury to *L's* possessory interest and *P's* reversionary interest, but *L* would be liable to *P* for the portion of the recovery that represented damage to the reversionary interest. *See* EDMUND M. MORGAN & FRANCIS X. DWYER, AN INTRODUCTION TO THE STUDY OF LAW 107 (2d ed. 1948).

101. For example, a husband, master, or father could eventually sue in case for loss of services or society of his wife, servant, or daughter (instead of trespass per quod servitium amisit) by treating the loss as the injury rather than the defendant's implied forceful act of enticing away, seducing, or debauching his wife, servant, or daughter. *See* BENJAMIN J. SHIPMAN, HANDBOOK OF COMMON-LAW PLEADING § 39, at 89 (3d ed. 1923).

Illustration 1-28. Assume that the defendant negligently drove a vehicle into the plaintiff's vehicle. In situations involving an immediate injury to persons or property attributable to negligence like this one, the courts eventually allowed plaintiffs to sue either in trespass (focusing on the immediate crash as the injury) or in case (focusing on the negligence of the wrongdoer as the cause of action).[102]

* * * * *

When forms of action were concurrent, some of the peril involved in choosing the wrong form was removed. Even then, however, the plaintiff was not always free of such peril.

Illustration 1-29. In the example of the crash in *Illustration 1-28*, assume the plaintiff sued in case. If the evidence ultimately showed that the defendant had not been negligent but instead had intentionally hit the plaintiff, the plaintiff would lose because only trespass would lie for intentional injuries. Similarly, assume that a vehicle had been negligently left standing on the highway and it was later hit by another vehicle at night. If the plaintiff sued in trespass, the plaintiff would lose if the court found the injury to be consequential rather than immediate.[103]

(b) Assumpsit

Debt, covenant, and account would not lie to enforce unsealed, executory promises. During the sixteenth century, assumpsit developed to provide this remedy. Assumpsit originated as a variant of trespass on the case. It covered a defendant's active misfeasance, such as (1) when the defendant undertook ("assumpsit") to perform some act, but did so negligently or (2) when the defendant undertook through an express promise to care for goods entrusted to the defendant, but did so improperly. Courts then extended assumpsit to situations in which a seller promised to sell goods to a buyer, but instead sold them to someone else. Courts considered the seller's action to be an active misfeasance in breach of the undertaking. Finally, early in the sixteenth century, courts extended assumpsit to a seller's nonfeasance (the refusal to perform the unsealed promise). This form of action was known as *special assumpsit*. It became the basis of modern contract law.[104]

Up to this point, plaintiffs still could not use assumpsit to recover for simple debts arising from the receipt of benefit or value because debt covered such half-completed transactions. Courts viewed the promise to repay the debt as a "grant," and not as an undertaking. The courts began to permit assumpsit actions in this situation when the debtor had made a second promise to pay.[105] In 1602, courts finally held that a second promise would be *implied*. This form of assumpsit, known as *indebitatus* or *general assumpsit*, became concurrent with debt.[106]

---

102. *See* Williams v. Holland, 131 Eng. Rep. 848 (C.P. 1833); *see also* M.J. Prichard, *Trespass, Case and the Rule in* Williams v. Holland, 1964 CAMBRIDGE L.J. 234 (discussing the historical evolution of this rule).

103. *See* JOSEPH H. KOFFLER & ALISON REPPY, HANDBOOK OF COMMON LAW PLEADING § 81, at 165-66 (1969).

104. EDMUND M. MORGAN & FRANCIS X. DWYER, AN INTRODUCTION TO THE STUDY OF LAW 108-09 (2d ed. 1948).

105. *Id.* at 110.

106. *See* Slade's Case, 76 Eng. Rep. 1072 (K.B. 1602); *see also* 1 DAN B. DOBBS, LAW OF REMEDIES § 4.2(3), at 578-79 (2d practitioner ed. 1993).

Courts also extended general assumpsit to cover other situations in which the defendant, in good conscience, was bound to pay the plaintiff.[107]

Illustration 1-30. Assume that the plaintiff rendered services or sold goods with the reasonable expectation of receiving fair value for them. Because the sum (reasonable value) was not fixed, debt could not be brought. Because no express promise to pay had been made, special assumpsit could not be used. Nevertheless, based upon the defendant's conduct creating the belief that reasonable value would be paid, the courts began to imply a promise to pay. When the law implied such a promise, the court referred to this implied obligation as a *quasi-contract.*

* * * * *

Because special and general assumpsit were variants of the same form of action, plaintiffs sometimes used both special and general assumpsit in the same action. For example, plaintiffs often used a count declaring in special assumpsit based upon an express contract and a count in general assumpsit based upon an implied promise to pay the reasonable value of the delivered goods or services. This approach alleviated the risk that the plaintiff might fail to prove that a binding express contract existed in special assumpsit. For example, an express contract might be voidable or the plaintiff might be found not to have substantially performed the contract. Nevertheless, the plaintiff's proof might still reveal the necessary elements for an implied undertaking to pay the reasonable value for the benefits conferred.[108]

Illustration 1-31. Assume that the parties exchanged promises and formed an express contract. When the plaintiff had delivered goods or conveyed a parcel of land as promised, the plaintiff could declare in special assumpsit, based on the express promise. If nothing remained to be performed except for the defendant to pay the monetary amount, the plaintiff could also add a count in general assumpsit to recover the reasonable value of the benefits received—based on the "debt" arising from the passage of a *quid pro quo.*

(c) Trover

About the same time that assumpsit split off from trespass on the case, trover also did so. Trover originally provided an action against the finder of lost goods who used or disposed of the goods instead of returning them. Courts then allowed trover to be used against any person who obtained possession of another's personal property by any means and then (1) sold or used it without the consent of the owner or (2) refused to deliver it when demanded.

In trover, the plaintiff recovered as damages the entire value of the chattel at the time and place of the wrongful act of conversion (a substantial interference with the plaintiff's "dominion" over the property). The plaintiff did not recover for the act of taking as in trespass (the actual harm to the chattel and loss of its use).[109]

---

107. *See* DAN B. DOBBS, LAW OF REMEDIES § 4.2(3), at 385-88 (2d student ed. 1993).

108. *See* JOSEPH H. KOFFLER & ALISON REPPY, HANDBOOK OF COMMON LAW PLEADING § 173, at 340 (1969).

109. *Id.* § 97, at 207.

When the defendant had satisfied the judgment in trover, the defendant received title to the converted chattel. Trover thus amounted to a "forced sale."[110]

Illustration 1-32. Assume that *D* found *P's* cart on the side of the road and that *D* refused to return it to *P*. *P* could sue in detinue. In detinue, the defendant had the option of returning the cart or paying its value to the plaintiff. Furthermore, in detinue, *P* might have to accept the return of the cart even if it was damaged. More likely, if *P* wanted the cart back, *P* would use replevin.[111] If *P* did not want it back, *P* would sue in trover. In trover, *P* would recover the value of the cart at the time and place of its conversion.

* * * * *

When the defendant secured possession of a chattel by a trespass, the plaintiff could elect between trover and trespass. Furthermore, if the converter had sold the chattel, the plaintiff could *waive the tort* (trespass) and sue in general assumpsit to recover the proceeds of the sale.[112]

Illustration 1-33. Assume that *D* stole *P's* horse, which was worth $100 at that time. Assume that the price of the horse then rose and that *D* was able to sell it to *C* for $200. *P* could sue in general assumpsit to recover the entire $200 which, in good conscience, belonged to *P*. *P's* pleading would use the common count of "money had and received."[113]

(d) Ejectment

Around the year 1500, ejectment branched off from trespass. Ejectment became the common means of establishing title and recovering possession of land. The reasons for its success included the availability of a jury trial and the more efficient procedure offered by the trespass action.[114] Originally, a lessee used ejectment to recover for damages resulting from an ouster from an estate for a term of years. Through an elaborate fiction, courts allowed plaintiffs to use ejectment to recover not only possession of a term, but also to assert the right of possession based upon title to a freehold estate (one for life or in fee simple).

Illustration 1-34. Assume that *D* was in possession of a tract of land and claimed to own it in fee simple. *P* also claimed to own the same land in fee simple. Because ejectment was technically available only to a tenant for a term of years, *P* would pretend that the land had been demised (leased) a few days earlier to John Doe. An action would then be commenced in John Doe's name. Doe's action would allege an entry, lease, and ouster by a fictitious "casual ejector," Richard Roe. *P's*

---

110. *See* DAN B. DOBBS, THE LAW OF TORTS § 59, at 121-22 (2000).

111. *See* subsection D(3)*(b)* (discussing detinue) and subsection D(3)*(c)(ii) supra* (discussing replevin).

112. *See* Lamine v. Dorrell, 92 Eng. Rep. 303 (K.B. 1706) (recognizing waiver of tort and suit in assumpsit); *see also* DAN B. DOBBS, LAW OF REMEDIES § 4.2(3), at 388-90 (2d student ed. 1993); JOSEPH H. KOFFLER & ALISON REPPY, HANDBOOK OF COMMON LAW PLEADING § 176, at 351-52 (1969).

113. For a discussion of the common counts, see Chapter 6(A)(2) *infra* ("Stating the Plaintiff's Claim in the Declaration").

114. Real actions such as a writ of right, an assize of novel disseisin, and the writ of entry used a "highly technical system of pleading which [set] many traps for the litigant" and were extremely slow. FREDERIC W. MAITLAND, THE FORMS OF ACTION AT COMMON LAW 46 (1936); *see also* JOSEPH H. KOFFLER & ALISON REPPY, HANDBOOK OF COMMON LAW PLEADING § 10, at 47 (1969) (noting that there were about sixty ancient real actions, "the distinction between them being highly technical and refined"); section D(3)*(a) supra* ("Real Actions").

title would also be alleged. Notice would then be given to the actual tenant (*D*) by the casual ejector (the fictitious Richard Roe). This notice offered *D* the opportunity to defend. If *D* wanted to defend, *D* would appear and ask to be substituted.[115] By means of a court rule (the "Common Consent Rule"), *D* would be substituted for Roe only if *D* consented to admit the entry, lease, and ouster. This consent left the issue of title between *P* and *D* as the only issue to be tried.[116] If *D* refused to defend, default would be entered in favor of the fictitious lessee and the plaintiff. The sheriff would then dispossess *D* pursuant to a writ of execution.[117] *D* thus had no practical choice but to enter the suit and defend on the ground that *D*, and not *P*, had title.

5. Modes of Trial Under the Writ System

One early mode of trial in England was the *ordeal*.[118] Accused persons who persisted in maintaining their innocence would be bound by a rope and let down into water. If the water accepted them (*i.e.*, they sank), they would be deemed innocent and, ideally, pulled from the water in time to be saved. If the water rejected them (*i.e.*, they floated), they would be deemed guilty. This mode of trial was abolished by the Lateran Council in 1215.[119]

Another early mode of trial, *battle*, was introduced by the Normans. It permitted litigants to challenge adverse witnesses to defend their veracity using combat. Certain witnesses could employ "champions" to represent them. These witnesses included women, infants, and persons over sixty years of age. The power to appoint champions was later extended to able-bodied litigants.[120]

Wager of law (also called "*compurgation*"), another early mode of trial, required one of the parties to swear a formal oath to the justice or injustice of the opposing party's claim and to produce several "oath helpers," usually twelve. The oath helpers did not swear to the facts. Instead, the oath helpers swore that a party's oath was trustworthy. A party lost if a party was unable to get the required number of oath helpers. A party also lost if the party or any of the oath helpers made an error in the formal oath.[121]

A legal historian has observed that "if we are to understand the history of the forms of action, we must be mindful of these things; a long chapter that might

---

115. The action would be styled *Doe ex dem.* (ex demissione, meaning "upon the demise") *P v. D. See generally* David Mellinkoff, *Who Is "John Doe"?* 12 UCLA L. REV. 79 (1964).

116. JOSEPH H. KOFFLER & ALISON REPPY, HANDBOOK OF COMMON LAW PLEADING § 106, at 229-30 (1969); *see also* FREDERIC W. MAITLAND, THE FORMS OF ACTION AT COMMON LAW 47-48 (1936).

117. A writ of execution evidenced the plaintiff's right to possession of the property and directed the sheriff to put the plaintiff in possession. When the plaintiff secured a money judgment in a common-law action, the writ of execution evidenced the "debt" that the defendant owed to the plaintiff. In that situation, the writ directed the sheriff to seize and sell the defendant's property to satisfy the debt (judgment). *See* BERNARD C. GAVIT, CASES AND MATERIALS ON AN INTRODUCTION TO LAW AND THE JUDICIAL PROCESS 11 (1936).

118. *See* THEODORE F.T. PLUCKNETT, A CONCISE HISTORY OF THE COMMON LAW 114 (5th ed. 1956).

119. *See* FREDERIC W. MAITLAND, THE FORMS OF ACTION AT COMMON LAW 14 (1936) ("We must not suppose that the unreasonableness of these archaic institutions was suddenly perceived; . . . the remembrance of the ordeal was dear to the people; they would 'swim a witch' long centuries after the Lateran Council . . . .").

120. *See* 1 WILLIAM S. HOLDSWORTH, A HISTORY OF ENGLISH LAW 140-41 (1903).

121. *See id.* at 138; 1 FREDERICK POLLOCK & FREDERIC W. MAITLAND, THE HISTORY OF ENGLISH LAW 38-39 (2d rev. ed. 1968).

be entitled 'Dodges to evade Wager of Battle', a still longer chapter, 'Dodges to evade Wager of Law'."[122] Thus, much of the development of the forms of action is attributable to the desire to secure a trial by jury, which was available in trespass and its derivatives. Although the jury trial did not take the form it does today,[123] it nevertheless provided a more rational method of trial.

Illustration 1-35. On the facts of *Illustration 1-32*, detinue and trover were concurrent forms of action. *P* would surely sue in trover because, *inter alia*, wager of law was available in detinue, at the defendant's option. As a derivative of trespass (on the case), trover provided a jury trial.

6. Development of Equity Jurisdiction

"Equity" was another important aspect of the traditional English system.[124] Equity jurisdiction and procedure have significantly influenced modern procedural reform. The English chancellor, the king's secretary, prepared and issued the original writs by which actions were commenced in the three royal courts.[125] In this capacity, the chancellor presided over a staff of professional clerks who drafted and issued the writs. This writ-issuing function allowed the chancellor to develop a system of courts (separate from the three royal courts) ultimately known as "equity" courts. Like the development of the common-law forms of action, the development of "equity" courts from "common-law" or "law" courts did not occur in a planned fashion. Rather, a separate equity system emerged as a result of the slow disappearance of "equitable powers" from the common-law courts.

As the practice in the common-law courts became less flexible, the royal courts became unable to supply the quality of relief litigants desired in all cases. Lawyers began to apply to the chancellor for the desired relief. The new procedures and judicial machinery brought to England at the Norman Conquest were, in a sense, thought to be the king's private property. Unlike the preexisting local courts, they were not part of the public machinery of the state to which individuals might apply to vindicate their private interests.[126] The procedures were thus available at the king's discretion and applied only to those cases that interested the king.

Linked with the specific procedures and judicial machinery of the royal courts was a particular conception of the king. The king was regarded not only as "the lord paramount of the realm," but also as owing a duty to the country to preserve order and see that justice was done.[127] This duty, coupled with the king's prerogative power, was an early precursor to equity. This early power, however,

---

122. FREDERIC W. MAITLAND, THE FORMS OF ACTION AT COMMON LAW 14 (1936).

123. *See* Chapter 4(A) *infra* ("Transitory and Local Actions") and Chapter 11(C) *infra* ("Trial by Jury in Anglo-American Law").

124. The term "equity" is used in Anglo-American law in different senses. In a "general juristic" sense, equity is sometimes referred to as the power to do justice in the individual case. In a more technical sense, however, equity refers to the system of law—substantive, remedial, and procedural—that was applied by the English chancery courts and their successors. *See* HENRY L. MCCLINTOCK, HANDBOOK OF THE PRINCIPLES OF EQUITY 1 (2d ed. 1948).

125. *See* section D(2)-(3) *supra* ("Issuance of Writs by the Chancellor" and "The Initial Development of the Forms of Action").

126. *See* George B. Adams, *The Origin of English Equity*, 16 COLUM. L. REV. 87, 89 (1916).

127. *See id.* at 89-91.

was originally a part of the ordinary justice provided in the royal courts. All common-law "actions in the eleventh and twelfth centuries . . . began with a petition asking the king to interfere to secure justice where it would not be secured by the ordinary and existing processes of law."[128]

At first, the chancellor freely issued the writs permitting actions in the royal courts. The courts granted flexible relief—later called "equitable relief" or "specific relief"—suited to the nature of the individual case. This relief included orders compelling the defendant to do or refrain from doing certain acts (in addition to granting money damages, the remedy most often associated with the common-law courts today).[129] As the forms of action developed, however, the common-law system became inflexible. Specific relief (as opposed to money damages) became the exception rather than the rule.[130]

In 1258, the Provisions of Oxford exacerbated this lack of flexibility. The Provisions forbade the chancellor from framing new writs without permission from the king and the king's council, which was a collection of the officers of the state and other advisers of the king.[131] In 1285, the Statute of Westminster II somewhat improved the circumstances. It allowed the law to develop through an expansion of the trespass action.[132] Nevertheless, specific relief was largely eliminated from common-law remedies. This development resulted in many cases in which royal courts provided no relief or only ineffective relief.[133] The decay in the equitable powers of the common-law courts was slow and was not complete until after the middle of the fourteenth century.[134]

The inflexibility of the common law prompted lawyers to apply to the "reserve of justice in the king"—*i.e.*, the power to do justice in all cases in which justice was demanded.[135] These applications were made to the king's council.[136] Because the chancellor was the prime minister and an especially learned member of the council, the chancellor read and considered a large share of the petitions.[137]

About the middle of the fourteenth century, the Chancery was recognized as a separate court. The chancellor, however, was still acting essentially as the representative of the council, not on his own authority.[138] The cases submitted to the Chancery were ones in which the ordinary mechanisms of the common-law courts would not work, so-called cases of "outrage." In these cases, petitioners alleged that

---

128. *Id.* at 91.

129. WILLIAM F. WALSH, A TREATISE ON EQUITY 5-6 (1930). *Compare* George B. Adams, *The Origins of English Equity*, 16 COLUM. L. REV. 87 (1916) *with* William S. Holdsworth, *The Relation of the Equity Administered by the Common Law Judges to the Equity Administered by the Chancellor*, 26 YALE L.J. 1 (1916), George B. Adams, *The Continuity of English Equity*, 26 YALE L.J. 550 (1917) *and* THEODORE F.T. PLUCKNETT, A CONCISE HISTORY OF THE COMMON LAW 681-82 (5th ed. 1956).

130. *See* WILLIAM F. WALSH, A TREATISE ON EQUITY 7-8 (1930).

131. *Id.* at 8; *see* subsection D(4) *supra* ("Subsequent Development of the Forms of Action").

132. *See* WILLIAM F. WALSH, A HISTORY OF ANGLO-AMERICAN LAW 70 (2d ed. 1932); *see* subsection D(4) *supra* ("Subsequent Development of the Forms of Action").

133. *See* WILLIAM F. WALSH, A TREATISE ON EQUITY 10 (1930).

134. *See id.*

135. *See* FREDERIC W. MAITLAND, EQUITY 3 (1929); WILLIAM F. WALSH, A TREATISE ON EQUITY 12 (1930).

136. *See* WILLIAM F. WALSH, A TREATISE ON EQUITY 13 (1930).

137. *See* FREDERIC W. MAITLAND, EQUITY 3 (1929).

138. *See* WILLIAM F. WALSH, A TREATISE ON EQUITY 16 (1930).

they were poor, that their adversaries were rich or powerful, and that their adversaries would intimidate or corrupt the jury.[139]

In the fifteenth century, these cases of outrage continued to occupy a large part of the chancellor's business. They diminished in the latter part of the century "as a more settled state of law and order was established."[140] Moreover, the power of the chancellor to interfere in cases of outrage provoked both the common-law judges and parliament. The chancellor "[was] warned off the field of common law—he [was] not to hear cases which might go to the ordinary courts, he [was] not to make himself a judge of torts and contracts, of property in lands and goods."[141]

However, the chancellor's power could not be dispensed with entirely because the chancellor had begun to do some valuable things, especially the enforcement of uses (trusts).[142] In the fourteenth century, certain landowners had conveyed their lands to friends to hold for their own use and benefit or for some third person.[143] These uses (trusts) were utilized for several reasons. For example, the common law did not permit disposition of land by will at that time. Uses (trusts) could evade this restriction. Legal title could be transferred to a trustee who would hold the title for the benefit of the landowner for a term measured by the landowner's life. Upon the landowner's death, the trustee would transfer the land according to the landowner's will. The same process of transferring title could also be used to avoid creditors or forfeiture.[144]

Such landowners, however, faced a potentially serious problem. If the trustee turned out to be dishonest, the common-law courts would not recognize any rights in the landowner (called the *cestui que use*) because the trustee possessed the legal title. The chancellor protected the *cestui que use* as a matter of conscience—because "a man ought to keep his promises, and should not be allowed profit by his own breach of faith."[145] The chancellor's enforcement of uses "assured the development of equity as a separate system outside of the common law."[146]

In addition to enforcing uses, the chancellor acted in other cases in which common-law relief was unavailable or inadequate.

Illustration 1-36. In the fifteenth century, the form of action known as covenant would lie for breach of a contract under seal. Debt would lie if an obligation to pay a specific sum existed. In the absence of a debt for a fixed sum, no remedy existed for breach of a contract not under seal. The chancellor would give relief in such cases either by awarding damages or by decreeing specific performance. In the sixteenth century, the form of action of assumpsit developed in

---

139. *See* FREDERIC W. MAITLAND, EQUITY 4 (1929); STROUD F.C. MILSOM, HISTORICAL FOUNDATIONS OF THE COMMON LAW 74-75 (1969).

140. WILLIAM F. WALSH, A TREATISE ON EQUITY 18 (1930).

141. FREDERIC W. MAITLAND, EQUITY 6 (1929).

142. *Id.*

143. *See* SHELDON F. KURTZ, MOYNIHAN'S INTRODUCTION TO THE LAW OF REAL PROPERTY 231-32 (5th ed. 2011).

144. The ability to avoid forfeiture was particularly important during the War of the Roses. *See* WILLIAM F. WALSH, A HISTORY OF ANGLO-AMERICAN LAW 198-99 (2d ed. 1932). For an excellent treatment of the relationship between law and equity during the Tudor period and a critical examination of the justification by Christopher St. Germain for equitable intervention to mitigate the "rigors" of the common law, see Georg Behrens, *An Early Tudor Debate on the Relation Between Law and Equity*, 19 J. LEGAL HIST. 143 (1998).

145. SHELDON F. KURTZ, MOYNIHAN'S INTRODUCTION TO THE LAW OF REAL PROPERTY 233 (5th ed. 2011).

146. WILLIAM F. WALSH, A TREATISE ON EQUITY 19 (1930).

the "law" courts to provide adequate relief by way of damages in simple contract cases. Equity then relinquished its jurisdiction over such matters. Equity retained only such power as was necessary to decree specific performance when damages constituted an inadequate remedy.[147]

* * * * *

Five other principal areas existed in which the chancellor gave relief because of inadequacies in the remedy at law. First, equity would provide relief when the owner of chattels sought relief against a person in possession of the chattels and either no relief or inadequate relief at law existed.

Second, equity would provide relief in certain cases involving fraud and mistake. For example, the common-law courts would enforce contracts under seal even when they had been procured by fraud. Equity would provide relief from such contracts.

Third, equity in the fifteenth century granted relief against penalties enforced by the common-law courts. For example, equity would reduce a bond for double the amount of a debt (enforceable at law) to the amount of the debt.

Fourth, equity would act when the petitioner sought an injunction to restrain waste or some other wrongful act.[148]

Fifth, equity would also enforce assignments of "choses in action" (the right to sue to recover a debt or claim). Such assignments were not enforceable in the common-law courts.[149] Indeed, during the fifteenth century, equity "interfered to give relief in many other cases where because of technicality of procedure, defective methods of proof, and other shortcomings in the common law, adequate relief could be had only in equity."[150] By the early part of the sixteenth century, the "Chancery had developed into a distinct court, primarily of equity, and equity as administered by this court, had grown to be a great system of law, outside of the common law, competing with it in many ways."[151]

As might be expected, the common-law courts came to resent competition from equity courts. The chancellor had been warned off the field of the common law at one time. Thus, the chancellor's powers had been achieved largely by indirection. The equity courts did not act in direct opposition to the common law. Instead, equity courts enforced their decrees on the defendant's person. This mode of enforcement contrasted sharply with the common-law "in rem" mode of execution against the defendant's property by the sheriff.[152]

This conflict was finally resolved during the reign of James I (1603-1625) in the Coke-Ellesmere dispute (so-named after Chief Justice Coke and Lord Chancellor Ellesmere). The equity courts enjoined the enforcement of the judgments of the common-law courts under certain circumstances—for example, when a judgment had been procured by fraud. Equity courts used their "contempt power" to imprison persons who enforced such common-law judgments. The

---

147. *See id.* at 23-25.

148. Such cases, though not common, did occur, though equitable relief against torts developed mainly in the eighteenth and nineteenth centuries. *Id.* at 27.

149. *See id.*

150. *Id.*

151. *Id.*

152. *See id.*

common-law courts, however, began releasing those persons on habeas corpus.[153] Worse, Chief Justice Coke asserted that petitioners in equity who obtained such injunctions were violating the Statutes of Praemunire. These statutes made it illegal to question the judgments of the king's courts in other courts.[154]

The King appointed Francis Bacon to head a commission to resolve the conflict. The commission approved the traditional formula. The equity courts could enjoin a person from enforcing a common-law judgment, but the action did not affect the judgment itself or act directly against the common-law court that rendered it. This formula effectively resolved the dispute in favor of the equity courts.[155] "From this time forward the Chancery had the upper hand. It did not claim to be superior to the courts of law, but it could prevent men from going to those courts, whereas those courts could not prevent men from going to it."[156]

7. Equitable Relief

The victory of the Chancery cleared the way for a highly developed system of equitable relief.[157] In contrast to the procedure in the common-law courts, the final disposition of an equity case took the form of a *decree* rather than a *judgment*. Ordinarily, the decree ordered the defendant to do or stop doing some specific act. Under the "clean-up" doctrine, equity avoided a multiplicity of suits by awarding money damages that would otherwise have to be recovered in a separate common-law action. As a result, the plaintiff did not have to bring an additional action in the common-law courts.[158] Failure to obey an equity decree was punishable by *contempt* (a fine or imprisonment). Thus, the enforcement of equity decrees differed from that of common-law judgments (which were enforced by a writ of execution).[159]

8. Colonial Procedure and Procedure After Independence

Compared to the English system, the early history of the American colonies reveals a far less formal approach to litigation. In the earliest stages, the colonies were relatively primitive societies. Consequently, it was difficult for them to incorporate substantive or procedural common-law principles except in the most general way. The English common law was a sophisticated body of principles that had evolved with English society. Implementing that body of law required a trained lawyer class as well as the accouterments of that class—law books and institutions

---

153. *See, e.g.*, Courtney v. Glanvil, 79 Eng. Rep. 294, 294-95 (K.B. 1615).

154. These statutes had originally been aimed at the Papal curia. FREDERIC W. MAITLAND, EQUITY 10 (1929).

155. The controversy and the judgment of the king are described in 21 Eng. Rep. 576-88. *See generally* HENRY L. MCCLINTOCK, HANDBOOK OF THE PRINCIPLES OF EQUITY 11 (2d ed. 1948).

156. FREDERIC W. MAITLAND, EQUITY 10 (1929).

157. Equity built this system upon the foundations laid in the fourteenth and fifteenth centuries.

158. *See* Chapter 7(A) *infra* ("Joinder of Claims by Plaintiffs at Common Law and in Equity") and *Illustration 7-6 infra*.

159. *See* BERNARD C. GAVIT, CASES AND MATERIALS ON AN INTRODUCTION TO LAW AND THE JUDICIAL PROCESS 9 (1936); CHRISTOPHER C. LANGDELL, A SUMMARY OF EQUITY PLEADING xxii-xxiii (1877).

suitable for legal training. These were largely absent in the colonies. Indeed, a general hostility existed toward lawyers during the colonial period.

This hostility, coupled with the primitive state of colonial legal institutions, resulted in an attempt to codify the law. The codifications departed from the English common law in many respects. Furthermore, they did not cover every matter that came to be the subject of a dispute. Although the common law was declared to be subsidiary law in cases not covered by local codes, the absence of a trained lawyer class rendered such declarations largely ineffective. As a result, the courts had great discretion in supplying a rule that satisfied local conditions in areas not covered by the codes. Therefore, while the English common law was sometimes used as a model, it played a relatively minor role in the early administration of colonial justice.[160]

Judicial proceedings were informal during this early period, especially in the "popular courts" that grew up in the colonies. These courts were composed of a relatively large number of judges. Trials resembled a community deliberation. The judges of these courts were not trained professionals. Instead, they were representatives of the community who enforced a popular sense of justice and local custom. In this way, the popular courts were reminiscent of the very early English courts. Pleading was simple compared to the English system. In the popular courts, litigants pleaded their own cases. Although the labels of the English forms of action were often used, the English rigidity of enforcing the forms was absent. In general, the jury system was retained in the colonies, sometimes with modifications.[161]

The administration of equity jurisprudence varied widely. Sometimes, the governor and council of a colony administered it. At other times, the colonial legislatures administered it. Special courts were sometimes given equity powers. At other times, equity powers were delegated to the regular courts. Despite this irregular pattern, the need for Chancery power was recognized. Before the Revolutionary War, courts of equity—or at least courts with equity powers—existed in some form in every colony.[162]

By 1800, the colonies—now states—had reached a more highly developed stage. State legal systems increasingly absorbed common-law institutions at both the substantive and procedural levels. By the nineteenth century, the United States had incorporated much of the technicality of English procedure. Although some procedural reforms had occurred in America, significant reform of the common-law system did not come until the middle of the nineteenth century. In addition, the structure of the state appellate courts did not resemble modern systems (in which a single court of last resort exists whose principal function is to review inferior court decisions).[163] Rather, both "superior" and "inferior" courts were often trial

---

160. *See* Paul S. Reinsch, *The English Common Law in the Early American Colonies*, *in* 1 SELECT ESSAYS IN ANGLO-AMERICAN LEGAL HISTORY 367 (1907).

161. *See id.* at 411-12.

162. *See generally* Sydney G. Fisher, *The Administration of Equity Through Common Law Forms*, 1 L.Q. REV. 455 (1885); Ellen E. Sward, *A History of the Civil Trial in the United States*, 51 U. KAN L. REV. 347 (2003); William F. Walsh, *The Growing Function of Equity in the Development of the Law*, *in* 3 LAW: A CENTURY OF PROGRESS 139, 145-55 (1937); Solon D. Wilson, *Courts of Chancery in America—Colonial Period*, 18 AM. L. REV. 226 (1884); Edwin H. Woodruff, *Chancery in Massachusetts*, 5 L.Q. REV. 370 (1889).

163. *See* WILFRED J. RITZ, REWRITING THE HISTORY OF THE JUDICIARY ACT OF 1789, at 27-52 (Wythe Holt & J.H. LaRue eds., 1993).

courts. Successive trials whose aim was to reach the single "correct result" were common.[164] In these proceedings, judges, lawyers, and juries all conducted a search for "the true rule of law."[165] Modern hierarchical systems of appellate review were not established until the nineteenth (and in some instances the twentieth) century.[166]

As part of the adoption of English procedure, equity jurisprudence had become a fairly regular feature of American judicial practice.[167] Unlike the English system, however, the same court that exercised common-law power often also exercised equity jurisdiction in America—though the common-law and equity activities of the courts were kept formally distinct.[168] In a few states, law and equity courts were separate. In two, Pennsylvania and Massachusetts, equity did not exist in any ordinary form.[169]

9. The Field Code and Reform of Procedure in the States

The first significant reform in American procedure came in New York around the middle of the nineteenth century. The New York Constitution of 1846 abolished the New York Court of Chancery.[170] The constitution also directed the Legislature, at its first session after the adoption of the constitution, to appoint three commissioners. Their duty "shall be to revise, reform, simplify, and abridge the rules of practice, pleading, forms, and proceedings of the courts . . . of this State, and to report thereon to the legislature, subject to their adoption and modification from time to time."[171]

The Legislature appointed the commission, which rendered its report in 1848.[172] In accord with the commissioners' recommendations, the Legislature enacted the *Field Code*, so-named after David Dudley Field, the most prominent commissioner.[173] The Field Code embodied numerous reforms, including (1) the merger of law and equity, (2) the simplification and limitation of the pleading process, (3) the broadening of claim and party joinder, and (4) the liberalization of amendments to pleadings (and the corresponding deemphasis of variances between pleading and proof). By 1900, almost thirty states had adopted some version of the Field Code. More adopted it in the twentieth century.[174]

Despite the laudable aims of the "codes," reform did not, and in certain respects has not yet, come easily. For example, although the codes merged law and equity, troublesome questions remained about the interaction between the rules that were formerly administered in separate systems. Of particular concern was (1) a

---

164. *Id.* at 35.

165. *See id.* at 28-30.

166. *See id.* at 41-49; *see generally* ROSCOE POUND, ORGANIZATION OF COURTS (1940).

167. *See* William F. Walsh, *The Growing Function of Equity in the Development of the Law*, *in* 3 LAW: A CENTURY OF PROGRESS 139, 151 (1937).

168. *See id.*

169. *See* Sydney G. Fisher, *The Administration of Equity Through Common Law Forms*, 1 L.Q. REV. 455 (1885); Edwin H. Woodruff, *Chancery in Massachusetts*, 5 L.Q. REV. 370 (1889).

170. N.Y. CONST. OF 1846, art. VI, § 3.

171. *Id.* § 24.

172. FIRST REPORT OF THE NEW YORK COMMISSIONERS ON PRACTICE AND PLEADINGS (1848).

173. Act of Apr. 12, 1848, ch. 379, 1848 N.Y. Laws 497.

174. *See* GEOFFREY C. HAZARD, JR. ET AL., CIVIL PROCEDURE § 1.7, at 22 (6th ed. 2011); ROBERT W. MILLAR, CIVIL PROCEDURE OF THE TRIAL COURT IN HISTORICAL PERSPECTIVE 54-55 (1952).

party's constitutional right to a jury trial in a merged system and (2) the status of rules previously used to determine when a court would grant equitable relief.[175]

10. Early Procedure in the Federal Courts

Article III of the U.S. Constitution vests the judicial power of the federal government in "one supreme Court, and in such inferior Courts as the Congress may from time to time ordain and establish."[176] The Constitution extends that power to "all Cases, in Law and Equity" within certain limited categories.[177] In 1789, Congress implemented the provisions of Article III by establishing a Supreme Court and a system of circuit and district courts.[178] Congress has always directly regulated many procedural subjects. For example, Congress has always regulated in detail subject-matter jurisdiction and venue, which are treated in Chapters 2 and 4. Of primary interest here, however, is the historical development of the procedural rules of the federal trial courts. These rules govern the manner of conducting the civil actions which Congress has authorized the federal courts to hear.

Law and equity were not administered in separate federal courts. Nonetheless, the traditional distinction between equity and common-law jurisdiction was maintained in the federal courts until 1938. The First Process Act (1789) provided

> [t]hat until further provision shall be made . . . the forms of writs and executions, except their style, and modes of process and rates of fees, except fees to judges, in the circuit and district courts, in suits at common law, shall be the same in each state respectively as are now [1789] used or allowed in the supreme courts of the same. And the forms and modes of proceedings in causes of equity . . . shall be according to the course of the civil law.[179]

In 1792, Congress modified this provision. Although the provision remained the same in suits at common law, procedure in equity cases was henceforth declared to be "according to the principles, rules and usages which belong to courts of equity . . . as contra-distinguished from courts of common law."[180] However, Congress made both common-law and equity cases in federal courts subject to a rulemaking power in the U.S. Supreme Court and the lower federal courts.[181]

---

175. *See* DAN B. DOBBS, LAW OF REMEDIES § 2.6 (2d student ed. 1993); *see also* Glen S. Koppel, *Toward a New Federalism in State Civil Justice: Developing a Uniform Code of State Civil Procedure Through a Collaborative Rule-Making Process,* 58 VAND. L. REV. 1167 (2005) (arguing that the top-down model for developing uniform state procedural rules on the basis of the Federal Rules of Civil Procedure has failed and arguing for a new approach to developing uniform state procedural rules); Thomas O. Main, *Reconsidering Procedural Conformity Statutes,* 35 W. ST. U. L. REV. 75 (2007). Michael Moffitt, *Customizing Litigation: The Case for Making Civil Procedure Negotiable,* 75 GEO. WASH . L. REV. 461 (2007) (arguing in favor of treating procedural rules as default rules from which parties can mutually negotiate deviations).

176. U.S. CONST. art. III, § 1.

177. *Id.* § 2.

178. Judiciary Act of 1789, ch. 20, §§ 1-4, 1 Stat. 73, 73-75.

179. Act of Sept. 29, 1789, ch. 21, § 2, 1 Stat. 93, 93-94.

180. Act of May 8, 1792, ch. 36, § 2, 1 Stat. 275, 276.

181. *See id.*; *see also* Judiciary Act of 1789, ch. 20, § 17, 1 Stat. 73, 83; Act of Aug. 23, 1842, ch. 188, § 6, 5 Stat. 516, 518.

The result of these process acts was to establish a *static conformity* to state procedure in common-law cases. Thus, the federal courts were obligated to use the procedural law of the state in which they were sitting as the procedural law appeared in 1789. Even though state procedural laws might change, as indeed they did, federal procedure continued to exist as it had in the states in 1789. This arrangement was made even worse because the original process acts did not apply to states admitted to the Union after 1789. Congress partially remedied the latter difficulty by enacting process acts in 1828 and 1842. These acts, however, primarily dealt with the problem of newly admitted states. For the most part, the federal courts in the older states were bound by the 1789 procedures.[182]

The courts did not use their rulemaking power to minimize the difficulties of static conformity, though they certainly could have. In the Conformity Act of 1872, Congress repealed the rulemaking authority and established a *dynamic conformity* to state procedures in common-law actions.[183] Thus, in common-law cases, federal procedure conformed to state procedures that existed at the time the federal court heard the case. This dynamic conformity lasted until the Federal Rules of Civil Procedure were adopted in 1938.

Federal equity procedure was quite different. The process acts did not require conformity, static or otherwise, to state procedure in equity cases. Furthermore, the U.S. Supreme Court showed no reluctance to utilize its rulemaking power for equity cases. The Court promulgated equity rules in 1822, 1842, and 1912.[184] In 1915, Congress provided that "equitable defenses" could be raised in actions at law. Congress also abolished the objection that a party had brought the suit on the wrong "side" of the court. Prior to this change, the objection would have caused a dismissal of the action.[185] With a few modifications, the 1912 equity rules lasted until the Federal Rules of Civil Procedure merged law and equity in 1938.

11. Promulgation of the Federal Rules of Civil Procedure

Despite dynamic conformity and extensive use of the rulemaking power for equity cases, widespread dissatisfaction with the federal procedural scheme remained. By the twentieth century, most states had established a uniform procedure for law and equity cases. In addition, interpretation of the Conformity Act produced numerous areas in which the federal courts could disregard state procedure in favor of independent federal practices.[186] The result was a system that did not achieve uniformity between state and federal courts in the same state. Nor was there uniformity between federal courts sitting in different states. Under the American Bar Association's leadership, a movement to reform federal procedure finally

---

182. *See* Act of May 19, 1828, ch. 68, 4 Stat. 278; Act of Aug. 1, 1842, ch. 109, 5 Stat. 499.

183. Act of June 1, 1872, ch. 255, § 5, 17 Stat. 196, 197.

184. In 1822, the Court promulgated 33 equity rules. 20 U.S. (7 Wheat.) xvii-xxi (1822). In 1842, the Court replaced the 1822 rules with 92 rules. 42 U.S. (1 How.) xli-lxx (1842). The 1842 rules, in turn, were replaced by 81 rules in 1912. 226 U.S. 627, 649-73 (1912).

185. Law and Equity Act, ch. 90, 38 Stat. 956 (1915).

186. *See* RICHARD H. FALON ET AL., HART & WECHSLER'S THE FEDERAL COURTS AND THE FEDERAL SYSTEM 539 (6th ed. 2003).

produced the Rules Enabling Act of 1934.[187] Pursuant to this authority, the U.S. Supreme Court appointed an Advisory Committee to draft new rules.[188] After the legal profession examined the Committee's proposed rules, some changes were made. The Court approved the Federal Rules of Civil Procedure with the changes. The Rules took effect on September 16, 1938.[189]

The principal purposes of the Federal Rules of Civil Procedure were similar to those of the codes: (1) the merger of law and equity, (2) the simplification and limitation of pleading, (3) the broadening of claim and party joinder, (4) the liberalization of amendments to pleadings, and (5) the deemphasis of variances between pleading and proof. The Federal Rules differ in several important respects from the codes in how they achieve these purposes. In addition, the Federal Rules established comprehensive procedures for "discovery" before trial—a major improvement over the limited discovery provided under the codes.[190] The Federal Rules are designed to be "trans-substantive" in nature: that is, the Rules govern procedures in all civil actions, regardless of the substantive nature of the claims or defenses in the suit.[191]

12. Amendments to Federal Rules of Civil Procedure

Since 1938, the Federal Rules of Civil Procedure have been amended numerous times on a piecemeal basis. Major changes included the 1966 amendment of Rule 23 dealing with class actions and Rule 19 dealing with required joinder of parties; the 1970 amendment of the discovery rules; the 1980 amendment of Rule 26 empowering the court to require lawyers to participate in a discovery conference to narrow discovery and to lead to a discovery plan and timetable; further amendments of the discovery process in 1983, 1993, 2000, 2006, and 2010; the

---

187. Rules Enabling Act of 1934, ch. 651, 48 Stat. 1064 (codified as amended at 28 U.S.C. §§ 2072-2074). This Act provided

> [Sec. 1.] . . . [T]he Supreme Court of the United States shall have the power to prescribe, by general rules, for the district courts of the United States and for the courts of the District of Columbia, the forms of process, writs, pleadings, and motions, and the practice and procedure in civil actions at law. Said rules shall neither abridge, enlarge, nor modify the substantive rights of any litigant. They shall take effect six months after their promulgation, and thereafter all laws in conflict therewith shall be of no further force or effect.
>
> Sec. 2. The court may at any time unite the general rules prescribed by it for cases in equity with those in actions at law so as to secure one form of civil action and procedure for both: *Provided, however,* That in such union of rules the right of trial by jury as at common law and declared by the [S]eventh [A]mendment to the Constitution shall be preserved to the parties inviolate. . . .

188. 295 U.S. 774 (1935).

189. *See* 308 U.S. 645, 645-766 (1937).

190. *See* FLEMING JAMES, JR. ET AL., CIVIL PROCEDURE § 1.8, at 25 (5th ed. 2001); *see also* David Marcus, *The Federal Rules of Civil Procedure and Legal Realism as a Jurisprudence of Law Reform*, 44 GA. L. REV. 433 (2010); Stephen N. Subrin, *How Equity Conquered the Common Law: The Federal Rules of Civil Procedure in Perspective*, 135 U. PA. L. REV. 1873 (1987).

191. *See* Richard L. Marcus, *Of Babies and Bathwater: The Prospects for Procedural Progress*, 59 BROOK. L. REV. 761, 776-79 (1993); *see also* Thomas O. Main, *Traditional Equity and Contemporary Procedure,* 78 WASH. L. REV. 429 (2003) (discussing how traditional equity powers can mitigate the inequitable results that can occur by the technical application of a modern procedural rule); Stephen N. Subrin, *The Limitations of Transsubstanive Procedure: An Essay on Adjusting the "One Size Fits All" Assumption*, 87 DENV. U. L. REV. 2010). *See generally* Robert G. Bone, *Who Decides? A Critical Look at Procedural Discretion,* 28 CARDOZO L. REV. 1961 (2007) (discussing the discretion of judges to design procedures for particular lawsuits); Richard L. Marcus, *Modes of Procedural Reform,* 31 HAST. INT'L & COMP. L. REV. 157 (2008); Richard Marcus, *Confessions of a Federal "Bureaucrat": The Possibilities of Perfecting Procedural Reform,* 35 W. ST. U. L. REV. 103 (2007).

amendment of Rule 15 in 1991 and again in 2009; the amendment of Rule 11 dealing with good-faith pleading in 1983 and 1993, a revision of Rule 56 dealing with summary judgment in 2010, and the amendment of 21 federal rules as part of a comprehensive "time computation project" (intended to make the method of computing time periods simpler and more consistent) in 2009.[192]

13. "Restyling" of Federal Rules of Civil Procedure

In 2007, all Federal Rules of Civil Procedure underwent a complete "restyling" to improve the formatting of the rules to achieve clearer presentation; to reduce inconsistent, ambiguous, redundant, repetitive, and inconsistent words or phrases; and to remove redundant cross-references within the rules.[193] To minimize the impact on research, the restyled rules retained their same numbers.[194] However, caution must still be exercised in conducting research because many of the restyled rules rearranged or eliminated subdivisions within particular rules.

Illustration 1-37. Federal Rule 19(a) enumerates the parties who must be joined in a lawsuit when feasible. Many court opinions frequently referred to particular types of these parties by using the relevant subdivision of Rule 19(a) that set out the circumstances when such a party must be joined. For example, prior to restyling, a person whose absence would prevent "complete relief" from being accorded among existing parties was commonly referred to as a "Rule 19(a)(1)" party. After restyling, such a person would now be a "Rule 19(a)(1)(A)" party. Similarly, prior to restyling, Rule 15(c)(3)(A) dealt with relation back of an amendment when the amendment changed the party or the naming of a party against whom a claim was asserted. That provision is now contained in restyled Rule 15(c)(1)(c).

* * * * *

The restyled rules improved their readability and removed potential ambiguities arising from inconsistent use of terminology. Furthermore, the minor errors in the restyling process are unlikely to cause any real practical difficulties.

Illustration 1-38. Prior to restyling, Federal Rule 9(a) provided that it was unnecessary to allege the capacity or authority of a party to sue or be sued or the legal existence of an entity. If a party wanted to raise such an issue, the party had to do so "by specific negative averment, which shall include such supporting particulars as are peculiarly within the pleader's knowledge."[195] Restyled Rule

---

192. These changes and numerous others are discussed at the appropriate instance in subsequent chapters.

193. *See* FED. R. CIV. P. 1 advisory committee's note to the 2007 amendment. The restyled rules break the rules down into constituent parts, use progressive indented subparagraphs, and change textual lists into vertical ones. A simple example of using consistent terminology is changing "infant" in many rules to "minor" in all of them. The restyling also removed "intensifiers"—"expressions that attempt to add emphasis, but instead state the obvious and create negative implications for other rules." As a result of restyling, "[t]he court in its discretion may" has been changed to "the court may" and "unless the order expressly directs otherwise" has been changed to "unless the court orders otherwise." *Id.*

194. *Id.* Only in one instance—the transfer of former Rule 25(d)(2) to Rule 17(d)—was a provision moved from one rule to another. *Id.*

195. FED. R. CIV. P. 9(a) (prior to the 2007 restyling). The Federal Rules carried forward the "specific negative averment" procedure that was generally employed under the codes and at the common law. 5A CHARLES ALAN WRIGHT & ARTHUR R. MILLER, FEDERAL PRACTICE AND PROCEDURE: CIVIL §1294 (3d ed. 2004).

9(a)(2) changed the method of raising a capacity issue from a "specific negative averment" to "a specific denial, which must state any supporting facts that are peculiarly within the party's knowledge."[196] Rule 8(b)(3) provides that when "[a] party that does not intend to deny all the allegations [of a pleading] must either specifically deny *designated* allegations or generally deny all except those specifically admitted."[197] Assuming that a plaintiff follows Rule 9(a) and does not allege capacity to sue in the complaint, there will be no allegations in the complaint that can be *designated* for denial. The solution here is simply to continue to raise the issue using the traditional format (a specific negative averment).

* * * * *

The Advisory Committee Notes accompanying the restyled rules repeatedly indicate that the changes in the rules were "intended to be stylistic only" and that "no changes in substantive meaning" were intended.[198] Nevertheless, language rephrasing, by its very nature, can create differences in substantive meaning and trigger possible unintended changes in the application of the rules.[199]

Illustration 1-39. An "unmatured" or "contingent" claim,[200] such as one for attorney's fees or contribution, is not a compulsory counterclaim because Rule 13(a) requires that the claim exist at the time of the serving of the pleading.[201] Prior to restyling of the Federal Rules, the lower courts were split on the issue such claims could be asserted as permissive counterclaims.[202] Prior to restyling, Rule 13(b) provided that permissive counterclaims were ones "*not* arising out of the transaction or occurrence that is the subject of the opposing party's claim."[203] Such claims obviously did arise out of the transaction or occurrence that was the subject of the opposing party's claim. Restyled Rule 13(b), however, now simply states as follows: "A pleading may state as a counterclaim against an opposing party *any claim* that is not compulsory."[204] In making this change, the Advisory Committee was clearly focused on permitting counterclaims that were recognized as two exceptions to compulsory counterclaims in Rule 13(a)(2)—the claim was already pending in another action and the opposing party sued on its claim by attachment or other process that did not establish personal jurisdiction over the pleader on that

---

196. FED. R. CIV. P. 9(a)(2).

197. FED. R. CIV. P. 8(b)(3) (emphasis added). A denial can be general or specific. A general denial controverts all the allegations of a pleading. *Id.* The prevailing view is that "an issue of capacity, authority, or legal existence cannot be raised by a general denial." 5A CHARLES ALAN WRIGHT & ARTHUR R. MILLER, FEDERAL PRACTICE AND PROCEDURE: CIVIL §1294 (3d ed. 2004).

198. *See, e g,.* FED. R. CIV. P. 1 advisory committee's note to the 2007 amendment. A few minor technical amendments were approved separately from the restyled rules, which became effective at the same time. *Id.*

199. *See, e.g.*, Edward A. Hartnett, *Against (Mere) Restyling*, 82 NOTRE DAME L. REV. 155, 156-71 (2006) (discussing "The Near Impossibility of Changing Text Without Changing Meaning," citing five examples that were identified and resolved during the comment process, and illustrating future potential problems with a further illustration in the application of Rule 68).

200. In general, a claim is "mature" only when it is presently enforceable and is not dependent on a contingency. For example, a claim for contribution, being contingent on a verdict and judgment establishing liability, is not a matured claim. *See* 20 AM. JUR. 2D *Counterclaim, Recoupment, and Setoff* § 22 (2005).

201. Federal Rule 13(a) requires that a pleader state "as a counterclaim any claim—at the time of its service—the pleader *has* against an opposing party if the claim . . . arises out of the transaction or occurrence that is the subject matter of the opposing party's claim . . . ." FED. R. CIV. P. 13(a)(1) (emphasis added).

202. Tenneco Oil Co. v. Templin, 201 Ga. App. 30, 32, 410 S.E.2d 154, 156 (1991) (so stating); *see In re* Oil Spill by Amoco Cadiz, 491 F. Supp. 161, 165 (N.D. Ill. 1979) (citing cases).

203. FED. R. CIV. P. 13(b) (prior to restyling) (emphasis added).

204. FED. R. CIV. P. 13(b) (emphasis added).

claim.[205] However, the language of the restyled rule now lends strong support that unmatured or contingent claims are also permissible. While such a result may not necessarily be incorrect, such a decision should be made consciously in light of the potential differing policy considerations involved.

14. Influence of the Federal Rules on State Court Procedure

The influence of the Federal Rules of Civil Procedure has been widespread. Every state has modified its procedures to accord with the Federal Rules in some ways. About half of the states have adopted the Federal Rules almost unchanged.[206] Furthermore, lawyers can use federal precedents as persuasive authority in construing state court rules of procedure modeled on the Federal Rules.[207] The dominance of the Federal Rules in the United States has also influenced the structure and content of the modern Civil Procedure course, which this book is designed to accompany. Consequently, while relevant common-law, equity, and code procedure is examined in later chapters, the Federal Rules constitute the main focus of each procedural topic covered in this book.

SECTION E. ALTERNATIVE DISPUTE RESOLUTION

Adjudication of disputes in civil actions described in the proceeding section is the traditional form of dispute resolution. However, parties to disputes have long had other alternatives available, such as arbitration, mediation, and negotiation. In recent years, concern has mounted about court congestion, spiraling costs, increasing delays, and other negative effects of litigation.[208] These concerns have led to an increased use of these and other means of "alternative dispute resolution" (ADR). Parties often find that these alternatives meet their need for a more satisfactory way of resolving disputes. Federal and state legislation has encouraged

---

205. The Advisory Committee Note indicates that this restyling change was made to make clear "as a matter of intended meaning and current practice" that it should be permissible for a party to "state as a permissive counterclaim a claim that does grow out of the same transaction or occurrence as an opposing party's claim even though one of the exceptions in Rule 13(a) means the claim is not a compulsory counterclaim." FED. R. CIV. P. 13 advisory committee's note to the 2007 amendment.

206. *See* CHARLES A. WRIGHT & MARY KAY KANE, HANDBOOK OF THE LAW OF FEDERAL COURTS § 62, at 431 (7th ed. 2011); John B. Oakley, *A Fresh Look at the Federal Rules in State Courts*, 3 NEV. L.J 354 (2002/2003); *cf.* Glen S. Koppel, *Toward a New Federalism in State Civil Justice: Developing a Uniform Code of State Civil Procedure Through a Collaborative Rule-Making Process,* 58 VAND. L. REV. 1167 (2005); Thomas O. Main, *Traditional Equity and Contemporary Procedure,* 78 WASH. L. REV. 429 (2003) (providing extensive background on the development of law and equity as well as the merger of law and equity and arguing that as the Federal Rules become more elaborate and technical, "equity remains a source of authority for district judges to avoid the application of a procedural rule when technical compliance [with the rule] would produce an inequitable result"); Thomas O. Main, *Procedural Uniformity and the Exaggerated Role of Rules: A Survey of Intra-State Uniformity in Three States That Have Not Adopted the Federal Rules of Civil Procedure*, 46 VILL. L. REV. 311, 319 (2001) ("Based upon a review of hundreds of judicial opinions, the [author's] survey presents evidence of uniform procedural standards within the federal and state courts of each state [not adopting the Federal Rules] in practice, notwithstanding fundamental differences in the texts of those federal and state procedural rules.").

207. *See, e.g., Ex parte* Dorsey Trailers, Inc., 397 So. 2d 98, 103 (Ala. 1981) ("cases construing the Federal Rules of Civil Procedure are authority for construction of the Alabama Rules of Civil Procedure").

208. *See, e.g.,* RICHARD A. POSNER, THE FEDERAL COURTS: CRISIS AND CHALLENGE 53-189 (1996).

this use of ADR.[209] ADR processes can be set in motion through the parties' mutual agreement or through court-annexed procedures. This section provides an overview of the major ADR processes.

1. Negotiation

Negotiation involves consensual bargaining in an attempt to reach a mutually satisfactory settlement of an actual or potential dispute. The autonomy of the parties and the lack of third-party intervention in the process during negotiation distinguish it from other forms of dispute resolution. A negotiated settlement avoids the "winner-take-all" nature and limited scope of most legal remedies available in court, which allows the parties the opportunity to fashion a package meeting their specific goals and interests. A negotiated settlement avoids the vagaries and uncertainties of trial and appeal. It also avoids the substantial economic, social, and psychological costs of litigation. These costs include the anxiety and stress of trial, possible embarrassment or adverse publicity, and further damage to any relationship between the parties.[210]

2. Mediation

Mediation is a "facilitated negotiation." In a mediation, neutral third parties—mediators—assist the parties or their representatives in resolving their disputes themselves.[211] Mediation is usually a voluntary process. In some jurisdictions, however, statutes, rules, or court orders may mandate participation in mediation. The disputants and their mediator ordinarily control the process. They decide when and where the mediation will occur, who will be involved, how the cost of the mediation will be paid, whether the mediator will meet individually with the disputants, and other details of the process. The mediator assists the settlement process by (1) providing the forum for the parties' negotiations; (2) supervising the exchange of information and the bargaining process; (3) helping the parties find common ground and dealing with unrealistic expectations; (4) offering alternatives and creative solutions; and (5) assisting in the drafting of the final settlement.[212]

3. Arbitration

Arbitration involves submitting a dispute to a neutral third person for a decision. Traditionally, the decision to arbitrate is based on a voluntary agreement between the parties. This agreement may be the result of a preexisting contractual

---

209. *See, e.g.*, Alternative Dispute Resolution Act of 1998, Pub. L. No. 105-315, 112 Stat. 2993 (codified at 28 U.S.C. §§ 651-658) (requiring all federal trial courts to implement ADR programs for litigants and allowing courts to mandate participation in those programs).

210. *See* LARRY L. TEPLY, LEGAL NEGOTIATION IN A NUTSHELL 2-3 (2d ed. 2005).

211. *See* CARRIE J. MENKEL-MEADOW ET AL., DISPUTE RESOLUTION: BEYOND THE ADVERSARIAL MODEL 223 (2d ed. 2011).

212. *See generally* SARAH R. COLE ET AL., MEDIATION: LAW, POLICY AND PRACTICE (2010).

provision. It may also be the result of an ad hoc agreement after the dispute has arisen. Such agreements typically provide (1) a mechanism for selecting the arbitrator; (2) the manner in which the arbitral hearing will be held; (3) the procedural and evidentiary rules to be used; and (4) the controlling law.

A party initiates the arbitration process by notifying the other party. Usually, a party makes a written demand for arbitration. Typically, only one arbitrator conducts the arbitration. Some agreements call for a panel of three arbitrators, two of whom are chosen by the parties. The two arbitrators chosen by the parties, in turn, choose a third arbitrator by mutual agreement. The arbitration hearing usually resembles a judicial hearing. The parties make opening and closing statements, present testimony, and offer documentary proof. Typically, arbitrators have wide discretion in admitting evidence and in making decisions. Sometimes, the arbitration agreement will require the arbitrator to choose between "final offers" submitted by the parties. This procedure militates against a possible tendency of the arbitrator to make a compromise decision. It also pressures each party to make a reasonable offer. Judicial review of the arbitration award is limited.[213]

In contrast to the traditional arbitration model based on a voluntary agreement to arbitrate, compulsory arbitration has been widely adopted for critical public sector employees, such as firefighters, police, and teachers. Some jurisdictions have also required arbitration of other types of disputes, such as medical malpractice. In addition, "court-annexed" arbitration has become compulsory for certain categories of civil cases in several state and federal district courts. In some jurisdictions, however, court-annexed arbitration is simply offered as an option. The arbitrators in court-annexed arbitrations are usually lawyers or retired judges. In a mandatory court-annexed arbitration, a party dissatisfied with the arbitrator's decision has a right to a trial *de novo*. Some jurisdictions provide a disincentive to exercising that right. If the dissatisfied party fails to secure a better outcome at trial, that party must pay the arbitrator's fees or court costs.[214]

4. Summary Jury Trial

In a summary jury trial, the litigants' lawyers present a capsulized version of the case to a jury. This presentation usually occurs after the parties have completed discovery and the judge has resolved any pending motions. Particular proceedings vary, but can include voir dire (a preliminary examination to test the qualifications of prospective jurors), opening statements, summarized presentation of admissible evidence, live witness testimony, rebuttal, closing arguments, and jury instruction. The jury then renders a nonbinding, advisory decision. If the jury is unable to reach a consensus, each juror provides an opinion on liability and

---

213. *See generally* THOMAS E. CARBONNEAU, ARBITRATION IN A NUTSHELL 10-281 (2d ed. 2009); JACQUELINE M. NOLAN-HALEY, ALTERNATIVE DISPUTE RESOLUTION IN A NUTSHELL 153-220 (3d ed. 2008); STEPHEN J. WARE, PRINCIPLES OF ALTERNATIVE DISPUTE RESOLUTION §§ 2.1-2.55 (2d ed. 2007).

214. *See generally* JACQUELINE M. NOLAN-HALEY, ALTERNATIVE DISPUTE RESOLUTION IN A NUTSHELL 220-22 (3d ed. 2008); STEPHEN J. WARE, PRINCIPLES OF ALTERNATIVE DISPUTE RESOLUTION § 4.30 (2d ed. 2007).

damages. Lawyers may question the jurors in a debriefing session. After attending this summary jury trial, the parties then attempt to settle the case.[215]

5. Early Neutral Evaluation

"Early neutral evaluation" ordinarily occurs after the first status conference. The court chooses a private lawyer who is experienced in the substantive area of the law involved in the dispute. That lawyer then holds a confidential evaluation session. Before the session, the court orders the litigants' lawyers to submit written statements identifying (1) the issues in dispute and (2) the discovery that would be useful in fashioning a settlement. The court also orders the parties to identify the names of any opposing parties whose presence might assist in settling the case. These parties, in turn, are ordered by the court to attend the session. The session typically includes an opening statement by the neutral evaluator and narrative presentations by the litigants' lawyers. The evaluator then identifies areas of agreement. The evaluator assesses each side's strengths and weaknesses, estimates the likelihood of liability and damages, and may propose stipulations and facilitate the planning for discovery.[216]

6. Mini-Trial and Other Hybrid Processes

The mini-trial is a hybrid of adversarial case presentation, negotiation, and mediation. A mini-trial consists of a discovery phase, a hearing phase, and a post-hearing settlement discussion between the parties. A mini-trial is initiated by an agreement of the parties on the procedures that will govern the process. Typically, if the agreement requires a neutral adviser, a lawyer or retired judge will be chosen. The agreement will also provide for limited exchanges, such as introductory statements, key exhibits, and summaries of testimony. At the hearing, usually lasting one day, each side's lawyers present a summary of their "best cases" to individuals from each party's organization—ordinarily, senior executives with full settlement authority. The neutral advisor may ask questions, comment on the evidence or arguments, and evaluate the probable outcome of the case. The representatives on the mini-trial panel then enter into post-hearing settlement discussions. The neutral advisor may mediate these discussions.[217]

Other hybrid dispute resolution processes include "med-arb" and private judging. In med-arb, the same individual typically serves as both a mediator and then as the arbitrator if the parties do not settle their dispute.[218] Private judging involves the submission of a dispute to a referee, often a retired judge. Its principal advantages are the speed in which a decision is rendered, privacy, ability to select the referee, and the right to a full review of the decision.[219]

---

215. *See* JACQUELINE M. NOLAN-HALEY, ALTERNATIVE DISPUTE RESOLUTION IN A NUTSHELL 223-32 (3d ed. 2008).

216. *See id.* at 232-35.

217. *See id.* at 246-53.

218. *See id.* at 255-56.

219. *See id.* at 254-55 ("Reference Procedures").

Chapter 2

SUBJECT-MATTER JURISDICTION

SECTION A. GENERAL PRINCIPLES OF SUBJECT-MATTER JURISDICTION

1. The Mandatory Nature of Subject-Matter Jurisdiction

The allocation of judicial authority to adjudicate cases and controversies in their first instance is referred to as "original" jurisdiction. It contrasts with "appellate" jurisdiction in which a superior court reviews or controls actions taken by an inferior court.[1] In the United States, this authority is vested in particular courts through constitutional and legislative provisions. In doing so, these provisions typically give courts original jurisdiction over *categories* of cases.[2]

Illustration 2-1. *H* and *W* are married and live in Arizona. *W* is considering divorce. The Arizona Constitution would be the starting point for determining which Arizona court has original subject-matter jurisdiction over divorce actions. The Arizona Constitution allocates jurisdiction over divorce matters as follows: "The superior court shall have original jurisdiction of . . . [d]ivorce and for annulment of marriage."[3]

Illustration 2-2. Article III, § 1 of the U.S. Constitution provides that the judicial power of the United States "shall be vested" in a Supreme Court "and in such inferior Courts as the Congress may from time to time ordain and establish."[4] Section 2 of Article III limits the judicial power to specific categories of cases:

---

1. Thus, "trial" courts ordinarily exercise original jurisdiction and "appellate" courts ordinarily exercise appellate jurisdiction. However, in some instances, courts that are primarily trial courts (and thus usually exercise only original jurisdiction) also have appellate jurisdiction over other trial courts. For example, in some states, the courts of general jurisdiction might exercise appellate jurisdiction over certain types of decisions made by the courts of limited jurisdiction. Likewise, some appellate courts also possess original jurisdiction over certain kinds of cases. *See, e.g.*, 28 U.S.C. § 1251(a) (providing that the U.S. "Supreme Court shall have original and exclusive jurisdiction over all controversies between two or more States").

2. *See, e.g.*, Goodrum v. Goodrum, 283 Ga. 163, 657 S.E.2d 192 (2008) (subject-matter jurisdiction refers to whether a court has jurisdiction to decide a particular class of cases); State Farm Mut. Auto. Ins. Co. v. Kunz, 2008 WY71, 186 P.3d 378 (subject-matter jurisdiction refers to the power of a court to hear and determine cases of the general class to which the proceedings belong); K.S. v. State, 849 N.E.2d 538 (Ind. 2006) (subject-matter jurisdiction is the power to hear and determine cases of the general class to which any particular proceeding belongs); Harshberger v. Harshberger, 2006 ND 245, 724 N.W.2d 148 (subject-matter jurisdiction is the court's power to hear and decide the general subject in the action).

3. ARIZ. CONST. art. VI, § 14.

4. U.S. CONST. art. III, § 1. This language has been interpreted as requiring Congress to establish a Supreme Court, but giving Congress the discretion to create inferior courts. *See generally* CHARLES A. WRIGHT & MARY KAY KANE, THE LAW OF FEDERAL COURTS § 10 (7th ed. 2011) (discussing congressional control of jurisdiction); *cf.* Bowles v. Russell, 551 U. S. 205, 127 S. Ct. 2360, 168 L. Ed. 2d 96 (2007) (because Congress decides whether lower federal courts can hear cases at all, it can also determine when and under what conditions the courts can hear them; discussing lack of appellate jurisdiction for failure to file a timely notice of appeal).

> The judicial Power shall extend to all Cases, in Law and Equity, arising under this Constitution, the Laws of the United States, and Treaties made, or which shall be made, under their Authority;—to all Cases affecting Ambassadors, other public Ministers and Consuls;—to all Cases of admiralty and maritime Jurisdiction;—to Controversies to which the United States shall be a Party;—to Controversies between two or more States;—between a State and Citizens of another State;—between Citizens of different States;—between Citizens of the same State claiming Lands under Grants of different States, and between a State, or the Citizens thereof, and foreign States, Citizens or Subjects.[5]

This section further provides that

> [i]n all Cases affecting Ambassadors, other public Ministers and Consuls, and those in which a State shall be Party, the supreme Court shall have original Jurisdiction. In all the other Cases before mentioned, the supreme Court shall have appellate Jurisdiction, both as to Law and Fact, with such Exceptions, and under such Regulations as the Congress shall make.[6]

Congress implemented the provisions of Article III in the Judiciary Act of 1789 by establishing a Supreme Court and a system of inferior federal courts.[7] Congress has greatly expanded the jurisdiction of the lower federal courts over the years, but it has never conferred upon them the full scope of Article III jurisdiction. Today, the principal trial courts in the federal system are the U.S. District Courts, which are located in "judicial districts" throughout the United States.[8] Congress has also created a system of specialized courts and intermediate appellate courts.[9]

* * * * *

Courts in the United States consider it obligatory to hear cases within their grants of constitutional and legislative subject-matter jurisdiction. This obligation

---

5. U.S. CONST. art. III, § 2. It is generally agreed that this latter part of § 2 prevents Congress from depriving the Supreme Court of its original jurisdiction in any of the cases listed. However, disagreement exists about the extent to which Congress can limit the Court's appellate jurisdiction through "exceptions and regulations." *See* 13 CHARLES A. WRIGHT ET AL., FEDERAL PRACTICE AND PROCEDURE: JURISDICTION AND RELATED MATTERS § 3525, at 517-26 (3d ed. 2008).

6. U.S. CONST. art. III, § 2.

7. Judiciary Act of 1789, ch. 20, §§ 1-4, 1 Stat. 73, 73-75.

8. Each state has at least one judicial district, and some states have more than one. With one unimportant exception, *see* 28 U.S.C. § 131 (establishing the district lines for the U.S. District Court of Wyoming), the district lines do not extend across state lines. The number and exact boundaries of districts within a particular state are set out in §§ 81-131 of Title 28 of the *United States Code*. *See, e.g.,* 28 U.S.C. § 84 (dividing California into four judicial districts to be known as the Northern, Eastern, Central, and Southern Districts of California). In addition, these sections indicate where court will be held within the district. *See, e.g., id.* (stating that the Northern District of California comprises the counties of Alameda, Contra Costa, Del Norte, Humboldt, Lake Marin, Mendocino, Monterey, Napa, San Benito, Santa Cruz, San Francisco, San Mateo, and Sonoma; and designating that court for the Northern District shall be held at Eureka, Oakland, San Francisco, and San Jose).

9. The federal intermediate appellate courts are today called courts of appeals. Thirteen federal courts of appeals exist. Most of these courts hear appeals taken from federal district courts within a specific geographical area. For example, the U.S. Court of Appeals for the Second Circuit covers appeals from federal district courts in Vermont, New York, and Connecticut; the Fifth Circuit covers Texas, Louisiana, and Mississippi; and the Eighth Circuit covers North Dakota, South Dakota, Nebraska, Minnesota, Iowa, Missouri, and Arkansas. The Court of Appeals for the Federal Circuit hears appeals from all district courts involving patent litigation and certain claims against the federal government. Examples of specialized federal courts include the Court of International Trade, the Court of Federal Claims, and the Tax Court.

is the product of principles of legislative supremacy embedded in the separation-of-powers doctrine. The courts disregard this obligation only for the most compelling reasons.[10] If a dismissal results from a court's refusal to hear a case within its subject-matter jurisdiction, the proper course is an appeal.[11] If a judge refuses to schedule a case for trial or to render a decision, the proper course is to seek a writ of mandamus from a superior court.[12] The court of superior jurisdiction will command the inferior court to exercise its authority. The counterpart to a writ of mandamus is a writ of prohibition. A writ of prohibition directs the judge and the parties to a suit in an inferior court to cease litigating matters outside the inferior court's jurisdictional authority.[13]

In some instances, the U.S. Constitution imposes an obligation on state courts to hear cases.

Illustration 2-3. In *Hughes v. Fetter*,[14] an administrator commenced an action in a Wisconsin state court to recover damages for the death of a decedent who was fatally injured in an automobile accident in Illinois. The action was based on the Illinois wrongful death statute. The Wisconsin trial court dismissed the complaint. The court found that a Wisconsin statute created a right of action for death caused in Wisconsin and established a local policy against Wisconsin courts entertaining suits brought under the wrongful death acts of other states. On appeal, the U.S. Supreme Court held that "Wisconsin cannot escape [this] constitutional obligation to enforce rights and duties validly created under the laws of other states by the simple device of removing jurisdiction from courts otherwise competent."[15] The Court explained that Wisconsin had no public policy against wrongful death actions because it had a wrongful death statute of its own. Wisconsin had no other legitimate reason for dismissing the action, such as a lack of any connection between the state and the case. Consequently, the Court concluded that the Full Faith and Credit Clause obligated the Wisconsin state court to hear the action.[16]

Illustration 2-4. In *McKnett v. St. Louis & San Francisco Railway Co.*,[17] a resident of Tennessee commenced an action in an Alabama state court. The plaintiff sued a railroad for injuries occurring in Tennessee. The plaintiff based the case on a right of action created by the Federal Employers' Liability Act. That Act is the federal workers' compensation law covering employees of railroads engaged in interstate and foreign commerce. The Alabama court dismissed this action. No Alabama court had jurisdiction of any suit against a foreign corporation (in this

---

10. *But see* David L. Shapiro, *Jurisdiction and Discretion*,. 60 N.Y.U. L. REV 543 (1985).

11. *See, e.g.*, Buckman v. United Mine Workers, 80 Wyo. 199, 339 P.2d 398 (1959).

12. *See, e.g.*, Lyons v. Westinghouse Elec. Corp., 222 F.2d 184 (2d Cir. 1955).

13. *See* Chapter 12(B)(2)*(d) infra* ("Extraordinary Writs").

14. 341 U.S. 609, 71 S. Ct. 980, 95 L. Ed. 1212 (1951).

15. *Id.* at 611, 71 S. Ct. at 982, 95 L. Ed. at 1216.

16. *Id.* at 612-13, 71 S. Ct. at 982-83, 95 L. Ed. at 1216-17. The Full Faith and Credit Clause requires, *inter alia*, that "[f]ull faith and credit shall be given in each State to the public Acts . . . of every other State." U.S. CONST. art. IV, § 1. For criticism of the result in *Hughes*, see RUSSELL J. WEINTRAUB, COMMENTARY ON THE CONFLICT OF LAWS § 9.3A, at 708-10 (6th ed. 2010). The Court's reference to dismissal because of lack of connections between Wisconsin and the case was part of a discussion of the doctrine of forum non conveniens, which is examined in Chapter 4(D)(1)*(a) infra* ("Forum Non Conveniens"). The Full Faith and Credit Clause is discussed further in conjunction with the doctrine of personal jurisdiction in Chapter 3(A)(1)*(c)-(e) infra* (dealing with the development of the territorial rules of personal jurisdiction).

17. 292 U.S. 230, 54 S. Ct. 690, 78 L. Ed. 1227 (1934).

instance, a railroad incorporated outside of Alabama) unless the cause of action had arisen in Alabama. The Alabama Supreme Court affirmed. The court held that the Alabama Legislature had modified this rule only to the extent of allowing plaintiffs to bring actions based on the common law or the statutes of another *state* in Alabama, not those arising under *federal* law. On certiorari, the U.S. Supreme Court reversed. The Supreme Court pointed out that the Alabama court would have had jurisdiction if the accident had occurred in Alabama or the plaintiff had sued under Tennessee law. Under these circumstances, the U.S. Constitution prohibited Alabama from discriminating against rights created by federal law.[18]

2. The "No-Waiver, No-Consent" Rule

The parties to an action cannot consent to allow a court to hear a case beyond its subject-matter competence as defined by the relevant constitutional and statutory provisions.[19] Under conventional rules, a party also cannot waive an objection to subject-matter jurisdiction.[20] As a result, a party may successfully object to subject-matter jurisdiction at late stages of a proceeding or sometimes in wholly separate proceedings.[21] Furthermore, a court of original jurisdiction must raise the lack of subject-matter jurisdiction on its own initiative (*sua sponte*), even when the parties do not. Likewise, in reviewing a lower court judgment, an appellate court must raise objections to the subject-matter jurisdiction of the lower court even if neither the lower court nor the parties have objected.[22]

This strict *"no-waiver, no-consent" rule* for subject-matter jurisdiction originated in English common-law practice. It arose out of a conflict between the king's courts and various other courts of limited jurisdiction. Three superior royal courts evolved through a process of delegation and specialization: the Court of Exchequer for revenue matters; the Court of Common Pleas for ordinary civil litigation; and the Court of King's Bench for criminal matters and wrongs done *vi et armis* (by force of arms). By the time of Edward I (1272-1307), these three royal courts "had become in one way or another courts of first instance for almost all

---

18. Specifically, the Court stated that the U.S. Constitution forbids

> state courts of general jurisdiction from refusing to [hear actions] solely because the suit is brought under a federal law. The denial of jurisdiction by the Alabama court is based solely upon the source of law sought to be enforced. The plaintiff is cast out because he is suing to enforce a federal act. A state may not discriminate against rights arising under federal laws.

Id. at 233-34, 54 S. Ct. at 692, 78 L. Ed. at 1229. In addition, a state cannot confer rights upon private parties and require that litigation between those parties must be confined to the state's own courts. If federal jurisdiction exists, as where the parties are citizens of different states, they may sue on the state rights in federal court. *See, e.g.*, BNSF Ry. Co. v. O'Dea, 572 F.3d 785 (9th Cir. 2009).

19. *See, e,g.*, Harshberger v. Harshberger, 2006 ND 245, 724 N.W.2d 148 (subject-matter jurisdiction cannot be conferred by agreement, consent, or waiver, and subject-matter jurisdiction objections may be raised by the court at any time).

20. *See, e.g.*, Springfield City Sch. Support Personnel v. State Employment Relations Bd., 84 Ohio App. 3d 294, 616 N.E.2d 983 (1992).

21. *See* FED. R. CIV. P. 12(h)(3). The ability to attack a judgment in a subsequent proceeding because of a lack of subject-matter jurisdiction is discussed in Chapter 13(E) *infra* ("Claim and Issue Preclusion on Questions of Subject-Matter and Personal Jurisdiction").

22. *See, e.g.*, Louisville & Nashville R.R. Co. v. Mottley, 211 U.S. 149, 151, 29 S. Ct. 42, 43, 53 L. Ed. 126, 127 (1908).

litigation."[23] However, a few kinds of cases were not within the jurisdiction of the three superior royal courts. For example, the ecclesiastical courts handled certain types of cases. Other minor courts existed, including the Court of the Marshalsea, the court of the king's household.

In the leading *Case of the Marshalsea*,[24] Richard Hall was imprisoned for three months pursuant to process issued by the Marshalsea Court. The Court of the King's Bench permitted Hall to bring a trespass action for false imprisonment against (1) the party who had sued him in the Marshalsea Court, (2) the marshal who directed the execution of the process, and (3) the officer who executed it. The King's Bench held that the Marshalsea Court lacked jurisdiction over the case because neither the plaintiff nor the defendant was of the king's household. The marshal and officer defended by asserting that they had acted in good faith pursuant to the process issued. The King's Bench stated that if the Marshalsea Court would have had jurisdiction over the "cause" (which is referred to today as the "subject matter") and had merely proceeded "erroneously," no action would lie against them. However, because the Marshalsea Court did not have jurisdiction over the action, the whole proceeding was *coram non judice* (not before a judge) and absolutely void. Acting in good faith pursuant to process was not a defense in such a void action.[25]

Although England subsequently limited the no-waiver, no-consent rule, the United States accepted the rule as part of the jurisprudence inherited from England. The rule fit well with the allocation of authority among the three branches of the federal government. It also fit well with the division of authority between federal and state court systems in the U.S. Constitution.[26]

The determination whether the no-waiver, no consent rule applies must take into the account the fact that jurisdictional "categories" can be drawn in an infinite variety of ways and that not all apparent limitations should be considered subject-matter jurisdiction limits. These questions cannot be solved by reference to any general formula, but require careful analysis of the context in which a limit appears, the purposes of the legislatively mandated restriction, and the consequences of holding the limit to be jurisdictional or not.[27]

Illustration 2-5. Under Title VII of the Civil Rights Act of 1964,[28] a business must have fifteen or more employees to be an "employer" subject to suit

---

23. FREDERIC W. MAITLAND, THE CONSTITUTIONAL HISTORY OF ENGLAND 114 (1908); *see* Chapter 1(D)(1) *supra* ("Origin of the Common-Law Courts").

24. 77 Eng. Rep. 1027 (K.B. 1613).

25. *Id.* at 1038-40; *see* Dan B. Dobbs, *The Decline of Jurisdiction by Consent,* 40 N.C. L. REV. 49, 67-68 (1961) (discussing the *Marshalsea* decision). The same rule was applied in English law when the plaintiff sought prohibition (a writ prohibiting an inferior court from acting outside its jurisdiction). For example, the common-law courts issued writs of prohibition to the ecclesiastical courts, even after a defendant had been forced to admit jurisdiction and judgment had been entered. *Id.* at 66-67.

26. *See id.* at 77-78. For a more complete discussion of the limitations of and exceptions to the "no-waiver, no-consent" rule, see Dan B. Dobbs, *The Validation of Void Judgments: The Bootstrap Principle* (pts. 1 & 2), 53 VA. L. REV. 1003, 1241 (1967); Dan B. Dobbs, *Beyond Bootstrap: Foreclosing the Issue of Subject-Matter Jurisdiction Before Final Judgment,* 51 MINN. L. REV. 491 (1967).

27. For an excellent examination of the nature and consequences of jurisdictional labels, see Alex Lees, Note, *The Jurisdictional Label: Use and Misuse,* 58 STAN. L. REV. 1457 (2006).

28. 42 U.S.C. § 2000e(b).

under the Act. In *Arbaugh v. Y & H Corp.*,[29] the U.S. Supreme Court held that this restriction was not a subject-matter jurisdiction restriction, but a restriction on the ability of a plaintiff to assert a claim for relief. Consequently, the restriction could not be raised at any stage of the litigation, but was subject to waiver.[30]

Illustration 2-6. In *Henderson v. Shinseki*,[31] the U.S. Supreme Court held that the 120-day deadline for filing appeals to the U.S. Court of Appeals for Veterans Claims was not jurisdictional.[32]

Illustration 2-7. In *John R. Sand & Gravel Co. v. United States,*[33] the U.S. Supreme Court held that the special statute of limitations governing actions in the court of claims was jurisdictional and should be raised by the courts on their own motion. The Court reasoned that ordinary statutes of limitations are designed to protect the parties from stale claims and are, therefore, waivable affirmative defenses. Some statutes of limitations, however, are designed to achieve broader systemic goals. This was the case with the statute of limitations governing Court of Claims actions, which was designed to facilitate the administration of claims against the United States.[34]

3. "General" vs. "Limited" Jurisdiction

State court subject-matter configurations vary widely. In all states, however, a court of *general jurisdiction* exists to handle all cases not exclusively delegated to another court within the state. Courts of general jurisdiction always possess the broadest subject-matter authority within a state. When no other courts within the system have subject-matter jurisdiction over a particular action, courts of general jurisdiction, as "repository" courts, have subject-matter authority over such actions.

Illustration 2-8. The Arizona Constitution provides that "[t]he superior court shall have original jurisdiction of . . . [c]ases and proceedings in which exclusive jurisdiction is not vested by law in another court" and "[s]pecial cases and proceedings not otherwise provided for, and such other jurisdiction as may be provided by law."[35] Thus, in Arizona, the court of general jurisdiction, the repository court, is the superior court.[36]

* * * * *

Typically, each state also has one or more courts of *limited jurisdiction*. The law circumscribes the authority of these courts in a variety of ways. For example, the law may limit the subject-matter jurisdiction of a court according to amount in

---

29. 546 U.S. 500, 126 S. Ct. 1235, 163 L. Ed. 2d 1097 (2006).

30. *Id.* at 516, 126 S. Ct. at 1245, 163 L. Ed. 2d at 1110-11.

31. 562 U. S. __, 131 S. Ct. 1197, 179 L. Ed. 2d 159 (2011).

32. *Id.* at __, 131 S. Ct. at 1202-06, 179 L. Ed. 2d at 166-71.

33. 552 U.S. 130, 128 S. Ct. 750, 169 L. Ed. 2d 591 (2008).

34. *Id.* at 133-39, 128 S. Ct. at 753-57, 169 L. Ed. 2d at 595-99; *see also* T.L. *ex rel.* Ingram v. United States, 443 F.3d 956 (8th Cir. 2006) (compliance with the Federal Tort Claims Act's two-year statute of limitations for filing administrative claims is a jurisdictional prerequisite to the commencement of an FTCA lawsuit).

35. ARIZ. CONST. art. VI, § 14.

36. *See id.* The name of the court designated as the court of general jurisdiction varies from state to state. For example, in Illinois, the court of general jurisdiction is called the circuit court. *See* ILL. CONST. art. VI, § 9. In New York, it is the supreme court. N.Y. CONST. art. VI, § 7. In Iowa, it is the district court. *See* IOWA CONST. art. V, § 6. *See generally* Jeffrey A. Parness, *American General Jurisdiction Trial Courts: New Visions, New Guidelines,* 55 KAN. L. REV. 189 (2006).

controversy or geographical area. Likewise, the law may prohibit a court from hearing cases involving certain subjects, such as title to land.

In contrast with the organization of the state courts, all federal courts are courts of limited jurisdiction. As a result, restrictive rules exist in the federal system concerning how federal subject-matter jurisdiction must be pleaded and established. For example, a plaintiff who wants to invoke some branch of federal jurisdiction must plead its existence in the complaint.

Illustration 2-9. Federal Rule 8(a)(1) requires that a complaint contain a short and plain statement of the grounds for the court's jurisdiction. The first paragraph of the complaint usually sets forth this statement. The following two allegations illustrate how federal subject-matter jurisdiction is typically pleaded:

(a) "This action arises under the United States Copyright Act, United States Code, Title 17, §§ 101 *et seq.*"[37]

(b) "Plaintiff *P-1* is a citizen of the State of Ohio and plaintiff *P-2* is a citizen of the State of Florida. Defendant *D-1* is a citizen of the State of New York, defendant *D-2* is a citizen of the State of California, and defendant *D-3* is a citizen of the State of Arkansas. The amount in controversy, without interest and costs, exceeds the sum or value specified by 28 U.S.C. § 1332." This allegation pleads jurisdiction over the action based on diversity of citizenship involving multiple natural persons.[38]

* * * * *

If federal subject-matter jurisdiction is not pleaded properly, the district court must dismiss the case on its own motion without waiting for the defendant to object.[39] If the defendant objects to subject-matter jurisdiction, the plaintiff has the burden of proving its existence, even if the plaintiff has properly pleaded it.[40] Even when no objection to subject-matter jurisdiction occurs at the district court level and the case proceeds to judgment, the federal appellate courts must raise any apparent objections to the district court's or their own subject-matter jurisdiction. Thus, an action can be fully tried and judgment rendered without anyone objecting to subject-matter jurisdiction, but the case may be reversed on appeal when the appellate court or a party objects to subject-matter jurisdiction.[41]

---

37. *Cf.* Form 7(b) ("For federal-question Jurisdiction") in the Appendix of Forms following the Federal Rules of Civil Procedure. Section 1338 authorizes copyright claims to be brought in federal court. *See* 28 U.S.C. § 1338(a).

38. *Cf.* Form 7(a) (diversity of citizenship jurisdiction) in the Appendix of Forms following the Federal Rules of Civil Procedure.

39. Jurisdictional defects have long been raised by federal courts on their own motion. *See, e.g.*, Capron v. Van Noorden, 6 U.S. (2 Cranch) 126, 2 L. Ed. 229 (1804).

40. Assume that the diversity allegation in *Illustration 2-9* inadvertently stated that each of the parties was a "resident" rather than a "citizen" of each of the states listed. Rule 15 of the Federal Rules of Civil Procedure permits amendments either as of right or by leave of the district court. Thus, the plaintiff ordinarily has the opportunity to amend a defective allegation of jurisdiction prior to a complete dismissal of the claim. Section 1653 of Title 28 also specifically provides that "[d]efective allegations of jurisdiction may be amended, upon terms, in the trial or appellate courts." 28 U.S.C. § 1653; *see* section D(10) *infra* ("Correcting Defects in Diversity Jurisdiction and Adjudicating Disputes Over Diversity"); *cf.* Michael G. Collins, *Jurisdictional Exceptionalism,* 93 VA. L. REV. 1829 (2007) (examining the history of the pleading and raising of federal jurisdiction objections).

41. *See* Louisville & Nashville R.R. Co. v. Mottley, 211 U.S. 149, 29 S. Ct. 42, 53 L. Ed. 126 (1908); *see generally* Gil Seinfeld, *Article I, Article III, and the Limits of Enumeration,* 108 MICH. L. REV. 1389 (2010) (discussing how, despite the enumeration of cases in Article III, the Supreme Court has "shown little interest" in keeping the federal courts within the limits of Article III, Section 2).

4. Presumptions in Favor of and Against Jurisdiction

It is commonly said that the subject-matter jurisdiction of a court of general jurisdiction is presumed to exist, but that the subject-matter jurisdiction of a court of limited jurisdiction is presumed not to exist and must be demonstrated.[42] If this statement were literally true, the "no-waiver, no-consent" rule, as a universal proposition, would only apply to courts of limited jurisdiction. The "presumption" in favor of the subject-matter jurisdiction of courts of general jurisdiction would supply authority when none actually existed.[43] In reality, of course, these presumptions do not prevent the operation of the "no-waiver, no-consent" rule in courts of general jurisdiction. Rather than being true presumptions, they actually express other differences between the subject-matter authority of courts of general and limited jurisdiction. Some of those differences are valid elements of practice today while others are now obsolete.

Plaintiffs in courts of limited jurisdiction must ordinarily demonstrate the basis for the court's subject-matter jurisdiction.[44] Even if subject-matter jurisdiction actually exists under the existing facts, the failure to demonstrate the jurisdictional basis of the action will result in dismissal or transfer. In contrast, plaintiffs in courts of general jurisdiction do not ordinarily have to affirmatively demonstrate the existence of subject-matter jurisdiction.[45] However, even if a plaintiff demonstrates jurisdiction by a statement in the complaint, a court of limited jurisdiction will be required by the "no-waiver, no-consent" rule to dismiss the action if facts come to light showing that no subject-matter jurisdiction actually exists. Similarly, the presumption of subject-matter jurisdiction in courts of general jurisdiction does not eliminate the court's obligation to question subject-matter jurisdiction on its own initiative if it appears affirmatively that jurisdiction may be lacking.[46]

---

42. *See, e.g.*, 13 CHARLES A. WRIGHT ET AL., FEDERAL PRACTICE AND PROCEDURE: JURISDICTION AND RELATED MATTERS § 3522, at 100-03 (3d ed. 2008).

43. For example, assume the plaintiff commences an action in a court of general jurisdiction. Assume also, however, that the action actually belongs to the exclusive jurisdiction of another court within the state. If the defendant does not raise the issue of subject-matter jurisdiction and come forward with sufficient evidence to destroy the presumption, the court of general jurisdiction might enter a valid judgment against the defendant. Presumptions normally operate in this way. *See* Chapter 11(H)(3) *infra* ("Presumptions"). The court of general jurisdiction could rely on the presumption to provide it with subject-matter jurisdiction instead of being required by the "no-waiver, no-consent" rule to raise the objection to subject-matter jurisdiction on its own motion. Moreover, an appellate court would not be able to reverse the judgment for lack of jurisdiction. The presumption would provide the necessary jurisdictional predicate for the lower court's action.

44. *See, e.g.*, State *ex rel.* Smilack v. Bushong, 93 Ohio App. 201, 209-10, 112 N.E.2d 675, 680 (1952), *aff'd on other grounds*, 159 Ohio St. 259, 111 N.E.2d 918 (1953); State v. Vijil, 784 P.2d 1130, 1133 (Utah 1989). The cases usually state that the "record" must affirmatively demonstrate the jurisdiction of the court. *See, e.g.*, Hall v. Franklin Cnty., 184 Miss. 77, 86-87, 185 So. 591, 594-95 (1939); Colagirovanni v. District Court, 47 R.I. 323, 324, 133 A. 1, 2 (1926). Thus, if the action moves past the pleading stage—for example, if a judgment is rendered which is then appealed—the court may rely on the entire record to establish the necessary jurisdictional facts. However, at the commencement of the action, the plaintiff's initial pleading is, of necessity, the only vehicle for demonstrating jurisdiction. *See* Blount Cnty. Bank v. Barnes, 218 Ala. 230, 232, 118 So. 460, 461 (1928).

45. *See, e.g.*, Broom v. Board of Supervisors, 171 Miss. 586, 593, 158 So. 344, 345 (1934); Dougherty v. Matthews, 35 Mo. 520 (1865); State *ex rel.* Smilack v. Bushong, 93 Ohio App. 201, 112 N.E.2d 675 (1952), *aff'd on other grounds*, 93 Ohio St. 259, 111 N.E.2d 918 (1953); Peek v. Equipment Serv. Co., 779 S.W.2d 802 (Tex. 1989); State v. Vijil, 784 P.2d 1130 (Utah 1989); Slater v. Melton, 119 W. Va. 259, 262, 193 S.E. 185, 186 (1937).

46. *Compare* Richardson v. First Nat'l Life Ins. Co., 419 S.W.2d 836 (Tex. 1967) (specific pleading controls over general pleading for determining jurisdiction) *with* Peek v. Equipment Serv. Co., 779 S.W.2d 802, 804 (Tex. 1989) (liberal construction of pleadings appropriate; lack of allegation of jurisdictional amount cured at trial); *cf.* Johnson v. South Carolina Dep't of Prob., Parole, & Pardon Servs., 372 S.C. 279, 641 S.E.2d 895

Illustration 2-10. Assume that the county court in State *X* is a court of limited jurisdiction. State *X* law authorizes county courts to adjudicate actions in which the amount in controversy is not less than $500 and not more than $2,000. *P* sues *D* in the county court for property damage arising from an automobile accident. *P's* complaint does not contain a jurisdictional statement or demonstrate in any other way the amount in controversy. *P* is actually seeking $900 in damages, an amount within the jurisdiction of the court. *D* does not object to subject-matter jurisdiction. The usual rules governing the authority of courts of limited jurisdiction do not authorize the county court to adjudicate the action. *P* must include a jurisdictional statement in a pleading or make some other appropriate demonstration of the amount in controversy. Even though *D* has not objected to the court's jurisdiction, the court should raise the jurisdictional objection on its own motion.

Illustration 2-11. On the facts of *Illustration 2-10*, assume that *P's* complaint does contain a jurisdictional statement. *P* alleges that the amount in controversy is not less than $500 and does not exceed $2,000. Under the usual rules governing the authority of courts of limited jurisdiction, this statement satisfies the special jurisdictional pleading requirements applicable to those courts. However, assume that *P* is actually seeking only $200 in damages from *D*. This fact becomes clear during the trial. *D* again does not object to subject-matter jurisdiction. Despite the jurisdictional statement in *P's* initial pleading, the court should raise the issue of subject-matter jurisdiction on its own motion and take appropriate action to dismiss or transfer the action, whichever the state's statutes require.

Illustration 2-12. Assume that the superior court is the court of general jurisdiction in State *Y*. Assume that *P* sues *D* for patent infringement in the superior court. Patent infringement actions are within the exclusive jurisdiction of the federal courts.[47] *D* does not object to the court's subject-matter jurisdiction. The superior court should raise the objection to its subject-matter jurisdiction on its own motion and dismiss the action. If the superior court fails to do so and the judgment is appealed, the appellate court should raise the objection on its own motion if the parties fail to do so. In this situation, the action will have to be dismissed. State courts cannot transfer cases to federal courts.

* * * * *

At one time, the traditional presumptions concerning courts of general and limited jurisdiction produced another distinction. This distinction concerned challenges to the validity of judgments of the two kinds of courts in subsequent proceedings, as opposed to challenges raised in the original proceeding in which the judgment was rendered (such as by appeal). Traditionally, the presumption in favor of the jurisdiction of courts of general jurisdiction prevented a party from attacking the judgment of such a court in a later action on the ground of lack of subject-matter jurisdiction. However, the judgments of courts of limited jurisdiction, not having

---

(2007) (court of appeals is only required to address the issue of lower court's subject-matter jurisdiction if it appears that the lower court did not possess subject-matter jurisdiction).

47. *See* 28 U.S.C. § 1338(a). Because the federal courts are provided by statute with exclusive jurisdiction over patent infringement actions, if any such action is commenced in the state courts, it appears affirmatively in the record that the state court lacks jurisdiction.

the benefit of the presumption, could be "impeached" for lack of subject-matter jurisdiction in a subsequent action.[48] Today, no such distinction is drawn.[49]

Illustration 2-13. Assume that the State *Y* superior court is the court of general jurisdiction in the state. State *Y* statutes expressly forbid the superior court from adjudicating automobile accident cases. State *Y* has exclusively allocated those actions to the jurisdiction of a special automobile claims court. *P-1* sues *D* in the superior court for $100,000 in damages for personal injuries received in an automobile accident. Neither the court nor the parties raise an issue of subject-matter jurisdiction. After a trial, the court enters judgment for *P-1* on an express finding that *D's* negligence caused *P-1's* injuries. Subsequently, *P-2* sues *D* for personal injuries received in the same accident. *P-2's* action is brought in the special automobile claims court in State *Y*. To establish *D's* negligence in *P-2 v. D*, *P-2* wishes to use the finding of *D's* negligence in *P v. D-1* against *D*. *P-2* can use the judgment to establish *D's* negligence only if it is immune from attack on subject-matter jurisdiction grounds. In determining whether the judgment is immune from attack today, it would be irrelevant that a court of general jurisdiction rendered the judgment.[50]

5. "Concurrent" vs. "Exclusive" Jurisdiction

A court may possess *concurrent* or *exclusive* subject-matter jurisdiction over certain kinds of cases. If the court has exclusive jurisdiction over a class of cases, no other court within the system has authority to hear cases within that class. If the court has concurrent jurisdiction, at least one other court in the state may also hear cases within the class. If concurrent jurisdiction exists, the plaintiff will be able to decide in which court to commence the action. A court of limited jurisdiction may also possess exclusive jurisdiction over certain classes of cases.

Illustration 2-14. In Nebraska, the district court is the court of general jurisdiction. County courts are courts of limited jurisdiction. The district court has "general, original and appellate jurisdiction in all matters, both civil and criminal, except where otherwise provided."[51] On the other hand, the county court exercises exclusive jurisdiction in certain types of cases, such as decedents' estates.[52] In other types of cases, the county court exercises concurrent jurisdiction with the district court—for example, "in all civil actions of any type when the amount in controversy does not exceed fifteen thousand dollars."[53] In the latter category of cases, the plaintiff may sue in either a district or county court.

* * * * *

---

48. *See* RESTATEMENT (SECOND) OF JUDGMENTS § 12 cmt. e (1982).

49. *See id.*

50. *See id.* Under modern rules governing the ability to attack judgments on subject-matter jurisdiction grounds in later actions, the judgment in *P-1 v. D* would probably be invalid because the subject-matter of the action was so plainly beyond the superior court's jurisdiction that entertaining the action in that court was a "manifest abuse of authority." *See id.* § 12(1); *see also* Chapter 13(E) *infra* ("Claim and Issue Preclusion on Questions of Subject-Matter and Personal Jurisdiction"), which fully discusses the grounds for attacking a judgment for lack of subject-matter jurisdiction in a subsequent action.

51. NEB. REV. STAT. § 24-302 (2008).

52. *Id.* § 24-517(1).

53. *Id.* § 24-517(4).

In addition to concurrent jurisdiction with the state courts, a certain portion of the jurisdiction of the federal district courts is exclusive of the state courts.

Illustration 2-15. Federal courts have exclusive jurisdiction over admiralty, patent, and copyright cases.[54]

* * * * *

When federal jurisdiction is exclusive, the state courts may not hear cases included within the exclusive grant. Any such actions commenced in state courts must be dismissed for lack of subject-matter jurisdiction. However, because Congress excludes the state courts from hearing cases within the federal judicial power only for compelling reasons, exclusive federal jurisdiction is the exception rather than the rule. Usually, those reasons involve a perceived need for an unbiased or uniform interpretation of some federal law of great national importance.

6. Transfer to Cure Subject-Matter Jurisdiction Deficiencies

Except in rare instances, when a federal court lacks subject-matter jurisdiction, the court must dismiss the action.[55] In the states, statutes often authorize transfer from a court without subject-matter jurisdiction to a court possessing subject-matter jurisdiction. While transfer schemes avoid the inconvenience of dismissal, they sometimes produce their own special complications.[56]

Transfer issues often arise in the context of an action properly commenced in a court of limited jurisdiction when the defendant asserts a counterclaim that is beyond the court's jurisdiction—or would have been if the counterclaim had been asserted as an original claim in the same court. Under these circumstances, several procedural interests may compete with each other. One such interest is the plaintiff's interest in choosing the forum. The plaintiff may prefer the court of limited jurisdiction to prosecute the action. If a counterclaim beyond the jurisdiction of the court results in transfer of the case to a different court, the transfer will deprive the plaintiff of the natural forum preference that plaintiffs ordinarily possess.[57] In addition, if the state permits transfer upon the assertion of counterclaims that are factually unrelated to the plaintiff's claim,[58] the transfer will

54. *See* 28 U.S.C. §§ 1333, 1338.

55. *See* 28 U.S.C. § 1631 (providing for transfers in limited circumstances, such as transfers from U.S. District Courts to the U.S. Claims Court); Kier Bros. Invs. Inc. v. White, 943 F. Supp. 1, 4 (D.D.C. 1996) (dismissal only appropriate remedy when court lacks subject-matter jurisdiction in a diversity case; section 1631 does not allow a federal court to transfer actions to state courts); Jeffrey W. Tayon, *The Federal Transfer Statute: 28 U.S.C. § 1631*, 29 S. TEX. L. REV. 189 (1987).

56. For a discussion of the transfer systems in two states, see Lee Blalack, Comment, *Civil Procedure*—Flowers v. Dyer County: *The Death of the Motion to Dismiss for Lack of Subject Matter Jurisdiction*, 23 MEMPHIS ST. U. L. REV. 409 (1993); Joseph M. Lynch, *Lack of Jurisdiction of the Subject Matter in the New Jersey Courts: Application of N.J.R. 1:13-4, the Transfer of Causes Rule*, 6 SETON HALL L. REV. 1 (1974). For a discussion of additional jurisdictional and other problems related to the state courts, see Edson R. Sunderland, *Problems Connected with the Operation of a State Court System*, 1950 WIS. L. REV. 585.

57. Of course, the plaintiff may have brought the claim in the court of limited jurisdiction because it was the only court with subject-matter jurisdiction over the claim. In such circumstances, it is unrealistic to speak of the plaintiff having a forum choice. Nevertheless, even if the plaintiff does not have a forum choice, the plaintiff may still have a forum preference for the court in which the action was commenced. Furthermore, in some cases the plaintiff *can* frame the claim for relief so that it fits within the jurisdiction of one court rather than another.

58. This type of counterclaim would normally be classified as a permissive counterclaim under state procedural rules patterned on the Federal Rules of Civil Procedure. *See* FED. R. CIV. P. 13(b).

undermine the plaintiff's forum preference for reasons having little to do with the convenient resolution of claims in the same proceeding. Indeed, in the latter situation, the defendant may have asserted the factually unrelated claim purely as a forum shopping tactic rather than as a result of considerations of procedural convenience.

Countervailing considerations exist for the defendant. When the plaintiff's claim factually relates to the defendant's counterclaim, the plaintiff may have consciously engaged in a "race to the courthouse" to trap the defendant in the court of the plaintiff's choosing—at least in those states that do not permit transfer to another court on the basis of the counterclaim. If the action is not transferred, but the defendant is required to assert the claim in a separate action, other difficulties may result. Procedural inconvenience may result from having to litigate factually related claims in different proceedings. Additionally, the doctrine of issue preclusion may preclude certain factual or legal matters determined against the defendant in the court of limited jurisdiction from relitigation in the action on the defendant's claim in another court. Furthermore, even if the defendant's counterclaim is not factually or legally related to the plaintiff's claim, many procedural systems permit the assertion of the counterclaim on the assumption that it may be convenient for parties to resolve all claims existing between them in a single action.[59] To require the defendant to assert the counterclaim in a separate proceeding would deprive the defendant of this potential procedural convenience.

The manner in which any given procedural system resolves transfer issues depends upon how it balances this complex mix of factors. No single solution is inherently better than another. The following illustrations demonstrate some possible solutions.

Illustration 2-16. *P* sued *D* in a magistrate court in State *X* for $1,016.79. State *X* law limits the jurisdiction of the magistrate court to actions in which the sum demanded does not exceed $1,500. *D's* answer contained a counterclaim for $7,308.13 arising out of the same facts as the plaintiff's claim. After serving the answer containing the counterclaim, *D* sought a mandatory injunction from the circuit court to prevent the magistrate court from proceeding with the action. The circuit court issued an injunction restraining the magistrate court from proceeding and ordered the case to be certified to the circuit court for decision. On appeal, the court of appeals reversed. The court of appeals held that asserting a counterclaim in excess of the jurisdictional amount did not deprive the magistrate court of jurisdiction, even though the magistrate court had no power to enter judgment in favor of *D* for an amount in excess of $1,500.[60] The court of appeals noted that the magistrate court could enter judgment for *D* in an amount that did not exceed the jurisdictional amount. The court also noted that *D* could pursue the claim in a separate action in the circuit court. In a separate action, the doctrine of claim preclusion would not prevent *D* from asserting the claim, although the doctrine of

---

59. State procedural systems based on the Federal Rules of Civil Procedure permit unlimited joinder of claims at the pleading stage of the litigation; they provide other procedural mechanisms for separating and resolving the claims at later stages of the litigation if it turns out that the hoped-for procedural convenience is not actually present. *See* Chapter 7(F) *infra* ("Counterclaims and Crossclaims Under the Federal Rules").

60. *See* State *ex rel.* St. Louis Boiler & Equip. Co. v. Gabbert, 241 S.W.2d 79, 82 (Mo. Ct. App. 1951).

issue preclusion could result in *D* being bound in the circuit court action by findings made against *D* in the magistrate court.[61] By resolving the transfer issue in this manner, the court of appeals in State *X* weighed the inefficiencies of resolving factually related claims and counterclaims in separate proceedings as less than depriving the plaintiff of a possible forum preference for the magistrate court. It also gave little weight to the danger of forum shopping by the plaintiff through a "race to the courthouse" and the potential difficulties posed for the defendant by the operation of the doctrine of issue preclusion.

Illustration 2-17. Assume that county courts in State *Y* are authorized to hear any case involving amounts up to $5,000. *P* sued *D* in a county court of State *Y* to recover $2,000 on a promissory note *D* gave to *P*. *D's* answer contained defenses to *P's* claim. *D's* answer also contained a counterclaim for $7,000 based on an alleged conversion of *D's* property by *P*. *D* then sought a transfer of the action to a circuit court in State *Y*. The county court reasoned that only compulsory counterclaims exceeding the jurisdictional limit required transfer of the action; *D's* claim was a permissive counterclaim because it was unrelated to *P's* claim. Thus, the county court concluded that the action need not be transferred and that the counterclaim could not be asserted in the county court because it was beyond the jurisdiction of the county court. The court of appeals in State *Y* granted a writ of prohibition to prevent the county court from exercising jurisdiction in the action. The appellate court interpreted the transfer provision in State *Y* as requiring transfer of an action when either a compulsory or a permissive counterclaim exceeded the jurisdictional amount limit of the county court.[62] In contrast to the case described in *Illustration 2-13*, the court of appeals in State *Y* has given great weight to the convenience of resolving even factually unrelated claims in the same proceeding and more weight to the defendant's interests than to the plaintiff's preference.

7. Order in Which Courts Consider Subject-Matter Jurisdiction Objections When Other Objections Are Raised at the Same Time

Given the significance of subject-matter jurisdiction in American judicial systems, it follows that courts should ordinarily consider and dispose of objections

---

61. *See id.* at 81-82. The court did not indicate whether the doctrine of claim preclusion would allow the defendant to assert part of the claim in the magistrate court and the excess in the circuit court. However, in Brother International Corp. v. Southeastern Sales Co., 234 S.C. 573, 109 S.E.2d 444 (1959), the court indicated that the defendant could assert the counterclaim in the court of limited jurisdiction and waive the amount in excess of the jurisdictional limit or assert the entire claim in a separate action. *See id.* at 575, 109 S.E.2d at 445. This approach is consistent with the modern law of claim preclusion. *See* Chapter 13(B) *infra* ("Claim Preclusion"). However, in McDaneld v. Lynn Hickey Dodge, Inc., 1999 OK 30, 979 P.2d 252, the Oklahoma Supreme Court held that when a defendant who is sued in a small claims court possesses a compulsory counterclaim in excess of the court's jurisdictional competence, the defendant must plead the counterclaim and seek transfer of the action to a court that possesses subject-matter jurisdiction. Failure to plead the counterclaim and seek transfer will result in preclusion of a separate action on the claim. *See also* Rogers v. Bailey, 2011 OK 69, 261 P.3d 1150 (small claims procedure provides for a transfer of case to general docket when a defendant presses a counterclaim that exceeds the statutory limit upon the amount in controversy).

62. *See* State *ex rel.* Rosenfeld v. Boyer, 145 So. 2d 547, 549 (Fla. Dist. Ct. App. 1962); *see also* Elliott v. Roach, 409 N.E.2d 661, 669 (Ind. Ct. App. 1980); State *ex rel.* Moore v. Morrison, 1964 OK 154, ¶ 10, 401 P.2d 484, 486.

based on subject-matter jurisdiction *before* considering other issues in a case. Several recent U.S. Supreme Court decisions illustrate the considerations involved in determining whether subject-matter jurisdiction objections should be given priority over other threshold objections.

Illustration 2-18. In *Steel Co. v. Citizens for a Better Environment*,[63] the Supreme Court held that federal district courts must first decide whether they have subject-matter jurisdiction before deciding whether an action should be dismissed on the ground that the complaint fails to state a claim upon which relief can be granted—even though the failure-to-state-a-claim issue might be easier to decide under available authorities.[64] In addition to the high importance of subject-matter jurisdiction, this priority is also justified by the potential operation of issue preclusion in a subsequent action on the failure-to-state-a-claim issue. If a federal court could dismiss on the ground of failure to state a claim without first considering whether it has subject-matter jurisdiction, one of two unfortunate consequences might follow. Either the plaintiff would be prevented by the doctrine of issue preclusion from commencing a second action on the same complaint in another court,[65] or the second court would have to disregard the first dismissal as "void" because the first court did not have subject-matter jurisdiction to make the dismissal.[66] In the latter case, the second court, which might be a state court, would find itself in the awkward position of determining whether the federal court lacked subject-matter jurisdiction over the action, when the federal court is in a better position to determine that question for itself.[67]

Illustration 2-19. In *Ruhrgas AG v. Marathon Oil Co.*,[68] the Supreme Court distinguished *Steel Co.* by holding that in removed actions,[69] no absolute bar exists

---

63. 523 U.S. 83, 118 S. Ct. 1003, 140 L. Ed. 2d 210 (1998).

64. *Id.* at 92-101, 118 S. Ct. at 1011-16, 140 L. Ed. 2d at 225-32. Note that because a dismissal on subject-matter jurisdiction grounds is not "on the merits," the plaintiff would not be prevented from bringing a second action by the doctrine of "claim preclusion," which only precludes a suit on the same claim when a prior judgment in an action on the claim is "on the merits" or "with prejudice." *See* FED. R. CIV. P. 41(b); Chapter 13(B) *infra* (discussing the doctrine of claim preclusion); *see also* Brereton v. Bountiful City Corp., 434 F.3d 1213 (10th Cir. 2006) (dismissal on jurisdictional ground that plaintiff lacked standing to sue should have been without prejudice).

65. This result would occur because the judgment of dismissal in the first federal action might be held to preclude relitigation of the failure to state a claim issue in a subsequent action in another court. *See* Chapter 13(B)(2) *infra* (discussing the doctrine of direct estoppel).

66. *See* Chapter 13(E) *infra* (discussing exceptions to preclusion when the court in an initial action lacked subject-matter jurisdiction).

67. *See also* Hernandez v. Conriv Realty Assocs., 182 F.3d 121 (2d Cir. 1999) (dismissal with prejudice as a procedural sanction is improper when court lacks subject-matter jurisdiction); University of S. Ala. v. American Tobacco Co., 168 F.3d 405 (11th Cir. 1999) (although voluntary dismissal may normally precede any analysis of subject-matter jurisdiction because voluntary dismissal is self-executing and moots all pending motions, district court must nevertheless reach subject-matter jurisdiction issues first when ruling on the notice of dismissal requires court to reach complex, important questions of state substantive law). For a discussion of the issues of "hypothetical jurisdiction" as applied to issues of appellate jurisdiction, see Joan Steinman, *After* Steel Co.: *"Hypothetical Jurisdiction" in the Federal Appellate Courts,* 58 WASH. & LEE L. REV. 855 (2001); *see also* Ely Todd Chayet, Comment, *Hypothetical Jurisdiction and Interjurisdictional Preclusion: A "Comity" of Errors,* 28 PEPP. L. REV. 75 (2000).

68. 526 U.S. 574, 119 S. Ct. 1563, 143 L. Ed. 2d 760 (1999); *see also* Ortiz v. Fibreboard Corp., 527 U.S. 815, 119 S. Ct. 2295, 144 L. Ed. 2d 715 (1999) (Rule 23 class certification issues are logically antecedent to Article III standing issues and themselves pertain to statutory standing, which may properly be treated before Article III standing; therefore, class certification issues would be treated first). *Steel Co.*, *Ruhrgas*, and *Ortiz* are discussed in Richard D. Freer, *Observations on the Scope of the Supreme Court's Rejection of "Hypothetical Jurisdiction,"* 8 FED. LITIG. GUIDE REP. 247 (1999).

69. *See* section F *infra* (discussing removal jurisdiction).

to considering and disposing of personal jurisdiction[70] issues before taking up questions of subject-matter jurisdiction. Although the Court stated that a federal court customarily resolves issues of subject-matter jurisdiction before questions on the merits (such as failure of the complaint to state a claim on which relief can be granted), no absolute necessity existed for the courts to give priority to subject-matter jurisdiction questions over personal jurisdiction questions. Unlike subject-matter jurisdiction, personal jurisdiction is a "waivable" defect, but it is still an essential element of a court's power to proceed to an adjudication on the merits. When an inquiry into subject-matter jurisdiction would involve a difficult and novel question, but the federal district court is faced with a straightforward issue of personal jurisdiction involving no complex questions of state law, the court may, in its discretion, resolve the personal jurisdiction issue first.[71]

Illustration 2-20. In *Sinochem International Co. v. Malaysia International Shipping Corp.*,[72] the Supreme Court held that the United States District Courts are not obligated to establish their subject-matter jurisdiction before dismissing an action on grounds of forum non conveniens.[73] The Court reasoned that *Sinochem* was a "textbook case" for dismissal on grounds of forum non conveniens, while the issue of subject-matter jurisdiction was more difficult. District courts have discretion to choose among threshold grounds for refusing to decide a case on the merits. If a district court can readily determine that it lacks subject-matter or personal jurisdiction, the proper course would be to dismiss on that ground. However, when subject-matter jurisdiction or personal jurisdiction is difficult to determine and forum non conveniens is easy, as in this case, the court may take the less burdensome course of dismissing on the latter ground.[74]

SECTION B. FEDERAL QUESTION JURISDICTION

As indicated in the preceding section, the Judiciary Act of 1789 created federal trial courts. At an early date, Congress conferred subject-matter jurisdiction on those courts over particular matters arising under federal statutes through specific statutory grants. For example, Congress specifically conferred federal

---

70. *See* Chapter 3 *infra* (discussing personal jurisdiction).

71. 526 U.S. at 583-87, 119 S. Ct. at 1569-72, 143 L. Ed. 2d at 770-73. Nevertheless, the Court's decision leaves troubling questions. If the plaintiff recommences the dismissed action in a state court in the same state, will the state court be permitted to second guess the personal jurisdiction determination if it finds that the federal court acted without subject-matter jurisdiction, or will it be prevented from doing so on the ground that issue preclusion prevents reconsideration of the federal court's dismissal? *See* Chapter 13(E) *infra* (discussing claim and issue preclusion on questions of subject-matter and personal jurisdiction). *Cf.* Norris v. Six Flags Theme Parks, Inc., 102 Haw. 203, 74 P.3d 26 (2003) (personal jurisdiction question must be decided before the merits of a statute of limitations defense).

72. 549 U.S. 422, 127 S. Ct. 1184, 167 L. Ed. 2d 15 (2007).

73. Forum non conveniens is a discretionary venue doctrine that is discussed below in Chapter 4(D)(1)*(a)*.

74. 549 U.S. at 429, 432-34, 127 S. Ct. at 1190, 1192-93, 167 L. Ed. 2d at 15-16, 26-27; *See also* David W. Feder, Note, *The Forum Non Conveniens Dismissal in the Absence of Subject-Matter Jurisdiction,* 74 FORDHAM L. REV. 3147 (2006); *cf.* Davis Int'l, LLC v. New Start Group Corp., 488 F.3d 597 (3d Cir. 2007) (district court held that the issue of forum non conveniens had already been litigated and determined in a prior federal action and could not be relitigated under the doctrine of issue preclusion (discussed in Chapter 13, *infra*), even though the appellees had asserted subject-matter and personal jurisdiction issues in defense as well as issue preclusion on the forum non conveniens question; court of appeals, citing *Sinochem* as controlling, affirmed).

question jurisdiction over actions for patent infringement.[75] However, Congress did not give lower federal courts subject-matter jurisdiction over all cases arising under the Constitution, laws, or treaties of the United States ("general federal question jurisdiction") until 1875.[76] Today, the general federal question statute confers on the district courts "original jurisdiction of all civil actions arising under the Constitution, laws, or treaties of the United States."[77] This general federal question jurisdiction is concurrent with the state courts.

The conventional justification for conferring general federal question jurisdiction on the federal district courts, rather than leaving cases arising under federal law to the state courts, is that the federal courts will provide a more expert, more uniform, and more sympathetic interpretation of federal law.[78] Several empirically unsupported assumptions underlie this conventional justification. The structure of Article III and the Supremacy Clause of the Constitution also undermine the justification.[79] The Supremacy Clause assumes that state courts are fully competent to deal with matters of federal law; and they are bound to uphold the supremacy and validity of that law, notwithstanding anything to the contrary that may exist in their own constitutions and laws.[80] In addition, even if all assumptions supporting conferral of the federal question jurisdiction on the district courts are valid, the achievement of an expert, uniform, and sympathetic interpretation of federal law is left to the discretion of the parties in most cases because of the concurrent nature of much of the jurisdiction.

1. The Constitutional Scope of Federal Question Jurisdiction

The seminal U.S. Supreme Court decision defining the scope of Congress' power to create federal question jurisdiction is *Osborn v. Bank of the United States*.[81] In an opinion written by Chief Justice Marshall, the Supreme Court interpreted Article III to allow Congress to confer jurisdiction on the federal courts whenever federal law forms some "ingredient" in the case, even if no actual issue of federal law exists in the case and even if no federal law confers the basic right of action. The *Osborn* case contained a federal question because the Bank of the United States relied on the U.S. Constitution to invalidate a state law that had levied

---

75. *See* Root v. Railway Co., 105 U.S. 189, 26 L. Ed. 975 (1882).

76. Act of Mar. 3, 1875, ch. 137, § 1, 18 Stat. 470, 470. Originally, this grant of jurisdiction was subject to a jurisdictional amount requirement, but that requirement no longer exists. *See* 28 U.S.C. § 1331.

77. 28 U.S.C. § 1331.

78. *See* ALI STUDY OF THE DIVISION OF JURISDICTION BETWEEN STATE AND FEDERAL COURTS 164-68 (1969); Paul M. Bator, *The State Courts and Federal Constitutional Litigation*, 22 WM. & MARY L. REV. 605, 607, 623 (1981); *see also* Anthony J. Bellia, Jr., *The Origins of Article III "Arising Under" Jurisdiction*, 57 DUKE L.J. 263 (2007); John F. Preis, *Reassessing the Purposes of Federal Question Jurisdiction*, 42 WAKE FOREST L. REV. 247 (2007).

79. *See* U.S. CONST. art. III, VI.

80. *See* THE FEDERALIST No. 82 (Alexander Hamilton) (Jacob E. Cooke ed., 1961); Paul M. Bator, *The State Courts and Federal Constitutional Litigation*, 22 WM. & MARY L. REV. 605, 606, 624, 627-29 (1981). The question whether the state courts are, in fact, in parity with federal courts in the enforcement of federal rights is hotly contested. *See, e.g.*, Burt Neuborne, *The Myth of Parity*, 90 HARV. L. REV. 1105 (1977).

81. 22 U.S. (9 Wheat.) 738, 6 L. Ed. 204 (1824).

a tax on the Bank.[82] However, the opinion in *Osborn* supported a much broader theory. According to Chief Justice Marshall, the federal act incorporating the Bank formed an original ingredient in every case in which the Bank was a party, even if no question of the interpretation or validity of the act was ever raised in the case.[83]

The *Osborn* ingredient theory has sometimes been viewed as a kind of "but for" test. "But for" the federal act creating the Bank, the Bank could not legitimately engage in any transactions or sue or be sued. However, under this view, it is sometimes questionably asserted that the *Osborn* decision authorizes Congress to confer jurisdiction over cases in which federal law is a less active ingredient in a case than was the act incorporating the Bank in *Osborn*.

Illustration 2-21. *Osborn* is sometimes said to authorize Congress to create federal question jurisdiction over virtually every case involving the title to land in the western states because title to land in those states originated in a grant from the United States.[84] This view assumes that the *Osborn* holding extends to any situation in which a right originated remotely in a law of the United States, even if the federal law has exhausted its original force and has no current effect or operation. In other words, "but for" the original grant of land, the current title would not exist. However, in *Osborn*, the act incorporating the Bank was an essential part of the Bank's daily ability to operate. If the act had ceased to exist, the Bank would have ceased to exist. In contrast, after the passage of sufficient time, the original federal law under which a title was granted ceases to have any force or effect, and the title depends entirely on state law for its current viability.[85]

Thus, suppose the United States invalidly conveys title to *A* when *P* is actually entitled to receive title under federal law. *A* then enters the land and conveys to *B*. *B* lives on the land for eighty years and dies. *B* bequeaths the land to *D*, who lives on the land another fifty years. Under these circumstances, state limitations law will preclude *P's* heirs from challenging *D's* title based on title defects in the original grant to *A* under federal law. For Congress to have the power

---

82. *See* CHARLES A. WRIGHT & MARY KAY KANE, THE LAW OF FEDERAL COURTS § 17, at 104 (7th ed. 2011). It is sometimes asserted that the Bank was asserting a "claim under the federal Constitution." *See id.* at 104. However, this assertion is incorrect on the facts of the case. Technically, the Bank's claim was an injunction against trespass. The defense asserted to the claim was that the state statute authorized the levy of the tax. In effect, the federal constitutional issue came into the action as a reply to this defense, not as a part of the plaintiff's "claim," which arose under state law. *See Osborn*, 22 U.S. at 836-37, 6 L. Ed. at 833. Nevertheless, a *case* still arises under the laws of the United States for purposes of Article III when the federal issue in the case comes into the action as a defense or a reply to a defense. *See* subsection 2*(b) infra* (discussing the "well-pleaded complaint" rule). For a discussion of the nature of trespass, see Chapter 1(D)(3)-(4) *supra*; *see also* Carlos M. Vázquez, *The Federal "Claim" in the District Courts:* Osborn, Verlinden, *and Protective Jurisdiction,* 95 CAL. L. REV. 1731 (2007).

83. *See* 22 U.S. (9 Wheat.) at 823-24, 6 L. Ed. at 820; *see also* CHARLES A. WRIGHT & MARY KAY KANE, THE LAW OF FEDERAL COURTS § 17, at 104 (7th ed. 2011). The Act incorporating the Bank was the only basis for federal jurisdiction in Bank of the United States v. Planters' Bank, 22 U.S. (9 Wheat.) 904, 6 L. Ed. 244 (1824), in which no issues of federal law were involved in the case.

84. *See* CHARLES A. WRIGHT & MARY KAY KANE, THE LAW OF FEDERAL COURTS § 17, at 104 (7th ed. 2011); *see also* Shulthis v. McDougal, 225 U.S. 561, 569-70, 32 S. Ct. 704, 706, 56 L. Ed. 1205, 1211 (1912); Shoshone Mining Co. v. Rutter, 177 U.S. 505, 507, 20 S. Ct. 726, 726, 44 L. Ed. 864, 865 (1900), which discuss why the title-to-western-land cases do not fit within the statutory federal question jurisdiction.

85. Ordinarily, when a title is granted by the United States, the incidents of the title are not thereafter forever controlled by federal law. Instead, state law controls subsequent transfers of title as well as other rights to hold and enjoy peaceable possession. Thus, even if a defect existed in the original title that could be challenged by someone at the time the title had been granted to the original purchaser, state adverse possession statutes operating on the title would, after the passage of sufficient time, eliminate the ability to assert a valid challenge to the title based on "federal" defects. Thus, the force of federal law would be eliminated from any dispute about the title.

to grant federal question jurisdiction in a case between *D* and *P's* heirs, *Osborn* would have to be extended beyond its facts to circumstances in which federal law could not possibly have any current force. This example demonstrates that if Article III is interpreted to establish a "but for" test of Congress' power to establish federal question jurisdiction, the holding of *Osborn* cannot be its basis.

* * * * *

Whatever the scope of the *Osborn* holding, the decision permits Congress to create federal question jurisdiction in cases in which a federally chartered corporation is a party.

Illustration 2-22. In *American National Red Cross v. S.G.*,[86] a blood recipient sued the Red Cross, a federally chartered corporation, in state court. The recipient alleged that blood supplied by the Red Cross had caused the recipient to contract AIDS. The Red Cross removed the action to a U.S. District Court on the basis of federal question jurisdiction. The district court upheld jurisdiction based on a provision in the Red Cross charter authorizing the Red Cross "to sue and be sued in courts of law and equity, State or Federal, within the jurisdiction of the United States." The U.S. Court of Appeals reversed. It held that Congress did not intend the "sue and be sued" provision of the charter to be a grant of subject-matter jurisdiction. The U.S. Supreme Court granted certiorari and reversed the court of appeals. Relying on *Osborn* and other decisions, the Court held the "sue and be sued" provision granted federal question jurisdiction within Article III of the Constitution. The Court interpreted its prior decisions as establishing the rule that a congressional charter's "sue and be sued" provision may be read to confer federal jurisdiction "if, but only if, it specifically mentions the federal courts."[87]

2. The Scope of the Statutory Grant of Federal Question Jurisdiction

Osborn (discussed in the preceding subsection) establishes how far Congress may go in creating jurisdiction for cases arising under Article III. The rule established by *Osborn* must be distinguished from the rules that apply to the statutory grant of general federal question jurisdiction in 28 U.S.C. § 1331. Because the language of the general federal question statute is substantially the same as the language of the Constitution, one might think that Congress has conferred on the district courts the full scope of the "federal question" jurisdiction permitted under Article III. However, Congress need not confer the full scope of the jurisdiction authorized by any clause of Article III on the inferior federal courts. In fact, the constitutional scope of federal question jurisdiction has always been much broader

---

86. 505 U.S. 247, 112 S. Ct. 2465, 120 L. Ed. 2d 201 (1992).

87. *Id.* at 255, 112 S. Ct. at 2471, 120 L. Ed. 2d at 211. In most cases involving congressionally chartered corporations, federal jurisdiction has been limited by statute to cases in which the United States owns more than one-half the capital stock of the federally chartered corporation. *See* 28 U.S.C. § 1349. However, the Court held that the Red Cross charter conferred jurisdiction independently of this statutory restriction. *See* 505 U.S. at 251 n.3, 112 S. Ct. at 2469 n.3, 120 L. Ed. 2d at 209 n.3; *cf.* Adair v. Lease Partners, Inc., 587 F.3d 238 (5th Cir. 2009) (statute providing that suits in which FDIC are a party are deemed to arise under federal law provides for federal question jurisdiction even after FDIC is dismissed from an action).

than the jurisdiction conferred by the general federal question statute. This difference means, *inter alia*, that Congress has a significant repository of power to draw upon in expanding the statutory jurisdiction to meet future requirements in the administration of federal law.

The U.S. Supreme Court has interpreted the statutory grant of general federal question jurisdiction much more narrowly than the constitutional grant to prevent "a flood of litigation" based on some remote federal "ingredient" in the cases.[88] This restrictive interpretation of the general federal question statute has given rise to a set of complex rules for determining whether a case arises under federal law for purposes of jurisdiction in the federal district courts.[89] The following subsections explore (1) the analytical categories of cases in which federal question jurisdiction has been found to exist, (2) a frequently stated test for federal question jurisdiction called the *"well-pleaded complaint" rule*, and (3) special problems of determining whether federal question jurisdiction exists in actions seeking the remedy of declaratory judgment.

(a) The Categories of Cases That Arise Under Federal Law Within the Meaning of 28 U.S.C. § 1331

Section 1331 has been read to grant jurisdiction in three general situations. First, § 1331 grants jurisdiction when *federal law expressly creates a remedy*.[90]

Illustration 2-23. Civil rights actions under 42 U.S.C. § 1983 vindicate infringements of constitutional rights by persons acting under color of state law.

---

88. CHARLES A. WRIGHT & MARY KAY KANE, THE LAW OF FEDERAL COURTS § 17, at 104 (7th ed. 2011). Professors Wright and Kane have explained the reason for the differing interpretation of the Constitution and the statute:

> What . . . had not always been kept in mind . . . is that there is a difference between construing the Constitution, as Marshall was obliged to do in Osborn, and construing a statute. The very expansive reading Marshall gave to the "cases arising under" language of the Constitution is appropriate in dealing with a constitution. It leaves room for Congress to grant such particular jurisdiction as may in the future be seen to be necessary. But to hold that [§ 1331] gives federal jurisdiction wherever some element of federal law is an "ingredient" of the cause of action would mean, for example, that virtually every case involving the title to land in the western states, where title descends from a grant from the United States, could be litigated in federal court. If Congress in fact meant to open the door of the federal courthouse to such a flood of litigation, the Osborn case shows that it had the power to do so. Actually both the language of [§ 1331], following so closely the constitutional language, and such skimpy legislative history as exists, do support the view that Congress meant to give all the jurisdiction it could constitutionally confer, but this is not an inevitable conclusion, and the courts acted understandably in giving a restrictive reading to the statute.

Id. (footnotes omitted). Although these conclusions about the western land title cases has been questioned in the preceding subsection, Professors Wright and Kane are nevertheless correct that interpreting 28 U.S.C. § 1331 to confer the full scope of the constitutionally permissible jurisdiction would undoubtedly open the doors of the federal courts to an excess of litigation only remotely related to substantial federal interests.

89. The classic works on federal question jurisdiction are James H. Chadbourn & A. Leo Levin, *Original Jurisdiction of Federal Questions*, 90 U. PA. L. REV. 639 (1942); William Cohen, *The Broken Compass: The Requirement That a Case Arise "Directly" Under Federal Law*, 115 U. PA. L. REV. 890 (1967); Paul J. Mishkin, *The Federal "Question" in the District Courts*, 53 COLUM. L. REV. 157 (1953).

90. *See* 13D CHARLES A. WRIGHT ET AL., FEDERAL PRACTICE AND PROCEDURE: JURISDICTION § 3562, at 183 (3d ed. 2008). In Milan Express, Inc. v. Averitt Express, Inc., 208 F.3d 975 (11th Cir. 2000), a suit was commenced on an injunction bond issued under Federal Rule 65, and a claim for damages was asserted in excess of the amount of the bond. The court of appeals upheld the district court's jurisdiction under 28 U.S.C. § 1352, which authorizes suit on any bond executed under "any law of the United States." Rule 65 was held to be a "law of the United States" for the purposes of this jurisdictional provision.

Section 1983 expressly authorizes legal and equitable remedies when a person's federal constitutional rights have been deprived.[91]

* * * * *

Second, § 1331 grants jurisdiction when *federal law imposes a duty from which a remedy may be implied.*[92]

Illustration 2-24. Assume that a federal official violates the plaintiff's right not to be subjected to unreasonable searches and seizures under the Fourth Amendment to the U.S. Constitution. No federal law expressly creates a remedy for a Fourth Amendment violation. Rather, federal law in the form of the Fourth Amendment imposes a duty upon the federal official. The U.S. Supreme Court has implied the remedy of damages for violation of that duty.[93]

* * * * *

These first two situations in which federal question jurisdiction exists are sometimes referred to as "Category 1" cases. Category 1 cases are cases that "arise under" federal law for purposes of the general federal question statute because "the plaintiff asserts a federally created cause of action."[94] This statement is accurate and can be relied on without harm, provided it is recognized that not every federal "duty" is of the sort that is appropriate for the implication of a remedy that will produce a federal "cause of action."[95]

Third, § 1331 grants jurisdiction when *state law creates both the right and the remedy, but an important question of federal law is an essential element in the plaintiff's case.*[96] This third situation is often referred to as "Category 2" of the federal question jurisdiction. This category may seem quite broad. In fact, however, it is seldom the basis for federal question jurisdiction. The case authority supporting this basis for jurisdiction is narrow. As discussed below, it may be used to establish jurisdiction only in cases in which (1) the federal interest in the action is sufficiently substantial to justify the exercise of federal jurisdiction and (2) the increased caseload to the federal courts of hearing cases of the same sort would not be severe.

For a significant period of time, the Supreme Court authorities approving and disapproving Category 2 jurisdiction were in a state of confusion. Recently, however, the Court has attempted to clarify the considerations that are important to the exercise of Category 2 federal question jurisdiction. An examination of the two

---

91. *Cf.* Mims v. Arrow Fin. Servs., L.L.C., 565 U.S. __, 132 S. Ct. 740, 181 L. Ed. 2d 881 (2012) (Telephone Consumer Protection Act creates federal claim for relief and permissive grant of jurisdiction to state courts did not deprive federal courts of jurisdiction over such claim, but only provided for concurrent jurisdiction); Cotroneo v. Shaw Env't & Infrastructure, Inc., 639 F.3d 186 (5th Cir. 2011) (federal Price-Anderson Act explicitly provided that substantive rules of decision shall be derived from state law of state in which a nuclear incident occurs and thus provided that state law operate as federal law, thereby creating a new cause of action that supplanted prior state cause of action).

92. *See* 13D CHARLES A. WRIGHT ET AL., FEDERAL PRACTICE AND PROCEDURE: JURISDICTION § 3562, at 210-11 (3d ed. 2008).

93. *See* Bivens v. Six Unknown Named Agents of Fed. Bureau of Narcotics, 403 U.S. 388, 91 S. Ct. 1999, 29 L. Ed. 2d 619 (1971).

94. RICHARD H. FALLON ET AL., HART & WECHSLER'S THE FEDERAL COURTS AND THE FEDERAL SYSTEM 782 (6th ed. 2009).

95. *See generally id.* at 812-25 (5th ed. 2003).

96. *See* 13D CHARLES A. WRIGHT ET AL., FEDERAL PRACTICE AND PROCEDURE: JURISDICTION AND RELATED MATTERS § 3562, at 187-99 (3d ed. 2008).

leading authorities (the *Smith* and *Merrell* Dow cases) prior to the Court's clarification will indicate the nature of the confusion that formerly existed.

In *Smith v. Kansas City Title & Trust Co.*,[97] state law prohibited the directors of a corporation from investing in illegally issued securities and provided shareholders a remedy against the directors for breach of this duty. The U.S. Supreme Court found that federal question jurisdiction existed because the directors wanted to invest in securities that had allegedly been issued in violation of federal law. In this case, state law created the plaintiff's basic right of action—the right to sue to prevent directors from investing in illegal securities. However, federal law was essential to the existence of this right because only federal law allegedly made the issuance of the securities illegal. In addition, the question of federal law in the case was an important one: the constitutionality of a federal statute authorizing the issuance of the securities that the plaintiff claimed were illegally issued. In this situation, the impact of an erroneous state court decision on the question of federal law was potentially severe. If a state court incorrectly decided that the statute was unconstitutional, all the federal securities issued under the statute would, as a practical matter, become unmarketable until the state court decision was corrected on appeal. Thus, not only was federal law essential to the plaintiff's claim, the federal interest in a correct decision was great. As stated earlier, the justification for conferring federal question jurisdiction on the district courts is that those courts will provide a more expert, sympathetic, and uniform interpretation of federal law than the state courts. If so, the federal interest in such an interpretation in *Smith* clearly justified the exercise of jurisdiction.

In *Merrell Dow Pharmaceuticals Inc. v. Thompson*,[98] the U.S. Supreme Court held federal jurisdiction improper when the federal interest in the case was not as strong as in the *Smith* case. In *Merrell Dow*, the plaintiffs sought damages for the birth of deformed children that resulted from the mothers' ingestion during pregnancy of a drug manufactured by the defendant. Five of six counts in each complaint were based entirely on state law. One count, however, alleged that the drug had been misbranded in violation of the Federal Food, Drug, and Cosmetic Act (FDCA).[99] If this allegation proved to be correct, a rebuttable presumption would arise under state law that the defendant had been negligent. Thus, a federal law would contribute to the plaintiffs' state claims for negligence. However, the Court held that the failure of Congress to create a federal right of action in damages for violation of the FDCA made the exercise of federal jurisdiction improper. In effect, the Court held that since Congress failed to provide a remedy for the violation of the FDCA, the federal interest in the case was too weak to justify the exercise of federal question jurisdiction.[100]

It was possible to read *Merrell Dow* as meaning that whenever Congress fails to provide a remedy, the strength of the federal interest is too weak to justify the exercise of federal jurisdiction. However, under this reading of the case, *Smith*,

---

97. 255 U.S. 180, 41 S. Ct. 243, 65 L. Ed. 577 (1921).
98. 478 U.S. 804, 106 S. Ct. 3229, 92 L. Ed. 2d 650 (1986).
99. 21 U.S.C. §§ 301-393.
100. *See Merrell Dow*, 478 U.S. at 814-17, 106 S. Ct. at 3235-36, 92 L. Ed. 2d at 662-64.

which involved no congressionally created right of action, would no longer be good law. Yet, the Court cited and discussed *Smith* with approval in *Merrell Dow*.[101] The facts of *Merrell Dow* and *Smith*, when read in conjunction, suggested plausible alternative readings of the former case that would have produced the same result without placing such emphasis on the failure of Congress to provide a right of action in damages under the FDCA.

In *Merrell Dow*, the Court explicitly rejected the view that federal question jurisdiction was improper because the plaintiff could also recover on the exclusively state-law claims.[102] Thus, the fact that in *Smith* federal law was the only basis upon which the plaintiff could win is not a viable distinction between *Merrell Dow* and *Smith*. Nevertheless, violation of federal law would have produced only a rebuttable presumption of negligence in *Merrell Dow*. In contrast, violation of federal law in *Smith* would have produced *automatic* victory. Therefore, the contribution of federal law in *Smith* was, in a sense, more important than in *Merrell Dow*. In addition, the court in *Merrell Dow* distinguished *Smith* by observing: "In *Smith* . . . the issue was the constitutionality of an important federal statute."[103] This observation suggested either that federal question jurisdiction will exist (1) when a federal constitutional question contributes to a state right of action, (2) when an "important" federal statute contributes to the state right of action, or (3) when the state claim involves the federal constitutionality of an important federal statute.[104]

A more satisfactory distinction would be one based on the degree of impact that an erroneous state-court decision might have on the enforcement of federal law in each case. In *Merrell Dow*, the impact of an erroneous decision on the federal issue was not nearly as severe as in *Smith*. If a state court erroneously decided that the defendant's drug had been mislabeled in violation of the FDCA, the erroneous decision might result in the defendant and others similarly situated having to exercise more care than the FDCA really requires during the time necessary to overturn the state decision on appeal. However, a defendant who exercises more care than legally required does not really undermine the purpose of the FDCA, which requires care in labeling to protect consumers. On the other hand, if a state court erroneously determined that the defendant's drug was *not* misbranded in violation of federal law, the decision would not bind the Federal Food and Drug Administration. The law could still be enforced by that agency against the defendant independently of the state court decision. On this view, *Merrell Dow* was an easy case in which the federal issue was neither an essential component of the state claim nor important enough to warrant the exercise of federal jurisdiction.[105]

Nevertheless, it was obvious that to clarify the distinction between *Merrell Dow* and *Smith*, the Court needed, at least, to establish what weight federal courts

---

101. *See* 478 U.S. at 814 n.12, 106 S. Ct. at 3235 n.12, 92 L. Ed. 2d at 662 n.12.

102. *See id.* at 817 n.15, 106 S. Ct. at 3236 n.15, 92 L. Ed. 2d at 664 n.15.

103. *See id.* at 814 n.12, 106 S. Ct. at 3235 n.12, 92 L. Ed. 2d at 662 n.12.

104. *See also* Note, *Mr. Smith Goes to Federal Court: Federal Question Jurisdiction over State Law Claims Post-*Merrell Dow, 115 HARV. L. REV. 2272, 2288, 2290-93 (2002) (criticizing the distinction between statutory and constitutional claims and arguing for a test that focuses on the state's interest in restricting the *Smith*-type of claim to state court).

105. For a complete discussion and criticism of *Merrell Dow*, see Note, *The Supreme Court, 1985 Term—Leading Cases*, 100 HARV. L. REV. 100, 230-40 (1986).

should give to (1) the importance of the contribution made by federal law to the state claim, (2) the significance of a federal constitutional contribution to the state claim (or of inclusion in the state claim of the federal constitutionality of an important federal statute), and (3) the danger to the administration of federal law of an erroneous state-court decision. Because of the existing ambiguities of the test, the lower federal courts applied it in divergent ways.[106]

In *Grable & Sons Metal Products, Inc. v. Darue Engineering & Manufacturing,*[107] the Supreme Court attempted to clarify the *Merrell Dow* test. In *Grable,* the Internal Revenue Service (IRS) seized land from the plaintiff for a federal tax deficiency. The plaintiff sued in state court to quiet title to land that the IRS conveyed to the defendant by quitclaim deed. The plaintiff contended that the notice of the seizure given by the IRS, although received by him, did not comply with federal statutory requirements. Thus, although state law created the right of action, the entire claim turned on the interpretation of the federal statute providing for notice to the plaintiff. The defendant removed the action, the district court refused to remand, and the court of appeals affirmed. The Supreme Court granted certiorari and affirmed.[108]

The Court made it clear that the failure of Congress to create a right of action was not to be given conclusive weight under the *Merrell Dow* test.

> . . . *Merrell Dow* should be read in its entirety as treating the absence of a federal private right of action as evidence relevant to, but not dispositive of, the "sensitive judgments about congressional intent" that § 1331 requires. The absence of any federal cause of action affected *Merrell Dow's* result two ways. The Court saw the fact as worth some consideration in the assessment of substantiality. But its primary importance emerged when the Court treated the combination of no federal cause of action and no preemption of state remedies for misbranding as an important clue to Congress's conception of the scope of jurisdiction to be exercised under § 1331. The Court saw the missing cause of action not as a missing federal door key, always required, but as a missing welcome mat, required in the circumstances, when exercising federal jurisdiction over a state

---

106. *See, e.g.,* Douglas v. E.G. Baldwin & Assocs., Inc., 150 F.3d 604 (6th Cir. 1998) (violation of the policies of the federal Family and Medical Leave Act, 29 U.S.C. § 2601 *et seq.*, which had been voluntarily adopted by an employer to whom the Act did not apply, did not produce a case arising under federal law); Torres v. Southern Peru Copper Corp., 113 F.3d 540 (5th Cir. 1997) (Peruvian government protested suit against the copper company, which removed an action commenced by Peruvian citizens on state claims in state court; the federal court of appeals held federal question jurisdiction appropriate because it raised substantial questions of federal common law by implicating important foreign policy concerns, but the court never identified the precise way in which federal law contributed to the plaintiff's claim); Guardian Nat'l Acceptance Corp. v. Swartzlander Motors, Inc., 962 F. Supp. 1137 (N.D. Ind. 1997) (finance company sued car dealer alleging that it breached contract warranties in assignment of contract with car buyer by violating the federal Truth in Lending Act, resulting in the finance company being sued by the car buyer and incurring litigation costs in the action, which it won; although the action was based on state contract law, the district court held that the federal contribution was sufficient to create Category 2 jurisdiction, even though the right of action created by Congress in the federal Act was on behalf of the car buyer and not the finance company).

107. 545 U.S. 308, 125 S. Ct. 2363, 162 L. Ed. 2d 257 (2005).

108. *Id.* at 310, 125 S. Ct. at 2366, 162 L. Ed. 2d at 262-63.

> misbranding action would have attracted a horde of original filings and removal cases raising other state claims with embedded federal issues. For if the federal labeling standard without a federal cause of action could get a state claim into federal court, so could any other federal standard without a federal cause of action. And that would have meant a tremendous number of cases.[109]

In contrast, the Court observed that the application of the federal interest test to the case before it would not produce the same consequences. Even though Congress had not created a federal right of action in the case before the Court, "it is the rare state quiet title action that involves contested issues of federal law."[110] As a result,

> jurisdiction over actions like [the plaintiff's] would not materially affect, or threaten to affect, the normal currents of litigation. Given the absence of threatening structural consequences and the clear interest the Government, its buyers, and its delinquents have in the availability of a federal forum, there is no good reason to shirk from federal jurisdiction over the dispositive and contested federal issue at the heart of the state-law title claim.[111]

In addition, the Court explicitly rejected the plaintiff's argument that, after *Merrell Dow*, federal question jurisdiction over state-law claims would be proper in the absence of a federal right of action only when a federal constitutional question existed in the case. Although, "[a]s *Merrell Dow* itself suggested, constitutional questions may be the more likely ones to reach the level of substantiality that can justify federal jurisdiction," the Court observed that "a flat ban on statutory questions would mechanically exclude significant questions of federal law like the one this case presents."[112]

The Court's clarification of the *Merrell Dow* test in *Grable* is welcome and answers several of the questions examined earlier about the distinctions between *Smith* and *Merrell Dow*. However, whether the clarification will suitably resolve the confusion among the lower federal courts about the proper extent of federal jurisdiction over state claims involving essential federal questions is doubtful. As Justice Thomas noted in his concurrence, "[j]urisdictional rules should be clear."[113] It is questionable whether the test that the Court announces meets this criterion.

Decisions subsequent to *Grable* confirm this judgment. In *Empire Healthchoice Assurance, Inc. v. McVeigh,*[114] Empire sued McVeigh, a federal

---

109. *Id.* at 318, 125 S. Ct. at 2370, 162 L. Ed. 2d at 267.

110. *Id.* at 319, 125 S. Ct. at 2371, 162 L. Ed. 2d at 268.

111. *Id.*

112. *Id.* at 320 n.7, 125 S. Ct. at 2371 n.7, 162 L. Ed. 2d at 268 n.7; *cf.* Palkow v. CSX Transp., Inc., 431 F.3d 543 (6th Cir. 2005) (an independent action collaterally attacking a prior federal judgment on grounds that it was based on perjured testimony and seeking compensatory damages does not allege a substantial federal question of great federal interest and may not be entertained by a federal court without independent subject-matter jurisdiction).

113. 545 U.S. at 321, 125 S. Ct. at 2372, 162 L. Ed. 2d at 269; *see also* Andrew D. Bradt, Grable *on the Ground: Mitigating Unchecked Jurisdictional Discretion*, 44 U.C. DAVIS L. REV. 1153 (2011); Rory Ryan, *No Welcome Mat, No Problem?: Federal-Question Jurisdiction After* Grable, 80 ST. JOHN'S L. REV. 621 (2006).

114. 547 U.S. 677, 126 S. Ct. 2121, 165 L. Ed. 2d 131 (2006).

worker, in United States District Court to seeking reimbursement of insurance benefits on the grounds that McVeigh had recovered damages for his injuries in a state tort action. A federal law, the Federal Employees Health Benefits Act of 1959 ("FEHBA") displaced state law on questions relating to coverage or benefits afforded by health care plans of federal employees such as McVeigh, but contained no provision addressing the subrogation or reimbursement of health care carriers. FEHBA also specifically authorized federal question jurisdiction over civil actions or claims against the United States, but did not expressly authorize federal jurisdiction to carriers seeking reimbursement from beneficiaries or tortfeasors. Empire argued, among other things, that federal question jurisdiction was proper under *Grable* because federal law was a necessary element of Empire's claim for relief.

The Supreme Court rejected this argument. The Court distinguished *Grable* on several grounds. First, it noted that *Grable* centered on the action of a federal agency (the IRS) and the compatibility of that action with a federal statute, whereas the case before it concerned action triggered not by the action of a federal agency, but by settlement of a personal-injury action in state court and the proportion of that settlement that was properly payable to Empire. Second, the Court observed that *Grable* concerned a "pure issue of law," whereas the case before it was highly fact dependent. Third, although a claim for reimbursement might involve as an issue the extent, if any, to which the reimbursement should take into account attorney's fees expended to obtain the tort recovery, an issue the Court implied might be governed by federal law, the Court reasoned that there was no reason why a proper federal-state balance should place such a non-statutory issue under the complete control of a federal court. Finally, the Court stated that even though the United States has a strong interest in attracting able federal workers to the federal workforce and in the health and welfare of those workers, those interests did not warrant turning an insurer's contract claim for reimbursement into a discrete and costly federal case.[115]

The Court's judgments about federal jurisdiction in *Empire* may be correct, but the conclusory and seemingly ad hoc nature of the distinctions drawn between *Empire* and *Grable* do not significantly clarify how Category 2 federal question cases should be identified. Nevertheless, together, *Grable* and *Empire* make it possible to discern an outline of how a Category 2 case should be analyzed. To be appropriate for Category 2, the federal issue of law contributing to the state claim (1) must be essential to the plaintiff's claim, essential probably meaning that resolution of the issue will be dispositive of the case; (2) must actually be contested in the case;[116] (3) must be a "pure" question of law and not highly fact-dependent in that the application of the federal law will often change with a variety of fact situations likely to be presented under the law; and (4) must be an issue that is "substantial," or "important," probably in the sense that the decision will affect the

---

115. *Id.* at 699-701, 126 S. Ct. at 2136-37, 165 L. Ed. 2d at 149-50.

116. Note that it is unclear whether this requirement will prevent a federal court from taking jurisdiction to enforce a federal law whose meaning is settled and that contributes to a state claim when the settled meaning of the federal law has been ignored or disregarded by one of the parties.

ability to administer the law in a uniform, national manner; the importance of the issue will be enhanced if the way in which the federal law is administered affects the interests of the federal government in a significant way. Finally, (5) the adjudication of the federal issue must not present a danger that large numbers of cases involving basically state-law claims will be adjudicated in federal court within the federal question jurisdiction.[117]

The lower federal court decisions since *Grable* and *Empire* have not significantly eliminated the remaining ambiguities in the Category 2 test. However, it is also true that the lower courts have not had much difficulty administering the *Grable* test, perhaps indicating that the ambiguities of the test discussed above do not present major problems. For example, in *Eastman v. Marine Mechanical Corp.,*[118] the plaintiff brought an action in Ohio state court against his former employer for retaliatory discharge under Ohio law, which provided a remedy for such a discharge "in violation of public policy." The complaint alleged violation of both Ohio public policy and public policy embodied in federal statutes, the latter of which did not create federal rights of action on behalf of the plaintiff. The defendant removed the action to federal court on the basis of federal question jurisdiction, the plaintiff moved to remand for lack of subject-matter jurisdiction, and the district court denied remand. Subsequently, the district court granted summary judgment against the plaintiff, and the plaintiff appealed.

The Sixth Circuit Court of Appeals held that the district court lacked federal question jurisdiction and the action should have been remanded. Interpreting *Grable*, the court held that there was no substantial federal question because the meaning of none of the federal statutes was in doubt, in contrast to the federal statute in *Grable.* In addition, the court held that accepting jurisdiction would be disruptive of the sound division of labor between state and federal courts envisioned by Congress. This was because employment litigation is a frequent occurrence in both federal and state courts, and Congress had provided access to the federal courts by employees under specifically delineated circumstances. The balance established by Congress would be upset "drastically" if state public policy claims could be converted into federal claims by "the simple expedient of referencing federal law as the source of that public policy." The court's analysis seems sound.[119]

In *Mikulski v. Centerior Energy Corp.,*[120] plaintiffs commenced state litigation breach of contract and fraudulent misrepresentation that caused them to overpay federal and state income taxes. The defendant removed the action on the basis of federal question jurisdiction, contending that although the plaintiffs' claims were based on state law, they raised a substantial question of federal law because of the need to interpret the federal income tax laws. The district court refused to remand, but the Sixth Circuit Court of Appeals reversed, holding that the plaintiffs had not raised a substantial federal question. The court held that when a federal

---

117. This factor is related to factor 3 above and may, in fact, be indistinguishable from it; this factor may also trump all the other factors in the sense that even an essential, contested, important issue of federal law contributing to a state claim will not sustain federal question jurisdiction if it creates a significant caseload problem.

118. 438 F.3d 544 (6th Cir. 2006).

119. *Id.* at 546-55.

120. 435 F.3d 666 (6th Cir. 2006).

issue is raised in a state claim, federal jurisdiction exists only if the federal issue is substantial, disputed, of great federal interest, and necessary to the decision of the state claim. In the case before it, the court of appeals viewed the federal income tax issues as involving only insubstantial analysis or interpretation of federal law, making the federal interest weak in adjudicating the issue in federal court.[121]

However, in *Nicodemus v. Union Pacific Corp.*,[122] the Tenth Circuit Court of Appeals concluded that federal question jurisdiction existed in a state action for trespass, unjust enrichment, and slander of title. The action was by landowners against a railroad based on the railroad's licensing to telecommunications providers of the right to install and maintain fiber-optic cable in its rights-of-way on the landowners' property. The landowners contended, among other things, that the railroad's actions exceeded the scope of its rights under the federal land-grant statute. The court of appeals concluded that there was a contested interpretation of the federal land-grant statute in the action that constituted a substantial federal question under *Grable*. The court also concluded that the United States had a direct interest in the determination of property rights granted to the railroad, even though there was no federal right of action under the statute. Additionally, the court opined that providing a federal forum would not disrupt the sound division of labor between state and federal courts, because it would be the rare state trespass action that would so uniquely turn on a matter of federal law.[123]

Note that the difference in result in *Mikulski* and *Nicodemus* turned in part on the evaluation by the respective courts of the importance of the federal issue, although *Nicodemus* also turned on the lack of a significant caseload impact. There is likely to be significant room for difference of opinion on the question of the importance of the federal issue from case to case, creating substantial lack of predictability about when Category 2 jurisdiction will be held appropriate. Furthermore, although *Nicodemus* seems to suggest that the caseload factor can trump even important federal interests, only time will tell whether this should be taken seriously. The probability that there will have to be extensive litigation over the weight to be given to the *Grable* factors and how they should interact with each other indicates the wisdom of Justice Thomas's suggestion that Category 2 jurisdiction should be reconsidered.

Finally, *Bennett v. Southwest Airlines Co.*,[124] is an illustration of an easy case in which none of the *Grable* factors pointed toward the exercise of jurisdiction. The Seventh Circuit Court of Appeals held that federal jurisdiction did not exist over state claims arising out of aircraft accidents simply because federal law plays an important role in air transportation. There was no contention that a disputed issue of federal law governed any particular aspect of the plaintiffs' claims, and it was possible that federal statutes and regulations would play no role at all in resolving

---

121. *Id.* at 668-70, 674-66.

122. 440 F.3d 1227 (10th Cir. 2006).

123. *Id.* at 1230-37; *see also* Richard D. Freer, *Of Rules and Standards: Reconciling Statutory Limitations on "Arising Under" Jurisdiction,* 82 IND. L.J. 309 (2007); Douglas D. McFarland, *The True Compass: No Federal Question in a State Law Claim,* 55 KAN. L. REV. 1 (2006); Jason Pozner, *The More Things Change, the More They Stay the Same:* Grable & Sons v. Darue Engineering *Does Not Resolve the Split Over* Merrell Dow v. Thompson, 2 SETON HALL CIR. REV. 533 (2006).

124. 484 F.3d 907 (7th Cir. 2007).

the claims. In addition, the claims would require fact-specific application of both state law and any federal law that would be involved, not a "context free" inquiry into the meaning of federal law.[125]

One additional question that has been presented in Category 2 cases is how the category operates in situations in which the federal law contributing to the state claim is the subject of a grant of exclusive jurisdiction to the federal courts. In *Christianson v. Colt Industries Operating Corp.*,[126] the Supreme Court considered which of two appellate courts, the Federal Circuit or the Seventh Circuit Court of Appeals, had appellate jurisdiction over a case. This issue depended on whether the action was one "arising under the patent statutes" for purposes of 28 U.S.C. § 1338(a), which provides for exclusive jurisdiction in the federal district courts over patent, plant variety protection, and copyright cases. If the case arose under § 1338(a), then the appeal was exclusively in the Federal Court of Appeals under 28 U.S.C. § 1295(a)(1); otherwise, appellate jurisdiction was in the Seventh Circuit. In deciding this action, the Court analogized jurisdiction under § 1338 to jurisdiction under § 1331, the general federal question statute. This meant that the plaintiff's claim had to depend on federal patent law; it was not sufficient that an issue of patent law be raised in defense. At one point, the Court stated:

> A district court's federal-question jurisdiction, we recently explained, extends over "only those cases in which a well-pleaded complaint establishes either that federal law creates the cause of action or that the plaintiff's right to relief necessarily depends on resolution of a substantial question of federal law . . . in that "federal law is a necessary element of one of the well-pleaded . . . claims.[127]

This statement by the Court seems to envision that both Category 1 and Category 2 cases are possible under § 1338(a). If this is so, of course, then not only would the United States District Courts have the power to hear a Category 2 case in which patent law contributed to a state-law claim in the appropriate way, but, because of the grant of exclusive jurisdiction to those courts in the statute, the state courts might be excluded from hearing the case.

In fact, such cases have occurred in the lower federal (and state) courts. For example, in *Air Measurement Technologies, Inc.* v. *Akin Gump Strauss Hauer & Feld, L.L.P.*,[128] a former client brought a malpractice action against an attorney in state court for legal malpractice based on alleged mistakes made by the attorney in prior patent litigation. The action was removed to U.S. District Court, which denied a motion to remand, but certified the case for an interlocutory appeal to the Federal Court of Appeals. That court, following the dictum in *Christianson* quoted above, held that the action arose under the patent laws for purposes of § 1338(a), because it was an essential part of the state malpractice claim for the plaintiff to

---

125. *See id.* at 909-12.
126. 486 U.S. 800, 108 S. Ct. 2166, 100 L. Ed. 2d 811 (1988).
127. *Id.* at 808, 108 S. Ct. at 2173-74, 100 L. Ed. at 825.
128. 504 F.3d 1262 (Fed. Cir. 2008).

establish that it would have prevailed in the prior action, which meant that it had to prove patent infringement.[129]

Subsequently, in *Minton v. Gunn*,[130] a legal malpractice claim was brought in a state court based on prior patent infringement litigation. The action was not removed to federal court, and the state trial court granted summary judgment for the defendant. After the plaintiff appealed to the Texas Court of Appeals in Fort Worth, the Federal Court of Appeals decided the *Air Measurement* case discussed above, and the plaintiff moved to dismiss for lack of subject-matter jurisdiction on the ground that the action was within the exclusive jurisdiction of the federal courts. The court of appeals refused to follow *Air Measurement* and affirmed the judgment below. On appeal, the Texas Supreme Court reversed, holding that this was a Category 2 case within the meaning of *Grable*, and that the federal courts had exclusive jurisdiction over the case.

The result in the *Minton* case is questionable. First, it is questionable whether the court applied the *Grable* criteria properly.[131] This is especially so with regard to the caseload factor in *Grable*. It seems likely that many basically state-law malpractice claims will eventually be drawn into federal court by holding that these cases satisfy the criteria for Category 2 jurisdiction due to a patent law contribution to the state claim. More broadly, however, it is arguable that all Category 2 jurisdiction should be considered concurrent with the state courts. In such cases, if an action is commenced in or removed to a federal court, the federal court can conduct the delicate balancing process necessary to determine whether the Category 2 criteria are satisfied. However, in cases in which an action is commenced in and not removed from a state court, if the state court must conduct an evaluation to determine whether it has subject-matter jurisdiction or jurisdiction lies exclusively in the federal courts, one may expect that the state courts will not be as attuned to the nuances that pervade Category 2 jurisdiction as will the federal courts.

In addition, there is the interesting question of what happens if a state court dismisses the action because it believes a Category 2 case is within the exclusive jurisdiction of the federal courts and a federal court disagrees with the state court in a subsequently commenced federal action. Normally, federal courts must give the same effect to state-court judgments as those judgments would receive in the courts that rendered them.[132] If the jurisdictional determination in the state court would have an issue preclusion effect in other state courts, will that mean that the federal court is also bound by the determination, even if it disagrees with it and believes it has no subject-matter jurisdiction over the case under the *Grable* criteria? If so, the federal court will literally be forced to hear a case that it considers beyond its

---

129. *See also* USPPS, Ltd. v. Avery Dennison Corp., 647 F.3d 274 (5th Cir. 2011) (Federal Circuit had exclusive jurisdiction over appeal involving state law claim because of essential issue of patent law contributing to state claim); Immunocept, LLC v. Fulbright & Jaworski, LLP, 504 F.3d 1281 (Fed. Cir. 2001) (district court had jurisdiction over malpractice claim because of contribution of issue of patent law to claim).

130. 355 S.W.3d 634 (Tex. 2011), *cert. granted*, __ U.S. __, 133 S. Ct. 420, 184 L. Ed. 2d 251 (2012).

131. The dissent in *Minton* observed that it was questionable in that case whether the federal legal issue was in dispute and whether it was sufficiently substantial, in that the determination before the court was one of fact rather than law, the case will not result in a precedent that controls numerous other cases, and the issue was one of federal common law rather than a statutory issue. In addition, the dissent questioned whether the caseload factor had been properly evaluated by the majority. *See id.* at 650-53.

132. *See* 28 U.S.C. § 1738; Chapter 13(F)(1)*(c)(ii) infra* ("Federal Law").

statutory power. If not, and if the federal court dismisses the action, what will the plaintiff do? Will the state court then be expected to give way and disregard its prior judgment of dismissal, or will the plaintiff simply be left without a remedy? Questions like these counsel that all Category 2 cases, even ones in which patent issues contribute to state claims, should be considered concurrent jurisdiction cases.

(b) The "Well-Pleaded Complaint" Rule

In both categories of cases in which jurisdiction is appropriate under § 1331, the focus is on the plaintiff's claim for relief. This focus has resulted in a "well-pleaded complaint" test for jurisdiction under the statute. This test is often stated separately from the tests described in the preceding subsection, but it is actually complementary to them: in all situations in which jurisdiction is based on § 1331, the federal question must appear on the face of the plaintiff's *well-pleaded complaint*.[133] In other words, federal law must contribute to the plaintiff's original claim. The basis of federal jurisdiction may not be federal defenses, even if the federal defenses are the only important issues in the case and the plaintiff correctly anticipates in the complaint that the defendant will raise them. Nor may federal question jurisdiction be based on federal laws that would negate a defense or provide for counterclaims by defendants.

Illustration 2-25. In *Louisville & Nashville Railroad Co. v. Mottley*,[134] a railroad settled a personal injury claim by agreeing to issue passes for free transportation on the railroad as long as E.L. Mottley and his wife lived. In 1906, Congress passed a law prohibiting railroads from giving free transportation or passes.[135] The railroad issued the Mottleys their passes and renewed them annually from 1871 until 1907, but then refused to renew the passes. The Mottleys sued in federal court to compel the railroad's performance of its contract. They alleged that the railroad's refusal to renew the passes was based solely on the Act of Congress. They maintained that the Act did not prohibit the railroad from issuing passes under the circumstances of their case, but if it did, the Act deprived them of their property without due process of law in violation of the Fifth Amendment. The U.S. Supreme Court held that the Mottleys' action did not fit within the federal question jurisdiction. The Mottleys' claim was a state breach-of-contract claim. The Act of Congress was a defense that the railroad might be expected to raise to this state breach of contract claim. The question of the Act's constitutionality was a reply to this defense that the Mottleys might raise. It was not part of the Mottleys' original

---

133. For a criticism of the "well-pleaded complaint" rule, see Donald L. Doernberg, *There's No Reason For It; It's Just Our Policy: Why the Well-Pleaded Complaint Rule Sabotages the Purposes of Federal Question Jurisdiction*, 38 HASTINGS L.J. 597 (1987); *see also* F. Andrew Hessick III, *The Common Law of Federal Question Jurisdiction*, 60 ALA. L. REV. 895 (2009) (discussing in the context of the "well-pleaded complaint" rule and other examples how the Supreme Court rather than Congress has become the "primary regulator" of federal question jurisdiction).

134. 211 U.S. 149, 29 S. Ct. 42, 53 L. Ed. 126 (1908).

135. *See* Act of June 29, 1906, ch. 3591, 34 Stat. 584.

claim for relief. Thus, no federal law contributed in any way to the Mottleys' original claim, and federal question jurisdiction was lacking.[136]

Illustration 2-26. In *Federated Department Stores v. Moitie*,[137] the U.S. Supreme Court permitted federal question jurisdiction in a case in which the only apparent federal question was a defense based on a plea of res judicata under a prior federal judgment.[138] This decision led many lower federal courts to sustain removal jurisdiction predicated on res judicata defenses based on prior federal judgments. However, in *Rivet v. Regions Bank*,[139] the Court directly held that a res judicata defense based on a prior federal judgment does not provide a proper basis for federal question jurisdiction under the *Mottley* principle.[140]

Illustration 2-27. In *Holmes Group, Inc. v. Vornado Air Circulation Systems, Inc.*,[141] the plaintiff ("Holmes Group") and the defendant ("Vornado") manufactured household fans and heaters with a "spiral grill design." The Holmes Group commenced a declaratory judgment action in the U.S. District Court for the District of Kansas, seeking, *inter alia*, a declaration of non-liability under 15 U.S.C.

---

136. *Mottley*, 211 U.S. at 152, 29 S. Ct. at 43, 53 L. Ed. at 127-28. In rejecting the Mottleys' action, the Court stated that:

> [i]t is the settled interpretation of these words, as used in this statute, conferring [general federal question] jurisdiction, that a suit arises under the Constitution and laws of the United States only when the plaintiff's statement of his own cause of action shows that it is based upon those laws or that Constitution. It is not enough that the plaintiff alleges some anticipated defense to his cause of action and asserts that the defense is invalidated by some provision of the Constitution of the United States. Although such allegations show that very likely, in the course of the litigation, a question under the Constitution would arise, they do not show that the suit, that is, the plaintiff's original cause of action, arises under the Constitution.

Id. But cf. Freeman v. Burlington Broadcasters, Inc., 204 F.3d 311 (2d Cir. 2000) (local zoning board found a radio station in violation of a zoning permit that required RF interference to be remedied, but determined that its authority to enforce the ordinance had been preempted by the federal government's occupation of the field of RF interference; homeowners and the town sought review of that determination before a state environmental court; before the decision of the environmental court, the case was removed to federal district court; that court dismissed the case for lack of jurisdiction on preemption grounds; the federal court of appeals held that even though federal preemption had been raised defensively at the administrative level, when the homeowners appealed to the state court, the issue had already been adjudicated and the federal defense was no longer speculative, but the entire action depended on it; therefore, federal question jurisdiction existed!).

137. 452 U.S. 394, 101 S. Ct. 2424, 69 L. Ed. 2d 103 (1981).

138. *Id.* at 394, 397 n.2, 101 S. Ct. at 2427 n.2, 69 L. Ed. 2d at 108 n.2.

139. 522 U.S. 470, 118 S. Ct. 921, 139 L. Ed. 2d 912 (1998); *see* Arthur R. Miller, *Artful Pleading: A Doctrine in Search of Definition*, 76 TEX. L. REV. 1781 (1998).

140. Subsequent to *Rivet*, the U.S. Court of Appeals for the Eighth Circuit considered a case removed from state to federal court by a defendant; after removal, the defendant moved to dismiss the action on the basis that it was precluded under a prior federal judgment, a consent decree. The court acknowledged that *Rivet* precluded removal based on the res judicata effect of the prior federal judgment. However, the court held that removal was proper under 28 U.S.C. § 1651(a), the "All Writs Act." This Act authorizes federal courts to "issue all writs necessary or appropriate in aid of their respective jurisdictions and agreeable to the usages and principles of law." The court reasoned that the All Writs Act authorized removal based on the district court's continuing supervisory power over the consent decree. However, other courts have held removal of similar cases improper under the All Writs Act. *See, e.g.*, Hillman v. Webley, 115 F.3d 1461 (10th Cir. 1997); *cf.* 28 U.S.C. § 2283 (precluding federal injunctions against state-court proceedings except, *inter alia*, "to protect or effectuate [their] judgments"). In Syngenta Crop Protection, Inc. v. Henson, 537 U.S. 28, 123 S. Ct. 366, 154 L. Ed. 2d 368 (2002), the Supreme Court resolved this split among the circuits over whether the All Writs Act, 28 U.S.C. § 1651(a), could provide a basis for removal independent of whether the federal courts would have original jurisdiction over the action. The Court held that the Act did not provide authority for removal of a state-court case to prevent frustration of previous orders of a federal court unless the federal court would have had independent subject-matter jurisdiction of the state action. *See generally* Lonny Sheinkopf Hoffman, *Removal Jurisdiction and the All Writs Act,* 148 U. PA. L. REV. 401 (1999); Joan Steinman, *The Newest Frontier of Judicial Activism: Removal Under the All Writs Act,* 80 B.U. L. REV. 773 (2000). For further discussion of the circumstances under which federal injunctions are appropriate against state proceedings, see CHARLES A. WRIGHT & MARY KAY KANE, LAW OF FEDERAL COURTS § 47 (7th ed. 2011).

141. 535 U.S. 826, 122 S. Ct. 1889, 153 L. Ed. 2d 13 (2002).

§ 1125(a) (which protects "trade dress" as part of the federal trademark laws) and an injunction restraining the defendant from accusing it of trade-dress infringement in promotional materials. In addition to seeking this declaratory judgment, the plaintiff asserted several related claims, including defamation, unfair competition, injurious falsehood, and tortious interference with prospective economic advantage. The plaintiff's complaint invoked jurisdiction under 28 U.S.C. §§ 1331 and 1332(a), 15 U.S.C. § 1121 (providing original jurisdiction for trademark, including "trade dress," claims in the federal district courts without regard to the amount in controversy or to diversity or lack of diversity of the citizenship of the parties), and supplemental jurisdiction.[142]

The plaintiff, Holmes Group, did not seek a declaratory judgment that the plaintiff's products did not infringe the defendant's patent, even though before the commencement of the action, the defendant, Vornado, had lodged a complaint with the U.S. International Trade Commission against the Holmes Group, claiming that the Holmes Groups' sale of fans and heaters did infringe Vornado's patent and trade dress. However, the defendant's answer asserted a compulsory counterclaim alleging patent infringement. Relying on the issue preclusion effect of prior litigation in which another manufacturer had successfully defeated Vornado's assertion of a "trade dress" protection, the district court granted the plaintiff the declaratory judgment of non-liability under 15 U.S.C. § 1125(a) ("trade dress") and the injunction it had sought. The court also stayed all proceedings related to the defendant's patent counterclaim, adding that the counterclaim would be dismissed if the declaratory judgment were affirmed on appeal.[143]

The defendant appealed to the U.S. Court of Appeals for the Federal Circuit, which has appellate jurisdiction under 28 U.S.C. § 1295(a)(1) if the district court's jurisdiction was based on 28 U.S.C. § 1338, which confers jurisdiction over civil actions "arising under" the federal patent laws. The U.S. Court of Appeals for the Federal Circuit vacated the district court's judgment and remanded the case. The U.S. Supreme Court reversed, holding that the U.S. Court of Appeals for the Federal Circuit lacked appellate subject-matter jurisdiction. The Court reasoned that the Federal Circuit's appellate jurisdiction is fixed by reference to the district court's jurisdiction, and the basis of the district court's jurisdiction must be a claim "arising under" the patent laws. According to the Court, the *plaintiff's* claim must "arise under" the patent laws in a manner that satisfies 28 U.S.C. § 1338. The Court pointed out that § 1338 uses the "same operative language" as § 1331 and that "linguistic consistency" requires the Court to apply the same "arising under" test to both §§ 1331 and 1338. The Court observed that the plaintiff's well-pleaded complaint did not assert any claim arising under federal patent law. Even though the Court's prior cases dealing with the "well-pleaded complaint" rule involved federal defenses, the Court indicated that the same underlying principles should be applied to federal counterclaims.[144] The Court thus "decline[d] to transform the longstand-

---

142. Brief for Petitioner at 2, *id.* Supplemental jurisdiction is examined in Section E *infra.*
143. 535 U.S. at 828, 122 S. Ct. at 1892, 153 L. Ed. 2d at 18-19.
144. *Id.* at 829-31, 122 S. Ct. at 1893-94, 153 L. Ed. 2d at 20.

ing well-pleaded-complaint rule" into the "well-pleaded-complaint-*or-counterclaim* rule" urged by the defendant.[145]

It is important to note that *Holmes Group* does not mean that the district court did not have federal question jurisdiction. The district court had subject-matter jurisdiction over the plaintiff's "trade dress" declaratory claim under 15 U.S.C. § 1121, but it was insufficient to confer *appellate jurisdiction* on the Federal Circuit under 28 U.S.C. § 1295(a)(1) because original jurisdiction was not based on 28 U.S.C. § 1338. In addition, the district court *would have had* subject-matter jurisdiction under 28 U.S. C. § 1338, based on the precedents discussed in subsection *(iii)*, below, if the plaintiff had sought a declaratory judgment that the defendant's patent was not being infringed or was invalid. In this latter event, presumably appellate jurisdiction would have existed under § 1295(a)(1). However, the plaintiff did not seek a declaratory judgment of non-infringement or non-validity.

Illustration 2-28. To further illustrate how the "well-pleaded complaint" rule operates, consider the following pleadings:

(a) Form 18 in the Appendix of Forms to the Federal Rules of Civil Procedure illustrates a complaint for patent infringement. Paragraph 1 of the complaint (alleging subject-matter jurisdiction) would state that the action arises under 35 U.S.C. §§ 1-376 (the patent laws). This allegation, however, does not alone satisfy the well-pleaded complaint rule. It must appear from the body of the complaint that the plaintiff's right of action is the sort conferred by the federal patent laws. Paragraphs 2, 3, and 4 of the complaint reveal that this complaint, in fact, alleges a right of action authorized by the federal patent laws; however, it is possible to reach this conclusion only *if one possesses some knowledge of the patent laws and, therefore, of the kinds of actions that they authorize*.

(b) Form 10(a) in the Appendix of Forms to the Federal Rules of Civil Procedure illustrates a complaint on a promissory note. By reading Form 10*(a) and by possessing the knowledge that the laws generally governing promissory notes are state (not federal) laws*, one can see that the plaintiff's action arises under state law and does not come within federal court jurisdiction under 28 U.S.C. § 1331.

(c) Suppose, however, that a plaintiff filed the following complaint in a U.S. District Court:

1. The action arises under 51 U.S.C. § 1 [a hypothetical federal statute] and the Fifth Amendment to the U.S. Constitution, as hereinafter more fully appears.

---

145. *Id.* at 832, 122 S. Ct. at 1894, 153 L. Ed. 2d at 21; *see generally* Christopher A. Cotropia, *Counterclaims, The Well-Pleaded Complaint, and Federal Jurisdiction,* 33 HOFSTRA L. REV. 1 (2004); Christopher A. Cotropia, *"Arising Under" Jurisdiction and Uniformity in Patent Law,* 9 MICH. TELECOMM. & TECH. L. REV. 253 (2003) (discussing *Holmes Group*). The Leahy-Smith America Invents Act of 2011 changed the specific result in *Holmes Group* by amending 28 U.S.C. § 1295(a)(1) to authorize appellate jurisdiction in the Court of Appeals for the Federal Circuit "in any civil action in which a party has asserted a compulsory counterclaim arising under any Act of Congress relating to patents or plant variety protection." However, the Leahy-Smith America Invents Act of 2011 does not alter the "well-pleaded complaint" rule in any type of action other than those involving a counterclaim relating to federal patent or plant variety protection laws. Thus, in other kinds of cases, the "well-pleaded complaint" rule is only satisfied if the claim asserted by the plaintiff properly arises under federal law, and federal question jurisdiction cannot be predicated on the existence of a federal defense or federal counterclaim.

2. Defendant on or about [date], executed and delivered to plaintiff a promissory note, a copy of which is hereto attached as Exhibit A, whereby defendant promised to pay to plaintiff on [date], the sum of $100,000 with interest thereon at the rate of eighteen percent per annum.

3. Defendant refused to pay the amount of said note or interest when due, asserting as an excuse for nonpayment that 51 U.S.C. § 1 nullified defendant's obligation to pay because the interest rate charged by the note exceeded the legally permitted maximum rate of twelve percent per annum.

4. Plaintiff alleges that the defendant's interpretation of 51 U.S.C. § 1 is erroneous in the following respects:

a. 51 U.S.C. § 1 is inapplicable to the note made by defendant because the statute applies only to notes given as part of a transaction in interstate commerce, and the note made by defendant was given in payment for a transaction wholly intrastate in nature.

b. Even if 51 U.S.C. § 1 is applicable to the note made by defendant, it does not wholly nullify the defendant's obligation to pay principal and interest. At most, it nullifies the defendant's obligation to pay amounts of interest in excess of twelve percent per annum.

5. Alternatively, plaintiff alleges that if 51 U.S.C. § 1 is applicable to the note made by defendant and if the statute wholly nullifies defendant's obligation to pay principal and interest, the statute violates the Fifth Amendment of the U.S. Constitution by depriving plaintiff of property without due process of law.

6. Therefore, defendant owes to plaintiff the principal amount of said note and interest.

Wherefore plaintiff demands judgment against defendant for the sum of $118,000.00, interest, and costs.

This complaint violates the well-pleaded complaint rule. To state a claim for relief, all the plaintiff had to allege was the facts in paragraph 2, paragraph 6, and the introductory clause of the sentence that makes up paragraph 3. The remainder of the complaint attempts to anticipate certain defenses under federal law that defendant will raise to plaintiff's action and to counter those defenses. Assuming, therefore, that the hypothetical federal statute (51 U.S.C. § 1) and the Fifth Amendment do not confer a right of action on plaintiff for the amount of the note—an eventuality unlikely in the extreme given the structure of the complaint—the only pertinent federal law in the case will come up by way of defenses or counters to defenses.

* * * * *

The "well-pleaded complaint" rule will be satisfied whenever the action fits within either of the two categories of cases discussed in the preceding subsection that are appropriate for jurisdiction under § 1331. Analytically, if one determines that an action fits one of the categories, one need not separately consider whether the "well-pleaded complaint" rule is satisfied. In this sense, the rule is a superfluity. Often, however, the courts apply the rule without specific analytical reference to any one of the situations in which § 1331 jurisdiction is proper. Sometimes, courts intertwine the rule with the analysis of the jurisdictional category in such a fashion as to be inseparable from it. Ordinarily, this approach will cause no harm. However, considering the "well-pleaded complaint" rule without specific reference to the analytical categories in which federal question jurisdiction is proper does pose some danger of confusion.

Illustration 2-29. The plaintiffs' statement of their claim in the *Merrell Dow* case, discussed in section C(1)*(b)(i)*, above, seems to satisfy the "well-pleaded complaint" rule; the plaintiffs did allege a violation of federal law as an element contributing to their claim. Yet the Court held jurisdiction improper in *Merrell Dow* because the federal interest was not sufficiently substantial to justify exercising jurisdiction. Thus, the "well-pleaded complaint" rule cannot be safely applied to determine the propriety of jurisdiction without referring to the analytical categories of cases in which the Court has held jurisdiction to be proper under § 1331.[146]

(c) Determining Federal Question Jurisdiction in Declaratory Judgment Actions

When the plaintiff seeks a declaratory judgment, special problems arise in determining federal question jurisdiction. A declaratory judgment action seeks a judicial declaration of the rights and liabilities of the parties to a dispute. Declaratory judgments cannot be executed against a party's person or property. They are useful when the parties to a transaction are involved in a dispute over their legal rights and need an authoritative statement from a court about the nature and extent of those rights. In declaratory judgment actions, parties will usually obey court decrees voluntarily, so no need exists for a decree that can be executed against the loser.[147] In federal courts, declaratory judgments are authorized by 28 U.S.C. §§ 2201-2202. A precondition of such an action is an actual controversy within the subject-matter jurisdiction of a federal court.[148] When enacting these provisions, however, Congress did not intend for them to have a "jurisdictional effect."[149]

A person who might have been a defendant in an action for some other kind of remedy may bring a declaratory judgment action as a plaintiff. In that situation, the declaratory plaintiff's complaint may state a dispute or controversy about a proposition of federal law. Such a statement would seem to satisfy the "well-pleaded complaint" rule; in order to state a claim for declaratory relief, a plaintiff must describe some sort of dispute or controversy that a declaratory

---

146. For a useful examination of the bases of "arising under" jurisdiction discussed in this section, see John B. Oakley, *Federal Jurisdiction and the Problem of the Litigative Unit: When Does What "Arise Under" Federal Law*, 76 TEX. L. REV. 1829 (1998).

147. *See* Gulf Beach Hotel, Inc. v. State *ex rel.* Whetstone, 935 So.2d 1177 (Ala. 2006) (no justiciable controversy existed in declaratory judgment action because complaint did not allege any controversy between parties whose legal interests were adverse); Wilmans v. Sears, Roebuck & Co., 355 Ark. 668, 144 S.W.3d 245 (2004) (declaratory relief will lie where (1) there is a justiciable controversy, (2) that controversy exists between parties with adverse interests, (3) those seeking relief have a legal interest in the controversy, and (4) the issues involved are ripe for decision); Director of the Office of State Lands & Invs. v. Merbanco, Inc., 2003 WY 73, 70 P.3d 241 (declaratory judgments statute designed to enable parties to obtain judicial determinations prior to an injury rather than requiring them to wait until the damage is done); *see also* EDWIN BORCHARD, DECLARATORY JUDGMENTS 4, 13, 25-28 (2d ed. 1941). Of course, if a declaratory judgment is not voluntarily obeyed, the party obtaining the judgment can seek other remedies based on the judgment. *See id.* at 13-14.

148. *See* 28 U.S.C. § 2201(a).

149. *See* Skelly Oil Co. v. Phillips Petroleum Co., 339 U.S. 667, 671, 70 S. Ct. 876, 879, 94 L. Ed. 1194, 1199 (1950).

judgment will serve a useful purpose in resolving.[150] If the only dispute or controversy in the case is over a proposition of federal law, then the declaratory plaintiff's proper statement of the claim for declaratory relief will necessarily contain a federal question. The difficulty is, of course, that if an action had been brought for some other kind of relief, the defendant in the declaratory judgment action often would have brought it rather than the declaratory plaintiff, and the action would not have involved a claim based on federal law at all. Instead, the federal question would have been a matter of defense or, perhaps, a reply to a defense.

The U.S. Supreme Court has addressed the problem of federal question jurisdiction in the context of declaratory judgment actions several times. In determining how the "well-pleaded complaint" rule should be applied, the Court has focused on the relationship between the declaratory action and the action that would have been brought had the declaratory judgment action not been brought. In essence, the Court has held that an action for declaratory relief may not be brought within the federal question jurisdiction unless one of the parties to the action could have brought an action as a plaintiff for some other kind of relief in federal court.[151] However, the facts of the cases decided by the Court in this area may support a broader rule. Thus, the Court may some day reinterpret its decisions to allow more declaratory actions than have yet been permitted. The following illustrations examine the operation of the well-pleaded complaint rule in declaratory judgment actions and discuss the broader rule that may be derived from the Court's decisions.

Illustration 2-30. (a) Two individuals, *P* and *D*, enter into a contract that requires each individual to perform at different times. Before the time arrives for *D* to perform, *P* and *D* dispute the validity of the contract. *D* contends that the contract is void, and *P* contends that it is valid. *P* threatens to sue *D* for damages if, at the time performance is due, *D* refuses to perform. Obviously, if the threatened suit were actually brought, *P* would be the plaintiff and *D* would be the defendant. Assume that *D* relies on federal law to support *D's* view that the contract is void. *P* relies on state law to support *P's* claim. *P* also disputes *D's* view of federal law. *P's* threatened action would not be within the federal question jurisdiction of the federal district courts. The action is, in all respects, like *Louisville & Nashville Railroad v. Mottley*, discussed in *Illustration 2-25*. The "well-pleaded complaint"

---

150. UNIF. DECLARATORY JUDGMENTS ACT § 6, 12A U.L.A. 391 (2008) provides as follows: "The court may refuse to render or enter a declaratory judgment or decree where such judgment or decree, if rendered or entered, would not terminate the uncertainty or controversy giving rise to the proceeding." In effect, this standard is often said to involve a determination whether a declaratory judgment will serve a "useful purpose" in resolving the controversy between the parties. *See* EDWIN BORCHARD, DECLARATORY JUDGMENTS 293 (2d ed. 1941); Edwin Borchard, *Discretion to Refuse Jurisdiction of Actions for Declaratory Judgments*, 26 MINN. L. REV. 677, 678 (1942); *see also* Zab, Inc. v. Berenergy Corp., 136 P.3d 252 (Colo. 2006) (court may exercise discretion to issue declaratory judgment when (1) the judgment would serve a useful purpose in clarifying and settling the legal relations at issue and (2) would terminate the uncertainty, insecurity, or controversy giving rise to the dispute; if neither result can be accomplished, court should decline to render the declaration).

151. The decisions discussed below have, in effect, adopted the rule advocated in *Developments in the Law: Declaratory Judgments—1941-1949*, 62 HARV. L. REV. 787, 802-03 (1949); *see also* Community State Bank v. Strong, 485 F.3d 597 (11th Cir. 2007) (in arbitration declaratory judgment action, district court had subject-matter jurisdiction because plaintiffs' complaint demonstrated that defendant could bring federal RICO action, even though defendant had sued only on state claims in state court and state action had not been amended to include federal claim); Commercial Union Ins. Co. v. United States, 999 F.2d 581 (D.C. Cir. 1993) (federal question jurisdiction in declaratory judgment and interpleader actions determined in the same way).

rule prevents *P*, who is suing on a state breach of contract claim, from anticipating the issue of federal law that is the basis of *D's* defense. Thus, no federal question jurisdiction exists because the federal question would not appear as part of the plaintiff's well-pleaded complaint.

(b) Assume that in the above situation, *P* sought a declaratory judgment to resolve the dispute instead of waiting to sue for breach of contract after *D* refused to perform. Such a judgment would seek to establish the validity of *P's* state claim and the invalidity of *D's* federal defense. In this situation, when the plaintiff in the declaratory judgment action also would have been the plaintiff in the action for a nondeclaratory remedy, the Supreme Court has clearly indicated that no jurisdiction exists under § 2201 because no jurisdiction would have existed in the action for the nondeclaratory remedy (see (a) above).[152]

Illustration 2-31. (a) Assume that *P* is threatening to sue *D* for patent infringement, an action over which the federal courts would have exclusive jurisdiction.[153] Assume that instead of waiting for *P* to sue, *D* sues in federal court for a declaratory judgment that *P's* patent is invalid—an issue that would have been raised as a defense in *P's* infringement suit. In this situation, federal question jurisdiction under § 2201 *exists* because the *declaratory defendant*, *P*, could have sued as a plaintiff in federal court within the federal question jurisdiction to obtain non-declaratory relief.[154] The difference between this situation and that in *Illustration 2-30* is that here one of the parties—*P*, the declaratory judgment defendant—could have litigated the action in a federal court action for a nondeclaratory remedy. In the example in *Illustration 2-30*, *neither* party could have sued within the federal question jurisdiction for a nondeclaratory remedy.

(b) A qualification must be added. Not all suits in which the declaratory judgment defendant could have sued in federal court for a nondeclaratory remedy will fit within the federal question jurisdiction. In *Franchise Tax Board v. Construction Laborers Vacation Trust*,[155] the Supreme Court held that the declaratory judgment plaintiff also must have "a clear interest" in a swift *federal*

---

152. *See* Skelly Oil Co. v. Phillips Petroleum Co., 339 U.S. 667, 70 S. Ct. 876, 94 L. Ed. 1194 (1950). However, the "well-pleaded complaint" rule, applied in a straightforward manner to the plaintiff's complaint, would seem to be satisfied. To state a claim for declaratory relief, the plaintiff must describe a live dispute or controversy with the defendant. When the plaintiff describes such a controversy here, the plaintiff describes a dispute or controversy over federal law. *See also* Webster Cnty. Lumber Co. v. Wayne, No. 02-1429, 2003 WL 1465391, 2003 U.S. App. LEXIS 5573 (4th Cir. Mar. 24, 2003) (action by private plaintiffs against other private parties for declaratory judgment that tax deeds and tax sale of property to defendants were invalid under the Due Process Clause of the Fourteenth Amendment; holding action must be dismissed for lack of jurisdiction under the *Skelly* rule because of plaintiffs' failure to demonstrate any federal claim on their own part or the part of the defendants that would be sufficient to confer federal jurisdiction in a nondeclaratory action); Norfolk S. Ry. Co. v. Guthrie, 233 F.3d 532 (7th Cir. 2000) (no statutory federal question jurisdiction in case in which federal jurisdiction would not exist in a nondeclaratory action by the declaratory judgment defendant against the plaintiff); Northeast Ill. Reg'l Commuter R.R. Corp. v. Hoey Farina & Downes, 212 F.3d 1010 (7th Cir. 2000) (no federal question jurisdiction in declaratory judgment action in which federal question would arise only as a defense to a state claim in absence of federal declaratory judgment procedure).

153. *See* 28 U.S.C. § 1338.

154. 13D CHARLES A. WRIGHT ET AL., FEDERAL PRACTICE AND PROCEDURE: JURISDICTION AND RELATED MATTERS § 3566, at 280-82 (3d ed. 2008); *see also* Household Bank v. JFS Group, 320 F.3d 1249 (11th Cir. 2003) (district court had subject-matter jurisdiction over declaratory judgment action in which plaintiffs' well-pleaded complaint demonstrated that the defendants could commence a nondeclaratory action against the plaintiffs in federal court that arises under federal law).

155. 463 U.S. 1, 103 S. Ct. 2841, 77 L. Ed. 2d 420 (1983).

resolution of the issue of federal law upon which the parties disagree.[156] A clear interest exists in the patent case discussed in (a), above, because the alleged patent infringer, who is suing for federal declaratory relief, will be liable for damages if it turns out the patent is being infringed, and also because the alleged infringer's contractual relations with other parties may be disrupted by the allegations of infringement.[157] However, in *Franchise Tax Board*, the Court held that a suit by a state to declare that the defendant has no valid federal claim against the enforcement of the state's tax laws is not within the federal question jurisdiction—even though the declaratory judgment defendant could have sued for an injunction against enforcement of the tax laws in federal court within the federal question jurisdiction. The Court reasoned that the state's interests in a swift resolution of the question of federal law were insufficient to support federal question jurisdiction.[158]

Illustration 2-32. (a) Assume again the basic facts of *Illustration 2-30*, in which *P* and *D* entered into a contract that required future performance. Recall that before the time for performance arrived, *D* claimed that the contract was void under federal law. If *D* refused to perform at the appointed time, *P* could attempt to sue for breach of contract under state law. However, *P* could not sue for breach of contract or for a declaratory judgment in federal court because *P's* claim was based on state law. The only federal issue in the case would be *D's* federal defense, and the "well-pleaded complaint" rule would preclude jurisdiction based on a federal defense. What would happen if *D*, instead of *P*, brought an action for a declaratory judgment on the ground that federal law rendered the contract void? If *D* is the plaintiff, the entire basis of *D's* claim for the declaratory judgment is based upon federal law. Should the court apply the well-pleaded complaint rule in a straightforward fashion and conclude that federal jurisdiction exists on the theory that *D* only has to plead the dispute over federal law to state a claim for declaratory relief? Or should the court instead conclude that to allow the action to be brought in federal court would result in an *expansion* of the federal question jurisdiction, something that is not supposed to result from the enactment of the declaratory judgment statute? Extensive dicta in U.S. Supreme Court cases indicate that no federal question jurisdiction would exist over *D's* declaratory judgment action against *P*.[159]

---

156. *See Franchise Tax Bd.*, 463 U.S. at 20, 21 n.23, 103 S. Ct. at 2851-52 n.23, 77 L. Ed. 2d at 437-38 n.23.

157. *See id.* at 21 n.23, 103 S. Ct. at 2852 n.23, 77 L. Ed. 2d at 438 n.23.

158. *Id.* at 21, 103 S. Ct. at 2852, 77 L. Ed. 2d at 438. The Supreme Court explained that

> [s]tates are not significantly prejudiced by an inability to come to federal court for a declaratory judgment in advance of a possible injunctive suit by a person subject to federal regulation. They have a variety of means by which they can enforce their own laws in their own courts, and they do not suffer if the [preemption] questions such enforcement may raise are tested there.

Id.

159. For example, the Court has stated that

> [i]f the cause of action, which the declaratory defendant threatens to assert, does not itself involve a claim under federal law, it is doubtful if a federal court may entertain an action for a declaratory judgment establishing a defense to that claim. This is dubious even though the declaratory complaint sets forth a claim of federal right, if that right is in reality in the nature of a defense to a threatened cause of action.

Public Serv. Comm'n v. Wycoff Co., 344 U.S. 237, 248, 73 S. Ct. 236, 242-43, 97 L. Ed. 291, 298 (1952); *see also* Skelly Oil Co. v. Phillips Petroleum Co., 339 U.S. 667, 673-74, 70 S. Ct. 876, 880, 94 L. Ed. 1194, 1199-1200 (1950); *cf.* Franchise Tax Bd. v. Construction Laborers Vacation Trust, 463 U.S. 1, 19, 103 S. Ct. 2841, 2851, 77 L. Ed. 2d 420, 437 (1983).

(b) However, the Court has never directly held that *D's* suit is not a proper case for federal question jurisdiction. The Court indicated in the *Franchise Tax Board* case that "[p]arties subject to conflicting state and federal regulatory schemes . . . have a clear interest in sorting out the scope of each government's authority, especially [when] they face a threat of liability if the application of federal law is not quickly made clear."[160] *D* is precisely in this situation. Therefore, although the *Franchise Tax Board* decision applied the "clear interest" test to *exclude* from federal court a case that would have fallen within the federal question jurisdiction under the test described in *Illustration 2-31(a)*, the "clear interest" test could conceivably be applied affirmatively in the future to *allow* a case such as *D's* to be brought in federal court. If the Court adopts this approach, the "clear interest" test of *Franchise Tax Board* could become the exclusive test for federal questions in declaratory judgment actions.[161]

* * * * *

One question about the *Franchise Tax Board* "clear interest" test is whether it is the same as the test used in *Merrell Dow*[162] to determine the substantiality of the federal interest necessary to confer federal question jurisdiction in cases in which federal law contributes to a state claim for relief. *Merrell Dow* was decided after *Franchise Tax Board*. The Court in *Merrell Dow* cited and discussed *Franchise Tax Board* with approval.[163] However, in *Merrell Dow*, the Court did not state that the "federal interest" tests were identical. Rather, it cited *Franchise Tax Board* for the more general proposition that, in areas of "uncertain jurisdiction," there was a "need for careful judgments about the exercise of federal judicial power."[164] Furthermore, while the "federal interest" test of each case has been used to *exclude* actions from federal court that involve contributions of federal law that would otherwise make federal question jurisdiction appropriate, the focus of the two tests is very different. The *Merrell Dow* test, as refined in *Grable* and *Empire Health Choice*, seems designed to vindicate the general policies of § 1331, which are aimed not merely at party protection, but also at the proper administration of federal law in the national interest. In contrast, the *Franchise Tax Board* test seems to focus on the need of the party seeking declaratory relief for a swift federal adjudication of the issue of federal law upon which the controversy depends. So focused, the test appears to focus primarily, if not exclusively, upon party protection.[165]

If, indeed, the *Franchise Tax Board* and *Merrell Dow* tests are different, there may be cases in which each test must be applied separately to determine whether a case is appropriate for federal question jurisdiction.

---

160. 463 U.S. at 21 n.21, 103 S. Ct. at 2852 n.21, 77 L. Ed. 2d at 438 n.21.

161. Concededly, however, the test has been used thus far only to exclude cases from federal jurisdiction that would otherwise be appropriate. *See* the discussion below.

162. The *Merrell Dow* test is discussed in subsection 2*(a), supra*.

163. *See* 478 U.S. at 813-14, 106 S. Ct. at 3234-35, 92 L. Ed. 2d at 661-62.

164. *Id.* at 814, 106 S. Ct. at 3235, 92 L. Ed. 2d at 662.

165. As noted below, the *Franchise Tax Board* test seems to be no more than a recasting into a jurisdictional rule of the usual standard for whether declaratory judgment complaint states a claim upon which relief can be granted.

Illustration 2-33. Reconsider the discussion of federal question jurisdiction in the Category 2 case of *Smith v. Kansas City Title & Trust Co.* Assume that instead of suing the bank and its directors for an injunction to prevent them from investing in the (allegedly) unconstitutionally issued federal securities, the shareholders simply threaten to sue. The directors then sue the shareholders for a declaratory judgment that the federal securities are valid. *Grable* confirmed that *Smith* is still good law after *Merrell Dow*. Thus, the first step in determining the existence of federal question jurisdiction in declaratory judgment cases is satisfied. The shareholders could sue for nondeclaratory relief (an injunction) within the federal question jurisdiction because they would be asserting a state claim for relief to which federal law made an essential and important contribution. In such an action, the federal interest would be sufficiently substantial under the *Smith-Merrell Dow-Grable* cases to justify the exercise of federal question jurisdiction.

However, whether the "clear interest" test of *Franchise Tax Board* would be satisfied is more problematic. The bank and its directors, who would be the defendants in an injunction suit, are not precisely in the same position as the alleged patent infringer, who could demonstrate the necessary interest to justify federal declaratory judgment jurisdiction. The alleged patent infringer is subject to conflicting state and federal regulatory schemes and may incur a damage judgment if it continues to manufacture the allegedly infringing product. The alleged infringer will also lose profits if it stops manufacturing the product in response to threats of an infringement action. It is far from clear that the bank or its directors are subject to the same perils. They face no threat of a damages judgment. There could, of course, be adverse consequences to the bank if it invested in securities that were later determined to be illegal. However, these consequences are produced by the constitutional doubt that exists about the validity of the securities issue. This doubt would exist even if there had been no threat of an injunction suit by the shareholder. The bank is not committed to a single course of investment and can, therefore, dispel the doubt by buying different securities.[166] It is, therefore, unclear whether the bank can demonstrate a sufficient interest to justify the exercise of federal declaratory judgment jurisdiction under the *Franchise Tax Board* test.

* * * * *

Apart from the problem of coordinating *Merrell Dow* and *Franchise Tax Board*, additional, unnecessary confusion exists in the Supreme Court's decisions on federal question jurisdiction in declaratory judgment actions. First, the Court

---

166. The bank's dilemma in this illustration should not be confused with the problem of whether the mere existence of a *penal* or *regulatory* statute should enable a party subject to the statute to obtain a declaratory judgment of its validity in a suit against the person charged with its administration in the absence of a threat of enforcement. *See* Edwin Borchard, *Challenging "Penal" Statutes by Declaratory Action*, 52 YALE L.J. 445, 459, 467-75 (1943); Note, *Developments in the Law-Declaratory Judgments* 1941-1949, 62 HARV. L. REV. 787, 870-71 (1949); Note, *Official Threat of Enforcement as a Requisite of Justiciability in Declaratory Judgment Actions*, 50 YALE L.J. 1278 (1941). In such cases, the peril and insecurity arising from the mere existence of a statute applicable to the declaratory judgment plaintiff's activities should be sufficient to justify the issuance of the remedy against the statute's administrator. *See* Ralph U. Whitten, *Federal Declaratory and Injunctive Interference with State Court Proceedings: The Supreme Court and the Limits of Judicial Discretion*, 53 N.C. L. REV. 591, 618-19 (1975) (and authorities there cited). The bank's situation is different in the above illustration. It is not compelled to invest in the questionable securities. To be entitled to a federal declaratory remedy, the *Franchise Tax Board* test would have to be extended to cases of lesser peril than that of the alleged patent infringer, which parallels that of the person whose ongoing activities are potentially subject to as the yet unenforced penal or regulatory statute.

may be correct that the Federal Declaratory Judgment Act was not designed to expand the jurisdiction of the federal courts.[167] However, allowing a declaratory judgment action in federal court that could not be brought there by one of the parties for nondeclaratory relief should not be considered a "jurisdictional" expansion. For example, the Federal Rules of Civil Procedure are also not supposed to have a jurisdictional effect.[168] Yet, no one supposes that federal jurisdiction has been expanded by those rules because it is possible under the liberalized pleading standards of Rule 8 to bring an action in federal court that could not have been brought there under the more restrictive pleading standards that existed prior to the advent of the Rules. The Court has never adequately explained why a simple increase in the number of cases that can be brought within the federal question jurisdiction should be considered an expansion of federal jurisdiction when the standards for determining jurisdiction have remained constant. Indeed, the better argument would be that there is no jurisdictional effect as long as the rules of jurisdiction, applied to declaratory judgment actions straightforwardly, have not changed. Instead, all that has happened is that the old jurisdictional rules are operating within a new procedural context.[169]

Second, even accepting the premise that allowing additional cases into federal court constitutes an expansion of the federal question jurisdiction, the Court's approach is internally inconsistent. *Illustration 2-31(a)* demonstrates that when a person is threatened with a nondeclaratory action in federal court, the Court allows that person to sue for a declaratory judgment that the threatened claim in the federal action is invalid under federal law. In the Court's view, such an action does not constitute an expansion of jurisdiction because the declaratory judgment defendant could bring an action for nondeclaratory relief in federal court. Thus, no additional case is being allowed within federal jurisdiction because the declaratory judgment defendant could have sued within the federal question jurisdiction. This position, however, is flawed. Absent the declaratory judgment remedy, the declaratory judgment plaintiff would have had no access to federal court at all. Indeed, the declaratory judgment plaintiff would not have a remedy in any court, unless a state-created right of action happened to exist for the threats to sue being made by the opposing party in the case.[170] Furthermore, no guarantee exists that the declaratory judgment defendant would ever have brought the threatened federal action. A threat to sue is not, after all, a suit. By analyzing the jurisdictional question hypothetically, the Court is allowing the declaratory judgment statute to have a jurisdictional impact under the very test it has embraced.[171]

Illustration 2-34. *P* believes that *D* is infringing *P's* patent by manufacturing and selling an item covered by the patent without permission. *D* believes that

---

167. *But see* Paul J. Mishkin, *The Federal "Question" in the District Courts*, 53 COLUM. L. REV. 157, 178 n.99 (1953).

168. *See* FED. R. CIV. P. 82 ("These rules do not extend or limit the jurisdiction of the district courts . . . .").

169. *See* Paul J. Mishkin, *The Federal "Question" in the District Courts*, 53 COLUM. L. REV. 157, 178 (1953).

170. *See* American Well Works Co. v. Layne & Bowler Co., 241 U.S. 257, 36 S. Ct. 585, 60 L. Ed. 987 (1916).

171. *Cf.* Paul J. Mishkin, *The Federal "Question" in the District Courts*, 53 COLUM. L. REV. 157, 181 (1953).

P's patent is invalid. *P* threatens to sue *D* and all persons purchasing the item from *D* for patent infringement in federal court. Without waiting for *P* to sue, *D* commences an action in federal court for slander of title to the item in question. *D's* action seeks an injunction to prevent *P* from threatening *D* and *D's* customers with suit and damages for the past injuries caused by the threats. Prior to the enactment of the Federal Declaratory Judgment Act, the Supreme Court held that *D's* action could not be brought in federal court because slander of title is a claim arising wholly under state law, even though the only significant issue in the action is the validity of *P's* patent.[172] This situation is very similar to that in *Illustration 2-31*. That illustration demonstrated that today, after the enactment of the Federal Declaratory Judgment Act, *D* could bring an action for a declaratory judgment against *P* in federal court to determine the issue of patent validity. Under the modern doctrine of supplemental jurisdiction, discussed in subsection 4, below, *D* could join the state slander of title claim with the federal declaratory judgment claim and have both claims decided by the federal court. Thus, the Supreme Court precedents that allowed *D* to sue *P* for a federal declaratory judgment can result in a claim being brought in federal court (the state slander of title claim) that could not be brought there in the absence of the declaratory judgment remedy.

* * * * *

Finally, the Court's attempt in *Franchise Tax Board* to restrict federal question jurisdiction in declaratory judgment actions is unnecessarily vague. In that case, the Court held that even if an action for declaratory judgment was otherwise appropriate for federal question jurisdiction, if the declaratory plaintiff cannot demonstrate a clear interest in a swift federal resolution of the issue of federal law, the declaratory judgment action may be disqualified from federal jurisdiction. Although delineating the categories of cases in which the federal courts will exercise discretion to decline jurisdiction is arguably both desirable and inevitable,[173] the way in which the Court delineates those discretionary categories is important. In *Franchise Tax Board*, the Court seemingly did no more than adopt as a jurisdictional rule the usual standard for determining whether the plaintiff's complaint for a declaratory judgment states a claim for relief, with the qualification that the demonstration must include a showing that relief is necessary from a *federal* court. This rule, however, gives no clear guidance to the district courts about how strong the plaintiff's interest in *federal* relief must be before federal jurisdiction is appropriate. Thus, it violates one of the cardinal principles of procedure—reiterated by Justice Thomas's concurrence in *Grable*—that jurisdictional rules should be as clear as possible to avoid the waste of time and energy that results when they are not.[174] Furthermore, as noted in *Illustration 2-32(b)*, the *Franchise Tax Board*

---

172. *See* American Well Works Co. v. Layne & Bowler Co., 241 U.S. 257, 36 S. Ct. 585, 60 L. Ed. 987 (1916).

173. *See* David L. Shapiro, *Jurisdiction and Discretion*, 60 N.Y.U. L. REV. 543 (1985).

174. *See* ZECHARIAH CHAFEE, JR., SOME PROBLEMS OF EQUITY 311-12 (1950). When jurisdictional rules are not clear, some cases in which the trial courts have subject-matter jurisdiction will be erroneously dismissed, and the dismissal will be reversed on appeal after much expense and waste of time. Other cases in which the trial courts do not have subject-matter jurisdiction will be erroneously retained, with the result that a dismissal on appeal will produce even more waste. In the latter situation, the action will have to be tried over again in a proceeding commenced in a court that possesses subject-matter jurisdiction.

standard could logically produce an expansion of federal question jurisdiction in situations that the Court has indicated in dictum to be inappropriate for jurisdiction. The overall picture is, therefore, one of unfortunate and unnecessary confusion that a clearer standard would avoid.[175]

SECTION C. CIVIL ACTIONS TO WHICH THE UNITED STATES IS A PARTY

Federal courts have subject-matter jurisdiction over civil actions in which the United States Government is a party.[176] Section 1345 of Title 28 grants the district courts original jurisdiction, except as otherwise provided, over all civil actions commenced by the United States, its agencies, and officers expressly authorized by Congress to sue.[177] In such cases, the district courts usually have concurrent jurisdiction with the state courts. The federal courts, however, have exclusive jurisdiction over suits involving seizures, recovery of fines, penalties, and forfeitures incurred under acts of Congress.[178] The federal district courts also have jurisdiction when the United States is named as a party defendant.[179] The most notable precondition to such actions is that the federal government must have waived its sovereign immunity to suit.[180]

SECTION D. DIVERSITY AND ALIENAGE JURISDICTION

Article III of the U.S. Constitution authorizes jurisdiction in "Controversies . . . between citizens of different States" and "between a State, or the Citizens thereof, and foreign States, Citizens, or Subjects."[181] Congress gave the lower federal courts jurisdiction of actions between citizens of different states and between citizens of a state and citizens or subjects of a foreign state—so-called diversity jurisdiction and alienage jurisdiction—in the Judiciary Act of 1789.[182] Since then, diversity and alienage jurisdiction have continued in varying forms. The existing grant of diversity jurisdiction is found in § 1332 of Title 28 of the *United States Code*. Diversity jurisdiction is concurrent with the state courts.

---

175. Another difficult problem of determining the existence of federal question jurisdiction occurs in cases in which federal law has preempted the operation of state law. This problem is discussed in section F on removal jurisdiction *infra*.

176. Article III of the Constitution extends the judicial power to "Controversies to which the United States shall be a party." U.S. CONST. art. III, § 2.

177. *See* 28 U.S.C. § 1345.

178. *See* 28 U.S.C. §§ 1355, 1356.

179. Over 15% of the civil cases filed in the federal district courts involved the United States either as a party plaintiff or defendant, which makes the United States the most frequent litigant in those courts. *See* CHARLES A. WRIGHT & MARY KAY KANE, THE LAW OF FEDERAL COURTS § 22, at 127 & n.2 (7th ed. 2011).

180. *See* 28 U.S.C. § 1346. Section 1346(a)(1) permits suits to recover internal revenue taxes. Section 1346(a)(2) lists several situations in which the federal government has consented to suit (derived from the 1855 Act creating the Court of Claims and the 1887 Tucker Act). Section 1346(b) is the jurisdictional grant for the Federal Tort Claims Act, which was enacted in 1946.

181. U.S. CONST. art. III, § 2.

182. *See* Act of Sept. 24, 1789, § 11, 1 Stat. 73, 78-79.

The historical justification for conferring diversity jurisdiction on the federal district courts was the fear of prejudice in state courts against citizens of other states—prejudice which would manifest itself against out-of-staters in state court proceedings.[183] The continuing vitality of this justification has been questioned today.[184] Indeed, it has been questioned whether significant prejudice against out-of-state citizens in state courts ever really existed.[185] However, repeated attempts to abolish or significantly curtail diversity jurisdiction have failed.[186]

1. Complete Diversity Requirement

Like the grant of general federal question jurisdiction, the general diversity statute does not confer the full scope of diversity jurisdiction permissible under the Constitution. For one thing, courts have always interpreted the general diversity statute to require complete diversity of citizenship between the adverse parties to the suit. This "complete diversity" requirement means that all the persons who join as plaintiffs must not have any overlapping citizenship with the persons joined as defendants.[187] This restriction on the exercise of diversity jurisdiction may result in the very kind of bias or prejudice in state court that the jurisdiction was designed to guard against.

---

183. *See* ALI STUDY OF THE DIVISION OF JURISDICTION BETWEEN STATE AND FEDERAL COURTS 101 (1969). The actual statement of the traditional justification is more complex than mere fear of prejudice against out-of-state citizens:

> On a broader theory, potential deterrence to free movement and business activity throughout the several states lay in the risk, or the fear of the risk, that the courts of the states other than one's own could not be relied upon to render adequate justice. On this view, the possible reasons for concern included protracted delay, inefficient or untrained personnel, and procedural complexities and restrictions, as well as prejudice against strangers. From either aspect, the availability of a federal forum away from home for litigation with strangers served to provide a guarantee of efficient, competent, and disinterested justice that, by its reassurance to one considering movement or business in another state, contributed to the expansion of trade and intercourse throughout the nation.

Id. But see Robert L. Jones, *Finishing A Friendly Argument: The Jury and the Historical Origins of Diversity Jurisdiction,* 82 N.Y.U. L. REV. 997 (2007) (arguing that existing accounts of the origins of the diversity jurisdiction are inadequate and that the purpose of the jurisdiction was to funnel politically sensitive litigation into the federal courts because federal officials would have the power to dictate the composition of federal juries, which had far more power than the bench in deciding cases in the eighteenth century).

184. *See* ALI STUDY OF THE DIVISION OF JURISDICTION BETWEEN STATE AND FEDERAL COURTS 106 (1969); *see also* Debra Lyn Bassett, *The Hidden Bias in Diversity Jurisdiction,* 81 WASH. U. L.Q. 119 (2003) (arguing that diversity jurisdiction's continued existence in its current form perpetuates a continuing form of discrimination based on the idea that rural courts and juries are inferior to those found in more urbanized areas); Stone Grissom, *Diversity Jurisdiction: An Open Dialogue in Dual Sovereignty,* 24 HAMLINE L. REV. 372 (2001) (tracing the historical origins of diversity jurisdiction and its continued impact on federalism in the United States).

185. *See* Henry J. Friendly, *The Historic Basis of Diversity Jurisdiction*, 41 HARV. L. REV. 483, 493 (1928). In addition, the diversity jurisdiction is configured more broadly than necessary to prevent bias or prejudice against out-of-state citizens. A plaintiff who is a citizen of the forum state may commence a diversity action in a federal court within the plaintiff's "home" state. The American Law Institute has recommended that this possibility be eliminated. *See* ALI STUDY OF THE DIVISION OF JURISDICTION BETWEEN STATE AND FEDERAL COURTS § 1302(a) (1969).

186. *See* CHARLES A. WRIGHT & MARY KAY KANE, THE LAW OF FEDERAL COURTS § 23 (7th ed. 2011); *see also* Thomas D. Rowe, Jr., *Abolishing Diversity Jurisdiction: Positive Side Effects and Potential for Further Reforms*, 92 HARV. L. REV. 963 (1979). The latest recommendation to limit the diversity jurisdiction has not been implemented by Congress. *See* REPORT OF THE FEDERAL COURTS STUDY COMMITTEE 38-43 (1990); 1 FEDERAL COURTS STUDY COMMITTEE WORKING PAPERS AND SUBCOMMITTEE REPORTS 418-67 (1990).

187. *Compare* Strawbridge v. Curtiss, 7 U.S. (3 Cranch) 267, 2 L. Ed. 435 (1806) ("complete diversity" required under statutory grant of jurisdiction) *with* State Farm Fire & Cas. Co. v. Tashire, 386 U.S. 523, 87 S. Ct. 1199, 18 L. Ed. 2d 270 (1967) ("incomplete diversity" permitted by the Constitution).

Illustration 2-35. *P-1* (a citizen of Vermont), *P-2* (a citizen of Kentucky), and *P-3* (a citizen of Alabama) sue *D-1* (a citizen of California), *D-2* (a citizen of Florida), and *D-3* (a citizen of Kentucky) in a U.S. District Court for $500,000. Complete diversity does not exist because a citizen of Kentucky is present on both sides of the lawsuit. Thus, if all of the plaintiffs are going to bring the action against all of the defendants, the plaintiffs will have to bring the action in a state court. However, if the plaintiffs bring the action in a state court, bias and prejudice against out-of-state citizens might operate in a variety of ways. Assume that *P-1*, *P-2*, and *P-3* are suing *D-1*, *D-2*, and *D-3* on claims in the alternative for personal injuries arising from an automobile accident. A trier of fact could find any combination of *D-1*, *D-2*, and *D-3*, or only one of them, liable to *P-1*, *P-2*, and *P-3* for their injuries. If the plaintiffs bring the action in a Kentucky state court, a Kentucky trier of fact might find in favor of *P-1*, *P-2*, and *P-3* and against *D-1* or *D-2*, but exonerate *D-3* (the defendant from Kentucky). If the plaintiffs bring the action in a Vermont state court, a Vermont trier of fact could find in favor of *P-1*, the Vermont plaintiff, and against one or more of the out-of-state defendants, even if the defendants had strong, but not conclusive, factual defenses against *P-1*, such as contributory negligence. Thus, if bias or prejudice actually exists against out-of-staters, the complete diversity rule may allow that bias or prejudice to operate in many cases.[188]

* * * * *

Congress has, for specific cases, enacted special grants of diversity jurisdiction that do not require complete diversity between all of the adverse parties to the action. For example, in interpleader cases, Congress has provided for jurisdiction in cases in which there are "[t]wo or more adverse claimants, of diverse citizenship."[189] Also, in the Multiparty, Multiforum Trial Jurisdiction Act of 2002, discussed below, Congress provided for minimal diversity jurisdiction in certain mass disaster cases. In the Class Action Fairness Act of 2005,[190] also discussed below in this chapter and in Chapter 8, Congress provided for jurisdiction in certain class actions in which (1) "any member of a class of plaintiffs is a citizen of a [s]tate different from any defendant," (2) "any member of a class of plaintiffs if a foreign state or a citizen or subject of a foreign state and any defendant is a citizen of a [s]tate," and (3) "any member of a class of plaintiffs is a citizen of a [s]tate and any defendant is a foreign state or a citizen or subject of a foreign state."[191]

2. Determination of State Citizenship

Diversity of citizenship must exist at the time that the action is commenced.[192] In *Grupo Dataflux v. Atlas Global Group, L.P.*,[193] the Supreme

---

188. *See* David P. Currie, *The Federal Courts and the American Law Institute* (pt. 1), 36 U. CHI. L. REV. 1, 18-19 (1968).

189. *See* 28 U.S.C. § 1335. This "statutory interpleader" is examined in Chapter 8(D)(2), below.

190. Pub. L. No. 109-2, 119 Stat. 4 (2005) (codified as 28 U.S.C. § 1332(d)(2)).

191. *See* 28 U.S.C. § 1332(d)(2)(A)-(C).

192. *See, e.g.*, Symes v. Harris, 472 F.3d 754 (10th Cir. 2006) (if allegations of the complaint were true and requested relief were granted, plaintiffs would be part owners of partnership that was one of defendants, and diversity of citizenship would be incomplete; nevertheless, under the commencement rule, diversity was complete on date on which action commenced and jurisdiction thus existed). In the Class Action Fairness Act of 2005,

Court held that a post-filing change in citizenship by a party could not cure a lack of diversity of citizenship between the parties at the commencement of the action. The Court distinguished *Caterpillar Inc. v. Lewis*,[194] a removal case discussed below in section C(5)*(e)*, on the ground that the defect in diversity in *Caterpillar* had been cured by dismissal of a party, a method that had long been considered an exception to the rule that diversity must be determined at the time the action is commenced. In contrast, *Grupo Dataflux* involved a situation in which non-diverse members of a partnership were dropped from the partnership after commencement. Because the partnership was the "party" whose citizenship counted, the elimination of the non-diverse partners placed the case within the rule that a party may not change citizenship after commencement to create (or destroy) diversity.

The First Circuit Court of Appeals correctly refused to extend the *Grupo Dataflux* rule to an action in which the plaintiffs amended their complaint as a matter of right under Rule 15(a) shortly after commencement to change the basis of subject-matter jurisdiction from diversity to federal question jurisdiction. Citing, *inter alia*, the Supreme Court's decision in *Rockwell International Corp. v. United States*,[195] (holding that when a plaintiff amends a complaint in federal court, the court looks to the amended complaint to determine jurisdiction), the court held that *Grupo Dataflux* was inapplicable to the plaintiff's entitlement to sue within the federal question jurisdiction, because it did "not depend on a manipulation of its business membership in order to fabricate complete diversity."[196]

Two general requirements must be met for a person to be a citizen of a state within the meaning of 28 U.S.C. § 1332. First, a person must be a citizen of the United States. Second, the person must be "domiciled" within some state.[197] Domicile is a common-law concept drawn from the subject of conflict of laws. To acquire a domicile within a state, one must be physically present within the state. Simultaneous with this physical presence, one must intend to remain in the state indefinitely or permanently or to make the state one's home.[198] Everyone has a domicile, and no one has more than one.

Illustration 2-36. A person's "domicile of origin" is the domicile that the person has at birth.[199] A child's domicile is that of the parent with whom the child lives. If the parent's domicile changes, the domicile of the minor also changes.[200]

* * * * *

Congress created new jurisdictional and removal provisions to apply to at least some diversity class actions. New § 1332(d)(7) provides that in determining citizenship of the proposed plaintiff classes under the Act, citizenship shall be determined as of the date of filing of the complaint or amended complaint, or, if the case stated by the initial pleading is not subject to federal jurisdiction, as of the date of service by plaintiffs of an amended pleading, motion, or other paper, indicating the existence of federal jurisdiction. This Act is discussed at various points in this chapter and in Chapter 8, below.

193. 541 U.S. 567, 124 S. Ct. 1920, 158 L. Ed. 2d 866 (2004).

194. 519 U.S. 61, 117 S. Ct. 467, 136 L. Ed. 2d 437 (1996). For a discussion and criticism of *Grupo*, see Note, *The Supreme Court 2003 Term,* 118 HARV. L. REV. 386, 386-96 (2004).

195. 549 U.S. 457, 127 S. Ct. 1397, 167 L. Ed. 2d 190 (2007).

196. *See* Connectu LLC v. Zuckerberg, 522 F.3d 82 (1st Cir.2008).

197. *See* RICHARD H. FALLON ET AL., HART & WECHSLER'S THE FEDERAL COURTS AND THE FEDERAL SYSTEM 1361 (6th ed. 2009).

198. *See* RESTATEMENT (SECOND) OF CONFLICT OF LAWS §§ 15-18 (1971).

199. *See id.* § 14.

200. *See id.* § 22; *see also* McCann v. Newman Irrevocable Trust, 458 F.3d 281 (3d Cir. 2006) (discussing how the burden of proof works on the issue of domicile in diversity actions).

Once a person has acquired a domicile, that domicile continues until the person acquires a new one.

Illustration 2-37. If an adult's domicile is in Texas, that domicile continues in Texas until the adult acquires a new "domicile of choice" by being physically present within the borders of another state and *simultaneously* possessing the intent to remain in the new state indefinitely or permanently.[201]

* * * * *

The domicile requirement produces several difficulties in determining state citizenship for purposes of the diversity statute. If a party's domicile is disputed, the main problem arises in determining whether that party really intends to make a particular state that party's home. Two common situations present this question. One situation exists when a party moves from one state to another, and the issue is whether the party really intends to make the new state home. The other situation exists when a party has substantial day-to-day relationships with more than one state, and a court must determine which state is the party's domicile. No mathematical formula exists to resolve the domicile issue in either kind of case. Courts consider a variety of factors in each situation that bear on the party's intent to make one or another state home. The totality of the facts must be taken into account.

Illustration 2-38. *P's* domicile of origin is Massachusetts. *P* moved from Massachusetts to Nebraska to attend law school. *P* lived in Nebraska only during the school year. Each summer, *P* returned to Massachusetts. While in Massachusetts during the summer after *P's* second year of law school, *D* allegedly assaulted *P*. *D* is a citizen of Massachusetts. *P* sued *D* in a U.S. District Court to recover damages for the assault. The jurisdictional statement in *P's* complaint alleged that *P* was a citizen of Nebraska and that *D* was a citizen of Massachusetts. *D* moved to dismiss the action for lack of subject-matter jurisdiction on the ground that *P* was really a citizen of Massachusetts. On similar facts, a federal district court agreed with *D* and dismissed the action. In addition to returning to Massachusetts each summer to work, *P* had retained a Massachusetts driver's license, had never obtained a Nebraska automobile registration, and had never registered to vote in Nebraska. The totality of the circumstances indicated that *P's* domicile had never shifted from Massachusetts to Nebraska. Therefore, no diversity of citizenship was present between the parties.[202]

Illustration 2-39. *P* sued *D* for libel in a U.S. District Court in Nevada. The jurisdictional statement in *P's* complaint alleged that *P* was a citizen of

---

201. *See* RESTATEMENT (SECOND) OF CONFLICT OF LAWS §§ 11-23 (1971); *see also* Padilla-Mangual v. Pavía Hosp., 516 F.3d 29 (1st Cir. 2008) (when a party expressly declares the intent to effectuate a change of domicile, there must be an evidentiary hearing to determine the domicile issue if evidence submitted in opposition to the declaration does not demonstrate the falsity of the declaration with reasonable certainty; this is because the declarant's credibility will be an essential element of the district court's determination, and this cannot be evaluated without a hearing); McCann v. Newman Irrevocable Trust, 458 F.3d 281 (3d Cir. 2006) (when it is established that a party was domiciled in a particular state, there is a presumption that the party remains domiciled in that state; if a litigant asserting that diversity exists claims the established domicile has changed, the litigant must rebut the presumption by a preponderance of the evidence); *cf.* Smith v. Cummings, 445 F.3d 1254 (10th Cir. 2006) (because domicile is a voluntary status, prisoner is presumed to be a citizen of the state of which he was a citizen before he was incarcerated, even if he is subsequently incarcerated in another state; however, this presumption is rebuttable, and case was reversed and remanded for prisoner to be given an opportunity to demonstrate his citizenship).

202. *See* Murphy v. Newport Waterfront Landing, Inc., 806 F. Supp. 322 (D.R.I. 1992), *aff'd without opinion*, 13 F.3d 409 (11th Cir. 1994).

California and that *D* was a citizen of Nevada. *D* moved to dismiss the action on the ground that *P* was really a citizen of Nevada and, therefore, diversity of citizenship was lacking. The facts developed at an evidentiary hearing on the jurisdictional issue indicated that *P* had maintained a residence in California about fifteen miles from the Nevada border. *P* lived in this residence with *P's* spouse and children for eight years before commencement of the lawsuit. After commencement of the action, the IRS seized the residence, and it later burned. However, *P* was licensed to practice law in Nevada, and *P's* law practice had always been based there. *P* also maintained an apartment in the same building in Nevada where *P* practiced law. *P's* automobiles had Nevada registrations. *P* possessed a Nevada driver's license, banked exclusively in Nevada, and listed a Nevada mailing address on federal income tax returns. *P* never filed a California income tax return. Although *P* registered to vote in California, *P* never actually voted there. *P* had voted in at least one presidential election in Nevada. On these facts, a federal district court held that *P* was domiciled in California and that diversity of citizenship existed. The court emphasized that *P* and *P's* family had lived at the California address for eight years before the action was commenced and had considered the residence to be their home.[203]

* * * * *

A United States citizen can be domiciled in a foreign country. As a result, it is possible for a United States citizen to have no state citizenship for diversity purposes.[204]

Illustration 2-40. *P* was born in Virginia. *P* abandons *P's* home in Virginia and travels to Paris, France. *P* intends to remain there permanently. However, *P* does not become a naturalized citizen of France, but retains U.S. citizenship. *P* cannot sue or be sued in federal court based upon diversity jurisdiction. *P* is a citizen of the United States. However, because *P* is not domiciled within any *state*, *P* cannot be a citizen of a state. In any suit *P* brings against a citizen of a state as well as in any suit brought against *P* by a citizen of a state, the action would not be "between citizens of different states."[205]

* * * * *

Few problems exist with determining whether a party is physically present in a state. However, in rare circumstances, the physical presence requirement and the rule that diversity is determined at the commencement of the action can combine to create or defeat diversity.

Illustration 2-41. *D's* domicile is Michigan. *D* abandons that domicile, moves to Pennsylvania, and intends to make Pennsylvania *D's* permanent home. However, after *D* left Michigan but before *D* arrived in Pennsylvania, *P* sued *D* in a U.S. District Court for breach of contract. *P* is a citizen of Michigan. *D* moved to

---

203. *See* Abbott v. United Venture Capital, Inc., 718 F. Supp. 823 (D. Nev. 1988).

204. *See, e.g.*, Newman-Green, Inc. v. Alfonzo-Larrain, 490 U.S. 826, 828, 109 S. Ct. 2218, 2220-21, 104 L. Ed. 2d 893, 899 (1989); Sadat v. Mertes, 615 F.2d 1176 (7th Cir. 1980); *cf.* King v. Cessna Aircraft Co., 505 F.3d 1160 (11th Cir. 2007) (a United States citizen does not lose his or her state domicile when citizen is sent abroad by his or her employer to work).

205. Nor, since *P* retained United States citizenship, could there be a suit between a citizen of a state and a citizen or subject of a foreign state. *See* 28 U.S.C. § 1332(a)(2); subsection 4 *infra*.

dismiss on the ground that no diversity of citizenship existed. On the facts, a federal district court agreed and dismissed the action. *P* had not arrived in Pennsylvania on the date the action was commenced. Thus, *D* still retained *D's* Michigan domicile. Diversity of citizenship did not exist even though *D* intended to make Pennsylvania home.[206] If a citizen of any state other than Michigan, including Pennsylvania, had sued *D*, diversity would have existed. After *P's* action is dismissed, *P* may commence a new action in federal court based on diversity of citizenship. Assuming that *D* has reached Pennsylvania in the interim and thus established a new domicile, diversity of citizenship would exist in the new action.[207] If a citizen of Pennsylvania had sued *D* before *D* reached Pennsylvania, *D's* arrival in Pennsylvania and shift of domicile to that state would not destroy jurisdiction. This result is attributable to the rule that federal jurisdiction, once it has attached, will not be ousted by subsequent events.[208]

3. Citizenship of Corporations and Associations

For some time, the general diversity statute has conferred multiple citizenship upon corporations.[209] Except in direct actions against liability insurers,[210] a corporation has been treated as a citizen of any state where it is incorporated *and* the state where it has its principal place of business.[211] Until 2012, the provisions of 28 U.S.C. § 1332(c)(1) creating this multiple citizenship only used the word "State" to describe the places where corporations would be citizens. This gave rise to doubt and confusion about the application of the dual citizenship requirement when corporations were either incorporated in a foreign nation or had their principal place of business there. In the Federal Courts Jurisdiction and Venue Clarification Act of 2011, effective in January 2012, § 1332(c)(1) was amended to clarify that the

---

206. *See* Linardos v. Fortuna, 157 F.3d 945 (2d Cir. 1998) (district court erred in concluding that the plaintiff's domicile changed as soon as the plaintiff formed the intent to move from one state to the other, but before the plaintiff actually moved and was physically present in the new state).

207. Of course, other obstacles may arise to prevent *P* from successfully maintaining the action, such as the running of the relevant statute of limitations before the second action is commenced.

208. *See* CHARLES ALAN WRIGHT & MARY KAY KANE, LAW OF FEDERAL COURTS § 28 (7th ed. 2011).

209. *See* 28 U.S.C. § 1332(c)(1). The diversity statute has not always explicitly conferred citizenship on corporations. *See* John McCormack, Comment, Carden v. Arkoma Associates: *The Citizenship of Limited Partnerships, Associations, and Juridical Entities—A Chilling Future for Federal Diversity Jurisdiction*, 27 NEW ENG. L. REV. 505, 514-19 (1992) (detailing the history of the diversity jurisdiction for corporations).

210. As amended in 1964, § 1332(c)(1) provides a special rule for a direct action against an insurer when the insured has not been joined as a party defendant. Besides being deemed a citizen of any state where the insurer is incorporated as well as the state where it has its principal place of business, a liability insurer is also deemed to be a citizen of the state where the insured is a citizen. This provision was amended effective January 2012 to include provisions providing for multiple citizenship in case of insureds and corporations that were citizens of foreign nations. *See* Federal Courts Jurisdiction and Venue Clarification Act of 2011, Pub. L. No. 112-63, § 102, 125 Stat. 758, 759 (codified in 28 U.S.C. § 1332(c)(1)); *see also* National Athletic Sportswear, Inc. v. Westfield Ins. Co., 528 F.3d 508 (7th Cir. 2008) (action by insured against insurer is not a direct action); Lee-Lipstreu v. Chubb Group of Ins. Cos., 329 F.3d 898 (6th Cir. 2003) (plaintiff sued employer's insurance company to recover underinsured motorist benefits under policy that covered employee; holding that in this type of action, the employee is, in effect, the insured, and is claiming benefits as the insured party even though the employer purchased the policy; therefore, the action is not a direct action; to apply direct action provision to actions between an insured and the insured's carrier would effectively eliminate these kinds of suits from federal court, since the insured and the carrier would always be considered citizens of the same state).

211. *See* 28 U.S.C. § 1332(c)(1).

section created dual citizenship for corporations with appropriate relationships to foreign nations. The section now reads:

> (c) For the purposes of this section and section 1441 [the general removal statute] of this Title—
>
> > (1) a corporation shall be deemed to be a citizen of every State and foreign state by which it has been incorporated and of the State or foreign state where it has its principal place of business, except that in any direct action against the insurer of a policy or contract of liability insurance, whether incorporated or unincorporated, to which action the insured is not joined as a party-defendant, such insurer shall be deemed a citizen of—
> >
> > (A) every State and foreign state of which the insured is a citizen;
> >
> > (B) every State and foreign state where the insurer has been incorporated; and
> >
> > (C) the State or foreign state where the insurer has its principal place of business; . . . .[212]

Corporations are sometimes incorporated in more than one state,[213] but a corporation can have only one principal place of business. This multiple citizenship limits diversity jurisdiction to cases in which no party opposing a corporation is a citizen of any state in which the corporation is incorporated or has its principal place of business. Note that other statutes may alter this rule in specific kinds of cases. For example, in 2002, Congress enacted 28 U.S.C. § 1369, the Multiparty, Multiforum Trial Jurisdiction Act, which is discussed in subsection *(e)* below. For purposes of the Act, a corporation is deemed to be a citizen of "any State, and a citizen or subject of any foreign state, in which it is incorporated or has its principal place of business."[214]

Illustration 2-42. Assume that *P*, a citizen of Utah, sues *D Corporation*. *D* is incorporated in Delaware and has its principal place of business in Utah. Under the prevailing view of § 1332(c)(1), complete diversity is not present. *P* cannot allege only *D's* state of incorporation to establish diversity. *D* is a citizen of

---

212. Pub. L. No. 112-63, § 102, 125 Stat. 758, 758 (codified as 28 U.S.C. § 1332(c)(1)).

213. *See, e.g.*, Bell v. United Cities Gas Co., No. 90-0479-R, 1991 U.S. Dist. LEXIS 15811 (W.D. Va. Apr. 26, 1991). Federally chartered corporations whose activities are limited to one state are citizens of that state, but if their activities are spread over more than one state, it has been held that they are national citizens only and not citizens of any state, with the result that they cannot sue or be sued within the diversity jurisdiction. *See* Little League Baseball, Inc. v. Welsh Publ'g Group, Inc., 874 F. Supp. 648 (M.D. Pa. 1995). In Wachovia Bank v. Schmidt, 546 U.S. 303, 126 S. Ct. 941, 163 L. Ed. 2d 797 (2006), the Supreme Court interpreted 28 U.S.C. § 1348, which provides that national banks are citizens of "the States in which they are respectively located," as making national banks citizens only of the states in which their main offices are located; *see also* Wells Fargo Bank v. WMR e-Pin, LLC, 653 F.3d 702 (8th Cir. 2011); Paul E. Lund, *Federally Chartered Corporations and Federal Jurisdiction*, 36 FLA. ST. U. L. REV. 317 (2009); Paul E. Lund, *National Banks and Diversity Jurisdiction,* 46 U. LOUISVILLE L. REV. 73 (2007).

214. 28 U.S.C. § 1369(c)(2).

Delaware *and* Utah. Thus, the overlap with *P's* Utah citizenship is fatal to diversity jurisdiction.[215]

* * * * *

At one time, there was a dispute about how to determine the principal place of business of a corporation whose activities were dispersed among different states. In *Hertz Corp. v. Friend*,[216] the Supreme Court adopted the so-called "nerve center test" for determining principal place of business. Under the nerve center test, a corporation's principal place of business is determined by where its corporate headquarters are located. Although even this test may present problems in cases in which a corporation's command and coordinating functions are dispersed throughout different locations, the test nevertheless focuses the courts on the center of overall direction, control, and coordination and will presumably simplify the principal place of business inquiry in many cases.

Illustration 2-43. *P Corporation* is incorporated in Illinois. Its sole manufacturing plant is in Mississippi. *P* sued *D*, a citizen of Mississippi, in a U.S. District Court in Mississippi. *D* moved to dismiss the action on the ground that diversity of citizenship was lacking. *D* contended that *P's* principal place of business was in Mississippi. *P* argued that its principal place of business should be considered to be Illinois because its executive offices were located in Illinois. On these facts, the nerve center test clearly points to Illinois as *P's* principal place of business and diversity jurisdiction exists.

Illustration 2-44. *P*, a citizen of Kentucky, sued *D Corporation* in a state court in Kentucky. *D* is incorporated in New York. *D* removed the action to a U.S. District Court in Kentucky.[217] *P* moved to remand the action to the Kentucky state court on the ground that diversity jurisdiction was lacking. *P* contended that *D* was a citizen of Kentucky because its principal place of business was in Kentucky. *D's* plant in Kentucky employed over 9,000 employees. In addition, *D's* activities are spread over several states. Furthermore, some of *D's* operations in other states generated more income for *D* than its Kentucky operations. However, *D's* basic corporate and personnel records are maintained in New York. Under the nerve center test, the corporation's principal place of business is in New York and diversity again exists.[218]

* * * * *

Unlike corporations, unincorporated associations do not have artificial citizenship under the general diversity statute. Thus, labor unions, partnerships,

---

215. *See also* Holston Invs., Inc. v. Lanlogistics Corp., 677 F.3d 1068 (11th Cir. 2012); Grand Union Supermarkets, Inc. v. H.E. Lockhart Mgmt., Inc., 316 F.3d 408 (3d Cir. 2003) (corporation that had ceased doing business for two years did not have a principal place of business and was citizen of state of its incorporation only); Dawn Levy, *Where Do Dead Corporations Live? Determining the Citizenship of Inactive Corporations for Diversity Jurisdiction Purposes,* 62 BROOK. L. REV. 663 (1996).

216. 559 U.S. __, 130 S. Ct. 1181, 175 L. Ed. 2d 1029 (2010); *see generally* Connor D. Deverell, *Defining A Corporation's "Principal Place of Business": The United States Supreme Court's Decision in* Hertz Corp. v. Friend, 56 LOY. L. REV. 733 (2010).

217. Removal jurisdiction is discussed in section F *infra.*

218. *See also* Central W. Va. Energy Co. v. Mountain State Carbon, LLC, 636 F.3d 101 (4th Cir. 2011) (merely filing a document for listing a principal place of business without more is insufficient to establish a corporation's nerve center for diversity jurisdiction purposes; however, here filing agreed with facts that nerve center was in Michigan).

joint stock companies, trade groups, governing boards of institutions, societies, and other unincorporated associations are deemed, for diversity purposes, to be citizens of *each* state where one of their members is a citizen.[219]

Illustration 2-45. *F* fraternal society, an unincorporated association, has members in all fifty states. Thus, *F* cannot sue or be sued in federal court within the diversity jurisdiction by another U.S. citizen because complete diversity can never exist.[220]

* * * * *

In the Class Action Fairness Act of 2005, Congress created new jurisdictional provisions to govern at least some diversity class actions.[221] In new 28 U.S.C. § 1332(d)(1), the citizenship of an unincorporated association is defined, for purposes of subsection (d), to be that of the state where the association has its principal place of business and the state under whose laws it is organized.[222] This definition does not, however, apply to diversity actions by or against associations under other provisions of § 1332. Other provisions of the Act are discussed in subsection 6 and other appropriate parts of this chapter, below.[223]

4. Alienage Jurisdiction

The general diversity statute includes within its scope more than jurisdiction of suits between citizens of different states. Section 1332(a) also allows jurisdiction of suits between (a) citizens of a state and citizens or subjects of a foreign state, (b) citizens of different states in which citizens or subjects of a foreign

---

219. *See, e.g.*, Carden v. Arkoma Assocs., 494 U.S 185, 110 S. Ct. 1015, 108 L. Ed. 2d 157 (1990); United Steelworkers v. R.H. Bouligny, Inc., 382 U.S. 145, 86 S. Ct. 272, 15 L. Ed. 2d 217 (1965); D.B. Zwirn Special Opportunities Fund, L.P. v. Mehrotra, 661 F.3d 124 (1st Cir. 2011) (in a diversity action in which a limited liability company is a party, the complaint or notice of removal must specifically identify the citizenship of each of the L.L.C.'s members); Underwriters at Lloyd's London v. Osting-Schwinn, 613 F.3d 1079 (11th Cir. 2010) (unincorporated association as plaintiff is required to plead citizenship of each of its members in order to establish diversity jurisdiction); Emerald Investors Trust v. Gaunt Parsippany Partners, 492 F.3d 192 (3d Cir. 2007) (citizenship of unincorporated investment trust must be determined by looking to the citizenship of both the trustee and the beneficiaries); Debra R. Cohen, *Limited Liability Company Citizenship: Reconsidering an Illogical and Inconsistent Choice,* 90 MARQ. L. REV. 269 (2006); Christine M. Kailus, Note, *Diversity Jurisdiction and Unincorporated Businesses: Collapsing the Doctrinal Wall,* 2007 U. ILL. L. REV. 1543 (arguing that unincorporated businesses should be treated like corporations for purposes of the diversity jurisdiction).

220. It is sometimes possible for an unincorporated association to sue or be sued as a class. *See* FED. R. CIV. P. 23.2. When the prerequisites for a class action have been met, only the citizenship of the named representative of the class is taken into account in determining diversity of citizenship. *See, e.g.*, Deloitte Noraudit A/S v. Deloitte Haskins & Sells, 148 F.R.D. 523 (S.D.N.Y. 1993). Diversity requirements in class actions are discussed in Chapter 8(D)(4) *infra* ("Class Actions").

221. *See* Pub. L. No. 109-2, 119 Stat. 4 (codified as 28 U.S.C. § 1332(d)); Amanda Coney, Comment, *Defining "Primary Defendants" in the Class Action Fairness Act of 2005,*67 LA. L. REV. 903 (2007); C. Douglas Floyd, *The Inadequacy of the Interstate Commerce Justification for the Class Action Fairness Act of 2005,* 55 EMORY L.J. 487 (2006); Heather Scribner, *Protecting Federalism Interests After the Class Action Fairness Act of 2005: A Response to Professor Vairo,* 51 WAYNE L. REV. 1417 (2005); Edward F. Sherman, *Class Actions After the Class Action Fairness Act of 2005,* 80 TUL. L. REV. 1593 (2006); Patrick Woolley, Erie *and Choice of Law After the Class Action Fairness Act,* 80 TUL. L. REV. 1723 (2006).

222. Ferrell v. Express Check Advance, LLC, 591 F.3d 698 (4th Cir. 2010) (limited liability was an unincorporated association within meaning of CAFA deeming an unincorporated association to be a citizen of the state under whose laws it was organized, and principal place of business was in South Carolina).

223. For a discussion of whether a corporation's dual citizenship can create the minimal diversity necessary under the Class Action Fairness Act when the representative party in the class action is a citizen of either the state where the corporation is incorporated or the state where it has its principal place of business, see Kimberly Nakamaru, Comment, *Touching a Nerve:* Hertz v. Friend's *Impact on the Class Action Fairness Act's Minimum Diversity Requirement,* 44 LOY. L.A. L. REV. 1019 (2011).

state are additional parties, and (c) a foreign state as plaintiff and citizens of a state or of different states.[224]

Illustration 2-46. *P*, a citizen of Texas, sues *D*, a citizen of France. This action can be brought in a U.S. District Court under 28 U.S.C. § 1332(a)(2), which permits suits between citizens of a state and citizens or subjects of a foreign state.[225]

Illustration 2-47. *P-1*, a citizen of Florida, and *P-2*, a citizen of Canada, sue *D*, a citizen of Oregon. This action can be brought in a U.S. District Court under 28 U.S.C. § 1332(a)(3), which permits suits between "citizens of different states and in which citizens or subjects of a foreign state are additional parties."[226]

* * * * *

In some instances, a person will possess dual United States and foreign citizenship. When confronted with this situation, most courts only recognize the U.S. nationality of the party.[227] This approach will result in a denial of jurisdiction when the party possessing dual citizenship is domiciled within a state and the opposing party is a citizen of the same state. This result probably coincides with the purposes of the alienage jurisdiction. No bias or prejudice will be likely against the party with dual citizenship in a state court where the party is domiciled. In addition, the foreign state is not likely to be affronted by the treatment of its citizen in state court because its citizen is also a citizen of the United States.[228]

Illustration 2-48. *P*, a citizen of the United States, also possesses Swiss citizenship. *P* is domiciled in California. *D* is a citizen of California. *P* cannot sue *D* in a U.S. District Court because *P* is considered to be a citizen of California, not Switzerland. Consequently, no diversity of citizenship exists between *P* and *D*.

* * * * *

In 1988, Congress modified the "alienage" jurisdiction authorized by 28 U.S.C. § 1332. Under this modification, section 1332(a) provided that "an alien admitted to the United States for permanent residence shall be deemed a citizen of the State in which such alien is domiciled."[229] This amendment was designed to

---

224. 28 U.S.C. § 1332(a)(2)-(4).

225. The use of the plural "citizens of a state" does not mean that all of the domestic parties in the action must be citizens of the same state. *See* Iraola & CIA, S.A. v. Kimberly-Clark Corp., 232 F.3d 854, 858 (11th Cir. 2000).

226. *See, e.g.*, Zurich Ins. Co. v. Sigourney, 278 F.2d 826 (9th Cir. 1960); Hunter v. Shell Oil Co., 198 F.2d 485 (5th Cir. 1952). Under 28 U.S.C. § 1332(a)(2) and (3), suits in which an alien and a citizen of a state are on one side and an alien is on the other are usually held beyond the jurisdiction of the district courts. *See, e.g.*, Ed & Fred, Inc. v. Puritan Marine Ins. Underwriters Corp., 506 F.2d 757 (5th Cir. 1975); Engstrom v. Hornseth, 959 F. Supp. 545 (D.P.R. 1997). However, actions may fit within 28 U.S.C. § 1332(a)(3) when (1) citizens of different states are plaintiff and defendant and (2) aliens are also joined on both sides of the suit. *See* Dresser Indus., Inc. v. Underwriters at Lloyd's, 106 F.3d 494 (3d Cir. 1997).

227. *See, e.g.*, Swiger v. Allegheny Energy, Inc., 540 F.3d 179 (3d Cir. 2008); Frett-Smith v. Vanterpool, 511 F.3d 396 (3d Cir. 2008) (party who had dual citizenship could not invoke alienage jurisdiction; only party's U.S. Citizenship could be counted, with the result that she was a U.S. citizen domiciled abroad).

228. *See* 13E CHARLES A. WRIGHT ET AL., FEDERAL PRACTICE AND PROCEDURE: JURISDICTION AND RELATED MATTERS § 3621 (3d ed. 2009).

229. Judicial Improvements and Access to Justice Act of 1988, Pub. L. No. 100-702, § 203, 102 Stat. 4642, 4646 (codified at 28 U.S.C. § 1332(a)). For an alien to be admitted to the United States for permanent residence, the alien must be admitted to permanent residence under the immigration laws—*i.e.*, have a "green card." Thus, if the alien has simply lived in the United States for a number of years on a temporary work permit without being formally admitted to permanent status, the alien retains his or her status as a citizen or subject of a foreign state for purposes of the alienage jurisdiction. *See* Foy v. Schantz, Schatzman & Aaronson, P.A., 108 F.3d 1347 (11th Cir. 1997) (jurisdiction sustained). Given the fact that federal subject-matter jurisdiction must be affirmatively alleged, one might think that the "permanent resident alien" provision would now require plaintiffs to allege that any foreign citizens are *not* permanent resident aliens domiciled in a state where any opposing party is a citizen,

destroy jurisdiction between citizens of states who sue or are sued by aliens domiciled in the same state. However, one other potential effect of the amendment was to create jurisdiction between an alien admitted to permanent residence within the United States who is domiciled within a state and another alien not domiciled within the state. Although Congress probably did not intend this effect, it was a possible result under the wording of the amendment. Such a result would arguably be unconstitutional because Article III of the Constitution does not authorize jurisdiction over suits between two citizens or subjects of foreign states.[230] In the Federal Courts Jurisdiction and Venue Clarification Act of 2011, effective in January 2012, Congress rectified this problem. The Act deleted the "resident alien" language from the end of § 1332(a) and then modified § 1332(a)(2) to make it clear that the provision applied only to that section, as well as clarifying the language of the provision:

> (a) The district courts shall have original jurisdiction of all civil actions where the matter in controversy exceeds the sum or value of $75,000, exclusive of interests and costs, and is between—
>
> . . . .
>
> (2) citizens of a State and citizens or subjects of a foreign state, except that the district courts shall not have original jurisdiction under this subsection of an action between citizens of a State and citizens or subjects of a foreign state who are lawfully admitted for permanent residence in the United States and are domiciled in the same state[.][231]

This language should make it clear that the "resident alien" provision is designed (1) to contract the alienage jurisdiction of the federal courts rather than expand it, and (2) is constitutional.

Illustration 2-49. *P*, a citizen of Nevada, and *D*, a citizen of Canada admitted to the United States for permanent residence and domiciled in Nevada, have an automobile accident in Nevada. Prior to the 1988 amendment to § 1332, *P* could sue *D* in a U.S. District Court under 28 U.S.C § 1332(a)(2), which permits actions between citizens of a state (*P*) and citizens or subjects of a foreign state (*D*).[232] After the 1988 amendment, *P* cannot sue *D* in federal court within the alienage jurisdiction because both parties would be considered citizens of Nevada.

---

but at least one court has refused to impose such a requirement. *See* Karazanos v. Madison Two Assocs., 147 F.3d 624 (7th Cir. 1998).

230. *See* Larry Kramer, *Diversity Jurisdiction*, 1990 B.Y.U. L. REV. 97, 122; John B. Oakley, *Recent Statutory Changes in the Law of Federal Jurisdiction and Venue*, 24 U.C. DAVIS L. REV. 735, 745 (1991); David D. Siegel, *Changes in Federal Jurisdiction and Practice Under the New Judicial Improvements and Access to Justice Act*, 123 F.R.D. 399, 408-09 (1989).

231. Pub. L. No. 112-63, § 101, 125 Stat. 758, 758 (codified at 28 U.S.C. § 1332(a)(2)).

232. Unlike the requirement of state citizenship for diversity purposes—*i.e.*, that a person be (1) a citizen of the United States *and* (2) domiciled within some state to be a citizen of a state—a party does not have to be domiciled in a foreign state to be considered a citizen or subject of the foreign state for purposes of the alienage jurisdiction. This absence of a domicile requirement is still true, except when the alien in question is admitted to the United States for permanent residence and is domiciled within a state. Thus, a citizen of France domiciled in England is still considered a citizen of France for purposes of the alienage jurisdiction, even after the 1988 amendment to 28 U.S.C. § 1332.

Illustration 2-50. *P*, a citizen of France admitted to permanent residence in the United States and domiciled in Texas, is involved in an automobile accident in Texas with *D*, a citizen of Great Britain domiciled in Great Britain. On the face of the 1988 amendment to § 1332, *P* could sue *D* in a U.S. District Court within the alienage jurisdiction. Under the wording of that amendment, *P* is treated as a citizen of Texas, and *D* is a subject of Great Britain. Thus, jurisdiction appeared to exist under 1332(a)(2), because the action is between a citizen of a state and a subject of a foreign state. Under the 2011 amendment to § 1332(a), this interpretation is no longer possible and no jurisdiction would exist in this case.

* * * * *

The 1988 amendment's use of the term "alien" presented another difficulty. The general diversity statute, tracking Article III, section 2 of the Constitution, confers jurisdiction in certain controversies involving "citizens or subjects of a foreign state." However, the 1988 amendment spoke of "an alien admitted to the United States for permanent residence" who is domiciled within a state. Before the amendment, rare cases arose that involved persons who were "stateless aliens"—persons who were not citizens or subjects of any foreign state because they had lost their national citizenship.[233] For the most part, the federal courts declined jurisdiction over actions involving stateless aliens because they were not "citizens or subjects of a foreign state."[234] The wording of the 1988 amendment could have been read as conferring state citizenship upon stateless aliens admitted to the United States for permanent residence and domiciled within a state. Although such persons are not "citizens or subjects of a foreign state," they are "aliens." Thus, the amendment literally applied to them. Nevertheless, Congress no more intended this result than it intended to authorize actions between two parties who are citizens of foreign states. The 2011 amendment to § 1332(a)(2) does not use the word "alien," but the phrase citizens or subjects of a foreign state. The amendment thus clarifies that there is no jurisdiction in the situation described in this illustration.

Illustration 2-51. *P* is a Cuban refugee who is no longer a citizen of Cuba. However, *P* has not acquired any other national citizenship. *P* has been admitted to permanent residence in the United States and is domiciled in Florida. Before the 1988 amendment, most decisions held that *P* could not sue or be sued within the diversity or alienage jurisdiction. Because *P* was not a citizen of the United States, *P* was not a citizen of a state within the meaning of the diversity statute. Because *P* possessed no national citizenship, *P* was also not a citizen or subject of a foreign state within the meaning of the statute. The word "alien" in the 1988 amendment literally made it appear as if the stateless alien described in this illustration would

---

233. Unlike domicile, national citizenship can be lost without acquiring new national citizenship.

234. *See* 13E CHARLES A. WRIGHT ET AL., FEDERAL PRACTICE AND PROCEDURE: JURISDICTION AND RELATED MATTERS § 3621 (3d ed. 2009). In National City Bank v. Aronson, 474 F. Supp. 2d 925 (S.D. Ohio 2007), the court applied the "stateless" terminology to a U.S. citizen domiciled abroad and denied jurisdiction. Although the court was correct to deny the existence of diversity, a U.S. citizen domiciled abroad is not "stateless" because he or she is, in fact, a citizen of the United States. The term "stateless" should be reserved for parties who have lost their national citizenship and not acquired new national citizenship.

be given state citizenship for purposes of the diversity jurisdiction. The 2011 amendment to § 1332(a) makes it clear that this is not so.

* * * * *

Before 2012, a similar interpretive problem existed in determining the citizenship of "alien" corporations because of the wording of 28 U.S.C. § 1332(c)(1). That section provided that a corporation shall be deemed a citizen of any "State" by which it has been incorporated and the "State" where it has its principal place of business. The use of the word "State" in the statute led some courts to conclude that it did not apply to a corporation incorporated in the United States with its principal place of business in a foreign country or to a corporation incorporated in a foreign country with its principal place of business in a state of the United States.[235] However, other courts held that 28 U.S.C. § 1332(c)(1) conferred dual citizenship on all corporations.[236] The Federal Courts Jurisdiction and Venue Clarification Act of 2011, effective in January 2012, amended § 1332(c)(1) to make it clear that corporations incorporated in or with their principal place of business in foreign countries also have dual citizenship for purposes of the provisions of § 1332(a).[237] This amendment was quoted in subsection (3), above.

In *JP Morgan Chase Bank v. Traffic Stream (BVI) Infrastructure Ltd.*,[238] the Supreme Court resolved the question whether a corporation incorporated under the laws of a dependent territory of a foreign country could be considered a citizen or subject of a foreign state within the meaning of the diversity statute. In *JP Morgan*, the Court held that a corporation of a foreign state is considered that state's citizen for jurisdictional purposes. In addition, the Court held that a

---

235. *See, e.g.*, MAS Capital, Inc. v. Biodelivery Scis. Int'l, Inc., 524 F.3d 831 (7th Cir. 2008) (domestic corporation with its principal place of business in a foreign country is a citizen of its state of incorporation only); Torres v. Southern Peru Copper Corp., 113 F.3d 540 (5th Cir. 1997). Note, however, that corporations organized under the laws of countries that the United States does not formally recognize may not be considered citizens of a "foreign state" within the meaning of § 1332(a)(2). *See* Matimak Trading Co. v. Khalily, 118 F.3d 76 (2d Cir. 1997). Note also that even if alien corporations can have dual citizenship, there will be the same problems with determining their principal place of business as exist with domestic corporations. *See* Bel-Bel Int'l Corp. v. Community Bank, 162 F.3d 1101 (11th Cir. 1998) (corporation incorporated in Panama had its only investment in Florida where it also had a bank account and attorneys and was designed as an investment vehicle whereby Venezuelan citizens could make loans to a Florida tomato farm; all shareholders of corporation were Venezuelan citizens; the corporation's principal place of business was in Venezuela); *see also* Universal Licensing Corp. v. Paola del Lungo S.P.A., 293 F.3d 579 (2d Cir. 2002) (§ 1332 does not distinguish between corporations incorporated in the United States and those incorporated outside the United States; even if a corporation incorporated in a foreign country has its principal place of business in the United States and is considered a citizen of the state where the principal place of business is located, diversity is defeated if another alien party is present on the other side of the litigation); Rosenblatt v. Ernst & Young Int'l, Ltd., No. 00-56099, 2002 WL 115577, 2002 U.S. App. LEXIS 1575 (9th Cir. Jan. 29, 2002) (§ 1332 does not distinguish between corporations incorporated within the United States and those incorporated outside the United States; Cayman Islands corporation could also be citizen of California if its principal place of business is there).

236. *See, e.g.*, Danjaq, S.A. v. Pathe Communications Corp., 979 F.2d 772 (9th Cir. 1992); Cabalceta v. Standard Fruit Co., 883 F.2d 1553 (11th Cir. 1989); Jerguson v. Blue Dot Inv., Inc., 659 F.2d 31 (5th Cir. Unit B Oct. 1981). This interpretation accords with the American Law Institute's recommendations for revision of the diversity jurisdiction statute. *See* ALI STUDY OF THE DIVISION OF JURISDICTION BETWEEN STATE AND FEDERAL COURTS § 1301(b)(1) (1969).

237. *See* Pub. L. No. 112-63, § 102, 125 Stat. 758, 758 (codified as 28 U.S.C. § 1332(c)(1)).

238. 536 U.S. 88, 122 S. Ct. 2054, 153 L. Ed. 2d 95 (2002).

corporation incorporated under the laws of the British Virgin Islands was a "citizen or subject" of the United Kingdom for purposes of 28 U.S.C. § 1332(a).[239]

5. Multiparty, Multiforum Trial Jurisdiction Act of 2002

In 2002, Congress enacted 28 U.S.C. § 1369, the Multiparty, Multiforum Trial Jurisdiction Act. The Act confers jurisdiction on the district courts of civil actions involving minimal diversity between adverse parties in cases arising from a single accident, as long as at least 75 "natural persons" have died in the accident "at a discrete location" and either (1) a defendant resides in a state and a substantial part of the accident occurred in another state or location, regardless of whether that defendant is also a resident of the state where a substantial part of the accident took place; (2) any two defendants reside in different states, regardless of whether such defendants are also residents of the same state or states; or (3) substantial parts of the accident took place in different states.[240] "Minimal diversity" exists under the Act if "any party is a citizen of a State and any adverse party is a citizen of another State, a citizen or subject of a foreign state, or a foreign state as defined in [§] 1603(a) of [Title 28]."[241] Even if minimal diversity exists and the other threshold requirements of the Act are satisfied, the district court in which the action is commenced is directed to abstain from hearing the action if (1) the substantial majority of all plaintiffs are citizens of a single state of which the primary defendants are also citizens and (2) the claims asserted will be governed primarily by the laws of that state.[242]

Other provisions of the Act define corporate citizenship and residence,[243] prescribe rights of intervention for plaintiffs in cases arising out of the same accident as a case filed in district court within the jurisdiction conferred by the Act,[244] prescribe rights of removal for defendants sued in state court on claims that could have been brought originally in federal court under the Act or that arise from the same accident as a case pending against the defendant in federal court under the Act,[245] prescribe venue for actions brought under the Act,[246] and create nationwide

---

239. *See also* Stiftung v. Plains Mktg., L.P., 603 F.3d 295 (5th Cir. 2010) (foreign entity, a "stifung," created under Liechtenstein law, was a juridical person and thus a foreign citizen for purposes of diversity); Slavchev v. Royal Caribbean Cruises, Ltd., 559 F.3d 251 4th Cir. (2009) (Liberian corporation had dual citizenship for purposes of diversity jurisdiction). Note that in 28 U.S.C. § 1369(c)(2), the Multiparty, Multiforum Trial Jurisdiction Act of 2002, discussed in the next subsection, Congress specifically dealt with the dual citizenship problem in cases within the purview of the Act, by making a corporation "a citizen of any State, and a citizen of subject of any foreign state, in which it is incorporated or has its principal place of business."

240. *See* 28 U.S.C. § 1369(a); *see generally* Peter Adomeit, *The Station Nightclub Fire and Federal Jurisdictional Reach: The Multidistrict, Multiparty, Multiforum Jurisdiction Act of 2002,* 25 W. N. ENG. L. REV. 243 (2003) (discussing the Act in the context of a particular case); Joseph M. Creed, Note, *Choice of Law Under the Multiparty, Multiforum Trial Jurisdiction Act of 2002,* 17 REGENT U. L. REV. 157 (2004); Angela J. Rafoth, Note, *Congress and the Multiparty, Multiforum Trial Jurisdiction Act of 2002: Meaningful Reform or a Comedy of Errors?,* 54 DUKE L.J. 255 (2004).

241. 28 U.S.C. § 1369(c)(1).

242. *Id.* § 1369(b)(1) & (2).

243. *Id.* § 1369(c)(2).

244. *Id.* § 1369(d).

245. *Id.* § 1441(e)(1)(A) & (B).

246. *Id.* § 1391(g).

long-arm jurisdiction for cases brought under the Act.[247] These provisions are discussed in later parts of this book.

The objective of the Act is to "streamline the process by which multidistrict litigation governing disasters are adjudicated."[248] However, the Act is complex, and some of its terms are not defined, perhaps inviting excessive threshold litigation over unimportant procedural matters. For example, as noted above, the Act directs district courts to abstain from hearing any civil action within the jurisdictional provisions of the Act if "the substantial majority of all plaintiffs are citizens of a single state of which the primary defendants are also citizens" and the claims asserted will be governed "primarily" by the laws of that state.[249] However, the Act does not define what it takes to make a "substantial majority," how the court is to determine who the "primary defendants" are, or when the claims asserted are governed "primarily" by the laws of a state.

In *Passa v. Derderian*,[250] five civil actions arising out of a nightclub fire were commenced in Rhode Island. Two of the actions were commenced originally in the U.S. District Court for the District of Rhode Island, and three of the actions were removed to that court from a Rhode Island state court. In all of the cases, jurisdiction was predicated on 28 U.S.C. § 1369. Jurisdictional objections were raised in both the original and removed actions. The parties and the court agreed that the minimal diversity required by § 1369(a) was present. The court also held that the provision of § 1369(b) providing for abstention did not constitute a limitation on subject-matter jurisdiction, but rather was a mandatory abstention provision.[251] So viewed, the court held that § 1369(b) requires a court to abstain from hearing any case in which the conditions of the statute are satisfied. As applied to the case before it, the court held that the requirement in § 1369(b) that a substantial majority of "all plaintiffs" were citizens of the same state as the state in which the primary defendants are citizens had to be interpreted to mean "all potential plaintiffs," as opposed to only those plaintiffs who had commenced actions. Although Rhode Islanders made up the largest group of potential plaintiffs, it could not be said that they were a majority of all plaintiffs under the court's reading of the statute. Then, in an extended dictum, the court indicated that the phrase "primary defendants" meant parties facing direct liability in the litigation as opposed to defendants who were sued under theories of vicarious liability or joined for purposes of indemnification or contribution. Under this definition, the primary defendants were not all from a single state, and, therefore, abstention would also not be proper for this reason.[252]

---

247. *Id.* § 1697.

248. *See* H.R. CONF. REP. NO. 107-685, at 199 (2002).

249. 28 U.S.C. § 1369(b)(1) & (2); *see* Wallace v. Louisiana Citizens Prop. Ins. Corp., 444 F.3d 697 (5th Cir. 2006) (Multiparty, Multiforum Trial Jurisdiction Act's abstention provisions do not apply to actions removed under Act's removal provision).

250. 308 F. Supp. 2d 43 (D.R.I. 2004).

251. *Id.* at 56-57. The court considered this distinction important because a decision as to the propriety of subject-matter jurisdiction remains open throughout a proceeding, whereas the decision whether to abstain is not normally revisited after it is made.

252. *Id.* at 59-63; *see also* Joshua A. DeCuir, Comment, *A Federal Tête-à-Tête? The Multiparty, Multiforum Trial Jurisdiction Act and Hurricane Katrina: Past, Present, and Future Considerations*, 68 LA. L. REV. 681 (2008).

6. The Class Action Fairness Act

In the Class Action Fairness Act of 2005 ("CAFA"), Congress created new provisions governing original and removal jurisdiction of certain class actions.[253] Among other things, the Act authorizes minimal diversity jurisdiction when "any member of a class of plaintiffs is a citizen of a State different from any defendant,"[254] when "any member of a class of plaintiffs is a foreign state or a citizen or subject of a foreign state and any defendant is a citizen of a State,"[255] or when any member of a class of plaintiffs is a citizen of a State and any defendant is a foreign state or a citizen or subject of a foreign state."[256] Minimal diversity is also created for so-called "mass actions," which are defined as civil actions in "which monetary relief claims of more than 100 or more persons are proposed to be tried jointly on the grounds that the plaintiffs' claims involve common questions of law or fact."[257] The Act also possesses special removal provisions, special jurisdictional amount provisions, "abstention" provisions, and other complicated provisions.[258] The Act is discussed in appropriate parts of this chapter above and below and in Chapter 8 as it is relevant to particular topics.

7. The Amount-in-Controversy Requirement

The diversity jurisdiction has always been subject to an amount-in-controversy requirement.[259] Congress has raised the amount in controversy from time to time in an attempt to reduce the volume of diversity actions in federal court. In 1996, Congress raised the amount from more than $50,000 to its current level of more than $75,000.[260] Even though the dollar amount has changed, however, the rules for determining the amount in controversy remain unchanged.

---

253. *See* Pub. L. No. 109-2, 119 Stat. 4 (codified as 28 U.S.C. §§ 1332(d) & 1453).

254. 28 U.S.C. § 1332(d)(2)(A); *see also* Mark Moller, *A New Look at the Original Meaning of the Diversity Clause*, 51 WM. & MARY L. REV. 1113 (2009); Denise Mazzeo, *Securities Class Actions, CAFA, and a Countrywide Crisis: A Call for Clarity and Consistency*, 78 FORDHAM L. REV. 1433 (2009); Diane P. Wood, *The Changing Face of Diversity Jurisdiction*, 82 TEMP. L. REV. 593 (2009).

255. 28 U.S.C. § 1332(d)(2)(B).

256. *Id.* § 1332(d)(2)(C).

257. *Id.* § 1332(d)(11)(B)(i); *see also* Tanoh v. Dow Chem. Co., 561 F.3d 945 (9th Cir. 2009) (separate state toxic tort actions each with less than 100 plaintiffs could not be treated as a single "mass action" eligible for removal under CAFA); Guyon Knight, *The CAFA Mass Action Numerosity Requirement: Three Problems with Counting to 100*, 78 FORDHAM L. REV. 1875 (2010).

258. LG Display Co. v. Madigan, 665 F.3d 768 (7th Cir. 2011) (a "parens patriae" action brought by the attorney general of a state is not removable as a class action or a mass action under CAFA).

259. 14AA CHARLES A. WRIGHT ET AL., FEDERAL PRACTICE AND PROCEDURE: JURISDICTION AND RELATED MATTERS § 3701 (4th ed. 2011). Other provisions of the Judicial Code have also been subject to an amount-in-controversy requirement. The general federal question jurisdiction was subject to a jurisdictional amount until 1980, when Congress eliminated the requirement. *See* Federal Question Jurisdictional Amendments Act of 1980, Pub. L. No. 96-486, 94 Stat. 2369. For a nondiversity statute containing an amount-in-controversy limit in the current Judicial Code, see 28 U.S.C. § 1346(a)(2) ("Tucker Act" claims).

260. *See* Federal Courts Improvement Act of 1996, Pub. L. No. 104-317, § 205, 110 Stat. 3847, 3850 (codified at 28 U.S.C. § 1332(a)). The Judiciary Act of 1789 set the amount at $500. Congress raised it to $2,000 in 1887, to $3,000 in 1911, to $10,000 in 1958, and to $50,000 in 1988. *See* RICHARD H. FALLON ET AL., HART & WECHSLER'S THE FEDERAL COURTS AND THE FEDERAL SYSTEM 1376 (6th ed. 2009). The amount must be *more than* $75,000. *See, e.g.,* Freeland v. Liberty Mut. Fire Ins. Co., 632 F.3d 250 (6th Cir. 2011) (action seeking declaratory judgment that policy provided coverage of up to $100,000 per accident rather than only $25,000 involved exactly $75,000 in controversy and jurisdiction was lacking).

(a) Single Plaintiff with a Single Claim or Multiple Claims Against a Single Defendant

In actions for damages, when a single plaintiff asserts a single claim against a single defendant, the amount claimed by the plaintiff controls—if it is apparently made in good faith. It must appear to a legal certainty that the plaintiff cannot recover more than $75,000 before a court can dismiss the case.[261] However, only the "direct effect" of the judgment will be considered, not collateral effects that the judgment may have by way of res judicata or stare decisis.[262] Interests and costs are excluded in calculating the amount in controversy.

Illustration 2-52. *P*, a citizen of State *X*, sues *D Bank*, a corporation incorporated and with its principal place of business in State *Y*, in a U.S. District Court. *P* seeks damages of $137,000 from *D* for negligent failure to pay a check. *P* alleges that *D* negligently failed to credit *P's* account for $37,000, the amount of a check that *P* had deposited with *D*. *P* also seeks $100,000 in punitive damages. Assume that the substantive law applicable to the case prohibits the recovery of punitive damages under the allegations in *P's* complaint. Thus, it appears to a legal certainty that *P* cannot recover more than $37,000. As a result, the court should dismiss *P's* complaint.[263]

Illustration 2-53. *P*, a citizen of State *X*, sues *D*, a citizen of State *Y*, in a U.S. District Court. *P* seeks damages for the conversion of a negotiable instrument with a face value of $75,000, interest at the legal rate, attorney's fees, and costs. Assume that the substantive law applicable to the action does not allow the recovery of attorney's fees. Under the express prohibition in 28 U.S.C. § 1332, costs are not a permissible element in calculating the jurisdictional amount. In addition, interest may not be included in calculating the jurisdictional amount when interest is simply the result of delay in payment, as it appears to be from *P's* claim for relief.[264] The face amount of the negotiable instrument ($75,000) is the only permissible element of damages. This amount fails to meet the amount-in-controversy requirement.

---

261. *See* St. Paul Mercury Indem. Co. v. Red Cab Co., 303 U.S. 283, 58 S. Ct. 586, 82 L. Ed. 845 (1938); Clark v. Matthews Int'l Corp., 639 F.3d 391 (8th Cir. 2011) (amount-in-controversy requirement satisfied by claim by employee for back pay when he would have earned at least $168,000 from time of his termination to present); *see generally* Robert A. Hurstak, *The Uncertain Status of the Legal Certainty Test: The Need for Consistency Among Federal Courts When Determining the Amount-in-Controversy*, 14 SUFFOLK J. TRIAL & APP. ADVOC. 78 (2009).

262. *See* Healy v. Ratta, 292 U.S. 263, 54 S. Ct. 700, 78 L. Ed. 1248 (1934); Esquilin-Mendoza v. Don King Productions, 638 F.3d 1 (1st Cir. 2011) (amount in controversy not satisfied when plaintiff's claim for emotional distress not recoverable under the applicable substantive law and damages that were recoverable did not exceed $22,5000).

263. *See* D'Amato v. Rhode Island Hosp. Trust Nat'l Bank, 772 F. Supp. 1322 (D.R.I. 1991), *aff'd*, 951 F.2d 361 (table), No. 91-2041, 1992 WL 55890, 1992 U.S. App. LEXIS 15186 (1st Cir. Mar. 25, 1992).

264. When interest is simply the result of delay in payment, such as when a statute provides for the recovery of interest at a certain rate from the date a claim matures, it is not permissible to take it into account in calculating the jurisdictional amount. However, when interest is an essential element of the claim for relief, it may be taken into account. Thus, in the illustration, if *P* had claimed $80,000, which included $75,000 in principal and $5,000 in interest that were both part of the face amount of the note due at maturity, the amount-in-controversy requirement would have been met. The purpose of this distinction is to prevent plaintiffs from delaying suit in order to inflate the claim above the amount in controversy by interest that accrues after the claim matures. *See* 14AA CHARLES A. WRIGHT ET AL., FEDERAL PRACTICE AND PROCEDURE: JURISDICTION AND RELATED MATTERS 3712, at 817-18 (4th ed. 2011).

Section 1332 requires that *more than* $75,000 be in controversy. Thus, the court should dismiss *P's* action for failure to meet the jurisdictional amount.[265]

Illustration 2-54. *P*, a citizen of State *X*, sues *D*, a citizen of State *Y*, in a U.S. District Court. *P* seeks damages for personal injuries received in an automobile accident. *P's* only injury in the accident was a broken thumb. *P* claimed $1,026 in lost wages and medical expenses. *P* also claimed $80,000 for pain and suffering. On similar facts, a federal district court dismissed *P's* action. The court held that it appeared to a legal certainty that *P's* claim did not meet the amount-in-controversy requirement because if a jury had awarded damages that met the amount requirement, the trial judge would have been bound to set the award aside as excessive.[266]

* * * * *

The rules governing the determination of the amount in controversy in single-plaintiff, single-defendant damage actions may seem straightforward enough, but there is still uncertainty in the area. The uncertainty is produced by the interaction of a number of subsidiary rules governing amount-in-controversy disputes and the failure of the courts to recognize that they are violating these rules, or some of them, in the very cases in which they purport to be applying them.

First, it is settled that the amount in controversy is determined as of the commencement of the action.[267] A second rule follows from the first: if the proper amount in controversy exists at the commencement of the action, subsequent events may not oust the jurisdiction by reducing the amount below its level at commencement.[268] For example, the plaintiff may not reduce the amount in controversy after commencement to defeat federal jurisdiction (as, for example, in a case removed by the defendant from state to federal court).[269] Nor may a valid defense to part or all

---

265. *See* Bradford Nat'l Life Ins. Co. v. Union State Bank, 794 F. Supp. 296 (E.D. Wis. 1992); *see also* Gardynski-Leschuck v. Ford Motor Co., 142 F.3d 955 (7th Cir. 1998), in which the plaintiff claimed $51,000 in damages plus $25,000 in attorney's fees, the fees representing the plaintiff's estimate of the amount the attorney would have to be paid after full litigation of the suit. The court of appeals held that the amount-in-controversy requirement had been violated. Even if attorney's fees were recoverable under the applicable substantive law, the amount in controversy had to be calculated as of the commencement of the action. At that time, the fees had not been incurred and might not be. For example, the fees might be avoided by the defendant's prompt payment or settlement of the plaintiff's claim. *Compare* Manguno v. Prudential Prop. & Cas. Ins. Co., 276 F.3d 720 (5th Cir. 2002) (in class action removed from state court, amount-in-controversy requirement was satisfied by defendant's undisputed affidavit that the aggregate attorney fees for the putative class would likely exceed $75,000 and applicable state law allowed recovery of such fees) *with* Kanter v. Warner-Lambert Co., 265 F.3d 853 (9th Cir. 2001) (potential attorney fee awards under applicable state law could not be attributed solely to representative of class, but had to be divided among class members in determining amount-in-controversy requirement).

266. *See* Burns v. Anderson, 502 F.2d 970 (5th Cir. 1974). The *Burns* approach represents a trend in which the lower federal courts have been willing to scrutinize cases involving unliquidated damages more carefully than in earlier cases in which the plaintiff's claim was virtually conclusive on the question.

267. *See* 14AA CHARLES A. WRIGHT ET AL., FEDERAL PRACTICE AND PROCEDURE: JURISDICTION AND RELATED MATTERS § 3702.4, at 457 (4th ed. 2011).

268. *See id.* at 461-75; *cf.* Choice Hotels Int'l, Inc. v. Shiv Hospitality, L.L.C., 491 F.3d 171 (4th Cir. 2007) (action commenced in federal court and stayed pending arbitration; after arbitration, application was made to district court to confirm arbitration award, which was less than amount-in-controversy requirement; holding amount in controversy is to be determined by amount requested in original complaint, not amount of award; events subsequent to commencement that reduce amount below jurisdictional minimum do not result in loss of jurisdiction).

269. *See* St. Paul Mercury Indem. Co. v. Red Cab Co., 303 U.S. 283, 58 S. Ct. 586, 82 L. Ed. 845 (1938). *But cf.* Zurich Am. Ins. Co. v. Integrand Assurance Co., 178 F. Supp. 2d 47 (D.P.R. 2001) (after settling with all defendants except one, plaintiff amended complaint to assert claim against remaining defendant for $48,839.00 and defendant moved to dismiss for lack of subject-matter jurisdiction; an amended pleading supersedes the original pleading, which is treated thereafter as nonexistent; therefore, the amendment had the effect of creating an action claiming an amount less than $75,000 and depriving court of jurisdiction).

of the claim defeat jurisdiction.[270] The difficulty in administering these rules consistently with each other can be illustrated by various decisions in the U.S. Courts of Appeals.

In *Tongkook America, Inc. v. Shipton Sportswear Co.*,[271] the plaintiff sued the defendant for $117,621.05, plus interest, for breach of contract. The amount represented a balance that both parties believed was due on a sale of goods by the plaintiff to the defendant. During discovery, the parties learned that the plaintiff had, prior to commencement of the action, drawn $80,760.00 on a letter of credit that had been provided by the defendant to the plaintiff. As a result, the actual amount of the plaintiff's claim at commencement was $36,861.05, which was below the amount-in-controversy requirement of $50,000 existing at the time of the action. The defendant amended its answer to raise the defense of partial payment. After the district court raised the issue of jurisdictional amount, the defendant sought dismissal for lack of subject-matter jurisdiction. However, the district court retained jurisdiction and ultimately entered judgment for the plaintiff in the amount of $38,861.05.

The Second Circuit Court of Appeals reversed. The court held that the "good-faith, legal-certainty" rule, discussed above, had been violated. The court's opinion acknowledged (1) the rule that the amount in controversy is determined as of commencement; (2) the rule that events subsequent to commencement cannot defeat jurisdiction; and (3) the rule that valid defenses cannot defeat jurisdiction. Nevertheless, the court held that the record demonstrated to a legal certainty that the requisite amount in controversy *never* existed.

The problem with the court's conclusion is that payment is a defense.[272] It is clear, therefore, that the court allowed the assertion of a valid defense to defeat jurisdiction. It has been observed that "[c]ourts have distinguished between subsequent events that cannot destroy subject-matter jurisdiction, and subsequent events that require the dismissal or remand of the case because they reveal that the necessary dollar amount was not actually in controversy at the commencement of the action in federal court or when it was removed from state court."[273] However, this distinction cannot realistically be viewed as consistent with the subsidiary rules governing jurisdictional amount when the subsequent event in question is the revelation of a valid defense during the discovery stage of litigation.

Furthermore, there are cases that do not follow the "never-in-controversy" rule. For example, in *Coventry Sewage Associates v. Dworkin Realty Co.*,[274] a mistaken calculation by a third party upon whom the parties had no choice but to rely resulted in the inflation of the amount in controversy above the required minimum. In effect, as in *Tongkook*, the objective facts existing at commencement demonstrated that the required amount in controversy *never* existed. Nevertheless,

---

270. *See* 303 U.S. at 289, 58 S. Ct. at 590, 82 L. Ed. at 848; 14AA CHARLES A. WRIGHT ET AL., FEDERAL PRACTICE AND PROCEDURE: JURISDICTION AND RELATED MATTERS § 3702.4, at 492 (4th ed. 2011).

271. 14 F.3d 781 (2d Cir. 1994).

272. *See* FED. R. CIV. P. 8(c)(1) (listing payment as one of a number of affirmative defenses).

273. 14AA CHARLES A. WRIGHT ET AL., FEDERAL PRACTICE AND PROCEDURE: JURISDICTION AND RELATED MATTERS § 3702.4, at 483-87 (4th ed. 2011) (citing authorities).

274. 71 F.3d 1 (1st Cir. 1995).

the First Circuit Court of Appeals upheld jurisdiction. The court distinguished *Tongkook* on the ground that the plaintiff in *Tongkook* should have discovered that its claim did not meet the amount-in-controversy requirement. On the other hand, the third-party's error in *Coventry Sewage* was not obvious, and the parties could not have discovered it prior to commencement. Nevertheless, if the governing rule is that discovery of objective facts after commencement can reveal that the required amount at commencement *never* existed, *Coventry Sewage* is both wrong *and* inconsistent with *Tongkook*.

Tongkook, *Coventry Sewage*, and other cases administering the amount-in-controversy requirement[275] cannot be reconciled with each other under the rules they purport to apply. Nevertheless, the results of the cases may be justifiable according to a rule not yet fully articulated by the courts. The cases discussed above, as well as others,[276] seem to be aimed at preventing the negligent or manipulative creation of federal jurisdiction through inflation of the amount in controversy. If the plaintiff has not conducted a reasonable investigation that would have uncovered facts prior to commencement showing that the amount-in-controversy requirement was not met, jurisdiction should be declined. Conversely, if a reasonable pre-commencement investigation could not have uncovered the relevant facts bearing on jurisdictional amount, discovery of those facts after commencement should not defeat jurisdiction. This approach reconciles *Tongkook* and *Coventry Sewage*.[277]

The same approach should be taken when there is a danger that the amount in controversy has been intentionally inflated or otherwise illegitimately manipulated to meet the amount-in-controversy requirement.

---

275. *See, e.g.*, Wolde-Meskel v. Vocational Instruction Project Cmty. Servs., Inc., 166 F.3d 59 (2d Cir. 1999), in which Second Circuit upheld jurisdiction after the amount in controversy was reduced below the required level by a grant of summary judgment produced by the addition to the case of certain legal defenses by the defendant and the inability of the plaintiff to adduce evidence to establish the claim. The court distinguished *Tongkook* on the ground that the partial payment in that case meant the requisite amount in controversy never existed. The problem is that a grant of summary judgment can only occur when there is no genuine issue of material fact and the moving party is entitled to judgment as a matter of law. The inability of the plaintiff to produce evidence in support of his claim would seem to mean that it was invalid on the objective facts as of commencement. *Accord* Herremans v. Carrera Designs, Inc., 157 F.3d 1118 (7th Cir. 1998) (claims eliminated by summary judgment did not defeat jurisdiction); *see also* McNulty v. Travel Park, 853 F. Supp. 144 (E.D. Pa. 1994) (during discovery, plaintiff's attorney concluded on the basis of certain medical information that the plaintiffs could not recover an amount sufficient to meet the amount in controversy and moved to dismiss; the court refused, holding that jurisdiction had to be determined without regard to success on the merits).

276. Of course, not *all* cases in this area can be reconciled on the basis of the policies discussed in the text. However, a large number of cases can be understood if the rules the courts purport to be enforcing are ignored and one focuses instead on whether there is a danger of negligent or manipulative creation of jurisdiction.

277. In *Tongkook*, there was no excuse for the plaintiff's failure to learn about the partial payment before commencement, and jurisdiction was properly declined. However, in *Coventry Sewage* there was no realistic way that either party could have learned of the miscomputation by the third party prior to commencement, and jurisdiction was properly upheld. *See also* McNulty v. Travel Park, 853 F. Supp. 144 (E.D. Pa. 1994), in which plaintiff discovered medical information that appeared to be inaccessible prior to commencement and that demonstrated the plaintiff could not recover the required amount. Jurisdiction was upheld. Cases that superficially appear inconsistent with the approach suggested in the text can often be reconciled with it. For example, in Zacharia v. Harbor Island Spa, Inc., 684 F.2d 199 (2d Cir. 1982), the court held it was error for the district court to dismiss the plaintiff's action against a hotel for lack of proper jurisdictional amount based on the hotel's defense under an applicable statute limiting its liability to $1,000 for loss of a guest's valuables. Parts of the court's opinion spoke in absolute terms about the impermissibility of taking defenses into account. However, throughout the opinion, the court discussed facts indicating that there was real doubt about whether the defense was valid on the facts. Therefore, there was no certainty at the time of commencement that the plaintiff was not entitled to recover the amount requested and no danger of negligent or manipulative creation of jurisdiction as a result.

Illustration 2-55. In *Indiana Hi-Rail Corp. v. Decatur Junction Railway Co.*,[278] the plaintiff sued the defendant in U.S. District Court for the conversion of a locomotive. Under the applicable substantive law of conversion, the plaintiff was entitled to recover damages measured by the value of the locomotive at the time of the conversion, which exceeded the amount-in-controversy requirement. However, if the property converted had been returned, the plaintiff's damages were limited to any amount the plaintiff had lost by reason of the detention of the property. Despite the fact that the locomotive had been returned before commencement of the federal action, the plaintiff sought damages measured by the value of the locomotive at the time of conversion. The Seventh Circuit Court of Appeals held that the amount-in-controversy requirement was not met, even though the plaintiff did not have to say anything in the complaint about failure to return the locomotive to state a claim for relief and the issue of return was thus clearly a defense to be pleaded by the defendant. To allow the plaintiff to claim an amount to which it clearly was not entitled under clear and knowable substantive rules would be to allow the manipulative creation of federal jurisdiction because of the fortuitous allocation of the burden of pleading under state law. Note that if the locomotive had been returned *after* the commencement of the federal action, the result should be different. The plaintiff would then have been suing for an amount to which it was entitled under the applicable substantive law, and return of the locomotive by the defendant after commencement should not be allowed to defeat federal jurisdiction.

* * * * *

It should be understood that the guidelines discussed above concerning negligent and manipulative creation of jurisdiction are designed only for cases in which matters come to light after commencement that bear directly upon the amount in controversy, as opposed to the underlying substantive validity of the plaintiff's claim. Jurisdiction should never be defeated by elimination of an entire claim due to the inability of the plaintiff to establish an essential element of the claim or because of a valid substantive defense asserted by the defendant not bearing specifically on the amount of the claim.[279] It would be administratively complex and wasteful to extend the negligent and manipulative creation of jurisdiction policies to all substantive disposition of claims. There are other effective tools available to the federal courts with which to discourage frivolous factual and legal presentations on the merits of claims.[280] The case law generally, though not explicitly, embraces this distinction.

Illustration 2-56. *P*, a citizen of State *X*, sues *D*, a citizen of State *Y*, in a U.S. District Court in State *Y*. *P* seeks $100,000 in damages for breach of an oral contract. *D's* answer contains a defense that *P's* claim for relief is barred under the applicable statute of frauds. If this defense is valid, *P's* action should be dismissed on the merits. It should not be dismissed for lack of jurisdiction, even though the validity of the statute of frauds defense means that, on the objective facts existing

---

278. 37 F.3d 363 (7th Cir. 1994).

279. *See, e.g.*, Johnson v. Wattenbarger, 361 F.3d 991 (7th Cir. 2004) (district court erred in dismissing action for lack of proper amount in controversy after first dismissing some claims on the merits).

280. *See* Chapter 6(F) *infra* (discussing Federal Rule 11).

at the time of commencement, the plaintiff was entitled to recover nothing. The statute-of-frauds defense addresses the substantive merits of the plaintiff's claim, not the ability of the plaintiff to recover the amount of damages requested, or any portion of it. To permit dismissal for lack of the proper jurisdictional amount whenever a defendant raises a valid affirmative defense directed to the merits of the plaintiff's claim rather than the amount requested would result in many jurisdictional dismissals at late stages of federal actions. Such a result would be wasteful and would not directly address the problem of illegitimate inflation of the amount in controversy to create federal jurisdiction. If *P* has frivolously resisted *D's* statute-of-frauds defense, the district court has power to impose appropriate sanctions on *P*.[281]

Illustration 2-57. *P*, a citizen of State *X*, sues *D*, a citizen of State *Y*, in a U.S. District Court in State *Y*. *P* seeks $1,000,000 in damages due to the exposure of *P* to an asbestos product manufactured by *D*. After a full opportunity for discovery, *P* is unable to develop any proof that the product to which *P* was exposed belonged to *D*, which is an essential element that *P* must prove to establish the claim. *D* moves for summary judgment. To defeat *D's* motion, *P* must come forward with some evidence to show that *D* manufactured the product to which *P* was exposed. If *P* cannot do so, the court should grant summary judgment.[282] However, *P's* action should not be dismissed for lack of jurisdiction, even though the objective facts available after full opportunity for discovery indicate that *P* is entitled to recover nothing. For the same reasons given in *Illustration 2-56*, it would be wasteful to dismiss actions like *P's* for lack of jurisdiction. Furthermore, it would not directly address the problem of illegitimate inflation of the amount-in-controversy requirement. If *P* has asserted a claim for relief against *D* without proper pre-commencement investigation of the facts, the district court has the power to impose an appropriate sanction on *P* or *P's* attorney.[283]

* * * * *

When the benefit to the plaintiff of the relief requested has a different value than the cost that the relief will impose on the defendant—for example, as in some injunction suits—a split of authority exists about how to determine whether the amount in controversy has been satisfied. The cases variously hold that (1) the value to the plaintiff, (2) the value to the defendant, (3) the value to either plaintiff or defendant if one or the other, but not both, satisfies the amount-in-controversy requirement, or (4) the value to the person who invokes federal jurisdiction (the plaintiff in an original action or the defendant in an action removed from state court) controls.[284]

---

281. *See id.*

282. See the discussion of *Celotex v. Catrett* in *Illustration 10-12* in Chapter 10(C)(2) *infra* ("Applying the Summary Judgment Standard").

283. *See* FED. R. CIV. P. 11(b)(2), (3); Chapter 6(F) *infra* ("Good Faith Pleading").

284. Ericsson GE Mobile Commc'ns v. Motorola Commc'ns, Inc., 120 F.3d 216 (11th Cir. 1997) (plaintiff's viewpoint controls; no jurisdiction); Grinnell Mut. Reins. Co. v. Shierk, 121 F.3d 1114 (7th Cir. 1997) (insured was sued in state court for damages "in excess of $15,000"; insurance company brought declaratory judgment action that it was not obligated to defend or indemnify the insured in the state action under a policy with a limit of $100,000; later judgment was rendered in the state action against the insured for $14,045; court of appeals reverses district court's dismissal for lack of jurisdiction, holding that the commencement of the federal action, the insurance company could have incurred liability of up to $100,000 and later event of state judgment

Illustration 2-58. *P*, a citizen of State *X*, seeks an injunction in federal court requiring *D*, a citizen of State *Y*, to remove a building partially constructed on *P's* land. Assume that the encroachment decreases the value of *P's* land by $5,000. Removing the encroaching part of the building would cost *D* over $100,000. Courts following the "value to the plaintiff" rule or the "person who invokes jurisdiction" rule would hold that the amount-in-controversy requirement is not satisfied. On the other hand, courts following the "value to the defendant" rule or the "value to either" rule would allow the action to proceed.[285]

* * * * *

When a single plaintiff sues a single defendant on two or more claims, the plaintiff may aggregate the plaintiff's claims to meet the requirement, no matter how unrelated the claims are.[286] This right of aggregation exists even when one or more of the plaintiff's claims is based on diversity jurisdiction and others are based on federal question jurisdiction.[287]

Illustration 2-59. Assume that *P* has three unrelated claims against *D*. The first is for negligence for $30,000. The second is for breach of contract for $35,000. The third is for slander for $25,000. *P* may join all three claims in a single action against *D*. Because a total of $90,000 is sought, the amount-in-controversy requirement is satisfied.

* * * * *

---

did not oust jurisdiction); Guardian Life Ins. Co. of Am. v. Muniz, 101 F.3d 93 (11th Cir. 1996) (amount in controversy met in action by an insurance company to cancel a life insurance policy of $100,000, even though the insured party was still alive); *see also* Macken *ex rel.* Macken v. Jensen, 333 F.3d 797 (7th Cir. 2003) (in action against trustee for accounting and unredacted copies of trust documents, plaintiff failed to establish that the value of the relief met the amount-in-controversy requirement; impermissible to use the value of the assets of the trust, since the value of those assets was not in controversy); *In re* Ford Motor Co./Citibank (S.D.), N.A., 264 F.3d 952 (9th Cir. 2001) (refusing to extend "either viewpoint" rule to multiple plaintiff case (class action); cost to defendant of complying with injunction cannot be used to satisfy the amount in controversy in such a case when the plaintiff class members are not uniting to enforce a single title or right in which they have a common and undivided interest); Morrison v. Allstate Indem. Co., 228 F.3d 1255 (11th Cir. 2000) (effectively refusing to take into account the cost to the defendant of complying with an injunction in a class action case); Hoffman v. Vulcan Materials Co., 19 F. Supp. 2d 475, 481-82 (M.D.N.C. 1998) ("flexible approach" that takes into account defendant's viewpoint applied; jurisdiction upheld); Crawford v. American Bankers Ins. Co., 987 F. Supp. 1408 (M.D. Ala. 1997) (plaintiff's viewpoint must be used in injunction case); *see generally* 14AA CHARLES A. WRIGHT ET AL., FEDERAL PRACTICE AND PROCEDURE: JURISDICTION AND RELATED MATTERS § 3703 (4th ed. 2011). Cases involving arbitration orders or awards also present some special difficulties. *See, e.g.*, Karsner v. Lothian, 532 F.3d 876 (D.C. Cir. 2008) (in proceeding to confirm arbitration award, "award approach" would determine whether amount in controversy is met by amount of award in arbitration proceeding; "demand approach" determines issue by reference to amount sought in underlying arbitration, regardless of amount awarded; "remand approach," which applies if petition includes a request to remand and reopen arbitration, determines issue by reference to amount sought in underlying proceeding; here district court correctly determined issue by reference to amount sought in underlying arbitration); Advance Am. Servicing v. McGinnis, 526 F.3d 1170 (8th Cir. 2008) (when a defendant in a state-court law suit petitions a federal diversity court for arbitration, the value to defendant of avoiding state-court litigation may not be taken into account in meeting the amount in controversy; Caudle v. American Arbitration Ass'n, 230 F.3d 920 (7th Cir. 2000) (in diversity action seeking an order to require arbitration association to provide arbitration services at a reasonable cost, plaintiff contended that amount in controversy was satisfied by the stakes of his dispute with the defendant; held that amount in controversy was determined by the cost of the arbitration fees ($5,800) that the plaintiff was being required to pay).

285. *See, e.g.*, Correspondent Servs. Corp. v. First Equities Corp., 442 F.3d 767 (2d Cir. 2006) (in declaratory judgment action to declare that plaintiff had no liability on certificate of deposit, amount in controversy, measured from plaintiff's viewpoint, was not satisfied; CD was object of suit, and all agreed that it was worthless).

286. *See, e.g.*, Bullard v. City of Cisco, 290 U.S. 179, 54 S. Ct. 177, 78 L. Ed. 254 (1933).

287. 14AA CHARLES A. WRIGHT ET AL., FEDERAL PRACTICE AND PROCEDURE: JURISDICTION AND RELATED MATTERS § 3704 (4th ed. 2011).

Removal jurisdiction is generally discussed in section F, below. That section discusses new provisions contained in the Federal Courts Jurisdiction and Venue Clarification Act of 2011[288] that clarify jurisdictional amount practice in removed cases.

As discussed in section F, below, removal can sometimes be based on facts revealed after a state court action has been pending for some time. This can give rise in the removal context to some unusual approaches to evaluating cases. For example, in *Rising-Moore v. Red Roof Inns, Inc.*,[289] the plaintiff brought an action in state court against the motel to recover for personal injuries sustained in a slip and fall accident. The plaintiff was not required to reveal the amount of damages claimed in state court, but when the plaintiff's attorney revealed in settlement negotiations that the claim was worth between $180,000 and $200,000, the defendant removed. The district court granted summary judgment for the defendant, and the plaintiff appealed, arguing that the amount in controversy was not satisfied because his damages were not more than about $35,000. The Seventh Circuit Court of Appeals rejected this argument, holding that the fact that the defendant ultimately offered to settle for $60,000 could be admitted to establish that the amount-in-controversy requirement was satisfied. This was because, in the court's words, an offer to settle for $60,000 is an offer to take $60,000 with certainty, whereas if the case had gone to trial, the amount claimed probably would have been twice this amount. Because plaintiffs win about half of all tort suits that go to trial, the amount sought in settlement was being discounted by 50%, and the higher amount represents the amount in controversy.[290]

Other problems in removed cases will be presented by the recent enactment of the Class Action Fairness Act, discussed in subsection 6, above. These problems are discussed at the end of subsection *(b)*, below.

(b) Aggregation of Claims with Multiple Parties: The "Common and Undivided Interest" Test

Multiple parties may aggregate claims to satisfy the amount-in-controversy requirement only "if the several parties have a common undivided interest and a single title or right is involved."[291] This test requires much more than simply a legal and factual relationship between the claims.

Illustration 2-60. Assume that two plaintiffs, *P-1* and *P-2*, each have a $56,000 claim for personal injuries arising out of the same automobile accident against *D*. Because the plaintiffs' claims involve injuries to rights possessed

---

288. Pub. L. No. 112-63, § 103(b)(3)(C), 125 Stat. 758, 760-61 (codified at 28 U.S.C. § 1446(c)(2) & (3)(A)).

289. 435 F.3d 813 (7th Cir. 2006) (Easterbrook, J.).

290. The Federal Courts Jurisdiction and Venue Clarification Act of 2011, Pub. L. No. 112-63, § 103, codified as 28 U.S.C. § 1446(c), now deals specifically with cases in which the amount in controversy is not revealed at the beginning of the action, but at a later time, and also codifies the preponderance of the evidence standard discussed in the text prior to the illustration. This provision will be examined in detail in section F(4), *infra*.

291. CHARLES A. WRIGHT & MARY KAY KANE, THE LAW OF FEDERAL COURTS § 36, at 211 (7th ed. 2011); *see also* Snyder v. Harris, 394 U.S. 332, 89 S. Ct. 1053, 22 L. Ed. 2d 319 (1969).

separately by each plaintiff, the plaintiffs may not aggregate their claims against a defendant to meet the amount-in-controversy requirement.[292]

* * * * *

When would the "common and undivided interest" test be satisfied? A comparison of two cases will illustrate how difficult this question is to answer. In *Manufacturers Casualty Insurance Co. v. Coker*,[293] the Fourth Circuit held that a common and undivided interest was present when an insurance company sued for a declaratory judgment asserting that it was not liable under an insurance policy to several persons who had obtained judgments against the insured party. The aggregate amount of the judgments was more than the required jurisdictional amount, but no single judgment exceeded that amount. The parties who had obtained the judgments were held to have a common and undivided interest against the insurance company arising out of the policy of insurance.

On the other hand, in *Aetna Insurance Co. v. Chicago, Rock Island & Pacific Railroad Co.*,[294] the Tenth Circuit held that no common and undivided interest was present when forty-seven insurance companies had joined in issuing a single policy of insurance to a railroad and sued for a declaration that a certain loss suffered by the railroad was not covered by the policy. The court stated that

> [h]ere the claims of the plaintiffs are common in the sense of a community of interest in the rights asserted, but they are not undivided in the sense that they "constitute in their totality an integrated right." Instead they are separate and distinct having only a common basis of fact and law arising from a single instrument.[295]

There has been vigorous criticism of applying the "common and undivided interest" test in a modern procedural context in which joinder of parties and claims is permitted much more liberally than when the test originated over one hundred fifty years ago. Nevertheless, recent U.S. Supreme Court decisions indicate that the test will continue to govern aggregation in the absence of congressional action to modify it.[296] As the discussion of the *Aetna* and *Coker* cases indicates, no single

---

292. *See, e.g.*, McMillian v. Sheraton Chi. Hotel & Towers, 567 F.3d 839 (7th Cir. 2009) (amount in controversy not satisfied where several hotel guests joined as plaintiffs in seeking damages from hotel for personal injuries received when escalator malfunctioned and none of guests' individual claims for damages met amount-in-controversy requirement).

293. 219 F.2d 631 (4th Cir. 1955).

294. 229 F.2d 584 (10th Cir. 1956).

295. *Id.* at 586; *see also* Lovell v. State Farm Mut. Auto. Ins. Co., 466 F.3d 893 (10th Cir. 2006) (in removed class action, defendant could not demonstrate that costs of complying with declaratory and injunctive relief satisfied the amount-in-controversy requirement on the theory that the relief benefitted the entire class because "common and undivided interest" test not met; however, defendant could meet the amount requirement by demonstrating that the costs of compliance would exceed $75,000 as to each named plaintiff and class member!). The *Aetna* and *Coker* cases are discussed in CHARLES A. WRIGHT & MARY KAY KANE, THE LAW OF FEDERAL COURTS § 36, at 214-15 (6th ed. 2002). For a discussion of additional cases applying the aggregation rule, see 14AA CHARLES A. WRIGHT ET AL., FEDERAL PRACTICE AND PROCEDURE: JURISDICTION AND RELATED MATTERS § 3704 (4th ed. 2011).

296. *See* Zahn v. International Paper Co., 414 U.S. 291, 94 S. Ct. 505, 38 L. Ed. 2d 511 (1973); Snyder v. Harris, 394 U.S. 332, 89 S. Ct. 1053, 22 L. Ed. 2d 319 (1969); *cf.* Crawford v. American Bankers Ins. Co., 987 F. Supp. 1408 (M.D. Ala. 1997) ("common and undivided interest" test satisfied in injunction action in which an injunction would prevent defendant from engaging in a certain form of business and the injunction had no separable value to each member of the class); 14AA CHARLES A. WRIGHT ET AL., FEDERAL PRACTICE AND PROCEDURE: JURISDICTION AND RELATED MATTERS § 3704, at 607-09 (4th ed. 2011). Recent decisions in the lower

approach to administering the test will reconcile all the decisions. For example, if the *Aetna* view had been applied to the *Coker* facts, the result in the latter case would have differed.

To simplify the test, the following question should be asked: Must the parties sue or be sued together to obtain the relief sought in the action? If they must, courts should permit aggregation. If separate actions might have been brought by or against the parties, courts should still permit aggregation if the amount in controversy would be the same in either a single or multiple party action. This situation will sometimes occur when the relief given to one plaintiff or against one defendant will, as a practical matter, result in relief to the other plaintiff(s) or against the other defendant(s). However, courts should not permit aggregation merely because the relief requested for or against one party will result in relief for or against another. Rather, an action by or against one of the multiple parties must involve the same amount in controversy as a multiple party action. Thus, courts should not permit aggregation when separate actions might have been brought by or against the multiple parties and the jurisdictional amount would not be the same in the (hypothetical) separate action(s) and the multiple party action.

Illustration 2-61. *A*, a citizen of State *X*, sold land to *D*, a citizen of State *Y*. *A* took two separate notes, each for $40,000, in return for the land. *A* also reserved a vendor's lien on the land. Subsequently, *A* validly assigned one of the notes to *P-1* and the other to *P-2*. *P-1* and *P-2* are also citizens of State *X*. When the notes matured, *D* failed to pay them. *P-1* and *P-2* sued *D* in a U.S. District Court to enforce the vendor's lien. *P-1* and *P-2* may aggregate the amount of the notes to meet the amount-in-controversy requirement. Although their claims on the notes are "separate and distinct," their claim under the vendor's lien is "common and undivided." The lien is common security for the payment of both notes, and neither *P-1* nor *P-2* could sue to enforce the lien without joining the other.[297]

Illustration 2-62. *A*, a citizen of State *Y*, died. *A's* will provided that a certain amount of *A's* personal estate should be held in trust by the *D Bank*, a

---

federal courts have divided on the issue of whether, in a class action in which none of the individual claimants have compensatory damages claims that meet the amount-in-controversy requirement, the class may use a punitive damages claim to meet the requirement on the theory that each class member has an undivided interest in the punitive damages. *Compare* Ard v. Transcontinental Gas Pipe Line Corp., 138 F.3d 596 (5th Cir. 1998) (claims cannot be aggregated), Gilman v. BHC Sec., Inc., 104 F.3d 1418 (2d Cir. 1997) (no aggregation unless underlying claim is common and undivided), *and* Johnson v. Gerber Prods. Co., 949 F. Supp. 327 (E.D. Pa. 1996) (no aggregation) *with* Tapscott v. MS Dealer Serv. Corp., 77 F.3d 1353 (11th Cir. 1996); Allen v. R & H Oil & Gas Co., 63 F.3d 1326 (5th Cir. 1995) *and* Sharrow v. General Motors Acceptance Corp., 938 F. Supp. 518 (C.D. Ill. 1996) (punitive damages may be taken into account, but punitive damages are not recoverable in the particular case); *see also* Crawford v. F. Hoffman-La Roche Ltd., 267 F.3d 760 (8th Cir. 2001) (class members may not aggregate punitive damages to meet amount-in-controversy requirement); *In re* Ford Motor Co./Citibank (S.D.), N.A., 264 F.3d 952 (9th Cir. 2001) (punitive damages may not be aggregated to meet the amount-in-controversy requirement when the class members do not have a common and undivided interest); Kirkland v. Midland Mortg. Co., 243 F.3d 1277 (11th Cir. 2001) (multiple plaintiffs cannot aggregate punitive damages for purposes of establishing amount in controversy; purpose of punitive damages is deterrence and punishment of defendant, not compensation of plaintiff, and amount of award is not based on injury to particular plaintiff, but on behavior of defendant); Smith v. GTE Corp., 236 F.3d 1292 (11th Cir. 2001) (punitive damages may not be aggregated to establish jurisdictional amount-in-controversy requirement); *see generally* Christopher J. Willis, *Aggregation of Punitive Damages in Diversity Class Actions: Will the Real Amount in Controversy Please Stand Up?*, 30 LOY. L.A. L. REV. 775 (1997).

297. *See* Troy Bank v. G.A. Whitehead & Co., 222 U.S. 39, 41, 32 S. Ct. 9, 9-10, 56 L. Ed. 81, 82-83 (1911).

corporation incorporated and with its principal place of business in State *Y*. The beneficiaries of the trust were *A's* children, *P-1* and *P-2*, both citizens of State *X*. *P-1* and *P-2* sue *D* in a U.S. District Court. *P-1* and *P-2* claimed that the bank breached its fiduciary duty through improper investments. As a result, *D* lost $80,000 of the estate funds. *P-1* and *P-2* seek to have *D* restore the $80,000 to the trust. Assume that either *P-1* or *P-2* could have brought this action without joining the other. Under these circumstances, the amount-in-controversy requirement is satisfied. In this situation, relief granted to one beneficiary will result in relief to the other, but the amount-in-controversy requirement is not satisfied for this reason. The requirement is satisfied because, even if a single trust beneficiary had sued, the amount in controversy would have been the same as in a multiple plaintiff action. A single plaintiff action would seek to have the principal amount of $80,000 restored to the trust by *D*.[298]

Illustration 2-63. *D*, a citizen of State *Y*, operates a manufacturing plant in State *X*. The plant emits fumes that are damaging separate parcels of land owned by *P-1* and *P-2*, both citizens of State *X*. This "nuisance" is reducing the value of *P-1's* land by $40,000 and of *P-2's* land by the same amount. If *P-1* and *P-2* join in an action against *D* in a U.S. District Court to have the nuisance abated, the amount-in-controversy requirement will not be met. Either *P-1* or *P-2* could sue separately to abate the nuisance. If that suit were successful, the relief granted to one plaintiff would also result in relief to the other. However, the amount in controversy in a suit by only one of the plaintiffs would be $40,000, the amount by which that plaintiff's land is being reduced in value by the nuisance.[299]

Illustration 2-64. *D* is *A's* executor. Both *A* and *D* are citizens of State *Y*. *A's* will provided bequests for all of *A's* children except *P-1* and *P-2*. *P-1* and *P-2* are citizens of State *X*. *P-1* and *P-2* sue *D* in a U.S. District Court to set aside *A's* will. They claim that they were omitted from the will by mistake. If this claim is

---

298. *See* Hyde v. First & Merchants Nat'l Bank, 41 F.R.D. 527 (W.D. Va. 1967); *cf.* Packard v. Provident Nat'l Bank, 994 F.2d 1039 (3d Cir. 1993) (jurisdictional amount not satisfied in suit by beneficiaries of separate trusts managed by trustee).

299. This conclusion is based on the assumption that the amount in controversy is measured from the plaintiff's viewpoint. If the amount is measured from the defendant's viewpoint, and if the cost of abating the nuisance to the defendant exceeds $75,000, the amount-in-controversy requirement would be met in either a single or a multiple party action. In Friedman v. New York Life Ins. Co., 410 F.3d 1350 (11th Cir. 2005), an insured brought a class action against her insurer in state court. She alleged that the class members' premiums were raised in violation of applicable state law that was incorporated into the insurance contract. The action was removed by the defendant, and the district court denied the plaintiff's motion to remand. The court of appeals reversed, holding that the claims of the class members could not be aggregated because they had separate and distinct claims, which did not constitute common and undivided claims. In addition, although the plaintiff sought an injunction against the defendant insurance company that the company argued would affect payment of future premiums, the court held that the cost of the injunction to the defendant could not be added to the value of the compensatory damages. The court stated that the prayer for an injunction was a "tag-along" request and that the defendant's emphasis on it ignored that the primary claim was for reimbursement of premiums, which asserted a "separate and distinct right." However, even if the request for an injunction was to be given more significance, it was not against a common res, nor did it convert the class claims from separate and distinct ones into common and undivided claims. In addition, it was speculative what kind of action the insurance company would take with regard to rate structuring if the plaintiffs won, and this fact, combined with the fact that the plaintiff had not requested any particular injunctive relief, made it an inappropriate basis for satisfying the amount-in-controversy requirement that the defendant had the burden of demonstrating in this removed case. *See also* LM Ins. Co. v. Spaulding Enters. Inc., 533 F.3d 542 (7th Cir. 2008) (when there are two or more defendants, plaintiff may aggregate amount against defendants only if they are jointly liable; however, if they are severally liable, plaintiff must satisfy the amount requirement separately against each defendant; fraud claim against one defendant measured by loss to plaintiff could not have exceeded $20,000; therefore, amount requirement not met as to that defendant).

correct, *P-1* and *P-2* will each be entitled to a share in *A's* estate in the amount they would have received if *A* had died intestate (without a will)—$40,000 each. However, *P-1* and *P-2* may not aggregate their claims to meet the amount-in-controversy requirement. The question whether one child has been omitted from a will by mistake is entirely distinct from the question whether the other has been omitted by mistake. For example, the testator could have mistakenly omitted *P-1* and intentionally omitted *P-2*. *P-1* and *P-2* may assert their claims in separate actions. They need not join in a single suit. In each of the separate actions, however, the amount in controversy would only be $40,000, and thus they would not be within the diversity jurisdiction.[300]

* * * * *

In the Class Action Fairness Act of 2005 ("CAFA"),[301] Congress provided special aggregation rules for class actions covered by the Act. In new subsection 1332(d)(6), Congress provided that "[i]n any class action, the claims of the individual class members shall be aggregated to determine whether the matter in controversy exceeds the sum or value of $5,000,000, exclusive of interest and costs."[302] One interesting question about this provision concerns its relationship with previous law. The language "[i]n any class action" is clearly designed to apply to class actions covered by new § 1332(d), but it could be read to apply to all class actions, even those not governed by the other provisions of the new Act. This result would present no problem in certain kinds of class actions because of the Supreme Court's recent decision in *Exxon Mobil Corp. v. Allapattah Services, Inc.*,[303] discussed in section E(5)(*a*) and other places in this book, below. *Exxon Mobil* has made aggregation much easier in class actions in which one or more of the representative parties has a claim in excess of $75,000, while some or all of the other members of the class have claims that do not meet the $75,000 requirement. In such actions, *Exxon Mobil* has effectively held that the supplemental jurisdiction statute, discussed in section E, below, permits aggregation of the claims of the class as long as they are factually related, effectively abolishing the "common and undivided interest" test for those kinds of class actions. However, *Exxon Mobil* has no application to a case in which all of the members of the class have claims below the $75,000 requirement. In the latter kinds of class actions, the liberalized aggregation rules of the Class Action Fairness Act might now be interpreted to permit aggregation, assuming, again that the language of the Act is interpreted broadly to apply to all class actions and not just to those governed by the other provisions of § 1332(d).

Even more curious results are possible. The Act provides for a jurisdictional amount in controversy of $5,000,000. Some class actions will involve an amount lower than $5,000,000, but higher than the +$75,000 amount requirement

---

300. *See* Pinel v. Pinel, 240 U.S. 594, 36 S. Ct. 416, 60 L. Ed. 817 (1916).

301. Pub. L. No. 109-2, 119 Stat. 4 (codified as 28 U.S.C. § 1332(d)).

302. *Id.* (codified as 28 U.S.C. § 1332(d)(6)); *cf.* Rolwing v. Nestle Holdings, Inc., 666 F.3d 1069 (8th Cir. 2012) (shareholder's stipulation that he would not accept damages in excess of $4,999,999 on behalf of class and would only accept attorney's fees on a contingency fee basis out of the damage award were enforceable under Missouri law and precluded removal under CAFA's $5,000,000 jurisdictional threshold).

303. 545 U.S. 546, 125 S. Ct. 2611, 162 L. Ed. 2d 502 (2005).

of § 1332(a). If the language, "in any class action," found in new § 1332(d)(6) is interpreted to apply to all class actions, not just to those governed by the other (non-aggregation) provisions of § 1332(d), this would result in the disqualification from the federal diversity jurisdiction of any class action involving an amount in controversy *below* $5,000,000, even those that would otherwise have satisfied diversity and amount-in-controversy requirements in the absence of the 2005 Act.

In *Brill v. Countrywide Home Loans, Inc.*,[304] the recipient of a faxed advertisement brought a class action in state court against the advertiser under the federal Telephone Consumer Protection Act. The defendant removed the action under the Class Action Fairness Act, 28 U.S.C. §§ 1332(d) & 1453, and the plaintiff moved to remand. The district court ordered the action remanded on the grounds, in part, that the defendant had not carried its burden of demonstrating that the amount in controversy exceeded $5,000,000. The defendant sought interlocutory review of the remand order under 28 U.S.C. § 1453(c)(1), and the Seventh Circuit Court of Appeals accepted the appeal and summarily reversed. The court of appeals agreed with the district court that the defendant, as the proponent of federal jurisdiction, had the burden of demonstrating that the amount-in-controversy requirement was satisfied. However, the court of appeals held that the defendant had discharged its burden by admitting that one of its employees had sent at least 3,800 fax ads. This gave rise to the possibility under the federal act that treble damages of $1,500 per fax might be awarded if the violation of the act was demonstrated to be willful. The court of appeals held that this was sufficient to satisfy the "good-faith, legal-certainty" test of *St. Paul Mercury Indemnity Co. v. Red Cab Co.*[305] The court of appeals also rejected the district court's conclusion that the action was not removable on the grounds that the state courts have exclusive jurisdiction over actions under the Telephone Consumer Protection Act. The court of appeals held instead that jurisdiction of the state and federal courts was concurrent under the Act, thus making the action removable on the basis of federal question jurisdiction as well as under the Class Action Fairness Act.[306]

Section 1332(d)(6) specifically states that "[i]n any class action, the claims of the individual class members shall be aggregated to determine whether the amount in controversy exceeds the sum or value of $5,000,000 . . . ."[307] This language would seem pretty clearly to eliminate any requirement that at least one

---

304. 427 F.3d 446 (7th Cir. 2005); *see also* Morgan v. Gay, 471 F.3d 469 (3d Cir. 2006) (when complaint in action removed under Class Action Fairness Act requests relief of less than $5 million, the burden is on the defendant to prove to a legal certainty that the amount in controversy exceeds the Act's $5 million jurisdictional threshold); Strawn v. AT & T Mobility, Inc., 513 F. Supp. 2d 599 (S.D. W. Va. 2007) (when damages sought in state court complaint do not limit actual recovery, a request for damages of less than $5,000,000 does not necessarily preclude satisfying the amount-in-controversy requirement of CAFA); Standard Fire Ins. Co. v. Knowles, __ U.S. __, 133 S. Ct. 90, 193 L. Ed. 2d 730 (2012) (granting certiorari to review whether a state class representative may stipulate to damages of less than $5 million to prevent removal).

305. 303 U.S. 283, 58 S. Ct. 586, 82 L. Ed. 845 (1938).

306. *See also* Pretka v. Kolter City Plaza II, Inc., 608 F.3d 744 (11th Cir. 2010) (developer removing class action in which prospective purchasers sought to obtain release of their contracts of purchase met burden of proof on amount-in-controversy under CAFA by including in notice of removal that it had collected more than $5,000,000 in purchase deposits); Amoche v. Guarantee Trust Life Ins. Co., 556 F.3d 41 (1st Cir. 2009) (insurance company failed on removal to demonstrate that class action brought in state court for refund of premiums met +$5,000,000 amount-in-controversy requirement).

307. 28 U.S.C. § 1332(d)(6).

class member have a claim in excess of the ordinary amount-in-controversy of $75,000 in order to aggregate class claims. Despite this language, a panel of the Eleventh Circuit Court of Appeals initially held that one member of the class (at least) have a claim in excess of $75,000 for the class to be able to aggregate claims under CAFA.[308] Fortunately, however, this result was reversed on rehearing, with the result that aggregation was permitted to meet the +$5,000,000 requirement under CAFA even though all class claims were less than $75,000.[309]

Under 28 U.S.C. § 1332(d)(11)(B)(i), a "mass action" is a civil action in which 100 or more plaintiffs assert monetary claims that are proposed to be tried jointly on the ground that the plaintiff's claims involve common questions of law or fact. Jurisdiction exists over mass actions if it would otherwise exist over a class action under 28 U.S.C. § 1332(d)(2)-(10). However, § 1332(d)(11)(B)(i) provides that in a mass action, jurisdiction shall exist only over those plaintiffs whose claims in a mass action satisfy the + $75,000 jurisdiction amount requirement of § 1332(a). In *Lowery v. Alabama Power Co.*,[310] the Eleventh Circuit Court of Appeals held that the amount-in-controversy requirement for individual plaintiffs in mass actions was not a threshold jurisdictional requirement that would prevent removal even if the other jurisdictional requirements of § 1332(d) were met. Rather, it was an exception to jurisdiction to be determined on a plaintiff-by-plaintiff basis. As indicated in the discussion of the *Exxon Mobil* case in section E(5), below, however, the Supreme Court's interpretation of the supplemental jurisdiction statute now allows multiple plaintiffs properly joined under Federal Rule 20 to aggregate their claims to meet the amount-in-controversy requirement, as long as at least one of the plaintiffs has a claim in excess of $75,000. If the supplemental jurisdiction statute applies in CAFA mass actions (which is by no means certain), this would mean that the *Lowery* interpretation of the statute would, if correct, practically apply only to cases in which no plaintiff has a claim in excess of $75,000.

(c) The Effect of Counterclaims on the Amount in Controversy

When a counterclaim is involved in the action, the question arises whether the amount of the counterclaim can be aggregated with the plaintiff's claim to meet the amount-in-controversy requirement. This question arises when the plaintiff sues for $75,000 or less, but the defendant possesses a counterclaim that exceeds $75,000. It also arises when the plaintiff sues for $75,000 or less and the defendant possesses a counterclaim that is also less than $75,000, but the plaintiff's claim combined with the defendant's counterclaim exceed $75,000. Because of a peculiar U.S. Supreme Court decision, doubt exists about the extent to which counterclaims

---

308. *See* Cappuccitti v. DirecTV, Inc., 611 F.3d 1252 (11th Cir. 2010).

309. *See* Cappuccitti v. DirecTV, Inc., 623 F.3d 1118 (11th Cir. 2010). *But cf.* Marple v. T-Mobile Cent., L.L.C., 639 F.3d 1109 (8th Cir. 2011) (consumers' amounts in controversy for ten separate class actions could not be aggregated to satisfy the jurisdictional requirements of CAFA; CAFA does not permit aggregation between actions).

310. 483 F.3d 1184 (11th Cir. 2007).

can be taken into account in satisfying the jurisdictional amount requirement.[311] This matter is discussed in Chapter 7.[312]

8. Creating and Destroying Diversity of Citizenship

Because diversity of citizenship is determined in part by reference to an individual's domicile, an individual can change home states to create or destroy diversity of citizenship with a potential adversary. In addition, diversity jurisdiction may be created or destroyed in other ways. For example, a claim owned by one person may be "assigned" to another person to create or destroy diversity. Likewise, the representative of a deceased person's estate may be selected because of the representative's citizenship to create or destroy diversity. To what extent should such attempts to create or destroy diversity be successful?

When creation of diversity is at issue, 28 U.S.C. § 1359 must be considered. Section 1359 deprives federal district courts of subject-matter jurisdiction whenever "any party, by assignment or otherwise, has been improperly or collusively made or joined to invoke the jurisdiction of such court."[313] Acting under this section, the U.S. Supreme Court has concluded that a colorable rather than a real assignment will not result in the creation of diversity jurisdiction.[314] Some federal courts have also held that if the motive for making the assignment is primarily to create diversity, this motive can be taken into account as a negative factor in determining whether jurisdiction exists.[315]

Illustration 2-65. *P Corp.* is incorporated and has its principal place of business in State *X*. *P-Sub Corp.* is a wholly owned subsidiary of *P*. *P-Sub* is incorporated with its principal place of business in State *Y*. *P* possesses a claim against *D*, a citizen of State *X*, for $100,000. *P* assigns the claim to *P-Sub*. *P-Sub* sues *D* in a diversity action in a U.S. District Court. Under these circumstances, some federal courts will presume that the assignment was improper and made primarily to create diversity jurisdiction. In these courts, unless *P-Sub* can show that the assignment was made for legitimate business purposes, the courts will dismiss the action.[316]

* * * * *

In determining whether appointment of a representative will be allowed to create diversity jurisdiction, the federal courts have examined (1) the nature of the representative's duties, (2) the relationship of the representative to the parties

---

311. *See* Horton v. Liberty Mut. Ins. Co., 367 U.S. 348, 81 S. Ct. 1570, 6 L. Ed. 2d 890 (1961). A full understanding of the problem requires a familiarity with federal pleading, motion practice, and counterclaim rules.

312. *See* Chapter 7(F)(4)*(d) infra* ("Effect of a Counterclaims on the Amount in Controversy").

313. 28 U.S.C. § 1359.

314. *See* Kramer v. Caribbean Mills, Inc., 394 U.S. 823, 89 S. Ct. 1487, 23 L. Ed. 2d 9 (1969); *see also* Slater v. Republic-Vanguard Ins. Co., 650 F.3d 1132 (8th Cir. 2011) (interpreting *Kramer* as providing that an absolute noncollusive assignment creates diversity jurisdiction).

315. *See* 6 CHARLES A. WRIGHT ET AL., FEDERAL PRACTICE AND PROCEDURE: CIVIL § 1557 (3d ed. 2010); 13F CHARLES A. WRIGHT ET AL., FEDERAL PRACTICE AND PROCEDURE: JURISDICTION AND RELATED MATTERS § 3639 (3d ed. 2009).

316. *See* Prudential Oil Corp. v. Phillips Petroleum Co., 546 F.2d 469 (2d Cir. 1976). *But see* Ambrosia Coal & Const. Co. v. Pages Morales, 482 F.3d 1309 (11th Cir. 2007) (under § 1359, an assignment between closely related entities that creates diversity will not be presumed to be collusive).

being represented, (3) the existence of alternative representatives who are not of diverse citizenship, (4) whether the motive for selecting the representative was the creation of diversity jurisdiction, and (5) other similar factors.[317] In the Judicial Improvements and Access to Justice Act of 1988, Congress amended § 1332 to deal directly with appointments of representatives creating diversity.[318] Section 1332(c)(2) provides that "the legal representative of the estate of a decedent shall be deemed to be a citizen only of the same State as the decedent, and the legal representative of an infant or incompetent shall be deemed to be a citizen only of the same State as the infant or incompetent."[319] Thus, § 1332 now prevents appointments that create diversity jurisdiction in the classes of cases covered by the amendment. It is, therefore, no longer necessary to refer to the factors developed under § 1359 to evaluate the legitimacy of such appointments.[320]

Amended § 1332(c)(2), however, has not solved all problems related to creation of diversity jurisdiction by appointment of representatives. First, appointments of representatives who are not representatives of estates, infants, or incompetents are not covered by the amendment and will continue to be governed by § 1359. Second, there is some question about who qualifies as the "legal representative of the estate of a decedent" within the meaning of the statute. Third, the normal rules governing pleading and proof of federal subject-matter jurisdiction may cause problems in some cases for the representatives of decedents' estates when they are unable to establish the citizenship of decedents. Finally, there is a split of authority over the ability of the representative of an incompetent to change the domicile of the incompetent in a way that creates diversity jurisdiction.[321]

Illustration 2-66. *S*, a citizen of North Carolina, was electrocuted while *S* was working for *D-1 Corp.*, which is incorporated and has its principal place of business in North Carolina. *D-2* is incorporated and has its principal place of business in Pennsylvania. *D-2* manufactured a crane upon which *S* was working

---

317. *See, e.g.*, Bianca v. Parke-Davis Pharm. Div., 723 F.2d 392 (5th Cir. 1984); Vaughan v. Southern Ry. Co., 542 F.2d 641 (4th Cir. 1976); Groh v. Brooks, 421 F.2d 589, 595 (3d Cir. 1970).

318. Judicial Improvements and Access to Justice Act of 1988, Pub. L. No. 100-702, § 202, 102 Stat. 4642, 4646 (codified at 28 U.S.C. § 1332(c)(2)).

319. 28 U.S.C. § 1332(c)(2).

320. In addition to the provisions discussed in the text, one other provision of the Judicial Code will influence whether diversity exists in certain actions against insurance companies. Section 1332(c)(1) of Title 28 provides that in a direct action against an insurer to which the insured is not joined as a party defendant, the insurer will be considered a citizen of the state of which the insured is a citizen, as well as any state by which the insurer is incorporated and the state where it has its principal place of business. Thus, if *P*, a citizen of State *X*, is injured in an automobile accident with *D*, a citizen of State *X*, but sues *D's* insurance company, which is incorporated and has its principal place of business in State *Y*, there would be no diversity of citizenship in the action. However, not every action against an insurance company is a direct action within the meaning of § 1332(c)(1). For example, an action by an insured party against the party's own insurer for bad faith refusal of the insurer to indemnify the insured is not a direct action. *See, e.g.*, Searles v. Cincinnati Ins. Co., 998 F.2d 728 (9th Cir. 1993); Warth v. State Farm Fire & Cas. Co., 792 F. Supp. 101 (M.D. Fla. 1992); Kelly v. State Farm Mut. Auto. Ins. Co., 764 F. Supp. 1337 (S.D. Iowa 1991); Kimball Small Props. v. American Nat'l Fire Ins. Co., 755 F. Supp. 1465 (N.D. Cal. 1991); *see also* Rosa v. Allstate Ins. Co., 981 F.2d 669 (2d Cir. 1992) (action by passenger against driver's insurance company not a direct action because no-fault laws prevented driver from being sued directly). *But cf.* Boston v. Titan Indem. Co., 34 F. Supp. 2d 419, 423-24 (N.D. Mass. 1999) (holding a garnishment proceeding by a judgment creditor to obtain the proceeds of an insurance policy owned by the judgment debtor to be a direct action within the meaning of § 1332(c)(1)).

321. This problem is discussed in Chapter 8(C)(2)*(b) infra* ("Subject-Matter Jurisdiction Problems in Administering Rule 17(b)"); *see also* Heather N. Hormel, Comment, *Domicile for the Dead: Diversity Jurisdiction in Wrongful Death Actions*, 2001 U. CHI. LEGAL F. 519 (discussing the need for a uniform rule in wrongful death actions based on diversity).

when *S* was electrocuted. *M*, a citizen of Louisiana, is *S's* mother. *M* was appointed *S's* personal representative. *M* sued *D-1* and *D-2* in a U.S. District Court to recover for the wrongful death of *S*. On these facts, a federal district court held that *M* had to be deemed a citizen of North Carolina pursuant to 28 U.S.C. § 1332(c)(2). Therefore, diversity of citizenship did not exist between *M* and *D-1*.[322]

Illustration 2-67. *M* is *S's* mother. *M* and *S* are citizens of Minnesota. *F*, a citizen of Illinois, is *S's* father. *S* was killed in an automobile accident with *D*, a citizen of Minnesota. *F* was appointed trustee for *S's* next of kin under the Minnesota wrongful death statute. *F* sued *D* for the wrongful death of *S* in a U.S. District Court, invoking the diversity jurisdiction. *F* claimed to be suing as the trustee of an express trust, not as the legal representative of the estate of a decedent. Thus, *F* contended that *F's* Illinois citizenship, rather than *S's* citizenship, should control in determining diversity of citizenship. A federal district court rejected this argument and held § 1332(c)(2) applied to *F*.[323] However, the Eight Circuit Court of Appeals subsequently held that a Minnesota wrongful death trustee was not a representative of an estate within the meaning of the statute.[324]

Illustration 2-68. Similarly, in *Tank v. Chronister*,[325] the Tenth Circuit Court of Appeals held that § 1332(c)(2) does not apply to a person who is authorized by a wrongful death statute to sue for damages, but who is not a representative of the decedent's estate bringing the action for the benefit of the estate. Other, but not all, federal courts have reached similar results.[326]

---

322. *See* Janeau v. Pitman Mfg. Co., No. 92-1923, 1993 WL 280354, 1993 U.S. App. LEXIS 19646 (4th Cir. July 27, 1993); *see also* Fox v. Mandelbaum, No. 92-1352-FGT, 1993 WL 338728, 1993 U.S. Dist. LEXIS 12091 (D. Kan. July 12, 1993); Tilyou v. Carroll, No. CV-92-0750 (CPS), 1992 WL 170916, 1992 U.S. Dist. LEXIS 10204 (E.D.N.Y. July 2, 1992); Koss v. Metropolitan Ins. & Annuity Co., No. 1: CV-92-0177, 1992 U.S. Dist. LEXIS 8534 (M.D. Pa. June 8, 1992); Warth v. State Farm Fire & Cas. Co., 792 F. Supp. 101 (M.D. Fla. 1992); Snyder v. Pleasant Valley Finishing Co., 756 F. Supp. 725 (S.D.N.Y. 1990).

323. *See* Green v. Lake of the Woods Cnty., 815 F. Supp. 305 (D. Minn. 1993).

324. *See* Steinlage *ex rel.* Smith v. Mayo Clinic Rochester, 435 F.3d 913 (8th Cir. 2006) (Minnesota wrongful death trustee is not a representative of an estate as required for applicability of § 1332(c)(2); therefore, trustee's own citizenship controls for purposes of diversity); *see also* Zebley v. Heartland Indus., 625 F.3d 449 (8th Cir. 2010) (suit by trustee of heirs under North Dakota wrongful death statute was not suit by representative of estate). Other problems of interpretation are presented by the use of the word "State" in § 1332(c)(2) when the administrator of the decedent's estate is an alien. At least one court has held that § 332(c)(2) applies to alien administrators. *See* Geler v. National Westminster Bank USA, 763 F. Supp. 722 (S.D.N.Y. 1991). A parallel problem exists when the decedent is an alien and the administrator is a citizen of a state. At least one court has applied § 1322(c)(2) to this situation. *See* Nolan v. Boeing Co., 736 F. Supp. 120 (E.D. La. 1990). Note that this problem was not addressed in the Federal Courts Jurisdiction and Venue Clarification Act of 2011, effective in 2012, as were some other problems of use of the term "State" in the diversity statute, giving rise to a possible interpretive inference that Congress really wants to limit the operation of § 1332(c) to citizens of "States." *See* Pub. L. No. 112-63, §§ 102 & 103, 125 Stat. 758, 759 (2011) (providing amendments to 28 U.S.C. § 1332, but not to § 1332(c)(2)); *cf.* Jones v. Petty-Ray Geophysical Geosource, Inc., 954 F.2d 1061 (5th Cir. 1992) (holding that the plaintiff, a Texas administrator, could not defeat diversity by using § 1332(c)(2) to assume the citizenship of the decedent, a subject of Great Britain, because the action was filed prior to the effective date of § 1332(c)(2)).

325. 160 F.3d 597 (10th Cir. 1998).

326. *See, e.g.*, Webb v. Banquer, 19 F. Supp. 2d 649, 652 (S.D. Miss. 1998) (when wrongful death action is brought by beneficiary of the action rather than the court-appointed representative of the estate, § 1332(c)(2) is inapplicable and the relevant citizenship is that of the beneficiary); Winn v. Panola-Harrison Elec. Coop., Inc., 40 F. Supp. 2d 850 (E.D. Tex. 1998) ("plain language" of § 1332(c)(2) refers to claims under a survival statute, which is created in favor of heirs, legal representative, and estate of a decedent, not a claim under a wrongful death statute for the benefit of survivors). *But see* Gustafson v. Zumbrunnen, 546 F.3d 398 (7th Cir. 2008) (although beneficiary of grandfather's will was not the personal representative of deceased grandfather's estate, the beneficiary was the "legal representative" of decedent's estate for diversity purposes because Wisconsin law permitted any person having an interest in the decedent's estate to sue on behalf of the estate to recover estate property).

Illustration 2-69. *R*, the representative of the estate of a decedent, *A*, commences an action against *D*, a citizen of State *Y*, on behalf of the estate. *R's* complaint alleges that *A* was a citizen of State *X*. *D* moves to dismiss on the ground that *A* was not a citizen of State *X*. In this situation, at least one federal court has held that the action must be dismissed if *R* cannot prove that *A* was a citizen of State *X*, even if there is no indication that *A* was a citizen of the same state as *D*.[327]

* * * * *

When a person changes domiciles to create diversity, it is strained to conclude that someone has been "improperly or collusively made or joined" to create subject-matter jurisdiction within the meaning of 28 U.S.C. § 1359. Thus, if one of the motives for the change of domicile, even the predominant motive, is to create diversity jurisdiction, that motive will not destroy subject-matter jurisdiction as long as the change of domicile is otherwise genuine. In other words, if the party invoking federal jurisdiction actually intends to remain in the new state indefinitely or permanently, subject-matter jurisdiction should exist. However, the fact that the change was made to create diversity can be considered as evidence indicating that the change was not real—the party did not intend to remain in the new state indefinitely or permanently. Thus, motive will be examined along with all other factors to decide if there has been a real, or only pretended, change of domicile.[328]

No statute like 28 U.S.C. § 1359 prohibits parties from destroying diversity jurisdiction by assigning claims. The only formal word from the Supreme Court indicates that devices destroying diversity will be effective.[329] However, some federal courts have reasoned that modern Supreme Court cases under § 1359 have rendered this traditional view obsolete. These courts have begun to evaluate attempts to destroy diversity of citizenship in the same way they evaluate attempts to create it.[330] If this approach prevails, a court will not give effect to devices used to destroy diversity when the real controversy is between citizens of different states.

In addition, the 1988 amendment to § 1332 discussed earlier will probably prevent the destruction of diversity jurisdiction by the appointment of a nondiverse representative of an estate, an infant, or an incompetent person. On its face, the amendment does not distinguish between appointments designed to create diversity and those designed to destroy diversity. Furthermore, the wording of the amendment has its roots in a 1969 recommendation made by the American Law Institute. That recommendation was explicitly designed to prevent the destruction, as well as the creation, of diversity jurisdiction.[331]

---

327. *See* Davis v. Morganti Nat'l, Inc., No. 2:95-CV256, 1997 U.S. Dist. LEXIS 5014 (W.D.N.C. Jan. 27, 1997).

328. *See, e.g.*, Korn v. Korn, 398 F.2d 689 (3d Cir. 1968); O'Brien v. Delta Gas, Inc., 486 F. Supp. 810 (E.D. La. 1980).

329. *See* Mecom v. Fitzsimmons Drilling Co., 284 U.S. 183, 52 S. Ct. 84, 76 L. Ed. 233 (1931). However, *Mecom* involved an appointment to destroy diversity rather than an assignment. Appointments are now largely controlled by 28 U.S.C. § 1332(c)(2). *See Illustrations 2-66* and *2-67 supra*. There is no direct Supreme Court authority on assignments to destroy diversity. *See generally* Brent Caslin, Provident Savings Life Assurance Society v. Ford: *120 Years of Shenanigans Designed to Destroy Diversity Jurisdiction*, 42 WILLAMETTE L. REV. 439 (2006).

330. *See, e.g.*, Miller v. Perry, 456 F.2d 63 (4th Cir. 1972).

331. *See* ALI STUDY OF THE DIVISION OF JURISDICTION BETWEEN STATE AND FEDERAL COURTS § 1301(b)(4), commentary at 117 (1969).

9. Judicial Exceptions to Federal Diversity Jurisdiction

Two judicially created exceptions to federal jurisdiction exist. The federal courts will not take jurisdiction in suits between citizens of different states involving (1) domestic relations and (2) probate matters. The courts created these exceptions when the statute conferring diversity jurisdiction on the federal courts granted jurisdiction over civil suits "in law or in equity." Because the federal courts believed that the English ecclesiastical courts, rather than the common-law and equity courts, handled domestic relations and probate matters, the federal courts read the statute as excluding these subject areas. Although 28 U.S.C. § 1332(a) now extends diversity jurisdiction to all civil actions, courts have nevertheless continued to read these exceptions into the current statute.[332]

In *Ankenbrandt v. Richards*,[333] the Supreme Court held that the domestic relations exception is only an interpretation of the general diversity statute, not an exception compelled by Article III of the Constitution.[334] However, the Court also held that the exception is limited to actions seeking to grant or modify a divorce, alimony, or child custody decree.[335]

Illustration 2-70. *M* is the mother of *A* and *B*. *M*, *A*, and *B* are all citizens of State *X*. *F*, a citizen of State *Y*, is the father of *A* and *B* and the former spouse of *M*. *M*, acting as the representative of *A* and *B*, sued *F* in a U.S. District Court for $100,000 in damages. *M* alleged that *F* physically and sexually abused *A* and *B* while they were in *F's* custody under an order of a state court granting *F* visitation rights with *A* and *B*. The federal district courts have diversity jurisdiction over this action because the action does not seek the granting or modification of a divorce, alimony, or custody decree.[336]

---

332. *See* 13E CHARLES A. WRIGHT ET AL., FEDERAL PRACTICE AND PROCEDURE: JURISDICTION AND RELATED MATTERS § 3609 (3d ed. 2009).

333. 504 U.S. 689, 112 S. Ct. 2206, 119 L. Ed. 2d 468 (1992).

334. *Id.* at 695-96, 112 S. Ct. at 2210-11, 119 L. Ed. 2d at 477.

335. *Id.* at 701-04, 112 S. Ct. at 2213-15, 119 L. Ed. 2d at 481-83.

336. *See generally id.* at 704, 112 S. Ct. at 2215, 119 L. Ed. 2d at 482; *see also* Dunn v. Cometa, 238 F.3d 38 (1st Cir. 2001) (court agrees that placing "tort" label on an action will not avoid application of the domestic relations exception, but refuses to apply exception to action in which father of husband disabled in accident sued wife for breach of fiduciary duty, negligence, and waste for allowing husband's health insurance to expire and wrongfully transferring marital assets to herself while caring for husband; wife was seeking divorce, and claim may have been relevant to the amount of alimony the wife would have to pay in the divorce; though not applying the domestic relations exception, the court indicated that the best course of action would be for the district court to abstain from decision because state law was unclear and claims were based on conduct occurring in a family context); McLaughlin v. Cotner, 193 F.3d 410 (6th Cir. 1999) (plaintiff and husband entered into a separation agreement providing for the sale of a house they held in joint tenancy; the agreement was incorporated in a divorce decree; later, plaintiff sued the former husband for breach of the separation agreement and tortious interference with contract because he had failed to sell the house; the court of appeals affirmed the dismissal of the action under the domestic relations exception, holding that the exception applies to actions that appear to be tort or contract actions, but are really domestic relations disputes; court viewed obligations of the parties as having been imposed by the divorce decree rather than general contract or tort law); Stone v. Wall, 135 F.3d 1438 (11th Cir. 1998) (diversity action by father and minor daughter against daughter's maternal grandmother, aunt, and their attorney to recover damages for interference with father's custody of daughter not within domestic relations exception). In United States v. Johnson, 114 F.3d 476 (4th Cir. 1997), the court held in a federal question criminal prosecution that the domestic relations exception is only a judicially implied limit on diversity jurisdiction, but the exception did not limit the federal question jurisdiction. In *Johnson*, the prosecution was under the federal Child Support Recovery Act, 18 U.S.C. § 228; Emily J. Sack, *The Domestic Relations Exception, Domestic Violence, and Equal Access to Federal Courts*, 84 WASH. U. L. REV. 1441 (2006).

Illustration 2-71. *P*, a citizen of State *X*, sued *D*, a citizen of State *Y*, in a U.S. District Court seeking enforcement of the judgment of a state court ordering *D* to pay alimony to *P*. *P* seeks payment of $80,000 of back alimony awarded but unpaid under the state judgment. The U.S. District Court has diversity jurisdiction over this action. The domestic relations exception does not apply because the action does not seek an award of alimony or a modification of the state alimony decree. Instead, it seeks enforcement of the state judgment that awarded the alimony.[337]

* * * * *

In *Marshall v. Marshall*,[338] the Supreme Court clarified the operation of the probate exception to federal jurisdiction. In *Marshall*, probate proceedings were instituted in Texas state court to settle the estate of J. Howard Marshall. Vicki Lynn Marshall (a.k.a. Anna Nicole Smith), Marshall's widow, subsequently instituted a federal bankruptcy proceeding in the U.S. Bankruptcy Court for the Central District of California. Marshall's son, E. Pierce Marshall, filed a claim in the bankruptcy proceeding, alleging that Vicki had defamed him. Vicki, in turn, filed counterclaims asserting that Pierce had tortiously interfered with a gift that J. Howard had intended to make to her. Vicki won in the bankruptcy court, and the bankruptcy court was affirmed by the U.S. District Court. Both the bankruptcy court and the district court rejected the son's assertion that Vicki's claim fell within the probate exception to federal jurisdiction. However, the Ninth Circuit Court of Appeals reversed, holding the probate exception applicable. The Supreme Court, in turn, granted certiorari and reversed the Ninth Circuit.

Employing reasoning similar to that in *Ankenbrandt*, the Court held that the probate exception only applied to prevent federal courts from probating or annulling a will, administering a decedent's estate, or endeavoring to dispose of property that is in the custody of a state probate court. Because Vicki's claim was for a widely recognized tort, the probate exception was not applicable. The Court expressly refused to determine whether provisions of the federal bankruptcy act that had been waived by the son would have required the bankruptcy court to abstain in the action. Nor did the Court suggest that the probate exception was inapplicable because the case was a federal question case arising under the bankruptcy act, or that the probate exception would be inoperative if it somehow interfered with the operation of the federal bankruptcy act, or federal bankruptcy proceedings,[339] in a

---

337. *See* Barber v. Barber, 62 U.S. (21 How.) 582, 16 L. Ed. 226 (1859). *Barber* was cited and discussed with approval in *Ankenbrandt*. *See* 504 U.S. at 693-703, 112 S. Ct. at 2209-14, 119 L. Ed. 2d at 475-82. In two subsequent cases, federal courts of appeals have allowed parties to use federal declaratory judgment proceedings to adjudicate the federal constitutional validity of prior state divorce judgments. Both opinions rejected the application of the domestic relations exception to the case. *See* Rash v. Rash, 173 F.3d 1376 (11th Cir. 1999); Catz v. Chalker, 142 F.3d 279 (6th Cir. 1998), *amended*, 243 F.3d 234 (6th Cir. 2001). These cases pose the danger that the declaratory judgment procedure could undermine the policy supporting exclusion of divorce cases from federal jurisdiction.

338. 547 U.S. 293, 126 S. Ct. 1735, 164 L. Ed. 2d 480 (2006).

339. The Court remanded for a determination of whether the proceeding before the bankruptcy court was a "core proceeding." A federal bankruptcy court may enter final judgment only in so-called "core proceedings" under the bankruptcy act. The district court held the proceeding to be a non-core proceeding and reviewed the determinations of fact and law made by the bankruptcy judge de novo. This review in theory resulted in some differences of result between the bankruptcy and district court proceedings, particularly on the amount of damages that Vicki received from the two courts. Thus, if the proceeding had been held on remand to be a valid "core proceeding," Vicki could theoretically have received the benefit of a larger damage award made by the bankruptcy judge. *See id.* at 314-15, 126 S. Ct. at 1750, 164 L. Ed. 2d at 500.

particular case. The Court remanded the case for determination, *inter alia,* of whether claim or issue preclusion would bar Vicki's counterclaim because of the judgment of the Texas probate court, which had become final one month earlier than the District Court's judgment reviewing the bankruptcy court's decision.[340] Note that *Marshall* seems to mean that the probate exception, and by inference the domestic relations exception, are not simply exceptions to the diversity jurisdiction, but to the federal question jurisdiction as well.[341]

Marshall makes it clear that the probate exception, like the domestic relations exception, does not deprive the federal courts of jurisdiction over every action that somehow involves a decedent's estate. The district courts may entertain actions that involve estates as long as the actions do not interfere with state probate proceedings or assume control of property in a state court's custody."[342] Unfortunately, even after the clarification, the exception produces some subtle distinctions between the kinds of relief that courts can and cannot award against executors and administrators.

Illustration 2-72. *P*, a citizen of State *X*, sued *D*, a citizen of State *Y*, in U.S. District Court. *D* is the executor of *T's* will. *T* was a citizen of State *Y*. *P's* action sought a declaration that certain gifts under *T's* will had lapsed and that *P* was the sole party entitled to share in *T's* residuary estate. In addition, *P* sought to obtain an accounting for all the decedent's assets coming into *D's* hands as well as the amount of the residuary estate. *P's* claims under the will exceed $90,000. The district court has jurisdiction to determine whether the gifts have lapsed. The court also has jurisdiction to determine whether *P* is the sole party entitled to the

---

340. In a later decision, Stern v. Marshall, 562 U.S. __, 131 S. Ct. 2494, 180 L. Ed. 2d 475 (2011), the Supreme Court considered whether a bankruptcy judge, not protected by the tenure and salary guarantees of Article III, had the power to enter judgment on Vicki's counterclaim, which was governed entirely by state law. The significance of the issue was this: if the bankruptcy judge had the power to enter judgment on the counterclaim, that judgment would control and Vicki's estate would recover. If the bankruptcy judge did not have such power, then a later decision of the U.S. District Court in review of the bankruptcy judge's decision would control, and by the time the district judge acted, the decision of a Texas probate court had been rendered deciding issues that would preclude Vicki's ability to recover in the district court. The Supreme Court held that although the bankruptcy code gave the bankruptcy judge the power to enter the judgment, the judge lacked power under Article III of the Constitution to do so. As a result, the Texas probate court's decision on critical issues against Vicki had a preclusive effect in the district court and prevented that court from rendering a judgment in her favor. Presumably *Stern* is the final act in this drama, but one can never be certain. *See* Aneil Kovvali, Recent Development, *State Law Claims and Article III in* Stern v. Marshall, 131 S. Ct. 2594 (2011), 35 HARV. J. L. & PUB. POL'Y 423 (2012).

341. *See also* Wisecarver v. Moore, 489 F.3d 747 (6th Cir. 2007) (probate exception did not apply to federal diversity action against primary beneficiaries of a will alleging undue influence to persuade the decedent to sign testamentary documents; exception does not apply to in personam claims for relief that do not interfere with property over which a state probate court has jurisdiction or that do not seek to probate or annul a will); Jones v. Brennan, 465 F.3d 304 (7th Cir. 2006) (judgment vacated for consideration of whether any of plaintiff's federal claims fell outside the probate exception; court opined that plaintiff was complaining for the most part about the maladministration of her father's estate; court added, however, that if district court found even one colorable federal claim that fell outside the probate exception, supplemental jurisdiction would exist over the state claims under 28 U.S.C. § 1367).

342. In some cases, the existence of federal jurisdiction depends on state practice. For example, the probate exception generally applies to disallow federal jurisdiction over actions to set aside a will, but if the state where the will is being probated has given its own courts of general jurisdiction authority over such actions, the federal courts may also entertain them under the diversity jurisdiction. *See Marshall*, 547 U.S. at 313-15, 126 S. Ct. at 1749, 164 L. Ed. 2d at 499-500; Rienhardt v. Kelly, 164 F.3d 1296 (10th Cir. 1999) (standard for determining whether probate exception applies is whether the claim in question could be adjudicated under state law only in state probate court; if so, the exception applies; if not, the exception is inapplicable); *see also Illustration 2-64 supra*; Storm v. Storm, 328 F.3d 941 (7th Cir. 2003) (federal court had no jurisdiction to entertain an action for tortious interference with an inheritance expectancy that was in essence a will contest).

residuary estate under the will. These determinations will bind the executor in the state probate proceeding. However, the district court does not have the power to order an accounting because such an order would directly interfere with an exclusive function of the state probate court.[343]

Illustration 2-73. *P*, a citizen of State *X*, suffered personal injuries in an automobile accident with *C*, a citizen of State *Y*. *C* was killed in the accident. *D*, a citizen of State *Y*, was appointed administrator of *C's* estate. *P* sues *D* in a U.S. District Court to recover $100,000 for the personal injuries *P* received in the accident. The district court has diversity jurisdiction over this action. The action does not directly affect any probate proceeding being conducted for the purposes of distributing *C's* estate. If *P* wins the action, *D* will be bound in *D's* capacity as administrator to pay the judgment out of the proceeds of *C's* estate.

* * * * *

In summary, it is sufficient to say that the historical foundation for the domestic relations and probate exceptions to federal jurisdiction has been seriously questioned,[344] and the current statutory language no longer supports their existence.[345] A suggested modern justification for these exceptions is that domestic relations and probate are matters of peculiar state interest and competence.[346] Some federal practitioners, however, believe that the exceptions continue because federal judges do not like to deal with domestic relations and probate matters.

10. Correcting Defects in Diversity Jurisdiction and Adjudicating Disputes Over Diversity Jurisdiction

Section 1653 of Title 28 of the *United States Code* states that "[d]efective allegations of jurisdiction may be amended, upon terms, in the trial or appellate courts."[347] Thus, if the plaintiff makes a mistake in pleading jurisdictional facts, § 1653 allows the plaintiff to amend the complaint to allege the facts correctly. However, § 1653 only applies to defective allegations of jurisdiction. The statute does not apply when, under the objective facts, diversity jurisdiction does not actually exist.[348] Under these circumstances, when complete diversity of citizenship does not exist between all the parties to the action, a U.S. District Court can employ

---

343. *See* Waterman v. Canal-Louisiana Bank & Trust Co., 215 U.S. 33, 44-46, 30 S. Ct. 10, 12-13, 54 L. Ed. 80, 84-85 (1909).

344. *See* Spindel v. Spindel, 283 F. Supp. 797 (E.D.N.Y. 1968).

345. *See* Ankenbrandt v. Richards, 504 U.S. 689, 706, 112 S. Ct. 2206, 2217, 119 L. Ed. 2d 468, 485 (1992) (Blackmun, J., concurring).

346. *See* 13E CHARLES A. WRIGHT ET AL. FEDERAL PRACTICE AND PROCEDURE: JURISDICTION AND RELATED MATTERS § 3609 (3d ed. 2009).

347. 28 U.S.C. § 1653; *see* McCready v. eBay, Inc., 453 F.3d 882 (7th Cir. 2006) (failure to allege principal place of business was jurisdictional defect that required dismissal; although amendment would ordinarily be allowed to correct defective allegation, no purpose would be served in allowing frivolous suit to continue); Novak v. Capital Mgmt. & Dev. Corp., 452 F.3d 902 (D.C. Cir. 2006) (allegation of residence rather than citizenship is defective, as is failure to allege states of incorporation and principal place of business of corporate defendants).

348. *See* Newman-Green, Inc. v. Alfonzo-Larrain, 490 U.S. 826, 109 S. Ct. 2218, 104 L. Ed. 2d 893 (1989); *see also* Franceskin v. Credit Suisse, 214 F.3d 253 (2d Cir. 2000) (diversity jurisdiction improperly pleaded, but amendment was impossible because alienage jurisdiction was actually absent; claims against nondiverse defendant ordered dismissed); Whitmire v. Victus Ltd., 212 F.3d 885 (5th Cir. 2000) (abuse of discretion not to allow amendment to allege diversity jurisdiction when federal question jurisdiction failed).

Federal Rule 21 to drop a nondiverse party.[349] The U.S. Supreme Court has also held that the courts of appeals may use Rule 21 to drop nondiverse parties. However, the court of appeals may drop such a party only if dismissing the nondiverse party will not prejudice the remaining parties to the action.[350]

Illustration 2-74. *P*, a citizen of State *X*, commences an action in U.S. District Court against *D*, a citizen of State *Y*. *P's* complaint alleges that *D* is a "resident" of State *Y*. This allegation is defective because it alleges *D's* residence, but not *D's* citizenship. Section 1653 of Title 28 authorizes *P* to amend the complaint to allege that *D* is a "citizen of State *Y*." The amendment may be permitted by the U.S. District Court or, if the case reaches the appellate stage before anyone recognizes the defect, by the U.S. Court of Appeals.[351]

Illustration 2-75. *P*, a citizen of State *X*, sues *D-1*, a citizen of State *Y*, and *D-2*, a citizen of State *X*, in a U.S. District Court. No diversity jurisdiction exists. Citizens of State *X* are on both sides of the action. This problem cannot be corrected under the authority of 28 U.S.C. § 1653. That statute applies only to defective allegations of jurisdiction. On these facts, no allegation of jurisdiction can save the case. Instead, the district court must drop *D-2* from the action under Federal Rule 21. If the action reaches the appellate stage before the jurisdictional defect is recognized, the court of appeals must take that action.

* * * * *

Like all other defects in federal jurisdiction, defects in diversity jurisdiction are raised by the parties or the court on its own motion. However, the procedures employed to determine the existence of diversity can be more elaborate than the procedures employed in other kinds of cases in which federal jurisdiction is questioned.[352] Questions such as the determination of the domicile of an individual or the principal place of business of a corporation cannot be resolved on the face of the pleadings. In determining such questions, the U.S. District Courts have broad discretion over the procedures they employ.

Illustration 2-76. Assume that (a) the plaintiff's complaint alleges diversity of citizenship between plaintiff and defendant; (b) the defendant believes that the plaintiff's allegation of citizenship is incorrect because the plaintiff and defendant are both U.S. citizens domiciled in the same state; and thus (c) no diversity jurisdiction exists. Typically, the plaintiff's allegation of diversity

---

349. Rule 21 states that "[o]n motion or on its own, the court may at any time, on just terms, add or drop a party." FED. R. CIV. P. 21. For a party to be dropped, the party must not be a required party under Rule 19. *See* FED. R. CIV. P. 19; Chapter 8(C)(3) *infra* ("Joinder of Persons Needed for Just Adjudication") (discussing Rule 19).

350. *See* Newman-Green, Inc. v. Alfonzo-Larrain, 490 U.S. 826, 832-38, 109 S. Ct. 2218, 2223-26, 104 L. Ed. 2d 893, 902-06 (1989).

351. *See* Kanter v. Warner-Lambert Co., 265 F.3d 853 (9th Cir. 2001) (removal improper when defendant alleged that plaintiff was "resident" of particular state rather than a "citizen" of the state; however, defendants could potentially cure defective allegations of jurisdiction under § 1653 by amending notice of removal jurisdiction); Tylka v. Gerber Prods. Co., 211 F.3d 445 (7th Cir. 2000) (failure of defendant to correct reference to plaintiff's residence to a reference to plaintiff's citizenship after warning by appellate court results in lack of jurisdiction and necessity of remand of removed case to state court); *cf.* W.N.J. v. Yocom, 257 F.3d 1171 (10th Cir. 2001) (plaintiff wishing to commence an action in an anonymous name must receive permission of the court; otherwise, the court lacks jurisdiction over the action).

352. For instance, in federal question cases, it is usually apparent from the face of the plaintiff's complaint whether an action fits within one of the appropriate categories of cases in which an action will be deemed to arise under federal law. Likewise, in diversity actions, it will be readily apparent when an allegation of diversity jurisdiction is defective or missing from the complaint.

jurisdiction will be put in issue by either a preanswer motion pursuant to Federal Rule 12(b)(1) or a challenge to jurisdiction in the defendant's answer.[353] However, if the lack of diversity should come to the attention of the district court in any other way, the court must raise the issue of subject-matter jurisdiction on its own motion. The court has broad discretion over the manner in which it determines the issue of citizenship. For example, the district judge may decide the question based on the pleadings, affidavits of the parties, and available depositions. The court may hold a full-scale evidentiary hearing or, at its discretion, submit the issue to a jury.[354]

SECTION E. SUPPLEMENTAL JURISDICTION

The doctrines of "pendent" and "ancillary" jurisdiction traditionally allowed federal courts to hear claims that were not otherwise within the original jurisdiction of those courts. This expansion of federal jurisdiction occurred only when (1) the pendent or ancillary claims were asserted in an action containing other claims over which the federal courts had original jurisdiction (freestanding claims); and (2) a close factual relationship existed between the freestanding claims and the pendent or ancillary claims.

In 1990, Congress codified and expanded the doctrines of pendent and ancillary jurisdiction. In the Judicial Improvements Act of 1990,[355] Congress added a new § 1367 to Title 28 of the *United States Code*.[356] This new section substitutes the term "supplemental jurisdiction" for the terms "pendent" and "ancillary" jurisdiction. Supplemental jurisdiction has raised several new and difficult interpretative issues for the federal courts. In order to understand these issues and the operation of supplemental jurisdiction statute, it is first necessary to examine the general nature of pendent and ancillary jurisdiction as well as the constitutional and statutory bases of these doctrines. With this background, supplemental jurisdiction as authorized by § 1367 will then be examined in detail.

1. The General Nature of Pendent and Ancillary Jurisdiction

The doctrine of *pendent jurisdiction* applied only to federal question cases. Furthermore, it applied only to original claims asserted by plaintiff(s) against

---

353. *See also* Herrick Co. v. SCS Commc'ns, Inc., 251 F.3d 315 (2d Cir. 2001) (party invoking jurisdiction has burden of establishing diversity; if party challenges jurisdiction on the basis of lack of diversity due to a change in domicile, the party has the burden of proving that a change occurred only if the party asserting jurisdiction first establishes a specific initial domicile).

354. *See* 13E CHARLES A. WRIGHT ET AL., FEDERAL PRACTICE AND PROCEDURE: JURISDICTION AND RELATED MATTERS) § 3612 (3d ed. 2009). In determining whether diversity of citizenship exists in an action, the court must also employ the doctrine of "realignment." This doctrine simply provides that the parties to an action, regardless of how they are aligned in the pleadings, must be arranged according to their true interests in the action. Realignment can result in diversity being preserved where it appears to be absent on the face of the pleadings or destroyed where it appears to be present. Realignment is discussed in Chapter 8(C)(3)*(c) infra* ("Problems of Subject-Matter Jurisdiction, Personal Jurisdiction, and Venue Under Rule 19") in conjunction with practice under Federal Rule 19.

355. Pub. L. No. 101-650, 104 Stat. 5089.

356. *See id.* § 310, 104 Stat. 5089, 5113-14.

defendant(s) in an action.[357] For example, if a U.S. District Court had federal question jurisdiction over a plaintiff's claim, the doctrine of pendent jurisdiction would allow the court to exercise jurisdiction over all state claims originally asserted by the plaintiff which were *factually related* to the federal claim. Thus, without a federal claim in an action, pendent jurisdiction would not allow a federal court to obtain jurisdiction over a case involving nondiverse opposing parties. Jurisdiction over such cases was restricted by the rule requiring complete diversity of citizenship between the parties under 28 U.S.C. § 1332.[358] Likewise, when diversity of citizenship between the parties was the exclusive basis for jurisdiction, pendent jurisdiction did not allow a federal court to obtain jurisdiction over claims that did not independently meet the jurisdictional amount requirement of § 1332. Jurisdiction over such claims had to be determined by reference to the restrictive aggregation rules developed under § 1332 (discussed above).[359] The term "pendent jurisdiction" was thus properly applied only to cases under 28 U.S.C. § 1331 (and other federal question jurisdiction statutes) in which state claims could be asserted because they arose out of the same facts as the federal question claim that conferred subject-matter jurisdiction.

Illustration 2-77. *P*, a citizen of State *X*, sued *D*, also a citizen of State *X*, in a U.S. District Court in State *X*. Assume that *P* asserted two claims against *D*, one under a federal statute and the other based on the same facts, but arising under state law. Because no diversity of citizenship existed between the parties, the district court had no independent basis for exercising subject-matter jurisdiction over the state claim. Nevertheless, because the state and federal claims arose from the same facts, the district court was said to have "pendent jurisdiction" over the state claim—which simply meant that the court's unquestioned jurisdiction over the federal claim under 28 U.S.C. § 1331 gave the federal district court authority to adjudicate the state claim as well.

Illustration 2-78. *P*, a citizen of State *X*, sued *D-1*, a citizen of State *Y*, and *D-2*, a citizen of State *X*, in a federal district court in State *X*. *P's* claims arose under state law and were for $1,000,000 in the alternative against *D-1* and *D-2*.[360] The doctrine of pendent jurisdiction did not allow *P* to join *D-2* in the action. Pendent jurisdiction applied only to federal question cases. Jurisdiction in *P's* action against *D-1* and *D-2* was based solely on diversity of citizenship. Consequently, the complete diversity rule of 28 U.S.C. § 1332 barred jurisdiction over the action. However, if *D-1* and *D-2* both had been citizens of State *Y* and *P* had asserted alternative claims against them arising out of the same automobile accident, the

---

357. *Cf.* 1 FEDERAL COURTS STUDY COMMITTEE WORKING PAPERS AND SUBCOMMITTEE REPORTS 546 (1990). The definitions of "pendent" and "ancillary" jurisdiction in the text are generally accurate for the federal courts. However, state courts may use the terms in a different manner. *See* Entergy Miss., Inc. v. Burdette Gin Co., 726 So. 2d 1202 (Miss. 1998) (using the term "pendent" jurisdiction to apply to a third-party claim in which a person not originally a party is brought into the action by the defendant).

358. *See* Owen Equip. & Erection Co. v. Kroger, 437 U.S. 365, 98 S. Ct. 2396, 57 L. Ed. 2d 274 (1978).

359. *See* Zahn v. International Paper Co., 414 U.S. 291, 94 S. Ct. 505, 38 L. Ed. 2d 511 (1973); Snyder v. Harris, 394 U.S. 332, 89 S. Ct. 1053, 22 L. Ed. 2d 319 (1969); section D(7)*(b) supra* ("Aggregation of Claims with Multiple Parties: the 'Common and Undivided Interest' Test").

360. A claim in the alternative asserts that either *D-1* or *D-2* is liable to *P* for a specific amount of damages. As long as the specific amount claimed exceeds $75,000, claims in the alternative satisfy the amount-in-controversy requirement.

complete diversity rule and the amount-in-controversy requirement would have been satisfied. On the other hand, if, instead of asserting claims in the alternative, *P's* claim against *D-1* was for $80,000 and *P's* claim against *D-2* was for only $10,000, *P* could not join *D-2*. The restrictive aggregation rules of 28 U.S.C. § 1332 (discussed in the preceding subsection) would not allow *D-2's* claim to be added to *D-1's* claim to satisfy the jurisdictional amount requirement.[361]

* * * * *

The doctrine of *ancillary jurisdiction* applied to both federal question and diversity actions. However, it applied only to claims coming into an action *after* the plaintiff's original claims, not to those original claims themselves.[362] Thus, ancillary jurisdiction enabled a federal court to exercise subject-matter jurisdiction over claims asserted by the defendant that were closely related to the principal claim in the action, even if no independent subject-matter jurisdiction existed over the claims.

Illustration 2-79. *P*, a citizen of State *X*, sued *D*, a citizen of State *Y*, in a U.S. District Court in State *Y*. *P* asserted a claim against *D* arising under state law for $80,000. *D's* answer contained a compulsory counterclaim against *P* for $1,000, which also arose under state law. The counterclaim did not meet the amount-in-controversy requirement of § 1332, and no other basis for federal subject-matter jurisdiction existed over the claim. Nevertheless, the federal district court could adjudicate the counterclaim. By definition, a compulsory counterclaim arises out of the same transaction or occurrence as the opposing party's claim.[363] Thus, because of the close factual relationship between the plaintiff's claim and the defendant's counterclaim, the court had "ancillary jurisdiction" over the counterclaim.

Illustration 2-80. *P*, a citizen of State *X*, sued *D*, a citizen of State *X*, in a U.S. District Court in State *X*, asserting a federal claim against *D*. *D's* answer contains a compulsory counterclaim against *P* under state law for $1,000. As in *Illustration 2-79*, *D's* counterclaim is within the ancillary jurisdiction of the district court because of its close factual relationship with *P's* federal claim, even though there is no diversity of citizenship between the parties and *D's* claim is for only $1,000.

2. The Constitutional Basis of Pendent and Ancillary Jurisdiction

Pendent and ancillary jurisdiction share a common constitutional basis. When Article III of the Constitution authorized Congress to give federal courts jurisdiction over cases enumerated in § 2 of that Article, it authorized Congress to

---

361. Under these circumstances, the "common and undivided interest" test is not satisfied because *P* is claiming that *D-1* damaged *P* in the amount of $80,000 and that *D-2* inflicted separate damage in the amount of $10,000. Neither defendant is liable for the damage inflicted by the other. *See* section D(7)*(b) supra* ("Aggregation of Claims with Multiple Parties: the 'Common and Undivided Interest' Test").

362. *See* 1 FEDERAL COURTS STUDY COMMITTEE WORKING PAPERS AND SUBCOMMITTEE REPORTS 546 (1990).

363. *See* FED. R. CIV. P. 13(a).

confer jurisdiction over *entire* cases, not just the "federal" parts of the cases.[364] Therefore, in the case of pendent jurisdiction, when the events giving rise to a federal claim over which the federal district courts have independent subject-matter jurisdiction also give rise to a claim under state law, both claims are considered to be a part of the same case for purposes of Article III.[365] This same theory provides the constitutional basis of ancillary jurisdiction, at least in federal question cases.[366] For example, when a defendant possesses a state counterclaim arising out of the same facts as the plaintiff's federal claim, both claims are considered to be a part of the same case or controversy under Article III of the Constitution.

In *United Mine Workers v. Gibbs*[367] and later cases,[368] the U.S. Supreme Court strongly suggested in dicta that Article III of the Constitution not only permits, but requires, the federal and nonfederal claims to be *factually related—i.e.*, to arise from a "common nucleus of operative fact." These Supreme Court dicta[369] have led to a general belief that federal and nonfederal claims *must* be factually related to satisfy Article III.[370] Nevertheless, caution would seem in order on this question. Nothing in the language of Article III explicitly requires that the scope of a "case" or "controversy" be defined by reference to the factual relationship between the joined claims, as opposed to, for example, the entire relationship between the parties to an action, which may include factually unrelated claims. Furthermore, the history of joinder-of-claims practice at common law, in equity, and

---

364. This theory is derived from *Osborn v. Bank of the United States*, discussed in section B(1), *supra*. *See generally* Finley v. United States, 490 U.S. 545, 109 S. Ct. 2003, 104 L. Ed. 2d 593 (1989).

365. *See* United Mine Workers v. Gibbs, 383 U.S. 715, 725, 86 S. Ct. 1130, 1138, 16 L. Ed. 2d 218, 227-28 (1966); Osborn v. Bank of the United States, 22 U.S. (9 Wheat.) 738, 6 L. Ed. 204 (1824).

366. As discussed earlier in conjunction with diversity jurisdiction, Article III does not require complete diversity of citizenship between the parties and, of course, mentions nothing about an amount-in-controversy requirement. As discussed below in conjunction with the supplemental jurisdiction statute, the "Article III relationship test" of that statute was drawn from pendent jurisdiction cases. It may be inapplicable to the constitutional requirements for diversity jurisdiction.

367. 383 U.S. 715, 725, 86 S. Ct. 1130, 1138, 16 L. Ed. 2d 218, 227-28 (1966). In Diamler Chrysler Corp. v. Cuno, 547 U.S. 332, 164 S. Ct. 1854, 164 L. Ed. 2d 589 (2006), the Supreme Court held that *Gibbs* does not permit a federal court to exercise supplemental jurisdiction over a claim that does not satisfy the Article III standing requirement based on its factual relationship with a claim that does satisfy the requirement. *See also* C. Douglas Floyd, *Three Faces of Supplemental Jurisdiction After the Demise of* United Mine Workers v. Gibbs, 60 FLA. L. REV. 277 (2008).

368. *See, e.g.*, Finley v. United States, 490 U.S. 545, 548, 109 S. Ct. 2003, 2006, 104 L. Ed. 2d 593, 601 (1989) (interpreting *Gibbs* as extending pendent jurisdiction as far as the Constitution permits—*i.e.*, to state claims that arise out of the same facts as federal claims).

369. In United Mine Workers v. Gibbs, 383 U.S. 715, 86 S. Ct. 1130, 16 L. Ed. 2d 218 (1966), the Court held that federal and nonfederal claims arising from the same facts were part of the same Article III case or controversy. However, the Court did not have before it a case in which factually unrelated federal and state claims had been joined. Therefore, the Court's references to Article III of the Constitution technically cannot be read as holding that factually unrelated federal and state claims can never be part of the same case or controversy. In Finley v. United States, 490 U.S. 545, 548, 109 S. Ct. 2003, 2006, 104 L. Ed. 2d 593, 601 (1989), the Court stated that *Gibbs* had extended pendent claim jurisdiction "to the full extent permitted by the Constitution." This statement was also unnecessary to the decision of that case, which, again, did not involve factually unrelated claims. Thus, there is technically no direct authority that Congress lacks the power in an appropriate case to provide for pendent jurisdiction over factually unrelated state claims in a federal question case. Nevertheless, the strong statement in *Finley* may well indicate the Court's current view of the scope of Article III.

370. *See, e.g.*, CHARLES A. WRIGHT & MARY KAY KANE, THE LAW OF FEDERAL COURTS § 39, at 239 n.33 (7th ed. 2011) (discussing the constitutionality of removing factually unrelated federal and state claims under 28 U.S.C. § 1441(c)).

under modern procedural codes supports the theory that a single case may include factually unrelated claims.[371]

Historical practice aside, sound reasons may sometimes exist for defining the scope of a case or controversy to include unrelated claims—reasons grounded in policies designed to protect or enhance the operation of federal subject-matter jurisdiction. When such policies can be seen to support a statute, a conferral of jurisdiction over factually unrelated federal and state claims arguably should be held to be within the power of Congress under Article III of the Constitution and the Necessary and Proper Clause.[372] This interpretation of Article III conforms to the flexible approach that the U.S. Supreme Court has traditionally taken to Congress's power to confer jurisdiction on the federal courts.[373]

Illustration 2-81. *P*, a citizen of State *X*, sues *D*, a citizen of State *X*, in a State *X* court. *P* asserts against *D* a claim arising under a federal statute. *P* joins with this federal claim a factually unrelated claim under state law, as permitted by State *X* joinder of claim rules.[374] Congress might wish to allow *D* to "remove"[375] this entire case to federal district court, both to protect the policies supporting the grant of removal jurisdiction under 28 U.S.C. § 1441 *and* to protect the plaintiff, *P*. If *D* is not allowed to remove at least the federal claim, *P* can "trap" *D* in state court by joining a factually unrelated state claim solely to prevent removal under the general removal statutes.[376] If *D* is permitted to remove only the federal claim to federal court, *P* may be treated unfairly. The liberal State *X* joinder of claim rules may be based on a policy of allowing *P* to adjudicate factually unrelated claims in the same action when it will be convenient for *P* to do so. Thus, *P* may have sound reasons of convenience for joining the unrelated claims and may not be joining them simply to prevent removal by *D*. By permitting *D* to remove the entire case, perhaps with discretion in the district court to remand the state claim if *P* does not have good convenience-based reasons for joining it, the policies of removal jurisdiction in

---

371. At common law, it was possible to join factually unrelated claims as long as the claims fell within the same form of action. *See* Chapter 7(A) *infra* ("Joinder of Claims by Plaintiffs at Common Law and in Equity"). Equity courts would permit a defendant to set off a claim arising out of a different transaction or occurrence than the plaintiff's claim, and this equitable practice was later extended to the common-law courts by statute. *See* Chapter 7(D) *infra* ("Joinder of Claims by Defendants at Common Law and in Equity"). The federal courts have actually entertained set-off claims. *See* Richard A. Matasar, *Rediscovering "One Constitutional Case": Procedural Rules and the Rejection of the* Gibbs *Test for Supplemental Jurisdiction*, 71 CAL. L. REV. 1399, 1474-75 (1983). Under the codes, joinder of factually unrelated claims by the plaintiff is permitted when the claims fall within certain legal categories. *See* Chapter 7(B) *infra* ("Joinder of Claims by Plaintiffs under the Codes"). Similarly, code counterclaim joinder practice permits joinder of factually unrelated contract counterclaims in actions in which the plaintiff's claim is also based on contract. *See* Chapter 7(E) *infra* ("Counterclaims and Crossclaims Under the Codes"). Early federal joinder-of-claims practice in common-law cases was governed by the conformity acts, which would have incorporated common-law and code joinder rules prevalent in the states. *See* Chapter 1(D)(10) *supra* ("Early Procedure in the Federal Courts"). Furthermore, the Federal Equity Rules specifically recognized the practice of equitable set off, discussed in Chapter 7. *See* Chapter 7(F) *infra* ("Counterclaims and Crossclaims Under the Federal Rules").

372. *See* U.S. CONST. art. I, § 8, cl. 18.

373. *See* section B(1) *supra* (where the "ingredient theory" propounded by Chief Justice Marshall in Osborn v. Bank of the United States, 22 U.S. (9 Wheat.) 738, 6 L. Ed. 204 (1824), is discussed); *see also* State Farm Fire & Cas. Co. v. Tashire, 386 U.S. 523, 87 S. Ct. 1199, 18 L. Ed. 2d 270 (1967) (incomplete diversity permitted by the U.S. Constitution).

374. *See* FED. R. CIV. P. 18(a) (permitting unlimited joinder of claims).

375. Removal is discussed in section F *infra*.

376. *See* 28 U.S.C. § 1441(a) & (b). These statutes are discussed in section F *infra*.

federal question cases could be protected while also avoiding unfairness to the plaintiff.[377]

Illustration 2-82. *P*, a citizen of State *X*, sues *D*, a citizen of State *X*, in a federal district court in State *X*. *P* asserts a claim for damages against *D* under a federal statute. *D* possesses a permissive counterclaim against *P* arising under state law. By definition, a permissive counterclaim is one that does not arise out of the same facts as the opposing party's claims.[378] Congress might wish to allow *D* to assert this permissive counterclaim in the action against *P* to avoid potential unfairness to *D*. For example, if *P* is insolvent, refusing to allow *D* to assert *D's* state claim in *P's* federal action might, as a practical matter, mean that *D* will never be able to collect the state claim. Delays in the state courts may mean that *P's* claim will be adjudicated in federal court long before *D's* claim is adjudicated in state court. Furthermore, if *P* wins in federal court and collects a judgment from *D*, the funds collected under the federal judgment may be dissipated before *D* wins a judgment against *P* in state court and can collect it. Allowing *D* to join the permissive counterclaim will thus prevent the exercise of federal jurisdiction over *D* from working an unfairness—a purpose that is arguably a necessary and proper incident of establishing federal jurisdiction.

* * * * *

Because Congress might have legitimate policy reasons for conferring pendent or ancillary jurisdiction over factually unrelated nonfederal claims, it is unwise to conclude that the scope of an Article III "case or controversy" can never be extended to such claims. Instead, the determination whether Congress has such power should await each specific instance in which the issue is directly presented.

3. The Statutory Basis of Pendent and Ancillary Jurisdiction

The U.S. Supreme Court has made it clear that the exercise of pendent jurisdiction requires a statutory basis as well as a constitutional one.[379] The Court's earliest modern decisions seemed to stand for the proposition that federal jurisdictional statutes would be presumed to allow the assertion of pendent or ancillary jurisdiction.[380] Although some decisions allowed this presumption to be rebutted,[381] the burden seemed to rest on the party opposing pendent or ancillary jurisdiction to demonstrate that an affirmative statutory policy against the exercise

---

377. *See* 28 U.S.C. § 1441(c). As discussed in section F, *infra*, the policies described in this illustration may, in fact, be the policies that formerly supported "separate and independent" claim removal under 28 U.S.C. § 1441(c). However, as also discussed in section F, the Federal Courts Jurisdiction and Venue Clarification Act of 2011 has amended § 1441(c) to eliminate the ability of a federal court to remove and keep a factually unrelated state claim joined with a federal claim in a state court.

378. *See* FED. R. CIV. P. 13(b).

379. *See* Finley v. United States, 490 U.S. 545, 109 S. Ct. 2003, 104 L. Ed. 2d 593 (1989); Owen Equip. & Erection Co. v. Kroger, 437 U.S. 365, 98 S. Ct. 2396, 57 L. Ed. 2d 274 (1978); Aldinger v. Howard, 427 U.S. 1, 96 S. Ct. 2413, 49 L. Ed. 2d 276 (1976).

380. *See, e.g.*, United Mine Workers v. Gibbs, 383 U.S. 715, 86 S. Ct. 1130, 16 L. Ed. 2d 218 (1966); 1 FEDERAL COURTS STUDY COMMITTEE WORKING PAPERS AND SUBCOMMITTEE REPORTS 549-52 (1990).

381. *See* Owen Equip. & Erection Co. v. Kroger, 437 U.S. 365, 98 S. Ct. 2396, 57 L. Ed. 2d 274 (1978); Aldinger v. Howard, 427 U.S. 1, 96 S. Ct. 2413, 49 L. Ed. 2d 276 (1976).

of jurisdiction existed.[382] In *Finley v. United States*,[383] the Court reversed this burden and required the demonstration of the existence of an affirmative statutory grant of pendent or ancillary jurisdiction before such jurisdiction could be exercised.[384]

Finley involved "pendent party" jurisdiction—*i.e.*, jurisdiction that would, if valid, allow the plaintiff to join a federal claim against one defendant with a factually related state claim in which a separate, nondiverse party is a defendant. While indicating that pendent party jurisdiction would be improper in the absence of an affirmative grant of authority from Congress, the Court in *Finley* did not disturb its previous decisions approving pendent and ancillary claim jurisdiction.[385] Thus, after *Finley*, pendent and ancillary claim jurisdiction was still proper under the general statutory grants of subject-matter jurisdiction in § 1331 and § 1332, even before the recent codification of those doctrines in § 1367.[386]

Illustration 2-83. *P*, a citizen of State *X*, sues *D-1*, a citizen of State *X*, asserting a claim against *D-1* under a federal statute. *P* also joins *D-2*, a citizen of State *X*, in the action. *P* asserts a state claim against *D-1* arising out of the same facts as *P's* federal claim against *D-1*. Under *Finley*, this assertion of pendent party jurisdiction over *D-2* is invalid unless Congress has affirmatively granted authority to the federal courts to hear the claim in the statute that confers federal jurisdiction over *P's* claim against *D-1*. If the jurisdiction is based on 28 U.S.C. § 1331, the assertion of pendent party jurisdiction is invalid, because § 1331 does not affirmatively authorize pendent party jurisdiction.

Illustration 2-84. On the facts of *Illustration 2-83*, the assertion of pendent jurisdiction over the state claim would be proper, even after *Finley*, if *P* asserted a state claim against *D-1* alone arising out of the same facts as *P's* federal claim against *D-1*.

* * * * *

At the statutory level, the policy reasons supporting the doctrine of pendent jurisdiction are different from those supporting ancillary jurisdiction. Pendent jurisdiction is based largely on the fear that if the plaintiff is unable to assert a factually related state claim in a federal question case, the plaintiff might be deterred from asserting the federal claim in federal court.[387] The inability to sue on both claims in federal court would leave the plaintiff with several unacceptable choices.

---

382. *See* 1 FEDERAL COURTS STUDY COMMITTEE WORKING PAPERS AND SUBCOMMITTEE REPORTS 549-52 (1990).

383. 490 U.S. 545, 109 S. Ct. 2003, 104 L. Ed. 2d 593 (1989).

384. *See id.*; 1 FEDERAL COURTS STUDY COMMITTEE WORKING PAPERS AND SUBCOMMITTEE REPORTS 552-53 (1990).

385. *See* 1 FEDERAL COURTS STUDY COMMITTEE WORKING PAPERS AND SUBCOMMITTEE REPORTS 553 (1990). The Court's decision in *Finley* also casts doubt upon ancillary *party* jurisdiction because such jurisdiction is not explicitly authorized by § 1331 and § 1332 of Title 28. *See id.* at 554-55. However, given that the Court drew an explicit distinction between "pendent claim" and "pendent party" jurisdiction, it seems far fetched to assert, as some have, that *Finley* also casts doubt on pendent and ancillary claim jurisdiction. *See id.* at 555-56.

386. As discussed in subsection 4 *infra*, the primary purpose of 28 U.S.C. § 1367 was to overrule *Finley* and thereby render pendent and ancillary party jurisdiction proper.

387. *See, e.g.*, ALI STUDY OF THE DIVISION OF JURISDICTION BETWEEN STATE AND FEDERAL COURTS 209 (1969).

The plaintiff might bring two actions, one in federal court on the federal claim and one in state court on the state claim—with the wasteful duplication of effort and the danger of issue preclusion[388] that dual proceedings entail.[389] Alternatively, the plaintiff might choose to bring both claims in state court to avoid the perils and burdens of dual federal and state proceedings. The result of this choice would be that the policies supporting the creation of subject-matter jurisdiction over federal claims would be undermined by the lack of authority in the federal courts to hear the factually related state claim. If the federal courts have exclusive jurisdiction over the federal claim, the plaintiff might even be induced by the inconvenience of dual actions to abandon the federal claim and sue only on the state claim in state court.[390] Such difficulties have traditionally been thought to justify the exercise of pendent jurisdiction over factually related state claims in federal question cases.

In cases originally brought in federal court, the policies supporting ancillary jurisdiction are different than the policies supporting pendent jurisdiction. By definition, ancillary jurisdiction applies only to claims coming into an action after the plaintiff's original claim. Therefore, there will normally be no danger that anyone will be deterred from resorting to federal court by a denial of ancillary jurisdiction in an original action commenced in federal court. For example, in *Illustrations 2-79* and *2-80*, above, if ancillary jurisdiction were denied over the defendant's compulsory counterclaim, no one would be deterred from resorting to federal court. The plaintiff who invoked jurisdiction would be delighted that the defendant could not assert the counterclaim and might even file in federal court to obtain the benefit of a denial of ancillary jurisdiction. The defendant has no choice but to be in federal court and can do nothing to get the case to a state court to have both claims tried there.[391]

In cases originally commenced in federal district court, ancillary jurisdiction must be based on policies of fairness to the party asserting the ancillary claim. Again, to use the example of ancillary jurisdiction over compulsory counterclaims in *Illustrations 2-79* and *2-80*, if jurisdiction were denied over the counterclaim, the defendant would be subjected to substantial burdens by having to try two actions arising out of the same facts when one would suffice.[392] It is legitimate to interpret the grants of general federal question and diversity

---

388. The danger of issue preclusion exists because the federal and state claims are factually related. Under these circumstances, issues of fact may be adjudicated in the first action that proceeds to judgment. That adjudication also effectively terminates the other action because the losing party will be precluded from relitigating the facts in the second action. Issue preclusion is fully discussed in Chapter 13(C) *infra* ("Issue Preclusion").

389. *See* ALI STUDY OF THE DIVISION OF JURISDICTION BETWEEN STATE AND FEDERAL COURTS 209 (1969).

390. *Cf. id.* at 209-10; 1 FEDERAL COURTS STUDY COMMITTEE WORKING PAPERS AND SUBCOMMITTEE REPORTS 556-58 (1990).

391. In the discussion of removal jurisdiction in section F *infra*, it will be seen that if a defendant is sued in a state court action that the plaintiff could have brought in federal court, the defendant can sometimes remove the action. In cases in which removal is possible, a denial of ancillary jurisdiction to the defendant might deter the defendant from resorting to the right of removal. Thus, in removal cases, the policies supporting pendent and ancillary jurisdiction may conform more closely to each other. However, they do not so conform in actions originally filed in federal court.

392. In Owen Equip. & Erection Co. v. Kroger, 437 U.S. 365, 376, 98 S. Ct. 2396, 2404, 57 L. Ed. 2d 274, 284 (1978), the Supreme Court hinted at this policy of fairness when it stated that ancillary jurisdiction "typically involves claims by a defending party haled into court against his will, or by another person whose rights might be irretrievably lost unless he could assert them in an ongoing action in federal court."

jurisdiction to avoid these burdens on the defendant, who, after all, has not chosen the federal forum.

The differing policy bases of pendent and ancillary jurisdiction may make no difference in the way in which the two doctrines operate.[393] However, when interpreting federal jurisdictional grants, it is important to recognize the limits on the kinds of evils that can be prevented by interpreting the grants one way or the other. It is also important to understand the kinds of policies that support pendent and ancillary jurisdiction, to judge whether Congress has legitimate reasons for expanding those doctrines to new kinds of cases.

4. The Codification of Pendent and Ancillary Jurisdiction

In the Judicial Improvements and Access to Justice Act of 1988, Congress established the Federal Courts Study Committee to study and recommend possible reforms in federal court jurisdiction.[394] In 1990, the Committee published its study, which recommended extensive revisions of federal jurisdiction.[395] The Committee recommended that Congress specifically authorize federal courts "to hear any claim arising out of the same 'transaction or occurrence' as a claim within federal jurisdiction, including claims within federal question jurisdiction, that require the joinder of additional parties, namely, defendants against whom . . . plaintiff has a closely related state claim."[396] In addition to codifying the doctrines of pendent and ancillary claim jurisdiction, this recommendation was designed to overrule the Supreme Court's decision in *Finley v. United States*[397] and thus allow the federal courts to exercise pendent party jurisdiction.[398]

In the Judicial Improvements Act of 1990, Congress responded to the Committee's recommendation by enacting 28 U.S.C. § 1367.[399] Section 1367 combines both pendent and ancillary jurisdiction under the label "supplemental jurisdiction."[400] This approach reflects the Federal Courts Study Committee's belief that no functional difference exists between the two doctrines.[401] The Federal Courts

---

393. Indeed, it has been said that "the distinction between ancillary and pendent jurisdiction has no functional significance and merely confuses matters." 1 FEDERAL COURTS STUDY COMMITTEE WORKING PAPERS AND SUBCOMMITTEE REPORTS 546 (1990). It would seem wise, however, to bear in mind the different policy bases when legislating in the area, so that a grant or restriction of pendent or ancillary authority will be based on policies designed to support or enhance the operation of the basic grants of federal subject-matter jurisdiction.

394. *See* Judicial Improvements and Access to Justice Act of 1988, Pub. L. No. 100-702, §§ 101-109, 102 Stat. 4642, 4644-45.

395. *See generally* REPORT OF THE FEDERAL COURTS STUDY COMMITTEE (1990).

396. *Id.* at 47; *see also* 1 FEDERAL COURTS STUDY COMMITTEE WORKING PAPERS AND SUBCOMMITTEE REPORTS 559-68 (1990).

397. 490 U.S. 545, 109 S. Ct. 2003, 104 L. Ed. 2d 593 (1989).

398. *Finley* and "pendent party" jurisdiction were discussed briefly in subsection 3 *supra*. They are also discussed in Chapter 8(C)(4) *infra* ("Permissive Joinder of Parties").

399. *See* Pub. L. No. 101-650, § 310, 104 Stat. 5089, 5113-14 (codified at 28 U.S.C. § 1367).

400. Note that the enactment of the supplemental jurisdiction statute did not codify the entirety of the doctrine of ancillary jurisdiction that existed prior to the statute, producing a question about whether the uncodified portion has been abolished or survives as a sort of "common law" ancillary jurisdiction. *See, e.g.*, Robb Evans & Assocs., LLC v. Holibaugh, 609 F.3d 359 (4th Cir. 2010) (§ 1367 did not codify all of ancillary jurisdiction, but left some intact as a common law of ancillary jurisdiction, such as ancillary jurisdiction over an action brought by a federally appointed receiver).

401. *See* 1 FEDERAL COURTS STUDY COMMITTEE WORKING PAPERS AND SUBCOMMITTEE REPORTS 546 (1990).

Study Committee recommended that Congress provide for supplemental jurisdiction over any claim arising out of the same transaction or occurrence as a claim within federal jurisdiction.[402] However, Congress did not use that recommended language. Instead, Congress enacted the following provision:

> (a) Except as provided in subsections (b) and (c) or as expressly provided otherwise by Federal statute, in any *civil action* of which the district courts have *original jurisdiction*, the district courts shall have *supplemental jurisdiction over all other claims that* are so related to claims in the action within such original jurisdiction that they *form part of the same case or controversy under Article III of the United States Constitution.* Such supplemental jurisdiction shall include claims that involve the joinder or intervention of additional parties.[403]

The failure of Congress to use the language recommended by the Federal Courts Study Committee in § 1367(a) has produced difficult interpretative problems.[404] In addition, serious interpretive problems also exist with both

---

402. *See* REPORT OF THE FEDERAL COURTS STUDY COMMITTEE 47 (1990). In fact, the working papers of the Committee contained a recommendation as to the precise statutory language that Congress should use:

> (a) Except as provided in subsections (b) and (c) or in another provision of this Title, in any civil action on a claim for which jurisdiction is provided, the district court shall have jurisdiction over all other claims arising out of the same transaction or occurrence, including claims that require the joinder of additional parties.

1 FEDERAL COURTS STUDY COMMITTEE WORKING PAPERS AND SUBCOMMITTEE REPORTS 567 (1990).

403. *See* Judicial Improvements Act of 1990, Pub. L. No. 101-650, § 310, 104 Stat. 5089, 5113-14 (codified at 28 U.S.C. § 1367) (emphasis added). The legislative history of the statute can be found in H.R. REP. NO. 734, 101st Cong., 2d Sess. 27-30 (1990); *Hearing Before the Subcommittee on Courts, Intellectual Property, and the Administration of Justice of the Committee on the Judiciary House of Representatives on H.R. 5381 to Implement Certain Proposals of the Federal Courts Study Committee, and for Other Purposes and H.R. 3898 Civil Justice Reform Act of 1990*, 101st Cong., 2d Sess. 28-32, 87, 92-96, 102, 147, 155-56, 185, 201, 216-17, 224-28, 686-722, 735-36 (1990). In Handberry v. Thompson, 436 F.3d 52 (2d Cir. 2006), the court held that the Prison Litigation Reform Act's restriction on prospective relief to remedy state law violations (18 U.S.C. § 3636(a)(1)(A)) was a "Federal statute" within the meaning of 28 U.S.C. § 1367(a) that "expressly provided" that supplemental jurisdiction over state claims would be limited. *But see* Lindsay v. Government Employees Ins. Co., 448 F.3d 416 (D.C. Cir. 2006) (opt-in class certification provision of the Fair Labor Standards Act did not expressly prohibit exercise of supplemental jurisdiction).

404. The literature on § 1367 is already extensive and reflects the controversy surrounding the drafting and interpretation of the statute. Two early articles discussing the enactment and scope of § 1367 are Thomas M. Mengler et al., *Congress Accepts Supreme Court's Invitation to Codify Supplemental Jurisdiction*, 74 JUDICATURE 213 (1991); David D. Siegel, *Changes in Federal Jurisdiction and Practice Under the New (Dec. 1, 1990) Judicial Improvements Act*, 133 F.R.D. 61, 62-69 (1991). Criticism and defense of the new statute erupted in full, but bitter, flower in the pages of the *Emory Law Journal. See* Richard D. Freer, *Compounding Confusion and Hampering Diversity: Life After* Finley *and the Supplemental Jurisdiction Statute*, 40 EMORY L.J. 445 (1991); Thomas D. Rowe, Jr. et al., *Compounding or Creating Confusion About Supplemental Jurisdiction? A Reply to Professor Freer*, 40 EMORY L.J. 943 (1991); Thomas C. Arthur & Richard D. Freer, *Grasping at Burnt Straws: The Disaster of the Supplemental Jurisdiction Statute*, 40 EMORY L.J. 963 (1991); Thomas D. Rowe, Jr. et al., *A Coda on Supplemental Jurisdiction*, 40 EMORY L.J. 993 (1991); Thomas C. Arthur & Richard D. Freer, *Close Enough for Government Work: What Happens When Congress Doesn't Do Its Job*, 40 EMORY L.J. 1007 (1991). Although the primary antagonists in the debate were Professors Arthur and Freer (for the prosecution) and Professors Burbank, Mengler, and Rowe (for the defense), other voices were soon heard. *See* Erwin Chemerinsky, *Rationalizing Jurisdiction*, 41 EMORY L.J. 3 (1992); Rochelle Cooper Dreyfuss, *The Debate Over § 1367: Defining the Power to Define Federal Judicial Power*, 41 EMORY L.J. 13 (1992); Karen Nelson Moore, *The Supplemental Jurisdiction Statute: An Important But Controversial Supplement to Federal Jurisdiction*, 41 EMORY L.J. 31 (1992); Joan Steinman, *Section 1367—Another Party Heard From*, 41 EMORY L.J. 85 (1992). Useful analyses apart from that combat are found in Marilyn J. Ireland, *Supplemental Jurisdiction Over Claims in Intervention*, 23 N.M. L. REV. 57 (1993); Denis F. McLaughlin, *The Federal Supplemental Jurisdiction Statute—A Constitutional and Statutory Analysis*, 24 ARIZ. ST. L.J. 849 (1992); John B. Oakley, *Recent Statutory Changes in the Law of Federal Jurisdiction and Venue: The Judicial Improvements Acts of 1988 and 1990*, 24 U.C. DAVIS L. REV. 735 (1991); Joan Steinman, *Supplemental Jurisdiction in § 1441 Removed Cases: An Unsurveyed Frontier of Congress'*

§ 1367(b), which contains provisions designed to preserve the policies of the diversity jurisdiction, and § 1367(c), which is designed to guide the district court's discretion in retaining and dismissing supplemental claims. The remainder of this section explores these problems. The subsections below also discuss the American Law Institute's proposed revision of § 1367.

5. The Scope of Supplemental Jurisdiction: Section 1367(a)

(a) The Language of the Statute: "Claim-Specific" or "Action-Specific"

Section 1367 states that "in any civil action of which the district courts have original jurisdiction," the federal district courts shall also have supplemental jurisdiction over "all other claims that are so related to claims in the action within such original jurisdiction" that they form part of the same case or controversy under Article III.[405] This wording suggests an "action-specific" interpretation of § 1367(a).[406] That is, it suggests that before supplemental jurisdiction will be proper, there must *first* be a "civil action"—as opposed to simply a "claim for relief"—within the original jurisdiction of the district courts. Section 1367(a) does not itself confer jurisdiction over the "civil action" that its language seems to require as a prerequisite to supplemental jurisdiction. One must thus refer outside the statute to other jurisdictional provisions, such as 28 U.S.C. § 1331, to satisfy the "action-specific" prerequisite.

This approach seems straightforward enough until one realizes that the *Finley* interpretation governs statutes such as 28 U.S.C. § 1331. *Finley* holds that jurisdictional provisions must explicitly authorize pendent party jurisdiction before such jurisdiction may be permissibly exercised.[407] Because § 1331 does not explicitly authorize pendent party jurisdiction, a civil action commenced under § 1331 by a plaintiff who asserts a federal claim against one nondiverse party and a state claim against another nondiverse party is not within the original jurisdiction of the district courts. Thus, if the courts applied the language of § 1367(a) literally, it would defeat the main purpose of the statute—overruling *Finley*.[408]

Handiwork, 35 ARIZ. L. REV. 305 (1993).

405. 28 U.S.C. § 1367(a).

406. The expressions "action-specific" and "claim-specific" used in the discussion that follows have been adapted from terminology used by Professor John Oakey, the Reporter for the American Law Institute's Federal Judicial Code Revision Project. *See, e.g.*, ALI FEDERAL JUDICIAL CODE REVISION PROJECT at 5 (2004). The ALI's proposed revision is discussed later in this subsection.

407. See the discussion of *Finley* in subsection 3 *supra*.

408. Several commentators expressed fear that § 1367 may be interpreted in accord with its "plain language." *See* Thomas C. Arthur & Richard D. Freer, *Grasping at Burnt Straws: The Disaster of the Supplemental Jurisdiction Statute*, 40 EMORY L.J. 963, 986 (1991); Denis F. McLaughlin, *The Federal Supplemental Jurisdiction Statute—A Constitutional and Statutory Analysis*, 24 ARIZ. ST. L.J. 849, 942 n.480, 973 (1992). However, the statute in its totality cannot be given a "plain meaning" interpretation. Section 1367(a)'s "plain meaning" (as explained above in the text) is that plaintiffs may not join a federal claim against one party with a related state claim against a separate, nondiverse party within the supplemental jurisdiction. Yet, as demonstrated in subsection 6 *infra*, § 1367(b) is specifically aimed at exempting from § 1367(a) multiple claims by plaintiffs against nondiverse parties in diversity actions. If § 1367(a) does not confer supplemental jurisdiction over such claims, § 1367(b) is unnecessary.

Illustration 2-85. *P*, a citizen of State *X*, sues *D-1*, a citizen of State *X*, and *D-2*, a citizen of State *X*, in a U.S. District Court. *P* asserts a claim against *D-1* under a federal statute and a factually related claim against *D-2* under state law. This case is thus like *Finley v. United States*, which 28 U.S.C. § 1367(a) was designed to overrule. However, the wording of § 1367(a), read literally, would not provide for jurisdiction over this action. As a prerequisite to supplemental jurisdiction, § 1367(a) seems to require that there be a "civil action" over which there is original jurisdiction under some provision of the Judicial Code other than § 1367. The action of *P v. D-1 & D-2* is a "civil action," but no original jurisdiction exists over this civil action under other provisions of the Judicial Code, such as 28 U.S.C. § 1331, because those other provisions do not explicitly authorize pendent party jurisdiction.[409]

* * * * *

Even under a literal interpretation, however, § 1367(a) would not be meaningless in isolation. Rather, a literal interpretation would result in a codification of the doctrine of ancillary jurisdiction (including ancillary party jurisdiction). The wording of the statute suggests that once a civil action has been commenced over which there is original jurisdiction, supplemental claims that are sufficiently related to the civil action can then be *added* to the action. The doctrine of ancillary jurisdiction precisely encompassed this situation prior to the enactment of § 1367.[410]

Illustration 2-86. *P*, a citizen of State *X*, sues *D*, a citizen of State *X*, in a U.S. District Court. *P* asserts a claim against *D* under a federal statute. *D's* answer contains a state counterclaim arising out of the same facts as *P's* federal claim. *D* joins *C*, a citizen of State *X*, as an additional party on the state counterclaim as permitted by Federal Rules 13(h) and 20. Under a literal reading of § 1367(a), supplemental jurisdiction would exist over *D's* counterclaim. *P v. D* is a civil action over which there is original jurisdiction under 28 U.S.C. § 1331. Once such an action exists, the last clause of § 1367(a)'s first sentence allows the assertion of an additional claim (*D's* counterclaim) that is part of the same Article III case or controversy as the civil action over which there is original jurisdiction.[411] The second sentence of § 1367(a) permits the joinder of *C* as an additional party on the supplemental claim.[412] Thus, § 1367(a), read literally, would codify and preserve ancillary party jurisdiction.

* * * * *

---

409. There is, of course, a claim for relief in the action over which the district courts would have original jurisdiction if the claim were asserted alone—the claim by *P* against *D-1*. However, the language of § 1367, read literally, would not allow supplemental jurisdiction simply because there is a claim in the case over which the district courts would have original jurisdiction. Rather, the language literally requires a "civil action" over which there is original jurisdiction. The action by *P v. D-1 & D-2* does not qualify as such a civil action. Thus, the initial prerequisite for the operation of § 1367(a) does not seem to be present. *See* James E. Pfander, *Supplemental Jurisdiction and Section 1367: The Case for a Sympathetic Textualism*, 148 U. PA. L. REV. 109, 142 (1999) (agreeing with this text that a literal reading of § 1367 would not overrule *Finley*).

410. In section 1, *supra*, ancillary jurisdiction was described as encompassing claims that come into the action after the plaintiff's original claim or claims.

411. The relevant language of the sentence confers supplemental jurisdiction "over all other claims that are so related to claims in the action within such original jurisdiction that they form part of the same case or controversy under Article III of the United States Constitution." 28 U.S.C. § 1367(a).

412. The second sentence provides that "[s]uch supplemental jurisdiction shall include claims that involve the joinder or intervention of additional parties." *Id.*

Note that the language of § 1367(a) would technically also apply to a case in which the plaintiff first commenced a "civil action" against one nondiverse defendant on a federal claim and then later *amended the complaint* to add a factually related state claim against another nondiverse defendant. There would be original jurisdiction over the first "civil action" under 28 U.S.C. § 1331, and the later state claim would then be added to the action in a manner similar to an ancillary claim. However, in this kind of situation the courts have traditionally insisted that the amended complaint satisfy the same jurisdictional standards as the original complaint. To do otherwise would be to invite evasion of jurisdictional requirements by the simple expedient of amendments adding new parties to an action. Section 1367(a) cannot reasonably be interpreted to have abolished this longstanding practice. Thus, amendments to complaints should still be evaluated for jurisdictional purposes as if they were original complaints, and the courts have continued to do this since the enactment of § 1367.[413]

Note also that the doctrine of pendent claim jurisdiction would continue to operate as an interpretation of statutes such as 28 U.S.C. § 1331, because *Finley* did not purport to disturb the interpretation of statutes permitting pendent claim jurisdiction.

Illustration 2-87. *P*, a citizen of State *X*, sues *D*, a citizen of State *X*, in a U.S. District Court. *P* asserts a claim against *D* under a federal statute and a factually related state claim. Pendent claim jurisdiction exists over *P's* state claim against *D* under 28 U.S.C. § 1331 without the need to resort to 28 U.S.C. § 1367(a). As discussed in subsection 4*(c)*, above, *Finley* does not affect the validity of pendent *claim* jurisdiction.

* * * * *

Of course, interpreting § 1367(a) as exclusively a codification of ancillary jurisdiction would break down when one reaches § 1367(b), which is framed in such a fashion as to deny jurisdiction over certain claims *by plaintiffs* that violate the policies of the diversity jurisdiction. If § 1367(a) had been designed only to codify ancillary jurisdiction, there would be no need for § 1367(b), because ancillary jurisdiction does not apply to original claims by plaintiffs. In addition, a literal interpretation of 28 U.S.C. § 1367(a) that would allow only pendent claim jurisdiction in federal question cases would defeat the primary purpose of the statute, which was to overrule *Finley v. United States* and authorize pendent party jurisdiction. Therefore, it was clear from the beginning that the statute could not be read literally. Instead, it seemed likely that it would have to be interpreted as if it read "in any civil action in which a claim is asserted over which the district courts would have original jurisdiction if that claim were asserted alone, the district courts shall have supplemental jurisdiction over all other claims that are so related to

---

413. *See, e.g.*, Sta-Rite Indus., Inc. v. Allstate Ins. Co., 96 F.3d 281 (7th Cir. 1996); Wellness Cmty.-Nat'l v. Wellness House, 70 F.3d 46 (7th Cir. 1995); *cf.* R.F. Barron Corp. v. Nuclear Fields (Austl.) Pty. Ltd., No. 91 C 7610, 1992 U.S. Dist. LEXIS 9612 (N.D. Ill. July 6, 1992) (diversity jurisdiction cannot be created where there is none by the simple expedient of amendments adding nondiverse defendants to the action); *cf.* Pintando v. Miami-Dade Hous. Agency, 501 F.3d 1241 (11th Cir. 2007) (when an amendment to a pleading eliminates the federal claim that gives the district court original jurisdiction, the court may not exercise supplemental jurisdiction over any remaining related state law claims).

claims within the original jurisdiction that they form part of the same case or controversy under Article III." Such a reading would conform to the legislative history of the statute, even though it would not conform to its wording.[414]

(b) The Interpretation of the Statute: "Claim-Specific" or "Action-Specific" or Both?

Before the Supreme Court's resolution of the statute's interpretation in 2005, the vast majority of federal courts did, indeed, interpret § 1367(a) in a "claim specific" fashion.[415] However, the interpretations cannot be said to have completely recognized all of the problems that the language of the statute presents, and there was some reluctance to resort to the legislative history of the statute as a justification for the "claim specific" interpretation.

In *City of Chicago v. International College of Surgeons*,[416] the U.S. Supreme Court indirectly endorsed a "claim-specific" view of § 1367(a), but it did not resolve the statute's interpretive problems comprehensively. In *City of Chicago*, the defendants removed state actions to federal court in which the plaintiffs were seeking judicial review of decisions made by the Chicago Landmark Commission. The actions contained claims that certain city ordinances violated the federal and state constitutions and also sought judicial review of the Landmarks Commission's decisions under the ordinances on the record of the Commission, a type of review known as "deferential review." The U.S. District Court to which the action was removed ruled in favor of the City, but the Seventh Circuit reversed.

The Seventh Circuit held that the district court did not have subject-matter jurisdiction over an action for deferential review of a state agency decision. The Seventh Circuit reasoned that such review involved an appellate function that is

---

414. *See* H.R. REP. NO. 734, 101st Cong., 2d Sess. 28-29 (1990) ("[Section 1367(a)] generally authorizes the district court to exercise jurisdiction over a supplemental claim whenever it forms part of the same constitutional case or controversy as the claim or claims that provide the basis of the district court's original jurisdiction").

415. Many courts simply transform the language of § 1367(a) to eliminate the expression "civil action" and substitute the term "claim" or an equivalent expression. *See, e.g.*, Detroit Edison Co. v. Michigan Dep't of Envtl. Quality, 29 F. Supp. 2d 786 (E.D. Mich. 1998) (once district court has original jurisdiction over a claim, it may exercise supplemental jurisdiction over all other claims that are so related to that claim as to form part of the same case or controversy under Article III); Miller Parts Co. v. Joe Self Chevrolet, Inc., No. 93-1035-PFK, 1993 WL 246071, 1993 U.S. Dist. LEXIS 9700 (D. Kan. June 14, 1993) (§ 1367 gives district courts supplemental jurisdiction over all state claims which are related to claims over which the court has original jurisdiction); Leith v. Lufthansa German Airlines, 793 F. Supp. 808 (N.D. Ill. 1992) (once jurisdiction over the main claim is established, the statute mandates that the district court shall have supplemental jurisdiction over all other claims that are so related to claims in the action within such original jurisdiction as to form part of the same case or controversy under Article III); *see also* David D. Siegel, *Changes in Federal Jurisdiction and Practice Under the New (Dec. 1, 1990) Judicial Improvements Act*, 133 F.R.D. 61, 65 (1991) (under § 1367(a), as long as a district court has original jurisdiction of a claim, it shall have supplemental jurisdiction over the related claims). Other courts simply ignore the significance of the phrase "civil action" and interpret the statute in a claim-specific fashion. *See, e.g.*, Stromberg Metal Works, Inc. v. Press Mech., Inc., 77 F.3d 928 (7th Cir. 1996) (§ 1367(a) provides that district courts shall have supplemental jurisdiction over all other claims that are so related to claims in the action within such original jurisdiction that they form part of the same case or controversy within Article III); Free v. Abbott Labs., 51 F.3d 524 (5th Cir. 1995) (§ 1367 grants district courts jurisdiction over related claims generally). Note, however, that the courts have not been willing to allow removal of a case from state court based on a relationship between the claim in the state action and a claim in an action already pending in federal court. Supplemental jurisdiction requires that the freestanding and supplemental claims be joined in the same action. *See, e.g.*, Halmekangas v. State Farm Fire & Cas. Co., 603 F.3d 290 (5th Cir. 2010).

416. 522 U.S. 156, 118 S. Ct. 523, 139 L. Ed. 2d 525 (1997).

inconsistent with the function of a court of original jurisdiction. Thus, the action was not a "civil action" within the district court's "original jurisdiction" under the removal statute, 28 U.S.C. § 1441(a). The U.S. Supreme Court reversed. It held that the district court had original jurisdiction over the federal claims and could exercise supplemental jurisdiction over the state claims under § 1367(a). The Court's language seemed to adopt the claim-specific interpretation of § 1367(a) described above:

> [O]nce the case was removed, the District Court had original jurisdiction over ICS's claim arising under federal law, and thus could exercise supplemental jurisdiction over the accompanying state law claims so long as those claims constitute "other claims that . . . form part of the same case or controversy." [28 U.S.C.] § 1367(a). We think it's clear that they do.[417]

Despite the suggestive language of the *City of Chicago* opinion, it was essentially a pendent-claim case.[418] As noted above,[419] § 1367(a) did not alter the status of pendent claim jurisdiction, which operates the same way after its codification in § 1367(a) as it did before codification. Putting it differently, in simple pendent-claim cases, there is a "claim" within the jurisdiction of the district courts under § 1331, and there is also a "civil action" within federal jurisdiction under § 1331. Therefore, whether a "claim-specific" or "action-specific" interpretation of § 1367 is adopted, supplemental jurisdiction exists in pendent-claim cases.

Illustration 2-88. *P*, a citizen of State *X*, sues *D*, a citizen of State *X*, in a U.S. District Court of State *X*. *P* asserts a claim for relief under a federal statute and a factually related claim for relief under state law. *P's* action against *D* is an example of pendent-claim jurisdiction. If § 1367(a) requires the entire "civil action" that *P* has commenced against *D* to be within the original jurisdiction of the district court under some provision of the Judicial Code other than § 1367(a), the requirement is satisfied. Under the Supreme Court's interpretation of 28 U.S.C. § 1331 existing before § 1367(a) was enacted, there is original jurisdiction over *P's* entire action.[420] Of course, if § 1367(a) only requires a federal claim over which there would be original jurisdiction in order to confer supplemental jurisdiction over *P's* related state claim against *D*, that requirement is also satisfied: *P's* federal claim would be within the original jurisdiction of the district court under 28 U.S.C. § 1331 if it were asserted alone.

* * * * *

A truly authoritative determination of whether § 1367(a) embodied an "action-specific" or a "claim-specific" interpretation had to await a case involving multiple party joinder. As noted above,[421] § 1367(a) was specifically designed to overrule *Finley v. United States*. The *Finley* rule governs the exercise of pendent

---

417. *Id.* at 165, 118 S. Ct. at 530, 139 L. Ed. 2d at 535-36.

418. Although there were two plaintiffs and multiple defendants in the case, which involved several consolidated actions, the plaintiffs were asserting the same federal and state claims in both actions, and the court treated the defendants as a single entity, designating them "the City." *See id.* at 161, 118 S. Ct. at 527, 139 L. Ed. 2d at 533. Thus, the case is indistinguishable from a single-plaintiff, single-defendant case.

419. *See* subsection 4 *supra*.

420. *See* subsection 3, *Illustration 2-84, supra*.

421. *See* subsection 4 *supra*.

party jurisdiction under § 1331 and other federal question jurisdiction statutes.[422] Therefore, pendent party cases directly present the "action-specific-claim-specific" question. However, diversity actions involving multiple party joinder under Federal Rules 19 and 20 and class actions under Rule 23 also present this question.

Before 2005, only a few federal courts recognized that § 1367's language required original jurisdiction over a "civil action" as a prerequisite to the exercise of supplemental jurisdiction, and, for the most part, those cases did not recognize the full implications of the statute's wording.[423] Furthermore, as noted earlier, many cases in which the interpretive issue might have been raised simply ignored the significance of the "civil action" language of the statute.[424] A notable exception is the decision of the Tenth Circuit in *Leonhardt v. Western Sugar Co.*[425] In *Leonhardt*, the Tenth Circuit was reacting to certain decisions of the Fifth and Seventh Circuits under Federal Rule 23 and 28 U.S.C. § 1367(b).[426] These decisions interpreted § 1367(b) expansively, but ignored the wording of § 1367(a). The Tenth Circuit responded, as follows:

> In our view, a literal and textually faithful reading of § 1367(a) leads to the opposite conclusion from that of the Fifth and Seventh Circuits. Section 1367(a) specifically addresses "any civil action of which the district courts have *original jurisdiction*." . . . It then provides for *supplemental jurisdiction* over transactionally related claims. Section 1332 is what confers original jurisdiction over diversity cases and it expressly requires that the "matter in controversy exceed[] the sum or value of $75,000." . . . Thus, Congress in § 1367(a) expressly excepted claims brought under § 1332 and its well-understood definition of "matter in controversy." . . .[427]

The court's literal reading of § 1367(a) corresponded closely to the literal reading described in the text, above. The result of the court's literal interpretation of § 1367(a) was to avoid a difficult problem of interpretation under § 1367(b). However, the court in *Leonhardt* failed to see that a literal "action-specific"

---

422. *See Illustration 2-83 supra.*

423. *See* Moore v. Rosenthal & Schanfield, P.C., No. 92 C 7460, 1992 WL 346422, 1992 U.S. Dist. LEXIS 17874 (N.D. Ill. Nov. 19, 1992) ("By its own terms the statute applies only 'in any civil action of which the district courts have original jurisdiction' and only then may the case-or-controversy claims be added in the action"); ZB Holdings, Inc. v. White, 144 F.R.D. 42, 47 (S.D.N.Y. 1992) ("The fundamental question for this [c]ourt to resolve is what the term 'original jurisdiction' means in . . . this statute. . . . This [c]ourt understands 'original jurisdiction' to mean jurisdiction in the first instance over a viable lawsuit, without regard to parties to be joined later. Stated differently, the term 'original jurisdiction' presupposes a viable lawsuit"); *cf.* Noble v. White, 996 F.2d 797, 799 (5th Cir. 1993) (district court has supplemental jurisdiction over state claims that are part of the same case or controversy over which the district court has original jurisdiction).

424. The interpretive issue would be central to the typical pendent parties jurisdiction case. *See, e.g.*, Stromberg Metal Works, Inc. v. Press Mech., Inc., 77 F.3d 928 (7th Cir. 1996); Free v. Abbott Labs., 51 F.3d 524 (5th Cir. 1995); Godfrey v. Perkin-Elmer Corp., 794 F. Supp. 1179 (D.N.H. 1992); Arnold v. Kimberly Quality Care Nursing Serv., 762 F. Supp. 1182 (M.D. Pa. 1991).

425. 160 F.3d 631 (10th Cir. 1998).

426. *See* Stromberg Metal Works, Inc. v. Press Mech., Inc., 77 F.3d 928 (7th Cir. 1996); Free v. Abbott Labs., 51 F.3d 524 (5th Cir. 1995); Chapter 8(D) *infra* ("Special Joinder Devices").

427. 160 F.3d at 640. Out of caution, the court went on to examine the legislative history of § 1367, which it found to support the same result produced by its textual analysis. *Leonhardt* was followed by the Third Circuit Court of Appeals in Meritcare, Inc. v. St. Paul Mercury Ins. Co., 166 F.3d 214 (3d Cir. 1999); *see also* City of San Francisco v. Hartford Life Ins. Co., No. C99-0225 CRB ARB, 1999 WL 354522 (N.D. Cal. May 17, 1999).

interpretation of § 1367(a) would undermine the central purpose of the statute to overrule the Supreme Court's *Finley* decision and codify the doctrine of pendent-party jurisdiction.[428]

In *Exxon Mobil Corp. v. Allapattah Services, Inc.*,[429] the Supreme Court addressed the "civil action" language in § 1367(a) as part of an opinion concerned primarily with two issues under § 1367(b) (discussed in subsection 4*(f)* and in Chapter 8, below). *Exxon Mobil* involved two diversity actions consolidated before the court. The cases posed aggregation questions under § 1332 's requirement that more than $75,000 be in controversy. One action was a class action under Rule 23 in which some of the class members met the amount-in-controversy requirement but others did not. The other action involved a permissive joinder of plaintiffs under Rule 20, in which one of the plaintiffs independently met the amount-in-controversy requirement, but the other plaintiffs did not. Thus, in both cases, the issue was whether § 1367 had eliminated the traditional restrictions on aggregation discussed in section D(7)*(b)* of the text, above. An exception would be created to the traditional aggregation rules if (1) § 1367(a) provided for supplemental jurisdiction over the claims not meeting the amount-in-controversy requirement independently and (2) § 1367(b) did not override the conferral of supplemental jurisdiction and restore the amount-in-controversy requirement on the facts of the two cases. As part of its inquiry into the first question, the Court examined the "civil action" language of § 1367(a) discussed in this subsection of the text.

In an opinion written by Justice Kennedy, the Court concluded that when the district courts have original jurisdiction over one claim in an action, § 1367(a) confers supplemental jurisdiction over all other claims in a diversity action that do not meet the jurisdictional requirements independently because they do not satisfy the amount-in-controversy requirement. In drawing this conclusion, Justice Kennedy eschewed reliance on the legislative history of the statute,[430] which indicated that in both Rule 20 and Rule 23 joinder situations, the intent of Congress was to retain the traditional restrictive aggregation rules discussed in section D(7)*(b)*, above.[431] The opinion stated that

> [w]hen the well-pleaded complaint contains at least one claim that satisfies the amount-in-controversy requirement, *and there are no other relevant jurisdictional defects*, the district court,

---

428. Likewise, as observed in the text above, a literal interpretation of § 1367(a) would collide with the language of § 1367(b). This point is explored further in subsection 6 *infra* and in Chapter 8 in conjunction with an examination of jurisdictional problems under the multiple-party joinder provisions of the Federal Rules of Civil Procedure. Even though the federal courts have generally interpreted § 1367(a) in a nonliteral, or "claim-specific," fashion, they have not altogether ignored the phrases "in any civil action" and "in the action" in the statute. They have universally insisted that supplemental jurisdiction can only be exercised over state claims joined in the same action with federal claims, as opposed to state claims that are factually related to federal claims, but which are asserted in a completely separate state proceeding that the defendant is trying to remove to federal court. *See, e.g.*, Ortolf v. Silver Bar Mines, 111 F.3d 85 (9th Cir. 1997); Ahern v. Charter Twp., 100 F.3d 451 (6th Cir. 1996); George v. Borden Chems. & Plastics Operating Ltd. P'ship, 960 F. Supp. 92 (M.D. La. 1997); Emerson Power Transmission Corp. v. Roller Bearing Co. of Am., 922 F. Supp. 1306 (N.D. Ind. 1996); *In re* Estate of Tabas, 879 F. Supp. 464 (E.D. Pa. 1995); Veeder v. Omaha Tribe, 864 F. Supp. 889 (N.D. Iowa 1994); Holt v. Lockheed Support Sys., Inc., 835 F. Supp. 325 (W.D. La. 1993); Zewe v. Law Firm of Adams & Reese, 852 F. Supp. 516 (E.D. La. 1993).

429. 545 U.S. 546, 125 S. Ct. 2611, 162 L. Ed. 2d 502 (2005).

430. *Id.* at 567-71, 125 S. Ct. at 2625-27, 162 L. Ed 2d at 526-28.

431. *See also* Chapter 8(C)(4)*(b)* & D(4)*(c)*, *infra*.

> beyond all question, has original jurisdiction over that claim. The presence of other claims in the complaint, over which the district court may lack original jurisdiction, is of no moment. If the court has original jurisdiction over a single claim in the complaint, it has original jurisdiction over a "civil action" within the meaning of § 1367(a), even if the civil action over which it has jurisdiction comprises fewer claims than were included in the complaint. Once the court determines it has original jurisdiction over the civil action, it can turn to the question whether it has a constitutional and statutory basis for exercising supplemental jurisdiction over the other claims in the action.[432]

Although this interpretation of § 1367(a) is consistent with the "claim specific" interpretation that Congress intended, as an exercise in textual exegesis, it is unpersuasive.[433] As pointed out above, the terms "civil action" and "claim for relief" are not coterminous in the law of federal procedure. The quoted passage from the majority opinion does not attempt to show otherwise. The explanation for the majority's *ipse dixit* is that if it had departed from a pure textual approach to interpretation and relied on congressional intent and the materials comprising the legislative history of § 1367, it could not have reached the later conclusions that it did with regard to the provisions of § 1367(b) that were the main focus of the opinion.

It is also clear that Justice Kennedy means, by the qualifying statement "and there are no other relevant jurisdictional defects," to eliminate from the reach of § 1367(a) cases involving incomplete diversity of citizenship, allowing only supplemental jurisdiction over claims involving an inadequate amount in controversy. Throughout his opinion for the majority, Justice Kennedy attempted to draw a distinction between the aggregation requirement of § 1332 and the complete diversity requirement, with the intent of preserving the latter. He explained this in terms of the "contamination theory." That is, defects in jurisdictional amount did not, under § 1367(a) "contaminate" the entire case and prevent supplemental jurisdiction from attaching to the jurisdictionally insufficient claim. However, defects in diversity of citizenship do "contaminate" the case, preventing supplemental jurisdiction from operating under § 1367(a) over claims against non-diverse parties.[434] In effect, this read § 1367(a) as "claim-specific" with regard to jurisdictional amount problems and as "action-specific" with regard to incomplete

---

432. *Id.* at 559, 125 S. Ct. at 2620-21, 162 L. Ed. 2d at 521.

433. *See generally* Shawn Doyle, Note, *Weaving the Cloth of Supplemental Jurisdiction: The Role of Dialogue in Tailoring Judicial Power* (Exxon Mobil Corp. v. Allapattah Servs., Inc., 126 S. Ct. 2611 (2005)), 82 NOTRE DAME L. REV. 843 (2006); Note, *The Supreme Court, 2004 Term,* 119 HARV. L. REV. 28, 317-27 (2005) (criticizing *Allapattah*). The "common and undivided interest" test will still apply if no plaintiff's claim satisfies the amount requirement, because there must exist at least one claim that satisfies subject-matter jurisdiction requirements for § 1367(a) to provide supplemental jurisdiction over all other claims that are factually related. *Cf.* Everett v. Verizon Wireless, Inc., 460 F.3d 818 (6th Cir. 2006) (plaintiff's claims for unjust enrichment and punitive damages could not be aggregated because they did not meet the "common and undivided interest" test; in removed action, the cost of complying with an injunction could not be used to satisfy the requirement because defendant did not make an adequate showing that its costs of compliance would meet the requirement).

434. *See* 545 U.S. at 562, 125 S. Ct. at 2622, 162 L. Ed. 2d at 523.

diversity problems.[435] However, a distinction between the aggregation and complete diversity requirements cannot be justified on the basis of the text of either § 1332 or § 1367, because the text of neither statute textually treats one kind of problem as more fundamental than the other.[436] Since there is no apparent textual difference between supplemental jurisdiction over claims by or against non-diverse parties and supplemental jurisdiction over claims not meeting the amount-in-controversy requirement, the distinction drawn by Justice Kennedy is simply incoherent as textual exegesis.

In addition, the majority opinion was disingenuous in the way in which it dealt with the impact of § 1367(a) on the *Finley* decision. As indicated above, the opinion specifically rejected resort to the legislative history of the statute. However, this left the majority with the problem of how to deal with *Finley* under the language of the statute. Would it conclude that the presence of a pendent, non-diverse party in a federal question case would fit within the "claim-specific" rationale that it applied to aggregation problems? Or would it treat the pendent party jurisdiction the way in which it treated incomplete diversity of citizenship and conclude that the presence of the pendent party "contaminated" the entire action? In fact, Justice Kennedy avoided the problem of discussing the statutory language as applied to *Finley* by simply stating that "[a]ll parties to this litigation and all courts to consider the question agree that § 1367 overturned the result in *Finley*"[437] The difficulty with Justice Kennedy's statement is that it is not possible to know that the purpose of the statute was to overturn *Finley* without resort to something other than the text of the statute. The statute, of course, does not mention *Finley*. In addition, as observed above, when one limits the process of interpretation to the text of the statute, § 1367(a) standing alone is most sensibly read as a perfect codification of the doctrine of ancillary jurisdiction. Thus, Justice Kennedy's statement was an artifice designed to avoid having to consider whether a non-diverse pendent party would "contaminate" an action in a federal question case in the same manner that it would in a pure diversity case.[438]

---

435. Justice Kennedy attempted to justify this conclusion by pointing to 28 U.S.C. § 1331 and the Court's prior interpretation of that statute as allowing pendent jurisdiction. He argued that an "indivisibility," or "contamination," theory that would destroy jurisdiction over cases involving claims insufficient in amount under § 1332 would make no sense, given that under § 1331 a factually related state claim does not destroy jurisdiction over a case involving a jurisdictionally sufficient federal claim. However, this ignores the structure of § 1367(a). As observed in the text above, the "civil action" language of the latter statute refers outside § 1367(a) to other statutes conferring subject matter jurisdiction. In the case of § 1331, the statute and its prior interpretation by the Court confer jurisdiction over an entire civil action containing factually related federal and state claims. The presence of the state claim does not destroy jurisdiction. However, in the case of § 1332, factually related state claims that are jurisdictionally deficient do destroy jurisdiction over the case (until the deficient claims are dismissed) under the Court's prior interpretations of the statute. If this makes no sense, it is because the Court has not found the policies of §§ 1331 & 1332 to be identical in its prior interpretations of those statutes. In addition, Justice Kennedy ignores the fact that in cases of defects in diversity, his interpretation does destroy jurisdiction over the entire case under § 1332. This preserves the very indivisibility theory that he rejects under § 1331, but only for part of § 1332.

436. It should be noted that the grant of diversity jurisdiction has contained an amount in controversy restriction from the Judiciary Act of 1789 forward, and both the restrictive aggregation rules and the complete diversity requirement are judicial interpretations of the statute that do not appear on the face of the text and never have.

437. 545 U S. at 558, 125 S. Ct. at 2620, 162 L. Ed. 2d at 520.

438. This may be considered too harsh by some readers, especially since Justice Ginsburg, in dissent, adopted the "action-specific" interpretation of § 1367(a) discussed in the text above, but also stated that "[s]ection 1367, all agree, was designed to overturn this Court's decision in *Finley* . . . ." *Id.* at 577, 125 S. Ct. at 2361, 162 L. Ed. 2d at 532 (Ginsburg, J., with whom Stevens, J., O'Connor, J., & Bryer, J., joined, dissenting). In Justice

Exxon Mobil was a 5-4 decision. The observations about *Finley* and the "contamination theory" as applied to defects in diversity were unnecessary to the decision of the case. Given the illogic of the Court's justifications, it is possible that the decision will turn out to be unstable and will have to be reconsidered. Nevertheless, decisions in the lower federal courts after *Exxon Mobil* indicate that the claim specific interpretation of § 1367(a) applied to jurisdictional amount problems will not be applied to defects in diversity of citizenship.

In *Merrill Lynch & Co. v. Allegheny Energy, Inc.*,[439] the plaintiff failed to join a non-diverse Rule 19(a) party in the action.[440] The district court ordered joinder of the party, aligned it as a defendant, and exercised supplemental jurisdiction over the claim against it under § 1367(a) prior to *Exxon Mobil*. The court of appeals, after the decision in *Exxon Mobil*, held this to be error. The court stated that under the "contamination theory" of *Exxon Mobil*, a defect in diversity involving a Rule 19(a) party prevents the exercise of supplemental jurisdiction. The court explained:

> The Supreme Court [in *Exxon Mobil*] does not define the reach of the contamination theory and does not purport to announce a new standard for assessing diversity defects but instead relies on the Court's consistent construction of the complete diversity rule. . . . However, even if we read *Exxon* as preserving certain well-established exceptions to the complete diversity rule . . . [the Rule 19(a) party's] joinder does not fall within any such exception.[441]

Similarly, in *Picciotto v. Continental Casualty Co.*,[442] the district court dismissed the action because of failure to join an indispensable, non-diverse party. On appeal, the plaintiffs argued that it was permissible to exercise supplemental jurisdiction over the non-diverse party under the language of § 1367(b) as long as the plaintiffs did not assert a claim against the party once the party was joined as a defendant, a theory discussed in Chapter 8 of this text.[443] The court of appeals disagreed, holding that § 1367(b) is irrelevant because of the "contamination theory" of *Exxon Mobil*. Under that theory, the court held, failure to join an indispensable, non-diverse party fails the § 1367(a) threshold test by eliminating any "suit" over which the district court has original jurisdiction. Thus, the result was produced by Justice Kennedy's schizophrenic distinction between the need for a "civil action," or "suit," over which the district court has original jurisdiction insofar as complete diversity is concerned, and the mere need for a "claim" over

---

Ginsburg's case, the statement allowed her to avoid considering the literal effect of an "action-specific" interpretation of the statute on *Finley*. Had such an effect been considered, she would not have been able to conclude that *Finley* was overruled under the language of the statute and would have had to adopt a "claim-specific" reading to avoid undermining the principal purpose of the provision. Whether dishonesty or incompetence is a harsher judgment about the opinions in the case we will leave for others to decide. It is one or the other.

439. 500 F.3d 171 (2d Cir. 2007).

440. Rule 19 is examined in Chapter 8(C)(3) *infra* ("Joinder of Claims Needed for Just Adjudication").

441. 500 F.3d at 179. However, the court went on to hold that the Rule 19(a) party was not indispensable under Rule 19(b) and could be dropped as a party under Rule 21 to preserve diversity.

442. 512 F.3d 9 (1st Cir. 2008).

443. *See* Chapter 8(C)(3)*(c)* *infra* ("Problems of Subject-Matter Jurisdiction, Personal Jurisdiction, and Venue Under Rule 19").

which the district court has original jurisdiction insofar as jurisdictional amount is concerned.[444]

Justice Kennedy's opinion in *Exxon Mobil* also stated that the recent enactment of the Class Action Fairness Act, discussed in section D(7)*(b)* of this text, above, and in Chapter 8, had no bearing on his analysis of the issues in the *Exxon Mobil* case.[445] However, as also discussed in section D(7)*(b)*, it is now possible under the language of the aggregation provision of the Class Action Fairness Act, which states that the provision applies "in any class action,"[446] that class actions not appropriate for diversity jurisdiction under the old "common and undivided interest" test for aggregation will now fall within the diversity jurisdiction, even though they are for an aggregate amount less than the new Act's $5,000,000 amount-in-controversy requirement. This fact raises the question whether other restrictions in the new Act should be applied to such actions. Alternatively, it raises the question whether the new Act should be interpreted as the exclusive provision governing diversity class actions, with the result that actions for less than $5,000,000 may not be brought in or removed to federal court at all, even though aggregation in some such actions is, after *Exxon Mobil,* easier than under the old common-and-undivided-interest test.[447] For example, will the $5,000,000 amount-in-controversy requirement under the new Act now prevent a class action from being brought in or removed to federal court when the representative party's claim exceeds $75,000, the class members' claims do not, but the aggregate amount of all class claims is less than $5,000,000? This problem is discussed further in Chapter 8(D)(4)*(c)*.

Apart from the potential effect of the Class Action Fairness Act, it is important to remember that *Exxon Mobil* does not entirely eliminate the restrictive aggregation rules discussed in section D(7)*(b)*. There must be at least one claim in the action that meets the amount-in-controversy requirement before § 1367(a) can operate in accord with the *Exxon Mobil* interpretation. Thus, for example, in a case in which no plaintiff (in a multiple plaintiff action) possesses a claim that meets the amount requirement, the old common-and-undivided-interest test will still control aggregation, because § 1367(a) requires at least one claim in the action that independently meets the amount-in-controversy requirement before other claims can be aggregated with the jurisdiction-conferring claim.[448]

---

444. *See also In re* Lorazepam & Clorazepate Antitrust Litig., 631 F.3d 537 (D.C. Cir. 2011) (following the contamination theory of *Exxon Mobil*).

445. *See Exxon Mobil,* 545 U.S. at 571-72, 125 S. Ct. at 2627-28, 162 L. Ed. 2d at 529.

446. *See* 28 U.S.C. § 1332(d)(6).

447. *See also* Stephen B. Burbank, *Litigation Reform Since the PSLRA: A Ten-Year Retrospective: Panel Four: Class Action Fairness Act: Aggregation on the Couch: The Strategic Uses of Ambiguity and Hypocrisy,* 106 COLUM. L. REV. 1924 (2006) (criticizing Nagareda and Issacharoff articles, below); Samuel Issacharoff, *Settled Expectations in a World of Unsettled Law: Choice of Law After the Class Action Fairness Act,* 106 COLUM. L. REV. 1839 (2006); Richard A. Nagareda, *Aggregation and its Discontents: Class Settlement Pressure, Class-Wide Arbitration, and CAFA,* 106 COLUM. L. REV. 1872 (2006).

448. *See* Oshana v. Coca-Cola Co., 472 F.3d 506 (7th Cir. 2006) (plaintiff-representative of class refused to admit that she could not recover more than $75,000, making removal proper; court's discussion makes it clear that aggregation would be improper if representative could not recover more than $75,000); Lovell v. State Farm Mut. Auto. Ins. Co., 466 F.3d 893 (10th Cir. 2006) (class members cannot aggregate unless they are uniting to enforce a single title or right unless one class member's claim is for more than $75,000); *see also* Shawn Doyle, Note, *Weaving the Cloth of Supplemental Jurisdiction: The Role of Dialogue in Tailoring Judicial Power,* 82 NOTRE DAME L. REV. 843 (2006) (discussing *Exxon Mobil*); Gunnar Gundersen, Note, *The Wrath of* Zahn: *The Supreme Court's Requiem for "Sympathetic Textualism,"* 34 PEPP. L. REV. 835 (2007). On a related issue, the

It is possible that Congress may again address the question of supplemental jurisdiction in order to resolve the "claim-specific-action-specific" dilemma textually. The American Law Institute has proposed a revision of § 1367 that would explicitly make the supplemental jurisdiction statute "claim-specific":

> § 1367. Supplemental jurisdiction
>
> (a) *Definitions*. As used in this section:
>
> (1) A "freestanding" claim means a claim for relief that is within the original jurisdiction of the district courts independently of this section.
>
> (2) A "supplemental" claim means a claim for relief, not itself freestanding, that is part of the same case or controversy under Article III of the Constitution as a freestanding claim that is asserted in the same civil action.
>
> . . . .
>
> (b) *General grant of supplemental jurisdiction.* Except as provided by subsection (c) or as otherwise expressly provided by statute, a district court shall have original jurisdiction of all supplemental claims, including claims that involve the joinder or intervention of additional claiming or defending parties.[449]

If Congress follows the ALI's recommendation and adopts this revision, § 1367(a) would, through introduction of the concept of a freestanding claim, make the operation of supplemental jurisdiction depend explicitly on the presence in a federal action of a claim over which the federal courts would have subject-matter jurisdiction independently of § 1367. Supplemental claims would, by definition, be claims asserted in the same civil action as a freestanding claim, but over which the district courts would not have subject-matter jurisdiction independently of § 1367—*i.e.*, under some other provision of the Judicial Code. If these supplemental claims are part of the same Article III case or controversy as a freestanding claim, § 1367(b) would confer jurisdiction over them. This revision would thus textually validate a "claim-specific" approach to supplemental jurisdiction.[450]

Second Circuit Court of Appeals considered the application of §1367 to a copyright action brought under federal law. The court held that a requirement in the federal Copyright Act that an infringement suit may not be brought until preregistration or registration of the copyright was jurisdictional. The court then held that this requirement applied to each claim within a purported class and thus required each class member's claim to arise out of a registered copyright. Section 1367 did not allow supplemental jurisdiction over jurisdictionally insufficient federal claims joined with jurisdictionally sufficient federal claims. This was because § 1367(a) excepts from its reach jurisdictionally insufficient claims related to jurisdictionally sufficient claims when "expressly provided otherwise by federal statute." The court interpreted the restriction in the copyright act to be a federal statute that "provide[s] otherwise" within the meaning of § 1367(a). The court observed that the restriction in the Copyright Act was another "relevant jurisdictional defect[ ]" of the sort to which the Supreme Court alluded in *Exxon Mobil*. *See In re* Literary Works in Elec. Databases Copyright Litig., 509 F.3d 116 (2d Cir. 2007).

449. ALI FEDERAL JUDICIAL CODE REVISION PROJECT § 1367, at 13 (2004).

450. The ALI has made other suggestions for improvements in § 1367. These will be discussed as they become pertinent, *infra*. *See also* Symposium, *A Reappraisal of the Supplemental Jurisdiction Statute: Title 28 U.S.C. § 1367*, 74 IND. L.J. 1 (1998). One contributor to the symposium has objected to the process whereby § 1367 and other jurisdictional statutes are being made longer and more complex; instead, he argues that the statute should be simplified and the federal courts given more discretion to determine whether supplemental claims should be adjudicated. *See* David L. Shapiro, *Supplemental Jurisdiction: A Confession, An Avoidance, and a Proposal*, 74 IND. L.J. 211 (1998).

(c) Same Article III Case or Controversy

In addition to the question whether § 1367(a) should be read literally or in a "claim-specific" fashion, the language in the statute providing for supplemental jurisdiction over claims that fall within "the same case or controversy under Article III of the Constitution" presents practical difficulties. Congress believed that the "same transaction or occurrence" test proposed by the Federal Courts Study Committee was coextensive with the scope of an Article III case or controversy. The portion of the House Report explaining 28 U.S.C. § 1367 stated that § 1367

> implements a recommendation of the Federal Courts Study Committee . . . . The doctrines of pendent and ancillary jurisdiction, in this section jointly labeled supplemental jurisdiction, refer to the authority of the federal courts to adjudicate, without an independent basis of subject matter jurisdiction, claims that are so related to other claims within the district court's original jurisdiction that they form part of the same case or controversy under Article III of the United States Constitution.[451]

Federal and nonfederal claims arising from the same transaction or occurrence *are unquestionably* part of the same Article III case or controversy. It also *may be* true that the scope of an Article III case or controversy extends no further than freestanding and supplemental claims arising out of the same transaction or occurrence. Subsection 4*(b)*, above, discussed U.S. Supreme Court decisions containing pronouncements to this effect. However, subsection 4*(b)* also noted that (1) no U.S. Supreme Court decision has ever directly *held* that factually unrelated federal and nonfederal claims fall outside the same Article III case or controversy; (2) Article III of the Constitution does not contain any explicit direction that the scope of a constitutional case or controversy be defined by reference to the factual relatedness of the claims asserted in the action; (3) the history of joinder-of-claims practice at common law, in equity, and under the Codes supported the theory that factually unrelated claims can be part of the same case; and (4) Congress might have good reasons, linked to policies designed to protect or enhance the operation of basic federal subject-matter jurisdiction grants, to define the scope of a case or controversy to include factually unrelated claims. These reasons suggest that Article III and the Necessary and Proper Clause should be interpreted to allow Congress to provide for jurisdiction over nonfederal claims joined with factually unrelated federal claims in some cases.[452]

Ironically, if the constitutional power does exist to provide for jurisdiction over factually unrelated federal and state claims, § 1367(a), read literally, would

---

451. H.R. REP. NO. 734, 101st Cong., 2d Sess. 27-28 (1990). In a later passage the Report stated that § 1367(a) "generally authorizes the district court to exercise jurisdiction over a supplemental claim whenever it forms part of the same constitutional case or controversy as the claim or claims that provide the basis of the district court's original jurisdiction." *Id.* at 28-29. In a footnote appended to this sentence, the Report added: "In so doing, subsection (a) codifies the scope of supplemental jurisdiction first articulated by the Supreme Court in *United Mine Workers v. Gibbs . . . .*" *See id.* at 29 n.15.

452. *See* subsection 2 & *Illustrations 2-81* and *2-82 supra. But cf.* Copeland v. Penske Logistics L.L.C., 675 F.3d 1040 (7th Cir. 2012) (plaintiff did not argue that contract claim was part of same controversy as claim under Labor Management Relations Act).

constitute an exercise of that power. The language of the statute would allow a plaintiff asserting a federal claim in an action to join a factually unrelated state claim against the same party, even in the absence of diversity of citizenship, and even, perhaps, if the state claim required the joinder of additional nondiverse parties as defendants. Likewise, a defendant sued on a federal claim could assert a factually unrelated counterclaim against the plaintiff arising under state law, even in the absence of diversity of citizenship, and even, perhaps, if the counterclaim required the joinder of additional nondiverse parties.

Nevertheless, the legislative history of § 1367 demonstrates that Congress did not intend to authorize jurisdiction over factually unrelated claims when it used the same Article III case or controversy language in 28 U.S.C. § 1367(a). Instead, Congress was under the (perhaps mistaken) impression that Article III requires a factual relationship between claims before they may be deemed part of the same case or controversy. The question now is whether there is any reasonable way to interpret the statute to prevent the results described. One way would be for the Supreme Court to simply recognize that while Article III sometimes permits Congress to provide for jurisdiction over factually unrelated federal and nonfederal claims, Congress did not actually intend to do so in § 1367(a). Rather, Congress intended to provide for supplemental jurisdiction only over claims that arise out of the same transaction or occurrence as the claims in the action that are within original federal jurisdiction. The only real issue is whether the courts should disregard the clear language of the statute in favor of a construction based on legislative intent.[453]

Fortunately, a time-honored practice exists on the part of federal courts of disregarding both the language and legislative history of jurisdictional provisions when otherwise "inconvenient" results would occur. As noted earlier, the language of the general federal question statute seems to confer the full scope of the federal question jurisdiction permitted by Article III of the Constitution. However, the Supreme Court has never interpreted the language of the statute this broadly because of the enormous amount of litigation that such an interpretation would produce in the federal courts.[454] Furthermore, in the case of the general federal question statute, the legislative history indicates that Congress intended to confer the full scope of the federal question jurisdiction permissible under Article III.[455] In contrast, the language and legislative history of 28 U.S.C. § 1367(a) point in different directions. Therefore, it is even more justifiable for the courts to disregard the language of § 1367(a) than it has been for them to disregard the language of 28 U.S.C. § 1331(a).[456]

---

453. Unfortunately, the American Law Institute's proposed revision of § 1367 will not, even if adopted by Congress, solve this problem. The revision continues to use the "Article III case or controversy" language, rather than specifying the degree of factual relationship that must exist between freestanding and supplemental claims.

454. *See* section B(2) *supra* ("The Scope of the Statutory Grant of Federal Question Jurisdiction").

455. *See* CHARLES A. WRIGHT & MARY KAY KANE, THE LAW OF FEDERAL COURTS § 17, at 104-05 (7th ed. 2011); Ray Forrester, *Federal Question Jurisdiction and Section 5*, 18 TUL. L. REV. 263, 276-78 (1943).

456. In addition, as later discussed in section F, *infra*, this construction of § 1367(a) solves a knotty problem that Congress created when it enacted that section and simultaneously amended 28 U.S.C. § 1441(c)—the separate and independent claim removal provision—to apply only in federal question cases.

In fact, the existing court decisions under § 1367 almost all agree that a factual relationship between claims is essential for supplemental jurisdiction to exist.[457] The decisions do not always reveal whether the courts believe this result is compelled by the Constitution or only the statute. However, they appear to be premised on the U.S. Supreme Court dicta discussed earlier, which stated that a factual relationship between federal and nonfederal claims is necessary to satisfy Article III.[458] Thus, until the Supreme Court reviews a case in which the Article III and statutory issues are directly presented, the prevailing view will be, contrary to this text, that both the Constitution and the statute necessitate a factual relationship.

Assuming that the Supreme Court concludes that some factual relationship between freestanding and supplemental claims is necessary to satisfy Article III (or § 1367(a)), how close must the factual relationship be? Many federal courts have held a "loose" factual relationship between the federal and nonfederal claims to be sufficient to satisfy the "common nucleus of operative fact" test of the *Gibbs* case.[459] However, other courts have required a closer factual relationship—for example, rejecting supplemental jurisdiction over state claims simply because they arise out of the same employer-employee relationship as a federal claim but involve no overlapping facts.[460] They have also rejected supplemental jurisdiction over non-overlapping state claims that are part of a continuing, festering dispute between the parties.[461] A few cases have even rejected supplemental jurisdiction when some facts overlap between the federal and state claims and the claims arise out of the same events.

---

457. Apparently, only one case has indicated that factually unrelated claims will be within the supplemental jurisdiction of the district court under § 1367(a). *See* Wesley v. General Motors Acceptance Corp., No. 91 C 3368, 1991 WL 169204, 1991 U.S. Dist. LEXIS 11745 (N.D. Ill. Aug. 20, 1991) (permissive counterclaim not arising out of the same transaction or occurrence as plaintiff's claim is within supplemental jurisdiction); *cf.* Winn v. North Am. Philips Corp., 826 F. Supp. 1424 (S.D. Fla. 1993) (court assumes that "common nucleus of operative fact" test and § 1367(a) test are different). Numerous courts have dismissed claims that they perceived to be lacking the necessary factual relationship with claims within the original jurisdiction. *See, e.g.*, Hudson v. Delta Air Lines, Inc., 90 F.3d 451 (11th Cir. 1996) (state breach of contract claim arising out of same employer-employee relationship not part of same case or controversy as federal ERISA claim when contract was not part of ERISA plan and was administered by different department of employer); Lyon v. Whisman, 45 F.3d 758 (3d Cir. 1995) (federal Fair Labor Standards Act claim against employer for failure to pay overtime not part of same case or controversy as state tort claim for failure to pay employee a bonus); Bullock v. Barham, 957 F. Supp. 154 (N.D. Ill. 1997) (federal and state claims cannot simply arise from same event, but must arise from a common nucleus of operative fact; no jurisdiction where plaintiff's federal claim against one defendant shares no overlapping facts with state claims against other defendant); Hunt v. Up N. Plastics, Inc., 980 F. Supp. 1042 (D. Minn. 1997) (no supplemental jurisdiction when no overlapping facts); Ginsberg v. Valhalla Anesthesia Assocs., P.C., 971 F. Supp. 144 (S.D.N.Y. 1997) (no supplemental jurisdiction over counterclaim when its only relationship with principal claim is that it arose out of same employer-employee relationship); *see also In re* Prudential Ins. Co. of Am. Sales Practices Litig. Agent Actions, 148 F.3d 283 (3d Cir. 1998) (district court may not assert supplemental jurisdiction over state claims that are totally unrelated to the federal claims that form the bases of the court's jurisdiction, citing *Lyon*, but necessary relationship satisfied here by common scheme to defraud class); Axel Johnson, Inc. v. Carroll Carolina Oil Co., 145 F.3d 660 (4th Cir. 1998) (plaintiff, in arguing for Federal Rule 54(b) certification, contended federal claims were factually distinct from dismissed state claims; court of appeals used this argument against plaintiff in holding claims were not part of the same case or controversy).

458. Numerous decisions explicitly rely on the Supreme Court dicta discussed earlier. *See, e.g.*, Rolex Watch, U.S.A., Inc. v. Bulova Watch Co., 820 F. Supp. 60 (E.D.N.Y. 1993); Carlucci v. United States, 793 F. Supp. 482 (S.D.N.Y. 1992).

459. *See* 13D CHARLES A. WRIGHT ET AL., FEDERAL PRACTICE AND PROCEDURE: JURISDICTION AND RELATED MATTERS § 3567.1, at 337 (3d ed. 2008) (and authorities there cited).

460. *See, e.g.*, Hudson v. Delta Air Lines, Inc., 90 F.3d 451 (11th Cir. 1996); Lyon v. Whisman, 45 F.3d 758 (3d Cir. 1995); Ginsberg v. Valhalla Anesthesia Assocs., P.C., 971 F. Supp. 144 (S.D.N.Y. 1997).

461. *See, e.g.*, Council of Unit Owners of Wisp Condo., Inc. v. Recreational Indus., Inc., 793 F. Supp. 120 (D. Md. 1992).

Illustration 2-89. In *Doe v. Neal*,[462] a police officer kidnaped and raped the plaintiff in a parking lot. The plaintiff sued the city and a number of city officials. The plaintiff asserted federal claims against the defendants under the civil rights laws for the policeman's actions. The plaintiff also joined the owner of the parking lot as a defendant. The plaintiff asserted a state claim against the owner for negligently failing to secure the parking lot from trespassers. Despite the fact that the federal and state claims all originated in the rape committed by the police officer, the court held that the claims did not arise from a "common nucleus of operative fact."

Illustration 2-90. In *Obendorfer v. Gitano Group, Inc.*,[463] the plaintiff sued the company for which she worked in U.S. District Court. The plaintiff asserted federal sex harassment and sex discrimination claims against the company arising out of the behavior of her supervisor toward her. The plaintiff's fiancé, a lawyer, joined with her as a plaintiff in the federal action. He asserted a state claim for slander against the supervisor. The slander claim was based on remarks the supervisor made to the plaintiff to the effect that her fiancé was a cheat and a liar, like all lawyers. Despite the fact that the allegedly slanderous remarks were part of the ongoing harassment of the plaintiff, the court held that the slander claim was insufficiently related to the federal claim to be part of the same case or controversy.

* * * * *

Even if Article III requires some kind of factual relationship between federal and nonfederal claims, the cases requiring more than a loose factual relationship between federal and state claims seem wrong. There is no basis in the text or history of Article III that justifies the decisions, and they impose an inflexible barrier to the power of Congress to define the scope of a constitutional case in a reasonable way. Their rationale should be rejected by the Supreme Court in an appropriate case.

One final problem with the "same Article III case or controversy" language of the statute concerns the possibility that the language may be interpreted differently in federal question and diversity actions. Textually, the § 1367(a) does not distinguish between federal question and diversity actions, and it might, therefore, be assumed that if a factual relationship between claims is required in federal question cases, it should also be required in diversity cases to satisfy Article III. However, to date, the Supreme Court has specifically refused to hold that the same constitutional test applies in both federal question and diversity actions.[464] Furthermore, it is demonstrably false that a factual relationship test should be held

---

462. No. 94-4294, 1994 WL 702876, 1994 U.S. Dist. LEXIS 17746 (E.D. Pa. Dec. 12, 1994).

463. 838 F. Supp. 950 (D.N.J. 1993).

464. In Owen Equipment & Erection Co. v. Kroger, 437 U.S. 365, 98 S. Ct. 2396, 57 L. Ed. 2d 274 (1978), the Court stated:

> Federal jurisdiction in *Gibbs* was based upon the existence of a question of federal law. The Court of Appeals in the present case believed that the "common nucleus of operative fact" test also determines the outer boundaries of constitutionally permissible federal jurisdiction when that jurisdiction is based upon diversity of citizenship. We may assume, *without deciding*, that the Court of Appeals was correct in this regard. *See also* n.13 [in the Court's opinion].

Id. at 371, n.10, 98 S. Ct. at 2401, n.10, 57 L. Ed. 2d at 281, n.10 (emphasis added). In Note 13 in *Kroger*, the Court later observed that the complete diversity requirement was not a constitutional one. *See id.* at 373, n.13, 98 S. Ct. at 2402, n.13, 57 L. Ed. 2d at 282, n.13.

to govern the scope of an Article III case or controversy in diversity actions. In diversity cases, Article III requires only that citizens of different states be present on both sides of the action. As observed in section C(3), above, the constitutional requirement is satisfied even if diversity is "incomplete" and the action also contains non-diverse opposing parties. Whether one applies a "claim-specific" or an "action-specific" interpretation to § 1367(a), it is possible to envision situations in which Article III would permit jurisdiction over factually unrelated claims between co-citizens.

Illustration 2-91. *P*, a citizen of State *X*, sues *D*, a citizen of State *Y*, in a U.S. District Court for the District of State *Y*, asserting a state-law claim against *D* for $100,000 in tort. *D's* answer contains a state-law permissive counterclaim under Rule 13(a) in which *D* sought $10,000 from *P* for breach of contract. Pursuant to Rule 13(h), *D* joins *A*, a citizen of State *Y*, as an additional party to the counterclaim. The counterclaim against *P* and *A* is, of course, factually and legally unrelated to *P's* claim against *D*. It seems clear, nevertheless, that *D's* counterclaim satisfies the requirements of Article III of the Constitution. As observed in section D(3), complete diversity of citizenship between the parties is not required under Article III. Nor is any particular amount in controversy required under Article III. Clearly, therefore, Congress could, if it chose to do so, authorize the federal courts to entertain *D's* claim against *P* and *A* as an original matter in federal court. Thus, the only question is whether § 1367(a) should be read to authorize supplemental jurisdiction over the claim. Even read literally, there is a "civil action" within the jurisdiction of the federal courts sufficient to satisfy the introductory language of § 1367(a): the civil action commenced by *P* against *D*. There is also a "claim" over which the federal courts have independent subject-matter jurisdiction under Article III and § 1332(a): *P's* claim against *D*. Therefore, whether read in an "action-specific" or a "claim-specific" manner, the statute is satisfied.

The only question is whether, in diversity actions, *D's* claim against *P* and *A* is "so related" to *P's* claim against *D* "that they form part of the same case or controversy under Article III of the United States Constitution." Given that *D's* claim, evaluated independently of *P's* claim, satisfies Article III, the answer would clearly seem to be, "yes." Only if the Article III relational language in § 1367(a) is interpreted in all cases to mean "same transaction or occurrence" or same "common nucleus of operative" fact would there not be supplemental jurisdiction over the counterclaim. It is impossible to discern any rational reason why the statutory language should be so read *if the statute's purpose is interpreted to be an extension of the scope of supplemental jurisdiction under § 1367(a) to the full limits of Article III.* Only if it is concluded that Congress really did *not* mean to extend the scope of supplemental jurisdiction under § 1367(a) to the limits of Article III would such an interpretation be reasonable.

(d) "Ancillary" or "Supplemental" Jurisdiction Independent of § 1367(a)

It is important to recognize that the Supreme Court has, in limited circumstances, approved of the exercise of ancillary jurisdiction by the federal district courts independent of § 1367(a). In *Kokkonen v. Guardian Life Insurance*

Co.,[465] the Supreme Court held that the federal courts do not have ancillary jurisdiction to enforce a dismissal by stipulation unless the federal court in its order dismissing the case either retains jurisdiction to enforce the agreement or the agreement is embodied in the order. The Court stated that there was no federal statute conferring such jurisdiction, the facts underlying the breach of the settlement agreement had nothing to do with the facts of the principal claim, and automatic jurisdiction over settlement agreements is not necessary to the conduct of federal court business. However, the clear implication of the Court's opinion was that ancillary jurisdiction *would be proper* if a federal court retained jurisdiction to enforce the settlement agreement, and the lower federal courts have recognized the propriety of jurisdiction when this is so, as well as in other appropriate circumstances.[466] Of course, this raises the possibility that other kinds of "ancillary" or "supplemental" jurisdiction might also be recognized outside the scope of § 1367(a), though to date, the Supreme Court has not given encouragement to this thought.

6. Exceptions to the Scope of Supplemental Jurisdiction in Diversity Cases: Section 1367(b)

In 28 U.S.C. § 1367(b), Congress attempted to limit the operation of supplemental jurisdiction. Congress provided that supplemental jurisdiction must

---

465. 511 U.S. 375, 114 S. Ct. 1673, 128 L. Ed. 2d 391 (1994); *see also* Peacock v. Thomas, 516 U.S. 349, 116 S. Ct. 862, 133 L. Ed. 2d 817 (1996) (on similar facts, ancillary jurisdiction did not exist because of the lack of any factual relationship between the original suit and the second suit).

466. T St. Dev., LLC v. Dereje, 586 F.3d 6 (D.C. Cir. 2009) (district courts have jurisdiction to enforce settlement agreements after dismissal of a case when the court either incorporated the agreement's terms into the dismissal order or expressly retained jurisdiction over the agreement); IFC Interconsult, AG v. Safeguard Int'l Partners, LLC, 438 F.3d 298 (3d Cir. 2006) (district court had ancillary jurisdiction over separate garnishment proceeding under Rule 69; *Peacock*, cited in the preceding footnote, distinguishable because it recognized that when a party has obtained a valid federal judgment, the Federal Rules govern proceedings on execution; Rule 69 permits separate proceeding if in accord with practice and procedure under state law); Myers v. Richland Cnty., 429 F.3d 740 (8th Cir. 2005) (holding that the district court had ancillary enforcement jurisdiction, apart from supplemental jurisdiction statute, to adjudicate plaintiff's contract claim based on settlement agreement because district court had expressly retained jurisdiction to enforce settlement agreement); Fafel v. DiPaola, 399 F.3d 403 (1st Cir. 2005) (holding that the district court's exercise of jurisdiction to enforce "Rule 68" judgment complied with *Kokkonen* because Rule 68 judgment incorporates the offer of settlement that leads to the judgment and the court may later be required to interpret the terms of the offer); Ellis v. All Steel Constr., Inc., 389 F.3d 1031 (10th Cir. 2004) (when a judgment holder attempts to hold a non-party liable in a judgment enforcement proceeding, independent jurisdictional grounds are necessary if the theory of liability is significantly different from that supporting the judgment); Hudson v. Coleman, 347 F.3d 138 (6th Cir. 2003) (after dismissal of dog owner's claim and entry of consent decree against the officers who had stolen the dog, ancillary enforcement jurisdiction against the city who was not an original party was not within the court's authority, even though the garnishment action was proceeding under same case number as original action, because the relief was sought relied on an entirely independent legal theory, *i.e.*, indemnity; citing *Peacock* as authority); Ortolf v. Silver Bar Mines, 111 F.3d 85 (9th Cir. 1997) (no supplemental jurisdiction to enforce settlement agreement when court did not retain jurisdiction to do so); Jeffrey A. Parness & Daniel J. Sennott, *Expanded Recognition in Written Laws of Ancillary Federal Court Powers: Supplementing the Supplemental Jurisdiction Statute,* 64 U. PITT. L. REV. 303 (2003); Jeffrey A. Parness & Matthew R. Walker, *Enforcing Settlements in Federal Civil Actions,* 36 IND. L. REV. 33 (2003) (discussing the difficulties faced by lower federal courts in determining whether they have enforcement jurisdiction after *Kokkonen*); Jeffrey A. Parness & Daniel J. Sennott, *Recognizing Party and Nonparty Interests in Written Civil Procedure Laws,* 20 REV. LITIG. 481 (2001) (discussing *Kokkonen*); *cf.* Palkow v. CSX Transp., Inc., 431 F.3d 543 (6th Cir. 2005) (an independent action collaterally attacking a federal judgment on grounds of perjury and seeking affirmative relief in the form of compensatory damages does not allege a claim under federal law and requires an independent basis of subject-matter jurisdiction).

be exercised consistently with the requirements of 28 U.S.C. § 1332, the general diversity statute. Section 1367(b) provides:

> (b) In any civil action of which the district courts have original jurisdiction founded solely on section 1332 of this title, the district courts shall not have supplemental jurisdiction under subsection (a) over claims by plaintiffs against persons made parties under Rule 14, 19, 20, or 24 of the Federal Rules of Civil Procedure, or over claims by persons proposed to be joined as plaintiffs under Rule 19 of such rules, or seeking to intervene as plaintiffs under Rule 24 of such rules, when exercising supplemental jurisdiction over such claims would be inconsistent with the jurisdictional requirements of section 1332.[467]

The clear import of this provision is to prevent plaintiffs invoking diversity jurisdiction from evading the restrictions of 28 U.S.C. § 1332. The House Report confirms this interpretation. The Report explained the purpose of § 1367(b) as follows:

> In diversity-only actions the district courts may not hear plaintiffs' supplemental claims when exercising supplemental jurisdiction would encourage plaintiffs to evade the jurisdictional requirement of 28 U.S.C. § 1332 by the simple expedient of naming initially only those defendants whose joinder satisfies section 1332's requirements and later adding claims not within original federal jurisdiction against other defendants who have intervened or been joined on a supplemental basis. In accord with case law, the subsection also prevents the joinder or intervention of persons [as] plaintiffs if adding them is inconsistent with section 1332's requirements.[468]

Section 1367(b) restricts supplemental jurisdiction more than the Federal Courts Study Committee recommended. The statutory language proposed in the Committee's working papers only prohibited supplemental jurisdiction as to parties joined under Rules 14 and 19 of the Federal Rules of Civil Procedure and as to claims by parties who intervened permissively under Federal Rule 24(b).[469] In addition, the Committee proposed that, even as to parties joined under Federal Rules 14, 19, and 24(b), the federal courts be permitted to exercise supplemental jurisdiction when "necessary to prevent substantial prejudice to a party or third party."[470] In contrast, § 1367(b) precludes supplemental jurisdiction over claims asserted against persons joined under Rules 14, 19, 20, or 24(a) *or* (b) of the Federal Rules. Furthermore, § 1367(b) also precludes supplemental jurisdiction over claims asserted *by* persons who are joined and aligned as plaintiffs under Federal Rule

---

467. Judicial Improvements Act of 1990, Pub. L. No. 101-650, § 310, 104 Stat. 5089, 5113-14 (codified at 28 U.S.C. § 1367(b)).

468. H.R. REP. NO. 734, 101st Cong., 2d Sess. 29 (1990).

469. *See* 1 FEDERAL COURTS STUDY COMMITTEE WORKING PAPERS AND SUBCOMMITTEE REPORTS 567-68 (1990).

470. *Id.* at 568.

19[471] and *by* persons who intervene on the plaintiff's side of the litigation under Federal Rule 24. Section 1367(b) also eliminates the recommended discretion to exercise supplemental jurisdiction to prevent injustice.[472]

The interpretive problems with § 1367(b) cannot be fully understood apart from joinder of claims and parties practice under the Federal Rules of Civil Procedure. Therefore, a complete discussion of this section of the statute will be deferred until Chapters 7 and 8, where federal claim and party joinder are examined. As seen in those chapters, drafting mistakes have produced a number of serious interpretive issues under § 1367(b). These issues will have to be resolved either by the Supreme Court or by Congress.

Two of those issues have already been mentioned in subsection *(e)*, above: the problem of the Rule 20 and Rule 23 "gaps" in § 1367(b), which the Supreme Court in the *Exxon Mobil* case held did indeed exist. Further discussion of the Court's opinion on these two issues will also be found in Chapter 8. For the time being, it is important simply to remember that *Exxon Mobil's* "contamination theory" applicable to incomplete diversity situations has rendered § 1367(b) superfluous in many of the circumstances that its language appears to control.

For example, assume *P-1*, a citizen of State *X*, sues *D-1*, a citizen of State *Y* and *D-2*, a citizen of State *X*, in a U.S. District Court in State *Y*, properly joining the defendants under Rule 20 and asserting claims against them in the alternative for $200,000 in tort. Prior to *Exxon Mobil*, the proper way to analyze this case would be to conclude that § 1367(a) conferred supplemental jurisdiction over the claim against *D-2* because of its factual relationship with the claim against *D-1*, over which there existed independent jurisdiction. However, § 1367(b)'s language would then destroy supplemental jurisdiction because the claims were against defendants "made parties" under Rule 20, and the joinder would be inconsistent with the jurisdictional policies of 28 U.S.C. § 1332 in the form of the complete diversity requirement of the latter statute. After *Exxon Mobil*, the proper way to analyze the same case would be to conclude that no supplemental jurisdiction exists in the first place over the claim against *D-2* because the lack of complete diversity "contaminates" the entire case and deprives the court of jurisdiction over the action until *D-2* is dismissed. Thus, § 1367(b) now withdraws jurisdiction over claims against multiple defendants that are defective in jurisdictional amount, but is irrelevant to claims against non-diverse parties, despite the fact that the language of the section does not distinguish between incomplete diversity and amount-in-

---

471. The language of § 1367(b) precludes supplemental jurisdiction "over claims by persons proposed to be joined as plaintiffs under [Federal] Rule 19." This wording is peculiar, since as demonstrated in Chapter 8(C)(3)*(c)*, the standard procedure in cases under Rule 19 is to join a party whose joinder is necessary for just adjudication as a defendant and then, if necessary, to realign the party for jurisdictional purposes. Except in rare cases within the "involuntary plaintiff" clause of the rule, Rule 19 parties are not "joined as plaintiffs." The best interpretation of the phrase "persons . . . joined as plaintiffs" in § 1367(b), therefore, would seem to be "persons . . . joined as defendants under Rule 19 and realigned as plaintiffs for jurisdictional purposes." The peculiar wording of § 1367(b) may have been derived from a portion of the Federal Study Committee's working papers in which the case of Acton Co. v. Bachman Foods, Inc., 668 F.2d 76 (1st Cir. 1982), was discussed in terms of joinder of a Rule 19 party as a plaintiff. *See* 1 FEDERAL COURTS STUDY COMMITTEE WORKING PAPERS AND SUBCOMMITTEE REPORTS 564 (1990). The *Acton* case, however, spoke in very conventional terms of defendant joinder and realignment. *See Acton*, 668 F.2d at 79.

472. *See* 28 U.S.C. § 1367(b).

controversy problems. In Chapter 8, we will see that this same analysis now must be employed under other multiple-party joinder rules as well as under Rule 20.

One proposal to cure the problem with § 1367(b) has been made by the American Law Institute. The ALI's proposal to reform § 1367(a) was discussed above.[473] The ALI also proposes to reform § 1367(b) by substituting for it the following provision:

> (c) *Restriction of supplemental jurisdiction in diversity litigation.* When the jurisdiction of a district court over a supplemental claim depends upon a freestanding claim that is asserted in the same pleading and that qualifies as a freestanding claim solely on the basis of the jurisdiction conferred by section 1332 of this title, the court shall have jurisdiction of the supplemental claim only if it—
>
> (1) is asserted representatively by or against a class of additional unnamed parties; or
>
> (2) would be a freestanding claim on the basis of section 1332 of this title but for the value of the claim; or
>
> (3) has been joined to the action by the intervention of a party whose joinder is not indispensable to the litigation of the action.[474]

When examining the interpretive problems that have arisen under § 1367(b) in Chapters 7 and 8, below, it will be useful to return to this proposed reform to determine how it addresses the problems. For now, it is sufficient to note that the language of the subsection is framed in the same "claim-specific" manner as the ALI's proposed revisions to § 1367(a).

7. The Discretion to Decline Supplemental Jurisdiction: Section 1367(c)

Under both the pendent and the ancillary jurisdiction doctrines, courts had a certain amount of discretion to decline to exercise jurisdiction over pendent and ancillary claims—even though the courts had the *power* to exercise jurisdiction.[475] The Supreme Court articulated the factors that should guide a district court's discretion in deciding whether to retain or dismiss a pendent state claim in federal question cases in *United Mine Workers v. Gibbs*.[476] The Court listed five considerations that would point toward dismissal of the state claim: (1) the absence of judicial economy, convenience, and fairness to litigants; (2) the avoidance of needless decisions of state law; (3) the dismissal of federal claims before trial; (4) the predominance of state issues in terms of proof, scope of the issues raised, or comprehensiveness of the remedy sought; and (5) the likelihood of jury confusion

---

473. *See* subsection 5*(b) supra* ("The Interpretation of the Statute: 'Claim-Specific' or 'Action-Specific' or Both?").

474. ALI FEDERAL JUDICIAL CODE REVISION PROJECT § 1367(c), at 14 (2004). The ALI's amendment of § 1367(b) is found in subsection (c) of the proposed revision because the revision of current § 1367(a) now occupies two subsections of the proposed new statute, (a) and (b).

475. *See* 13 CHARLES A. WRIGHT ET AL., FEDERAL PRACTICE AND PROCEDURE: JURISDICTION AND RELATED MATTERS § 3523 (3d ed. 2008).

476. 383 U.S. 715, 86 S. Ct. 1130, 16 L. Ed. 2d 218 (1966).

in treating divergent legal theories.[477] In addition, the Court stated that if the state claim is closely tied to federal policy, retaining jurisdiction over the claim would be justifiable.[478]

In 28 U.S.C. § 1367(c), Congress attempted to codify the factors that the Supreme Court had previously recognized as legitimate bases for declining to exercise "supplemental jurisdiction":

> (c) The district courts may decline to exercise supplemental jurisdiction over a claim under subsection (a) if—
>
> (1) the claim raises a novel or complex issue of state law,
>
> (2) the claim substantially predominates over the claim or claims over which the district court has original jurisdiction,
>
> (3) the district court has dismissed all claims over which it has original jurisdiction, or
>
> (4) in exceptional circumstances, there are other compelling reasons for declining jurisdiction.[479]

On the face of the statute, the factors in subsection (c) apply to all exercises of "supplemental jurisdiction," including those that would formerly have been covered by the doctrine of "pendent jurisdiction" and those that would have been covered by the doctrine of "ancillary jurisdiction." However, before § 1367 was enacted, the federal courts did not exercise their discretion exactly the same in pendent and ancillary jurisdiction cases. Dismissal of the action prior to trial based on a lack of subject-matter jurisdiction would result in dismissal of both pendent and ancillary claims in the vast majority of cases.[480] Likewise, under both pendent and ancillary jurisdiction, the district courts had discretion to dismiss or retain pendent and ancillary claims when the jurisdiction conferring, or freestanding, claim was dismissed, even when it was dismissed prior to trial on the merits.[481]

However, dismissal of a state claim because it raises a novel or complex issue of state law[482] or because it substantially predominates over the jurisdiction conferring claim[483] are grounds of dismissal that are applicable only to certain

---

477. *See id.* at 726-27; 86 S. Ct. at 1139, 16 L. Ed. 2d at 228.

478. *See id.* at 727, 86 S. Ct. at 1139, 16 L. Ed. 2d at 228.

479. 28 U.S.C. § 1367(c); *see* H.R. REP. NO. 734, 101st Cong., 2d Sess. 29 (1990).

480. *See* 13 CHARLES A. WRIGHT ET. AL., FEDERAL PRACTICE AND PROCEDURE: JURISDICTION AND RELATED MATTERS § 3523 (3d ed. 2008); Rosado v. Wyman, 397 U.S. 397, 90 S. Ct. 1207, 25 L. Ed. 2d 442 (1970); *see also* Avila,v. Pappas, 591 F.3d 552 (7th Cir. 2010) (when federal claims are insubstantial, state claims may not be retained under § 1367(c)); Arena v. Graybar Elec. Co., 669 F.3d 214 (5th Cir. 2012) (if federal claims are frivolous, federal court lacks jurisdiction over those claims and consequently also lacks supplemental jurisdiction over any state claims joined with the federal claims unless there is diversity jurisdiction); Estate of Harshman v. Jackson Hole Mountain Resort Corp., 379 F.3d 1161 (10th Cir. 2004) (when a district court dismisses federal claims for lack of subject-matter jurisdiction, it has no supplemental jurisdiction over related state law claims); Herman Family Revocable Trust v. Teddy Bear, 254 F.3d 802 (9th Cir. 2001) (when federal claims are dismissed for lack of subject-matter jurisdiction, state claims must be dismissed; court has no discretion to retain them); Scarfo v. Ginsberg, 175 F.3d 957 (11th Cir. 1999) (federal courts of appeals uniformly agree state claims should be dismissed when federal claims dismissed for lack of jurisdiction). *But cf.* Trustees of Constr. Indus. & Laborers Health & Welfare Trust v. Desert Valley Landscape & Maint., Inc., 333 F.3d 923 (9th Cir. 2003) (default judgment on federal claim is not a dismissal that allows dismissal of state claims under § 1367(c)(3)).

481. *See, e.g.*, Albingia Versicherungs A.G. v. Schenker Int'l Inc., 344 F.3d 931 (9th Cir. 2002) (supplemental jurisdiction over state claim is not eliminated by dismissal of nonfrivolous federal claim), *amended* 350 F.3d 916 (9th Cir. 2003); 13 CHARLES A. WRIGHT ET AL., FEDERAL PRACTICE AND PROCEDURE: JURISDICTION AND RELATED MATTERS § 3523.1 (3d ed. 2008).

482. *See* 28 U.S.C. § 1367(c)(1).

483. *See* 28 U.S.C. § 1367(c)(2).

situations: (1) those formerly covered by the doctrine of pendent jurisdiction; and (2) perhaps to ancillary jurisdiction cases in which the basis of federal jurisdiction is a claim arising under federal law.[484] It would be highly improper to dismiss a state claim in a pure diversity case on the grounds that "it predominates" or "raises a novel or complex issue of state law." As discussed in Chapter 5, most diversity actions involve *only* issues of state law. Therefore, it would constitute a serious abdication of the district courts' responsibility in diversity actions to allow dismissal on the grounds listed in § 1367(c)(1) & (2).[485] Rather than apply the factors in § 1367(c) blindly to all cases of supplemental jurisdiction, courts should therefore interpret § 1367(c) with an eye toward the prior operation of the doctrines of pendent and ancillary jurisdiction.[486]

Since the enactment of § 1367(c), the vast majority of dismissals have occurred under § 1367(c)(3) after the claims conferring federal jurisdiction have been eliminated from the action.[487] However, the courts do not always dismiss the supplemental claims when the jurisdiction conferring claims go out of the case. Courts have retained supplemental claims in the following situations: when a large amount of effort has already gone into the case and it is almost ready for trial;[488] when extensive discovery has been completed on the state claims and they can be disposed of on summary judgment along with the federal claims;[489] when it is clear

---

484. *See* United Mine Workers v. Gibbs, 383 U.S. 715, 725-27, 86 S. Ct. 1130, 1138-39, 16 L. Ed. 2d 218, 227-28 (1966); 13D CHARLES A. WRIGHT ET AL., FEDERAL PRACTICE AND PROCEDURE: JURISDICTION AND RELATED MATTERS § 3567.3 (3d ed. 2008); *cf.* 13 *id.* § 3523.

485. Only one court seems to have applied § 1367(c) in a diversity action to dismiss a state-law claim. In Crown Life Insurance Co. v. Harris Bank Hinsdale, No. 91 C 4222, 1992 WL 3699, 1992 U.S. Dist. LEXIS 31 (N.D. Ill. Jan. 2, 1992), the court dismissed a third-party claim in a diversity action because state law predominated. However, the third-party claim was probably not proper under Federal Rule 14 because it did not assert liability against the third-party defendant that was dependent on the defendant/third-party-plaintiff's liability to the plaintiff. Third-party claims are discussed in Chapter 8(D)(1) *infra* ("Impleader").

486. *See* Robinson v. Alter Barge Line, Inc., 513 F.3d 668 (7th Cir. 2008) (Posner, J.) (state claims in federal court because of federal jurisdiction would normally be dismissed in the district court's discretion if the federal claims go out before trial, but in present case that would be improper because there is diversity of citizenship between the parties). There seems no problem with applying 28 U.S.C. § 1367(c)(3) and (4) to all cases of supplemental jurisdiction.

487. *See, e.g.*, RWJ Mgmt. Co., Inc. v. BP Prods. N. Am., Inc., 672 F.3d 476 (7th Cir. 2012) (district court acted within its discretion in dismissing state claims after federal claims dismissed, even though there had been extensive pretrial activity prior to dismissal); Price v. FCC Nat'l Bank, 4 F.3d 472 (7th Cir. 1993); Noble v. White, 996 F.2d 797 (5th Cir. 1993); Packett v. Stenberg, 969 F.2d 721 (8th Cir. 1992); Ashland Oil, Inc. v. Sonford Prods. Corp., 810 F. Supp. 1057 (D. Minn. 1993); ZB Holdings, Inc. v. White, 144 F.R.D. 42 (S.D.N.Y. 1992); Procopio v. Johnson, 785 F. Supp. 1317 (N.D. Ill. 1992), *aff'd on other grounds*, 994 F.2d 325 (7th Cir. 1993); *see also* Nightingale Home Health Care, Inc. v. Anodyne Therapy, LLC, 589 F.3d 881 (7th Cir. 2009) (failure to exercise discretion to determine whether to retain state claims or not constitute's abuse of discretion); Kolari v. New York Presbyterian Hosp., 455 F.3d 118 (2d Cir. 2006) (error for district court to exercise supplemental jurisdiction over state claims after federal claims dismissed; district court failed to identify federal interest in state claims and no other factors justified exercising supplemental jurisdiction); Trustees of the Constr. Indus. & Laborers Health & Welfare Trust v. Desert Valley Landscape & Maint., Inc., 333 F.3d 923 (9th Cir. 2003) (when district court granted default judgment on federal claim for plaintiff, it could not use § 1367(c)(3) as basis for dismissing state claims because federal claim had not been dismissed). *But cf.* Motorola Credit Corp. v. Uzan, 388 F.3d 39 (2d Cir. 2004) (holding that the district court did not err in retaining state claims after federal claims dismissed when the court had spent substantial time dealing with the claims and had also conducted a trial on the merits). Although the federal courts generally have discretion to retain jurisdiction over state claims even when the federal claim is dismissed early in the action, the courts must dismiss the claim for lack of jurisdiction when the federal claim itself is dismissed for lack of jurisdiction, as opposed to being dismissed on the merits. *See, e.g.*, Estate of Harshman v. Jackson Hole Mountain Resort Corp., 379 F.3d 1161 (10th Cir. 2004).

488. *See, e.g.*, Nowak v. Ironworkers Local 6 Pension Fund, 81 F.3d 1182 (2d Cir. 1996) (state claim properly retained when federal claim dismissed only nine days before trial); Roche v. John Hancock Mut. Life Ins. Co., 81 F.3d 249 (1st Cir. 1996) (litigation had matured beyond discovery stages).

489. *See, e.g.*, Roche v. John Hancock Mut. Life Ins. Co., 81 F.3d 249 (1st Cir. 1996).

that the state claim lacks merit or its proper disposition is otherwise clear;[490] and when retaining jurisdiction over the supplemental claims would be efficient and would preserve the resources of the litigants and the court system.[491]

When the district courts dismiss under § 1367(c)(1) on the ground that novel and complex issues of state law exist in the action, often it is because no authoritative state precedents exist on the state-law issues involved in the case.[492] It is more difficult to generalize about dismissals under § 1367(c)(2) on the ground that state law predominates. Sometimes, the sheer number of the state issues in comparison to the federal issues will lead the courts to conclude that state law predominates.[493] In other instances, discovery reveals that the state-law issues are the true focus of the case, and the federal issues are secondary.[494] However, some district courts, in clearly improper actions, have dismissed entire cases, including federal claims, because state law predominated.[495] The explicit terms of § 1367(c) only permit the district courts to dismiss "a claim under subsection (a)," if one or

---

490. *See, e.g.*, Rothman v. Emory Univ., 123 F.3d 446 (7th Cir. 1997) (decisions on federal claim also dispositive of state counterclaim); Korzen v. Local Union 705, Int'l Bhd. of Teamsters, 75 F.3d 285 (7th Cir. 1996) (state claim plainly without merit); Wright v. Associated Ins. Cos., 29 F.3d 1244 (7th Cir. 1994) (correct disposition of state claims is clear).

491. *See* Rothman v. Emory Univ., 123 F.3d 446 (7th Cir. 1997) (decisions on federal claim also dispositive of state counterclaim); Roche v. John Hancock Mut. Life Ins. Co., 81 F.3d 249 (1st Cir. 1996) (action had matured beyond discovery stage, summary judgment record was complete, and federal and state claims were intertwined); Parks v. Hayward's Pit, Inc., No. 93-2387-JWL, 1993 WL 545231, 1993 U.S. Dist. LEXIS 18529 (D. Kan. Dec. 21, 1993) (state claim against one defendant had evidentiary overlap with federal claim against another defendant); Daniels v. Board of Trustees of Herington Mun. Hosp., 841 F. Supp. 363 (D. Kan 1993) (retention of jurisdiction because of time expended by parties on issue); *see also* Crosby v. City of Gastonia, 635 F.3d 634 (4th Cir. 2011) (district court did not err in retaining state claims after erroneously dismissing federal claims on subject-matter jurisdiction grounds, because court should have dismissed for failure to state a claim and could have correctly retained jurisdiction over state claims under those circumstances); Parker v. Scrap Metal Processors, Inc., 468 F.3d 733 (11th Cir. 2006) (error for district court not to exercise supplemental jurisdiction over state claims after parties had already litigated liability questions to final judgment that had been upheld on appeal).

492. *See, e.g.*, Women Prisoners of D.C. Dep't of Corrections v. District of Columbia, 93 F.3d 910 (D.C. Cir. 1996); Winn v. North Am. Philips Corp., 826 F. Supp. 1424 (S.D. Fla. 1993); Schwartz v. System Software Assocs., Inc., 813 F. Supp. 1364 (N.D. Ill. 1993); Support Ministries for Persons with AIDS, Inc. v. Village of Waterford, 799 F. Supp. 272 (N.D.N.Y. 1992); *see also* Seabrook v. Jacobson, 153 F.3d 70 (2d Cir. 1998) (state issue not only undecided, but depended on balancing of important state policies; if federal courts decide issue, their decision might soon be replaced by state adjudication); O'Connor v. Nevada, 27 F.3d 357 (9th Cir. 1994) (difficult issue of state constitutional law); Lane v. Calhoun-Liberty Cnty. Hosp. Ass'n, 846 F. Supp. 1543 (N.D. Fla. 1994) (new state statutory cause of action presents novel issue); Mars, Inc. v. Nippon Conlux Kabushiki-Kaisha, 825 F. Supp. 73 (D. Del. 1993) (claims presenting complex issues of Japanese law dismissed), *aff'd on other grounds*, 24 F.3d 1368 (Fed. Cir. 1994); *cf.* H. Salt, Inc. v. Wen Lung Yu, No. 92-55430, 1993 WL 306153, 1993 U.S. App. LEXIS 20636 (9th Cir. Aug. 11, 1993) (dismissal refused because California law settled); Atkinson v. B.C.C. Assocs., Inc., No. 91 Civ. 4443 (MBM), 1992 WL 51568, 1992 U.S. Dist. LEXIS 2824, (S.D.N.Y. Mar. 9, 1992) (remand on grounds of complex and unsettled issues of state law refused when plaintiff admits there is direct authority on state issues from state supreme court); *see also* De Asencio v. Tyson Foods, Inc., 342 F.3d 301 (3d Cir. 2003) (in action in which federal claims had not been dismissed, federal district court abused its discretion in exercising supplemental jurisdiction over Pennsylvania Wage Payment and Collection Law claims because case presented novel and complex questions of state law and the scope of the state issues might substantially predominate over the federal Fair Labor Standards Act claims; issue of whether an implied contract could give rise to a claim under the Pennsylvania statute had never been addressed by the Pennsylvania courts).

493. *See, e.g.*, Town of Jaffrey v. Town of Fitzwilliam, 846 F. Supp. 3 (D.N.H. 1994); James v. Sun Glass Hut, Inc., 799 F. Supp. 1083 (D. Colo. 1992); Anspec Co. v. Johnson Controls, Inc., 788 F. Supp. 951 (E.D. Mich. 1992).

494. *See* Freer v. Mayer, 796 F. Supp. 89 (S.D.N.Y. 1992); Elb-Mattison, Inc. v. M/V Kosciuszko, No. 91 C 5449, 1992 WL 132538, 1992 U.S. Dist. LEXIS 7992 (N.D. Ill. June 8, 1992); *see also* Lassiter v. Kulp, No. 93-1176, 1993 WL 364694, 1993 U.S. Dist. LEXIS 12720 (E.D. Pa. Sept. 13, 1993) (state claims involving entirely different threshold issues, burdens of proof, and evidentiary proffers).

495. *See, e.g., In re* City of Mobile, 75 F.3d 605 (11th Cir. 1996); Borough of W. Mifflin v. Lancaster, 45 F.3d 780 (3d Cir. 1995); Bodenner v. Graves, 828 F. Supp. 516 (W.D. Mich. 1993). The *Bodenner* court cited a decision of another district court involving remand of a removed case to state court when state issues predominated. As section F *infra* on removal demonstrates, remand of an entire removed case on these grounds is also improper.

more of the factors under § 1367(c) is present. Section 1367(c) does not authorize the courts to dismiss the entire case. Furthermore, dismissal of federal as well as state claims deprives the plaintiff of the congressionally granted privilege of suing on the federal claims in federal court. When state issues predominate, the plaintiff may have a difficult choice if the district court dismisses the plaintiff's state claims. Nevertheless, the choice to keep the federal claim in federal court, take it to state court, or drop either the federal or state claims should always reside with the plaintiff.

One issue that has split the courts of appeals under § 1367(c) is the extent to which the statute is intended to confine the open-ended discretion of the *Gibbs* decision, discussed above. In *Executive Software North America, Inc. v. United States District Court*,[496] the Ninth Circuit held that the factors listed in § 1367(c) were the exclusive bases for discretionary dismissals of supplemental claims:

> It is clear that, once it is determined that the assertion of supplemental jurisdiction is permissible under sections 1367(a) and (b), section 1367(c) provides the only valid basis upon which the district court may decline jurisdiction .... Moreover, we conclude that although subsections (c)(1)-(3) appear to codify most preexisting applications of the *Gibbs* doctrine, subsection (c)(4), which also permits a court to decline jurisdiction when, "in exceptional circumstances, there are other compelling reasons," channels the district court's discretion to identify new grounds for declining jurisdiction more particularly than did preexisting doctrine. Accordingly, we conclude that the district court erred to the extent that it relied on a basis for [declining jurisdiction over] pendent claims not permitted under section 1367(c).[497]

Other courts of appeals have disagreed with the *Executive Software* approach and concluded that the *Gibbs* open-ended discretionary approach has survived the codification of the factors in § 1367(c).[498]

In *Funkhouser v. Wells Fargo Bank, N.A.*,[499] the Ninth Circuit Court of Appeals confronted the interesting question of whether a district court has jurisdiction to rule on a federal preemption issue when it declined to exercise supplemental jurisdiction over a state law breach-of-contract claim. The court held that when a district court chooses not to exercise supplemental jurisdiction over a claim, it ordinarily lacks power to adjudicate the merits of the claim, including affirmative defenses of federal preemption. However, as observed in subsection (5), below, dealing with removal, preemption is not always simply a defense. Under the "complete preemption" doctrine, federal law can sometimes preempt state law so thoroughly that the claim arises under federal law, despite the fact that the plaintiff relies only on state law in the statement of the claim. In such a situation, federal

---

496. 24 F.3d 1545 (9th Cir. 1994).

497. *Id.* at 1551-52; *see also* McLaurin v. Prater, 30 F.3d 982 (8th Cir. 1994) (§ 1367(a) is mandatory unless § 1367(b) or (c) apply).

498. *See* Edmondson & Gallagher v. Alban Towers Tenants Ass'n, 48 F.3d 1260 (D.C. Cir. 1995) (*Gibbs* determines the framework within which § 1367 factors are to be considered); Diven v. Amalgamated Transit Union Int'l, 38 F.3d 598 (D.C. Cir. 1994) (statute fairly exudes discretion under the exceptions in § 1367(c)).

499. 289 F.3d 1137 (9th Cir. 2002).

question removal jurisdiction exists over the resulting federal claim. As the court correctly recognized, the consequence of complete preemption would be that the district court would lack power to dismiss the completely preempted claim under § 1367(c), because only supplemental claims can be dismissed under the statute, not freestanding (or jurisdiction-conferring) claims. Thus, the district court had to consider the preemption claim in order to determine whether it had power to dismiss the claim under § 1367(c).

The American Law Institute's proposed revision of § 1367(c), addresses some of the questions that have arisen under the existing statute:

> (d) *Discretion to decline to exercise jurisdiction.* This section does not permit a district court to decline to exercise jurisdiction of any freestanding claim except as provided by subsection (e). A district court may decline to exercise jurisdiction of a supplemental claim under subsection (b) if—
>
> (1) all freestanding claims that are the basis for its jurisdiction of a supplemental claim have been dismissed before trial of that claim; or
>
> (2) the supplemental claim raises a novel or complex issue of State law that the district court need not otherwise decide; or
>
> (3) the exercise of supplemental jurisdiction would substantially alter the character of the litigation; or
>
> (4) in exceptional circumstances, there are other compelling reasons for declining supplemental jurisdiction.[500]

The first sentence of this proposal would clarify that the district courts do not ordinarily have discretion to dismiss federal claims when they exercise their discretion to dismiss supplemental state claims.[501] In addition, the proposal reorders and, in some respects, reframes the existing § 1367(c) factors. The reordering is designed to reflect "the increasingly subjective nature of each ground for declining supplemental jurisdiction."[502] In addition, the terms of subsections (d)(1)-(3) of the statute have narrowed the degree to which the district courts may exercise discretion to dismiss supplemental claims. New subsection (d)(1) only permits dismissal of supplemental claims when the freestanding claim that is the basis of jurisdiction has been dismissed "before trial," as opposed to existing subsection (c)(3), which does not contain this restriction.[503]

Proposed § 1367(d)(2) incorporates a restriction not contained in existing § 1367(c)(1) to which it corresponds: declining supplemental jurisdiction over claims involving novel or complex issues of state law is impermissible unless it would avoid the need to decide the novel or complex issue of state law. This

---

500. ALI FEDERAL JUDICIAL CODE REVISION PROJECT § 1367(d), at 14 (2004). The ALI revision is designated subsection (d) because the revisions of § 1367(a) and (b) occupy subsections (a)-(c) in the proposal.

501. The reference to subsection (e) in this opening sentence deals with certain problems involving joinder of additional defendants whose presence would otherwise destroy diversity and are within the prohibition of subsection (c) of the proposal, discussed in subsection 5*(b) supra* ("The Interpretation of the Statute: 'Claim-Specific' or 'Action-Specific' or Both?"). Subsection (e) of the ALI proposal is discussed in section F(1) *infra* ("General Rule of Removal Jurisdiction: Section 1441(a)").

502. ALI FEDERAL JUDICIAL CODE REVISION PROJECT § 1367(d), at 19, expl. note (2004).

503. *See id.* at 113, cmt. d-6.

provision is designed primarily to prevent the district courts from declining jurisdiction over state issues in diversity actions that they would still have to decide as freestanding claims.[504] However, as indicated above, it is still not clear that it is ever justifiable for a district court to refuse to decide a novel and complex issue of state law in a diversity case, and it might have been better for the ALI to forbid this ground of dismissal altogether except in federal question cases.

Proposed subsection (d)(3) corresponds with existing § 1367(c)(2), but has been reformulated to narrow the permissible grounds for dismissal. The supplemental claims would have to "predominate" by "substantially" altering the character of the litigation.

> The gist of [the *Gibbs'*] reasoning is not, as present § 1367(c)(2) would suggest, that a district court should attempt to weigh the "relative importance" or compare the number of supplemental and freestanding *claims* that must be determined in order to render judgment. Even though a supplemental claim is based on state law, its adjudication may require reference to federal law, or may require resolution of substantially the same disputed facts as must be determined incident to adjudicating freestanding claims. Thus, new § 1367(d)(3) is articulated in terms of the effect of exercising supplemental jurisdiction on "the character of the litigation" as it would otherwise be shaped in the exercise of the jurisdiction that the district court has no discretion to decline.[505]

Finally, proposed § 1367(d)(4), while differing only slightly from existing § 1367(c)(4), makes it clear that "compelling reasons" and "exceptional circumstances" can only justify declining supplemental jurisdiction, not jurisdiction over freestanding claims.[506] The overall effect of the ALI's proposal would be to create a "modestly more restrictive" provision than existing § 1367(c).[507]

8. Tolling of Limitations for Dismissed Claims: Section 1367(d)

Section 1367(d) provides a tolling period for any statute of limitations that might apply to claims dismissed under § 1367:

> (d) The period of limitations for any claim asserted under subsection (a), and for any other claim in the same action that is voluntarily dismissed at the same time as or after the dismissal of the claim under subsection (a), shall be tolled while the claim is pending and for a period of 30 days after it is dismissed unless State law provides for a longer tolling period.[508]

This provision protects parties who choose to assert supplemental claims in federal court from finding that state statutes of limitation bar their claims if the

504. *See id.* at 114, cmt. d-7.
505. *Id.* at 117, cmt. d-8; *see generally id.* at 114, cmt. d-7.
506. *See id.* at 118, cmt. d-9.
507. *See id.* cmt. d-10.
508. 28 U.S.C. § 1367(d).

claims are dismissed or if the parties choose to dismiss other claims voluntarily after dismissal of their supplemental claims. In the absence of § 1367(d), a party might find that state law would not toll the applicable statute of limitations as to a dismissed supplemental claim or as to a voluntarily dismissed claim over which original jurisdiction existed. Thus, § 1367(d) is a valuable provision because it prevents injustice to parties asserting supplemental claims.[509]

Illustration 2-92. *P*, a citizen of State *X*, sues *D*, a citizen of State *X*, in U.S. District Court. *P* asserts a federal claim against *D* and joins a factually related state law claim. After the lapse of a substantial period of time within which the parties and the court are occupied with various pretrial matters, the court dismisses *P's* state claim under 28 U.S.C. § 1367(c)(1) because it raises a novel and complex issue of state law. The state statute of limitations applicable to the dismissed claim expired after commencement of the federal action, but before dismissal of the state claim. Assume that under state law, the statute would not be considered tolled by the pendency of the federal action. By virtue of 28 U.S.C. § 1367(d), however, the state period of limitations was tolled during the pendency of the federal action. *P* has thirty days after dismissal to commence an action on the state claim in state court.[510]

Illustration 2-93. In *Illustration 2-92*, assume that after dismissal of the state claim, *P* wishes also to dismiss the federal claim voluntarily to pursue both claims in state court. The statute of limitations applicable to the federal claim would also be considered tolled under 28 U.S.C. § 1367(d) during the pendency of the federal action and for a period of thirty days after the voluntary dismissal of the federal claim.[511]

Illustration 2-94. In both *Illustrations 2-92* and *2-93*, if state law provides a longer tolling period than thirty days, *P* will have the benefit of the longer tolling period under state law in which to commence a state action on the federal and state claims.[512]

* * * * *

---

509. Section 1367(d) appears to have been patterned after § 1386(b) of the American Law Institute's 1969 proposals. *See* ALI STUDY OF THE DIVISION OF JURISDICTION BETWEEN STATE AND FEDERAL COURTS 651 (1969). The constitutionality of provisions like § 1367(d) are discussed in *id.* at 453-57; *see also* Denis F. McLaughlin, *The Federal Supplemental Jurisdiction Statute—A Constitutional and Statutory Analysis*, 24 ARIZ. ST. L.J. 849, 985-89 (1992). For an article arguing that § 1367(d) is unconstitutional, *see* Brian Augustus Beckcom, *Pushing the Limits of the Judicial Power: Tolling State Statutes of Limitations Under 28 U.S.C. § 1367(d)*, 77 TEX. L. REV. 1049 (1999).

510. *See* H.R. REP. NO. 734, 101st Cong., 2d Sess. 30 (1990).

511. *See id.*

512. For a discussion of various minor issues of interpretation under § 1367(d), see Denis F. McLaughlin, *The Federal Supplemental Jurisdiction Statute—A Constitutional and Statutory Analysis,* 24 ARIZ. ST. L.J. 849, 984-85 (1992). In Kolani v. Gluska, 64 Cal. App. 4th 402, 75 Cal. Rptr. 2d 257 (1998), the California Court of Appeals, in a curious opinion, considered what § 1367(d) means by "tolled while the claim is pending" plus 30 days. The state statute of limitations was two years. The plaintiff commenced a federal action on the claim, as a supplemental claim, after one year. Two years later, the federal court dismissed the federal action under § 1367(c). One issue considered by the court of appeals was whether the plaintiff had one year and thirty days after the federal dismissal to commence an action in state court in these circumstances. The issue is presented because, literally, "tolled while the action is pending" can be read to mean "stops running while the action is pending." This reading would, again literally, give the plaintiff the one-year remaining on the state statute of limitations plus the additional 30 days provided by § 1367(d). The Court of Appeals correctly rejected this interpretation of § 1367(d) as unreasonable. *See also* Rester v. McWane, Inc., 962 So.2d 183 (Ala. 2007) (tolling provision of § 1367(d) applies only to the same state-law claims asserted within the supplemental jurisdiction of the federal courts; where party attempted to assert different claims, state statute of limitations was not tolled by § 1367(d)).

In *Raygor v. Regents of University of Minnesota*,[513] the U.S. Supreme Court held that § 1367(a) did not provide supplemental jurisdiction over claims against a state barred by the Eleventh Amendment when the state had not consented to the suit. The Court also held that § 1367(d) did not toll the state statute of limitations applicable to the claims against the state. Both interpretations were designed to avoid a potential collision between the Eleventh Amendment and the supplemental jurisdiction statute. However, the decision casts no light on the general question of the constitutionality of § 1367(d) in other cases.

More recently, the South Carolina Supreme Court declared § 1367(d) unconstitutional under the Tenth Amendment to the U.S. Constitution. In *Jinks v. Richland County*,[514] the plaintiff sued the county, its detention center director, and the detention center physician in a federal action under 42 U.S.C. § 1983, seeking damages for the death of her husband while he was in custody. She also asserted supplemental state claims in the action. The district court granted the defendants' motions for summary judgment on the § 1983 claims and dismissed the state claims under § 1367(c)(3). Although the two-year South Carolina statute of limitations on the state claims under the South Carolina Tort Claims Act had run, the plaintiff refiled the action on the state claims in South Carolina state court within the tolling period provided under § 1367(d). The South Carolina Supreme Court held § 1367(d) unconstitutional.

The court conceded that § 1367(d)(3) was a "necessary" exercise of power under Article III and the Necessary and Proper Clause, in that it allowed litigants to pursue actions in federal courts without giving up access to state court in the event the federal jurisdictional basis fails, and the statute governed federal practice and procedure in that it eliminated the need for federal judges to retain supplemental claims that would be dismissed as time-barred in state court. Nevertheless, the court held that the statute was not "proper" within the meaning of the Necessary and Proper Clause, because, as applied to the states and their political subdivisions in tort actions, it interferes with the State's sovereign authority to establish the extent to which its political subdivisions are subject to suit.

In *Jinks v. Richland County*,[515] the U.S. Supreme Court reversed the South Carolina Supreme Court and held § 1367(d) both applicable to the case and constitutional. The Court held that § 1367(d) is a necessary and proper exercise of congressional authority under Article III of the Constitution because it eliminates "a serious impediment to access to the federal courts on the part of plaintiffs pursuing federal-law and state-law claims" arising from the same facts. In particular, the Court held that the tolling provision eliminates the inadequate choices posed to the plaintiff of (1) filing a single federal action and risking that the state claims would be dismissed after the applicable statute of limitations has run, (2) filing a single state action on the federal and state claims, thus abandoning their right to a federal forum, and (3) filing separate actions in federal and state courts

---

513. 534 U.S. 533, 122 S. Ct. 999, 152 L. Ed. 2d 27 (2002); *see also* Joseph F. Cascio, *Are All Roads Tolled? State Sovereign Immunity and the Federal Supplemental Jurisdiction Tolling Provision,* 73 U. CHI. L. REV. 965 (2006).

514. 349 S.C. 298, 563 S.E.2d 104 (2002), *rev'd*, 538 U.S. 456, 123 S. Ct. 1667, 155 L. Ed. 631 (2003).

515. 538 U.S. 456, 123 S. Ct. 1667, 155 L. Ed. 2d 631 (2003).

and asking that the state litigation be stayed until the federal action is resolved. The Court also held that the fact that the action was filed against a state political subdivision, as opposed to a private party, did not make § 1367(d) inapplicable. The Court's previous decisions prohibiting legislation that abrogates state sovereign immunity in the state's own courts did not apply to actions against political subdivisions of the state and thus did not require an interpretation of § 1367(d) that would eliminate doubts about the statute.[516]

In *Zhang v. Department of Labor & Immigration,*[517] a district court declined to exercise jurisdiction over state claims because they raised novel issues under the law of the Commonwealth of the Northern Mariana Islands, but the plaintiff's federal claims remained pending. The court dismissed the state claims in November 1998, the statute of limitations on the Commonwealth claims expired on January 22, 1999, and the plaintiff commenced suit in a Commonwealth court on the claims in March 1999. The Commonwealth court dismissed the claims because the statute of limitations had expired and the plaintiff had not commenced the Commonwealth action within the time prescribed in § 1367(d). The plaintiff then returned to the federal court and attempted to amend the complaint to once again assert the Commonwealth claims in the federal action. The district court gave a claim preclusive effect to the Commonwealth judgment and refused to permit the amendment. The court of appeals reversed, holding that a dismissal on statute-of-limitations grounds generally does not bar a second action in a different forum when the limitations period in the second forum is longer than the first and has not expired. The court held that the statute of limitations would not bar the plaintiff's claims in the second forum (the federal court) because the plaintiff had a timely complaint still pending there, her Commonwealth claims arose out of the same facts, and, therefore, the amended complaint would relate back to the commencement of the action under Federal Rule 15(c).

Zhang is clearly wrong. There was no separate statute of limitations in federal court. Rather, the statute of limitations applicable to the Commonwealth claims was that of the Commonwealth in both the federal and Commonwealth court action. Section 1367(d) created a narrow exception to the Commonwealth statute of limitations that the plaintiff did not meet.[518] Therefore, the claims should have been deemed barred under the Commonwealth limitations period whether or not claim preclusion applied. The court's relation back discussion was also wrong. Federal Rule 15(c) was not designed to allow plaintiffs to disregard time limits under the applicable law that the plaintiff was aware of and chose to ignore. It was designed to allow plaintiffs to correct omissions and assert claims that were revealed after the commencement of the action (through the processes of discovery or otherwise). The court should have held the amendment impermissible under Rule 15(a) in the discretion of the court because of the plaintiff's sloth in asserting the

---

516. *See also* Bergemann v. Rhode Island Dep't of Envtl. Mgmt., 665 F.3d 336 (1st Cir. 2011).

517. 331 F.3d 1117 (9th Cir. 2003).

518. Indeed, it is not even clear that §1367(d) has any pertinence to the facts of *Zhang*. When the Commonwealth claims were dismissed, the statute of limitations had not run and did not run for more than 30 days after the dismissal. In other words, the plaintiff had more than 30 days under state law to commence an action, so there was nothing for § 1367(d) to toll.

claims in Commonwealth court. Relation back should have had no bearing on the outcome of the case.

In the Class Action Fairness Act ("CAFA"), discussed earlier in this chapter and in Chapter 8, Congress expanded the original and removal jurisdiction over certain diversity actions.[519] Section § 1332(d)(11)(D) of Title 28 provides that "[t]he limitations periods on any claims asserted in a mass action[520] that is removed to [f]ederal [c]ourt pursuant to this subsection shall be deemed tolled during the period that the action is pending in [f]ederal [c]ourt." Unlike the tolling provision in § 1367(d), however, this provision does not provide a grace period of 30 days (or any other time period) after dismissal of a class action under the new Act. Consequently, there is a danger that dismissal will take place after the statute of limitations has run and even prompt refiling by the plaintiff(s) will not be able to avoid the bar of the applicable limitations period. This is because "tolling" is usually interpreted to prevent the running of the statute of limitations for purposes of the action in which the statute is tolled, but not necessarily to produce an extension of the statute for the period of time the action is pending when the action is later dismissed.[521] Thus, if a federal action is filed (or removed) under the Act on day 1, the applicable period of limitations expires on day 2, the action is dismissed on day 3, and the action is refiled in state court on day 4, the state court may, in the absence of a federally mandated grace period, deem the statute of limitations period to have run on day 2. One possible solution to this problem would be for the federal courts to delay dismissal of the statute until the joined plaintiffs have an opportunity to file individual actions in state court. Another possible solution would be to interpret the action as permitting a reasonable period of time within which to commence individual actions after dismissal of a federal diversity class action.

The American Law Institute's proposed revision of § 1367(d) would clarify and somewhat expand the provisions of the existing statute.[522]

---

519. *See* Pub. L. No. 109-2, 119 Stat. 4 (codified as 28 U.S.C. § 1332(d) & 1453).

520. A "mass action" is deemed in 28 U.S.C. § 1332(d)(11)(A) to be "a class action removable under paragraphs (2) through (10) if it otherwise meets the provisions of those paragraphs." Section 1332(d)(11)(B)(I) then defines a "mass action" as an action "in which monetary claims of 100 or more persons are proposed to be tried jointly on the ground that the plaintiffs claims involve common question of law or fact." Curiously, however, § 1332(d) does not provide for "removal" of class actions at all, but instead for original jurisdiction over such actions. Removal is provided for by new § 1453. This makes the interpretation of the tolling provision discussed in the text problematic. Does it only apply to removed actions as opposed to actions originally filed in federal court?

521. *See, e.g.*, Stewart-Veal v. District of Columbia, 896 A.2d 232 (D.C. 2006) (once a suit is dismissed, even if without prejudice, the tolling effect of the filing of the suit is wiped out and the statute of limitations is deemed to have continued running from whenever the cause of action accrued, without interruption by the filing); *see also In re* WorldCom Sec. Litig., 496 F.3d 245 (2d Cir. 2007) (class action tolling rule applied in federal question cases tolls statute of limitations for claims asserted by members of class in individual actions prior to commencement of class action, even though those claims would have been untimely if the class action had not been commenced).

522. ALI FEDERAL JUDICIAL CODE REVISION PROJECT § 1367(f), at 15-16 (2004):

> *(f) Disposition of supplemental claims; tolling of limitations period.* When a district court lacks or declines to exercise supplemental jurisdiction, the court shall dismiss the supplemental claim unless it was joined before removal of the action, in which case the district court shall remand the claim to the State court from which it was removed. The period of limitations for the following claims shall be tolled until 30 days after their dismissal becomes final, unless the applicable law provides for a longer tolling period:
>
> (1) any supplemental claim dismissed because the district court lacks or declines to exercise supplemental jurisdiction; and
>
> (2) any other claim in the same civil action that is voluntarily dismissed as the result of a notice or stipulation of dismissal, or motion for order of dismissal, filed within 30 days after—

SECTION F. REMOVAL JURISDICTION

In the first Judiciary Act, Congress gave defendants a limited right to "remove" cases from state to federal court. Congress has steadily expanded this right.[523] Today, the general removal statute is 28 U.S.C. § 1441. Section 1441(a) sets out the general rule on removal jurisdiction. Section 1441(b) and (c) describe exceptions to the general rule.[524] Several other statutes provide for removal of specific kinds of cases from state to federal court.[525] Section 1445 of Title 28 sets out certain cases that are not removable, even if they fall within the terms of one of the removal statutes.[526] Finally, §§ 1446-1450 deal with the procedures for removal and the procedures after removal, including remand of improperly removed cases.[527] The following subsections discuss removal under 28 U.S.C. § 1441, the procedures governing removal, and remand.

1. General Rule of Removal Jurisdiction: Section 1441(a)

Section 1441(a) states the general rule of removal jurisdiction for the U.S. District Courts. A civil action may be removed from a state court to a U.S. District Court whenever the U.S. District Court would have original jurisdiction of the action. Removal under § 1441 is limited to defendants.[528] Usually, in actions

---

(A) the dismissal or remand of a supplemental claim because the district court lacks or declines to exercise supplemental jurisdiction; or

(B) the court's decision under subsection (e) to refuse to permit the joinder of a supplemental claim against an additional defendant.

See also id. at 131-33, cmts. f-1 to f-3.

523. *See* CHARLES A. WRIGHT & MARY KAY KANE, THE LAW OF FEDERAL COURTS § 38, at 224 (7th ed. 2011); *cf.* Erica B. Haggard, *Removal to Federal Courts From State Administrative Agencies: Reevaluating the Functional Test*, 66 WASH. & LEE L. REV. 1831 (2009) (discussing the rule followed by some federal courts that cases can be removed from state administrative agencies that "function as courts" to federal court).

524. 28 U.S.C. § 1441(a)-(c).

525. *See, e.g.*, 28 U.S.C. § 1442 (involving federal officers or agencies sued or prosecuted), § 1442a (involving members of armed forces sued or prosecuted), § 1443 (civil rights cases), § 1444 (foreclosure actions against the United States), § 1452 (involving claims related to bankruptcy cases); *see also* Watson v. Phillip Morris Cos., 551 U. S. 142, 127 S. Ct. 2301, 168 L. Ed. 2d 42 (2007) (the fact that a federal regulatory agency directs, supervises, and monitors a private company's activities does not mean that the company is "acting under" a federal officer within the meaning of 28 U.S.C. § 1442(a)(1)); Isaacson v. Dow Chem. Co., 517 F.3d 129 (2d Cir. 2008) (the term "person" in the federal officer removal statute includes corporations, thus allowing removal by corporate defendants acting under federal officers).

526. 28 U.S.C. § 1445 (involving certain civil actions against railroads or carriers; claims arising under state workers' compensation laws; and civil actions based on the Violence Against Women Act of 1994).

527. 28 U.S.C. § 1446 ("Procedure for removal"), § 1447 ("Procedure after removal generally"), § 1448 ("Process after removal"), § 1449 (state court record for use in removed action), § 1450 (status of attachments, injunctions, orders, bonds issued prior to removal).

528. *See* Shamrock Oil & Gas Corp. v. Sheets, 313 U.S. 100, 61 S. Ct. 868, 85 L. Ed. 1214 (1941) (plaintiff may not remove on the basis of defendant's counterclaim). The *Shamrock* case was a diversity action, but it has also been held applicable to federal question counterclaims. *See* General Elec. Capital Auto Lease, Inc. v. Mires, 788 F. Supp. 948 (E.D. Mich. 1992); *cf.* Holmes Group, Inc. v. Vornado Air Circulation Sys., Inc., 535 U.S. 826, 122 S. Ct. 1889, 153 L. Ed. 2d 13 (2002) (federal counterclaim does not produce a case arising under federal law for purposes of original jurisdiction) (discussed in section B(2)*(b), Illustration 2-27 supra*); Palisades Collections, L.L.C. v. Shorts, 552 F.3d 327 (4th Cir. 2008) (Class Action Fairness Act does not alter traditional rule that only original defendant may remove). In its proposed revision of the Judicial Code, the American Law Institute retains these basic rules in revised language:

§ 1441. Right of removal of civil actions—in general

(a) *Basic right of removal.*

involving multiple defendants, all defendants must be willing to remove, or removal will not be allowed.[529]

Illustration 2-95. *P*, a citizen of California, sues *D-1*, a citizen of New Jersey, and *D-2*, a citizen of New York, in a New York state court on a claim based on federal law. *D-1* and *D-2* can remove the case to a New York federal district court. Removal jurisdiction exists because the federal district courts would have original jurisdiction of the action as a case arising under federal law pursuant to 28 U.S.C. § 1331.[530]

* * * * *

Because removal jurisdiction is generally based on the existence of original jurisdiction in the district courts, the "well-pleaded complaint" rule also applies when a case is removed from state to federal court on the basis of federal question jurisdiction. Thus, removal ordinarily cannot be based on a federal defense to a state claim for relief even if the plaintiff anticipates the federal defense in the complaint.[531] Nor can removal ordinarily be based on the existence of a federal counterclaim in an action.[532] An exception to this rule exists when federal law has

---

> (1) Except as provided in subsection (f), for purposes of this section a removable claim is any claim that is within the subject-matter jurisdiction of the district courts.
>
> (2) Except as otherwise expressly provided by Act of Congress, a civil action brought in a State court may be removed by the defendant or defendants to the district court of the United States for the district in which the action is pending if every claim asserted in the complaint or other initial pleading is a removable claim, disregarding any claim against a party not properly joined or aligned as a defendant with respect to that claim.

ALI FEDERAL JUDICIAL CODE REVISION PROJECT § 1441, at 333 (2004). In contrast to the claim-specific nature of the ALI's proposed revision of the supplemental jurisdiction statute, discussed in subsection 4 *supra*, the removal provision remains action-specific as it is under current law. However, a claim-specific analysis must precede the determination whether the entire action is removable. *See id.* at 348-51 (cmt.). Thus, for a civil action to be removable under proposed § 1441(a), every claim in the action must be within the original or supplemental subject-matter jurisdiction of the district courts.

529. *See* 14C CHARLES A. WRIGHT ET AL., FEDERAL PRACTICE AND PROCEDURE: JURISDICTION AND RELATED MATTERS § 3730, at 440 (3d ed. 2009). An exception to this rule exists when a case is removed under 28 U.S.C. § 1441(c), discussed below. In § 1441(c) cases, only the defendant against whom the removable claim is asserted need seek removal. *See id.* at 469. *See also* Casey v. Federal Deposit Ins. Corp., 583 F.3d 586 (8th Cir. 2009) (rule of unanimity did not limit FDIC's authority to unilaterally remove case); Proctor v. Vishay Intertechnology, Inc., 584 F.3d 1208 (9th Cir. 2009) (filing of notice of removal effective even though not accompanied by individual consent documents on behalf of each defendant). Another exception exists when removal is based on diversity of citizenship and it is alleged and proved that the plaintiff has "fraudulently joined" a resident defendant to prevent removal. Under such circumstances, the nonresident defendant alone can remove upon a proper allegation and proof of the fraudulent joinder. *See, e.g.*, Wilson v. Republic Iron & Steel Co., 257 U.S. 92, 42 S. Ct. 35, 66 L. Ed. 144 (1921); Green v. Amerada Hess Corp., 707 F.2d 201 (5th Cir. 1983). Fraudulent joinder is discussed in 14B CHARLES A. WRIGHT ET AL., FEDERAL PRACTICE AND PROCEDURE: JURISDICTION AND RELATED MATTERS § 3723, at 787-878 (3d ed. 2009). In the Class Action Fairness Act of 2005, Congress provided special jurisdictional and removal provisions for at least some class actions. *See* Pub. L. No. 109-2, 119 Stat. 4 (codified as 28 U.S.C. § 1332(d) & 28 U.S.C. § 1453). This Act has been discussed earlier in this chapter and is further discussed in subsection 2 *infra* and in Chapter 8 *infra*.

530. Cases involving federal claims and supplemental state claims within the district court's original jurisdiction under § 1367 are, of course, also removable. For an excellent discussion of problems involving the interplay of § 1367 and removal, see Joan Steinman, *Crosscurrents: Supplemental Jurisdiction, Removal, and the ALI Revision Project*, 74 IND. L.J. 75 (1998).

531. *See also* Holmes Group, Inc. v. Vornado Air Circulation Sys., Inc., 535 U.S. 826, 122 S. Ct. 1889, 153 L. Ed. 2d 13 (2002) (federal counterclaim does not produce a case arising under federal law for purposes of original jurisdiction) (discussed in section B(2)*(b)*, *Illustration 2-27 supra*)

532. Under the removal provisions of the Leahy-Smith American Invents Act, a provision was added to the removal statutes, 28 U.S.C. § 1454, which authorizes removal of state actions in which any party, including the defendant, asserts a counterclaim relating to patents, plant variety protection, or copyrights, even when the plaintiff's claim is based entirely on state law. New § 1454 provides:

> A civil action in which any party asserts a claim for relief arising under any Act of Congress relating to patents, plant variety protection, or copyrights may be removed to the district may be removed to the district court of the United States for the district and division embracing the place where the

completely preempted state law within an area. When state law has been completely preempted, any claim purportedly based on the preempted state law is considered federal from its inception. Therefore, the claim arises under federal law for purposes of removal even if the complaint does not in any way rely on federal law. However, when federal law does not completely preempt an area of state law, but leaves the plaintiff a choice whether to base the claim on federal or state law, the plaintiff can prevent removal from state court by simply pleading a claim for relief based on state law alone.[533]

In determining whether the so-called "complete preemption" doctrine allows removal of an action commenced in state court, it is important to determine whether federal law simply negates the plaintiff's state claims for relief. If it does, preemption is only a defense, and the action is not removable. On the other hand, if federal law so occupies the field as to create a federal claim for relief that displaces state remedies, the action is removable.

Illustration 2-96. *U*, a labor union, enters into a collective bargaining agreement with *D*, a corporation. Subsequently, *P*, an employee of *D*, brings an action in state court against *D* to recover damages for rights allegedly violated by *D* under the agreement. *D* files a timely notice of removal to federal court. Even though *P's* complaint does not rely explicitly on federal law, the action is removable. The U.S. Supreme Court has held that when a state complaint relies on the provisions of a collective bargaining agreement, the complaint arises under federal law. The Court has also held that the federal labor laws have entirely preempted state law as a source of private rights to enforce collective bargaining agreements.[534]

Illustration 2-97. If, in *Illustration 2-96*, *P* had brought a state action to enforce an individual employment contract with *D*, rather than to enforce the provisions of a collective bargaining agreement, the action could be brought under state law and would be nonremovable. The federal labor laws completely preempt only state remedies for violations of collective bargaining agreements. Even if *P* possesses substantial rights under the collective bargaining agreement, *P* can choose

---

action is pending.

Thus, this new provision constitutes an exception to the ordinary rule that a federal counterclaim may not be the basis of removal.

533. *See* Caterpillar Inc. v. Williams, 482 U.S. 386, 107 S. Ct. 2425, 96 L. Ed. 2d 318 (1987); Metropolitan Life Ins. Co. v. Taylor, 481 U.S. 58, 107 S. Ct. 1542, 95 L. Ed. 2d 55 (1987). In Beneficial National Bank v. Anderson, 539 U.S. 1, 123 S. Ct. 2058, 156 L. Ed. 2d 1 (2003), the plaintiff sued in Alabama state court asserting claims for usury under state law. The defendants removed the case to federal court, asserting in their notice of removal that federal law provided the exclusive provision governing the rate of interest that a national bank could charge and that federal law also provided the exclusive remedies against a national bank charging an excessive rate of interest. The district court denied a motion to remand, but certified the case for interlocutory appeal under 28 U.S.C. § 1292(b) on the issue of subject-matter jurisdiction. The Eleventh Circuit Court of Appeals reversed, holding that the "well-pleaded complaint" rule did not permit removal and that it could find no clear congressional intent to permit removal under the federal statutes cited by the defendants. The Supreme Court granted certiorari and reversed, holding that the National Bank Act completely preempted state remedies against national banks for usury and, therefore, that removal was permitted despite the fact that the complaints relied only on state law. *See also* Bernhard v. Whitney Nat'l Bank, 523 F.3d 546 (5th Cir. 2008) (boilerplate request for attorneys' fees that does not refer to federal law does not provide the basis for removal jurisdiction, even though such fees are only available under federal law).

534. *See* Avco Corp. v. Aero Lodge No. 735, 390 U.S. 557, 88 S. Ct. 1235, 20 L. Ed. 2d 126 (1968).

not to rely on that agreement in framing the complaint. In that event, *P* may prevent removal because the complaint will be based entirely on state law.[535]

* * * * *

Removal under § 1441(a) is of "civil actions." Recall from subsection 4*(e)(ii)*, above, that in *City of Chicago v. International College of Surgeons,*[536] the U.S. Supreme Court held that a state action for deferential judicial review of a state agency's action was a removable "civil action" within the meaning of § 1441(a). The Court reached this conclusion because (1) there were federal claims within the original jurisdiction of the district courts present in the action and (2) § 1367 provided supplemental jurisdiction over the state claims in the action. In *Wisconsin Department of Corrections v. Schacht,*[537] the Court sustained removal jurisdiction over a case in which claims barred by the Eleventh Amendment[538] to the U.S. Constitution were joined with claims not barred by the Amendment. Citing the *City of Chicago* case, the Court held that the presence of even one federal claim over which there is original jurisdiction suffices to make the action a "civil action . . . of which the district courts . . . have original jurisdiction" within the meaning of § 1441(a). The Court distinguished diversity removal cases in which nondiverse defendants had been joined on the ground that the complete diversity rule of § 1332 cannot be waived, while the Eleventh Amendment defense can be.[539]

When removal is based on diversity of citizenship, diversity must exist at the time the action was commenced in state court as well as when the petition for removal is filed. Thus, a nondiverse defendant cannot change domiciles after commencement to create diversity and make the action removable.[540] If a nondiverse defendant is eliminated by voluntary action of the plaintiff, however, the remaining defendant(s) can remove.[541]

---

535. *See* Caterpillar Inc. v. Williams, 482 U.S. 386, 107 S. Ct. 2425, 96 L. Ed. 2d 318 (1987); *see also* Beneficial Nat'l Bank v. Anderson, 539 U.S. 1, 123 S. Ct. 2058, 156 L. Ed. 2d 1 (2003) (holding federal removal of a usury action against a national bank proper on the grounds that the National Bank Act provided the exclusive basis for usury claims against national banks and thus that despite the plaintiffs' attempt to frame the claim as one under state law, the claims could only arise under federal law); *see generally* Karen A. Jordan, *The Complete Preemption Dilemma: A Legal Process Perspective*, 31 WAKE FOREST L. REV. 927 (1996); Garrick B. Pursley, *Rationalizing Complete Preemption After* Beneficial National Bank v. Anderson: *A New Rule, A New Justification,* 54 DRAKE L. REV. 371 (2006); Margaret Tarkington, *Rejecting the Touchstone: Complete Preemption and Congressional Intent After Beneficial National Bank v. Anderson,* 59 S.C. L. REV. 225 (2008).

536. 522 U.S. 156, 118 S. Ct. 523, 139 L. Ed. 2d 525 (1997).

537. 524 U.S. 381, 118 S. Ct. 2047, 141 L. Ed. 2d 364 (1998).

538. U.S. Const. amend. XI.

539. 524 U.S. at 390-91, 118 S. Ct. at 2053, 141 L. Ed. 2d at 373-74; *see also* Motion Control Corp. v. Sick, Inc., 354 F.3d 702 (8th Cir. 2003) (action not removable on the basis of grant of supplemental jurisdiction under 28 U.S.C. § 1367 on the theory that it is related to a separate action pending before the district court).

540. *See, e.g.*, Kellam v. Keith, 144 U.S. 568, 12 S. Ct. 922, 36 L. Ed. 544 (1892); Kanzelberger v. Kanzelberger, 782 F.2d 774 (7th Cir. 1986); 14B CHARLES A. WRIGHT ET AL., FEDERAL PRACTICE AND PROCEDURE: JURISDICTION AND RELATED MATTERS § 3723, at 696 (3d ed. 2009). Of course, the rule that jurisdiction may not be ousted by subsequent events prevents plaintiff from reducing the claim below the amount-in-controversy requirement and then successfully moving to remand. *See* Poore v. American-Amicable Life Ins. Co., 218 F.3d 1287 (11th Cir. 2000) (after removal, plaintiffs eliminated claims for punitive damages and then moved to remand; district court remands; court of appeals reverses, holding that jurisdiction is determined as of time of removal); *see also* Salazar v. Allstate Texas Lloyd's, Inc., 455 F.3d 571 (5th Cir. 2006) (district court cannot create removal jurisdiction in a single defendant case based on diversity by substituting another defendant).

541. *See* 14B CHARLES A. WRIGHT ET AL., FEDERAL PRACTICE AND PROCEDURE: JURISDICTION AND RELATED MATTERS § 3723, at 701 (3d ed. 2009). If a nondiverse defendant is dropped by order of the court, rather than by voluntary action by the plaintiff, the cases are divided on whether the action can be removed. The best result is that the case should not be considered removable. The "distinction [between voluntary action by the plaintiff making an action removable and action by the court that does not make the action removable has] merit

Congress has also provided that the citizenship of defendants sued under fictitious names shall be disregarded for purposes of removal.[542] If, after removal, the plaintiff seeks to join additional defendants whose joinder would destroy subject-matter jurisdiction, the court has discretion to deny the joinder or to allow it and remand the case to the state court.[543] The purpose of the latter provision is to give the district court flexibility when a party must be joined under Federal Rule 19 after removal. It permits joinder and remand, instead of only dismissal or denial of joinder, when the party to be joined would destroy diversity.[544]

In *Lincoln Property Co. v. Roche,*[545] an action was removed from state to federal court in Virginia. After denying the plaintiffs' motion to remand, the U.S. District court granted summary judgment for the defendants in the action. The U.S. Court of Appeals reversed with instructions to remand because the defendant had failed to show the nonexistence of an affiliated Virginia defendant that was "a real party in interest" which should be joined as a defendant. The U.S. Supreme Court granted certiorari and reversed the court of appeals. The Court held that neither Rule 17, Rule 19, nor any provision of the jurisdictional or removal statutes

---

in that it prevent[s] removal when the nondiverse party [is] eliminated by a court order that might be [subject to] revers[al] on appeal." *Id.* at 581-82; *see also* Crockett v. R.J. Reynolds Tobacco Co., 436 F.3d 529 (5th Cir. 2006) (when a state court severs claims against improperly joined defendants and the severance order is not appealed, post-severance removal is not subject to the "voluntary-involuntary" rule); *cf.* Williams v. Costco Wholesale Corp., 471 F.3d 975 (9th Cir. 2006) (elimination of federal claim after removal does not require new removal notice to demonstrate diversity removal jurisdiction; post-removal amendment does not affect removability of action); Harper v. AutoAlliance Int'l, Inc., 392 F.3d 195 (6th Cir. 2004) (elimination of federal claim by amendment after removal does not deprive court of subject-matter jurisdiction; whether to retain or remand pendent state claim is a matter of discretion with the district court). The American Law Institute's proposed revisions of the Judicial Code would essentially preserve this rule in its proposed § 1446(b)(2). This proposal would allow removal of actions not removable at commencement only when they have become removable by the "voluntary act of the plaintiff or plaintiffs." *See* ALI FEDERAL JUDICIAL CODE REVISION PROJECT § 1446(b)(2), at 437 (2004). The reporter has acknowledged that this provision might permit removal if the plaintiff changes citizenship to create diversity after commencement of the state action. *See id.* at 367 (cmt. on § 1441(b)). However, this result could only occur if the defendant is not a citizen of the state in which the action is brought. *See id.* § 1441(b)(2); subsection 2 *infra*. Thus, the situations in which a change of domicile by the plaintiff would create removal jurisdiction would be rare.

542. *See* The Judicial Improvements and Access to Justice Act of 1988, Pub. L. No. 100-702, § 1016(a), 102 Stat. 4642, 4669 (codified at 28 U.S.C. § 1441(a)). This amendment was intended to overrule the Ninth Circuit's decision in Bryant v. Ford Motor Co., 832 F.2d 1080 (9th Cir. 1987). *Bryant* held that naming fictitious defendants under California law destroys diversity jurisdiction and thus the ability to remove to federal court. In the Federal Courts Jurisdiction and Venue Clarification Act of 2011, Pub. L. No. 112-63, § 103, 125 Stat. 758, 759 (codified at 28 U.S.C. § 1441(b)(1)), the text of this provision was shifted from the end of § 1441(a) to new § 1441(b)(1) for purposes of clarity. The American Law Institute would preserve this rule under its proposed revision of § 1441. *See* ALI FEDERAL JUDICIAL CODE REVISION PROJECT § 1441(b)(1), at 345 (2004).

543. *See* The Judicial Improvements and Access to Justice Act of 1988, Pub. L. No. 100-702, § 1016(e), 102 Stat. 4642, 4669 (codified at 28 U.S.C. § 1447(e)); *see also* Schur v. L.A. Weight Loss Ctrs., Inc., 577 F.3d 752 (7th Cir. 2009) (permitting joinder of nondiverse parties and remanding action to state court was warranted).

544. *See* H.R. REP. NO. 889, 100th Cong., 2d Sess. 72-73, *reprinted in* 1988 U.S.C.C.A.N. 5982, 6033; *see also* Yniques v. Cabral, 985 F.2d 1031 (9th Cir. 1993) (Rule 19 and § 1447(e) give district courts three options: (1) deny joinder, conclude the nonjoined party is indispensable, and dismiss; (2) deny joinder, conclude the nonjoined party is not indispensable, and allow the action to continue; or (3) allow joinder and remand) (the district court may *not* permit joinder and *dismiss*). If a district court does allow joinder of such a party and then adjudicates the action, the court of appeals may be able to cure the error by allowing a nondiverse, nonindispensable party to be dismissed at the appellate level. *See* Ingram v. CSX Transp., Inc., 146 F.3d 858 (11th Cir. 1998). In Doleac *ex rel.* Doleac v. Michalson, 264 F.3d 470 (5th Cir. 2001), a plaintiff sued several defendants, identifying some of the defendants under fictitious names. The defendants not fictitiously named removed the action, after which the plaintiff amended the complaint to substitute nonfictitiously named co-citizens for the fictitiously named defendants. The court held that the action had to be remanded because the amendment destroyed diversity. In its proposed revision of the Judicial Code, the American Law Institute would also give district courts the option of retaining the action and exercising supplemental jurisdiction over the claim against the newly joined nondiverse defendant. *See* ALI FEDERAL JUDICIAL CODE REVISION PROJECT § 1367(e), at 15 (2004); *Id.* § 1447[e], at 465 (2004).

545. 546 U.S. 81, 126 S. Ct. 606, 163 L. Ed. 2d 415 (2005).

required a defendant to "propose as additional defendants persons the [plaintiffs], as masters of their complaint, permissively might have joined."[546]

In addition, if a plaintiff "fraudulently joins" a nondiverse defendant with a diverse defendant to prevent removal, the diverse defendant will be permitted to remove and the fraudulently joined defendant will be dismissed[547] A defendant is fraudulently joined when a plaintiff "has not or cannot" state a claim for relief against that defendant,[548] although some courts have recognized other grounds for fraudulent joinder.[549] The fraudulent joinder doctrine is inapplicable to actions containing a single claim against a single defendant. The Fifth Circuit Court of Appeals has held that after removal of an action against a single nondiverse defendant, the district court may not, on fraudulent joinder grounds, substitute a diverse defendant against whom a claim exists for the non-diverse defendant against whom no claim exists.[550]

Before 1986, a strange rule in the area of removal provided that removal jurisdiction was "derivative." If the state court in which the action had been commenced had no jurisdiction over the case, the federal court to which removal was sought had no jurisdiction either because the federal court's jurisdiction was derived from that of the state court. Thus, curious as it may seem, if the federal courts had exclusive subject-matter jurisdiction of a case and the case was erroneously commenced in state court, it could not be removed to federal court. In such a situation, the state court had no jurisdiction because of the grant of exclusive jurisdiction to the federal courts. Because the state court had no jurisdiction and the

---

546. *Id.* at 94, 126 S. Ct. at 616, 163 L. Ed. 2d at 428.

547. *See* 14B CHARLES A. WRIGHT, ET AL., FEDERAL PRACTICE AND PROCEDURE: JURISDICTION AND RELATED MATTERS § 3523, at 787-878 (3d ed. 2009); Aaron Burke, *Confusion Now Hath Made His Masterpiece! But When Does the Removal Countdown Begin? A Discussion on the Fifth Circuit's Recent Fraudulent Joinder Decisions and their Potential to Trap the Unwary Litigator*, 63 BAYLOR L. REV. 237 (2011); Paul Rosenthal, *Improper Joinder Confronting Plaintiffs' Attempts to Destroy Federal Subject Matter Jurisdiction*, 59 AM. U. L. REV. 49 (2009).

548. *See* 14B CHARLES A. WRIGHT, ET AL., FEDERAL PRACTICE AND PROCEDURE: JURISDICTION AND RELATED MATTERS § 3523, 787-866 (3d ed. 2009).

549. *See id.* at 867-78 (procedural misjoinder); *see also* Cuevas v. BAC Home Servicing, L.P., 648 F.3d 242 (5th Cir. 2011); Travis v. Irby, 326 F.3d 644 (5th Cir. 2003) (when plaintiff's complaint states a claim for relief, but defendant contends that there is no factual basis for liability, the defendant cannot establish fraudulent joinder by demonstrating that the plaintiff has no evidence to support the claim against the allegedly fraudulently joined defendant; instead, defendant must show evidence that negates liability); *compare* Smallwood v. Illinois Cent. R.R. Co., 385 F.3d 568 (5th Cir. 2004) (en banc) (when removing nonresident defendant's showing that there is no reasonable basis for predicting that state law would allow recovery against an in-state defendant equally disposes of claims against all defendants, there is no fraudulent joinder and entire suit must be remanded to state court) *with* Boone v. Citigroup, 416 F.3d 382 (5th Cir. 2005) ("common defense rule," applied in *Smallwood*, above, is inapplicable when defense does not equally and necessarily compel dismissal of all claims against all diverse defendants; here, limitations defense that applied to non-diverse defendants did not necessarily apply to diverse defendants; therefore, district court correctly refused to remand, considering non-diverse defendants to have been fraudulently joined); *cf.* Purdue Pharrna, L.P. v. Estate of Heffner, 904 So. 2d 100 (Miss. 2004) (federal district court's finding that there was no fraudulent joinder is not the same as a finding of proper joinder for an action in state court). *See also* Laura I. Asbury, Comment, *A Practical Guide to Fraudulent Joinder in the Eighth Circuit*, 57 ARK. L. REV. 913 (2005); Matthew J. Richardson, *Clarifying and Limiting Fraudulent Joinder*, 58 FLA. L. REV. 119 (2006). Professors Hines and Gensler have advocated an exception to the complete diversity rule in removal cases for cases in which there is "procedural misjoinder" in the state courts. The purpose of the doctrine is similar to the fraudulent joinder doctrine and is designed to prevent plaintiffs from joining in state court largely unrelated claims against or on behalf of non-diverse parties in order to prevent removal. *See* Laura J. Hines & Steven S. Gensler, *Driving Misjoinder: The Improper Party Problem in Removal Jurisdiction*, 57 ALA. L. REV. 779 (2006).

550. Salazar v. Allstate Tex. Lloyd's, Inc., 455 F.3d 571 (5th Cir. 2006); *see also* Borden v. Allstate Ins. Co., 589 F.3d 168 (5th Cir. 2009) (once a court permits post-removal joinder of a non-diverse defendant, the fraudulent joinder doctrine is not applicable and the court loses subject-matter jurisdiction).

federal court's removal jurisdiction was derivative, the case could not be removed.[551]

In 1986, Congress abolished the derivative jurisdiction rule, at least in cases removed under § 1441, by adding what is now[552] subsection (f) to 28 U.S.C. § 1441: "The court to which such civil action is removed is not precluded from hearing and determining any claim in such civil action because the State court from which such civil action is removed did not have jurisdiction over that claim."[553]

Illustration 2-98. *P* sues *D* in a Massachusetts state court for treble damages under the federal antitrust laws based upon an alleged scheme to fix the price of dynamite sold in interstate and foreign commerce with the United States. Prior to 1986, *D* could not remove the action to a Massachusetts federal district court because of the derivative-jurisdiction rule. The Massachusetts state court lacked jurisdiction because Congress has vested exclusive authority to hear federal antitrust claims in federal district courts. Instead, *D* could have had the state court action dismissed for lack of subject-matter jurisdiction. Today, however, *D* may remove the case.

* * * * *

The defendant may waive the right to remove by taking substantial defensive action in the state court, such as the filing of an answer on the merits.[554] Given the thirty-day time limit that exists on removal (discussed in subsection *(d)*, below), the waiver doctrine is of minor significance today.[555] A party will seldom be able to take substantial defensive action in a state court before the thirty-day time

---

551. *See* RICHARD H. FALLON ET AL., HART & WECHSLER'S THE FEDERAL COURTS AND THE FEDERAL SYSTEM 1440 (6th ed. 2009).

552. When originally added, the subsection was lettered (e). It was relettered after insertion of a provision added by the Multiforum Trial Jurisdiction Act of 2002, which is discussed in subsection 5 *infra*.

553. 28 U.S.C. § 1441(f) (In the Federal Courts Jurisdiction and Venue Clarification Act of 2011, Pub. L. No. 112-63, § 103(7), 125 Stat. 758, 759, retained this provision in § 1441(f) and clearly labeled the subsection "DERIVATIVE REMOVAL JURISDICTION."). Today, therefore, the district courts may hear removed cases over which they have exclusive jurisdiction as well as other cases properly falling within subsections (a)-(d) of 28 U.S.C. § 1441 that have been commenced in a state court lacking subject-matter jurisdiction as a matter of state law. However, state-court jurisdiction will not always be irrelevant to the right to remove. In Sheppard v. Exxon Co. U.S.A., 760 F. Supp. 92 (M.D. La. 1990), the court held that an action could not be removed from state court on the basis that original jurisdiction existed under 28 U.S.C. § 1332, because the amount-in-controversy requirement of that statute was not satisfied. Plaintiff had filed suit in a state court that had a statutory jurisdictional amount limitation of $10,000. Thus, even though the plaintiff was seeking punitive damages, the amount in controversy could not exceed $10,000 because that was the largest amount for which the state court could render a judgment. Furthermore, a number of cases have held that the abolition of the derivative jurisdiction rule only applies to cases removed under § 1441 and that jurisdiction is still derivative under other removal statutes. *See, e.g.*, Rodas v. Seidlin, 656 F.3d 610 (7th Cir. 2011) (derivative jurisdiction rule is applicable to removal under § 1442; however, rule is a procedural rather than a jurisdictional requirement that does not prevent a district court from entering judgment in a case when it has subject-matter jurisdiction at the time of the judgment); Palmer v. City Nat'l Bank, 498 F.3d 236 (4th Cir. 2007) (derivative jurisdiction rule applies to removal under 28 U.S.C. § 1442); *In re* Elko Cnty. Grand Jury, 109 F.3d 554 (9th Cir. 1997) (removal under § 1442); Edwards v. United States Dep't of Justice, 43 F.3d 312 (7th Cir. 1994) (removal under § 1442). *But see* North Dakota v. Fredericks, 940 F.2d 333 (8th Cir. 1991) (removal under § 1444; although derivative jurisdiction rule has explicitly been abolished only in § 1441 removal cases, rule is judicially abolished in all other cases). The American Law Institute's proposed revision of § 1441 would clarify that the derivative jurisdiction rule is abolished in all cases. *See* ALI FEDERAL JUDICIAL CODE REVISION PROJECT § 1441(e), at 346 (2004).

554. *See* 14B CHARLES A. WRIGHT ET AL., FEDERAL PRACTICE AND PROCEDURE: JURISDICTION AND RELATED MATTERS AND RELATED MATTERS § 3721, at 97-117 (3d ed. 2009). *But cf.* Aqualon Co. v. MAC Equip., Inc., 149 F.3d 262 (4th Cir. 1998) (no waiver by conduct when defendant filed motion for judgment against third party the same day notice of removal filed because waiver by conduct does not occur when removal precedes any action by the state court).

555. *See* RICHARD H. FALLON ET AL., HART & WECHSLER'S THE FEDERAL COURTS AND THE FEDERAL SYSTEM 1433 (6th ed. 2009).

limit for removing the action expires.[556] Waiver of the right to remove may also occur by entering into a valid forum selection clause.[557]

Illustration 2-99. *P*, a citizen of State *X*, contracts with *D*, a citizen of State *Y*. The contract contains a forum selection clause in which *D* agrees to submit to a forum selected by *P*. The clause also prohibits *D* from removing the action to federal court. Subsequently, *P* sues *D* in a state court in State *X*. *D* removes the action to federal court. The action should be remanded. *D* has waived the right to remove by entering into a valid forum selection clause.[558]

2. Exception to the General Rule of Removal Jurisdiction in Diversity Cases: Section 1441(b)(2)

Section 1441(b)(2) excepts certain diversity cases from the removal jurisdiction conferred by § 1441(a). When removal is based entirely on diversity of citizenship, a case may not be removed if *any* of the defendants is a citizen of the state in which the action is brought. This restriction reflects the policies of the diversity jurisdiction. If a state court is satisfactory to a noncitizen plaintiff, the defendant may not remove because no danger of bias or prejudice exists against the defendant as an outsider in the courts of the defendant's own state.[559]

However, § 1441(b)(2) creates a curious imbalance between original jurisdiction and removal jurisdiction in diversity cases. A plaintiff who is a citizen of the state in which the action is brought may sue an out-of-state citizen within the diversity jurisdiction under 28 U.S.C. § 1332, but a defendant who is a citizen of the state in which the action is brought may not remove an action brought in state court by an out-of-state citizen. Furthermore, in multiple defendant actions in which only one of the defendants is a citizen of the state in which the action is brought, the restriction on removal in § 1441(b)(2) can potentially result in the out-of-state defendant being subjected to the kind of bias or prejudice that the diversity jurisdiction was designed to guard against. In this respect, however, § 1441(b)(2) is no worse that the rule requiring complete diversity of citizenship for original (and removal) jurisdiction. As indicated in section D, above, that rule can also result in the operation of bias or prejudice against noncitizens.[560]

---

556. *But see* Scholz v. RDV Sports, Inc., 821 F. Supp. 1469 (M.D. Fla. 1993).

557. *See, e.g.,* Snapper, Inc. v. Redan, 171 F.3d 1249 (11th Cir. 1999); Excell, Inc. v. Sterling Boiler & Mech., Inc., 106 F.3d 318 (10th Cir. 1997); Travelers Ins. Co. v. Keeling, 996 F.2d 1485 (2d Cir. 1993); *see also* American Soda, LLP v. U.S. Filter Wastewater Group, Inc., 428 F.3d 921 (10th Cir. 2005) (when a forum selection clause refers to courts "of a state," venue is not proper in federal district court in the state in removed action; action remanded). *But see* City of New Orleans v. Municipal Admin. Servs., Inc., 376 F.3d 501 (5th Cir. 2004) (contract clause may defeat right to removal only if it is unambiguous).

558. *See, e.g.,* Foster v. Chesapeake Ins. Co., 933 F.2d 1207 (3d Cir. 1991); *see also* David S. Coale, et al., *Contractual Waiver of the Right to Remove to Federal Court: How Policy Judgments Guide Contract Interpretation*, 29 REV. LIT. 327 (2010).

559. The American Law Institute's proposed revision of § 1441 retains this restriction, but it broadens the language of the restriction to make it clear that it applies to defendants who have voluntarily appeared without being served with process and to plaintiffs who have been realigned as defendants. (The doctrine of realignment is examined in Chapter 8(C)(3)*(c) infra.*) *See* ALI FEDERAL JUDICIAL CODE REVISION PROJECT § 1441(b)(2), at 345 (2004); *id.* at 365-66 (cmt.).

560. *See Illustration 2-35* and accompanying text *supra*.

Illustration 2-100. *P*, a citizen of State *X*, sues *D*, a citizen of State *Y*, for $500,000 in a State *Y* state court. *P's* claim arises under state law. *D* may not remove the action to a U.S. District Court in State *Y* because of the restriction in § 1441(b) on removal jurisdiction. *D* is a citizen of the state in which the action is brought and the claim is based entirely on state law. However, if a citizen of the forum state possesses a claim for relief against a noncitizen meeting the amount-in-controversy requirement, the citizen can sue the noncitizen in a U.S. District Court in the forum state notwithstanding the fact that the plaintiff is a citizen of the state in which the action is brought.[561]

Illustration 2-101. In *Illustration 2-100*, if *P's* claim had been based on federal law, the § 1441(b)(2) restriction would not prevent removal. Section 1441(b) provides only that when removal is based exclusively on the fact that the district court would have had original jurisdiction based on diversity, the presence of a resident defendant will defeat removal.[562]

Illustration 2-102. *P*, a citizen of State *X*, sues *D-1*, a citizen of State *Y*, and *D-2*, a citizen of State *Z*, in a state court in State *Y*. *P* asserts a state claim in the alternative for $500,000 against *D-1* and *D-2* arising out of an automobile accident. The action cannot be removed even though a U.S. District Court would have had original jurisdiction over the action. *D-1* is a citizen of State *Y*. Thus, § 1441(b)(2) prevents removal. Note that the State *Y* trier of fact may find in favor of *P* and against *D-2* while exonerating *D-1*, the State *Y* citizen, on the basis of bias or prejudice. *D-2's* position is different from *P's*. If a State *Y* trier of fact discriminates against *P*, it is because *P* did not sue in a U.S. District Court in State *Y* where the bias or prejudice is (presumably) absent or can be controlled. However, because of *D-1's* presence in the action, *D-2* may not remove to a federal forum. *D-2* is thus deprived of a choice by § 1441(b) that *P* possessed, but chose to relinquish.

* * * * *

Sections 1441(e)(1)(A) & (B) provide for removal of cases in two additional situations. First, an action may be removed if it could have been brought originally in a federal district court under § 1369. Second, it may be removed if "the defendant is a party to an action which is or could have been brought, in whole or in part, under [§] 1369 in a [U.S.] District Court and arises from the same accident as the action in State Court," even if the action to be removed could not have been brought in a district court as an original matter.[563] These provisions trump the restriction in 28 U.S.C. § 1441(b)(2) that prohibits removal by defendants in diversity actions who are citizens of the state in which the action is brought.

---

561. If, after *P* sues *D* in the state court, *D* asserts a counterclaim against *P*, *P* cannot remove to federal court; only defendants can remove and *P* is a plaintiff. *See* Shamrock Oil & Gas Corp. v. Sheets, 313 U.S. 100, 61 S. Ct. 868, 85 L. Ed. 1214 (1941).

562. Prior to 2012, this provision was found in § 1441(b), which was not then divided into separate subsections (1) & (2). At that time the provision led off with a statement that civil actions in which the district courts had original jurisdiction based on a federal claim could be removed without regard to the citizenship or residence of the parties. In the Federal Courts Jurisdiction and Venue Clarification Act of 2011, Pub. L. No. 112-63, § 103(3), 125 Stat. 758, 759, this sentence was removed. Now § 1441(b)(2) simply states:

> A civil action otherwise removable solely on the basis of the jurisdiction under section 1332(a) of this title may not be removed if any of the parties in interest properly joined and served as defendants is a citizen of the State in which such action is brought.

563. *See* 28 U.S.C. § 1441(e)(1)(A) & (B) (enacted as part of the Multiparty, Multiforum Trial Jurisdiction Act of 2002, discussed in section C(3)(e), above).

In *Passa v. Derderian,*[564] discussed in section D(5) of this chapter, the court held that the action was properly removed under 28 U.S.C. § 1441(e)(1)(B) because one of the defendants who was sued originally in both actions in the district court was also a defendant in the removed actions. Thus, as to this defendant, it was "a party to an action which is . . . brought" originally in the district court and could, therefore, remove even if the removed actions could not have been brought originally in a district court.

As discussed earlier in this chapter in section D(6) and other appropriate places and in Chapter 8, below, in 2005 Congress enacted the Class Action Fairness Act, which established special jurisdiction and removal provisions for at least some class actions. New 28 U.S.C. § 1453(b) provides that class actions governed by the Act may be removed "without regard to whether any defendant is a citizen of the State in which the action is brought," and also provides that "such action may be removed by any defendant without the consent of all defendants." Thus, for actions covered by the Act, the resident defendant and unanimity requirements[565] for removal have been eliminated. However, certain class actions are eliminated from the coverage of the removal provisions by 28 U.S.C. § 1453(d).

Specifically, certain securities claims[566] and claims relating to the internal affairs or governance of a corporation or other business enterprise that arise under the laws of the state in which the corporation or other business enterprise is incorporated or organized[567] are exempted from the new removal provisions. It is unclear whether removal would nevertheless be prohibited by the exemption from removal granted in § 1453(d) if these exempt actions would be removable under the general removal provisions of Title 28. The ambiguity is created because the language of § 1453(d) specifically states that "[t]his section shall not apply" to the exempted actions, seeming to leave it open whether other sections might permissibly provide for removal.

3. Removal of Separate and Independent Claims: Section 1441(c)

Section 1441(c) provides for removal of a category of cases over which no original jurisdiction may exist in the district courts. Thus, § 1441(c) encompasses

---

564. 308 F. Supp. 2d 43 (D.R.I. 2004).

565. The unanimity requirement is that normally all defendants joined in the state court action must join in the removal notice. This requirement, including amendments to clarify when and when it is not applicable made in the Federal Courts Jurisdiction and Venue Clarification Act of 2011, Pub. L. No. 112-63, 125 Stat. 758, are discussed below in conjunction with the topic of removal procedure in subsection 4.

566. *See* 28 U.S.C. § 1453(d)(1) & (3); *see also* Farina v. Nokia, Inc., 625 F.3d 97 (3d Cir. 2010) (commencement for purposes of Class Action Fairness Act ("CAFA") is determined by state law); Admiral Ins. Co. v. Abshire, 574 F.3d 267 (5th Cir. 2009) (commencement for purposes of CAFA determined by state law; court questions whether using concept of relation back, as done by some other courts, is ever illuminating); Springman v. AIG Mktg., Inc., 523 F.3d 685 (7th Cir. 2008) (amendment to pleading in state court that adds federal claim where only state claims had been framed before opens a new window of removal under CAFA); Ford Motor Credit Co. v. Jones, No.1:07 CV 728, 2007 WL 2236618, 2007 U.S. Dist. LEXIS 55336 (N.D. Ohio July 31, 2007) (Class Action Fairness Act does not allow removal by a third-party defendant); Lonny Sheinkopf Hoffman, *Burdens of Jurisdictional Proof,* 59 ALA. L. REV. 409 (2008) (discussing the attempt in the courts to reverse the normal burden of proof on jurisdictional issues under CAFA's exceptions).

567. *See* 28 U.S.C. § 1453(d)(2).

certain cases that are not removable under § 1441(a). Prior to 2012, § 1441(c) was worded in a manner that raised substantial problems of coordination with the supplemental jurisdiction statute discussed in subsection (4) of this chapter, as well as substantial problems of constitutionality. In the Federal Courts Jurisdiction and Venue Clarification Act of 2011 (effective in January 2012),[568] § 1441(c) was extensively amended. The amendments have eliminated the constitutional doubts about the operation of § 1441(c), though at some cost to plaintiffs' joinder prerogatives. However, it is doubtful that they have eliminated the doubts about the coordination of the provision with the supplemental jurisdiction statute. This subsection will discuss the law prior to 2012 and the difficulties that it raised. It will then discuss the recent amendments to § 1441(c).

(a) The History of Section 1441(c)

Before 1990, 28 U.S.C. § 1441(c) had provided that when a "separate and independent" claim or cause of action, which would be removable if sued on alone, was joined with a nonremovable claim, the entire action could be removed to federal court.[569] In the Judicial Improvements Act of 1990, § 1441(c) was amended to eliminate its application to diversity actions.[570] After the amendment, section 1441(c) read:

> (c) Whenever a separate and independent claim or cause of action within the jurisdiction conferred by section 1331 of this title is joined with one or more otherwise non-removable claims or causes of action, the entire case may be removed and the district court may determine all issues therein, or, in its discretion, may remand all matters in which State law predominates.[571]

The stated purpose of the 1990 amendment was to implement, "in modified form," a recommendation of the Federal Courts Study Committee.[572] However, the Federal Courts Study Committee had recommended outright repeal of § 1441(c).[573] The Committee recognized that the principal purpose of § 1441(c) was to prevent a defendant's right of removal from being defeated by the joinder of an unrelated nonremovable claim[574] and that most § 1441(c) applications occurred in diversity actions.[575] The Committee felt that the statute caused "much litigation apart from the merits as defendants try and mostly fail to qualify for separate claim removal."[576] The Committee's only reference to federal question cases was the following passage:

---

568. Pub. L. No. 112-63, § 103(4), 125 Stat. 758, 759 (codified at 28 U.S.C. § 1441(c)).

569. *See generally* William T. Goglia, Annotation, *What Is "A Separate and Independent Claim or Cause of Action" Within 28 U.S.C.S. § 1441(c) Which Permits Nonresident Codefendant to Remove Case From State to Federal Court*, 58 A.L.R. FED. 458 (1982).

570. Pub. L. No. 101-650, § 312, 104 Stat. 5089, 5114 (codified at 28 U.S.C. § 1441(c)).

571. *Id.*

572. *See* H.R. REP. NO. 734, 101st Cong., 2d Sess. 22 (1990).

573. *See* REPORT OF THE FEDERAL COURTS STUDY COMMITTEE 94-95 (1990).

574. *See id.* at 94.

575. *See id.* at 94-95.

576. *Id.* at 95.

> In the small number of federal question cases in which the statute might apply . . . it can work fairly well as a backstop to the general removal provisions (§§ 1441(a) & (b)). Hence we recommend its repeal only if Congress retains the general diversity jurisdiction, in which most of the difficulties with § 1441(c) arise.[577]

Congress did retain the general diversity jurisdiction. So why was § 1441(c) modified and not repealed as the Committee recommended? The House Report accompanying the amendment § 1441(c) explained:

> The amendment would . . . retain the opportunity for removal in the one situation in which it seems clearly desirable. The joinder rules of many states permit a plaintiff to join completely unrelated claims in a single action. The plaintiff could easily bring a single action on a federal claim and a completely unrelated state claim. The reasons for permitting removal of federal question cases [apply] with full force. In addition, the amended provision could actually simplify determination of removability. In many cases the federal and state claims will be related in such a way as to establish pendant [sic] jurisdiction over the state claim. Removal of such cases is possible under Sec. 1441(a). *The amended provision would establish a basis for removal that would avoid the need to decide whether there is pendant* [sic] *jurisdiction.*[578]

In summary, after 1990, but prior to 2012, § 1441(c) provided for removal of civil actions in which a claim was asserted within 28 U.S.C. § 1331 (the general

---

577. *Id.*

578. H.R REP. NO. 734, 101st Cong., 2d Sess. 23 (1990) (emphasis added). The legislative history in the Senate is similar, but contains a reference to the need to remand "state claims" that do not form part of the same case or controversy as federal claims with which they are joined:

> The amendment would . . . retain the opportunity for removal in the one situation in which it seems clearly desirable. The joinder rules of many states permit a plaintiff to join completely unrelated claims in a single action. The plaintiff could easily bring a single action on a federal claim and a completely unrelated state claim. The reasons for permitting removal of federal question cases applies with full force. In addition, the amended provision could actually simplify determinations of removability. In many cases the federal and state claims will be related in such a way as to establish pendant [sic] jurisdiction over the state claim. Removal of such cases is possible under 28 U.S.C. § 1441(a).
>
> The further amendment to 28 U.S.C. § 1441(c) that would permit remand of all matters in which state law predominates also should simplify administration of the separate and independent claim removal. Of course, a district court must remand state claims that are so unrelated to the federal claim that they do not form part of the same Article III case or controversy.

136 CONG. REC. 517, 581 (Oct. 27, 1990) (statement of Sen. Grassley). The Senate history thus eliminates a reference in the House Report that indicates § 1441(c) would avoid the need to determine whether there is pendent jurisdiction. The Senate history then adds a sentence (in the second paragraph quoted above) indicating that state claims which are not part of the same Article III case or controversy as the removable federal claims would have to be remanded. One commentator has read this change as specific evidence that "Congress" chose to address the constitutional difficulties with § 1441(c) (discussed in subsection *(c), infra*) by "counting on federal courts to use the power of remand." *See* Edward Hartnett, *A New Trick From an Old and Abused Dog: Section 1441(c) Lives and Now Permits the Remand of Federal Question Cases*, 63 FORDHAM L. REV. 1099, 1150 (1995). This conclusion, however, ignores the fact that amended § 1441(c) only provides for remand of state claims when they "predominate." In any event, the reference by Senator Grassley to remand of "state claims" does not support Professor Hartnett's position that § 1441(c) permitted the remand of entire cases. Indeed, remand of federal claims as well as state claims would have gutted the central purpose of removal under § 1441(c), something that the legislative history in both the House and Senate indicated as applying in "full force." *See* subsection *(c) infra*; *see also* REED DICKERSON, THE INTERPRETATION AND APPLICATION OF STATUTES 154-59 (1975) (discussing the lack of reliability of floor statements when compared with committee reports).

federal question statute) when those actions also contain nonfederal claims that were, to some degree, factually unrelated to the federal claim in the action. Actions containing factually related (to some degree) federal and nonfederal claims were removable under § 1441(a) & (b), because they were within the original jurisdiction of the district courts under § 1331 and § 1367 (the supplemental jurisdiction statute). Consequently, § 1441(c) provided for removal of federal question cases containing state claims that were too unrelated to the federal claims in the action to fall within the supplemental jurisdiction of the district courts. When a claim was removable under § 1441(c), only the defendant against whom the removable claim is asserted must seek removal. This result is contrary to the usual rule that all defendants must agree to remove the action.[579]

Numerous and severe problems existed with the pre-2012 text of § 1441(c). Equally severe problems existed with the explanation given in the legislative history of the 1990 amendment to the section. These problems are explored below. Specifically, three issues of interpretation will be discussed: (1) when claims should have been considered "separate and independent" within the meaning of § 1441(c); (2) how § 1367 and § 1441(c) could have been reconciled with each other and the U.S. Constitution; and (3) the scope of the remand provision of § 1441(c) prior to 2012.

(b) The Meaning of "Separate and Independent"

Before the 1990 amendment, it was not entirely clear what kinds of cases were removable under the statute. In *American Fire & Casualty Co. v. Finn*,[580] the U.S. Supreme Court held that when the plaintiff sought to recover for a single wrong resulting from an interlocked series of transactions, no separate and independent claims existed under § 1441(c).

Illustration 2-103. *P*, a citizen of Texas, sued *D-1 Insurance Corp.*, which is incorporated and with its principal place of business in Indiana, and *D-1's* agent *D-2*, a citizen of Texas, in a state court in Texas. *P* sought to recover for a fire loss allegedly covered by *D-1*. *P's* complaint sought recovery in the alternative against *D-1* and *D-2*. The claim against *D-1* was under a policy of insurance issued by *D-2*. The claim against *D-2* alleged that if recovery under the policy was impossible because the policy had lapsed, *D-2* was liable to *P* for the amount of the loss because *D-2* had a duty to notify *P* of any cancellation or expiration of the policy and did not do so. Under these circumstances, the action would not be removable to federal court under former § 1441(c). The claim against *D-1* was a claim which would be removable if sued on alone because it was within the diversity jurisdiction, and, before the 1990 amendment, § 1441(c) applied to diversity cases. In addition, the removable diversity claim was joined with a nonremovable claim, the claim against *D-2*. However, *Finn* held that claims are not separate and independent

---

579. *See* 14C CHARLES A. WRIGHT ET AL., FEDERAL PRACTICE AND PROCEDURE: JURISDICTION AND RELATED MATTERS § 3730, at 469-70 (3d ed. 2009).

580. 341 U.S. 6, 14, 71 S. Ct. 534, 540, 95 L. Ed. 702, 708-09 (1951).

within the meaning of § 1441(c) when the plaintiff seeks a recovery for a single loss against multiple defendants based on a single event.

* * * * *

Finn was the only Supreme Court decision directly construing § 1441(c) before the 1990 amendment. However, in *Carnegie-Mellon University v. Cohill*,[581] the Supreme Court stated in dictum that § 1441(c) "is not directly applicable to suits involving pendent [today supplemental] claims, because pendent claims are not 'separate and independent' within the meaning of the removal statute."[582] This statement confirms the strong impression left by *Finn* and the language of § 1441(c) that to be separate and independent, claims must be factually unrelated. Factually related claims fit within the scope of pendent (today supplemental) jurisdiction. Furthermore, if the federal and state claims do not arise out of the same facts, they will surely seek separate recoveries. Taking *Finn* and *Carnegie-Mellon* together, therefore, claims would be "separate" when separate recoveries are sought and "independent" when the claims arise from different facts.

Illustration 2-104. Assume that *P*, a citizen of State *X*, sues *D*, also a citizen of State *X*, in a State *X* state court. *P's* suit consists of two claims, one arising under federal law for $500,000 and one arising under state law for $30,000. The claims seek separate recoveries and are unrelated, factually and legally. Thus, they are "separate and independent." The claim arising under federal law would be removable if sued upon alone. The state claim would not be removable if sued upon alone. Thus, the entire case was removable both under the language of § 1441(c) and the precedents interpreting it.

* * * * *

Nevertheless, a difficult question of interpretation existed under former § 1441(c) involving cases falling between those exemplified by *Illustrations 2-103* and *2-104*. In particular, when a plaintiff sued multiple defendants for multiple losses (rather than a single recovery) arising from the same or a related set of facts, or multiple plaintiffs seek separate recoveries against a single defendant for losses arising from a single or related set of facts, are the claims asserted "separate and independent" within the meaning of § 1441(c)? *Finn* and *Carnegie-Mellon* suggest not. However, some lower federal court decisions before the amendment of § 1441(c) permitted removal in these kinds of cases despite the Supreme Court's suggestion that removal was improper.[583]

Illustration 2-105. *P-1*, a citizen of State *X*, and *P-2*, a citizen of State *Y*, sued *D Airline*, a corporation incorporated and with its principal place of business in State *Y*. *P-1* and *P-2* brought the action in a state court in State *X*. *P-1* sought $100,000 in damages for personal injuries resulting from the crash of a *D* airliner. *P-2* also sought $100,000 in damages for personal injuries received in the same crash. Before the 1990 amendment of § 1441(c), some lower federal courts

---

581. 484 U.S. 343, 108 S. Ct. 614, 98 L. Ed. 2d 720 (1988).

582. *Id.* at 354, 108 S. Ct. at 621, 98 L. Ed. 2d at 732.

583. *See, e.g.*, Twentieth Century-Fox Film Corp. v. Taylor, 239 F. Supp. 913 (S.D.N.Y. 1965) (action against Richard Burton and Elizabeth Taylor for breach of their employment contracts during the filming of the movie "Cleopatra") (disapproved in Gardner & Florence Call Cowles Found. v. Empire Inc., 754 F.2d 478, 482 n.5 (2d Cir. 1985)); Herrmann v. Braniff Airways, Inc., 308 F. Supp. 1094 (S.D.N.Y. 1969) (action by multiple plaintiffs arising from a single aircraft accident).

permitted *D* to remove this action under the section. *P-1's* claim would be removable if sued on alone. *P-2's* claim was not removable if sued on alone. Even though the claims arose from the same event, the courts that permitted removal considered the claims to be both separate and independent merely because separate recoveries were sought.[584]

* * * * *

The structure and probable purpose of § 1441(c), together with the legislative history of the 1990 amendment to the section, should dispel any doubt about the meaning of the terms "separate and independent." Only claims that arise from entirely unrelated facts and seek separate recoveries should be removable under the section. In deciphering the statute, several questions should be considered: (1) Why did Congress make removability contingent upon the joined claims being sufficiently unrelated to each other? (2) When the claims meet the relationship test of the statute, why is the entire action, as opposed to only the claim over which the district court has original jurisdiction, made removable? (3) Once the action has been removed, why was the district court given discretion to keep the entire case or to remand the nonremovable claim before 1990?

Focusing first on the requirement that the joined claims must be unrelated, note that even prior to the 1990 amendment to § 1441(c), Congress was probably attempting to prevent the joinder of removable and nonremovable claims in state court simply for the purpose of preventing removal by the defendant. This danger is greatest in that category of cases in which joinder by the plaintiff is least likely to be for legitimate procedural reasons—cases in which the claims are factually and legally unrelated to each other. In other cases, when some factual relationship exists between the claims, plaintiffs are less likely to join claims simply to prevent removal.[585]

Nevertheless, some plaintiffs may join factually unrelated claims for legitimate reasons. In joinder systems patterned on Federal Rule 18, unlimited joinder of claims is permitted even if no factual or legal relationship exists between the claims. The theory of this kind of system is that no harm results from unlimited joinder of claims at the pleading stage of the litigation, but only, sometimes, by trying unrelated claims together. However, if inconvenience will result from trying unrelated claims together, the inconvenience can be dealt with under provisions, such as Federal Rule 42(b), which allow separate trials of the claims to be ordered.[586] Thus, the policy of modern unlimited joinder practice is to leave to the plaintiff in the first instance the decision whether it will be convenient to resolve

---

584. *See* Herrmann v. Braniff Airways, Inc., 308 F. Supp. 1094 (S.D.N.Y. 1969).

585. The textual discussion is applicable only to situations in which joinder of the claims in question is not "fraudulent." Whenever a plaintiff collusively or fraudulently joins a claim against a resident defendant in a diversity action to prevent removal, the nonresident defendant may remove by alleging and proving the fraudulent joinder. Thus, the textual discussion here is limited to cases in which the joinder does not meet the fraudulent joinder standards, but may be primarily intended to defeat removal nonetheless. Fraudulent joinder is discussed in 14B CHARLES A. WRIGHT ET AL., FEDERAL PRACTICE AND PROCEDURE: JURISDICTION AND RELATED MATTERS § 3723, at 787-878 (3d ed. 2009). The most common situation in which fraudulent joinder is found is when the plaintiff has failed to state a claim for relief against a nondiverse defendant. *See, e.g.*, Brown v . Jevic, 575 F.3d 322 (3d Cir. 2009) (joinder of debtor who had declared bankruptcy to state court action was fraudulent because plaintiff could not recover against debtor due to automatic stay issued in bankruptcy proceedings prohibiting suits against debtor); Green v. Amerada Hess Corp., 707 F.2d 201 (5th Cir. 1983).

586. 6A CHARLES A. WRIGHT ET AL., FEDERAL PRACTICE AND PROCEDURE: CIVIL § 1586 (23 ed. 2010).

all claims the plaintiff possesses against the defendant in one proceeding, subject to later discretion in the court to sever the claims for trial.

The original § 1441(c) drafters' decision can be seen as an attempt to accommodate the policy of unlimited joinder of claims that is found in many modern procedural systems with the policy of avoiding the joinder of unrelated claims simply to prevent removal. By limiting removal to situations in which wholly unrelated claims were joined, the drafters protected against joinder designed to prevent removal. Plaintiffs are less likely to join completely unrelated claims for reasons of litigation convenience than they are to join related claims for these same reasons. Allowing removal of the entire case, rather than only the removable claim, accommodated the policy of unlimited joinder that is found in modern procedural systems. Finally, giving discretion to the district court to remand the nonremovable claim allowed the court to determine whether the plaintiff's reasons for joinder were legitimate or whether joinder was effectuated simply to prevent removal. Therefore, before the 1990 amendment, to conform removal to both the language and the structure of the statute, the courts should have limited the application of § 1441(c) to cases in which no factual relationship existed between the claims.[587]

The legislative history of the 1990 amendment to the statute should resolve any doubt about the kinds of cases that are removable under § 1441(c). That history confirms that the words "separate and independent" require factually unrelated claims seeking separate recoveries. The House Report explains that Congress retained separate and independent claim removal to prevent the defendant's right of removal from being destroyed when the plaintiff joins federal and state claims that are completely unrelated to each other, factually and legally.[588]

Unfortunately, the court decisions construing § 1441(c) after the 1990 amendment did not entirely dispel the pre-1990 confusion about the statute's interpretation. Several decisions since the amendment have allowed removal of factually related federal and state claims. A few of these decisions seem to confuse the relationship between § 1441(a), § 1441(c), and § 1367 of Title 28. Some courts combine the different statutes, despite their language, to allow removal of factually related claims.[589] Nevertheless, even courts that show an awareness of the proper

---

587. Unfortunately, the legislative history of the statute prior to 1990 adds little to the understanding of the meaning of the words "separate and independent." *See* RICHARD H. FALLON ET AL., HART & WECHSLER'S THE FEDERAL COURTS AND THE FEDERAL SYSTEM 1443 (6th ed. 2009). However, candor requires the admission that the history of the statute, to the extent it adds anything, works against the interpretation in the text. Under the textual interpretation, few diversity actions would be removable. Thus, the section had its primary value in federal question cases. Yet it may be that in the 1948 revision of the Judicial Code, Congress did not think that § 1441(c) would be applicable to federal question cases. *See* 1 FEDERAL COURTS STUDY COMMITTEE WORKING PAPERS AND SUBCOMMITTEE REPORTS 534 (1990), and authorities there discussed in note 59; *see also* CHARLES A. WRIGHT & MARY KAY KANE, THE LAW OF FEDERAL COURTS § 39, at 236-37 (7th ed. 2011).

588. Recall that the House Report accompanying the amendment to § 1441(c) stated that when, as permitted by joinder rules like Federal Rule 18, the plaintiff joined a federal claim "and a completely unrelated state claim," "[t]he reasons for permitting removal of federal question cases [apply] with full force." H.R. REP. NO. 734, 101st Cong., 2d Sess. 23 (1990). The legislative history in the Senate was identical on this point. *See* 136 Cong. Rec. at 5.17,581 (Oct. 27, 1990) (statement of Sen. Grassley).

589. *See, e.g.*, Newton v. Coca-Cola Bottling Co. Consol., 958 F. Supp. 248 (W.D.N.C. 1997) (Title VII claim that plaintiff fired in retaliation for complaining about sexual violence committed against her by former employee and nonremovable Violence Against Women Act claim against employee are separate and independent); Richmond v. American Sys. Corp., 792 F. Supp. 449 (E.D. Va. 1992); *see also* Scianna *ex rel.* Urso v. Furlong, 56 F. Supp. 2d 1000 (N.D. Ill. 1999) (stating that "[i]t is not the facts that the court focuses upon to determine whether the claims are separate and independent," but rather the legal rights involved (citing *Finn* as authority!);

differences between the statutes sometimes allow removal of factually related claims seeking separate recoveries.[590]

Illustration 2-106. *P*, a citizen of State *X*, had a flat tire. P sought the assistance of *D-1*, who was a police officer and citizen of State *X*. *D-1* called an agent of *D-2*, a corporation incorporated and with its principal place of business in State *X*, to assist *P*. After *D-2's* agent had changed *P's* flat tire, the agent demanded payment in cash. When *P* could not pay, the agent called *D-1*, who arrested *P*. *P* sued *D-1* and *D-2* in a state court of State *X*. *P* asserted a claim against *D-1* under 42 U.S.C. § 1983, the Civil Rights Act of 1871. *P* asserted only a state-law claim against *D-2* for unfair and deceptive trade practices. *D-1* attempted to remove the action to a U.S. District Court in State *X* under § 1441(c). Because *D-1* alone sought removal, § 1441(a) and (b), which require all defendants to seek removal, could not be used. On these facts, a federal district court allowed removal under § 1441(c). The court stated that the harm allegedly caused by *D-2* was separate and distinct from the harm caused by *D-1*. The court's opinion was based on the fact that separate recoveries were sought on the claims against *D-1* and *D-2*. However, the claims arose from the same facts and would have been within the supplemental jurisdiction of the district court under § 1367. Therefore, had both defendants joined in seeking removal of the action, jurisdiction would have been proper under § 1441(a). Under the pre-1990 U.S. Supreme Court precedents interpreting § 1441(c), and given the probable purposes of the statute and the legislative history of the 1990 amendment, it is highly likely that the action was improperly removed.[591]

* * * * *

Despite the persistence of decisions allowing removal under § 1441(c) when joined federal and state claims are factually related, other decisions after 1990 correctly hold that removal under § 1441(c) requires factually unrelated claims. Under this view, which accords with the language, structure, and the 1990 legislative history of § 1441(c), few cases are removable under the statute. Thus, numerous decisions deny removal because the federal and state claims are factually related.[592] Some cases have allowed removal on the basis that the federal and state

---

Dobiecki v. Palacios, 829 F. Supp. 229 (N.D. Ill. 1993) (describing § 1441(c) and § 1367(c) as alternative provisions allowing removal whenever there is a federal question in the case).

590. *See* Alexander v. Goldome Credit Corp., 772 F. Supp. 1217 (M.D. Ala. 1991) (separate recoveries, related facts); Rey v. Classic Cars, 762 F. Supp. 421 (D. Mass. 1991); Moore v. DeBiase, 766 F. Supp. 1311, 1318-19 n.13 (D.N.J. 1991) (separate recoveries, related facts; action removed under §§ 1441(a) & (b), remanded under § 1441(c); court stated that § 1441(c) allows removal of federal question cases in which state claims are somewhat related to federal claims, but not sufficiently related to be within pendent jurisdiction); *see also* Joan Steinman, *Supplemental Jurisdiction in § 1441 Removed Cases: An Unsurveyed Frontier of Congress' Handiwork*, 35 ARIZ. L. REV. 305 (1993); *cf.* Patel v. Del Taco, Inc., 446 F.3d 996 (9th Cir. 2006) (removal of action under § 1441(c) improper where no federal claim exists; joinder of a federal claim and a claim for removal of a state court action in a federal complaint cannot effectuate § 1441(c) removal); Lannes v. Operators Int'l, No. Civ.A 04-584, 2004 WL 2984327, 2004 U.S. Dist. LEXIS 25781 (E.D. La. Dec. 20, 2004) (allowing removal on the basis of a crossclaim, under Fifth Circuit authorities stating that a federal question claim is separate and independent if it involves an obligation distinct from the nonremovable claims in the case).

591. *Cf.* Rey v. Classic Cars, 762 F. Supp. 421 (D. Mass. 1991) (facts simplified for purposes of illustration).

592. *See, e.g.*, Scott v. Ditto, No. 1:11-CV-227, 2011 WL 5921432, 2011 U.S. Dist. LEXIS 136139 (E.D. Tenn. Nov. 28, 2011) (to be separate and independent, federal and state claims must be completely disassociated); Mullins v. Hinkle, 953 F. Supp. 744 (S.D. W. Va. 1997); Texas Hosp. Ass'n v. National Heritage Ins. Co., 802 F. Supp. 1507 (W.D. Tex. 1992); Lang v. American Elec. Power Co., 785 F. Supp. 1331 (N.D. Ind. 1992); Allsup v.

claims were unrelated, but the courts in those cases may have mistakenly perceived that the federal and state claims were sufficiently disassociated to be "separate and independent" within the meaning of § 1441(c).[593]

Illustration 2-107. *P*, a citizen of State *X*, sued *D*, a citizen of State *X* who was *P's* former employer, in a state court of State *X*. *P* asserted two claims against *D*. One claim was a federal claim for failure to pay *P* overtime for certain work performed by *P* while *P* was employed by *D*. The second claim was a state-law claim for breach of an implied contract of employment when *D* fired *P*. *P* did not allege that the firing was related to *P's* complaints about *D's* failure to pay overtime. *D* removed the action under § 1441(c). In allowing removal, the district court reasoned that *P's* federal claim would turn on whether *P* had devoted more than half *P's* time to supervisory duties when employed by *D*, while the second claim would depend on establishing an implied contract of employment and its breach. Because proving one claim would be of no assistance in proving the other, the court considered the claims separate and independent. However, although *P* sought separate recoveries from *D*, the federal and state claims were probably not sufficiently disassociated to be separate and independent. Both claims arose out of the same employment relationship between *P* and *D*. The claims were thus sufficiently related to justify removal on the basis of supplemental jurisdiction under 28 U.S.C. § 1367 and § 1441(a).[594] Under the pre-1990 U.S. Supreme Court precedents construing § 1441(c), claims sufficiently related to fall within supplemental jurisdiction are not separate and independent.

Illustration 2-108. *P*, a citizen of State *X*, is a merchant. *P* was assaulted by *D-1*, a police officer who is also a citizen of State *X*. The assault occurred when *D-1* stopped *P's* automobile for speeding. Several months before the assault, *D-1* had purchased goods on a time payment plan from *P's* store. The entire transaction had been handled by one of *P's* sales representatives, and *D-1* did not even know the store was owned by *P*. Later, *D-1* stopped making payments on the goods. The assault had nothing to do with the sale of goods or *D-1's* failure to make payments.

Liberty Mut. Ins. Co., 782 F. Supp. 325 (N.D. Tex. 1991); Sullivan v. Leaf River Forest Prods., Inc., 791 F. Supp. 627 (S.D. Miss. 1991); *cf.* Borough of W. Mifflin v. Lancaster, 45 F.3d 780 (3d Cir. 1995) (district court had pendent jurisdiction under § 1367; therefore, claims could not be separate and independent and could not be remanded under § 1441(c)).

593. *See, e.g.*, Moralez v. Meat Cutters Local 539, 778 F. Supp. 368 (E.D. Mich. 1991); Nesbitt v. Bun Basket, Inc., 780 F. Supp. 1151 (W.D. Mich. 1991).

594. *See* Nesbitt v. Bun Basket, Inc., 780 F. Supp. 1151, 1152 (W.D. Mich. 1991). In section E(5)*(c) supra*, it was argued that only a loose factual relationship is necessary to satisfy the requirements for pendent jurisdiction. *See* 13D CHARLES A. WRIGHT ET AL., FEDERAL PRACTICE AND PROCEDURE: JURISDICTION AND RELATED MATTERS § 3567.1, at 349 (3d ed. 2008). Note, however, that if the cases hold something more than a "loose factual relationship" necessary to bring federal and state claims within the scope of the same case, two possibilities for the interpretation of § 1441(c) arise. One possibility, supported by the pre-amendment interpretation of § 1441(c) by the U.S. Supreme Court and by the legislative history of amended § 1441(c), is that complete factual disassociation between the removable and nonremovable claims will be required. Thus, there could be federal removable claims joined with claims that would be nonremovable under §§ 1367(a) and 1441(a) because they were only "loosely" related to the federal claim, but which would be too closely related to the federal claims to be removable under § 1441(c). *See* CHARLES A. WRIGHT & MARY KAY KANE, LAW OF FEDERAL COURTS § 39, at 239 (7th ed. 2011) (discussing this possibility under the pre-1990 version of the statute). The second possibility, which would contradict the U.S. Supreme Court's interpretation of the statute and the legislative history of the 1990 amendment, would treat claims as separate and independent if they are "loosely" related *or* totally unrelated. This approach would allow removal under § 1441(c) of all cases in which the federal removable claims and the nonremovable claims are not closely enough related to fit within the supplemental jurisdiction conferred by § 1367(a). This approach would, of course, be subject to the constitutional restrictions discussed in subsection *(c) infra*.

P sued *D-1* in a State *X* court. *P* asserted a federal civil rights claim against *D-1* and a state-law claim for breach of the contract for sale of goods. This kind of action is one in which removal would be proper under § 1441(c). *P* asserts claims that seek separate recoveries and are factually unrelated in time, space, origin, and motivation.

Illustration 2-109. On the facts of *Illustration 2-108*, assume that *P* was assaulted by *D-1* and *D-2*. Both *D-1* and *D-2* are police officers and citizens of State *X*. All other facts remain the same. *P* sues *D-1* and *D-2* in a state court of State *X*. *P* asserts federal civil rights claims against both *D-1* and *D-2*. *P* joins with these claims the state-law claim against *D-1* for breach of the contract to sell goods.[595] This action is also removable under § 1441(c). The civil rights claims are within the jurisdiction conferred by 28 U.S.C. § 1331. They are separate and independent from the breach of contract claim on the facts described.

(c) The Relationship Between Supplemental Jurisdiction and Separate and Independent Claim Removal

In retaining separate and independent claim removal for federal question cases, Congress overlooked a problem created by the interaction of § 1441(c) and § 1367 of the Judicial Code dealing with supplemental jurisdiction.[596] Recall from subsection 4*(d)*, above, that Congress provided for "supplemental jurisdiction" over claims that were joined in a federal action when those claims "are so related" to claims over which the district court has original jurisdiction as to "form part of the same case or controversy under Article III of the United States Constitution."[597] This language (from 28 U.S.C. § 1367(a)) produces an immediate difficulty. If wholly unrelated federal and state claims are within the same constitutional case or controversy, original jurisdiction exists over such claims under 28 U.S.C. § 1331 (the general federal question statute) and § 1367(a), with the result that a case involving such claims would be removable under 28 U.S.C. § 1441(a) and (b). In this event, 28 U.S.C. § 1441(c) would be superfluous. On the other hand, if joined federal and state claims must arise from the same facts to be within the same constitutional case or controversy, amended § 1441(c) can have no constitutional applications.[598]

---

595. Under joinder of claims and parties rules like Rules 18 and 20 of the Federal Rules of Civil Procedure, these claims would be properly joined. *See* Chapter 8(C)(4) *infra* ("Permissive Joinder of Parties").

596. Some commentators have argued that the legislative history of § 1441(c) in the Senate indicates that "Congress" intended to handle the constitutional problems with § 1441(c) by remand. *See* Edward Hartnett, *A New Trick From an Old and Abused Dog: Section 1441(c) Lives and Now Permits the Remand of Federal Question Cases*, 63 FORDHAM L. REV. 1099, 1150 (1995). However, the House and Senate history is contradictory on this point. *See* subsection 3*(a)* and accompanying notes *supra*. Furthermore, if Congress intended to require remand in cases of constitutional difficulty under § 1441(c), "why does the text of § 1441(c) speak only of 'discretion' to remand?" RICHARD H. FALLON ET AL., HART AND WECHSLER'S THE FEDERAL COURTS AND THE FEDERAL SYSTEM 1443 (6th ed. 2009).

597. *See* Judicial Improvements Act of 1990, Pub. L. No. 101-650, § 310, 104 Stat. 5089, 5113-14 (codified at 28 U.S.C. § 1367(a)).

598. At least two federal district courts have held § 1441(c) unconstitutional to the extent that it permits removal of factually unrelated federal and state claims. *See* Fullin v. Martin, 34 F. Supp. 2d 726 (E.D. Wis. 1999); Salei v. Boardwalk Regency Corp., 913 F. Supp. 993 (E.D. Mich. 1996); *cf.* 1 FEDERAL COURTS STUDY COMMITTEE WORKING PAPERS AND SUBCOMMITTEE REPORTS 537 (1990); CHARLES A. WRIGHT & MARY KAY KANE, THE LAW OF FEDERAL COURTS § 39, at 240 (7th ed. 2009). Recall that the House Report accompanying the

This dilemma can be avoided if the courts interpret the scope of a constitutional case or controversy and the scope of 28 U.S.C. § 1367(a) as this text recommended earlier. Subsection 4*(b)*, above, asserted that Article III should be interpreted to permit joinder of factually unrelated federal and state claims when Congress has a legitimate reason for authorizing such joinder linked to policies designed to protect or enhance the operation of federal jurisdictional grants within Article III. Congress has such legitimate purposes in precisely the situation now governed by 28 U.S.C. § 1441(c).[599] In addition, subsection 4*(e)(iii)* asserted that, despite the Article III case or controversy language found in 28 U.S.C. § 1367(a), Congress did not mean to extend jurisdiction under that section to factually unrelated claims. Rather, Congress intended only to provide for "supplemental jurisdiction" over cases in which the federal and nonfederal claims arise out of the same facts.[600] If § 1367(a) is limited in its operation to factually related claims, and if Article III of the Constitution is interpreted to permit jurisdiction over factually unrelated claims in the situation now covered by 28 U.S.C. § 1441(c), the latter section will be neither superfluous nor unconstitutional.

(d) Remand Under Section 1441(c)

Section 1441(c) contains its own remand provision. Before the 1990 amendment to § 1441(c), this section simply provided that the district court might "remand all matters not otherwise within its original jurisdiction." Under the 1990 amendment, the district courts are authorized to "remand all matters in which state

---

amendment to 28 U.S.C. § 1441(c) stated that "[t]he amended provision would establish a basis for removal that would avoid the need to decide whether there is pendant [sic] jurisdiction." H.R. REP. NO. 734, 101st Cong., 2d Sess. 23 (1990). This statement is clearly not true if the "constitutional case or controversy" language in 28 U.S.C. § 1367(a) means what it says. For in every case brought to federal court, originally or by removal, the courts are obligated to determine whether the jurisdiction conferred by Congress is constitutional. Therefore, in every federal question case involving joined claims, the courts must determine whether the joined claims fit within the same case or controversy under Article III of the Constitution. In Porter v. Roosa, 259 F. Supp. 2d 638 (S.D. Ohio 2003), *P-1* sued *D* in state court asserting federal and state claims against *D*. *P-2* joined with *P-1* in the action, asserting only state claims against *D*. *D* removed the action to federal court. The court held that with regard to *P-1*, there was no need to invoke § 1441(c), because the federal and state claims arose from a common nucleus of operative fact and were, therefore, all removable under § 1441(a) because within the pendent jurisdiction of the federal court. Indeed, the court's analysis indicated that these claims could not be removed under § 1441(c), because to be separate and independent, there had to be a complete disassociation between the federal and state claims, which could not be true when they arise out of the kind of common nucleus of operative fact required by pendent (or supplemental) jurisdiction. As far as *P-2's* state claims were concerned, the court found them to be identical to those stated by *P-1* insofar as the legal theory upon which they were based, but were completely factually independent. They therefore met the statutory requirement for removal as "separate and independent" claims under § 1441(c). However, the court held that § 1441(c) was unconstitutional as applied to these claims, because they did not fall within the same constitutional case or controversy as *P-1's* federal claims. The court then ordered *P-2's* claims, but not the entire case, remanded to state court. Note that this interprets § 1441(a) as allowing removal of part of a case in which (presumably) the claims of all parties were properly joined in state court. Although §§ 1441(a) & 1367(c) would allow remand of state claims properly removed under the combined authority of that section (in the discretion) of the court, and § 1441(c) would allow remand of the separate and independent state claims in a case that was properly removed under § 1441(c), no section apparently allows removal of that part of a case that is removable under §§ 1441(a) & 1367(a) and remand of part of the case that is not removable under § 1441(c).

599. *See* section E(2), *Illustration 2-81 supra*. The argument in favor of interpreting Article III to permit joinder of some factually unrelated federal and state claims conforms to the reasons, discussed above, why Congress decided to retain separate and independent claim removal in federal question cases, rather than to repeal § 1441(c) as recommended by the Federal Courts Study Committee.

600. Furthermore, only a "loose" factual relationship should be required by the statute. *See* section E(5)*(c)* and accompanying notes *supra*.

law predominates."[601] Several problems of interpretation existed with this change in wording.

Early commentary suggested that this new wording might justify remand of an entire case in which the state claim(s) predominated over the federal claim(s).[602] Despite the lack of support for this position in the legislative history of the statute[603] and only the barest justification in the statutory language,[604] several early decisions followed this suggestion and remanded entire cases in which they perceived that state law predominated over federal law.[605] However, permitting the remand of an entire case undermines the primary purpose of § 1441(c). The statute was designed to prevent defendants against whom federal claims were asserted from being trapped in federal court by having an unrelated state claim joined against them. Allowing remand of both federal and state claims would undermine this purpose anytime a plaintiff could join an unrelated state claim that somehow "predominated" over the federal claim. The better, and majority, interpretation of § 1441(c) was that only nonremovable claim(s) could be remanded.[606]

Some courts also applied the remand provision of § 1441(c) to cases that were removed under § 1441(a) and (b).[607] This approach was improper. The remand provision of § 1441(c) was not designed to provide additional remand authority to the district courts in non-§ 1441(c) cases. Furthermore, no support in the language or legislative history exists for this interpretation of § 1441(c). Fortunately, most courts rejected this view.[608]

---

601. *See* 28 U.S.C. § 1441(c).

602. *See* EDWARD HARTNETT, *A New Trick From An Old and Abused Dog: Section 1441(c) Lives and Now Permits the Remand of Federal Question Cases*, 63 FORDHAM L. REV. 1099 (1995); David D. Siegel, *Changes in Federal Jurisdiction and Practice Under the New (Dec. 1, 1990) Judicial Improvements Act*, 133 F.R.D. 61, 78 (1991).

603. *See* H.R. REP. NO. 734, 101st Cong., 2d Sess. 23 (1990) (which simply states that the new wording should simplify administration of separate and independent claim removal); 136 CONG. REC. 517, 581 (Oct. 27 1990) (statement of Sen. Grassley) (indicating that district courts must remand state "claims" that are so unrelated to the federal claim that they do not form part of the same case or controversy).

604. The entire position depends upon the interpretation of the word "matters" in the statute to include entire "cases." However, the word "matters" was also used in the pre-1990 version of the statute and it did not authorize remand of entire "cases" then.

605. *See, e.g.*, Cotton v. South Dakota *ex rel.* South Dakota Dep't of Soc. Servs., 843 F. Supp. 564 (D.S.D. 1994) (dictum); Administaff, Inc. v. Kaster, 799 F. Supp. 685 (W.D. Tex. 1992); Alexander v. Goldome Credit Corp., 772 F. Supp. 1217 (M.D. Ala. 1991); Moore v. DeBiase, 766 F. Supp. 1311 (D.N.J. 1991); Martin v. Drummond Coal Co., 756 F. Supp. 524 (N.D. Ala. 1991); Holland v. World Omni Leasing, Inc., 764 F. Supp. 1442 (N.D. Ala. 1991). *But see In re* City of Mobile, 75 F.3d 605, 607 (11th Cir. 1996) (overruling *Alexander*, *Martin*, and *Holland*).

606. *See, e.g.*, Poche v. Texas Air Corps, Inc., 549 F.3d 999 (5th Cir. 2008); Eastus v. Blue Bell Creameries, L.P., 97 F.3d 100 (5th Cir. 1996); *In re* City of Mobile, 75 F.3d 605 (11th Cir. 1996); Brockman v. Merabank, 40 F.3d 1013 (9th Cir. 1994).

607. *See, e.g.*, Ward v. County of Ingham, No. 5:94-CV-28, 1994 U.S. Dist. LEXIS 8612 (W.D. Mich. Apr. 25, 1994); Land & Lakes Co. v. Henderson, No. 94 C 1815, 1994 WL 124876, 1994 U.S. Dist. LEXIS 4514 (N.D.Ill. Apr. 11, 1994); Neal v. Fairman, No. 92 C 6785, 1992 U.S. Dist. LEXIS 18540 (N.D. Ill. Dec. 1, 1992); Moore v. DeBiase, 766 F. Supp. 1311 (D.N.J. 1991).

608. *See, e.g.*, Borough of W. Mifflin v. Lancaster, 45 F.3d 780 (3d Cir. 1995); John G. & Marie Stella Kenedy Mem. Found. v. Mauro, 21 F.3d 667 (5th Cir. 1994); Surprise v. GTE Serv. Corp., 47 F. Supp. 2d 240 (D. Conn. 1999); Thaxtton v. International Bhd. of Painters, 933 F. Supp. 560 (S.D.W. Va. 1996); McGilvray v. Hallmark Fin. Group, Inc., 891 F. Supp. 265 (E.D. Va. 1995). Of course, remand of state claims is permitted in cases removed under § 1367 and § 1441(a) after the federal claims have been dismissed, but otherwise remand of the entire case, including the federal claims, is not proper. *See, e.g.*, Williams v. Ragnone, 147 F.3d 700 (8th Cir. 1998) (district court has no power to remand case removed under §§ 1331, 1367(a), and 1441(a)); Choice Hotels Int'l, Inc. v. Bonham, No. 96-2717, 1997 WL 600061, 1997 U.S. App. LEXIS 26909 (4th Cir. Sept. 30, 1997) (*Carnegie Mellon* permits remand of state claims after federal claims dismissed).

The 1990 change in § 1441(c)'s wording can also be interpreted to mean that no discretion exists to remand state claims that do not "predominate," even if the district court finds that those claims were joined solely to prevent removal. Likewise, the language, though discretionary, can be read to encourage the district courts to remand state claims that do "predominate," even if the remand will cause substantial inconvenience to a plaintiff who joined them in good faith. However, this reading was not inevitable.

Illustration 2-110. *P*, a citizen of State *X*, sues *D*, a citizen of State *X*, in a state court in State *X*. *P* asserts a claim against *D* under a federal statute and a factually and legally unrelated claim under state law. The claims are not properly joined under state law. State joinder law requires either that claims be factually related or that they fall within the same legal category, such as contract, tort, etc.[609] Instead of objecting to joinder in the state court, *D* removes the entire action to a U.S. District Court in State *X* under § 1441(c). The state claim does not predominate over the federal claim and is, in fact, relatively minor in terms of the complexity of the issues and the relief sought. Nevertheless, the district court should have the discretion to remand the state claim under § 1441(c) if the state and federal claims do not form a convenient trial unit.[610]

(e) The 2011 Amendments to § 1441(c)

In the Federal Courts Jurisdiction and Venue Clarification Act of 2011,[611] effective in January 2012, Congress attempted to address some of the difficulties discussed with § 1441(c). The new subsection reads, as follows:

---

609. Joinder-of-claims provisions in code pleading states often contain provisions restricting joinder in the manner described in this illustration. *See* Chapter 7(B) *infra* ("Joinder of Claims by Plaintiffs Under the Codes"). Some courts have held that procedural misjoinder of certain kinds constitutes "fraudulent joinder," which would allow removal without regard to the misjoined claim. *See* 14B CHARLES A. WRIGHT, FEDERAL PRACTICE AND PROCEDURE: JURISDICTION AND RELATED MATTERS § 3723, at 788-878 (3d ed. 2009). If this doctrine extends to the facts of this illustration, there would be no need to resort to the remand provisions of § 1441(c).

610. Practice under § 1441(c) has given rise to a number of problems other than the major ones discussed in the text. For example, the courts are split on the question whether third-party defendants joined under Federal Rule 14 can remove under § 1441(c). *Compare, e.g.*, Jones v. Petty-Ray Geophysical Geosource, Inc., 954 F.2d 1061, 1066 (5th Cir. 1992); Hayduk v. United Parcel Serv., 930 F. Supp. 584 (S.D. Fla. 1996) *with* Monmouth-Ocean Collection Serv., Inc. v. Klor, 46 F. Supp. 2d 385 (D.N.J. 1999) (third-party defendants may not remove under § 1441(c), but third-party claim is not separate and independent in any event); Galen-Med, Inc. v. Owens, 41 F. Supp. 2d 611 (W.D. Va. 1999) (third-party defendant may not remove under either §§ 1441(a) or 1441(c)); Lane v. Mitchell, Civ. No. 1:97CV278, 1997 U.S. Dist. LEXIS 20853 (W.D.N.C. Dec. 1, 1997) (no removal on basis of third-party claim); Rosario v. Witchin Co., No. Civ. A. 97-702, 1997 WL 313221 (E.D. La. June 5, 1997) (third-party claim not removable because not separate and independent); New Venture Gear, Inc. v. Fonehouse, 982 F. Supp. 892 (N.D.N.Y. 1997) (third-party claim involves overlapping facts, so not separate and independent). Also, the Fifth Circuit Court of Appeals allowed a party to remove under § 1441(c) who had been added to a case as an additional party to a federal counterclaim against the original plaintiffs. *See* Texas *ex rel.* Board of Regents v. Walker, 142 F.3d 813 (5th Cir. 1998). In addition to the question whether the additional party qualifies for removal at all, there was a question whether the federal counterclaim and state claims were separate and independent, because they both arose from the same general, festering dispute between the parties, even though they did not involve common elements of proof. At least one court has allowed removal under § 1441(c) by a co-defendant based on a crossclaim for indemnity asserted by another co-defendant. *See* Acme Brick Co. v. Agrupacion Exportadora de Maquimaria Ceramica, 855 F. Supp. 163 (N.D. Tex. 1994). But note that crossclaims, by definition, must arise out of the same transaction or occurrence as the subject matter of the original action or a counterclaim therein. *See* FED. R. CIV. P. 13(g). They cannot possibly be "separate and independent" under such circumstances. *See generally* Michael C. Massengale, Note, *Riotous Uncertainty: A Quarrel with the "Commentators' Rule" Against Section 1441(c) Removal for Counterclaim, Cross-Claim, and Third-Party Defendants*, 75 TEX. L. REV. 659 (1997).

611. Pub. L. No. 112-63, 125 Stat. 758.

(c) JOINDER OF FEDERAL LAW CLAIMS AND STATE LAW CLAIMS—(1) If a civil action includes—

(A) a claim arising under the Constitution, laws, or treaties of the United States (within the meaning of section 1331 of this title), and

(B) a claim not within the original or supplemental jurisdiction of the district court or a claim that has been made nonremovable by statute,

the entire action may be removed if the action would be removable without the inclusion of the claim described in subparagraph (B).

(2) Upon removal of an action described in paragraph (1), the district court shall sever form the action all claims described in paragraph (1)(B) and shall remand the severed claims to the State court from which the action was removed. Only the defendants against whom a claim described in paragraph (1)(A) has been asserted are required to join in or consent to the removal under paragraph (1).[612]

It is clear that the purposes of the 2011 amendments to § 1441(c) were to solve some of the problems discussed above with the operation of the subsection. The House Report accompanying the amendments stated, in part:

> Some Federal district courts have declared [§ 1441(c)] unconstitutional or raised constitutional concerns because, on its face, subsection 1441(c) purports to give courts authority to decide state law claims for which the [f]ederal courts do not have original jurisdiction . . . . Other courts have chosen simply to remand the entire case to state court, thereby defeating access to [f]ederal court . . . .
>
> This section of the bill is intended to make changes to better serve the purpose for which the statute was originally designed, namely to provide a [f]ederal forum for the resolution of [f]ederal claims that fall within the original jurisdiction of the [f]ederal courts. The amendment to subsection 1441(c) would permit the removal of the case but require that a district court remand unrelated state law matters. This sever-and-remand approach is intended to cure any constitutional problems while preserving the defendant's right to remove claims arising under [f]ederal law.[613]

The House Report seems correct to conclude that the amendment to § 1441(c) eliminates any constitutional problems with the section. It is well within the prerogatives of Congress under Article III and the Necessary and Proper Clause to provide for removal to protect state-court defendants against whom federal claims are asserted, and there can clearly be no serious constitutional question with a remand procedure designed to eliminate removal jurisdiction over claims that would not have an independent jurisdictional basis in federal court. Likewise, the

---

612. Pub. L. No. 112-63, § 103(4), 125 Stat. 758, 759 (codified at 28 U.S.C. § 1441(c)).
613. H.R. Rep. No. 112-10, at 8 (2011).

section properly clarifies that a district court cannot remand an entire case removed under the provision, but only the claim over which no jurisdiction would exist but for its joinder with the removable federal claim. The section also codifies the previously accepted rule that, in a multiple defendant action, only the defendant against whom the removable claim was asserted needs to consent to the removal. Nevertheless, the amendment has not eliminated all problems.

First, recall that the prior structure of § 1441(c) could be interpreted as an attempt to preserve both the defendant's removal rights *and* the plaintiff's joinder prerogatives. That is, in those cases in which the plaintiff had good reason for joining factually unrelated federal and state claims, the statue arguably preserved the power of the district court to retain the entire case. This was clearly so under the wording of the statute prior to 1990, and even after the 1990 amendments, there was arguably sufficient play in the joints to allow the district courts to conclude that unrelated state law claims could be retained to protect plaintiff's joinder prerogatives, at least when those claims did not predominate. Under the current version of the statute, plaintiffs' joinder rights are entirely sacrificed, and as the prior discussion of both § 1441(c) and § 1367 have indicated, those rights may have been sacrificed because of bogus constitutional fears.

Second, the second paragraph of the House Report only refers to the power to remand "unrelated state law matters." However, the amendments potentially include within the removal and remand power more than "unrelated" matters and more than "state law" manners. The new provision clearly encompasses joined claims "not within the original or supplemental jurisdiction of the district court" or claims that have "been made nonremovable by statute." It is quite possible that a plaintiff may join removable federal claims with other federal claims that have been made nonremovable by statute, but which are factually related to each other. By requiring remand of the nonremovable claims in such cases, the amendment sacrifices plaintiffs joinder prerogatives even when there may exist strong reasons of convenience and judicial economy for adjudicating factually related claims together.

Third, the amendments do nothing to address the problem of the proper scope of an Article III case or controversy that was discussed above in conjunction with the topic of supplemental jurisdiction and the history of removal under § 1441(c). This problem has two aspects. First, despite consistent dicta in U.S. Supreme Court decisions that federal and state claims must be factually related to be within the same constitutional case or controversy, there is no square holding on facts requiring such a decision that a factual relationship is necessary between federal and state claims for Article III to be satisfied. The language of Article III contains no such requirement, and the general history of joinder practice at the time the Constitution was formed and consistently thereafter has allowed the formation of cases in which unrelated claims were joined. Indeed, the configuration of § 1441(c) after 1990 suggested a legitimate congressional purpose in allowing removal and retention of factually unrelated federal and state claims that satisfies the Constitution—the purpose of protecting defendant's removal rights *and* plaintiffs' joinder prerogatives in appropriate cases. Note that if Article III really does permit the joinder of factually unrelated federal and state claims, the text of

§ 1367(a) and § 1441(a) would literally permit a case containing such claims to be removed. Such a result would, again, raise the question of what purpose § 1441(c) serves.

A second part of the problem also concerns the coordination of § 1441(c) and §§ 1367(a) and 1441(a). If a factual relationship is required to satisfy Article III and § 1367(a), how close must the factual relationship be? This problem is important for purposes of the administration of § 1441(c) because of the courts that hold a "loose factual relationship" between federal and state claims to be insufficient to satisfy the requirements of supplemental jurisdiction. After the 2011 amendments, those courts would presumably hold cases involving a loose factual relationship to be removable under § 1441(c), but would remand the state claims under the (now) mandatory remand provision. This would, again, impair the joinder prerogatives of plaintiffs in many more cases in which there exist good reasons of efficiency and judicial economy for adjudicating federal and state claims together.

4. Removal Procedure

Under 28 U.S.C. § 1446(a), a civil action[614] is removed by filing a notice of removal signed pursuant to Federal Rule 11. The notice must contain a short and plain statement of the grounds for removal, together with a copy of all process, pleadings, and orders that have been served upon the defendant in the state action.[615] After 1988, a removal bond is no longer required.[616] The notice must be filed within thirty days of the defendant's receipt of the initial pleading, or within thirty days after service of the summons if the initial pleading is filed in court but not required to be served on the defendants, whichever period is shorter.[617]

---

614. In the Federal Courts Jurisdiction and Venue Clarification Act of 2011, Pub. L. No. 112-63, § 103, 125 Stat. 758, 760, § 1446(a) was amended to eliminate its application to criminal prosecutions. Under the Act, a new § 1455 was added at the end of Chapter 89, Title 28, to govern removal of criminal prosecutions. *See id.* at 761-62.

615. *See* 28 U.S.C. § 1446(a); Cook v. Randolph Cnty., 573 F.3d 1143 (11th Cir. 2009) (failure to include all state court pleadings and process with the notice of removal is procedurally incorrect but is not a jurisdictional defect). In the Judicial Improvements and Access to Justice Act of 1988, Congress amended 28 U.S.C. § 1446(a) to provide for a notice of removal signed pursuant to Rule 11 rather than the verified petition for removal required under the former version of the statute. *See* Judicial Improvements and Access to Justice Act of 1988, Pub. L. No. 100-702, § 1016(b), 102 Stat. 4642, 4669 (codified at 28 U.S.C. § 1446(a)).

616. Section 1446(d) formerly required that the defendant file a bond to assure that the defendant would pay all costs incurred by the removal proceedings if they are later determined to be improper. In 1988, Congress eliminated subsection (d) and, thus, eliminated the bond requirement. *See* The Judicial Improvements and Access to Justice Act of 1988, Pub. L. No. 100-702, § 1016(b)(3), 102 Stat. 4642, 4670. Subsections (e) and (f) of § 1446 were relettered (d) and (e), respectively. *See id.* (codified at 28 U.S.C. § 1446).

617. *See* 28 U.S.C. § 1446(b); Destfino v. Reiswig, 630 F.3d 952 (9th Cir. 2011) (each defendant was entitled to thirty days after service to exercise removal right); Bailey v. Janssen Pharmaceutica, Inc., 536 F.3d 1202 (11th Cir. 2008) (under "last-served defendant rule," each defendant is permitted to file a timely motion for removal within thirty days of receipt of service by that individual defendant in multi-defendant litigation; earlier served defendants who may have waived their right to independently seek removal may consent to a timely motion by a later served defendant); McKinney v. Board of Trustees, 955 F.2d 924 (4th Cir. 1992) (when multiple defendants served on different dates, each defendant has thirty days from date of service to join otherwise valid petition for removal). *But see* Barbour v. International Union, 640 F.3d 599 (4th Cir. 2011) (removal is untimely if first-served defendant does not seek removal within thirty days after being served). *See generally* Lindsay E. Hale, Comment, *Triggering Removal Under 28 U.S.C. § 1446: The Eleventh Circuit's Adoption of the Last-Served Defendant Rule in* Bailey v. Janssen Pharmaceutica, Inc., 32 AM. J. TRIAL ADVOC. 363 (2008).

In *Murphy Bros. v. Michetti Pipe Stringing, Inc.*,[618] the U.S. Supreme Court held that the 30-day removal period is triggered either by simultaneous service of the summons and complaint or by receipt of the complaint after and apart from service of the summons. The Court made it clear that mere receipt of the complaint without any formal service would not trigger the removal period. This decision resolved a dispute among the lower federal courts about whether a receipt of a "courtesy copy" of the complaint before service could start the 30-day period.[619]

In the Federal Courts Jurisdiction and Venue Clarification Act of 2011,[620] § 1446(b) was extensively amended. The first paragraph of the section remains substantively the same, but was renumbered "(b)(1)." However, the second paragraph was deleted and a new paragraph (b)(2) inserted:

> (2)(A) When a civil action is removed solely under section 1441(a), all defendants who have been properly joined and served must join in or consent to the removal of the action.
>
> (B) Each defendant shall have 30 days after receipt by or service on that defendant of the initial pleading or summons described in paragraph (1) to file the notice of removal.
>
> (C) If defendants are served at different times, and a later served defendant files a notice of removal, any earlier served defendant may consent to the removal even though that earlier-served defendant did not previously initiate or consent to removal.[621]

This new paragraph reiterates the previously accepted rule of unanimity—*i.e.,* that all defendants properly joined and served must join in the removal of the action. However, the new provision now clarifies what should occur in a situation that had previously been uncertain: what happens if the thirty-day removal period runs for an earlier served defendant and then a later served defendant want to remove within thirty days of being served. The new provision makes it clear that the unanimity provision still applies, but that the later served defendant can remove as long as the earlier served defendant consents to the removal.

---

618. 526 U.S. 344, 119 S. Ct. 1322, 143 L. Ed. 2d 448 (1999). The American Law Institute has proposed a revision of § 1446 that would require the notice of removal to be filed within 30 days after receipt or possession by a defendant of a copy of the complaint "at or after the time of service or waiver of effective summons of that defendant" or within 30 days "after the service of effective summons upon a defendant" if the complaint has been filed in state court and is not required to be served. *See* ALI FEDERAL JUDICIAL CODE REVISION PROJECT § 1446(b)(1), at 436-37 (2004).

619. *See also* Harris v. Bankers Life & Cas. Co., 425 F.3d 689 (9th Cir. 2005) (removability is determined by the defendant's receipt of the initial pleading only when that pleading affirmatively reveals the facts necessary for federal court jurisdiction on its face, not by the existence of knowledge on the part of the defendant, actual or constructive, of facts that would make the case removable); Sikirica v. Nationwide Ins. Co., 416 F.3d 214 (3d Cir. 2005) (a summons by itself is not an initial pleading whose service triggers the 30-day removal period; summons coupled with demand letter did not give sufficient notice to defendant that case was removable; defendant did not have such notice until served with the complaint over 60 days after service of summons); *see generally* Robert P. Faulkner, *The Courtesy Copy Trap: Untimely Removal from State to Federal Court*, 52 MD. L. REV. 374 (1993); Donna Rohwer, Comment, *The Forty-Year Dispute: What Triggers the Start of the Removal Period Under 28 U.S.C. § 1441(b)?*, 61 UMKC L. REV. 359 (1992); *cf.* Jordan Bailey, *Giving State Courts the Ol' Slip: Should a Defendant Be Allowed to Remove an Otherwise Irremovable Case to Federal Court Solely Because Removal Was Made Before Any Defendant Is Served?*, 42 TEX. TECH. L. REV. 181 (2009).

620. Pub. L. No. 112-63, § 103(b), 125 Stat. 758, 760.

621. *Id.*

"Promptly" after filing the notice of removal, the defendant is directed to give written notice to all adverse parties and to file a copy of the notice with the state court clerk. This action effects removal, and the state court is directed to proceed no further in the action.[622]

Even if the case stated by the initial pleading is not removable, the defendant still may remove within thirty days after receipt of an amended pleading (or other paper[623]) from which it can first be ascertained that the case is removable.[624] In 1988, Congress provided that when removal is based on diversity of citizenship, a case may not be removed more than one year after commencement of the action.[625] This provision provided unscrupulous plaintiffs with a weapon with which to prevent the removal of some diversity actions.[626] A plaintiff who could manipulate joinder of parties or the jurisdictional amount to prevent the existence of diversity jurisdiction for more than a year could effectively thwart removal of the action.

Illustration 2-111. *P*, a citizen of State *X*, sues *D-1*, a citizen of State *Y*, and *D-2*, a citizen of State *X*, in a state court in State *X*. *P* asserts claims in the alternative against *D-1* and *D-2* for $1,000,000 arising out of an automobile

---

622. *See* 28 U.S.C. § 1446(d); *see also* ALI FEDERAL JUDICIAL CODE REVISION PROJECT § 1446, at 436-37 (2004) (clarifying and revising § 1446); *cf.* Fulford v. Transport Servs. Co., 412 F.3d 609 (5th Cir. 2005) (state class action removed to federal court; thereafter, identical state class action filed in state court by different plaintiffs against same defendant plus a co-citizen defendant; in removed action, court refused to certify the action as a class action; court also refused to enjoin the later commenced state action; court of appeals affirmed refusal to grant injunction on the ground that once class certification was refused in federal action, state plaintiffs had no connection with federal suit).

623. In the Federal Courts Jurisdiction and Venue Clarification Act of 2011, effective in January 2012, Pub. L. No. 112-63, § 103(b)(3)(C) (codified as 28 U.S.C. § 1446(c)(3)(A)) dealt with the term "other paper" for purposes of this provision in cases in which the amount in controversy is initially uncertain in a state action:

> (3)(A) If the case stated by the initial pleading is not removable solely because the amount in controversy does not exceed the amount specified in section 1332(a), information relating to the amount in controversy in the record of the State proceeding, or in responses to discovery, shall be treated as an "other paper" under subsection (b)(3).

See infra for discussion of subsection (b)(3).

624. This provision was formerly found in the second paragraph of 28 U.S.C. § 1446(b). However, in the Federal Courts Jurisdiction and Venue Clarification Act of 2011, Pub. L. No. 112-63, § 103(b), 125 Stat. 758, 760, the provision was moved to a new subsection (b)(3). *See* Dahl v. R.J. Reynolds Tobacco Co., 478 F.3d 965 (8th Cir. 2007) (a court decision in another case is not an order or other paper within meaning of § 1446(b)). In the Class Action Fairness Act of 2005, Congress created new jurisdictional and removal provisions to govern at least some diversity class actions. *See* Pub. L. No. 109-2, 119 Stat. 4 (codified as 28 U.S.C. §§ 1332(d) & 1453). In § 1332(d)((7) of the Act, Congress provided that citizenship of the membership of proposed plaintiff classes "shall be determined [for purposes of the Act] as of the date of the filing of the complaint or amended complaint, or, if the case stated by the initial pleading is not subject to federal jurisdiction, as of the date of service by plaintiffs or an amended pleading, motion, or other paper, indicating the existence of federal jurisdiction. Presumably, this provision will have its principal, if not exclusive, operation in cases removed under new § 1453 and will, therefore, govern those cases instead of the provision discussed in the principal text. *But see* Springman v. AIG Mktg., Inc., 523 F.3d 685 (7th Cir. 2008) (state class action removed to federal court under CAFA and remand denied; court of appeals states that an amendment to pleadings that adds a claim under federal law where only state claims had been framed before or that adds a new defendant opens a new window of removal, citing both old § 1446(b) and § 1453(b)); *see also* Moffitt v. Residential Funding Co., L.L.C., 604 F.3d 156 (4th Cir. 2010) (even if state actions removed at a time when they did not satisfy federal subject-matter jurisdiction, plaintiffs independently conferred subject-matter jurisdiction on federal court by filing an amended class actions that gave rise to federal jurisdiction under CAFA before filing their motion to remand); Debra Lyn Bassett & Rex R. Perschbacher, *The Roots of Removal*, 77 BROOK. L. REV. 1 (2011) (discussing three difficult problems in cases that become removable after the initial thirty day period).

625. *See* The Judicial Improvements and Access to Justice Act of 1988, Pub. L. No. 100-702, § 1016(b)(2)(B), 102 Stat. 4642, 4669 (codified at 28 U.S.C. § 1446(b)).

626. Katherine L. Floyd, *The One-Year Limit on Removal: An Ace Up the Sleeve of the Unscrupulous Litigant?*, 24 GA. ST. U. L. REV. 1073 (2008); Michael W. Lewis, *Comedy or Tragedy: The Tale of Diversity Jurisdiction Removal and the One-Year Bar*, 62 S.M.U. L. REV. 201 (2009).

accident. One year and a day after *P* commenced the action, *P* voluntarily dismisses *D-2* from the action. Under the time limit for removal established in 1988, *D-1* literally could not remove the action.

* * * * *

The U.S. Courts of Appeals, led by the Ninth Circuit, tried to limit some of the more absurd applications of the one-year provision. In *Ritchey v. Upjohn Drug Co.*,[627] the plaintiff joined three defendants in a state action, two of whom were nondiverse to the plaintiff. The plaintiff did not serve or notify the defendants of the state action until more than a year had passed and previously commenced federal litigation had been resolved against the plaintiff. When notified of the action, the diverse defendant removed the action. The diverse defendant contended that the two nondiverse defendants had been fraudulently joined. The plaintiff invoked the one-year limit, but the court of appeals held the limit applicable only to cases that are not removable from the outset. Because the two nondiverse defendants were fraudulently joined, the action was removable at commencement. Thus, the diverse defendant had 30-days after receiving a copy of the initial pleading within which to remove,[628] even though receipt occurred more than a year after commencement.

The result in the *Ritchey* case is clearly correct and was uniformly followed by the other U.S. Courts of Appeals.[629] Other solutions to manipulation of the one-year limit that were suggested by the lower federal courts are more problematic. For example, in *Norman v. Sundance Spas, Inc.*,[630] the plaintiff had joined one nondiverse defendant with several diverse defendants. Some of the diverse defendants had been joined at the commencement of the action, but some were added to the action by amendment one month after commencement. The nondiverse defendant was eliminated from the action over a year after commencement (along with some of the diverse defendants), leaving two diverse defendants, one of whom had been joined at commencement and one of whom had been added a month after commencement. The defendants removed within thirty days after the elimination of the nondiverse defendant, and the plaintiff moved to remand on the basis of the one year limit. The district court ordered the case remanded, even though one defendant was seeking removal within a year of being added to the action. The presence of the diverse defendant who had been joined at commencement prevented removal, because that defendant was seeking removal more than one year after commencement.

The court expressed concern that plaintiffs might delay removal beyond the one-year period by manipulating the liberal joinder and amendment provisions of the Federal Rules of Civil Procedure. The court suggested that the federal courts might develop fraudulent delay in joinder rules that were analogous to the

---

627. 139 F.3d 1313 (9th Cir. 1998); *see also* E. Farish Percy, *The* Tedford *Equitable Exception Permitting Removal of Diversity Cases After One Year: A Welcome Development or the Opening of Pandora's Box*, 63 BAYLOR L. REV. 146 (2011).

628. *See* 28 U.S.C. § 1446(b)(1).

629. *See* Brown v. Tokio Marine & Fire Ins. Co., 284 F.3d 871 (8th Cir. 2002) (one-year limitation applies only to actions not removable based on initial pleadings); Brierly v. Alusuisse Flexible Packaging, Inc., 184 F.3d 527 (6th Cir. 1999) (one-year limit applies only to cases not originally removable); New York Life Ins. Co. v. Deshotel, 142 F.3d 873 (5th Cir. 1998) (one-year limit applies only to cases not originally removable).

630. 844 F. Supp. 355 (W.D. Ky. 1994).

fraudulent joinder doctrine already existing in removal cases. However, it is not apparent, given the unclear boundaries of the fraudulent joinder doctrine itself,[631] that a "fraudulent delay in joinder" doctrine would be a useful solution to the problem of later-joined defendants.[632]

In the Federal Courts Jurisdiction and Venue Clarification Act of 2011, effective in January 2012, Congress amended the one-year limit in an attempt to take care of the problems of manipulation described above. In new § 1446(c)(1):

> (c) REQUIREMENTS; REMOVAL BASED ON DIVERSITY OF CITIZENSHIP.—(1) A case may not be removed under subsection (b)(3) [containing the provisions governing cases that become removable after the initial pleading] on the basis of jurisdiction conferred by section 1332(a) more than 1 year after commencement of the action, unless the district court finds that the plaintiff has acted in bad faith in order to prevent a defendant from removing the action.[633]

The "bad faith" language of the statute now provides a textual authorization for the district courts to prevent manipulation of the one-year limit. Unfortunately, the failure to define "bad faith" generally invites collateral litigation over that issue at threshold of removal. However, Congress did specifically define "bad faith" in one situation. New subsection (c)(3)(B) provides:

> (B) If the notice of removal is filed more than 1 year after commencement of the action and the district court finds that the plaintiff deliberately failed to disclose the actual amount in controversy to prevent removal, that finding shall be deemed bad faith under paragraph (1).[634]

---

631. *See* 14B CHARLES A. WRIGHT ET AL., FEDERAL PRACTICE AND PROCEDURE: JURISDICTION AND RELATED MATTERS § 3723, at 787-878 (3d ed. 2009) (discussing the variations in the fraudulent joinder doctrine); subsection 1 *supra* ("General Rule of Removal Jurisdiction: Section 1441(a)").

632. *See* 14C CHARLES A. WRIGHT ET AL., FEDERAL PRACTICE AND PROCEDURE: JURISDICTION AND RELATED MATTERS § 3731, at 600-15 (3d ed. 2009) (discussing the fairness of this rule in the context of the 30-day time limit). Plaintiffs also attempt to manipulate the amount in controversy to prevent removal, and sometimes, even in the absence of manipulation, it is difficult to determine the amount in controversy because some state pleading rules do not require or allow the amount of damages requested to be set out by the plaintiff. The result is a large number of federal decisions dealing with how to cope with these problems in various contexts. *See, e.g.*, Singer v. State Farm Mut. Auto. Ins. Co., 116 F.3d 373 (9th Cir. 1997) (state law prohibited plaintiffs from setting out a monetary amount of damages, but plaintiff's admission before the federal court that the case was worth considerably more than the amount in controversy established that the requirement was satisfied); Sheppard v. Exxon Co., U.S.A., 760 F. Supp. 92 (M.D. La. 1990) (action in a state court with a jurisdictional limit of $10,000; amount-in-controversy requirement not satisfied because court could not render judgment for more than $10,000); Jack E. Karns, *Removal to Federal Court and the Jurisdictional Amount in Controversy Pursuant to State Statutory Limitations on Pleading Damage Claims*, 29 CREIGHTON L. REV. 1091 (1996); Alice M. Noble-Allgire, *Removal of Diversity Actions When the Amount in Controversy Cannot Be Determined From the Face of the Plaintiff's Complaint: The Need for Judicial and Statutory Reform to Preserve Defendant's Equal Access to Federal Courts*, 62 MO. L. REV. 681 (1997); *see also* Benson v. SI Handing Sys., Inc., 188 F.3d 780 (7th Cir. 1999) (case removed and remanded because defendant failed to show amount in controversy met; after developing information during discovery showing the amount requirement met, defendant removed again, but the district court held that successive removal is not permissible; court of appeals disagreed and reversed); Marano Enters. v. Z-Teca Rests., L.P., 254 F.3d 753 (8th Cir. 2001) (in multiple defendant cases, each defendant has 30 days after being served to file a notice of removal, even if defendants who were earlier served did not file a removal notice within 30 days of being served).

633. Pub. L. No. 112-63, § 103(b), 125 Stat. 758, 760.

634. *Id*, at 761.

The American Law Institute has also recommended a modification of the one-year limit to provide a solution to the problems produced by the one-year limit. The ALI has proposed to confer discretion on the U.S. District Courts to remand diversity actions removed after one year "in the interest of justice."[635] Although the "interest of justice" standard "clearly invites the district court to weigh the equities when deciding whether to exercise this special remand power, [the preconditions built into the statute] substantially curtail the scope of this discretionary power."[636] In addition, the solution provided by the 2011 amendments to the statute make it unlikely that the ALI proposal will be adopted.

In addition to the amount-in controversy provision that Congress enacted to prevent manipulation of the one-year limit on removal (quoted above), the Federal Courts Jurisdiction and Venue Clarification Act of 2011 also contained additional provisions to deal with difficulties caused by cases in which the amount in controversy in state actions is not clear. New subsection (c)(2) deals with this problem:

> (2) If removal of a civil action is sought on the basis of the jurisdiction conferred by section 1332(a), the sum demanded in good faith in the initial pleading shall be deemed to be the amount in controversy, except that—
>
> (A) the notice of removal may assert the amount in controversy if the initial pleading seeks—
>
> (i) nonmonetary relief; or
>
> (ii) a money judgment, but the State practice either does not permit demand for a specific sum or permits recovery of damages in excess of the amount demanded; and
>
> (B) removal of the action is proper on the basis of an amount in controversy asserted under subparagraph (A) if the district court finds, by a preponderance of the evidence, that the amount in controversy exceeds the amount specified in section 1332(a).[637]

---

635. ALI FEDERAL JUDICIAL CODE REVISION PROJECT § 1447(b), at 463 (2004):

> (b) *Remand in interest of justice.* If a civil action has been removed under sections 1441(a) and 1446(b)(2) of this chapter more than one year after the commencement of the action, and if the sole basis for removal is the jurisdiction conferred by sections 1332 or 1367 of this title, the district court may in the interest of justice remand the action to the State court from which it was removed. No such remand shall be ordered except upon motion of a party filed within the time permitted for a motion to remand under subsection (c)(1).

636. *Id.* at 467 (cmt. on § 1447). Note that under the statute prior to 2012, the courts were split over whether, if the one-year limit was violated, they could nevertheless employ "equitable considerations" in determining whether to remand. *Compare* Jenkins v. Sandoz Pharm. Corp., 965 F. Supp. 861 (N.D. Miss. 1997) (impermissible to employ equitable considerations) *with* Davis v. Merck & Co., 357 F. Supp. 2d 974 (E.D. Tex. 2005) (intentional attempt to manipulate joinder of non-diverse defendant to prevent removal justified an equitable exception to the one-year limit); Ferguson v. Security Life Ins. Co., 996 F. Supp. 597 (N.D. Tex. 1998) (equitable principles may be employed), *aff'd without opinion*, 162 F.3d 1160 (5th Cir. 1998), Kinabrew v. Emco-Wheaton, Inc., 936 F. Supp. 351 (M.D. La. 1996) (equitable principles employed), *and* Morrison v. National Benefit Life Ins. Co., 889 F. Supp. 945 (S.D. Miss. 1995) (equitable principles employed; *see also* Tedford v. Warner-Lambert, Co., 327 F.3d 423 (5th Cir. 2003) (one-year time limit is not jurisdictional and is subject to an equitable exception to prevent forum manipulation by plaintiff).

637. Pub. L. No. 112-63, § 103(b)(2)(C), 125 Stat. 758, 760 (codified as 28 U.S.C. § 1446(c)(2)).

The initial paragraph of this amendment simply codifies the good-faith, legal certainty rule discussed in section C(3)*(g)(i)* above (with all its ambiguities and uncertainties). Paragraph (A) permits the defendant to assert an amount in controversy in situations in which it is not clear from the complaint what the amount is, and subsection 2(B) states the burden of proof applicable to establishing that the amount claimed is true. The House report accompanying the Act explains the need for this new provision:

> First, circuits have adopted differing standards governing the burden of showing that the amount in controversy is satisfied. The "sum claimed" and "legal certainty" standards that govern the amount[-] in[-] controversy requirement when a plaintiff originally files in [f]ederal court have not translated well to removal, where the plaintiff often may not have been permitted to assert in state court a sum claimed or, if asserted, may not be bound by it. Second, many defendants faced with uncertainty regarding the amount in controversy remove immediately—rather than waiting until future developments provide needed clarification—out of a concern that waiting and removing later will result in the removal's being deemed untimely. In these cases, [f]ederal judges often have difficulty ascertaining the true amount in controversy, particularly when removal is sought before discovery occurs. As a result, judicial resources may be wasted and the proceedings delayed when little or no objective information accompanies the notice to remove.
>
> Proposed new paragraph 1446(c)(2) allows a defendant to assert an amount in controversy in the notice of removal if the initial pleading seeks non-monetary relief or a money judgment, in instances where the state practice either does not permit demand for a specific sum or permits recovery of damages in excess of the amount demanded. The removal will succeed if the district court finds by a preponderance of the evidence that the amount in controversy exceeds the amount specified in 28 U.S.C. [§] 1332(a), presently $75,000.
>
> . . . .
>
> In adopting the preponderance standard, new paragraph 1446(c)(2) would follow the lead of recent cases. . . . As those cases recognize, defendants do not need to prove to a legal certainty that the amount[-] in[-] controversy requirement has been met. Rather, defendants may simply allege or assert that the jurisdictional threshold has been met. Discovery may be taken with regard to that question. In case of a dispute, the district court must make findings of jurisdictional fact to which the preponderance standard applies. If the defendant establishes by a preponderance of the evidence that the amount exceeds $75,000, the defendant, as

proponent of Federal jurisdiction, will have met the burden of establishing jurisdictional facts.[638]

In the Multiparty, Multiforum Trial Jurisdiction Act of 2002, discussed in section D(5) and other appropriate parts of this text, above, Congress provided for original and removal jurisdiction of cases falling within the Act. The Act also contains provisions dealing with the procedure for removal. Specifically, new 28 U.S.C. § 1441(e)(1) provides:

> The removal of an action under this subsection shall be made in accordance with [§] 1446 of [Title 28], except that a notice of removal may also be filed before trial of the action in State court within 30 days after the date on which the defendant first becomes a party to an action under [§] 1369 in a United States district court that arises from the same accident as the action in State court, or a later time with leave of the district court.[639]

As explained in subsection C(3)*(e)*, actions under § 1369 are based on minimal diversity of citizenship. Because a defendant against whom a nonremovable action is brought in state court might become a party to an action under § 1369 in a U.S. District Court more than one year after the state action is commenced against the defendant, this provision will presumably trump the one-year limitation on removal of diversity actions discussed above in this subsection.

In the Class Action Fairness Act of 2005, discussed in section D(5) and other appropriate parts of this text, above, Congress provided special jurisdictional provisions for at least some kinds of class actions.[640] In addition, Congress enacted a special removal provision, 28 U.S.C. § 1453, to govern removal of class actions under the new Act. New 28 U.S.C. § 1453(b) specifically eliminates the one-year restriction that applies to removal of other kinds of actions under § 1446. This Act will be discussed further in Chapter 8 below.

5. Remand of Removed Cases

The district court must remand any case removed without jurisdiction prior to final judgment in the case.[641] In 1988, Congress provided that a motion to remand a case to state court based on a defect in removal procedure, as opposed to a defect of jurisdiction, must be made within thirty days after filing the notice of removal.[642]

---

638. H.R. Rep. No. 112-10, at 10 (2011).

639. 28 U.S.C. § 1441(e)(1).

640. Pub. L. No. 109-2, 119 Stat. 4 (codified as 28 U.S.C. § 1332(d)). The Act is discussed in section D(5) & F(2), above, and Chapter 8(D)(4)*(b)(vi) & (c)*, below. *See also* Preston v. Tenet Healthsystem Mem'l Med. Ctr., Inc., 485 F.3d 804 (5th Cir. 2007) (district court properly remanded under CAFA's "local controversy" and "home state" exceptions and its discretionary jurisdiction provision); *In re* Burlington N. Santa Fe Ry. Co., 606 F.3d 379 (7th Cir. 2010) (federal removal jurisdiction existed under Class Action Fairness Act even though plaintiffs amended their complaint to eliminate class allegations after removal).

641. *See* 28 U.S.C. § 1447(c).

642. *See* Judicial Improvements and Access to Justice Act of 1988, Pub. L. No. 100-702, § 1016(c), 102 Stat. 4262, 4670 (codified at 28 U.S.C. § 1447(c)); *see also* Snapper, Inc. v. Redan, 171 F.3d 1249 (11th Cir. 1999) (remand on basis of forum selection clause not jurisdictional; clause constitutes absolute waiver of right to remove); Ragas v. Tennessee Gas Pipeline Co., 136 F.3d 455 (5th Cir. 1998) (limitation on removal jurisdiction waived by not moving to remand within thirty days as long as district court would have had original jurisdiction over case); Archuleta v. Lacuesta, 131 F.3d 1359 (10th Cir. 1997) (removal statutes do not set forth principles of subject-matter jurisdiction); Harmon v. OKI Sys., 115 F.3d 477 (7th Cir. 1997) (failure of defendant to allege basis for

In 1996, the language of § 1447(c) was amended again, this time to provide that "[a] motion to remand the case on the basis of any defect other than lack of subject-matter jurisdiction" must be made within 30 days after the notice of removal is filed.[643] These various changes in language are obviously designed to distinguish between defects in "subject-matter" jurisdiction and lesser "procedural" defects. Nevertheless, Congress has not been notably successful in clarifying what it considers to be a "defect . . . of subject-matter jurisdiction." The most likely meaning of "subject-matter jurisdiction" in § 1447(c) is "original subject-matter" jurisdiction, such as that conferred by provisions of the Judicial Code such as §§ 1331 and 1332. Other limitations on removal, such as those found in § 1446, would not be considered jurisdictional.[644]

Illustration 2-112. *P*, a citizen of State *X*, sues *D-1*, a citizen of State *Y*, and *D-2*, a citizen of State *Y*, in a state court in State *X*. *P* asserts claims in the alternative against *D-1* and *D-2* for $1,000,000 arising out of an automobile accident. *D-1* files a timely notice of removal, but *D-2* does not join in the removal notice. Subsequently, *D-2* also files a notice of removal, but *D-2's* notice is not timely under 28 U.S.C § 1446(b). Sixty days after *D-1's* notice of removal is filed, *P* moves to remand the action because both defendants did not join in removing the action in a timely fashion. This defect in removal procedure cannot be asserted as the basis of remand more than thirty days after the notice of removal is filed.[645]

* * * * *

However, a problem exists with limiting the meaning of "subject matter jurisdiction" to defects in original jurisdiction. This limited meaning treats as nonjurisdictional some very important limitations on removal. For example, the restrictions in § 1441(b) on the ability of citizens of the forum state to remove is not a limit on the original diversity jurisdiction of the federal courts.[646] Likewise, the one-year limit on removal in diversity cases in § 1446(b) is also not a limit on original federal jurisdiction.[647] Furthermore, 28 U.S.C. § 1445, entitled "Non-removable Actions," contains a whole list of cases that Congress has declared nonremovable, but which can be brought originally in federal court. It is not clear from the text of § 1447(c) whether Congress really wishes to treat all of these limitations on removal as "nonjurisdictional."[648]

---

subject-matter jurisdiction in notice of removal is procedural, not jurisdictional).

643. Pub. L. No. 104-219, § 1, 110 Stat. 3022 (1996) (codified at 28 U.S.C. § 1447(c)).

644. *See, e.g.*, Ragas v. Tennessee Gas Pipeline Co., 136 F.3d 455 (5th Cir. 1998); Baris v. Sulpicio Lines, Inc., 932 F.2d 1540, 1544-45 (5th Cir. 1991); *see also* Tedford v. Warner-Lambert, Co., 327 F.3d 423 (5th Cir. 2003) (one-year time limit is not jurisdictional and is subject to an equitable exception to prevent forum manipulation by plaintiff).

645. *See* Moore v. North Am. Sports, Inc., 623 F.3d 1325 (11th Cir. 2010) (procedural defect in timeliness of notice of removal not fatal to adjudication); Miller v. National Brokerage Servs., Inc., 782 F. Supp. 1440 (D. Nev. 1991).

646. *See In re* 1994 Exxon Chem. Fire, 558 F.3d 378 (5th Cir. 2009) (forum-defendant rule is procedural). *But cf.* Balzer v. Bay Winds Fed. Credit Union, 622 F. Supp. 2d 628 (W.D. Mich. 2009) (*sua sponte* remand of action based on forum defendant rule). *See generally* Theodore P. "Jack" Metzler, Jr., *A Lively Debate: The Eighth Circuit and the Forum Defendant Rule*, 36 WM. MITCHELL L. REV. 1638 (2010).

647. *See* Music v. Arrowood Indem. Co., 632 F.3d 284 (6th Cir. 2011) (one-year limit is procedural not jurisdictional).

648. *See* Rodas v. Seidlin, 656 F.3d 610 (7th Cir. 2011) (doctrine of derivative jurisdiction did not constitute essential ingredient of federal subject-matter jurisdiction over removed action that precluded district court from exercising jurisdiction after removal when it would have had original jurisdiction over action); Holmstrom v. Peterson, 492 F.3d 833 (7th Cir. 2007) (forum defendant rule is a "defect other than lack of subject-

If a case is removed in a procedurally proper and timely fashion, but without jurisdiction under the removal statute, situations exist in which it will not have to be remanded. If "after removal a case is tried on the merits without objection and the federal court enters judgment, the issue . . . on appeal is not whether the case was properly removed, but whether the federal district court would have had original jurisdiction of the case had it been filed in that court."[649]

Illustration 2-113. *P*, a citizen of State *X*, sues *D-1*, a citizen of State *Y*, and *D-2*, a citizen of State *Z*, in a state court in State *Z*. *P* asserts claims in the alternative against *D-1* and *D-2* for $1,000,0000 arising out of an automobile accident. *D-1* and *D-2* remove the action to a U.S. District Court in State *Z*. Neither the court nor the parties realize that the action is not removable because *D-2* is a citizen of the state in which the action is brought. Therefore, no one objects to removal and the action is tried on the merits. A judgment is rendered for *P* against *D-2* but in favor of *D-1*. *D-2* appeals, raising as error that the case was not removable under § 1441(b). The case before the district court was one over which it would have had original jurisdiction had it been initially commenced in that court. Thus, *D-2's* objection will not prevail because it is untimely.[650]

* * * * *

In *Caterpillar Inc. v. Lewis*,[651] a state court defendant removed an action to federal court, even though there was another nondiverse defendant joined in the action. The district court erroneously refused to remand on plaintiff's motion, but the nondiverse defendant was dismissed prior to trial, thus making diversity of citizenship complete. The Supreme Court held that the district court's error was not fatal to the validity of the judgment because diversity existed at the time judgment was rendered. This holding considerably extends the principle exemplified by the case described in *Illustration 2-113*. There, neither the parties nor the court

---

matter jurisdiction for purposes of § 1447(c)); Lively v. Wild Oats Mkt., Inc., 456 F.3d 933 (9th Cir. 2006) (forum defendant rule is nonjurisdictional and can be waived if not raised in a timely remand motion); Shapiro v. Logistec USA, Inc., 412 F.3d 307 (2d Cir. 2005) (an untimely motion to remand cannot be granted on the basis of 28 U.S.C. § 1441(b)'s "forum defendant" restriction because it is not jurisdictional); Hurley v. Motor Coach Indus., 222 F.3d 377 (7th Cir. 2000) (resident defendant limitation is procedural, not jurisdictional). *But see* Horton v. Conklin, 431 F.3d 602 (8th Cir. 2005) (resident defendant limitation is jurisdictional defect and not procedural defect capable of being waived); Aaron E. Hankel, Note, *On the Road to the Merits in the Federal System: Is the "Forum Defendant Rule" a Procedural Speed Bump or a Jurisdictional Road Block?*, 28 WASH. U. L.J. & POL'Y 427 (2008) (arguing that the restriction in § 1441(b) should be jurisdictional); *see also* Albarado v. Southern Pac. Transp. Co., 199 F.3d 762 (5th Cir. 1999) (limits on removal in 28 U.S.C. § 1445 are procedural, not jurisdictional); Scott Dodson, *In Search of Removal Jurisdiction*, 102 NW. U. L. REV. 55 (2008) (discussing the jurisdictional characterization in removal cases); ALI FEDERAL JUDICIAL CODE REVISION PROJECT § 1447, at 589-97, rptr's note K (2004) (discussing statutory restrictions on the right of removal and the distinctions between "procedural" and "jurisdictional" defects in removal). The American Law Institute's proposed revision of § 1447 would retain the procedural-jurisdictional distinction of current § 1447(c) and would clarify that, indeed, "restriction[s] on the right of removal" and "procedure[s] for exercising" the right of removal are waivable unless made the subject of a motion to remand within 30 days after removal. *See id.* § 1447(c)(1), (3).

649. *See* Grubbs v. General Elec. Credit Corp., 405 U.S. 699, 702, 92 S. Ct. 1344, 1347, 31 L. Ed. 2d 612, 617 (1972); Moffitt v. Residential Funding Co., L.L.C., 604 F.3d 156 (4th Cir. 2010) (even assuming state actions removed before jurisdictional prerequisites exist, plaintiffs cured defect after removal by amending complaint to bring action within federal jurisdiction under the Class Action Fairness Act).

650. It has been held that removal of a case over which there is original jurisdiction under 28 U.S.C. § 1332, but in which one of the defendants is a citizen of the state in which the action is brought, is a defect in removal procedure under 28 U.S.C. § 1447(c) that must be raised within thirty days after the notice of removal is filed. *See In re* Shell Oil Co., 932 F.2d 1518 (5th Cir. 1991). Under this holding, an objection to removal would be untimely in the illustration long before judgment was rendered at the district court level.

651. 519 U.S. 61, 117 S. Ct. 467, 136 L. Ed. 2d 437 (1996).

recognized the absence of removal authority under § 1441(b). In *Caterpillar*, there was an absence of original jurisdiction under § 1332 at the time of removal, the parties and the district court recognized the lack of jurisdiction, the court and defendant improperly ignored it, and the plaintiff challenged jurisdiction at the district court level and on appeal. Thus, in the absence of some clarification by the court, *Caterpillar* contains the seeds for wholesale evasion of jurisdictional restrictions in removal cases.[652]

Except in removal of civil rights cases under 28 U.S.C. § 1443, an order remanding a case to the state court from which it was removed is not reviewable on appeal or otherwise.[653] However, this limitation on the reviewability of remand orders applies only if the remand is on a ground specified in 28 U.S.C. § 1447(c), which covers remand based on defects in removal procedure and lack of jurisdiction.[654] If the remand is for any other reason, the remand order may be reviewed by a writ of mandamus.[655]

---

652. *See also* Gentek Bldg. Prods., Inc. v. Sherwin-Williams Co., 491 F. 3d 320 (6th Cir. 2007) (removal was improper based on complete preemption doctrine, but defendant waived objection by failing to move to remand; because court had subject-matter jurisdiction at time of judgment, remand was not required); AmSouth Bank v. Dale, 386 F.3d 763 (6th Cir. 2004) (in case originally filed in federal court seeking a declaratory judgment, jurisdiction was predicated on the existence of a federal question; the court of appeals held that federal question jurisdiction was improper, but that voluntary dismissal of a non-diverse party after commencement allowed the court to exercise diversity jurisdiction under *Caterpillar*). *But see, e.g.,* Waste Control Specialists, LLC v. Envirocare, Inc., 207 F.3d 225 (5th Cir. 2000) (post-removal amendment of a complaint to allege a federal claim does not waive the right to object to removal by a timely objection; under *Caterpillar*, a timely objection to remand preserves the jurisdictional objection despite subsequent amendment of complaint to state a federal claim; here, there was no trial on the merits and the case only consumed a minimum of the district court's resources). In Atlas Global Group, L.P. v. Grupo Dataflux, 312 F.3d 168 (5th Cir. 2002), the *Caterpillar* exception was held applicable to an action in federal court in which diversity was incomplete at the time of the filing, but the defect was cured prior to a verdict or dispositive ruling. According to the court, a case should not be dismissed if constitutional or statutory jurisdictional requirements are not met at the time a case is filed or removed, neither the parties nor the judge challenges jurisdiction, but the jurisdictional defect is corrected before a verdict or dispositive ruling.

653. *See* 28 U.S.C. § 1447(d).

654. *See In re* Shell Oil Co., 932 F.2d 1518 (5th Cir. 1991); *cf.* Price v. Johnson, 600 F.3d 460 (5th Cir. 2010) (only remand orders based on defects in removal procedure or lack of subject-matter jurisdiction are non-reviewable); Hamilton v. Aetna Life & Cas. Co., 5 F.3d 642 (2d Cir. 1993) (order remanding case removed by *plaintiff* construed as based on procedural reasons; order reviewed and affirmed; no federal subject-matter jurisdiction existed!).

655. *See* Thermtron Prods., Inc. v. Hermansdorfer, 423 U.S. 336, 96 S. Ct. 584, 46 L. Ed. 2d 542 (1976); *see also* Carlsbad Tech. v. HIF Bio, Inc., 556 U.S. 635, 129 S. Ct. 1862, 173 L. Ed. 2d 843 (2009) (remand after district court has refused to exercise supplemental jurisdiction over state claims is not a remand for lack of subject-matter jurisdiction that precludes review); Powerex Corp. v. Reliant Energy Servs., Inc., 551 U.S. 224, 127 S. Ct. 2411, 168 L. Ed. 2d 112 (2007) (when a district court remands a removed case because it lacks subject-matter jurisdiction, the remand order is not reviewable, and appellate courts must take this jurisdictional restriction seriously). In Mitskovski v. Buffalo & Ft. Erie Public Bridge Authority, 435 F.3d 127 (2d Cir. 2006), the plaintiff moved to remand a removed case on the basis of a procedural defect. The district court granted the remand motion, but on a procedural ground different from ones identified by the plaintiff in its motion to remand. Under these circumstances, the Second Circuit Court of Appeals held the remand order appealable because it was identified by the district court on its own motion more than thirty days after removal. However, the court of appeals assumed that the district court had the power to remand on its own motion on the basis of a procedural defect it had identified because the plaintiff had made a timely motion to remand, albeit on other grounds; *cf.* College of Dental Surgeons v. Connecticut Gen. Life Ins. Co., 585 F.3d 33 (1st Cir. 2009) (remand of case based on determination that district court lacked jurisdiction under Class Action Fairness Act because complaint did not sufficiently define the plaintiff class was premature and justified returning case to district court); Gentek Bldg. Prods., Inc. v. Sherwin-Willliams Co., 491 F.3d 320 (6th Cir. 2007) (when a jurisdictional defect in removal, no motion to remand, and a cure of the jurisdictional defect before entry of a final judgment, failure to move to remand waives objection to jurisdiction); Burr & Forman v. Blair, 470 F.3d 1019 (11th Cir. 2006) (by remanding removed claim and then exercising supplemental jurisdiction over it, district court was, in a sense, reviewing its own remand order, which runs afoul of the prohibitions in § 1447(d)); *see generally* Michael E. Solimine, *Removal, Remands, and Reforming Federal Appellate Review*, 58 MO. L. REV. 287 (1993).

Illustration 2-114. *P*, a citizen of State *X*, sues *D*, a citizen of State *Y*, in a state court of State *X*. *P* asserts a claim for $1,000,000 against *D* based on state law. *D* removes the action to the U.S. District Court for State *X* under 28 U.S.C. § 1441(a) & (b). The district judge remands the action because the docket of the court is too crowded. The order of remand is reviewable by a writ of mandamus in the court of appeals.[656]

* * * * *

Even though express authorization does not exist in 28 U.S.C. § 1447(c), the U.S. Supreme Court has held that the district courts may remand state claims that have been removed on the basis of pendent (today supplemental) jurisdiction when the federal claims that are the source of jurisdiction over the action have been dismissed from the case.[657] Under these circumstances, remand is more efficient than dismissal, which would be the appropriate procedure in a case originally commenced in federal court on the basis of supplemental jurisdiction. This power to remand state claims removed on the basis of supplemental jurisdiction has survived the enactment of 28 U.S.C. § 1367.[658] However, some courts have remanded entire cases under the authority of § 1367(c), including the federal claims in the cases.[659] Such remands are improper. As noted in subsection 4*(g)* above, 28 U.S.C. § 1367(c) only permits dismissal of supplemental claims, not entire cases. The power to remand should not be broader than the power to dismiss under the statute. Furthermore, remand of an entire action unjustifiably deprives the defendant of the right to a federal forum on the federal claim. For these reasons, the better rule

---

656. Review by writ of mandamus is discussed in Chapter 12(B)(3) *infra* ("The Final Judgment Rule and Its Exceptions"). *See also* Thomas C. Goodhue, Note, *Appellate Review of Remand Orders: A Substantive/ Jurisdictional Conundrum,* 91 IOWA L. REV. 1319 (2006). In the Class Action Fairness Act of 2005, Congress provided for special jurisdictional and removal provisions to govern at least some class actions. *See* Pub. L. No. 109-2, 119 Stat. 4 (codified as 28 U.S.C. §§ 1332(d) & 1453). In new 28 U.S.C. § 1453(c), Congress provided that while 28 U.S.C. § 1447 would generally apply to the removal of a case under § 1453, the provisions of § 1447(d) would not apply, but instead "a court of appeals may accept an appeal from an order of a district court granting or denying a motion to remand a class action to the [s]tate court from which it was removed if application is made to the court of appeals *not less than* 7 days after entry of the order." 28 U.S.C. § 1453(c)(1) (emphasis added). Congress obviously meant to say "not more than," rather than "not less than." Most, but not all courts, have so concluded. *See* Chapter 8(D)(4)*(c) infra* ("Subject-Matter Jurisdiction Problems Under Rule 23"). Section 1453 also provides that if the court of appeals accepts such an appeal, the court must complete all action on it, including the rendition of judgment, not later than 60 days after the date on which the appeal is filed unless an extension is granted upon agreement of all of the parties (for any period of time) or it is shown that an extension of not more than 10 days is justified on a showing of "good cause and in the interests of justice." *See* 28 U.S.C. § 1453(c)(2) & (3). If a final judgment on such an appeal is not issued before the period prescribed, including any extension, the appeal "shall be denied." *See* 28 U.S.C. § 1453(c)(4). One court has held that the 60-day period for the court of appeals to enter its judgment is triggered by the order granting leave to appeal the remand order, not by the parties' filing of an application for leave to appeal. *See* Patterson v. Dean Morris, L.L.P., 444 F.3d 365 (5th Cir. 2006); *see also* Preston v. Tenet Healthsystem Mem'l Med. Ctr., Inc., 485 F.3d 804 (5th Cir. 2007) (district court did not clearly err in finding that one-third of class members were citizens of Louisiana at time suit was filed and in remanding on basis of Class Action Fairness Act's "local controversy" and "home state" exceptions); Lowery v. Alabama Power Co., 483 F.3d 1184 (11th Cir. 2007) (CAFA does not shift burden of proof on removal; removing party failed to demonstrate that CAFA's amount-in-controversy requirement was satisfied).

657. *See* Carnegie-Mellon Univ. v. Cohill, 484 U.S. 343, 108 S. Ct. 614, 98 L. Ed. 2d 720 (1988). This remand is not on the ground of a "defect in removal procedure" within the meaning of 28 U.S.C. § 1447(c); *see also* David D. Siegel, *Commentary on 1988 Revision*, 28 U.S.C.A. § 1447 (West 1993 Supp. at 61-62).

658. *See, e.g.,* Noble v. White, 996 F.2d 797 (5th Cir. 1993).

659. *See, e.g.,* Administaff, Inc. v. Kaster, 799 F. Supp. 685 (W.D. Tex. 1992); 14C CHARLES A. WRIGHT, ET AL., FEDERAL PRACTICE AND PROCEDURE: JURISDICTION AND RELATED MATTERS § 3739, at 503-04 (3d ed. 1998).

is that an entire case can be remanded only when the federal claims have first been dismissed, leaving the case comprised entirely of state claims.[660]

Section 1447(c) provides that "[a]n order remanding the case may require payment of just costs and any actual expenses, including attorney fees, incurred as a result of the removal." In *Martin v. Franklin Capital Corp.*,[661] the Supreme Court held that § 1447(c) does not require an award of attorney's fees on remand as a matter of course. The Court stated that attorney's fees should not be awarded when the removing party had an objectively reasonable basis for removal. On the facts of the case, the defendant had removed a case that did not meet the amount-in-controversy requirement for diversity actions, but the defendant had relied on case law governing the requirement that was only subsequently held unsound. Therefore, it was not error for the district court to deny, in its discretion, an award of fees, because at the time of removal there was an objectively reasonable basis for concluding that the amount requirement was satisfied.[662]

Under § 1447(e), if after removal on the basis of diversity of citizenship a defendant seeks to add new parties whose joinder would destroy subject-matter jurisdiction, the court has two options. It may deny joinder, or it may permit joinder and remand the action. These options allow the court to make the inquiry dictated by Rule 19 in order to determine whether it is mandatory to join the party. Although § 1447(e) speaks in terms of joinder, it also applies when a plaintiff attempts to substitute newly identified non-diverse defendants for previously joined "John Doe" defendants.[663]

In the Multiparty, Multiforum Trial Jurisdiction Act of 2002, discussed in section C(3)*(e)* and other portions of this text, above, Congress enacted special remand provisions for civil actions removed under the new removal provisions of the Act. Specifically, Congress provided in 28 U.S.C. § 1441(e)(2) that whenever an action is removed under subsection (e)(1) and the district court to which it is

---

660. *See, e.g.*, Williams v. Ragnone, 147 F.3d 700 (8th Cir. 1998) (no power to remand entire case removed under §§ 1331, 1367 and 1441(a)); Kabealo v. Davis, 829 F. Supp. 923 (S.D. Ohio 1993) (§ 1367 does not permit remand of federal claims); *cf.* Bradgate Assocs., Inc. v. Fellows, Read & Assocs., Inc., 999 F.2d 745 (3d Cir. 1993) (removed case consolidated with one originally filed in federal court; later determined court had no jurisdiction over removed case; remand of case originally filed in federal court with removed case improper).

661. 546 U.S. 132, 126 S. Ct. 704, 163 L. Ed. 2d 547 (2005); *see also* Warthman v. Genoa Twp. Bd. of Trustees, 549 F.3d 1055 (6th Cir. 2008) (in determining whether to award attorneys fees, the district court abused its discretion by simply determining that plaintiff's complaint referenced federal law instead of determining whether removal was objectively reasonable); Admiral Ins. Co. v. Abshire, 574 F.3d 267 (5th Cir. 2009) (attorneys fees associated with seeking remand should ordinarily not be awarded when the removing party had an objectively reasonable basis for removal).

662. 546 U.S. at 137-41, 126 S. Ct. at 709-12, 163 L. Ed. 2d at 553-56; *see also* Knop v. Mackall, 645 F.3d 381 (D.C. Cir. 2011) (court of appeals reviews district court's award of attorney's fees for abused of discretion); Durham v. Lockheed Martin Corp., 445 F.3d 1247 (9th Cir. 2006) (award of attorney fees upon remand because removal was untimely was error; even though complaint disclosed basis for removal at commencement, basis required removing defendant to convince co-defendants to remove; later-disclosed basis for removal on grounds that defendant was a "federal officer" under § 1442 did not require consent of co-defendants and started time for removal again; thus, basis for removal was reasonable and attorney fees were improper); *cf.* Micrometl Corp. v. Tranzact Techs., Inc., 656 F.3d 467 (7th Cir. 2011) (although attorneys fees under § 1447 are normally awarded to plaintiffs, there is no party-based limit in the statute and a defendant can be awarded fees upon remand; however, district court properly exercised its discretion not to award fees in this case); Calabro v. Aniqa Halal Live Poultry Corp., 650 F.3d 163 (2d Cir. 2011) (court of appeals has jurisdiction to review award of attorney's fees and costs, even though it had no jurisdiction to review remand order).

663. *See, e.g.*, Curry v. U.S. Bulk Transp., Inc., 462 F.3d 536 (6th Cir. 2006).

removed or transferred[664] has made a liability determination requiring further proceedings as to damages, the district court shall remand the action to the state court from which it had been removed for the determination of damages, unless the court finds that, for the convenience of the parties and witnesses and in the interest of justice, the action should be retained in the district court for the determination of damages.

In addition, 28 U.S.C. § 1441(e)(3) provides that any remand under subsection (e)(2) shall not be effective until 60 days after the district court has issued an order determining liability and has certified its intention to remand the removed action for the determination of damages. During the 60-day period, an appeal can be taken from the liability determination of the district court. If such an appeal is taken, the remand shall not be effective until the appeal has been finally disposed of, but once the remand has become effective, the liability determination "shall not be subject to further review by appeal or otherwise."[665] Finally, 28 U.S.C. § 1441(e)(4) provides that any decision to remand for the determination of damages under § 1441(e)(3) shall not be reviewable by appeal or otherwise.[666]

---

664. The actual text of subsection (e)(2) states "removed or transferred under § 1407(j)." However, there is no § 1407(j) and this appears to be a drafting error. An earlier House Report, H.R. Rep. 107-14, at 9 (2001) states:

> New § 1407(j)(2)-(3) sets forth the terms by which an action is remanded, as well as the criteria for an appeal of decisions governing liability and punitive damages. Any decision concerning remand for the determination of damages is not reviewable under new § 1407(j)(4). The transferee court is also empowered to transfer or dismiss an action on the ground of inconvenient forum pursuant to new § 1407(j)(5).

The provisions referred to in the quoted paragraph now appear in 28 U.S.C. § 1441(e)(2)-(6).

665. *See* 28 U.S.C. § 1441(e)(3).

666. *See* 28 U.S.C. § 1441(e)(4).

Chapter 3

PERSONAL JURISDICTION AND SERVICE OF PROCESS

Personal jurisdiction is the power of a court to impose its decisions on the particular parties in a lawsuit. In modern procedural systems, personal jurisdiction is acquired over defendants by serving them with "process."[1] This service also provides the defendant with notice of the lawsuit. The notice contained in the process directs the defendant to appear and defend the suit or else the court will enter a "default judgment" against the defendant. Rules of personal jurisdiction determine when service of process can authorize a court to enter a *valid* judgment against the defendant.

In the United States, modern rules of personal jurisdiction are the end product of an evolutionary process that stretches over more than two centuries. Today, the landscape of personal jurisdiction is dominated by rules derived from provisions of the U.S. Constitution that restrict the authority of the state and federal governments to adjudicate cases against nonresidents. Originally, these restrictions were based on the concept that governments had *territorial* power over persons and things within their boundaries.

Under this territorial theory, the courts of a state could not constitutionally secure personal jurisdiction over defendants if they (1) were not present within the state when served with process, (2) did not consent to suit there, or (3) did not own property there. The first two bases allowed the sovereign to exercise what is known as *in personam* jurisdiction. The third basis allowed the sovereign to exercise what is known as *in rem* jurisdiction. The territorial rules functioned to protect sovereignty—the characteristic of governments which distinguish and preserve their power and independence from other governments.

Today, courts have relaxed the traditional territorial restrictions on acquiring personal jurisdiction over nonresident defendants. States may constitutionally compel nonresidents to defend suits in the state if they have relationships with the state that make the assertion of jurisdiction "reasonable." The underlying focus of these rules is on the protection of individuals from overreaching by governments—the restriction of the power to enter judgments against persons unless an adequate opportunity to be heard in defense is first afforded to them.

The traditional territorial rules, however, have not been entirely abandoned. Furthermore, sovereignty-oriented policies have been so strong that they have received explicit recognition in some modern cases interpreting the Due Process

1. *See, e.g.*, Semenza v. Kniss, 2005 MT 268, 329 Mont.115, 122 P.3d 1203 (court acquires personal jurisdiction over a defendant by service of process; rules of process are mandatory and must be strictly followed; if service of process is flawed, the court acquires no jurisdiction over the party).

Clause of the Fourteenth Amendment, a provision undeniably aimed at protection of individuals from state governmental power. This chapter discusses the basic rules of personal jurisdiction, their evolution over time, and modern procedures for serving process.

SECTION A. DEVELOPMENT OF TERRITORIAL RULES OF PERSONAL JURISDICTION

1. Personal Jurisdiction Restrictions Prior to the Adoption of the Fourteenth Amendment

(a) The Forms of Action in Suits on Foreign Judgments and the "International" Rules of Jurisdiction

At the time the U.S. Constitution was ratified, the method for enforcing a judgment that was not capable of direct execution was to bring an action of debt on a record.[2]

Illustration 3-1. Assume that *P* sued *D* in an English common-law court and recovered a judgment for money. By means of a writ of execution, *P* could have *D's* property sold to satisfy the judgment. Under the law of England, however, the plaintiff's right to have the judgment directly executed (by obtaining a writ of execution) ceased if the judgment had not been executed within a year and a day of its recovery. After that time, the plaintiff had to commence a new action using the form of action known as debt on a record. In this new action, the plaintiff did not have to prove the original claim again. The domestic judgment (one rendered by a court of record in England) was res judicata. Thus, the plaintiff had only to plead and prove the prior judgment to win. Similarly, if the defendant in the original action won and the plaintiff attempted to sue the defendant again on the same claim, the defendant could plead the original judgment in defense as res judicata.[3]

* * * * *

When a judgment of a court of a foreign country was involved, debt on a record was not the proper form of action. The judgment of a foreign court was not considered to be a "record" because the judgment had not been rendered by a court deriving its authority from the same sovereign as the judgment-enforcing court. Thus, the plaintiff had to employ either debt on a simple contract or general assumpsit, rather than debt on a record.[4] Furthermore, the foreign judgment was not

---

2. *See generally* Ralph U. Whitten, *The Constitutional Limitations on State-Court Jurisdiction: A Historical Interpretative Reexamination of the Full Faith and Credit and Due Process Clauses* (pt. 1), 14 CREIGHTON L. REV. 499, 509-14 (1981).

3. *See* JOSEPH H. KOFFLER & ALISON REPPY, HANDBOOK OF COMMON LAW PLEADING § 142, at 297-99 (1969); Chapter 1(D)(3)*(b) supra* ("*Ex Contractu* Personal Actions").

4. *See* Gage v. Bulkeley, 27 Eng. Rep. 824 (Ch. 1744); Chapter 1(D)(13*(b) supra* ("*Ex Contractu* Personal Actions") & Chapter 1(D)(4)*(b)* ("Assumpsit"). *See generally* Ralph U. Whitten, *The Constitutional Limitations on State-Court Jurisdiction: A Historical Interpretative Reexamination of the Full Faith and Credit and Due Process Clauses* (pt. 1), 14 CREIGHTON L. REV. 499, 511-14 (1981).

res judicata because it was not a record. Rather, it was only prima facie evidence of the debt being sued on, and the defendant could rebut it.[5]

The English decisions eventually evolved away from this prima facie evidence rule. In the earliest stages of the evolutionary process, the English courts drew a distinction between foreign judgments sued on affirmatively and those pleaded defensively. Foreign judgments sued on affirmatively were treated as prima facie evidence. Foreign judgments pleaded defensively were given a res judicata (conclusive) effect.[6] Later, the English rule evolved into its modern form, in which all foreign judgments rendered with jurisdiction are given a res judicata effect.[7] However, the important point is that at the time the U.S. Constitution was framed and ratified, and for some time before, foreign judgments were *not* treated the same as domestic judgments in English and American law.

To be given any effect, a foreign judgment had to have been rendered in compliance with certain "international" rules of jurisdiction.[8] These rules were part of a larger body of common-law rules known as private international law. As such, they governed the relations between the courts of separate sovereigns.[9] Three bases for international judicial jurisdiction were traditionally recognized: (1) presence of the person within the territory of the sovereign; (2) consent by the person to the jurisdiction of the courts of a sovereign; and (3) presence of something belonging to the person within the territory of the sovereign.[10]

Illustration 3-2. If a court in France obtained jurisdiction over an English citizen in compliance with the international rules of jurisdiction, the judgment of the French court would be enforceable in an English court. Thus, the French plaintiff only had to sue on the judgment in England. Today, such a judgment will be given a "res judicata" effect by the English courts—even if the French court committed nonjurisdictional errors of fact or law in the case.[11] On the other hand, if no jurisdiction in the "international sense" exists, the French judgment will be considered void and unenforceable in England—even if the French court accurately determined the merits of the case and the French plaintiff complied with all the

---

5. *See* Gage v. Bulkeley, 27 Eng. Rep. 824 (Ch. 1744); Walker v. Witter, 99 Eng. Rep. 1 (K.B. 1778); Galbraith v. Neville, 99 Eng. Rep. 5 (K.B. 1789) (*Galbraith* appears as a note to *Walker v. Witter*).

6. *See* Geyer v. Aguilar, 101 Eng. Rep. 1196, 1205 (K.B. 1789); Phillips v. Hunter, 126 Eng. Rep. 618, 622 (C.P. 1795) (Eyre, C.J. dissenting).

7. *See* J.J. FAWCETT & J.M. CARRUTHERS, CHESHIRE, NORTH & FAWCETT'S PRIVATE INTERNATIONAL LAW 514-15 (14th ed. 2008) and authorities there cited.

8. *See id.* at 348.

9. In the United States, private international law rules are usually referred to as conflict-of-law or choice-of-law rules. Today, the rules of jurisdiction that govern the power of courts in different nations to adjudicate cases that affect the interests of other nations are considered to be part of customary international law, while the rules that govern the power of state courts of the United States to adjudicate cases that affect the interests of other states are part of the national law of the United States. *See* RESTATEMENT (THIRD) OF THE FOREIGN RELATIONS LAW OF THE UNITED STATES 304 (1987); RESTATEMENT (SECOND) OF CONFLICT OF LAWS §§ 24-79 (1971 & Supp. 1988).

10. The grounds stated in the text are the traditional grounds recognized in English and early American practice. Today, the recognized bases for jurisdiction to adjudicate in international law are more numerous. *See* RESTATEMENT (THIRD) OF THE FOREIGN RELATIONS LAW OF THE UNITED STATES § 421 (1987). Furthermore, the modern international rules governing jurisdiction to adjudicate differ in important respects from the traditional bases and from some of the modern American bases. Notably, the modern international rules do not recognize jurisdiction based on transient presence or on the presence of property unconnected with the claim, whereas the traditional rules did recognize these bases, and modern American law still recognizes transient presence as a proper basis for asserting personal jurisdiction. *See id.* § 421(2)(a), (k).

11. *See* J.J. FAWCETT & J.M. CARRUTHERS, CHESHIRE, NORTH & FAWCETT'S PRIVATE INTERNATIONAL LAW 539 (14th ed. 2008).

French domestic rules governing service of process and acquisition of personal jurisdiction.[12]

Illustration 3-3. *D*, a citizen of Belgium, punched *P*, a citizen of England, in the nose. The punch occurred in Germany while *P* and *D* were in Germany on vacation. *P* sued *D* in an English court by serving *D* with process in England while *D* was traveling there. Under the presence theory, the English court acquired in personam jurisdiction in compliance with the international rules of personal jurisdiction by the service of process on *D* while *D* was in England. Thus, even if *D* left England and did not defend the action, the English court could enter a judgment against *D* that would be recognized and enforced by courts in other nations. Under the presence theory, it was irrelevant whether the event that was the subject of the action occurred in the country where process was served on the defendant. Although it is fairer to require a more substantial connection between the country where the action is brought and the subject matter of the action or the parties, the presence theory did not require anything more than transient presence of the defendant when process was served.[13] However, even when a ground such as transient presence was recognized as a valid basis for jurisdiction in the international sense, a country might have certain domestic rules, such as the doctrine of forum non conveniens,[14] which would produce dismissal of an action that was only remotely connected with the country.

(b) Colonial Developments and the Articles of Confederation

Several American colonies statutorily dealt with judgments of other colonies. The statutes seemed primarily aimed at problems of authentication and proof, rather than the effect to be given to a judgment of another colony. Only one colony, Massachusetts, seems to have elevated the judgments of other colonies to a higher level than foreign judgments.[15] Thus, as far as can be determined from these statutes, the colonies considered themselves to be independent sovereigns in relation to other colonies.

The Articles of Confederation contained a Full Faith and Credit Clause stating that "[f]ull faith and credit shall be given in each of these states to the records, acts, and judicial proceedings of the courts and magistrates of every other State."[16] Unlike the later Full Faith and Credit Clause of the U.S. Constitution, this provision did not contain any requirement that the "public acts" of other states be

---

12. *Cf.* RESTATEMENT (THIRD) OF THE FOREIGN RELATIONS LAW OF THE UNITED STATES § 421 (Jurisdiction to Adjudicate), § 481 (Recognition and Enforcement of Foreign Judgments), § 482 (Grounds for Nonrecognition of Foreign Judgments) (1987).

13. The tenuous connection upon which the "presence" theory allows the forum country to exercise jurisdiction makes the theory controversial. *See* J.J. FAWCETT ET AL., CHESHIRE, NORTH & FAWCETT'S PRIVATE INTERNATIONAL LAW 517 (14th ed. 2008). As a result, the theory has been generally discarded as a basis of jurisdiction to adjudicate in modern international law. *See* RESTATEMENT (THIRD) OF THE FOREIGN RELATIONS LAW OF THE UNITED STATES § 421(2)(a) (1987); *see also* UNIF. FOREIGN MONEY-JUDGMENTS RECOGNITION ACT § 5 (1962), 13 U.L.A. pt. II, at 73 (2002).

14. *See* Chapter 4(D) *infra* ("Forum Non Conveniens and Change of Venue").

15. *See generally* Ralph U. Whitten, *The Constitutional Limitations on State Court-Jurisdiction: A Historical-Interpretative Reexamination of the Full Faith and Credit and Due Process Clauses* (pt. 1), 14 CREIGHTON L. REV. 499, 527-35 (1981).

16. ARTS. OF CONFED. art. IV.

given full faith and credit; nor did it authorize the Continental Congress to prescribe rules of authentication or the effect of state judgments. The history of the framing and interpretation of this Clause adds little to the understanding of how the expression "full faith and credit shall be given" should be understood.[17] However, at least one decision rejected an argument that the Full Faith and Credit Clause of the Articles of Confederation required a conclusive effect to be given to the judgments of other states. Instead, the court held that the Clause only required the states to receive the judgments of other states into evidence as "full evidence of . . . such judicial proceedings"—*i.e.*, as conclusive proof that the proceeding embodied in the judgment occurred and adjudicated the matters described in the judgment.[18] If the states viewed the judgments of other states as "foreign judgments," the international rules of jurisdiction would have controlled the validity of the judgments in courts of other states.

(c) The Full Faith and Credit Clause of the U.S. Constitution

When the United States was formed, the states were essentially considered to possess the status of independent sovereigns. When they ratified the U.S. Constitution, the states ceded some of their sovereignty to the federal government. This relationship created two potential sources of restrictions on state-court jurisdiction. First, each state still might create "local" or "domestic" restrictions on the power of its courts to render valid judgments against residents and nonresidents of the state.[19] In theory, these domestic restrictions might appear in statutory, constitutional, or common-law form. Second, the U.S. Constitution itself might provide direct restrictions on state-court jurisdiction or authorize Congress to create such restrictions.[20]

In the original Constitution, the provision having the most direct bearing on the obligation of a state court to enforce the judgments of other states was the Full Faith and Credit Clause of Article IV, § 1: "Full Faith and Credit shall be given in each State to the public Acts, Records, and judicial Proceedings of every other State. And the Congress may by general Laws prescribe the Manner in which such Acts, Records and Proceedings shall be proved and the Effect thereof."[21] Like the identical language in the Articles of Confederation, the expression "full faith and credit" originated in English evidence law. The expression was interpreted to mean simply that each state was obliged, when asked to enforce a judgment rendered by a court in another state, to admit the judgment into evidence as conclusive proof that the judgment had been rendered and the court had adjudicated the matters described

---

17. *See* Ralph U. Whitten, *The Constitutional Limitations on State-Court Jurisdiction: A Historical Interpretative Reexamination of the Full Faith and Credit and Due Process Clauses* (pt. 1), 14 CREIGHTON L. REV. 499, 523-27, 535-41 (1981).

18. *See* James v. Allen, 1 Dall. 188, 190 (Pa. 1786).

19. For example, "local" or "domestic" rules of personal jurisdiction would include rules governing the procedures for issuing summons, subpoenas, and writs of attachment.

20. *See generally* Ralph U. Whitten, *The Constitutional Limitations on State-Court Jurisdiction: A Historical Interpretative Reexamination of the Full Faith and Credit and Due Process Clauses* (pt. 1), 14 CREIGHTON L. REV. 499, 542-46 (1981); Ralph U. Whitten, *The Constitutional Limitations on State Choice of Law: Full Faith and Credit*, 12 MEM. ST. U. L. REV. 1 (1981).

21. U.S. CONST. art. IV, § 1.

in the judgment.[22] In other words, the Full Faith and Credit Clause did not require directly that one state give a res judicata effect to the judgments of other states rendered with jurisdiction.[23] Similarly, the Full Faith and Credit Clause did not limit the power of states to choose their own law over the law of other states. As far as state statutes were concerned, all the Clause required was that the states admit properly authenticated "public acts" of other states into evidence as conclusive proof of their existence and contents.[24]

Illustration 3-4. Assume that *P* sued *D* in State *X* and recovered a judgment against *D*. Assume further that *P* was forced to take the judgment rendered in State *X* to another state to enforce it. *P* would do so by commencing an action on the judgment in the other state. In the suit to enforce the judgment, the first sentence of the Full Faith and Credit Clause would require of its own force that the enforcing state admit the judgment into evidence to prove that it had been rendered and had adjudicated the matters described in the judgment record. However, as originally understood, the Clause did not require that the court give the judgment a res judicata effect. In the absence of a statute enacted by Congress or the judgment-enforcing state requiring a greater effect, the result would be that the enforcing state would treat the judgment as a "foreign" judgment and give the judgment an effect only as rebuttable evidence of the plaintiff's claim. This result did not follow from the Full Faith and Credit Clause itself, but from the common-law rules derived from English practice that applied to the judgments of foreign nations.[25]

(d) The 1790 Implementing Statute

The Full Faith and Credit Clause granted Congress the power to declare the "effect" that state judgments and statutes would have in other states.[26] Thus,

---

22. Many historical sources indicate that the words "faith" and "credit" in English law were evidentiary terms. *See generally* Ralph U. Whitten, *The Constitutional Limitations on State-Court Jurisdiction: A Historical Interpretative Reexamination of the Full Faith and Credit and Due Process Clauses* (pt. 1), 14 CREIGHTON L. REV. 499, 508-23 (1981). The words were flexible enough to mean, standing alone, that a conclusive effect should be given to some item of evidence, or that some effect less than a conclusive effect should be given to the item. Likewise, when the words were modified with a term such as "full," "entire," or "implicit," they were usually meant to convey that a conclusive effect should be given to a piece of evidence. *See id.* at 519.

23. *See id.* at 508-55.

24. *See generally* Ralph U. Whitten, *The Original Understanding of the Full Faith and Credit Clause and the Defense of Marriage Act*, 32 CREIGHTON L. REV. 255 (1998); Ralph U. Whitten, *The Constitutional Limitations on State Choice of Law: Full Faith and Credit*, 12 MEM. ST. U. L. REV. 1 (1981).

25. *See* Ralph U. Whitten, *The Constitutional Limitations on State-Court Jurisdiction: A Historical Interpretative Reexamination of the Full Faith and Credit and Due Process Clauses* (pt. 1), 14 CREIGHTON L. REV. 499, 508-55 (1981).

26. When the Full Faith and Credit Clause of the Constitution was being framed, a clause was reported to the constitutional convention which provided that "[f]ull faith and credit ought to be given in each State to the public acts, records, and Judicial proceedings of every other State, and the Legislature shall by general laws prescribe the manner in which such acts, Records & proceedings shall be proved, and the effect which Judgments obtained in one State, shall have in another." 2 THE RECORDS OF THE FEDERAL CONVENTION OF 1787, at 485 (Max Farrand ed. 1911). In the debate over this clause, it was moved that the power of Congress be expanded, so that it would have the authority to declare the effect of public acts and records as well as judicial proceedings. *See id.* at 488. One delegate objected to this motion. James Wilson replied "that if the Legislature were not allowed to *declare the effect* the provision would amount to nothing more than what now takes place among all Independent Nations." *Id.* Wilson's remark indicates as clearly as any evidence available that the expression "full faith and credit shall be given" was not being used to give direct commands to the states about conflict of laws or jurisdictional matters. If the "full faith and credit" language of the Constitution had no greater effect "than what now takes place among independent nations," it could not be elevating state judgments to a higher level than foreign nation judgments or supplanting state conflict-of-laws doctrine with a constitutional command. Rather, Wilson's statement

Congress has the authority to promulgate both nationwide conflict-of-laws rules and interstate jurisdictional standards to determine the effect of state-court judgments. In 1790, pursuant to this authority, the first Congress passed "An Act to prescribe the mode in which the public Acts, Records, and Judicial Proceedings in each State shall be authenticated so as to take effect in every other state."[27] This "implementing" statute provided:

> That the acts of the legislatures of the several states shall be authenticated by having the seal of their respective states affixed thereto: That the records and judicial proceedings of the courts of any state, shall be proved or admitted in any other court within the United States, by the attestation of the clerk, and the seal of the court annexed, if there be a seal, together with a certificate of the judge, chief justice, or presiding magistrate, as the case may be, that the said attestation is in due form. And the said records and judicial proceedings authenticated as aforesaid, shall have such faith and credit given to them in every court within the United States, as they have by law or usage in the courts of the state from whence the said records are or shall be taken.[28]

Several things should be noted about this statute. First, its title does not say that its purpose is to *declare* the effect that the records and judicial proceedings of one state should have when taken to another state. Instead, the title indicates that the Act prescribes the mode by which state statutes, records, and judicial proceedings shall be authenticated "so as to take effect" in other states. Thus, the Act is a provision that will allow state acts, records, and judgments to be authenticated so as to take effect in accordance with some set of rules outside the statute.[29] Second, Congress used the faith-and-credit language of the Constitution to provide that "such faith and credit" should be given to state records and judicial proceedings as they would have in the courts of the state from which they were taken. If this language was intended to prescribe an effect, why did Congress not use the word "effect"? Alternatively, if the language of the Constitution prescribes an effect, why was it necessary to duplicate the language in the implementing statute?

The debate in the early decisions over the interpretation of the implementing statute concerned the "such faith and credit" language of the Act. Some courts held that Congress had intended to declare the effect that the judgments of one state should have when taken to another state by using the "such faith and credit" language. Other courts believed that the terms "faith" and "credit" in the Constitution prescribed only an evidentiary (or admissibility) effect, not a res judicata effect. To the latter courts, it was unreasonable to suppose that Congress had used the words in the statute in a different sense than it had used them in the Constitution.[30]

---

indicates that the important authority under the clause was being given to Congress through the power to declare the "effect" of public acts, records, and judicial proceedings.

27. Act of May 26, 1790, ch. 11, 1 Stat. 122 (now codified as 28 U.S.C. § 1738).

28. *Id.*

29. *See* Ralph U. Whitten, *The Constitutional Limitations on State-Court Jurisdiction: A Historical Interpretative Reexamination of the Full Faith and Credit and Due Process Clauses* (pt. 1), 14 CREIGHTON L. REV. 499, 556 (1981).

30. *See generally id.* at 559-70.

Significantly, however, even when the courts construed the Act as prescribing a non-evidentiary effect for state judgments and records, they sometimes agreed that the language of the Constitution was *not* designed, of its own force, to give more than an evidentiary command. Thus, in *Green v. Sarmiento*,[31] Justice Washington, sitting as a circuit judge, interpreted the "such faith and credit" language of the statute as designed to declare the effect of the judgments of a state court in other states. However, throughout the opinion, Justice Washington was careful to distinguish between the use of the "faith and credit" language in the Constitution and its use in the statute.[32] In *Peck v. Williamson*,[33] Chief Justice Marshall, sitting as a circuit judge, interpreted the implementing statute contrary to Justice Washington's interpretation in *Green*. Importantly, however, Chief Justice Marshall agreed with Justice Washington on the evidentiary character of the Constitution's language. To Marshall, it appeared "very clear" that the Constitution made "a pointed distinction between the faith and credit, and the effect, of a record in one state when exhibited in evidence in another."[34]

---

31. 10 F. Cas. 1117 (C.C.D. Pa. 1810) (No. 5760).

32. At one point, Justice Washington stated that the Full Faith and Credit Clause of the Constitution had three objectives: (1) to declare that faith and credit should be given in each state to the public acts, records, and judicial proceedings of other states; (2) to provide a method of authenticating the acts, records, and proceedings of the states; and (3) to declare the effect of acts, records, and judicial proceedings of the state courts in other states. The first objective, stated Washington, "is declared and established by the Constitution itself, and was to receive no aid." *Id.* at 1118. However, "the second and third objects of the section, were expressly referred to the legislature of the Union, to carry them into effect in such manner, as to that body might seem right." *Id.* Washington also drew a distinction between "full faith and credit" and effect when commenting on the differences between the Full Faith and Credit Clauses of the Articles of Confederation and the Constitution. The Articles of Confederation clause "goes no farther than to declare that 'full faith and credit shall be given in each state, to the records, acts, and judicial proceedings of the courts and magistrates of every other state;' whereas the constitution proceeds to add, that congress may declare . . . the effect of such records, acts, and judicial proceedings." *Id.* at 1118-19. Thus, Washington viewed the direct effect of the Constitution's language, which was basically the same as the language of the Full Faith and Credit Clause of the Articles of Confederation, as relatively unimportant. What was important was the power that had been given to Congress under the Constitution. Finally, Washington answered an argument that the language of the implementing statute was designed only to mean "no more than that full faith and credit shall be given to the record, so authenticated; as evidence, that such proceedings were had, and such judgment rendered, as the record imports." *Id.* at 1119. "But the sentence does not go so far as this; for it does not give full faith and credit, but such faith and credit as the record has in the state from whence it is taken." *Id.* Washington was here arguing that the Constitution already provided full faith and credit "as a matter of evidence" and Congress could not qualify that command. Thus, Congress had to be declaring "effect" in the "same faith and credit" language of the statute. *See id.* This conclusion, however, seems questionable. An evidentiary effect is still an effect. Therefore, it seems clear that Congress had the right in the "effects" clause to declare evidentiary as well as other effects. As demonstrated *infra*, this is likely what Congress was really attempting to do in the statute. Thus, while Washington's opinion is a good indication that the direct effect of the Full Faith and Credit Clause was to impose only a limited rule of evidence, it is not a sound guide to the scope of the powers of Congress under the Clause. Nevertheless, Washington's opinion is a very clear statement that the constitutional language was understood as evidentiary language and that evidentiary effects were distinguished from other kinds of effects.

33. 19 F. Cas. 85 (C.C.D.N.C. 1813) (No. 10,896).

34. Chief Justice Marshall stated that "[u]nless Congress had prescribed its effect, it should be allowed only such as it possesses on common-law principles. In our opinion, Congress have not prescribed its effect. To suppose that they have is to believe that they use the words "faith and credit" in a sense different from that which they have in the clause of the constitution upon which they were legislating." *Id.* For other decisions also interpreting the Constitution as Marshall interpreted it in *Peck*, see Bartlet v. Knight, 1 Mass. 401, 404-05, 405-07, 409 (1805); Hitchcock v. Aicken, 1 Cai. R. 460, 475-77, 479-81, 483 (N.Y. Sup. Ct. 1803); Wright v. Tower, Browne's R. App. i, x-xii (Pa. 1801) (Court of Common Pleas of Luzerne County, Third Judicial District); Hammond v. Smith, 2 S.C.L. (2 Bay) 52, 54 (1802). For a discussion of these cases, as well as the minority of decisions reaching the opposite conclusion before 1813 when the Supreme Court resolved the issue, see Ralph U. Whitten, *The Original Understanding of the Full Faith and Credit Clause and the Defense of Marriage Act*, 32 CREIGHTON L. REV. 255, 297-327 (1998); Ralph U. Whitten, *The Constitutional Limitations on State-Court Jurisdiction: A Historical Interpretative Reexamination of the Full Faith and Credit and Due Process Clauses* (pt. 1), 14 CREIGHTON L. REV. 499, 559-64 (1981); Ralph U. Whitten, *The Constitutional Limitations on State Choice of Law: Full Faith and Credit*, 12 MEM. ST. U. L. REV. 1, 41-49 (1981).

In 1813, in *Mills v. Duryee*,[35] the U.S. Supreme Court interpreted the last sentence of the implementing statute to be an attempt by Congress to declare the effect state-court judgments should have in other states. In *Mills*, an action of debt was brought in the U.S. Circuit Court for the District of Columbia on the judgment of a New York state court. The defendant pleaded *nul tiel record*, which denies the existence of the record and was the proper defensive plea in an action of debt on a record. The issue in the case turned on whether this plea was proper, or whether a plea of *nil debet*, the proper plea in an action on a foreign judgment, was the proper plea.[36] The resolution of the pleading issue depended on whether the implementing statute had elevated the status of state judgments to domestic judgments in other states.[37] The U.S. Supreme Court held that it had.[38] Thus, according to *Mills*, if a judgment would be given a res judicata effect by the judgment-rendering state, the judgment would have to be given a res judicata effect by other states as well.

Illustration 3-5. Assume that *P* obtained a judgment against *D* for $100,000 from a State *X* court that possessed no personal jurisdiction under State *X* law and thus was void in State *X*. Under the 1790 implementing statute, as interpreted in *Mills*, the judgment would be entitled to no effect in State *Y* if *P* attempted to enforce the judgment there against *D*. This conclusion followed under the *Mills* interpretation of the statute because State *X* itself would give no effect to the judgment. Since State *Y* was required only to give the same effect to the judgment that State *X* would give it, State *Y* also would treat the judgment as void. Therefore, a violation of the judgment-rendering state's *domestic rules of jurisdiction* could render a judgment unenforceable in other states.

* * * * *

The U.S. Supreme Court's interpretation of the implementing statute in *Mills* was surely incorrect,[39] but it caused no appreciable problems in the

---

35. 11 U.S. (7 Cranch) 481, 3 L. Ed. 411 (1813).

36. *See* Chapter 6(A)(3)*(f) infra* ("The General Issue").

37. Recall the discussion of the forms of action appropriate to actions on domestic and foreign judgments in subsection *(a)*, *supra*.

38. Justice Johnson dissented on the ground that the statute had not elevated the judgments of one state to the status of records in another. He observed that faith and credit were terms strictly applicable to evidence. *See* 11 U.S. (7 Cranch) at 304-05, 3 L. Ed. at 413-14.

39. As Chief Justice Marshall had written in *Peck v. Williamson*, 19 F. Cas. 85 (C.C.D.N.C. 1813) (No. 10,896), to suppose that Congress was trying to declare the effect of a judgment rendered in one state when taken to another was to suppose that it had used the terms "faith and credit" in the statute differently than they had been used in the Constitution. It is more likely that Congress was also giving a kind of evidentiary command in the statute to deal with a rather obvious problem that would be produced by the language of the Constitution. There were courts within the states that were courts of inferior jurisdiction. These courts were not courts of record, and their judgments would probably not be admitted into evidence in the other courts of the same state, much less given a res judicata effect. However, the unadulterated language of the Full Faith and Credit Clause would have commanded the courts of other states to admit the judgments of these inferior courts into evidence as conclusive proof that they had been rendered and adjudicated the matters described in the judgment. To prevent the anomaly of a judgment inadmissible in the state where it was rendered from having to be admitted in the courts of other states because of the Full Faith and Credit Clause, Congress provided in the implementing statute that the admissibility of state judgments would depend upon their admissibility in the state from which they were taken. *See* Ralph U. Whitten, *The Original Understanding of the Full Faith and Credit Clause and the Defense of Marriage Act*, 32 CREIGHTON L. REV. 255, 330-32 (1998); Ralph U. Whitten, *The Constitutional Limitations on State-Court Jurisdiction: A Historical Interpretative Reexamination of the Full Faith and Credit and Due Process Clauses* (pt. 1), 14 CREIGHTON L. REV. 499, 557-59 (1981); Ralph U. Whitten, *The Constitutional Limitations of State Choice of Law: Full Faith and Credit*, 12 MEM. ST. U. L. REV. 1, 52-53 (1981). This reading also explains the absence from the statute of a command that the public acts of one state be given "such faith and credit" as they would have in the state from which they were taken. There would have been no problem of statutory admissibility under the Full Faith and Credit Clause that would parallel the potential problems with judgments and records.

enforcement of state judgments in other states. Making the enforceability of judgment in another state depend upon its enforceability in the state where it was rendered is a sensible rule, with few complicating features.[40] However, the *Mills* interpretation has produced two other problems.

First, many years after *Mills* was decided and the dispute over the meaning of the implementing statute and the Constitution had been forgotten, the Supreme Court utilized *Mills* as authority for construing the Full Faith and Credit Clause to contain a command to the states that they apply the *law* of other states under certain circumstances. In *Chicago & Alton Railroad v. Wiggins Ferry Co.*,[41] Chief Justice Waite stated:

> Without doubt the constitutional requirement, Art. IV, § 1, that "full faith and credit shall be given in each state to the public acts, records, and judicial proceedings of every other state," implies that the *public acts* of every state shall be given the same effect by the courts of another state that they have by law and usage at home. This is clearly the logical result of the principles announced as early as 1813 in *Mills v. Duryee* . . . and steadily adhered to ever since.[42]

In this passage, Chief Justice Waite failed to appreciate the nature of the controversy over the implementing statute. Waite concluded that because the language of the statute and the Constitution were the same, they must mean the same thing. This conclusion was correct as an original matter because both the language of the statute and of the Constitution had been intended to give limited evidentiary commands. However, Chief Justice Waite failed to realize that *Mills* interpreted the language of the implementing statute to mean something *different* than the language of the Constitution. This misunderstanding led to a more expansive view of the Full Faith and Credit Clause of the Constitution than was justifiable under its language and history.[43] Worse, it seemed to establish a constitutional rule that, had it persisted, would have been insensible.[44]

Illustration 3-6. If the *Mills* interpretation of the "faith and credit" language is read into the Full Faith and Credit Clause of the Constitution, that interpretation

---

Domestic statutes did not have to be proved to courts in the state where the statute was enacted. The courts of the enacting state would take judicial notice of the statutes of their own states. Statutes only had to be proved when they were brought into issue in the courts of other states. Thus, the command of the Full Faith and Credit Clause produced no anomaly in the case of statutes. There would never be a case in which the Clause commanded a state to admit a statute of another state into evidence when the statute would not be admitted into evidence in the state where it was enacted. The implementing statute thus provided how to authenticate statutes so they could be admitted in other states, but it was unnecessary for Congress to limit their admissibility in the "such faith and credit" passage. *See id.* at 53.

40. The question whether the *Mills* interpretation of the statute eliminated the ability to refuse enforcement of a judgment that violated the international rules of jurisdiction is discussed in the next subsection. Other issues under the statute are discussed in Chapter 13(F)(1) *infra* ("Enforcement of State Judgments").

41. 119 U.S. 615, 7 S. Ct. 398, 30 L. Ed. 519 (1887).

42. *Id.* at 622, 7 S. Ct. at 401-02, 30 L. Ed. at 522 (emphasis added).

43. *See* Ralph U. Whitten, *The Constitutional Limitations on State Choice of Law: Full Faith and Credit*, 12 MEM. ST. U. L. REV. 1, 4-5, 55-56 (1981).

44. Chief Justice Waite's understanding of the constitutional rule did not persist, probably because it became apparent that it would produce an unintelligible constitutional command. *See Illustration 3-6 infra*. However, an expansive view of the Full Faith and Credit Clause as applied to choice-of-law matters did persist. *See* Ralph U. Whitten, *The Constitutional Limitations on State Choice of Law: Full Faith and Credit*, 12 MEM. ST. U. L. REV. 1, 4-11 (1981).

would require that each state apply the law of some other state instead of its own in multistate disputes. Thus, assume that *P*, a citizen of State *X*, has an automobile accident in State *Y* with *D*, a citizen of State *Y*, and is killed. States *X* and *Y* both have wrongful death statutes with limits on the amount that can be recovered, but the limit in each state is different. The *Mills* rule, applied to public acts, would seem to require State *X* to apply the wrongful death limit of State *Y* if the suit is commenced in State *X*. Similarly, it would seem to require State *Y* to apply the wrongful death limit of State *X* if the suit is commenced in State *Y*. This is the logical result of commanding each state to give the same effect to the statutes of another state that the statute would have in the state that enacted it.[45]

* * * * *

Second, in 1948, Congress for the first time added "public acts" to the faith and credit command of the implementing statute.[46] The only explanation for this change in the statute's language was found in the Revisers' Notes, which stated that public acts were added to follow the language of the Constitution.[47] The difficulty is, of course, that the *Mills* interpretation of the statute would now apply to public acts in addition to records and judicial proceedings. The revisers obviously did not grasp the implications of such an application, nor of the fact that *Mills* had interpreted the "faith and credit" language of the statute to mean something different than the same language in the Constitution. The result is that, as with Chief Justice Waite's mistaken reliance on *Mills* as an interpretation of the constitutional Clause, the modern implementing statute gives an unintelligible command with regard to public acts.[48]

Illustration 3-7. On the facts of *Illustration 3-6*, the implementing statute appears to require (1) State *X* to apply the wrongful death limit of the "public act" of State *Y* if the suit is commenced in State *X* and (2) State *Y* to apply the wrongful death limit of the "public act" of State *X if* the suit is commenced in State *Y*.

* * * * *

Properly, however, the U.S. Supreme Court has ignored the requirement of full faith and credit to public acts in the statute,[49] although the Court has incorporated limited choice-of-law commands to the states through the first sentence of the Full Faith and Credit Clause.[50]

---

45. *Cf.* Ralph U. Whitten, *The Constitutional Limitations on State Choice of Law: Full Faith and Credit*, 12 MEM. ST. U. L. REV. 1, 61-62 (1981) (discussing the modern implementing statute).

46. The 1948 language has been retained to the present. After providing for the authentication of public acts, records, and judicial proceedings, the statute reads:

> Such *Acts*, records and judicial proceedings or copies thereof, so authenticated, shall have the same full faith and credit in every court within the United States and its Territories and Possessions as they have by law or usage in the courts of such State, Territory, or Possession from which they are taken.

28 U.S.C. § 1738 (emphasis added).

47. *See* Ralph U. Whitten, *The Constitutional Limitations on State Choice of Law: Full Faith and Credit*, 12 MEM. ST. U. L. REV. 1, 60-61 (1981).

48. There is general agreement on this point. *See id.* at 61-62.

49. *See id.* at 62.

50. *See id.* at 4-5, 55-56.

(e) The Status of the Territorial Rules of Jurisdiction Under the Full Faith and Credit Clause and the Implementing Statute

After *Mills*, the status of the territorial "international" rules of jurisdiction was still in doubt. The *Mills* interpretation of the statute required a reference to the domestic jurisdictional rules of the judgment-rendering state to determine the effect that the state-court judgment should have. Did either the Constitution or the implementing statute require, permit, or forbid an additional reference to the territorial rules of jurisdiction to determine the effect that the judgments of one state should have in another?

In 1851, the Supreme Court answered this question in *D'Arcy v. Ketchum*.[51] In *D'Arcy*, the Court held that neither the Constitution nor the implementing statute dealt with the territorial jurisdictional rules. Instead, those rules of jurisdiction remained as they were in 1789—although Congress had the power to modify them under the Full Faith and Credit Clause if Congress decided to do so. This conclusion had been drawn by the state courts both before and after *Mills v. Duryee*.[52] The Court's reasoning in *D'Arcy* explains the relationship between the Constitution and implementing statute on the one hand, and the territorial jurisdictional rules on the other:

> In construing the Act of 1790, the law as it stood when the act was passed must enter into that construction; so that the existing defect in the old law may be seen, and its remedy by the act of Congress comprehended. Now it was most reasonable, on general principles of comity and justice, that, among States and their citizens united as ours are, judgments rendered in one should bind citizens of other States, where defendants had been served with process, or voluntarily made defence.
>
> As these judgments, however, were only *prima facie* evidence, and subject to be inquired into by plea where sued on in another State, Congress saw proper to remedy the evil, and to provide that such inquiry and double defence should not be allowed. To this extent, it is declared in the case of *Mills v. Duryee*, Congress has gone in altering the old rule. Nothing more was required.
>
> On the other hand, the international law as it existed among the States in 1790 was, that a judgment rendered in one State, assuming to bind the person of a citizen of another, was void within the foreign State, when the defendant had not been served with process or voluntarily made defence, because neither the legislative jurisdiction, nor that of courts of justice, had binding force.
>
> Subject to this established principle, Congress also legislated; and the question is, whether it was intended to overthrow this principle, and to declare a new rule, which would bind the citizens

---

51. 52 U.S. (11 How.) 165, 174, 13 L. Ed. 648, 652 (1851).

52. *See, e.g.*, Bissell v. Briggs, 9 Mass. 462, 466-67 (1813); Ralph U. Whitten, *The Constitutional Limitations on State-Court Jurisdiction: A Historical Interpretative Reexamination of the Full Faith and Credit and Due Process Clauses* (pt. 1), 14 CREIGHTON L. REV. 499, 571-72, 578 (1981).

> of one State to the laws of another; as must be the case if the laws of New York bind this defendant in Louisiana. There was no evil in this part of the existing law, and no remedy called for, and in our opinion Congress did not intend to overthrow [the] old rule by the enactment that such faith and credit should be given to records of judgments as they had in the State where made.[53]

Thus, neither the U.S. Constitution nor the implementing statute touched the preexisting customary international territorial rules of jurisdiction.[54] Furthermore, the Supreme Court did not describe the international territorial rules as *constitutional* rules. Instead, the Court referred to the rules as based on international law as it existed among the States in 1790.[55] Some of the state courts that had adopted an interpretation of the implementing statute identical to that in *Mills* had also stated explicitly that neither the Constitution nor the implementing statute had incorporated or otherwise touched the preexisting jurisdictional rules.[56]

Illustration 3-8. Assume that *P*, a citizen and resident of State *X*, sued *D*, a citizen and resident of State *Y*, in a State *X* court. *P* seeks to recover $100,000. *D* was served with process in State *Y* under a State *X* statute allowing mail service on nonresidents outside State *X*. *D* did not appear and defend. The State *X* court then entered a default judgment against *D* for $100,000. Assume that State *X* would consider this judgment valid and binding under its domestic law. Nevertheless, the courts of State *Y*, or of any other state, would refuse to enforce the State *X* judgment on the ground that the judgment was rendered in violation of the international

---

53. 52 U.S. (11 How.) at 175-76, 13 L. Ed. at 653.

54. Today, the recognized bases for jurisdiction to adjudicate in international law are more numerous. *See* RESTATEMENT (THIRD) OF THE FOREIGN RELATIONS LAW OF THE UNITED STATES § 421 (1987). For excellent discussions of the territorial nature of jurisdictional rules in the early nineteenth century, see Michael M. O'Hear, *"Some of the Most Embarrassing Questions": Extraterritorial Divorces and the Problem of Jurisdiction Before* Pennoyer, 104 YALE L.J. 1507 (1995); James Weinstein, *The Early American Origins of Territoriality in Judicial Jurisdiction*, 37 ST. LOUIS U. L.J. 1 (1992).

55. Nevertheless, despite this evidence, some commentators have argued that the Clause incorporated the international territorial rules of jurisdiction as constitutional commands to the states, the violation of which would invalidate state-court judgments under the Clause. *See* FLEMING JAMES, JR. ET AL., CIVIL PROCEDURE § 2.4, at 64 (5th ed. 2001); Geoffrey C. Hazard, Jr., *A General Theory of State-Court Jurisdiction*, 1965 SUP. CT. REV. 241. For a view of the historical record that is contrary to the view presented in this section, see also Douglas Laycock, *Equal Citizens of Equal and Territorial States: The Constitutional Foundations of Choice of Law*, 92 COLUM. L. REV. 249, 295-305 (1992). *But see* Ralph U. Whitten, *The Original Understanding of the Full Faith and Credit Clause and the Defense of Marriage Act*, 32 CREIGHTON L. REV. 255, 346-72 (1998) (disputing Laycock's interpretation).

56. For example, in Bissell v. Briggs, 9 Mass. 462 (1813), the Supreme Judicial Court of Massachusetts held that the implementing statute required a res judicata effect to be given to the judgments of other states, and then stated:

> But neither . . . the federal constitution, nor the act of Congress, had any intention of enlarging, restraining, or in any manner operating upon, the jurisdiction of the legislatures, or of the courts of any of the *United States*. The jurisdiction remains as it was before; and the public acts, records, and judicial proceedings contemplated, and to which full faith and credit are to be given, are such as were within the jurisdiction of the state whence they shall be taken. Whenever, therefore, a record of a judgment of any court of any state is produced as conclusive evidence, the jurisdiction of the court rendering it is open to inquiry; and if it should appear that the court had no jurisdiction of the cause, no faith or credit whatever will be given to the judgment.

Id. at 466-67. Given the explicit statements about the nonconstitutional nature of the international rules of jurisdiction, it is difficult to see how anyone can interpret the case law as holding that the constitutional clause incorporated the rules, but some commentators have tried. *See* Douglas Laycock, *Equal Citizens of Equal and Territorial States: The Constitutional Foundations of Choice of Law*, 92 COLUM. L. REV. 249, 298-301 (1992). *But see* Ralph U. Whitten, *The Original Understanding of the Full Faith and Credit Clause and the Defense of Marriage Act*, 32 CREIGHTON L. REV. 255, 346-72 (1998) (disputing Laycock's interpretation).

territorial rules of jurisdiction. Those rules were not satisfied. *D* was not served with process while physically present in State *X*, *D* did not consent to suit there, and *D* owned no property there. Neither the Full Faith and Credit Clause of the Constitution nor its implementing statute altered or incorporated the international jurisdictional rules. Consequently, they operated after the formation of the Constitution in the same way that they had operated before.

2. Territorial Rules and the Due Process Clause of the Fourteenth Amendment of the U.S. Constitution

(a) Interpretation of State Due Process Clauses Prior to the Fourteenth Amendment

The states could impose restrictions on the jurisdictional reach of their *own* courts, either by common-law, statutory, or constitutional rules. Each state had adopted a due process clause or its equivalent, even before the Fourteenth Amendment imposed a federal due process requirement on the states.[57] Because the federal Due Process Clause has been so important in limiting the jurisdictional authority of state courts after 1868, it is important to consider whether the *state* due process clauses were interpreted to impose domestic restrictions on the states' own courts prior to the Fourteenth Amendment. The interpretation of the state due process clauses before the Civil War constitutes a significant source of evidence about how the Fourteenth Amendment would have been understood.

The evidence indicates that prior to the adoption of the Fourteenth Amendment, "due process" was interpreted to require that persons had to be provided a judicial proceeding with an adequate opportunity to defend before they could be deprived of life, liberty, or property. Also, it was thought that due process required the proceeding to be a "regular" proceeding with "regular allegations, opportunity to answer, and a trial according to some settled course of judicial proceedings."[58] Nevertheless, Congress and the state legislatures were thought to have wide latitude to dispense with "ordinary" judicial proceedings.[59]

Embodied in the basic concept of a "regular" judicial proceeding was the opportunity to be heard in defense before a state could take life, liberty, or property. Several pre-Fourteenth Amendment cases dealt with an essential precondition of the opportunity-to-be-heard principle: notice of the pending action. These decisions revealed a broad power in the legislative branches of the state and federal governments to dispense with personal notice to a defendant by in-hand service of process. The cases approved *constructive notice*—by publication of notice of the

---

57. *See generally* Ralph U. Whitten, *The Constitutional Limitations on State-Court Jurisdiction: A Historical Interpretative Reexamination of the Full Faith and Credit and Due Process Clauses* (pt. 2), 14 CREIGHTON L. REV. 735 (1981); *see also* Ralph U. Whitten, *The Constitutional Limitations on State Choice of Law: Due Process*, 9 HASTINGS CONST. L.Q. 851 (1982).

58. *See* Murray's Lessee v. Hoboken Land & Improvement Co., 59 U.S. (18 How.) 272, 280, 15 L. Ed. 372, 376 (1856).

59. *See* Ralph U. Whitten, *The Constitutional Limitations on State-Court Jurisdiction: A Historical Interpretative Reexamination of the Full Faith and Credit and Due Process Clauses* (pt. 2), 14 CREIGHTON L. REV. 735, 796-98 (1981) (summary proceedings approved in tax cases and other situations).

suit in a newspaper instead of in-hand service. The cases indicated that the choice of a particular form of notice by the legislature would be upheld unless the legislature had provided for a type of proceeding in which it was not plausible to believe that notice would reach the defendant.[60]

The due process rules concerning notice and an opportunity to defend should be contrasted with the international territorial rules of jurisdiction. The latter rules reflected traditional notions of the territorial authority of a sovereign to control persons or property within its borders.[61] Such sovereignty-oriented rules were not related to the traditional due process concept of an opportunity to be heard in defense, although rules requiring adequate notice to the defendant obviously relate to a fair opportunity to defend. For example, a state could not, under the international rules, compel a defendant outside the state to appear when the defendant did not own property within the state and could not be served with process in the state. Under those circumstances, the state could not render a judgment against the defendant enforceable in another state. This result would follow even if the forum state was a perfectly convenient place of trial for the defendant and would not adversely affect the defendant's opportunity to be heard. Conversely, if a defendant were served with process while temporarily in a state, the state could enter a judgment against the defendant that would be enforceable in other states under the international rules. This result would follow even if the judgment-rendering state was so inconvenient a place to maintain the action that the defendant literally could not afford to defend the suit there. Therefore, before the Fourteenth Amendment, it is not surprising that the due process clauses of the state constitutions usually were *not* interpreted to require the states to follow the international rules of jurisdiction, but they *were* interpreted to require adequate notice.[62]

(b) Incorporation of the Territorial Rules into the Due Process Clause of the Fourteenth Amendment

Pennoyer v. Neff[63] was the first Supreme Court decision to indicate that the Due Process Clause of the Fourteenth Amendment limited the power of the states

---

60. *See, e.g.*, Mason v. Messenger & May, 17 Iowa 261 (1864); United States Trust Co. v. United States Fire Ins. Co., 18 N.Y. 199 (1858); *see also* Davidson v. Farrell, 8 Minn. 258 (1863); Jack v. Thompson, 41 Miss. 49 (1866).

61. For an excellent discussion of sovereignty in the law of the personal jurisdiction before the Fourteenth Amendment, see Michael M. O'Hear, *"Some of the Most Embarrassing Questions": Extraterritorial Divorces and the Problem of Jurisdiction Before* Pennoyer, 104 YALE L.J. 1507, 1534-35 (1995).

62. *See generally* Ralph U. Whitten, *The Constitutional Limitations on State-Court Jurisdiction: A Historical Interpretative Reexamination of the Full Faith and Credit and Due Process Clauses* (pt. 2), 14 CREIGHTON L. REV. 735, 774-804 (1981). It is, of course, true that the states usually did follow the traditional rules because they were the accepted common-law procedures of the day. *See, e.g.*, JOSEPH STORY, COMMENTARIES ON THE CONFLICT OF LAWS § 554 (1834).

63. 95 U.S. 714, 24 L. Ed. 565 (1878). For an excellent analysis of *Pennoyer*, see Patrick J. Borchers, *The Death of the Constitutional Law of Personal Jurisdiction: From* Pennoyer *to* Burnham *and Back Again*, 24 U.C. DAVIS L. REV. 19 (1990). For a spirited debate provoked by Professor Borchers' article, see Patrick J. Borchers, *Jurisdictional Pragmatism:* International Shoe's *Half-Buried Legacy*, 28 U.C. DAVIS L. REV. 561 (1995); John B. Oakley, *The Pitfalls of "Hint and Run" History: A Critique of Professor Borchers' "Limited View" of* Pennoyer v. Neff, 28 U.C. DAVIS L. REV. 591 (1995); Patrick J. Borchers, Pennoyer's *Limited Legacy: A Reply to Professor Oakley*, 29 U.C. DAVIS L. REV. 115 (1995); *see also* Harold L. Korn, *Rethinking Personal Jurisdiction and Choice of Law in Multistate Mass Torts*, 97 COLUM. L. REV. 2183, 2190-93 (1997); Wendy Collins Perdue, *Sin, Scandal, and Substantive Due Process: Personal Jurisdiction and* Pennoyer *Reconsidered*, 62 WASH. L. REV. 479 (1987).

to adjudicate cases involving nonresident defendants. The significance of *Pennoyer* was that a case decided by a state court in excess of its jurisdiction could be reviewed directly by the Supreme Court on the ground that the state-court judgment violated due process.[64] As noted in section A(1), before the ratification of the Fourteenth Amendment and *Pennoyer's* interpretation of it, a state judgment rendered without jurisdiction under the international territorial rules could be invalidated only when the judgment was taken to the courts of another state or to the federal courts for enforcement. Ironically, although *Pennoyer* established that the Due Process Clause of the Fourteenth Amendment limited state-court jurisdiction over nonresidents, the Due Process Clause was not the basis of the Court's holding in the case.

In *Pennoyer*, Neff claimed a tract of land in Oregon under a "land patent" issued to him by the United States in 1866. Pennoyer claimed the land by virtue of an execution sale made by a local sheriff pursuant to a judgment of an Oregon state court rendered in 1866. Neff was a nonresident defendant in the state action leading to the sheriff's sale. He had been served with process in the state action by publication of notice in a newspaper, as provided for by Oregon law. Neff brought an action against Pennoyer in the U.S. Circuit Court in Oregon to recover possession of the land. In that action, he attacked the validity of the Oregon state judgment, but not on federal due process grounds.[65] The U.S. Circuit Court held the state judgment invalid because of certain defects in an affidavit that was necessary under state law to obtain the service by publication. However, the U.S. Supreme Court did not regard the defects in the affidavit found by the circuit court to be the kind of error that could be raised in a subsequent proceeding brought to attack the judgment. Rather, such errors could be raised only on appeal of the state judgment to a higher Oregon state court.[66] Nevertheless, the Supreme Court affirmed the judgment of the circuit court on other grounds.

The Court held that the state judgment was void because the defendant had not been personally served with process while present in Oregon and the property which was the subject of the action had not been seized prior to judgment. Thus, the state judgment violated the international rules of jurisdiction. Under well-settled principles, no other state or federal court had to give effect to the judgment under the full-faith-and-credit implementing statute. In addition, the Court, in an extended

---

64. *See* Philip B. Kurland, *The Supreme Court, The Due Process Clause and the In Personam Jurisdiction of State Courts—From* Pennoyer *to* Denckla*: A Review*, 25 U. CHI. L. REV. 569, 585 (1958). The availability of direct review on due process grounds assumes that the state possesses a "special appearance" procedure or its equivalent that allows nonresident defendants to challenge a court's assertion of personal jurisdiction over them. Special appearance procedures are discussed in subsection B(3) *infra*.

65. No due process argument was made or discussed in the lower federal court that decided *Pennoyer*. *See* Neff v. Pennoyer, 17 F. Cas. 1279 (C.C.D. Or. 1875) (No. 10,083), *aff'd*, 95 U.S. 714, 24 L. Ed. 565 (1878). Furthermore, no due process argument appears in the appellate brief of Neff, the defendant in error, who would have been the party to raise it, nor anywhere else in the record on appeal. *See generally* Brief for Defendant in Error, Pennoyer v. Neff, 95 U.S. 714, 24 L. Ed. 565 (1878); Transcript of Record, *id.*; *see also* Ralph U. Whitten, *The Constitutional Limitations on State-Court Jurisdiction: A Historical Interpretative Reexamination of the Full Faith and Credit and Due Process Clauses* (pt. 2), 14 CREIGHTON L. REV. 735, 821 (1981).

66. *See* Pennoyer v. Neff, 95 U.S. at 720-21, 24 L. Ed. at 567-68.

dictum,[67] indicated that the violation of the international rules of jurisdiction would produce a due process violation in the future:

> Since the adoption of the Fourteenth Amendment to the Federal Constitution, the validity of such judgments [judgments rendered in violation of the international rules] may be directly questioned, and their enforcement in the State resisted, on the ground that proceedings in a court of justice to determine the personal rights and obligations of parties over whom that court has no jurisdiction do not constitute due process of law. Whatever difficulty may be experienced in giving to those terms a definition which will embrace every permissible exertion of power affecting private rights, and exclude such as is forbidden, there can be no doubt of their meaning when applied to judicial proceedings. They mean a course of legal proceedings according to those rules and principles which have been established in our systems of jurisprudence for the protection and enforcement of private rights. To give such proceedings any validity, there must be a tribunal competent by its constitution—that is, by the law of its creation—to pass upon the subject-matter of the suit; and, if that involves merely a determination of the personal liability of the defendant, he must be brought within its jurisdiction by service of process within the State, or his voluntary appearance.[68]

The Court was erroneous in at least two important respects. First, in order to invalidate the Oregon judgment, the Court had to conclude that the international rules of jurisdiction had been violated. The Court reasoned that the defendant either had to be served with process personally while present within the state or, if the presence of property was to be the basis of a court's jurisdiction, the property had to be brought under the control of the court by seizure of the property *before* judgment.[69] However, a requirement of seizure before judgment was not a part of the international rules before *Pennoyer*.[70] Thus, prejudgment seizure of the property as the basis for the court's power should have been considered merely a matter of municipal choice by the state.

Second, the Court erroneously concluded that a violation of the international rules per se was a violation of the Due Process Clause of the Fourteenth Amendment. Violation of the international territorial rules had not generally been

---

67. The due process portion of the Supreme Court's opinion in *Pennoyer* could not have been part of the Court's holding. The state judgment under consideration in *Pennoyer* had been rendered in 1866. The Fourteenth Amendment was not ratified until 1868. Thus, the Fourteenth Amendment could not have been the basis for voiding the judgment. *See* Ralph U. Whitten, *The Constitutional Limitations on State-Court Jurisdiction: A Historical Interpretative Reexamination of the Full Faith and Credit and Due Process Clauses* (pt. 1), 14 CREIGHTON L. REV. 499, 504-05 (1981); *id.* (pt. 2) at 821.

68. Pennoyer v. Neff, 95 U.S. at 733, 24 L. Ed. at 572.

69. *See id.* at 727-28, 24 L. Ed. at 570-71.

70. *See* Adrian M. Tocklin, Pennoyer v. Neff: *The Hidden Agenda of Stephen J. Field*, 28 SETON HALL L. REV. 75 (1997); Ralph U. Whitten, *The Constitutional Limitations on State-Court Jurisdiction: A Historical Interpretative Reexamination of the Full Faith and Credit and Due Process Clauses* (pt. 1), 14 CREIGHTON L. REV. 499, 507 n.30 (1981); *id.* (pt. 2) at 826. The lack of authority for this part of the opinion was noted by Justice Hunt in dissent. *See* Pennoyer v. Neff, 95 U.S. at 736-48, 24 L. Ed. at 573-78; *see also* Cooper v. Reynolds, 77 U.S. (10 Wall.) 308, 19 L. Ed. 931 (1870); Cleland v. Tavernier, 11 Minn. 194 (1866).

considered to be a violation of the due process clauses of the states prior to the ratification of the Fourteenth Amendment. Thus, violation of such rules would not void a judgment *within* a state, even though other states would not recognize or enforce a judgment rendered without jurisdiction in the "international sense."[71]

Despite these errors, the *Pennoyer* opinion became the basis for the development of the modern law of personal jurisdiction.[72] As later sections will demonstrate, the Supreme Court has moved away from the international territorial rules of personal jurisdiction embraced by *Pennoyer* to more justifiable rules of due process that focus on the burdens placed on the defendant by a state's assertion of personal jurisdiction. However, all vestiges of *Pennoyer's* territorialism have not been eliminated from the Due Process Clause.

SECTION B. THE OPERATION OF THE TERRITORIAL RULES

As indicated in the preceding section, the territorial rules of jurisdiction contained two basic grounds upon which in personam jurisdiction could be exercised—physical presence of the person within the borders of the sovereign and consent. In addition, the international rules recognized the presence of property or the alteration of an inhabitant's status as valid grounds for the exercise of in rem (or quasi in rem) jurisdiction.[73] After the incorporation of these rules into the Due

---

71. *See generally* Ralph U. Whitten, *The Constitutional Limitations on State-Court Jurisdiction: A Historical Interpretative Reexamination of the Full Faith and Credit and Due Process Clauses* (pt. 2), 14 CREIGHTON L. REV. 735 (1981). Although the territorial rules were not suited to the protection of the defendant's opportunity to be heard in defense, compliance with the rules would have been deemed consistent with the due process clauses of the states prior to the Fourteenth Amendment. For example, if a state asserted jurisdiction over a defendant by serving the defendant with process while the defendant was temporarily within the state, or attaching the defendant's property within the state, the resulting judgment would be valid both in the judgment-rendering state and elsewhere. *See, e.g.*, RESTATEMENT (FIRST) OF CONFLICT OF LAWS §§ 77-84 (1934); JOSEPH STORY, COMMENTARIES ON THE CONFLICT OF LAWS §§ 539, 543, 554 (1834). Yet such assertions of jurisdiction are inconsistent with the opportunity-to-be-heard principle of the due process clauses, in that they allow defendants to be subjected to jurisdiction in cases in which the claim has nothing to do with the state and it would be terribly burdensome for the defendant to defend within the state. The deeply rooted acceptance of the territorial rules at common law, together with the inability to acquire personal jurisdiction over absent defendants by other procedural means, probably obscured the impropriety of the rules in a due process sense. Nevertheless, *Pennoyer's* incorporation of the international rules into the Due Process Clause of the Fourteenth Amendment has been defended on the ground that "the restriction on state sovereign power [imposed on the states by *Pennoyer*] is a function of the individual liberty interest preserved by the due process clause." John N. Drobak, *The Federalism Theme in Personal Jurisdiction*, 68 IOWA L. REV. 1015, 1033 (1983). However justifiable it may be to impose some due process limitations on the sovereignty of the states to protect individual liberty interests, it was not justifiable to incorporate the international rules into the clause for that purpose because the international rules permit much more infringement of individual liberty interests than they prohibit. *See also* James Weinstein, *The Federal Common Law Origins of Judicial Jurisdiction: Implications for Modern Doctrine*, 90 VA. L. REV. 169 (2004) (arguing that the current unsatisfactory state of personal jurisdiction doctrine can be traced to *Pennoyer's* mismatch between the source of authority for federal restrictions on state-court jurisdiction and the content of the rules).

72. *Pennoyer* continues to excite scholarly commentary. *See, e.g.*, Nicholas R. Spampata, Note, *King* Pennoyer *Dethroned: A Policy Analysis-Influenced Study of the Limits of* Pennoyer v. Neff *in the Jurisdictional Environment of the Internet*, 85 CORNELL L. REV. 1742 (2000).

73. "Pure" in rem jurisdiction should be distinguished from a kind of jurisdiction that has come to be known as *quasi in rem* jurisdiction. Quasi in rem jurisdiction involves the seizure of property as a means of compelling the appearance of the defendant to litigate a dispute that does not concern the property. *See* ROBERT L. FELIX & RALPH U. WHITTEN, AMERICAN CONFLICTS LAW § 8 (6th ed. 2011) (discussing, *inter alia*, the traditional types of jurisdiction, including quasi in rem). Quasi in rem jurisdiction is a term that is also used to describe jurisdiction in an action that seeks to determine the interest of particular persons, as opposed to the entire world, in a thing. *See*

Process Clause in *Pennoyer*, their evolution continued. In addition, a peculiarly American rule permitting a sovereign to exercise jurisdiction over its absent citizens or domiciliaries also evolved.

1. In Rem Jurisdiction

After *Pennoyer v. Neff*, the Supreme Court developed important principles governing in rem jurisdiction. On the affirmative side, *Pennoyer's* conception of state power allowed a state to exercise control over property located within the state. On the restrictive side, *Pennoyer* prevented states from directly exercising power over property located in other states. In addition, the problems posed for defendants whose property was attached by a state court in a quasi in rem proceeding caused some states to authorize "limited appearance" procedures.

(a) Affirmative Principles of In Rem Jurisdiction

On the affirmative side of *Pennoyer*, the most important problem concerned the location, or *situs*, of intangible property. One issue concerned the location of a debt for purposes of seizure of the debt through attachment or garnishment procedures. In *Harris v. Balk*,[74] Harris, a North Carolina resident, owed a debt of $180 to Balk, also a North Carolina resident. Epstein, a Maryland resident, asserted Balk owed him over $300. On August 6th, Epstein garnished the debt owed by Harris to Balk while Harris was in Maryland on business. Harris consented to garnishment of the $180 debt and paid Epstein $180 on August 11th.

On the same day, Balk sued Harris in North Carolina state court. Harris' defense was the payment of the Maryland judgment. The lower North Carolina court and the North Carolina Supreme Court rejected this defense. The North Carolina courts maintained that the Maryland court lacked jurisdiction to attach or garnish the debt due from Harris to Balk because Harris was only temporarily in Maryland and the situs of the debt was in North Carolina. The North Carolina courts reasoned that the situs of a debt is at the domicile of either the creditor or debtor. Thus, the debt did not follow the debtor, Harris, into Maryland on his temporary visit. Therefore, there was no "property" in Maryland that could be attached or garnished.[75]

The U.S. Supreme Court reversed. The Court held that the Maryland judgment was valid and had to be given effect in North Carolina. The Court explained that attachment (and presumably other methods of seizing property) was a matter of local law. As long as state law provided for seizure of the debt based on personal service of process on the debtor within the state, the state court could validly acquire in rem jurisdiction. The debt followed the debtor, even on temporary visits to other states. As long as the debtor could be sued by the creditor in the state,

---

id. This form of quasi in rem jurisdiction is, so far as American jurisdictional theory is concerned, identical to pure in rem jurisdiction.

74. 198 U.S. 215, 25 S. Ct. 625, 49 L. Ed. 1023 (1905).

75. *See id.* at 216-17, 25 S. Ct. at 626, 49 L. Ed. at 1023-24.

which was beyond dispute in *Harris*, the creditor's creditor (Epstein) could garnish the debt. The garnishee (Harris) could thus set up the Maryland judgment as a defense, provided proper notice of the garnishment proceeding had been given to the garnishee's creditor (Balk). Such notice had indisputably been given in the case. Furthermore, the Court noted that Balk had a year and a day after entry of judgment in the Maryland proceeding to litigate the question of his liability to Epstein in the Maryland courts, but had not done so.[76]

The decision in *Harris v. Balk*, like that in *Pennoyer v. Neff*, was heavily dependent upon the distinction between in rem and in personam proceedings. The force of this distinction became evident in the Supreme Court's decision in *New York Life Insurance Co. v. Dunlevy*,[77] decided nine years after *Harris v. Balk*. In 1907, Boggs & Buhl recovered a valid personal judgment against Dunlevy in a Pennsylvania Court of Common Pleas. In 1909, New York Life Insurance Co. became liable to Gould, Dunlevy's father, for $2,479.70 under a life insurance policy held by Gould. Dunlevy claimed that Gould had assigned the proceeds of the policy to her, but the validity of the assignment was disputed by Gould. In November, 1909, Boggs & Buhl garnished the debt allegedly owed by New York Life to Dunlevy in an action in the Pennsylvania Court of Common Pleas. Both Gould and New York Life were summoned as garnishees.

In January 1910, Dunlevy sued New York Life and Gould in California. Both New York Life and Gould were served properly with process in that state. In February, 1910, New York Life answered Boggs & Buhl's garnishment process in Pennsylvania by setting up the conflicting claims and requesting interpleader. Pursuant to this answer, New York Life admitted the debt and paid the money into the court. Notice was given to Dunlevy in California, but she did not appear or plead in the Pennsylvania interpleader proceeding. The Pennsylvania jury found that the assignment was invalid, and the proceeds were paid to Gould.

New York Life then set up the Pennsylvania judgment as a bar to Dunlevy's action in California. The California court rejected this defense. The court found the assignment to be valid and awarded the proceeds to Dunlevy. On appeal to the U.S. Supreme Court, the Court held that California did not have to give effect to the Pennsylvania judgment:

> Beyond doubt, without the necessity of further personal service of process upon Mrs. Dunlevy, the Court of Common Pleas at Pittsburgh had ample power through garnishment proceedings to inquire whether she held a valid claim against the insurance company, and, if found to exist then to condemn and appropriate it so far as necessary to discharge the original judgment. Although herself outside the limits of the State, such disposition of the property would have been binding on her [citing *Harris v. Balk*].

---

76. *See id.* at 222-23, 227-28, 25 S. Ct. at 626-29, 49 L. Ed. at 1027-29; *cf.* Koehler v. Bank of Bermuda, Ltd., 12 N.Y.2d 533, 911 N.E.2d 825, 883 N.Y.S.2d 763 (2009) (court in New York with personal jurisdiction over garnishee bank could order bank to produce stock certificates located outside New York); Michael A. McGarry Jr., *Vestiges of Jurisdiction: On the In Rem Nature of Pre-Judgment Attachment in New York*, 32 CARDOZO L. REV. 1581 (2011); Damien H. Weinstein, Comment, *New York: The Next Mecca for Judgment Creditors? An analysis of* Koehler v. Bank of Bermuda, Ltd., 78 FORDHAM L. REV. 3161 (2010).

77. 241 U.S. 518, 36 S. Ct. 613, 60 L. Ed. 1140 (1916).

> But the interpleader initiated by the company was an altogether different matter. This was an attempt to bring about a final and conclusive adjudication of her personal rights, not merely to discover property and apply it to debts. And unless in contemplation of law she was before the court, and required to respond to that issue, its orders and judgments in respect thereto were not binding on her. . . .
>
> . . . .
>
> The established general rule is that any personal judgment which a state court may render against one who did not voluntarily submit to its jurisdiction, and who is not a citizen of the State, nor served with process within its borders, no matter what the mode of service, is void, because the court had no jurisdiction over his person.[78]

The result of cases like *Harris* and *Dunlevy* was that litigants had to exercise extreme care in determining the proper categorization of the different kinds of proceedings they wished to bring and the effect of the procedural steps they took within them. In *Dunlevy*, had New York Life simply allowed itself to be garnished in aid of execution of the original judgment that Boggs & Buhl had obtained against Dunlevy in 1907, there would, under the Court's opinion, have apparently been no difficulty. The Supreme Court would have considered the garnishment to be a continuation of the original proceeding against Dunlevy, in which in personam jurisdiction had already been validly acquired over her. Alternatively, the garnishment could have been considered a valid exercise of in rem jurisdiction over property located within the state. In either case, Mrs. Dunlevy would have been bound by the garnishment,[79] which also would have bound Gould because he had been summoned as a garnishee in aid of execution. The Court, however, conceptualized New York Life's petition for interpleader as "collateral" to the original proceeding and not supported by the original acquisition of personal jurisdiction over Dunlevy.[80] As a result, because interpleader was considered an "in personam" action, it required a new acquisition of personal jurisdiction over Dunlevy, who could no longer be served with process because she had left Pennsylvania. Thus, even though the practical effect of the interpleader proceeding on Dunlevy's rights was no different than the practical effect of garnishment in aid of execution, the Court held the interpleader proceeding to be void.[81]

---

78. *Id.* at 520, 522-23, 36 S. Ct. at 613-14, 60 L. Ed. at 1142-43.

79. This point is indicated by the Court's statement that the Pennsylvania court had "ample power through garnishment proceedings" to determine the ownership of the policy proceeds and, if the court determined Mrs. Dunlevy to be the owner, "to condemn and appropriate [the proceeds of the policy] so far as necessary to discharge the original judgment." Even though Mrs. Dunlevy was "outside the limits of the State," the Court indicated that "such disposition of the property would have been binding on her." *See id.* at 520, 36 S. Ct. at 613-14, 60 L. Ed. at 1142-43.

80. *See id.* at 521-22, 36 S. Ct. at 614, 60 L. Ed. at 1142.

81. The difficulty that the *Dunlevy* decision produced for insurance companies caused Congress to enact a federal interpleader statute, which, among other things, authorized federal courts in cases within the subject-matter jurisdiction provisions of the statute to exercise nationwide personal jurisdiction over rival claimants to insurance policies. *See* 7 CHARLES A. WRIGHT ET AL., FEDERAL PRACTICE AND PROCEDURE: CIVIL § 1701, at 526-27 (3d ed. 2001). Interpleader at both the state and federal level is discussed in Chapter 8(D)(2) *infra* ("Interpleader").

(b) Restrictive Principles of In Rem Jurisdiction

On the restrictive side of the in rem jurisdiction concept, the U.S. Supreme Court recognized the rule that only the state where land was located had jurisdiction to deal directly with the title to the land. Again, however, this principle was dramatically affected by the distinction between in personam and in rem jurisdiction.

In *Fall v. Eastin*,[82] a Washington state court awarded real property located in Nebraska to a wife in a divorce action. The husband refused to execute a deed to her. The court subsequently appointed a commissioner to issue a deed to the wife, as authorized by a Washington state statute. The wife went into possession of the Nebraska land under the commissioner's deed. Subsequently, the husband conveyed the same land to his sister (Eastin) in repayment of a debt. After the conveyance, the wife brought a quiet title action in Nebraska. The issue was whether the commissioner's deed had to be recognized by the Nebraska courts. Emphasizing Nebraska's sovereignty over real property located in Nebraska, the U.S. Supreme Court held that the attempt by the Washington state court to transfer title to the land directly to the wife by the commissioner's deed was ineffective and that the Full Faith and Credit Clause did not require Nebraska to accept it.[83]

If a court, such as the Washington court in *Fall v. Eastin*, had in personam jurisdiction over the defendant, the court could order the defendant to convey land located in another state by a deed that would be recognized there. If the defendant refused to convey the land, the defendant could be held in contempt and jailed, if necessary, to obtain compliance with the court's decree. What a court could not do was affect the title to the foreign land *directly* by its judgment—for example, under a statute authorizing the court to transfer title from *D* to *P* by decree or under a statute such as the one in *Fall* that authorized the appointment of an official to transfer title from *D* to *P*. The court's action in the contempt example was conceptually viewed to be limited to the defendant's person, even though it effectively resulted in transfer of title. However, the court's action in the examples involving direct transfer by decree or appointment was viewed as operating directly on the property. Thus, it was thought to violate the exclusive jurisdiction over the land possessed by the courts of the situs state.[84]

Illustration 3-9. *P*, a citizen of State *X*, enters into a contract with *D*, a citizen of State *X*, to purchase land owned by *D* located in State *Y*. When the time for performance arrives, *D* refuses to convey the land. *P* sues *D* in a state court of State *X*. *P* seeks a decree of specific performance to force *D* to convey the land. *D* is personally served with process in this action in State *X*. The State *X* court issues a decree of specific performance ordering *D* to convey the land in accordance with

---

82. 215 U.S. 1, 30 S. Ct. 3, 54 L. Ed. 65 (1909).

83. *Id.*; *see also* Durfee v. Duke, 375 U.S. 106, 84 S. Ct. 242, 11 L. Ed. 2d 186 (1963); Clarke v. Clarke, 178 U.S. 186, 20 S. Ct. 873, 44 L. Ed. 1028 (1900); Carpenter v. Strange, 141 U.S. 87, 11 S. Ct. 960, 35 L. Ed. 640 (1891).

84. *See* DAN B. DOBBS, THE LAW OF REMEDIES § 2.7, at 128-29 (2d student ed. 1993); *see also* ALBERT A. EHRENZWEIG, A TREATISE ON THE CONFLICT OF LAWS 209-13 (1962); ROBERT L. FELIX & RALPH U. WHITTEN, AMERICAN CONFLICTS LAW § 44 (6th ed. 2011); RUSSELL J. WEINTRAUB, COMMENTARY ON THE CONFLICT OF LAWS §§ 8.3-8.4 (6th ed. 2010).

the contract. *D* refuses. The court holds *D* in contempt. The court then orders *D* placed in jail until *D* complies with the decree of specific performance. After spending some time in jail, *D* complies with the court's order and executes a deed to the land sufficient under the law of State *Y* to convey ownership to *P*. *P* has obtained good title to the land. *P* may record the deed in the land records of the county in State *Y* where the land is located. No due process or full faith and credit problems existed with this procedure because the court did not act directly on the land with its decree. However, if State *X* had possessed a statute allowing the State *X* courts to directly decree the title to the land out of *D* and into *P*, that procedure could not validly have been employed under *Fall v. Eastin*. The court's decree would have been considered as operating directly on the land. Thus, the court's decree would have been invalid.

* * * * *

It is important to appreciate that *Fall v. Eastin* appeared to establish a due process restriction on the power of the state courts even though the Court never mentioned the Due Process Clause. Before *Pennoyer*, the objection to the Washington court's judgment would have been made under the international rules of jurisdiction. Those rules were specifically framed in terms of state territorial sovereignty. The objection would have been available only on collateral attack of the Washington court's judgment when the judgment was taken to Nebraska for enforcement, as in *Fall* itself. After *Pennoyer*, the international rules were incorporated into the Fourteenth Amendment as due process restrictions on the power of the states. The effect of this incorporation was to render the judgment void in the state where it was rendered as a matter of due process as well as void in other states on collateral attack of the judgment. Presumably, therefore, if a state such as Washington had an appropriate procedure for raising jurisdictional objections of the *Fall v. Eastin* sort, the objection could have been raised in the original Washington proceeding. If the Washington courts denied the objection, an appeal might ultimately be taken to the U.S. Supreme Court. Thus, after *Pennoyer* and *Fall*, the possibility of attacking state judgments affecting foreign land titles directly as well as collaterally (in the state where the land is located) appeared to exist.[85]

Nevertheless, great doubt exists about whether (1) the restrictive principles of in rem jurisdiction are due process principles and (2) whether such principles can be used as the basis of direct attack on a judgment involving the title to land located elsewhere. The doubt is created in part because the U.S. Supreme Court has described the restrictive principles of in rem jurisdiction as *subject-matter jurisdiction* principles.[86] It is not clear whether a lack of subject-matter jurisdiction of this sort in a state court ought to be considered a violation of due process. Recall that in *Pennoyer v. Neff*, the Supreme Court stated in dictum that due process required "a tribunal competent by its constitution—that is by the law of its creation—to pass upon the subject-matter of the suit."[87] This statement seems to require only that state courts have subject-matter jurisdiction as a matter of their

---

85. *Cf.* Eckard v. Eckard, 333 Md. 531, 636 A.2d 455 (1994) (appeal from a civil contempt order on ground that the court had no jurisdiction to enter an order affecting realty outside the state).

86. *See, e.g.*, Durfee v. Duke, 375 U.S. 106, 84 S. Ct. 242, 11 L. Ed. 2d 186 (1963).

87. 95 U.S. at 733, 24 L. Ed. at 572; *see* section (A)(2)(*b*), *supra*.

own law to satisfy the Due Process Clause of the Fourteenth Amendment.[88] If so, a lack of "territorial subject-matter jurisdiction" would not constitute a violation of the Due Process Clause of the Fourteenth Amendment. Thus, unless *Pennoyer's* incorporation of the traditional territorial rules of jurisdiction into the Due Process Clause encompasses the restrictive in rem principles, no other apparent source of federal law would obligate the states to follow them.[89] The possibility that the rules still may be enforced as nonfederal, sovereignty-based rules is explained below.[90]

In the preceding subsection, it was observed in conjunction with the *Dunlevy* case that the practical effect of the interpleader action was no different than the practical effect of the garnishment in aid of execution. However, it is possible to envision some practical difficulties for the state where land is located if other states are allowed to adjudicate title issues. In *Fall*, the Nebraska Supreme Court had identified a potential practical problem for purchasers of Nebraska land that might be caused by the Washington judgment:

> If the Washington decree bound the conscience of [the husband], so that when he left the jurisdiction of that state any deed that he might make would be absolutely void, and had he sold the land to an innocent purchaser, who had inspected the records and found that [the husband owned the land], such purchaser, though relying on the laws of this state for his protection, would receive no title. . . . [I]f this is correct, the action of the court of another state directly interferes with the operation of the laws of this state over lands within its sovereignty.[91]

The practical difficulties identified by the Nebraska Supreme Court can be eliminated if the plaintiff who obtains title to land through a proceeding in a nonsitus state is required to follow a specific procedure. The plaintiff would have to institute a proceeding in the situs state based upon the judgment of the nonsitus court and obtain a judgment of the situs court confirming the plaintiff's title.[92] Once a judgment of the situs court is obtained by the plaintiff, the situs court judgment can be recorded in the land records to protect bona fide purchasers of the land. If the plaintiff is required to follow such a procedure, no serious practical problems

---

88. Even this subject-matter jurisdiction requirement is open to question today. There is no apparent reason why a state should not be able to limit a defendant's objections to its courts' subject-matter jurisdiction to direct attack or make them waivable objections. *See* Chapter 13(E) *infra*. If this can be done, however, it is difficult to see how subject-matter jurisdiction deficiencies rise to the level of a federal due process concern.

89. Recall from section A(1)*(e)*, *supra*, that the traditional territorial rules were, prior to the Fourteenth Amendment, considered to be "international" rules that operated between independent sovereigns. They were not incorporated either in the Full Faith and Credit Clause or its implementing statute as commands against the states, although the Constitution and statute, in failing to touch or otherwise modify the rules, allowed the states to refuse enforcement to the judgments of other states that violated the rules. However, *Pennoyer* purported to base its holding on "two principles of public law," one of which was "that no State can exercise direct jurisdiction and authority over persons and property without its territory." 95 U.S. at 722, 24 L. Ed. at 568. This principle, of course, encompasses the restrictive principles of in rem jurisdiction and may have been incorporated with the Due Process Clause by the *Pennoyer* dictum.

90. *See* section G(3) *infra* ("Sovereignty-Based Restrictions on State-Court Jurisdiction"). For a discussion of the preclusive effect that a judgment in the non-situs state either litigating or ignoring the subject-matter jurisdiction issue, see ROBERT L. FELIX & RALPH U. WHITTEN, AMERICAN CONFLICTS LAW § 44, at 162-64 (6th ed. 2011).

91. Fall v. Fall, 75 Neb. 104, 106 N.W. 412 (1905), *vacated on rehearing*, 75 Neb. 120, 133, 113 N.W. 175, 180 (1907), *aff'd*, 215 U.S. 1, 30 S. Ct. 3, 54 L. Ed. 2d 65 (1909).

92. *See* RUSSELL J. WEINTRAUB, COMMENTARY ON THE CONFLICT OF LAWS § 8.4, at 582 (6th ed. 2010).

would be created for the situs state or people in the situs state resulting from a nonsitus judgment affecting the land. Consequently, all legitimate sovereignty-based interests of the situs state would be protected.

Illustration 3-10. *P*, a citizen of State *X*, enters into a contract with *D*, a citizen of State *Y*, to purchase land owned by *D* and located in State *Y*. When *D* refuses to perform the contract, *P* sues *D* in a state court in State *X* to obtain specific performance. The State *X* court renders judgment for *P*. Under a statute of State *X*, State *X* courts are allowed to directly convey the land from *D* to *P* in the decree, instead of relying on the contempt proceeding described in *Illustration 3-9*, above. The State *X* court employs this procedure. *P* takes the State *X* decree to State *Y* and there commences an action on the decree to quiet title to the land. *P* requests the State *Y* court give a res judicata effect to the State *X* judgment transferring title to *P*. No legitimate practical concerns on the part of State *Y* appear to exist if this procedure is followed. State *Y* cannot complain that subsequent purchasers of the land in State *Y* will be misled into believing that *D* has good title to the land. The familiar procedure of filing a notice of lis pendens prevents any such deception. No other considerations appear to justify preventing State *X* from transferring the title to the land located in State *Y* to *P*.[93]

* * * * *

Despite the fact that following an appropriate procedure would eliminate any legitimate objections that the situs state could have to a nonsitus proceeding, it is doubtful whether the U.S. Supreme Court in the era of *Pennoyer v. Neff* would have agreed.[94] In effect, therefore, *Fall v. Eastin* and similar decisions may have elevated a venue rule known as "the local action rule" into a constitutional limitation under the Due Process Clause of the Fourteenth Amendment, when the "local action" involved an adjudication of the title to land (as opposed, for example, to a request for damages to land located in another state).[95] In later sections, it will be important to determine whether the *Fall* rule has survived the modern decisions articulating due process limits on the power of state courts to assert personal jurisdiction over nonresidents.[96]

---

93. Although this example does not involve any interpretation of State *Y* land title law by the State *X* court, if such an interpretation were required, no significant practical difficulties would exist that would justify refusing enforcement of the State *X* judgment. The courts of State *Y* are not bound, as a matter of stare decisis, to follow the interpretation of State *Y* law by the State *X* court. The decision of the State *X* court, if erroneous, may create some difficulties for persons in State *Y* who wish to engage in similar transactions, but no more so than an erroneous decision on an issue of State *Y* real property law by an inferior court in State *Y* that is not appealed. In either case, the erroneous precedent will have to be clarified by the highest court of State *Y* in a later case. Thus, in both instances the direct effect of the decision is exhausted on the parties, just as in non-land title cases. *But see* Clarke v. Clarke, 178 U.S. 186, 20 S. Ct. 873, 44 L. Ed. 1028 (1900); Carpenter v. Strange, 141 U.S. 87, 11 S. Ct. 960, 35 L. Ed. 640 (1891). Both *Clarke* and *Carpenter* were fully litigated probate cases involving the title to land located in other states. The U.S. Supreme Court appeared to declare flatly that the courts of the non-situs state had no jurisdiction to directly affect the title to land located elsewhere. Passages in both opinions can be read as stating that the situs state is entitled to the opportunity to apply its own law to the title question. *See Clarke*, 178 U.S. at 194-95, 20 S. Ct. at 876, 44 L. Ed. 2d at 1032-33; *Carpenter*, 141 U.S. at 105-06, 11 S. Ct. at 966, 35 L. Ed. 2d at 647-48. This reading flows from the Court's position, discussed in the text, *supra*, that a court in one state has no *subject-matter jurisdiction* over the title to land located in another state.

94. *See* RUSSELL J. WEINTRAUB, COMMENTARY ON THE CONFLICT OF LAWS § 8.4, at 582 (6th ed. 2010); Guyon Knight, Note, *The CAFA Mass Action Numerosity Requirement: Three Problems with Counting to 100*, 78 FORDHAM L. REV. 1875 (2010).

95. *See* Chapter 4(A) *infra* ("Transitory and Local Actions").

96. *See* section E(1) *infra* ("Quasi in Rem and Related Jurisdictional Doctrines") & section G(3) *infra* ("Sovereignty-Based Restrictions on State-Court Jurisdiction").

(c) Limited Appearance Procedures

A dilemma existed for defendants whose property was attached or garnished in a quasi in rem proceeding brought to satisfy a claim unrelated to the property. If the defendant appeared in the action to defend the property, the appearance would constitute a "general appearance" that would allow the court to enter judgment against the defendant for an amount in excess of the value of the property. On the other hand, if the defendant did not appear, a default judgment would be entered against the defendant and the property would be sold to satisfy the judgment, as in *Pennoyer v. Neff.*

To alleviate this dilemma, some states recognized a device known as the *limited appearance*. In a limited appearance, defendants appeared in the action and defended on the merits. However, the appearance for this purpose did not constitute a *general appearance* that would allow the court to render a judgment against the defendant for an amount in excess of the property attached. Rather, the judgment had a limited effect—if the defendant lost, the plaintiff was able to execute the judgment on the property seized, but if the plaintiff's claim exceeded the amount of the property, the remainder had to be satisfied by a subsequent suit against the defendant in which the plaintiff would again have to prove the claim on the merits.[97] This subsequent proceeding would have to be brought in a state where personal jurisdiction could be obtained over the defendant (or where the defendant owned additional property). Not all courts recognized the limited appearance procedure, but in those that did, the rigors of quasi in rem jurisdiction were mitigated.[98]

2. In Personam Jurisdiction: Physical Presence

Under *Pennoyer*, jurisdiction based upon a person's presence within the sovereign's territorial limits could be achieved by service of process within the state. No other connection between the state, the defendant, and the claim was required. The mere transient presence of the defendant within the state, plus service on the defendant while the presence continued, was sufficient to sustain jurisdiction.[99]

---

97. *See* Cheshire Nat'l Bank v. Jaynes, 224 Mass. 14, 112 N.E. 500 (1916); RESTATEMENT (FIRST) OF JUDGMENTS § 40 cmt. a (1942).

98. Whether a state permits limited appearances is less important today than it was prior to 1977. The limited appearance procedure is primarily valuable to defendants in quasi in rem actions, when property located within the state is seized as a means of compelling the defendant's appearance in a proceeding brought to adjudicate a claim unrelated to the property. As discussed in a later section, this type of jurisdiction was held unconstitutional by the U.S. Supreme Court in *Shaffer v. Heitner*, 433 U.S. 186, 97 S. Ct. 2569, 53 L. Ed. 2d 683 (1977). After *Shaffer*, the need for the limited appearance procedure has virtually been eliminated.

99. In Grace v. MacArthur, 170 F. Supp. 442 (E.D. Ark. 1959), for example, personal jurisdiction was held to have been properly acquired over a defendant by serving the defendant with process over the Eastern District of Arkansas on a nonstop flight from Memphis, Tennessee, to Dallas, Texas. *Cf.* Darrah v. Watson, 36 Iowa 116 (1872) (personal jurisdiction validly acquired after in-hand service of process on the defendant, even though the defendant was in the state only for a few hours on business). This basis of acquiring jurisdiction has been recognized by the RESTATEMENT (SECOND) OF CONFLICT OF LAWS § 28 (1971) ("A state has power to exercise judicial jurisdiction over an individual who is present within its territory, whether permanently or temporarily."). However, developments in the law of personal jurisdiction, discussed later in this chapter, seemed to undermine the physical presence basis of jurisdiction, leading the authors of the *Restatement (Second)* to propose a modification of the presence test: "A state has power to exercise judicial jurisdiction over an individual who is

However, two self-imposed limitations on this manner of acquiring jurisdiction should be noted.[100] First, a state may immunize nonresidents from service when they voluntarily enter the state to attend litigation. Under this rule, a nonresident party, that party's counsel, and witnesses are immune from service when they are present in the forum to attend litigation and for a reasonable time in transit.[101] Second, if someone is brought into the state by fraud or unlawful force for the purpose of service of process, a state may not, as a matter of its own domestic law, exercise jurisdiction over the person.[102]

(a) Immunity from Service of Process

The usual justification for granting immunity to nonresident parties, attorneys, and witnesses is that the administration of justice requires the grant of immunity.[103] To encourage the attendance of these nonresidents at judicial proceedings pending within the state, they are granted immunity from service of process in other actions that might be brought against them while they are present to attend the litigation and for a reasonable time to travel to and from the litigation.[104] However, the justification for a grant of immunity to serve the needs of judicial administration will vary, depending upon whether the immunity is being granted to a nonresident plaintiff, a nonresident defendant, a witness, or an attorney.

For a nonresident plaintiff to be granted immunity to serve the needs of judicial administration, it must be assumed that the nonresident would not physically attend litigation within the state for fear that process would be served on the plaintiff in an unrelated[105] action. However, if the plaintiff's attendance at

---

present within its territory unless the individual's relationship to the state is so attenuated as to make the exercise of such jurisdiction unreasonable." *Id.* (Supp. 1988). Section E(2) *infra* discusses the Supreme Court's decision in Burnham v. Superior Court, 495 U.S. 604, 110 S. Ct. 2105, 109 L. Ed. 2d 631 (1990). *Burnham* revives the physical presence test as a valid basis for acquiring jurisdiction over nonresident defendants independent of the developments in the law of personal jurisdiction that caused the *Restatement's* drafters to impose a "reasonableness" limitation on the test. Thus, the modern utility of the self-imposed limitations discussed in the text *infra* must be evaluated in light of *Burnham*.

100. These limitations are not constitutional requirements; a state may decide to exercise jurisdiction in these circumstances if it so desires. If a state chooses not to follow these rules or to limit or qualify their application, its judgments must be recognized and given effect in other states. *See* RESTATEMENT (SECOND) OF CONFLICT OF LAWS § 82 cmt. f, § 83 cmt. b (1971).

101. *See id.* § 83 cmt. b.

102. *See id.* § 82; *see also* RESTATEMENT (SECOND) OF JUDGMENTS § 4(1)(b) (1982).

103. *See* RESTATEMENT (SECOND) OF CONFLICT OF LAWS § 83 (1971). Many of the other reasons often given for granting immunity are far less persuasive than the "needs of judicial administration rationale." *See generally* Arthur J. Keefe & John J. Roscia, *Immunity and Sentimentality*, 32 CORNELL L.Q. 471 (1947); Note, *Immunity of Non-Resident Participants in a Judicial Proceeding From Service of Process—A Proposal for Renovation*, 26 IND. L.J. 459 (1951).

104. *See* RESTATEMENT (SECOND) OF CONFLICT OF LAWS § 83 cmt. b (1971); *see also In re* B.J., 917 A.2d 86 (D.C. 2007) (exception exists to immunity from process rule when party to action is being served in another action that is closely related in subject matter to action in which service of process is made).

105. It must be assumed that the threatened service is in an unrelated action, since under modern procedural rules, related claims can be asserted in a variety of ways against the plaintiff in the action that the plaintiff has commenced within the state. Thus, the defendant can assert both related and unrelated counterclaims against the plaintiff in the action commenced by the plaintiff. *See* Chapter 7(E) *infra* ("Counterclaims and Crossvlaims Under the Codes") & Chapter 7(F) *infra* ("Counterclaims and Crossclaims Under the Federal Rules"). Similarly, third parties who may wish to become defendants to defend against the plaintiff's claims and assert counterclaims against the plaintiff may be able to intervene in the action. *See* Chapter 8(D)(3) *infra* ("Intervention"); *see also* Adam v. Saenger, 303 U.S. 59, 58 S. Ct. 454, 82 L. Ed. 649 (1938). In any event, the convenience of resolving all related matters in a single proceeding may outweigh the needs of judicial administration in cases where related actions are commenced against the plaintiff in the state that could be consolidated with the plaintiff's action.

discovery proceedings or trial is necessary to the litigation that the plaintiff has commenced, the court has ample power to compel that attendance by forbidding the plaintiff from prosecuting the claim if the plaintiff does not attend. Similarly, if a nonresident defendant refuses to attend proceedings within the state that have been validly commenced against the defendant, a default judgment can be rendered against the defendant which can be enforced in another state under the full faith and credit implementing statute.[106] Thus, the needs of judicial administration do not require a grant of immunity to a nonresident defendant over whom personal jurisdiction has been properly acquired. For a grant of immunity to be justified in the case of either a nonresident plaintiff or defendant, therefore, a justification other than the needs of judicial administration, such as fairness to the plaintiff or defendant, must support the grant. However, the traditional justification for immunity is only the needs of judicial administration, not fairness to the party immunized.[107]

Immunity for nonresident witnesses and attorneys is more justifiable than immunity for parties. If a party to pending litigation within the state cannot persuade a nonresident witness to attend the litigation, the ability of the party to prosecute a claim or defense may be impaired. Similarly, if a party cannot freely choose counsel of the party's choice to prosecute or defend an action within the state, the party's ability to conduct the litigation successfully may also be impaired. Because nonresident witnesses and attorneys are not parties to the case pending within the state, the court does not possess the same coercive powers to compel their attendance at litigation within the state that it possesses over parties. As a result, a grant of immunity may be necessary to prevent witnesses and attorneys from being deterred from entering the state by the fear that litigation will be commenced against them while they are present there. On the other hand, modern procedural rules may be able to alleviate the absence of a witness by devices such as videotape depositions.[108] To the extent that such devices are available under the state's procedural rules, it may be unjustifiable to grant a witness immunity from process to attend trial within the state.

Illustration 3-11. *P*, a citizen of State *X*, commences an action against *D*, a citizen of State *Y*, in a state court in State *Y*. *P* seeks damages from *D* for personal injuries received in an automobile accident in State *Y*. While *P* is attending pretrial proceedings in State *Y*, *P* is served with process by *C*, a citizen of State *Y*, in an action for breach of a contract made and to be performed in State *X*. Traditionally, *P* could plead immunity from process in the action by *C* and have the action dismissed. However, it is highly questionable whether the needs of judicial administration in the action by *P* justify the grant of immunity. *P* can be compelled to attend the proceedings in *P v. D* in State *Y* on pain of losing the claim for relief if *P* does not attend. The situation would not differ if *D* were the nonresident who

---

106. *See* 28 U.S.C. § 1738; section A(1)*(d) supra* (discussing the implementing statute).

107. *See* RESTATEMENT (SECOND) OF CONFLICT OF LAWS § 83 (1971).

108. *See* Chapter 9(E) *infra* ("Oral Depositions"); *see also* Moch v. Nelsen, 239 Mich. App. 681, 609 N.W.2d 848 (2000) (Michigan statute granting immunity from process to persons going to, attending, or returning from any court proceedings in any action if service could not otherwise have been made on them is inapplicable to attorney present in the state to attend administrative proceedings in disciplinary action).

was served in the unrelated action. By hypothesis, *D* has been validly subjected to personal jurisdiction in State *Y*. Therefore, if *D* does not participate in the litigation as needed, the court can render a default judgment against *D* that will be enforceable in other states.

Illustration 3-12. On the facts of *Illustration 3-11*, assume that *P*, *D*, and *C* are all citizens and residents of State *Y*. However, *D* wants to summon *W*, a citizen of State *X*, as a witness in the action. Assume that *C's* breach of contract claim is against *W*, rather than *P* or *D*. If the court cannot compensate for *W's* absence under its procedural rules through some device such as a videotape deposition, *W* should be granted immunity in any action brought by *C* while *W* is in State *Y* to attend the litigation between *P* and *D* and for a reasonable period to travel to and from the litigation.

Illustration 3-13. On the facts of *Illustration 3-12*, assume that *C* possesses the breach of contract claim against *L*, a lawyer who is a citizen of State *X*. *D* wishes to hire *L* to defend the action by *P*. *L* should be granted immunity from process in the action by *C* for the period of time *L* is in State *Y* to participate in the litigation and for a reasonable period to travel to and from the litigation. If *L* is not immunized from process and is deterred from representing *D* as a result, no procedural rule can compensate for *L's* absence and the deprivation of *D's* freedom to choose counsel. Although this justification may be valid, note that if *L* is a heart surgeon who *D* wishes to have perform a life-saving operation in the state there is no immunity rule that would protect *L* from service. Given that there will be other lawyers in the state who can represent *D* adequately, one may wonder, even here, whether a grant of immunity is justifiable. This situation differs from *Illustration 3-12*, in that *W* may be the only witness to a critical event affecting *D's* liability, while other lawyers are surely available to *D* in the forum state.

Illustration 3-14. On the facts of *Illustration 3-13*, assume that after *L* successfully represents *D*, *L* does not leave State *Y* with reasonable dispatch, but remains in the state to attend a football game that is played two days after the action between *P* and *D* is completed. During the football game, *C* has *L* served with process in the breach of contract action. *L* is not immune from process because *L* did not leave State *Y* within a reasonable period of time.

* * * * *

The immunity rules described above depend on the need to serve a defendant with process while the defendant is physically present within the state. As discussed below, modern due process restrictions on personal jurisdiction permit nonresidents to be summoned to defend actions based on their relationships with the forum state. Such assertions of jurisdiction are accomplished under state "long-arm" statutes.[109] To the extent that the defendant can be validly summoned under modern standards, service of process within the state is irrelevant. Therefore, it would be unjustifiable to grant immunity to a nonresident who is constitutionally subject to personal jurisdiction under a state long-arm statute.

---

109. *See* section F *infra* (discussing modern long-arm statutes).

(b) Acquisition of Jurisdiction by Fraud or Unlawful Force

The rule prohibiting the acquisition of jurisdiction by fraud or unlawful force is based on the policy of preventing a plaintiff from profiting by inequitable conduct.[110] Like the immunity rules, this rule is premised on the need to serve the defendant while the defendant is physically present within the state. If another basis exists for acquiring jurisdiction over the defendant, the fraud and force rule becomes irrelevant.

Illustration 3-15. Assume that *D* is a resident of State *X* and that *P* is a resident of State *Y*. *P* and *D* have had a meretricious relationship for several years. *P* writes *D* that *P* is leaving the country to go to *P's* dying mother in Ireland and that *P* will not return. *P* professes undying love for *D* and entreats *D* to come to State *Y* for one last visit. Upon *D's* arrival at an airport in State *Y*, *D* is served with process by *P* in a State *Y* action for money loaned and for seduction under promise to marry. *D* does not appear in the State *Y* action. The court then enters a default judgment against *D*. In an action brought on the State *Y* default judgment in State *X*, the State *X* court should determine whether the law of State *Y* would make the default judgment void because *D* was induced to enter State *Y* by *P's* misrepresentations.[111] If so, the judgment should be held to be unenforceable in State *X*.[112] If *D* were subject to personal jurisdiction on some other basis than service while physically present in State *Y*, *P* would use that basis to acquire jurisdiction and would not need to trick *D* into entering the state.

3. In Personam Jurisdiction: Consent, Appearance, and Waiver

As observed in the earlier discussion of the international rules of jurisdiction, individuals may consent to the jurisdiction of a sovereign's courts, even though they could not validly be subjected to a suit in the state absent their consent. A person may manifest consent by (1) agreeing to jurisdiction in a contract prior to suit, (2) accepting or waiving service of process with the intent to consent to jurisdiction, even though the acceptance or waiver occurs outside the state, or (3) designating an agent within the state to receive service of process.[113]

Closely related to jurisdiction by consent is jurisdiction conferred by appearance. Defendants who voluntarily appear in an action, even though they are not compelled to do so, consent in a real sense to the jurisdiction of the court over them. However, even if the defendant's appearance in the action is not "voluntary"

---

110. *See* RESTATEMENT (SECOND) OF CONFLICT OF LAWS § 82 cmt. a. (1971).

111. *See* Wyman v. Newhouse, 93 F.2d 313 (2d Cir. 1937). *But see* Warner v. Houghton, 43 A.D.3d 376, 841 N.Y. S.2d 499 (2007) (husband was not fraudulently induced to consent to divorce jurisdiction in New York by wife's representations that the action was to be merely an uncontested divorce, when wife was also seeking property division).

112. The rule against acquiring jurisdiction by fraud and force can be contrasted with the duty of persons voluntarily present within the jurisdiction to submit to service. In the latter instance, the courts will permit a process server to engage in subterfuge to accomplish service. *See* Gumperz v. Hofmann, 245 A.D. 622, 283 N.Y.S. 823 (1935), *aff'd*, 271 N.Y. 544, 2 N.E.2d 687 (1936).

113. *See* RESTATEMENT (SECOND) OF CONFLICT OF LAWS § 32 cmts. a, d, e & f (1971).

in this sense, the appearance still may confer jurisdiction on the court. Defendants wanting to object to a court's assertion of personal jurisdiction over them traditionally had to make what is called a *special appearance* in the action—an appearance made for the *sole* purpose of objecting to personal jurisdiction. If the defendant made such a special appearance, and if the court had no jurisdiction over the defendant, the court would dismiss the action.[114]

The procedures for making special appearances were strictly circumscribed. If a defendant "either enters an appearance in an action without limiting the purpose for which he appears or . . . asks for relief which the court may give only if it has jurisdiction over him," the defendant makes what is known as a *general appearance*.[115] A general appearance conferred jurisdiction on the court. Thus, if defendants did not carefully follow the procedures set out in a state for making a special appearance to challenge jurisdiction, they could find that they had appeared generally and conferred jurisdiction on the court.[116]

The U.S. Supreme Court has held that a state is not constitutionally required to provide a method, such as a special appearance procedure, by which the defendant may raise objections to the state's assertion of jurisdiction. The defendant's ability to ignore the assertion of jurisdiction and challenge the validity of a default judgment on jurisdictional grounds when the plaintiff seeks to enforce the judgment against the defendant in another state—to *collaterally attack* the judgment—is considered constitutionally sufficient.[117]

This holding presents no problem today because every state now provides for a special appearance procedure or its equivalent.[118] Before these procedures

---

114. *See id.* § 81.

115. *Id.* § 33 cmt. d.

116. The same result can occur today under procedural systems governed by the Federal Rules of Civil Procedure, which provide for challenges to personal jurisdiction by motion, rather than by special appearance. If the procedure prescribed by the Federal Rules is not followed exactly, the defendant will have "waived" the objection to the court's jurisdiction. *See* FED. R. CIV. P. 12(g) & (h). "Waiver" and "general appearance" are equivalent expressions which signify that the defendant has submitted to the court's jurisdiction, whether or not the defendant intended to do so. Waiver under the Federal Rules is discussed more fully in Chapter 6(D)(3)*(g) infra* ("Consolidation and Waiver of Defenses"). Because some states still have the old special appearance schemes, while others follow the more modern Federal Rules motion scheme, practitioners must examine the law of the state in which they are challenging jurisdiction carefully to determine which procedure is appropriate. *See, e.g.*, Rhino Metals, Inc. v. Craft, 146 Idaho 319, 193 P.3d 866 (2008) (Idaho Rule 4(i) provides that the voluntary appearance or service of any pleading by a party constitutes voluntary submission to the personal jurisdiction of the court, with three exceptions: (1) filing a motion under Rule 12(b)(2), (4), or (5) does not constitute a voluntary appearance; (2) filing a motion asserting any other defense does not constitute a voluntary appearance if it is joined with a motion under Rule 12(b)(2), (4), or (5); and (3) filing a pleading and defending the lawsuit does not constitute a voluntary appearance if it is done after the trial court has denied the party's motion under Rule 12(b)(2), (4), or (5); thus, under Idaho rules, serving a motion to strike amended complaint constituted a general appearance).

117. *See* York v. Texas, 137 U.S. 15, 11 S. Ct. 9, 34 L. Ed. 604 (1890).

118. The trend continues toward abolishing special appearance procedures in favor of motion procedures patterned after those of the Federal Rules. *See* Hansen v. Eighth Judicial Dist. Court *ex. rel.* County of Clark, 116 Nev. 650, 6 P.3d 982 (2000) (general and special appearance abolished by adoption of state rule identical to Federal Rule 12). Under the motion procedures patterned after those of Federal Rule 12, a defendant still has the option to default and collaterally attack the judgment as void because rendered for lack of jurisdiction when the plaintiff seeks to enforce the judgment against the defendant in another state. When this option is selected, however, the defendant is obligated to raise the defense that the judgment is void in the enforcement proceeding by an appropriate procedure. *See, e.g.*, *In re* Knight, 208 F.3d 514 (5th Cir. 2000) (defendant obligated to raise defense that judgment is void as an affirmative defense in enforcement action or defense will be waived in accordance with the rule governing affirmative defenses); *cf.* CIBC Mellon Trust Co. v. Mora Hotel Corp. N.V., 100 N.Y.2d 215, 792 N.E.2d 155, 762 N.Y.S.2d 5 (2003) (New York statute governing recognition of foreign nation money judgments provided that judgment should not be denied enforcement for lack of personal jurisdiction if the defendant voluntarily appeared in the foreign proceedings other than for the purpose of protecting property seized

existed in all the states, however, defendants could be placed in an uncomfortable position. If a defendant failed to appear and litigate the action in a state that did not provide for a special appearance, a default judgment would be rendered. When the plaintiff sought to enforce the default judgment against the defendant in another state, the defendant could challenge the validity of the judgment on the ground that it had been rendered without jurisdiction. But if the defendant's jurisdictional objection was invalid, the default judgment would be valid and enforceable against the defendant, even though the defendant had never litigated the merits of the case.[119]

A scheme of special appearances would not help the defendant in quasi in rem or in rem cases, in which the court's power was based on the presence of property owned by the defendant within the state. Under the rule of *Pennoyer v. Neff*, a state could validly acquire jurisdiction to adjudicate up to the limits of the property if the property had been properly seized. A special appearance would fail if the property was attached in the manner prescribed in *Pennoyer* and later cases. As a practical matter, therefore, the attachment of property might compel the defendant to enter a general appearance to defend the property from loss. Unless the state provided for the kind of limited appearance discussed in section B(1)*(c)*, above, a defendant was posed with an even greater dilemma than in an in personam action. If the defendant did not appear and defend on the merits, the defendant would lose the property attached. However, if the defendant did appear and defend, the defendant made a general appearance that might result in a binding judgment for an amount far in excess of the value of the property—a judgment that could be enforced against the defendant in another state.

---

or threatened with seizure).

119. Though this dilemma is eased for the defendant when a state provides a special appearance procedure or its equivalent, it may not be eliminated entirely. If a defendant specially appears to challenge the jurisdiction of the court, the court may overrule the objection. At that point, the defendant may or may not be able to appeal the jurisdictional determination of the trial court, depending on whether the state permits interlocutory appeals. If the state does not permit the defendant to appeal immediately, the defendant will have to defend the action on the merits. The defendant may not refuse to defend further, allow a default judgment to be entered, and defend on jurisdictional grounds when the default judgment is enforced in another state. The determination of the jurisdictional issue against the defendant in the special appearance procedure will be res judicata in the subsequent action on the default judgment, and again the defendant will have lost the ability to defend on the merits. Thus, the defendant's only alternative is to defend on the merits and if the defendant loses, to appeal, raising the objection to the court's jurisdiction along with any errors allegedly occurring in the trial of the merits. *See* RESTATEMENT (SECOND) OF JUDGMENTS § 10(2) cmt. d (1982). This *direct attack* on the judgment will preserve the jurisdictional objection, but the defendant may encounter substantial inconvenience in trying the merits before obtaining appellate review on the jurisdictional point. Yet this pattern of review is followed in most states and the federal courts. *See* RESTATEMENT (SECOND) OF CONFLICT OF LAWS § 81 cmt. c (1971); Harkness v. Hyde, 98 U.S. 476, 25 L. Ed. 237 (1879). Even if a state permits interlocutory appeals from adverse jurisdictional determinations in special appearance proceedings, all of the defendant's difficulties may not be eliminated. A problem may arise if the state *requires* defendants to appeal the jurisdictional question before litigating the merits of the case. *See* RESTATEMENT (SECOND) OF CONFLICT OF LAWS § 81 cmt. c (1971). Under this approach, a failure to take an interlocutory appeal will result in loss of the right to litigate the jurisdictional question later in the proceedings. The interlocutory appeal on the jurisdictional issue may fail, however, and the defendant will be forced to litigate the merits of the case in the state. This process may produce wasted expense for the defendant, but the problems of a plaintiff faced with an unscrupulous defendant who uses the interlocutory appeal only for purposes of delay may be worse.

4. In Personam Jurisdiction: Domicile

Substantial doubt exists whether either nationality or domicile traditionally constituted a sufficient basis for jurisdiction in private international law. The theory that nationality is a sufficient basis is predicated on the notion that a citizen of a nation is bound to obey the commands of that citizen's sovereign and thus the judgments of the courts of that sovereign.[120] However, it does not necessarily follow that other sovereigns ought to enforce a judgment rendered on the basis of nationality.[121] Furthermore, strong support still exists for the proposition that domicile is not a ground of jurisdiction recognized at the international level.[122]

Nevertheless, after *Pennoyer v. Neff*, the U.S. Supreme Court recognized that nationality and domicile were bases for the exercise of in personam jurisdiction that would not violate the Due Process Clauses of the U.S. Constitution. In *Blackmer v. United States*,[123] the Court held that service of a subpoena on an American citizen abroad as authorized by a federal statute was consistent with the Due Process Clause of the Fifth Amendment. The Court stated the underlying principle for the exercise of state-court jurisdiction based on a person's domicile in *Milliken v. Meyer*:[124] "[T]he authority of a state over one of its citizens is not terminated by the mere fact of his absence from the state. The state which accords him privileges and affords protection to him and his property by virtue of his domicile may also exact reciprocal duties."[125]

Domicile has never been a common-law basis of jurisdiction. In other words, unlike presence and consent, a specific statutory authorization had to exist before a court would assert jurisdiction over a nonresident domiciliary of the state.[126] For example, in *Milliken*, the Court upheld jurisdiction acquired under a Wyoming statute that provided for service by publication in actions when resident defendants had departed from the county of their residence with the intent to delay or defraud their creditors or to avoid service of a summons. The defendant had been personally served with process outside the state pursuant to another provision of the Wyoming statutes that allowed such service in all cases in which service could be made by publication. Because jurisdiction had been acquired properly, the Court required other states to give effect to the judgment entered pursuant to these statutes.[127]

In private international law, the absence of domicile as a recognized ground of international jurisdiction means that a judgment rendered by a United States court under the *Blackmer* and *Milliken* principles might not be enforceable in the courts of a foreign country. This result is unexceptional in international practice. It

---

120. *See* J.J. FAWCETT & J.M. CARRUTHERS, CHESHIRE, NORTH & FAWCETT'S PRIVATE INTERNATIONAL LAW 527-28 (14th ed. 2008).

121. *See id.*

122. *See id.* at 360. *But see* Note, *Developments in the Law—State-Court Jurisdiction*, 73 HARV. L. REV. 909, 913 (1960); RESTATEMENT (THIRD) OF THE FOREIGN RELATIONS LAW OF THE UNITED STATES § 421(2)(b) (1987); UNIF. FOREIGN MONEY-JUDGMENTS RECOGNITION ACT § 5(4) (1962), 13 U.L.A. pt. II, at 73 (2002).

123. 284 U.S. 421, 52 S. Ct. 252, 76 L. Ed. 375 (1932).

124. 311 U.S. 457, 61 S. Ct. 339, 85 L. Ed. 278 (1940).

125. *Id.* at 463, 61 S. Ct. at 343, 85 L. Ed. at 283.

126. *See* RESTATEMENT (SECOND) OF CONFLICT OF LAWS § 29 cmt. d (Supp. 1988).

127. *Milliken*, 311 U.S. at 458-63, 61 S. Ct. at 340-43, 85 L. Ed. at 281-83.

has long been recognized that the courts of one country may render judgments that comply with their own domestic rules, but which are unenforceable in foreign courts because they are not based on an accepted ground of international jurisdiction.[128] Thus, federal and state statutes authorizing jurisdiction based on nationality and domicile are domestic rules of the United States, not necessarily binding in international practice, even though the statutes comply with the Due Process Clauses of the U.S. Constitution.

The unusual feature of American jurisprudence produced by *Pennoyer v. Neff* is that a judgment rendered by one state based on the domicile of the defendant *must be* recognized and enforced by other states. This conclusion results because (1) *Pennoyer* incorporated the international rules of jurisdiction into the Due Process Clause as constitutional rules; (2) after *Pennoyer*, the jurisdictional rules that operated through the Due Process Clause and in full-faith-and-credit cases came to be viewed as identical; and (3) the Court treated domicile as a sufficient basis of jurisdiction under the Due Process Clause, making it also a sufficient basis in cases in which a judgment rendered by one state is taken for enforcement to another state under the full-faith-and-credit implementing statute.

Illustration 3-16. *D*, who is domiciled in State *X*, departed from State *X* to roam the world. *D* never returned to State *X*, but *D* also never acquired a new domicile by being physically present in any other state or country and having the intention to make that state or country *D's* home indefinitely or permanently. Consequently, under the rules of domicile traditionally applied in the United States, *D* technically retained a domicile in State *X*. *P*, who is also domiciled in State *X*, sued *D* in a State *X* court to recover damages for personal injuries received in an automobile accident with *D* in State *Y*, where *P* and *D* were temporarily present. *D* was served with process in State *Z*, where *D* was temporarily present, under a statute of State *X* authorizing State *X* to assert personal jurisdiction over nonresident domiciliaries of State *X* who are absent from the state. Under the rules that evolved in the United States after *Pennoyer v. Neff*, State *X* could validly assert personal jurisdiction over *D* based on *D's* technical domicile in State *X*.

* * * * *

To this point, domicile has been spoken of as a basis of jurisdiction over an individual who is absent from the state. However, domicile in the United States also became an important prerequisite for jurisdiction to alter status under certain circumstances. The best example of this basis of jurisdiction occurs in divorce cases. A state has jurisdiction to divorce a married couple if either or both spouses are domiciled within the state.[129] Traditionally, this rule was, like jurisdiction over property, a species of in rem jurisdiction over status.[130] However, the portion of the

---

128. *See* J.J. FAWCETT & J.M. CARRUTHERS, CHESHIRE, NORTH & FAWCETT'S PRIVATE INTERNATIONAL LAW 516-17 (14th ed. 2008).

129. *See* RESTATEMENT (SECOND) OF CONFLICT OF LAWS §§ 70-71 (1971).

130. *See* RESTATEMENT (FIRST) OF CONFLICT OF LAWS § 110 cmt. a (1934). The in rem theory of status resembled in many ways the theory propounded by the Court in *Harris v. Balk*, discussed in section B(1)*(a) supra*. Recall that the presence of a person within the state gave power to the state to garnish a debt owed by the person to another nonresident. The theory was that the debt followed the debtor wherever the debtor went. In the divorce cases, the status follows the person and is treated as modifiable wherever the person is domiciled. The only difference is that in the divorce cases, a more substantial relationship between the state and the plaintiff is required—domicile rather than mere presence.

rule allowing divorce based on the domicile of only one spouse is of relatively recent origin. The traditional approach was that the domicile of a single spouse was insufficient, without more, to satisfy due process in a divorce case.[131]

Illustration 3-17. *H* and *W* are a married couple who have lived all their lives in State *X*. *H* abandons *W* and travels to State *Y*, where *H* establishes a new domicile. *H* sues *W* for divorce in a State *Y* court. Under the domicile rule that evolved in the United States after *Pennoyer v. Neff*, the State *Y* court could constitutionally divorce *H* and *W*, even though *W* has never been near State *Y* and *W* does not appear and defend the divorce action. If the State *Y* judgment is later attacked in a proceeding in State *X* or another state, it must be given effect insofar as it changes the marital status of *H* and *W*. However, *W* can resist enforcement of the divorce decree on the ground that *H* did not acquire a legitimate domicile in State *Y* and that, as a result, State Y did not have jurisdiction to grant the divorce.

SECTION C. FICTIONAL EVOLUTION OF THE PRESENCE AND CONSENT TESTS FOR PERSONAL JURISDICTION

1. Jurisdiction over Corporations

The preceding section only discussed jurisdiction over nonresident individuals. But much of the law of personal jurisdiction after *Pennoyer* developed in cases in which corporations were defendants. One of the theories used to justify state-court jurisdiction over corporations—the implied consent theory—was then adapted to certain kinds of actions over individuals. The landmark Supreme Court decision[132] establishing the modern test governing state-court jurisdiction under the Fourteenth Amendment was a reaction to the fictional adaptations of the presence and consent theories to actions against corporate and individual defendants. Thus, a brief discussion of the development of the *Pennoyer* doctrines in these cases will be useful in understanding modern theories of state-court jurisdiction.

A corporation, like an individual, could consent to suit in a forum where it would otherwise not have been amenable to suit. In the absence of *actual* consent, the traditional rule was that a corporation could not be sued outside the state that chartered it.[133] To circumvent this rule, states began to require that a *foreign*

---

131. *See* RESTATEMENT OF CONFLICT OF LAWS § 71 cmt. a (1934); Michael M. O'Hear, *"Some of the Most Embarrassing Questions": Extraterritorial Divorces and the Problems of Jurisdiction Before* Pennoyer, 104 YALE L.J. 1507, 1525-34 (1995). *Compare* Haddock v. Haddock, 201 U.S. 562, 26 S. Ct. 525, 50 L. Ed. 867 (1906) *with* Williams v. North Carolina, 317 U.S. 287, 63 S. Ct. 207, 87 L. Ed. 279 (1942); *see also* RESTATEMENT (THIRD) OF THE FOREIGN RELATIONS LAW OF THE UNITED STATES § 484 (1987) (providing that U.S. courts will recognize foreign divorce decrees of a state where both parties were domiciled and may, but need not, recognize foreign divorce decrees of states where only one party was domiciled).

132. *See* the discussion of the *International Shoe* decision in section D *infra*.

133. St. Clair v. Cox, 106 U.S. 350, 354, 1 S. Ct. 354, 358, 27 L. Ed. 222, 224 (1882) ("[A] foreign corporation could not be sued in an action for the recovery of a personal demand outside of the State by which it was chartered. The principle that a corporation must dwell in the place of its creation, and cannot . . . migrate to another sovereignty, coupled with the doctrine that an officer of the corporation does not carry his functions with him when he leaves his State, prevented the maintenance of personal actions against it. There was no mode of compelling its appearance in the foreign jurisdiction. Legal proceedings there against it were, therefore, necessarily

corporation—one incorporated in another state—appoint an agent upon whom service could be made as a condition of conducting local business of the corporation in the state. If the corporation did not make an actual appointment, the state statutes generally provided for service upon the secretary of state, another public official, or an agent of the corporation in the state. A state could require such an appointment on the theory that the state had the sovereign authority to exclude a foreign corporation from doing local (as opposed to interstate) business altogether. Thus, the state could condition its permission to do local business on the foreign corporation's consent to the appointment of an agent to receive process.[134]

When a foreign corporation conducted only interstate commerce within the state, for example by shipping goods into the state, the state could not exclude the foreign corporation from transacting that interstate commerce. Thus, the consent theory would not work. To subject foreign corporations to jurisdiction under these circumstances, the courts resorted to the presence theory: "A foreign corporation is amenable to process to enforce a personal liability, in the absence of consent, only if it is doing business within the State in such a manner and to such extent as to warrant the inference that it is present there."[135] In the absence of corporate "presence," service on a corporate agent was deemed to be ineffective.[136]

Under either theory—consent or presence—the foreign corporation had to be "doing business." Therefore, the central question in each case became whether, in fact, it was doing such business as would subject it to jurisdiction under the theory upon which the state's assertion of jurisdiction was based.[137] A large body of case law grew up on the question of what constituted "doing business" for jurisdictional purposes. The cases drew distinctions that tended to focus on the quantity or level of activity without focusing on practical considerations, such as the burden on the defendant of suit in a particular state or the need for adjudication there.[138]

Although an individual who was present within a state could be served with process and subjected to jurisdiction even in cases in which the claim arose outside the state, it was unclear whether a corporation could likewise be subjected to

---

confined to the disposition of such property belonging to it as could be there found; and to authorize them legislation was necessary"); *see also* Bank of Augusta v. Earle, 38 U.S. (13 Pet.) 519, 588, 10 L. Ed. 274, 308 (1839).

134. Even before *Pennoyer*, this manipulation of the concept of consent had been approved by the Supreme Court in Lafayette Insurance Co. v. French, 59 U.S. (18 How.) 404, 407, 15 L. Ed. 451, 452-53 (1856).

135. Philadelphia & Reading Ry. Co. v. McKibbin, 243 U.S. 264, 265, 37 S. Ct. 280, 280, 61 L. Ed. 710, 711-12 (1917). The presence theory offered a loophole through which a corporation could escape jurisdiction. If the claim against the corporation arose out of its activities within the state, it could still avoid jurisdiction by ceasing to do business within the state before an action was commenced. Under such circumstances, it would cease to be "present" within the state. *See* Robert Mitchell Furniture Co. v. Selden Breck Constr. Co., 257 U.S. 213, 42 S. Ct. 84, 66 L. Ed. 201 (1921). However, if the corporation was found to have consented to jurisdiction, ceasing business prior to suit would not vitiate the consent. *See* Washington *ex rel.* Bond & Goodwin & Tucker, Inc. v. Superior Court, 289 U.S. 361, 53 S. Ct. 624, 77 L. Ed. 1256 (1933).

136. *See, e.g.*, Riverside & Dan River Cotton Mills v. Menefee, 237 U.S. 189, 35 S. Ct. 579, 59 L. Ed. 910 (1915) (a state cannot acquire jurisdiction over a corporation by in-hand service on one of the corporate directors residing in the state when the corporation had no other connection with that state).

137. *See* Philip B. Kurland, *The Supreme Court, The Due Process Clause and the In Personam Jurisdiction of State Courts—From* Pennoyer *to* Denckla*: A Review*, 25 U. CHI. L. REV. 569, 584 (1958).

138. *See id.*; *see also* John A. Swain & Edwin E. Aguilar, *Piercing the Veil to Assert Personal Jurisdiction over Corporate Affiliates: An Empirical Study of the* Cannon *Doctrine*, 84 B.U. L. REV. 445 (2004) (discussing the application of one early doctrine in a modern context); *Developments in the Law—State-Court Jurisdiction*, 73 HARV. L. REV. 911, 922-23 (1960).

jurisdiction based on presence when the claim arose elsewhere. Some cases denied jurisdiction. Others upheld jurisdiction when the claim did not arise out of the activities of the corporation in the state. The distinction between the decisions may have turned upon the level of corporate activity within the state, with "continuous and systematic" activity resulting in jurisdiction over cases involving claims unrelated to the state.[139]

2. Implied Consent Extended Beyond Corporations

In addition to employing implied consent as a means of establishing jurisdiction over foreign corporations, the states utilized the implied consent theory to gain personal jurisdiction over individual nonresidents under certain circumstances.

Illustration 3-18. In *Hess v. Pawloski*,[140] the Supreme Court upheld a Massachusetts statute deeming nonresident motorists' use of the state's highways to be equivalent to the motorists' appointment of the registrar of motor vehicles as their agent upon whom process could be served in any action arising out of an accident on the state's highways. The statute conditioned the sufficiency of service upon the nonresident motorists' actual receipt of process by registered mail and the granting of continuances to afford them a reasonable opportunity to defend.[141] Because the state had the power to regulate use of its highways, the state could exclude nonresidents from operating motor vehicles on its highways unless an appointment of an agent to receive process had been made. In the absence of a formal appointment, one could be implied by the Massachusetts Legislature from a nonresident's decision to use its highways.[142]

* * * * *

The implied consent theory was sufficiently broad to allow the states to imply the consent of an individual to suit any time the state possessed the power to regulate, and thus place conditions on, the defendant's activity within the state. For example, the states were held to have the power to make the use, ownership, or possession of real estate situated in the state by a nonresident a ground for

---

139. *Compare* Simon v. Southern Ry. Co., 236 U.S. 115, 35 S. Ct. 255, 59 L. Ed. 492 (1915) (jurisdiction denied), Louisville & Nashville R.R. Co. v. Chatters, 279 U.S. 320, 328, 49 S. Ct. 329, 331-32, 73 L. Ed. 711, 717-18 (1929) (same; dictum) *and* Takacs v. Philadelphia & Reading Ry. Co., 228 F. 728 (S.D.N.Y. 1915) (same) *with* Tauza v. Susquehanna Coal Co., 220 N.Y. 259, 115 N.E. 915 (1917) (jurisdiction upheld) (Cardozo, J.). An anomalous result occurred under the consent theory because the courts applied the theory both when the corporation actually appointed an agent to receive service of process as required by statute and when the corporation violated the statute by not appointing an agent. When the corporation actually appointed an agent as required by statute, the cases held that it had consented to suit both as to claims arising from its activities within the state and as to claims arising outside the state. *See* Pennsylvania Fire Ins. Co. v. Gold Issue Mining & Milling Co., 243 U.S. 93, 37 S. Ct. 344, 61 L. Ed. 610 (1917). However, even if the corporation did not comply with a state statute requiring it to appoint an agent to receive service, the courts concluded it had consented to suits arising from its activities within the state by doing business within the state. "The rationale of the latter result was that a corporation which did not appoint an agent but did business within the state should not be in a better position than one which complied with the statute." *Developments in the Law—State-Court Jurisdiction*, 73 HARV. L. REV. 911, 920 (1960). Nevertheless, an advantage still accrued to the noncomplying corporation because the courts held that such a corporation only consented as to claims that arose out of its activities within the state. *See* Simon v. Southern Ry. Co., 236 U.S. 115, 35 S. Ct. 255, 59 L. Ed. 492 (1915).

140. 274 U.S. 352, 47 S. Ct. 632, 71 L. Ed. 1091 (1927).

141. *Id.* at 354, 47 S. Ct. at 632-33, 71 L. Ed. at 1093-94.

142. *Id.* at 356-57, 47 S. Ct. at 633-34, 71 L. Ed. at 1094-95.

exercising personal jurisdiction over the nonresident on claims arising out of such use, ownership, or possession.[143] Thus, a jurisdictional theory that had been stretched to fit corporations was stretched even further to fit actions against individuals. The result was a morass of fictional rules that were ill-suited to the society that had evolved in the United States by the middle of the twentieth century.[144]

SECTION D. THE DEVELOPMENT OF MODERN RESTRICTIONS ON STATE-COURT JURISDICTION: THE MINIMUM CONTACTS TEST

In *International Shoe Co. v. Washington,*[145] the U.S. Supreme Court began to evolve a new test for determining personal jurisdiction over foreign corporations and other defendants: the *minimum contacts* test. International Shoe was a Delaware corporation having its principal place of business in St. Louis, Missouri. International Shoe manufactured and sold shoes and other footwear. The business conducted by International Shoe in Washington was purely interstate commerce. However, to conduct this business, International Shoe employed salesmen who resided and worked within the state. As a result, Washington assessed International Shoe for contributions to the state unemployment compensation fund. International Shoe was properly notified of the administrative proceeding brought to assess the tax against it and specially appeared to challenge Washington's authority to assert personal jurisdiction over it. The Washington administrative agency before which the proceeding was pending and the Washington courts reviewing the agency's action all rejected this challenge.[146]

---

143. *See* Dubin v. City of Philadelphia, 34 D. & C. 61 (C.P. Phila. Co. 1938); RESTATEMENT (SECOND) OF CONFLICT OF LAWS § 38(1) (1971). There was some indication that the question whether a state had power to adjudicate based on the implied consent theory depended on whether the state had manifested its interest in the subject matter in a formalized way. In *Dubin*, above, the rules of liability were common law in nature, but the state had a specific long-arm statute by which it manifested its interest in the subject of nonresident owners and users of real estate. In Flexner v. Farson, 248 U.S. 289, 39 S. Ct. 97, 63 L. Ed. 250 (1919), the Court invalidated an assertion of jurisdiction over a partnership in a suit for breach of contract to sell bonds. The state did not regulate the securities business, and jurisdiction was asserted under a general "doing business" long-arm statute. However, in Henry L. Doherty & Co. v. Goodman, 294 U.S. 623, 55 S. Ct. 553, 79 L. Ed. 1097 (1935), the Supreme Court sustained jurisdiction over a nonresident individual in a suit for damages arising out of a stock sale. The state regulated the securities business extensively by statute, although jurisdiction was again asserted under a general long-arm statute. Assuming the validity of the assertion of jurisdiction in *Dubin*, the cases might be read as standing for the proposition that the state must either have a specific long-arm statute or a specific regulatory scheme expressing its formalized interest in the case before the implied consent theory would work. This possible reading is important in light of the Court's emphasis in modern cases on the "state's interest" as a factor militating in favor of jurisdiction and the view that interest can be enhanced by a formalized statutory expression of the interest. *See* sections G(2)*(b)(iv) infra* ("The Reasonableness Test").

144. *See* Philip B. Kurland, *The Supreme Court, The Due Process Clause and the In Personam Jurisdiction of State Courts—From* Pennoyer *to* Denckla*: A Review*, 25 U. CHI. L. REV. 569, 585-86 (1958).

145. 326 U.S. 310, 66 S. Ct. 154, 90 L. Ed. 95 (1945). The approach adopted in *International Shoe* was essentially that articulated by Judge Learned Hand in Hutchinson v. Chase & Gilbert, Inc., 45 F.2d 139 (2d Cir. 1930). For an article discussing the development and application of the *Pennoyer* and *International Shoe* decisions, see Douglas D. McFarland, *Drop the* Shoe*: A Law of Personal Jurisdiction,* 68 MO. L. REV. 753 (2003); *see also* Lonny Sheinkopf Hoffman, *The Case Against Vicarious Jurisdiction,* 152 U. PA. L. REV. 1023 (2004).

146. *See International Shoe*, 326 U.S. at 313-15, 66 S. Ct. at 156-57, 90 L. Ed. at 100-01.

On appeal to the U.S. Supreme Court, International Shoe relied on cases in which it had been held that the mere solicitation of orders for the purchase of goods within a state, to be accepted outside the state and filled by shipment of the purchased goods interstate, did not render the corporate seller amenable to suit within the state. International Shoe also argued that "since it was not present within the state, it [was] a denial of due process to subject [the company] to taxation or other money exaction."[147] The Court rejected International Shoe's contentions.

Although it might have sustained Washington's assertion of jurisdiction over International Shoe under the presence test,[148] the Court instead chose to articulate a new test for personal jurisdiction. The Court stated that the presence test as applied to corporations was merely "symbolic" of the activities within the state that would be deemed sufficient under the Due Process Clause to allow the state to subject the corporation to jurisdiction.[149] To satisfy the demands of due process, the corporation must have such "contacts" with the forum state "as make it reasonable, in the context of our federal system of government, to require the corporation to defend the particular suit which is brought there."[150] This "minimum contacts" test would be satisfied when the "quality and nature of the activity" of the defendant within the state was sufficient "in relation to the orderly administration of the laws that it was the purpose of the [D]ue [P]rocess [C]lause to insure."[151] The Due Process Clause would not permit an assertion of jurisdiction "against an individual or corporate defendant with which the state has no contacts, ties, or relations."[152] In applying the test, "[a]n 'estimate of the inconveniences' which would result to the corporation from a trial away from its 'home' or principal place of business is relevant."[153]

Since the decision in *International Shoe*, the minimum contacts test has dominated the landscape of personal jurisdiction in the United States. However, in addition to being ambiguous on several points, the Court's decision left several issues for resolution in the future. The following five sections explore the development and application of the minimum contacts test in the more than sixty years since the Court decided *International Shoe*. Specifically, those sections will explore (1) the status of the territorial rules of *Pennoyer v. Neff* after the advent of the minimum contacts test; (2) the enactment by the states of new "long-arm" statutes in reaction to the minimum contacts test; (3) the content of the minimum contacts test; (4) the application of the minimum contacts test in particular categories of cases; and (5) the possible development of a concept of "jurisdiction by necessity." The final three sections of the chapter will examine (1) the due process requirement of notice, which is a separate requirement from the minimum

---

147. *Id.* at 316, 66 S. Ct. at 158, 90 L. Ed. at 101.

148. The Court cited and discussed its prior decisions under the presence and consent tests that would have sustained jurisdiction over International Shoe. *See id.* at 317-19, 66 S. Ct. at 159, 90 L. Ed. at 102-03.

149. *See id.* at 316-17, 66 S. Ct. at 158, 90 L. Ed. at 102.

150. *Id.* at 317, 66 S. Ct. at 158, 90 L. Ed. at 102. The Court had earlier stated that "due process requires only that in order to subject a defendant to a judgment *in personam*, if he be not present within the territory of the forum, he have certain minimum contacts with it such that the maintenance of the suit does not offend 'traditional notions of fair play and substantial justice.' " *Id.* at 316, 66 S. Ct. at 158, 90 L. Ed. at 102 (citations omitted).

151. *Id.* at 319, 66 S. Ct. at 160, 90 L. Ed. at 104.

152. *Id.*

153. *Id.* at 317, 66 S. Ct. at 158, 90 L. Ed. at 102.

contacts test; (2) the mechanics of service of process in state and federal courts; and (3) special problems of amenability to process in federal courts.

SECTION E. THE STATUS OF THE TERRITORIAL RULES OF JURISDICTION AFTER *INTERNATIONAL SHOE*

The effect of the Court's decision in *International Shoe* on the territorial rules of *Pennoyer v. Neff* was not immediately apparent. On one hand, as indicated above, the Court could have decided the case under the old presence test. The fact that the Court went out of its way to develop a new test might have meant that the new test replaced the old tests used under *Pennoyer*. This interpretation of the case was reinforced by the derogatory way in which the Court described the presence and consent tests in its opinion.[154] Furthermore, the new test focused on contacts between the defendant and the forum. The Court's statement about an "estimate of the inconveniences" of a trial in the forum being relevant to the administration of the test seemed to indicate that the new test replaced the territorial rules of *Pennoyer*. As observed in the earlier discussion of those rules, the territorial rules did not aim at preserving, as due process rules arguably should, an effective opportunity to be heard for the defendant. The new minimum contacts test, however, did seem to be aimed at this goal.

On the other hand, the tone of the Court's opinion in *International Shoe* was expansive. The minimum contacts test seemed to afford the states more leeway in asserting jurisdiction over nonresidents than the old territorial rules, even as those rules had evolved under the fictional presence and consent tests. Thus, it was possible to read *International Shoe* as if the minimum contacts test constituted an additional justification for an assertion of jurisdiction over nonresidents when the territorial rules could not be used to acquire jurisdiction over a defendant. This reading of the Court's opinion was reinforced by its statement that due process would be satisfied by an assertion of jurisdiction over a defendant who had minimum contacts with the state "if he be not present within the territory of the forum."[155]

Finally, the Court took care to analyze its prior decisions to indicate the consistency of their results with the new minimum contacts approach. Thus, while the new test was replacing *Pennoyer's* territorial analysis, it could mean that the results under the new test would be the same as under the old territorial rules. Under this reading of the opinion, the minimum contacts test would be neither expansive nor contractive. Rather, it would simply represent a more rational, nonfictional way

---

154. The Court stated that to say a corporation is present in a state "is to beg the question to be decided" and that the terms "present" or "presence" are used merely to symbolize the activities of the corporation within the state that will justify an assertion of jurisdiction over the corporation under the Due Process Clause of the Fourteenth Amendment. *See International Shoe*, 326 U.S. at 316-17, 66 S. Ct. at 158, 90 L. Ed. at 102. In addition, the Court described its decisions subjecting the corporation to suit based on consent as a "legal fiction." *See id.* at 318, 66 S. Ct. at 159, 90 L. Ed. at 103.

155. *Id.* at 316, 66 S. Ct. at 158, 90 L. Ed. at 102.

of analyzing the due process validity of a state's assertion of jurisdiction over nonresidents.

Amazingly, in the more than fifty years since *International Shoe* was decided, the Supreme Court has not completely resolved the status of the territorial rules. In 1977, the Court appeared to say that the territorial rules were no longer valid bases for state-court jurisdiction. However, a Supreme Court decision in 1990 again threw doubt on the issue.

1. Quasi In Rem and Related Jurisdictional Doctrines

In *Shaffer v. Heitner*,[156] the Supreme Court appeared to clarify the respective roles of the minimum contacts test of *International Shoe* and the territorial rules of *Pennoyer*. In *Shaffer*, the plaintiff was the owner of one share of stock in the Greyhound Corporation. The plaintiff sued Greyhound and twenty-eight present or former officers of Greyhound in a Delaware state court. The plaintiff alleged that the individual defendants had violated their duties to Greyhound by causing the company to engage in actions that resulted in it being held liable for substantial antitrust damages and criminal contempt fines. The actions that allegedly led to the damages and contempt fines occurred in Oregon. Greyhound was a Delaware corporation. However, both the plaintiff and the individual defendants were nonresidents of Delaware.[157]

At the time the plaintiff filed the complaint, the plaintiff sequestered the property of the individual defendants, which constituted a substantial number of shares of stock and stock options. The sequestration was accomplished pursuant to a Delaware statute by placing "stop transfer" orders on the books of the Greyhound Corporation. The stock and options were not physically present in Delaware. However, the stock was considered to be subject to seizure in the state because of a Delaware statute that made Delaware the situs of ownership of all stock in Delaware corporations. In effect, the Delaware sequestration procedure was the equivalent of the garnishment to achieve quasi in rem jurisdiction that had occurred in *Harris v. Balk*, discussed above.[158]

The defendants entered a special appearance to challenge Delaware's assertion of quasi in rem jurisdiction over them. The defendants asserted that they lacked sufficient contacts with the state to sustain jurisdiction under the minimum contacts test of *International Shoe*. The Delaware trial court rejected this jurisdictional challenge. The Delaware Supreme Court affirmed the judgment of the trial court on the ground that an assertion of quasi in rem jurisdiction was not subject to the limitations of the minimum contacts test.[159]

The U.S. Supreme Court reversed the judgment of the Delaware Supreme Court. The Court stated "that all assertions of state-court jurisdiction must be

---

156. 433 U.S. 186, 97 S. Ct. 2569, 53 L. Ed. 2d 683 (1977).

157. *See id.* at 189-91, 97 S. Ct. at 2572-73, 53 L. Ed. 2d at 688-90.

158. *See id.* at 190-92, 97 S. Ct. at 2572-73, 53 L. Ed. 2d at 688-90. *Harris v. Balk* is discussed in section B(1)*(a) supra* ("Affirmative Principles of In Rem Jurisdiction").

159. *See Shaffer*, 433 U.S. at 190-95, 97 S. Ct. at 2572-75, 53 L. Ed. 2d at 689-92.

evaluated according to the standards set forth in *International Shoe* and its progeny."[160] The extension of the *International Shoe* standards to "all" assertions of state-court jurisdiction logically seemed to invalidate more than simply quasi in rem jurisdiction of the *Harris v. Balk* variety. Also placed in jeopardy by this part of the Court's opinion were the traditional rules permitting jurisdiction based on (1) service of process on a defendant who is only transitorily present in the state, (2) the domicile of the defendant, when the domicile is only "technical" and the defendant no longer has a substantial relationship with the state, and (3) the domicile of the plaintiff in ex parte divorce cases, even though the defendant has no contacts with the state.

In a cryptic footnote in *Shaffer*, however, the Court created doubt whether it really meant to subject "all" assertions of state-court jurisdiction to the minimum contacts test: "We do not suggest that jurisdictional doctrines other than those discussed in [the] text, such as the particularized rules governing the adjudications of status, are inconsistent with the [*International Shoe*] standard of fairness."[161] This statement appears to be a direct reference to ex parte divorce cases, in which the states are allowed to divorce two parties based on the domicile of only the plaintiff in the state.[162] The *International Shoe* test focused on the fairness of the jurisdictional assertion to the defendant. Thus, it was not immediately apparent how the ex parte divorce jurisdiction could be consistent with the test. In ex parte divorce cases, the defendant often has no contact at all with the forum state. In addition, the forum state would usually also be a burdensome place for the defendant to litigate.

The explanation for the Court's footnote may lie in the substantive nature of most ex parte divorce proceedings. If a plaintiff commences an ex parte divorce action in a state with a no fault divorce law, there is realistically no defense to the action. Because the Due Process Clause is designed to insure the defendant an adequate opportunity to be heard in defense, it is possible to reason that when no defense exists under the applicable substantive law, the defendant is not deprived of anything by the state's assertion of jurisdiction. A problem exists, of course, if the forum state has a no fault divorce law that it will apply to the action, while the state of the marital domicile has a fault divorce law that would prevent the plaintiff from obtaining the divorce. But this problem should not be addressed through due process limits on the state's ability to assert personal jurisdiction. Instead, it is a problem of determining whether the state should be permitted to apply its substantive divorce law to dissolve a marriage between a domiciliary of the state and a nonresident who has no connections with the state.

---

160. *Id.* at 212, 97 S. Ct. at 2584, 53 L. Ed. 2d at 703.

161. *Id.* at 208 n.30, 97 S. Ct. at 2582 n.30, 53 L. Ed. 2d at 700 n.30. In another footnote (36), the Court indicated that there would be no unfairness in allowing suit in a state where a defendant has property after judgment in another state against the defendant rendered by a court with proper jurisdiction, even if the state where the property was located would not have had minimum contacts to determine the action as an original matter. *Cf.* Aristides Diaz-Pedrosa, Shaffer's *Footnote 36*, 109 W. VA. L. REV. 17 (2006) (discussing footnote 36 as applied to arbitral awards).

162. *See, e.g.*, Williams v. North Carolina, 317 U.S. 287, 63 S. Ct. 207, 87 L. Ed. 279 (1942) (*Williams I*); Williams v. North Carolina, 325 U.S. 226, 65 S. Ct. 1092, 89 L. Ed. 1577 (1945) (*Williams II*); *see also* E. Roy Hawkens, *The Effect of* Shaffer v. Heitner *on the Jurisdictional Standard in Ex Parte Divorces*, 18 FAM. L.Q. 311 (1984).

Illustration 3-19. *H* and *W* are a husband and wife who are domiciled in State *X*. *H* abandons *W* and travels to State *Y*, where *H* establishes a new domicile. After acquiring a domicile in State *Y*, *H* commences a divorce action in a State *Y* court under the State *Y* no-fault divorce law. *W* is served with mail process in this action in State *X*. *W*, who has never been near State *Y*, does not appear and defend the action. The court then enters a default judgment granting the divorce. The State *Y* judgment is arguably valid under the minimum contacts test. The minimum contacts test is designed to assure that the defendant has an adequate opportunity to be heard in defense before life, liberty, or property is taken from the defendant. Because there is no defense to the State *Y* divorce action, there is nothing for *W* to be heard about in the proceeding. Therefore, the Due Process Clause arguably does not protect *W* against an assertion of no-fault divorce jurisdiction by State *Y*. However, if State *X* is a "fault" divorce state, *W* may possess a valid constitutional objection to the *State Y's* application of its divorce law to the action.[163]

* * * * *

The impact of ex parte divorce jurisdiction on the defendant has been mitigated by the concept of "divisible divorce" developed by the U.S. Supreme Court. Under the divisible divorce concept, the right of a defendant spouse to support or alimony cannot be cut off by a judgment of divorce unless the state where the divorce proceeding is pending has personal jurisdiction consistent with the minimum contacts test over the defendant.[164] Thus, while the domicile of the plaintiff alone will suffice to permit a state to terminate the marital status of the plaintiff and the defendant, domicile of the plaintiff alone will not allow the state to cut off the personal rights of the defendant to support or alimony.[165]

Although the Court in *Shaffer* clearly indicated that traditional in rem jurisdiction based on property within the state would be subject to the *International Shoe* standard, the Court carefully pointed out that nothing precluded the state where property was located from asserting jurisdiction to adjudicate claims directly

---

163. More recent Supreme Court decisions under the Full Faith and Credit Clause and the Due Process Clause have held that a state must have a significant contact with a case that creates a legitimate interest on the part of a state in applying its law. *See* Allstate Ins. Co. v. Hague, 449 U.S. 302, 101 S. Ct. 633, 66 L. Ed. 2d 521 (1981). However, long established and still subsisting conflict-of-laws practices do not violate either the Full Faith and Credit Clause or the Due Process Clause. *See* Sun Oil Co. v. Wortman, 486 U.S. 717, 108 S. Ct. 2117, 100 L. Ed. 2d 743 (1988). Under either of these standards, the state of the plaintiff's domicile may be able to apply its divorce law constitutionally to the case described in this illustration. Nevertheless, there is reason to believe that the Due Process Clause should be interpreted to prohibit the application by a state of its law that will unfairly surprise the defendant. *See* Ralph U. Whitten, *The Constitutional Limitations on State Choice of Law: Due Process*, 9 HAST. CONST. L.Q. 851 (1982). Under an unfair surprise standard, the defendant in an ex parte divorce proceeding might have a valid constitutional objection to the application by the forum state of its no-fault divorce law, if the defendant lives in a fault-based divorce state.

164. *See* Vanderbilt v. Vanderbilt, 354 U.S. 416, 77 S. Ct. 1360, 1 L. Ed. 2d 1456 (1957); Estin v. Estin, 334 U.S. 541, 68 S. Ct. 1213, 92 L. Ed. 1561 (1948).

165. *See* ROBERT L. FELIX & RALPH U. WHITTEN, AMERICAN CONFLICTS LAW § 183 (6th ed. 2011); RUSSELL J. WEINTRAUB, COMMENTARY ON THE CONFLICT OF LAWS § 5.2E2 (6th ed. 2010); *see also* David E. Seidelson, *Jurisdictional Reach and Choice-of-Law Determinations in Divorce Actions and Proceedings Incident Thereto: The Illusion of Tradition and the Significance of Finality and Efficacy*, 6 WIDENER J. PUB. L. 423 (1997). However, the divisible divorce concept does not protect all personal rights of the defendant spouse. For example, the Supreme Court has held that a husband's ex parte divorce can terminate a wife's dower rights in the husband's estate. *See* Simons v. Miami Beach First Nat'l Bank, 381 U.S. 81, 85 S. Ct. 1315, 14 L. Ed. 2d 232 (1965).

related to the property, as opposed to claims such as the one in *Shaffer* that were unrelated to the property.[166]

Illustration 3-20. *P*, a citizen of State *X*, sues *D*, a citizen of State *Y*, in a state court in State *X*. *P* seeks to quiet title to land located in State *X*. *D* has no contacts with State *X* other than a claim to the ownership of the land. Under *Shaffer*, the location of the land in the state is sufficient contact for the state to assert jurisdiction over *D* to adjudicate the title to the land consistent with due process.

* * * * *

The concept of divisible divorce sometimes collides with the language in *Shaffer* indicating that the states have the constitutional power to adjudicate claims to property located within the state. For example, in *Abernathy v. Abernathy*,[167] a husband and wife were married in Florida and resided in Louisiana until their separation. Upon separation, the husband moved to Georgia and purchased real property there, apparently with assets accumulated during the marriage and taken by the husband from Louisiana to Georgia. After about a year, the husband commenced a divorce proceeding against the wife in Georgia. As part of the divorce proceeding, the husband requested that the property located in Georgia be awarded to him. The wife objected to personal jurisdiction, but the Georgia trial court asserted jurisdiction over the "res of the marital relationship" and "in rem jurisdiction with respect to [the] property located within this state."[168]

The Georgia Supreme Court affirmed. According to the court, the Georgia courts had jurisdiction to divorce based on the plaintiff's domicile in Georgia. The assertion of in rem jurisdiction to dispose of the property did not violate the minimum contacts test of *International Shoe*. The language in *Shaffer* preserved the jurisdiction of state courts to adjudicate claims to property within the state. Presiding Justice Fletcher dissented on the ground that the divisible divorce concept compelled the opposite conclusion:

> The majority's opinion opens the doors of Georgia's courts to any citizen of this country who wants to divorce and to obtain an unfair advantage over his or her spouse in the division of marital property. All any citizen need do is leave his or her marital home, take any or all assets of the couple, move to Georgia and file for divorce. . . . The non-resident spouse is then forced to litigate his or her claim to those marital assets in a foreign jurisdiction.[169]

Also in dissent, Justice Sears observed that the Georgia Legislature had, in the Georgia long-arm statute, specifically required personal jurisdiction over a non-resident spouse in actions for division of marital property.[170] In the alternative,

---

166. *See Shaffer*, 433 U.S. at 207-08, 97 S. Ct. at 2581-82, 53 L. Ed. 2d at 699-700; *see also* Cass County Joint Water Res. Dist. v. 1.43 Acres of Land, 2002 ND 83, 643 N.W.2d 685 (holding condemnation actions are proceedings in rem; persons are made parties to condemnation actions not to confer jurisdiction on the court to render a personal judgment, but to enable the condemnor to acquire the property free from all claims; minimum contacts must exist between the parties joined and the state, but *Shaffer* states that location of property in the state can provide adequate contacts when the property itself is the subject of the action).

167. 267 Ga. 815, 482 S.E.2d 265 (1997).

168. *Id.* at 816, 482 S.E.2d at 266.

169. *Id.* at 819, 482 S.E.2d at 269.

170. *See id.* at 821-22, 482 S.E.2d at 270-71. The majority had held the Georgia long-arm statute irrelevant because the trial court was exercising in rem jurisdiction over the property.

Justice Sears argued that the minimum contacts test was violated by Georgia's assertion of jurisdiction over the wife. Justice Sears observed that the U.S. Supreme Court had, in *Shaffer*, also given an example of when property located within the state would *not* support jurisdiction to adjudicate a claim to the property. That example was taken from comment c of the *Restatement (Second) of Conflict of Laws* § 60.[171] The example provided that a state will not *usually* exercise jurisdiction over personal property brought into its territory without the owner's consent.[172]

The debate between the majority and the dissenters in *Abernathy* may have a broad impact on cases in which personal property is brought into a state without the consent of all the persons who claim the property. The citation by the U.S. Supreme Court in *Shaffer* of the *Restatement (Second) of Conflict of Laws* § 60 is ambiguous: Section 60 deals with the personal-property equivalent of the rules governing the acquisition of jurisdiction by fraud or force over persons.[173] Thus, the citation could simply be an innocuous reference to non-constitutional fraud-and-force rules. Alternatively, it could be a suggestion by the Supreme Court that the fraud-and-force rules as applied to property will have constitutional status, at least in some circumstances.[174] What is clear is that cases like *Abernathy* bring to the forefront a latent problem with the U.S. Supreme Court's dictum in *Shaffer*. The solution to that problem depends upon whether the Court interprets the minimum contacts test as applicable to the kind of claim in *Abernathy*, as well as to other claims involving personalty brought into a state without the consent of all claimants to the property.

As discussed earlier,[175] traditional notions of state control over property involved not only affirmative powers to deal with property located within the state, but also restrictions on the ability of states to deal with land located in other states. The Court's statement in *Shaffer* that all assertions of state-court jurisdiction would be governed by *International Shoe* suggested that a state with sufficient contacts to make it fair to assert jurisdiction over the defendant could render a judgment that directly affects the title to land located in another state. However, this position was contradicted by the Court's footnote aimed at preserving traditional ex parte divorce jurisdiction. It was also contradicted by later statements in the opinion focusing on the importance of the state's interest in the minimum contacts analysis.[176] The requirement that the state have a sufficient interest in adjudicating a particular

---

171. RESTATEMENT (SECOND) OF CONFLICT OF LAWS § 60, cmt. c (1971).

172. *See id.*

173. *See id.* cmts. c, d (stating that the limits are not based on "any principle of jurisdiction"; *cf.* section B(2)(*b*), *supra* (discussing the nonjurisdictional limits on state jurisdiction acquired by fraud or force).

174. *See* RESTATEMENT (SECOND) OF CONFLICT OF LAWS § 60, cmt. a (1971) (stating that, while a state "may exercise judicial jurisdiction" to affect interests in a chattel within its territory, if the chattel is situated in a state that has no relation to the parties or the occurrence in question, the assertion of jurisdiction "might be thought inconsistent with the basic principle of reasonableness which underlies the field of judicial jurisdiction"). The reference to reasonableness is clearly a reference to the *International Shoe* standard, and the RESTATEMENT (SECOND) cited § 24 and § 56 as references to the reasonableness principle. These sections are based on the minimum contacts test. *See id.* § 24 cmt. b, § 56 cmt. c.

175. *See* section B(1)*(b) supra* ("Restrictive Principles of In Rem Jurisdiction").

176. In responding to an argument by the plaintiff, the Court stated that the defendants' positions as officers and directors of Greyhound did not, of itself, give Delaware a sufficient "interest" in asserting jurisdiction in the case. *See Shaffer*, 433 U.S. at 214-15, 97 S. Ct. at 2585, 53 L. Ed. at 704. The role of the state's interest in the minimum contacts analysis is discussed further in section G(2)*(b)(iv) infra*.

dispute might result in the preservation of the exclusive jurisdiction of the state where land is located over matters that directly affect the title to the land.

Before *Shaffer*, some states, following the lead of *Seider v. Roth*,[177] had approved of a form of quasi in rem jurisdiction in automobile accident cases against insured defendants. In these cases, the plaintiff would garnish the obligation of the defendant's insurance company to defend and indemnify the defendant. In this way, the plaintiff could bring the action in any state where the insurance company was doing business and thus subject to personal jurisdiction. The theory of these actions was obviously based on *Harris v. Balk*, which the states had assumed survived the decision in *International Shoe*.[178]

After *Shaffer*, there was reason to believe that the form of quasi in rem jurisdiction exercised in *Seider v. Roth* would still be valid. *Seider* jurisdiction had been limited in important ways to assure fairness to both the insurer and the insured. Specifically, the judgment in a *Seider* action was limited to the face amount of the insurance policy, the defendant had the right to a limited appearance,[179] and the plaintiff either had to reside in the forum state or the claim had to arise there.[180] These protections made the *Seider* jurisdiction appear much like a direct action against the insurance company, which some states authorize by statute. Nevertheless, in 1980, the Supreme Court invalidated *Seider* jurisdiction in *Rush v. Savchuk*.[181]

In *Rush*, the Supreme Court stated that *Seider* actions were not the equivalent of direct actions against the insurer. The Court held that the state's ability to assert power over the insured was "analytically prerequisite" to the insurer's entry into the case.[182] Furthermore, the Court held that the "assumption" that the insured party had no real stake in the litigation was "far from self-evident."[183] In support of this last conclusion, the Court cited (1) the potential economic impact on the insured when multiple plaintiffs sued in different states for an aggregate amount in excess of the policy limits; (2) the potential that an adverse decision might affect the defendant's insurability; and (3) the potential noneconomic impact that might occur in professional malpractice actions, in which the insured's professional competence and integrity are questioned.[184] Finally, the Court stated that it was improper to attribute the insurer's contacts to the insured to satisfy the minimum contacts test because "[t]he requirements of *International*

---

177. 17 N.Y.2d 111, 216 N.E.2d 312, 269 N.Y.S.2d 99 (1966).

178. *See, e.g.*, Minichiello v. Rosenberg, 410 F.2d 106 (2d Cir.), *aff'd on rehearing en banc*, 410 F.2d 117 (2d Cir. 1968).

179. Limited appearance is discussed in section B(1)*(c) supra* ("Limited Appearance Procedures").

180. *See, e.g.*, O'Connor v. Lee-Hy Paving Corp., 579 F.2d 194, 200-02 (2d Cir. 1978); Minichiello v. Rosenberg, 410 F.2d 106 (2d Cir.), *aff'd on rehearing en banc*, 410 F.2d 117 (2d Cir. 1968); Simpson v. Loehmann, 21 N.Y.2d 305, 234 N.E.2d 669, 287 N.Y.S.2d 633 (1967). *See generally* Napoleon B. Williams, Jr., *The Validity of Assuming Jurisdiction by the Attachment of Automobile Liability Insurance Obligations: The Impact of* Shaffer v. Heitner *Upon* Seider v. Roth, 9 RUT.-CAM. L.J. 241 (1977).

181. 444 U.S. 320, 100 S. Ct. 571, 62 L. Ed. 2d 516 (1980).

182. *See id.* at 330-31, 100 S. Ct. at 578, 62 L. Ed. 2d at 526.

183. *Id.* at 331, 100 S. Ct. at 579, 62 L. Ed. 2d at 527.

184. *See id.* at 331 n.20, 100 S. Ct. at 579 n.20, 62 L. Ed. 2d at 527 n.20. None of these factors was actually present in the *Rush* case itself, raising the question whether the Court should have invalidated *Seider* jurisdiction in a case in which no adverse effects on the actual insured involved in the case could be identified.

Shoe . . . must be met as to each defendant over whom a state court exercises jurisdiction."[185]

Rush casts substantial doubt on the constitutionality of direct action statutes. Those statutes possess many of the same flaws that the Court deemed present in *Seider* quasi in rem jurisdiction. Specifically, the hypothetical adverse effects on the insured party that the Court said were involved in *Seider* cases are seemingly also present in direct actions.[186] Nevertheless, the Court's statement that *Seider* jurisdiction is not the equivalent of a direct action against the insurer may save the constitutionality of direct action statutes.[187] Of greater concern is the Court's exaltation of form over substance in *Rush*. For example, although the Court stated that jurisdiction over the insured was an analytical prerequisite to jurisdiction over the insurer, it gave no persuasive reason for this conclusion. Given the protections that had evolved in *Seider* actions to assure fairness to both the insured and the insurer, no significant due process problem seemed to exist with the jurisdiction.

2. Transient Presence Jurisdiction

As discussed above, the Court's apparent willingness in *Shaffer* to preserve ex parte divorce jurisdiction from attack under the *International Shoe* standard also raised questions about whether the Court would be willing to preserve other traditional grounds of jurisdiction, such as transient presence, from attack. Only one Supreme Court decision since *Shaffer* has addressed the status of the other traditional territorial rules of jurisdiction. In *Burnham v. Superior Court*,[188] the Court unanimously sustained the rule permitting jurisdiction to be acquired over a defendant who is temporarily within the state when served with process. Although the Court was unanimous in upholding transient presence as a basis of jurisdiction, a majority could not agree on why the rule of transient presence is valid. The *Burnham* decision is, therefore, of limited value in predicting the Court's approach to the validity of other features of the territorial system. The primary value of the case lies in what it reveals about the divisions among the members of the Court (as then constituted) over the philosophy of interpretation that should govern applications of the Due Process Clause to questions of personal jurisdiction.

Burnham involved a divorce action in California. The Burnhams were married in 1976 in West Virginia. They later moved to New Jersey, where their two children were born. They separated in 1987. At the time of the separation, they

---

185. *Id.* at 332, 100 S. Ct. at 579, 62 L. Ed. 2d at 527.

186. *See id.* at 331 n.20, 100 S. Ct. at 579 n.20, 62 L. Ed. 2d at 527 n.20.

187. *Cf.* APC Commodity Corp. v. Ram Dis Ticaret A.S., 965 F. Supp. 461 (S.D.N.Y. 1997) (holding that quasi in rem jurisdiction existed over funds held by an importer-defendant's New York bank where the funds were related to contracts between the plaintiff and defendant that called for a series of exchanges in New York City, which gave rise to a reason why the defendant should have been expected to be sued in New York; however, the court had previously held the defendant subject to personal jurisdiction in New York under the New York long-arm statute. Under such circumstances, there was no real reason to sustain jurisdiction on a quasi in rem theory); *see also* Koehler v. Bank of Bermuda Ltd., 577 F.3d 497 (2d Cir. 2009) (court need not have in rem jurisdiction over property if it has personal jurisdiction over defendant, who can be validly ordered to turn over property located outside the state).

188. 495 U.S. 604, 110 S. Ct. 2105, 109 L. Ed. 2d 631 (1990).

agreed that the wife would take custody of the children and move to California, while the husband would remain in New Jersey. The plan was for the wife to file suit for divorce on the ground of irreconcilable differences. After the wife moved, the husband commenced a divorce action in New Jersey on the ground of desertion, but the wife was never served in this action.

In 1988, after the husband refused to abide by the agreement to submit to an irreconcilable differences divorce, the wife commenced a divorce action in California. Shortly after the wife commenced the action, the husband was served with process while he was temporarily present in California on business and was visiting his children. The husband specially appeared to object to personal jurisdiction in this action on the ground that he did not have sufficient contacts with California to justify an assertion of jurisdiction under the Due Process Clause.[189] The California Superior Court denied the husband's motion to quash the service of process. The California Court of Appeal denied a writ of mandamus on the ground that service while physically present within the state was a valid basis for asserting personal jurisdiction under the Due Process Clause. The U.S. Supreme Court granted certiorari and affirmed.[190]

All nine Justices of the Court agreed that California's assertion of personal jurisdiction over the husband was valid. However, they disagreed concerning the proper standard for judging the validity of the jurisdictional assertion. Writing for four members of the Court,[191] Justice Scalia distinguished between the Due Process Clause as a limitation on the introduction of "novel procedures" and as a limitation on traditionally accepted procedures.[192] Essentially, the opinion stated that the minimum contacts test of *International Shoe* is a standard designed to measure the due process validity of assertions of state-court jurisdiction over defendants who are not served while physically present within the state.[193] According to Justice Scalia, the minimum contacts test does not apply to a traditionally accepted method of obtaining personal jurisdiction.

But what of *Shaffer v. Heitner*, in which the minimum contacts test had been used to invalidate a traditional method of acquiring jurisdiction to adjudicate? Justice Scalia's opinion attempted to distinguish *Shaffer* on the ground that *Shaffer* recognized that quasi in rem jurisdiction was really a fictional way of acquiring in

---

189. The significance of this objection was not directed to the ability of the wife to obtain a California divorce. Recall from the discussion of *Shaffer* that the Court, in footnote 30 of that decision, appeared to preserve the validity of traditional ex parte divorce jurisdiction in cases in which the defendant has no contacts at all with the forum state. *See* Shaffer v. Heitner, 433 U.S. 186, 208 n.30, 97 S. Ct. 2569, 2582 n.30, 53 L. Ed. 2d 683, 700 n.30 (1977). Rather, the significance of the defendant's challenge to California's assertion of jurisdiction must be seen as relevant to issues of support and alimony, which require valid personal jurisdiction over the defendant. *See* the discussion of "divisible divorce" in the text accompanying the discussion of *Shaffer v. Heitner* in section E(1) *supra* ("Quasi in Rem and Related Jurisdictional Doctrines").

190. *Burnham*, 495 U.S. at 608, 110 S. Ct. at 2109, 109 L. Ed. 2d at 638.

191. Justice White concurred in those portions of Justice Scalia's opinion that articulated the standard by which the constitutionality of the traditional territorial rules should be measured under the Due Process Clause. Along with Justice Scalia, the Chief Justice, and Justice Kennedy, Justice White made up the four-member plurality in favor of that standard. Justice White did not concur in sections II-D or III of Justice Scalia's opinion, however. Section II-D of the opinion attempted to distinguish *Shaffer v. Heitner*. Section III responded to Justice Brennan's concurring opinion. Justice White also filed a separate concurring opinion. *See id.* at 626-27, 110 S. Ct. at 2119, 109 L. Ed. 2d at 650. Justice White's concurrence is discussed in the text *infra*.

192. *Id.* at 619, 110 S. Ct. at 2115, 109 L. Ed. 2d at 644-45.

193. *See id.* at 618, 110 S. Ct. at 2114, 109 L. Ed. 2d at 644.

personam jurisdiction over a defendant who is *absent* from the state.[194] Thus, *Shaffer* simply placed "all suits against absent nonresidents on the same constitutional footing, regardless of whether a separate Latin label is attached to one particular basis of contact."[195] Perhaps uneasy with this ground of distinction, Justice Scalia added that the plurality's basic approach to the Due Process Clause in *Burnham* was different than in *Shaffer*. In *Burnham*, the plurality refused to make an independent inquiry into the fairness of the transient presence rule, while in *Shaffer* just such an inquiry was used to invalidate quasi in rem jurisdiction. Furthermore, under the plurality's approach in *Burnham*, the application of the minimum contacts test would be reserved to judge the constitutionality of "new procedures hitherto unknown," while doctrines accepted when the Due Process Clause was adopted and still generally observed would automatically satisfy due process.[196]

Justice White, who concurred in most of Justice Scalia's opinion, filed a separate opinion.[197] While agreeing that jurisdiction based on physical presence was and is too well accepted to be invalid, Justice White nevertheless indicated that "the Court has the authority under the [Fourteenth Amendment] to examine even traditionally accepted procedures and declare them invalid."[198] However, Justice White was unwilling to invalidate the transient presence rule because no showing had been made "that as a general proposition the rule is so arbitrary and lacking in common sense in so many instances that it should be held violative of Due Process in every case."[199] Until such a general showing is made, Justice White indicated that "claims in individual cases that the rule would operate unfairly as applied to the particular nonresident involved need not be entertained."[200]

Justice Brennan filed a concurring opinion, in which Justices Marshall, Blackmun, and O'Connor joined.[201] While the concurring Justices believed that tradition was relevant to the due process inquiry, they did not deem it to be dispositive.[202] Rather, they argued that the minimum contacts test of *International Shoe* should be applied to every case, even those involving traditional methods of acquiring jurisdiction over nonresidents.[203] However, in applying the minimum contacts test to the facts of the case, the concurring Justices felt that the test was

---

194. *Id.* at 620-21, 110 S. Ct. at 2115-16, 109 L. Ed. 2d at 645-46.

195. *Id.* at 621, 110 S. Ct. at 2116, 109 L. Ed. 2d at 646.

196. *Id.* at 622, 110 S. Ct. at 2116-17, 109 L. Ed. 2d at 646-67 (footnote omitted). In a footnote, Justice Scalia suggested that *Shaffer* may have involved a unique state procedure, in that Delaware was the only state that treated the place of incorporation as the situs of corporate stock. *See id.* at 622, n.4, 110 S. Ct. at 2116, n.4, 109 L. Ed. 2d at 646, n.4. This may be true, but it is certainly disingenuous. Quasi in rem jurisdiction based solely on the attachment of property located in the state was a widespread feature of American jurisprudence when the Fourteenth Amendment was adopted *and* when *Shaffer* was decided. Yet *Shaffer* appeared to invalidate quasi in rem jurisdiction as practiced in all states, not just in its Delaware form.

197. *See id.* at 628, 110 S. Ct. at 2119, 109 L. Ed. 2d at 650.

198. *See id.*

199. *Id.* at 628, 110 S. Ct. at 2119-20, 109 L. Ed. 2d at 650.

200. *Id.* at 628, 110 S. Ct. at 2120, 109 L. Ed. 2d at 650. It is mystifying, to say the least, how a showing that the rule operates unfairly in "so many instances" could be made in the course of litigation without reference to the specific facts of the case under adjudication, which Justice White said need not be considered in any event.

201. *See id.*

202. *See id.* at 629-34, 110 S. Ct. at 2120-22, 109 L. Ed. 2d at 650-53.

203. *See id.* at 630-32, 110 S. Ct. at 2121-22, 109 L. Ed. 2d at 651-53. Justice Brennan's opinion also questioned the historical pedigree of the transient presence rule, which Justice Scalia had accepted. *See id.* at 633-37, 110 S. Ct. at 2122-24, 109 L. Ed. 2d at 653-56.

satisfied for several reasons. First, "[t]he transient rule is consistent with reasonable expectations and is entitled to a strong presumption that it comports with due process"[204] because when individuals visit another state, they knowingly assume the risks that the state will exercise some power over their person or property while they are there.[205] The presence of the individual in a state enhances the foreseeability of suit there.[206] Second, by visiting a state, individuals avail themselves of "significant benefits" provided by the state, including police, fire, emergency medical services, freedom of travel on the state's roads and waterways, and the "fruits of the state's economy."[207] Finally, the concurring Justices argued that the burdens on the transient defendant were slight because of modern means of transportation and communication and the availability of procedural devices with which to mitigate inconvenience.[208] Moreover, the fact that the defendant has journeyed once to the forum is itself an indication that suit in the forum would not be prohibitively inconvenient.[209]

The effect of *Burnham* on other "traditional" rules is made especially unclear by Justice Stevens' concurrence. As indicated above, four Justices were willing to rely on the historical pedigree of a rule in sustaining its validity, while four others believed traditional rules must, like others, be justified under the *International Shoe* test. Justice Stevens refused to join in any of the other opinions. However, Justice Stevens agreed that the considerations articulated in all other opinions justified affirming the California judgment.[210]

The task now confronting practitioners and scholars is to decipher the meaning of *Burnham* for other cases. It is difficult to determine which opinion will

---

204. *Id.* at 637, 110 S. Ct. at 2124, 109 L. Ed. 2d at 656.

205. *See id.*

206. *See id.*

207. *See id.* at 637-38, 110 S. Ct. at 2124-25, 109 L. Ed. 2d at 656-57. Justice Brennan added that without transient presence jurisdiction, "an asymmetry would arise" because nonresidents could sue as plaintiffs within the state while remaining immune from suit as defendants. *See id.* at 638, 110 S. Ct. at 2125, 109 L. Ed. 2d at 657 (citing Earl M. Maltz, *Sovereign Authority, Fairness, and Personal Jurisdiction: The Case for the Doctrine of Transient Jurisdiction*, 66 WASH. U. L.Q. 671, 698-99 (1988)). However, there is symmetry in the fact that all nonresidents can sue in the courts of all residents' states while remaining immune from jurisdiction within the state. Thus, California residents can sue New York residents in New York, while remaining immune from suit in New York (unless they have minimum contacts with New York) and New York residents can sue California residents in California while remaining immune from suit in California (unless they have minimum contacts with California). What is "asymmetrical" about this? Even if it is "asymmetrical," the Due Process Clause guarantees an adequate opportunity to be heard in defense before life, liberty, or property is taken from someone. It doesn't guarantee "symmetry."

208. *See Burnham*, 495 U.S. at 638, 110 S. Ct. at 2125, 109 L. Ed. 2d at 657.

209. *See id.* at 639, 110 S. Ct. at 2125, 109 L. Ed. 2d at 657.

210. *See id.* at 640, 110 S. Ct. at 2126, 109 L. Ed. 2d at 658. In *Shaffer*, Justice Stevens had concurred on the ground that the Due Process Clause should be interpreted to require not only adequate notice of the existence of the action, but also fair warning that a particular kind of activity might subject the defendant to the jurisdiction of "a foreign sovereign." *See* Shaffer v. Heitner, 433 U.S. 186, 218, 97 S. Ct. 2569, 2587, 53 L. Ed. 2d 683, 706 (1977) (Stevens, J., concurring). Because such fair warning was, in his view, absent in *Shaffer*, Justice Stevens concurred in the judgment. *See id.* at 218-19, 97 S. Ct. at 2587, 53 L. Ed. 2d at 706-07. However, Justice Stevens agreed with Justice Powell that the Court's opinion should not be read to invalidate quasi in rem jurisdiction when real estate is involved. *See id.* at 219, 97 S. Ct. at 2587, 53 L. Ed. 2d at 707. Justice Stevens also stated that he would not invalidate other long-established methods of acquiring jurisdiction over persons with notice that their local activities might subject them to suit. *See id.* One may extrapolate from Justice Stevens' opinion in *Shaffer*, then, that he agrees with the four members of the Court led by Justice Brennan that transient presence provides adequate foreseeability that the defendant may be sued within the state without more, even if the claim arises outside the state. If the defendant's activities within the state give rise to the claim, transient presence is unnecessary. The defendant can be served outside the state, if necessary, and subjected to jurisdiction consistent with the Due Process Clause under the *International Shoe* test.

prevail due to Justice Stevens' concurrence. Furthermore, the Court's due process methodology outside the personal jurisdiction area has been inconsistent.[211] If Justice Brennan's approach prevails, the validity of the other traditional grounds for and limits on personal jurisdiction would remain in doubt. The main problem in that event would be sorting out how the different Justices would choose to apply the minimum contacts test to particular facts—a daunting task, given that the concurring Justices in *Burnham* were willing to validate transient presence under the test.

If Justice Scalia's position ultimately prevails, there would be different problems. The question in each instance would be (1) whether a traditional ground of jurisdiction existed that was sufficiently accepted at the time the Due Process Clause was formed and (2) whether the states have continued to follow that ground. "Technical domicile"[212] might survive under this test, for example, if it is found that domicile was recognized as a basis of jurisdiction by a sufficient number of states at the time the Fourteenth Amendment was ratified for it to be considered a valid historical basis of asserting jurisdiction—as long as, of course, the states have continued to recognize it. On the other hand, technical domicile does involve an attempt to acquire jurisdiction over a defendant who is absent from the state, a basis that Justice Scalia relied on for distinguishing *Shaffer* from *Burnham*. Furthermore, the Court's decisions recognizing domicile as a valid basis of jurisdiction were not decided until after the Fourteenth Amendment was ratified,[213] giving rise to the possibility that the rule's historical pedigree would not be found adequate under Justice Scalia's approach.[214]

SECTION F. THE REACTION OF THE STATES TO THE MINIMUM CONTACTS TEST: LONG-ARM STATUTES

After *International Shoe* was decided, the states reacted to the new minimum contacts jurisprudence by enacting statutes to extend the reach of their

---

211. In Sun Oil Co. v. Wortman, 486 U.S. 717, 108 S. Ct. 2117, 100 L. Ed. 2d 743 (1988), a majority of the Court, in an opinion by Justice Scalia, validated a traditional conflict-of-laws rule on the grounds that it was accepted at the time the Fourteenth Amendment was adopted and its acceptance had continued into the present. However, in Pacific Mutual Life Insurance Co. v. Haslip, 499 U.S. 1, 111 S. Ct. 1032, 113 L. Ed. 2d 1 (1991), the Court, in validating the common-law method of assessing punitive damages, gave the historical pedigree of the rule substantial weight, but refused to consider it conclusive. Justice Scalia protested this methodology. *See id.* at 24-40, 111 S. Ct. at 1046-54, 113 L. Ed. 2d at 24-34 (Scalia, J., concurring). *Haslip* was decided after *Burnham* and may indicate that Justice Scalia's opinion will not command a majority of the Court in the future.

212. "Technical domicile" is domicile that continues because the defendant has not acquired a new domicile, even though the defendant has left the domiciliary state and no longer has substantial connections with the state. Technical domicile should be distinguished from domicile that is accompanied by substantial connections with the state, such as when the defendant continues to reside in the domiciliary state.

213. *See* section B(4) *supra* ("In Personam Jurisdiction: Domicile").

214. Similarly, if a state attempted to depart from the restrictive in rem principles of jurisdiction discussed in section B(1)*(b) supra*, it might be considered a novel assertion of personal jurisdiction to be judged by reference to the minimum contacts test assuming that, as "subject-matter jurisdiction" limits, these restrictions were incorporated into the Due Process Clause by *Pennoyer*. Thus, despite the long historical pedigree of the restrictions, they could be supplanted by a minimum contacts analysis. On the other hand, in rem restrictions might be considered valid, traditional bases upon which the situs state might refuse to enforce the judgment of another state directly affecting the title to land.

jurisdiction over nonresidents. Just as the "long-arm" statutes enacted by the states between *Pennoyer* and *International Shoe* had relied for their structure on the territorial theories of the former case—notably on the implied consent theory—so did the statutes enacted after *International Shoe* begin to generalize the grounds upon which the states could assert jurisdiction over nonresident defendants under the minimum contacts theory. The first of these generalized long-arm statutes was enacted by Illinois in 1955. The Illinois Act provided that the courts of the state could assert jurisdiction over a nonresident defendant on a "cause of action" arising from any one of four kinds of acts performed in the state: (1) transacting any business within the state; (2) committing a tortious act within the state; (3) owning, using, or possessing any real estate in the state; or (4) contracting to insure any person, property or risk located within the state at the time that the contract was made.[215] When jurisdiction was based on this Act, only causes of action enumerated in the statute could be asserted against the defendant in the action.[216] The Act authorized process to be served on the defendant personally outside the state.[217]

In addition to the issues of constitutional validity that arise whenever any long-arm statute is applied to the facts of a specific case, there also exist questions of statutory applicability that must be worked out on a case-by-case basis. The Illinois statute was designed to extend the reach of Illinois state-court jurisdiction to the limits permitted by *International Shoe*.[218] However, at the time the Illinois statute was enacted, the limited experience with the minimum contacts test had not necessarily revealed the full range of situations in which the Due Process Clause would permit a state to exercise jurisdiction. As a result, the courts had to interpret the statutory language based on what they perceived *International Shoe* would permit.

The statutory requirement that the "commission of a tortious act [be] within this state" presented one such interpretative problem. In *Gray v. American Radiator & Standard Sanitary Corp.*,[219] a hot water heater had been purchased in the ordinary course of commerce. The hot water heater exploded in Illinois. The injured plaintiff commenced an action in Illinois against the Pennsylvania manufacturer of the hot water heater and one of its suppliers. The plaintiff alleged that the supplier negligently constructed the safety valve of the heater in Ohio and sold it to the manufacturer. The supplier objected to jurisdiction on the ground that it had not committed a tortious act within the state of Illinois. The supplier claimed that whatever negligent acts were performed by it occurred in Ohio. In response, the Illinois Supreme Court relied on the legislative intent as well as the general purpose and effect of the long-arm statute rather than the "technicalities" of the definition of a "tortious act." The court concluded that the alleged negligence in manufactur-

---

215. 1955 Ill. Laws 2283, § 1. The current version of this statute is found in ILL. COMP. STAT. ANN. ch. 735, § 5/2-209 (West 2003).

216. 1955 Ill. Laws 2283, § 3.

217. *Id.* § 2.

218. *See* Baltimore & Ohio R.R. Co. v. Mosele, 67 Ill. 2d 321, 328, 368 N.E.2d 88, 91 (1977) (Illinois expanded the in personam jurisdiction of its courts to what was in 1955 understood to be the limits permitted under the Due Process Clause of the Fourteenth Amendment).

219. 22 Ill. 2d 432, 176 N.E.2d 761 (1961).

ing could not be separated from the resulting injury in Illinois. Thus, a tortious act had been committed within Illinois within the meaning of the statute.[220]

In *Gray*, the court held that a reasonable inference could be drawn from the supplier's general commercial transactions that the substantial use and consumption of its valves in Illinois satisfied *International Shoe's* requirement of "minimum contacts" with the state. When the defendant had made no sales or deliveries in the state and had no agent or office there, the complaint had to show affirmatively that the defendant's distribution pattern or volume was such that a reasonable inference could be drawn that the defendant had chosen to operate in national channels of commerce.[221] However, once a showing of contact had been made and a cause of action in tort had been stated in the complaint, the defendant could not demand proof of all the facts necessary to establish ultimate liability in tort in order for the court to have jurisdiction. Otherwise, it was feared, a preliminary hearing on jurisdictional issues would involve a "full-dress" trial on the merits.[222]

Seven years after the enactment of the Illinois long-arm statute, the National Conference of Commissioners on Uniform State Laws approved a Uniform Long-Arm Act. Several states have adopted this Act. The Act attempts to solve some of the problems of interpretation involved in the Illinois statute. Section 1.03 provided:

> (a) A court may exercise personal jurisdiction over a person, who acts directly or by an agent, as to a [cause of action] [claim for relief] arising from the person's
>
> (1) transacting any business in this state;
>
> (2) contracting to supply services or things in this state;
>
> (3) causing [a] tortious injury by an act or omission in this state;
>
> (4) causing [a] tortious injury in this state by an act or omission outside this state if he regularly does or solicits business, or engages in any other persistent course of conduct, or derives substantial revenue from goods used or consumed or services rendered, in this state; [or]
>
> (5) having an interest in, using, or possessing real property in this state[; or

---

220. *Id.* at 435-36, 176 N.E.2d at 762-63; *see also* Vlasak v. Rapid Collection Sys., Inc., 962 F. Supp. 1096 (N.D. Ill. 1997) (telephone calls and letters from Arizona to Illinois that violated Fair Debt Collections Practices Act constituted commission of a "tortious act" in Illinois); Rivera v. Bank One, 145 F.R.D. 614, 619-21 (D.P.R. 1993) (Puerto Rican long-arm statute authorizing jurisdiction over a person who "[p]articipated in tortious acts within Puerto Rico" interpreted to apply to defendant who committed tortious acts outside Puerto Rico that had an effect in the jurisdiction); Green v. USF & G Corp., 772 F. Supp. 1258 (S.D. Fla. 1991) (Florida long-arm statute authorizing jurisdiction over a defendant who commits tortious acts within the state applicable to defendant who made slanderous remarks over the telephone in Maryland to a person in Florida); Wendt v. Horowitz, 822 So. 2d 1252 (Fla. 2002) (making telephone, electronic, or written communications into Florida from outside state can constitute a tortious act for purposes of the Florida long-arm statute if cause of action arises from those communications); Alonso v. Line, 846 So. 2d 745 (La. 2003) (in malpractice action against Alabama attorney, failure of attorney to file suit in Alabama for client constituted an "omission" within Louisiana's long-arm statute). Not all "tortious act" provisions have been given the broad interpretation found in *Gray* and the cases cited above in this note. *See, e.g.*, Bensusan Restaurant Corp. v. King, 126 F.3d 25 (2d Cir. 1997) (interpreting, on the basis of prior authority, New York's tortious act provision to require physical activities in New York by defendant).

221. Keckler v. Brookwood Country Club, 248 F. Supp. 645 (N.D. Ill. 1965).

222. Nelson v. Miller, 11 Ill. 2d 378, 143 N.E.2d 673 (1957).

(6) contracting to insure any person, property, or risk located within this state at the time of contracting].[223]

Subsections (a)(3) and (4) of this Act separate tortious acts committed entirely within the state from tortious acts committed outside the state that have an impact within the state. The latter situations require greater activity on the part of the defendant within the state to permit an assertion of jurisdiction. Obviously, the Act was drafted under the impression that tortious acts committed outside the state would require greater contact to satisfy the *International Shoe* test.[224]

In contrast to the approach of the Illinois and Uniform Acts, which establish specific categories of cases over which the state's courts may exercise jurisdiction, California has simply authorized its courts to "exercise jurisdiction on any basis not inconsistent with the Constitution of this state or of the United States."[225] California also provides for service of process outside the state in cases in which jurisdiction is asserted pursuant to this statute.[226] A provision like the California statute eliminates questions of statutory construction that may arise under the Illinois and Uniform Acts. The inquiry in each case becomes whether an assertion of jurisdiction by the state satisfies the minimum contacts test.[227]

These approaches illustrate the most common ways in which the states have responded to the *International Shoe* test. However, they do not exhaust the responses of the states to long-arm jurisdiction. There are many variations. Cases presenting specific kinds of substantive problems are often treated individually by the state legislatures rather than being left to resolution under a general long-arm

---

223. UNIF. INTERSTATE & INTERNATIONAL PROCEDURE ACT § 1.03 (1962), 13 U.L.A. 361-62 (1986) (Personal Jurisdiction Based upon Conduct) (withdrawn due to obsolescence in 1977, *see* 13 U.L.A. pt. II, at 127 (2002)); *see also* N.Y. C.P.L.R. § 302 (2010); Brunner v. Hampson, 441 F.3d 457 (6th Cir. 2006) (American hunters who were injured or killed in cabin explosion and fire in Canada sued Canadian outfitter in Ohio, alleging that the outfitter provided inadequate and unsafe facilities; held: claim did not arise out of outfitter's contacts with Ohio, which were limited to advertising and solicitation of business in Ohio; therefore, contacts were insufficient under Ohio long-arm statute to allow assertion of jurisdiction; although defendant's solicitations were "but for" cause of injuries, Ohio statute requires that conduct in Ohio be a proximate cause of injuries).

224. *But cf.* Crane v. Carr, 814 F.2d 758, 762 (D.C. Cir. 1987) (Ginsburg, Cir. J.) (subsection (a)(4) may stop short of outer constitutional limits); Fogle v. Ramsey Winch Co., 774 F. Supp. 19, 23 (D.D.C. 1991) (subsection (a)(4) is more restrictive than the Due Process Clause); *see also* Bensusan Restaurant Corp. v. King, 126 F.3d 25 (2d Cir. 1997) (interpreting an identical provision of New York's long-arm statute as inapplicable to actions by a Missouri defendant that may have had an impact in New York because the Missouri defendant did not apparently derive substantial revenue from interstate commerce).

225. CAL. CIV. PROC. CODE § 410.10 (West 2004).

226. *See id.* § 415.40.

227. However, the U.S. Supreme Court has indicated that a particularized statutory declaration of interest may strengthen the case for jurisdiction. *See, e.g.*, Keeton v. Hustler Magazine, Inc., 465 U.S. 770, 775-77, 104 S. Ct. 1473, 1479, 79 L. Ed. 2d 790, 798-99 (1984); Shaffer v. Heitner, 433 U.S. 186, 214-15, 97 S. Ct. 2569, 2585, 53 L. Ed. 2d 683, 704 (1977); *see* section G(2)*(b)(iv) infra* ("The Reasonableness Test"). It is also important to note that states with particularized long-arm statutes often construe the statutes to extend the jurisdiction of the states' courts as far as due process will permit, thus, in effect, treating the statutes as if they read like the California statute. *See* Douglas D. McFarland, *Dictum Run Wild: How Long-Arm Statutes Extended to the Limits of Due Process,* 84 B.U. L. REV. 491 (2004) (arguing that enumerated long-arm statutes are better than general ones and that the courts in states with enumerated statutes should interpret the statutes as written instead of holding that the statutes extend to the limits of due process in spite of the limited language); Jeffrey A. Van Detta & Shiv K. Kapoor, *Extraterritorial Personal Jurisdiction for the Twenty-First Century: A Case Study Reconceptualizing the Typical Long-Arm Statute to Codify and Refine* International Shoe *After its First Sixty Years*, 3 SETON HALL CIR. REV. 339 (2007); *cf.* LinkAmerica Corp. v. Cox, 857 N.E.2d 961 (Ind. 2006) (amendment to long-arm provision adding California-type language to enumeration of specific category provision; retention of enumerated acts of original rule served only as a handy checklist of activities that usually supported jurisdiction). *But see* Diamond Crystal Brands, Inc. v. Food Movers Int'l, Inc., 593 F.3d 1249 (11th Cir. 2010) (Georgia long-arm statute has been interpreted by the Georgia Supreme Court not to be coextensive with due process).

statute. Therefore, the statutes of each state must be consulted to determine how personal jurisdiction issues have been addressed.

Illustration 3-21. *D*, a citizen of State *Y*, contracted with *P*, a citizen of State *X*, to purchase four boat engines from *P*. The engines were to be shipped by *P* from State *X* to *D* in State *Y*. *P* subsequently sued *D* in a state court of State *X*. *P* alleged that *D* had failed to fulfill *D's* obligations under the contract. *D* was served with process under a provision of the State *X* long-arm statute, which authorized personal jurisdiction over nonresidents in any action which "[r]elates to goods, documents of title, or other things of value shipped from this state by the plaintiff to the defendant on the defendant's order or direction." In *Riggs Marine Service, Inc. v. McCann*,[228] the court held that the contract between *P* and *D* was precisely the kind of transaction covered by the long-arm statute.

* * * * *

In addition, the advent of modern long-arm statutes that generalize the bases for asserting jurisdiction over nonresident defendants has not necessarily eliminated the possibility of asserting jurisdiction under one of the pre-*International Shoe* methods. For example, in *State ex rel. K-Mart Corp. v. Holliger*,[229] the defendant was served in Missouri through its registered agent there. The defendant conceded that it was doing substantial and continuous business in the state. However, the defendant objected to personal jurisdiction on the ground that the action did not fit within any of the categories in the Missouri long-arm statute. The Missouri Supreme Court rejected this argument. The court held that the long-arm statute applied only when service outside the state was necessary.[230] The enactment of the long-arm statute did not preclude assertion of jurisdiction under one of the pre-*International Shoe* forms, as long as the minimum contacts test was satisfied.[231]

SECTION G. THE CONTENT OF THE MINIMUM CONTACTS TEST

Since *International Shoe*, the U.S. Supreme Court has decided a significant number of cases that attempt to define the content of the minimum contacts test. The approach of these cases has not always been consistent, as the discussion of the *Shaffer* and *Burnham* cases in section E, above, has indicated. However, the decisions do articulate the factors that will determine the constitutionality of a state's assertion of jurisdiction over nonresidents under the minimum contacts test. This section examines the content of the minimum contacts test as it has evolved

---

228. 160 Wis. 2d 846, 467 N.W.2d 155 (Ct. App. 1991).

229. 986 S.W.2d 165 (Mo. 1999).

230. *See id.* at 168.

231. *See id.* at 168-69; *see also* Ehrenfeld v. Mahfouz, 518 F.3d 102 (2d Cir. 2008) (question of law certified to state's highest court as to whether personal jurisdiction could be exercised over Saudi Arabian citizen in state under "doing business" provision of state long-arm statute in declaratory judgment action to hold default judgment in libel action in England unenforceable in United States; New York Court of Appeals answer to question is that New York long-arm statute does not extend to this action); Merriman v. Crompton Corp., 282 Kan. 433, 146 P.3d 162 (2006) (Kansas statute requiring consent to personal jurisdiction as a condition of doing business provided basis for exercising general jurisdiction over nonresident corporation).

since *International Shoe*. The next section then examines the application of the test to specific categories of cases.

1. Cases to Which the Minimum Contacts Test Applies

Because of the *Burnham* decision, discussed in section E, above, evaluations of a state's assertion of jurisdiction over a nonresident must first consider whether the state is applying a traditional or novel rule of personal jurisdiction. If the state is applying a traditional rule, one must consider whether, under Justice Scalia's opinion in *Burnham*, the historical pedigree of the rule and its continuing acceptance by the states are sufficient to make it constitutional.[232] However, because there was no majority opinion in *Burnham*, it cannot be certain that Justice Scalia's test will be used to determine the validity of even traditional rules in the future. Consequently, until the Court provides further guidance on this question, an alternative analysis under the minimum contacts test must be employed to determine whether the assertion of jurisdiction will satisfy that test. If the assertion passes muster under both the historical and minimum contacts tests, there is obviously no difficulty. However, if the tests point in different directions on the constitutional issue, the Court will have to make a difficult decision about which test is controlling.

Fortunately, the circumstances in which *Burnham* is likely to cause difficulties are few. *Burnham* did not purport to disturb *Shaffer's* holding that quasi in rem jurisdiction is unconstitutional.[233] Furthermore, *Burnham* upheld the constitutionality of transient presence jurisdiction under both the historical and minimum contacts tests. *Shaffer* stated that the state where property is located will have sufficient contacts to adjudicate claims directly involving the property.[234] However, this statement must be qualified because of the problem raised by the *Abernathy* case, discussed in section E(1), above: if property is brought within the state without the consent of the claimants to the property, it is unclear whether the state will have jurisdiction to adjudicate claims to the property consistent with due process.

The only traditional rules upon which the Court has not generally pronounced are (1) consent, (2) domicile, and (3) the rule restricting states from directly affecting the title to land located in other states. Undoubtedly, the Court would not constitutionally invalidate consent as a basis of jurisdiction under any

---

232. *See* William M. Richman, *Understanding Personal Jurisdiction*, 25 ARIZ. ST. L.J. 599, 638, 641 (1993).

233. In a footnote, Justice Scalia suggested that *Shaffer* might be distinguished from other quasi in rem cases because the Delaware statute declaring the situs of corporate stock to be in the state of incorporation was unique. This observation may indicate that some members of the Court are prepared to uphold other kinds of quasi in rem jurisdiction that are more "traditional." *See Burnham*, 495 U.S. at 622, n.4, 110 S. Ct. at 2116, n.4, 109 L. Ed. 2d at 646, n.4. In addition, Justice Stevens had indicated in *Shaffer* that the decision should not be read to invalidate quasi in rem jurisdiction when real estate was the property involved. *See Shaffer*, 433 U.S. at 218, 97 S. Ct. at 2587, 53 L. Ed. 2d at 706 (Stevens, J., concurring).

234. *See Shaffer*, 433 U.S. at 207-08, 97 S. Ct. at 2581-82, 53 L. Ed. 2d at 699-700.

test—whether it is true consent or consent by appearance or waiver.[235] *Shaffer* preserved domicile of the plaintiff in ex parte divorce actions from attack under the minimum contacts test. For the reasons given in section E(1), above, this conclusion does not seem to be vulnerable to reversal. Domicile of the defendant will never be an unconstitutional basis for asserting jurisdiction if the defendant actually resides in the state of domicile or has other substantial relations with the state. The problem case will be that of the nonresident domiciliary who no longer has any substantial contacts with the state, but who has not acquired a domicile in another state or nation. Such cases of "technical domicile" will be rare, if not nonexistent. Finally, the restriction on the power of states to directly affect the title to land located in other states will rarely be a problem either. Venue rules in the forum state will often preclude the state from adjudicating such actions apart from constitutional restrictions.[236] State forum non conveniens doctrines may also produce the dismissal of many such cases. Consequently, while the distinction between traditional and novel assertions of jurisdiction must be addressed when relevant, it seems unlikely to be of great significance in the jurisprudence of state-court jurisdiction.

2. General and Specific Jurisdiction

In a path-breaking article, Professors Von Mehren and Trautman argued that the traditional terminology used to discuss multistate personal jurisdiction was not helpful.[237] They recommended that the expression "jurisdiction to adjudicate" be substituted for the traditional categories of jurisdiction.[238] They suggested the term "specific jurisdiction" to describe power to adjudicate issues arising out of "the very controversy that establishes jurisdiction to adjudicate."[239] They suggested the term "general jurisdiction" to describe "power to adjudicate any kind of controversy when jurisdiction is based on relationships, direct or indirect, between the forum and the person or persons whose legal rights are to be affected."[240] U.S. Supreme Court decisions have adopted this terminology.[241]

---

235. The Court's recent decisions on the validity of jurisdiction acquired under forum selection clauses suggest that something less than true consent will suffice to satisfy constitutional standards. *See* Chapter 4(C)(12) *infra* ("Raising and Waiving Federal Venue Objections").

236. *See* Chapter 4(A) *infra* (discussing the local action rule).

237. *See* Arthur T. Von Mehren & Donald T. Trautman, *Jurisdiction to Adjudicate: A Suggested Analysis*, 79 HARV. L. REV. 1121, 1135 (1966).

238. *See id.* at 1135-36.

239. *See id.* at 1136.

240. *See id.*

241. The first decision to adopt the terminology explicitly was Helicopteros Nacionales de Colombia, S.A. v. Hall, 466 U.S. 408, 414 nn.8-9, 104 S. Ct. 1868, 1872 nn.8-9, 80 L. Ed. 2d 404, 411 nn.8-9 (1984). The Court's definition of the terms specific and general jurisdiction was somewhat different than that of Professors Von Mehren and Trautman. The Court defined specific jurisdiction as an exercise of personal jurisdiction "over a defendant in a suit arising out of or related to the defendant's contacts with the forum." *Id.* at n.8, 104 S. Ct. at 1872 n.8, 80 L. Ed. 2d at 411 n.8. It defined general jurisdiction as the exercise of jurisdiction "over a defendant in a suit not arising out of or related to the defendant's contacts with the forum." *Id.* at n.9, 104 S. Ct. at 1872 n.9, 80 L. Ed. 2d at 411 n.9. *Hall* involved an attempt by Texas to exercise general jurisdiction because the assertion of jurisdiction was to adjudicate a claim arising out of events that occurred outside Texas. Thus, in the Court's definition, the suit did not arise out of the defendant's contacts with Texas, but with the defendant's contacts with Peru. In Von Mehren and Trautman's definition, Texas was attempting to assert jurisdiction based on the relationship between the defendant and the state, not the relationship between the controversy and the state. *Hall* is discussed in the text *infra*. For recent commentary on the scope of general and specific jurisdiction, see Robert

The distinction between general and specific jurisdiction must be addressed at the threshold of the minimum contacts analysis because the validity of each kind of jurisdiction is determined differently under the Supreme Court's decisions. Subsection *(a)* will discuss general jurisdiction and the standards that apply to determine its validity. Subsection *(b)* will similarly discuss specific jurisdiction. Subsection *(c)* will examine recent decisions indicating confusion about the distinction between general and specific jurisdictions. It will also examine cases suggesting that the general and specific jurisdiction doctrines may be converging. Subsection *(d)* will then question why the two kinds of jurisdiction should be analyzed differently and suggest a common test for both.

(a) General Jurisdiction

The U.S. Supreme Court has decided only three cases involving general jurisdiction since *International Shoe*. The first, *Perkins v. Benguet Consolidated Mining Co.*,[242] was decided before the Court had divided the universe under the Due Process Clause into "general" and "specific" jurisdiction cases. The second, *Helicopteros Nacionales de Colombia, S.A. v. Hall*,[243] was the decision in which the

---

Banks, Jr., *The Future of General Jurisdiction in Tennessee*, 27 U. MEM. L. REV. 559 (1997); Mary Twitchell, *The Myth of General Jurisdiction*, 101 HARV. L. REV. 610 (1988); Lea Brilmayer, *Related Contacts and Personal Jurisdiction*, 101 HARV. L. REV. 1444 (1988); Mary Twitchell, *A Rejoinder to Professor Brilmayer*, 101 HARV. L. REV. 1465 (1988).

242. 342 U.S. 437, 72 S. Ct. 413, 96 L. Ed. 485 (1952). In *Perkins*, the plaintiff sued a Philippine corporation in an Ohio state court. The plaintiff sought to recover $68,400 in dividends and $2,500,000 in damages due to the failure of the corporation to issue certain shares of stock to her. The corporation was served with process by service of a summons on its president in Ohio. The U.S. Supreme Court held that "no requirement of federal due process . . . either *prohibits* Ohio from opening its courts to the cause of action . . . presented or *compels* Ohio to do so." 342 U.S at 446, 72 S. Ct. at 418, 96 L. Ed. at 493. The Court characterized the activities of the corporation in Ohio as "continuous and systematic." *See id.* at 445, 72 S. Ct. at 418, 96 L. Ed. at 492. This level of activities made it valid under the minimum contacts test for Ohio to assert jurisdiction over the corporation, even though the claim against the corporation did not arise out of the corporation's activities within the state. *See id.* at 445-46, 72 S. Ct. at 418, 96 L. Ed. at 492-93; *see also id.* at 447-48, 72 S. Ct. at 419-20, 96 L. Ed. at 493-94 (describing the activities of the corporation within Ohio). *International Shoe* had recognized that foreign corporations could be sued on claims arising outside the state if the activities of the corporations were "continuous" and sufficiently "substantial." *See International Shoe*, 326 U.S. at 318, 66 S. Ct. at 159, 90 L. Ed. at 103. Nothing in the Court's opinion in *International Shoe* had cast doubt on the continuing ability of the states to summon foreign corporations to defend suits on this basis. *See* Philip B. Kurland, *The Supreme Court, the Due Process Clause, and the In Personam Jurisdiction of State Courts—From* Pennoyer *to* Denckla*: A Review*, 25 U. CHI. L. REV. 569, 601 (1958). Therefore, it was unsurprising to find jurisdiction sustained in *Perkins*, given the substantial nature of the corporate activity in Ohio. However, the Court's application of the minimum contacts test to the facts in *Perkins* did nothing to clarify how the test would be applied in future cases. After indicating that corporations conducting systematic and continuous activities within a state could be sued there on claims arising outside the state, the Court simply recited the activities of the defendant in *Perkins* and stated that they were sufficient to sustain an assertion of jurisdiction against a due process challenge. *See id.* at 447-48, 72 S. Ct. at 419-20, 96 L. Ed. at 493-94. The Court gave no indication how low the level of corporate activity might fall before an exercise of jurisdiction to adjudicate a claim arising outside the state would be considered invalid.

243. 466 U.S. 408, 104 S. Ct. 1868, 80 L. Ed. 2d 404 (1984). *Hall* was a wrongful death action brought in a Texas state court. Hall sued Helicol, Bell Helicopter, and Consorcio to recover for the death of her husband that occurred in a helicopter crash in the Peruvian jungle. Helicol was a Colombian corporation with its principal place of business in Bogota, Colombia. Helicol provided helicopter transportation for oil and construction companies in South America. It purchased $4,000,000 worth of helicopters, spare parts, and accessories from Bell Helicopter in Fort Worth, Texas from 1970-77. During the same period, its pilots were also trained by Bell in Fort Worth and ferried helicopters from Fort Worth to Colombia. Bell also trained Helicol management and maintenance personnel from 1970-77. Consorcio was the Peruvian alter-ego of a joint venture among Williams International Sudamericana, Ltd., a Delaware Corporation, Sedco Construction Corporation, a Texas corporation, and Horn International, Inc., a Texas corporation. The purpose of the joint venture was to construct an oil pipeline from the interior of Peru to the Pacific Ocean. Consorcio was formed because Peruvian law forbade construction of the pipeline by a non-Peruvian entity. Consorcio, in turn, contracted with Helicol to obtain helicopter transportation

Court adopted the terms "general" and "specific" jurisdiction. The third, *Goodyear Dunlop Tires Operations v. Brown*,[244] dealt with an attempt by a state court to import a concept from the doctrine of specific jurisdiction to satisfy the requirements of general jurisdiction and revealed little further about how the doctrine of general jurisdiction should be administered. All three cases applied the same test to determine the validity of an assertion of general jurisdiction—the "systematic

---

for the construction project. The claim arose when a helicopter owned by Helicol crashed in Peru, killing, among others, four United States citizens. None of the four was a citizen of Texas, though all were hired by Consorcio in Houston to work on the pipeline project. The claim asserted against Helicol was negligence in the form of pilot error. In addition to the contacts already mentioned, Helicol had sent its chief executive officer to Houston for a contract negotiating session with Consorcio and accepted payments into its New York and Florida bank accounts from Consorcio drawn upon Consorcio's Houston bank. Helicol challenged the jurisdiction of the Texas state courts, but its challenge was overruled at the trial-court level. A verdict was directed in favor of Bell Helicopter and Consorcio, but a general jury verdict of $1,141,200 was entered against Helicol. Consorcio also obtained judgment on a cross-claim against Helicol for $70,000. The Texas Supreme Court ultimately sustained jurisdiction over Helicol and affirmed, construing its long-arm statute to extend as far as due process permits. The U.S. Supreme Court granted certiorari and reversed. *See Hall*, 466 U.S. at 409-13, 104 S. Ct. at 1869-72, 80 L. Ed. 2d at 408-10. In evaluating the case, the Court placed primary emphasis on two prior decisions: *Perkins* and *Rosenberg Bros. & Co. v. Curtis Brown Co.*, 260 U.S. 516, 43 S. Ct. 170, 67 L. Ed. 372 (1923), the latter of which antedated *International Shoe*. The Court first compared the defendant's contacts with those of the defendant in the *Perkins* case to determine whether the contacts in *Hall* were of the "systematic and continuous" sort that sustained jurisdiction in *Perkins*. The Court concluded that they were not. *See Hall*, 466 U.S. at 414-17, 104 S. Ct. at 1872-74, 80 L. Ed. 2d at 410-13. The Court relied on *Rosenberg* for the proposition that purchases and related trips are not sufficient to sustain jurisdiction to adjudicate an action based on a claim arising outside the state. *See id.* at 417-18, 104 S. Ct. at 1873-74, 80 L. Ed. 2d at 413.

244. 564 U.S. ___, 131 S. Ct. 2846, 180 L. Ed. 2d 796 (2011). In *Goodyear*, two minor children who resided in North Carolina were killed in a bus accident on a highway outside of Paris, France. The accident occurred allegedly due to a defect in a tire manufactured by a Goodyear subsidiary in Turkey. The plaintiffs sued Goodyear USA, and three Goodyear subsidiaries located and operating respectively in Luxembourg, Turkey, and France. Goodyear USA did not challenge jurisdiction, but the other defendants did. The North Carolina courts sustained jurisdiction over the foreign defendants on the grounds that they had put their tires in the stream of interstate commerce without any restriction on the extent to which those tires could be sold in North Carolina. As we will see in section 2*(b)(iii)*, below, this is a test that has been used, albeit unsuccessfully at the U.S. Supreme Court level, to sustain jurisdiction over defendants in specific jurisdiction cases, in which the claim arises out of the defendant's contacts with the state. In *Goodyear*, the Supreme Court rejected its use to sustain jurisdiction over the foreign defendants by North Carolina. The defendants did not distribute their tires in North Carolina in the regular course of business, although a small percentage (which the court described as tens of thousands out of tens of millions manufactured between 2004 and 2007) had been distributed in North Carolina through special orders from other Goodyear distributors. The Supreme Court rejected this activity as sufficient to sustain personal jurisdiction over the defendants under the systematic and continuous contacts test, stating that the North Carolina courts' "stream of commerce analysis elided the essential difference between" specific and general jurisdiction. *See* 564 U.S. at __, 131 S. Ct. at 2855, 180 L. Ed. 2d at 808. The Court also rejected North Carolina's attempt to sustain jurisdiction based on its strong interest in providing a forum in which its residents could obtain redress for their injuries, stating that "'[g]eneral jurisdiction to adjudicate has in [United States] practice never been based on the plaintiff's relationship to the forum.'" *See* 564 U.S. at __ n.5, 131 S. Ct at 2857 n.5, 180 L. Ed. 2d at 809. Finally, the Court rejected an argument by the plaintiffs that Goodyear and its subsidiaries should be considered a single enterprise, so that jurisdiction over the parent would produce jurisdiction over the subsidiaries as well, on the ground that this contention had been raised for the first time in their brief before the Supreme Court and waived by failure to raise it earlier. On this point, as Professor Borchers has noted, the Court cited commentary indicating that the question should be decided in the same way that one would determine whether to pierce the corporate veil, which is a state law matter governed by state standards. However, Professor Borchers observes that even if the corporate veil cannot be pierced for liability purposes, there may be cases in which the activities of the subsidiary are sufficiently directed by the parent to justify an assertion of jurisdiction. *See* Patrick J. Borchers, J. McIntyre Machinery, Goodyear, *and the Inconherence of the Minimum Contacts Test*, 44 CREIGHTON L. REV. 1245, 1268-69 (2011); Symposium, *Personal Jurisdiction for the Twenty-First Century: The Implications of* McIntyre *and* Goodyear Dunlop Tires, 63 S.C. L. REV. 463 (2012) (containing articles by Professors Brilmayer & Smith, Carrington, Citron, Feder, Freer, Miller, Peddie, Perdue, Stein, Steinman, Silberman, Stravitz, and Vail); *see also* Rasmussen v. General Motors Corp., 2011 WI 52, 335 Wis. 2d 1, 803 N.W.2d 623 (although subsidiary had sufficient contacts to sustain assertion of general jurisdiction over it, there was insufficient demonstration of control over subsidiary by parent to justify disregarding separate corporate identities and subjecting parent to general jurisdiction on the basis of activities of subsidiary).

and continuous contacts" test.[245] None of the cases provides much guidance about how to determine whether the level of contacts in a case is "systematic and continuous" or something less.[246] All that is clear is that the systematic and continuous contacts test for general jurisdiction requires a higher overall level of contacts, quantitatively and qualitatively, than the test for specific jurisdiction.

In *Perkins*, *Hall*, and *Goodyear*, the defendants were corporations. One question that arises after the *Burnham* decision discussed in section E(2), above, is whether the concept of general jurisdiction has any meaningful application to individual defendants. Justice Scalia's opinion in *Burnham* suggested that the systematic and continuous contacts test might be applicable only to corporate defendants.[247] It is difficult to see what purpose the rule serves in cases in which individual defendants are being sued on claims arising outside the state. Presumably individuals who are currently engaging in systematic activities within the state can easily be served personally inside the state while they are there conducting those activities. Personal service on an individual defendant in the state validly subjects the defendant to jurisdiction under the Due Process Clause without regard to the level of the defendant's activities within the state.[248]

The only situation in which the systematic-and-continuous-activities test might be relevant to suits against individuals is when an individual is alerted to the possibility of an action within the state and ceases the activities or otherwise remains outside the state. In that situation, the plaintiff would have to use a long-arm statute to serve the defendant, giving rise to a possible challenge on ground that the defendant's (former) activities are insufficient to justify suit on a claim arising outside the state.

However, it is unclear from the reported decisions whether general jurisdiction may be asserted over a defendant whose activities within the state have ceased by the time the action has been commenced. Furthermore, even if systematic and continuous contacts may be established by past activities, it is not clear how far in the past a court may reach to determine whether systematic and continuous activities exist. For example, in *Serafini v. Superior Court*,[249] the California Court of Appeals held an assertion of general jurisdiction over an individual defendant invalid. The court's opinion linked the general jurisdiction concept as applied to

---

245. *Hall* basically listed the contacts in the case and compared them with the contacts in *Perkins*, and stated in a conclusory fashion that they were not systematic and continuous. *Goodyear* compared the contacts in the case with both those in *Perkins* and *Hall*, with an additional discussion of how *International Shoe* discussed the categories, and found the contacts insufficient.

246. Professor Borchers has commented that *Goodyear*, while not the disaster that its companion case, J. McIntyre Mach., Ltd. v. Nicastro, 564 U.S. __, 131 S. Ct. 2780, 180 L. Ed. 2d 765 (2011), was in the specific jurisdiction area, did not give the hoped for guidance on the question of the quantum of contacts necessary to create general jurisdiction. *See* Patrick J. Borchers, J. McIntyre Machinery, Goodyear, *and the Incoherence of the Minimum Contacts Test*, 44 CREIGHTON L. REV. 1245 (2011).

247. *See Burnham*, 495 U.S. at 610 n.1, 110 S. Ct. at 2110 n.1, 109 L. Ed. 2d at 639 n.1. The Court's opinion in *Goodyear* left this question still up in the air. *See* Patrick J. Borchers, J. Mcintyre Machinery, Goodyear, *and the Incoherence of the Minimum Contacts Test*, 44 CREIGHTON L. REV. 1245, 1266-68 (2011) (suggesting that language in *Goodyear's* repeated references to corporate defendants plus its references suggesting that general jurisdiction is only proper when defendants are "at home" in the forum, may mean that general jurisdiction is not applicable to individuals).

248. Presumably, this will be true not only under Justice Scalia's historical analysis, but also under the minimum contacts test, which the concurring Justices found satisfied by the transient presence of the defendant in *Burnham*.

249. 68 Cal. App. 4th 70, 80 Cal. Rptr. 2d 159 (1998).

both corporate and individual defendants to the old "presence" test of jurisdiction that was used prior to *International Shoe*.[250] Under that test, cessation of activities destroyed the basis for jurisdiction.[251] In this regard, *Serafini* is clearly wrong. Even though general jurisdiction was originally based on the theory that a corporation "doing business" in the state was "present" there,[252] that is no longer the basis of the doctrine after *International Shoe*. Today, general jurisdiction is justified on the basis that a defendant's systematic and continuous contacts with the state makes an assertion of jurisdiction "reasonable" in terms of the burdens imposed on the defendant by suit on an unrelated claim.[253]

A more justifiable approach was taken by the Second Circuit in *Metropolitan Life Insurance Co. v. Robertson-Ceco Corp.* (*"Met Life"*).[254] In *Met Life*, the court considered whether an assertion of general jurisdiction over a corporate defendant would be proper. Although the Second Circuit ultimately held that general jurisdiction would be improper on the facts of the case,[255] it indicated that the appropriate procedure was to "examine a defendant's contacts with the forum state over a period that is reasonable under the circumstances—up to and including the date the suit was filed—to assess whether they satisfy the 'continuous and systematic' standard."[256] Implicit in the court's holding is the notion that systematic and continuous contacts can be based on past activities that have now ceased, as long as they have not ceased so long in the past as to make an assertion of jurisdiction based on them "unreasonable."[257]

It is important to note that particular long-arm statutes of the Illinois or Uniform Act variety are worded in such a manner as to limit jurisdiction of the enacting state's courts to cases in which the claim arises out of the defendant's activities within the state.[258] When states interpret such statutes to the limits of due process, thus treating them as if they were worded like the California statute, they will include the power to exercise general jurisdiction. If not, there is a danger that states with particularized statutes will not be able to exercise general jurisdiction

---

250. *Id.* at 79-80, 80 Cal. Rptr. 2d at 165.

251. *See id.*

252. *See* section C(1) *supra* ("Jurisdiction over Corporations").

253. *See* subsection *(c) infra.*

254. 84 F.3d 560 (2d Cir. 1996).

255. This aspect of the decision is discussed in subsection *(c) infra.*

256. 84 F.3d at 569-70. The court drew strength for its holding from the fact that the U.S. Supreme Court, in *Helicopteros*, had evaluated the defendant's contacts over a seven-year period. *See id.* at 569. In the *Goodyear* case, discussed above, the Court focused on the number of tires manufactured by the subsidiary of Goodyear that made their way into North Carolina between 2004, when the accident occurred, and 2007, when presumably the suit was commenced. *See* 564 U.S. at __, 131 S. Ct. at 2852, 180 L. Ed. 2d at 804; *see also* Todd David Peterson, *The Timing of Minimum Contacts* 79 GEO. WASH. L. REV. 101 (2010).

257. *See also* Choice Healthcare, Inc. v. Kaiser Found. Health Plan, 615 F.3d 364 (5th Cir. 2010) (defendants' intermittent payments to Louisiana over the course of more than three years were insufficient to establish the systematic and continuous contacts required for general jurisdiction); Autogenomics, Inc. v. Oxford Gene Tech., Ltd., 566 F.3d 1012 (Fed. Cir. 2009) (district court correctly held that it lacked general jurisdiction in California over defendant even though it was reasonable to infer that it met potential customers four conferences it attended there over five years). For recent discussions and criticisms of the concept of general jurisdiction, see Patrick J. Borchers, *The Problem with General Jurisdiction*, 2001 U. CHI. LEGAL F. 119; Walter W. Heiser, *Toward Reasonable Limitations on the Exercise of General Jurisdiction*, 41 SAN DIEGO L. REV. 1035 (2004); Friedrich K. Juenger, *The American Law of General Jurisdiction*, 2001 U. CHI. LEGAL F. 141; Charles W. "Rocky" Rhodes, *Clarifying General Jurisdiction*, 34 SETON HALL L. REV. 807 (2004); Mary Twitchell, *Why We Keep Doing Business with Doing-Business Jurisdiction*, 2001 U. CHI. LEGAL F. 171.

258. *See* section F *supra.*

under such a statute unless some other provision exists to allow service of a nonresident defendant on the basis of out-of-state activities. It might be well for the states to specifically address general jurisdiction in a separate statutory provision to deal with this problem. At least one state, Florida, has done so. Florida has enacted a long-arm statute that authorizes its courts to exercise jurisdiction over a defendant "who engages in substantial and not isolated activity within this state, whether such activity is wholly interstate, intrastate, or otherwise, . . . whether or not the claim arises from that activity."[259] Thus, the statute expressly authorizes the state's courts to exercise general jurisdiction. In *Stubbs v. Wyndham Nassau Resort*,[260] the court held that the statute constitutionally authorized general jurisdiction to be exercised over a Bahamian corporation based on an out-of-state tort. The court found that a Florida corporation operated solely for the purposes of national marketing and scheduling for the defendant and that the defendant realized all the revenues generated by the in-state corporation, which the court found to be the agent of the defendant. In addition to these direct contacts with Florida, the defendant maintained numerous other commercial relationships with Florida entities and vendors, as well as maintaining at least six bank accounts in the state for purposes of disbursements to entities and persons in the U.S., including Florida.[261]

(b) Specific Jurisdiction

(i) Claims Arising Out of or Related to the Defendant's Contacts with the State

In determining whether a case involves general or specific jurisdiction, it is obviously important to determine whether the defendant's actions in the state gave rise to the claim for relief. If the claim arose from the defendant's contacts with the state, the case is one of specific jurisdiction. However, even if the claim arose out of the defendant's activities in another state, the case still may be a specific jurisdiction case, which requires something less than "systematic and continuous" contacts by the defendant to justify the state's assertion of jurisdiction. A case may be deemed a specific jurisdiction case even though the claim technically arose elsewhere if the claim is "related to" the defendant's activities within the forum state.

The Court originally suggested in *Hall* that there might be a distinction drawn between controversies that arise out of the defendant's contacts with the state

---

259. FLA. STAT. ANN. § 48.193(2) (West 2006).

260. 447 F.3d 1357 (11th Cir. 2006).

261. *See also* Bauman v. DiamlerChrysler Corp., 644 F.3d 909 (9th Cir. 2011) (in action under Alien Tort Victims Protection Act arising out of activities in Argentina that wholly owned subsidiary of defendant allegedly collaborated in with state, wholly owned U.S. subsidiary that served as general distributor of German manufacturer's automobiles in the U.S. was the defendant's agent for purposes of general jurisdiction in the United States); Snow v. DirecTV, Inc., 450 F.3d 1314 (11th Cir. 2006) (neither specific nor general jurisdiction existed under Florida's long-arm statute; general jurisdiction did not exist over Washington law-firm under long-arm statute because its negotiations on defendant's behalf with some Florida residents, seven appearances as counsel of record for client, and representation of four Florida clients in Washington were insufficient contacts when balanced against lack of physical presence in Florida, non-solicitation of Florida clients, and derivation of less than one percent of its revenue from matters connected with Florida).

and controversies that are merely related to the defendant's contacts with the state.[262] However, the Court refused to address the distinction because it had not been raised or briefed in the case.[263] In a decision after *Hall*, the Court stated that "specific jurisdiction" involves "injuries that 'arise out of or relate to'" the defendant's activities within the forum state,[264] while general jurisdiction involves an exercise of "personal jurisdiction over a defendant in a suit not arising out of or related to the defendant's contacts with the forum."[265] This statement indicates that a claim arising out of the defendant's activities in another state but related to the activities in the forum state will indeed present a case of specific jurisdiction. As yet, the Court has not defined what it means for a claim to be "related to" the defendant's contacts with the forum.[266]

---

262. This distinction was initially raised by Justice Brennan in dissent and then answered by the majority. Justice Brennan objected to the majority's refusal "to consider any distinction between controversies that 'relate to' a defendant's contacts with the forum and causes of action that 'arise out of' such contacts . . . ." *Hall*, 466 U.S at 420, 104 S. Ct. at 1875, 80 L. Ed. 2d at 415 (Brennan, J., dissenting). Justice Brennan was actually objecting to the implication, which he saw in the majority opinion, that a distinction might be drawn between controversies "related to" the defendant's contacts with the state and causes of action "arising out" of the defendant's contacts with the state. His fear was that the Court would approve of specific jurisdiction only in cases in which the controversy arose out of the defendant's contacts with the state and would require the level of contacts necessary to sustain *general* jurisdiction in cases in which the controversy was only "related to" the defendant's contacts with the state. *See id.* Justice Brennan viewed Helicol's contacts with Texas to be related to its activities within the state because the plaintiff claimed that Helicol was legally responsible for the pilot's negligence, and Helicol had negotiated the contract to provide transportation services in Texas, had purchased the helicopter involved in the crash in Texas, and had the pilot trained in Texas. *See id.* at 425-26, 104 S. Ct. at 1877-78, 80 L. Ed. 2d at 418-19. To Justice Brennan, these factors made the Texas contacts directly related to the negligence that caused the accident and also should have made it foreseeable to Helicol that it could be sued in Texas. *See id.* at 426, 104 S. Ct. at 1878, 80 L. Ed. 2d at 418-19.

263. Thus, the Court withheld decision on whether the expressions "arising out of" and "related to" describe different connections between the claim and the state. It also reserved judgment on what kind of relationship between the defendant and the state would determine whether either connection exists. Likewise, the Court refused to determine whether cases involving claims "related to" the defendant's contacts with the state should be analyzed as specific or general jurisdiction cases, assuming that "arising out of" and "related to" describe different relationships with the state. *Id.* at 415-16 n.10, 104 S. Ct. at 1872-73 n.10, 80 L. Ed. 2d at 411-12 n.10.

In Daynard v. Ness, Motley, Loadholt, Richardson & Poole, P.A., 290 F.3d 42 (1st Cir. 2002), the plaintiff, a law professor, sued South Carolina and Mississippi law firms to recover fees generated by tobacco litigation. The South Carolina law firm conceded personal jurisdiction over it in Massachusetts, but the Mississippi law firm challenged personal jurisdiction. The district court concluded that it did not have personal jurisdiction over the Mississippi firm based on its direct contacts with Massachusetts and also that jurisdiction could not be asserted over it based on contacts imputed to the Mississippi defendant from the South Carolina defendant. The court of appeals disagreed with this latter conclusion. The court held that the breach-of-contract claim that was the basis of the suit arose from a course of dealing between the parties that started in Massachusetts and that called for interaction between the Massachusetts, South Carolina, and Mississippi defendants. These contacts satisfied the "relatedness" requirement of specific jurisdiction. The "purposeful contacts" test was satisfied by actions by the South Carolina defendants that could be imputed to the Mississippi defendants by virtue of the fact that the plaintiff reasonably understood the two defendants to be engaged in a joint venture or other agency relationship and that the plaintiff was providing services to both defendants. The court held that the "reasonableness test" did not defeat jurisdiction because the burden of appearing in Massachusetts to defend the suit was not "unusual," and the plaintiff's interest in bringing the action in the forum, "given the traditional deference accorded to a plaintiff's choice of forum, weighs in favor of personal jurisdiction."

264. Burger King Corp. v. Rudzewicz, 471 U.S. 462, 472, 105 S. Ct. 2174, 2182, 85 L. Ed. 2d 528, 540-41 (1985); *see also* Jonathan P. Diffley, *Spa-cific Jurisdiction: A Massage In Barbados Perpetuates Improper Analysis of Personal Jurisdiction in U.S. Courts*, 58 CATH. U. L. REV. 305 (2008) (discussing the sliding scale test for relatedness).

265. *Burger King*, 471 U.S. at 473, n.15, 105 S. Ct. at 2182, n.15, 85 L. Ed. 2d at 541, n.15.

266. In Goodyear Dunlop Tires Operations, S.A. v. Brown, 564 U.S. __, 131 S. Ct. 2846, 180 L. Ed. 2d 796 (2011), discussed in section 2((a), above, the Court dealt with a general jurisdiction case without addressing the "related to" factor. Even though the defendants had distributed some products inside the state by special order that were similar to or identical to the product that injured the plaintiffs outside the state, the Court said nothing about relatedness. In J. McIntyre Machinery, Ltd. v. Nicastro, 564 U.S. __, 131 S. Ct. 2780, 180 L. Ed. 2d 765 (2011), discussed in subsection *(b)(iii)*, below, dealt with a specific jurisdiction case in which it was unnecessary to consider the relatedness factor because the claim clearly arose out of the defendant's contacts with the forum. *See*

A proper determination of when a claim is "related to" the defendant's contacts with the forum can only be made in conjunction with the test employed by the Court for specific jurisdiction and the purposes of that test. The specific jurisdiction test will be discussed fully in subsections *(b)(ii)-(iv)*, below. However, only the first step in the specific jurisdiction test appears to be relevant to the question whether a claim arising outside the forum state should be considered "related to" the defendant's contacts with the forum. The Supreme Court has indicated that the first step in analyzing specific jurisdiction is to determine whether the defendant's contacts with the state have been "purposeful."[267] The requirement of purposeful contacts is designed to fulfill the objective of the Due Process Clause. That objective is to protect the defendant's individual liberty interest by assuring that the defendant has fair warning that the activity being conducted within the state can subject the defendant to suit there. This fair warning gives the legal system a degree of predictability that allows potential defendants to structure their activity with some minimum assurance as to where it may subject them to suit. Defendants possessing this knowledge can protect themselves by (1) ceasing the jurisdiction-producing activity, or (2) if this is not possible, taking steps such as purchasing insurance to defray the burdens of suit that the activity may produce.[268]

Under the purposeful contacts step, the most important factor in determining whether a claim is "related to" the defendant's activities within the forum state is the notice-giving quality of the activities. If the activities are such that the defendant can expect lawsuits within the forum based on its activities, and if preparation for the lawsuits that might arise from the defendant's forum activity would also protect the defendant from lawsuits based on the claim actually sued on, the claim should be considered "related to" the defendant's contacts with the state. On the other hand, if the defendant's activities in the forum state would not enable the defendant to protect against an action brought by the plaintiff on a claim arising elsewhere, the claim should be considered "unrelated to" the defendant's contacts with the forum. Under the latter circumstances, the assertion of jurisdiction should be considered general, with the corresponding necessity that a higher level of contacts with the state should be required to satisfy due process.[269]

---

also Oldfield v. Pueblo de Bahia Lora, S.A., 558 F.3d 1210 (11th Cir. 2009) (claim of plaintiff who was injured on a boat operated by an out-of-country resort did not arise out of or relate to defendant's contacts with the United States; plaintiff, a Florida resident, had read an advertisement for the resort on the Internet and had submitted an online reservation request through the resort's website, a credit card authorization form to secure a room, and made arranged with a charter service for a fishing trip; the court held the injury suffered was not a foreseeable consequence of these contacts).

267. *See Burger King*, 471 U.S. at 471-72, 105 S. Ct. at 2181-82, 85 L. Ed. 2d at 540; *see also* TH Agric. & Nutrition, LLC v. Ace European Group Ltd., 488 F.3d 1282 (10th Cir. 2007) (insurer issued insurance policies that contained a worldwide territory-of-coverage clause and an option to defend Kansas insured; this resulted in injury that arose out of or was related to insurer's contacts with Kansas and established purposeful contacts with Kansas; however, it would violate traditional notions of fair play and substantial justice under reasonableness test to subject Dutch owners of insurers to jurisdiction in Kansas). In J. McIntyre Machinery, Inc. v. Nicastro, 564 U.S. __, 131 S. Ct. 2780, 180 L. Ed. 2d 765 (2011), the plurality opinion by Justice Kennedy attempted to shift the description of the function of the purposeful contacts test from foreseeability to the assurance that the state was validly exercising sovereign power. However, this idea does not at this time have majority support in the Court.

268. *See Burger King*, 471 U.S. at 471-76, 105 S. Ct. at 2181-84, 85 L. Ed. 2d at 540-43.

269. *See* ITL Int'l, Inc. v. Constenla, S.A., 669 F.3d 493 (5th Cir. 2012) (state long-arm statute provided for jurisdiction over defendant because by receiving goods from candy manufacturer in Gulfport for shipment to Costa Rica it performed "any character of work" in Mississippi within the meaning of the doing business provision of the statute; contacts of receiving candy shipments were purposeful; however, contacts did not relate to claims

With this understanding of when a claim should be considered "related to" the defendant's contacts with the state, it is possible to make some critical judgments about the kinds of facts that will produce a specific jurisdiction case when the claim arises outside the forum state. In his dissent in *Hall*, Justice Brennan argued that a claim should be considered "related to" the defendant's activities within the state when the defendant has engaged in some acts within the state in preparation for later activities outside the state that give rise to the claim for relief. Under these circumstances, the state where the preparatory acts occurred could validly assert jurisdiction to adjudicate the claim, even if none of the preparatory acts made up an element of the claim.[270]

The problem with this position is that if the activity being conducted by the defendant in the state is not of the sort that would give rise to some kind of liability, the activity may not give sufficient notice to the defendant to allow the defendant to defray the burdens of a suit within the state. Therefore, if the goal of the purposeful contacts step in the jurisdictional test is to be fulfilled, "related to" must be given a meaning that will allow the defendant to avoid or defray the burdens of suit within the state. Thus, the defendant's activities in the forum will normally have to be of a liability-producing sort.[271]

The most likely situation in which a claim should properly be considered related to the defendant's contacts with the state is when the defendant is engaging in activity within the forum that is similar or identical to liability-producing conduct that the defendant conducts elsewhere. The conduct within the state may be of the sort that should alert the defendant to the possibility of a suit within the state based on the conduct. Furthermore, the defense of a suit based in the state arising from liability-producing activities occurring outside the state may be no more burdensome than defense of a suit arising from the defendant's conduct within the state. This will be so when, if the defendant had done those things necessary to protect itself against a suit in the state based on its conduct within the state, it would also have protected itself against the suit brought based on its conduct elsewhere.[272]

---

because claims were trademark claims and general contract issues, and contacts did not give defendants notice that they could be sue on these claims in Mississippi).

270. *See Hall*, 466 U.S. at 427, 104 S. Ct. at 1879, 80 L. Ed. 2d at 419. The quoted passage thus argues that specific jurisdiction ought to be valid based on nonliability-producing acts of the sort that are connected with the liability-producing acts that occur outside the state in a rather loose chain of events.

271. In Aylward v. Fleet Bank, 122 F.3d 616 (8th Cir. 1997), the court held that the defendant's contacts were related to the activity about which the plaintiff was complaining; nevertheless, they were insufficient to establish jurisdiction because they were not liability producing. However, the court did not identify how the contacts were related in order to determine whether the case was one of specific or general jurisdiction; instead, they were part of a three-factor test for personal jurisdiction that did not correspond to the Supreme Court's decisions on specific and general jurisdiction. In addition, note that the court's conclusion does *not* conform to the analysis recommended in the text, *supra*. After the claim has arisen (by definition in another state), acts that are "related to" the claim will always be non-liability producing in the particular case before the court. The recommendation in the text is that, viewed as of the time the "related to" acts are conducted, they must have the potential of producing liability of some sort. If they do, they may, depending on the circumstances, have the capacity to give the quality of warning to the defendant that due process requires.

272. Thus, Justice Brennan's argument in *Hall* should be effective only if it can be seen that Helicol's activity in Texas was of the sort that might produce liability in itself. If the activity was potentially liability producing, Helicol should have taken steps to defray the burdens of suit that the activity might produce. If the preparation for suit that Helicol should have undertaken would also have defrayed the burdens of the suit that was actually brought against Helicol, the claim should be considered "related to" Helicol's activity within the state, and Texas' assertion of jurisdiction should be considered specific. For example, if Helicol's activities in Texas would ordinarily lead a prudent business to purchase liability insurance providing for the defense of actions based on

Under these circumstances, an assertion of jurisdiction over the defendant to adjudicate the claim arising outside the state should be sustained.

Illustration 3-22. Assume that *D Co.* manufactures products *Q* and *R*, which are similar, but not identical. *P* purchases product *Q* in State *X*, where it explodes and injures *P*. Subsequently, *P* moves to State *Y*. *D* does not sell product *Q* in State *Y*, but does sell product *R* there. *P* sues *D* in State *Y* for the personal injuries that *P* received in State *X* due to the explosion of product *Q* in State *X*. As long as the court in State *Y* can see that the sales of product *R* in State *Y* should have led to preparations by *D* to defend the sort of suit brought by *P*, the court should consider the "purposeful contacts" test satisfied. Those preparations assure that *D* will not be deprived of an adequate opportunity to be heard in defense in State *Y*, even though *P's* claim is based entirely on events occurring in State *X*. *D's* preparations for potential lawsuits over sales of product *R* in *Y* should defray the burdens of *P's* suit based on the sales of product *Q* in State *X*.

* * * * *

In administering the specific jurisdiction test, the courts must remember that the test is not simply designed to allow the defendant to defray the burdens of suit within a state, but also to avoid jurisdiction altogether by ceasing the jurisdiction-producing activity within the state. Thus, the mere fact that the defendant is conducting some kind of activity within the state should not lead to the conclusion that a claim arising outside the state is related to that activity—even if the activity within the forum would normally cause the defendant to take steps, such as purchasing insurance, that would defray the burdens of any kind of suit within the state. As long as the U.S. Supreme Court maintains that the defendant is entitled to avoid the jurisdiction of a state by ceasing jurisdiction-producing activities within the state, it will be necessary to inquire whether the defendant has reasonably taken steps to do so.[273]

---

activities and events within and outside of Texas, the claim against Helicol, though technically arising in Peru, should be considered related to the Texas activities.

273. In American Type Culture Collection, Inc. v. Coleman, 83 S.W.3d 801 (Tex. 2002), the Texas Supreme Court held that even though the defendant made 3.5% of its total sales and 5% of its U.S. sales in Texas, these sales plus purchases from a Texas vendor were insufficient to sustain an assertion of general jurisdiction by Texas. The court emphasized that the defendant had purposefully structured its sales and services so as to complete them in Maryland, where it had its principal place of business. For example, all sales were made F.O.B. Maryland. To the court, this indicated that the defendant was structuring its business in such a way as to avoid jurisdiction in Texas by structuring its activities so as not to afford itself the benefits and protections of Texas law. This decision is highly questionable. In the first place, it is not clear that the foreseeability test of specific jurisdiction applies to an assertion of general jurisdiction. Even if the test is applicable to assertions of general jurisdiction, it seems highly questionable to allow a defendant who ships a large volume of products into a state to avoid an assertion of jurisdiction by the state just by the technical step of making its sales F.O.B. the state of its principal place of business. For other discussion of the "related contacts" requirement, including the application of a "but for" test and a test requiring the forum contacts to have "substantive relevance" to the cause of action, see Lea Brilmayer, *Related Contacts and Personal Jurisdiction*, 101 HARV. L. REV. 1444 (1988); Mark M. Maloney, Note, *Specific Jurisdiction and the "Arise from or Relate to" Requirement . . . What Does It Mean?* 50 WASH. & LEE L. REV. 1265 (1993); Lea Brilmayer, *How Contacts Count: Due Process Limitations on State Court Jurisdiction*, 1980 SUP. CT. REV. 77; William M. Richman, *Casad's Jurisdiction in Civil Actions* (pt. 1), *A Sliding Scale to Supplement the Distinction Between General and Specific Jurisdiction* (pt. 2), 72 CAL. L. REV. 1328, 1338 (1984). In subsection *(d)*, below, the possibility of establishing a unified test for general and specific jurisdiction is discussed. Under a unified test, there will be some cases in which jurisdiction is valid, even though the defendant has done nothing at all within the state, because the defendant will not be able to demonstrate significantly greater burdens of suit within the state than exist elsewhere. Thus, the discussion in the text is premised on the retention by the U.S. Supreme Court of the existing analysis of state-court jurisdiction problems under the Due Process Clause.

Illustration 3-23. *P*, a State *X* corporation, and *D*, a Scottish corporation, had enjoyed a long-term relationship in which *P* sold engine parts from time to time to *D*. The parts were shipped from State *X* to wherever *D* wanted. *D* notified *P* that *C*, another Scottish corporation, had engines to sell that *P* might want to buy for resale in the U.S. *P* negotiated a contract with *C* to buy the engines. Subsequently, *P* and *D* agreed that *D* would obtain the engines from *C*, take certain parts off the engines that *D* wanted for itself, and then send the engines to *P* in State *Y*, where *P* intended to store them. During the shipments of the engines to State *Y*, two of the engines were damaged, allegedly because *D* had improperly packed them. *P* sued *D* in State *X*. *P* asserted personal jurisdiction over *D* under the State *X* long-arm statute, which extends as far as the Due Process Clause permits.

In *RAR, Inc. v. Turner Diesel, Ltd.*,[274] the Seventh Circuit held that *D's* contacts with State *X* did not give rise to an assertion of specific jurisdiction. The court held that the prior contacts between the parties had nothing to do with the specific contract for shipment of the engines.[275] Because that specific contract had no relationship to State *X* other than the fact that it arose out of the general business relationship between the parties, it could not give rise to an assertion of specific jurisdiction.[276] The court was concerned that a less-restrictive standard for specific jurisdiction would leave potential defendants "uncertain as to what causal connections courts might draw between past contacts and current litigation."[277] To avoid unfair surprise, therefore, the court indicated that "[u]nless their contacts are continuous and systematic enough to rise to the level of general jurisdiction, individuals and corporations must be able to conduct interstate business confident that transactions in one context will not come back unexpectedly to haunt them in another."[278]

---

274. 107 F.3d 1272 (7th Cir. 1997).

275. *See id.* at 1278-80.

276. *See id.* at 1278. The court stated:

> Admittedly, [*P's*] suit is, in a certain sense, related to [*D's*] contacts with [State *X*], if only because [*D*] never would have come to handle the engines in Scotland had it not previously dealt with [*P*] in [State *X*]. We do not think, however, that using such a loose causal connection between a suit and a defendant's forum contacts as the basis for personal jurisdiction comports with fair play and substantial justice. . . . [S]pecific jurisdiction is not appropriate "merely because a plaintiff's cause of action arose out of the general relationship between the parties; rather, the action must *directly arise* out of the specific contacts between the defendant and the forum state."

Id. at 1278 (citing and quoting Sawtelle v. Farrell, 70 F.3d 1381, 1389 (1st Cir. 1995)). Because the plaintiff did not allege systematic and continuous contacts with State *X*, the court held that it had "waived any general jurisdiction argument." 107 F.3d at 1277.

277. 107 F.3d at 1278-79.

278. *Id.* at 1278. The court's test, while not precisely like the test stated in the text, *supra*, is very close. Note that the nature of the shipment contract between *P* and *D* was different than the nature of their prior contracts. Therefore, preparation to defray the burden of suits in State *X* on those prior contracts would not necessarily have defrayed the burdens of suit on the particular contract involved in the suit. Likewise, the court seems correct that the defendant should be able to avoid suit in State *X* unless its activities are so substantial as to alert it that it can be sued in State *X* for anything. *Cf.* African Dev. Co. v. Keene Eng'g, Inc., 963 F. Supp. 522 (E.D. Va. 1997) (specific jurisdiction proper over seller in breach of contract action, where seller shipped defective mining dredges from California to Virginia; in addition to shipping the dredges into Virginia, the court emphasized that the defendant had engaged in extensive telephone negotiations and had solicited the plaintiff's business by mailing catalogues to plaintiff). It has been suggested that provisions in long-arm statutes authorizing personal jurisdiction over defendants who cause tortious injury in a state by an act or omission outside the state if the defendants regularly do or solicit business in the state or engage in any other persistent cause of conduct in the state authorize a kind of hybrid jurisdiction that is neither "general" or "specific." *See* Linda Sandstrom Simard, *Hybrid Personal Jurisdiction: It's Not General Jurisdiction, or Specific Jurisdiction, But Is It Constitutional?* 48 CASE W. RES. L. REV. 559 (1998).

Illustration 3-24. In *Von Cos. v. Seabest Foods, Inc.*,[279] a franchiser sued a meat supplier in California state court for selling the franchiser contaminated meat. The meat supplier, in turn, asserted claims against nonresident franchisees. The supplier alleged that the nonresident franchisee's failure to cook the meat properly caused the plaintiff's harm. The California Supreme Court held that an assertion of specific jurisdiction over the franchisees was appropriate because the meat supplier's claim against them was related to their franchise arrangements with the California franchiser. The court held that it was sufficient that the plaintiff's claim had a substantial connection with the franchisee's business contacts with California. The court observed that specific jurisdiction would exist in a suit by the franchiser against the franchisee for any liability that the franchiser suffered as a result of the franchisee's undercooking of the meat because the franchise agreement provided that the franchisees would prepare their products in conformance with the franchiser's regulations. Failure to do so would produce a breach of contract claim that would arise from the franchisee's contacts with California.[280] Under these circumstances, the court was correct to conclude that the franchisee's contacts with California were sufficiently related to the meat supplier's claim against them to sustain an assertion of specific jurisdiction. The franchisee's could not claim a lack of fair warning that they might be sued in California based on their activities outside the state. Nor had they attempted to structure their activities so as to avoid the jurisdiction of California's courts on claims that would be virtually identical to the ones asserted against them.

(ii) The Two-Step Test for the Validity of Specific Jurisdiction

The test currently employed by the U.S. Supreme Court for specific jurisdiction is the product of an evolutionary process. During most of that process, the Court took a very loose, unstructured approach to determining whether "minimum contacts" existed between the defendant and the forum. In *Burger King Corp. v. Rudzewicz*,[281] the Court began to add structure to the specific jurisdiction part of the minimum contacts test.[282] Specifically, the Court stated that when the

---

279. 14 Cal. 4th 434, 926 P.2d 1085, 58 Cal. Rptr. 2d 899 (1996).

280. *See id.* at 451, 926 P.2d at 1095-96, 58 Cal. Rptr. 2d at 909; *see also* the discussion of *Burger King Corp. v. Rudzewicz*, in subsection *(ii)* and section H(2), *infra*.

281. 471 U.S. 462, 105 S. Ct. 2174, 85 L. Ed. 2d 528 (1985).

282. The test articulated in *Burger King* was actually created in World-Wide Volkswagen Corp. v. Woodson, 444 U.S. 286, 100 S. Ct. 559, 62 L. Ed. 2d 490 (1980). However, after using the test in *World-Wide Volkswagen*, the Court's next several decisions did not apply it, but returned to the loose analysis of prior cases. *See* Calder v. Jones, 465 U.S. 783, 104 S. Ct. 1482, 79 L. Ed. 2d 804 (1984); Keeton v. Hustler Magazine, Inc., 465 U.S. 770, 104 S. Ct. 1473, 79 L. Ed. 2d 790 (1984); *see also* Rush v. Savchuk, 444 U.S. 320, 100 S. Ct. 571, 62 L. Ed. 2d 516 (1980) (decided the same day as *World-Wide Volkswagen*, in which the Court also did not apply the *World-Wide Volkswagen* test). For cases prior to *World-Wide Volkswagen* employing the unstructured approach to the minimum contacts test described in the text, see McGee v. International Life Ins. Co., 355 U.S. 220, 78 S. Ct. 199, 2 L. Ed. 2d 223 (1957); Mullane v. Central Hanover Bank & Trust Co., 339 U.S. 306, 70 S. Ct. 652, 94 L. Ed. 865 (1950). Three cases suggest a more structured approach to minimum contacts, although not the one ultimately adopted by the Court in *Burger King*, are Kulko v. Superior Court, 436 U.S. 84, 98 S. Ct. 1690, 56 L. Ed. 2d 132 (1978); Shaffer v. Heitner, 433 U.S. 186, 97 S. Ct. 2569, 53 L. Ed. 2d 683 (1977) (discussed above); and Hanson v. Denckla, 357 U.S. 235, 78 S. Ct. 1228, 2 L. Ed. 2d 1283 (1958). For a discussion of the analysis in *Kulko* and *Shaffer*, see Catherine T. Dixon, Note, *Constitutional Law—Jurisdiction—A New Minimum Contacts Analysis*—Kulko v. Superior Court, *98 S. Ct. 1690 (1978)*, 12 CREIGHTON L. REV. 905 (1979). The cases cited in this footnote are discussed *infra* in conjunction with specific topics in this section and in the next section on the

forum is asserting specific jurisdiction, a two step analysis is necessary to determine the validity of the jurisdictional assertion. As noted in subsection *(b)(i)*, above, the first step in the analysis requires the court to determine whether the defendant has conducted purposeful activities within the forum state. Even if purposeful contacts are found present in a case, however, jurisdiction can still be defeated under the second step in the test.

The second step in the analysis involves a balancing test, referred to as the "reasonableness" test. This step requires the court to take into account (1) the burdens on the defendant of a suit within the forum (2) the forum state's interest in adjudicating the dispute, (3) the plaintiff's interest in obtaining convenient and effective relief, (4) the interstate judicial system's interest in the most efficient resolution of controversies, and (5) the shared interests of the several states in furthering fundamental substantive social policies.[283] However, the Court has made it clear that once purposeful contacts are established between the defendant and the forum, there will be a heavy burden imposed on the defendant to defeat the state's assertion of jurisdiction with the reasonableness test.[284] In *Burger King*, the Court also indicated that the reasonableness test may be used "to establish the reasonableness of jurisdiction upon a lesser showing of minimum contacts than would otherwise be required."[285]

To understand the operation of the two-step test, it will be useful to examine each step and element of the test separately. Many of the Supreme Court cases applying the different elements of the test were decided before *Burger King*. However, these cases are still good authority for the purpose of determining how these elements should be applied today. After examining the operation of the test, an evaluation can then be made of whether the Court's approach to either general or specific jurisdiction cases properly addresses the concerns of the Due Process Clause of the Fourteenth Amendment.

(iii) The Purposeful Contacts Test

The first U.S. Supreme Court decision to emphasize that the defendant must engage in purposeful activities within the state was *Hanson v. Denckla*.[286] In *Hanson*, a Pennsylvania settlor established a trust in Delaware and later moved to Florida. The settlor executed a will in Florida and died there in 1952. However, at the time the will was executed, the settlor also executed two appointments from the Delaware trust to certain legatees. In the Florida proceeding brought to probate the settlor's will, the Florida court held these powers of appointment void. The U.S. Supreme Court held the Florida probate judgment invalid because the Florida court

---

application of the minimum contacts test to specific cases.

283. *See Burger King*, 471 U.S. at 476-77, 105 S. Ct. at 2184-85, 85 L. Ed. 2d at 543-44.

284. *See id.* at 476-78, 105 S. Ct. at 2184-85, 85 L. Ed. 2d at 543-44.

285. *Id.* at 477, 105 S. Ct. at 2184, 85 L. Ed. 2d at 543-44. The Court cited Keeton v. Hustler Magazine, Inc., 465 U.S. 770, 104 S. Ct. 1473, 79 L. Ed. 2d 790 (1984) and McGee v. International Life Insurance Co., 355 U.S. 220, 78 S. Ct. 199, 2 L. Ed. 2d 223 (1957), in conjunction with this statement. As discussed in the next section, these cases both emphasized the state's interest in asserting jurisdiction, indicating that it will be the most important factor in enhancing jurisdiction under the *Burger King* analysis.

286. 357 U.S. 235, 78 S. Ct. 1228, 2 L. Ed. 2d 1283 (1958).

did not have personal jurisdiction over the Delaware trustee and certain other Delaware defendants consistent with the Due Process Clause. The Court stated that "[t]he unilateral activity of those who claim some relationship with a nonresident defendant cannot satisfy the requirement of contact with the forum [s]tate."[287] Rather, the minimum required before a state might exercise jurisdiction over a nonresident defendant was that "there be some act by which the defendant purposefully avails itself of the privilege of conducting activities within the forum State, thus invoking the benefits and protections of its laws."[288] Because the Delaware defendants had been essentially passive in the relationships and transactions leading to the controversy, there was no activity that would satisfy the purposeful contact requirement.

In *Shaffer v. Heitner*,[289] the Court indicated that the purposeful contacts test was linked to the foreseeability of suit within the state. In addition, the Court indicated that a properly framed state long-arm statute might enhance that foreseeability.[290] The Court then observed that Delaware had not enacted a statute treating the acceptance of a directorship in a Delaware corporation as consent to jurisdiction in the state.[291] This statement suggested that a properly framed long-arm statute could, by alerting the defendants that their actions would subject them to suit within the state, satisfy the purposeful contact component of the Due Process Clause.[292]

In *World-Wide Volkswagen Corp. v. Woodson*,[293] the Court addressed the operation of the purposeful contacts test in the context of a products liability action. The issue before the Court was whether Oklahoma could properly exercise personal jurisdiction over a nonresident automobile retailer and its wholesale distributor whose only connection with the state was that an automobile sold in New York to

---

287. *Id.* at 253, 78 S. Ct. at 1239-40, 3 L. Ed. 2d at 1298.

288. *Id.*

289. 433 U.S. 186, 97 S. Ct. 2569, 53 L. Ed. 2d 683 (1977).

290. In *Shaffer*, the Court held that Delaware could not assert personal jurisdiction over the nonresident directors and officers of a Delaware corporation in a shareholders' derivative action. Among other reasons, the Court stated that the defendants, who had no contacts with Delaware other than the acceptance of positions as officers and directors in the corporation, had not, by their actions, established the purposeful contacts with the state required by *Hanson*. *See Shaffer*, 433 U.S. at 216, 97 S. Ct. at 2586, 53 L. Ed. 2d at 705.

291. *See id.* at 416, 97 S. Ct. at 2586, 53 L. Ed. 2d at 705. In addition, the Court stated that the absence of a specific expression of statutory interest on the part of Delaware in the kind of action brought in *Shaffer* rendered the state's interest in maintaining the action in Delaware weak. The state's interest factor is now employed in the second step of the due process analysis—the reasonableness test. This aspect of *Shaffer* is discussed in subsection *(iv) infra*.

292. This suggestion was promptly followed by the Delaware Legislature. *See* DEL. CODE ANN. tit. 10, § 3114 (Supp. 2006) (effective Sept. 1, 1977). The constitutionality of the statute was upheld in Armstrong v. Pomerance, 423 A.2d 174, 176-79 (Del. 1980). *See* Susan Stuckert, Note, *A Constitutional Analysis of the New Delaware Director-Consent-to-Service Statute*, 70 GEO. L.J. 1209 (1982); *see also* David L. Ratner & Donald E. Schwartz, *The Impact of* Shaffer v. Heitner *on the Substantive Law of Corporations*, 45 BROOK. L. REV. 641 (1979). However, it is difficult to accept that a state long-arm statute alone will be sufficient to provide the purposeful contacts required by the minimum contacts test, when, as in *Shaffer*, the defendants "have simply had nothing to do with the state" asserting jurisdiction. *See Shaffer*, 433 U.S. at 216, 97 S. Ct. at 2586, 53 L. Ed. 2d at 705. As discussed below, the purposeful contacts test, as it has evolved, insures that the defendant will have fair warning that the defendant's *conduct* may produce an assertion of jurisdiction by the state. It is the notice-giving quality of the conduct that provides the defendant with the opportunity to avoid the state's jurisdiction or to defray the burdens of a suit within the state. A long-arm statute detached from conduct will not necessarily give the requisite fair warning to the defendant. Thus, it seems safer to read *Shaffer* as saying that a long-arm statute can buttress the case for jurisdiction in marginal cases in which the defendant's conduct alone is almost, but not quite, sufficient to provide the necessary fair warning that a suit might be brought within the state.

293. 444 U.S. 286, 100 S. Ct. 559, 62 L. Ed. 2d 490 (1980).

New York residents became involved in an accident in Oklahoma. The Court held that the necessary purposeful contact was not present under these circumstances. The Court found that the dispute was based on one isolated occurrence, which fortuitously occurred in Oklahoma. It rejected the argument that because an automobile is mobile by its very design and purpose, it was "foreseeable" that it would cause injury in Oklahoma. Rather, the Court stated that foreseeability alone had never been sufficient to satisfy the Due Process Clause.[294] The kind of foreseeability that is relevant to the due process analysis is the kind which assures that "the defendant's conduct and connection with the forum State are such that he should reasonably anticipate being haled into court there."[295] This kind of foreseeability is important because it "gives a degree of predictability to the legal system that allows potential defendants to structure their primary conduct with some minimum assurance as to where that conduct will and will not render them liable to suit."[296]

Significantly, the Court distinguished the situation of the local retailer and regional distributor from that of the manufacturer and importer of the automobile, who were also defendants in the action. The manufacturer and importer purposefully availed themselves of the privilege of conducting activities in the forum by attempting to serve the national market. This attempt to serve the national market was relevant because a state does not violate the Due Process Clause if it asserts "personal jurisdiction over a corporation that delivers its products into the stream of commerce with the expectation that they will be purchased by consumers in the forum [s]tate."[297] In contrast, the Court noted that the retailer's sales were made in Massena, New York, and that the regional distributor's market, although substantially larger, was limited to dealers in New York, New Jersey, and Connecticut. Thus, while it might be foreseeable that the purchasers of automobiles sold by the distributor and the retailer would take them to Oklahoma, "the mere 'unilateral activity of those who claim some relationship with a nonresident defendant cannot satisfy the requirement of contact with the forum [s]tate' [citing *Hanson v. Denckla*]."[298]

Illustration 3-25. *D*, a citizen of State *Y*, is in the business of selling tires from a retail outlet located adjacent to an interstate highway in State *Y*. *P*, a citizen of State *X*, is vacationing in State *Y* when two of *P's* tires require replacement. *P* purchases two tires from *D*, who installs them on *P's* automobile. *D* is aware that *P* is from State *X* and will drive back to State *X* in the automobile. After *P* returns to State *X*, *P* is seriously injured in an accident due to defects in the tires sold and

---

294. *See id.* at 295-96, 100 S. Ct. at 566-67, 62 L. Ed. 2d at 500-01.

295. *Id.* at 297, 100 S. Ct. at 567, 62 L. Ed. 2d at 501.

296. *Id.*

297. *Id.* at 298, 100 S. Ct. at 567, 62 L. Ed. 2d at 502 (citing Gray v. American Radiator & Standard Sanitary Corp., 22 Ill. 2d 432, 176 N.E.2d 761 (1961)).

298. *Id.* at 298, 100 S. Ct. at 567, 62 L. Ed. 2d at 502. The Court also rejected the argument that jurisdiction could be supported by the fact that petitioners earned substantial revenue from goods used in Oklahoma. The Court noted that "[t]his argument seems to make the point that the purchase of automobiles in New York, from which the petitioners earn substantial revenue, would not occur *but for* the fact that the automobiles are capable of use in distant [s]tates like Oklahoma." *Id.* at 298, 100 S. Ct. at 568, 62 L. Ed. 2d at 502. The Court, however, found that "whatever marginal revenues" Seaway and World-Wide may have received by virtue of the fact that their products were capable of use in Oklahoma was "far too attenuated a contact to justify that [s]tate's exercise of *in personam* jurisdiction over them." *Id.* at 299, 100 S. Ct. at 568, 62 L. Ed. 2d at 502.

installed by *D*. *P* sues *D* in a state court of State *X*. *P* asserts jurisdiction over *D* under the State *X* long-arm statute that extends as far as the U.S. Constitution permits. If *D* objects to State *X's* assertion of personal jurisdiction over *D*, the court should dismiss the action. *D* lacks the purposeful contact with State *X* required by the minimum contacts test. Even though *D* knew that *P* was from State *X* and was returning there, *D* was not attempting to serve the market encompassed by State *X*. *D's* activities were entirely local to State *Y*.[299]

* * * * *

Despite the Court's apparent approval of a "stream of commerce" test to establish purposeful contacts with the state in *World-Wide Volkswagen*,[300] doubt remains about the degree of contact that is necessary to subject a manufacturer to jurisdiction under such a test. In *Asahi Metal Industry Co. v. Superior Court*,[301] four Justices indicated that placing a product into the stream of commerce alone would not be sufficient to satisfy the purposeful contact portion of the minimum contacts test.[302] To satisfy that part of the test, "additional conduct" of the defendant would have to indicate an "intent or purpose" to serve the market in the forum state. Such additional conduct could include designing the product for the market in the forum state, advertising in the forum state, establishing channels for providing regular advice to customers in the forum state, or selling the product through a distributor who has agreed to be a sales agent in the forum state. However, merely placing the product in the stream of commerce with the awareness that it would wind up in the forum state would not alone satisfy the purposeful contact requirement.[303]

Four other Justices disagreed with this conclusion.[304] Instead, they concluded that placing a product into the stream of commerce alone was sufficient

---

299. *See id.* at 296, 100 S. Ct. at 566, 62 L. Ed. at 500-01; *see also* Erlanger Mills, Inc. v. Cohoes Fibre Mills, Inc., 239 F.2d 502, 507 (4th Cir. 1956).

300. In *World-Wide Volkswagen*, the Court cited Gray v. American Radiator & Standard Sanitary Corp., 22 Ill. 2d 432, 176 N.E.2d 761 (1961), with seeming approval at the end of its statement about the stream of commerce, quoted above. *See* 444 U.S. at 297-98, 100 S. Ct. at 567, 62 L. Ed. 2d at 501-02. *Gray* involved the explosion of a water heater due to a defective component part. Jurisdiction was sustained in the case over the component part manufacturer that had sold the part to the manufacturer outside the forum state. *Gray* is discussed in section F *supra* ("The Reaction of the States to the Minimum Contacts Test: Long-Arm Statutes").

301. 480 U.S. 102, 107 S. Ct. 1026, 94 L. Ed. 2d 92 (1987). The *Asahi* case arose out of a California motorcycle accident in which the driver of a Honda motorcycle collided with a tractor when one of the tires on the motorcycle exploded. The motorcycle driver commenced a products liability action in a California state court against the Taiwanese tire manufacturer, among others. The tire manufacturer sought indemnity from its codefendants and from Asahi Metal Industry Co., a Japanese corporation that manufactured the valve stem for the tire. Asahi was served with process pursuant to California's long-arm statute, which authorizes jurisdiction on any basis that is not inconsistent with the U.S. Constitution. Ultimately, the motorcycle driver settled with all of the original defendants, leaving only the indemnity claim between the tire manufacturer and Asahi still pending. *See id.* at 105-06, 101 S. Ct. at 1029-30, 94 L. Ed. 2d at 100, 100-01. Asahi asserted that California could not exercise jurisdiction over it consistent with the Due Process Clause of the Fourteenth Amendment. Based on information that Asahi's valve stems were incorporated extensively in the manufacturer's tires and distributed throughout the United States with Asahi's knowledge, the California trial court sustained jurisdiction. The California Court of Appeal ordered the service quashed. It believed that it would be unreasonable for Asahi to have to defend an action in California based simply on the foreseeability that its product would wind up there. The California Supreme Court reversed the Court of Appeal, holding that Asahi's act of placing its product into the stream of commerce with knowledge of distribution in California was sufficient to satisfy the Fourteenth Amendment. The U.S. Supreme Court granted certiorari and reversed. *See id.* at 106-08, 101 S. Ct. at 1029-31, 94 L. Ed. 2d at 100-02.

302. Justices O'Connor, Powell, Scalia, and Chief Justice Rehnquist agreed that placing a product in the stream of commerce alone is not enough to satisfy the purposeful contacts portion of the test. *See Asahi*, 480 U.S. at 105, 109-13, 101 S. Ct. at 1029, 1031-33, 94 L. Ed. 2d at 100, 102-05.

303. *See id.* at 112, 101 S. Ct. at 1033, 94 L. Ed. 2d at 104.

304. *See id.* at 116-21, 101 S. Ct. at 1035-38, 94 L. Ed. 2d at 107-10 (Brennan, J., with whom White, J., Marshall, J., and Blackmun, J. joined, concurring).

to satisfy the purposeful contact portion of the test. In addition, Justice Stevens, joined by Justices White and Blackmun, stated that even under the plurality's theory, the "stream of commerce plus" test had been satisfied, though they also indicated that it was unnecessary to formulate the theory for this case.[305] While the plurality would require something more than a significant quantity of sales of the product in the forum state, these Justices took the view that "a regular course of dealing that results in deliveries of over 100,000 units annually over a period of several years would constitute 'purposeful availment' even though the item delivered to the forum State was a standard product marketed throughout the world."[306] Thus, even were the Court to approve of the "stream of commerce plus" theory in the future, the Justices may disagree on how it should be applied to particular facts.[307] Nevertheless, the Court's most recent pronouncement on the effect of putting a product into the stream of commerce suggests that the concept may have limited utility in the future.

In *J. McIntyre Machinery, Ltd. v. Nicastro*,[308] the Supreme Court again addressed the "stream of commerce" test in a suit involving a defendant from a foreign nation. In *McIntyre*, a worker was injured in New Jersey by a metal shearing machine manufactured in England by McIntyre. The worker commenced a products

---

305. *See id.* at 121-22, 101 S. Ct. at 1038, 94 L. Ed. 2d at 100, 110-11.

306. *Id.* at 122, 101 S. Ct. at 1038, 94 L. Ed. 2d at 111. However, eight Justices in *Asahi* agreed that on the facts of the case the reasonableness test would defeat the state's assertion of jurisdiction. Only Justice Scalia did not join in the Court's opinion on the reasonableness test. *See id.* at 105, 101 S. Ct. at 1029, 94 L. Ed. 2d at 100. In addition, three Justices indicated that it was unnecessary to examine whether purposeful contacts existed in the case when it could be seen that the reasonableness test would defeat jurisdiction. Thus, these Justices would not require that the purposeful contacts analysis precede the reasonableness analysis. *See id.* at 121-22, 101 S. Ct. at 1038, 94 L. Ed. 2d at 100, 110-11 (Stevens, J., with whom White, J. and Blackmun, J. joined, concurring).

307. The plurality's "stream of commerce plus" requirement seems at odds with the Court's reasons for requiring purposeful contact under the Due Process Clause. In *World-Wide Volkswagen*, the Court had carefully explained why the purposeful contact component was essential to protect the defendant from unreasonable burdens of suit in the forum: "When a corporation 'purposefully avails itself of the privilege of conducting activities within the forum State' . . . it has clear notice that it is subject to suit there, and can act to alleviate the risk of burdensome litigation by procuring insurance, passing the expected costs on to customers, or, if the risks are too great, severing its connection with the State." *See* 444 U.S. at 297, 100 S. Ct. at 567, 62 L. Ed. 2d at 501 (1980); *see also Asahi*, 480 U.S. at 119, 101 S. Ct. at 1036, 94 L. Ed. 2d at 108-09 (Brennan, J., concurring). This description certainly fits a component parts manufacturer like Asahi. It is difficult to see why it is unfair to subject a defendant to suit in a state where the defendant knows its product will be distributed and may cause harm, given the options available to alleviate the burdens of suit in the state. As discussed in subsection *(b)(iv)*, *infra*, it is likely that if the injured plaintiff had sued Asahi directly, jurisdiction could not have been defeated under the reasonableness test. Therefore, because there are circumstances under which Asahi could clearly be sued within the state, it should have anticipated and prepared for litigation in California. If it had done so, it would probably have defrayed the burdens of the actual indemnity action brought against it in the case, as well as the burdens of a direct action against it by the plaintiff. Under these circumstances, it would seem clear that placing a product into the stream of commerce without more gives a manufacturer all the warning that due process requires to protect it from the burdens of suit within a state; *see also* Nuance Commc's, Inc. v. Abbyy Software House, 626 F.3d 1222 (Fed. Cir. 2010) (in patent infringement action, personal jurisdiction established by fact that defendant purposefully ships software products into forum with the expectation that copies of those products will be sold there); Merriman v. Crompton Corp., 282 Kan. 433, 146 P.3d 162 (2006) (stream-of-commerce theory does not apply to general jurisdiction; jurisdiction sustained over suppliers of rubber processing chemicals to tire manufacturers on grounds of specific jurisdiction based on knowledge of and participation in price-fixing conspiracy that caused plaintiff class to pay more for tires in Kansas); *cf.* Dever v. Hentzen Coatings, Inc., 380 F.3d 1070 (8th Cir. 2004) (presence of manufacturer's products in state was insufficient by itself to support general personal jurisdiction under a stream-of-commerce theory); *see generally* Diane S. Kaplan, *Paddling Up the Wrong Stream: Why the Stream of Commerce Theory Is Not Part of the Minimum Contacts Doctrine*, 55 BAYLOR L. REV. 503 (2003); S. Wilson Quick, *Staying Afloat in the Stream of Commerce:* Goodyear, McIntyre, *and the Ship of Personal Jurisdiction*, 37 N.C. J. INT'L L. & COM. REG. 547 (2011); Andrew Kurvers Spalding, Note, *In the Stream of the Commerce Clause: Revisiting* Asahi *in the Wake of* Lopez *and* Morrison, 4 NEV. L.J. 141 (2003).

308. 564 U.S. __, 131 S. Ct. 2780, 180 L. Ed. 2d 765 (2011).

liability action in New Jersey state court to recover damages from the injury. McIntyre challenged personal jurisdiction over it, but the New Jersey Supreme Court ultimately sustained jurisdiction relying in part on the "stream of commerce" test. McIntyre had not sent either the machine that injured the worker or any other machine directly into New Jersey. Instead, it had distributed its products through an independent distributor in another state. The New Jersey Supreme Court felt that this justified the assertion of jurisdiction under the Due Process Clause, because it amounted to a conscious decision by McIntyre to distribute its products through a nationwide distribution system that might lead the products to be sold in any of the fifty states, and McIntyre had not taken any reasonable steps to prevent its products from being sold in New Jersey.

The Supreme Court of the United States disagreed. In an opinion by a plurality of the Court written by Justice Kennedy, four members of the Court indicated that the purposeful contacts portion of the minimum contacts test was designed to limit the exercise of jurisdiction over nonresidents to situations in which it is permissible for a state to exercise lawful sovereign authority:

> The Due Process Clause protects an individual's right to be deprived of life, liberty, or property only by the exercise of lawful power. . . . This is no less true with respect to the power of a sovereign to resolve disputes through judicial process than with respect to the power of a sovereign to prescribe rules of conduct for those within its sphere. . . .
>
> A court may subject a defendant to judgment only when the defendant has sufficient contacts with the sovereign "such that the maintenance of the suit does not offend 'traditional notions of fair play and substantial justice.'" . . . Freeform notions of fundamental fairness divorced from traditional practice cannot transform a judgment rendered in the absence of authority into law. As a general rule, the sovereign's exercise of power requires some act by which the defendant "purposefully avails itself of the privilege of conducting activities within the forum State, thus invoking the benefits and protections of its laws," . . . though in some cases, as with an intentional tort, the defendant might well fall within the State's authority by reason of his attempt to obstruct its laws. In products-liability cases like this one, it is the defendant's purposeful availment that makes jurisdiction consistent with "traditional notions of fair play and substantial justice."
>
> A person may submit to a State's authority in a number of ways. [The Court here discusses explicit consent, presence within the state when served with process, citizenship (or domicile), and incorporation or principal place of business as examples of actions from which it is proper to infer an intention to benefit from and thus an intent to submit to the laws of a state.] These examples support exercise of the general jurisdiction of the State's courts and allow the State to resolve both matters that originate within the State and those based on activities and events elsewhere. . . . By

> contrast, those who live or operate primarily outside a [s]tate have a due process right not to be subjected to judgment in its courts as a general matter.
>
> There is also a more limited form of submission to a State's authority for disputes that "arise out of or are connected with the activities within the state." . . . Where a defendant "purposefully avails itself of the privilege of conducting activities within the forum [s]tate, thus invoking the benefits and protections of its laws," . . . it submits to the judicial power of an otherwise foreign sovereign to the extent that power is exercised in connection with the defendant's activities touching on the State. . . .[309]

However, the plurality then rejected the position of the plaintiff and the New Jersey Supreme Court that purposeful contacts could be established on the facts before it by the "stream of commerce" test. Significantly, the plurality stated that "[t]he defendant's transmission of goods permits the exercise of jurisdiction only where the defendant can be said to have targeted the forum; as a general rule, it is not enough that the defendant might have predicted that its goods will reach the forum State."[310]

The plurality's sovereignty oriented analysis was arguably a withdrawal from the Court's previous position on the function of the Due Process Clause, which it had earlier described as designed to protect the individual liberty interest of the defendant.[311] However, neither the plurality's "sovereignty-based" reasoning, nor its position on the ability of the "stream of commerce" test to satisfy the purposeful contacts requirement of the minimum contacts test in specific jurisdiction cases constituted a majority position of the Supreme Court.[312] Justice Bryer, in a concurrence with which Justice Alito joined, was reluctant "to announce a rule of broad applicability without full consideration of the modern-day consequences."[313] Rather, the concurring Justices attempted to adhere tightly to the Court's previous precedents, which they viewed as not supporting jurisdiction based on a single isolated sale, even when the claim arose from the defendant's contact

---

309. *Id.* at __, 131 S. Ct. at 2786-88, 180 L. Ed. 2d at 772-75.

310. *Id.* at __, 131 S. Ct. at 2788, 180 L. Ed. 2d at 775. This test, of course, is considerably more restrictive than even the *Asahi* plurality's "stream of commerce plus" requirement. *See* Patrick J. Borchers, J. McIntyre Machinery, Goodyear, *and the Incoherence of the Minimum Contacts Test*, 44 CREIGHTON L. REV. 1245, 1255 (2011).

311. *See* Insurance Corp. of Ir., Ltd. v. Compagnie des Bauxites de Guinee, 456 U.S. 694, 702-03, 102 S. Ct. 2099, 2101-03, 72 L. Ed. 2d at 492, 497-500 (1982). *Insurance Corp. of Ireland* and the notion of incorporating sovereignty protection into the Due Process Clause are discussed more fully in section G(3), below, where this aspect of *McIntyre* is also explored more fully. In addition, the plurality in *McIntyre* indicated that Congress might be able to authorize federal courts to exercise long-arm jurisdiction over foreign defendants based on their contacts with the United States under circumstances in which state courts could not do so based on contacts with the states. *See McIntyre* 564 U.S. __, 131 S. Ct. at 2789, 2790, 180 L. Ed. 2d at 777; Patrick J. Borchers, J. McIntyre Machinery, Goodyear, *and the Incoherence of the Minimum Contacts Test*, 44 CREIGHTON L. REV. 1245, 1255 (2011); Symposium, *Personal Jurisdiction for the Twenty-First Century: The Implications of* McIntyre *and* Goodyear Dunlop Tires, 63 S.C. L. REV. 463 (2012) (containing articles by Professors Brilmayer & Smith, Carrington, Citron, Feder, Freer, Miller, Peddie, Perdue, Stein, Steinman, Silberman, Stravitz, and Vail).

312. As the dissenters pointed out, the fact that the defendant was from a foreign nation rendered the plurality's meandering reasoning about the danger of one state illegitimately encroaching on the sovereignty of another irrelevant on the facts of the case. *See* 564 U.S. at __, 131 S. Ct. at 2798, 180 L. Ed. 2d at 786 (Ginsburg, J., dissenting); Patrick J. Borchers, J. McIntyre Machinery, Goodyear, *and the Incoherence of the Minimum Contacts Test*, 44 CREIGHTON L. REV. 1245, 1258-59 (2011).

313. 564 U.S. at __, 131 S. Ct. at 2791, 180 L. Ed. 2d at 778.

with the state.[314] The concurring Justices emphasized the plaintiff had the burden of establishing the facts necessary to sustain New Jersey's exercise of jurisdiction and had failed to show "no 'regular . . . flow' or 'regular course' of sales in New Jersey; and there is no 'something more,' such as special state-related design, advertising, advice, marketing, or anything else."[315] The concurrence added:

> The plurality seems to state strict rules that limit jurisdiction where a defendant does not "inten[d] to submit to the power of a sovereign" and cannot "be said to have targeted the forum." . . . But what do those standards mean when a company targets the world by selling products from its [website]? And does it matter if, instead of shipping the products directly, a company consigns the products through an intermediary (say, Amazon.com) who then receives and fulfills the orders? And what if the company markets its products through popup advertisements that it knows will be viewed in a forum? Those issues have serious commercial consequences but are totally absent in this case.
>
> . . . .
>
> But though I do not agree with the plurality's seemingly strict no-jurisdiction rule, I am not persuaded by the absolute approach adopted by the New Jersey Supreme Court . . . . Under that view, a producer is subject to jurisdiction for a products-liability action so long as it "knows or reasonably should know that its products are distributed through a nationwide distribution system that *might* lead to those products being sold in any of the fifty states."
>
> For one thing, to adopt this view would abandon the heretofore accepted inquiry of whether, focusing upon the relationship between "the defendant, the *forum*, and the litigation," it is fair, in light of the defendant's contacts *with that forum*, to subject the defendant to suit there. . . .
>
> For another, I cannot reconcile so automatic a rule with the constitutional demand for "minimum contacts" and "purposedfu[l] avail[ment]," each of which rest upon a particular notion of defendant-focused fairness. . . . A rule like the New Jersey Supreme Court's would permit every State to assert jurisdiction in a products-liability suit against any domestic manufacturer who sells it products (made anywhere in the United States) to a national distributor, no matter how large or small the manufacturer, no matter how distant the forum, and no matter how few the number of items that end up in the particular forum at issue. What might appear fair in the case of a large manufacturer which specifically seeks, or expects, an equal-sized distributor to sell its product in a distant State might seem unfair in the case of a small manufacturer (say an Appalachian potter) who sells his product (cups and

---

314. *Id.* at __, 131 S. Ct. at 2792, 180 L. Ed. 2d at 779.
315. *Id.*

> saucers) exclusively to a large distributor, who resells a single item (a coffee mug) to a buyer from a distant state (Hawaii). I know too little about the range of these or in-between possibilities to abandon in favor of the more absolute rule what has previously been this Court's less absolute approach.[316]

Taken together, the plurality and concurrence leave the state of the "stream of commerce" test, along with the general ability to sustain and exercise of specific jurisdiction over nonresident domestic and foreign manufacturers in products liability cases, in a state of uncertainty. Certainly, it is reasonable to ask, as did Justice Ginsburg in dissent, what sensible view of adjudicatory authority would make "the place of [the plaintiff's] injury within the United States . . . off limits for his products liability claim against a foreign manufacturer who targeted the United States (including all the States that constitute the Nation) as the territory it sought to develop."[317]

It should not escape notice that the Court's decision may leave an injured plaintiff with nowhere in the United States to sue.[318] If the plaintiff is unable to sue where the injury occurred, the next most likely location for suit in the United States is probably the state where the importer/distributor of the foreign manufacturer's products is located. Even if that location is possible, what sense does it make to force the plaintiff to sue there, given that the defendant is not likely to be burdened less by a suit there than in the state where witnesses and other evidence are located?

Further, the statements by both the plurality and the concurrence seem to indicate, contrary to the emphasis in *Ashai* on the foreign nature of the defendant, that a restrictive view may be taken about jurisdiction over domestic manufacturers who distribute through middlemen rather than making direct sales to customers within the states. This would open a rather large loophole in the ability to assert specific jurisdiction over nonresident defendants in products liability cases. It would

---

316. *Id.* at __, 131 S. Ct. at 2793, 180 L. Ed. 2d at 780-81. The concurrence also added that the fact that the defendant was a foreign rather than a domestic manufacturer made the basic fairness of an absolute rule yet more uncertain, and cast in doubt the position of the New Jersey Supreme Court that the nature of international commerce had changed so significantly as to require a new approach to personal jurisdiction. *See id.* at __, 131 S. Ct. at 2793-94, 180 L. Ed. at 781. Justice Breyer did not state how he proposed to cure the absence of knowledge from which he (and by implication Justice Alito) suffered with regard to the realities of domestic and international commerce. Furthermore, as Professor Borchers has observed:

> [F]ollowing Justice Breyer's concurrence in the judgment is no straightforward matter. That opinion gives no hint as to whether it favors the Brennan or the O'Connor view of the stream of commerce, leaving lower courts marooned as before. Perhaps the only thing one can say for certain is that the stream of commerce cannot be fulfilled by a single drop, even if that drop comes in the form of a $24,000 industrial machine. Some regular and substantial number of sales needs to occur in the forum, but when and where that threshold is crossed is impossible to say.

Patrick J. Borchers, J. McIntyre Machinery, Goodyear, *and the Incoherence of the Minimum Contacts Test*, 44 CREIGHTON L. REV. 1245, 1265 (2011).

317. 564 U.S. at __, 131 S. Ct. at 2797, 180 L. Ed. 2d at 785 (Ginsburg, J., with whom Sotomayor, J., and Kagan, J., concurred). The dissenting Justices also rejected the plurality's sovereignty-based analysis of due process. *See id.* at __, 131 S. Ct. at 2798, 180 L. Ed. 2d at 785-86. Professor Borchers has justifiably called the *McIntyre* case a "disaster." *See* Patrick J. Borchers, J. McIntyre Machinery, Goodyear, *and the Incoherence of the Minimum Contacts Test*, 44 CREIGHTON L. REV. 1245 (2011). He added: "The plurality opinion in *J. McIntyre Machinery v. Nicastro* is quite possibly the most poorly reasoned and obtuse decision of the entire minimum contacts era." *Id.* at 1263.

318. *Cf.* Patrick J. Borchers, J. McIntyre Machinery, Goodyear, *and the Incoherence of the Minimum Contacts Test*, 44 CREIGHTON L. REV. 1245, 1265 (2011) (observing that even Ohio, where the U.S. Distributor for J. McIntyre was located, might not even have the ability to assert jurisdiction under the plurality's theory).

also arguably encourage manufacturers to adopt modes of product distribution in order to evade personal jurisdiction rather than for reasons of economic efficiency.

The concurrence's suggestion that distinctions might in the future be drawn between large and small product manufacturers is also disturbing. The ability of manufacturers to protect themselves from suits within a forum by virtue of the fact that their distribution makes a suit there foreseeable in the abstract may differ due to their situations, including their size. This, in turn, may require different jurisdictional results depending upon the ability of different manufacturers to defray the burdens of suit on the basis of foreseeability. Nevertheless, the Court has heretofore not suggested that size per se should insulate a defendant from suit in a forum where the defendant causes harm. Given that such harm is often inflicted on one who has never left the forum, it would seem improper to do so in the name of "fairness."

On the whole, *McIntyre* is an unsatisfactory case that leaves the law of specific jurisdiction more unsettled than before the case was decided. Although it is still technically legitimate for a state to sustain jurisdiction over a manufacturer who sends a product directly into the state when the product causes harm there, even that situation is cast in doubt by the decision. Given that the only reason to grant certiorari in these kinds of cases is to clarify the applicable standards, one wonders, when a split of this nature between the Court's members becomes apparent during deliberations, whether it would not have been better to dismiss the writ of certiorari as improvidently granted rather than make things worse than they were before.[319]

Most of the decisions applying the purposeful contact requirement discussed thus far found jurisdiction to be lacking under the test. The only case explicitly finding the test satisfied was *Burger King*.[320] *Burger King* was a diversity action in the U.S. District Court for the Southern District of Florida. In this action, Burger King sought damages and injunctive relief against two individual defendants. Burger King alleged that the defendants had failed to make certain payments under a franchise agreement to Burger King in Florida. Burger King also asserted that the defendants were infringing its trademarks by continuing to operate as a Burger King franchise. The defendants were Michigan residents operating the Burger King franchise in Michigan.[321] Jurisdiction was asserted over them under a

---

319. *Cf. id.* at 1271 (suggesting that the Court should have denied certiorari in both *J. McIntyre* and its companion general jurisdiction case *Goodyear* rather than muddy the waters of state-court jurisdiction further).

320. Numerous other cases exist in which the Court found jurisdiction to be constitutional but did not explicitly discuss the purposeful contact requirement. These cases are consistent with the test. They will be discussed in section H *infra* ("Application of the Minimum Contacts Test to Specific Cases").

321. Burger King was a Florida corporation with its principal place of business in Florida. *See* 471 U.S. at 464, 105 S. Ct. at 2178, 85 L. Ed. 2d at 535. The controversy leading to the action arose out of a franchise granted by Burger King to the defendants in Michigan. The defendants had jointly applied to Burger King's Birmingham, Michigan, office for the franchise in 1978. That office forwarded the application to Burger King's Miami office. Extensive negotiations ensued, leading to the execution of a franchise agreement between the parties and the commencement of the franchise operation in 1979. Although the franchise enjoyed early success, a recession in 1979 curtailed its business, with the result that the defendants fell behind in payments that they had agreed to make under the franchise agreement. After notices of default from the Florida office and extensive, but unsuccessful, negotiations between that office and the defendants, Burger King terminated the franchise and ordered the defendants to vacate the premises of the franchise location. They refused and continued to operate the facility as a Burger King franchise, whereupon Burger King commenced the Florida action. *See id.* at 464-68, 105 S. Ct. at 2178-80, 85 L. Ed. 2d at 535-38.

provision of Florida's long-arm statute. That provision authorized jurisdiction over anyone who breaches a contract in Florida by failing to perform acts required by the contract in the state, provided the cause of action arises from the alleged contract breach.[322]

In evaluating the district court's assertion of jurisdiction over the defendants, the Court found that purposeful contacts existed between the defendants and Florida. The Court recognized that the existence of a contract with a resident of the forum state alone cannot automatically satisfy the purposeful contact requirement. Nevertheless, a combination of factors, such as prior negotiations, contemplated future consequences, the terms of the contract, and the parties actual course of dealing, can establish purposeful contacts.[323] Thus, the fact that the defendants had voluntarily reached out beyond their home state of Michigan to negotiate a franchise arrangement with a Florida corporation produced the necessary purposeful conduct.[324] The Court emphasized that the contract documents and the parties' actual course of dealing should have indicated to the defendants that ultimate decision-making authority was vested in Burger King's Miami office. Consequently, it was foreseeable that an action might be brought there to enforce the agreement.[325]

Illustration 3-26. *M Manufacturing Co.* is incorporated with its sole place of business in State *X*. *M* manufactures various types of springs to the special order of its customers. *D Manufacturing Co.* is incorporated with its sole place of business in State *Y*. *D* is contacted by a sales representative of *M* about the possibility of placing an order for springs from *M*. After negotiations with *M*, all of which took place by telephone between States *X* and *Y*, *D* entered into a contract with *M*. The contract provided that *M* would manufacture an order of springs for *D* according to *D's* specifications. The contract contained a choice-of-law clause providing that the law of State *X* would govern the contract. After the springs were manufactured and shipped, *D* refused to pay for them because they were allegedly defective. *M* sued *D* in a state court of State *X*. *M* asserted jurisdiction over *D* under a provision of the State *X* long-arm statute that permits jurisdiction to be asserted over defendants who enter into contracts to be performed in whole or part in State *X*. The assertion of jurisdiction over *D* satisfies the purposeful contact requirement.

---

322. *See id.* at 463-64, 468-69, 105 S. Ct. at 2177, 2180, 85 L. Ed. 2d at 535, 538. Jurisdiction was asserted over the trademark infringement claim under the tortious act provisions of the Florida long-arm statute, but this assertion of jurisdiction was not before the Supreme Court because the trademark claim was the subject of a compromise, which resulted in waiver of the right to appeal the claim. Thus, the Supreme Court reserved the question whether the tortious act provision of the Florida statute could extend to out-of-state trademark infringements. *See id.* at 469 n.11, 105 S. Ct. at 2180 n.11, 85 L. Ed. 2d at 539 n.11.

323. *See id.* at 478-79, 105 S. Ct. at 2185, 85 L. Ed. 2d at 544-45; *see also* Kugler Co. v. Growth Prods. Ltd., 265 Neb. 505, 658 N.W.2d 40 (2003) (defendant's establishment of ongoing relationship with plaintiff in which plaintiff was to distribute defendant's products in Nebraska was sufficient to satisfy the purposeful contacts test).

324. *See Burger King*, 471 U.S. at 480, 105 S. Ct. at 2186, 85 L. Ed. 2d at 545-46.

325. *See id.* at 480-81, 105 S. Ct. at 2186-87, 85 L. Ed. 2d at 545-46. Furthermore, the contract itself provided that it would be governed by Florida substantive law and permitted Burger King to bring suit either in Florida or elsewhere in controversies arising out of the agreement. Although the Court had indicated in prior cases that the ability of a state to apply its law to a controversy did not automatically establish personal jurisdiction, the Court held in *Burger King* that the fact that a contract contained a choice-of-law provision could, when combined with other factors, help establish that a defendant possesses purposeful contact with the state. *See id.* at 481-82, 105 S. Ct. at 2187, 85 L. Ed. 2d at 546-47.

D negotiated a contract with a resident of State *X*. The contract was to be performed in part in State *X*. The contract also contained a choice-of-law clause providing that the law of State *X* would govern the contract. Under the *Burger King* test, it was foreseeable to *D* that an action might be brought in State *X* to enforce the contract.[326]

* * * * *

The purposeful contact requirement has evolved into a major protection for defendants under the minimum contacts analysis. Nevertheless, the purposeful contact requirement does not seem indispensable to protect the defendant's opportunity to be heard. As discussed in subsection *(c)*, below, it may be possible to develop a unified test for jurisdiction in both general and specific jurisdiction cases. Under this test, it will be important to inquire whether the defendant's conduct would cause a reasonable person to take steps to defray the kinds of burdens that will be imposed on the defendant by a state's assertion of jurisdiction. It is possible that these burdens may reasonably be defrayed in some cases even though the defendant has never engaged in the kind of purposeful activity that the Court has thus far required under the Due Process Clause of the Fourteenth Amendment. Under such circumstances, the absence of purposeful contacts should not defeat jurisdiction.

(iv) The Reasonableness Test

The Court has only applied the reasonableness test once to defeat a state's assertion of jurisdiction under the minimum contacts test. Furthermore, the Court has never explicitly used the test to create jurisdiction when the purposeful contacts requirement has not been satisfied. Despite the sparse use of the test, however, it is possible to make some general observations about how the factors in the test should operate based on the Court's decisions.

The single decision in which the Court has used the reasonableness test to defeat jurisdiction is *Asahi Metal Industry Co. v. Superior Court*.[327] As noted in subsection *(b)(iii)*, above, majority support for reversing the judgment of the California Supreme Court existed in *Asahi* only because eight members of the Court

---

326. *See* Quality Pork Int'l v. Rupari Food Servs., Inc., 267 Neb. 474, 675 N.W.2d 642 (2004) (plaintiff's claim arose out of defendant's contacts with state because the defendant had induced the plaintiff to send products from Nebraska to Florida; therefore, purposeful contacts existed; the fact that the defendant had no physical contacts with state was irrelevant);. Springmasters, Inc. v. D & M Mfg., 303 S.C. 528, 402 S.E.2d 192 (Ct. App. 1991); *see also* Alonso v. Line, 846 So. 2d 745 (La. 2003) (attorney's agreement to represent client in case based on automobile accident in Louisiana constituted purposeful contacts with Louisiana for purposes of malpractice action against attorney for failure to file action within statute of limitations). In Gonzalez v. Internacional De Elevadores, S.A., 891 A.2d 227 (D.C. 2006), the District of Columbia Court of Appeals held that the district could not constitutionally assert either general or specific personal jurisdiction over a Mexican elevator repair company for injuries received by an employee of the American embassy in Mexico in an elevator accident in Mexico. However, in analyzing the issue of general jurisdiction, the court stated that a defendant corporation must "purposely avail itself of the privilege of conducting activities within the forum state, and its continuing contacts with the District of Columbia must provide it with clear notice that it is subject to suit here." This is a questionable importation of the purposeful availment rhetoric into the analysis of general jurisdiction, which the Supreme Court has never approved. *See also* Daniel E. Wanat, *Copyright Infringement Litigation and the Exercise of Personal Jurisdiction Within Due Process Limits: Judicial Application of Purposeful Availment, Purposeful Direction, or Purposeful Effects Requirements to Finding that a Plaintiff Has Established a Defendant's Minimum Contacts Within the Forum State*, 59 MERCER L. REV. 553 (2008).

327. 480 U.S 102, 107 S. Ct. 1026, 94 L. Ed. 2d 92 (1987).

agreed that the reasonableness portion of the specific jurisdiction test defeated jurisdiction. Justice O'Connor's opinion for these members of the Court emphasized the burdens that would be placed upon Asahi by the action in California. These burdens included not only the distance from Japan to California, but also the fact that the dispute between the foreign tire manufacturer and Asahi would be adjudicated by "a foreign nation's judicial system."[328]

The other elements in the reasonableness test were not sufficient to overcome these burdens. The state's and the tire manufacturer's interest in litigating its indemnity claim in California was considered slight. The transaction that was the basis of the claim occurred in Taiwan, and the tire valves had been shipped from Japan to Taiwan.[329] Finally, the Court addressed the shared interests of the several states in efficient procedural resolution of the controversy and in furthering fundamental substantive social policies. On the facts of the case, this factor required consideration of "the procedural and substantive policies of other nations" affected by California's assertion of jurisdiction. The Court concluded that these interests, as well as the foreign-relations interests of the United States, would be "best served by a careful inquiry into the reasonableness of the assertion of jurisdiction in the particular case, and an unwillingness to find serious burdens on an alien defendant outweighed by minimal interests on the part of the plaintiff or the forum State."[330]

The result in *Asahi* was a product, in part, of the peculiar procedural posture of the case. A change in that posture would likely produce a different result under the reasonableness test. Under the Court's analysis, if Asahi had been sued directly by the California motorcycle driver, both California and the plaintiff would probably have sufficiently strong interests in the case to counterbalance the burdens that a suit in California would impose on Asahi. In addition, if Asahi had been one of a number of defendants sued by the driver, it would be procedurally efficient to resolve the relative liabilities of all of the multiple defendants in the California proceeding. Furthermore, it would arguably be in the interests of the interstate and international community to assure that substantive tort liability was imposed on the correct party through proceedings in California. Thus, in a changed procedural context, the Court would probably not be able to justify dismissing Asahi under the reasonableness test.

Illustration 3-27. *P*, a citizen of State *X*, sues *D-1*, a citizen of State *X*, and *D-2*, a citizen of State *Y*, in a state court in State *X*. *P* asserts a claim in the alternative against *D-1* and *D-2* in tort. *P* was injured when a machine manufactured by *D-2* exploded in State *X*. *D-1* is the doctor who treated *P* for *P's* injuries. *P*

---

328. *Id.* at 114, 107 S. Ct. at 1034, 94 L. Ed. 2d at 105.

329. *See id.* California's interest in entertaining the indemnity claim in its courts was also weak, because none of the parties to the indemnity claim was a resident of California. Although the California Supreme Court had argued that California had an interest in protecting its consumers by assuring that foreign manufacturers complied with the state's safety standards, the U.S. Supreme Court held that, for several reasons, this definition of the state's interest was overly broad. The dispute was mainly about indemnity, not safety standards. It was also unclear whether it was appropriate for California law to govern an indemnity claim between two foreign manufacturers based on a foreign transaction. Furthermore, while the possibility of a suit in California might create some additional deterrence, the Court felt that Asahi would receive similar pressures from the manufacturers who incorporated its products into their tires as long as those manufacturers were subject to California tort law. *See id.* at 114-15, 101 S. Ct. at 1034, 94 L. Ed. 2d at 100, 105-06.

330. *See id.* at 115, 107 S. Ct. at 1034-35, 94 L. Ed. 2d at 106.

asserts that the negligence of either *D-1* or *D-2* or both contributed to certain permanent injuries received by *P*. *D-1* and *D-2* are not indispensable parties to the action. Thus, *P* could sue *D-1* in State *X* and *D-2* in State *Y*. However, if *P* sued *D-2* in State *Y*, *D-1* could not be subjected to jurisdiction in State *Y* because all of *D-1's* actions occurred in State *X*. If *P* is forced to bring separate actions against *D-1* in State *X* and *D-2* in State *Y*, each defendant may defend on the ground that the other defendant is exclusively liable for *P's* permanent injuries. A trier of fact in State *X* might find in favor of *D-1* on the ground that *D-2* was exclusively responsible for *P's* injuries, and a trier of fact in State *Y* might find that *D-1* was exclusively responsible for *P's* injuries. Thus, two triers of fact would have agreed that one of the defendants was liable for *P's* permanent injuries, but *P* would not recover from either defendant. Under these circumstances, the state's and plaintiff's interests in conducting the action in State *X*, the only state where both defendants can possibly be joined, are strong. Likewise, it will be procedurally more efficient to resolve the relative liability of *D-1* and *D-2* in the State X proceeding than to conduct separate actions for this purpose. Finally, the interstate system has an interest in assuring that tort liability is not avoided by the parties through inconsistent judgments.[331]

* * * * *

Further examination of how the elements of the reasonableness test operate will be reserved until section H, below, where the test will be applied to specific categories of cases. However, one aspect of the test is important enough to explore briefly here. In *Shaffer v. Heitner*,[332] the Supreme Court rejected an argument that the state's interest in adjudicating the suit was high. In so doing, the Court stated that the argument was "undercut by the failure of the [state legislature] to assert the state interest [plaintiff] finds so compelling."[333] Thus, the Court suggested that the state's interest could be enhanced by the enactment of a particularized long-arm statute, as opposed to the general kind of statute involved in *Shaffer*.[334] Since *Shaffer*, the Court has explicitly addressed enhancement of the state's interest by statute only once. In *Keeton v. Hustler Magazine, Inc.*,[335] a libel action, the Court found the state's interest enhanced by two features of the statutory scheme. First, the state had not limited its criminal defamation statute to libels aimed at the state's

---

331. In this example, one must now assume that to satisfy the dissenters and the concurrence in the *J. McIntyre* case, discussed above in the preceding subsection, the manufacturer would either have to have sold the machine directly in the state or distributed more than one machine in the state through a distributor for jurisdiction to be proper under the "stream of commerce" test. In addition, the failure of the Court to discuss the reasonableness test in the case probably should not be interpreted to mean that the test is abolished. *See* Patrick J. Borchers, J. McIntyre Machinery, Goodyear, *and the Incoherence of the Minimum Contacts Test*, 44 CREIGHTON L. REV. 1245, 1265-66 (2011). However, the failure to mention the test may cast doubt on the dictum in the *Burger King* case that the reasonableness test, especially the state interest factor, could enhance the case for jurisdiction even when purposeful contacts were absent. *See* section H(2) *infra*.

332. 433 U.S. 186, 97 S. Ct. 2569, 53 L. Ed. 2d 683 (1977).

333. *Id.* at 214, 97 S. Ct. 2585, 53 L. Ed. 2d at 704. The Court added that "[i]f Delaware perceived its interest in securing jurisdiction over corporate fiduciaries to be as great as [plaintiff] suggests, we would expect it to have enacted a statute more clearly designed to protect that interest." *Id.* at 214-15, 97 S. Ct. at 2585, 53 L. Ed. 2d 704.

334. Recall that the statute in *Shaffer* was a generalized sequestration statute applicable to many kinds of cases. The Court also indicated that the foreseeability of suit within the state was adversely affected by the absence of a statute treating acceptance of a directorship in a Delaware corporation as consent to jurisdiction. *See* section G(2)*(b)(iii) supra* ("The Purposeful Contacts Test"). Thus, the presence of a focused long-arm statute can enhance both the likelihood of purposeful contacts with the state and the state's interest in adjudicating the action.

335. 465 U.S. 770, 104 S. Ct. 1473, 79 L. Ed. 2d 790 (1984).

residents. Second, the state had amended its long-arm statute to eliminate a requirement that torts falling within the statute be committed against residents of the state. These statutory features were said to constitute a clear expression of the state's interest in protecting nonresident victims of libel.[336]

Shaffer and *Keeton*, taken together, do not provide adequate guidance to the states about the kinds of statutes that will enhance their interests for purposes of the reasonableness test. *Keeton* has a particularly clouding effect. In that decision, the criminal defamation statute said to be a "clear" expression of the state's interest was inapplicable to the case before the Court. In addition, the expression of the state's interest was discovered in an omission of a limitation from the statute. Furthermore, the amendment of the state's long-arm statute eliminated a restriction on suits by nonresidents in *all* tort cases, not just in libel cases. *Keeton* thus raises the interesting prospect that a state's interest can be increased by (1) the absence of limitations in inapplicable statutes or (2) amendments to long-arm statutes that eliminate restrictions that are applicable to broad categories of cases. The philosophy of *Keeton* thus seems to be at odds with the insistence in *Shaffer* on a rather precise declaration of the state's interest by means of a tightly focused long-arm statute. Because of the apparent inconsistency in the approach of the two cases, therefore, clarification of the precise way in which a state's interest may be enhanced by statute will obviously have to await future decisions.[337]

In addition, *Keeton* described the state interest factor of the reasonableness test as a "surrogate" for other factors in the due process analysis.[338] This description clouds the operation of the reasonableness test even further by suggesting that a high state interest in adjudicating a dispute may, by itself, justify an assertion of specific jurisdiction. The Supreme Court has not returned to this suggestion since reviving the two-step test for the validity of specific jurisdiction in *Burger King*. However, at least one lower federal court has held that if the forum state has "an appreciable interest in the litigation" because issues in the litigation either would be affected by or would impact on policies expressed in the state's "substantive, procedural, or remedial laws," an assertion of jurisdiction by the state is "prima facie constitutional,"[339] even if there is no territorial connection between the state and the events giving rise to suit.[340] Only a demonstration of an inability by the defendant to "mount a defense in the state without suffering relatively substantial hardship" can defeat this prima facie case.[341]

---

336. *See id.* at 777, 104 S. Ct. at 1479, 79 L. Ed. 2d at 799.

337. One of the interesting questions about statutory enhancement is whether a statute such as the Uniform Interstate and International Procedure Act, discussed *supra* section F, contains sufficiently precise categories of jurisdiction to give the state's interest a boost. Presumably, a general long-arm statute of the California variety, discussed *supra* section F, will not enhance the state's interest. However, such a statute apparently will not detract from the state's interest if the interest is otherwise sufficient. In Calder v. Jones, 465 U.S. 783, 104 S. Ct. 1482, 79 L. Ed. 2d 804 (1984), another libel case decided the same day as *Keeton*, the Court sustained an exercise of jurisdiction by California under its general long-arm statute without discussing the state's interest or the absence of a precise long-arm statute. *Keeton* and *Calder* are discussed further *infra* in section H(1) ("Tort Cases").

338. *See Keeton*, 465 U.S. at 776, 104 S. Ct. at 1479, 79 L. Ed. 2d at 798.

339. *In re* DES Cases, 789 F. Supp. 552, 587 (E.D.N.Y. 1992). Recall that in Goodyear Dunlop Tires Operations, S.A. v. Brown, 564 U.S. __, 131 S. Ct. 2846, 180 L. Ed. 2d 796 (2011), discussed in section G(2), above, the Court indicated that a high state interest produced by injured plaintiff's domicile in the state would not sustain an exercise of *general* jurisdiction.

340. *See* 789 F. Supp. at 577-87.

341. *Id.* at 587.

(c) Confusion and Possible Convergence

Not all cases in the state and lower federal courts have fully appreciated the U.S. Supreme Court's distinction between general and specific jurisdiction or applied it in a sensible fashion. For example, in *Roxas v. Marcos*,[342] the plaintiff, a Philippine national, sued former President of the Philippines Ferdinand Marcos and his wife in Hawaii state court for conversion. In determining whether Marcos, who had died during the pendency of the action, was subject to personal jurisdiction in Hawaii, the Hawaii Supreme Court indicated that, although Marcos had not established a domicile in Hawaii, he had lived there for 3½ years and had thus purposely availed himself of the forum. It is clear that the assertion of jurisdiction over Marcos was "general" in the case. The court did not rely on the existence of any traditional territorial rule, such as presence or domicile. Furthermore, the claim clearly "arose" in the Philippines and did not "relate to" anything Marcos had done in Hawaii. Yet the court did not consider whether the assertion of jurisdiction was "general" or "specific" and applied the "purposeful availment" step of the specific jurisdiction test, but not the "reasonableness" analysis.

Cases such as *Roxas* are unfortunately sloppy, but they do not necessarily reach incorrect results.[343] It is not uncommon to see courts ignore the issue whether an assertion of jurisdiction is general or specific, or apply only the first step in the specific jurisdiction analysis.[344] Sometimes, when jurisdiction is asserted under a state long-arm statute that requires the claim to arise out of a particular kind of activity conducted within the state, it will be completely justifiable for a court to treat the general jurisdiction category as irrelevant.[345] However, when a state has a long-arm statute that, explicitly or as construed, extends jurisdiction as far as the U.S. Constitution permits, it is analytically preferable for the courts to first determine whether the assertion of jurisdiction is "general" or "specific" before proceeding to determine whether it is valid.[346]

Furthermore, in any case involving an assertion of specific jurisdiction, the courts should address the reasonableness factors. When purposeful contacts have been established, the courts should at least comment on whether the defendant has

---

342. 89 Haw. 91, 969 P.2d 1209 (1998).

343. Under the authority of the *Burnham* decision, discussed in section E(2), *supra*, the court could have exercised jurisdiction based on Marcos' physical presence in Hawaii. Likewise, if general jurisdiction is a category applicable to individuals, *see* section G(2)*(a) supra*, it could have been sustained based on Marcos' 3½ year residence in Hawaii, even if Marcos had not established a domicile there. *Cf.* RESTATEMENT (SECOND) OF CONFLICT OF LAWS § 30 (1971) (state has power to exercise jurisdiction over an individual who is a resident unless the individual's relationship is so attenuated as to make the exercise of jurisdiction unreasonable).

344. *See, e.g.*, Northwest Airlines, Inc. v. Astraea Aviation Servs., Inc., 111 F.3d 1386 (8th Cir. 1997); Generadora de Electricidad del Caribe v. Foster Wheeler Corp., 30 F. Supp. 2d 196 (D.P.R. 1998).

345. Thus, in the *Generadora* case, cited in the preceding note, jurisdiction was asserted under a provision of the Puerto Rican long-arm statute allowing "personal jurisdiction over nonresident defendants . . . when the litigation arises out of transactions in Puerto Rico." 30 F. Supp. 2d at 199.

346. Thus, in Northwest Airlines, Inc. v. Astraea Aviation Services, Inc., 111 F.3d 1386 (8th Cir. 1997), the court observed that Minnesota's long-arm statute "is applied to the fullest extent permitted under the [D]ue [P]rocess [C]lause of the [F]ourteenth [A]mendment." *Id.* at 1390. The court did not directly consider whether the assertion of jurisdiction was general or specific, but at one point in its opinion it did identify several contacts with Minnesota "which related to the disputed contracts under which [the plaintiff] brought its breach of contract claims." *Id.* Nevertheless, it is unclear from the opinion whether the court made this reference to establish the assertion of jurisdiction as specific or as the first step in the test for determining validity—*i.e.*, the purposeful contacts test. *See id.* at 1391-92.

met its burden of overcoming the presumption of validity established by the purposeful contacts.[347] If purposeful contacts have not been established, the court should at least briefly discuss whether the plaintiff has overcome the lack of purposeful contacts by the reasonableness factors.[348] Only by addressing the elements of the jurisdictional tests in a systematic way can the courts hope to clarify their operation over time.

A separate question that has arisen in recent years is the role of the "reasonableness factors" in assessing the validity of an assertion of general jurisdiction. As the discussion in preceding subsections has demonstrated, the U.S. Supreme Court has thus far addressed the reasonableness factors only in specific jurisdiction cases. By implication, this suggests that it is not proper to employ those factors to defeat an assertion of general jurisdiction when systematic and continuous contacts have been established, or to enhance the validity of an assertion of general jurisdiction when the defendant's contacts with the forum are less than systematic and continuous. Nevertheless, some courts have considered the reasonableness factors to be relevant to assertions of general jurisdiction.

The leading case is *Metropolitan Life Insurance Co. v. Robertson-Ceco Corp.* (*"Met Life"*).[349] In *Met Life*, an insurance company sued a manufacturer of building materials in the U.S. District Court for the District of Vermont. The claim was based on breach of contract and negligence in conjunction with materials supplied for the construction of a building owned by the insurance company in Miami, Florida. The defendant moved to dismiss the action for lack of personal jurisdiction. The district court dismissed the action. The court found that the activities of the defendant in Vermont did not rise to the "systematic and continuous" level necessary to sustain an assertion of general jurisdiction. The district court also applied the "reasonableness test" of the Supreme Court's specific jurisdiction cases and stated that even if systematic and continuous contacts had been established, that test would make the assertion of jurisdiction over the defendant unreasonable.[350]

On appeal, the Second Circuit disagreed with the conclusion of the district court that the defendant did not have systematic and continuous contacts with Vermont.[351] However, the Second Circuit agreed with the district court that the "reasonableness factors" could be used to test the validity of general jurisdiction and that those factors defeated jurisdiction on the facts of the case.[352] Although the Second Circuit acknowledged that the Supreme Court had not specifically applied the reasonableness test to general jurisdiction cases,[353] it felt justified in doing so by the uniform view of other courts of appeals,[354] as well as by the absence of any

---

347. *See* section G(2)*(b)(ii) supra* ("The Two-Step Test for the Validity of Specific Jurisdiction").

348. *See id.* (discussing the statement in *Burger King* indicating that the reasonableness factors can be used to sustain jurisdiction upon a lesser showing of "minimum contacts" than would otherwise be required).

349. 84 F.3d 560 (2d Cir. 1996). *Met Life* was also discussed in section G(2)*(a)* ("General Jurisdiction") *supra*.

350. *See id.* at 566.

351. *See id.* at 570-73.

352. *See id.* at 573-76.

353. *See id.* at 573.

354. *See id.* (citing and discussing Donatelli v. National Hockey League, 893 F.2d 459, 465 (1st Cir. 1990) and Bearry v. Beech Aircraft Corp., 818 F.2d 370, 377 (5th Cir. 1987)).

indication from the Supreme Court that the reasonableness inquiry is inappropriate in general jurisdiction cases.[355] In evaluating the factors, the court found that the "burden on the defendant" factor cut "slightly" in favor of the defendant on the facts,[356] but that Vermont had no interest in the suit,[357] the plaintiff's interest in suing in Vermont was weak,[358] no witnesses or evidence were located in Vermont,[359] and no "shared interests of the several states" or "substantive social policies" had been shown by the plaintiff to exist in favor of Vermont as a forum.[360] Thus, the Second Circuit found that the first factor weighed slightly against jurisdiction, while the second through fourth factors weighed heavily against it, in combination defeating jurisdiction.[361]

The majority's approach in *Met Life* provoked a strong dissent from Judge Walker.[362] The dissenting opinion canvassed many of the Supreme Court's decisions discussed in this text in preceding and following sections. It provides an admirable summary and evaluation of the minimum contacts test as well as the confusion it has produced in the lower federal and state courts.[363] As to the use of the reasonableness test in general jurisdiction cases, Judge Walker stated:

> In the wake of *Burger King* and *Asahi*, we are bound to adhere to the Supreme Court's adoption of a reasonableness inquiry in the specific jurisdiction context. In the general jurisdiction context, however, we are not so bound . . . . Unless and until the Supreme Court instructs us in a general jurisdiction case that interests other than those of the defendant are implicated by due process in the personal jurisdiction analysis, we should not rush to make them so. I believe that these ancillary interests, which have nothing to do

---

355. *See Met Life*, 84 F.3d at 573.

356. *See id.* at 573-74.

357. *See id.*

358. The plaintiff had sued in Vermont because it had a long statute of limitations. The court, on the authority of Keeton v. Hustler Magazine, Inc., 465 U.S. 770, 778, 104 S. Ct. 1473, 1480, 79 L. Ed. 2d 790, 799 (1984), discussed in section H(1) *infra*, considered this fact irrelevant. *See Met Life*, 84 F.3d at 574.

359. *See Met Life*, 84 F.3d at 574-75.

360. *See id.* at 575.

361. *See id.*

362. *See id.* at 576 (Walker, J., dissenting).

363. Judge Walker provided the following summary:

> The Supreme Court's opinion in *International Shoe*, which implicated only the interests of the defendant and not the interests of the plaintiff or of the forum state, made it clear that whether due process is satisfied turns exclusively on the fairness to the defendant in being made to defend a suit in a particular forum.
>
> The majority's holding is, in part, an accommodation of the Supreme Court's more recent jurisprudence which reconfigures the jurisdictional underpinning of *International Shoe*. Thirty-five years after the Supreme Court hailed "minimum contacts" as the constitutional touchstone of the due process analysis, it espoused, albeit in dicta, an additional due process consideration concerning the protection of interstate federalism. *World-Wide Volkswagen* . . . . This supplemental function of due process is the precursor to the majority's "reasonableness" inquiry in the present case. Only two years later, however, in *Insurance Corp. of Ireland* . . . , the Supreme Court reaffirmed its earlier course, recognizing that the personal jurisdiction requirement "represents a restriction on judicial power not as a matter of sovereignty, but as a matter of individual liberty" . . . . In spite of this reassertion, in *Burger King* . . . and later in *Asahi* . . . the Supreme Court doubled-back to its holding in *World-Wide Volkswagen* by defining the test for specific jurisdiction to include both a "minimum contacts" and a "reasonableness" component. In other words, the concept of "traditional notions of fair play and substantive justice," which was defined in *International Shoe* only by the "contacts" of the defendant with the forum state, has been transformed into the notion of reasonableness apart from the contacts.

Id. at 577.

with whether it is fair and just for a foreign defendant to be haled into an out-of-state court, are properly accounted for under the doctrine of forum non conveniens.

The fact that other circuits have chosen the course embarked on by the majority, if anything, reinforces my concerns. The sprouting like weeds of multi-pronged tests for the reasonableness inquiry in the circuits in both specific and general jurisdiction cases has left this legal garden in disarray.[364]

The majority's approach in *Met Life* represents a strong trend.[365] Nevertheless, the dissent has by far the better case. As discussed in the next subsection, there are great difficulties with the minimum contacts test as it has evolved in U.S. Supreme Court decisions. Although a unified test for general and specific jurisdiction cases is desirable, it cannot be coherently formulated by grafting the reasonableness factors onto the general jurisdiction test. To mention but one problem, it is impossible to see how a defendant who has systematic and continuous contacts with a state should ever be able to complain that the state is such a burdensome place to adjudicate any claim as to deprive the defendant of due process. Judge Walker was entirely correct in arguing that residual problems of inconvenience that may exist in such cases should be dealt with through transfers of venue or discretionary dismissal on forum non conveniens grounds. Recall, also, that in *Goodyear Dunlop Tires Operations, S.A. v. Brown*,[366] discussed in section G(2), above, the Supreme Court rejected the notion that general jurisdiction could be predicated on a strong state interest in providing a forum in which a resident plaintiff could obtain redress for injuries that were inflicted outside the state and not related to the defendant's in-state contacts.[367] *Goodyear* may be taken as some evidence that the reasonableness test is not an appropriate standard in general jurisdiction cases.

The distinction between general and specific jurisdiction, particularly the difference between claims that are and claims that are not "related to" the defendant's activities within the forum state, continues to cause difficulties for litigants. For example, in *Williams v. Lakeview Co.*,[368] the plaintiffs were injured in Arizona as the result of the service of liquor to an Arizona resident by the defendant in Nevada. The plaintiffs were riding with the intoxicated person, who lost control

---

364. *Id.* The doctrine of forum non conveniens mentioned in Judge Walker's dissent and the related problem of transfer of venue in federal court under 28 U.S.C. § 1404(a) are discussed in Chapter 4(D) *infra* ("Forum Non Conveniens and Change of Venue"). The role of sovereignty interests in the Supreme Court's decisions and in jurisdictional analysis more generally is discussed in section G(3) *infra* ("Sovereignty-Based Restrictions on State-Court Jurisdiction").

365. In addition to the cases cited and discussed by the majority, *supra*, see, *e.g.*, Harlow v. Children's Hosp., 432 F.3d 50 (1st Cir. 2005) (even if defendant's contacts with Maine were sufficient to support an exercise of specific or general jurisdiction, assertion of jurisdiction would be unreasonable); *Ex parte* United Bhd. of Carpenters, 688 So. 2d 246 (Ala. 1997) (after systematic and continuous contacts established, reasonableness test applied to sustain jurisdiction); *see also* Shannon McGhee-Hernandez, *Civil-Procedure*-Metropolitan Life Insurance Co. v. Robertson-Ceco Corp.: *The Reasonableness Inquiry in the Context of General Jurisdiction*, 27 U. MEM. L. REV. 723 (1997); Note, *Civil Procedure-Personal Jurisdiction-Second Circuit Applies "Reasonableness" Test for General Personal Jurisdiction*-Metropolitan Life Ins. Co. v. Robertson Ceco Corp., 84 F.3d 560 (2d Cir. 1996), 110 HARV. L. REV. 1328 (1997).

366. 564 U.S. __, 131 S. Ct. 2846, 180 L. Ed. 2d 796 (2011).

367. *Id.* at __ n.5, 131 S. Ct. at 2857 n.5, 180 L. Ed. 2d at 809 n.5.

368. 199 Ariz. 1, 13 P.3d 280 (2000).

of the automobile after it crossed from Nevada into Arizona. The defendant (a casino) advertised in Arizona, had made an offer involving incentives to Arizona tour bus companies to induce them to stop at the defendant's casino on the way into Nevada, and employed 23 Arizona residents. However, the plaintiffs conceded that their visit to the defendant's casino did not arise out of or relate to any of the defendant's contacts with Arizona. Because the court found that "systematic and continuous" contacts between Arizona and the defendant did not exist, Arizona's assertion of personal jurisdiction was invalid. Although it seems clear that the claim did not "arise out of" the defendant's contacts with the state, it is not as clear that the plaintiffs were correct to concede (as they did) that the claim did not "relate to" those contacts. The defendant was actively seeking customers from Arizona. Had it attracted such a customer and served the customer too much alcohol, with the result that the customer drove into Arizona and injured another Arizona citizen, the situation before the court would not have differed in any material respect from the plaintiffs' case. In both instances, the defendant's ability to anticipate a suit in Arizona and protect itself from the burdens of that suit is the same.

(d) Toward a Unified Test for General and Specific Jurisdiction

Serious difficulties exist with the minimum contacts analysis evolved by the U.S. Supreme Court. The Court has never explained why a different standard is applied to general and specific jurisdiction cases. In other words, why is the validity of general jurisdiction judged by whether "systematic and continuous" contacts with the forum exist, while specific jurisdiction is judged by whether "purposeful contacts" between the defendant and the forum state exist that are not outweighed by reasonableness factors? Why does the Court not use the two-tiered approach to jurisdiction in both general and specific jurisdiction cases as suggested by the *Met Life* case discussed in the preceding subsection. Alternatively, why is a territorial nexus required between the state and either the claim or the defendant?[369]

The separate tests used in general and specific jurisdiction cases seem to be aimed at achieving the same goal. The objective of the Due Process Clause is to assure an adequate opportunity to be heard in defense before a valid judgment may be entered against the defendant. Jurisdictional tests that restrict the location of suit serve this purpose by assuring that the defendant may not be subjected to an

---

369. For additional commentary on and criticism of the minimum contacts test, along with proposals for change, see Stephanie M. Chaissan, Comment, *"Minimum Contacts" Abroad: Using the* International Shoe *Test to Restrict the Extraterritorial Exercise of United States Jurisdiction Under the Maritime Drug Law Enforcement Act,* 38 U. MIAMI INTER-AM. L. REV. 641 (2006-07); Robert J. Condlin, *"Defendant Veto" or "Totality of the Circumstances"? It's Time for the Supreme Court to Straighten Out the Personal Jurisdiction Standard Once Again,* 54 CATH. U. L. REV. 53 (2004); Walter W. Heiser, *A "Minimum Interest" Approach to Personal Jurisdiction,* 35 WAKE FOREST L. REV. 915 (2000) (proposing a new constitutional test for personal jurisdiction similar to the test currently employed by the Supreme Court in choice-of-law determinations); Charles W. "Rocky" Rhodes, *Nineteenth Century Personal Jurisdiction Doctrine in a Twenty First Century World,* 64 FLA. L. REV. 387 (2012); Linda Sandstrom Simard, *Meeting Expectations: Two Profiles for Specific Jurisdiction,* 38 IND. L. REV. 343 (2005); A. Benjamin Spencer, *Jurisdiction to Adjudicate: A Revised Analysis,* 73 U. CHI. L. REV. 617 (2006); *cf.* Ralf Michaels, *Two Paradigms of Jurisdiction,* 27 MICH. J. INTL L. 1003 (2006) (discussing the differences between European and United States jurisdictional doctrine). *But see* Charles W. "Rocky" Rhodes, *Liberty, Substantive Due Process, and Personal Jurisdiction,* 82 TULANE L. REV. 567 (2007) (defending the view that constitutional limits on personal jurisdiction arise from substantive due process principles).

unreasonably burdensome place of suit. By requiring that systematic and continuous contacts exist between the defendant and the forum when the claim does not arise out of or relate to the defendant's forum activities, the Court may be trying to assure that the forum will not be unreasonably burdensome. When a defendant's forum activities are "systematic and continuous," the defendant cannot be heard to complain that any suit brought against the defendant in the forum is so burdensome that it violates due process. A helpful illustration is the case of an action brought in the state of the defendant's domicile on a claim arising outside the state. If the domicile is substantial, rather than technical, the defendant can hardly complain that the plaintiff has chosen to sue the defendant at the defendant's home rather than in a distant forum where the claim arose.[370] To be sure, there may be inconvenience in a trial at the defendant's domicile if important witnesses and evidence are located where the claim arose. However, any such inconvenience does not rise to the level of a due process violation and can often be accommodated by a forum non conveniens dismissal, a transfer of the litigation, or other procedural means.[371]

Similarly, in specific jurisdiction cases, the requirement of purposeful contacts is aimed at protecting the defendant from unreasonable burdens that might be imposed by a suit in a particular state. By assuring that the defendant can predict where its activities may result in a suit, the purposeful contacts test assures that the defendant can avoid jurisdiction-producing activities in states where the burdens of suit will be too great, or take steps to defray the burdens with insurance or other measures. A test that allowed the defendant to object to the burdens of suit in a state even when the defendant might have avoided or defrayed the burdens would be unjustifiable. Insistence on reasonable efforts to anticipate the consequences of one's forum-related activity are not unjust under the Due Process Clause, given the options open to potential defendants to avoid or alleviate the burdens of suit.[372] Of

---

370. Significantly, in Goodyear Dunlop Tires Operations v. Brown, 564 U.S. __, 131 S. Ct. 2846, 180 L. Ed. 2d 796 (2011), the Court described "the paradigm" for an individual for the exercise of jurisdiction as being the individual's domicile and "for a corporation, it is an equivalent place, one in which the corporation is fairly regarded as at home." *Id.* at __, 131 S. Ct. at 2853-54, 180 L. Ed. 2d at 806.

371. *See* Chapter 4(D) *infra* ("Forum Non Conveniens and Change of Venue").

372. While the purposeful contacts test reasonably accommodates the competing interests of the defendant, the forum, and the plaintiff, it is difficult to say the same about the reasonableness test. The reasonableness test allows a defendant to defeat jurisdiction when, by definition, the defendant has had an opportunity to anticipate a suit in the state and avoid or defray its burdens. If the defendant has had an adequate ability to predict a suit based on the defendant's activities within the state, the defendant should take the steps available to defray or avoid the burdens the suit would impose. If the defendant does not do so, the reasonableness test suggests that there will be cases, however rare, in which the defendant can still defeat jurisdiction by demonstrating significant objective burdens coupled with, for example, weak state and plaintiff interests in maintaining the suit in the forum. However, if a defendant has failed to take steps necessary to protect itself from foreseeable suits in the forum, it is difficult to see why weak state and plaintiff interests should allow the defendant to escape jurisdiction. Why not afford the defendant an adequate opportunity to predict the suit and alleviate its burdens and let the state and the plaintiff be the judge of their own interests? The jurisdiction-enhancing function of the reasonableness test is even more questionable. If a defendant's activities are not sufficiently purposeful to provide warning that the defendant can be subjected to suit within the state, it is difficult to understand how it can possibly be "fair" to subject the defendant to a suit within the state if the burdens of suit are significant. Furthermore, as noted in section G(2)*(b)(iv)*, *supra*, many Supreme Court decisions suggest that the "state interest" factor may be the most important jurisdiction-enhancing element in the reasonableness test. *See, e.g.*, Burger King Corp. v. Rudzewicz, 471 U.S. 462, 477, 105 S. Ct. 2174, 2184, 85 L. Ed. 2d 528, 543 (1985); Keeton v. Hustler Magazine, Inc., 465 U.S. 770, 104 S. Ct. 1473, 79 L. Ed. 2d 790 (1984); McGee v. Int'l Life Ins. Co., 355 U.S. 220, 78 S. Ct. 199, 2 L. Ed. 2d 223 (1957). This emphasis is especially objectionable because the state's interest seems to have nothing to do with the core objective of the Due Process Clause, which is to provide defendants with an adequate opportunity to be heard in defense. If defendant's activities are not such as to provide fair warning of the possibility of a suit within the state, and if the burdens of suit are substantial, it would seem that due process should protect the defendant from

course, after *J. McIntyre Machinery, Ltd. v. Nicastro*,[373] discussed in section G(2)*(b)(iii)*, above, this may have to be qualified, given the unsettling force of the plurality and concurring opinions on the application of the purposeful contacts in products liability test. Nevertheless, until a majority position emerges among the members of the Court on this issue, the discussion here remains valid.

Because the goal of the general and specific jurisdiction tests is arguably the same, the Court can, by returning to first principles, create a unified test for the two kinds of jurisdiction. The Court could focus in each case on the function of the Due Process Clause to ensure an adequate opportunity to be heard in defense. Under such an approach, a state would always be allowed to exercise jurisdiction over a defendant unless it could be demonstrated that the objective burdens of defending the action within the state are so great that the defendant would, as a practical matter, have to relinquish the opportunity to be heard rather than incur the burdens. A defendant who engages in activity within the state of the sort that should alert the defendant of the possibility of a suit within the state could never make the required demonstration, because such a defendant should act to defray the burdens of the suit before the suit occurs. In addition, a defendant should never be allowed to defeat a state's assertion of jurisdiction if it can be seen that the forum is no more burdensome to the defendant as a practical matter than some other state in which the defendant concededly might be sued. Under this approach, the state's interest, the plaintiff's interest, and other interests would be adequately accommodated without the necessity of emphasizing them separately as part of a vague reasonableness test.

Furthermore, the suggested approach, although it might expand the reach of state-court jurisdiction somewhat, would do so while retaining the focus on the defendant's right to an adequate opportunity to be heard that it is the purpose of the Due Process Clause to assure. Any additional protections for the defendant that are necessary should be imposed through due process limitations on the ability of a state to apply its substantive law in a manner that produces unfair surprise,[374] or by self-imposed limits on a state-court's jurisdiction under doctrines such as forum non conveniens.[375]

---

jurisdiction no matter how high the state's interest happens to be; *cf. Ex parte* Unitrin, Inc., 920 So. 2d 557 (Ala. 2005) (regardless of whether jurisdiction is alleged to be general or specific, the nexus between the defendant and the forum state must arise out of an action of the defendant that was purposefully directed toward the forum).

373. 564 U.S. __, 131 S. Ct. 2780, 180 L. Ed. 2d 765 (2011).

374. *See* Ralph U. Whitten, *The Constitutional Limitations on State Choice of Law: Due Process*, 9 HASTINGS CONST. L.Q. 851, 913, 917 (1982).

375. *See* Chapter 4(D) *infra* ("Forum Non Conveniens and Change of Venue"). The standard recommended should also not preclude the development of reasonable modern sovereignty-based restrictions on the enforcement of sister-state judgments to replace the sovereignty-oriented "international" rules that existed prior to *Pennoyer v. Neff* and which were eliminated with the development of the minimum contacts test of *International Shoe*. A judgment should not necessarily have to be enforced by another state simply because the judgment does not offend the Due Process Clause or domestic rules of the judgment-rendering state. The development of sovereignty-based restrictions is discussed in subsection 3, *infra*; *see also* Stephen B. Burbank, *Jurisdiction to Adjudicate: End of the Century or Beginning of the Millennium?*, 7 TUL. J. INT'L & COMP. L. 111 (1999) (discussing personal jurisdiction in the United States in a historical and comparative context); Robert C. Casad, *Jurisdiction in Civil Actions at the End of the Twentieth Century: Forum Conveniens and Forum Non Conveniens*, 7 TUL. J. INT'L & COMP. L. 91 (1999) (making suggestions for how the law of personal jurisdiction should develop in the twenty-first century); Kevin C. McMunigal, *Desert, Utility, and Minimum Contacts: Toward a Mixed Theory of Personal Jurisdiction*, 108 YALE L.J. 189 (1998) (discussing how the Supreme Court might make better use of the ingredients it has identified as relevant under the minimum contacts analysis by developing a "mixed" theory of

Illustration 3-28. *D*, a citizen of Texas, collides with *P*, a citizen of Omaha, Nebraska, in Council Bluffs, Iowa, which is a city separated from Omaha by the Missouri River. *P* sues *D* in a Nebraska state court in Omaha. *D* is served with process in Texas under a Nebraska long-arm statute extending the jurisdiction of Nebraska courts as far as the U.S. Constitution will permit. *D* should have no valid due process objection to an action in Omaha because Omaha is no more burdensome a forum than would be a court in Council Bluffs, where the accident occurred. The absence of a due process objection to jurisdiction does not preclude *D* from objecting on due process grounds to the application of Nebraska substantive law to the accident, if such an application would produce unfair surprise to *D*. Nor does it preclude *D* from moving to dismiss the action under the doctrine of forum non conveniens.

3. Sovereignty-Based Restrictions on State-Court Jurisdiction

When *Pennoyer v. Neff* incorporated the international rules of jurisdiction into the Due Process Clause of the Fourteenth Amendment, the Supreme Court's decision effectively constitutionalized rules that previously had not been constitutional rules. As previously noted,[376] these rules were not suitable due process rules because they did not focus on the effectuation of the defendant's opportunity to be heard in defense. Instead, the rules reflected the authority of the states as independent sovereigns, at least as this authority was understood at the time the Constitution was formed. However, although the international rules were not appropriate due process rules, *Pennoyer's* incorporation of them into the Due Process Clause did nothing to impair their value as safeguards of state sovereign interests. After *Pennoyer* but before *International Shoe*, therefore, a judgment that violated the state sovereignty interests reflected in the rules was unenforceable both in the state where it was rendered and in other states.

When *International Shoe* began replacing the territorial rules with the minimum contacts test, especially after *Shaffer* indicated that the latter test would govern all assertions of state-court jurisdiction, it was not recognized that this replacement might obliterate the protection that the territorial rules had afforded to state sovereignty interests. While the minimum contacts test, with its focus on fairness to the defendant, was certainly a better due process test than the territorial rules, the minimum contacts test was not concerned with safeguarding state sovereign prerogatives.[377] Thus, the combined effect of *Pennoyer* and *International Shoe* is that a judgment that satisfies the minimum contacts test must be enforced

---

personal jurisdiction that blends notions of desert, utility, and proportionality); Michael E. Solimine, *The Quiet Revolution in Personal Jurisdiction*, 73 TUL. L. REV. 1 (1998) (empirically examining whether federal and state courts have responded differently to the Supreme Court's personal jurisdiction decisions and how often plaintiffs leave their home states to shop for more favorable fora).

376. *See* section A(2)*(b) supra* ("Incorporation of the Territorial Rules into the Due Process Clause of the Fourteenth Amendment").

377. *Burnham's* potential preservation of the validity of some territorial rules did not restore the sovereign authority of the states as it had existed under *Pennoyer*. All *Burnham* suggested was that an assertion of jurisdiction under (some) traditional rules would not *violate* due process. "Novel" assertions of state-court jurisdiction that would have violated state sovereign interests under *Pennoyer* and earlier decisions are still governed by the minimum contacts test after *Burnham*.

in other states under the full-faith-and-credit implementing statute. There is apparently no room for a state to refuse enforcement of another state's judgment on the ground that it violates the sovereignty of the judgment-enforcing state as long as the judgment satisfies due process.

In *World-Wide Volkswagen Corp. v. Woodson,*[378] the Supreme Court appeared ready to restore some protection for state sovereign interests under the minimum contacts test. On review of an Oklahoma decision, the Court stated that

> [t]he concept of minimum contacts . . . can be seen to perform two related, but distinguishable functions. It protects the defendant against the burdens of litigating in a distant or inconvenient forum. And it acts to ensure that the States through their courts, do not reach out beyond the limits imposed on them by their status as coequal sovereigns in a federal system.[379]

In *World-Wide Volkswagen*, the Court indicated that the sovereignty component of the minimum contacts test was an independent standard that had to be met in addition to a "convenience" or burdens component (based upon a balancing of the interests of the defendant, the plaintiff, the state asserting jurisdiction, and other factors). Thus, the first step in the minimum contacts analysis was to determine whether the state asserting jurisdiction possessed the sovereign power to do so by estimating whether the defendant had engaged in activity that was sufficiently "purposeful."[380]

Two years after *World-Wide Volkswagen*, the Court reversed course and held that the minimum contacts test was not, in fact, designed to perform a sovereignty-protection role. In *Insurance Corp. of Ireland, Ltd. v. Compagnie des Bauxites de Guinee*,[381] the defendant refused to cooperate in discovery proceedings aimed at determining whether the necessary minimum contacts with the state existed to satisfy due process. As a sanction for the defendant's failure to make discovery, the district court imposed a finding under Federal Rule of Civil Procedure 37(b)(2)(A) that minimum contacts existed. The defendant contended that it was impermissible to apply Rule 37(b)(2)(A) to jurisdictional facts because to do so might establish judicial power when such power did not exist in fact.[382]

In rejecting this argument, the Supreme Court distinguished between objections based on subject-matter and personal jurisdiction. The Court described federal subject-matter jurisdiction limits as sovereignty-based separation-of-powers restrictions, but stated that the "personal jurisdiction requirement . . . represents a restriction on judicial power not as a matter of sovereignty, but as a matter of

---

378. 444 U.S. 286, 100 S. Ct. 559, 62 L. Ed. 2d 490 (1980).

379. *Id.* at 291-92, 100 S. Ct. at 564, 62 L. Ed. 2d at 498; *see also id.* at 293, 100 S. Ct. at 565, 62 L. Ed. 2d at 497-98, in which the Court stated that the framers had intended for the states to retain many of the attributes of independent sovereigns and that sovereign limits on the power of state courts was inherent both in the plan of the original Constitution and the Fourteenth Amendment.

380. *See id.* at 293-99, 100 S. Ct. at 565-68, 62 L. Ed. 2d at 498-502.

381. 456 U.S. 694, 102 S. Ct. 2099, 72 L. Ed. 2d 492 (1982).

382. *See id.* at 696-701, 102 S. Ct. at 2101-03, 72 L. Ed. 2d at 497-500; *cf.* Walk Haydel & Assocs., Inc. v. Coastal Power Prod. Co., 517 F.3d 235 (5th Cir. 2008) (when court does not allow discovery on personal jurisdiction issue, plaintiff must make only a prima facie showing of jurisdictional facts, and this burden is satisfied by plaintiff's allegation of jurisdictional facts pleaded in good faith; but when discovery on personal jurisdiction issue is allowed, plaintiff's burden increases, and required prima facie showing must be based on specific record evidence in the form of affidavits and written submissions).

individual liberty."[383] In discussing *World-Wide Volkswagen*, the Supreme Court stated:

> The restriction on state sovereign power described in *World-Wide Volkswagen Corp.* . . . must be seen as ultimately a function of the individual liberty interest preserved by the Due Process Clause. That clause is the only source of the personal jurisdiction requirement and the Clause itself makes no mention of federalism concerns. Furthermore, if the federalism concept operated as an independent restriction on the sovereign power of the court, it would not be possible to waive the personal jurisdiction requirement: Individual actions cannot change the powers of sovereignty, although the individual can subject himself to powers from which he may otherwise be protected.[384]

Thus, as quickly as the Court had brought the state sovereignty function of the minimum contacts test into existence, the Court eliminated it. After *Insurance Corp. of Ireland*, the only components of the minimum contacts test that may function to protect state sovereignty are found in the reasonableness test. The state's interest, the interstate judicial system's interest in the most efficient resolution of controversies, and the shared interests of the several states in furthering fundamental substantive social policy may afford some protection to state sovereign interests. However, these components are, at best, indirect and inefficient standards with which to protect state sovereignty.[385]

The Supreme Court's more recent decision in *J. McIntyre Machinery, Ltd. v. Nicastro*,[386] discussed in section G(2)*(b)(iii)*, above, has technically not undermined the authority of *Insurance Corp. of Ireland.*[387] Although, as discussed above, the plurality opinion attempted to move back toward a sovereignty-based analysis of due process, this view was not adopted by a majority of the court and was explicitly rejected by the three dissenting Justices. For the sake of a rational view of the Due Process Clause as applied to jurisdictional questions, one devoutly hopes the plurality's view does not become law in the future.

A better approach would be for the Supreme Court to recognize directly that protection for state sovereign interests has been undermined radically by the *International Shoe* test. The Court should hold that a judgment which satisfies the Due Process Clause does not, for that reason alone, deserve enforcement in another state. Instead, the states should be able to employ reasonable sovereignty-based jurisdictional restrictions to refuse enforcement to the judgments of other states.

---

383. 456 U.S. at 702, 102 S. Ct. at 2104, 72 L. Ed. 2d at 501.

384. *Id.* at 702-03 n.10, 102 S. Ct. at 2104 n.10, 72 L. Ed. 2d at 501 n.10. Despite the fact that the Supreme Court in *Insurance Corp. of Ireland* withdrew from *World-Wide Volkswagen's* statement about the Due Process Clause being an instrument of interstate federalism, some courts continue to treat the statement as good law. *See, e.g.*, Williams v. Lakeview Co., 199 Ariz. 1, 13 P.3d 280, 285 (2000).

385. *But see* Tracy O. Appleton, Note, *The Line Between Liberty and Union: Exercising Personal Jurisdiction Over Officials From Other States,* 107 COLUM. L. REV. 1944 (2007) (arguing that federalism concerns should be considered under the reasonableness factors of *Burger King*, especially the factor focusing on the "shared interests of the several states in furthering fundamental substantive social policies").

386. 564 U.S. __, 131 S. Ct. 2780, 180 L. Ed. 2d 765 (2011).

387. Professor Borchers has described *J. McIntyre* as "nothing short of a bull-headed attempt to ground personal jurisdiction in a sovereignty theory." *See* Patrick J. Borchers, J. McIntyre Machinery, Goodyear, *and the Incoherence of the Minimum Contacts Test*, 44 CREIGHTON L. REV. 1245, 1263 (2011).

The Court can, as it did prior to the Fourteenth Amendment, supervise the states' administration of sovereignty-based jurisdictional restrictions through the use of its appellate jurisdiction over the state courts. A refusal to enforce a judgment of another state presents a federal question under the full-faith-and-credit implementing statute, even if the refusal is based on the violation of a nonconstitutional sovereignty-based rule. In cases within the appellate jurisdiction on these grounds, the Court has the authority to assure that the reasons given by the state courts are justifiable.[388]

If the Court were to adopt this approach, modern sovereignty-based rules would have to be developed. How often would the states be able to refuse the enforcement of other states' judgments under those rules? Sensible restrictions on the development of modern sovereignty-based rules can readily be envisioned. One restriction should be that a state could never refuse enforcement of another state's judgment on the ground that the judgment was rendered in violation of a nonconstitutional jurisdictional rule if the judgment-enforcing state would itself exercise jurisdiction under the same circumstances. Given the existence of broad long-arm statutes in virtually every state, this restriction alone would prevent wholesale refusals by the states to enforce the judgments of other states.

A second, complementary restriction should be that a state could not refuse enforcement to another state's judgment if the refusal does not accord with generally accepted jurisdictional principles. Thus, even if a state has a very narrow long-arm statute, it could not refuse enforcement to the judgments of other states if the jurisdictional rule on which it relied was not generally accepted throughout the states. This last restriction parallels pre-Fourteenth Amendment practice under the full-faith-and-credit implementing statute, when the international rules used to determine the validity of state judgments were the restrictions on state sovereign power that were generally accepted at the time.

Given the restrictions that would necessarily attend the development and administration of modern sovereignty-based rules of jurisdiction, only one situation is immediately apparent in which the states would justifiably be able to refuse enforcement to other states' judgments. If a state judgment directly affects the title to land located in another state, the situs state should be able to refuse enforcement of the judgment, even if no due process defect exists in the judgment. Even if no practical problems would be created for the situs state or its citizens, the situs state should still be able to refuse enforcement of the judgment. Although no rational basis exists for preventing states from directly affecting the title to land located in other states if no practical problems would be created by the adjudication, the tradition is still strong in the United States that such adjudications infringe the

---

388. *See* Ralph U. Whitten, *The Constitutional Limitations on State-Court Jurisdiction: A Historical-Interpretative Reexamination of the Full Faith and Credit and Due Process Clauses* (pt. 1), 14 CREIGHTON L. REV. 499, 596-99 (1981) (discussing the Court's exercise of appellate jurisdiction in implementing act cases prior to the Fourteenth Amendment and the concept of "jurisdiction of" the common law); *see also* Austen L. Parrish, *Sovereignty, Not Due Process: Personal Jurisdiction Over Nonresident Alien Defendants*, 41 WAKE FOREST L. REV. 1 (2006); Allan Erbsen, *Impersonal Jurisdiction*, 60 EMORY L.J. 1 (2010) (criticizing the modern law of personal jurisdiction as being muddled because not connected to a coherent purpose and arguing for conceptualizing constitutional limits on personal jurisdiction as a manifestation of horizontal federalism).

sovereignty of the situs state.[389] A jurisdictional rule so firmly established in the states constitutes a justifiable basis for refusing enforcement of a judgment. When nonconstitutional sovereignty-based rules are at issue, the states must ultimately be the judges of their own interests.[390]

Illustration 3-29. *P* and *D* are citizens of State *X*. They both claim title to the same plot of land in State *Y*. *P* sues *D* in a state court of State *X* to quiet the title to the land in State *Y*. Although *D* is personally served with process in this action in State *X*, *D* fails to appear and defend the action. The court enters a default judgment quieting the title to the land located in State *Y*. This procedure should not be deemed to violate the Due Process Clause because all necessary protections under that Clause have been afforded to the defendant, *D*.

Illustration 3-30. On the facts of *Illustration 3-29*, if *P* sues on the State *X* judgment in State *Y* to establish title, no apparent practical problems would be created for the situs state or its citizens. The State *Y* court in which the action is brought can investigate any matters that would render the judgment void under State *X* law before enforcing the judgment. Once a State *Y* judgment has been rendered in favor of *P*, that judgment can be recorded in the land records in the county of State *Y* where the land is located. A State *Y* judgment appearing in the land records will not cause any greater practical problems in this kind of case than in a purely domestic land title action in State *Y* in which a judgment is rendered.

Nevertheless, State *Y* should still be able to refuse enforcement to the judgment because of the strong tradition against such judgments in the United States. The tradition gives rise to a legitimate sovereignty-based limitation on State *X's* jurisdiction, even though the rule may make no practical sense. Congress could, under the second sentence of the Full Faith and Credit Clause, require enforcement of judgments of nonsitus states in the described circumstances, or condition the enforcement of such judgments on the presence of jurisdictional prerequisites other than the traditional restriction.[391]

Illustration 3-31. On the facts of *Illustration 3-30*, if *D* appears in the State *X* action and litigates the title issue on the merits, *D* should be foreclosed from raising the issue of jurisdiction in accordance with the ordinary rules governing the raising and foreclosure of jurisdictional issues examined in section B(3), above, and section H(3) and Chapter 13(E), below, as long as the State *X* court applies State *Y* substantive land title law to resolve the dispute. However, if State *X* applies its own substantive title law to resolve the dispute, the State *Y* court should be able to disregard the State *X* judgment, whether or not *D* objected to State *X's* lack of

---

389. *See* section B(1)*(b) infra* ("Restrictive Principles of In Rem Jurisdiction") & section H(3) *infra* ("Property Cases"). As discussed, in the latter section, however, this jurisdictional restriction must be limited by the Supreme Court's holdings on raising and foreclosure of jurisdictional questions.

390. It would, of course, be possible for Congress to require enforcement of such judgments in the situs state under the second sentence of the Full Faith and Credit Clause, given that it has the power to declare the effect that state judgments must be given in other states. Congress could, under the same power, condition the enforcement of state judgments of this sort on the presence of jurisdictional prerequisites in the judgment-rendering state that differ from the traditional restriction. *See Illustration 3-30 infra.*

391. *See* section A(1) *supra* and authorities there cited, especially section A(1)*(e)* discussing the Supreme Court's decision in *D'Arcy v. Ketchum*, which indicated that Congress could have altered or eliminated the traditional rules under the power conferred upon it in the Full Faith and Credit Clause, though it had not done so in the original (1790) implementing statute.

jurisdiction to adjudicate the issue under State *X* law. This result also accords with the Supreme Court's modern decisions on raising and foreclosure of jurisdictional issues.

SECTION H. THE APPLICATION OF THE MINIMUM CONTACTS TEST TO SPECIFIC TYPES OF CASES

Many of the U.S. Supreme Court's decisions applying the minimum contacts test were decided before the *Burger King* decision had established the two-step analysis for specific jurisdiction cases. Nevertheless, these cases remain good authority for determining the due process validity of state-court jurisdiction in specific categories of cases. By examining the situations in which the Court has approved and disapproved of jurisdictional assertions by the states, it will be possible to obtain a better picture of how the minimum contacts test should be applied to future cases. The discussion that follows will describe the results in the categories of cases thus far addressed by the Court and also analyze whether the results are still justified under the *Burger King* test. When pertinent, the discussion will also address whether jurisdiction would be justified under the unified test for jurisdiction recommended in section G(2)*(d)* or the modern sovereignty-based restrictions discussed in section G(3), above.

One word of caution is in order about the following discussion. The discussion assumes in the situations examined that it is appropriate to apply the minimum contacts analysis. It does not address the question whether jurisdiction can be exercised based on one of the traditional territorial rules of *Pennoyer v. Neff*. The possibility that one of the traditional rules will provide a valid basis of jurisdiction must be left open after *Burnham v. Superior Court*, discussed in sections E(2) and G(1), above. Thus, one of the threshold inquiries in every case today must be whether the state is exercising jurisdiction under a "traditional" or "novel" rule. If under a "traditional" rule, the disagreement among the members of the Supreme Court about the proper mode of analysis must be confronted and resolved.

1. Tort Cases

Section C(2), above, discussed the extension of state implied consent statutes beyond corporations to individuals under the doctrine of *Pennoyer v. Neff*. In that section it was observed that the states had asserted jurisdiction over nonresident motorists under statutes implying the consent of the motorists to suit in the state by the act of driving an automobile within the state. These assertions of jurisdiction were upheld by the Supreme Court under the Due Process Clause of the Fourteenth Amendment. Nothing in *International Shoe* or the later evolution of the minimum contacts test casts doubt on the ability of the states to assert jurisdiction in this kind of case today. A person who drives an automobile into another state engages in the kind of purposeful conduct required under *Burger King* to give fair warning that litigation in the state may result if the motorist has an accident there. The motorist should take steps either to protect against the burdens of suit by purchasing insurance or by not driving in the state. Any objective burdens on a nonresident motorist forced to litigate within the state will always be outweighed by the other factors in the reasonableness test, particularly the interest of the state in providing a forum for its injured resident and the interest of the injured plaintiff in litigating within the state. It is, of course, also likely that the state of the accident will often be a convenient place to resolve the dispute because of the location of witnesses and evidence there.

The case of a nonresident motorist sued in the state of the accident must be carefully distinguished from the case in which a defendant is sued based on a claim arising outside the state, as in *Helicopteros Nacionales de Colombia, S.A. v. Hall*, and *Goodyear Dunlop Tires Operations, S.A.*, discussed in section G(2)*(a)*, above. In such cases, if the defendant has no activities within the forum that can be considered "related to" the activities outside the state that gave rise to the claim,[392] the state will be asserting general jurisdiction over the defendant and "systematic and continuous" contacts will be required. If the defendant's contacts with the forum are "related to" the activity giving rise to the claim outside the state, the state will be asserting specific jurisdiction, and the analysis in the preceding paragraph will be applicable.

Illustration 3-32. *D*, a citizen and resident of State *Y*, operates a delivery service. The service delivers packages to customers in States *Y*, *X*, and *Z*. While driving a delivery truck in State *Z*, *D* collided with *P*, a citizen and resident of State *X*. *P* sued *D* in a state court of State *X* to recover damages for personal injuries received in the accident. *D* was served under the State *X* long-arm statute, which extends jurisdiction of the State *X* courts as far as the Due Process Clause permits. *D* specially appears and objects that State *X's* assertion of personal jurisdiction violates the Due Process Clause of the Fourteenth Amendment. If *D's* activities in State *X* are not considered "related to" the activities that gave rise to the claim in State *Z*, State *X's* assertion of jurisdiction is general. Thus, *D's* activities in State *X* must be of a "systematic and continuous" nature for jurisdiction to be valid. If *D's* activities in State *X* are considered "related to" the activities in State *Z* that gave rise to the claim, State *X's* assertion of jurisdiction is specific. Under the latter circumstances, *D's* action in purposefully operating a delivery truck in State *X* should give fair warning to *D* that a suit might result in the state if an accident occurs there. *D* should purchase insurance or take other action to defray the burdens of suit in State *X*. If *D* has taken such action, it will defray the burden of suit on the claim arising in State *Z*. If *D* has not taken action to defray the burdens of suit, *D* should not be excused from jurisdiction on the ground that the burdens of suit are

---

392. *See* section (G)(2)*(b)(i) supra* ("Claims Arising Out of or Related to the Defendant's Contacts with the State"). It must be kept in mind that a threshold inquiry in every case in which a defendant is sued on a claim arising outside the state is whether the defendant is engaging in activities related to the claim within the state. If related activities exist, the case is one of specific jurisdiction, which requires application of the purposeful contacts-reasonableness test analysis of *Burger King*. *See* section (G)(2)*(b)(ii)-(iv) supra*.

heavy in State *X* and the state and plaintiff interests are less than they would be if the accident had actually occurred in State *X*.[393]

* * * * *

In two decisions after *International Shoe*, the Supreme Court sustained exercises of state-court jurisdiction over nonresident defendants in libel actions. In *Keeton v. Hustler Magazine, Inc.*,[394] the Court sustained an exercise of jurisdiction by New Hampshire over a publisher who had committed a nationwide libel. Jurisdiction was proper not only for that part of the claim arising from the distribution of the defendant's magazines in New Hampshire, but also for that part of the claim resulting from distribution in other states.[395] The Court did not use the two-step test for jurisdiction established later in *Burger King*. However, the elements of that test would seem to be satisfied on the facts of *Keeton*. The defendant's actions in distributing magazines in New Hampshire were purposeful and gave clear warning that a suit might result in New Hampshire.[396] In addition, the activities conducted in other states would seem to fit the definition of activities that are "related to" the defendant's contacts with New Hampshire—publication and

---

393. Depending on the facts, the objective burdens of a suit in State *X* may be no greater than the objective burdens of a suit in State *Z*, where the accident occurred. For example, States *X*, *Y*, and *Z* may be adjacent states. It may be as easy for *D* to defend a suit in State *X* as in State *Z*. Under these circumstances, whether the assertion of jurisdiction is general or specific would be irrelevant if the test suggested in section (G)(2)(c) *supra* ("Toward a Unified Test for General and Specific Jurisdiction") is adopted. Under that test, a defendant would never be able to object to an assertion of jurisdiction on due process grounds if the objective burdens of suit are no greater in the forum than they would be in some other state where the defendant could concededly be sued. *But cf.* Felch v. Transportes Lar-Mex SA de CV, 92 F.3d 320 (5th Cir. 1996), in which the plaintiff sued the defendant, a Mexican corporation, in Texas for the wrongful death of the plaintiff's mother in an automobile accident in Mexico. The defendant transports cargo in Mexico to Nuevo Laredo, a city on the Mexican side of the Texas-Mexico border. Normally, the defendant drops the cargo off on the Mexican side and has others deliver the cargo into Texas. Occasionally, but rarely, the defendant delivers the cargo into Texas. Under these circumstances, the Fifth Circuit held that the defendant's contacts with Texas were insufficient to establish either specific or general jurisdiction; *see also* Employers Mut. Cas. Co. v. Bartile Roofs, Inc., 618 F.3d 1153 (10th Cir. 2010) (roofing subcontractor established purposeful contacts with forum necessary for specific jurisdiction by negotiating and entering into work order for construction project and working on project for three years; suit was by insurer seeking declaratory judgment on duty to defend and indemnify subcontractor in suit on construction project); Harlow v. Children's Hosp., 432 F.3d 50 (1st Cir. 2005) (plaintiff sued Massachusetts hospital for negligence in Maine after Massachusetts statute of limitations had run; the court held that (1) Maine could not assert specific jurisdiction over the hospital on the theory that the claim was related to its forum-based contacts; the relatedness requirement necessitates a showing that the defendant's in-state conduct forms an important or at least material element of proof in the plaintiff's case, which is not true in this case; a broad "but for" argument is insufficient because "but for" events can be very remote; in addition, post-tort contacts cannot be taken into account in evaluating specific jurisdiction, only contacts that existed at the time the claim arose because otherwise the fair warning function of the purposeful availment component of the specific jurisdiction test would be undermined; (2) Maine could not assert general jurisdiction over the hospital; in considering general jurisdiction, unrelated contacts that occurred after the cause of action arose can be taken into account in determining whether systematic and continuous contacts exist; however, treating patients from Maine in Massachusetts, even on a regular basis, is not the same as engaging in systematic and continuous activity in Maine; (3) even if hospitals contacts were sufficient to support an assertion of either specific or general jurisdiction, the exercise of jurisdiction here would be unreasonable).

394. 465 U.S. 770, 104 S. Ct. 1473, 79 L. Ed. 2d 790 (1984).

395. Although the Court did not discuss it, this might be a case within the specific jurisdiction category in which the defendant's out-of-state activities could be considered "related to" its in-state activities, with the twist that the in-state activities in the case were also liability producing. *See* section G(2)*(b)(i)*, *Illustration 3-22 supra*.

396. In *Keeton*, the Court stated that Hustler, because of its continuous and deliberate exploitation of the New Hampshire market, and because it could "be charged with knowledge of 'the single publication rule,'" (described in the text *infra*) should reasonably have anticipated being haled into court within the state. *See id.* at 781, 104 S. Ct. at 1481-82, 79 L. Ed. 2d at 801-02. The "continuous and systematic" language makes it appear as if the case was a general jurisdiction case, although it must be remembered that the Court was not applying the current two-step test at the time. *See also* Addison Ins. Co. v. Knight, Hoppe, Kurnik & Knight, L.L.C., 734 N.W.2d 473 (Iowa 2007) (out-of-state law firm's contacts with Iowa in the form of representation of plaintiff in Iowa declaratory judgment action were sufficient to sustain exercise of specific jurisdiction in Iowa in malpractice suit arising out of representation).

distribution of the same libelous article. Consequently, New Hampshire's assertion of jurisdiction is properly classified as specific as to the entire claim, and the first step in the specific jurisdiction analysis is satisfied.

Furthermore, the elements of the reasonableness test would not allow the defendant to defeat jurisdiction on the facts of *Keeton*. Even if the objective burdens of suit are great in New Hampshire, the state had compensatory and deterrent interests in providing a forum for the plaintiff, even though she was a nonresident.[397] In addition, the plaintiff sued under the "single publication rule." This rule allowed recovery for the damages done to the plaintiff nationwide by the libel in a single forum. The interstate judicial system's interests in efficiently resolving the claim for libel in a single action, rather than multiple actions, weighs in favor of the validity of jurisdiction in cases like *Keeton*.[398] Similarly, the shared interests of the several states in furthering fundamental substantive social policy was furthered in *Keeton* by an action in New Hampshire in which damages for the nationwide libel could be recovered.[399]

A second libel case was decided the same day as *Keeton*. In *Calder v. Jones*,[400] Jones commenced a libel action in a California state court against the *National Enquirer*, the California distributor of the *National Enquirer*, Calder (the president and editor of the *Enquirer*), and South (a reporter for the *Enquirer*). The *Enquirer* and the local distributor appeared and answered the complaint, but Calder and South, both residents of Florida, objected to the court's assertion of personal jurisdiction over them. Calder's contacts with California consisted of two trips to California, one for pleasure and one to testify in an unrelated case. As president and editor, Calder supervised all the functions of the *Enquirer*. Calder reviewed and approved the subject of the article about Jones, edited the article in its final form, and declined a request by Jones to print a retraction. South frequently traveled to California on business, but did most, if not all, of the research on the Jones article from Florida by phone. The Court concluded that the relationship between the defendants, the state, and the litigation was sufficient to sustain California's assertion of jurisdiction under the minimum contacts test. Particularly important in *Calder* was the fact that California was the focal point of the allegedly libelous article as well as the location of the harm suffered. For this reason, the Court was easily able to sustain jurisdiction in California because of the effects that the article had caused there.[401] The Court also rejected an argument that special First

---

397. In *Keeton*, the Court concluded that New Hampshire's interest was strong in part because the libel was committed partly within New Hampshire. This fact gave the state deterrent and compensatory interests in awarding damages to protect both the nonresident "subject of the falsehood" and its own citizens who were deceived by the libel. *See* 465 U.S. at 776-77, 104 S. Ct. at 1479, 79 L. Ed. 2d at 799.

398. On the facts of *Keeton*, there could be only one action because the statutes of limitation of all other states had run. However, in this class of cases, the single publication rule clearly affords the possibility of an efficient single-suit recovery that will avoid a multiplicity of suits even when other fora are available.

399. The Court observed that New Hampshire had an interest in cooperating with other states through the single publication rule to provide an efficient forum in which to litigate interstate libel cases. *See id.* at 777-78, 104 S. Ct. at 1480, 79 L. Ed. 2d at 799.

400. 465 U.S. 783, 104 S. Ct. 1482, 79 L. Ed. 2d 804 (1984).

401. *See id.* at 788-89, 104 S. Ct. at 1485, 79 L. Ed. 2d at 810. In one of the more ironic arguments to be made in American jurisprudence, the editor and reporter of the National Enquirer likened themselves to boiler workers who had worked on a boiler in Florida which later exploded in California due to the workers' negligence. Their notion was that while it might be fair to subject the manufacturer of the boiler to jurisdiction in California in such a case, it would not be appropriate to subject the workers to jurisdiction there because of their lack of

Amendment jurisdictional limitations should be placed on libel cases. Because special substantive First Amendment limits were already placed on the ability of a plaintiff to recover in libel cases, the Court felt that any additional jurisdictional limits would be a form of "double counting."[402]

Calder is arguably good authority for asserting jurisdiction in any case in which the defendant commits an intentional wrong against a citizen of the forum state.[403] Thus, *Calder* has been cited as authority for assertions of jurisdiction in trademark infringement actions[404] and antitrust cases,[405] among others.[406] However, some courts have considered even intentional torts committed against a resident of the forum state inadequate to sustain jurisdiction when the facts revealed a more passive relationship between the defendants and the forum than was present in

---

control over the distribution of the boiler and the absence of any benefit to them from its distribution in the state. *See id.* at 789, 104 S. Ct. at 1487, 79 L. Ed. 2d at 812. The Supreme Court rejected this argument. Unlike the hypothetical boiler workers, the editor and reporter were not charged with "untargeted negligence," but rather with an intentional tort whose focal point was California. *See id.* at 789-90, 104 S. Ct. at 1487, 79 L. Ed. 2d at 812-13. *But cf.* Young v. New Haven Advocate, 315 F.3d 256 (4th Cir. 2002) (accessibility of an out-of-state newspaper's website by forum residents does not provide sufficient contacts to sustain an exercise of jurisdiction in a libel action brought by a forum resident based on newspaper stories published outside the forum and available on the paper's website; no manifest intent on the part of defendant to target website activity at the forum); *see also* Dudnikov v. Chalk & Vermillion Fine Arts, Inc., 514 F.3d 1063 (10th Cir. 2008) (*Calder* does not require harmful intentional act to be wrongful as long as it is directed at the state).

402. *See* Calder, 465 U.S. at 790-91, 104 S. Ct. at 1487-88, 79 L. Ed. 2d at 813.

403. *See, e.g.*, Fiore v. Walden, 657 F.3d 838 (9th Cir. 2011) (the court of appeals found the *Calder* test satisfied in an action against a police officer based on a false affidavit of probable cause and false reference of a case for forfeiture proceedings against plaintiffs property that took place in the Atlanta airport in Georgia at a time when the police officer knew the plaintiffs were residents of the forum, Nevada, and would be impacted there by the illegal seizure of their cash); Menken v. Emm, 503 F.3d 1050 (9th Cir. 2007) (in action alleging negligence, wrongful interference with contractual relations, civil extortion, and violation of Arizona statute prohibiting improper recording of documents claiming interest in real property, *Calder* "effects test" supports exercise of specific jurisdiction over out-of-state judgment creditor who wrongfully recorded judgment in Arizona and used judgment to attempt to exact more than was due under judgment); Bickford v. Onslow Mem'l Hosp. Found., Inc., 2004 ME 111, 885 A.2d 1150 (*Calder* and *Keeton* support constitutionality of assertion of long-arm jurisdiction over out-of-state creditor who refused to correct allegedly false statement that it made to credit-reporting agencies; creditor had engaged in exchange with plaintiff about report and, thereafter, was on notice that it was injuring a Maine resident by failing to take steps to correct the statement; Maine's interest in providing forum for its injured resident also emphasized; assertion of jurisdiction was reasonable because of Maine's strong interest coupled with the fact that while it would be inconvenient for creditor to litigate in Maine, it would be more burdensome for plaintiff to prosecute the claim in North Carolina); Horne v. Mobile Area Water & Sewer Sys., 897 So. 2d 972 (Miss. 2004) (Alabama city and board of water commissioners were subject to long-arm jurisdiction in Mississippi consistent with due process because they released water from reservoir in a manner that they knew would flow into the Mississippi River, and the Mississippi property owners claim arose out of the release of the water, which damaged their property in Mississippi).

404. *See* Dakota Indus., Inc. v. Dakota Sportswear, Inc., 946 F.2d 1384 (8th Cir. 1991) (trademark infringement in which defendant's actions were "uniquely" aimed at the forum state).

405. VDI Techs. v. Price, 781 F. Supp. 85 (D.N.H. 1991) (antitrust and unfair competition claims; jurisdiction sustained on authority of *Calder* because New Hampshire was location of injury).

406. *See* Rothstein v. Carriere, 41 F. Supp. 2d 381 (E.D.N.Y. 1999) (jurisdiction appropriate in New York in action for malicious prosecution and intentional infliction of emotional distress against defendant who made false statements outside the forum resulting in a criminal prosecution of the plaintiff outside the forum, because plaintiff was located in the forum at the time of the statements and thus harm was caused there and was a foreseeable consequence of defendant's actions); Lowry v. Owens, 621 So. 2d 1262 (Ala. 1993) (nonresident automobile dealer and salesman fraudulently sold used automobile as new to a resident of the state; dealer advertised extensively in the state and solicited business there, even though sale did not occur in the state). *But see* Bils v. Bils, 200 Ariz. 45, 22 P.3d 38 (2001) (Arizona resident sued his brother, a California resident, and his brother's lawyer, an Oregon resident, in Arizona state court for malicious prosecution, abuse of process, and intentional infliction of emotional distress arising from the probate of the plaintiff's mother's estate in California court; plaintiff had been served twice in Arizona with copies of papers in the California probate proceeding; the court rejected the argument that *Calder* justified an assertion of jurisdiction by Arizona on the theory that the defendants had committed intentional acts that had a harmful effect on the plaintiff in Arizona; court observes that plaintiff was an active participant in the probate proceeding in California, that the defendants did not aim anything at Arizona, and that the only connection Arizona had with the case was that the plaintiff lived there).

Calder.[407] It should also be noted that in *J. McIntyre Machinery v., Ltd. v. Nicastro*,[408] a products liability case discussed below in this subsection and above in section G(2)*(B)(iii)*, the plurality opinion cryptically stated:

> As a general rule, the sovereign's exercise of power requires some act by which the defendant "purposefully avails itself of the privilege of conducting activities within the forum State, thus invoking the benefits and protections of its laws," . . . though in some cases, as with an intentional tort, the defendant might well fall within the State's authority by reason of his attempt to obstruct its laws.[409]

The plurality gave no examples to illustrate the meaning of this statement, and the meaning is not apparent upon significant reflection. It would thus be inappropriate to interpret the statement as undermining the standards established in the Court's preceding intentional tort cases.

Illustration 3-33. *P*, a citizen and resident of State *X*, is a collector of Civil War memorabilia. *P* purchased a rare Confederate battle flag from *C*, a citizen and resident of State *Z*, in State *Z*. Subsequently, *D*, a citizen of State *Y*, asserted that the flag had belonged to *D* and was stolen from *D* at a date long prior to the time that *P* had purchased it from *C*. *D's* assertions were made outside State *X* to a number of collectors attending events on Civil War antiques. However, some collectors in State *X* also learned of the assertions indirectly. *P* contends that the assertions are false and that *D* sold the flag along with a number of other Civil War artifacts to a person unknown, who later sold them to *C*. *P* commences an action against *D* in

---

407. *See* Mobile Anesthesiologists Chi. v. Anesthesia Assocs., P.A., 623 F.3d 440 (7th Cir. 2010) (no specific jurisdiction in Illinois based on mainenance of website in Texas with domain name allegedly similar to Illinois plaintiff's trademark; Texas defendant was not licensed outside Texas, and maintenance of website after receiving cease and desist letter did not establish that defendant expressly aimed its conduct at Illinois); Clemens v. McNamee, 615 F.3d 374 (5th Cir. 2010) (in suit for defamation by former professional baseball player against his trainer, statements made by trainer in New York to media reporter and commission investigating use of performance-enhancing substances by professional baseball players were not aimed or directed at forum state of Texas, so minimum contacts did not exist); Green v. USF & G Corp., 772 F. Supp. 1258 (S.D. Fla. 1991) (slanderous telephone calls from Maryland to Florida not sufficient to justify assertion of jurisdiction under the Due Process Clause); *see also* Michiana Easy Livin' Country, Inc. v. Holten, 168 S.W.3d 777 (Tex. 2005) (*Calder* did not support jurisdiction over the seller of out-of-state recreational vehicle based on theory that it had committed tortious act within the state based on a misrepresentation made in conjunction with sale of vehicle to Texas purchaser; Texas purchaser of vehicle had initiated contact with seller in Indiana, had sent payment to Indiana, had paid for delivery from Indiana, and had agreed to resolve all disputes in Indiana; seller, therefore, had no purposeful contacts with Texas based on either *Calder* or a stream-of-commerce theory). *But see* Collegesource, Inc. v. Academyone, Inc., 653 F.3d 1066 (9th Cir. 2011) (defendant committed intentional acts targeting forum by downloading plaintiff's catalogs and republishing them on its own website knowing that the plaintiff was a resident of the forum); Mavrix Photo, Inc. v. Brand Techns., Inc., 647 F.3d 1218 (9th Cir. 2011) (in copyright infringement case, display of plaintiff's photographs by defendant on passive website sufficient to establish purposeful contacts necessary for specific jurisdiction; where defendant used photos to exploit market in forum for its own purposes, it intentionally targeted forum); Yahoo! Inc. v. La Ligue Contre Le Racisme et L'Antisemitisme, 433 F.3d 1199 (9th Cir. 2006) (the *Calder* case supports specific jurisdiction over defendants who engage in non- wrongful conduct targeted at a plaintiff whose principal place of business is in California; defendants' contacts consisted of sending a cease and desist letter to the plaintiff in California, service of process on the plaintiff in California in a French proceeding, and the impact and potential impact on the plaintiff of a French court's orders in the action brought by the defendant; nevertheless, jurisdiction was not allowed over the French associations that obtained order from French court to block French citizens' access to Nazi material displayed or offered for sale on a United States website); Michelle Feldman, Note, *Putting the Brakes on Libel Tourism: Examining the Effects Test as a Basis for Personal Jurisdiction Under New York's Libel Terrorism Protection Act*, 31 CARDOZO L. REV. 2457 (2010).

408. 546 U.S. __, 131 S. Ct. 2780, 180 L. Ed. 2d 765 (2011).

409. *Id.* at __, 131 S. Ct. at 2787, 180 L. Ed. 2d at 774.

State *X*. *P* seeks damages for slander of *P's* title to the flag. *D* is served with process in State *Y* under the provisions of the State *X* long-arm statute, which extends jurisdiction as far as permitted by the U.S. Constitution.

Calder supports the State *X* assertion of jurisdiction because *D* made the assertions in question knowing of *P's* possession of the flag in State *X* and claims of ownership to it. Thus, *D* could reasonably foresee the impact of the assertions on *P* in State *X*. Nevertheless, *Calder* is distinguishable from this case, in that *D* did not make the assertions in State *X*. Furthermore, the assertions were only indirectly learned of by collectors in State *X*. Thus, *D's* contact with State *X* is less direct and immediate than the contact of the defendants in *Calder* and might be considered too tenuous to satisfy the purposeful contact test. If the foreseeability of the impact on *P's* title in State *X* is sufficient to produce the conclusion that *D* has engaged in purposeful conduct with regard to State *X*, *Keeton* is authority that *P* can sue *D* in State *X* for damages incurred throughout the United States produced by the assertions.[410]

* * * * *

The Supreme Court has dealt with products liability cases three times since *International Shoe*. In all three cases, the Court invalidated state-court assertions of jurisdiction. As discussed in section G(2)*(b)(iii)*, above, the important issue in this kind of case will be whether placing a product into the stream of commerce alone is enough to satisfy the purposeful contacts portion of the due process test, as suggested in *World-Wide Volkswagen Corp. v. Woodson*, or whether stream of commerce activity "plus" other actions by the defendant will be necessary, as suggested by the plurality opinion in *Asahi Metal Industry Co. v. Superior Court*. After *J. McIntyre Machinery, Ltd. v. Nicastro*,[411] one must assume that the "stream of commerce plus" test will be the minimum necessary to satisfy a majority of the Supreme Court that purposeful contacts are present. The two concurring Justices took the position that the injured New Jersey worker might be able to demonstrate activities by the defendant other than selling a single product in the state through a middleman that would justify the exercise of jurisdiction.[412] However, no such

---

410. *See* Fielding v. Hubert Burda Media, Inc., 415 F.3d 419 (5th Cir. 2005) (defendant's circulation of magazines in Texas was insufficient to sustain specific jurisdiction in libel action under *Keeton* because that case requires substantial circulation; furthermore, defendant's circulation of magazines in Texas was insufficient to sustain specific jurisdiction in libel action under *Calder* because that case requires that the subject matter of and sources relied on in the article to be in the forum; here, the focus of the articles was on activities in Germany and Switzerland, with minimal research in Texas; fact that plaintiff resided in Texas was not sufficient to show that effects of articles would be felt there); IMO Indus., Inc. v. Kiekert AG, 155 F.3d 254 (3d Cir. 1998) (intentional tort having impact in forum does not justify assertion of jurisdiction over defendant when tort was not specifically directed at forum); Noonan v. Winston Co., 135 F.3d 85 (1st Cir. 1998) (inadvertent tort committed through an advertisement that included a picture of plaintiff without permission; tort had impact on forum, but was not specifically directed at forum and did not, as a consequence, justify jurisdiction).

411. 564 U.S. __, 131 S. Ct. 2780, 180 L. Ed. 2d 765 (2011).

412. The concurring opinion stated:

> . . . [The plaintiff], who here bears the burden of proving jurisdiction, has shown no specific effort by the British Manufacturer to sell in New Jersey. He has introduced no list of potential New Jersey customers who might, for example, have regularly attended trade shows [in another state to which the defendant sent representatives]. And he has not otherwise shown that the British Manufacturer "purposefully avail[ed] itself of the privilege of conducting activities" within New Jersey, or that it delivered its goods in the stream of commerce "with the expectation that they will be purchased" by New Jersey users. . . .
>
> There may well have been other facts that Mr. Nicastro could have demonstrated in support of jurisdiction. The dissent considers some of those facts. . . . (describing the size and scope of New

activities had actually been demonstrated by the plaintiff on the record in the case. However, clear cases at each extreme exist in which jurisdiction can easily be judged valid or invalid.

Illustration 3-34. *D Corp.* is incorporated and has its principal place of business in State *Y*. *D* manufactures machine tools and sells the tools nationwide through distributors in each of the fifty states. *D* also advertises extensively in trade magazines circulated in each state and by direct mail sent to companies in each state known to be potential purchasers of the kind of machine tools that *D* manufactures. *D* has also established a toll-free number for purchasers of its products to call for technical advice on the operation of its products. For problems that cannot be efficiently addressed over the telephone, *D* has established a practice of sending engineers to the plants of any customers encountering problems with its products. Through the distribution process described above, *D* sells approximately $9,000,000 worth of machine tools each year in State *X*. *C Corp.* is incorporated with its principal place of business in State *X*. *C* purchased a number of machine tools from *D*. One of the machines malfunctioned, seriously injuring *P*, an employee of *C*. *P* sued *D* in a state court of State *X* to recover damages for the personal injuries received in the accident. *D* was served with process under the State *X* long-arm statute, which extends jurisdiction as far as permitted by the U.S. Constitution.

The assertion of jurisdiction would be valid. Even under the "stream of commerce plus" theory of *Asahi*, as it would be applied by the concurring and dissenting Justices in *McIntyre* the defendant has engaged in the kind of purposeful contacts with the forum that justify an assertion of state-court jurisdiction. In addition to placing its products into the stream of commerce, *D* has advertised in the forum state, established regular channels for providing advice to customers in the forum state, and marketed its products through distributors in the forum state who have agreed to serve *D's* sales agents there. These are all actions that *Asahi* indicated would sufficiently indicate a purpose to serve the market encompassed by the forum state.[413] The actions would certainly satisfy the concurring and dissenting Justices in *McIntyre* and would probably even satisfy the Justices in the plurality in that case. In addition, jurisdiction cannot be defeated through use of the reasonableness test, as in *Asahi*. Whatever the burdens on the defendant of a suit in the forum, the state's interest in providing a forum for its injured resident and the plaintiff's interest in suing at home are strong in this case because the plaintiff is suing the defendant directly. The defendant is not, as in *Asahi*, being pulled into the case by the action of another defendant asserting an indemnity claim.

Illustration 3-35. *P*, a citizen and resident of State *X*, is vacationing by automobile in State *Y* when *P* stops at a roadside store operated by *D*, a citizen and resident of State *Y*. *P* purchases a canned soft drink. When the sale is made, *D* knows that *P* is from State *X* and is returning there by automobile. *P* does not immediately open the soft drink, but places it in a cooler and resumes the trip. After returning to State *X*, *P* removes the soft drink from the cooler and drinks it,

---

Jersey's scrap-metal business). But the plaintiff bears the burden of establishing jurisdiction, and here I would take the facts precisely as the New Jersey Supreme Court stated them.

564 U.S. at __, 131 S. Ct. at 2792, 180 L. Ed. 2d at 780.

413. *See Asahi*, 480 U.S. 102, 112, 107 S. Ct. 1026, 1033, 94 L. Ed. 2d 92, 104 (1987).

ingesting a decomposed mouse in the process. *P* sues *D* in a state court of State *X* to recover damages for the injuries received when *P* ingested the mouse. *D* is served with process under the State *X* long-arm statute, which extends as far as the U.S. Constitution permits. The assertion of jurisdiction is invalid because *D* has not engaged in purposeful contact with State *X*. *D's* activities are entirely localized. *D* in no way attempts to serve the market encompassed by State *X*. Even if a simple "stream of commerce" test is ultimately adopted by the Supreme Court, *D* could not be subjected to jurisdiction in State *X*.[414]

* * * * *

In categories of tort actions not directly addressed by the Supreme Court, the state courts and lower federal courts must, of necessity, evaluate particular cases under the tests for general and specific jurisdiction established in the Supreme Court's decisions. Most cases present straightforward problems that can easily be solved by the courts. As the minimum contacts test continues to evolve, however, difficult problems will often be presented about the analysis that is appropriate in different fact situations.

Illustration 3-36. *D*, a physician, is a citizen and resident of State *Y*. *D* owns a clinic that is located in State *Y*. *D's* practice is territorially limited to State *Y*. However, *D* advertises in a newspaper published in State *Y*, but circulated in states adjoining State *Y*, including State *X*. The newspaper advertisements include a toll-free number for prospective patients to call in order to make appointments at *D's* clinic. *P*, a citizen of State *X*, read an advertisement by *D* printed in one of the editions of the newspaper published in State *Y*, but circulated in State *X*. *P* called the toll-free number and made an appointment at *D's* clinic in State *Y*. Subsequently, *D* treated *P* on several occasions at the clinic in State *Y*. *P* contends that this treatment was negligent and caused *P* permanent injuries. *P* sued *D* in a state court of State *X* to recover for the injuries inflicted on *P* by *D's* malpractice. *D* was served with process in this action under the State *X* long-arm statute, which extends jurisdiction as far as permitted under the U.S. Constitution. The claim arose from *D's* activities in State *Y*.

The advertisements in State *X* might be classified as activities "related to" *D's* actions in State *X* giving rise to the claim, but this classification is uncertain. If the advertisements are not "related to" *D's* claim-producing conduct in State *Y*, the case is one of general jurisdiction, which will require "systematic and continuous" contacts between *D* and State *X*. Whether such contacts exist will depend on the extent of the solicitation of patients through advertising that *D* does in State *X*. If *D's* advertising in State *X* is considered "related to" *D's* claim-producing activity in State *Y*, which seems appropriate, the assertion of jurisdiction will be specific. In this event, the solicitation of patients through advertising in State *X* will have to constitute "purposeful contact" with State *X*. If purposeful contacts exist, jurisdiction will only be defeated if the burdens of suit in State *X* outweigh State *X's*

---

414. *See World-Wide Volkswagen*, 444 U.S. 286, 296, 100 S. Ct. 559, 566, 62 L. Ed. 2d 490, 500-01 (1980); *see also* Jennings v. AC Hydraulic A/S, 383 F.3d 546 (7th Cir. 2004) (plaintiff sued manufacturer of floor jack that caused death of plaintiff's husband in Indiana; fact that manufacturer placed product in stream of commerce was not sufficient to satisfy jurisdiction; sales to distributors in Florida, without demonstration of how product got to Indiana, insufficient).

interest in providing a forum for *P*, *P's* interest in suing in State *X*, the interstate judicial system's interest in the most efficient resolution of controversies, and the shared interest of the several states in furthering fundamental substantive social policies. At least one court has viewed this kind of case as involving an assertion of specific jurisdiction by State *X* that is valid under the Due Process Clause.[415]

* * * * *

Mass tort cases arising out of the national or international marketing of a product can produce special jurisdictional problems. Although the Supreme Court has not yet addressed the appropriate due process standards in such cases, at least one U.S. District Court has done so. In the *DES Cases*,[416] Judge Weinstein noted that the due process standards developed by the Supreme Court to control state personal jurisdiction had been developed in cases "almost all of which involved one or a few parties on each side."[417] Accordingly, Judge Weinstein asserted that those standards were inapt for mass tort cases. Judge Weinstein argued that a "territorial nexus" requirement "is arguably least pressing in mass torts [and] the continued reliance on such protections creates significant obstacles to their resolution."[418] Instead, Judge Weinstein substituted a two-step test. In the first step, the court must determine whether the forum state has an "appreciable interest" in the litigation.[419] This inquiry focuses on whether the "litigation raises issues whose resolution would be affected by, or have a probable impact on the vindication of, policies expressed in the substantive, procedural, or remedial laws of the forum."[420] If an "appreciable state interest" is established, the assertion of jurisdiction is "prima facie constitutional." It will be considered valid unless "given the actual circumstances of the case, the defendant is unable to mount a defense in the forum."[421] Evidence bearing on the latter question includes (1) the defendant's available assets; (2) whether the defendant has or is engaged in substantial interstate commerce; (3)

---

415. *See* Sanders v. Hunter, 253 N.J. Super. 666, 602 A.2d 809 (Law Div. 1991). The court clearly viewed the defendant's actions in soliciting patients through advertising within the state as purposeful. This seems correct. The solicitation should have given the defendant fair warning that an action might be brought by a disgruntled patient from another state. However, the effect of advertising in establishing purposeful contacts is currently the subject of controversy in the lower federal and state courts. *Compare* Nowak v. Tak How Invs., Ltd., 94 F.3d 708 (1st Cir. 1996) (business sends representatives to Hong Kong regularly; on one trip an executive negotiates special rates with hotel for business's executives in future; hotel then sends information about special corporate rates and other promotional literature to the business in the forum; based on the information received, one of business's executives makes reservations for himself and wife at hotel; wife killed in drowning accident; contacts of hotel with forum are sufficient to sustain specific jurisdiction over hotel in forum) *with* Lott v. J.W. O'Connor & Co., 991 F. Supp. 785 (N.D. Miss. 1998) (no general jurisdiction in forum over a shopping mall in another state where plaintiff was injured; jurisdictional assertion based on general, untargeted out-of-state advertising reaching consumers in forum) *and* Gardemal v. Westin Hotel Co., 186 F.3d 588 (5th Cir. 1999) (no specific or general jurisdiction in Texas action over corporate manager of beachfront hotel in Mexico in suit to recover damages based on drowning accident at hotel when victim learned of seminar at hotel through promotion by a third party rather than hotel; the hotel did not purposefully direct its activities at Texas nor did it have systematic and continuous contacts with Texas); *see generally* Keith H. Beyler, *Personal Jurisdiction Based on Advertising: The First Amendment and Federal Liberty Issues*, 61 MO. L. REV. 61 (1996). Special problems of jurisdiction based on internet activities are discussed in subsection 7, *infra*.

416. *In re* DES Cases, 789 F. Supp. 552 (E.D.N.Y. 1992).

417. *Id.* at 585.

418. *Id.* at 586.

419. *Id.* at 587.

420. *Id.* "The notion that a forum state ought to have an interest in litigation before asserting jurisdiction over the parties is based on the idea that a state may not impose obligations on nonresidents without a reason." *Id.* at 585.

421. *Id.* at 587.

whether the defendant is being represented by an indemnitor or is sharing the cost of defense with someone else; (4) the comparative hardship the defendant will incur in defending the suit in a different forum; and (5) the comparative hardship to the plaintiff if the action is dismissed.[422] Whether Judge Weinstein's standards can be squared with cases like *Asahi* is doubtful. Whether the Supreme Court will adopt this analysis for mass tort cases, only time will tell. What is clear, in mass torts and elsewhere, is that more workable standards than those yet developed under *International Shoe* are greatly to be desired.

2. Contract Cases

The Supreme Court has decided two significant contract cases under the minimum contacts test since *International Shoe*. One of these, *Burger King Corp. v. Rudzewicz*, was discussed in section G(2)*(b)(ii)* and *(iii)*, above. *Burger King* established the two-step analysis that must now be applied to all cases of specific jurisdiction. The other decision, *McGee v. International Life Insurance Co.*,[423] was one of the early decisions under the minimum contacts test. Taken together, *McGee* and *Burger King* provide general guidance about the kinds of situations in which states may validly assert jurisdiction in contract cases.[424]

In *McGee*, a resident of California purchased an insurance policy from an Arizona insurance corporation in 1944. In 1946, the defendant, a Texas corporation, assumed all of the Arizona company's insurance obligations. The defendant mailed a reinsurance certificate to the California insured, offering to reinsure him in accordance with the policy he held with the Arizona corporation. This offer was accepted. The insured paid premiums on the policy by mailing the premiums from California to Texas until his death in 1950. Other than this contact with California, there was no evidence that either the defendant or the Arizona insurance company had any offices or agents in California or had ever done any other insurance business there. The defendant refused to pay the proceeds of the policy to the beneficiary upon the insured's death, claiming the insured had committed suicide. The beneficiary sued in a California court, asserting jurisdiction under a California statute subjecting foreign insurance companies to suit in California on insurance contracts with residents of California, even though the companies could not be served within the state. A default judgment was ultimately entered against the defendant. The plaintiff sued on the judgment in Texas to enforce it there. The defendant challenged the validity of the judgment on the ground that California's assertion of jurisdiction violated the Due Process Clause of the Fourteenth Amendment.

The U.S. Supreme Court sustained the validity of the California judgment. The Court stated that it was "sufficient for purposes of due process that the suit was

---

422. *Id.*; *see* Scott Fruehwald, *Judge Weinstein on Personal Jurisdiction in Mass Tort Cases: A Critique*, 70 TENN. L REV. 1047 (2003).

423. 355 U.S. 220, 78 S. Ct. 199, 2 L. Ed. 2d 223 (1957).

424. For a comprehensive evaluation of personal jurisdiction in contracts cases, see Martin B. Louis, *Jurisdiction Over Those Who Breach Their Contracts: The Lessons of* Burger King, 72 N.C. L. REV. 55 (1993).

based on a contract which had substantial connection with [California]."[425] The Court emphasized that modern means of transportation and communication made it much less burdensome for a party to defend an action where the party engages in economic activity.[426] The Court also stated that "California [had] a manifest interest in providing effective means of redress for its residents," who "would be at a severe disadvantage if they were forced to follow the insurance company to a distant State in order to hold it legally accountable."[427]

Applying the two-step *Burger King* analysis to the facts of *McGee* produces the conclusion that California's assertion of jurisdiction was proper. The defendant's solicitation of an insurance contract with the plaintiff and acceptance of premiums constitutes purposeful contacts with the state, even if the insurance agreement is the only one ever solicited in the state. For the reasons given by the Court, it would seem impossible to defeat jurisdiction with the reasonableness test. The burdens on the defendant of a suit in California are probably not great and should, in any event, have been taken into account before the defendant entered into business in the state. The state's and plaintiff's interests in maintaining the action in California are strong. Furthermore, it would seem more efficient to resolve the dispute in California than anywhere else, because the witnesses and evidence pertinent to determine whether the insured committed suicide are most likely present there. Finally, if shared interests of the several states in furthering fundamental substantive social policies exist, they must surely focus on assuring that interstate insurance companies meet their obligations to the people that they insure in the state where they insure them.

Given the clear propriety of jurisdiction in *McGee* under the two-step test, it is curious that the Supreme Court cited *McGee* in *Burger King* as an example of a situation in which the reasonableness test might *create* jurisdiction even in the face of less than optimal purposeful contacts between the defendant and the forum state.[428] The citation of *McGee* for this proposition suggests that it was a case in which the defendant did not have "adequate" purposeful contacts with the state, which seems clearly wrong. The better interpretation is that the Court was simply illustrating the kind of state and plaintiff interests that would serve to enhance jurisdiction if purposeful contacts are absent, without meaning to suggest that they were actually absent in *McGee*.

Burger King itself made it clear that an extensive course of negotiations by the defendant with a plaintiff located in the forum state will help establish the kinds of purposeful contacts that are necessary to sustain jurisdiction under the Due Process Clause. In *Burger King*, extensive negotiations led to a contract that was to

---

425. 355 U.S. at 223, 78 S. Ct. at 201, 2 L. Ed. 2d at 226; *see also* Helmer v. Doletskaya, 393 F.3d 201 (D.C. Cir. 2004) (personal jurisdiction proper under District of Columbia long-arm statute and minimum contacts test because contract in case had substantial connection to D.C.; plaintiff and former Russian girlfriend agreed, while visiting plaintiff's home in D.C., that the girlfriend would arrange for the purchase of a Moscow apartment in plaintiff's name and that plaintiff would support her until her career was established, at which time she would repay him, with the support partially consisting of her use of plaintiff's credit cards issued in D.C., the monthly billing statements for which would be sent to him in D.C.).

426. 355 U.S. at 222-23, 78 S. Ct. at 200, 2 L. Ed. 2d at 226.

427. *Id.* at 223, 78 S. Ct. at 201, 2 L. Ed. 2d at 226; *see also* Traveler's Health Ass'n v. Virginia *ex rel.* State Corp. Comm'n, 339 U.S. 643, 648-49, 70 S. Ct. 927, 929-30, 94 L. Ed. 1154, 1161-62 (1950) (dictum).

428. *See Burger King*, 471 U.S at 476, 105 S. Ct. at 2184, 85 L. Ed. 2d at 543.

be performed in part in the forum state and that contained a choice-of-law clause stating that the forum state's law would be applied to resolve disputes under the contract. Taken together, these factors established the kind of fair warning necessary under the Due Process Clause that an action on the contract might be brought in the forum.[429] The Court made it clear that when these kinds of factors are present, the fact that the defendant never entered the forum state will be irrelevant.[430] Furthermore, the reasonableness test could not be used to defeat jurisdiction. The state and plaintiff's interests in maintaining the action in the forum were strong, and the burdens on the defendant could be addressed short of a jurisdictional dismissal through procedural means, such as a change of venue.[431]

Taken together, *McGee* and *Burger King* seem to establish that an assertion of jurisdiction to adjudicate a contract case will always be valid if the defendant has taken an active role in forming a contract to be performed, at least in part, in the forum.[432] In cases in which the defendant is an interstate business, such as an insurance company, it may be sufficient that the company enters into a contract to be performed in the forum without more.[433] For example, in *McGee*, if the plaintiff had purchased the insurance in Texas without a prior solicitation from the defendant, but at the time of contracting the defendant had knowingly undertaken to insure a risk in California and accepted premiums from the plaintiff in that state over a number of years, it would seem that the purposeful contact portion of the

---

429. *See id.* at 478-82, 105 S. Ct. at 2185-87, 85 L. Ed. 2d at 544-47.

430. *See id.* at 476, 105 S. Ct. at 2184, 85 L. Ed. 2d at 543.

431. *See id.* at 482-84, 105 S. Ct. at 2187-88, 85 L. Ed. 2d at 547-48; *see also* Angelou v. African Overseas Union, 33 S.W.3d 269 (Tex. Ct. App. 2000) (sustaining an exercise of specific jurisdiction over Maya Angelou on a claim for breach of a contract based on her failure to appear in Texas to attend an award ceremony and receive an award; court found that the defendant's active participation in forming the contract constituted purposeful contacts with Texas; in addition, the defendant was unable to demonstrate that defending the action in Texas would be unduly burdensome because she admitted that she frequently came to Texas). *But see* Johnson v. Woodcock, 444 F.3d 953 (8th Cir. 2006) (in action for royalties, Minnesota could not exercise specific jurisdiction over defendant based on relationship with plaintiff that resulted in claim for royalties, but that occurred 15 years before, defendant having moved out of the state; Minnesota also could not exercise general jurisdiction over defendant based on correspondence with plaintiff, collaboration with plaintiff during relevant time frame, and publishing relationship with Minnesota company).

432. *See also* Marcus Food Co. v. DiPanfilo, 671 F.3d 1159 (10th Cir. 2011) (assertion of specific jurisdiction in Kansas over Canadian independent sales and purchasing agent was valid in suit for breach of contract, fraud, and breach of fiduciary duty; agent had ongoing ten year relationship with Kansas company that was sufficient to establish minimum contacts).

433. *But cf.* OMI Holdings, Inc. v. Royal Ins. Co. of Can., 149 F.3d 1086 (10th Cir. 1998) (defendant insurers agreed to defend the plaintiff whenever it was sued, but declined to defend action in Kansas on the ground that it was not covered by the policy; after losing in Kansas, plaintiff sued defendants there to recover attorney's fees and costs incurred in defending the suit; court held that the agreement to defend the plaintiff anywhere satisfied the purposeful contacts portion of the specific jurisdiction test, but that the burden of litigating in Kansas made the assertion of jurisdiction unreasonable). In Corporate Waste Alternatives, Inc. v. McLane Cumberland, Inc., 896 So. 2d 410 (Ala. 2004), an Alabama corporation solicited an out-of-state corporation to perform waste management services for the out-of-state corporation outside Alabama. The parties entered into a contract providing for the services and that Alabama law would govern the contract, but the contract did not contain a choice-of-forum clause. After a time, the out-of-state corporation terminated the contract. The Alabama corporation contended that payments were due under the contract that had not been made and sued in Alabama. The Alabama Supreme Court held that the out-of-state corporation was subject to personal jurisdiction in Alabama, which had extended the reach of its long-arm jurisdiction as far as the Constitution permits. The court stated that the out-of-state corporation knew the plaintiff was an Alabama corporation and that any failure to make payments under the contract would create a hardship on the plaintiff. Also, the defendant had entered into an ongoing relationship. Thus, it was foreseeable that the defendant could be haled into court in Alabama. However, given that the relationship was solicited by the plaintiff and all of the services under the contract were to be performed out of state, this case comes very close to the line drawn in *Burger King* between merely forming a contract with an out-of-state citizen and other contracts with more substantial relationships between the defendant and the forum. Indeed , the court may have crossed that line.

minimum contacts test would still be satisfied. Other situations in which the defendant is only tenuously connected with the state will present greater difficulties.

Illustration 3-37. *D Corp.* is a large catalog order business that sells popular electronic products and novelty items to consumers. *D* obtains the names of potential customers by purchasing mailing lists from other catalog companies. It then mails catalogs unsolicited to the potential customers, who are located in all fifty states. *D* is incorporated with its principal place of business in State *Y*. *D* obtains *P's* name as a potential customer from a mailing list. *P* is a citizen and resident of State *X*. *D* mailed a copy of one of its catalogs to *P* in State *X*. *P* subsequently purchased an expensive electronic item from *D* by mail. When the product arrived, it did not function properly. *D* refused to accept a return of the product or to return *P's* money. *P* sued *D* in a state court of State *X* for breach of contract. *D* was served under the State *X* long-arm statute, which extends jurisdiction as far as permitted by the U.S. Constitution. State *X* should be able to assert jurisdiction over *D* in the breach of contract action. *D's* action in mailing the catalog to *P* and shipping goods to *P* in State *X* was purposeful contact of the sort sufficient under *McGee* and *Burger King* to establish jurisdiction over *D*. Even if the burdens of litigating in State *X* are substantial, the state and plaintiff's interests are strong in maintaining the action in State *X* to protect consumers in *P's* position, and the shared interests of the several states in furthering fundamental substantive social policy are arguably implicated by the need to provide consumers throughout the states with protection from mail order products that turn out not to be as advertised. The fact that the defendant has no sales representatives in the state and maintains no sales outlets in the state is irrelevant.[434]

Illustration 3-38. Assume the facts of *Illustration 3-37*, except that after *D* extends credit to *P* and ships the product to *P* in State *X*, *P* refuses to pay for it. *D* sues *P* in a state court of State *Y* to recover the purchase price of the product. *P* is served under the State *Y* long-arm statute, which extends jurisdiction as far as permitted by the U.S. Constitution. State *Y's* assertion of jurisdiction should be considered invalid. Even if *P's* action in ordering the product from *D* in State *Y* and agreeing to pay *D* for the product there is purposeful contact of the sort necessary to satisfy the first step in the minimum contacts analysis, the reasonableness test

---

434. *See* Quill Corp. v. North Dakota *ex rel.* Heitkamp, 504 U.S. 298, 112 S. Ct. 1904, 119 L. Ed. 2d 91 (1992), discussed in subsection 6 *infra* ("State Tax Cases"); *see also* Leventhal v. Harrelson, 723 So. 2d 566 (Ala. 1998) (plaintiffs, Alabama citizens, were trustees of a pension plan who sued a Georgia resident who had influenced their decision to invest in a limited partnership in investment property in Georgia; plaintiffs traveled to Georgia to discuss the investment with defendant; defendant's partner recommended the investment to the plaintiffs, and defendant sent a letter agreement to Alabama to dispel misgivings the plaintiffs had about the investment, but never entered Alabama; jurisdiction in Alabama upheld); Spectrum Pool Prods., Inc. v. MW Golden, Inc., 1998 MT 283, 291 Mont. 439, 968 P.2d 728 (contract negotiated by phone between Colorado swimming pool installation contractor and Montana swimming pool component manufacturer for Montana party to provide component for pool in Colorado; all contacts and correspondence initiated by Colorado party; contract provided for manufacture of component in Montana, shipping to Colorado, and, later, repair of product in Montana; when full payment was not made, Montana party sued Colorado party in Montana; defendant's contacts with Montana held to be purposeful and jurisdiction upheld); *cf.* Breckenridge Pharm., Inc. v. Metabolite Labs., Inc., 444 F.3d 1356 (Fed. Cir. 2006) (jurisdiction existed over Rule 19 party under provision of Florida long-arm statute authorizing jurisdiction over a party who causes injury to persons or property within state by an act or omission outside state and who is on or about the date of the injury engaged in solicitation or service in state; specific jurisdiction existed over party in action for patent holder because the holder established a relationship with its exclusive licensee in state that was sufficient under *Burger King* in action for declaratory judgment of non-infringement).

should defeat jurisdiction in this case. The burdens of litigating in State *Y* will be substantial for *P*, and the countervailing interests are not strong. *D* can protect itself by requiring credit card payment at the time the order is placed or by arranging for c.o.d. payment. Given the means available to *D* to structure its business in a way as to protect itself in case of disputes with its customers, *D* should not be allowed to sue *P* in State *Y*.

3. Property Cases

The Supreme Court's position on jurisdiction to adjudicate property cases is derived from *Shaffer v. Heitner*, discussed in section E(1), above. *Shaffer* made it clear that the presence of property within the state could not be used as the basis for adjudicating a claim having nothing to do with the property. However, the Court also made it clear that the states have power consistent with the Due Process Clause to adjudicate disputes over the ownership of property located in the state. As indicated in the discussion of *Abernathy v. Abernathy* in section E(1), above, questions still exist about the power of the states to adjudicate claims to property brought into the state without the consent of the property's owner.[435] Another important issue remaining open under the Court's decisions is whether a state will have jurisdiction under the Due Process Clause to directly affect the title to land located in another state. The resolution of this issue may depend on how the dispute between different minorities of the Court in *Burnham v. Superior Court*, discussed in section E(2), above, is resolved. If Justice Scalia's view of the Due Process Clause prevails, and if the restriction on state jurisdiction to affect the title to land located elsewhere is classified as a traditional rule, only the situs state will be able to deal directly with the title to land. To this it may be added that if the view of the plurality opinion in *J. McIntyre Machinery, Ltd. v. Nicastro*,[436] discussed in sections G(2)*(b)* and H(1), above, ever commands a majority of the Supreme Court, the sovereignty-based views of personal jurisdiction expressed there may well reinforce the impulse to reaffirm the traditional restriction on the ability of a non-situs state to deal directly with the title to land. If Justice Brennan's view prevails, the minimum contacts test will be applied to determine the validity of a state's assertion of jurisdiction to adjudicate title to land located elsewhere. This issue has been adequately discussed elsewhere and need not be treated further here.[437]

If the restrictive principles of in rem jurisdiction persist, either as due process, full faith and credit, or common-law sovereignty restrictions, they should be subject to the ordinary rules developed by the U.S. Supreme Court to govern raising and foreclosure of jurisdictional issues. Recall from section B(1)*(b)*, above, that the Supreme Court has characterized these principles as subject-matter jurisdiction restrictions.[438] Nevertheless, it is clear from the Court's decisions that even subject-matter jurisdiction limitations can be foreclosed from consideration

---

435. *See* section E(1) *supra* ("Quasi In Rem and Related Jurisdictional Doctrines").
436. 564 U.S. __, 131 S. Ct. 2780, 180 L. Ed. 2d 765 (2011).
437. *See* section G(1) *supra* ("Cases to Which the Minimum Contacts Test Applies").
438. *See* section B(1)*(b)* *supra* ("Restrictive Principles of In Rem Jurisdiction").

if they are raised and determined against the losing party in an initial proceeding, and even if they are not raised at all in a fully litigated action. In *Durfee v. Duke*,[439] the defendant in a Nebraska state action fully litigated the issue of whether land claimed by the defendant was located in Nebraska or Missouri. The Nebraska courts determined that the land was located in Nebraska, and the defendant lost. Subsequently, the defendant in the Nebraska proceeding commenced an action in Missouri to quiet title to the same land. The U.S. Supreme Court held that, despite the fact that Nebraska only had power to determine the merits of an action if it had subject-matter jurisdiction over the land, the question of subject-matter jurisdiction itself was foreclosed by prior litigation of the issue in Nebraska. In *Chicot County Drainage District v. Baxter State Bank*,[440] the Court had previously held that an issue of subject-matter jurisdiction could be foreclosed if not raised in a fully litigated action.[441] Taken together, these decisions should preclude relitigation of subject-matter jurisdiction issues concerning the power of courts over extrastate land that have been fully and fairly litigated in an initial action. They should also preclude, in most cases, litigation of subject-matter jurisdiction issues concerning the power of courts over extrastate land when those issues are not raised in an initial action that is otherwise fully litigated on the merits.[442]

Unfortunately, not all courts have recognized the significance for land cases of the Supreme Court's modern decisions on foreclosure of subject-matter jurisdiction issues. For example, in the case of *In re Estate of Hannan*,[443] a Virginia domiciliary died leaving as part of her residual estate land located in Nebraska, which she devised to her surviving children and the "issue" of her children per stirpes. The decedent's will was probated in Virginia. The Virginia Supreme Court held that under Virginia law the word "issue" did not include adopted children. In an ancillary probate proceeding in Nebraska, the adopted child of one of the decedent's deceased children attempted successfully to relitigate the question whether "issue" included adopted children under Nebraska law. Ultimately, the Nebraska Supreme Court applied Nebraska law to this question and held that the word "issue" included adopted children. The court did not discuss the effect of the judgment in the Virginia probate proceeding, in which the adopted child had participated, noting simply that Nebraska followed the conflict-of-law rule that the law of the state where real property is located governs devises of such property by will.[444] However, the Nebraska Court of Appeals had discussed the effect of the

---

439. 375 U.S. 106, 84 S. Ct. 242, 11 L. Ed. 2d 186 (1963).

440. 308 U.S. 371, 60 S. Ct. 317, 84 L. Ed 329 (1940). *Chicot*, however, did not involve a question of jurisdiction over land.

441. Foreclosure of subject-matter jurisdiction questions in fully litigated proceedings should be distinguished from foreclosure of such issues in cases in which the defendant defaults. In Thompson v. Whitman, 85 U.S. (18 Wall.) 457, 21 L. Ed. 897 (1874), the Court allowed an issue of subject-matter jurisdiction to be raised in a subsequent action when the defendant had not appeared in the first proceeding.

442. Foreclosure of subject-matter jurisdiction and personal jurisdiction by the doctrines of claim and issue preclusion are discussed fully in Chapter 13(E) *infra*. While the same rules of preclusion normally apply to both personal and subject-matter jurisdiction questions, there are some exceptions to preclusion in the case of subject-matter jurisdiction questions. *See* RESTATEMENT (SECOND) OF JUDGMENTS § 12 (1982).

443. 246 Neb. 828, 523 N.W.2d 672 (1994).

444. *Id.* at 831, 523 N.W.2d at 674.

Virginia proceeding.[445] Relying on the old U.S. Supreme Court decision of *Clarke v. Clarke*,[446] the Nebraska Court of Appeals held that the Virginia courts did not have jurisdiction to control the devolution of real property located in another state.[447] Therefore, the Virginia probate judgment was not entitled to full faith and credit in Nebraska.

Standing alone, the *Clarke* decision would indeed support denial of full faith and credit to the Virginia judgment in *Hannan*. In *Clarke*, the South Carolina courts, in a litigated proceeding, held that a will had worked an "equitable conversion" of real property located in Connecticut into personal property. This conversion allowed the courts to determine how the property should pass under the will because it was no longer realty; instead it was personalty over which the courts in the decedent's domicile had "jurisdiction."[448] In a subsequent proceeding in Connecticut, the South Carolina judgment was denied full faith and credit. The U.S. Supreme Court affirmed. The Court held that the South Carolina courts did not have subject-matter jurisdiction over the Connecticut land. Thus, *Clarke* parallels in many respects the facts of *Hannan*. The difficulty is that the holding of *Clarke* has arguably been modified by the Court's later decisions in *Durfee* and *Chicot County*, discussed above. If a question concerning the title to land is fully litigated on the merits in a nonsitus forum without anyone raising the question of the forum's subject-matter jurisdiction, it is difficult to see why the situs state should be permitted to deny effect to the nonsitus state's judgment. Similarly, if an issue of subject-matter jurisdiction is actually litigated and determined in the nonsitus state, there is no apparent reason why relitigation of the issue should be permitted, at least in the absence of a gross disregard of the interests of the situs.[449] In both instances, the policies supporting finality in litigation support foreclosure of the jurisdictional issue, as well as issues concerning the merits.[450]

---

445. *See In re* Estate of Hannan, 2 Neb. App. 636, 513 N.W.2d 339, *rev'd*, 246 Neb. 828, 523 N.W.2d 672 (1994).

446. 178 U.S. 186, 20 S. Ct. 873, 44 L. Ed. 1028 (1900).

447. 2 Neb. App. at 642, 513 N.W.2d at 344.

448. *See* ROBERT L. FELIX & RALPH U. WHITTEN, AMERICAN CONFLICTS LAW § 44, at 160-63 (6th ed. 2011) (discussing *Clarke*); *id.* § 140, at 468-70 (discussing conflict-of-law issues with equitable conversion).

449. *But see id.* § 44, at 163 (arguing that it would be more in accord with precedent *not* to foreclose the issue on collateral attack when it is not raised in the non-situs state). In practice, an exception exists to issue preclusion on questions of subject-matter jurisdiction when "[t]he subject-matter of the action was so plainly beyond the court's jurisdiction that . . . entertaining the action was a manifest abuse of authority." RESTATEMENT (SECOND) OF JUDGMENTS § 12(1) (1982). Thus, one might draw a distinction between cases like *Durfee*, which involved questions of fact concerning the physical location of land, and cases like *Clarke* and *Hannan*, which involved conceded applications of the non-situs state's substantive law to determine a question involving devolution of land elsewhere. The difficulty is that, while there are cases in which it is so clear that the situs states' substantive law should be applied to a title question that failure to do so might constitute "manifest abuse of authority," of which *Clarke* may be one, *Hannan* does not seem to involve such a situation. Indeed, in *Hannan*, the Nebraska Court of Appeals held that, in determining the intent of a nonresident testator as to a term in a will, Nebraska should follow the law of the testator's domicile as to devises of both real and personal property and that it did not violate Nebraska's public policy to do so in the case. *See Hannan*, 2 Neb. App. at 644-49, 513 N.W.2d at 345-47; *see also* Chapter 13(E) *infra* ("Claim and Issue Preclusion on Questions of Subject-Matter and Personal Jurisdiction"); *cf. Illustrations 3-29* to *3-31* in section G(3) *supra*. It is also relevant that Nebraska follows the "most significant contacts analysis" of the RESTATEMENT (SECOND) OF CONFLICT OF LAWS (1971). Under the *Restatement (Second)'s* scheme, it is permissible to place a choice-of-law clause in a will designating the state whose rules of construction are to be applied to the will, even as to issues concerning real property. *See id.* § 240. Under these circumstances, it is difficult to see how it is justifiable to classify this type of question as beyond the subject-matter competence of a court of another state and thus falling within the land title jurisdictional restriction, even if that restriction is still good law.

450. *See* Chapter 13 ("Finality in Litigation").

In general, the *Shaffer* decision controls the jurisdiction of the states to adjudicate disputes in which either real or personal property is involved. *Shaffer* itself involved the seizure of personal property in an attempt to obtain jurisdiction to adjudicate a dispute having nothing to do with the property. However, there is one major difference between jurisdiction over personal and real property. Even assuming that there are constitutional restrictions on the power of states to adjudicate disputes involving the title to land located in other states, there have never been comparable restrictions on the power to adjudicate the title to personalty located elsewhere. Similarly, there are no sufficient sovereign interests to justify a refusal to enforce the judgment of another state's courts adjudicating the title to personalty in which the judgment-enforcing state has an interest. Therefore, if a state can acquire jurisdiction over the defendant under conventional standards, the state will be able to adjudicate an action validly even though it involves the title to personalty located elsewhere.

Illustration 3-39. *P*, a citizen and resident of State *X*, claims ownership of a valuable painting in the possession of *D*, a citizen and resident of State *Y*. *D* also claims ownership of the painting. *D* is temporarily present in State *X* when *P* has *D* personally served with process in an action in a State *X* court for a declaratory judgment that *P* is the true owner of the painting. Assuming that the personal service on *D* is valid under the *Burnham* decision discussed in section E(2), above, or that jurisdiction can validly be asserted against *D* under the minimum contacts test, State *X* may enter a valid judgment determining the ownership of the painting, even though the painting is located in State *Y*. If the judgment determines that *P* owns the painting, a State *Y* court will be obligated to enforce the judgment under the implementing statute to the Full Faith and Credit Clause.[451]

4. Trust and Estate Cases

The U.S. Supreme Court has adjudicated two cases involving trust assets. In *Hanson v. Denckla*,[452] discussed in section G(2)*(b)(iii)* above, the Court held that a state had no authority to adjudicate the interests of nonresidents in trust assets located in another state when the nonresidents did not have minimum contacts with the state. *Hanson* was based on the absence of purposeful contacts between the defendants and the forum state. The defendants were essentially passive with regard to the forum and could not have anticipated and defrayed the burdens of a suit there. Furthermore, there was an alternate forum where the action could be conveniently adjudicated against all parties.

The other trust case was *Mullane v. Central Hanover Bank & Trust Co.*[453] In *Mullane*, New York enacted "common trust fund" legislation, which permitted numerous small trust estates to be pooled into a single fund for purposes of

---

451. Of course, if other claimants to the painting are "indispensable parties" to the action and are not subject to the jurisdiction of the court, the action might not be maintainable for that reason. *See* Chapter 8(C)(3) *infra* ("Joinder of Persons Needed for Just Adjudication").

452. 357 U.S. 235, 78 S. Ct. 1228, 2 L. Ed. 2d 1283 (1958).

453. 339 U.S. 306, 70 S. Ct. 652, 94 L. Ed. 865 (1950).

investment administration. Provisions were made for accountings twelve to fifteen months after a bank had established such a fund and triennially thereafter. In such accounting proceedings, the judicial decree was made binding and conclusive upon all persons having any interest in the common fund or any participating estate, trust, or fund. Central Hanover Bank & Trust established such a common trust fund in January1946. In March 1947, the bank petitioned the New York Surrogate's Court for settlement of its first account as common trustee. In this accounting proceeding, the power of the state of New York to adjudicate as to nonresident beneficiaries of the trust was raised. The argument was made that the New York court did not have power to adjudicate the interests of nonresident beneficiaries without personal service of process on them within the state. The authority for this argument was, of course, *Pennoyer v. Neff.*[454] The U.S. Supreme Court stated that whether the proceedings were classified by the New York court as in rem or in personam, the state had the power to adjudicate the interests of the nonresidents due to its strong interests in providing means to close trusts that are established under its laws and are administered under the supervision of its courts.[455]

Mullane was decided prior to *Shaffer v. Heitner* and *Burger King Corp. v. Rudzewicz*, at a time when the minimum contacts test was still maturing. Therefore, with the exception of the Court's emphasis on the state's interest, *Mullane* did not apply any element of the modern two-step minimum contacts analysis. However, the modern analysis also supports the result in *Mullane*. *Shaffer* confirmed that a state has power to adjudicate claims to property located within the state. Therefore, the location of the trust assets in New York provides ample basis for New York to assert jurisdiction over nonresident beneficiaries of the trust.

In addition, the nonresident beneficiaries' claims to the trust assets present a case of specific jurisdiction. Under a specific jurisdiction analysis, the possibility of litigation in the state to supervise the administration of the trust was foreseeable to the party investing in the common trust. However, the original investors in the common trust would not always, or even often, have been the beneficiaries of the trust whose interests were being affected by the adjudication. It may be, therefore, that the beneficiaries of the trust would not have been in a position to foresee and, therefore, to protect themselves from the burdens of litigation in New York. Nevertheless, even if the beneficiaries could do nothing to defray the burdens of suit within the state, it would seem that New York was the most convenient location in which an action for an accounting by the trustee might be brought, thus enhancing the case for personal jurisdiction under the *Burger King* reasonableness test.

The Court in *Mullane* emphasized the strong state interest in supervising trusts established under its laws. In addition, no other state could probably assert jurisdiction over all the nonresident beneficiaries, thus creating strong plaintiff's interests in a suit in New York because of the absence of a convenient alternative forum. The prevention of multiple suits in different states also creates an interest on the part of the interstate judicial system in having the action adjudicated in New York. Furthermore, New York had established a procedure in which a representa-

---

454. *See id.* at 311-12, 70 S. Ct. at 655-56, 94 L. Ed. at 871-72.
455. *Id.* at 313, 70 S. Ct. at 656, 94 L. Ed. at 872.

tive was appointed to safeguard the interests of the nonresident beneficiaries of the trust. Finally, it would seem that states share a substantive interest in establishing procedures whereby trustees will be required to account for their management of trust assets. The state where the trust is established and the assets are managed would seem to be the most logical place to conduct such an accounting.[456]

Hanson and *Mullane* taken together may indicate a preference by the Supreme Court for an action in the state where the trust is established and the assets are located, if a single action in that state is feasible between the contestants. However, it is also arguable that *Hanson* was wrongly decided under the modern due process analysis. In *Hanson*, Florida asserted jurisdiction over the nonresident defendants in a proceeding to probate the will of a deceased domiciliary of the state. The state where a decedent is domiciled at death certainly has an interest in probating the will and disposing of the estate's assets in an efficient manner. Furthermore, Florida seems as logical a forum to settle all claims pertaining to the decedent's assets as Delaware. It was no more inconvenient for the Delaware parties to litigate in Florida than it was for the Florida parties to litigate in Delaware.

Under the Court's holding in *Hanson*, it will be necessary for an executor or administrator of an estate to bring ancillary proceedings in every state where personal property of the decedent is located when residents of the situs state assert claims to the property and lack purposeful contacts with the state where the probate proceeding is being conducted. Separate proceedings will result in the possibility of conflicting holdings on matters of fact and applicable law that may impede the process of administration.[457] It seems no more necessary or desirable to require multiple proceedings to protect nonresident beneficiaries of an estate than it would be to insist on separate accounting proceedings in each state where the beneficiary of a trust is located. Given these problems with *Hanson*, it would seem desirable to limit the holding of the case as much as possible.

Illustration 3-40. *R*, a citizen and resident of State *X*, is the representative of the employees of certain motion picture and record companies. *R* sues *T*, a citizen and resident of State *Y*. *T* is the trustee of a trust established to receive payment of certain royalties from the employers of the employees that *R* represents. The action is brought in a state court of State *X*. The action seeks to invalidate collective bargaining and related trust agreements between the employers and the employee's union. The allegation is that the union violated its duty as the employee's collective bargaining agent by agreeing with the employers that the royalty payments should be paid into the trust rather than to the employees as wages. *R* seeks a declaratory judgment of the invalidity of the agreement, the appointment of a receiver to collect future royalty payments, and preliminary injunctive relief against payment of further royalties to the trust by the employers. In *Atkinson v. Superior Court*,[458] jurisdiction was sustained over the nonresident trustee in an action of this sort after

---

456. *Mullane* is also a possible example of a case in which, even if ordinary due process standards are not satisfied, the doctrine of "jurisdiction by necessity" may allow a state such as New York to assert jurisdiction. *See* section I *infra* ("Jurisdiction by Necessity").

457. *See, e.g.*, *In re* Estate of Crichton, 20 N.Y.2d 124, 228 N.E.2d 799, 281 N.Y.S.2d 811 (1967).

458. 49 Cal. 2d 338, 316 P.2d 960 (1957).

Hanson was decided, and the U.S. Supreme Court denied certiorari to review the state court decision.

Hanson and *Atkinson* can be distinguished on several grounds. First, the trustee in *Atkinson* had established a continuing relationship with nonresidents in which the assets of the trust were constantly being enhanced by payments from out of state. In contrast, *Hanson* involved a continuing relationship in which the corpus of the trust was not being enhanced by the settlor, but the Delaware trustee was instead paying amounts to the settlor from time to time in Florida. Second, the nonresident trustee in *Atkinson* established a relationship with residents of a state who remained residents of the same state. That state turned out to be the forum. In *Hanson*, the settlor of the trust was a resident of Pennsylvania when she established the trust and later moved to Florida. Thus, the trustee in *Atkinson* could anticipate litigation in the state where the employees lived at the time the trust was formed, while the trustee in *Hanson* could not anticipate litigation in Florida when the trust was formed. Finally, the action in *Atkinson* sought in part to prevent the future transfer of assets out of the forum to the trustee. Surely the forum had jurisdiction to grant this relief based on the presence of the property (wages) in the state. Under these circumstances, combining the other relief against the trustee with this relief against the employers seems to be an efficient and convenient litigation package.

5. Domestic Relations Cases

As discussed in section E(1), above, *Shaffer v. Heitner* preserved ex parte interstate divorce jurisdiction from attack under the minimum contacts test. However, the Supreme Court did not explain how the ex parte divorce cases could be justified under the test. A possible explanation, also offered in section E(1), is that in a no fault divorce action, the defendant has no substantive rights that the Due Process Clause can effectively protect through the imposition of location-of-suit rules. However, it must be remembered that this rationale applies only to claims for divorce. Under the concept of "divisible divorce," a nonresident spouse's rights to support and alimony cannot be cut off without minimum contacts between the defendant and the forum.[459] Since *Shaffer*, the Supreme Court has decided only two domestic relations cases under the minimum contacts test: *Kulko v. Superior Court*[460] and *Burnham v. Superior Court*.[461] These cases illustrate the operation of the test in domestic relations cases well.

---

459. *See* Vanderbilt v. Vanderbilt, 354 U.S. 416, 77 S. Ct. 1360, 1 L. Ed. 2d 1456 (1957); Estin v. Estin, 334 U.S. 541, 68 S. Ct. 1213, 92 L. Ed. 1561 (1948); RUSSELL J. WEINTRAUB, COMMENTARY ON THE CONFLICT OF LAWS § 5.2E2 (6th ed. 2010); *see also* Von Schack v. Von Schack, 2006 ME 30, 893 A.2d 1004 (minimum contacts test does not apply to divorce jurisdiction; because Maine has a unique interest in assuring that its citizens are not compelled to remain in such personal relationships involuntarily and because no personal or real property interests would be determined in the proceeding, Maine courts have jurisdiction to enter a divorce judgment without personal jurisdiction over the defendant as long as the due process requirements of notice of the action have been complied with).

460. 436 U.S. 84, 98 S. Ct. 1690, 56 L. Ed. 2d 132 (1978).

461. 495 U.S. 604, 110 S. Ct. 2105, 109 L. Ed. 2d 631 (1990).

In *Kulko v. Superior Court*,[462] the Court invalidated an assertion of personal jurisdiction by California over a nonresident father who was sued for increased child support. The jurisdictional assertion was defective because of the absence of purposeful contact between the father and California. The fact that the father, who had custody of the children in New York, allowed them to go to California to live permanently with their mother was not sufficient to establish purposeful contacts with the forum.[463]

In *Burnham v. Superior Court*,[464] discussed in section E(2), above, the Court sustained an assertion of jurisdiction by California over a nonresident husband-father for divorce, custody, and alimony. Jurisdiction was sustained on the basis that the husband-father was personally served within the state while temporarily present there. This "transient presence" jurisdiction was obviously not relevant to the ability of the plaintiff-wife to obtain a divorce, which could have been granted ex parte on the basis of *Shaffer*. Rather, the jurisdictional assertion enabled California to make support and alimony awards that would not otherwise have been possible in the absence of minimum contacts between the husband-father and the state.

In *Burnham*, the plaintiff did not attempt to obtain jurisdiction over the defendant under the California long-arm statute. An obvious obstacle to asserting jurisdiction over the defendant under a long-arm statute was *Kulko*. However, it is interesting to consider whether the facts in *Kulko* and *Burnham* are sufficiently distinguishable to allow a valid assertion of jurisdiction under the minimum contacts test in the latter case. In *Burnham*, the couple was residing in New Jersey at the time of their separation. They agreed that the wife would take the two

---

462. 436 U.S. 84, 98 S. Ct. 1690, 56 L. Ed. 2d 132 (1978).

463. In *Kulko*, a married couple domiciled in New York decided to divorce. The couple entered into a separation agreement which provided that the couple's two children would reside with the husband in New York during the school year, but would spend Christmas, Easter, and summer vacations with the wife. The wife waived any claim for her own support, but the agreement provided that the husband was to pay $3,000 per year in child support for the periods that the children resided with the wife. The wife then obtained a Haitian divorce that incorporated the terms of the separation agreement. Subsequently, each of the children expressed a desire to live permanently with the wife in California, and the husband permitted them to do so. After the children had taken up residence in California, the wife instituted a California proceeding to establish the Haitian divorce as a California judgment, to modify the judgment to award her permanent custody of the children, and to increase the support obligations of the father. The husband was served with long-arm process in this action under the general California long-arm statute, providing that the state's courts could exercise jurisdiction on any basis not inconsistent with the Constitution. The husband specially appeared to challenge the jurisdiction of the California courts over him under the Due Process Clause. The California courts held that due process was not violated by the state's assertion of jurisdiction. The California Supreme Court concluded that jurisdiction was proper because the husband had caused an "effect" in California by purposely sending at least one of the children to live with the wife. *See id.* at 86-90, 98 S. Ct. at 1694-95, 56 L. Ed. 2d at 138-40. The U.S. Supreme Court reversed the California judgment. The Court held that the mere act of sending a child to live with his or her mother did not demonstrate an intent to obtain nor an expectancy of receiving a corresponding benefit from the state that would make it fair to assert jurisdiction over the husband. *See id.* at 92-94, 98 S. Ct. at 1696-98, 56 L. Ed. 2d at 141-43. After determining that there was no "purposeful act" by the defendant that would sustain an exercise of jurisdiction by California, the Court weighed California's interest in adjudicating the action in its courts against the burdens that would be imposed on the husband by litigation in California and concluded under this balancing process that California was not a fair forum. *See id.* at 92-97, 98-101, 98 S. Ct. at 1696-99, 1700-01, 56 L. Ed. 2d at 141-45, 145-47. This two-step process resembles the analysis established in *Burger King*. Under *Burger King*, the absence of purposeful contacts will defeat jurisdiction, unless the reasonableness test can be used to enhance the case for jurisdiction. As discussed in subsection G(2)*(b)(iv) supra* ("The Reasonableness Test"), the factor in the reasonableness test that appears to be most important in enhancing the case for jurisdiction is the state's interest in adjudicating the action in its courts. Assuming that *Kulko* was anticipating the *Burger King* decision, therefore, *Kulko* can be read as a case in which the state's interest was inadequate to overcome the absence of purposeful contacts.

464. 495 U.S. 604, 110 S. Ct. 2105, 109 L. Ed. 2d 631 (1990).

children and move to California while the husband would remain in New Jersey. In addition, they agreed that the wife would commence an action in California for divorce based on irreconcilable differences and that the husband would submit to this proceeding. However, after the wife and children moved to California, the husband not only refused to submit to the California divorce proceeding, but also commenced a New Jersey divorce proceeding on grounds of desertion.

In contrast, the wife and husband in *Kulko* entered into a separation agreement providing for custody of the children in the husband and for payment of limited support amounts by the husband during short periods when the children resided with the mother in California. The husband complied fully with the terms of this agreement. Although the husband later allowed the children to go to California to live with the mother permanently, he did not, as did the father in *Burnham*, contrive to send the entire family to California to live in the first instance and then breach an agreement that he had made with the wife to submit to proceedings in California.

These factual differences between *Kulko* and *Burnham* seem significant in light of the goal of the minimum contacts test. That test is structured to allow a defendant to anticipate litigation in a distant state in order to either avoid jurisdiction-conferring actions or defray the burdens of a suit away from home. The husband in *Kulko* cooperated in a plan that resulted in divorce, custody, and support awards without litigation in a distant forum. Indeed, it is difficult to see what else the father could have done to protect himself from distant litigation, except to prevent the children from migrating to live with their mother, an action that seems extreme under the circumstances of the case. Given that he acted prior to the action to avoid burdensome litigation and complied with all obligations assumed in the agreement he entered into, it would seem unjustified to subject him to jurisdiction in California. In contrast, the husband in *Burnham* contrived to send his entire family to California to live and, rather than forming an agreement with the wife that would have protected him from distant litigation, actively breached an agreement to submit to divorce jurisdiction in California. These actions seem sufficiently purposeful to justify an assertion of jurisdiction over the husband-father under a long-arm statute.

If this distinction between *Kulko* and *Burnham* is valid, the wife could have asserted jurisdiction over the husband-father in the latter case under California's long-arm statute. There was thus no need to establish transient presence jurisdiction over the defendant to award support and alimony. Minimum contacts were satisfied not, as Justice Brennan argued, because of the defendant's transient presence in the state, but because of the defendant's prior actions in sending the family to live in California and breaching an agreement with the plaintiff that would have resulted in jurisdiction over the defendant in California.

Some controversies arising out of broken family relations, and which thus might be labeled "domestic relations" cases, really fit under the category of tort actions for purposes of jurisdictional analysis. For example, in *S.L. ex rel. Susan L.v. Steven L.*,[465] the Nebraska Supreme Court upheld an assertion of jurisdiction

---

465. 274 Neb. 646, 742 N.W.2d 734 (2007).

over a father, who was a resident of Canada, in an action for child abuse allegedly committed by the father during periods in which the child was visiting with the father in Canada. On these occasions, the father had transported the child from Nebraska and returned her to Nebraska pursuant to court-ordered visitation. In a separate proceeding, the Nebraska Supreme Court had held that the Canadian courts had exclusive continuing jurisdiction under the Uniform Custody Jurisdiction and Enforcement Act over a custody dispute between the mother and father over the child.

The court treated the case as involving an assertion of specific jurisdiction and held that the father had minimum contacts with Nebraska and that the assertion of jurisdiction comported with fair play and substantial justice. Citing both *Kulko* and *Calder v. Jones*, discussed in subsection 1, above ("Tort Cases"), the court stated that the father's trips to Nebraska were not random, fortuitous, or attenuated and were part of the means used to inflict harm upon a Nebraska resident (albeit out of state). This behavior gave the father fair warning that he might be summoned to defend a tort suit in the state. Furthermore, the fact that the father had previously traveled to the state to pick up the child and participate in court proceedings diminished any inconvenience that he might incur by defending a suit here, witnesses were either available in Nebraska or their testimony could be obtained without undue burden, and Nebraska had a high interest in providing its resident with a forum to redress her injuries. Although Canada had an interest in the fair adjudication of the controversy, its interest did not outweigh that of Nebraska.[466]

6. State Tax Cases

International Shoe itself involved an assertion of jurisdiction by Washington to impose a tax on the defendant. The Supreme Court's decision in the case thus stands for the proposition that a state can subject a nonresident defendant to jurisdiction in order to collect taxes levied on the basis of the defendant's activities within the state. In *International Shoe*, the defendant had sales representatives within the state and maintained both temporary and permanent outlets within the state where samples of its merchandise could be viewed. All of its business, however, was interstate commerce because all sales of its goods were made on the basis of orders sent by the sales representatives to the defendant in St. Louis, Missouri, and the goods were shipped from that location to Washington.

Subsequently, in *Quill Corp. v. North Dakota ex rel. Heitkamp*,[467] the Supreme Court considered the power of North Dakota to require an out-of-state retailer to collect a state use tax from its customers within the state. Unlike the defendant in *International Shoe*, the retailer in *Quill* maintained no outlets or sales representatives within the state. All of its sales were made through catalogs, flyers, advertisements in national publications, and telephone calls. Through these processes, the defendant sold approximately $1,000,000 worth of goods annually

---

466. *Id.* at 652-59, 742 N.W.2d at 741-45.
467. 504 U.S. 298, 112 S. Ct. 1904, 119 L. Ed. 2d 91 (1992).

in North Dakota. The Supreme Court held that the Due Process Clause did not restrict North Dakota's power to collect the use tax from the defendant, although the Court also held that the Commerce Clause of the Constitution did prohibit the tax. The due process holding was predicated on the Court's analysis in judicial jurisdiction cases.[468] The Court stated that "there is no question that Quill has purposefully directed its activities at North Dakota residents, that the magnitude of those contacts is more than sufficient for due process purposes, and that the use tax is related to the benefits that Quill receives from access to the State."[469] Under these circumstances, it is irrelevant that the defendant had no physical presence in the state.

Because of the Court's reliance on the judicial jurisdiction cases, *Quill* stands for the proposition that the state has power to subject a nonresident defendant to jurisdiction to adjudicate the validity of a tax, as well as for the proposition that the Due Process Clause imposes no obstacle to the state's power to levy the tax. In addition, it is arguable that *Quill* is also authority for the proposition that a defendant such as Quill can be subjected to jurisdiction within the state by one of its customers in a breach of contract action. The activity of the defendant is no less purposeful in such a case than in the case of the state's power to tax. Thus, the fact that the defendant has no physical presence in the state should not matter.[470]

7. Internet Activities

In recent years, the rise of internet activities has produced difficult issues of personal jurisdiction. The U.S. Supreme Court has not yet addressed these issues, but internet activities have produced significant litigation in other courts.[471] They have also spawned an extensive academic literature.[472] In general, the decided cases

---

468. *See id.* at 306-08, 112 S. Ct. at 1910-11, 119 L. Ed. 2d at 103-04.

469. *Id.* at 308, 112 S. Ct. at 1911, 119 L. Ed. 2d at 104.

470. *Cf. Illustrations 3-37* and *3-38 supra*; Tracy O. Appleton, Note, *The Line Between Liberty and Union: Exercising Personal Jurisdiction Over Officials From Other States,* 107 COLUM. L. REV. 1944 (2007).

471. *See, e.g.*, Jason H. Eaton, Annotation, *Effect of Use, or Alleged Use, of Internet on Personal Jurisdiction, or Venue of, Federal Court Case*, 155 A.L.R. FED. 535 (1999).

472. The academic literature is so vast that it cannot all be cited here. This note contains citations to the most important literature published since the last edition of this text. Previous articles may be found cited in the corresponding footnote in the last edition of the text. *See* Brian D. Boone, *Bullseye!: Why A "Targeting" Approach to Personal Jurisdiction in the E-Commerce Context Makes Sense Internationally,* 20 EMORY INT'L L. REV. 241 (2006); Andrew Cabasso, Note, *Piercing* Pennoyer *with the Sword of a Thousand Truths*: *Jurisdictional Issues in the Virtual World,* 22 FORDHAM INTELL. PROP. MEDIA & ENT. L.J. 383 (2012); Danielle Keats Citron, *Minimum Contacts in a Borderless World: Voice over Internet Protocol and the Coming Implosion of Personal Jurisdiction Theory,* 39 U.C. DAVIS L. REV. 1481 (2006); John Di Bari, *A Survey of the Internet Jurisdiction Universe,* 18 N.Y. INT'L L. REV. 123 (2005); Cindy Chen, Comment, *United States and European Union Approaches to Internet Jurisdiction and Their Impact on E-Commerce,* 25 U. PA. J. INT'L ECON. L. 423 (2004); Emily Ekland, Comment, *Scaling Back* Zippo: *The Downside to the* Zippo *Sliding Scale and Proposed Alternatives to Its Uses,* 5 ALB. GOV'T L. REV. 380 (2012); William E. Frazier, Jr., Note, *When the* International Shoe *Doesn't Fit: Online Auctions and the Jurisdictional Problems that Follow,* 25 T. JEFFERSON L. REV. 493 (2003); Fred Galves, *Virtual Justice as Reality: Making the Resolution of E-Commerce Disputes More Convenient, Legitimate, Efficient, and Secure,* 2009 U. ILL. J. TECH. & POL'Y 1; Tim Gerlach, Note, *Using Internet Content Filters to Create E-Borders to Aid in International Choice of Law and Jurisdiction,* 26 WHITTIER L. REV. 899 (2005); Richard K. Greenstein, *The Action Bias in American Law: Internet Jurisdiction and the Triumph of* Zippo Dot Com, 80 TEMP. L. REV. 21 (2007); Derek J. Illar, *Unraveling International Jurisdictional Issues on the World Wide Web,* 88 U. DET. MERCY L. REV. 1 (2010); Jeffery M. Jensen, *Developments in the Law: Transnational Litigation: VI. Personal Jurisdiction in Federal Courts Over International E-Commerce Cases,* 40 LOY. L.A. L. REV. 1507 (2007); Kyle D. Johnson,

have struggled, with only limited success, to fit internet activities within the models supplied by the U.S. Supreme Court for other cases. This subsection will illustrate the problems involved through a discussion of several lower federal court decisions that have dealt with the issues in different factual contexts.

One of the leading decisions in the area is *CompuServe, Inc. v. Patterson.*[473] In *CompuServe*, a Texas resident subscribed to a network service based in Ohio. He also entered into a separate agreement with the service to sell his software over the internet. He regularly sent software to the service in Ohio and advertised the software through the service. Later, he claimed the service, by marketing a similar software product, had infringed his trademarks and engaged in deceptive trade practices. After he demanded $100,000 to settle his claims, the service sued him in Ohio. The service sought a declaratory judgment that it had not infringed his trademarks or engaged in deceptive trade practices.

The U.S. District Court in which the action was brought dismissed it for lack of personal jurisdiction, but the Sixth Circuit reversed. Because the service had based its action on the behavior of the defendant in sending his software to Ohio for sale on the service, the Sixth Circuit considered the case one of specific jurisdiction.[474] It also concluded that the purposeful contact requirement of the specific jurisdiction test was satisfied by the user's behavior in subscribing to the service and entering into an agreement designed to market his software through the service in other states (which contained a choice-of-law clause providing that Ohio law would govern the agreement). The court emphasized that the defendant *both* formed a contract with the plaintiff *and* placed a product into the stream of commerce. The court held that entering into this ongoing relationship with the

---

Note, *Measuring Minimum Contacts Over the Internet: How Courts Analyze Internet Communications to Acquire Personal Jurisdiction Over the Out-of-State Person,* 46 U. LOUISVILLE L. REV. 313 (2007); Moritz Keller, *Lessons for the Hague: Internet Jurisdiction in Contract and Tort Cases in the European Community and the United States,* 23 J. MARSHALL J. COMPUTER & INFO. L. 1 (2004); Kevin F. King, *Personal Jurisdiction, Internet Commerce, and Privacy: The Pervasive Legal Consequences of Modern Geolocation Technologies*, 21 ALB. L.J. SCI. & TECH. 61 (2011); Kevin A. Meehan, Note, *The Continuing Conundrum of International Internet Jurisdiction,* 31 B.C. INT'L & COMP. L. REV. 345 (2008); Jeffrey Hunter Moon, *New Wine, Old Wineskins: Emerging Issues in Internet-Based Personal Jurisdiction,* 42 CATH. LAW. 67 (2002); Quinn K. Nemeyer, Comment, *Don't Hate the Player, Hate the Game: Applying the Traditional Concepts of General Jurisdiction to Internet Contacts,* 52 LOY. L. REV. 147 (2006); Erin F. Norris, *Why the Internet Isn't Special: Restoring Predictability to Personal Jurisdiction*, 53 ARIZ. L. REV. 1013 (2011); James R. Pielemeier, *Why General Personal Jurisdiction over "Virtual Stores" Is a Bad Idea,* 27 QUINNIPIAC U. L. REV. 625 (2009); Joel R. Reidenberg, *Technology and Internet Jurisdiction,* 153 U. PA. L. REV. 1951 (2005); Carlos J.R. Salvado, *An Effective Personal Jurisdiction Doctrine for the Internet,* 12 U. BALT. INTELL. PROP. L.J. 75 (2003); Tracie E. Wandell, *Geolocation and Jurisdiction: From Purposeful Availment to Avoidance and Targeting on the Internet*, 16 J. TECH. L. & POL'Y 275 (2011); Brian P. Werley, Note, *Aussie Rules: Universal Jurisdiction over Internet Defamation,* 18 TEMP. INT'L & COMP. L.J. 199 (2004); Symposium, *Personal Jurisdiction in the Internet Age,* 98 NW. U. L. REV. 409 (2004) (containing articles by Professors Stein, Perdue, Borchers, and Matwyshyn); Note, *A "Category-Specific" Legislative Approach to the Internet Personal Jurisdiction Problem in U.S. Law,* 117 HARV. L. REV. 1617 (2004); Note, *Developments in the Law—The Law of Media: V. Internet Jurisdiction: A Comparative Analysis,* 120 HARV. L. REV. 1031 (2007).

473. 89 F.3d 1257 (6th Cir. 1996); *see* Michael J. Sikora III, Note, *Beam Me Into Your Jurisdiction: Establishing Personal Jurisdiction Via Electronic Contacts in Light of the Sixth Circuit's Decision in* CompuServe, Inc. v. Patterson, 27 CAP. U. L. REV. 163 (1998); David D. Tyler, Case Note, *Personal Jurisdiction Via E-Mail: Has Personal Jurisdiction Changed in the Wake of* CompuServe, Inc. v. Patterson*?*, 51 ARK. L. REV. 429 (1998).

474. The court considered the contacts of the defendant described in the text to be "related to" the claims of trademark infringement and deceptive trade practices that he asserted. *See* 89 F.3d at 1267. His action in threatening to sue for an injunction and damages also gave rise, in part, to the service's declaratory judgment claim. *See id.*

service provided adequate notice that he could be sued in Ohio. Applying the reasonableness step of the specific jurisdiction test, the court found that the defendant could not overcome the presumption of jurisdiction raised by the existence of purposeful contacts, largely because the state and plaintiff's interests were high in maintaining the suit in Ohio.

There are many similarities between *CompuServe* and *Burger King*. In particular, the Sixth Circuit seemed influenced by the entrepreneurial nature of the defendant's activities,[475] as well as the fact that the defendant had initiated an ongoing relationship with the service.[476] Although the court did not draw the parallel explicitly, the defendant's activities in *CompuServe* are very similar to those of the Michigan franchisees in *Burger King.*[477] This analogy breaks down somewhat, however, because of the procedural posture of the case. In *Burger King,* the franchisor was suing for breach of a franchise agreement into which the nonresident defendants had entered. In *CompuServe*, the affirmative claims for relief were possessed by the nonresident defendant, and the plaintiff had anticipated the claims by a declaratory judgment action in Ohio. *Burger King* would be on all fours with *CompuServe* if the franchisees in the former case had entrusted property (*e.g.*, recipes for a new food product) to Burger King in Florida, Burger King had allegedly misappropriated the property, and, when the franchisees threatened to sue in Michigan, Burger King had sought a declaratory judgment in Florida that the property had not been misappropriated. Even in the face of an ongoing franchise relationship, an assertion of jurisdiction over the Michigan franchisees would be troublesome in such a case.

One dispute that has arisen in the decisions in whether a so-called "passive" website in one state can justify an assertion of jurisdiction over the owner of the site in a distant state where the site has caused damage to a plaintiff. The cases are split. In *Cybersell, Inc. v. Cybersell, Inc.*,[478] an Arizona corporation sued a Florida corporation for trademark infringement in Arizona. The Arizona corporation alleged that it had been damaged by the defendant's use of its mark on the defendant's home page in Florida. The Ninth Circuit held that the actions of the Florida corporation were not sufficient to establish personal jurisdiction over it in Arizona. The court acknowledged that the Florida home page could be accessed by anyone in the world, but opined that posting "an essentially passive home page on the web" was insufficient to establish the purposeful contacts that were necessary to validate an assertion of specific jurisdiction.[479] The court also noted that there was no

---

475. *See id.* at 1268.

476. *See id.* at 1266-67.

477. *See* section G(2)*(b)(iii)* & H(2) *supra* (discussing *Burger King)*.

478. 130 F.3d 414 (9th Cir. 1997).

479. *See id.* at 419. The plaintiff had conceded that the plaintiff did not "exist" in Arizona, so only specific jurisdiction was appropriate. *See id.* at 416. However, when a party establishes a website with the knowledge, and probably the desire, that it be accessed by persons everywhere, there is a sense in which it is conducting activities wherever other parties are located who access it. This "general jurisdiction" possibility has yet to be sufficiently explored in the decisions. Among other problems, it raises the question whether access by a third party—*i.e.*, a "hit"—from a distant state should be considered activity of the defendant "in" that state based on the knowledge and desire of the defendant that the hit, and many others like it, would take place.

evidence that any part of the defendant's business had occurred in Arizona or with people from Arizona.[480]

In contrast to *Cybersell*, the U.S. District Court for the Eastern District of Missouri rejected the notion that a "passive" website could not create jurisdiction. In *Maritz, Inc. v. CyberGold, Inc.*,[481] a trademark infringement action was brought in Missouri against a California corporation. As in *Cybersell*, the claim was based on a website maintained by the defendant in another state, California. The district court concluded that the defendant was subject to jurisdiction under Missouri's "tortious act" provision of its long-arm statute. The court held this assertion of jurisdiction constitutional:

> Although CyberGold characterizes its activity as merely maintaining a "passive website," its intent is to reach all internet users, regardless of geographic location. Defendant's characterization of its activity as passive is not completely accurate . . . . With CyberGold's website, CyberGold automatically and indiscriminately responds to each and every internet user who accesses its website. Through its website, CyberGold has consciously decided to transmit advertising information to all internet users, knowing that such information will be transmitted globally. Thus, CyberGold's contacts are of such a quality and nature, albeit a very new quality and nature for personal jurisdiction, that they favor the exercise of personal jurisdiction over the defendant.[482]

---

480. *See id.* at 419; *see also* Gator.com Corp. v. L.L. Bean, Inc., 398 F.3d 1125 (9th Cir. 2005) (out-of-state vendor's highly interactive website that generates multimillion dollar merchandise sales to forum residents is enough to subject the vendor to general jurisdiction in the state); Jennings v. AC Hydraulic A/S, 383 F.3d 546 (7th Cir. 2004) (assertion of long-arm jurisdiction based only on passive website that only provided information about manufacturer and products insufficient to satisfy due process); Panavision Int'l, L.P. v. Toeppen, 141 F.3d 1316 (9th Cir. 1998) (simply registering another party's trademark as a domain name and posting a website on the internet is not sufficient to subject a nonresident to jurisdiction; jurisdiction sustained, however, because defendant's actions were in pursuit of a scheme to extract money from plaintiff that the defendant knew would adversely affect plaintiff in the forum); Millennium Enters., Inc. v. Millennium Music, L.P., 33 F. Supp. 2d 907 (D. Or. 1999) (for an interactive website to provide a basis for jurisdiction defendant must engage in deliberate action within the forum through the site or purposefully direct its activities at forum residents; fact that someone accessing the site could buy a product not enough; action was trademark infringement action in which there had been only one sale of a product to a forum resident); Zippo Mfg. Co. v. Zippo Dot Com, Inc., 952 F. Supp. 1119 (W.D. Pa. 1997) (leading case establishing a "sliding scale" test for internet jurisdiction based on the interactivity of the website).

481. 947 F. Supp. 1328 (E.D. Mo. 1996); *see* Brian K. Epps, Recent Developments, Maritz, Inc. v. CyberGold, Inc.: *The Expansion of Personal Jurisdiction in the Modern Age of Internet Advertising*, 32 GA. L. REV. 237 (1997).

482. 947 F. Supp. at 1333; *see also, e.g.*, Toys "R" Us, Inc. v. Step Two, S.A., 318 F.3d 446 (3d Cir. 2003) (defendant's maintenance of interactive website plus two sales to forum residents was not sufficient to sustain exercise of specific jurisdiction in trademark infringement action; mere operation of interactive website should not subject operator to jurisdiction anywhere in the world; rather, evidence must exist that defendant purposefully availed itself of conducting activity in forum by directly targeting its website to the state, knowingly interacting with residents of the state through site, or other related contacts); Quick Techs., Inc. v. Sage Group PLC, 313 F.3d 338 (5th Cir. 2002) (advertisements do not establish personal jurisdiction where there is no evidence that the claim arises out of or is related to the advertisements; website that is no more than a passive advertisement that provides product information, toll-free telephone numbers, e-mail addresses, and mail-in order forms does not support the exercise of personal jurisdiction); GTE New Media Servs. Inc. v. BellSouth Corp., 199 F.3d 1343 (D.C. Cir. 2000) (personal jurisdiction may not be based solely on the ability of the forum's residents to access the defendant's website); Soma Med. Int'l v. Standard Chartered Bank, 196 F.3d 1292 (10th Cir. 1999) (passive website that does little more than make information available to those who are interested is insufficient to justify an assertion of personal jurisdiction); Mink v. AAAA Dev. LLC, 190 F.3d 333 (5th Cir. 1999) (defendant who posted a passive website, which only advertised defendant's product, but which did not accept orders over the internet, was not subject to personal jurisdiction in the forum based on the website); Threlkeld v. Colorado, 2000 MT 369, 303

The court in *Maritz* correctly rejected the notion that a "passive" website cannot result in personal jurisdiction in another state. However, it cannot be said that the case otherwise established a workable test for distinguishing between internet activities that should, and those that should not, result in jurisdiction. One possible distinction between *Maritz* and *Cybersell* is that, in the latter case, there was no past or apparent future commercial benefit to the defendant in the forum resulting from the nonforum website, while in *Maritz* there had been 131 out-of-state "hits" from Missouri on the defendant's out-of-state website.[483] Although the website had not yet become operational, and thus there had been no actual commercial benefit to the defendant from these hits, the plaintiff was seeking injunctive relief to prevent the future damage to its interests that the defendant's activities would cause. No similar evidence, even of future harm, appeared to exist in *Cybersell.*

One frequently cited and discussed decision in the area of Internet jurisdiction is *Zippo Mfg. Co. v. Zippo Dot Com, Inc.*[484] The Zippo Manufacturing Company filed an action in the Western District of Pennsylvania alleging trademark dilution, trademark infringement, and false designation under the Federal Trademark Act.[485] The claims were based on the operation of a website and an internet news service by Zippo Dot Com (Dot Com), which had obtained the exclusive right to use the domain names "zippo.com," "zippo.net," and "zipponews.com." Dot Com's contacts with Pennsylvania occurred almost exclusively over the internet, although the company also had about two percent (3,000) of its paying news subscribers in Pennsylvania. Dot Com moved to dismiss for lack of personal jurisdiction, but the district court sustained jurisdiction. The plaintiff did not urge the court to assert general jurisdiction, so the court's focus was limited to specific jurisdiction.

After discussing a number of cases, including *Compuserve* and *Maritz*, the court concluded that "[t]his is a 'doing business over the Internet' case in the line of *Compuserve* . . . ."[486] The court concluded that Dot Com had purposefully availed itself of doing business in Pennsylvania, not only by advertising over the Internet,

---

Mont. 432, 16 P.3d 359 (fact that Colorado defendant had website and advertised in national magazines, both of which reach Montana, are insufficient contacts to establish general jurisdiction; promotional activities did not give rise to specific jurisdiction over tort claim in Montana).

483. *See* 947 F. Supp. at 1333; *see also* Licciardello v. Lovelady, 544 F.3d 1280 (11th Cir. 2008) (allegations by a nationally known musician and entertainer that his former manager created a website in Tennessee containing an allegedly infringing and deceptive use of the entertainer's trademark were sufficient to authorize jurisdiction over the nonresident manager under provisions of the Florida long-arm statute permitting a Florida court to assert jurisdiction over any person who committed a tortious act with the state when the manager's website was accessible in Florida); Gary Scott Int'l, Inc. v. Baroudi, 981 F. Supp. 714 (D. Mass. 1997) (personal jurisdiction for trademark infringement claim sustained in Massachusetts over California seller who advertised over internet nationwide and intended to sell large amounts of product—cigar humidors—in Massachusetts, even though only 12 humidors had actually been sold there).

484. 952 F. Supp. 1119 (W.D. Pa. 1997). *See* Bunmi Awoyemi, Zippo *Is Dying, Should It Be Dead?: The Exercise of Personal Jurisdiction by U.S. Federal Courts Over Non-Domiciliary Defendants in Trademark Infringement Lawsuits Arising Out of Cyberspace,* 9 MARQ. INTELL. PROP. L. REV. 37 (2005); Catherine Ross Dunham, Zippo-*ing the Wrong Way: How the Internet Has Misdirected the Federal Courts in Their Personal Jurisdiction Analysis*, 43 U.S.F. L. REV. 559 (2009); Pavan Mehrotra, *Back to the Basics: Why Traditional Principles of Personal Jurisdiction Are Effective Today and Why* Zippo *Needs to Go,* 12 N.C. J. L & TECH. 229 (2010).

485. 15 U.S.C. §§ 1051-1127.

486. *Zippo*, 952 F. Supp. at 1125.

but also by signing up a significant number of subscribers in Pennslyvania.[487] In addition, the court concluded that the contacts by Dot Com with Pennsylvania were not fortuitous, and that the claims arose out of those contacts.[488] A cause of action for trademark infringement occurs where the passing off occurs, and the object of Dot Com's business is the transmission of messages partly into Pennsylvania that allegedly infringe and dilute the plaintiff's trademark there.[489] Finally, the court concluded that the assertion of jurisdiction was not unreasonable on the facts of the case, because Pennsylvania had a strong interest in adjudicating disputes involving the alleged infringement of trademarks owned by resident corporations, the plaintiff had an interest in suing in Pennsylvania (where it was incorporated and had its principal place of business), and these factors outweighed any burdens imposed on Dot Com of defending in the state, "especially when Dot Com consciously chose to conduct business in Pennsylvania, pursuing profits from the actions that are now in question."[490]

Whatever course the decisions take in the future, one sound result would be to deny jurisdiction over non-forum websites that are advertising for purely local commercial benefits. For example, in *Bensusan Restaurant Corp. v. King,*[491] the defendant was an operator of a small club in Columbia, Missouri. He established a local website to advertise the club. The plaintiff, who operated a club with an identical name in New York, sued the defendant in the U.S. District Court for the Southern District of New York for trademark infringement. The district court dismissed the action for lack of personal jurisdiction. The court held that jurisdiction did not exist under New York's long-arm statute. It also held that even if jurisdiction existed under the statute, it would violate due process.[492] The court was correct, given the localized nature of the defendant's activities and the fact that benefits from the website advertising would result to the defendant, if at all, in Missouri. As the court observed:

> There are no allegations that [the defendant] actively sought to encourage New Yorkers to access his site, or that he conducted any business—let alone a continuous and systematic part of its business—in New York. There is in fact no suggestion that [the defendant] has any presence of any kind in New York other than the [website] that can be accessed worldwide. [The plaintiff's] argument that [the defendant] should have foreseen that users

---

487. *Id.* at 1126.

488. *Id.* at 1126-27.

489. *Id.* at 1127.

490. *Id.*; *see also* uBid, Inc. v. Godaddy Group, Inc., 623 F.3d 421 (7th Cir. 2010) (in action against Arizona domain name registration corporation under Anti-Cybersquatting Consumer Protection Act, specific jurisdiction was sustained over the defendant in Illinois; court held that defendant deliberately and successfully exploited Illinois market through extensive national advertising campaigns as well as celebrity and sports sponsorships, together with physical ads in Illinois sporting venues, even though the court admitted that the defendant did not deliberately target Illinois customers in its advertising and the process whereby customers entered into transactions with the defendant was completely automated); Chloe v. Queen Bee, LLC, 616 F.3d 158 (2d Cir. 2010) (sustaining an assertion of specific jurisdiction in a trademark infringement action based on the advertising of counterfeit merchandise for sale on the internet and the physical shipment of the merchandise into the forum).

491. 937 F. Supp. 295 (S.D.N.Y. 1996), *aff'd*, 126 F.3d 25 (2d Cir. 1997).

492. The Second Circuit Court of Appeals affirmed only on the long-arm statute issue. *See* 126 F.3d at 26-29.

could access the site and be confused as to the relationship of the two . . . clubs is insufficient to satisfy due process.[493]

Another difficult application of personal jurisdiction principles arises when jurisdiction is asserted over *users*—as opposed to owners—of websites, such as eBay. To date, most cases have concluded that a one-time user of eBay does not satisfy the minimum contacts test but that a regular user does.[494] However, the courts have not developed a consistent method of analysis for such cases.[495]

Ultimately, it is difficult to determine what course the decisions will take in cases involving internet activities. The reasonableness test may be the most feasible means of resolving the myriad of factually diverse cases involving internet activities. However, the downside of this suggestion is that the degree of judicial discretion involved in applying the reasonableness test does not offer the prospect of significant certainty and predictability.

As stated above, the Supreme Court has not yet addressed the due process limits on personal jurisdiction based on internet activities. It may be waiting for some edifying principle to emerge from the state and lower federal court decisions. However, the difficulty with a "hands off" approach, whatever its motivation, is that the state and lower federal courts will probably continue trying to draw analogies from general minimum contacts analysis in the internet jurisdiction area. As indicated in the preceding sections of this chapter minimum contacts analysis has not, even outside the internet area, proven to be a particularly coherent approach to interstate limits on personal jurisdiction. That analysis seems even more inadequate in the internet area. It must be added that the bizarre nature of the result in the *McIntyre* decision, discussed in section G(2)*(iii)*, above, together with the multiple opinions by the members of the Court in that case, may be expected to produce unpredictable results in the internet area. In any event, given the diversity of problems in both general and internet jurisdiction, a case-by-case approach may be doomed to failure. Internet jurisdiction may, therefore, be an area in which comprehensive legislation based on the Commerce and/or the Full Faith and Credit Clause is particularly desirable.[496]

---

493. 937 F. Supp. at 301.

494. Recent Case, 122 HARV. L. REV. 1014, 1018 & n.49 (2009) (citing illustrative cases and discussing Boschetto v. Hansing, 539 F.3d 1011 (9th Cir. 2008), which involved a suit by a distant, successful bidder for a vehicle on eBay based on alleged violation of the California Consumer Protection Act, breach of contract, misrepresentation, and fraud).

495. Recent Case, 122 HARV. L. REV. 1014, 1018-19 (2009). As the student author points out, "courts have presented a confused picture of the proper way to approach these cases. . . . [S]everal courts . . . have . . . attempted to use [tests developed for owners of websites]. By stretching to apply an unrelated test, these courts have introduced unnecessary complexity and confusion into jurisdictional analyses involving eBay. Other courts have added to the confusion by relying on different specific aspects of the cases: some have emphasized that the seller had no control over the winning bidder, some have analogized the case to long-range advertising, and some have discussed technical aspects of eBay. Similarly, other opinions [have] discussed a number of factual and theoretical rationales without specifying which were determinative in the case." *Id.* at 1019 (footnotes omitted). In contrast, in Boschetto v. Hansing, 539 F.3d 1011 (9th Cir. 2008), the Ninth Circuit's panel opinion discounted the internet dimension of the case and treated it like any other long-distance transaction under traditional specific jurisdiction standards. *See id.* at 1016-19.

496. The companion case to *McIntyre*, *Goodyear*, which was discussed above in conjunction with general jurisdiction, may indicate that any notion that the establishment of an online "virtual store" would result in general jurisdiction is dead. *See* Patrick J. Borchers, J. McIntyre Machinery, Goodyear, *and the Incoherence of the Minimum Contacts Test*, 44 CREIGHTON L. REV. 1245, 1267 (2011).

SECTION I. JURISDICTION BY NECESSITY

U.S. Supreme Court decisions under the Due Process Clause suggest that there may be a doctrine of "jurisdiction by necessity." The basic notion supporting jurisdiction by necessity is that there must be at least one forum somewhere with power to adjudicate every case. Within this notion, however, there are at least two distinguishable kinds of "jurisdiction by necessity" cases.[497] One kind of case is represented by *Mullane v. Central Hanover Bank & Trust Co.*, discussed in section H(4), above. In this kind of "jurisdiction by necessity" case, strong practical considerations point to a particular state as the only realistic forum in which to settle a dispute. The second kind of "jurisdiction by necessity" case is one in which no forum possesses the necessary relationships with all of the defendants to assert jurisdiction under conventional due process standards. In this kind of "jurisdiction by necessity" case, the forum selected by the plaintiff would be allowed to exercise jurisdiction over the defendants simply because there is no other available forum that is any better.

There is little difficulty with the doctrine of jurisdiction by necessity when dealing with examples like the absent beneficiaries of the trust in the *Mullane* case or a dispute involving conflicting claims to land located within a state. In such cases, strong practical considerations dictate that defendants who do not have contacts with the state be subject to the jurisdiction of the state for purposes of settling their claims. Otherwise, absent defendants could, simply by refusing to consent to the jurisdiction of the state's courts, paralyze the ability of others also interested in the subject matter of the suit to settle their own claims to the property or assets located within the state. It would be no answer to require a suit in an absent defendant's home state to settle the defendant's claim. Such an approach would require actions in every state where potential claimants resided, with the attendant danger of conflicting judgments to the property or assets that would bind no other claimant. Under these circumstances, the state where the subject matter of the suit is located is simply the most convenient place to settle the dispute.

Thus, even if these kinds of cases are viewed as ones in which the "conventional standards" of the minimum contacts test are not met, jurisdiction by necessity would seem to be a justifiable concept to prevent the burdens of multiple suits and attendant dangers of substantive paralysis that might follow. However, as discussed in section H(4) in conjunction with the *Mullane* decision, the application of the modern minimum contacts analysis does seem to justify the result in the case. Specifically, even if the purposeful contacts portion of the test is not satisfied in a case like *Mullane* because of the inability of the trust beneficiaries to anticipate and defray the burdens of litigation in New York, the *Burger King* reasonableness test applied to the facts, especially the strong state interest factor emphasized by the Court, enhances the case for jurisdiction sufficiently to satisfy due process. Therefore, it would seem unnecessary to resort to a doctrine of jurisdiction by

---

497. *See* Arthur T. Von Mehren & Donald T. Trautman, *Jurisdiction to Adjudicate: A Suggested Analysis*, 79 HARV. L. REV. 1121, 1173-74 (1966); *see also* George B. Fraser, Jr., *Jurisdiction By Necessity—An Analysis of the* Mullane *Case*, 100 U. PA. L. REV. 305 (1951).

necessity in this kind of case, because "conventional standards" sustain jurisdiction to adjudicate.

Much more difficult is the notion that the doctrine of jurisdiction by necessity should be extended to situations in which there are multiple defendants, but no conflicting claims to property or assets located within the state. This concept of jurisdiction by necessity receives some support from recent Supreme Court decisions. In *Shaffer v. Heitner*, the Court reserved decision on whether jurisdiction would exist in the state where the defendant owned property,if no other forum were available to the plaintiff. This statement cannot sensibly be read as a reference to the power of a state court to settle claims to the property itself, a power which the Court made it clear elsewhere in the *Shaffer* opinion the states possess.[498] Rather, it must be read as a reference to the potential power of the states to exercise jurisdiction to adjudicate claims that have nothing to do with the property when the defendant lacks minimum contacts with the state and cannot be sued elsewhere. It is, however, difficult to imagine such a case. If the claim arose elsewhere, why can the defendant not be sued where the claim arose or where the defendant resides?[499]

It is possible that the Court had in mind cases in which the only alternate forum is in a foreign country. However, in *Helicopteros Nacionales de Colombia v. Hall*, discussed in section G(2)*(a)*, above, the Court stated:

> As an alternative to traditional minimum-contacts analysis, respondents suggest that the Court hold that the State of Texas had personal jurisdiction over Helicol under a doctrine of "jurisdiction by necessity" [citing footnote 37 in *Shaffer v. Heitner*]. We conclude, however, that respondents failed to carry their burden of showing that all three defendants could not be sued together in a single forum. It is not clear from the record, for example, whether suit could have been brought against all three defendants in either Colombia or Peru.[500]

Based on this passage, if all defendants could be sued in Columbia or Peru, it would be inappropriate for Texas to exercise jurisdiction by necessity. Thus, if the availability of a forum in a foreign nation defeats jurisdiction by necessity, the statement in *Shaffer* remains cryptic. However, the statement in *Hall* of the possible parameters of a doctrine of jurisdiction by necessity also raises other problems. If the plaintiff in *Hall* had demonstrated that it was impossible to sue all defendants in a single foreign court, the statement suggests that it *might* have been appropriate for Texas to exercise jurisdiction by necessity. This suggestion raises troubling questions of its own.

First, why should jurisdiction by necessity extend to this fact situation at all? Even if the defendants cannot be sued together in a single foreign forum, they can surely be sued individually in separate actions. True, such multiple actions would involve the danger of conflicting judgments, but the problem here is not as grave as the situation discussed above in which a court needs to settle conflicting

---

498. *See* Shaffer v. Heitner, 433 U.S. 186, 207-08, 97 S. Ct. 2569, 2581, 53 L. Ed. 2d 683, 700 (1977).

499. Or, after *Burnham*, discussed in sections E(2) and H(5) *supra*, where the defendant can be served.

500. Helicopteros Nacionales de Colombia, S.A. v. Hall, 466 U.S. 408, 419 n.13, 104 S. Ct. 1868, 1874 n.13, 80 L. Ed. 2d 404, 414 n.13 (1984).

claims to property or assets located within the state. In the latter situation, an individual suit against a claimant will not bind the other claimants if they do not participate in the action. The result is that unless all claimants are brought together in a single proceeding (or unless separate suits against each claimant happen, fortuitously, to result in judgments in one claimant's favor), the title to the property or assets subject to the conflicting claims may effectively be clouded forever. In the *Hall* situation, however, individual actions against multiple defendants in different courts will settle the dispute with those defendants one way or the other. Of course, the plaintiff is at a tactical disadvantage if multiple actions must be brought because each defendant may successfully convince a trier of fact that one of the absent defendants is the party actually responsible for the plaintiff's injuries. But the result is simply that the plaintiff will not recover. This result is unfortunate if the plaintiff might have won a judgment by bringing all defendants together in a single proceeding. However, unfortunate or not, the dispute will be settled by the multiple judgments. The question is why a tactical disadvantage to the plaintiff should outweigh the defendants' ordinary due process rights to a reasonably nonburdensome forum?

A second question is, why Texas? Even assuming that jurisdiction by necessity extends to the *Hall* facts, how does one determine which of all the places in the universe of fora gets to exercise jurisdiction under the doctrine? In *Hall* itself, there were factors that probably made Texas the most logical state of the United States in which to bring an action. Bell Helicopter was one of the defendants and was located in Fort Worth. The decedents in the crash had been hired in Texas by another of the defendants, even though the decedents and their survivors were not residents of Texas, and so forth.[501] Thus, if jurisdiction by necessity is a viable doctrine, the plaintiff may have to bear the burden of selecting the most logical forum of all those possessing contacts with the parties and the transaction. But at this juncture, the Court's skimpy references to the doctrine have provided little guidance on this and other questions.[502]

---

501. *See id.* at 409-12, 104 S. Ct. at 1869-71, 80 L. Ed. 2d at 408-10.

502. Another case that may have jurisdiction-by-necessity implications is Phillips Petroleum Co. v. Shutts, 472 U.S. 797, 105 S. Ct. 2965, 86 L. Ed. 2d 628 (1985). *Phillips* was a class action brought to recover interest on certain royalty payments withheld from the plaintiff class members. The defendants objected that the Kansas courts did not have sufficient contacts with nonresident members of the plaintiff's class to justify adjudicating their claims as part of the class action. The Supreme Court rejected this contention. The Court held that absent members of a plaintiff class did not face the same burdens as nonresident defendants given the protections afforded to the class by the Kansas class action rules. The reason *Phillips* may be an example of jurisdiction by necessity is that the claims of each individual member of the class were so small as to make pursuit of the claims in individual actions by the class members uneconomical. Unless a state that does not have contacts with all the class members can entertain the class action, often no action at all may be possible to vindicate the plaintiffs' claims. Another twist to the jurisdiction-by-necessity doctrine concerns the kinds of factors that will legitimately render a forum the only logical, available one. In Keeton v. Hustler Magazine, Inc., 465 U.S. 770, 104 S. Ct. 1473, 79 L. Ed. 2d 790 (1984), New Hampshire was selected as the forum because the statutes of limitation of all other states had run. Likewise, in the *Phillips* litigation, the Supreme Court in a later decision held that it was constitutional for Kansas to apply its longer statute of limitations to interest claims that had arisen in other states and were barred by the statutes of limitation of those states. *See* Sun Oil Co. v. Wortman, 486 U.S. 717, 108 S. Ct. 2117, 100 L. Ed. 2d 743 (1988). In both *Keeton* and *Sun Oil*, the states asserting jurisdiction had some contact with the events giving rise to suit. The question is, would a state be allowed to assert jurisdiction by necessity if it had no contacts with the parties or the event giving rise to suit merely because it is the only state whose statute of limitations has not run? For an argument that it should not be able to do so, see LEA BRILMAYER, AN INTRODUCTION TO JURISDICTION IN THE AMERICAN FEDERAL SYSTEM 36 (1986).

Illustration 3-41. *P*, a citizen and resident of State *X*, sues *D*, a citizen of a foreign nation, in State *Y*, by attaching property located in State *Y* owned by *D*. Other than the ownership of the property, *D* has no contacts with State *Y*. *P's* claim is based on an automobile accident that occurred in Canada between *P* and *D*. *D* has returned to *D's* home country, which would not permit its courts to entertain an action by *P* and would not enforce a judgment against *D* obtained in any court of the United States or any court of any other nation. These facts may represent a valid case for jurisdiction by necessity in State *Y*. If *P* is not allowed to assert the claim in State *Y* and use the property owned by *D* there as a means of satisfying a judgment obtained against *D*, *P* will, practically speaking, be deprived of *P's* claim for relief. It would be senseless to require *P* to proceed first in a Canadian court to obtain a judgment against *D* and then enforce the judgment against the land located in State *Y*. In addition to posing risks to *P* that *D* will dispose of the property in State *Y* to avoid the potential Canadian judgment, there is no reason to believe that proceeding first in Canada to obtain a judgment would place fewer burdens on *D* than would a suit in State *Y*.[503]

Illustration 3-42. On the facts of *Illustration 3-41*, but assuming that *D* is a citizen of Great Britain, a proper case of jurisdiction by necessity would not seem to be presented under the *Hall* dictum. *P* can either sue *D* in Great Britain or in Canada and obtain an enforceable judgment. There is no justification for *P* to use the presence of property in State *Y* as the basis of jurisdiction under these circumstances.

Illustration 3-43. *P*, a citizen of State *X*, sues *D-1*, a citizen of State *X*, and *D-2*, a citizen of State *Y*, in a state court of State *X*. *D-1* has no contacts, ties, or relations with State *Y* and *D-2* has no contacts, ties, or relations with State *X*. Neither *D-1* nor *D-2* has any contacts, ties, or relations with a state where the other party has contacts, ties, or relations. Neither *D-1* nor *D-2* owns property outside the states where they are citizens. *D-1* and *D-2* are required ("indispensable") parties to an action against either of them. Because *D-1* and *D-2* are required parties, *P* may not prosecute separate actions against *D-1* in State *X* and *D-2* in State *Y*.[504] These facts may present a jurisdiction-by-necessity case. To deny *P* the right to sue both parties in either State *X* or State *Y* will effectively deny *P* the right to recover on *P's* claim. However, to give *P* the right to suit will deprive either *D-1* or *D-2* the conventional protections afforded to defendants by the Due Process Clause. It is not clear why the rights of *P*, the plaintiff, should be preferred to the rights of either *D-1* or *D-2* in this situation under a doctrine of jurisdiction by necessity.

Illustration 3-44. On the facts of *Illustration 3-43*, but assuming that *D-1* and *D-2* are not indispensable parties to actions against the other, a jurisdiction-by-necessity case would not seem to be present. *P* can pursue separate actions against *D-1* in State *X* and *D-2* in State *Y*. Although *P* may encounter tactical problems in maintaining separate actions against *D-1* and *D-2*, especially if *P* is asserting claims

---

503. The same would be true if the accident had occurred in another state of the United States and the question is whether to make *P* proceed in the state of the accident first.

504. The indispensable party doctrine is discussed in Chapter 8(C)(3) *infra* ("Joinder of Persons Needed for Just Adjudication").

in the alternative against the two defendants,[505] those tactical problems are not sufficient to justify depriving one of the defendants of the conventional due process protections afforded by the minimum contacts test.

SECTION J. NOTICE

Due process has always been seen as a guarantee to the defendant of an opportunity to be heard in defense before the defendant's life, liberty, or property may be taken. The minimum contacts test discussed in the preceding sections supports this opportunity-to-be-heard principle by securing a reasonably nonburdensome place of trial for the defendant. Obviously, if the location of trial places great burdens of expense or inconvenience on defendants, they might well relinquish their opportunity to be heard rather than incur those burdens. However, as the earlier discussion indicated, due process restrictions on the permissible locations of suit are an innovation that occurred subsequent to the adoption of the Fourteenth Amendment. Far older is the due process requirement that the defendant receive adequate notice that an action has been commenced. Indeed, the notice requirement is not only older, but more basic, than the location-of-suit restrictions of the Due Process Clause. Obviously, even if litigation is conducted in the most convenient possible location from the defendant's point of view, the defendant will not be able to defend the action adequately if no notice is provided that the action has been commenced.[506]

In addition to being older and more fundamental than the location-of-suit rules imposed under the rubric of the minimum contacts test, the notice requirements of the Due Process Clause are simpler and more consistent. Recall from section A(2)*(a)*, above, that the pre-Fourteenth Amendment due process decisions of the state courts established that state legislatures had wide latitude to dispense with personal service of process as a form of notice and to provide alternate forms of notice. The decisions indicated that the form of notice chosen by the legislature would be upheld unless it was not plausible to believe that the form would reach the defendant. In effect, given the options available, the legislature had to choose a form of notice that was reasonably likely to reach the defendant. Often, this standard allowed the legislature to choose notice by publication in a newspaper because under the relatively crude conditions existing in most of the country, notice by publication was as likely to reach the defendant as an alternate form of notice.

The modern due process notice decisions by the Supreme Court follow the same fundamental principle as the pre-Fourteenth Amendment decisions of the state courts under their own due process clauses. Although the modern Fourteenth Amendment notice requirements may superficially appear inconsistent with early

---

505. When claims in the alternative are asserted, each defendant may defend by "pointing the finger" at the other defendant. Triers of fact in separate actions may absolve the defendant before them on the theory that the other defendant is responsible for the plaintiff's injuries. Therefore, two triers of fact in different actions may conclude that someone is liable to the plaintiff, but the plaintiff will not recover. *Cf. Illustration 3-27 supra.*

506. Certain other rules, concerning the opportunity to be heard in defense before a person's property may be taken by a provisional remedy such as attachment or garnishment, are examined in Chapter 6(F) ("Provisional Remedies"). These rules concern the timing of the opportunity to be heard, which does not always have to be provided prior to the taking that is the subject of the due process challenge.

due process jurisprudence, they in fact apply the same rule: the form of notice provided must, given the options available to the legislature, be a form that is reasonably likely to provide the defendant with actual notice of the action.

Recall that in *Mullane v. Central Hanover Bank & Trust Co.*,[507] discussed in section H(4) above, the Supreme Court sustained the power of New York to settle a trust account with regard to nonresident beneficiaries of the trust. The *Mullane* case also contained an important holding on the quality of notice that had to be provided to the beneficiaries of the trust. In *Mullane*, the only notice that had been given to beneficiaries of the trust account was notice by publication in a newspaper, as provided by statute. The Supreme Court held this notice to be inadequate under the Due Process Clause as to beneficiaries whose whereabouts were known, although it was adequate as to beneficiaries whose interests or whereabouts could not be ascertained.[508] As to known, present beneficiaries, the Court stated that mail notice was the least form of notice permissible under the Due Process Clause.[509] The general standard the Court articulated for notice under that Clause was a form of notice which "within the limits of practicability" was "reasonably calculated to reach interested parties."[510]

In *Pennoyer v. Neff*,[511] the Supreme Court had, in part, connected a requirement of seizure of the property before judgment to the due process requirement of notice. The Court conditioned the sufficiency of notice by publication upon the seizure of the property or some other equivalent act.[512] A passage in *Mullane* seemed to indicate that this part of *Pennoyer* was still good law.[513] Subsequent decisions have, however, confirmed that even in actions concerning property within the state, the *Mullane* decision requires the best form of notice that is practicable under the circumstances. This standard will usually

---

507. 339 U.S. 306, 70 S. Ct. 652, 94 L. Ed. 865 (1950).

508. *See id.* at 317-18, 70 S. Ct. at 658-59, 94 L. Ed. at 875.

509. *Id.* at 318, 70 S. Ct. at 659, 94 L. Ed. at 875-76.

510. *Id.*; *see also id.* at 314-20, 70 S. Ct. at 657-60, 94 L. Ed. at 873-77. That actual notice to the defendant is not required to satisfy due process was recently confirmed by the U.S. Supreme Court. In Dusenbery v. United States, 534 U.S. 161, 122 S. Ct. 694, 151 L. Ed. 2d 597 (2002), the F.B.I. disposed of property seized pursuant to the federal Controlled Substances Act. The Act required that notice be provided to each party who appeared to have an interest in the property, which was done by sending a letter of the intent to forfeit by certified mail addressed to Dusenbery in federal prison. Subsequently, Dusenbery challenged this notice under the Due Process Clause of the Fifth Amendment. The Court upheld the notice under the *Mullane* test. The certified mail notice, plus the procedures followed by the prison to assure delivery of the mail, satisfied *Mullane's* requirement that the notice be reasonably calculated under all the circumstances to notify Dusenbery of the action. The Court noted that its cases have never required actual notice. *See also* State Dep't of Human Servs. v. Fargo, 771 So. 2d 935 (Miss. Ct. App. 2000) (mailing of service to last known address of defendant when mailer has knowledge that last known address is no longer defendant's actual address was not sufficient under Alaska rule governing service of process and did not afford defendant due process in the absence of evidence that mailer had made a good faith effort to obtain a more current address for defendant). For an argument that service of process by internet will satisfy due process, see Rachel Cantor, Comment, *Internet Service of Process: A Constitutionally Adequate Alternative?* 66 U. CHI. L. REV. 943 (1999); *see also* Rio Props., Inc. v. Rio Int'l Interlink, 284 F.3d 1007 (9th Cir. 2002) (after initial attempts at service of process had failed, district court ordered service by regular mail and e-mail on internet business in foreign country in trademark infringement action under Federal Rule 4(f)(3); court of appeals held that method of service was proper under Rule 4(f)(3) and did not violate due process).

511. 95 U.S. 714, 24 L. Ed. 565 (1878).

512. *See id.* at 727, 24 L. Ed. at 570. For a criticism of this portion of Justice Field's opinion for the Court in *Pennoyer*, see Ralph U. Whitten, *The Constitutional Limitations on State-Court Jurisdiction: A Historical-Interpretative Reexamination of the Full Faith and Credit and Due Process Clauses* (pt. 2), 14 CREIGHTON L. REV. 735, 828-35 (1981).

513. *See Mullane*, 339 U.S. at 316, 70 S. Ct. at 658, 94 L. Ed. at 874.

require at least mail notice to interested persons whose whereabouts are known or reasonably ascertainable.[514]

The *Mullane* standard thus governs all attempts by the legislative branch of government to provide notice to defendants in civil actions. The standard is connected in a straight line with the pre-Fourteenth Amendment decisions of the state courts governing notice restrictions under their own due process clauses.[515] Compared with the complexities of the minimum contacts test of *International Shoe*, the standard is simple and easy to apply.

Illustration 3-45. *P* possesses a claim against *D* for money lent to *D*. *D* refuses to pay. *P* sues *D* in a state court of proper subject-matter jurisdiction and venue in the state where the parties reside. The statutes in the state where the action is brought provide that the normal method of serving process on a defendant in a civil action is by delivering a copy of the summons and complaint to the defendant. This method is unsuccessful in *P v. D*, because *D*, having become aware that *P* has commenced the action, successfully evades numerous attempts at service. A statute of the state authorizes service of process on defendants by publication of a notice in a newspaper for several successive weeks when ordinary means of serving process on the defendant fail or the plaintiff is able to demonstrate that the whereabouts of the defendant are unknown. *P* uses this statute to serve *D* by publication. After notice has been published for the necessary statutory period, *P* obtains a default judgment against *D*. The judgment is valid under the *Mullane* test. The statutory forms of notice provided by the state are the best that are practicable under the circumstances. They are reasonably calculated to provide actual notice of the action to *D* and no better forms of notice are available.[516]

* * * * *

In *Jones v. Flowers*,[517] the Supreme Court considered the operation of the *Mullane* test in a situation in which the plaintiff knew that the defendant had not received the notice of suit. In *Jones*, the plaintiff and his wife divorced, and the wife

---

514. *See, e.g.*, Mennonite Bd. of Missions v. Adams, 462 U.S. 791, 103 S. Ct. 2706, 77 L. Ed. 2d 180 (1983); Walker v. City of Hutchinson, 352 U.S. 112, 77 S. Ct. 200, 1 L. Ed. 2d 178 (1956); *see also* Tulsa Prof'l Collection Servs., Inc. v. Pope, 485 U.S. 478, 108 S. Ct. 1340, 99 L. Ed. 2d 565 (1988); *see also* Andersen v. Monforton, 2005 MT 310, 329 Mont. 460, 125 P.3d 614 (service by publication was insufficient to acquire personal jurisdiction over landowner who had a possible claim to disputed acreage); W.S. Frey Co. v. Heath, 158 N.J. 321, 729 A.2d 1037 (1999) (acknowledging that due process does not require actual notice, but holding the mail notice used in the case inadequate under the circumstances; the notice violated the Virginia long-arm statute under which it was sent because it was not sent to the defendant's last known address, which was easily determinable); Dispensa v. University State Bank, 987 S.W.2d 923 (Tex. Ct. App. 1999) (default judgment against nonresident who was not served was not void under Due Process Clause, when nonresident learned of judgment in time to take remedial measures under forum law, such as file a motion for new trial, but did not do so and when, also, the nonresident had minimum contacts with the state). *But see* Miserandino v. Resort Props., Inc., 345 Md. 43, 691 A.2d 208 (1997) (first-class mail notice permitted by Virginia statute on Maryland defendants violates due process).

515. It has sometimes been stated that the *Mullane* decision "radically modified" the traditional notice requirements. *See* RESTATEMENT (SECOND) OF JUDGMENTS at 27 (1982). This statement is based on *Mullane's* rejection of notice by publication, which had been traditionally approved under the Due Process Clause. However, rejection of notice by publication in *Mullane* was based on the availability of better forms of notice at the time the case was decided. At the time of the pre-Fourteenth Amendment decisions, notice by publication may well have been the best available form in most situations. Thus, the principle enforced in *Mullane* arguably was the same principle being enforced in the earlier cases.

516. *But cf.* Jennifer Lee, Note, *EXTRA! Read All About It: Why Notice by Newspaper Publication Fails to Meet* Mullane's *Desire-to-Inform Standard and How Modern Technology Provides a Viable Alternative*, 45 GA. L. REV. 1095 (2011).

517. 547 U.S. 220, 126 S. Ct. 1708, 164 L. Ed. 2d 415 (2006).

continued to live in the house that the plaintiff had purchased prior to the divorce. The plaintiff continued to pay the mortgage on the house, which meant that the mortgage holder paid the taxes that periodically came due out of an escrow account. However, when the mortgage was paid, plaintiff ceased paying the taxes. In the course of time, the state land commissioner attempted to notify the plaintiff by certified mail of the tax delinquency, but no one was at home to receive the letter, and it remained unclaimed at the post office. Subsequently, the commissioner published a notice of public sale in a local newspaper, and a purchaser submitted a purchase offer for the house. The commissioner then sent another certified letter notifying the plaintiff that the house would be sold if the plaintiff did not pay the delinquent taxes. This letter was also returned "unclaimed." The state then sold the house, and the purchaser caused an unlawful detainer notice to be delivered to the property. This notice was served on the plaintiff's daughter, who notified the plaintiff of the sale. The plaintiff then commenced an action in state court against the purchaser and the commissioner, contending that the failure to provide notice of the sale and his right to redeem violated due process. The state courts ruled against the plaintiff, but the Supreme Court granted certiorari and reversed.

The Court essentially held that, although the due process clause does not require that a defendant actually receive notice of an action, the *Mullane* test requires that additional steps be taken to provide notice when there is affirmative evidence that the plaintiff has not received notice. The Court stated that the *Mullane* test had been violated by the procedure employed by the state, because "[w]e do not think that a person who actually desired to inform a real property owner of an impending tax sale of a house he owns would do nothing when a certified letter sent to the owner is returned unclaimed." The Court indicated that there were a number of steps that the state could have taken to rectify the lack of notice other than giving notice by publication. For example, the state might have sent notice to the plaintiff by ordinary mail, which does not require a signature and which thus could have been delivered without being returned to the post office. Alternatively, the state might have posted a notice on the front door of the house.

In dissent, Justice Thomas, joined by Justices Scalia and Kennedy, protested that, under *Mullane*, the constitutionality of the method prescribed by the state to provide notice should be judged "*ex ante, i.e.,* from the viewpoint of the government agency at the time its notice is sent." So judged, Justice Thomas argued that the method prescribed by the state was reasonably calculated to inform the plaintiff of the proceedings affecting his property, especially given that the plaintiff was under a legal obligation to inform the state of a change in his mailing address, and that due process, as the majority conceded, does not require that an affected party actually receive the notice.[518]

Sometimes a lack of notice to a person can be overcome if the person's interests are adequately represented in an action, such as a class action, or there is

---

518. *See id.* at 242-44, 126 S. Ct. at 1723-24, 164 L. Ed. 2d at 435-36.; *see also* Patrick J. Borchers, Jones v. Flowers: *An Essay on a Unified Theory of Procedural Due Process,* 40 CREIGHTON L. REV. 343 (2007); Note, *The Supreme Court, 2005 Term,* 120 HARV. L. REV. 125, 233 (2006) (discussing *Jones*).

a special substantive relationship between the parties to the actions—often called a "privity" relationship—that justifies binding the unnotified party's interests.[519]

However, the U.S. Supreme Court has made it clear that actions in which the interests of outsiders are alleged to have been represented will be scrutinized closely to assure that the representation actually occurred and was adequate. For example, in *Richards v. Jefferson County*,[520] plaintiffs sued in Alabama state court to challenge the federal constitutionality of a state tax. The Alabama courts held the suit precluded by the judgment in a prior action. The plaintiffs were not parties to the prior action and had not received any notice that an action was pending in which their rights would be adjudicated.[521] Nevertheless, the Alabama Supreme Court held that the judgment bound the plaintiffs because their interests were adequately represented by the plaintiffs in the prior action.

The U.S. Supreme Court reversed. The Court held that there was insufficient indication that the court in the prior action had taken care to protect the plaintiffs' interests. There was no "privity" between the parties, the first action was not brought as a class action, and the plaintiffs in that action showed no intent to represent the interests of outsiders or awareness that they were doing so. In addition, the judgment in the prior action did not purport to bind any nonparties.[522] Under these circumstances, the Supreme Court was unable to conclude that the plaintiffs in the prior action provided "representation sufficient to make up for the fact that [plaintiffs in the second suit] neither participated in . . . nor had the opportunity to participate in, the [prior] action. Accordingly, due process prevents [plaintiffs] from being bound by the . . . judgment."[523]

Richards indicates that to bind nonparties on the theory that their interests are adequately represented in an action, the "representatives" in the first action, as well as the court, must be aware of the representative nature of the proceeding and take steps to assure that the non-parties' interests are adequately protected. However, the case does not specify further the kinds of protections, including possible notice to the nonparties, that must be afforded to satisfy due process in a representational proceeding. These issues are examined in Chapter 8(D)(4), dealing with "class actions," below.

---

519. Privity is discussed in Chapter 13(D)(1)*(b) infra* ("Substantive Relationships Binding Nonparties").

520. 517 U.S. 793, 116 S. Ct. 1761, 135 L. Ed. 2d 76 (1996).

521. *See id.* at 799, 116 S. Ct. at 1766, 135 L. Ed. 2d at 84.

522. *See id.* at 801-02, 116 S. Ct. at 1767-68, 135 L. Ed. 2d at 86.

523. *Id.* at 802, 116 S. Ct. at 1768, 135 L. Ed. 2d at 86; *see also* South Cent. Bell Tel. Co. v. Alabama, 526 U.S. 160, 119 S. Ct. 1180, 143 L. Ed. 2d 258 (1999). In *South Central Bell*, corporations had sued to challenge the constitutionality of an Alabama tax under the Commerce Clause. After this suit was commenced, other corporations instituted an action to challenge the tax on the same grounds, but for additional tax years. The first action resulted in a holding that the tax was constitutional, whereupon the trial court in the second action appeared to hold that action barred by the res judicata effect of the judgment in the first. The U.S. Supreme Court found the case indistinguishable from *Richards*, even though the plaintiffs in the second action were aware of the first action, one of their lawyers was representing the plaintiffs in the first action, and they had requested their action to be held in abeyance until the first action was decided. The plaintiffs in the second action were still strangers to the first action, the first action was not a class action in which the interests of the plaintiffs in the second action were being represented, and there was no special relationship that would create "privity" between the parties.

SECTION K. SERVICE OF PROCESS

1. Service of Process in English and Early United States Practice

One of the functions of the original writ at common law was to order the sheriff to compel the defendant's appearance. The appearance of the defendant was essential to further proceedings. The plaintiff did not have to appear or plead until the defendant had appeared, nor could there be a trial or judgment.[524] Under this system, the means available to compel the defendant to appear were of great importance. At a relatively early date,[525] statutes authorized writs of *capias ad respondendum* to be issued in almost all actions at law.[526] Pursuant to these writs, the sheriff was commanded to arrest the defendant and to hold the defendant until either security for the defendant's appearance ("safe pledges") was provided or the date for appearance arrived. This process worked if the defendant was subject to arrest. If the defendant was not subject to arrest—for instance, when the defendant was absent from the country—a writ of attachment commanding the seizure of the defendant's property was available to compel appearance.[527]

Appearance of the defendant was as necessary in equity as in common-law actions. However, the procedure for compelling appearance of the defendant was different. An equity proceeding was commenced by a bill, which was the initial pleading in the action. In form, this bill was a prayer for a *subpoena ad respondendum* to issue to compel the defendant's appearance.[528] The subpoena served the same function as the summons at common law: to notify the defendant of the action and compel the defendant to appear or suffer a penalty.[529] The form of the subpoena differed from the summons because a subpoena was directed to the defendant rather than an officer of the court. If the defendant failed to appear, the court considered the defendant in contempt of court and issued a writ of attachment.

Early United States procedures for service of process and commencement of common-law actions did not follow a uniform pattern. Some states, such as New York, used the *capias ad respondendum* as the usual method of commencing personal (principally contract and tort) actions. The initial process in other states

---

524. ROBERT W. MILLAR, CIVIL PROCEDURE OF THE TRIAL COURT IN HISTORICAL PERSPECTIVE 74 (1952).

525. At common law, the first process for the purpose of securing the defendant's appearance was the summons, which was simply a warning to the defendant to appear. If a defendant failed to appear in response to the summons or offer any excuse ("essoin") for nonappearance, other means were used to compel appearance. In the earliest times, these means involved a lengthy series of ever more serious penalties, including seizure of the defendant's land, seizure of the defendant's body, seizure of the defendant's goods, and outlawry. As Pollock and Maitland state, this "mesne process" "[v]ery slowly . . . turn[ed] the screw which [brought] pressure to bear upon . . . defendant[s]." 2 FREDERICK POLLOCK & FREDERIC W. MAITLAND, THE HISTORY OF ENGLISH LAW 591 (2d ed. 1968).

526. ROBERT W. MILLAR, CIVIL PROCEDURE OF THE TRIAL COURT IN HISTORICAL PERSPECTIVE 75-76 (1952) (Statute of Marlbridge (1267), Statute of Westminster II (1285), and others).

527. *See* JOSEPH H. KOFFLER & ALISON REPPY, HANDBOOK OF COMMON LAW PLEADING § 16, at 73-74 (1969).

528. *See* ROBERT W. MILLAR, CIVIL PROCEDURE OF THE TRIAL COURT IN HISTORICAL PERSPECTIVE 78 (1952).

529. The subpoena was also used in the common-law courts to compel the attendance of witnesses and was probably introduced into equity from the common-law practice. *See* JOSEPH STORY, COMMENTARIES ON EQUITY PLEADINGS § 45 (9th ed. 1879).

was a summons, often combined with an attachment of property. In equity cases, the states generally followed the method used in English chancery actions. Suits were normally commenced by filing a bill and issuing a subpoena.[530]

In the later English and early American practice, actual appearance of the defendant was not required. Instead, if the defendant failed to appear after being properly served with a summons in a common-law action or a subpoena in an equity action, a "default" would be entered, and the case would proceed to judgment against the defendant.[531] The default judgment could then be enforced like a judgment entered after an appearance by the defendant.

2. Modern Methods of Serving Process

Under modern systems of procedure, the process for notifying the defendant of the action and securing jurisdiction to adjudicate the proceeding is the service of a summons, whether the suit was formerly one at law or in equity. The subpoena is the name given to the process to compel the attendance of witnesses at trial and pretrial proceedings. The content of the summons is regulated by statute or by rule,[532] as is the time and method of its proof,[533] by whom the summons may be served,[534] upon whom it may be served,[535] and so forth.

Methods of serving process in the states vary widely, but include the traditional methods of service already discussed in earlier sections, such as in-hand service, service by leaving a copy of the process at the defendant's home, usual residence, or place of business, and service by publication under circumstances where other methods fail or are unavailable.[536] Rule 4 of the Federal Rules of Civil Procedure prescribes the requirements of service of process for the federal courts and states operating under provisions identical to the Federal Rules. An examination of Rule 4 will provide a good illustration of the technical aspects of service of process rules in both federal and state courts.

Rule 4 has been amended several times since it first became effective in 1938. In particular, amendments of Rule 4 in 1983 and 1993 made extensive changes in the operation and structure of the rule in the federal courts. Before 1993, Rule 4 governed not only service of the summons, but also service of certain other kinds of process. The 1993 amendments to Rule 4 restrict its application to service of the summons.[537] A new rule, Rule 4.1, was created in 1993 to govern service of

---

530. *See* ROBERT W. MILLAR, CIVIL PROCEDURE OF THE TRIAL COURT IN HISTORICAL PERSPECTIVE 74-84 (1952).

531. *See id.* at 82-84.

532. *See, e.g.*, CAL. CIV. PROC. CODE § 412.20 (West 2004).

533. *See, e.g.*, FED. R. CIV. P. 4(*l*); CAL. CIV. PROC. CODE § 417.10 (West Supp. 2012).

534. *See, e.g.*, CAL. CIV. PROC. CODE § 414.10 (West 2004).

535. *See, e.g.*, FED. R. CIV. P. 4(*h*)(1) (specifying service on an officer, a managing or general agent, or any other agent authorized by appointment or by law for purposes or serving corporations or associations).

536. The advance of technology, of course, affects methods of service of process. *See, e.g.*, Majorie A. Shields, Annotation, *Service of Process Via Computer or Fax*, 30 A.L.R.6TH 413 (2008).

537. For a general review of amended Rule 4, see Kent Sinclair, *Service of Process: Amended Rule 4 and the Presumption of Jurisdiction*, 14 REV. LITIG. 159 (1994).

process other than the summons or a subpoena.[538] Service of a subpoena is governed by Federal Rule 45. In addition, Federal Rule 5 governs service of pleadings and papers other than process. As discussed in Chapter 1(D)(12), above, the Federal Rules of Civil Procedure were amended in 2007 to restyle the rules, make them easier to read, and insure that the terminology of the Rules is consistent throughout. In many instances, this restyling has resulted in internal renumbering and relettering of the Rules. In the following discussion, references are made to the restyled designations, even though the text may be discussing amendments to the rules that may have had different designations prior to 2007.

(a) Form of the Summons

Rule 4(a) provides that the summons must be signed by the clerk, bear the seal of the court, identify the court and the parties, be directed to the defendant, and state either the name and address of the plaintiff's attorney or of an unrepresented plaintiff.[539] The summons must also state the time within which the defendant must appear and defend and notify the defendant that failure to do so will result in a default judgment for the relief demanded in the complaint. The 1993 amendments to Rule 4 eliminated a requirement that a federal summons conform as nearly as possible to the form required by state law when state law was utilized under other provisions of Rule 4 to serve process. The change was designed to make the form of a federal court summons uniform in all cases.[540] If the content of the summons does not conform to the requirements of Rule 4(a), the defendant may object pursuant to Rule 12(b)(4) based on insufficient process. However, Rule 4(a)(2) provides that the court may allow the summons to be amended.

Illustration 3-46. *P* commences an action against *D* in a U.S. District Court. *P* presents a summons to the clerk as required by Rule 4(b).[541] The clerk signs, seals, and issues the summons. However, the summons is defective because it fails to state the time within which the defendant must appear and defend the action. Under Federal Rule 12(b)(4), *D* may move to dismiss the action for insufficient process. Alternatively, *D* may make an insufficient process objection in *D's* answer, as permitted by Rule 12(b).[542] However, the court may permit *P* to amend the summons under Rule 4(a)(2).[543]

---

538. For example, Federal Rule 69(a) states that "[p]rocess to enforce a judgment for the payment of money shall be a writ of execution, unless the court directs otherwise." FED. R. CIV. P. 69(a). After the 1993 amendments to the Federal Rules, it would appear that service of a writ of execution will be governed by Federal Rule 4.1. *But see* Apostolic Pentecostal Church v. Colbert, 169 F.3d 409 (6th Cir. 1999) (service of writ of garnishment pursuant to state law valid; Rule 69 governs, not Rule 4.1(a)). Rule 4.1(a) provides that process other than a summons or subpoena shall be served by a U.S. marshal, deputy marshal, or a person specially appointed to serve process. The person serving process under Rule 4.1 must make proof of service as provided in Rule 4(*l*). Proof of service under Rule 4(*l*) is discussed in the text *infra*. Process under Rule 4.1 may be served anywhere within the territorial limits of the state in which the district court is located, or beyond the limits of the state when authorized by a federal statute. Rule 4.1(b) provides for service of orders of commitment for civil contempt. *See* FED. R. CIV. P. 4.1.

539. Prior to 1993, Rule 4(a) governed the issuance of the summons and Rule 4(b) governed the form of the summons. These provisions were switched in the 1993 amendment to Rule 4. *See* FED. R. CIV. P. 4 advisory committee's note to the 1993 amendment.

540. *See id.*

541. Rule 4(b) is discussed in the text *infra*.

542. Federal Rule 12(b) is discussed in Chapter 6(D)(3)*(d) infra* ("Motions to Dismiss").

543. *See* FED. R. CIV. P. 4(a).

(b) Issuance of the Summons

Rule 4(b) provides that on or after the complaint is filed, the plaintiff may present a summons to the clerk for the signature and seal required by Rule 4(a)(1)(F) & (G). If the summons is in the form prescribed by Rule 4(a)(1), the clerk must sign, seal, and issue it to the plaintiff for service on the defendant. If there are multiple defendants, a separate summons or a copy of an original summons must be issued for each defendant. The 1993 amendments to the rule provided that it is the plaintiff's responsibility to fill in the summons, not the responsibility of the clerk.[544]

(c) What Must Be Served with the Summons and Who May Serve the Summons

Rule 4(c)(1) requires that a copy of the complaint be served with the summons. The plaintiff must serve the summons and complaint within the time allowed by Rule 4(m). The plaintiff must also furnish the process server with the necessary copies of the summons and complaint. Rule 4(c)(2) states that service may be effected by any person who is not a party and who is at least 18 years of age. However, Rule 4(c)(3) also provides that, under certain circumstances, the court may direct that service be made by a U.S. marshal or other person specially appointed by the court.

Before 1983, Rule 4(a) directed the clerk to deliver the summons to the marshal or to anyone else authorized by Rule 4 to serve process. Rule 4, in turn, provided for service by the marshal, by some person specially appointed by the court to serve process, or by anyone authorized to serve process in an action brought in the courts of general jurisdiction of the state in which the district court is held. The 1983 amendments to Rule 4 relieved marshals of most of the duty of serving process in civil litigation.[545] After 1983, Rule 4 placed the primary responsibility for securing service on the plaintiff or the plaintiff's attorney. The 1993 amendments to Rule 4 continued this trend by further reducing the obligations of the marshal to serve process in actions in which the United States is seeking service. Like other litigants, the United States may now employ any nonparty who is 18 years of age to serve process. Service by the marshal or other specially appointed process server is today mandatory only in situations in which the plaintiff is authorized to proceed in forma pauperis under 28 U.S.C. § 1915 or as a seaman under 28 U.S.C. § 1916.[546]

---

544. *See id.* advisory committee's note to the 1993 amendment.

545. The 1983 amendment to Rule 4 was not accomplished in the ordinary fashion by promulgation under the Rules Enabling Act by the Supreme Court. *See* Chapter 1(D)(11) *supra* ("Promulgation of the Federal Procedure of Civil Procedure") (describing the rulemaking process under the Rules Enabling Act); *see also* Chapter 5(F) *infra* ("The Evolution of the *Erie* Doctrine: Conflicts Between State Law and Federal Rules of Civil Procedure"). Rather, Congress, dissatisfied with changes in the rule proposed by the Advisory Committee and adopted by the Supreme Court, acted directly to amend the rule into its 1983 form. *See* 4 CHARLES A. WRIGHT & ARTHUR R. MILLER, FEDERAL PRACTICE AND PROCEDURE: CIVIL § 1061, at 316 (3d ed. 2002).

546. *See* FED. R. CIV. P. 4(c)(1); *see also* FED. R. CIV. P. 4 advisory committee's note to the 1993 amendment. Lawyers must take care when hiring private process servers in some jurisdictions. For example, in New York, it has been held that if a lawyer hires a private process server and the process server negligently fails to serve the defendant before the statute of limitations runs, the lawyer can be held vicariously liable to the client for the negligence of the process server. *See* Kleeman v. Rheingold, 81 N.Y.2d 270, 614 N.E.2d 712, 598 N.Y.S.2d 149 (1993).

(d) Waiver of Service of Process

Rule 4(d) contains the most important portion of the 1993 amendments to Rule 4. Rule 4(d) is designed to reduce the costs of service of process by encouraging certain classes of defendants to waive the service of the summons.[547] The waiver provisions of Rule 4(d) are only applicable to defendants who are competent, adult individuals, or corporations, partnerships, or unincorporated associations.[548] The waiver provisions are not applicable to individual defendants who are infants or incompetent persons, to the United States, its agencies, corporations, or officers, or to foreign, state, or local governments. Rule 4(g), (i), and (j) contain provisions prescribing the manner in which the latter classes of defendants must be served.

With regard to the classes of defendants governed by Rule 4(d), the rule provides that the plaintiff may notify the defendant in writing that the action has been commenced and request that the defendant waive the service of a summons.[549] The notice and request must be addressed directly to individual defendants.[550] If the defendant is a corporation, partnership, or unincorporated association, the notice and request must be addressed to an officer, a managing or general agent, or an agent otherwise authorized by appointment or law to receive service of process.[551] The notice and request must be sent by first-class mail or "other reliable means." They also must be accompanied by a copy of the complaint and identify the court in which the action has been filed.[552] The notice and request must correspond to Form 5 in the Appendix of Approved Forms to the Federal Rules of Civil Procedure.[553] That form requests the defendant to return a waiver of service of summons.[554] The form must be enclosed with the notice and request.[555] The form also notifies the defendant that return of the waiver will mean that the summons will

---

547. The text of Rule 4(d) is new, but was substantially derived from the provisions of former Federal Rule 4(c)(2)(C) & (D). *See* FED. R. CIV. P. 4 advisory committee's note to the 1993 amendment.

548. *See* FED. R. CIV. P. 4(d)(1). In Estate of Darulis v. Garate, 401 F.3d 1060 (9th Cir. 2005), the plaintiff brought tort actions against multiple individual defendants and the City and County of San Francisco. The plaintiff requested the defendants to waive service, which they did not do. After having them served with process, the plaintiff ultimately lost the action and sought to recover the costs of service. The defendants resisted on the ground that the plaintiff had lost. The district court denied costs, but the court of appeals reversed and ordered costs reimbursed, holding that Rule 4(d) was a free-standing provision that operated independently of Rule 54(d)(1). However, the court of appeals apparently failed to notice that while the individual defendants were subject to the waiver provisions of Rule 4(d), the City and County of San Francisco were not, because service of the latter defendants was governed by Rule 4(j). *See also* Moore v. Hosemann, 591 F.3d 741 (5th Cir. 2009) (waiver provisions of Rule 4 did not apply to Mississippi Secretary of State when secretary served in his official capacity and not as an individual).

549. *See* FED. R. CIV. P. 4(d)(A)(i).

550. In D'Orange v. Feely, No. 95-7904, 1996 WL 446254, 1996 U.S. App. LEXIS 20495 (2d Cir. Aug. 8, 1996), the plaintiff sent a notice and request for waiver to the defendant's attorney in a related action. The attorney refused to accept the waiver for the defendant, but the defendant was aware of the service on the attorney, obtained the waiver, and returned it within 30 days from the date it was sent to the attorney. However, the plaintiff, instead of directing a new waiver to the defendant, had the defendant served with a summons and complaint. The defendant did not answer the complaint within the time period required by Rule 12(a), and a default was entered against the defendant. The defendant moved to set aside the default, claiming that the return of the waiver meant there was 60 days in which to answer. The district court refused to set aside the default, and entered a default judgment. The court of appeals affirmed on the ground that the defendant had not shown good cause for the default.

551. *See* FED. R. CIV. P. 4(d)(1)(A)(ii).

552. *See* FED. R. CIV. P. 4(d)(1)(B)-(C).

553. *See* FED. R. CIV. P. 4(d)(1)(D).

554. *See* Form 5 in the Appendix of Forms following the Federal Rules of Civil Procedure.

555. *See* FED. R. CIV. P. 4(d)(1)(C) (providing that the defendant must be provided with two copies of the waiver form and a prepaid means of compliance in writing).

not be served on the defendant and the action will proceed as if the defendant had been served on the date that the waiver is filed with the court by the plaintiff.[556] The defendant must be given a reasonable time to return the waiver. The amount of time cannot be less than 30 days from the date on which the request is sent, or 60 days if the defendant is served outside the United States.[557]

If the defendant returns the waiver of service as requested, the normal 21 day period within which to answer the complaint after normal service of a summons is extended to 60 days, or 90 days if the defendant is outside the United States.[558] If the defendant does not waive service, the notice and request inform the defendant that service will be effectuated in another manner authorized by the Federal Rules of Civil Procedure and that the plaintiff will request the court to impose the full costs of the alternative service on the defendant.[559] The rule provides that the court must impose costs on a defendant located within the United States unless the defendant shows good cause for the failure to return the waiver.[560] These costs include not only the expenses incurred in effecting service under Rule 4(e), (f), or (h), but also a reasonable attorney's fee for any motion that must be filed to collect the fee.[561] Rule 4(d) thus imposes a duty on the defendant to avoid unnecessary costs of serving the summons.[562] One court has held that Rule 4(d)(2) is a free-standing cost provision that requires payment of the costs of service by a defendant who prevails in the action, but who inappropriately failed to waive service, even though such a defendant is generally entitled to recover the costs of the action under Federal Rule 54(d)(1).[563] However, the rule explicitly provides that the waiver of a service of summons does not thereby waive any objection that the defendant has to venue or personal jurisdiction.[564]

Illustration 3-47. *P*, a citizen of State *X*, sues *D*, a citizen of State *Y*, in a U.S. District Court in State *X* for $500,000. *P's* claim is for personal injuries received in an automobile accident with *D* in State *Z*. *D* has no contacts, ties, or relations with State *X*. After commencement of the action, *P's* attorney sends the notice and request prescribed by Rule 4(d) to *D*. After consulting an attorney, *D* returns the form waiving service of a summons, and the waiver is filed with the U.S. District Court in State *X*. Subsequently, *D* moves under Federal Rule 12(b)(2) and (3) to dismiss the action for lack of personal jurisdiction and improper venue. *D's* motion should be granted. The return of the waiver of service of summons pursuant to Rule 4(d) does not waive *D's* personal jurisdiction and venue objections, which are valid on the facts of this illustration.

---

556. *See* FED. R. CIV. P. 4(d)(1)(D).

557. *See* FED. R. CIV. P. 4(d)(1)(F).

558. *See* FED. R. CIV. P. 4(d)(3), 12(a)(1)(A)(ii).

559. *See* Form 5 in the Appendix of Forms following the Federal Rules of Civil Procedure.

560. *See* FED. R. CIV. P. 4(d)(2)(A)-(B); *see also* FED. R. CIV. P. 4 advisory committee's note to the 1993 amendment.

561. *See* FED. R. CIV. P. 4(d)(2)(B); Double "S" Truck Line, Inc. v. Frozen Food Express, 171 F.R.D. 251 (D. Minn. 1997).

562. *See* FED. R. CIV. P. 4(d)(1).

563. *See* Estate of Darulis v. Garate, 401 F.3d 1060 (9th Cir. 2005). *But cf.* Andrew v. Clark, 561 F.3d 261 (4th Cir. 2009) (refusal to award costs and fees for refusal to waive service is reviewed for abused of discretion; no error here because plaintiff did not give defendant reasonable time within which to waive service under circumstances of case).

564. *See* FED. R. CIV. P. 4(d)(5).

Illustration 3-48. Assume on the facts of *Illustration 3-47* that after returning the waiver of service, *D* does not appear further in the action and a default judgment is rendered against *D*. When *P* attempts to enforce the judgment against *D* in State *Y*, *D* may resist the enforcement of the judgment on the ground that it is void because the U.S. District Court in State *X* did not have personal jurisdiction over *D*.[565] However, even though the rule provides that venue is not waived by returning a waiver, *D* may not attack the judgment of the State X federal court in a subsequent action in a state or federal court in another state, because venue is not the kind of objection that is available on "collateral attack" of a judgment in another court as are defects of subject-matter or personal jurisdiction.[566]

Illustration 3-49. Assume on the facts of *Illustration 3-47* that *D* does not return the waiver of service as requested. Subsequently, *P* has *D* personally served with the summons and complaint under the law of State *Y* where *D* resides, as authorized by Rule 4(e)(1). *P* then moves to have *D* pay the costs of service, as required by Rule 4(d). The court orders *D* to show cause why the costs of the alternative service should not be imposed on *D*. *D* argues that personal jurisdiction and venue were plainly improper and that the failure to return the waiver was justified as a consequence. The fact that jurisdiction and venue were lacking is not good cause for the failure to return the waiver and will not exempt *D* from having to pay the costs of service.[567] However, the fact that personal jurisdiction and venue were clearly improper may give *D* the right to move for sanctions against *P* under Federal Rule 11 at some point in the action.[568]

Illustration 3-50. Assume on the facts of *Illustration 3-49* that *D* argues that the cost of having process personally served on *D* in State *Y* where *D* lives is unjustified because *P* had less expensive ways of effectuating service on *D* and instead employed the more expensive method of personal service under the law of the state where *D* resides. Specifically, *D* points to the State *X* long-arm statute, which authorizes service on *D* by first class mail and which was available to *P* under Rule 4(e)(1). Neither the text of Rule 4 nor the accompanying Advisory Committee's note indicate whether *P* is obligated to employ the least expensive form of alternative service when *D* refuses to return the waiver of service of summons. However, it is arguable that the use of a more expensive form of notice than was necessary under the circumstances should be taken into account in determining the costs that *D* must pay under Rule 4(d). *P* should be required to show why the more expensive form of notice was used. If *P* cannot offer a reasonable explanation for use of the more expensive form, *D* should not have to pay more than the costs of the least expensive form of notice.

Illustration 3-51. Assume on the facts of *Illustration 3-47* that the statute of limitations of State *X* where the action is commenced requires that an action be commenced by personal service of summons on the defendant within the statutory

---

565. *See* FED. R. CIV. P. 4 advisory committee's note to the 1993 amendment.

566. *See* Chapter 4 *infra* (Venue and Related Matters), introductory material preceding section A.

567. *See id.*

568. Rule 11 is discussed in Chapter 6(F) *infra* ("Good Faith Pleading: Rule 11"). It is also not a sufficient excuse for failure to return the waiver that the plaintiff's complaint is baseless. *See* Morales v. SI Diamond Tech, No. 98-CIV.-8309 CSH, 1999 WL 144469, 1999 U.S. Dist. LEXIS 2964 (S.D.N.Y. Mar. 17, 1999).

period. At the time *D* receives the notice and request for waiver of service of summons, the statute has not yet run. However, by the time that *D* returns the waiver and it is filed by *P*, the statute has run. *D* answers the complaint in the action in part by asserting the affirmative defense of the statute of limitations. *D's* defense is good, and the action should be dismissed. Rule 4(d)(4) makes it clear that upon the filing of the waiver with the court by *P*, "these rules apply as if a summons and complaint had been served at the time of filing the waiver."[569] Thus, the State *X* statute of limitations was not tolled by the receipt of the notice and request by *D*. Obviously, if *D* had not returned the waiver at all, the same result would follow if *P* were unable to have *D* personally served before the expiration of the statute of limitations. If an applicable statute of limitations is about to run, a plaintiff must attempt to serve process in a way that will toll the statute effectively. The notice and request for waiver cannot safely be used when the applicable statute of limitations does not toll upon receipt by the defendant of notice of the action.[570]

(e) Manner of Service

Assuming that a defendant does not waive service of process or that the defendant is a member of one of the classes to which waiver does not apply, Rule 4(e)-(j) provide the manner in which service must be made on the defendant. A few examples will suffice to indicate how the rule operates. If service is to be made on a competent, adult individual located within the United States,[571] Rule 4(e) provides several methods of service. The defendant may be served pursuant to the law of the state in which the district court is located or pursuant to the law of the state in which service is made.[572] However, the state law in question must be applicable to the service of a summons in the state's courts of general jurisdiction.[573] In addition, Rule 4(e)(2) provides that the defendant may be served (1) by delivering a copy of the summons and complaint to the defendant personally;[574] (2) by leaving a copy of

---

569. *See* FED. R. CIV. P. 4(d)(4); *see also* FED. R. CIV. P. 4 advisory committee's note to the 1993 amendment.

570. *See* Larsen v. Mayo Med. Ctr., 218 F.3d 863 (8th Cir. 2000) (defendant did not return initial waiver of service; plaintiff then sent amended complaint with another request for waiver, and the defendant again refused to execute the waiver; plaintiff eventually had defendant served with process in a proper fashion, but the statute of limitations had run by the time the service was complete; court of appeals held the action time-barred); *see also* Blaney v. West, 209 F.3d 1027 (7th Cir. 2000) (plaintiff's attorney misunderstood right-to-sue letter and did not serve the government properly under Rule 4(i), but attempted service under Rule 4(e); although informed of the mistake, the service was not corrected, with the result that the action was dismissed and the claim was time-barred). The interaction between state statutes of limitation and federal procedural rules is discussed in Chapter 5(E) *infra* ("The Evolution of the *Erie* Doctrine: Applicability of State "Substantive Law" Under the Rules of Decision Act").

571. For provisions governing service on competent adults located outside the United States, see FED. R. CIV. P. 4(f).

572. *See* FED. R. CIV. P. 4(e)(1); Williams v. Moody, No. Civ. A. 98-1211, 1999 WL 79535 (E.D. Pa. Jan. 22, 1999) (defendant, a member of U.S. Navy stationed in Spain, was involved in an auto accident in Sicily; process served pursuant to Rule 4(e)(1) by mailing a copy of the complaint to defendant in care of the Navy Department in Washington, D.C., on the theory, under Pennsylvania law, that was defendant's usual place of business; because defendant is not a resident of any judicial district, Rule 4(f) must be used; service improper); *see also* Caisse v. DuBois, 346 F.3d 213 (1st Cir. 2003) (service of process on public employees sued in their official capacities is governed by the provisions of Rule 4(e) for service on individuals).

573. *See* FED. R. CIV. P. 4(e)(1).

574. *See* FED. R. CIV. P. 4(e)(2)(A). When a rule such as Rule 4(e) provides for delivery to an individual personally, there is the possibility of differences of opinion over the meaning of "personally." In particular, does "personally" mean that process must actually be handed to the defendant, or, under appropriate circumstances, may it be left somewhere in the defendant's vicinity. *See, e.g.*, CRB v. Wyoming Dep't of Family Servs., 974 P.2d 931

the summons and complaint at the defendant's dwelling house or usual place of abode with someone of suitable age and discretion residing there;[575] or (3) by delivering a copy of the summons and complaint to an agent authorized by appointment or law to receive service.[576] Rule 4(e) allows service to be made in any judicial district of the United States. However, mere service does not establish personal jurisdiction. Whether service establishes personal jurisdiction is governed by Rule 4(k), discussed below.[577] Service on individuals who are infants or incompetent persons located in the United States is made in the manner prescribed by the law governing service of a summons on those categories of individuals in the courts of general jurisdiction in the state where service is made.[578]

Domestic or foreign corporations, partnerships, and unincorporated associations not waiving service are served within the United States (1) in the manner prescribed by state law for service of the summons in the courts of general jurisdiction of the state or (2) by delivering a copy of the summons and complaint to an officer, a managing or general agent, or any other agent authorized by appointment or law to receive service.[579] If service is made on an agent authorized by statute to receive service, a copy of the summons and complaint must also be mailed to the defendant if the statute so requires.[580] Service on these same categories of defendants outside the United States is made in the manner prescribed for service on individuals outside the United States under Rule 4(f), except that corporations, partnerships, and unincorporated associations may not be served by personal delivery pursuant to Rule 4(f)(2)(C)(i).[581]

(Wyo. 1999) (sufficient to deposit process in mailbox outside defendant's apartment after process server phoned defendant while outside defendant's apartment and defendant refused to open door); Freund Equip., Inc. v. Fox, 301 Ill. App. 3d 163, 703 N.E.2d 542 (1998) (placing the process in the general vicinity of defendant and announcing the nature of the papers was sufficient).

575. *See* FED. R. CIV. P. 4(e)(2)(B); Stars' Desert Inn Hotel & Country Club, Inc. v. Hwang, 105 F.3d 521 (9th Cir. 1997) (defendant, a citizen of Taiwan, was residing in a state of the U.S. when process served at his U.S. residence by leaving the process with a security guard; service proper; defendant did not have to be served pursuant to Rule 4(f) because he was not a citizen of the U.S.); Beane v. Dailey, 226 W. Va. 445, 701 S.E. 2d 848 (2010) (under provision identical to Rule 4(e)(2)(B), providing for service at defendant's dwelling place or usual place of abode, service on defendant's mother at her home was not valid where there was no proof defendant lived with his mother).

576. *See* FED. R. CIV. P. 4(e)(2)(C); *In re* Focus Media Inc., 387 F.3d 1077 (9th Cir. 2004) (in an adversary proceeding brought in district court related to bankruptcy case, attorney could be an agent "impliedly authorized" to receive service of process if the attorney is representing the party in the related bankruptcy proceeding and the totality of the surrounding circumstances demonstrate the intent of the client to convey such authority).

577. *See* FED. R. CIV. P. 4 advisory committee's note to the 1993 amendment.

578. *See* FED. R. CIV. P. 4(g). An infant or incompetent person located outside the United States is served pursuant to the provisions of Federal Rule 4(f)(2)(A) or (B), or (f)(3) *See id.*

579. FED. R. CIV. P. 4(h)(1)(A) & (B); *see* Mommaerts v. Hartford Life & Accident Ins. Co., 472 F.3d 967 (7th Cir. 2007) (service on a corporate officer may occur anywhere).

580. *See* FED. R. CIV. P. 4(h)(1)(B); Ayres v. Jacobs & Crumplar, P.A., 99 F.3d 565 (3d Cir. 1996) (service on office manager not authorized by appointment or by law was improper); Baade v. Price, 175 F.R.D. 403 (D.D.C. 1997) (service on receptionist of individual codefendant was not service on university when receptionist not an agent by appointment or by law); *see also* Jones v. Automobile Club, 26 Fed. App'x 740 (9th Cir. 2002) (service improperly made on security guard employed by corporate defendant; held that service on improper person could sometimes be excused, but not in this case); David P. Stewart & Anna Conley, *E-Mail Service on Foreign Defendants: Time for an International Approach?* 38 GEO. J. INT'L L. 755 (2007).

581. *See* FED. R. CIV. P. 4(h)(2); *see also* Brockmeyer v. May, 383 F.3d 798 (9th Cir. 2004) (Hague convention on the Service Abroad of Judicial and Extrajudicial Documents does not interfere with the freedom to send judicial documents to persons abroad); Hunter Douglas Metals v. Aluminio Conesa, S.A. de C.V., No. 96 C 6853, 1997 WL 282880, 1997 U.S. Dist. LEXIS 7344 (N.D. Ill. May 16, 1997) (service on alien corporation in foreign country by registered mail under Rule 4 invalid if foreign country does not recognize service by registered mail); Rio Props., Inc. v. Rio Int'l Interlink, 284 F.3d 1007 (9th Cir. 2002) (alternative service by regular mail and e-mail ordered by district court under Rule 4(f)(3) on defendant in foreign country; service valid and did not deny

Failure to follow the provisions governing manner of service in Rule 4(e)-(j) can be raised as an insufficiency of service of process objection under Federal Rule 12(b)(5).

Illustration 3-52. *P* sues *D*, a competent adult, in a U.S. District Court. *P* has *D* served under Rule 4(e)(2)(B), but the process server leaves a copy of the summons and complaint at *D's* home with *D's* child, who is four years old. *D* may move to dismiss the complaint under Federal Rule 12(b)(5) for insufficiency of service of process because process was not left with someone of "suitable age and discretion" as required by Rule 4(e)(2)(B).

(f) Territorial Limits of Effective Service

Rule 4(k)(1) provides that service of a summons or waiver of service is effective to establish personal jurisdiction over a defendant (1) who could be subjected to the jurisdiction of a court of general jurisdiction in the state in which the district court is located, (2) who is a party joined under Rule 14 or 19 and is served at a place within a judicial district of the United States that is not more than 100 miles from the place where the summons issues, (3) when authorized by a federal statute. The provision authorizing personal jurisdiction over a defendant who is subject to jurisdiction under state law, when combined with the manner of service provisions found in Rule 4(e)-(j), allows the federal courts to use state long-arm statutes to acquire personal jurisdiction over nonresident defendants. However, as discussed in section L, below, the federal courts adhere to the Fourteenth Amendment limitations on the power of state courts when asserting personal jurisdiction under state law. Therefore, the due process restrictions of the minimum contacts test discussed in earlier sections of this chapter are applicable to cases in which state long-arm statutes are used to acquire personal jurisdiction over nonresidents in federal actions.

Rule 4(k)(2) is an independent "federal long-arm rule" added by the 1993 amendments to Rule 4.[582] Rule 4(k)(2) provides that service of the summons or filing a waiver of service will be effective to establish personal jurisdiction over a defendant "[f]or a claim arising under federal law"[583] when the defendant is not subject to personal jurisdiction of the courts of general jurisdiction of any state and the assertion of jurisdiction will not violate the Constitution or laws of the United States. This rule was added to close a gap in the ability to obtain personal

---

due process). *But see* Dee-K Enters., Inc. v. Heveafil Sdn. Bhd., 174 F.R.D. 376 (E.D. Va. 1997) (fact that the form of service employed is not authorized by foreign law does not mean that it is "prohibited" by foreign law within the meaning of Rule 4(f)(2)(C)); *but see In re* Estate of Vischering, 782 N.W.2d 141 (Iowa 2010) (district court erred in determining that Hague Convention did not apply in this case; Iowa rule could not be used contrary to Hague Convention to serve defendant personally abroad). *See generally* Yvonne A. Tamayo, *Sometimes the Postman Doesn't Ring at All: Serving Process by Mail to a Post Office Box Abroad,* 13 WILLAMETTE J. INT'L L. & DISP. RESOL. 269 (2005).

582. *See generally* Jeffrey R. Armstrong, *Guaranteed Jurisdiction: The Emerging Role of Fed. R. Civ. P. 4(k)(2) in the Acquisition of Personal Jurisdiction of Foreign Nationals in Internet Intellectual Property Disputes,* 5 MINN. INTELL. PROP. REV. 63 (2003); Gary B. Born & Andrew N. Vollmer, *The Effect of the Revised Federal Rules of Civil Procedure on Personal Jurisdiction, Service, and Discovery in International Cases,* 150 F.R.D. 221, 222-29 (1993).

583. *See, e.g.,* Getz v. Boeing Co., 654 F.3d 852 (9th Cir. 2011) (claims for products liability, negligence, wrongful death, and loss of consortium did not arise under federal law for purposes of Rule 4(k)(2).

jurisdiction when the defendant is a nonresident of the United States who has sufficient contacts with the United States to justify an assertion of personal jurisdiction under the Constitution, but lacks sufficient contacts with any single state to meet the requirements of the Fourteenth Amendment.[584]

The Advisory Committee on the Federal Rules of Civil Procedure had doubts about the validity of Rule 4(k)(2). In a special note, the Advisory Committee called the attention of the Supreme Court and Congress to Rule 4(k)(2). In doing so, the Committee cited concerns that the rule might be invalid under the Rules Enabling Act, 28 U.S.C. § 2072.[585] The Committee's only constitutional concerns were addressed to the limitations that may exist on the territorial reach of the federal court's jurisdiction under the Due Process Clause of the Fifth Amendment.[586] As discussed in Chapter 5, however, a Federal Rule of Civil Procedure extending the territorial reach of the district courts' jurisdiction probably does not violate the Rules Enabling Act, the Advisory Committee's concerns

---

584. *See* FED. R. CIV. P. 4 advisory committee's note to the 1993 amendment; *see also* Omni Capital Int'l, Ltd. v. Rudolf Wolff & Co., 484 U.S. 97, 108 S. Ct. 404, 98 L. Ed. 2d 415 (1987). Of course, in the situations covered by Rule 4(k)(2), there is also no federal long-arm statute in existence that would authorize the federal courts to assert jurisdiction over the nonresident. If such a long-arm statute existed and could be applied consistently with the Constitution, Rule 4(k)(1)(D) would authorize the use of the federal statute and use of Rule 4(k)(2) would be unnecessary.

In administering Rule 4(k)(2), the courts insist upon a demonstration that the defendant cannot be subjected to the jurisdiction of any state court of general jurisdiction. *See, e.g.*, Doe v. Unocal Corp., 248 F.3d 915 (9th Cir. 2001) (listing of stock on various exchanges is insufficient to subject defendant to personal jurisdiction in the United States under Rule 4(k)(2); if contacts of defendant's subsidiaries are imputed to defendant, several states would have jurisdiction over defendant and thus Rule 4(k)(2) would be inapplicable); United States v. Swiss Am. Bank, Ltd., 191 F.3d 30 (1st Cir. 1999) (plaintiff seeking to invoke Rule 4(k)(2) must show (a) that the claim asserted arises under federal law; (b) that personal jurisdiction is not available under any situation-specific federal statute; and (c) that the defendant's contacts with the nation as a whole satisfy constitutional requirements; in addition, (d) the plaintiff must "certify" that, based on information readily available to the plaintiff, the defendant is not subject to suit in the courts of general jurisdiction of any state; once these showings are made, the burden shifts to the defendant to produce evidence that one or more specific states exist in which it can be sued or that its contacts with the United States make an assertion of jurisdiction over it constitutionally insufficient; if the defendant produces evidence that it is subject to personal jurisdiction in one or more states and the plaintiff chooses to contest that matter further, the defendant will be deemed to have waived any claim that it is subject to personal jurisdiction in states other than the ones it has identified). *But see* ISI Int'l, Inc. v. Borden Ladner Gervais LLP, 256 F.3d 548 (7th Cir. 2001) (when defendant's counsel was asked at oral argument whether defendant was subject to personal jurisdiction in any state, counsel indicated that more discovery would be needed; defendant does not need discovery to know its own actions; therefore, appellate court concluded that jurisdiction was appropriate under Rule 4(k)(2) in Illinois; burden on defendant to show it is subject to personal jurisdiction to suit somewhere other than the forum state in order to preclude jurisdiction).

In Central States, Southeast & Southwest Areas Pension Fund v. Reimer Express World Corp., 230 F.3d 934 (7th Cir. 2000), a federal statute authorized nationwide, but not worldwide, service of process. The defendant argued that Rule 4(k)(2) could not be used to assert jurisdiction over defendants outside the United States under these circumstances because the absence of an authorization for worldwide service in the federal long-arm statute would make Rule 4(k)(2) inconsistent with the laws of the United States. The court disagreed, holding that Rule 4(k)(2) was "consistent" with the federal long-arm statute because it did not contradict or oppose the statutory language. However, the plaintiff had not demonstrated the existence of minimum contacts with the United States sufficient to satisfy due process, and the court also held that the district court had not abused its discretion in refusing to allow discovery against the defendant to establish minimum contacts.

585. *See* FED. R. CIV. P. 4(k)(2) special advisory committee's note. The promulgation and operation of the Rules Enabling Act is discussed in Chapter 1(D)(11) *supra* ("Promulgation of the Federal Rules of Civil Procedure") and in Chapter 5(F) *infra* ("The Evolution of the *Erie* Doctrine: Conflicts Between State Law and Federal Rules of Civil Procedure").

586. *See* FED. R. CIV. P. 4 advisory committee's note to the 1993 amendments. The Fifth Amendment limitations on the territorial reach of federal process are discussed in section L *infra* ("Special Problems of Amenability to Process in Federal Court").

notwithstanding.[587] Nevertheless, even though such a rule does not violate the Rules Enabling Act, a strong argument can be made that it violates separation of powers restrictions on judicial rulemaking.[588]

Illustration 3-53. *P*, a citizen of State *X*, sues *D*, a citizen of France, in a U.S. District Court in State *X* for $10,000 on a claim arising under a federal statute. The events giving rise to the claim occurred in State *Z*. After commencement of the action, *P* sends *D* the notice and request for waiver of service prescribed by Rule 4(f). *D* returns the waiver, and *P* files it with the court. Subsequently, *D* appears and moves to dismiss the action for lack of personal jurisdiction. Rule 4(k)(2) does not afford a basis for personal jurisdiction over *D*, even assuming that the Due Process Clause of the Fifth Amendment would not be violated by an assertion of jurisdiction in State *X* on the facts of this illustration. Rule 4(k)(2) is inapplicable if the defendant in an action is subject to personal jurisdiction in the courts of general jurisdiction in any state. Here, *D* would surely be subject to personal jurisdiction in State *Z*, where the events giving rise to the suit occurred.

(g) Proof of Service

As provided by Rule 4(l), proof of service must be made by the person making the service. When that person is someone other than a U.S. marshal or deputy marshal, the proof of service must be made by affidavit. When service is made outside the United States by internationally agreed means calculated to give notice, as authorized by Rule 4(f)(1), proof of service must be made pursuant to the treaty or international convention under which service is authorized. When service outside the United States is made under other provisions of Rule 4(f), proof of service must include a receipt signed by the addressee or other evidence of delivery to the addressee that is satisfactory to the court.[589] Failure to make proof of service does not invalidate the service, and the court may allow proof of service to be amended under Rule 4(l).[590]

(h) Time Limits on Effectuating Service

Pursuant to Rule 4(m), if service is not made within 120 days after the filing of the complaint, the court may, on motion or on its own initiative and after notice to the plaintiff, dismiss the action without prejudice as to any defendant not served. Alternatively, the court may order that service be effectuated within a specified time. If the plaintiff shows good cause for failing to make service within the 120 day period, the court must extend the time for "an appropriate period." However,

---

587. *But see* Stephen B. Burbank, *The World in Our Courts*, 89 MICH. L. REV. 1456, 1484 n.164 (1991) (reviewing GARY B. BORN & DAVID WESTIN, INTERNATIONAL CIVIL LITIGATION IN UNITED STATES COURTS: COMMENTARY AND MATERIALS (1989)).

588. *See* Ralph U. Whitten, *Separation of Powers Restrictions on Judicial Rulemaking: A Case Study of Federal Rule 4*, 40 ME. L. REV. 41, 103-06 (1988). For further discussion of the validity of Rule 4(k)(2) under the Rules Enabling Act and the separation-of-powers doctrine, see Chapter 5 *infra*, where the subject can be placed in the context of a full discussion of the Supreme Court's rulemaking authority.

589. *See* FED. R. CIV. P. 4(l)(2)(A) & (B).

590. *See* Russell v. City of Milwaukee, 338 F.3d 662 (7th Cir. 2003) (absence of a certificate of service does not preclude a finding that service has been made).

it is not good cause for failure to serve the defendant within the time limits that the plaintiff mailed the defendant a proper request for waiver and the defendant did not return it.[591] The time limits do not apply to service in a foreign country under Rule 4(f) or 4(j)(1) (dealing with service on a foreign state or its subdivisions, agencies, or instrumentalities).[592]

Illustration 3-54. *P*, a citizen of State *X*, sues *D*, a citizen of State *Y*, in a U.S. District Court for $500,000. *P's* claim is for personal injuries received in an automobile accident with *D* in State *X*. The State *X* statute of limitations applicable to *P's* claim will run 20 days after commencement of the action. The statute requires that an action such as *P's* be commenced by personal service of process on the defendant within the statutory period. Under these circumstances, *P* should not use the notice and request for waiver of service provisions of Rule 4(d), but should, with celerity, have *D* served personally in State *Y* before the statutory time period runs. Rule 4(d)(2)(F) requires that a defendant be given at least 30 days from the date on which the request is sent to return the waiver. Thus, a severe danger exists that the statute of limitations will have run before *D* returns the waiver and *P* files it with the court.[593]

* * * * *

Rule 4(m) provides that if the plaintiff shows good cause for the failure to serve the defendant within 120 days, the court shall extend the time for service. In *Coleman v. Milwaukee Board of School Directors,*[594] the plaintiff ineffectively attempted to serve the defendant twice. The result of the ineffective attempts at service was that service was not accomplished within 120 days. The district court dismissed the action. On appeal, the court of appeals stated that when the defendant does not show any harm to its ability to defend as a consequence of the delay in service, and when, as here, dismissal without prejudice has the effect of dismissal

---

591. *See* Troxell v. Fedders of N. Am., Inc., 160 F.3d 381 (7th Cir. 1998). An objection that service is untimely under Rule 4(m) is an insufficiency of process objection under Rule 12(b)(5) that can be waived under Rule 12(h)(1) if not included in a preanswer motion. *See* McCurdy v. American Bd. of Plastic Surgery, 157 F.3d 191 (3d Cir. 1998); *see also* United States v. McLaughlin, 470 F.3d 698 (7th Cir. 2006) (a showing of "excusable neglect" is not necessary to obtain an extension of time for service); Bolden v. City of Topeka, 441 F.3d 1129 (10th Cir. 2006) (period for service of process is not restarted by filing of amended complaint except as to defendants newly added to action by amendment); Betty K Agencies, Ltd. v. M/V Monada, 432 F.3d 1333 (11th Cir. 2005) (dismissal with prejudice for failure to perfect service was improper; dismissal with prejudice is a drastic sanction that should be applied only when lesser sanctions would be inadequate to correct any defect in service); Romo v. Gulf Stream Coach, Inc., 250 F.3d 1119 (7th Cir. 2001) (in action removed from state to federal court, it was discovered that defendant had never been served with process; district court dismissed action for failure to comply with the 120-day limit in Rule 4(m) and because plaintiff refused to exercise reasonable diligence in serving process as required by state law; court of appeals holds that the 120-day limit is not applicable to cases commenced in state court, even if they are later removed to federal court; however, court agreed that district court could apply state procedural rules to pre-removal conduct and affirmed); City of Merced v. Fields, 997 F. Supp. 1326 (E.D. Cal. 1998) (new time period to serve begins for defendants added to the action after 120 days).

592. *See* Nylok Corp. v. Fastener World Inc., 396 F.3d 805 (7th Cir. 2005) (120-day time limit under Rule 4(m) does not apply to service of foreign defendants).

593. *See, e.g.*, Cruz v. Louisiana *ex rel.* Dep't of Pub. Safety, 528 F.3d 375 (5th Cir. 2008) (dismissal was without prejudice under Rule 4(m), but state law applied to determine whether dismissed action suspended running of state statute of limitations for purposes of later-filed action); Roberts v. Georgia, 228 Fed. App'x 851 (11th Cir. 2007) (dismissal without prejudice for failure to timely serve defendants; action refiled, but barred by statute of limitations under Georgia law);

594. 290 F.3d 932 (7th Cir. 2002); *see also* Bowling v. Hasbro, Inc., 403 F.3d 1373 (Fed. Cir. 2005) (dismissal with prejudice under Rule 4(m) was improper; invocation of Rule 41(b) as justification for dismissing "on the merits" was not a proper justification where there was inadequate evidence that plaintiff had notice that dismissal with prejudice was about to occur); Horenkamp v. Van Winkle & Co., 402 F.3d 1129 (11th Cir. 2005) (district court has discretion to extend 120-day period even in the absence of a showing of good cause).

with prejudice because the statute of limitations has run, the district court's discretion to extend the time for service should normally be exercised in favor of the plaintiff. However, the court found no abuse of discretion in the district court's refusal to extend the time for service. The plaintiff's attorney had waited until almost the last minute to serve the defendant and had then failed to do so in accordance with the rules. The plaintiff stated that the reason for waiting until the 115th day to attempt service was that the plaintiff wanted to add a claim to the complaint and had to wait for a right-to-sue letter to do so. The plaintiff feared that if the defendant was served and answered the complaint promptly, the plaintiff's right to amend to add the claim would be cut off under Rule 15(a) and the plaintiff would have to ask the court for permission. The court held this reason was not a good one because no real danger existed that the district court would deny permission to amend.[595]

(i) In Rem and Quasi in Rem Jurisdiction

Rule 4(n) is a curious provision that authorizes the assertion of in rem and quasi in rem jurisdiction in the federal courts. Rule 4(n)(1) states that the court can assert jurisdiction over property if authorized by a federal statute. When such jurisdiction is exercised, notice must be sent to claimants of the property either in the manner authorized by the statute or by service of a summons under Rule 4. Section 1655 of Title 28 provides for nationwide long-arm jurisdiction in actions in the district courts to enforce liens upon or claims to, or to remove encumbrances or liens or clouds upon, the title to real and personal property within the district. Section 1655 is the kind of statute incorporated by reference in Rule 4(n).[596] Any constitutional issues concerning the application of this federal statute would be determined by reference to the Fifth Amendment due process limits on the power of Congress.[597] However, under *Shaffer v. Heitner*, discussed in section E(1), above, an assertion of jurisdiction by a court where property is located to adjudicate a matter directly concerning the property does not violate the Due Process Clause of the Fourteenth Amendment. Because the Fifth Amendment due process restrictions on the power of Congress are not narrower than the Fourteenth Amendment due process restrictions on the power of the states, there should be no constitutional difficulties with the application of § 1655 or similar statutes under Rule 4(n)(1).[598]

---

595. *See also* Zapata v. City of New York, 502 F.3d 192 (2d Cir. 2007) (district court did not abuse discretion in dismissing for failure to comply with time limit of Rule 4(m) without a discretionary extension of time, even though action would be time-barred absent such an extension); Lepone-Dempsey v. Carroll Cnty. Comm'rs, 476 F.3d 1277 (11th Cir. 2007) (when plaintiff fails to show good cause for not completing timely service, district court must still consider whether any circumstances, including whether action would be barred by statute of limitations, warranted giving plaintiff additional time); Efaw v. Williams, 473 F.3d 1038 (9th Cir. 2007) (error to grant extension of time to plaintiff to serve defendant after delay of seven years, given lack of reasonable explanation for delay).

596. *See* FED. R. CIV. P. 4 advisory committee's note to the 1993 amendment.

597. *See* the discussion of the Fifth Amendment limits on federal jurisdiction in section L *infra* ("Special Problems of Amenability to Process in Federal Court").

598. Rule 4(n)(1) states that "[t]he court may assert jurisdiction over property if authorized by a federal statute." In Porsche Cars N.A., Inc. v. Porsch.com, 51 F. Supp. 2d 707 (E.D. Va. 1999), the plaintiff attempted to use Rule 4(n)(1) to assert in rem jurisdiction to cancel internet domain names that allegedly diluted protected trademarks. The court held that the Trademark Dilution Act, 15 U.S.C. § 1125(c), under which the action was brought, did not permit in rem jurisdiction. The court was influenced by the fact that to interpret the Act to provide

More troublesome is the authorization of quasi in rem jurisdiction in Rule 4(n)(2). Rule 4(n)(2) states that a district court may exercise jurisdiction over a defendant's assets located within the district by seizing the assets under the circumstances and in the manner authorized by the law of the state in which the district court is located. The only qualification of this authority in the text of Rule 4(n)(2) is that there must be a showing that personal jurisdiction cannot be obtained over the defendant in the district where the action is brought "by reasonable efforts to serve a summons under this rule." Thus, the rule appears to authorize the acquisition of jurisdiction based on the presence of property alone, without regard to whether the defendant can be constitutionally subjected to personal jurisdiction within the state under the minimum contacts test.

The Advisory Committee's note to this portion of Rule 4 states that it is, indeed, the intention of Rule 4(n)(2) to authorize quasi in rem jurisdiction, but only under "exigent circumstances." The Committee's note also states that the occasion to use quasi in rem jurisdiction of this sort should be rare, such as when the defendant is a fugitive or the assets are in imminent danger of disappearing.[599] This statement appears to suggest that seizure of property under the rule can only occur in accord with the accepted constitutional restrictions on the use of state provisional remedies.[600] If this is the meaning of Rule 4(n)(2), the rule does not really constitute an attempt to authorize the acquisition of jurisdiction based only on property contrary to *Shaffer v. Heitner*. However, the text of the rule does not contain this limitation. It is bothersome that the Advisory Committee has placed such an important qualification of the rule in its note rather than in the text itself. In several instances, the Supreme Court has insisted on interpreting Federal Rules of Civil Procedure in accordance with their "plain language," even when this approach has produced a seemingly unreasonable result.[601] Under the plain text of Rule 4(n)(2), quasi in rem jurisdiction of the sort outlawed by *Shaffer* seems to be authorized. Therefore, the rule, as phrased, raises unfortunate constitutional questions.

Illustration 3-55. *P*, a citizen of State *X*, sues *D*, a citizen of State *Y*, in a U.S. District Court in State *X* for $500,000. *P's* claim is based on an automobile accident that occurred between *P* and *D* in State *Z*. *D* owns a parcel of land in State *X* worth $1,000,000, but has no other contacts with State *X*. *P* has no evidence that

---

for in rem jurisdiction would bring the constitutionality of the statute into doubt. "Although *in rem* proceedings purport to affect nothing more than the disposition of property, they necessarily affect the interests of persons as well [citing *Shaffer v. Heitner*]. As a result, courts generally cannot exercise *in rem* jurisdiction to adjudicate the status of property unless the Due Process Clause would have permitted *in personam* jurisdiction over those who have an interest in the *res* [citing *Shaffer* again]." *Id.* at 712. The court's suggestion seems to be that Congress cannot, given the restrictions imposed by the Fifth Amendment, give the federal courts nationwide long-arm jurisdiction to adjudicate the interests of persons in the United States over property located in the United States. This suggestion may be incorrect in any case, but in any event it cannot be correct if the question pertains to property located in or connected to the district in some substantial way because *Shaffer* explicitly preserved the power of the *state courts* to adjudicate claims related to property located in the states, and the power of Congress to provide for long-arm jurisdiction in the federal courts certainly cannot be less than that of the state legislatures. The Fourth Circuit Court of Appeals, in the same case, later confirmed that an assertion of in rem jurisdiction is constitutional under *Shaffer* when the property itself is the source of the controversy. *See* Porsche Cars N.A., Inc. v. Porsche.net, 302 F.3d 248 (4th Cir. 2002).

599. *See* FED. R. CIV. P. 4 advisory committee's note to the 1993 amendment.

600. These restrictions are discussed in Chapter 6(G)(7) *infra* ("Constitutional Limitations on Provisional Remedies").

601. *See, e.g.*, Delta Air Lines, Inc. v. August, 450 U.S. 346, 101 S. Ct. 1146, 67 L. Ed. 2d 287 (1981). *Delta Air Lines* is discussed in Chapter 10(F)(2) *infra* ("Settlement: Rule 68").

D is about to dispose of the land. Assume that State *X* has a statute allowing property owned by a nonresident defendant to be attached merely *because* the defendant is a nonresident. Rule 4(n)(2) would seem to allow *P* to institute a quasi in rem action against *D* in State *X* by attaching the land owned by *D* under the State *X* statute. However, if the U.S. District Court follows the usual approach of the federal courts to personal jurisdiction acquired pursuant to state law, the court would enforce the Fourteenth Amendment limitations on the ability to utilize quasi in rem jurisdiction announced by *Shaffer v. Heitner*. These limitations would require the court to dismiss *P's* action on *D's* motion. Rule 4(n) should not be read to override the normal constitutional restrictions on personal jurisdiction that would be enforced in diversity actions. To do so would require that the court treat Rule 4(n)(2) as a kind of federal long-arm rule of procedure, whose validity would have to be evaluated under the Due Process Clause of the Fifth Amendment and the separation of powers restrictions on judicial rulemaking referred to above. The text and Advisory Committee note do not clearly indicate that Rule 4(n)(2) was intended to operate this broadly.

SECTION L. SPECIAL PROBLEMS OF AMENABILITY TO PROCESS IN FEDERAL COURT

In determining whether a defendant can be subjected to personal jurisdiction by a federal court, one must confront two separate sets of problems. First, there exists a question about the proper constitutional standard to apply to assertions of long-arm jurisdiction under federal statutes. Second, there exists a question about the proper constitutional standard to use when the federal courts assert jurisdiction under a state long-arm statute. The Supreme Court has never authoritatively resolved these questions. Furthermore, general agreement among the federal courts exists on only a few of the questions, although there is an emerging pattern in the U.S. Courts of Appeals in cases involving federal long-arm statutes and rules.

1. The Constitutional Standard Under Federal Long-Arm Statutes and Rules

There is universal agreement that the Due Process Clause of the Fifth Amendment limits the power of Congress to enact federal long-arm statutes, while the Due Process Clause of the Fourteenth Amendment limits the power of the state legislatures to enact state long-arm statutes. As demonstrated in earlier sections of this chapter, when the constitutionality of applying a state long-arm statute is in issue, the minimum contacts test of *International Shoe v. Washington* is applied.

When Congress enacts a long-arm statute that allows the federal courts to serve process nationwide, what standard does the Fifth Amendment impose on the power to apply the statute to nonresidents of the district or state in which the action is brought? The traditional assumption has been that Congress has absolute power to extend long-arm jurisdiction throughout the United States without restriction by the Due Process Clause of the Fifth Amendment.[602] This traditional view evolved when *Pennoyer v. Neff's* territorial understanding of the Fourteenth Amendment's due process restrictions on state court jurisdiction prevailed.[603] Under *Pennoyer*, the Due Process Clause of the Fourteenth Amendment only limited the power of the states to assert personal jurisdiction when the states reached outside their borders. Applied to the Due Process Clause of the Fifth Amendment, this theory would only limit the power of federal courts to assert personal jurisdiction when those courts are authorized to reach outside the borders of the United States. Thus, Congress might authorize a district court to assert jurisdiction over any defendant within the country, despite the lack of any contact between the defendant and the particular place within the country where the district court is located.[604] Such a conferral of long-arm jurisdiction would be valid because Congress would not be extending the reach of process beyond the territorial limits of the United States.

Illustration 3-56. *P*, a citizen of State *X*, and *D*, a citizen of State *Y*, collide in their automobiles in State *Z*. State *X* is a state on the East Coast of the United States. State *Y* is a state on the West Coast of the United States. State *Z* is a state in the Mid-West. *D* has no contacts with State *X*. Under the traditional view of Congress' power under the Due Process Clause of the Fifth Amendment, Congress may validly authorize a U.S. District Court in State *X* to assert jurisdiction over *D* to adjudicate a claim for personal injuries by *P* arising out of the automobile accident, despite the fact that *D* has no contacts with State *X* and defending the action there would be very burdensome.[605]

* * * * *

The traditional view of Congress' power under the Due Process Clause of the Fifth Amendment is at odds with the purposes of the minimum contacts test of the Fourteenth Amendment. The latter test seeks to preserve the defendant's opportunity to be heard in defense by allowing the defendant to anticipate the burdens of suit in a particular location and avoid or defray those burdens. Even if

---

602. *See* ALI STUDY OF THE DIVISION OF JURISDICTION BETWEEN STATE AND FEDERAL COURTS 437 (1969); RICHARD H. FALLON ET AL., HART & WECHSLER'S THE FEDERAL COURTS AND THE FEDERAL SYSTEM 1420-22 (6th ed. 2009). Numerous cases have stated in dictum that Congress' power to provide for nationwide long-arm jurisdiction is absolute. *See, e.g.*, Mississippi Publ'g Corp. v. Murphree, 326 U.S. 438, 442, 66 S. Ct. 242, 245, 90 L. Ed. 185, 190 (1946); Robertson v. Railroad Labor Bd., 268 U.S. 619, 622, 45 S. Ct. 621, 622, 69 L. Ed. 1119, 1121 (1925); United States v. Union Pac. R.R. Co., 98 U.S. 569, 603-04, 25 L. Ed. 143, 151 (1879); Toland v. Sprague, 37 U.S. (12 Pet.) 300, 328, 9 L. Ed. 1093, 1105 (1838).

603. *See* RICHARD H. FALLON ET AL., HART & WECHSLER'S THE FEDERAL COURTS AND THE FEDERAL SYSTEM 1420-22 (6th ed. 2009).

604. Under the influence of the minimum contacts test of *International Shoe*, federal courts operating under the traditional view often state that minimum contacts with the United States are required for an assertion of jurisdiction under a federal long-arm statute to be valid. *See, e.g.*, Lorelei Corp. v. County of Guadalupe, 940 F.2d 717, 720 (1st Cir. 1991); New Eng. Health Care Employees Union, Dist. 1199 v. Fall River Nursing Home, Inc., 802 F. Supp. 674, 677 (D.R.I. 1992); Duckworth v. Medical Electro-Therapeutics, Inc., 768 F. Supp. 822, 826 (S.D. Ga. 1991); *see also* Dakota Indus., Inc. v. Dakota Sportswear, Inc., 946 F.2d 1384 (8th Cir. 1991); *cf.* Jackie Gardina, *The Bankruptcy of Due Process: Nationwide Service of Process, Personal Jurisdiction and the Bankruptcy Code*, 16 AM. BANKR. INST. L. REV. 37, 37-42 (2008).

605. In this illustration, venue would not be proper under 28 U.S.C. § 1391(a). Thus, it must be assumed that Congress, in addition to authorizing personal jurisdiction in the district court for State *X*, also authorizes venue there. Furthermore, under 28 U.S.C. § 1404(a), *D* could move for a transfer of venue for the convenience of the parties and witnesses and in the interests of justice, and a transfer would surely be granted. Under the *Burger King* decision, discussed in section G(2)*(b)(ii) supra* ("The Two-Step Test for the Validity of Specific Jurisdiction"), the availability of transfer could be taken into account in evaluating the due process validity of an assertion of jurisdiction under the minimum contacts test of the Fourteenth Amendment. Thus, Congress might also have to repeal § 1404(a) to present a pure case under the Fifth Amendment.

the defendant has "purposeful contacts" with the forum, the defendant is still allowed to show that the burdens of suit are unreasonable under the *Burger King* reasonableness test. It makes no sense to suppose that the Fourteenth Amendment imposes restrictions on the power of the states designed to protect defendants from unreasonably burdensome places of trial, but the Fifth Amendment allows Congress to impose such burdens without restraint. Perhaps for this reason, it has been suggested that the Fifth Amendment restrictions on the power of Congress may contain restrictions similar to those imposed on the states under the Fourteenth Amendment.[606]

Some lower federal courts have agreed that the Fifth Amendment must be read to contain standards protecting the defendant from burdensome litigation similar to those contained in the Fourteenth Amendment. For example, in *Republic of Panama v. BCCI Holdings (Luxembourg) S.A.*,[607] the court held that the Fifth Amendment standard governing federal long-arm service over a domestic defendant included the same reasonableness standards as the Fourteenth Amendment and allowed defendants to demonstrate that a forum is excessively burdensome. Although the Fifth Amendment standard required evaluation of the defendant's contacts with the United States, those contacts would not automatically satisfy due process. The defendant was entitled to demonstrate that an assertion of jurisdiction in the forum will make litigation so gravely difficult that the defendant is at a severe disadvantage in comparison to the plaintiff. Once this showing is made, due process will only be satisfied if the federal interest in having the action litigated in the forum outweighs the burdens on the defendant.

In *Republic of Panama*, the defendants were large corporations providing banking services to customers in major metropolitan areas along the eastern seaboard of the United States.[608] The court held that the fact that they did not have significant contacts with Florida, where the action was brought, was insufficient to show that Florida was an unreasonably inconvenient forum.[609] In addition, the fact that discovery in the action would be conducted throughout the world suggested to the court that Florida would not be substantially more inconvenient than other districts in the United States.[610] Thus, the court held that the defendants challenging personal jurisdiction had not met their threshold burden of making a compelling case that their ability to defend the action would be severely compromised if they had to litigate in Florida.[611] Because this threshold burden had not been met, the

---

606. *See* FED. R. CIV. P. 4(k)(2) advisory committee's note to the 1993 amendment; *see also* Maryellen Fullerton, *Constitutional Limits on Nationwide Personal Jurisdiction in the Federal Courts*, 79 NW. U. L. REV. 1, 39-60 (1984); Jackie Gardina, *The Bankruptcy of Due Process: Nationwide Service of Process, Personal Jurisdiction and the Bankruptcy Code*, 16 AM. BANKR. INST. L. REV. 37, 41-42, 68 (2008); Ralph U. Whitten, *The Constitutional Limitations on State-Court Jurisdiction: A Historical-Interpretative Reexamination of the Full Faith and Credit and Due Process Clauses* (pt. 2), 14 CREIGHTON L. REV. 735, 850 (1981).

607. 119 F.3d 935 (11th Cir. 1997).

608. *See id.* at 948.

609. *See id.*

610. *See id.*

611. *See id.*

court found it unnecessary to balance the federal interest in providing for long-arm jurisdiction against the burdens on the defendants.[612]

Because the court in *Republic of Panama* did not find it necessary to reach the balancing portion of the test it articulated, it is not possible to determine how the court will attach weight to the different elements of the test or otherwise analyze the case. However, in *ESAB Group, Inc. v. Centricut, Inc.*,[613] the court followed *Republic of Panama*, but indicated that when defendants are located within the United States, they must look primarily to federal venue requirements for protection from onerous litigation. This echos the statement in the Supreme Court's *Burger King* decision that the reasonableness test under the Fourteenth Amendment could not be used to defeat jurisdiction in that case in part because of the availability of procedural mechanisms such as a change of venue.[614]

If the combined analysis of these two cases takes root, it may be impossible for a defendant to defeat an assertion of long-arm jurisdiction under the Fifth Amendment if a transfer of venue is possible under 28 U.S.C. § 1404(a). However, as we will see in the next chapter, transfer under § 1404(a) takes into account more factors than simply the burdens on the defendant, such as the convenience of all the parties and the witnesses, the interests of the public and the court system, and so forth.[615] Therefore, it is conceivable, especially in a multiple defendant case, that a transfer might be denied, but that one of the defendants might be so significantly burdened as to meet *Republic of Panama's* threshold test. This would present directly the question of how much weight the federal interest in providing for nationwide long-arm jurisdiction in the forum would be over *all* the defendants.[616]

---

612. Professor Borchers has suggested that one remedy for the Supreme Court's decisions in the *McIntyre* and *Goddyear* cases discussed in previous sections would be to amend Rule 4(k)(2) to eliminate the requirement of a federal claim, thus extending the nationwide long-arm reach over foreign defendants to diversity actions governed by state law as the plurality opinion in *McIntyre* suggested the federal government might have power to do. *See* Patrick J. Borchers, J. McIntyre Machinery, Goodyear, *and the Incoherence of the Minimum Contacts Test*, 44 CREIGHTON L. REV. 1245, 1275 (2011). However, if the Fifth Amendment Due Process test evolving in the lower federal courts prevails, this approach might not work. Balancing the federal interest in long-arm jurisdiction against the burdens on the defendant will presumably produce jurisdiction more easily when Congress (or the rulemakers) are attempting to provide a forum for the vindication of federal rights—*i.e.*, because the federal interest will weigh more heavily when federal rights are involved than when state rights are involved. Thus, jurisdiction might be more easily be defeated in diversity and alienage cases under the test than in federal question cases.

613. 126 F.3d 617, 627 (4th Cir. 1997).

614. This and other aspects of *Burger King* are discussed in section H(2) *supra*.

615. Section 1404(a) is examined in Chapter 4(D)(2)*(a) infra*.

616. *See also* Denny's, Inc. v. Cake, 364 F.3d 521 (4th Cir. 2004) (assertion of personal jurisdiction by a U.S. District Court in South Carolina over California Labor Commissioner under long-arm provisions of ERISA would not violate the Due Process Clause of the Fifth Amendment in the absence of a demonstration by the Commissioner that the assertion of jurisdiction would result in such extreme inconvenience or unfairness as would outweigh congressionally articulated policy of nationwide long-arm jurisdiction in ERISA); Quick Techs., Inc. v. Sage Group PLC, 313 F.3d 338 (5th Cir. 2002) (exercise of specific jurisdiction under Rule 4(k)(2) must be consistent with the Due Process Clause of the Fifth Amendment, which requires that defendant have purposeful contacts with the United States; here, claims do not sufficiently arise out of or relate to the defendant's contacts with the United States); Peay v. BellSouth Med. Assistance Plan, 205 F.3d 1206 (10th Cir. 2000) (rejecting the view adopted by the Fifth and Eighth Circuits that national contacts alone are sufficient to satisfy the Due Process Clause of the Fifth Amendment and holding that the Fifth Amendment requires the same reasonableness inquiry as does the Fourteenth Amendment; jurisdiction sustained under the test). *But see* SEC v. Bilzerian, 378 F.3d 1100 (D.C. Cir. 2004) (due process requirement that there be minimum contacts with the forum state is inapplicable when court exercises jurisdiction under federal long-arm statute; in such circumstances, minimum contacts with the United States suffice); Action Embroidery Corp. v. Atlantic Embroidery, Inc., 368 F.3d 1174 (9th Cir. 2004) (when a federal statute authorizes nationwide service of process, due process is satisfied if the defendant has minimum contacts with the United States).

When a defendant must be served outside the United States, similar issues exist. Some federal courts hold that national, rather than state, contacts are the only relevant inquiry under the Fifth Amendment.[617] Other cases seem more willing to use standards closer to the Fourteenth Amendment restrictions on state-court jurisdiction. These cases tend to follow the analytical pattern of the Fourteenth Amendment minimum contacts decisions, inquiring whether the assertion of jurisdiction is specific or general and then analyzing the case accordingly, depending on which category is relevant. The latter decisions represent a strong trend in the U.S. Courts of Appeals,[618] and the reason seems obvious. In a case in

---

617. *See, e.g.*, Holland Am. Line Inc. v. Wärtsilä N. Am., Inc., 485 F.3d 450 (9th Cir. 2007) (although defendant did not allege it was subject to personal jurisdiction in any state, it had insufficient national contacts to satisfy due process in an assertion of personal jurisdiction under Rule 4(k)(2); Pebble Beach Co. v. Caddy, 453 F.3d 1151 (9th Cir. 2006) (defendant's use of "Pebble Beach" in passive website advertising was insufficient to subject him to personal jurisdiction under Rule 4(k)(2) under national contacts test); SEC v. Carrillo, 115 F.3d 1540 (11th Cir. 1997); Szafarowicz v. Gotterup, 68 F. Supp. 2d 38 (D. Mass. 1999); Miller Pipeline Corp. v. British Gas PLC, 901 F. Supp. 1416 (S.D. Ind. 1995); *see also* Graduate Mgmt. Admission Council v. Raju, 241 F. Supp. 2d 589 (E.D. Va. 2003) (in copyright and trademark infringement action against citizen of India, plaintiff attempted to assert jurisdiction over defendant under state long-arm statute; court held that long-arm statute applied to case, but that defendant did not have sufficient contacts with state to satisfy the Due Process Clause of the Fourteenth Amendment; however, court also held that jurisdiction could be asserted under Rule 4(k)(2) because defendant's internet activities provided sufficient contacts with United States as a whole to satisfy the Due Process Clause of the Fifth Amendment).

618. *See, e.g.*, Porina v. Marward Shipping Co., 521 F.3d 122 (2d Cir. 2008) (assertion of general jurisdiction under Rule 4(k)(2); defendant did not have systematic and continuous contacts with the United States); Saudi v. Northrop Grumman Corp., 427 F.3d 271 (4th Cir. 2005) (under Rule 4(k)(2), foreign corporation was not subject to either specific or general jurisdiction in United States; only contacts were a single short-term contract and had a wholly-owned subsidiary in Texas; seaman's personal injury claim did not arise out of corporation's contacts with the United States and the contacts were not enough to constitute systematic and continuous contacts that were necessary to sustain an assertion of general jurisdiction); R & B Falcon Drilling, Inc. v. Noble Denton Group, 91 Fed. App'x 317 (5th Cir. 2004) (in action against worldwide engineering consulting firm for damages to drilling rig at sea, Texas could not exercise general or specific jurisdiction over defendant, and no jurisdiction existed under Rule 4(k)(2) because contacts between defendant and United States were insufficient to satisfy Due Process Clause of Fifth Amendment); Chew v. Dietrich, 137 F.3d 748 (2d Cir. 1998) (jurisdiction proper under Rule 4(k)(2) in Rhode Island where defendant assembled crew in Rhode Island for round trip yacht voyage to Bermuda and plaintiff's decedent killed on return leg; contacts with Rhode Island "related to" claim and satisfied Fifth Amendment); Doe v. Unocal Corp., 27 F. Supp. 2d 1174 (C.D. Cal. 1998) (jurisdiction asserted under Rule 4(k)(2) over French corporation invalid, *inter alia*, because contract with California citizen inadequate by itself under *Burger King* to establish purposeful contacts and reasonableness test need not be reached); Nissho Iwai Corp. v. M/V Star Sapphire, No. Civ. A. H-94-1599, 1995 WL 847172, 1995 U.S. Dist. LEXIS 21443 (S.D. Tex. Aug. 24, 1995) (claim arising outside U.S. requires systematic and continuous contacts with U.S. as a whole to satisfy assertion of federal long-arm jurisdiction); *see also* Adams v. Unione Mediterranea di Sicurta, 364 F.3d 646 (5th Cir. 2004) (Italian cargo insurer that had insured hundreds of shipments to United States and covered numerous United States companies, had sufficient ties to United States as a whole to satisfy due process, as required for exercise of personal jurisdiction under Rule 4(k)(2) when foreign defendant was not subject to personal jurisdiction in any particular state); Glencore Grain Rotterdam B.V. v. Shivnath Rai Harnarain Co., 284 F.3d 1114 (9th Cir. 2002) (jurisdiction asserted under Rule 4(k)(2) invalid; defendant's California contacts were not sufficient to satisfy the national contacts requirement of the Due Process Clause of the Fifth Amendment); Base Metal Trading, Ltd. v. OJSC "Novokuznetsy Aluminum Factory," 283 F.3d 208 (4th Cir. 2002) (assertion of jurisdiction under Rule 4(k)(2) invalid because plaintiff has not demonstrated that defendant is not subject to personal jurisdiction in any state or that defendant has sufficient contacts with the United States to satisfy general jurisdiction test); Submersible Sys., Inc. v. Perforadora Cent., S.A. de C.V., 249 F.3d 413 (5th Cir. 2002) (defendant vessel owner's contacts with Mississippi were wholly unrelated to plaintiff's claim that defendant converted plaintiff's equipment in Mexico; therefore, under Fifth Amendment, contacts of defendant with United States had to be systematic and continuous to satisfy the validity test for general jurisdiction); BP Chems. Ltd. v. Formosa Chem. & Fibre Corp., 229 F.3d 254 (3d Cir. 2000) (service under Rule 4(k)(2) did not establish personal jurisdiction over defendant whose contacts with the United States were insufficient to sustain either specific or general jurisdiction; contracts with United States party were unrelated to tort claim, which arose from actions outside the United States that had their impact outside the United States); Consolidated Dev. Corp. v. Sherritt, Inc., 216 F.3d 1286 (11th Cir. 2000) (jurisdiction asserted under Rule 4(k)(2) invalid; claim does not arise out of defendant's activities with United States; thus, assertion of jurisdiction is general; defendant's limited and sporadic contacts with United States are not substantial enough to sustain assertion of jurisdiction); Associated Transp. Line, Inc. v. Productos Fitosanitarios Proficol El Carmen, S.A., 197 F.3d 1070 (11th Cir. 1999) (national contacts of defendant insufficient to sustain exercise of general jurisdiction over defendant under Rule 4(k)(2)).

which the defendant must be served abroad, the specific and general jurisdiction analysis of the Fourteenth Amendment seems more directly relevant to the Fifth Amendment analysis. In contrast, federal long-arm jurisdiction over resident defendants, if analogized directly to Fourteenth Amendment doctrine, would always, under the *Burnham* decision,[619] result in the assertion of jurisdiction being valid, because the defendant would always be served within the territory of the United States and the minimum contacts test would either be irrelevant or automatically satisfied. Indeed, the label "long-arm" jurisdiction would arguably be inappropriate under such an analogy. Nevertheless, the strong pull of *International Shoe's* logic is that due process, insofar as it places restrictions on the location of suit, should focus on the burdens that the particular location places on the defendant's opportunity to be heard in defense. That logic has begun to result in cases like *Republic of Panama* and *ESAB Group*, which struggle with how to create reasonable Fifth Amendment restrictions on location of suit under long-arm statutes that probably reflect nineteenth century assumptions about territorial power.

Oddly, the Supreme Court has not directly confronted the question of the power of Congress to confer long-arm jurisdiction on the federal courts since *International Shoe* was decided.[620] In the Court's recent decision of *J. McIntyre Machinery, Ltd. v. Nicastro*,[621] discussed in section G(2)*(b)(iii)*, above, the plurality opinion at one point stated:

> It may be that, assuming it were otherwise empowered to legislate on the subject, the Congress could authorize the exercise of jurisdiction in appropriate courts. That circumstance is not presented in this case, however, and it is neither necessary nor appropriate to address here any constitutional concerns that might be attendant to that exercise of power.[622]

To say that this cryptic statement is not clear is an understatement. The Court's reference to "appropriate courts," rather than to "federal courts," suggests that the statement may not be referring to the power of Congress to confer long-arm jurisdiction on the latter, but rather to some power of Congress to confer long-arm jurisdiction on the state courts under one of its "substantive" powers in Article I of the Constitution, such as the Commerce Clause.[623] This reading is reinforced by an earlier statement by the plurality that did seem directly address the power of Congress to confer long-arm jurisdiction on the federal courts:

> Because the United States is a distinct sovereign, a defendant may in principle be subject to the jurisdiction of the courts of the United

---

619. *Burnham* is discussed in sections (E) and (G)(1) *supra*.

620. For discussions of Fifth Amendment restrictions on assertions of jurisdiction by federal courts, see Robert C. Casad, *Personal Jurisdiction in Federal Question Cases*, 70 TEX. L. REV. 1589 (1992); Maryellen Fullerton, *Constitutional Limits on Nationwide Personal Jurisdiction in the Federal Courts*, 79 NW. U. L. REV. 1 (1984); Irene D. Sann, *Personal Jurisdiction in Federal Question Suits: Toward a Unified and Rational Theory for Personal Jurisdiction Over Non-Domiciliary and Alien Defendants*, 16 PAC. L.J. 1 (1984); David E. Seidelson, *The Jurisdictional Reach of a Federal Court Hearing a Federal Cause of Action: A Path Through the Maze*, 23 DUQ. L. REV. 323 (1985); Pamela J. Stephens, *The Federal Court Across the Street: Constitutional Limits on Federal Court Assertions of Personal Jurisdiction*, 18 U. RICH. L. REV. 697 (1984); *see also* Gerald Abraham, *Constitutional Limitations Upon the Territorial Reach of Federal Process*, 8 VILL. L. REV. 520 (1963).

621. 564 U.S. __, 131 S. Ct. 2780, 180 L. Ed. 2d 765 (2011).

622. *Id.* at __, 131 S. Ct at 2790, 180 L. Ed. 2d at 777.

623. *See* U.S. CONST. art. I § 8 cl. 2.

> States but not of any particular State. This is consistent with the premises and unique genius of our Constitution. Ours is "a legal system unprecedented in form and design, establishing two orders of government, each with its own direct relationship, its own privity, its own set of mutual rights and obligations to the people who sustain it and are governed by it." . . . For jurisdiction, a litigant may have the requisite relationship with the United States Government but not with the government of any individual State. That would be an exceptional case, however. If the defendant is a domestic domiciliary, the courts of its home State are available and can assert general jurisdiction. And if another State were to exercise jurisdiction in an inappropriate case, it would upset the federal balance which posits that each State has a sovereignty that is not subject to unlawful intrusion by other States. Furthermore, foreign corporations will often target or concentrate on particular States, subjecting them to specific jurisdiction in those forums.[624]

Whatever the intent of the two quoted statements, neither of them addresses the content of the Fifth Amendment's due process test, and the Court has not authoritatively addressed that test in any other modern decision.

Perhaps the Court is waiting for a coherent pattern to develop in the cases in the lower federal courts before dealing with the content of the Fifth Amendment. Given the view articulated in the Court's decisions under the Fourteenth Amendment, however, it is difficult to believe that the Court will allow Congress to confer long-arm jurisdiction on the federal courts without restriction. The case of *Insurance Corp. of Ireland v. Compagnie des Bauxites de Guinee*, discussed in section G(3), above, presents a strong argument against the traditional view.[625] *Insurance Corp. of Ireland* emphasized that the purpose of the Due Process Clause of the Fourteenth Amendment is to protect the defendant's individual liberty interest in civil actions. If the Due Process Clause of the Fourteenth Amendment is designed for that purpose, it is difficult to understand how the Fifth Amendment cannot be aimed at the same goal. Under this reasoning, surely the traditional view of Congress' power must give way to a test that focuses on the burdens that the forum places on the defendant's opportunity to be heard. Indeed, this was the reasoning of the *Republic of Panama* case, discussed above.[626]

Nevertheless, a contrary inference about the content of the Fifth Amendment can be derived from *Burnham v. Superior Court*, discussed in section E(2) and (G)(1), above. In *Burnham*, the Court indicated that the assertion by the states of transient presence jurisdiction would not violate the Due Process Clause of the Fourteenth Amendment. The plurality opinion by Justice Scalia relied on the basis

---

624. *McIntyre*, 564 U.S. at __, 131 S. Ct. at 2789-90, 180 L. Ed. 2d at 776-77.

625. *Cf.* Robert C. Casad, *Personal Jurisdiction in Federal Question Cases*, 70 TEX. L. REV. 1589, 1602 (1992) (discussing commentators and authorities relying on *Insurance Corp. of Ireland* to stand for the proposition that a "basic fairness" test, rather than simply a "national contacts" test should be applied under the Fifth Amendment).

626. *See Republic of Panama*, 199 F.3d at 942-44. Recall from the discussion of *McIntyre* in section G(2)*(b)(iii)*, above, that the plurality opinion in latter case, with its emphasis on state sovereignty, may have undermined the rational of *Insurance Corp. of Ireland* if the opinion ever commands a majority.

of the historical pedigree of the transient presence rule and its continuing acceptance in the states rather than under the minimum contacts test. If a majority of the Court adopts Justice Scalia's view of due process, the Court might also hold that the Due Process Clause of the Fifth Amendment is not violated whenever a defendant can be served with process within the United States.[627] Thus, the resolution of questions about the scope of Congress' power to confer nationwide long-arm jurisdiction on the federal courts may depend on whether the philosophy of *Insurance Corp. of Ireland* or the philosophy of *Burnham* will control the application of the Fifth Amendment.

In 2002, Congress enacted the Multiparty, Multiforum Trial Jurisdiction Act of 2002,[628] which was discussed in Chapter 2(C)(3)*(e)*, above. As part of the Act, Congress also enacted new 28 U.S.C. § 1697, which provides that when the jurisdiction of a district court is based "in whole or in part upon [§] 1369 of [Title 28], process, other than subpoenas, may be served at any place within the United States, or anywhere outside the United States if otherwise permitted by law."[629] This section is obviously designed to create nationwide long-arm jurisdiction for actions brought under the Act, which involve mass accidents in which at least 75 persons are killed at a "discrete location" and certain other requirements are met. The venue provisions of the Act are found in new 28 U.S.C. § 1391(g). These provisions allow actions in which jurisdiction is based on § 1369 to be brought in any district in which any defendant resides or in which a substantial part of the accident giving rise to the action took place. Although these venue provisions may eliminate some of the Fifth Amendment Due Process issues discussed above, they will not eliminate them all. For example, the venue provisions would, in a multiple defendant action, allow the plaintiffs to bring suit in a district where one of the defendants resides, but in which no part of the accident occurred and with which other defendants have no contacts. This situation would thus raise the issue of whether an assertion of long-arm jurisdiction over the nonresidents would satisfy the Due Process Clause of the Fifth Amendment.

2. Restrictions on Federal Jurisdiction to Adjudicate Imposed by Use of State Long-Arm Statutes and Other Methods of Service

The number of federal long-arm statutes is limited. In most cases in federal court, the courts utilize state long-arm statutes to assert jurisdiction over nonresidents under the authority provided in Federal Rule 4.[630] In addition, federal courts can acquire jurisdiction to adjudicate if a defendant is served personally with process within the state where the district court is located. When federal courts

---

627. *See id.* at 1605.

628. 28 U.S.C. § 1369.

629. *Id.* § 1697.

630. After the 1993 amendments to Rule 4, discussed in section K(2) *supra* ("Modern Methods of Serving Process"), this authority will exist, for example, with regard to competent, adult individuals under Rule 4(e)(1). Before the 1993 amendments, the provisions of Rule 4(e) authorized service on all nonresidents "under the circumstances and in the manner" provided by state law.

utilize state long-arm statutes to assert jurisdiction, or when the defendant is served personally with process in the state where the district court is located, what constitutional standard do the federal courts use to determine the validity of the jurisdictional assertion?

After the discussion in the preceding subsection, one might think that the answer to this question would be easy. The reach of federal jurisdiction to adjudicate should be judged by reference to the standards of the Fifth Amendment. Whatever the standards of the Fifth Amendment turn out to be, the federal courts should apply them to determine whether they may exercise jurisdiction under state long-arm statutes or in any other circumstances. Fortunately or unfortunately, this simple answer is not the one that the courts have given to amenability questions in either federal question or diversity cases.

(a) Service Pursuant to State Long-Arm Statutes

Before 1993, Federal Rule 4(e) authorized the federal courts to use state long-arm statutes to acquire jurisdiction over nonresidents. However, Rule 4(e) only authorized service to be made under state long-arm statutes "under the circumstances and in the manner prescribed by the statute."[631] This language clearly limited the use of state long-arm statutes to the situations described in the statutes. However, the language of the rule said nothing about the constitutional standards that would limit the application of the statutes. Nevertheless, given the tendency of the states to enact statutes that, either explicitly or as construed, extend state court jurisdiction as far as the Fourteenth Amendment permits, it is understandable that the federal courts held that they may apply state long-arm statutes only as far as the Fourteenth Amendment would permit state courts to apply them. Thus, whether the case was based on federal question or diversity jurisdiction, when a federal court used a state long-arm statute, the court was confined in its application of the statute by the minimum contacts test of *International Shoe*.[632]

In the 1993 amendments to Federal Rule 4, Rule 4(e) was repealed and other provisions substituted for it. These new provisions textually confirmed the prior limitations on federal long-arm jurisdiction under state statutes. Thus, under the current provisions of Rule 4, the federal courts will still be confined by the Fourteenth Amendment limitations on state-court jurisdiction when exercising authority under state long-arm provisions.[633] While other provisions of amended

631. *See* 146 F.R.D. 550 (1993) (amendment eliminating former Rule 4(e)).

632. *See, e.g.*, Dakota Indus., Inc. v. Dakota Sportswear, Inc., 946 F.2d 1384 (8th Cir. 1991); Lorelei Corp. v. County of Guadalupe, 940 F.2d 717 (1st Cir. 1991); United Elec. Workers of Am. v. 163 Pleasant St. Corp., 960 F.2d 1080 (1st Cir. 1992); New Eng. Health Care Employees Union, Dist. 1199 v. Fall River Nursing Home, Inc., 802 F. Supp. 674 (D.R.I. 1992); *see also* Robert C. Casad, *Personal Jurisdiction in Federal Question Cases*, 70 TEX. L. REV. 1589, 1594-95 (1992).

633. Cases applying the Due Process Clause of the Fourteenth Amendment to assertions of jurisdiction through use of state long-arm statutes are legion. *See, e.g.*, Wiwa v. Royal Dutch Petroleum Co., 226 F.3d 88 (2d Cir. 2000) (assertion of jurisdiction under New York's long-arm statute over two foreign companies accused of human rights violations under the Alien Tort Claims Act did not violate due process, even though events in question occurred in Nigeria, because companies controlled a vast and wealthy oil empire and had a physical presence in New York through an investor relations office); Ciena Corp. v. Jarrard, 203 F.3d 312 (4th Cir. 2000) (assertion of jurisdiction under Rule 4(k)(1)(A) looks to the law of the state in which the district court sits and the limits on the jurisdiction of that state's courts imposed by the Fourteenth Amendment).

Rule 4 may widen the federal court's ability to assert long-arm jurisdiction, the preexisting practice under state long-arm statutes remains unaffected.

Illustration 3-57. Federal Rule 4(e)(1) provides that service on a competent, adult individual may be made under the state law "in courts of general jurisdiction in the state where the district court is located or where service is made." Federal Rule 4(k)(1)(A), in turn, states that service of a summons or filing a waiver of service establishes personal jurisdiction over a defendant "who is subject to the jurisdiction of a court of general jurisdiction in the state where the district court is located." Putting these two provisions together, if a defendant is served under the circumstances and in the manner provided by a state long-arm statute, as authorized by Federal Rule 4(e)(1), the defendant can be subjected to personal jurisdiction if the courts of general jurisdiction in the state would be able to do so under the Fourteenth Amendment. Federal Rule 4(k)(1)(A) thus explicitly incorporates the Fourteenth Amendment Due Process limits as limits on the power of federal courts whenever those courts use state long-arm statutes to assert personal jurisdiction.

Note, however, that even if service is made under the independent federal service provisions of Rule 4(e)(2), say by leaving a copy of the summons and complaint at the defendant's dwelling or usual place of abode with someone of suitable age and discretion who resides there, Rule 4(k)(1)(A) still makes personal jurisdiction valid if it could be validly exercised by a state court of general jurisdiction within the state where the federal district court is located. Therefore, a federal court does not have to use the provisions of state law to serve process in order to assert long-arm jurisdiction. Rather, it may do so either by using state provisions or independent federal provisions and, in either case, thereby acquire personal jurisdiction if a state court of general jurisdiction in the state where the federal court is located could do so under its long-arm provisions consistent with the Fourteenth Amendment.

(b) Service Under Rule 4 when the State Courts Would Not Assert Jurisdiction: Federally Created Rights Cases

More difficult questions are presented when federal process is served on a defendant within the state where the federal action is pending, but the state courts would not assert jurisdiction over the defendant. Before 1993, this problem arose because of the interaction of Federal Rule 4(d) and (f). Before 1993, Rule 4(d) prescribed the manner in which process could be served on a defendant who was an inhabitant of or found within the state. Rule 4(f) provided that process could be served anywhere within the territorial limits of the state in which the district court was held. Thus, the question arose whether the federal courts could acquire jurisdiction by serving the defendant within the state, as prescribed in Rule 4(f), in a manner prescribed by Rule 4(d), even though no federal statute authorized the court to assert *jurisdiction* over the defendant, and even though the state courts of the state in which the district court is held would refuse to exercise *jurisdiction* over the defendant. Depending on whether the plaintiff's claim was created by federal or state law, the answer differed.

When the plaintiff was suing on a federally created right, the cases generally agreed that a federal amenability standard should limit the reach of personal jurisdiction under Rule 4.[634] Disagreement existed, however, about the proper content of the federal standard. Some cases attempted to measure whether the defendant had minimum contacts with the state in which the district court was sitting, thus applying the Fourteenth Amendment due process restrictions on the power of the states as the federal test of amenability.[635] Other cases stated that the Due Process Clause of the Fifth Amendment should determine the content of the federal standard. Under this standard, the test was stated to be whether the defendant had minimum contacts with the United States.[636] Finally, some cases applied a *state* standard of amenability even in cases where the plaintiff's action was based on a federally created right, when service was made under former Rule 4 in a *manner* prescribed by state law.[637] The principle of the latter cases did not permit the federal courts to assert jurisdiction when the courts of the state in which the district court was held would not assert jurisdiction over the defendant.

The use of a federal amenability standard in federally created rights cases means that there were situations prior to 1993 in which federal courts would assert personal jurisdiction over defendants pursuant to Rule 4(d) and (f), even though the state courts would not have asserted jurisdiction over the defendant as a matter of state law. Of course, before the federal courts could apply a federal amenability standard, there had to be some federal statute, state statute, or Federal Rule of Civil Procedure that authorized service of process on the defendant. The Supreme Court made it clear that federal courts do not have the power to create common-law service of process rules.[638] However, in the cases discussed thus far, Rule 4 provided authority to serve the defendant. The question was, once served, could the defendant be subjected to jurisdiction.

---

634. *See, e.g.*, Fraley v. Chesapeake & Ohio Ry. Co., 397 F.2d 1 (3d Cir. 1968); Volkswagen Interamericana, S.A. v. Rohlsen, 360 F.2d 437 (1st Cir. 1966); *see also* 4A CHARLES A. WRIGHT & ARTHUR R. MILLER, FEDERAL PRACTICE AND PROCEDURE: CIVIL § 1075, at 389 (3d ed. 2002).

635. *See, e.g.*, Fraley v. Chesapeake & Ohio Ry. Co., 397 F.2d 1 (3d Cir. 1968); PPS, Inc. v. Jewelry Sales Representatives, Inc., 392 F. Supp. 375 (S.D.N.Y. 1975); Goldberg v. Mutual Readers League, Inc., 195 F. Supp. 778 (E.D. Pa. 1961).

636. *See* Volkswagen Interamericana, S.A. v. Rohlsen, 360 F.2d 437 (1st Cir. 1966); Holt v. Klosters Rederi A/S, 355 F. Supp. 354 (W.D. Mich. 1973); Edward J. Moriarty & Co. v. General Tire & Rubber Co., 289 F. Supp. 381 (S.D. Ohio 1967). These cases seemed to assume that the standards under the Fifth and Fourteenth Amendments were identical. *See, e.g.*, Holt v. Klosters Rederi A/S, 355 F. Supp. 354 (W.D. Mich. 1973). That is, the assumption seemed to be that due process limits are *only* a product of territorial limitations on the power of a government, so that minimum contacts with the relevant government's territory (the state's territory in the case of the Fourteenth Amendment and the United States' territory in the case of the Fifth) is all that is necessary to satisfy due process. This approach rejected the view, discussed in subsection 1, above, that the minimum contacts test serves the function of protecting the defendant's individual liberty interest by assuring the defendant a reasonably nonburdensome place of trial. If the Supreme Court should someday hold that the Due Process Clause of the Fifth Amendment contains protections for the defendant's individual liberty interest, the federal courts holding the contrary view would have to alter the results of their decisions accordingly. *Cf.* Goldberg v. Mutual Readers League, Inc., 195 F. Supp. 778 (E.D. Pa. 1961). *See generally* Gerald Abraham, *Constitutional Limitations Upon the Territorial Reach of Federal Process*, 8 VILL. L. REV. 520 (1963); Pamela J. Stephens, *The Federal Court Across the Street: Constitutional Limits on Federal Court Assertions of Personal Jurisdiction*, 18 U. RICH. L. REV. 697 (1984). However, as also noted in the previous subsection, the *Burnham* decision might be applied by the Court to validate federal power to extend jurisdiction nationwide, regardless of the burdens that may be imposed on the defendants thereby.

637. *See* Gkiafis v. S.S. Yiosonas, 342 F.2d 546 (4th Cir. 1965); Scott Paper Co. v. Scott's Liquid Gold, Inc., 374 F. Supp. 184 (D. Del. 1974).

638. *See* Omni Capital Int'l, Ltd. v. Rudolf Wolff & Co., 484 U.S. 97, 108 S. Ct. 404, 98 L. Ed. 2d 415 (1987).

After 1993, the question of what amenability standard to apply in federally created right cases will arise under amended Rule 4. The former provisions of Rule 4(d) and (f) have been reorganized and supplemented with new provisions governing the manner of service and the territorial reach of the district courts' jurisdiction. Whether it was intended or not by the drafters, these new provisions can be read to prohibit the use of a federal "common-law" amenability standard in the situations described above. Before 1993, Rule 4(d) and (f) did not specifically address problems of amenability. Instead, Rule 4(d) provided for the manner of service on different categories of defendants, while Rule 4(f) simply provided where process might be served. Neither provision specifically attempted to authorize jurisdiction to be asserted over the different categories of defendants to be served. Left with this ambiguity, the courts evolved amenability standards such as those discussed in the text above to govern questions of personal jurisdiction under Rule 4(d) and (f).

After 1993, Rule 4(e)-(j) govern the manner of serving process on different categories of defendants. Like the pre-1993 Rule 4(d), these provisions do not establish personal jurisdiction over defendants. Instead, they merely provide for the manner of service on particular kinds of defendants.[639] However, as indicated in *Illustration 3-57,* above, unlike former Rule 4(f), which was silent on questions of amenability, Rule 4(k) now specifically addresses these questions. Rule 4(k)(1) begins by stating that service of a summons or filing a waiver of service "establishes jurisdiction over the person of a defendant" under the circumstances described in the rule. Rule 4(k)(1) then follows with three situations in which jurisdiction will be established: (1) when the defendant is subject to the jurisdiction of a court of general jurisdiction in the state where the district court is located; (2) when a Rule 14 or 19 party is served within a judicial district of the United States and not more than 100 miles from where the summons was issued; (3) when authorized by a federal statute. In addition, Rule 4(k)(2) explicitly creates a narrow federal long-arm rule applicable to cases involving claims based on federal law.[640]

The specific reference by Rule 4(k) to questions of personal jurisdiction gives rise to a strong inference that Rule 4(k) articulates the exclusive standards for determining the territorial reach of the district courts' jurisdiction. If this interpretation of Rule 4(k) is correct, the courts can no longer create or apply federal amenability standards that do not exist in Rule 4(k).

---

639. For example, Federal Rule 4(e) now provides for service on competent, adult individuals. In its comments on Rule 4(e), the Advisory Committee stated: "Service of the summons under this subdivision does not conclusively establish the jurisdiction of the court over the person of the defendant. A defendant may assert the territorial limits of the court's reach set forth in subdivision (k) . . . ." FED. R. CIV. P. 4(e) advisory committee's note to the 1993 amendment.

640. *See generally* Dora A. Corby, *Putting Personal Jurisdiction Within Reach: Just What Has Rule 4(k)(2) Done for the Personal Jurisdiction of Federal Courts?* 30 MCGEORGE L. REV. 167 (1998). Several federal courts have held that admiralty law is "federal" law for purposes of Rule 4(k)(2). *See* World Tanker Carriers Corp. v. M/V Ya Mawlaya, 99 F.3d 717 (5th Cir. 1996); West Afr. Trading & Shipping Co. v. London Int'l Group, 968 F. Supp. 996 (D.N.J. 1997); Western Equities, Ltd. v. Hanseatic, Ltd., 956 F. Supp. 1232 (D.V.I. 1997); Sarah S. Nickerson, World Tanker Carriers Corp. v. M/V Ya Mawlaya: *The Fifth Circuit Finds Rule 4(k)(2) Applicable to Admiralty Claims,* 72 TUL. L. REV. 1047 (1997). This conclusion is interesting, given that the U.S. Supreme Court has held that admiralty law is not federal law for purposes of federal question jurisdiction under 28 U.S.C. § 1331. *See* Romero v. International Terminal Operating Co., 358 U.S. 354, 79 S. Ct. 468, 3 L. Ed. 2d 368 (1959).

Illustration 3-58. *P*, a citizen of State *X*, is an employee of *D Corp.*, a corporation incorporated with its principal place of business in State *X*. *P* is injured while working for *D* in State *X*. Subsequently, *P* moves to State *Z*, where *P* commences an action against *D* to recover damages for the injuries received while working for *D*. *P's* claim is based on a federal statute and is commenced in a U.S. District Court in State *Z*. *D* is served with process under Federal Rule 4(h)(1)(B) by delivering a copy of the summons and complaint to an officer of *D Corp.* in State *Z*. No federal long-arm statute authorizes the federal courts to assume personal jurisdiction over *D* under the circumstances described. The courts of State *Z* would not, as a matter of their own law, assert jurisdiction over *D* under these circumstances. Before the 1993 amendments to Rule 4, whether *D* could be subjected to personal jurisdiction in State *Z* would be determined by a federal amenability standard of the sort described in the text, above. After the 1993 amendments to Rule 4, it is probably not possible to use a federal amenability standard to justify an assertion of jurisdiction. Rule 4(k)(1)(A) does not allow an assertion of jurisdiction unless the defendant is subject to jurisdiction in the courts of general jurisdiction in the state where the action is brought, which is not possible here. Rule 4(k)(1)(B) only applies to cases in which Rule 14 or 19 parties are served within 100 miles from the place where the summons was issued. *D* is not a Rule 14 or 19 party. Rule 4(k)(1)(C) only applies to cases in which a federal statute authorizes personal jurisdiction, and this is not such a case. Rule 4(k)(2) only applies to actions in which the defendant is not subject to personal jurisdiction in the courts of general jurisdiction of any state. *D* could be sued in State *X*. Therefore, if the provisions of Rule 4(k) are given their natural meaning, *P's* action must be dismissed.[641]

* * * * *

It is unclear whether the drafters of the 1993 amendments to Rule 4 intended to prevent the creation and application of federal amenability standards beyond the circumstances described in Rule 4(k).[642] The Advisory Committee's note to the 1993 amendments to Rule 4 does not directly address this question. It does seem strange that the drafters of the rule would produce such a significant result without explanatory commentary. Nevertheless, the text of Rule 4(k) is compelling and should not be departed from lightly. Unless the courts identify ambiguities in the rule that would justify the creation of federal amenability standards, Rule 4(k) should be treated as excluding the creation of federal amenability standards beyond the circumstances described in the text of the rule.

A separate question is who bears the burden of showing whether the criteria of Rule 4(k)(2) are met. In *United States v. Swiss American Bank, Ltd.*,[643] the First Circuit held that a plaintiff who seeks to invoke Rule 4(k)(2) must make a prima facie case for the applicability of the rule by showing that (1) the claim arises under federal law; (2) personal jurisdiction is not available under any federal statute; and (3) the defendant's contacts with the United States are sufficient to satisfy the

---

641. Of course, when jurisdiction is asserted under Federal Rule 4(k)(2), the Fifth Amendment Due Process Standards will have to be satisfied. *See* section L(1), *supra*, for a discussion of these standards.

642. *But see, e.g.*, Mavrix Photo, Inc. v. Brand Techs., Inc., 647 F.3d 1218 (9th Cir. 2011) (in the absence of a federal long-arm statute, federal courts apply the law of the state in which they are sitting).

643. 191 F.3d 30 (1st Cir. 1999).

Constitution. In addition, the plaintiff must certify that, based on the information readily available to the plaintiff and the plaintiff's attorney, the defendant is not subject to personal jurisdiction in any state. Upon making this showing, the burden shifts to the defendant to produce evidence which would either show that the defendant is subject to personal jurisdiction in one or more specific states, or that its contacts with the United States are constitutionally insufficient.[644]

(c) Service Under Rule 4 when the State Courts Would Not Assert Jurisdiction: Diversity Actions

Before 1993, when the jurisdiction of a federal court was based solely on diversity of citizenship, the appellate cases unanimously held that a state, rather than a federal, standard of amenability should be applied when service was effectuated under Rule 4 on a defendant within the state.[645] Thus, if the state in which the district court was held would not assert jurisdiction over the defendant, even if it could do so under the Fourteenth Amendment, the federal court would not assert jurisdiction through the use of former Federal Rule 4(d) and (f). This result was the product of Judge Friendly's opinion for the Second Circuit Court of Appeals in *Arrowsmith v. United Press International*.[646]

In *Arrowsmith*, a citizen of Maryland sued United Press International, a New York corporation, in the U.S. District Court for Vermont. The plaintiff asserted a claim for libel based on a U.P.I. story about the dynamiting of a synagogue in Atlanta, Georgia. Apparently, the action was brought in Vermont because Vermont had a longer statute of limitations than other states on libel claims. The defendant was served with process under Federal Rule 4(d)(3) by serving the manager of the defendant's Montpelier news bureau in Vermont. The defendant moved to dismiss the action under Federal Rule 12(b) for lack of personal jurisdiction, improper venue, and failure to state a claim upon which relief could be granted.

The district court dismissed on the latter ground, and the plaintiff appealed. The Second Circuit Court of Appeals held that the district court erred in dismissing for failure to state a claim upon which relief could be granted without first

---

644. *Id.* at 41. If the defendant successfully shows that it is subject to personal jurisdiction in one or more states, the plaintiff may (a) move for a transfer to one of those states; (b) discontinue the action and refile it in one of those states; or (c) contest the defendant's evidence, in which case the defendant will be deemed to have waived any contention that it is subject to personal jurisdiction in a state other than the ones the defendant has identified. *Id.* at 42; *see also* Synthes (U.S.A.) v. GMReis, 563 F.3d 1285 (Fed. Cir. 2009) (if defendant contends that he cannot be sued in the forum state and refuses to identify any other state in which suit is possible, a federal court is entitled to use Rule 4(k)(2); Fifth Amendment test is whether sufficient contacts exist with the United States to subject defendant to general or specific jurisdiction and, if specific, whether the assertion of jurisdiction is appropriate under the five-factor reasonableness test); Touch Com, Inc. v. Bereskin & Parr, 574 F.3d 1403 (Fed. Cir. 2009) (defendants were not subject to personal jurisdiction in Virginia's courts of general jurisdiction and did not name another state in which they would be subject to jurisdiction; thus, assertion of jurisdiction under Rule 4(k)(2) proper; under Fifth Amendment, defendants purposefully directed activities to the United States and assertion of jurisdiction did not violate fair play and substantial justice under five-factor reasonableness test); *but see* Getz v. Boeing Co., 654 F.3d 852 (8th Cir. 2011) (claims by crash survivors and heirs of military personnel killed in Army helicopter crash did not arise under federal law; therefore, jurisdiction could not be asserted under Rule 4(k)(2)).

645. *See* 4A CHARLES A. WRIGHT & ARTHUR R. MILLER, FEDERAL PRACTICE AND PROCEDURE: CIVIL § 1075, at 398, n.33 (3d ed. 2002) and authorities there cited.

646. 320 F.2d 219 (2d Cir. 1963).

considering the issue of personal jurisdiction. The court thus vacated the district court's judgment of dismissal and remanded for consideration of the jurisdictional question. In so doing, the court considered it necessary to decide what standard should govern the district court's determination of the jurisdictional issue.

The Second Circuit held that when the subject-matter jurisdiction of a federal court is based solely on diversity of citizenship, the court cannot acquire personal jurisdiction pursuant to Rule 4(d) and (f) when the state in which the district court is held would not assert jurisdiction over the defendant. The court based its decision in part on the failure of Rule 4 to address questions of amenability to suit, as opposed to manner of service. In addition, the court refused to read into the statutes conferring diversity jurisdiction a congressional mandate to disregard state jurisdictional restrictions.[647]

The *Arrowsmith* rule seems secure after the 1993 amendments to Rule 4. Rule 4(k)(1)(A) now specifically states that service of a summons under Rule 4 will establish personal jurisdiction over a defendant "who is subject to the jurisdiction of a court of general jurisdiction in the state where the district court is located." The remaining provisions of Rule 4(k) authorize jurisdiction over defendants in special situations and do not contradict the *Arrowsmith* rule. Therefore, it would seem that in diversity actions in which no state or federal long-arm statute authorizes jurisdiction over a defendant, amenability to process will be determined by reference to the ability of the forum state to assert jurisdiction, just as before 1993.

(d) Amenability Questions Under the 100-Mile Bulge Rule

In addition to the amenability questions that existed when process is served pursuant to Rule 4(d) and (f) within the state in which the federal district court sits, a similar amenability problem existed under the so-called 100-mile bulge provision of Rule 4. Rule 4(f) was amended in 1963 to allow federal process to be served outside the territorial limits of the state, but within the United States, at any place that was not more than 100 miles from the place in which the action is commenced, or to which it is assigned or transferred for trial. This 100-mile bulge rule only applied when (1) process is being served on a person who is being brought in as a party under Rule 14, (2) process is being served on a person who is being brought in as an additional party to a pending action or a counterclaim or crossclaim therein pursuant to Rule 19, or (3) process is being served on a person required to respond to an order of commitment for civil contempt.

In explaining the purpose of the 100-mile provision, the Advisory Committee stated:

> The bringing in of parties under the 100-mile provision in the limited situations enumerated is designed to promote the objective of enabling the court to determine entire controversies. In the light of present-day facilities for communication and travel, the territorial range of the service allowed . . . can hardly work hardship on the parties summoned. The provision will be especially

---

647. *See id.* at 225-27.

> useful in metropolitan areas spanning more than one State. Any requirements of subject-matter jurisdiction and venue will still have to be satisfied as to the parties brought in. . . .[648]

Although the Advisory Committee's note implied that anyone who was served with federal process within the 100-mile area would be subjected to the personal jurisdiction of the district court, the courts did not reach this result under Rule 4(f). Like defendants served within the state pursuant to Rule 4(d) and (f), restrictive amenability standards were also read into the 100-mile provision. Generally, the courts insisted that for personal jurisdiction to exist, the party served with process had to have minimum contacts with the bulge area.[649] Most courts holding that minimum contacts had to exist with the "bulge" area seem to be adopting a suggestion by Professor Kaplan that the 100-mile provision should be interpreted to contain such a limitation on amenability—an interpretation that, in effect, incorporated the Fourteenth Amendment minimum contacts test as part of the rule.[650] Some courts, however, concluded that the "minimum contacts" amenability standard of the 100-mile provision was compelled by the Constitution. Of these courts, some indicated that it was the Due Process Clause of the Fourteenth Amendment that compelled the result.[651] This conclusion is clearly wrong because the Fourteenth Amendment limits state-court jurisdiction, not federal-court jurisdiction. Other courts cited the Fifth Amendment Due Process Clause as the source of the amenability restriction.[652]

After the 1993 amendment to Rule 4, the amenability problems discussed in the previous paragraph have probably been eliminated. Rule 4(k)(1)(B) now contains the 100-mile bulge provision. However, as noted in subsection (2)(*b*), above, Rule 4(k) now specifically addresses questions of personal jurisdiction. The rule provides that service of a summons is effective to establish personal jurisdiction over a defendant "who is a party joined under Rule 14 or 19 and is served within a judicial district of the United States and not more than 100 miles from where the summons was issued."[653] Thus, the rule now explicitly provides that

---

648. FED. R. CIV. P. 4(f) advisory committee's note to the 1963 amendment. In measuring the 100-mile distance for service under Rule 4(k)(1)(B), one court has held that "as the crow flies" is the proper method rather than road miles. *See* Bellum v. PCE Constructors, Inc., 407 F.3d 734, 740 n.7 (5th Cir. 2005).

649. *See* Sprow v. Hartford Ins. Co., 594 F.2d 412, 416 (5th Cir. 1979); Drames v. Milgreva Co. Maritima, S.A., 571 Supp. 737, 738-39 (E.D. Pa. 1983); Jacobs v. Flight Extenders, Inc., 90 F.R.D. 676, 679 (E.D. Pa. 1981) (minimum contacts with either forum state or bulge must exist; here contacts with bulge existed); Paxton v. Southern Pa. Bank, 93 F.R.D. 503, 505 (D. Md. 1982); School Dist. v. Missouri, 460 F. Supp. 421, 436 (W.D. Mo. 1978); Lee v. Ohio Cas. Ins. Co., 445 F. Supp. 189, 193-94 (D. Del. 1978) (court need not determine whether amenability by law of forum or only contacts with bulge necessary, since both are present); Pillsbury Co. v. Delta Boat & Barge Rental, Inc., 72 F.R.D. 630, 632 (E.D. La. 1976); McGonigle v. Penn-Central Transp. Co., 49 F.R.D. 58, 62-63 (D. Md. 1969). *But see* Coleman v. American Export Isbrandtsen Lines, Inc., 405 F.2d 250, 252 (2d Cir. 1968) (process can be validly served in bulge only on persons over whom bulge state has jurisdiction and, very likely, only on persons over whom it has chosen to exercise jurisdiction); Spearing v. Manhattan Oil Transp. Corp., 375 F. Supp. 764, 771 (S.D.N.Y. 1974) (jurisdiction can only be asserted over persons over whom the bulge state has chosen to exercise jurisdiction).

650. *See* Benjamin Kaplan, *Amendments of the Federal Rules of Civil Procedure, 1961-1963 (I)*, 77 HARV. L. REV. 601, 632-33 (1964).

651. *See* Paxton v. Southern Pa. Bank, 93 F.R.D. 503, 505 (D. Md. 1982); McGonigle v. Penn-Central Transp. Co., 49 F.R.D. 58, 63 (D. Md. 1969).

652. *See* Jacobs v. Flight Extenders, Inc., 90 F.R.D. 676, 679 (E.D. Pa. 1981).

653. FED. R. CIV. P. 4(k)(1)(B).

personal jurisdiction is acquired by simple service of process within the "bulge" area.

Illustration 3-59. *P*, a citizen of State *X*, sues *D*, a citizen of State *Y*, in a U.S. District Court for the Western District of State *Y*, where *D* resides. *P's* claim is for personal injuries received in an automobile accident in State *R*. The accident was caused when *T*, who was *D's* employee, driving *D's* truck on *D's* business, collided with *P* in State *R*. *D* asserts that if *D* is liable to *P*, *T* is liable to *D* for any damages that *D* must pay to *P*. *T* is a citizen of State *Z* who resides in the Southern District of State *Z*. The Southern District of State *Z* abuts the northern side of the Western District of State *Y*. However, *T* lives more than 100 miles from the city in the Southern District of State *Y* where the action is pending and the summons was issued. Thus, *T* cannot be served with process in State *Z*. However, *D* has *T* served with a summons and third-party complaint under Rule 14 while *T* is passing through the Eastern District of State *Q*, which abuts the western side of the Western District of State *Y*. *T* is served 30 miles from the city in the Western District of State *Y* where the action is pending and the summons was issued. Under the terms of Rule 4(k)(1)(B), the U.S. District Court in the Western District of State *Y* acquires personal jurisdiction over *T* by the service of process on *T* in the Eastern District of State *Q*. Because the 100-mile rule is a mini-federal long-arm rule, the constitutionality of an assertion of personal jurisdiction under the rule must be tested under the Due Process Clause of the Fifth Amendment. Under the evolving standards in the courts of appeals exemplified by the *Republic of Panama* and *ESAB Group* decisions, it seems unlikely that third-party defendants such as *T* will be able to demonstrate the quality of severe burden that would violate the Fifth Amendment, especially given that they would be subject to suit within the state where they were served personally in a court that is no more than 100 miles from where they are actually being sued.[654]

---

654. See the discussion of *Republic of Panama* and *ESAB Group* in section L(1) *supra*.

Chapter 4

VENUE AND RELATED MATTERS

Venue rules determine the location where the action will be conducted. Legislatures establish venue rules primarily for the *convenience* of the parties.[1] The rules define those places where the legislature believes the parties can try certain categories of cases most fairly and efficiently. Frequently, a procedural system will allow a change of venue for the convenience of the parties or witnesses. Unlike subject-matter jurisdiction,[2] defendants may waive venue objections by not raising them promptly in the manner prescribed by individual procedural systems.[3]

Like venue, personal jurisdiction also limits the geographical areas in which civil actions may be brought to assure a nonburdensome place of adjudication for the defendant. Thus, venue restrictions obviously overlap with personal jurisdiction restrictions. However, venue is different from personal jurisdiction in two important respects. First, venue either is or is not proper in the court in which an action is commenced. In contrast, personal jurisdiction, even if properly obtainable, still must be acquired by service of process on the defendant. Second, venue restrictions do not ordinarily render judgments void and subject to collateral attack in subsequent proceedings; however, exceeding the limits on the reach of a court's personal jurisdiction can void a judgment and subject it to collateral attack in a separate action.[4] Thus, if an action is commenced in an improper venue within a state against a nonresident defendant, the defendant may not default and collaterally attack the judgment in another state for lack of proper venue.[5]

SECTION A. TRANSITORY AND LOCAL ACTIONS

The most important venue concept produced by English law was the distinction between *local* and *transitory* actions. If the events giving rise to the action could have occurred only in a particular place, the courts characterized the action as local. Local actions always have something to do with land, but not all actions having to do with land are local actions.[6] Examples of traditional local

---

1. In contrast, subject-matter jurisdiction rules are supported by separation-of-powers considerations. *See* Chapter 2(A)(2) *supra* ("The 'No-Waiver, No-Consent' Rule").

2. Subject-matter jurisdiction may not be waived or conferred on a court by consent of the parties. *See id.*

3. *See, e.g.*, FED. R. CIV. P. 12(h)(1) (waiver of venue under the Federal Rules).

4. *See* Chapter 3(B)(3) *supra* ("In Personam Jurisdiction: Consent, Appearance, and Waiver") (discussing the option of collaterally attacking a judgment for lack of personal jurisdiction).

5. Note, however, that a case fully tried on the merits can be reversed on appeal if venue is improper and the venue objection is properly raised, even if the absence of proper venue does not produce any error on the merits of the disposition. *See* SEC v. Johnson, 650 F.3d 710 (D.C. Cir. 2011).

6. *See, e.g.*, Cooper v. Amerada Hess Corp., 2000-NMCA-100, 129 N.M. 710, 13 P.3d 68 (2000) (damage action by landowners against oil and gas producers for negligence, trespass, nuisance, unjust enrichment, and infliction of emotional distress did not involve an "interest in lands" within the meaning of the New Mexico general venue statute and, therefore, did not have to be brought in the county where the land was located), *aff'd sub nom.* Cooper v. Chevron U.S.A., 2002-NMSC-020, 132 N.M. 382, 49 P.3d 61 (2002).

actions include actions for the recovery of land or for damages for injury to land. Transitory actions were actions based on events that could have occurred anywhere. Examples include actions to recover damages for slander or assault and battery.[7]

The distinction between local and transitory actions remains important today. However, understanding the distinction requires some historical background. The distinction is a product of the evolution of trial by jury in England. The Norman kings began to allow juries to decide cases in the king's courts. Before the fifteenth century, however, these juries based their decisions chiefly on their own knowledge of the case. The jurors acquired this knowledge by simply being neighbors of the litigants or by searching out evidence before trial.[8]

Illustration 4-1. The court of the mesne lord[9] normally tried the question of ownership of land. The usual method of trial was battle.[10] The Grand Assize, enacted during the reign of Henry II (1154-1189), gave the defendant the option to refuse battle. Instead, the defendant could remove the action to the king's court. The court then tried the case through the oath of twelve neighbors who "knew by their own eyes and ears" who had the better title.[11] Similarly, a plaintiff could use the writ of novel disseisin to determine the immediate right to possession of land.[12] This writ required the sheriff to obtain "twelve men of the neighborhood to view the land."[13] They then had "to attend the king's court at a day named, prepared to deliver their verdict."[14] In the field of criminal law, oaths of neighbors formed the basis of indictments for robberies and other violent misdeeds.[15]

* * * * *

The courts considered these situations (as well as others) to be "local" in nature because the jurors would ordinarily have to be from the vicinity where the events or misdeeds at issue actually occurred. This need to secure a local jury prompted the courts to require the parties to allege with great particularity the location where the events giving rise to the suit had occurred. When factual issues existed, the court could then summon jurors from that location to Westminster to decide them.[16] English courts could not try an action arising outside of England because it was impossible to secure a jury with knowledge of the facts.[17]

In the thirteenth century, the common-law courts began to sit en banc at Westminster during four terms each year (the Easter, Trinity, Michaelmas, and Hilary terms, each of which lasted only a few weeks). Individual judges held jury

---

7. *See* JOSEPH H. KOFFLER & ALISON REPPY, HANDBOOK OF COMMON LAW PLEADING § 29, at 103-04 (1969).

8. *See* W.H. Wicker, *The Development of the Distinction Between Local and Transitory Actions*, 4 TENN. L. REV. 55 (1926).

9. A mesne lord was an intermediate lord who stood between the tenant and a superior lord.

10. *See* 1 WILLIAM S. HOLDSWORTH, A HISTORY OF ENGLISH LAW 140-41 (1903); *see also* Chapter 1(D)(5) *supra* ("Modes of Trial Under the Writ System").

11. ALBERT T. CARTER, A HISTORY OF THE ENGLISH COURTS 29-30 (5th ed. 1927).

12. *See* Chapter 1(D)(3)*(a) supra* ("Real Actions").

13. WILLIAM F. WALSH, A HISTORY OF ANGLO-AMERICAN LAW 60 (2d ed. 1932).

14. *Id.*

15. FREDERIC W. MAITLAND, THE CONSTITUTIONAL HISTORY OF ENGLAND 108-09 (1908).

16. W.H. Wicker, *The Development of the Distinction Between Local and Transitory Actions*, 4 TENN. L. REV. 55, 59 (1926); *see* 5 WILLIAM S. HOLDSWORTH, A HISTORY OF ENGLISH LAW 117 (1924).

17. W.H. Wicker, *The Development of the Distinction Between Local and Transitory Actions*, 4 TENN. L. REV. 55, 59 (1926).

trials away from the courts at Westminster.[18] The judge did not enter judgment on a jury verdict immediately. Instead, judgment was delayed until after commencement of the next term—at which time the losing party could present motions designed to prevent entry of the judgment. Under this *nisi prius* system, an allegation of venue thus determined the place of trial. It also determined the location from which the jury was selected.[19]

The jury's function ultimately evolved into judging the truth of testimony presented at trial. As a result, the need for a local jury ceased because jurors' personal knowledge was no longer needed to determine the facts. Consequently, the courts gradually relaxed venue rules.[20] In most actions, the courts permitted plaintiffs to state the county where the action arose in the margin of the declaration. The courts selected the jury based on this *marginal venue*. The courts held that this allegation of venue was not material, and the defendant could thus not dispute ("traverse") it in most personal actions.[21] One commentator has suggested, however, that the courts "innate conservatism" may have been the reason why the courts did not apply this view to actions involving real estate.[22]

As the law developed, local actions became those that sought one of the following: (1) the recovery of land—for example, ejectment actions; (2) the establishment or enforcement of a right arising out of land—for example, enforcement of covenants running with the land based upon privity of estate; or (3) the recovery of damages for injury to land—for example, trespass or nuisance actions for damage to real estate.[23] The plaintiff had to try these actions where the land was located.[24]

In contrast, other common-law actions became transitory. When the plaintiff brought a transitory action in a place where the events giving rise to the action had not occurred, the courts permitted the plaintiff, after stating the true location, to use a *videlicet* (viz. or to wit) to allege a place within the court's jurisdiction.[25] In this way, the courts were able to maintain in England actions arising outside of England if they were not "local" in nature.[26] Thus, in *Doulson v. Matthews*,[27] Justice Buller of the Court of King's Bench stated that:

> [i]t is now too late for us to inquire whether it were wise or politic to make a distinction between transitory and local actions: it is sufficient for the Courts that the law has settled the distinction, and

---

18. *Id.* at 61.

19. *Id.* at 60.

20. *Id.*

21. *Id.* at 61; *see also* Chapter 6(A)(3)*(d) infra* ("Traverses") and Chapter 6(A)(6) *infra* ("Relation of Pleading to Proof at Trial").

22. W.H. Wicker, *The Development of the Distinction Between Local and Transitory Actions*, 4 TENN. L. REV. 55, 60-62 (1926) (the old precedents caused the courts "to refuse to swallow the fiction that land was situated somewhere other than where it was in fact").

23. *See, e.g.*, L.S. Rogers, Annotation, *Venue of Action for the Cutting, Destruction, or Damage of Standing Timber or Trees*, 65 A.L.R.2D 1268 (1959); F.T. Woods, Annotation, *Venue of Suit to Enjoin Nuisance*, 7 A.L.R.2D 481 (1949).

24. If the plaintiff alleged a false location to gain a favorable venue and the defendant showed the land to be located elsewhere, the court could dismiss the action. JOSEPH H. KOFFLER & ALISON REPPY, HANDBOOK OF COMMON LAW PLEADING § 29, at 103-05 (1969).

25. *Id.* at 106; *see also* Chapter 6(A)(6) *infra* ("Relation of Pleading to Proof at Trial").

26. W.H. Wicker, *The Development of the Distinction Between Local and Transitory Actions*, 4 TENN. L. REV. 55, 61-62 (1926).

27. 100 Eng. Rep. 1143 (K.B. 1792).

> that an action [for trespass] *quare clausum fregit* is local. We may try actions here which are in their nature transitory, though arising out of a transaction abroad, but not such as are in their nature local.[28]

Equity courts did not use jurors. Equity courts ordinarily based their jurisdiction on the defendant's presence before the court. Therefore, plaintiffs did not have to bring equity suits in particular counties. When an equity court ordered a change of possession of land located in England, the court could assist the plaintiff by issuing a writ. Such a writ directed the sheriff of the county where the land was located to help the plaintiff take possession.[29] When the defendant was before the court but the land was located abroad, the court had to rely upon contempt and other measures to enforce its decree.[30]

State venue rules in the United States commonly preserve the distinction between local and transitory actions.

Illustration 4-2. Section 103 of the Field Code of 1848, for example, provided as follows:

> § 103. Actions for the following causes, must be tried in the county where the cause or some part thereof arose, or in which the subject of the action or some part thereof is situated, subject to the power of the court to change the place of trial, in the cases provided by statute.
>
> 1. For the recovery of real property or of an estate or interest therein, or for the determination, in any form, of such right or interest, and for injuries to real property;
> 2. For the partition of real property;
> 3. For the foreclosure of a mortgage of real property.[31]

This section classified actions for injuries to real property as local in nature. It required that they be brought in the county where the land was located. The current New York statute eliminates specific reference to actions for injuries to real property:

> § 507. Real Property actions.
>
> The place of trial of an action in which the judgment demanded would affect the title to, or the possession, use or enjoyment of, real property shall be in the county in which any part of the subject of the action is situated.[32]

The New York courts could have interpreted this statute as eliminating a local action venue requirement in actions for trespass to land. However, New York

---

28. *Id.* at 1144 (dismissing trespass action demanding money damages in England for entering plaintiff's dwelling house in Canada and expelling the plaintiff); *see also* Chapter 1(D)(3)*(c) supra* ("*Ex Delicto* Personal Actions").

29. William W. Blume, *Place of Trial of Civil Cases*, 48 MICH. L. REV. 1, 27 (1949).

30. *Id.* at 27-28; *see* Penn v. Baltimore, 27 Eng. Rep. 1132 (Ch. 1750) (holding specific performance decree proper for land outside England); *see also* Bergeron v. Boyle, 2003 VT 89, 176 Vt. 78, 838 A.2d 918 (action for declaratory relief and specific performance of contract for sale of farm property was not an action "concerning real estate" within the meaning of the state's statutory local action rule and did not have to be brought in the county in which the land was located; the action did not require the court to directly establish, quiet, attach, transfer, or bestow property to real estate).

31. Act of Apr. 12, 1848, ch. 379, § 103, 1848 N.Y. Laws 497, 517.

32. N.Y. C.P.L.R. § 507 (McKinney 2006).

decisions continue to classify actions involving injury to land as local in nature.[33] These decisions demonstrate the resiliency of the local action rule, even in a time when the premises of the rule have come into question.[34]

* * * * *

A few courts have discarded the local action rule when a statute does not compel its application.

Illustration 4-3. In *Reasor-Hill Corp. v. Harrison*,[35] for example, the Arkansas Supreme Court held that the Arkansas courts could entertain a suit for injuries to real property located in Missouri. The court examined the reasons given in support of the local action rule and found them unpersuasive. It concluded that the local action rule, as applied to the case before it, had "no basis in logic or equity and rests solely upon English cases that were decided before America was discovered and in circumstances that are not even comparable to those existing in our Union."[36]

* * * * *

The courts have abandoned the local action rule mainly in actions seeking to recover damages for injuries to real property located outside the state.[37] In actions directly involving the title to land located outside the state, courts apparently have not relaxed the rule.[38] Likewise, with regard to land located within the state, most states have retained the local action rule as it traditionally operated.[39] The justifications for retaining the rule include the following:

> [T]he court of the county in which the res, which is the subject matter of the suit, is located is best able to deal with the problem. The local sheriff can attach, deliver, or execute upon the property. The local clerk can make the necessary entries with a minimum of red tape where title to land is affected. Trial convenience is served

---

33. *See, e.g.*, Town of Hempstead v. City of N.Y., 88 Misc. 2d 366, 388 N.Y.S.2d 78 (Sup. Ct. 1976); Geidel v. Niagara Mohawk Power Corp., 46 Misc. 2d 990, 261 N.Y.S.2d 379 (Sup. Ct. 1965).

34. *See, e.g.*, Brainerd Currie, *The Constitution and the "Transitory" Cause of Action*, 73 HARV. L. REV. 36, 67-69 (1959); *see also In re* Applied Chem. Magnesias Corp., 206 S.W.3d 114 (Tex. 2006) (declaratory judgment action to determine the rights of contracting parties to acquire surface and mineral leases was an action involving an interest in real property subject to mandatory, statutory venue provision requiring that action be filed in county where property located).

35. 220 Ark. 521, 249 S.W.2d 994 (1952).

36. *Id.* at 525, 249 S.W.2d at 996.

37. *See, e.g.*, Reasor-Hill Corp. v. Harrison, 220 Ark. 521, 249 S.W.2d 994 (1952); Candlewood Timber Group, LLC v. Pan Am. Energy, LLC, 859 A.2d 989 (Del. Super. 2004) (action for damages to land in foreign country is transitory); Little v. Chicago St. Paul, Minneapolis & Omaha Ry. Co., 65 Minn. 48, 67 N.W. 846 (1896); Ingram v. Great Lakes Pipe Line Co., 153 S.W.2d 547 (Mo. Ct. App. 1941). New York has abolished the local action rule by statute in actions to recover damages for injury to land located outside the state and in actions for breach of contract or covenants relating to land outside the state. *See* N.Y. REAL PROP. ACTS § 121 (2009). Most states have retained the local action rule in this category of cases. *See* RUSSELL J. WEINTRAUB, COMMENTARY ON THE CONFLICT OF LAWS § 4.39 (6th ed. 2010).

38. *See* RUSSELL J. WEINTRAUB, COMMENTARY ON THE CONFLICT OF LAWS §§ 8.4-8.5 (6th ed. 2010). As discussed in Chapter 3, *supra*, and in the text, *infra*, this situation may involve due process restrictions on the power of courts to affect the title to land located outside the state. *See* Chapter 3(B)(1)*(b) supra* ("Restrictive Principles of In Rem Jurisdiction").

39. *See, e.g.*, S.D. CODIFIED LAWS ANN. §§ 15-5-1(1) to (3) (action for recovery of realty, partition of realty, foreclosure of mortgage on realty, and damages for injury to realty must be brought in county where subject of the action, or some part thereof, is situated), § 15-5-8 (action for damages to property may, at plaintiff's option be brought in county where damages were inflicted or cause of action arose) (2004); June F. Entman, *Abolishing Local Action Rules: A First Step Toward Modernizing Jurisdiction and Venue in Tennessee*, 34 U. MEM. L. REV. 251 (2004); *cf.* SDDS, Inc. v. State, 502 N.W.2d 852 (S.D. 1993) (action by solid waste developer challenging initiative and referendum resulting in denial of permit was not a suit in which the subject of action was land).

> where "a view" is necessary or of value in reaching a determination. Third parties can readily ascertain, at a logical point of inquiry, the status of a res in which they may be interested.
>
> . . . [T]hese factors are of sufficient importance in this type of case to outweigh other considerations such as convenience of parties or witnesses in the selection of place of trial. Consequently, in actions of the type generally referred to as local, venue based upon where the subject of action or part thereof is situated makes sense and should be preserved.[40]

Regardless whether these justifications made sense in the past, they do not make sense today. Local officials can attach, deliver, or execute upon land based on the judgment of a court located in another county, if the law authorizes them to do so. There should be few administrative problems involved if the clerk in the county where land is located is authorized to make entries concerning the title based on an action pending in some other county. A view of the property is seldom necessary, even when land is the subject of the action. When a view is necessary, the court can transfer the action under an appropriate statute to the county where the land is located.[41] In addition, while other kinds of actions exist in which a view is sometimes necessary, those actions are not, as a consequence, classified as local actions.[42] Finally, third parties can ascertain the status of land in which they are interested in the county where the land is located, even if actions concerning the land are allowed in other counties. For example, a notice of lis pendens can be entered in the records of the county where the land is located based on an action concerning the land in another county, as long as the law authorizes such an entry.

For these reasons, retention of the local action rule is questionable today. Nevertheless, as noted in *Illustration 4-2*, above, the rule has shown great resilience. Furthermore, no strong nationwide legislative movement is afoot today to abolish the rule.

One issue concerning the local action rule is whether the courts should treat it as a rule of venue or subject-matter jurisdiction. Some courts consider the local action objection to be waivable like other venue objections.[43] However, other courts, sometimes influenced by state constitutional provisions classifying certain actions as local, consider the objection to be jurisdictional in nature.[44] Absent a specific legislative or constitutional classification recognizing that a case is beyond a court's subject-matter jurisdiction when it is brought somewhere other than where land is situated, little justification exists for considering the objection to be jurisdictional in nature.

Chapter 3 discussed decisions of the U.S. Supreme Court holding that states do not have subject-matter jurisdiction to entertain actions that directly affect the

---

40. George N. Stevens, *Venue Statutes: Diagnosis and Proposed Cure*, 49 MICH. L. REV. 307, 310 (1951).

41. *See* section D *infra* ("Forum Non Conveniens and Change of Venue").

42. *See* RUSSELL J. WEINTRAUB, COMMENTARY ON THE CONFLICT OF LAWS § 4.39, at 331 (6th ed. 2010).

43. *See, e.g.*, Cirillo Bros. Petroleum Co. v. Kyne Realty Corp., 30 Misc. 2d 702, 216 N.Y.S.2d 269 (City Ct. 1961); *see also* Hallaba v. Worldcom Network Servs. Inc., 196 F.R.D. 630 (N.D. Okla. 2000) (trespass to land is a local action, the local action is a venue doctrine not a subject-matter jurisdiction doctrine, and defendant had waived the objection by answering the plaintiff's complaint without raising a venue objection).

44. *Compare* Maguire v. Cunningham, 64 Cal. App. 536, 222 P. 838 (1923) *with* Childs v. Eltinge, 29 Cal. App. 3d 843, 851, 105 Cal. Rptr. 864, 869 (1973).

title to land located in other states.[45] It may be that the courts holding the local action rule to be a rule of subject-matter jurisdiction generally have confused ordinary local actions with these out-of-state actions directly affecting the title to land. In any event, as discussed in Chapter 3, it is clear that this restrictive principle of jurisdiction was not, prior to the Fourteenth Amendment, considered a matter of constitutional law. Rather, the principle was one of a number of sovereignty-based rules of international law that the states were entitled to enforce in order to protect their prerogatives from the encroachment of other states.[46] After the adoption of the Fourteenth Amendment, the status of these rules as "constitutional" rules or "nonconstitutional" sovereignty-based rules is unclear.[47] However, the Supreme Court has continued to enforce them.

For purposes of this chapter, it is important to note that some local actions in state courts will overlap with the principle prohibiting actions that directly affect the title to land located elsewhere while other actions will not. For example, actions to recover damages for trespass to land located in another state will surely not be held to "directly" affect the title to the land in a way that would entitle the situs state to refuse to enforce the forum's judgment.[48] Note, however, that if the forum state not only classifies such an action as "local," but treats the local action rule as a subject-matter jurisdiction restriction generally, the same result would follow as if the restriction were encompassed in the rules enforced by the Supreme Court in land title cases. The situs state could refuse enforcement to the judgment under the latter circumstances because it would be void under the law of the state where it was rendered and, therefore, entitled to no effect under the full-faith-and-credit implementing statute examined in Chapter 3.[49] Thus, when dealing with actions concerning land located in other states, litigants must be alert to the nature and scope of the forum's local action rule. In addition, they must be alert to principles

---

45. *See* Chapter 3(B)(1)*(b) supra* ("Restrictive Principles of In Rem Jurisdiction") & Chapter 3(H)(3) *supra* ("Property cases").

46. *See* Chapter 3(A)(1) *supra* ("Personal Jurisdiction Restrictions Prior to the Adoption of the Fourteenth Amendment").

47. *See* Chapter 3(B)(1)*(b) supra* ("Restrictive Principles of In Rem Jurisdiction"); *see also* Chapter 3(G)(3) *supra* ("Sovereignty-Based Restrictions on State-Court Jurisdiction"). For a complete discussion of this question, see ROBERT L. FELIX & RALPH U. WHITTEN, AMERICAN CONFLICTS LAW § 44 (6th ed. 2011).

48. In addition, the states may issue equitable decrees such as injunctions or decrees of specific performance against defendants over whom they have personal jurisdiction, even though the injunction or decree will affect foreign land. The reason is that these kinds of decrees act "in personam," that is, on the person of the defendant instead of "directly" on the land. *See* the discussion of the equity courts power in the text, *supra*. Actions seeking such orders have traditionally not been considered "local" in nature; nor were they restricted by the traditional, territorial, international rules. *Cf.* RESTATEMENT (SECOND) OF CONFLICT OF LAWS § 55 (1971) (court has power to order a person subject to its jurisdiction to do an act in the state, even if carrying out the order will affect a thing in another state). There may, of course, be actions in between the situations described in the text that the Supreme Court will have to determine as either being within the "direct effect on title" principle or not. *See, e.g.*, Farha v. Signal Cos., 216 Kan. 471, 532 P.2d 1330 (1975), in which the Kansas Supreme Court permitted the adjudication of an action for damages in Kansas for the use and occupation of land in Texas. The action involved an issue of adverse possession to the Texas land, which one would think would "directly affect" the title. Nevertheless, the court held that an action for damages for use and occupation of the land was "transitory" in nature and that the Kansas courts had jurisdiction to adjudicate the issue of title by adverse possession as an incidental matter. It is interesting to speculate whether a Texas court should be permitted to deny issue preclusion effect to the adverse possession determination in a subsequent action in Texas where the title was directly involved. Note that this sort of issue can also arise in the trespass-to-land case when lack of title in the plaintiff is asserted as a defense.

49. *See* Chapter 3(A)(1)*(d) supra* ("The 1790 Implementing Statute") & Chapter 13(E) *infra* ("Claim and Issue Preclusion on Questions of Subject-Matter and Personal Jurisdiction").

that the U.S. Supreme Court has allowed the situs state to enforce apart from the forum's own rules.[50]

The federal courts traditionally observed the distinction between local and transitory actions. Although federal statutes never made more than oblique references to the local action concept,[51] judicial interpretation settled that the local action rule existed in the federal courts.[52] However, as discussed in section C(4)*(c)*, below, the Federal Courts Jurisdiction and Venue Clarification Act of 2011,[53] effective in 2012, repealed the local action rule in federal court.

SECTION B. VENUE IN STATE COURTS

In areas that do not concern local actions, state venue schemes vary widely. The specific makeup of state venue schemes reflect "historical developments and piecemeal legislative tinkering."[54] Proper venue in a particular state will depend on one or more of the following factors: (1) the theory of the claim; (2) the subject matter of the claim; and (3) the parties involved. Most states provide the plaintiff with a narrower range of venue choices than the English common law did in transitory actions. These choices typically include: (1) where the cause of action arose or accrued;[55] (2) where the defendant resides; (3) where the plaintiff resides; (4) where the defendant is doing business; (5) where the defendant has an office or a place of business or where one of its agents or officers resides; (6) where the defendant may be found; (7) where the defendant may be summoned or served; and (8) where the seat of government is located.[56]

When a state venue statute allows the plaintiff to bring an action in the county "where the cause of action arose" or "where the damages were sustained," a conceptual problem may exist. This problem may arise when time and space separate the defendant's actions from the ultimate injury suffered by the plaintiff.

---

50. It should also be noted that, in theory, the states possess power to extend their local action rules to encompass any kind of civil action, whether or not the action involves land. As long as the local action designation is a restriction that the state would be imposing on its own authority, no federal constitutional objection exists, whether the state designates the restriction as one of venue or as a subject-matter jurisdiction limit. However, a state cannot necessarily bind other states to adhere to novel forms of local actions that would preclude them from adjudicating actions if the actions are otherwise within the scope of the subject-matter and personal jurisdiction authority of the other states. Other states may honor such restrictions on their authority as a matter of comity, but they would not be obligated to do so. For example, in Wilson v. Celestral Greetings, Inc., 896 S.W.2d 759 (Mo. Ct. App. 1995), a shareholder of a Delaware corporation dissented from a merger decision and commenced an action in Missouri state court under Delaware statutory law to have her shares appraised and to obtain compensation. The Missouri Court of Appeals held that the action was a local action that could only be brought in Delaware. The court agreed that the action was basically a contract action that would be transitory in nature, but it interpreted the Delaware statutes as requiring that the action be brought in Delaware. Clearly, even if the court's interpretation of Delaware law is correct, Delaware has no power by classifying an action as local to *force* other states to dismiss the action. Thus, unless the court of appeals decision is viewed as based on comity with Delaware, it is incorrect. Only if an action classified as "local" fits within constitutional or other rules that restrict state power can the states be forced to refuse jurisdiction of the action.

51. *See* 28 U.S.C. § 1392, *repealed by* Pub. L. 112-63, § 203, 125 Stat. 758, 764 (2011).

52. *See, e.g.*, Livingston v. Jefferson, 15 F. Cas. 660 (C.C.D. Va. 1811) (No. 8411).

53. Pub. L. 112-63, § 202(1), 125 Stat. 758, 763 (2011) (codified in 28 U.S.C. § 1391(a)(2); *id.* § 203, 125 Stat. at 764 (2011) (repealing 28 U.S.C. § 1392, which contained a reference to the local action rule).

54. George N. Stevens, *Venue Statutes: Diagnosis and Proposed Cure*, 49 MICH. L. REV. 307, 307 (1951).

55. *See* Jay M. Zitter, Annotation, *Place Where Claim or Cause of Action "Arose" Under State Venue Statute*, 53 A.L.R.4TH 1104 (1987).

56. *See* George N. Stevens, *Venue Statutes: Diagnosis and Proposed Cure*, 49 MICH. L. REV. 307, 309-16 (1951).

Illustration 4-4. *P-1* and *P-2* are the parents of *C*. *P-1*, *P-2*, and *C* reside in County *X*. *D* is a doctor who resides and practices medicine in County *Y*. *P-1* and *P-2* take *C* to County *Y*, where *D* negligently treats *C*. *P-1*, *P-2*, and *C* return to County *X*. *C* then dies due to the negligent treatment. *P-1* and *P-2* sue *D* in a court in County *X*. The venue statutes provide that a plaintiff may bring an action for wrongful death in the county "where the damages were sustained." On similar facts, the Louisiana Court of Appeal held venue improper in County *X*.[57] The court stated that *C*, the patient, sustained the damages where the negligent treatment occurred, not where *C* died.[58]

Illustration 4-5. Assume that *D-1* injures *P* in a construction accident in County *X*, where both *P* and *D-1* reside. *P* sues *D-1* in County *X* to recover for *P's* personal injuries. After *P* commences this action, *P* has an automobile accident in County *Y* with *D-2*, a resident of County *Y*. After this accident with *D-2*, *P* amends the complaint in *P's* action against *D-1* in County *X*. *P's* amended complaint adds *D-2* as a defendant in that action. The amended complaint alleges that *D-2's* negligence caused the automobile accident and aggravated injuries suffered by *P* in the construction accident. Assume that the venue statute allows the plaintiff to sue in the county of residence "of any defendant who is joined in good faith and with probable cause for the purpose of obtaining a judgment against the defendant and not solely for the purpose of fixing venue in that county." On similar facts, the Illinois Appellate Court held venue proper in County *X*.[59] *P* did not join *D-2* merely to establish venue in County *X*. *P's* action against *D-1* and *D-2* in County *X* sought a correct apportionment of damages between the two defendants.[60]

SECTION C. VENUE IN FEDERAL COURTS

The general federal venue provisions are found in 28 U.S.C. §§ 1391-1407. These sections reveal the basic pattern of federal venue.

1. Plaintiffs' Residence as Proper Venue

Before 1990, the federal venue statutes contained several peculiarities. Congress addressed many of these peculiarities in the Judicial Improvements Act

---

57. Keele v. Knecht, 621 So. 2d 106 (La. Ct. App. 1993) (statute provided for venue in parish where wrongful conduct occurred or where the damages were sustained; if any damage occurs in same parish where wrongful conduct occurred, that parish is the only proper venue).

58. This construction is, of course, far from inevitable. The situation in this illustration is a variation of the problem discussed in section C(3), *infra*, under the former language of 28 U.S.C. § 1391 providing for venue where the "cause of action arose." The language suggests the cause of action can arise in only one place. Under the state statute in *Keele*, the language suggests that the damages can occur in only one county, though the court did not hold this construction to be true in every case. In products liability actions in which the wrongful conduct and damages usually occur in entirely different counties, venue would be proper where the damages occur. *See* 621 So. 2d at 110-11.

59. Hall v. Keating, 246 Ill. App. 3d 538, 616 N.E.2d 683 (1993).

60. *Id.* at 539, 616 N.E.2d at 684; *see also* R & D Transp., Inc. v. A.H., 859 N.E.2d 332 (Ind. 2006) (venue rule that provided for venue in county where chattels or some part thereof were regularly located did not control over venue rule that provided automobile accident cases should be adjudicated in the county where the accident occurred, even though chattel, an automobile, was damaged in the accident; venue rule for chattels was designed for cases in which ownership of property was in question).

of 1990.[61] Before the 1990 amendments, actions based on diversity of citizenship could be brought only in the district (1) where all the plaintiffs resided, (2) where all the defendants resided, or (3) where the claim arose.[62] However, when jurisdiction was based in part on the existence of a federal question in the action, venue was proper only in either the district (1) where all the defendants resided or (2) where the claim arose, but it was not proper in the district where all plaintiffs resided.[63] No defensible reason existed for this difference.[64]

In 1990, the Federal Courts Study Committee recommended extensive changes in the general venue statute.[65] One of these recommendations was that "Congress [should] eliminate the century-old anomaly . . . providing for venue in diversity but not federal question cases 'in the judicial district where all plaintiffs . . . reside.'"[66] Following a 1969 recommendation of the American Law Institute,[67] the Committee recommended[68] and Congress enacted[69] amendments to 28 U.S.C. § 1391(a) & (b). These amendments eliminated plaintiffs' residence as a basis for venue in diversity actions.

In 2011, Congress enacted the Federal Courts Jurisdiction and Venue Clarification Act of 2011,[70] effective in January 2012, to clarify certain aspects of the operation of § 1391. Subsection (a)(1) provides that (except as otherwise provided by law) "this section shall govern the venue in all civil actions brought in the district courts of the United States. This makes it clear that the statute provides the general requirements for venue in the federal courts, but does not displace special venue rules that govern under particular federal statutes.[71] However, Congress expressed the hope that by providing greater uniformity of venue, the amended statute would lessen the need for special venue provisions in titles other than Title 28.[72] The 2011 amendments will be discussed as they are pertinent to particular categories of venue examined in later subsections.

2. Defendants' Residence as Proper Venue

The Judicial Improvements Act of 1990 provided for venue in both federal questions and diversity cases in "a judicial district where any defendant resides, if all defendants reside in the same *state*."[73] These amendments may appear to have expanded the permissible locations for suit based on defendants' residence. As noted in the preceding subsection, before 1990, § 1391(a) & (b) provided for venue at defendants' residence only when all the defendants resided in the same *district*.

---

61. *See* Pub. L. No. 101-650, § 311, 104 Stat. 5089, 5114.
62. This standard was found in former 28 U.S.C. § 1391(a).
63. This standard was found in former 28 U.S.C. § 1391(b).
64. *See* REPORT OF THE FEDERAL COURTS STUDY COMMITTEE 94 (1990).
65. *Id.*
66. *Id.*
67. ALI STUDY OF THE DIVISION OF JURISDICTION BETWEEN STATE AND FEDERAL COURTS §§ 1303(a)(2), 1314(a)(2) (1969).
68. *See* REPORT OF THE FEDERAL COURTS STUDY COMMITTEE 94 (1990).
69. Judicial Improvements Act of 1990, Pub. L. No. 101-650, § 311, 104 Stat. 5089, 5114 (codified at 28 U.S.C. §§ 1391(a)(1) & (b)(1)).
70. Pub. L. 112-63, § 202, 125 Stat. 758, 763 (2011) (codified at 28 U.S.C. § 1391(a)-(e)).
71. *See* H.R. Rep. No. 112-10, at 11 (2011).
72. *See id.* n. 8.
73. *See id.* (emphasis added).

However, even before the 1990 amendments, § 1392(a) of Title 28 allowed plaintiffs to bring non-local actions against defendants residing in different districts in the same state "in any of such districts."[74] For a time, Congress did not repeal or amend § 1392(a) to conform to the 1990 amendments of § 1391(a) & (b). Thus, two separate statutes made venue proper in a district within a state in which "any defendant resides" as long as "all defendants reside in the same state." However, it was clear that the amendments to § 1391(a) & (b) made 28 U.S.C. § 1392(a) superfluous, and the section was repealed in 1996.[75]

In 2011, Congress enacted the Federal Courts Jurisdiction and Venue Clarification Act of 2011,[76] effective in January 2012. The Act combined former sections 1391(a) & (b) into a new section 1391(b) applicable to both diversity and federal question cases. New subsection 1391(b)(1) reworded the provision governing venue based on defendants' residence, as follows:

> (b) VENUE IN GENERAL.—A civil action may be brought in—
>
> (1) a judicial district in which any defendant resides, if all defendants are residents of the State in which the district court is situated;

This new wording is designed to take care of a problem under former § 1391(a)(1) & (b)(1). Those provisions stated that venue was proper in "a judicial district in which any defendant resides, if all defendants reside in the same state." Read literally, this would make venue proper in a district within a state where one defendant only resides if both defendants also reside in another state. As a practical matter, this problem only existed if one of the defendants was a corporation. The House Report accompanying the amendment explained:

> . . . [C]onsider a suit brought against both a resident (natural person) in Illinois and a corporation that does substantial business in every state, including Illinois and the litigation arose from events that occurred in Illinois. Under current subsection 1391(c) [governing the residence of corporations], the corporation could be considered a resident of Illinois and every other state, by virtue of its being subject to personal jurisdiction in all those states. A plaintiff might sue both defendants in any other district where the corporation happens to reside, such as the Southern District of New York, on the theory that, because all defendants reside in the same state (Illinois) as provided in 28 U.S.C. Sec. 1391(a) and (b), venue is proper in any other district where "any defendant resides."

The language of the new provision makes it clear that all defendants must be residents of the state in which the district court in which the action is brought is "situated," thus eliminating this problem with the language.

Also contained in the 2011 amendments is a new subsection (c)(1), defining the residence of a natural person to be the judicial district in which that person is

---

74. 28 U.S.C. § 1392(a) (repealed 1996).

75. *See* Act of Oct. 1, 1996, Pub. L. No. 104-220, § 1, 110 Stat. 3023, 3023.

76. Pub. L. 112-63, § 202(1), 125 Stat. 758, 763 (2011) (codified as 28 U.S.C. § 1391(b)(1)).

domiciled.[77] Although prior to the 2011 amendment, it had generally been understood that citizenship and residence were synonymous, some courts had interpreted the term residence to mean something less than "permanent residence" or domicile, giving rise to the possibility that an individual defendant might have multiple residences for purpose of the venue statute.[78] The amendment makes it clear that this interpretation is wrong.

Illustration 4-6. *P*, a citizen of State *X*, wishes to sue *D-1* and *D-2* for $500,000 in damages resulting from an automobile accident. *D-1* and *D-2* are both citizens of State *Y*. However, *D-1* resides in the Northern District and *D-2* resides in the Southern District of State *Y*. Under § 1391(b)(1) *P* may sue *D-1* and *D-2* in either the Northern or the Southern District of State *Y*.

Illustration 4-7. *P*, a citizen of State *X*, wishes to sue *D-1* and *D-2* in a federal diversity action for $500,000 in damages resulting from an automobile accident. *D-1* is a citizen of State *Y* who resides in the Northern District of State *Y*. *D-2* is a citizen of State *Z* who resides in the Northern District of State *Z*. *P* cannot base federal venue on the defendants' residence. The Judicial Code does not authorize venue based on the defendants' residence when the defendants reside in different districts in different states. Thus, *P* will have to establish venue on some other basis than defendants' residence, such as where the events giving rise to suit occurred, or, in an appropriate case, under the "fallback" provisions of § 1391(b)(3), discussed below.

* * * * *

One question that has sometimes arisen under the "defendants' residence" provisions is whether a defendant who resides in the state and district in which the action is brought can raise a venue objection for a nonresident as to whom venue is improper. The language of the venue statute literally makes venue improper in such cases, and it might be reasoned that any defendant should be able to raise the defect. However, some courts have held that resident defendants cannot raise venue objections for nonresidents.[79] This result seems correct. Venue is a defense personal to the party to whom it applies and can be waived,[80] just like a personal jurisdiction objection. Thus, if one defendant resides in a district and state and another does not, the nonresident should be able to legitimize venue that would otherwise be defective by either consenting to suit within the district or waiving the venue objection, just as would be the case with personal jurisdiction.[81]

---

77. *See id.*

78. *See* H.R. Rep. 112-10, at 13.

79. *See* Gerety v. Sunrise Express, Inc., 95 Civ. 2090 (NB), 1996 WL 19047, 96 U.S. Dist. LEXIS 378 (S.D.N.Y. Jan. 18, 1996); Pratt v. Rowland, 769 F. Supp. 1128 (N.D. Cal. 1991), *rev'd on other grounds*, 65 F.3d 802 (9th Cir. 1995).

80. However, note that least one federal court, incorrectly, thinks venue is an objection that can be raised by the court on its own motion. *See, e.g.,* California Advocates for Nursing Home Reform v. Creekside Care Convalescent Hosp., Inc., No. C-94-3519-VRW, 1994 WL 589459, 1994 U.S. Dist. LEXIS 14761 (N.D. Cal. Oct. 6, 1994). *But see* Woodke v. Dahm, 70 F.3d 983 (8th Cir. 1995) (no rule requires district court to dismiss defendant *sua sponte* to preserve venue).

81. The ALI would make this rule explicit by providing that "[o]nly a defendant as to whom venue would be improper absent joinder of any other defendant may object." ALI FEDERAL JUDICIAL CODE REVISION PROJECT § 1406(b), at 219 (2004).

3. Venue Proper Where Events Giving Rise to Suit Occur

Before 1963, the general venue statutes based federal venue wholly on the residence of the parties.[82] In 1963, Congress added a special venue provision for "tort claims arising out of the manufacture, assembly, repair, ownership, maintenance, use, or operation of an automobile."[83] In such civil actions, Congress permitted venue in the district where the act or omission occurred.[84] In 1966, Congress repealed this provision.[85] Instead, Congress provided for venue in the district where "the claim arose" in both diversity and federal question cases.[86] The "claim arose" language of § 1391 seemed to assume that a claim could arise in only one district. In some cases, this language presented no problem.

Illustration 4-8. Assume that *P* and *D* are involved in an automobile accident. *P* claims that *P* was injured as a result of *D's* negligent operation of a motor vehicle. This claim clearly arises in the district where the accident occurred and *P* was injured.[87]

* * * * *

When the transaction or event that was the subject of the action had connections with more than one district, the issue was whether the claim could be deemed to arise in more than one district. If so, the plaintiff would have a choice among several districts having connections with the claim. The U.S. Supreme Court never resolved this issue. However, in *Leroy v. Great Western United Corp.*,[88] the Court did indicate that if the plaintiff had such a choice, it would be limited to those "districts that with approximately equal plausibility—in terms of the availability of witnesses, the accessibility of other relevant evidence, and the convenience of the defendant (but *not* [the convenience] of the plaintiff)—may be assigned as locus of the claim."[89]

In 1990, the Federal Courts Study Committee recommended replacing "the claim arose" language. The Committee proposed permitting venue in "any judicial district in which a substantial part of the events or omissions giving rise to the claim occurred, or a substantial part of [the] property that is the subject of the action is situated."[90] The Committee patterned its recommendation on a 1969 proposal of the American Law Institute.[91] Congress followed this recommendation in the Judicial Improvements Act of 1990.[92] Congress thus eliminated the interpretive difficulties

---

82. *See* 14D CHARLES A. WRIGHT ET AL., FEDERAL PRACTICE AND PROCEDURE: JURISDICTION AND RELATED MATTERS § 3806, at 157 (3d ed. 2007).

83. Act of Dec. 23, 1963, Pub. L. No. 88-234, 77 Stat. 473 (adding subsection (f) to 28 U.S.C. § 1391).

84. *Id.*

85. Act of Nov. 2, 1966, Pub. L. No. 89-714, 80 Stat. 1111.

86. *See* 14D CHARLES A. WRIGHT ET AL., FEDERAL PRACTICE AND PROCEDURE: JURISDICTION AND RELATED MATTERS § 3806, at 159 (3d ed. 2007).

87. *See* Annotation, *What Is the Judicial District "In Which the Claim Arose" for Venue Purposes Under 28 U.S.C. § 1391(a) and (b)*, 59 A.L.R. FED. 320, 324 (1982).

88. 443 U.S. 173, 99 S. Ct. 2710, 61 L. Ed. 2d 464 (1979).

89. *Id.* at 185, 99 S. Ct. at 2717, 61 L. Ed. 2d at 475 (emphasis added).

90. REPORT OF THE FEDERAL COURTS STUDY COMMITTEE 94 (1990).

91. ALI STUDY OF THE DIVISION OF JURISDICTION BETWEEN STATE AND FEDERAL COURTS §§ 1303(a)(1), 1314(a)(1) (1969).

92. *See* Pub. L. No. 101-650, § 311, 104 Stat. 5089, 5114 (codified at 28 U.S.C. § 1391(a)(2) & (b)(2)).

of the "claim arose" language.[93] This language was retained in the 2011 amendments to § 1391 that were made in the Federal Courts Jurisdiction and Venue Clarification Act of 2011,[94] effective in 2012 and now found in 28 U.S.C. § 1391(b)(2).

Nevertheless, some commentators have suggested that this language in the venue statute will result in as much litigation as the previous "claim arose" language.[95] One difficulty lies in developing a test to determine whether the events or omissions occurring within a district are "substantial." If all of the events giving rise to the claim occur in one district, the events are obviously substantial and venue is proper in the district.[96] Similarly, if no events giving rise to the claim occur within a district, the plaintiff obviously cannot predicate venue in the district on § 1391(b)(2).[97] Presumably, also, if the plaintiff brings an action in a district where a majority (over 50%) of the events or omissions giving rise to suit occurred, no one would disagree that the events in the district are substantial.

The problem cases will be those in which the plaintiff brings the action in a district in which some, but less than a majority, of the events or omissions giving rise to the suit occurred. Both the language and the legislative history of "substantial events" based venue indicate that a substantial part of the events giving rise to the suit can occur in more than one district.[98] Therefore, the test established cannot make venue proper only where most (*i.e.*, 51% or more) of the events occurred.[99] Nor can venue be made proper only where the largest portion of the events occurred (*e.g.*, 34% in the proper district as opposed to 33% and 33% in each of two other districts).[100]

---

93. *See id. See also* Mitchell G. Page, Comment, *After the Judicial Improvements Act of 1990: Does the General Federal Venue Statute Survive as a Protection for Defendants?* 74 U. COLO. L. REV. 1153, 1156 (2003) (arguing that the 1990 amendments have not only afforded plaintiffs in diversity cases a greater choice of places in which to sue, but a greater choice in selecting the applicable substantive law that will govern the claim and, as a consequence, § 1391 should be construed in favor of defendants).

94. Pub. L. 112-63, § 202(1), 125 Stat. 758, 763 (2011) (codified in 28 U.S.C. § 1391(b)(2).

95. *See* John B. Oakley, *Recent Statutory Changes in the Law of Federal Jurisdiction and Venue: The Judicial Improvements Acts of 1988 and 1990*, 24 U.C. DAVIS L. REV. 735, 775 (1991); David D. Siegel, *Changes in Federal Jurisdiction and Practice Under the New (Dec. 1, 1990) Judicial Improvements Act*, 133 F.R.D. 61, 72 (1991). *See also* Mitchell G. Page, Comment, *After the Judicial Improvements Act of 1990: Does the General Federal Venue Statute Survive as a Protection for Defendants?* 74 U. COLO. L. REV. 1153 (2003).

96. *See, e.g.*, Jenkins Brick Co. v. Bremer, 321 F.3d 1366 (11th Cir. 2003) (Alabama company hired individual to sell products in Savannah, Georgia territory; contract contained noncompetition clause; employee resigned and went to work for competitor in Savannah; company sued to enforce noncompetition clause in Alabama; held: all the events giving rise to the claim occurred in Georgia; therefore, venue improper in Alabama).

97. Numerous cases have dismissed or transferred actions that were commenced in a district where none of the events giving rise to suit occurred and where venue was not proper on the basis of the defendants' residence. *See, e.g.*, Krain v. Devich, No. 91-15758, 1992 WL 129195, 1992 U.S. App. LEXIS 13546 (9th Cir. June 4, 1992); Banque de la Mediterranee-Fr., S.A. v. Thergen, Inc., 780 F. Supp. 92 (D.R.I. 1992); Berube v. Brister, 140 F.R.D. 258 (D.R.I. 1992); Lahm v. Wagner, 776 F. Supp. 114 (E.D.N.Y. 1991); Sani-Dairy v. Yeutter, 782 F. Supp. 1060 (W.D. Pa. 1991).

98. *See* H.R. REP. NO. 734, 101st Cong., 2d Sess. 23 (1990) (language "avoids the problem created by the frequent cases in which substantial parts of the underlying events have occurred in several districts"). *See, e.g.*, Bates v. C & S Adjusters, Inc., 980 F.2d 865, 867 (2d Cir. 1992).

99. *See* First of Mich. Corp. v. Bramlet, 141 F.3d 260 (6th Cir. 1998) (majority of events need not take place in district to be substantial).

100. *See, e.g.*, Gulf Ins. Co. v. Glasbrenner, 417 F.3d 353 (2d Cir. 2005) (under substantial events test, venue may be proper in more than one district as long as significant events or omissions material to a claim occurred in multiple districts; venue would have been proper in District of New Jersey where injury occurred and resulting judgment was rendered; however, venue in insurer's declaratory judgment action for nonliability was also proper in the Southern District of New York because policy was negotiated, approved, and executed at company's headquarters there and court held that submission, approval, and issuance of the policy constituted substantial part of the company's claim of nonliability); Mitrano v. Hawes, 377 F.3d 402 (4th Cir. 2004) (substantial part of events

(a) Fixed Minimum Percentage Test

One approach to creating a workable test would be to establish a fixed minimum percentage of the events or omissions that must occur within the district before venue is proper. Under this type of test, if the percentage dropped below the minimum level, the plaintiff could not base venue in the district. The difficulty in formulating such a test is setting the appropriate percentage. In some actions, a large number of events in a district could constitute a relatively small percentage of the total activity giving rise to suit. Therefore, establishing a minimum percentage risks eliminating as a proper venue a district where a considerable amount of activity took place and where no substantial inconvenience would result in conducting the action. When the total activity is large but only a small percentage of the activity occurred in any one district, establishing a fixed minimum could also mean that venue would not be proper anywhere based on a substantial part of the events or omissions. Thus, courts should reject this approach.[101]

Illustration 4-9. *P*, a citizen of State X residing in the Southern District of State *X*, sues *D*, a citizen of State *Y*, seeking damages for trademark infringement under federal law. *P* brought this action in the U.S. District Court for the Southern District of State *X*. *D's* infringing activity occurred in the form of sales of a product throughout the United States. The total sales of the product were $500,000,000. The sales in the Southern District of State *X* were $4,000,000. The largest amount of sales in any district was $15,000,000. If the court establishes a fixed minimum percentage, venue might not be proper in the Southern District of State *X*. The activity in State *X* is less than 1% of the total. Indeed, if courts establish a fixed percentage without regard to the facts of different cases, venue might not be proper in any district under § 1391(b)(2). For example, if the fixed minimum is established as 33%, under § 1391(b)(2) venue would not be proper anywhere. The largest amount of infringing activity occurring in any district is only 3% ($15,000,000).[102]

(b) Relative Activity Test

An alternative approach would apply a "relative activity" test under § 1391(a)(2) & (b)(2). This approach would not fix a minimum percentage that all cases must meet. Instead, it would permit venue in districts in which a relatively

---

can take place in more than one district; services lawyer performed in the Eastern District of Virginia may constitute a substantial part of the events giving rise to the claim under a contract centered in Massachusetts; remanded).

101. *See* Imagineering, Inc. v. Lukingbeal, No. 94 Civ. 2589 (RLC), 1996 WL 148431, 1996 U.S. Dist. LEXIS 3939 (S.D.N.Y. Apr. 1, 1996) (no minimum percentage necessary).

102. *See* Alcoholics Anonymous World Servs., Inc. v. Friedman, No. 91 Civ. 8741 (RLC), 1992 WL 150633, 1992 U.S. Dist. LEXIS 8939 (S.D.N.Y. June 17, 1992) (holding that less than 1% of the defendant's nationwide sales was not a substantial amount, but the court failed to examine sales in other districts; no fixed minimum percentage established); *cf.* Time Prods., PLC v. J. Tiras Classic Handbags, Inc., No. 93 CIV. 7856 (RWS), 1997 WL 139525 (S.D.N.Y. Mar. 26, 1997) (2.52% of defendant's sales constituted a substantial part of the events); Halsoprodukter Labs Karnerud Ab. v. Gero Vita Int'l, No. 93 C 2129, 1993 WL 384525, 1993 U.S. Dist. LEXIS 13519 (N.D. Ill. Sept. 28, 1993) (3% of sales and 5% of advertising in state sufficient to constitute substantial part of events). At this writing, no case has attempted to establish a fixed minimum percentage requirement under the statute. *But cf.* Telamerica Media, Inc. v. AMN Television Mktg., No. 99-25-72, 1999 WL 1244423, 1999 U.S. Dist. LEXIS 19423 (E.D. Pa. Dec. 21, 1999) (events so spread out across U.S. that no district contained substantial part; because multiple defendants residing in different states were involved, fallback provision of § 1391 applicable).

small, but significant, amount of activity had occurred. However, this approach fails to establish clear guidelines for determining what part of the events or omissions are substantial. Thus, such a test would breed litigation. In many cases, the defendant could legitimately dispute whether a "substantial part" of the events or omissions had occurred in the district.[103]

(c) Linking the Test to Minimum Contacts

Another approach would link the definition of "substantial part of the events or omissions" to the minimum contacts test for personal jurisdiction.[104] This test would regard the events or omissions giving rise to the claim to be "substantial" for venue purposes any time they are sufficient to permit long-arm jurisdiction over the defendant consistent with the Due Process Clause of the Fourteenth Amendment. Personal jurisdiction consistent with the Constitution must exist in every case. Otherwise, the court, on the defendant's motion, will dismiss the action. In many cases, the plaintiff will establish personal jurisdiction in a federal court through the use of a state long-arm statute based on the defendant's claim-producing activities within the state.[105] Thus, the inquiry into personal jurisdiction would also determine whether venue was proper under § 1391(b)(2).

A venue test linked to personal jurisdiction offers substantial advantages. The substantial events or omissions rule for venue and the minimum contacts test for personal jurisdiction involve similar inquiries.[106] In addition, both venue and personal jurisdiction requirements are meant to assure that the action will be conducted in a reasonably convenient place. Furthermore, while satisfying personal jurisdiction requirements will not always result in satisfying venue rules, this result will occur in a significant number of cases. Therefore, courts could reasonably

---

103. This approach is consistent with most of the opinions interpreting § 1391. The courts tend to approach the statute generally, without attempting to establish any fixed minimum percentage of events or omissions that will be required to make venue proper in a district. *See, e.g.*, Miller v. Meadowlands Car Imports, Inc., 822 F. Supp. 61 (D. Conn. 1993). One case rejecting a relative activity approach is Joint Stock Society "Trade House of Descendants of Peter Smirnoff" v. Heublein, Inc., 936 F. Supp. 177 (D. Del. 1996). The court refused to measure "substantial activity" by examining the percentage of the defendant's national sales that took place in the district, Delaware, because this approach would understate the effect of the products in question on Delaware consumers due to the fact that Delaware is a small state. Instead, the court examined other factors, such as the revenue from Delaware, the number of products sold in Delaware, and the use of sales agents in Delaware. Although the defendants' Delaware sales only amounted to 113th of 1% of its national sales, annual sales of the product (vodka) in Delaware totaled $1,000,000, and the defendants had two distributors and six sales representatives serving the state. On the basis of these factors, the court concluded that a substantial part of the sales giving rise to the claim occurred in Delaware. *See also* Lumpkin v. Land, CV No. 1:97CV00753, 1997 U.S. Dist. LEXIS 20846 (M.D.N.C. Nov. 5, 1997) (1/3 of events in district were not substantial because they were tangential to the dispute).

104. The minimum contacts test is discussed in Chapter 3(D) & (G) *supra*.

105. *See* Chapter 3(L) *supra* ("Special Problems of Amenability to Process in Federal Court").

106. Only one court has explicitly rejected a test for substantial activities linked to the minimum contacts test. *See* Ware v. Hedges, Nos. 4:92:CV:98 & 4:93:CV:21, 1993 U.S. Dist. LEXIS 11830 (W.D. Mich. July 12, 1993). In *Ware*, the court relied on a statement from Shapiro v. Republic of Bol., 930 F.2d 1013, 1019 (2d Cir. 1991), interpreting the term "substantial contact" in the Foreign Sovereign Immunities Act, 28 U.S.C. § 1603(e). *Shapiro* stated that "substantial contact" meant more than minimum contacts. However, the "substantial contact" language of the Foreign Sovereign Immunities Act is used to define when a foreign state can be sued within the "commercial activity" exception to the rule of sovereign immunity. *See* 28 U.S.C. § 1605(a)(2). This objective is far different than the one that supports the "substantial events" language of § 1391(b)(2). Additionally, the *Ware* opinion appears to be based on a verbal confusion. The fact that "minimum contacts" are required to satisfy the Due Process Clause of the Fourteenth Amendment does not mean that the requisite contacts will not be "substantial." The minimum contacts label is a term of art that encompasses the whole inquiry whether a nonresident's relationship with a state is sufficient to satisfy the Due Process Clause.

deem the events or omissions giving rise to the claim to be substantial anytime they may obtain personal jurisdiction over the defendant.[107]

Illustration 4-10. *P*, a citizen of State *X*, sued *D*, a citizen of State *Y*. *P* seeks $2,000,000 damages resulting from a libel of *P* in a national magazine published by *D*. *P* brought the action in a U.S. District Court in State *Z*, a single district state. *P* sued in State *Z* because it was the only state whose statute of limitations had not run on *P's* claim. *P* seeks damages from *D* for the harm caused throughout the United States by the publication of the article. *D* sells 10,000 to 15,000 copies of the magazine per month in State *Z*, but sells many more copies elsewhere. Under these circumstances, courts may constitutionally assert personal jurisdiction over *D* in State *Z* based on *D's* activity in State *Z*.[108] Under § 1391(b)(2), venue should be deemed proper because a substantial part of the events giving rise to the claim occurred in State *Z*.

Illustration 4-11. *P*, a citizen of State *X* residing in the Central District of State *X*, sued *D*, a citizen of State *Y*, in the U.S. District Court for the Central District of State *X*. *P* seeks to recover on a life insurance policy issued to *P's* spouse by *D*. *P's* spouse originally purchased the policy from *C*, a citizen of State *Z*. Later, *C* sold the insurance business to *D*. *D* sent a reinsurance notice to *P's* spouse in the Central District of State *X* offering to reinsure the spouse in accordance with the policy previously held with *C*. *P's* spouse signed this agreement and subsequently sent premiums to *D* in State *Y* until the spouse died. *D* refused to pay the insurance benefits to *P*, asserting that *P's* spouse had committed suicide. *D's* actions in sending the reinsurance agreement to *P's* spouse and accepting premiums are sufficient to subject *D* to personal jurisdiction in State *X*.[109] Therefore, venue should be considered proper in the Central District of State *X* under § 1391(b)(2) on the ground that a substantial part of the events giving rise to the claim occurred there.

* * * * *

A venue test linked with personal jurisdiction would have to avoid several pitfalls. As Chapter 3 discusses, the plaintiff can establish personal jurisdiction over a defendant without regard to the defendant's claim-producing activities within the state. For example, the plaintiff can establish personal jurisdiction by personally serving the defendant within the state, even when the events giving rise to suit occurred outside the state. Similarly, the plaintiff can sometimes base personal

---

107. Several courts have either explicitly linked the personal jurisdiction test discussed in the text with the venue rule in § 1391(b)(2), or found personal jurisdiction and venue to be proper because of the same activities within the district. *See, e.g.*, Alternative Pioneering Sys., Inc. v. Direct Innovative Prods., Inc., No. 4-92-278, 1992 WL 510190, 1992 U.S. Dist. LEXIS 21762 (D. Minn. Aug. 20, 1992) (amenability to long-arm jurisdiction in district satisfies substantial events test); Gould, Inc. v. Alter Metals Co., No. 91 C 20371, 1992 WL 170567, 1992 U.S. Dist. LEXIS 10483 (N.D. Ill. July 16, 1992) (defendant shipped hazardous materials to plaintiff in state; personal jurisdiction proper; venue proper under § 1391(b)(2) because personal jurisdiction proper); Fogle v. Ramsey Winch Co., 774 F. Supp. 19 (D.D.C. 1991) (injury within district from product sold by out-of-state defendant sustains personal jurisdiction and venue under § 1391; Sidco Indus., Inc. v. Wimar Tahoe Corp., 768 F. Supp. 1343 (D. Or. 1991) (trademark infringement action in which personal jurisdiction and venue under § 1391(b)(2) established by same action of defendant sending brochures into state); *see also* Magic Toyota, Inc. v. Southeast Toyota Distribs., Inc., 784 F. Supp. 306 (D.S.C. 1992) (personal jurisdiction and venue improper because of lack of contacts between defendants and forum). The test proposed in the text is similar to the statutorily imposed test for a corporate defendant's residence under 28 U.S.C. § 1391(c), discussed in subsection 6, *infra*.

108. *See* Keeton v. Hustler Magazine, Inc., 465 U.S. 770, 104 S. Ct. 1473, 79 L. Ed. 2d 790 (1984). The *Keeton* case is discussed in Chapter 3(H)(1) *supra* ("Tort Cases").

109. *See* McGee v. International Life Ins. Co., 355 U.S. 220, 78 S. Ct. 199, 2 L. Ed. 2d 223 (1957). The *McGee* case is discussed in Chapter 3(H)(2) *supra* ("Contract Cases").

jurisdiction on a high level of the defendant's general activities within the state, even when the event giving rise to the claim occurred elsewhere. Section 1391(b)(2), however, requires that venue be based on claim-producing activities within the district. Therefore, when personal jurisdiction is based on something other than the defendant's claim-producing activities, a court would have to make a separate venue inquiry. This inquiry would have to assure that sufficient claim-producing events or omissions occurred within the district where the action is commenced to sustain venue.[110]

Illustration 4-12. *P*, a citizen of State *X* residing in the Northern District of State *X*, sues *D*, a citizen of State *Y* residing in the Southern District of State *Y*. *P* commences this action in the U.S. District Court for the Northern District of State *X*. *P's* action seeks $500,000 in damages against *D* for personal injuries received in an automobile accident in State *Z*. The plaintiff acquires personal jurisdiction over *D* in the Northern District of State *X* by personally serving *D* with process while *D* is present in the Northern District. The basis of personal jurisdiction is not *D's* claim-producing activities. In fact, no claim-producing events or omissions occurred in the Northern District. Thus, despite the existence of valid personal jurisdiction over *D*, venue is not proper under § 1391(b)(2).

* * * * *

Another pitfall for a venue test linked with personal jurisdiction arises when the plaintiff bases personal jurisdiction on the claim-producing activities of the defendant within the state. For personal jurisdiction, the activities within the *entire state* are relevant to the jurisdictional inquiry. In contrast, the general venue statutes require substantial claim-producing events or omissions within the *district* where the action is brought. In multiple district states, the activities of the defendant giving rise to the claim can occur entirely within one district. If the plaintiff commences an action in a district within the state in which none of the claim-producing activities occur, venue will obviously not be proper in that district. If the defendant's claim-producing activities occur in more than one district within the state, the court in the district where the action is commenced will have to inquire whether the amount of those activities occurring within that district would have sustained

---

110. In Lohman v. Township of Oxford, No. 91-7037, 1992 WL 95914, 1992 U.S. Dist. LEXIS 5276 (E.D. Pa. Apr. 22, 1992), the court viewed the defendants' activities alternatively as forum related and non-forum related, and sustained personal jurisdiction under both viewpoints. The court then went on to state that venue was proper under § 1391(b)(2): "As can be seen from the personal jurisdiction analysis above, a sufficiently substantial part of the events in this case occurred in the Eastern District of Pennsylvania." It is unclear whether the court believed that forum activity by the defendant that was not claim producing, but which satisfied personal jurisdiction standards, would satisfy the venue test under § 1391(b)(2). *See also* Pecoraro v. Sky Ranch for Boys, Inc., 340 F.3d 558 (8th Cir. 2003), in which a victim of alleged sexual abuse at a camp in South Dakota sued the camp and the foundation that assisted the camp with fund raising in Nebraska. The court first found sufficient minimum contacts to sustain personal jurisdiction, apparently on a theory of specific jurisdiction, though the court's opinion did not focus on the exact nature of the relationship between the claim and events occurring in Nebraska. The court then found venue proper under old § 1391(a)(2) (now § 1391(b)(2) after the 2011 amendments to § 1391). Although the court admitted that South Dakota's relationship "to the defendants" was much stronger than Nebraska's, the court stated that Nebraska also had a substantial connection to the claim based on the court's prior analysis of minimum contacts. It did appear that the party who operated the camp and was accused of the abuse did enter Nebraska to take the plaintiff out of the state to Wyoming on false pretenses. However, in another part of its opinion, the court held that a South Dakota diocese to whom the alleged abuser was assigned was not subject to personal jurisdiction even if the diocese could be held vicariously liable for the abuser's conduct, since it could not reasonably be held to be haled into court "based solely on its activity as the Diocese and not on the activity of administrators of related entities acting in other capacities."

personal jurisdiction over the defendant. The activities in the other districts within the state are irrelevant to this inquiry.

Illustration 4-13. *P*, a citizen of State *X* residing in the Western District of State *X*, sues *D*, a citizen of State *Y*. *P's* claim is for damages under the Fair Debt Collection Practices Act, a federal statute.[111] The action is brought in the Western District of State *X*. *P* had incurred a debt while residing in the Western District of State *Y*. *P's* creditor referred the debt for collection to *D*. Meanwhile, *P* had moved to the Western District of State *X*. *D* mailed a collection notice to *P* at *P's* former address in the Western District of State *Y*. The U.S. Postal Service forwarded the collection notice to *P* in the Western District of State *X*. *P's* claim is based on the contents of this collection notice. Assume that placing the collection notice in the mail without an instruction to the Postal Service not to forward the notice, together with *P's* actual receipt of the notice, are sufficient to subject *D* to personal jurisdiction in the Western District of State *X*. Under such circumstances, venue should be considered proper under § 1391(b)(2) on the basis that substantial events giving rise to the claim occurred in the Western District of State *X*.[112]

On the other hand, if these acts are insufficient themselves to sustain personal jurisdiction over *D*, venue should be deemed improper under § 1391(b)(2), even if personal jurisdiction is acquired over *D* on some other basis. For example, *D* might waive any personal jurisdiction objection that *D* possesses. Likewise, *D's* general level of activities in State *X*, apart from the sending and receipt of the notice, might be sufficiently high to sustain jurisdiction over *D* on any claim. Nonetheless, even if personal jurisdiction is asserted over *D* on some basis other than the acts giving rise to the claim, the court should not *assume* that venue is improper under § 1391(b)(2). Instead, the court should make an independent inquiry to determine whether the nature and quality of *D's* actions in the district would be sufficient to sustain personal jurisdiction over *D*.[113]

* * * * *

The facts of the preceding illustration are based on *Bates v. C & S Adjusters, Inc.*[114] In *Bates*, the court held venue proper under § 1391(b)(2) on these facts. However, the defendant did not challenge personal jurisdiction, so it is impossible to know what the court would have held if such a challenge had been raised. Nevertheless, there is reason to believe that the sending and receiving of the collection notice would have been sufficient to sustain personal jurisdiction.[115]

---

111. 15 U.S.C. §§ 1692-1692*o*.

112. *Cf.* Bates v. C & S Adjusters, Inc., 980 F.2d 865 (2d Cir. 1992) (the text following this illustration discusses *Bates*).

113. *But cf.* United Liberty Life Ins. Co. v. Pinnacle W. Capital Corp., 149 F.R.D. 558 (S.D. Ohio 1993) (substantial events occurred where misleading financial statements created, not where they were received). As in determining a corporate defendant's residence under 28 U.S.C. § 1391, discussed *infra* subsection 6, it is theoretically possible for the defendant's claim-producing activities to be spread thinly across several districts of a multiple district state. Thus, it might be feared that while the total activities in the state are sufficient to sustain personal jurisdiction, the activities within any one district would not be sufficient to do so. However, given the structure of the minimum contacts test, such a case is not likely to occur. When the defendant's activities within the district give rise to part of the claim, it is highly likely that the contacts with the district will be sufficient to sustain personal jurisdiction. *See* Chapter 3(G)(2)*(b) supra* ("Specific Jurisdiction"); *cf.* Keeton v. Hustler Magazine, Inc., 465 U.S. 770, 104 S. Ct. 1473, 79 L. Ed. 2d 790 (1984); *Illustration 4-10 supra.*

114. 980 F.2d 865 (2d Cir. 1992).

115. *Cf.* Calder v. Jones, 465 U.S. 783, 104 S. Ct. 1482, 79 L. Ed. 2d 804 (1984) (sustaining jurisdiction over nonresident defendants in a libel action on the basis that the tort was intentionally directed at the defendant in the forum state). *Calder* is discussed in Chapter 3(H)(1) *supra*.

However, *Bates* should be compared with *Daniel v. American Board of Emergency Medicine.*[116] In *Daniel*, emergency medicine physicians brought suit in the U.S. District Court for the Western District of New York against a medical specialty certification board for emergency medicine and hospitals operating residency programs in emergency medicine, alleging that the defendants conspired to restrict competition in the market for emergency medicine physicians in violation of the Sherman and Clayton Antitrust Acts. The Second Circuit Court of Appeals held that venue was improper in the district.

According to the court, an events based venue inquiry under § 1391(b)(2) requires a two-step inquiry. First, the court should identify the nature of the claims and the acts and omissions that the plaintiff alleges give rise to those claims. Second, the court should determine whether a substantial part of those acts and omissions occurred in the district where suit was filed. The court described the substantiality inquiry as "more a qualitative than a quantitative inquiry."[117] The vast majority of the acts giving rise to the claims of the plaintiffs occurred outside the State of New York. The plaintiffs were able to point to only six of the numerous plaintiffs who had been notified of adverse certification decisions in the Western District of New York. In addition, of the hospitals sued, none were located in the Western District of New York. Thus, the court stated:

> Viewed in this context, [the certification board's] transmittal into the Western District of New York of a half-dozen letters rejecting applications to sit for its certification examination outside New York constitutes only an insignificant and certainly not "a substantial part of the events or omissions giving rise to the [plaintiff's antitrust] claim[s]." We conclude that these coincidental contacts are insufficient to afford venue in the Western District of New York pursuant to § 1391(b)(2).[118]

Note, however, that under the *Bates* facts, the individual defendants who had received rejection notices in the Western District of New York could probably have subjected the board defendant to jurisdiction there, if not the hospital defendants. In addition, under the test favored in the principal text, those plaintiffs could have predicated events-based venue in the Western District. The multiple plaintiff and defendant nature of the case, however, correctly required the court to scrutinize the contacts in a more rigorous fashion than in *Bates*.

(d) When Do Events Give Rise to the Claim?

For venue to be proper under § 1391(b)(2), the "substantial" events occurring within a district must give rise to the claim. Literally, therefore, non-claim producing activities are irrelevant to the inquiry under the statute. As a result, the district courts must engage in careful analysis. For example, in *Daleus v. Kovelesky*,[119] the plaintiff, a citizen of New York, sued the defendant, a citizen of

---

116. 428 F.3d 408 (2d Cir. 2005).
117. *Id.* at 432-33.
118. 428 F.3d at 434.
119. No. 98 Civ. 9628 (JSR), 1998 WL 856077, 1998 U.S. Dist. LEXIS 19331 (S.D.N.Y. Dec. 7, 1998).

New Jersey, in a U.S. District Court in New York. *P* sought damages for personal injuries received in an automobile accident in New Jersey. The plaintiff contended that venue was proper in the Southern District of New York because the medical care and treatment the plaintiff received in New York after the accident were substantial events occurring in New York. The district court held that these events were not sufficient to make venue proper because they did not give rise to the claim. The court stated that "[t]he subsequent remedial actions taken in New York may have contributed to the amount of damages, but can in no meaningful way be said to have given rise to the claim itself."[120] Although this common-sense result prevents manipulation of the venue statutes, it is not literally true that damages are not part of the claim itself. The medical expenses did accrue in New York; consequently, they were, in a sense, partially involved in "giving rise to the claim." Thus, a literal interpretation of the venue statutes might produce a different result.[121]

Another difficulty exists in multiple defendant cases when the events giving rise to the claim against some defendants occur in the district and the events giving rise to claims against other defendants occur entirely outside the district. In *Kaplan v. Reed*,[122] the district court held that venue was improper as to the defendants whose acts occurred entirely outside the district. Note, however, that if a combination of events by some defendants in the district and by some outside are sufficient to produce personal jurisdiction over all defendants in the district, venue could be considered proper under the test suggested in subsection *(c)*, above. Under the test for specific jurisdiction discussed in Chapter 3, a defendant neither has to act within the state nor ever enter the state to be subject to personal jurisdiction. Unlike the situation discussed in subsection *(c)*, above, concerning general jurisdiction, the impact of the defendant's activities in the district, especially if they are part of a combined course of action with other defendants who have acted within the district, may be enough to sustain both personal jurisdiction and venue.[123]

---

120. *Id.* at *1, 1998 U.S. Dist. LEXIS at *2; *accord* Labranche v. Embassy Suites, Inc., No. Civ. A. 97-3721, 1999 WL 58841, 1999 U.S. Dist. LEXIS 1495 (E.D. La. Feb. 3, 1999) (plaintiff injured in defendant's hotel in Iowa received medical treatment that contributed to his damages in Louisiana, his home state; the court held that the medical treatment did not give rise to the claim).

121. In Fiore v. Walden, 657 F.3d 838 (9th Cir. 2011), a police officer seized a large amount of money from the plaintiffs, who were citizens of Nevada, at the Atlanta, Georgia airport. The seizure was based on a false probable cause affidavit and a false reference of the case for forfeiture of the property at a time when the defendant officer knew the defendants were from Las Vegas. After sustaining personal jurisdiction, the court of appeals also found venue to be proper in Nevada. The court reasoned that because the harms suffered by the plaintiffs were felt in Nevada, including loss of use of and interest on the funds seized for seven months, and the return of the funds in Nevada caused the plaintiffs' claims to "mature," a substantial part of the events or omissions giving rise to the claim occurred in Nevada. *See id.* at 859.

122. 28 F. Supp. 2d 1191 (D. Colo. 1998).

123. *Cf.* Schomann Int'l Corp. v. Northern Wireless, Ltd., 35 F. Supp. 2d 205 (N.D.N.Y. 1999) (both personal jurisdiction and substantial events venue proper over nonresident defendant who entered into contract to be performed outside the forum when the contract required defendant to maintain regular communication with plaintiff's forum office and plaintiff received purchase orders in and made regular payments from the district; contract negotiated by phone and fax and defendant's representatives never entered forum).

(e) Miscellaneous Issues

Several federal district courts in New York have held that if venue is proper in a district where all of the defendants reside under 28 U.S.C. § 1391(b)(1), the plaintiff cannot sue in another district where a substantial part of the events giving rise to the claim occurred under § 1391(b)(2).[124] This position is based on pre-1990 authority interpreting the "claim arose" language of old § 1391(b) in cases in which the court was struggling to apply the U.S. Supreme Court's decision in *Leroy v. Great Western United Corp.*, discussed in the introduction to this section.[125] However, *Leroy* and the pre-1990 New York authority interpreting it were attempting to determine when it was appropriate to allow an action to be brought in a district where some, but not all, the claim(s) arose at a time when § 1391 appeared to assume that a claim could only arise in one place. The rationale of the New York cases is that the 1966 amendment inserting the "claim arose" language into the old § 1391 was only intended to close venue gaps and should not be read more broadly than necessary to do so. Because there is no venue gap when venue can be predicated upon defendants' residence, the plaintiff should not have the option to choose an alternative forum under such circumstances.[126] In the view of these courts, the 1990 amendment was simply a "revision" of this original gap-closing measure and did not alter the rationale of pre-1990 authorities.[127]

Whatever may be said for the rationale of the pre-1990 New York cases, and much may be said against it, the rationale cannot survive the 1990 amendments to § 1391. As can be seen from the wording of the "fallback" provision in § 1391(b)(3) discussed in subsection 5, below, when Congress wanted to make the applicability of one subsection of the venue statute depend on the inapplicability of another, it knew how to do so. Yet the terms of the statute do not make § 1391(b)(2) dependent on the inapplicability of § 1391(b)(1).

4. Presence of Property as a Basis of Venue

Sections 1391(b)(2)[128] also provides that venue is proper in a district where "a substantial part of the property that is the subject of the action is situated." Like venue based on the occurrence of substantial events or omissions, this provision poses several problems of interpretation.

---

124. *See* Dashman v. Peter Letterese & Assocs., Inc., 999 F. Supp. 553 (S.D.N.Y. 1998); Cobra Partners L.P. v. Liegl, 990 F. Supp. 332 (S.D.N.Y. 1998); Welch Foods, Inc. v. Packer, 93-CV-0811E(F), 1994 WL 665399, 1994 U.S. Dist. LEXIS 16974 (W.D.N.Y. Nov. 22, 1994).

125. *See* Canaday v. Koch, 598 F. Supp. 1139 (E.D.N.Y. 1984).

126. *See, e.g.,* Welch Foods, Inc. v. Packer, 93-CV-0811E(F), 1994 WL 665399 at *2, 1994 U.S. Dist. LEXIS 16974 at *6 (W.D.N.Y. Nov. 22, 1994).

127. *See id.* at *3, 1994 U.S. Dist. LEXIS at *7. *But see* Gregory v. Pocono Grow Fertilizer Corp., 35 F. Supp. 2d 295 (W.D.N.Y. 1999) (rejecting the view described in the text and holding that §§ 1391(b)(1) & (2) are alternatives to each other).

128. The property based provisions were, before 2011, found in §§ 1391(a)(2) & (b)(2). The Federal Courts Jurisdiction and Venue Clarification Act combined these provisions in a new § 1391(b)(2), which now governs both diversity and federal question cases. *See* Pub. L. 112-63, § 202(1), 125 Stat. 758, 763 (2011).

(a) When Property Should Be Considered to Be the "Subject of the Action"

An issue of interpretation that has already arisen under the location-of-property provisions is when property should be considered to be "the subject of the action." The language of the statute was drawn from a 1969 American Law Institute proposal.[129] However, the commentary to the proposal gives no clue about how to determine when property is "the subject of the action."[130] The legislative history of § 1391 is also silent on this question.[131]

(i) Ownership of Property Directly at Issue

The property must be directly, rather than tangentially, involved in the action to satisfy "the subject of action" requirement.[132] This requirement will surely be met when the controversy directly concerns the ownership of specific property.

(ii) Actions for Damages for Injury to Land or to Prevent Future Harm to Land

The "subject of the action" requirement will also probably be met when the action seeks to recover damages for injury to land or to prevent future harm to land.[133]

Illustration 4-14. *P*, a citizen of State *X*, sues *D*, a citizen of State *Y*. *P* seeks to obtain specific performance of a contract between *P* and *D* to convey land worth $2,000,000. The action is brought in the Western District of State *Z*, where the land is located. The land is clearly property that is "the subject of the action." Venue is, therefore, proper in the Western District.

Illustration 4-15. *P*, a citizen of State *X*, sues *D*, a citizen of State *Y*. *P* seeks to recover $80,000 damages for injuries to land owned by *P*. The action is brought in the Southern District of State *Z*, where the land is located. In an action

---

129. *See* ALI STUDY OF THE DIVISION OF JURISDICTION BETWEEN STATE AND FEDERAL COURTS §§ 1303(a)(1), 1314(a)(1).

130. *See id.* at 135-37, 216.

131. *See* H.R. REP. NO. 734, 101st Cong., 2d Sess. 23 (1990).

132. *See* United States v. Selland, No. 93-1719, 1993 WL 347197, 1993 U.S. App. LEXIS 23396 (8th Cir. Sept. 14, 1993) (action to foreclose on property is proper in district where property is located); *cf.* Anderson v. FDIC, 1996 U.S. Dist. LEXIS 19907 (E.D. Mich. Nov. 25, 1996), in which the F.D.I.C. denied applications for deposit insurance sent to Washington, D.C. and Chicago, Illinois. The plaintiffs sued in the Eastern District of Michigan on the theory that the bank in question would have been located in Pontiac, Michigan, in the Eastern District. Thus, the "property" that was the "subject of the action" was arguably located in the Eastern District. However, the court held that property was not the subject of the action. *See also* Pfeiffer v. Insty Prints, No. 93 C 2937, 1993 WL 443403, 1993 U.S. Dist. LEXIS 15317 (N.D. Ill. Oct. 29, 1993) (action for breach of contract to produce play did not involve ownership of play; therefore, property not the subject of the action).

One question that has not yet directly arisen is whether, and if so how, § 1391(b)(2) will apply to intangible property, such as the debt in *Harris v. Balk*, discussed in Chapter 3(B)(1)*(a) supra* ("Affirmative Principles of In Rem Jurisdictions"). At least one court has raised the possibility that such property may not be included within the statute at all. *See* Pfeiffer v. Insty Prints, No. 93 C 2937, 1993 WL 443403, n.4, 1993 U.S. Dist. LEXIS 15317, n.4 (N.D. Ill. Oct. 29, 1993). Thus, venue would have to be predicated on defendant's residence or the events giving rise to suit. If intangible property is included within the statute, the courts will have to struggle with the situs of such property, as in *Harris*.

133. When the claim is for damages to land or to prevent future harm to land, venue will usually also be proper on the basis that a substantial part of the events giving rise to the claim occurred in the district where the land is located.

for injury to land, the land is central to the action and should be considered "the subject of the action." Thus, the court should consider venue to be proper in the Southern District.[134]

Illustration 4-16. *P*, a citizen of State *X*, sues *D*, a citizen of State *Y*. *P* seeks to force *D* to abate a nuisance. *P* claims that the nuisance is reducing the value of *P's* land in the Eastern District of State *Z* by $1,000,000. The source of the nuisance is a manufacturing plant that emits noxious fumes. The plant is located in State *Y*, which is adjacent to the border of State *Z*. In an action to abate a nuisance that decreases the value of land, the land being harmed is central to the action. The court should consider it to be "the subject of the action." Thus, the court should rule venue to be proper in the Eastern District.[135]

(iii) Damages for Injury to Specific Personal Property

Actions seeking damages for injury to specific personal property must be approached more cautiously. The mobility of personal property presents the danger that the property might be located in a district that has no relationship to the focus of the action brought. In addition, a danger exists that the plaintiff might attempt to manipulate the venue of the action by removing the property to a district where venue would otherwise be improper. When administering the statute, courts should prevent such manipulation.

Illustration 4-17. *P*, a citizen of State *X*, sues *D*, a citizen of State *Y*. *P* seeks to recover $100,000 for property damage to *P's* truck in an accident between *P* and *D*. *P* has brought the action in the Northern District of State *X*, where the truck is located and where *P* resides. The accident occurred in the Southern District of State *Z*. The truck was then towed to a repair shop in the Northern District of State *X* and has been located there ever since. Venue should not be considered proper in the Northern District of State *X*. Although the action seeks to recover damage to a truck, which is "property," the court should not regard the truck as "the subject of the action" and allow venue to be established in the district of *P's* residence. The 1990 amendments to § 1391(a) specifically repealed plaintiff's residence as a proper venue. The district of the plaintiff's residence has no connection with the events or omissions giving rise to the claim.

(iv) Money

Money is property, but the courts should not consider all cases involving money to be ones in which property is the "subject of the action."[136] Instead, courts

---

134. Venue would also be proper here on the ground that the events giving rise to the claim occurred in the Southern District.

135. Because the impact of the nuisance occurs in the district where the land is located, venue would also be proper because a substantial part of the events giving rise to the claim occurred there.

136. *See* David D. Siegel, *Changes in Federal Jurisdiction and Practice Under the New (Dec. 1, 1990) Judicial Improvements Act*, 133 F.R.D. 61, 72 (1991).

should consider money to be property that is the subject of the action only when the claim relates to a specific fund or source of money within the district.[137]

Illustration 4-18. Assume the same facts as in *Illustration 4-17*, except that *P* seeks to recover $100,000 in damages for personal injuries received in the accident. *P* brings the action in the Western District of State *Q*, where *D* has a $100,000 bank account. *P* contends that venue is proper because the bank account is property that *P* seeks to recover in the action and is, therefore, the "subject of the action." The court should not consider venue to be proper in the Western District. *P* has no specific claim to the money in the bank account, as opposed to $100,000 of *D's* general assets. The court should not permit *P* to use the property-as-subject-of-the-action provision to establish venue in a district that has nothing to do with the central focus of the action, the accident between *P* and *D*.

Illustration 4-19. *P*, a citizen of State *X*, sues *D*, a citizen of State *Y*. *P* seeks to recover $85,000 from *D* for breach of *D's* fiduciary duty in managing a trust of money. *P* is the beneficiary of the trust, and *D* is the trustee of the trust. The action is brought in the Northern District of State *Z*, where the trust assets are deposited in a bank. Venue should be considered proper in the Northern District of State *Z* because the property that is the subject of the action is located there. The action directly concerns a specific fund of money located within the district.[138]

Illustration 4-20. *P*, a citizen of State *X*, sues *D*, a citizen of State *Y*. *P* seeks to recover rents in the amount of $650,000. *D* assigned the rents to *P* as security for a mortgage and promissory note that *D* had given to *P*. The land that *D* mortgaged to *P* is located in the Eastern District of State *Z*. *P* has brought the action in that district. Venue is proper in the Eastern District of State *Z* for two reasons. First, the mortgaged property is located there and is properly considered the "subject of the action." Second, even if no mortgage existed, the property is the source of the assigned rents.[139]

(v) Other Cases

Other cases will, of necessity, depend on whether property is central to the controversy or only remotely involved. No mechanical test will resolve all the cases.

Illustration 4-21. *P*, a citizen of State *X*, sues *D*, a citizen of State *Y*. *P* seeks $10,000,000 for common-law fraud. *P* brings the action in the Western District of State *Z*. *P* bases the claim on a transaction between *P* and *D* in which *D* sold a manufacturing plant located in the Western District to *P*. As part of the transaction, *D* provided *P* with an affidavit stating that no hazardous wastes had been stored on the plant site and no hazardous substances had been released in violation of the law. *P* asserts that this affidavit was false. *P* also asserts that *P* will incur $10,000,000 in clean-up costs. Venue is proper in the Western District of

---

137. *See* Jackson Nat'l Life Ins. Co. v. Stillman Land Co., No. 5:92-CV-66, 1993 U.S. Dist. LEXIS 14218 (W.D. Mich. Sept. 22, 1993) (suit on an insurance claim does not involve property as subject of the action; suit is not for a specific fund; contrary ruling would mean any suit for damages would be one in which property would be the subject of the action).

138. *See* Brady v. Capital Grp., Inc., No. CIV.A.91-3873, 1992 WL 46337, 1992 U.S. Dist. LEXIS 2478 (E.D. La. Mar. 4, 1992).

139. *See* Travelers Ins. Co. v. Swolsky, No. CIV.A.91-7537, 1992 WL 150698, 1992 U.S. Dist. LEXIS 8408 (E.D. Pa. June 17, 1992).

State *Z*. The action seeks to recover the costs of cleaning a contaminated plant located within the district. The plant, which is property, is correctly considered the "subject of the action," even though the claim is for common-law fraud.[140]

Illustration 4-22. *P*, a citizen of State *X*, sued *D*, a citizen of State *Y*, in the U.S. District Court for State *X*. *P's* claim is for $1,000,000 for fraud and negligent misrepresentation. *P's* claim arose out of the sale of an apartment complex located in the District of State *X*. *P* sold the complex to *C*, a citizen of State *Y*. *D* is an accountant who prepared *C's* financial statement. *P* alleges that the financial statement contained false statements. *D* sent the financial statement to *M* in State *Q* to obtain *M's* consent to the sale. *M* is a mortgagee of the apartment complex. *D* performed all services in State *Y*. *P* never saw the financial statement or knew about the misrepresentations in it until after the sale. It is questionable whether venue is proper in the District of State *X* on the ground that the apartment complex is located there. In *Illustration 4-21*, the plaintiff sought to recover the expenses that the plaintiff would incur to clean up specific property located within the district. In this illustration, the defendant's alleged fraud is more remote from the property. On these facts, one court has held venue to be improper in the district where the apartment complex was located because the complex was not "the subject of the action."[141]

(b) When a "Substantial Part" of the Property Should Be Considered Located Within the District

When property is concededly the "subject of the action," problems may arise in determining when a "substantial part" of the property is located within the district. As in venue based on events or omissions within the district, § 1391(b)(2) provides for venue in more than one district when the amount of property located in multiple districts is "substantial." If the amount of property located in a given district is not "substantial," however, venue cannot be proper in that district based on the location of property.

Obviously, if no property is located within the district, the amount is not substantial. Conversely, if all the property is located within a district, the amount of property is substantial. Furthermore, if more than half the property is located in a district, the amount of property is substantial. Therefore, as in venue based on events or omissions giving rise to the claim, the problem case concerns situations in which less than half of the property is located in a district.

As with events-or-omission-based venue, it is inappropriate to establish an irreducible minimum percentage of property that must be present in the district to support venue. A large amount of property located within a district might be only a small percentage of the total amount of property involved in the action. Yet no inconvenience may occur in basing venue on the location of the small percentage of property.

---

140. *See* Samuel G. Keywell Co. v. Weinstein, No. CIV.A.HAR-91-659, 1991 WL 149894, 1991 U.S. Dist. LEXIS 10570 (D. Md. July 31, 1991).

141. *See* Monarch Normandy Square Partners v. Normandy Square Assocs. Ltd. P'ship, 817 F. Supp. 896 (D. Kan. 1993).

Illustration 4-23. *P*, a citizen of State *X*, sues *D*, a citizen of State *Y*. *P* seeks specific performance of a contract to convey land located in the Southern District of State *Z* and the Northern District of State *Q*. *P* has brought the action in the Northern District of State *Q*. Ninety-five thousand acres of the land are located in the Southern District of State *Z* and five thousand acres of the land are located in the Northern District of State *Q*. Even though the amount of land located in the Northern District of State *Q* is only 5% of the total amount, the court should not disqualify the Northern District as a proper venue based on the amount of property located there.

* * * * *

With respect to events-or-omissions-based venue, it was suggested that a test linked to the minimum contacts test for personal jurisdiction would be the best approach to determine when events or omissions within the district were substantial. In the context of venue based on the location of property, however, a test linked to whether the presence of a certain amount of property within the district would sustain personal jurisdiction is not appropriate. If a claim directly concerns property, personal jurisdiction will often exist regardless of how little property is located in the district.[142] However, § 1391(b)(2) envisions that the amount of property located within a district can be too insubstantial to support venue. Thus, when property is involved, a venue test linked to personal jurisdiction should not be adopted because such a test might result in finding venue proper regardless of how small the amount of property within the district might be.[143] Thus, in the case of property-based venue, there seems to be no escape from a fluid test for substantiality that will depend on the facts of particular cases. Nevertheless, since the venue statutes are designed to provide convenient locations for trial, courts should consider whether the particular district chosen by the plaintiff is substantially less convenient than other districts in which the property is also located.

Illustration 4-24. In *Illustration 4-23*, the court should not consider a substantial amount of property to be located in the Northern District of State *Q* if that district is substantially less convenient than the Southern District of State *Z*.[144]

---

142. Recall from Chapter 3 that in Shaffer v. Heitner, 433 U.S. 186, 97 S. Ct. 2569, 53 L. Ed. 2d 683 (1977), the Supreme Court held that the presence of property unrelated to the claim would not, of itself, sustain personal jurisdiction. This sort of case presents no problem under the venue statutes, since property that is unrelated to the claim will not be "the subject of the action." However, *Shaffer* made it clear that when a claim directly concerns property located within the state, the state will be able to assert jurisdiction to adjudicate the claim, at least if the property has not been brought within the state without the consent of all the claimants. *See Shaffer*, 433 U.S. at 207-08, 97 S. Ct. at 2581-82, 53 L. Ed. 2d at 699-700; *see also* Chapter 3(E)(1) *supra* ("Quasi in Rem and Related Jurisdictional Doctrines").

143. In contrast, under the substantial events test of § 1391(a)(2) & (b)(2) and the minimum contacts test for personal jurisdiction, a defendant's activities within the state can be too tenuous to support personal jurisdiction and, therefore, venue.

144. Even if this test is not adopted by the courts, an action brought in a proper, but substantially inconvenient, venue can be transferred to a more convenient venue under 28 U.S.C. § 1404(a). Transfer under § 1404(a) is discussed in section D(2)*(a) infra* ("Section 1404(a) Transfers").

(c) Abolition of the Local Action Rule in Federal Court

A now resolved problem of interpretation concerned the interaction of the pre-2011 property based venue provisions (in old § 1391(a)(2) & (b)(2), now found in § 1391(b)(2) with former § 1392 of Title 28 (repealed in 2011). Old section 1392 (formerly § 1392(b)) dealt with local actions involving property located in different districts in the same state. Section 1392 allowed the plaintiff to bring such a local action in any of the districts where the property is located.[145] Congress did not repeal or amend § 1392 when it enacted the 1990 amendments to old § 1391(a) & (b). The retention of § 1392 thus gave rise to a problem of construction. Should § 1391(a)(2) and (b)(2) have been read as overriding § 1392? Indeed, should § 1391(a)(2) and (b)(2) have been read as repealing the local action rule altogether? Alternatively, should the courts have attempted to reconcile § 1391(a)(2) & (b)(2) with § 1392?

These problems were solved by the Federal Courts Jurisdiction and Venue Clarification Act of 2011,[146] effective in 2012. New section 1391(a)(2) abolishes the local action rule in federal courts:

> (2) The proper venue for a civil action shall be determined without regard to whether the action is local or transitory in nature.

It is important to note that this provision now allows federal courts to entertain (say in diversity actions), suits that would be classified as local actions in the courts of the state in which the action is brought. Thus, if federal jurisdiction exists in such an action, a United States District Court will be able to hear it, even if the courts of the state in which the action is brought would dismiss the action under the state's local action rule.

Illustration 4-25. *P*, a citizen of State *X*, sues *D*, a citizen of State *Y*, for $500,000 for trespass to land located in State *X*. The action is brought in a United States District Court for the District of State *Y*. Under the law of State *Y*, the action would be classified as a local action and, if brought in the courts of State *Y*, dismissed under the State *Y* local action rule. Nevertheless, venue is proper in the action in the U.S. District Court for the District of State *Y* under 28 U.S.C. § 1391(b)(1) because *D* resides in the district and 28 U.S.C. § 1391(a)(2) makes the local or transitory nature of the action irrelevant in federal court.

* * * * *

It is also important to remember that the local action rule is not the only restriction on the authority of courts to entertain actions involving land. Recall from Chapter 3(B)(1)*(b)* and section (A) of this chapter that a rule has traditionally existed prohibiting a court from "directly affecting" the title to land located in another state. This rule is usually invoked when a judgment is rendered in the state courts of one state that directly affects the title to land located in another state and then enforcement of the judgment is sought in the courts of the state where the land is located. The traditional rule stated that the situs state need not give full faith and credit to the judgment because it was rendered without "subject matter jurisdiction,"

---

145. *See* 28 U.S.C. § 1392(b).

146. Pub. L. 112-63, § 202(1), 125 Stat. 758, 763 (2011) (codified at 28 U.S.C. § 1391(a)(2)); *id.*, § 203, 125 Stat. at 764 (repealing 28 U.S.C. § 1392).

the land being the "subject matter" of the action and being located outside the territorial authority of the judgment-rendering court.[147] It is not clear today whether this rule is rule embodied in the Due Process Clause of the Fourteenth Amendment, the Full Faith and Credit Clause of the Constitution, or 28 U.S.C. § 1738, the general implementing statute to the Full Faith and Credit Clause. Indeed, the rule may be embodied in none of these provisions, but may be a vestige of the old common-law rules of international jurisdiction discussed in Chapter 3(A)(1)*(e)*, (B)(1)*(b)* &(G)(3) above.[148] Perhaps unfortunately, the Supreme Court of the United States has recently cited one of the old cases involving the subject-matter rule with approval, indicating that, whatever the source of the rule is, it still exists.[149]

The abolition of the local action rule in the federal courts does not mean that the subject-matter jurisdiction restriction discussed in the previous paragraph is also abolished, though, as observed in section (A) of this chapter, above, the two rules have often been confused with each other. Nevertheless, depending on the nature and source of the subject-matter rule, it may be a rule that is only binding on state courts. As observed in the sections of Chapter 3 cited above, the rule was clearly designed to protect the sovereignty of one state from encroachment by other states.[150] The theory underlying the traditional rules was that the states retained their status as separate sovereigns relative to each other when the Constitution was formed, except as they gave away to the national government the power to affect their sovereign relations, as, for example, in the second sentence of the Full Faith and Credit Clause, which allows Congress to declare the effect that state public acts, records, and judicial proceedings will have in other states.[151] The subject-matter restriction operates in accord with this traditional theory.

However, the U.S. Government is not in this same sense a separate sovereign from the states when acting within its delegated powers, including its judicial powers.[152] Therefore, it is arguable that federal courts in one state should be able to entertain actions that directly affect the title to land located in other states without running afoul of territorial subject-matter jurisdiction restrictions that operate on the states. Of course, there may be self-imposed restrictions on the power of federal courts to entertain such cases. For example, as discussed in Chapter 3(K)(2)*(f)*, Federal Rule 4(k)(1)(A) generally limits the ability of federal courts to assert personal jurisdiction to cases in which state courts of general jurisdiction within the state can do so. The traditional subject-matter restriction is related to personal jurisdiction restrictions in that it had its genesis in the sovereignty-based restrictions of the old international, territorial rules. Thus, if the phrase "personal

---

147. *See* ROBERT L. FELIX & RALPH U. WHITTEN, AMERICAN CONFLICTS LAW § 44 (6th ed. 2011) (discussing the cases extensively); *id.* § 31 (discussing the relationship between the local action rule and the subject-matter jurisdiction rule).

148. *See id.* § 44 (discussing the possibilities).

149. *See* Baker *ex rel.* Thomas v. General Motors Corp., 522 U.S. 222, 235, 118 S. Ct. 657, 665, 139 L. Ed. 580, 593 (1998) (citing with approval Fall v. Eastin, 215 U.S. 1, 30 S. Ct. 3, 54 L. Ed. 65 (1909)).

150. *See also* ROBERT L. FELIX & RALPH U. WHITTEN, AMERICAN CONFLICTS LAW § 44 (6th ed. 2011) (extensively discussing the nature and sources of the rule).

151. *See* U.S. Const., art. IV, § 1.

152. *See* Testa v. Katt, 330 U.S. 386, 67 S. Ct. 810, 91 L. Ed. 967 (1947) (stating that the states cannot refuse to enforce the laws of the United States on the traditional conflict of laws ground that they are "penal in the international sense" the United States is not foreign to the states in the same sense as another state or a foreign country).

jurisdiction" in Rule 4(k)(1)(A) is broad enough to include the subject-matter rule, the ability of federal courts to render judgments that directly affect title to land located in another state may be limited accordingly.[153]

5. The "Fallback" Provisions of § 1391

In addition to the amendments to § 1391(a) & (b) discussed above, Congress added two other provisions to the statute in 1990. Section 1391(a) provided for venue in actions in which jurisdiction is based only on diversity of citizenship. In that provision, Congress originally provided that venue would be proper in "a judicial district in which the defendants are subject to personal jurisdiction at the time the action is commenced."[154] This addition seemed to be patterned after a 1988 amendment to 28 U.S.C. § 1391(c), discussed below, which deals with venue when corporations are defendants. However, the amendment was curious for two important reasons. First, unlike the two previous amendments discussed above, the Federal Courts Study Committee had not recommended it.[155] Second, this provision seemed to make the other provisions of 28 U.S.C. § 1391(a) superfluous. As demonstrated in Chapter 3, it is always necessary to obtain personal jurisdiction over the defendants in an action. If venue is proper whenever personal jurisdiction can be obtained, it is unnecessary to provide for venue on any other basis, such as defendants' residence. Conversely, in the unlikely event that personal jurisdiction could not be obtained over the defendants—for example, in the district where one of them resided or in the district where a substantial part of the events giving rise to the claim occurred—then the fact that venue was proper in those districts would be irrelevant.

The legislative history of § 1391(a)(3) indicated that Congress intended the amendment to be a "fallback" provision. It was to apply only when § 1391(a)(1) & (2) were inapplicable.[156] In other words, § 1391(a)(3) would apply only to actions in which no substantial part of the events giving rise to the claim occurred in the United States and the defendants resided in different districts in different states. Because the language of the statute did not restrict venue to fallback cases, however, some district courts interpreted the provision to apply to any action in which plaintiffs could obtain personal jurisdiction over the defendants.[157] In 1992, Congress amended § 1391(a)(3) to make it clear that the provision was indeed a

---

153. This, however, depends on many other things. Depending what the Supreme Court ultimately holds the source of the subject-matter rule to be, there are questions about whether an objection based on the rule can be made directly in the initial action in the non-situs state or only on collateral attack in the situs state. *See* ROBERT L. FELIX & RALPH U. WHITTEN, AMERICAN CONFLICTS LAW § 44 (6th ed. 2011) (fully discussing these issues).

154. Judicial Improvements Act of 1990, Pub. L. No. 101-650, § 311(1), 104 Stat. 5089, 5114 (codified at 28 U.S.C. § 1391(a)(3)).

155. *See* REPORT OF THE FEDERAL COURTS STUDY COMMITTEE 94 (1990).

156. H.R. REP. NO. 734, 101st Cong., 2d Sess. 23 (1990) stated:

> Subsection 3 is meant to cover the cases in which no substantial part of the events happened in the United States and in which all the defendants do not reside in the same state. This provision would act as a safety net by allowing venue in a "judicial district in which the defendants are subject to personal jurisdiction at the time the action is commenced.["] If personal jurisdiction cannot be brought in a single federal court, this proposal does not create any new basis for personal jurisdiction. Instead two actions must be brought in separate courts.

157. *See, e.g.*, Bartle v. Capy, No. 91-2308, 1991 WL 152955, 1991 U.S. Dist. LEXIS 10954 (E.D. Pa. Aug. 6, 1991); Siemion v. USX Corp., No. 90 C 7092, 1991 WL 125933, 1991 U.S. Dist. LEXIS 8669 (N.D. Ill. June 27, 1991).

fallback provision.[158] Thus, after the amendment, § 1391(a)(3) provided that venue is proper in "a judicial district in which the defendants are subject to personal jurisdiction at the time the action is commenced, if there is no district in which the action may otherwise be brought."[159]

In 1995, § 1391(a)(3) was again amended to provide that venue would be proper in a district in which "any defendant" is subject to personal jurisdiction at the time the action is commenced.[160] This amendment made it clear that only one defendant had to be subject to personal jurisdiction at commencement for venue to be proper, as was the case with old § 1391(b)(3), discussed below.[161]

Illustration 4-26. *P*, a citizen of State *X*, *D-1*, a citizen of State *Y*, and *D-2*, a citizen of State *Z*, collided in automobiles they were driving in France. *P* brought an action for $500,000 to recover for personal injuries received in the accident. *P* brought the action in a U.S. District Court for the District of State *Y* against *D-1* and *D-2*. *D-1* is subject to personal jurisdiction in State *Y* because it is *D-1's* domicile. *D-2* is subject to personal jurisdiction in State *Y* because *D-2* conducts substantial activities within the state. Under these circumstances, venue is proper in the District of State *Y* under § 1391(a)(3).

Illustration 4-27. On the facts of *Illustration 4-26*, assume that *D-2* was not subject to personal jurisdiction in the District of State *Y* when *P* commenced the action because *D-2* was not present in the district and had never conducted any activities there. After commencement of the action, however, *D-2* is served with process while passing through the district. Venue is still proper under these circumstances, though it would not have been before 1995. After the 1995 amendment to the statute, only one defendant need be subject to personal jurisdiction at the commencement of the action (here *D-1*) for venue to be proper.

* * * * *

In 1990, Congress also added a fallback provision to § 1391(b), which then governed actions in which jurisdiction is not based entirely on diversity of citizenship. In § 1391(b)(3), Congress provided that venue would be proper in "a judicial district in which any defendant may be found, if there is no district in which the action may otherwise be brought."[162] Again, the Federal Courts Study Committee made no such recommendation.[163] Thus, unless the legislative history accompanying the amendment to § 1391(a)(3) is also applicable to this amendment, there is no explanation at all in the legislative history as to why Congress added the provision.[164] However, the language of the provision was similar to the language of a 1969 American Law Institute (ALI) proposal.[165] The ALI's explanation for its

---

158. Federal Courts Administration Act of 1992, Pub. L. No. 102-572, § 504, 106 Stat. 4506, 4513 (codified at 28 U.S.C. § 1391(a)(3)).

159. 28 U.S.C. § 1391(a)(3).

160. *See* Act of Oct. 3, 1995, Pub. L. 104-34, § 1, 109 Stat. 293, 293.

161. However, as discussed below, other differences in language between § 1391(a)(3) and (b)(3) were, mysteriously given the criticism of the statute that had already occurred, not eliminated.

162. Judicial Improvements Act of 1990, Pub. L. No. 101-650, § 311, 104 Stat. 5089, 5114 (codified at 28 U.S.C. § 1391(b)(3)).

163. *See* REPORT OF THE FEDERAL COURTS STUDY COMMITTEE 94 (1990).

164. *See* H.R. REP. NO. 734, 101st Cong., 2d Sess. 23 (1990).

165. *See* ALI STUDY OF THE DIVISION OF JURISDICTION BETWEEN STATE AND FEDERAL COURTS § 1314(a)(3) (1969). The language of the ALI proposal provided for venue in a district in which "any defendant may be found, if there is no district within the United States in which the action may otherwise be brought under this subsection." *Id.*

recommendation parallels the explanation in the House Report for the amendment to § 1391(a)(3): "In the rare case where the events occurred outside the United States, and there is a defendant not resident within the United States, venue may be laid where any defendant may be found . . . ."[166]

The difficulty is that while the venue portion of the ALI proposal did not attempt to make personal jurisdiction and venue coextensive, a separate subsection of the ALI proposal did authorize nationwide long-arm jurisdiction in federal question cases.[167] Thus, under the ALI proposal, in a case where the events giving rise to suit occurred outside the United States, but the defendants were scattered throughout the United States, venue would be proper where any defendant could be "found." Personal jurisdiction could then be asserted over the remaining defendants in that district under the nationwide long-arm provision. Therefore, because personal jurisdiction could be obtained over all the defendants in any district (so long as they could be served somewhere in the United States), venue and personal jurisdiction were, in effect, coextensive under the ALI proposal.

However, under the amendment to 28 U.S.C. § 1391(b)(3), it venue and personal jurisdiction are not coextensive. As discussed in Chapter 3, it may be possible to obtain personal jurisdiction over a defendant wherever the defendant is found. However, if other defendants in the action cannot be subjected to personal jurisdiction in the district where the action is brought, venue will be proper under the wording of § 1391(b)(3), but it will still have to be dismissed as to the defendants not subject to personal jurisdiction upon proper objection.

The central question about § 1391(a)(3) & (b)(3) was why Congress worded the two provisions differently. That is, why did § 1391(a)(3) make venue proper in a district in which any defendant "is subject to personal jurisdiction" at the commencement of the action, while § 1391(b)(3) makes venue proper in a district in which any defendant "may be found"? The difference in language held the potential for different results under the two subsections. For example, under the language of § 1391(a)(3) venue would be proper in a district where one of several nonresident defendants was subject to personal jurisdiction at commencement because the defendant had minimum contacts with the state in which the action was brought. However, § 1391(b)(3)'s use of the phrase "may be found" suggests that the defendant would have to be physically present within the jurisdiction, not merely subject to personal jurisdiction under a long-arm statute. On the other hand, § 1391(b)(3) did not require that the defendant be "found" within the district at commencement. Thus, under § 1391(b)(3), if a defendant could be served within the district *after* commencement, the court would have personal jurisdiction over the defendant and venue would be proper, but the same was not true under § 1391(a)(3).

There was no apparent reason why Congress would want to treat venue differently under § 1391(a)(3) & (b)(3). Thus, the difference in wording appears to have been a byproduct of extremely poor drafting. The American Law Institute proposed that in both diversity and federal question cases, the fallback provision should make venue proper "in any judicial district in which any defendant is subject

---

166. *See id.* at 31, reporter's note to § 1314(a)(3); *see also id.* at 218-19.
167. *See id.* § 1314(d).

to personal jurisdiction."[168] In 2011, Congress adopted this suggestion in the Federal Courts Jurisdiction and Venue Clarification Act.[169] New 28 U.S.C. § 1391(b) eliminates old §§ 1391(a) & (b) and applies the same rules of venue to both diversity and federal question cases in a new § 1391(b). Subsection (3) of new § 1391(b) provides that

> if there is no district in which an action may otherwise be brought as provided in this section, [venue is proper in] any judicial district in which any defendant is subject to personal jurisdiction with respect to such action.

Note that in addition to eliminating the differences in language between old sections 1391(a)(3) and (b)(3), this new section also eliminates the requirement that a defendant be subject to personal jurisdiction at the commencement of the action.

Illustration 4-28. *P*, a citizen of State *X*, sues *D-1*, a citizen of State *X*, and *D-2*, a citizen of State *Y*, in the U.S. District Court for the District of State *X*. The events giving rise to the claim occurred outside the United States. *D-1* is personally served with process in State *X*, where *D-1* is domiciled. *D-2* is not subject to personal jurisdiction in State *X*. Venue is proper in State *X* under the wording of new § 1391(b)(3). However, *D-2* will have to be dismissed from the action because there is no personal jurisdiction over *D-2*. *P* may be able to bring the action in another federal court, if *P* can find a district somewhere in which either *D-1* or *D-2* are subject to personal jurisdiction. However, the action would still have to be dismissed against the other defendant unless personal jurisdiction could also be acquired over that defendant. Note that if the action had been brought in the U.S. District Court for the District of State *Q* and *P* had served either *D-1* or *D-2* in the district after commencement of the action, thus acquiring personal jurisdiction over the defendant served, venue would also now be proper.

6. Residence of Corporations and Associations

Before 1988, another peculiarity of the venue statute was found in 28 U.S.C. § 1391(c), which defined venue for suits against corporations. It provided that "[a] corporation may be sued in any judicial district in which it is incorporated or licensed to do business or is doing business, and such judicial district shall be regarded as the residence of such corporation for venue purposes." The language "and such judicial district shall be regarded as the residence of such corporation for venue purposes" might have been read as making the section applicable to the venue of corporate plaintiffs as well as corporate defendants. However, even before 1988, it was generally settled that this section was intended only to broaden venue for suits against corporate defendants and did not fix venue for corporate plaintiffs. Before 1990, a corporation predicating venue on the plaintiff's residence had to sue where it was incorporated.[170] After 1990, the plaintiff's residence is no longer a proper venue under 28 U.S.C. § 1391.

---

168. *See* ALI FEDERAL JUDICIAL CODE REVISION PROJECT § 1391(e), at 167 (2004).

169. Pub. L. 112-63, § 202, 125 Stat. 758, 763 (2011) (codified in 28 U.S.C. § 1391(b)(3)).

170. *See* 14D CHARLES A. WRIGHT ET AL., FEDERAL PRACTICE AND PROCEDURE: JURISDICTION AND RELATED MATTERS § 3811, at 292 (3d ed. 2007).

In 1988, § 1391(c) was amended to expressly apply only to corporate defendants.[171] In the Federal Courts Jurisdiction and Venue Clarification Act of 2011, effective in 2012,[172] Congress moved this provision to § 1391(d), but did not alter its text. Section 1391(d) provides that a corporate defendant "shall be deemed to reside in any judicial district in which it is subject to personal jurisdiction at the time the action is commenced."[173] However, in states containing more than one judicial district, corporate defendants can be sued only in those judicial districts in which their activities would be sufficient to subject them to personal jurisdiction if the districts were separate states.[174] This restriction was designed to protect corporations that conduct activities primarily or exclusively in only one district of a state from being sued in another district in the state with which they have little or no contact, unless venue would be proper in that other district on a different basis than defendant's residence.[175] In addition, § 1391(d) provides that if there is no district, evaluated as a separate state, in which a corporate defendant has sufficient contacts to subject it to personal jurisdiction, the corporation may be sued in the district "within which it has the most significant contacts."[176] This unwieldy provision is designed to take care of the rare case in which a corporate defendant may have sufficient contacts with an entire state to subject it to personal jurisdiction within the state, but lacks sufficient contacts with any one of the federal districts in that state to subject it to personal jurisdiction within a particular district.

Illustration 4-29. *P*, a citizen of State *X*, sued *D Corporation*, a corporation incorporated and with its principal place of business in State *Y*. *P* brings the action in a U.S. District Court for the Northern District of State *Z*. *P* asserts a claim based

---

171. *See* Judicial Improvements and Access to Justice Act of 1988, Pub. L. No. 100-702, § 1013, 102 Stat. 4642, 4669 (originally codified at 28 U.S.C. § 1391(c), now codified at 28 U.S.C. § 1391(d)). Section 1391(d) defines residence of a corporate defendant "[f]or purposes of venue under this chapter," which means that the definition of a corporate defendant's residence applies not only for purposes of venue under §§ 1391(b)(1), but also for purposes of any venue statute in Chapter 87 of Title 28 that provides for proper venue at defendant's residence. *See, e.g.*, Astro-Med, Inc. v. Nihon Kohden Am., Inc., 591 F.3d 1 (1st Cir. 2009); *In re* Regents of Univ. of Cal., 964 F.2d 1128 (Fed. Cir. 1992) (patent infringement); Dakota Indus., Inc. v. Dakota Sportswear, Inc., 946 F.2d 1384 (8th Cir. 1991) (trademark infringement); Milwaukee Concrete Studios, Ltd. v. Fjeld Mfg. Co., 795 F. Supp. 277 (E.D. Wis. 1992) (copyright infringement); *see also* Bass v. Energy Transp. Corp., 787 F. Supp. 530 (D. Md. 1992) (definition of corporate residence applied to venue under the Jones Act, 46 U.S.C § 688).

172. Pub. L. 112-63, § 202(1), 125 Stat. 758, 764 (2012) (codified at 28 U.S.C. § 1391(d)).

173. *See* 28 U.S.C. § 1391(d). This portion of § 1391(d) is straightforward and poses no special difficulties of administration apart from, perhaps, a complicated inquiry into whether personal jurisdiction is proper in a given case. *See* Dakota Indus., Inc. v. Dakota Sportswear, Inc., 946 F.2d 1384 (8th Cir. 1991). *But see* Davies Precision Machining, Inc. v. Defense Logistics Agency, 825 F. Supp. 105 (E.D. Pa. 1993) (Defense Logistics Agency, federal agency, is not a corporation for purposes of § 1391(d)); Variable-Parameter Fixture Dev. Corp. v. Morpheus Lights Co., 832 F. Supp. 643 (S.D.N.Y. 1993) (venue proper as to majority shareholders of corporation in district where corporation is subject to personal jurisdiction).

174. *See* 28 U.S.C. § 1391(d). Under this portion of the statute, a court must focus on the contacts with the district, not simply on contacts with the state. *See* Bicicletas Windsor, S.A. v. Bicycle Corp. of Am., 783 F. Supp. 781 (S.D.N.Y. 1992) (focusing on contacts with the entire state for purposes of personal jurisdiction, but focusing on contacts with the district for purposes of venue). Some courts, however, have simply assumed that contacts with a state sufficient to confer personal jurisdiction automatically satisfy the venue test. *See, e.g.*, Kaufman v. First Wachovia Corp., No. C-91-4456 MHP ARB, 1992 U.S. Dist. LEXIS 5617 (N.D. Cal. Apr. 3, 1992) (contacts with California sustain personal jurisdiction; these contacts simultaneously created venue in the district).

175. *See* H.R. REP. NO. 889, 100th Cong., 2d Sess. 70, *reprinted in* 1988 U.S.C.C.A.N. 5982, 6031. Thus, because personal jurisdiction is measured by reference to the contacts between the defendant and an entire state, the general language of the amendment to § 1391(d) would have subjected a corporation conducting activities only in the southern district of a state to suit in the northern district. The qualification in § 1391(d) prevents this result unless venue is proper on other grounds, such as when the northern district is the place where the events giving rise to the action occurred. *See id.*

176. *See* Judicial Improvements and Access to Justice Act of 1988, Pub. L. No. 100-702, § 1013, 102 Stat. 4642, 4669 (originally codified at 28 U.S.C. § 1391(c) now codified at 28 U.S.C. § 1391(d)).

on state law for $500,000. The events giving rise to the claim occurred in State *Q*. *D* does extensive business in the Southern District of State *Z* and is subject to personal jurisdiction in State *Z* as a result. *D* conducts no activities in the Northern District of State *Z*. Venue is, therefore, improper in the Northern District of State *Z*. In multiple district states, § 1391(d) requires that the activities of a corporate defendant be evaluated with regard to each district in order to determine corporate residence. If the activities in one district would be sufficient to subject the defendant to personal jurisdiction if that district were a separate state, the defendant is deemed to reside there for purposes of § 1391(b)(1). However, if the defendant's activities in a district would not be sufficient to subject it to personal jurisdiction if that district were a separate state, the defendant does not reside there under § 1391(d). Here, *D* conducts no activities in the Northern District of State *Z* and, therefore, that district cannot be deemed to be its residence.

Illustration 4-30. On the facts of *Illustration 4-29*, assume that *P* brought the action against both *D Corp.* and *D-2*, a citizen of State *Z* who resides in the Northern District of State *Z*. Under these circumstances, venue is proper in the Northern District of State *Z* under § 1391(b)(1). Because of its activities in the Southern District of State *Z*, *D Corp.* is deemed to reside there under § 1391(d). *D-2* is a resident of the Northern District of State *Z*. Therefore, the action is against multiple defendants who reside in different districts in the state in which the action is brought. Section 1391(b)(1) provides that, under these circumstances, venue is proper in a district where any defendant resides and the district court is located.

Illustration 4-31. *P*, a citizen of State *X*, sues *D Corp.*, a corporation incorporated and with its principal place of business in State *Y*, in a U.S. District Court for the Northern District of State *Z*. *P* asserts a claim based on state law for $500,000. The events giving rise to the claim occurred entirely in State *Q*. *D* does sufficient business in State *Z* to subject it to personal jurisdiction there, but its activities are spread over the Northern and Southern Districts of State *Z*. The activities in each district, viewed alone, would not be sufficient to subject *D* to personal jurisdiction in either of the districts if they were separate states. Whether the venue is proper in the Northern District of State *Z* depends upon whether *D's* activities there are more significant than its activities in the Southern District.[177]

* * * * *

The difficult hypothetical inquiry required by § 1391(d) means that the district courts will, in some cases, have to go through specific and general jurisdiction analyses with regard to activities of a corporate defendant within the district, even though it is clear that the corporation's activities would be subject to personal jurisdiction within the state where the district is located. Although the problem has seldom arisen, the cases thus far have not reached results that would command unanimous agreement.[178] It is hard to believe that transfer to another

---

177. Some courts evaluating venue under § 1391(c) have erroneously focused on the defendant's activities in the state, rather than the district. *See, e.g.*, Halsoprodukter Labs. Karnerud Ab. v. Gero Vita Int'l, No. 93 C 2129, 1993 WL 384525, 1993 U.S. Dist. LEXIS 13519 (N.D. Ill. Sept. 27, 1993).

178. *See* Zinn v. Gichner Sys. Grp., Civ. No. 93-5817, 1994 WL 116014, 1994 U.S. Dist. LEXIS 4076 (E.D. Pa. Apr. 5, 1994), in which the corporation, which had ample activities to subject it to jurisdiction in Pennsylvania under both the general and specific jurisdiction doctrines, was sued in the Eastern District on a claim arising in the Middle District. After employing general jurisdiction analysis to the corporation's activities in the Eastern District, the court concluded that it would not be able to assert general jurisdiction if the district were a

district in the same state, which will often be the result of an inquiry under this part of the statute, is worth in convenience to defendants the costs it will impose in judicial administration.

In 1967, the U.S. Supreme Court held that unincorporated associations could be sued wherever they were doing business.[179] No statute dictated this result.[180] Instead, the Court reached the result by analogy to corporate venue in the old version of § 1391(d).[181] In the Federal Courts Jurisdiction and Venue Clarification Act of 2011, effective in 2012, Congress enacted a new provision to govern the venue of unincorporated associations.[182] New 28 U.S.C. § 1391(c)(2) now provides:

> (c) RESIDENCY.—For all venue purposes—
>
> . . . .
>
> (2) an entity with the capacity to sue and be sued in its common name under applicable law, whether or not incorporated, shall be deemed to reside, if a defendant, in any judicial district in which such defendant is subject to the court's personal jurisdiction with respect to the civil action in question, and, if a plaintiff, only in the judicial district in which it maintains its principal place of business; . . .[183]

Note that this provision literally applies both to corporations and to unincorporated associations. The provision applicable to corporations obviously operates the same as § 1391(d), discussed above, when dealing with corporate residence in single district states. However, new § 1391(d) is of value when determining corporate defendants' residence in multiple district states. As applied to the residence of unincorporated association defendants, § 1391(c)(2) now makes it clear that they reside in any district where they are subject to personal jurisdiction for purposes of § 1391(b)(1) and other provisions of the venue chapter of Title 28 dealing with venue on the basis of residence. However, this is only true if an unincorporated association can otherwise sue and be sued as an entity under the law governing the association. If it cannot, the provisions applicable to individuals will still govern venue in which the entity is a party, and this will mean that residence will be determined by reference to the residence of the individual members of the association. The language governing plaintiffs' residence in the new provision is

---

separate state. The court did not employ a specific jurisdiction analysis because the claim for personal injuries clearly "arose" in the Middle District. However, the court failed to consider whether the defendant's activities in the Eastern District "related to" the claim. *See* Chapter 3(G)(2)*(b)(i) supra* ("Claims Arising Out of or Related to the Defendant's Contacts with the State"); *see also* LG Elecs. Inc. v. Advance Creative Computer Corp., 131 F. Supp. 2d 804 (E.D. Va. 2001) (personal jurisdiction over a corporation for purposes of § 1391(d) is not proper in a district just because a corporation is incorporated in the state in which the district is located; instead, there must be minimum contacts with the particular district in which venue is laid); Sanders v. Seal Fleet, Inc., 998 F. Supp. 729 (E.D. Tex. 1998) (insufficient to show that a corporation is incorporated in a district of a multidistrict state; defendant must have sufficient contacts with district in which the action is brought). *But see* Lisseveld v. Marcus, 173 F.R.D. 689 (M.D. Fla. 1997) (defendant's contacts with Middle District of Florida sufficient to subject defendant to personal jurisdiction because, although the defendant's products were sold in South Florida, defendant expected the products to enter the stream of commerce of the entire state), *aff'd sub nom.* Enviro Response v. Marcus, 268 F.3d 1066 (11th Cir. 2001) (table).

179. *See* Denver & Rio Grande W. R.R. Co. v. Brotherhood of R.R. Trainmen, 387 U.S. 556, 87 S. Ct. 1746, 18 L. Ed. 2d 954 (1967).

180. *See* 14D CHARLES A. WRIGHT ET AL., FEDERAL PRACTICE AND PROCEDURE: JURISDICTION AND RELATED MATTERS § 3812, at 348-49 (3d ed. 2007).

181. *See id.* at 135.

182. *See* Pub. L. 112-63, § 202(1), 125 Stat. 758, 763 (2011) (codified at 28 U.S.C. § 1391(c)(2)).

183. *Id.*

designed to deal with cases "in which other laws provide that venue may be based on the residence of the plaintiff."[184] This also applies only to unincorporated associations that can sue as entities. Associations that cannot do so under the applicable law will, again, have venue determined by reference to the domiciles of their individual members.[185]

Note, however, that unlike corporations, the new provisions do not deal separately with situations in which unincorporated entities are subject to personal jurisdiction in a multiple district state when they have minimum contacts with the state based on activities that occur entirely within a single district of the state. Under such circumstances, venue presumably be proper in any district in the state, even a district in which the entity-defendant conducts no activities, because the entity will literally be subject to personal jurisdiction there based on its activities in another district.

7. Venue in Actions Involving Aliens

Before 2012, section 1391(d) stated that an "alien may be sued in any district."[186] Thus, when an alien was a defendant, venue was proper anywhere. The alien could be sued wherever personal jurisdiction could be obtained. The 1988 amendment to 28 U.S.C. § 1332(a), discussed in Chapter 2, did not alter this rule.[187] That amendment provided that an alien admitted to permanent residence in the United States would be considered a citizen of the state in which the alien is domiciled.[188] However, that provision was expressly applicable only to §§ 1332, 1335, and 1441. Therefore, it was inapplicable to the venue statutes.

In the Federal Courts Jurisdiction and Venue Clarification Act of 2011,[189] effective in 2012, Congress modified alienage venue substantially. Sections (c)(1) and (c)(3) of section 1391 now deal with venue over resident and nonresident aliens (*i.e.*, resident and nonresident citizens and subjects of foreign states) differently:

> (c) RESIDENCY.— For all venue purposes—
>
> (1) a natural person, including an alien lawfully admitted for permanent residence in the United States, shall be deemed to reside in the judicial district in which that person is domiciled;
>
> . . . .
>
> (3) a defendant not resident in the United States may be sued in any judicial district, and the joinder of such a defendant shall be disregarded in determining where the action may be brought with respect to other defendants.

---

184. *See* H.R. Rep. No. 112-10, at 14 (2011).

185. *See id.* Note that both in the case of unincorporated association defendants and plaintiffs, the ability to sue and be sued is normally determined by state law. However, a partnership or unincorporated association that lacks the ability to sue and be sued under state law can sue and be sued in their common name for purposes of enforcing federal rights. *See id.*; FED. R. CIV. P. 17(b)(3)(A).

186. 28 U.S.C. § 1391(d). The ALI has recommended that this provision be expanded to include all defendants "not resident in the United States." *See* ALI FEDERAL JUDICIAL CODE REVISION PROJECT § 1391(d), at 167 (2004).

187. *See* Chapter 2(D)(4) *supra* ("Alienage Jurisdiction").

188. *See* 28 U.S.C. § 1332(a).

189. Pub. L. No. 112-63, § 202(a), 125 Stat. 758, 763 (2011) (codified as 28 U.S.C. § 1391(c)(1) & (3)).

New subsection(c)(1) now treats permanent resident aliens the same as citizens for purposes of venue, thus making their treatment for this purpose the same as their treatment for citizenship in determining whether subject-matter jurisdiction exists on the basis of diversity of citizenship. Subsection (c)(3) now applies the rule that an alien may be sued in any district only to nonresident aliens and makes it clear that their joinder does not affect the determination of proper venue with regard to other defendants.

Illustration 4-32. *P*, a citizen of State *X*, sues *D*, a citizen of France admitted to permanent residence in the United States and domiciled in State *Y*, in the U.S. District Court for the District of State *X* based on residence. *P's* claim is for $500,000 and is based on state law. The events giving rise to the claim occurred entirely in State *Q*. Venue is proper in States *Q* and *Y*, not in State *X*. Section 1391(c)(1) now provides that the residence of an alien admitted to permanent residence in the U.S. is to be determined on the basis of where the alien is domiciled, here State *Y*.

Illustration 4-33. On the facts of *Illustration 4-32*, if the events giving rise to suit had occurred in State *X*, *P* could bring the action against *D* there under 28 U.S.C. § 1391(b)(2), based on the "substantial events" that had occurred in the district.

Illustration 4-34. Assume that on the facts of *Illustration 4-32*, *D* was not admitted to permanent residence in the United States and domiciled in State *Y*, but was domiciled abroad. Under these circumstances, *P* could sue *D* in the United States District Court for the District of State *X* even if the events giving rise to the claim occurred entirely in State *Q*, and venue would be proper there by virtue of new 28 U.S.C. § 1391(c)(3).

8. Venue in Removed Actions

Section 1441(a) of Title 28 provides that civil actions can be removed "to the district court of the United States for the district and division embracing the place where [the state] action is pending."[190] This language has always been understood as establishing special venue for removed actions.[191] However, in the Federal Courts Jurisdiction and Venue Clarification Act of 2011,[192] effective in 2012, a new provision was added to the Judicial Code to make it clear that the general venue provisions apply only to actions commenced originally in federal court. New 28 U.S.C. § 1390(c) now provides:

> (c) CLARIFICATION REGARDING CASES REMOVED FROM STATE COURTS.—This chapter shall not determine the district court to which a civil action pending in a State court may be removed, but shall govern the transfer of an action so removed as between districts and divisions of the United States district courts.

---

190. *See* 28 U.S.C. § 1441(a).

191. *See* 14D CHARLES A. WRIGHT ET AL., FEDERAL PRACTICE AND PROCEDURE: JURISDICTION AND RELATED MATTERS § 3804, at 136 (3d ed. 2007).

192. Pub. L. No. 112-63, § 201(a), 125 Stat. 758, 762-63 (2011) (codified at 28 U.S.C. § 1390(c)).

Therefore, even if an action is brought in a state court within a district where venue would have been improper if the action had been commenced in the U.S. District Court, venue will be proper in the district if the action is removed to the district court.[193]

Illustration 4-35. *P*, a citizen of State *X*, sues *D*, a citizen of State *Y*, in a state court in State *X*. *P's* claim is for $500,000 and is based on state law. The events giving rise to the claim occurred entirely in State *Q*. *D* removes the action to the U.S. District Court for the District of State *X*. Even though venue would not have been proper if the action had been commenced in the U.S. District Court for the District of State *X* originally, venue is proper over the removed action by virtue of § 1441(a).

Illustration 4-36. On the facts of *Illustration 4-35*, if the action is to be transferred to a district court in another district, the transfer must be made to another district in which venue would have been proper if the action had been commenced in federal court originally, or all the parties must consent to the transfer, as further discussed in subsection D(2), below.

9. Divisional Venue

Before 1988, 28 U.S.C. § 1393(a) required non-local actions against a single defendant in districts with more than one division to be brought in the division where the defendant resided. Under § 1393(b), non-local actions against multiple defendants residing in different divisions of the same district could be brought in any of the divisions.[194] In 1988, § 1393 was repealed. Thus, divisional venue in civil cases was generally eliminated.[195] However, § 1441(a) still contains language referring to divisional venue, which may result in its retention for purposes of removed cases.[196]

---

193. *Id.*; *see also* Peterson v. BMI Refractories, 124 F.3d 1386 (11th Cir. 1997) (if action is removed to a district court in *wrong district* in a state, the defect is procedural only, not one of subject-matter jurisdiction, and concerns venue; venue is waivable and was waived by *plaintiff* in the action). The ALI would repeal this rule and provide that a removing defendant could raise a venue objection that could have been asserted if the action had been brought in the district originally. *See* ALI FEDERAL JUDICIAL CODE REVISION PROJECT § 1406(c), at 219 (2004).

194. *See* Judicial Improvements and Access to Justice Act of 1988, Pub. L. No. 100-702, § 1001, 102 Stat. 4642, 4664.

195. *See* H.R. REP. NO. 889, 100th Cong., 2d Sess. 66-67, *reprinted in* 1988 U.S.C.C.A.N. 5982, 6027.

196. Subsection (a) of 28 U.S.C. § 1441, which provides for removal of civil actions from state to federal court, continues to require removal "to the district court of the United States for the district *and division* embracing the place where such action is pending." *See* 28 U.S.C. § 1441(a) (emphasis added). The failure to amend § 1441 to eliminate divisional venue in removed cases was probably inadvertent. Nevertheless, the presence of the quoted language may result in divisional venue being retained for such cases. Note that the Federal Courts Jurisdiction and Venue Clarification Act of 2011, effective in 2012, and discussed throughout this section, Congress did not deal with the "divisional venue" language in the statue. *See* Pub. L. No. 112-63, § 103(a)(2), 125 Stat. 758, 759 (2011). The American Law Institute has proposed to reform the general removal provision to make it clear that divisional venue is also abolished in removed cases. *See* ALI FEDERAL JUDICIAL CODE REVISION PROJECT § 1441(a)(2), at 345 (2004) (making civil actions removable "to the district court of the United States for the district in which the civil action is pending").

10. Special Venue Provisions

Special federal venue provisions also exist. These special provisions are sometimes contained in separate statutes[197] or in the statutes that create the right to sue.[198] In some instances, these special federal venue provisions have been interpreted to displace the general federal venue provisions.[199] Usually, the special provisions broaden the choice of venue available under the general venue provisions.[200] In some instances, however, the choice is narrowed.[201]

In 2002, Congress enacted the Multiparty, Multiforum Trial Jurisdiction Act of 2002, 28 U.S.C. § 1369, to provide the district courts with subject-matter jurisdiction based on minimal diversity of citizenship between the parties in certain kinds of mass disaster actions.[202] As part of the Act, Congress created new 28 U.S.C. § 1391(g), to provide for special venue under the Act. Section 1391(g) provides that when jurisdiction is based on § 1369, venue will be proper in any district in which any defendant resides or in which a substantial part of the accident giving rise to the action took place.

In addition, § 1369(c)(2) provides that a corporation will be deemed to be a resident of any state in which it is incorporated or licensed to do business or is doing business.[203] Note, however, that to the extent that § 1391(g) refers to residence generally, the definitions of residence (discussed above) in § 1391(c) will control what residence means for purposes of the Act. Since corporate residence is defined to include any district in which a corporation can be subjected to personal jurisdiction, and since all of the places listed in § 1369(c)(2) are places where personal jurisdiction will normally be proper, § 1369(c)(2) is probably superfluous.

---

197. *See, e.g.*, 28 U.S.C. § 1400 (patent and copyright suits).

198. *See, e.g.*, 46 U.S.C. § 688 (allowing seamen who are injured in the course of their employment to sue for damages for the negligence of the owner, master, or fellow crew members). Special venue statutes can be found by using the subject index to the *United States Code*.

199. *Compare* 28 U.S.C. § 1391(e) (special venue provision controls actions against officers, employees, or agencies of the federal government) *and* Jean F. Rydstrom, Annotation, *Construction and Application of 28 USC § 1391(e) Providing for Venue and Process in Civil Actions Against Federal Officers, Employees, or Agencies*, 9 A.L.R. FED. 719 (1971) *with* 45 U.S.C. § 56 (general venue provisions render largely superfluous the special venue provision for Federal Employer's Liability Act cases governing railroad employees engaged in interstate and foreign commerce); *see also* Sunbelt Corp. v. Noble, Denton & Assocs., Inc., 5 F.3d 28 (3d Cir. 1993) (admiralty cases not governed by 28 U.S.C. § 1391). *See generally* 14D CHARLES A. WRIGHT ET AL., FEDERAL PRACTICE AND PROCEDURE: JURISDICTION AND RELATED MATTERS § 3803 (3d ed. 2007) (special venue statutes that expressly cover a particular kind of action "will control over general venue statutes"; however, the general venue statutes will be "read as supplementing the special statute in absence of contrary restrictive indications in the special statute").

200. *See, e.g.*, 15 U.S.C. §§ 15, 22 (allowing antitrust suits to be brought wherever the defendant "resides or is found or has an agent"). In Cortez Byrd Chips, Inc. v. Bill Harbert Constr. Co., 529 U.S. 193, 120 S. Ct. 1331, 146 L. Ed. 2d 171 (2000), the Supreme Court held that the venue provisions of the Federal Arbitration Act were permissive and allowed suit to enforce an arbitration award either where it was made or in any district proper under the general federal venue statutes.

201. *See, e.g.*, 12 U.S.C. § 94 (allowing suits against national banks to be brought only in the district where the banks' principal office and place of business are located, as specified in their certificates); Richard Cordero, Annotation, *Venue Provisions of National Bank Act (12 USCS § 94), as Affected by Other Federal Venue Provisions and Doctrines*, 111 A.L.R. FED. 235 (1993).

202. This Act was previously discussed in Chapter 2(C)(3)*(e)* and at other appropriate places in the text.

203. *See* 28 U.S.C. §§ 1391(g) & 1369(c)(2).

11. Interaction of Venue, Subject-Matter Jurisdiction and Personal Jurisdiction Rules

The inability to satisfy the requirements of the federal venue provisions may mean that a suit must be brought in a state court. Furthermore, interaction of the venue requirements with those of subject-matter and personal jurisdiction may also mean that certain actions cannot be brought in any federal court.

Illustration 4-37. *P* suffered personal injuries in a four-car automobile accident involving drivers *D-1*, *D-2*, and *D-3*. *P* is a citizen of State *X*; *D-1* is a citizen of State *Y*; *D-2* is a citizen of State *Z*; and *D-3* is a citizen of State *X*. The accident occurred on a highway in England. If *P* wishes to sue *D-1*, *D-2*, and *D-3* in a single federal court action, *P* may not do so. A suit joining *D-3* as a defendant would violate the complete diversity requirement because *P* and *D-3* are both citizens of State *X*.

Illustration 4-38. On the facts of *Illustration 4-37*, if *P* wishes to join only *D-1* and *D-2* in a federal court action for *P's* injuries, *P* likewise may not do so if a proper objection is made. Complete diversity of citizenship, and therefore subject-matter jurisdiction, would exist in such a case. However, in an action against *D-1* and *D-2*, venue (and personal jurisdiction) would probably not be proper anywhere. *D-1* and *D-2* do not live in the same state, so venue could not be predicated on the defendants' residence under 28 U.S.C. § 1391(b)(1). The events giving rise to the action occurred outside the United States, so venue could not be predicated on 28 U.S.C. § 1391(b)(2). Because personal jurisdiction can be obtained over *D-1* and *D-2* individually in the districts in which they live, venue will be proper under 28 U.S.C. § 1391(b)(3) in those districts in an action against both defendants. However, for the action to proceed against the other defendant, personal jurisdiction would also have to be obtained over that defendant in the forum. Even if *P* sued only *D-1* in a federal diversity action in the District of State *Y*, where subject-matter jurisdiction, venue, and personal jurisdiction would be proper, *D-1* might be able to obtain a dismissal under the doctrine of forum non conveniens, discussed in section D, below. And the same might be true of a diversity action against *D-2* in the District of State *Z*.

12. Raising and Waiving Federal Venue Objections

In contrast to actions at common law in which venue had to be alleged in the declaration (the plaintiff's initial pleading), venue need not be alleged in a complaint filed in federal court. Under the Federal Rules of Civil Procedure, improper venue is a matter of *defense* which the defendant must raise.[204] If the defendant fails to object to the venue in a timely and proper fashion, venue objections are waived.[205] Waiver can also occur through contractual provisions

---

204. *See* Notes to former Form 2 ("Allegation of Jurisdiction") prior to restyling in the Appendix of Forms following the Federal Rules of Civil Procedure.

205. *See* FED. R. CIV. P. 12(h)(1); The precise mechanics of waiver under the Federal Rules of Civil Procedure are discussed in Chapter 6(D)(3)*(g) infra* ("Consolidation and Waiver of Defenses"). Some courts have held that it is proper for a district court to raise a venue issue *sua sponte*. *See, e.g.*, Algodonera de las Cabezas, S.A. v. American Suisse Capital, Inc.,432 F.3d 1343 (11th Cir. Dec. 19, 2005) (although court has previously made clear

entered into before a dispute arises.[206] Many contracts include a "forum selection" clause. A forum selection clause will usually provide that suit on the contract may be brought only in the courts in a particular place. Courts generally enforce forum selection clauses unless they are deemed unreasonable either in themselves or in the effects that they have on the rights of the litigants.[207]

The U.S. Supreme Court has held forum selection clauses in contracts of adhesion (an unbargained for contract in which one of the parties is an unsophisticated consumer not in bargaining parity with the party who drafted the contract) are enforceable. In *Carnival Cruise Lines, Inc. v. Shute*,[208] a Washington State couple purchased tickets on a cruise ship operated by Carnival Cruise Lines. The tickets contained a forum selection clause requiring that all disputes be litigated in Florida. While on the cruise, one of the plaintiffs suffered personal injuries on the ship. The plaintiffs sued Carnival Cruise Lines in the U.S. District Court for the Western District of Washington. The district court dismissed the action for lack of personal jurisdiction. The Ninth Circuit reversed, holding that Carnival Cruise Lines had sufficient contacts with Washington to sustain personal jurisdiction. In addition, the Ninth Circuit held that the forum selection clause was unenforceable because it was not freely bargained for and operated to deny the plaintiffs their day in court. The Supreme Court reversed, holding the forum selection clause enforceable.

---

that a district court may raise a venue objection *sua sponte*, it may not dismiss the suit without first giving the parties an opportunity to present their views on the issue; this approach gives the defendants an opportunity to waive the venue defense and the plaintiffs an opportunity to present argument as to why venue is proper before the case is dismissed); Zhu v. Whinery, 109 Fed. App'x 137 (9th Cir. July 20, 2004) (defendant does not waive an improper venue objection by not raising it as long as defendant has not filed a responsive pleading to the complaint and the time for doing so has not expired; district court may raise venue objection *sua sponte*). This practice is clearly wrong. It deprives the plaintiff of the benefit of a waiver of venue produced by the defendant's noncompliance with the waiver process described in the Federal Rules of Civil Procedure.

206. *See* Robert Force, *The Position in the United States on Foreign Forum Selection and Arbitration Clauses, Forum Non Conveniens, and Antisuit Injunctions*, 35 TUL. MARITIME L.J. 401 (2011).The ALI has recommended a codification that would provide that venue may be "conferred by conduct or by reasonable contract." *See* ALI FEDERAL JUDICIAL CODE REVISION PROJECT § 1406(c), at 219 (2004). The provision for waiver by conduct is unfortunate in that it provides no standards for determining what conduct will constitute waiver.

207. *See, e.g.*, M/S Bremen v. Zapata Off-Shore Co., 407 U.S. 1, 12-19, 92 S. Ct. 1907, 1914-18, 32 L. Ed. 2d 513, 521-26 (1972) (contractual forum selection designating disputes to be brought only before the High Court of Justice in London, England, enforced; no compelling, countervailing reason making enforcement unreasonable); National Equip. Rental, Ltd. v. Szukhent, 375 U.S. 311, 315-16, 84 S. Ct. 411, 415, 11 L. Ed. 2d 354, 357 (1964) (diversity action upholding appointment of an agent for service of process); *see also* Albemarle Corp. v. Astrazeneca UK, Ltd., 628 F.3d 643 (4th Cir. 2010) (forum selection clause providing contract was subject to jurisdiction of the English High Court was not unreasonable); American Soda, LLP v. U.S. Filter Wastewater Grp., Inc., 428 F.3d 921 (10th Cir. 2005) (when forum selection clause refers to courts "of a state," venue is not proper in federal district court in designated state); F.L. Crane & Sons v. Malouf Constr. Corp., 953 So. 2d 366 (Ala. 2006) (forum selection clause not enforced because serious inconvenience would arise if case arising from same construction project had to be litigated against different parties in different fora); Reiner, Reiner & Bendett, P.C. v. Cadle Co., 278 Conn. 92, 897 A.2d 58 (2006) (forum selection clause does not oust courts of jurisdiction, but simply allow them to decline to exercise jurisdiction under certain circumstances); Secure Fin. Serv., Inc. v. Popular Leasing USA, Inc., 391 Md. 274, 892 A.2d 571 (2006) (forum selection clause should be enforced unless unreasonable; party opposing the clause should be given the chance to show that the clause was induced by fraud or overreaching or is otherwise unreasonable); Polk Cny. Recreational Ass'n v. Susquehanna Patriot Com. Leasing Co., 273 Neb. 1026, 734 N.W.2d 750 (2007) (forum selection clause in equipment lease executed by golf course providing that any action concerning lease would be brought in Pennsylvania was mandatory and enforceable under both Nebraska and Pennsylvania law); Caperton v. A.T. Massey Coal Co., 690 S.E.2d 322 (W. Va. 2009) (forum selection clauses not contrary to public policy); Durdahl v. National Safety Assocs., Inc., 988 P.2d 525 (Wyo. 1999) (forum selection clauses prima facie valid). *But see, e.g.*, Omne Fin., Inc. v. Shacks, Inc., 226 Mich. App. 397, 573 N.W.2d 641 (1997) (contract agreeing to venue in a specific court is unenforceable because legislature has not approved such a rule; allowing parties to contract around venue statutes would undermine the power of the legislature, and contract agreeing to venue would conflict with court rules allowing trial court to change venue).

208. 499 U.S. 585, 111 S. Ct. 1522, 113 L. Ed. 2d 622 (1991).

The Court found it irrelevant that the forum selection clause was not negotiated between the parties. Rather, the Court held it reasonable, given the business context involved in the case, that (1) the forum selection clause would be included in a form contract (the ticket); (2) the clause would not be the subject of negotiation between the parties; and (3) the purchaser would not have bargaining parity with the cruise line. The Court noted that the forum selection clause served several important purposes: (1) limiting the fora in which the cruise line, which carries passengers from many locales, can be sued; (2) dispelling confusion about where actions arising from the contract may be brought, thus saving litigants the time and expense of pretrial motions to determine the correct forum and conserving the judicial resources that would be devoted to that subject; and (3) reducing the fares charged to passengers because of the savings that the cruise line enjoys by limiting where it can be sued.[209]

After *Carnival Cruise Lines*, a forum selection clause controlled by federal law[210] will not be held unenforceable simply because it appears in a contract of adhesion.[211] Instead, a forum selection clause of which the plaintiff has adequate notice[212] will be valid if sufficient reasons can be given for including the clause in the contract.

The reasons given in *Carnival Cruise* for holding the forum selection clause enforceable have been criticized as imposing no real limitations on the enforcement of such clauses.[213] However, the result in the *Carnival Cruise Lines*, as well as the

---

209. *See id.* at 593, 111 S. Ct. at 1527, 113 L. Ed. 2d at 633.

210. *Carnival Cruise Lines* was an admiralty case, in which federal law controlled the enforceability of the forum selection clause. *See id.* at 589, 111 S. Ct. at 1525, 113 L. Ed. 2d at 630-31. In Schaff v. Sun Line Cruises, Inc., 999 F. Supp. 924 (S.D. Tex. 1998), the court invalidated a forum selection clause in a cruise ticket. The court distinguished *Carnival Cruise Lines* on the grounds that the ticket in *Schaff* required litigation in a foreign country, the ticket was nonrefundable, and the plaintiff did not have an adequate option to reject the contract.

211. In 1992, Congress overruled *Carnival Cruise Lines* on its facts by amending 46 U.S.C. app. § 183c (which is now codified at 46 U.S.C. §30509(a) after Title 46 was enacted into positive law). *See* Oceans Act of 1992, Pub. L. No. 102-587, § 3006, 106 Stat. 5039, 5068 (making it "unlawful" for any operator of a vessel transporting passengers between ports of the United States or between ports of the United States and foreign ports to insert "any provision or limitation" into a transportation agreement "purporting . . . to lessen, weaken, or avoid the right of any claimant to a trial by *any* court of competent jurisdiction on the question of liability for . . . loss or injury") (emphasis added). The legislative history indicated that it was "needed because of the Supreme Court ruling in *Carnival Cruise Lines* [and that] [t]he amendment . . . would overturn the result in *Carnival*." 138 CONG. REC. H11,785 (daily ed. Oct. 5, 1992) (statement of Rep. Studds). However, in 1993, Congress deleted the word "any." *See* Kurt A. Franklin & David A. Weldy, Note, *Dark of Night Legislation Takes Aim at Forum Selection Clauses: Statutory Revisions in Reaction to* Carnival Cruise Lines, Inc. v. Shute, 6 U.S.F. MAR. L.J. 259 (1994) (pointing out that the 1993 change restored the language to be identical that considered by the Court in *Carnival Cruise Lines* and thus making it appear that Congress intended to restore the law to its former state). Subsequently, that result has been confirmed. *See* Smith v. Doe, 991 F. Supp. 781, 782 (E.D. La. 1998) (so holding).

212. It was conceded in *Carnival Cruise Lines* that the plaintiffs had notice of the forum selection clause in the ticket. The Court's discussion of this point suggested that it might have been significant if the plaintiffs had no notice of the clause. *See Carnival*, 499 U.S. at 589-90, 111 S. Ct. at 1525-26, 113 L. Ed. 2d at 631. For a criticism of the Court's reasoning on the notice issue, see Patrick J. Borchers, *Forum Selection Agreements in the Federal Courts After* Carnival Cruise*: A Proposal for Congressional Reform*, 67 WASH. L. REV. 55, 75-77 (1992); *see also* Edward A. Purcell, Jr., *Geography as a Litigation Weapon: Consumers, Forum-Selection Clauses, and the Rehnquist Court*, 40 UCLA L. REV. 423 (1992); David H. Taylor, *The Forum Selection Clause: A Tale of Two Concepts*, 66 TEMPLE L. REV. 785 (1993). For a proposal for a federal statute to insure the enforcement in federal and state courts of forum selection clauses that select a foreign nation's forum, see Young Lee, Note, *Forum Selection Clauses: Problems of Enforcement in Diversity Cases and State Courts,* 35 COLUM. J. TRANSNAT'L L. 663 (1997).

213. Professor Richman has suggested that the reasoning of *Carnival Cruise* may be limited to situations where the drafter of the clause faces a threat of multiple litigation in many different fora, while also suggesting that this limit may not be significant, since many interstate and international commercial enterprises face such a threat. *See* William M. Richman, Carnival Cruise Lines: *Forum Selection Clauses in Adhesion Contracts*, 40 AM. J. COMP. L. 977, 983 (1992). Professor Richman argues that the remainder of the reasons given by the Court were

value of forum selection clauses generally, has also been well defended. "A healthy but not blind deference to forum selection clauses can serve the values of enhancing the parties' contractual expectations, reducing litigation over jurisdictional issues, and of respecting procedural due-process protections."[214] In addition, one feature of *Carnival Cruise Lines*, not mentioned by the Court, deserves emphasis. The contract in which the forum selection clause appeared was a contract for a luxury, not a contract for a necessity. This aspect of the case may impose an important limitation on the future application of the *Carnival Cruise Lines* principles.[215]

SECTION D. FORUM NON CONVENIENS AND CHANGE OF VENUE

Even if the plaintiff commences a civil action in a court of proper venue, conducting the action elsewhere may be desirable. A more desirable venue may be in (1) another court within the judicial system in which the plaintiff originally commenced the action or (2) a court in a different judicial system. When the more desirable venue is within the same judicial system, statutes often provide for transfer to that venue. The basis for such a transfer is usually for the convenience

---

flawed. *See id.* 983-84. Professor Borchers argues that the reasons given by the Court amount to no real limitation on enforcement of forum selection clauses and agrees with Professor Richman that the multiple suits threat is something suffered by every large enterprise. *See* Patrick J. Borchers, *Forum Selection Agreements in the Federal Courts After* Carnival Cruise*: A Proposal for Congressional Reform*, 67 WASH. L. REV. 55, 74 (1992).

214. Michael E. Solimine, *Forum-Selection Clauses and the Privatization of Procedure*, 25 CORNELL INT'L L.J. 51, 101 (1992); *see id.* at 81-85, for a defense of the result in *Carnival Cruise Lines*.

215. *See also* Publicis Commc'n v. True N. Commc'ns, Inc., 132 F.3d 363 (7th Cir. 1997) (compulsory counterclaim should not be entertained in violation of a forum selection clause). In Marra v. Papandreou, 216 F.3d 1119 (D.C. Cir. 2000), the Greek Ministry of Tourism awarded to a consortium a license to operate a casino in Greece. The license contained a forum selection clause requiring all disputes arising from its application, interpretation, or performance to be litigated in Greek courts. Subsequently, the Ministry of Tourism revoked the license, and Marra, one member of the consortium, commenced an action in the U.S. District Court for the District of Columbia for breach of contract. The district court found the forum selection clause enforceable, and the court of appeals affirmed. The plaintiff argued that the defendant should not be able to repudiate the contract and at the same time rely on the forum selection clause, which was a part of the contract. However, the court of appeals held that while the repudiation of the contract relieved the plaintiff of carrying out the obligations to the defendant, it did not preclude enforcement of the clause. Otherwise, such clauses would have little value, because one party or the other to a contract can often plausibly assert that the other party's nonperformance constitutes a repudiation that would preclude reliance on the clause. *See also* J. Brian Beckham, *Forum Selection Clauses in Clickwrap Agreements,* 14 U. BALT. INTELL. PROP. L.J. 151 (2006); Paul Hartman Cross & Hubert Oxford, IV, *"Floating" Forum Selection and Choice of Law Clauses,* 48 S. TEX. L. REV. 125 (2006) (discussing forum selection and choice-of-law clauses that allow selection of the forum by one of the contracting parties after a controversy arises under the contract, rather than designating a single forum ahead of time within which an action may be brought); J. Zachary Courson, Yavuz v. 61 MM, Ltd.*: A New Federal Standard—Applying Contracting Parties' Choice of Law to the Analysis of Forum Selection Agreements,* 85 DENV. U. L. REV. 597 (2008); Axel Gehringer, *After* Carnival Cruise *and* Sky Reefer*: An Analysis of Forum Selection Clauses in Maritime and Aviation Transactions,* 66 J. AIR L. & COM. 633 (2001); David Marcus, *The Perils of Contract Procedure: A Revised History of Forum Selection Clauses in the Federal Courts,* 82 TUL. L. REV. 973 (2008); Kendra Johnson Panek, *Forum Selection Clauses in Diversity Actions,* 36 J. MARSHALL L. REV. 941 (2003); Daniel Tan, *Damages for Breach of Forum Selection Clauses, Principled Remedies, and Control of International Litigation,* 40 TEX. INT'L L.J. 623 (2005); Jason Webb Yackee, *Choice of Law Considerations in the Validity & Enforcement of International Forum Selection Agreements: Whose Law Applies?,* 9 UCLA J. INT'L L. & FOREIGN AFF. 43 (2004). The effect of forum selection clauses in cases in which a transfer of venue is sought from one federal court to another under 28 U.S.C. § 1404(a) is discussed in section D(2)*(a) infra*. In Ameritas Investment Corp. v. McKinney, 269 Neb. 564, 694 N.W.2d 191 (2005), the Nebraska Supreme Court held that a choice-of-forum clause was valid under the Model Choice of Forum Act. Although, in the absence of the clause, the state could not constitutionally exercise personal jurisdiction over the defendant, the enforcement of the clause would not result in serious inconvenience to the defendant in violation of the Act.

of the parties and witnesses or for the interests of justice.[216] Traditionally, if the more desirable venue is in a court of a different judicial system, transfer has not been possible. Instead, a common-law[217] doctrine known as forum non conveniens allows a court to dismiss an action in its discretion when a court in another judicial system would provide a more appropriate forum.[218] After dismissal under the doctrine of forum non conveniens, the plaintiff commences a new action in the courts of the more convenient judicial system.

As applied to American courts, this structure produces varying results: (1) statutes or common-law rules often authorize a state court to transfer a case to another court in the same state where the action can be more conveniently conducted;[219] (2) state courts using the doctrine of forum non conveniens will dismiss an action when it can be conducted in a substantially more convenient court in another state or a foreign country; (3) federal statutes authorize the federal courts to transfer actions to other federal courts where they might have been brought for the convenience of parties and witnesses and in the interests of justice; and (4) the federal courts dismiss actions under the doctrine of forum non conveniens when the action can be conducted in a substantially more convenient court in a foreign country.

---

216. *See, e.g.*, NEB. REV. STAT. § 25-410 (2008).

217. *But see In re* Ensco Offshore Int'l Co., 311 S.W.3d 921 (Tex. 2010) (Texas statute spelling out factors to take into account in determining whether forum non conveniens dismissal proper).

218. For an argument that properly conducted personal jurisdiction and choice of law inquiries eliminate the need for forum non conveniens doctrine, see Margaret G. Stewart, *Forum Non Conveniens: A Doctrine in Search of a Role*, 74 CAL. L. REV. 1259 (1986). For an argument that the doctrine of forum non conveniens provides a mechanism for courts to reach desirable forum selection results without distorting the doctrine of personal jurisdiction, see Alex Wilson Albright, *In Personam Jurisdiction: A Confused and Inappropriate Substitute for Forum Non Conveniens*, 71 TEX. L. REV. 351 (1992).

219. *See Ex parte* Price, 47 So. 3d 1221 (Ala. 2010) (Alabama forum non conveniens statute did not permit transfer to another county because substantial part of events giving rise to claim occurred in county where action filed); State *ex rel.* Riffle v. Ranson, 195 W. Va. 121, 464 S.E.2d 763 (1995) (transfer statute is exclusive authority for intrastate transfers). *But see* First Am. Bank v. Guerine, 198 Ill. 2d 511, 764 N.E.2d 54 (2002) (holding that intrastate forum non conveniens transfer is appropriate only when the litigation has no practical connection with the plaintiff's chosen forum; in the case before the court, it held the trial court abused its discretion in granting an intrastate forum non conveniens transfer when the potential trial witnesses were scattered among several counties, including the plaintiff's chosen forum, and no single county enjoyed a predominant connection to the litigation); Peile v. Skelgas, Inc., 163 Ill. 2d 323, 645 N.E.2d 184 (1994) (recognizing common-law doctrine of intrastate forum non conveniens); Stevens v. Blevins, 1995 OK 6, 890 P.2d 936. In Beaven v. McAnulty, 980 S.W.2d 284 (Ky. 1998), the Kentucky Supreme Court reviewed a case in which the trial court had transferred an action to a court in another county under the common-law doctrine of forum non conveniens. Although the court recognized that Oklahoma and Illinois had adopted an intrastate forum non conveniens doctrine, it held that the power to transfer must be conferred by statute. Forum non conveniens, in contrast, only permits courts to dismiss or stay an action. However, the court did not hold that forum non conveniens only applies when the alternative forum is in another state or in a foreign country, leaving open the possibility that an intrastate case might be dismissed or stayed under the doctrine in an appropriate situation; *cf. Ex parte* Miller, Hamilton, Snider & Odom, LLC, 978 So. 2d 12 (Ala. 2007) (intrastate forum non conveniens transfer inapplicable to suit commenced in improper venue and transferred to proper venue); Vulcan Materials Co. v. Alabama Ins. Guar. Ass'n, 985 So. 2d 376 (2007) (dismissal under Alabama forum non conveniens statute of declaratory judgment action in preference to California forum where declaratory judgment action involving identical issues was pending); Malsch v. Bell Helicopter Textron, Inc., 916 So. 2d 600 (Ala. 2005) (plaintiffs sued Bell in Alabama for injuries received in helicopter crash in California; Alabama Supreme Court affirmed dismissal of plaintiff's action under Alabama forum non conveniens statute because a California forum was available to them; California trial court had decided statute of limitations issue in favor of plaintiffs, and Alabama Supreme Court rejected their argument that a California appellate court could reverse that decision, thus leaving them without an alternative forum); Langenhorst v. Norfolk So. Ry. Co., 219 Ill. 2d 430, 848 N.E. 2d 927 (2006) (defendant's motion for intrastate transfer under state doctrine of forum non conveniens denied because defendants did not meet their burden of proof); Jill E. Adams, Dawdy *and the Future of Intrastate Forum Non Conveniens in Illinois,* 92 ILL. B.J. 246 (2004).

When an action is commenced in an improper venue, statutes in both state and federal courts authorize dismissal or transfer to a proper venue within the respective systems. State courts may not transfer cases to federal courts. Federal courts may not transfer cases to state courts. Traditionally, state courts could not transfer cases to the courts of other states. However, the Uniform Transfer of Litigation Act, proposed by the National Conference of Commissioners on Uniform State Laws, will allow adopting states to transfer litigation to courts in other states instead of dismissing them under the doctrine of forum non conveniens.

The following subsections discuss the forum non conveniens doctrine and transfer of venue. The first subsection discusses the forum non conveniens doctrine as it operates in both state and federal courts. In addition, it discusses the Uniform Transfer of Litigation Act. Although this legislation would authorize transfer between the courts of different states, it is properly discussed in conjunction with the doctrine of forum non conveniens because it would replace that doctrine in the state courts when the more convenient forum is a court of another state. The second subsection then discusses transfer of venue in the federal courts.

1. Forum Non Conveniens and the Uniform Transfer of Litigation Act

(a) Forum Non Conveniens

In general, the defendant may invoke the doctrine of forum non conveniens when the action in question has little or no connection with the place where the plaintiff has commenced the action.[220] Under such circumstances, the burden on the

---

220. The historical pedigree of the doctrine of forum non conveniens is the subject of scholarly dispute. The original American treatment of the doctrine is Paxton Blair, *The Doctrine of Forum Non Conveniens in Anglo-American Law*, 29 COLUM. L. REV. 1, 2 (1929). Blair's historical view generally accords with Robert Braucher, *The Inconvenient Federal Forum*, 60 HARV. L. REV. 908, 909-18, 920-21 (1947). The Paxton-Braucher view is disputed in David W. Robertson & Paula K. Speck, *Access to State Courts in Transnational Personal Injury Cases: Forum Non Conveniens and Antisuit Injunctions*, 68 TEX. L. REV. 937, 948 n.68 (1990); Allan R. Stein, *Forum Non Conveniens and the Redundancy of Court-Access Doctrine*, 133 U. PA. L. REV. 781, 796-99 (1985); *see also* Ann Alexander, *Forum Non Conveniens in the Absence of an Alternative Forum*, 86 COLUM. L. REV. 1000, 1001-02 (1986); E.E. Daschbach, *Where There's a Will, There's a Way: The Cause for a Cure and Remedial Prescriptions for Forum Non Conveniens as Applied in Latin American Plaintiffs' Actions Against U.S. Multinationals*, 13 L. & Bus. Rev. Am. 11 (2007); John P. Dobrovich, *Dismissal Under Forum Non Conveniens: Should the Availability Requirement be a Threshold Issue When Applied to Nonessential Defendants*, 12 WIDENER L. REV. 561 (2006); David W. Feder, *The Forum Non Conveniens Dismissal in the Absence of Subject-Matter Jurisdiction*, 74 FORD. L. REV. 3147 (2006); Dante Figueroa, *Conflicts of Jurisdiction Between the United States and Latin America in the Context of Forum Non Conveniens Dismissals*, 37 U. MIAMI INTER-AM. L. REV. 119 (2005); Walter W. Heiser, *Forum Non Conveniens and Choice of Law: The Impact of Applying Foreign Law in Transnational Tort Actions*, 51 WAYNE L. REV. 1161 (2005); Elizabeth T. Lear, *National Interests, Foreign Injuries, and Federal Forum Non Conveniens*, 41 U.C. DAVIS L.REV. 559 (2007); Elizabeth T. Lear, *Congress, the Federal Courts, and Forum Non Conveniens: Friction on the Frontier of the Inherent Power*, 91 IOWA L. REV. 1147 (2006); Helen E. Mardirosian, Note, *Developments in the Law: Federal Jurisdiction and Forum Selection: Forum Non Conveniens*, 37 LOY. L.A. L. REV. 1643 (2004); Allan I. Mendelsohn, *International Litigation: The U.S. Jurisdiction to Prescribe and the Doctrine of Forum Non Conveniens*, 73 J. AIR L. & COM. 17 (2008); Jeffrey A. Van Detta, *The Irony of Instrumentalism: Using Dworkin's Principle-Rule Distinction to Reconceptualize Metaphorically A Substance-Procedure Dissonance Exemplified by Forum Non Conveniens Dismissals in International Product Injury Cases*, 87 MARQ. L. REV. 425 (2004); Russell J. Weintraub, *International Litigation and Forum Non Conveniens*, 29 TEX. INT'L L.J. 321 (1994); Christopher A. Whytock & Cassandra Burke Robertson, *Forum Non Conveniens and the Enforcement of Foreign Judgments*, 111 COLUM. L. REV. 1444 (2011); Symposium, *Forum Non Conveniens: Development and Issues over the Past Seven Years*, 35 U. MIAMI INTER-AM. L. REV. 1 (2003); Note, *Cross-Jurisdictional Forum Non Conveniens Preclusion*, 121 HARV. L. REV. 2178 (2008) (discussing the preclusive effect that a dismissal on forum non conveniens grounds in one court should have on

judicial system in which the plaintiff originally commenced the action and the inconvenience to the parties and witnesses of the trial in that system may dictate that the action be dismissed and tried elsewhere.

Forum non conveniens is a discretionary doctrine.[221] In exercising this discretion, courts consider several factors. These factors focus on the convenience of the parties and the public interest in having the action tried elsewhere. In *Gulf Oil Corp. v. Gilbert*,[222] the U.S. Supreme Court summarized these factors. The Court first addressed the private interests of the litigants:

> An interest to be considered, and the one likely to be most pressed, is the private interest of the litigant. Important considerations are the relative ease of access to sources of proof; availability of compulsory process for attendance of unwilling, and the cost of obtaining attendance of willing, witnesses; possibility of view of premises, if view would be appropriate to the action; and all other practical problems that make trial of a case easy, expeditious and inexpensive. There may also be questions as to the enforceability of a judgment if one is obtained. The court will weigh relative advantages and obstacles to fair trial. It is often said that the plaintiff may not, by choice of an inconvenient forum, "vex," "harass," or "oppress" the defendant by inflicting upon him expense or trouble not necessary to his own right to pursue his remedy. But unless the balance is strongly in favor of the defendant, the plaintiff's choice of forum should rarely be disturbed.[223]

The Supreme Court then addressed the factors relating to the public interest:

> Factors of public interest also have [a] place in applying the doctrine. Administrative difficulties follow for courts when litigation is piled up in congested centers instead of being handled at its origin. Jury duty is a burden that ought not to be imposed upon the people of a community which has no relation to the litigation. In cases which touch the affairs of many persons, there is reason for holding the trial in their view and reach rather than in remote parts of the country where they can learn of it by report only. There is a local interest in having localized controversies decided at home. There is an appropriateness, too, in having the trial of a diversity case in a forum that is at home with the state law that must govern the case, rather than having a court in some other forum untangle problems in conflict of laws, and in law foreign to itself.[224]

---

an action in another forum).

221. *See* David W. Robertson, *The Federal Doctrine of Forum Non Conveniens: "An Object Lesson in Uncontrolled Discretion,"* 29 TEX. INT'L L.J. 353 (1994).

222. 330 U.S. 501, 67 S. Ct. 839, 91 L. Ed. 1055 (1947).

223. *Id.* at 508, 67 S. Ct. at 843, 91 L. Ed. at 1062 (footnote omitted).

224. *Id.* at 508-09, 67 S. Ct. at 843, 91 L. Ed. at 1062-63; *see also* State *ex rel.* Wyeth v. Grady, 262 S.W.3d 216 (Mo. 2008) (although many of the factors in the forum non conveniens test pointed to a lack of relationship between Missouri and the litigation, the court held that the trial court had not "[u]nder the special circumstances of this case" abused its discretion in refusing dismissal; the relevant factors were not found to weigh

In evaluating the private interest factors described in *Gulf Oil Corp. v. Gilbert*, the courts usually give the plaintiff's interest great weight.[225] However, in *Piper Aircraft Co. v. Reyno*,[226] the U.S. Supreme Court held that a distinction should be drawn between plaintiffs who have chosen their home forums and foreign plaintiffs. When a plaintiff chooses a home forum, it is reasonable to assume the choice is convenient. Thus, the courts should give the plaintiff's choice deference unless the balance of convenience is heavily in favor of the alternative forum. On the other hand, when the plaintiff is foreign, it is much less reasonable to assume that the plaintiff has chosen a convenient forum. In such circumstances, the courts may give the plaintiff's choice less weight in the balancing process.[227]

---

heavily in favor of dismissal and the defendants failed to show that keeping the cases in Missouri would be oppressive or impose an undue burden on Missouri courts); Kedy v. A.W. Chesterton Co., 946 A.2d 1171 (R.I. 2008) (in suit by Canadian citizens alleging claims for personal injury and wrongful death, Rhode Island holds doctrine of forum non conveniens, previously applied only in child-custody cases, generally applicable in state and court holds that private and public interest factors call for dismissal on facts of case); Peterson v. Feldmann, 2010 SD 53, 784 N.W.2d 493 (circuit court correctly dismissed on grounds of forum non conveniens where private interests factors weighed in favor of dismissal, even though public interest factors did not heavily favor either forum or alternative forum).

225. *See, e.g.*, Duha v. Agrium, Inc., 448 F.3d 867 (6th Cir. 2006) (U.S. citizen sued former employer based on employment in foreign country; district court erred in failing to apply proper deference to plaintiff's choice of forum in its weighing of the private interest factors of the forum non conveniens test); SME Racks, Inc. v. Sistemas Mecanicos para Electronica, S.A., 382 F.3d 1097 (11th Cir. 2004) (domestic plaintiff; district court abused discretion by failing to apply strong presumption in favor of plaintiff's choice of forum in forum non conveniens analysis); Baypack Fisheries, L.L.C. v. Nelbro Packing Co., 992 P.2d 1116 (Alaska 1999) (plaintiff's choice of forum should rarely be disturbed on grounds of forum non conveniens unless balance of private and public interest factors weighs strongly in favor of dismissal); *see also* Emily J. Derr, *Striking a Better Public-Private Balance in Forum Non Conveniens*, 93 CORNELL L. REV. 819 (2008).

226. 454 U.S. 235, 102 S. Ct. 252, 70 L. Ed. 2d 419 (1981); *see also* Yavuz v. 61 MM, Ltd., 576 F.3d 1166 (10th Cir. 2009) (foreign plaintiff's choice of forum deserves less deference); Quixtar, Inc. v. Signature Mgmt. Team, LLC, 315 S.W.3d 28 (Tex. 2010) (nonresident plaintiff's forum choice receives substantially less deference); *cf.* Abad v. Bayer Corp., 563 F.3d 663 (7th Cir. 2009) (when forum non conveniens dismissal would send plaintiffs to their home court, presumption in favor of plaintiff's choice of forum is little more than a tie breaker). For an excellent discussion of the forum non conveniens analysis in *Piper Aircraft* and its development over the decade following the decision, see William L. Reynolds, *The Proper Forum for a Suit: Transnational Forum Non Conveniens and Counter-Suit Injunctions in the Federal Courts*, 70 TEX. L. REV. 1663 (1992); *see also* Richard D. Freer, *Refracting Domestic and Global Choice-of-Forum Doctrine Through the Lens of a Single Case*, 2007 B.Y.U. L. REV. 959 (discussing *Piper Aircraft*); Don G. Rushing & Ellen Nudelman Adler, *Some Inconvenient Truths About Forum Non Conveniens Law in International Aviation Disasters*, 74 J. AIR L. & COM. 403 (2009).

227. *See* 454 U.S. at 255-56, 102 S. Ct. at 266, 70 L. Ed. 2d at 436; *see also* Pollux Holding Ltd. v. Chase Manhattan Bank, 329 F.3d 64 (2d Cir. 2003) (Liberian corporations' decision to sue in the United States was not due the same degree of deference for forum non conveniens purposes as such a decision by a United States citizen suing in his or her home forum, even though plaintiff sued defendant in defendant's home district); Radeljak v. Daimlerchrysler Corp., 475 Mich. 598, 719 N.W.2d 40 (2006) (trial court correctly dismissed action in favor of forum in foreign country where none of public or private interests factors pointed to Michigan as more convenient than foreign forum; trial court correctly afforded less deference to a foreign plaintiff's choice of forum than to a domestic plaintiff's choice); 3M Co. v. Johnson, 926 So. 2d 860 (Miss. 2006) (doctrine of forum non conveniens required dismissal of out-of-state plaintiffs whose claims arose outside state and as to which evidence was located outside the state and not subject to state court's compulsory subpoena power); *cf.* Adelson v. Hananel, 510 F.3d 43 (1st Cir. 2007) (district court correctly recognized strong presumption in favor of American plaintiff's choice of forum, but then erroneously ignored that presumption on grounds that parallel litigation was pending in Israel, even though court found American litigation not vexatious); Rothluebbers v. Obee, 2003 SD 95, 668 N.W.2d 313 (presumption in favor of the plaintiff's choice of forum applies with less force when the plaintiff or parties are foreign, but public and private interest factors did not weigh in favor of Germany as forum in action based on accident in South Dakota). Not all courts give plaintiffs' choice less weight when the plaintiffs are foreign nationals. *See, e.g.*, Ison v. E.I. DuPont de Nemours & Co., 729 A.2d 832 (Del. Super. 1999) (fact that plaintiffs are foreign nationals does not deprive them of the presumption that their choice of forum should be respected). *But see* Tazoe v. Airbus S.A.S., 631 F.3d 1321 (11th Cir. 2011) (dismissal of American citizens action on grounds of forum non conveniens was correct when other factors weighed in favor of dismissal). *See generally* Martin Davies, *Time to Change the Federal Forum Non Conveniens Analysis*, 77 TUL. L. REV. 309 (2002); Douglas W. Dunham & Eric F. Gladbach, *Forum Non Conveniens and Foreign Plaintiffs in the 1990s*, 24 BROOK. J. INT'L L. 665 (1999); Lonny Sheinkopf Hoffman & Keith A. Rowley, *Forum Non Conveniens in Federal Statutory Cases*, 49 EMORY L.J. 1137 (2000); Anne McGinness Kearse, *Forfeiting the Home-Court Advantage: The Federal Doctrine*

Illustration 4-39. *P*, a citizen of Scotland, is the administrator of the estate of *A*, also a citizen of Scotland. *A* died in an aircraft crash in Scotland. *P* sues *D Corp.*, a corporation incorporated and with its principal place of business in State *X* of the United States, in a U.S. District Court for the District of State *X*. *P* seeks $1,000,000 in damages for the wrongful death of *A*. *D* Corp. is the manufacturer of the aircraft in which *A* was a passenger at the time of the crash. If *D Corp.* moves for dismissal on grounds of forum non conveniens, *P's* choice of forum is due less deference that it would be if *P* had chosen *P's* home forum.

* * * * *

The doctrine of forum non conveniens presupposes that the plaintiff can bring the action in another forum.[228] The courts often condition a forum non conveniens dismissal on the defendant submitting to personal jurisdiction in the alternative forum or waiving other obstacles to suit there, such as the statute of limitations.[229] Dismissing an action on the ground of forum non conveniens would be unfair to the plaintiff if no other forum existed in which the defendant could be sued.[230] However, this "adequate alternative forum" doctrine is complex and can involve a variety of inquiries. For example, in *Figueiredo Ferraz E Engenharia de Projeto Ltda. v. Republic of Peru*,[231] the plaintiff, a Brazilian corporation, brought suit in the Southern District of New York, seeking to enforce a foreign arbitration award. As part of its action, the plaintiff ultimately sought to attach assets of the defendant in New York. When the defendant moved to dismiss on grounds of forum

---

of Forum Non Conveniens, 49 S.C. L. REV. 1303 (1998); Allan I. Mendelsohn & Renee Lieux, *The Warsaw Convention Article 28, The Doctrine of Forum Non Conveniens, and the Foreign Plaintiff*, 68 J. AIR L. & COM. 75 (2003); Emma Suarez Pawlicki, Comment, Stangvik v. Shiley *and Forum Non Conveniens Analysis: Does a Fear of Too Much Justice Really Close California Courtrooms to Foreign Plaintiffs?*, 13 TRANSNAT'L LAW. 175 (2000); Daniel J. Dorward, Comment, *The Forum Non Conveniens Doctrine and the Judicial Protection of Multinational Corporations from Forum Shopping Plaintiffs*, 19 U. PA. J. INT'L ECON. L. 141 (1998); Charles Eric Ruhr, Comment, *Forum Non Conveniens: A Review of Its Application in Past and Recent Cases*, 6 TULSA J. COMP. INT'L L. 247 (1999); Recent Case, *Civil Procedure – Forum Non Conveniens – Fifth Circuit Holds Mexico to Be an Adequate Alternative Forum Despite Its $2500 Cap on Damages for a Child's Death.* – Gonzalez v. Chrysler Corp., *301 F.3d 377 (5th Cir. 2002)*, Petition for Cert. Filed, *71 U.S.L.W. 3489 (U.S. Jan. 7, 2003) (No. 02-1044)*, 116 HARV. L. REV. 1905 (2003).

228. *See* Vicknair v. Phelps Dodge Indus., Inc., 2009 ND 113, 767 N.W.2d 171 (alternative forum is a necessity for forum non conveniens analysis and does not exist when statute of limitations has run in potential alternative forum); Walter W. Heiser, *Forum Non Conveniens and Retaliatory Legislation: The Impact on the Available Alternative Forum Inquiry and on the Desirability of Forum Non Conveniens as a Defense Tactic*, 56 U. KAN. L. REV. 609 (2008); Note, *Requirement of a Second Forum for Application of Forum Non Conveniens*, 43 MINN. L. REV. 1199 (1959). *But see* Ann Alexander, *Forum Non Conveniens in the Absence of an Alternative Forum*, 86 COLUM. L. REV. 1000 (1986) (arguing for dismissal on forum non conveniens grounds in the absence of an alternative forum in some circumstances).

229. *See, e.g.*, Vasquez v. Bridgestone/Firestone, Inc., 325 F.3d 665 (5th Cir. 2003) (it is error for a district court to dismiss on grounds of forum non conveniens without including within its order a "return jurisdiction" clause that allows the plaintiff to return to the dismissing court if the defendant refuses to submit to the jurisdiction of the foreign court); Mace v. Mylan Pharm., Inc., 227 W. Va. 666, 714 S.E.2d 223 (2011); Abbott v. Owens-Corning Fiberglas Corp., 191 W. Va. 198, 444 S.E.2d 285 (1994); John Bies, Comment, *Conditioning Forum Non Conveniens*, 67 U. CHI. L. REV. 489 (2000); *see also* Virginia A. Fitt, *The Tragedy of Comity: Questioning the American Treatment of Inadequate Foreign Courts*, 50 VA. J. INT'L L. 1021 (2010); Finity E. Jernigan, *Forum Non Conveniens: Whose Convenience and Justice?*, 86 TEX. L. REV. 1079 (2008); Julius Jurianto, *Forum Non Conveniens: Another Look at Conditional Dismissals*, 83 U. DET. MERCY L. REV. 369 (2006); Joel H. Samuels, *When Is an Alternative Forum Available? Rethinking the Forum Non Conveniens Analysis*, 85 IND. L.J. 1059 (2010); Christopher M. Marlowe, Comment, *Forum Non Conveniens Dismissals and the Adequate Alternative Forum Question: Latin America*, 32 U. MIAMI INTER-AM. L. REV. 295 (2001).

230. *See, e.g.*, William L. Reynolds, *The Proper Forum for a Suit: Transnational Forum Non Conveniens and Counter-Suit Injunctions in the Federal Courts*, 70 TEX. L. REV. 1663, 1666 (1992). *But cf.* Vulcan Materials Co. v. Alabama Ins. Guar. Ass'n, 985 So. 2d 376 (Ala. 2007) (California was an available alternative forum despite the fact that personal jurisdiction did not exist there over one defendant).

231. 665 F.3d 384 (2d Cir. 2011).

non conveniens, the plaintiff argued that an alternative forum in a foreign country would be inadequate, because only a court in New York could order attachment of assets located in NewYork. The district court refused to dismiss, but the Second Circuit Court of Appeals reversed. On the attachment issue, the court of appeals held that a forum was adequate if the defendant is subject to personal jurisdiction there and the forum permits litigation of the subject matter of the dispute. When the suit ultimately seeks execution on the defendant's assets, the question of adequacy depends on whether there are some assets of the defendant in the forum, not whether the particular assets located in the United States can be executed on in the alternative forum.

When a court dismisses an action on the ground of forum non conveniens and the plaintiff recommences the action in a new forum, the substantive law applied to resolve the dispute will often change. The courts of the new forum will apply their own conflict-of-laws rules to select the applicable law. A defendant will seldom move for a forum non conveniens dismissal if the dismissal will result in a disadvantageous substantive law being applied to the defendant. Thus, any change in applicable substantive law will usually be to the plaintiff's disadvantage. In fact, a plaintiff's initial choice of forum often will be motivated by an advantage in the substantive law that will be applied to the action.

Under the federal doctrine of forum non conveniens, a change in the applicable substantive law will not ordinarily affect the court's decision whether to dismiss the action. In *Piper Aircraft Co. v. Reyno*,[232] discussed above, the U.S. Supreme Court held that the possibility of an unfavorable change in the substantive law applicable to the plaintiff's claim "should ordinarily not be given conclusive or even substantial weight in the forum non conveniens inquiry."[233] However, the Court left open the possibility that a change in law that would deprive the plaintiff of a remedy altogether, rather than simply making it harder to win, could be given substantial weight.[234] The latter possibility is an aspect of the policy that a forum non conveniens dismissal is inappropriate unless an adequate alternative forum exists in which the action can be conducted.[235] However, this aspect of the alternative forum doctrine may simply be a disguised preference for applying the forum state's substantive law to resolve the dispute. There are good arguments both against and for this result. If the plaintiff's home nation would not provide the plaintiff with a remedy, the plaintiff should arguably be made to live with that result. On the other hand, the forum state's substantive law permitting recovery may

---

232. 454 U.S. 235, 102 S. Ct. 252, 70 L. Ed. 2d 419 (1981).

233. *See id.* at 247, 102 S. Ct. at 261, 70 L. Ed. 2d at 430 (italics deleted).

234. *See id.* at 254-55, 102 S. Ct. at 265, 70 L. Ed. 2d at 435.

235. *See id.* at 254 n.22, 102 S. Ct. at 265 n.22, 70 L. Ed. 2d at 435 n.22; William L. Reynolds, *The Proper Forum for a Suit: Transnational Forum Non Conveniens and Counter-Suit Injunctions in the Federal Courts*, 70 TEX. L. REV. 1663, 1670 (1992); *see also* Gutierrez v. Advanced Med. Optics, Inc., 640 F.3d 1025 (9th Cir. 2011) (intervening case in forum country that dismissed similar action for lack of jurisdiction warranted remand for reconsideration of forum non conveniens dismissal to determine whether alternative forum was still available); Parex Bank v. Russian Sav. Bank, 116 F. Supp. 2d 415 (S.D.N.Y. 2000) (refusing to dismiss in favor of a Russian forum when Russia would not consider the particular contract in question enforceable, stating that under such circumstances, a Russian court was not an adequate alternative forum); Joel H. Samuels, *When Is an Alternative Forum Available? Rethinking the Forum Non Conveniens Analysis*, 85 IND. L. J. 1059 (2010). In Leon v. Millon Air, Inc., 251 F.3d 1305 (11th Cir. 2001), the court held that, on a motion to dismiss based on forum non conveniens, the defendant has the burden of proving the adequacy of the foreign forum, but only after the plaintiff has substantiated allegations that the forum is inadequate.

be supported by policies that would be furthered if the defendant is held liable, even to an undeserving plaintiff.

Illustration 4-40. On the facts of *Illustration 4-39*, assume that if the action remained in a federal court of State *X*, the substantive law of State *X* would be applied to resolve the dispute under State *X* conflict-of-laws rules.[236] State *X* follows a strict liability theory in this kind of case. Thus, for *P* to recover, *P* would only have to prove that a defect in the aircraft caused the crash. *P* would not have to prove that the defect was the result of *D Corp.'s* negligence. If the action is dismissed on the ground of forum non conveniens in favor of a court in Scotland, the Scottish courts would apply Scottish substantive law to resolve the action. Scottish substantive law would require *P* to prove that the crash was the result of *D Corp.'s* negligence. Under *Piper Aircraft*, the federal court cannot refuse to dismiss the action on forum non conveniens grounds because the dismissal would result in an unfavorable change in law to the plaintiff. Furthermore, in evaluating whether to dismiss, the federal court may not even give substantial weight to the fact that a change in the applicable substantive law would occur if the action is dismissed.

Illustration 4-41. On the facts of *Illustration 4-39*, assume that the alternative forum is in a foreign country that does not recognize the action for wrongful death and would apply its own substantive law to the dispute. If the action remains in the federal court in State *X*, the federal court in State *X* would apply State *X* substantive law. State *X* recognizes the right to recover for wrongful death. Furthermore, State *X* would apply strict liability principles to the plaintiff's claim and allow recovery based on proof that a defect in the aircraft caused the crash. Under these circumstances, the federal court in State *X* may give substantial weight to the fact that the plaintiff would have no remedy at all if the action is dismissed. Based on this factor, the action should probably not be dismissed. It would not be unfair to the plaintiff to dismiss the action and leave the plaintiff without a remedy because the plaintiff's home nation would not provide a remedy. However, the policies of State *X's* strict liability rule may be furthered by holding the defendant liable. If State *X's* law is meant to deter manufacturers from producing and selling defective products, that policy will be furthered by holding the defendant liable. To the extent that State *X* manufacturers exercise greater care, the citizens of State *X*, as well as citizens of other states and nations, will benefit.[237]

* * * * *

If a legitimate preference for the application of the forum state's law is indeed the basis for part or all of the alternative forum doctrine, it would be desirable for the courts to recognize the preference openly as part of the forum non conveniens inquiry. However, in *Piper Aircraft*, the Supreme Court actually discouraged forum non conveniens analysis that involved complex choice-of-law inquiries. The Court stated that if the possibility of a change in law were given

---

236. As Chapter 5 discusses, the federal court in State *X* would be obligated, in this kind of case, to apply the conflict-of-laws rules of State *X* to select the substantive law that would be applied to the dispute.

237. *Cf.* Kamel v. Hill-Rom Co., 108 F.3d 799 (7th Cir. 1997) (permissible to dismiss on the ground of forum non conveniens if the alternative forum provides some remedies for plaintiff's loss, but not the complete range of remedies as the forum); Burke v. Quartey, 969 F. Supp. 921 (D.N.J. 1997) (burden on defendant to show that potential alternative fora permit recovery by plaintiff).

substantial weight in the inquiry, the trial court would have to make a comparative appraisal of the law that would be applied by the chosen forum and the alternative forum. It would also have to evaluate the rights, remedies, and procedures available in each forum. In the Court's view, "[t]he doctrine of forum non conveniens . . . is designed in part to help courts avoid conducting complex exercises in comparative law."[238]

Yet, despite the Court's discouragement of a choice-of-law analysis, such an analysis is inevitable. A choice-of-law inquiry is, by the Court's own admission, relevant to determine whether the plaintiff would be left with any remedy in the alternative forum if dismissal is granted. In addition, when evaluating the public interest factors of *Gulf Oil Corp. v. Gilbert*, it is relevant to inquire whether the chosen forum will have to apply foreign law if a dismissal is not granted and whether the foreign court will have to apply American law if a dismissal is granted.[239] This inquiry cannot be made without a choice-of-law analysis. Therefore, because choice-of-law analysis is an inevitable part of every forum non conveniens determination, the courts should make certain that preferences for the application of forum law are openly stated as part of their evaluative process.

In recent years, some foreign countries have enacted statutes denying their courts of subject-matter jurisdiction over any claim that has previously been the subject of an action in a foreign country that has been dismissed on grounds of forum non conveniens. At least one court in the United States has held that the adequate alternative forum doctrine is not satisfied when such a statute is applicable to the case.[240] The statutes in question are obviously designed to thwart foreign non conveniens dismissals in the United States, even where the balance of private and public interest factors heavily weighs in favor of dismissal, in order to give foreign plaintiffs access to United States' courts and United States' substantive law. Given that the forum non conveniens doctrine protects both defendants and courts in extreme cases from the unwarranted burdens of suit that would be imposed upon them by a suit in the state or federal courts of this country, it is questionable whether United States' courts should honor these foreign statutes.[241]

Forum non conveniens determinations are committed to the discretion of the trial court. Therefore, an appellate court should not reverse a decision to dismiss an action on forum non conveniens grounds unless the trial court has abused its discretion. This standard limits the appellate court to a review of whether the trial court's analysis of the forum non conveniens factors was reasonable. The appellate

---

238. 454 U.S. at 251, 102 S. Ct. at 263, 70 L. Ed. 2d at 433 (italics deleted).

239. *See* William L. Reynolds, *The Proper Forum for a Suit: Transnational Forum Non Conveniens and Counter-Suit Injunctions in the Federal Courts*, 70 TEX. L. REV. 1663, 1671, 1677-79 (1992); *see also* Sidney K. Smith, *Forum Non Conveniens and Foreign Policy: Time for Congressional Intervention?*, 90 TEX. L. REV. 743 (2012) (arguing for congressional preemption of state forum non conveniens doctrine in transnational cases).

240. *See* Paulownia Plantations de Pan. Corp. v. Rajamannan, 757 N.W.2d 903 (Minn. Ct. App. 2008) (reversing grant of forum non conveniens dismissal on the grounds that Panamanian statute deprived its courts of subject-matter jurisdiction and thus that there was no alternative forum). The Court of Appeals decision in *Paulownia* was reversed by the Minnesota Supreme Court on the ground that the Panamanian statute was inapplicable due to the fact that a Panamanian plaintiff was not involved in the action. *See* Paulownia Plantations de Panama Corp. v. Rajamannan, 793 N.W.2d 128 (Minn. 2009). *See also* Don G. Rushing & Ellen Nudelman Adler, *Some Inconvenient Truths About Foreign Non Conveniens Law in International Aviation Disasters*, 74 J. AIR. L. & COM. 403 (2009).

241. *See* ROBERT L. FELIX & RALPH U. WHITTEN, AMERICAN CONFLICTS LAW § 35, at 115-16 (6th ed. 2011).

court may not substitute its own judgment for that of the trial court by independently weighing each of the factors that are relevant to the analysis.[242]

In *Sinochem Int'l Co. Ltd. v. Malaysia Int'l Shipping Corp.*,[243] the Supreme Court held that a district court does not err in dismissing on grounds of forum non conveniens without first determining that it has subject-matter or personal jurisdiction. The question of subject-matter jurisdiction was difficult, presenting an issue of first impression. In addition, the question of personal jurisdiction would have involved burdensome discovery. In contrast, the forum non conveniens question was described by the Court as "a textbook case for immediate . . . dismissal."[244] (An action was pending abroad involving the same subject at the time the federal action was filed and the nub of the controversy was the arrest in admiralty of a foreign ship in foreign waters pursuant to the orders of a foreign court.)

(b) The Uniform Transfer of Litigation Act

Transfer of cases between different judicial systems has not been possible because no law has existed authorizing such transfers. However, in 1991, the National Conference of Commissioners on Uniform State Laws approved the Uniform Transfer of Litigation Act,[245] which would permit transfers between state courts in different states.[246] Nevertheless, to date, no state has adopted this Act. Thus, it appears unlikely that this Act will provide parties with a significant alternative to forum non conveniens dismissals.

2. Transfer of Venue Between Federal Courts

(a) Section 1404(a) Transfers

In the 1948 revision of the Judicial Code, Congress largely replaced the doctrine of forum non conveniens in the federal courts. Section 1404(a) originally provided for a change of venue "[f]or the convenience of parties and witnesses, in the interest of justice" to "any other district or division" where the action "might have been brought."[247] In *Hoffman v. Blaski*,[248] the Supreme Court held that the "where it might have been brought" language of the statute prevents transfer to a district where venue or personal jurisdiction would have been improper as an original matter. Thus, under *Hoffman*, if the defendant moved for a change of venue

---

242. *See Piper Aircraft*, 454 U.S. at 257-61, 102 S. Ct. at 266-68, 70 L. Ed. 2d at 436-38.

243. 549 U.S.422, 127 S. Ct. 1184, 167 L. Ed. 2d 15 (2007).

244. *Id.* at 435, 127 S. Ct. at 1194, 167 L. Ed. 2d at 26; *see also* Nathan Viavant, Recent Developments, Sinochem International Co. v. Malaysia International Shipping Corp.: *The United States Supreme Court Puts Forum Non Conveniens First*, 16 TUL. J. INT'L & COMP. L. 557 (2008).

245. 14 U.L.A. 661 (2005).

246. The specific provisions of this Uniform Act are discussed in prior editions of this book. *See, e.g.*, LARRY L. TEPLY & RALPH U. WHITTEN, CIVIL PROCEDURE 398-401 (4th ed. 2009).

247. *See* 28 U.S.C. § 1404(a). *See generally* Edmund Kitch, *Section 1404(a) of the Judicial Code: In the Interests of Justice or Injustice?*, 40 IND. L.J. 99 (1965); David E. Steinberg, *The Motion to Transfer and the Interests of Justice*, 66 NOTRE DAME L. REV. 443 (1990); Stowell R. Kelner, Note, *"Adrift on an Uncharted Sea": A Survey of Section 1404(a) Transfer in the Federal System*, 67 N.Y.U. L. REV. 612 (1992).

248. 363 U.S. 335, 80 S. Ct. 1084, 4 L. Ed. 2d 1254 (1960).

under § 1404(a) to a location where venue or personal jurisdiction would have been improper, the defendant could not be deemed to have "consented" to the transfer or "waived" the venue or personal jurisdiction objections. In essence, this holding treated the "where it might have been brought" language as if it were a subject-matter jurisdiction restriction.[249]

In the Federal Courts Jurisdiction and Venue Clarification Act of 2011,[250] effective in 2012, Congress overruled *Hoffman*. Section 1404(a) now reads, as follows:

> (a) For the convenience of the parties and witnesses, in the interests of justice, a district court may transfer any civil action to any other district or division where it might have been brought *or to any district or division to which all parties have consented*; . . .[251]

The amendment was made to allow transfers to districts in which venue and personal jurisdiction would not have been proper originally in those cases in which the district to which the action is transferred would be more convenient to the litigqants.[252] Note, however, that a transfer by consent can only be made if all the parties consent *and* the transferor district court finds the transfer to be for the convenience of the parties and witnesses and in the interests of justice.[253]

After the enactment of § 1404(a), transfer to another federal district court under the terms of this section is the appropriate mode of disposition in a case where the other federal district court is more suitable for the trial of the case. Thus, today, dismissal on forum non conveniens grounds is appropriate only in rare instances where the alternative forum is a state court or the court of a foreign country, both instances in which § 1404(a), by its terms, is inoperative.[254] Dismissal on forum non conveniens grounds in preference of a state court in another location will rarely be appropriate, considering that transfer to another federal court in the same location will usually be possible. As a practical matter, therefore, the federal

---

249. For a criticism of the result in *Hoffman* and a recommendation that transfers be permitted when the moving party could have sued the non-moving party in the transferee district, see Michael J. Waggoner, *Section 1404(a), "Where It Might Have Been Brought": Brought by Whom?*, 1988 B.Y.U. L. REV. 67.

250. Pub. L. No. 112-63, § 204, 125 Stat. 758, 764 (2011) (codified as 28 U.S.C. § 1404(a)).

251. *Id.* (emphasis added). In addition, the amendment added a restriction to 28 U.S.C. § 1404(d), which defines the term "district court" to include the district courts of Guam, the Northern Mariana Islands, and the district court for the Virgin Islands, as well as stating that the word "district" includes the territorial jurisdiction of such courts. The restriction appears at the beginning of the subsection, and the subsection now reads, in its entirety:

> Transfers from a district court of the United States to the District Court of Guam, the District Court for the Northern Mariana Islands, or the District Court of the Virgin Islands shall not be permitted under this section. As otherwise used in this section, the term "district court" includes the District Court of Guan, the District Court for the Northern Mariana Islands, and the District Court for the Virgin Islands, and the term "district" includes the territorial jurisdiction of each such court.

The courts in question are non-Article III territorial courts, and the amendment was designed to eliminate "possible constitutional doubts from arising" about transfers to such courts from Article III courts. *See* H.R. Rep. 112-10, at 15 (2011). Note, however, that the restriction does not affect the ability of the designated courts to transfer actions to Article III courts or to each other.

252. *See* H.R. Rep. 112-10, at 15 (2011).

253. *See id.*

254. 14D CHARLES A. WRIGHT ET AL., FEDERAL PRACTICE AND PROCEDURE: JURISDICTION AND RELATED MATTERS § 3828, at 620-23 (3d ed. 2007).

doctrine of forum non conveniens is limited to dismissal in favor of foreign nation tribunals.[255]

Transfer under § 1404(a) presents some complicated choice-of-law problems. In *Van Dusen v. Barrack*,[256] the Supreme Court held that after a transfer granted on the defendant's motion, the transferee district court must apply the same substantive law that the transferor district court would have applied under the transferor state's conflict-of-laws rules. In *Ferens v. John Deere Co.*,[257] the Court held that the same rule would be applied to a transfer granted on motion of the plaintiff. In *Ferens*, the Court also indicated in a dictum that the *Van Dusen* rule would be applied to transfers when (1) both the defendant and the plaintiff move for transfer; (2) a district court grants a transfer on its own initiative; (3) the plaintiff moves for transfer after the defendant removes an action from state to federal court; (4) only one of several plaintiffs moves for transfer; or (5) through no fault of the plaintiff, circumstances change, making a once desirable forum inconvenient.[258]

Illustration 4-42. *P*, a citizen of State *X*, is injured in State *X* when a machine manufactured by the *D Corp.* malfunctions. *D Corp.* is incorporated with its principal place of business in State *Y*. *P* waits too long to commence an action for damages in State *X*, and the statute of limitations runs. *P* commences an action for personal injuries against *D Corp.* in a U.S. District Court for the District of State *Z*, where the statute of limitations has not run. *D Corp.* does extensive business in State *Z* and is, therefore, subject to personal jurisdiction there under the doctrine of general jurisdiction examined in Chapter 3. Federal venue is also proper in State *Z* under 28 U.S.C. § 1391(b)(1) & (c)(2) because *D Corp.* is subject to personal jurisdiction in State *Z* and thus "resides" in the state. After commencing the action, *P* moves to transfer the case to the District of State *X* under § 1404(a). The district court in State *Z* grants the motion. After transfer, the district court in State *X* must apply the State *Z* statute of limitations and consider the action timely, assuming that under State *Z* conflict-of-laws rules the courts of State *Z* would consider their limitations period rather than that of State *X* to be applicable.

* * * * *

Van Dusen removed an incentive for defendants to use § 1404(a) to obtain a different applicable substantive law, rather than simply a more convenient forum. As *Illustration 4-42* demonstrates, however, under *Ferens*, the existence of § 1404(a) constitutes an incentive for a plaintiff to engage in interstate forum shopping for a federal court to obtain, first, a desirable substantive law, and, subsequently, a convenient place of trial. The *Ferens* result might be justified if it were based on important policies supporting the exercise of federal jurisdiction. In fact, both *Van Dusen* and *Ferens* purported to be based on such policies—the limits on the power of federal courts to make law in diversity cases. These policies will be discussed in Chapter 5. There, it will be demonstrated that *Van Dusen* articulated

---

255. *See* C.P. Jhong, Annotation, *Application of Common-Law Doctrine of Forum Non Conveniens in Federal Courts After Enactment of 28 USC § 1404(a) Authorizing Transfer to Another District*, 10 A.L.R. FED. 352 (1972).

256. 376 U.S. 612, 84 S. Ct. 805, 11 L. Ed. 2d 945 (1964).

257. 494 U.S. 516, 110 S. Ct. 1274, 108 L. Ed. 2d 443 (1990).

258. *See id.* at 529, 110 S. Ct. at 1283, 108 L. Ed. 2d at 456.

a rule correctly based on the policies limiting federal court lawmaking, but *Ferens* did not.[259]

The factors taken into account in determining whether to transfer a case under § 1404(a) are generally the same as are taken into account in determining whether a forum non conveniens dismissal is appropriate.[260] However, because transfer of an action is not as harsh on the plaintiff as dismissal under the doctrine of forum non conveniens, the discretion of the district courts to transfer under the statute is broader than the discretion to dismiss under the forum non conveniens doctrine.[261] In *Stewart Organization, Inc. v. Ricoh Corp.*,[262] the Supreme Court held that the existence of a forum selection clause would not absolutely control the question whether a case should be transferred under § 1404(a). Rather, a forum selection clause is simply one factor to be weighed in the balance to determine whether a transfer is appropriate.[263]

As discussed above, in *Van Dusen*, the Supreme Court held that the district court where the action is commenced should consider the effect of the law that will be applied after transfer on the convenience of the parties and witnesses.[264] Under the *Van Dusen* rule, the transferee district court must apply the law that the transferor district court would have applied. Thus, if the transferor court determines that it would apply the substantive law of the state in which it is sitting under that state's conflict-of-laws rules, the transferee district court will have to do likewise. If the laws of the transferor state involve complexities that will cause inconvenience

---

259. *See* Chapter 5(D)(2)*(b) infra* ("Special *Erie* Doctrine Problems in Cases of Transfer Under 28 U.S.C. § 1404(a)"); *see also* Phillip F. Cramer, Note, *Constructing Alternative Avenues of Jurisdictional Protection: Bypassing* Burnham's *Roadblock Via § 1404(a)*, 53 VAND. L. REV. 311 (2000). However, even if plaintiffs are able to obtain a choice-of-law advantage by selecting an inconvenient (though proper) forum in which to commence an action, there is empirical evidence that transfer counterbalances the forum shopping and diminishes the plaintiff's chances of winning the action. Thus, some or all of the burden of pretrial litigation over transfer motions may be outweighed by the diminution of inaccurate results that transfer produces. *See* Kevin M. Clermont & Theodore Eisenberg, *Exorcising the Evil of Forum-Shopping,* 80 CORNELL L. REV. 1507 (1995). For a defense of forum shopping in various forms, see Mary Garvey Algero, *In Defense of Forum Shopping: A Realistic Look at Selecting Venue*, 78 NEB. L. REV. 79 (1999).

260. *See, e.g., In re* Acer Am. Corp., 626 F.3d 1252 (Fed. Cir. 2010) (in determining convenience on motion to transfer, court applies public and private interest factors used in forum non conveniens analysis).

261. *See* Norwood v. Kirkpatrick, 349 U.S. 29, 32, 75 S. Ct. 544, 546-47, 99 L. Ed. 789, 793 (1955); *see also* Piper Aircraft Co. v. Reyno, 454 U.S. 235, 253, 258 n.26, 102 S. Ct. 252, 264-65, 267 n.26, 70 L. Ed. 2d 419, 434, 437 n.26 (1981); *In re* Volkswagen of Am., Inc., 506 F.3d 376 (5th Cir. 2007) (§ 1404(a) allows transfer based on lesser showing than dismissal on grounds of forum non conveniens; plaintiff's choice of forum is given less deference on a § 1404(a) transfer than on a forum non conveniens dismissal), *on rehearing en banc*, 545 F.3d 304 (5th Cir. 2008) (mandamus granted and transfer ordered); *see also In re* Volkswagen AG, 371 F.3d 201 (5th Cir. 2004) (nothing in § 1404(a) limits the application of the terms "parties" and "witnesses" to those involved in an original complaint; such terms contemplate consideration of the parties and witnesses in all claims and controversies properly joined in a proceeding); *cf. In re* Apple, Inc., 602 F.3d 909 (8th Cir. 2010) (because of lack of connection between parties, witnesses, and dispute with the forum, plaintiff's choice of forum was entitled to minimum weight). For a complete discussion of the cases applying the factors under § 1404(a), see 15 CHARLES A. WRIGHT ET AL., FEDERAL PRACTICE AND PROCEDURE: JURISDICTION AND RELATED MATTERS §§ 3847-3854 (3d ed. 2007).

262. 487 U.S. 22, 108 S. Ct. 2239, 101 L. Ed. 2d 22 (1988).

263. *See id.* at 29-30, 108 S. Ct. 2239, 2244, 101 L. Ed. 2d 22, 31 (1988); *see also* Tradecomet.com, LLC v. Google, Inc., 647 F.3d 472 (2d Cir. 2011) (district court is not required to enforce a forum selection clause only by transferring a case when the clause specifies that suit may be brought in an alternative federal forum; court may enforce clause through a motion to dismiss); Kerobo v. Southwestern Clean Fuels Corp., 285 F.3d 531 (6th Cir. 2002) (venue in removed action is controlled by removal statute and is proper in district and division embracing the place where the state action was pending; district court erred in dismissing a removed action for improper venue, notwithstanding a forum selection clause in the parties' agreement; whether forum selection clause should be enforced is a matter of contract, not an issue of proper venue; motion to transfer controlled by federal statute when action properly removed to federal court, notwithstanding forum selection clause).

264. *See Van Dusen*, 376 U.S. at 643-46, 84 S. Ct. at 823-24, 11 L. Ed. 2d at 965-67.

to the transferee court, then, under *Van Dusen*, that is one factor militating against transfer. Conversely, if the transferor district court determines that the conflict-of-laws rules of the transferor state require application of the transferee state's substantive law, no inconvenience would occur after transfer in administering the applicable substantive law. Even if inconvenience would result after transfer due to the applicable law, other factors bearing on the convenience of the parties and witnesses and the interests of justice may still justify the transfer.[265]

One other question that has arisen under § 1404(a) is whether the *Van Dusen-Ferens* rule governs in cases where federal law supplies the rule of decision. The issue arises because conflicts can exist among different federal circuits about the meaning and application of that law. Thus, if an action is commenced in a U.S. District Court with proper venue and personal jurisdiction and transferred to a district court in another circuit under § 1404(a), the issue would be whether the transferee district court should follow the view of its own circuit about the content of federal law or that of the transferor circuit, assuming that the two differ.[266]

As discussed in Chapter 5,[267] below, the *Van Dusen-Ferens* rule is based in part on the obligations of federal courts in diversity actions to follow state law under the *Erie* doctrine. The *Erie* doctrine has no application where federal substantive law governs the case. Rather, federal law is, in theory, uniform and supreme throughout the entire country. Although there may be temporary disagreement about the content of federal law among the circuits, there is, in theory, only one correct answer to the issue of its meaning. In contrast, under state law, the meaning of even identically worded statutes may permissibly differ from state to state. Thus, federal courts should attempt in every case to resolve issues of federal law as they should be resolved; although they may consider the decisions of other federal courts to be persuasive authority, they are not bound to follow them after a § 1404(a) transfer.[268] In addition, it is important to note that application of the transferor circuit's view of federal law would produce a different interpretation of

---

265. *Cf.* Houk v. Kimberly-Clark Corp., 613 F. Supp. 923 (W.D. Mo. 1985) (fact that forum will have to apply foreign law given little weight in determining whether to grant transfer where foreign law is uncomplicated); *see also In re* Hoffman-La Roche, Inc., 587 F.3d 1333 (Fed. Cir. 2009) (no connection between forum and litigation; plaintiff's attmpt to transfer litigation documents to district prior to filing should be disregarded as an attempt to manipulate venue).

266. *See, e.g.*, McMasters v. United States, 260 F.3d 814 (7th Cir. 2001) (transferee court not bound by erroneous conclusion of transferor court about proper interpretation of Federal Rule 4 concerning whether government had been properly served). For a discussion of this problem, *see, e.g.*, *In re* Korean Airlines Disaster, 829 F.2d 1171 (D.C. Cir. 1987) (Ginsburg, J.), *aff'd on other grounds sub nom.* Chan v. Korean Airlines, Ltd., 490 U.S. 122, 109 S. Ct. 1676, 104 L. Ed. 2d 113 (1989); Richard L. Marcus, *Conflicts Among Circuits and Transfers Within the Federal Judicial System*, 93 YALE L.J. 677, 721 (1984); Joan E. Schaffner, *Federal Circuit "Choice of Law": Erie Through the Looking Glass*, 81 IOWA L. REV. 1173 (1996); Joan Steinman, *Law of the Case: A Judicial Puzzle in Consolidated and Transferred Cases and in Multidistrict Litigation,* 135 U. PA. L. REV. 595, 662-706 (1987).

267. *See* Chapter 5(D)(2)*(b) infra* ("Special *Erie* Doctrine Problems in Cases of Transfer Under 28 U.S.C. § 1404(a)").

268. The vast majority of federal courts and commentators take this approach. *See, e.g.*, *In re* Korean Airlines Disaster, 829 F.2d 1171 (D.C. Cir. 1987) (Ginsburg, J.), *aff'd on other grounds sub nom.* Chan v. Korean Airlines, Ltd., 490 U.S. 122, 109 S. Ct. 1676, 104 L. Ed. 2d 113 (1989); Richard L. Marcus, *Conflicts Among Circuits and Transfers Within the Federal Judicial System*, 93 YALE L.J. 677, 721 (1984); Joan E. Schaffner, *Federal Circuit "Choice of Law": Erie Through the Looking Glass*, 81 IOWA L. REV. 1173 (1996); Joan Steinman, *Law of the Case: A Judicial Puzzle in Consolidated and Transferred Cases and in Multidistrict Litigation,* 135 U. PA. L. REV. 595, 662-706 (1987); 15 CHARLES A. WRIGHT ET AL., FEDERAL PRACTICE AND PROCEDURE: JURISDICTION AND RELATED MATTERS § 3846, at 91-92, and authorities there cited in n.37 (3d ed. 2007); for contrary authority, *see id.* at 93 n.38.

federal substantive rights to different litigants in the transferee circuit, depending on whether an action is commenced in the circuit or transferred there.[269] This problem was not present in *Van Dusen* and *Ferens*. Under those cases, the transferee court will apply the view of the highest authority in the transferor state about the meaning of the transferor state's law.[270] Similarly, if an action is originally commenced in the transferee state and that state selects another state's law as applicable to the case, it will apply the view of the highest authority in the other state to determine the meaning of that law.

(b) Section 1406 Transfers

Transfer under § 1404(a) is possible only if venue is proper in the district in which the action is originally brought.[271] If venue is improper in the district where the action is brought, transfer is controlled by § 1406. Section 1406 provides that in such circumstances, the district court "shall dismiss, or if it be in the interest of justice, transfer such case to any district or division in which it could have been brought."[272] Transfer is possible under § 1406 even if personal jurisdiction over the defendant is also lacking in the transferor district.[273] Transfers under § 1406 must be to a district where venue would be proper and personal jurisdiction would be obtainable over the defendant.[274]

The Supreme Court's decision in *Stewart Organization* (examined in subsection *(a)* above) did not discuss whether an action brought in a statutorily proper venue, but in contravention of a forum selection clause, should be treated as

---

269. *See In re* Korean Airlines Disaster, 829 F.2d 1171, 1175 (D.C. Cir. 1987), *aff'd on other grounds sub nom.* Chan v. Korean Airlines, Ltd., 490 U.S. 122, 109 S. Ct. 1676, 104 L. Ed. 2d 113 (1989).

270. *See Korean Airlines*, 829 F.2d at 1174-75. In some federal question cases, the *Van Dusen-Ferens* rule should control. For example, Congress sometimes enacts statutes creating federal claims, but does not provide a statute of limitations to govern such claims. In such cases, the federal courts apply the state statute of limitations that is most analogous to the federal claim. Thus, this situation is indistinguishable from the one in *Ferens*, in which the limitations periods of the transferor and transferee state differed. *See generally* Kimberly Jade Norwood, *Double Forum Shopping and the Extension of* Ferens *to Federal Claims that Borrow State Limitation Periods*, 44 EMORY L.J. 501 (1995).

271. *See* 15 CHARLES A. WRIGHT ET AL., FEDERAL PRACTICE AND PROCEDURE: JURISDICTION AND RELATED MATTERS § 3844, at 33 (3d ed. 2007), and cases there cited. However, numerous cases hold that if venue is proper, but personal jurisdiction is lacking in the district where the action is originally commenced, the action may be transferred under § 1404(a). *See* 15 *id.* at 34 and cases there cited in note 15.

272. 28 U.S.C. § 1406(a). In Farmer v. Levenson, 79 Fed. App'x 918 (7th Cir. Oct. 30, 2003), the district court dismissed the action with prejudice for improper venue after the plaintiffs repeatedly failed to respond to motions to dismiss for improper venue. The court of appeals reversed, holding that the district court should have transferred the action to a proper venue rather than dismiss. The court also stated, in agreement with other circuits (and Rule 41(b)), that a dismissal for improper venue should be without prejudice). Chapter 5 discusses complicated questions of the applicable law in § 1404 and § 1406 transfer cases.

273. *See* Goldlawr, Inc. v. Heiman, 369 U.S. 463, 82 S. Ct. 913, 8 L. Ed. 2d 39 (1962). Some courts have held that if venue is proper and personal jurisdiction is lacking, transfer is still appropriate under § 1406(a). *See* 14D CHARLES A. WRIGHT ET AL., FEDERAL PRACTICE AND PROCEDURE: JURISDICTION AND RELATED MATTERS (VENUE) § 3827, at 576 (3d ed. 2007) and cases there cited in note 15. Other cases hold transfer proper in these circumstances under § 1404(a). *See id.* § 3844, at 34 and cases there cited in note 15.

274. *See* 14D CHARLES A. WRIGHT ET AL., FEDERAL PRACTICE AND PROCEDURE: JURISDICTION AND RELATED MATTERS § 3827, at 606 (3d ed. 2007). *But see* Wild v. Subscription Plus, Inc., 292 F.3d 526 (7th Cir. 2002) (Posner, J.) (holding that it was not erroneous to transfer a multiple defendant action under § 1406 from a district in which venue was improper to one in which it was proper, even though one of the defendants could not be subjected to personal jurisdiction in the transferee district; inability to transfer to transferee district would have meant that there was no venue in which all defendants could be sued under the general venue statutes and action would have had to be dismissed in its entirety; such a result was the kind of injustice that Congress was seeking to avoid in § 1406; after transfer, defendant who cannot be subjected to personal jurisdiction in the transferee district must be severed from action and the suit against that defendant either dismissed or retransferred).

one in which venue is proper or improper. Yet this question has an important bearing on whether transfer should be under § 1404(a) or § 1406. It also has a bearing on whether the transferor or transferee's law should be applied after transfer (discussed below). It is actually arguable that neither § 1404(a), nor § 1406 was applicable to the issue in *Stewart Organization*.[275] The question may be foreclosed by stare decisis in § 1404(a) transfer cases due to the Supreme Court's holding in the case. However, it has not been deemed foreclosed in § 1406 transfer cases, when forum selection clauses have controlled if they are otherwise enforceable.[276]

The *Van Dusen-Ferens* rule is inapplicable in cases in which venue is improper and the action is transferred under § 1406. After transfer, the law of the transferee state governs in such cases.[277] It would be unconscionable to allow a plaintiff to fix the applicable law by initially selecting an improper forum. However, not all matters may be governed by the law of the transferee forum after transfer under § 1406. In *Lafferty v. St. Riel*,[278] an action was transferred from the United States District Court for the District of New Jersey to the United States District Court for the Eastern District of Pennsylvania under § 1406 because federal venue was improper in New Jersey. Both New Jersey and Pennsylvania had identical two-year periods of limitations applicable to the plaintiff's claim. However, the Pennsylvania district court dismissed the action as time barred because the transfer occurred after the running of the statute of limitations. The United States Court of Appeals reversed, holding that for purposes of calculating the limitations period of the transferee forum after transfer, the initial filing date in the transferor forum applies. Thus, because the action was timely under the transferee state's limitations period on the date that it was commenced in the transferor state, the action could not be dismissed as time barred. In reaching its conclusion, the court of appeals reviewed the history of § 1406, particularly the purpose of authorizing transfer rather than dismissal in order not to unfairly disadvantage a plaintiff who might have to evaluate facts bearing on venue that present close questions.

Lafferty probably represents a special case, with other similar problems governed by the law of the transferee state after transfer under § 1406. For example, in *Eggleton v. Plasser & Theurer Export Von Bahnbaumaschinen Gesellschaft*,[279] an action was transferred from the Eastern District of Virginia to the District of

---

275. *See* Richard D. Freer, Erie's *Mid-Life Crisis*, 63 TUL. L. REV. 1087, 1117-21 (1989); Walter W. Heiser, *Forum Selection Clauses in Federal Courts: Limitations on Enforcement After* Stewart *and* Carnival Cruise, 45 FLA. L. REV. 553, 590-95 (1993); Allan R. Stein, Erie *and Court Access*, 100 YALE L.J. 1935, 1961-65 (1991).

276. *See, e.g.*, Servewell Plumbing, LLC v. Federal Ins. Co., 439 F.3d 786 (8th Cir. 2006) (action dismissed for improper venue based on a forum selection clause; appellate court stated that there was no need to determine whether the *Erie* doctrine, examined in Chapter 5, required application of state law to the issue of the validity of the forum selection clause, because both the applicable state and federal law were the same on that issue in this case); International Software Sys., Inc. v. Amplicon, Inc., 77 F.3d 112 (5th Cir. 1996) (*Stewart Organization* does not control in cases involving motions to dismiss based on forum selection clauses; uniform approach among circuits discussed); *cf.* AmerMed Corp. v. Disetronic Holding AG, 6 F. Supp. 2d 1371 (N.D. Ga. 1998) (provision governing dismissal for improper venue, § 1406, is silent as to dismissal on any ground other than statutorily deficient venue).

277. *See* Nationwide Bi-Weekly Admin., Inc. v. Belo Corp., 512 F.3d 137 (5th Cir. 2007) (statute of limitations of transferee state applied after transfer under § 1406 as a matter of transferee's state's conflict-of-laws rules); Adam v. J.B. Hunt Transp., Inc., 130 F.3d 219, 230 (6th Cir. 1997) (law of transferee state applies after a § 1406 transfer); Wisland v. Admiral Beverage Corp., 119 F.3d 733 (8th Cir. 1997) (same); *cf.* Gerena v. Korb, 617 F.3d 197 (2d Cir. 2010) (district court must determine whether transfer is under § 1404(a) or § 1406 before determining whether transferor or transferee state's choice-of-law doctrine should be applied).

278. 495 F.3d 72 (3d Cir. 2007).

279. 495 F.3d 582 (8th Cir. 2007).

Nebraska under § 1406 because of lack of personal jurisdiction in Virginia over the defendant. The action was timely under Virginia limitations and tolling provisions, but would have been untimely if commenced under the same circumstances in Nebraska. The district court agreed with the plaintiff that the filing in Virginia was done in good faith and not for reasons of forum shopping and refused to dismiss. The court of appeals, however, reversed, holding that the law of the transferee state, Nebraska, should be applied to bar the action. The court confronted two precedents in the Eighth Circuit that conflicted on the issue before it.[280] Acknowledging that it had no power to overrule a prior decision of another panel of the circuit, the court nevertheless held that it could choose which of two conflicting precedents to follow within the circuit. The court, in accord with the weight of authority in other circuits, elected to apply the rule that the transferee court's law applied. The court stated:

> Our sister circuits' apparently universal agreement on this general rule is grounded in well-established choice-of-law principles. The plaintiff has the choice of the initial forum. If he chooses an improper venue or one that lacks personal jurisdiction over the defendants, then application of the law of the original, legally defective forum upon transfer to a legally appropriate forum carries dual risks. First, it may create unfairness to defendants. A defendant in such a situation does not expressly or impliedly consent to suit in the defective forum, yet she would be made to suffer the choice-of-law consequences of a plaintiff's mistake in choosing such a forum to file his lawsuit. Second, a rule calling for application of the law of the defective forum may encourage procedural gamesmanship among plaintiffs generally. Such a rule creates an incentive for plaintiffs to engage in undue forum shopping; that is, it opens the possibility for a plaintff to intentionally file a case in a forum with advantageous law (but without venue and/or personal jurisdiction), with the knowledge that he will receive the benefits of the law so long as he can convince the original district court to transfer the case rather than dismiss it outright.[281]

(c) Section 1407 Transfers

Another transfer provision, 28 U.S.C. § 1407, authorizes the transfer of civil actions pending in different districts "to *any* district for coordinated or consolidated *pretrial* proceedings" and also establishes a Judicial Panel on Multidistrict Litigation.[282] For transfer, the actions must involve "one or more common questions

---

280. Mayo Clinic v. Kaiser, 383 F.2d 653 (8th Cir. 1967) (law of transferor state applied) and Wisland v. Admiral Beverage Corp., 119 F.3d 733 (8th Cir. 1997) (law of transferee state applied).

281. *Eggleton*, 495 F.3d at 588-89.

282. 28 U.S.C. § 1407(a), (d) (emphasis added); *see* George T. Conway III, Note, *The Consolidation of Multistate Litigation in State Courts*, 96 YALE L.J. 1099 (1987) (proposing that Congress confer upon the Judicial Panel the power to direct litigation to and from the state courts as well). *See generally* 15 CHARLES A. WRIGHT ET AL., FEDERAL PRACTICE AND PROCEDURE: JURISDICTION AND RELATED MATTERS §§ 3861-3868 (3d ed. 2007); Wilson W. Herdon & Ernest R. Higginbotham, *Complex Multidistrict Litigation—An Overview of 28 U.S.C.A. § 1407*, 31 BAYLOR L. REV. 33 (1979); Mark A. Hill, *Opening the Door for Bias: The Problem of Applying Transferee Forum Law in Multidistrict Litigation*, 85 NOTRE DAME L. REV. 341 (2009); Richard L. Marcus, *Cure-All for an Era of Dispersed Litigation? Toward a Maximalist Use of the Multidistrict Litigation Panel's Transfer*

of fact."[283] Also, the panel must determine that the transfer "will be for the convenience of parties and witnesses and will promote the just and efficient conduct of such actions."[284] Generally speaking, the kind of case transferred involves complex litigation, such as antitrust or securities actions. After the pretrial proceedings have been completed, the actions are then remanded back to the districts from which they were transferred.[285] In *Lexecon, Inc. v. Milberg Weiss Bershad Hynes & Lerach*,[286] the Supreme Court held that after transfer of a case under § 1407 for pretrial proceedings, the transferee court could not permanently transfer the case to itself under § 1404(a) for trial.[287] However, this result will be affected by the new transfer by consent provisions added to § 1404(a) by the Federal Courts Jurisdiction and Venue Clarification Act of 2011,[288] effective in 2012, discussed above. The legislative history of the Act indicates that "mutually agreed upon and judicially approved transfers would be proper in any action, including actions that have been centralized for pre-trial proceedings by the Judicial Panel on Multidistrict Litigation under 28 U.S.C. [§] 1407."[289]

SECTION E. INJUNCTIONS AGAINST EXTRASTATE LITIGATION AND OTHER DEVICES FOR CONTROLLING THE LOCATION OF THE SUIT

In addition to the methods discussed in earlier sections for controlling the location of suit, there are other devices available for controlling the location of the suit. For example, when multiple actions have been commenced (or are threatened) in different states or countries concerning the same subject matter, it is sometimes possible to obtain an injunction in one forum preventing litigation in another or a stay of proceedings in one court in deference to the other. In effect, these devices, when available, allow litigants to limit the venue of an action to a single forum.

Power, 82 TULANE L. REV. 2245 (2008); Note, *The Judicial Panel and the Conduct of Multidistrict Litigation*, 87 HARV. L. REV. 1001 (1974). The panel is appointed by the Chief Justice of the United States. The panel consists of seven circuit or district judges. No more than one judge from a circuit may be appointed. *Id.* Upon its own motion or on motion by any party involved in one of the actions sought to be consolidated, the panel determines whether a transfer should be made, which district should be the transferee forum, and who should preside as the transferee judge. 28 U.S.C. § 1407(c). The concurrence of four of the seven members of the panel is required for any action to be taken. 28 U.S.C. § 1407(d).

283. 28 U.S.C. § 1407(a).

284. *Id.* Even if these requirements are met, transfer is not automatic. *See, e.g.*, *In re* Truck Accident Near Alamagordo, 387 F. Supp. 732 (J.P.M.L. 1975).

285. 28 U.S.C. § 1407(a). *See generally* ALI COMPLEX LITIGATION: STATUTORY RECOMMENDATIONS AND ANALYSIS WITH REPORTER'S STUDY ch. 3 (1994) (discussing federal intrasystem consolidation).

286. 523 U.S. 26, 118 S. Ct. 956, 140 L. Ed. 2d 62 (1998).

287. *In re* Carbon Dioxide Indus. Antitrust Litig., 229 F.3d 1321 (11th Cir. 2000), distinguished *Lexecon* and refused to retransfer an action when the plaintiffs had stipulated in the final pretrial order that the transferee court had proper subject-matter jurisdiction and venue over all claims and had consistently urged the transferee court to try the case until the day scheduled for jury selection. The court held that a party may not challenge a ruling that the party has induced the court to make. It has also been held that, after a transfer under § 1407, a district court should apply the law of the state that would have been applied to the individual cases if they had not been transferred. *See In re* Temporomandibular Joint (TMJ) Implants Prods. Liab. Litig., 97 F.3d 1050 (8th Cir. 1996).

288. Pub. L. 112-63, § 204, 125 Stat. 758, 764 (2011) (codified in 28U.S.C. § 1404(a)).

289. H.R. Rep. No. 112-10, at 15 (2011).

1. Injunctions Against Suit

The general rule is that parallel actions in different jurisdictions are allowed to proceed until a judgment is reached in one jurisdiction that can be pleaded as res judicata in the other.[290] However, under appropriate circumstances, injunctions against foreign litigation, which were prohibited in some early decisions, are now widely considered to be proper.[291] An injunction against prosecuting or commencing an action in another jurisdiction is not directed against the court or judge in the other state or nation. Instead, it is directed against the party who brought, or is threatening to bring, the foreign action.[292]

There are two general approaches to injunctions against foreign litigation.[293] The "restrictive" approach only permits injunctions to protect the jurisdiction of the forum court or to prevent evasion of important public policies of the forum.[294] Protection of the forum's jurisdiction by an injunction against a foreign suit is most justified in cases in which jurisdiction is based on the presence of property within the court's jurisdictional boundaries—*i.e.,* in-rem or quasi-in-rem actions. In that situation, concurrent proceedings in a foreign jurisdiction pose "the danger that the foreign court will order the transfer of the property out of the jurisdictional boundaries of the first court, thus depriving it of jurisdiction over the matter."[295] When the proceedings are in personam, as opposed to in rem or quasi in rem, an injunction against a foreign suit will be justifiable when the foreign court is attempting to assert exclusive jurisdiction over an action. Under such circumstances, the foreign proceeding is not merely following a "parallel track," but threatens to deprive the forum proceeding of validity.[296] In addition, it seems settled that once the forum has rendered a judgment on the merits of an action, a parallel proceeding in another jurisdiction dealing with the same claim may be enjoined to

---

290. *See, e.g.,* Gau Shan Co. v. Bankers Trust Co., 956 F.2d 1349, 1352 (6th Cir. 1992); Golden Rule Ins. Co. v. Harper, 925 S.W.2d 649, 651 (Tex. 1996); Margarita Trevino de Coale, *Stay, Dismiss, Enjoin, or Abstain?: A Survey of Foreign Parallel Litigation in the Federal Courts of the United States*, 17 B.U. INT'L L.J. 79, 80-81 (1999). *But cf.* Bank of Okla., N.A. v. Tharaldson Motels, Inc., 743 F. Supp. 2d 1080 (D.N.D. 2010) (federal Anti-Injunction Act, 28 U.S.C. § 2283, imposes an absolute ban upon the issuance of a pending parallel state-court proceeding in same state where federal court is sitting).

291. *See* J.E. Macy, Annotation, *Injunction by State Court Against Action in Court of Another State*, 6 A.L.R.2d 896, 899 (1949); *see also* Kurtis A. Kemper, Annotation, *Propriety Under Circumstances of State Court Injunction Against Nonmatrimonial Action in Court of Sister State*, 20 A.L.R.6TH 211 (2006); Robin Cheryl Miller, Annotation, *Propriety of Federal Court Injunction Against Suit in Foreign Country*, 78 A.L.R. FED. 831 (1986); Milton Roberts, Annotation, *Propriety of Injunction by Federal Court in Civil Action Restraining Prosecution of Later Civil Action in Another Federal Court Where One or More Parties or Issues Are, or Allegedly Are, Same,* 42 A.L.R. FED. 592 (1979).

292. *See* Annotation, *Injunction by State Court Against Action in Another State,* 6 A.L.R.2D 896, 899 (1949). In Baker *ex rel.* Thomas v. General Motors Corp., 522 U.S. 222, 118 S. Ct. 657, 139 L. Ed. 2d 580 (1998), the Supreme Court held that full faith and credit did not require Missouri to give effect to a Michigan injunction restraining a former employee of G.M. from testifying as an expert witness against G.M. However, the case appears merely to confirm the settled proposition that a state judgment may not ordinarily bind nonparties to the judgment; and the Court indicated that the judgment would be preclusive between the employee and G.M., who were parties. Thus, *Baker* appears not to undermine the results of the cases discussed in this subsection.

293. *See, e.g.,* Gau Shan Co. v. Bankers Trust Co., 956 F.2d 1349, 1353-54 (6th Cir. 1992) (discussing the different standards applied in the U.S. Courts of Appeals).

294. *See id.* at 1353; Sea Containers Ltd. v. Stena AB, 890 F.2d 1205 (D.C. Cir. 1989); China Trade & Dev. Corp. v. M.V. Choong Yong, 837 F.2d 33 (2d Cir. 1987); Laker Airways Ltd. v. Sabena, Belgian World Airlines, 731 F.2d 909 (D.C. Cir. 1984).

295. Gau Shan Co. v. Bankers Trust Co., 956 F.2d 1349, 1356 (6th Cir. 1992); *see also* China Trade & Dev. Corp. v. M.V. Choong Yong, 837 F.2d 33 (2d Cir. 1987).

296. *See* Laker Airways Ltd. v. Sabena, Belgian World Airlines, 731 F.2d 909, 929-30 (D.C. Cir. 1984).

prevent "evasion [of the judgment] through vexatious or oppressive relitigation."[297] The latter situation, however, should be limited to relitigation in the courts of foreign countries, because within the states of the United States, a plea of res judicata in the "foreign" court will preclude the action under the full-faith-and-credit implementing statute, 28 U.S.C. § 1738.[298]

The ability to issue an injunction to protect important public policies of the forum may seem broad enough to undermine completely the principle allowing parallel proceedings in different jurisdictions. However, courts following the "restrictive" view do not enforce the "public policy" rule simply to prevent duplicative foreign litigation involving the same parties and issues.[299] Indeed, one federal court has indicated that a simple "advantage in law" in the forum suit will not warrant invoking the public policy justification for an injunction,[300] and that while "evasion of an important national policy might outweigh certain principles of international comity," it is questionable "whether the public policy of one state could ever outweigh those principles."[301]

Some courts have articulated a more liberal standard for granting injunctions against foreign litigation than the "restrictive" view described above. In addition to the "protection of jurisdiction" and "public policy" justifications, these courts add two additional rationales for such injunctions: (1) prevention of vexation and oppression; and (2) prevention of prejudice to "other equitable considerations."[302] In effect, decisions by these courts seem to stand for the proposition that a duplication of parties and issues alone is sufficient to justify an injunction against foreign litigation.[303] However, not all courts articulating this "liberal" view of foreign antisuit injunctions apply the standards broadly. For example, in *Golden Rule Insurance Co. v. Harper*,[304] the Texas Supreme Court stated that an antisuit injunction is appropriate in the four circumstances encom-

---

297. *Id.* at 928.

298. *See* Chapter 13(F)(1) *infra* ("Enforcement of State Judgments").

299. *See* Gau Shan Co. v. Bankers Trust Co., 956 F.2d 1349, 1357 (6th Cir. 1992).

300. *Id.* at 1357.

301. *Id.* at 1358. This statement implies that injunctions against litigation in foreign nations may be controlled by "federal common law" in diversity and alienage actions. *See* Chapter 5(I) *infra* ("Federal Common Law"); *see also* Paramedics Electromedicina Comercial, Ltda. v. GE Med. Sys. Info. Techs., Inc., 369 F.3d 645 (2d Cir. 2004) (antisuit injunction was appropriate measure to enforce and protect judgment compelling arbitration; antisuit injunction against parallel litigation is proper only if parties are the same in both proceedings and resolution of case before the enjoining court is dispositive of action to be enjoined; once past this threshold, court should consider such additional factors as whether foreign action threatens jurisdiction or strong public policies of enjoining forum); Quaak v. Klynveld Peat Marwick Goerdeler Bedrijfserevisoren, 361 F.3d 11 (1st Cir. 2004) (auditor obtained order from Belgian court concerning records that were the subject of a motion to compel discovery by opposing party of auditor in federal antitrust litigation; injunction against auditor to prevent auditor from pursuing further litigation in Belgium affirmed; considerations of international comity that give rise to a rebuttable presumption against the issuance of an order that halts foreign judicial proceedings may be counterbalanced by such things as the nature of the two actions, the posture of the proceedings in the two countries, the conduct of the parties, the importance of the policies at stake in the litigation, and the extent to which the foreign judicial proceeding has the potential to undermine the forum court's ability to reach a just and speedy result).

302. *See, e.g.*, Kaepa, Inc. v. Achilles Corp., 76 F.3d 624 (5th Cir. 1996); Seattle Totems Hockey Club, Inc. v. National Hockey League, 652 F.2d 852, 855 (9th Cir. 1981); *In re* Unterweser Reederei GMBH, 428 F.2d 888, 890 (5th Cir. 1970); Golden Rule Ins. Co. v. Harper, 925 S.W.2d 649 (Tex. 1996).

303. *See* Gau Shan Co. v. Bankers Trust Co., 956 F.2d 1349, 1352-53 (6th Cir. 1992) (describing the views of the Fifth and Ninth Circuits in this way).

304. 925 S.W.2d 649 (Tex. 1996); *see also* Allendale Mut. Ins. Co. v. Bull Data Sys., Inc., 10 F.3d 425 (7th Cir. 1993) (Posner, J.) ("lax" standard takes account of international comity, but requires some tangible evidence that it will be impaired before injunction will be refused).

passed by the "liberal" view.[305] However, the court then reversed the judgment of a lower court granting an injunction against parallel litigation in another state:

> [W]e have never accepted the notion that a mirror image proceeding is sufficiently different from an ordinary single parallel proceeding to justify an injunction. We reject the implicit distinction of the court below between single parallel proceedings and mirror image proceedings .... This approach fails to give adequate weight to the principle of comity and threatens to allow the exception to swallow the rule.[306]

Golden Rule thus suggests that courts articulating the "liberal" standard for foreign antisuit injunctions may actually administer the standard in a way that is nearer to the restrictive standard. If so, mere duplicative parallel proceedings in another jurisdiction will seldom justify an injunction.[307]

2. Stays of Forum Proceedings in Deference to Out-of-State Litigation

Many state courts follow a rule that they will abate a proceeding involving the same parties and subject matter in favor of a prior pending action in the same state.[308] If the prior pending action is in a different venue within the same state, the plea of prior pending action gives a litigant some control over the venue of the action. However, the abatement of a proceeding in favor of a prior pending action usually does not extend to proceedings in other states.[309]

---

305. *See Golden Rule*, 925 S.W.2d at 651.

306. *Id.* The "mirror image" proceeding the court referenced was a declaratory judgment action brought in Illinois that "mirrored" an action for damages brought in Texas; *see also* Mercury Mktg. Techs., Inc. v. State *ex rel.* Beebe, 358 Ark. 319, 189 S.W.3d 414 (2004) (injunction to prevent defendant from conducting telemarketing business in Arkansas did not violate judicial comity simply because order existed in federal action in Pennsylvania that was being administered by the FTC; parties were not the same in the federal and state proceedings, and same conduct could violate both federal and state law).

307. Many articles discuss the use of injunctions against suit in international litigation. *See, e.g.*, George A. Bermann, *The Use of Anti-Suit Injunctions in International Litigation*, 28 COLUM. J. TRANSNAT'L L. 589 (1990); *See also* N. Jansen Calamita, *Rethinking Comity: Towards a Coherent Treatment of International Parallel Proceedings*, 27 U. PA. J. INT'L ECON. L. 601 (2006); Robert Force, *The Position in the United States on Foreign Forum Selection and Arbitration Clauses, Forum Non Conveniens, and Antisuit Injunctions*, 35 TUL. MARITIME L.J. 401 (2011); Trevor C. Hartley, *Comity and the Use of Antisuit Injunctions in International Litigation*, 35 AM. J. COMP. L. 487 (1987); Markus Lenenbach, *Antisuit Injunctions in England, Germany and the United States: Their Treatment Under European Civil Procedure and the Hague Convention*, 20 LOY. L.A. INT'L & COMP. L.J. 257 (1998); Haig Najarian, Note, *Granting Comity Its Due: A Proposal to Revive the Comity-Based Approach to Transnational Antisuit Injunctions*, 68 ST. JOHN'S L. REV. 961 (1994); Eric Roberson, Comment, *Comity Be Damned: The Use of Antisuit Injunctions Against the Courts of a Foreign Nation*, 147 U. PA. L. REV. 409 (1998); Steven R. Swanson, *The Vexatiousness of a Vexation Rule: International Comity and Antisuit Injunctions*, 30 GEO. WASH. J. INT'L L. & ECON. 1 (1996).

308. *See* Annotation, *Stay of Civil Proceedings Pending Determination of Action in Another State or Country*, 19 A.L.R.2D 301, 305-06 (1951).

309. *See id.* at 305-06. *But see* First Midwest Corp. v. Corporate Fin. Assocs., 663 N.W.2d 888 (Iowa 2003), in which a Nebraska corporation sued an Iowa corporation in Nebraska state court to recover a fee for consulting services. After discovery, both parties moved for summary judgment, but the Nebraska court denied the motions, holding that there were genuine issues of material fact that made a trial necessary and scheduling the case for trial. At that point, the Iowa corporation filed a "mirror image" action for declaratory judgment against the Nebraska corporation in an Iowa state court to determine the extent of its obligations to the Nebraska corporation. The Iowa trial court refused to stay the action in deference to the Nebraska proceeding. On appeal, the Iowa Supreme Court held that it was error to deny the stay. The court, relying on Waicker v. Colbert, 347 Md. 108, 699 A.2d 426 (1997), held that in the absence of compelling circumstances, it is inappropriate for a court to entertain a declaratory judgment action where identical issues are pending in another proceeding, even when the other

Some courts will exercise discretion to stay (as opposed to abate or dismiss) an action in favor of an action in another jurisdiction. Though other reasons are sometimes given, the principal reason for granting such a stay is to prevent vexation of the defendant when there is no apparent reason for the plaintiff to bring the same suit in two different states.[310] When an action in the forum is stayed in favor of an action in another state, a judgment on the merits in the other state will control the forum proceeding under the ordinary principles of res judicata. Under the full-faith-and-credit implementing statute, 28 U.S.C. § 1738, the states are obligated to give the same effect to the judgments of other states as they would receive in the state where the judgments are rendered.[311] When the judgment is rendered by the courts of a foreign nation, however, neither the Full Faith and Credit Clause nor its implementing statute require United States courts to enforce the judgment.[312] Nevertheless, most state courts today give the same effect to foreign nation judgments as they give to judgments of other states.[313]

---

proceeding is in another state. The court then rejected the reasons given by the Iowa trial court for refusing the stay, stating in conclusion:

> In the face of proof that the Nebraska court was capable of and ready to render complete justice to these parties within weeks, the decision by the Iowa court to derail that course at the behest of an Iowa plaintiff can only be described as arbitrary and capricious. It resulted in forum shopping that is contrary to the most basic notions of comity.

See First Midwest, 663 N.W.2d at 893. *But cf.* Manuel v. Convergys Corp., 430 F.3d 1132 (11th Cir. 2005) (declaratory judgment action filed in anticipation of suit in another forum; anticipatory nature of suit is an equitable consideration that can be taken into account in determining whether compelling circumstances exist to warrant an exception to the rule that forum preference be given to first filed action; however, no compelling circumstances exist in this case to prefer Ohio forum over Georgia forum where action first filed); Sensient Colors, Inc. v. Allstate Ins. Co., 193 N.J. 373,939 A.2d 767 (2008) (under first-filed rule, New Jersey state court ordinarily will stay or dismiss a civil action in deference to an already pending, substantially similar lawsuit in another state, unless compelling reasons exist to retain jurisdiction; in this case, special equities favored New Jersey exercising jurisdiction over insured's action for declaratory judgment that insurance policy covered liability for clean up of contaminated property in New Jersey).

310. *See* Annotation, *Stay of Civil Proceedings Pending Determination of Action in Another State or Country*, 19 A.L.R.2D 301, 306 (1951); *see also* RUSSELL J. WEINTRAUB, COMMENTARY ON THE CONFLICT OF LAWS § 4.38, at 326-27 (6th ed. 2010).

311. *See* Chapter 13(F)(1) *infra* ("Enforcement of State Judgments").

312. *See* Chapter 13(F)(3) *infra* ("Enforcement of Foreign Judgments").

313. *See id.* Sometimes, parties have options whether to seek injunctions against foreign litigation or to move for abatement or dismissal of the forum action. For example, in Shell Offshore, Inc. v. Heeremac, 33 F. Supp. 2d 1111 (S.D. Tex. 1999), an antitrust action was commenced in Texas in contravention of a forum selection clause that required litigation arising out of contracts between the parties to be adjudicated in London. Some of the defendants commenced an action in London against the Texas plaintiffs, seeking to prevent the plaintiffs from adjudicating their claims in Texas. The Texas plaintiffs, in turn, applied for a "temporary injunction" from the Texas court, arguing that the defendants should have to raise the forum selection clause defensively as a matter of "abatement" in the Texas proceeding rather than simply commencing parallel litigation in London. The Texas federal court issued the injunction, stating that the plaintiff's position was in accord with both English and American law.

For a discussion of various devices with which parties seek to stop parallel litigation in United States and foreign courts, see Margarita Trevino de Coale, *Stay, Dismiss, Enjoin, or Abstain?: A Survey of Foreign Parallel Litigation in the Federal Courts of the United States*, 17 B.U. INT'L L.J. 79 (1999); *see also* James P. George, *Parallel Litigation*, 51 BAYLOR L. REV. 769 (1999); Jody Kerwin, Note, *A Choice of Law Approach for International Antisuit Injunctions*, 81 TEX. L. REV. 927 (2003); Edwin A. Perry, *Killing One Bird With One Stone: How the United States Federal Courts Should Issue Foreign Antisuit Injunctions in the Information Age*, 8 U. MIAMI BUS. L. REV. 123 (1999); John Ray Phillips, III, Comment, *A Proposed Solution to the Puzzle of Antisuit Injunctions*, 69 U. CHI. L. REV. 2007 (2002).

Chapter 5

SOURCES OF LAW

As discussed in the previous three chapters, lawyers must select a court that possesses subject-matter jurisdiction, venue, and personal jurisdiction before commencing an action. In addition, before selecting a court, lawyers must consider what rules of law a court will apply to resolve the dispute between the parties. However, predicting what law courts will apply can be a difficult task. If the legal system has never confronted and directly resolved a dispute like the one presented in the case, no rule of law may exist that exactly fits the circumstances of the dispute. Under such conditions, lawyers will have to predict whether the courts will (1) extend a rule of law previously applied in a similar, but not identical, case to the facts of the present one or (2) create an entirely new rule. Even when prior decisions have "settled" the law, lawyers must consider whether those prior decisions remain on a sound footing or whether they are subject to attack. Changed conditions may convince an appellate court to overrule even settled decisions.[1]

In the United States, two structural features of the legal system complicate the task of predicting or determining the applicable law. First, the doctrine of separation of powers allocates primary lawmaking authority to the legislative branches of government. It also restrains the power of the courts to make and revise the law. Second, the existence of the federal system complicates the selection of the applicable rules of law. Each of the fifty states and the national government possess lawmaking power within a limited sphere of authority. In actions based on events that occur in more than one state, or in actions involving parties from more than one state, lawyers must determine which state's law the court will select to resolve the dispute. Furthermore, there is an ever-present need to determine whether the national government has promulgated rules that preempt state law and thereby control the outcome of the case.

Many problems of legal interpretation concern the respective lawmaking roles of the legislative and judicial branches of government. Section A briefly examines these "separation of powers" problems. Section B introduces some basic problems of selecting the applicable law in multistate disputes. The remaining sections are devoted to a special source-of-law problem created by the existence of separate state and national courts within each state that possess concurrent authority to adjudicate some of the same disputes.[2]

---

1. Difficult questions of applicable law are not only presented to plaintiffs trying to decide whether to commence an action. The same questions exist on the defendant's side of the case and bear on whether settlement or litigation is the most viable option.

2. Recall the discussion in Chapter 2(A)(5) of the concurrent subject-matter jurisdiction of federal and state courts in diversity and federal question cases, *supra*.

SECTION A. THE SEPARATION-OF-POWERS DOCTRINE

Ideally, the rule of law presupposes the traditional doctrine of separation of powers. Separation of powers limits each branch of government to its appropriate function. The legislative branch must enact only general laws and not acts of attainder or retroactive laws. The executive must act only with the approval of the judiciary in enforcing the laws against individuals. The courts are not to make law, but only to "find" it.[3]

This ideal rule of law is only an "approximation" of what actually occurs.[4] In reality, courts perform lawmaking functions, but their lawmaking authority is not as broad as that of legislatures. While judges inevitably create law when they articulate the rules of law applicable to the dispute before them, simple fairness dictates that judges limit their lawmaking. Courts should not unfairly surprise the parties to a dispute by applying rules of decision that did not exist, at least in an inchoate form, when the parties engaged in their primary behavior. In addition, limitations on the judicial lawmaking authority perform broader political functions. Fundamental policy issues should be reserved for determination by the legislative branch of government. Courts should refrain from taking sides on partisan political issues. The administration of law by the courts should "exhibit coherence of principle" and should not be a process of ad hoc decision making. Values transcending partisan political differences should be recognized in a society's laws. Although these principles potentially conflict, they can be reconciled by maintaining the distinction between legislative and judicial powers. Thus, while judges will inevitably make law when engaged in the process of adjudication, they should take care to make it only interstitially.[5]

Within an individual state, making law "only interstitially" depends on the source of the law. When the courts enforce a constitutional provision, they should be bound by the meaning of the provision as understood by the framers and ratifiers of the provision, including the boundaries of the provision's operation. When enforcing a statute, the courts must determine the meaning communicated by, and objectives of, the legislators. Difficult problems of "interstitial" lawmaking also are posed when the courts enforce common-law principles. It is tempting to conclude that the lawmaking constraints on courts are fewer, or perhaps nonexistent, when courts apply common-law rules. After all, the rules originated with the courts in the first instance. Thus, perhaps they should be subject to repeal or modification by the courts in a policy-oriented fashion. In addition to the serious problems of unfair surprise to the parties such a process would entail, this view oversimplifies the origins of common-law rules and the role of the courts in enforcing those rules in a modern society.

In its earliest stages, English law was customary in nature. The oldest customs were not handed down from central institutions to individuals and local communities. Instead, they originated in the localities and "reflected not different

---

3. *See* JOHN R. LUCAS, THE PRINCIPLES OF POLITICS 113-14 (1966).

4. *See id.*

5. *See* NEIL MACCORMICK, LEGAL REASONING AND LEGAL THEORY 187-88 (1978).

answers to the same problem but different ways of life."[6] After the Norman Conquest, this system of local customary institutions was taken over by the Conqueror. The product of the centralization of justice that took place after the Conquest with the rise of the king's court became known as the "common law."[7]

As the common law developed, the courts limited the operation of local custom.[8] The courts placed a "heavy burden of proof" upon persons who contended that local custom should control instead of common-law rules. In effect, the proponents of local custom had to establish the existence of a local custom that favored their side of the dispute. They also had to demonstrate that the custom "has borne fruit in actual practice and governed the decisions of the local courts."[9] The process of identifying the existence and extent of a local custom was similar to fact finding today.[10] This fact-finding process was not limited to the establishment of local custom that would control instead of a common-law rule. It was also used when local custom was incorporated into the common law as the national rule of decision.

Illustration 5-1. (a) An illustration of how the common-law processes operated in conjunction with local custom is found in the history of the "law merchant" or "mercantile law." The information in this illustration is also relevant to an understanding of the doctrine of *Swift v. Tyson*, discussed in section C, below. The law merchant originated in the local customs of particular places where substantial commercial activity occurred.[11] Despite its character as local custom, the law merchant was conceived of as international in scope and "known to merchants throughout Christendom."[12] Indeed, long before the English common law incorporated it, the law merchant existed not only at the local level in England, but also as European local custom.[13]

(b) Much of the law merchant was customary maritime law, spread by seaborne commerce along shipping routes.[14] Indeed, the bodies of law that came to be separately known as "Admiralty" and "Commercial Law" were not originally distinguished from each other.[15] "The custom of merchants on land [in Europe] seems to have been more varied [than in the seaport towns]. Every town tended to develop a more or less comprehensive body of merchant custom . . . . Divergences in detail are very numerous, but even here attempts were made to achieve some sort of uniformity."[16] The "international character of commerce" that brought merchants

---

6. S.F.C. MILSOM, HISTORICAL FOUNDATIONS OF THE COMMON LAW 1 (1969).

7. *Id.* "The custom of the king's court is the custom of England and becomes the common law." 1 FREDERICK POLLOCK & FREDERIC W. MAITLAND, THE HISTORY OF ENGLISH LAW 184 (2d ed. 1968).

8. *See* 1 FREDERICK POLLOCK & FREDERIC W. MAITLAND, THE HISTORY OF ENGLISH LAW 184 (2d ed. 1968).

9. *Id.* at 184-85.

10. *See* RANDALL BRIDWELL & RALPH U. WHITTEN, THE CONSTITUTION AND THE COMMON LAW: THE DECLINE OF THE DOCTRINES OF SEPARATION OF POWERS AND FEDERALISM 14 (1977).

11. *See* THEODORE F.T. PLUCKNETT, A CONCISE HISTORY OF THE COMMON LAW 314, 657 (5th ed. 1956).

12. 1 FREDERICK POLLOCK & FREDERIC W. MAITLAND, THE HISTORY OF ENGLISH LAW 467 (2d ed. 1968).

13. *See* THEODORE F.T. PLUCKNETT, A CONCISE HISTORY OF THE COMMON LAW 657-58 (5th ed. 1956).

14. *See id.*

15. GRANT GILMORE & CHARLES L. BLACK, THE LAW OF ADMIRALTY § 1-3, at 5 n.13 & accompanying text (2d ed. 1975); Thomas E. Scrutton, *General Survey of the History of the Law Merchant*, *in* 3 SELECT ESSAYS IN ANGLO-AMERICAN LEGAL HISTORY 7, 11-12 (1909).

16. THEODORE F.T. PLUCKNETT, A CONCISE HISTORY OF THE COMMON LAW 658 (5th ed. 1956).

from different countries into contact with each other promoted deliberate attempts to make the mercantile law uniform.[17]

(c) Both on the continent and in England, local maritime tribunals and merchants' courts enforced the law merchant.[18] In England, the inland courts were called "piepowder" courts, so named because of the dusty feet of the wandering merchants who used them.[19] English seaport towns had their own maritime courts.[20] Later, the central admiralty courts took over the administration of the law merchant from the local maritime courts. In the fourteenth century, statutory "courts of the staple" were set up in competition with the piepowder courts.[21] Later, the common-law courts took over the administration of the law merchant.

(d) When the common-law courts first began to incorporate the law merchant into the common law, a jury of merchants had to establish the alleged existence of a commercial custom in each case.[22] However, "by the close of the seventeenth century the constant repetition of finding mercantile custom in each case that arose was seen to be unnecessary, and the courts began to take notice of some of the more notable mercantile customs without requiring proof of them, and this policy was finally adopted as a general practice by Lord Mansfield [in the eighteenth century]."[23]

(e) Incorporating the law merchant into the common law subjected the commercial law to the common-law process of analogical reasoning. This process was, of course, the familiar one of arguing "from one case to another case which is similar though not precisely similar."[24] Taking judicial notice of a mercantile custom resembled a fact-finding task in many respects, as judicial notice does today, while the analogical reasoning process resembled more what would be called lawmaking today, though it was not so considered in the eighteenth and nineteenth centuries.

(f) When custom was used as a source of law, the particular rules of law that formed the content of the customs were not created by the courts that enforced the customs. Instead, the rules were created by the interaction of private parties to suit the needs of the parties. As a consequence, when a court enforced a particular rule, no legislative-like policy choice was made—whether the decision about the content of the rule was made by judicial notice or by allegation and proof to a jury. If any policy choice was involved, the choice was to follow custom in the first place. Thus, when the common-law courts decided to incorporate the law merchant as national common law, the courts may have been making a significant policy choice. Thereafter, when they engaged in the process of establishing what the particular rules of the law merchant were, they were merely engaged in fact finding, not in creation of the particular rule for legislative-like policy reasons.

---

17. *See id.* at 659.

18. *See* THEODORE F.T. PLUCKNETT, A CONCISE HISTORY OF THE COMMON LAW 660 (5th ed. 1956); GRANT GILMORE & CHARLES L. BLACK, THE LAW OF ADMIRALTY § 1-3, at 5 (2d ed. 1975).

19. *See* THEODORE F.T. PLUCKNETT, A CONCISE HISTORY OF THE COMMON LAW 660 (5th ed. 1956).

20. *Id.*

21. *See id.*

22. *See id.* at 663.

23. *Id.* at 664.

24. 1 FREDERICK POLLOCK & FREDERIC W. MAITLAND, THE HISTORY OF ENGLISH LAW 183 (2d ed. 1968).

(g) When custom was enforced as law, an important policy underlying the separation-of-powers restriction on lawmaking by judges was preserved. The parties to the dispute were not unfairly surprised by the creation and retroactive application of a legal rule that did not exist when they engaged in the transaction that gave rise to the dispute. Thus, if the court performed the fact-finding task accurately and identified the custom correctly, the rule applied to resolve the dispute was, by definition, the one in existence when the parties entered into their transaction.

(h) When courts properly applied the analogical reasoning process of the common-law method, the courts observed the same separation-of-powers policy. The analogical reasoning process permitted the application of legal rules to disputes only when the disputes had features in common with past applications of the rules that made them substantially identical to the situations giving rise to those applications. This process prevented unfair surprise to the parties because, by hypothesis, the parties ought to have been aware of the similarities between their transaction and the substantially identical transaction to which the legal rule had been applied in the past.

(i) The description in this illustration involves planned transactions, as opposed to unplanned events such as torts. Unfair surprise is often absent in tort cases when common-law rules are extended to new situations because the parties relied on no legal rule in formulating their behavior. Because the tort was not planned or anticipated, the application of one legal rule rather than another defeated no one's expectations. This premise should not be *assumed*, however, because parties may rely on tort rules as well as commercial rules. For example, a charity may rely on a rule of charitable immunity by not purchasing insurance to indemnify itself against tort liability. To avoid unfair surprise in unplanned situations, a court must examine the facts of each case.[25]

* * * * *

When the doctrine of separation of powers was formalized in the state and national constitutions in the United States, the common-law method or process described in *Illustration 5-1* represented an accepted feature of "judicial power." The combined processes of fact-finding, judicial notice, and analogical reasoning that had allowed the English courts to develop and adapt the common law to new situations also satisfied separation-of-powers restrictions on judicial lawmaking by limiting the policy choices of judges and preventing the creation of rules that unfairly surprised the parties to a dispute.[26]

Even in today's substantially different legal system, arguments derived from analogy and preexisting principle are considered vital to the proper performance of the judicial function in a system of separation of powers. Arguments from analogy

---

25. *See* A.W.B. Simpson, *The Common Law and Legal Theory*, *in* OXFORD ESSAYS IN JURISPRUDENCE (SECOND SERIES) 77 (A.W.B. Simpson ed. 1973); *see also* Celia Wasserstein Fassberg, *The Empirical and Theoretical Underpinnings of the Law Merchant: Lex Mercatoria—Hoist With Its Own Petard?* 5 CHI. J. INT'L L. 67 (2004). The view of the law merchant as a body of uniform law produced by an autonomous merchant class has recently been challenged. *See* Stephen E. Sachs, *From St. Ives to Cyperspace: The Modern Distortion of the Medieval "Law Merchant,"* 21 AM. U. INT'L REV. 685 (2006).

26. *See* RANDALL BRIDWELL & RALPH U. WHITTEN, THE CONSTITUTION AND THE COMMON LAW: THE DECLINE OF THE DOCTRINES OF SEPARATION OF POWERS AND FEDERALISM 21 (1977).

and preexisting principle permit judges to make law only "interstitially."[27] Thus, while a judge's lawmaking power is more readily conceded today than in the eighteenth and nineteenth centuries, judges are still obligated to avoid encroachment on legislative prerogatives by keeping their lawmaking activities within appropriate boundaries.

Nevertheless, the legitimate scope of the lawmaking power of the courts is disputed today. The lawmaking power of courts has expanded from the narrow scope permissible under the traditional common-law process accepted in the eighteenth and nineteenth centuries. This expansion raises serious, complex questions about the nature and extent of the separation of powers between the legislative and judicial branches of government today. No mathematical formula exists by which proper judicial lawmaking can be distinguished from improper judicial "legislation." The task requires a sensitivity both to historical form and the function of courts in a modern political democracy. For the time being, it is sufficient to note that because a legal rule is "common law," rather than statutory or constitutional in nature, judges are not completely free from constraints on their lawmaking power.

SECTION B. CONFLICT-OF-LAWS PROBLEMS IN A FEDERAL SYSTEM

As described in section A, above, the task of staying within proper lawmaking limits is difficult, even when the courts are only concerned with determining the content of the law of their own government. The task can become much more complex when the judges must determine whether to apply the law of some other government to a dispute, and if so, what that law is. Such cases commonly are said to present "conflict-of-laws" problems.

Illustration 5-2. Assume that *P*, a citizen of State *X*, is injured in an automobile accident in State *X* with *D*, a citizen of State *Y*. Pursuant to a proper long-arm statute, State *X* obtains jurisdiction over *D* in a suit brought by *P*. Should a court in State *X* apply the law of State *X*, of State *Y*, or some other state? If the issue is whether *D* has violated the rules of the road in producing *P's* injuries, the answer will probably be the law of State *X*, which is where the accident occurred. The "conflict of laws" or "choice-of-law" rules of State *X* and most other states would point to *X's* substantive rules under such circumstances. Suppose, however, that State *X* has a guest statute that bars recovery by a guest-passenger in an automobile driven by a host-driver unless gross negligence can be established. Suppose further that *P* was a guest-passenger in a car driven by *D*, that the trip originated and was to end in State *Y*, and that State *Y* has no guest statute. Suddenly,

---

27. *See* NEIL MACCORMICK, LEGAL REASONING AND LEGAL THEORY 188 (1978):

> [T]here must be criterion for distinguishing interstitial from architectural legislation. One possible criterion is that either a relevant analogy or an established principle is a necessary element of justification of an innovative decision. So if we seek a reason why arguments from analogy or from principle have the force they have in legal argument, the answer is the existence of a highly desirable conventional rule conferring power on judges to extend the law to cover circumstances not directly or unambiguously governed by established mandatory rules, but imposing limits on the extent of that power.

the considerations relevant to a determination of the conflict-of-laws problem have multiplied. The substantive law of State *X* no longer clearly applies to the guest-host relationship formed in another state between a resident host and a foreign guest.

* * * * *

The conflict-of-laws problem described in *Illustration 5-2* is typical of the kinds of problems that can arise in a federal system. A detailed examination of such problems must be reserved for treatises on Conflict of Laws.[28] However, one kind of choice of law problem is directly relevant to Civil Procedure. What law should a federal court apply in cases in which the court's subject-matter jurisdiction is based on diversity of citizenship between the parties? Section 34 of the Judiciary Act of 1789 (the Rules of Decision Act) provided "[t]hat the law of the several states, except where the Constitution, treaties, or statutes of the United States shall otherwise require or provide, shall be regarded as rules of decision in trials at common law in the Courts of the United States, in cases where they apply."[29] Over the two hundred years it has existed, the Rules of Decision Act has undergone differing interpretations. The next three sections of this chapter examine these interpretations.

SECTION C. THE DOCTRINE OF *SWIFT V. TYSON*

The modern interpretation of the Rules of Decision Act is embodied in the *Erie* doctrine—so named for the case of *Erie Railroad v. Tompkins*[30] decided by the U.S. Supreme Court in 1938. To understand the Rules of Decision Act and the *Erie* decision, however, one must begin at a much earlier date, with the decision in *Swift v. Tyson*,[31] decided by the Supreme Court in 1842. That decision is the source of the "*Swift*" doctrine.

1. The *Swift* Decision

The *Swift* case involved a suit on a negotiable instrument brought within the diversity jurisdiction of the federal courts.[32] Two individuals, Norton and Keith, represented themselves to be the owners of land in Maine. Tyson contracted with them to purchase the land. As part of the consideration for the purchase, Norton drew a bill of exchange on Tyson, which Tyson accepted in New York.[33] Norton endorsed the bill to Swift in return for Swift's cancellation of a preexisting debt.

---

28. *See, e.g.*, ROBERT L. FELIX & RALPH U. WHITTEN, AMERICAN CONFLICTS LAW (6th ed. 2011); PETER HAY, ET AL., CONFLICT OF LAWS (5th ed. 2010); RUSSELL J. WEINTRAUB, COMMENTARY ON THE CONFLICT OF LAWS (6th ed. 2010).

29. § 34, 1 Stat. 73, 92. The current version of the Rules of Decision Act is found in 28 U.S.C. § 1652.

30. 304 U.S. 64, 58 S. Ct. 817, 82 L. Ed. 1188 (1938).

31. 41 U.S. (16 Pet.) 1, 10 L. Ed. 865 (1842).

32. For an excellent discussion of the negotiable instruments aspects of *Swift*, as well as the view of law embodied in the case, see William P. LaPiana, Swift v. Tyson *and the Brooding Omnipresence in the Sky: An Investigation of the Idea of Law in Antebellum America*, 20 SUFFOLK U.L. REV. 771 (1986).

33. A bill of exchange is a written order from one person directing another person to pay a sum of money to a specified third person, to the drawer of the instrument, or to the bearer of the instrument. If the bill is accepted by the person ordered to pay, it becomes a valid obligation owed by the acceptor. If, as is normally the case, the bill is framed so as to be negotiable, the drawer of the bill can then transfer it to a third party in accord with the rules governing negotiable instruments, and the acceptor of the bill will have to pay the amount owed to the transferee of the bill when it becomes due.

When the bill became due, Tyson refused to pay Swift because Norton and Keith had fraudulently misrepresented that they owned the land in Maine. Swift sued Tyson in the U.S. Circuit Court for the Southern District of New York to collect the amount of the bill. Tyson attempted to raise the defense that there was fraud in the original transaction between Tyson and Norton and Keith. Swift objected that this defense was not valid as to him because he was a bona fide purchaser for value (today, a holder in due course) of the bill and thus immune from defenses between the original parties. There was no question that Swift had taken the bill before it became due with no knowledge of the fraud practiced by Norton and Keith in the original transaction with Tyson. However, the judges of the circuit court divided on another question. Did cancellation of a preexisting debt constitute valuable consideration for the transfer of the bill of exchange? If it did, Swift was a bona fide purchaser for value. If it did not, Swift was not a bona fide purchaser and was subject to the defenses that would have existed in a suit by Norton and Keith against Tyson.

The circuit court judges certified the question of negotiable instruments law to the U.S. Supreme Court. In his opinion for the Court, Justice Joseph Story first addressed Tyson's contention that because the bill of exchange was accepted in New York, it was a New York contract and thus controlled by the laws of New York. Under the New York decisions, Tyson contended, a preexisting debt did not constitute valuable consideration for the transfer of a negotiable instrument. Story first examined the New York decisions and concluded that they were unsettled on the question certified.[34] Then, in a memorable and often misunderstood passage, Justice Story held for a unanimous Court[35] that even if the New York decisions had been settled, those decisions would not control the case.

To reach this conclusion, Justice Story had to interpret § 34 of the Judiciary Act of 1789—the Rules of Decision Act. Significantly, Story first observed that the "Courts of New York" were not basing their decisions on any local law, but were attempting to "deduce the doctrine from the general principles of commercial law."[36] Nevertheless, it had been argued that the Rules of Decision Act required the federal courts to follow the decisions of the state courts "in all cases to which they apply."[37] This argument was based on an interpretation of the word "laws" in the Rules of Decision Act as including state court decisions.[38] Story rejected this interpretation. The Court held that the word "laws" did not, "[i]n the ordinary use

---

34. *See Swift*, 41 U.S. (16 Pet.) at 16-18, 10 L. Ed. at 870-71.

35. Despite later criticism of Story's opinion in *Swift*, it is significant that on the point of interpretation of the Rules of Decision Act for which *Swift* became famous, the Court was unanimous. Justice Catron concurred, objecting to a dictum by Story on a point of negotiable instruments law not before the Court, *see* 41 U.S. (16 Pet.) at 23-24, 10 L. Ed. at 872. However, no Justice objected to Story's interpretation of the Rules of Decision Act, which, as is demonstrated below, had long been accepted by the time *Swift* was decided.

36. Justice Story stated:

> But, admitting the doctrine to be fully settled in New York, it remains to be considered, whether it is obligatory upon this Court, if it differs from the principles established in the general commercial law. It is observable that the Courts of New York do not found their decisions upon this point upon any local statute, or positive, fixed, or ancient local usage: but they deduce the doctrine from the general principles of commercial law.

41 U.S. at 18, 10 L. Ed. at 871.

37. *See id.*

38. *See id.*

of language," include court decisions.[39] However, his opinion stated that the "laws of a state" were usually understood to include statutes and long-established local customs having the force of law. The Rules of Decision Act, said Story, had been uniformly interpreted to apply only to state laws of a local nature, such as statutes "and the construction thereof adopted by the local tribunals, and to rights and titles to things having a permanent locality, such as the rights and titles to real estate, and other matters immovable and intraterritorial in their nature and character," but not to "questions of a more general nature," such as questions of general commercial law.[40]

The statement that the Rules of Decision Act includes court decisions construing statutes (and other local laws), but not court decisions on matters of general commercial law seems contradictory. It would appear that court decisions should either constitute laws within the meaning of the Rules of Decision Act or they should not. As discussed below, however, the statements are not contradictory when read in the full context of the jurisprudence of the time. A significant factor in explaining the statements is Story's further explanation that when determining questions of general commercial law, "the state tribunals are called upon to perform the like functions as ourselves, that is, to ascertain upon general reasoning and legal analogies . . . what is the just rule furnished by the principles of commercial law to govern the case."[41]

Critics of *Swift* have focused on Story's view of the nature of law expressed in the decision. In particular, Justice Story has been criticized for his view that court decisions were not law and that general commercial law transcended the authority of any specific government. Nevertheless, the best historical scholarship has confirmed that Story's view of law was widely shared at the time *Swift* was decided.[42] In the discussion that follows, it will be demonstrated that the *Swift* decision was fully compatible with principles of separation of powers and federalism. The discussion will necessarily be far ranging because the *Swift* decision was only a component of a larger body of jurisprudence in the federal courts. In understanding that jurisprudence, it is important to keep in mind two aspects of the *Swift* decision. First, at the beginning of the discussion of the Rules of Decision Act, Justice Story pointed out that the New York decisions were not founded on any

---

39. Justice Story stated:

> In order to maintain the argument, it is essential, therefore, to hold, that the word "laws," in this section, includes within the scope of its meaning the decisions of the local tribunals. In the ordinary use of language it will hardly be contended that the decisions of Courts constitute laws. They are, at most, only evidence of what the laws are; and are not of themselves laws. They are often reexamined, reversed, and qualified by the Courts themselves, whenever they are found to be either defective, or ill-founded, or otherwise incorrect.

41 U.S. at 18, 10 L. Ed. at 871.

40. *See* 41 U.S (16 Pet.) at 18-19, 10 L. Ed. at 871.

41. 41 U.S.(16 Pet.) at 19, 10 L. Ed. at 871. Having reasoned that the U.S. Supreme Court was entitled to make an independent judgment on the content of the general commercial law, Justice Story then concluded that the cancellation of a preexisting debt did constitute valuable consideration for the transfer of a negotiable instrument. *See id.* at 19-22, 10 L. Ed. at 871-72.

42. *See, e.g.*, WILFRED J. RITZ, REWRITING THE HISTORY OF THE JUDICIARY ACT OF 1789, at 28-30 (Wythe Holt & L.H. LaRue eds., 1989) (discussing the eighteenth century function of judges to "find" law); William P. LaPiana, Swift v. Tyson *and the Brooding Omnipresence in the Sky: An Investigation of the Idea of Law in Antebellum America*, 20 SUFFOLK U.L. REV. 771 (1986); *see also* William A. Fletcher, *The General Common Law and Section 34 of the Judiciary Act of 1789: The Example of Marine Insurance*, 97 HARV. L. REV. 1513 (1984) (finding the *Swift* holding to be a restatement of settled law).

local rule of common law, but were attempts to deduce the correct principle of general commercial law. In other words, New York courts themselves agreed that cases like *Swift* should be governed by something called *general commercial law*. Second, Justice Story did not say federal courts would never treat state court decisions as binding. Rather, Story said the federal courts would not be bound by such decisions on matters of general law, as opposed to local law. When these two aspects of the opinion are combined with a number of well-accepted principles drawn from the jurisprudence of the time, the *Swift* decision will be seen to be a rather ordinary example of antebellum jurisprudence, acceptable under all potentially applicable constitutional doctrines.

2. The *Swift* Doctrine

The doctrine that has taken its name from *Swift v. Tyson* was, in fact, a complex body of rules governing all aspects of the power of the federal courts to administer law. What became known as the *Swift* doctrine was, in reality, a mixture or interaction of principles derived from at least four different sources: (1) the concepts of sovereignty that governed the power of the states relative to each other and to the federal government during the early nineteenth century; (2) the doctrine of stare decisis, which governed the precedential value of the decisions of courts in a common-law system; (3) the concept of separation of powers between the legislative and judicial branches of the federal government that prevailed in the early nineteenth century; and (4) the early nineteenth-century understanding of the purposes of the diversity jurisdiction exercised by the federal courts.

Once one understands the interaction of the principles derived from these sources, Justice Story's opinion in *Swift* becomes more comprehensible. It also becomes possible to understand how many critics of the *Swift* doctrine have been misled by the opinion. These critics failed to read the opinion in the context of the nineteenth century, law-administering power of the federal courts. Others also failed to recognize that the *Swift* doctrine did not remain static over time, but began to change radically in the latter part of the nineteenth century. The later expansion of the law-administering power of the federal courts, which modern courts and commentators have found objectionable, was not a part of the original *Swift* approach.

(a) Sovereignty

By the time *Swift v. Tyson* was decided, it had long been established that § 34 of the Judiciary Act of 1789 was a conflict-of-laws directive to the federal courts. The portion of § 34 that produced this directive was the Act's "in cases where they apply" language.[43] In this regard, a warning is in order to those reading

---

43. *See* Hawkins v. Barney's Lessee, 30 U.S. (5 Pet.) 457, 464, 8 L. Ed. 190, 192-93 (1831); Society for Propagation of Gospel v. Wheeler, 22 F. Cas. 756, 767 (C.C.D.N.H. 1814) (No. 13,156) (Story, J.); Van Reimsdyk v. Kane, 28 F. Cas. 1062, 1065 (C.C.D.R.I. 1812) (No. 16,871), *rev'd on other grounds sub nom.* Clark's Ex'rs v. Van Riemsdyk, 13 U.S. (9 Cranch) 153, 3 L. Ed. 688 (1815); RANDALL BRIDWELL & RALPH U. WHITTEN, THE CONSTITUTION AND THE COMMON LAW: THE DECLINE OF THE DOCTRINES OF SEPARATION OF POWERS AND

the modern commentaries on the Rules of Decision Act. Some commentators who attempt to read the Act without benefit of historical research into how it was originally interpreted become befuddled by the "in cases where they apply" language.[44] Specifically, the "in cases where they apply" language directed the federal courts to make an independent conflict-of-laws decision about which state's law was applicable when no federal statutory, constitutional, or treaty provision existed to control the case before the court. However, the Supreme Court also had made it clear that § 34 was merely declarative of the rule that would have been followed even if the section had never been included as part of the original Judiciary Act.[45] Thus, even in the absence of § 34, it would have been implied from the grant of diversity jurisdiction that (1) federal courts were required to administer state law when no controlling federal law existed and (2) because diversity cases by definition involved disputes between citizens of different states, the federal courts were obligated as a matter of necessity to choose which state's law "applied." The rules by which this independent conflict-of-laws decision were to be made were the accepted "territorial" conflict-of-laws rules of the time, which incorporated the nineteenth century notions of the power of respective sovereigns to control various events with their laws.

As discussed in Chapter 3(A)(1)*(c)*, the international rules of jurisdiction governing the enforceability of the judgments of the courts of one nation in other nations remained in effect after the formation of the U.S. Constitution. By entering into the constitutional system, the states ceded a certain portion of their sovereignty to the national government. However, the states otherwise retained their status as independent sovereigns. Consequently, the international rules of jurisdiction continued in existence. The body of "private international law" containing the rules of jurisdiction also contained conflict-of-laws rules dictating when the courts of one sovereign would apply the substantive law of another sovereign. Like the jurisdictional rules, these conflict-of-laws rules were "territorial" in nature. They focused upon some event occurring, or object or person located, within the borders of a state or nation as the significant indicator of which state or nation's substantive law should be applied. The existence of the territorial conflict-of-laws rules

---

FEDERALISM 110-11 (1977); 2 WILLIAM W. CROSSKEY, POLITICS AND THE CONSTITUTION IN THE HISTORY OF THE UNITED STATES 832-34, 867 (1953); William F. Baxter, *Choice of Law and the Federal System*, 16 STAN. L. REV. 1, 41 (1963).

44. Consider, for example, the following excerpt from MARTIN REDISH, FEDERAL JURISDICTION: TENSIONS IN THE ALLOCATION OF JUDICIAL POWER 121 (2d ed. 1990): "[T]he Act's language contains within it a circularity which renders it all but useless. To say that state laws shall serve as the rules of decision 'in cases where they apply' ultimately fails to tell us to which cases state laws specifically 'apply'"; *see also* Note, *The Federal Common Law*, 82 HARV. L. REV. 1512, 1515 (1969).

45. *See, e.g.*, Hawkins v. Barney's Lessee, 30 U.S. (5 Pet.) 457, 464, 8 L. Ed. 190, 193 (1831). Research by the late Professor Wilfred J. Ritz into the history of the Judiciary Act of 1789 has indicated that *Swift* may have misinterpreted § 34 of the Act. Specifically, Professor Ritz argues that § 34 was probably a temporary measure designed to provide an applicable American law for national prosecutions brought in federal courts before Congress enacted statutory criminal provisions. The historical proof of Professor Ritz's thesis is complex and includes the position of § 34 in the Judiciary Act of 1789, the use of the wording "laws of the several states" instead of "laws of the respective states," and other evidence. *See* WILFRED J. RITZ, REWRITING THE HISTORY OF THE JUDICIARY ACT OF 1789, at 126-48, 149-63 (Wythe Holt & L.H. LaRue eds., 1989). If Professor Ritz is correct, the Supreme Court was incorrect in *Swift* and other cases to read § 34 as a requirement that state local law be applied in diversity actions. However, this does not mean that *Swift* and other decisions were incorrect in their results. As *Hawkins, supra*, and the text indicate, the same results would have been reached by the federal courts in diversity actions even if § 34 had not existed.

governing the relations of independent sovereigns explains how the federal courts arrived at the independent conflict-of-laws decisions they were obligated to make by the "in cases where they apply" language of the Rules of Decision Act. Those courts simply followed the generally accepted, international territorial rules of conflict of laws that governed the relations between independent sovereigns. The "in cases where they apply" language implied that the conflict-of-laws decision required by the language would be made in accord with those principles that governed the relationships between independent governments. At the time, those principles were the territorial rules.

In *Swift v. Tyson*, the territorial conflict-of-laws rule governing contract cases like *Swift* was that the substantive law of the place where the contract was made governed the rights and obligations of the parties under the contract.[46] Because the bill of exchange had been accepted in New York, the contract was considered to have been "made" there. Under this rule, all other states and nations at that time would have applied New York substantive law to resolve any dispute that arose under the contract. New York followed the general commercial law in *Swift*, so other states and nations would apply the general commercial law to resolve disputes under the contract—exactly what the Supreme Court did in *Swift*. Had the New York courts refused to follow the general commercial law and instead grounded their decisions on the issue in question on some rule of local law, the federal courts would have been obliged to do likewise. This conclusion is implied in *Swift* by Justice Story's observation that the New York courts were basing their decisions in the area on general commercial law rather than local custom. The point that has confused modern readers of *Swift* is Justice Story's refusal to consider the federal courts bound by state court *decisions* on general commercial law matters, as opposed to local matters. This result, however, was dictated by the nature of the sovereign choice that New York had made in deciding to follow general commercial law rather than local law.

Recall *Illustration 5-1* in section A, above. There, the law merchant, or general commercial law, was described as a body of worldwide customary rules. When a state decided to apply the general commercial law, the state elected to follow rules that were not uniquely local, but were considered to be the law of the entire civilized world. Thus, once a state had decided to apply the general commercial law, federal courts were not obligated to follow state decisions absolutely because the state had, in fact, made a sovereign decision to apply a body of uniform international custom also followed by all, or most, other states. As part of this decision, the state voluntarily relinquished a certain amount of control over the content of the commercial law that it had decided to enforce. While the state retained the right to determine for itself the content of the general commercial law administered in its own courts, the state's decision to adhere to general commercial law also meant that the courts of all other sovereigns would reserve the right to do likewise in their own courts. Had New York in *Swift v. Tyson* chosen to administer

---

46. Professor Ritz has argued that the prevailing conflict-of-laws rule required Maine law to apply in *Swift*. *See* WILFRED J. RITZ, REWRITING THE JUDICIARY ACT OF 1789, at 158 (Wythe Holt & L.H. LaRue eds. 1989). However, his argument appears to be incorrect insofar as the state of the law at the time *Swift* was decided is concerned. *See id.* at 158 n.42 (editors' note).

a body of *local* commercial law, whether statutory or common law, the federal courts, New Jersey courts, Maine courts, and all other courts would have considered themselves bound by New York's decisions on the content of that local law. As a result, they would have applied the New York local commercial rule whenever international conflict-of-laws rules would permit New York as a sovereign to control the transaction that gave rise to the dispute.

However, by deciding to follow the general commercial law instead of a local commercial rule and by deciding that the relevant commercial rule was that a preexisting debt did not constitute valuable consideration, New York sent essentially two messages to the courts of other sovereigns: (1) New York wished to follow the general commercial law, and (2) New York believed the general commercial law to be that a preexisting debt did not constitute valuable consideration. If the courts of other sovereigns saw the second message as incorrect, they were faced with a dilemma—should they disregard the first message and conclude that New York did not wish to follow general commercial law due to its "incorrect" understanding of the content of that law? Alternatively, should they accept the first message and disregard the second, on the assumption that New York really did wish to adhere to the general commercial law, but had (temporarily) misunderstood its content?

In fact, the dilemma was easily resolved because the first message was vastly more important from a policy standpoint. Consequently, the U.S. Supreme Court applied the general commercial law in *Swift* as New York indicated it wished to do. However, the Court made its own independent determination of the content of that law, as New York's decision to follow the general commercial law had given all courts the right to do. By adopting this approach, the U.S. Supreme Court gave New York's sovereignty and the principle of federalism all the respect they were due.

Illustration 5-3. Assume that during the *Swift* era New York enacted a statute providing that cancellation of a preexisting debt would not constitute valuable consideration for the transfer of a bill of exchange. Thereafter, *D*, a citizen of New York, accepts a bill of exchange in New York City drawn by *C*, a citizen of Maine, on *D*. The bill is given in payment for lands located in Maine sold by *C* to *D*. Subsequently, *C* endorses the bill to *P*, a citizen of Maine, in Portland, Maine. In return, *P* cancels a preexisting debt that *C* owes to *P*. When the bill of exchange comes due, *D* refuses to pay it on the ground that the original transaction between *D* and *C* was fraudulent, in that *C* did not have title to the Maine lands that *C* purported to sell to *D*. *P* sues *D* in a federal court in New York to recover the amount of the bill of exchange, jurisdiction being based on diversity of citizenship. *D* defends on the ground that there was fraud in the original transaction. *P* contends that *D's* defense is invalid, because *P* is a bona fide purchaser for value of the bill of exchange. *P's* claim should fail. The only difference between facts of this illustration and the facts of *Swift v. Tyson* is that here New York has "localized" its rule of commercial law by enacting a statute. Because the bill of exchange was accepted in New York, the contract was "made" there, and thus New York had the right to control the transaction with its law under the traditional territorial conflict-of-laws rules. Here, unlike *Swift*, New York law is local, and the federal courts, as well as all other courts, would have been obliged to apply it.

Illustration 5-4. Assume the same facts as in *Illustration 5-3*, except that the bill of exchange was accepted by *D* in Maine. Assume further that Maine decisions indicate that Maine follows the general commercial law. However, the Maine decisions also indicate that the Maine courts believe that the correct general commercial law rule is that cancellation of a preexisting debt does not constitute valuable consideration for the transfer of a bill of exchange. In the federal action in New York, the court should apply general commercial law, but should make an independent judgment about what the correct rule of general commercial law is. Because the bill of exchange was accepted in Maine, Maine had the power to control the transaction with its substantive law under the prevailing territorial conflict-of-laws rules. Maine follows the general commercial law. Therefore, the federal court in New York is obligated to apply the general commercial law also, the New York statute notwithstanding. However, Maine's decision to follow the general commercial law gave authority to any court that was adjudicating a case under Maine law to make an independent judgment about what the correct rule of general commercial law was. Because there was broad agreement that cancellation of a preexisting debt did constitute valuable consideration for the transfer of a bill of exchange under the general commercial law, *P* would win on the facts of this illustration.

(b) Stare Decisis

In *Swift*, Justice Story interpreted the word "laws" in the Rules of Decision Act as not including court decisions—a pronouncement that led later commentators, such as Professor John Chipman Gray, to ridicule Story's opinion.[47] Gray and others who have examined *Swift* were confused because they neglected to take account of how the doctrine of stare decisis interacted with principles of sovereignty and the Rules of Decision Act to produce different degrees of respect owed to state-court decisions by federal courts and other state courts.

The best explanation of this interaction appears in the case of *Carroll v. Carroll's Lessee*.[48] In *Carroll*, Michael B. Carroll executed a will on September 10,

---

47. Justice Story stated:

> Among the causes which led to the decision in *Swift v. Tyson*, the chief seems to have been the character and position of [Justice] Story. He was then by far the oldest judge in commission on the bench; he was a man of great learning, and of reputation for learning greater even than the learning itself; he was occupied at the time in writing a book on bills of exchange, which would, of itself, lead him to dogmatize on the subject; he had had great success in extending the jurisdiction of the Admiralty; he was fond of glittering generalities; and he was possessed by a restless vanity. All these things conspired to produce the result.
>
> . . . .
>
> If "the laws of a State" in the 34th section of the Judiciary Act mean its statutes only, then the decisions of the State courts should stand alike, and none of them should have the binding weight that is now given to some of them. If, on the other hand, "the laws" are to include "decisions," the Judiciary Act would allow no difference between them and statutes. On the general question, therefore, whether decisions are sources of the law, the doctrine of the Supreme Court of the United States in *Swift v. Tyson* throws no light. If they are sources of Law, they should be followed even when dealing with non-statutory commercial matters. If they are not, then they are not binding when dealing with real estate or the construction of statutes. The doctrine of *Swift v. Tyson* is an anomaly, and does not lend a support to either theory.

JOHN C. GRAY, THE NATURE AND SOURCES OF THE LAW 253, 255 (2d rev. ed. 1921; Peter Smith reprint 1972).

48. 57 U.S. (16 How.) 275, 14 L. Ed. 936 (1854).

1837, disposing of his real and personal property. Subsequently, he acquired land in Maryland that he had not owned on the date the will was executed. The Maryland Legislature then enacted a statute providing that wills should be construed to speak and take effect as of the date of the testator's death. The statute altered the Maryland common-law rule that a will could not devise property acquired after the date of the will's execution. However, the statute was to take effect on June 1, 1850. It was not to apply to wills executed before its enactment unless it appeared from the will that the testator intended it to speak as of the date of his death. The issue was whether the statute applied to Carroll's will.

When the case reached the U.S. Supreme Court, the Court determined that the statute did not apply to Carroll's will. In reaching this decision, the Court had to consider the force that should be given to a decision of the Maryland Court of Appeals adjudicating the effect of the same will. The U.S. Supreme Court stated:

> If the Court of Appeals had found it necessary to construe a statute of that State in order to decide upon the rights of parties subject to its judicial control, such a decision, deliberately made, might have been taken by this [C]ourt as a basis on which to rest our judgment. But it must be remembered that we are bound to decide a question of local law, upon which the rights of parties depend, as well as every other question, as we find it ought to be decided. In making the examination preparatory to this finding, this [C]ourt has followed two rules, one of which belongs to the common law, and the other is a part of our peculiar judicial system. The first is the maxim of the common law, stare decisis. The second grows out of the thirty-fourth section of the Judiciary Act, . . . which makes the laws of the several States the rules of decision in trials at the common law; and inasmuch as the States have committed to their respective judiciaries the power to construe and fix the meaning of the statutes passed by their legislatures, this [C]ourt has taken such constructions as part of the law of the State, and has administered the law as thus construed. But this rule has grown up and been held with constant reference to the other rule, stare decisis; and it is only so far and in such cases as this latter rule can operate, that the other has any effect.[49]

Based on basic principles of stare decisis, the Court then explained that the Maryland decision would not be given effect because it was dictum on the point in question.[50]

As far as the general commercial law is concerned, the important aspect of this passage is the Court's statement that, because the states had committed to their respective judiciaries the power to fix the meaning of the statutes passed by their legislatures, "this court has taken such constructions as part of the law of the state, and has administered the law as thus construed." This statement meant that federal courts would be *bound* by settled state decisions interpreting state statutes.

---

49. *Id.* at 286, 14 L. Ed. at 285.
50. *Id.* at 286-87, 14 L. Ed. at 285.

Likewise, as Justice Story had indicated in *Swift*, the settled decisions of the state courts on *local* common-law issues bound the federal courts. Justice Story's opinion carefully pointed out that on the issue involved in *Swift*, the New York courts did not base their decisions on "any local statute, or positive, fixed or ancient local usage."[51] The reason that the state decisions were considered binding on "local" matters was simply that the state decisions were the highest evidence of the meaning and content of local law because the states had committed final authority to "fix" the meaning of local law to their courts.

However, the states could not confer authority on their courts to "fix" the content of the general commercial law in a way that bound other states. The general commercial law was, by definition, a body of world-wide custom. A state choosing to follow the general commercial law was, therefore, choosing to follow law whose content had been "fixed" over centuries by the practices of merchants trading internationally. Therefore, the task for the state courts in general commercial law cases was one of identifying the worldwide custom. A single state's opinion on a general commercial law matter could not bind all other states and nations, for a single state had no sovereign authority to fix the content of world custom "finally" as it did to fix the content of local law "finally." As Justice Story observed in *Swift*, on general commercial law matters, "the State tribunals are called upon to perform the like functions as ourselves, that is, to ascertain upon general reasoning and legal analogies, what is the . . . just rule furnished by the principles of commercial law to govern the case."[52]

This scheme honored all relevant principles of federalism. On those issues (of local law) over which the state had the ultimate sovereign power, the federal courts considered themselves *bound* to follow settled state decisions on the content of the law. When the state did not have absolute sovereign power (on issues of the content of general commercial law), however, the federal courts were not bound by state-court decisions in determining the law. The state's sovereign authority was respected fully by the federal court's absolute adherence to whatever decision the state had made about *whether* to follow the general commercial law. If the state chose to do so, as in *Swift*, the federal courts would respect the state's decision.

It is important to understand a second aspect of the doctrine of stare decisis, involved in both *Swift* and *Carroll*. In *Swift*, Justice Story indicated two reasons why the federal courts were not bound by New York decisions on the issue of substantive law disputed in the case. One reason, the one for which *Swift* is famous, was that federal courts were *not bound* by state decisions on issues of general commercial law. The other reason was that the New York decisions on the substantive issue were "unsettled." Thus, even if New York had indicated that it did *not* follow the general commercial law and, therefore, that the substantive issue was controlled by New York local law (either statutory or common law), the federal courts would not have been bound by the unsettled New York decisions on the point of local law.

---

51. *See Swift*, 41 U.S. (16 Pet.) at 18, 10 L. Ed. at 871.
52. *Id.* at 19, 10 L. Ed. at 16.

The reasons for this conclusion were explained in *Carroll*. Recall that the Court there stated that state decisions were binding only to the extent that they were given force by the common-law doctrine of stare decisis. When state-court opinions on a point of law were either contradictory (as in *Swift*) or dictum (as in *Carroll*), the doctrine of stare decisis did not give the opinions binding force. As the Supreme Court observed in *Carroll,* "this [C]ourt and other courts organized under the common law" would not be bound by decisions except in accord with the common-law principles of stare decisis.[53]

This approach did not violate principles of federalism. The state courts, like the federal courts, were "organized under the common law." Consequently, the state courts did not hold themselves obligated to follow their own decisions when those decisions were not rendered binding by traditional principles of stare decisis. Thus, even if a point of local law had been in dispute in *Swift*, the New York courts might not have considered themselves bound to follow the previous New York decisions on the point because those decisions were contradictory.

Likewise, in *Carroll*, the Maryland Court of Appeals decision would not have been considered binding by Maryland's own courts because the opinion on the relevant substantive point was dictum. Why should the federal courts have considered themselves bound by state decisions that would not be considered binding in the state's own courts? The answer is that the federal courts should not have considered, and did not consider, themselves bound by such decisions.[54]

When were state decisions considered unsettled? In *Swift* itself, the decisions were contradictory and the contradictions had not been resolved clearly by the state courts. Therefore, state law was unsettled. In *Carroll v. Carroll's Lessee*, the state decision was not on point. Consequently, state law was considered to be unsettled. State law also could be unsettled if there were no state cases dealing with the issue in question.[55] Finally, if the state decisions were by a court, such as an inferior state court, without authority finally to "fix" the meaning of state law, state law might be considered unsettled.[56]

---

53. *Carroll*, 57 U.S. (16 How.) at 287, 14 L. Ed. at 287.

54. Some glaring mistakes have been made by commentators on the *Swift* doctrine who have incorrectly read U.S. Supreme Court decisions refusing to follow *unsettled* state authorities as decisions *overriding settled* state authorities. *Compare, e.g.*, 2 WILLIAM W. CROSSKEY, POLITICS AND THE CONSTITUTION IN THE HISTORY OF THE UNITED STATES 719-53 (1953) (analyzing Huidekoper's Lessee v. Douglass, 7 U.S. (3 Cranch) 1, 2 L. Ed. 347 (1805)) *with* RANDALL BRIDWELL & RALPH U. WHITTEN, THE CONSTITUTION AND THE COMMON LAW: THE DECLINE OF THE DOCTRINES OF SEPARATION OF POWERS AND FEDERALISM 101-05 (1977) (disputing Crosskey's interpretation of *Huidekoper's Lessee*).

55. *See* Wilson v. Mason, 5 U.S. (1 Cranch) 45, 2 L. Ed. 29 (1801); RANDALL BRIDWELL & RALPH U. WHITTEN, THE CONSTITUTION AND THE COMMON LAW: THE DECLINE OF THE DOCTRINES OF SEPARATION OF POWERS AND FEDERALISM 101 (1977).

56. *Cf.* Huidekoper's Lessee v. Douglass, 7 U.S. (3 Cranch) 1, 2 L. Ed. 347 (1805); RANDALL BRIDWELL & RALPH U. WHITTEN, THE CONSTITUTION AND THE COMMON LAW: THE DECLINE OF THE DOCTRINES OF SEPARATION OF POWERS AND FEDERALISM 104-05 (1977). Professor Ritz's excellent work on the Judiciary Act of 1789 has pointed out that most states in the eighteenth century did not have modern systems of appellate review with a single court of last resort charged with the responsibility of fixing the meaning of state law. *See* WILFRED J. RITZ, REWRITING THE JUDICIARY ACT OF 1789, at 27, 35-49 (Wythe Holt & L.H. LaRue eds., 1989). To the extent that a state did not have a modern system of appellate review, the federal courts obviously could not refuse to follow state court decisions that were properly "settled" under the system that the state did have. However, one must approach Professor Ritz's findings with caution. The fact that a state had not established a "pure" system of appellate review along modern lines does not mean that the state did not have a court with final authority to fix the meaning of state law. For example, Professor Ritz points out that Maryland authorized a modern court of appeals in 1776, but did not establish that the Maryland Court of Appeals was to have appellate jurisdiction until 1851.

Illustration 5-5. In 1789, State *X* had a system of trial courts with general original jurisdiction to determine all civil actions. State *X* did not have an appellate system organized along modern lines. Instead, the trial judges in the state would get together from time to time to consider questions appropriate for decision by a tribunal exercising the functions of appellate review.[57] If the trial judges exercising their appellate function decided a matter of local state law, it would be binding on the federal courts—assuming that the decision was necessary to the decision of a case in the common-law sense and that the decision was published in a reliable form available to the federal courts.[58]

Illustration 5-6. *P*, a citizen of State *X*, sued *D*, a citizen of State *Y*, in a federal court in State *X*. *P* sought to quiet title to land located in State *X*. The issue in the case concerned the method by which title to land could be acquired by adverse possession in State *X*. The highest court in State *X* had rendered several decisions on the issue in the case. However, the decisions were conflicting. The latest statement on the issue was contained in a case in which it was unnecessary to the decision. The issue in the action is an issue of local law on which the federal courts under *Swift* were bound to follow the decisions of the state courts. Nevertheless, the federal court would have had to make its own independent determination of the adverse possession issue because the decisions in State *X* on the issue were unsettled.

(c) Separation of Powers

The doctrine of *Swift v. Tyson* has often been criticized as a violation of principles of federalism.[59] The preceding discussion of the concepts of sovereignty and stare decisis prevailing in the early nineteenth century has demonstrated that the *Swift* decision itself involved no such difficulties. In addition to federalism restrictions, however, the Constitution also contains separation-of-powers restrictions. As noted in section A, the traditional doctrine of separation of powers presupposes that the courts' lawmaking activities will be limited. While couched in federalism terms, much of the modern criticism of *Swift* really appears to be based on the theory that the Court was making law in too broad a fashion, thus violating implicit separation-of-powers restrictions on its authority. If the basic lawmaking powers in a case like *Swift* resided either in the sovereign state of New York or in Congress, where did the Supreme Court get the authority in *Swift* to enforce a rule prescribed by neither of those bodies?

The flaw in this criticism lies in a misperception of what the courts were doing when they administered the general commercial law. The most important feature of that law in terms of separation-of-powers principles was its characteristic as a body of private international *custom*. As custom, the commercial law had not

---

See id. at 36, 43-44, 45. This obviously does not mean that, as in *Carroll*, the Maryland Court of Appeals, when it was exercising appellate functions before 1851, would not have been treated as authoritative by the federal courts.

57. *Cf.* WILFRED J. RITZ, REWRITING THE JUDICIARY ACT OF 1789, at 43 (Wythe Holt & L.H. LaRue eds., 1989) (discussing the early judicial systems of North and South Carolina).

58. *See id.* at 46-48 (discussing the dates that modern systems of law reporting were established and the relationship between courts of appellate review and modern systems of law reporting).

59. *See, e.g.*, the discussion of *Erie Railroad v. Tompkins* in section D, *infra*.

been "created" by any one sovereign—*i.e.*, no institution within a government had made a conscious policy choice to make up particular rules for the convenience of its merchants. Rather, general commercial custom originated in the behavior of individuals—merchants—trading among seafaring nations. Indeed, the separate bodies of law now referred to as admiralty and commercial law were at one time a single body of "private international law" and only later separated into distinct subject areas.[60]

Substantively, therefore, the important policy choice involved when a state or nation decided to follow general commercial law was the choice to follow it, not the sovereign's approval or creation of the law's content, which had already been established by the interaction of private individuals. This "legislative" policy choice was respected in cases like *Swift* by the federal courts' adherence to whatever decision the relevant sovereign had made about *whether* to follow the general commercial law; and, of course, which sovereign was the "relevant" one to make the policy choice was determined by the international conflict-of-laws rules enforced under the "in cases where they apply" language of the Rules of Decision Act.

The content that needed to be added to the relatively mature body of commercial law rules in existence by the time of the *Swift* decision was added through the processes of analogical reasoning familiar to the common law and would be called today (as discussed in section A above) "interstitial lawmaking," which involved no separation-of-powers violation. Nevertheless, the separation-of-powers doctrine did impose limitations on the federal courts' ability to administer common-law rules. A comparison of the most important situation in which these limitations were present with cases in which separation of powers was not an obstacle to administration of common-law principles will further illustrate why the *Swift* decision did not involve proscribed lawmaking.

Early cases dealing with the common law of crimes and civil admiralty best illustrate how the separation-of-powers doctrine affected the common-law authority of the federal courts. Section 9 of the Judiciary Act of 1789 conferred exclusive subject-matter jurisdiction on the federal courts over federal crimes. Section 11 of the Act conferred exclusive jurisdiction of civil admiralty cases. Yet in the area of criminal jurisdiction, the Supreme Court refused to permit the administration of a common law of crimes, while in the area of admiralty the courts always and without question have applied "common-law" rules of admiralty.[61]

The distinction between these two kinds of cases was rooted in the separation-of-powers doctrine, which dictated that only the primary lawmaking branch of the government could decide whether a particular act was a crime and

---

60. *See* RANDALL BRIDWELL & RALPH U. WHITTEN, THE CONSTITUTION AND THE COMMON LAW: THE DECLINE OF THE DOCTRINES OF SEPARATION OF POWERS AND FEDERALISM 61 (1977); *see also* GRANT GILMORE & CHARLES L. BLACK, THE LAW OF ADMIRALTY § 1-3, at 5 (2d ed. 1975); THEODORE F.T. PLUCKNETT, A CONCISE HISTORY OF THE COMMON LAW ch. 5 (5th ed. 1956); Thomas E. Scrutton, *General Survey of the History of the Law Merchant*, *in* 3 SELECT ESSAYS IN ANGLO-AMERICAN LEGAL HISTORY 7, 11-12 (1909).

61. *See generally* RANDALL BRIDWELL & RALPH U. WHITTEN, THE CONSTITUTION AND THE COMMON LAW: THE DECLINE OF THE DOCTRINES OF SEPARATION OF POWERS AND FEDERALISM ch. 3 (1977).

affix a punishment to it.[62] Such a fundamental policy choice was beyond the scope of the judicial power because of the nature of the choices that the judiciary would have had to make in adopting common-law crimes as "federal" crimes. Although there were many acts that constituted crimes in the English common law and the common law of the states, it was inconceivable that *all* such acts would be adopted as federal crimes, given the limited power of the federal government. Yet if some, but not all, common-law crimes were to be adopted as "federal" crimes, how would the courts make the selection? It was apparent to the judges of the time that any process of picking and choosing among common-law crimes would amount to the kind of policy-making that was reserved to Congress. As Justice Johnson explained in the *Trial of William Butler for Piracy*:[63]

> [I]f the courts of the United States are to be at liberty to select such parts [of the common-law of crimes] as in their judgment are applicable, what is this but giving as much force to one part as to another? By what rule or principle are they to be governed in the selection? I know of none; and the consequence is, either that they find the whole system in force, or what is worse, erect themselves into legislators in the selection.[64]

The distinction between the common law of crimes and the civil admiralty was clear. It was not at all ridiculous to suppose that the whole body of "common-law" principle composing admiralty and maritime jurisprudence should be enforced by the federal courts within the exclusive grant of subject-matter jurisdiction to them. The constitutional and statutory grants of subject-matter jurisdiction in admiralty and maritime cases presupposed the existence of a body of rules that the courts would enforce within the jurisdictional grants.[65] As noted earlier, admiralty and maritime rules were private international customary rules that predated the Constitution. These rules were not created by any sovereign, in the first instance, but by seafaring merchants. The grant of admiralty jurisdiction presupposed that the federal courts would administer the whole body of these private rules *without* needing to make any legislative selection of which rules would be enforced. Of course, the question *whether* the United States should enforce the traditional admiralty principles did involve a legislative-like policy choice, but that choice had been made by the constitutional and statutory authorization of admiralty subject-matter jurisdiction itself. The *administration* of the rules of admiralty jurisprudence within the jurisdictional grant did not involve any additional policy choices forbidden to the judges, as would an enforcement of a federal common law of crimes. Moreover, the admiralty and maritime rules remained customary rules, created by private parties; whereas adoption of a common law of crimes would have

---

62. *See* United States v. Hudson & Goodwin, 11 U.S. (7 Cranch) 32, 33-34, 3 L. Ed. 259, 260 (1812); United States v. Coolidge, 14 U.S. (1 Wheat.) 415, 4 L. Ed. 124 (1816); JOHN M. GOODENOW, HISTORICAL SKETCHES OF THE PRINCIPLES AND MAXIMS OF AMERICAN JURISPRUDENCE 32 (Arno ed. 1972).

63. This case is an unreported pamphlet decision of a special circuit court for the trial of crimes against the United States.

64. *See also* JOHN M. GOODENOW, HISTORICAL SKETCHES OF THE PRINCIPLES AND MAXIMS OF AMERICAN JURISPRUDENCE 21 (Arno ed. 1972).

65. *Cf.* GRANT GILMORE & CHARLES L. BLACK, THE LAW OF ADMIRALTY § 1-16, at 45 (2d ed. 1975); DAVID W. ROBERTSON, ADMIRALTY AND FEDERALISM 148 (1970).

amounted to a sovereign policy choice to create distinctly federal law, a prerogative reserved to Congress.[66]

No separation-of-powers problem was involved when the federal courts administered general commercial law. Like admiralty, general commercial law was a private international body of customary rules. The adoption of the diversity jurisdiction coupled with the decision by an individual state to follow general commercial principles exhausted the legislative-like policy choices that were involved in the administration of commercial rules. Thus, the federal courts were able to enforce general commercial rules, when appropriate, without violating the principles of separation of powers.

Indeed, refusal to enforce the general commercial-law rules would, in its own right, have amounted to a violation of the separation-of-powers doctrine. Grants of subject-matter jurisdiction are not simply authorizations that allow the courts to exercise authority when and if they choose. They are, to an extent at least, legislative commands to exercise jurisdiction in the categories of cases included within the grant.[67] Take, for example, diversity jurisdiction. The purpose of the legislative authorization traditionally has been understood to be the protection of noncitizens from the bias or prejudice that they might encounter in state courts. This purpose would have been undermined if, each time a case involving general commercial law was instituted within the diversity jurisdiction, the federal courts had dismissed the case or adhered to the view of the states in which they were sitting about the content of the law. In either instance, the parties to the action would have been deprived of the benefits Congress had elected to give them. Had there been a dismissal, the parties would have been deprived completely of a federal court; and had the federal court retained jurisdiction but followed state decisions on the content of general commercial law, the parties would have been deprived of the independent judgment of a court about the content of the legal principles controlling their transaction—something they would have had in any other court and which is, arguably, an essential ingredient of judicial power.[68]

(d) The Functions of the Diversity Jurisdiction

One aspect of the law-administering power of the federal courts under *Swift* that has sometimes appeared to violate principles of federalism is the power, under certain circumstances, to disregard *settled* state decisions on *local* matters to preserve the integrity of the congressional grant of diversity jurisdiction. Such decisions were disregarded when the application of the settled state decisions posed a danger that state-court bias in lawmaking would adversely and retroactively affect noncitizens of the state. The principle is illustrated by a line of cases from Mississippi.

---

66. *Cf.* DAVID W. ROBERTSON, ADMIRALTY AND FEDERALISM 148 (1970); GRANT GILMORE & CHARLES L. BLACK, THE LAW OF ADMIRALTY § 6-58, at 456 (2d ed. 1975); *see also* Ernest A. Young, *The Last Brooding Omnipresence:* Erie Railroad Co. v. Tompkins *and the Unconstitutionality of Preemptive Federal Maritime Law*, 43 ST. LOUIS U. L.J. 1349, 1359 (1999) (abundant research shows that the law merchant was not federal in nature).

67. *See* Chapter 2(A)(1) *supra* ("The Mandatory Nature of Subject-Matter Jurisdiction").

68. Recall the statement in *Carroll v. Carroll's Lessee*, above, that the Supreme Court was "bound to decide . . . every . . . question, as we find it ought to be decided."

The Mississippi Constitution of 1832 declared that "[t]he introduction of slaves into this state, as merchandise, or for sale, shall be prohibited, from and after the first day of May, eighteen hundred and thirty-three." Despite this provision, a noncitizen of Mississippi imported slaves in 1835 and 1836 and sold them, taking a note in exchange for the slaves. The note was not paid when due, and the holder instituted an action in the U.S. Circuit Court for the District of Louisiana. The sole defense was the illegality of consideration for the note under the Mississippi constitutional provision. The plaintiff won a judgment, and the defendant brought the case to the U.S. Supreme Court. In *Groves v. Slaughter*,[69] the Supreme Court held that the consideration was not illegal because the Mississippi constitutional provision was not self-executing and no legislation had been enacted to make it effective. There were certain Mississippi decisions dealing with the construction of the constitutional provision, but the Court did not consider them binding because all discussion of the issue had been dicta and the state judges had disagreed among themselves about the proper interpretation of the constitutional provision.[70]

After the Supreme Court's decision in *Groves*, the Mississippi Supreme Court held that the constitutional provision in question was self-executing and rendered all sales of slaves made after May 1, 1833, void. An action was then brought in the U.S. Circuit Court for the District of Mississippi to recover on a note given for the purchase of slaves sold in 1836. Under instructions from the circuit court that the note was void if given for slaves imported after May 1, 1833, the jury found for the defendant. Plaintiff brought the case to the U.S. Supreme Court. In *Rowan v. Runnels*,[71] the Court reversed. The Court held that it would give full effect to the Mississippi decision from the time it was made, but would not give it retroactive effect. To do so, said the Court, might render "utterly useless and nugatory" that provision of the U.S. Constitution "which secures to the citizens of another state the right to sue in the courts of the United States."[72]

The Court's concern in *Rowan* was to prevent the operation of possible state-court bias in lawmaking against noncitizens, who had the most to lose from the Mississippi court's interpretation of its constitution. That this possible state-court bias in lawmaking was the limit of the doctrine can be seen by a comparison of *Rowan* with *Nesmith v. Sheldon*.[73] In *Nesmith*, the dispute involved a Michigan constitutional provision that required a two-thirds vote of each house of the state legislature to pass any act of incorporation. The Michigan Legislature enacted two statutes that authorized persons to form banking associations in corporate form and made the stockholders of the corporations liable for the debts the corporations incurred. The U.S. Circuit Court for the District of Michigan held these legislative acts valid. However, the Michigan Supreme Court later declared them invalid under the constitutional provision described above.

---

69. 40 U.S. (15 Pet.) 449, 10 L. Ed. 800 (1841).

70. *See id.*; RANDALL BRIDWELL & RALPH U. WHITTEN, THE CONSTITUTION AND THE COMMON LAW: THE DECLINE OF THE DOCTRINES OF SEPARATION OF POWERS AND FEDERALISM 74 (1977).

71. 46 U.S. (5 How.) 134, 12 L. Ed. 85 (1847).

72. *Id.* at 139, 12 L. Ed. at 87; *see* RANDALL BRIDWELL & RALPH U. WHITTEN, THE CONSTITUTION AND THE COMMON LAW: THE DECLINE OF THE DOCTRINES OF SEPARATION OF POWERS AND FEDERALISM 74-75 (1977).

73. 48 U.S. (7 How.) 812, 12 L. Ed. 925 (1849).

The U.S. Supreme Court followed the state court's interpretation of the Michigan Constitution without question. The Court stated that *Groves* and *Rowan* "in relation to the construction of the constitution of Mississippi, stand on very different grounds, as will be seen by a reference to the cases."[74] The difference between cases was that in *Rowan*, the state interpretation would primarily have harmed noncitizens, who were the largest class of importers and sellers of slaves. In *Nesmith*, however, the state decision would harm equally both citizens and noncitizens of Michigan. The suit in *Nesmith* was brought to hold stockholders of a banking corporation liable for its debts. There was no reason to believe that more stockholders were noncitizens than citizens of Michigan.

Thus, despite broad interpretations of the *Rowan* decision as a case permitting "state precedents interpretative of state written law to be disregarded, in the national courts, when necessary 'to establish justice,'"[75] the operative principle was much narrower. Federal courts could refuse to give a *retroactive* effect to state decisions when it appeared that there was a potential for the state decisions to operate more harshly against noncitizens than against citizens of the state. The justification for the principle was the function of the federal courts in suits between citizens of different states to prevent state bias from operating against noncitizens.[76]

In addition to the *Rowan* principle, the U.S. Supreme Court also refused to allow state laws to limit noncitizens' access to federal courts.[77] One case applying this principle, but which has, at times, been read incorrectly to permit the federal courts to disregard state attempts to "localize" the general commercial law, is *Watson v. Tarpley*.[78] In *Watson*, an action was brought on a bill of exchange by a citizen of Tennessee against a citizen of Mississippi in a Mississippi federal court. The trial court instructed the jury that even after presentment of the bill for acceptance, regular protest, and notice of nonacceptance, an action could not be maintained until after the maturity of the bill. Acting under the lower court's instruction, which appeared to be required by a Mississippi statute, the jury gave a verdict for the defendant. The U.S. Supreme Court held the instruction to be erroneous. At one point in its opinion, the Court stated that the Mississippi statute was a "violation of the general commercial law, which a state would have no power to impose, and which the courts of the United States would be bound to

---

74. *Id.* at 818, 12 L. Ed. at 928.

75. *See, e.g.*, 2 WILLIAM W. CROSSKEY, POLITICS AND THE CONSTITUTION IN THE HISTORY OF THE UNITED STATES 862 (1953).

76. *See* RANDALL BRIDWELL & RALPH U. WHITTEN, THE CONSTITUTION AND THE COMMON LAW: THE DECLINE OF THE DOCTRINES OF SEPARATION OF POWERS AND FEDERALISM 73-76 (1977). It is, of course, possible to disagree with the principle announced in *Rowan*. For example, it is possible to reason that the principle was unnecessary to protect noncitizens from bias within the diversity jurisdiction, or that even if it did afford them important protections, the cost of the principle in terms of encroachment on state lawmaking prerogatives was too great. However, disagreement with the necessity or utility of the principle should not be extended to a distortion of the principle itself. It was a highly limited one and did not represent some vast repository of power in the federal courts to disregard state-court decisions with which the federal courts disagreed.

77. *See* Union Bank v. Jolly's Adm'rs, 59 U.S. (18 How.) 503, 507, 15 L. Ed. 472, 474 (1856); RANDALL BRIDWELL & RALPH U. WHITTEN, THE CONSTITUTION AND THE COMMON LAW: THE DECLINE OF THE DOCTRINES OF SEPARATION OF POWERS AND FEDERALISM 76 (1977).

78. 59 U.S. (18 How.) 517, 15 L. Ed. 509 (1856); *see* 2 WILLIAM W. CROSSKEY, POLITICS AND THE CONSTITUTION IN THE HISTORY OF THE UNITED STATES 861-62 (1953); TONY A. FREYER, HARMONY & DISSONANCE: THE *Swift* & *Erie* CASES IN AMERICAN FEDERALISM 51-55 (1981); MORTON J. HORWITZ, THE TRANSFORMATION OF AMERICAN LAW, 1780-1860, at 225 (1977).

disregard."[79] This passage, however, does not mean that the states could not "localize" rules of commercial law. There was no doubt that general commercial law would determine the primary rights and liabilities of the parties in *Watson*. The Mississippi statute thus did not alter the substantive right to recover on the bill of exchange, but only the time when the action could be brought. It was to this impairment of the right to resort to the diversity jurisdiction to which the Court objected.

The Court stated that while "the laws of the several states are of binding authority upon their domestic tribunals," they could not "affect, either by enlargement or diminution, the jurisdiction of the courts of the United States . . . nor destroy or control the rights of parties litigant to whom the right of resort to these courts has been secured by the laws and [C]onstitution."[80] Because the Constitution and the Judiciary Act of 1789 had given noncitizens "the power or privilege of litigating and enforcing their rights acquired under and defined by [the] general commercial law before the judicial tribunals of the United States," the Court concluded that state laws, "the effect of which would be to impair the rights thus secured, or to divest the federal courts of cognizance thereof, in their fullest acceptation under the commercial law, must be nugatory and unavailing."[81] Despite some broad language in *Watson*, therefore, the decision appears consistent with the much narrower principle that state laws will not be permitted to impair a suitor's access to the federal courts.[82]

(e) Equity and Admiralty Cases

Until 1948, the Rules of Decision Act prescribed that state laws were to be regarded as rules of decision only in "trials at common law."[83] Thus, at the time *Swift* was decided, equity and admiralty cases were excluded from the Act's coverage. As noted in the earlier discussion of the separation-of-powers doctrine, the federal courts were granted exclusive jurisdiction over admiralty cases by the first Judiciary Act. When acting within that grant of jurisdiction, the courts applied general maritime law.[84] In equity cases, the pattern was more complex.

In common-law cases in the federal courts, a "static conformity" to state procedure was required from 1789 to 1872. Then a "dynamic conformity" was

---

79. *Watson*, 59 U.S. (18 How.) at 521, 15 L. Ed. at 511.

80. *Id.* at 520, 15 L. Ed. at 511.

81. *Id.* at 521, 15 L. Ed. at 511; *see* RANDALL BRIDWELL & RALPH U. WHITTEN, THE CONSTITUTION AND THE COMMON LAW: THE DECLINE OF THE DOCTRINES OF SEPARATION OF POWERS AND FEDERALISM 77-78 (1977). As in *Rowan*, this result may have been, on balance, unnecessary to protect the policies supporting the diversity jurisdiction. However, as discussed above, like the *Rowan* principle, disagreement with the principle should not be extended to distortion of it.

82. *See* RANDALL BRIDWELL & RALPH U. WHITTEN, THE CONSTITUTION AND THE COMMON LAW: THE DECLINE OF THE DOCTRINES OF SEPARATION OF POWERS AND FEDERALISM 70 (1977). Note that it is possible to criticize the *Watson* decision as wrong, in that it was unnecessary to protect the access of noncitizens to the diversity jurisdiction. Similar criticism can be made of *Rowan*. Even if the decisions were incorrect applications of the "*Swift* doctrine," however, they should not be interpreted as something that they clearly were not. They were not statements of a broad principle that federal diversity courts had the power to override state local laws when they contradicted the federal courts' opinions of what the general commercial law was.

83. In the 1948 revision of the Judicial Code, the Act was amended to apply to all "civil actions." *See* 28 U.S.C. § 1652.

84. *See* GRANT GILMORE & CHARLES L. BLACK, THE LAW OF ADMIRALTY § 1-16, at 45 (2d ed. 1975); DAVID W. ROBERTSON, ADMIRALTY AND FEDERALISM 148 (1970).

required from 1872 to 1938, when the Federal Rules of Civil Procedure were adopted.[85] However, in equity cases, conformity to state procedure was not required. The Supreme Court from time to time prescribed equity rules to govern the practice and procedure in equity cases. Taken together with the omission of equity cases from the coverage of the Rules of Decision Act, it might appear that the federal courts were free in all equitable proceedings to follow their own procedural and substantive rules. Nonetheless, the federal courts were not entirely free to do so.

The independent federal equity power was necessary because some states did not have equity courts.[86] In such states, there might be no equity procedures that federal courts could follow, making procedural conformity impossible. Similarly, because equity contained remedial "rules of decision," there might be an absence of equitable "rules of decision" in states without equity courts, making it necessary to omit equity cases from the Rules of Decision Act to ensure that the grant of jurisdiction to the federal courts in "law and equity" cases would be effective. Nevertheless, by providing effective remedies, equity often operated on "legal" rights when the remedies at law were inadequate. Thus, the federal courts could not disregard state law entirely just because they were sitting in equity. In fact, they did not do so.

Federal courts sitting in equity enforced primary rights defined by state law. The only effect of the independent federal equity power was that the states would not be allowed to destroy the division between law and equity that existed in the federal courts by (1) enacting laws that enlarged or limited the powers of those courts or (2) providing forms of remedies enforceable in federal equity proceedings that were inconsistent with traditional equitable principles. Nor could state-court decisions bind federal courts on matters of general equity jurisprudence.[87] The overall result was that the federal courts in both law and equity cases generally followed state-court decisions defining local primary rights, but not on issues of general commercial law. In addition, the federal courts conformed to state procedure in common-law cases. However, the federal courts had an independent federal equity procedure and independent federal equity remedial power. That power could sometimes override state "substantive" law when necessary for the effective exercise or integrity of the independent equity power.

Illustration 5-7. State *X* and State *Y* settled a boundary dispute between the two states by compact. The compact stated that land titles granted previous to the compact by either state would be as secure as in the state that granted them and not be affected by the compact. After the compact had settled the two states' boundaries, certain land that formerly had been in State *X* fell in State *Y*. *P*, a citizen of State *X*, claims title to this land under the law of State *X*. *D*, a citizen of State *Y*, also claims title to this land under the law of State *X*. *P* sues *D* in a federal court in State *Y* to eject *D* from the land. *P's* claim in the action is based on legal title, while *D's* claim is based on equitable title. Under the procedures followed by State *X* courts,

---

85. *See* Chapter 1(D)(10) *supra* ("Early Procedure in the Federal Courts") (discussing the Conformity Acts).

86. CHARLES A. WRIGHT & MARY KAY KANE, HANDBOOK OF THE LAW OF FEDERAL COURTS § 54, at 373 (7th ed. 2011).

87. *See* RANDALL BRIDWELL & RALPH U. WHITTEN, THE CONSTITUTION AND THE COMMON LAW: THE DECLINE OF THE DOCTRINES OF SEPARATION OF POWERS AND FEDERALISM 172-73 n.46, 186-87 n.43 (1977) (citing cases).

an equitable title cannot be set up as sufficient in an action at law, such as ejectment, but must be established in a separate equitable proceeding. Under the procedures followed by the State *Y* courts, an equitable title can be set up as a defense in an action at law for ejectment. Under the procedures followed by the federal courts, an equitable title could not be set up in an action at law. On facts similar to these, the U.S. Supreme Court held that *D* could not set up the equitable title in the federal action in State *Y*.[88] However, under the traditional practice governing separate actions at law and equity, defenses that were recognized exclusively in equity were sometimes made into legal defenses by statute and thereafter recognized by the common-law courts.[89] Even if the State *Y* procedures are based on statutes in State *Y* converting the equitable title into legal title, they would not be recognized by the federal courts on these facts, because the law controlling the title dispute is State *X* law by virtue of the compact. However, the Supreme Court made it clear that, on a matter that State *Y* law controlled, statutes converting an equitable title into a legal title would be recognized as fully in federal courts as in the courts of the state.[90]

(f) The **Swift** *Doctrine Changes*

The doctrine taking its name from *Swift v. Tyson* changed radically in the latter part of the nineteenth century. The changes that occurred in the doctrine transformed the power of the federal courts in ways that violated both separation-of-powers and federalism restrictions in the U.S. Constitution. These later alterations in the *Swift* doctrine, not the manner in which the doctrine had operated in the early nineteenth century, produced major objections by courts and commentators and the eventual transformation of the federal courts' source-of-law authority in *Erie Railroad v. Tompkins*.[91]

The transformation of *Swift* was complex and touched many kinds of cases. Two of the earliest, and most grievous, departures from the original *Swift* doctrine occurred in cases involving municipal bonds and torts. From the previous discussion of the *Swift* doctrine, two propositions should be clear. First, the states were not obligated to follow the general commercial law. Instead, they were free to "localize" their commercial law, for example, by enacting statutes to govern commercial transactions. If a state did so, and if under the prevailing territorial conflict-of-law rules the state had the authority to control a dispute with its law, the federal courts had no authority to apply general commercial law instead of the local law. The *Swift* decision itself implied as much.

Second, distinct limits to "general" law existed. There was a "general commercial law" and "general admiralty law" because those bodies of law were comprised of international customary rules. However, all property law was local to

---

88. *See* Robinson v. Campbell, 16 U.S. (3 Wheat.) 212, 4 L. Ed. 372 (1818).

89. *See* Chapter 7(D)(2) *infra* (discussing the recognition of "set-off" in equity courts, the subsequent enactment of "set-off" statutes, and the recognition of set-off thereafter in the common-law courts).

90. *See* Robinson v. Campbell, 16 U.S. (3 Wheat.) 212, 223, 4 L. Ed. 372, 376 (1818).

91. 304 U.S. 64, 58 S. Ct. 817, 82 L. Ed. 1188 (1938).

the sovereign where the property was located. Likewise, all tort law was local to the sovereign where the alleged tort was committed.

In municipal bond cases, the U.S. Supreme Court departed from *Swift* by disregarding explicit state statutory limitations on the power of localities to issue negotiable bonds.[92] Yet nothing could have been clearer under *Swift* than a state's right to limit negotiable transactions by statute. All who engaged in such transactions within the state were bound to know whatever limitations the state had imposed, at their peril.[93] Thus, the Court was making law in disregard of the sovereign rights of the states to control transactions within their borders.

In tort cases, the Court departed from *Swift* by applying a "general" law of torts.[94] Quite clearly there was no international body of customary tort law that deserved the label "general." The Court simply made the "general tort law" up as it went along. This approach violated restrictions (observed under *Swift*) on its lawmaking authority. It also violated the sovereign right of the states to impose their own tort law in cases arising within their borders.[95]

SECTION D. THE *ERIE* DOCTRINE

Incursions upon the prerogatives of Congress and the states such as those in the municipal bond and tort cases produced the reaction known today as the "*Erie* doctrine"—so named after *Erie Railroad v. Tompkins*.[96] In *Erie*, the U.S. Supreme Court reinterpreted the Rules of Decision Act to require that the federal courts follow state-court decisions on all matters of state law.[97] The Court overruled *Swift* and eradicated the distinction drawn under the *Swift* doctrine between matters of local and general law. The Court in *Erie* established a new distinction between substantive matters, upon which the federal courts were bound to follow state decisions if no controlling federal statute existed, and procedural matters, which could be controlled by federal decisions.[98] In addition, after *Erie*, the federal courts were empowered to fashion federal substantive common-law rules on some matters that would control the outcome of cases in both federal and state courts.

---

92. *See, e.g.*, Board of Comm'rs v. Aspinwall, 62 U.S. (21 How.) 539, 16 L. Ed. 208 (1859).

93. *See* RANDALL BRIDWELL & RALPH U. WHITTEN, THE CONSTITUTION AND THE COMMON LAW: THE DECLINE OF THE DOCTRINES OF SEPARATION OF POWERS AND FEDERALISM 116-19 (1977).

94. *See id.* 199-222.

95. Compare the discussion above of the Court's decisions in the common law of crimes and civil admiralty areas during the early nineteenth century. *See also* TONY A. FREYER, HARMONY & DISSONANCE: THE *SWIFT* & *ERIE* CASES IN AMERICAN FEDERALISM ch. III (1981); RICHARD H. FALLON ET AL., HART & WECHSLER'S THE FEDERAL COURTS AND THE FEDERAL SYSTEM 555-56 (6th ed. 2009).

96. 304 U.S. 64, 58 S. Ct. 817, 82 L. Ed. 1188 (1938).

97. *See* Ralph U. Whitten, Erie *and the Federal Rules: A Review and Reappraisal After* Burlington Northern Railroad v. Woods, 21 CREIGHTON L. REV. 1, 2 (1987); *cf.* Thomas O. Mann, *The Procedural Foundation of Substantive Law*, 87 WASH. U. L. REV. 801 (2010) (discussing how substantive law entails assumptions about the procedures that will apply when the substantive law is ultimately enforced); Michael Steven Green, Erie's *Suppressed Premise*, 95 MINN. L. REV. 1111 (2011) (discussing the "suppressed premise" in *Erie* that a state court may not free federal courts of the duty to follow their decisions on matters of the state's own law).

98. *See* Ralph U. Whitten, Erie *and the Federal Rules: A Review and Reappraisal After* Burlington Northern Railroad v. Woods, 21 CREIGHTON L. REV. 1-4 (1987).

1. The *Erie* Decision

In *Erie*, the plaintiff, Tompkins, a citizen of Pennsylvania, was walking along a railroad right of way in Pennsylvania. Tompkins was struck by something protruding from the car of one of the defendant's trains. Tompkins sued the Erie Railroad in a federal district court in New York. Tompkins alleged that Erie's negligence caused the accident. Erie's defense was that under Pennsylvania law, its duty to Tompkins was no greater than that owed to a trespasser. Under Pennsylvania law, unless its negligence were wilful or wanton, it could not be held liable. The district judge refused to instruct the jury that the applicable law precluded recovery. The jury brought in a verdict for Tompkins. On appeal, the Second Circuit held that it was unnecessary to consider whether the law of Pennsylvania required wilful or wanton negligence because the question was one of general law upon which the federal courts could make an independent judgment. Under this "general tort law," the Second Circuit held that the railroad could be held liable for ordinary negligence. The U.S. Supreme Court granted certiorari and reversed.[99]

Despite the fact that no one had argued that *Swift* should be overruled,[100] the opening sentence of Justice Brandeis' opinion for the Court stated: "The question for decision is whether the oft-challenged doctrine of *Swift v. Tyson* shall now be disapproved."[101] The Court seemed to treat the problem created by the *Swift* doctrine as exclusively one of federalism.[102] The Court also asserted that the *Swift* doctrine created a problem of forum shopping. According to the Court, the diversity jurisdiction was designed to provide a nondiscriminatory forum for the noncitizen.[103] The *Swift* doctrine, however, had resulted in discrimination by noncitizens against citizens. Because noncitizens were able to choose either state or federal court, they were able to survey the state and federal decisions on the substantive matters at issue in the case and select the court that would apply the most favorable substantive law.[104] However, the Court indicated that the forum shopping problem would not, in itself, have caused *Swift* to be overruled if the issue were merely one of a longstanding misconstruction of the Rules of Decision Act.

---

99. *See Erie*, 304 U.S. at 69-70, 58 S. Ct. at 818, 82 L. Ed. at 1189-90.

100. *See id.* at 66 (argument for petitioner did not question the finality of the doctrine of *Swift v. Tyson*; petitioner argued that state decisions were controlling if "sufficiently established"); *id.* at 68 (argument for respondent contending that the question was one of general law and that there was no doctrine that a matter was one of local law if "sufficiently established" in local decisions).

101. 304 U.S. at 69, 58 S. Ct. at 818, 82 L. Ed. at 1189.

102. "The federal courts assumed in the broad field of 'general law,' the power to declare rules of decision which Congress was confessedly without power to enact as statutes." *Id.* at 72-73, 58 S. Ct. at 819, 82 L. Ed. at 1191 (footnotes omitted).

103. *See id.* at 74, 58 S. Ct. at 820, 82 L. Ed. at 1192.

104. *See id.* at 74-75, 58 S. Ct. at 820-21, 82 L. Ed. at 1192. The reason that the noncitizen has the choice of forum, of course, is due to the configuration of the diversity and removal jurisdiction. Recall from Chapter 2(F) *supra* ("Removal Jurisdiction") that the noncitizen plaintiff can choose to sue in either federal or state court. If the noncitizen plaintiff chooses federal court, the citizen defendant is obligated to defend there. However, if the noncitizen plaintiff chooses state court, the citizen defendant must defend there if diversity of citizenship is the only basis of federal jurisdiction, because a citizen of the state in which the action is brought may not remove such a case. *See* 28 U.S.C. § 1441(b)(2). However, a noncitizen defendant may remove on the basis of diversity alone. *See id.* The Court did not consider the problem of the plaintiff who is a citizen of the state in which the action is brought who picks a federal court in the state based on a desire to obtain a more favorable substantive law, even though such a plaintiff could forum shop in the same offensive way as a noncitizen defendant under the *Swift* doctrine. Indeed, in such a case, the plaintiff must have some motive for picking the federal court other than fear of discrimination against noncitizens that might occur in the state courts.

Rather, the Court was compelled to overrule *Swift* because "the unconstitutionality of the course pursued" had become clear to it.[105]

The result in *Erie* was undoubtedly correct for at least two reasons. First, the dispute was controlled by substantive tort principles. As noted in section C(2)*(f)*, above, the Court had distorted the *Swift* doctrine when it concluded that there existed a general law of torts upon which the federal courts had a right, in diversity cases, to make a judgment independent of state decisions. All tort law should have been considered local in nature. Second, by the time *Erie* was decided, it was probably true that there was not anything that could reasonably be labeled "general" law in any area, even the commercial law area. The notion of a customary law whose content transcended the control of any given government while being accepted by all (or most) governments had been discarded.[106] In its place, American courts had generally accepted the notion that all law, from the general corpus of a subject area (such as torts or contracts) to the content of the individual rules within the area, must be the product of some sovereign's will. Under this view, judges were seen as active participants in the policy-making processes of lawmaking. They did not "find" law even in the limited sense described and accepted in *Swift*. If this attitude about law had not been entirely accepted by the time *Erie* was decided, at least its acceptance was well underway and has undeniably been completed today.[107] Under such circumstances, even Justice Story would have agreed that the federal courts would be bound by settled state court decisions on all "substantive" matters not directly controlled by federal law.[108]

As a criticism of *Swift* and as a justification for a change of course, however, the *Erie* opinion was an intellectual disaster. Justice Brandeis had cited

---

105. *See id.* at 77-78, 58 S. Ct. at 822, 82 L. Ed. at 1195.

106. The jurisprudential developments that resulted in this view were complex and cannot be described fully here. For good descriptions of those developments, see WILLIAM L. TWINING, KARL LLEWELLYN AND THE REALIST MOVEMENT (1973); G. Edward White, *From Sociological Jurisprudence to Realism: Jurisprudence and Social Change in Early Twentieth-Century America, in* PATTERNS OF AMERICAN LEGAL THOUGHT 99 (1978); *see also* JEROME FRANK, LAW AND THE MODERN MIND (1930); KARL N. LLEWELLYN, THE COMMON LAW TRADITION: DECIDING APPEALS (1960); Patrick J. Borchers, *The Origins of Diversity Jurisdiction: The Rise of Legal Positivism, and a Brave New World for* Erie *and* Klaxon, 72 TEX. L. REV. 79, 115-17 (1993); Karl N. Llewellyn, *A Realistic Jurisprudence—The Next Step*, 30 COLUM. L. REV. 431 (1930).

107. It has often been argued that *Erie's* rejection of *Swift* was the result of the rejection of *Swift's* philosophy of law and the acceptance of the philosophy of legal positivism. *See, e.g.*, Bradford R. Clark, *Ascertaining the Laws of the Several States: Positivism and Judicial Federalism After* Erie, 145 U. PA. L. REV. 1459 (1997). For a dissenting view, see Jack Goldsmith & Steven Walt, Erie *and the Irrelevance of Legal Positivism*, 84 VA. L. REV. 673 (1998); *cf.* Caleb Nelson, *The Presence of General Law,* 106 COLUM. L. REV. 503 (2006) (discussing the continuing relevance of rules of general law, meaning rules whose content is not dictated entirely by any single decision maker, but results from patterns followed in many different jurisdictions, and related matters).

108. *Cf.* RANDALL BRIDWELL & RALPH U. WHITTEN, THE CONSTITUTION AND THE COMMON LAW: THE DECLINE OF THE DOCTRINES OF SEPARATION OF POWERS AND FEDERALISM xiv, 2, 4, 11, 136-37 (1977). For an excellent history of the developments leading up to *Erie*, the history of the construction of the opinion (including the influence of various members of the Court on the content of the opinion), and the later development of the *Erie* doctrine, see EDWARD A. PURCELL, JR., BRANDEIS AND THE PROGRESSIVE CONSTITUTION: *ERIE*, THE JUDICIAL POWER, AND THE POLITICS OF THE FEDERAL COURTS IN TWENTIETH-CENTURY AMERICA (2000). It is important to note that the *Erie* doctrine does not apply only in diversity actions. It applies in any federal action in which state law supplies the rule of decision. *See, e.g.*, AIG Baker Sterling Heights, LLC v. American Multi-Cinema, Inc., 508 F.3d 995 (11th Cir 2007) (amount of prejudgment interest is governed by state law in a diversity action involving the Federal Arbitration Act); *In re* Exxon Valdez, 484 F.3d 1098 (9th Cir. 2007) (*Erie* applies in case removed under 28 U.S.C. § 1441 to question of what law governs prejudgment interest; issue is substantive for purposes of *Erie* and state law controls when state law provides rule of decision on other issues).

the "recent research of a competent scholar" to the effect that Justice Story's interpretation of the Rules of Decision Act in *Swift* was incorrect. The research referred to was that of Professor Charles Warren, who had discovered an original draft of the Judiciary Act of 1789, in which the Rules of Decision Act originally read:

> And be it further enacted, that the statute law of the several states in force for the time being and their unwritten or common law now in use, whether by adoption from the common law of England, the ancient statutes of the same or otherwise, except where the constitution, treaties or statutes of the United States shall otherwise require or provide, shall be regarded as rules of decision in the trials at common law in the courts of the United States in cases where they apply.[109]

In the final version of the Act, the phrase "the laws of the several states" was substituted for "the statute law of the several states in force for the time being and their unwritten or common law now in use, whether by adoption from the common law of England, the current statutes of the same or otherwise." Professor Warren concluded that the change was intended to be stylistic only and that, as a consequence, decisions of state tribunals on common-law matters were intended to be included within the word "laws."[110]

Professor Warren's interpretation of the Rules of Decision Act has been criticized.[111] For present purposes, it is sufficient to note that Warren simply assumed that expressions such as "unwritten or common law" were the equivalent of "court decisions" in the minds of those who drafted and enacted the original Rules of Decision Act. As the discussion of the *Swift* doctrine in the last section indicated, however, in the late eighteenth and early nineteenth century, "common law" and "judicial decisions," or "law" and "decisions of courts," were simply not equivalent expressions.[112] Thus, it is quite plausible to believe that the drafters of the First Judiciary Act intended to require the federal courts to adhere to state

---

109. Charles Warren, *New Light on the History of the Federal Judiciary Act of 1789*, 37 HARV. L. REV. 49, 86 (1923).

110. *See id.*

111. *See* WILFRED J. RITZ, REWRITING THE JUDICIARY ACT OF 1789, at 165-179 (Wythe Holt & L.H. LaRue eds. 1989); 2 WILLIAM W. CROSSKEY, POLITICS AND THE CONSTITUTION IN THE HISTORY OF THE UNITED STATES 866-867 (1953); HENRY J. FRIENDLY, IN PRAISE OF Erie AND THE NEW FEDERAL COMMON LAW 383, 389-91 (1964); Patrick J. Borchers, *The Origins of Diversity Jurisdiction: The Rise of Legal Positivism, and a Brave New World for* Erie *and* Klaxon, 72 TEX. L. REV. 79, 103-06 (1993). As Professor Crosskey pointed out, one is immediately impressed with the similarity in wording between the original draft that Warren found and the wording of the provision of the First Process Act that established a "static conformity" to state law in matters of procedure. *See* Chapter 1(D)(10) *supra* ("Early Procedure in the Federal Courts") for a description of the First Process Act and static conformity. Thus, if the change were merely stylistic, as Warren contended, then the more plausible interpretation of the Act would be that it was intended to establish a "static conformity" to state law as that law existed in 1789. For a theory of how this static conformity would have made sense, see 2 WILLIAM W. CROSSKEY, POLITICS AND THE CONSTITUTION IN THE HISTORY OF THE UNITED STATES (1953), whose conclusions, however, have been widely rejected. *See also* Craig Green, *Repressing* Erie's *Myth,* 96 CAL. L. REV. 595 (2008) (criticizing *Erie's* constitutional reasoning and modern commentary resting the decision on separation-of-powers norms); Thomas E. Plank, *The* Erie *Doctrine in Bankruptcy,* 79 NOTRE DAME L. REV. 633 (2004); Robert A. Schapiro, *Interjurisdictional Enforcement of Rights in a Post-*Erie *World,* 46 WM. & MARY L. REV. 1399 (2005).

112. *Cf.* WILFRED J. RITZ, REWRITING THE JUDICIARY ACT OF 1789, at 28-30 (Wythe Holt & L.H. LaRue eds., 1989) (discussing the eighteenth century view that law was "found" rather than "made"); *see also* Patrick J. Borchers, *The Origins of Diversity Jurisdiction: The Rise of Legal Positivism, and a Brave New World for* Erie *and* Klaxon, 72 TEX. L. REV. 79, 111-15 (1993).

common-law rules in the absence of controlling federal statutory, treaty, or constitutional provisions. However, the weight to be given to state decisions interpreting that common law was to be determined in light of the traditional common-law doctrine of stare decisis.

Furthermore, Warren's interpretation does not solve the dilemma of a federal court faced with the kind of problem involved in *Swift*. Even if one assumes that the federal courts are obligated to follow settled[113] state decisions, what were those courts to do when given contradictory commands by the decisions, as New York had given in *Swift*? Recall that New York had indicated that it wished to follow the general commercial law, but its conclusion about the content of that law was at odds with the view of the federal courts and other states. Which New York "decision" was the U.S. Supreme Court supposed to follow, the decision of New York to follow the general commercial law or New York's decision about that law's content? As noted in the last section, the resolution of this problem for those who understand the relative importance of each of New York's "decisions" in the jurisprudence of the time was easy. Only a perverse refusal to understand that jurisprudence could result in the conclusion that New York's decision on the content of commercial law should be treated as more important than the decision to follow the general commercial law and, therefore, as controlling in the federal courts and the courts of other states.

In addition to Justice Brandeis' mistaken reliance upon Professor Warren's conclusions, there were other problems with the opinion in *Erie*. For one, Brandeis indicated that the practice of the federal courts under *Swift* had been unconstitutional because Congress had no power to enact the kinds of rules involved in *Swift* and *Erie* and the Constitution gave the courts no greater powers than Congress. This approach treated the *Swift-Erie* problem simply as one of federalism. If Congress has the power to enact a rule into law, then the federal courts can make up a rule to govern diversity actions within the same area. If Congress does not have such power, then the federal courts do not have lawmaking power either. This view is flatly wrong. In the first place, Congress did have the power to enact both the rule in *Swift* and the rule in *Erie*. The matter at issue in *Swift* concerned a bill of exchange negotiated between citizens of different states. The matter in *Erie* involved the tort obligations of an interstate railroad. Justice Brandeis failed to explain why Article I, § 8 of the Constitution (the Commerce Clause) does not give Congress power to enact rules of decision to regulate both these subjects.[114]

Additionally, Justice Brandeis' willingness to equate the lawmaking power of Congress and the lawmaking power of the courts ignores potential separation-of-powers restrictions on the ability of the courts to create law. In fact, if the powers that the federal courts assumed in the name of the *Swift* doctrine were to be held

---

113. Presumably even Professor Warren would have agreed that the federal courts would have to have some powers of independent judgment when state decisions were unsettled or contradictory or rendered by a state court of less than final authority.

114. *See* RANDALL BRIDWELL & RALPH U. WHITTEN, THE CONSTITUTION AND THE COMMON LAW: THE DECLINE OF THE DOCTRINES OF SEPARATION OF POWERS AND FEDERALISM 3 (1977); CHARLES A. WRIGHT & MARY KAY KANE, THE LAW OF FEDERAL COURTS § 56, at 383 n.17 (7th ed. 2011). One need not resort to the more troublesome proposition advanced by Justice Reed in concurrence in *Erie* that Article III plus the necessary and proper clause may authorize Congress to provide substantive rules of decision to govern diversity actions. *See Erie*, 304 U.S. at 92, 58 S. Ct. at 828, 82 L. Ed. at 1201-02.

unconstitutional, a far better ground for so holding is separation of powers, rather than federalism. The notion that the federal courts have lawmaking powers as broad as those of Congress had been rejected long before *Erie*, at least as early as the common law of crimes cases discussed in the preceding section. When the federal courts expanded the coverage of "general law" into areas in which there was no international or interstate body of customary law to which the states were attempting to adhere—*i.e.*, into areas that were purely local—the federal courts arguably were exceeding their proper lawmaking grasp. As observed in the last section, although a federalism violation was also produced, the violation was not the result of the lack of congressional power to regulate some of the matters being dealt with by the federal courts. Instead, the violation was the result of the constitutional delegation of primary lawmaking responsibility to Congress. Congress' decision to leave areas within its lawmaking authority unregulated should ordinarily mean that the state lawmaking will control those areas.[115] Thus, separation-of-powers restrictions on court lawmaking, operating through political processes that restrict the willingness of Congress to supplant state authority, actually afford valuable federalism protections to the states.[116]

Finally, Justice Brandeis stated in *Erie* that "[t]here is no *federal* general common law."[117] This statement implies that under the *Swift* doctrine, there was such law. But the use of the adjective "federal" was clearly improper, either to describe the law being applied in *Swift*, or to describe the illegitimate general law rules that were applied after *Swift* had been expanded in the latter part of the nineteenth and early twentieth centuries. For, although the federal courts disregarded state court decisions on general law matters—legitimately in *Swift* and illegitimately under the later decisions—the state courts were not bound to follow the general law decisions of the U.S. Supreme Court. The proof that the federal

---

115. The notion that separation-of-powers restrictions on judicial lawmaking afford protections to the states occurs in numerous areas in constitutional law. *See* 1 LAURENCE H. TRIBE, AMERICAN CONSTITUTIONAL LAW § 2-3, at 126 (3d ed. 2000). *See generally* Adam N. Steinman, *What Is the* Erie *Doctrine? (And What Does It Mean for the Contemporary Politics of Judicial Federalism?)*, 84 NOTRE DAME L. REV. 245 (2008) (arguing that *Erie* sets a constitutional principle that federal judicial lawmakers cannot dictate substantive rights where that lawmaking has only the justification that there is federal authority to adjudicate a dispute or provide procedural for such adjudication).

116. *See* Henry J. Friendly, *In Praise of Erie and the New Federal Common Law*, 39 N.Y.U. L. REV. 383, 392-98 (1964). Perhaps Justice Brandeis' seeming equation of congressional and judicial lawmaking powers had another, more legitimate meaning than the one discussed in the text. Perhaps Brandeis was saying that if Congress wishes to act within its delegated powers, it must do so in an accepted "legislative" manner. It is not acceptable "legislation" to provide rules of decision whose applicability become apparent only when parties whose conduct the rules govern find out in which court they have been sued. Thus, an implicit separation-of-powers restriction on Congress' ability to enact statutes within its expressly delegated powers is that Congress must provide rules of decision whose operation on primary conduct does not depend upon fortuitous or arbitrary facts such as the plaintiff's choice of courts. Such a restriction would, at least, have respectable antecedents in due process restrictions on retroactive legislation. *See generally* JOHN E. NOWAK & RONALD D. ROTUNDA, CONSTITUTIONAL LAW § 11.9(a) (8th ed. 2010). Indeed, the retroactivity limitation of the Due Process Clauses appears to be rooted in a separation-of-powers function of those clauses as applied to legislative action. *See generally* Ralph U. Whitten, *The Constitutional Limitations on State Choice of Law: Due Process*, 9 HAST. CONST. L.Q. 851 (1982). The idea that valid legislation must operate in this manner is suggested by a close reading of Friendly, *supra*, though Judge Friendly's article does not elaborate the idea in precisely the manner done here; *cf.* Justin D. Forlenza, Note, *CAFA and* Erie: *Unconstitutional Consequences?* 75 FORDHAM L. REV. 1065 (2006) (arguing that the recent Class Action Fairness Act, discussed in Chapter 2 and elsewhere in this text, conflicts with *Erie* by forcing certain kinds of class actions governed by state law into federal court, thus forcing the federal courts to create federal common law to govern those actions in areas where the primary role of developing common law resides with the state courts).

117. *Erie*, 304 U.S. at 78, 58 S. Ct. at 822, 82 L. Ed. at 1194.

courts' decisions under the *Swift* doctrine cannot be properly characterized as decisions on matters of "federal" law is that the Court consistently refused to entertain appeals from the state courts when those courts rendered decisions that conflicted with the Supreme Court's general law pronouncements. Such appeals could not be heard by the Court because no "federal" question existed in the case.[118]

2. The *Erie* Doctrine Applied to Conflict-of-Laws Issues

(a) The Klaxon *Decision*

As discussed in the preceding section, under *Swift v. Tyson*, the federal courts in diversity cases made conflict-of-laws decisions independent of the state courts. The "in cases where they apply" language of the Rules of Decision Act dictated this result. In *Erie*, the Court seemed to assume that the New York federal court would apply Pennsylvania law in the case. However, the Court's opinion was unclear whether (1) the federal courts continued to have independent choice-of-law authority and should exercise it in favor of Pennsylvania law or (2) after *Erie*, the federal courts had to follow the conflict-of-laws doctrine of the states in which they were sitting and New York would apply Pennsylvania law.[119]

In *Klaxon Co. v. Stentor Electric Manufacturing Co.*,[120] the Court held that *Erie* required federal courts in diversity cases to follow the conflict-of-laws rules prevailing in the states in which the courts sit. The purpose, said the Court, was to prevent "the accident of diversity of citizenship" from disturbing the "equal administration of justice in coordinate state and federal courts sitting side by

---

118. *See, e.g.*, New York Life Ins. Co. v. Hendren, 92 U.S. 286, 286-87, 23 L. Ed. 709, 709-10 (1876); Rockhold v. Rockhold, 92 U.S. 129, 130, 23 L. Ed. 507, 507 (1876); Tarver v. Keach, 82 U.S. (15 Wall.) 67, 67-68, 21 L. Ed. 82, 82 (1873); Bethell v. Demaret, 77 U.S. (10 Wall.) 537, 540, 19 L. Ed. 1007, 1008 (1871); *see also* Ralph U. Whitten, *The Constitutional Limitations on State-Court Jurisdiction—A Historical-Interpretative Reexamination of the Full Faith and Credit and Due Process Clauses (Part One)*, 14 CREIGHTON L. REV. 499, 597-98 (1981); Ernest A. Young, *The Last Brooding Omnipresence:* Erie Railroad Co. v. Tompkins *and the Unconstitutionality of Preemptive Federal Maritime Law*, 43 ST. LOUIS U. L.J. 1349, 1359 (1999) (abundant research shows that the law merchant was not viewed as federal in nature). It has been commonplace to characterize what was going on in *Swift* as the development of "federal common law." For example, consider the following passage from Professor Chemerinsky's treatise:

> In *Swift v. Tyson*, in 1842, the Supreme Court held that in diversity cases, in the absence of a state statutory or constitutional provision, or a particular local interest, federal courts should fashion federal common law. . . .
>
> . . . Story, writing for the Court in *Swift* . . . concluded that the Rules of Decision Act only required federal courts to apply state constitutional and statutory provisions, not state common law.

ERWIN CHEMERINSKY, FEDERAL JURISDICTION § 5.3, at 321-22 (5th ed. 2007). The quoted passage is, like many other current descriptions of the *Swift* doctrine, a curious mixture of accuracy and inaccuracy. The use of the expression "particular local interest" is especially curious, as it seems to represent a recognition that the federal courts would feel bound to follow "state common law" in some instances. But the expression is not explained and is contradicted by the other flat statements that the federal courts would not feel bound to follow state common law. As the discussion of *Swift* in section C *supra* has indicated, however, the federal courts *were* following state common law in cases like *Swift* by adhering to the decision made by the state to follow the general commercial law or not to follow it. The difference between general commercial law and local law was in the degree of deference that the federal courts would pay to state precedents constituting the content of these respective areas of law. However, it is clear that in no realistic sense were the federal courts fashioning "federal" common law. How can common law be deemed "federal" when ultimate control over whether to follow the law remains with the state?

119. *See* CHARLES A. WRIGHT & MARY KAY KANE, THE LAW OF FEDERAL COURTS § 57, at 387-88 (7th ed. 2011).

120. 313 U.S. 487, 61 S. Ct. 1020, 85 L. Ed. 1477 (1941).

side."[121] The *Klaxon* decision flatly disregarded a clear and direct congressional command embodied in the Act. The "in cases where they apply" language of the Act was uniformly interpreted under *Swift* as a directive to the federal courts to make judgments on matters of conflict of laws independent of the state courts' decisions on the same matters.[122] The power to make independent conflict-of-laws decisions was a valuable protection against biased law application afforded by the diversity jurisdiction under the *Swift* doctrine. The result in *Klaxon* eliminated much of the utility of the diversity jurisdiction to litigants.[123]

The substance-procedure distinction of *Erie* can interact in some tricky ways with *Klaxon's* requirement that federal courts apply the conflict-of-laws doctrine of the state in which they are sitting. Sometimes, evaluation of a state rule will indicate that it is "substantive" for *Erie* purposes, but the rule will be treated as "procedural" for purposes of a state's conflict-of-laws doctrine.[124] If a state classifies an issue as procedural, it will apply its own law to resolve the issue under traditional conflicts practice.[125] In this situation, if the issue is characterized as substantive for purposes of *Erie*, the federal court must apply state law regardless of the state's characterization of the issue. Conversely, a state may treat a particular issue as substantive under its conflict-of-laws doctrine. Thus, the state may or may not apply its own law, depending upon what its conflict-of-laws doctrine tells it to do. In this situation, there is a question posed for a federal court exercising diversity jurisdiction. Should the federal court ask first how the issue is characterized for *Erie* purposes and only then, if *Erie* requires the application of state law, ask which

---

121. 313 U.S. at 496, 61 S. Ct. at 1021, 85 L. Ed. at 1480; *see also* Day & Zimmermann, Inc. v. Challoner, 423 U.S. 3, 96 S. Ct. 167, 46 L. Ed. 2d 3 (1975); Griffin v. McCoach, 313 U.S. 498, 61 S. Ct. 1023, 85 L. Ed. 1481 (1941); *In re* Gaston & Snow, 243 F.3d 599 (2d Cir. 2001) (*Klaxon* requires a federal court in a bankruptcy case to apply the forum state's choice-of-law rules when state law is in issue; nevertheless, a significant federal policy may call for the imposition of a federal conflicts rule).

122. *See* RANDALL BRIDWELL & RALPH U. WHITTEN, THE CONSTITUTION AND THE COMMON LAW: THE DECLINE OF THE DOCTRINES OF SEPARATION OF POWERS AND FEDERALISM 110-11 (1977); 2 WILLIAM W. CROSSKEY, POLITICS AND THE CONSTITUTION IN THE HISTORY OF THE UNITED STATES 832-34, 867 (1953); William F. Baxter, *Choice of Law and the Federal System*, 16 STAN. L. REV. 1, 41 (1963).

123. *See* RANDALL BRIDWELL & RALPH U. WHITTEN, THE CONSTITUTION AND THE COMMON LAW: THE DECLINE OF THE DOCTRINES OF SEPARATION OF POWERS AND FEDERALISM 135 (1977); *see also* CHARLES A. WRIGHT & MARY KAY KANE, THE LAW OF FEDERAL COURTS § 57, at 389-90 (7th ed. 2011) (discussing criticisms of *Klaxon* on the grounds that the federal courts are in a "uniquely favorable position to develop a rational body" of conflicts law); Patrick J. Borchers, *The Origins of Diversity Jurisdiction: The Rise of Legal Positivism, and a Brave New World for* Erie *and* Klaxon, 72 TEX. L. REV. 79, 124-33 (1993) (advocating the development of independent choice-of-law rules in diversity cases); Scott Fruehwald, *Choice of Law in Federal Courts: A Reevaluation*, 37 BRANDEIS J. FAM. L. 212 (1998-99) (arguing that *Klaxon* should be overruled and a federal choice-of-law method substituted that would first determine which states have created legal relations applicable to the controversy and then select the applicable law on the basis of which state has the closest connection to the controversy). Under *Swift*, for example, the independent conflict-of-laws authority provided a valuable protection against biased selection of a state's own law over that of another state through the application of forum-oriented, conflict-of-laws systems. After *Klaxon*, this valuable protection has been lost at a time when conflict-of-laws doctrine within the states is particularly confused, but substantially forum oriented. *See* Ralph U. Whitten, *U.S. Conflict-of-Laws Doctrine and Forum Shopping, International and Domestic (Revisited)*, 37 TEX. INT'L L.J. 557 (2002) (discussing the tendency of modern conflicts systems to result in the application of forum law and the implications of this fact for forum shopping); Ralph U. Whitten, *Curing the Deficiencies of the Conflicts Revolution: A Proposal for National Legislation on Choice of Law, Jurisdiction, and Judgments*, 37 WILLAMETTE L. REV. 259 (2001) (describing the deficiencies of modern conflicts law).

124. This kind of result can occur because "substance" and "procedure" are defined in different ways for purposes of state conflicts doctrine and the *Erie* policies against forum shopping and discrimination against citizens of the forum state. *See* section E *infra* (discussing the evolution of the *Erie* substance-procedure distinction).

125. *See, e.g.*, ROBERT L. FELIX & RALPH U. WHITTEN., AMERICAN CONFLICTS LAW § 65 (6th ed. 2011) (discussing, *inter alia*, the characterization of matters as substantive or procedural for conflict-of-laws purposes).

state's law the forum's conflict-of-laws rule requires the federal court to apply? Alternatively, should the court ask the state conflicts question first, and then make the *Erie* determination based on the law that would be applied by the forum state? A few courts have adopted the first of these approaches.[126] With all due respect to the courts reaching this result, however, the result is clearly incorrect. As will be shown in sections E and F, below, a federal court cannot determine for *Erie* purposes whether a matter is substantive or procedural until it knows the content of the state law it is being asked to apply. Therefore, it is clear that federal diversity courts should ask the state conflicts question first and the *Erie* categorization question second.[127]

(b) Special Erie *Doctrine Problems in Cases of Transfer Under 28 U.S.C. § 1404(a)*

The *Klaxon* rule has produced difficulties when more than one federal court deals with a single case. The most important example of these difficulties occurs when a transfer of venue is made for the convenience of parties and witnesses and in the interests of justice from one federal court to another under 28 U.S.C. § 1404(a).[128] The Supreme Court first considered this issue in the context of a defendant's motion to transfer the action. In *Van Dusen v. Barrack*,[129] the Court held that the court to which the action was transferred (transferee court) must apply the same substantive law that would have been applied by the court that transferred the action (transferor court). The Court reached this result to prevent the defendant from moving for the transfer of venue in order to obtain a different applicable law,

---

126. *See* Chin v. Chrysler LLC, 538 F.3d 272 (3d Cir. 2008) (in diversity actions, first determine whether a matter is substantive or procedural for *Erie* purposes, and then, if choice-of-law decisions is called for, which state's substantive law should be applied); Schwan's Sales Enters., Inc. v. SIG Pack, Inc., 476 F.3d 594 (8th Cir. 2007) (stating that prejudgment interest is a substantive matter for purposes of *Erie*, but that under Minnesota conflict-of-laws doctrine it is a procedural matter to be governed by the law of the forum state); Ferrell v. West Bend Mut. Ins. Co., 393 F.3d 786 (8th Cir. 2005) (first holding that whether attorney fees were available is a "substantive" matter under *Erie* requiring the matter to be controlled by state law, but then holding that the matter was procedural under state conflict-of-laws doctrine, making the controlling law that of the forum state); Servicios Comerciales Andinos, S.A. v. General Elec. Del Caribe, Inc., 145 F.3d 463 (1st Cir. 1998) (first determine whether matter is substantive or procedural for *Erie* purposes; then ask which law the forum state would apply under its conflicts rule); *see also* Boyd Rosene & Assocs., Inc. v. Kansas Mun. Gas Agency, 174 F.3d 1115 (10th Cir. 1999) (following *Servicios*); *compare* MRO Commc'ns, Inc. v. American Tel. & Tel. Co., 197 F.3d 1276 (9th Cir. 1999) (holding that a choice-of-law clause in a contract selecting New Jersey law only applied to "substantive issues," and that the question in the case, which was whether to award attorney's fees under state law, was a "procedural issue," to be decided under the law of the forum, "Nevada") *with* All Underwriters v. Weisberg, 222 F.3d 1309 (11th Cir. 2000) (federal court may apply state law allowing attorney's fees in federal admiralty case involving maritime insurance contract); *cf.* McMahan v. Toto, 311 F.3d 1077 (11th Cir. 2002) (under authority of state intermediate appellate court opinion, court holds that Florida's offer of judgment statute is applicable to cases that are tried in Florida even if the substantive law that governs the case is that of another state, but does not then consider whether offer of judgment statute conflicts with any Federal Rule of Civil Procedure or could legitimately be disregarded under the Rules of Decision Act because it deals with a matter of procedure in the *Erie* sense that the federal courts may decide for themselves).

127. *In re* Cedant Corp. Sec. Litig., 139 F. Supp. 2d 585 (D.N.J. 2001) (holding that while they have held state "affidavit of merit" statute both substantive and procedural, New Jersey courts would classify it as substantive for choice-of-law purposes; under state choice-of-law rules, applied under the mandate of *Klaxon*, New Jersey would apply the substantive law of Connecticut; therefore, "affidavit of merit" statute inapplicable).

128. *See* Chapter 4(D) *supra* ("Forum Non Conveniens and Change of Venue").

129. 376 U.S. 612, 84 S. Ct. 805, 11 L. Ed. 2d 945 (1964).

as opposed to simply a more convenient venue.[130] The Court stated that the result in *Van Dusen* "fully accords with and is supported by the policy underlying *Erie [Railroad] v. Tompkins*."[131] The *Erie* policy "should ensure that the 'accident' of federal diversity jurisdiction does not enable a party to utilize a transfer to achieve a result in federal court which could not have been achieved in the courts of the State where the action was filed."[132]

Illustration 5-8. *P*, a citizen of State *X*, sues *D Corp.*, a corporation incorporated and with its principal place of business in State *Y*. *P* seeks $500,000 for the wrongful death of *P's* spouse received in an automobile accident in State *Y*. The action is brought in the U.S. District Court for State *X*. *D* is subject to personal jurisdiction in State *X* because *D* does extensive business there. Thus, venue is also proper under 28 U.S.C. § 1391(a)(1) and (c). *D* moves for a transfer of venue under 28 U.S.C. § 1404(a) to State *Y*, where the accident occurred. *D's* motion is granted. Assume that State *X* would apply its own law to determine the amount of any wrongful death recovery to which *P* is entitled and that State *X* law permits unlimited damages to be recovered for wrongful death. On the other hand, State *Y* limits the amount of damages that can be recovered for wrongful death to $100,000. If the action had been commenced in a State *Y* court, the State *Y* wrongful death limit would have been applied under State *Y* conflict-of-laws rules. Under the *Klaxon* decision, if the action had not been transferred, the U.S. District Court in State *X* would have been obligated to apply State *X* conflict-of-laws rules to determine the applicable law, and those rules would have required the application of the State *X* unlimited recovery rule in the federal diversity action. Under the *Van Dusen* rule, the U.S. District Court in State *Y* must apply the same law that would have been applied had there been no transfer. Thus, the State *X* unlimited recovery rule would have to be applied after transfer to the State *Y* federal district court.

* * * * *

After *Van Dusen*, it was still possible to argue that if a transfer was made on the motion of the plaintiff, the transferee court should apply the law that it would have applied under *Klaxon* if the action had been commenced originally in the transferee court. When the plaintiff is seeking the transfer, it is arguably improper to give the plaintiff a choice-of-law advantage resulting from the plaintiff's initial choice of a forum that the plaintiff is, in the transfer motion, arguing to be inconvenient.[133] The Supreme Court rejected this seemingly sensible rule in *Ferens v. John Deere Co.*[134] In *Ferens*, the plaintiffs filed a tort action in Mississippi to

---

130. The situation is actually more complicated. In determining whether to transfer, the district court must consider the applicable law as well as other factors bearing on the convenience of the transferee forum. If the court decides that the conflict-of-laws rule of the state in which it sits would select the substantive law of the transferee state, then that is one factor favoring the transfer. On the other hand, if the conflict-of-laws rule of the transferor state would result in the application of the substantive law of the transferor state under *Klaxon*, then that is one reason not to transfer, because upon transfer (under the *Van Dusen* rule) the transferee district court would have to apply the transferor state's law, with which it is less familiar. Thus, the choice-of-law decision under *Klaxon* and § 1404(a) has become an integral part of the decision whether to transfer, along with all other factors bearing on the convenience of the transfer. *See Van Dusen*, 376 U.S. at 643-46, 84 S. Ct. at 823-24, 11 L. Ed. 2d at 965-67.

131. 376 U.S. at 637, 84 S. Ct. at 820, 11 L. Ed. 2d at 961.

132. *Id.* at 638, 84 S. Ct. at 820, 11 L. Ed. 2d at 962 (citing Guaranty Trust v. York, 326 U.S. 99, 65 S. Ct. 1464, 89 L. Ed. 2d 2079 (1945), discussed in section E(1) *infra*).

133. ALI STUDY OF THE DIVISION OF JURISDICTION BETWEEN STATE AND FEDERAL COURTS 155 (1969) (comment to § 1306(c)).

134. 494 U.S. 516, 110 S. Ct. 1274, 108 L. Ed. 2d 443 (1990).

obtain the benefit of the Mississippi statute of limitations. The plaintiffs then moved to transfer the action under § 1404(a) to the Western District of Pennsylvania, where the accident had occurred and where a related breach of contract and warranty action was pending. The district court granted the motion to transfer to the Western District of Pennsylvania. However, the Pennsylvania federal district court held that the *Van Dusen* rule did not apply when the action was transferred on the plaintiff's motion. The Pennsylvania federal court dismissed the tort action under the Pennsylvania statute of limitations. The Third Circuit affirmed. The U.S. Supreme Court granted certiorari and reversed.

In *Ferens*, the Court stated that the advantages the defendant would lose by applying the *Van Dusen* rule to plaintiff's transfer cases would be slight, while applying the transferee state's law would undermine the *Erie* rule in a serious way by allowing the initiation of a transfer to result in a change of law. The Court further reasoned that the contrary rule would simply cause plaintiffs either not to sue defendants when they would have no choice but to litigate in an inconvenient forum, or to sue them and hope that the defendants would move to transfer. The Court also felt that the opportunities for forum shopping that the *Van Dusen* rule sought to avoid would not be enhanced by the application of that rule to plaintiffs' transfer motions. Because the plaintiffs would have been able to forum shop in the state courts in any event, the diversity jurisdiction and the application of the transferor state's law merely duplicated the results of that forum shopping.[135] The Court was also concerned that if the applicable law were to change following a transfer, the district court might be reluctant to grant a transfer motion that would disadvantage defendants. Such a disadvantage could occur because plaintiffs might find as many ways to exploit application of the transferee state's law as they would the transferor state's law.[136] In any event, the transferor court would have to make complex inquiries to assure that prejudice did not occur to the defendant. Finally, the Court noted that punishing the plaintiffs for their choice of forum would be improper because § 1404(a) was not only for the benefit of the moving party, but also for the benefit of the witnesses and the interests of justice.[137]

Numerous problems exist with the Court's reasoning in *Ferens*, but the most serious is the Court's failure to appreciate that its holding will encourage an abuse of the federal diversity jurisdiction that is similar to the kind *Erie* sought to eliminate. Under the Court's holding in *Ferens*, a plaintiff faced with a choice of a federal or state court in a state like Mississippi will always pick the federal court. While the state court will apply its longer statute of limitations to the action, it would not transfer the case on the motion of the plaintiff because no transfer

---

135. *See id.* at 525-26, 110 S. Ct. at 1280-81, 108 L. Ed. 2d at 454-55. The Court also expressed the fear that if the transferee state's law were applied on plaintiffs' transfer motions, many states would enact long statutes of limitation like Mississippi's statute. Why? Because if the transferee state law were applied, plaintiffs would not move for transfer, and thus the states, knowing this rule, would enact long statutes of limitation in the hope of getting tort business for their lawyers. *See id.* at 528, 110 S. Ct. at 1282, 108 L. Ed. 2d at 456. It is, of course, just as likely that if all or lots of states enacted long statutes of limitation, then plaintiffs would not have to shop for a forum with a long statute because they would likely have one in their home states.

136. *Id.* at 529, 110 S. Ct. at 1283, 108 L. Ed. 2d at 457. But why wouldn't the plaintiff just file in the transferee state in the first place if its law were more favorable and it was also more convenient?

137. *Id.*

mechanism exists between state courts.[138] Thus, unless the action is dismissed under the doctrine of forum non conveniens, the action would remain in the state, with whatever inconveniences that might entail to the plaintiff. However, the option of federal court under the rule in *Ferens* offers the possibility of a favorable applicable law *and* a more convenient place for the litigation. Had the Court instead held that the transferee state's law would be applicable when a case is transferred on the plaintiff's motion, the plaintiff would have no similar incentive to pick a federal court over a state court, because no advantage would be gained by choosing a federal forum. Thus, the rule in *Ferens* encourages abuse of the diversity jurisdiction and the federal transfer mechanism with no seeming gain to the goals of *Erie*.

The Court in *Ferens* indicated that the *Van Dusen* rule would be applied to all sorts of transfers under § 1404(a), including cases that were not before the Court for decision.[139] However, open questions still exist. For one, the *Van Dusen-Ferens* rule should not control transfers under 28 U.S.C. § 1406(a), when plaintiff initially commences the action in the wrong venue. "[W]henever the original venue is improper, so that transfer is under § 1406(a), the transferee court should apply whatever law it would have applied had the action been properly commenced there."[140] The same is arguably true when the transfer is from a district where venue is proper, but personal jurisdiction cannot be obtained over the defendant, regardless of whether the transfer is under § 1404(a) or § 1406(a).[141]

In addition to these obvious questions, litigation in the lower federal courts continues to produce other difficult administrative problems with § 1404(a). For

---

138. This situation may be about to change. As discussed in Chapter 4(D)(1)*(b) supra* ("The Uniform Transfer of Litigation Act"), that the National Conference of Commissioners on Uniform State Law has recommended the adoption by the states of the Uniform Transfer of Litigation Act. If this A ct is widely adopted, the state courts would be able to transfer litigation such as that involved in *Ferens* to another state. Furthermore, § 209 of the Uniform Act provides that a receiving court cannot dismiss an action based on statute of limitations if the matter would not be barred by limitations in the transferring state, provided the transferring state had subject-matter and personal jurisdiction over the action. *See id.* This section would not necessarily place the state and federal law of transfer in parity, however, because a receiving court can refuse a transfer for any reason under § 204 of the Uniform Act. *See id.* Thus, a receiving court that believed that the plaintiff had inappropriately engaged in forum shopping for a longer statute of limitations could presumably refuse to accept a transfer for that reason.

139. Thus, the Court indicated that the same rule would be applied when (1) both plaintiff and defendant move for a transfer, (2) the court transfers on its own motion, (3) a plaintiff moves for a transfer after a removed action, (4) only one of several plaintiffs moves for transfer, or (5) the circumstances change through no fault of the plaintiff, making a transfer desirable. *See Ferens*, 494 U.S. at 529, 110 S. Ct. at 1283, 108 L. Ed. 2d at 457.

140. 15 CHARLES A. WRIGHT ET AL., FEDERAL PRACTICE AND PROCEDURE: JURISDICTION AND RELATED MATTERS § 3827, at 581 (3d ed. 2007); *see, e.g.*, Adam v. J.B. Hunt Transp., Inc., 130 F.3d 219, 230 (6th Cir. 1997) (law of transferee state applies after transfer under § 1406); Wisland v. Admiral Beverage Corp., 119 F.3d 733 (8th Cir. 1997) (same).

141. *See* 15 CHARLES A. WRIGHT ET AL., FEDERAL PRACTICE AND PROCEDURE: JURISDICTION AND RELATED MATTERS § 3827, at 576-79 (3d ed. 2007). Recall from Chapter 4 that when venue is proper, but personal jurisdiction cannot be obtained over the defendant, the cases are divided over whether transfer should be made under § 1404(a) or § 1406(a). *See* Chapter 4(D) *supra* ("Forum Non Conveniens and Change of Venue"). The *Klaxon* decision also creates problems in areas other than transfers of venue. For example, Rule 501 of the Federal Rules of Evidence provides that the privilege of a witness in a civil action in which state law provides the rule of decision must be determined in accordance with state law. This means that a federal diversity court must generally apply the privilege law of the state in which it is sitting. However, it is possible for a federal action to be pending in one district based on an event occurring in another district and a deposition in the action may be taken in still another district, with perhaps the parties raising the privilege claim having a more substantial relationship to still a fourth district than they have with any of the first three. For a discussion of how the cases have addressed the problem of what state's privilege law to apply in such situations, see 23 CHARLES A. WRIGHT & KENNETH W. GRAHAM, JR., FEDERAL PRACTICE AND PROCEDURE: EVIDENCE § 5435 (1980).

example, in *Boardman Petroleum, Inc. v. Federated Mutual Insurance Co.*,[142] an insurance company instituted a diversity action in a U.S. District Court to obtain a declaratory judgment that a policy issued to the insured did not cover a particular occurrence. The insured commenced a separate diversity action in another district to recover under the policy. The insurer's action was transferred under § 1404(a) to the district where the insured's action was pending. The conflict-of-laws rules of the transferor and transferee states pointed to a different applicable substantive law for each action. In this situation, it is obvious that the choice-of-law problem cannot be solved by applying a different state's substantive law to each case, because both cases involve the same issue. The Eleventh Circuit, in effect, applied an independent federal conflict of laws approach to resolve the problem, *Klaxon, Van Dusen*, and *Ferens* notwithstanding. Under this approach, the court balanced the interests of the concerned states in having their law applied and applied the law of the state that, in the court's view, had the greater interest. In contrast, the U.S. District Court for the Eastern District of Pennsylvania, in a similar case, applied the law of the transferor state to both actions, although the court had some misgivings about this approach because the action in the transferee district had been commenced first. However, the court ultimately concluded that the substantive law of all the concerned states was the same, making the choice-of-law decision irrelevant to the result.[143] Other alternatives available to courts in these situations might include (1) the court in the second-filed action deferring to the first filed action, instead of transferring and consolidating the suits;[144] (2) the court in the declaratory judgment action exercising its discretion to defer to the damage action;[145] and (3) one of the courts enjoining the defendant from proceeding as a plaintiff in the other action, as discussed in Chapter 4.[146]

Another problem under 28 U.S.C. § 1404(a) concerns the effect of state law on a forum selection clause relied on by a party seeking transfer. In Chapter 4(D)(2)*(a)*, above, it was observed that the Supreme Court has established that a forum selection clause would not absolutely control the question of transfer under 28 U.S.C. § 1404(a), but would be weighed in the balance along with all other factors bearing on the convenience of the parties and witnesses and the interests of justice. This was the holding of *Stewart Organization, Inc. v. Ricoh Corp.*[147] However, in *Stewart Organization*, the forum selection clause in question would not have been enforceable under the applicable state law controlling the contract

---

142. 135 F.3d 750 (11th Cir. 1998).

143. Computer Aid, Inc. v. Hewlett-Packard Co., 56 F. Supp. 2d 526 (E.D. Pa. 1999).

144. *See* Kerotest Mfg. Co. v. C-O-Two Fire Equip. Co., 342 U.S. 180, 72 S. Ct. 219, 96 L. Ed. 2d 200 (1952).

145. *See id.*; *see also* Wilton v. Seven Falls Co., 515 U.S. 277, 115 S. Ct. 2137, 132 L. Ed. 2d 214 (1995) (discussing the discretion of federal courts to defer to pending state actions in declaratory judgment suits).

146. *See* Chapter 4(E) *supra* ("Injunctions Against Extrastate Litigation and Other Devices for Controlling the Location of Suit"); *see also* International Bus. Machs. Corp. v. Bajorek, 191 F.3d 1033 (9th Cir. 1999) ("substantive" action commenced in New York federal court and transferred to California, where declaratory judgment action pending; district court dismisses "substantive" action; court of appeals refuses to resolve whether district court must exercise its discretion to dismiss earlier filed declaratory judgment action in favor of "substantive" action because parties agree that New York and California would apply same conflict-of-laws rule to case); *cf.* Johnson v.Nextel Commc'ns, Inc., 660 F.3d 113 (2d Cir. 2011) (after transfer from New Jersey to New York, New Jersey's conflict-of-laws rules applied; however, New York substantive law, as forum law, applied to law of the case because there was no conflict between New York and New Jersey law).

147. 487 U.S. 22, 108 S. Ct. 2239, 101 L. Ed. 2d 22 (1988).

between the parties. As the dissent pointed out, there was no apparent reason to have the question of the validity of the forum selection clause controlled by federal law rather than state law, which would control all other issues of the validity of the contract.[148] Certainly, there is nothing in the language, history, or purposes of 28 U.S.C. § 1404(a) that would indicate that federal law was designed to control such an issue under the statute.[149] Additionally, the application of a federal judge-made rule, rather than state law, to determine the validity of the forum selection clause would produce both forum shopping by the party seeking to rely on the clause and discrimination against a citizen of the forum state who is deprived of the benefit of a valuable rule of law that would be applied by the state courts.[150] The majority's only response in *Stewart Organization* to these serious difficulties was to state that the dissent's analysis "makes the applicability of a federal statute depend upon the content of state law."[151] However, it is quite common for the application of federal statutes to depend on the operation of state law. For example, in determining whether the jurisdictional amount requirement of 28 U.S.C. § 1332 is satisfied, it must always be determined whether state law will permit a recovery of more than $75,000.[152]

In addition to the question of whether federal or state law should control the validity of the forum selection clause in *Stewart Organization*, the majority also did not explain why 28 U.S.C. § 1404(a) rather than § 1406 was the controlling federal statute. At the district court level, the defendant had moved in the alternative to transfer under § 1404(a) or to dismiss under § 1406.[153] However, the Supreme Court did not provide an adequate explanation why § 1404(a), which controls transfers of venue when an action is commenced in a correct venue, should govern the case rather than § 1406, which controls dismissal and transfer when an action is commenced in an incorrect venue.[154] Indeed, it has been persuasively argued that

---

148. *See* 487 U.S. at 33-38, 108 S. Ct at 2246-48, 101 L. Ed. 2d at 33-39 (Scalia, J., dissenting).

149. As discussed in section F *infra*, the first obligation of a federal court faced with a contention that a federal statute or Federal Rule of Civil Procedure controls a case is to determine whether the statute or rule is broad enough to cover the question in issue. *See also* 487 U.S. at 34, 108 S. Ct. at 2246, 101 L. Ed. 2d at 34 (Scalia, J., dissenting). However, it has been persuasively argued that if a statute such as § 1404(a) is not "plainly on point," the federal courts should disregard the statute and decide the case under the general *Erie* doctrine discussed in section E *infra*. *See* Richard D. Freer, Erie's *Mid-Life Crisis*, 63 TUL. L. REV. 1087, 1117-20 (1989).

150. *See* 487 U.S. at 38-41, 108 S. Ct. at 2248-50, 101 L. Ed. 2d at 37-39 (Scalia, J., dissenting). As discussed in the next section, forum shopping and discrimination against citizens of the forum state are important factors in judging the validity of "federal common-law rules of practice and procedure" under the *Erie* doctrine.

151. *See id.* at 31 n.10, 108 S. Ct. at 2244 n.10, 101 L. Ed. 2d at 32 n.10.

152. *See* Chapter 2(D)(7) *supra* ("Amount-in-Controversy Requirement").

153. *See Stewart Organization*, 487 U.S. at 24, 108 S. Ct at 2241, 101 L. Ed. 2d at 28.

154. *See* Allan R. Stein, Erie *and Court Access*, 100 YALE L.J. 1935, 1961-64 (1991). In Kerobo v. Southwestern Clean Fuels Corp., 285 F.3d 531 (6th Cir. 2002), the district court dismissed an action properly removed from state court for improper venue because of a forum selection clause in the parties' agreement. The court of appeals reversed, holding that venue in a properly removed action is controlled by the removal statute, which makes venue proper in the district and division embracing the place where the state action is pending. Thus, because venue was proper, the court of appeals found the action indistinguishable from *Stewart Organization*. Under the latter precedent, § 1404(a) governed the transfer to another venue and was broad enough to control the issue of whether the forum selection clause should be given effect. In cases not involving transfer under § 1404(a), the federal courts of appeals are split over whether state or federal law controls the enforceability of a forum selection clause in a diversity action. *See, e.g.*, Huffington v. T.C. Group, LLC, 637 F.3d 18 (1st Cir. 2011) (no need to determine whether *Erie* requires use of state law to determine validity of forum selection clause because state law is same as federal common law in this case); Rucker v. Oasis Legal Fin. L.L.C., 632 F.3d 1231 (11th Cir. 2011) (no *Erie* conflict between federal and state law on validity of forum selection clause; clause valid); Albemarle Corp. v. Astrazenca UK Ltd., 628 F.3d 643 (4th Cir. 2010) (appropriate venue of an action is a procedural matter governed by federal rule and statute; therefore, federal law governed interpretation of forum selection clause);

there was no reason for the Supreme Court to pick either § 1404(a) or § 1406 as applicable to the problem before it, as opposed to deciding the case under the general *Erie* doctrine discussed in the next section.[155]

SECTION E. THE EVOLUTION OF THE *ERIE* DOCTRINE: APPLICABILITY OF STATE "SUBSTANTIVE LAW" UNDER THE RULES OF DECISION ACT

The decisions developing the *Erie* doctrine group themselves into two separate categories. One category of cases involves actual or potential conflicts between state law and Federal Rules of Civil or Appellate Procedure created under the Rules Enabling Act, 28 U.S.C. § 2072. The second category of cases involves the Rules of Decision Act, 28 U.S.C. § 1652, under which *Swift* and *Erie* were decided. These categories must be examined separately because different considerations ultimately determine whether a conflict should be resolved in favor of state law or federal law under each statute. This section examines the problems involved in Rules of Decision Act cases, but a caveat is in order before examining the cases. Differentiating the decided cases on the basis of whether they are controlled by the Rules of Enabling Act or the Rules of Decision Act is analytically proper. However, as demonstrated in the next section, it was not always clear that the cases under the two statutes should be analyzed under different standards. In the

---

Rafael Rodriguez Barril, Inc. v. Conbraco Indus., Inc., 619 F.3d 90 (1st Cir. 2010) (same); Preferred Capital, Inc. v. Sarasota Kennel Club, Inc., 489 F.3d 303 (6th Cir. 2007) (*Erie* compels use of state law to govern interpretation of forum selection clause when no motion to transfer made in order to avoid undercutting the twin aims of *Erie* in diversity action); Servewell Plumbing, LLC v. Federal Ins. Co., 439 F.3d 786 (8th Cir. 2006) (court need not decide whether federal or state law governs the enforceability of a forum selection clause, since state law and federal standards are the same in this case); M.B. Restaurants, Inc. v. CKE Restaurants, Inc., 183 F.3d 750, 752 n.4 (8th Cir. 1999) (citing cases evidencing split of authorities); Kelly Amanda Blair, Note, *A Judicial Solution to the Forum-Selection Clause Enforcement Circuit Split: Giving* Erie *a Second Chance*, 46 GA. L. REV. 799 (2012).

In Jackson v. West Telemarketing Corp. Outbound, 245 F.3d 518 (5th Cir. 2001), the court held that the transferee court properly applied the choice-of-law rules of its forum state rather than the choice-of-law rules of the transferor court's state, because the action had been transferred for improper venue. The court stated that *Stewart Organization* did not mandate that whenever a forum selection clause is present the transfer must be treated as one under § 1404(a). In transferring the case, it appeared that the transferor court had based the transfer on the forum selection clause and accepted the argument that the clause made venue in the transferor state improper. In AmerMed Corp. v. Disetronic Holding AG, 6 F. Supp. 2d 1371 (N.D. Ga. 1998), the court, in a case involving a permissive forum selection clause and a motion to dismiss under § 1406 for improper venue, held that the federal provisions governing "improper" or "wrong" venue were silent as to dismissal on any ground other than statutorily deficient venue, and, therefore, that there was no controlling statute or Federal Rule of Civil Procedure to dictate the result in the case, unlike *Stewart Organization*. However, in 2215 Fifth Street Associates, LP v. U-Haul International, Inc., 148 F. Supp. 2d 50 (D.D.C. 2001), the court enforced a forum selection clause on a motion to dismiss, or in the alternative to transfer, under § 1406. In Tri-State Foundation Repair & Waterproofing, Inc. v. Permacrete Systems, Inc., No. 99-1132-CV-W-6, 2000 WL 245824, 2000 U.S. Dist. LEXIS 2390 (W.D. Mo. Mar. 1, 2000), the court, following Eighth Circuit precedent, indicated that a forum selection clause that would have called for dismissal in preference to a forum in Nova Scotia had to be disregarded in a federal diversity action because it was unenforceable under the law of the forum state. The court did not discuss the *Erie* policies against forum shopping and discrimination against citizens of the forum state. *See also* Kendra Johnson Panek, *Forum Selection Clauses in Diversity Actions*, 36 J. MARSHALL L. REV. 941 (2003).

155. *See* Richard D. Freer, Erie's *Mid-Life Crisis*, 63 TUL. L. REV. 1087, 1117-21 (1989); *see also* AmerMed Corp. v. Disetronic Holding AG, 6 F. Supp. 2d 1371 (N.D. Ga. 1998) (holding federal provisions governing improper venue were silent as to dismissal on any ground other than statutorily deficient venue and, therefore, unlike *Stewart Organization*, there was no controlling federal statute or Federal Rule of Civil Procedure to dictate the result in a case involving a permissive forum selection clause); Walter L. Heiser, *Forum Selection Clauses in Federal Courts: Limitations on Enforcement After* Stewart Organization *and* Carnival Cruise, 45 FLA. L. REV. 553, 590-95 (1993); Allen R. Stein, Erie *and Court Access*, 100 YALE L.J. 1935, 1961-65 (1991).

early days of the *Erie* doctrine, the Supreme Court appeared to use the same standard under both statutes. Thus, until the case of *Hanna v. Plumer*,[156] discussed in the next section, the Court did not make it clear that the validity of Federal Rules of Civil Procedure were to be judged differently than general *Erie* problems under the Rules of Decision Act.

In *Erie*, the U.S. Supreme Court indicated that the Rules of Decision Act required the federal courts to follow state court decisions on matters of substantive law.[157] Implicit in the Court's description of the obligations of the federal courts was the suggestion that they were *not* bound to follow state law on matters of procedure.[158] Neither the language of the Rules of Decision Act nor the jurisprudence of the *Swift* doctrine distinguished "substantive" matters from "procedural" matters.[159] Under the Conformity Acts,[160] federal courts generally followed the procedural rules of the state in which they were sitting in common-law actions.[161] In 1938, when the Federal Rules of Civil Procedure became effective, this pattern changed. Federal courts now had their own uniform procedure. Thus, when *Erie* stated that the federal courts were obligated to follow state law on substantive matters under the Rules of Decision Act, it seemed that a dichotomy had been established between substance and procedure that would have the effect of allowing the federal courts to have their own uniform procedural system.[162]

However, the Federal Rules of Civil Procedure and the Federal Rules of Appellate Procedure do not cover all matters of federal practice and procedure. Numerous issues that can, in some sense, be described as "procedural" are simply not dealt with by the Federal Rules.[163] Furthermore, even before the Federal Rules, a considerable amount of case law had built up a body of independent federal procedural rules and practices, mainly in equity actions in which the federal courts were not obliged by the Conformity Acts to follow state procedural law.[164] One

---

156. 380 U.S. 460, 85 S. Ct. 1136, 14 L. Ed. 2d 8 (1965).

157. *See* Erie R.R. Co. v. Tompkins, 304 U.S. 64, 78, 58 S. Ct. 817, 822, 82 L. Ed. 1188, 1194 (1938) (stating that "Congress has no power to declare substantive rules of common law applicable in a State"); *see also* Lawrence B. Solum, *Procedural Justice,* 78 SO. CAL. L. REV. 181 (2004) (discussing, *inter alia*, the substance-procedure distinction under *Erie*).

158. *See* CHARLES A. WRIGHT & MARY KAY KANE, THE LAW OF FEDERAL COURTS § 55, at 377 (7th ed. 2011); Ralph U. Whitten, Erie *and the Federal Rules: A Review and Reappraisal After* Burlington Northern Railroad v. Woods, 21 CREIGHTON L. REV. 1, 3-4 (1987).

159. *See* Ralph U. Whitten, Erie *and the Federal Rules: A Review and Reappraisal After* Burlington Northern Railroad v. Woods, 21 CREIGHTON L. REV. 1, 3 (1987).

160. The Conformity Acts are discussed in Chapter 1(D)(10) *supra* ("Early Procedure in the Federal Courts"); *see also* Ralph U. Whitten, Erie *and the Federal Rules: A Review and Reappraisal After* Burlington Northern Railroad v. Woods, 21 CREIGHTON L. REV. 1, 3 n.13 (1987).

161. *See* Ralph U. Whitten, Erie *and the Federal Rules: A Review and Reappraisal After* Burlington Northern Railroad v. Woods, 21 CREIGHTON L. REV. 1, 3 (1987).

162. *See id.* at 1-4.

163. For example, while some issues concerning the effect to be given to federal judgments are covered by the Federal Rules, *see* FED. R. CIV. P. 13(a), 41(b), most such issues are governed by common-law rules. *See* RESTATEMENT (SECOND) OF JUDGMENTS § 87 (1982); *see also* Chapter 13*infra* ("Finality in Litigation").

164. *See* Ralph U. Whitten, Erie *and the Federal Rules: A Review and Reappraisal After* Burlington Northern Railroad v. Woods, 21 CREIGHTON L. REV. 1, 8 (1987). The independent equity power of the federal courts is described in Chapter 1(D)(10) *supra* ("Early Procedure in the Federal Courts"). In addition to the independent federal equity practice, federal judge-made rules of practice also grew up in common-law actions because of a requirement in the 1872 Conformity Act that the federal courts only conform "as near as may be" to state procedural law. "Partly in reliance on this latter phrase and partly by a restrictive interpretation of the three categories of 'practice, pleadings, and forms and modes of proceedings', the Court withdrew from the operation of the [Conformity] Act a wide area of particularly important matters affecting the administration of federal justice." RICHARD H. FALLON ET AL., HART & WECHSLER'S THE FEDERAL COURTS AND THE FEDERAL SYSTEM 607

question after *Erie* was whether the federal courts would be able to continue to apply this body of independent "common law"[165] rules of practice and procedure, in the face of conflicting state law.

1. The *Guaranty Trust* Case: Independent Federal Equity Powers and the "Outcome Determinative" Test

The Court first addressed the *Erie* substance-procedure distinction in the case of *Guaranty Trust Co. v. York*.[166] A federal class action was brought against Guaranty Trust for breach of trust. The district court granted summary judgment in favor of the defendant. However, that judgment was reversed by the court of appeals. The court of appeals held that in a suit brought on the equity side of a federal court, the court was not obliged to apply the statute of limitations that would govern in the state courts of the same state, even though federal jurisdiction was based exclusively on diversity of citizenship.[167] The U.S. Supreme Court granted certiorari and reversed. In an opinion by Justice Frankfurter, the Court held that the *Erie* doctrine required the application of the state statute of limitations even in an "equity" action.[168]

In deciding that *Erie* required the application of state law on the facts of *Guaranty Trust*, the Court had to address both the substance-procedure distinction and the question of whether the federal courts possessed an independent equity power after *Erie*. On the question of independent federal equity power, Justice Frankfurter's opinion was not clear. First, Justice Frankfurter stated correctly[169] that "[i]n giving federal courts 'cognizance' of equity suits in cases of diversity jurisdiction, Congress never gave, nor did the federal courts ever claim, the power to deny substantive rights denied by State law."[170] However, Justice Frankfurter then suggested that there might be some room left for independent equity power after *Erie*. His opinion stated that (1) the federal courts were obligated to follow explicit restrictions placed on their equity powers by Congress and the Constitution; (2) the federal courts were not obligated to give "whatever equitable remedy is available in a State court"; and (3) the federal courts might give an equitable remedy

---

(5th ed. 2003).

165. The expression "common law" is used hereafter to include rules drawn from equity that are not embodied in the Federal Rules of Civil Procedure.

166. 326 U.S. 99, 65 S. Ct. 1464, 89 L. Ed. 2079 (1945).

167. *See id.* at 100-01, 65 S. Ct. at 1465, 89 L. Ed. at 2081. The equitable doctrine of laches, applied by the court of appeals, is more flexible than most statutes of limitations and, for example, does not depend entirely on the passage of time, but whether the plaintiff is chargeable with lack of diligence in bringing the action. *See* Burch v. Bricker, 2006 SD 101, 724 N.W.2d 604.

168. Of course, by the time *Guaranty Trust* had been decided, law and equity had been merged in the federal courts by the Federal Rules of Civil Procedure. *See* FED. R. CIV. P. 2. However, the Rules of Decision Act still applied only to "common-law" actions; it was not amended to apply to all civil actions until the 1948 revision of the judicial code. *See* 28 U.S.C. § 1652 reviser's note. Neither of these facts seemed to affect the Court's decision in *Guaranty Trust*.

169. See the discussion of the independent federal equity power under *Swift* in section C *supra*.

170. *Guaranty Trust*, 326 U.S. at 105, 65 S. Ct. at 1468, 89 L. Ed. at 2084. This statement appears at the end of a lengthy passage in which Justice Frankfurter recounted the history of federal equity. That history is, in all essential respects, in agreement with the history of federal equity under the *Swift* doctrine set out in section C(2)*(e) supra*.

for the violation of a state substantive right, even though the state courts could not give the remedy.[171]

No difficulty exists with the observation that federal courts must abide by explicit congressional restrictions on equity powers. When Congress acts within its delegated powers to restrict the jurisdiction or remedial authority of the federal courts, the congressionally mandated restrictions must be obeyed. Likewise, explicit constitutional commands applicable to the federal courts, such as the Seventh Amendment right to a trial by jury, must also be obeyed. However, the remainder of the Court's discussion of federal equitable power is much more troublesome.

In observing that federal equity was subject to restrictions that might not apply to the states, the Court stated that federal "suits must be within the traditional scope of equity as historically evolved in the English Court of Chancery."[172] This statement suggests that a historical test will be applied to determine whether a federal court in diversity can hear an action that would be adjudicated by the courts of the state in which the federal court is sitting. In some ways, this suggestion is unexceptional. For example, a state might authorize its courts to give advisory opinions on pending legislation, a kind of case that would not be justiciable under the requirements of Article III of the Constitution.[173] Certainly a federal court sitting in diversity could not entertain such a proceeding. However, to require that a justiciable case within one of the Article III categories (here, the diversity category) also conform to historic equitable forms is unjustifiable. It would presumably mean that if new remedies were authorized at the state level and labeled "equitable," the federal courts could not hear cases in which those remedies were requested if the remedies were not within the historic scope of equity on the date the Constitution was formed. If this conclusion is correct, however, Congress also could not authorize new remedies unknown to the categories "Law" and "Equity" described in Article III. Statutes such as the federal Declaratory Judgment Act would be unconstitutional because they create a remedy that was, strictly speaking, known neither to law or equity at the time the Constitution was formed.[174] The terms "Law" and "Equity" are more reasonably interpreted as encompassing all judicial actions that otherwise fall within the justiciability and category requirements of Article III.[175]

---

171. *See id.* at 105-06, 65 S. Ct. at 1468-69, 89 L. Ed. at 2084-85.

172. *See id.* at 105, 65 S. Ct. at 1468, 89 L. Ed. at 2084.

173. *See* U.S. CONST. art. III, § 2; Hayburn's Case, 2 U.S. (2 Dall.) 409, 1 L. Ed. 436 (1792); RICHARD H. FALLON ET AL., HART & WECHSLER'S THE FEDERAL COURTS AND THE FEDERAL SYSTEM 50 - 58 (6th ed. 2009) (describing the correspondence of the Justices).

174. *See* 28 U.S.C. §§ 2201-2202.

> Although it is sometimes said that an action for a declaratory judgment is "equitable in nature," other cases have spoken of an action for a declaratory judgment as "essentially legal." The truth is that "a declaratory judgment action is a statutory creation, and by its nature is neither fish nor fowl, neither legal nor equitable." The new remedy may be sought both in cases that historically would have been legal and those that historically would have been equitable.

CHARLES A. WRIGHT & MARY KAY KANE, THE LAW OF FEDERAL COURTS § 100, at 718 (7th ed. 2011).

175. In *Guaranty Trust*, the Court did cite cases that seemed to support a historical limit on the equity powers of federal courts in diversity actions. *See, e.g.*, Pusey & Jones Co. v. Hanssen, 261 U.S. 491, 43 S. Ct. 454, 67 L. Ed. 763 (1923); Payne v. Hook, 74 U.S. (7 Wall.) 425, 19 L. Ed. 260 (1869). However, the doctrines announced in those cases should have become obsolete with the change in context brought about by the merger of law and equity by the Federal Rules of Civil Procedure and the decision in *Erie*. *See, e.g.*, Sprague v. Ticonic Nat'l Bank, 307 U.S. 161, 169-70, 59 S. Ct. 777, 781-82, 83 L. Ed. 1184, 1188-89 (1939) (the new Federal Rules of Civil Procedure have rendered anachronistic the technical niceties pertaining to terms of court as to both law

In addition to suggesting that historic equity forms might confine the powers of federal diversity courts to follow state law, the Court also suggested that federal courts might still be able to give equitable remedies that were not available under state law.[176] Like the Court's discussion of the confining power of historic equity forms, this discussion also seems erroneous after *Erie*. Besides being infected by a view of independent federal equity power that should have become obsolete after *Erie*, this suggestion by the Court was supported by an erroneous view of the nature of remedies. The modern thinking about remedies is that "remedies are the means of carrying into effect the substantive right."[177] Thus, subject to some qualifications, "the remedy should reflect the right or the policy behind that right as precisely as possible."[178] If this approach is proper—and it seems analytically irrefutable—it is difficult to see how the federal courts could give a remedy for the violation of a state right that the state courts would not give. Likewise, it is hard to see how a federal court could justifiably deny a remedy authorized by the state for the violation of a state right, assuming that neither Congress nor the Constitution has forbidden the grant of the remedy.[179] Even if the policies of the *Erie* doctrine do not forbid the federal denial of a remedy the state courts would give, the policies supporting the diversity jurisdiction would be undermined by such a denial. Plaintiffs needing the remedy would be forced to abandon the possibility of suing

---

and equity, but the ruling of the district court was made prior to the operation of the new rules). Certainly, the Court's later discussion in *Guaranty Trust* of the standard for resolving conflicts between state and federal law under the *Erie* doctrine seems inconsistent with the older "independent equity" authorities cited by the Court in its opinion. Furthermore, there has been no case after *Guaranty Trust* decided by the Court in which the historic forms of equity jurisprudence have prevented a federal diversity court from adjudicating an action that would be heard by the state courts. *But cf.* Grupo Mexicano de Desarrollo S.A. v. Alliance Bond Fund, Inc., 527 U.S. 308, 119 S. Ct. 1961, 144 L. Ed. 2d 319 (1999), in which the Supreme Court held that U.S. District Courts do not have the power under Federal Rule 65 to issue preliminary injunctions to prevent defendants from disposing of their assets before the plaintiff has obtained a judgment from the defendant "fixing the debt" owed. The court reasoned that such power was not part of the power possessed by equity at the time the federal courts first obtained jurisdiction over equity cases in the Judiciary Act of 1789. The merger of law and equity by the Federal Rules of Civil Procedure pursuant to the Rules Enabling Act, *see* section F *infra*, had not expanded federal equity power because (1) the historic restriction on equity's power to issue this type of injunction, while partly procedural, was also partly substantive and (2) the Rules Enabling Act preserved substantive rights from abridgement or enlargement by the Federal Rules. However, the Court indicated that Congress could give the federal courts this power. Because the argument was not properly raised in the lower courts, the Supreme Court refused to consider whether, if the forum state's law permitted such injunctions, *Erie* would require that the power to issue the remedy be determined by state law. *See* 527 U.S. at 319 n.3, 119 S. Ct. at 1968 n.3, 144 L. Ed. 2d at 330 n.3. *Grupo* is discussed further in Chapter 6(G)(4)*(a)*, *infra*. *But cf.* United States *ex rel.* Rahman v. Oncology Assocs., P.C., 198 F.3d 489 (4th Cir. 1999) (*Grupo* does not prevent equitable order freezing assets in a case in which final relief requested is partly equitable, but Federal Rule 64 adopts state law permitting such an order in any event). *See also* Cendant Corp. v. Forbes, 70 F. Supp. 2d 339 (S.D.N.Y. 1999) (there may be settings in which equitable remedial rights doctrine can still be applied, but when it conflicts with *Erie*, *Erie* must prevail); John T. Cross, *The* Erie *Doctrine in Equity*, 60 LA. L. REV. 173 (1999).

176. *See Guaranty Trust*, 326 U.S. at 106, 65 S. Ct. at 1468-69, 89 L. Ed. at 2084-85.

177. DAN B. DOBBS, LAW OF REMEDIES § 1.7, at 22 (2d student ed. 1993).

178. *Id.*

179. Perhaps one circumstance which could cause a federal district court to consider not giving a remedy authorized by a state might be when such relief would "unduly" strain the resources of the federal district court. For example, a federal district court might have such a concern when a state would provide injunctive relief that would require extensive, detailed, time-consuming, and continuing "supervisory" regulation. *Cf.* DAN B. DOBBS, LAW OF REMEDIES § 2.9(1), at 164 (2d student ed. 1993) (describing "structural injunctions" that "are typically complex and invasive [and] are likely to involve the judge in tasks traditionally considered to be non-judicial, that is, less about rights and duties and more about management"). However, if a federal court dismissed a diversity action on such a ground, the dismissal would surely have to be without prejudice to a future action in state court. *See* Chapter 13(B)(2) *infra* (discussing the effect of dismissals "on the merits"); Clausen v. M/V New Carissa, 339 F.3d 1049 (9th Cir. 2003) (right to attorney fees that is part of state damages remedy is substantive for purposes of *Erie* doctrine).

in a diversity action and sue in state court to have any possibility of obtaining the remedy.[180]

Illustration 5-9. *M Corp.* is incorporated with its principal place of business in State *X*. *M* does extensive business in State *Y*. *M* sues *D*, a citizen of State *Y* who is also the attorney general of State *Y*, in a U.S. District Court in State *Y*. *M* seeks an injunction to prevent *D* from enforcing a State *Y* statute against *M* that *M* contends is unconstitutional under the State *Y* constitution. Assume that under the traditional equity principles followed by the federal courts, an injunction would be justified, but that under the equity principles followed by the State *Y* courts no injunction would be permissible. It is difficult to imagine a federal interest that would justify the federal court granting an injunction to enforce state rights when the state courts would not grant the injunction under similar circumstances.[181] If the courts did grant such an injunction, it would encourage plaintiffs such as *M* to forum shop for federal courts to obtain a different result than could be obtained under state law, and this consequence would seem to run counter to the *Erie* policies.

Illustration 5-10. Assume the same facts as in *Illustration 5-9*, except that traditional federal equitable principles would not permit the award of an injunction, while State *X* principles would permit the injunction. In this situation, denial of the injunction by the federal courts will not encourage the noncitizen plaintiff to forum shop for a different result because the federal result would disfavor the plaintiff. Likewise, if the plaintiff brings the action in state court, the defendant cannot remove the action (and thus forum shop for a different result) because a citizen of the forum state cannot remove an action based solely on diversity of citizenship.[182] Similarly, application of the federal equitable principles would not discriminate against a citizen of the forum, because those principles favor the defendant who is the citizen of the forum state. Thus, if avoidance of forum shopping and discrimination against forum citizens are the only policies supporting the *Erie* doctrine, that doctrine might not be violated by a refusal of the federal injunction. Nevertheless, the federal court should not refuse an injunction in this situation, because to do so would undermine the policies supporting the diversity jurisdiction. To refuse injunctions under these circumstances would cause plaintiffs such as *M* to abandon their congressionally granted privilege of resorting to the diversity jurisdiction and sue in state court. In the state court, the plaintiffs might be subjected to the very kind of fact-finding bias and prejudice that the diversity jurisdiction was designed to guard against. Therefore, even if the *Erie* doctrine does not compel the duplication of the result that would be reached by the state courts, the policies supporting the diversity jurisdiction require the federal court to grant the injunction on these facts.

* * * * *

---

180. No Supreme Court decision since *Guaranty Trust* has approved of a federal diversity court granting a remedy the state courts would deny or denying a remedy the state courts would grant in the absence of a statute or a Federal Rule of Civil Procedure dictating the result.

181. *But cf.* Beal v. Missouri Pac. R.R. Corp., 312 U.S. 45, 61 S. Ct. 418, 85 L. Ed. 577 (1941) (Supreme Court appeared to decide case under federal equitable principles without any reference to what rules of decision existed under state law).

182. *See* 28 U.S.C. § 1441(b)(2).

The major contribution of *Guaranty Trust* to the *Erie* jurisprudence was the enunciation of a new test to deal with the substance-procedure dichotomy. Justice Frankfurter observed for the Court that "substance" and "procedure" are not mutually exclusive categories. They vary in content depending upon the purpose for which they are being used. As far as the *Erie* doctrine is concerned, the important question is not whether a state statute of limitations can be considered a matter of procedure in some sense—for example, for purposes of conflict-of-laws doctrine. Rather, the important question is whether disregard of the state statute in federal court would significantly affect the result of the litigation.[183] This so-called "outcome determinative test"[184] of *Guaranty Trust*, far from alleviating all problems of distinguishing between substantive and procedural matters, created substantial problems of its own. "[A]lmost every procedural rule may have a substantial effect on the outcome of a case," but "[i]f the test was not to be carried to its literal limits, . . . there was confusion as to how far it was to go."[185] As discussed in the next section, the main difficulty presented by the test was that it was believed to be applicable to conflicts between Federal Rules of Civil Procedure and state law, with the possibility that many of the Federal Rules would be held invalid because they could substantially affect the outcome of cases.[186] However, even as applied to conflicts between federal common-law rules of practice or procedure and state law, the test was, on its face, too extreme.[187]

Nevertheless, the results produced by the outcome determinative test were eminently justifiable. In *Woods v. Interstate Realty Co.*,[188] the Supreme Court considered whether a federal court sitting in diversity was required to apply a Mississippi statute that closed the doors of the state's courts to foreign corporations that failed to qualify under state law to do business within the state. A pre-*Erie* decision had indicated that such statutes did not apply in federal court because it was impermissible for the states to prescribe the qualifications of suitors in federal courts.[189] In *Woods*, the Court held that *Erie* and *Guaranty Trust* now required the application of such door-closing statutes.

After *Woods*, fear was expressed that application of state door-closing statutes in diversity cases may frustrate "the full exercise of [the federal courts'] congressionally invested diversity jurisdiction."[190] This fear is misplaced. If diversity jurisdiction is only designed to prevent bias from operating against out-of-

---

183. *See Guaranty Trust*, 326 U.S. at 108-09, 65 S. Ct. at 1469-70, 89 L. Ed. at 2085-86; *see also* Novak v. Capital Mgmt. & Dev. Corp., 452 F.3d 902 (D.C. Cir. 2006) (*Erie* is also applicable to the District of Columbia and requires federal courts in District to reach same outcome as D.C. Court of Appeals would reach).

184. "In essence, the intent of [*Erie*] was to insure that, in all cases where a federal court is exercising jurisdiction solely because of the diversity of citizenship of the parties, the outcome of the litigation in the federal court should be substantially the same, so far as legal rules determine the outcome of a litigation, as it would be if tried in a State court." *Id.* at 109, 65 S. Ct. at 1470, 89 L. Ed. at 2086.

185. CHARLES A. WRIGHT & MARY KAY KANE, THE LAW OF FEDERAL COURTS § 55, at 378 (7th ed. 2011).

186. *See id.*; John H. Ely, *The Irrepressible Myth of* Erie, 87 HARV. L. REV. 693, 727-28 (1974).

187. *See* Charles E. Clark, *Federal Procedural Reform and States' Rights; to a More Perfect Union*, 40 TEX. L. REV. 211, 220 (1961).

188. 337 U.S. 535, 69 S. Ct. 1235, 93 L. Ed. 1524 (1949).

189. *See* David Lupton's Sons Co. v. Automobile Club of Am., 225 U.S. 489, 500, 32 S. Ct. 711, 714, 56 L. Ed. 1177, 1181-82 (1912). The Court did seem to recognize that if the state law was interpreted as one that voided the contract altogether, rather than simply preventing suit on the contract in the state's courts, it would be enforced. *See id.* at 495-500, 32 S. Ct. at 712-15, 56 L. Ed. at 1179-82.

190. *See* Martin H. Redish & Carter G. Phillips, Erie *and the Rules of Decision Act: In Search of the Appropriate Dilemma*, 91 HARV. L. REV. 356, 378 (1977).

state citizens in state courts, a conclusion that *Erie* seems to mandate, then closing the doors of both the state and federal courts within a state to a litigant will not undermine the diversity policies. Under such circumstances, no out-of-state citizen will be forced into a state court within the state. If the plaintiff can obtain personal jurisdiction over the defendant in another state, then both the federal and state courts in that state will be available to the out-of-state citizen. If personal jurisdiction cannot be obtained over the defendant in another state and the plaintiff is the out-of-stater, the plaintiff may be effectively deprived of a right of action. Nevertheless, this result is not a concern of the policies supporting the diversity jurisdiction after *Erie* and *Guaranty Trust*. The deprivation of the plaintiff's right of action has occurred as the result of the operation of state law. It has not occurred as the result of bias operating through the state-court system, which is the only concern of the general grant of diversity jurisdiction after *Erie*.[191] Thus, given the premises of *Erie* and *Guaranty Trust*, the decision in *Woods* is correct.

2. The *Byrd* Decision: Categorization of State Rules and Balancing

The U.S. Supreme Court mitigated the effect of the *Guaranty Trust* outcome determinative test in *Byrd v. Blue Ridge Rural Electric Cooperative, Inc.*[192] In *Byrd*, a state common-law rule required that, in a personal injury action, the affirmative defense that the plaintiff was an employee of the defendant for purposes of the state worker's compensation statute should be submitted for resolution to the judge. A federal common-law rule of procedure required submission of the defense to the jury. The Court held that the federal practice should govern in diversity actions.[193]

In reasoning that the federal practice should prevail, the Court divided the universe of state laws into the following three categories: (1) rules defining state rights and obligations;[194] (2) rules "bound up" with state-created rights and obligations;[195] and (3) rules of "form and mode."[196] If a state rule either defines state rights and obligations or is bound up with state-created rights and obligations, the federal courts must apply the state rule.[197] However, if the state rule is classified as

---

191. *See* Ralph U. Whitten, Erie *and the Federal Rules: A Review and Reappraisal After* Burlington Northern Railroad v. Woods, 21 CREIGHTON L. REV. 1, 40 n.181 (1987).

192. 356 U.S. 525, 78 S. Ct. 893, 2 L. Ed. 2d 953 (1958).

193. For an excellent criticism of the Court's holding that the federal courts were obligated to submit the issue in *Byrd* to the jury, see Peter Westen & Jeffrey S. Lehman, *Is There Life for* Erie *After the Death of Diversity?*, 78 MICH. L. REV. 311, 344-52 (1980).

194. *See Byrd*, 356 U.S. at 535, 78 S. Ct. at 899-900, 2 L. Ed. 2d at 961-62. The Court stated that "[i]t was decided in *Erie [Railroad] v. Tompkins* that the federal courts in diversity cases must respect the definition of state-created rights and obligations by the state courts." *Id.*

195. The Court stated: "We must, therefore, first examine the rule in *Adams v. Davison-Paxon Co.* to determine whether it is bound up with these state rights and obligations in such a way that its application in the federal court is required." *Id.*

196. *See id.* at 536-37, 78 S. Ct. at 900, 2 L. Ed. 2d at 962-63.

197. This conventional interpretation of *Byrd* conforms to the structure of the Court's opinion better than any other interpretation. *See* Szantay v. Beech Aircraft Corp., 349 F.2d 60, 63-64 (4th Cir. 1965); Ralph U. Whitten, Erie *and the Federal Rules: A Review and Reappraisal After* Burlington Northern Railroad v. Woods, 21 CREIGHTON L. REV. 1, 35 (1987). However, it cannot be pretended that all the case law conforms to this interpretation. *See* Martin H. Redish & Carter G. Phillips, Erie *and the Rules of Decision Act: In Search of the Appropriate Dilemma*, 91 HARV L. REV. 356, 364-66 (1977) (discussing other interpretations of *Byrd*). Because

one of "form and mode," its application by the federal courts is not absolutely mandated. Instead, the state rule of form and mode must be applied only when failing to do so would produce a substantial likelihood of different outcomes in the state and federal courts.[198] Furthermore, even if there is a substantial likelihood of a different outcome if the state rule is disregarded, the federal courts do not have to apply the state rule if federal countervailing considerations exist that are sufficient to outweigh the general *Erie* policies of duplicate outcomes between state and federal actions.[199] In *Byrd* itself, the Court felt that the need to duplicate the outcome between state and federal court was outweighed by federal countervailing considerations in the form of a "strong federal policy against allowing state rules to disrupt the judge-jury relationship in the federal courts."[200]

In applying the *Byrd* decision to new facts, classifying the state rule in the first instance is important. Rules defining state rights and obligations are easy to identify. These are the "purely substantive" rules like the ones involved in *Swift* and *Erie*. The federal courts are not given the discretion to balance federal countervailing considerations against the need to apply these rules. Given that the federal countervailing policies that would be balanced against the application of state rules defining state rights will always be procedural policies, the Court wisely established a flat prohibition against application of federal law.[201]

Rules "bound up" with the definition of state rights and obligations are more difficult to define. The Court cited *Cities Service Oil Co. v. Dunlap*[202] as an example of a case involving a rule bound up with the definition of state rights and obligations. In *Cities Service*, a lower federal court disregarded a settled state burden-of-proof rule and instead applied what it deemed to be a better rule, reasoning that the suit was in equity and the burden of proof was a matter of practice and procedure not governed by *Erie*. The Supreme Court reversed, holding that the federal courts must apply the state burden-of-proof rule.

Although the citation to *Cities Service* in *Byrd* may appear to establish that state burden-of-proof rules are bound up with the definition of state rights and obligations in a way that requires the federal courts to enforce them, this conclusion may not always be correct.[203] This possible uncertainty disappears, however, when the burden-of-proof rule in *Cities Service* is examined closely. The rule required that on an issue of bona fide purchase for value without notice, the person attacking the legal title to land and asserting a superior equity must bear the burden of proof.[204] As to this issue, the Court stated that the state rule was more than simply

---

the interpretation in the text conforms best to the structure of the Court's opinion, it will be assumed to be correct for purposes of further discussion.

198. 356 U.S. at 537, 78 S. Ct. at 900, 2 L. Ed. 2d at 962.

199. *See id.*; *see also* Szantay v. Beech Aircraft Corp., 349 F.2d 60, 64 (4th Cir. 1965).

200. *Byrd*, 356 U.S. at 538, 78 S. Ct. at 901, 2 L. Ed. 2d at 963.

201. It must be remembered that here only conflicts between state law and federal procedural law are being discussed. In section I ("Federal Common Law") *infra*, it will be seen that the federal courts after *Erie* do have the power to supplant state substantive law rules with substantive federal common-law rules in appropriate cases.

202. 308 U.S. 208, 60 S. Ct. 201, 84 L. Ed. 196 (1939).

203. The uncertainty is created by the failure of *Byrd* to cite Palmer v. Hoffman, 318 U.S. 109, 63 S. Ct. 477, 87 L. Ed. 645 (1943). The *Palmer* case involved, in part, a holding that the question of the burden of establishing contributory negligence is a matter of local law on which the federal courts are bound to follow state practice under *Erie*. *See id.* at 117-19, 63 S. Ct. at 482-83, 87 L. Ed. at 651-53. However, *Palmer* involved a general burden-of-proof rule not specifically designed to "affect decision of the issue."

204. *See Cities Serv.*, 308 U.S. at 210, 60 S. Ct. at 202, 84 L. Ed. at 197.

a rule of practice in courts of equity. Rather, it constituted a valuable assurance to the recorded title holder of state land.[205] This description of the burden-of-proof rule in *Cities Service* suggests a workable distinction between rules bound up with the definition of state rights and obligations and state rules of form and mode. Rules bound up with the definition of state rights and obligations are procedural rules supported by specific policies designed to advance the purposes of the substantive rights to which the "bound up" rules are linked. Rules of form and mode are procedural rules that might dramatically affect the enforcement of substantive rights, but which cannot be seen to be supported by specific policies designed to advance the purposes of the substantive right in question.[206]

Burden-of-proof rules offer good examples of these different kinds of rules. Some burden-of-proof rules, such as the one at issue in *Cities Service*, are designed "to affect decision of the issue rather than to regulate the conduct of the trial."[207] When federal courts are confronted with the former sort of rule, they should be forbidden from identifying and balancing federal countervailing considerations against the need to duplicate the result that would be reached in state court. Such rules are so closely related to the substantive rights at issue in the case as to be virtually identical to those substantive rights for purposes of the policies of the *Erie* doctrine. The strength of the *Erie* policy is as great in this category of cases as it would be in a case in which a rule defining state rights and obligations is directly involved (as in *Erie* itself). Therefore, *Byrd* should be viewed as holding that no federal countervailing policies ever exist that would justify disregarding this kind of state rule.[208]

If the state burden-of-proof rule is concerned solely with matters of trial administration, the situation is different. Under such circumstances, applying the outcome determinative test of *Guaranty Trust* will protect the *Erie* policies. However, because both state and litigant interests are of lesser strength when rules of trial administration are at issue, *Byrd* allows the identification and weighing of appropriate federal interests against the outcome determinative policy. The reason that such rules are of lesser strength from the standpoint of litigants is that they are less likely than "bound up" rules to be taken into account at the planning stage of

---

205. *See id.* at 212, 60 S. Ct. at 203, 84 L. Ed. at 198.

206. *Cf.* Northon v. Rule, 637 F.3d 937 (9th Cir. 2011) (attorneys fees statute attached to substantive state law statutory claim for relief enhanced the statutory claim's protection of important state substantive interests and is applicable in federal court); Bourbon v. Kmart Corp., 223 F.3d 469 (7th Cir. 2000) (Posner, J., concurring) (practical way of determining whether a rule of state law is substantive or procedural is to ask whether it is limited to a particular substantive area or whether it applies "across the board"); S.A. Healy Co. v. Milwaukee Metro. Sewerage Dist., 60 F.3d 305, 310 (7th Cir. 1995) (stating that state procedural rules that are limited to particular substantive areas are "substantive" for *Erie* purposes).

207. RESTATEMENT (SECOND) OF CONFLICT OF LAWS §§ 133-134 (1971).

208. If federal countervailing considerations of sufficient strength to outweigh the need to duplicate the outcome in state court do exist in this situation, they are probably of sufficient strength to justify the creation of a preemptive, substantive federal common-law rule of the sort discussed in section I *infra* ("Federal Common Law"). In Knievel v. ESPN, 393 F.3d 1068 (9th Cir. 2005), the court first held that the Montana Constitution did not establish a rule that defamation plaintiffs are entitled to a jury trial in state court, and then held that even if it did, under *Erie* and *Hanna*, the federal courts were obligated to apply the Federal Rules of Civil Procedure, which allowed them, *inter alia*, to grant summary judgment in actions in which there are no disputed issues of fact. However, the Montana rule, as articulated in state cases, looked very much like a burden-of-proof rule, *i.e.*, the issue of whether statements were true or false are to be submitted to a jury unless the evidence is so overwhelming that any other conclusion would be unreasonable. Assuming that this would preclude summary judgment even if a federal court determined under Rule 56 that there were "no genuine issue of material fact," it is questionable whether the federal court could nevertheless override the state standard and grant summary judgment.

activity, as opposed to the litigational stage. The reason that rules of "form and mode" are of lesser strength from the standpoint of the states is that their main utility is in litigation in the state's own courts. When the litigation is in federal court, the states do not have the same interest in enforcing their own views of what rules are best to promote the interests of efficient trial administration as they do when the action is in their own courts. Still, in such circumstances, the *Erie* policy remains strong enough to justify some deference to the state rules, subject to the *Byrd* balancing test.[209]

In addition to the cryptic nature of the state-rule categories discussed in *Byrd*, the opinion contained other difficulties. For one, neither *Byrd* nor *Guaranty Trust* clearly state what kind of outcome difference ought to be taken into account by the federal courts when they are trying to decide whether to apply a state rule of form and mode or a conflicting federal common-law rule of practice or procedure. Both *Guaranty Trust*, which involved a statute-of-limitations issue, and *Byrd*, which involved a question of judge-jury relations, spoke in terms of ultimate differences in outcome on the merits of the case.[210] However, the Court has never addressed whether outcome differences of a lesser nature than an outcome difference on the ultimate merits of the case will invoke the outcome determinative test. An argument that such lesser differences will justify application of the outcome rule can be derived from *Woods v. Interstate Realty Co.*,[211] discussed above. Recall that *Woods* held that the federal courts were obligated to apply state door-closing statutes that prohibit suits from being brought by certain categories of litigants in the state courts. If a plaintiff barred from the courts of a state by such a statute can obtain personal jurisdiction over the defendant in another state, the plaintiff may still be able to win a judgment on the merits. The *Woods* holding thus seems to indicate that outcome differences of less than an ultimate difference on the merits can be considered by the federal courts in administering the *Guaranty Trust-Byrd* rule.[212]

---

209. The *Erie* policies will be protected by this process in most instances because there simply will be no federal countervailing interests to balance against the need to duplicate the outcome. For example, in burden-of-proof cases, the Court has never identified any such policies. This fact does not mean that there are no problems with the balancing portion of *Byrd*, however. The balancing test invites abuse through the identification of spurious federal interests, as discussed *infra*.

210. In *Byrd*, the Court stated as follows: "It may well be that in the instant personal-injury case the outcome would be substantially affected by whether the issue of immunity is decided by a judge or jury." *Byrd*, 356 U.S. at 537, 78 S. Ct. at 900, 2 L. Ed. 2d at 962.

211. 337 U.S. 535, 69 S. Ct. 1235, 93 L. Ed. 1524 (1949).

212. In *Woods*, the Court considered the case controlled by *Guaranty Trust*. *See id.* at 538, 69 S. Ct. at 1237, 93 L. Ed. at 1527. The Court did not discuss whether it would have been possible for the corporate plaintiff to obtain personal jurisdiction over the defendant in another state, though it was clear that the court of appeals had held that the state door-closing statute did not void the contract on which the action was brought, but simply deprived the plaintiff of the benefits of the state's courts. *See id.* at 536, 69 S. Ct. at 1236, 93 L. Ed. at 1525-26. The Supreme Court did not question that part of the court of appeals' holding.

Another problem with *Woods* after *Byrd* is determining how the state door-closing statute should be classified. The statute was not tied to any specific substantive right. Rather, it was a general statute depriving corporate plaintiffs who failed to designate an agent for service of process of the benefits of the state's courts. Thus, it does not seem to be a rule "bound up" within the definition of state rights and obligations in the sense meant by *Byrd*. It does not seem exactly aimed at trial administration either, however. Nevertheless, it is probably best categorized as a rule of "form and mode" because it seems aimed at assuring that resident plaintiffs will be able to sue foreign corporations in the state's courts and removing the privilege of the foreign corporation to sue in the state's courts when such a suit is not possible—*i.e.*, when the foreign corporation has not appointed the statutorily required agent.

This interpretation was reinforced by the later decision of the Court in *Hanna v. Plumer*.[213] In *Hanna*, a conflict existed between a Federal Rule of Civil Procedure and state law. Therefore, this decision will be discussed more fully in the next section. In the process of deciding the issue before it, however, the Court in an extended dictum provided some additional guidance on the administration of the outcome determinative test. According to the Court, not just any difference in outcome would produce the obligation to apply state law under *Guaranty Trust*. Rather, only outcome differences that cause "forum shopping" or "inequitable administration of the laws" are prohibited.[214]

Hanna's elaboration of the outcome determinative test requires a further inquiry in each instance where a state rule of form and mode is involved in a case. To determine whether a court must apply a state rule of form and mode, one must now ask whether failure to apply the state rule in federal court would cause someone to choose a federal court over a state court or would result in unfair discrimination against a citizen of the forum state by depriving the citizen of the benefit of a valuable rule of law that would be applied in the state court. Since many rules might have either one of these effects but would not necessarily produce a difference in outcome on the merits, the outcome determinative test would seem to extend to lesser outcome differences.

Illustration 5-11. *P*, a citizen of Ireland, sues *D*, a citizen of State *X*, U.S.A., in a federal court in State *X*. *D* moves to dismiss the action under the doctrine of forum non conveniens,[215] on the ground that Ireland is a more convenient forum. The State *X* Supreme Court has interpreted a State *X* constitutional provision as forbidding the State *X* courts from applying a doctrine of forum non conveniens. Therefore, if suit were in State *X* court, *D's* motion would be denied. If the State *X* rule defines state rights and obligations or is a rule bound up with state rights and obligations, the federal courts must apply it.[216] If the state rule is one of "form and mode," the federal court may consider whether the action should be dismissed under the federal doctrine of forum non conveniens or whether such a dismissal will offend the *Erie* policies. The plaintiff certainly would not commence suit in federal court to obtain the benefit of the federal doctrine of forum non conveniens. Such action could only result in dismissal of the action and trial in a location that the plaintiff does not prefer (Ireland). Similarly, if the action had

---

213. 380 U.S. 460, 85 S. Ct. 1136, 14 L. Ed. 2d 8 (1965).

214. *See id.* at 468, 85 S. Ct. at 1142, 14 L. Ed. 2d at 15. In a footnote, the Court added:

> *Erie* and its progeny make clear that when a federal court sitting in a diversity case is faced with a question of whether or not to apply state law, the importance of a state rule is . . . relevant . . . only in the context of asking whether application of the rule would make so important a difference to the character or result of the litigation that failure to enforce it would unfairly discriminate against citizens of the forum State, or whether application of the rule would have so important an effect upon the fortunes of one or both of the litigants that failure to enforce it would be likely to cause a plaintiff to choose the federal court.

Id. n.9, 85 S. Ct. at 1142 n.9, 14 L. Ed. 2d at 15 n.9.

215. *See* Chapter 4(D) *supra* ("Forum Non Conveniens and Change of Venue").

216. It is possible that such a rule may define state rights and obligations if the constitutional provision in question is interpreted to be a guarantee to both residents and nonresidents of access to a forum for reasons of substantive constitutional policy. The fact that a rule appears procedural in form should not result in automatic classification as a "bound up" rule or a "form and mode" rule. Such rules can confer valuable rights on residents and nonresidents alike. *See* Ralph U. Whitten, Erie *and the Federal Rules: A Review and Reappraisal After* Burlington Northern Railroad v. Woods, 21 CREIGHTON L. REV. 1, 36 (1987).

been filed in a State *X* court, the defendant would not have been able to forum shop for a federal forum because a citizen of the state in which the action is brought may not remove an action in which jurisdiction is based solely on diversity of citizenship. Therefore, disregard of the state rule could not result in forum shopping by either the plaintiff or the defendant. Nor will disregard of the state rule result in discrimination against citizens of the forum state. It is *D*, the citizen of the forum state, who is asking for the state rule to be disregarded. Therefore, none of the *Erie* policies, as redefined through *Hanna*, will be offended by application of the federal doctrine of forum non conveniens. For the *Erie* policies to be offended in the situation described in this illustration, they would have to be more broadly defined. The policies would have to be redefined to include discrimination against *noncitizens* by application of a different law than would be applied in state court.[217]

Illustration 5-12. Although the Court's currently defined *Erie* policies do not preclude dismissal under the federal doctrine of forum non conveniens in *Illustration 5-11*, other federal policies may nevertheless prevent dismissal. The effect of dismissing actions such as the one described in *Illustration 5-11* will be to drive plaintiffs who want to resort to the alienage jurisdiction out of federal court into state court, where no dismissal will be possible. As a result, a federal forum non conveniens dismissal would be improper in the situation described. Forum non conveniens is a federal common-law procedural doctrine that is less important than the subject-matter jurisdiction policies supporting the alienage jurisdiction.

Illustration 5-13. Assume that the citizenship of the parties in *Illustration 5-11* is reversed. Thus, *P* is a citizen of State *X*, and *D* is a citizen of Ireland. In this situation, a federal forum non conveniens dismissal would clearly produce the sort of outcome difference with which *Erie* was concerned. While *P* would still not choose a federal court in State *X* to get the benefit of a doctrine that would result in dismissal of the action, *D* might well remove the action to get the benefit of that doctrine if *P* commenced the action in a State *X* court. Thus, disregard of the state rule might cause forum shopping by the noncitizen defendant.[218] In addition, dismissal of the action would deprive *P* of a valuable rule that would be applied to prevent dismissal in the State *X* courts, resulting in discrimination against a citizen of the forum state. The question whether the federal doctrine of forum non conveniens could be applied, therefore, would depend on whether the policies

---

217. The situation described in *Illustration 5-11* will not necessarily result in an ultimate outcome difference because the plaintiff might win a judgment either in Ireland or in State *X*. However, there may nonetheless be ultimate outcome-difference implications. The plaintiff may have chosen an American court to get the benefit of the applicable substantive law in State *X*. If so, and if a dismissal will result in a change in that substantive law to the disadvantage of the plaintiff, an outcome difference that favors the defendant may become more likely. Piper Aircraft Co. v. Reyno, 454 U.S. 235, 102 S. Ct. 252, 70 L. Ed. 2d 419 (1981), cited and discussed in Chapter 4(D)(1)*(a) supra*, allows a forum non conveniens dismissal even in the face of such a possibility, but *Piper* reserved judgment on whether state law must control the question of forum non conveniens dismissals in diversity actions where it differs from federal law. *See id.* at 248 n.13, 102 S. Ct. at 262 n.13, 70 L. Ed. 2d at 431 n.13; *see also* Koster v. Lumbermens Mut. Cas. Co., 330 U.S. 518, 529, 67 S. Ct. 828, 834, 91 L. Ed. 1067, 1076-77 (1947); Gulf Oil Corp. v. Gilbert, 330 U.S. 501, 509, 67 S. Ct. 839, 843, 91 L. Ed. 1055, 1062-63 (1947); Williams v. Green Bay & W. R.R. Co., 326 U.S. 549, 558-59, 66 S. Ct. 284, 288-89, 90 L. Ed. 311, 317-18 (1946). *But see* DTEX, L.L.C. v. BBVA Bancomer, S.A., 508 F.3d 785 (5th Cir. 2007) (federal court in diversity applies the federal doctrine of forum non conveniens).

218. Although the Court from *Erie* to present has phrased the forum shopping policy in terms of plaintiff forum shopping, there is no apparent policy reason to exclude defendant forum shopping from the *Erie* prohibitions. *But see* Ashley S. Deeks, Comment, *Raising the Cost of Lying: Rethinking* Erie *for Judicial Estoppel*, 64 U. CHI. L. REV. 873, 887 (1997).

supporting that doctrine outweighed the *Erie* policies favoring duplication of outcomes between state and federal courts. The policies supporting the federal forum non conveniens doctrine are to prevent the vexation of defendants that would result from litigation in an inconvenient forum and to prevent the burden on the federal court system that would result from imposing litigation unrelated to the forum on that system.[219] Because the Supreme Court has never indicated how to attach weight to federal countervailing interests, it is unclear whether these policies would outweigh the outcome determinative policies.

* * * * *

Another problem with the *Byrd* opinion is the vagueness of the Court's balancing test when state rules of "form and mode" are involved. The Court gave the lower courts no guidance on how to identify legitimate federal countervailing considerations.[220] Nor, as indicated in *Illustration 5-13*, did the Court state how to attach weight to such considerations once they had been properly identified. The predictable result was that some lower federal courts recognized demonstrably spurious federal interests and attached substantial weight to interests that should have received little, if any, consideration.[221]

Illustration 5-14. In *Szantay v. Beech Aircraft Corp.*,[222] a Beech aircraft was purchased in Nebraska. It was flown to Miami, Florida and then to Columbia, South Carolina, where Dixie Aviation Co. serviced the aircraft. It then left Columbia bound for Chicago, Illinois, but crashed en route in Tennessee. All of its occupants were killed. The decedents were all Illinois citizens. Their personal representatives commenced a diversity action in South Carolina federal court against Dixie Aviation, a South Carolina corporation, and Beech Aircraft, which is a Delaware corporation with its principal place of business in Kansas. Beech moved to be dismissed from the suit on the ground that the South Carolina door-closing statute prohibited an action against it in the state. The door-closing statute forbade actions against foreign corporations by nonresident plaintiffs unless the cause of action arose in South Carolina. The district court denied Beech's motion. Beech appealed to the Fourth Circuit Court of Appeals. That court held the South Carolina door-closing statute inapplicable under the *Byrd* analysis.

In applying the *Byrd* test to the action,[223] the Fourth Circuit identified "explicit and numerous" countervailing federal interests.[224] First, the court argued

---

219. *See* Chapter 4(D)(1)*(a) supra* ("Forum Non Conveniens").

220. *Cf.* 19 CHARLES A. WRIGHT ET AL., FEDERAL PRACTICE AND PROCEDURE: JURISDICTION AND RELATED MATTERS (ERIE DOCTRINE) § 4504, at 36-38 (2d ed. 1996) (discussing the ambiguity in the way the Court derived the federal interests in *Byrd*).

221. *See* CHARLES A. WRIGHT & MARY KAY KANE, THE LAW OF FEDERAL COURTS § 59, at 402-03 (7th ed. 2011).

222. 349 F.2d 60 (4th Cir. 1965).

223. The court identified the door-closing statute as one of form and mode. *See id.* at 64. It then concluded that no citizen of the forum state would be discriminated against if the state statute were not applied. *See id.* However, the court did not evaluate whether forum shopping would occur if the statute were not applied by the federal courts. This failure was a clear error because plaintiffs would be encouraged to forum shop if the state statute is applied by state, but not federal, courts. *See id.*

224. *Id.* at 65. The court apparently thought *Byrd* required it to balance the federal considerations against the state policies involved in the door-closing statute. This conclusion was incorrect at the time because, as demonstrated in the text above, *Byrd* requires that the countervailing federal considerations be balanced against the *Erie* policy of duplicate outcomes between state and federal courts. However, even on its own terms, the court did not give the state interests all they were due. The court interpreted the state statute as a statutory formulation of the doctrine of forum non conveniens, which would not be undermined by disregard of the statute by the federal

that applying the door-closing statute would undermine the constitutional grant of diversity jurisdiction to the federal courts.[225] However, no one would have been deprived of the benefits of the diversity jurisdiction in *Szantay* if the South Carolina federal court had dismissed Beech from the action under the state door-closing statute. The Illinois plaintiffs could have sued Dixie Aviation in South Carolina federal court and Beech in a federal court elsewhere—for example, in Kansas, where Beech had its principal place of business. Although this might have been less convenient for, or tactically disadvantageous to, the plaintiffs, it would not deprive the plaintiffs of the benefits of the diversity jurisdiction.

Second, the court argued that the Full Faith and Credit Clause of the Constitution expressed a "national interest 'looking toward maximum enforcement in each state of the obligations or rights created or recognized by the statutes of sister states.'"[226] This federal countervailing consideration was also spurious. As the court itself acknowledged, applying the South Carolina door-closing statute would not violate the Full Faith and Credit Clause.[227] It is difficult to see how a constitutional clause that concededly permits the application of a statute can be the source of a "policy" that prohibits the application of the statute.

Third, the court stated that a federal policy encouraging "efficient joinder in multi-party actions" existed under statutes like the federal interpleader statute and the Federal Rules of Civil Procedure governing joinder of multiple claims and parties.[228] Nevertheless, the federal interpleader statute and most of the federal multiparty joinder rules cited by the court were inapplicable to the case before it. Certain other rules, particularly Federal Rule 20, which permitted joinder of multiple defendants in *Szantay*, were applicable to the case. However, those rules were not designed specifically to override state door-closing statutes. Furthermore, while the Federal Rules governing joinder of multiple claims and parties express important federal efficiency policies, these policies only operate when the federal courts have before them cases which are otherwise within the proper scope of their authority. When a case is outside the subject-matter jurisdiction of the federal courts or when the courts are deprived of power to act by other fundamental doctrines that govern the relationship between state and federal courts, such as the *Erie* doctrine,

---

courts. *See id.* at 65. Given the structure of the statute, this conclusion is not persuasive. Beech's argument seems much more plausible. Beech argued that the statute was designed to encourage foreign corporations to do business in the state by freeing them of the fear that they would be sued in the state by nonresidents on causes of action having nothing to do with the state. *See* Arrowsmith v. United Press Int'l, 320 F.2d 219, 226 (2d Cir. 1963) ("State statutes determining what foreign corporations may be sued, for what, and by whom, are not mere whimsy; like most legislation they represent a balancing of various considerations—for example, affording a forum for wrongs connected with the state and conveniencing resident plaintiffs, while avoiding the discouragement of activity within the state by foreign corporations."). In addition, if the policies supporting the state statute in *Szantay* were unclear, as the court supposed, *see Szantay*, 349 F.2d at 65, it would seem more in accord with the *Erie* policies to assume a significant state policy rather than a less significant one. *Cf.* Martin H. Redish & Carter G. Phillips, Erie *and the Rules of Decision Act: In Search of the Appropriate Dilemma*, 91 HARV. L. REV. 356, 395-96 (1977) (arguing that when legislative history is absent, the federal courts should assume the existence of some state interest).

225. *See Szantay*, 349 F.2d at 65.

226. *Id.* at 65.

227. *See id.* at 65-66.

228. *Id.* at 66 & n.12.

the policies supporting the Federal Rules surely cannot "outweigh" the more fundamental doctrines.[229]

3. Subsequent Developments: Imprecision and Confusion

For many years after the *Hanna* dictum discussed in the previous subsection, the Supreme Court did not address the problem of conflicts between federal common-law rules of procedure and state law.[230] In the 1990's, the Court twice considered such conflicts in *Chambers v. NASCO, Inc.*[231] and *Gasperini v. Center for Humanities, Inc.*[232] Far from clarifying the analytical structure that its previous decisions seemed to establish, the Court's opinions in *Chambers* and *Gasperini* ignored key steps in and distinctions established by earlier precedents. The result is an intensification of the confusion about how the *Erie* analysis should be conducted, a confusion that has infected the operation of the doctrine in the lower federal courts.[233]

In *Chambers*, a federal diversity action was brought to obtain specific performance of a contract. The defendant engaged in a substantial amount of bad-faith conduct before and during the course of the litigation, some of which was sanctionable under Federal Rule 11 and some of which was not. For the conduct not sanctionable under Rule 11, the district court imposed a substantial sanction against the defendant under the court's "inherent powers." The court of appeals affirmed this use of inherent powers to impose sanctions. The court of appeals rejected the argument that a federal court sitting in diversity must look to state law to determine the circumstances under which sanctions may be assessed.[234] The Supreme Court granted certiorari and affirmed.

---

229. *Cf.* FED. R. CIV. P. 82. The multiparty joinder policy was the only basis that the court found to distinguish *Woods v. Interstate Realty Co.*, discussed above, in which the Supreme Court had required the application of a state door-closing statute. In AXA Corporate Solutions v. Underwriters Reinsurance Corp., 347 F.3d 272 (7th Cir. 2003), the district court refused to dismiss an action under the abstention doctrine articulated in Colorado River Water Conservation District v. United States, 424 U.S. 800, 96 S. Ct. 1236, 47 L. Ed.2d 483 (1976), which sometimes allows abstention in favor of parallel state court proceedings. An Illinois statute also allowed dismissal in favor of prior pending actions between the same parties on the same claim, however, and the district court held this statute had to be applied in a diversity action and dismissed on that ground. The court of appeals reversed, holding that the Illinois statute was not the kind of state law that a federal diversity court had to follow. Although the court acknowledged that failure to follow the state statute in a federal diversity action would result in forum shopping, it stated that not everything that might lead to forum shopping requires the application of state law, pointing to the fact that preference for Federal Rules of Civil Procedure, differences in venue rules, jury rules, discovery rules, and "countless other procedural rules that are found in the federal Constitution, statutes, and rules, also influence forum choice." The court also observed that the problem addressed by the state statute "is closely akin to topics such as forum non conveniens, lis pendens, and venue statutes," all of which were organizational matters that are governed by the law of the sovereign that established the court, here the United States. By mixing federal statutory and constitutional matters with federal common-law procedural matters such as abstention and forum non conveniens, the court seems to have disregarded the core of the *Erie* doctrine. It is difficult to know what kinds of federal common-law (or equity) matters the court thinks are included within *Erie* and what kinds are not and what the distinction between the two kinds is. The court did not mention the *Byrd* federal countervailing considerations test.

230. *See* Ralph U. Whitten, *Developments in the* Erie *Doctrine: 1991*, 40 AM. J. COMP. L. 967, 970 (1992).

231. 501 U.S. 32, 111 S. Ct. 2123, 115 L. Ed. 2d 27 (1991).

232. 518 U.S. 415, 116 S. Ct. 2211, 135 L. Ed. 2d 659 (1996).

233. *See* section G *infra* ("The *Erie* Doctrine in the Lower Federal Courts").

234. *See Chambers*, 501 U.S. at 43, 111 S. Ct. at 2131, 115 L. Ed. 2d at 43.

The Court rejected the argument that federal statutes and rules of procedure had displaced the inherent power of the district court to impose sanctions.[235] The Court then confirmed that, under the dictum in *Hanna*, "the 'outcome determinative' test of *Erie* and *Guaranty Trust* . . . 'cannot be read without reference to the twin aims of the *Erie* rule: discouragement of forum shopping and avoidance of inequitable administration of the law.'"[236] There existed no danger of forum shopping because the imposition of sanctions under the district court's inherent power does not depend upon who wins the litigation, but "on how the parties conduct themselves during the litigation."[237] This conclusion was correct. A party will not be able to shop for a federal court to obtain a different applicable rule of law unless the party not only is aware of a different federal rule, but can anticipate its application. Normally, this will not be possible if the conduct giving rise to the application of the rule cannot occur until after litigation has been commenced.[238] However, the Court's reference to rules that affect "which party wins the lawsuit"[239] could be read as a requirement that only outcome differences on the ultimate merits of the case are prohibited by *Erie*. This interpretation would be unfortunate. As discussed in the preceding subsection, there exist differences between federal and state procedures that will produce forum shopping, but not necessarily a difference on the ultimate merits of the case. These differences are substantial enough to be included within the policy of the outcome determinative rule. Therefore, the holding of *Chambers* should be limited to rules that apply to behavior of the parties after commencement of the action.[240]

The Court also held that inequitable administration of the law was not involved in the case because it is not inequitable to utilize inherent sanctioning power to impose sanctions on "citizens and noncitizens alike, when the party, by controlling his or her conduct in litigation, has the power to determine whether sanctions will be assessed."[241] This part of the Court's opinion is unclear. The "inequitable administration of the law" factor evolved from that part of *Erie* objecting to *Swift v. Tyson* on the ground that *Swift* produced discrimination against citizens of the forum state. This discrimination occurred because in diversity actions the federal courts sometimes applied different substantive rules than would have been applied in the state courts, and the noncitizen plaintiff or defendant was in control of the choice of forum under the rules of subject-matter jurisdiction.

---

235. *See* 501 U.S. at 42-50, 111 S. Ct. at 2131-36, 115 L. Ed. 2d at 43-49. The Court also rejected the argument that its decision in Alyeska Pipeline Service Co. v. Wilderness Society, 421 U.S. 240, 95 S. Ct. 1612, 44 L. Ed. 2d 141 (1975), prohibited a federal court sitting in diversity from awarding attorney's fees as a sanction. The Court held that *Alyeska* only applies to fee-shifting rules "that embody a substantive policy, such as a statute which permits a prevailing party in certain classes of litigation to recover fees." 501 U.S. at 52, 111 S. Ct. at 2136, 115 L. Ed. 2d at 49-50.

236. 501 U.S. at 52, 111 S. Ct. at 2137, 115 L. Ed. 2d at 50.

237. *Id.* at 53, 111 S. Ct. at 2137, 115 L. Ed. 2d at 50.

238. It is, of course, possible for a plaintiff to anticipate that a defendant will engage in sanctionable conduct during litigation that has not yet been commenced. Such a plaintiff might find a federal diversity court more attractive than a state court that could not levy sanctions for the conduct anticipated. However, to the extent that such "forum shopping" occurs, it does not rise in seriousness to the level of forum shopping for a federal court to obtain the benefit of highly predictable results based on preexisting rules of law. Many differences in procedure exist between federal and state courts that may make the federal courts more attractive in the same way.

239. *See* 501 U.S. at 53, 111 S. Ct. at 2137, 115 L. Ed. 2d at 50.

240. *But see* Canada Life Assurance Co. v. LaPeter, 563 F.3d 837 (9th Cir. 2009) (federal standard for appointing receiver does not offend *Erie* because it does not affect the ultimate outcome of the action).

241. *Id.*

However, *Guaranty Trust* and *Byrd* extended the *Erie* doctrine beyond pure substantive rules to rules of "form and mode." After those decisions, as elaborated in the *Hanna* opinion, it appeared that the inequitable administration of the law factor would be implicated by a federal court's refusal to apply any state rule of law that would confer valuable benefits on a litigant if the action were in state court. This description seems to fit the rule in *Chambers*. A state law that refuses to recognize a bad-faith exception to the traditional rule against fee shifting would certainly have produced valuable benefits to the defendant in the case. *Chambers* can, therefore, be read as a rejection of the view that disregard of any law conferring a valuable benefit on a litigant will produce inequitable administration of the laws. In fact, the Court's opinion can be read as saying that inequitable administration of the law is never involved when a federal rule applies equally to both citizens and noncitizens alike, a reading with potentially far-reaching effects.

Nevertheless, it would seem safer to interpret *Chambers* more narrowly. In addition to emphasizing that the federal sanctioning power was applicable to citizens and noncitizens alike, the Court also observed that every litigant could avoid the application of sanctions by adopting appropriate behavior during the litigation. Thus, the case should probably be read as holding only that application of independent federal rules to post-commencement behavior does not violate the *Erie* doctrine. The flaw in *Swift* was the ability of the noncitizen to control the application of rules of law to the disadvantage of the citizen of the forum. Post-commencement rules that allow all parties to control the application of legal rules by adopting appropriate litigation behavior are not similarly flawed. Thus, in the case of post-commencement rules, the forum shopping and inequitable administration of the laws factors seem to coincide, with neither factor being applicable under the *Erie* policies.

A final, and potentially more serious, difficulty with *Chambers* was the Court's failure to discuss why the state rule in the case should be considered a rule of form and mode subject to the outcome determinative test. The district court had awarded sanctions in part for conduct by the defendant that had occurred outside the formal confines of the litigation, but which clearly affected it. The dissenting Justices in *Chambers* argued that such an award constituted an expansion of the scope of the remedy for breach of contract that would have existed in state court.[242] The majority's only response was conclusory: the defendant was not sanctioned for breach of contract, but in order to vindicate judicial authority.[243] However, if the dissenters' argument is correct, the state rule in *Chambers* would appear to be a rule "bound up" with state rights and obligations. As demonstrated in the previous subsection, state rules "bound up" with the definition of state rights and obligations are rules that are specifically linked with particular substantive rights or obligations and designed to support their policies. Remedies rules often fall within this

---

242. *See* 501 U.S. at 58-60, 111 S. Ct. at 2140-41, 115 L. Ed. 2d at 53-55 (Scalia, J., dissenting); 501 U.S. at 75-76, 111 S. Ct. at 2148-49, 115 L. Ed. 2d at 64-65 (Kennedy, J., with whom Rehnquist, C.J., and Souter, J., joined, dissenting).

243. *See id.* at 54-55, 111 S. Ct. at 2138, 115 L. Ed. 2d at 52; *see also* Goya Foods, Inc. v. Wallack Mgmt. Co., 290 F.3d 63 (1st Cir. 2002) (relying on *Chambers* and holding that an award of prejudgment interest as a civil contempt sanction is within the district court's inherent power, and holding that the district court erroneously relied on state law in determining whether and in what amount prejudgment interest should be granted as a sanction).

description. If the state rule in question was really a rule prescribing the remedies for breach of contract, it would be plausible to consider it a rule "bound up" and, therefore, obligatory on the federal courts. Thus, it would have been preferable for the majority to address directly the question of the state rule's characterization in order to dispel the dissenters' arguments.

Nevertheless, the majority's classification appears to have been correct. The state rule in question was the traditional American rule against fee shifting. The state simply did not recognize an exception to this rule for bad faith conduct on the part of the defendant during the course of litigation. The traditional American rule is not a rule linked to specific substantive rights or obligations. Rather, it is a rule that cuts across all substantive categories and operates unless there is a specific exception to the rule.[244] Therefore, it cannot plausibly be classified as a rule "bound up" with the definition of state substantive rights. Other remedies rules will have to be evaluated on a case-by-case basis to determine whether they are sufficiently linked to state substantive rights or obligations so as to be considered "bound up" with those rights and obligations.

Illustration 5-15. In *Illustration 5-9*, traditional federal equity principles were assumed to justify an injunction for the threatened violation of a state right, while state equity principles would forbid the injunction. If the state rule is linked to the specific kind of case brought by the plaintiff—for example, if a state statute forbids injunctions against state officers—the rule should probably be considered bound up with state substantive rights and obligations and thus obligatory on the federal courts. On the other hand, if the state rule is a general rule of equity jurisprudence applicable to any kind of case brought for an injunction, it should probably be classified as a rule of form and mode.[245] If the rule is a rule of form and mode, federal disregard of it will produce forum shopping by plaintiffs for a federal court, as discussed in *Illustration 5-9*. As stated in that illustration, no apparent federal countervailing interest seems to exist that would justify granting an injunction for the threatened violation of state rights that state law would deny.

Illustration 5-16. *P*, a citizen of State *X*, sues *D Corp.*, a corporation incorporated and with its principal place of business in State *Y*, in a U.S. District Court in State *X*. *P's* claim is based on an insurance policy issued by *D* to *P*. *P* allegedly incurred a loss covered by the policy that *D* refuses to pay. *P* seeks the amount of the covered loss plus attorney's fees from *D* as damages. By statute, State *X* provides that in any case in which an insurer denies payment of a claim under a policy and the insured successfully sues to recover for the loss, the insurer must pay the insured's reasonable attorney's fees in the action. The State *X* rule prescribing payment of attorney's fees is specifically linked to state substantive rights in

---

244. As discussed in subsection 1 *supra*, remedies rules are closely linked to substantive rights. However, the traditional American rule, because of its peculiar history may not qualify as "substantive" in the same way as other remedies. *See* DAN B. DOBBS, LAW OF REMEDIES § 3.10, at 277 (2d student ed. 1993).

245. An example of such a rule might be the traditional inadequate-remedy-at-law rule, which must, in theory, be satisfied in any case in which the plaintiff requests an injunction. The inadequate-remedy-at-law rule, although still applied after the merger of law and equity, is a rule that is historically linked with the existence of separate law and equity courts. Its retention in modern merged systems of law and equity is a product of both inertia and the failure of the legislatures that enacted merger statutes to instruct the courts what rule to apply in its place. *See* Ralph U. Whitten, *Federal Declaratory and Injunctive Interference With State Court Proceedings: The Supreme Court and the Limits of Judicial Discretion*, 53 N.C. L. REV. 591, 600-04, 611-16 (1975).

insurance cases. Therefore, it is a rule "bound up" with the definition of state rights and obligations and obligatory on the U.S. District Court in State *X*.

* * * * *

In *Gasperini v. Center for Humanities, Inc.*,[246] the plaintiff, a photographer who was a citizen of California, commenced an action in the U.S. District Court for the Southern District of New York to recover damages from the defendant, a New York corporation. The plaintiff's claims were for breach of contract, conversion, and negligence resulting from the loss by the defendant of certain slides that the plaintiff had supplied to the defendant for use in an educational videotape. After a trial, a jury awarded the plaintiff $450,000 in compensatory damages, which represented $1,500 for each of 300 slides. The district court denied the defendant's motion for a new trial without comment. The Court of Appeals for the Second Circuit vacated the judgment as excessive, applying a New York statute that required trial and appellate courts in the state to determine whether verdicts "materially deviate from what is reasonable compensation."[247] The Second Circuit applied the New York statute because the action was a diversity action in which New York substantive law governed the controversy. However, in both state and federal courts, the standard which had controlled prior to the statute was whether the verdict was so exorbitant that it shocked the conscience of the court.[248] The statute thus called for closer supervision of jury verdicts by both trial and appellate courts in New York. Thus, the question was raised whether application of the New York statute at the federal appellate level "would be out of sync with the federal system's division of trial and appellate court functions, an allocation weighted by the Seventh Amendment."[249]

In considering this question, the Supreme Court, in an opinion written by Justice Ginsburg, found Rule 59 of the Federal Rules of Civil Procedure, which generally governs the granting of new trials in federal court, inapplicable to the issue before it.[250] Thus, the issue was whether the Court's precedents under the Rules of Decision Act compelled the application of the New York statute. A majority of the Court found that disregarding the "deviates materially" standard of the statute would violate the policies of the *Erie* doctrine. First, the Court held that if federal courts were to ignore the statutory standard and apply instead the "shock the conscience test" applied before the statute was enacted, substantial variations between state and federal money judgments would result—with the federal judgments being larger because of the lesser scrutiny that would be given to such judgments. This variation, the Court stated, implicated the *Erie* prohibitions against forum shopping and inequitable administration of the laws.[251]

The Court then examined whether application of the state statute would be inconsistent with the Seventh Amendment. On this issue, the Court held that

---

246. 518 U.S. 415, 116 S. Ct. 2211, 135 L. Ed. 2d 659 (1996).

247. *See* N.Y. C.P.L.R. § 5501(c) (McKinney Supp. 2012).

248. *See* 518 U.S. at 422, 116 S. Ct. at 2217, 135 L. Ed. 2d at 670.

249. *Id.* at 426, 116 S. Ct. at 2219, 135 L. Ed. 2d at 673.

250. *See id.* at 437 n.22, 116 S. Ct. at 2224 n.22, 135 L. Ed. 2d at 680 n.22. This aspect of the case is discussed in section F *infra* ("The Evolution of the *Erie* Doctrine: Conflicts Between State Law and Federal Rules of Civil Procedure").

251. *See* 518 U.S. at 429-31, 116 S. Ct. at 2220-21, 135 L. Ed. 2d at 675-76.

nothing in the Seventh Amendment absolutely precludes appellate review of a district court's denial of a motion to set aside a jury verdict as excessive.[252] Nevertheless, the question remained whether application of the New York statute would, in the *Byrd* sense, unduly disrupt the proper relationship between the federal trial and appellate courts. In applying an apparent variation of the *Byrd* balancing test, the Court found that New York's "dominant" substantive interest could be respected without disrupting the federal court system by requiring the district courts to follow the New York statute, but subjecting the district court's decisions to appellate review under the abuse of discretion standard applied throughout the U.S. Courts of Appeals.[253]

There are numerous problems with the *Gasperini* opinion. First, the Court paid no attention to the *Byrd* categorization process. The New York statute applied to review of money judgments in which an itemized verdict was required by another New York statute.[254] The latter provision requires itemized verdicts in tort actions of particular sorts, and it was part of a general reform effort to control the level of damages awarded in tort cases by juries.[255] Thus, the statute appears to be the kind of provision that the *Byrd* opinion would treat as "bound up" with state substantive rights, in that it is designed to affect the decision of the damages issue in specific kinds of substantive cases only. Nevertheless, the Court never considered whether the statute was a rule "bound up" with substantive rights or a rule of form and mode. It simply applied the outcome determinative test to determine whether the federal courts were obligated to apply the rule.

The Court's failure in both *Chambers* and *Gasperini* to consider the proper categorization of the state rule may mean that the *Byrd* categorization process is no longer viable and that the outcome determinative test applies both to rules previously denominated as "bound up" with state substantive rights and to rules of

---

252. *See id.* at 431-36, 116 S. Ct. at 2221-24, 135 L. Ed. 2d at 676-79.

253. *See id.* at 436-39, 116 S. Ct. at 2224-25, 135 L. Ed. 2d at 679-81. Justice Stevens dissented. While Justice Stevens agreed that the Seventh Amendment does not limit the power of federal appellate courts in diversity cases to decide whether a verdict exceeds the limits established by state law, he disagreed that *Byrd* required the court of appeals to apply a different damage control standard than the district courts. *See id.* at 439-48, 116 S. Ct. at 2225-30, 135 L. Ed. 2d at 681-87. Justice Scalia, with whom the Chief Justice and Justice Thomas joined, also dissented. In part, Justice Scalia's dissent was based on the view that the Seventh Amendment's re-examination clause prevented the kind of appellate review of which the majority approved. *See id.* at 448-61, 116 S. Ct. at 2230-36, 135 L. Ed. 2d at 688-95. However, Justice Scalia also disagreed with the majority's *Erie* analysis. He was of the opinion that Rule 59 of the Federal Rules of Civil Procedure governed the standard for granting new trials in federal court, a conclusion that is discussed in section F *infra* ("The Evolution of the *Erie* Doctrine: Conflicts Between State Law and Federal Rules of Civil Procedure"). However, he also disagreed with the majority's general *Erie* analysis, finding that "[t]he Court commits the classic *Erie* mistake of regarding whatever changes the outcome as substantive." *Id.* at 465, 116 S. Ct. at 2238, 135 L. Ed. 2d at 697. Rather, he stated, "the Court exaggerates the difference that the state standard will make" at the trial when compared with the standard actually used by the federal courts, and he was of the opinion that forum shopping was much more likely to be encouraged by "the consistent difference between the state and federal appellate standards," a conclusion that seems unlikely in the extreme, given that litigants are not likely to plan litigation on the basis that a federal appellate court will sustain an excessive verdict in their favor that has not been overturned by a federal trial court. *See id.* at 465-67, 116 S. Ct. at 2238-39, 135 L. Ed. 2d at 697. Finally, Justice Scalia appeared to argue that the *Byrd* countervailing considerations test required application of a federal standard at the trial level rather than the New York statute to prevent destruction of the uniformity of federal practice. *See id.* at 467, 116 S. Ct. at 2239, 135 L. Ed. 2d at 698.

254. *See* N.Y. C.P.L.R. § 5501 (McKinney Supp. 2012).

255. *See id.* §§ 4111(d) (itemized verdict required in medical, dental, or podiatric malpractice actions), 4111(e) (itemized verdict required in certain actions against public employees for personal injury and wrongful death), 4111(f) (itemized verdict required in actions for personal injury, injury to property, or wrongful death).

"form and mode."[256] If so, the Court's failure to explain why the treatment of the two kinds of rules is to be the same is disturbing. As discussed earlier,[257] a close evaluation of "bound up" rule indicates that they are of the same quality and strength as rules defining state rights and obligations, which are, and should be, absolutely obligatory on the federal courts unless the interests of the federal government in the issue are strong enough to justify the creation of substantive federal common law.[258] Alternatively, the Court could simply have considered it obvious that the state rules in *Chambers* and *Gasperini* were rules of "form and mode" governed by the outcome determinative test. However, given the nature of the state statute in *Gasperini*, this approach is hardly more satisfactory. If the "bound up" category of rules is to survive, it is not appropriate for the Court to refuse to reveal the kinds of cases that it covers.

Worse than the Court's failure to address the *Byrd* categorization process was its application of the outcome determinative test. Although, as indicated above, the majority stated that failure to apply the state rule would violate the "twin aims" of *Erie* to prevent forum shopping and inequitable administration of the law, the opinion did not address some potential problems with this conclusion. The majority's notion was that failure to apply the state statute would result in higher verdicts in federal court than in state court because of the lesser scrutiny that "excessive" verdicts would receive from federal judges after they were rendered. To reach this conclusion, one must reason that plaintiffs, who would be the category of litigants to shop for a federal forum to obtain the higher verdicts, are motivated to forum shop by the vision of obtaining an "excessive" verdict that the federal courts would not set aside after it is rendered, but which the state courts would set aside. However, if Justice Scalia is correct that the majority was exaggerating the difference that the federal and state standards governing excessive verdicts would make to outcomes,[259] it is a proposition that is at least worth more discussion than the majority gave it. It is true that, in *Gasperini* itself, the defendant citizen of the forum state would have been deprived of a rule of law valuable to it in the particular case if the state statute had been disregarded. Therefore, the "inequitable administration of the laws" policy of the *Erie* doctrine may have been violated by disregard of the state statute on the facts of the case. However, this conclusion again depends on the degree of difference that the state and federal standards actually make to the

---

256. *But cf* Shropshire v. Laidlaw Transp., Inc., 550 F.3d 570 (6th Cir. 2008) (Michigan statute made a "closed-head" injury a question of fact for the jury as part of its no-fault insurance scheme; in response to the plaintiff's attempt to avoid summary judgment, court quotes *Byrd's* "bound up" language and holds—without detailed analysis—that the Michigan statute was "procedural" rather than substantive; court also observed the statute "overlaps" with Federal Rule 56); Kampa v. White Consol. Indus., Inc., 115 F.3d 585 (8th Cir. 1997) (state law provided that certain claims were to be decided by a judge without a jury; court examines this law to determine whether it is bound up with the substantive rights being enforced as *Byrd* requires; held: law not bound up with substantive rights, but Seventh Amendment requires jury trial in any event); Cendant Corp. v. Forbes, 70 F. Supp. 2d 339 (S.D.N.Y. 1999) (state statutory equitable rule must be applied in diversity action because it is both bound up with the rights of parties and potentially outcome determinative); Matthew M. Petersen, *The* Erie *Doctrine &* McDonnell Douglas *Framework: Much Ado About Nothing or an Issue Worth Analyzing*, 53 St. L. U. L.J. 927 (2009) (analyzing the *Erie* obligations in the context of a burden-shifting standard used in federal employment discrimination cases when state and federal standards differ).

257. *See* subsection E(2) *supra*.

258. *See* section I *infra* ("Federal Common Law").

259. *See* 518 U.S. at 465-66, 116 S. Ct. at 2238-39, 135 L. Ed. 2d at 697-98 (Scalia, J., dissenting).

outcome of the particular case, as well as the meaning of "inequitable administration of the laws," which the Court has never extensively addressed.

Finally, while both the majority and dissent considered the *Byrd* "federal countervailing considerations" test, the treatment of that test by both sides creates more uncertainty in its application than ever before. It is not clear whether the majority was saying that federal countervailing considerations *required* a less stringent standard of appellate review of district court decisions on excessive verdict issues, or whether the majority avoided the issue altogether by "accommodating" state and federal interests in the case. If it is the latter, the majority's approach represents a potentially far-reaching modification of the test. As observed earlier,[260] the *Byrd* opinion indicated that federal countervailing considerations, when present, should be balanced against the outcome determinative policies of the general *Erie* doctrine. The "accommodationist" approach of the majority seems to suggest that federal countervailing considerations can be balanced against state interests, a notion that seems likely to assure that the federal interests will virtually always win. In addition, the notion of accommodating state and federal interests may be even fuzzier than the notion of balancing federal countervailing policies against outcome determinative policies, creating further, unnecessary uncertainty in the administration of the *Erie* doctrine.

Nor was the dissent's approach to the countervailing considerations question much better. Justice Scalia indicated that federal countervailing considerations of the same strength as in the *Byrd* case were present.[261] However, in *Byrd* the question was whether shifting a question from the jury to the judge altogether would unduly disrupt the federal judge-jury relationship. In *Gasperini*, the question was whether requiring the judge to review a jury's verdict by a more stringent standard would unduly disrupt that relationship. It is questionable whether the latter practice would produce the same degree of disruption as the former. More importantly, neither Justice Scalia's opinion, nor the majority's, discussed how federal countervailing considerations may legitimately be derived and how they should be weighted once they are identified. For all that can be determined under Justice Scalia's opinion, *any* effect of a state law on the judge-jury relationship will be sufficient to outweigh outcome determinative policies.[262]

---

260. *See* subsection E(2) *supra*.

261. *See* 518 U.S. at 467, 116 S. Ct at 2239, 135 L. Ed. 2d at 698 (Scalia, J., dissenting).

262. For decisions explicitly applying *Gasperini*, see ,*e.g.*, Continental Trend Res., Inc. v. OXY USA, Inc., 101 F.3d 634 (10th Cir. 1996) (*Gasperini* applies to punitive damage awards); Medcom Holding Co. v. Baxter Travenol Labs., Inc., 100 F.3d 1241 (7th Cir. 1996) (state law governs substantive assessment of whether the evidence supports the damages award when liability based on state law); *see also* Central Office Tel. v. American Tel. & Tel. Co., 108 F.3d 981 (9th Cir. 1997) (state law determines whether evidence supports plaintiff's claim); Acme Inv., Inc. v. Southwest Tracor, Inc., 105 F.3d 412 (8th Cir. 1997) (federal court with diversity jurisdiction should, in a specific performance action, apply the de novo standard of appellate review that would be applied by Nebraska state courts because it is an issue of substantive rather than procedural law, comparable to the standard for reviewing the sufficiency of evidence to support a jury verdict); *cf.* Miskis v. Howard, 106 F.3d 754 (7th Cir. 1997) (federal standards used to determine excessiveness of verdict in a diversity case); Torres v. Wendco, Inc., Civil No. 95-1544 (CCC) JA, 1997 WL 135682, 1997 U.S. Dist. LEXIS 3182 (D.P.R. Jan. 15, 1997) (in the absence of a state statute governing awards that "materially deviate" from awards in similar cases, Puerto Rico has no substantive law governing limitations on jury awards and federal case law provides guidance). For an example of a federal district court case attempting to apply the New York statute involved in *Gasperini*, see Geressy v. Digital Equip. Corp., 950 F. Supp. 519 (E.D.N.Y. 1997); *see also* Smith v. Louisville Ladder Co., 237 F.3d 515 (5th Cir. 2001) (employing a federal standard for determining the sufficiency of the evidence in a diversity action). *But cf.* Broadcast Satellite Int'l, Inc. v. National Digital Television Ctr., Inc., 323 F.3d 339 (5th Cir. 2003) (in

Semtek International, Inc. v. Lockheed Martin Corp.[263] is the latest case in which a majority of the Supreme Court has pronounced on the Rules of Decision Act side of the *Erie* doctrine. In *Semtek*, the Court took up the question of whether the effect of a federal judgment in a diversity action was to be determined by state or federal law. The action was commenced in a state court in California and removed by the defendant to the U.S. District Court for the Central District of California. The defendant then moved to dismiss the action on the ground that the California statute of limitations had run. The district court granted this motion and dismissed the action, specifying that the dismissal was "on the merits and with prejudice."[264] The plaintiff appealed to the Ninth Circuit Court of Appeals, which affirmed the judgment of the district court. In addition, the plaintiff commenced a new action against the defendant in a Maryland state court, Maryland possessing a longer statute of limitations that had not yet run on the plaintiff's claims.[265] The Maryland state court dismissed the action, holding that the California federal judgment had a claim preclusive effect and barred the action.[266] The Maryland Court of Special Appeals affirmed, and the U.S. Supreme Court granted certiorari.

The Court, in a tortured opinion, first held that Federal Rule 41(b)[267] was inapplicable to the case.[268] It then held that while the scope of a federal judgment, including a diversity judgment, is to be determined by federal law, federal law in diversity cases will normally adopt state law to determine the scope of a federal judgment in diversity actions.[269] This will not be so only when state law is "incompatible with federal interests," which was not true in the case before the Court.[270] Because California law might not make a dismissal on statute of limitations grounds claim preclusive in an action in another state under the latter's longer statute of limitations, the Court reversed the determination by the Maryland Special Court of Appeals that the federal judgment necessarily precluded the Maryland action.[271]

It is important to note that in the part of its opinion holding that federal law would normally adopt state law to control the scope of federal diversity judgments, the Court relied on the *Erie* doctrine only in passing. The Court stated that any other rule would produce the kind of forum shopping and inequitable administration of

---

diversity actions, the substance of jury instructions is controlled by state law, but the form or manner of giving the instruction is controlled by federal law; *Erie* does not require federal diversity courts to follow state pattern jury instructions).

263. 531 U.S. 497, 121 S. Ct. 1021, 149 L. Ed. 2d 32 (2001).

264. *Id.* at 499, 121 S. Ct. at 1024, 149 L. Ed. 2d at 37.

265. The plaintiff obviously hoped to invoke the rule that statute of limitations are "procedural" for purposes of conflict-of-laws determinations. Under this rule, the Maryland court would be able to apply its own longer statute of limitations, and the action would not be barred, so long as the federal diversity judgment did not preclude the action.

266. The procedural history is somewhat more complicated than stated here. *See Semtek,* 531 U.S. at 499-500, 121 S. Ct. at 1023-24, 149 L. Ed. 2d at 37-38.

267. Rule 41(b) makes all dismissals except three specific types "on the merits" and thus, apparently, claim preclusive. The three specified exceptions do not appear to include dismissals on statute of limitations grounds. *See* FED. R. CIV. P. 41(b). However, as observed in Chapter 10(E) *infra*, the Supreme Court has interpreted an exception to Rule 41(b) for jurisdictional dismissals in a very broad fashion, to include dismissals that do not appear to be in any way jurisdictional in nature.

268. *See Semtek*, 531 U.S. at 501-06, 121 S. Ct. at 1024-27, 149 L. Ed. 2d at 38-41. This aspect of *Semtek* is discussed below in this chapter, in Chapter 10, and in Chapter 13.

269. *See Semtek,* 531 U.S. at 506-09, 121 S. Ct. at 1024-27, 149 L. Ed. 2d at 38-41.

270. *See id.* at 509, 121 S. Ct. at 1028, 149 L. Ed. 2d at 41.

271. *See id.*

the laws that *Erie* seeks to avoid, because filing in or removing to federal court would be encouraged by the divergent effects that the litigants would anticipate from likely grounds of dismissal.[272]

Since *Semtek*, a majority of the Supreme Court has not spoken on the operation of the Rules of Decision Act side of the *Erie* doctrine. However, a dissenting minority in *Shady Grove Orthopedic Associates v. Allstate Insurance Co.*[273] did attempt to apply the Rules of Decision Act test. In *Shady Grove*, New York had enacted a statute that prohibited class actions in suits for penalties. The plaintiff, seeking a penalty from the defendant Allstate, commenced an action in federal court in New York and attempted to qualify the action as a class action under Federal Rule of Civil Procedure 23. The Second Circuit Court of Appeals held that Rule 23 did not control the issue of which substantive causes of action could be brought as class actions and thus left room for the operation of the New York law. The court of appeals then held that *Erie* required application of the New York law.[274] The Supreme Court granted certiorari and reversed.

A majority of the Court held Rule 23 applicable to the case and in conflict with the statute.[275] A plurality of the Court also found Rule 23, as so interpreted, to be valid under the Rules Enabling Act.[276] However, Justice Stevens, concurring, viewed the state statute to be supported only by procedural policies. Thus, he did not, as a consequence, believe that the application of Rule 23 instead of the state law "abridge[d], enlarge[d], or modifie[d]" any substantive right within the meaning of the Rules Enabling Act.[277] In dissent, Justice Ginsburg, for herself and three other members of the Court, found Rule 23 inapplicable to the case and determined that *Erie* required application of the New York law.[278] To evaluate the dissenters' analysis of the *Erie* issue in *Shady Grove*, it is important first to understand some important features of the case that differentiate it from previous cases discussed in this section.

---

272. *See id.* at 508-09, 121 S. Ct. at 1028, 149 L. Ed. 2d at 41. *But cf.* State v. Lemmer, 736 N.W.2d 650 (Minn. 2007) (collateral estoppel is a procedural rule that is not necessarily outcome determinative); Vasquez v. Bridgestone/Firestone, Inc., 325 F.3d 665 (5th Cir. 2003) (*Semtek* does not require federal diversity court to incorporate state law to define the effect of a federal forum non conveniens dismissal; unlike a dismissal based on state "substantive law," the threats of forum shopping and inequitable administration of the law that *Erie* seeks to avoid are not present where a dismissal is based on federal procedure); Stephanie Moser Goins, Comment, *Beware the Ides of Marchington: The* Erie *Doctrine's Effect on Recognition and Enforcement of Tribal Court Judgments in Federal and State Courts,* 32 AM. INDIAN L. REV. 189 (2008).

273. 559 U.S. __, 130 S. Ct. 1431, 176 L. Ed. 2d 311 (2010).

274. *See* Shady Grove Orthopedic Assocs. P.A. v. Allstate Ins. Co., 549 F.3d 137 (2d Cir. 2008).

275. *See Shady Grove*, 559 U.S. at __, 130 S. Ct. at 1436-42, 176 L. Ed. 2d at 315-22 (Scalia, J., for the Court).

276. *See id.* at __, 130 S. Ct. at 1442-44, 176 L. Ed. 2d at 322-25 (Scalia, J., with whom Roberts, C.J., Thomas, J., & Sotomayor, J., concurred).

277. *See id.* at __, 130 S. Ct. at 1448-60, 176 L. Ed. 2d at 329-41 (Stevens, J., concurring). At least one circuit views Justice Steven's opinion as constituting the holding of the case. *See* James River Ins. Co. v. Rapid Funding, LLC, 648 F.3d 1134 (10th Cir. 2011); Garman v. Campbell Cnty. Sch. Dist. No. 1, 630 F.3d 977 (10th Cir. 2010); *see also* Andrew J. Kazakes, *Relatively Unguided: Examining the Precedential Value of the Plurality Decision in* Shady Grove Orthopedic Associates v. Allstate Insurance Co., *and Its Effects on Class Action Litigation*, 44 LOY. L.A. L. REV. 1049 (2011). *But see* Craig T. Cagney, *O Sonia, Where Art Thou?: Why Justice Sotomayor's Silent "Opinion" Should Serve as* Shady Grove's *Holding*, 80 FORDHAM L. REV. 189 (2011) (discussing Justice Sotomayor's unexplained failure to join in the part of Justice Scalia's opinion arguing in favor of the validity of Federal Rules of Civil Procedure that conflict with state rules "bound up" with state substantive rights). The Rules Enabling Act side of *Erie* is discussed in the next section of this Chapter.

278. *See Shady Grove*, 559 U.S. at __, 130 S. Ct. at 1460-73, 176 L. Ed. 2d 341-55 (Ginsburg, J., with whom Kennedy, J., Bryer, J., & Alito, J., joined, dissenting).

As discussed in section F, below, when neither a Federal Rule of Civil Procedure nor any other federal law controls a case, the federal courts must consider the case under the Rules of Decision Act to determine whether the state law is "substantive" or "procedural" under that Act and the general *Erie* doctrine. Previously, this section has identified two kinds of cases under the Rules of Decision Act. In one kind of case, exemplified by *Guaranty Trust* and *Byrd*, there is present in the case a federal common-law or equity rule of practice that conflicts with state law, but there is no Federal Rule of Civil Procedure even remotely in the background of the case. In this kind of case, the issue is whether the federal common-law or equity rule instead of state law will produce the kinds of evils the general *Erie* doctrine is designed to prevent. If the state rule defines state rights or is bound up with the definition of state rights and obligations, the federal courts are obligated to apply the state rule rather than the federal common-law or equity rule (assuming that the *Byrd* categorization process survives the later cases discussed in the text above). However, even if the state rule is a rule of "form and mode," the federal courts are to apply the rule if application of the federal common-law or equity rule of practice instead of the state rule would produce an outcome difference that would cause forum shopping or inequitable administration of the laws in the *Erie* sense, unless sufficient weighty "federal countervailing considerations" exist to justify application of the federal law instead.

A second kind of Rules of Decision Act case is exemplified by the *Woods* decision, discussed earlier in section E(1). In this kind of case, there is no existing federal common-law or equity rule of practice or procedure present that conflicts with state law. Instead, one of the litigants is simply arguing that the state law is "substantive" in the general *Erie* sense and the other is arguing that it is "procedural." However, which *Byrd* category of cases the state rule fits within is determined in the same manner as in the first kind of case. If the state rule defines state rights or is bound up with state rights and obligations, its application is mandatory in federal court (unless, as discussed above, the *Byrd* categorization process has fallen into desuetude after the *Gasperini* decision). If the state rule is one of form and mode, the question is still whether disregard of the rule would produce forum shopping and inequitable administration of the law in violation of the *Erie* policies as redefined in *Hanna*). If so, unless there are sufficiently weighty federal countervailing considerations to justify disregard of the state rule, *Erie* requires the federal courts to follow the state law. In the absence of a federal common-law or equity rule, it will usually be more difficult to find such countervailing considerations, because the policies supporting a federal rule will usually be necessary to produce federal countervailing considerations. Nevertheless, the analytical process is structurally the same in the first and second kind of case.

Shady Grove arguably involves a third kind of case, in which precisely the same kinds of questions cannot be asked as in the first two kinds of examples. If, as the dissenters argued, Rule 23 is inapplicable to the case, the situation may appear to be like the second category of cases discussed above. This is because, Rule 23 being the only rule of any kind that authorizes class actions in federal court, finding the rule inapplicable would mean there is no federal law that conflicts with state law in the action. However, in this (third) kind of case, as opposed to the *Woods* kind of case, it is never permissible for a federal court to disregard the state law in the case. This is so regardless of the *Byrd* category that the state law falls into, and, if it is a rule of form and mode, forum shopping and federal countervailing considerations inquiries are irrelevant to the case. This is because, in cases like *Shady Grove*, disregard of the state law would literally mean allowing a class action for the penalties sought by the plaintiff. However, because Rule 23 has been found inapplicable to the case in order to reach the Rules of Decision Act question, this is not possible. Thus, the proper conclusion is that state law must be applied, because under the analytical process that produced the conclusion that Rule 23 is inapplicable, there is no other law to apply. There is no need to make forum shopping or federal countervailing consideration inquiries, because to do so suggests that Rule 23, which has previously been determined to be inapplicable, might nevertheless be applied, a logical absurdity.[279]

Given the fact that *Shady Grove* involved this third kind of case, how well or poorly did the dissenting opinion evaluate the problem. As noted earlier, Justice Ginsburg first interpreted Rule 23 and concluded that it was inapplicable to the issue before the Court.[280] This part of the dissent will be discussed in the next section of this chapter. However, it should be noted that Justice Ginsburg considered both Rule 23 and the state law in determining the applicability of the latter rule, and she did so specifically so that Rule 23 could be construed with "sensitivity to state interests."[281] This resulted in the conclusion that Rule 23 did not create a right to use the class-action procedure in the face of a state law providing otherwise. After concluding that Rule 23 did not apply to the case, Justice Ginsburg turned to the Rules of Decision Act side of the doctrine. She began:

> Because I perceive no unavoidable conflict between Rule 23 and [the state law], I would decide this case by inquiring "whether application of the [state] rule would have so important an effect upon the fortunes of one or both of the litigants that failure to [apply] it would be likely to cause a plaintiff to choose the federal court."[282]

Based on the previous discussion of the case, one can see that Justice Ginsburg is off on the wrong foot in this passage. There can be no failure to apply the state rule after concluding that Rule 23 was inapplicable because it did not control the right of a litigant to use the class action procedure. Moreover, Justice Ginsburg drew this

---

279. A distinguishable case is involved when a Federal Rule is found applicable to the case, but state law contains an additional substantively based procedural requirement that can be applied alongside the Federal Rule. This was arguably the case in Cohen v. Beneficial Industrial Loan Corp., 337 U.S. 541 (1949), in which the Court held that part of Rule 23 governing shareholder derivative actions (now Rule 23.1) as not in conflict with a state law that provided an additional requirement that shareholders owning less than a certain amount of stock post a bond as a condition of bringing such an action. The problem in this kind of case is really one of determining whether the Federal Rule in question is all encompassing, so as to negate the ability to apply any additional requirements found in state law. In *Shady Grove*, it was not possible to apply both Rule 23 and the state law after Rule 23 was interpreted by the majority as giving a right to the plaintiff to bring a class action in federal court. *See also* Ralph U. Whitten, Shady Grove Orthopedic Associates, P.A. v. Allstate Insurance Co.: *Justice Whitten Nagging in Part and Declaring a Pox on All Houses*, 44 CREIGHTON L. REV. 115, 123-26 (2010) (discussing the bearing that *Cohen* should have had on *Shady Grove*).

280. *See Shady Grove*, 559 U.S. at __, 130 S. Ct. at 1465-69, 176 L. Ed. 2d at 351-55 (Ginsburg, J., dissenting).

281. *See id.*

282. *Id.* at __, 130 S. Ct. at 1469, 176 L. Ed. 2d at 351 (quoting *Hanna v. Plumer*, 380 U.S. at 468 n.9, 85 S. Ct. at 1142 n.9, 14 L. Ed. 2d at 15 n.9, which is discussed in section F(3) *infra* ("The *Hanna* Decision: Return to the *Sibbach* Test").

conclusion specifically to avoid a conflict between state law and Rule 23. Thus, disregard of the state rule after her previous analysis would mean considering whether a plaintiff would forum shop to obtain the benefit of an inapplicable Federal Rule of Civil Procedure that has been construed as inapplicable explicitly to make room for the operation of a potentially conflicting state law—an absurd proposition.

After beginning badly, Justice Ginsburg's opinion continued for some time refuting Shady Grove's argument that the state rule was procedural, a refutation that need not have take up the amount of space devoted to it and that contained additional confusing references to the incentive to forum shop to get the benefit of the federal class action procedure. For example, Justice Ginsburg's opinion stated:

> In short, Shady Grove's effort to characterize [the state law] as simply "procedural" cannot successfully elide this fundamental norm: When no federal law or rule is dispositive of an issue, and a state statute is outcome affective in the sense our cases on *Erie* . . . develop, the Rules of Decision Act commands application of the State's law in diversity suits. . . . As this case starkly demonstrates, if federal courts exercising diversity jurisdiction are compelled by Rule 23 to award statutory penalties in class actions while New York courts are bound by [the state statute], "substantial variations between state and federal [money judgments] may be expected. . . . The "variation" here is indeed "substantial." Shady Grove seeks class relief that is *ten thousand times* greater than the individual remedy available to it in state court. Forum shopping will undoubtedly result if a plaintiff need only file in federal instead of state court to seek a massive monetary award explicitly barred by state law.[283]

Of course, no forum shopping would take place at all by the plaintiff to obtain the benefit of a procedural right not provided by federal law. Justice Ginsburg failed to observe that the premise established by the first part of her opinion rendered an inquiry into forum shopping irrelevant. She should simply have recognized that her previous analysis rendered further inquiry into the ability to disregard the state rule irrelevant and held the state rule applicable because there was no other rule to apply.

On the whole, the Supreme Court's jurisprudence under the *Erie* doctrine leaves much to be desired. The Court has failed to pay attention to the distinctions that its own opinions suggest should be drawn between different kinds of cases. The Court has also demonstrated a general lack of attention to how the standards that it has articulated should operate. As a result, the Court has created much confusion in the lower federal courts.[284] The Court's excursions into *Erie* jurisprudence in the

---

283. *Id.* at __, 130 L. Ed. 2d at 1471, 176 L. Ed. 2d at 353.

284. The operation of the general *Erie* doctrine in the lower federal courts will be explored in section G *infra*.

Gasperini and *Semtek* cases are particularly disturbing,[285] and Justice Ginsburg's dissent in *Shady Grove* is bound to create further confusion about the proper role of the forum shopping prohibition in cases involving Federal Rules of Civil Procedure.[286] The Court seldom addresses *Erie* questions. It would not seem too much to ask that when it does, it not create more confusion than it dispels.[287]

SECTION F. THE EVOLUTION OF THE *ERIE* DOCTRINE: CONFLICTS BETWEEN STATE LAW AND FEDERAL RULES OF CIVIL PROCEDURE

The Rules of Decision Act governed all the cases discussed in the preceding section. However, when dealing with conflicts between Federal Rules of Civil Procedure and state law, the relevant statute is not the Rules of Decision Act, but the Rules Enabling Act, 28 U.S.C. § 2072. The Rules Enabling Act gives the Federal Rules of Civil Procedure the force and effect of statutory law. Because state law is not to apply in the face of a controlling federal statute, valid Federal Rules control any case to which they apply even if contrary state law exists. This conclusion, however, simply pushes the inquiry to a different level. In each case, it must be determined (1) whether a Federal Rule exists which is applicable to the case; (2) if so, whether the Federal Rule is valid under the Rules Enabling Act; and

---

285. For an excellent critique of *Gasperini*, raising many of the same issues as the text, *supra*, see C. Douglas Floyd, Erie *Awry: A Comment on* Gasperini v. Center for Humanities, Inc., 1997 B.Y.U. L. REV. 267; *see also* Donald L. Doernberg, *The Unseen Track of* Erie Railroad: *Why History and Jurisprudence Suggest a More Straightforward Form of* Erie *Analysis*, 109 W. VA. L. REV. 611 (2007); Richard D. Freer, *Some Thoughts on the State of* Erie *After* Gasperini, 76 TEX. L. REV. 1637 (1998); J. Benjamin King, Note, *Clarification and Disruption: The Effect of* Gasperini v. Center for Humanities, Inc., *on the* Erie *Doctrine*, 83 CORNELL L. REV. 161, 183 (1997); Eva Madison, Case Note, *The Supreme Court Sets New Standards of Review for Excessive Verdicts in Federal Court in* Gasperini v. Center for Humanities, Inc., 50 ARK. L. REV. 591 (1997). For an article defending (for the most part) the Court's *Erie* jurisprudence, see Thomas D. Rowe, Jr., *Not Bad For Government Work: Does Anyone Else Think the Supreme Court Is Doing a Halfway Decent Job in Its* Erie-Hanna *Jurisprudence*?, 73 NOTRE DAME L. REV. 963 (1998). The worst aspects of the *Semtek* case are discussed later in this chapter and in Chapters 10 and 13.

286. *Shady Grove* is discussed in Stephen B. Burbank & Tobias Barrington Wolff, *Redeeming the Missed Opportunities of* Shady Grove, 159 U. PA. L. REV. 17 (1020); Helen Hershkoff, Shady Grove: *Duck-Rabbits, Clear Statements, and Federalism*, 74 ALB. L. REV. 1703 (2010-11); Jay Tidmarsh, *Procedure, Substance, and* Erie, 64 VAND. L. REV. 877 (2011); *Synmposium:* Erie *Under Advisement: The Doctrine after* Shady Grove, 44 AKRON L. REV. 897 (2011) (containing articles by Provessors Doernberg, Genetin, Koppel, Stempel, and Tidmarsh); *Symposium on* Shady Grove Orthopedic Associates v. Allstate Insruance: *A Collection of Opinions*, 44 CREIGHTON L. REV. 1 (2010) (containing articles by Professors Bassett, Borchers, Cox, Freer & Arthur, Oakley, Rensberger, Rowe, and Whitten); *Symposium*, 86 NOTRE DAME L. REV. 939 (2011) (containing articles by Professors Bauer, Clermont, Ides, Nagareda, Sternman, and Struve).

287. It has recently been argued that *Erie* cases should be treated like "classic federal common-law cases" and, therefore, that courts should ask (1) whether a source of common-law authority exists that will justify the creation of a federal common-law procedural rule and (2) if so, whether the national interest requires a federal rule or the need for uniformity outweighs the need for uniformity within a state. *See* Wendy Collins Perdue, *The Sources and Scope of Federal Procedural Common Law: Some Reflections on* Erie *and* Gasperini, 46 U. KAN. L. REV. 751 (1998). The problem with this suggestion is that there are two kinds of cases on the Rules of Decision Act "side" of the *Erie* doctrine. In one kind of case, an affirmative "federal common-law procedural rule" or "practice" exists (or someone is asking the federal courts to create one). This kind of case is the sort Professor Perdue's suggestion addresses. However, the other kind of case is one in which there is no federal common-law procedural rule (and no one is asking the federal courts to create one), but one of the litigants is simply arguing that a state law should be disregarded because it is "procedural" in the *Erie* sense. As cases discussed in previous subsections have demonstrated, the policies supporting *Erie* can be offended as much by disregard of state law in the latter kind of case as in the former. Professor Perdue's recommendation, however, does not seem to address the second kind of case. *See generally* Jerome A. Hoffman, *Thinking Out Loud About the Myth of* Erie: *Plus a Good Word for Section 1652*, 70 MISS. L.J. 163 (2000).

(3) if so, whether the Federal Rule is constitutional. This section considers the standards that govern these issues.

The Rules Enabling Act was enacted in 1934. Under the authority of the Act, the Federal Rules of Civil Procedure became effective in 1938.[288] When the Supreme Court promulgated the Federal Rules, law and equity were merged. The preexisting requirement of conformity to state procedure was also ended in areas covered by the Federal Rules. However, Congress did not delegate the power to promulgate rules of procedure under the Rules Enabling Act to the Supreme Court without restriction. The Act provided that the rules promulgated "shall neither abridge, enlarge, nor modify the substantive rights of any litigant."[289] This restriction has given rise to serious problems of interpretation.

The best examination of the legislative history of the Rules Enabling Act is by Professor Stephen Burbank.[290] Professor Burbank concludes that the "substantive rights" restriction was designed to allocate regulatory power over procedure between Congress and the Supreme Court in such a way that the Supreme Court would not be able to exercise "legislative power."[291] The "substantive rights" restriction, in this sense, merely restated limitations on the Court's rulemaking power embodied in the basic delegation by the first sentence of the Rules Enabling Act. That sentence authorizes the Court to make only rules governing "the forms of process, writs, pleadings, and motions, and the practice and procedure in civil actions."[292] The objective of the Act was thus to prevent the Court's rulemaking power from extending to "'matters involving substantive legal and remedial rights affected by considerations of public policy.'"[293] In light of the matters later discussed in this section, it is interesting to note that among the kinds of rules *excluded* from the Supreme Court's rulemaking power were rules governing the admissibility of evidence and discovery rules providing for the compulsion of physical and mental examinations by the imposition of contempt sanctions.[294]

1. The *Sibbach* Decision

The U.S. Supreme Court first construed the Rules Enabling Act in *Sibbach v. Wilson & Co.*[295] Mrs. Sibbach instituted an action in the U.S. District Court for the Northern District of Illinois. She sought to recover damages for personal injuries suffered in an accident in Indiana. The district court ordered Mrs. Sibbach to undergo a physical examination under Rule 35 of the Federal Rules of Civil Procedure to determine the nature and extent of her injuries. When she refused to obey this order, the district court found her in contempt and directed that she be

---

288. *See* Chapter 1(D)(11) *supra* ("Promulgation of the Federal Rules of Civil Procedure").

289. The current version of the Act is worded similarly. *See* 28 U.S.C. § 2072(b); *see also* Chapter 1(D)(10) *supra* ("Promulgation of the Federal Rules of Civil Procedure").

290. Stephen B. Burbank, *The Rules Enabling Act of 1934*, 130 U. PA. L. REV. 1015 (1982).

291. *See id.* at 1106.

292. *See id.* at 1107.

293. *Id.* at 1121 (quoting S. REP. NO. 1174, 69th Cong., 1st Sess. 9 (1926)).

294. *See id.* at 1129-30, 1137-43, 1176-84.

295. 312 U.S. 1, 61 S. Ct. 422, 85 L. Ed. 479 (1941).

imprisoned until she complied with the order. On appeal, the court of appeals affirmed. The Supreme Court granted certiorari and reversed.

Mrs. Sibbach argued that Rule 35, which authorizes physical examinations, and Rule 37, which deals with sanctions for failure to obey discovery orders, were invalid under the substantive rights restriction of the Rules Enabling Act. Ultimately, the Supreme Court found that the lower courts had erred in interpreting Rule 37 as authorizing the imposition of contempt for failure to comply with an order to submit to a physical examination.[296] However, the Court rejected Mrs. Sibbach's argument that the rules were invalid under the Rules Enabling Act. In so doing, the Court opted for an interpretation of the substantive rights restriction that treated "substantive" and "procedural" matters as entirely distinct. Substantive rights were held to include "rights conferred by law to be protected and enforced by the adjective law of judicial procedure."[297] However, the Court rebuffed Mrs. Sibbach's argument that "substantive rights" within the meaning of the Rules Enabling Act included "important and substantial rights theretofore recognized."[298] "The test," stated the Court, "must be whether a rule really regulates procedure—the judicial process for enforcing rights and duties recognized by substantive law and for justly administering remedy and redress for disregard or infraction of them."[299]

The Court's references to "rights conferred by law to be protected and enforced in accordance with the adjective law of judicial procedure" and to procedure as "judicial process for enforcing rights and duties recognized by substantive law" strongly suggest that the Rules Enabling Act divided the legal universe into two parts: (1) rules of decision found in areas such as contracts, torts, and property that would be deemed purely substantive by anyone's definition; and (2) all other rules, which would be considered procedural, even if they had some effect on the enforcement of pure substantive rules. This bifurcation was reinforced by an example of "substantive rights" given by the Court: "the right not to be injured in one's person by another's negligence."[300]

This view, which treated substance and procedure as mutually exclusive categories, seemed to contradict the structure of the Rules Enabling Act. The Act first authorized the Supreme Court to "prescribe by general rules the forms of process, writs, pleadings, and motions and the practice and procedure of the district

---

296. *See id.* at 16, 61 S. Ct. at 427-28, 85 L. Ed. at 486. Rule 37(b)(2)(iv), which is today Rule 37(b)(2)(D), specifically exempted failures to comply with physical or mental examinations from the contempt sanction, although other substantial sanctions can be imposed for such a failure under Rule 37(b)(2).

297. *See* 312 U.S. at 13, 61 S. Ct. at 426, 85 L. Ed at 484.

298. *See id.* at 13-14, 61 S. Ct. at 426, 85 L. Ed. at 484-85.

299. *Id.* at 14, 61 S. Ct. at 426, 85 L. Ed. at 485. In a cryptic portion of its opinion, the Court had also indicated that there were other restrictions on the rulemaking power of the courts: "There are other limitations upon the authority to prescribe rules which might have been, but were not, mentioned in the Act; for instance, the inability of a court, by rule, to extend or restrict the jurisdiction conferred by a statute." *Id.* at 10, 61 S. Ct. at 424-25, 85 L. Ed. at 483. This language seems to refer to separation-of-powers restrictions on the rulemaking authority, but without elaboration by the Court, the kind of restrictions it had in mind cannot be precisely determined. Potential separation-of-powers restrictions on the rulemaking power are discussed in subsection 6 *infra*. *See generally* Ralph U. Whitten, *Separation of Powers Restrictions on Judicial Rulemaking: A Case Study of Federal Rule 4*, 40 ME. L. REV. 41 (1988).

300. *Sibbach*, 312 U.S. at 13, 61 S. Ct. at 426, 85 L. Ed. at 485.

courts and courts of appeals of the United States in civil actions."[301] The Act then provided that "[s]aid rules shall neither abridge, enlarge, nor modify the substantive rights of any litigant."[302] On the face of the Act, the expressions "rules of practice and procedure" and "substantive rights" were apparently not mutually exclusive. Had they been so intended, both clauses of the Act would not have been necessary. Instead, Congress might simply have authorized the Court to regulate the practice and procedure of the district courts without any reference to substantive rights. The mutual exclusivity of substance and procedure would have assured that the Court would not have the power to create substantive rules. By using two expressions, Congress suggested that procedure and substance were overlapping categories and that there are procedural rules within the meaning of the statute that could affect substantive rights. A plausible facial interpretation of the Act was, therefore, that the Court might prescribe uniform procedural rules for the lower federal courts. However, in applying those rules, the courts should take care not to abridge, enlarge, or modify substantive rights.[303]

Mrs. Sibbach, in fact, argued before the Supreme Court that "[i]f rules of 'procedure' could not be construed to involve 'substantive rights,' the second sentence in the Act would be surplusage."[304] Some commentators have likewise concluded that the substantive rights restriction of the Act should be given a meaning different, and more restrictive, than the phrase "practice and procedure" in the first sentence of the Act.[305] Nevertheless, Professor Stephen Burbank's research into the legislative history of the Act has indicated that the substantive rights restriction was indeed designed only to emphasize a limitation inherent in the use of the words "practice and procedure" in the first sentence of the Act.[306] However, as discussed below, the real problem with the Court's interpretation of the Rules Enabling Act in *Sibbach* and later cases is that it recognizes virtually no restrictions on the rulemaking authority at all. This interpretation is the one that would seem wholly implausible under either the language or history of the Act.[307]

Sibbach's view of the Enabling Act was followed five years later in *Mississippi Publishing Corp. v. Murphree*.[308] In *Murphree*, the defendant challenged the validity of original Rule 4(f) of the Federal Rules of Civil Procedure. Prior to the promulgation of Rule 4(f), the personal-jurisdiction reach of the federal district courts was limited to the territorial limits of the district. Rule 4(f) permitted a district court in a multidistrict state to summon a defendant from anywhere within a state. In evaluating the validity of Rule 4(f), the Court confirmed *Sibbach's*

---

301. *See* Act of June 19, 1934, ch. 651, 48 Stat. 1064 (codified as amended at 28 U.S.C. § 2072(a)). The current version of the Act simply authorizes the Supreme Court to prescribe "rules of practice and procedure and rules of evidence." *See* 28 U.S.C. § 2072(a). In addition, the Judicial Improvements Act of 1990 added a new subsection (c) to 28 U.S.C. § 2072: "Such rules may define when a ruling of a district court is final for purposes of appeal under section 1291 of this title." Pub. L. No. 101-650, § 315, 104 Stat. 5089, 5115 (codified at 28 U.S.C. § 2072(c)).

302. Act of June 19, 1934, ch. 651, 48 Stat. 1064 (codified as amended at 28 U.S.C. § 2072(b)).

303. *See* Ralph U. Whitten, Erie *and the Federal Rules: A Review and Reappraisal After* Burlington Northern Railroad v. Woods, 21 CREIGHTON L. REV. 1, 5 (1987).

304. *Sibbach*, 312 U.S. at 3 (argument of petitioner).

305. *See* John H. Ely, *The Irrepressible Myth of* Erie, 87 HARV. L. REV. 693, 718-40 (1974).

306. *See* Stephen B. Burbank, *The Rules Enabling Act of 1934*, 130 U. PA. L. REV. 1015, 1107-08 (1982).

307. Professor Burbank, for example, argues that the restrictions of the Act were designed to allocate lawmaking power between the Supreme Court and Congress. *See id.* at 1106.

308. 326 U.S. 438, 66 S. Ct. 242, 90 L. Ed. 185 (1946).

interpretation of the substance-procedure dichotomy of the Act. Congress, stated the Court, did not aim the substantive rights restriction of the Rules Enabling Act at "such incidental effects as necessarily attend the adoption of the prescribed new rules of procedure upon the rights of litigants who, agreeably to rules of practice and procedure, have been brought before a court authorized to determine their rights."[309] Rule 4(f) would operate to affect the rights of the defendant by subjecting those rights to adjudication by the district court for the Northern District of Mississippi, rather than the district court for the Southern District of Mississippi. However, the rule would "not operate to abridge, enlarge, or modify the rules of decision by which [the district court] will adjudicate its rights."[310] Consequently, the rule related only to the manner and means by which a right to recover was enforced.[311]

2. The Outcome Determinative Test and the Federal Rules of Civil Procedure

After *Erie* but before *Sibbach*, the Supreme Court held that the lower federal courts could not, under the guise of *Erie's* substance-procedure distinction, apply burden-of-proof rules that state courts would not apply in a similar case.[312] Then, in *Guaranty Trust*, the Court established the outcome determinative test to govern when the federal courts had to follow state rules that were in some sense classified as "procedural."[313] In retrospect, it probably should have been clear that the outcome determinative test did not apply to determine the validity of Federal Rules of Civil Procedure under the Enabling Act. Nevertheless, later events made *Guaranty Trust* appear to govern conflicts between state law and Federal Rules of Civil Procedure. The main difficulty was that the Court itself seemed to think that *Guaranty Trust* governed such conflicts.[314]

In *Murphree*, the Court cited *Guaranty Trust* as authority for sustaining Federal Rule 4(f) under the Enabling Act.[315] In *Ragan v. Merchants Transfer & Warehouse Co.*,[316] an apparent conflict existed between Federal Rule 3, which provides that an action is commenced by filing a complaint with the court,[317] and a Kansas provision that required commencement by service of a summons in order

---

309. *Id.* at 445, 66 S. Ct. at 246, 90 L. Ed. at 191.

310. *Id.* at 446, 66 S. Ct. at 246, 90 L. Ed. at 192.

311. *Id.*

312. *See* Palmer v. Hoffman, 318 U.S. 109, 117, 63 S. Ct. 477, 482, 87 L. Ed. 645, 651 (1943); Cities Serv. Oil Co. v. Dunlap, 308 U.S. 208, 210-12, 60 S. Ct. 201, 202-03, 84 L. Ed. 196, 197-98 (1939).

313. *Guaranty Trust* is discussed in section E(1) *supra* ("The *Guaranty Trust* Case: Independent Equity Powers and the 'Outcome Determinative' Test").

314. One reason may have been that the Court had by "essentially obliterating the Enabling Act in *Sibbach* . . . created a need for limits on the Rules." John H. Ely, *The Irrepressible Myth of* Erie, 87 HARV. L. REV. 693, 698 (1974). Another reason was that, despite being warned by Justice Frankfurter that the terms "substantive" and "procedural" were not words of unvarying content, the temptation to treat them the same for purposes of both the Rules of Decision Act and the Rules Enabling Act proved too great even for the Court. *See* Guaranty Trust Co. v. York, 326 U.S. 99, 108, 65 S. Ct. 1464, 1469, 89 L. Ed. 2079, 2085 (1945); *see also* WALTER W. COOK, THE LOGICAL AND LEGAL BASES OF THE CONFLICT OF LAWS ch. VI (1942).

315. *See Murphree*, 326 U.S. at 446, 66 S. Ct. at 246, 90 L. Ed. at 192.

316. 337 U.S. 530, 69 S. Ct. 1233, 93 L. Ed. 1520 (1949).

317. *See* FED. R. CIV. P. 3.

to toll the running of the statute of limitations.[318] The Court held that the Kansas method of commencement by service had to be applied in a federal diversity action. Throughout the *Ragan* opinion, the Court employed the *Erie-Guaranty Trust* line of decisions to analyze the issue before it,[319] even though the argument was explicitly made that Rule 3 governed commencement for purposes of the Kansas statute.[320] One cannot read *Ragan* without concluding that the Court believed *Erie* required the application of state law because of a conflict between Rule 3 and the Kansas statute.[321] The Court did not cite *Sibbach* in its opinion.[322]

In *Cohen v. Beneficial Industrial Loan Corp.*,[323] the Court held that a federal court sitting in diversity had to apply a state statute governing shareholder derivative actions. The statute required that a plaintiff owning less than 5% of the par value of the corporation's outstanding shares had to provide security for the reasonable expenses, including attorney's fees, that the corporation might incur in its successful defense of the derivative action.[324] In considering the applicability of Rule 23 of the Federal Rules of Civil Procedure, which governed derivative actions in federal district court,[325] the Court explicitly stated that the provisions of Rule 23 did not conflict with the state statute.[326] However, the dissenters considered Rule 23 applicable and, like the majority, seemed to consider *Erie* and *Guaranty Trust* to be the only relevant precedents.[327]

Ragan and *Cohen* were widely interpreted to mean that the *Guaranty Trust* outcome determinative test governed the validity of Federal Rules of Civil Procedure.[328] Thus, when the Court decided *Byrd v. Blue Ridge Rural Electric*

---

318. *See Ragan*, 337 U.S. at 531 n.4, 69 S. Ct. at 1234 n.4, 93 L. Ed. at 1522 n.4.

319. *See id.* at 532-34, 69 S. Ct. at 1234-35, 93 L. Ed. at 1522-24.

320. *See id.* at 532-33, 69 S. Ct. at 1234-35, 93 L. Ed. at 1522-23.

321. *See id.* at 532-34, 69 S. Ct. at 1234-35, 93 L. Ed. at 1522-24.

322. *See id.* at 531-34, 69 S. Ct. at 1234-35, 93 L. Ed. at 1521-24. The Kansas commencement rule continues to wreak havoc with litigants. *See, e.g.*, Burnham v. Humphrey Hospitality REIT Trust, Inc., 403 F.3d 709 (10th Cir. 2005) (plaintiff filed complaint on March 19, 2003, but failed to effectuate service appropriate under Federal Rule 4 either in the manner prescribed by state law or in the manner prescribed by Federal Rule within 90 days as required by Kansas commencement rule; therefore, action time barred because statute of limitations had run by the time service was made; United States *ex rel.* Conner v. Salina Reg. Health Ctr., Inc., 543 F.3d 1211 (10th Cir. 2008) (no conflict between Federal Rule 15(c) and Kansas service provisions; Kansas service provisions controls and cause limitation period to run). *But cf.* S.J v. Issaquah Sch. Dist. No. 411, 470 F.3d 1288 (9th Cir. 2006) (in federal question case in which district court adopted state statute of limitations, it was incorrect for court to also borrow state's time limit for serving process, which should be controlled by Rule 4(m)).

323. 337 U.S. 541, 69 S. Ct. 1221, 93 L. Ed. 1528 (1949).

324. *Id.* at 544 n.1, 69 S. Ct. at 1224 n.1, 93 L. Ed. at 1535 n.1.

325. The Rules were amended in 1966, and today derivative actions are governed by Rule 23.1 of the Federal Rules of Civil Procedure.

326. *See Cohen*, 337 U.S. at 556, 69 S. Ct. at 1230, 93 L. Ed. at 1541-42.

327. *See id.* at 557, 69 S. Ct. at 1230-31, 93 L. Ed. at 1542 (Douglas, J. & Frankfurter, J., dissenting); *id.* at 558-61, 69 S. Ct. at 1231-32, 93 L. Ed. at 1542-44 (Rutledge, J., dissenting). In Woods v. Interstate Realty Co., 337 U.S. 535, 69 S. Ct. 1235, 93 L. Ed. 1524 (1949), discussed in the preceding section of this chapter, the Court confronted the question whether a federal diversity court was required to apply a Mississippi door-closing statute. The Court held that *Erie* required application of the state statute. Although the Court did not consider any potential conflict between the state law and a Federal Rule of Civil Procedure, others have observed that Federal Rule 17(b), governing capacity to sue and be sued in federal court, may have been applicable to the case. *See* John H. Ely, *The Irrepressible Myth of* Erie, 87 HARV. L. REV. 693, 727-28 (1974); *cf.* Kona Enters., Inc. v. Estate of Bishop, 179 F.3d 767 (9th Cir. 1999) (court, on the authority of *Cohen*, held the requirement of continuous ownership in Rule 23.2 applicable in federal court, even if state law was to the contrary, without discussing any Rules Enabling Act problem).

328. *See* CHARLES A. WRIGHT & MARY KAY KANE, THE LAW OF FEDERAL COURTS § 55, at 378, § 59, at 401-02 (7th ed. 2011).

Cooperative Inc.,[329] discussed in the preceding section of this chapter, it appeared to open an escape valve that might save the Federal Rules: the *Byrd* balancing test might allow the "interest of the federal system in having a uniform procedure in its courts"[330] to outweigh the need to duplicate the outcome between state and federal courts. However, *Byrd* did not turn out to be the savior of the Federal Rules. That role was to be played by the Court's decision in *Hanna v. Plumer*.[331]

3. The *Hanna* Decision: Return to the *Sibbach* Test

In *Hanna*, the issue was a potential conflict between Rule 4(d)(1)[332] of the Federal Rules of Civil Procedure and a state statute. Rule 4(d)(1) provided for service of process upon competent, adult individuals by leaving a copy of the summons and complaint at their home with someone of suitable age and discretion. The state statute required in-hand service under the circumstances of the case. Service had been made in accord with Rule 4(d)(1) rather than the state statute. The defendant thus apparently received actual notice of the action within the limitations period.[333] Nevertheless, in-hand service had not been made within the period required by the state statute of limitations. Therefore, if the state method of service had to be employed in federal court to toll the statute of limitations, the statute would have expired. The district court granted summary judgment for the defendant on the authority of *Guaranty Trust* and *Ragan*. The court of appeals affirmed.[334] The Supreme Court granted certiorari and reversed.

The defendant—plausibly given the history of the Court's decisions dealing with Federal Rule-state law conflicts—argued that the *Guaranty Trust* outcome determinative test required the federal courts to apply the state rule.[335] As noted in section E(2), above, the Court first analyzed the case as if Federal Rule 4(d)(1) were a federal common-law rule of practice or procedure. The Court rejected the argument that, under such a supposition, *Guaranty Trust* required application of the conflicting state rule.[336] However, the Court then held that the *Erie-Guaranty Trust-Byrd* line of cases did not apply to conflicts between Federal Rules of Civil Procedure and state law. Instead, the Court pointed to a separate line of cases, beginning with *Sibbach*, involving the validity of Federal Rules under the Enabling Act. The Court stated that it was this line of cases that had to be consulted when the validity of a Federal Rule of Civil Procedure is questioned. The Court interpreted *Ragan* and *Cohen* as holding only that the Federal Rules in question were not broad enough to cover the case before the federal court. Under such circumstances, of course, no conflict between federal and state law existed. Thus, both could be applied to the case within their respective spheres.[337]

---

329. 356 U.S. 525, 78 S. Ct. 893, 2 L. Ed. 2d 953 (1958).

330. CHARLES A. WRIGHT & MARY KAY KANE, THE LAW OF FEDERAL COURTS § 59, at 402 (7th ed. 2011).

331. 380 U.S. 460, 85 S. Ct. 1136, 14 L. Ed. 2d 8 (1965).

332. The provisions of Rule 4(d)(1) in effect at the time *Hanna* was decided are now found in Federal Rule 4(e)(2).

333. *See Hanna*, 380 U.S. at 463 n.1, 85 S. Ct. at 1139 n.1, 14 L. Ed. 2d at 12 n.1.

334. *See id.* at 462-63, 85 S. Ct. at 1138-39, 14 L. Ed. 2d at 11-12.

335. *See id.* at 465, 85 S. Ct. at 1140-41, 14 L. Ed. 2d at 13.

336. *See id.* at 466-69, 85 S. Ct. at 1141-43, 14 L. Ed. 2d at 13-16.

337. *See id.* at 470, 85 S. Ct. at 1143, 14 L. Ed. 2d at 16.

Hanna clarified the analysis used to determine the validity of Federal Rules. The Court's reinterpretation of *Ragan* and *Cohen* indicated that the first step in any analysis of a Federal Rule-state law conflict is to (1) determine whether the Federal Rule in question is broad enough to cover the issue in the case and (2) when possible, avoid the conflict. In addition, by making it clear that the generalized *Erie* analysis does not apply to issues of Federal Rules validity, the Court focused the lower federal courts on the proper source of statutory authority with which to determine Rule validity: the Rules Enabling Act rather than the Rules of Decision Act.[338]

Nevertheless, *Hanna* contained significant flaws. In *Hanna* itself, the Court missed an opportunity to avoid the conflict between federal and state law. At one point in the decision, the Court stated as follows: "Here, of course, the clash [between state law and the Federal Rule of Civil Procedure] is unavoidable. Rule 4(d)(1) states . . . that in-hand service is not required in federal courts."[339] Earlier, however, the Court had observed that the state statute's purpose was to insure that executors would receive actual notice of claims, which was also the purpose of Federal Rule 4(d)(1). The Federal Rule simply reflected a determination that this purpose could be accomplished by a "less cumbersome" method than prescribed by the state statute. Importantly, the Court noted that the purposes of both the Federal Rule and the state statute had apparently been accomplished because the defendant did not contend that actual notice of the action had not been received.[340] If the purposes of the state statute had indeed been fully achieved by applying the Federal Rule, no real conflict existed in the case.[341]

The Court also might have enhanced the conflict-avoidance process for future cases by discussing the need to evaluate the scope of state law. Conflicts between state law and Federal Rules of Civil Procedure can be avoided if either the Federal Rule or the state law does not apply to the case before the federal court. Some state laws are limited by their terms, policies, or purposes to enforcement only in state courts. Such laws cannot be said to conflict with Federal Rules because the states have limited the operation of their laws to their own judicial systems. Furthermore, it would be inappropriate for a federal court to invalidate a Federal Rule of Civil Procedure that conflicted with state substantive policies if the state substantive policies supported a rule applicable only in the state's own courts.[342]

Illustration 5-17. Assume that a state rule sets the time limits within which pleadings must be filed. Such a rule should not be interpreted as in conflict with the time limit provisions of Federal Rule 12(a) because the state rule is designed to prescribe time limits only for actions in the state courts. A state statute or rule

---

338. *See* Ralph U. Whitten, Erie *and the Federal Rules: A Review and Reappraisal After* Burlington Northern Railroad v. Woods, 21 CREIGHTON L. REV. 1, 13-14 (1987).

339. 380 U.S. at 470, 85 S. Ct. at 1143, 14 L. Ed. 2d at 16.

340. *See id.* at 462 n.1, 85 S. Ct. at 1139 n.1, 14 L. Ed. 2d at 12 n.1.

341. *See* Ralph U. Whitten, Erie *and the Federal Rules: A Review and Reappraisal After* Burlington Northern Railroad v. Woods, 21 CREIGHTON L. REV. 1, 15 (1987).

342. The failure of the Court in *Hanna* to point this out was, however, much more justifiable than its failure to avoid the conflict in the case by acknowledging that service pursuant to the Federal Rule had satisfied the purposes of the state statute. The underlying policy of the state service provision in Hanna—*i.e.*, the achievement of actual notice within the statutory period—was clearly applicable to the case before the Court. *See* Ralph U. Whitten, Erie *and the Federal Rules: A Review and Reappraisal After* Burlington Northern Railroad v. Woods, 21 CREIGHTON L. REV. 1, 16 (1987).

whose policies or purposes extend only to actions in the state's own courts is, for purpose of conflict-avoidance analysis, essentially no different than a statute that does not apply to the factual occurrences in the case. It is never appropriate for a federal court to apply such a state statute or rule in a federal action when a Federal Rule of Civil Procedure governs the issue.

* * * * *

It is important to note that the form of conflict avoidance discussed in the text and *Illustration 5-17—i.e.*, conflict avoidance by determining that the policies of the state rule are applicable only in state-court actions—is inappropriate under the general *Erie* (or Rules of Decision Act) analysis. For example, if a state has a policy supporting its door-closing statute that indicates that the statute is applicable only in actions brought in the state's own courts, the federal courts under the *Erie-Guaranty Trust-Byrd* analysis must still apply the statute. Under the Rules of Decision Act, failure to do so would violate the policies against forum shopping and inequitable administration of the law. Thus, all the federal court can do by way of conflict avoidance with state law under the general *Erie* analysis is to determine whether the state rule is applicable to the facts of the case before the court. If it is, then the court must apply the general *Erie* analysis to determine whether the state law can be disregarded. Thus, Justice Jackson was incorrect in his dissent in *Woods v. Interstate Realty Co.*[343] in taking the majority of the Court to task for failure to observe that the state door-closing statute in that case appeared to be limited in its applicability to actions in the state's own courts. Once it has been determined that a Federal Rule of Civil Procedure is applicable to the case, however, a federal court should examine whether the policies supporting the state rule are, even if "substantive" in some sense, applicable only in the state's own courts in order to avoid the conflict with the Federal Rule.[344]

The most serious difficulty with the *Hanna* opinion was the Court's failure to give content to the substantive rights restriction of the Rules Enabling Act. As Professor Ely has observed, "the text of the opinion did little more, so far as the interpretation of the Enabling Act was concerned, than point to *Sibbach*."[345] As noted above, *Sibbach* suggested that the Enabling Act's restrictions prohibit only Federal Rules that are purely substantive by anyone's definition, an interpretation that is not supported by either the language, the structure, or the legislative history

---

343. 337 U.S. 535, 539, 69 S. Ct. 1235, 1237-38, 93 L. Ed. 1524, 1527-28 (1949); *See also* Joseph P. Bauer, *The* Erie *Doctrine Revisited: How a Conflicts Perspective Can Aid the Analysis*, 74 NOTRE DAME L. REV. 1235, 1264-65 (1999) (arguing, *inter alia*, that the conflict-of-laws process of distinguishing between true and false conflicts could be useful in determining when Federal Rules really conflict with state law).

344. Contrary to this argument, one federal court has held that a state procedure that is limited in its operation to the state courts can make a general *Erie* analysis unnecessary under the Rules of Decision Act. In Swaim v. Fogle, 68 F. Supp. 2d 703 (E.D. Va. 1999), a Virginia procedure in medical malpractice cases allowed either party to request review by a medical malpractice review panel after commencement of a malpractice action, but limited the exercise of that right to actions commenced in state court. The court held that the federal court did not have to apply the procedure, noting that another federal court had reached a contrary conclusion. The procedure in question required submission of a request for a review panel to the clerk of the state court, who then forwarded it to the Virginia Supreme Court, which designated the review panel. Thus, to apply the procedure in federal court, the party requesting the panel would have to submit the request to the clerk of the federal court, who would then forward it to the Virginia Supreme Court in a similar manner, and the Virginia Supreme Court would have to designate a review panel in response to the request.

345. John H. Ely, *The Irrepressible Myth of* Erie, 87 HARV. L. REV. 693, 720 (1974).

of the Act.[346] Worse, taken together, the *Sibbach* and *Hanna* opinions suggest that the power delegated to the Court in the Enabling Act is the whole power of Congress to regulate the practice and procedure of the federal courts.[347] However, as discussed below, some procedural matters are so fundamental that they should be beyond the power of Congress to delegate to the Court. In addition, the Court cannot exercise some fundamental procedural powers that, while they are delegable, are beyond the rulemaking power in the face of an active policy by Congress regulating the procedural matter in question.[348]

4. The *Burlington Northern* Decision: Establishing Content for the Substantive Rights Restriction

After *Hanna*, no significant decision addressed a Federal Rule-state law conflict until 1987.[349] In that year, the Court decided *Burlington Northern Railroad*

---

346. The Court did state that "in measuring a Federal Rule against the standards contained in the Enabling Act and the Constitution" a court "need not wholly blind itself to the degree to which the Rule makes the character and result of the litigation stray from the course it would follow in state courts." 380 U.S. at 473, 85 S. Ct. at 1145, 14 L. Ed. 2d at 18. Given the Court's other remarks in the opinion, this statement cannot seriously be interpreted as designed to import an outcome determinative test of the *Guaranty Trust* variety into the Enabling Act. But if this is not the purpose of the statement, it is not clear what the Court had in mind. The Court's citation at this point to a portion of the *Sibbach* opinion, 312 U.S. 1, 13-14, 61 S. Ct. 422, 426-27, 85 L. Ed. 479, 484-85 (1941), is mystifying. Professors Wright and Kane's assessment of the decision seems most accurate: *Hanna* "provides the [Federal] Rules with a presumptive validity if not quite an automatic seal of approval." CHARLES A. WRIGHT & MARY KAY KANE, THE LAW OF FEDERAL COURTS § 59, at 404 (7th ed. 2011).

347. In *Sibbach*, the Court at one point stated: "Congress has undoubted power to regulate the practice and procedure of federal courts, and may exercise that power by delegating to this or other federal courts authority to make rules not inconsistent with the statutes or constitution of the United States . . . ." 312 U.S. at 9-10, 61 S. Ct. at 424-25, 85 L. Ed. at 482-83. The Court's citations of authority for this statement indicate that by its references to the constitutional limits on the rulemaking power, it may have had in mind separation-of-powers limitations, but this conclusion is uncertain. *See id.* nn.6-7, 61 S. Ct. at 424 nn.6-7, 85 L. Ed. at 483 nn.6-7; *see also* Ralph U. Whitten, *Separation of Powers Restrictions on Judicial Rulemaking: A Case Study of Federal Rule 4*, 40 ME. L. REV. 41, 51-53 (1988). However, *Hanna's* statements indicating that Congress had delegated all of its rulemaking power to the Court seemed to be more unqualified. *See Hanna*, 380 U.S. at 472-74, 85 S. Ct. at 1144-45, 14 L. Ed. 2d at 17-18. The startling feature of the statements in *Hanna* is that there is no distinction drawn between the power of Congress to regulate procedure directly and the power that Congress has delegated to the Court to regulate procedure in the Enabling Act, suggesting that Congress has delegated all the rulemaking power it can exercise.

348. *See generally* Ralph U. Whitten, *Separation of Powers Restrictions on Judicial Rulemaking: A Case Study of Rule 4*, 40 ME. L. REV. 41 (1988).

349. In 1980, the Court decided Walker v. Armco Steel Corp., 446 U.S. 740, 100 S. Ct. 1978, 64 L. Ed. 2d 659 (1980), in which it reaffirmed the *Hanna* interpretation of Ragan—*i.e.*, that the scope of Rule 3 of the Federal Rules of Civil Procedure is not broad enough to cover problems of commencement of an action for purposes of state statutes of limitations. That holding made it unnecessary for the Court to discuss the restrictions of the Enabling Act, and it did not do so. *See id.* at 752 n.14, 100 S. Ct. at 1986 n.14, 64 L. Ed. 2d at 669 n.14; *see also* Snow v. WRS Group, Inc., 73 Fed. App'x 2 (5th Cir. 2003) (state statute of limitations provided that if complaint served within 60 days of commencement, action is deemed commenced on date of filing, but if not, action is considered commenced on date service is effected; state service provisions do not conflict with Federal Rule 4(m), which provides complaint must be served within 120 days of commencement; Federal Rule merely provides procedural maximum time for service, while state statute is a substantive decision by the state that is an integral part of the several policies served by the statute of limitations; action time-barred under state statute); Torre v. Brickey, 278 F.3d 917 (9th Cir. 2001) (under Oregon statute of limitations, summons must be served within 60 days of the filing of the complaint in order for the action to commence as of the date the complaint is filed; plaintiffs failed to serve defendants within this period, though they did serve the defendant within the 120-day period permitted by Federal Rule 4(m); district court held the action time-barred and the court of appeals affirmed; court held that there was no conflict between Rule 4(m) and state law because Rule 4(m) does not control service for purposes of the statute of limitations); Larsen v. Mayo Med. Ctr., 218 F.3d 863 (8th Cir. 2000) (plaintiff sent the defendant a request for a waiver of service of process under Rule 4, but the defendant refused to execute the waiver, and by the time the plaintiff served the defendant in the ordinary way, the statute of limitations had run; plaintiff argued that the Federal Rules of Civil Procedure determined when an action was commenced in federal court, but the court of

v. Woods.[350] In *Burlington Northern*, the issue was the applicability in federal diversity actions of an Alabama statute imposing a fixed 10% penalty on appellants who obtain stays of damage judgments pending unsuccessful appeals. A personal injury action was brought against the railroad in Alabama state court and removed to the U.S. District Court in Alabama. The action resulted in a judgment for damages in favor of the plaintiffs. The railroad posted bond to stay the judgment pending appeal, but the judgment was affirmed without modification by the court of appeals. Upon motion of the plaintiffs-appellees, the court of appeals imposed a 10% penalty under the Alabama statute. The U.S. Supreme Court granted certiorari and reversed.

The Court held that the Alabama statute conflicted with Rule 38 of the Federal Rules of Appellate Procedure. Rule 38 provides that "[i]f a court of appeals shall determine that an appeal is frivolous, it may award just damages and single or double costs to the appellee." The Court also held that under the *Hanna* analysis, the Alabama statute had to give way to the Federal Rule. According to the Court, a Federal Rule that conflicts with state law is valid if it comports with both the constitutional restrictions on Congress' rulemaking power and the "substantive rights" restriction of the Rules Enabling Act.[351] In the Court's view, the constitutional limitations "define a test of reasonableness." "Rules regulating matters indisputably procedural are *a priori* constitutional. Rules regulating matters 'which, though falling within the uncertain area between substance and procedure, are rationally capable of classification as either,' also satisfy this constitutional standard."[352] The substantive rights restriction of the Rules Enabling Act is not violated by "[r]ules which incidentally affect litigants' substantive rights," as long as the rules are "reasonably necessary to maintain the integrity" of the "uniform and consistent system of rules governing federal practice and procedure."[353] Furthermore, "the study and approval given each proposed rule by the Advisory Committee, the Judicial Conference, and this Court, and the statutory requirement that the Rule be reported to Congress for a period of review before taking effect . . . give the Rules presumptive validity under both the constitutional and statutory constraints."[354]

Applying these standards, the Court concluded simply that "Federal [Appellate] Rule 38 regulates matters which can reasonably be classified as procedural, thereby satisfying the constitutional standard for validity."[355] The Court also found that the "displacement of the Alabama statute" by Appellate Rule 38 satisfied the statutory limits of the Rules Enabling Act because the selection "of a discretionary procedure" for penalizing unsuccessful litigants under Appellate Rule 38 "affects only the process of enforcing litigants' rights and not the rights themselves."[356]

---

appeals rejected the argument under the *Walker* case, holding that the state requirement of service within the limitations period did not conflict with the Federal Rules and that the action was time barred).

350. 480 U.S. 1, 107 S. Ct. 967, 94 L. Ed. 2d 1 (1987).

351. *See id.* at 5, 107 S. Ct. at 969-70, 94 L. Ed. 2d at 7.

352. *Id.* (quoting *Hanna*, 380 U.S. at 472, 85 S. Ct. at 1144, 14 L. Ed. 2d at 17).

353. *Id.*

354. *Id.* at 6, 107 S. Ct. at 970, 94 L. Ed. 2d at 7-8.

355. *Id.* at 8, 107 S. Ct. at 971, 94 L. Ed. 2d at 9.

356. *Id.*

The Court's opinion in *Burlington Northern* was flawed in many respects. It will suffice here to discuss two problems with the opinion.[357] First, the Court should have construed Federal Appellate Rule 38 as inapplicable to the case before it. Second, in evaluating Rule 38's validity under the Enabling Act, the Court's analysis was entirely conclusory. The analysis failed to (1) examine the Alabama statute carefully to determine whether it created a "substantive" right, (2) examine the impact of Rule 38 carefully to determine whether its impact was only "incidental," and (3) evaluate whether Rule 38 was "reasonably necessary" to the integrity of the uniform scheme of procedure that is the purpose of the Rules Enabling Act.

Although the Court correctly addressed the interpretation of Appellate Rule 38 as the first analytical step in the case,[358] the Court incorrectly interpreted Rule 38. In discussing the Rule's applicability, the Court observed that it was discretionary, rather than mandatory, in nature and that it only authorized the courts of appeals to penalize frivolous appeals and appeals interposed for delay, rather than all unsuccessful appeals.[359] From these correct observations, however, the Court proceeded to conclude that the Rule was broad enough to cover the case before it and conflicted with the Alabama statute. The Court observed that the "discretionary mode of operation [of Rule 38] unmistakably conflicts with the mandatory provision of Alabama's affirmance penalty statute."[360] Even though the Court was aware that Alabama possessed a rule allowing an appellate court the discretion to penalize frivolous appeals,[361] it nevertheless concluded that the discretion afforded under Rule 38 would be impaired if the federal court was obliged to follow the Alabama statute.[362]

The problem with the Court's analysis was that Federal Appellate Rule 38, by the Court's own admission, applies only to frivolous appeals. Rule 38 does not apply to unsuccessful, but nonfrivolous appeals. In the latter kind of case, Rule 38 confers no discretion at all on the courts of appeals. Therefore, it cannot confer any discretion with which the Alabama statute would interfere.[363] Thus, if the Court felt that the Alabama statute interfered with the discretion afforded the courts of appeals to penalize frivolous appeals, the Court should have directed that the statute could not be applied in cases in which a frivolous appeal is taken. The case then should

---

357. For a more complete critical evaluation of *Burlington Northern*, see Ralph U. Whitten, Erie *and the Federal Rules: A Review and Reappraisal After* Burlington Northern Railroad v. Woods, 21 CREIGHTON L. REV. 1 (1987).

358. *See Burlington Northern*, 480 U.S. at 4-5, 107 S. Ct. at 969-70, 94 L. Ed. 2d at 6-7. The Court was correct to interpret the Rule first, rather than state law, because the interpretation of the Federal Rule will determine the next appropriate analytical step in the case. If the Rule is determined to be inapplicable, the case must be analyzed under the *Erie-Guaranty Trust-Byrd* line of cases. If the Rule is determined to be applicable, the next step is to determine whether there is a conflict between the Rule and state law by interpreting the state law; if there is a conflict, the validity of the Rule under constitutional and statutory standards must be determined. Thus, in any case involving a potential Federal Rule-state law conflict, the interpretation of the Federal Rule is analytically prior to all other steps.

359. *Burlington Northern*, 480 U.S. at 6-7, 107 S. Ct. at 970, 94 L. Ed. 2d at 7-8.

360. *Id.* at 7, 107 S. Ct. at 970-71, 94 L. Ed. 2d at 8-9.

361. *See id.* Rule 38 of the Alabama Rules of Appellate Procedure provides: "In civil cases, if the appellate court shall determine on motion or ex mero motu that an appeal is frivolous, it may award just damages and single or double costs to the appellee." ALA. R. APP. P. 38.

362. *See Burlington Northern*, 480 U.S. at 7-8, 107 S. Ct. at 970-71, 94 L. Ed. 2d at 8-9.

363. *See* Ralph U. Whitten, Shady Grove Orthopedic Associates, P.A. v. Allstate Insurance Co.: *Justice Whitten Nagging in Part and Declaring a Pox on All Houses*, 44 CREIGHTON L. REV. 115, 122 (2010).

have been remanded for a determination whether the appeal in *Burlington Northern* was frivolous.[364]

The Court could only have concluded that the Alabama statute interfered with the operation of Rule 38 by interpreting Rule 38 as an implied negation of any other authority to levy penalties in cases of unsuccessful appeals in federal courts. But the Court did not construe Rule 38 in this manner. The Court's discussion was limited to the discretionary mode of the Rule's operation and its purpose to penalize only frivolous appeals.[365] Furthermore, had the Court construed the Rule as an implied negation of all other authority to impose penalties for unsuccessful appeals, it would have had to contend with its prior decision in *Cohen v. Beneficial Industrial Loan Corp.*[366] Recall that in *Cohen* the Court dealt with a potential conflict between Rule 23 of the Federal Rules of Civil Procedure and a state security-for-expenses statute. The Court held that the state statute had to be applied in federal diversity actions, finding that the statute did not conflict with Rule 23.[367] Despite the fact that Rule 23 said nothing about security for expenses, the Court did not interpret it as an implied negation of additional requirements for derivative actions that might be imposed by state law. If Rule 38 were to be interpreted as an implied negation of power to impose penalties under other sources of law, the Court would need to distinguish *Cohen* in some reasoned fashion. No such reasoned distinction was provided by the Court.[368]

Even if the Court's conclusions about the meaning of Federal Appellate Rule 38 had been correct, the Court's reasoning concerning its validity under the Rules Enabling Act was flawed. The Court explicitly acknowledged that the substantive rights restriction of the Act imposes "an additional requirement" over and above the constitutional test of whether a rule "falling within the uncertain area

---

364. *See* Ralph U. Whitten, Erie *and the Federal Rules: A Review and Reappraisal After* Burlington Northern Railroad v. Woods, 21 CREIGHTON L. REV. 1, 22 (1987).

365. *See Burlington Northern*, 480 U.S. at 6-8, 107 S. Ct. at 969-71, 94 L. Ed. 2d at 7-9. The Court had, correctly, interpreted the Alabama statute as having (1) the purpose of penalizing frivolous appeals and appeals taken for purposes of delay and (2) providing additional damages as compensation to appellees for having to suffer the ordeal of defending the judgments on appeal. It attempted to buttress its conclusion about the coextensive purposes of Rule 38 and the Alabama statute by pointing to Rule 37 of the Federal Rules of Appellate Procedure, which provides for an award of post-judgment interest to successful appellees, and 28 U.S.C. § 1961, which does likewise. The Court's conclusion was that these provisions operated to provide the compensation to the victorious appellee that was the second objective of the Alabama statute. *See id.* at 7 n.5, 107 S. Ct. at 971 n.5, 94 L. Ed. 2d at 8 n.5. However, this conclusion neglected the fact that Alabama also possesses a rule of appellate procedure authorizing an award of post-judgment interest on money judgments that are successfully affirmed, as well as a separate rule providing for discretionary penalties for frivolous appeals. *See* ALA. R. APP. P. 37, 38. Thus, the structure of Alabama law provided for post-judgment interest, penalties for frivolous appeals that might be imposed in addition to the 10% affirmance penalty under the statute, and the 10% penalty, which could all operate in the same case. *See* McAnnally v. Levco, Inc., 456 So. 2d 66 (Ala. 1984). Given these additional Alabama laws, it is impossible to see how the Supreme Court could have interpreted the purposes of Rule 38 and Alabama law to be coextensive. And if the Court was interpreting Rule 37 and 28 U.S.C. § 1961 to be implied negations of power to compensate for unsuccessful appeals drawn from other sources, its reasoning was as flawed as its reasoning about the scope of Federal Rule 38. *See* Ralph U. Whitten, Erie *and the Federal Rules: A Review and Reappraisal After* Burlington Northern Railroad v. Woods, 21 CREIGHTON L. REV. 1, 23-25 (1987).

366. 337 U.S. 541, 69 S. Ct. 1221, 93 L. Ed. 1528 (1949).

367. *Id.* at 556, 69 S. Ct. at 1230, 93 L. Ed. at 1541-42. Recall, also, that in *Hanna* the Court interpreted *Cohen* as a case in which the Federal Rule involved was not broad enough to cover the issue in the case. *See* Hanna v. Plumer, 380 U.S. 460, 470 n.12, 85 S. Ct. 1136, 1143 n.12, 14 L. Ed. 2d 8, 16 n.12 (1965); *see also* Kamen v. Kemper Fin. Servs., Inc., 500 U.S. 90, 111 S. Ct. 1711, 114 L. Ed. 2d 152 (1991) (holding, in part, that Federal Rule 23.1 is not broad enough to control the content of the demand requirement in shareholder derivative actions).

368. *See* Ralph U. Whitten, Erie *and the Federal Rules: A Review and Reappraisal After* Burlington Northern Railroad v. Woods, 21 CREIGHTON L. REV. 1, 25 (1987).

between substance and procedure, [is] rationally capable of classification as either."[369] Furthermore, the Court stated that the substantive rights restriction does not invalidate rules that "incidentally affect litigant's substantive rights . . . if [the rules are] reasonably necessary to maintain the integrity of [the uniform and consistent system of federal rules that it was the purpose of Congress to authorize under the Act]."[370] The standard articulated by the Court thus focuses in part on the state rules and in part on the extent to which a Federal Rule affects the operation of the state rule. Federal Rules may wholly supplant state procedural "rights" or rules. However, a Federal Rule can only "incidentally" affect state substantive rights, and even then such an incidental effect can only be justified if the Federal Rule in question is reasonably necessary to maintain the integrity of the uniform system of procedure that is the purpose of the Rules Enabling Act.

Under this standard, the Court incorrectly concluded that the application of Federal Appellate Rule 38 did not abridge, enlarge, or modify any substantive right within the meaning of the Enabling Act. By the Court's own admission, the Alabama statute was designed in part to provide additional damages as compensation for the appellee's ordeal of having to successfully defend an appeal. This provision is best characterized as creating a claim for relief for perceived harm done to the appellee by appellate litigation—harm that the state deems significant enough to justify relief. So viewed, the state's policies obviously extend beyond the usual procedural policies that exist for supplementing an appellee's damage award—*i.e.*, the policies of penalizing frivolous appeals and of compensating the appellee for loss of use of the judgment proceeds during the appeal through an award of post-judgment interest. Thus, even though the Alabama statute was aimed at a party's unsuccessful resort to a procedure, it was, like most other remedies, created for a seemingly substantive reason—compensation for harm thought to be significant by the state.

Furthermore, Federal Appellate Rule 38, as interpreted by the Court, did not have a mere "incidental effect" on the right created by the Alabama statute. It obliterated the right in all federal actions. It is difficult to see how a rule that altogether prevents a damage recovery allowed by state law can be described as only "incidentally" affecting the right that the recovery aims at vindicating. Nor is it apparent how a rule that effectively negates a right to the remedy of money damages in the circumstances covered by the Alabama statute is necessary to the integrity of the uniform system of federal procedure that the Enabling Act sought to insure. The system of federal procedure could operate both effectively and uniformly if discretion were afforded to the federal courts to impose penalties in whatever amounts are deemed desirable, but only in cases in which appeals are found to be frivolous.[371]

---

369. *Burlington Northern*, 480 U.S. at 5, 107 S. Ct. at 969-70, 94 L. Ed. 2d at 7.

370. *Id.*; *see also* Mississippi Publ'g Corp. v. Murphree, 326 U.S. 438, 445-46, 66 S. Ct. 242, 246-47, 90 L. Ed. 185, 191-92 (1946).

371. *See* Ralph U. Whitten, Erie *and the Federal Rules: A Review and Reappraisal After* Burlington Northern Railroad v. Woods, 21 CREIGHTON L. REV. 1, 30-35 (1987). The *Burlington Northern* test is applied in later chapters to specific Federal Rules. *See, e.g.*, Chapter 6(D)(5)*(b) infra* ("Relation Back of Amendments Changing a Claim or Defense"). *But see* Martin H. Redish & Dennis Murashko, *The Rules Enabling Act and the Procedural-Substantive Tension: A Lesson in Statutory Interpretation*, 93 MINN. L. REV. 26, 89-92 (2008) (arguing that "incidental" should not be interpreted to mean "unimportant").

5. Further Confusion: *Business Guides*, *Gasperini*, and *Semtek*

After *Burlington Northern*, discussed in the preceding subsection, but before the Court's latest decision under the Rules Enabling Act,[372] the Supreme Court decided three additional significant cases concerning the validity of a Federal Rule: *Business Guides, Inc. v. Chromatic Communications Enterprises, Inc.*,[373] *Gasperini v. Center for Humanities, Inc.*,[374] and *Semtek International, Inc. v. Lockheed Martin Corp.*[375] None of these cases provided much guidance about how the Rules Enabling Act branch of the *Erie* doctrine should operate. Furthermore, the *Gasperini* case created more confusion about the proper method of conflict avoidance in cases in which Federal Rules potentially conflict with state law.

In *Business Guides*, the Court considered a challenge to Rule 11 of the Federal Rules of Civil Procedure as applied to a represented party who had signed a document in violation of the rule, but in good faith.[376] The Court upheld the validity of Rule 11 under the Rules Enabling Act. In *Business Guides*, the president and director of research of the plaintiff corporation signed an application for a temporary restraining order and an affidavit in support of the application, both of which contained false information. The corporate plaintiff and the law firm representing the plaintiff were sanctioned by the district court for violating Rule 11. The sanctions were upheld by the Court of Appeals for the Ninth Circuit, and the Supreme Court affirmed. The Court held that Rule 11's objective standard of reasonable inquiry into the facts applied to represented parties as well as attorneys. The plaintiff argued that imposing sanctions on represented parties who had not acted in bad faith violated the Rules Enabling Act in two ways: (1) by authorizing fee shifting in a manner not approved by Congress; and (2) by creating a federal tort of malicious prosecution that encroached on various state causes of action. The Supreme Court rejected both of these arguments.

Following its previous decision in *Cooter & Gell v. Hartmarx Corp.*,[377] the Court held that Rule 11 of the Federal Rules of Civil Procedure did not constitute an impermissible fee shifting rule or effectively create a federal tort of malicious prosecution. In its Rules Enabling Act analysis, the Court repeated a statement it had first made in *Hanna v. Plumer* that the Federal Rules are to be judged as "prima facie" valid because of the participation by the Supreme Court, Congress, and the

---

372. Shady Grove Orthopedics Ass'n v. Allstate Ins. Co., 559 U.S. __, 130 S. Ct. 1431, 176 L. Ed. 2d 311 (2010), discussed in subsection 6, below.

373. 498 U.S. 533, 111 S. Ct. 922, 112 L. Ed. 2d 1140 (1991); *see also* Kamen v. Kemper Fin. Servs., Inc., 500 U.S. 90, 111 S. Ct. 1711, 114 L. Ed. 2d 152 (1991) (holding that Federal Rule 23.1, governing derivative actions in federal court, is not broad enough to control the content of the demand requirement in such actions and, therefore, that state law controls the content of the demand requirement in actions under the Investment Company Act of 1940). *See generally* Ralph U. Whitten, *Developments in the* Erie *Doctrine: 1991*, 40 AM. J. COMP. L. 967 (1992).

374. 518 U.S. 415, 116 S. Ct. 2211, 135 L. Ed. 2d 659 (1996). The Rules of Decision Act part of *Gasperini* was discussed in section E(3), *supra*.

375. 531 U.S. 497, 121 S. Ct. 1021, 149 L. Ed. 2d 32 (2001).

376. Federal Rule 11 is discussed in Chapter 6(F) *infra* ("Good Faith Pleading").

377. 496 U.S. 384, 110 S. Ct. 2447, 110 L. Ed. 2d 359 (1990).

Advisory Committee in the rulemaking process.[378] To overcome the "presumptive validity" that this process establishes for rules promulgated under the Enabling Act,[379] litigants must establish that the *Burlington Northern* test, discussed in the preceding subsection, has been violated. In applying this test in *Business Guides*, the Court stated that "[t]here is little doubt that Rule 11 is reasonably necessary to maintain the integrity of the system of federal practice and procedure and that any effect on substantive rights is incidental."[380] The Court concluded that Rule 11 did not inappropriately shift fees because (1) Rule 11 sanctions are not keyed to the outcome of litigation, but to specific filings within the litigation; (2) Rule 11 sanctions do not shift the entire cost of litigation, but only the cost of a discrete event; and (3) Rule 11 only mandates an "appropriate sanction," not necessarily attorney's fees.[381] Likewise, the Court held that Rule 11 did not impermissibly create a federal tort of malicious prosecution because the main objective of the rule is not to reward parties who are victimized by litigation, but to deter baseless filings and curb abuses. "Imposing monetary sanctions on parties that violated the Rule may confer a benefit on other litigants, but the Rules Enabling Act is not violated by such incidental effects on substantive rights."[382]

Justices Kennedy, Marshall, Stevens, and Scalia dissented. However, only the first three of these Justices felt that a Rules Enabling Act question was raised by the majority's interpretation of Rule 11. The dissenters stated that the majority's interpretation of Rule 11 raised "troubling concerns with respect to both separation of powers and federalism."[383] The dissenters argued that the majority's distinction between fee shifting and Rule 11 sanctions for "discrete events" within the litigation was improper where the "discrete event" was the filing of a lawsuit and the "appropriate sanction" was the payment of the opposing party's attorney's fees.[384] In addition, the dissenters argued that the majority's interpretation of Rule 11 did indeed create a federal tort of "negligent prosecution" or "accidental abuse of process" by placing duties on represented parties who sign papers under the rule that exceeded the duties imposed by state tort law.[385] However, the dissenters were

---

378. *See* 498 U.S. at 552, 111 S. Ct. at 933, 112 L. Ed. 2d at 1159. However, there exist the most serious possible reasons to question whether the participation by these groups in the rulemaking process assure rule validity. For a statement that the Court does not engage in meaningful independent review of the rules, see 146 F.R.D. 501-06 (1993) (statement of Justice White made upon the Court's promulgation of the 1993 amendments to the Federal Rules). For evidence supporting the Court's inattention to the rules, see Gene R. Shreve, *Eighteen Feet of Clay: Thoughts on Phantom Rule 4(m)*, 67 IND. L.J. 85 (1991). Furthermore, Justice Frankfurter warned years ago that the participation by Congress in the rulemaking process cannot be given significant weight in determining rule validity. "Plainly," wrote Frankfurter, "the rules are not acts of Congress and can not be treated as such. Having due regard to the mechanics of legislation and the practical conditions surrounding the business of Congress . . . to draw any inference of tacit approval from non-action by Congress is to appeal to unreality." Sibbach v. Wilson & Co., Inc., 312 U.S.1, 18, 61 S. Ct. 422, 428, 85 L. Ed. 479, 487 (1941). For documentation of confusion on the part of the Advisory Committee on the limits of the rulemaking power under the Rules Enabling Act, see Stephen Burbank, *The Rules Enabling Act of 1934*, 130 U. PA. L. REV. 1015, 1027, 1135-37 (1982); Ralph U. Whitten, *Separation of Powers Restrictions on Judicial Rulemaking: A Case Study of Federal Rule 4*, 40 ME. L. REV. 41, 73-81 (1988). On the whole, therefore, whatever the "presumption of validity" means, it would seem to be unjustified.

379. *See* Burlington N. R.R. Co. v. Woods, 480 U.S. 1, 6, 107 S. Ct. 967, 970, 94 L. Ed. 2d at 7-8 (1987).

380. 498 U.S. at 552, 111 S. Ct. at 934, 112 L. Ed. 2d at 1160.

381. *See id.* at 553, 111 S. Ct at 934, 112 L. Ed. 2d at 1160.

382. *Id.*

383. *Id.* at 565, 111 S. Ct. at 940, 112 L. Ed. 2d at 1168.

384. *See id.* at 566, 111 S. Ct. at 940, 112 L. Ed. 2d at 1168.

385. *See id.* at 567, 111 S. Ct. at 941, 112 L. Ed. 2d 1169.

reluctant to draw the conclusion that the flaws in the majority's reasoning actually produced a Rules Enabling Act violation. Rather, they argued that the Rules Enabling Act concerns raised by the plaintiff counseled strongly against an interpretation of Rule 11 that would avoid questions of validity.[386]

Business Guides provides little additional instruction about how to determine the validity of Federal Rules of Civil Procedure under the *Burlington Northern* test. For example, the decision does not indicate how to determine whether a Federal Rule impacts on a state right that is considered "substantive,"[387] or what kind of an impact a Federal Rule may have on such substantive rights before the impact is more than "incidental." Nor did the decision indicate how to determine when a Federal Rule is or is not "reasonably necessary to the uniform system of federal practice and procedure." The Court did not even provide guidance on the most general elements of the test. For example, what does it mean to say that the Federal Rules have "presumptive validity"? Clearly, this presumptive validity is not a factual presumption of the sort that normally aids a litigant in meeting its burden of proof at trial.[388] Yet, if it is not an ordinary "evidentiary presumption," it is unclear what it is. Given the Court's refusal *ever* to invalidate a Federal Rule under the Rules Enabling Act, the "presumption of validity" would seem to be simply a truism. The Federal Rules are not subject to successful attack under the Rules Enabling Act.[389]

As discussed in section E(3), above, the *Gasperini* case was decided under the Rules of Decision Act. However, to reach the Rules of Decision Act question, the Court had to determine whether Rule 59 of the Federal Rules of Civil Procedure, which governs the granting of new trials in federal court, was applicable to the case. The Court determined that Rule 59 did not apply to the case. Although conceding that one ground for a new trial under Rule 59 is that the damages awarded are excessive, the majority stated that "[w]hether damages are excessive for the claim-in-suit must be governed by some law. And there is no candidate for that governance other than the law that gives rise to the claim for relief here, the law of New York."[390] In other words, because Rule 59 did not provide a standard for determining whether damages were excessive, the case was thrown to the Rules of Decision Act side of the *Erie* doctrine, where the question was whether the federal courts could disregard the applicable state statute under that doctrine.

The Court's interpretation of Rule 59 was sensible, though it is not entirely free from doubt. Rule 59 states that new trials may be granted when a jury has

---

386. *See id.* at 568, 111 S. Ct. at 942, 112 L. Ed. 2d at 1170.

387. For example, when the Federal Rule conflicts with a state rule, does the state rule itself have to embody a "right" that can somehow be classified as "substantive"? Alternatively, does the Federal Rule impact on state substantive rights even if the state rule with which it conflicts is purely procedural, if application of the Federal Rule instead of the state rule would expand or contract a state right in some more general sense, as long as the expanded or contracted right could somehow be classified as "substantive"? For example, if a state rule governing relation back of amendments to avoid the bar of the statute of limitations is supported by purely procedural policies, but would bar relation back, would application of Rule 15(c) of the Federal Rules of Civil Procedure to allow relation back impact on a state substantive right because it would allow a claim to be prosecuted in federal court that would be barred in state court? *See* Chapter 6(D)(5)*(d) infra* ("Rules Enabling Act Issues with Rule 15(c)").

388. For a discussion of evidentiary presumptions, see Chapter 11(H)(3) *infra* ("Presumptions").

389. However, for additional discussion of how *Business Guides* might be interpreted, see Chapter 7(F)(5) *infra* ("Rules Enabling Act Issues Under Rule 13").

390. *Gasperini*, 518 U.S. at 437 n.22, 116 S. Ct. at 2224 n.22, 135 L. Ed. 2d at 680 n.22.

returned a verdict "for any of the reasons for which new trials have heretofore been granted in actions at law in the Courts of the United States."[391] This provision can be interpreted as incorporating the traditional reasons used by the federal courts for determining whether new trials should be granted because the damages awarded were excessive.[392] However, it is also plausible to read the rule as not listing the content of the grounds for which a new trial can be granted.[393] In choosing between the two interpretations, however, the method of conflict avoidance that the Court had established since *Hanna* is relevant, and that method has been employed by the Court inconsistently.

As discussed in subsections 3 & 4, above, in *Hanna* and *Burlington Northern*, the Court gave excessively broad interpretations to Federal Rules of Civil and Appellate Procedure, producing conflicts with state law when narrower, and arguably more plausible, interpretations would have avoided the conflicts. However, in the *Ragan* and *Cohen* cases, discussed in subsection 2, above, the Court had given narrow interpretations to Federal Rules of Civil Procedure that avoided conflicts between the rules and state law.[394] Furthermore, after *Hanna*, a case identical to *Ragan* arose involving a potential conflict between the provision in Federal Rule 3 that an action is commenced by filing a complaint with the court and a state rule that required commencement by service of process to toll the running of the state statute of limitations. In *Walker v. Armco Steel Corp.*,[395] the Court followed the *Ragan* approach to Federal Rule interpretation rather than that in *Hanna* and *Burlington Northern* and held that Rule 3 was not broad enough to cover commencement for purposes of the state statute of limitations. Curiously, in *Gasperini* the Court cited *Hanna*, *Burlington Northern*, and *Walker* all in the same footnote as if they were consistent with each other. After citing *Hanna* and *Burlington Northern* for the proposition that when a Federal Rule is on point and is "consonant" with the Rules Enabling Act and the Constitution, it "applies regardless of contrary state law,"[396] the Court then cited *Walker* for the proposition

---

391. FED. R. CIV. P. 59(a).

392. This was, in effect, the way that Justice Scalia interpreted the rule. *See* 518 U.S. at 467-68, 116 S. Ct. at 2239, 135 L. Ed. 2d at 698-99 (Scalia, J., dissenting).

393. *Cf.* CHARLES A. WRIGHT & MARY KAY KANE, LAW OF FEDERAL COURTS § 95, at 680 (6th ed. 2002) (Rule 59 does not list grounds for new trial, but only states that the usual grounds, including excessive damages, are permissible).

394. At least, this was Court's own view of what it had been doing when it viewed the *Ragan* and *Cohen* cases in retrospect in *Hanna*. *See* subsection 3 *supra*.

395. 446 U.S. 740, 100 S. Ct. 1978, 64 L. Ed. 2d 659 (1980); *see also* Habermehl v. Potter, 153 F.3d 1137 (10th Cir. 1998) (state law provided that filing a complaint with the court would toll the statute of limitations, but only if process served within 60 days after commencement; this was argued to conflict with 120-day period for service in Federal Rule 4(m); holding that Rule 4(m) and state law do not conflict and state law must be used to determine whether the limitations period had run). In Powell v. Jacor Commc'ns Corporate, 320 F.3d 599 (6th Cir. 2003), a plaintiff filed a pro se complaint in a personal injury diversity action. A federal statute required that her complaint be scrutinized to determine whether she was entitled to in forma pauperis status. As a result of the screening process, the summons was not issued until more than a year after she was injured, and the applicable Kentucky statute of limitations required that actions for personal injury be commenced by issuance of summons within one year of accrual of the action. The court of appeals held that the statute of limitations was tolled during the period when the plaintiff's in forma pauperis status was being determined. The court reasoned that the this was consistent with *Erie*, since the summons would have been issued immediately in state court and have been timely and the same would have been true in federal court had it not been for the in forma pauperis determination. Thus, the court reasoned that the federal court should not bar an action that would have been timely in state court.

396. 518 U.S. at 427 n.7, 116 S. Ct. at 2219 n.7, 135 L. Ed. 2d at 674 n.7.

that "[f]ederal courts have interpreted the Federal Rules . . . with sensitivity to important state interests and regulatory policies."[397]

The Court's overall approach to rule interpretation in *Gasperini*, together with its citation to its former cases employing incompatible methods of Rule interpretation, clouds the manner in which the lower federal courts should approach potential conflicts between Federal Rules and state law.[398] It may be that the Court's citation to *Walker* was a signal to the lower courts that the "more sensitive" method of interpretation is now back in vogue. Such a change would certainly be desirable. However, it would have been preferable for the Court to acknowledge the inconsistency in its past interpretive methodology and clearly mark the path to a new way. In the absence of such a straightforward rejection of the method used in cases like *Hanna* and *Burlington Northern*, inconsistency in the conflict-avoidance method of the lower federal courts was bound to persist.[399] Moreover, as we will see in the next subsection, if the Court was giving a signal that Federal Rules should be interpreted with sensitivity to state interests, the signal was short-lived.

In *Semtek International, Inc. v. Lockheed Martin Corp.*,[400] the Supreme Court held that federal law controls the scope of a federal diversity judgment, but that normally federal law will adopt the res judicata law of the judgment-rendering state to define the scope of the judgment. In the process, the Court confronted the applicability of Federal Rule 41(b) to the judgment in the case. A California federal district court had dismissed the action as time-barred under California limitations law, explicitly specifying that the judgment was on the merits. The plaintiff commenced a new action in Maryland state court, contending that the scope of the California judgment should be controlled by California state law, which would make the judgment of dismissal without prejudice. The Maryland Court of Special Appeals held that federal law controlled the scope of the federal judgment and precluded the action, and the Supreme Court granted certiorari and reversed.

The Court first considered the applicability of Federal Rule 41(b), which provides that all dismissals in federal court are on the merits unless they are otherwise specified to be without prejudice or fall within one of three specified exceptions. The Court reasoned that the expression "on the merits" in Rule 41(b) originally meant an adjudication that actually passed on the substance of a particular

---

397. *Id.*

398. Apparently, the *Gasperini* decision has created more confusion than even suggested in the text. On remand in *Gasperini*, the district court stated:

> The Supreme Court decision in this case represents an extension of *Erie* . . . or more likely a reversion by the Supreme Court to prior *Erie* doctrine since abandoned, of which *Guaranty Trust* . . . is the outstanding example. The Supreme Court in *Guaranty Trust* and again in *Gasperini* seems to have endorsed the outcome determinative test to determine whether a disputed point of law is procedural, and therefore governed by the Federal Rules of Civil Procedure, or substantive so as to be governed by state law.

Gasperini v. Center for Humanities, Inc., 972 F. Supp. 765, 767 (S.D.N.Y. 1997). Not in the wildest dreams of the authors of this treatise would they read *Gasperini* as holding that the outcome determinative test governs the applicability or validity of a Federal Rule of Civil Procedure.

399. *See generally* Joseph P. Bauer, *The* Erie *Doctrine Revisited: How a Conflicts Perspective Can Aid the Analysis*, 74 NOTRE DAME L. REV. 1235, 1264-65 (1999) (arguing, *inter alia*, that the process of distinguishing true from false conflicts used in the area of conflict of laws could be useful in determining when Federal Rules really conflict with state law); *see also* Bernadette Bollas Genetin, *Expressly Repudiating Implied Repeals Analysis: A New Framework for Resolving Conflicts Between Congressional Statutes and Federal Rules,* 51 EMORY L.J. 677 (2002).

400. 531 U.S. 497, 121 S. Ct. 1021, 149 L. Ed. 2d 32 (2001).

claim.[401] The Court noted, however, that the meaning of "judgment on the merits" had changed over the years and had "come to be applied to some judgments . . . that do *not* pass upon the substantive merits of the claim and hence do *not* (in many jurisdictions) entail claim-preclusive effect."[402] The Court then concluded that "it is no longer true that a judgment 'on the merits' is necessarily a judgment entitled to claim-preclusive effect."[403] This conclusion clearly does not follow from the Court's premises. The fact that more matters are today made "on the merits" than in former times does not mean that "on the merits" does not mean "claim preclusive." The reason that more dismissals are today considered "on the merits" is a byproduct of the extensive opportunities afforded in modern procedural systems for dealing with dismissals on procedural grounds.[404] If litigants do not avail themselves of those opportunities, but allow dismissals on procedural grounds to become final and do not appeal, there is no reason not to treat the judgment as claim preclusive just because it is on a ground that does not go (to use the Court's words) directly to the substantive merits of the case.

The Court also reasoned that Rule 41(b) "sets forth nothing more than a default rule for determining the import of a dismissal (a dismissal is 'upon the merits,' with the three stated exceptions, unless the court 'otherwise specifies')."[405] "This," reasoned the Court, "would be a highly peculiar context in which to announce a federally prescribed rule on the complex question of claim preclusion, saying in effect, 'All federal dismissals (with three specified exceptions) preclude suit elsewhere, unless the court otherwise specifies.'"[406] Further, the Court reasoned that "even apart from the purely default character of Rule 41(b), it would be peculiar to find a rule governing the effect that must be accorded federal judgments by other courts ensconced in rules governing the internal procedures of the rendering court itself."[407] The Court added that if Rule 41(b) did have a claim preclusive effect in other courts, it would arguably violate the Rules Enabling Act.[408] In addition, the Court stated that interpreting Rule 41(b) to have a claim preclusive effect in other courts

> would in many cases violate the federalism principle of *Erie Railroad Co. v. Tompkins* . . . by engendering "substantial variations [in outcomes] between state and federal litigation" which would "[l]ikely . . . influence the choice of a forum . . . ." With regard to the claim-preclusion issue involved in the present case, for example, the traditional rule is that expiration of the applicable statute of limitations merely bars the remedy and does not extinguish the substantive right, so that dismissal on that ground does not have claim-preclusive effect in other jurisdictions with longer, unexpired limitation periods. . . . Out-of-state defendants sued on

---

401. *See id.* at 501-02, 121 S. Ct. at 1024-25, 149 L. Ed. 2d at 38-39.

402. *Id.* at 502, 121 S. Ct. at 1025, 149 L. Ed. 2d at 39.

403. *Id. at* 503, 121 S. Ct. at 1025, 149 L. Ed. 2d at 39.

404. *See* Chapter 10(E) and Chapter 13(B)(2) discussing reasons for the expansion of the category of "on the merits" dismissals under modern procedural systems.

405. *Semtek,* 531 U.S. at 503, 121 S. Ct. at 1025, 149 L. Ed. 2d at 39.

406. *Id.*

407. *Id.*

408. *Id.*

> stale claims in California and in other States adhering to this traditional rule would systematically remove state-law suits brought against them to federal court—where, unless otherwise specified, a statute-of-limitations dismissal would bar suit everywhere.[409]

Thus, the Court concluded that "[t]he primary meaning of 'dismissal without prejudice' [in Rule 41(b)] is dismissal without barring the defendant from returning later, to the same court, with the same underlying claim."[410]

The Court's tortured interpretation of Rule 41(b) can only be explained by its expressed fear that an alternative interpretation would violate the Rules Enabling Act, though the Court's explanation of why this would be so under the prevailing test (derived from the *Burlington Northern* case discussed in the principal text) is nonexistent. Thus, the interpretation seemed to confirm that the Court has returned to a method of Rule interpretation that is designed to avoid conflicts with state law and avoid Rules Enabling Act issues.[411] However, restrictive rule interpretation can be justified only to a point. There is no question that the expression "on the merits" is designed to signify that a judgment should have a claim-preclusive effect in all courts. The Court's reasoning to the contrary casts in doubt a number of other rules that are designed to have claim-preclusive effects in other courts. Specifically, *Semtek* casts doubt on whether failure to plead a compulsory counterclaim under Rule 13(a) will produce claim preclusion in a successive action in another federal or a state court. Similarly, *Semtek* also casts doubt on whether the "second dismissal" rule of Rule 41(a)(1) will produce a claim-preclusive effect in a court other than the federal court in which the second dismissal occurs. Under the Court's decision, each of these rules is as susceptible as Rule 41(b) to interpretation as a rule designed for the regulation of the "internal proceedings" of the district courts. The doubt cast on the operation of these rules is a substantial price to pay for a

---

409. *Id.* at 504, 121 S. Ct. at 1026, 149 L. Ed. 2d at 40.

410. *Id.* at 505, 121 S. Ct. at 1027, 149 L. Ed. 2d at 41. The Court added that inability to return to the same court with the same claim "will ordinarily (though not always) have the consequence of not barring the claim from *other* courts . . . ." *Id.* However, the Court did not indicate what else would be necessary to make a dismissal claim preclusive in another court. *Semtek* was discussed in Styskal v. Weld Cnty. Bd. of Cnty. Comm'rs, 365 F.3d 855 (10th Cir. 2004). There, the district court dismissed supplemental state claims with prejudice under 28 U.S.C. § 1367(a) on the ground that they were insufficiently related to the federal claims in the action. The plaintiff appealed, arguing that the state claims should have been dismissed without prejudice. The court of appeals held that after *Semtek*, all the "with prejudice" designation meant was that the plaintiff could not refile the claims in the same district court that dismissed them, but that the plaintiff was not precluded from refiling the claims in state court. In Brereton v. Bountiful City Corp., 434 F.3d 1213 (10th Cir. 2006), the Tenth Circuit again confronted the *Semtek* problem in a case in which federal court dismissed a plaintiff's complaint with prejudice for lack of standing. The plaintiff did not refile an action in state court, but instead appealed, in part because of the "with prejudice" designation. The appellate court held that standing was a jurisdictional dismissal under Rule 41(b) and that the "with prejudice" designation was in error. Clarifying *Styskal*, the court interpreted *Semtek* as not designed to do away with the general rule, "reflected in Rule 41(b)," that a dismissal for lack of jurisdiction should be without prejudice. "We specifically *decline* to read *Styskal* as abrogating our duty to correct a district court disposition erroneously entered 'with prejudice' on jurisdictional grounds." *See also* Boyle v. American Auto Serv., 571 F.3d 734 (8th Cir. 2009) (finding Rule 41(b) applicable rather than potentially conflicting state law and affirming a district court's dismissal of an action for lack of prosecution with prejudice, without discussing what "with prejudice" meant).

411. *See* the discussion of *Gasperini supra.*

restrictive interpretation of Rule 41(b) simply to avoid Rules Enabling Act problems.[412]

How might the Court have interpreted Rule 41(b) in *Semtek* to avoid the Rules Enabling Act problem without distorting the operation of the rule or casting doubt on other Federal Rules of Civil Procedure containing preclusion doctrines, such as Rule 13(a)? One answer might simply be to recognize that Rule 41(b) was not designed to operate in cases involving dismissals under state statutes of limitations, where the conflict-of-laws context of the dismissals does not afford the ordinary procedural protections that attend other kinds of involuntary dismissals in federal court. When a federal court dismisses under a state statute of limitations, the plaintiff may, of course, appeal the dismissal if it is erroneous and obtain a reversal. If the dismissal is correct, however, the plaintiff cannot remain in the initial forum by resorting to the sorts of procedural devices that are available when the dismissal is on some other ground. For example, it is usually very easy for the plaintiff to state a claim upon which relief can be granted under the federal system of notice pleading embodied in Rule 8(a).[413] If the plaintiff's complaint is dismissed for failure to state a claim upon which relief can be granted, the plaintiff can amend the complaint or appeal if the plaintiff believes the district court erred in dismissing. If a plaintiff does not take advantage of amendment or appeal in these circumstances, but allows a judgment to become final and commences a new action on the same claim in another court, making the judgment claim preclusive under Rule 41(b) would not seem to violate any imaginable proscription imposed on the rulemaking power under the Rules Enabling Act.

Requiring a plaintiff to use the procedural opportunities given by the federal court system to correct error cannot plausibly be considered an abridgement of the plaintiff's substantive rights.[414] In comparison, however, if a plaintiff mistakenly sues in a forum in which the limitations period has run, there are no procedural steps the plaintiff can take to correct the mistake other than to file suit in another forum with a longer statute. If this would be permitted under the law of the state providing the shorter limitations period, it is difficult to see how there is any federal interest in providing otherwise in the Federal Rules. Thus, an interpretation of Rule 41(b) that would recognize that the rule only applies to cases in which the ordinary procedural protections afforded by the Federal Rules system can operate would resolve all Rules Enabling Act difficulties. Indeed, the three exceptions to the "on the merits" effect set out in Rule 41(b) exemplify this principle. Dismissals for lack of jurisdiction, improper venue, or failure to join a party under Rule 19 all represent situations in which the plaintiff will usually have to go to another court to sue if the

---

412. *Cf.* Boyle v. American Auto Serv., Inc., 571 F.3d 734 (8th Cir. 2009) (Rule 41(b) controls dismissals for failure to prosecute in federal court rather than conflicting state law that does not provide for dismissal on the merits).

413. This may be changing, but the point in the text remains valid even so. *See, e.g.*, Ashcroft v. Iqbal, 556 U.S. 662, 129 S. Ct. 1937, 173 L. Ed. 2d 868 (2009); Bell Atl. Corp. v. Twombly, 550 U.S. 544, 127 S. Ct. 1955, 167 L. Ed. 2d 929 (2007). These cases are discussed in Chapter 6(D)(2)*(b)(i) & (ii) infra.*

414. *See, e.g.*, Kamelguard v. Macura, 585 F.3d 334 (7th Cir. 2009) (Rule 12(b)(6) dismissal is on the merits under Rule 41(b) unless the court otherwise specifies; no citation of *Semtek*).

dismissals are correct.[415] If that is so, the usual procedural avenues for remaining in the court in which the action was originally commenced, such as amendment, are ordinarily of no use. Thus, reading an additional "statute of limitations" dismissal exception into the rule would do no violence to its operation—far less that the Supreme Court's interpretation of the rule in *Semtek*.[416]

Perhaps the worst part of the Court's opinion in *Semtek* was its statement that a claim-preclusive interpretation of Rule 41(b) would violate the policies of the general *Erie* doctrine—the avoidance of forum shopping and discrimination against citizens of the forum state. Although many questions had previously remained open about the operation of both the Rules Enabling Act and Rules of Decision Act, the one matter believed to be settled since the *Hanna* decision was that the general *Erie* policies do not control Rules Enabling Act questions. The Court's discussion of the *Erie* policies in conjunction with an issue concerning the validity of a Federal Rule of Civil Procedure now casts even that matter in doubt. Indeed, it was fair to ask, given that the *Semtek* decision was unanimous, whether any member of the current Supreme Court understands even the most basic propositions about the scope of the *Erie* doctrine.[417] After the Court's latest decision, discussed in the next subsection,[418] the question seems even more cogent.

6. The *Shady Grove* Decision

The Supreme Court's latest excursion into the Rules Enabling Act side of the *Erie* doctrine occurred in *Shady Grove Orthopedic Associates v. Allstate Insurance Co.*[419] The Rules of Decision Act portion of *Shady Grove*, as reflected in the dissenting opinion of Justice Ginsburg for four members of the Court, was discussed above in section E(3) of this chapter. In *Shady Grove*, New York had enacted a statute prohibiting class actions in suits for statutory penalties. Shady Grove commenced an action for such penalties in U.S. District Court in New York

---

415. This is obvious with regard to dismissals for lack of personal or subject-matter jurisdiction or improper venue. However, if a Rule 19 party is not joined, but can be, and the plaintiff refuses to effectuate the joinder, the action would be dismissed. This parallels the failure to state a claim example in the text. However, if a Rule 19 party cannot be joined because the party is not subject to personal jurisdiction, or because joinder would destroy subject-matter jurisdiction or venue, the plaintiff may have to sue elsewhere, which parallels the jurisdiction and venue exceptions in Rule 41(b), as well as the statute of limitations example. *See* Chapter 8(C)(3) *infra* ("Joinder of Persons Needed for Just Adjudication").

416. *See* ROBERT L. FELIX & RALPH U. WHITTEN, AMERICAN CONFLICTS LAW § 107, at 354-55 (6th ed. 2011).

417. For a discussion of *Semtek*, including many of the issues examined in the text, above, see Stephen B. Burbank, Semtek, *Forum Shopping, and Federal Common Law*, 77 NOTRE DAME L. REV. 1027 (2002). *See also* Earl C. Dudley, Jr. & George Rutherglen, *Deforming the Federal Rules: An Essay on What's Wrong With the Recent* Erie *Decisions*, 92 VA. L. REV. 707 (2006); June F. Entman, *Federalism, Claim Preclusion, Statutes of Limitations, and the Dilution of a Federal Rule*, 4 TENN. J. PRAC. & PROC. 9 (2002); Thomas Sciacca, Case Note, *Has the Supreme Court Sacrificed Stare Decisis to Clarify Res Judicata? An "On the Merits" Evaluation of Federal Common Law Jurisprudence After* Semtek, 23 PACE L. REV. 313 (2002); Justin Sobey, Note, Semtek International Inc. v. Lockheed Martin Corp.: *An* Erie *Solution to Interjurisdictional Preclusion Choice of Law*, 54 BAYLOR L. REV. 555 (2002); Howard M. Wasserman, *The Roberts Court and the Civil Procedure Revival*, 31 REV. LITIG. 313 (2012); Patrick Woolley, *The Sources of Federal Preclusion Law After* Semtek, 72 U. CINN. L. REV. 527 (2003) (arguing, in spite of *Semtek*, that Federal Rules of Civil Procedure can, except in narrow circumstances, provide rules of preclusion and that even in diversity actions there should be uniform federal rules of preclusion).

418. *See* Shady Grove Orthopedic Assocs. v. Allstate Ins. Co., 559 U.S. __, 130 S. Ct. 1431, 176 L. Ed. 2d 311 (2010). *Shady Grove* was also discussed in section E(3), above, where Justice Ginsburg's opinion on the Rules of Decision Act aspects of the case was examined.

419. 559 U.S. __, 130 S. Ct. 1431, 176 L. Ed. 2d 311 (2010).

and sought to have it certified as a class action under Rule 23 of the Federal Rules of Civil Procedure. On motion of the defendant Allstate, the district court dismissed, and the Second Circuit Court of Appeals affirmed, construing Rule 23 as inapplicable to the case. The Supreme Court granted certiorari and reversed.

A majority of the Court concluded that Rule 23 was applicable to the case and that the Rule was valid under the Rules Enabling Act. However, Justice Stevens, concurring, made up a majority of five for the conclusion that Rule 23 was applicable to the case, but his opinion differed on the question of the proper standard to determine whether Rule 23 conflicted with state law and violated the Rules Enabling Act's substantive rights restriction. This meant that there was no majority on the interpretation of the scope of the substantive rights restriction, because, as discussed in section E(3), above, Justice Ginsburg, for herself and three members of the Court, dissented, finding Rule 23 inapplicable and the New York law thus obligatory under the Rules of Decision Act.

On the applicability of Rule 23, the Second Circuit Court of Appeals had construed Rule 23 and the New York statute as not in conflict. Rather, the court of appeals had held that Rule 23 only dealt with the question whether a given class was certifiable under Rule 23's criteria, while the New York statute dealt with an antecedent question: whether the type of claim in the case is eligible for class treatment in the first place. Justice Scalia, writing for a majority of the Court, disagreed with this interpretation of Rule 23. The majority refused to read Rule 23 as empowering a federal court to certify an action as a class action only when some other law has made the class's claims eligible for class treatment.[420] Rather, the majority read the rule as allowing class actions in all United States District Courts when Rule 23's criteria are met.[421]

Similarly, the majority refused to read the state law as affecting only the remedy the plaintiff can get if it wins, a position taken by the dissenters.[422] In this last regard, the dissent cited legislative history that indicated the limitation on class actions in the state statute was designed for defendant-protection purposes—to prevent ruinous recoveries against defendants in single suits for penalties.[423] The majority described this legislative history as "sparse,"[424] but a plurality of the Court stated that even if it were credited, the New York statute conflicted with Rule 23.[425] The majority rejected an approach to interpretation of Federal Rules of Civil Procedure that it described as "state friendly."[426] The majority's concern was that the so-called "state friendly" approach would involve examination of the "subjective intentions" of state legislatures in numerous cases, making the task of Federal Rule interpretation arduous and confusing.[427] Furthermore, the result of the process, even were it to avoid conflict between Rule 23 and the New York law,

---

420. *See id.* at __, 130 S. Ct. at 1438, 176 L. Ed 2d at 318.

421. *See id.*

422. *See id.* at __, 130 S. Ct. at 1440-41, 176 L. Ed 2d at 320-21.

423. *See id.* at __, 130 S. Ct. at 1464-67, 176 L. Ed 2d at 345-49 (Ginsburg, J., dissenting).

424. *See id.* at __, 130 S. Ct. at 1440, 176 L. Ed 2d at 320.

425. *See id.* This part of the opinion must be considered a plurality opinion only, because Justice Stevens ultimately concluded that Rule 23 and state law did not conflict because the state law was supported only by procedural policies. Justice Stevens' opinion is discussed *infra*.

426. *See id.* at __, 130 S. Ct. at 1440, 176 L. Ed 2d at 320-21.

427. *See id.* at __, 130 S. Ct. at 1440-41, 176 L. Ed 2d at 320-21.

would do so by invalidating Rule 23 as applied to the case on the grounds the rule conflicted with the substantive policies supporting the state law,[428] a concern that was later addressed by Justice Scalia's opinion (for himself and three other members of the Court) interpreting the proper standard for judging the validity of a Federal Rule under the substantive rights restriction of the Rules Enabling Act (discussed below).

The majority's approach to the interpretation of Rule 23 is supported by two of the principal policies supporting the Rules Enabling Act: to establish a system of procedural rules for the federal courts that is (1) uniform throughout the nation and (2) trans-substantive—*i.e.,* that results in the application of the same procedural rules regardless of the source of the substantive law being enforced in an action.[429] An interpretation of Rule 23 that wold have held it inapplicable would have meant that the availability of class actions in the federal courts would depend throughout the nation on state substantive restrictions in class action cases, which even the dissent recognized were numerous.[430] However, the interpretive approach of the majority did not square with the Court's approach to Federal Rule interpretation in two most recent decisions prior to *Shady Grove*. Recall that in the *Gasperini* case, examined in section F(5), above, the Court had interpreted Rule 59 with "sensitivity to state interests," rendering it inapplicable to the issue before the Court, with the result that state law was held to control under the Rules of Decision Act.[431] It is perhaps understandable that Justice Scalia's opinion did not embrace the *Gasperini* method of Federal Rule interpretation, given that his dissenting opinion in that case was based in part on the interpretation of Rule 59 as applicable to the case. However, there can be no adequate explanation for Justice Scalia's interpretation of Rule 23 in *Shady Grove* when it is compared with his tortured interpretation of Rule 41(b) in the *Semtek* case, also discussed in section F(5), above. Candor requires that the difference in rule interpretation in the two cases be explained. However, the only place in Justice Scalia's opinion where any such explanation appeared was the following passage:

> If the Rule were susceptible of two meanings—one that would violate § 2072(b) [the substantive rights restriction of the Enabling Act] and another that would not—we would [interpret Rule 23 to avoid overstepping its authorizing statute] . . . ; *cf. Semtek Int'l, Inc. v. Lockheed Martin Corp.* . . .[432]

Given the position that Justice Scalia took on the content of the substantive rights restriction of the Enabling Act in *Shady Grove* (discussed below), this explanation is inadequate. For under that position, it is hard to see how Rule 41(b) could have been treated as invalid in *Semtek*, or, for that matter, how any other Federal Rule could be treated as invalid.

Having interpreted Rule 23 as applicable to the case, Justice Scalia's opinion turned to the question of whether the rule was valid under the substantive

---

428. *See id.* at __, 130 S. Ct. at 1441-42, 176 L. Ed 2d at 321-22.

429. *See* Chapter 1(D)(11) *supra* (discussing the purposes of the Federal Rules).

430. *See Shady Grove*, 559 U.S. at __ n.11, 130 S. Ct. at 1468 n.11, 176 L. Ed. 2d at 349 n.11 (Ginsburg, J., dissenting).

431. *See Gasperini*, 518 U.S. 415, 426 n.7, 116 S. Ct. 2211, 2220 n.7, 135 L. Ed. 2d at 674 n.7(1996).

432. *Shady Grove*, 559 U.S. at __, 130 S. Ct. at 1441-42, 176 L. Ed. 2d at 321-22.

rights restriction of the Rules Enabling Act. Because Justice Stevens did not concur in this portion of the opinion, it constitutes a plurality opinion for four members of the Court only, the dissenters having found Rule 23 inapplicable and also having found that the New York statute should control under the Rules of Decision Act.[433] Technically, this means that the *Burlington Northern* test is still the controlling authority on the meaning of the substantive rights restriction as a matter of stare decisis, because the test articulated in the latter case has not been overruled. Nevertheless, the possibility that in a future case another justice of the Court will join with the plurality's view creates great uncertainty on the standard that will be used to judge the validity of Federal Rules of Civil Procedure that conflict with state law.

In essence, Justice Scalia's opinion for the plurality returned to the *Sibbach* standard for determining whether a Federal Rule of Civil Procedure "abridges, enlarges, or modifies" a litigant's substantive rights.[434] In the process, the plurality made it absolutely clear that this standard focused on the procedural character of the Federal Rule and not on whether the state rule with which the Federal Rule conflicted was supported by "substantive policies." The plurality opinion stated:

> We have long held that this limitation means that the Rule must "really regulat[e] procedure,—the judicial practice for enforcing rights and duties recognized by substantive law and for justly administering remedy and redress for disregard or infraction of them." *Sibbach* . . . .; see *Hanna* . . . . The test is not whether the rule affects a litigant's substantive rights; most procedural rules do. . . . What matters is what the rule itself regulates. If it governs only "the manner and means" by which the litigants' rights are "enforced," it is valid; if it alters the rules of decision by which [the] court will adjudicate those rights, " it is not. . . .
>
> Applying that test, we have rejected every statutory challenge to a Federal Rule that has come before us. . . .
>
> [W]e think it obvious that rules allowing multiple claims (and claims by or against multiple parties) to be litigated together are . . . valid. . . .
>
> . . . .
>
> Allstate argues that Rule 23 violates § 2072(b) because the state law it displaces, . . . creates a right that the Federal Rule abridges—namely, a "substantive right . . . not to be subjected to aggregated class-action liability" in a single suit. . . . As a fallback argument, Allstate argues that even if [the state statute] is a procedural provision, it was enacted "for *substantive reasons*," . . . . Its end was not to improve "the conduct of the litigation process itself" but to alter "the outcome of that process." . . .

---

433. *See supra* section (E)(3). It should also be noted that Justice Sotomayor did not concur in that portion of Justice Scalia's opinion arguing in favor of the validity of Federal Rules that conflict with state rules "bound up" with state substantive rights. *See* Craig T. Cagney, *O Sonia Where Art Thou?: Why Justice Sotomayor's Silent "Opinion" Should Serve as* Shady Grove's *Holding*, 80 FORDHAM L. REV. 189 (2011)

434. *See supra* section F(1), discussing *Sibbach*.

> The fundamental difficulty with both these arguments is that the substantive nature of New York's law, or its substantive purposes, *makes no difference*. A Federal Rule of Procedure is not valid in some jurisdictions and invalid in others—or valid in some cases and invalid in others—depending upon whether its effect is to frustrate a state substantive law (or a state procedural law enacted for substantive purposes). That could not be clearer in *Sibbach* . . . .[435]

Under this view, a federal rule of procedure created under the Rules Enabling Act will not be invalid unless it embodies what the *Byrd* case described as a rule "defining state rights and obligations,"—*i.e.,* a pure substantive rule.[436] This is unlikely in the extreme to occur. Therefore, as observed earlier in discussing *Sibbach,*[437] should the plurality's view of the substantive rights restriction be adopted by a majority of the Court in the future, it will be virtually impossible to invalidate any Federal Rule of Civil Procedure under the Rules Enabling Act. For the plurality's view literally equates the power given to the Supreme Court under the Act with the power possessed by Congress to regulate procedure under Article III and the Necessary and Proper Clause of the Constitution.[438]

Justice Stevens, concurring in the judgment, took a different view of the Rules Enabling Act analysis than the plurality. Under his view, if a Federal Rule created under the Act unavoidably conflicts with a state law, a federal court must not assume the Federal Rule is valid simply because Congress could have created the rule.[439] Rather, it must pay attention to whether the conflicting state rule is, though procedural in form, an attempt to define the scope of the state substantive right being enforced in the case or is significantly bound up with that right.[440] If it is, the federal rule may not validly be applied to adversely affect the state substantive policies in the particular case. Importantly, this view, along with the Federal Rule interpretive method employed by the dissenters, discussed in section

---

435. *Shady Grove*, 559 U.S. at __, 130 S. Ct. at 1442-44, 176 L. Ed. 2d at 322-24. The plurality's view of the substantive rights restriction of the Rules Enabling Act was further described in its rejection of Justice Stevens' view of the restriction in concurrence. *See id.* at __, 130 S. Ct. at 1444-47, 176 L. Ed. 2d at 325-28. Justice Stevens' view is discussed *infra*.

436. *See supra* section E(2), describing the *Byrd* categorization process.

437. *See supra* section F(1).

438. *See* U.S. Const. Art III, § 2; art. I, § 8, cl 18. Note, however, that under the plurality's focus on the nature of the Federal Rule of Civil Procedure to the exclusion of the state law involved in the case, there is a danger that a state rule cast in procedural form that is really designed to create or abolish a state claim or defense would be ignored, thus violating even the power of Congress to regulate procedure under Article III. *Cf.* ROBERT L. FELIX & RALPH U. WHITTEN, AMERICAN CONFLICTS LAW § 110, at 371 -72 (6th ed. 2011) (discussing the problem of state seat belt statutes).

439. *Shcdy Grove*, 559 U.S. at __, 130 S. Ct. at 1451, 176 L. Ed. 2d at 332 (Stevens, J., concurring): "Congress may have the constitutional power 'to supplant state law with rules that are 'rationally capable of classification as procedure,' . . . but we should generally presume that it has not done so." *See also id.* at __, 130 S. Ct. at 1452, 176 L. Ed. 2d at 333-34 (footnotes omitted):

> Justice Scalia believes that the sole Enabling Act question is whether the federal rule "really regulates procedure," . . . . I respectfully disagree. This interpretation of the Enabling Act is consonant with the Act's first limitation to "general rules of practice and procedure," . . . but it ignores the second limitation that such rules also not "abridge, enlarge, or modify *any* substantive right," . . . (emphasis added), and in so doing ignores the balance that Congress struck between uniform rules of procedure and respect for a State's construction of its own rights and remedies. It also ignores the separation-of-powers presumption . . . and federalism presumption that counsel against judicially created rules displacing state substantive law.

440. *See id.* at __, 130 S. Ct. at 1448-50, 176 L. Ed. 2d at 329-31, especially notes 8-9.

E(3), above, produces a five-member majority of the Court for focusing on the policies supporting a state law that potentially conflicts with a Federal Rule of Civil Procedure. While the dissenters focus on those policies in order to avoid conflicts with Federal Rules and state law, Justice Stevens focuses on the policies to determine whether a Federal Rule can be validly applied in a particular case without affecting state rights in violation of the Enabling Act.[441]

However, Justice Stevens concluded that the New York law did not embody policies that are "intimately bound up in the scope of a substantive right or remedy."[442] In his view, therefore, for a Federal Rule to abridge state substantive rights, the conflicting state procedural rule must not just be supported by substantive policies, but must be the kind of rule that *Byrd* described as "bound up" with the definition of state substantive rights and obligations.[443] The difficulty is, of course, that the New York rule looks a lot like the kind of rule that should be considered bound up with substantive rights in the *Byrd* sense. As Justice Ginsburg's opinion argued, the rule seems aimed at protection of defendants from ruinous liability in single suits for penalties.[444] As such, it appears to fit the definition of a bound up rule suggested in *Byrd*: a procedural rule designed to advance or retard the enforcement of the "pure substantive rights" involved in the action.[445] Clearly, the ability to bring a class action will influence whether some plaintiffs with penalty claims will proceed with their actions at all, and the inability to seek penalties in a class format provides a valuable protection for defendants subject to such claims. Justice Stevens' view seems to be that because the New York statute did not "serve[] to define who can obtain a statutory penalty or that certifying such a class would enlarge New York's remedy," it did not fit the category of cases that would require a Federal Rule to give way.[446] Thus, Rule 23 simply conflicted with a state rule supported by procedural rather than substantive policies and was, consequently, valid. Left unclear was exactly what kind of state law would fit Justice Stevens' version of the "bound up" category of state rules.[447]

---

441. *But see* Godin v. Schencks, 629 F.3d 79 (1st Cir. 2010) (canvassing the Scalia and Stevens' opinions and then citing the Stevens opinion at the end of a process in which the court avoided the conflict between Federal Rules 12(b)(6) and 56, on the one hand, and state law, on the other, by considering both the Federal Rules and the state law).

442. *Id.* at __, 130 S. Ct. at 1457-60, 176 L. Ed. 2d at 338-41.

443. *See* section E(2) *supra*, discussing *Byrd* and the bound-up category of state rules.

444. *See Shady Grove*, 559 U.S. at __, 130 S. Ct. at 1464-65, 176 L. Ed. 2d at 345-47 (Ginsburg, J., dissenting).

445. *See id.*; *see also* section E(2) *supra*, discussing the scope of the bound-up category of state rules.

446. *See Shady Grove*, 559 U.S. at __, 130 S. Ct. at 1458, 176 L. Ed. 2d at 340 (Stevens, J., concurring). Justice Stevens continued with an analysis of the state statute's history that indicated that it might only be supported by "a classically procedural calibration of making it easier to litigate a claim in New York courts . . . only when it is necessary to do so, and not making it *too* easy when the class tool is not required." *See id.* at __, 130 S. Ct. at 1459, 176 L. Ed. 2d at 340. This, if true, would remove the New York law from the bound up category altogether.

447. *See also* Craig T. Cagney, *O Sonia Where Art Thou?: Why Justice Sotomayor's Silent "Opinion" Should Serve as* Shady Grove's *Holding*, 80 FORDHAM L. REV. 189 (2011) (discussing Justice Sotomayor's failure to concur in the part of Justice Scalia's opinion that argued that Federal Rules were valid even when they conflicting with state laws bound up with substantive rights); Jennifer S. Hendricks, *In Defense of the Substance-Procedure Dichotomy*, 89 WASH. U. L. REV. 103 (2011) (arguing in favor of an approach that emphasizes federal procedure so that state lawmakers can act with knowledge of the procedures through which state policy will be enforced and to encourage those lawmakers to act openly through the substantive law rather than manipulate outcomes with special procedures).

On the whole, the several opinions in *Shady Grove* constitute an unfortunate excursion into both the Rules of Decision Act and the Rules Enabling Act areas of the *Erie* doctrine. As discussed in both this subsection and in section E(3), above, there are numerous questions in both parts of the doctrine that call out for clarification. It cannot be said that *Shady Grove* has produced that clarification. Of perhaps more importance is the danger that one additional member of the Court will join Justice Scalia's view of the substantive rights restriction of the Enabling Act in a future case. Although this would have the benefit of making the analysis under that restriction easier, it would be at the expense of validating all Federal Rules promulgated under the Act at the expense of a broad range of substantive interests. It would do well for the Court to consider the admonition of Justice Harlan, concurring in the *Hanna* case, that *Erie* established fundamental propositions concerning the role of the federal courts in the constitutional order.[448] These propositions are not confined to Rules of Decision Act cases, or even to cases in which federal courts are supplanting "pure" state substantive laws with federal rules of decision, as under *Swift*. They also require a proper respect for state substantive lawmaking power when it is exercised in the form of procedural rules supported by substantive policies. This respect should also produce deference to such state lawmaking power when it comes into conflict with procedural rules created under the Enabling Act. Proper respect in this regard is not demonstrated by an approach under the Act that thwarts the ability of the states to make substantive policy in procedural form. Nor is proper respect demonstrated for the prerogatives of Congress to control federal procedure when the Court interprets the scope of its rulemaking power under the Act to be coextensive with that of Congress. A uniform, trans-substantive scheme of procedure for the federal courts is not so important that it should overwhelm all other policy considerations.

7. Separation-of-Powers Restrictions on Judicial Rulemaking

In addition to the restrictions on the rulemaking power that may exist under the Rules Enabling Act, separation-of-powers restrictions may exist on the Supreme Court's authority to make even purely procedural rules under certain circumstances. The Court has seldom addressed the separation-of-powers restrictions that may exist on judicial rulemaking. However, one important early decision, *Wayman v. Southard*,[449] did address these restrictions. The Process Act of 1789[450] established a static conformity to state law on procedural matters. The Process Act of 1792[451] continued this static conformity, but provided power in the federal courts to make "such alterations and additions" as the courts would "deem expedient." It also gave the Supreme Court power to prescribe supervisory rules for the lower federal

448. *See* Hanna v. Plumer, 380 U.S. 460, 474-75, 85 S. Ct. 1136, 1145-46, 14 L. Ed. 2d 8, 18-19(1965) (Harlan, J., concurring).

449. 23 U.S. (10 Wheat.) 1, 6 L. Ed. 253 (1825); *see also* Robert P. Wasson, Jr., *Resolving Separation of Powers and Federalism Problems Raised by the Rules of Decision Act, and the Rules Enabling Act: A Proposed Solution*, 32 CAP. U. L. REV. 519 (2004).

450. ch. 21, § 2, 1 Stat. 93, 93-94; *see* Chapter 1(D)(10) *supra* ("Early Procedure in the Federal Courts").

451. ch. 36, § 2, 1 Stat. 275, 276; *see* Chapter 1(D)(10) *supra* ("Early Procedure in the Federal Courts").

courts.[452] In *Wayman*, the Supreme Court addressed the validity of this congressional delegation of rulemaking power as applied to a rule made by a lower federal court:

> It will not be pretended that Congress can delegate to the Courts, or to any other tribunals, powers which are strictly and exclusively legislative. But Congress may certainly delegate to others, powers which the legislature may rightfully exercise itself. . . . The Courts . . . may make rules directing the returning of writs and processes, the filing of declarations and other pleadings, and other things of the same description. It will not be contended, that these things might not be done by the legislature, without the intervention of the Courts; yet it is not alleged that the power may not be conferred on the judicial department.
>
> The line has not been exactly drawn which separates those important subjects, which must be entirely regulated by the legislature itself, from those of less interest, in which a general provision may be made, and power given to those [persons] who are to act under such provisions to fill up the details. . . .
>
> . . . .
>
> . . . The power given to the Court to vary the mode of proceeding in this particular [*i.e.*, to regulate whether the officer proceeding under a writ of execution shall leave the property taken by the officer in the hands of the debtor until the day of the sale], is a power to vary minor regulations, which are within the great outlines marked out by the legislature in directing the execution. To vary the terms on which a sale is to be made, and declare whether it shall be on credit, or for ready money, is certainly a more important exercise of the power of regulating the conduct of the officer, but is one of the same principle. It is, in all its parts, the regulation of the conduct of the officer of the Court in giving effect to its judgments. A general superintendence over this subject seems to be properly within the judicial province, and has always been so considered.[453]

Several important principles can be derived from this passage. First, Congress has the power to regulate the procedure of the federal courts. Second, Congress may delegate some of its power to regulate procedure to the federal courts. Third, Congress may not delegate any power to regulate procedure that is "strictly and exclusively legislative." Fourth, the line between procedural regulations that are within the exclusive power of Congress and regulations that Congress may delegate the power to the courts to make is not precisely drawn by the Constitution. However, the line should be drawn by separating "important subjects" from those of "less interest," which involve only the "details" of procedure. Fifth, it is relevant in drawing the line between important matters and

452. *See* Process Act of 1792, ch. 36, § 2, 1 Stat. 275, 276.
453. *Wayman*, 23 U.S. (10 Wheat.) at 42-45, 6 L. Ed. at 262-63.

matters of detail to determine whether a "general superintendence" over the subject has traditionally been considered "properly within the judicial province."[454]

The Supreme Court has never materially clarified the boundaries between those procedural matters that only Congress can regulate and those which Congress can delegate to the courts.[455] Nevertheless, several factors can be identified that should be taken into account in determining whether a delegation of rulemaking power to the courts is valid. First, it is relevant to determine whether Congress has legislated within a procedural area. If it has not done so, and if it has given general rulemaking power to the courts, there will be greater power in the courts to regulate the area than if Congress has extensively dealt with a procedural matter.[456] Nevertheless, some procedural matters are so fundamental that they must be dealt with by Congress.

Illustration 5-18. Assume that Congress establishes a Supreme Court and delegates to it the following rulemaking authority: "The Supreme Court shall have the power by rule to ordain and establish courts inferior to itself and to define the subject-matter jurisdiction that such courts shall exercise within the limits of Article III, § 2 of the Constitution." Such a delegation of rulemaking authority would be unconstitutional because it would contravene the express language of Article III, § 1, which provides that the "judicial power of the United States, shall be vested . . . in such inferior courts as the Congress may from time to time ordain and establish." The constitutional language implies that only Congress can determine whether there will be inferior federal courts, and this reading is supported by the historic compromise that led to the establishment of § 1 in the Constitutional Convention. Thus, both the text and the history of Article III reveal that the decision whether to create inferior federal courts cannot be delegated, even when Congress has not previously legislated to create such courts.[457]

* * * * *

A more difficult problem, but one of greater relevance to today's statutory context, is what separation-of-powers restrictions exist on the rulemaking power of the courts when Congress *has* extensively regulated a procedural area, but also delegated rulemaking authority to the courts of such a general nature as also to encompass the area, with an additional proviso that any court rules made within the

---

454. *See* Ralph U. Whitten, *Separation of Powers Restrictions on Judicial Rulemaking: A Case Study of Federal Rule 4*, 40 ME. L. REV. 41, 52 (1988); *see also* Michael Blasie, *A Separation of Powers Defense of Federal Rulemaking Power*, 66 N.Y.U. ANN. SURV. AM. L.593 (2011); Amy Coney Barrett, *The Supervisory Power of the Supreme Court,* 106 COLUM. L. REV. 324 (2006) (discussing the possibility that the Supreme Court possesses supervisory power over the lower federal courts to prescribe rules of procedure and evidence because of its constitutional supremacy over those courts); Bernadette Bollas Genetin, *The Powers That Be: A Reexamination of the Federal Courts' Rulemaking and Adjudicatory Powers in the Context of a Clash of a Congressional Statute and a Supreme Court Rule,* 57 BAYLOR L. REV. 587 (2005); *cf.* Leslie M. Kelleher, *Taking "Substantive Rights" (In the Rules Enabling Act) More Seriously*, 74 NOTRE DAME L. REV. 47 (1998) (reviewing the constitutional and statutory allocation of rulemaking authority between Congress and the Supreme Court and proposing a multifactor analysis for the Court and the Advisory Committee to use when evaluating the validity of rules created under the Rules Enabling Act).

455. The other early decisions cast little light on the separation-of-powers restrictions because they were based on existing statutory restrictions on judicial rulemaking, rather than on constitutional limits. *See* Ralph U. Whitten, *Separation of Powers Restrictions on Judicial Rulemaking: A Case Study of Federal Rule 4*, 40 ME. L. REV. 41, 52-53 (1988).

456. *See generally id.* at 54-60.

457. *See id.* at 54 and authorities there cited. *See also id.* at 55-60.

delegated authority shall supersede inconsistent statutes.[458] As long as Congress has delegated none of its fundamental powers to the courts, any court rule made within the delegated powers might seem to be valid, even if the rule supersedes an inconsistent statute. However, this approach is too simplistic. Even when Congress has delegated general rulemaking authority to the courts with the power to supersede inconsistent statutes, Congress may wish to exercise exclusive control over certain areas. These areas might not be so fundamental that Congress could not delegate them to the courts if it explicitly chose to do so. However, the areas may traditionally have been of great concern to the legislative branch, and Congress may have consistently exercised legislative control over the areas. To paraphrase *Wayman v. Southard*, such areas would *not* be ones in which general superintendence over the subject has been considered properly within the judicial province.

Under these circumstances, to determine whether court rules created pursuant to a general delegation of rulemaking authority, such as the Rules Enabling Act, are valid, several factors should be evaluated: (1) the detail with which Congress has regulated the area; (2) the length of time that Congress has exercised exclusive control over the area before the courts make a rule within the area; (3) the apparent importance of the statutory policies prescribed by Congress within the area to both Congress and litigants; (4) the timing and purpose of the delegation of general rulemaking power to the courts in relation to the statutory scheme; (5) the extent to which the court-made rules will impact on the statutory scheme; and (6) the extent to which a court-made rule will support or protect statutory policies that are more important than the statutory policies replaced or affected by the court rule.[459]

Illustration 5-19. An example of a valid court-made rule under this analysis is original Rule 4(f) of the Federal Rules of Civil Procedure. Rule 4(f) expanded the personal jurisdiction authority of the U.S. District Courts from the limits of the district to the limits of the state in which the federal district court sits. Before Rule 4(f) became effective in 1938, a federal district court sitting in one district of a state could not summon a defendant residing in another district of the same state to defend an action in the district in which the court was sitting. After the effective date of Rule 4(f), however, a district court in one district could summon a defendant anywhere within the state to defend an action in the district. Rule 4(f) thus expanded the territorial power of the district courts. At the time Rule 4(f) was promulgated, Congress had long regulated the personal jurisdiction authority of the district courts in some detail. It had not only limited that authority to the limits of the districts as a general matter, but had paid close attention to matters of personal jurisdiction by expanding the authority of the district courts itself when it thought such an expansion was necessary. In addition, this detailed regulation of federal personal jurisdiction dated from 1789. Thus, the specificity and duration of the congressional regulation of jurisdiction both weighed against the validity of Rule 4(f).

---

458. The Rules Enabling Act contains such a proviso. *See* 28 U.S.C. § 2072(b).

459. *See* Ralph U. Whitten, *Separation of Powers Restrictions on Judicial Rulemaking: A Case Study of Rule 4*, 40 ME. L. REV. 41, 60-66 (1988).

Furthermore, although personal jurisdiction is not one of those matters that is so fundamental that power may not be delegated to the Court to affect it, it is not far removed in importance from those fundamental matters and has been treated as of great importance by Congress. In addition, because personal jurisdiction affects the location of suit, it is also of substantial importance to litigants, especially to defendants, though the slight expansion of personal jurisdiction accomplished by Rule 4(f) is not as burdensome as other possible modifications might be. Also weighing against the validity of Rule 4(f) is the fact that the Supreme Court never exercised its rulemaking power under the original Conformity Acts to affect personal jurisdiction. The purpose of the delegation of rulemaking authority to the Court in the Enabling Act—to end conformity to state law and establish a uniform system of procedure for the federal courts—could have been fulfilled completely without any regulation of personal jurisdiction.

Nevertheless, favoring the validity of Rule 4(f) are two factors (in addition to the fact, mentioned above, that the burdens of the expansion of personal jurisdiction on litigants are slight). One is the fact that Rule 4(f) only expanded the jurisdiction of the district courts to the limits of the state in which they are sitting. Rule 4(f) did not, therefore, encroach on the power, long and exclusively exercised by Congress, to choose when to create federal interstate long-arm jurisdiction. More importantly, the factor that tips the balance in favor of the Rule's validity is that it prevents the defeat of federal subject-matter jurisdiction policies in an important way. The inability to assert personal jurisdiction over defendants located in different districts in the same state prior to Rule 4(f) meant that plaintiffs seeking to sue such defendants might have to sue them in state, rather than federal court, to obtain personal jurisdiction over them. For example, a plaintiff residing in the northern district of a state seeking to sue a nonresident defendant over whom personal jurisdiction could be obtained only in the southern district of the state would either have to go to the defendant's state and district of permanent residence and sue the defendant there, where personal jurisdiction would exist *and* venue would be proper, or sue in a state court in the northern or southern district of the state which had the capacity to obtain personal jurisdiction over the defendant. The inconvenience of suing in the defendant's home state would often mean that the plaintiff would abandon the federal courts for the state courts, thus relinquishing the privilege of suing in federal court that had been granted by the subject-matter jurisdiction statutes. Because subject-matter jurisdiction policies are among the most important to the operation of the federal courts, the validity of Rule 4(f) is sustained by the fact that it prevents the defeat of these policies.[460]

Illustration 5-20. Suppose, however, that the Supreme Court had promulgated a rule expanding the venue of the federal courts to allow actions to be brought in either district of a state by multiple plaintiffs residing in different districts in that state. The rationale of such a rule might be similar to that of Rule 4(f)—multiple plaintiffs unable to join in a federal action in their home state because of federal venue restrictions might decide to sue in a state court within the state instead of suing the defendant in the defendant's state of residence, thus

---

460. *See id.* at 86-92.

abandoning their congressionally granted privilege of resorting to the diversity jurisdiction. Nevertheless, such a modification of the venue statutes by rule would be invalid. Although venue and personal jurisdiction are similar, in that they both govern the location of the action, Congress has regulated general venue in the judicial code in much more detail than it has regulated general intrastate personal jurisdiction for the federal courts. Personal jurisdiction restrictions existing at the time Rule 4(f) was promulgated under the Enabling Act generally limited process to the limits of the district in which the district court sat. However, venue was regulated separately for diversity and all other actions, for actions against multiple defendants residing in different districts in the same state and residing in different divisions in the same district, for local actions, and others. Thus, the detail with which Congress has addressed venue in the Judicial Code would make it improper for the courts to address the question by rule, even to remove obstacles to federal subject-matter jurisdiction.[461]

Illustration 5-21. Not all modifications of federal personal jurisdiction authority would be valid under the analysis in *Illustration 5-19*. For example, Federal Rule 4(k)(2) provides nationwide long-arm jurisdiction for the federal courts in a small category of cases. As amended in 1993, Rule 4(k)(2) authorizes the federal courts to assert personal jurisdiction over defendants in cases arising under federal law whenever the defendants are not subject to the courts of general jurisdiction of any state.[462] This amendment was designed to "correct a gap" in the enforcement of federal law in cases where a defendant has contacts with the United States sufficient to justify the assertion of jurisdiction over the defendant under the Due Process Clause of the Fifth Amendment, but insufficient contacts with any state to permit the assertion of jurisdiction under state law.[463] However, this amendment to Rule 4 raises serious separation-of-powers questions. The detail with which Congress has regulated federal long-arm jurisdiction parallels the detail with which it has regulated federal venue. Establishing nationwide or international long-arm jurisdiction independent of the states has, therefore, not traditionally been considered a matter fit for the general superintendence of the judiciary through court rulemaking.

In addition, Rule 4(k)(2) cannot be justified as necessary to prevent the defeat of federal subject-matter jurisdiction policies.[464] The amended rule does not eliminate a discrepancy between the personal jurisdiction authority of the federal and state courts that would encourage litigants to abandon their federally granted privilege of resorting to federal court. On the contrary, it creates a discrepancy between the personal jurisdiction authority of state and federal courts that will

---

461. *See id.* at 92-93. It may be no accident, therefore, that Federal Rule 82 forbids a construction of the Federal Rules of Civil Procedure that would extend or limit the venue of the district courts. *See* FED. R. CIV. P. 82. Rule 82 also prohibits constructions that extend or limit "jurisdiction," but this reference has always been understood to be limited to subject-matter jurisdiction. *See* Ralph U. Whitten, *Separation of Powers Restrictions on Judicial Rulemaking: A Case Study of Rule 4*, 40 ME. L. REV. 41, 73 (1988).

462. *See* FED. R. CIV. P. 4(k)(2); *see also* Chapter 3(L) *supra* ("Special Problems of Amenability to Process in Federal Court").

463. *See* FED. R. CIV. P. 4(k)(2) advisory committee's note to the 1993 amendment.

464. *See* Ralph U. Whitten, *Separation of Powers Restrictions on Judicial Rulemaking: A Case Study of Rule 4*, 40 ME. L. REV. 41, 103-06 (1988); *see also id.* at 93-103; *see also* JACK B. WEINSTEIN, REFORM OF COURT RULE-MAKING PROCEDURES 4-5 (1977) (comparing the processes of adjudication and rulemaking).

encourage litigants to forum shop for federal courts to obtain the benefit of long-arm jurisdiction that does not exist at the state level. An effect of this sort arguably involves a policy judgment that only Congress can make in the absence of an explicit grant of rulemaking authority to the courts over the subject. Balanced against these considerations are the facts that the extension of jurisdiction by Rule 4(k) is small and that the extension allows litigants in some federal claims cases to sue in federal court within the United States, rather than suing in the courts of a foreign nation. Whether these considerations are sufficient to save the constitutionality of the new rule is questionable.

* * * * *

In *Sibbach*, the Supreme Court stated that "[t]here are other limitations upon the authority to prescribe rules which might have been, but were not, mentioned in the [Rules Enabling] Act; for instance, the inability of a court, by rule, to extend or restrict the jurisdiction conferred by a statute."[465] This statement, in combination with the Court's discussion of the limits on judicial rulemaking in *Wayman*, suggest that one of the "important" subjects reserved for Congress may be the subject of jurisdiction—presumably meaning "subject-matter jurisdiction." As *Illustration 5-18*, above, suggests, surely the Supreme Court could not be given the entire power to define the subject-matter jurisdiction that the federal courts will exercise within the limits of Article III. Such a power would involve policy decisions that the language and history of Article III, fairly construed, reserve to Congress. The question remains, however, whether lesser judicial rulemaking power over subject-matter jurisdiction would be permissible.

In 1992, Congress delegated to the Supreme Court the power to provide for interlocutory appeals from the U.S. District Courts to the U.S. Courts of Appeals in cases not otherwise provided for in 28 U.S.C. § 1292, the statute that currently authorizes appeals from interlocutory orders.[466] In 1998, the Supreme Court exercised this power by creating a new Rule 23(f) under the Rules Enabling Act. Rule 23(f) authorizes the courts of appeals, in their discretion, to permit an appeal from an order of a district court granting or denying class action certification under Rule 23.[467] Rule 23(f) is a clear regulation of appellate subject-matter jurisdiction under a delegation of authority from Congress. It thus squarely raises the separation-of-powers issue posed by *Sibbach* and *Wayman*.

In the language of *Wayman*, Rule 23(f) concerns a matter—subject-matter jurisdiction—whose "general superintendence" has *not* traditionally been considered "properly within the judicial province." Similarly, in the language of

---

465. *Sibbach*, 312 U.S. at 10, 61 S. Ct. at 425, 85 L. Ed. at 483.

466. 28 U.S.C. § 1292(e). Congress added subsection (e) to § 1292 in 1992. *See* Federal Courts Administration Act of 1992, Pub. L. No. 102-572, § 101, 106 Stat. 4506, 4506. This enactment had been recommended by the Federal Courts Study Committee, along with a recommendation concerning rulemaking power to define what constitutes a final judgment under 28 U.S.C. § 1291. The Committee recommended that the Court be permitted "to add to—but not subtract from—the list of categories of interlocutory appeal permitted . . . in 28 U.S.C. § 1292." REPORT OF THE FEDERAL COURTS STUDY COMMITTEE 96 (1990). Section 1292(e) conforms to this recommendation. *But see* Bolin v. Sears, Roebuck & Co., 231 F.3d 970 (5th Cir. 2000) (holding § 1292(e) to be a "permissible delegation of rulemaking authority with the judiciary's central mission"); Carey M. Erhard, Note, *A Discussion of the Interlocutory Review of Class Certification Orders Under Federal Rule of Civil Procedure 23(f)*, 51 DRAKE L. REV. 151, 179 (2002) (arguing that Rule 23(f) is constitutional and consistent with the Rules Enabling Act because it affects only the timing of appeals).

467. *See* FED. R. CIV. P. 23(f).

Sibbach, Rule 23(f) certainly appears to be an "extension" of "jurisdiction" by "rule." Under existing 28 U.S.C. § 1292(b), an interlocutory appeal can be taken from a district court to a court of appeals only (1) if the district court certifies (2) that an order otherwise not appealable involves "a controlling question of law as to which there is substantial ground for difference of opinion and that an immediate appeal from the order may materially advance the ultimate termination of the litigation," and (3) the court of appeals, in its discretion, permits the appeal. By removing the first two requirements of § 1292(b), Rule 23(f) seems clearly to expand the appellate jurisdiction over class action certification orders.[468] The Advisory Committee suggested that "[t]he expansion of appeal opportunities effected by subdivision (f) is modest."[469] Perhaps the limited nature of the expansion saves the validity of the rule on the theory that it amounts only to a regulation of procedural detail and is, therefore, one of those subjects of "less interest" that *Wayman* suggested was properly within the judicial rulemaking authority. Nevertheless, § 1292(e) and Rule 23(f) raise troubling questions about the ability of Congress to delegate its authority validly over fundamental questions of judicial power to the courts.[470]

SECTION G. THE *ERIE* DOCTRINE IN THE LOWER FEDERAL COURTS

Given the lack of clarity in both the Rules of Decision Act and the Rules Enabling Act branches of the *Erie* doctrine, it is not surprising to find that the lower federal courts have taken different approaches to the application of state law in federal courts. *Erie* issues are numerous in diversity actions because of the wide range of matters upon which Federal Rules of Civil Procedure can potentially conflict with state procedural law, and also because of the abundance of state laws that can be argued to have outcome determinative consequences that violate the *Erie* policies under the Rules of Decision Act. Most frequently, these kinds of conflicts involve the pleading and motion provisions of Federal Rules 8, 9, and 12 (governing pleading, motion practice),[471] Federal Rule 11 (governing the standard of factual and

---

468. *See* Advisory Committee Note to Proposed Rule 23(f), 167 F.R.D. at 565 (1996).

469. *Id.* at 566; *see also* David L. Shapiro, *Federal Diversity Jurisdiction: A Survey and Proposal*, 91 HARV. L. REV. 317, 346-47 (1977) (arguing for the validity of judicial regulation of subject-matter jurisdiction under a properly circumscribed grant of power from Congress).

470. *See also* 28 U.S.C. § 2072(c) (authorizing the Supreme Court to define by procedural rule "when a ruling of a district court is final for the purposes of appeal under [28 U.S.C. § 1291]").

471. *See, e.g.*, Windy City Metal Fabricators & Supply, Inc. v. CIT Tech. Fin. Servs., Inc., 536 F.3d 663 (7th Cir. 2008) (Federal Rule 8 governs pleading of unfair conduct claim under Illinois Consumer Fraud Act rather than Rule 9(b) or Illinois fact-pleading standard); United States *ex rel.* Newsham v. Lockheed Missiles & Space Co., 190 F.3d 963 (9th Cir. 1999) (state statute provided special procedures for dealing with meritless actions designed to chill the exercise of freedom of speech; statute provided for special motion to strike the offending suit upon a prima facie showing by the offended party and shifted the burden of proof to the other side to demonstrate by a reasonable probability that the plaintiff will prevail on the claim and that the defendant's constitutional defenses are either not applicable as a matter of law or under a prima facie factual showing; prevailing party on motion entitled to attorney's fees and costs; court holds that statute does not directly collide with Federal Rules such as Rules 8, 11, 12, and 16 and that disregard of the statute would encourage plaintiffs to bring meritless suits covered by the statute to federal court, thus violating the "twin aims" of *Erie*); Richard Henry Seamon, *An* Erie *Obstacle to State Tort Reform*, 43 IDAHO L. REV. 37 (2007) (discussing state provisions limiting the plaintiff's ability to plead punitive damages). *But see* Metabolife Int'l, Inc. v. Wornick, 264 F.3d 832 (9th Cir. 2001) (if provision of California statute allowing defendant to file motion and put plaintiff to proof immediately without

legal investigation that plaintiffs must conduct before bringing a federal action),[472] Federal Rules 26-37 (governing discovery),[473] and Federal Rule 56 (summary judgment).[474] However, almost any Federal Rule of Civil Procedure can potentially conflict with state law.[475] Thus, all of the situations in which Rules Enabling Act or Rules of Decision Act issues arise cannot be examined in this section. Instead, a few

---

discovery were applied in federal court, it would conflict with Federal Rule 56; therefore, it cannot be applied; *Lockheed Missiles* distinguished on the ground that different portions of California statute were involved in that case; no discussion of whether Rule 56 could be validly applied to prevent application of state statute).

472. *See, e.g.*, *In re* Larry's Apartment, L.L.C., 249 F.3d 832 (9th Cir. 2001) (Arizona law providing for sanctions held inapplicable in diversity actions; court stated that the *Erie* doctrine does not require otherwise because federal courts must be in control of their own proceedings and federal sanction law is the body of law to be considered in that regard; Rule 11 contains "prerequisites and protections for parties who are accused of violating its strictures, and parties should be able to rely upon those in federal court proceedings").

473. *See, e.g.*, Fagin v. Gilmartin, 432 F.3d 276 (3d Cir. 2005) (New Jersey procedural rule making limited discovery a mandatory part of procedure in shareholder derivative action in which corporation's board refused shareholder demand did not directly conflict with Federal Rule 23.1 because federal rule did not deal with discovery; this necessitated application of *Erie* test to determine whether New Jersey law was substantive or procedural; under application of that test, New Jersey rule was not per se outcome determinative and the use of federal discovery law would "probably" not lead to forum shopping; no discussion of whether state rule conflicted with Federal Rules of Civil Procedure governing discovery); Ellingson v. Walgreen Co., 78 F. Supp. 2d 965 (D. Minn. 1999) (Minnesota statutory expert disclosure requirement must be applied in federal diversity action; plaintiffs contend that statute conflicts with Federal Rule 26, which should control; court, without discussing the potential conflict or whether a Rules of Decision Act or Rules Enabling Act analysis is appropriate, holds that the statute must be applied in federal court).

474. *See, e.g.*, Snead v. Metropolitan Prop. & Cas. Ins. Co., 237 F.3d 1080 (9th Cir. 2001) (plaintiff sued defendant in an Oregon state court under state law for disability discrimination; defendant removed the action to federal district court on the basis of diversity and subsequently moved for summary judgment; under state summary judgment practice, all the defendant had to do to avoid summary judgment was demonstrate a prima facie case under state law, which had been done; under federal summary judgment practice in federal discrimination cases, after the employee establishes a prima facie case, the employer can offer a nondiscriminatory reason for firing the plaintiff and the burden shifts to the plaintiff to demonstrate that the explanation for the firing is pretextual; because the plaintiff did not do this, summary judgment was granted by the district court; the court of appeals affirmed, employing the "twin aims" analysis of the general *Erie* doctrine to conclude that the difference between the state and federal standards would not be outcome determinative; even though summary judgment would not be granted against the plaintiff, when the action went to trial the standard applied to determine whether the plaintiff would suffer either a nonsuit or a judgment notwithstanding the verdict would be the same as the federal summary standard; thus, the ultimate outcome would be identical in both the state and federal court, and the only result of applying different standards would be one of timing; given that the ultimate outcome would be the same, the difference between the state and federal summary judgment standards did not, in the court of appeals' view, create the kind of forum shopping or discrimination against citizens of the forum state that were the concern of *Erie* as redefined in *Hanna*; the court did not consider the issue before it to be controlled by Federal Rule 56, dealing with summary judgment).

475. Bass v. First Pac. Networks, Inc., 219 F.3d 1052 (9th Cir. 2000) (federal jurisdiction based on federal question plus supplemental jurisdiction over state claims; district court dismissed the federal claim, but retained the state claims; judgment was for the plaintiff, and as a condition of granting a supersedeas pending appeal, the defendant was required to post a supersedeas bond pursuant to Federal Rule 62(d); after the parties subsequently settled, the plaintiff moved pursuant to Rule 65.1 to enforce the supersedeas bond, the district court granted the motion, and the court of appeals affirmed; the plaintiff then sought attorney's fees incurred in enforcing the bond contract as provided for under state law; district court found a conflict between state law and Rule 65.1 and held that attorney's fees were not recoverable; court of appeals affirms, holding that Rule 62(d) is a purely procedural mechanism to preserve the status quo during a stay pending appeal and creates no "choice-of-law concerns"; Rule 65.1 only provides for an enforcement mechanism for bonds posted under Rule 62(d); thus, federal law did not allow for the recovery of attorney's fees and was applicable; no explanation of how, if state law was supported by substantive policies as the plaintiff argued, the application of the Federal Rules in question in the way that the court applied them did not violate those substantive policies); Garcia v. Wal-Mart Stores, Inc., 209 F.3d 1170 (10th Cir. 2000) (state cost-shifting statute provides for the shifting of certain "actual litigation costs" to the defendant based on the defendant's failure to accept a pretrial settlement offer that was lower than the original judgment; Federal Rule 68 provides only for shifting certain kinds of costs to plaintiffs; Federal Rule 54(d)(2) provides that claims for attorney's fees and related nontaxable expenses shall be made by motion unless the substantive law governing the action provides for the recovery of such fees as an element of damages to be proved at trial; held, neither rule conflicts with the state statute and, therefore, the general *Erie* analysis applies and requires application of the state statute because otherwise forum shopping for a federal court and inequitable administration of the law would result; Rule 68 was held not to conflict with state law because it dealt only with shifting defendants' costs to plaintiffs).

prominent examples will be taken up here to illustrate the kinds of difficulties that the Supreme Court's *Erie* decisions pose for the lower federal courts. Other issues will be examined in later chapters as they arise in conjunction with the procedural topics there discussed.

As a general proposition, it can be said that issues in which conflicts arise between Federal Rules of Civil Procedure and state law tend to be resolved in favor of the Federal Rules, either because the rules in question are found not to conflict with state law,[476] or because, when they do, the lower federal courts find the Federal Rules valid under the Rules Enabling Act and Constitution.[477] Given the discussion of the Supreme Court's approach to Federal Rule validity in section F, above, such results are not surprising. In cases in which no Federal Rule is applicable and the lower federal courts must decide the case under the Rules of Decision Act branch of *Erie*, state law is more often found applicable. However, even under the Rules of Decision Act, the tendency to honor state law is not universal. Furthermore, in both Rules Enabling Act and Rules of Decision Act cases, the approach of the lower federal courts is often not sophisticated, and is, indeed, frequently confused about the proper analysis to be used.[478] Such results are also not surprising, however, given the lack of clarity in the Supreme Court's decisions under the two acts, as well as the tendency of the Court to ignore both branches of the *Erie* doctrine for long periods of time.

One illustrative line of cases that may offer the Supreme Court the opportunity to clarify the workings of one or both branches of the *Erie* doctrine arises out of state tort reform efforts. As the *Gasperini* case, discussed in section E, above, indicated, the states sometimes tend to curb litigation abuses in the tort area by adopting procedural rules that are designed to create barriers of one sort or another to plaintiffs without altogether precluding recovery or limiting the amount that can be recovered. Thus, some states have imposed requirements that plaintiffs seeking to recover in certain kinds of tort actions supply expert affidavits to demonstrate a factual basis for their suits, or have introduced special pleading requirements that require the plaintiff to demonstrate a factual basis for certain

---

476. *See, e.g.*, Scottsdale Ins. Co. v. Tolliver, 636 F.3d 1273 (10th Cir. 2011) (Rule 68 applies to the procedural method of making an offer of judgment, even though it conflicts with the method provided for under state law, but Rule 68, which does not provide for recovery of attorneys' fees, does not conflict with state law, which does and which is substantive in the general *Erie* sense); Torres v. Bayer Corp., 616 F.3d 778 (8th Cir. 2010) (Rule 25 is a procedural rule setting forth the proper method of substituting a successor for a decedent, but state law determines who may prooperly constitute a successor); Wade v. Danek Med., Inc., 182 F.3d 281 (4th Cir. 1999) (Rule 23 does not incorporate an equitable tolling rule; state tolling rule applies); Vaught v. Showa Denko, K.K., 107 F.3d 1137 (5th Cir. 1999) (same); *cf.* Canada Life Assurance Co. v. LaPeter, 557 F.3d 1103 (9th Cir. 2009) (appointment of a Receiver under Rule 66 does not implicate *Erie* because it has no affect on the outcome of the underlying action); Freund v. Nycomed Amersham, 347 F.3d 752 (9th Cir. 2003) (California rule providing that appealability of punitive damages is not waivable was not a rule that created any substantive right; therefore, Federal Rule 50, which requires that a party making a motion for judgment as a matter of law after verdict must have moved for such a judgment prior to verdict can be applied without abridging any substantive right).

477. *See, e.g.*, Goldberg v. Pacific Indem. Co., 627 F.3d 752 (9th Cir. 2010) (Rule 68 does not permit defendants to recover costs when they make an offer of judgment under the rule and win a take nothing judgment, but Arizona's offer of judgment rule does; the rule conflict and Rule 68 prevails in federal court).

478. *See, e.g.*, Jones v. United Parcel Serv., Inc., 674 F.3d 1187 (10th Cir. 2011) (issue is whether jury was properly allowed to determine punitive damages when Kansas statute provided judge should do so; court treats case as involving application of Rule 38, which declares right to trial by jury as declared by Seventh Amendment is preserved; holding that Rule 38 controls and, under *Shady Grove*, discussed in sections E(3) and F(6), answers the question in dispute because the Seventh Amendment requires a right to jury trial on the punitive damages issue).

kinds of tort claims without first being able to obtain discovery from defendants on the claims. For example, Florida has provided that when a plaintiff seeks punitive damages, "no claim for punitive damages shall be permitted unless there is a reasonable showing by evidence in the record or proffered by the claimant which would provide a reasonable basis for recovery of such damages."[479] Although the statute also provides that the claimant can move to amend the complaint to assert a claim for punitive damages, and that the rules of civil procedure should be liberally construed to allow the claimant discovery of evidence "which appears reasonably calculated to lead to admissible evidence on the issue of punitive damages," it also provides that no discovery of the defendant's financial worth can be allowed until "after the pleading concerning punitive damages is permitted."[480] The U.S. District Courts in Florida initially split on the question whether this statute is applicable in federal diversity actions.

In *Neill v. Gulf Stream Coach, Inc.*,[481] the U.S. District Court for the Middle District of Florida found that the statute did not conflict with any Federal Rule of Civil Procedure and that failure to apply the statute in a federal diversity action would create forum shopping and inequitable administration of the law in violation of the Rules of Decision Act. In an extensive opinion, the court concluded that it was possible to give both Federal Rule 8(a), which establishes a liberal notice pleading standard for the federal courts,[482] and the Florida statute their full field of operation.[483] In the court's view, Federal Rule 8(a) contained no requirement that all claims be pleaded in the first complaint on pain of being lost forever if they are not; rather, Rule 8(a) only provides that when claims are pleaded, the pleading in which they are contained need only contain a short and plain statement showing that the pleader is entitled to relief.[484] Thus, Rule 8(a) and the Florida statute could both be applied, because once the plaintiff made the showing required, the complaint could be amended to add claims for punitive damages that comported in form to Rule 8(a).[485] In addition, the court pointed out that even if Rule 8(a)(2) was "understood as governing when the pleading of certain matters is to occur," it would not conflict with the state statute, because

> [a] "claim" showing that the pleader is entitled to relief—within the meaning of the rule—refers to the pleader's cause of action or legal theory of recovery, as opposed to a specific component of the relief that may be available should the claim be proved. Thus, there can be no such thing as a free[-]standing "claim" for punitive damages. . . . As such . . . the only basis for conflict would be Rule

---

479. *See* FLA. STAT. ANN. § 768.72 (West 2011).

480. *Id.*

481. 966 F. Supp. 1149 (M.D. Fla. 1997); *see also* Teel v. United Techs. Pratt & Whitney, 953 F. Supp. 1534 (S.D. Fla. 1997) (applying same analysis as *Neill*).

482. *See* Chapter 6(D)(2)*(b) infra* (discussing federal notice pleading).

483. *See Neill*, 966 F. Supp. at 1153-54.

484. *See id.* at 1153.

485. *See id.* at 1154.

8(a)(3)'s requirement that the pleading contain a demand for judgment for the relief the pleader seeks.[486]

The court also held that the Florida statute did not conflict with Federal Rule 9(g), which requires that when special damages are claimed, they shall be specifically stated in the pleading in which they are claimed.[487] In the court's view, Rule 9(g) says nothing about when items of special damage may be pleaded, but only requires that when they are pleaded they be stated with specificity. In contrast, the Florida statute has nothing to say about the content of a pleading concerning punitive damages, but speaks only to when an entitlement to such damages can be pleaded. Each provision could thus operate side-by-side and be given its intended sphere of operation.[488]

Turning to the Rules of Decision Act side of the *Erie* doctrine, the court concluded that the failure to apply the Florida statute would cause inequitable administration of the law because the statute was part of a tort reform effort that was designed to "create a positive legal right on the part of those sued in tort under Florida law to be free from punitive damages claims absent a threshold judicial determination of a reasonable basis for their assertion."[489] As such, the statute "represents a means of achieving a substantive legislative goal."[490] Thus, to deny a federal defendant its protection in federal court would be "to thwart one of the twin aims of *Erie*, namely, the avoidance of inequitable administration of the laws."[491] In addition, the court found that the plaintiff's incentive to shop for a federal forum would "increase significantly" if the federal courts disregarded the Florida statute, thus producing the forum shopping that *Erie* sought to avoid.

Other Florida federal district courts reached different results. For example, in *Tutor Time Child Care Systems, Inc. v. Franks Investment Group, Inc.*,[492] the U.S. District Court for the Southern District of Florida disagreed with *Neill*. Essentially, the court's view of the statute was that it required "satellite pleading"[493] in cases in which the plaintiff wishes to claim punitive damages. This satellite-pleading requirement conflicted with both Rules 8(a) and 9(g), which contain no such requirement.[494] Having found a conflict between the state statute and the Federal Rules, the court concluded summarily that the conflict should be resolved in favor of the Federal Rules, which had been "constitutionally promulgated pursuant to the

---

486. *Id.* at 1153 n.8. However, the court did not point out why this conflict with Rule 8(a)(3) would not produce a Rules Enabling Act issue. In Cohen v. Office Depot, Inc., 184 F.3d 1292 (11th Cir. 1999), the court of appeals found a conflict between the Federal Rules of Civil Procedure and the Florida statute on this basis. *Cohen* is discussed in the text, *infra*.

487. *See* Chapter 6(D)(2)*(e)(iii) infra* (discussing the requirements of Rule 9(g)).

488. *Neill*, 966 F. Supp. at 1154. The court did not discuss possible conflicts between the Florida statute and Federal Rule 11 or the provisions of the Federal Rules governing discovery. *Cf.* Hogan v. Wal-Mart Stores, Inc., 167 F.3d 781 (2d Cir. 1999) (Federal Rule 9(g) requires that when items of "special damage" are claimed, "they shall be specifically stated"; however, Rule 9(g) does not define what special (as opposed to "general") damages are; held, it is not settled in the circuit whether the law defining general or special damages is procedural; answer may depend on relation of damages to the claim for relief; question does not have to be answered in this case).

489. *Neill*, 966 F. Supp. at 1154.

490. *Id.* at 1155.

491. *Id.* at 1156.

492. 966 F. Supp. 1188 (S.D. Fla. 1997).

493. *See id.* at 1191-92.

494. *See also* Primerica Fin. Servs., Inc. v. Mitchell, 48 F. Supp. 2d 1363 (S.D. Fla. 1999) (following *Tutor Time*).

Rules Enabling Act."[495] Similarly, in *Alexander v. University/Gainesville Healthcare Center, Inc.*,[496] the U.S. District Court for the Northern District of Florida concluded that to apply the Florida statute in federal court would be to "convert the pleading of punitive damages from the requirement of mere notice to a quasi-adjudication of plaintiff's claim, requiring evidentiary inquiry and discovery, argumentation of counsel, and a judicial ruling. Such an application would subvert not only the intent of Rule 8, but the entire system of the Federal Rules."[497] Furthermore, the court construed the Florida statute as not having created any new substantive rights (contrary to *Neill*), but as having merely added a pleading requirement.[498] Thus, the application of the Federal Rules instead of the state statute did not violate the Constitution or the Rules Enabling Act.[499]

In *Cohen v. Office Depot, Inc.*,[500] the Eleventh Circuit Court of Appeals adopted the view of the Florida district courts that had found the Florida statute in conflict with the Federal Rules of Civil Procedure and, therefore, inapplicable in federal diversity actions. *Cohen* found the statute in conflict with Federal Rule 8(a)(3) on two grounds. First, the court held that under Rule 8(a)(3), a pleading that sets forth a claim for relief must contain a request for a remedy. Because the Florida statute prohibits a request for punitive damages, the court held that it conflicted with Rule 8(a)(3). Alternatively,[501] the court held that even if Rule 8(a)(3) does not require that the complaint request a remedy, it permits the complaint to do so. Thus, the Florida statute conflicted with the rule by forbidding the complaint from containing a demand for punitive damages. However, after finding a conflict between Rule 8(a)(3) and the Florida statute, the court's analysis of whether the Rules Enabling Act was violated by Rule 8(a)(3) was purely conclusory. The court relied on the statement in *Sibbach* that Federal Rules are valid if they "really regulate procedure" and a statement from *Mississippi Publishing Corp. v. Murphree* that "incidental effects" by Federal Rules on substantive rights do not violate the Act.[502] Although decided prior to the Supreme Court's decision in *Shady Grove*,

---

495. 966 F. Supp. at 1193.

496. 17 F. Supp. 2d 1291 (N.D. Fla. 1998).

497. *Id.* at 1292.

498. *See id.* at 1293.

499. *See id.*

500. 184 F.3d 1292 (11th Cir. 1999).

501. The defendant argued that there was no real conflict between Rule 8(a)(3) and the Florida statute because Rule 8(a)(3) was effectively rendered a nullity by Rule 54(c), which states that, except in the case of default judgments, "every final judgment shall grant the relief to which the party in whose favor it is rendered is entitled, even if the party has not demanded such relief in the party's pleadings." The court did not view Rule 54(c) as nullifying Rule 8(a)(3), and, in fact, viewed the provision of Rule 54(c) dealing with default judgments as reinforcing the direction in Rule 8(a)(3) that a pleading stating a claim include a demand for relief. That part of Rule 54(c) states that the relief awarded in the case of a default judgment "shall not be different in kind from or exceed in amount that prayed for in the demand for judgment." *See* 184 F.3d at 1298; *see also* Andresen v. Diorio, 349 F.3d 8 (1st Cir. 2003) (state heightened pleading standards for defamation not applicable in federal court; detail required in pleading governed by Federal Rule 8).

502. *See* 184 F.3d at 1299. *But see* Liggon-Redding v. Estate of Sugarman, 659 F.3d 258 (3d Cir. 2011) (Rules 7, 8, 9, 11, and 41(b) do not conflict with Pennsylvania affidavit of merit statute; statute is obligatory on federal diversity courts under the Rules of Decision Act); *cf.* Newton v. Clinical Reference Lab., Inc., 517 F.3d 554 (8th Cir. 2008) (U.S. District court found Arkansas statutory requirement that expert affidavit be filed within thirty days after commencement applicable in federal diversity action and dismissed with prejudice as required by Arkansas law; while case was on appeal, Arkansas Supreme Court invalidated the affidavit requirement as inconsistent with Arkansas procedural Rule 3 on commencement of an action because it was a procedural rule that added a "legislative encumbrance" to commencing a cause of action not found in Rule 3; thereafter, the Eighth Circuit Court of Appeals held that it was obligated to reverse under this new view of Arkansas law and so did not

examined in sections E and F, above, the decision in *Cohen* seems consistent with the majority's method of determining whether Federal Rules are broad enough to cover a case, as well as with the plurality's interpretation of the substantive rights restriction of the Rules Enabling Act.

Cohen notwithstanding, even brief reflection on the standards discussed in previous sections will illustrate how difficult it is to determine which of the above approaches is correct. For example, section F(5), above, observed that the Supreme Court's approach to the problem of avoiding conflicts between Federal Rules of Civil Procedure and state law has varied. Under the Court's interpretation of Federal Rule 59(a) in the *Gasperini* case, in which Court now followed an approach that is more sensitive to "important state interests and regulatory policies,"[503] as well as the interpretive method of the dissenters in *Shady Grove,* the approach taken in *Neill* would probably be correct. Certainly, neither Rule 8(a) nor 9(g) explicitly negate other requirements that may exist under state law for asserting a particular kind of claim, although it would have been desirable if the court had considered possible conflicts with Rule 11 and the federal discovery rules as well as Rules 8 and 9.

Nevertheless, it is also possible to sympathize with the courts in *Tutor Time* and *Alexander* that application of the state statute would create satellite pleading and a mini-adjudication requirement for punitive damages claims, neither of which exists under the Federal Rules. Treating punitive damages in this way would undoubtedly violate the spirit of the liberal notice pleading philosophy of Rule 8(a). If the *Burlington Northern* method of Federal Rule interpretation, or that of the majority in *Shady Grove,* discussed in section F(4) - (6), above, is correct, the Florida statute was correctly interpreted as in conflict with Federal Rules 8(a) & 9(g). However, even if the rules are in conflict with state law, the courts' approach to the Rules Enabling Act problem is arguably inadequate in *Tutor Time*, *Alexander*, and *Cohen*. The approach would, of course, be correct under the plurality's return to the *Sibbach* standard in *Shady Grove*, because that standard focuses only on the procedural nature of a Federal Rule itself. However, the court in *Neill* had the better case that the state statute embodied "substantive rights." *Tutor Time*, *Alexander,* and *Cohen* did not examine this issue adequately, much less determine in anything more than a conclusory fashion whether the application of the Federal Rules instead of the state law would abridge the statutory rights more than "incidentally."[504] Which approach ultimately turns out to be correct, of course, depends on the resolution of the difference between the plurality and other justices in *Shady Grove* about the proper interpretation of the Enabling Act's restriction. Because there was no majority on the interpretation of the Act in *Shady Grove*, however, the *Burlington Northern* test remains the authoritative standard.

If the court was correct in *Neill* that there is no conflict between a Federal Rule of Civil Procedure and state law, it was undoubtedly also correct that disregard

---

reach the question of whether the affidavit requirement was obligatory on federal diversity courts).

503. *See Gasperini*, 518 U.S. at 427 n.7, 116 S. Ct. at 2219 n.7, 135 L. Ed. 2d at n.7.

504. *Cf.* Chamberlain v. Giampapa, 210 F.3d 154 (3d Cir. 2000) (New Jersey "affidavit of merit" statute does not conflict with Federal Rules 8 or 9, and under general *Erie* analysis, statute must be applied in federal diversity action to prevent forum shopping and inequitable administration of the laws).

of the state statute would create forum shopping and inequitable administration of the law. There seems to be no question that defendants would be deprived of valuable benefits that they would enjoy in state court if federal courts disregard the state statute in diversity actions. Moreover, as the court pointed out in *Neill*, plaintiffs will surely shop for a federal forum if the federal courts disregard the requirements of the state statute in diversity cases. On the other hand, the court failed to consider whether federal countervailing considerations existed that might outweigh the outcome determinative policies.[505]

One of the problems in the Florida cases discussed above is that the state legislature may have been framing a procedural restriction for substantive policy purposes. As is evident from the discussion of the *Shady Grove* case in sections E(3) and F(6), above, when legislatures act in this way, as they often seem to do, the task of a federal court in determining the purposes of the state laws in order to perform the *Hanna* conflict avoidance analysis becomes more complicated. In addition, the problem of determining whether the state laws should be considered "substantive" for Rules Enabling Act purposes is also enormously complicated. Nevertheless, even when state laws are cast in a procedural form, they are sometimes more clearly substantive than the Florida punitive damages restriction discussed above (or the class-action restriction in *Shady Grove*). As state laws progress toward the substantive end of the substance-procedure spectrum, the federal courts tend to apply them in spite of potentially conflicting federal procedural law.

Good examples of procedural restrictions with a substantive purpose are state "seat-belt statutes." These statutes prohibit the introduction of evidence that a plaintiff in an automobile accident case was not wearing a seat belt in order to prove the plaintiff was contributorily negligent. Although such statutes are framed as rules of evidence, they are often actually provisions designed to eliminate the defense of contributory negligence under state law for the particular omission covered by the statutes. Nothing could be more substantive. In cases in which

---

505. *See generally* Jeffrey A. Parness et al., *The Substantive Elements in the New Special Pleading Laws*, 78 NEB. L. REV. 412, 428-38 (1999); Rhett Traband, *An* Erie *Decision: Should State Statutes Prohibiting the Pleading of Punitive Damages Claims Be Applied in Federal Diversity Actions*? 26 STETSON L. REV. 225 (1996); *see also* Clark v. Sarasota Cnty. Pub. Hosp. Bd., 65 F. Supp. 2d 1308 (M.D. Fla. 1999) (federal diversity court must apply Florida medical malpractice mediation requirements; those requirements do not conflict with Federal Rule 8 and disregard of them would violate the twin aims of *Erie*); Baird v. Celis, 41 F. Supp. 2d 1358 (N.D. Ga. 1999) (Georgia expert affidavit requirement conflicts with notice pleading standards in federal court and is, therefore, inapplicable in federal diversity action); McKenzie v. Hawaii Permanente Med. Group, Inc., 29 F. Supp. 2d 1174 (D. Haw. 1998) (state medical claims conciliation procedure, which must be pursued before a state medical malpractice action may be filed, is "procedural" for *Erie* purposes; thus, plaintiff need not pursue the procedure before commencing a federal diversity action); Oakes v. Halvorsen Marine, Ltd., 179 F.R.D. 281 (C.D. Cal. 1998) (California statute establishing procedures for pleading exemplary or punitive damages and obtaining information relevant to such claims is inapplicable because it is "procedural" law that conflicts with Federal Rules); RTC Mortgage Trust 1994 N-1 v. Fidelity Nat'l Title Ins. Co., 981 F. Supp. 334 (D.N.J. 1997) (New Jersey affidavit-of-merit statute does not conflict with any Federal Rule of Civil Procedure or notice pleading policies and must be applied by federal courts in diversity actions because it is outcome determinative and there are no federal countervailing considerations); Robert K. Harris, Brown v. Nichols: *The Eleventh Circuit Refuses to Play the* Erie *Game With Georgia's Expert Affidavit Requirement*, 29 GA. L. REV. 291 (1994); Note, *Tort Law—Products Liability—Illinois Imposes Certificate of Merit Requirement on Products Liability Actions—Civil Justice Reform Amendments of 1995, Pub. Act 89-7, sec. 15, § 2-623, 1995 Ill. Legis. Serv. 224, 229-30 (West) (to be codified at Ill. Comp. Stat. ch. 735, § 5/2-623)*, 109 HARV. L. REV. 705, 708 (1996). For a general discussion of certificate-of-merit laws, see Jeffrey A. Parness & Amy Leonetti, *Expert Opinion Pleading: Any Merit to Special Certificates of Merit?* 1997 B.Y.U. L. REV. 537.

defendants have argued that seat-belt laws are inconsistent with the Federal Rules of Evidence[506] governing relevant evidence, the federal courts have universally recognized the substantive character of the laws and held them applicable in federal diversity actions.[507]

Occasionally, in applying a state law to comply with the general *Erie* policies, a federal court will dismiss a diversity action, not seeing that it may be undermining the policies that support the diversity jurisdiction.[508] For example, Illinois has a statute that, at least in the absence of special circumstances, requires dismissal of actions in favor of prior pending actions between the same parties on the same claim. Some Illinois federal decisions have held that *Erie* requires the application of this statute in diversity actions to produce dismissal in favor of prior pending actions commenced in other courts, including Illinois courts and the courts of other states and nations.[509] The problem with this view is that it may represent an abdication of the federal courts' responsibilities to provide an unbiased forum in diversity actions.

Illustration 5-10 in section E(1), above, stated that it would be improper for a federal diversity court to refuse the plaintiff a remedy that would be given by a state court in the same state, because to do so would be literally to drive the plaintiff

---

506. The Federal Rules of Evidence were originally promulgated by the Supreme Court under the Rules Enabling Act, but, due to objections to certain of the rules, Congress prevented them from going into effect and later enacted them in revised form as statutes. *See* Chapter 11(I) *infra* ("Evidence"). Thus potential conflicts between the rules and state substantive law raise the issue of the power of Congress to override state substantive provisions.

507. *See, e.g.*, Gardner *ex rel.* Gardner v. Chrysler Corp., 89 F.3d 729 (10th Cir. 1996) (state rule is substantive and must be excluded to prove contributory negligence of plaintiff or failure to mitigate damages, but may be admitted for other purposes permitted by state law); Dillinger v. Caterpillar, Inc., 959 F.2d 430 (3d Cir. 1992) (evidence of failure to use seat belt must be excluded under state law); Barron v. Ford Motor Co. of Can., 965 F.2d 195 (7th Cir. 1992) (state law precluding admissibility of failure to use seat belt is substantive and cannot be admitted to show contributory negligence); Potts v. Benjamin, 882 F.2d 1320 (8th Cir. 1989) (state law precluding evidence of failure to use seat belt is substantive and must be applied by federal court in diversity case); Morton v. Brockman, 184 F.R.D. 211 (D. Me. 1999) (state statute excluding evidence of failure to wear seat belt is substantive and must be applied in federal diversity action); *see also* Fitzgerald, P.P.A. v. Expressway Sewerage Constr., Inc., 71 F.3d 71 (1st Cir. 1999) (state law called the "collateral source rule" provided that compensation received from a third party, such as plaintiff's insurance company, will not diminish the plaintiff's recovery from a tortfeasor; this gave rise to a corresponding state rule that evidence of collateral source payments are inadmissible for purpose of reducing damages; held, state law controlled the admissibility of evidence for the purposes of reducing damages, but Federal Rules of Evidence controlled whether evidence was unduly prejudicial when admitted for other purposes); *see also* Sims v. Great Am. Life Ins. Co., 469 F.3d 870 (10th Cir. 2006) (*Erie* does not apply to Federal Rules of Evidence because they are statutes, but diversity court must inquire whether statute excluding evidence of seat belt non use is motivated by evidentiary purpose to exclude evidence because jury will attach too much weight to it or by motivation not to penalize persons who fail to fasten seat belts, in which case it is substantive; here, evidence admitted to prove driver's suicidal state of mind, not to show that driver could have minimized injuries by wearing seat belt); Blue Cross & Blue Shield, Inc. v. Philip Morris, Inc., 133 F. Supp. 2d 162 (E.D.N.Y. 2001) (court held that admissibility of statistical evidence under the Federal Rules of Evidence is permissible in a diversity action, even if it would be impermissible under state law (though the court also held that the evidence would be admissible under state law); court distinguished between the substantive elements of a claim and the methods of proving the claim; even though the use of statistical evidence made it easier for the plaintiff to satisfy its burden of proof, it did not alter the substantive elements of the claim under state law).

508. *See* section E, *Illustration 5-10, supra.*

509. *See, e.g.*, Praxair, Inc. v. Slifka, 61 F. Supp. 2d 753 (N.D. Ill. 1999) (following earlier decisions holding the Illinois statute to be "substantive" for *Erie* purposes); Brach & Broch Confections, Inc. v. Redmond, 988 F. Supp. 1106 (N.D. Ill. 1997) (*Erie* requires dismissal under statute because of prior pending action in California state court, subsequently removed to California federal court on basis of diversity); Northbrook Prop. & Cas. Ins. Co. v. Allendale Mut. Ins. Co., 887 F. Supp. 173 (N.D. Ill. 1995) (statute must be applied in diversity cases and requires dismissal in favor of prior pending Canadian action); *cf.* Locke v. Bonello, 965 F.2d 534, 538 n.3 (7th Cir. 1992) (suggesting that the statute must be applied in federal courts to require dismissal in favor of prior pending actions in Illinois courts).

out of federal court into a state court to obtain the remedy. When the plaintiff is a noncitizen of the forum, this problem is particularly serious because the plaintiff might encounter in the state court the very bias in fact-finding that the diversity jurisdiction is designed to eliminate. The cases applying the Illinois prior pending action statute do not undermine the diversity policy as seriously as refusal of a remedy in *Illustration 5-10*, however, because even if a federal court *refuses* to dismiss a case in favor a prior pending state action, a parallel action will still be pending in state court in which state fact-finding bias could potentially operate against the noncitizen. Furthermore, if the state action reaches judgment before the federal action, the state judgment will be res judicata.[510]

However, the application of the state statute is also not as clearly demanded under *Erie* as the state statute in the *Woods* case, also discussed in section E(1), above. In *Woods*, the Supreme Court held that *Erie* required application of state "door-closing" statutes in federal diversity actions. However, in the door-closing situation, dismissal of the federal diversity action will not result in a state action in the same state because the doors of the state courts are also closed to the action. Because the diversity jurisdiction is designed to provide an alternative, unbiased tribunal to a state court, the absence of the possibility of a state action eliminates any danger that subject-matter jurisdiction policies will be undermined. There can be no room for bias to operate in state court if the state courts are closed to the action.

Thus, the Illinois prior-pending action statute represents an intermediate situation, in which, no matter what result the federal court reaches, important federal policies will be undermined. If the federal court refuses to dismiss under the state statute, plaintiffs will surely forum shop for a federal court to obtain whatever procedural advantages the second federal action will afford them, and defendants will be deprived of the valuable benefit, which would be available in an Illinois state court, of avoiding duplicative litigation. Retention of the case will thus undermine the *Erie* policies. On the other hand, dismissal of diversity actions will deprive noncitizens of the benefit of a presumptively unbiased tribunal in those cases in which the federal court would reach judgment first and thus control the outcome of both actions through the doctrine of res judicata.[511] On balance, the courts should probably resolve the issue in favor of retention rather than dismissal. *Erie* should be viewed as a subordinate policy to subject-matter jurisdiction policies. Therefore, when *Erie* and subject-matter jurisdiction policies cannot both be vindicated in an action, subject-matter policies should control. The question in this situation is a close one, however, and the Illinois federal courts cannot be seriously faulted for reaching the opposite result.

However, they can be faulted for not understanding the proper questions to ask. In *AXA Corporate Solutions v. Underwriters Reinsurance Corp.*,[512] the district court dismissed under the Illinois statute, but the court of appeals disagreed that the statute's application in federal court was obligatory. The court agreed that disregard of the statute would create forum shopping, but stated that not everything that

---

510. *See* Chapter 13(F)(1) *infra* ("Enforcement of State Judgments").
511. *See* Chapter 13(F)(2) *infra* ("Enforcement of Federal Judgments").
512. 347 F.3d 272 (7th Cir. 2003).

creates forum shopping requires the application of state law. "Parties might prefer the notice-pleading regime of the Federal Rules of Civil Procedure over the fact-pleading approach that prevails in Illinois courts, but no one thinks that the Illinois rules of pleading are binding on the federal courts."[513] The court went on to hold that the problem addressed by the Illinois statute was "closely akin" to topics such as forum non conveniens, lis pendens, and venue statutes, each of which addresses an organizational matter that is governed by the law that establishes the forum. Note, however, that the court's examples mixed problems under the Rules Enabling Act with problems of conflict between federal common-law rules and state law under the Rules of Decision Act and problems governed directly by federal statute without acknowledging the analytical differences between such problems. Nor did the court address questions that the Supreme Court has left open, such as whether outcome differences less than differences on the merits count at all under the *Erie* doctrine. The decision thus does not adequately resolve the *Erie* issues posed by the Illinois statute.

Numerous other problems exist with the administration of the *Erie* doctrine in the lower federal courts. A few courts do not understand *Hanna's* message that the validity and applicability of Federal Rules of Civil Procedure do not depend on whether the general *Erie* policies of forum shopping and inequitable administration of the laws would be violated.[514] Such decisions are inexcusable. However, other problems of administering the *Erie* doctrine are the byproduct of the Supreme Court's failure to clarify the operation of the doctrine. For example, forum shopping for a federal diversity court can be encouraged by refusals to apply state laws that will not necessarily produce an ultimate outcome difference on the merits, as opposed to some "lesser" outcome difference. The failure of the Supreme Court to clarify whether such "lesser" outcome differences count under *Erie* has led the federal courts to different results. In the Illinois cases discussed above, retention of federal diversity actions rather than dismissal on prior pending action grounds will not necessarily produce an ultimate outcome difference on the merits of the case, but the Illinois federal district courts applied the *Erie* doctrine to require dismissal anyway, and, as noted above, the Seventh Circuit Court of Appeals did not address the issue in *AXA Corporate Solutions*.

Other courts seem to require an ultimate difference on the merits before a state law may be classified as "substantive" for *Erie* purposes, even though disregard of the law will clearly cause forum shopping or inequitable administration of the law. Thus, in *McKenzie v. Hawaii Permanente Medical Group, Inc.*,[515] the federal district court considered whether plaintiffs were required to proceed in a medical claim conciliation requirement before commencing a federal diversity action, as they would have to do before commencing a state action on the claim. The court held that the state requirement was "procedural" for *Erie* purposes and not obligatory in federal court, despite the fact that plaintiffs will clearly go to federal

---

513. *Id.* at 277.

514. *See, e.g.*, Wester v. Crown Controls Corp., 974 F. Supp. 1284 (D. Ariz. 1996) (Federal Rule 26(a) applicable, constitutional, and valid under the Rules Enabling Act, but state rule should be applied because otherwise forum shopping and discrimination against citizens of the forum state would result).

515. 29 F. Supp. 2d 1174 (D. Haw. 1998).

court to avoid the medical conciliation procedure when they wish, for any reason, to commence an action immediately. The court stated:

> [T]he [medical claim conciliation] requirement is procedural and not substantive, because it does not "materially [affect] the character or result of a litigation.". . . [T]he requirement "does not affect the merits of the parties' positions under state law, and . . . imposes no additional method for parties in state court to have their cases conclusively adjudicated."[516]

One final example will illustrate the kind of confusion that exists in the lower federal courts about the *Erie* doctrine. In *Kohlrautz v. Oilmen Participation Corp.,*[517] the court engaged in a prolonged ratiocination in an action that deserved far simpler treatment. The issue was whether state or federal law governed an immunity defense to a state claim. The court first recognized correctly that no Federal Rule of Civil Procedure applied to the case. Then, however, it employed alternative analyses to (1) determine that use of federal law rather than state law could create an outcome difference that would produce forum shopping in some cases (though it did not discuss what would happen on the facts before it) and appeared to hold (under an "interest balancing" test) that no federal countervailing considerations were present justifying use of the federal immunity law that would apply in federal claim cases and (2) hold that a Federal Rule of Civil Procedure could not be promulgated to control the immunity issue without violating the Rules Enabling Act, with the result that the outcome determinative and "interest balancing" tests contemplated by *Hanna* could also not be employed. Therefore, the court stated that it was confronted with "a straightforward [!] choice between the substantive official immunity law of a state and the analogous substantive federal immunity law" under the Rules of Decision Act. This resulted in application of state law because the federal government had absolutely no interest in applying federal immunity law to a state claim.[518] The court's confused analysis can, in large part, be attributed to the fact that the Supreme Court has not mentioned the *Byrd* categorization process since *Byrd* was decided. Under that process, it is hard to see how a state immunity defense to a state claim could be classified as anything other than a rule defining state rights and obligations that is absolutely obligatory on federal courts under the Rules of Decision Act. Having decided that no Federal Rule of Civil Procedure existed to govern the case, this is all the court had to say to justify the application of state law.

Other issues concerning the administration and application of the *Erie* doctrine in the lower federal courts will be discussed in later chapters as they become pertinent to the topics there examined.

---

516. *Id.* at 1177, *quoting* Hum v. Dericks, 162 F.R.D. 628 (D. Haw. 1995); *see also* General Elec. Co. v. Latin Am. Imports, S.A.,127 Fed. App'x 157 (6th Cir. 2005) (classifying the type and amount of documentation needed to support a request for attorneys' fees in a diversity action as "procedural" without applying either the Rules of Decision Act or Rules Enabling Act tests). For a discussion of how a number of highly regarded Civil Procedure casebooks present the *Erie* doctrine, including how they deviate from what the Supreme Court has said in its opinions under the doctrine, see Robert J. Condlin, *"A Formstone of Our Federalism": The* Erie/Hanna *Doctrine & Casebook Law Reform*, 59 U. MIAMI L. REV. 475 (2005).

517. 441 F.3d 827 (9th Cir. 2006).

518. *Id.* at 830-33.

SECTION H. DETERMINATION OF STATE LAW

Under the *Swift* doctrine, federal courts had to follow state-court decisions interpreting state constitutions and statutes and articulating state rules of decision on "local" matters. Under *Erie*, federal courts are obligated to follow state decisions on all matters of state law, when state law provides the rule of decision.[519] Because of this broadened obligation, it is important to understand how the federal courts are to determine state law.

Early in the history of the *Erie* doctrine, the federal courts appeared to be obligated to follow even the decisions of lower state courts in the absence of other evidence of what state common law would be—even though the lower state court decisions would not have been binding on another court of the same state in a similar case.[520] The Supreme Court has since retreated from this inflexible doctrine.[521] As Professors Wright, Miller, and Cooper have observed, this retreat was essential if the *Erie* doctrine was not to substitute one kind of forum shopping for another. State precedents that might not be followed by the highest court of a state would, under the earlier practice, be binding in the federal courts, tempting litigants who would be favored by the precedents to pick a federal forum. The

---

519. *But cf.* Vacation Village, Inc. v. Clark Cnty., 497F.3d 902 (9th Cir. 2007) (when state statutes have been interpreted by state courts to comply with federal constitution, but state courts have proceeded under an erroneous view of federal constitutional law, federal courts in diversity are not bound by state decisions).

520. *See, e.g.*, Fidelity Union Trust Co. v. Field, 311 U.S. 169, 61 S. Ct. 176, 85 L. Ed. 109 (1940); Edwards v. HOVENSA, LLC, 497 F.3d 355 (3d Cir. 2007) (*Erie* governs whether federal district court is bound to follow decisions of the Superior Court of the Virgin Islands; district court did not err in determining that it was not bound by such decisions, but it could rely on them as a datum).

521. *See* Commissioner v. Estate of Bosch, 387 U.S. 456, 87 S. Ct. 1776, 18 L. Ed. 2d 886 (1967); Bernhardt v. Polygraphic Co. of Am., 350 U.S. 198, 76 S. Ct. 273, 100 L. Ed. 199 (1956); King v. Order of United Commercial Travelers of Am., 333 U.S. 153, 68 S. Ct. 488, 92 L. Ed. 608 (1948); *see also* Reiser v. Residential Funding Corp., 380 F.3d 1027 (7th Cir. 2004) (district court refused to follow prior federal court of appeals decision on issue of state law after finding two later state intermediate court of appeals decisions to the contrary; the Seventh Circuit held that the district court made a fundamental error; just as the court of appeals must follow decisions of the Supreme Court whether or not it agrees with decisions, so must district courts follow court of appeals decisions; a decision by a state's supreme court will terminate the authoritative force of a federal court of appeals decision on an issue of state law; but decisions of state intermediate court of appeals decisions do not have the same force and cannot liberate a district court from the force of a court of appeals decision); Weber v. GAF Corp., 15 F.3d 35, 37 (3d Cir. 1994) (refusing to rely on lower state court decision on the grounds that the plain language of the law dictated a contrary result and it was not persuaded by the lower state decision); *In re* Orso, 214 F.3d 637 (5th Cir. 2000) (prior precedent of court of appeals on state issue should not be disregarded on the basis of subsequent intermediate state appellate court precedent unless such precedent comprises unanimous or nearly unanimous holdings from several—preferably a majority—of the intermediate state appellate courts of the state in question). *But cf.* Kurczi v. Eli Lilly & Co., 113 F.3d 1426 (6th Cir. 1997) (decision of state intermediate court of appeals constitutes datum from which state law can be determined and is not to be disregarded by federal court in the absence of other persuasive evidence that the state's highest court would decide otherwise). It has been held that if a federal court of appeals has rendered a decision on a state issue, but the state's highest court has not, a district court should follow the court of appeals decision rather than the decision of a state intermediate court of appeals. *See* FDIC v. Abraham, 137 F.3d 264 (5th Cir. 1998) (*Erie* does not require abandonment of a federal court of appeals decision in deference to a subsequent holding by a state intermediate court of appeals); Perez v. Brown & Williamson Tobacco Corp., 967 F. Supp. 920 (S.D. Tex. 1997) (district court must follow federal court of appeals decision). For an excellent article discussing the problems with the attempts by the lower federal courts to "predict" what rule the highest court of a state would adopt if a question were before it, see Bradford R. Clark, *Ascertaining the Laws of the Several States: Positivism and Judicial Federalism After* Erie, 145 U. PA. L. REV. 1459 (1997); *see also* Michael C. Dorf, *Prediction and the Rule of Law*, 42 UCLA L. REV. 651, 695-715 (1995) (discussing, *inter alia*, the "radical realist roots" of *Erie* as a source of the "prediction model" of determining state law in diversity cases); Benjamin C. Glassman, *Making State Law in Federal Court,* 41 GONZ. L. REV. 237 (2006); Doug M. Keller, Comment, *Interpreting Foreign Law Through an* Erie *Lens: A Critical Look at* United States v. McNab, 40 TEX. INT'L L.J. 157 (2004).

federal courts, in turn, would be unable to assure that the outcome in federal diversity actions would be the same as in the state courts.[522]

Under the accepted practice today, a federal court determining state law can use any available sources to predict how the state's highest court would decide a case.[523] Such sources include, but are not limited to, lower state-court decisions, which constitute persuasive, but not binding, authority in federal diversity actions.[524] Similarly, if no state judicial precedents exist with which to predict how the state's highest court will decide a case, the federal courts can look to persuasive authorities from other states on the same issue, scholarly works, and other similar sources, just as lawyers within the state would do. Old decisions of the state's highest court are binding in diversity actions if no evidence exists that they have been undermined by later cases. When confronted with such precedents, the federal courts will examine them to determine whether "clear evidence" exists that they would no longer be followed. In the absence of such evidence, however, the old precedents will be followed.[525]

Illustration 5-22. *P*, a citizen of State *X*, was traveling on a train operated by *D Railroad*, a corporation incorporated with its principal place of business in State *Y*. *P* was assaulted by *C*, an employee of *D*, who was not acting within the scope of *C's* employment by *D* at the time of the assault. *P* sues *D* and *C* in a U.S. District Court for State *X*. *C* defaults, and a judgment is rendered against *C*. *D* defends on the ground that it is not liable for the intentional torts of an employee who is not acting within the scope of employment when the assault is committed. The U.S. District Court determines that under the *Klaxon* doctrine, State *X* would apply the substantive law of State *Y* to resolve the dispute. Under the State *Y* precedents, a sixty-year-old decision holds that because of the special relationship between a common carrier, such as *D*, and its passengers, carriers are liable for the intentional torts of their employees committed against passengers, even if the

---

522. *See* 19 CHARLES A. WRIGHT ET AL., FEDERAL PRACTICE AND PROCEDURE: JURISDICTION AND RELATED MATTERS (ERIE DOCTRINE) § 4507, at 140-41 (2d ed. 1996) (footnotes omitted).

523. *See id.*; *cf.* Primrose Operating Co. v. National Am. Ins. Co., 382 F.3d 546 (5th Cir. 2004) (refusing to follow two unpublished lower court decisions on Texas law because (1) such unpublished decisions were not precedent in Texas and (2) neither announced a persuasive argument suggesting how the Texas Supreme Court would decide the issue). In Ileto v. Glock Inc., 349 F.3d 1191, 1218 (9th Cir. 2003) (Hall, J., dissenting), the dissenting judge chastised the majority for violating the *Erie* doctrine in disregarding a state statute barring the claim, in adopting a negligence theory that was specifically rejected by the California Supreme Court, and in adopting a nuisance theory that contradicted relevant California authority.

524. *But cf.* Bravo v. United States, 577 F.3d 1324 (11th Cir. 2009) (federal courts obligated to follow decisions of intermediate state appellate court on point unless there is persuasive evidence that the highest state court would rule otherwise); *see also* Beeman v. Anthem Prescription Mgmt., LLC, 652 F.3d 1085 (9th Cir. 2011) (intermediate state appellate decisions are binding on federal courts in the absence of authority from the state's highest court, even when they construe a state constitutional provision by relying exclusively on federal precedents; however, here intermediate state precedents can be disregarded because court convinced that California Supreme Court would interpret state constitutional provision by relying on First Amendment to U.S. Constitution, and First Amendment not violated!).

525. *See, e.g.*, Gilstrap v. Amtrak, 998 F.2d 559 (8th Cir. 1993); *see also* United Fire & Cas. Ins. Co. v. Garvey, 328 F.3d 411 (8th Cir. 2003) (decisions of state's intermediate courts of appeals are persuasive, but not binding, authority on United States Court of Appeals); Allstate Ins. Co. v. Menards, Inc., 285 F.3d 630 (7th Cir. 2002) (district court faced with a conflict between state intermediate appellate courts was not obliged to follow the decision of the appellate court with jurisdiction over the place where the suit would have been brought if it had been brought in state court; rather, district court is obliged to make a prediction as to how the highest court of the state would decide the matter if it were presented to that court); Data Specialties, Inc. v. Transcontinental Ins. Co., 125 F.3d 909 (5th Cir. 1997) (relying on dicta in Texas Supreme Court and Court of Appeals decisions, decisions from other states, and commentary in treatises and law reviews).

employees are not acting within the scope of their employment. *D* offers several more recent State *Y* precedents indicating that employers are not liable for the intentional torts of their employees acting outside the course of their employment. However, these precedents do not involve torts committed by the employees of common carriers against passengers of the carriers. The federal court should follow the sixty-year-old decision under these circumstances, unless there is other evidence that the State *Y* Supreme Court would no longer follow the decision. The old decision was a case specially predicated on the relationship between common carriers and their passengers. The newer decisions do not involve common carrier cases. Therefore, the newer decisions are not on point and do not indicate that the old case is obsolete.[526]

Illustration 5-23. *P*, a citizen of State *X*, sues *D*, a citizen of State *Y*, in a U.S. District Court in State *Y*. *P* seeks $500,000 for breach of contract. The district court grants a motion to dismiss *P's* complaint on the ground that contracts of the kind in question are invalid in State *Y*. This decision is based on a decision of the State *Y* Supreme Court in existence at the time the district court rules on the motion. *P* appeals to the court of appeals. While the case is on appeal, the State *Y* Supreme court overrules the decision relied on by the district court and holds contracts of the kind between *P* and *D* valid and enforceable in State *Y*. The court of appeals must apply the later State *Y* Supreme Court decision because it represents the most accurate picture of State *Y* law at the time the court of appeals must make its decision.[527]

* * * * *

Ordinarily, federal courts must decide questions of state law themselves, without seeking answers directly from the state courts. However, some states have adopted a procedure called *certification*, whereby federal courts may obtain answers

---

526. *See* Gilstrap v. Amtrak, 998 F.2d 559 (8th Cir. 1993); *see also* Memorial Hermann Healthcare Sys., Inc. v. Eurocopter Deutschland, GMBH, 524 F.3d 676 (5th Cir. 2008) (in making an *Erie* guess, federal court's task is to predict state law, not to create or modify it; appellant carries heavy burden in assuring court that it would not be making state law when practical effect of adopting exception to Texas economic loss rule would be to create a previously nonexistent state cause of action; federal court will rely on intermediate state appellate court decisions unless convinced by other persuasive data that highest court of state would decide otherwise, but here there is no Texas decision supporting appellant's position; therefore, appellant has not carried its burden).

527. *See* Vandenbark v. Owens-Illinois Glass Co., 311 U.S. 538, 61 S. Ct. 347, 85 L. Ed. 327 (1941). *But cf.* Cincinnati Ins. Co. v. Flanders Elec. Motor Serv., Inc., 131 F.3d 625 (7th Cir. 1997) (appellant moved to stay proceedings before court of appeals until state supreme court decided a case involving the identical issue in the federal action; court of appeals denied stay and affirmed district court; a year and a half later, state supreme court decision indicated that court of appeal's decision of state issue was incorrect; appellant's motion for relief under Federal Rule 60(b) denied by district court; court of appeals affirms denial on the ground that use of Rule 60(b) to obtain relief from erroneous interpretations of state law in diversity cases would unduly undermine the principle of finality in litigation); *see also* United States *ex rel.* Garibaldi v. Orleans Parish Sch. Bd., 397 F.3d 344 (5th Cir. 2005) (change in controlling authority after judgment becomes final is ordinarily not an "extraordinary circumstance" justifying relief under Federal Rule 60(b)); Kansas Pub. Employees Ret. Sys. v. Reimer & Koger Assocs., Inc., 194 F.3d 922 (8th Cir. 1999) (Rule 60(b) relief from judgment improper on basis of decision of state's highest court indicating that state statute of limitations had not run on claim; state decision made one week after mandate of court of appeals issued in case holding that state statute of limitations barred action); Willis v. Roche Biomedical Labs., Inc., 21 F.3d 1368, 1372-75 (5th Cir. 1994), *withdrawn after decision of the highest state court and new opinion substituted*, 61 F.3d 313 (5th Cir. 1995) (relying on intermediate state court of appeals decisions even though state's highest court had granted review and then correcting decision after highest court ruled). The *Vandenbark* rule should not apply if the state court would hold that the new rule applies only prospectively to cases not yet commenced. *Cf.* Albano v. Shea Homes Ltd. P'ship, 662 F.3d 1120 (9th Cir. 2011) (court of appeals holds that state rule would be applied retrospectively after state's highest court answers certified question).

to unsettled questions of state law from the state's highest court. The U.S. Supreme Court has approved of the use of these certification procedures by the federal courts in diversity cases when the procedures exist.[528] However, certification is discretionary with the federal court.[529] The possibility that certification will produce significant delay, the difficulty of certifying a question to the state court in a manner that will result in an authoritative answer,[530] the sensitivity or importance of the question to the state, and the danger of abdicating the federal judicial function all are taken into account in determining whether to certify.[531] When a question is

---

528. *See* Lehman Bros. v. Schein, 416 U.S. 386, 94 S. Ct. 1741, 40 L. Ed. 2d 215 (1974); *see also* UNIF. CERTIFICATION OF QUESTIONS OF LAW ACT (1995), 12 U.L.A. 64 (1996). For a discussion of certification as a means of making the determination of state law required by *Erie*, see Bradford R. Clark, *Ascertaining the Laws of the Several States: Positivism and Judicial Federalism After* Erie, 145 U. PA. L. REV. 1459, 1544-63 (1997); Larry M. Roth, *Certified Questions From the Federal Courts: Review and Re-Proposal*, 34 U. MIAMI L. REV. 1 (1979); *see also* Stanton S. Kaplan, *Certification of Questions From Federal Appellate Courts to the Florida Supreme Court and Its Impact on the Abstention Doctrine*, 16 U. MIAMI L. REV. 413 (1962); Vincent L. McKuzick, *Certification: A Procedure for Cooperation Between State and Federal Courts*, 16 ME. L. REV. 33 (1964).

529. *But cf.* Royal Capital Dev. LLC v. Maryland Cas. Co., 659 F.3d 1050 (11th Cir. 2011) (language stating that if there is any doubt about the application of state law, court should certify question, but that certification is discretionary and should never be automatic or unthinking).

530. *See, e.g., In re* Vasquez, 228 Ariz. 357, 266 P.3d 1053 (2011) (Arizona Supreme Court answers one of two certified questions from federal court, but refuses to answer the second on the grounds that it is not determinative of the cause pending in the certifying court).

531. *See* City of Houston v. Hill, 482 U.S. 451, 470-71, 107 S. Ct. 2502, 2514-15, 96 L. Ed. 2d 398, 417-18 (1987); Florida *ex rel.* Shevin v. Exxon Corp., 526 F.2d 266, 274-75 (5th Cir. 1976); Barnes v. Atlantic & Pac. Life Ins. Co. of Am., 514 F.2d 704, 705 n.4 (5th Cir. 1975); *see also* Albano v. Shea Homes Ltd. P'ship, 662 F.3d 1120 (9th Cir. 2011) (court of appeals holds new rule of state law applies retrospectively after Arizona Supreme Court answered certified question); Reddington v. Staten Island Univ. Hosp., 511 F.3d 126 (2d Cir. 2007) (in determining whether to certify, court considers the absence of authoritative precedents interpreting the state statute, the importance of the issue to the state, including whether the issue implicates issues of state public policy, and the capacity of certification to resolve the issue: split of authority between state and federal courts on issue is particularly important, because it could result in the kind of forum shopping that *Erie* was designed to eliminate); International Interests, L.P. v. Hardy, 448 F.3d 303 (5th Cir. 2006) (certifying a question of law to the Texas Supreme Court concerning whether choice-of-law clause in Ohio contract would be given effect in action for a deficiency judgment resulting from foreclosure sale of Texas real property); Stichting Ter Behartiging Van De Belangen Van Oudaandeelhouders in Het Kapitaal Van Saybolt Int'l B.V. v. Schreiber, 407 F.3d 34 (2d Cir. 2005) (conflict-of-laws question about whether New York law, which permitted assignment of tort malpractice claim, or New Jersey law, which did not permit assignment, certified to New York Court of Appeals under New York's conflict-of-laws system); Gulfstream Park Racing Ass'n v. Tampa Bay Downs, Inc., 399 F.3d 1276 (11th Cir. 2005) (case raised question as to whether plaintiff's contracts were enforceable under state's pari-mutuel wagering act; the issue was one of first impression that was an integral part of the state's extensive regulatory scheme; therefore, question was certified); Volvo Cars of N. Am. v. Ricci, 122 Nev. 146, 137 P.3d 1161 (2006) (refusing to answer certified questions from federal court because questions would not produce answers that would be determinative of the federal action as required by Nevada rule of appellate procedure); 17A CHARLES A. WRIGHT ET AL., FEDERAL PRACTICE AND PROCEDURE: JURISDICTION AND RELATED MATTERS § 4248 (3d ed. 2007); Deborah J. Challenger, *Distinguishing Certification From Abstention in Diversity Cases: Postponement Versus Abdication of the Duty to Exercise Jurisdiction,* 38 RUTGERS L.J. 847 (2007); Rebecca A. Cochran, *Federal Court of Questions of State Law to State Courts: A Theoretical and Empirical Study,* 29 J. LEGIS. 157 (2003); Jonathan Remy Nash, *Examining the Power of Federal Courts to Certify Questions of State Law,* 88 CORNELL L. REV. 1672 (2003); *cf.* Arizonans for Official English v. Arizona, 520 U.S. 43, 117 S. Ct. 1055, 137 L. Ed. 2d 170 (1997) (lower federal courts should have used Arizona's certification procedure to obtain a state-court interpretation of a novel state constitutional question in order to possibly avoid a federal constitutional question concerning the validity of the state constitutional provision). For a questionable use of the certification procedure, see Prodigy Ctrs./Atlanta No. 1 L.P. v. T-C Assocs., Ltd., 127 F.3d 1021 (11th Cir. 1997), in which the court of appeals certified a question of Georgia law to the Georgia Supreme Court concerning whether a partnership interest in a limited partnership constituted a "chose in action." The court of appeals considered Georgia law ambiguous on the issue because of uncertainty about whether this question had been before the Georgia Supreme Court in a prior case in which the latter court had relied on Georgia chose in action law in considering whether a judgement lien attached to a partnership interest sold to a good faith purchaser. However, the court of appeals did not consider factors such as how important the question was in Georgia law in determining whether to certify. Other questionable uses of certification include Union Planters Bank, N.A. v. New York, 436 F.3d 1305 (11th Cir. 2006) (certifying three questions to the Alabama Supreme court simply because there were no cases interpreting the Alabama statutes at

certified to the highest court of a state, the proceedings after certification are governed by the statutes and rules of the state court to which the certification is made.[532]

An interesting example of a certified question that did not resolve, but will present, an *Erie* problem to the federal courts is *Lewis v. Waletzky*.[533] In *Lewis*, the United States Court of Appeals for the Fourth Circuit certified a question to the Court of Appeals of Maryland. The action was a medical malpractice case that had been commenced in United States District Court in Maryland. Maryland follows the traditional vested rights system of conflict of laws that would apply the law of the place of the injury to determine all substantive matters in a malpractice case.[534] However, Maryland had a statute that provided for certain specific administrative filing requirements, including a expert certificate of merit requirement, which had to be complied with to avoid an alternative dispute resolution requirement that would otherwise be required as a prerequisite to a malpractice action. The plaintiff did not comply with these requirements, and the U.S. District Court dismissed the action as a result. However, the court of appeals, in its certified question, queried whether Maryland would recognize a "public policy" exception to the law of the state of the injury test, or any other exception to that test, that would require the plaintiff to adhere to the Maryland procedure in this case, even though the substantive law of the District of Columbia, where the malpractice induced injury occurred, was otherwise controlling under Maryland's conflicts rules. The Court of Appeals of Maryland ignored the "public policy" query, but answered the certified question by indicating that the Maryland statute was "procedural" for purposes of Maryland conflicts law and would have to be applied in a Maryland state court even though Maryland would ultimately apply the substantive malpractice law of the District of Columbia to the case.[535]

The interesting point about the answer to this question is that it now presents the *Erie* questions discussed in previous sections to the federal courts for decision. Had the Court of Appeals of Maryland held that the provision was "substantive" for conflict-of-laws purposes and inapplicable in Maryland, no Rules Enabling Act or Rules of Decision Act issue would have been presented. The Maryland requirement would have been inapplicable because District of Columbia substantive law controlled the case, and the District of Columbia has no such requirement. By holding the requirement "procedural" and thus applicable in Maryland courts, the federal courts will now have to determine whether the

---

issue and because the court did not find clear guidance in the statutes themselves); CSX Tranp., Inc. v. City of Garden City, 325 F.3d 1236 (11th Cir. 2003) (when there is any doubt as to the application of state law, federal court should certify question to state supreme court to avoid making mistake); *In re* Genesys Data Techs., Inc., 204 F.3d 124 (4th Cir. 2000) (question certified to the Hawaii Supreme Court concerning whether a $1.2 million default judgment was void under Hawaii Rule of Civil Procedure 54(c) because it was different in kind from, or exceeded in amount of, the relief requested by the complaint).

532. *See, e.g.*, NEB. REV. STAT. § 24-224 (2008) (providing for an expedited briefing and hearing procedure so that the certified question can be answered promptly); *see also* Scottsdale Ins. Co. v. Tolliver, 2005 OK 93, 127 P.3d 611 (refusing to answer a certified question under the Oklahoma Uniform Certification of Questions of Law Act on the ground that controlling authority existed on the issue certified).

533. 422 Md. 647, 31 A.3d 123 (2011).

534. For a description of the vested rights system, see ROBERT L. FELIX & RALPH U. WHITTEN, AMERICAN CONFLICTS LAW §§ 54-55 (generally), §§ 111-114 (torts) (6th ed. 2011).

535. *See* 422 Md. at 656-66, 31 A.3d at 129-35.

requirement conflicts with any Federal Rule of Civil Procedure. If so, a Rules Enabling Act issue will be presented. If, on the other hand, the federal courts determine that no Federal Rule of Civil Procedure of sufficient breadth exists to cover the case, a Rules of Decision Act question will be presented—*i.e.,* whether disregard of the state law would be obligatory under the general *Erie* doctrine because the state law is either bound up with state substantive rights or, if a rule of form and mode, would produce forum shopping or inequitable administration of the law. The holding by the Court of Appeals of Maryland that the state law is "procedural" for state conflicts purposes does not produce the conclusion that it is also procedural for *Erie* purposes.[536]

An additional device for obtaining answers to unsettled state-law questions is the doctrine of *abstention.* In reality, several different doctrines of abstention exist, all of which are complicated subjects reserved for treatment in treatises on Federal Courts.[537] For present purposes, it is only relevant to determine whether a federal court sitting in diversity may abstain from making a decision to obtain an answer to an unsettled question of law from a state court. If abstention is proper in these circumstances, the federal court would postpone decision of the diversity action until such time as the parties had commenced and completed state litigation to obtain an answer to the state-law question. However, the Supreme Court disapproved of abstention for these purposes in *Meredith v. City of Winter Haven,*[538] a case which the Court has subsequently cited with approval.[539] Thus, while *certification* may be available in an ordinary diversity action to obtain an answer to an unsettled issue of state law, *abstention* is improper in such a case in the absence of special factors making one of the other (nondiversity) abstention doctrines proper.[540]

Traditionally, determinations of issues of state law by U.S. District Courts have been paid great deference when diversity cases are appealed to the U.S. Courts of Appeals.[541] However, in *Salve Regina College v. Russell,*[542] the Supreme Court held, contrary to a majority of the courts of appeals, that litigants in diversity actions are entitled to plenary appellate review of matters of state law. In *Salve Regina College,* the plaintiff was asked to withdraw from a nursing program because she was excessively obese. After completing her education at another

---

536. *See also* Southeast Floating Docks, Inc. v. Auto-Owners Ins. Co., 82 So. 3d 73 (Fla. 2012) (answering certified question about Florida "offer of judgment" statute by stating (1) that the statute was substantive for conflict-of-laws purposes, (2) that it did not involve such a strong public policy that it would override the parties' freedom to agree contractually to be governed by the law of another state and (3) that the statute was inapplicable when the parties have agreed that their contractual rights are governed by the substantive law of another state).

537. *See, e.g.,* CHARLES A. WRIGHT & MARY KAY KANE, THE LAW OF FEDERAL COURTS § 52 (7th ed. 2011).

538. 320 U.S. 228, 64 S. Ct. 7, 88 L. Ed. 9 (1943).

539. *See* Colorado River Water Conservation Dist. v. United States, 424 U.S. 800, 816, 96 S. Ct. 1236, 1245-46, 47 L. Ed. 2d 483, 497 (1976).

540. *See* 17A CHARLES A. WRIGHT ET AL., FEDERAL PRACTICE AND PROCEDURE: JURISDICTION AND RELATED MATTERS (FEDERAL AND STATE COURTS) § 4246 (3d ed. 2007).

541. *See* 19 CHARLES A. WRIGHT ET AL., FEDERAL PRACTICE AND PROCEDURE: JURISDICTION AND RELATED MATTERS (ERIE DOCTRINE) § 4507, at 211 (2d ed. 1996).

542. 499 U.S. 225, 111 S. Ct. 1217, 113 L. Ed. 2d 190 (1991); *see also* B.E.L.T., Inc. v. Wachovia Corp., 403 F.3d 474 (7th Cir. 2005) (cases cited by plaintiffs were U.S. District court decisions, which have no authoritative force under *Erie*); *see generally* Ralph U. Whitten, *Developments in the* Erie *Doctrine: 1991*, 40 AM. J. COMP. L. 967, 973-75 (1992).

institution, she filed a federal diversity action against the college from which she was forced to withdraw, asserting claims for intentional infliction of emotional distress, invasion of privacy, and breach of contract. After the close of the plaintiff's case, the district court directed a verdict against the plaintiff on all claims except the breach of contract claim. The refusal to direct a verdict on the latter claim was based on the district court's "intuition" that the Rhode Island Supreme Court would recognize the doctrine of substantial performance in the academic context, even though it had theretofore been limited to commercial contexts. The jury returned a verdict for the plaintiff on the breach of contract claim, and the defendant appealed. In affirming, the court of appeals deferred to the district court's determination of state law rather than exercising an independent judgment about the content of that law. The Supreme Court granted certiorari and reversed.

The Court held that "[n]othing about the exercise of diversity jurisdiction . . . warrants the departure from a rule of independent appellate review."[543] The Court held that deferential appellate review was inconsistent with the aims of the *Erie* doctrine, in that it invited divergent development of state law among the federal courts within a single state and created a dual system of enforcement of state-created rights in which the substantive rule applied to a dispute might depend upon the choice of a federal or state court.[544]

Salve Regina College presented a strong case for requiring independent appellate review. The district court's determination that state law was not grounded in existing state supreme court decisions or other authoritative sources, but was based on the district judge's lengthy experience as a state trial judge and his "feel" for what the state supreme court would do based on that experience. A majority of the Supreme Court seemed to find this intuitive approach to state law distasteful.[545] However, the Court might better have established a requirement of nondeferential appellate review only for cases in which the district court's determination of state law was based on no traditional, preexisting legal sources, but merely, as in *Salve Regina College*, on raw intuition. Such cases present a peculiar danger of arbitrariness by the district courts, justifying a heightened standard of appellate review. In other cases, requiring the parsing of traditional legal materials, a deferential standard of appellate review might have been approved based on the presumptively greater familiarity of the district judge with state law. It is possible to reason otherwise, as did the dissenters in *Salve Regina College*, who concluded that in the face of unsettled state law, the "insights" of an experienced district judge might be deemed particularly valuable in predicting how the state supreme court would resolve the issue in question.[546] Nevertheless, it seems more appropriate to

---

543. 499 U.S. at 233-34, 111 S. Ct. at 1222, 113 L. Ed. 2d at 199.

544. *See id.* at 234, 111 S. Ct. at 1222, 113 L. Ed. 2d at 200.

545. [T]he proposition that a district judge is better able to "intuit" the answer to an unsettled question of state law is foreclosed by our holding in *Erie* doctrine is that the bases of state law are presumed to be communicable by the parties to a federal judge no less than to a state judge. . . . Similarly, the bases of state law are as equally communicable to the appellate judges as they are to the district judge. To the extent that the available state law on a controlling issue is so unsettled as to admit of no reasoned divination, we can see no sense in which a district judge's prior exposure or nonexposure to the state judiciary can be said to facilitate the rule of reason. *Id.* at 238-39, 111 S. Ct. at 1225, 113 L. Ed. 2d at 202-03.

546. *See id.* at 240-43, 111 S. Ct. at 1225-27, 113 L. Ed. at 204 (Rehnquist, C.J., with whom White, J., and Stevens, J., join, dissenting).

recognize that traditional legal authorities, where they exist, confine the ability of district judges acting in good faith to depart from the likely outcome that would be reached by the state courts. A more deferential standard of review that focuses on the reasonableness of the district court's interpretation of existing authorities seems appropriate in cases where authority exists. When the district court does not rely on preexisting authority, but on raw intuition, heightened appellate scrutiny is called for to assure that the result is based on a good faith attempt to interpret state law, rather than the individual policy predilections of the district judge.[547]

An interesting question that has arisen in recent years is what effect a federal court within one federal circuit should give to a precedent from a federal court of appeals of another circuit on a question of state law arising within the latter circuit. This issue was presented for decision in *Factors Etc., Inc. v. Pro Arts, Inc.*[548] *Factors* was a diversity action in a New York federal district court in which Factors sought to prevent Pro Arts and others from making any use of Elvis Presley's name or likeness. Factors contended that it had the exclusive right to use Presley's name and likeness under a grant of authority from Boxcar Enterprises, a Tennessee corporation formed by Presley before his death, to which Presley had assigned the exclusive ownership rights to his persona. Pro Arts argued that a decision of the Sixth Circuit Court of Appeals holding that Presley's right of publicity was not descendible was binding on the New York federal court. This argument was rejected by the district court. The case was ultimately appealed to the U.S. Court of Appeals for the Second Circuit. The issue posed by the Second Circuit for decision was whether the federal courts of one circuit are bound to follow the decisions of the federal courts of appeals of another circuit on a question of state law arising from a state within the latter circuit.

The Second Circuit first reasoned that under the *Erie-Klaxon* doctrine, the courts of New York would apply the law of Tennessee to determine whether Presley's right of publicity was descendible. Then the court reasoned that although the courts of appeals are not absolutely bound to follow the decisions of the courts of appeals of other circuits on matters of state law within the other circuit, they should nevertheless do so in the absence of a clear basis in the law of the pertinent state for predicting that the relevant state courts would reach a different result. The court stated that this approach should be followed in order to prevent diversity actions from disrupting the orderly development of state law. The court's fear was

---

547. It has been argued that predictive precedents by the courts of appeals on state issues should be presumptively binding on the district courts, but that a litigant should be able to overcome such precedents with substantial evidence of a change in state law. *See* Jed I. Bergman, Note, *Putting Precedent in Its Place: Stare Decisis and Federal Predictions of State Law*, 96 COLUM. L. REV. 969 (1996). This approach seems consistent with the dual obligations of the district courts to *Erie* and court of appeals precedents. However, the argument that district courts are under *no* statutory or constitutional obligation to follow "outrageously wrong" court of appeals decisions and treat court of appeals decisions as, at most, persuasive authority, goes too far. *See* Nififoros Mathews, *Circuit Court* Erie-*Errors and the District Court's Dilemma: From* Roto-Lith *and the Mirror Image Rule to* Octagon Gas *and Asset Securitization*, 17 CARDOZO L. REV. 739 (1996). The latter argument gives too little weight to the position and function of the courts of appeals and the district courts in the federal hierarchy. Indeed, it could be equally applied to U.S. Supreme Court decisions on matters of state law that are "outrageously wrong."

548. 652 F.2d 278 (2d Cir. 1981); *see* James Balog, Note, Factors etc., Inc. v. Pro Arts, Inc.: *Deference to Circuit Court Rulings on State Law*, 15 J. MARSHALL L. REV. 499 (1982); William F. Jestings, Note, Factors etc. v. Pro Arts, Inc., 16 SUFFOLK U. L. REV. 787 (1982).

that such disruption would be more likely if there existed divergent federal decisions on the same issue of state law in different circuits.[549]

As the dissent pointed out, however, it seems curious to follow the Sixth Circuit's view of Tennessee law when, as in *Factors*, that view is based on raw speculation, or, perhaps more accurately, was based on the Sixth Circuit's view of what Tennessee law *should* be. Likewise, there is not as much reason for deferring to a court of appeals' view of state law as there is for deferring to the opinion of a district court sitting in the state whose law is at issue, especially where the court of appeals' view is at odds with the view of the district court, as it was in *Factors.*[550] Furthermore, after the *Salve Regina College* decision, discussed above, the rule announced in *Factors* seems even more suspect. If a court of appeals cannot defer to the decisions of the U.S. District Courts on matters of state law, it is difficult to see the justification for allowing them to defer to the judgments of other courts of appeals.[551]

It has also been suggested that the critical question that should be asked in a case like *Factors* "is what weight New York's highest court would have given to the Sixth Circuit's construction of Tennessee common law."[552] This view assumes that the *Erie-Klaxon* doctrine requires federal courts to adhere not only to the conflict-of-laws rules or approach of the state in which they are sitting, but also to parrot the forum's understanding of the content of the law of the other state. This approach carries *Klaxon* too far. It is one thing to hold that federal courts must defer to the courts of the states in which they sit to determine whether the forum state's law or some other state's law is applicable to the dispute. It is quite another to hold that litigants in federal courts do not even have the right to an independent judgment about the content of another state's law. The courts of the state in which a federal court is sitting are in no better position to determine the content of another state's law than are the federal courts. The *Klaxon* decision did not hold that federal courts must duplicate the view of the forum state about the content of the law of another state, and there is no apparent reason to impose such a requirement on the speculation that doing so will prevent forum shopping for a federal court. Therefore, once it has been determined that the forum state has effectively disclaimed any sovereign interest in applying its own substantive law to the dispute, the federal

---

549. *See* 652 F.2d at 282-83.

550. *See* 652 F.2d at 284-85 (Mansfield, J., dissenting); *see also* Northwest Forest Res. Council v. Dombeck, 107 F.3d 897 (D.C. Cir. 1997) (error to give stare decisis effect to a decision of a district court in another circuit on an issue of *federal law*).

551. In fact, other courts of appeals have not shown this deference. In Rick v. Wyeth, 662 F.3d 1067 (8th Cir. 2011), the Eighth Circuit Court of Appeals was faced with the issue of whether a prior dismissal of a case before it under the New York statute of limitations was claim preclusive. The court, parsing the New York authorities, determined that a decision of New York's highest court had not been undermined by a later case by the same court, and provided that statutes of limitation dismissals were claim preclusive. This contradicted a decision of the Second Circuit Court of Appeals, which had held to the contrary. *See* Cloverleaf Realty, Inc. v. Town of Wawayanda, 572 F.3d 93, 95 (2d Cir. 2009). The Eighth Circuit indicated that it was "troubled" by this, but examined the Second Circuit authorities and seemed to hint that they were deficient on the question. *See Rick*, 662 F.3d at 1071; *cf.* Hall v. Pennsylvania Bd. of Prob. & Parole, 578 Pa. 245, 851 A.2d 859 (2004) (state courts not bound by decisions of lower federal courts on issues of federal law); State v. Greger, 1997 SD 14, 559 N.W.2d 854 (state's highest court not bound by decision of federal court of appeals covering the state on an issue of *federal law*).

552. 19 CHARLES A. WRIGHT ET AL., FEDERAL PRACTICE AND PROCEDURE: JURISDICTION AND RELATED MATTERS (ERIE DOCTRINE) § 4507, at 220 (2d ed. 1996).

courts should feel free to determine for themselves the content of the relevant state's law, including the proper weight to give different kinds of precedents interpreting state law.[553]

A 2006 Texas Supreme Court decision on an issue of conflict-of-laws may pose some difficult problems for Texas federal courts in diversity actions. In *Coca-Cola Co. v. Harmar Bottling Co.*,[554] the plaintiffs sued Coke in Texas state court under the Texas antitrust statute. Some of the behavior alleged to violate the Texas statute had occurred in Arkansas, Louisiana, and Oklahoma. Therefore, the plaintiffs alleged in the alternative that (1) Texas law governed all the behavior, wherever it occurred and (2) that the law of the other states where the behavior occurred was identical to Texas law. The Texas Supreme Court rejected the argument that Texas law should govern all the behavior, and held that as a matter of "comity" it would not interpret the law of the other states. According to the court, the content of antitrust law was so dependent on the "social needs and values" of each state and also so heavily dependent on policy determinations that would have to be made by the courts of other states in the process of interpretation that it would be unduly intrusive on the other state's prerogatives to try to apply their law. Although Coke had not denied that Texas law and the law of the other states was identical, the court refused to presume that the other states' laws were the same (as it would have done in other cases) for similar reasons.

What should a federal diversity court do in a case brought partly under Texas antitrust law and partly under the law of another state after *Harmar*? One view of the decision might be that it is simply a conflict-of-laws rule that is binding on a federal diversity court under the *Klaxon* doctrine. However, it is difficult to believe that the *Erie* doctrine should be interpreted to disable a federal diversity court in Texas from applying another state's law, not because Texas considers the other state's law inapplicable as a matter of ordinary conflict-of-laws policy, but because the Texas Supreme Court finds the interpretive difficulties of figuring out the other state's law to be too much for it. It is, of course, true that disregard by a Texas federal court of the comity part of the Texas Supreme Court's decision would create forum shopping of the sort that *Erie* and *Klaxon* were designed to avoid. Nevertheless, it is carrying the doctrine of those cases too far to require federal courts that feel capable of understanding the law of another state to refuse to behave like courts just because the Texas Supreme Court refuses to do so.

Furthermore, the potential problems posed by *Harmar* extend considerably beyond its facts. For example, the Texas Supreme Court's approach raises the possibility that litigants in Texas will begin identifying other areas heavily dependent on the "social needs and values" and judicially formulated "policies" of other states that it would be too intrusive for Texas to involve itself with. Indeed, under contemporary views of the nature of law, it is questionable whether there are

---

553. *See also* Camacho v. Texas Workforce Comm'n, 445 F.3d 407 (5th Cir. 2006) (district court did not err under *Erie* doctrine in refusing to apply fee award provision of Texas Declaratory Judgment Act; prior circuit court panel decision had held that fee award provision was procedural for *Erie* purposes; two subsequent panel decisions reached the opposite result; two panel decisions subsequent to the contradictory panel decisions upheld the first panel decision; the earliest of conflicting panel decisions controls; this is true, even though the earliest decision did not conduct a proper *Erie* analysis!).

554. 218 S.W.2d 671 (Tex. 2006).

any areas *not* heavily dependent on the "social needs and values" and judicially determined policies of a state. Thus, the potential effect of the case could have major effects on the operation of the diversity jurisdiction.

Other technical problems can also be imagined. For example, would the decision of the Texas Supreme Court have been the same if there had existed better authority in the other states on the issue involved in the action? If a precedent directly on point had existed in one of other states interpreting that state's antitrust laws on the facts of the case, would the Texas Supreme Court have agreed to apply that state's law? Would it matter if the other state's precedent were recent or old (so that new "social needs and values" might have intervened to render the precedent obsolete)? What if the other state had held that its courts were bound to follow federal precedents under federal antitrust laws in interpreting the state's antitrust laws, as states sometimes do, and there were ample federal precedents?[555] Could the Texas Supreme Court then possibly reason that the state's interpretation of its antitrust laws would be too dependent on local values and needs to be applied by Texas courts? These and other imaginable difficulties should at least cause federal diversity courts to refuse to extend *Harmar* to other fact situations, even if they feel compelled to follow it on its precise facts by the *Klaxon* doctrine.

SECTION I. FEDERAL COMMON LAW

Well, one thing is for sure. The Court in *Erie* definitely decided that there is no substantive federal common law, right? Wrong. On the same day it decided *Erie*, the Court held in another case that "federal common law" governed the question whether the water of an interstate stream must be apportioned between two states.[556] This section is devoted to an examination of how this "new federal common law" works.[557] However, it is important to remember that the federal common law discussed in this section differs from the federal common law discussed in section E, above. Section E discussed the circumstances in which it is justifiable under the Rules of Decision Act for the federal courts to apply federal common-law rules of practice and procedure. This section discusses when it is appropriate for the federal courts to create and apply substantive federal common-law rules. As section E demonstrated, even the power to apply federal common law rules of procedure is restricted under the *Erie* doctrine. Because of both separation

---

555. *See* Kessel v. Monogalia Cnty. Gen. Hosp. Co., 648 S.E.2d 367 (W. Va. 2007) (state courts must apply federal decisional law interpreting Sherman Act to parallel West Virginia antitrust statute).

556. *See* Hinderlider v. La Plata River & Cherry Creek Ditch Co., 304 U.S. 92, 58 S. Ct. 803, 82 L. Ed. 1202 (1938).

557. *See* Henry J. Friendly, *In Praise of* Erie—*And of the New Federal Common Law*, 39 N.Y.U. L. REV. 383 (1964). Useful discussions of federal common law include Bradford R. Clark, *Federal Common Law: A Structural Reinterpretation*, 144 U. PA. L. REV. 1245 (1996); Martha Field, *Sources of Law: The Scope of Federal Common Law*, 99 HARV. L. REV. 881 (1986); Stewart Jay, *Origins of Federal Common Law* (pts. 1 & 2), 133 U. PA. L. REV. 1003, 1231 (1985); Thomas W. Merrill, *The Common Law Powers of Federal Courts*, 52 U. CHI. L. REV. 1 (1985); Martin H. Redish, *Federal Common Law, Political Legitimacy, and the Interpretive Process: An "Institutionalist" Perspective*, 83 NW. U. L. REV. 761 (1989); *see also* Martin H. Redish, *Federal Common Law and American Political Theory: A Response to Professor Weinberg*, 83 NW. U. L. REV. 853 (1989); Louise Weinberg, *Federal Common Law*, 83 NW. U. L. REV. 853 (1989); Louise Weinberg, *The Curious Nation That the Rule of Decision Act Blocks Supreme Federal Common Law*, 83 NW. U. L. REV. 860 (1989); *see also* Anthony J. Bellia Jr., *State Courts and the Making of Federal Common Law*, 153 U. PA. L. REV. 825 (2005).

of powers and federalism restrictions, the justifiability of federal courts creating substantive federal common-law rules is even more controversial.

In addition to distinguishing federal substantive common law from the federal procedural common law discussed in section E, two features of the "new federal common law" should be distinguished from the general law applied by the Supreme Court in *Swift v. Tyson*.[558] First, if the plaintiff possesses a claim for relief under the "new federal common law," that claim is one arising under federal law for purposes of the federal-question jurisdiction.[559] Recall from the discussion of the *Swift* doctrine in section C, however, that the general commercial law enforced in that case was not "federal" law that would provide a basis for federal-question jurisdiction.[560] Second, when it is created, the "new" substantive federal common law controls the disputes it covers in both federal and state courts.[561] Under the *Swift* doctrine, federal and state courts were each entitled to their own view of the content of the general commercial law. The states also had the right to localize the rule of decision in the general commercial law area and thus to control decisions in both state and federal courts.[562]

1. A Conceptual Framework for Evaluating Federal Common-Law Decisions

The Rules of Decision Act provides that state law shall be the rule of decision except where the Constitution, treaties, or Acts of Congress otherwise require or provide.[563] The Act does not mention "federal common law." Under a literal interpretation of the provision, therefore, it would seem inappropriate for the federal courts to create "federal common law."[564] As noted in section A, however, it is inevitable that judges will engage in lawmaking when they articulate the rules of decision applicable to a dispute before them—even when the judges are interpreting a statutory or constitutional provision. It is widely believed today that no bright line exists between statutory and constitutional interpretation on the one hand and common-law decision making on the other. Thus, "[a]s specific evidence of legislative purpose to the issue at hand attenuates, interpretation shades into

---

558. *See* section C *supra* ("The Doctrine of *Swift v. Tyson*").

559. *See* Illinois v. City of Milwaukee, 406 U.S. 91, 92 S. Ct. 1385, 31 L. Ed. 2d 712 (1972).

560. Derivation of subject-matter jurisdiction from general common-law rules would probably have been considered a separation-of-powers violation in its own right under the *Swift* doctrine. For there existed at that time a concept that distinguished between the common law as a source of judicial power and the common law as a means of exercising judicial power conferred by other sources. The idea was that the courts had "jurisdiction of the common law," but could not obtain "jurisdiction from the common law." *See* RANDALL BRIDWELL & RALPH U. WHITTEN, THE CONSTITUTION AND THE COMMON LAW: THE DECLINE OF THE DOCTRINES OF SEPARATION OF POWERS AND FEDERALISM 31-33, 46 (1977). Modern commentators have had difficulty understanding this phraseology. *See, e.g.*, Note, Swift v. Tyson *Exhumed*, 79 YALE L.J. 284, 297-98 (1969).

561. *See, e.g.*, Hinderlider v. La Plata River & Cherry Creek Ditch Co., 304 U.S. 92, 58 S. Ct. 803, 82 L. Ed. 1202 (1938); *see also* Dice v. Akron, Canton & Youngstown R.R. Co., 342 U.S. 359, 72 S. Ct. 312, 96 L. Ed. 398 (1952); Brown v. Western Ry., 338 U.S. 294, 70 S. Ct. 105, 94 L. Ed. 100 (1949).

562. *See* section C *supra* ("The Doctrine of *Swift v. Tyson*").

563. 28 U.S.C. § 1652.

564. *See* ERWIN CHEMERINSKY, FEDERAL JURISDICTION § 6.1, at 364 (5th ed. 2007); MARTIN A. REDISH, FEDERAL JURISDICTION: TENSIONS IN THE ALLOCATION OF JUDICIAL POWER 127 (2d ed. 1990). *But see* Louise Weinberg, *The Curious Notion That the Rules of Decision Act Blocks Supreme Federal Common Law*, 83 NW. U. L. REV. 860 (1989).

judicial lawmaking on a spectrum."[565] Nevertheless, from the terms of the Rules of Decision Act and from the general separation-of-powers obligation of the judges to make law only "interstitially," the creation of federal common law decreases in justifiability as the judges move away from the process of interpreting the will of Congress or the framers and ratifiers of the Constitution toward the promulgation of rules of decision that have only the barest support in any articulated, nonjudicially created policy. The following discussion illustrates the general nature of the problems involved.

(a) "Interpretation"

At the most basic level, judges perform activities that are classified under the labels "statutory interpretation" or "statutory construction." However, different sorts of interpretive activity raise different separation of powers issues. Suppose, first, that the problem confronting a federal court is one of determining the meaning of a particular word or words in a statute or constitutional provision. In other words, the court is attempting in good faith to determine what Congress or the Framers of the Constitution meant when they used a word or phrase and will follow the communicated meaning once it has been determined. This kind of problem has been traditionally defined as one of statutory or constitutional interpretation. The court simply is trying to understand a formal communication made to it by a superior lawmaking institution. The court may do a poor job of determining meaning, because the judges are stupid, lazy, or careless, or because the form of expression chosen by Congress or the Framers was so poor that the meaning is indecipherable. Nevertheless, the performance of the task of interpretation is appropriate for the judges and raises no separation-of-powers problems unless the judges insincerely read their own personal predilections into the words of the statute instead of trying to determine the meaning communicated by the lawmakers.

One step removed from the task of determining statutory meaning is the more creative task of filling in gaps left in a statute or constitutional provision when the court believes Congress or the framers meant a certain rule of decision to be included but, for some reason, did not put the rule of decision explicitly into the text. This task raises no serious separation-of-powers problems as long as it is done sincerely—*i.e.*, if the court simply is attempting to discern and enforce the will of Congress or the framers, not making up law according to its own policy preferences—and, in the case of statutory gaps, so long also as the gaps left by Congress are not so broad as to involve an unconstitutional delegation of legislative power to the courts. Separation-of-powers difficulties are created when Congress delegates lawmaking authority to the courts in a wholesale manner, not because the courts are usurping functions given to Congress that Congress wishes to retain, but because Congress itself is attempting to give away more of its legislative authority than the Constitution permits.

---

565. RICHARD H. FALLON ET AL., HART & WECHSLER'S THE FEDERAL COURTS AND THE FEDERAL SYSTEM 755 (4th ed. 1996) (quotation removed from later editions).

(b) "Supplementation"

More serious separation-of-powers difficulties exist in what might be called statutory or constitutional "supplementation" cases. Such cases exist when the courts create rules of decision not explicitly found in statutory or constitutional provisions and which the courts cannot sincerely say that Congress or the framers meant, though inadvertently failed, to create explicitly. Sometimes, the courts will create rules of decision in such cases to prevent unforeseen circumstances from undermining the principal purposes of a statute or constitutional provision.[566] This situation is the most justifiable of the supplementation cases, but separation-of-powers dangers exist here nevertheless.

A court appropriately may create supplementary rules of decision that will prevent the main objects of Congress or the framers from being defeated, on the reasonable assumption that those lawmaking bodies would have approved of the creation of the supplementary law so that their legislative acts would not be exercises in futility. However, the courts may go only so far as they think the superior lawmaking institutions would have gone in preserving the statutory or constitutional scheme. Otherwise, the judges effectively elevate themselves into legislators by choosing to vindicate policies that the legislators might have rejected.[567] In addition, the courts must be on guard, in the process of protecting statutory purposes, not to indirectly accept delegations of lawmaking authority that more appropriately belong to Congress.

A second "supplementation" case, distinguishable from the example discussed above, occurs when the judges seek not to prevent the objectives of a statutory or constitutional provision from being undermined, but to further the purposes of a statutory or constitutional scheme by creating rules of decision that the judges deem to be a desirable *extension* of the policies supporting the law. The distinction between this case and the first "supplementation" case is that here the rules created by the judges are not essential to protect the objectives of Congress or the framers. Rather, they are rules that the courts themselves deem to be desirable extensions of the law. The separation-of-powers problems with this kind of judicial activity are severe. By extending a law to situations that the creators of the law did not extend them, the courts may go beyond the legislators' policy choices and make the policy choices themselves. Thus, there is a danger that the lawmaking in which the judges are engaging will not be merely "interstitial" in nature.

(c) "Policy Making"

The final category of problems concerns cases in which the courts create rules of decision based on policies identified or created by the judges themselves. Here, some distant statutory or constitutional provision exists, but the articulated congressional or constitutional policies are remote from the immediate issues under litigation. The justifiability of federal court lawmaking in this category of cases

---

566. *See* ERWIN CHEMERINSKY, FEDERAL JURISDICTION § 6.3.1 (5th ed. 2007).

567. *See* Learned Hand, *Is a Judge Free in Rendering a Decision? in* THE SPIRIT OF LIBERTY 103, 109 (3d ed. 1974).

depends on the reality and strength of the national policies identified by the courts compared with the strength of any existing state interests in controlling the issues with state law. The stronger the national interest in controlling the case with uniform national law, the more justifiable is the creation of "federal common law" to govern the case.[568]

2. Examples of Federal Common-Law Decisions

The federal courts have actually created "federal common law" in all of the ways described in the preceding subsection, but not always justifiably. Professors Wright, Miller, and Cooper have identified three categories of cases that are "neither exhaustive nor analytically precise" in which federal common law has been developed. Each of these categories can involve "interpretation," "supplementation," or "policy making": (1) cases involving significant conflict between a federal policy or interest and state law in which a federal rule of decision is required to protect federal interests; (2) cases in which legal policy is so dominated by federal statutory or constitutional provisions that it may be inferred that federal courts should provide rules of decision to govern issues not explicitly controlled by the statutory or constitutional provisions; and (3) cases in which there is a strong national concern with an area, and state law would not be sufficiently sensitive to federal concerns, would not be uniform, and would develop at various rates of speed.[569]

The best-known example of the first category of cases described by Professors Wright, Miller, and Cooper is *Clearfield Trust Co. v. United States*.[570] In *Clearfield*, a check issued by the United States was stolen and cashed by the thief. The United States sued a bank that had guaranteed all prior endorsements on the check when it presented the check for payment. Under the law of Pennsylvania where the federal district court was sitting, the delay of the United States in notifying the bank that the endorsement was a forgery would have prevented recovery. The U.S. Supreme Court, however, held that federal common law governs the rights and duties of the United States on its commercial paper. The Court's decision was based on the fact that when the United States disburses funds or pays its debts, it exercises a constitutional function, which is not dependent on the laws of any state. Therefore, the Court believed that even in the absence of a controlling federal statute, it was the federal courts' obligation to formulate the governing rule of decision according to their own standards.[571] In the *Clearfield* category of cases, it is the extent to which the rights and liabilities of the United States are implicated in the action that justifies the creation of federal common law, not simply the fact

---

568. *See generally* ERWIN CHEMERINSKY, FEDERAL JURISDICTION § 6.2 (5th ed. 2007).

569. *See* 19 CHARLES A. WRIGHT ET AL., FEDERAL PRACTICE AND PROCEDURE: JURISDICTION AND RELATED MATTERS (ERIE DOCTRINE) § 4514, at 463-73 (2d ed. 1996); *see also* ERWIN CHEMERINSKY, FEDERAL JURISDICTION §§ 6.1-6.3 (5th ed. 2007).

570. 318 U.S. 363, 63 S. Ct. 573, 87 L. Ed. 838 (1943).

571. *See* 318 U.S. at 366-67, 63 S. Ct. at 574-76, 87 L. Ed. at 841-42.

that the United States is a party to the action.[572] Indeed, in *Empire Healthchoice Assurance, Inc. v. McVeigh*,[573] the Supreme Court recently stated that "in post-*Clearfield* decisions, and with the benefit of enlightened commentary . . . the Court has 'made clear that uniform federal law need not be applied to all questions in federal government litigation, even in cases involving government contracts . . . .'"[574] Although the Court distinguished the case before it from prior decisions and did not overrule *Clearfield* or any other decision, the quoted statement may indicate that *Clearfield* will be limited to its facts in future cases.

The second category of cases described by Professors Wright, Miller, and Cooper is one in which the federal courts are filling in the gaps "of a pervasively federal framework" with federal common law.[575] This situation generally occurs when the courts are filling in the gaps of a federal statutory scheme, but it is obvious that gaps can be lesser or greater depending upon whether the courts are attempting to construe the terms of a statute or to exercise wholesale lawmaking power under a broad delegation of authority from Congress.[576] As noted in subsection (1)*(b)*, above, the former situation presents an ordinary problem of statutory supplementation that the courts are perfectly suited to perform, while the latter presents an extremely serious separation-of-powers problem.

An example of justifiable federal common-law creation in the second category of cases is *Wilson v. Garcia*,[577] in which the Supreme Court held that in actions brought under 42 U.S.C. § 1983 (the Civil Rights Act of 1871), the federal courts should apply the state statute of limitations applicable to personal injury actions to determine whether the actions are time barred. Thus, the Court established a relatively simple, uniform rule for all § 1983 actions that assures that the limitations period cannot be fixed in a way that discriminates against federal law.[578] *Wilson* constitutes a justifiable case of supplementation because Congress failed to provide a federal limitations period for § 1983 actions, and a period of limitations obviously had to be supplied by the courts.

Perhaps the classic example of a separation-of-powers violation occurring in the second category of federal common law cases occurred in *Textile Workers*

---

572. *See* 19 CHARLES A. WRIGHT ET AL., FEDERAL PRACTICE AND PROCEDURE: JURISDICTION AND RELATED MATTERS (ERIE DOCTRINE) § 4515, at 485-95 (2d ed. 1996); *see also In re* Gaston & Snow, 243 F.3d 599 (2d Cir. 2001) (before federal courts may create federal common law, a significant conflict between some federal policy or interest and use of state law must first be specifically shown); Woodward Governor Co. v. Curtiss-Wright Flight Sys., Inc., 164 F.3d 123 (2d Cir. 1999) (in suit by sub-subcontractor against a contractor on a defense procurement contract related to national defense, federal common law does not control the claim when there was no allegation that the United States could incur liability if the sub-subcontractor was not paid, there was no allegation that national security would be imperiled if the sub-subcontractor was not paid, and there was no showing that application of state law would conflict with a significant federal policy or interest).

573. 547 U.S. 677, 126 S. Ct. 2121, 165 L. Ed. 2d 131 (2006).

574. *Id.* at 691, 126 S. Ct. at 2132, 165 L. Ed. 2d at 144.

575. *See* 19 CHARLES A. WRIGHT ET AL., FEDERAL PRACTICE AND PROCEDURE: JURISDICTION AND RELATED MATTERS (ERIE DOCTRINE) § 4516, at 500 (2d ed. 1996).

576. *See id.* at 500-02.

577. 471 U.S. 261, 105 S. Ct. 1938, 85 L. Ed. 2d 254 (1985).

578. *See id.* at 279, 105 S. Ct. at 1949, 85 L. Ed. 2d at 269. For a discussion of the cases after *Wilson* dealing with the appropriate limitations period when a state has one statute of limitations for personal injury actions resulting from intentional torts and another for negligent torts, see 19 CHARLES A. WRIGHT ET AL., FEDERAL PRACTICE AND PROCEDURE: JURISDICTION AND RELATED MATTERS (ERIE DOCTRINE) § 4519, at 610-15 (2d ed. 1996).

Union of America v. Lincoln Mills.[579] *Lincoln Mills* is an excellent example of improper "supplementation" because it involves the acceptance by the Supreme Court of an overbroad delegation of lawmaking authority by Congress. In *Lincoln Mills*, Congress had given the federal courts jurisdiction to determine disputes between employers and labor organizations representing employees in industries affecting commerce.[580] However, Congress had not provided any substantive rules for the determination of the disputes that would arise within the jurisdictional grant. The Supreme Court concluded that the jurisdictional grant authorized the federal courts to create a federal common law of labor-management contracts. The Court's decision has been criticized as essentially unreasoned.[581] Worse than the unreasoned nature of the Court's opinion, however, was the violation of the separation-of-powers doctrine that resulted from the decision. As observed by Justice Frankfurter in dissent, when Congress casts "upon the federal courts, with no guides except 'judicial inventiveness,' the task of applying a whole industrial code that is as yet in the bosom of the judiciary," the courts cannot perform their job by using the ordinary process of interpretation. "For the vice of the statute here lies in the impossibility of ascertaining, by any reasonable test, that the legislature meant one thing rather than another. . . ."[582]

Among other kinds of cases, the third category described by Professors Wright, Miller, and Cooper involves the derivation from federal statutes and constitutional provisions of private rights of action that help to effectively implement the statutes and constitutional provisions.[583] The most important factor in this area, especially as it concerns the derivation of federal common-law rules from statutes, is some indication that Congress would desire the federal courts to fashion such rules. The Supreme Court has vacillated over the years in its willingness to permit the creation of private rights of action from silent federal statutes.[584] The Court's current approach is to allow the creation of a private right of action only when there is "affirmative evidence that Congress intended to create a private right of action."[585] This approach seems to be based on the theory that the separation-of-powers doctrine vests the primary policy-making role in Congress, not

---

579. 353 U.S. 448, 77 S. Ct. 912, 1 L. Ed. 2d 972 (1957).

580. *See* 29 U.S.C. § 185(a).

581. *See* Alexander M. Bickel & Harry H. Wellington, *Legislative Purpose and the Judicial Process: The* Lincoln Mills *Case*, 71 HARV. L. REV. 1, 35-37 (1957).

582. 353 U.S. at 464-65, 77 S. Ct. at 925, 1 L. Ed. 2d at 985 (Frankfurter, J., dissenting); *see* RANDALL BRIDWELL & RALPH U. WHITTEN, THE CONSTITUTION AND THE COMMON LAW: THE DECLINE OF THE DOCTRINES OF SEPARATION OF POWERS AND FEDERALISM 133-34 (1977) (comparing the *Lincoln Mills* approach to the approach of the Court in the common law of crimes cases, discussed in section C(2)*(c) supra* ("Separation of Powers")).

583. *See* 19 CHARLES A. WRIGHT ET AL., FEDERAL PRACTICE AND PROCEDURE: JURISDICTION AND RELATED MATTERS (ERIE DOCTRINE) § 4517, at 538 (2d ed. 1996).

584. *Compare* J.I. Case Co. v. Borak, 377 U.S. 426, 84 S. Ct. 1555, 12 L. Ed. 2d 423 (1964) *with* Cort v. Ash, 422 U.S. 66, 95 S. Ct. 2080, 45 L. Ed. 2d 26 (1975) *and* Touche Ross & Co. v. Redington, 442 U.S. 560, 99 S. Ct. 2479, 61 L. Ed. 2d 82 (1979). For an excellent discussion of this area, see ERWIN CHEMERINSKY, FEDERAL JURISDICTION § 6.3.3 (5th ed. 2007).

585. ERWIN CHEMERINSKY, FEDERAL JURISDICTION § 6.3.3, at 397 (5th ed. 2007); *see, e.g.*, Herman & MacLean v. Huddleston, 459 U.S. 375, 103 S. Ct. 683, 74 L. Ed. 2d 548 (1983); Merrill Lynch, Pierce, Fenner & Smith, Inc. v. Curran, 456 U.S. 353, 102 S. Ct. 1825, 72 L. Ed. 2d 182 (1982); Texas Indus., Inc. v. Radcliff Materials, Inc., 451 U.S. 630, 101 S. Ct. 2061, 68 L. Ed. 2d 500 (1981); Northwest Airlines, Inc. v. Transport Workers Union of Am., 451 U.S. 77, 101 S. Ct. 1571, 67 L. Ed. 2d 750 (1981); Transamerica Mortgage Advisors, Inc. v. Lewis, 444 U.S. 11, 100 S. Ct. 242, 62 L. Ed. 2d 146 (1979); Touche Ross & Co. v. Redington, 442 U.S. 560, 99 S. Ct. 2479, 61 L. Ed. 2d 82 (1979).

the courts, and that the courts are unsuited for the resolution of complex policy issues.[586]

As noted in the discussion of *Wilson Garcia*, above, when federal courts have the power to create federal common law, they sometimes adopt state law as the rule of decision. State law is adopted not because *Erie* or the Constitution requires the federal courts to do so, but as a matter of the courts' discretion in determining the content of federal rules of decision.[587] In cases like *Wilson*, it is easy to understand how federal common law can adopt state law and still be "federal." Congress has left a gap in a statutory scheme that must be filled, and state law is the natural and most available source of law with which to fill the gap. Nevertheless, the controlling principle is still "federal" because it is clearly a federal rule of decision that tells the courts which state limitations period controls the federal right of action. However, in other situations, saying that state law is being adopted as federal common-law is curious. When federal common law can appropriately control an area, but state law is adopted as the federal common law, what is the significance of calling the law "federal"?[588]

It is clear, of course, that the Court will not adopt state law as federal law unless there is little or no need for a uniform federal rule in a category of cases.[589] But this statement does not tell us why, when state law is adopted, it is appropriate to say that "federal" law controls the area. It is also true that state law will not be adopted if it is hostile to federal interests or otherwise inconsistent with federal law.[590] But this statement, again, does not tell us the significance of saying that

---

586. *See* Sosa v. Alvarez-Machain, 542 U.S. 692, 724, 124 S. Ct. 2739, 159 L. Ed.2d 718 (2004) (Alient Tort Statute is a jurisdictional provision that creates no new federal causes of action); Texas Indus., Inc. v. Radcliff Materials, Inc., 451 U.S. 630, 101 S. Ct. 2061, 68 L. Ed. 2d 500 (1981); Northwest Airlines, Inc. v. Transport Workers Union of Am., 451 U.S. 77, 101 S. Ct. 1571, 67 L. Ed. 2d 750 (1981); *see also* Ali v. Rumsfeld, 649 F.3d 762 (D.C. Cir. 2011) (following *Sosa supra*); Ungaro-Benages v. Dresdner Bank AG, 379 F.3d 1227 (11th Cir. 2004) (exception to *Erie* doctrine applies to litigation that implicates nation's foreign relations; federal common law applies in such cases); 19 CHARLES A. WRIGHT ET AL., FEDERAL PRACTICE AND PROCEDURE: JURISDICTION AND RELATED MATTERS (ERIE DOCTRINE) § 4517, at 547 (2d ed. 1996). For a debate concerning the question whether customary international law should have the status of federal common law, see Curtis A. Bradley & Jack L. Goldsmith, *Federal Courts and the Incorporation of International Law*, 111 HARV. L. REV. 2260 (1998); Curtis A. Bradley & Jack L. Goldsmith, *Customary International Law as Federal Common Law: A Critique*, 110 HARV. L. REV. 815 (1997); Curtis A. Bradley, *The Status of Customary International Law in U.S. Courts—Before and After* Erie, 26 DEN. J. INT'L L. & POLICY 807 (1988). *But see* F. Giba-Matthews, *Customary International Law Acts as Federal Common Law in U.S. Courts*, 20 FORDHAM INT'L. L.J. 1839 (1997); Harold Hongju Koh, *Is International Law Really State Law?* 111 HARV. L. REV. 1824 (1998); Beth Stephens, *The Law of Our Land: Customary International Law as Federal Law After* Erie, 66 FORDHAM L. REV. 393 (1997). *See also* Hans Smit, *Federalizing International Civil Litigation in the United States: A Modest Proposal*, 8 TRANSNAT'L L. & CONTEMP. PROBS. 57 (1998) (arguing for wholesale overruling of *Erie*, but, in any event, for overruling *Erie* insofar as it requires application of state law in conflicts cases with international aspects); William H. Theis, *United States Admiralty Law as an Enclave of Federal Common Law*, 23 TUL. MAR. L.J. 73 (1998). *See also* Robert Force, *An Essay on Federal Common Law and Admiralty*, 43 ST. LOUIS U. L.J. 1367 (1999); Joel K. Goldstein, *Federal Common Law in Admiralty: An Introduction to the Beginning of an Exchange*, 43 ST. LOUIS U. L.J. 1337 (1999); Ernest A. Young, *The Last Brooding Omnipresence:* Erie Railroad Co. v. Tompkins *and the Unconstitutionality of Preemptive Federal Maritime Law*, 43 ST. LOUIS U. L.J. 1349 (1999).

587. 19 CHARLES A. WRIGHT ET AL., FEDERAL PRACTICE AND PROCEDURE: JURISDICTION AND RELATED MATTERS (ERIE DOCTRINE) § 4518, at 566-67 (2d ed. 1996). *See, e.g.*, United States v. Kimbell Foods, Inc., 440 U.S. 715, 99 S. Ct. 1448, 59 L. Ed. 2d 711 (1979).

588. *See* Ernest A. Young, *Preemption and Federal Common Law*, 83 NOTRE DAME L. REV. 1639 (2008) (discussing, *inter alia*, what happens when a court chooses to use state law under this doctrine).

589. *See, e.g.*, Wilson v. Omaha Indian Tribe, 442 U.S. 653, 673, 99 S. Ct. 2529, 61 L. Ed. 2d 153, 170 (1979); United States v. Kimbell Foods, Inc., 440 U.S. 715, 728, 99 S. Ct. 1448, 1458, 59 L. Ed. 2d 711, 723-24 (1979).

590. *See, e.g.*, United States v. Little Lake Misere Land Co., 412 U.S. 580, 93 S. Ct. 2389, 37 L. Ed. 2d 187 (1973).

federal common law controls an area when the law adopted *is* state law. It may be that the Court will someday reject the *Klaxon* approach (in cases in which federal law adopts state law) and apply an independent federal conflict-of-laws rule to determine which state's law will be adopted.[591] But this possibility, too, does not tell us the significance of saying that federal law controls when the law ultimately selected by the federal conflict of laws rule is state law. After all, federal courts exercised independent conflict-of-laws authority under *Swift*, but the applicable law was never characterized as "federal" when they did so. A federal court might feel free to reject state precedents interpreting the state law adopted as federal law, but this would raise the question whether the federal court was, in any realistic sense, adopting "state" law at all.

The most plausible explanation for the Court's way of expressing doctrine in this area is as follows: when federal law controls an area, but state law is adopted as federal law, the Court is simply saying that federal interests are sufficient to allow the creation of federal law in an area if state law is in any way insufficient. In addition, when the law in question creates a claim for relief on behalf of the plaintiff, the case is appropriate for federal question jurisdiction. In all other respects, the law in question is state law, and state precedents defining the content of that law should be followed unless and until they become inconsistent with the federal interests in the area. In the latter eventuality, federal courts should develop independent federal common-law rules to govern the issue.

3. Federal Procedural Common Law in State Courts

As noted in Chapter 2, most of the federal question jurisdiction conferred upon the U.S. District Courts is concurrent with the state courts. When the state courts are adjudicating federal claims within their concurrent jurisdiction, the Supreme Court has sometimes denied them the right to use procedures that they would employ in similar actions under state law. In effect, this requires the state courts to follow the procedures that would exist if the plaintiff had sued on the federal claim in federal court.[592]

Illustration 5-24. *P* sues *D Railroad* in a state court of State *X* in an action under the Federal Employers Liability Act ("F.E.L.A."). *D* defends on the ground that *P* had released all claims that *P* possessed against *D*. *P* contends that the release is void because it was procured by fraud. If the action had been brought in federal court, the issue of whether the release is fraudulent would have been tried to a jury. The practice in the courts of State *X* is to split the issue of fraud in parts, with the judge trying some parts and the jury trying others. *P* contends that it is impermissible for State *X* to split the fraud issue in this manner in an F.E.L.A. action. In these circumstances, the Supreme Court held in *Dice v. Akron, Canton & Youngstown Railroad Co.*,[593] that federal common law controls the validity of the release *and*

---

591. *See* UAW v. Hoosier Cardinal Corp., 383 U.S. 696, 705 n.8, 86 S. Ct. 1107, 113 n.8, 16 L. Ed. 2d 192, 199 n.8 (1966).

592. *See generally* Joseph R. Olivert, *Converse-*Erie: *The Key to Federalism in an Increasingly Administrative State*, 76 GEO. WASH. L. REV. 1372 (2008).

593. *See* 342 U.S. 359, 72 S. Ct. 312, 96 L. Ed. 398 (1952).

that the fraud issue must be submitted entirely to the jury, because jury trial is part and parcel of the remedy afforded under the F.E.L.A.

Illustration 5-25. *P* sues *D* railroad in a state court of State *X* under the F.E.L.A. *D* demurs to *P's* complaint under state rules of procedure on the grounds that the complaint fails to state facts sufficient to constitute a cause of action. The State *X* court in which the action is pending sustains the demurrer and dismisses the action, despite *P's* contention that it is impermissible for State *X* to use its strict local pleading rules in F.E.L.A. actions. *P* contends that a more liberal "notice pleading" approach, such as that employed under the Federal Rules of Civil Procedure, should be used by the State *X* courts. Under these circumstances, the Supreme Court held in *Brown v. Western Ry.*,[594] that the strict local pleading rules unnecessarily burdened the federal right of action and could not be used by the state courts in the F.E.L.A. action.

* * * * *

The principle of these decisions does not require the state courts to abandon their own rules of procedure across the board when adjudicating federal claims. Rather, only state procedures that interfere with the policy embodied in the federal statute being enforced must be discarded. This will occur in cases such as *Illustration 5-24* when Congress has embodied procedural rights in a statute conferring a federal right of action. It will occur in cases such as *Illustration 5-25* when state procedures unnecessarily burden the adjudication of the federal claim. This last proposition has been most recently illustrated by the Supreme Court's decision in *Felder v. Casey*.[595] In *Felder*, a state "notice of claim" statute provided that plaintiffs wishing to sue state or local governments or their officers had to notify the defendant of the claim and the intent to hold the defendant liable for it. The notice had to be provided within 120 days after the occurrence of the event giving rise to the claim or the claim would be barred, unless the defendant had actual notice of the claim and the plaintiff could show that the defendant was not prejudiced by failure to provide the notice. After notification, the plaintiff had to refrain from suing for 120 days in order to give the defendant a chance to consider the relief requested. Failure to comply with the statute constituted grounds for dismissing an action based on the claim. The plaintiff commenced an action in state court under 42 U.S.C. § 1983 (the Civil Rights Act of 1871) against a city and certain of its police officers. The action was dismissed for failure to comply with the notice of claim statute. The state's highest court held the statute applicable to cases in which the plaintiff was asserting federal civil rights claims. The Supreme Court held the statute preempted in federal civil rights actions because it unnecessarily burdened the right of recovery afforded by federal law.[596]

---

594. *See* 338 U.S. 294, 298-99, 70 S. Ct. 105, 108, 94 L. Ed. 100, 104 (1949).

595. 487 U.S. 131, 108 S. Ct. 2302, 101 L. Ed. 2d 123 (1988); *cf.* Hardy v. New York City Health & Hosps. Corp., 164 F.3d 789 (2d Cir. 1999) (New York notice of claims statute applicable to federal claim under the Emergency Medical Treatment and Active Labor Act, 42 U.S.C. § 1395dd, because of language in Act indicating that notice-of-claim provision should be considered as part of the applicable law of the state under the Act).

596. *See* 487 U.S. at 150-51, 108 S. Ct. at 2313, 101 L. Ed. 2d at 145-46 (alternative holding).

In *Johnson v. Fankell*,[597] the Supreme Court held that in civil rights actions under 42 U.S.C. § 1983, state courts are not obligated to provide interlocutory appeals from denials of defendants' motions to dismiss on the basis of "qualified immunity," even though immediate appeals from such denials are available in federal court.[598] The Court interpreted *Brown* and *Felder* as cases in which the ultimate outcome of the state case would have been affected adversely by the application of the state procedures in question. The Court interpreted *Dice* as a case in which the jury trial procedure was a statutory right of plaintiffs suing on claims under the F.E.L.A. This may mean that states can use their own procedures when adjudicating federal claims as long as the procedures will not necessarily affect the outcome of the action or Congress has not mandated an alternative procedure. However, it may also be significant that *Fankell* involved a procedure for adjudicating a federal defense to a federal claim, while all the other cases involved procedures that directly burdened the claims themselves. State procedural burdens on federal claims may represent a more serious encroachment on federal interests than state procedural burdens on federal defenses to federal claims. This may especially be true in cases like *Fankell*, where state officials are likely to be the defendants in civil rights actions under § 1983. There is little danger that the states will not be vigilant in protecting the ability of such parties to assert federal defenses through adequate state procedures.

Even if the *Dice, Brown*, and *Felder* line of cases is narrow, it can be criticized. When Congress provides plaintiffs access to either federal or state courts for the adjudication of federal claims, it is arguable that plaintiffs should have to take the state courts as they find them, as long as the state courts do not discriminate against federal rights. If a plaintiff believes the procedures in state court are unreasonably restrictive or burdensome, the plaintiff should bring the action in federal court. This approach would accommodate both the interests of the federal government in providing for adjudication of federal claims without unnecessary restrictions or burdens on the plaintiff, as well as the interests of the states in providing uniform, nondiscriminatory procedures for all actions in their courts.

---

597. 520 U.S. 911, 117 S. Ct. 1800, 138 L. Ed. 2d 108 (1997); *see also* Hardy v. New York City Health & Hosps. Corp., 164 F.3d 789 (2d Cir. 1999) (holding New York notice-of-claims statute applicable to a federal claim under the Emergency Medical Treatment & Active Labor Act, 42 U.S.C. § 1395dd, because of language in the statute indicating that the notice-of-claim provision should be treated as part of the applicable law of the state under the statute).

598. *See* Chapter 12(B)(3)*(d) infra* ("The Collateral Order Rule"); *see also* Amy Coney Barrett, *Procedural Common Law,* 94 VA. L. REV. 813 (2008) (discussing the sources of authority for federal courts to create federal procedural common law); Kevin M. Clermont, *Reverse*-Erie, 82 NOTRE DAME L. REV. 1 (2006).

Chapter 6

PLEADING AND RELATED MATTERS

Pleading is the "branch of legal science . . . governing the formal written statements made to the court by the parties to a suit of their respective claims and defenses."[1] Because modern pleading is strongly influenced by its historical antecedents, this chapter begins by reviewing common-law pleading. It then examines the reforms embodied in code pleading and the Federal Rules of Civil Procedure. It also discusses verification and good faith pleading. Lastly, it examines the remedies available at the outset of a lawsuit—called "provisional remedies."

SECTION A. COMMON-LAW PLEADING

1. Commencing the Action

A plaintiff commenced a common-law action by obtaining an original writ. This writ ordered the sheriff to compel the defendant to appear. It also gave the court subject-matter jurisdiction over the suit and determined the nature of the action (trespass, case, debt, etc.).[2]

2. Stating the Plaintiff's Claim in the Declaration

After the defendant had appeared, the plaintiff had to state the claim in more detail in the *declaration*.[3] The declaration was a formal statement of the specific facts and circumstances on which the plaintiff's action was based. Some declarations, such as ones based on trespasses, set forth the events in a relatively direct and straightforward manner. Conversely, others, such as ejectment, reflected elaborate fictions developed in certain common-law actions.[4] General assumpsit developed standard, generalized allegations known as *common counts.*[5]

Illustration 6-1. The common count for *money had and received* was available when (1) the defendant obtained the plaintiff's money or goods by fraud,

---

1. CHARLES E. CLARK, HANDBOOK OF THE LAW OF CODE PLEADING § 1, at 1 (2d ed. 1947).

2. *See* Chapter 1(E)(1)*(b)* ("Issuance of Writs by the Chancellor and the Initial Development of the Forms of Action") *supra*.

3. Originally, the plaintiff or someone on the plaintiff's behalf would orally state the factual basis of the action, and the court would call for the defendant's response. A change to formal, written pleadings began in the late thirteenth century and extended into the second half of the sixteenth century. *See* EDMUND M. MORGAN & FRANCIS DWYER, INTRODUCTION TO THE STUDY OF LAW 116-17 (2d ed. 1948).

4. *See* Chapter 1(E)(1)*(c)(iv)* ("Ejectment") *supra*.

5. *See* Chapter 1(E)(1)*(c)(ii)* ("Assumpsit") *supra*. Provided the declaration showed that the "debt" owed to the plaintiff was not one under seal or on a record, the courts permitted the plaintiff to make a generalized statement of the claim. *See generally* 1 DAN B. DOBBS, LAW OF REMEDIES § 4.2(3), at 581-84 (2d practitioner ed. 1993); JOSEPH H. KOFFLER & ALISON REPPY, HANDBOOK OF COMMON LAW PLEADING § 176, at 347-60 (1969).

duress, or another tort and then converted the money or the proceeds to the defendant's use; (2) the plaintiff paid money to the defendant by mistake believing it was due, but in fact it was not; or (3) the plaintiff paid money for a consideration that failed, such as when the seller refused to deliver the bargained-for goods.[6]

* * * * *

Other important common counts were *(1) quantum meruit* (used when the plaintiff performed services in consideration for the defendant's "promise" to pay so much as the plaintiff deserved); *(2) quantum valebant* (used when the plaintiff sold goods in consideration for a "promise" to pay so much as the goods were worth); (3) goods sold and delivered;[7] (4) work, labor, and services;[8] (5) board and lodging;[9] and (6) use and occupation of land.[10]

Common-law pleading required the parties, through a series of pleadings, to disclose the issues between them. The final result was a *single issue* of law or fact. By means of several restrictive pleading rules, the parties often had to elect a set of facts and a legal theory at the outset of the action and had to plead with certainty. The plaintiff could not plead in the alternative ("either-or"). Nor was hypothetical pleading ("if-then") permitted. Common-law pleading also prohibited duplicity: stating different grounds to enforce a single right of recovery.[11]

Illustration 6-2. Assume that the plaintiff alleged as follows: "On [date], on a [named] public highway, defendant C.D. or defendant E.F. or both C.D. and E.F. willfully or recklessly or negligently drove or caused to be driven a motor vehicle against plaintiff who was then crossing said highway." This allegation would violate the rule against pleading in the alternative. It would also be considered to be duplicitous because it raised different grounds (willfulness, recklessness, or negligence) to enforce a single right of recovery.[12]

* * * * *

---

6. *See* JOSEPH H. KOFFLER & ALISON REPPY, HANDBOOK OF COMMON LAW PLEADING § 176, at 351-53 (1969). Money had and received was known as a money count. Other money common counts included (1) money paid to the defendant's use (available when the plaintiff became a surety for the defendant's debt at the defendant's request and was subsequently compelled to pay the debt, or when the plaintiff discharged a legal obligation of the defendant based upon an express or implied request of the defendant to make the payment for defendant); (2) money lent (used when the plaintiff loaned money to the defendant); and (3) money due on an account stated (used when the plaintiff and defendant had transactions resulting in matured debts, the parties by agreement had computed a balance that the defendant promised to pay, and the plaintiff agreed to accept in full payment for the items covered by the account). *See id.* at 349.

7. The common count for goods sold and delivered was used when goods had been actually or constructively delivered to the defendant and the defendant refused to pay. *Id.* at 357-58.

8. The common count for work, labor, and services was used when the plaintiff performed services for the defendant under such circumstances that the law would imply a promise to pay what they were worth, or when the plaintiff fully performed services pursuant to a contract with the defendant, who did not compensate the plaintiff for them. Originally, the common counts for work, labor, and services and for goods sold and delivered (unlike the value counts of quantum meruit and quantum valebant) could not be used when the sum claimed was of an uncertain amount. As the law developed, however, these counts could be used when the evidence would reduce an uncertain sum to a certainty; thus, they became concurrent with the value counts. *See id.* at 359.

9. The common count for board and lodging was used when the plaintiff furnished the defendant board, lodging, or other "necessaries" at the defendant's special request. *See id.* at 357.

10. The common count for use and occupation of land was used when the defendant (tenant) in possession of land agreed to pay the plaintiff (landlord) either a reasonable sum or fixed sum of money for use and occupation of the land. This action was not available against a trespasser. *Id.* at 354-55; *see also* 1 DAN B. DOBBS, LAW OF REMEDIES § 4.2(3), at 582, § 5.9, at 801-03 (2d practitioner ed. 1993) (citing a few cases that now allow an assumpsit measure of recovery for trespasses that involve actual use and occupation of land).

11. *See generally* BENJAMIN J. SHIPMAN, HANDBOOK OF COMMON-LAW PLEADING §§ 294-327 (3d ed. 1923); HENRY J. STEPHEN, PRINCIPLES OF PLEADING IN CIVIL ACTIONS 434-35 (2d ed. 1901).

12. *See* CHARLES E. CLARK, HANDBOOK OF THE LAW OF CODE PLEADING § 42 (2d ed. 1947).

If the declaration contained internally inconsistent or unintelligible allegations, it could be challenged, respectively, as repugnant or insensible. Allegations had to be positive and not by way of "recital."[13]

Illustration 6-3. Assume that the plaintiff alleged: "*P*, as agent of *D*, . . ." This allegation would be a prohibited recital. To cure this defect, the plaintiff should use positive terms: "*P* was *D's* agent."[14]

Illustration 6-4. Assume that the plaintiff alleged the following in a declaration: "By written agreement dated [date], plaintiff and defendant agreed to plaintiff's occupancy and cultivation of [certain described lands], for a term of twenty years, commencing [date]. As a result, defendant granted plaintiff a freehold interest in said lands. . . ." The plaintiff has alleged a lease for a specific term, followed by the conclusion that the defendant granted the plaintiff a "freehold interest" in the lands. This pleading would be repugnant (internally inconsistent) because it was legally impossible to obtain a freehold interest (a fee simple or a life estate) from such a lease.[15]

* * * * *

At common law, plaintiffs could not, in the declaration, anticipate defenses that the adversary might raise. Any such allegations were regarded as immaterial. Fraud, mistake, and the performance of conditions precedent (acts that must be performed before an agreement becomes effective) had to be pleaded with particularity.[16] The common law also required the pleading of jurisdictional facts supporting a prior judgment, regardless of the type of judgment.[17]

3. Challenges to the Declaration

(a) General Demurrers

A party could challenge a declaration by contending that the alleged facts did not constitute a legally recognized obligation even if they could be proved. This objection was raised by a *general demurrer*. The decision on the demurrer terminated the action: either (1) the demurrer was sustained and the plaintiff's action was dismissed or (2) the demurrer was overruled and judgment was entered against the defendant based on the defendant's admission of the facts. The defendant could not later challenge the truth of the allegations. Nor did the plaintiff have the right to amend the declaration except to correct formal defects and errors of oversight.[18]

---

13. *See* JOSEPH H. KOFFLER & ALISON REPPY, HANDBOOK OF COMMON LAW PLEADING § 55, at 130 (1969).

14. *See id.* at 130-31.

15. *See id.* § 69, at 145.

16. CHARLES E. CLARK, HANDBOOK OF THE LAW OF CODE PLEADING § 45, at 280, § 48, at 312 (2d ed. 1947).

17. 5A CHARLES A. WRIGHT & ARTHUR R. MILLER, FEDERAL PRACTICE AND PROCEDURE: CIVIL § 1306, at 335 (3d ed. 2004).

18. *See* 5B *id.* § 1355, at 352.

(b) Special Demurrers

A *special demurrer* raised formal defects in a party's pleading. At common law, all special demurrers were also general demurrers. Thus, special demurrers also raised defects in substance.

(c) Dilatory Pleas

If the defendant did not file a general or special demurrer, the defendant could enter a *plea*. One type of plea was a *dilatory plea*. It objected to the venue or to the court's jurisdiction over the person or the subject-matter of the suit. A defendant could also use a dilatory plea to raise other objections: nonjoinder or misjoinder of parties, defects in the original writ, misnomer of the defendant, lack of capacity to sue or be sued, prematurity of bringing the action, and the pendency of another action for the same cause.[19] A dilatory plea sought to delay or defeat the particular suit without destroying the plaintiff's right to sue elsewhere. Such a plea had to be presented before the defendant pleaded to the merits (such as by denying the plaintiff's allegations).[20]

The common law rigidly prescribed the order of pleading. For example, the defendant had to make a plea to the jurisdiction over the person before the defendant demurred or offered any other plea. Otherwise, the defendant was deemed to have submitted to the court's jurisdiction.[21] The parties waived defects of form unless the parties raised them by special demurrer.

(d) Traverses

Assuming that the defendant did not file a dilatory plea, the defendant could deny the allegations of the declaration by means of a *traverse*. A traverse had to be directed to an essential element of the plaintiff's claim, and it had to be specific. It could not be *argumentative*.

Illustration 6-5. Assume that *P*, the plaintiff, alleged that *D*, the defendant, was in State *X* on a particular day. Assume that *D* traversed by alleging that *D* was in State *Y* on that day. *D's* traverse is argumentative and would have been improper. The proper form of pleading would be to deny that *D* was in State *X* on that day.[22]

* * * * *

A traverse could not contain a *negative pregnant*. A negative pregnant is a negative expression that implies an affirmative. It can result from framing the denial in the exact language of the opposing party's averment.

Illustration 6-6. Assume *P* alleged that *D* hit *P* over the head with a lead pipe. If *D* traversed by alleging that "*D* did not hit *P* over the head with a lead pipe,"

---

19. These pleas were called dilatory pleas in abatement. *See* BENJAMIN J. SHIPMAN, HANDBOOK OF COMMON-LAW PLEADING § 225 (3d ed. 1923).

20. *See id.* at § 220, at 382-83; JOSEPH H. KOFFLER & ALISON REPPY, HANDBOOK OF COMMON LAW PLEADING §§ 203-206, at 410-20 (1969).

21. *See* JOSEPH H. KOFFLER & ALISON REPPY, HANDBOOK OF COMMON LAW PLEADING § 204, at 411 (1969).

22. *See id.* § 230, at 467-69.

the traverse would contain a negative pregnant. Did *D* intend to deny that *D* had not hit *P* at all or to admit that *D* did hit *P*, but not with a lead pipe? *D's* response would be taken to have admitted the battery.[23]

(e) Pleas in Confession and Avoidance

If the defendant chose not to demur generally or traverse an allegation of fact in the declaration, the defendant could enter a *plea in confession and avoidance*. Such a plea admitted the allegations of the prior pleading and presented new matter to avoid the legal effect of those allegations (for example, self-defense).[24] Thus, the defendant could not deny an allegation of the declaration or demur generally and, at the same time, raise new matters of defense.[25]

(f) The General Issue

The defendant had the alternative of denying the legal conclusion sought to be drawn from the declaration by means of the *general issue*. The form of the general issue varied according to the form of action—"not guilty" in trespass, case, and trover or "nil debet" in debt. The general issue enabled the defendant to contest most of the plaintiff's factual allegations and, in some actions, to raise various defenses. The defendant could also raise some affirmative defenses under the general issue.[26]

(g) Bills of Particulars

If a pleader showed by affidavit that the pleader was not fairly informed of the details of the opposing party's claim, the court frequently granted a bill of particulars. It required the opposing party to make a general allegation more specific, especially when the plaintiff had used a common count in general assumpsit in the declaration.[27]

4. Subsequent Pleading

If the defendant demurred generally, traversed, or responded by pleading the general issue, the pleadings were complete because a single issue had been produced. On the other hand, if the defendant entered a plea of confession and

---

23. *See id.* § 221, at 445; 5 CHARLES A. WRIGHT & ARTHUR R. MILLER, FEDERAL PRACTICE AND PROCEDURE: CIVIL § 1267, at 553 (3d ed. 2004).

24. The rule requiring the defendant to rely on only a single matter of defense was first evaded by fictitious pleading ("express color") and eventually changed by statute, which allowed defendants to plead as many defenses as they had. *See* 4 & 5 Anne, ch. 16, § 4 (1705); CHARLES E. CLARK, HANDBOOK OF THE LAW OF CODE PLEADING § 91, at 576 & nn.3-4 (2d ed. 1947).

25. *See* JOSEPH H. KOFFLER & ALISON REPPY, HANDBOOK OF COMMON LAW PLEADING §§ 215, 225-226 (1969).

26. *See id.* § 224; BENJAMIN J. SHIPMAN, HANDBOOK OF COMMON-LAW PLEADING §§ 169, 189 (3d ed. 1923).

27. *See* CHARLES E. CLARK, HANDBOOK OF THE LAW OF CODE PLEADING § 54, at 338 (2d ed. 1947); JOSEPH H. KOFFLER & ALISON REPPY, HANDBOOK OF COMMON LAW PLEADING § 372 (1969).

avoidance, the pleadings did not yet produce an issue, so the plaintiff had to respond. If the plaintiff believed the plea was insufficient as a matter of law, the plaintiff would demur to the plea. If not, the plaintiff filed a *replication* either (1) traversing a material allegation in the plea or (2) admitting the truth of the plea and raising a new matter of confession and avoidance. If the plaintiff raised a new matter of confession and avoidance in the replication, the defendant had to either demur or file a *rejoinder* containing either a traverse or a new matter of confession and avoidance. This process continued until a single issue of law or fact was reached when one side traversed or demurred.[28]

During this pleading process, the parties had several opportunities to demur. Whenever a party demurred, it had the effect of "opening up" or *searching the record.* Thus, a demurrer tested not only the legal sufficiency of the pleading to which it was addressed, but also the legal sufficiency of all prior pleadings.

Illustration 6-7. Assume that the defendant demurred to the plaintiff's replication. In addition to considering the legal sufficiency of the replication, the court would examine the legal sufficiency of the plaintiff's declaration and the defendant's plea.[29]

5. Amendments, "Pleading Over," and Pleas Puis Darrein Continuance

When oral pleading prevailed, courts allowed parties to correct and adjust their pleadings.[30] As written pleadings replaced oral pleadings, formalism increased. Courts began to reject pleadings containing minor errors of form and to arrest and reverse judgments on this basis.[31] Beginning in 1340, Statutes of Jeofails permitted the parties to amend their pleadings to correct formal defects and errors of oversight.[32] However, a party could not change the form of action by an amendment (for example, from trespass to case or covenant to assumpsit).[33] Substantive defects might be "aided by pleading over," (*i.e.*, by supplying the omitted allegation in a subsequent pleading).

Illustration 6-8. If the defendant, rather than demurring, pleaded facts by way of confession and avoidance that supplied an omission in the declaration, the defect in the declaration would be cured.[34]

* * * * *

---

28. *See* BERNARD C. GAVIT, CASES AND MATERIAL ON AN INTRODUCTION TO LAW AND THE JUDICIAL PROCESS 10 (1936). Assuming that matters of confession and avoidance were raised each time, the subsequent pleadings were called a surrejoinder, a rebutter, and a surrebutter. *See* JOSEPH H. KOFFLER & ALISON REPPY, HANDBOOK OF COMMON LAW PLEADING § 191, at 380 (1969).

29. *See* CHARLES E. CLARK, HANDBOOK OF THE LAW OF CODE PLEADING § 83, at 524-25 (2d ed. 1947).

30. BENJAMIN J. SHIPMAN, HANDBOOK OF COMMON-LAW PLEADING § 163, at 294 (3d ed. 1923).

31. CHARLES E. CLARK, HANDBOOK OF THE LAW OF CODE PLEADING § 114, at 703-04 (2d ed. 1947); *see also* Chapter 12(A) *infra* (discussing post-trial motions in common-law practice).

32. BENJAMIN J. SHIPMAN, HANDBOOK OF COMMON-LAW PLEADING § 163, at 294-95 (3d ed. 1923) (the term "jeofails" was derived from the expression "*J'ai failé*"; early pleaders used this expression when they "perceived a slip in [their] proceedings."); 1 WILLIAM S. HOLDSWORTH, A HISTORY OF ENGLISH LAW 223 (6th ed. 1938) ("if the pleader saw and acknowledged the error (J'ai failé), [the pleader] was allowed to amend.").

33. JOSEPH H. KOFFLER & ALISON REPPY, HANDBOOK OF COMMON LAW PLEADING § 301, at 559 (1969).

34. *See id.* § 298.

The defendant also had the opportunity to enter a *plea puis darrein continuance*. This plea raised a new matter of defense that arose *after* the defendant had entered a plea.[35]

6. Relation of Pleading to Proof at Trial

If the evidence at trial disclosed a valid claim covered by another form of action, the plaintiff could not recover. The allegations in the pleadings were ordinarily "material" and the evidence had to *conform to the pleadings*. Otherwise, a fatal *variance* occurred. Even minor variances could be fatal.

Illustration 6-9. For instance, a fatal variance occurred when the note received in evidence was a half cent larger than the amount alleged in the declaration. In an assumpsit action based on a note allegedly signed by "William Becker," a fatal variance occurred when the note introduced in evidence showed it was signed by "Wilhelm Becker."[36]

* * * * *

Common-law pleading also required certainty in pleading time and place. However, matters laid under a *videlicet* ("to wit" or "viz."), did not give rise to fatal error if the evidence varied from the stated facts under it.[37] In other respects, a pleader who alleged immaterial facts was ordinarily compelled to prove them literally, even though it was unnecessary to set them out.[38]

SECTION B. PLEADING IN EQUITY

A plaintiff commenced an equity action by filing a bill of complaint with the court. The bill, which originally simply stated the grievance, was also the first pleading in equity. In contrast, pleading in common-law actions did not occur until after the original writ had been issued. The nature of equity jurisdiction explains this difference. The bill petitioned the chancellor for relief when legal remedies were inadequate or nonexistent. In such cases, the chancellor did not act automatically—unlike the common-law courts in which the original writ was issued according to established methods to vindicate settled legal rights. Relief was in the discretion of the chancellor. Therefore, the plaintiff had to make it apparent at the outset that grounds for the relief existed. The bill enabled the chancellor to make this determination before compelling the defendant to appear by means of a subpoena.[39]

By the sixteenth century, bills had become more stylistically intricate. Typically, they consisted of three parts: (1) the stating part (stating the grounds for

---

35. BENJAMIN J. SHIPMAN, HANDBOOK OF COMMON-LAW PLEADING § 208 (3d ed. 1923).

36. JOSEPH H. KOFFLER & ALISON REPPY, HANDBOOK OF COMMON LAW PLEADING § 68, at 145 (1969).

37. Parties frequently used videlicets to detail time, place, or manner that they had previously stated in general language (for example, "on a certain day, *viz.*, September 1, [year]"). Furthermore, common-law courts held that the allegations of place for purposes of venue were not material in transitory actions. *See* Chapter 4(A) ("Transitory and Local Actions") *supra*.

38. JOSEPH H. KOFFLER & ALISON REPPY, HANDBOOK OF COMMON LAW PLEADING § 68, at 144 (1969).

39. *See* Chapter 1(E)(2) ("Equity Jurisdiction and Procedure") *supra*.

relief), (2) the charging part (stating the evidence in detail), and (3) the interrogative part (propounding interrogatories designed to obtain admissions and discover evidence from the opposing party).[40] After the defendant appeared, the chancellor required the defendant to answer the bill. The evidence was largely documentary, contained in or attached to the pleadings. Pleading in equity cases never achieved the rigidity of common-law pleading. Nor did it embrace the fictions embodied in common-law pleading.

In equity, the plaintiff could file a pleading called a *supplemental bill* in addition to the original bill. A supplemental bill remedied either some defect or omission in the original bill or introduced related matters happening since the commencement of the suit.[41]

SECTION C. CODE PLEADING

In 1848, the Field Code abolished the forms of action in New York. In their place, the Field Code established a single form of action known as the *civil action*. Code pleading reforms quickly followed in many states.[42]

1. Commencing the Action

Section 106 of the original Field Code of New York provided that "[c]ivil actions in the courts of record in this state, shall be commenced by the service of a summons."[43] Other sections prescribed the content of the summons and required a copy of the complaint to be served with the summons in most cases.[44]

2. The Code Complaint

The Field Code, as amended in 1851, required the plaintiff to file a complaint—called a "petition" in some code states. This initial pleading had to contain (1) a formal introductory part or "caption" that specified the names of the parties and the court, (2) "[a] plain and concise statement of the facts constituting a cause of action without unnecessary repetition," and (3) a demand for the judgment.[45] If the plaintiff demanded monetary relief, the plaintiff had to state the

---

40. *See* Chapter 9(A) ("Development of Modern Discovery") *infra*.

41. BENJAMIN A. SHIPMAN, HANDBOOK OF THE LAW OF EQUITY PLEADING 290 (1897).

42. *See* Chapter 1(E)(4) ("The Field Code and the Reform of Procedure in the States") *supra*.

43. Act of Apr. 12, 1848, ch. 379, § 106, 1848 N.Y. Laws 497, 518.

44. *See id.* §§ 107-109, 1848 N.Y. Laws 497, 518. Not all code-pleading systems, however, required a copy of the complaint to be served with the summons. *See, e.g.*, S.C. CODE ANN. §§ 15-9-10 to 15-9-40 (Law. Coop. 1976) (summons only) (repealed 1985) (complaint is now served with the summons in South Carolina); CHARLES E. CLARK, HANDBOOK OF THE LAW OF CODE PLEADING § 14, at 76 (2d ed. 1947). In systems that served only the summons, it could be quite difficult for a layperson to determine the nature of the suit or what action to take. *See, e.g.*, Jolley v. Jolly, 265 S.C. 594, 220 S.E.2d 882 (1975).

45. Act of July 10, 1851, ch. 479, § 142, 1851 N.Y. Laws 876, 887. Originally, the Field Code had provided that the plaintiff's complaint had to contain, *inter alia*, "[a] statement of the facts constituting the cause of action, in ordinary and concise language, without repetition, and in such a manner as to enable a person of common understanding to know what is intended." Act of Apr. 12, 1848, ch. 379, § 120, 1848 N.Y. Laws 497, 521. The thrust of both the original 1848 provision and the amended 1851 provision was to insure that all the elements of

amount.[46] Furthermore, the codes required plaintiffs to include in the complaint only those matters on which they would have the initial burden of production of proof at trial, which constituted the prima facie case or cause of action.[47]

(a) Pleading "Facts"

By requiring a plain and concise statement of "facts" constituting a "cause of action,"[48] the codes produced a requirement that plaintiffs should state "ultimate facts" in the complaint, avoiding conclusions of law and evidentiary facts.[49] This requirement posed several difficulties.

Illustration 6-10. Assume that the plaintiff alleged in a complaint in a code-pleading jurisdiction that the plaintiff was "entitled to possession" of specific property. This allegation could be challenged on the ground that the plaintiff had pleaded a conclusion of law. On the other hand, assume that the plaintiff alleged that "the defendants [had] agreed to convey realty to the plaintiff, that the defendants delivered the deed to the plaintiff, and that the defendants now refuse to deliver possession to the plaintiff." This allegation could be challenged on the ground that the plaintiff was pleading evidence rather than the ultimate facts of ownership and right to possession.[50]

Illustration 6-11. Assume that the plaintiff alleges that "*D* is the wife of *P*."[51] Is this allegation a conclusion of law, an ultimate fact, or an evidentiary fact? Professor Clark has suggested that the particularity of an allegation should vary with the question at issue. The allegation would probably suffice in a suit for personal injuries to one of the persons (either the husband or the wife). However,

---

the cause of action would be pleaded as clearly and concisely as possible. However, the first version of the Code appeared to require that pleadings be intelligible to the ordinary layperson. The second version eliminated this requirement. It was probably recognized that it was impractical to require both that a cause of action be stated in all its possible technical detail and that the complaint still be intelligible to a layperson. The second version thus simply required as concise, clear, and short a statement of the cause of action as possible.

46. Act of Apr. 12, 1848, ch. 379, § 120, 1848 N.Y. Laws 497, 521.

47. One court has aptly pointed out that "the allocation of an element to the plaintiff's case or to the defendant's affirmative pleading is not determined by abstract logic. There is no logic, for instance, why a plaintiff should not be compelled as an element of [the plaintiff's] case to establish that [the plaintiff] was free of contributory negligence or did not induce a particular contract by fraud; or that an assertedly subsisting claim has not been paid or released. Considerations of fairness and convenience, of the ease or difficulty of making proof, of the comparative likelihood that a particular defensive situation may exist in a reasonable proportion of the cases presented to the court, and even of handicapping disfavored contentions, have contributed to the" allocation of the burden of pleading. *See* Greathouse v. Charter Nat'l Bank-S.W., 851 S.W.2d 173, 175-76 (Tex. 1992); *see also* Chapter 11(H) ("Involuntary Dismissals, Directed Verdicts, Burden of Proof, and Presumptions") *infra*; *see generally* Edward W. Cleary, *Presuming and Pleading: An Essay on Juristic Immaturity*, 12 STAN. L. REV. 5 (1959).

48. The Field Code did not define "cause of action." Three general views reflect varying shades of meaning. First, some courts defined a cause of action as simply a right of action, referring to the legal right of the plaintiff. Second, some courts defined a cause of action as a group of facts relied on by the litigant as entitling the litigant to relief. Third, some courts defined a cause of action as a group of facts entitling the litigant to relief, but limited as a layperson would to a single occurrence or affair, without particular reference to the resulting legal right or rights. CHARLES E. CLARK, HANDBOOK OF THE LAW OF CODE PLEADING § 19, at 129-30 (2d ed. 1947).

49. *See id.* § 38, at 225.

50. *See id.* § 38, at 229. *Compare* Sheridan v. Jackson, 72 N.Y. 170 (1878) (pleading conclusions) *with* McCaughey v. Schuette, 117 Cal. 223, 46 P. 666 (1896) (pleading evidence). A similar problem arose concerning the allegation of consideration for a contractual promise. Some courts regarded the simple allegation of a "valuable consideration" to be a legal conclusion. These courts wanted the consideration exactly specified as at common law. CHARLES E. CLARK, HANDBOOK OF THE LAW OF CODE PLEADING § 45, at 279-80 (2d ed. 1947).

51. *See* CHARLES E. CLARK, HANDBOOK OF THE LAW OF CODE PLEADING § 38, at 232 (2d ed. 1947) (providing this example).

suppose *D* is claiming an individual statutory share of *P's* estate on the ground that *D* is *P's* common-law wife. *D's* allegation would probably be insufficient.[52]

* * * * *

The availability of challenges to pleading evidence and conclusions of law led to wasteful litigation. This problem was exacerbated both by the tendency of pleaders to try to conceal information as well as by the possible lack of information about the facts at the time of pleading.[53] As Clark has pointed out, the codifiers' "ideal of pleading [ultimate] facts, as it has been worked out, has proved probably the most unsatisfactory part of their reform."[54] Clark attributes this result to (1) the reality that the distinction between fact, law, and evidence, "if existent at all, is not clear-cut and obvious," (2) the codifiers "attempt[ed] to apply rigid rules to a matter in which flexibility is a necessity," and (3) the "inherent difficulties" of this general problem.[55]

The "common counts" at common law were generalized statements of the claim.[56] Even though code pleading required the allegation of "facts" and § 118 of the Field Code specifically provided that "[a]ll the forms of pleading heretofore existing, inconsistent with the provisions of this act, are abolished,"[57] courts accepted the common counts as proper under code pleading.[58]

(b) Alternative, Hypothetical, and Inconsistent Pleading

Code practice generally continued the common-law pleading prohibition on pleading facts in the alternative or hypothetically. However, recognizing that "pleader[s] often cannot know, and cannot reasonably be expected to know, which of two or more alternatives is the correct one" at the time of pleading, several states modified this rule.[59] Traditional code practice also continued to condemn inconsistent pleading.[60]

(c) Anticipating Defenses

Under the codes, plaintiffs did not have to anticipate in the complaint defenses that the adversary would raise. Indeed, as at common law, the plaintiff

---

52. *Id. See generally* Walter W. Cook, *"Facts" and "Statements of Fact,"* 4 U. CHI. L. REV. 233 (1937); Bernard C. Gavit, *Legal Conclusions*, 16 MINN. L. REV. 378 (1932); Nathan Isaacs, *The Law and the Facts*, 22 COLUM. L. REV. 1 (1922); Clarence Morris, *Law and Fact*, 55 HARV. L. REV. 1303 (1942); Carl C. Wheaton, *Manner of Stating Cause of Action*, 20 CORN. L.Q. 185 (1935).

53. *See* CHARLES E. CLARK, HANDBOOK OF THE LAW OF CODE PLEADING § 38, at 226-27 (2d ed. 1947).

54. *Id.* at 226.

55. *Id.*; *see also* Walter W. Cook, *"Facts" and "Statements of Fact,"* 4 U. CHI. L. REV. 233 (1937); Clarence Morris, *Law and Fact*, 55 HARV. L. REV. 1303 (1942).

56. *See* section A(2) ("Stating the Plaintiff's Claim in the Declaration") *supra*.

57. Act of Apr. 12, 1848, ch. 379, § 118, 1848 N.Y. Laws 497, 521.

58. *See, e.g.*, Abadie v. Carrillo, 32 Cal. 172, 176 (1867).

59. *See* CHARLES E. CLARK, HANDBOOK OF THE LAW OF CODE PLEADING § 42, at 255 (2d ed. 1947) (allowing allegations in the alternative is "one of the most simple, desirable, and effective improvements upon the common-law rules").

60. *See id.* § 43; 5 CHARLES A. WRIGHT & ARTHUR R. MILLER, FEDERAL PRACTICE AND PROCEDURE: CIVIL § 1282, at 714, § 1283, at 725 (3d ed. 2004); Gregory Hankin, *Alternative and Hypothetical Pleadings*, 33 YALE L.J. 365 (1924); *see also* section A(2) ("Stating the Plaintiff's Claim in the Declaration") *supra*.

could not do so because the courts regarded any such allegations to be immaterial.[61] Some codes, however, allowed plaintiffs to anticipate defenses in the complaint if the complaint contained matter answering the anticipated defense.[62]

(d) Pleading Special Matters

Like the common law,[63] the codes required fraud and mistake to be pleaded with particularity.[64] In some code states, corporate existence had to be alleged. However, in many code states, no such allegation was necessary.[65] If the caption of the complaint clearly identified the capacity in which they were suing, many (but not all) code states did not require fiduciary plaintiffs acting as administrators, executors, guardians, or receivers to allege their appointment.[66] In the absence of an express code provision to the contrary, courts interpreted the codes as continuing the common-law requirement that the performance of conditions precedent had to be alleged with particularity.[67] However, many codes contained specific provisions permitting a general allegation of performance of conditions precedent.[68] Many code states also eliminated the common-law requirement of pleading jurisdictional facts supporting a prior judgment regardless of the type of judgment.[69]

3. Responding to the Complaint

(a) Motions for More Definite Statements and Bills of Particulars

Assuming that the defendant did not default, the defendant had to prepare some type of defense. In doing so, the defendant could face a real difficulty: the complaint might be so vague or ambiguous that the defendant could not reasonably be expected to respond. The Field Code provided that the defendant could present a motion to require the plaintiff to make the complaint "more definite and certain." Frequently, the codes also required an affidavit specifying the allegations in question.[70]

A similar request, known as a *bill of particulars*, was utilized for a different purpose: to determine the particulars of an opposing party's claim so that the moving party could prepare for trial. It was also used to prevent surprise and limit issues. However, several codes limited the use of bills of particulars to actions of

---

61. *See* section A(2) ("Stating the Plaintiff's Claim in the Declaration") *supra*.

62. CHARLES E. CLARK, HANDBOOK OF THE LAW OF CODE PLEADING § 82, at 524 (2d ed. 1947); *see also id.* § 40, at 250-52 (indicating that there was a conflict among the courts whether allegations anticipating defenses should be considered to be immaterial or should be considered a proper part of the complaint).

63. *See* section A(2) ("Stating the Plaintiff's Claim in the Declaration") *supra*.

64. CHARLES E. CLARK, HANDBOOK OF THE LAW OF CODE PLEADING § 48, at 312 (2d ed. 1947).

65. *Id.* § 50, at 323. Apparently, at common law, no such allegation was necessary. *Id.*

66. *Id.* at 324-26.

67. *Id.* § 45, at 280 (2d ed. 1947); *see* section A(2) ("Stating the Plaintiff's Claim in the Declaration") *supra*.

68. 5A CHARLES A. WRIGHT & ARTHUR R. MILLER, FEDERAL PRACTICE AND PROCEDURE: CIVIL § 1302, at 323 (3d ed. 2004).

69. *Id.* § 1306, at 335-36.

70. CHARLES E. CLARK, HANDBOOK OF THE LAW OF CODE PLEADING § 87, at 548 (2d ed. 1947).

account or contract claims for damages. In some states, bills of particulars and motions to make more definite and certain became interchangeable.[71]

(b) Demurrers

The codes continued the common-law practice of using a demurrer to challenge the legal sufficiency of a pleading.[72] The codes also allowed a party to use a demurrer to raise other matters formerly raised by common-law dilatory pleas.[73] However, such matters could be raised by demurrer only when they appeared on the face of the complaint.[74] Specifically, the Field Code provided for demurrers on six grounds if they appeared on the face of the complaint: (1) the complaint failed to state sufficient facts to constitute a cause of action; (2) the court did not have (a) personal jurisdiction over the defendant or (b) subject-matter jurisdiction; (3) the plaintiff lacked the legal capacity to sue; (4) a defect of parties, either plaintiff or defendant, existed; (5) the plaintiff had improperly united several causes of action; and (6) another action was pending between the parties for the same cause.[75] Virtually all codes repeated these grounds without additions.[76] Some codes later permitted these objections to be raised by a motion to dismiss.[77] Improper venue was often handled by a motion to transfer.[78] The codes also provided that "[s]ham, irrelevant, or frivolous answers . . . , may on motion be stricken out."[79]

In some code states, a defendant could use a demurrer to challenge the complaint's failure to use a consistent theory in stating the facts.[80] Most code states repudiated this "theory-of-the-pleadings" doctrine as "inconsistent with the code plan of pleading facts only, leaving the legal conclusions to be drawn by the court."[81]

(c) The Code Answer

The defendant had to raise defenses and objections not appearing on the face of the complaint in the answer. For example, the defendant had to raise the

---

71. *See id.* §§ 54, 87; *see also* section A(3)*(g)* ("Bills of Particulars") *supra*.

72. At common law, a general demurrer put in issue the legal sufficiency of the declaration. *See* section A(3)*(a)* ("General Demurrers") *supra*.

73. *See* section A(3)*(c)* ("Dilatory Pleas") *supra*.

74. A defense appears on the face of a complaint when it is possible to read the complaint alone and determine that the defense exists. This, of course, assumes that the reader of the complaint has a complete knowledge of the substantive law. Thus, the reader perceives the facts alleged in the complaint, compares the fact to the situations in which the substantive law provides for relief (or remedies), and judges whether a cause of action or defense exists.

75. Act of Apr. 12, 1848, ch. 379, § 122, 1848 N.Y. Laws 497, 521.

76. CHARLES E. CLARK, HANDBOOK OF THE LAW OF CODE PLEADING § 79, at 505 (2d·ed. 1947). Some codes included misjoinder of parties as a separate ground. *Id.*

77. *Id.*

78. *See, e.g.*, SMITH-HURD ILL. COMP. STAT. ANN. ch. 735, § 5/2-104 (West 2003).

79. CHARLES E. CLARK, HANDBOOK OF THE LAW OF CODE PLEADING § 87, at 551 (2d ed. 1947).

80. This approach is called the "theory-of-the-pleadings" doctrine:

> [A] complaint in the first instance and where challenged by demurrer, may [not] be uncertain and ambulatory, purposely so made, now presenting one face to the court and now another, at the mere will of the pleader, so that it may be regarded as one in tort, or one on contract, or equity as he is pleased to name it and the necessities of argument require.

Supervisors of Kewaunee County v. Decker, 30 Wis. 624, 629 (1872) (Dixon, C.J.).

81. CHARLES E. CLARK, HANDBOOK OF THE LAW OF CODE PLEADING § 43, at 259 (2d ed. 1947).

following objections in the answer (rather than by demurrer) when those objections did not appear on the face of the complaint: (1) an objection to improper service; (2) a challenge to the recitals in the officer's return of service; or (3) a question of the plaintiff's lack of capacity to sue.[82]

The codes carried forward the common-law traverse and general issue[83] in the form of the specific denial and the general denial. The typical code provision stated that the answer must contain "[a] general or specific denial of each material allegation of the complaint controverted by the defendant, or of any knowledge or information thereof sufficient to form a belief."[84] In addition, the codes typically required the answer to contain "[a] statement of any new matter constituting a defense or counterclaim, in ordinary and concise language without repetition."[85] The codes usually continued by stating that the "defendant may set forth in [the] answer as many defenses or counterclaims, or both, as [the defendant] has."[86] Several codes added a list of defenses that the defendant had to raise affirmatively by specific averment in the answer. Difficult questions often arose whether the defendant had to raise a particular defense (1) affirmatively as a "new matter" in the answer or (2) by way of a denial of the plaintiff's allegations.[87]

Illustration 6-12. Assume that *P* sued *D* for breach of contract. *D* answered by denying the contract. The code states were "thoroughly divided" on the question whether *D's* denial was sufficient to allow *D* to assert that the contract violated the statute of frauds. Some states held that the defendant had to raise this defense by pleading it affirmatively in the answer.[88]

(d) Waiver of Defenses

As noted in subsection *(b)*, above, the codes utilized demurrers as the means for challenging certain enumerated defenses that appeared on the face of the complaint (*i.e.*, failure to state sufficient facts to constitute a cause of action, lack of personal jurisdiction, lack of subject-matter jurisdiction, lack of capacity to sue, defects of parties, improperly joined causes of action, and prior pending action). Failure to raise "such an objection" by demurrer resulted in a waiver of the objection.[89] However, the codes provided two exceptions to this rule. First, failure to state facts sufficient to constitute a cause of action could be made at trial.[90] Furthermore, as at common law, defects of substance could be cured by supplying

---

82. *Id.* at § 81, at 517, § 95, at 601-04.

83. *See* section A(3)*(d)* ("Traverses") and section A(3)*(f)* ("The General Issue") *supra*.

84. CHARLES E. CLARK, HANDBOOK OF THE LAW OF CODE PLEADING § 91, at 577 (2d ed. 1947).

85. *Id.*

86. *Id.* at 578. In some states, however, the courts interpreted the codes to prohibit the defendant from denying matter alleged in the complaint and at the time inconsistently making the same matter part of an affirmative defense. 5 CHARLES A. WRIGHT & ARTHUR R. MILLER, FEDERAL PRACTICE AND PROCEDURE: CIVIL § 1270, at 559 (3d ed. 2004).

87. *See* CHARLES E. CLARK, HANDBOOK OF THE LAW OF CODE PLEADING §§ 96-97 (2d ed. 1947).

88. *Id.* § 97, at 613 (citing cases and noting that conflicts also existed as to contributory negligence, assumption of risk, and inherent illegality).

89. *Id.* § 85, at 532.

90. *Id.* at 532-33.

the omitted fact in a subsequent pleading.[91] Second, lack of subject-matter jurisdiction could be raised for the first time as late as the appellate stage.[92]

Illustration 6-13. Assume that the plaintiff's lack of capacity to sue is apparent on the face of the complaint (*e.g.*, the complaint indicates that the plaintiff is twelve years old and the plaintiff has sued in the plaintiff's name alone). Virtually all codes permitted the defendant to raise this defense by demurrer.[93] The defendant waived this defense if the defendant failed to demur before answering the complaint.

Illustration 6-14. Assume that the defendant failed to demur to the complaint on the ground the plaintiff had omitted an essential allegation from the complaint. The defendant did not waive this defense. The defendant could raise this defense as late as the trial stage. After trial, however, the defendant waived the defense.

* * * * *

As noted in subsection *(c)*, above, the defendant had to raise defenses and objections not appearing on the face of the complaint in the answer. Failure to include "such an objection" in the answer was deemed to waive the objection. Again, however, objections to the lack of subject-matter jurisdiction could be raised for the first time on appeal.[94]

Illustration 6-15. Assume the facts of *Illustration 6-13*, except that the lack of capacity to sue did *not* appear on the face of the complaint (*e.g.*, the allegations of the complaint did not indicate that the plaintiff was a minor). Instead, the defendant had personal knowledge that the plaintiff was twelve years old and thus lacked the legal capacity to sue. The defendant could not raise this defense by demurrer because it did not appear on the face of the complaint. Assuming that the burden of pleading was on the defendant in this situation, the proper method for the defendant to raise lack of capacity would be an affirmative defense in the answer.[95] If the defendant failed to do so, the defense would be waived—unless the court permitted the defendant to amend the answer later to add the defense.[96] However, one caveat is in order. If the state placed the burden of pleading capacity on the plaintiff, the absence of an allegation of capacity would make the complaint subject to demurrer for legal insufficiency. In theory, the same could be true for many issues that are normally considered affirmative defenses, such as contributory negligence. Thus, one would always need to know where the burden of pleading resided on an issue before it would be possible to determine whether defendant should raise the matter by demurrer or affirmative defense *if the matter were omitted from a pleading altogether*.[97]

---

91. *See* section A(5) ("Amendments, 'Pleading Over,' and Pleas Puis Darrein Continuance") *supra*.

92. *See* CHARLES E. CLARK, HANDBOOK OF THE LAW OF CODE PLEADING § 85, at 532-33 (2d ed. 1947).

93. *See* subsection *(b)* ("Demurrers") *supra*.

94. CHARLES E. CLARK, HANDBOOK OF THE LAW OF CODE PLEADING § 85, at 532-33 (2d ed. 1947).

95. *See id.* § 97, at 616. Under the codes, issues such as the statutes of limitations, accord and satisfaction, payment, release, estoppel, conditions subsequent, truth, and justification could generally be raised only by affirmative plea by the defendant. *Id.*

96. *See* subsection 5 ("Amendments and Supplemental Pleadings") *infra*.

97. *See also Illustration 6-17 infra*.

Illustration 6-16. Assume that *P* loaned *D* $50,000. *P* sued *D* for repayment of the loan. *D* maintained that *P* had released *D* from the obligation to repay the loan. *D* could not raise this defense (release) by demurrer because it was not a defense that the codes permitted to be raised in that manner. Instead, the proper method of raising this defense was as an affirmative defense in *D's* answer. If the defendant failed to do so, the defense would be waived—unless the court permitted the defendant to amend the answer later to add the defense.

4. The Plaintiff's Reply

Many codes required the plaintiff to reply to any "new matter" contained in the answer. If there was no reply, the new matter would be taken as admitted.[98] However, code practice typically permitted a party to demur to a defense in an answer (or reply).[99] The reply ended the pleading process.

Illustration 6-17. Assume that the defendant alleges in the answer that the plaintiff's negligence contributed to an accident. Under the applicable substantive law, the plaintiff's contributory negligence would bar the plaintiff's recovery for injuries sustained in the accident. The plaintiff would have to reply if this allegation is "new matter." Whether something is "new matter" depends on who has the burden of pleading *and* on what appears in the complaint. This allegation would be a new matter if the jurisdiction places the burden of pleading contributory negligence on the defendant. Thus, if the answer contains matter raising the issue of contributory negligence, a reply would be required. On the other hand, some jurisdictions require the plaintiff to plead freedom from contributory negligence. In these jurisdictions, the absence of such an allegation in the complaint is demurrable. However, if the plaintiff pleads freedom from contributory negligence, the defendant's response negating that allegation in the complaint is a denial, not "new matter." Thus, a reply is not necessary.

5. Amendments and Supplemental Pleadings

The codes provided for amendment of pleadings without leave of court within a certain time and for amendments with leave of court thereafter. Generally, a pleading could be amended once as a matter of course (1) at any time before the defendant served a demurrer or answer or (2) within twenty days after demurrer and before determination of the issue raised by the demurrer. The amended pleading simply was filed and served on the opposing party. The opposing party then typically had twenty days to answer, reply, or demur to the amended pleading.[100] After the time allowed for amendments as a matter of course, the court could permit an amendment in its discretion "in furtherance of justice" and "on such terms as may be proper."[101]

---

98. CHARLES E. CLARK, HANDBOOK OF THE LAW OF CODE PLEADING §§ 107-109 (2d ed. 1947).
99. *Id.* § 79, at 509.
100. *Id.* § 115, at 708-09.
101. *Id.* at 710.

Illustration 6-18. Assume that before the defendant responded to the complaint, the plaintiff wanted to amend the complaint to correct a mistake in the name of a party. This amendment would be permitted without leave of court.

Illustration 6-19. Assume that after the defendant served a demurrer on the ground that the complaint failed to state a cause of action, the plaintiff served an amended complaint curing the defect—for example, alleging consideration for the contract set forth in the initial pleading. This amendment would be permitted. If the amendment was timely (usually within 20 days after the demurrer) and the court had not held a hearing on the issues raised by the demurrer, the plaintiff could serve the amendment without leave of court. Thereafter, the plaintiff had to seek leave of court.

* * * * *

Either by explicit provisions or by judicial decision, the codes originally did not permit amendments "changing the cause of action." However, most code states eventually eliminated this restriction. Furthermore, from the outset, the courts in code-pleading states appear to have taken a liberal approach in permitting defendants to raise new defenses by amendments of their answers.[102] When amendments were permitted, courts allowed them to "relate back" for purposes of satisfying the statute of limitations.

Illustration 6-20. Assume that before the defendant responded, the plaintiff wanted to amend the complaint to allege that the defendant negligently, rather than intentionally, drove a vehicle against the plaintiff. A traditional code-pleading state would not permit this amendment because it changed the cause of action from battery to negligence. The plaintiff would have to take a voluntary dismissal and commence a new action.

* * * * *

The codes also permitted *supplemental pleadings*. However, most codes limited such pleadings to "a supplemental complaint, answer or reply, alleging facts material to the case occurring *after* the filing of the former complaint, answer or reply."[103] When a party was ignorant of certain facts at the time of the filing of an earlier pleading, a few codes permitted the supplemental pleading of those facts.[104] The codes did not permit supplemental pleadings to cure certain defects, such as prematurity of the claim.[105]

6. Code Motions to Expunge or Strike

A party could use the code motion to expunge to strike out irrelevant, immaterial, redundant, impertinent, or scandalous matter. When the entire pleading or an entire claim in a pleading was a sham, irrelevant, or frivolous, a code motion to strike was proper.[106]

---

102. *Id.* § 116.
103. *Id.* § 121, at 741 (emphasis added).
104. *Id.* at 742.
105. *Id.* § 121, at 743.
106. *Id.* § 87, at 550-52.

SECTION D. FEDERAL RULES PLEADING

The Federal Rules of Civil Procedure apply to practice in the federal district courts. Many states have also adopted the Federal Rules.[107] They have been described as "one of the greatest contributions to the free and unhampered administration of law and justice ever struck off . . . since the dawn of civilized law."[108] Not everyone, however, is convinced that all aspects of the Federal Rules represent a panacea.[109]

1. Commencing the Action

Federal Rule 3 provides that "[a] civil action is commenced by filing a complaint with the court."[110] The mechanics of filing a complaint are simple. Rule 5(d)(2) defines filing with the court as filing with the clerk of the court[111] unless the judge permits the papers to be filed with the judge.[112]

2. The Federal Rules Complaint

Federal Rule 8(a) provides that the plaintiff's initial pleading in federal court is a *complaint*. In setting forth a claim for relief, Rule 8(a) indicates that the complaint must contain three basic items. First, the plaintiff must provide "a short and plain statement of the grounds for the court's jurisdiction, unless the court already has jurisdiction and the claim needs no new jurisdictional support."[113]

---

107. *See* Chapter 1(E)(5)*(d)* ("Influence of the Federal Rules on State Court Procedure") *supra*.

108. B.H. Cary, *In Favor of Uniformity*, 3 F.R.D. 505, 507 (1943).

109. *See generally* Maurice Rosenberg, *The Federal Civil Rules After Half a Century*, 36 ME. L. REV. 243 (1984); Stephen N. Subrin, *Fireworks on the Fiftieth Anniversary of the Federal Rules of Civil Procedure*, 73 JUDICATURE 4 (1989); Symposium, *The Fiftieth Anniversary of the Federal Rules of Civil Procedure*, 63 NOTRE DAME L. REV. 597 (1988); Symposium, *The Fiftieth Anniversary of the Federal Rules of Civil Procedure*, 62 ST. JOHN'S L. REV. 399 (1988); Symposium, *The 50th Anniversary of the Federal Rules of Civil Procedure, 1938-1988*, 137 U. PA. L. REV. 1873 (1989); Symposium, The Future of Federal Litigation, 50 U. PITT. L. REV. 701 (1989); Symposium, *Issues in Civil Procedure: Advancing the Dialogue*, 69 B.U. L. REV. 467 (1989); Symposium, *Modern Civil Procedure: Issues in Controversy*, 54 LAW & CONTEMP. PROBS., Summer 1991, at 1.

110. FED. R. CIV. P. 3. After the complaint has been filed, service of process occurs pursuant to Rule 4. *See* Chapter 3(K) ("Service of Process") *supra*.

111. FED. R. CIV. P. 5(d)(2). Upon receiving the complaint, the clerk "time-dates" it. The party instituting a civil action in federal court must pay a $350 filing fee. *See* 28 U.S.C. § 1914(a). In addition, a civil cover sheet must be filed. This cover sheet identifies, *inter alia*, the names of the plaintiff and the defendant, their residences, the names of the attorneys, the basis of jurisdiction, the nature of suit, and the relief requested.

112. If the complaint or other papers are filed with the judge, the judge is required to note thereon the filing date and transmit them to the clerk's office. FED. R. CIV. P. 5(d)(2)(B).

113. FED. R. CIV. P. 8(a)(1). Pleading jurisdiction is simple. Assume, for example, that *P*, a citizen of California, sues *D*, a citizen of Texas. To demonstrate subject-matter jurisdiction based upon diversity, *P* would allege in the complaint: "Plaintiff is a citizen of California. The defendant is a citizen of Texas." Official Form 7 illustrates how *P* would plead the jurisdictional amount: "The amount in controversy, without interest and costs, exceeds the sum or value specified by 28 U.S.C. § 1332." Form 7 in the Appendix of Forms following the Federal Rules of Civil Procedure. For corporations, Form 7 suggests the following: "The defendant is a corporation incorporated under the laws of New York with its principal place of business in New York." *Id.* No overlap can exist between the plaintiff's citizenship and that of the corporation (determined by both its state of incorporation and its principal place of business). *See* Chapter 2(C)(3)*(c)* ("Citizenship of Corporations and Associations") and *Illustration 2-41 supra*. However, prior to restyling, the official forms suggested that the plaintiff should allege the state in which the defendant is incorporated but need only allege that the corporation's principal place of business is in a state other than the plaintiff's state of citizenship. *See* Form 2 in the Appendix of Forms prior to the 2007 restyling. The reason for this approach is that the plaintiff may have difficulty ascertaining the location of the

Second, the plaintiff must provide "a short and plain statement of the claim showing that the pleader is entitled to relief."[114] Third, the plaintiff must make "a demand for the relief sought . . . ."[115] Rule 8(d)(1) adds that each allegation in the pleading "must be simple, concise, and direct."[116]

(a) Captions, Numbered Paragraphs, Separate Counts, and Incorporation by Reference

All pleadings, motions, and other papers filed in a federal court must have a caption. The caption consists of the name of the court, the title of the action, the names of all the parties, the file number, and a designation of the type of document (*i.e.*, "Complaint," "Answer," etc.)[117] In subsequent pleadings and other documents served after the complaint, only the name of the first party on each side is required.[118] The clerk supplies the file number of the complaint when the plaintiff commences the action.[119]

When a party makes a claim (or defense) in a federal pleading, the pleader must use numbered paragraphs. Each paragraph should be "limited as far as practicable to a single set of circumstances."[120] The requirement of numbered paragraphs provides "an easy mode of identification for referring to a particular paragraph in a prior pleading or for cross-referencing within a single pleading."[121]

Rule 10(b) provides that "[e]ach claim founded on a separate transaction or occurrence . . . must be stated in a separate count . . . ."[122] However, as Professors Wright and Miller point out, "[d]espite the express language of Rule 10(b) that more than one transaction must be involved before separate statements of claims are necessary, the federal courts consistently have required separate statements when separate claims are pleaded, notwithstanding the fact that the claims arose from a

---

defendant's principal place of business. *See* 5 CHARLES A. WRIGHT & ARTHUR R. MILLER, FEDERAL PRACTICE AND PROCEDURE: CIVIL § 1208, at 133 (3d ed. 2004). Obviously, if a plaintiff is uncertain about a corporation's principal place of business, following the form prior to restyling would be a much wiser course. Otherwise, the plaintiff may be met with a denial in the answer if the plaintiff is not correct. Part (b) of Form 7 illustrate how federal question jurisdiction is pleaded.

114. FED. R. CIV. P. 8(a)(2); Davis v. Ruby Foods, Inc., 269 F.3d 818 (7th Cir. 2001) (holding that the district court abused its discretion by dismissing a complaint that appeared to state a claim merely because of the presence of superfluous matter). Several forms in the Appendix of Forms following the Federal Rules of Civil Procedure illustrate statements of claims. *See, e.g.*, Form 10 ("Complaint to Recover a Sum Certain"); Form 11 ("Complaint for Negligence"); Form 12 ("Complaint for Negligence When the Plaintiff Does Not Know Who Is Responsible"); Form 15 ("Complaint for Conversion of Property"); Form 17 ("Complaint for Specific Performance of a Contract to Convey Land"); Form 20 ("Complaint for Interpleader and Declaratory Relief"); Form 21 ("Complaint on Claim for Debt and to Set Aside a Fraudulent Conveyance Under Rule 18(b)") in the Appendix of Forms following the Federal Rules of Civil Procedure.

115. FED. R. CIV. P. 8(a)(3). The official forms give some illustrations of such demands. *See, e.g.*, Form 11 (damages), Form 17 (specific performance and damages), Forms 18 and 19 (injunction, accounting, and other remedies), Form 20 (declaratory relief), and Form 21 (damages and to set aside fraudulent conveyance) in the Appendix of Forms following the Federal Rules of Civil Procedure.

116. FED. R. CIV. P. 8(d)(1).

117. *See* FED. R. CIV. P. 10(a); *see also* FED. R. CIV. P. 7(a) (listing the names of the pleadings permitted in federal court).

118. FED. R. CIV. P. 10(a).

119. *See* FED. R. CIV. P. 79(a).

120. FED. R. CIV. P. 10(b); *see, e.g.*, Form 20 in the Appendix of Forms following the Federal Rules of Civil Procedure.

121. 5A CHARLES A. WRIGHT & ARTHUR R. MILLER, FEDERAL PRACTICE AND PROCEDURE: CIVIL § 1323, at 400 (3d ed. 2004).

122. FED. R. CIV. P. 10(b).

single transaction."[123] Rule 10(c) permits a party to "adopt by reference" (or "incorporate by reference") prior allegations.[124] Parties may raise defects of form by motion.[125]

(b) "Notice" Pleading

Federal Rule 8(a)(2) omits the code requirement that the complaint state the "facts" constituting the "cause of action." Instead, what is required is "a short and plain statement of the claim showing that the pleader is entitled to relief."[126] In this way, federal rules pleading avoids the distinctions between factual and legal

---

123. 5A CHARLES A. WRIGHT & ARTHUR R. MILLER, FEDERAL PRACTICE AND PROCEDURE: CIVIL § 1324, at 410 (3d ed. 2004). *But see* Form 19 in the Appendix of Forms following the Federal Rules of Civil Procedure (claims for copyright infringement and unfair competition stated in a single count); *cf.* Bautista v. Los Angeles County, 216 F.3d 837 (9th Cir. 2000). In *Bautista*, the Ninth Circuit reversed the district court's dismissal of the plaintiff's second amended complaint with prejudice for failure to comply with (1) Rules 8(a)'s requirement that the complaint contain a short and plain statement of the claim showing that the pleader is entitled to relief and (2) Rule 10(b)'s requirement that each claim based on a separate transaction or occurrence be stated in a separate count. The second amended complaint was not substantially different from the earlier complaint, and the court of appeals held that the district court had power to dismiss the complaint for failure to comply with the rules, but erred in dismissing the complaint with prejudice. The principal opinion by Judge Schwarzer indicated that the "sudden death" response was an abuse of discretion because the deficiencies in the complaint were readily curable with some guidance from the district court. Judge Reinhardt concurred, but objected to Judge Schwarzer addressing "procedural matters never before raised in the litigation" and expressing "views on those matters which I believe to be incorrect." Judge Reinhardt agreed that the district court should have been reversed, but objected to Judge Schwarzer's extended discussion of the requirements of Rules 8(a) and 10(b), which he believed to be incorrect. Judge O'Scannlain concurred in part and dissented in part. Judge O'Scannlain indicated that the district court had correctly dismissed the complaint "after entertaining two previous efforts to fashion a viable complaint," but rejected Judge Schwarzer's direction that the district judge should give guidance to the plaintiffs concerning how to frame it properly, stating:

> District courts are in the business of judging, not editing. The majority's directive belies its assumption that the district court knew what the plaintiffs were trying to say and should therefore have "specif[ied] what it required in the pleading.". . . As every law student knows, it is Rule 8 that sets forth the standard for pleadings, not customized orders from district courts. The litigation explosion cannot sustain a world in which plaintiffs can simply toss incomprehensible documents before the district court and have the court do the work of sorting out what should be pled.

Id. at 845.

124. *See* FED. R. CIV. P. 10(c). Incorporation by reference was permitted in common-law pleading with respect to allegations in separate counts of the same pleading, but not to allegations in separate pleadings (or motions) as Rule 10(c) permits. 5A CHARLES A. WRIGHT & ARTHUR R. MILLER, FEDERAL PRACTICE AND PROCEDURE: CIVIL § 1326, at 426 (3d ed. 2004). Many code states likewise permitted incorporation by reference. CHARLES A. CLARK, HANDBOOK OF THE LAW OF CODE PLEADING § 37, at 223-24 (2d ed. 1947).

125. At common law, formal defects in a party's pleading could be challenged by a special demurrer. All special demurrers were general demurrers and thus would also raise defects in substance. In code and federal practice, courts traditionally have entertained motions to correct defects of form, even though the codes or the Federal Rules may not authorize such motions specifically. Such motions are permitted on the ground that they are necessary to effectuate specific provisions of the rules. For example, motions have been used as a means of making the pleadings conform to the formal requirements of Federal Rule 10 (caption, names of parties, paragraphs, etc.). *See* 5C CHARLES A. WRIGHT & ARTHUR R. MILLER, FEDERAL PRACTICE AND PROCEDURE: CIVIL § 1360 (3d ed. 2004).

126. FED. R. CIV. P. 8(a)(2). The counterargument against notice pleading focuses on practical implications of the differences between pleading facts under the codes and providing notice of the claim under the Federal Rules:

> When only notice pleading is required, reputedly, practicing lawyers often complain that they do not become fully aware of the issue in many cases until after prolonged discovery. This results in increased costs to the litigants and untoward delay in cases reaching the trial stage. Under code pleading, if the pleadings are properly prepared, the issues are apparent immediately upon the filing of a petition and the filing of an answer. If either a petition or an answer does not clearly set forth a litigant's issues, sustaining a motion to make more definite and certain will expeditiously clarify the issues, save the litigants unwarranted expense, promote judicial economy, and avoid unnecessary delay in a case reaching the trial stage.

Christianson *ex rel.* Christianson v. Educational Serv. Unit No. 16, 243 Neb. 553, 560, 501 N.W.2d 281, 287-88 (1993).

conclusions and the specificity requirements of code pleading.[127] The Federal Rules have also abolished the theory-of-the-pleadings doctrine prevailing in some code-pleading systems.[128] As explained by Charles Clark, the reporter of the committee that drafted the Federal Rules of Civil Procedure, pleadings in federal court

> must sufficiently differentiate the situation of fact which is being litigated from all other situations to allow of the application of the doctrine of res judicata, whereby final adjudication of this particular case will end the controversy forever. As a natural corollary, they will also show the type of case brought, so that it may be assigned to the proper form of trial, whether by the jury in negligence or contract, or to a court, referee, or master, as in foreclosure, divorce, accounting, and so on. . . . These minimal requirements . . . emphasize only the setting forth of the factual situation as a whole; they do not force a pleader to allege all the fine details or to include a series of legal epithets or conclusions as to the defendant's conduct.[129]

As developed by the Supreme Court, two requirements must be satisfied in order to meet the standards of Rule 8(a)(2): (1) providing *fair notice* of the claim and (2) showing that the pleader is *plausibility* entitled to relief. These requirements are discussed in the following two subsections.

(i) The "Fair Notice" Requirement

In *Conley v. Gibson*,[130] the complaint alleged that a railroad had wrongfully discharged the plaintiffs based on racial discrimination and that the plaintiffs' union, acting according to plan, refused to protect their jobs as it did those of white employees or help the plaintiffs with their grievances.[131] If these allegations were proven, there was a "manifest breach" of the union's statutory duty of fair

---

127. Pleading facts constituting a cause of action in a code-pleading system contrasts with pleading facts and circumstances on which the claim is based in sufficient detail to give notice of the claim, but not necessarily alleging a specific fact to cover every substantive element of the claim. *See* section C(2)*(a)* ("Pleading 'Facts' ") *supra*.

128. *See, e.g.*, FED. R. CIV. P. 8(e), 15(b), 54(c); *see also* section C(3)*(b)* ("Demurrers") *supra*.

129. Charles E. Clark, *Simplified Pleading*, 2 F.R.D. 456, 456-57 (1943).

130. 355 U.S. 41, 78 S. Ct. 99, 2 L. Ed. 2d 80 (1957).

131. Specifically, the Court summarized the relevant allegations as follows:

> [The plaintiffs] were employees of the Texas and New Orleans Railroad at its Houston Freight House. Local 28 of the Brotherhood was the designated bargaining agents under the Railway Labor Act for the bargaining unit to which [the plaintiffs] belonged. A contract existed between the Union and the Railroad which gave the employees in the bargaining unit certain protection from discharge and loss of seniority. In May 1954, the Railroad purported to abolish 45 jobs held by [the plaintiffs,] all of whom were either discharged or demoted. In truth the 45 jobs were not abolished at all but instead filled by whites . . . , except for a few instances where [the plaintiffs] were rehired to fill their old jobs but with loss of seniority. Despite repeated pleas by [the plaintiffs], the Union, acting according to plan, did nothing to protect them against these discriminatory discharges and refused to give them protection comparable to that given white employees. The complaint then went on to allege that the Union had failed in general to represent [the plaintiffs] equally and in good faith. It charged that such discrimination constituted a violation of [the plaintiffs'] right under the Railway Labor Act to fair representation from their bargaining agent. And it concluded by asking for relief in the nature of declaratory judgment, injunction and damages.

Id. at 43, 78 S. Ct. at 100-01, 2 L. Ed. 2d at 83.

representation without hostile discrimination under the Railway Labor Act.[132] In reversing and remanding the dismissal of the complaint, the U.S. Supreme Court described the simplified pleading permitted by the Federal Rules and emphasized the requirement of "fair notice":

> The respondents also argue that the complaint failed to set forth specific facts to support its general allegations of discrimination . . . . The decisive answer to this is that the Federal Rules of Civil Procedure do not require a claimant to set out in detail the facts upon which [the pleader] bases [the] claim. To the contrary, all the Rules require is "a short and plain statement of the claim" that will give the defendant *fair notice of what the plaintiff's claim is and the grounds upon which it rests*. The illustrative forms appended to the Rules plainly demonstrate this. Such simplified "notice pleading" is made possible by the liberal opportunity for discovery and the other pretrial procedures established by the Rules to disclose more precisely the basis of both claim and defense and to define more narrowly the disputed facts and issues. Following the simple guide of Rule 8(f) that "all pleadings shall be so construed as to do substantial justice," we have no doubt that petitioners' complaint adequately set forth a claim and gave the respondents fair notice of its basis. The Federal Rules reject the approach that pleading is a game of skill in which one misstep by counsel may be decisive to the outcome and accept the principle that the purpose of pleading is to facilitate a proper decision on the merits.[133]

Besides the general policy statement in *Conley*, what specific guidance has the Court given on pleading to achieve "fair notice"? First, in *Atchison, Topeka & Santa Fe Railway Co. v. Buell*,[134] a railroad carman commenced an action alleging a violation of a Federal Employers Liability Act (FELA) in federal court. The carman alleged that the railroad failed "to provide [the plaintiff] with a safe place to work, including, but not limited to, having fellow employees harass, threaten, intimidate [the plaintiff], and in particular, [the] foreman . . . threatened, harassed,

---

132. *Id.* at 46, 78 S. Ct. at 102, 2 L. Ed. 2d at 84.

133. *Id.* at 47-48, 78 S. Ct. at 103, 2 L. Ed. 2d at 85-86 (footnotes omitted and emphasis added); *see also, e.g.*, Rannels v. S.E. Nichols, Inc., 591 F.2d 242, 245 (3d Cir. 1979) (rejecting the infusion of the technical requirements of code pleading into pleading under the Federal Rules). The pleading in *Conley* would have certainly meet the standards set out by Clark, above:

> The notice [required by Rule 8(a)(2)] is [provided by stating] *the general nature of the case and the circumstances or events upon which it is based*, so as to differentiate it from other acts or events, to inform the opponent of the affair or transaction to be litigated—but not of details which he should ascertain for himself in preparing his defense—and to tell the court of the broad outlines of the case. Thus it serves the purposes referred to above of routing the case through proper court channels for the choice of jury or other form of trial and the like, and, ultimately, for the application of res judicata to the final judgment rendered. The latter may perhaps be considered the final test, for if the pleadings isolate the events in question from others sufficiently to show the affair which the judgment settles, then the parties will have the protection they are entitled to against relitigation of the same matter.

Charles E. Clark, *Simplified Pleading*, 2 F.R.D. 456, 460-61 (1943) (emphasis added). Thus, the principal drafter of the Federal Rules and the Court in *Conley* both indicate that "fair notice" is essentially directed to two areas: (1) what the plaintiff's claim is; and (2) the grounds upon which it rests.

134. 480 U.S. 557, 107 S. Ct. 1410, 94 L. Ed. 2d 563 (1987).

and intimidated [him] maliciously and oppressively, negligently, and intentionally, in order to cause personal injury to [the plaintiff] and to cause mental and emotional suffering."[135] In response to an argument that emotional injury was not cognizable under the Act (raised by the defendant on appeal), the Court specifically stated that "[u]nder the Federal Rules of Civil Procedure, [the plaintiff] had no duty to set out all of the relevant facts in [the] complaint," citing *Conley*, and indicated that the method for raising that issue would have been through summary judgment.[136]

Second, in *Swierkiewicz v. Sorema N.A.*,[137] the plaintiff brought an employment discrimination action based on an alleged violation of Title VII of the Civil Rights Act of 1964. The plaintiff could prove a violation through two different "routes" at trial: either by (1) offering direct evidence of discrimination or (2) proving circumstances that indirectly supported an inference of discrimination.[138] In that case, the Court held that the plaintiff did not have to choose one of those specific "routes" and plead "facts" establishing all elements of a prima facie case for the chosen route in order to give fair notice and withstand a motion to dismiss for failure to state a claim.[139]

Third, by specifically amending Federal Rule 84, the Court has established that the official forms appended to the Federal Rules "suffice" under these rules—in other words, they meet the requirements of Rule 8(a)(2), including fair notice.[140] Thus, the forms themselves provide authoritative insight into how the plaintiff can permissibly inform the defendant of what the plaintiff's claim and the grounds upon which it rests.[141]

---

135. *Id.* at 559, 107 S. Ct. at 1412, 94 L. Ed. 2d at 569.

136. *Id.* at 568 n.15, 107 S. Ct. at 1417 n.15, 94 L. Ed. 2d at 574 n.15. The Court pointing out that "[h]ad [the defendant] moved for summary judgment on the ground that FELA does not recognize claims for [a particular] type of injury, [the plaintiff] would have had the opportunity to supplement the record with relevant facts to contest that motion." *Id.*

137. 534 U.S. 506, 122 S. Ct. 992, 152 L. Ed. 2d 1 (2002).

138. *Id.* at 511-12, 122 S. Ct. at 997, 152 L. Ed. 2d at 9.

139. Justice Thomas explained:

> [U]nder a notice pleading system, it is not appropriate to require a plaintiff to plead facts establishing a prima facie case because the [inferential] framework [required by the Second Circuit] does not apply in every employment discrimination case. For instance, if a plaintiff is able to produce direct evidence of discrimination, he may prevail without proving all the elements of a prima facie case. Under the Second Circuit's . . . pleading standard, a plaintiff without direct evidence of discrimination at the time of his complaint must plead a prima facie case of discrimination, even though discovery might uncover such direct evidence. It thus seems incongruous to require a plaintiff, in order to survive a motion to dismiss, to plead more facts than he may ultimately need to prove to succeed on the merits if direct evidence of discrimination is discovered.
>
> Moreover, the precise requirements of a prima facie case can vary depending on the context and were "never intended to be rigid, mechanized, or ritualistic." Before discovery has unearthed relevant facts and evidence, it may be difficult to define the precise formulation of the required prima facie case in a particular case. Given that the prima facie case operates as a flexible evidentiary standard, it should not be transposed into a rigid pleading standard . . . .

Id. at 511-12, 122 S. Ct. 992, 997-98, 152 L. Ed. 2d at 9 (citations omitted).

140. *Swierkiewicz*, 534 U.S. at 513 n.4, 122 S. Ct. at 998 n.4, 152 L. Ed. 2d at 10 n.4 (quoting the complaint for negligence, restyled at Form 11).

141. With regard to the form for the Complaint for Negligence, Clark pointed out that

> if one were merely to claim "damages for X for $10,000 for personal injuries" [in the complaint], there would be little to afford a basis for res judicata in the case. On the other hand, under Federal Form [for negligence], as under its progenitor in the old declaration in trespass on the case, we have the claim particularized to a running-down accident with the defendant's automobile while the plaintiff was crossing a certain street on a particular date. That this affords adequate basis for res judicata is clear; plaintiff will not have many accidents of that kind at that time and place. But to a trained mind the kind of case it is, with respect to trial or calendar practice, is quite clear; and there are only certain kinds and numbers of misdeeds—speed, signals, position on the highway, failure to

Despite the Supreme Court's statements regarding "fair notice" and the policies embodied in the official forms, lower courts have consistently attempted to develop stricter, more detailed pleading of "facts" ("heightened pleading requirements") for certain types of cases.[142] As long as the complaint gave fair notice, the Court has consistently rejected these attempts.[143] For example, in *Leatherman v. Tarrant County Narcotics Intelligence & Coordination Unit*,[144] the Court unanimously rejected a "heightened pleading" requirement for civil rights cases alleging municipal liability under section 1983 of Title 42.[145] The Court emphasized "that it is impossible to square the "heightened pleading standard" applied in this case with the liberal system of 'notice pleading' set up by the Federal Rules."[146] The Court pointed out that the Federal Rules do provide exceptions to the liberal pleading requirement in Rule 8(a)(2).[147] Specifically, Rule 9(b) requires pleaders to state with particularity the circumstances constituting fraud or mistake.[148] Relying on the traditional maxim providing that the expression of one exception to the general rule excludes other unspecified exceptions, the Court refused to create a heightened pleading exception by judicial interpretation.[149]

> look, and so on—which either party can commit. These each party should prepare himself to face; even if they be unstated, a wise counsel will not face trial without considering their contingency.

Charles E. Clark, *Simplified Pleading*, 2 F.R.D. 456, 461-62, 464 (1943) ("Careful examination of [the official] forms will, it is believed, convince the reader that they state all the necessary details which an intelligent lawyer needs to prepare his defense, while they inform the court adequately of all matters needed for calendar adjustments, and furnish full basis for res judicata").

142. *See* Richard L. Marcus, *The Revival of Fact Pleading Under the Federal Rules of Civil Procedure*, 86 COLUM. L. REV. 433 (1986) (pointing out that fact pleading was "enjoying a revival" in several areas, such as securities fraud and civil rights cases); *see also* Douglas A. Blaze, *Presumed Frivolous: Application of Stringent Pleading Requirements in Civil Rights Litigation*, 31 WM. & MARY L. REV. 935 (1990); C. Keith Wingate, *A Special Pleading Rule for Civil Rights Complaints: A Step Forward or A Step Back?* 49 MO. L. REV. 677 (1984); Edward Cavanagh, *Pleading Rules in Antitrust Cases: A Return to Fact Pleading?* 21 REV. LITIG. 1 (2002) (condemning the lower court development of judge-made specificity requirements for pleading in antitrust cases); Christopher M. Fairman, *Heightened Pleading*, 81 TEX. L. REV. 551 (2002) (extensive review of heightened pleading practice in the federal courts and strongly supporting a transsubstantive approach to pleading).

143. *See, e.g.*, Hospital Bldg. Co. v. Trustees of Rex Hosp., 425 U.S. 738, 96 S. Ct. 1848, 48 L. Ed. 2d 338 (1976); Conley v. Gibson, 355 U.S. 41, 78 S. Ct. 99, 2 L. Ed. 2d 80 (1957).

144. 507 U.S. 163, 113 S. Ct. 1160, 122 L. Ed. 2d 517 (1993).

145. The defendants argued that a municipality's freedom from *respondeat superior* liability necessarily included immunity from suit. Thus, the more relaxed pleading standard of the Federal Rule 8(a)(2) "would subject municipalities to expensive and time-consuming discovery in every § 1983 case, eviscerating their immunity from suit and disrupting municipal functions." *Id.* at 166, 113 S. Ct. at 1162, 122 L. Ed. 2d at 523. The Court rejected this argument, refusing to equate freedom from liability with immunity from suit. According to the Court, municipalities, unlike various government officials, are not immune from suit. "[A] *municipality* can be sued under § 1983, but it cannot be held liable unless a municipal policy or custom caused the constitutional injury." *Id.* at 166-67, 113 S. Ct. at 1162, 122 L. Ed. 2d at 523(emphasis added). The Court did not "consider whether [its] qualified immunity jurisprudence would require a heightened pleading in cases involving *individual* government officials" who are sometimes immune from suit. *Id.* (emphasis added). The federal courts of appeals are now divided on whether to follow *Leatherman* in suits against individuals. *See* Gary T. Lester, Comment, Schultea II—*Fifth Circuit's Answer to* Leatherman—*Rule 7 Reply: More Questions than Answers in Civil Rights Cases?* 37 S. TEX. L. REV. 413, 439-41 (1996).

146. 507 U.S. at 168, 113 S. Ct. at 1160, 122 L. Ed. 2d at 523.

147. *Id.* at 168, 113 S. Ct. at 1160, 122 L. Ed. 2d at 524.

148. *See* subsection 2*(e)(i)* ("Fraud and Mistake") *infra* (discussing special pleading requirements imposed by Federal Rule 9).

149. "[T]he Federal Rules do address in Rule 9(b) the question of the need for greater particularity in pleading certain actions, but do not include among the enumerated actions any reference to complaints alleging municipal liability under § 1983. *Expressio unius est exclusio alterius.*" *Id.* at 168, 113 S. Ct. at 1163, 122 L. Ed. 2d at 524. However, it is likely that lower courts will continue to seek more detailed pleading. *See, e.g.*, Ersek v. Township of Springfield, 822 F. Supp. 218 (E.D. Pa. 1993) (requiring the defendant to file a more definite statement to plaintiff's claims for conspiracy, defamation, false light, and § 1983 and attempting to distinguish *Leatherman* on the ground that the redrafting of the complaint ordered in *Ersek* was not designed to preempt any potential defenses or to require plaintiff to plead with any special care because this action involved § 1983; a more

Likewise, in *Swierkiewicz v. Sorema, N.A.*,[150] applying a heightened pleading standard in an employment discrimination case, the Second Circuit had affirmed the district court's dismissal of a complaint because the plaintiff had failed to specifically allege each of the elements of a prima facie case. Reversing, the Supreme Court stated that a prima facie case is "an evidentiary standard, not a pleading requirement."[151] Using the same reasoning as in *Leatherman*, the Court emphasized that Rule 8 provides a "simplified pleading standard [that] applies to all civil actions, with limited exceptions," such as averments of fraud and mistake under Rule 9(b), and that the express mention of heightened pleading in Rule 9 for some kinds of claims meant that other claims must be governed by the more liberal requirements of Rule 8.[152] Applying this standard, the Court concluded that the "complaint easily satisfies the requirements of Rule 8(a) because it gives respondent fair notice of the basis for petitioner's claims."[153]

---

definite statement was ordered "to make the claims in a straightforward way because the complaint is rife with unsupportable generalizations"); Paul J. McArdle, *A Short and Plain Statement: The Significance of* Leatherman v. Tarrant County, 72 U. DET. MERCY L. REV. 19, 38-42 (1994) (discussing lower court cases responding to *Leatherman*); Richard L. Marcus, *The Puzzling Persistence of Pleading Practice*, 76 TEX. L. REV. 1749 (1998) (discussing the persistence of traditional pleading practice in spite of the notice pleading philosophy of the Federal Rules and cases like *Leatherman*); *cf.* Marsh v. Butler Cnty., 268 F.3d 1014 (11th Cir. 2001) (holding that it was proper to advance an immunity defense in a Rule 12(b)(6) motion and that the court had to determine from the face of the complaint (even if a claim is otherwise sufficiently stated) whether the law supporting the existence of that claim was or was not clearly established and prohibited what the government official was alleged to have done before the defendant acted); *see also* Doe v. Cassel, 403 F.3d 986 (8th Cir. 2005) (district court erred in imposing heightened pleading requirement in § 1983 actions against individual defendants, but dismissal on the merits under Rule 41(b) sustained on the alternative ground of plaintiff's refusal to comply with discovery orders); McKenna v. Wright, 386 F.3d 432 (2d Cir. 2004) (qualified immunity defense can be raised by a Federal Rule 12(b)(6) motion to dismiss under limited circumstances when facts supporting the defense appear on the face of the complaint); Wynder v. McMahon, 360 F.3d 73 (2d Cir. 2004) (district court improperly dismissed plaintiff's complaint for failure to comply with order to supply a complaint that substantially exceeded the requirements of Federal Rule 8); Andresen v. Diorio, 349 F.3d 8 (1st Cir. 2003) (Rule 8, not more detailed state requirements for stating a claim in defamation, apply in federal diversity action); Christopher M. Fairman, *The Myth of Notice Pleading,* 45 ARIZ. L. REV. 987 (2003); Laurens Walker, *The Other Federal Rules of Civil Procedure,* 25 REV. LITIG. 79 (2006) (discussing other rules, such as heightened pleading requirements, that interact with the Federal Rules in such a way as to counter their progressive character).

Furthermore, in Schultea v. Wood, 47 F.3d 1427 (5th Cir. 1995), the Fifth Circuit held that, *Leatherman* notwithstanding, Federal Rule 7(a) can be used to order a plaintiff to reply to a defendant's affirmative defense of limited immunity. To the extent that the defendant has pleaded factual details in the defense, the plaintiff can be required to plead details in the reply on the ground that notice pleading under Federal Rule 8(a) applies only to complaints; according to the court, the only rule governing the content of a Rule 7 reply is Federal Rule 8(e)(1), which requires pleadings to be "simple, concise, and direct"; Rule 8(e)(1) would not prohibit a detailed court-ordered reply. However, the Fifth Circuit failed to consider whether Federal Rules 8(b) ("Defenses; Form of Denials") and (c) ("Affirmative Defenses") applied to the plaintiff's reply if it asserted denials and defenses to the defendant's immunity defense. These provisions are worded generally to apply to defenses asserted in all pleadings, and Rules 8(b) and (c) embody the notice pleading standards of the Federal Rules. *See* 5 CHARLES A. WRIGHT ET AL., FEDERAL PRACTICE AND PROCEDURE: CIVIL §§ 1261, 1274 (3d ed. 2004). Nevertheless, Rule 8(b) requires that denials must "fairly meet the substance of the averments denied," and this provision may sometimes produce the result that the Fifth Circuit wants when the defense is pleaded properly. *See* sections D(3)*(f)(ii)* ("Admissions and Denials") & D(4) ("The Plaintiff's Reply and Motions to Strike an Insufficient Defense") *infra*.

150. 534 U.S. 506, 122 S. Ct. 992, 152 L. Ed. 2d 1 (2002). *But cf.* Crawford-El v. Britton, 523 U.S. 574, 118 S. Ct. 1584, 140 L. Ed. 2d 759 (1998) (leaving open the possibility of heightened pleading requirements in § 1983 actions against governmental officials for damages when the governmental official's improper motive is an essential element of the claim); Elaine M. Korb & Richard A. Bales, *A Permanent Stop Sign: Why Courts Should Yield to the Temptation to Impose Heightened Pleading Standards in § 1983 Cases,* 41 BRANDEIS L.J. 267 (2002).

151. *Swierkiewicz*, 534 U.S. at 510, 122 S. Ct. at 997, 152 L. Ed. 2d at 8. The Court pointed out that not all employment discrimination cases require proof of a prima facie case at trial, such as when a plaintiff has direct (*e.g.*, the employer states to a third-party that the employee was fired because of the employee's age) rather than circumstantial evidence of discrimination.

152. *Id.* at 513-14, 122 S. Ct. at 998-99, 152 L. Ed. 2d at 10.

153. *Id.* at 514, 122 S. Ct. at 999, 152 L. Ed. 2d at 11.

In *Bell Atlantic Corp. v. Twombly*,[154] also discussed in the next subsection dealing with the plausibility requirement, the U.S. Supreme Court again rejected the judicial creation of "heightened pleading" standards for specific cases. In *Twombly*, the plaintiff had sued under § 1 of the Sherman Antitrust Act, which requires "a contract, combination . . . , or conspiracy, in restraint of trade or commerce."[155] The plaintiff's complaint (as interpreted by the majority of the Court) alleged that major telecommunications providers engaged in parallel conduct in their respective service areas to inhibit the growth of competition. In addition, the plaintiff alleged that the defendants refrained from competing against one another by a failure to pursue attractive business opportunities in contiguous markets in which they possessed substantial competitive advantages. However, the complaint did not "directly allege an illegal agreement," but instead "proceed[ed] exclusively via allegations of parallel conduct."[156] In this context, the Court held that the allegations failed to meet the pleading standard of Rule 8(e)(2). Nor was it intending to broaden the scope of Rule 9, citing *Leatherman* and *Swierkiewicz*.[157] However, the allegations failed to meet the plausibility standard discussed in the next subsection.

The Court in *Twombly* pointed out, hypothetically, that had the plaintiffs' complaint not rested on parallel conduct but simply alleged a conspiracy in violation of § 1 of the Sherman Act, "we doubt that the complaint's references to an agreement among [the defendants] would have given the notice required by Rule 8."[158] In other words, the problem would not have been plausibility, discussed in the next subsection; rather, it would have been that the lack of detail failed to satisfy the "fair notice" requirement. In so stating, the Court pointed out the sharp contrast to the Complaint for Negligence in the official forms: "the pleadings mentioned no specific time, place, or person involved in the alleged conspiracies [and thus] furnishes no clue as to which of the four [defendants] (much less which of their employees) supposedly agreed, or when and where the illicit agreement took place." The Court also added that defendants "seeking to respond to [those] conclusory allegations . . . would have little idea where to begin."[159]

---

154. 550 U.S. 544, 127 S. Ct. 1955, 167 L. Ed. 2d 929 (2007).

155. 15 U.S.C. § 1.

156. 550 U.S. at 565 & n.11, 127 S. Ct. at 1970-71 & n.11, 167 L. Ed. 2d at 946 & n.11.

157. *Id.* at 569 n.14, 127 S. Ct. at 1973 n.14, 167 L. Ed. 2d at 948 n.14. Two weeks after *Twombly* was decided, the Court decided Erickson v. Pardus, 551 U.S. 89, 127 S. Ct. 2197, 167 L. Ed. 2d 1081 (2008). In that case, a pro se prisoner's action under 42 U.S.C. § 1983 seeking medical treatment was dismissed by a U.S. District Court because the allegations of the complaint were deemed conclusory. The court of appeals affirmed, which found that the plaintiff's complaint for denial of medical treatment made "only conclusory allegations" in alleging that the plaintiff had suffered a "cognizable independent harm." Under the applicable substantive law, such a harm was necessary to give rise to an actionable claim. In vacating the judgment and remanding the case, the Court held that the allegations of the complaint complied with the requirements of Rule 8(a)(2). The plaintiff had alleged that the defendants' denial of prescribed medication and treatment for his hepatitis C was "endangering [his] life." According to the Court, "[t]his alone" was sufficient to state a claim under Rule 8(a)(2) and concluded that the allegations gave fair notice of the claim and the grounds upon which it rested. *Id.* at 90-95, 127 S. Ct. at 2198-2200, 167 L. Ed. 2d at 1083-86.

158. *Id.* at 565 n.10, 127 S. Ct. at 1973 n.10, 167 L. Ed. 2d at 945 n.10.

159. *Id.* Furthermore, while not pointed out by the Court, there would also be little to afford a sufficient basis for res judicata based on the allegations in the case. *See* Charles E. Clark, *Simplified Pleading*, 2 F.R.D. 456, 461 (1943) (suggesting this res judicata factor is another important function of notice pleading).

Of course, in cases in which a statute imposes a heightened pleading standard, the statute governs rather than the notice pleading standard in Rule 8(a)(2).[160]

(ii) "Entitled to Relief": The "Plausibility" Requirement

In order for a claim to be legally sufficient, *i.e.*, to withstand a motion to dismiss under Rule 12(b)(6), Rule 8(a)(2) requires a pleader to provide "a short and plain statement of the claim *showing that the pleader is entitled to relief*."[161] In *Conley v. Gibson*,[162] the U.S. Supreme Court stated that

> [i]n appraising the [legal] sufficiency of the complaint we follow, of course, the accepted rule that a complaint should not be dismissed for a failure to state a claim unless it appears beyond doubt that the plaintiff can prove no set of facts in support of [the plaintiff's] claim which would entitle [the plaintiff] to relief.[163]

In *Bell Atlantic Corp. v. Twombly*,[164] discussed in the preceding subsection, the U.S. Supreme Court repudiated this "no set of facts" standard.[165] In *Twombly*, the district court had dismissed the complaint for failure to state a claim on the ground that allegations of parallel anti-competitive conduct without more do not support the Sherman Act's requirement of a "contract, combination, or conspiracy."[166] The Second Circuit Court of Appeals reversed under the *Conley* "no set of facts" standard quoted above, indicating that parallel conduct could be the product of collusion rather than independent action and thus that the defendants had not shown that the plaintiff could prove no set of facts that would entitle him to relief.[167]

The U.S. Supreme Court, in turn, reversed the Second Circuit. In discussing the *Conley* standard, the Court stated:

> On . . . a . . . literal reading of *Conley's* "no set of facts [standard]," a wholly conclusory statement of [a] claim would survive a motion to dismiss whenever the pleadings left open the possibility that a plaintiff might later establish some "set of [undisclosed] facts" to support recovery. So here, the Court of Appeals specifically found the prospect of unearthing direct

---

160. *See* Tellabs, Inc. v. Makor Issues & Rights, Ltd., 551 U.S. 308, 127 S. Ct. 2499, 168 L. Ed. 2d 179 (2007) (to meet requirements of Private Securities Litigation Reform Act, plaintiff alleging fraud in § 10(b) securities action must plead facts rendering scienter at least as likely as any plausible opposing inference); *see also Marvin Lowenthal, Revitalizing Motive and Opportunity Pleading after* Tellabs, 109 MICH. L. REV. 625 (2011).

161. FED. R. CIV. P. 8(a)(2) (emphasis added).

162. 355 U.S. 41, 78 S. Ct. 99, 2 L. Ed. 2d 80 (1957).

163. 355 U.S. at 45-46, 78 S. Ct. at 102, 2 L. Ed. 2d at 84. This statement cannot, of course, be taken literally. Otherwise, a complaint stating only that the "defendant is legally liable to the plaintiff" would be legally sufficient because it does not appear beyond doubt that the plaintiff can prove no set of facts in support of the claim that would entitle the plaintiff to relief. *See* FLEMING JAMES, JR. ET AL., CIVIL PROCEDURE § 3.6, at 190 (5th ed. 2001).

164. 550 U.S. 544, 127 S. Ct. 1955, 167 L. Ed. 2d 929 (2007).

165. *Id.* at 563, 2127 S. Ct. at 1969, 167 L. Ed. 2d at 945; *see The Supreme Court: 2006 Term; Leading Cases*, 121 HARV. L. REV. 185, 305 (2007) (interpreting *Twombly* as having abandoned the above pleading standard in *Conley*).

166. *Id.* at 552, 127 S. Ct. at 1963, 167 L. Ed. 2d at 938.

167. *Id.* at 552, 127 S. Ct. at 1963, 167 L. Ed. 2d at 938-39.

> evidence of conspiracy sufficient to preclude dismissal, even though the complaint does not set forth a single fact in a context that suggests an agreement. . . . It seems fair to say that this approach to pleading would dispense with any showing of a "reasonably founded hope" that a plaintiff would be able to make a case.[168]

In *Twombly*, the Court observed that a literal reading of *Conley's* "no set of facts" standard had puzzled courts and commentators and had been widely criticized. The Court then indicated that a literal reading of the statement was not permissible:

> [T]here is no need to pile up further citations to show that *Conley's* "no set of facts" language has been questioned, criticized, and explained away long enough. To be fair to the *Conley* Court, the passage should be understood in light of the opinion's preceding summary of the complaint's concrete allegations, which the Court quite reasonably understood as amply stating a claim for relief. But the passage so often quoted fails to mention this understanding on the part of the Court, and after puzzling the profession for 50 years, this famous observation has earned its retirement. The phrase is best forgotten as an incomplete, negative gloss on an accepted pleading standard: once a claim has been stated adequately, it may be supported by showing any set of facts consistent with the allegations in the complaint. . . . *Conley,* then, described the breadth of opportunity to prove what an adequate complaint claims, not the minimum standard of adequate pleading to govern a complaint's survival.[169]

In the course of its opinion, the Court emphasized that a proper pleading must provide not only fair notice of the claim, but also must state the grounds upon which the claim rests in order to showing that the pleader is *plausibility* entitled to relief. The Court indicated that "[f]actual allegations must be enough to raise a right to relief above the speculative level";[170] "more than labels and conclusions" are required;[171] "a formulaic recitation of the elements of a cause of action will not do";[172] the statement must "possess enough heft" to show the pleader is entitled to relief;[173] "we do not require heightened fact pleading of specifics, but only enough facts to state a claim to relief that is *plausible* on its face";[174] and that the allegations must "nudge[]" the claims "across the line from conceivable to *plausible*" and must not stop "short of the line between possibility and *plausibility*."[175] In establishing the "plausibility" requirement, however, the Court stated that "[a]sking for plausible

---

168. *Id.* at 561-62, 127 S. Ct. at 1968-69, 167 L. Ed. 2d at 944 (citation omitted).
169. *Id.* at 562-63, 127 S. Ct. at 1969, 167 L. Ed. 2d at 944-45.
170. *Id.* at 555, 127 S. Ct. at 1965, 167 L. Ed. 2d at 940.
171. *Id.*
172. *Id.*
173. *Id.* at 557, 127 S. Ct. at 1966, 167 L. Ed. 2d at 941.
174. *Id.* at 570, 127 S. Ct. at 1974, 167 L. Ed. 2d at 949 (emphasis added).
175. *Id.* at 557, 127 S. Ct. at 1966, 167 L. Ed. 2d at 941 (emphasis added).

grounds . . . does not impose a probability requirement at the pleading stage."[176] Indeed, "a well-pleaded complaint may proceed even if it strikes a savvy judge that actual proof of those facts is improbable."[177]

In *Twombly*, the Court correctly rejected a literal interpretation of *Conley*. The language of the Rule 8(a)(2) requires a "statement of the claim showing that the pleader is *entitled to relief*."[178] In other words, the complaint must be based on a plausible legal theory in the complaint. The factual allegations of parallel conduct in *Twombly* were a description of legally innocent behavior of oligopolists that, without some kind of "plus" factor, does not violate the Sherman Act and thus do not show the pleader entitled to relief.[179] In judging allegations covering a wide range of possible conduct, much of it innocent and possibly highly unlikely, the allegations must be specific enough to move down the continuum to "plausible": impossible ➜ conceivable ➜ possible ➜ plausible ➜ probable ➜ highly likely ➜ certain. In other words, the allegations must be enough that, if assumed to be true, the plaintiff plausibly—not just speculatively—has a claim for relief. In *Twombly*, "the complaint warranted dismissal because it failed *in toto* to render [the] plaintiffs' entitlement to relief plausible."[180]

Two years after *Twombly*, the Court decided *Ashcroft v. Iqbal*,[181] in which a Muslim Pakistani pretrial 9/11 detainee sued 53current and former government officials, including the former Attorney General of the United States, John Ashcroft, and the Director of the Federal Bureau of Investigation ("FBI"), Robert Mueller. Iqbal claimed that the defendants took a series of unconstitutional actions against him after being separated from the general prison population and forced to undergo harsh conditions.[182]

With regard to Ashcroft and Mueller, Iqbal specifically alleged that (1) the FBI, under Mueller's direction, "arrested and detained thousands of Arab Muslim men . . . as part of its investigation of the events of September 11"; (2) Ashcroft and Mueller, in discussions in the weeks after September 11, 2001, approved "[t]he policy of holding post-September 11th detainees in highly restrictive conditions of confinement until they were 'cleared' by the FBI"; (3) Ashcroft and Mueller "each

---

176. *Id.* at 556, 127 S. Ct. at 1965, 167 L. Ed. 2d at 940.

177. *Id.*

178. FED. R. CIV. P. 8(a)(2) (emphasis added).

179. Areeda and Hovenkamp point out that "[w]ith rare exceptions, the courts have held that mere parallelism, including interdependent conscious parallelism, cannot support a conspiracy finding unless there are additional or 'plus' factors." 7 PHILLIP E. AREEDA & HERBERT HOVENKAMP, ANTITRUST LAW ¶ 1434, at 241 (2d ed. 2003). Those plus factors include those emphasized in the simple refusal to deal cases, parallelism of a much more elaborate and complex nature, or a web of circumstantial evidence pointing out very convincingly to the ultimate fact of agreement. *See id.* ¶ 1433, at 241 (citation omitted). They also point out that "[t]he meaning of the term "plus factor" is clear enough when the additional evidence is sufficient to imply a traditional conspiracy. But the courts also say that conspiratorial motivation and acts against self-interest are plus factors. This could mean that interdependent parallelism, which is synonymous with interdependence, is conspiratorial, but [there are] persuasive reasons to reject that reading." *Id.* ¶ 1434, at 242.

180. *Twombly*, 550 U.S. at 569 n.14, 127 S. Ct. at 1973 n.14, 167 L. Ed. 2d at 948-49 n.14. The Court pointed out that "[a] statement of parallel conduct, even conduct consciously undertaken, needs some setting suggesting the agreement necessary to make out a § 1 claim; without that further circumstance pointing toward a meeting of the minds, an account of a defendant's commercial efforts stays in neutral territory." Thus, "[a]n allegation of parallel conduct is . . . much like a naked assertion of conspiracy in a § 1 complaint: it gets the complaint close to stating a claim, but without some further factual enhancement it stops short of the line between possibility and plausibility of 'entitle[ment] to relief.' " *Id.* at 557, 127 S. Ct. at 1966, 167 L. Ed. 2d at 941.

181. 556 U.S. 662, 129 S. Ct. 1937, 173 L. Ed. 2d 868 (2009).

182. *Id.* at 666-71, 129 S. Ct. at 1942-44, 173 L. Ed. 2d at 876-80.

knew of, condoned, and willfully and maliciously agreed to subject" Iqbal "to harsh conditions of confinement 'as a matter of policy, solely on account of [Iqbal's] religion, race, and/or national origin and for no legitimate penological interest"; (4) Ashcroft was the "principal architect" of the policy; and (5) Mueller was "instrumental in [its] adoption, promulgation, and implementation."[183]

Ashcroft and Mueller raised the defense of qualified immunity and moved to dismiss the complaint on ground that it failed to state sufficient allegations to show their own involvement in clearly established unconstitutional conduct. Relying on *Conley*, the district court denied their motion.[184] On appeal, the Second Circuit recognized that the no-set-of-facts test relied upon by the district court had been retired by *Twombly*.[185] In attempting to apply *Twombly*, the Second Circuit applied a flexible plausibility standard that requires "a pleader to amplify a claim with some factual allegations in those contexts [in which] such amplification is needed to render the claim *plausible*" and that this claim was not one.[186] As a result, the Second Circuit held that the pleading adequately alleged the defendants' personal involvement in discriminatory decisions which, if true, violated clearly established constitutional law."[187]

In a 5-4 decision, the U.S. Supreme Court reversed. Agreeing with the Second Circuit, the Court indicated that "[d]etermining whether a complaint states a plausible claim for relief will . . . be a *context-specific task* that requires the reviewing court to draw on its *judicial experience and common sense*."[188] Only a complaint that states a plausible claim for relief can survive a motion to dismiss.[189] It also made it clear that *Twombly* rationale applies to all civil actions, not just antitrust cases.[190]

According to the majority opinion, authored by Justice Kennedy, the starting point is the substantive elements of the claim.[191] Those elements then are assessed in relation to the well-pleaded facts.[192] In carrying out this task, the Court used a "two-pronged" approach: the judge must first exclude "legal conclusions" ("Prong 1") before applying the plausibility standard to the remaining factual allegations ("Prong 2").[193] The majority explained that

> a court considering a motion to dismiss can choose to begin by identifying pleadings that, because they are no more than conclusions, are not entitled to the assumption of truth. While legal

---

183. *Id.* at 669, 129 S. Ct. at 1944, 173 L. Ed. 2d at 878 (as summarized by the U.S. Supreme Court in the majority opinion).

184. *Id.* at 666-71, 129 S. Ct. at 1942-44, 173 L. Ed. 2d at 876-80.

185. *Id.* at 670, 129 S. Ct. at 1944, 173 L. Ed. 2d at 878.

186. Iqbal v. Hasty, 490 F.3d at 143, 157-58, 174 (2d Cir. 2007).

187. *Id.* at 174.

188. 556 U.S. at 679, 129 S. Ct. at 1950, 173 L. Ed. 2d at 884 (emphasis added).

189. *Id.*

190. *Id.* at 684, 129 S. Ct. at 1953, 173 L. Ed. 2d at 887.

191. *Id.* at 675, 129 S. Ct. at 1947, 173 L. Ed. 2d at 882 (pointing out that the Court in *Twombly* also began with discussing the antitrust principles implicated by the complaint in that case).

192. *Id.* at 679, 129 S. Ct. at 1950, 173 L. Ed. 2d at 884.

193. This approach marks a significant departure from what the Court did in *Twombly*. *See* Robert G. Bone, *Plausibility Pleading Revisited and Revised: A Comment on* Ashcroft v. Iqbal, 85 NOTRE DAME L. REV. 849, 867-69 (2010) (pointing out that the Court in *Twombly* "did not simply dismiss the questionable allegations of agreement as conclusory and then subject the remaining allegations to the plausibility standard, as the *Iqbal* [majority] claims it did"; instead, the Court in *Twombly* "interpreted the complaint as a whole.").

> conclusions can provide the framework of a complaint, they must be supported by factual allegations. When there are well-pleaded factual allegations, a court should assume their veracity and then determine whether they plausibly give rise to an entitlement to relief.[194]

It is at this point the majority and dissenters in *Iqbal* diverged: which allegations in the complaint constituted "legal conclusions"?[195] The majority concluded that Iqbal's allegations regarding the purpose of adopting the harsh conditions policy was "solely on account of [his] religion, race, and/or national origin and for no legitimate penological interest," that "Ashcroft was the 'principal architect' of this invidious policy," and that "Mueller was 'instrumental' in adopting and executing it."[196] The majority deemed these allegations to be "bare assertions, much like the pleading of conspiracy in *Twombly*" and regarded them as "amount[ing] to nothing more than a 'formulaic recitation of the elements' of a constitutional discrimination claim."[197] As such, these allegations were "disentitle[d] . . . to the presumption of truth."[198]

Limited to the allegations the majority found to be entitled to the presumption of truth (and excluding those it found to be legal conclusions), the majority then found two different interpretations possible in much the same way as the Court did in *Twombly*: one unlawful and the other lawful. The majority readily recognized that Iqbal's allegations could indeed be consistent with constitutionally prohibited behavior.[199] On the other hand, those allegations could also be consistent with legitimate law enforcement efforts: "It should come as no surprise that a legitimate policy directing law enforcement to arrest and detain individuals because of their suspected link to the attacks would produce a disparate, incidental impact on Arab Muslims, even though the purpose of the policy was to target neither Arabs nor Muslims."[200] Thus, the majority concluded that the inference that Ashcroft and Mueller had engaged in unconstitutional conduct could not be plausibly be drawn from what Iqbal had alleged.[201]

According to the majority, another important function of its pleading standard is to foreclose discovery,[202] especially when defendants are government officials entitled to assert qualified immunity as a defense.[203] Justice Breyer

---

194. 556 U.S. at 679, 129 S. Ct. at 1950, 173 L. Ed. 2d at 884.

195. *Compare id.* at 680-81, 129 S. Ct. at 1951-52, 173 L. Ed. 2d at 885-86 (Justice Kennedy's majority opinion) *with id.* at 694-99, 129 S. Ct. at 1958-61, 173 L. Ed. 2d at 894-61 (Justice Souter's dissenting opinion).

196. *Id.* at 680-81, 129 S. Ct. at 1951, 173 L. Ed. 2d at 885-86.

197. *Id.* The majority also emphasized that these allegations were rejected because of their "conclusory nature . . . rather than their extravagantly fanciful nature . . . ." *Id.*

198. *Id.* at 681, 129 S. Ct. at 1951, 173 L. Ed. 2d at 885.

199. *See id.* at 681, 129 S. Ct. at 1951, 173 L. Ed. 2d at 886 ("Taken as true, these allegations are consistent with [Ashcroft and Mueller's] purposefully designating detainees 'of high interest' because of their race, religion, or nation origin" in violation of the law.)

200. *Id.* at 682, 129 S. Ct. at 1951, 173 L. Ed. 2d at 886.

201. *Id.* at 681-83, 129 S. Ct. at 1951-52, 173 L. Ed. 2d at 886-87 ("As between th[e] 'obvious alternation explanation' for the arrest, . . . and the purposeful, invidious discrimination [Iqbal] asks us to infer, discrimination is not a plausible conclusion.").

202. *Id.* at 685-86, 129 S. Ct. at 1953-54, 173 L. Ed. 2d at 888-89. *See* Edward D. Cavanagh, *Making Sense of* Twombly, 63 S.C. L. REV. 97, 134 (2010) (suggesting that "[t]he level of factual content in a pleading required by *Twombly* and *Iqbal* is directly proportional to the complexity of the case and the likely costs of pretrial discovery").

203. 556 U.S. at 685, 129 S. Ct. at 1953, 173 L. Ed. 2d at 888.

particularly took issue with the majority on this point, asserting that a trial judge has "other legal weapons" (case management tools) to prevent unwarranted interference with that immunity, including limited or staged discovery.[204]

The majority's approach also raises potential, although not insurmountable, inconsistencies with the official forms, which are deemed to be sufficient and in compliance with the Federal Rules.[205] In this regard, most of the focus has been on the allegations in Form 18 related to patent infringement.[206] In addition, the majority's approach raises questions about how this approach should apply, if at all, to pleading affirmative defenses.[207] Furthermore, it has implications for the relationship between Federal Rule 8(a) prescribing what a pleading must contain to state a claim for relief and Rule 9(b)'s permission to allege "[m]alice, intent, knowledge, and other conditions of a person's mind . . . generally."[208]

In conclusion, *Twombly* and *Iqbal* provide a more rational standard than *Conley* did, especially for situations involving claims based on allegations of conduct that encompass a wide range of conduct, much of which is legally permissible. *Iqbal* properly indicates that the analysis is "context specific." On the other hand, to the extent that *Twombly* and *Iqbal* encourage (or force) lower courts to actively engage in classifying allegations as "conclusory" or "nonconclusory," that effort is likely to encounter the same problems that such classifications faced under code pleading.[209] Thus, it is not surprising that even in *Iqbal* itself, the dissenting Justices found that the majority inconsistently classified similar (in their view) allegations in the complaint.[210] Furthermore, to the extent that the real

---

204. *Id.* at 699-700, 129 S. Ct. at 1961-62, 173 L. Ed. 2d at 897 (Justice Souter's dissenting opinion); *see generally* Jonah B. Gelbach, Note, *Locking the Doors to Discovery? Assessing the Effects of* Twombly *and* Iqbal *on Access to Discovery*, 121 YALE L.J. 2270 (2012).

205. *See* FED. R. CIV. P. 84.

206. *See, e.g.*, Rex Mann, *What the Federal Rules of Civil Procedure Forms Say About* Twombly *and* Iqbal: *Implications of the Forms on the Supreme Court's Standard*, 41 U. MEM. L. REV. 501 (2011); Damon C. Andrews, Note, Iqbal-*ing* Seagate: *Plausibility Pleading of Willful Patent Infringement*, 25 BERKELEY TECH. L.J. 1955, 1970-72 (2010).

207. *See* Leslie Paul Machado & C. Matthew Haynes, *Do* Twombly *and* Iqbal *Apply to Affirmative Defenses?*, 59 FED. LAW., July 2012, at 56 (recognizing a developing split); James V. Bilek, Comment, Twombly, Iqbal, *and Rule 8(c): Assessing the Proper Standard to Apply to Affirmative Defenses*, 15 CHAP. L. REV. 377, 386 (2011) (concluding cases are in a "state of disarray"; courts have developed a multitude of standards; due to lack of uniformity, the majority of courts do not apply the plausibility standard); Ryan Mize, Comment, *From Plausibility to Clarity: An Analysis of the Implications of* Ashcroft v. Iqbal *and Possible Remedies*, 58 U. KAN. L. REV. 1245, 1260-61 (2010) (stating that the majority view endorses applying the *Twombly-Iqbal* standard to affirmative defenses).

208. *See Iqbal*, 556 U.S. at 686, 129 S. Ct. at 1954, 173 L. Ed. 2d at 889 (asserting that "'generally' is a relative term[, which] [i]n the context of Rule 9, . . . is to be compared to the particularity requirement applicable to fraud and mistake" and concluding that "Rule 9 merely excuses a party from pleading discriminatory intent under an elevated pleading standard [and] [i]t does not give [a party] license to evade the less rigid—though still operative—strictures of Rule 8"); Robert G. Bone, *Plausibility Pleading Revisited and Revised: A Comment on* Ashcroft v. Iqbal, 85 NOTRE DAME L. REV. 849, 860-67 (2010) (pointing out the majority's statements about "threadbare" and "formulaic" recitals of the "defendant-unlawfully-harmed me" seem to "point to some defect or deficiency intrinsic to the allegation[s]" themselves, but the key allegations actually at issue "describe[d] mental states, link[ed] those mental states to a discriminatory policy described in some detail elsewhere in the complaint, and refer [red] to more particular types of involvement by Ashcroft and Miller"; thus, the majority's statements "suggest a different problem: not that the allegations track formulaic language, but that they state facts at too high a level of generality"; the practical difficulty with this approach, as highlighted by Justice Souter's dissenting opinion, is straightforward and well-known: "There is no obvious way to draw a line along the generality-specificity continuum.").

209. *See* Chapter 6(C)(2)(a) ("Pleading Facts"); *Illustrations 6-10 & 6-11 supra.*

210. *Id.* at 699, 129 S. Ct. at 1961, 173 L. Ed. 2d at 896-97 (Justice Souter) ("majority's holding that the statements it selects are conclusory cannot be squared with its treatment of certain other allegations in the complaint as nonconclusory [and] unprincipled") (providing examples).

problem is that the facts are alleged at too high a level of generality, lower courts are going to encounter serious difficulties. More likely, lower courts will simply ignore the issue of plausibility in most cases. *Twombly* and *Iqbal*, however, will also allow lower court judges to seize upon the "plausibility" requirement to force detailed "fact pleading" and to dismiss cases at the pleading stage based on their own judicial experience with that type of case or their own personal perception of common sense.[211]

As might be expected, the *Twombly* and *Iqbal* decisions have evoked an outpouring of commentary and lower court reaction. The commentary first focused on initial reactions to the *Twombly* decision and its significance;[212] then it turned to attempts to define the rationale, theoretical underpinnings, and scope of *Iqbal*;[213] it

---

211. *See* Robert G. Bone, *Plausibility Pleading Revisited and Revised: A Comment on* Ashcroft v. Iqbal, 85 NOTRE DAME L. REV. 849, 869-70 (2010) (arguing that the majority's two-pronged approach "facilitates overly aggressive screening at the pleading stage and inappropriately makes it much easier for judges to do so).

212. *See, e.g.*, Charles B. Campbell, *A "Plausible" Showing After* Bell Atlantic Corp. v. Twombly, 9 NEV. L.J. 1 (2008); Richard A. Epstein, Bell Atlantic v. Twombly: *How Motions to Dismiss Become (Disguised) Summary Judgments*, 25 WASH. U. J. L. & POL'Y 61 (2007); Daniel R. Karon, *"'Twas Three Years After* Twombly *and All Through the Bar, Not a Plaintiff Was Troubled From Near or From Far"—The Unremarkable Effect of the U.S. Supreme Court Re-Expressed Pleading Standard in* Bell Atlantic Corp. v. Twombly, 44 U. S.F. L. REV. 571 (2010); Collen McMahon, *The Law of Unintended Consequences: Shockwaves in the Lower Courts After* Bell Atlantic Corp. v. Twombly, 41 SUFFOLK U. L. REV. 851 (2008); Douglas G. Smith, *The* Twombly *Revolution?*, 36 PEPP. L. REV. 1063 (2009); A. Benjamin Spenser, *Understanding Pleading Doctrine*, 108 MICH. L. REV. 1 (2009); Symposium, *The Future of Pleading in the Federal System: Debating the Impact of* Bell Atlantic v. Twombly, 82 ST. JOHN'S L. REV. 893 (2008); Z.W. Julius Chen, Note, *Following the Leader:* Twombly, *Pleading Standards, and Procedural Uniformity*, 108 COLUM. L. REV. 1431 (2008); Ryan Gist, Note, *Transactional Pleading: A Proportional Approach to Rule 8 in the Wake of* Bell Atlantic Corp. v. Twombly, 2008 WIS. L. REV. 1013; Jason G. Gottesman, Comment, *Speculating as to the Plausible: Pleading Practice After* Bell Atlantic Corp. v. Twombly, 17 WIDENER L.J. 973 (2008); Matthew A. Josephson, Note, *Some Things Are Better Left Said: Pleading Practice After* Bell Atlantic Corp. v. Twombly, 42 GA. L. REV. 867 (2008); Saritha Komatireddy Tice, Recent Development, *A "Plausible" Explanation of Pleading Standards*, 31 HARV. J. L. & PUB. POL'Y 827 (2008); *The Supreme Court: 2006 Term; Leading Cases,* 121 HARV. L. REV. 185, 305 (2007).

213. *See, e.g.*, Victor E. Schwartz & Chrisopher E. Appel, *Rational Pleading in the Modern World of Civil Litigation: The Lessons and Public Policy Benefits of* Twombly *and* Iqbal, 33 HARV. J.L. & PUB. POL'Y 1107 (2010); Robert G. Bone, *Plausibility Pleading Revisited and Revised: A Comment on* Ashcroft v. Iqbal, 85 NOTRE DAME L. REV. 849 (2010); Edward D. Cavanagh, *Making Sense of* Twombly, 63 S.C. L.REV. 97 (2011); Kevin M. Clermont & Stephen C. Yeazell, *Inventing Tests, Destabilizing Systems*, 95 IOWA L. REV. 821 (2010); Benjamin P. Cooper, Iqbal's *Retro Revolution*, 46 WAKE FOREST L. REV. 937 (2011) (examining parallels between pleading under the 1983 version of Rule 11 and pleading in the post-*Iqbal* era); John M. Greabe, Iqbal, Al-Kidd *and Pleading Past Qualified Immunity: What the Cases Mean and How They Demonstrate a Need to Eliminate the Immunity Doctrines from Constitutional Tort Law*, 20 WM. & MARY BILL RTS. J. 1 (2011); Luke Meier, *Why* Twombly *Is Good Law (But Poorly Drafted) and* Iqbal *Will Be Overturned*, 87 IND. L.J. 709 (2012); Arthur R. Miller, *From* Conley *to* Twombly *to* Iqbal: *A Double Play on the Federal Rules of Civil Procedure*, 60 DUKE L.J. 1 (2010) (contending that "too much attention [has been] paid to claims by corporate and other defense interests of expense and possible abuse and too little to citizen access, a level litigation playing filed, and the other values of civil litigation"); Michael S. Pardo, *Pleadings, Proof, and Judgment: A Unified Theory of Civil Litigation*, 51 B.C. L. REV. 1451 (2010) (proposing a "procedural accuracy" theory to explain and justify, *inter alia*, dismissals at the pleading stage in light of the evidentiary proof rules that implement underlying policy choices regarding accurate outcomes and allocations of the risk of adjudicative error); Alex Reinert, *The Impact of* Ashcroft v. Iqbal *on Pleading*, 43 URB. LAW. 559 (2011); Daniel W. Robertson, *In Defense of Plausibility:* Ashcroft v. Iqbal *and What the Plausibility Standard Really Means*, 38 PEPP. L. REV. 111, 127 (2010) (pointing out, *inter alia*, that "[f]actual allegations tend to be those specific to the factual setting out of which the case arose [and are not] generally applicable to every case of its type" and asserting that "it is reasonable to conclude that the Court means only to exclude legal conclusions of the fact-conclusion continuum."); Joseph A. Seiner, *After* Iqbal, WAKE FOREST L. REV. 179 (2010); Steve Subrin, Ascroft v. Iqbal: *Contempt for Rules, Statutes, the Constitution, an45d Elemental Fairness*, 12 NEV. L.J. 571 (2012); Suja A. Thomas, *Oddball* Iqbal *and* Twombly *and Employment Discrimination*, 2011 U. ILL. L. REV. 215; Ryan Charlson, Comment, *Flying Blind: The Lack of Uniformity in Federal Pleading after* Twombly *and* Iqbal, 44 J. Marshall L. Rev. 485 (2011); Trisha Chokshi, Note, *A Pleading Problem: Seventh Circuit Decision in* Swanson v. Citibank *Illustrates the Unstable State of Federal Pleading Standards in the Post-*Iqbal *Era*, 32 N. ILL. U. L. REV. 103 (2011); Ryan Mize, Comment, *From Plausibility to Clarity: An Analysis of the Implications of* Ashcroft v. Iqbal *and Possible Remedies*, 58 U. KAN. L. REV. 1245 (2010) (good analysis of alternatives); Allison Sirica, Comment, *The New Federal Pleading Standard*, 62 FLA. L.

has also stimulated empirical studies[214] and assessments of how the plausibility standard impacts particular types of cases.[215]

In additional, several states following the Federal Rules model have refused to adopt the plausibility standard.[216] Typical of the concerns of these states are those articulated by the Tennessee Supreme Court. Its views provide a good reflection of the negative commentary that *Twombly* and *Iqbal* have evoked. The court first recognized that these "decisions reflect a significant and substantial departure from the United States Supreme Court's prior interpretations of [Federal Rule] 8 and the seventy-year history of a liberal notice pleading standard as envisioned by the Federal Rules of Civil Procedure and . . . *Conley*,"[217] which has resulted in "a loss of clarity, stability, and predictability in federal pleadings practice."[218] In the court's view, "the plausibility pleading standard incorporates an evaluation and determination of likelihood of success on the merits—a judicial weighing of the facts pleaded to see if they "plausibly" present a claim for relief—at the earliest stage of the proceedings, before a sworn denial is even required."[219] In its view, this approach was "at odds with the well-established principle in Tennessee that a Rule [12(b)(6) equivalent] motion [to dismiss for failure to state a claim] challenges only the legal sufficiency of the complaint, not the strength of the plaintiff's proof or evidence."[220]

REV. 547 (2010); Devon J. Stewart, *Note, Take Me Home to* Conley v. Gibson, *Country Roads: An Analysis of the Effect of* Bell Atlantic Corp. v. Twombly *and* Ashcroft v. Iqbal *on West Virginia's Pleading Doctrine*, 113 W. VA. L. REV. 167 (2010) (arguing that *Twombly-Iqbal* should not be adopted in West Virginia); Carly R. Wilson, Recent Decision, *Complaints Must Plead Non-Conclusory Facts that Manifest Plausibility to Survive a Motion to Dismiss in All Civil Cases*: Ashcroft v. Iqbal, 48 DUQ. L. REV. 173 (2010).

214. *See, e.g.*, REPORT OF THE JUDICIAL CONFERENCE COMMITTEE ON RULES OF PRACTICE AND PROCEDURE, Mar. 2012, at 6 (reporting that the Federal Judicial Center's study found that motions to dismiss for failure to state a claim were being made more frequently after *Twombly* and *Iqbal*, but that there "was no statistically significant increase in the rate of granting motions to dismiss"); Patricia Hatamyar Moore, *An Updated Quantitative Study of* Iqbal's *Impact on 12(b)(6) Motions*, 46 U. RICH. L. REV. 603 (2012); Alexander A. Reinert, *The Costs of Heightened Pleading*, 86 IND. L.J. 119 (2011) (summarizing empirical research and suggesting that there is no correlation between the "heft of a pleading" and the ultimate success of a case and that "the costs imposed by heightened pleading may be substantial and may not create the assumed benefits"); Jonah B. Gelbach, Note, *Locking the Doors to Discovery? Assessing the Effects of* Twombly *and* Iqbal *on Access to Discovery*, 121 YALE L.J. 2270 (2012); Colleen McNamara, Note, Iqbal *as Judicial Rorschach Test: An Empirical Study of District Court Interpretations of* Ashcroft v. Iqbal, 105 NW. U. L. REV. 401 (2011).

215. *See, e.g.*, Raymond H. Brescia, *The* Iqbal *Effect: The Impact of New Pleading Standards in Employment and Housing Discrimination Litigation*, 100 KY. L.J. 235 (2012); Richard A. Epstein, *Of Pleading and Discovery: Reflections on* Twombly *and* Iqbal *with Special Reference to Antitrust*, 2011 U. ILL. L. REV. 187; William M. Janssen, Iqbal *"Plausibility" in Pharmaceutical and Medical Device Litigation*, 71 LA. L. REV. 541 (2011); Goutam U. Jois, Pearson, Iqbal, *and Procedural Judicial Activism*, 37 FLA. ST. U. L. REV. 901 (2010) (effect on civil rights cases and sovereign immunity); Meryl J. Thomas, *The Merits of Procedure vs. Substance*: Erie, Iqbal, *and Affidavits of Merit as Medmal Reform*, 52 ARIZ. L. REV. 1135 (2010) (effect on diversity cases); Tanvir Vahora, *Working Through a Muddled Standard: Pleading Discrimination Cases After* Iqbal, 44 COLUM. J.L. & SOC. PROBS. 235 (2010); Carol L. Zeiner, *When* Kelo *Met* Twombly-Iqbal: *Implications for Pretext Challenges to Eminent Domain*, 46 WILLAMETTE L. REV. 201 (2009) Damon C. Andrews, Note, Iqbal-*ing* Seagate: *Plausibility Pleading of Willful Patent Infringement*, 25 BERKELEY TECH. L.J. 1955 (2010); Brook Detterman, Note, *Rumors of* Conley's *Demise Have Been Greatly Exaggerated: The Impact of* Bell Atlantic Corporation v. Twombly *on Pleading Standards in Environmental Litigation*, 40 ENVTL. L. 295 (2010); Jordan D. Shepherd, Note, *When* Sosa *Meets* Iqbal: *Plausibility Pleading in Human Rights Litigation*, 95 MINN. L. REV. 2318 (2011) (effect on litigation under the Alien Tort Statute); Geoffrey C. Westbrook, Note, *Evolutionary Pleading: Should Congress Override the Supreme Court's Unnatural Selection in* Ashcroft v. Iqbal *to Prevent the Extinction of Civil Rights Cases?*, 45 NEW ENG. L. REV. 205 (2010).

216. *See, e.g.*, Cullen v. Auto-Owners Ins. Co.,218 Ariz. 417, 189 P.3d 344 (2008); Colby v. Umbrella, Inc., 184 Vt. 1, 955 A.2d 1082 (2008); Webb v. Nashville Area Habitat for Humanity, Inc., 346 S.W.3d 422 (Tenn. 2011); McCurry v. Chevy Case Bank, FSB, 169 Wash. 2d 96, 233 P.3d 861 (2010) (en banc).

217. Webb v. Nashville Area Habitat for Humanity, Inc., 346 S.W.3d 422, 430 (Tenn. 2011).

218. *Id.* at 431.

219. *Id.* at 431-32.

220. *Id.* at 432.

Furthermore, the court was concerned that "the *Twombly/Iqbal* standard . . . raises potential concerns implicating the Tennessee constitutional mandate that "the right of trial by jury shall remain inviolate."[221]

With regard to the tests formulated by *Twombly* and *Iqbal* in attempting to guide courts how to determine the plausibility of a claim based on the pleading alone, the court viewed them to be "problematic."[222] In particular, the court had great reservations about the first prong of *Iqbal's* approach because "the distinction between whether an allegation is a 'fact' or a 'conclusion' is fine, blurry, and hard to detect."[223] The court pointed out that "[t]he differing viewpoints of the *Iqbal* majority and dissent illustrate [this] fundamental problem with the fact/conclusion dichotomy: many, if not most, allegations can be fairly described as at least having a 'conclusory' aspect"[224] and this problem "is generally avoided by adhering to the principles that are already well established in Tennessee for ruling on a motion to dismiss."[225]

The court also was concerned about the impact of the *Twombly/Iqbal* standard on cases involving "information asymmetry."[226] In the court's view, the required "a demonstration of plausibility at the pre-discovery phase of the case result[ed] in the disproportionate dismissal of certain types of potentially meritorious claims that require discovery to be proven, including actions for violations of civil rights, employment discrimination, antitrust, and conspiracy."[227] Furthermore, the court agreed that "[t]he policy concerns cited by the [U.S. Supreme] Court in *Twombly*—the threat of expensive and/or abusive discovery practices leading to the settlement of 'even anemic cases' . . . should not be lightly dismissed."[228] However, in its view, "such a broad and sweeping change in the procedural landscape . . . should come by operation of the normal rule-making process, not by judicial fiat in the limited context of a single case."[229]

(c) Alternative, Hypothetical, and Inconsistent Pleading

Common-law pleading requirements forced a party to elect a set of facts and a legal theory at the outset of the action and to plead them with certainty.[230] In contrast, Federal Rule 8(d)(2) expressly permits a plaintiff to set forth two or more statements of a claim alternatively or hypothetically, either in a single count or in separate ones. A plaintiff may also set forth claims inconsistently.[231]

---

221. *Id.*

222. *Id.*

223. *Id.* at 432-33.

224. *Id* at 434. In this regard, see *Illustration 6-11* (discussing the allegation that "*D* is the wife of *P*") *supra*.

225. *Id.* The court reserved using the "legal conclusion" determination for "legal argument couched as a factual assertion," which are not required to be taken as true. *Id.* The example the court gave was an allegation that "a statute was unconstitutional." *Id.*

226. *Id.*

227. *Id.* (primarily relying on commentators and observers).

228. *Id.* at 436.

229. *Id.*

230. The prohibition against pleading in the alternative at common law was eventually circumvented by using different counts to state the same cause of action in alternative ways. *See* CHARLES E. CLARK, HANDBOOK OF THE LAW OF CODE PLEADING § 70, at 459-60 (2d ed. 1947).

231. *See* FED. R. CIV. P. 8(d)(2), (3).

Illustration 6-21. The Federal Rules would permit the alternative and hypothetical allegations in *Illustration 6-2*.[232]

(d) Anticipating Defenses

The Federal Rules do not require the plaintiff to anticipate defenses. If the plaintiff does anticipate a defense, the plaintiff should be permitted to do so—particularly when the plaintiff offers a justification for a defense appearing on the face of the complaint.[233] However, the plaintiff cannot use such an anticipation to satisfy federal jurisdiction.[234]

Illustration 6-22. Assume that the dates alleged in *P's* complaint appear to indicate that the applicable statute of limitations has run on *P's* claim. *P* can anticipate the statute of limitations defense by alleging information demonstrating a recognized basis for tolling the statute (*e.g.*, *P's* mental incompetency or fraudulent concealment of a conspiracy that prevented its discovery).

(e) Pleading Special Matters

Historically, several pleading problems have been dealt with in special ways. The Federal Rules have addressed these matters by a series of special provisions—sometimes preserving common-law and code-pleading requirements.

(i) Fraud and Mistake

Like the common law and codes, Federal Rule 9(b) requires that "[i]n alleging fraud or mistake, a party must state with particularity the circumstances constituting fraud or mistake."[235]

---

232. The allegation tracks the allegation in Federal Form 12. *Cf.* PAE Gov't Servs., Inc. v. MPRI, Inc., 514 F.3d 856 (9th Cir. 2007) (allegations may not be stricken from an amended complaint because they contradict allegations in earlier complaint); Schwartz v. Rockey, 593 Pa. 536, 932 A.2d 885 (2007) (complaint with claim for breach of contract damages does not foreclose an amendment substituting an inconsistent equitable remedy).

233. The fact that no reply is permitted in federal court unless the court orders one points in favor of allowing anticipation.

234. *See, e.g.*, Louisville & Nashville R.R. Co. v. Mottley, 211 U.S. 149, 29 S. Ct. 42, 53 L. Ed. 126 (1908); Chapter 2(C)(1)*(b)(ii)* ("The Well-Pleaded Complaint Rule"); *Illustration 2-23, supra.*

235. FED. R. CIV. P. 9(b); *see also* Form 10(e) ("Complaint to Recover a Sum Certain [f]or Money Paid by Mistake") and Form 21 ("Complaint on a Claim for a Debt and to Set Aside a Fraudulent Conveyance Under Rule 18(b)") in the Appendix of Forms following the Federal Rules of Civil Procedure. *See generally* Barney J. Finberg, Annotation, *Construction and Application of Provision of Rule 9(b), Federal Rules of Civil Procedure, that Circumstances Constituting Fraud or Mistake Be Stated with Particularity*, 27 A.L.R. FED. 407 (1976). The following reasons have been advanced in support of the requirement of pleading fraud and mistake with particularity. The requirement is necessary to safeguard potential defendants from lightly made claims charging commission of acts that involve some degree of moral turpitude. Allegations of fraud or mistake frequently are advanced only for their nuisance or settlement value and with little hope that they will be successful. Further, since assertions of fraud or mistake often are involved in attempts to reopen completed transactions or set aside previously issued judicial orders, courts are unwilling to entertain charges of this type unless they are based on allegations that are sufficient to show whether the alleged injustice is severe enough to warrant the risks and difficulties inherent in a re-examination of old and settled matters. Also, fraud and mistake embrace such a wide variety of potential conduct that a defendant needs a substantial amount of particularized information about plaintiff's claim in order to enable him to understand it and effectively prepare his response. Finally, as has been pointed out by the commentators, the old cliche that actions or defenses based upon fraud are disfavored and are scrutinized by the courts with great care because they often form the basis of "strike suits" still retains considerable vitality. 5A CHARLES A. WRIGHT & ARTHUR R. MILLER, FEDERAL PRACTICE AND PROCEDURE: CIVIL § 1296, at

Illustration 6-23. Assume that *P* sued *D* based upon certain fraudulent misrepresentations made to induce *P* to purchase a tract of land. To satisfy the pleading requirements of Rule 9(b), *P* could allege the following "circumstances": (1) time, (2) place, (3) content of the false representations, (4) identity of the person making the representations, and (5) what was obtained thereby (reliance).[236]

* * * * *

The Private Securities Litigation Reform Act of 1995 imposed additional requirements for pleading fraud and fraudulent intent in investor securities litigation.[237]

31-51 (3d ed. 2004). Nevertheless, it is doubtful whether these reasons are sufficient to support a specialized pleading requirement today. Other types of allegations, such as assault and battery, involve moral turpitude, but no specialized pleading rule applies to them. In any event, this rationale can, at best, apply to fraud, but certainly not to mistake. Negligence allegations are often "advanced only for their nuisance or settlement value," but no specialized pleading requirement applies to them. Negligence also embraces a wide variety of conduct, but the defendant is not thought to need particularized information from the plaintiff at the pleading stage to prepare a response to an allegation of negligence. Old and settled matters will not have to be reopened if there is no evidence to justify reopening them, but this does not provide a persuasive reason for a particularized *pleading* requirement. Finally, there is no justifiable reason for a Federal Rule to "disfavor" any particular kind of action or defense. Indeed, that would seem to be a "substantive" matter from which the rulemakers are prohibited under 28 U.S.C. § 2072. Similarly, "strike suits" can be dealt with under Federal Rule 11. *See* section F ("Good Faith Pleading") *infra*; *see also* Christopher M. Fairman, *An Invitation to the Rulemakers—Strike Rule 9(b)*, 38 U.C. DAVIS L. REV. 281 (2004).

236. *See* 5A CHARLES A. WRIGHT & ARTHUR R. MILLER, FEDERAL PRACTICE AND PROCEDURE: CIVIL § 1297 (3d ed. 2004); Alternative Sys. Concepts, Inc. v. Synopsys, Inc., 374 F.3d 23 (1st Cir. 2004) (misrepresentation claim subject to special pleading requirements of Federal Rule 9(b); claim improperly pleaded because allegations were wholly conclusory and lacking in any semblance of specific detail); Benchmark Elecs., Inc. v. J.M. Huber Corp., 343 F.3d 719 (5th Cir. 2003) (complaint setting forth the who, what, when, and where of fraud allegations and explaining why the assertions were fraudulent met the Rule 9(b) requirements of pleading fraud with specificity); Williams v. WMX Techs., Inc., 112 F.3d 175 (5th Cir. 1997) (holding that to plead fraud with particularity, the plaintiff must specify the statements that were fraudulent and why they were fraudulent, identify who made the statements, identify when the statements were made, and identify where the statements were made; furthermore, all this must be done before the plaintiff has access to discovery); *cf.* Wasco Prods., Inc. v. Southwall Techs., Inc., 435 F.3d 989 (9th Cir. 2006) (tolling a statute of limitations on the basis of a conspiracy to commit fraud requires that the elements of the conspiracy be pleaded with particularity under Rule 9(b)). *But cf.* Form 21 in the Appendix of Forms following the Federal Rules of Civil Procedure (specificity of allegations will vary depending on circumstances).

237. *See* Pub. L. No. 104-67, 109 Stat. 737 (codified at 15 U.S.C. § 78u-4 *et seq.*). If the plaintiff alleges that (a) the defendant made an untrue statement of a material fact or (b) failed to state a material fact necessary to make the statements not misleading under the circumstances, the Act requires that the complaint "specify each statement alleged to have been misleading, the reason or reasons why the statement is misleading, and, if an allegation regarding the statement or omission is made on information and belief, the complaint shall state with particularity all facts on which that belief is formed." *Id.* § 101(b), Pub. L. No. 104-67, 109 Stat. 737, 747. In addition, with regard to the defendant's fraudulent intent, the Act requires that the complaint, "with respect to each act or omission alleged to violate this title, state with particularity facts giving rise to a *strong inference* that the defendant acted with the required state of mind." *Id.* (emphasis added). *Compare In re* Advanta Corp. Sec. Litig., 180 F.3d 525 (3d Cir. 1999) (Private Securities Litigation Reform Act's requirement for pleading scienter can be satisfied by alleging with particularity facts establishing motive and opportunity to commit fraud or facts constituting circumstantial evidence of reckless or conscious behavior that raise a strong inference of fraudulent intent) *and* Press v. Chemical Inv. Servs. Corp., 166 F.3d 529 (2d Cir. 1999) (same) *with* Bryant v. Avado Brands, Inc., 187 F.3d 1271 (11th Cir. 1999) (allegations of motive and opportunity insufficient to allege scienter), *In re* Comshare, Inc. Sec. Litig., 183 F.3d 542 (6th Cir. 1999) (same), *and In re* Silicon Graphics Inc. Sec. Litig., 183 F.3d 970 (9th Cir. 1999) (same); *see also* Tellabs, Inc. v. Makor Issues & Rights, Ltd., 551 U.S. 308, 127 S. Ct. 2499, 168 L. Ed. 2d 179 (2007) (plaintiff alleging fraud in § 10(b) securities action must plead facts rendering scienter at least as likely as any plausible opposing inference to meet Private Securities Litigation Reform Act requirements); Belizan v. Hershon, 434 F.3d 579 (D.C. Cir. 2006) (Private Securities Litigation Reform Act does not mandate dismissal with prejudice when an original complaint fails to satisfy its heightened pleading requirements); Rombach v. Chang, 355 F.3d 164 (2d Cir. 2004) (requirements of Rule 9(b) concerning the pleading of fraud were not met in securities action; plaintiffs' complaint did not explain why information defendants provided to analysts was fraudulent and did not identify any materially false statements in a registration statement). *See generally* 5A CHARLES A. WRIGHT & ARTHUR R. MILLER, FEDERAL PRACTICE AND PROCEDURE: CIVIL § 1301.1 (3d ed. 2004); Patricia J. Meyer, Note, *What Congress Said About the Heightened Pleading Standard: A Proposed Solution to the Securities Fraud Pleading Confusion,* 66 FORDHAM L. REV. 2517 (1998).

(ii) Conditions of the Mind

Federal Rule 9(b) permits "[m]alice, intent, knowledge, and other conditions of a person's mind" to be "alleged generally."[238] Detailed descriptions of such conditions of mind would be prolix and unworkable. Also, no need exists for more detailed descriptions in light of the general goal of providing notice.[239] However, in investor securities litigation involving fraudulent intent, the Private Securities Litigation Reform Act of 1995 imposes more stringent standards.[240]

(iii) Special Damages

Like the common-law and code-pleading systems, the Federal Rules require *special damages* to be stated specifically.[241] The courts have divided damages into two basic categories: (1) *general damages*, which are presumed to flow in the natural course of events from the specific injuries alleged; and (2) *special damages*, which are unusual or peculiar and are not presumed to have occurred.[242] Court decisions over a long period established the dividing line between special damages and general damages. To some extent, this division is an arbitrary classification. Furthermore, the courts are not always completely in accord on how a particular item of damage should be classified.

General damages often are based on either of the following: (1) market measures, such as the difference between the contract price and the market price; or (2) naturally expected consequences, such as pain and suffering resulting from injuries in an automobile accident. General damages need not be alleged at all, except to the extent that damages (actual injury) are part of the statement of a cause of action, as in a negligence claim. On the other hand, special damages must be specifically stated and must be proved at trial with reasonable certainty. Examples include the loss of profits resulting from a contract breach, expenses incurred in pursuing converted property in order to recover it, and statutory double or treble damages.[243]

---

238. FED. R. CIV. P. 9(b).

239. An interesting comparison can be drawn between the Federal Rules and current English practice, which requires the particulars of the facts for malice, fraudulent intention, or other conditions of the mind. *See* 5A CHARLES A. WRIGHT & ARTHUR R. MILLER, FEDERAL PRACTICE AND PROCEDURE: CIVIL § 1296, at 30 n.2 (3d ed. 2004) (citing English Order 18, Rule 12(15)).

240. *See* Pub. L. No. 104-67, 109 Stat. 737 (codified at 15 U.S.C. § 77a *et seq.*). The Act goes beyond Rule 9(b) by introducing the *standard* by which the allegation should be judged: "with respect to each act or omission alleged to violate this title, [the pleader must] state with particularity facts giving rise to a *strong inference* that the defendant acted with the required state of mind." *Id.* § 101(b), Pub. L. No. 104-67, 109 Stat. 737, 747 (emphasis added). This standard surely overrides the provision in Rule 9(b) allowing knowledge and intent to be pleaded generally.

241. *See* FED. R. CIV. P. 9(g); CHARLES E. CLARK, HANDBOOK OF THE LAW OF CODE PLEADING § 51 (2d ed. 1947); JOSEPH H. KOFFLER & ALISON REPPY, HANDBOOK OF COMMON LAW PLEADING § 54, at 129 (1969).

242. *See* Cotton Bros. Baking Co. v. Industrial Risk Insurers, 102 F.R.D. 964, 965-67 (W.D. La. 1984) (discussing the definitions of general and special damages; claims for interest due on loans taken out as the result of fire and for loss of sales and accelerated equipment usage were not claims for special damages that had to be alleged specifically).

243. *See* DAN B. DOBBS, THE LAW OF REMEDIES § 3.2 (2d student ed. 1993); *see also* Fowler v. Curtis Publ'g Co., 182 F.2d 377 (D.C. Cir. 1950) (disparagement claim; when special damage is part of the substantive claim, a specific statement is required, such as the loss of particular customers by name or a general diminution of business if specific customers cannot be alleged; it is not sufficient to allege that the plaintiff has suffered special damages or that the party has been put to great costs and expenses); Diaz Irizarry v. Ennia, N.V., 678 F. Supp. 957,

(iv) Conditions Precedent

Unlike the common law, Federal Rule 9(c) permits a general allegation of performance of conditions precedent.[244] This approach is justified because the satisfaction of conditions precedent is usually not an issue.[245] However, if conditions precedent are not usually at issue, perhaps the Federal Rules should not have required any allegation of their performance. The Federal Rules take this approach with regard to other types of allegations, such as capacity to sue or be sued.[246] The probable explanation for treating conditions precedent and capacity differently is the existence of a strong pleading custom in contract cases.

(v) Official Documents, Official Acts, and Judgments

Federal Rule 9(d) provides that "[i]n pleading an official document or official act, it suffices to allege that the document was legally issued or the act [was] legally done."[247] Like prior code practice, Rule 9(e) permits a general allegation of any judicial or quasi-judicial judgment or decision "without showing jurisdiction to render it."[248]

(vi) Capacity of a Party to Sue or Be Sued

Federal Rule 9(a) provides that a pleader does not have to allege the capacity of a party to sue or be sued or the authority of a party to sue or be sued in representative capacity or the legal existence of an organized association of persons

---

959 (D.P.R. 1988) (purpose of requiring that special damages be specifically pleaded is to notify the defendant that damages other than those that are presumed to exist are going to be sought; no requirement that special damages must be pleaded with the same level of particularity as fraud or mistake); Lebeda v. A.H. Robins Co., 101 F.R.D. 689, 690 (D. Me. 1984) (although great particularity is not required in pleading special damages, a specific statement is required). *Compare* Comeau v. Rupp, 762 F. Supp. 1434, 1449 (D. Kan. 1991), Citron v. Armstrong World Indus., Inc., 721 F. Supp. 1259, 1261 (S.D. Fla. 1989) *and* Barton v. Barnett, 226 F. Supp. 375, 378 (N.D. Miss. 1964) (punitive damages are special damages that must be pleaded specially under Rule 9(g)) *with* American Sur. Co. v. Franciscus, 127 F.2d 810 (8th Cir. 1942) *and* Nelson v. G.C. Murphy Co., 245 F. Supp. 846, 847 (N.D. Ala. 1965) (punitive damages are not special damages and need not be specially stated). *See generally* Note, *The Definition and Pleading of Special Damage Under the Federal Rules of Civil Procedure*, 55 VA. L. REV. 542 (1969).

244. 5A CHARLES A. WRIGHT & ARTHUR R. MILLER, FEDERAL PRACTICE AND PROCEDURE: CIVIL § 1302, at 323 (3d ed. 2004).

245. Professors Wright and Miller aptly point out that "it seems doubtful that even the usually perfunctory allegation of performance . . . serves any significantly useful function . . . ." *See id.* at 324; *cf.* William V. Dorsaneo III & C. Paul Rogers III, *The Flawed Nexus Between Contract Law and the Rules of Procedure: Why Rules 8 and 9 Must Be Changed*, 31 REV. LITIG. 233, 257-64 (2012) (urging Rule 9(c) be amended to restore it to its original purpose by broadening its current language focusing on the performance of conditions precedent to cover all performance of all contractual obligations and promises and the occurrence of all conditions to liability; a general averment under Rule 9(c) would then oblige the defendant to specifically plead the matters which have not been performed or occurred in the form of a denial; also urging that "failure of consideration" be removed from the list of affirmative defenses and instead be more appropriately handled pursuant to amended provisions of Rule 9(c)).

246. *See* subsection *(vi)* ("Capacity of a Party to Sue or Be Sued") *infra*.

247. FED. R. CIV. P. 9(d). With respect to pleading official documents or acts, see Form 18 and paragraph 4 of Form 19 in the Appendix of Forms following the Federal Rules of Civil Procedure.

248. FED. R. CIV. P. 9(e). In an action to recover on the judgment of a domestic court of record at common law, *see* Chapter 1(E)(1)*(b)(ii)* ("*Ex Contractu* Personal Actions") *supra*; *Illustration 3-1* in Chapter 3(A)(1) ("Personal Jurisdiction Restrictions Prior to the Fourteenth Amendment") *supra*, the plaintiff did not have to allege facts demonstrating that the court rendering the judgment had jurisdiction. However, the contrary was true when the action was based on a judgment of a domestic court of limited or inferior jurisdiction or a judgment of a foreign court. *See* Chapter 3(A)(1)*(a)* ("The Forms of Action in Suits on Foreign Judgments and the "International" Rules of Jurisdiction") *supra*.

that is made a party, except to the extent required to show the jurisdiction of the court.[249] In proposing Rule 9(a), the Advisory Committee thought that capacity was rarely in issue.[250]

(vii) Time and Place

Unlike the common law, Federal Rule 9(f) provides that "[a]n allegation of time or place is material when testing the sufficiency of a pleading."[251] Rule 9(f) does not address whether specific allegations of time and place have to be alleged at all, but merely their significance when alleged.[252] Making allegations of time and place material helps to identify the particular occurrence or transaction at issue for purposes of providing the opposing party with notice. It also may facilitate early adjudication of statute-of-limitations defenses.[253]

(viii) Nonjoinder of Certain Parties

Rule 19(c) requires a pleader to state the names, if known, of any persons who ought to have been made parties pursuant to Rule 19(a), but who were not. The pleader must also state the reason or reasons for not joining such parties.[254] As demonstrated in Chapter 8, Rule 19(a) requires certain kinds of parties to be joined. If Rule 19(a) parties are not joined, there must be an adequate reason for their nonjoinder. In addition, a specialized inquiry must be made under Rule 19(b) to determine whether the action can continue without the nonjoined parties or the action must be dismissed.[255]

3. Responding to the Complaint

(a) Default

After the defendant has been notified of the lawsuit, the defendant is required to respond. If the defendant fails to respond in the appropriate manner,

---

249. *See* FED. R. CIV. P. 9(a).

250. *See* 5A CHARLES A. WRIGHT & ARTHUR R. MILLER, FEDERAL PRACTICE AND PROCEDURE: CIVIL § 1292 (3d ed. 2004).

251. FED. R. CIV. P. 9(f).

252. 5A CHARLES A. WRIGHT & ARTHUR R. MILLER, FEDERAL PRACTICE AND PROCEDURE: CIVIL § 1309, at 341 (3d ed. 2004).

253. *Id.* § 1308, at 340-41; Kincheloe v. Farmer, 214 F.2d 604 (7th Cir. 1954) (reason for making time and place averments material is to help determine whether the statute of limitations bars an action). Courts have allowed the statute-of-limitations defense to be raised through a preanswer motion under Rule 12(b)(6) or a motion for judgment on the pleadings under Rule 12(c) if the complaint demonstrates on its face that the action is time-barred. *See* subsection *3(d)* ("Motions to Dismiss") & Chapter 10(B) ("Judgment on the Pleadings") *infra*; *see also* subsection 2*(d)* ("Anticipating Defenses") *supra*.

254. *See* FED. R. CIV. P. 19(c). Federal Form 8 illustrates how this allegation may be made: "The complaint does not join as a party *name* who [is not subject to the jurisdiction of this court] [cannot be made a party to the action without depriving this court of subject-matter jurisdiction] because *state the reason*."

255. *See* Chapter 8(C)(3) ("Joinder of Persons Needed for Just Adjudication") *infra*.

"judgment by default will be entered against [the defendant] for the relief demanded in the complaint."[256]

(b) Motions for More Definite Statements and Bills of Particulars

Federal Rule 12(e) provides for a "Motion for a More Definite Statement." Rule 12(e) requires that the motion identify "the defects complained of and the details desired."[257] A motion for a *more definite statement* under the Federal Rules deals with the problem of the moving party's inability to frame a responsive pleading.[258] The original version of Rule 12(e) also permitted bills of particulars.[259] In 1948, Rule 12(e) was amended to eliminate the bill of particulars from federal practice. The Advisory Committee noted that Rule 12(e) "as originally drawn has been the subject of more judicial rulings than any other part of the rules, and has been much criticized by commentators, judges and members of the bar."[260]

Given the general notice pleading philosophy of the Federal Rules, it will seldom be the case that a complaint that states a claim upon which relief may be granted will be so vague that a Rule 12(e) motion is appropriate. As long as the complaint is sufficiently definite to allow the defendant to prepare a responsive pleading, a Rule 12(e) motion is improper. Given the options available to the defendant under Rule 8(b), therefore, there should seldom be an occasion to use Rule 12(e).

(c) Motions to Strike

Rule 12(f) permits motions to strike "redundant, immaterial, impertinent, or scandalous matter" from a pleading. Rule 12(f) performs the same function as the code motion to expunge.[261] Under Federal Rule 12(f), a motion to strike must be made before responding to a pleading (for example, before serving an answer to the

---

256. Form 3 ("Summons") in the Appendix of Forms following the Federal Rules of Civil Procedure. *See* Chapter 10(A) ("Default Judgment") *infra*.

257. FED. R. CIV. P. 12(e). The general nature of motions in federal court is described in Federal Rule 7(b).

258. Under the codes, a motion to make more definite and certain deals with this problem. *See* section C(3)*(a)* ("Motions for More Definite Statements and Bills of Particulars") *supra*.

259. *See* sections A(3)*(g)* ("Bills of Particulars") & C(3)*(a)* ("Motions for More Definite Statements and Bills of Particulars") *supra*.

260. The Advisory Committee set forth the reasons for this change:

> Rule 12(e) . . . . The tendency of some courts freely to grant extended bills of particulars has served to neutralize any helpful benefits derived from Rule 8, and has overlooked the intended use of the rules on depositions and discovery. [Original Rule 12(e) provided that "a party may move for a more definite statement or for a bill of particulars of any matter which is not averred with sufficient definiteness or particularity to enable [the pleader] properly to prepare [a] responsive pleading or to prepare for trial."] The words "or to prepare for trial" . . . have sometimes been seized upon as grounds for compulsory statement in the opposing pleading of all the details which the movant would have to meet at trial.

FED. R. CIV. P. 12(e) advisory committee's note to the 1946 Amendment. The principal reasons for its excessive use appeared to be delay, harassment, and an attempt to put a burden on the plaintiff. *See* CHARLES E. CLARK, HANDBOOK OF THE LAW OF CODE PLEADING § 40, at 250-52 (2d ed. 1947); 5C CHARLES A. WRIGHT & ARTHUR R. MILLER, FEDERAL PRACTICE AND PROCEDURE: CIVIL § 1376 (3d ed. 2004). *See generally* Stefan F. Tucker, Comment, *Federal Rule 12(e): Motion for More Definite Statement—History, Operation and Efficacy*, 61 MICH. L. REV. 1126 (1963).

261. CHARLES E. CLARK, HANDBOOK OF THE LAW OF CODE PLEADING § 87, at 550-52 (2d ed. 1947); *see also* section C(6) ("Code Motions to Expunge or Strike") *supra*.

complaint) or within 21 days after service of the pleading if no responsive pleading is allowed (for example, to attack a scandalous answer).

Illustration 6-24. Assume that *D* wants the court to strike out certain scandalous allegations in *P's* complaint prior to filing an answer. *D* can use a motion to strike under Rule 12(f) for this purpose.[262]

Illustration 6-25. *D* denies the allegations of the complaint in the answer. *D* then moves to strike scandalous matter from the complaint. Rule 12(f) technically bars the motion because *D* has already answered. The court, however, may strike the matter on its own initiative.[263]

(d) Motions to Dismiss

The defendant can move to dismiss an action prior to serving an answer. Rule 12(b) provides seven grounds for such motions: (1) lack of subject-matter jurisdiction; (2) lack of personal jurisdiction; (3) improper venue; (4) insufficient process (failure to conform the contents of the summons to the requirements of Rule 4(a) regulating that content); (5) insufficient service of process (use of an improper manner of service or the failure to deliver the summons at all); (6) failure to state a claim upon which relief can be granted; and (7) failure to join a required party (as defined by Rule 19).[264] Misjoinder of parties is not a ground for dismissal of the action.[265]

Illustration 6-26. Assume that *P* has served a complaint alleging certain facts. *D* believes that the facts stated, assuming that they could be proved, do not give rise to a recognized legal obligation. At common law and under the Field Code, *D* raised this defense by a demurrer.[266] The Federal Rules have abolished

---

262. If the motion is denied, Rule 12(a)(4)(A) states that the responsive pleading shall be served within 14 days after notice of the court's action. If the motion is granted, Rule 12(a)(4) does not specifically provide a time period for serving the answer. Technically, the defendant might be in default if the defendant did not serve the answer within 21 days after the complaint was filed. This apparent result may reflect defective drafting in Rule 12(a)(4). However, the theory could be that there is no need to delay the answer to obtain the result of a Rule 12(f) motion. *See* 5B CHARLES A. WRIGHT & ARTHUR R. MILLER, FEDERAL PRACTICE AND PROCEDURE: CIVIL § 1346 (3d ed. 2004); Davis v. Ruby Foods, Inc., 269 F.3d 818, 821 (7th Cir. 2001) (indicating in dictum that motions to strike extraneous matter should not be made unless the presence of such material "in the complaint is actually prejudicial to the defense"). A more likely reason for the absence of a time limit in Rule 12(a)(4) is that granting a motion to strike should result in an order to amend the complaint to eliminate the offensive matter, bringing into play the time limits in Rule 15(a) within which to respond to an amended pleading.

263. *See* FED. R. CIV. P. 12(f)(1).

264. FED. R. CIV. P. 12(b).

265. *See* FED. R. CIV. P. 21. Federal Rule 12 does not require that the objection appear on the face of the complaint, and it does not list lack of capacity to sue as a matter that can be raised by preanswer motion. *See* FED. R. CIV. P. 12(b). As noted in subsection D(2)*(e)(vi)* ("Capacity of a Party to Sue or Be Sued") *supra*, Federal Rule 9(a) does not require a plaintiff to plead capacity to sue. The federal rule contrasts with the practice in some code states, which requires allegations of the legal existence of a corporate plaintiff. Rule 9(a) further provides that a party who wants to raise capacity issues "must do so by a specific denial, which must state any supporting facts that are peculiarly within the party's knowledge." FED. R. CIV. P. 9(a)(2). Before restyling, the rule required a "specific negative averment." This restyling error is discussed in *Illustration 1-38* in Chapter 1(E)(5)*(c) supra*. FED. R. CIV. P. 9(a). Despite this express language, some federal courts have permitted defendants to raise this objection in a Rule 12(b)(6) motion (failure to state a claim upon which relief can be granted) when the defect appears on the face of the complaint. 5C CHARLES A. WRIGHT & ARTHUR R. MILLER, FEDERAL PRACTICE AND PROCEDURE: CIVIL § 1360, at 80-81 (3d ed. 2004). In federal court, the pendency of another action between the same parties for the same cause and the prematurity of bringing the action must be raised by answer. *See* 5 *id.* § 1271; FED. R. CIV. P. 8(c).

266. *See* section A(3)*(a)* ("General Demurrers"); section C(3)*(b)* ("Demurrers") *supra*.

demurrers.[267] The equivalent challenge to the legal sufficiency of the complaint under the Federal Rules is a Rule 12(b)(6) defense of "failure to state a claim upon which relief can be granted."[268] Like common-law pleading and the codes, the Federal Rules assume for purposes of this motion that all well-pleaded facts in the complaint are admitted.[269] In ruling on the motion, the court may not consider matters outside the complaint, except matters of public record, court orders, items present in the record, and exhibits attached to the complaint.[270]

Illustration 6-27. Assume that *P* serves a summons and complaint on *D*. *D* believes that *P* failed to serve process properly, that venue is improper, and that the court lacks subject-matter jurisdiction of *P's* action. Rule 12(b) permits *D* to raise all of these defenses in a preanswer motion to dismiss.[271]

(e) The Mechanics of Motion Practice

Federal Rule 5 governs service of papers after original service of process on the defendant, including service of motions.[272] Rule 5(a) requires that a written motion, except one that may be heard ex parte, must be served on every party.[273] Rule 5(b) states that if a party is represented by an attorney, service must be made by serving the attorney (unless the court orders service on the party).[274] Service upon attorneys or parties may be made in several ways: (1) handing it to the person;[275] (2) leaving it at the person's office with a clerk or other person in charge (or if no one is in charge, in a conspicuous place in the office);[276] (3) leaving at the person's dwelling of usual place of abode with someone of suitable age and discretion who resides there if the person has no office or the office is closed;[277] (4)

---

267. See FED. R. CIV. P. 7 advisory committee's note to 2007 restyling amendments (deleting former Rule 7(c) "because it has done its work").

268. FED. R. CIV. P. 12(b)(6).

269. At common law, a decision on the demurrer terminated the action: either the demurrer was sustained and judgment was entered against the plaintiff, or the demurrer was overruled and judgment was entered against the defendant. The defendant did not have an opportunity to challenge the truth of the allegations subsequently, nor did the plaintiff have the right to amend the declaration except to correct formal defects and errors of oversight. *See* 5B CHARLES A. WRIGHT & ARTHUR R. MILLER, FEDERAL PRACTICE AND PROCEDURE: CIVIL § 1355, at 352 (3d ed. 2004). Code and federal practice allow further pleading and amendments. *See, e.g.*, NEB. REV. STAT. §§ 25-811, 25-812 (1995) (repealed 2003); S.C. CODE § 15-13-340 (Law. Coop. 1976) (repealed 1985) (pleading after demurrer permitted); FED. R. CIV. P. 12(a) & 15(a).

270. Breliant v. Preferred Equities Corp., 109 Nev. 842, 858 P.2d 1258 (1993); *see also* Berk v. Ascott Inv. Corp., 759 F. Supp. 245, 249 (E.D. Pa. 1991) (documents incorporated by reference into the complaint considered); Hollymatic Corp. v. Holly Sys., Inc., 620 F. Supp. 1366, 1367 (N.D. Ill. 1985) (contract attached to complaint and admissions in answer and in reply to counterclaim considered).

271. *See* Form 40 ("Motion to Dismiss Under Rule 12(b) for Lack of Jurisdiction, Improper Venue, Insufficient Service of Process, or Failure to State a Claim") in the Appendix of Forms following the Federal Rules of Civil Procedure. As noted in Chapter 2 *supra* and more fully discussed in subsection *(g)(ii)* ("Waiver") *infra*, a subject-matter jurisdiction objection may be made subsequently, for example, at trial or even thereafter.

272. *See, e.g.*, Employee Painters' Trust v. Ethan Enters., Inc., 480 F.3d 993 (9th Cir. 2007) (Rule 4 governs original service of summons and complaint, but Rule 5 governs service of amended complaint). As amended in 1993, Rule 4 governs service of the summons. Rule 4.1 governs the service of other process. *See* FED. R. CIV. P. 4, 4.1 & advisory committee's note accompanying the 1993 amendments.

273. FED. R. CIV. P. 5(a)(1)(D).

274. FED. R. CIV. P. 5(b)(1).

275. FED. R. CIV. P. 5(b)(2)(A).

276. FED. R. CIV. P. 5(b)(2)(B)(i).

277. FED. R. CIV. P. 5(b)(2)(B)(ii).

mailing it to the person's last known address;[278] (5) leaving it with the court clerk if the person has no known address;[279] (6) sending it by electronic means if the person has consented in writing;[280] or (7) delivering it by any other means which has be consented to in writing.[281]

At the hearing on the motion, the judge will listen to the arguments of counsel.[282] An oral hearing may be dispensed with as provided in Rule 78.[283] The judge will then issue an order ruling on the motion. If the court denies the motion or postpones its disposition until trial, Rule 12(a)(4) requires the responsive pleading (answer) be served within 14 days after notice of the court's action.[284] If a motion for a more definite statement is granted, the responsive pleading (answer) must be served within 14 days after the service of the more definite statement.[285] Rule 6(a) provides the method for calculating time periods.[286] Rule 6(d) adds three additional days when service is made by mailing it to the person's last known address, leaving it with the court clerk, sending it by electronic means, or delivering it by any other means which has been consented to in writing.[287]

(f) The Federal Rules Answer

Assuming that the action is not dismissed or the defendant's obligation to respond is not otherwise suspended pursuant to the hearing of a preanswer motion,[288] the defendant must serve an answer within 21days.[289] However, if service of the summons has been waived pursuant to Rule 4(d), the defendant must serve an answer within 60 days after the date when the request for waiver was sent (or 90 days after that date if the defendant was addressed outside any judicial district of the United States).[290] The answer in federal practice functions as the means of setting forth the defendant's position—the defendant must "state in short and plain terms [the party's] defenses to each claim asserted against it" and must "admit or deny the allegations asserted against [the party] by an opposing party."[291]

---

278. FED. R. CIV. P. 5(b)(2)(C). Service is complete upon mailing. *Id.*; *see* Greene v. WCI Holdings Corp., 136 F.3d 313 (2d Cir. 1998) ("mailing" occurs when placed in the mailbox, not when postmarked).

279. FED. R. CIV. P. 5(b)(2)(D).

280. FED. R. CIV. P. 5(b)(2)(E). Service is complete upon transmission, but it is not effective according to the rule if the serving party learns that the transmission did not reach the person to be served. *Id.*

281. FED. R. CIV. P. 5(b)(2)(F). Service is complete when the person making the service delivers it to the agency designated to make delivery. *Id.*

282. Rule 6(c)(1) provides a 14-day time period as a minimum between service of a motion and notice of the hearing and the date of the hearing. Rule 6(d) provides an additional three days when service has been made by mail. Rule 78 provides for a motion day. *See* FED. R. CIV. P. 6(c), 6(d), 78. In general, local rules should be consulted to determine how and when the motion will be heard or whether oral argument is permitted at all. *See, e.g.*, NEB. LOCAL R. 7(e) (oral argument permitted only on order of the court).

283. FED. R. CIV. P. 78(b).

284. FED. R. CIV. P. 12(a)(4)(A) (unless a different time is fixed by court order).

285. FED. R. CIV. P. 12(a)(4)(B) (unless a different time is fixed by court order).

286. FED. R. CIV. P. 6(a).

287. FED. R. CIV. P. 6(d).

288. A partial motion to dismiss some, but not all, of the claims of the plaintiff extends the time for answering. *See* Oil Express Nat'l Inc. v. D'Alessandro, 173 F.R.D. 219 (N.D. Ill. 1997).

289. FED. R. CIV. P. 12(a)(1)(A)(i) (unless a different time is fixed by court order). *See generally* Chapter 3(K) ("Service of Process") *supra*.

290. FED. R. CIV. P. 12(a)(1)(A)(ii) (unless a different time is fixed by court order). The United States and its officers and agencies have 60 days to respond. FED. R. CIV. P. 12(a)(3). *See generally* Chapter 3(K) ("Service of Process") *supra*.

291. FED. R. CIV. P. 8(b)(1)(A) & (B).

(i) Defenses that Were Not Raised by Preanswer Motions

Rule 12(b) gives the defendant two options at the pleading stage: (1) to raise certain objections by motion prior to serving an answer or (2) to raise the objections as defenses in the defendant's answer.[292]

Illustration 6-28. Assume that the defendant has all the defenses listed in *Illustration 6-27*. If the defendant does not want to serve a preanswer motion, Federal Rule 12 permits the defendant to raise these defenses in the answer.[293]

(ii) Admissions and Denials

Federal Rule 8(b) requires a party to admit or deny the allegations that the opposing party asserts against the party.[294] Denials must fairly respond to the substance of the allegations.[295] Furthermore, when a party intends in good faith to deny only a part of the allegation, the party "must admit the part that is true and deny the rest."[296]

Illustration 6-29. Assume that *P* has alleged in the complaint that *D's* negligent conduct caused *P* injury. *D*, however, wants to show that *D* was somewhere other than where the accident happened. *D* would raise this defense by a denial. The denial should be specific.[297] Thus, it should specify that *D* was not negligent and did not cause the accident because *D* was not present at the time and place of the collision.[298]

Illustration 6-30. Assume that *P* alleges that *D* converted *P's* car. *P* alleges that the car has a value that exceeds $60,000. *D* responds that the car "does not have a value that exceeds $60,000." Under the traditional "negative pregnant" doctrine,[299] *D* has technically denied the immaterial word "exceeds" but has admitted that the car is worth at least $60,000.[300] Rule 8(e) requires that the pleadings be construed to do substantial justice. Similarly, Rule 1 requires that the Federal Rules be construed to secure the just, speedy, and inexpensive determination of every action. Rule 8(e) and Rule 1 would thus probably eliminate the technical objections to the phraseology that caused the negative pregnant to be an ineffective denial at common law. However, Rule 8(b) requires denials to fairly meet the substance of the allegations denied. Likewise, Rule 8(b) provides that when a pleader intends in

---

292. *See, e.g.*, the last ground listed in Form 40 ("Motion to Dismiss Under Rule 12(b) for Lack of Jurisdiction, Improper Venue, Insufficient Service of Process, or Failure to State a Claim") and the fourth paragraph in Form 30 ("Answer Presenting Defenses Under Rule 12(b)") in the Appendix of Forms following the Federal Rules of Civil Procedure. Later, it will be explained how these objections may also be made subsequently, for example, at trial. *See* Chapters 10 ("Disposition of the Action Without Trial") & 11 ("Trial") *infra*.

293. *See, e.g.*, Form 30 ("Answer Presenting Defenses Under Rule 12(b)") in the Appendix of Forms following the Federal Rules of Civil Procedure.

294. FED. R. CIV. P. 8(b)(1)(B).

295. FED. R. CIV. P. 8(b)(2).

296. FED. R. CIV. P. 8(b)(4).

297. At common law, a traverse raised this defense. *See* section A(3)*(d)* ("Traverses") *supra*. Under the codes, it would be raised by a denial. *See* section C(3)*(c)* ("The Code Answer") *supra*.

298. At common law, such a "specific denial" would have been improper because it was argumentative. *See* section A(3)*(d)* ("Traverses"), *Illustration 6-5*, *supra*.

299. *See* section A(3)*(d)* ("Traverses") and *Illustration 6-6 supra*.

300. *See* Freedom Nat'l Bank v. Northern Ill. Corp., 202 F.2d 601, 605 (7th Cir. 1953); 5 CHARLES A. WRIGHT & ARTHUR R. MILLER, FEDERAL PRACTICE AND PROCEDURE: CIVIL § 1207 (3d ed. 2004).

good faith to deny only a part of an allegation, the pleader must admit the part that is true. Thus, it is arguable that a negative pregnant would be effective only if the pleader intended to deny all aspects of the allegations, Rule 8(e) and Rule 1 notwithstanding.[301] The better practice is to avoid the negative pregnant by specifying the truth or falsity of each allegation.

* * * * *

Federal Rule 8(b) further provides, as did the practice under many codes, that when a party "lacks knowledge or information sufficient to form a belief about the truth of an allegation," the party "must so state, and the statement has the effect of a denial."[302] In general, one's own conduct and matters of public record are presumed to be within the knowledge of the pleader.

Illustration 6-31. Assume that *D* is considering answering the following allegations on the ground that the pleader is without knowledge or information sufficient to form a belief as to the truth of an averment: (1) that *D* was negligent; (2) that *D* is married; (3) that the plaintiff foreign corporation has qualified to do business in the state by registration; or (4) that a street became a one-way street in a certain direction at a particular time of day. Whether the pleader was negligent, whether the pleader is married, or whether the plaintiff is qualified to do business would be matters to which *D* would not normally be able to respond with the "without knowledge" response. Under some circumstances, however, such a response would be appropriate, *e.g.*, lapse of memory or destroyed records.[303] The one-way street allegation may be a matter of general knowledge in the community, but even if it is not, it may be a matter of law under a city ordinance.

* * * * *

Allegations not denied (other than those relating to the amount of damages) are admitted.[304] Federal Rule 8(b) also permits a general denial: "Defendant denies each and every allegation of the complaint." However, Rule 8(b) provides that a general denial may not be used unless the pleader intends in good faith to controvert the entire complaint, "including the jurisdictional grounds."[305]

Illustration 6-32. Assume that *P* has served a complaint on *D* similar to Federal Form 21 in federal court. *P's* complaint contains (1) a statement of subject-matter jurisdiction. *P* alleges that (2) "On [date], defendant *D* signed a note promising to pay to the plaintiff on [date] the sum of one hundred thousand dollars with interest at the rate of six percent per annum." *P* also alleges that (3) "Defendant *D* owes to the plaintiff the amount of the note and interest." *P* then alleges that (4) "On [date], Defendant *D* conveyed all of *D's* real property to Defendant *C* for the purpose of defrauding the plaintiff and hindering or delaying

---

301. *See* 5 CHARLES A. WRIGHT & ARTHUR R. MILLER, FEDERAL PRACTICE AND PROCEDURE: CIVIL § 1207 (3d ed. 2004).

302. FED. R. CIV. P. 8(b)(5). See the denials set forth in the second and third paragraphs in Form 30 in the Appendix of Forms following the Federal Rules of Civil Procedure.

303. *See* 5 CHARLES A. WRIGHT & ARTHUR R. MILLER, FEDERAL PRACTICE AND PROCEDURE: CIVIL § 1263 (3d ed. 2004). The same results would occur under the codes. The codes required an affidavit in support of such a response. CHARLES E. CLARK, HANDBOOK OF THE LAW OF CODE PLEADING § 93, at 596 (2d ed. 1947).

304. FED. R. CIV. P. 8(b)(6).

305. FED. R. CIV. P. 8(b)(3); *see* 5 CHARLES A. WRIGHT & ARTHUR R. MILLER, FEDERAL PRACTICE AND PROCEDURE: CIVIL § 1265 (3d ed. 2004).

the collection of the debt."[306] *D* serves an answer denying the allegation that *D* owes *P* the amount of the note. *D's* answer also admits that *D* conveyed property to *C*. However, *D* denies that the conveyance was fraudulent. Because *D* has denied paragraphs 3 and 4, they are in dispute. Because *D* was required to respond to the complaint, the allegations in paragraphs 1 and 2 are admitted because *D* made no response to them.[307]

(iii) Affirmative Defenses

Federal Rule 8(c) requires that a pleader "affirmatively state any avoidance or affirmative defense." It then lists eighteen specific affirmative defenses: accord and satisfaction; arbitration and award; assumption of risk; contributory negligence; duress; estoppel; failure of consideration; fraud; illegality; injury by fellow servant; laches; license; payment; release; res judicata; statute of frauds; statute of limitations; and waiver.[308] Rule 8(d) permits a party to set forth defenses alternatively or hypothetically, regardless of their consistency.[309]

Illustration 6-33. Assume that *D* wants to bring forward facts to show that *P* is an infant and thus lacks capacity to sue. *D* also wants the action dismissed because another action is pending between the same parties for the same cause. Even though lack of capacity and prior pending action are not listed as affirmative defenses in Rule 8(c), they would be matters constituting "avoidance." *D* would have to raise these defenses affirmatively in the answer.[310] Furthermore, Rule 9(a) requires that lack of capacity be raised by a specific denial. *D* would have to state "any supporting facts that are peculiarly within the party's knowledge."[311]

* * * * *

Affirmative defenses that are not pleaded normally may not be relied on by the defendant. Unlike waiver of certain defenses by omitting them from a motion under Rule 12, discussed below, affirmative defenses omitted from an original answer may be added by amendment in accord with the procedure described in Rule 15. However, unless such a defense is raised by an original pleading or an

---

306. *See* Form 21 in the Appendix of Forms following the Federal Rules of Civil Procedure.

307. Rule 8(b) provides that "[a]n allegation—other than one relating to the amount of damages—is admitted if a responsive pleading is required and the allegation is not denied." FED. R. CIV. P. 8(b)(6).

308. FED. R. CIV. P. 8(c). See the illustration of how to plead an affirmative defense, given in the sixth paragraph in Form 30 in the Appendix of Forms following the Federal Rules of Civil Procedure. *See also* Clark Cnty. Sch. Dist. v. Richardson Constr., Inc., 123 Nev. 382, 168 P.3d 87 (2007) (for purposes of determining what falls within catchall provision of Rule governing affirmative defenses, allegations must raise new facts and arguments that, if true, will defeat the plaintiff's claim, even if the allegations in the complaint are true).

309. FED. R. CIV. P. 8(d)(2), (3); *see, e.g.*, Little v. Texaco, Inc., 456 F.2d 219, 220 (10th Cir. 1972) (answer may contain inconsistent defenses; defendant can deny and at the same time advance an affirmative defense; parties fail to plead inconsistent defenses at their peril).

310. *See* 5 CHARLES A. WRIGHT & ARTHUR R. MILLER, FEDERAL PRACTICE AND PROCEDURE: CIVIL § 1271 (3d ed. 2004).

311. FED. R. CIV. P. 9(a)(2). Before restyling, the Federal Rule 9(a) required a "specific negative averment." This restyling error is discussed in *Illustration 1-38* in Chapter 1(E)(5)*(c) supra*. At common law, lack of capacity to sue would have been raised by a dilatory plea in abatement. *See* section A(3)*(c)* ("Dilatory Pleas") *supra*. Under the codes, it would be raised as an affirmative defense in the answer (assuming that the matter did not appear on the face of the complaint). *See* section C(3)*(c)* ("The Code Answer") *supra*.

amendment, it will usually be lost—but not always.[312] In *Day v. McDonough*,[313] a prisoner petitioned a federal court for habeas corpus. The defendant's answer admitted that the petition was timely filed, but a magistrate judge determined that the defendant had miscalculated the time period for the statute of limitations and that the petition was untimely. Despite the fact that the state had not pleaded the statute of limitations in the original answer or an amendment, the U.S. Supreme Court affirmed the dismissal of the petition. The Court acknowledged that "[o]rdinarily in civil litigation, a statutory time limitation is forfeited if not raised in a defendant's answer or an amendment thereto" pursuant to Rules 8(c) and 15. Nevertheless, the Court excused the state's failure to plead the defense because it was not an "intelligent waiver" on the defendant's part, but "only an evident miscalculation." This provoked a dissent by Justice Scalia, who was joined by Justices Thomas and Breyer. The dissent argued that there was no good reason for departing from the ordinary rules of civil procedure in the case, and the majority had not identified, because it could not, any inconsistency between habeas corpus practice and ordinary civil litigation. The dissent seems correct, and the majority's position raises troubling questions about when the federal courts may raise on their own motion affirmative defenses that have been omitted by mistake.[314]

(iv) Counterclaims and Crossclaims

A defendant may want to assert a claim against the plaintiff. At common law and in equity, the defendant could do so in certain limited situations by means of *recoupment* or *set-off*. Like the codes, the Federal Rules permit *counterclaims* and *crossclaims*.[315] Generally, a counterclaim is asserted when a party serves a pleading against an opposing party and possesses a claim for relief against that party. Crossclaims are asserted against co-parties. Counterclaims and crossclaims appear in pleadings served after the complaint. They are pleaded just like original claims for relief. However, new jurisdictional allegations may not be required. Recoupment, set-offs, counterclaims, and crossclaims are discussed in detail in the next chapter.

(g) Consolidation and Waiver of Defenses

(i) Consolidation

If the defendant decides to make a preanswer motion rather than waiting to raise all defenses in the answer, Federal Rule 12(g) requires the defendant to consolidate the defenses listed in Rule 12(b) in one motion. If the defendant moves

---

312. *Cf.* Strickland v. Strickland, 375 S.C. 76, 650 S.E.2d 465 (2007) (party's pleading only asserted as affirmative defense the doctrine of latches, not equitable estoppel; nevertheless, because the latches defense was indistinguishable from equitable estoppel on the facts, the defense would be considered on appeal, though not technically preserved on appeal).

313. 547 U.S. 198, 126 S. Ct. 1675, 164 L. Ed. 2d 376 (2006).

314. *Cf.* Eriline Co. v. Johnson, 440 F.3d 648 (4th Cir. 2006) (district courts may not raise statute-of-limitations defense on its own motion).

315. *See* Form 30 in the Appendix of Forms following the Federal Rules of Civil Procedure.

in a preanswer motion on any of the grounds provided in Rule 12 which are then available, the defendant may not make a second preanswer motion based upon any grounds omitted from the motion. This consolidation requirement is subject to the following exception: Rule 12(h)(3) provides that lack of subject-matter jurisdiction may be suggested at any time.[316]

Illustration 6-34. *P* sues *D* in federal court for personal injuries received in an automobile accident. *D* moves to dismiss *P's* action on the ground that venue is improper. The court denies the motion. *D* may not raise by preanswer motion any of the other grounds provided in Rule 12 that were available at the time the first motion was served, except lack of subject-matter jurisdiction.

Illustration 6-35. *D* moves for a more definite statement of the claim. The motion is granted. *P* then serves an amended complaint containing a more definite statement, showing for the first time possible grounds for a challenge that the complaint fails to state a claim upon which relief may be granted. *D* then moves under Rule 12(b)(6) to dismiss. This motion would be proper because the Rule 12(b)(6) objection was not "available" at the time of the first motion. It only became available when *P* amended the complaint.[317]

(ii) Waiver

Rule 12(h) keys waiver to the consolidation requirement in Rule 12(g), discussed in the preceding subsection. If the "available" defense omitted from a preanswer motion is (1) lack of personal jurisdiction, (2) improper venue, (3) insufficiency of process, or (4) insufficiency of service of process, Rule 12(h)(1)(A) provides that the omitted defense or defenses are waived.[318] Even if they are not waived in this manner, Rule 12(h)(1)(B) provides that these same defenses will be waived if they are not included in the defendant's answer or in an amendment permitted by Rule 15(a)(1) as a matter of course.[319] Rule 15(a)(1) provides, in effect, that the defendant may amend the answer once without the court's permission within 21 days after the defendant has served it.[320]

Illustration 6-36. On the facts of *Illustration 6-34*, *D* waived any personal jurisdiction defense that *D* possessed at the time *D* moved to dismiss for improper venue because *D* failed to include the personal jurisdiction objection in the motion. *D* may not raise the personal jurisdiction objection in *D's* answer. The interaction of Rules 12(g) and (h)(1) produces waiver of the personal jurisdiction objection by *D's* failure to consolidate it with the improper venue defense in the first motion.

---

316. *See* FED. R. CIV. P. 12(g), (h)(3).

317. *See* FED. R. CIV. P. 12(g).

318. FED. R. CIV. P. 12(b)(1)(A); *see, e.g., Ex parte* Harper, 934 So. 2d 1045 (Ala. 2006) (venue objection waived by failing to include it in motion to dismiss for failure to state a claim).

319. *See* FED. R. CIV. P. 12(h)(1)(B)(ii); *see also* Vax-D Med. Techs., LLC v. Texas Spine Med. Ctr., 485 F.3d 593 (11th Cir. 2007) (although service of process was improper under Rule 4(e)(1) in the manner provided by the law of the state where service was made, defendants had waived insufficiency of service, insufficiency of process, and personal jurisdiction objections by answering complaint without raising objections); *cf.* Heard v. Remy, 937 So. 2d 939 (Miss. 2006) (failure to use "magic words" "insufficiency of process" or "insufficiency of service of process" does not produce waiver when defendant specifically pleads that process was served after both time limit for service and statute of limitations had expired).

320. *See* section 5 ("Amendments Before Trial") *infra*.

Illustration 6-37. *P* sues *D* in federal court for breach of contract. *D* does not serve a preanswer motion under Rule 12. Instead, *D* serves an answer containing only admissions and denials of *P's* allegations. *D* waives the defenses of lack of personal jurisdiction, improper venue, insufficiency of process, and insufficiency of service of process by failing to include them in *D's* answer—unless *D* serves an amended answer containing these defenses within the time permitted for amending as a matter of course by Rule 15(a). Waiver here is not produced by failure to raise the objection in a preanswer motion. Rule 12 does not require waivable objections to be raised by preanswer motion *unless* the defendant chooses to make such a motion and omits a waivable objection from the motion. Instead, Rule 12 gives the defendant an option to raise certain defenses by motion or answer. If, as in this illustration, the defendant chooses not to make a preanswer motion, waiver will only occur if the defendant fails to include waivable defenses in the answer and does not discover the error until the time for amendment as a matter of course has expired under Rule 15(a).[321]

Illustration 6-38. *D* moves to strike redundant and impertinent matter from *P's* complaint. The court grants this motion. *D* then answers challenging venue and personal jurisdiction. *D* has waived any existing venue and personal jurisdiction objections. Rule 12(g) provides that "a party who makes a motion under this rule" [*e.g.*, a motion to strike under Rule 12(f)] is not permitted to "make another motion under this rule raising a defense or objection that was available to the party but omitted from its earlier motion."[322] Rule 12(h)(1)(A) thus produces waiver in such circumstances.[323]

Illustration 6-39. *D* moves before answering to drop a misjoined party. The court grants this motion. *D* then moves to dismiss the complaint on the ground that the court lacks personal jurisdiction over *D*. In this situation, the first motion is "under" Rule 21, not Rule 12. Thus, under the terms of Rule 12(g), the second motion is proper and *D* has not waived the personal jurisdiction objection under Rule 12(h).

* * * * *

The policy of making personal jurisdiction, venue, and process objections waivable at an early stage is sound. These objections primarily involve the personal convenience of the defendant. If the defendant does not care sufficiently about the defenses to raise them promptly, it is appropriate that they be waived.

Other defenses, however, involve institutional considerations or the interests of third parties. Thus, Rule 12(h)(2) and (3) appropriately preserve them from waiver. For example, the defense of failure to state a claim upon which relief may be granted and the defense of failure to join a required party are not waived by omitting them from a pre-answer motion or the answer. They may be presented later, including at the trial. Thereafter, however, these defenses are thereafter waived.[324] Lack of subject-matter jurisdiction may be raised even after the

---

321. *See id.*

322. FED. R. CIV. P. 12(g)(2).

323. Rule 12(h)(1)(A) specifically provides that "[a] party waives any defense listed in Rule 12(b)(2)-(5) by . . . omitting it from a motion in the circumstances described in Rule 12(g)(2). *See* FED. R. CIV. P. 12(h)(1).

324. *See* FED. R. CIV. P. 12(h)(2).

conclusion of the trial.[325] Omitting affirmative defenses such as those listed in Rule 8(c) can produce waiver after the time for serving amendments as a matter "of course" under Rule 15(a)(1) expires. However, after that, the defendant may still seek the permission of the court ("leave of court") to add such a defense. The court will usually freely grant permission to amend.

Illustration 6-40. On the facts of *Illustration 6-37*, *D* still may raise at trial the failure to join a required party.[326]

Illustration 6-41. On the facts of *Illustration 6-37*, *D* has waived the affirmative defenses of failure of consideration, release, and accord and satisfaction, unless the court permits *D* to amend the answer to include those defenses.

* * * * *

Although Rule 12 specifies the circumstances under which waiver of defenses will take place, some courts have recognized waiver of defenses by the defendants' "conduct" of the litigation, such as a failure to press for a ruling on an otherwise properly raised defense of lack of personal jurisdiction.[327] These

---

325. *See* FED. R. CIV. P. 12(h)(3); Chapter 2(A)(2) ("The 'No-Waiver, No-Consent' Rule") *supra*.

326. *Cf.* Nationwide Bi-Weekly Admin., Inc. v. Belo Corp., 512 F.3d 137 (5th Cir. 2007) (defendant did not lose Rule 12(b)(6) motion by failing to consolidate it with preanswer motion to dismiss for lack of personal jurisdiction because Rule 12(g) did not, because of Rule 12(h)(2), require consolidation of 12(b)(6) motion with other motion); Gilmour v. Gates, McDonald & Co., 382 F.3d 1312 (11th Cir. 2004) (claim may not be raised for the first time in a brief submitted in opposition to a motion for summary judgment).

327. *See, e.g.*, Lybbert v. Grant Cnty., 141 Wash. 2d 29, 1 P.3d 1124 (2000) (defendant entered an appearance indicating that the defendant was not "waiving objections to improper service or jurisdiction"; for nine months thereafter, the defendant acted as if it were preparing to litigate the merits and had indicated that it would fully cooperate in providing a response to the plaintiff's interrogatory asking whether it intended to rely on the insufficiency of service of process defense; when the defendant served its answer, the defendant raised the defense of insufficiency of process; the court held that the defendant waived this objection by failing to raise it in answer or responsive pleading in a timely manner, by engaging in discovery over course of several months, and by asserting the defense after the statute of limitations had apparently extinguished plaintiffs' claim; the court concluded that its "holding today merely underscores the importance of preventing the litigation process from being inhibited by inconsistent or dilatory conduct on the part of litigants. We are satisfied, in short, that the doctrine of waiver complements our current notion of procedural fairness and believe its application, in appropriate circumstances, will serve to reduce the likelihood that the 'trial by ambush' style of advocacy, which has little place in our present-day adversarial system, will be employed."); *cf.* N.J. CT. R. 4:6-3 (requiring the defendant to raise the defenses of lack of personal jurisdiction, insufficiency of process, and insufficiency of service of process by motion within 90 days after service of an answer including one or more of those defenses); *see also* East Miss. State Hosp. v. Adams, 947 So. 2d 887 (Miss. 2007) (insufficiency of process and service of process objections raised in timely fashion, but waived by participation in litigation and failure to "pursue" the defenses for two years after raising them). *But cf.* Democratic Republic of Congo v. FG Hemisphere Assocs., LLC, 508 F.3d 1062 (D.C. Cir. 2007) (personal jurisdiction defense is waived by defaulting defendant's participation in post-default litigation without raising the defense); Stichting Ter Behartiging Van De Belangen Van Oudaandeelhouders in Het Kapitaal Van Saybolt Int'l B.V. v. Schreiber, 407 F.3d 34 (2d Cir. 2005) (no waiver of real party in interest objection raised after more than three years of litigation; motion disputing validity of assignment bearing on question raised late, but defense raised in answers to complaint and issue was promptly raised in response to district court's order following remand from the court of appeals that parties submit motions on any ground not previously raised). Hamilton v. Atlas Turner, Inc., 197 F.3d 58 (2d Cir. 1999) (defendant who preserved personal jurisdiction defense in answer and raised it one additional time by motion nevertheless "forfeited" the defense by failing to raise it thereafter except after trial); Continental Bank, N.A. v. Meyer, 10 F.3d 1293 (7th Cir. 1993) (holding that although the defendants had properly raised their objection to personal jurisdiction in their answer, they had waived it by participating in the action for over two and one-half years without actively contesting jurisdiction); Yeldell v. Tutt, 913 F.2d 533, 539 (8th Cir. 1990) (holding that the defendants failed to "comply with the spirit of Rule 12" when they included a personal jurisdiction defense in their answer but failed to reassert the issue until appeal); Network Prof'ls, Inc. v. Network Int'l Ltd., 146 F.R.D. 179 (D. Minn. 1993) (the court considered raising lack of personal jurisdiction to be part of a "calculated strategy of delay and deception" which "violated the spirit of Rule 12"; the court concluded that "defendants have waived their personal jurisdiction defense by raising it again after the court considered the merits or quasi-merits of the case in the preliminary injunction motion and more than one year after the action commenced); Marquest Med. Prods., Inc. v. EMDE Corp., 496 F. Supp. 1242 (D. Colo. 1980) (waiver held to occur because the defendants requested extensions of time to answer and to respond to discovery as well as entered into stipulation granting preliminary injunctive relief before raising lack of personal jurisdiction and

decisions are questionable. Waiver is a serious matter. It should not be produced without a clear textual basis in the governing rules or statutes. Waiver by conduct has no textual basis in the rules. Nor do the rules provide for waiver for seeking court-approved extensions of time or responding on the merits to motions for preliminary injunctions prior to answering. Although waiver should perhaps be recognized in clear cases of abuse as a matter of policy, the policy should be articulated by Congress or the proper rulemaking authority, not on a case-by-case basis.[328]

4. The Plaintiff's Reply and Motions to Strike an Insufficient Defense

The principal function of common-law pleading was to reach a single issue, either of law or fact. The process of pleading continued until the parties reached such an issue.[329] In contrast, the codes and the Federal Rules of Civil Procedure do not attempt to force the definition of a single issue. In federal court, pleading ceases after the defendant serves an answer unless (1) the defendant includes a counterclaim in the answer or (2) the court orders a reply.[330] Although a reply is not ordinarily used in federal court, Federal Rule 12(f) allows the plaintiff to move to strike a defense in an answer as "insufficient." This motion is a partial analogue of a Rule 12(b)(6) motion (failure to state a claim upon which relief may be granted) directed to the complaint.

Illustration 6-42. Assume that *P* sues *D* in federal court. *P* asserts *D's* negligence. *D's* answer denies *D's* negligence, asserts *P's* contributory negligence, and "counterclaims" for damages that *D* suffered in the accident.[331] Federal Rule 12(a)(1) requires *P* to serve an answer (a "reply" prior to the restyling of the Federal Rules) to the counterclaim within 21 days after service of the answer.[332]

Illustration 6-43. On the facts of *Illustration 6-42*, assume that *D* is obviously attempting to set forth a counterclaim but fails to label it a counterclaim.

---

venue).

328. The American Law Institute has proposed a waiver-by-conduct provision for venue objections. Unfortunately, the provision does not provide any standards by which to determine what constitutes "waiver by conduct." *See* ALI FEDERAL JUDICIAL CODE REVISION PROJECT § 1406(c) (2004).

329. *See* section A(2) ("Stating the Plaintiff's Claim in the Declaration") *supra*.

330. *See* FED. R. CIV. P. 7(a), 12(a). The court may order a reply to an answer, a reply to a third-party answer, or a crossclaim answer. FED. R. CIV. P. 7(a)(7) & advisory committee's note to the 2007 restyling amendment. In common-law pleading, the parties had several opportunities to demur. Whenever a party generally demurred, the demurrer had the effect of opening-up or "searching the record"; it thus tested not only the legal sufficiency of the pleading to which it was addressed, but also all prior pleadings. *See* section A(4) ("Subsequent Pleading") *supra*; *Illustration 6-7 supra*. The codes generally applied a similar rule to code demurrers. For example, the plaintiff's demurrer to the defendant's answer would "search the record" and would test the legal sufficiency of the complaint. CHARLES E. CLARK, HANDBOOK OF THE LAW OF CODE PLEADING § 83, at 524-25 (2d ed. 1947). The Federal Rules have abolished demurrers and have limited the pleadings. Thus, the concept of searching the record is not relevant in federal practice except in certain limited circumstances involving judgment on the pleadings under Federal Rule 12(c). *See* Chapter 10(B) ("Judgment on the Pleadings") *infra*.

331. *See* Form 30 in the Appendix of Forms following the Federal Rules of Civil Procedure (stating that under the heading "Counterclaim" the pleader would "[s]et forth any counterclaim in the same way a claim is pleaded in a complaint." It also directs the pleader to "[i]Include a further statement of jurisdiction if need.").

332. FED. R. CIV. P. 12(a)(1)(B).

Under these circumstances, *P* does not have to answer. An answer is due only when the counterclaim is "designated as a counterclaim."[333]

Illustration 6-44. On the facts of *Illustration 6-32*, assume that *D* also asserts as an affirmative defense that *P* released the claim on the promissory note for a valuable consideration. *P* is not required or permitted to reply in the absence of a court order. Rule 8(b) provides that if "a responsive pleading is not required, an allegation is considered denied or avoided."[334] Thus, the affirmative defense is taken as denied or avoided. *P* would thus be allowed to take any one of several positions at trial with respect to *D's* affirmative defense. For example, *P* may (1) deny there was such a release or (2) assert an affirmative defense, *e.g.*, fraud in securing the release. A court-ordered reply to the answer would be useful under these circumstances if a reply would enable the court to dispose of the action on the pleadings. For example, *P* may not be able to deny or otherwise defend against the affirmative defense.[335]

5. Amendments Before Trial

(a) Amendments as a Matter of Course and with Leave of Court

Federal Rule 15(a) permits a party to amend the party's pleading once "as a matter course" (*i.e.*, without the court's permission) within 21 days after serving it;[336] or if the pleading is one to which a responsive pleading is required (*i.e.*, a complaint, an answer containing a counterclaim designated as a counterclaim, a crossclaim, or a third-party complaint), then the pleading may be amended once as a matter of course either (a) 21 days after service of the responsive pleading or (b) 21 days after service of a motion under Rule 12(b) seeking to dismiss the action, 12(e) seeking to require a more definite statement, or 12(f) seeking to strike an insufficient defense or redundant, immaterial, impertinent, or scandalous matter—whichever is first.[337] These latter 21-day periods are not cumulative. For example, if a responsive pleading is served after one of these motions has been served, there is no new 21-day period.[338]

To amend thereafter, a party must obtain leave of court (or the written consent of the opposing party). However, the court is directed to permit amendments freely "when justice so requires."[339] Rule 15(a) does not specify the

---

333. *See* FED. R. CIV. P. 7(a)(3).

334. FED. R. CIV. P. 8(b)(6).

335. *See* CHARLES E. CLARK, HANDBOOK OF THE LAW OF CODE PLEADING § 108, at 692 (2d ed. 1947).

336. *See* FED. R. CIV. P. 15(a)(1)(A) (as amended in 2009).

337. *See* FED. R. CIV. P. 15(a)(1)(B) (as amended in 2009).

338. *See* FED. R. CIV. P. 15(a)(1) advisory committee's note to the 2009 amendment.

339. FED. R. CIV. P. 15(a)(2); *see also* United States *ex rel.* Mathews v. HealthSouth Corp., 332 F.3d 293 (5th Cir. 2003) (when leave of court is required to amend a complaint, an amended complaint filed without first obtaining permission of the court is ineffective and would not toll a limitations period). Time limits for serving amendments under Rule 15(a) can be fixed by a scheduling order under Federal Rule 16(b). If amendments are not made within the time specified in the scheduling order, permission to amend thereafter can be denied. *See* Nourison Rug Corp. v. Parvizian, 535 F.3d 295 (4th Cir. 2008) (after the deadlines provided in scheduling order have passed, "good cause" standard of the pretrial conference and scheduling rule must be satisfied to justify leave to amend pleadings); S & W Enters., L.L.C. v. SouthTrust Bank, 315 F.3d 533 (5th Cir. 2003) (when a deadline set by a scheduling order for amending pleadings has expired, Rule 16(b) governs and requires a showing of good cause

procedure for obtaining leave to amend. Ordinarily, leave to amend is sought by motion pursuant to Rule 7(b). To satisfy the requirements of Rule 7(b), the moving party should submit the proposed amendment with the motion.[340]

If a pleading has been amended, Rule 15(a) further provides that any required response to it must be made either within the time remaining to respond to the original pleading or within 14 days after service of the amended pleading, whichever is later—unless the court orders otherwise.[341]

(b) Relation Back of Amendments Changing a Claim or Defense

Rule 15(c)(1)(A) allows an amendment to relate back to the date of the original pleading when the law providing the statute of limitations permits relation back. Thus, if state law provides the statute of limitations in a diversity action, a claim *not* arising from the same facts as the claim in the original pleading can relate back if state law so provides.[342]

Rule 15(c)(1)(B) allows relation back of pleadings changing a claim or defense, but not a party, when the claim or defense in the amended pleading arose out of the same conduct, transaction, or occurrence as the claim or defense set out—or attempted to be set out—in the original pleading.[343] The "same transaction or occurrence" rule governing relation back of amendments changing claims and defenses reflects the underlying policy of the Federal Rules to provide maximum opportunity for each claim to be decided on its merits rather than on the basis of procedural technicalities.[344] The rule also reflects the limited role of the pleadings under the Federal Rules—the role of providing notice rather than fact revelation or issue formation. These latter functions are now handled by the discovery process.[345]

The assumption is that when an amended claim or defense arises out of the same transaction or occurrence as an original claim or defense, the party opposing the amendment cannot be unfairly surprised or prejudiced. Rather, a party should always be prepared to meet as many claims or defenses as may arise from a single set of facts. Nor can a party reasonably rely on a repose policy supporting the statute of limitations. As long as the party is sued on a claim arising from a

---

to modify the scheduling order; if good cause is shown, then the "when justice so requires" standard of Rule 15(a) applies).

340. 6 CHARLES A. WRIGHT & ARTHUR R. MILLER, FEDERAL PRACTICE AND PROCEDURE: CIVIL § 1485 (3d ed. 2010); *see also* Reier Broad. Co. v. Montana State Univ.-Bozeman, 2005 MT 240, 328 Mont. 471, 121 P.3d 549 (proposed amendment of complaint properly denied because it would be futile).

341. FED. R. CIV. P. 15(a)(3).

342. FED. R. CIV. P. 15(c)(1)(A).

343. FED. R. CIV. P. 15(c)(1)(B).

344. Professors Wright and Miller point out that

> [t]his is demonstrated by the emphasis Rule 15 places on the permissive approach that the district courts are to take to amendment requests, no matter what their character may be; the rule is in sharp contrast to the common law and code restriction that amendments could not change the original cause of action. No longer is a party to be irrevocably bound to the legal or factual theory of the party's first pleading. The thrust of the rule also is reinforced by the elimination of the wooden cause of action test for determining whether an amended pleading should relate back.

6 CHARLES A. WRIGHT & ARTHUR R. MILLER, FEDERAL PRACTICE AND PROCEDURE: CIVIL § 1471, at 587-89 (3d ed. 2010) (footnotes omitted). *See also* Douglas D. McFarland, *Seeing the Forest for the Trees: The Transaction or Occurrence and the Claim Interlock Civil Procedure*, 12 FLA. COSTAL L. REV. 247, 279-86 (2011) (discussing the same transaction or occurrence standard for relation back).

345. *See id.*

particular set of facts before the statute runs and the amended claim arises out of those same facts, relation back will not violate the repose policies of the statute of limitations.[346]

In *Mayle v. Felix,*[347] the Supreme Court considered the application of Rule 15(c)'s "same transaction or occurrence" requirement in the context of a federal habeas corpus proceeding brought to challenge the constitutional validity of a state criminal conviction. In *Mayle*, the prisoner was convicted in a California state court of first-degree murder and second-degree robbery and sentenced to life imprisonment. After exhausting his remedies on direct review in the state court, he filed a petition in U.S. District Court for habeas corpus to challenge the constitutionality of the procedures that led to his conviction. His initial petition was timely and alleged a claim under the Sixth Amendment's Confrontation Clause based on the admission against him of videotaped statements of a witness telling the police that he had overheard a conversation in which the prisoner had described the planned robbery just before it occurred. Subsequently, the prisoner filed an amended petition asserting an additional claim under the Fifth Amendment based on statements that the prisoner himself made at a pretrial police interrogation. This amended petition was, however, filed after the one-year limitation period on habeas corpus petitions

---

346. *Cf.* Tho Dinh Tran v. Alphonse Hotel Corp., 281 F.3d 23 (2d Cir. 2002) (initial complaint by a former hotel employee asserted overtime claims under the Fair Labor Standards Act, along with state law claims; the amended complaint sought to add a violation of the Racketeer Influenced and Corrupt Organizations Act (RICO), based on the allegations that the hotels and their owners bribed union officials as part of a scheme to pay their employees wages below the union rate; the court held that the "same transaction or occurrence" test was not met because the original complaint made no reference to acts of bribery, which was the only predicate act that could give rise to a RICO violation). In City of Saint Paul v. Evans, 344 F.3d 1029 (9th Cir. 2003), the court held that when a claim is time barred, it may not be used as an affirmative defense to a counterclaim. This may provide a clue as to how a defense might, as suggested by Rule 15(c), be time-barred. The policies supporting statutes of limitation are discussed more fully below in conjunction with amendments changing parties. *See also* Johnson v. Crown Enters., Inc., 398 F.3d 339 (5th Cir. 2005) (district court erred in denying relation back to claim added to action in amended complaint on the grounds that the claim in the original complaint and the new claim involved different elements of proof and different procedural requirements; test is whether claims involved the same conduct, transaction, or occurrence, which they did); USX Corp. v. Barnhart, 395 F.3d 161 (3d Cir. 2004) (in action against Commissioner of Social Security to challenge assignment of health benefit premium responsibilities to plaintiff, amendment to include assignments of additional miners related back; although each assignment was a separate transaction or occurrence, all assignments were made under same (now invalidated) legal doctrine and Commissioner had notice from original complaint that all assignments made on basis of that theory were questionable); Bensel v. Allied Pilots Ass'n, 387 F.3d 298 (3d Cir. 2004) (claims in amended complaint related back to original complaint because they merely expounded upon and further detailed factual scenario of claims in original complaint); Brzozowski v. Correctional Physician Servs., Inc., 360 F.3d 173 (3d Cir. 2004) (Rule 15(c) relation back provisions apply only to statutes of limitation, not to the 90-day filing provision in Title VII of the Civil Rights Act). *But cf.* Scarborough v. Principi, 541 U.S. 401, 124 S. Ct. 1856, 158 L. Ed. 2d 674 (2004) (relation back applied to an amendment to a fee application made to cure an initial defect in the application, even though the application was not a pleading). It is important to note that doctrines other than relation back may permit assertion of late filed claims. *See* Muhammed v. Welch, 2004 ND 46, 675 N.W.2d 402 (doctrine of equitable estoppel can excuse delay in bringing an action if the delay is induced by the defendant's promises, suggestions, or assurances that, if carried into effect, would result in a solution or adjustment without litigation); *cf.* Popp Telecom, Inc. v. American Sharecom, Inc., 361 F.3d 482 (8th Cir. 2004) (Private Securities Litigation Reform Act (PSLRA) provision amending RICO to preclude assertion of RICO claims based on securities fraud applied to all claims commenced after enactment of PSLRA; RICO claims asserted by amendment did not relate back, even though claims arose from same transaction or occurrence, because the plaintiffs attempted to add them by amendment after the date on which the PSLRA was enacted). Sometimes parties attempt, improperly, to apply the doctrine of relation back to issues other than the statute of limitations. *See, e.g.*, Harper v. AutoAlliance Int'l, Inc., 392 F.3d 195 (6th Cir. 2004) (after removal, motion to remand was denied and plaintiff amended complaint to drop federal claims and asserted that amendment related back to beginning of action and thus deprived court of subject-matter jurisdiction; the filing of amended complaint did not deprive court of subject-matter jurisdiction, notwithstanding elimination of federal claims; jurisdiction is determined as of time of removal).

347. 545 U.S. 644, 125 S. Ct. 2562, 162 L. Ed. 2d 582 (2005).

found in the Antiterrorism and Effective Death Penalty Act.[348] The issue was, therefore, whether the amended petition related back under Rule 15(c) so as to allow the prisoner to assert the Fifth Amendment claim.

The district court dismissed the Fifth Amendment claim as time-barred, but the Ninth Circuit Court of Appeals reversed. Under the rule followed by the Ninth and Seventh Circuits, an amended habeas petition would relate back as long as it asserted a claim that was derived from the prisoner's trial, conviction, and sentence. The majority of circuits required that the original and amended claims in the habeas petition derive from a common core of facts and prohibited relation back when the new claims depended upon events separate in time and type from the original ones. The Supreme Court reversed the Ninth Circuit and adopted the view of the majority of circuits.[349]

The majority in *Mayle* was influenced by the fact that Habeas Corpus Rule 2(c) was more demanding than Rule 8 of the Federal Rule of Civil Procedure in providing what the prisoner's petition for habeas must contain. Rule 8 requires only a short and plain statement of the claim showing that the pleader is entitled to relief, and, as observed in section D(2)*(b)* above, Rule 8 requires only sufficient allegations to give "fair notice" of what the plaintiff's claim is. This standard has been interpreted to allow a very general statement of the facts, but not to require any allegation of a particular legal theory. The result is that when the plaintiff alleges a claim under Rule 8, the defendant is on notice that the plaintiff may recover on any legal theory supported by the general facts alleged, even if that theory has not been specified in the complaint. In contrast, Habeas Corpus Rule 2(c) requires a petitioner to "specify all the grounds for relief available to the petitioner" and "state the facts supporting each ground." This more stringent pleading requirement for habeas cases caused the majority in *Mayle* to conclude that the incidents alleged in the amended petition arose from different transactions and occurrences—one the pretrial interview of a witness against the prisoner and the other the pretrial interrogation of the prisoner.[350]

Because of its reliance on Habeas Rule 2(c), *Mayle* does not affect the relation back doctrine as it was administered prior to *Mayle*. Significantly, in *Mayle*, the Supreme Court cited and discussed with approval its prior decision in *Tiller v. Atlantic Coast Line R.R. Co.*,[351] an ordinary civil action in which the plaintiff's amended complaint stating a claim based on the same facts as the original complaint, but based on a new legal theory, was allowed to relate back.[352]

---

348. 28 U.S.C. § 2241(d)(1).

349. *See* 545 U.S. at 648-54, 125 S. Ct. at 2566-69, 162 L. Ed. 2d at 589-92.

350. *See id.* at 654-64, 125 S. Ct. at 2569-75, 162 L. Ed. 2d at 592-99; *see also* United States *ex rel.* Miller v. Bill Harbert Int'l Constr., Inc., 608 F.3d 871 (D.C. Cir. 2010) (no relation back of claims under separate contracts just because contracts involve construction of sewer systems in Egypt and were funded by the USAID, citing *Mayle*); United States v. Gonzalez, 592 F.3d 675 (5th Cir. 2009) (following *Mayle*; new claims of ineffective assistance of counsel do not relate back simply because they involve the same constitutional provision); Hebner v. McGrath, 543 F.3d 1133 (9th Cir. 2008) (amended habeas corpus petition did not relate back, following *Mayle*).

351. 323 U.S. 574, 65 S. Ct. 421, 89 L. Ed. 465 (1945).

352. 545 U.S. at 659-70, 125 S. Ct. at 2572, 162 L. Ed. 2d at 595-96 (discussing *Tiller*); *see also* Hall v. Spencer Cnty., 583 F.3d 930 (6th Cir. 2009) (amended complaint can relate back when party adds a new legal theory as long as it arises out of the same transaction or occurrence as the original claim); Williams v. Boeing Co., 517 F.3d 1120 (9th Cir. 2008) (amendment adding a compensation discrimination claim to action originally alleging that plaintiffs had been discriminated against in promotion, subjected to hostile work environment, and

(c) Relation Back of Amendments Changing Parties

A specific provision governing amendments changing parties was added to Rule 15(c) in 1966.[353] Under this provision, when an amendment changed the party against whom a claim was asserted, the amendment would relate back if it arose from the same transaction or occurrence as the original claim and certain other requirements were satisfied. First, the party to be brought in by amendment had to receive "such notice of the institution of the action that the party would not be prejudiced in maintaining a defense on the merits."[354] Second, this notice had to be received "within the period provided by law for commencing the action against the party to be brought in by amendment." Finally, it had to be shown that the party brought in "knew or should have known that, but for a mistake concerning the identity of the proper party, the action would have been brought against the party."

These additional requirements reflect the policies of statutes of limitations.[355] These policies are twofold: (1) a desire to protect the courts and parties from the danger of inaccurate determination of claims based on stale evidence;[356] and (2) the assurance of a period of repose that will benefit parties in ordering their affairs free from the fear that claims arising from long-past events may be asserted against them.[357] By requiring that a defending party receive a quality of notice that would prevent the party from being prejudiced in defending the claim on the merits, the drafters of the 1966 amendment addressed the policies against stale claims. Furthermore, by requiring that the defending party receive the notice within the period provided by law for commencing the action against the party, the drafters also addressed the policies of repose.

(i) Schiavone v. Fortune

In 1986, the U.S. Supreme Court construed the "change of parties" provisions of Federal Rule 15(c). In *Schiavone v. Fortune*,[358] the plaintiff

---

retaliated against because of race did not relate back because there was no common core of operative facts between claims in amended and original complaint, despite the fact that they arose from the same employer-employee relationship); Moross Ltd. P'ship v. Fleckenstein Capital, Inc., 466 F.3d 508 (6th Cir. 2006) (amendment did not relate back where it did not just change legal theory of recovery or allege added events leading up to the same injury, but involved a completely different set of factual disputes); Oja v. United States Army Corps of Eng'rs, 440 F.3d 1122 (9th Cir. 2006) (plaintiff's amendment of complaint alleging that employer published private information on Internet without his consent in violation of Privacy Act did not relate back to filing of original complaint; original complaint was based on claim that employer published identical information at a later time; fact that language in the two disclosures was identical did not produce relation back, because each act of disclosure was separate and distinct in time and place, if not substance).

353. Before 1966, amendments changing parties were governed by the same test that governed relation back of amendments changing claims only, the same transaction or occurrence test.

354. The words "institution of" were deleted as part of the 2007 restyling amendments as "potentially confusing." The Advisory Committee stated that "[w]hat counts is that the party to be brought in have notice of the existence of the action, whether or not the notice includes details as to its 'institution.' " FED. R. CIV. P. 15(c) advisory committee's note to the 2007 restyling amendment.

355. The Advisory Committee's note to the 1966 amendment to Rule 15(c) stated that "[r]elation back is intimately connected with the policy of the statute of limitations." *See* FED. R. CIV. P. 15(c) advisory committee's note to the 1966 amendment.

356. *See* RESTATEMENT (SECOND) OF CONFLICT OF LAWS § 142 cmt. f (Supp. 1989).

357. *See, e.g.*, John Hart Ely, *The Irrepressible Myth of* Erie, 87 HARV. L. REV. 693, 726 (1974); *see also In re* Sharps Run Assocs., L.P., 157 B.R. 766, 775 (D.N.J. 1993).

358. 477 U.S. 21, 106 S. Ct. 2379, 91 L. Ed. 2d 18 (1986).

commenced a diversity action on May 9, 1983. The plaintiff named "Fortune" magazine as the defendant. However, "Fortune" is only a trademark of Time, Inc. Thus, the plaintiff should have sued Time. The statute of limitations ran on May 19th, and Time was served with process after this date. Time refused service because it was not properly named as the defendant in the action. The plaintiff then amended the complaint to name Time as the defendant and effectuated new service of process on July 21, 1983. The Supreme Court held that the one-year statute of limitations applicable to the action had run. Thus, the amendment to the complaint did not relate back. According to the Court, although Time had received notice of the action within the 120 day period for serving process prescribed by Rule 4, the party to be brought in had to receive notice of the action within the limitations period, not simply within the period for service of process.[359]

Commentators strongly criticized the Court's interpretation of Rule 15(c) in *Schiavone*.[360] If Time had been properly named in the complaint and had been served after the one-year period had run, the action would have been timely. Yet, under such circumstances, Time would still not have received notice of the action within the limitations period. Furthermore, when Time did receive notice of the action, it understood perfectly that the plaintiff had made a mistake in naming the defendant and that it was the defendant who should have been sued. Under these circumstances, it is difficult to understand how the policies of the statute of limitations would have been undermined if the amended complaint had been allowed to relate back.[361]

(ii) The 1991 Amendment to Rule 15(c)

In 1991, Rule 15(c) was amended to overrule *Schiavone*.[362] Revised Rule 15(c) allows amendments to relate back under three circumstances: (1) as provided by Rule 15(c)(1)(A), when relation back is permitted by the law that provides the statute of limitations applicable to the action;[363] *or* (2) as provided by Rule 15(c)(1)(B), when the claim or defense asserted in the amended pleading arises out of the same conduct, transaction, or occurrence as the claim or defense in the

---

359. *See id.* at 29-32, 106 S. Ct. at 2384-85, 91 L. Ed. 2d at 27-29. Prior to the Supreme Court's decision in *Schiavone*, the courts were split on this issue. *Compare, e.g.*, Hendrix v. Memorial Hosp., 776 F.2d 1255 (5th Cir. 1985) (action had to be filed within the statutory limitations period and notice given within the time for service) *with* Weisgal v. Smith, 774 F.2d 1277 (4th Cir. 1985) (notice had to be received before the statute of limitations had run).

360. *See, e.g.*, Joseph P. Bauer, Schiavone*: An Un-*Fortune*-ate Illustration of the Supreme Court's Role as Interpreter of the Federal Rules of Civil Procedure*, 63 NOTRE DAME L. REV. 720 (1988); Robert D. Brussack, *Outrageous* Fortune*: The Case for Amending Rule 15(c) Again*, 61 S. CAL. L. REV. 671 (1988); Lawrence A. Epter, *An Un-*Fortune*-Ate Decision: The Aftermath of the Supreme Court's Eradication of the Relation-Back Doctrine*, 17 FLA. ST. U. L. REV. 713 (1990); Laurie Helzick, Note, *Looking Forward: A Fairer Application of the Relation Back Provisions of Federal Rule of Civil Procedure 15(c)*, 63 N.Y.U. L. REV. 131 (1988).

361. Some state courts have not followed the *Schiavone* reasoning. *See, e.g.*, West v. Buchanan, 981 P.2d 1065 (Alaska 1999) (rejecting *Schiavone* and holding that the words "within the period provided by law for commencing the action" encompass the reasonable time for service of process when the complaint is timely filed); Hughes v. Water World Slide, Inc., 314 S.C. 211, 442 S.E.2d 584 (1994); Ritchie v. Grand Canyon Scenic Rides, 165 Ariz. 460, 799 P.2d 801 (1990).

362. *See* FED. R. CIV. P. 15(c) advisory committee's note to the 1991 amendment.

363. *See* FED. R. CIV. P. 15(c)(1) (restyled as 15(c)(1)(A) by the 2007 restyling amendments).

original pleading;[364] *or* (3) as provided by Rule 15(c)(1)(C), when the amendment changes the party or the naming of the party against whom a claim is asserted and (a) the "same transaction or occurrence test" of Rule 15(c)(1)(B) is satisfied; (b) the party to be brought in by amendment receives notice within the 120 day period for service of process provided in Rule 4(m); (c) the notice is sufficient to prevent the party from being prejudiced in maintaining a defense on the merits; and (d) the party knew or should have known that, but for a mistake concerning the identity of the proper party, the action would have been brought against the party.[365]

(iii) Relationship Between Amended Rule 15(c)(1)(A) and (C)

The structure of the 1991 amendments to Rule 15(c) has given rise to several problems of interpretation.[366] As restyled, Rule 15(c)(1)(A) provides that relation back will occur when "the law that provides the statute of limitations allows relation back." Should Rule 15(c)(1)(A) be applied to amendments changing parties because the rule's language is, on its face, applicable to all amendments and such an application would not render any other provision of Rule 15(c) superfluous? Alternatively, should Rule 15(c)(1)(A) be deemed inapplicable to amendments changing parties because it does not specifically state that it is applicable to such amendments and Rule 15(c)(1)(C) does specifically deal with them?

The Advisory Committee apparently intended for Rule 15(c)(1)(A) to apply to amendments changing parties. The Advisory Committee's note to the 1991 amendment states that "[w]hatever may be the controlling body of limitations law, if that law affords a more forgiving principle of relation back than the one provided in this rule, it should be available to save the claim. . . ." In addition, the Advisory Committee stated that "[i]f *Schiavone v. Fortune* . . . implies the contrary, this paragraph is intended to make a material change in the rule."[367]

Nevertheless, there is some danger that the courts will not interpret the rule in this fashion. Since the 1991 amendment, courts have interpreted the Rule 15(c) on numerous occasions. A substantial number of courts have applied Rule 15(c)(1)(C) to amendments changing parties without first inquiring whether Rule 15(c)(1)(A) would provide relation back. It is difficult to determine whether these courts consider the provisions of Rule 15(c)(1)(A) inapplicable to amendments changing parties. The courts in question may have considered Rule 15(c)(1)(A) and determined it to be inapplicable without specifically stating as such in their

---

364. *See* FED. R. CIV. P. 15(c)(2) (restyled as 15(c)(1)(B) by the 2007 restyling amendments).

365. *See* FED. R. CIV. P. 15(c)(3) (restyled as 15(c)(1)(C) by the 2007 restyling amendments).

366. In addition to the problem discussed in the text, a less significant question of the proper relationship between Rule 15(c)(1)(B) and (C) exists. The provisions of Rule 15(c)(1)(C) are clearly designed to apply to amendments changing parties to the action because Rule 15(c)(1)(C) specifically addresses the problem of amendments changing parties. Just as clearly, the same transaction or occurrence test of Rule 15(c)(1)(B), standing alone, is not designed to apply to amendments changing parties. Although each of the subdivisions are worded in the alternative ("or"), it would be unreasonable to interpret Rule 15(c)(1)(B) to allow an amendment changing parties to relate back just because the amendment arises out of the same transaction or occurrence as the original claim. Rule 15(c)(1)(C) specifically incorporates the same transaction or occurrence test as one of several conditions that must be met before an amendment changing parties may relate back. Thus, Rule 15(c)(1)(C) would be rendered superfluous if an amendment changing a party could relate back merely by satisfying the same transaction or occurrence test of Rule 15(c)(1)(B).

367. *See* FED. R. CIV. P. 15(c) advisory committee's note to the 1991 amendment.

opinions. Alternatively, some other explanation may exist for their failure to address Rule 15(c)(1)(A). However, because many of the cases dealing specifically with Rule 15(c)(1)(C) *deny* relation back, it strongly appears that the courts, in those cases at least, believe Rule 15(c)(1)(A) to be inapplicable to amendments changing parties. Otherwise, when the courts find relation back inappropriate under Rule 15(c)(1)(C), they would consider the applicability of Rule 15(c)(1)(A).[368]

Fortunately, however, several decisions also hold that amendments changing parties may relate back if either Rule 15(c)(1)(A) or Rule 15(c)(1)(C) is satisfied. These decisions generally recognized that the Advisory Committee intended relation back to occur under either provision of the rule.[369] This position is better reasoned and should ultimately prevail.[370]

Illustration 6-45. *P*, a citizen of State *X*, sues *D*, a citizen of State *Y*, on January 1st in federal court. *P* asserts a claim for relief for $80,000 arising out of an automobile accident. On February 1st, *P* amends the complaint to add a claim for relief based on a contract that is factually and legally unrelated to *P's* automobile accident claim. The state contract statute of limitations applicable to the latter claim expired on January 15th. Under these circumstances, Rule 15(c)(1)(B) does not provide for relation back of the contract claim. The claim does not arise out of the

---

368. *See, e.g.*, Worthington v. Wilson, 8 F.3d 1253 (7th Cir. 1993) (no relation back under Rule 15(c)(3), restyled as 15(c)(1)(C); Rule 15(c)(1), restyled as 15(c)(1)(A), not mentioned); Woods v. Indiana Univ.-Purdue Univ., 996 F.2d 880 (7th Cir. 1993) (same); Richardson v. John F. Kennedy Mem'l Hosp., 838 F. Supp. 979 (E.D. Pa. 1993) (same); Hunt v. Department of Air Force, 149 F.R.D. 657 (M.D. Fla. 1993) (same; alternative holding); Gardner *ex. rel.* Gardner v. Toyota Motor Sales, Inc., 793 F. Supp. 287 (D. Kan. 1992) (no relation back under Rule 15(c)(3), restyled as 15(c)(1)(C)); *cf.* Desanctis v. Hastings, No. 95-2403, 1997 WL 9765 (4th Cir. Jan. 13, 1997) (holding that Rule 15(c)(3), restyled as 15(c)(1)(C), controlled and prohibited the substitution of the estate of a defendant who had died unknown to the plaintiff before the action was commenced; the court seemed to acknowledge that state law would have provided for relation back, but did not consider the possible effect of Rule 15(c)(1), restyled as 15(c)(1)(A)); *see also* DeRienzo v. Harvard Indus., Inc., 357 F.3d 348 (3d Cir. 2004) (New Jersey tolling rule applied to permit relation back of amendments substituting actual defendant for fictitiously named defendant in diversity action because the plaintiff exercised due diligence in ascertaining the identity of the defendant and the defendant would not be prejudiced by allowing amendment to substitute defendant for fictitiously named party).

A related problem, present even with amendments concerning defendants, is when does an amendment "change" a party. It is possible to reason, both with regard to plaintiffs and defendants, that amendments that simply "add" new parties without dropping old ones or substituting new for old ones, do not "change" the parties within the meaning of Rule 15(c)(1)(C). *But see* Goodman v. Praxair, Inc., 494 F.3d 458 (4th Cir. 2007) (amendment adding a defendant changes the party against whom the claim is asserted within the language of Rule 15(c)(3), restyled as 15(c)(1)(C); focus is not on the nature of plaintiff's mistake, but on the quality of the notice received by the added party and whether relation back will cause prejudice).

369. *See, e.g.*, Coons v. Indus. Knife Co., 620 F.3d 38 (1st Cir. 2010) (relation back of amendment changing party possible if either Rule 15(c)(1)(A) or (c)(1)(C) satusfied); Saxton v. ACF Indus., Inc., 254 F.3d 959 (11th Cir. 2001) (holding that Rule 15(c)(1), restyled as 15(c)(1)(A), permitted relation back when relation back was provided for under state law, even though the relation back rules were not found in the same state statute that set the limitations period and even though analysis under Rule 15(c)(3), restyled as 15(c)(1)(C), might have prevented relation back); Lundy v. Adamar, Inc., 34 F.3d 1173 (3d Cir. 1994); Lovelace v. O'Hara, 985 F.2d 847 (6th Cir. 1993); Cruz v. City of Camden, 898 F. Supp. 1100 (D.N.J. 1995); Bryan v. Associated Container Transp., 837 F. Supp. 633 (D.N.J. 1993); Jones v. Wysinger, 815 F. Supp. 1127 (N.D. Ill. 1993); Rae v. Klusak, 810 F. Supp. 983 (N.D. Ill. 1993); Bordner v. FDIC, 145 F.R.D. 13 (D.N.H. 1992); Crowe v. Mullin, 797 F. Supp. 930 (N.D. Ala. 1992); Jordan v. Tapper, 143 F.R.D. 575 (D.N.J. 1992); Wilson v. City of Atlantic City, 142 F.R.D. 603 (D.N.J. 1992); *cf.* Ocasio Ortiz v. Betancourt Lebron, 146 F.R.D. 34 (D.P.R. 1992) (both provisions applicable to amendments changing parties; however, court suggests that Rule 15(c)(1), restyled as 15(c)(1)(A), should only be used when Rule 15(c)(3), restyled as 15(c)(1)(C), is inapplicable).

370. When a federal statute provides the limitations period applicable to the action, a relation back period will seldom be built into the federal statute. Therefore, Federal Rule 15(c)(1)(A) will not operate, and Federal Rule 15(c)(1)(C) will govern by default. *See, e.g.*, Hamm v. Frank, 985 F.2d 563 (7th Cir. 1993); Skoczylas v. Federal Bureau of Prisons, 961 F.2d 543 (5th Cir. 1992); Hill v. United States Postal Serv., 961 F.2d 153 (11th Cir. 1992); *In re* Convertible Rowing Exerciser Patent Litig., 817 F. Supp. 434 (D. Del. 1993).

same transaction or occurrence as the automobile accident claim. Nevertheless, if the law of the state that provides the contract statute of limitations would allow relation back under these circumstances, the court should permit relation back under Rule 15(c)(1)(A).

Illustration 6-46. *P*, a citizen of State *X*, wishes to sue *D-1*, a citizen of State *Y*, for personal injuries received in an accident suffered on property owned by *D-1* in State *Y*. *P* commences an action in the U.S. District Court in State *Y*, but mistakenly names *D-2* as the defendant in the action. *D-2* is served with process in the action within the 120 day period provided in Rule 4(m). However, *D-1* receives no notice of the action within the 120 day period. After the 120 day period under Rule 4(m) expires and the state statute of limitations applicable to *P's* claim has run, *P* discovers that *P* has mistakenly named and served *D-2* instead of *D-1* as the defendant in the action. *P* moves to amend the complaint to drop *D-2* from the action and name *D-1* as the defendant. Under these circumstances, Rule 15(c)(1)(C) would not permit the amendment to relate back. *D-1* did not receive any notice of the action within the 120 day time period provided under Rule 4(m). Nevertheless, if the law of the state that provides the statute of limitations applicable to *P's* claim would allow relation back, Rule 15(c)(1)(A) permits relation back.

(iv) Nature, Quality, and Timing of Notice

Rule 15(c)(1)(C) permits an amendment changing a party or the naming of a party to relate back only when the party to be brought in has received "such notice of the action" that the party "will not be prejudiced in defending on the merits." This provision was originally added to the rule by the 1966 amendments to Rule 15(c). As indicated above, the language is obviously designed to support the policy of the statute of limitations to protect a party from inaccurate determination of stale claims. The Advisory Committee's note to the amendment stated that "the notice need not be formal."[371] Clearly, therefore, the notice provided does not have to be by service of process, although this method of notice will often be used after the plaintiff has discovered a mistake in the party named as defendant. The question is, what sort of "informal notice" should suffice? The cases do not give a consistent answer to this question.[372]

One approach allows relation back when the quality of notice assures that the party to be brought in will not be prejudiced in maintaining a defense on the merits. This situation will sometimes occur when the party is aware of the incident giving rise to the claim, even if the party is not aware that the plaintiff has mistakenly commenced an action against another defendant based on the incident.[373] Prior to the 2007 restyling amendments, the rule required that the party to be brought in have "received such notice of the *institution of* the action . . . ." The

---

371. *See* FED. R. CIV. P. 15(c) advisory committee's note to the 1966 amendment.

372. *See* 6A CHARLES A. WRIGHT ET AL., FEDERAL PRACTICE AND PROCEDURE: CIVIL § 1498, at 124-28 (3d ed. 2010); *cf.* O'Brien v. Indiana Dep't of Correction *ex rel.* Turner, 495 F.3d 505 (7th Cir. 2007) (failure of plaintiff to address question of whether new parties were on notice of the original suit or had knowledge that they were the rightful defendants justified district court denying relation back).

373. For a complete discussion of the cases, see 6A CHARLES A. WRIGHT ET AL., FEDERAL PRACTICE AND PROCEDURE: CIVIL § 1498, 124-28 (3d ed. 2010).

words "institution of" were deleted as part of the 2007 restyling amendments as "potentially confusing." The Advisory Committee indicated that "[w]hat counts is that the party to be brought in have notice of the existence of the action, whether or not the notice includes details as to its 'institution.'"[374] Thus, the Advisory Committee appears to believe that there still must be notice of "the action." While still concededly contrary to the literal wording of Rule 15(c)(1)(C), the better approach would be to ask directly whether the notice received by the party is of the sort that would enable the party to maintain a defense on the merits without prejudice. The emphasis should be on whether the party to be brought in had sufficient notice under the circumstances. This notice must alert the party that a defense on the merits of the plaintiff's claim will ultimately be necessary.[375]

A separate problem concerning the notice requirement of Rule 15(c)(1)(C) involves the time period for giving notice. Prior to the 1991 amendment, the rule required that a defendant receive the requisite quality of notice "within the period provided by law for commencing the action."[376] The amended language of the rule now provides that the notice must be received "within the period provided by Rule 4(m) for serving the summons and complaint."[377] Rule 4(m) provides for dismissal of an action if the summons and complaint are not served within "120 days after the complaint is filed," unless the court extends the time limit.[378] This linkage of relation back to the Rule 4(m) time period has created a significant ambiguity in the operation of the rule. The question is how the 120-day time period should be measured in different factual circumstances.

One interpretation of the language would be that relation back is impermissible after 120 days has expired from commencement of the action, even if the statute of limitations of the state has not yet run at that time.[379] Literally, this is what the rule says, but this interpretation would seem to be the least justifiable interpretation of the 1991 amendment. Relation back is a concept that only applies after a pertinent limitations period has expired. If the pertinent limitations period has not yet run, relation back is irrelevant. In addition, this interpretation would effectively create an independent federal statute of limitations that would bar the assertion of a claim against a new defendant even if the claim would be permitted

---

374. FED. R. CIV. P. 15(c) advisory committee's note to the 2007 restyling amendment.

375. *See* 6A CHARLES A. WRIGHT ET AL., FEDERAL PRACTICE AND PROCEDURE: CIVIL § 1498, at 124-28 (3d ed. 2010). Professors Wright, Miller, and Kane suggest also that the notice provision of Rule 15(c)(1)(C) will interact with the provision requiring the party to realize that, but for a mistake, the party would have been sued originally. Obviously, if the quality of the notice is such that the party understands that the party should have been made a defendant in a civil action based on a particular incident, the party cannot complain that the notice was insufficient to allow the party to maintain a defense on the merits. *Cf. id.* at 128; *see also In re* Color Tile Inc., 475 F.3d 508 (3d Cir. 2007) (imputed knowledge from subagent to agent of prior complaint must be analyzed according to principles of actual notice rather than principles of constructive or imputed notice; this prevents summary judgment on grounds of the statute of limitation).

376. *See* FED. R. CIV. P. 15(c)(2) (1966 amendment).

377. *See* FED. R. CIV. P. 15(c)(1)(C).

378. *See* FED. R. CIV. P. 4(m).

379. *See* Cruz v. City of Camden, 898 F. Supp. 1100, 1110 (D.N.J. 1995) (seeming to interpret the rule in this fashion). In *Cruz*, the court had previously interpreted Rule 15(c)(1), restyled as 15(c)(1)(A), as not permitting relation back because state law did not do so. *See id.* at 1107-10. Thus, the interpretation of Rule 15(c)(3), restyled as 15(c)(1)(C), by the court did no harm in the actual case. However, under the court's apparent reading of the rule, that provision might prohibit an amendment changing defendants before relation back even becomes relevant under state law—*i.e.*, prior to the running of the statute of limitations. *See also* Aslanidis v. United States Lines, Inc., 7 F.3d 1067, 1075 (2d Cir. 1993) (reading the rule in a similar fashion).

under state law. It is difficult to see how Rule 15(c)(1)(C) could withstand a Rules Enabling Act challenge under these circumstances.[380]

A second interpretation is that the defendant to be brought into the action must receive the required notice within 120 days after the running of the statute of limitations, even if the action has been commenced long prior to that time.[381] For example, if the statute of limitations runs six months after the federal action is commenced, this reading would allow relation back if the defendant to be brought in by amendment received the required notice within 120 days after the statute of limitations runs, even though this might be, *e.g.*, ten months after commencement. This interpretation also seems off the mark, as it ignores the limiting language of Rule 4(m), which keys the 120 day time period to the filing of the complaint. Although the reference in Rule 15(c)(1)(C) to Rule 4(m) could be interpreted to exclude the reference to filing, there seems to be no reason to do so. In addition, reading the reference to Rule 4(m) to exclude filing runs the risk of unduly extending state statutes of limitations in diversity cases long beyond their expiration date, a questionable result under the Rules Enabling Act.

A third interpretation has occurred in factual contexts similar to the *Schiavone* case. In that case, the statute of limitations had not run at the time the action was commenced, but ran shortly thereafter and before the defendant to be brought in had received the notice required by the rule. However, the defendant did receive notice within the 120-day limit for serving process under Rule 4. Under the amended rule, the notice would be timely received in the *Schiavone* case, and the amendment would relate back. Some courts have interpreted the Rule 15(c)(1)(C) time limit as providing for relation back in this situation.[382] This result is justifiable, and it suggests an interpretation of the rule that will avoid the pitfalls of the other interpretations discussed above.

The ambiguities in the rule can be resolved by adhering closely to the purpose of the 1991 amendment to overrule *Schiavone*, and also by exercising a little common sense. First, relation back should never be permitted when the statute of limitations has run against the defendant to be brought in prior to the commencement of the action.[383] Under these circumstances, even if the defendant had been joined in the original complaint, the action would not have been deemed timely, and thus there should also be no relation back, even if the defendant receives the requisite notice within 120 days of commencement. Second, if the statute of limitations has not run at the time of the amendment, relation back should be deemed irrelevant, and Rule 15(c)(1)(C) should not preclude the amendment just because it is made more than 120 days after commencement.[384] As discussed above, relation back is a concept that is only relevant when a limitations period has run at

---

380. *See* section D(5)*(d) infra* (discussing Rules Enabling Act problems with Rule 15(c)).

381. *See* Colbert v. City of Philadelphia, 931 F. Supp. 389, 392 (E.D. Pa. 1996).

382. *See* Lundy v. Adamar, Inc., 34 F.3d 1173, 1181-82 (3d Cir. 1994) (holding the notice timely where the defendant to be brought in received the notice after commencement and after the statute of limitations, but within the 120-day period, but also holding the quality of the notice inadequate).

383. *See* Jermosen v. Coughlin, No. 89 Civ. 1866 (RJW), 1992 WL 131786 n.9 (S.D.N.Y. June 3, 1992) (relation back if required notice received within the statute of limitations or within 120 days after filing, whichever is longer).

384. This statement assumes that the action is commenced by the method provided for in the state statute of limitations in a diversity action, as required by the *Ragan* case, discussed in Chapter 5(F)(2), *supra*.

the time an amendment is sought. When the appropriate limitations period has not run, relation back has no pertinence. Thus, Rule 15(c)(1)(C) relation back should be limited to situations in which the statute of limitations applicable to the defendant to be brought in runs after the federal complaint has been filed but before 120 days from the filing of the complaint has expired—the *Schiavone* situation. Under these circumstances if the defendant to be brought in has received the necessary quality of notice, either before the limitation period runs, or after it runs but before 120 days from the filing of the complaint has expired, the amendment should relate back, but not otherwise.[385]

In *Krupski v. Costa Crociere S. p. A.*,[386] the Supreme Court dealt with another aspect of the notice problem. In *Krupski*, a passenger of a cruise line sued for injuries sustained while aboard a cruise ship. The passenger's complaint erroneously named "Costa Cruises" as the defendant in the action instead of the correct defendant, "Costa Crociere." An amended complaint after the statute of limitations ran corrected this error, but the district court held that the amendment did not relate back under Rule 15(c), because Costa Crociere had identified itself as the correct defendant in several filings, but the plaintiff nevertheless delayed amending the complaint for several months. In the district court's view, this meant that she had not made a "mistake" within the meaning of the Rule. The court of appeals affirmed on the grounds that the plaintiff either knew or should have known of Costa Crociere's identity and therefore it was fair to treat her as having decided to sue one party rather than another.[387]

The Supreme Court granted certiorari and reversed. The Court held that the knowledge requirement of Rule 15(c)(1)(C) depends on what the party to be added to the action knew before the limitations period ran rather than what the plaintiff knew. Under the circumstances of the case, it was clear that Costa Crociere should have realized from the original complaint that it was the proper defendant and that it was not sued simply because the plaintiff had mistaken belief about which entity was in charge of the ship.[388]

(v) Mistake and Knowledge Requirements

Rule 15(c)(1)(C) permits an amendment changing a party or the naming of a party only when the party to be brought in "knew or should have known that the action would have been brought against it, but for a mistake concerning the proper party's identity."[389] This language contains at least two requirements. First, it requires that the plaintiff have made a "mistake." Second, it requires that the party to be added know that the party would have been sued in the absence of the mistake.

---

385. Obviously, a full 120 days should not be tacked onto the limitations period when it runs after the complaint is filed, as in the second interpretation discussed in the text, *supra*. *See* Coons v. Industrial Knife Co., 620 F.3d 38 (1st Cir. 2010) (no relation back because party to be brought in did not receive any notice of the action within the required 120-day time period). *See also* Yanez v. Columbia Coastal Transp., Inc., 68 F. Supp. 2d 489 (D.N.J. 1999) (discussing the various interpretations in the decided cases).

386. 560 U.S. __, 130 S. Ct. 2485, 177 L. Ed. 2d 48 (2010).

387. *Id.* at __, 130 S. Ct. at 2489-92, 177 L. Ed. 2d at 53-56.

388. *Id.* at __, 130 S. Ct. at 2490, 2493, 177 L. Ed. 2d at 53, 57.

389. FED. R. CIV. P. 15(c)(1)(C)(ii).

Many courts have read this language literally and prohibited relation back when the plaintiff's failure to name a defendant in the action was not based on a "mistake." Thus, when the plaintiff knew the identity of the defendant to be added, but did not join the defendant originally, courts have denied relation back on the ground that this mistake was not the kind of mistake within Rule 15(c)(3).[390] Furthermore, when the plaintiff simply lacked knowledge of the identity of certain defendants and, therefore, omitted them in the original complaint, many courts have denied relation back.[391] Sometimes, plaintiffs have attempted to deal with this lack

---

390. *See, e.g.*, Hall v. Norfolk So. Ry. Co., 469 F.3d 590 (7th Cir. 2006) (no mistake when failure to join defendant was based on lack of knowledge of identity of proper defendant); Locklear v. Bergman & Beving AB, 457 F.3d 363 (4th Cir. 2006) (no mistake where plaintiff simply lacked knowledge of the correct defendant's identity; to allow amendment would erode the distinction between misidentification and lack of knowledge that is inherent in the meaning of Rule 15(c)(3)(B), restyled as 15(c)(1)(C)(ii); also, allowing amendment would create a paradoxical result in which a plaintiff with no knowledge of the proper defendant could file a timely complaint naming any entity as defendant and then amend to add the correct defendant after the statute of limitations has run); *In re* Enterprise Mortgage Acceptance Co. Sec. Litig., 391 F.3d 401 (2d Cir. 2004) (no mistake when plaintiff chose not to name party in original complaint); Yerushalayim v. United States Dep't of Corrections, 374 F.3d 89 (2d Cir. 2004) (a plaintiff is not considered to have made a mistake if the plaintiff knew that the plaintiff was required to join individual defendants and did not do so); Garrett v. Fleming, 362 F.3d 692 (10th Cir. 2004) (prisoner's lack of knowledge regarding identities of corrections officials was not a mistake concerning the identity of a proper party and thus amendment substituting such officials for unidentified officials did not relate back); Henglein v. Colt Indus. Operating Corp. Informal Plan, 91 Fed. App'x 762 (3d Cir. 2004) (no relation back when defendant did not know, nor should it have known, that but for mistake it would have been sued by additional plaintiffs); Mishler v. Avery, 90 Fed. App'x 230 (9th Cir. 2004) (amendment adding a plaintiff did not relate back because plaintiff failed to show that the defendant would not suffer prejudice and also failed to show that defendant knew or should have known that she was a proper party for the action); Garvin v. City of Philadelphia, 354 F.3d 215 (3d Cir. 2003) (notice to added defendants may be imputed under Rule 15(c)(3), restyled as 15(c)(1)(c), if they share the same attorney or, under the "identity of interest" theory, they are so closely related to the defendant that an action against the defendant is notice to them; neither theory was satisfied here because individual police officers plaintiff sought to add were not represented by city's attorneys and their interests as employees were not sufficiently related to the interests of the city as an employer to satisfy the "identity of interest" theory); Powers v. Graff, 148 F.3d 1223 (11th Cir. 1998) (relation back not applicable under Rule 15(c)(3), restyled as 15(c)(1)(c), when plaintiff made a deliberate decision not to sue a defendant in the original complaint); Whittaker v. United Airlines, Inc., No. 94-1262, 1995 WL 309022 (10th Cir. May 18, 1995) (tactical decision not to join defendant initially is not a mistake); Cabrera v. Lawlor, 252 F.R.D. 120 (D. Conn. 2008) (no mistake when the plaintiffs had always known the defendant's identity; failure to name defendant was not a mistake, but a choice); Gardner *ex rel.* Gardner *ex rel.* Gardner v. Toyota Motor Sales, Inc., 793 F. Supp. 287 (D. Kan. 1992); *see also* Murray v. Town of Mansura, 76 Fed. App'x 547 (5th Cir. 2003) (untimely claim against defendants added to the action did not relate back because plaintiff did not demonstrate that he failed to bring claims against these defendants originally because of a mistake about their identity).

391. *See, e.g.*, Baskin v. City of Des Plaines, 138 F.3d 701 (7th Cir. 1998) (no mistake where plaintiff did not know identity of added defendant); Jacobsen v. Osborne, 133 F.3d 315 (5th Cir. 1998) (no mistake where defendant did not know identity of added defendant); Worthington v. Wilson, 8 F.3d 1253 (7th Cir. 1993); Sealey v. Fishkin, No. 96 CV 6303 (RR), 1998 WL 1021470, 1998 U.S. Dist. LEXIS 20142 (E.D.N.Y. Dec. 2, 1998) (either a mistake of fact or law will suffice, but a plaintiff's lack of knowledge of the identity of a defendant cannot constitute a mistake). *But see* Malesko v. Correctional Servs. Corp., 229 F.3d 374 (2d Cir. 2000) (no mistake when plaintiff knew additional defendants had to be joined but did not know their identities), *rev'd on other grounds*, 534 U.S. 61, 122 S. Ct. 515, 151 L. Ed. 2d 456 (2001); Shea v. Esensten, 208 F.3d 712 (8th Cir. 2000) (lack of knowledge about relationship between defendant to be brought in and other persons is not a mistake concerning identity); King v. One Unknown Fed. Correctional Officer, 201 F.3d 910 (7th Cir. 2000) (no mistake when defendant was unable to establish the identity of the proper party to sue); Barnes v. Prince George's Cnty., 214 F.R.D. 379 (D. Md. 2003) (after removal, plaintiff attempted to amend complaint to substitute officer for Doe defendant; amendment did not relate back, because plaintiff's failure to give name of offending officer in her complaint was not a "mistake" within the meaning of Rule 15(c)); Arthur v. Maersk, Inc., 434 F.3d 196 (3d Cir. 2006) (a mistake is no less a mistake when it flows from lack of knowledge as opposed to inaccurate description). *But see* Brink v. First Credit Res., 57 F. Supp. 2d 848 (D. Ariz. 1999) (mistake requirement satisfied when plaintiff did not know at time complaint was filed the names of the defendants the plaintiff later sought to add by amendment and had to obtain the names during discovery; named defendant resisted discovery of names of later-added defendants because named defendant knew they would be added to the action, and this knowledge was imputed to added defendants). *See generally* Rebecca S. Engrav, Comment, *Relation Back of Amendments Naming Previously Unnamed Defendants Under Federal Rule of Civil Procedure 15(c)*, 89 CALIF. L. REV. 1549 (2001) (noting that the "mistake" clause has produced inconsistent results when applied to situations in which, at the time the suit was filed, the plaintiff made no factual mistake but just did not know the identity of the correct defendant;

of knowledge by using fictitious names for the unknown defendants before the statute of limitations runs; the courts have then refused to allow the plaintiff to amend the complaint to insert the actual names after the statute has run.[392] In addition, some courts have refused to allow the plaintiff to change the capacity in which the defendant has been sued on the ground that no mistake has been made.[393]

These applications of the "mistake" language may be incorrect. The language of Rule 15(c)(1)(C) seems to be aimed at assuring that the party brought in by amendment has knowledge that the party could, or should, have been sued based on a particular event to (1) protect the party from prejudice in maintaining a defense on the merits and (2) satisfy the repose policies of the statute of limitations. The "mistake" language should arguably be administered in this light. Thus, courts should allow relation back whenever the defendant to be added will not be prejudiced in maintaining a defense and it would have been unreasonable for the defendant to rely on the statute of limitations for repose. Often, this interpretation will also satisfy the second requirement of Rule 15(c)(1)(C)—the requirement that the added defendant have knowledge that the defendant would have been sued "but for" the mistake. As long as the party to be brought in is aware that the party could have been sued based on a set of events, the party's knowledge will often be sufficient to allow the preparation of a defense on the merits. Frequently, the party will also have sufficient knowledge of the probability of an action to make it unreasonable to rely on the statute of limitations for repose.[394]

Cases refusing relation back on the "no mistake" ground often seem to be based on the notion that the plaintiff has been at fault for failure to join the party originally.[395] However, if the plaintiff is somehow at fault for failing to join the

---

and arguing that the language of Rule 15(c) should be amended to correct this inconsistency and to allow relation back in such situations, provided the defendant being brought in has had notice of the suit and that it is an intended defendant).

392. *See, e.g.*, Gomez v. Randle, 680 F.3d 859 (7th Cir. 2012) (plaintiff's lack of knowledge about a defendant's identity is not a "mistake" within the meaning of the rule); Barrow v. Wethersfield Police Dep't, 74 F.3d 1366 (2d Cir. 1996), *modifying*, 66 F.3d 466 (2d Cir. 1995) (initial complaint named some John Doe defendants because plaintiff did not know the identities of all the parties; not a mistake within the rule); Bauer v. Ohio Adult Parole Auth., No. 97-3510, 1999 WL 191334, 1999 U.S. App. LEXIS 4792 (6th Cir. Mar. 18, 1999) (substitution of named defendants for John Doe defendants is an amendment changing parties and does not relate back because there was no mistake); *see also* Steven S. Sparling, *Relation Back of "John Doe" Complaints in Federal Court: What You Don't Know Can Hurt You,* 19 CARDOZO L. REV. 1235 (1997); Carol M. Rice, *Meet John Doe: It Is Time for Federal Civil Procedure to Recognize John Doe Parties*, 57 U. PITT. L. REV. 883 (1996).

393. *See, e.g.*, Lovelace v. O'Hara, 985 F.2d 847 (6th Cir. 1993) (refusing to allow relation back when the complaint was amended to assert claims against police officers in their individual rather than their official capacity). *But see* Brown v. Shaner, 172 F.3d 927 (6th Cir. 1999) (permitting relation back of an amendment suing officers in their individual capacities; unlike *Lovelace*, the initial complaint named the officers as defendants but did not specify the capacity in which they were being sued; the amended complaint did so specify; the court held that a reading of the complaint indicated that the defendants could not be sued in their official capacities which satisfied the mistake and knowledge requirements of Rule 15(c)(3)). Note that it has been held that the complaint in a § 1983 action for money damages against state officials need not explicitly allege that the defendants are being sued in their individual capacity if this fact is clear from the "course of proceedings." *See* Moore v. City of Harriman, 272 F.3d 769 (6th Cir. 2001).

394. *See, e.g.*, Jackson v. Kotter, 541 F.3d 688 (7th Cir. 2008) (permitting the plaintiff to add the United States as a defendant in a negligence claim under the Federal Tort Claim Act when the plaintiff mistakenly sued federal prison employees and the United States had received actual notice within the limitations period and was not prejudiced; "the legal mistake [the plaintiff] made (which appears to be somewhat of a common mistake . . .) is the very type of mistake Rule 15 contemplates.").

395. *See, e.g.*, Eison v. McCoy, 146 F.3d 468 (7th Cir. 1998) (the plaintiff's original civil rights complaint identified defendant police officers only by their nicknames; the amended complaint identified them by their correct names; the court held that the amendments were not mere corrections of "misnomers" that were not subject to Rule 15(c)(3), restyled as 15(c)(1)(C), but were amendments changing parties; thus, the amendment did not relate back

defendant originally, the best remedy is to deny permission to amend in the court's discretion under Rule 15(a), rather than to pervert the objectives of Rule 15(c)(1)(C).[396] When administering Rule 15(c)(1)(C), it is preferable to maintain a tight focus on the policies of the statute of limitations to assure that those policies are not undermined. This view receives some support from the Supreme Court's decision in *Krupski v. Costa Crociere S. p. A.*,[397] discussed in the preceding subsection. In *Krupski*, the focus was on the "knowledge" requirement of the rule. However, in the process of deciding that issue, the Court also commented on the "mistake" requirement. The Court stated:

> That a plaintiff knows of a party's existence does not preclude her from making a mistake with respect to that party's identity. A plaintiff may know that a prospective defendant—call him party A—exists, while erroneously believing him to have the status of party B. Similarly, a plaintiff may know generally what party A does while misunderstanding the roles that party A and party B played in the "conduct, transaction, or occurrence" giving rise to her claim. If the plaintiff sues party B instead of party A under these circumstances, she has made a "mistake concerning the proper party's identity" notwithstanding her knowledge of the existence of both parties. The only question under Rule 15(c)(1)(C)(ii), then, is whether party A knew or should have known that, absent some mistake, the action would have been brought against him.[398]

The Court's emphasis on the posture of the party to be added is consistent with the policies of the statute of limitations to enable that party to be able to make an adequate defense and enjoy the benefits of repose.[399]

Illustration 6-47. *P* sues the United States for the death of *P's* spouse in the midair collision of two aircraft. At the time the action was commenced, *P* was unaware that the aircraft owned by the United States was being piloted by an employee of *D Corp.* Therefore, *P* did not join *D Corp.* as a defendant. *D Corp.* became aware of *P's* claim when it was required to participate in an administrative proceeding brought to investigate the accident shortly after it occurred. During this administrative proceeding, it was necessary for *D Corp.* to prepare evidence to defend the conduct of *D Corp.'s* employee in piloting the aircraft. After the statute

---

because the rule only allowed amendments to relate back when there is a mistake about the identity of the proper party and the mistake is chargeable to that party).

396. *Cf.* 6A CHARLES A. WRIGHT ET AL., FEDERAL PRACTICE AND PROCEDURE: CIVIL § 1498, at 128 (3d ed. 2010).

397. 560 U.S. __, 130 S. Ct. 2485, 177 L. Ed.2d 48 (2010).

398. *Id.* at __, 130 S. Ct. at 2494, 177 L. Ed.2d at 57-58; *see also* Joseph v. Elan Motorsports Techs. Racing Corp., 638 F.3d 555 (7th Cir. 2011) (defendant to be brought in knew that plaintiff intended to sue entity that was party to contract with plaintiff, which was it).

399. *See also* Robinson v. Clipse, 602 F.3d 605 (4th Cir. 2010) (amendment changing capacity in which defendant sued from official capacity to individual capacity related back because defendant received notice within the required period and would not be prejudiced); Sanders-Burns v. City of Plano, 594 F.3d 366 (5th Cir. 2009) (amended complaint changing the capacity in which a party is being sued can relate back if the mistake and knowledge requirements are satisfied; naming of defendant in his official capacity was a mistake instead of a strategic decision and complaint gave adequate notice to defendant that plaintiff intended to obtain a judgment against him in his individual capacity).

of limitations and the 120-day period for service of process under Rule 4(m) expired, *P* moved to amend the complaint to add *D Corp.* as a defendant to the action. The court should grant *P's* motion. The amendment should relate back to the commencement of the action. *P's* "mistake" appears to be due to *P's* lack of knowledge that *D Corp.'s* employee was piloting the aircraft. Nevertheless, the real reason the amendment should be allowed is that the policies of the statute of limitations are satisfied by the quality of notice that *D Corp.* possessed concerning the events giving rise to the suit and *P's* claim. The administrative proceeding alerted *D Corp.* to the need to prepare a defense on the merits and, indeed, involved the actual preparation of such a defense. In addition, given *D Corp.'s* knowledge of the events and *P's* claim gained through the administrative proceeding, it would be unreasonable for *D Corp.* to rely on the statute of limitations for repose.[400]

Illustration 6-48. *P* sued *D-1* for the death of *P's* spouse, who was piloting an aircraft at the time that it crashed. *P's* claim was based on manufacturing defects in certain equipment made by *D-1* and used in landing the aircraft. *P* did not name *D-2*, one of the other manufacturers of the equipment, as a defendant. *D-2* was aware of the incident giving rise to *P's* suit because *D-2* conducted an investigation shortly after the crash in order to prepare a defense to another action brought by a person injured in the crash. However, *D-2* was not aware of *P's* action against *D-1*. After the statute of limitations and the 120-day period for service of process under Rule 4(m) expired, *P* moved to amend the complaint and add *D-2* as a party defendant. Whether or not there has been a "mistake" on *P's* part in failing to name *D-2* originally, the amendment should not relate back because the requirements of Rule 15(c)(1)(C) have not been fulfilled. Preparation by *D-2* to defend a claim by a party injured in the crash would not necessarily include the preparation necessary to defend a claim for the death of the pilot. Thus, *D-2's* knowledge of the event did not necessarily provide *D-2* with the ability to maintain a defense on the merits. Furthermore, knowledge that a party injured in the crash had decided to sue *D-1* would not necessarily produce knowledge that the representative of the pilot would also choose to sue *D-2*. Thus, *D-2* could reasonably rely on the repose policies of the statute of limitations with regard to the claim by the pilot's representative.[401]

(vi) Amendments Changing Plaintiffs

Rule 15(c)(1)(C) does not specifically apply to amendments changing *plaintiffs*. Literally, the rule only applies to amendments changing the party or the naming of a party "against whom a claim is asserted." This language was added in 1966. At that time, the Advisory Committee observed that, while the rule did not

---

400. *See* Graham v. Gendex Med. X-Ray, Inc., 176 F.R.D. 288 (N.D. Ill. 1997) (fact that defendant was a party to an administrative proceeding preceding lawsuit should have alerted it to the fact that it would have been sued but for a mistake concerning the identity of the proper party); Meredith v. United Air Lines, 41 F.R.D. 34 (S.D. Cal. 1966); *see also* Nichols v. Greater S.E. Cmty. Hosp., No. Civ. A. 03-2081 (JDB), 2005 WL 975643 (D.D.C. Apr. 22, 2005) (defendant who was added by amendment after statute of limitations had run was the administrator of defendant who had been originally sued and, therefore, not only had notice of the original action, but knew itself to be the proper party); 6A CHARLES A. WRIGHT ET AL., FEDERAL PRACTICE AND PROCEDURE: CIVIL § 1498.1, at 152-53 (3d ed. 2010) (discussing *Meredith*).

401. *See* Craig v. United States, 413 F.2d 854 (9th Cir. 1969); *see also* 6A CHARLES A. WRIGHT ET AL., FEDERAL PRACTICE AND PROCEDURE: CIVIL § 1498.1, at 153-55 (3d ed. 2010) (discussing *Craig*).

literally apply to amendments changing plaintiffs, the policies articulated in Rule 15 "toward change of defendants extends by analogy to amendments changing plaintiffs."[402] Based on this comment, many courts have applied the changing parties provisions of Rule 15(c) to plaintiffs.[403] Nevertheless, as discussed below, while some amendments changing plaintiffs should clearly be allowed to relate back, relation back of other such amendments would violate the policies of the statute of limitations. A close application of the criteria of Rule 15(c)(1)(C) is necessary to assure that this does not occur.

When Rule 15(c)(1)(C) is applied "by analogy" to an amendment changing a plaintiff, caution must be exercised. There are certainly circumstances in which allowing relation back of amendments changing plaintiffs is appropriate. For example, when an action is not brought in the name of the real party in interest and an amendment is necessary to substitute the real party in interest for the originally named plaintiff, relation back is permissible. Indeed, the language of Rule 17(a) would seem to compel this result.[404] Furthermore, no discernable prejudice to the defendant or offense to the repose policies of the statute of limitations would seem to be involved in such a case. Similarly, when a plaintiff suing in an individual capacity seeks to add a claim in a representative capacity, or when a plaintiff suing in a representative capacity seeks to add a claim in an individual capacity, the amendment should be allowed to relate back for the same reasons.[405]

However, it is highly questionable whether the policies of the statute of limitations will always be satisfied when one plaintiff sues a defendant and another plaintiff seeks to be added to the action by amendment after the running of the statute of limitations.[406] A danger of prejudice to the defendant exists in such

---

402. *See* FED. R. CIV. P. 15(c) advisory committee's note to the 1966 amendment.

403. *See* 6A CHARLES A. WRIGHT ET AL., FEDERAL PRACTICE AND PROCEDURE: CIVIL § 1501 (3d ed. 2010); *see also* Jerald J. Director, Annotation, *Amendment of Pleading to Add, Substitute, or Change Capacity of, Party Plaintiff as Relating Back to Date of Original Pleading, Under Rule 15(c) of Federal Rules of Civil Procedure, So as to Avoid Bar of Limitations*, 12 A.L.R. FED. 233 (1972). *But cf.* Caprin v. Simon Transp. Servs., Inc., 99 Fed. App'x 150 (10th Cir. 2004) (plain language of Rule 15(c)(2), restyled as 15(c)(1)(B), does not address the addition of new plaintiffs with legal claims based upon the same general course of conduct asserted but arising under a different statute; no mention of Rule 15(c)(3), restyled as 15(c)(1)(C)). After the 1991 amendments to Rule 15(c), it will also be possible to rely on the provisions of Rule 15(c)(1)(A) to allow relation back of amendments changing or adding plaintiffs whenever the law that provides the statute of limitations would permit relation back. Unlike the language of Rule 15(c)(1)(C), the language of Rule 15(c)(1)(A) literally applies to all amendments and is not restricted to amendments changing parties against whom claims are asserted. The language of Rule 15(c)(1)(B) would also literally allow an amendment changing plaintiffs to relate back if the claim asserted by the plaintiff brought into the action arises from the same transaction or occurrence set forth in the original complaint. However, for the same reasons that it would be inappropriate to allow an amendment changing a defendant solely on the basis that the claim satisfied the same transaction or occurrence test, it would also be inappropriate to allow an amendment changing a plaintiff for that reason. *See* subsection *(iii)* ("Relationship Between Amended Rule 15(c)(1)(A) and (C)") *supra*.

404. *See* FED. R. CIV. P. 17(a); Advanced Magnetics, Inc. v. Bayfront Partners, Inc., 106 F.3d 11 (2d Cir. 1997) (holding an amendment substituting shareholders as the real parties in interest in an action related back under Rule 17, independently of Rule 15(c)); Scheufler v. General Host Corp., 126 F.3d. 1261 (10th Cir. 1997); Beal *ex rel.* Martinez v. City of Seattle, 134 Wash. 2d 769, 954 P.2d 237 (1998) (amendment substituting real party in interest related back under state equivalent of Rules 15(c) & 17(a)); *see also* 6A CHARLES A. WRIGHT ET AL., FEDERAL PRACTICE AND PROCEDURE: CIVIL § 1501, at 222 (3d ed. 2010).

405. *See* 6A CHARLES A. WRIGHT ET AL., FEDERAL PRACTICE AND PROCEDURE: CIVIL § 1501, at 222-26 (3d ed. 2010) and authorities there cited.

406. *See* Fleck v. Cablevision VII, Inc., 807 F. Supp. 824 (D.D.C. 1992); Dayton Monetary Assocs. v. Donaldson, Lufkin, & Jenrette Sec. Corp., No. 91 Civ. 2050 (LLS), 1992 WL 204374, 1992 U.S. Dist. LEXIS 12283 (S.D.N.Y. Aug. 11, 1992); *see also* Cliff v. Payco Gen. Am. Credits, Inc., 363 F.3d 1113 (11th Cir. 2004) (amended class complaint attempting to assert claims on behalf of class members outside state did not relate back because, when statute of limitations had run, defendant had been put on notice only of its obligation to defend itself

circumstances because the defendant may not be able to maintain an adequate defense on the merits against the new plaintiff if the defendant has not been alerted to the claim and preserved evidence necessary to defend against it. Even if this situation has not occurred, however, allowing amendments adding plaintiffs in these circumstances risks undermining the repose policies supporting the statute of limitations. As *Illustration 6-48*, above, indicates, a defendant sued by one plaintiff should not, without more, necessarily be expected to realize that another plaintiff will also choose to sue the defendant based on the same incident after the statute of limitations has run. Furthermore, if the courts rigidly enforce the requirement that there be a "mistake" by the plaintiff who did not sue within the limitations period, amendments adding plaintiffs after the statute of limitations will seldom be allowed.[407]

Illustration 6-49. *P-1*, *D*, and *P-2* are involved in a three car collision. Presuit investigation by all three parties indicates that *D* and *P-2* were driving in excess of the speed limit. *P-1* sues *D* for personal injuries resulting from the automobile accident. After the statute of limitations and the 120-day period for service of process under Rule 4(m) expire, *P-1* moves to amend the complaint to add *P-2* as a plaintiff. The amendment should not relate back to avoid the bar of the statute of limitations. Preparation to defend an action by *P-1* would not necessarily lead *D* to prepare for an action by *P-2*. Therefore, "by analogy" to amendments changing parties against whom claims are asserted under Rule 15(c)(3), the amendment should not relate back because the quality of notice possessed by *D* would not prevent prejudice in maintaining a defense on the merits against *P-2's* claim. Furthermore, knowledge of the event and of the action by *P-1* would not necessarily alert *D* that *P-2* also intends to sue. "By analogy" to amendments adding defendants under Rule 15(c)(1)(C), *D* did not know, nor should *D* have known, that *P-2* would have sued *D* "but for a mistake" in the identity of the proper party. Therefore, *D* should reasonably be able to rely on the repose policies of the statute of limitations. Furthermore, there does not appear to have been a "mistake" in the identity of the proper party in the first place. *P-2* simply failed to bring the action in a timely fashion.[408]

---

against claims of in-state class members); Henglein v. Colt Indus. Operating Corp. Informal Plan, 91 Fed. App'x 762 (3d Cir. 2004) (no relation back when defendant did not know, nor should it have known, that but for mistake it would have been sued by additional plaintiffs).

407. *See* Asher v. Unarco Material Handling, Inc., 596 F.3d 313 (6th Cir. 2010) (as a matter of first impression, amendment of a pleading adding otherwise untimely plaintiffs did not relate back); Dayton Monetary Assocs. v. Donaldson, Lufkin, Jenrette Sec. Corp., No. 91 Civ. 2050 (LLS), 1992 WL 204374, 1992 U.S. Dist. LEXIS 12283 (S.D.N.Y. Aug. 11, 1992); *cf.* United States v. Baylor Univ. Med. Ctr., 469 F.3d 263 (2d Cir. 2006) (complaint in intervention does not relate back under Rule 15(c)(2) to avoid bar of statute of limitations).

408. It should be added that there is a more fundamental argument against allowing amendments adding plaintiffs. The drafters of Rule 15 did not textually provide for such amendments except in Rule 15(c)(1). As noted in the text, *supra*, the Advisory Committee's notes to the 1966 amendments suggested that such amendment would be appropriate "by analogy" to amendments changing defendants, which were textually provided for. It is highly questionable whether the Advisory Committee should be able to bring into existence a rule through its notes that it is unwilling to write into textual form. Scrutiny of such extra-textual rules under the process prescribed by the Rules Enabling Act may not be the same as scrutiny of the text of rule amendments. Moreover, if the Supreme Court and Congress find the text of an amendment acceptable, those institutions may not, given the time-consuming nature of the amendment process, be willing to send a rule back to the Advisory Committee for revision of its notes. Finally, to the extent that the Supreme Court adopts a "plain language" interpretation of the civil rules, such textual notes may be ineffective in any event. *See, e.g.*, Delta Air Lines v. August, 450 U.S. 346, 101 S. Ct. 1146, 67 L. Ed. 2d 287 (1981). *But see* Karen N. Moore, *The Supreme Court's Role in Interpreting the Federal*

(d) Rules Enabling Act Issues with Rule 15(c)

The application of Rule 15(c)(1)(A) or (B) in the face of conflicting state relations back law can sometimes raise problems of rule validity under the Rules Enabling Act.[409] As yet, the Supreme Court has never addressed these problems.[410] However, the 1991 amendments to Rule 15(c) have solved half the validity problems that previously existed. Formerly, a conflict between Rule 15(c) and state relations back doctrine could occur in two situations: (1) Rule 15(c) might deny relation back when it was permitted by state law; or (2) Rule 15(c) might permit relation back when it was denied by state law. Under the 1991 amendments, Rule 15(c)(1)(A) now provides for relation back whenever it is permitted by the law that furnishes the statute of limitations. Thus, there should no longer be a conflict between Rule 15(c) and state relations back law when state law permits relation back.

When state law denies relation back, however, relation back in some cases may still be permitted under Rules 15(c)(1)(B) and (C). In such circumstances, the question is whether a Federal Rule of Civil Procedure can validly allow an action to continue that would be barred by the state relations back doctrine. Under the *Burlington Northern* decision, discussed in Chapter 5,[411] if Rule 15(c) applies,[412] it can validly operate in this way only if it has no more than an incidental impact on state substantive rights and it is reasonably necessary to the operation of the uniform scheme of procedure that it was the purpose of Congress to establish under the Rules Enabling Act. Assuming that the *Burlington Northern* test has survived the Supreme Court's most recent decision under the Rules Enabling Act in the *Shady Grove* case (see below), the validity of relation back under Rule 15(c) in the face of conflicting state law will have to satisfy that test.

The Supreme Court has not indicated how to determine whether a Federal Rule impacts on a state "substantive right." However, in the case of Rule 15(c), there are at least two possible ways in which an impact on substantive rights might occur. First, a state statute of limitations might be supported by policies of repose designed to allow parties to order their affairs free from the fear that claims arising from long past events may be asserted against them. Repose policies are universally viewed as substantive and usually support state statutes of limitations, perhaps

---

Rules of Civil Procedure, 44 HAST. L.J. 1039 (1993) (arguing against the plain meaning rule).

409. For a discussion of problems of rule validity under the Rules Enabling Act, 28 U.S.C. § 2072, see Chapter 5(F) ("The Evolution of the *Erie* Doctrine: Conflicts Between State Laws and Federal Rules of Civil Procedure") *supra*.

410. *See* CHARLES A. WRIGHT & MARY KAY KANE, THE LAW OF FEDERAL COURTS § 56, at 386 (6th ed. 2002); Harold S. Lewis, Jr., *The Excessive History of Federal Rule 15(c) and its Lessons for Civil Rules Revision*, 85 MICH. L. REV. 1507, 1554 (1987).

411. *See* Chapter 5(F)(4) ("The *Burlington Northern* Decision: Establishing Content for the Substantive Rights Restriction") *supra*.

412. *See* United States *ex rel.* Conner v. Salina Reg. Health Ctr., Inc., 543 F.3d 1211 (10th Cir. 2008) (finding no "direct conflict" between Rule 15 governing relation back of pleadings and the Kansas service requirement requiring service of an amended complaint within 90 days of the original timely complaint and thus creating an actual notice requirement; Kansas itself had a rule that was essentially identical to Rule 15(c) and had applied that "rule in conjunction with, not instead of," the Kansas service requirement).

among other policies.[413] Therefore, if Rule 15(c) permits relation back when a state statute supported by repose policies would not, the rule would arguably conflict with a state substantive right. Second, Rule 15(c) might conflict with a state substantive right by allowing an action to continue that would be precluded by state law—*i.e.*, by producing a different outcome on the ultimate merits of the case than would state law. It seems clear that Rule 15(c) will at least impact state substantive rights in the latter way, and it may, in a given case, impact state substantive rights in both ways. Therefore, the question remains whether Rule 15(c) will impact on state substantive rights more than "incidentally" within the meaning of *Burlington Northern*.

The Supreme Court has also not made it clear how to evaluate when the impact of a Federal Rule on substantive rights is "incidental." One view might be that an impact is more than incidental whenever a Federal Rule (1) entirely forecloses an action that would be permitted under state law or (2) permits an action that would entirely be foreclosed under state law. If this view is correct, Rule 15(c) could not validly allow an action to continue that would be barred by state relations back doctrine. Alternatively, the Court might take the view that a Federal Rule has only an incidental impact on state substantive rights (1) if the Federal Rule does not conflict with state law in a significant number of cases or (2) if the differences between the operation of the Federal Rule and state law result in only a short extension of the state limitations period. If one of these views is taken, the first part of the *Burlington Northern* test will be satisfied by allowing relation back under Rule 15(c) when state law does not.

Under the second part of the *Burlington Northern* test, Federal Rule 15(c) must be reasonably necessary to the uniform scheme of procedure that it was the purpose of Congress to establish under the Rules Enabling Act. Providing a more liberal relation back doctrine under Rule 15(c) than would be provided by state law is important to the uniform operation of the Federal Rules of Civil Procedure. The liberal notice pleading philosophy of the Federal Rules requires an amendment policy of equivalent liberality. Otherwise, a party pleading a claim for relief would be required to observe all the pleading niceties that might exist under state law in order to avoid the operation of a harsh state amendment policy. Thus, if Rule 15(c) passes the first part of the *Burlington Northern* test, it will easily pass the second.

Illustration 6-50. *P*, a citizen of State *X*, sues *D*, a citizen of State *Y*, in a U.S. District Court for State *Y*. *P* seeks to recover $100,000 for personal injuries received by *P* from a product manufactured by *D*. *P's* original complaint asserts a claim based on strict liability. After the State *Y* statute of limitations expires, *P* moves to amend the complaint to change the claim for relief to a claim based on *D's* negligence in manufacturing the product. Under the law of State *Y*, such an amendment would not be permitted and, therefore, would not relate back because

---

413. *See, e.g.*, *In re* Sharps Run Assocs., 157 B.R. 766, 775 (D.N.J. 1993); John Hart Ely, *The Irrepressible Myth of* Erie, 87 HARV. L. REV. 693, 726 (1974); RESTATEMENT (SECOND) OF CONFLICT OF LAWS § 142 cmt f. (Supp. 1989). "The periods chosen for different kinds of claims reflect judgments as to the relative difficulties of litigation when time has passed, the importance of repose, and the value of enforcing a particular type of right." ALI COMPLEX LITIGATION: STATUTORY RECOMMENDATIONS AND ANALYSIS WITH REPORTER'S STUDY § 6.04 cmt. a, at 384 (1994).

it changes the cause of action.[414] Under Rule 15(c)(1)(B), the amendment would relate back because the claim in the amended complaint arises from the same transaction or occurrence as the claim in the original complaint. It is unclear whether the Supreme Court would take the view that Rule 15(c)(1)(B) has more than an incidental impact on state substantive rights in these circumstances. If the rule's impact on substantive rights *is* more than incidental, it is invalid under the *Burlington Northern* test. However, if the impact of the rule on state substantive rights is no more than incidental, the rule is reasonably necessary to the uniform operation of the Federal Rules of Civil Procedure. *P's* original complaint gave *D* adequate notice that *P* was claiming damages for injuries received from a product manufactured by *D*. If, during discovery or otherwise, *P* learns of a basis for a claim based on an additional or different theory, the liberal amendment policies of Rule 15(a) allow *P* to amend the complaint to assert claims based on the theory. Thus, the liberal pleading, discovery, and amendment policies of the Federal Rules would be undermined if *P's* amendment could not relate back to the date of the original complaint.

As discussed in conjunction with the *Shady Grove* decision in Chapter 5, the *Burlington Northern* test is still technically good law, because Justice Scalia's opinion in *Shady Grove* reverting to the more liberal standard in the *Sibbach* case was not for a majority of the court.[415] Therefore, until a majority of the Court speaks more clearly on the question, the above analysis should be performed in determining the validity of relation back under Rule 15(c). However, the validity of Rule 15(c) has never been questioned by the lower federal courts, and even prior to *Shady*

---

414. Chapter 5(F) ("The Evolution of the *Erie* Doctrine: Conflicts Between State Laws and Federal Rules of Civil Procedure"), *supra*, discusses the conflict-avoidance policy that must be applied when a potential conflict between a Federal Rule of Civil Procedure and state law is present in a case. Under that process, the first step is to determine whether the Federal Rule in question is broad enough to apply to the issue before the court. It might be possible to interpret Rule 15(c) as inapplicable to relation back when state law provides an inconsistent rule, just as Rule 3 has been held not to provide for commencement for purposes of state statutes of limitations. *See* Harold S. Lewis, Jr., *The Excessive History of Federal Rule 15(c) and its Lessons for Civil Rules Revision*, 85 MICH. L. REV. 1507, 1554 (1987). However, given the presence of Rule 15(c)(1)(A) in the rule after 1991, this is more difficult to do than it formerly would have been. If the drafters of Rule 15(c) did not wish for relation back when it would not be permitted by the law providing the statute of limitations, they could have included a provision that so stated, just as they did in Rule 15(c)(1) when they wanted to codify the opposite policy. Nevertheless, Chapter 5(F) suggested that it is legitimate in the conflict-avoidance process also to ask whether the state rule is one that the state would want applied outside its court system. Although the Supreme Court's existing decisions do not authorize such a step at this time, it is arguably proper whenever a Federal Rule of Civil Procedure has been found applicable to a case and potentially conflicts with state law. *See* Chapter 5(F)(3) ("The *Hanna* Decision: Return to the *Sibbach* Test") *supra*. In this illustration, it may be possible to interpret the state rule as inapplicable. The rule appears to be a typical code state relation back rule, which is based on an interpretation of the strict code pleading and amendment provisions disallowing amendments that change the cause of action. *See* section C(5) ("Amendments and Supplemental Pleadings") *supra*. It may well be that the state has no interest in applying its relation back rule in a system of procedure governed by a more liberal pleading and amendment policy.

In Pacific Employers Insurance Co. v. Sav-a-Lot, 291 F.3d 392 (6th Cir. 2002), an action was commenced in Kentucky state court, and the plaintiff amended the complaint to correct a mistake in the defendant originally sued. The Kentucky state court repeatedly refused to dismiss this claim as time-barred against the substituted defendant. However, during discovery, it was revealed that the amount-in-controversy requirement for diversity jurisdiction was satisfied, and the defendant removed the action. After further discovery, the U.S. District Court to which the action had been removed dismissed the action as time-barred under the Kentucky rule. On appeal, the Sixth Circuit Court of Appeals affirmed, holding that the Kentucky rule applied because the amendment was made before removal to the federal court, and holding also that the Kentucky rule clearly precluded relation back. The court also held that the doctrines of law of the case, claim preclusion, and issue preclusion did not require the U.S. District Court to give effect to the Kentucky state trial court's rulings on the relation back issue.

415. Chapter 5(E)(3), *supra*, discussing the impact of *Shady Grove* on the Rules Enabling Act test.

Grove, lower federal court decisions have validated relation back under Rule 15(c) in the face of conflicting state law without reference to *Burlington Northern*.[416]

6. Supplemental Pleadings

Upon a proper motion, Federal Rule 15(d) permits "supplemental pleadings." As under most codes, such pleadings must be directed toward transactions, occurrences, or events that have happened *after* the date of the pleading sought to be supplemented.[417] Unlike the codes, the Federal Rules also permit supplemental pleadings to cure defects such as prematurity of the claim. However, an amendment, not a supplemental complaint, should be used to raise matters that the pleader was ignorant of at the time of pleading.[418]

Illustration 6-51. Examples of proper matters for supplemental pleading include (1) new defenses, *e.g.*, res judicata arising after commencement of the action, or (2) new damages, *e.g.*, additional breaches of a contract occurring after commencement. An example of a matter that is appropriate for an amended pleading, but not a supplemental pleading, is a mature claim omitted from the plaintiff's complaint.

SECTION E. VERIFICATION

Verification is a statement under oath that a pleading is true.[419] The Field Code introduced the requirement that the complaint, answer, and reply must be *verified* in most circumstances.[420] A year later, the Field Code was amended to give the plaintiff the option of verifying and to give any party the authority, by verifying a pleading, to force the verification of subsequent pleadings subject to certain exceptions.[421] Other code states adopted various versions of these two New York

---

416. *See* Morel v. DiamlerChrysler, AG, 565 F.3d 20 (1st Cir. 2009) (validating Rule 15(c) without any reference to *Burlington Northern*).

417. *See* FED. R. CIV. P. 15(d). If the defendant engages in new actionable conduct after the lawsuit has been commenced, however, the plaintiff is not obligated to add such conduct to the action by a supplemental pleading to prevent the new conduct from being barred by the doctrine of claim preclusion even though the new actionable conduct is part of the same transaction or occurrence as the conduct for which the original action was brought. *See* SEC v. First Jersey Sec., Inc., 101 F.3d 1450 (2d Cir. 1996); *see also* Chapter 13(B) ("Claim Preclusion") *infra*. *See generally* Annotation, *Construction and Application of Rule 15(d) of Federal Rules of Civil Procedure Providing for Allowance of Supplemental Pleadings Setting Forth Transactions, Occurrences, or Events Subsequent to Original Pleadings*, 28 A.L.R. FED. 129 (1976).

418. *See* 6A CHARLES A. WRIGHT ET AL., FEDERAL PRACTICE AND PROCEDURE: CIVIL § 1504 (3d ed. 2010).

419. *See In re* Doe, 91 Haw. 166, 981 P.2d 723 (Ct. App. 1999) (holding a requirement that a petition be verified satisfied by a declaration under penalty of perjury that the matters therein were "true" and "correct" based on the swearer's "knowledge, information and belief").

420. Act of Apr. 12, 1848, ch. 379, § 133, 1848 N.Y. Laws 497, 523. The pleadings also had to be signed by the attorney.

421. Act of Apr. 11, 1849, ch. 438, § 157, 1849 N.Y. Laws 613, 648. Verification of a pleading can also have other effects, depending on the state in question. *See In re* Marriage of O'Brien, 247 Ill. App. 3d 745, 617 N.E.2d 873 (1993) (verified pleading remains part of the record upon the filing of an amended pleading, and any admissions in the verified pleading which were not the product of mistake or inadvertence remain binding after amendment; however, verified statements in a pleading in one case are ordinary statements against interest when used in another case and may be controverted).

Code provisions. When verification is required, unverified pleadings may be treated as a nullity.[422]

In federal practice, verification is the exception rather than the rule. Federal Rule 11 provides that verification by a party is not required except when a rule or statute requires it.[423] Federal Rules that require verification are Rule 23.1 (derivative actions), Rule 27(a) (petitions to perpetuate testimony before an action is commenced), Rule 65 (ex parte request for a temporary restraining order), and Rule 66 (appointment of receivers).[424]

SECTION F. GOOD FAITH PLEADING

Federal Rule 11 is the primary source of sanctions for abuses of the litigation process in federal court and states operating under the Federal Rules of Civil Procedure. Defects in the operation of Rule 11 before 1983 produced certain amendments designed to deter and sanction abuses of the litigation process more effectively.[425] Additional dissatisfaction with the rule after 1983 produced further amendments in 1993. The 1983 and 1993 amendments will be discussed separately below. One should keep in mind that the 1993 amendments to Rule 11 do not change all the results that occurred under the 1983 version of the rule. Therefore, even in the federal courts, some of the pre-1993 decisions interpreting the rule remain good authority.

---

422. CHARLES E. CLARK, HANDBOOK OF THE LAW OF CODE PLEADING § 36, at 216-20 (2d ed. 1947). A typical verification states that "I am the plaintiff in the above-entitled action; I have read the foregoing Complaint and know the contents thereof; the same is true to my own knowledge, except as to those matters which are therein stated upon my information or belief, and as to those matters, I believe them to be true." It is signed by the party and then acknowledged, signed, and sealed by a notary public. In many states, a signed and dated declaration (for example, "I declare under penalty of perjury that the foregoing is true and correct.") may be used in lieu of a sworn affidavit. When a complaint has been verified, a number of states prohibit a general denial. *Id.* § 92, at 582-83.

423. FED. R. CIV. P. 11(a).

424. *See* FED. R. CIV. P. 23.1, 27(a), (b), 65 & 66 (by inference). Federal statutes that require verification include 28 U.S.C. § 1734(b) (replacement of lost or destroyed court records), 28 U.S.C. § 1915 (proceedings in forma pauperis), and 28 U.S.C. § 1924 (bill of costs); *see also* 28 U.S.C. § 1746 (form of the verification).

425. The amendments were circulated to the bench and bar in June 1981 by the Committee on Rules of Practice and Procedure of the Judicial Conference of the United States. *See* Preliminary Draft of Proposed Amendments to the Federal Rules of Civil Procedure, 90 F.R.D. 451, 462 (1981). After public hearings and comments from the legal profession, Rule 11 was modified. *See* 97 F.R.D. at 190-94 (explaining the modifications). The Supreme Court then promulgated the amendments under the Rules Enabling Act, 28 U.S.C. § 2072 on April 28, 1983. The amendments became effective on August 1, 1983. The literature on the rule as amended in 1983 is voluminous. In addition to commentary cited in conjunction with textual material presented below, some of the most important literature is as follows: Roger M. Baron, *Stepping on Board the Rule 11 Bandwagon*, 35 CLEV. ST. L. REV. 249 (1987); Richard H. Battey & John S. Dorsey, *Rule 11 Sanctions: Some Current Observations*, 33 S. DAK. L. REV. 207 (1988); Adam H. Bloomenstein, *Developing Standards for the Imposition of Sanctions Under Rule 11 of the Federal Rules of Civil Procedure*, 21 AKRON L. REV. 289 (1988); Stephen B. Burbank, *The Report of the Third Circuit Task Force on Federal Rule of Civil Procedure 11: An Update*, 19 SETON HALL L. REV. 511 (1989); Mark S. Cady, *Curbing Litigation Abuse and Misuse: A Judicial Approach*, 36 DRAKE L. REV. 483 (1986-87); John M. Johnson & G. Edward Cassady III, *Frivolous Lawsuits and Defensive Responses to Them—What Relief is Available*, 36 ALA. L. REV. 927 (1985); William W. Schwarzer, *Rule 11 Revisited*, 101 HARV. L. REV. 1013 (1988); Georgene M. Vairo, *Rule 11: A Critical Analysis*, 118 F.R.D. 189 (1988); Kim M. Rubin, Note, *Has a "Kafkaesque Dream" Come True? Federal Rule of Civil Procedure 11: Time for Another Amendment*, 67 B.U. L. REV. 1019 (1987); Alan E. Untereiner, Note, *A Uniform Approach to Rule 11 Sanctions*, 97 YALE L.J. 901 (1988); Kathleen M. Dorr, Annotation, *Comment Note—General Principles Regarding Imposition of Sanctions Under Rule 11, Federal Rules of Civil Procedure*, 95 A.L.R. FED. 107 (1989). Additional literature, including studies of the operation of Rule 11, are cited and discussed in 5A CHARLES A. WRIGHT & ARTHUR R. MILLER, FEDERAL PRACTICE AND PROCEDURE: CIVIL § 1332 (3d ed. 2004).

1. Original Rule 11

In form, original Rule 11 applied when an attorney or party signed a "pleading." It required that all pleadings be signed by an attorney representing a party or, in the case of *pro se* litigants, by the party acting *pro se*. It also provided that the signature of an attorney constituted a certificate that the attorney had read the pleading, that there was good ground to support it to the best of the attorney's knowledge, information, and belief and that it was not interposed for delay. The rule further provided if the pleading was not signed, or was signed with the intent to defeat the purposes of the rule, the pleading could be stricken as a sham or false. If an attorney "willfully" violated the rule, the attorney could be subjected to "appropriate" disciplinary action. Similar action was possible if "scandalous" or "indecent" matter were inserted in a pleading. The rule then provided for sanctions when pleadings, motions, or other papers were not signed, or when they were signed in violation of the standards imposed by the rule.

2. The 1983 Amendments to Rule 11

One problem with original Rule 11 was that its terms applied only to pleadings, leading to confusion about the applicability of the rule to motions and other papers.[426] The 1983 amendments explicitly extended the certification requirement to motions and other papers, as well as to pleadings.[427]

Another problem with original Rule 11 was that the terms of the rule made the certification requirement applicable only to attorneys, not to parties unrepresented by attorneys. The 1983 amendments required parties not represented by an attorney to sign all pleadings, motions, and other papers. This requirement made the certification requirements of the rule explicitly applicable to unrepresented parties.[428]

With regard to the certification aspect of original Rule 11, the "good ground to support" standard was unclear—for example, was there a duty to investigate the facts and the law before signing a pleading and, if so, what quality of investigation

---

426. *Cf.* 5A CHARLES A. WRIGHT & ARTHUR R. MILLER, FEDERAL PRACTICE AND PROCEDURE: CIVIL § 1331, at 472 (3d ed. 2004).

427. *See* FED. R. CIV. P. 11, 97 F.R.D. at 196 (1983) (containing 1983 amendments and original text of rule). Technically, the standards of Rule 11 were always applicable to motions and other papers. FED. R. CIV. P. 7(b)(2) provided, prior to 1983, that the rules applicable to captions, signing, and other matters of the form of pleadings applied to all motions and other papers provided for by the rules. This provision made the standards of Rule 11 applicable to motions and other papers, such as discovery papers. *See* FED. R. CIV. P. 7 advisory committee's note to the 1983 amendment. However, because Rule 11 itself only mentioned pleadings, some confusion arose about the propriety of sanctions in cases of improper motion practice. To eliminate this confusion, Rule 11 was amended to apply explicitly to motions and other papers. In addition, Rule 7(b) was amended to add the following subsection (3): "All motions shall be signed in accordance with Rule 11." *See id.* The reference to "other papers" in amended Rule 11 literally included discovery papers, but the certification requirements applicable to discovery papers are governed by a new Federal Rule 26(g), also added in 1983. *See* FED. R. CIV. P. 11 & 26(g) advisory committee's note to the 1983 amendment.

428. *See* 5A CHARLES A. WRIGHT & ARTHUR R. MILLER, FEDERAL PRACTICE AND PROCEDURE: CIVIL § 1331, at 471-73 (3d ed. 2004). However, in determining whether an unrepresented party has violated the certification standard, the court has discretion to take account of the problems that may confront an unrepresented subscribing party. *See* FED. R. CIV. P. 11 advisory committee's note to the 1983 amendment.

was required?[429] Under the 1983 amendments, the signature of an attorney or party constituted a certificate that to the best of the signer's "knowledge, information, and belief formed after reasonable inquiry" the pleading, motion, or other paper "is well grounded in fact and is warranted by existing law or a good faith argument for the extension, modification, or reversal of existing law" and that the pleading, motion, or other paper "is not interposed for any improper purpose, such as to harass or to cause unnecessary delay or needless increase in the cost of litigation."[430] This new standard made it clear that the signing party had an affirmative duty to investigate the facts and the law before filing a pleading, motion, or other paper. "The standard is one of reasonableness under the circumstances."[431]

In addition to imposing a reasonable duty of investigation upon a person signing a litigation paper, the 1983 amendments provided that a person's signature constituted a certificate that the paper was not interposed for any improper purpose. The rule then gave three examples of such a purpose: delay (which was included in the original Rule 11), harassment, and needless increase in the cost of litigation. The wording of the rule was open-ended. Thus, the courts had the power to identify improper purposes other than the specific examples.

The 1983 amendments removed the provision in original Rule 11 that a pleading might be stricken as sham or false if the pleading was not signed, or was signed with the intent to defeat the purposes of the rule. The provision was removed because it was rarely used and the decisions under the provision tended to confuse the issue of attorney honesty with the merits of the action. Thus, it was felt that the issues that arose under the old provision could better be dealt with under other rules, such as the general rules governing pleading (Rule 8) and summary judgment (Rule 56).[432] The 1983 amendments provided that if a litigation paper was not signed, it should be stricken unless signed promptly after the omission was called to the attention of the person filing the paper.

The reference in original Rule 11 to scandalous and indecent matter was also removed from the amended rule because the reference was unnecessary. Rule 12(f) already provided for a motion to strike scandalous or indecent matter. However, as the Advisory Committee's note to the amended rule indicated, the presence of scandalous or indecent matter in a litigation paper is a strong indication that it has been interposed for an improper purpose.[433]

---

429. The original rule simply required that an attorney not act in bad faith when signing a pleading. This old "bad faith" standard did not necessarily involve any affirmative duty of investigation. *See* Nemeroff v. Abelson, 620 F.2d 339 (2d Cir. 1980).

430. *See* FED. R. CIV. P. 11 advisory committee's note to the 1983 amendment.

431. However, although the new standard could be triggered by a greater range of circumstances than the old one, the Advisory Committee's note to the amended rule made it clear that the standard was not designed "to chill an attorney's enthusiasm in pursuing factual or legal theories."

> The court is expected to avoid using the wisdom of hindsight and should test the signer's conduct by inquiring what was reasonable to believe at the time the pleading, motion, or other paper was submitted. Thus, what constitutes a reasonable inquiry may depend on such factors as how much time for investigation was available to the signer; whether he had to rely on a client for information as to the facts underlying the pleading, motion, or other paper; whether the pleading, motion, or other paper was based on a plausible view of the law; or whether he depended on forwarding counsel or another member of the bar.

See FED. R. CIV. P. 11 advisory committee's note to the 1983 amendment.

432. *See id.*

433. *See id.*

One of the most important revisions to Rule 11 in 1983 was the amendment setting out the sanctions that could be imposed on an attorney or party for violating the rule. The amendment provided that if a litigation paper had been signed in violation of the rule, the court, upon motion or its own initiative, had to impose upon the person who signed it, a represented party, or both, an appropriate sanction. That sanction could include an order to pay to the opposing party the reasonable expenses incurred resulting from the filing of the paper, including a reasonable attorney's fee. The 1983 amendments thus required the imposition of a sanction if the rule were violated, though the nature of the sanction, as well as on whom it would be imposed, was left to the discretion of the court. Although the reference to the willfulness of an attorney's conduct was removed from the amended rule, the court could still take willfulness into account in determining upon whom the sanction should be imposed and how severe it should be.[434] The specific mention of the costs and fees sanction explicitly encouraged the use of this sanction for violations of the rule, although other sanctions also remained proper.[435] The time when sanctions should be imposed was left to the discretion of the district judge, but "it is anticipated that in the case of pleadings the sanctions issue under Rule 11 normally will be determined at the end of the litigation, and in the case of motions at the time when the motion is decided or shortly thereafter."[436] The procedure utilized in imposing sanctions was also left to the discretion of the trial judge. Obviously, the procedure utilized had to comport with due process, but the particular format to be followed depended upon the circumstances of the particular case.[437] The judge's participation in the proceedings would often provide full knowledge of the relevant facts "and little further inquiry [would] be necessary."[438]

Under the rule as amended in 1983, fewer decisions imposed sanctions for failure to make a reasonable factual investigation than for failure to investigate the applicable law. The reasons for this result are several. When the Federal Rules were promulgated and became effective in 1938, one of their primary purposes was to institute a system of simplified "notice pleading."[439] The idea was, partly, that the pleading stage of the litigation should be deemphasized as a means of exchanging factual information between the parties about the details of the case because discovery could do this job much more efficiently and effectively. One aspect of this idea, as applied to plaintiffs, was that there would be situations in which the plaintiff and the plaintiff's attorney would have a good faith belief that a valid claim for relief existed based on the facts in their possession before the commencement of the litigation. However, they could not be certain because essential facts necessary to determine the validity of the claim would be in the possession of the defendant. Therefore, the Federal Rules allowed plaintiffs to institute actions and proceed to the discovery stage of the litigation to develop the details of their claims

---

434. *See id.*

435. *See* 5A CHARLES A. WRIGHT & ARTHUR R. MILLER, FEDERAL PRACTICE AND PROCEDURE: CIVIL § 1336.1 (3d ed. 2004).

436. *See* FED. R. CIV. P. 11 advisory committee's note to the 1983 amendment.

437. *See generally* Kathleen M. Dorr, Annotation, *Comment Note—Procedural Requirements for Imposition of Sanction Under Rule 11, Federal Rules of Civil Procedure*, 100 A.L.R. FED. 556 (1990).

438. *See* FED. R. CIV. P. 11 advisory committee's note to the 1983 amendment.

439. *See* section D(2) ("The Federal Rules Complaint") *supra*.

as long as they are doing the best that they can under the circumstances to investigate the facts of the claim.

Nothing in the 1983 amendments to Rule 11 altered this notice pleading philosophy of the Federal Rules. Thus, the reasonable pre-filing investigation requirement of the amended rule had to be interpreted in light of the overall pleading philosophy of the Rules. Rule 11 could not realistically mandate a factual investigation that would, in all cases, require the plaintiff's attorney to confirm absolutely the existence of all the facts necessary to prove the claim before commencing the action. At least in situations in which critical information was in the exclusive possession of the defendant, the overall philosophy of the Federal Rules dictated that no sanctions be imposed for merely filing a complaint that turned out to be factually unmeritorious. In addition, other situations exist in which an attorney who signs a pleading should not be sanctioned for filing a factually unmeritorious pleading. The most common situation arises when the attorney must rely on information provided by the attorney's client that turns out to be erroneous.[440]

Nevertheless, courts can and did impose sanctions for failure to make the reasonable factual investigation required by Rule 11.

Illustration 6-52. Sanctions were approved for failure to make a factual investigation that would have indicated that the action was barred by the statute of limitations,[441] for failure to inquire into facts that would have indicated that the plaintiffs lacked standing for much of the relief that they requested in the action,[442] and for failure to make a reasonable investigation into the facts or the law supporting the exercise of personal jurisdiction over the defendant.[443]

* * * * *

Failure to make a reasonable investigation into the applicable law violated Rule 11, and sanctions were often imposed upon an attorney representing a party for this kind of failure.

Illustration 6-53. Attorneys have been sanctioned for failing to investigate the limitations law applicable to plaintiff's claims;[444] for failing to make a "minimal effort" to discover the law on claims of bad faith, intentional infliction of mental distress, and punitive damages asserted against an insurance company;[445] for filing a frivolous motion to dismiss the plaintiff's complaint on grounds of failure to state a claim upon which relief can be granted, lack of proper jurisdictional amount in controversy, improper venue, lack of personal jurisdiction, and forum non conveniens;[446] for failing to make a proper pre-filing inquiry as to whether venue would be proper in the district in which the action was filed;[447] and for attempting to base subject-matter jurisdiction on the existence of diversity of citizenship when

---

440. *See* FED. R. CIV. P. 11 advisory committee's note to the 1983 amendment.

441. *See, e.g.*, Aetna Cas. & Sur. Co. v. Fernandez, 830 F.2d 952 (8th Cir. 1987); Van Berkel v. Fox Farm & Road Mach., 581 F. Supp. 1248 (D. Minn. 1984); Fisher v. CPC Int'l, Inc., 591 F. Supp. 228 (W.D. Mo. 1984).

442. *See* Baker v. Citizens State Bank, 661 F. Supp. 1196 (D. Minn. 1987).

443. *See* Hasty v. PACCAR, Inc., 583 F. Supp. 1577 (E.D. Mo. 1984).

444. *See* Baker v. Citizens State Bank, 661 F. Supp. 1196 (D. Minn. 1987).

445. *See* Glenn v. Farmers & Merchants Ins. Co., 649 F. Supp. 1447 (W.D. Ark. 1986).

446. *See* Lucha, Inc. v. Goeglein, 575 F. Supp. 785 (E.D. Mo. 1983).

447. *See* Saturn Sys., Inc. v. Saturn Corp., 659 F. Supp. 868 (D. Minn. 1987).

the jurisdictional statement in the plaintiff's complaint alleged that both plaintiffs and two defendants were citizens of New York.[448]

* * * * *

In contrast to the objective requirement of a reasonable pre-filing investigation into the facts and the law, amended Rule 11's requirement that a pleading, motion, or other paper not be interposed "for any improper purpose" focused on the signer's subjective intent. Most cases involving an improper purpose also seemed to involve violations of the reasonable investigation requirement of the rule. Nevertheless, the rule clearly made the improper purpose requirement an independent basis for sanctions, which could theoretically result in liability even when a litigation paper was well grounded in fact and law.[449]

Illustration 6-54. One court imposed sanctions on the plaintiff and the plaintiff's attorney for filing a motion to amend the complaint with the intention of withdrawing the motion if the defendant opposed it. The court classified this action as an improper purpose, even though the court recognized that there was a legal basis for the claim asserted in the amended complaint.[450] In another case, the court sanctioned both the defendant and the defendant's counsel for filing an answer in which the defendant attempted to delay the disposition of the action. The answer did not respond to the jurisdictional allegations of the complaint in order to conceal the absence of diversity of citizenship from the court and the plaintiff.[451]

* * * * *

As stated earlier, amended Rule 11 gave the court discretion to impose sanctions upon either a party or the attorney representing a party or both. This discretion included authorization to impose sanctions on *pro se* litigants when appropriate. Numerous cases imposed sanctions on these categories of persons.[452] Subsequently, however, in *Pavelic & LeFlore v. Marvel Entertainment Group*,[453] the Supreme Court held that sanctions could only be imposed upon the attorney who

---

448. *See* Solloway v. Ellenbogen, 121 F.R.D. 29 (S.D.N.Y. 1988).

449. As noted earlier, the language of amended Rule 11 was open-ended. Any improper purpose could be the basis for sanctions. However, the text of the amended rule gave harassment, delay, and needless increase in the cost of litigation as specific examples of improper purposes for which a pleading, motion, or other paper could not be interposed. Numerous cases involve sanctions for these improper purposes. *See, e.g.*, *In re* TCI Ltd., 769 F.2d 441 (7th Cir. 1985) (increase in costs); Miller v. Affiliated Fin. Corp., 600 F. Supp. 987 (N.D. Ill. 1984) (delay); United States v. Allen L. Wright Dev. Corp., 667 F. Supp. 1218 (N.D. Ill. 1987) (delay).

450. *See* Cohen v. Virginia Elec. & Power Co., 788 F.2d 247 (4th Cir. 1986).

451. *See* Itel Containers Int'l Corp. v. Puerto Rico Marine Mgmt., Inc., 108 F.R.D. 96 (D.N.J. 1985).

452. Sanctions on parties: *See, e.g.*, Ident Corp. of Am. v. Wendt, 638 F. Supp. 116 (E.D. Mo. 1986). Sanctions on attorneys: *See, e.g.*, Baker v. Citizens State Bank, 661 F. Supp. 1196 (D. Minn. 1987); Glenn v. Farmers & Merchants Ins. Co., 649 F. Supp. 1447 (W.D. Ark. 1986); Hasty v. PACCAR, Inc., 583 F. Supp. 1577 (E.D. Mo. 1984); Hearld v. Barnes & Spectrum Emergency Care, 107 F.R.D. 17 (E.D. Tex. 1985). Sanctions on both parties and attorneys: *See, e.g.*, Bastien v. R. Rowland & Co., 116 F.R.D. 619 (E.D. Mo. 1987), *aff'd*, 857 F.2d 482 (8th Cir. 1988); Deretich v. City of St. Francis, 650 F. Supp. 645 (D. Minn. 1986); Itel Containers Int'l Corp. v. Puerto Rico Marine Mgmt., Inc., 108 F.R.D. 96 (D.N.J. 1985). Sanctions on pro se litigants: *See, e.g.*, Kurkowski v. Volcker, 819 F.2d 201 (8th Cir. 1987); Mullen v. Galati, 843 F.2d 293 (8th Cir. 1988); Bigalk v. Federal Land Bank Ass'n, 107 F.R.D. 210 (D. Minn. 1985) (sanctions not imposed on pro se litigant who was "sincere"); Eckert v. Lane, 678 F. Supp. 773 (W.D. Ark. 1988); Miller v. United States, 604 F. Supp. 804 (E.D. Mo. 1985).

453. 493 U.S. 120, 110 S. Ct. 456, 107 L. Ed. 2d 438 (1989).

signs the paper that violates Rule 11, not the law firm in which the attorney is a partner.[454]

3. The 1993 Amendments to Rule 11

Amended Rule 11 gave rise to a substantial amount of litigation over the question whether sanctions should be imposed for filing meritless papers and, if so, what quality of sanctions was justified. This increased use of the rule prompted criticism on numerous grounds.[455] It will suffice to mention here only two of the most important criticisms. First, Professor Burbank suggested that Rule 11 might violate the Rules Enabling Act, 28 U.S.C. § 2072, because (1) it mandated sanctions, contrary to traditional equitable doctrines allowing the award of attorney's fees in the discretion of the court and (2) it allowed the award of attorney's fees for nonwillful violations of the rule, contrary to the policy judgment made by Congress in 28 U.S.C. § 1927 that such sanctions should be awarded only for willful conduct.[456] Second, it was argued that the federal courts applied amended Rule 11 so broadly that they undermined the liberal pleading system established by the Federal Rules of Civil Procedure.[457] Because of these and other criticisms, the Advisory Committee proposed, and the Supreme Court adopted, additional amendments to Rule 11 in 1993.[458] These amendments aroused a great deal of controversy,[459] and attempts to roll back these changes have continued.[460]

The 1993 amendments to Rule 11 made extensive changes in the practice under the rule.[461] The changes render some of the case law developed under the 1983 amendment irrelevant, while other decisions remain good authority under the

---

454. *See id.* at 123-27, 110 S. Ct. at 458-60, 107 L. Ed. 2d at 443-45; *see also* Cooter & Gell v. Hartmarx Corp., 496 U.S. 384, 110 S. Ct. 2447, 110 L. Ed. 2d 359 (1990) (holding that a voluntary dismissal of the action by the plaintiff did not deprive the district court of jurisdiction to levy Rule 11 sanctions).

455. The criticisms are surveyed and discussed thoroughly in 5A CHARLES A. WRIGHT & ARTHUR R. MILLER, FEDERAL PRACTICE AND PROCEDURE: CIVIL § 1332 (3d ed. 2004). For a useful survey of the impact of the 1983 amendments on the practice of lawyers and on particular kinds of cases, see Lawrence C. Marshall et al., *The Use and Impact of Rule 11*, 86 NW. U. L. REV. 943 (1992).

456. *See* Stephen B. Burbank, *Sanctions in the Proposed Amendments to the Federal Rules of Civil Procedure: Some Questions About Power*, 11 HOFSTRA L. REV. 997, 1001-04, 1008-11 (1983). However, the Supreme Court held that Rule 11 permitted the imposition of a fee-shifting sanction on a represented party who signed a paper in violation of Rule 11's objective standard of reasonable investigation. As so interpreted, the Court held that Rule 11 was valid under the Rules Enabling Act. *See* Business Guides, Inc. v. Chromatic Communications Enters., Inc., 498 U.S. 533, 111 S. Ct. 922, 112 L. Ed. 2d 1140 (1991).

457. *See* Note, *Plausible Pleadings: Developing Standards for Rule 11 Sanctions*, 100 HARV. L. REV. 630, 632-44 (1987).

458. These amendments took effect on December 1, 1993; they govern proceedings after that date in the U.S. District Courts and in states which adopted this amendment.

459. When the Supreme Court promulgated the amendments to Rule 11 under the Rules Enabling Act, two Justices dissented. *See* 146 F.R.D. at 507-10 (1993) (dissenting opinion of Justice Scalia, with whom Justice Thomas joined); *see also* James R. Simpson, Note, *Why Change Rule 11? Ramifications of the 1992 Amendment Proposal*, 29 CAL. W.L. REV. 495 (1993); Kimberly A. Stott, *Proposed Amendments to Federal Rule of Civil Procedure 11: New, But Not Necessarily Improved*, 21 FLA. ST. U. L. REV. 111 (1993); Comment, *Practice and Procedure: The "Safe Harbor" Amendment to Rule 11 . . . Any Port in a Storm*, 47 OKLA. L. REV. 319 (1994).

460. *See* Lonny Hoffman, *The Case Against the Lawsuit Abuse Reduction Act of 2011*, 48 HOUS. L. REV. 545, 546-63 (2011) (noting that bills have been regularly introduced to "toughen Rule 11, but to date, none have been successfully enacted" and arguing, *inter alia*, that returning to the 1983 version would increase costs, delays, and litigation abuse rather than lessen it).

461. *See* Ridder v. City of Springfield, 109 F.3d 288 (6th Cir. 1997) (discussing the history of the 1993 amendments to Rule 11).

amended rule. This subsection discusses the changes made by the 1993 amendments and their effect on the prior operation of the rule.

The 1993 amendments divide Rule 11 into four subsections. Rule 11(a) requires that litigation papers be signed and dictates the effect of a failure to sign. Rule 11(b) contains the provisions that determine when violations of the rule have occurred. Rule 11(c) provides for the sanctions that may be imposed for violating Rule 11(b), including how imposition of sanctions may be initiated and the nature and limitations that are imposed on sanctions under the amended rule. Rule 11(d) provides for the inapplicability of Rule 11 to discovery matters.

(a) Signature Requirements

Rule 11(a) retains, with changes in language, the requirement that an attorney or an unrepresented party must sign litigation papers. Added to the rule is a requirement that all litigation papers must state the signer's address and telephone number, "if any."[462] The Advisory Committee's notes accompanying the amendment to Rule 11(a) state that the district courts can require by local rule that additional information be provided, "such as telephone numbers to facilitate facsimile transmissions."[463] Rule 11(a) also retains the requirement that an unsigned paper must be stricken unless the omission of the signature is promptly corrected after being called to the attorney's or party's attention.[464] The sentence in former Rule 11 providing that signing a litigation paper constituted a certificate that the signer had read the paper was eliminated from Rule 11(a). The certification requirements are now contained in Rule 11(b), and the provisions of that portion of the rule "obviously require that pleading, written motion, or other paper be read before it is filed or submitted to the court."[465]

(b) Certification Requirements

The 1993 amendments to Rule 11(b) have substantially altered the certification requirements of the prior rule. Rule 11(b) now provides that an attorney or unrepresented party certifies certain matters to the court by presenting to the court a pleading, written motion, or other paper—whether by signing, filing, submitting, or later advocating it. Formerly, the rule only provided that certification occurred when a litigation paper was signed. Therefore, the 1993 amendments have expanded the responsibilities that attorneys and unrepresented parties have to the court.[466] The certification now applies not only to initial factual and legal

---

462. *See* FED. R. CIV. P. 11(a).

463. *See* FED. R. CIV. P. 11(a) advisory committee's note to the 1993 amendment.

464. *See* FED. R. CIV. P. 11(a). The former rule stated: "The rule in equity that the averments of an answer under oath must be overcome by the testimony of two witnesses or of one witness sustained by corroborating circumstances is abolished." This provision was repealed by the 1993 amendments. According to the Advisory Committee, the sentence was no longer needed. *See* FED. R. CIV. P. 11(a) advisory committee's note to the 1993 amendment.

465. *See* FED. R. CIV. P. 11(a) advisory committee's note to the 1993 amendment.

466. *See id.*

contentions, but also imposes a continuing duty not to insist upon a contention after it has become untenable.[467]

Illustration 6-55. *P's* attorney commences an action against *D* in a U.S. District Court. At the time the attorney files the complaint, good ground exists to believe that factual allegations in the complaint will have evidentiary support after a reasonable opportunity is given to the plaintiff to engage in discovery from the defendant. However, after discovery has been completed, no evidentiary support for the allegations is developed. Nevertheless, at a pretrial conference, *P's* attorney continues to advocate the validity of the claim. The attorney has presented to the court the now untenable factual contentions within the meaning of Rule 11(b).[468]

Illustration 6-56. *P's* attorney commences an action against *D* in a state court. There is no basis in existing law for a claim for relief based on the factual allegations in the complaint and no nonfrivolous argument that can be made for the extension, modification, or reversal of existing law or the establishment of new law that would make the complaint nonfrivolous. *D* validly removes the action to a U.S. District Court and moves to dismiss the complaint for failure to state a claim upon which relief can be granted. If *P's* attorney resists the motion to dismiss—for example, by filing a brief in opposition—the attorney has presented to the court the frivolous legal contentions within the meaning of Rule 11(b).[469]

* * * * *

Under the 1993 amendments, an attorney or party presenting a pleading, written motion, or other paper to the court certifies four things. First, under Rule 11(b)(1), the attorney or party certifies that the paper "is not being presented for any improper purpose, such as to harass, cause unnecessary delay, or needlessly increase the cost of litigation."[470] This provision retains the identical requirement of former Rule 11 but, of course, expands the requirement to papers presented to the court, as opposed to papers merely signed by the party. Thus, the cases under the 1983 version of Rule 11 determining what constitutes an "improper purpose" will still be good authority under the amended rule.[471]

Second, under Rule 11(b)(2), the attorney or party also certifies that "the claims, defenses, and other legal contentions" in the paper presented "are warranted by existing law or by a nonfrivolous argument for extending, modifying, or reversing existing law or for establishing new law."[472] The certification of former Rule 11 literally applied only to "pleadings, motions, and other papers," while the

---

467. *See id.*

468. *See id.*

469. *See id.*

470. FED. R. CIV. P. 11(b)(1) (as restyled in 2007).

471. *See In re* DeVille, 361 F.3d 539 (9th Cir. 2004) (Bankruptcy Appellate Panel properly sanctioned attorney and client for series of bankruptcy filings and removals from state court designed to maximize delay of state civil proceedings); Whitehead v. Food Max, Inc., 332 F.3d 796 (5th Cir. 2003) (en banc; court of appeals affirms district court's imposition of sanctions against attorney for suing out a writ of execution against defendant and orchestrating a media event in which attorney was trying to promote himself and embarrass the defendant; court assumes that existing law at the time the attorney obtained the writ permitted the attorney to obtain it and that the defendant was not entitled to an automatic stay of execution under Rule 62(a) without a motion); *see also* Marissa L. Bracke, Note, *Where Improper Purposes Lead, Inadequate Protections Follow: Integrating the Rule 11 Improper Purpose Inquiry With the Rule 23 Protections for Absent Class Members,* 41 VAL. U. L. REV. 353 (2006).

472. FED. R. CIV. P. 11(b)(2) (as restyled in 2007).

language of the amended rule applies to "claims, defenses, and other legal contentions." Under the former rule, some courts had held that an entire litigation paper, as opposed to only a portion of the paper, had to be frivolous to violate Rule 11.[473] The language of the amended rule makes it clear that presenting even one frivolous claim or defense violates the rule, even if the pleading, written motion, or other paper contains other nonfrivolous contentions.[474] However, the 1993 amendments added language to Rule 11(b)(2) that allows a legal contention to be based on a nonfrivolous argument for the establishment of new law, as well as arguments for the extension, modification, or reversal of existing law, which had been allowed by the former rule.[475]

Third, under Rule 11(b)(4), an attorney or a party denying factual contentions certifies that "the denials . . . are warranted on the evidence or, if specifically so identified, are reasonably based on belief or a lack of information."[476] The Advisory Committee noted that denials of factual allegations must be treated more leniently under Rule 11(b)(4) than the allegations themselves are treated under Rule 11(b)(3).[477] Denials can be based on evidence that affirmatively contradicts the allegations. However, denials may also permissibly be based on an absence of information, or reasonable doubts about the credibility of the evidence supporting the allegations. Of course, a reasonable investigation must be made to determine whether there is support for a denial. In addition, a party may not deny an allegation the party knows to be true. Nevertheless, a party is not required to admit an allegation simply because the party lacks evidence to contradict the allegation.[478] When a denial is based on a lack of information or belief, the party must specifically identify it as such. This requirement appears to force a party who denies a factual allegation on the basis that the evidence supporting the allegation is not credible to state specifically the lack of credibility as the basis of the denial. Failure to do so will apparently constitute a violation of Rule 11(b)(4). Furthermore, if a denial later proves to be untenable after further investigation or discovery, the denying party may not continue to insist on the denial.[479]

---

473. *See, e.g.*, Golden Eagle Distrib. Corp. v. Burroughs Corp., 801 F.2d 1531 (9th Cir. 1986); *see also* Sommer v. Unum Life Ins. Co. of Am., 35 Fed. App'x 489 (9th Cir. 2002) (district court did not err in imposing sanctions under Rule 11 in case that was clearly precluded by res judicata); Christian v. Mattel, Inc., 286 F.3d 1118 (9th Cir. 2002) (complaint alleging copyright infringement was legally and factually frivolous under Rule 11 when allegedly infringing work was created six years before the infringing work; attorney's failure to investigate fell below requisite standard under Rule 11).

474. *See* Letter to the Honorable Robert E. Keeton, Chairman of the Standing Committee on Rules of Practice and Procedure of the Judicial Conference of the United States from Sam C. Pointer, Jr., Chairman of the Advisory Committee on the Civil Rules, Attachment B, 146 F.R.D. 521, 524 (1993); *see also* Kearney v. Dimanna, 195 Fed. App'x 717 (10th Cir. 2006) (assertion of federal claims that violated Rule 11 justified sanctions even if state claims asserted in action did not).

475. *See* Hartmarx Corp. v. Abboud, 326 F.3d 862 (7th Cir. 2003) (Rule 11 sanctions inappropriate under new rule of law when party was taking a reasonable legal position); *see also* Phonometrics, Inc. v. Economy Inns of Am., 349 F.3d 1356 (Fed. Cir. 2003) (district court properly sanctioned attorney for continuing to present to court claims after the issuance of an appellate decision indicating that they were without merit); Marguerite L. Butler, *Rule 11 Sanctions and a Lawyer's Failure to Conduct Competent Legal Research*, 29 CAP. U. L. REV. 681 (2001) (a synthesis of cases reveals that Rule 11 sanctions have been imposed when lawyers (1) ignore an unbroken line of contrary authority, (2) fail to offer even remote analogies, (3) do not cite any cases or only cite a single, wholly inapposite authority, and (4) fail to argue for the modification, extension, or reversal of existing law).

476. FED. R. CIV. P. 11(b)(4) (as restyled in 2007).

477. *See* FED. R. CIV. P. 11(b)(4) advisory committee's note to the 1993 amendment.

478. *See id.*

479. *See id.*

Illustration 6-57. *P* sues *D* in federal district court. *P* alleges that *D* made slanderous remarks about *P* to *C*. *D* tells *D's* attorney that *D* never made any such remarks. Furthermore, *D* tells the attorney that *P* and *C* are *D's* lifelong enemies. *D* thinks *P* and *C* are conspiring against *D* to bring the slander claim. *D* provides information to the attorney that will allow *P* and *C* to be impeached effectively at trial if they falsely testify that *D* made the slanderous remarks. *D's* attorney denies in the answer that *D* made the remarks, but without specifying that the denial is based on lack of belief. No violation of Rule 11(b)(4) has occurred. *D's* testimony at trial that *D* never made the slanderous remarks is affirmative contradictory evidence to the allegations that makes a specification under Rule 11(b)(4) unnecessary.

Illustration 6-58. *P* sues *D* in federal district court. *P* alleges that *C*, *D's* employee, negligently ran *P* down with a motor vehicle while *P* was crossing a highway. Shortly after the alleged accident, *C* was killed in a motor vehicle crash with another party. There is no witness to the accident other than *P*. *D* has no evidence that would indicate whether *C* ran *P* down. However, *D* does provide *D's* attorney with information indicating that *P* is not a credible witness and can be effectively impeached at trial. Based on this information, *D's* attorney denies the allegation that *C* ran *P* down, but does not specify in the answer that this denial is based on a lack of "belief." The denial apparently violates Rule 11(b)(4) because of the failure to specify that it is based on a lack of belief.

Illustration 6-59. On the facts of *Illustration 6-58*, assume that *D's* attorney specified in the answer that the denial was based on a lack of belief. Subsequently, however, the attorney's investigation turns up a neutral witness who witnessed *P* being run down by *C*. Thereafter, the attorney may not continue to insist on the denial without violating Rule 11(b)(4). It is not necessary that the attorney amend *D's* answer to eliminate the denial in order to avoid a violation of the rule, as long as the attorney does not continue to insist on the denial. However, amendment of the answer to withdraw the allegation might be helpful to avoid any implication that the attorney is continuing to rely on the denial.[480]

Illustration 6-60. *P* sues *D* and *C's* estate. *P* alleges in the alternative that either *D* or *C* was driving a motor vehicle that ran *P* down as *P* was crossing a highway. *D* tells *D's* attorney that *D*, not *C*, was driving the motor vehicle, but *D* does not think that *P* can prove who was driving because *D* and *C* were the only witnesses to the accident, and *C* is dead. Under the circumstances, if *D's* attorney denies in the answer that *D* was driving the motor vehicle, Rule 11(c)(4) is violated. It is not permissible in a civil action to deny a fact the party knows to be true on the basis that the other party has the burden of proof and cannot meet it.

* * * * *

Fourth, under Rule 11(b)(3), an attorney or party presenting a paper to the court certifies that "the factual contentions are warranted on the evidence or, if specifically so identified, are reasonably based on belief or a lack of information."[481] As with legal contentions under Rule 11(b)(2), this certification

---

480. *See id.*
481. FED. R. CIV. P. 11(b)(3) (as restyled in 2007).

requirement applies to all factual contentions. Thus, if a pleading contains some factual allegations that comply with the certification requirement and some that do not, the pleading violates Rule 11.

Former Rule 11 provided that the signer of a litigation paper certified that, based on a reasonable investigation, the paper was, to the best of the signer's knowledge, "well grounded in fact." The certification requirement of Rule 11(b)(3) was revised to make it clear that a party may have good ground to believe that an allegation is true, but may need discovery to "gather and confirm" the evidentiary basis for the allegation.[482] However, the 1993 revisions are not intended to relieve an attorney or party from the duty to conduct a factual investigation that is reasonable under the circumstances before making an allegation. Furthermore, if evidentiary support is not acquired after further opportunity for investigation and discovery, the attorney or party may not persist in advocating the contention.[483] In addition, the text of the rule clearly states that a party basing an allegation on a good faith belief of its truth, but without evidentiary support, must so state in the party's pleading or a violation of the certification requirement will occur.[484]

Illustration 6-61. *P* sues *D* in a federal district court. *P* alleges in the complaint that *D* negligently ran *P* down with a motor vehicle while *P* was crossing a specific street. At the time *P* files the complaint, *P's* investigation of the facts has not produced any evidence of *D's* negligence because *P* has, despite reasonable efforts, been unable to interview *C*, who was a witness to the accident. *P's* complaint does not specifically identify the allegation of negligence as one that is dependent upon further investigation or discovery. Under these circumstances, the allegation violates the certification requirement of Rule 11(b)(3).

Illustration 6-62. *P* sues *D* in a federal district court. *P* alleges that *D* slandered *P* in certain remarks made to *C*. *P* specifically identifies the allegation of slander as one that is dependent upon further investigation and discovery for confirmation. *P* is given a reasonable opportunity for further investigation and discovery, during which *P* takes the depositions of *D* and *C*. *D's* deposition states that *D* never made slanderous remarks to *C*. *C's* deposition states that *D* never made slanderous remarks to *C*. *D* and *C* are the only possible witnesses to the slanderous remarks. *D* moves for summary judgment against *P*, supporting the motion with the depositions of *D* and *C*. *P* resists the motion for summary judgment by arguing that *D* and *C* are lying. *P* wants to place *D* and *C* on the stand at trial, cross-examine them, and ask the trier of fact to disbelieve their denials that the slanderous utterances were made. Parties bearing the burden of proof on an issue may not

---

482. *See* FED. R. CIV. P. 11(b)(3) advisory committee's note to the 1993 amendment.

483. *See id.* The party need not formally amend the pleadings to withdraw the allegation, as long as the party does not further advocate an allegation that turns out after discovery to be untenable. *See id.*

484. *See, e.g.*, *In re* Taylor, 655 F.3d 274, 288 (3d Cir. 2011) ("Rule 11 requires more than rubber-stamping of the results of an automated process by a person who happens be a lawyer"; no reasonable inquiry when "a lawyer systematically fails to take any responsibility for seeking adequate information from her client, makes representations without any factual basis because they are included in a 'form pleading' [the lawyer] has been trained to fill out . . . and ignores obvious indications that [the lawyer's] information may be incorrect"); Top Entm't Inc. v. Ortega, 285 F.3d 115 (1st Cir. 2002) (complaint violated Rule 11, given plaintiffs' about-face regarding the very basis on which the complaint was founded, first alleging that the defendant was falsely claiming to be plaintiffs' concert promoter and then alleging that the parties did have an agreement and that the defendant breached it; miscommunication between counsel and the plaintiffs did not excuse misconduct in filing complaint with false allegations).

ordinarily satisfy that burden of proof by impeachment evidence alone. Thus, if *P* attempted to satisfy the burden of proof on slander by impeaching *D* and *C* at trial, the court would be obligated to grant a judgment as a matter of law against *P*. On this state of the evidence before trial, *D* is entitled to summary judgment against *P*.[485] Therefore, the court grants *D's* motion for summary judgment. *P* has violated the certification requirement of Rule 11(b)(3). The mere fact that a motion for summary judgment is granted against a party does not mean that there is no evidence for the party's position.[486] However, *P* has been given a reasonable opportunity to support the factual allegations of slander and has been unable to do so with evidence that would allow *P* to win the summary judgment motion. Thus, *P's* resistance of the summary judgment motion violated *P's* duty under Rule 11(b)(3) not to persist with unsupportable contentions.

* * * * *

The Court's decision in *Bell Atlantic Corp. v. Twombly*,[487] discussed in section D(2)*(b)* above, presents a potential interrelationship between Rule 11(b)(3) and the notice pleading requirements of Rule 8(a). In *Twombly*, the Court recognized the *in terrorem* effect of discovery in terms of incremental settlement value.[488] Assume that the plaintiff in *Twombly* had simply alleged an "agreement" (without identifying whether the agreement was actual or tacit) to divide the market among the parties using standard conclusory "form book" language[489] and then specifically identified this allegation as one that would likely have evidentiary support after a reasonable opportunity for further discovery. Would the plaintiff in *Twombly* have been able to achieve what it apparently had wanted: a chance to depose the executives under oath, to probe for communications or evidence showing "plus" factors required to prove a tacit agreement, etc.? (Of course, if the plaintiff came up with no evidence to support a viable theory of liability, then Rule 11 would mandate that the plaintiff not resist a motion for summary judgment.) Or would the Rule 11 approach fail on the ground that the allegation was one that would not "*likely* have evidentiary support" after discovery because the plaintiff at present could only show parallel conduct that may or may not evidence an agreement?[490] At present, there are no clear answers to these questions. However, given the Supreme Court's position in *Twombly* that an agreement cannot be inferred from parallel conduct alone, it seem unlikely that the Court would approve of an allegation that evidentiary support would exist for an agreement after discovery when that

---

485. *See* Chapter 10(C)(2) ("Applying the Summary Judgment Standard") & *Illustration 10-12 infra*.

486. *See* FED. R. CIV. P. 11(b)(3) advisory committee's note to the 1993 amendment.

487. 550 U.S.544, 127 S. Ct. 1955, 167 L. Ed. 2d 929 (2007).

488. *Id.* at 557, 127 S. Ct. at 1966, 167 L. Ed. 2d at 941-42 (citing Dura Pharm., Inc. v. Broudo, 544 U.S. 336, 347, 125 S. Ct. at 1627, 161 L. Ed. 2d at 589, which quoted, in part, Blue Chip Stamps v. Manor Drug Stores, 421 U.S. 723, 741, 95 S. Ct. 1917, 1928, 44 L. Ed. 2d 539, 552 (1975)).

489. The majority interpreted the complaint as relying exclusively on allegations of parallel conduct (contrary to the dissent's view) rather than directly alleging an illegal agreement. *Twombly*, 550 U.S. at 565 n.11, 127 S. Ct. at 1971 n.11, 167 L. Ed. 2d at 946 n.11. The Court also doubted the more general references to an agreement in the complaint would have given the notice required by Rule 8. *Id.* at 565 n.10, 127 S. Ct. at 1971 n.10, 167 L. Ed. 2d at 946 n.10, but it did not address whether Rule 11 could have been used in that context.

490. For excellent guidance on this general inquiry, see Lisa Pondrom, Comment, *Predicting the Unpredictable Under Rule 11(b)(3): When Are Allegations Likely to Have Evidentiary Support?*, 43 UCLA L. REV. 1393 (1996).

allegation itself is based only on an investigation that has revealed nothing more than parallel conduct.

(c) Sanctions and the "Safe Harbor" Provision

Rule 11(c) contains the most important part of the 1993 amendments to Rule 11. Rule 11(c) sets out the circumstances in which sanctions may be imposed for a violation of Rule 11(b). Rule 11(c) also clarifies the philosophy of sanctions and provides for important limitations on the imposition of sanctions.

Initially, Rule 11(c) provides that an alleged violator of the rule must be given notice and a reasonable opportunity to respond to the allegation of violations. After notice and an opportunity to respond have been given, the rule provides that the court may impose "an appropriate sanction" upon the attorneys, law firms, or parties that have violated the rule or are responsible for the violation.[491] The provision allowing the imposition of sanctions upon law firms overrules the Supreme Court's decision in *Pavelic & LeFlore v. Marvel Entertainment Group*.[492] As noted in the preceding subsection, *Pavelic* interpreted prior Rule 11 to preclude the imposition of sanctions on a law firm for the violation of the rule by one of its attorneys. This alteration of the rule was thought justifiable because of the so-called "safe harbor" provisions of Rule 11(c)(2), discussed below.[493] More importantly, the use of the word "may" in Rule 11(c)(1) (as restyled) eliminates the former provision of Rule 11 mandating sanctions for a violation of the rule. In addition, the nature of any sanction imposed also remains discretionary with the court, subject to the limitations imposed by Rule 11(c)(4) (as restyled).[494]

Rule 11(c)(2) (as restyled) contains the so-called "safe harbor" provisions of the rule. Rule 11(c)(2) provides that a motion for sanctions under the rule shall be made separately from other motions or requests and must describe the specific conduct that is alleged to violate Rule 11(b). That "motion must be served as provided in Rule 5, but it must not be filed or be presented to the court if the challenged paper, claim, defense, contention, or denial is withdrawn or appropri-

---

491. FED. R. CIV. P. 11(c)(1); *see* Jeffrey A. Parness, *Sanctioning Legal Organizations Under the New Federal Civil Rule 11: Radical Changes Loosen More Unforeseeable Forces*, 14 REV. LITIG. 63 (1994). Rule 11(c)(6) provides that when the court imposes sanctions, it must describe the sanctioned conduct and explain the basis for the sanction. However, when the court denies sanctions, "it should ordinarily not have to explain its denial." *See* FED. R. CIV. P. 11(c) advisory committee's note to the 1993 amendment; *see also* Nuwesra v. Merrill Lynch, Fenner & Smith, Inc., 174 F.3d 87 (2d Cir. 1999) (district court's orders must apprise party of the specific conduct alleged to be sanctionable to give party adequate notice and opportunity to defend); L.B. Foster Co. v. America Piles, Inc., 138 F.3d 81 (2d Cir. 1998) (court must enter an order to show cause or otherwise give notice to attorney as to whether he is being sanctioned under Rule 11 or § 1927); Thornton v. General Motors Corp., 136 F.3d 450 (5th Cir. 1998) (court's order indicated that the attorney was to produce evidence supporting claim, but did not give notice that the court was contemplating sanctions under the pre-filing investigation standard of the rule).

492. 493 U.S. 120, 110 S. Ct. 456, 107 L. Ed. 2d 438 (1989).

493. *See* FED. R. CIV. P. 11(c) advisory committee's note to the 1993 amendment. The last sentence of Rule 11(c)(1) also states that "[a]bsent exceptional circumstances, a law firm must be held jointly responsible for a violation committed by its partner, associate, or employee." FED. R. CIV. P. 11(c)(1) (as restyled in 2007).

494. *See* FED. R. CIV. P. 11(c) advisory committee's note to the 1993 amendment.

ately corrected within 21 days after service or with another time the court sets."[495] However, if the moving party violates the "safe harbor" provision and fails to serve the motion at least 21 days before filing it with the court, but the party against whom the motion is filed fails to raise the "safe harbor" provision as a defense, this defense may possibly be waived.[496] The rule also provides that the court may award to the prevailing party the reasonable expenses incurred in presenting or opposing the motion, including reasonable attorney's fees.

Under the "safe harbor" provisions of Rule 11(c)(2), a party may no longer be sanctioned unless the party insists on relying on matter that violates the rule after the violation has been called to the party's attention. The Advisory Committee observed that under the prior rule parties were sometimes reluctant to abandon matter that violated the rule for fear that the abandonment would itself be considered evidence of a violation.[497] There will no longer be justification for such a fear under the amended rule. The safe harbor period runs from the time that service of the motion for sanctions is made. Nevertheless, the Advisory Committee opined that "[i]n most cases . . . counsel should be expected to give informal notice to the other party, whether in person or by a telephone call or letter, of a potential violation before proceeding to prepare and serve a Rule 11 motion."[498] However, the Advisory Committee did not say what should happen to an attorney or party who fails to give such informal notice. Presumably, the court may take into account such a failure in determining whether to award sanctions for a violation, the severity of the sanctions to be awarded, or whether to award expenses to the moving party who prevailed on the Rule 11 motion.

Whatever difficulties may be involved with the "safe harbor" provision, it has solved one difficult conceptual problem that existed under the prior rule. When a "waivable" matter was involved in a case, it was not clear how the 1983 version of Rule 11 should have been applied. For example, if a plaintiff brought an action in a place where personal jurisdiction or venue was clearly improper, there was a real sense in which the action did not violate Rule 11. Personal jurisdiction and venue will be proper anywhere if they are not raised in accord with the procedures

---

495. *See* FED. R. CIV. P. 11(c)(2) (as restyled in 2007); *see also, e.g.*, Roth v. Green, 466 F.3d 1179 (10th Cir. 2006) (a letter informing an opposing party of intent to seek sanctions does not comply with the safe-harbor provision; provision requires service of a motion, and a warning letter may not be substituted for formal motion); Barber v. Miller, 146 F.3d 707 (9th Cir. 1998) (safe harbor provision precludes a motion for sanctions after dismissal of the complaint, because the plaintiff has no opportunity to withdraw the complaint voluntarily; however, court can award sanctions on its own motion after judgment); Morganroth & Morganroth v. DeLorean, 123 F.3d 374 (6th Cir. 1997) (safe harbor provision prohibits imposition of sanctions pursuant to a motion raised after verdict, even if lawsuit clearly frivolous); Gordon v. Unifund CCR Partners, 345 F.3d 1028 (8th Cir. 2003) (party's request for sanctions did not comply with Rule 11 because it was not made as a separate motion and was not served on opposing party to give opposing party 21 days to withdraw challenged motion).

496. Rector v. Approved Fed. Sav. Bank, 265 F.3d 248 (4th Cir. 2001) ("safe harbor" protection is not a jurisdictional rule and thus can be waived); *see also* Nyer v. Winterthur Int'l, 290 F.3d 456 (1st Cir. 2002) (nonparties may not ordinarily seek sanctions under Rule 11, but nonparty in this case was forced to prepare a possible defense against a claim and thus qualifies as a kind of nonparty who has standing to file a Rule 11 motion). *But see* Brickwood Contractors, Inc. v. Datanet Eng'g, Inc., 369 F.3d 385 (4th Cir. 2004) (safe harbor provisions are not jurisdictional and can be waived, but court would exercise its discretion to review improperly imposed sanctions; district court erred by imposing sanctions because defendants did not serve their Rule 11 motion on the plaintiff before filing it with district court and because defendants waited until after they were granted summary judgment to file it).

497. *See* FED. R. CIV. P. 11(c) advisory committee's note to the 1993 amendment.

498. *See id.*

prescribed in Rule 12. In other words, the defendant can waive such defenses. Thus, it was arguably proper for the plaintiff to bring the action in a location where personal jurisdiction and venue were clearly improper and wait to see whether the defendant would raise the defenses. Similar considerations were involved when the plaintiff asserted claims as to which there were clear affirmative defenses, such as the statute of limitations. The "safe harbor" provision solves the conceptual dilemma of the waivable defense. The plaintiff can now commence an action in which personal jurisdiction or venue is clearly improper, or which is clearly precluded by an affirmative defense, and rely on the safe harbor provision for protection from sanctions.[499]

Rule 11(c)(3) (as restyled) provides that the court may, on its own initiative, enter an order describing specific conduct that appears to violate Rule 11(b). The order must direct the attorney, law firm, or party to show cause why it has not violated Rule 11(b) as described in the order. Unlike Rule 11(c)(2), Rule 11(c)(3) does not contain a "safe harbor" provision. Thus, withdrawal of a contention that violates Rule 11(b) will not automatically insulate a violator from sanctions imposed by the court on its own motion. Nevertheless, the Advisory Committee stated that "corrective action" by a violator "should be taken into account in deciding what, if any, sanction to impose," if the court concludes that a violation has occurred after considering the alleged violator's response to the "show cause" order.[500]

Rule 11(c)(4) and (5) (as restyled) provide the nature of and limitations on the sanctions that may be imposed for a violation of Rule 11(b). Rule 11(c)(4) emphasizes that sanctions under the rule are designed to deter repetition of the violator's conduct or the conduct of those similarly situated. To this end, the rule prescribes that the sanction imposed shall be limited to what is sufficient for these deterrent purposes. Furthermore, subject to certain limitations imposed by Rule 11(c)(5), the rule provides that "[t]he sanction may include nonmonetary directives; an order to pay a penalty into court; or, if imposed on motion and warranted for effective deterrence, an order directing payment to the movant of part or all the reasonable attorney's fees and other expenses directly resulting from the violation."[501]

---

499. *Cf.* Professional Mgmt. Assocs., Inc. v. KPMG LLP, 345 F.3d 1030 (8th Cir. 2003) (district court abused its discretion in refusing to sanction plaintiff and his counsel for filing a lawsuit seeking to relitigate claims precluded by the doctrine of res judicata).

500. *See* FED. R. CIV. P. 11(c) advisory committee's note to the 1993 amendment; *see also* Clark v. United Parcel Serv., Inc., 460 F.3d 1004 (8th Cir. 2006) (district court did not err in citing six paragraphs of plaintiffs' pleading as examples of "misrepresentations and misstatements" that were unsupported by the record or blatantly non-responsive to defendants' summary judgment motion; court's notice based on the six paragraphs complied with Rule 11(c)(1)(B), restyled as 11(c)(3); plaintiff's attorney was properly notified that he should address why his "concise" listing of material facts spanned 948 paragraphs and why a 480 page pleading was justified under the circumstances); Brickwood Contractors, Inc. v. Datanet Eng'g, Inc., 369 F.3d 385 (4th Cir. 2004) (failure to comply with safe harbor provisions has no effect on the court's authority to impose sanctions sua sponte under Rule 11).

501. FED. R. CIV. P. 11(c)(4) (as restyled in 2007); *see also* Tropf v. Fidelity Nat'l Title Ins. Co., 289 F.3d 929 (6th Cir. 2002) (district court did not err in issuing a permanent injunction preventing the plaintiffs or their attorney from filing a civil action in any U.S. District Court based on the legal or factual claims in the action before the court without the written permission of the court; however, district court erred in enjoining the plaintiffs and their attorney from commencing actions in state court); Reinhardt v. Gulf Ins. Co., 489 F.3d 405 (1st Cir. 2007) (district court did not abuse discretion in imposing Rule 11 sanction of 10 hours of pro bono service on attorney as sanction for failure to enter into negotiations over stipulation); Hirczy v. Hamilton, 190 Fed. App'x 357 (5th Cir.

Rule 11(c)(4) and (5) are designed to work a major change in the way that Rule 11 operated under the 1983 amendments. As indicated in the preceding subsection, former Rule 11 specifically attempted to encourage the imposition of expenses and attorney's fees as a sanction. The encouragement was successful. An award of costs and attorney's fees became by far the most frequently awarded sanction by the courts. However, this result was criticized on the grounds that the costs and expenses sanction was too frequently selected, led to excessively large sanction awards, and created the incentive for many unnecessary Rule 11 motions.[502] The amendments to Rule 11(c)(2) are designed to make it clear that monetary sanctions imposed by the court should "ordinarily be paid into court as a penalty."[503]

Nevertheless, the language of the rule specifically recognizes that it will still be appropriate, albeit under fewer circumstances, to award expenses and fees to the moving party. The Advisory Committee stated that an award of fees and expenses would be particularly appropriate for violations of Rule 11(b)(1) when a paper has been presented for an improper purpose, such as harassment or delay.[504] When expenses and fees are awarded, they should not exceed the amount "directly and unavoidably caused by the violation of the certification requirement."[505] Likewise, the award should not provide compensation for services that could have been avoided by an earlier "disclosure of evidence or an earlier challenge to the groundless claims or defenses."[506] Special rules, however, apply to private securities litigation.[507]

Illustration 6-63. *P* files and serves a two-count complaint against *D*. One count of the complaint contains allegations with specific evidentiary support. The

---

2006) (trial court had authority under Rule 11 and various statutes and rules providing for sanctions, and inherent authority to issue permanent injunction against plaintiff forbidding him from filing suit in the district without written permission of the judge); Freeman v. Heiderich, 177 Fed. App'x 553 (9th Cir. 2006) (Rule 11 only allows court to impose sanctions on party that are paid to other party when motion is made for such sanctions; rule does not allow such sanctions on the court's own motion); Jimenez v. Madison Area Tech. Coll., 321 F.3d 652 (7th Cir. 2003) (sanction of dismissal was appropriate under Rule 11 for relying on fraudulent documents to bolster plaintiff's civil rights claims).

502. *See* Letter to the Honorable Robert E. Keeton, Chairman of the Standing Committee on Rules of Practice and Procedure of the Judicial Conference of the United States from Sam C. Pointer, Jr., Chairman of the Advisory Committee on the Civil Rules, Attachment B, 146 F.R.D. at 524 (1993).

503. *See* FED. R. CIV. P. 11(c)(2) advisory committee's note to the 1993 amendment.

504. *See id.*

505. *See id.*; *see also* Divane v. Krull Elec. Co., 319 F.3d 307 (7th Cir. 2003) (court may order attorney's fees to be paid to opposing party in an effort to deter future conduct, but when it does, court has an obligation to award only those fees that directly resulted from the sanctionable conduct).

506. *See* FED. R. CIV. P. 11(c)(2) advisory committee's note to the 1993 amendment. For a discussion of the problems involved with this aspect of the rule, see Jeffrey A. Parness, *Fines Under New Federal Civil Rule 11: The New Monetary Sanctions for the "Stop-and-Think-Again" Rule*, 1993 B.Y.U. L. REV. 879.

507. The Private Securities Litigation Reform Act of 1995, Pub. L. No. 104-67, 109 Stat. 737 (codified at 15 U.S.C. § 78u-4 *et seq.*), *inter alia*, added § 27(c) to the 1993 Securities Act and § 21D(c) to the 1934 Securities Exchange Act. Pursuant to these sections, upon final adjudication of the action, courts in private securities litigation shall include in the record specific findings regarding compliance by each party and each attorney representing any party with each requirement of Rule 11(b) as to any complaint, responsive pleading, or dispositive motion. These sections also establish a presumption that the appropriate sanction for filing a complaint in violation of Rule 11(b) is an award to the opposing party of the reasonable attorney's fees and other expenses incurred in the action. This presumption can be rebutted only upon proof that the award of attorney's fees and other expenses will impose an unreasonable burden on that party or attorney and would be unjust, and the failure to make such an award would not impose a greater burden on the party in whose favor sanctions are to be imposed. The presumption can also be rebutted by showing that the violation was de minimis. If the presumption is successfully overcome, the court is directed to award sanctions that the court deems appropriate pursuant to Federal Rule 11. *Id.* § 101(a), 109 Stat. 737, 742, 747-48.

other count contains allegations that violate Rule 11(b)(3) because *P* has no evidentiary support for the allegations and does not specify that the allegations are likely to have support after further investigation or discovery. After further investigation and discovery, *P* still has no support for the allegations. After informally notifying *P* of the Rule 11 violation with no results, *D* serves a motion for sanctions on *P* pursuant to Rule 11(c)(2). *P* refuses to withdraw the offending allegations within the time prescribed in the rule. *D* files the motion with the court. If the court concludes that a violation has occurred and that it is appropriate to impose sanctions on *P* in the form of a fees and expenses award to *D*, the court should award fees and expenses only for the costs and services that *D* has incurred with regard to the count of the complaint that violated the certification requirement of Rule 11. The court should not award fees and expenses for services attributable to responding to the non-violating count. In determining the appropriate amount to award, the court can consider whether earlier notice by *D* to *P* about the violation would have avoided some of the fees and expenses.[508] Of course, under Rule 11(c)(2), the court can also award *D* the fees and expenses involved in presenting the Rule 11 motion.[509]

* * * * *

Rule 11(c)(5)(A) (as restyled) provides that monetary sanctions may not be awarded against a represented party for a violation of Rule 11(b)(2), which involves frivolous legal contentions. The obvious rationale of this limitation is that monetary sanctions for frivolous legal contentions are "more properly placed solely on the party's attorneys." However, the court may impose nonmonetary sanctions, such as dismissal, that have "collateral financial consequences" to a party.[510]

Rule 11(c)(5)(B) (as restyled) provides that the court may not impose monetary sanctions on its own initiative unless the court issues its order to show cause before a voluntary dismissal or settlement of the claims "by or against the party which is, or whose attorneys are, to be sanctioned." This provision is designed to prevent parties who voluntarily dismiss or settle an action from being unexpectedly faced with sanctions that might have affected their willingness to settle or dismiss.[511]

---

508. There are substantial doubts about the effect that delay will have on the availability of sanctions under the new rule. The Advisory Committee's note states that "[o]rdinarily the motion should be served promptly after the inappropriate paper is filed, and, if delayed too long, may be viewed as untimely." *See* FED. R. CIV. P. 11 advisory committee's note to the 1993 amendment. Thus, on the facts of this illustration, *D's* motion might conceivably be held untimely because *D* waited until after discovery was complete to serve the motion. *D* may be able to justify this delay if it is necessary to wait for discovery in order to see that *P* had no evidentiary support for the second count in the complaint. The Advisory Committee's note also states that "[i]n other circumstances, it should not be served until the other party has had a reasonable opportunity for discovery." *Id.* However, the Advisory Committee does not state what should be done when a violation of the "specification requirement" occurs upon the filing of a litigation paper and the motion is served after discovery is complete. Under such circumstances, the violation may not be apparent to the moving party until both parties have completed discovery.

509. The Advisory Committee also stated, however, that a partial award of expenses and fees may suffice to deter persons of "modest financial resources," suggesting that even when fees and expenses are awarded to a moving party, the primary, if not exclusive, consideration should be deterrence, rather than compensation. *See id.*

510. *See id.*

511. *See id.* This provision overrules the Supreme Court's decision in Cooter & Gell v. Hartmarx Corp., 496 U.S. 384, 110 S. Ct. 2447, 110 L. Ed. 2d 359 (1990).

(d) Rule 11 Inapplicable to Discovery

Rule 11(d) (as restyled) provides that Rule 11 "does not apply to disclosures and discovery requests, responses, objections, and motions under Rules 26 through 37."[512] Rules 26(g) and 37 provide the certification standards and sanctions applicable to discovery matters.[513]

4. Section 1927 and the Court's Inherent Power to Sanction

Section 1927 of Title 28 provides that district courts may impose sanctions upon attorneys who multiply "the proceedings in any case unreasonably and vexatiously." The sanctions authorized are the payment of "the excess costs, expenses, and attorneys' fees reasonably incurred" because of the offending attorney's conduct.[514] In addition, the federal courts have "inherent power" to impose sanctions on litigants for bad faith conduct.[515] These two sources of authority can cover the same conduct as Rule 11 and can potentially conflict with each other.[516] For example, if a party violating Rule 11 withdraws the offending allegations or defenses during the safe harbor period of Rule 11, can sanctions nonetheless be imposed by the court under § 1927 or its inherent power? Some courts have taken the position that they have the power to impose sanctions even when the safe harbor provision has been utilized.[517]

---

512. FED. R. CIV. P. 11(d).

513. *See* FED. R. CIV. P. 11(d) advisory committee's note to the 1993 amendment.

514. 28 U.S.C. § 1927. *See generally* Debra T. Landis, Annotation, *What Conduct Constitutes Multiplying Proceedings Unreasonably and Vexatiously so as to Warrant Imposition of Liability on Counsel Under 28 U.S.C. § 1927 for Excess Costs, Expenses, and Attorney Fees*, 81 A.L.R. FED. 36 (1987).

515. *See, e.g.*, Mach v. Will Cnty. Sheriff, 580 F.3d 495, 502 (7th Cir. 2009) (recognizing inherent power to sanction); *see also* the discussion of the *Chambers* case in Chapter 5(E)(3) *supra*. *See generally* William A. Harrington, Annotation, *Award of Counsel Fees to Prevailing Party Based on Adversary's Bad Faith, Obduracy, or Other Misconduct*, 31 A.L.R. FED. 833 (1977).

516. Note that § 2072 of Title 28 provides that "[a]ll laws in conflict with [the Federal Rules of Civil Procedure] shall be of no further force or effect after such rules have taken effect." *See* 28 U.S.C. § 2072(b).

517. *See* Edward D. Cavanagh, *Rule 11 of the Federal Rules of Civil Procedure: The Case Against Turning Back the Clock*, 162 F.R.D. 383, 399-400 (1995) (citing an example from the Northern District of New York relying on the court's inherent powers to impose sanctions and concluding that "any attempts to manipulate the safe harbor provisions to the detriment of a rival litigant [are] amply dealt with in complementary sanction provisions under federal law). In Ridder v. City of Springfield, 109 F.3d 288 (6th Cir. 1997), the court held that the safe harbor requirement had not been complied with, so Rule 11 could not be the basis of sanctions. However, the court ordered the plaintiff's attorney sanctioned under § 1927. Nevertheless, the court noted that if an attorney is only guilty of inadvertence or negligence that frustrates the trial judge, a sanction is not appropriate under § 1927. In Corley v. Rosewood Care Ctr., Inc., 142 F.3d 1041 (7th Cir. 1998), sanctions were held improper under Rule 11 where the separate motion and safe harbor periods were not complied with; furthermore, sanctions were held improper under the court's inherent power because the district court did not make a finding of bad faith or explain why Rule 11 was inadequate to serve the court's purposes. *See also* Primus Auto. Fin. Servs., Inc. v. Batarse, 115 F.3d 644 (9th Cir. 1997) (sanctions requested under § 1927 and Rule 11; sanctions imposed on both attorney and client without allocating responsibility between them; totality of sanctions fell outside § 1927 and Rule 11, but were appropriate under the court's inherent power; however, sanctions required a finding of bad faith to be sustainable under inherent power); Trulis v. Barton, 107 F.3d 685 (9th Cir. 1995) (attempted bribery not sanctionable under Rule 11 but can be sanctioned under district court's inherent powers). *See generally* Ted Lapidus, S.A. v. Vann, 112 F.3d 91 (2d Cir. 1997) (discussing the differences in § 1927 and Rule 11); Robert G. Bone, *Modeling Frivolous Suits*, 145 U. PA. L. REV. 519 (1997).

Other statutory provisions also allow awards of costs and fees. *See, e.g.*, Martin v. Franklin Capital Corp., 546 U.S. 132, 126 S. Ct. 704, 163 L. Ed. 2d 547 (2005) (28 U.S.C. § 1447(c), which allows district court in its discretion to award costs, expenses, and attorney's fees when an improperly removed case is remanded, does not require such an award; attorney's fees should not be awarded when there was an objectively reasonable basis for removal); Wendt v. Leonard, 431 F.3d 410 (4th Cir. 2005) (district court had jurisdiction to award attorney fees

SECTION G. PROVISIONAL REMEDIES

This section concerns special procedures called *provisional remedies* that are sometimes important at the outset of litigation. The purpose of provisional remedies is to preserve the status quo pending the court's determination of the parties' rights or to insure that sufficient resources will be available to satisfy the plaintiff's claim if the plaintiff ultimately prevails. If such remedies—attachment, garnishment, sequestration, replevin, temporary restraining orders, preliminary injunctions, civil arrest—were not available, the litigation process could be substantially undermined.[518]

In federal court, "legal" provisional remedies, such as attachment, garnishment, and replevin, are controlled by the law of the state in which the district court is sitting. Rule 64 of the Federal Rules of Civil Procedure states that "[a]t the commencement of and throughout an action, every remedy is available that, under the law of the state where the court is located, provides for seizing a person or property to secure satisfaction of the potential judgment. But a federal statute governs to the extent it applies."[519] In contrast, federal district courts have independent equitable power, regulated by Federal Rule 65, to issue temporary restraining orders and preliminary injunctions. The difference in approaches under Rules 64 and 65 is attributable to the historical differences in the procedures followed by the federal courts in common law and equity actions before the Federal Rules of Civil Procedure were adopted. In common-law actions, the federal courts

---

under 42 U.S.C. § 1988(b) for an action dismissed for lack of subject-matter jurisdiction due to the Tax Injunction Act, 28 U.S.C. § 1341); Bryant v. Britt, 420 F.3d 161 (2d Cir. 2005) (citizen of forum removed action in violation of proscription against removal in 28 U.S.C. § 1441(b); provision in 28 U.S.C. § 1447(c) that a remand order may require payment of costs, including attorney's fees, incurred as a result of the removal (1) allowed award of costs and attorney's fees after remand and (2) did not require the award to be part of the remand order). *But cf. In re* Cardizem CD Antitrust Litig., 481 F.3d 355 (6th Cir. 2007) (Rule 54(d)(1) and 28 U.S.C. § 1920 permit "costs" to be charged to parties, not their attorneys; express authorization in Rule 11 and § 1927 would have little value if Rule 54 and § 1920 allowed such awards). In Smoot v. Mazda Motors of America, Inc., 469 F.3d 675 (7th Cir. 2006), a rule of the Court of Appeals required the parties in their briefs to include a jurisdictional statement. The parties did so incompetently. Judge Posner's remarks on this issue are worth reproducing:

> [T]he lawyers have wasted our time as well as their own and (depending on the fee arrangements) their clients' money. We have been plagued by the carelessness of a number of the lawyers practicing before the courts of this circuit with regard to the required contents of jurisdictional statements in diversity cases. . . . It is time . . . that this malpractice stopped. We direct the parties to show cause within 10 days why counsel should not be sanctioned for violating [our rule] and mistaking the requirements of diversity jurisdiction. We ask them to consider specifically the appropriateness, as a sanction, of their being compelled to attend a continuing education class in federal jurisdiction.
>
> Are we being fusspots and nitpickers in trying (so far with limited success) to enforce rules designed to ensure that federal courts do not exceed the limits that the Constitution and federal statutes impose on their jurisdiction? Does it really matter if federal courts decide on the merits cases that they are not actually authorized to decide? The sky will not fall if federal courts occasionally stray outside the proper bounds. But the fact that limits on subject-matter jurisdiction are not waivable or forfeitable—that federal courts are required to police their jurisdiction—imposes a duty of care that we are not at liberty to shirk. And since we are not investigative bodies, we need and must assure compliance with procedures designed to compel parties to federal litigation to assist us in keeping within bounds.

Id. at 677-78; *see also* Ratliff v. Stewart, 508 F.3d 225 (5th Cir. 2007) (attorneys unreasonably initiated litigation against wrong party and then unreasonably waited over a month to do anything about it once they had learned of their error; fees properly awarded under improper purpose standard of Rule 11 and § 1927).

518. In addition to the provisional remedies listed in the text, receivership is also considered a provisional remedy. Receivership is the appointment of a neutral third party to manage property that is the subject of the action in order to prevent it from ruin or dissipation by the parties to the action. *See, e.g.*, FED. R. CIV. P. 66.

519. FED. R. CIV. P. 64.

were governed by the conformity acts and generally followed the procedures under state law.[520] In equity cases, the federal courts possessed an independent equity power and were governed by federal equity rules.[521] The Federal Rules of Civil Procedure generally preserve this pattern,[522] with Rule 65 constituting a codification of the pre-Rules equity practice.[523]

1. Attachment and Garnishment

Assume that a defendant has been served with process in an action for money damages. What is to prevent the defendant from withdrawing money from the bank or selling assets and going to Las Vegas on a weekend fling? Or hiding the money? Or removing property from the state where the action is pending to another state or to a Swiss bank? Provisional remedies, such as attachment and garnishment, are designed to protect a plaintiff from these hazards. Attachment is the seizure of the defendant's property in advance of judgment, while garnishment makes an obligation owed by a third person to the defendant subject to the plaintiff's claim.

Statutes establish and regulate the right to attach or garnish property. The statutory grounds for attachment and garnishment usually focus on defendants who abscond, hide or convey assets, or leave the jurisdiction with the intent to defraud creditors.[524] The plaintiff must show that a proposed attachment or garnishment is based upon an appropriate statutory ground and that other statutory prerequisites have been met—for example, the action is one in which attachment is permitted, the property is not exempt from attachment, the plaintiff has posted a bond (undertaking) to cover the defendant's damages if the attachment is found to be improper, etc. If the plaintiff makes such a showing in support of an attachment, the court will order the sheriff (or some other officer) to seize a certain amount of the defendant's property. If the plaintiff makes such a showing in support of a garnishment, the court will order the sheriff (or some other officer) to serve the holder of the property owned by the defendant (for example, a bank) with notice not to pay the defendant (for example, not allow the defendant to withdraw funds from the defendant's account).

Illustration 6-64. *P* sues *D* in a state court. *P* seeks to recover $20,000 for personal injuries received in an automobile accident. Before the action, *P* and *D* had been involved in negotiations directed at settling the claim, but the negotiations broke down. *P* received reliable information that *D* was removing *D's* property from the jurisdiction in anticipation of an action by *P*. Upon commencing the action, *P*

---

520. For a discussion of the conformity acts, see Chapter 1(E)(5) ("Development of Federal Procedure and the Federal Rules of Civil Procedure") & Chapter 5(C)(2)*(e)* ("Equity and Admiralty Cases") *supra*.

521. *See* Chapter 5(C)(2)*(e)* ("Equity and Admiralty Cases") *supra* (discussing the federal equity power).

522. *See* 11A CHARLES A. WRIGHT & ARTHUR R. MILLER, FEDERAL PRACTICE AND PROCEDURE: CIVIL §§ 2931, 2941 (2d ed. 1995).

523. *See id.* § 2943, at 79. *But see, e.g.*, United States *ex rel.* Rahman v. Oncology Assocs., P.C., 198 F.3d 489 (4th Cir. 1999) (Rule 64 authorizes the use of state equitable remedies permitting seizures).

524. *See, e.g.*, NEB. REV. STAT. § 25-1001 (2008).; *see also* Af-Cap, Inc. v. Republic of Congo, 462 F.3d 417 (5th Cir. 2006) (Texas garnishment statute did not permit garnishment of nonmonetary obligations); Cahaly v. Benistar Prop. Exch. Trust Co., Inc., 268 Conn. 264, 842 A.2d 1113 (2004) (Connecticut prejudgment remedy statutes do not authorize attachment of defendant's assets to secure enforcement of an out-of-state judgment prior to the time that the judgment is rendered).

may proceed under the state attachment statute by having the sheriff seize an amount of *D's* property in *D's* possession that will satisfy *P's* claim against *D* if *P* wins the action.

Illustration 6-65. On the facts of *Illustration 6-64*, if *D* possesses bank accounts in the state where the action is commenced, *P* may proceed under the state garnishment statute to garnish the accounts. Under the garnishment statute, an order would issue from the court in which the action is pending to the bank where *D* had accounts, directing the bank to hold the money in the accounts secure for the further order of the court and to not pay the money to *D*. If the bank violates the order, the bank, as garnishee, can be held liable to *P* for the amount of the accounts.

* * * * *

Attachment and garnishment procedures (as well as those governing other provisional remedies) must afford the defendant due process. In general, the defendant must be served with notice of the proposed attachment or garnishment and be given the right to challenge the attachment or garnishment before it is ordered. However, in many situations, the nature of the grounds for attachment or garnishment are such that a prior notice and hearing would frustrate the purpose of these procedures. In such "emergency" situations, an ex parte order and writ may be issued, provided the defendant is given a *prompt* post-seizure opportunity to challenge the order and writ, to substitute a bond (undertaking) for the property attached or garnished, and to challenge the amount or sufficiency of the plaintiff's bond.[525]

Illustration 6-66. On the facts of *Illustrations 6-64* and *6-65*, the state attachment and garnishment statutes would normally provide for issuance of attachment and garnishment orders without a prior notice and an opportunity to be heard upon a proper showing by *P* that *D* was removing *D's* property from the state to avoid execution of a potential judgment against *D*. The statutes would usually also provide for a prompt postseizure hearing at *D's* request, in which *P* would have the burden of proving the existence of grounds for the provisional remedy issued. *P* would normally also have to post a bond sufficient to indemnify *D* for any economic losses *D* might suffer if the provisional remedy is eventually shown to have been erroneously issued. *D* would also have an opportunity to challenge the sufficiency of the bond after the provisional remedy is issued.

2. Sequestration

The writ of sequestration was used in English chancery actions as a provisional remedy to compel an answer to a bill and as a method of enforcing the final decree. As a provisional remedy today, it is employed primarily to preserve specific property from disposition pending the outcome of litigation. It was adopted by several states, but in many instances it has now been limited or abrogated by statute or court rule. It is directed generally at property or funds that are the subject of conflicting claims of ownership or liens. Sequestration also has been used to

---

525. *See* subsection 5 for a full discussion of the constitutional limitations on the operation of provisional remedies *infra*.

restore property that forcibly and unlawfully has been taken from a party. This use of sequestration is very similar to replevin, discussed in the next subsection.

3. Replevin

Replevin as a form of action at common law covered the wrongful seizure of chattels.[526] Today in the United States, the replevin procedure (also called in some states by other names, such as "claim and delivery") is regulated by statute but remains similar to the common-law practice. By claiming the right to immediate possession, the plaintiff can have the property returned to the plaintiff pending a trial on the merits. The plaintiff is required to post a bond to provide security to reimburse the defendant for damages if it is ultimately determined that the defendant is entitled to the property. Before the property is returned to the plaintiff, the defendant is given an opportunity to object to the bond's adequacy. Most states provide for a "re-delivery bond" or "counter bond," which provides security to protect the plaintiff. Such a bond permits a defendant to retain possession of the property until the final determination of the action.[527]

In addition to statutory replevin discussed above, many states have recognized "equitable replevin." Equitable replevin is accomplished by a mandatory injunction ordering the defendant to return property to the plaintiff. It is used when the statutory replevin procedure (the remedy at law) is inadequate for some reason. Often, the property that is the subject of the action is unique or irreplaceable. Under these circumstances, there is danger that the statutory replevin procedure will not produce a return of the property *in specie* because the defendant is able to post a redelivery bond. The redelivery bond will, by definition, be inadequate to protect the plaintiff because it will only substitute money for the unique or irreplaceable property.[528]

Both statutory and equitable replevin differ from attachment and garnishment in the extent to which the plaintiff is claiming an interest in the property seized. When a plaintiff utilizes attachment and garnishment, the plaintiff is simply attempting to seize general assets of the defendant in order to secure a potential judgment. The plaintiff is not claiming any property interest in the assets seized. In contrast, replevin is a provisional remedy used when the plaintiff is claiming an interest in specific personal property that is in the possession of the defendant.

Illustration 6-67. *P*, a merchant, sells a refrigerator to *D* under a contract requiring *D* to make installment payments for 24 months until the price of the refrigerator is paid. Under the contract, *P* retains ownership of the refrigerator as security that the payments will be made. If *D* does not make the payments required by the contract, *P* is entitled to repossess the refrigerator. After a time, *D* ceases making the payments required by the contract. *P* commences an action to obtain a judgment for the payments. Under these circumstances, many states would allow *P* to employ the provisional remedy of replevin to seize the refrigerator pending the

---

526. *See* Chapter 1(E)(1)*(b)(iii)* ("*Ex Delicto* Personal Actions") *supra*.
527. DAN B. DOBBS, LAW OF REMEDIES § 5.17(2), at 583-84 (2d student ed. 1993).
528. *See generally id.* § 5.17(3), at 586.

outcome of the litigation with *D*. The contract gives *P* a right to a return of the security if *D* does not make the payments. This interest makes the provisional remedy of replevin appropriate. By statute, *D* will usually have the right to post a redelivery bond to obtain the return of the refrigerator during the litigation with *P*.

Illustration 6-68. *P* claims ownership of an irreplaceable work of art. *P* asserts that *P* loaned the work of art to *D* and that *D* refuses to return the work of art. *P* sues *D* to obtain return of the work of art. Under these circumstances, the provisional remedy of equitable replevin may be available to *P* to obtain return of the work of art during the pendency of the litigation with *D*. The irreplaceable nature of the work of art arguably makes *P's* "remedy at law" in the form of statutory replevin inadequate because statutory replevin would allow *D* to obtain its return after seizure by posting a redelivery bond. Thus, equitable replevin will be the only provisional remedy that will assure *P* that the work of art will not be destroyed, sold, or removed from the jurisdiction by *D*.

4. Civil Arrest

The provisional remedies discussed in the preceding subsections are directed at the seizure of property as a means of securing the plaintiff's claim if the plaintiff ultimately should be successful. There are also provisional remedies directed at the seizure of the defendant for the same purpose: civil arrest and the writ of ne exeat, discussed in the next subsection. As noted in Chapter 3, certain actions at common law were commenced by *capias ad respondendum*. This writ directed the sheriff to arrest the defendant for the purpose of securing the defendant's court appearance on a certain day. A defendant could post security and thus secure release.[529] In most states, the use of civil arrest has been abolished or limited by state constitutional provisions prohibiting imprisonment for debt. However, it remains a proper provisional remedy in some states.[530]

5. Ne Exeat

The writ of ne exeat is similar to civil arrest. It was used in equity to restrain the impending departure of a defendant from the jurisdiction of the court with the intent to evade its jurisdiction or to defraud the plaintiff. The defendant could gain release by posting a bond or equitable bail securing the defendant's appearance and performance of the court's decree. While still available as a remedy in some states to secure equitable claims, it is rarely used, except in matrimonial actions. In many states, it has been abolished.[531]

---

529. *See* Chapter 3(K)(1) ("Service of Process in English and Early United States Practice") *supra*.

530. *See* 5 AM. JUR. 2D *Arrest* §§ 53-66 (2007); *see also* Eugene J. Morris & Hilton M. Wiener, *Civil Arrest: A Medieval Anachronism*, 43 BROOKLYN L. REV. 383 (1977). Curiously, arrest is still indirectly sanctioned in federal court under 28 U.S.C. § 1693, a statute preserved in the modern Judicial Code that traces its origins back to the Judiciary Act of 1789. For a discussion of the history of § 1693, see Ralph U. Whitten, *Separation of Powers Restrictions on Judicial Rulemaking: A Case Study of Federal Rule 4*, 40 ME. L. REV. 41, 71-72 (1988).

531. *See* 57 AM. JUR. 2D *Ne Exeat* §§ 1-33 (2001).

6. Temporary Restraining Orders and Preliminary Injunctions

(a) The Nature of Temporary Restraining Orders and Preliminary Injunctions

The development of equity as a separate system complementary to the common-law courts was described in Chapter 1.[532] As noted there, the development of equity has had a substantial impact on modern substantive law, procedures, and remedies, including limitations on the jurisdiction of the federal courts to issue particular types of relief. For example, in *Grupo Mexicano de Desarrollo, S.A. v. Alliance Bond Fund, Inc.*,[533] the Supreme Court held that the U.S. District Courts lack authority under Rule 65 to issue preliminary injunctions preventing defendants from disposing of their assets pending adjudication of claims for money damages in cases in which there has been no prior judgment fixing the amount of the debt. A majority of the Court agreed that the jurisdiction conferred by the Judiciary Act of 1789 over "all suits . . . in equity" gave the federal courts only the authority to administer in equity suits the "principles of the system of judicial remedies which had been devised and was being administered by the English Court of Chancery at the time of the separation of the two countries."[534] That power did not include the authority to issue the kind of preliminary injunction in question. This power was not altered by the merger of law and equity by the Federal Rules of Civil Procedure pursuant to the Rules Enabling Act, because "the rule requiring a judgment [fixing the amount of the debt before a preliminary injunction could issue] was historically regarded as serving, not merely the procedural end of assuring exhaustion of legal remedies (which the merger of law and equity could render irrelevant), but also the substantive end of giving the creditor an interest in the property which equity could then act upon."[535]

Interestingly, however, the majority indicated that "[t]he debate concerning this formidable power over debtors should be conducted and resolved where such issues belong in our democracy: in the Congress."[536] This implies that Congress could legislate to override state substantive rights with a remedial rule applicable only in federal courts without violating the constitutional restrictions on Congress's power potentially imposed by the *Erie* decision. However, in another part of its opinion, the Court also explicitly reserved judgment (because the parties had not raised the issue) as to whether, if state courts could issue the remedy in question, federal courts would be obliged to do so.[537] The Court also observed that no one in the case had raised the applicability of Federal Rule 18(b), which provided that multiple claims can be joined in an action even when one of them has been

---

532. *See* Chapter 1(E)(2) ("Equity Jurisdiction and Procedure") *supra*.
533. 527 U.S. 308, 119 S. Ct. 1961, 144 L. Ed. 2d 319 (1999).
534. *Id.* at 318, 119 S. Ct. at 1968, 144 L. Ed. 2d at 330.
535. *Id.* at 323, 119 S. Ct. at 1970, 144 L. Ed. 2d at 333-34.
536. *Id.* at 333, 119 S. Ct. at 1975, 144 L. Ed. 2d at 339.
537. *See id.* at 319, n.3, 119 S. Ct. at 1968, n.3, 144 L. Ed. 2d at 330, n.3.

"heretofore cognizable" after the other has been prosecuted to a conclusion,[538] but that the court can grant relief in the action only in accord with the "relative substantive rights of the parties." The Court also noted that Rule 18 said nothing about preliminary relief and specifically reserves substantive rights, as does the Rules Enabling Act.[539]

Equity courts usually act through personal orders to the defendant to do or refrain from doing some act. "Injunctive" orders and decrees for specific performance are enforced by contempt proceedings.[540] In the context of provisional remedies, such actions have taken the form of "temporary restraining orders" and "preliminary injunctions." Temporary restraining orders and preliminary injunctions are designed to preserve the status quo until final determination of the action. The primary difference between a temporary restraining order and a preliminary injunction is that the latter is granted only after a hearing while the former can be granted ex parte. In theory, a temporary restraining order should preserve the status quo only until there can be a hearing on a preliminary injunction, while the preliminary injunction is designed to remain in effect until the final determination of the action.[541] Federal Rule 65 sets out a uniform procedure for granting these two equitable remedies in federal court and in states that have adopted the Federal Rules. Rule 65 thus constitutes a useful example of how temporary restraining orders and preliminary injunctions are generally administered.

Temporary restraining orders are granted only in "emergency" situations. They are issued only when it clearly appears from a verified complaint, or from specific facts shown by affidavit, that the applicant will suffer "immediate and irreparable injury, loss, or damage" before notice can be served and a hearing can be held on a motion for preliminary injunction.[542] The steps that the applicant's attorney has taken (if any) to give notice must be specified and the reasons why

---

538. Note that Rule 18(b) has been substantially revised to eliminate this "heretofore cognizable" language. The Advisory Committee explained that its modification "avoids any uncertainty whether Rule 18(b)'s meaning is fixed by retrospective inquiry from some particular date." *See* FED. R. CIV. P. 18(b) advisory committee's note to the 2007 restyling amendment.

539. *See* 527 U.S. at 333, 119 S. Ct. at 1970, 144 L. Ed. 2d at 334; *cf.* Cahaly v. Benistar Prop. Exch. Trust Co., Inc., 268 Conn. 264, 842 A.2d 1113 (2004) (Connecticut prejudgment remedy statutes do not authorize attachment of defendant's assets to secure enforcement of an out-of-state judgment prior to the time that the judgment is rendered); United States *ex rel.* Rahman v. Oncology Assocs., P.C., 198 F.3d 489 (4th Cir. 1999) (holding it permissible for a federal court to issue an equitable order freezing assets when part of the final relief requested is also equitable; alternatively, Rule 64 allows federal courts to employ equitable orders freezing assets if state law so permits); *see also* Stephen B. Burbank, *The Bitter With the Sweet: Tradition, History, and Limitations on Federal Judicial Power—A Case Study*, 75 NOTRE DAME L. REV. 1291 (2000) (providing an excellent discussion of *Grupo*); Mary A. Nation, Comment, *Granting a Preliminary Injunction Freezing Assets Not Part of the Pending Litigation: Abuse of Discretion Or an Important Advance in Creditors' Rights?* 7 TUL. J. INT'L & COMP. L. 367 (1999); Jeffrey L. Wilson, Note, *Three If by Equity: Mareva Orders & the New British Invasion,* 19 ST. JOHN'S J. LEGAL COMMENT. 673 (2005).

540. *See* DAN B. DOBBS, LAW OF REMEDIES §§ 2.8(2)-2.8(7) (2d student ed. 1993) (discussing the differences between civil and criminal contempt).

541. Although temporary restraining orders can be issued without notice to the defendant, ex parte issuance must be justified by the circumstances. *See, e.g.,* Reno Air Racing Ass'n, Inc. v. McCord, 452 F.3d 1126 (9th Cir. 2006) (TRO improperly granted ex parte against accused trademark infringer when plaintiff offered no support that there was a significant risk that defendant would leave the area and did not advise court of plaintiff's prior dealings with defendant or that it had done nothing to enforce its rights following earlier contacts); *see also* Steffes v. City of Lawrence, 284 Kan. 380, 160 P.3d 843 (2007) (purposes of temporary restraining order or preliminary injunction are to prevent injury to a claimed right pending a final determination of the action on the merits; if the grant of a temporary restraining order or preliminary injunction would accomplish the entire objective of the action without bringing it to trial, the remedies would be improper).

542. *See* FED. R. CIV. P. 65(b)(1)(A).

notice should not be required also must be stated.[543] Local court rules often require specific efforts to give notice, such as telephoning the adverse party to inform that party of the facts and that an application for a temporary restraining order is being made so that oral counter-arguments might be made.[544] The applicant also must post security to indemnify the opposing party against economic harm that may occur due to an erroneous issuance of an order.[545] Rule 65(b)(2) provides that a temporary restraining "order expires at the time after entry—not to exceed 14 days—that the court sets, unless before that time the court, for good cause, extends it for a like period or the adverse party consents to a longer extension."[546] Ideally, within this time period, a hearing will be held to determine whether a preliminary injunction will be issued.[547]

Illustration 6-69. *P* awakens one morning to find *D Co.* present on *P's* property about to bulldoze a large number of ancient, ornamental trees. *D's* employees tell *P* that they are about to grade the land for the construction of an amusement park. Despite *P's* best attempts to convince the employees that they are in the wrong location, they persist in making preparations to destroy the trees. Under these circumstances, *P* should be able to obtain a temporary restraining order to prevent *D* from trespassing on the land and destroying the trees. *P* is faced with an emergency situation in which there is no time to provide notice and an opportunity to be heard to *D* before the order issues. Monetary damages will not adequately compensate *P* because of the age and ornamental character of the trees. Thus, *P* is threatened with "irreparable injury."[548]

* * * * *

Assume that a court has granted a temporary restraining order and a hearing is being held on the question of whether a preliminary injunction should be granted. What standard should the court use to decide this question? Rule 65 does not state a standard. Furthermore, the federal and state courts are not in full agreement on the proper standard. In general, courts take into account four factors: (1) the injury that will result to the applicant if the preliminary injunction is denied; (2) the likelihood of the applicant's success on the merits; (3) whether the threatened injury to the applicant outweighs the possible injury to the opposing party; and (4) whether the public interest would be harmed by issuance of a preliminary injunction.[549]

Illustration 6-70. *P* owns property that *P* uses as a residence. *P's* property is adjacent to property owned by *D*, which *D* uses as a manufacturing plant. *D's*

---

543. FED. R. CIV. P. 65(b)(2).

544. SHEPARD'S MANUAL OF FEDERAL PRACTICE 584 (2d ed. 1979).

545. *See* FED. R. CIV. P. 65(c). However, it has been held that the bond requirement is not a jurisdictional prerequisite to the validity of a preliminary injunction. Popular Bank v. Banco Popular, 180 F.R.D. 461 (S.D. Fla. 1998). *See generally* F.M. English, Annotation, *Furnishing of Bond as Prerequisite to Issuance of Temporary Restraining Order*, 73 A.L.R.2D 854 (1960).

546. *See* FED. R. CIV. P. 65(b)(2). The reasons for the extension must be entered in the record. *Id.*

547. *See In re* Cardizen CD Antitrust Litig., 329 F.3d 131 (2d Cir. 2003) (a temporary restraining order issued after notice and a hearing effectively becomes a preliminary injunction when the court extends it beyond the period prescribed by Rule 65(b); a party subject to an extended TRO cannot assume that it is no longer effective and violate it with impunity).

548. *See* DAN B. DOBBS, LAW OF REMEDIES § 2.11(2), at 193-94 (2d student ed. 1993).

549. SHEPARD'S MANUAL OF FEDERAL PRACTICE 583 (2d ed. 1979). *See generally* DAN B. DOBBS, LAW OF REMEDIES § 2.11(2) (2d student ed. 1993); 11A CHARLES A. WRIGHT & ARTHUR R. MILLER, FEDERAL PRACTICE AND PROCEDURE: CIVIL § 2948, at 127-38 (2d ed. 1995).

operations produce a small amount of pollution that is affecting the paint on *P's* house, causing it to deteriorate more rapidly than it would under natural conditions. *P* sues *D* for a preliminary injunction to stop *D* from emitting the pollution from *D's* plant. The only way to prevent the pollution over the short run is to close down the plant, which will throw 5,000 employees out of work and severely affect the economy of the local community in which the plant is located. Under these circumstances, it is unlikely that *P* will be able to obtain a preliminary injunction. The injury to *P's* house is minor compared to the effects on *D* and the public interest of granting the injunction. Indeed, the injury can probably be compensated adequately in damages. A full exploration of the merits may reveal some way that the pollution can be eliminated or diminished. Thus, the temporary harm to *P* does not justify the possibly massive harm to *D* and third parties that issuing the injunction would cause.

* * * * *

In *Gonzales v. Centro Espirita Beneficente Uniao Do Vegetal,*[550] the Supreme Court considered the relative burden of proof that the plaintiff and the defendant must carry on the probability of success on the merits inquiry. In *Gonzales,* the plaintiff sued under the Religious Freedom Restoration Act[551] ("RFRA") to invalidate a prohibition on the plaintiffs' use of a hallucinogenic substance in religious ceremonies. RFRA prohibits the federal government from substantially burdening a person's exercise of religion, even under a rule of general applicability, unless the government can demonstrate a compelling governmental interest and that the burden is the least restrictive means of furthering that interest. The prohibition on the use of the substance was conceded to impose a substantial burden on the plaintiffs' religious freedom. However, the government, which would have the burden of proof at trial on the other two issues because they were affirmative defenses, contended that the plaintiff, in order to demonstrate the probability of success necessary to obtain a preliminary injunction, had to bear the burden of showing no compelling state interest and that the means employed by the government was not the least restrictive alternative. The Supreme Court rejected this contention, holding that the burden of proof at the preliminary injunction stage mirrors the burden of proof at trial. Thus, the plaintiff bears the burden on elements of the plaintiff's claim, and the defendant bears the burden of proof on affirmative defenses that it would have to establish at trial. Because the evidence on the two affirmative defenses was in equipoise, this meant that the government lost and the plaintiff was entitled to the preliminary injunction. *Gonzalez* is an important clarification of preliminary injunction practice that has potentially far-reaching effects in other kinds of cases.

(b) Contempt

Temporary restraining orders and preliminary injunctions are enforced by means of the contempt sanction. There are two kinds of contempt: *civil contempt*

---

550. 546 U.S. 418, 126 S. Ct. 1211, 163 L. Ed. 2d 1017 (2006).
551. 42 U.S.C. § 2000bb-1(a).

and *criminal contempt*.[552] Violation of a temporary restraining order or preliminary injunction can result in the imposition of *both* civil and criminal contempt sanctions. Criminal contempt sanctions are imposed to punish someone for violating a court decree in order to vindicate the court's authority.[553] To this end, criminal contempt sanctions involve fixed fines or fixed jail sentences.[554] In contrast, civil contempt sanctions are designed to coerce compliance with the court's decree in the future.[555] Thus, a civil contempt fine will be assessed at a certain amount per day until the contemnor complies with the order, or a jail sentence of an indefinite term will be imposed until the contemnor agrees to comply with the court's order.[556] The nature and purpose of the sanction imposed, therefore, determines the kind of contempt involved in the case.[557]

When criminal contempt sanctions are imposed, the protections of a criminal trial must be afforded to the contemnor. For example, the criminal burden of proof applies in criminal contempt proceedings, and when "serious" penalties are imposed for criminal contempt, there is a constitutional right to a trial by jury.[558] In contrast, civil contempt sanctions do not ordinarily require the protections of a criminal proceeding and are not subject to the Sixth Amendment requirement of jury trials for criminal proceedings.[559] However, due process protections may be required in a civil proceeding to make them fundamentally fair.[560]

Illustration 6-71. *P* sues *D* for specific performance of a contract to convey land. The court issues a decree of specific performance against *D*. *D* refuses to comply with the decree. The court holds *D* in contempt in a proceeding that did not afford *D* the ordinary protections available in a criminal proceeding. The court sentences *D* to remain in jail until *D* agrees to execute a deed of the land covered by the contract and decree of specific performance. The court's action is valid. The sanction imposed on *D* is designed to coerce compliance with the court's decree, not to punish *D* for past violation of the decree. As a result, it is a civil contempt sanction that does not have to be accompanied by the protections of a criminal trial.

* * * * *

---

552. For a useful discussion of the differences between civil and criminal contempt, see Lawrence N. Gray, *Criminal and Civil Contempt: Some Sense of a Hodgepodge*, 72 ST. JOHNS L. REV. 337 (1998).

553. *See* DAN B. DOBBS, LAW OF REMEDIES § 2.8(3), at 139 (2d student ed. 1993).

554. *See id.*

555. *See id.*

556. *See id.*

557. *See id.* at 138.

558. *See id.* § 2.8(4), at 145-47.

559. There have been recent examples of cases in which the courts have held that it is possible for coercive sanctions imposed for civil contempt to become "criminal" in nature. *See id.* § 2.8(3), at 140-45. The alternative view is that the nature of the sanction should be measured at the time it is imposed. If it is civil then, it cannot become criminal. *Cf. id.* at 145.

560. *See, e.g.*, Turner v. Rogers, 564 U.S. __, 131 S. Ct. 2507, 180 L. Ed. 2d 452 (2011) (holding that the Due Process Clause of the Fourteenth Amendment does not automatically require the state to provide legal counsel at a civil contempt proceeding in the context of an indigent noncustodial parent who has failed o pay child support even though that parent faces incarceration to induce the parent to pay as long as the state provides alternative procedural safeguards equivalent to (1) adequate notice of the importance of the ability to pay, (2) the use of a form to elicit relevant financial information, (3) a fair opportunity to present or dispute evidence, and (4) the court makes express findings as to the supporting parent's ability to comply with the court order (because inability of a person who is unable to comply with the terms of the order is purged of civil contempt and is free) in order to reduce the risk of an erroneous deprivation of liberty; leaving open the issue when civil contempt proceedings involves money owed to the state or the case is unusually complex and thus the defendant can be fairly represented only by a trained advocate).

Traditionally, a party has been required to obey an injunctive order until it is overturned. Thus, a party can be punished for criminal contempt for disobeying a temporary restraining order or preliminary injunction, even if the order is ultimately reversed on appeal.[561] The ability to impose criminal contempt sanctions for violation of an erroneous order may depend on the availability to the defendant of adequate procedures to challenge the order before the time for disobedience to it arrives. If such procedures do not exist, a defendant may be able to violate the order and effectively challenge it on appeal from a criminal contempt conviction.[562] Nevertheless, it would take a bold lawyer to advise a client to disobey an injunctive order because the order is erroneous and might be reversed on appeal from a criminal contempt conviction. In addition to the fact that the state of the law in this area is unsettled, there is always the possibility that the order will be held correct, rather than erroneous, and the criminal contempt sentence upheld as a result.

There is also a potential escape from criminal contempt sanctions if an order is ultimately found to be "void," as opposed to only "erroneous." Void orders are ones issued without personal jurisdiction over the defendant or subject-matter jurisdiction over the action.[563] However, the "void order" exception is itself subject to an important exception. When a defendant raises a challenge to jurisdiction, the challenge must be determined by the court. This may require time, and the court may deem it proper to issue a temporary restraining order to preserve the status quo during the period of time necessary to determine the jurisdictional issue. It is said that a court always has jurisdiction to determine its own jurisdiction. Thus, if the defendant violates the temporary restraining order while the court is trying to determine whether it has ultimate jurisdiction over the action or the defendant's person, the defendant can be punished for criminal contempt even if the court ultimately holds that it lacks jurisdiction over the subject matter or the parties. The court's jurisdiction to determine jurisdiction gives it the power to enter an order that must be obeyed until the ultimate jurisdictional determination is made, at least if the jurisdictional issue is substantial and not frivolous.[564]

Illustration 6-72. *D* wants to conduct a civil rights march on Easter Sunday. *P*, a public official, obtains a temporary restraining order to prevent the march. *D* possesses notice of the order several days before the march, but does nothing to try to get the order overturned under the procedures available in the court that issued the order or the appellate courts of the state. Instead, when Easter Sunday arrives, *D* conducts the march in violation of the order. *D* attempts to defend a criminal contempt proceeding brought against *D* on the ground that the order violated *D's* First Amendment rights. Even if the order violates the First Amendment, *D* can be punished for criminal contempt. The order is only "erroneous," albeit constitutionally erroneous, and not "void." *D* did not attempt to get the order overturned, even

---

561. *See* DAN B. DOBBS, LAW OF REMEDIES § 2.8(6), at 153 (2d student ed. 1993). Obviously, however, a court cannot impose civil contempt sanctions on a person in violation of an order that is ultimately held to be in error. Once the order is held erroneous, there is nothing left with which a civil contempt sanction can coerce compliance.

562. *See id.* at 154-55.

563. *See id.*

564. *See id.* at 155-56.

though *D* had the time to do so and procedures were available to *D* to have the order reviewed by the court that issued it and the appellate courts of the state.[565]

Illustration 6-73. *D Labor Union* engaged in a strike during wartime when the government was operating the industry in which *D's* members worked. The government sought an injunction to prohibit the strike. *D* contended that the courts had no jurisdiction to issue injunctions in strike disputes. The court issued a temporary restraining order against *D* to prevent the strike during the period of time necessary to determine this jurisdictional issue. *D* violated the order. If the jurisdictional issue under the statute is substantial rather than frivolous, *D* can be punished for criminal contempt for violating the order, even if the courts ultimately hold that they have no jurisdiction to issue injunctions against strikes. The court's jurisdiction to determine jurisdiction gives it the power to issue a temporary restraining order to allow it to resolve the jurisdictional question.[566]

(c) The Bond Requirement

Ordinarily, temporary restraining orders and preliminary injunctions—as well as most other provisional remedies—cannot be issued without the plaintiff first providing security to protect the defendant from harm that may accrue if the provisional remedy is erroneously issued. This security is often provided in the form of a bond. The bond is quite important to the defendant. The predominant view is that, in the absence of security, the defendant cannot recover anything from the plaintiff for economic harm suffered as the result of an erroneous provisional order.[567] Furthermore, damages can normally be recovered under the bond only for economic losses actually incurred by the defendant as a result of the erroneous issuance of the order.[568] Depending upon the procedure in effect in the jurisdiction where recovery on the bond is sought, the injured party may have to proceed by independent action or may be allowed to recover against the surety on motion.[569]

7. Constitutional Limitations on Provisional Remedies

The procedures governing all provisional remedies presuppose circumstances under which the defendant will not receive notice and an opportunity to be heard in defense before the remedy issues. For example, the rules governing

---

565. *Cf.* Walker v. City of Birmingham, 388 U.S. 307, 87 S. Ct. 1824, 18 L. Ed. 2d 1210 (1967). *See generally* John R.B. Palmer, Note, *Collateral Bar and Contempt: Challenging a Court Order After Disobeying It,* 88 CORNELL L. REV. 215 (2002).

566. *See* United States v. United Mine Workers, 330 U.S. 258, 67 S. Ct. 677, 91 L. Ed. 884 (1947).

567. *See* DAN B. DOBBS, LAW OF REMEDIES § 2.11(3), at 197 (2d student ed. 1993). Sometimes, a plaintiff may be sanctionable under a rule, such as Federal Rule 11, for bringing a frivolous claim, and, rarely, the issuance of a provisional order may give rise to a claim for malicious abuse of civil process or restitution. *See id.* at 199. In addition, some courts have held that it is permissible to impose a condition on the provisional order that the plaintiff be personally liable to the defendant for economic harm suffered as a result of the order. *See id.* at 198. However, in the absence of such circumstances or conditions, the defendant must look to the bond as the sole source of compensation for economic harm suffered as a result of an erroneous provisional remedy.

568. *See id.* at 203-04.

569. *See* FED. R. CIV. P. 65.1. For a complete discussion of the security requirement, including questions such as the court's discretion to dispense with the bond, what will trigger the bond liability, and the measurement of damages recoverable, see DAN B. DOBBS, LAW OF REMEDIES § 2.11(3) (2d student ed. 1993).

temporary restraining orders envision that such orders can be issued without notice to the adverse party under limited circumstances.[570] It is obvious, however, that the availability of such remedies without prior notice and hearing can be the source of abuse. Abuse of the remedies has led the Supreme Court to place due process restrictions on availability of provisional remedies without prior notice and hearing. The Court's modern decisions have indicated the safeguards that a state's provisional-remedy scheme must have in order to meet constitutional standards. However, the Court's decisions have not yet completely clarified all of the elements of the constitutional test.

The Court's earliest modern decision was *Sniadach v. Family Finance Corp.*[571] In *Sniadach*, the Court invalidated Wisconsin's garnishment procedure under the Due Process Clause of the Fourteenth Amendment because it did not provide for notice and an opportunity to be heard before seizure. The property seized in *Sniadach* was wages, and the Court's opinion implied that wages deserved special protection under the Constitution.[572] However, this view was rejected in the Court's next decision, *Fuentes v. Shevin.*[573]

In *Fuentes*, the Court invalidated Florida's replevin procedure under circumstances where a creditor had utilized it to repossess consumer goods from a consumer who had stopped making payments on the goods.[574] The writ of replevin was issued on the ex parte application of the plaintiff, who was also required to file a bond in an amount double the value of the property. The Court recognized that extraordinary situations exist in which no notice or opportunity to be heard need be provided before a provisional remedy issues against a defendant. However, the Court held that the situations in which it had allowed postponement of notice and an opportunity to be heard shared certain common characteristics. In each case, (1) seizure was "directly necessary" to secure an important governmental or general public interest; (2) there was a "special need" for very prompt action; and (3) the state kept strict control over the seizure by requiring a government official to determine, "under the standards of a narrowly drawn statute" that the seizure was necessary under the circumstances of the case.[575]

In cases after *Fuentes*, the constitutional requirements for state provisional remedy statutes evolved into a more precise form. The Court's next two decisions, taken together, seemed to establish that a state provisional remedy statute would meet due process requirements if (1) it requires a factual affidavit or other sworn statement by someone with personal knowledge showing that the grounds for issuing the remedy exist; (2) a judge has to scrutinize the application to determine whether the remedy may properly issue; and (3) a prompt postseizure hearing is available in which the plaintiff has the burden of demonstrating the existence of the grounds for issuing the remedy. Furthermore, the constitutionality of an ex parte provisional remedy will be more secure if (1) it is sought for the seizure of property

---

570. *See, e.g.*, FED. R. CIV. P. 65(b).

571. 395 U.S. 337, 89 S. Ct. 1820, 23 L. Ed. 2d 349 (1969).

572. *See id.* at 340, 89 S. Ct. at 1822, 23 L. Ed. 2d at 353.

573. 407 U.S. 67, 92 S. Ct. 1983, 32 L. Ed. 2d 556 (1972).

574. The creditor had retained title to the goods as security for payment.

575. *See* 407 U.S. at 90-92, 92 S. Ct. at 1999-2000, 32 L. Ed. 2d at 575-77.

in which the plaintiff has a preexisting interest and (2) the plaintiff's claim is subject to documentary proof, rather than being dependent upon the testimony of witnesses about (perhaps complex) past events.[576]

In 1991, the Supreme Court clarified that the constitutionality of state provisional remedy schemes is to be determined by a balancing test. In *Connecticut v. Doehr*,[577] the Court held that due process validity of a provisional remedy depends upon a "threefold inquiry," requiring consideration of (1) the private interest that will be affected by the issuance of the provisional remedy; (2) the risk of an erroneous deprivation through the procedures under attack and the probable value of additional or alternative safeguards; and (3) the interest of the party seeking the provisional remedy with due regard for any ancillary interest the government may have in providing the procedure used or forgoing the added burden of providing greater protections.[578] Under this test, the Court found Connecticut's attachment statute unconstitutional. The statute allowed attachment of the defendant's real property without prior notice and an opportunity to be heard, but without a requirement that "exigent circumstances" exist for the attachment or that the plaintiff post a bond.[579] The Court held the statute invalid because it permitted ex parte seizure without a showing of exigent circumstances.[580] Four members of the Court also were of the opinion that a bond is an indispensable constitutional requirement, but the majority did not reach this issue.[581]

Nothing in *Doehr* suggested that the result of the case was affected by the fact that real property was the subject of the attachment. However, a subsequent decision of the Court under the Due Process Clause of the Fifth Amendment has suggested that the prejudgment seizure of real property may be more restricted than

---

576. *See* North Ga. Finishing, Inc. v. Di-Chem, Inc., 419 U.S. 601, 95 S. Ct. 719, 42 L. Ed. 2d 751 (1975); Mitchell v. W.T. Grant Co., 416 U.S. 600, 94 S. Ct. 1895, 40 L. Ed. 2d 406 (1974). In *Mitchell*, the Court upheld Louisiana's sequestration procedures, which had the safeguards described in the text. In addition, the sequestration procedure was used by a creditor to repossess consumer goods in which the creditor had a vendor's lien, and the creditor's claim was simple and could be resolved primarily on the basis of documentary proof. In *Di-Chem*, the provisional remedy was issued by the clerk based on a conclusionary affidavit by the plaintiff, and no way existed to dissolve the remedy except by the defendant filing a bond. In addition, the plaintiff garnished the defendant's bank account, in which the plaintiff had no preexisting interest. *Mitchell* is the only modern decision in which the Court has upheld a state provisional remedy statute against a challenge under the Due Process Clause of the Fourteenth Amendment. *But cf.* Matthews v. Eldridge, 424 U.S. 319, 96 S. Ct. 893, 47 L. Ed. 2d 18 (1976) (administrative procedures for terminating social security disability benefits constitutional, despite the fact that no evidentiary hearing was provided prior to termination).

577. 501 U.S. 1, 111 S. Ct. 2105, 115 L. Ed. 2d 1 (1991).

578. *See id.* at 10, 111 S. Ct. at 2112, 115 L. Ed. 2d at 13.

579. The application for attachment had to be made upon verified affidavit of the plaintiff or some other "competent affiant" that there was probable cause to sustain the validity of the plaintiff's claims. Based on this affidavit, a judge could issue the writ of attachment. The attachment notice had to inform the defendant that a right to a hearing existed in which the defendant could (1) litigate whether probable cause existed for the claim, (2) request that the attachment be vacated, modified, or that a bond be substituted, or (3) claim that the property was exempt from execution. The affidavit and notice complied with these requirements. *See id.* at 5-6, 111 S. Ct. at 2109-10, 115 L. Ed. 2d at 10.

580. The Court found that (1) the private interests affected by the seizure were significant, given the effects that attachment could have on the property owner; (2) the risk of erroneous deprivation was too great, given the highly fact-dependent nature of the plaintiff's claim and the lack of additional adequate safeguards under the statute; and (3) the plaintiff's interests in ex parte attachment were weak in the absence of a showing of exigent circumstances or a preexisting interest in the property on the part of the plaintiff. *See id.* at 11-17, 111 S. Ct. at 2112-15, 115 L. Ed. 2d at 14-16.

581. *See id.* at 18-24, 111 S. Ct. at 2116-19, 115 L. Ed. 2d at 18-21 (Justice White, with whom Justices Marshall, Stevens, and O'Connor joined). The Justices emphasized, however, that a bond requirement would not excuse the absence of exigent circumstances, a prompt post-seizure hearing, or other safeguards. *See id.* at 22-23, 111 S. Ct. at 2118-19, 115 L. Ed. 2d at 20-21.

the seizure of personalty. In *United States v. James Daniel Good Real Property*,[582] the Court invalidated an ex parte prejudgment seizure of the defendant's real property in a proceeding brought to forfeit the property because it had been used to facilitate the commission of a federal drug offense. Applying the *Doehr* balancing test, the Court found that the defendant's interests and the risk of erroneous deprivation outweighed the interests of the government in prejudgment seizure without additional safeguards.[583] The fact that real property "cannot abscond" impaired the government's ability to demonstrate the need for prompt action to seize the property.[584] In addition, the Court emphasized that "[i]ndividual freedom finds tangible expression in property rights," and that "security and privacy of the home and those who take shelter within it" are at stake when real property is seized.[585] These statements suggest that real property may receive an extra measure of protection from prejudgment seizure under the Due Process Clauses of the Constitution.

Based on the Court's decisions from *Sniadach* through *Good*, it is possible to summarize the elements that are indispensable to a state provisional remedy scheme in order for the scheme to meet constitutional requirements. In addition, it is possible to extrapolate at least one other likely requirement that the Court may add to the list of indispensable elements in the future. Finally, it is possible to point to certain other factors that will weigh heavily in the balance in determining whether a provisional remedy statute can be validly applied in specific cases.

To meet constitutional standards, a provisional remedy statute must contain at least four elements: (1) "exigent circumstances" must exist that somehow threaten to make the plaintiff's action an exercise in futility;[586] (2) the plaintiff must provide facts through an affidavit or other sworn statement by someone with personal knowledge showing that the grounds for issuing the provisional remedy

---

582. 510 U.S. 43, 114 S. Ct. 492, 126 L. Ed. 2d 490 (1993).

583. *See id.* at 62, 114 S. Ct. at 505, 126 L. Ed. 2d at 508-09.

584. *See id.* at 57, 114 S. Ct. at 502-03, 126 L. Ed. 2d at 505. The Court observed that a notice of lis pendens could be filed under state law when the government commences the forfeiture proceedings. *See id.* at 58, 114 S. Ct. at 503, 126 L. Ed. 2d at 506. Lis pendens is a notice filed on public records for the purpose of warning all persons that the title to certain property is in litigation and that they are in danger of being bound by an adverse judgment. Its purpose is to preserve rights pending litigation. However, lis pendens will often involve the same kind of interference with property rights that the Court previously found objectionable in *Doehr*. For example, lis pendens effectively clouds title and prevents the sale of the property until the action is resolved. Apparently, however, the Court is suggesting that this sort of interference with property rights would be legitimate. In addition, the Court stated that "[i]f there is evidence, in a particular case, that an owner is likely to destroy" the property "when advised of the pending action, the government may obtain an *ex parte* restraining order, or other appropriate relief, upon a proper showing in district court." *Id.* However, it may be difficult to obtain affirmative evidence that an owner intends to destroy property. The Court's pronouncement on this aspect of the case may have been affected by the fact that the government left the defendant's tenants in possession of the property. "The government's policy of leaving occupants in possession of real property under an occupancy agreement . . . demonstrates that there is no serious concern about destruction in the ordinary case." *Id.* at 59. Finally, the Court stated that the government could prevent the property from being used for further illegal activity "with search and arrest warrants obtained in the ordinary course." *Id.* at 59, 114 S. Ct. at 504, 126 L. Ed. 2d at 507. Again, this pronouncement may have been based on the four-year passage of time between the defendant's conviction and the commencement of the forfeiture action, as well as the fact that the defendant was not personally occupying the property.

585. *See id.* at 61, 114 S. Ct. at 505, 126 L. Ed. 2d at 508.

586. In the case of provisional remedies such as attachment or garnishment, the exigent circumstances will ordinarily be a tangible threat that the defendant is going to remove assets from the reach of the court's power of execution. In the case of temporary restraining orders, the threat will ordinarily be that the defendant is about to engage in action—*e.g.*, bulldozing ornamental trees on the plaintiff's property—that cannot be effectively remedied by a later damages judgment.

exist; (3) a judge must examine the application to determine that the grounds for issuing the provisional remedy exist; and (4) a prompt postseizure hearing must be available in which the plaintiff bears the burden of proving that the grounds for the provisional remedy exist.

In addition to these four "indispensable" elements of constitutionality, at least one other element will likely be considered indispensable to the validity of a provisional remedy statute. The plaintiff should have to demonstrate a possibility of success on the merits to the judge examining the application. Thus, it should not be possible, even on a showing of exigent circumstances, to obtain a provisional remedy unless the complaint demonstrates that the plaintiff possesses a claim upon which relief can be granted. No justification would exist for depriving the defendant of liberty or property, even temporarily, if the plaintiff cannot present a minimal case on paper that a judgment will ultimately be rendered against the defendant. Even a bond requirement would not suffice as an adequate substitute for such a showing, since the amount of the bond would be set initially in an ex parte proceeding and might not be sufficient to compensate the defendant for losses that would result from issuance of the provisional remedy.

It is more difficult to assess whether the Court will ultimately require a bond or other security as an indispensable constitutional requirement for the issuance of a provisional remedy. Four Justices made strong arguments in *Doehr* that a bond should be a constitutional requirement.[587] Nevertheless, it is far from certain that a bond will be held indispensable to the validity of a provisional remedy statute. One argument against a mandatory bond requirement is that it would often place an insurmountable obstacle in the path of an impecunious plaintiff's ability to obtain a provisional remedy, even when strong grounds exist for issuing the remedy. In addition, adequate substitutes for a bond may readily be imagined. For example, a state might provide a statutory cause of action that would allow a defendant to recover damages for the economic losses caused by a provisional remedy if the plaintiff's claim ultimately failed.[588] However, even if a bond is not held indispensable to the constitutionality of a provisional remedy, the bond is an important safeguard that could likely tip the balance in favor of validity in marginal cases.[589]

Two other factors will also weigh heavily in determining the validity of a provisional remedy when they are present in a particular case. First, when the plaintiff possesses an interest in the property seized, that interest will weigh in favor

---

587. *See Doehr*, 501 U.S. at 18-21, 111 S. Ct. at 2116-18, 115 L. Ed. 2d at 20 (Justice White, with whom Justices Marshall, Stevens, and O'Connor joined).

588. Connecticut provided such a procedure in *Doehr*, although it was hedged with restrictions and defenses that rendered it an inadequate substitute for a preseizure bond. *See id.* at 20-21, 111 S. Ct. at 2117-18, 115 L. Ed. 2d at 19-20.

589. *Cf.* McLaughlin v. Weathers, 170 F.3d 577 (6th Cir. 1999) (Tennessee statute differs from one in Connecticut and is constitutional; statute requires bond, provides for exigent circumstances, and defendant failed to take advantage of opportunities under state law to challenge the seizure in state court). Most states require a bond before issuance of a provisional remedy. *See* 501 U.S. at 24, 111 S. Ct. at 2119-20, 115 L. Ed. 2d at 22-23 (Appendix). It seems highly doubtful that the Court would ever hold that a *redelivery bond* is a mandatory constitutional requirement in every provisional remedy case. Such a requirement would render per se invalid the provisional remedy of equitable replevin, discussed in section F(2), *Illustration 6-68*, *supra*. Nevertheless, a redelivery bond requirement might also provide an additional safeguard to protect the defendant's interests in a particular case.

of the validity of seizure of the property without prior notice and an opportunity to be heard. The preexisting interest of the plaintiff bears on the existence of exigent circumstances. To leave the defendant in possession of property in which the plaintiff has an interest risks deterioration of the value of the property through the defendant's use, even when there is no additional risk that the defendant will transfer or destroy the property. However, a preexisting property interest cannot be considered an indispensable prerequisite to the validity of a provisional remedy. If it were, attachment or garnishment of the defendant's general assets when the defendant is removing them from the reach of a potential judgment would be impossible. Nothing in the Court's decisions suggests that attachment and garnishment are per se invalid.

Second, *Doehr* and *Good* taken together indicate that when seizure of real property is involved in an action, the plaintiff will have a more difficult time making a case for prejudgment seizure of the property. When real property is the subject of the seizure, it will be more difficult to demonstrate the necessary exigent circumstances because the property cannot be removed from the court's jurisdiction. In addition, the security and privacy values associated with realty will cause the Court to scrutinize real property cases carefully to determine whether less restrictive means of protecting the plaintiff's interests are available, as well as to assure that adequate safeguards are provided to protect the defendant's interests.[590]

---

590. For example, in a marginal case of prejudgment seizure of realty, the presence of an adequate bond requirement might tip the balance in favor of validity.

Chapter 7

JOINDER OF CLAIMS

SECTION A. JOINDER OF CLAIMS BY PLAINTIFFS AT COMMON LAW AND IN EQUITY

The common law restricted the joinder of claims by plaintiffs. The general rule allowed a plaintiff to join all claims within the same form of action. It made no difference if the claims were factually unrelated. Thus, a plaintiff could join a trespass claim with other unrelated trespass claims. Likewise, a plaintiff could join trespass-on-the-case claims with other unrelated trespass-on-the-case claims. However, a plaintiff could not join a trespass claim with a factually related trespass-on-the-case claim.[1]

Illustration 7-1. Assume that *P* wanted to sue *D* in a common-law court for damages, joining two counts. One count alleged an assault and battery. The other count alleged a breach of contract. *P* could not join these two causes of action because they did not fall within the same form of action.

Illustration 7-2. Suppose that *P* wanted to sue *D* in a common-law court for damages, joining two counts. One count alleged property damage due to *D's* negligence in colliding with *P's* wagon. The other count alleged an assault and battery committed by *D* against *P* on a wholly different occasion. Superficially, these causes of action appear to be unjoinable because the first arose in trespass on the case and the second arose in trespass. However, this illustration is unlike *Illustration 7-1*. As discussed in Chapter 1, the plaintiff had an option in negligent collision situations. The plaintiff could sue in trespass on the case, treating the defendant's negligence as the wrong; or instead, the plaintiff could sue in trespass, treating the immediate crash of the wagons as the wrong.[2] Thus, by electing this latter alternative, the plaintiff could join the two causes of action.

Illustration 7-3. Assume that *P* wanted to sue *D* in a common-law court for damages, joining three counts. One count alleged property damage due to *D's* negligence in colliding with *P* in *P's* wagon. The second count alleged an assault and battery occurring immediately after the collision when *D* jumped from the

---

1. *See* BENJAMIN J. SHIPMAN, HANDBOOK OF COMMON-LAW PLEADING § 80 (1923). Some exceptions to this rule existed. For example, a cause of action in debt could be joined with an unrelated cause of action in detinue. The reason was that

> anciently both were regarded as actions of debt and were found embodied in the same writ in the register of writs. Notwithstanding the modification and modern use of detinue, which relegates it to the classification of actions ex delicto [founded on tort], the courts have unaccountably continued the ancient practice of permitting its joinder with debt.

ALEXANDER MARTIN, CIVIL PROCEDURE AT COMMON LAW 184 (1905). Similarly, a cause of action for trespass on the case could be joined with a cause of action in trover, because a trover action was "in its nature a species of trespass on the case." *Id.*; *see also* Chapter 1(D)(4)*(c) supra* ("Trover").

2. *See* Chapter 1(D)(4)*(a) supra* ("Trespass on the Case") & *Illustration 1-28 supra*.

wagon and punched *P* in the nose. The third count alleged slander when, on the same occasion, *D* accused *P* of being a drunkard. *P* could not join *all* of these causes of action. Unlike *Illustration 7-2*, *P's* range of options was not broad enough to permit joinder of all three causes of action. As indicated in Chapter 1, the cause of action for assault and battery fell only within trespass, while the cause of action for slander fell only within trespass on the case.[3] *P* could join the cause of action for the damage to the wagon with either of these. However, *P* could not join all three causes of action together.

* * * * *

In addition to these joinder limitations, all the causes of action had to exist in favor of the plaintiff *in the same right* and against the defendant *in the same capacity* before the plaintiff could join them together. This requirement meant, for example, that a plaintiff could not join a claim brought as an individual with another claim brought as an executor. Nor could a defendant be sued in the same action on a claim against the defendant as an individual and on a claim against the defendant as a representative. Likewise, a *joint* claim on behalf of two plaintiffs could not be joined with a *several* claim on behalf of one of them. Furthermore, two plaintiffs could not join claims setting up separate rights against the same defendant.[4] A single plaintiff could not join different causes of action against different defendants. Nor could the plaintiff join a cause of action asserting the joint liability of two or more defendants with causes of action alleging the several liability of any or all the defendants.[5]

The plaintiff could include multiple statements of the same cause of action in the declaration, each of which represented the facts in a different way. Thus, when the plaintiff was uncertain whether one of the statements was legally sufficient or when the plaintiff feared that proof of one of the statements might fail, the plaintiff could plead the cause of action in a different way in separate counts in the declaration. In effect, this approach relaxed the rule against duplicity in pleadings.[6] However, the plaintiff still had to exercise care. As with so many situations at common law, the plaintiff could evade the rule against duplicity, but could not directly violate it. The plaintiff had to make each of the counts appear as if it actually stated an entirely different cause of action.[7]

Illustration 7-4. Assume that *D* entered into a bond with *P*. *D* promised in the bond to pay a penalty if *D* failed to pay a sum of money on the first of September and another sum on the first of October. If the defendant did not pay on both dates, either failure would entitle *P* to recover the penalty. If *P* stated both defaults in a single count, the declaration would be duplicitous. However, *P* could state each of the defaults in a separate count, prove a failure to pay on *either* date,

---

3. *See* Chapter 1(D)(3)*(c) supra* ("*Ex Delicto* Personal Actions") & Chapter 1(D)(4)*(a) supra* ("Trespass on the Case").

4. *Cf. Illustration 7-8 infra*.

5. *See* ALEXANDER MARTIN, CIVIL PROCEDURE AT COMMON LAW 184 (1905); BENJAMIN J. SHIPMAN, HANDBOOK OF COMMON-LAW PLEADING § 80 (1923); Edson R. Sunderland, *Joinder of Actions*, 18 MICH. L. REV. 571, 582-83 (1920).

6. The rule prohibiting duplicity in pleadings is discussed in Chapter 6(A)(2) *supra* ("Stating the Plaintiff's Claim in the Declaration").

7. *See* BENJAMIN J. SHIPMAN, HANDBOOK OF COMMON-LAW PLEADING § 81 (1923).

and still win the penalty. To do this, *P* had to allege the penal bond and a failure to pay on September 1st in the first count. *P* could then plead the same bond, describing it as "a certain other bond" in the second count. *D* then could allege a failure to pay on October 1st. This form of statement evaded the rule against duplicity. It thus allowed *P* to recover the penalty by proving failure of payment on either date.[8]

* * * * *

A plaintiff could use this same technique in other situations when possible variations in proof at trial clouded how a transaction or an event should be described in the complaint. Of course, when the plaintiff pleaded a single cause of action in different ways, the plaintiff could recover only once.

Illustration 7-5. Assume that *D* stole *P's* valuable work of art. *P* wanted to sue *D* for the value of the work of art in an action of assumpsit, but was uncertain whether *D* had sold the work of art to a third party or still had it. If the work of art had not been sold, the proper common count was goods sold and delivered. If *D* had sold the work of art and *P* wanted to recover the amount *D* received on the sale, the proper common count was money had and received.[9] If *P* selected goods sold and delivered and the work of art had been sold for an amount greater than its value, *P* would not be able to recover the greater amount from *D* at trial. On the other hand, if *P* selected money had and received and *D* had not sold the work of art, *P's* cause of action might fail altogether. To alleviate this problem, *P* could plead the cause of action in different ways in different counts. Of course, *P* could recover only once.[10]

* * * * *

The consequences of misjoining causes of action at common law were serious. Misjoinder impeached the validity of the entire declaration. The defendant could raise this defect by a general demurrer,[11] a motion in arrest of judgment, or a writ of error.[12] When the plaintiff correctly joined several counts, depending on the nature of the defense, the defendant could demur to all of them, plead to all, demur to one count and plead to another, or plead differently to each count.[13]

Equity was more flexible on matters of joinder than common law. The objective of equity was to determine in a single action as many controversies concerning the subject matter as was convenient.[14] The defendant could demur to a bill in equity as *multifarious*. However, this objection was unavailable unless the joined matters arose out of different transactions or occurrences *and* each matter constituted a complete cause of action in itself sufficient to sustain a bill in equity.[15] "Indeed, the objection of multifariousness, and the circumstances under which it [would] be allowed to prevail, or not, [was] in many cases, . . . a matter of

---

8. *See id.*
9. *See* Chapter 6(A)(2) *supra* ("Stating the Plaintiff's Claim in the Declaration") & *Illustration 6-1 supra*.
10. *See* BENJAMIN J. SHIPMAN, HANDBOOK OF COMMON-LAW PLEADING § 81 (1923).
11. *See* Chapter 6(A)(3)*(a) supra* ("General Demurrers").
12. *See* Chapter 12(A) *infra* ("Post-Trial Motions").
13. *See* ALEXANDER MARTIN, CIVIL PROCEDURE AT COMMON LAW § 229 (1905).
14. *See* HENRY L. MCCLINTOCK, HANDBOOK OF EQUITY § 9 (2d ed. 1948).
15. *See* BENJAMIN J. SHIPMAN, HANDBOOK OF THE LAW OF EQUITY PLEADING 340 (1897).

discretion, and no general rule can be laid down on the subject."[16] Equity also enforced a rule with the opposite effect of multifariousness: a plaintiff could not split a single cause of action into separate elements and thus unnecessarily multiply the number of suits. In such a situation, the court would force the plaintiff to join the omitted matter.[17]

Generally, a legal claim could not be joined with an equitable claim in an equity court. In certain cases, however, the *"clean-up doctrine"* allowed an equity court to grant its unique brand of relief and also award common-law damages, thus preventing a multiplicity of suits. In applicable cases, this doctrine had the practical effect of permitting the joinder of legal and equitable claims for relief.[18]

Illustration 7-6. Assume that *P* sued to enjoin *D* from repeatedly trespassing on *P's* land. The only dispute was whether the alleged trespasses were taking place. Under these circumstances, an equity court would take jurisdiction based on the request for an injunction and give damages for the past trespasses under the clean-up doctrine. However, if *D* defended by disputing *P's* title to the land, the equity court would not take the case under any doctrine. Equity would not try the title to land. As a result, there would have to be two actions. The first action would be in a common-law court to settle the title issue. If *P* was successful in that action, the second action would be in equity to obtain an injunction.[19]

SECTION B. JOINDER OF CLAIMS BY PLAINTIFFS UNDER THE CODES

One of the most important reforms instituted by the Field Code was the liberalization of claim joinder. The Code, however, did not permit unlimited joinder. The reformers believed some limitations on the scope of a lawsuit were necessary. As a result, they permitted joinder of claims that arose within limited categories.[20] Thus, a plaintiff could join all contract claims (express and implied). Likewise, a plaintiff could join all claims arising out of injuries by force to persons or property (such as trespass, false imprisonment, or assault and battery). However, the plaintiff could not join factually related contract and tort claims because torts and contracts were in different categories.

---

16. JOSEPH STORY, COMMENTARIES ON EQUITY PLEADINGS § 284 (9th ed. 1879).

17. *See id.* § 287.

18. *See* DAN B. DOBBS, THE LAW OF REMEDIES § 2.6(4), at 117 (2d student ed. 1993); *see* Chapter 1(D)(6) *supra* ("Development of Equity Jurisdiction"); Chapter 11(E) *infra* ("The Right to Trial by Jury in a Merged System: Operation of the Historical and Modern Federal Approaches").

19. *See* 1 DAN B. DOBBS, LAW OF REMEDIES § 2.7, at 180-81 (2d practitioner ed. 1993).

20. Section 143 of the 1848 Field Code provided as follows:

> The plaintiff may unite several causes of action in the same complaint, where they all arise out of,
> 1. Contract, express or implied; or
> 2. Injuries by force, to person or property; or
> 3. Injuries without force to person or property; or
> 4. Injuries to character; or
> 5. Claims to recover real property; with or without damages, for the withholding thereof; or,
> 6. Claims to recover personal property, with or without damages for the withholding thereof; or,
> 7. Claims against a trustee by virtue of a contract or by operation of law.
>
> But the causes of action, so united, must all belong to one only of these classes, and must equally affect all the parties to the action, and not require different places of trial.

Act of Apr. 12, 1848, ch. 379, § 143, 1848 N.Y. Laws 497, 525.

The joinder of claims provision in the Field Code of 1848 demonstrated a curious ambivalence. The Code followed the common-law pattern of allowing joinder of the causes of action that were thought to be similar in nature and did not require a factual relationship between the claims within a category. However, the Code contained an important, overriding restriction: the causes of action joined had to "equally affect" all the parties to the action and not require different places of trial.[21]

In 1852, the New York Legislature substantially liberalized claim joinder (§ 167). The amended joinder provision followed the former equity practice by permitting joinder of claims based on their factual relationship ("same transaction clause") (§ 167(1)). However, the amended section retained all the other joinder categories, which required no factual relationship between the claims (§ 167(2)-(7)).[22] The same transaction clauses of the codes have been subject to widely varying interpretations.[23]

Illustration 7-7. Assume that *P* assaulted and slandered *D* on the same occasion. Some courts held there were multiple causes of action, not joinable, arising out of different transactions. Some held that there were joinable multiple causes of action arising out of the same transaction. Some held there was only a single cause of action.[24] Obviously, the language of the same transaction clauses required some factual relationship between the causes of action joined. After the minimal factual relationship existed to satisfy the face of the statute, litigational efficiency should have determined whether the causes of action were properly joined.[25]

* * * * *

The 1852 amendment to the Field Code also retained the restriction that joined claims had to "affect" all parties to the suit and could not require different places of trial. However, the amendment altered the restriction so the claims no longer had to affect all parties "equally."[26]

Illustration 7-8. Assume that *H* and *W*, husband and wife, sued the *D Motel* for damages for being wrongfully ejected from the motel on the ground that they were not married. *H* and *W* attempted to join their individual claims in the same

---

21. *See id.*

22. The 1852 amendment (§ 167) to the Field Code provided:

> The plaintiff may unite in the same complaint several causes of action, whether they be such as have been heretofore denominated legal or equitable, or both, where they all arise out of,
>
> 1. The same transaction, or transactions connected with the same subject of action;
> 2. Contract, express or implied; or
> 3. Injuries with or without force, to person and property, or either; or
> 4. Injuries to character; or
> 5. Claims to recover real property, with or without damages, for withholding thereof, and the rents and profits of the same; or
> 6. Claims to recover personal property, with or without damages for the withholding thereof; or
> 7. Claims against a trustee, by virtue of a contract, or by operation of law.
>
> But the causes of action, so united must all belong to one of these classes, and must affect all the parties to the action, and not require different places of trial, and must be separately stated.

Act of Apr. 16, 1852, ch. 392, § 167, 1852 N.Y. Laws 651, 655; *see also* CHARLES E. CLARK, HANDBOOK OF THE LAW OF CODE PLEADING § 67, at 437-38 (2d ed. 1947).

23. *See* CHARLES E. CLARK, HANDBOOK OF THE LAW OF CODE PLEADING § 69, at 452 (2d ed. 1947).

24. *See id.* at 454 and authorities there cited.

25. *Cf. id.* at 455-56.

26. *Id.*

action under a joinder provision identical to § 167, as amended in 1852. The claims were improperly joined. Although both parties' causes of action arose out of the same transaction, the causes of action were "several," not joint. Thus, they did not "affect" all the parties to the action. In other words, under the substantive law, the husband "owned" his cause of action and the wife "owned" hers. Neither was entitled to share in the other's recovery.[27]

* * * * *

When claims were factually unrelated, they could still be joined, provided they all fit within a single category of the joinder provision. The result was a rather fortuitous joinder scheme, unrelated to any apparent considerations of litigational convenience.

Illustration 7-9. Assume that *P* sued *D* for damages. *P* joined in the complaint two causes of action. One was based on an automobile accident, in which *D* negligently collided with *P*. The other was based on an assault and battery committed by *D* against *P* on a wholly separate occasion. These causes of action could be joined under § 167(3) of the New York Code of 1852. That section provided for joinder of multiple causes of action when they all arose out of "injuries with or without force, to person or property or either." Assume that *P* also possessed a slander claim against *D* because *D* stated that *P* was an alcoholic immediately after the automobile accident. That claim could not be joined with the other two claims. Even if the slander and negligence claims arose from the same transaction or occurrence under § 167(1), the assault and battery arose from a different factual occurrence. Thus, all three causes of action did not fit within § 167(1). Likewise, the slander claim could not be joined with the other two under § 167(3), because it was not a cause of action for injuries "to person or property or either." Rather, the cause of action for slander fell within § 167(4), because it was an injury "to character." The other two causes of action did not fit within that section.

* * * * *

Measured by standards of practical convenience, this pattern was not well thought out.[28] Moreover, when the claim joinder sections were considered together with the party joinder provisions of the codes, joinder was further restricted in multiparty cases, discussed in the next chapter.

Illustration 7-10. *P* sued *D Bus Co.* for punitive damages for personal injuries received in an accident due to *D's* reckless conduct. *P* joined a cause of action against *I*, D's insurer, to recover compensatory damages for injuries negligently inflicted by *D* in the same accident. These causes of action were improperly joined. Although they both arose from the same transaction or occurrence, the cause of action against *D* did not affect *I*. Thus, both causes of action did not affect all the parties to the action.[29]

---

27. *See* Ryder v. Jefferson Hotel Co., 121 S.C. 72, 113 S.E. 474 (1922).
28. *See* CHARLES E. CLARK, HANDBOOK OF THE LAW OF CODE PLEADING § 69, at 455-56 (2d ed. 1947).
29. *See* Piper v. American Fidelity & Cas. Co., 157 S.C. 106, 154 S.E. 106 (1930).

SECTION C. JOINDER OF CLAIMS BY PLAINTIFFS UNDER THE FEDERAL RULES

1. Basic Operation of Federal Rule 18

Rule 18 of the Federal Rules of Civil Procedure vastly simplified the joinder of claims and remedies. Rule 18(a) allows a party to join as many claims as the party has against an opposing party, regardless of the relationship between the claims. Rule 18 permits unlimited joinder of claims at the pleading stage on the theory that any harm caused by joinder of unrelated claims occurs only at the trial stage.[30] If such harm exists, it can be eliminated in the discretion of the trial court under Rule 42(b), which permits severance and separate trial of joined claims in the interests of expedition and economy.[31] Rule 18 is permissive. It does not compel a party to join all claims that the party possesses against an opposing party. It merely allows joinder of the claims.

Federal Rule 18 was derived from former Equity Rule 26. The original version of Rule 18(a) attempted to liberalize former Equity Rule 26[32] by extending unlimited claim joinder to cases involving multiple parties.[33] Unfortunately, the lower federal courts restrictively interpreted the original version of Rule 18(a). Because the original version of Rule 18(a) referred to Rules 19, 20, and 22, the limitations on party joinder in those rules were read into Rule 18 as restrictions on claim joinder.[34] Rule 18(a) was amended in 1966 to clarify that this restrictive interpretation was incorrect

Illustration 7-11. Assume that *P* sues *D-1* and *D-2*. *P* asserts alternative claims for relief against *D-1* and *D-2* arising out of an automobile accident. Under Rule 18, *P* may join a claim against *D-1* alone for breach of contract arising out of a wholly separate event. As discussed in the next chapter, Rule 20 is satisfied in this situation because (a) a claim for relief arising out of the same occurrence is asserted against all the defendants and (b) questions of law or fact common to all the

---

30. *See* Edson R. Sunderland, *The New Federal Rules*, 45 W. VA. L.Q. 5, 13 (1938).

31. *See* FED. R. CIV. P. 18 advisory committee's note to the 1966 amendment.

32. Equity Rule 26 provided as follows:

> The plaintiff may join in one bill as many causes of action, cognizable in equity, as [the plaintiff] may have against the defendant. But when there is more than one plaintiff, the causes of action joined must be joint, and if there be more than one defendant the liability must be one asserted against all of the material defendants, or sufficient grounds must appear for uniting the causes of action in order to promote the convenient administration of justice. If it appear that any such causes of action cannot be conveniently disposed of together, the court may order separate trials.

226 U.S. at 655-56 (1912).

33. Original Rule 18(a) stated that

> [t]he plaintiff in his complaint or in a reply setting forth a counterclaim may join either as independent or as alternate claims as many claims either legal or equitable or both as he may have against an opposing party. There may be a like joinder of claims when there are multiple parties if the requirements of Rules 19, 20 and 22 are satisfied.

See FED. R. CIV. P. 18 advisory committee's note 2.

34. For example, suppose a plaintiff properly joined two defendants under Rule 20 by asserting against them claims arising out of the same transaction or occurrence and raising common questions of law or fact. The plaintiff was not permitted to join an additional factually unrelated claim against one of the defendants. *See, e.g.*, Federal Hous. Adm'r v. Christianson, 26 F. Supp. 419 (D. Conn. 1939).

defendants will exist in the action. Because Rule 20 is satisfied, *P* may join any other claims that *P* possesses against *D-1* or *D-2* by virtue of Rule 18.

* * * * *

Rule 18(b) allows a party to join two claims, even if one of them is contingent on the disposition of the other. The second sentence of Rule 18(b), allowing joinder of a claim for money and a claim to set aside a fraudulent conveyance, is merely an example of joinder of this sort.[35] Rule 18(b), in fact, applies to all sorts of contingent or conditional claims.[36]

It should be noted that Rule 18 was restyled in 2007 along with the other Federal Rules of Civil Procedure. One of the goals of the restyling project was to make the use of terminology consistent throughout the rules.[37] Before the restyling of the Rules, Rule 8(a)(1), in describing the the pleading requirements for a claim, spelled out that the requirements applied to "a claim for relief, whether an original claim, counterclaim, crossclaim, or third-party claim." Former Rule 18 duplicated this language, providing that "[a] party asserting a claim for relief as an original claim, counterclaim, crossclaim, or third-party claim," could join as many claims as the party has. Restyled Rule 8 now simply uses the phrase "claim for relief," obviously intending to include all claims (*e.g.*, counterclaims) within the term "claim." In contrast, restyled Rule 18 states that "[a] party asserting a claim, counterclaim, crossclaim, or third-party claim" may join as many claims as the party has. It is not clear why the restylers retained the former list of claims in Rule 18, while removing only the reference "original" at the beginning of the rule. It would appear that this part of the restyling project has failed to achieve the goal of consistent use of terminology throughout the rules.

2. Problems of Subject-Matter Jurisdiction, Venue, and Personal Jurisdiction Under Rule 18

The requirements of federal subject-matter jurisdiction, venue, and personal jurisdiction qualify the unlimited joinder of claims permitted by Rule 18.

(a) Subject-Matter-Jurisdiction Restrictions on Joinder

Subject-matter-jurisdiction restrictions on joinder depend both on the general statutes conferring jurisdiction on the lower federal courts, such as 28 U.S.C. §§ 1331 and 1332, and also on the scope of the supplemental jurisdiction conferred by 28 U.S.C. § 1367.

Illustration 7-12. *P*, a citizen of Sweden, sues *D*, a citizen of State *X*, in a U.S. District Court in State *X*. *P* asserts two claims against *D* arising under state law: a tort claim for $33,000 and a wholly unrelated contract claim for $33,000. Although Rule 18 does not restrict *P's* ability to join the tort and contract claims,

---

35. *See* FED. R. CIV. P. 18(b).

36. *See generally* E.H. Schopler, Annotation, *Construction, Application, and Effect of Federal Civil Rule 18(b) and Like State Rules or Statutes Pertaining to Joinder in a Single Action of Two Claims Although One Was Previously Cognizable Only After the Other Had Been Prosecuted to a Conclusion*, 61 A.L.R.2D 688 (1958).

37. *See* Chapter 1(D)(13) *supra* (discussing the goals of the restyling project).

the requirements of federal subject-matter jurisdiction are not satisfied because the two claims together do not meet the amount-in-controversy requirement.[38]

Illustration 7-13. If, on the facts of *Illustration 7-12*, *P* asserted a $33,000 claim arising under federal law and a totally unrelated state claim for $33,000, the federal court could entertain the federal claim, but probably could not entertain the state claim. Again, Rule 18 does not restrict joinder. The federal court would possess subject-matter jurisdiction over the federal claim because 28 U.S.C. § 1331 (the general federal question jurisdiction statute) does not contain an amount-in-controversy requirement. Before 1990, the district court clearly did not possess subject-matter jurisdiction over the state-law claim because (1) the jurisdictional amount requirement of 28 U.S.C. § 1332 was not satisfied[39] and (2) the state claim did not arise out of the same facts as the federal claim, which would have been necessary to bring the state claim within the pendent jurisdiction of the district court.

The 1990 enactment of 28 U.S.C. § 1367, the supplemental jurisdiction statute, has created doubt as to whether the state claim can be entertained today. Recall from the discussion in Chapter 2 that § 1367 extends the "supplemental jurisdiction" of the district courts to all claims that form part of the same constitutional case or controversy as a civil action over which the district courts have original jurisdiction. Recall, also, that a strong argument can be made that Congress has the power under Article III of the Constitution to extend the jurisdiction of the federal courts to factually unrelated state claims joined with federal claims over which the district courts have original jurisdiction.[40] If Article III is interpreted in this fashion, and if § 1367 is interpreted to mean what it says, jurisdiction will exist today over the state claim. However, if, as argued in Chapter 2,[41] § 1367 is construed to limit the "supplemental jurisdiction" of the district courts to state claims that arise from the same facts as federal claims over which the district courts have original jurisdiction, there will be no jurisdiction over the state claim.

Illustration 7-14. In *Illustration 7-13*, if *P's* federal and state claims had arisen out of the same facts, the federal district court, both before 1990 and today, would have jurisdiction over the state claim. Before 1990, this case would have been an appropriate one for pendent jurisdiction over the state claim under 28 U.S.C. § 1331.[42] The codification of the doctrine of "pendent claim jurisdiction" in 28 U.S.C. § 1367 would give the federal district court supplemental jurisdiction over the state claim today.[43]

---

38. *See* 28 U.S.C. § 1332; Chapter 2(D)(7)*(a) supra* ("Single Plaintiff with a Single Claim or Multiple Claims Against a Single Defendant").

39. *See id.*

40. *See* Chapter 2(E)(2) *supra* ("The Constitutional Basis of Pendent and Ancillary Jurisdiction").

41. *See* Chapter 2(E)(5) *supra* ("The Scope of Supplemental Jurisdiction: Section 1367(a)").

42. *See* Chapter 2(E)(1) *supra* ("The General Nature of Pendent and Ancillary Jurisdiction").

43. *See* Chapter 2(E)(5) *supra* ("The Scope of Supplemental Jurisdiction: Section 1367(a)").

(b) Venue Restrictions on Joinder

Venue restrictions depend not only on the operation of the general and special venue statutes in Title 28 of the *United States Code*, but also on whether the federal courts may, in some cases, exercise "pendent" or "supplemental" venue.

Illustration 7-15. On the facts of *Illustration 7-14*, if *P* had sued *D* in a U.S. District Court in State *Y* and the facts giving rise to *P's* claims had occurred entirely in State *X*, Rule 18 would permit joinder of the federal and state claims and the requirements of federal subject-matter jurisdiction would be satisfied (before 1990 under the doctrine of "pendent jurisdiction" and today under the doctrine of "supplemental jurisdiction"). However, venue would be improper under 28 U.S.C. § 1391(b). Under this venue section, venue proper only in a judicial district in which (1) the defendant resides, (2) a substantial part of the events or omissions giving rise to the claim occurred, or (3) any defendant is subject to personal jurisdiction if there is no district in which the action may otherwise be brought.[44] The defendant resides in State *X*, and all of the events giving rise to the claims occurred there. Consequently, even if the defendant can be subjected to personal jurisdiction in State *Y*, venue is improper there, because another district (in State *X*) exists where the action may be brought.

* * * * *

Occasionally, a case arises in which venue is proper for one claim under a special federal venue statute, but not as to a claim over which the U.S. District Court has supplemental jurisdiction. These cases raise the question whether the district courts may hear the supplemental claim under a doctrine of "pendent" or "supplemental" venue. Some courts have recognized the validity of such a doctrine,[45] while others have rejected it.[46] The venue question cannot be automatically decided on the basis that the requirements of subject-matter jurisdiction have been satisfied. The policies supporting supplemental jurisdiction are concerned with the scope of an Article III case or controversy and the statutory policies supporting grants of jurisdiction to the U.S. District Courts.[47] Satisfaction of these policies will not necessarily satisfy the policies of the federal venue statutes, which focus on the convenience of the particular location in which a suit is brought.

If "supplemental venue" is a viable concept at all, therefore, it should only be exercised under narrow circumstances. It might be justifiable for the district

---

44. *See* 28 U.S.C. § 1391(b)(1)-(3); *see also* Chapter 4(C) *supra* ("Venue in Federal Courts").

45. *See, e.g.*, Travis v. Anthes Imperial Ltd., 473 F.2d 515 (1973); *see also* 14D CHARLES A. WRIGHT ET AL, FEDERAL PRACTICE AND PROCEDURE: JURISDICTION AND RELATED MATTERS § 3808, at 256 n.5 (3d ed. 2007) (citing additional cases); Note, *Ancillary Process and Venue in the Federal Courts,* 73 HARV. L. REV. 1164, 1175-78 (1960).

46. *See, e.g.*, Reuber v. United States, 750 F.2d 1039 (D.C. Cir. 1984); Network Sys. Corp. v. Masstor Sys. Corp., 612 F. Supp. 438 (D. Minn. 1984); *see also* Berger Instruments, Inc. v. Northwest Instruments, Inc., No. 96 C 8393, 1997 WL 159377, 1997 U.S. Dist. LEXIS 3737 (N.D. Ill. Mar. 28, 1997) (must be an independent basis of venue for each claim in the complaint); 14D CHARLES A. WRIGHT ET AL., FEDERAL PRACTICE AND PROCEDURE: JURISDICTION AND RELATED MATTERS § 3808, at 259-61 n.8 (3d ed. 2007) (discussing cases disallowing pendent venue over claims governed by the general venue statute when they are added to a claim governed by a special venue statute in which venue is proper); *cf.* Geneva Furniture Mfg. Co. v. S. Karpen & Bros., 238 U.S. 254, 35 S. Ct. 788, 59 L. Ed. 1295 (1915) (holding venue proper as to some claims and improper as to other claims arising out of the same events).

47. *See* Chapter 2(E)(2)-(3) *supra* (discussing the constitutional and statutory bases of pendent and ancillary jurisdiction).

courts to exercise supplemental venue if it is necessary to do so in order to prevent the policies supporting a particular grant of subject-matter jurisdiction from being undermined.[48] Subject-matter-jurisdiction policies are higher-order policies than venue policies, and it is justifiable for the latter to give way in preference to the former in cases of conflict. Note that in *Illustration 7-15*, above, there is no need to exercise supplemental venue in order to protect subject-matter jurisdiction policies. Venue over the action will be proper in that illustration in State *X* and the action can be brought in a federal court there.

If an exercise of supplemental venue is not necessary to support subject-matter-jurisdiction policies, a district court should probably not exercise supplemental venue at all. However, if it does so, it should only exercise supplemental venue after assuring that the location of the suit on the supplemental claim will not be materially more burdensome to the defendant than a district where venue would be proper over the claim.[49] In addition, even if the forum would not be materially more burdensome than a proper venue, the court should not exercise supplemental venue if it determines that Congress has made a deliberate policy decision to limit venue over certain kinds of claims, of which the supplemental claim is one, to particular districts.[50]

It should also be noted that supplemental venue should be much harder to establish under the above criteria with regard to claims that are factually unrelated to the freestanding, or jurisdiction-conferring, claim in the action. Supplemental jurisdiction over such claims has traditionally not existed in federal practice and may not exist in the future. However, as discussed above and in Chapter 2, the extension of supplemental jurisdiction to the full limits of Article III by 28 U.S.C. § 1367(a) holds the possibility that factually unrelated federal and nonfederal claims existing between the same parties will someday be found to be within the scope of the same Article III case.[51] In that eventuality, if the events giving rise to the unrelated supplemental claim occurred in a district other than the forum, it would be difficult to imagine how the forum would not be a materially more burdensome place to litigate than a district where venue would be proper over the claim.

(c) Personal Jurisdiction Restrictions on Joinder

Personal jurisdiction requirements must normally be satisfied with regard to each claim joined in an action.[52] However, some courts have also held that it is

---

48. In particular, if the plaintiff in a federal question case would be deterred from resorting to federal court by having to adjudicate federal and state claims in different locations, it may be necessary to exercise supplemental venue in order to support the policies of the particular subject-matter jurisdiction grant in question. *See* Chapter 2(E)(3) supra (discussing, *inter alia*, the statutory policies supporting the doctrine of pendent jurisdiction).

49. *Cf.* Note, *Ancillary Process and Venue in the Federal Courts,* 73 HARV. L. REV. 1164, 1176 (1960) (additional inquiry beyond satisfaction of pendent jurisdiction policies requires balancing of the factors favoring retention of a claim against the added inconvenience to the defendant in defending against it).

50. *See, e.g.*, Bartel v. FAA, 617 F. Supp. 190, 198 n.33 (D.D.C. 1985) (no pendent venue because Congress has made deliberate decision to limit venue where Title VII claims may be brought).

51. *See* Chapter 2(E)(2) *supra* (discussing the constitutional bases of pendent and ancillary jurisdiction).

52. *See* Seiferth v. Helicopteros Atuneros, Inc, 472 F.3d 266 (5th Cir. 2006) (long-arm jurisdiction asserted under Mississippi long-arm statute; court holds that specific jurisdiction is "claim specific"; that is, a plaintiff bringing multiple claims that arise out of different forum contacts must separately establish specific jurisdiction for each claim as a matter due process).

possible to exercise "pendent" or "supplemental" personal jurisdiction over defendants on claims that fall within the supplemental jurisdiction of the U.S. District Courts. Such cases have sometimes arisen when a federal long-arm statute allows the district courts to exercise personal jurisdiction over a defendant for purposes of a federal claim, but the state where the action is brought would not allow an assertion of personal jurisdiction over the defendant for purposes of a supplemental state claim joined in the action.[53] Today, such a case might also arise under the 1993 amendments to Rule 4(k)(2), if a plaintiff sues a defendant on a federal claim and a closely related nonfederal claim in a federal court and the defendant is not subject to personal jurisdiction on the federal claim in any state court of general jurisdiction.[54] As discussed in *Illustration 7-16*, below, it may have been the intent of the drafters of Rule 4(k)(2) to confer supplemental personal jurisdiction over the nonfederal claim under these circumstances.

The federal courts should not assume supplemental personal jurisdiction over a defendant simply based on the fact that subject-matter-jurisdiction requirements have been satisfied. As with venue, the policies supporting supplemental subject-matter jurisdiction are not the same as the policies motivating a grant or denial of long-arm jurisdiction over particular claims. Contrary to the case of venue, however, subject-matter-jurisdiction policies are not always higher-order policies than policies supporting personal jurisdiction. When personal jurisdiction restrictions are based on the Due Process Clauses of the Fifth or Fourteenth Amendments, statutory subject-matter-jurisdiction policies should be considered subordinate to them. Therefore, it would only seem to be justified for the courts to assume supplemental personal jurisdiction to prevent the policies of a subject-matter-jurisdiction grant from being seriously undermined when the personal jurisdiction restrictions on adjudicating the supplemental claim are based on statutory limits.

As was the case with supplemental venue, if no subject-matter jurisdiction policy would be undermined by refusing supplemental personal jurisdiction, it would seem justifiable for the courts to assume supplemental personal jurisdiction over a defendant for purposes of the claim only when the burdens of suit in the forum would not be substantially greater than in another location where personal jurisdiction would be proper over the defendant. Finally, the courts should take care to scrutinize the reasons why state law has effectively immunized the defendant from suit in the forum in cases where the supplemental claim is a state claim. It would seem improper for the courts to assert supplemental personal jurisdiction over the defendant for purposes of adjudicating a state claim when the forum has

---

53. *See, e.g.*, Robinson v. Penn Cent. Co., 484 F.2d 553 (3d Cir. 1973) (long-arm jurisdiction over federal securities claim under securities long-arm statute and pendent personal jurisdiction exercised over pendent state claim over which securities long-arm statute does not authorize jurisdiction); *see also* 6A CHARLES A. WRIGHT ET AL, FEDERAL PRACTICE AND PROCEDURE: CIVIL § 1588, at 727 (3d ed. 2010); James S. Cochran, Note, *Personal Jurisdiction and the Joinder of Claims in the Federal Courts,* 64 TEX. L. REV. 1463 (1986); Jason A. Yonan, Note, *An End to Judicial Overreaching in Nationwide Service of Process Cases: Statutory Authorization to Bring Supplemental Personal Jurisdiction Within Federal Courts' Powers,* 2002 U. ILL. L. REV. 557; Note, *Ancillary Process and Venue in the Federal Courts,* 73 HARV. L. REV. 1164 (1960); *cf.* United States v. Botefuhr, 309 F.3d 1263 (10th Cir. 2002) (when an "anchor claim" is dismissed prior to trial, pendent personal jurisdiction should not be exercised over claims lacking an independent jurisdictional basis).

54. *See* Chapter 3(K)(2)*(f) supra* (discussing Rule 4(k)(2)).

made a conscious policy decision to immunize the defendant from suit on the claim within the state. On the other hand, if the inapplicability of a state long-arm statute results from an apparently inadvertent gap in the statute as opposed to a conscious policy decision, the inability to assert jurisdiction under state law can safely be disregarded.

Supplemental personal jurisdiction should be a doctrine that the federal courts rarely have occasion to use. Given the tendency of the state courts to extend their long-arm statutes as far as the Due Process Clause of the Fourteenth Amendment will permit, there should be few cases in which personal jurisdiction does not exist over factually related federal and state claims under state law, as well as under any federal long-arm statute that applies to the federal claim. However, as observed in Chapter 3,[55] it is possible that the Supreme Court will someday hold that the same due process standards do not govern Congress and the states in creating long-arm jurisdiction. If so, the federal courts may be able to assert jurisdiction over federal claims under federal long-arm statutes when the forum state's courts could not constitutionally exercise personal jurisdiction over the defendant for purposes of state or foreign claims joined within the supplemental subject-matter jurisdiction of the federal courts.

For example, Congress may be able to extend the jurisdiction of the federal courts to adjudicate federal claims nationwide, without regard to the relationship, or lack of relationship, between the defendant, the claims, and the forum. Such an extension would allow the federal courts to exercise jurisdiction over federal claims that have no relationship to the state in which the action is brought. Furthermore, supplemental state claims lacking any relationship with the state might be joined with the federal claims under Rule 18. Under these circumstances, the federal courts should probably not exercise supplemental personal jurisdiction over the state claims at all if the forum state's courts would be precluded from adjudicating them by Fourteenth Amendment limits. Congress may have power to extend federal long-arm jurisdiction to the state claims as well as the federal claims under such circumstances. However, if suit were in a state court, the defendant's lack of contacts with the state would result in litigational burdens so great as to violate the Due Process Clause of the Fourteenth Amendment. This fact should counsel the federal courts that the decision to extend personal jurisdiction over the claims is a major policy question that should only be decided by Congress itself.

For the same reasons given in the discussion of supplemental venue, extending supplemental personal jurisdiction to factually unrelated nonfederal claims should be difficult, if not impossible. If the supplemental jurisdiction statute, 28 U.S.C. § 1367(a), is some day interpreted to allow supplemental subject-matter jurisdiction over state claims that are factually unrelated to the freestanding, or jurisdiction-conferring, claims in the action, the same problems would exist with extending supplemental personal jurisdiction over the state claims as existed with extending supplemental venue over them. These problems should be resolved in the same manner. In the case of personal jurisdiction, however, the problems may be more serious because of the presence of due process considerations. If supplemental

---

55. *See* Chapter 3(L)(1) *supra* ("The Constitutional Standard Under Federal Long-Arm Statutes and Rules").

personal jurisdiction were to be asserted over a state claim which has no factual connection with the forum state, and which is also factually unrelated to the federal claim that confers subject-matter jurisdiction over the action, the burdens on the defendant of litigating the claim in the forum might be so substantial as to produce a due process violation if the suit were in a state court. Even if Congress could hypothetically create long-arm jurisdiction over the claim without violating the Fifth Amendment, the Fourteenth Amendment due process considerations should counsel against the courts themselves extending supplemental personal jurisdiction over the defendant for purposes of adjudicating the claim.

In *Action Embroidery Corp. v. Atlantic Embroidery, Inc.*,[57] the Ninth Circuit Court of Appeals adopted the doctrine of pendent personal jurisdiction in an antitrust case. The court first sustained personal jurisdiction over a federal antitrust claim, applying a "national contacts" test to determine the validity of asserting personal jurisdiction over the defendant on the claim under the Due Process Clause of the Fifth Amendment. The court then held that pendent personal jurisdiction existed over a state antitrust claim in the district court's discretion. The court reasoned that "[w]hen a defendant must appear in a forum to defend against one claim, it is often reasonable to compel that defendant to answer other claims in the same suit arising out of a common nucleus of operative facts."[58] The court did not conduct an independent inquiry to determine whether, if personal jurisdiction had been asserted over the state claim alone, the assertion of jurisdiction would have comported with the Due Process Clause of the Fourteenth Amendment, which would involve a "state contacts" test rather than a "national contacts" test. Nor did it examine whether there existed any state statutory policies that would have dictated that jurisdiction be refused over the state claim. Thus, the court did not demonstrate the sensitivity to the kinds of considerations recommended in this text when it evaluated the pendent, or supplemental, personal jurisdiction issue.

Illustration 7-16. *P*, a citizen of State *X*, sues *D*, a citizen and resident of Sweden, in a U.S. District Court in State *X*. *P* asserts a claim under a federal statute against *D* and joins a claim under Swedish law that is factually related to the federal claim against *D*. The events giving rise to both claims occurred in Sweden. Subject-matter jurisdiction is satisfied over the federal statutory claim under 28 U.S.C. § 1331 (the general federal question jurisdiction statute) and over the federal claim by 28 U.S.C. § 1367(a) (the supplemental jurisdiction statute). Venue is proper in State *X* under 28 U.S.C. 1391(c)(3), which provides that a defendant not resident in the United States can be sued in any district. *D* does not have sufficient contacts with any state to satisfy the Due Process Clause of the Fourteenth Amendment, but *D* does have sufficient contacts with the United States to satisfy the Due Process Clause of the Fifth Amendment. Because of the lack of minimum contacts with a state, personal jurisdiction cannot be asserted pursuant to Federal Rule 4(k)(1)(A), because *D* cannot be subjected to the jurisdiction of a court of general jurisdiction in any state, including State *X*. No federal long-arm statute authorizes the district court to assert personal jurisdiction over *D*. Therefore, personal jurisdiction cannot

---

57. 368 F.3d 1174 (9th Cir. 2004).
58. *Id.* at 1181.

be asserted pursuant to Federal Rule 4(k)(1)(C). The district court can assert personal jurisdiction over the federal claim under Rule 4(k)(2) because of *D's* minimum contacts with the United States. The language of Rule 4(k)(2) only authorizes the district court to assert personal jurisdiction over *D* for purposes of adjudicating the federal claim,[59] but the Advisory Committee Note to the rule makes a cryptic reference to cases in which supplemental subject-matter jurisdiction may be asserted over state or foreign claims.[60] This reference may mean that it was the intent of the drafters of Rule 4(k)(2) to confer supplemental personal jurisdiction over related state or foreign claims. If so, however, the jurisdictional conferral, like that of supplemental subject-matter jurisdiction, should be deemed to be discretionary. If substantial burdens would be imposed on *D* by having to litigate the Swedish claim in State *X*, the court should decline to exercise that jurisdiction in this case. If Rule 4(k)(2) does not specifically confer supplemental personal jurisdiction over the Swedish claim, the court should be reluctant to exercise that jurisdiction on its own for the same reason.[61]

3. Rules Enabling Act Problems Under Rule 18

Potential Rules Enabling Act problems with joinder of multiple claims sometimes occur when a plaintiff suing an insured party also attempts to join the party's insurer as a defendant in the action. State statutes often authorize an injured party to bring suit against a defendant's insurer, but only after obtaining a judgment against the defendant. Similarly, contracts of insurance often contain clauses precluding a suit directly against the insurer until a judgment is obtained against the insured. In contrast, Rule 18 on its face seems to authorize joinder of an insurer in both of these situations. As restyled in 2007, Rule 18(b) provides: "A party may join two claims even though one of them is contingent on the disposition of the other; but the court may grant relief only in accordance with the parties' relative substantive rights."[62] Some federal courts have held that these statutes and contract clauses are designed to protect "substantive rights" and that Rule 18 cannot authorize joinder of an insurance company in contravention of them.[63]

However, many of these cases were decided prior to the Supreme Court's development of standards under the Rules Enabling Act that distinguished problems

---

59. *See* Chapter 3(K)(2)*(f)* *supra* (discussing Rule 4(k)(2)).

60. This narrow extension of the federal reach applies only if a claim is made against the defendant under federal law. It does not establish personal jurisdiction if the only claims are those arising under state law or the law of another country, even though there might be diversity or alienage subject matter jurisdiction as to such claims. If, however, personal jurisdiction is established under this paragraph with respect to a federal claim, then 28 U.S.C. § 1367(a) provides supplemental jurisdiction over related claims against that defendant, subject to the court's discretion to decline exercise of that jurisdiction under 28 U.S.C. § 1367(c).

FED. R. CIV. P. 4(k)(2) advisory committee's note to the 1993 amendment.

61. Recall from Chapter 5 that there are also substantial separation-of-powers questions about the power of the Supreme Court to create Rule 4(k)(2) under the Rules Enabling Act. *See* Chapter 5(F)(6), *Illustration 5-21 supra*.

62. FED. R. CIV. P. 18(b).

63. *See* 6A CHARLES A. WRIGHT ET AL, FEDERAL PRACTICE AND PROCEDURE: CIVIL § 1594, at 747 n.5 (3d ed. 2010) (citing contract cases).

of the validity of the Federal Rules from general *Erie* doctrine problems under the Rules of Decision Act.[64] Other cases holding that Rule 18 cannot authorize joinder of an insurance company in these circumstances seem to violate Justice Frankfurter's admonition in *Guaranty Trust v. York* that substance and procedure do not mean the same thing everywhere the terms are used.[65] These cases sometimes confuse classifications of state joinder statutes as "substantive" for one purpose, such as conflict-of-laws doctrine, with classifications of the statutes as "substantive" for *Erie* or Rules Enabling Act purposes.[66]

It has been argued that the application of Rule 18 in the situation described above is valid because the rule only permits a federal court to render judgment in accordance with the substantive rights of the parties. That is, because the insured must be found liable before a judgment can be entered against the insurer, the ultimate substantive rights of the parties are preserved by Rule 18.[67] Under the *Burlington Northern* standard discussed in Chapter 5,[68] it is arguable that this is correct because any infringement of substantive rights, either under the states' limited direct action statutes or under the "no-joinder" contract clauses described above, would be no more than "incidental."[69]

If the state limited direct action statutes are designed to confer substantive rights of action against insurers only when judgments have been obtained against insured parties, these rights are protected fully as long as an insurer is not held liable until the insured has previously been found liable. The express language of Rule 18(b) assures that this relationship will be preserved. On the other hand, if the state statutes in question are designed to confer procedural protections on insurers by limiting their joinder in an action to prevent prejudice against them, the federal courts are arguably entitled to make their own judgments about the likelihood of prejudice and to use their own devices for assuring that the insurers are protected from the prejudice rather than the state device of limited joinder.[70]

---

64. *See, e.g.*, Headrick v. Smoky Mountain Stages, Inc., 11 F.R.D. 205 (E.D. Tenn. 1950) (Rule 18 inapplicable to joinder of different parties; to read it as authorizing joinder of insurer with insured would be to deprive insurer of a substantive right under its contract of insurance); *see also* Chapter 5(F) *supra* (discussing the Court's evolution of the Rules Enabling Act standards).

65. *See Guaranty Trust*, 326 U.S. at 108-09, 65 S. Ct. at 1469-70, 89 L. Ed. at 2085-86; *see also* Chapter 5(E)(1) *supra* (discussing Justice Frankfurter's opinion in *Guaranty Trust*).

66. For example, in Richards v. Select Insurance Co., 40 F. Supp. 2d 163, 167 (S.D.N.Y. 1999), the court held that New York's "limited direct action statute," which authorized suits directly against insurers only after a judgment against the insured, was "substantive" and had to be applied in a federal diversity action in which the injured party was seeking a declaratory judgment against the insurer and the insured prior to judgment against the insured. However, the court relied in part on cases evaluating similar statutes as "substantive" for non-*Erie* purposes. *See, e.g.*, State Trading Corp. of India, Ltd. v. Assuranceforeningen Skuld, 921 F.2d 409 (1990) (holding Connecticut's limited direct action statute substantive for conflict-of-laws purposes).

67. *See* 6A CHARLES A. WRIGHT ET AL., FEDERAL PRACTICE AND PROCEDURE: CIVIL § 1594, at 747-48 (3d ed. 2010) (discussing the purposes of the state statutes and contract clauses in question and describing why Rule 18(b) preserves the parties' substantive rights given these purposes).

68. *See* Chapter 5(F)(4) *supra* (discussing the *Burlington Northern* decision).

69. Recall that the *Shady Grove* decision, discussed in Chapter 5, by virtue of the absence of a majority on the interpretation of the Rules Enabling Act, has not technically overruled *Burlington Northern*. *See* Chapter 5(F)(6) *supra* (discussing *Burlington Northern*). Of course, if the *Sibbach* standard advocated by the plurality prevails as the interpretation of the "substantive rights" restriction of the Act, the Rule would be valid in the context being discussed because Rule 18(b) is undeniably "rationally classifiable as procedural."

70. *See* 6A CHARLES A. WRIGHT ET AL., FEDERAL PRACTICE AND PROCEDURE: CIVIL § 1594, at 748-49 (3d ed. 2010) (describing the likelihood of prejudice against the insurer and the devices available in federal court to prevent it).

As far as "no-joinder" contract clauses are concerned, it is arguable that the insurer has not, in these clauses, contracted for substantive rights at all, but for a kind of procedural protection. If this is an accurate way to view the clauses, allowing joinder of the insurer, but employing other means of protecting it from prejudice, would not impact on substantive rights, but on procedural ones. However, there is a broader sense in which substantive rights may be affected by disregarding the contract clauses in question. To the extent that the states allow the insurers to contract for procedural protections, they are following the traditional substantive contract policy of freedom of contract and enforceability of contractual arrangements. If a federal court overrides the no-joinder clauses by permitting joinder under Rule 18, it is arguably abridging this broader substantive right of freedom of contract, even though the insurer has employed the right to obtain a kind of procedural protection. Nevertheless, even if this is an accurate way to view what is happening, it is not clear that application of Rule 18 would be invalid. Under these circumstances, the validity of the Rule 18 will depend upon what the Supreme Court meant in *Burlington Northern* by "impact" on "substantive rights," something that the Court has yet to make clear. It will also depend on whether, if there is an impact on substantive rights, the impact is only "incidental" or more than incidental, something that the Court has also yet to clarify. Thus, if the Court holds either that the Rules Enabling Act does not protect this kind of substantive right, or that it does, but the impact of Rule 18 on the right is only incidental, Rule 18 may be validly applied in contravention of the no-joinder clauses.[71]

In addition, recall that a plurality of the Court in the *Shady Grove* decision, discussed in Chapter 5, returned to the interpretation of the "substantive rights" restriction of the Enabling Act first articulated in the *Sibbach* case. Should this interpretation of the Act prevail in the future, Rule 18(b) could be validly applied to permit joinder of insurers in the situation discussed above, because the rule is undeniably "rationally classifiable as procedural."[72]

SECTION D. JOINDER OF CLAIMS BY DEFENDANTS AT COMMON LAW AND IN EQUITY

In many instances, a defendant will possess an affirmative claim for relief against the plaintiff. Such a claim may either arise out of the same transaction or

---

71. Thus, it might be reasoned that the kinds of rights referred to in *Burlington Northern* as "substantive" are only the actual rights embodied in the provision with which a Federal Rule of Civil Procedure conflicts. In the contract cases, this would be the right not to be joined. This right, in turn, might not be considered "substantive" because it involves only guarantees pertaining to the configuration of litigation, as opposed to guarantees such as indemnity, assumption of the burdens and cost of defense, and so forth. In addition, even if freedom of contract and enforceability of contractual arrangements are included in the "substantive rights" referred to in *Burlington Northern*, the impact on that right might still be considered only incidental, on the theory that the impact only occurs in a narrow category of cases in which the federal courts employ Rule 18 to override anti-joinder clauses in insurance contracts. For the impact to be substantial, the rule would have to override freedom of contract in a much broader fashion, or in many more kinds of cases.

72. *See* Chapter 5(F)(1) *supra* (discussing *Sibbach*) & Chapter 5(F)(6) (discussing the *Shady Grove* plurality opinion). Recall that the *Shady Grove* decision, by virtue of the absence of a majority on the interpretation of the Rules Enabling Act, has not technically overruled *Burlington Northern*. *See* Chapter 5(F)(6) *supra* (discussing this aspect of *Burlington Northern*).

occurrence as the plaintiff's claim against the defendant or a separate transaction or occurrence. Should the defendant be permitted or required to assert this kind of claim against the plaintiff in the plaintiff's action? Today, *counterclaim* rules answer this question. At common law, nothing precisely like the modern counterclaim existed. Nevertheless, defendants used two devices, *recoupment* and *set-off*, to assert claims for relief against plaintiffs in certain cases. Equity also permitted defendants to use *cross-bills* to assert claims.

1. Recoupment

Recoupment allowed a defendant to assert a claim arising out of the same transaction or occurrence as the plaintiff's claim as a way to diminish or defeat the plaintiff's recovery. Thus, if the same transaction or occurrence rule were satisfied, a defendant could assert a contract claim against a plaintiff's tort claim. However, the defendant could only use the claim defensively. In other words, the claim could only diminish or defeat the plaintiff's claim, but no judgment for the surplus could be rendered in the defendant's favor when the defendant's claim exceeded that of the plaintiff. The claim did not have to be liquidated.[73]

Illustration 7-17. *P* sued *D* for $5,000 to recover for personal injuries incurred when *D's* automobile collided with *P*. *D* possesses a claim for $10,000 against *P* for an assault and battery occurring on the same occasion. At common law, *D* could assert this claim in *P's* action only through recoupment. The same transaction or occurrence rule was satisfied. The claim was not liquidated, but it did not have to be. However, the claim could be asserted only to the extent of $5,000. Recoupment only permitted the defendant's claim to diminish the plaintiff's award. The common-law courts would not allow an affirmative judgment for the surplus.

2. Set-Off

Originally, the common-law courts did not recognize set-off. However, equity courts permitted a defendant to set off a claim arising out of a different transaction or occurrence than the plaintiff's claim under certain circumstances. When set-off was available, the defendant obtained an affirmative judgment for the amount by which the defendant's claim exceeded the plaintiff's claim. By statute, the device of set-off was extended to the common-law courts.[74] After the passage of the set-off statutes, equity restricted set-off to cases in which some special equitable ground of relief was shown, or in which the claims, if they had been legal, could have been set off under the statutes and one of the claims provided a ground

---

73. *See generally* BENJAMIN J. SHIPMAN, HANDBOOK OF COMMON-LAW PLEADING §§ 209-210, at 365 (1923); *see also* Yim K. Cheung v. Wing Ki Wu, 2007 ME 22, 919 A.2d 619 (recoupment is a reduction of part of the plaintiff's damages because of a right in the defendant arising out of the same transaction; recoupment is an affirmative defense that must ordinarily be pleaded to be preserved; however, here the defense was preserved despite the defendant's failure to affirmatively plead it, because the trial court issued two pretrial orders giving defendant permission to proceed with the defense and both parties acknowledged unpleaded issue during trial).

74. *See* 4 & 5 Ann. ch. 4 (1705); 2 Geo. II, ch. 22, § 13 (1729), *as amended*, 8 Geo. II, ch. 24 (1735).

for equitable jurisdiction.[75] Normally, statutes restricted set-off to claims that were liquidated. Practically speaking, this restriction meant that set-off was unavailable in causes of action falling within case, trespass, and replevin, among others.[76]

Illustration 7-18. *P* sued *D* for nonpayment of a $5,000 debt. *D* possessed a claim against *P* for nonpayment of a wholly separate debt of $10,000. At common law, *D* could assert the claim against *P* only by set-off (or a separate action). Here both claims are liquidated. Because set-off permitted the defendant to obtain an affirmative judgment, *D* could not only diminish *P's* $5,000 claim to zero, but could also obtain an affirmative judgment for the $5,000 surplus.[77]

* * * * *

The English set-off statutes required that the defendant's claim be for a liquidated amount. Set-off was unavailable when a jury had to ascertain the damages.[78] In the United States, set-off statutes usually followed the English pattern.[79] However, some state statutes allowed unliquidated *contract* damages to be set off.[80]

The ability to set-off an unliquidated contract claim gave rise to the option of using *either* recoupment or set-off in a particular case, as a litigant desired. When set-off was available, it was ordinarily used because it did not, as recoupment did, require the litigant to grapple with the same transaction or occurrence rule, and set-off also allowed the litigant to obtain an affirmative judgment. Nevertheless, some courts permitted either set-off or recoupment to be used in an appropriate case.[81]

Illustration 7-19. In a suit on a promissory note given for goods sold to the defendant, the defendant might set-off a breach of warranty claim, even though the damages were unliquidated, when the set-off statute permitted unliquidated contract claims to be asserted.[82] Recoupment also would be appropriate in such a case: the same transaction or occurrence rule is satisfied and the breach of warranty would not produce damages in excess of the contract price.

3. Cross-Bills

Equity permitted cross-bills. A cross-bill allowed the defendant to assert a claim against the plaintiff or against codefendants. The cross-bill was treated as an auxiliary or dependent suit growing out of the original bill. Generally, it was

---

75. *See* CHARLES E. CLARK, HANDBOOK OF THE LAW OF CODE PLEADING § 100, at 636 (1947); 3 JOSEPH STORY, COMMENTARIES ON EQUITY JURISPRUDENCE §§ 1865-1876 (14th ed. 1886).

76. *See generally* 2 THEODORE SEDGWICK, A TREATISE ON THE MEASURE OF DAMAGES 265-70 (7th ed. 1880).

77. Because the same transaction or occurrence rule was not satisfied, recoupment would not have been proper. *See* subsection D(1) *supra* ("Recoupment").

78. *See* Morley v. Ingles, 132 Eng. Rep. 711, 713-14 (C.P. 1837); Hardcastle v. Netherwood, 106 Eng. Rep. 1127 (K.B. 1821).

79. *See* William H. Loyd, *The Development of Set-Off*, 64 U. PA. L. REV. 541, 561-63 (1916).

80. *See, e.g.*, Johnston v. Niemeyer, 10 Ind. 350, 351 (1858); Stevens v. Able, 15 Kan. 584, 586 (1875); Baltimore Ins. Co. v. M'Fadon, 4 H. & J. 31, 41-48 (Md. 1815); Raymond Bros. v. Greene & Co., 12 Neb. 215, 10 N.W. 709 (1881); Gellhaus v. Allemania Loan & Bldg. Ass'n, 6 Ohio. Dec. 443 (Super. Ct. 1897); Braden v. Gulf Coast Lumber Co., 89 Okla. 215, 215 P. 202 (1923); Fessler v. Love & Powell, 43 Pa. 313 (1862); Hubbard v. Fisher, 25 Vt. 539, 541 (1853).

81. *See* Davenport v. Hubbard, 46 Vt. 200, 207 (1873); *see also* Lehman v. Austin, 195 Ala. 244, 70 So. 653 (1915).

82. *See* Steigleman v. Jeffries, 1 Serg. & Rawle 477 (Pa. 1815).

available for the following purposes: (1) to obtain discovery of facts necessary to determine the action; (2) to obtain full relief for all parties to the action (as when a controversy arose between two defendants); (3) to bring a new matter before the court in aid of a defense that could not be raised by answer; and (4) to obtain affirmative relief against the plaintiff. When a cross-bill sought affirmative relief, the relief had to be within the jurisdiction of an equity court.[83]

Illustration 7-20. *P* sued *D* in an equity court for specific performance of a contract to convey land. *P* had taken possession of the land, but *D* refused to convey on the ground that *P* procured the contract by fraud. Under these circumstances, *D* could *not* assert a cross-bill against *P* to recover possession from *P*. Because the cross-bill would seek affirmative relief, it would have to be within the jurisdiction of an equity court. However, because ejectment was an adequate legal remedy for *D*, there would have been no "equity jurisdiction." *D* possessed the legal title and could demonstrate it in an ejectment action. *D* could, of course, defend the equitable action on the ground of fraud.[84]

SECTION E. COUNTERCLAIMS AND CROSSCLAIMS UNDER THE CODES

The original Field Code of 1848 did not contain a provision for counterclaims.[85] An 1852 amendment established the first counterclaim provision.[86] This amendment considerably liberalized the former practice. While including both recoupment and set-off, the counterclaim was broader than recoupment because it permitted an affirmative recovery by the defendant and broader than set-off because the defendant's claim did not have to be liquidated.[87] However, as with joinder of plaintiffs' claims, the drafters of the Code restricted the ability to assert counterclaims in order to limit the scope of the action. A counterclaim had to arise out of the same transaction as the plaintiff's claim. If it did not but was asserted in an

---

83. *See generally* BENJAMIN J. SHIPMAN, HANDBOOK OF THE LAW OF EQUITY PLEADING 303-308 (1897).

84. *See* JOSEPH STORY, COMMENTARIES ON EQUITY PLEADINGS § 398, at 345 (9th ed. 1879).

85. *See* Act of Apr. 12, 1848, ch. 379, § 128, 1848 N.Y. Laws 497, 522 (contents of the defendant's answer).

86. The 1852 amendment provided as follows:

§ 149. The answer of the defendant must contain:

. . . .

2. A statement of any new matter constituting a defense or counterclaim, in ordinary and concise language without repetition.

§ 150. The counterclaim mentioned in the last section, must be one existing in favor of a defendant, and against a plaintiff, between whom a several judgment might be had in the action, and arising out of one of the following causes of action:

1. A cause of action arising out of the contract or transaction set forth in the complaint, as the foundation of the plaintiff's claim, or connected with the subject of the action;

2. In an action arising on contract, any other cause of action arising also on contract, and existing at the commencement of the action;

The defendant may set forth by answer, as many defenses and counterclaims as he may have, whether they be such as have been heretofore denominated legal or equitable, or both. They must be separately stated. . . .

Act of Apr. 16, 1852, ch. 392, §§ 149-150, 1852 N.Y. Laws 651, 654; *see also id.* § 153, 1852 N.Y. Laws 651, 654-55 (allowing the plaintiff, within twenty days, to reply to an answer containing a counterclaim by denial, affirmative defense, or demurrer).

87. *See* CHARLES E. CLARK, HANDBOOK OF THE LAW OF CODE PLEADING § 100, at 637 (2d ed. 1947).

action of contract, the counterclaim had to be based on a contract theory. This latter provision was designed to continue the former practice of allowing set-off in cases in which the claim arose from a separate transaction.[88] Although the codes liberalized both recoupment and set-off, it is unclear why the drafters did not go further and allow joinder of any counterclaim, however unrelated to the plaintiff's cause of action. Such a step probably appeared too radical an expansion of the scope of the civil action. In any case, the modern codes following the Field Code pattern usually contained no separate provision for set-offs because the "contracts clause" eliminated the need for such a provision.[89]

Even though code provisions commonly declare that the defendant "must" or "shall" include a counterclaim in the action, the provisions are not read as compulsory unless a separate statute so provides.[90] Thus, the code counterclaim may, but need not, be included in the defendant's answer. If the defendant so chooses, it may be the subject of an entirely separate proceeding.[91]

The language of the code counterclaim provisions and the influence of the former common-law practice, produced some unfortunate interpretations.

Illustration 7-21. Assume that *P* contracted to sell land to *D*. *D* went into possession of the land under the contract. *P* then sued to eject *D* from the land. *P* alleged that *D* had forfeited the right to purchase because of a breach. *D* contended that *D* fully complied with the contract and counterclaimed for damages resulting from *P's* fraud in the sale. Some courts held that *D's* counterclaim was improperly joined under provisions like the amended Field Code. The courts reasoned that the transaction involved in the claim for ejectment was the plaintiff's right to possession. According to those courts, that right had nothing to do with the subject of the defendant's counterclaim—the alleged fraud of the plaintiff.[92] Clearly, however, the defendant's counterclaim arose out of the same basic factual occurrence as the plaintiff's claim and could be efficiently tried in the same action.[93]

Illustration 7-22. Assume that *P* sued *D* for damages for breach of contract. *D* counterclaimed for damages that occurred when *P* converted *D's* property and sold it to *C*. *D's* counterclaim might be held proper under the "contracts" clauses of the code counterclaim provisions. At common law, *D* could "waive the tort" of conversion and sue in assumpsit for money had and received. Assumpsit would be classified as a contract action.[94] However, the "contract" involved in the old assumpsit action for money had and received was often purely fictional. Such fictions should have no place in modern joinder.

* * * * *

---

88. *See id.*; BENJAMIN J. SHIPMAN, HANDBOOK OF COMMON-LAW PLEADING § 210, at 364 (1923). As a practical matter, the restrictions on set-offs limited them to contract cases.

89. *See* CHARLES E. CLARK, HANDBOOK OF THE LAW OF CODE PLEADING § 101, at 642-43 (2d ed. 1947). Some modern codes eliminated the contract clause and separately provided for set-offs. *See, e.g.*, NEB. REV. STAT. §§ 25-811, 25-813, 25-816 (1995) (repealed 2003).

90. *See* CHARLES E. CLARK, HANDBOOK OF THE LAW OF CODE PLEADING § 101, at 646-47 (2d ed. 1947).

91. *See, e.g.*, NEB. REV. STAT. § 25-814 (1995) (repealed 2003).

92. *See* Zettle v. Gillmeister, 64 Cal. App. 669, 222 P. 645 (1923).

93. *See* CHARLES E. CLARK, HANDBOOK OF THE LAW OF CODE PLEADING § 102, at 658 (2d ed. 1947), and authorities there cited; *see also Illustration 7-7 supra*.

94. *See* CHARLES E. CLARK, HANDBOOK OF THE LAW OF CODE PLEADING § 103, at 660-62 (2d ed. 1947); *see also* Chapter 1(D)(4)*(c) supra* ("Trover").

In addition to counterclaims against the plaintiff, modern codes often provide for crossclaims or cross-actions against coparties.[95] Typically, such provisions require that the crossclaim arise out of the same transaction or occurrence as the plaintiff's claim.[96]

SECTION F. COUNTERCLAIMS AND CROSSCLAIMS UNDER THE FEDERAL RULES

1. Basic Operation of Federal Rule 13

Federal Rule 13 provides for "counterclaims," which are claims for relief asserted against opposing parties after those parties assert a claim against the counterclaiming party. Rule 13 is derived from former federal Equity Rule 30.[97] However, Rule 13 considerably broadens the counterclaim practice from its scope under Equity Rule 30. Under Rule 13, a counterclaim may be either a legal or an equitable claim.[98] In addition, Rule 13 allows any pleader, not just a defendant serving an answer, to counterclaim against an opposing party.[99]

Rule 13 divides counterclaims into two general categories: *compulsory* counterclaims and *permissive* counterclaims. Rule 13(a) provides for compulsory counterclaims. Generally, a compulsory counterclaim arises out of the same transaction or occurrence as the opposing party's claim. A compulsory counterclaim must be asserted by the party possessing it if that party serves a pleading on the opposing party. It may not be the subject of an independent action.[100] The philosophy of the compulsory counterclaim rule is that all closely related claims

---

95. *See, e.g.*, NEB. REV. STAT. § 25-812 (1995) (repealed 2003).

96. *See id.* § 25-813 (repealed 2003). Some codes restricted crossclaim provisions even further. *See id.*

97. As applied to counterclaims, Equity Rule 30 stated:

> [t]he answer must state in short and simple form any counter-claim arising out of the transaction which is the subject matter of the suit, and may, without cross-bill, set out any set-off or counter-claim against the plaintiff which might be the subject of an independent suit in equity against him, and such set-off or counter-claim, so set up, shall have the same effect as a cross-suit, so as to enable the court to pronounce a final judgment in the same suit both on the original and crossclaims.

226 U.S. 657 (1912).

98. *See* 6 CHARLES A. WRIGHT ET AL., FEDERAL PRACTICE AND PROCEDURE: CIVIL § 1401, at 6 (3d ed. 2010).

99. *See id.*

100. *See* Robin Cheryl Miller, Annotation, *Effect of Filing Separate Federal Action Claim that Would Be Compulsory Counterclaim in Pending Federal Action*, 81 A.L.R. FED. 240 (1987); W.R. Habeeb, Annotation, *Failure to Assert Matter as Counterclaim as Precluding Assertion Thereof in Subsequent Action, Under Federal Rules or Similar State Rules or Statutes*, 22 A.L.R.2D 621 (1952); *see also* Bluegrass Hosiery, Inc. v. Speizman Indus., Inc., 214 F.3d 770 (6th Cir. 2000) (reversing a dismissal of an action on the ground that it was based on a claim that was an omitted counterclaim in a prior action; defendant in prior action had served a preanswer motion in the prior action that was denied, and the defendant had settled thereafter without answering; the court held correctly that under these circumstances, the claim was not a compulsory counterclaim because no pleading was ever served by the defendant); Allison v. Long, 336 Ark. 432, 985 S.W.2d 314 (1999) (compulsory counterclaim omitted from answer could be raised in supplemental pleading); *cf.* Orca Yachts, L.L.C. v. Mollicam, Inc., 287 F.3d 316 (4th Cir. 2002) (Orca's Virginia federal action dismissed for lack of personal jurisdiction and plaintiff appealed; Mollicam had sued Orca in Florida state action that had been removed to federal court; in latter action, Orca had asserted a counterclaim that was the same claim asserted in Virginia federal action; Federal Magistrate in Florida action found Orca in default for failure to file case management report as required by local rule and ordered Orca's answer, affirmative defense, and counterclaim stricken; held, this order resulted in claim preclusion in the Virginia action on appeal).

should be settled in a single action, so multiple litigation over the same basic dispute can be avoided.[101]

Illustration 7-23. *P* sued *D* in a U.S. District Court. *D* did not appear or defend the action. The court then entered judgment by default for *P*. Subsequently, *D* sued *P*. *D* asserted a claim against *P* arising out of the same transaction or occurrence as the claim *P* had asserted against *D* in the previous lawsuit. *P* objected that this claim was a compulsory counterclaim in the first action and that the failure to assert it should preclude *D* from asserting it in a separate action. *P's* objection should be considered unsound.[102] *D* never served a pleading on *P* in the first action. Rule 13(a) only operates when a party serves a pleading on an opposing party.[103] The same result would follow if *D* had appeared in the action and moved to dismiss *P's* complaint for failure to state a claim on which relief can be granted under Federal Rule 12(b)(6). If the court dismisses the complaint, *D* should be allowed to bring a later action on the claim that *D* possessed against *P*. A motion is not a pleading.[104] Thus, *D* never served a pleading in the action by *P* against *D*.

Illustration 7-24. *P* sued *D* in a U.S. District Court for damages resulting from an automobile accident. *D's* answer contained a permissive counterclaim for an assault and battery arising out of a wholly separate factual occurrence from *P's* claim. *P's* answer to the counterclaim denied the allegations of the counterclaim and asserted certain affirmative defenses to the counterclaim, but omitted a claim that *P* possesses for assault and battery arising out of the same events as *D's* counterclaim. *P* may not assert the assault and battery counterclaim in a separate action. In the first action, *P* served an answer to the counterclaim on *D*. The answer to the counterclaim is a pleading.[105] Therefore, the terms of Rule 13(a) obligate *P* to assert any claim arising out of the transaction or occurrence as *D's* counterclaim against *P*. The failure to do so precludes *P* from asserting the claim in a separate suit.[106]

* * * * *

---

101. *See* 6 CHARLES A. WRIGHT ET AL., FEDERAL PRACTICE AND PROCEDURE: CIVIL § 1403, at 10-11 (3d ed. 2010); *see also* Estate of Pearson *ex rel.* Latta v. Interstate Power & Light Co., 700 N.W.2d 333 (Iowa 2005) (defendant power company was sued on two wrongful death claims and judgment was entered against it on both claims; however, the jury found that each estate-plaintiff was fifteen percent responsible for the other estate's damages, and the company argued on appeal that the trial court should have offset the amounts awarded to each estate by the fifteen percent that the jury found each other estate was liable for the other's damages; however, because the defendant did not assert counterclaims for contribution against the estates, no offset was appropriate).

102. Reported decisions to the contrary can be found. *See* Todd David Peterson, *The Misguided Law of Compulsory Counterclaims in Default Cases*, 50 ARIZ. L. REV. 1107 (2008) (discussing and criticizing the cases).

103. *Cf.* Bluegrass Hosiery, Inc. v. Speizman Indus., Inc., 214 F.3d 770 (6th Cir. 2000) (reversing a dismissal of an action on the ground that it was based on a claim that was an omitted counterclaim in a prior action; defendant in prior action had served a preanswer motion in the prior action that was denied, and the defendant had settled thereafter without answering; the court held correctly that under these circumstances, the claim was not a compulsory counterclaim because no pleading was ever served by the defendant). Under certain rare circumstances, the doctrine of res judicata may prohibit a party from asserting a claim in a subsequent action, even if the compulsory counterclaim rule does not operate. *See* Chapter 13(B)(4)*(c) infra* ("Jurisdictions Without a Compulsory Counterclaim Rule"). That may provide a basis for explaining some of the reported cases appearing to reach a contrary result under Federal Rule 13(a).

104. *See* FED. R. CIV. P. 7(a).

105. *See* FED. R. CIV. P. 7(a). *But cf.* Robinson v. Texhoma Limestone, Inc., 2004 OK 50, 100 P.3d 673 (failure to assert compulsory counterclaim in answer in prior action did not preclude present action if final judgment on the merits was not rendered in prior action).

106. *See, e.g.*, Farmers Cooperative Ass'n v. Amsden, LLC, 2007 MT 287, 339 Mont. 452, 171 P.3d 684 (omission of compulsory counterclaim from reply to defendant's counterclaim in prior action precludes assertion of the counterclaim as an original claim in a subsequent action).

Rule 13 contains certain exceptions to the compulsory counterclaim requirement. An otherwise compulsory counterclaim does not have to be asserted if it requires "adding another party over whom the court cannot acquire jurisdiction."[107] Likewise, a party serving a pleading on an opposing party does not have to include a counterclaim arising out of the same transaction or occurrence as the opposing party's claim if, "when the action was commenced, the claim was the subject of another pending action."[108] In addition, an otherwise compulsory counterclaim does not have to be asserted if (1) the opposing party brought suit by attachment "or other process" that did not establish personal jurisdiction over the pleader on the claim asserted against the pleader and (2) the pleader does not assert any counterclaim under Rule 13.[109] Finally, a counterclaim that is not mature at the time a pleading is served need not be asserted, even if it arises out of the same transaction or occurrence as an opposing party's claim.[110]

Federal Rule 13(b) formerly defined permissive counterclaims as claims that do not arise out of the same transaction or occurrence as the opposing party's claim. Restyled Rule 13(b) now defines a permissive counterclaim as "any claim that is not compulsory." Under the restyled rule, factually unrelated counterclaims will still be permissive. As observed in Chapter 1,[111] the Advisory Committee did not intend for the restyling of the rules to change the way that they operated. However, as we will see in section F(3), below, the change in wording of Rule 13(b) presents some difficult problems of interpretation with regard to counterclaims that do not mature until the determination of other claims in the action.

Under both the old and the restyled rules, a pleader may assert permissive counterclaims, but the failure to assert a permissive counterclaim will not bar the pleader from asserting it in a separate action. The philosophy supporting permissive counterclaim rules is that it may be convenient for the parties to resolve all the claims that exist between them, however unrelated, in a single action.[112] Nevertheless, because of the unrelated nature of the claim, a party might be seriously prejudiced if the party were forced to assert it in an action. Furthermore, the consequences to the efficiency of the judicial system are less serious when a party fails to assert a counterclaim that is unrelated to an opposing party's claim, as

---

107. *See* FED. R. CIV. P. 13(a)(1)(B).

108. *See* FED. R. CIV. P. 13(a)(2)(A); *cf.* Mlynarik v. Bergantzel, 675 N.W.2d 584 (Iowa 2004) (compulsory counterclaim rule was statutorily inapplicable to actions in small claims court).

109. This provision was placed in the rule prior to the Supreme Court's decision in the case of *Shaffer v. Heitner*, discussed in Chapter 3(E)(1) *supra* ("Quasi In Rem and Related Jurisdictional Doctrines"). After *Shaffer* invalidated quasi in rem jurisdiction, the exception appears not to be necessary. *See* 6 CHARLES A. WRIGHT ET AL., FEDERAL PRACTICE AND PROCEDURE: CIVIL § 1411, at 101-02 (3d ed. 2010). *But cf.* FED. R. CIV. P. 4(n) (providing that upon a showing that personal jurisdiction cannot be obtained over a defendant the court may assert jurisdiction over the defendant's assets in the district by seizing them under the circumstances and in the manner provided by the law of the state in which the district court is located); Chapter 3(K)(2)(*i*) *supra* (discussing Rule 4(n)).

110. *See* 6 CHARLES A. WRIGHT ET AL., FEDERAL PRACTICE AND PROCEDURE: CIVIL § 1411, at 89-96 (3d ed. 2010). Counterclaims maturing after a pleading is served may be added to the action with the permission of the court by supplemental pleading under Rule 13(e). Supplemental pleadings are discussed in Chapter 6(D)(6) *supra* ("Supplemental Pleadings"). However, courts have held counterclaims to be altogether improper under Rule 13 when they do not mature until the outcome of the principal action is known. This problem is discussed further below. *See also* Allison v. Long, 336 Ark. 432, 985 S.W.2d 314 (1999) (compulsory counterclaim omitted from answer but asserted in supplemental pleading not precluded).

111. *See* Chapter 1(D)(13) *supra* (discussing the restyling project).

112. *See generally* 6 CHARLES A. WRIGHT ET AL, FEDERAL PRACTICE AND PROCEDURE: CIVIL § 1420 (3d ed. 2010).

opposed to a counterclaim that is closely related. Therefore, Rule 13(b) was drafted to give a party a choice whether to assert unrelated counterclaims on the assumption that this approach would best suit the convenience of the parties and the judicial system. For both compulsory and permissive counterclaims, Federal Rule 13(i) permits the court to order separate trials of the counterclaim under Rule 42(b). This approach reflects the general philosophy of federal claims joinder that inconvenience or prejudice does not result from the joinder of claims at the pleading stage of the litigation, but only, sometimes, by the trial of such claims together.[113]

The federal counterclaim rule encompasses the former procedures of recoupment and set-off. Thus, a counterclaim under Rule 13 "need not diminish or defeat the recovery sought by the opposing party," and it "may request relief that exceeds in amount or differs in kind from the relief sought by the opposing party."[114] Federal Rule 13(h) provides that "Rules 19 and 20 govern the addition of a person as a party to a counterclaim."[115]

In addition to counterclaims, Federal Rule 13 authorizes crossclaims against coparties.[116] A crossclaim must arise out of the transaction or occurrence that is the subject matter either of the original action or a counterclaim.[117] Otherwise, there are no limits on the kind of claims that may be asserted as cross-claims. Rule 13(h) provides that parties may be added to the action for purposes of a crossclaim if appropriate under Rules 19 or 20. Rule 13(i) permits severance and separate trial of cross-claims under Rule 42(b). The policy of federal crossclaim practice is similar to general federal joinder of claims policy: to settle as many related claims as possible in a single action, and thus avoid a multiplicity of suits.[118]

Crossclaims are *not compulsory*. Even though a party possesses a crossclaim arising out of the transaction or occurrence that is the subject matter of the action, the party may assert the crossclaim in a separate action. The decision not to make crossclaims compulsory was based on considerations similar to those bearing on the decision not to make all counterclaims compulsory. The possible prejudice to the parties resulting from a compulsory crossclaim rule, coupled with diminished consequences of failure to plead a crossclaim to the efficiency of the judicial system, dictated that the parties should be able to choose in the first instance whether to assert such claims. Moreover, the possibility that a party might be able to unduly complicate matters for other parties by adding claims collateral to the purposes of the suit dictated that crossclaims could not be joined unless factually related to the other claims in the action.

Under Rule 13(g), a crossclaim may only be asserted against a "coparty." Indeed, for purposes of counterclaim and crossclaim practice, Rule 13 appears to divide the universe of parties into "opposing parties" and "coparties." A litigant is

---

113. *See* section C *supra* ("Joinder of Claims by Plaintiffs Under the Federal Rules").

114. FED. R. CIV. P. 13(c).

115. FED. R. CIV. P. 13(h); *see also* FED. R. CIV. P. 13(e).

116. A crossclaim, of course, must be asserted in a "pleading." *See* Smith v. Eighth Judicial Dist. Court, 113 Nev. 1343, 950 P.2d 280 (1997) (defendant improperly filed and served a document labeled a "crossclaim" and a separate document called an "answer"; a crossclaim is not a pleading).

117. FED. R. CIV. P. 13(g).

118. *See* 6 CHARLES A. WRIGHT ET AL., FEDERAL PRACTICE AND PROCEDURE: CIVIL § 1431, at 267-68 (3d ed. 2010).

an "opposing party" if the litigant has previously asserted a claim against the pleader, as in *Illustration 7-24*, where *P* was obligated by Rule 13(a) to assert a counterclaim against *D* in *P's* answer to *D's* permissive counterclaim against *P*. Coparties are normally thought of as litigants who are aligned on the same side of an action against a common opposing party. Thus, if *P* sues *D-1* and *D-2*, *D-1* and *D-2* are thought of as coparties, although as soon as either *D-1* or *D-2* asserts a claim against the other, they also become opposing parties for purposes of administering the counterclaim provisions of Rule 13.[119]

The "opposing party" and "coparty" provisions of Rule 13 can sometimes cause confusion. For example, assume that *P* sues *D-1* and *D-2*. *D-1* then "impleads" *T* for indemnity against *P's* claim under Rule 14.[120] Assume further that *T* wishes to assert a claim against *D-2* arising out of the same facts as *P's* claims against *D-1* and *D-2*. The term "opposing party" does not describe the relationship between *T* and *D-2*, because neither *T* nor *D-2* has asserted a claim against the other. Thus, *T's* claim is not a counterclaim under Rule 13(a) or (b). However, the term "coparty" does not seem to describe the relations between *T* and *D-2* either, because they are not aligned against a common "opposing party." It is possible to reason that *T's* claim is simply a "claim" (formerly an "original claim" under the Federal Rules before they were restyled in 2007) possessed by *T* against *D-2* which *T* should be allowed to assert, but this classification would raise troublesome problems in cases in which parties such as *T* possess claims against other parties that are factually unrelated to the principal action. To avoid complicating the other parties' cases unjustifiably by joinder of such factually unrelated claims, it is preferable to limit joinder by the same transaction or occurrence rule that is applied to crossclaims. Some federal courts, administering joinder practice in a practical, common-sense manner, have recognized that parties like *T* should be allowed to assert factually related claims against parties like *D-2*, even if the terms used by Rule 13 do not exactly fit.[121]

2. Administration of the "Same Transaction or Occurrence" Test

Determining whether a claim arises out of the "same transaction or occurrence" as another party's claim is a frequent problem under Rule 13.[122] Though this determination must be made in several situations, two are of critical importance. One occurs when a defendant pleads a counterclaim for which no

---

119. *See Illustration 7-30*, section F(3), *infra*.

120. *See* Chapter 8(D)(1) *infra* (discussing Rule 14 impleader).

121. *See, e.g.*, Thomas v. Barton Lodge II, Ltd., 174 F.3d 636, 652 (5th Cir. 1999) (third-party defendants do not have to file an original complaint against an original defendant and move for consolidation, but may file a crossclaim against the defendant even if it would be inappropriate to characterize the third-party defendant as a coparty of the original defendant).

122. *See generally* Mary Kay Kane, *Original Sin and the Transaction in Federal Civil Procedure*, 76 TEX. L. REV. 1723 (1998) (discussing the different interpretations that the "same transaction test" does and should receive in the various places where it appears in the Federal Rules); Douglas D. McFarland, *Seeing the Forest for the Trees: The Transaction or Occurrence and the Claim Interlock Civil Procedure*, 12 FLA. COASTAL L. REV. 247 (2011) (discussing the administration of the transaction or occurrence test in a variety of procedural contexts, including in Federal Rules joinder situaions).

independent jurisdictional basis exists in federal court. As indicated below, if a court determines that the counterclaim is compulsory, it falls within the supplemental (ancillary) jurisdiction of the federal court. However, if a court determines that the counterclaim is permissive, the court will dismiss it for lack of jurisdiction. The issue of compulsoriness also can arise when a defendant fails to assert a counterclaim in a pending action and then later files suit independently on the claim. In that sort of case, if the counterclaim is compulsory, the party who failed to assert it will be barred from suing on the claim in the later action. A determination that it is permissive will allow the subsequently filed action to continue.

The courts have suggested four tests to determine when a counterclaim arises out of the "same transaction or occurrence" as the opposing party's claim. First, the claim and counterclaim are sometimes said to arise out of the same transaction or occurrence when they raise substantially the same issues of fact and law. Second, if the doctrine of res judicata would bar a subsequent suit on defendant's claim in the absence of a compulsory counterclaim rule, the counterclaim is sometimes said to be compulsory.[123] Third, if substantially the same evidence will support or refute both the claim and the counterclaim, some courts have held the counterclaim compulsory. Finally, a substantial number of decisions hold that if the claim and counterclaim are "logically related," the counterclaim is compulsory.[124] Each of these four tests can be criticized.[125] However, the "logical relationship" test is the most widely accepted of the four tests, despite its uncertainty.[126]

A better understanding of how the popular "logical relationship" test works can be attained by examining the different contexts in which the test is administered. Professors Wright, and Kane have noted that very few cases exist in which a party has been barred from asserting a claim on the ground that it was a compulsory counterclaim that should have been pleaded in a prior action.[127] However, many cases hold counterclaims to be compulsory under Rule 13.[128] Although these assertions appear inconsistent, the inconsistency disappears when it is recognized that most of the cases holding counterclaims to be compulsory deal with the issue of "supplemental jurisdiction" (formerly ancillary jurisdiction).[129] In the supplemental (ancillary) jurisdiction context, the courts must determine that the counterclaim in question is sufficiently related to the principal claim to satisfy

---

123. *See* Chapter 13 *infra* ("Finality in Litigation").

124. *See* 6 CHARLES A. WRIGHT ET AL, FEDERAL PRACTICE AND PROCEDURE: CIVIL § 1410 at 52-55 (3d ed. 2010) and authorities there cited; *see also* Copiah Med. Assocs. v. Mississippi Baptist Health Sys., 898 So. 2d 656 (Miss. 2005) (four prong test applied to determine whether counterclaim was compulsory: (1) whether same evidence or witnesses are relevant to both claims; (2) whether the issues of law and fact in the counterclaim are largely the same as those in the plaintiff's claim; (3) whether, if the counterclaim were asserted in a later lawsuit, it would be barred by res judicata; and (4) whether both claims are based on a "common nucleus of operative fact"; further, in applying this four-prong test, the logical relationship test is used to determine whether claim and counterclaim arise from same transaction or occurrence).

125. *See* 6 CHARLES A. WRIGHT ET AL, FEDERAL PRACTICE AND PROCEDURE: CIVIL § 1410 at 59-65 (3d ed. 2010).

126. *See id.* at 65.

127. *See* CHARLES A. WRIGHT & MARY KAY KANE, THE LAW OF FEDERAL COURTS § 79, at 568 (7th ed. 2011).

128. *See* 6 CHARLES A. WRIGHT ET AL., FEDERAL PRACTICE AND PROCEDURE: CIVIL § 1410, at 65 (3d ed. 2010) and authorities there cited.

129. *See id.*; *see also id.* § 1414.

constitutional and statutory subject-matter jurisdiction requirements. Thus, the consequence of concluding that a particular claim is compulsory in the jurisdictional context is to allow the federal courts to hear the claim. Although an erroneous decision in favor of hearing such a claim may undermine important policies pertaining to the constitutional and statutory limits on federal subject-matter jurisdiction, safeguards protect against wholesale evasions of jurisdictional requirements. In addition to the safeguard of appeal, the heavy caseload faced by the federal district courts assures that the judges will not cavalierly assume power over counterclaims that bear little relationship to the claim that provides the basis for federal jurisdiction.

On the other hand, when the issue concerns whether a party should be barred from asserting a claim on the ground that it should have been pleaded in a prior action, the courts will, correctly, be reluctant to apply the logical relationship test to produce the conclusion that the claim was a compulsory counterclaim. The severe consequences of such a conclusion dictate that the courts should label the claim a compulsory counterclaim in only the clearest cases of abuse, when the omitted claim obviously should have been raised in the first action.[130] Furthermore, because Federal Rule 13 allows a party to plead *any* counterclaim that the party possesses, "the careful attorney can and will plead all the client's claims as counterclaims if there is any reason at all to think that they may be compulsory."[131] This cautious and pragmatic approach further assures that there will be relatively few occasions in which the courts must invoke the bar of Rule 13 against a party, and the cases in which the rule is invoked will usually involve malpractice in the first action.

The "same transaction or occurrence test" appears in numerous procedural contexts in addition to compulsory counterclaim rules such as Rule 13(a). Proper operation of the test cannot be determined without judging in each context the consequences that flow from the test and the policies supporting the procedural rule that the test is designed to implement.

Illustration 7-25. *W* sued *H* for separate maintenance. *H's* answer contained a counterclaim for divorce on the ground of adultery, in which *H* named *A* as a coparty with *W* under a rule identical to Federal Rule 13(h). *W* and *A* replied by denying the allegations of adultery. Subsequently, *A* filed a separate action against *H* for defamation. *A* alleged that *H's* false allegations of adultery in the counterclaim for divorce were defamatory. *H* asserts that *A's* claim was a compulsory counterclaim in the divorce action because it arose from the same transaction or occurrence as *H's* counterclaim for divorce. Assume that the jurisdiction in question has a rule identical to Federal Rule 13(a). Thus, when *A* served the answer to the counterclaim for divorce, *H* claims that *A* should have asserted the defamation claim

---

130. This factor appears to be the primary motivating reason for the paucity of decisions holding a party barred by Federal Rule 13. *See id.* at 78-79; *see also* Morse Bros. v. Mason, 2001 ME 5, 764 A.2d 267 (claim for unpaid premiums from workers' compensation trust was a compulsory counterclaim in the trust's action against a member for unpaid premiums; claim was thus barred by failure to assert it in trust's action); Michael D. Conway, *Narrowing the Scope of Rule 13(a)*, 60 U. CHI. L. REV. 141 (1993).

131. CHARLES A. WRIGHT & MARY KAY KANE, THE LAW OF FEDERAL COURTS § 79, at 568 (7th ed. 2011).

in that answer. *H's* defense is valid if *A's* defamation claim arose out of the same transaction or occurrence as *H's* counterclaim for divorce.

In *Williams v. Robinson*,[132] the court considering *H's* defense held that *A's* counterclaim did not arise out of the same transaction or occurrence as *H's* counterclaim. The court stated that the same evidence would not support or refute the opposing claims.[133] This conclusion is demonstrably false. If *W* and *A* were guilty of adultery, *H's* divorce claim is valid. Likewise, if *W* and *A* were guilty of adultery, *A's* claim for defamation must fail, because truth is a defense. Conversely, if the allegation of adultery is false, the claim for divorce will fail and the claim of defamation will succeed. Therefore, both the claim for divorce and the claim for defamation turn on the truth of the allegation of adultery. The real reason that *A's* claim should not be considered a compulsory counterclaim to *H's* counterclaim for divorce is that omission of the counterclaim from *A's* answer is not a clear enough case of abuse on *A's* part to justify imposing the severe consequences of the compulsory counterclaim rule on *A*. Ordinarily, a lawyer preparing a response to a divorce claim will not consider a claim for defamation to be a compulsory counterclaim to the divorce claim. A more technical reason would be that the adultery, if any, occurred at a time before the serving of the pleading that allegedly defamed *A*. Therefore, the separation of the liability-producing events in time could also produce the conclusion that they are part of different transactions and occurrences.[134]

Illustration 7-26. On the facts of *Illustration 7-25*, assume that (1) *A* had attempted to assert the counterclaim for defamation in the action for maintenance and divorce and (2) the issue was whether the counterclaim was sufficiently related to the opposing party's claim to be within the supplemental jurisdiction of the court. In such a situation, the same transaction or occurrence test should be considered to be satisfied. The overlap between the facts necessary to establish *H's* counterclaim for divorce and *A's* counterclaim for defamation would probably be sufficient to place the two counterclaims within the same case or controversy for purposes of a supplemental jurisdiction statute, despite the time gap between the events giving rise to the two claims.[135] Therefore, even though the same transaction or occurrence

---

132. 1 F.R.D. 211 (D.D.C. 1940).

133. *See id.* at 213.

134. *See also* United-Bilt Homes, Inc. v. Sampson, 315 Ark. 156, 864 S.W.2d 861 (1993) (claim for foreclosure of mortgage not a compulsory counterclaim to third-party claim for wrongful refusal of mortgagee to release insurance proceeds to contractor who repaired mortgagor's house after a fire); Rebecca D. Hattabaugh, Case Note, United-Bilt Homes, Inc. v. Sampson: *A New Standard for Compulsory Counterclaims?* 48 ARK. L. REV. 1009, 1024-25 (1995) (concluding that *Sampson* abandoned the "logical relationship test" for a version of the "same evidence test"). With *United-Bilt Homes* compare Pomfret Farms Ltd. P'ship v. Pomfret Assocs., 174 Vt. 280, 811 A.2d 655 (2002) (in first action, vendors of real estate sued purchaser for foreclosure and on real estate promissory note and won; in second action, bank that loaned money to purchaser brought separate foreclosure action against purchaser and joined vendors as defendants; in second action, purchaser asserted crossclaim against vendors for fraud and negligent misrepresentation; held that purchaser's claim for fraud and misrepresentation was a compulsory counterclaim in the first action and was therefore precluded by the compulsory counterclaim rule in the second, because first action was not solely one for foreclosure, but one that involved personal liability of purchaser on note); *cf.* Davis v. Lowery, 228 Ill. App. 3d 660, 592 N.E.2d 1203 (1992) (third-party defendant impleaded for contribution in automobile accident case failed to assert counterclaim against third-party plaintiff for damages to the third-party defendant's vehicle; counterclaim was not precluded; even though it arose from the same accident as opposing party's claim, subject matter of first suit was damage to plaintiff's truck, while second suit involved claim for damage to third-party defendant's trailer; plaintiffs in both suits were different!).

135. *See* Chapter 2(E)(5) *supra* ("The Scope of Supplemental Jurisdiction: Section 1367(a)").

test should not be considered satisfied for purposes of the compulsory counterclaim rule, the altered context of the supplemental jurisdiction inquiry should produce the conclusion that the test is satisfied in the latter context.

Illustration 7-27. *P* sues *D* in a U.S. District Court. *P* asserts a claim under a federal statute and a related claim for unfair competition under state law. Various amendments to *P's* complaint and other extensions of time delay *D* from serving an answer for over two years from the date the action was commenced. *D's* answer contains a counterclaim for defamation. *D's* counterclaim alleges that the original complaint and certain statements made by *P* on the date the complaint was filed were libelous. *P's* answer to the counterclaim asserts the affirmative defense that the statute of limitations had run on the defamation claim. Assume on these facts that the U.S. District Court certifies the following question to the state's highest court: "Does the filing of a complaint suspend the running of the statute of limitations against permissive counterclaims which are pleaded in the answer under Federal Rule 13(b), and which accrued at the time of the filing of the complaint or thereafter, but before the answer was filed?"[136] In classifying the counterclaim as "permissive," the district court relied on the case whose facts form the basis of *Illustration 7-25*.[137] The certified question was improperly worded. There was no reason to classify the counterclaim as either compulsory or permissive under Rule 13. The issue does not concern the policies of the compulsory counterclaim rule, but the policies of the state statute of limitations applicable to defamation claims. It would have been sufficient to describe the circumstances of the plaintiff's claims and the counterclaim. That approach would have focused the state court on the relevant statute-of-limitations policy.

Illustration 7-28. *P*, an insurance company, sues *D-1*, its insured party, and *D-2*, a person injured by *D-1* in an automobile accident. *P* seeks a declaratory judgment of nonliability on the ground that the terms of the insurance policy issued to *D-1* do not cover the accident between *D-1* and *D-2*. *D-2's* answer contains a crossclaim against *D-1* under a rule identical to Federal Rule 13(g). The crossclaim seeks to recover for personal injuries received in the accident and allegedly inflicted by *D-1's* negligence. *D-2* should not be allowed to assert the crossclaim because the same transaction or occurrence requirement of the crossclaim rule has not been satisfied. Under Rule 13(g), the same transaction or occurrence requirement operates as a restriction on joinder to protect the plaintiff from having claims added to the action that are too remote from the plaintiff's claim. The factual inquiries involved in the plaintiff's claim and *D-2's* crossclaim are too dissimilar here to be conveniently litigated in the same action. Therefore, to protect *P*, the same transaction or occurrence requirement should not be deemed satisfied.[138]

Illustration 7-29. On the facts of *Illustration 7-28*, assume that *P's* action is for a declaratory judgment that *P* is not liable to *D-1* under the policy because the car was not under *D-1's* control at the time of the accident. Assume further that *D-1* also asserts as a defense to *D-2's* crossclaim that the car was not under *D-1's*

---

136. Certification is described in Chapter 5(H) *supra* ("Determination of State Law").

137. *See* Bose Corp. v. Consumers Union, Inc., 384 F. Supp. 600 (D. Mass. 1974).

138. *See* Allstate Ins. Co. v. Daniels, 87 F.R.D. 1 (W.D. Okla. 1978); *see also* 6 CHARLES A. WRIGHT ET AL., FEDERAL PRACTICE AND PROCEDURE: CIVIL § 1432, at 291-92 (3d ed. 2010).

control at the time of the accident. Now the overlap between the plaintiff's claim and the crossclaim is sufficient to conclude that no harm will result to *P* from the addition of the crossclaim to the action. Therefore, the same transaction or occurrence test should be deemed satisfied.[139]

3. Additional Problems of Administration Under Rule 13

Apart from the administration of the same transaction or occurrence test, relatively few difficulties exist in administering Federal Rule 13. In some situations, however, the language of Rule 13 has produced problems of interpretation that have yet to be entirely resolved. For example, counterclaims under Rule 13(a) and (b) can only be asserted against "opposing parties." Furthermore, they must be "mature" at the time the party serves the pleading that should contain the counterclaim.

Illustration 7-30. *H* and *W* are husband and wife. During an automobile trip in which *H* was driving and *W* was riding as a passenger, they are involved in an automobile accident with *D*. *W* is killed in the accident. *H* is appointed administrator of *W's* estate. Acting in the capacity as administrator of the estate, *H* sues *D* for the wrongful death of *W*. *D's* answer contains a counterclaim against *H* for personal injuries *D* received in the accident as the result of *H's* alleged negligence. When someone acting in a representative capacity, such as *H*, brings an action, the defendant in the action generally may not assert a counterclaim against the plaintiff as an individual because the counterclaim would not be asserted against an "opposing party."[140] However, if *W* had been driving the automobile at the time of the accident, *D* could then have asserted the counterclaim in an attempt to recover against *W's* estate. *H* would have been an opposing party in the latter situation because *H*, as administrator, is the representative of *W's* estate.[141]

Illustration 7-31. *P*, an insurance company, sues *D*, a party who has been insured by *P*. *P* seeks to obtain a declaratory judgment that the policy issued by *P* to *D* does not cover a certain loss. *D's* answer contains a counterclaim against *P* based on a state statute that allows insured parties to recover the expenses of successfully defending actions brought by insurance companies for declarations of nonliability. In this situation, it is arguable that *D's* counterclaim is premature and, therefore, improper under Rule 13. Courts have interpreted Rule 13 as precluding counterclaims that depend upon the outcome of the plaintiff's claim for their validity. The language of Rule 13 lends some validity to this result. Rule 13(a)

---

139. *See* Collier v. Harvey, 179 F.2d 664 (10th Cir. 1949); *see also* 6 CHARLES A. WRIGHT ET AL., FEDERAL PRACTICE AND PROCEDURE: CIVIL § 1432, at 292 (3d ed. 2010). In both *Illustration 7-28* and *Illustration 7-29*, if the question is whether the crossclaims are sufficiently related to the main claim to justify an assertion of supplemental jurisdiction under Article III of the Constitution or 28 U.S.C. § 1367, the answer is clearly yes.

140. *See* 6 CHARLES A. WRIGHT ET AL., FEDERAL PRACTICE AND PROCEDURE: CIVIL § 1404, at 15 (3d ed. 2010).

141. *See also* Fielder v. Credit Acceptance Corp., 175 F.R.D. 313 (W.D. Mo. 1997) (compulsory counterclaim rule not applicable in class actions; absent class members not opposing parties); Computer One, Inc. v. Grisham & Lawless P.A., 188 P.3d 1175 (N.M. 2008) (client's legal malpractice claim was not a compulsory counterclaim to the attorney's charging lien on settlement in original litigation because client and attorneys were not opposing parties). *Contra* Channell v. Citicorp Nat'l Servs., Inc., 89 F.3d 379 (7th Cir. 1996) (counterclaims against class members permissible); *Ex parte* Water Works & Sewer Bd., 738 So. 2d 783 (Ala. 1998) (defendant not precluded from asserting compulsory counterclaims in class action).

requires a pleader to assert any claim that the pleader "has" against an opposing party when it arises out of the same transaction or occurrence. Therefore, if *D* omitted the above described counterclaim from the answer, *D* should not be barred by the compulsory counterclaim rule from asserting it in a separate proceeding. The counterclaim arguably arises out of a different transaction or occurrence than *P's* claim, *i.e.*, the lawsuit rather than the event giving rise to the lawsuit. Furthermore, because the counterclaim has not matured, the pleader does not "have" it at the time of serving the pleading.[142] Rule 13(b) does not use the word "has." Instead, before it was restyled, Rule 13(b) spoke only of a "pleading" that states "as a counterclaim any claim against an opposing party" which does not arise out of the same transaction or occurrence that is the subject of the opposing party's claim. Arguably, the most sensible way to read Rule 13 is to conclude that counterclaims contingent on the outcome of the main action are permissive counterclaims. However, the courts considering this kind of question did not always draw this conclusion. Rather, they simply held unmatured counterclaims to be altogether improper under the Rule.[143] One argument in favor of this result is the absence in Rule 13 of a provision equivalent to Rule 18(b). Rule 18(b) allows a party to join a claim that is contingent upon the prosecution of another claim in the action to a successful conclusion.[144]

* * * * *

As noted earlier, the Federal Rules of Civil Procedure were restyled in 2007. The restyling of Rule 13(b) has produced a potential interpretive problem in the unmatured counterclaim situation exemplified by *Illustration 7-31*. The problem can be illustrated by the decision of the Georgia Court of Appeals in *Tenneco Oil Co. v. Templin*.[145] In *Tenneco*, Bullman and Bullman's wife-to-be sued Tenneco, Templin, and Tenneco's driver. Templin counterclaimed against Bullman for contribution on the contingency that Templin would be held liable to Bullman's wife. The jury awarded damages to Bullman's wife against Tenneco and Templin,

---

142. *See* Burlington N. R.R. Co. v. Strong, 907 F.2d 707 (7th Cir. 1990); Allstate Ins. Co. v. Valdez, 29 F.R.D. 479 (E.D. Mich. 1962). Rule 13(e) allows a party, with the permission of the court, to assert by supplemental pleading a counterclaim that matures after the party serves a pleading. However, a motion to assert a counterclaim in a supplemental pleading after the main action has terminated in the defendant's favor might be denied by the court as untimely; *cf.* Nameloc, Inc. v. Jack, Lyon & Jones, P.A., 362 Ark. 175, 208 S.W.3d 129 (2005) (defendant was not permitted to file a supplemental pleading asserting an omitted compulsory counterclaim when defendant was aware of counterclaim at time of serving the answer and waited until thirty minutes before trial to assert omitted counterclaim).

143. *See* Slaff v. Slaff, 151 F. Supp. 124 (S.D.N.Y. 1957); Union Nat'l Bank v. Universal-Cyclops Steel Corp., 103 F. Supp. 719 (W.D. Pa. 1952); Mennen Co. v. Krauss Co., 37 F. Supp. 161 (E.D. La. 1941), *rev'd on other grounds*, 134 F.2d 348 (5th Cir. 1943); Goodyear Tire & Rubber Co. v. Marbon Corp., 32 F. Supp. 279 (D. Del. 1940); Tenneco Oil Co. v. Templin, 201 Ga. App. 30, 410 S.E.2d 154 (1991) (claim for contribution did not accrue until after judgment; therefore, it did not exist when defendant served answer).

144. *See* section C *supra* ("Joinder of Claims by Plaintiffs under the Federal Rules"). Rule 18 itself is no help to a party trying to assert an unmatured counterclaim. Although Rule 18(a) speaks of a party asserting a claim to relief "as an original claim, counterclaim," etc., it applies only to situations in which a party is attempting to join two or more claims against an opposing party. Thus, a defendant asserting a compulsory counterclaim against a plaintiff is authorized by Rule 18(a) to join with that counterclaim any other counterclaim the defendant has against the plaintiff. Rule 18(b) similarly applies to situations in which a party is attempting to join a matured claim with an unmatured claim. Where, as in this illustration, the defendant is not joining two counterclaims, but simply attempting to assert a single unmatured counterclaim, Rule 18 has no application. *Cf.* Glaziers & Glassworkers Union Local 252 Annuity Fund v. Newbridge Sec., Inc., 823 F. Supp. 1188 (E.D. Pa. 1993) (language of Rule 13(g) allowing crossclaims to be asserted against party who "is or may be liable to the crossclaimant" permits the assertion of crossclaims that are not yet mature).

145. 201 Ga. App. 30, 410 S.E.2d 154 (1991).

but none to Bullman. Tenneco and Templin each satisfied one-half of the judgment against the wife, and Templin was awarded contribution against Bullman for what she had to pay to the wife. Subsequently, Tenneco sued Templin and Bullman for contribution in a separate action, and the trial court granted summary judgment against both Bullman and Templin.

On appeal, Bullman argued that Tenneco's claim against him was a compulsory counterclaim in the prior action.[146] The Georgia Court of Appeals rejected this argument, holding that while the claim did arise out of the same transaction or occurrence as Bullman's claim in the first action, Tenneco did not "have" it until judgment was rendered in the first action. As in *Illustration 7-31*, the counterclaim was thus premature. However, the court went on to opine in a dictum to address the issue of whether the claim by Tenneco could have been asserted in the prior action (as, indeed, Templin had asserted her claim for contribution against Bullman as a counterclaim). The court seemed to say that the better practice would be to consider claims like Tenneco's (and Templin's) to be permissive counterclaims that might be, but do not have to be, joined in the first action. The problem with this, of course, is that the Georgia permissive counterclaim rule was identical to Rule 13(b) before it was restyled. That rule provided that a permissive counterclaim was *not* one arising out of the same transaction or occurrence as the opposing party's claim, and the Georgia Court of Appeals had already stated that Tenneco's claim did arise out of the same transaction or occurrence as Bullman's claim in the first action.

It may seem as if restyled Federal Rule 13(b) solves the problem in *Tenneco*, since it now permits joinder of "any claim that is not compulsory." Since a premature counterclaim clearly is "not compulsory," the new wording of the rule raises the interesting question of whether Rule 13(b) now effectively overrules the cases holding that premature counterclaims may not be joined at all. On the one hand, the restyling project was not supposed to affect the operation of the restyled rules.[147] Thus, perhaps the conclusion should simply be that the holdings of the earlier cases are preserved, even though the wording of the restyled rule now literally would permit the joinder of premature counterclaims. On the other hand, the Supreme Court has never ruled on the premature counterclaim issue and there is, consequently, no final authoritative word on whether the lower court cases forbidding joinder of premature counterclaims are correct. Thus, the restyled rule could be considered "persuasive authority," in the form of the restylers' opinion, that the wording of the new rule reflects its "correct" historical meaning on the issue of premature counterclaims.

As noted above in *Illustration 7-31*, Rule 13 does not contain a provision like the provision in Rule 18(b) allowing joinder of contingent claims. However, Rule 13(e) gives the court discretion to permit a party to file a supplemental pleading asserting a counterclaim that matured or acquired by the party after serving the pleading. Rule 13(e) might, therefore, be thought to solve the interpretive

---

146. Tenneco's claim against Templin was clearly a crossclaim in the prior action and thus not compulsory, and the Georgia Court of Appeals so held.

147. *See* Chapter 1(D)(13) *supra* (discussing the restyling project).

problem discussed above by allowing a party to serve a supplemental pleading at the end of an action when a counterclaim has matured. However, it is at least questionable whether this solves the problem of counterclaims maturing at the end of an action. There are different kinds of counterclaims that might mature after commencement of an action. Some of these are counterclaims that will mature after commencement, but long before judgment. For example, assume that a plaintiff sues a defendant for a declaratory judgment that the interest provided for on a note that the plaintiff gave the defendant is usurious, and the defendant counterclaims for installments of interest due under the note at the time of serving the answer. Later in the course of the action, other installments of interest come due (mature) and the defendant seeks to add claims for these installments to the action by a supplemental answer. This is the kind of core situation in which Rule 13(e) was designed to operate. If, however, as in *Illustration 7-31* or *Tenneco*, a counterclaim does not mature until the end of an action, it seems less apt to allow the counterclaim to be added by supplemental answer before it matures, and a court might well be reluctant to do so if any delay in the final disposition of the action would result. Thus, it is doubtful whether Rule 13(e) should be held to solve the interpretive problem posed by the restyling of Rule 13(b), because literal interpretation of the latter rule would permit early joinder of counterclaims that mature at the end of the action.

4. Problems of Subject-Matter Jurisdiction, Venue, and Personal Jurisdiction Under Rule 13

(a) Supplemental (Ancillary) Subject-Matter Jurisdiction Over Counterclaims and Crossclaims

Like joinder of claims by plaintiffs, federal counterclaims and crossclaims must satisfy federal subject-matter jurisdiction, venue, and personal jurisdiction requirements. However, "ancillary jurisdiction" has always facilitated subject-matter jurisdiction over counterclaims and cross-claims. As discussed in Chapter 2, the doctrine of "ancillary jurisdiction" was, along with the doctrine of "pendent jurisdiction," codified by Congress in 1990 under the label "supplemental jurisdiction."[148] Before the codification, ancillary jurisdiction existed over compulsory counterclaims, but not over permissive counterclaims.[149] After the codification, 28 U.S.C. § 1367(a) still allows supplemental jurisdiction to be asserted over compulsory counterclaims.[150] However, as noted in Chapter 2, a

---

148. *See* Judicial Improvements Act of 1990, Pub. L. No. 101-650, § 310, 104 Stat. 5089, 5113-14 (codified at 28 U.S.C. § 1367); Chapter 2(E)(4) *supra* ("The Codification of Pendent and Ancillary Jurisdiction").

149. *See* Chapter 2(E)(3) *supra* ("The Statutory Basis of Pendent and Ancillary Jurisdiction").

150. *See, e.g.*, Greisbach Invs., Ltd. v. Compania Dominicana de Aviacion, C. Por. A., No. 90-CV-1931 (DHR), 1992 WL 390242, 1992 U.S. Dist. LEXIS 19078 (E.D.N.Y. Dec. 10, 1992) (factually related counterclaims adding additional parties are within the supplemental jurisdiction conferred by 28 U.S.C. § 1367); *see* Chapter 2(E)(4) *supra* ("The Codification of Pendent and Ancillary Jurisdiction"). *But see* Hot Springs Assocs., Inc. v. Kiesler, No. 90-0032-C, 1992 WL 88644, 1992 U.S. Dist. LEXIS 6042 (W.D. Va. Apr. 27, 1992), in which the court held that supplemental jurisdiction did not exist over factually related counterclaims adding additional parties, because the additional parties were added pursuant to Rules 19 and 20. The *Kiesler* decision is clearly incorrect. *See* Denis F. McLaughlin, *The Federal Supplemental Jurisdiction Statute—A Constitutional and Statutory Analysis*, 24 ARIZ. ST. L.J. 849, 931-32 (1992). Rules 19 or 20 must always be complied with when parties are

question exists whether the language of 28 U.S.C. § 1367 may result in the extension of supplemental jurisdiction to permissive counterclaims.[151] Section 1367(a) extends supplemental jurisdiction to claims that are so related to claims over which the district courts possess original jurisdiction "that they form part of the same case or controversy under Article III of the United States Constitution."[152] As argued in Chapter 2, the scope of an Article III case or controversy may be broad enough to allow the joinder of completely unrelated claims.[153] However, if 28 U.S.C. § 1367(a) is construed as Chapter 2 argued it should be, "supplemental jurisdiction" will be limited to claims that arise out of the same general facts as the claim over which the district courts have original jurisdiction.[154] In that event, permissive counterclaims will still have to independently satisfy all federal jurisdictional requirements.[155]

Generally, it can be said that § 1367(a) has been interpreted as described in the preceding paragraph. However, in *Channell v. Citicorp National Services, Inc.*,[156] the Seventh Circuit Court of Appeals held that the distinction between compulsory and permissive counterclaims has been rendered irrelevant by § 1367(a), and that the federal courts should today "use the language of the statute to define the extent of their powers."[157] However, although the court sustained supplemental jurisdiction over the defendant's counterclaims in the action, the counterclaims clearly arose out of the same facts as the plaintiff's claims and were, therefore, unquestionably a part of the same Article III case or controversy as those claims. The plaintiff's claims were class action claims alleging violation by the defendant of the federal Consumer Leasing Act. The defendant's counterclaims were claims seeking unpaid amounts under the very consumer leases that were the

---

added to a counterclaim under Rule 13(h). However, § 1367(b) only prohibits claims *by plaintiffs* against persons made parties under Rules 19 or 20 and claims by persons proposed to be joined *as plaintiffs* under Rule 19. *See* 28 U.S.C. § 1367(b); *see also* World Trade Ctr. Props., L.L.C. v. Hartford Fire Ins. Co., 345 F.3d 154 (2d Cir. 2003) (supplemental jurisdiction existed over counterclaims of defendants arising from same facts as principal action, even though some of the parties against whom counterclaims were asserted might be nondiverse); Murphy v. Florida Keys Elec. Coop. Ass'n, Inc., 329 F.3d 1311 (11th Cir. 2003) (maritime tort claim that could have been asserted in state court under the "savings to suitors" clause of 28 U.S.C. § 1333, but which was asserted in federal court without invoking exclusive admiralty jurisdiction was within supplemental jurisdiction).

151. *See* Chapter 2(E)(5) *supra* ("The Scope of Supplemental Jurisdiction: Section 1367(a)").

152. 28 U.S.C. § 1367(a); *see* Chapter 2(E)(4) *supra* ("The Codification of Pendent and Ancillary Jurisdiction").

153. *See* Chapter 2(E)(2) *supra* ("The Constitutional Basis of Pendent and Ancillary Jurisdiction").

154. *See* Chapter 2(E)(5) *supra* ("The Scope of Supplemental Jurisdiction: Section 1367(a)").

155. The majority of cases considering this question after the enactment of § 1367 have held that permissive counterclaims require an independent basis of jurisdiction. *See* Cameco Indus., Inc. v. Louisiana Cane Mfg., Inc., No. 92-3158, 1993 WL 62420, 1993 U.S. Dist. LEXIS 2686 (E.D. La. Mar. 4, 1993); Koprowski v. Wistar Inst. of Anatomy & Biology, No. 92-1132, 1992 WL 151302, 1992 U.S. Dist. LEXIS 9706 (E.D. Pa. June 18, 1992); Shamblin v. City of Colchester, 793 F. Supp. 831 (C.D. Ill. 1992); *see also* Unique Concepts, Inc. v. Manuel, 930 F.2d 573, 574 (7th Cir. 1991) (dictum). Only one case seems to have considered a permissive counterclaim to be within the supplemental jurisdiction conferred by § 1367. *See* Wesley v. General Motors Acceptance Corp., No. 91 C 3368, 1991 WL 169204, 1991 U.S. Dist. LEXIS 11745 (N.D. Ill. Aug. 23, 1991). The court in *Wesley* stated that the counterclaim was not compulsory in the sense that, had it been omitted from the action, it would have been precluded in a subsequent action by force of Rule 13(a). However, the court correctly recognized that this did not resolve the supplemental jurisdiction issue. That issue depended upon whether the counterclaim was sufficiently related to the plaintiff's claim to satisfy the policies of the supplemental jurisdiction statute. There seems no question that the counterclaim was sufficiently related to the plaintiff's claim for that purpose. Thus, at this writing, no case has clearly held a completely unrelated counterclaim to be within § 1367(a).

156. 89 F.3d 379 (7th Cir. 1996).

157. *Id.* at 385.

bases of the class action. In *Rothman v. Emory University,*[158] the Seventh Circuit was confronted with an action by a former law student against Emory University for violation of the Americans with Disabilities Act, a federal statute. The University asserted a counterclaim for the unpaid balance of student loans owed by the student, and the court, following *Channel,* upheld supplemental jurisdiction over the University's counterclaim. The court stated that "Emory's counterclaim, whether compulsory or permissive, was 'so related to' [the student's] original claims that they form the same case or controversy."[159]

The primary difference between *Channell* and *Rothman* is in the degree of relationship that existed between the original claims and counterclaims in both actions. In *Channell,* the original claims and counterclaims both arose out of the leases between the class members and the defendant. However, in *Rothman,* the original claim and counterclaim had in common only that they arose out of the same university-student relationship. Nevertheless, as discussed in Chapter 2, the claim and counterclaim in *Rothman* arose out of the same "loose factual relationship," which is probably sufficient to make the claims part of the same Article III case or controversy.[160] Thus, even though both cases discarded the distinction between compulsory and permissive counterclaims in making the jurisdictional determination, the actual factual relationship required for supplemental jurisdiction under § 1367(a) in the cases was actually no different than the relationship required for ancillary jurisdiction prior to the enactment of § 1367(a). Indeed, as discussed in section F(2), above, an actual examination of the contexts in which the same transaction or occurrence test has been administered in the past indicates that it has always varied in content depending upon the issue being considered in the particular case. Therefore, the Seventh Circuit's refusal to apply the unrevealing "compulsory" and "permissive" labels to determine jurisdiction under § 1367(a) is arguably a healthy development.[161]

---

158. 123 F.3d 446 (7th Cir. 1997).

159. *Id.* at 454. In Global NAPs, Inc. v. Verizon New Eng., Inc., 603 F.3d 71 (1st Cir. 2010), the First Circuit held that § 1367(a) had eliminated the prior distinction between compulsory and permissive counterclaims and provided supplemental jurisdiction over at least "some" permissive counterclaims. The court refused to address the outer limits of Article III, holding that whatever the limits, the counterclaims at issue fell within the limits of Article III.

160. *See* Chapter 2(E)(5)(*c*), *Illustrations 2-89* and *2-90, supra,* and accompanying text. However, it should be noted that the student argued in defense to the counterclaims that the university's violation of the ADA constituted a breach of contract that entitled him not to repay the loans. *See* 123 F.3d at 454-55. This argument was unsuccessful.

161. In Oak Park Trust & Savings Bank v. Therkildsen, 209 F.3d 648 (7th Cir. 2000), the Seventh Circuit held, without citing *Channell,* that no supplemental jurisdiction existed over a permissive counterclaim that was entirely unrelated to plaintiff's claim; *see also* Jones v. Ford Motor Credit Co., 358 F.3d 205 (2d Cir. 2004) (finance company's counterclaims for amounts due on named plaintiffs' loans and conditional counterclaims for amounts owed due to loan defaults by members of putative class were permissive counterclaims under Rule 13 in action under Equal Credit Opportunity Act for race discrimination; nevertheless, counterclaims were within supplemental jurisdiction); Leipzig v. AIG Life Ins. Co., 362 F.3d 406 (7th Cir. 2004) (dictum) (permissive counterclaims are within supplemental jurisdiction); Sea-Land Serv., Inc. v. Lozen Int'l, LLC, 285 F.3d 808 (9th Cir. 2002) (carrier sued shipper for money owed under shipping contract; shipper asserted counterclaims for breach of contract and for cargo loss and damage pursuant to Interstate Commerce Act; held that independent jurisdiction existed over counterclaim under Interstate Commerce Act and, consequently, supplemental jurisdiction existed over state-law counterclaims that arose out of same transaction as Interstate Commerce Act claim; although Interstate Commerce Act claim turned out to be unsuccessful, it was not insubstantial, and, therefore, court did not abuse its discretion under § 1367(c) in retaining state claims); Blue Dane Simmental Corp. v. American Simmental Ass'n, 952 F. Supp. 1399 (D. Neb. 1997) (holding that supplemental jurisdiction did not exist over a counterclaim when the claim and the counterclaim had only a single factual issue in common), *aff'd on other grounds*, 178 F.3d 1035

A separate issue concerning the application of § 1367 in Rule 13 cases involves additional parties to compulsory counterclaims under Rule 13(h). Specifically, the question is whether, if a defendant asserts a compulsory counterclaim against the plaintiff and joins an additional nondiverse party to the counterclaim under Rule 13(h), 28 U.S.C. § 1367(b) applies to defeat supplemental jurisdiction over the added party. The correct result is that § 1367(b) should not defeat jurisdiction over the additional party. The language of the statute applies only to defeat "claims by plaintiffs" that violate the policies of 28 U.S.C. § 1332 (the diversity jurisdiction statute). In addition, § 1367(b) nowhere lists Rule 13 among the Federal Rules of Civil Procedure to which the subsection applies. To the extent that authority exists on this issue, it generally agrees that supplemental jurisdiction exists over the additional party under § 1367(a) and that the jurisdiction is not defeated by § 1367(b).[162]

Illustration 7-32. *D* injured *P* in an automobile accident as a result of *D's* negligence. *P*, a citizen of State *X*, sued *D*, a citizen of State *Y*, in a U.S. District Court in State *Y* for $100,000 in damages. *D's* answer (1) denied negligence, (2) asserted the affirmative defense of contributory negligence, and (3) pleaded a counterclaim against *P* for $5,000 in property damage to *D's* automobile received in the same accident. Even though the amount of the counterclaim is less than the jurisdictional amount prescribed by 28 U.S.C. § 1332, the federal court has supplemental (ancillary) jurisdiction because the counterclaim arose out of the same facts as *P's* claim against *D*. If the accident had been a three-car collision in which *C*, a citizen of State *Y*, had also been involved, and if *D* had joined *C* as a party to the counterclaim against *P* under Rule 13(h), supplemental jurisdiction would also exist over the claim against *C* for the same reason.

(8th Cir. 1999); *cf.* Kaltman-Glasel v. Dooley, 82 Fed. App'x 244 (2d Cir. Nov. 21, 2003) (defendant's state law claims for unpaid legal fees was derived from a common nucleus of operative fact as plaintiff's claim for legal malpractice; therefore, when plaintiff's claim was dismissed, district court did not lose jurisdiction over counterclaim). *But cf.* Highway Equip. Co. v. FECO Ltd., 469 F.3d 1027 (Fed. Cir. 2006) (counterclaim for wrongful termination of dealership agreement did not arise out of common nucleus of operative fact with claim for patent infringement; dealership was terminated prior to issuance of patent that was subject of patent infringement claim); Iglesias v. Mutual Life Ins. Co., 156 F.3d 237 (1st Cir. 1998) (holding that the former distinction between compulsory and permissive counterclaims survives the enactment of § 1367 and denying supplemental jurisdiction over an employer's counterclaim for restitution of money that the employee obtained by submitting overstated expense reports in an action by the employee for discrimination and breach of contract; the court held that despite the fact that the counterclaim arose during the same period as the employee's claims, the original claims and counterclaim rested on different sets of facts). Note that the Seventh Circuit cases described in the text and the cases cited in this note differ primarily in their interpretation of the relationship between the claim and the counterclaim necessary to satisfy Article III of the Constitution. The disagreement over whether the test for Article III is the same as the test for compulsoriness under Rule 13(a) is a separate issue.

162. *See* Barefoot Architect, Inc. v. Bunge, 632 F.3d 822 (3d Cir. 2011) (§ 1367(b) does not deprive court of jurisdiction over counterclaims involving non-diverse parties, even though, had the counterclaims been asserted as original claims by plaintiffs and additional non-diverse parties had attempted to intervene under Rule 24 to prosecute those claims, § 1367(b) would have destroyed jurisdiction); State Nat'l Ins. Co. v. Yates, 391 F.3d 577 (5th Cir. 2004) (supplemental jurisdiction applied to claim against non-diverse party added to counterclaim because § 1367(b) only disqualifies claims by plaintiffs); United Capitol Ins. Co. v. Kapiloff, 155 F.3d 488 (4th Cir. 1998) (§ 1367(b) only limits jurisdiction over plaintiffs' efforts to join nondiverse parties, not over defendants' efforts to join nondiverse parties to a counterclaim under Rule 13(h)); Greisbach Invs., Ltd. v. Compania Dominicana de Aviacion, C. Por A, No. 90-CV-1931 (DHR), 1992 WL 390242, 1992 U.S. Dist. LEXIS 19078 (E.D.N.Y. Dec. 10, 1992) (factually related counterclaim adding additional parties is within supplemental jurisdiction); *contra* Hot Springs Assocs., Inc. v. Kiesler, No. 90-0032-C, 1992 WL 88644, 1992 U.S. Dist. LEXIS 6042 (W.D. Va. Apr. 27, 1992) (no supplemental jurisdiction over factually related counterclaims adding additional parties); *see also* Denis F. McLaughlin, *The Federal Supplemental Jurisdiction Statute—A Constitutional and Statutory Analysis*, 24 ARIZ. ST. L.J. 849, 931-32 (1992).

Illustration 7-33. Assume the same facts as in *Illustration 7-32*, except that *D's* $5,000 counterclaim is for breach of a contract wholly unrelated to *P's* tort claim. Before 1990, the federal district courts did not have jurisdiction over this kind of counterclaim because it was not related closely enough to the tort claim to be within the ancillary jurisdiction of the district courts. *D's* counterclaim was clearly permissive. As such, the counterclaim had to meet all requirements of federal jurisdiction independently, but it fails to do so because the counterclaim is for less than the jurisdictional amount prescribed by 28 U.S.C. § 1332. After 1990, if 28 U.S.C. § 1367(a) is construed to permit supplemental jurisdiction over any counterclaim that is so related to the plaintiff's claim as to be within the same constitutional case or controversy, this kind of counterclaim may be within the jurisdiction of the district courts. This construction depends on whether Article III is interpreted to allow wholly unrelated claims to fit within the same case or controversy, as Chapter 2 argued that it should be.[163] However, as Chapter 2 also argued, the better result would be for the courts to interpret the scope of an Article III case or controversy as broad enough to encompass factually unrelated claims, but to interpret 28 U.S.C. §1367(a) as authorizing supplemental jurisdiction only over claims that arise out of the same transaction or occurrence as the claim over which the district courts have original jurisdiction.[164] If that interpretation of § 1367(a) is adopted, there will still be no jurisdiction over the counterclaim described in this illustration. Thus, even if the enactment of § 1367(a) justifies the courts in discarding the former distinctions between compulsory and permissive counterclaims as a means of determining whether supplemental jurisdiction exists, the factual relationship necessary to justify supplemental jurisdiction should remain the same as it was prior to the enactment of § 1367.

Illustration 7-34. *P*, a citizen of State *X*, sues *D-1*, a citizen of State *Y*, and *D-2*, also a citizen of State *Y*, in a U.S. District Court in State *Y*. *P* seeks $100,000 in damages for personal injuries received in an automobile accident. *D-1's* answer contains a crossclaim against *D-2* for $5,000 for personal injuries received in the same accident. No diversity of citizenship exists between *D-1* and *D-2*. Also, *D-1's* cross-claim is for less than the jurisdictional amount prescribed by 28 U.S.C. § 1332. Nevertheless, before 1990, the cross-claim was within the ancillary jurisdiction of the district court because of its close factual relationship to the original claim in the action. After 1990, the crossclaim is still within the "supplemental jurisdiction" of the district court under 28 U.S.C. § 1367.

(b) Supplemental (Ancillary) Venue and Personal Jurisdiction Over Counterclaims and Crossclaims

When the federal courts have ancillary subject-matter jurisdiction over a counterclaim or cross-claim, the question arises whether supplemental (or ancillary) venue and personal jurisdiction should also exist. This question is easily answered when the issue concerns crossclaims. "[T]he venue statute is designed to test the

---

163. *See* Chapter 2(E)(2) *supra* ("The Constitutional Basis of Pendent and Ancillary Jurisdiction").
164. *See* Chapter 2(E)(5) *supra* ("The Scope of Supplemental Jurisdiction: Section 1367(a)").

appropriateness of the forum at the institution of a suit by the original plaintiff so that . . . the crossclaim . . . does not have to satisfy the statutory [venue] prerequisites."[165] Likewise, because (1) crossclaims are asserted between coparties to an action, such as codefendants who are already properly before the court, and (2) crossclaims must also arise out of the same facts as the original action, there ordinarily can be no personal jurisdiction questions about such claims.[166]

The same basic reasons normally support the conclusion that a plaintiff may not make venue or personal jurisdiction objections when a compulsory counterclaim is asserted against the plaintiff under Rule 13(a).[167] The exception is a case in which a third party is added under Rule 13(h) for purposes of a compulsory counterclaim under Rule 13(a) or a crossclaim under Rule 13(g). Rule 13(a) explicitly excludes from the compulsory category claims that require the presence of third parties over whom the court cannot acquire jurisdiction. This provision thus apparently preserves the third party's right to object to personal jurisdiction.[168] Indeed, even if Rule 13(a) did not explicitly preserve the third party's right to object, the Constitution might require that the personal jurisdiction objection be preserved in cases in which the third party added to the counterclaim does not have minimum contacts with the state where the action is brought.[169] The latter should also be true with regard to parties added to crossclaims under Rule 13(g), although since a crossclaim must arise out of the same facts as the original action or a counterclaim, it is difficult to imagine that personal jurisdiction would not exist over the additional party if it exists over the party asserting the crossclaim or against whom the counterclaim is asserted.

Illustration 7-35. *P*, a citizen of State *X*, sues *D*, a citizen of State *Y*, in a U.S. District Court for the District of State *Y*. *P* seeks $100,000 in damages for personal injuries received in an automobile accident in State *X*. *D's* answer contains a counterclaim for $250,000 for *D's* own personal injuries received in the same accident. *D* joins *C*, a citizen of State *X*, as a party on this counterclaim. *D* asserts in the alternative that either the negligence of *P*, or that of *C*, or both, caused *D's* injuries. *C* has no contacts with State *Y*. Under the language of Rule 13(a), *C* appears to have the right to object to the personal jurisdiction of the State *Y* district court over *C*.[170] However, even if the language of Rule 13(a) does not preserve this right, the Constitution may require that *C* be permitted to raise a personal jurisdiction objection based on the absence of contacts between *C* and the claim, on the one hand, and State *Y*, on the other. Clearly though, *P* has submitted to the jurisdiction of the State *Y* federal court for purposes of counterclaims arising from the same transaction or occurrence as *P's* claim against *D*.

* * * * *

As a general proposition, courts have also held that a plaintiff cannot raise venue and personal jurisdiction objections when a defendant asserts a permissive

---

165. 6 CHARLES A. WRIGHT ET AL., FEDERAL PRACTICE AND PROCEDURE: CIVIL § 1433, at 308 (3d ed. 2010). The same would be true, of course, if an additional party were added to the crossclaim under Rule 13(h).

166. *See id.*

167. *See id.* § 1416, at 140.

168. *See id.* § 1411, at 97, § 1416 at 142.

169. *See id.* § 1414, at 113; *see also* Chapter 3 *supra* ("Personal Jurisdiction and Service of Process").

170. *See* FED. R. CIV. P. 13(a).

counterclaim.[171] This result may be sound as an interpretation of the federal venue statutes.[172] However, to conclude that a plaintiff, by filing an action in a particular forum, "waives" all personal jurisdiction objections to whatever claims a defendant may possess against the plaintiff raises constitutional questions in some cases. The questions occur when the events giving rise to a permissive counterclaim happen outside the forum state and trial of the counterclaim in the forum would impose severe burdens on the plaintiff because of the lack of contact between the plaintiff and claim on the one hand, and the forum state, on the other.

Illustration 7-36. *P*, a citizen of State *X*, sued *D*, a citizen of State *Y*, in a U.S. District Court in State *Y*. *P* sought $250,000 in damages for breach of a contract made and to be performed in State *Y*. *D's* answer contained a permissive counterclaim in which *D* sought $400,000 in damages for personal injuries received in an automobile accident in State *Z*. The accident occurred while the parties were vacationing together in State *Z*. Under these circumstances, to conclude that *P* waived personal jurisdiction objections *P* would have otherwise possessed against a suit on *D's* tort claim in State *Y* raises serious constitutional questions. Although State *Y* seems to be the most appropriate place for suit on *P's* contract claim, no relationship exists between State *Y* and *D's* tort claim. If, under the minimum contacts test, it would be unconstitutional for a State *Y* federal court to assert jurisdiction over *P* in an original action on *D's* tort, *P* should be able to object on the same grounds to jurisdiction over *P* for purposes of the permissive counterclaim. This conclusion may have to be qualified in one respect. Recall from Chapter 3 that the U.S. Supreme Court sustained the validity of transient presence jurisdiction in *Burnham v. Superior Court*.[173] If the commencement of an action in a state is a sufficient relationship under *Burnham* to sustain jurisdiction over the plaintiff on a claim arising outside the state, then plaintiffs will not be able to successfully object to permissive counterclaims asserted against them on minimum contacts grounds. The plaintiff will be protected only if the state possesses an immunity rule that is broad enough in scope to insulate the plaintiff from the permissive counterclaim. However, the existence of such protection is highly unlikely.[174]

(c) Waiver by the Defendant of Venue or Personal Jurisdiction Objections when the Defendant Asserts a Compulsory or Permissive Counterclaim

A separate question in some federal actions is whether a defendant waives any venue and personal jurisdiction objections that the defendant possesses by asserting a compulsory or permissive counterclaim in the action. There is authority

---

171. *See* 6 CHARLES A. WRIGHT ET AL., FEDERAL PRACTICE AND PROCEDURE: CIVIL § 1424, at 217-19 (3d ed. 2010).

172. *See id.*

173. 495 U.S. 604, 110 S. Ct. 2105, 109 L. Ed. 2d 631 (1990); *see* Chapter 3(E)(2) *supra* ("Transient Presence Jurisdiction").

174. The immunity rules discussed in Chapter 3(B)(2)*(a) supra* ("Immunity From Service of Process") do not operate to immunize a party participating in litigation from the assertion of claims or counterclaims within the litigation. Rather, they insulate the party from separate litigation instituted by third parties. Thus, the states would have to expand their immunity rules considerably to encompass the kind of case described in this illustration.

that waiver occurs by asserting either a compulsory or a permissive counterclaim in an action.[175] These cases rely on the idea that a defendant possessing a counterclaim and a personal jurisdiction or venue objection should make a preanswer motion under Federal Rule 12(b) to challenge jurisdiction or venue rather than consolidating the venue or personal jurisdiction objections with a counterclaim in the answer.[176] This result is incorrect when applied to compulsory counterclaims. The defendant must plead such counterclaims or lose them. Furthermore, Federal Rule 12(h)(1) explicitly provides that venue and personal jurisdiction are waived only by omitting them from a preanswer motion or failing to include them in a responsive pleading.[177] Therefore, the better view, at least as to compulsory counterclaims, is that no waiver is produced by their consolidation with venue or personal jurisdiction objections in the answer.[178]

Some authorities have argued, however, that the assertion of a permissive counterclaim should produce waiver of venue and personal jurisdiction objections. This argument is supported by the theory that the defendant need not assert the permissive counterclaim. Thus, the defendant "is actually indicating a desire to use the forum for [the defendant's own] objectives" and "should not be able to object simultaneously to the inconvenience of that forum for purposes of defending against a claim by [the plaintiff]."[179] This view is also incorrect. Federal Rule 12(h) lists the circumstances under which waiver of venue and personal jurisdiction objections will occur. Waiver by assertion of a counterclaim is not among those circumstances. It is clearly contrary to the spirit of the Federal Rules to produce waiver by an action—*i.e.*, consolidation of venue or personal jurisdiction defenses with a permissive counterclaim in the answer—that is not listed in Rule 12(h) as one that will produce waiver. On the contrary, the Rule implicitly appears to permit such an action.

In addition, the view that waiver of venue and personal jurisdiction objections occurs by asserting a permissive counterclaim stems from an apparent inconsistency. It is regarded as inconsistent for a defendant to object to the forum based wholly or partly on the ground of inconvenience while simultaneously asserting a claim that the party does not have to assert, indicating that the forum is convenient. The answer to this argument is that there is no necessary inconsistency in objecting that the forum is inconvenient for purposes of the plaintiff's claim, but not for the permissive counterclaim. The relationship between the forum and the plaintiff's claim might well be so attenuated that it would impose a significant burden on the defendant to litigate the claim there. However, it also might be the case that the relationship between the parties, the permissive counterclaim, and the forum are substantial. Furthermore, the defendant's assertion of the permissive

---

175. *See* 6 CHARLES A. WRIGHT ET AL., FEDERAL PRACTICE AND PROCEDURE: CIVIL § 1416, at 142-46, § 1424, at 220-21 (3d ed. 2010), and cases there cited; *Comment Note—What Conduct Constitutes Waiver of Venue Privilege—Federal Cases*, 5 L. Ed. 2d 1056 (1960).

176. *See* 6 CHARLES A. WRIGHT ET AL., FEDERAL PRACTICE AND PROCEDURE: CIVIL § 1416, at 144-45 (3d ed. 2010), and authorities there cited.

177. *See id.* at 145.

178. *See, e.g.*, Dragor Shipping Corp. v. Union Tank Car Co., 378 F.2d 241, 244 (9th Cir. 1967); *see also* 6 CHARLES A. WRIGHT ET AL., FEDERAL PRACTICE AND PROCEDURE: CIVIL § 1416, at 142-47 (3d ed. 2010).

179. 6 CHARLES A. WRIGHT ET AL., FEDERAL PRACTICE AND PROCEDURE: CIVIL § 1424, at 220-21 (3d ed. 2010).

counterclaim may be viewed as conditional. If the defendant's venue and personal jurisdiction objections are overruled, thereby forcing the defendant to litigate the plaintiff's claim in the forum, *then* the defendant would find it convenient to litigate all the claims existing between the parties in the same proceeding, but not otherwise.[180]

If the defendant can bring a separate action in the forum on the claim that is the subject of the permissive counterclaim, it accomplishes little to force the defendant to make the claims the subject of an independent action rather than allowing assertion of the claim as a permissive counterclaim. Yet this result will be the practical consequence of a doctrine that produces waiver of personal jurisdiction and venue objections through the assertion of permissive counterclaims. If the claim can be litigated in the forum in any event, then no good reason exists to deter the defendant from litigating it as part of the existing action with the plaintiff, subject always to the power of the district court to order a separate trial of the counterclaim under Federal Rules 13(i) and 42(b) to prevent inconvenience.

Some courts have also held that waiver of a venue or personal jurisdiction defense by the assertion of either a compulsory or permissive counterclaim would undermine the right given in Federal Rule 12(b) to raise these defenses either by motion or in the answer. This view has recently been expressed by the United States Court of Appeals for the Federal Circuit:

> We hold that filing a counterclaim, compulsory or permissive, cannot waive a party's objections to personal jurisdiction, so long as the requirements of *Rule 12(h)(1)* are satisfied. Indeed, holding to the contrary would effectively eliminate the unqualified right provided by *Rule 12(b)* of raising jurisdictional defenses either by motion or answer. [Here the court quoted from the Third Circuit's opinion in *Neifeld v. Steinberg,* 438 F.2d 423, 428-29 (3d Cir. 1971), which stated that waiver by counterclaim would force a defendant to make waivable defenses by motion, thus undermining the option given in Rule 12(b).] We agree with this view, shared by several of our sister circuits . . . .[181]

Illustration 7-37. *P*, a citizen of State *X*, sues *D*, a citizen of State *Y*, in a U.S. District Court in State *X*. *P* seeks $400,000 in damages for personal injuries received in an automobile accident in State *Z*. The accident occurred while the parties were vacationing together in State *Z*. *D's* answer contains (1) an objection to venue; (2) an objection on minimum contacts grounds to the jurisdiction of the

---

180. *But cf.* Peterson v. Highland Music, Inc., 140 F.3d 1313 (9th Cir. 1998) (making a timely Rule 12 motion is sufficient to preserve personal jurisdiction objection after it was denied, even though defendant failed to raise issue further; other waiver by conduct cases in courts of appeals involved factors militating in favor of a waiver finding that are not present in this case); Continental Bank, N.A. v. Meyer, 10 F.3d 1293 (7th Cir. 1993) (although defendants had raised personal jurisdiction defense properly in answer, they waived it by participating in the action for over 2½ years without actively contesting jurisdiction); Yeldell v. Tutt, 913 F.2d 533 (8th Cir. 1990) (although defendants literally complied with Rule 12 by including personal jurisdiction defense in their answer, they violated spirit of rule by failing to reassert defense until appeal); *cf.* Vanvelzor v. Vanvelzor, 219 P.3d 184 (Alaska 2009) (when statutory basis for jurisdiction over wife in action for divorce or annulment did not exist, court would not conclude that wife, who properly objected to personal jurisdiction, waived objection by asserting counterclaim for support because wife was acting pro se).

181. Rates Tech., Inc. v. Nortel Networks Corp., 399 F.3d 1302, 1308 (Fed. Cir. 2005).

State *X* district court over *D*; and (3) a permissive counterclaim for $100,000 based on an alleged breach by *P* of a contract that was made and to be performed in State *X*. *D* should be able to object to venue and to the assertion of personal jurisdiction over *D* on the tort claim, while also asserting the permissive counterclaim without fear of waiver. Venue of the action is improper over the tort claim in State *X* under 28 U.S.C. § 1391(b). Moreover, the connection between *D* and the tort claim on the one hand, and State *X*, on the other, is attenuated, while the connection between the contract claim, the parties, and State *X* is substantial. Consequently, there is no inconsistency in *D* objecting to venue or personal jurisdiction in State *X* for purposes of the tort claim, while arguing that State *X* is a convenient place for litigation of the contract claim. *D* clearly could bring an independent action on the contract claim in State *X*, and there seems no reason under the Federal Rules or otherwise to deter *D* from asserting the claim as a permissive counterclaim in *P's* action by the imposition of a waiver rule.

Illustration 7-38. The only question that might legitimately arise in *Illustration 7-37* today would concern the effect of a dismissal of the tort claim on venue and personal jurisdiction grounds, but a retention of the contract counterclaim for adjudication in State *X* at *D's* request. If, after dismissal of the plaintiff's claim, *D* requests that the contract counterclaim be retained for adjudication, *D* is realistically in no different position than if *D* had commenced an original action on the contract claim against *P* in a State *X* federal court. However, suppose, as hypothesized in *Illustration 7-36*, it would be held under the *Burnham* decision that the assertion of an original claim within a state is sufficient to allow an assertion of personal jurisdiction over *D* on claims arising outside the state. Under those circumstances, *P* would be able to assert *P's* tort claim as a permissive counterclaim in an original action by *D* on the contract in State *X*. *D* would have no valid venue objection. As discussed in the text, the venue statutes only apply to original claims, not to counterclaims. *D* would also have no valid personal jurisdiction objection because of the effect of *Burnham*. Therefore, if *D* requests the federal district court to retain the contract counterclaim, and if *Burnham* would have the effect hypothesized above in an original action, it seems unfair to preclude *P* from asserting the tort claim. Instead, to avoid waiver, *D* should have to specify that the permissive counterclaim should be dismissed if *P's* tort claim is dismissed on venue or personal jurisdiction grounds.

(d) Effect of a Counterclaim on the Amount in Controversy

Another jurisdictional question concerning federal counterclaims arises because of a peculiar Supreme Court decision concerning the amount-in-controversy requirement of 28 U.S.C. § 1332. If the plaintiff asserts a claim for less than the jurisdictional amount requirement and the defendant asserts a compulsory counterclaim that is for more than $75,000, can the counterclaim be considered in determining whether federal jurisdiction exists? In *Horton v. Liberty Mutual Insurance Co.*,[182] the plaintiff asserted a worker's compensation claim for $14,035

---

182. 367 U.S. 348, 81 S. Ct. 1570, 6 L. Ed. 2d 890 (1961).

before the Texas Industrial Accident Board. The Board awarded the plaintiff $1,050. Under Texas law, either party could sue to set aside the award. In the action to set aside the award, the issues would be tried de novo. On the day the award was made, Liberty Mutual commenced a federal diversity action to set aside the $1,050 award. Liberty Mutual asserted that Horton's $14,035 claim was the amount in controversy.[183] (At that time, the jurisdictional amount requirement of 28 U.S.C. § 1332 was $10,000.) In fact, one week later, Horton, commenced an action in state court to set aside the $1,050 award and recover $14,035.

In the federal action, Horton moved to dismiss Liberty Mutual's claim. Horton argued that it did not satisfy the jurisdictional amount requirement. Horton also counterclaimed for $14,035, subject to this motion to dismiss.[184] The U.S. Supreme Court held that Liberty Mutual's action satisfied the amount-in-controversy requirement.[185] As Professors Wright, Miller, and Kane have observed, this holding results in the somewhat startling conclusion that "the amount-in-controversy requirement may be satisfied by the plaintiff simply alleging that defendant will interpose a counterclaim at a time when the defendant has not asserted it!"[186]

The most logical explanation of the *Horton* result is that the procedure for setting aside the worker's compensation award under Texas law appears to make the action similar to one for declaratory relief.[187] Because the Texas procedure provided for complete relitigation of the issues that were before the Texas Industrial Accident Board in a suit to set aside the Board's award, Liberty Mutual's action can be viewed as a request for a declaration of nonliability in which the opposing party was claiming the right to $14,035. In declaratory judgment actions, the amount that would be in controversy in any possible action for nondeclaratory relief determines the amount in controversy for purposes of the declaratory action.[188] In this case, Horton was the party who was seeking nondeclaratory relief, and he claimed $14,035. So viewed, *Horton* was not essentially different from a declaratory proceeding brought by the party who would have been the defendant in a nondeclaratory action in which the amount-in-controversy requirement would have been satisfied. Therefore, the *Horton* case probably should not be read to permit satisfaction of the amount-in-controversy requirement in any case in which the plaintiff anticipates that the defendant will assert a compulsory counterclaim for more than $75,000.

Illustration 7-39. *P*, a citizen of State *X*, sued *D*, a citizen of State *Y*, in a U.S. District Court in State *Y*, for $1,000 in property damages received in an automobile accident in State *Y*. *P* alleged in the complaint that *D* would counterclaim for $400,000 in damages for personal injuries received in the same accident.

---

183. Liberty Mutual, of course, asserted that Horton was entitled to nothing.

184. *Id.* at 349-50, 81 S. Ct. at 1571-72, 6 L. Ed. 2d at 892.

185. *Id.* at 350-55, 81 S. Ct. at 1572-74, 6 L. Ed. 2d at 893-95.

186. 6 CHARLES A. WRIGHT ET AL., FEDERAL PRACTICE AND PROCEDURE: CIVIL § 1415, at 138 (3d ed. 2010).

187. *See id.* at 121-22.

188. *See id.* at 122; *see also* Peebles v. Merrill Lynch, Pierce, Fenner & Smith Inc., 431 F.3d 1320 (11th Cir. 2005) (jurisdictional amount satisfied when the party suing in federal diversity action to set aside zero dollar arbitration award was also seeking a new arbitration hearing at which party would demand a sum that met the amount-in-controversy requirement).

In addition to an objection to subject-matter jurisdiction based on the absence of the proper jurisdictional amount, *D's* answer asserted a compulsory counterclaim for $400,000 for personal injuries. Unless the *Horton* case is extended beyond its facts to include anticipation of all compulsory counterclaims, *P's* action should be dismissed for lack of subject-matter jurisdiction.

5. Rules Enabling Act Issues Under Rule 13

Potential Rules Enabling Act issues can arise under Rule 13 when state courts do not possess compulsory counterclaim rules patterned after Rule 13(a) and federal courts are faced with the question whether to enforce the state rules or to preclude an omitted counterclaim in a prior federal diversity action under Rule 13. They can also arise when the state courts would either allow the assertion of a counterclaim in the initial action that Rule 13 would not permit to be joined or would preclude a counterclaim that Rule 13 would allow. Fortunately, however, at both a conceptual level and under the Supreme Court's authorities under the Rules Enabling Act examined in Chapter 5, the issues of validity in applying Rule 13 are easily resolved in favor of the rule.

In cases where the state procedure does not contain a compulsory counterclaim rule, courts should not hesitate to apply Rule 13(a) in appropriate cases to preclude assertion of a compulsory counterclaim omitted from a prior federal action. As argued in Chapter 5, there is no conflict between a Federal Rule of Civil Procedure and state law in either of two circumstances: (1) when the Federal Rule in question is not broad enough to apply to the case before the federal court; or (2) when the state rule in question was designed exclusively for use in the state's own court system.[189] Whenever a counterclaim arises out of the same transaction or occurrence as an opposing party's claim in a way that makes the counterclaim compulsory, as described in section F(2), above, it cannot be argued that Federal Rule 13(a) is inapplicable to the case. However, it can virtually always be argued that the state rule in question is designed for operation exclusively in the courts of the state in which the action is brought. For example, if the state has a code system of the sort described in section E, above, it cannot seriously be argued that the counterclaim rules of the system are designed to operate in courts other than those of the state itself. Therefore, it seems clear that in virtually every case involving a difference between Rule 13(a) and state permissive counterclaim practice, there will be no real conflict between the federal and state rules.

Even if such a conflict could be identified, however, the Supreme Court authorities discussed in Chapter 5 would validate Rule 13(a). In particular, the case of *Business Guides, Inc. v. Chromatic Communications Enterprises, Inc.*,[190] discussed in Chapter 5(F)(5), above, would validate the application of Rule 13(a) even in a case of assumed conflict with state law. In *Business Guides*, the Supreme Court validated the application of Rule 11 of the Federal Rules to a represented party who had signed a document in violation of the rule, but in good faith. As

---

189. *See* Chapter 5(F)(3), *Illustration 5-17* and accompanying text, *supra*.
190. 498 U.S. 533, 111 S. Ct. 922, 112 L. Ed. 2d 1140 (1991).

discussed in Chapter 5, the Court rejected arguments that Rule 11 involved impermissible fee shifting by observing, among other things, that the operation of the rule was not keyed to the ultimate outcome of the litigation, but to specific events within the litigation.[191] In addition, the Court observed that "[i]mposing monetary sanctions on parties that violated the Rule may confer a benefit on other litigants, but the Rules Enabling Act is not violated by such incidental effects on substantive rights."[192]

Business Guides assures that Rule 13(a) can be validly applied in any case of conflict with state rules that do not provide for compulsory counterclaims. This is so not simply because of what the Court said in the case, which, as indicated in Chapter 5, is ambiguous.[193] It is also true because of the configuration of the case and the resemblance of the Rule 11 problem in *Business Guides* to the compulsory counterclaim problem under Rule 13(a). Rule 11 does not directly affect the validity on the merits of a claim or defense in an action, but requires that the parties and their attorneys make reasonable investigations of the facts and the law before taking positions on those claims or defenses.[194] The application of Rule 13(a) to preclude a counterclaim that was omitted from a prior action will, indeed, affect the merits of a second action. However, it is clear that the party possessing the counterclaim can avoid the operation of Rule 13(a) by pleading the counterclaim in the initial proceeding. In this respect, Rule 13 is like Rule 11, in that the adverse effects of the rules can be avoided by compliance with the rules. In contrast, Rule 15(c) governing relation back of amendments, which was examined in Chapter 6(D)(5), above, can produce an adverse effect on a defendant's ability to win on the merits regardless of anything that the defendant does in the case. An amendment that relates back under Rule 15(c) that would not relate back under state law can cause a defendant to lose a case on the merits that the defendant would otherwise have won, and no post-commencement behavior by the defendant can affect this possibility. Thus, as seen in Chapter 6, Rule 15(c) presents much greater Rules Enabling Act problems than does either Rule 11 or Rule 13(a).[195]

Potential conflicts can also exist between Rule 13(a) and state law when state law would permit the assertion of a counterclaim that Rule 13 does not allow to be joined or would preclude the assertion of a counterclaim that Rule 13 would permit. For example, assume that under a state counterclaim rule, a party may assert a "contingent" counterclaim that will not mature until after judgment is rendered on the opposing party's claim, while under Federal Rule 13 this may not be done.[196] As with the problem discussed above where the state has no compulsory counterclaim rule, it does not seem appropriate to view this as a real case of conflict, because the state practice is highly likely to be designed only to operate in the state's own courts.

---

191. *See id.* at 553, 111 S. Ct. at 934, 112 L. Ed. 2d at 1160.
192. *Id.* at 553, 111 S. Ct. at 934, 112 L. Ed. 2d at 1160.
193. *See* Chapter 5(F)(5) *supra* (discussing *Business Guides*).
194. *See* Chapter 6(F) *supra* (discussing Rule 11).
195. *See* Chapter 6(D)(5)*(d) supra* (discussing the Rules Enabling Act issues with Rule 15(c)).
196. *See* section F(1)*(d) supra* (discussing this problem).

Even if this hypothetical situation is viewed as a case of conflict between the state rule and Rule 13, however, Rule 13 can be validly applied. At worst, the counterclaim would have to be asserted in an independent action due to the limitations in Rule 13, while under state law it could be joined in the initial action. This kind of difference, while perhaps producing procedural inconvenience to a federal litigant, will not necessarily affect substantive rights at all, and if any effect on substantive rights does exist, that effect will surely be only "incidental." General policies of efficient judicial administration arguably also support the rule against nonjoinder of premature counterclaims and assure that Rule 13 is reasonably necessary to the uniform scheme of procedure that it was the purpose of Congress to establish when it enacted the Rules Enabling Act. Thus, the nonexistent or incidental effect of Rule 13(a) on substantive rights, when coupled with the efficiency concerns described, should validate the rule as applied to this situation.[197]

A situation in which state law prohibits joinder of a counterclaim that Rule 13 would permit is illustrated by *Com/Tech Communication Technologies, Inc. v. Wireless Data Systems, Inc.*[198] In *Com/Tech,* New York had established a summary procedure applicable to actions based upon instruments "for the payment of money only or upon any judgment." Under this procedure, the plaintiff could file an appropriate action and serve the defendant with a motion for summary judgment and supporting papers in lieu of a complaint, and the defendant could not assert counterclaims against the plaintiff in the action.[199] The plaintiff commenced such an action on four notes totaling $150,000 in New York state court, and the defendant removed the action to federal court. However, when the defendant attempted to assert counterclaims against the plaintiff in the federal action, the district judge refused to entertain the counterclaims on the grounds that they were inconsistent with the New York summary procedure. The Second Circuit Court of Appeals vacated the district court's judgment and remanded the case, holding that it had to be conducted in accord with the Federal Rules, including Rule 13, which would permit the assertion of counterclaims by the defendant. The Second Circuit stated that the New York statute in question was only a procedural rule, which did not govern in the federal courts.[200]

Although the court's analysis of the case was unrevealing, the result was entirely correct. As with the other issues discussed above, it appears that there was no real conflict between the state procedure and Rule 13, because the state procedure was probably designed to operate only in the courts of New York. Even if it was intended to operate in other courts, however, it is difficult to see how the application of Rule 13 could affect the substantive rights of the parties. At best, Rule 13 would allow adjudication of the defendant's counterclaims in the same action with the plaintiff's claims, while the state procedure would require the adjudication of the defendant's claims in a separate proceeding. Thus, it might impose procedural burdens on the plaintiff in federal court that would not exist in

---

197. *See* Chapter 5(F)(4) *supra* (describing the *Burlington Northern* test for Federal Rule validity under the Rules Enabling Act).

198. 163 F.3d 149 (2d Cir. 1998).

199. *See id.* at 150.

200. *See id.* at 151.

state court, but it is difficult to see how it would affect the outcome on the merits of either the plaintiff's claims or the defendant's counterclaims. Therefore, in the absence of any indication that the New York law itself was supported by substantive policies—for example, such as those involved in the state tort reform effort in the *Gasperini* case, discussed in Chapter 5(F)(5), above—there was no reason for Rule 13 to give way to the state procedure.

It should be noted that the Supreme Court's decision in the *Shady Grove* decision, examined in Chapter 5,[201] does not affect the conclusions drawn above, which are that Rule 13 can be applied regardless of differences between the rule and state law. However, if the plurality's interpretation of the "substantive rights" restriction of the Rules Enabling Act in *Shady Grove* should prevail in the future, that interpretation would provide another reason for concluding that Rule 13 might be validly applied in the face of conflicting state law. Under the plurality's return to the test earlier articulated in the *Sibbach*[202] test, a Federal Rule of Civil Procedure that conflicts with state law will be valid if the Federal Rule is "rationally classifiable" as procedural.[203] Rule 13 clearly passes this test.

Chapter 5(F)(5) also examined the effect of the *Semtek* case on the interpretation of Federal Rules of Civil Procedure that provide preclusion rules, as does Rule 13(a). There it was suggested that *Semtek* may result in Rule 13(a) being interpreted to preclude assertion of omitted compulsory counterclaims only in the same federal court in which the original action was adjudicated and in which the counterclaim was omitted, and not in any other federal or state court. This possibility was adequately examined in Chapter 5, and will be examined further in Chapters 10(E) and 13(F)(2). Therefore, it will not be further discussed here.

---

201. *See* Chapter 5(F)(6) (discussing *Shady Grove*).
202. *See* Chapter 5(F)(1) (discussing the *Sibbach* case).
203. *See* Chapter 5(F)(6) (discussing the plurality's interpretation of the Act in *Shady Grove*).

Chapter 8

JOINDER OF PARTIES

SECTION A. BASIC JOINDER OF PARTIES RULES IN COMMON-LAW AND EQUITY ACTIONS

In modern procedural systems, rules on "real parties in interest" and "capacity to sue or be sued" govern who may sue as a plaintiff or be sued as a defendant. Rules on "permissive joinder of parties" and "joinder of persons needed for just adjudication" govern who may and must be joined with other parties in an action.[1] Like other modern procedural rules, these rules have antecedents in common law and equity practice. Typically, the common-law rules governing joinder tended to be rigid, while equity practice was more flexible. The more flexible equity practice provided the basis for modern codes and systems based on the Federal Rules of Civil Procedure.

1. Basic Joinder Rules in Common-Law Actions

The common law developed highly technical and restrictive rules governing joinder of parties.[2] In general, the plaintiff in a common-law action had to be a person who possessed the entire legal right or title involved in the action. Multiple plaintiffs each had to be equally entitled to the recovery before they could join in the suit. Multiple defendants had to be equally subject to a common liability. Even if it was possible to render a separate verdict against each defendant, a single judgment had to be rendered against all the defendants jointly. Otherwise, they could not be joined in the same action.[3]

2. Joinder of Parties in Equity

Compared to joinder rules in common-law actions, the joinder rules in equity cases were more flexible and reflected considerations of practical convenience to the parties. Two general principles governed equity proceedings. First, the real party in interest had to prosecute the suit, although other persons might join as plaintiffs if they had an interest in the subject matter or in obtaining the relief

---

1. *See, e.g.*, FED. R. CIV. P. 17, 19 & 20.

2. *See generally* ALEXANDER MARTIN, CIVIL PROCEDURE AT COMMON LAW §§ 181-225 (1904).

3. *See* JOHN N. POMEROY, CODE REMEDIES 77 (1904). The specific application of these common-law joinder rules differed depending upon whether the action was a personal action *ex contractu*, a personal action *ex delicto*, or a real action. *See* Chapter 1(D)(3)*(a)-(c) supra* (discussing these basic categories of common-law actions).

demanded. Second, all persons whose presence was necessary for a complete determination of the dispute had to be made parties to prevent a multiplicity of suits.[4]

Parties in equity were classified either as *necessary* (indispensable) or as *proper* (but not indispensable) parties. A person might be a necessary party either because the disposition of the lawsuit would affect the person's interests or because the person's absence might prevent final relief.[5]

Illustration 8-1. In a suit to rescind a contract between several persons, all parties to the contract were necessary parties to the action. A decree of rescission rendered against some, but not all, of the contracting parties would either destroy the absent persons' rights or leave the contract in effect as to the absentees and rescinded as to the parties joined in the action. If the decree would destroy the absentees' rights, the action would affect those rights without giving the absentees an opportunity to be heard. If the decree would leave the contract in effect as to the absentees and rescinded as to the parties to the action, complete relief—rescission as to all parties would not be afforded to the parties joined in the action.[6]

* * * * *

In some situations, all persons who were necessary parties could not be brought before the court. For example, when it was impossible to obtain jurisdiction over the absent persons, the court would determine whether a decree could be rendered without harming the absent parties. If it could, the action would proceed without them.[7] Such persons were not technically necessary (or indispensable) parties at all. Instead, they were "proper" parties whose interests were deemed to be "separable."[8] For example, in a suit to foreclose a mortgage, persons with liens on the property subordinate to the mortgage would be considered proper, but not indispensable, parties.[9] Another type of proper party was a "formal" party—a person who had a general interest in the subject matter that could be settled conveniently in the suit, but who had no interest in the particular question being litigated. Formal parties did not have to be joined, though they could be.[10]

Illustration 8-2. Assume that *D* mortgaged property to *C*. Subsequently, *C* assigned the debt and mortgage to *P*. If the debt was not paid and *P* sued the mortgagor to foreclose the mortgage, *C*, the mortgagee-assignor, did not have to be joined in the proceeding. By assigning the debt and mortgage, *C* divested *C's* interest absolutely and unconditionally. However, if *P* joined *C* in the action for some reason—for example, to obtain an admission in *C's* answer that the mortgage had been assigned—it would not be error. The mortgagee was a formal, proper party, but not a necessary (or indispensable) one.[11]

* * * * *

---

4. *See generally* BENJAMIN SHIPMAN, HANDBOOK OF THE LAW OF EQUITY PLEADING 13-19 (1897).

5. A necessary party possessed an interest in the dispute of such a nature that the final decree could not be made without affecting that interest or leaving the suit in such a condition that it could not be settled equitably. *See id.* at 19-21.

6. *See id.* at 21-22.

7. *See id.* 24-25.

8. *See id.* at 36.

9. *Id.* at 40.

10. *See id.* 36, 37, n.3.

11. *See* Merrill v. Bischoff, 3 A.D. 361, 38 N.Y.S. 194 (1896).

In both common-law and equity actions, all persons who had joint interests had to be joined in the suit. At common law, however, if a person possessed a joint interest with another and refused to join as a plaintiff, nothing could be done. In contrast, in equity, the party who refused to join as a plaintiff could be joined as a defendant.[12]

Illustration 8-3. Assume that *D-1* repeatedly trespassed on land that *P* and *D-2* owned as joint tenants. *P* wants to sue for an injunction to prevent *D-1's* trespasses. *D-2*, the other joint tenant, refuses to join as a plaintiff. Under these circumstances, *P* could bring the action. *D-2* would be joined as a defendant with the trespasser.

* * * * *

At common law, parties with separate interests had to sue separately. In equity, such persons could join as plaintiffs if they all had an interest in the suit and in obtaining the relief demanded.[13]

Illustration 8-4. Owners of separate parcels of property could join as plaintiffs in an equity action to abate a nuisance affecting their parcels. The parties had separate interests because of their separate ownership of the different parcels. However, all the parties had an interest in the action and in obtaining an abatement of the nuisance.[14]

* * * * *

Joinder of defendants in equity was based on similar standards. As at common law, all persons who had "joint interests" had to be joined as defendants. Such persons were "necessary" parties. In addition, any person who had an interest in the controversy or whose presence would enable the court to determine the dispute in its entirety could be made a defendant in equity.[15] This kind of joinder was in accord with the rules governing necessary and proper parties. An equity bill could be objectionable on grounds of *multifariousness* if one or more of the defendants had no interest in a matter involved in the suit.[16]

Illustration 8-5. Assume a lease contract stipulates that each of two tenants is liable for payment of only one-half of the rent. Two sureties join in the contract, each guaranteeing payment of only one tenant's portion of the rent. In such a case, joinder of the sureties in an action for the rent would be improper because each surety does not have an interest in the entire subject matter of the suit.[17]

Illustration 8-6. Assume that *P* sued to rescind contracts that *P* made with two defendants, *D-1* and *D-2*, on separate occasions. If each contract was induced by a separate and unrelated act of fraud, the bill would be multifarious. Neither of the defendants has any interest in the claim for rescission asserted against the other.[18]

---

12. *See* BENJAMIN SHIPMAN, HANDBOOK OF THE LAW OF EQUITY PLEADING 49-50 (1897).
13. *Id.* at 51.
14. *See id.* at 52.
15. *See id.* at 56.
16. *See id.* at 57.
17. *Id.* at 58, n.8.
18. *See* Woodruff v. Young, 43 Mich. 548, 6 N.W. 85 (1880).

SECTION B. BASIC PARTY JOINDER PROVISIONS OF THE CODES

The New York Field Code adopted the more flexible equity approach to joinder of parties. Section 91 provided that "[e]very action must be prosecuted in the name of the real party in interest, except as otherwise provided in [§] 93."[19] Section 93 stated that "[a]n executor or administrator, a trustee of an express trust, or a person expressly authorized by statute, may sue without joining with him the persons for whose benefit the suit is prosecuted."[20] In addition, § 97 of the Field Code provided that "[a]ll persons having an interest in the subject of the action, and in obtaining the relief demanded, may be joined as plaintiffs, except as otherwise provided in this title."[21] Section 98 stated that "[a]ny person may be made a party defendant, who has an interest in the controversy, adverse to the plaintiff."[22] Section 99 added that persons who were "united in interest must be joined as plaintiffs or defendants; but if the consent of any one, who should have been joined as plaintiff, cannot be obtained, [that person] may be made a defendant."[23] Finally, § 102 provided that "[w]hen a complete determination of the controversy cannot be had without the presence of other parties, the court may order them to be brought in, by an amendment of the complaint, or by a supplemental complaint, and a new summons."[24]

These changes removed many of the technical common-law restrictions on party joinder. For example, in a common-law action, an assignor was merely a nominal plaintiff. The assignee had to sue in the assignor's name to enforce the assignee's right of action, but the assignor was otherwise unimportant. When the codes merged law and equity, the substantive rights of the parties remained unchanged. The assignee still possessed the substantive right of action. However, the assignee now could sue in assignee's own name whether the assignee sought legal or equitable relief. Similarly, the equity rules on compulsory and permissive joinder applied to actions for legal or equitable relief under the codes, though the substantive rights of the parties remained the same.[25]

Some joinder problems remained, however. One problem concerned the ability to join parties in the alternative. Such alternative joinder had sometimes been permitted in equity, but not at common law. In the absence of a special statutory authorization, the courts often interpreted the codes to prohibit the joinder of

---

19. Act of Apr. 12, 1848, ch. 379, § 91, 1848 N.Y. Laws 497, 515.
20. *Id.* § 93, 1848 N.Y. Laws 497, 515.
21. *Id.* § 97, 1848 N.Y. Laws 497, 516.
22. *Id.* § 98, 1848 N.Y. Laws 497, 516.
23. *Id.* § 99, 1848 N.Y. Laws 497, 516.
24. *Id.* § 102, 1848 N.Y. Laws 497, 516. The Commissioners explained the purpose of these party provisions as follows:

> The rules respecting parties in the courts of law, differ from those in courts of equity. The blending of the jurisdiction makes it necessary to revise these rules, to some extent. In doing so, we have had a three-fold purpose in view: first, to do away with artificial distinctions existing in the courts of law, and to require the real party in interest to appear in court as such[;] second, to require the presence of such parties as are necessary to make an end of the controversy[;] and third, to allow otherwise great latitude in respect to the number of parties who may be brought in.

FIRST REPORT OF THE COMMISSIONERS ON PRACTICE AND PLEADINGS OF NEW YORK 123 (1848).
25. *See* CHARLES E. CLARK, HANDBOOK OF THE LAW OF CODE PLEADING § 22, at 161 (2d ed. 1947).

defendants in the alternative. For example, assume that a complaint alleged that either one or the other of two defendants, but not both, was liable to the plaintiff. Such a complaint was considered defective because the plaintiff had to state facts which constituted a cause of action against each defendant.[26] Thus, unless the plaintiff could allege a joint liability, the plaintiff had to sue the defendants separately. Separate suits produced a wasteful duplication of proceedings and a danger of losing both actions.[27]

Illustration 8-7. Assume that *P* was injured by the tortious behavior of *D-1* or *D-2*, but *P* did not know which one was responsible. It would be convenient to join both *D-1* and *D-2* in *P's* action, alleging their liability in the alternative. However, unless specially permitted by statute, courts often prohibited such joinder under the codes.[28]

* * * * *

Another joinder problem was produced by the requirement that all persons joined as plaintiffs had to have an interest in the subject of the action "*and*" in obtaining the relief demanded.[29] The use of the word "and" led some courts to restrict joinder of plaintiffs to situations in which each plaintiff was interested in *all* of the relief demanded. This interpretation contradicted the intent of the Field Code drafters, whose stated purpose was to employ equitable principles of joinder in the new statutes.[30] This restrictive interpretation disallowed joinder of parties who were interested in the same subject matter, but who did not benefit from all the relief demanded.

Illustration 8-8. Assume that an insurance policy designated *P-1* and *P-2* as beneficiaries. If each were to receive a separate amount under the policy, *P-1* and *P-2* might not be permitted to join as plaintiffs in a suit to recover the policy proceeds.[31] Some courts, however, "realizing that a multiplicity of suits may be avoided without inconvenience at trial or prejudice to the defendant, . . . allowed joinder in this situation, stressing that a lump sum recovery [was] sought."[32]

* * * * *

Even after statutes liberalized the party joinder rules in some states, the interaction between the party joinder and claim joinder provisions produced a serious joinder problem. The claim joinder provisions did not distinguish between single and multiple party cases. The courts should have interpreted the liberalized party joinder provisions as overriding the claim joinder sections in multiple party situations, but they did not always do so. When both sets of joinder requirements had to be satisfied, the liberal party joinder sections had no practical effect.[33]

---

26. Both defendants could admit the allegations and "still the court could not order judgment on the pleadings against either defendant." Casey Pure Milk Co. v. Booth Fisheries Co., 124 Minn. 117, 118, 144 N.W. 450, 451 (1913).

27. *See* CHARLES E. CLARK, HANDBOOK OF THE LAW OF CODE PLEADING § 62, at 393-96 (2d ed. 1947).

28. *See* Casey Pure Milk Co. v. Booth Fisheries Co., 124 Minn. 117, 144 N.W. 450 (1913); CHARLES E. CLARK, HANDBOOK OF THE LAW OF CODE PLEADING § 62, at 393-94 (2d ed. 1947).

29. *See* Act of Apr. 12, 1848, ch. 379, § 97, 1848 N.Y. Laws 497, 516; *see also* NEB. REV. STAT. § 25-311 (1995) (repealed and replaced 2003).

30. FIRST REPORT OF THE COMMISSIONERS ON PRACTICE AND PLEADING OF NEW YORK 123-24 (1848).

31. *See* Keary v. Mutual Reserve Fund Life Ass'n, 30 F. 359 (C.C.E.D. Mo. 1887).

32. CHARLES E. CLARK, HANDBOOK OF THE LAW OF CODE PLEADING § 57, at 366 (2d ed. 1947).

33. *See id.* § 67, at 438-39.

Illustration 8-9. At one time, § 211 of the New York Civil Practice Act provided that "[a]ll persons may be joined as defendants against whom the right to any relief is alleged to exist, whether jointly, severally or in the alternative; and judgment may be given against such one or more of the defendants as may be found to be liable, according to their respective liabilities."[34] In addition, § 212 of the Civil Practice Act stated that "[i]t shall not be necessary that each defendant shall be interested as to all the relief prayed for, or as to every cause of action included in any proceeding against him."[35] However, § 258(9) (the joinder of claims section of the New York Civil Practice Act) provided that the plaintiff might unite in a single complaint two or more causes of action when they were brought to recover "[u]pon claims arising out of the same transaction, or transactions connected with the same subject of action . . . ."[36] In *Ader v. Blau*,[37] the plaintiff sued two defendants for the wrongful death of a child. The plaintiff alleged that one of the defendants negligently maintained a picket fence that caused the death of the child. The plaintiff alleged in the alternative that the other defendant, a doctor, negligently treated the child, which caused the child's death. The New York Court of Appeals held that even if the party joinder provisions, standing alone, would permit joinder of the defendants, the claims joinder section prohibited the joinder because the causes of action asserted against the defendants did not arise out of the same transaction or transactions connected with the same subject of action.[38]

SECTION C. BASIC PARTY JOINDER PROVISIONS OF THE FEDERAL RULES

The basic party joinder provisions of the Federal Rules of Civil Procedure are found in Rule 17 (real party in interest and capacity to sue and be sued), Rule 19 (joinder of persons needed for just adjudication), and Rule 20 (permissive joinder of parties). Generally, the Federal Rules adopted the best features of party joinder under the codes, while avoiding the difficulties experienced under the code provisions.

1. Real Party in Interest

(a) In General

Federal Rule 17(a) requires that actions be prosecuted in the name of the real party in interest.[39] This rule was derived from former Equity Rule 37. The

34. *See* Ader v. Blau, 241 N.Y. 7, 13, 148 N.E. 771, 772 (1925).
35. *See id.*
36. *See id.* at 14, 148 N.E. at 773.
37. 241 N.Y. 7, 148 N.E. 771 (1925).
38. *See id.* at 16-21, 148 N.E. at 774-75.
39. FED. R. CIV. P. 17(a); *see also* Discover Bank v. Vaden, 489 F.3d 594 (4th Cir. 2007) (court finds plaintiff bank to be real party in interest on defendant's counterclaims; dissent correctly protests that "[a] defendant can never be a real party in interest").

equity rule, in turn, was derived from real-party-in-interest provisions under the codes. Before 1966, Rule 17(a) stated:

> Every action shall be prosecuted in the name of the real party in interest; *but* an executor, administrator, guardian, trustee of an express trust, a party with whom or in whose name a contract has been made for the benefit of another, or a party authorized by statute may sue in his own name without joining with him the party for whose benefit the action is brought . . . .[40]

The use of the word "but" in original Rule 17(a) to introduce the enumeration of specific instances gave rise to the interpretation that the specific instances were exceptions to the basic real-party-in-interest rule. In 1966, Rule 17(a) was amended to clarify that the specific instances set forth in the text of the rule were not exceptions to, but illustrations of, the rule.[41] The last sentence of Rule 17(a)(3) provides that an action may not be dismissed on the ground that it is not prosecuted in the name of the real party in interest until a reasonable time has been allowed after objection to cure the defect. This sentence was also added in 1966 to insure that an honest mistake in choosing the real party in interest will not result in dismissal of the action until a reasonable time has been given to correct the mistake. Note that Rule 17 (a) was restyled in 2007, but there were no material changes made in the wording of the rule that would change its operation.

Illustration 8-10. If *P Insurance Co.* pays its insured, *D*, for a loss in full, the substantive law of most states provides that *P* becomes subrogated to *D's* claim. *P* is the party that has the right to bring and control the action. If *P* mistakenly files suit in *D's* name and then seeks to correct its mistake by amendment, the court should permit *P* to do so under the last sentence of Rule 17(a).[42]

* * * * *

The real-party-in-interest rule has come under vigorous criticism in recent years.[43] It has been persuasively argued that Federal Rule 17(a) should be abolished because other procedural devices are available to resolve the issues that arise under that rule.[44] Specifically, a motion to dismiss for failure to state a claim upon which relief can be granted under Rule 12(b)(6), a motion to join a party needed for just adjudication under Rule 19(a), or a motion to dismiss for failure to join an

---

40. 308 U.S. 645, 685 (1937) (emphasis added).

41. *See* FED. R. CIV. P. 17(a) advisory committee's note to the 1966 amendment.

42. *See* Link Aviation, Inc. v. Downs, 325 F.2d 613 (D.C. Cir. 1963); *see also* Esposito v. United States, 368 F.3d 1271 (10th Cir. 2004) (when an honest mistake is made in naming someone other than the real party in interest, substitution under Rule 17 does not require a showing that the mistake was understandable); Krueger v. Cartwright, 996 F.2d 928, 931-32 (7th Cir. 1993) (insurance company that pays entire claim is real party in interest; when insurance company pays part of claim, it is only partly subrogated and both insured and company own part of the claim); IHP Indus., Inc. v. PermAlert, ESP, 178 F.R.D. 483 (S.D. Miss. 1997) (insurer is real party in interest when insured gives its right to recover damages to insurer, but retains right to share in any recovery by the insurer); Shaun P. Martin, *Substitution,* 73 TENN. L. REV. 545 (2006) (discussing substitution under Rule 25 in the real party in interest and other situations).

43. An analysis and criticism of this rule appears in the excellent article by Professor June F. Entman, *More Reasons for Abolishing Federal Rule of Civil Procedure 17(a): The Problem of the Proper Plaintiff and Insurance Subrogation*, 68 N.C. L. REV. 893 (1990); *see also* Thomas E. Atkinson, *The Real Party in Interest Rule: A Plea for Its Abolition*, 32 N.Y.U. L. REV. 926 (1957); John E. Kennedy, *Federal Rule 17(a): Will the Real Party in Interest Please Stand?* 51 MINN. L. REV. 675 (1967); Lewis M. Simes, *The Real Party in Interest*, 10 KY. L.J. 60 (1922).

44. *See generally* June F. Entman, *More Reasons for Abolishing Federal Rule of Civil Procedure 17(a): The Problem of the Proper Plaintiff and Insurance Subrogation*, 68 N.C. L. REV. 893 (1990).

indispensable party under Rule 12(b)(7)[45] can be used to deal with all situations in which proper plaintiff issues are present in an action.[46] Indeed, although proper application of Federal Rule 17(a) "produces results that are consistent with principles of diversity jurisdiction,"[47] manipulation of Rule 17(a) or confusion produced by its overlap with other rules can result in evasion of jurisdictional requirements.

Illustration 8-11. In *Virginia Electric & Power Co. v. Westinghouse Electric Corp.*,[48] an insurance company paid all but $150,000 of a $2,200,000 loss. The insured brought a diversity action on its own behalf and to recover for the amount paid by the insurer. The insurer provided counsel and had exclusive control over the action. No diversity of citizenship existed between the insurance company and the defendant. The Fourth Circuit held that both Rule 17(a) and Rule 19 were satisfied because the action was brought in the name of the insured. However, with regard to subject-matter jurisdiction, the traditional rule is that it is the citizenship of the real party in interest that counts in determining diversity. In *Virginia Electric*, the court did not consider whether the application of this principle should have required that the citizenship of the company be taken into account in determining whether jurisdiction existed.[49]

* * * * *

To avoid misapplication of Rule 17(a) to jurisdictional and other questions, the proper inquiry under the rule is whether the named plaintiff is the person upon whom the applicable substantive law confers the right to bring and control an action.[50] If so, the named plaintiff is the real party in interest. If not, the named plaintiff is not the real party in interest. This issue is not necessarily resolved in federal diversity actions by state statutes that give one person, such as an insurer, the right to sue in the name of another, such as an insured. Such provisions are usually considered "procedural" and do not really address the question of who has

---

45. Rule 19 objections are discussed in section C(3) of this chapter *infra*.

46. *See* June F. Entman, *More Reasons for Abolishing Federal Rule of Civil Procedure 17(a): The Problem of the Proper Plaintiff and Insurance Subrogation*, 68 N.C. L. REV. 893, 895-96 (1990).

47. *Id.* at 947.

48. 485 F.2d 78 (4th Cir. 1973). The *Virginia Electric* case is discussed in June F. Entman, *More Reasons for Abolishing Federal Rule of Civil Procedure 17(a): The Problem of the Proper Plaintiff and Insurance Subrogation*, 68 N.C. L. REV. 893, 947-48 (1990).

49. As Professor Entman states:

> [A] misapplication of Rule 17(a) allowed the litigation in federal court of a . . . claim between nondiverse parties on the basis of the citizenship of a merely nominal representative. This was a complete abrogation of principles of diversity jurisdiction . . . which might not have occurred if there were no Rule 17(a). Without the real party in interest rule, the court might have been forced to respond to the defendant's assertion that the insurer's interest defeated diversity by proceeding directly to the jurisdictional policies that ought to have governed.

See June F. Entman, *More Reasons for Abolishing Federal Rule of Civil Procedure 17(a): The Problem of the Proper Plaintiff and Insurance Subrogation*, 68 N.C. L. REV. 893, 948 (1990) (footnotes omitted). With *Virginia Electric* compare Louisiana v. Union Oil Co., 458 F.3d 364 (5th Cir. 2006) (State of Louisiana was real party in interest in action brought by parish school board as owner of mineral royalties on tract of land owned by state; therefore, diversity jurisdiction did not exist).

50. *See* June F. Entman, *More Reasons for Abolishing Federal Rule of Civil Procedure 17(a): The Problem of the Proper Plaintiff and Insurance Subrogation*, 68 N.C. L. REV. 893, 923-25 (1990).

the right to bring and control an action.[51] Nevertheless, state statutory provisions like these may complicate a federal court's task.[52]

The rule that an action should be brought in the name of the real party in interest should be distinguished from rules governing "standing" and "capacity to sue" (discussed below). A "real party in interest" is the person to whom the substantive law gives the right to bring and control the action.[53] "Standing" is a concept in the area of public law that serves a function similar to the real-party-in-interest requirement. When a person challenges governmental action on constitutional or other grounds, the doctrine of standing is used to determine the proper party to raise the challenge. Standing resembles real party in interest to the extent that standing requires a person challenging government action to be injured by that action. However, standing is a much broader concept than real party in interest. The standing requirement is an element of the "case or controversy" requirement of Article III of the Constitution and thus acts as a limitation on federal subject-matter jurisdiction. In addition to this constitutionally compelled component of the standing doctrine, which differs little, if at all, from the real-party-in-interest requirement, the Supreme Court has developed certain discretionary rules of standing to ensure that its exercise of the power of judicial review will be confined to proper cases. The result of these developments is that standing has become a

---

51. *See* subsection (c) *infra* (discussing the Rules Enabling Act issues raised by the interaction of provisions like these with Rule 17(a)).

52.

> [B]ecause of these provisions, it may be difficult to find state law decisions addressing the substantive rights of the insured and insurer to sue a third party. Insurers permitted to sue in the name of their insureds will do so; thus, there may be no decisions analyzing whether an insurer may enforce its claim directly against the third party. Similarly, unless some conflict between insured and insurer has been litigated, there might be no decisions discussing whether the insured may enforce the entire claim.

June F. Entman, *More Reasons for Abolishing Federal Rule of Civil Procedure 17(a): The Problem of the Proper Plaintiff and Insurance Subrogation*, 68 N.C. L. REV. 893, 923 (1990) (footnotes omitted). Because Rule 17(a) requires every action to be prosecuted in the name of the real party in interest, the rule might seem to prohibit suit by the plaintiff in a fictitious name. However, federal courts allow "John Doe" suits when necessary to protect plaintiffs from serious harm. *See* Doe v. Blue Cross & Blue Shield United, 112 F.3d 869 (7th Cir. 1997) (fictitious names are allowed when necessary to protect privacy of children, rape victims, and other potentially vulnerable parties, but not simply when a case involves a medical issue); W.N.J. v. Yocom, 257 F.3d 1171 (10th Cir. 2001) (if party wishes to litigate anonymously, party must obtain permission to do so from district court; otherwise, district court lacks jurisdiction); Roe v. Aware Woman Ctr. for Choice, Inc., 253 F.3d 678 (11th Cir. 2001) (district court reversed for not allowing plaintiff to proceed anonymously to protect her privacy rights; test is whether plaintiff has a substantial privacy right that outweighs the customary and constitutionally embedded presumption of openness in judicial proceedings; Rule 10(a) cited, but not Rule 17); *cf.* K.F.P. v. Dane Cnty., 110 F.3d 516 (7th Cir. 1997) (plaintiff permitted to name Doe defendants because she was at a disadvantage in obtaining information about identity; however, when plaintiff failed to isolate the individuals who were liable, summary judgment granted for defendants); Zocaras v. Castro, 465 F.3d 479 (11th Cir. 2006) (district court did not err in dismissing plaintiff's action with prejudice under Rule 41(b) as sanction for filing and litigating under a false name); Doe v. FBI, 218 F.R.D. 256 (D. Colo. 2003) (a plaintiff should be able to proceed anonymously only in exceptional cases involving matters of a highly sensitive and personal nature, real danger or physical harm, or when the injury litigated against would be incurred as a result of the disclosure of the plaintiff's identity); Unwitting Victim v. C.S., 273 Kan. 937, 47 P.3d 392 (2002) (plaintiff failed to demonstrate privacy interest of magnitude that would outweigh public interest in identity of plaintiff in suit by plaintiff to recover damages against his ex-fiancee for infecting him with herpes). *See generally* Joshua M. Dickman, *Anonymity and the Demands of Civil Procedure in Music Downloading Lawsuits*, 82 TULANE L. REV. 1049 (2008); Carol M. Rice, *Meet John Doe: It Is Time for Federal Civil Procedure to Recognize John Doe Parties*, 57 U. PITT. L. REV. 883 (1996).

53. *See* Lewis M. Simes, *The Real Party in Interest*, 10 KY. L.J. 60, 61 (1922).

complicated specialty of federal jurisdiction, whose examination is reserved for treatises on Administrative Law, Constitutional Law, and Federal Courts.[54]

An interesting case in which both real party in interest and standing objections were raised is *RK Co. v. See*.[55] In *See*, the court of appeals concluded that the defendant's real party in interest objection had been waived by failing to raise it at a time when it would be reasonably convenient to substitute the real party in interest for *RK Co.* (assuming that the real party in interest objection was valid). The court then considered whether the plaintiff had suffered the kind of injury necessary to satisfy the standing doctrine. It concluded that the plaintiff satisfied all constitutional standing requirements because it alleged that it lost $500,000 due to the defendant's violations of federal and state securities laws.[56] It then concluded that discretionary or "prudential" standing doctrines, such as restrictions on asserting the rights of third parties, were waiveable.[57] The court described Rule 17(a) as a codification of these prudential standing doctrines and concluded that the defendant had waived any prudential standing defenses along with its waiver of Rule 17(a) objections.[58]

(b) Subject-Matter Jurisdiction Problems in Administering Rule 17(a)

As observed in *Illustration 8-11* in the preceding subsection, Rule 17(a) sometimes obscures important subject-matter jurisdiction issues. In addition, it should be remembered that federal subject-matter jurisdiction in diversity actions can be affected by 28 U.S.C. § 1332(c)(2), discussed in Chapter 2.[59] For example, even though the representative of the estate of a decedent is the real party in interest, the citizenship of the decedent will be attributed to the representative for purposes of determining whether diversity jurisdiction exists. Also, when an assignee brings suit, 28 U.S.C. § 1359 must be taken into account in determining whether diversity of citizenship has been "improperly" or "collusively" created by the assignment.[60] In other words, even though the assignee may be the owner of the substantive right in question and, therefore, the real party in interest, a federal court may dismiss the action for lack of diversity jurisdiction if the assignment creates diversity in violation of the prohibition of § 1359.

Real party in interest questions do not always raise subject-matter jurisdiction issues, and when they do not, such questions are arguably subject to waiver. The question is, at what point should a real party in interest objection be deemed waived under the Federal Rules. In *RK Co. v. See*,[61] the defendant raised the objection during trial, seven years after the complaint was filed. The court of appeals held that the provision in Rule 17(a) allowing a reasonable time for the

---

54. *See generally* 6A CHARLES A. WRIGHT ET AL., FEDERAL PRACTICE AND PROCEDURE: CIVIL § 1542, at 471-75 (3d ed. 2010).

55. 622 F.3d 846 (7th Cir. 2010).

56. *See id.* at 851.

57. Presumably, if the court had concluded that the objection was a constitutional requirement in the case, it would also have concluded that the objection was not waiveable.

58. *See* is discussed further in the next subsection.

59. *See* Chapter 2(D)(8) supra (discussing § 1332(c)(2)).

60. *See id.* (discussing § 1359).

61. 622 F.3d 846 (7th Cir. 2010).

correct party to "step into the plaintiff's role" suggested that the objection must be raised when such joinder is practical and convenient. The court followed other courts of appeals in holding that the defense is waived if it is first raised during or shortly before trial.[62]

(c) Rules Enabling Act Problems in Administering Rule 17(a)

Rules Enabling Act issues can arise in administering Rule 17(a) if state substantive law confers the right of action on the plaintiff, but also provides that the plaintiff should bring an action in the name of someone else.[63] These problems are sometimes dealt with by the observation that, under the circumstances described, "the federal court will allow the claim to be asserted by plaintiff since [the plaintiff] has a right under state law, which makes [the plaintiff] the real party in interest for purposes of Rule 17(a)," and "the question of in whose name the action should be brought is a procedural one and should be governed by the federal rules."[64] This seems correct.

For example, suppose under state law that an insurer has become completely subrogated to the claim of an insured against the defendant, but that a state statute allows the insurer to bring the action in the name of the insured. In Chapter 7,[65] a similar problem was discussed concerning joinder of claims *against* insurers, where state law prohibited the joinder of such claims prior to obtaining a judgment against an insured and Rule 18 on its face allowed such joinder. Even in the face of such statutes, it was argued that Rule 18 could be validly applied, and the problem here is much simpler to resolve. There is only one conceivable purpose in allowing an insurer who is the real party in interest to sue in the name of an insured. That purpose is to prevent litigational prejudice that might occur to the insurer in the form of jury bias. The prejudice is avoided under the state law by making it appear that the action is brought by an individual rather than an insurance company. However, this objective is arguably a purely procedural one, because it focuses on the fairness and accuracy of the litigational process. Therefore, for two reasons, Rule 17 can be enforced without fear that any substantive rights of the insurer will be abridged. First, the state law in question neither embodies any "substantive" rights nor is supported by any substantive policies, and thus applying Rule 17(a) instead of the state law will not impinge on anything substantive contained in the state statute itself. However, in Chapter 7, it was also observed that substantive rights could be impacted in the Rule 18 joinder situation if the insurer

---

62. *See id.* at 850.

63. *See* 6A CHARLES A. WRIGHT ET AL., FEDERAL PRACTICE AND PROCEDURE: CIVIL § 1544, at 489 (3d ed. 2010).

64. *See id.*; *see also* Story v. Pioneer Hous. Sys., Inc., 191 F.R.D. 653 (M.D. Ala. 2000) (Rule 17 rather than state real-party-in-interest rule applies, but state law relevant to determine who owns the cause of action; no discussion whether state rule embodied substantive policies); Boosey & Hawkes Music Publishers, Ltd. v. Walt Disney Co., 53 U.S.P.Q.2d 2021 (S.D.N.Y. 2000) (plaintiff could not sue because the plaintiff was not the real party in interest, even though under the rules of the civil law jurisdictions where the damages in the case are asserted to have occurred, a "volunteer" could bring suit to vindicate the kind of claim the plaintiff is asserting; real party in interest is a procedural doctrine; no inquiry into the validity of Rule 17(a)).

65. *See* Chapter 7(C)(3) *supra* (discussing Rules Enabling Act problems with joinder of claims under Rule 18).

lost a case on the merits that it would otherwise win by virtue of a federal court's disregard of state procedural law. Nevertheless, to the extent that the federal courts apply their own measures for protecting against biased jury determinations rather than the measures provided for in state law, the ultimate substantive rights of the insured on the merits of the case will arguably be fully protected. Thus, it cannot be said that the application of Rule 17(a) will affect those ultimate substantive rights more than "incidentally," if at all.[66] Note also that under the plurality's opinion in the *Shady Grove* decision, examined in Chapter 5,[67] above, (should that opinion some day be adopted by a majority of the Court), Rule 17 would seem clearly to be a rule that is "rationally classifiable as procedural" and valid under the plurality's interpretation of the Rules Enabling Act.[68]

In *Stichting Ter Behartiging Van De Belangen Van Oudaandeelhouders in Het Kapitaal Van Saybolt Int'l B.V. v. Schreiber,*[69] the Second Circuit Court of Appeals considered a complicated question concerning the permissibility of assigning a tort claim for legal malpractice. In determining whether it could avoid making a choice-of-law decision between New York and New Jersey law, it had to consider whether the procedure provided for in Rule 17(a) for avoiding dismissal by "ratification" of the action by the real party in interest could be employed by the plaintiff. It decided that (1) if New Jersey law applied, it prohibited the assignment, and the named party would not be the real party in interest and (2) that to employ ratification by the real party in interest to avoid dismissal would expand substantive rights in violation of the Rules Enabling Act. Thus, the court had to determine the conflict-of-laws question, which it certified to the New York Court of Appeals.

2. Capacity to Sue and Be Sued

(a) In General

"Capacity" rules determine the ability of persons to sue and be sued. For example, a person may possess the right to be enforced in the action and may be injured sufficiently and otherwise qualified to possess standing to sue, but may lack the "capacity to sue" because of age, mental deficiency, or other impediments. The capacity requirement extends to both plaintiffs and defendants, unlike the real-party-in-interest rule, which restricts only plaintiffs.

Federal Rule 17(b) provides the basic standards for determining capacity to sue or be sued in federal court. The rule is unusual because it provides a federal-level, choice-of-law standard for determining capacity in several situations. Rule 17(b)(1) provides that the capacity of an individual not acting in a representative capacity is determined by the law of the individual's domicile. Rule 17(b)(2) provides that the capacity of a corporation is determined by the law under which it

---

66. *See* Chapter 5(F)(4) *supra* (discussing the *Burlington Northern* test for rule validity under the Enabling Act, which includes a determination of whether a Federal Rule impacts more than "incidentally" on state substantive rights).

67. *See* Chapter 5(E)(3), *supra.*

68. *See id.*

69. 407 F.3d 34 (2d Cir. 2005).

was organized. Rule 17(b)(3) states that for all other parties, capacity to sue or be sued shall be determined by the law of the state in which the district court is sitting. However, under Rule 17(b)(3)(A), a partnership or unincorporated association that has no capacity to sue or be sued under the law of the state where the district court is sitting may sue or be sued in its common name when a federal substantive right is being enforced by or against it. Rule 17(b)(3)(B) provides that federal law governs the capacity of a federal receiver.

Illustration 8-12. *R Corp.* is a bank incorporated in and has its principal place of business in State *X*, under which it has the capacity to sue. *R* is appointed the representative of *A's* estate. (*A* had been a citizen of State *X*.) *R* sues *D*, a citizen of State *Y*, in a U.S. District Court in State *Y* to recover $500,000 in damages for the wrongful death of *A*. Under the law of State *Y*, *R* does not have the capacity to sue. Rule 17(b)(2) states that the capacity of a corporation to sue shall be determined by the law under which it is organized. However, Rule 17(b)(3), which generally applies to suits by representatives, provides that the capacity of a representative to sue is determined by the law of the state in which the district court is held. Thus, Rule 17 appears to contain conflicting provisions about *R's* capacity to sue in this situation. Because there appears to be no reason to treat corporate representatives differently from individual representatives under Rule 17, this conflict should be resolved by applying the provisions governing representatives.[70] Thus, *R* should lack the capacity to sue *D* in State *Y* based on the law of State *Y*, where the district court is sitting.

* * * * *

Rule 17(c) outlines special rules governing the capacity of infants and incompetent persons to sue or be sued. If an infant or incompetent person has a representative, the representative may sue or defend on behalf of the infant or incompetent person. If the infant or incompetent person has no appointed representative, Rule 17(c)(2) provides that the action may be brought by the infant or incompetent's next friend or by a guardian ad litem—a guardian appointed by the court for purposes of the suit. Rule 17(c)(2) also expressly requires the court to appoint a guardian ad litem or take any other action the court deems proper to protect an infant or incompetent person who is unrepresented in an action.

Illustration 8-13. *A* is an infant who is a citizen of State *X*. *A* was injured in an automobile accident with *D*, a citizen of State *Y*. *R*, a citizen of State *X*, is appointed to represent *A* in an action for personal injuries against *D*. *R* has capacity to sue under the law of State *X*, but not under the law of State *Y*. Rule 17(b)(3) provides that the capacity of a representative shall be determined by the law of the state in which the district court is held. Rule 17(c) appears to state that the representative of an infant shall be able to sue for the infant in federal court. If *R* sues *D* on *A's* behalf in a U.S. District Court in State *Y*, there would be an apparent conflict between Rules 17(b)(3) and (c). This conflict should be resolved by applying the capacity provisions of Rule 17(b)(3). There is no apparent reason to

---

70. *See* 6A CHARLES A. WRIGHT ET AL., FEDERAL PRACTICE AND PROCEDURE: CIVIL § 1561, at 615-16 (3d ed. 2010).

allow the appointment of a representative who does not have capacity to sue under the relevant law designated by Rule 17(b)(3).[71]

(b) Subject-Matter Jurisdiction Problems in Administering Rule 17(b)

As noted in section C(1)*(a)*, above, the citizenship of the real party in interest is what counts in determining whether diversity jurisdiction exists.[72] When infants or incompetents do not have the capacity to sue, a representative must sue for them. In such circumstances, the substantive law gives the representative the right to bring the action, and the representative is the real party in interest. Prior to the enactment of § 1332(c)(2), this meant it was the citizenship of the representative that mattered in determining diversity, at least in the absence of any issue about whether the representative was "improperly" or "collusively" appointed to create diversity in contravention of 28 U.S.C. § 1359.[73] However, as observed above,[74] after the enactment of § 1332(c)(2), the citizenship of the infant or incompetent is attributed to the representative for purposes of determining diversity, which also eliminates any issues under § 1359. Nevertheless, one question remaining after the enactment of § 1332(c)(2) is whether the representative of an incompetent has the power to change the citizenship of the incompetent in a way that creates diversity of citizenship that would not otherwise exist.

In *Rishell v. Jane Phillips Episcopal Memorial Medical Center,*[75] the Tenth Circuit held that, under appropriate circumstances, the representative of a mentally incompetent person could, indeed, change the incompetent's domicile in a way that would create diversity jurisdiction. In *Rishell*, Ms. Lacey was hospitalized in the defendant institution when she attempted to commit suicide. As a consequence of the attempted suicide, she existed thereafter in a permanent vegetative state and was unable to make even basic life decisions for herself. Her domicile at the time she became incompetent was Oklahoma. She was then moved to Louisiana. In a court proceeding there, her brother-in-law was appointed as her guardian. Subsequently, the guardian commenced an action against the defendant in an Oklahoma federal court to recover damages from the defendant for negligence in allowing Ms. Lacey to receive the injuries leading to her incompetence. The defendant moved to dismiss on the ground of lack of jurisdiction. The defendant argued that Ms. Lacey was still domiciled in Oklahoma and, therefore, diversity of citizenship did not exist between the parties. The guardian contended that Ms. Lacey's domicile had been changed to Louisiana because she was under the jurisdiction of a Louisiana court and because the guardian and Ms. Lacey's husband, who was a kind of "co-guardian" (called an undercurator under Louisiana law), both intended Louisiana to be her permanent home.

---

71. *See* 6A CHARLES A. WRIGHT ET AL., FEDERAL PRACTICE AND PROCEDURE: CIVIL § 1571, at 680-82 (3d ed. 2010).

72. *See also, e.g.*, Certain Interested Underwriters at Lloyd's, London, Eng. v. Layne, 26 F.3d 39 (6th Cir. 1994).

73. *See* Chapter 2(D)(8) *supra* (discussing §§ 1332(c)(2) & 1359).

74. *See* section C(1)*(b)* ("Subject-Matter Jurisdiction Problems in Administering Rule 17(a)"), *supra*.

75. 12 F.3d 171 (10th Cir. 1993).

The district court dismissed the action for lack of jurisdiction, and the plaintiff appealed.[76] The Tenth Circuit reversed, holding that, under appropriate circumstances, the domicile of an incompetent could be changed by the incompetent's guardian:

> If the best evidence available shows the incompetent likely will never be restored to reason, the law must allow another, vested with legal authority, to determine domicile for the best interests of that person. To prohibit such determinations is to leave the incompetent in a never-ending limbo where the presumption against changing domicile becomes more important than the interests of the person the presumption was designed to protect.
>
> This case presents a situation ripe for consideration of that principle. Plaintiff alleges Ms. Lacey's present condition is permanent, which defendant apparently concedes. It is the expressed intent of both her husband and brother-in-law that Ms. Lacey's current hospitalization be permanent and that Ms. Lacey remain in Louisiana so she may obtain benefits from that state. Nothing in the record suggests that Ms. Lacey will ever return to Oklahoma, nor has defendant produced any evidence implying Ms. Lacey was moved to Louisiana simply to create diversity of citizenship.[77]

However, the Tenth Circuit remanded for a full evidentiary hearing in which it directed the district court to examine whether Ms. Lacey's domicile was changed in her best interests.[78]

In *Long v. Sasser,*[79] the Fourth Circuit rejected the holding in *Rishell.* The Fourth Circuit concluded that if the incompetent does not possess the capacity to effectuate a change of domicile, domicile remains the same for purposes of diversity jurisdiction regardless of where the guardian may move the incompetent:

> Jurisdictional rules should above all be clear. They are meant to guide parties to their proper forums with a minimum of fuss. While close cases may arise . . . regarding whether the ward possessed the necessary capacity to effect a change of domicile, *Rishell* requires a more speculative inquiry as to whether the ward will remain incompetent in the future, as well as inviting litigation over the "best interests" of the ward. . . .

---

76. After the dismissal, the plaintiff applied for an order from the Louisiana court that Ms. Lacey was domiciled there and received the order. The plaintiff then moved for reconsideration on the basis of the order, but the district court refused to take it into account. *See* 12 F.3d at 172.

77. *Id.* at 174; *see also* Acridge v. Evangelical Lutheran Good Samaritan Soc., 334 F.3d 444 (5th Cir. 2003) (following *Rishell*); Ryan S. Vincent, Comment, *As America Ages: Changing the Domicile of the Incompetent Challenges Diversity Jurisdiction*, 43 WASHBURN L.J. 513 (2004).

78. *See Rishell,* 12 F.3d. at 174. The court also directed the district court to determine whether Ms. Lacey's domicile was changed by operation of the Louisiana Code when the guardian was appointed for her by the Louisiana court. This ruling seems clearly wrong. As the court recognized earlier in its opinion, the question of domicile for purposes of diversity is controlled by federal principles, *see id.* at 172-73, and it is inconsistent to allow the issue to be controlled absolutely by operation of state law. Such an approach would give the persons in control of the incompetent a weapon with which to create diversity illegitimately simply by obtaining a state-court order.

79. 91 F.3d 645 (4th Cir. 1996).

> Inquiring whether the "best interests" of the ward are served by a guardian's attempt to effect a change in domicile to secure a federal forum strikes us as singularly unproductive. We note, for example, that this case does not raise the primary concern addressed by diversity jurisdiction—fear of local bias against litigants from out of state. This is essentially a local dispute . . . .[80]

Of the two cases, *Long* is the more persuasive. Even if it is necessary for a guardian to change the residence of an incompetent person for purposes of care and medical treatment, there is no reason to allow the change of residence, even if permanent, to affect the determination of domicile for purposes of diversity jurisdiction. No apparent policy of the jurisdictional grant will be served by doing so in cases like *Rishell* and *Long*. Furthermore, as observed in the latter case, the *Rishell* inquiry will simply complicate the jurisdictional question unnecessarily.[81]

The *Rishell-Long* problem is not limited to incompetents. Section 1332(c)(2) also attributes the citizenship of an infant to the "legal representative" of the infant. However, the problem of determining the domicile of an infant will usually be easier to solve than that of an incompetent. Ordinarily, a child's domicile is the domicile of the parent with whom the child lives.[82] As a result, the child's domicile can be changed by the custodial parent, but this change can only be done by the parent changing his or her own domicile. The inquiry therefore will focus on the intent of the parent to make a new state a permanent home, and this inquiry is no more complicated than the one involved in any ordinary diversity action involving an issue of the domicile of a competent, adult individual. More complicated problems of determining the domicile of a child will only occur when the child does not live with the person who is the child's guardian.[83] These kinds of cases can present problems similar to those in *Rishell* and *Long* and should probably be handled in the same manner—*i.e.*, the guardian should not be allowed to change

---

80. *Id.* at 647-48.

81. *See also* Acridge v. Evangelical Lutheran Good Samaritan Soc'y, 334 F.3d 444 (5th Cir. 2003) (court agreed with *Rishell* that guardian can change domicile of incompetent if change is made in best interests of incompetent; court finds that change was made in best interests of incompetent; result is that diversity was destroyed and case was remanded with instructions to dismiss action); Dakuras v. Edwards, 312 F.3d 256 (7th Cir. 2002) (guardian may change the domicile of an incompetent; however, change will be ineffective for diversity purposes if the sole or dominant reason for the change is to create federal jurisdiction; change in case was ineffective because guardian deceived incompetent into moving and thus acted improperly, even though move was not made to create diversity); McEachron v. Glans, 983 F. Supp. 330 (N.D.N.Y. 1997) (the court agreed with *Rishell* that a guardian could change the domicile of an incompetent in the best interests of the incompetent. However, on the facts of the case, the incompetent had been transferred to an institution in another state and was undergoing short-term therapy to determine the best long-term treatment that he should receive; when the long-term therapy issue was resolved, the incompetent might be transferred to an institution in another state. Therefore, the court concluded that the requisite permanent intent to establish a new domicile was not present). *But cf.* Angela K. Upchurch, *Can Granny Have a New Home? Resolving the Dilemma of Dementia and Domicile in Federal Diversity Jurisdiction Cases,* 79 U. COLO. L. REV. 545 (2008) (arguing that the "intent" portion of the domicile test should be deemed satisfied if an incompetent adult "himself or through his guardian establishes a residence in a new state and establishes indicia of permanency there").

82. *See* RESTATEMENT (SECOND) OF CONFLICT OF LAWS § 22 (1971). The issue should be resolved in the same way when the child's parents are dead or the child is otherwise in the custody of someone else standing *in loco parentis*, such as a grandparent. *See id.* cmt. i.

83. *Cf. id.* cmt. h (discussing the problems of changing a child's domicile when the child does not live with the guardian); Smith v. Cummings, 445 F.3d 1254 (10th Cir. 2006) (because acquisition of domicile must be voluntary, prisoner's domicile is presumed to be the state in which he was domiciled before incarceration, even if he is incarcerated in another state; however, presumption is rebuttable; case reversed and remanded for prisoner to be given attempt to demonstrate domicile).

the domicile of the child for purposes of the diversity jurisdiction by moving the child's residence.

(c) Rules Enabling Act Problems in Administering Rule 17(b)

Rules Enabling Act problems potentially exist with Rule 17(b) because it is an independent federal conflict-of-laws rule that may differ from the conflict-of-laws rule governing capacity in the courts of the forum state. The most general problem is whether it is legitimate for the Supreme Court to create a conflict-of-laws rule under the Enabling Act to govern any kind of issue. There may have been a time when conflicts issues were regarded as "procedural" in nature, but surely that view is outmoded today. Modern conflict-of-laws systems focus on the policies and purposes of the laws of the concerned states and the contacts of those states with the parties and the events giving rise to suit.[84] To the extent that a state's conflict-of-laws approach involves policy determinations of significance to a state that transcend actions in the courts of the state, it is questionable whether it is wise for the Supreme Court to override those considerations with Federal Rules of Civil Procedure, even if the particular issue in question can be characterized as "procedural" in some sense.

Indeed, even if the position of the plurality in the *Shady Grove* case, discussed in Chapter 5, is adopted, it might be possible to argue that a Federal Rule of Civil Procedure overriding state conflicts doctrine is not "rationally classifiable as procedural" and is thus invalid under even the plurality's liberal interpretation of the Act.[85] The argument would be, simply, that conflict-of-laws rules are in their nature inherently substantive and cannot be supplanted by rules under the Act. The problematic part of this argument is that, if the plurality's interpretation of the Act amounts to a conclusion that Congress has delegated all the power that it possesses to regulate procedure to the Supreme Court under the Act, the rule is valid because Congress would surely have the power to create such a rule for the federal courts under Article III and the Necessary and Proper Clause of the Constitution, even if the rule conflicts in some cases with state substantively based conflicts rules.[86]

Focusing particularly on the issue of capacity to sue, the issue under the prevailing majority interpretation of the Rules Enabling Act in the *Burlington Northern* case is whether the application of Rule 17(b) can ever impact on state substantive rights more than incidentally and whether the rule is reasonably necessary to the uniform scheme of procedure it was the intent of Congress to establish under the Act.[87] As discussed earlier, a Federal Rule may impact on state

---

84. *See, e.g.*, RESTATEMENT (SECOND) OF CONFLICT OF LAWS § 6 (1971); ROBERT L. FELIX & RALPH U. WHITTEN, AMERICAN CONFLICTS LAW ch. 4 (6th ed. 2011) (describing traditional and modern conflicts theories); RUSSELL J. WEINTRAUB, COMMENTARY ON THE CONFLICT OF LAWS § 1.5 (6th ed. 2010) (describing a number of modern conflicts theories).

85. *See* Chapter 5(F)(6) *supra* (discussing this aspect of the *Shady Grove* case).

86. *See id.* (discussing this aspect of the *Shady Grove* case).

87. This inquiry is the one demanded by the *Burlington Northern* case examined in Chapter 5(F)(4), *supra*.

"substantive" rights in two ways.[88] First, the rule may conflict with a state law that is configured as a procedural rule, but which is supported by discernable "substantive" policies—*i.e.,* policies that do not concern the efficiency or accuracy of the litigation process, but are aimed at achieving purposes outside that process or affecting the primary (non-litigation) behavior of parties. Second, even if a Federal Rule of Civil Procedure does not conflict with a state rule supported by specific substantive policies, the Federal Rule may impact substantive rights in a broader sense by affecting the outcome of the case. (Although the Supreme Court made it clear in the *Hanna* case that Rules Enabling Act issues are not to be resolved under the general *Erie* outcome determinative test evolved under the Rules of Decision Act, the Court also indicated that the extent to which a Federal Rule of Civil Procedure affects the outcome of the case may be relevant to its validity under the Enabling Act.[89]) Because the Court has not indicated which of these kinds of impacts on substantive rights is relevant under the Rules Enabling Act, it is necessary to examine Rule 17(b) under both kinds of impacts.

When Rule 17(b) conflicts with a capacity rule of the forum state, it will often be difficult to determine whether the state rule is supported by substantive or only procedural policies. For example, Rule 17(b) provides that the capacity of an individual not acting in a representative capacity is determined by the law of the individual's domicile. Thus, if the individual possesses capacity under the law of that individual's domicile, but lacks capacity under the law of the forum state, a potential conflict exists. As a general matter, rules of capacity are aimed at protecting the parties and the court system in the conduct of litigation. When the capacity of a plaintiff is at issue, a state has an interest in assuring that the plaintiff has the ability to participate in and conduct litigation in a prudent and efficient fashion so as not to lose rights the plaintiff validly possesses through poor judgment or to burden the court system with unwarranted litigation. Rules governing plaintiffs' capacity may also be designed to protect the defendant by assuring that the plaintiff can make prudent decisions about whether to litigate at all as well as decisions about the conduct of the litigation, such as whether to accept reasonable settlement offers, etc. Rules governing defendants' capacity may serve similar purposes, but will surely also be designed to assure that the defendant has sufficient maturity and mental capacity to protect the defendant's rights in the litigation. These policies seem to be a mixture of efficiency concerns and more serious party-protection goals that might legitimately be characterized as "substantive" in nature.

Thus, if a plaintiff is entitled to sue under the law of the plaintiff's domicile, but would, because of age, be considered an infant not entitled to sue under forum law, there could be an impact on a state substantive "right" in the first sense discussed above if the state rule is identified as being supported by plaintiff-protection or defendant-protection policies, as opposed to only litigational efficiency policies. Nevertheless, it is arguable that Rule 17(b) can be validly

---

88. *See* Chapter 5(F)(5) *supra* (discussing the *Business Guides* case); Chapter 6(D)(5)*(d) supra* (discussing Rules Enabling Act problems with Federal Rule 15(c); Chapter 7(C)(3) *supra* (discussing Rules Enabling Act problems with joinder under Federal Rule 18); section (C)(1)*(c) supra* (discussing Rules Enabling Act problems under Rule 17(a)).

89. *See* Chapter 5(F)(3) *supra* (discussing the *Hanna* case).

applied because a federal diversity court can take other procedural steps to protect parties other than disqualifying the plaintiff from suing (or requiring the plaintiff to sue by representation, as would probably be permitted under state law). For this reason, Rule 17(b) might be said to only "incidentally" affect state substantive rights, if it affects them at all.

A more serious question about the validity of Rule 17(b) may be whether the rule is reasonably necessary to the uniform scheme of procedure it was the intent of Congress to establish under the Rules Enabling Act. An inquiry into the reasonable necessity of the rule to the uniform scheme of rules is theoretically necessary any time a conflict is identified between Rule 17(b) and a forum's "substantively based" capacity rule of the sort discussed above, even if the impact of Rule 17 on the state rule is only "incidental." Unlike rules such as Rule 15(c), discussed in Chapter 6,[90] it is difficult to see how a rule like Rule 17(b) contributes to the uniformity of practice in federal court or to the effectiveness of the general scheme of Federal Rules. There would appear to be no loss to uniformity of federal practice if capacity issues were governed by the conflict-of-laws rules of the forum instead of by the independent choice-of-law rules contained in Rule 17(b). In either case, there will be disuniformity in determining the capacity of certain litigants to sue or be sued, because the domiciles of individual litigants will inevitably contain as many different capacity rules as will the states in which federal diversity courts are sitting. Furthermore, Rule 17(b) does not seem to contribute in any way to the effective operation of any other Federal Rule of Civil Procedure, or to the efficient or effective operation of the general scheme of Federal Rules. Therefore, if the Supreme Court is serious about this part of the Rules Enabling Act inquiry (always a question about the tests that the Court articulates), Rule 17(b) may be invalid. (Note also that these same considerations might well bear on whether the rule is rationally classifiable as procedural under the plurality's interpretation of the Rules Enabling Act in the *Shady Grove* decision in Chapter 5(F)(6), above.)

Assuming that conflict between Rule 17(b) and "substantively based" state capacity rules is no problem, there remains the question whether Rule 17(b) might impact on substantive rights in the broader, "outcome determinative," sense described earlier in this subsection. Such an impact seems unlikely. Even if forum state law would deprive an individual of capacity to sue or be sued contrary to the law of the individual's domicile, it is improbable that forum law would altogether preclude the assertion of a claim by or against the individual. Rather, it is far more likely that the forum state's law will allow suit if a representative or guardian is appointed to prosecute or defend against a claim for the individual. Under both Rule 17(b) and state law, therefore, suit will be permitted. The difference between the two sets of rules will simply be in the procedure required to maintain the suit. Thus, it seems likely that any effect on the ultimate outcome on the merits of the case by virtue of the application of Rule 17(b) rather than state law is unlikely.

Similar problems of Rule validity may exist in determining the capacity of corporations to be sued under Rule 17(b). However, there has been much unnecessary confusion about the corporate capacity issue because of a question

---

90. *See* Chapter 6(D)(5)*(d) supra* (discussing Rules Enabling Act problems with Rule 15(c)).

about how to classify state "door-closing" statutes. The Supreme Court held in *Woods v. Interstate Realty Co.*[91] that a state statute closing the doors of the forum state's courts to corporate plaintiffs which had not qualified to do business in the state was applicable in federal diversity actions under the Rules of Decision Act.[92] There has been some tendency to view the *Woods* problem as involving an issue of capacity to sue that should have been governed by Rule 17(b).[93] There is support for this view in the history of Rule 17(b).[94] The drafters of Rule 17(b) relied upon an old pre-Rules case, *David Lupton & Sons Co. v. Automobile Club of America*,[95] in which the Supreme Court held that a state statute precluding a nonregistering foreign corporation from suing in New York could not be applied in a federal diversity action because the states could not prescribe the qualifications of suitors in the courts of the United States.

However, *David Lupton* was a pre-*Erie* case that did not mention "capacity to sue," but was based on the notion that "despite its transaction of business without authority, the foreign corporation could sue upon its contracts in any court of competent jurisdiction other than a court of the state of New York," including a federal court.[96] As Chapter 5 demonstrated, this view became obsolete with *Erie*, which established that federal diversity courts are not independent of the state court systems on matters of state substantive law. Although the general *Erie* test under the Rules of Decision Act does not determine the validity of Federal Rules of Civil Procedure, *Erie* nevertheless changed the legal context in which federal diversity actions are conducted in ways that cannot be ignored in construing Federal Rules of Civil Procedure. As *Woods* indicated, after *Erie* state door-closing statutes cannot simply be viewed as "procedural" measures immune from application by federal diversity courts, even if other state courts would not apply the provisions as a matter of their conflict-of-laws doctrine.[97] Rather, door-closing statutes are, while procedurally configured, designed to effectuate the enacting state's substantive regulation of the activities of foreign corporations. Thus, after *Erie*, which the drafters of the Federal Rules had probably not fully absorbed when they created Rule 17(b),[98] the *David Lupton* view—that state door-closing statutes are simply

---

91. 337 U.S. 535, 69 S. Ct. 1235, 93 L. Ed. 1524 (1949).

92. *See* Chapter 5(E)(1) *supra* (discussing *Woods* and other decisions).

93. *See* 6A CHARLES A. WRIGHT ET AL., FEDERAL PRACTICE AND PROCEDURE: CIVIL § 1569 (3d ed. 2010); John H. Ely, *The Irrepressible Myth of* Erie, 87 HARV. L. REV. 693, 727-28 (1974).

94. *See, e.g.*, PROCEEDINGS OF THE INSTITUTE ON FEDERAL RULES, CLEVELAND OHIO, JULY 21, 22, 23, 1938 at 258 (William W. Dawson, ed., 1938) (statement of Charles Clark on Rule 17(b)).

95. 225 U.S. 489, 32 S. Ct. 711, 56 L. Ed. 1177 (1912).

96. *Id.* at 499, 32 S. Ct. at 714, 56 L. Ed. at 1181.

97. The *Klaxon* branch of *Erie* also significantly changed the viewpoint that was employed in *David Lupton*. In the latter case, the Court, in discussing a New Jersey case that had held the New York door closing statute inapplicable in a New Jersey proceeding to enforce a New York contract, stated:

> The court conceded the general rule both in New Jersey and New York to be that a contract void by the law of the state where made would not be enforced in the state of the forum. But it was held that the New York statute did not in terms declare the contract void; it provided that no such action should be maintained in that state.

See David Lupton, 225 U.S. at 499, 32 S. Ct at 714, 56 L. Ed. at 1181. However, after *Klaxon* established that federal courts are obligated to apply the conflict-of-laws rules of the state in which they are sitting, the fact that the courts of *another state* could disregard a statute of the forum under their conflicts rule became irrelevant. *Klaxon* is discussed in Chapter 5(D)(2)*(a)*, *supra*.

98. Recall from Chapter 5 that *Erie* was decided and the Federal Rules came into existence in 1938. However, the Rules Enabling Act was enacted in 1934, and the Advisory Committee on the Federal Rules had been working on the rules long prior to the time *Erie* was decided.

regulations of practice in the forum state's courts and are not obligatory in federal diversity cases—cannot be justified. Therefore, if the *David Lupton* holding is applied to Rule 17(b), the rule is arguably invalid because it has a significant impact on state substantive policy.

However, there was considerable confusion and inaccuracy in the way in which the drafters of the Federal Rules viewed the interaction of the concept of capacity and the incorporation of the *David Lupton* holding into Rule 17(b). The drafters seemed to view capacity as the general ability to sue and be sued,[99] and this view seems unquestionably correct. However, they viewed *David Lupton* as a case "holding that a state was not entitled to interfere with substantive rights of action against a corporation, once it had allowed the corporation to come within the borders of the state to do business,"[100] and also viewed it as a capacity decision.[101] Thus, they viewed *David Lupton* as being incorporated within Rule 17(b) as a statement of existing practice.[102] However, if capacity is merely the general ability to sue and be sued, it is hard to see how the state door-closing statutes in *David Lupton* and *Woods* had anything to do with the concept. There is no question that the corporations in both cases had the general ability to sue and be sued. The state door-closing statutes involved in the cases were not in any way designed to affect that general capacity. Rather, they were designed to effectuate the state's substantive regulatory power over foreign corporations that omitted to register in the state. Therefore, it was erroneous for the advisory committee to view *David Lupton* as involving a capacity problem in the first place, and certainly improper for

---

99. *See* PROCEEDINGS OF THE INSTITUTE ON FEDERAL RULES, CLEVELAND OHIO, JULY 21, 22, 23, 1938 at 258 (William W. Dawson, ed., 1938):

> The next sentence is: "The capacity of a corporation to sue or be sued shall be determined by the law under which it was organized." Some objectors asserted that that would give the state of incorporation the right of limiting the suability of a corporation in all other states. We felt clearly that that was a misuse of the term "capacity," that capacity dealt merely with suability, and that once a corporation was endowed with the general character of the corporate entity, such as we know it, that then it could not be provided that it was not subject to the liabilities of a corporation.

100. *Id.*

101. *See id.*

102. *See also Hearings Before the Committee on the Judiciary, House of Representatives, Seventy-Fifth Congress, 3d Sess., With Regard to The "Rules of Civil Procedure for the District Courts of the United States," Adopted by the Supreme Court of the United States Pursuant to the Act of June 19, 1934 (48 Stat. 1064) and on H.R. 8892, A Bill to Change and Modify the Rules of Procedure for the District Courts of the United States, Pursuant to the Act of June 19, 1934, Chapter 651, by Amending Sections 412 and 724 of Title 28 of the Code of Laws of the United States of American and by Adding Thereto Sections 430B, 430C, and 430D, Pertaining to Pleadings and Practice in the District Courts of the United States, Who May Sue and Be Sued, the Selection of Jurors, the Appointment of Court Stenographers, and For Other Purposes* at 10 (1938) (statement of Charles Clark):

> Mr. Clark. I wanted to call the attention of the committee to the case in the Supreme Court of *David Lupton's Sons Co.*, which is a case in which the Court held that when a corporation goes into another State to do business it cannot be prevented by the law of that State from suing. The State may prevent its doing business within the State except on the compliance with certain conditions; but if the State permits the corporation to do business it then cannot take away the right of suit, as a penalty when the corporation has done something that the State feels should not be permitted. That case is a decision of the Supreme Court, cited in the notes of the advisory committee as being stated in this section of the rules. It seems to me that this is a statement of the rule as it is worked out in that case.
>
> . . . .
>
> It seems to me, therefore, in the light of that leading case by the Supreme Court, that the rule just states the existing practice.

Among other curious things, it is hard to understand how a state can prevent a corporation from doing business in the state without complying with the conditions that the state puts on it unless the state can impose a penalty on the corporation, such as depriving it of the right to sue, if it does not comply with those conditions.

it to attempt to incorporate the holding of the case in Rule 17(b) by indirection—*i.e.*, through committee notes to the rule.[103]

The best way to avoid the dilemma created by the advisory committee's confusion is to disregard its reliance on *David Lupton* and treat "capacity" in Rule 17(b) as involving only the general authority to sue and be sued, and not any particular disqualification imposed by state law that depends on primary corporate behavior. *Woods* is authority for this interpretation because it treated the state-door closing statute involved in the case as presenting a Rules of Decision Act question rather than a Rules Enabling Act issue. Other federal courts have also interpreted Rule 17(b) in this fashion.[104] Furthermore, the interpretation will avoid all problems of rule invalidity that would otherwise occur due to conflict between Rule 17(b) and state statutes limiting the right of foreign corporations to sue in order to enforce substantive regulatory statutes of the state. Of course, the question whether Rule 17(b), as a general conflicts rule, is reasonably necessary to the uniform scheme of federal procedure exists as strongly here as it does in the case of individual capacity. However, the possibility of a clash between state rules governing general corporate capacity and Rule 17(b) will be limited, if not altogether eliminated, if courts follow the interpretation recommended above. In absence of a conflict between Rule 17(b) and state law, the federal courts will not be confronted with any issue of Rules Enabling Act validity.[105]

3. Joinder of Persons Needed for Just Adjudication

(a) History of Rule 19

The principles governing compulsory joinder of parties in the federal courts are found in Federal Rule 19. Existing Rule 19 is a model of outstanding drafting. Perhaps better than any other rule, it reflects the policies of practicality and convenience that should govern actions in a modern procedural system. However, Rule 19 has not always existed in its present form. It is a product of an evolutionary process having its roots in the principles of joinder developed in equity practice.

Much of the history of compulsory joinder in the federal courts is rooted in the case of *Shields v. Barrow*,[106] decided by the U.S. Supreme Court in 1854. In 1836, Barrow sold plantations located in Louisiana to Shields. Barrow and Shields were both citizens of Louisiana. The sale price of the plantations was to be paid in

---

103. *See* advisory committee note to original Rule 17(b) (citing *David Lupton* as an example of corporate capacity); *see also* Bernadette Bollas Genetin, *The Powers That Be: A Reexamination of the Federal Courts' Rulemaking and Adjudicatory Powers in the Context of a Clash of a Congressional Statute and a Supreme Court Rule,* 57 BAYLOR L. REV. 587 (2005) (discussing the conflict between the CERCLA statute and Rule 17).

104. *See, e.g.*, Joseph Muller Corp. Zurich v. Societe Anonyme De Gerance Et D'Armement, 314 F. Supp. 439 (S.D.N.Y. 1970) (restrictions on location of suit imposed by the nation under whose law the corporation is organized do not involve capacity; capacity is only general capacity to sue or be sued), *aff'd in part and rev'd in part on other grounds*, 451 F.2d 727 (2d Cir. 1971).

105. This assumes, of course, that the argument made above on the basis of the plurality opinion in the *Shady Grove* case discussed in section F(6) of Chapter 5 does not become the majority position of the Court.

106. 58 U.S. (17 How.) 130, 15 L. Ed. 158 (1855). For the manner in which equitable practice evolved—in an unfortunate way—and was incorporated into American Practice, see Geoffrey C. Hazard, Jr., *Indispensable Party: The Historical Origin of Procedural Phantom*, 61 COLUM. L. REV. 1254, 1256-71 (1961).

installments evidenced by notes. Each note was indorsed by six persons, two of whom were citizens of Mississippi and four of whom were citizens of Louisiana. After payment of $107,000 in installments, Shields defaulted on the remainder of the purchase price. A compromise was subsequently entered into whereby Shields and the six indorsers agreed to return the plantations to Barrow; the indorsers executed new notes in varying amounts to Barrow totalling $32,000, and Barrow retained the $107,000 already paid. In return, Barrow released Shields and the indorsers from their prior liabilities and discontinued the state-court litigation commenced against them.

Barrow subsequently sought to rescind this compromise agreement in a federal diversity action commenced in the U.S. Circuit Court for the Eastern District of Louisiana against the two Mississippi indorsers. The Supreme Court ultimately held that Shields and the four Louisiana indorsers were "indispensable parties," who had to be joined in the action. Because their joinder would destroy diversity of citizenship, the suit had to be dismissed. The Court explained that there were three classes of parties to a bill in equity: (1) formal parties; (2) persons interested in the controversy who ought to be made parties so that the court can determine the entire controversy by "adjusting all the rights in it"; and (3) persons who have an interest in the controversy of such a nature that a final decree cannot be made without affecting their interest or leaving the controversy in such a condition that its final determination would be "wholly inconsistent with equity and good conscience." *Shields* was an example of a controversy in which the parties were of the third class. If only some of the persons interested in the controversy were before the court, a decree of rescission would either destroy the rights of those who were absent or leave the contract in full force with respect to the absentees and set aside as to the parties before the court. The latter result could only be permitted in cases in which the rights of the parties before the court were completely "separable" from the rights of the absentees. *Shields* was not such a case. Thus, the absent parties were classified as indispensable.[107]

The Equity Rules of 1912 generally preserved the distinctions made by the *Shields* case.[108] When original Rule 19 was promulgated in 1938, the distinctions

---

107. *See* 58 U.S. (17 How.) at 139-40, 15 L. Ed. at 160. Nevertheless, the result in *Shields* was highly questionable even as of the time it was decided. The court was correct to be concerned about the absence of the Louisiana indorsers and Shields in the action. *See Illustration 8-14 infra*. However, the Court, even in the legal context of the time, should not have classified the absentees as indispensable parties. The Equity Rules of 1842 provided:

> In all cases where it shall appear to the court, that persons who might otherwise be deemed necessary or proper parties to the suit, cannot be made parties by reason of their being out of the jurisdiction of the court, or incapable of otherwise being made parties, or because their joinder would oust the jurisdiction of the court as to the parties before the court, the court may in their discretion proceed in the cause without making such persons parties; and in such cases the decree shall be without prejudice to the rights of the absent parties.

42 U.S. (1 How.) at lv (1842). The Court declared this rule to be declaratory of an act of Congress, Act of Feb. 28, 1839, ch. 36, § 1, 5 Stat. 321, 321-22, which clearly applied only to problems of personal jurisdiction. However, this view is, equally clearly, contrary to the plain language of Equity Rule 47. The language of Rule 47 stating "or because their joinder would oust the jurisdiction of the court as to the parties before the court" is clearly a reference to subject-matter jurisdiction. Joinder of absent parties never ousts the court of personal jurisdiction over parties who are present; it only ousts the court of diversity jurisdiction. Thus, Equity Rule 47 arguably provided a basis upon which the court could have resolved the case short of dismissal.

108. *See* Rules 25, 36 & 39, 226 U.S. at 655, 658-59 (1912).

were carried forward again.[109] Under the old equity rules and *Shields v. Barrow*, the courts attempted to determine whether rights were "joint," "common," or "separable," and whether parties were "united in interest," as a means of determining whether an absentee was "indispensable" to the action. Original Rule 19 could be read as preserving the notion that persons holding "joint" rights are indispensable parties. The result was sometimes a rather difficult and narrow application of the concepts of "joint" and "separable" interests to determine questions of compulsory joinder. Criticism of this approach centered on the fact that the courts under original Rule 19 tended to decide joinder questions thoughtlessly on the basis of labels rather than by pragmatically analyzing who, if anyone, would be harmed by nonjoinder of a party and whether the harm could be prevented by some means short of dismissal.[110]

The 1966 amendments to Rule 19 were designed to eliminate these problems. The amendments were structured to focus the decisionmaking process on the practical factors that should determine whether an action should be permitted to continue in the absence of a party. Not all courts had ignored these factors, either under original Rule 19 or the prior equity practice. The 1966 amendments to Rule 19 were designed to preserve the approach of these courts while eliminating the results sometimes produced by use of such terms as "joint interest" in the original rule.[111] Although Rule 19 was restyled in 2007, the rewording of the rule should not produce any change in its operation. However, one significant attempt by the restylers to affect the terminology of mandatory joinder practice should be noted. Old Rule 19(b) stated that if a person described in Rule 19(a) could not be made a party, the court should determine whether "in equity and good conscience" the action should proceed with the existing parties or should be dismissed, "the absent person being thus regarded as indispensable." The restyled rule does not use the term "indispensable," thus attempting to remove what has sometimes been considered a confusing term from the lexicon of federal practice. The restylers will be lucky, indeed, if this works.

---

109. Original Rule 19 provided as follows:

(a) Necessary Joinder. Subject to the provisions of Rule 23 and of subdivision (b) of this rule, persons having a joint interest shall be made parties and be joined on the same side as plaintiffs or defendants. When a person who should join as a plaintiff refuses to do so, he may be made a defendant or, in proper cases, an involuntary plaintiff.

(b) Effect of Failure to Join. When persons who are not indispensable, but who ought to be made parties if complete relief is to be accorded between those already parties, have not been made parties and are subject to the jurisdiction of the court as to both service of process and venue and can be made parties without depriving the court of jurisdiction of the parties before it, the court shall order them summoned to appear in the action. The court in its discretion may proceed in the action without making such persons parties, if its jurisdiction over them as to either service of process or venue can be acquired only by their consent or voluntary appearance or if, though they are subject to its jurisdiction, their joinder would deprive the court of jurisdiction of the parties before it, but the judgment rendered therein does not affect the rights or liabilities of absent persons.

(c) Same: Names of Omitted Persons and Reasons for Non-joinder to be Pleaded. In any pleading in which relief is asked, the pleader shall set forth the names, if known to him, of persons who ought to be parties if complete relief is to be accorded between those already parties, but who are not joined, and shall state why they are omitted.

308 U.S. at 687 (1938).

110. *See, e.g.*, John W. Reed, *Compulsory Joinder of Parties in Civil Actions*, 55 MICH. L. REV. 327, 483 (1957).

111. *See* FED. R. CIV. P. 19 advisory committee's note to the 1966 amendment.

(b) Application of Rule 19

Rule 19(a) lists three categories of persons who must be joined in an action if possible: (1) persons whose absence would prevent relief from being accorded among those already parties;[112] (2) persons who claim an interest in the subject of the action and are so situated that disposition of the action in their absence may, as a practical matter, impair or impede their ability to protect their interests;[113] and (3) persons who claim an interest in the subject of the action and are so situated that disposition of the action, in their absence, will leave any of the persons already parties subject to a substantial risk of incurring double, multiple, or otherwise inconsistent obligations by reason of the interest claimed by the absent parties.[114] If any such persons exist, Rule 19(a) directs that they should be joined, if possible.[115]

Joinder of the absentees may not be possible in some cases because of limitations on the court's power to obtain personal jurisdiction over them, or because of rules limiting the subject-matter jurisdiction of the court or the venue of the action. When joinder is impossible for one of these reasons, Rule 19(b) directs the court to determine whether the action may continue without the absent person. Rule 19(b) lists a number of factors that the court must consider in determining whether the action may go forward: (1) the extent to which a judgment rendered in the absence of a person might be prejudicial to the absent person or to those already parties; (2) the extent to which any prejudice due to the person's absence can be lessened by (A) protective provisions in the judgment, (B) shaping the relief, or (C) other measures; (3) whether a judgment rendered in the person's absence will be adequate; and (4) whether the plaintiff will have an adequate remedy if the action were dismissed for nonjoinder. These factors are not exhaustive. The court may also take into account other factors. Only after it is clear that (1) an absentee fits within one of the categories in Rule 19(a), (2) joinder of the absentee is impossible, *and* (3) no means are available under Rule 19(b) to protect against the harm caused by the party's absence should the court dismiss the action.

Illustration 8-14. Reconsider the facts of *Shields v. Barrow*, discussed in the previous subsection. How would the absent indorsers have been classified under Rule 19? Would the action be allowed to continue without them today? The absent indorsers do not appear to be Rule 19(a)(1)(A) parties. Complete relief could be granted between the original parties in their absence. Barrow sought rescission plus recovery on the original notes, which all the indorsers had signed. Thus, each indorser was liable for the entire amount of each note. The Mississippi indorsers who were joined in the action could have paid the entire amount of the notes and had the plantations returned. Similarly, the absent indorsers were probably not Rule

---

112. FED. R. CIV. P. 19(a)(1)(A).

113. FED. R. CIV. P. 19(a)(1)(B)(i).

114. FED. R. CIV. P. 19(a)(1)(B)(ii).

115. A Rule 19 objection is raised by a Rule 12(b)(7) defense in a preanswer motion or the defendant's answer. A Rule 12(b)(7) defense is, however, preserved from waiver through trial. *See* FED. R. CIV. P. 12(h)(2). *But cf.* Fireman's Fund Ins. Co. v. National Bank of Coops., 103 F.3d 888 (9th Cir. 1996) (Rule 12(b)(7) motion's timeliness within discretion of district courts and court may take into account whether defendant is interposing objection to protect absent party or protect defendant's own interests).

19(a)(1)(B)(i) parties. There would probably be no way that the federal action could practically affect the absent indorsers' interests. Barrow could not sue the absentees on the notes if the Mississippi indorsers paid them because Barrow would be forced to surrender the notes in return for payment. The federal judgment would not bind the absentees. Thus, if the absent indorsers were sued by the Mississippi indorsers for contribution, they would have available all defenses they would possess in an action against Barrow. Consequently, it is doubtful that the possibility of a suit by the Mississippi indorsers constitutes the kind of practical effect envisioned by Rule 19(a)(1)(B)(i). However, the absent indorsers are clearly Rule 19(a)(1)(B)(ii) parties. The joined Mississippi indorsers might incur inconsistent obligations unless the absentees are joined in the action. If the Mississippi indorsers lose the federal action, they would have to sue for contribution from the absent indorsers and Shields. In that action, they would have to establish the facts necessary to justify rescission and payment of the original notes again, with the danger that the facts found in favor of Barrow might be found against them. These are the kind of "inconsistent obligations" that Rule 19 seeks to prevent. Nevertheless, the absent indorsers probably would not be classified as "indispensable parties" today. The federal court in which the action is pending could withhold judgment until Barrow sued the absent Louisiana indorsers and Shields in state court for the same relief he sought in federal court. If Barrow loses against the state-court defendants, the federal court could refuse judgment in his favor in the action under the doctrine of res judicata.[116] If Barrow wins against the state-court defendants, the Mississippi defendants in the federal action could be made to pay their pro rata share. Thus, Rule 19(b) could be utilized to avoid dismissal of the action today.[117]

* * * * *

The proper analysis of joinder questions under Rule 19 is illustrated by the U.S. Supreme Court's decision in *Provident Tradesmens Bank & Trust Co. v. Patterson*.[118] The dispute in *Provident Tradesmens* arose out of an automobile accident. Dutcher owned an automobile, which he lent to Cionci. While driving the automobile with Lynch and Harris as passengers, Cionci collided with a truck driven by Smith. Cionci, Lynch, and Smith were killed, and Harris was injured. Several state and federal actions arose out of this incident. Lynch's estate sued Cionci's estate in a federal diversity action. This action was settled for $50,000, but the $50,000 was not paid because Cionci's estate had no assets. Smith's estate and Harris each sued Cionci's estate, Dutcher, and Lynch's estate in state court, but those actions never went to trial. Dutcher, the owner of the automobile, had a $100,000 insurance policy with Lumbermen's Mutual Casualty Company that covered Dutcher's liability as Cionci's principal and the liability of anyone driving

---

116. *See* Chapter 13(D) ("Parties Bound by Judgments") *infra*.

117. In contrast to joint contract obligors, the United States Supreme Court has held that joint tortfeasors are not Rule 19(a) parties, much less indispensable parties. *See* Temple v. Synthes Corp., 498 U.S. 5, 111 S. Ct. 315, 112 L. Ed. 2d 263 (1990). However, the Court did not parse the categories in Rule 19(a) to determine whether any of them fit the situation of joint tortfeasors. It relied instead on the historical fact that defendants have not been allowed to compel the joinder of joint tortfeasors and the fact that the advisory committee's note to the 1966 amendment to Rule 19(a) states that the revisions to the rule in that year were not designed to change this traditional rule. *See* W. PAGE KEETON ET AL., PROSSER AND KEETON ON TORTS § 47, at 327 (5th ed. 1984); 7 CHARLES A. WRIGHT ET AL., FEDERAL PRACTICE AND PROCEDURE: CIVIL § 1623, at 361 (3d ed. 2001).

118. 390 U.S. 102, 88 S. Ct. 733, 19 L. Ed. 2d 936 (1968).

the car with Dutcher's permission. However, Lumbermen's Mutual refused to defend the federal diversity action for Cionci's estate on the ground that Cionci was driving without permission.[119] Lynch's estate brought another federal diversity action against Cionci's estate and Lumbermen's Mutual for a declaratory judgment that Cionci had been driving with Dutcher's permission. Smith's estate and Harris were joined as plaintiffs in this action. Dutcher was not joined, however, because he was a citizen of Pennsylvania, as were all the plaintiffs.

The district court granted directed verdicts in favor of the two estate plaintiffs, on the ground that under the applicable state law the automobile was presumed to have been driven with permission. This presumption could not be rebutted as to the two estate plaintiffs because of the state "Dead Man Rule." This rule prevented Dutcher from testifying against the estates if he had an adverse interest to them. The district court found such an adverse interest because Dutcher might have to use the $100,000 insurance fund to pay judgments against him. Thus, he had an interest in seeing that the fund was not exhausted by the payment of claims against Cionci. Dutcher was allowed to testify against Harris, however, and the jury still returned a verdict that the automobile had been driven with Dutcher's permission. The court of appeals reversed the judgment of the district court on the ground that Rule 19 required Dutcher's joinder in the action. The court of appeals raised this Rule 19 objection on its own motion. The court based its decision on its view that Dutcher's right to be joined was a substantive right that could not be affected by the Federal Rules. In the court of appeal's view, the right to be joined existed because of the same adverse interests on the part of Dutcher that caused the state "Dead Man Rule" to be applicable. The Supreme Court granted certiorari and reversed.

The Court assumed that Dutcher was a person who should be joined if feasible under Rule 19(a). Because Dutcher could not be joined without destroying diversity jurisdiction, Rule 19(b) required that the court determine whether the action should be dismissed or proceed without him. However, the Rule 19 issue had been raised for the first time on appeal. Therefore, the court of appeals should have considered the effect of the parties' failure to raise the objection at the trial level, as well as the fact that a judgment binding on all the other parties, but not Dutcher, had already been entered after extensive litigation.[120]

The Court identified four interests that had to be considered under Rule 19(b) in determining whether the action could go on without Dutcher: (1) the plaintiff's interest in having a forum; (2) the defendant's interest in avoiding multiple litigation, inconsistent relief, or sole liability that the defendant actually shares with another; (3) the interest of the nonjoined party; and (4) the interests of the courts and the public in the complete, consistent, and efficient settlement of controversies.[121]

---

119. The insurance company's position was based on the fact that while Dutcher had loaned his automobile to Cionci, Cionci had deviated from the errand for which Dutcher had allowed the automobile to be taken. *See id.* at 105, 88 S. Ct. at 735, 19 L. Ed. 2d at 942.

120. *See id.* at 109, 88 S. Ct. at 737, 19 L. Ed. 2d at 942.

121. *See id.* at 109-11, 88 S. Ct. at 737-39, 19 L. Ed. 2d at 944-46.

As to the strength of the plaintiffs' interest in a forum, the Court observed that, before trial, the plaintiff's interest depends upon whether a "satisfactory" alternative forum exists. However, if the plaintiff wins, the judgment is appealed, and the joinder question is raised for the first time on appeal, the plaintiff has a strong additional interest in preserving the judgment.[122] While the Court was unable to determine whether the plaintiffs could have brought the same action against the same defendants plus Dutcher in a state court, this possibility was less adequate from the plaintiff's point of view after winning a successful judgment.[123] "[The plaintiffs'] interest in preserving a fully litigated judgment should be overborne only by rather greater opposing considerations than would be required at an earlier stage when the plaintiffs' only concern was for a federal rather than a state forum."[124] The countervailing interests were not sufficient to outweigh the plaintiffs' interest on the facts of the case.

As to the defendants' interests, they were foreclosed by the failure of the defendants to raise them at the trial level.[125] The Court found Dutcher's interest "more difficult to reckon."[126] Importantly, Dutcher's interest was not eliminated by the fact that any judgment rendered in Dutcher's absence would not be res judicata. Rather, Rule 19(a) requires the court to consider the practical effects that the judgment may have on the nonparty. The Supreme Court held that an appellate court should raise the joinder issue on its own motion if necessary to protect the interests of the nonparty.[127] Nevertheless, on the facts of the case, the Court considered that the adverse interest possessed by Dutcher against the plaintiffs was not enough to outweigh the interests of the plaintiffs in preserving the judgment.

> Dutcher had an "adverse" interest (sufficient to invoke the Dead Man Rule) because he would have been *benefited* by a ruling *in favor of* the insurance company; the question before the Court of Appeals . . . was whether Dutcher was *harmed* by the judgment *against* the insurance company.
>
> The two questions are not the same. If the three plaintiffs had lost to the insurance company on the permission issue, that loss would have ended the matter favorably to Dutcher. If, as has happened, the three plaintiffs obtain a judgment against the insurance company on the permission issue, Dutcher may still claim that as a nonparty he is not estopped by that judgment from relitigating the issue. At that point it might be argued that Dutcher should be bound by the previous decision because, although

---

122. *See id.* at 109-10, 88 S. Ct. at 738-39, 19 L. Ed. 2d at 945-46.

123. It has been held that the availability or unavailability of an alternative forum in the Rule 19 inquiry is primarily of negative significance. That is, the absence of an alternative forum is weighed heavily in favor of a classification of nonindispensability (and nondismissal), while the existence of an alternative forum does not have as significant an impact in favor of a classification of indispensability (and therefore in favor of dismissal). *See* Rishell v. Jane Phillips Episcopal Mem'l Med. Ctr., 94 F.3d 1407, 1413 (10th Cir. 1996).

124. *Provident Tradesmen*, 390 U.S. at 112, 88 S. Ct. at 739, 19 L. Ed. 2d at 946.

125. *See id.* at 109-10, 112, 88 S. Ct. at 737-39, 19 L. Ed. 2d at 945-46. The Court added that the insurance company would have the ability to litigate each claim against the fund in any event, and its only concern with the absence of Dutcher was to obtain a windfall escape from its defeat at trial. *See id.* at 112, 88 S. Ct. at 739, 19 L. Ed. 2d at 946.

126. *See id.* at 113, 88 S. Ct. at 739, 19 L. Ed. 2d at 947.

127. *See id.* at 110-11, 88 S. Ct. at 738-39, 19 L. Ed. 2d at 945-46.

> technically a nonparty, he had purposely bypassed an adequate opportunity to intervene . . . . If, however, Dutcher is properly foreclosed by his failure to intervene in the present litigation, then the joinder issue considered in the Court of Appeals vanishes, for any rights of Dutcher's have been lost by his own inaction.
>
> If Dutcher is not foreclosed by his failure to intervene below, then he is not "bound" by the judgment in favor of the insurance company . . . . There remains, however, the practical question whether Dutcher is likely to have any need and if so will have any opportunity, to relitigate. The only possible threat to him is that if the fund is used to pay judgments against Cionci the money may in fact have disappeared before Dutcher has an opportunity to assert his interest. Upon examination, we find this supposed threat neither large nor unavoidable.[128]

As for the interest of the courts and the public in efficient resolution of controversies, the Court stated that it might have been preferable at the trial level to dismiss the action and force the plaintiffs to sue elsewhere.[129] Nevertheless, there was no reason to disregard the judgment at the court of appeals level just because it did not theoretically settle the entire controversy.[130] Finally, the Court rejected the reasoning of the court of appeals that Dutcher's right to be joined was a "substantive right" that the Federal Rules could not permissibly affect. The court of appeals had reasoned that the substantive law defined the category of persons called indispensable parties and that substantive law could not be modified by rule. It followed that the right of a person falling within the category to participate in litigation was also substantive and absolute. To this reasoning, the Court responded:

> Rule 19 does not prevent the assertion of compelling substantive interests; it merely commands the courts to examine each controversy to make certain that the interests really exist. To say that a court "must" dismiss in the absence of an indispensable party and that it "cannot proceed" without him puts the matter the wrong way around: a court does not know whether a particular person is "indispensable" until it has examined the situation to determine whether it can proceed without him.[131]

Under the *Provident Tradesmens* opinion, few cases should be dismissed on the ground that a party is "indispensable" and, therefore, that the court cannot proceed without that party. The opinion invites—as does the text of Rule 19(b)both

---

128. *Id.* at 114-15, 88 S. Ct. at 740, 19 L. Ed. 2d at 947-48 (emphasis added). The Court further explained that the threat to Dutcher was not great because (1) the state court actions against him had lain dormant for years at the pleading stage; (2) Dutcher could defend the state actions in part on the grounds that no permission had been granted to Cionci and that payments made from the insurance fund on Cionci's behalf should be credited against Dutcher's liability; (3) the court of appeals could have phrased the decree so as to avoid any difficulty to Dutcher by ordering payment withheld from the plaintiffs until the state court suits against him were settled; and (4) the plaintiffs had indicated a willingness to accept a limitation on all claims to the amount of the insurance policy. *See id.* at 115-16, 88 S. Ct. at 741, 19 L. Ed. 2d at 948.

129. The Court considered even this possibility to be "highly problematical, however, for the actual threat of relitigation by Dutcher depended on there being judgments against him and on the amount of the fund, which was not revealed to the District Court." *Id.* at 116, 88 S. Ct. at 741, 19 L. Ed. 2d at 948.

130. *See id.*

131. *Id.* at 119, 88 S. Ct. at 743, 19 L. Ed. 2d at 950.

counsel and the federal courts to exercise the utmost ingenuity to protect the interests described in Rule 19(a) from harm without resorting to the severe action of dismissal. Under this flexible approach, the need to apply the indispensable party label should be rare.[132]

Illustration 8-15. *E*, the executor of a will and a citizen of State *X*, sues the *D* charity, a corporation incorporated and having its sole place of business in State *Y*, in a U.S. District Court in State *Y*. *E* seeks to have the residuary clause of a will declared invalid. Under the residuary clause, *D* would inherit a substantial sum of money. *A*, a citizen of State *X*, stands to lose $100,000 if the residuary clause is declared invalid. *A* is not joined in the action because *A's* joinder would destroy diversity jurisdiction. *A* is a Rule 19(a)(1)(B)(i) party. If the residuary clause under which *A* would inherit is declared void, *A* will have practical difficulty obtaining the inheritance. However, *A* should not be classified as an indispensable party. Under Rule 19(b), the court can create a protective provision in the judgment requiring the executor to retain the amount *A* would inherit to pay any judgment that might go against the executor in a state-court action by *A*.[133]

Illustration 8-16. *P* sues *D* to cancel a mineral lease. *D* counterclaims for a declaration confirming *D's* rights under the lease. If the lease is cancelled, *B* and *C* will lose the royalty interests they possess under the lease. The district court finds the lease invalid and cancels it. On appeal, *D* objects for the first time that *B* and *C* were Rule 19 parties who should have been joined in the action. *B* and *C* are clearly Rule 19(a)(1)(B)(i) parties who should have been joined in the action because the proceeding could adversely affect *B* and *C's* interests. This potential harm justifies allowing the Rule 19 objection to be raised for the first time on appeal, despite Federal Rule 12(h)(2), which appears to preserve the objection only through trial. The parties to an action cannot always be relied on to raise an objection that is aimed at protecting nonparties. Indeed, under *Provident Tradesmens*, it would be justifiable for the court of appeals to raise the Rule 19 objection on its own motion if *D* does not raise it.

Illustration 8-17. Assume on the facts of *Illustration 8-16* that the district court declares the lease valid. Under these circumstances, *Provident Tradesmens* would require the court of appeals to affirm. Although the judgment could have adversely affected the absentees' interest, the judgment that was *actually* rendered did not. Thus, the interest of the plaintiff in preserving a valid judgment that does not adversely affect the interests of the Federal Rule 19 parties must prevail.[134]

Illustration 8-18. *P*, a legatee under a will, sues *D* to set aside gifts made by the decedent to *D*. Other legatees do not join in the suit because their joinder will destroy diversity. *D* objects under Federal Rule 12(b)(7) that the absent legatees are

---

132. *See, e.g.*, Glancy v. Taubman Ctrs., Inc., 373 F.3d 656 (6th Cir. 2004) (Rule 19(a)(2)(i), restyled as Rule 19(a)(1)(B)(i), party could not be joined without destroying diversity; action remanded so that district court could determine under Rule 19(b) whether interests of absentee could be adequately represented by existing parties and, if not, to dismiss the action because action could not proceed in equity and good conscience without absentee because judgment would be prejudicial to its interests).

133. Note that the possibility of multiple actions here does not make *A* a Rule 19(a)(2)(ii) party. The possibility of a second action here is the possibility of a state-court action against the executor-plaintiff in the federal action. The executor ought to be willing to elect this option over dismissal.

134. In Calcote v. Texas Pac. Coal & Oil Co., 157 F.2d 216 (5th Cir. 1946), upon which this illustration is based, the court of appeals reversed. This result would not be justifiable after *Provident Tradesmens*.

Federal Rule 19 parties. The district court overrules this objection. Ultimately, the district court enters a judgment ordering *D* to pay the sum claimed by *P* to the estate. *D* appeals, raising only the Rule 19 objection on appeal. Despite the fact that the actual judgment entered by the district court did not adversely affect the absentees, the court of appeals should arguably reverse and order the action dismissed. This result is justified in order to force the district courts to obey the requirements of Rule 19.[135]

* * * * *

Not all situations in which an absentee cannot be joined are susceptible to an analysis under Rule 19(b) that will prevent dismissal, as the Supreme Court's recent decision in *Republic of the Phillippines v. Pimentel*[136] indicates. An absent claimant in an interpleader[137] proceeding is a Rule 19(a)(1)(B)(i) party, because the interpleader proceeding may award the money or property to another claimant, thus practically impairing or impeding the claimant's ability to recover the money or property. The absent claimant is also a Rule 19(a)(1)(B)(ii) party, because a separate action by the absent claimant against the stakeholder in interpleader might result in double liability to the stakeholder. In *Merrill Lynch, Pierce, Fenner & Smith, Inc. v. ENC Corp.*,[138] the court of appeals had held that while the Republic of the Philippines was a Rule 19(a) party in an interpleader action designed to resolve conflicting claims to assets transferred to the stakeholder by the former, late President of the Philippines, Ferdinand E. Marcos, the Republic was not an "indispensable" party under Rule 19(b). The Court relied on various factors, including delay on the part of the Republic in obtaining a judgment for the assets in a forum of its choice, the applicability of the statute of limitations to bar the Republic's claim in the most likely forum where it might bring suit, the presence of victims as claimants who had obtained judgments, and the fact that the assets were located in the United States and could only be disposed of by the order of a court located there. These factors eliminated prejudice against the Republic and the stakeholder (who had indicated no dissatisfaction with the judgment rendered by the district court in the absence of the Republic) and made a judgment rendered in the absence of the Republic adequate.[139]

In *Pimental*, the Supreme Court granted certiorari and reversed. The Court agreed that the absentees were Rule 19(a) parties because their interests might be impaired in their absence. However, the Court held that the court of appeals did not give enough weight to the prejudice that the absentees might incur. In addition, the Court saw no effective way to alleviate the prejudice under Rule 19(b). The Court additionally held that the Rule 19(b)(3) factor—the extent to which a judgment rendered without the absent party would be adequate—was not satisfied because the absentees would not be bound by any judgment and, therefore, that the judgment would not satisfy the public interest in settling disputes by wholes. The Court felt that the stakeholder would have an adequate remedy in any separate action by

---

135. *See* Young v. Powell, 179 F.2d 147 (5th Cir. 1950).
136. 553 U.S. 851, 128 S. Ct. 2180, 171 L. Ed. 2d 131 (2008).
137. Interpleader is examined in section D(2) *infra*.
138. 446 F.3d 1019 (9th Cir. 2006).
139. *Id.* at 1023-27.

moving to dismiss on Rule 19 grounds in the absence of all the parties who might sue it for the stake, thus satisfying the fourth Rule 19(b) factor (here favoring dismissal). Thus, the Court ordered the action dismissed.[140]

(c) Problems of Subject-Matter Jurisdiction, Personal Jurisdiction, and Venue Under Rule 19

As noted in the preceding subsection, Rule 19 only permits joinder of absent parties when subject-matter jurisdiction or venue would not be destroyed by the joinder and when personal jurisdiction can be obtained over the absent party. Ordinarily, the court must judge whether subject-matter jurisdiction, venue, and personal jurisdiction would have been proper if the absentee had been originally joined in the action. However, even when joinder of a Rule 19 party would apparently destroy subject-matter jurisdiction, the doctrines of realignment or supplemental jurisdiction may enable the court to avoid dismissal of the action.

Rule 19(a) applies to absent parties who should join as plaintiffs in an action, as well as those who should be joined as defendants. Following the traditional equity practice described in section A(2), above, Rule 19(a)(2) provides that if a person should join as a plaintiff but refuses to do so, that person may be named as a defendant in the action and served with process just like an ordinary defendant. When this action is taken, special problems of federal subject-matter jurisdiction may arise.

Illustration 8-19. *P*, a citizen of State *X*, wishes to sue *D*, a citizen of State *Y*, in a diversity action in federal court. Assume that *C*, who is a citizen of State *X*, is a Rule 19(a) party who should join with *P* in the suit, but *C* refuses to do so. If *P* joins *D* and *C* as defendants, there will be citizens of State *X* (*P* and *C*) on both sides of the lawsuit. Under the complete diversity of citizenship requirement, the federal court would have no subject-matter jurisdiction over the action—unless the parties are "realigned," as discussed below.

* * * * *

The doctrine of "realignment of parties" ordinarily deals with the problem of federal subject-matter jurisdiction created by overlapping citizenship of the parties discussed in *Illustration 8-19*. The doctrine of realignment is simply that in determining whether diversity of citizenship exists in an action, the court is not bound by the alignment of the parties in the pleadings, but must look beyond the pleadings and arrange the parties according to their true interests in the action.[141] In theory, this rule applies to all diversity actions, even though no question of improper alignment exists in most cases. Because the rule applies to joinder of defendants under Rule 19(a), an assessment of the parties' ultimate interests in the outcome of the action will often result in realignment of a person joined as a defendant under

---

140. 553 U.S. at 862-72, 128 S. Ct. at 2188-94, 171 L. Ed. 2d at 143-50.

141. *See* CHARLES A. WRIGHT & MARY KAY KANE, HANDBOOK OF THE LAW OF FEDERAL COURTS § 30 (7th ed. 2011).

Rule 19(a)(1)(B). Thus, on the facts given in *Illustration 8-19*, *C* may be realigned with *P* for purposes of determining whether diversity jurisdiction exists.[142]

Rule 19(a)(2) states that a person who should join as a plaintiff but refuses to do so "may be made either a defendant, or, in a proper case, an involuntary plaintiff." The "involuntary plaintiff" provision is designed to ameliorate the situation that occurs when a person who should join as a plaintiff is beyond the reach of service of process. In such circumstances, joining the absentee as a defendant is impossible because the court cannot acquire personal jurisdiction over the absent person. However, for the involuntary plaintiff portion of Rule 19(a) to be available, the plaintiff must notify the absentee of the action and the absentee must refuse to join. Furthermore, Rule 19(a)(2) states that an absentee may be made an involuntary plaintiff only in a "proper case."[143] A "proper case" exists only when the absentee has a duty to allow the plaintiff to use the absentee's name in the action. Consequently, use of the involuntary plaintiff provision has, as a practical matter, been limited to cases in which the exclusive licensees of patents, exclusive licensees of copyrights, or equitable owners of copyrights seek to join the owner of the patent or copyright as a plaintiff.[144]

In 1990, the doctrines of "pendent" and "ancillary" jurisdiction were codified in 28 U.S.C. § 1367 under the label "supplemental jurisdiction."[145] In 28 U.S.C. § 1367(b), Congress sought to preserve the jurisdictional requirements of 28 U.S.C. § 1332 from impairment. Section 1367(b) limits the ability of parties joined under certain multiple party joinder rules to assert claims, or to have claims asserted against them, that would violate the policies of § 1332. Among other things, § 1367(b) provides that the district courts will not have jurisdiction over claims asserted by plaintiffs against persons made parties under Rule 19 when the claims would violate the restrictions of § 1332.[146] This provision assures that a plaintiff may not fail to join a defendant who should be a party under Rule 19 and later assert a claim against that defendant after joinder of the defendant has been compelled under the rule. However, § 1367(b) also provides that claims may not be asserted *by* "persons proposed to be joined as plaintiffs under Rule 19"when the policies of

---

142. Maryland Cas. Co. v. W.R. Grace & Co., 23 F.3d 617 (2d Cir. 1994), in which the court applied a "collision of interests" test to refuse realignment that would have defeated diversity. The "collision of interests" test requires an actual, substantial controversy, or a collision of interests, though the conflict may concern an issue other than the primary issue in dispute. *See id.* at 622-24. In contrast, a test that would require alignment in accord with the parties' positions on the primary issue in dispute would ignore controversies on secondary issues in determining the realignment question. *See also* Hidey v. Waste Sys. Int'l, Inc., 59 F. Supp. 2d 543 (D. Md. 1999) (after realigning claimants in interpleader to oppose each other in accord with their positions on the "primary issue" in the action—the ownership of interpleaded funds, the court then considers whether the remaining claimant should be considered the defendant for purposes of the removal statute; court holds remaining claimant is defendant within removal statutes because if it had sued as plaintiff it could have sued in federal court and if it had been sued in state court by the other claimant, it could have removed). The operation of the doctrine of realignment has been criticized. *See* Jacob S. Sherkow, Note, *A Call for the End of the Doctrine of Realignment*, 107 MICH. L. REV. 525 (2008) (arguing that the "fractionated and free-form" doctrine is "wholly unworkable").

143. *See* FED. R. CIV. P. 19(a); *see also* Jean F. Rydstrom, Annotation, *What Constitutes "Proper Case" Within Meaning of Provision of Rule 19(a) of Federal Rules of Civil Procedure That When Person Who Should Join as Plaintiff Refuses to Do So, He May Be Made Involuntary Plaintiff "In a Proper Case,"* 20 A.L.R. FED. 193 (1974).

144. *See* Independent Wireless Tel. Co. v. Radio Corp. of Am., 269 U.S. 459, 46 S. Ct. 166, 70 L. Ed. 357 (1926); FED. R. CIV. P. 19 advisory committee's note to the original rule; 7 CHARLES A. WRIGHT ET AL., FEDERAL PRACTICE PROCEDURE: CIVIL § 1606, at 78-83 (3d ed. 2001).

145. *See* Chapter 2(E)(4) ("The Codification of Pendent and Ancillary Jurisdiction") *supra*.

146. *See* 28 U.S.C. § 1367(b).

28 U.S.C. § 1332 would be violated by the claim.[147] Under the traditional practice described above, persons are technically only "joined as plaintiffs" under the involuntary plaintiff provision of Rule 19. Thus, § 1367(b) might be read only to limit assertion of claims by involuntary plaintiffs, but not by persons joined as defendants under Rule 19 and realigned as plaintiffs for jurisdictional purposes. This interpretation would be unfortunate. As noted in Chapter 2, § 1367(b) was probably just clumsily worded and should be interpreted to apply to persons joined as defendants under Rule 19 and realigned as plaintiffs, as well as to persons joined as involuntary plaintiffs under the rule.[148]

The language in § 1367(b) prohibiting plaintiffs from asserting claims *against* "persons made parties under Rule . . . 19" also produces some interpretive problems. Read literally, the language does not prohibit joinder of a party as a defendant under Rule 19, even when the party, if joined originally in the action, would have destroyed subject-matter jurisdiction. It simply prohibits the plaintiff from asserting a claim against the party once the party has been joined. Persons who contributed to the drafting of the statute have suggested that this language in § 1367(b) purposely authorizes the joinder of Rule 19 defendants to take care of a particular kind of case. The case allegedly occurs when a plaintiff has no claim against a non-joined party, but the absentee is a Rule 19 party because the absentee's interests could be adversely affected by the suit.[149] Others disagree that there can be a case under § 1367 in which a Rule 19 defendant exists against whom the plaintiff asserts no claim.[150]

Two technical realities support the latter position. First, even if there are defendants who should be joined under Rule 19 because their interests would be adversely affected, but against whom the plaintiff possesses no "claim," these defendants will be bound by the judgment in the action once they have been joined.[151] Thus, they are, in all significant respects, in the position of persons against whom a "claim" for declaratory relief exists.[152] Second, but more importantly, 28 U.S.C. § 1367(b) is a provision that excludes certain cases from the jurisdiction conferred by § 1367(a). Section 1367(a), however, only confers

---

147. *See id.*

148. *See* Chapter 2(E)(6) ("Exceptions to the Scope of Supplemental Jurisdiction in Diversity Cases: Section 1367(b)") *supra*; *see also* Denis F. McLaughlin, *The Federal Supplemental Jurisdiction Statute—A Constitutional and Statutory Analysis*, 24 ARIZ. ST. L.J. 849, 958 (1992).

149. *See* Thomas D. Rowe, Jr. et al., *Compounding or Creating Confusion About Supplemental Jurisdiction? A Reply to Professor Freer*, 40 EMORY L.J. 943, 957-58 (1991); Thomas D. Rowe, Jr. *et al.*, *A Coda on Supplemental Jurisdiction*, 40 EMORY L.J. 993, 1000-01 (1991); *see also* Denis F. McLaughlin, *The Federal Supplemental Jurisdiction Statute—A Constitutional and Statutory Analysis*, 24 ARIZ. ST. L.J. 849, 954-57 (1992).

150. *See* Thomas C. Arthur & Richard D. Freer, *Grasping at Burnt Straws: The Disaster of the Supplemental Jurisdiction Statute*, 40 EMORY L.J. 963, 966-72 (1991); Thomas C. Arthur & Richard D. Freer, *Close Enough for Government Work: What Happens When Congress Doesn't Do Its Job*, 40 EMORY L.J. 1007, 1010-11 (1991); *see also* Wendy Collins Perdue, *The New Supplemental Jurisdiction Statute—Flawed but Fixable*, 41 EMORY L.J. 69, 80 (1992).

151. *See* Thomas C. Arthur & Richard D. Freer, *Close Enough for Government Work: What Happens When Congress Doesn't Do its Job*, 40 EMORY L.J. 1007, 1010 (1991); Thomas C. Arthur & Richard D. Freer, *Grasping at Burnt Straws: The Disaster of the Supplemental Jurisdiction Statute*, 40 EMORY L.J. 963, 969-70 (1991).

152. *See* Thomas C. Arthur & Richard D. Freer, *Close Enough for Government Work: What Happens When Congress Doesn't Do Its Job*, 40 EMORY L.J. 1007, 1010 (1991).

supplemental jurisdiction over "claims."[153] Therefore, if the plaintiff has no "claim" against a Rule 19 defendant, no provision of the judicial code authorizes jurisdiction to be asserted over the defendant, and § 1367(b) is irrelevant.

In addition, allowing joinder of Rule 19 defendants against whom a plaintiff could assert no claim would produce an anomalous result. A party who is of the same citizenship as the plaintiff could not be originally joined by the plaintiff in the action due to the complete diversity rule of 28 U.S.C. § 1332. However, the nonjoined person could be made a party defendant under Rule 19 on the motion of either the court or the original defendant in the action. Under a literal reading of § 1367(b), there is no restriction placed upon persons "made parties" under Rule 19 that would prevent them from asserting claims against the plaintiff. Thus, after being joined, the party could assert defenses or claims in the action.

Under the same literal wording, the plaintiff could not assert claims against the joined party. To avoid this difficulty, as well as the difficulties discussed in the preceding paragraph, the language of § 1367(b) should be interpreted to prohibit joinder of a party as a defendant when that party could not have been originally joined in the action due to the restrictions of 28 U.S.C. § 1332. As discussed below in conjunction with intervention under Rule 24, this interpretation accords with the legislative history of § 1367(b).[154] In the alternative, if § 1367 is interpreted to permit joinder by the plaintiff of Rule 19 defendants against whom no claims exist, the plaintiff should be prohibited from asserting claims against the Rule 19 defendant only as long as the Rule 19 defendant asserts no claims against the plaintiff.

Illustration 8-20. *D*, a citizen of State *Y*, leases store space in a mall to *P*, a citizen of State *X*. The lease agreement provides that *D* will not lease store space in the mall to any of *P's* competitors. Subsequently, *D* leases store space to *C*, a citizen of State *X* who is allegedly a competitor of *P*. *P* sues *D* in a U.S. District Court in State *Y* to enjoin enforcement of the lease between *D* and *C*. *C* is a person whose interests are adversely affected in a manner that appears to justify joinder under Rule 19(a)(1)(B)(i). However, if *C* is joined in the action, citizens of State *X* will be on both sides of the action, thus destroying complete diversity of citizenship. Therefore, unless supplemental jurisdiction exists over *C*, joinder is impermissible. If *P* does not possess a "claim" against *C*, 28 U.S.C. § 1367(a) does not authorize supplemental jurisdiction over *C*. If *P* does possess a "claim" against *C*, § 1367(a) permits joinder, but § 1367(b) disallows joinder. If § 1367(a) and (b) are read to permit joinder of *C*, *P* should only be prohibited from asserting a claim against *C* as long as *C* does not assert a claim against *P*. Thus, if after *C* is joined, *C* asserts a counterclaim against *P* for a declaratory judgment that the provision in the lease

---

153. *See* Wendy Collins Perdue, *The New Supplemental Jurisdiction Statute—Flawed but Fixable*, 41 EMORY L.J. 69, 80 (1992); *see also* Hayne Blvd. Campus Pres. Ass'n, Inc. v. Julich, 143 F. Supp. 2d 628, 632 (E.D. La. 2001) (stating that parties may not be joined as defendants under Rule 19 unless the plaintiff has a cause of action against them).

154. *See* subsection (D)(3) ("Intervention") *infra*; *see also* Denis F. McLaughlin, *The Federal Supplemental Jurisdiction Statute—A Constitutional and Statutory Analysis*, 24 ARIZ. ST. L.J. 849, 955 (1992).

between *P* and *D* is void, *P* should be able to assert a claim directly against *C* for injunctive or other appropriate relief.[155]

* * * * *

The future relevance of § 1367(b) as well as the significance of the interpretive problems discussed above will be affected by the Supreme Court's decision in *Exxon Mobil Corp. v. Allapattah Services, Inc.*,[156] discussed in Chapter 2(C)(4)*(e)(i)* & *(ii)*, above, and subsection (4)*(b)*, below. Recall that in *Exxon Mobil*, the Court indicated that while § 1367(a) would confer supplemental jurisdiction over claims that were factually related to claims within the diversity jurisdiction of the lower federal courts, but were deficient in jurisdictional amount, that section would not confer supplemental jurisdiction over claims asserted between co-citizens. This is the so-called "contamination theory" articulated by the Court and discussed earlier in Chapter 2. This theory effectively changes the analysis that must be used in Rule 19 as well as other situations. In circumstances like those described in *Illustration 8-20*, it may now be the case that § 1367(b) has become irrelevant because § 1367(a) does not confer supplemental jurisdiction over a claim asserted by one co-citizen against another. Thus, if *P* is asserting a claim against *C*, no supplemental jurisdiction would exist over the claim under the *Exxon Mobil* interpretation of § 1367(a). If *P* is not asserting a claim against *C* and somehow the Supreme Court concludes that this fact permits *C* to be joined without jurisdictional problems, the analysis should probably proceed as suggested in *Illustration 8-20* and *P* should be allowed to assert a claim against *C* if *C* asserts a claim against *P*.

Note also that the contamination theory would result in a lack of supplemental jurisdiction over a non-joined, non-diverse party who should be aligned as a plaintiff in the action, resulting in the quite specific language of § 1367(b) also being rendered irrelevant as to such parties. However, whether or not the contamination theory is applied to Rule 19 "plaintiffs," the results will not be changed. If the contamination theory applies, there will be no supplemental jurisdiction over Rule 19 plaintiffs under § 1367(a). If the contamination theory does not apply, supplemental jurisdiction will exist over a non-diverse plaintiff's claim under § 1367(a), but will be withdrawn under § 1367(b), because the language of the latter section is clear as applied to plaintiffs. Of course, if the defect in the Rule 19 plaintiff's claim is one of jurisdictional amount rather than diversity, the contamination theory does not apply. Rather, the *Exxon Mobil* "claim specific" interpretation of § 1367(a) applies to amount-in-controversy problems and confers supplemental jurisdiction over the Rule 19 plaintiff's claim, and that jurisdiction is, again, withdrawn by § 1367(b). The only time a diverse Rule 19 plaintiff with a claim below $75,000.01 will be able to join in the action is when the restrictive aggregation rules that controlled before § 1367 was enacted are satisfied.[157] Under such circumstances, the supplemental jurisdiction statute is irrelevant.

Lower federal courts considering how defects in diversity are affected by § 1367(a) & (b) after *Exxon Mobil* agree that the claim specific interpretation of

---

155. *See* Helzberg's Diamond Shops, Inc. v. Valley W. Des Moines Shopping Ctr., Inc., 564 F.2d 816 (8th Cir. 1977).

156. 545 U.S.546, 125 S. Ct. 2611, 162 L. Ed. 2d 502 (2005).

157. *See* Chapter 2(D)(7)*(b)* *supra* (discussing these rules).

§ 1367(a) applied to jurisdictional amount problems will not be applied to defects in diversity of citizenship. In *Merrrill Lynch & Co., Inc. v. Allegheny Energy, Inc.*,[158] the plaintiff omitted to join a non-diverse Rule 19(a) party in the action. The district court ordered joinder of the party, aligned it as a defendant, and exercised supplemental jurisdiction over the claim against it under § 1367(a) prior to *Exxon Mobil*. The court of appeals, after the decision in *Exxon Mobil*, held this to be error. The court stated that under the "contamination theory" of *Exxon Mobil*, a defect in diversity involving a Rule 19(a) party prevents the exercise of supplemental jurisdiction. The court explained:

> The Supreme Court [in *Exxon Mobil*] does not define the reach of the contamination theory and does not purport to announce a new standard for assessing diversity defects but instead relies on the Court's consistent construction of the complete diversity rule.... However, even if we read *Exxon* as preserving certain well-established exceptions to the complete diversity rule ... [the Rule 19(a) party's] joinder does not fall within any such exception.[159]

Similarly, in *Picciotto v. Continental Casualty Co.*,[160] the district court dismissed the action because of failure to join an indispensable, nondiverse party. On appeal, the plaintiffs argued that it was permissible to exercise supplemental jurisdiction over the non-diverse party under the language of § 1367(b) as long as the plaintiffs did not assert a claim against the party once the party was joined as a defendant. The court of appeals disagreed, holding that § 1367(b) is irrelevant because of the "contamination theory" of *Exxon Mobil*. Under that theory, the court held, failure to join an indispensable, non-diverse party fails the § 1367(a) threshold test by eliminating any "suit" over which the district court has original jurisdiction. If *Picciotto's* interpretation of the supplemental jurisdiction statute prevails, it will not matter whether, in the situation in *Illustration 8-20,* the plaintiff is asserting a claim against the Rule 19 party or not. In either case, if there is a defect of diversity of citizenship, no supplemental jurisdiction will exist. The only issue remaining in the situation covered by the illustration will be how defects in the amount in controversy requirement of the diversity statute will be handled.[161]

---

158. 500 F.3d 171 (2d Cir. 2007).

159. *Id.* at 179. However, the court went on to hold that the Rule 19(a) party was not indispensable under Rule 19(b) and could be dropped as a party under Rule 21 to preserve diversity.

160. 512 F.3d 9 (1st Cir. 2008).

161. In McLaughlin v. Mississippi Power Co., 376 F.3d 344 (5th Cir. 2004), the plaintiff brought a declaratory judgment action for a determination that it did not owe compensation to any owners of the property over which it was constructing fiber optic lines. Subsequently, the plaintiff sought an injunction against two nondiverse property owners who had commenced state-court litigation against the plaintiff. The district court determined that it did not have jurisdiction over the plaintiff's claims against the property owners. On appeal, the plaintiff, while conceding that diversity was not complete, contended that the property owners had been joined under Federal Rule 71A(b), which allows a plaintiff in a condemnation action to "join in the same action one or more separate pieces of property, whether in the same or different ownership and whether or not sought for the same use." Because Rule 71A is not listed as one of the exceptions in § 1367(b), the argument was that supplemental jurisdiction existed by virtue of § 1367(a) and was not taken away by § 1367(b). The Fifth Circuit Court of appeals disagreed, holding that Rule 71A permits joinder of properties, not parties. Thus, the nondiverse parties had to be joined under some other rule—either Rule 19 or 20—to which § 1367(b) applies. The court also held that while dispensable nondiverse parties may be dismissed to preserve diversity, in condemnation actions, known property owners must be joined under Rule 19. Note that after *Exxon Mobil,* the court's analysis, though not the result in the case, is wrong. Because diversity was incomplete, no supplemental jurisdiction existed under § 1367 (a) in the first place, making § 1367 (b) irrelevant. *See also* Merrill Lynch & Co. v. Allegheny Energy, Inc., 500 F.3d 171 (2d Cir. 2007)

Although there has been a substantial amount of case law concerning supplemental jurisdiction under other multiple party joinder rules (discussed below), apart from the dictum in *Exxon Mobil* and the lower court cases following it, there have been few cases examining the application of § 1367 to Rule 19 since the enactment of the supplemental jurisdiction statute.[162] What case law exists is not encouraging about the courts' understanding of § 1367(b). For example, in *Butcher v. Hildreth,*[163] the plaintiff's state-court action was removed to federal court on the basis of diversity of citizenship. The defendant's answer contained a compulsory counterclaim. The plaintiff objected under Rule 19 that a person named Barfield should be joined in the action as an indispensable party to the counterclaim. The district court ordered Barfield joined, but then remanded the action because Barfield's joinder had destroyed diversity of citizenship. This decision is clearly wrong. There is no reason to believe that *Exxon Mobil* intended to extend the "contamination" theory of § 1367(a) to counterclaims, as opposed only to plaintiff's original claims—the situation to which it has historically been limited. Furthermore, as discussed in Chapter 7 in conjunction with the operation of Rule 13(a), the language of 1367(b) applies only to claims asserted by plaintiffs, not to claims asserted by defendants.[164] Therefore, if supplemental jurisdiction existed over the counterclaim against the plaintiff and the nondiverse party under § 1367(a), as it surely did, § 1367(b) did not destroy diversity.[165]

Rule 19(a) only provides for joinder of parties who are "subject to service of process." Although service of process and personal jurisdiction are distinct, though related, concepts,[166] it seems clear that Rule 19(a)'s reference to service refers generally to the ability of the court to assert personal jurisdiction over the defendant. Thus, the rule itself seems to preserve the ability of a Rule 19(a) party to object to personal jurisdiction. Nevertheless, one must keep in mind that the doctrine of "supplemental" or "pendent" personal jurisdiction approved by some federal courts may provide a basis for asserting personal jurisdiction in some cases of Rule 19(a) joinder. For example, assume that a plaintiff wants to assert both a federal and a state claim against a Rule 19(a) party and that service can be made on

---

(under "contamination theory" of Supreme Court in *Exxon Mobil* decision , court not exercise supplemental jurisdiction over nondiverse Rule 19(a) defendant, but because party was not indispensable under Rule 19(b), party could be dropped under Rule 21 to preserve diversity).

162. *See* Krueger v. Cartwright, 996 F.2d 928, 932-34 (7th Cir. 1993) (refusing to allow joinder of a nondiverse Rule 19 party as a plaintiff, holding the party dispensable and refusing to dismiss the action, but directing parties in the future to consider the jurisdictional limits inherent in Rule 19 and 28 U.S.C. § 1367(b) to avoid jurisdictional anomalies); ZB Holdings, Inc. v. White, 144 F.R.D. 42 (S.D.N.Y. 1992) (holding that a derivative action in which an indispensable, nondiverse corporate defendant was not joined had to be dismissed; court relied exclusively on 28 U.S.C. § 1367(a), reasoning that in the absence of the indispensable party, the court never had the "original jurisdiction" over the lawsuit required by that section).

163. 992 F. Supp. 1420 (D. Utah 1998).

164. *See* Chapter 7(F)(4)*(a) supra* (discussing supplemental jurisdiction over additional nondiverse parties added to counterclaims under Rule 13(h)).

165. At one point in its opinion, the court held that § 1367(b) was applicable because the additional party to the counterclaim was joined pursuant to a Rule 19 motion, and Rule 19, in contrast to Rule 13, *is* specifically mentioned in § 1367(b). *See* 992 F. Supp. at 1422. However, the court failed to recognize that § 1367(b)'s reference to Rule 19 was made in conjunction with claims by plaintiffs, and there is no indication in the case that the added party was asserting a claim against the defendants, despite the fact that the court referred to the party as an "involuntary plaintiff."

166. As indicated in Chapter 3, the fact that a defendant may be served with process in a manner authorized by an appropriate statute or court rule of a court system does not mean that an assertion of jurisdiction over the defendant under the circumstances will also comply with separate statutory or constitutional requirements.

the party under a federal long-arm statute for purposes of the federal claim only, but that jurisdiction cannot be asserted under Federal Rule 4(k)(1)(A) because the forum's courts would not have minimum contacts over the defendant for purposes of an assertion of long-arm jurisdiction over the federal or state claims. Under these circumstances, federal courts recognizing the doctrine of "pendent" or "supplemental" personal jurisdiction might hold jurisdiction for purposes of the state claim proper under Federal Rule 4(k)(1)(D).[167]

The problems with "supplemental personal jurisdiction" have been discussed in Chapter 7 in conjunction with joinder of claims under Rule 18.[168] The problems with asserting "supplemental" or "pendent" personal jurisdiction over Rule 19 parties are even more severe than asserting "supplemental" or "pendent" personal jurisdiction for purposes of multiple claim joinder under Rule 18. The explicit reference in Rule 19(a) to a party's right to assert personal jurisdiction objections seems to require an independent basis of personal jurisdiction over Rule 19 parties.

Rule interpretation aside, however, there will be problems with asserting a kind of "supplemental *party*" or "pendent *party*" personal jurisdiction over Rule 19 parties that are more severe than the problems with asserting "supplemental" or "pendent" *claim* personal jurisdiction for purposes of supplemental claims joined under Rule 18. In the Rule 18 situation, the defendant will always be subject to personal jurisdiction in the forum on one claim (the federal claim) and the only question is whether to allow assertion of an additional, presumably related, state claim against the same defendant. In contrast, "supplemental" or "pendent" personal jurisdiction over a Rule 19 party may involve a situation in which the party is not independently subject to personal jurisdiction in the forum on any other claim. Rather, the party may be summoned to participate in an action because of the party's relationship to other parties already joined in the case who *are* subject to personal jurisdiction. As discussed in Chapter 2(C)(4)*(c)*, above, the Supreme Court refused to recognize the propriety of "supplemental" or "pendent" *party* subject-matter jurisdiction in the absence of an affirmative grant of authority from Congress. For similar reasons, it would seem appropriate for the courts to exercise restraint in subjecting Rule 19 parties to "supplemental" or "pendent" personal jurisdiction in a forum in which neither Congress nor federal rulemakers have explicitly authorized them to be sued.

Rule 4(k)(1)(B) provides that service of process on a party joined under Rule 19 "at a place within a judicial district of the United States and not more than 100 miles from the place from which the summons issues" is effective to establish personal jurisdiction over the party. Rule 4(k)(1)(B) is, in effect, a "mini" federal long-arm rule. By hypothesis, Rule 4(k)(1)(B) is not useful unless a defendant is neither subject to personal jurisdiction in a court of general jurisdiction in the state in which the action is pending, nor is subject to jurisdiction under a federal long-arm statute. As discussed in Chapter 3(L)(2)*(d)*, above, because Rule 4(k)(1)(B) is

---

167. *Cf.* ESAB Group, Inc. v. Centricut, Inc., 126 F.3d 617 (4th Cir. 1997) (holding pendent personal jurisdiction proper over state claim under RICO long-arm statute, even though jurisdiction could not be validly asserted over state claim under South Carolina long-arm statute).

168. *See* Chapter 7(C)(2)*(c) supra* ("Personal Jurisdiction Restrictions on Joinder").

an exercise of federal long-arm authority, the constitutionality of asserting personal jurisdiction over a Rule 19 party served within the "100-mile" bulge area will be determined by standards developed under the Fifth Amendment, and it is implausible to suppose that the Fifth Amendment would impose any serious restrictions on asserting jurisdiction over Rule 19 parties under the circumstances described in the rule, at least assuming that the parties could be constitutionally subjected to personal jurisdiction in the forum if there existed a state or federal long-arm statute that applied to them under the circumstances of the case.[169] However, the very existence of Rule 4(k)(1)(B) provides an additional reason to suppose that "supplemental" or "pendent" party jurisdiction over Rule 19 parties is improper. If Congress has not chosen to authorize jurisdiction over Rule 19 parties by statute (which would make jurisdiction over them proper under Rule 4(k)(1)(D)), and if the rulemakers have addressed long-arm jurisdiction over Rule 19 parties under Rule 4(k)(1)(B), but have chosen not to extend jurisdiction over such parties any further than the 100-mile area, it would seem improper for the courts to assert jurisdiction in circumstances not specifically authorized by statute or rule.

Rule 19(a) likewise preserves the right of an added party to object to venue, by stating that "[i]f the joined party objects to venue and joinder of that party would render the venue of the action improper, that party shall be dismissed from the action." Thus, only the joined party, and not the originally joined defendant, has the right to make the venue objection, which may be waived if the party so chooses.[170] As with personal jurisdiction, however, there is the possibility that the federal courts will recognize a doctrine of "supplemental" or "pendent" venue in cases in which supplemental subject-matter jurisdiction exists over the claim against the Rule 19 party. The issues concerning supplemental venue have also been discussed in Chapter 7, and will not be repeated here.[171] However, the language of Rule 19 with regard to the ability of a joined party to object to venue seems even stronger than the language of Rule 19 dealing with personal jurisdiction. Thus, venue objections should arguably be preserved despite the existence of supplemental subject-matter or personal jurisdiction in a case.[172]

---

169. It is possible that if the Fifth Amendment would preclude direct assertion of personal jurisdiction over the defendant in the forum—*e.g.*, because the defendant does not have "minimum contacts" with the United States—it would also be impermissible to assert jurisdiction over the defendant in the forum by serving the defendant in the 100-mile area. However, this may not be true if the *Burnham* case, discussed in Chapter 3(E)(2), *supra*, also permits personal jurisdiction to be asserted validly under the Fifth Amendment by personal service within the territory of the United States, as seems likely.

170. *See* 7 CHARLES A. WRIGHT ET AL., FEDERAL PRACTICE AND PROCEDURE: CIVIL § 1610, at 155-56 (3d ed. 2001).

171. *See* Chapter 7(C)(2)*(b)* ("Venue Restrictions on Joinder") *supra*.

172. *Cf.* 7 CHARLES A. WRIGHT ET AL., FEDERAL PRACTICE AND PROCEDURE: CIVIL § 1610, at 156 (3d ed. 2001) (express recognition of venue defense in Rule 19(a) may act as a restraining influence on the exercise of ancillary venue). In Askew v. Sheriff of Cook County, 568 F.3d 632 (7th Cir. 2009), the court recognized that a Rule 19 party brought into a case has the right to object to venue, but stated that venue objections would unlikely be invalid because of the provision in § 1391(a)(3) providing for proper venue when the defendant is subject to personal jurisdiction. This statement ignores the language in § 1391(a)(3) providing that the provision is a fallback section available only when venue is not proper in any other district. The statement also ignores that, on the facts of the case, the correct fallback provision was former § 1391(b)(3) rather than (a)(3) because the case was a federal question case, not a diversity action. This, of course, has been changed by the Federal Courts Jurisdiction and Venue Clarification Act of 2011, 125 Stat. 758, 763 (amending § 1391 to eliminate the distinction between diversity and federal question cases; now both kinds of cases are governed by § 1391(b)(1)-(3)).

(d) Rules Enabling Act Problems in the Application of Rule 19

There are no serious Rules Enabling Act problems with Rule 19. The interpretation of the rule in the *Provident Tradesmens* case, discussed in subsection 1*(b)*, above, requires the federal courts to refer to state substantive law in order to determine the interests of absentees for purposes of joinder under Rule 19. Therefore, Rule 19 fully preserves the substantive rights of all parties and Rule 19(a) nonparties. The fact that state law would require joinder when a Rule 19 analysis would not does not abridge the substantive rights of either parties or nonparties. A proper Rule 19 analysis assures that the interests of the existing parties to the action will be protected by the federal courts under Rule 19(b) or the case will be dismissed. The fact that the rule permits these interests to be protected by measures short of joinder does not adversely affect substantive rights. The federal courts are entitled to use their own independent procedural methods for preserving the substantive rights of the parties, rather than the procedural methods used by the state courts. In the same way, the rights of absent parties are equally protected by the analysis that federal courts are required to pursue under Rule 19(b).[173] In addition, nonparties are not normally bound by the judgment in a civil action, which provides additional protection for their substantive rights.[174]

Of course, if the plurality's position on the meaning of the Rules Enabling Act in the *Shady Grove* case, examined in Chapter 5, ultimately prevails, that would provide another reason for concluding that Rule 19 is valid.[175] Under that opinion, Rule 19 would surely be rationally classifiable as procedural and thus valid.

4. Permissive Joinder of Parties

(a) Application of Rule 20

Federal Rule 20 governs permissive joinder of parties in federal court. Original Rule 20 was derived from English practice and practice in those code states that had liberalized party joinder to free it from the restrictive interpretation placed on the original Field Code provisions (*i.e.*, the interpretation requiring plaintiffs who joined in an action to be interested in both the subject matter of the suit and all of the relief requested).[176] The Advisory Committee stated that Rule 20 represented "only a moderate expansion of the present federal equity practice to cover both law and equity actions."[177]

---

173. *See id.* § 1603.

174. *See id.* at 33; Chapter 13(D) *infra* (discussing the persons who are bound by judgments in civil actions); *cf.* Liberty Mut. Ins. Co. v. Treesdale, Inc., 419 F.3d 216 (3d Cir. 2005) (holding by state supreme court that certain absentees were indispensable parties to declaratory judgment action by insurance company was not obligatory on federal court under *Erie* outcome determinative analysis because ruling was a procedural and jurisdictional one, not a ruling based on substantive law).

175. *See* Chapter 5(F)(6) ("The *Shady Grove* Decision") *supra*.

176. *See* section B ("Basic Party Joinder Provisions of the Codes") *supra*.

177. *See* FED. R. CIV. P. 20 advisory committee's note to the 1938 rule; *see also* Rules 26, 37, 40, and 42 of the 1912 Equity Rules, 226 U.S. at 655, 659-60. The 1938 Version of Rule 20(a) was as follows:

> (a) Permissive Joinder. All persons may join in one action as plaintiffs if they assert any right to relief jointly, severally, or in the alternative in respect of or arising out of the same transaction,

Under the original version of Rules 18 and 20, some federal courts had erroneously concluded that Rule 20 was designed to limit joinder of claims under Rule 18. The language that produced this result was found in the second sentence of Rule 18(a) stating that joinder of claims was permitted "if the requirements of Rules 18, 20 and 22 are satisfied." From this language some courts concluded that when a complaint asserted some claims against all defendants and some claims against fewer than all the defendants, the claims could be joined *only* if they *all* arose out of the same transaction or occurrence and presented common questions of law or fact. If the claims arose out of different transactions and were not against all of the defendants, they could not be joined. The 1966 amendments to Rule 18 and 20 were designed to make it clear that this interpretation was erroneous.[178]

Illustration 8-21. Assume that *P* sued *D-1* and *D-2* on a claim arising out of a contract made with *D-1* and *D-2*. Under the pre-1966 interpretation of Rule 20, *P* could not join a claim arising out of a wholly separate contract made with *D-2*.[179] The 1966 amendments make it clear that *P* can join the claim against *D-2*.

* * * * *

Today, the most serious restrictions on joinder of parties in federal court arise because of the requirements of federal subject-matter jurisdiction, venue, and personal jurisdiction explored in Chapters 2-4, and discussed in subsection *(b)*, below. Rule 20 cannot override these restrictions.[180] Consequently, even when Rule 20 is satisfied, restrictions on subject-matter jurisdiction, venue, and personal jurisdiction may operate to prevent joinder. In cases of permissive joinder of parties under Rule 20, the consequences are not as serious as they can sometimes be in cases of compulsory joinder of parties under Rule 19. If a person is a Rule 19(a) party and that person's joinder is impossible because it would destroy federal subject-matter jurisdiction or venue, or because the absentee is not subject to personal jurisdiction, the action may have to be dismissed. In theory, the plaintiff may be deprived of any effective remedy for the deprivation of the plaintiff's rights because, in certain situations, no court may have authority over all the Rule 19 parties to an action. Because joinder under Rule 20 is permissive, however, inability to join a party because of subject-matter jurisdiction, venue, or personal jurisdiction restrictions simply means that plaintiffs will have to sue in separate actions, or that defendants will have to be sued separately.

Nevertheless, even though the operation of the Federal Rules themselves does not produce harsh consequences in cases of permissive party joinder, the inability to join parties under Rule 20 could have serious consequences for other

---

> occurrence, or series of transactions or occurrences and if any question of law or fact common to all of them will arise in the action. All persons may be joined in one action as defendants if there is asserted against them jointly, severally, or in the alternative, any right to relief in respect of or arising out of the same transaction, occurrence, or series of transactions or occurrences and if any question of law or fact common to all of them will arise in the action. A plaintiff or defendant need not be interested in obtaining or defending against all the relief demanded. Judgment may be given for one or more of the plaintiffs according to their respective rights to relief, and against one or more of the defendants according to their respective liabilities.

308 U.S. at 687-88.

178. *See* FED. R. CIV. P. 18, 20 advisory committee's note to the 1966 amendment.

179. *See* Federal Hous. Adm'r v. Christianson, 26 F. Supp. 419 (D. Conn. 1939).

180. *See* FED. R. CIV. P. 82.

reasons. For one thing, the inability to join parties in an action may result in multiple litigation over the same basic matter, which duplicates effort and expense. In addition, a party may be caught in a serious tactical bind if that party is unable to join others in the same suit.

Illustration 8-22. Assume that in a tort suit *P* wants to assert claims against *D-1* and *D-2* in the alternative. *P* is certain that either *D-1* or *D-2* is responsible for *P's* injuries, but is uncertain which one. If *P* is forced to sue each defendant in a separate proceeding, *P* may lose *both* suits because the defendant in each action may be able to convince the trier of fact that the absent defendant was solely responsible for *P's* injuries.

* * * * *

Finally, rules of issue preclusion, which are discussed in detail in Chapter 13,[181] may operate to the serious disadvantage of a party who sues or is sued in separate actions.

Illustration 8-23. Assume that a plaintiff is prevented by rules of subject-matter jurisdiction from joining two defendants in the alternative in a tort suit. The plaintiff sues the two defendants separately. One of the actions proceeds to judgment before the other and the plaintiff loses that action because of a finding of contributory negligence against the plaintiff. If that finding can be used against the plaintiff in the second action against the other defendant, the plaintiff will lose that action as well. This result may or may not be fair, depending on the circumstances surrounding the first suit. A plaintiff who anticipates that an action might be lost for reasons unrelated to the merits, such as the jury's sympathy for a particular defendant, might well decide to bring only one suit against the other defendant. Inability to join both defendants will pose difficult choices for the plaintiff, and, if plaintiff's judgment is wrong, the plaintiff may suffer significant costs. For these reasons, inability to join parties even when joinder is only "permissive" is of potentially great importance to litigants.

* * * * *

Rule 20 contains two restrictions on multiple party joinder. First the claims asserted by or against the multiple parties must arise out of the same transaction or occurrence or series of transactions or occurrences. Second, questions of law or fact common to the multiple plaintiffs or defendants must exist in the action.

Illustration 8-24. *P* sues *D-1* and *D-2* in a tort action. *P* alleges that *D-1* negligently collided with *P* in an automobile, severely injuring *P*. *P* also alleges that *D-2*, a physician, negligently treated *P* at the emergency room where *P* was taken after the accident thus aggravating *P's* injuries. Rule 20 is satisfied under these circumstances. Although the incidents in which *D-1* and *D-2* injured *P* are separated in time, Rule 20 permits joinder not only when the same transaction or occurrence is involved. It also permits joinder when the claims arise out of the same series of transactions or occurrences, which is the case here. In addition, common questions of fact will arise between the claims against *D-1* and *D-2*. Those issues will concern the extent to which *P's* injuries are attributable to *D-1's* negligence or *D-2's*

---

181. *See* Chapter 13(C) *infra* ("Issue Preclusion").

negligence.[182] A common question of law also exists on the claims against the two defendants in the form of the rule of negligence that will make each defendant liable or not on the facts of the case.

Illustration 8-25. *P-1*, *P-2*, and *P-3* sue *D*, a municipality. They seek an order to compel *D* to issue the plaintiffs a license to sell alcoholic beverages in their restaurants. *D* had refused licenses to each plaintiff on the same grounds, but on separate occasions. *P-1*, *P-2*, and *P-3* are not associated in any other way. Rule 20 is not satisfied under these circumstances. A common question of law exists between the claims of the plaintiffs. However, the claims asserted by *P-1*, *P-2*, and *P-3* are not factually connected. Therefore, the same transaction or occurrence or series of transactions or occurrences is not involved.[183]

Illustration 8-26. *P-1* and *P-2* were fraudulently induced to invest in a sham corporation by a false prospectus issued by *D*. Even though no relationship exists between *P-1* and *P-2* other than the fact that they were induced by the same false prospectus to invest in the sham corporation, *P-1* and *P-2* may join in an action against *D* under Rule 20. The common question requirement is satisfied by the question whether the prospectus was false and fraudulent. The same transaction or occurrence requirement is satisfied by the fact that the plaintiffs were defrauded by the same prospectus. Here, unlike the situation in *Illustration 8-25*, a factual connection exists between the plaintiffs claims because the issuance of the prospectus was the "transaction or occurrence" that defrauded them both.

(b) Problems of Subject-Matter Jurisdiction, Personal Jurisdiction, and Venue Under Rule 20

The 1990 codification of the doctrines of "pendent" and "ancillary" jurisdiction in 28 U.S.C. § 1367 has removed one obstacle to Rule 20 joinder in federal question cases that previously existed. In *Finley v. United States,*[184] the Supreme Court drastically limited the ability of the federal courts to exercise so-called "pendent party" jurisdiction (*i.e.*, jurisdiction that allows the plaintiff to join

---

182. *See* Lucas v. City of Juneau, 127 F. Supp. 730 (D. Alaska 1955).

183. *See* Erwin v. City of Dallas, 85 F. Supp. 103 (N.D. Tex. 1949); *see also* DirecTV v. Loussaert, 218 F.R.D. 639 (S.D. Iowa 2003) (multiple defendants were improperly joined under Rule 20; although plaintiff alleged that all defendants had violated the same federal statute by selling devices that allowed unauthorized receipt of satellite programming, the sales were not sufficiently related to satisfy the "same transaction" requirement); Purdue Pharma, L.P. v. Estate of Heffner, 904 So. 2d 100 (Miss. 2004) (claims of three patients against three different prescribing physicians and drug manufacturer did not arise out of the same transaction or occurrence or series of transactions or occurrences for purpose of state multiple party joinder rule identical to Rule 20; Rule 20 does not allow diverse plaintiffs to bring claims against diverse defendants when there is no transaction or occurrence common to them all); *cf.* DirecTV, Inc. v. Leto, 467 F.3d 842 (3d Cir. 2006) (district court properly severed misjoined claims rather than dismissing them to prevent running of statute of limitations on claims against misjoined defendants); Swan v. Ray, 293 F.3d 1252 (11th Cir. 2002) (inmate obtained a federal consent judgment granting a permanent injunction to require Georgia Board of Pardons to give annual reconsideration to his application for parole; inmate then filed a later action to enforce this judgment; a second inmate moved to join in the second action; held that district court properly denied joinder under Rule 20; second inmate was not a party to the first suit and was not eligible for injunctive relief sought by first inmate based on first judgment; in addition, second inmate may not be entitled to same relief granted first inmate in first action because the opinion in first suit indicated that a particularized inquiry was required; the first inmate's claim, therefore, cannot have a common factual basis with claims in second suit).

184. 490 U.S. 545, 109 S. Ct. 2003, 104 L. Ed. 2d 593 (1989); *see also* Aldinger v. Howard, 427 U.S. 1, 96 S. Ct. 2413, 49 L. Ed. 2d 276 (1976).

with a federal claim a factually related state claim in which a nondiverse party is a defendant).[185] In effect, the *Finley* case held that pendent party jurisdiction would be prohibited in the absence of an explicit, affirmative grant of authority to the federal courts by Congress.[186] The enactment of 28 U.S.C. § 1367(a) was designed to overrule *Finley*. Thus, today the federal courts may exercise "supplemental jurisdiction" over state claims that arise out of the same transaction or occurrence as federal claims over which the federal courts have original jurisdiction under 28 U.S.C. § 1331, even if those state claims are asserted entirely against additional nondiverse parties.[187]

Recall, however, that Congress authorized joinder of claims within the supplemental jurisdiction whenever the claims formed a part of the same constitutional case or controversy as claims over which the district courts have original jurisdiction. In Chapter 2(C)(4)*(e)(iii)*, above, it was suggested that Article III of the Constitution may permit Congress to treat factually unrelated federal and state claims as part of the "same case or controversy."[188] If so, once the joinder requirements of Rule 20 are satisfied, it might be possible to join an additional factually unrelated claim against a nondiverse defendant who has been brought within the supplemental jurisdiction of the district courts under 28 U.S.C. § 1367(a).

Illustration 8-27. *P*, a citizen of State *X*, sues *D-1* and *D-2*, who are also citizens of State *X*, in a U.S. District Court in State *X*. *P* asserts a federal claim against *D-1* and a factually related state claim against *D-2*. *P* also joins a factually unrelated state claim against *D-2*. Rule 20 is satisfied in this situation because the federal claim against *D-1* and the factually related state claim against *D-2* arise out of the same transaction or occurrence and involve common questions of fact. Recall from Chapter 7(C)(1), *Illustration 7-11* and section C(4)*(a)*, *Illustration 8-21*, above, that once Rule 20 is satisfied by the presence of any claims against multiple defendants that comply with the same transaction and common question requirements, Rule 18 permits joinder of any other claim, however unrelated, against either of the defendants.[189] If (1) Article III is interpreted to permit factually unrelated state and federal claims to become part of the same case or controversy and (2) 28 U.S.C. § 1367(a) is read to extend the "supplemental jurisdiction" of the federal courts as far as the Constitution permits, jurisdiction would exist over the factually unrelated state claim against *D-2*. However, as argued in Chapter 2(C)(4)*(b)* & *(e)(iii)*, above, while the Constitution should be interpreted flexibly to allow Congress to authorize joinder of factually unrelated state and federal claims, § 1367(a) should be construed to permit joinder only of factually related claims.

---

185. *See* Chapter 2(E)(3) *supra* ("The Statutory Basis of Pendent and Ancillary Jurisdiction").

186. *See id.*

187. *See* Chapter 2(E)(4) *supra* ("The Codification of Pendent and Ancillary Jurisdiction"); *see also* Arnold v. Kimberly Quality Care Nursing Serv., 762 F. Supp. 1182 (M.D. Pa. 1991) (section 1367 confers supplemental jurisdiction over pendent plaintiffs in federal question case).

188. *See* Chapter 2(E)(5)*(c) supra* ("Same Article III Case or Controversy").

189. As observed in Chapter 7, the case would not differ if the factually unrelated claim had been joined against *D-1*, rather than *D-2*, if the scope of an Article III case or controversy is broad enough to encompass factually unrelated federal and state claims.

Under this latter construction, no jurisdiction would exist over *P's* factually unrelated state claim against *D-2*.[190]

* * * * *

As discussed in Chapter 2(C)(4), above, § 1367(b) attempts to preserve the policies of the diversity jurisdiction, including the complete diversity rule of *Strawbridge v. Curtiss*,[191] and the rules limiting the ability of plaintiffs to aggregate claims in order to satisfy the jurisdictional amount requirement of § 1332.[192] Because of serious drafting problems, however, it initially appeared that there was a possibility that § 1367(b) had, in some permissive joinder cases under Rule 20, left unintentional gaps in the exceptions it attempted to create for diversity claims that fall within the supplemental jurisdiction conferred by § 1367(a). This possibility existed because the language of § 1367(b) prohibits "claims by plaintiffs against persons made parties under Rule . . . 20 of the Federal Rules of Civil Procedure." As discussed above, Rule 20 allows joinder of multiple defendants when claims are asserted against them that arise out of the same events and raise common questions of law or fact. Likewise, the rule permits joinder of multiple plaintiffs when the plaintiffs assert claims that arise out of the same events and raise common questions of law or fact.[193] The language of § 1367(b) thus appeared to preserve the requirement of complete diversity of citizenship when a plaintiff joins multiple defendants in federal court under Rule 20.[194] However, the wording of the statute did not literally preserve the complete diversity rule when multiple plaintiffs joined to sue a single defendant. Thus, the question was raised whether the wording of § 1367 expanded diversity jurisdiction beyond its previous boundaries.

Illustration 8-28. *P-1*, a citizen of State *X*, and *P-2*, a citizen of State *Y*, sue *D*, a citizen of State *Y*, in a U.S. District Court. *P-1* and *P-2* each seek damages of $100,000 against *D* for personal injuries received in an automobile accident. Under the wording of § 1367, this action originally appeared to be within the jurisdiction of the district court. Under the "claim-specific" interpretation of § 1367(a) discussed in Chapter 2 and endorsed by most federal courts, before the Supreme Court's decision in the *Exxon Mobil* case (discussed in Chapter 2 and in conjunction with Rule 19 in section C(3)*(c)*, above),[195] the district court appeared to have original jurisdiction over the claim between *P-1* and *D* because diversity of citizenship exists between those parties and the jurisdictional amount was satisfied. Under this same interpretation, § 1367(a) would then provide for supplemental jurisdiction over the claim between *P-2* and *D*. Even though there is no diversity of citizenship between those parties, the claim between *P-2* and *D* arises from the same facts as the claim between *P-1* and *D* and is, therefore, within the same Article III case or controversy. Furthermore, the wording of § 1367(b) does not appear to

---

190. *See* Denis F. McLaughlin, *The Federal Supplemental Jurisdiction Statute—A Constitutional and Statutory Analysis*, 24 ARIZ. ST. L.J. 849, 940-42 (1992).

191. 7 U.S. (3 Cranch) 267, 2 L. Ed. 435 (1806).

192. *See* Chapter 2(D)(7)*(b) supra* ("Aggregation of Claims with Multiple Parties: The Common and Undivided Interest Test").

193. *See* FED. R. CIV. P. 20(a).

194. *See, e.g.*, American Standard Ins. Co. v. Rogers, 123 F. Supp. 2d 461 (S.D. Ind. 2000) (single plaintiff may not aggregate claims against multiple defendants unless the defendants could be held jointly liable).

195. *See* Chapter 2(E)(5) *supra* ("The Scope of Supplemental Jurisdiction: Section 1367(a)").

preclude supplemental jurisdiction over the claim in this situation. Section 1367(b) prohibits claims by plaintiffs *against* persons made parties under Federal Rule of Civil Procedure 20. *P-1* and *P-2* are plaintiffs asserting claims, but they are the ones who are "made parties" under Rule 20. *D*, against whom the claims are asserted, is a single defendant and is not, therefore, "made a party" under Rule 20. To preserve the rule of complete diversity in this situation, it appeared that § 1367(b) would have to read to prohibit claims by *plaintiffs made parties* under Rule 20, as well as claims by plaintiffs *against* persons made parties under Rule 20.

Illustration 8-29. *P-1*, a citizen of State *X*, and *P-2*, a citizen of State *X*, sue *D*, a citizen of State *Y*, in a U.S. District Court. *P-1* seeks $100,000 in damages from *D* for personal injuries received in an automobile accident. *P-2* seeks $10,000 from *D* for property damage suffered in the same accident. Under these circumstances, the aggregation rules of 28 U.S.C. § 1332 are not satisfied. Therefore, *P-2* could not, before the enactment of § 1367, join with *P-1* in a suit against *C* in federal court because *P-2's* claim does not satisfy the amount-in-controversy requirement.[196] For the reasons given in *Illustration 8-28*, however, the language of § 1367(a) seemed to create supplemental jurisdiction over *P-2's* claim, and the language of § 1367(b) does not preclude jurisdiction in this case.

* * * * *

The drafters of § 1367 acknowledged the potentially serious gap in the language of § 1367(b) in multiple plaintiff actions.[197] However, the drafters acknowledged the problem only in cases in which a plaintiff commences an action against a diverse defendant and then by amendment attempts to add a non-diverse plaintiff to the action. In cases in which two plaintiffs sue originally, one of them diverse and one of them non-diverse to the defendant, the drafters stated that joinder of the non-diverse plaintiff would be prohibited by the complete diversity rule.[198] However, the only way this could be so is if § 1367(a) had been interpreted literally to require that the entire "civil action" commenced by the plaintiff or plaintiffs as an original matter be within the original jurisdiction of the district courts. As discussed in Chapter 2(C)(4)*(e)(i)*, however, if this interpretation is correct, it would destroy the central purpose of § 1367 to overrule the *Finley* case and authorize pendent party jurisdiction in federal question cases. On the other hand, if the "civil action" language of § 1367(a) were given a "claim-specific" meaning in federal question cases involving pendent parties (as opposed to an "action-specific" meaning), it would seemingly have to be given the same meaning in diversity actions, because the statute does not distinguish between diversity and federal question cases. The result would be that the statute provides supplemental jurisdiction over the claim of a nondiverse plaintiff joined originally under Rule 20. Early in the statute's history, at least one district court read § 1367(b) to be applicable only to nondiverse parties added to the action by amendment after the

---

196. *See* Zahn v. International Paper Co., 414 U.S. 291, 94 S. Ct. 505, 38 L. Ed. 2d 511 (1973); Chapter 2(D)(7)*(b)*, *Illustration 2-59*, *supra*.

197. *See* Thomas D. Rowe, Jr. et al., *Compounding or Creating Confusion About Supplemental Jurisdiction? A Reply to Professor Freer*, 40 EMORY L.J. 943, 961 n.91 (1991).

198. *See id.*

original action has been commenced.[199] However, there is a longstanding practice in the federal courts of reassessing federal subject-matter jurisdiction whenever amendments are made. Section 1367 does not appear to be designed to overrule that practice, and, it has continued unabated after the statute's enactment.[200] Thus, the district court decision, as well as the drafters' suggestion about how to read the statute, seems clearly wrong.

Because the "Rule 20 gap" was clearly the product of a drafting mistake, the sensible result would have been to disregard the gap and interpret § 1367(b) as preserving the complete diversity rule in cases in which multiple plaintiffs join in an action against a single defendant as well as in multiple defendant actions[201] Such a result would have conformed to the legislative history of the statute.[202] Prior to the Supreme Court's decision in the *Exxon Mobil* case, discussed below, the lower federal court decisions interpreting § 1367(b) generally, but not uniformly, interpreted the "Rule 20 gap" away. However, in *Stromberg Metal Works, Inc. v. Press Mechanical, Inc.*,[203] the Seventh Circuit held, in a Rule 20 joinder case involving an aggregation question, that § 1367(a) & (b) permit the district courts to entertain claims by plaintiffs that do not meet the amount-in-controversy require-

---

199. *See* First Nat'l Bancshares, Inc. v. Geisel, 853 F. Supp. 1333, 1336 n.5 (D. Kan. 1994).

200. *See* Scaccianoce v. Hixon Mfg. & Supply Co., 57 F.3d 582, 584-85 (7th Cir. 1995); Dieter v. MFS Telecom, Inc., 870 F. Supp. 561 (S.D.N.Y. 1994); Arnold v. Kimberly Quality Care Nursing Serv., 762 F. Supp. 1182, 1185 (M.D. Pa. 1991); Patrick D. Murphy, *A Federal Practitioner's Guide to Supplemental Jurisdiction Under 28 U.S.C. § 1367,* 78 MARQ. L. REV. 973, 1003 (1995); *cf.* Darren J. Gold, *Supplemental Jurisdiction Over Claims by Plaintiffs in Diversity Cases: Making Sense of 28 U.S.C. § 1367(b),* 93 MICH. L. REV. 2133, 2157-69 (1995); *see also In re* Wireless Tel. Fed. Cost Recovery Fees Litig., 396 F.3d 922 (8th Cir. 2005) (holding that an amended complaint supersedes the original complaint and requires subject-matter jurisdiction issues to be resolved under the amended complaint; however, court incorrectly relies on doctrine of relation back under the Federal Rules of Civil Procedure for this holding; relation back properly applies only to statute of limitations issues); Zurich Am. Ins. Co. v. Integrand Assurance Co., 178 F. Supp. 2d 47 (D.P.R. 2001) (an amended pleading supersedes the original, which is treated thereafter as nonexistent; therefore, when plaintiff settled with certain defendants for $330,000 and amended its complaint to eliminate those defendants from the action, the only claim left was for $48,839 and the court was deprived of jurisdiction because the amount in controversy fell below the $75,000 requirement). *But see* Sunpoint Sec., Inc. v. Porta, 192 F.R.D. 716 (M.D. Fla. 2000) (stating that because diversity jurisdiction was proper at the beginning of the action, amendment of the complaint to add a nondiverse plaintiff did not destroy diversity because supplemental jurisdiction applied to the added plaintiff; no mention of the Rule 20 gap; court just seemed to assume that the addition of a plaintiff did not require a new jurisdictional assessment); *cf.* Riley v. Fairbanks Capital Corp., 222 Fed. App'x 897 (11th Cir. 2007) (amended complaint eliminated federal claim; new jurisdictional assessment of complaint indicated that there was no federal subject-matter jurisdiction; therefore, court could not exercise supplemental jurisdiction over state claims); Scottsdale Ins. Co. v. Subscriptions Plus, Inc., 195 F.R.D. 640 (W.D. Wis. 2000) (insurer sued multiple parties, including another insurer, for a declaratory judgment that it had no duty to defend or indemnify two of the defendants in a suit arising out of an automobile accident; the plaintiff and defendant insurers were nondiverse, and the defendant insurer was asserting crossclaims against its co-defendants; the court refused to realign the nondiverse defendant-insurer as a plaintiff; the two insurers argued that it was unnecessary to drop the nondiverse insurer from the action, but instead that the plaintiff could simply drop its claim against that party and the party could remain in the action for purposes of asserting its crossclaims against the other insurers; the court correctly refused to do so and insisted on dropping the nondiverse defendant), *aff'd on other grounds*, 299 F.3d 618 (7th Cir. 2002).

201. *See* Denis F. McLaughlin, *The Federal Supplemental Jurisdiction Statute—A Constitutional and Statutory Analysis*, 24 ARIZ. ST. L.J. 849, 940-42 (1992).

202. The House Report accompanying the statute stated: "This section [§ 1367(b)] is not intended to affect the jurisdictional requirements of 28 U.S.C. § 1332 in diversity-only class actions, as those requirements were interpreted prior to *Finley*." H.R. REP. NO. 734, 101st Cong., 2d Sess. 29 (1990).

203. 77 F.3d 928 (7th Cir. 1996). *Stromberg* is discussed in Mark C. Cawley, Note, *The Right Result for the Wrong Reasons: Permitting Aggregation of Claims Under 28 U.S.C. § 1367 in Multi-Plaintiff Diversity Litigation,* 73 NOTRE DAME L. REV. 1045 (1998); Heather McDaniel, *Plugging the "Gaping Hole": The Effect of 28 U.S.C. § 1367 on the Complete Diversity Requirement of 28 U.S.C. § 1332,* 49 BAYLOR L. REV. 1069 (1997); Note, *Federal Civil Procedure—Supplemental Jurisdiction—Seventh Circuit Holds that 28 U.S.C. § 1367 Allows Supplemental Jurisdiction Over Permissively Joined Plaintiffs in Diversity Suits.*—Stromberg Metal Works, Inc. v. Press Mechanical, Inc., 77 F.3d 928 (7th Cir. 1996), 110 HARV. L. REV. 1173 (1997).

ment, but which are factually related to claims that do meet the requirement. *Stromberg* followed the decision of the Fifth Circuit in *Free v. Abbott Laboratories,*[204] a class action case discussed in section D(4)*(c)*, below. However, at least two other courts of appeals rejected the *Abbott* and *Stromberg* rationale,[205] and the district courts mostly, but not uniformly, held that the aggregation rules survived the enactment of § 1367.[206]

As discussed in Chapter 2(C)(4)*(e)(i)* & *(ii)*, above, in *Exxon Mobil Corp. v. Allapattah Services, Inc.*,[207] the Supreme Court held that when there is one claim asserted by a plaintiff in an action that meets the amount-in-controversy requirement and claims by other parties that do not independently meet the requirement, § 1367(a) confers supplemental jurisdiction over the factually related claims that do not meet the requirement. Thus, the Court held that the "Rule 20 gap" was real as applied to amount-in-controversy defects and, thus, that § 1367(b) does not withdraw the jurisdiction conferred by § 1367(a) in the Rule 20 gap situation. As stated in Chapter 2, this placed a claim-specific interpretation on § 1367(a) as applied to amount-in-controversy problems. However, as also discussed in Chapter 2, and in section C(3)*(c)*, above, in conjunction with Rule 19, the Court treated defects in diversity of citizenship differently than defects in jurisdictional amount under § 1367(a), even though the text of the statute does not draw any distinction between the two kinds of jurisdictional problems. When diversity is incomplete, the Court held, the defect "contaminates" the entire action, with the result that no supplemental jurisdiction is conferred by § 1367(a) over a claim by or against a nondiverse party properly joined under Rule 20. This places an "action-specific"

---

204. 51 F.3d 524 (5th Cir. 1995), *aff'd by an equally divided court*, 529 U.S. 333, 120 S. Ct. 1578, 146 L. Ed. 2d 306 (2000).

205. *See* Meritcare Inc. v. St. Paul Mercury Ins. Co., 166 F.3d 214 (3d Cir. 1999); Leonhardt v. Western Sugar Co., 160 F.3d 631 (10th Cir. 1998). In one curious case, the Fourth Circuit held that when multiple claims are joined by a single plaintiff against a single defendant and one of the claims is dismissed on summary judgment, thus reducing the amount requested by the plaintiff to less than the amount-in-controversy requirement, the district court has discretion to retain the other claims in the action. *See* Shanaghan v. Cahill, 58 F.3d 106 (4th Cir. 1995). The court held that the basis for the district court's discretion lies in the model of supplemental jurisdiction under § 1367. The district court should first look to the face of the complaint to determine whether the plaintiff's claims meet the amount requirement. If they do, but some subsequent event, such as dismissal of one of the claims, reduces the amount in controversy below the amount requirement in § 1332, the district court should be guided by the same kinds of factors that inform decisions about whether to dismiss supplemental claims in the court's discretion under § 1367(c). *Shanaghan* is clearly wrong. If the amount-in-controversy requirement is satisfied at the outset of the action, the district court has no discretion to dismiss the claims if a subsequent event reduces the amount below the statutorily required figure. *See* Wolde-Meskel v. Vocational Instruction Project Community Servs., Inc., 166 F.3d 59 (2d Cir. 1999) (rejecting *Shanaghan's* reasoning); Amanda Dalton, Note, Shanaghan v. Cahill: *Supplementing Supplemental Jurisdiction*, 1996 B.Y.U. L. REV. 281.

206. Numerous district court decisions addressed whether the aggregation rules under § 1332 have survived the enactment of § 1367. *See, e.g.*, Fairchild v. State Farm Mut. Auto. Ins. Co., 907 F. Supp. 969 (M.D. La. 1995) (aggregation rules overruled in some cases); Henkel v. ITT Bowest Corp., 872 F. Supp. 872 (D. Kan. 1994) (aggregation rules survive); Lindsay v. Kvortek, 865 F. Supp. 264 (W.D. Pa. 1994) (aggregation rules overruled in some cases); Tokarz v. Texaco Pipeline, Inc., 860 F. Supp. 563 (N.D. Ill. 1994) (aggregation rules survive); Fountain v. Black, 876 F. Supp. 1294 (S.D. Ga. 1994) (aggregation rules survive); Chouest v. American Airlines, Inc., 839 F. Supp. 412 (E.D. La. 1993) (aggregation rules survive); Durrett v. John Deere Co., 150 F.R.D. 555 (N.D. Tex. 1993) (aggregation rules survive); Mayo v. Key Fin. Servs., Inc., 812 F. Supp. 277 (D. Mass. 1993) (aggregation rules survive); Hairston v. Home Loan & Inv. Bank, 814 F. Supp. 180 (D. Mass. 1993) (aggregation rules survive); Averdick v. Republic Fin. Servs., Inc., 803 F. Supp. 37 (E.D. Ky. 1992) (aggregation rules survive); *see also* Congram v. Giella, No. 91 Civ. 1134 (LMM), 1992 WL 349845, 1992 U.S. Dist. LEXIS 17230 (S.D.N.Y. Nov. 10, 1992) (aggregation rules in multiple defendant actions remain the same after enactment of § 1367).

207. 545 U. S. 546, 125 S. Ct. 2611, 162 L. Ed. 2d 502 (2005).

interpretation on § 1367(a) for purposes of diversity of citizenship problems and makes § 1367(b) irrelevant to such problems in Rule 20 joinder cases.

Throughout the majority opinion, in *Exxon Mobil*, the Court insisted that § 1367 is not ambiguous, a patently preposterous proposition. Nevertheless, this insistence, coupled with a discussion of the pitfalls of relying on legislative history, allowed the majority to avoid any discussion of the legislative history or other sources outside the statute that would have contradicted its conclusion. In addition, though admitting that the omission of Rule 20 plaintiffs from the list of § 1367(b) exceptions "presents something of a puzzle on our view of the statute," the Court justified its view by arguing that the reference to Rule 19 plaintiffs in the latter subsection is at least as anomalous as the omission of Rule 20 plaintiffs—if the district court lacked original jurisdiction over a diversity action where any plaintiff's claims failed to satisfy the requirements of the diversity statute, there is no need for a special exception in § 1367(b) for Rule 19 plaintiffs who do not meet these requirements. Apparently, the Court did not understand (as explained in section C(3)*(c)*, above) that this provision was probably simply a clumsily drafted attempt to prevent assertion of claims by Rule 19 parties joined as defendants and later realigned as plaintiffs when those claims would be asserted against co-citizen defendants. Viewed in this fashion, had some kind of provision not been included in § 1367(b) concerning Rule 19 plaintiffs, another "gap" would have been created in the statute. Furthermore, in interpreting the Rule 20 gap to exist in multiple plaintiff joinder situations under Rule 20, the Court did not bother to ask why Congress would create such a gap in multiple plaintiff joinder situations under Rule 20, but not in multiple defendant joinder situations. No apparent reason exists why Congress would want to prefer plaintiff joinder over defendant joinder in supplemental jurisdiction cases involving only jurisdictional amount problems. This would seem at least as anomalous as the Court's confused evaluation of the Rule 19 plaintiff joinder language. Indeed, it would seem to be another good reason to consider the statute ambiguous and consult the legislative history.

Personal jurisdiction over each defendant joined under Rule 20 will ordinarily have to be proper under an applicable long-arm statute and the relevant constitutional standards governing the assertion of jurisdiction—*i.e.*, Fourteenth Amendment standards in the case of a state long-arm statute and Fifth Amendment standards in the case of a federal long-arm statute. Ordinarily, there will be no problem with one defendant being subject to personal jurisdiction while another defendant joined under Rule 20 is not. The fact that the claims against the joined defendants must arise out of the same transaction or occurrence or series of transactions or occurrences will assure that if a long-arm statute is constitutionally applicable to one defendant, it will also be constitutionally applicable to other defendants joined under Rule 20. Nevertheless, it is possible to envision situations in which one defendant may be subject to personal jurisdiction within a state, but another defendant joined under Rule 20 may not be. For example, a defendant may be subject to personal jurisdiction because the defendant is domiciled within the state, or because the defendant is personally served within the state, even though the claim arises outside the state. Another defendant joined under Rule 20 may not be subject to jurisdiction on the same basis and will also not be subject to long-arm jurisdiction within the state because the claim arose elsewhere and the defendant has no contacts with the state. In these circumstances, the action could not be maintained in the forum, even though the parties would be properly joined in the action. In addition, it should be noted that even if the parties could both be subjected to personal jurisdiction in the forum, venue restrictions (discussed below), would usually prevent the action from being maintained there over the objection of the defendants.

When a federal claim is being asserted against one defendant and a state claim is being asserted against a second, nondiverse defendant within a district court's supplemental jurisdiction, a question arises whether the federal court can assert "supplemental" or "pendent" party personal jurisdiction over the nondiverse defendant, assuming that the defendant against whom the federal claim is asserted is subject to personal jurisdiction under a federal long-arm statute or rule, but the nondiverse defendant is not explicitly subject to personal jurisdiction under any federal or state statute or rule. Although Rule 20, unlike Rule 19,[208] does not contain specific language that preserves a joined party's right to object to personal jurisdiction, the problems with asserting "supplemental" or "pendent" personal jurisdiction over Rule 20 defendants are otherwise similar to those under Rule 19. Indeed, it can be argued that the reasons for not recognizing a doctrine of "supplemental" or "pendent" personal jurisdiction in Rule 20 cases are even stronger than those in Rule 19 cases. If a Rule 19 party cannot be subjected to personal jurisdiction within the forum, and if the prejudice caused by the party's absence cannot be cured under Rule 19(b), the action will have to be dismissed. If there is no forum in which all such Rule 19 parties can be subjected to personal jurisdiction, the plaintiff will effectively be precluded from asserting a claim against anyone. Thus, the potential consequences to the plaintiff of a lack of personal jurisdiction over a Rule 19 party could be severe. However, Rule 20 parties do not all have to be joined for an action to proceed against other parties. Although, as noted in subsection *(a)*, above, a plaintiff can encounter serious tactical problems if the plaintiff is unable to join multiple defendants in some actions, these tactical problems are not as serious as having an action dismissed altogether. Therefore, if, as argued above, the courts should not recognize a doctrine of "supplemental" or "pendent" personal jurisdiction in Rule 19 cases in the absence of explicit statutory or rule authority to do so, it is even more arguable that they should not recognize such a doctrine in Rule 20 cases.

Venue must normally be proper for each defendant joined under Rule 20. Thus, if venue is predicated on defendant's residence, both defendants must reside in the same state or venue is improper under the general venue statutes. Likewise, if venue is predicated on the fact that substantial events giving rise to the claim occurred in the district, it should ordinarily have to be true as to all defendants joined under Rule 20 or venue ought to be held improper. Only when the action cannot be brought in any other district is it possible to predicate venue on the ability to assert personal jurisdiction over only one defendant in the district. In the latter

---

208. *See* section C(3)*(c) supra* (discussing the possibility of "pendent" or "supplemental" personal jurisdiction over Rule 19 parties).

cases, difficulties of obtaining personal jurisdiction over Rule 20 defendants who are *not* subject to personal jurisdiction in the district will often prevent the plaintiff from maintaining the action there in spite of the fact that venue is proper.

As was the case with Rule 19 joinder,[209] the possibility exists that when a federal claim is asserted against one Rule 20 defendant and a supplemental state claim is asserted against another defendant, a special federal statute may make venue proper for the federal claim, but not for the state claim. In such a case, the question arises whether the federal courts should recognize a kind of "supplemental" or "pendent" party venue over the defendant against whom the supplemental state claim is asserted. Unlike Rule 19, the text of Rule 20 does not seem to provide explicitly that each joined defendant may make a venue objection. However, as was the case with the issue of "pendent" or "supplemental" personal jurisdiction discussed above, it may be unjustifiable to deprive a defendant as to whom venue is not independently proper of a venue objection in the absence of express statutory or rule authority for doing so. The problem of "supplemental" or "pendent" venue in Rule 20 cases differs from the problem of "supplemental" or "pendent" venue in cases of multiple claim joinder under Rule 18, discussed in Chapter 7.[210] As with personal jurisdiction, a defendant against whom multiple federal and state claims are joined under Rule 18 must defend an action in the forum on the federal claim in any event, and it may not be much of a burden to require the defendant to defend an additional related state claim in the process. However, that situation may not exist for a defendant joined under Rule 20 as to whom no independent basis for proper venue exists. If a doctrine of "supplemental" or "pendent" party venue is recognized by the federal courts, such a defendant might be subjected to substantial burdens against which the general venue statutes were designed to protect.[211]

(c) Rules Enabling Act Issues in the Administration of Rule 20

There are no serious Rules Enabling Act issues with Rule 20. State laws that permit joinder of multiple defendants when Rule 20 does not, or which restrict joinder when it is permitted under Rule 20, are virtually always supported by different views of efficiency in judicial administration than those which motivated federal rulemakers. Such differences in viewpoint about efficiency do not result in any abridgement, enlargement, or modification of substantive rights within the meaning of the Rules Enabling Act. As indicated in subsection *(a)*, above, the ability to join multiple parties can result in important tactical advantages, especially to plaintiffs wishing to join multiple defendants in an action. Furthermore, such

---

209. *See* section C(2)*(c) supra* (discussing the possibility of "pendent" or "supplemental" venue in Rule 19 cases).

210. *See* Chapter 7(C)(2)*(b) supra* (discussing the possibility of "pendent" or "supplemental" venue in cases of multiple claim joinder under Rule 18).

211. The concept of pendent party venue has also infected the state courts. *See Ex parte* State Farm Mut. Auto. Ins. Co., 893 So. 2d 1111 (Ala. 2004) (plaintiff may join the plaintiff's uninsured/underinsured motorist carrier in an action against another motorist; proper venue for the claims against the tortfeasor is also proper venue for claims against insurer under the doctrine of pendent venue—*i.e.*, the rule that venue being good for one is good for all).

tactical differences can conceivably produce ultimate differences in the results of cases as between state and federal courts. However, even under such circumstances, it is hard to believe that tactical differences of this sort amount to more than an "incidental" effect on the substantive rights of parties. Thus, Rule 20 can validly be administered in the face of conflicting state law.[212] Indeed, as suggested in Chapter 5, state efficiency-based joinder rules should probably not be interpreted as in conflict with Rule 20 in the first place, because such rules are virtually never designed to control party joinder in cases outside the courts of the state that created the rules.[213]

Furthermore, if the interpretation of the Rules Enabling Act in the plurality opinion in the *Shady Grove* case, examined in Chapter 5,[214] someday becomes a majority view, Rule 20 would be valid under that view, because the rule is undeniably "rationally classifiable as procedural."

SECTION D. SPECIAL PARTY JOINDER DEVICES

In addition to the basic joinder rules discussed in the previous sections, special party joinder devices are found in every jurisdiction. These devices are (1) impleader, or third-party practice,[215] (2) interpleader,[216] (3) intervention,[217] and (4) class actions.[218]

1. Impleader

(a) History of Impleader

Impleader is a procedure that allows a party to bring into an action a new party who is allegedly liable to the original party for all or part of a claim asserted against the original party in the action. In equity actions all persons who were necessary to a complete determination of the proceeding would be joined in order to prevent a multiplicity of suits. The codes generally adhered to this equity practice and even sought to broaden it.[219] However, when joinder was optional with the plaintiff, the plaintiff could not be forced to add a new party to the action. Consequently, a defendant could not insist on joining a person who was obligated to indemnify the defendant for all or a part of the plaintiff's claim against the defendant.

At common law, a procedure known as *vouching to warranty* was the predecessor to modern impleader or third-party practice. In "vouching to warranty" situations, a defendant who was sued for the recovery of real property could "vouch

---

212. *See* Chapter 5(F)(4) *supra* (discussing the *Burlington Northern* test for Rules Enabling Act validity of Federal Rules of Civil Procedure).

213. *See* Chapter 5(F)(3), *Illustration 5-17* & accompanying text, *supra*.

214. *See* Chapter 5(F)(6) *supra* ("The *Shady Grove* Decision").

215. *See* FED. R. CIV. P. 14.

216. *See* FED. R. CIV. P. 22.

217. *See* FED. R. CIV. P. 24.

218. *See* FED. R. CIV. P. 23-23.2.

219. *See* sections A and B of this chapter *supra*.

in" a person who had given a warranty of title to the defendant. The person "vouched in" then had the opportunity to defend the suit. If the person vouched in refused to defend, and if a judgment ultimately was rendered that the defendant's title was invalid, the defendant could sue the warrantor in a second suit on the warranty. In the second suit, the judgment in the first action would bind the warrantor, provided that the defendant successfully proved the attempt to vouch the warrantor into the first action, the terms of the warranty, and the judgment in the first suit.[220] In nineteenth century England, the "vouching to warranty" practice was expanded to permit a defendant to bring in a third party who was obligated to indemnify the defendant against the plaintiff's claim. Based partly on this expanded procedure, the American states developed their own forms of third-party practice that permitted the joinder of third parties who were obligated to the defendant in whole or in part for the claim being litigated.[221]

The federal courts recognized a right of impleader in admiralty cases in the late nineteenth century.[222] In addition, the federal courts utilized impleader in actions at law prior to 1938 under the Conformity Act whenever the state in which the federal court was sitting had adopted a modern impleader rule.[223] When the Federal Rules of Civil Procedure were adopted in 1938, Rule 14 provided for impleader in appropriate cases brought in the district courts.[224] Rule 14 generally exemplifies modern impleader practice in both the state and federal courts.

(b) Application of Rule 14

Serious problems are posed when a defendant has been held liable on a claim and then must bring a separate suit against a third party who, in theory, is obligated to indemnify the defendant in whole or in part for the amount the defendant must pay under the judgment. The most serious problem is the danger of inconsistent results. Because the indemnitor is not a party to the suit against the defendant, the indemnitor is usually not bound by the judgment in that action. As a result, in the second action against the indemnitor, the defendant in the first action may have to relitigate the issues giving rise to the right of indemnity. Thus, there is a danger that the issues will be determined in a fashion inconsistent with their determination in the first proceeding. Second, even if the issues are determined the same way in both the first and second proceedings, the defendant in the first action is subjected to a useless multiplicity of actions over the same basic matter, with the attendant inconvenience and expense that multiple suits involve. Finally, even if the defendant in the first action is successful in the second action and is ultimately indemnified for the amounts that the defendant has been forced to pay under the first judgment, that success may not come until a substantial period of time has

---

220. *See* 6 CHARLES A. WRIGHT ET AL., FEDERAL PRACTICE AND PROCEDURE: CIVIL § 1441, at 335-37 (3d ed. 2010); Note, *Developments in the Law—Multiparty Litigation in the Federal Courts*, 71 HARV. L. REV. 874, 907 (1958).

221. *See* 6 CHARLES A. WRIGHT ET AL., FEDERAL PRACTICE AND PROCEDURE: CIVIL § 1441, at 336-37 (3d ed. 2010).

222. *See* The Hudson, 15 F. 162 (S.D.N.Y. 1883).

223. *See* 6 CHARLES A. WRIGHT ET AL., FEDERAL PRACTICE AND PROCEDURE: CIVIL § 1441, at 337 (3d ed. 2010).

224. *See* 308 U.S. at 681-82 (1938).

passed between payment of the first judgment and victory in the suit for indemnification. Throughout this time, the defendant in the first action will be deprived of the amount that has been paid to satisfy the judgment.[225]

The general purpose of Rule 14 is to eliminate these problems. Rule 14 permits a defending party to bring in the third person who is obligated to indemnify the defendant. Thus, the indemnity claim can be settled in the same action with the claim giving rise to the right of indemnity. Impleader is permissive, not compulsory. Impleader is available to any defending party, even a plaintiff against whom a counterclaim is asserted.[226] The person initiating the impleader is called the third-party plaintiff. Impleader is accomplished by serving a summons and "third-party complaint" on the third party. Before 1963, Rule 14 required a party seeking impleader to obtain leave of court before serving the summons and third-party complaint.[227] Rule 14 was amended in 1963 to permit the third party to be impleaded without leave of court if the third-party complaint is filed within ten days after the third-party plaintiff serves the original answer. However, the question whether a third-party may be impleaded is still discretionary with the court, even if the third-party complaint is filed within the ten-day period.[228] After the ten-day period, leave of court is still required. In exercising discretion under the rule, the courts will generally permit the impleader if it is within the scope of Rule 14 and will not significantly prejudice the plaintiff or the third-party defendant. "Prejudice" may be shown, for example, when the impleader is filed at a late stage of the proceeding and might delay the trial. Prejudice may also be shown when the impleader would introduce issues unrelated to the original claim. Such issues may excessively complicate the action.[229]

To be within the scope of Rule 14, the third-party plaintiff's claim must be that the third-party defendant is liable to the third-party plaintiff for all or part of the claim asserted against the third-party plaintiff. Typical of this type of claim is a claim for indemnity.

Illustration 8-30. Assume that *P* sues *D* for personal injuries received when *T*, *D's* employee operating *D's* car on *D's* business, collided with *P*. Under the substantive law often applicable to this type of case, if *T's* negligence caused the accident, both *T* and *D* are liable to *P*, and *P* can sue either or both of them for damages. If *D* must pay *P* because of *T's* negligence, *D* is entitled to indemnity from *T*. Therefore, if *P* sues only *D* for *P's* personal injuries, *D* may implead *T* on the indemnity claim under Rule 14. Note, however, that if *D's only* claim against *T* is that *T* owes *D* for damage done to *D's* car due to *T's* negligence, Rule 14 impleader

---

225. *See* 6 CHARLES A. WRIGHT ET AL., FEDERAL PRACTICE AND PROCEDURE: CIVIL § 1442 at 339-41 (3d ed. 2010).

226. *See* FED. R. CIV. P. 14(b).

227. *See* 308 U.S. at 681 (1938).

228. *See* FED. R. CIV. P. 14 advisory committee's note to the 1963 amendment.

229. *See* 6 CHARLES A. WRIGHT ET AL., FEDERAL PRACTICE AND PROCEDURE: CIVIL § 1443, at 348-60 (3d ed. 2010).

is improper. A Rule 14 claim must be dependent on *P's* claim against *D*. A direct claim by *D* against *T* does not meet this requirement.[230]

* * * * *

When a third-party complaint is filed, Federal Rule 5(a) requires that a copy be served on each of the parties to the original action. Rule 14(a)(2)(A)-(B) provides that the third-party defendant shall present any defenses to the third-party plaintiff's claim as provided in Rule 12 and counterclaims against the third-party plaintiff and cross-claims against other third-party defendants as provided in Rule 13. Rule 14(a)(2)(C)-(D) provide that the third-party defendant may assert any defenses that the third-party defendant has to the plaintiff's claim and also may assert any claims against the plaintiff arising out of the same transaction or occurrence as the principal claim in the action. Rule 14(a)(3) further permits the plaintiff to assert claims directly against the third-party defendant when the plaintiff's claims arise out of the transaction or occurrence that is the subject-matter of the principal claim in the action. In the latter event, the third-party defendant again must assert any defenses against the plaintiff's claims as provided in Rule 12 and counterclaims and cross-claims as provided in Rule 13. A third-party defendant also may implead persons who are liable for all or part of the claims asserted against the third-party defendant.

Illustration 8-31. On the facts of *Illustration 8-30*, once *D* has impleaded *T* under Rule 14, *P* can amend the complaint to add a claim directly against *T* for *T's* negligence. In addition, *D* can join with the impleader claim a claim against *T* for damages to *D's* car by virtue of Rule 18(a).[231] Under the terms of Rule 14(a)(2)(D), *T* may also assert a claim directly against *P* for personal injuries received in the accident.

* * * * *

In 2007, the Federal Rules of Civil Procedure, including Rule 14, were restyled to make them easier to read and make the terminology of the rules consistent throughout.[232] Before restyling, Rule 14 stated that "a defending party" as third-party plaintiff may bring in a nonparty who "is or may be liable to the third-party plaintiff for all or part of *the plaintiff's claim* against the third-party plaintiff." Restyled Rule 14 replaces the reference to "the plaintiff's claim" with the phrase "the claim against it" thus making it clear that any defending party may bring in a third-party defendant, not just an original defendant defending against a plaintiff's claim. However, the Advisory Committee did not similarly modify the language of restyled Rule 14(a)(2)(C) & (D), which still refer to a third-party defendant asserting defenses and claims against a plaintiff only and not against any other kind of party, such as a co-defendant asserting a crossclaim against the third-party plaintiff. Nor did the Advisory Committee modify Rule 14(a)(3), which only refers

---

230. *See, e.g.*, Evert v. Finn, No. Civ. A. 98-3293, 1999 WL 397401, 1999 U.S. Dist. LEXIS 9412, (E.D. La. June 15, 1999); Collini v. Wean United, Inc., 101 F.R.D. 408 (W.D. Pa. 1983). *Illustration 8-31, infra*, however, indicates that if *D* possesses a proper Rule 14 claim, Rule 18 authorizes *D* to join with that Rule 14 claim any other claim that *D* possesses against *T*. *See also* State Bd. of Regents. v. Skinner, 267 Kan. 808, 987 P.2d 1096 (1999) (third-party complaint is defective when it seeks an independent judgment against a third-party defendant that is not keyed to any liability of the third-party plaintiff).

231. *See* Chapter 7(C)(1) ("Basic Operation of Federal Rule 18") *supra*.

232. *See* Chapter 1(D)(13) ("'Restyling' the Federal Rules of Civil Procedure") *supra*.

to a plaintiff asserting claims against a third-party defendant, instead of another party (such, again, as a co-defendant) whose claim against the third-party plaintiff prompted the claim against the third-party defendant. This appears to be another instance in which the Advisory Committee failed in its goals by inadvertence or exhaustion. The rule should be interpreted to include within the label "plaintiff" any party whose claim prompted the third-party claim.

(c) Problems of Subject-Matter Jurisdiction, Personal Jurisdiction, and Venue Under Rule 14

Cases involving third-party claims can become complex. These complexities increase when problems of federal subject-matter jurisdiction, venue, and personal jurisdiction are considered.

Illustration 8-32. Assume that *P*, a citizen of State *X*, sues *D*, a citizen of State *Y*. *D* impleads *T*, a citizen of State *Y*, under Federal Rule 14. Under these circumstances, diversity of citizenship exists between the plaintiff, *P*, on the one hand, and *D* and *T*, on the other. However, there is no diversity between the third-party plaintiff, *D*, and the third-party defendant, *T*, because they are both citizens of State *Y*. Nevertheless, the federal courts have traditionally assumed jurisdiction of the impleader claim under the doctrine of ancillary jurisdiction (today supplemental jurisdiction), discussed in Chapter 2.[233] The concept of ancillary jurisdiction is based on the principle that when a federal court obtains jurisdiction of a case, the court obtains jurisdiction of the entire case, not just that part of the case for which there is a specific grant of subject-matter jurisdiction found in Article III and the judicial code. As this concept is applied to impleader cases, subject-matter jurisdiction over the principal claim between the plaintiff and the defendant (the claim asserted by *P* against *D*) gives a federal court ancillary (supplemental) jurisdiction over an impleader claim between the defendant (third-party plaintiff) and the third-party defendant (the claim asserted by *D* against *T*), because the impleader claim is an incidental part of the same case as the principal claim due to its close factual relationship to the principal claim.

* * * * *

For a claim to be within the ancillary (supplemental) jurisdiction of the federal courts, the claim must not only be a part of the same Article III constitutional case or controversy as a claim over which the federal courts have subject-matter jurisdiction. It also must not offend the *statutory* policies of the grant of subject-matter jurisdiction to the federal courts in Title 28 of the *United States Code*. The courts have assumed rather automatically (perhaps too automatically) that impleader claims meet both the constitutional requirements *and* the statutory policies necessary to sustain ancillary jurisdiction.[234] This assumption, however, is not true for all claims that may be asserted under Rule 14. In addition to authorizing the basic impleader claim, Rule 14 also authorizes the plaintiff to assert claims

---

233. *See* Chapter 2(E)(1) *supra* ("The General Nature of Pendent and Ancillary Jurisdiction") and Chapter 7(F) ("Counterclaims and Crossclaims Under the Federal Rules").

234. *See generally* 6 CHARLES A. WRIGHT ET AL., FEDERAL PRACTICE AND PROCEDURE: CIVIL § 1444, at 370-71 (3d ed. 2010).

directly against the third-party defendant if the claims arise out of the same transaction or occurrence as the plaintiff's claim against the defendant.

Illustration 8-33. Assume that *P*, a citizen of State *X*, sues *D*, a citizen of State *Y*. *D* impleads *T*, a citizen of State *X*. There is diversity between *P*, the plaintiff, and *D*, the defendant. There is also diversity between *D*, the third-party plaintiff, and *T*, the third-party defendant. Therefore, because there is complete diversity between all adverse parties, there is no need to resort to the concept of ancillary jurisdiction. However, assume that *P* asserts a claim directly against *T* arising out of the same transaction or occurrence as *P's* claim against *D*. Such a claim is permitted by Rule 14, but is it permitted by 28 U.S.C. § 1332, given the fact that *P* and *C* are both citizens of State *X*?

* * * * *

In 1978, the U.S. Supreme Court decided *Owen Equipment & Erection Co. v. Kroger,*[235] which held that the diversity statute forbids assertion of the plaintiff's claim under the circumstances described in *Illustration 8-33*. To allow the plaintiff's claim against the third-party defendant would be to circumvent the congressional command embodied in 28 U.S.C. § 1332, as interpreted in *Strawbridge v. Curtiss*.[236] The Court indicated that a close factual relationship between the claim over which there is jurisdiction and the putative ancillary claim satisfies the requirements of Article III of the Constitution, but not necessarily the statutory requirements of Title 28. The Court also emphasized that ancillary jurisdiction "typically involves claims by a defending party haled into court against [that party's] will, or by another person whose rights might be irretrievably lost unless [that person] could assert them in an ongoing action in a federal court."[237] This statement indicates that ancillary jurisdiction would still apply to claims asserted directly against the plaintiff by the third-party defendant, as permitted by Rule 14. It also suggests that ancillary jurisdiction might apply to compulsory counterclaims asserted by the plaintiff against a third-party defendant who, by directly asserting a claim against the plaintiff, has put the plaintiff in a defensive position.[238]

In 1990, Congress codified the doctrines of "ancillary" and "pendent" jurisdiction under the label "supplemental jurisdiction" in 28 U.S.C. § 1367(a).[239] However, in 28 U.S.C. § 1367(b), Congress sought to preserve the jurisdictional restrictions of 28 U.S.C. § 1332 from impairment by certain of the multiple party joinder rules. As applied to Rule 14 cases, § 1367(b) prohibits jurisdiction over claims asserted by plaintiffs against persons made parties under Rule 14 who are citizens of the same state as the plaintiffs.[240] Thus, § 1367(b) codifies the holding

---

235. 437 U.S. 365, 98 S. Ct. 2396, 57 L. Ed. 2d 274 (1978).

236. 7 U.S. (3 Cranch) 267, 2 L. Ed. 435 (1806); *see Kroger*, 437 U.S. at 377, 98 S. Ct. at 2404, 57 L. Ed. 2d at 284; Chapter 2(E) *supra* ("Supplemental Jurisdiction").

237. *Kroger*, 437 U.S. at 376, 98 S. Ct. at 2404, 57 L. Ed. 2d at 284.

238. The application of ancillary jurisdiction to compulsory counterclaims and crossclaims, as described in Chapter 7(F)(4)*(b) supra* ("Supplemental (Ancillary) Jurisdiction Over Counterclaims and Crossclaims"), satisfies this aspect of *Kroger*.

239. *See* Chapter 2(E)(4) *supra* ("The Codification of Pendent and Ancillary Jurisdiction").

240. *See* 28 U.S.C. § 1367(b).

of *Owen Equipment & Erection Co. v. Kroger*.[241] However, as discussed in Chapter 2(C)(4)*(e)(i)* & *(ii)*, and in subsections (C)(3)*(c)* and (C)(4)*(b)* of this chapter, discussing supplemental jurisdiction issues under Rules 19 and 20, respectively, the Supreme Court's decision in the *Exxon Mobil* case may have changed the analysis that applies to supplemental jurisdiction in Rule 14 cases in some respects, although it will not alter the results of the cases. Specifically, recall that when defects in diversity of citizenship exist as opposed to defects in jurisdictional amount, the "contamination theory" of *Exxon Mobil* eliminates the possibility of supplemental jurisdiction over claims by plaintiffs against nondiverse defendants. When this is coupled with the traditional practice requiring reassessment by federal courts of subject-matter jurisdiction when a plaintiff serves an amended complaint, discussed in section (C)(4)*(b)* in conjunction with supplemental jurisdiction in Rule 20 cases, this would seem to mean that on the facts of the *Owen Equipment* case and similar cases, § 1367(a) may not be interpreted to allow supplemental jurisdiction over claims by plaintiffs against nondiverse third-party defendants. As was the case with Rule 19 and 20 joinder, this makes the terms of § 1367(b) irrelevant as applied to the defective diversity situation. The only remaining relevance of the § 1367(b) language as applied to plaintiff's claims against persons joined under Rule 14 will be in cases, if any there be, in which the plaintiff amends the complaint to assert a claim against a diverse third-party defendant against whom the plaintiff has a claim that is under $75,000.01 and does not meet the traditional aggregation rules of the diversity statute, discussed in Chapter 2(C)(3)*(g)(ii)*, above.

However, the language of § 1367(b) creates several other problems that the federal courts will have to address. The statute flatly prohibits claims by plaintiffs against persons "made parties under Rule 14" when the restrictions of 28 U.S.C. § 1332 would be violated.[242] But what if a non-diverse third-party defendant asserts a claim directly against the plaintiff as permitted by Rule 14?[243] The language of § 1367(b) could be read to prohibit the plaintiff from asserting a factually related counterclaim against the third-party defendant under these circumstances. This

---

241. *See, e.g.*, ARE Sikeston Ltd. P'ship v. Weslock Nat'l, Inc., 120 F.3d 820 (8th Cir. 1997). After the enactment of § 1367, several courts have upheld supplemental jurisdiction over third-party claims. *See id.*; Estate of Bruce v. City of Middletown, 781 F. Supp. 1013 (S.D.N.Y. 1992); Whitney Nat'l Bank v. Chatelain, No. 91-2432, 1991 WL 213917 at * 5 n.8, 1991 U.S. Dist. LEXIS 15056 at * 16 n.8 (E.D. La. Oct. 15, 1991) (dictum). However, a few courts have shown a willingness to scrutinize third-party claims more carefully to determine whether they arise from the same facts as the principal claim in the action. *See* Fleming Cos. v. Hope Plaza, Inc., No. 90-6323, 1992 WL 30565, 1992 U.S. Dist. LEXIS 2274 (E.D. Pa. Feb. 12, 1992) (alternative holding; third-party claim was improper under Rule 14 and also did not arise out of a common nucleus of operative fact with the principal claim); *In re* Feifer Indus., 141 B.R. 450 (N.D. Ga. 1991) (third-party claim rejected as not sufficiently related to principal claim); *cf.* Molina v. Mallah Org., Inc., 817 F. Supp. 419 (S.D.N.Y. 1993) (defamation claim joined with third-party claim for contribution; third-party claim improper; defamation claim did not arise out of same transaction or occurrence as principal claim, thus no supplemental jurisdiction under § 1367). *But see* Bank Brussels Lambert v. Credit Lyonnais (Suisse) S.A., No. 93 Civ. 6876 (LMM), 1998 WL 91217, 1998 U.S. Dist. LEXIS 2280 (S.D.N.Y. Mar. 3, 1998) (plaintiff asserts federal claim and supplemental state claim against defendant; defendant impleads third-party defendant for indemnity on state claims and joins other claims against third-party defendant under Rule 18, but which post-date events that are the subject of the main action and the Rule 14 claim; court holds supplemental jurisdiction exists over Rule 14 and Rule 18 claims, but without closely examining the relationship between the Rule 18 claims and either the Rule 14 claims or the plaintiff's federal claim).

242. *See* 28 U.S.C. § 1367(b).

243. Rule 14 provides as follows: "The third-party defendant may also assert any claim against the plaintiff arising out of the transaction or occurrence that is the subject matter of the plaintiff's claim against the third-party plaintiff." FED. R. CIV. P. 14(a).

reading would be terribly unfair to the plaintiff. The courts might respond to this problem by preventing nondiverse third-party defendants from asserting claims against the plaintiff, but that also seems unfair. After all, the third-party defendant has no choice whether to be in the action. Consequently, there seems to be no reason to inflict dual proceedings on the third-party defendant with regard to factually related claims possessed against the plaintiff.[244]

The best result would be to interpret the language of § 1367(b) as preventing claims by the plaintiff against the third-party defendant *only* when the third-party defendant does not assert claims against the plaintiff. This interpretation will assure that the policy of § 1367(b)—to prevent evasion of the requirement of the diversity statute by plaintiffs[245]—will be effectuated, while preventing unfairness to the plaintiff, the defendant, and the third-party defendant.[246] Note that this result would comport with the policies of the diversity jurisdiction as they were defined in the *Owen* case, discussed above. In *Owen*, the Supreme Court approved of ancillary jurisdiction on behalf of parties who had been placed in defensive positions in a diversity action and who wished to assert jurisdictionally deficient claims. This describes both the nondiverse third-party defendant's position and the position of a plaintiff against whom a nondiverse third-party defendant asserts a claim.

Illustration 8-34. *P*, a citizen of State *X*, sues *D*, a citizen of State *Y*, in a U.S. District Court in State *Y*. *P* asserts a claim for $500,000 against *D* for personal injuries arising out of an automobile accident occurring in State *Y*. When the accident occurred, *P* was riding as a passenger in a car owned by *P*, but driven by *T*, a citizen of State *X*, and the car collided with a car driven by *D*. *D* impleads *T* in the action under Rule 14. *D* alleges that *T* was negligent and that *T's* negligence contributed to the accident. Under the law of State *Y*, *T* would be liable for all or part of *P's* claim as a joint tortfeasor with *D*. After being impleaded, *T* asserts a claim directly against *P* for personal injuries received in the accident. *T* alleges that *P* negligently maintained the brakes on the automobile in which *P* and *T* were riding. Under these circumstances, *P* should not be prohibited from counterclaiming against *T*, even though *P* and *T* are both citizens of State *X*. *P* has been put in a defensive position by *T's* claim. *P* did not assert a claim directly against *T* until *T*

---

244. Another alternative, even more unpalatable, would be to prevent joinder of third-party defendants altogether when they are citizens of the same state as the plaintiff. This approach, of course, would produce unfairness to the defendant in the action. Indeed, because complete diversity of citizenship might often exist between the defendant and third-party defendant, it would be anomalous to prevent joinder of the third-party defendant in many cases.

245. *See* H.R. REP. NO. 734, 101st Cong., 2d Sess. 29 (1990).

246. *See* Denis F. McLaughlin, *The Federal Supplemental Jurisdiction Statute—A Constitutional and Statutory Analysis*, 24 ARIZ. ST. L.J. 849, 942-49 (1992), and authorities there cited and discussed. *But cf.* Viacom Int'l, Inc. v. Kearney, 212 F.3d 721 (2d Cir. 2000). In *Viacom*, a plaintiff sued a defendant in a diversity action, and the defendant impleaded two third-party defendants. One of the third-party defendants, in turn, impleaded Taylor Forge. The defendant asserted counterclaims against the plaintiff and also moved to dismiss the action on the ground that Taylor Forge was an indispensable party to the counterclaims who could not be joined to them without destroying diversity. The district court dismissed the action, but the court of appeals reversed, holding that because Taylor Forge was already a party to the action, it could assert any counterclaims against the plaintiff that it possessed. The court concluded that § 1367(b) did not preclude Taylor Forge from doing so because it only prohibited plaintiffs' claims that violated the diversity statute, not claims by parties like Taylor Forge who were in defensive positions. However, the court cryptically noted that the case would have been different if the plaintiff had wanted to assert claims against Taylor Forge and could not do so.

first asserted a claim against *P*. Therefore, there is no reason to believe that *P* was attempting to evade the policies of the diversity jurisdiction.

* * * * *

In addition to the interpretive problems discussed above, at least one court has read § 1367(b) to preclude a plaintiff from impleading a nondiverse third-party defendant to indemnify plaintiff on a counterclaim asserted by the defendant. In *Guaranteed Systems, Inc. v. American National Can Co.*,[247] the plaintiff, a contractor, filed suit against American National Can in a North Carolina state court, alleging that American National had failed to pay it for construction work. American National removed the action to federal court on the basis of diversity and asserted a counterclaim against the plaintiff alleging negligence in the performance of the construction work. The plaintiff impleaded a nondiverse subcontractor under Rule 14, asserting claims for indemnity and contribution for any amount that the plaintiff owed to American National as a result of the counterclaim. The district court dismissed the third-party claim, holding that it was prohibited by the terms of § 1367(b). The court stated that "Guaranteed Systems is clearly a plaintiff in a diversity suit asserting a claim against a non-diverse third-party defendant made a party under Rule 14."[248] The court recognized that, if § 1367(b) had not been enacted, the plaintiff would not have been precluded by the Supreme Court's decision in the *Owen Equipment* case, discussed above, from impleading a nondiverse third-party defendant, because *Owen Equipment* only precluded plaintiffs from asserting claims against such third-party defendants impleaded by defendants.[249] Nevertheless, the court felt bound by the "plain terms" of § 1367(b).[250]

As discussed in Chapter 2,[251] the purposes of § 1367(b) were to preserve the policies of the diversity jurisdiction, not to change the results that would have been achieved in diversity actions had the supplemental jurisdiction statute not been enacted. There is little question that prior to the enactment of § 1367(b), ancillary jurisdiction would have existed over the plaintiff's third-party claim in *Guaranteed Systems*, as the court itself recognized. The correct rule in cases like *Guaranteed Systems* in which plaintiffs or other parties seek to employ Rule 14 impleader is that supplemental jurisdiction exists over the impleader claim as long as jurisdiction exists over the claim upon which impleader depends and the two claims form part of the same Article III case or controversy.

Illustration 8-35. *P*, a citizen of State *X*, sues *D*, a citizen of State *Y*, for $500,000 in a U.S. District Court in State *Y*. *D's* answer contains a permissive counterclaim against *P* for $100,000. *P* wants to implead *T*, a citizen of State *X*,

---

247. 842 F. Supp. 855 (M.D.N.C. 1994).

248. *Id.* at 857.

249. *See id.*

250. *See id.*; *cf.* Grimes v. Mazda N. Am. Operations, 355 F.3d 566 (6th Cir. 2004) (defendant's impleader of state agency entitled to Eleventh Amendment immunity did not destroy diversity; under state law, to receive apportionment jury instruction, defendant must assert a claim against third-party defendant, even if the third-party defendant cannot be held liable in the action; in the latter case, the third-party defendant is then dismissed, and the apportionment jury instruction is given).

251. *See* Chapter 2(E)(6) *supra* ("Exceptions to the Scope of Supplemental Jurisdiction in Diversity Cases: Section 1367(b)"). The American Law Institute has proposed extensive revisions of § 1367 to deal with the problems under Rule 14 and other areas.

under Rule 14, on the ground that *T* is liable to *P* for half of any amount that *P* must pay to *D* under the permissive counterclaim. The language in § 1367(b) prohibiting plaintiffs from asserting claims "against persons made parties under Rule 14" should not be read as prohibiting supplemental jurisdiction over Rule 14 claims asserted by plaintiffs. Therefore, *P* should be able to implead *T*.

* * * * *

Earlier sections have examined whether, if "supplemental" or "ancillary" subject-matter jurisdiction is established in an action, the federal courts should also recognize a doctrine of "ancillary" or "supplemental" personal jurisdiction.[252] Those sections concluded that a doctrine of "supplemental" personal jurisdiction would be less justifiable in cases of multiple party joinder than in cases of multiple claim joinder under Rule 18, which was discussed in Chapter 7.[253] The same conclusion is warranted, for the same reasons, in cases of Rule 14 joinder. In fact, in Rule 14 cases, the courts agree that personal jurisdiction must be established independently over third-party defendants.[254]

The result is different with venue, however. "According to [the] existing case law, the statutory venue limitations have no application to Rule 14 claims even if they would require the third-party action to be heard in another district had it been brought as an independent action."[255] As was the case with crossclaims and counterclaims (examined in Chapter 7), this result seems justifiable as an interpretation of the federal venue statutes, which seem aimed at measuring venue only by reference to original claims in the action.[256]

(d) Rules Enabling Act Problems in the Administration of Rule 14

As with claim joinder under Rule 18[257] and party joinder under the other Federal Rules of Civil Procedure discussed in this chapter, there will be cases in which joinder is possible under Rule 14 in a diversity action, but in which joinder of the third-party defendant would not be possible in the courts of the state in which the federal action is brought, which raises the question whether the application of Rule 14 violates the Rules Enabling Act in such cases.

One typical situation in which the Rules Enabling Act issue exists involves a tort action in which the defendant wishes to implead a joint tortfeasor in a federal diversity action for contribution under Rule 14, but state law would require the

---

252. *See* sections C(3)*(c) supra* (discussing supplemental personal jurisdiction in Rule 19 cases) & C(4)*(b) supra* (discussing supplemental personal jurisdiction in Rule 20 cases).

253. *See* Chapter 7(C)(2)*(c)* ("Personal Jurisdiction Restrictions on Joinder") *supra*.

254. *See* 6 CHARLES A. WRIGHT ET AL., FEDERAL PRACTICE AND PROCEDURE: CIVIL § 1445, at 404-06 (3d ed. 2010). In addition to the general unjustifiability of creating a doctrine of supplemental personal jurisdiction in Rule 14 cases, it should be noted that, as with Rule 19, Rule 4(k)(1)(B) contains a provision allowing third-party defendants to be subjected to personal jurisdiction when they are served outside a state and district, but within 100 miles of the place where the federal action is pending. As was the case with Rule 19, the existence of this provision, which demonstrates that federal rulemakers have considered the problem of long-arm jurisdiction over third-party defendants and not extended it further than the 100-mile area, militates against a doctrine of supplemental personal jurisdiction in Rule 14 cases.

255. *See* 6 CHARLES A. WRIGHT ET AL, FEDERAL PRACTICE AND PROCEDURE: CIVIL § 1445, at 407 (3d ed. 2010).

256. *See* Chapter 7(F)(4)*(b)* ("Supplemental (Ancillary) Venue and Personal Jurisdiction Over Counterclaims and Crossclaims") *supra*.

257. *See* Chapter 7(C)(3) *supra* ("Rules Enabling Act Problems Under Rule 18").

defendant to pursue the contribution claim in a separate action after paying the plaintiff more than the defendant's proportionate share of the plaintiff's claim. In this kind of case, it is generally agreed that Rule 14 may be applied notwithstanding the restrictions on joinder existing under state law. The restriction on joinder under state law is not likely to be based on any particular substantive policies, but instead is probably an outgrowth of the historical reluctance in tort cases to compel the joinder of joint tortfeasors.[258] Thus, in the absence of evidence that a particular state joinder restriction is supported by specific substantive policies, permitting joinder under Rule 14 will not undermine any substantive purpose inherent in the restriction. In addition, the broader substantive rights of the parties are fully protected by joinder under Rule 14, as long as the federal courts do not permit a judgment to be enforced against the third-party defendant for contribution unless the liability of the principal defendant to the plaintiff has been determined.[259] Thus, Rule 14 merely accelerates the determination of the third-party defendant's liability, but does not expand it.[260] As a result, Rule 14 should be immunized from any attack on the ground that it would result in an expansion or contraction of the substantive rights of the parties on the merits of the case. Other problems of conflict with state law and Rule 14, as in the case of state laws or enforceable contract provisions under state law that prohibit the joinder of insurers are similar to those discussed in Chapter 7(C)(3), where Rules Enabling Act issues with Rule 18 were examined. The discussion there also applies to Rule 14 joinder issues.

As with other Federal Rules of Civil Procedure dealing with joinder of claims and parties, discussed previously in Chapter 7 and this Chapter, an additional ground for finding Rule 14 valid when it conflicts with state law may someday exist if the plurality opinion's interpretation of the Rules Enabling Act in the *Shady Grove* decision, examined in Chapter 5,[261] ever becomes the majority view of the Court. Under the plurality's return to the *Sibbach* test for rule validity, Rule 14 is rationally classifiable as procedural and thus would be valid in all cases.

2. Interpleader

Interpleader allows a person in possession of money or property against which inconsistent claims are asserted to bring all the adverse claimants before a court in a single proceeding to resolve their claims. Like impleader, it is grounded in the policy of preventing a multiplicity of suits over the same subject matter, thus

---

258. *See* W. PAGE KEETON ET AL., PROSSER AND KEETON ON TORTS § 47, at 327 (5th ed. 1984). However, in cases in which Rule 14 is used to implead an insurer who is obligated under an insurance policy to indemnify the defendant for any amounts the defendant must pay the plaintiff, the same kinds of problems may exist as were discussed in Chapter 7(C)(3), *supra*, with joinder of contingent claims against insurers under Rule 18, when the insurer has contracted with the defendant for immunity from suit until a judgment has been rendered against the defendant, or when a state statute exists that prohibits joinder of the insurer until such time as a judgment has been rendered. In these situations, the Rules Enabling Act problems in Rule 18 cases are identical to those existing under Rule 14. The problems were adequately discussed in Chapter 7.

259. *See, e.g.*, Brown v. Shredex, Inc., 69 F. Supp. 2d 764 (D.S.C. 1999); 6 CHARLES A. WRIGHT ET AL., FEDERAL PRACTICE AND PROCEDURE: CIVIL § 1448, at 453-57 (3d ed. 2010).

260. *See* 6 CHARLES A. WRIGHT ET AL., FEDERAL PRACTICE AND PROCEDURE: CIVIL § 1448, at 453-57 (3d ed. 2010).

261. *See* Chapter 5(F)(6) *supra* ("The *Shady Grove* Decision").

protecting against the attendant inconvenience, expense, and danger of inconsistent results.

(a) History of Interpleader

(i) "Strict" Bills of Interpleader

Interpleader existed at common law in certain kinds of cases to protect a defendant from double liability.[262] Interpleader shifted from the law courts to the equity courts over time, and the remedy ultimately came to be viewed as exclusively equitable.[263] The common-law remedy of interpleader was available only to defendants, but the equitable remedy was also available to plaintiffs beset by multiple claimants.[264] Nevertheless, "strict" technical requirements circumscribed even equitable interpleader and limited its usefulness. The most often quoted summary of these "strict" requirements was made by Professor Pomeroy:

> 1. The same thing, debt, or duty must be claimed by both or all parties against whom the relief is demanded;
> 2. All their adverse titles or claims must be dependent, or be derived from a common source;
> 3. The person asking the relief—the plaintiff—must not have or claim any interest in the subject-matter;
> 4. He must have incurred no independent liability to either of the claimants; that is, he must stand perfectly indifferent between them, in the position merely of a stakeholder.[265]

Illustration 8-36. *S*, a student, has been eating at a college boarding house. *S* made no express agreement with anyone, but expected to pay the standard rates for the meals consumed. A quarrel breaks out between *C-1*, the cook in the boarding house, and *C-2*, the cook's spouse, about which of them owns the house. *C-1* claims that *S* should pay *C-1* $75.00 for the meals *S* has consumed. *C-2* claims that *S* should pay *C-2* $100.00 for the meals consumed. Under Pomeroy's statement of the requirements for interpleader, *S* could not force *C-1* and *C-2* to interplead because

---

262. *See generally* Zechariah Chafee, Jr., *Modernizing Interpleader*, 30 YALE L.J. 814 (1921); Ralph V. Rogers, *Historical Origins of Interpleader*, 51 YALE L.J. 924 (1942).

263. Professor Chafee stated that the shift of interpleader from the law to the equity courts was produced by the introduction of the jury in the common law courts. The jury "demanded a narrow issue and was unsuited to such old practices as interpleader and prohibition." *See* Zechariah Chafee, Jr., *Modernizing Interpleader*, 30 YALE L.J. 814, 822 (1921). Rogers, however, suggests that the shift may have been due to the fact that interpleader at common law was available only to defendants, not as an affirmative remedy, which was "its great weakness." *See* Ralph V. Rogers, *Historical Origins of Interpleader*, 51 YALE L.J. 924, 947-50 (1942).

264. *See* Ralph V. Rogers, *Historical Origins of Interpleader*, 51 YALE L.J. 924, 947-50 (1942).

265. 4 JOHN N. POMEROY, A TREATISE ON EQUITY JURISPRUDENCE § 1322, at 906 (5th ed. 1941); *cf.* St. Mary's Traditional Roman Catholic Church, Inc. v. Eight Hundred, Inc., 779 So. 2d 317 (Fla. Ct. App. 1999) (interpleader improper on the grounds that claimants held not to be claiming the same thing because one asserted a claim to payment based on ownership of property (a bingo hall) and the other asserted the right to payment based on a promissory note given by the church when it purchased the property; in addition, one of the claimants held the church's promissory note as an assignor of the seller of the bingo hall, which was purchased by the church subject to the rights of the other claimant and the plaintiff (the church) was thus not in a position of indifference between the claimants because it preferred that the claimant asserting adverse ownership rights lose); Southern Gen. Ins. Co. v. Crews, 253 Ga. App. 765, 560 S.E.2d 331 (2002) (insurer of insureds killed in automobile accident not entitled to petition for interpleader because of conflicting claims by the representatives of the insureds; claim did not involve multiple claimants to the same stake and insurer could not be held liable for more than policy limits).

the "same thing, debt, or duty" is not being claimed by all the claimants. *C-1* and *C-2* are claiming different amounts.[266]

Illustration 8-37. *S* is in possession of land. *C-1* claims title to the land under a deed and claims that *S* owes *C-1* $1,000 as the value of *S's* use and occupation of the land. *C-2* claims title to the same land by adverse possession and also claims that *S* owes *C-2* $1,000 as the value of *S's* use and occupation of the land. Under Pomeroy's statement of the requirements for interpleader, *S* could not force *C-1* and *C-2* to interplead. The titles of the claimants are not derived from a common source. *C-1* claims under a deed. *C-2* claims by virtue of adverse possession.

Illustration 8-38. *S Insurance Co.* issues a policy of automobile insurance to *A*. Subsequently, *A* is involved in an automobile accident with *C-1* and *C-2*, both of whom are injured in the accident. *C-1* and *C-2* both claim the $100,000 face amount of the insurance policy. *A's* negligence is conceded by everyone, but *S* refuses to pay the $100,000 on the ground that the policy issued to *A* does not cover the accident. *S* also wants to interplead *C-1* and *C-2*, so that *S* will not suffer double liability if *S's* position about the policy's coverage turns out to be unfounded. Under Pomeroy's statement of the requirements of interpleader, *S* may not force *C-1* and *C-2* to interplead. The stakeholder (*S*), is claiming an interest in the subject matter. *S* is disputing liability on the policy.

Illustration 8-39. *S Insurance Co.* issued a policy of fire insurance to *A*. Subsequently, a fire destroyed the insured property. The *C-1* loan company, a mortgagee of the property, claims that *S* should pay *C-1* the proceeds of the policy. *C-1* instituted a suit against *S* to recover the proceeds. *S* settled the suit with *C-1* and agreed to pay the proceeds of the policy to *C-1* provided that *C-1's* action against *S* was dismissed on the merits. *C-2* loan company, a creditor of *A*, then claimed the proceeds of the policy as the result of a judgment against *A* prior to *S's* settlement with *C-1*. *S*, which has not yet paid the proceeds to *C-1*, wants to commence an interpleader proceeding against *C-1* and *C-2*. Under Pomeroy's statement of the requirements for interpleader, *S* may not force *C-1* and *C-2* to interplead. *S* is potentially liable independently to *C-1* under the settlement agreement. In addition, the "common source" requirement may be violated because *C-1* is claiming under a mortgage and *C-2* is claiming as a judgment creditor. The "same debt" requirement may also be violated for this last reason.

(ii) Bills "in the Nature of Interpleader"

The restrictions summarized by Pomeroy applied to a "strict" bill of interpleader. However, in addition to the strict bill, a bill "in the nature of interpleader" existed, which could be used by a "stakeholder" threatened with double liability. The stakeholder had to show an independent basis for equitable jurisdiction—for example, a stakeholder's suit for reformation of a contract. If such an independent basis existed, the requirements of the strict bill were not rigidly enforced. However, a good deal of confusion existed about the difference between

---

266. *See* Zechariah Chafee, *Modernizing Interpleader*, 30 YALE L.J. 814, 824 (1921).

a "strict" bill and a "bill in the nature of interpleader." It has been suggested that there was no real difference except as to whether the restrictions of a strict bill would be applied or not.[267] This suggestion was undoubtedly true because even in cases in which a strict bill was appropriate, the courts tended to honor Pomeroy's restrictions "in name only."[268] In addition, it should also be noted that some courts do not insist that the stakeholder be faced with a threat of double liability for interpleader. For example, some courts recognize that so-called "pie-slicing" interpleader is appropriate when the stakeholder seeks to assure that a limited fund (the "pie") is fairly apportioned ("sliced") among multiple claimants.[269]

(iii) Interpleader in the State Courts

In state courts, the action of interpleader is usually provided for by statute or court rule. The Field Code, as amended in 1851, so provided in the second paragraph of § 122.[270] Curiously, the Field Code provision limited interpleader to defendants only, as at common law, while extending the remedy to claims against a fund, as in equity. The section also seemed to require that the claims relate to the same fund or thing.[271] This codification may well have impeded reform of interpleader in the states, because many code states copied the Field Code provision more or less verbatim, and some states still retain the provision more or less in this strict form.[272] Other states have modernized interpleader significantly.[273]

(b) Personal Jurisdiction Problems in Interpleader

The primary difficulty confronting American courts in interpleader cases was their inability to secure personal jurisdiction over adverse claimants to the money or property that was the subject of the dispute. In *New York Life Insurance Co. v. Dunlevy*,[274] the U.S. Supreme Court held that interpleader proceedings were

---

267. *See* Geoffrey C. Hazard Jr. & Myron Moskovitz, *An Historical and Critical Analysis of Interpleader*, 52 CAL. L. REV. 706, 745-49 (1964).

268. *See* 7 CHARLES A. WRIGHT ET AL., FEDERAL PRACTICE AND PROCEDURE: CIVIL § 1701, at 526 (3d ed. 2001).

269. *See, e.g.*, Lawhorne v. Employers Ins. Co., 343 Md. 111, 680 A.2d 518 (1996) (pie-slicing interpleader proper). However, it would seem that the declaratory judgment procedure, discussed below, would be the preferable procedure to employ in "pie-slicing" cases when it is available. *See* subsection *(h) infra* (discussing the declaratory judgment procedure as an alternative to interpleader); *cf.* Kearny Cnty. Hosp. v. Allstate Ins. Co., 38 Kan. App. 2d 641, 170 P.3d 900 (2007) (automobile liability insurer that brought interpleader action against accident victims to fairly apportion policy proceeds should have named hospitals as claimants in action; failure to do so meant that hospitals could recover against insurer under hospital lien statute in separate action).

270.

> A defendant, against whom an action is pending upon a contract, or for specific, real, or personal property, may at any time before answer, upon affidavit, that a person not a party to the action, and without collusion with him, makes against him a demand for the same debt, or property, upon due notice to such person, and the adverse party apply to the court for an order to substitute such person in his place, and discharge him from liability to either party on his depositing in court the amount of the debt, or delivering the property, or its value, to such person as the court may direct; and the court may, in its discretion, make the order.

Act of July 10, 1851, ch. 479, § 122, 1851 N.Y. Laws 876, 883.

271. *See* Geoffrey C. Hazard Jr. & Myron Moskovitz, *An Historical and Critical Analysis of Interpleader*, 52 CAL. L. REV. 706, 748-49 (1964).

272. *See* NEB. REV. STAT. § 25-325 (1995) (repealed 2003).

273. *See, e.g.*, CAL. CODE CIV. PROC. § 386 (West 2004).

274. 241 U.S. 518, 36 S. Ct. 613, 60 L. Ed. 1140 (1916).

"in personam" in nature and required personal service of process on the adverse claimants within the state. The general effect of *Dunlevy* was that a stakeholder who was subject to personal jurisdiction in a state where one of the claimants resided, but who could not obtain personal jurisdiction over all the other claimants in the state where the property that was the subject of the claims was located, could not escape the threat of double liability. After *Dunlevy*, an interpleader proceeding could not be treated as an in rem proceeding to settle the adverse claims, and the nonresident claimants could not be subjected to personal jurisdiction if they could not be served within the state. However, if the stakeholder was subject to personal jurisdiction in the claimants' home states, the stakeholder could be sued in separate actions and potentially lose all the actions.[275]

It is unlikely that the *Dunlevy* restriction still exists under the "minimum contacts test" of *International Shoe Co. v. Washington*.[276] The modern constitutional test has broadened the authority of the states to subject adverse claimants to personal jurisdiction in the state where the property that is the subject of the claims is located. In such cases, the adverse claimants will usually have minimum contacts with the state in which the action is brought. If they do not, jurisdiction would only exist if the Supreme Court someday approves of "jurisdiction by necessity."[277]

(c) "Statutory" Interpleader in Federal Courts

Even before *International Shoe* broadened the ability of the states to assert jurisdiction over nonresidents, Congress had extended the authority of federal courts over interstate interpleader cases to alleviate the *Dunlevy* problem. In response to the problem created by the *Dunlevy* case for multi-state businesses like insurance companies, Congress enacted interpleader statutes in 1917, 1925, 1926, and 1936.[278]

Section 1335 of Title 28 of the *United States Code* confers special subject-matter jurisdiction on federal courts in interpleader actions. A jurisdictional amount in controversy of only $500 must be involved in the action. Furthermore, jurisdiction exists if there are two or more adverse claimants of diverse citizenship as defined in § 1332 of Title 28. Thus, the citizenship of the stakeholder is irrelevant under § 1335. Two or more claimants can be citizens of the same state, as long as one claimant is a citizen of some other state.[279] Section 1335 also eliminates the rigid requirements of a strict bill in interpleader by stating that an action "of interpleader or in the nature of interpleader" may be entertained even though the titles of the claimants do not have a common origin, or are not identical,

---

275. *See* Chapter 3(B)(1)*(a)* *supra* ("Affirmative Principles of In Rem Jurisdiction") (discussing the *Dunlevy* case).

276. 326 U.S. 310, 66 S. Ct. 154, 90 L. Ed. 95 (1945); *see* Chapter 3(B)(1)*(a)* ("Affirmative Principles of In Rem Jurisdiction") *supra*; Chapter 3(D) ("The Development of Modern Restrictions on State-Court Jurisdiction: The Minimum Contacts Test") *supra*; Chapter 3(E) ("The Status of the Territorial Rules of Jurisdiction After *International Shoe*") *supra*.

277. *See* Chapter 3(I) ("Jurisdiction by Necessity").

278. *See* 7 CHARLES A. WRIGHT ET AL., FEDERAL PRACTICE AND PROCEDURE: CIVIL § 1701, at 526-32 (3d ed. 2001). The current version of these federal interpleader statutes is found in §§ 1335, 1397, and 2361 of Title 28 in the *United States Code*.

279. *See* 28 U.S.C. § 1335(a).

but are adverse and independent of one another.[280] This language abolishes the "common source" restriction and the "same debt" restriction. Although it is unclear from the wording of the statute, the requirement that the stakeholder be "disinterested" has also been abolished. In part, the section achieves this result by authorizing an action "in the nature of interpleader." Historically, however, a bill in the nature of interpleader required an independent ground of equity jurisdiction. The federal courts have generally eroded this requirement,[281] probably because of the merger of law and equity by the Federal Rules of Civil Procedure. The only traditional restriction that remains in doubt under § 1335 is the requirement that the stakeholder not have incurred any independent liability to one of the claimants. The cases are split on whether this requirement remains under the statute, but the trend is to reject it. The reasoning seems to be that the drafters of the 1936 version of the statute viewed the no-independent-liability requirement as merely a special application of the "common source" rule.[282]

In addition to a special grant of subject-matter jurisdiction, special provisions for venue and service of process for actions brought under § 1335 also exist. Section 1397 of Title 28 provides that venue in an action under § 1335 is proper in any district where one or more of the claimants resides.[283] Section 2361 provides for nationwide service of process on all claimants. It also provides that the district court may restrain the claimants from instituting any proceeding in any state or federal court affecting the property in the interpleader action.[284]

As noted in Chapter 3, the traditional assumption was that Congress had absolute power to give the federal courts nationwide long-arm jurisdiction in any case, without the same kinds of constitutional restrictions that apply to state legislatures under the Fourteenth Amendment.[285] This assumption was based on the territorial power theory of *Pennoyer v. Neff*. The idea was that the power of a state legislature was limited by the territorial boundaries of the state under the Fourteenth Amendment. The power of Congress, however, was limited under the Fifth Amendment only by the territorial boundaries of the United States. When the *International Shoe* line of cases substituted a constitutional test that focused on the burdens of the place of action on the defendant for the territorial power theory of *Pennoyer*, the traditional assumption that applied to Congress' power under the Fifth Amendment became questionable. When confronted with this issue, the Supreme Court could hold that Congress cannot enact nationwide long-arm statutes for the federal courts which impose unreasonable burdens on defendants.[286] If this

---

280. *See* 28 U.S.C. § 1335(b).

281. *See* 7 CHARLES A. WRIGHT ET AL., FEDERAL PRACTICE AND PROCEDURE: CIVIL § 1701, at 530-31 (3d ed. 2001).

282. *See id.* § 1706, at 561-62.

283. *See* 28 U.S.C. § 1397; *see also* Carolina Cas. Ins. Co. v. Mares, 826 F. Supp. 149 (E.D. Va. 1993) (actions of statutory interpleader need not be brought in a district designated in § 1391(b); section 1391(b) limits venue "except as otherwise provided by law"; in statutory interpleader, § 1391(b) must yield to § 1397).

284. *See* 28 U.S.C. § 2361. *See generally* David B. Levendusky, Annotation, *Federal Interpleader Proceeding as In Rem or In Personam in Context of Problem of Service of Process Upon Particular Claimant*, 17 A.L.R. FED. 447 (1973).

285. *See* Chapter 3(L) ("Special Problems of Amenability to Process in Federal Court") *supra*.

286. *See id.* (discussing lower federal court decisions which hold that the Fifth Amendment contains standards protecting the defendant from burdensome litigation similar to those imposed by the Fourteenth Amendment on the states).

result occurs, the long-arm jurisdiction provided for under § 2361 will have to be applied with a view to the contacts between the claimants and the location of the action.

However, the Supreme Court's decision in *Burnham v. Superior Court*[287] may make it more likely that the traditional view of the power of Congress will prevail. If the Court adopts Justice Scalia's position in *Burnham*, the critical factor may be that the longstanding assumption that Congress' power to confer nationwide jurisdiction on the federal courts is absolute. That traditional assumption is still accepted by many lower courts. Thus, continued acceptance by the courts along with the historical pedigree of the rule may serve to validate it. Even if the Court adopts the minimum contacts analysis advocated in Justice Brennan's opinion, absolute congressional power may still be validated. As noted in Chapter 3, the traditional acceptance of the rule may receive enough weight in the analysis to sustain its validity, or other factors such as the procedural mechanisms available in the federal courts to alleviate the burdens of suit in a particular action may result in its preservation.[288]

Illustration 8-40. *S*, a citizen of State *X*, is in possession of a $100,000 fund of money claimed by *C-1*, a citizen of State *Y*, and *C-2*, a citizen of State *Z*. *S* commences an action of interpleader against *C-1* and *C-2* in a U.S. District Court in State *Y*. *C-1* is personally served with process in State *Y*. *C-2* is served with process in State *Z* pursuant to 28 U.S.C. § 2361. Subject-matter jurisdiction is proper under 28 U.S.C. § 1335, because *C-1* and *C-2* are citizens of different states. Venue is proper under 28 U.S.C. § 1397 because the action was brought in a district where one of the claimants (*C-1*) resides. Statutory personal jurisdiction is proper under 28 U.S.C. § 2361. However, if *C-2* has no contacts, ties, or relations with State *Y*, the constitutional restrictions that exist under the Due Process Clause of the Fifth Amendment on the power of Congress to confer personal jurisdiction on the U.S. District Courts may be violated.[289]

(d) "Rule" Interpleader in Federal Courts

In addition to the special form of "statutory" interpleader provided in §§ 1335, 1397, and 2361 of Title 28 of the *United States Code*, federal "rule" interpleader also exists under Rule 22 of the Federal Rules of Civil Procedure. "Rule" interpleader differs from "statutory" interpleader (under § 1335) in several respects. Subject-matter jurisdiction in actions under Rule 22 must be found in the general grants of subject-matter jurisdiction in Title 28 of the *United States Code*. Thus, a "federal question" under 28 U.S.C. § 1331 or diversity of citizenship under

---

287. 495 U.S. 604, 110 S. Ct. 2105, 109 L. Ed. 2d 631 (1990). The *Burnham* decision is discussed in detail in Chapter 3(E)(2) ("Transient Presence Jurisdiction") *supra*.

288. *See* Chapter 3(E)(2) *supra* ("Transient Presence Jurisdiction"); Chapter 3(G)(1) *supra* ("Cases to Which the Minimum Contact Test Applies"); Chapter 3(G)(2)*(b)(iv) supra* ("The Reasonableness Test"); Chapter 3(L)(1) *supra* ("The Constitutional Standard Under Federal Long-Arm Statutes and Rules").

289. However, it may be possible, as discussed below, for *S* to commence an action of "rule" interpleader in some other federal court that would satisfy all constitutional requirements.

28 U.S.C. § 1332 usually must be present.[290] When diversity of citizenship is the sole basis of jurisdiction, more than $75,000 must be in controversy. Furthermore, complete diversity of citizenship must exist between the stakeholder on the one hand and all the claimants on the other.[291] In addition, actions under Rule 22 are governed by the general venue provision, 28 U.S.C. § 1391. Thus, venue is proper in rule interpleader actions only in a district where (1) one of the defendants resides, if all defendants reside in the same state, (2) a substantial part of the events or omissions giving rise to the claim occurred, or a substantial part of property that is the subject of the action is situated, or (3) personal jurisdiction may be obtained over any defendant, if there is no other district in which the action may be brought.[292] Personal jurisdiction in actions under Rule 22 must be acquired in the ordinary fashion provided in Rule 4. When nonresident claimants are involved, the state in which the district court is sitting will usually have to have a long-arm statute of some sort permitting jurisdiction to be asserted over the claimants consistent with the Fourteenth Amendment.[293]

Although the subject-matter jurisdiction, venue, and personal jurisdiction restrictions on statutory interpleader are generally more liberal than the restrictions on rule interpleader, circumstances exist in which rule interpleader is available and statutory interpleader is not. For example, subject-matter jurisdiction is proper in statutory interpleader cases only when two or more claimants are citizens of different states. Thus, if diversity exists between the stakeholder and the claimants, but not between the claimants, only rule interpleader is available. Likewise, if the stakeholder wishes to bring the action in a district where none of the claimants resides—for example, where the events giving rise to the claims occurred—rule interpleader must be used because of the venue restrictions of § 1397.[294] Finally, 28 U.S.C. § 2361 only permits service of the claimants in "the respective districts where the claimants reside or may be found." Therefore, if one or more claimants reside outside the United States and cannot be "found" in a district, § 2361 may not be used to assert personal jurisdiction over the claimant. Rule interpleader might still be available, however, by serving process on the claimant in one of the ways provided in Federal Rule 4.

Illustration 8-41. Assume the same facts as *Illustration 8-40*, with the additional fact that the events giving rise to the claims of *C-1* and *C-2* to the fund of money occurred entirely in State *Q*. If *S* wants to institute an action of federal interpleader in State *Q*, *S* can probably do so, assuming that State *Q* has an

---

290. *See* Commercial Union Ins. Co. v. United States, 999 F.2d 581 (D.C. Cir. 1993); *see also* Truck-A-Tune, Inc. v. Re, 23 F.3d 60 (2d Cir. 1994) (statutory interpleader improper because of interaction between "permanent resident alien" language of § 1332(a) and provisions governing representatives of estates in § 1332(c)(2); Rule 22 interpleader proper because complete diversity existed between stakeholder and claimants).

291. *See* Chapter 2(D)(1) *supra* ("Complete Diversity Requirement").

292. *See* Chapter 4(C) *supra* ("Venue in Federal Courts").

293. *See* Chapter 3(K) *supra* ("Service of Process"); Chapter 3(L) *supra* ("Special Problems of Amenability to Process in Federal Court").

294. *Cf.* Carolina Cas. Ins. Co. v. Mares, 826 F. Supp. 149 (E.D. Va. 1993) (section 1391 must yield to § 1397 in statutory interpleader actions).

appropriate long-arm statute that can be utilized under Rule 4.[295] Subject-matter jurisdiction is proper under 28 U.S.C. § 1332 because complete diversity of citizenship exists between *S*, on the one hand, and all of the claimants, on the other. The jurisdictional amount requirement is satisfied because the amount of the fund is $100,000. Venue is proper under 28 U.S.C. § 1391 because the action is brought in the district where all the events giving rise to the claim occurred. The Fourteenth Amendment restrictions on the authority of State *Q* to assert personal jurisdiction over the claimants are probably satisfied by the fact that the events giving rise to the claim occurred entirely in State *Q*. Therefore, minimum contacts probably exist between the claims and the claimants and State *Q*. *S* may also be able to maintain an action in the state where *S* resides—State *X*. Although the 1990 amendments to 28 U.S.C. § 1391(a) generally eliminated the ability of a plaintiff to predicate venue in the district where the plaintiff resides,[296] here the property that is the subject of the action is located in State *X*, where *S* lives. Thus, venue is proper under 28 U.S.C. § 1391(b)(2) in the district in State *X* where the fund is located. Furthermore, as observed in Chapter 3, while *Shaffer v. Heitner*[297] restricted the ability to assert personal jurisdiction over defendants based on "quasi in rem" jurisdiction (where ownership of property by the defendant in the state is not related to the claim), the Court was careful to preserve the authority of the state where property is located to adjudicate direct claims to the property.[298] Thus, if State *X* possesses an appropriate long-arm statute, the minimum contacts test may well be satisfied by an assertion of personal jurisdiction over *C-1* and *C-2* to settle their claims to the fund in that state.

* * * * *

Like statutory interpleader, Federal Rule 22 abolishes the requirements of the strict bill of interpleader. Rule 22(a)(1)(A) provides that actions under Rule 22 are not objectionable even though "the claims of the several claimants, or the titles on which their claims depend, lack a common origin or are adverse and independent rather than identical. Rule 22(a)(1)(B) provides that it also does not matter that the plaintiff denies liability in whole or in part to any or all of the claimants."[299] Thus, this language abolishes the "common-source," "same-debt," and "disinterested stakeholder" requirements. Some courts have held that the language allowing the plaintiff (stakeholder) to aver that there is no liability to one or more of the claimants abolishes the requirement that the stakeholder have incurred no independent liability to any of the claimants.[300] This result seems questionable. The language in Rule 22 seems to be a direct attempt only to abolish the "disinterested stakeholder" requirement. However, as suggested in the discussion of 28 U.S.C.

---

295. *S* may be able to commence an action of interpleader in state or federal court in State *Q*. If *S* wants to commence an action of state interpleader, *S* will have to comply with whatever restrictions State *Q* places on the action of interpleader under its own law, and State *Q* will have to have a long-arm statute that applies to the facts of the case.

296. *See* Chapter 4(C)(1) *supra* ("Plaintiff's Residence as Proper Venue").

297. 433 U.S. 186, 97 S. Ct. 2569, 53 L. Ed. 2d 683 (1977).

298. *See Shaffer*, 433 U.S. at 207-08, 97 S. Ct. at 258-82, 53 L. Ed. 2d at 699-700; *see also* Chapter 4(E)(1) *supra* ("Quasi in Rem and Related Jurisdictional Doctrines").

299. FED. R. CIV. P. 22.

300. *See* 7 CHARLES A. WRIGHT ET AL., FEDERAL PRACTICE AND PROCEDURE: CIVIL § 1706, at 563 (3d ed. 2001).

§ 1335, above, the no-independent-liability requirement may simply be a special application of the "common-source" requirement. If so, the abolition of the "common-source" restriction by Rule 22 will also have abolished the no-independent-liability requirement.

(e) The Effect of the Supplemental Jurisdiction Statute on Interpleader Jurisdiction

One interesting question is whether the supplemental jurisdiction statute has had any effect on interpleader practice in the federal courts. Considering federal question jurisdiction first, the statute will have no effect on jurisdiction under 28 U.S.C. § 1335 because jurisdiction under that statute is based entirely on diversity of citizenship. Obviously, if all of the claims to the money or property in question arise under federal law, federal question jurisdiction would exist in a Rule 22 interpleader case without the need to invoke the supplemental jurisdiction statute. Thus, in federal question cases, the only situation that could be affected by the supplemental jurisdiction statute is one in which at least one claim to the property arises under federal law and other claims arise under state law, with diversity of citizenship not existing between the parties to the action. Under the claim-specific interpretation of § 1367(a) discussed in Chapter 2(C)(4)*(e)(i)*, above, federal question jurisdiction would exist over the federal claim under § 1331, and supplemental jurisdiction would exist over the state claim by virtue of § 1367.[301]

Note that in the absence of § 1367(a), no jurisdiction would probably exist over the state claim in the example given above, because the claim would represent an example of "pendent" or "supplemental" party jurisdiction, which *Finley v. United States*, discussed in Chapter 2(C)(4)*(c)*, held was not permissible under statutes like § 1331 and which § 1367(a) was designed to overrule. Note also, however, that for supplemental jurisdiction to exist, the federal and state claims would have to be closely enough related to fall within the same Article III case or controversy as required by § 1367(a), which will probably mean that a factual relationship will have to exist between the federal and state claims.[302] As noted in the preceding subsection, Rule 22 abolishes the common source requirement for interpleader. It is possible to reason that the relationship between the federal question and state claims might not meet the case or controversy requirement if they do not arise from a common source, because the factual relationship between the claims would not be sufficient. However, the preferable conclusion is that the claims fall within the same constitutional case even if they do not arise from a common source, because they are claims to the same property.

Turning to interpleader based on diversity jurisdiction, the first point to make is that § 1367(b) does not exclude from the supplemental jurisdiction Rule 22 claims over which supplemental jurisdiction exists under § 1367(a). Unlike the

---

301. The cases subsequent to § 1367(a) generally support this interpretation, but without citation to the statute itself. *See* Commercial Union Ins. Co. v. United States, 999 F.2d 581 (D.C. Cir. 1993); Blackmon Auctions, Inc. v. Van Buren Truck Ctr., Inc., 901 F. Supp. 287 (W.D. Ark. 1995).

302. As discussed in Chapter 2(C)(4)*(e)(iii)*, an argument can be made, contrary to the existing dicta in U.S. Supreme Court cases, that no factual relationship between federal and state claims should be necessary to satisfy Article III, but that even if this is so, § 1367(a) should be construed to require such a relationship.

"Rule 20 gap," which was discussed in section (C)(4)*(b)*, above, and unlike the omission of a reference to Rule 23 from § 1367(b), which is discussed in section (D)(4)*(c)*, below, the omission of a reference to Rule 22 in § 1367(b) does not seem unintentional. It is likely that the drafters of the statute believed that there would be no consequences from such an omission because of the existence of § 1335, which creates jurisdiction based on incomplete diversity of citizenship between any two claimants. Thus, between Rule 22 interpleader under § 1332 and statutory interpleader under § 1335, all cases of interpleader depending on diversity of citizenship would be covered.

Note, however, that in a case of Rule 22 interpleader, the combined effect of § 1367(a) & (b) under the claim specific interpretation of the statute discussed in Chapter 2(C)(4)*(f)* would be to create supplemental jurisdiction over a claim by a nondiverse claimant in a case that also contains a claim by a diverse claimant that exceeds $75,000. Although jurisdiction in such a case would also exist under § 1335, the effect of the supplemental jurisdiction statute in this kind of case might be to broaden the venue in which an interpleader action could be brought. If the action is brought under § 1335, venue would be proper under § 1397 in a district in which one of the claimants resides. As observed in Chapter 4(C)(10), discussing special venue provisions, sometimes such provisions broaden and sometimes they narrow venue under the general venue statutes. If § 1397 is interpreted to be the exclusive venue provision for statutory interpleader under § 1335, then § 1391(b)(2) could not be used to predicate venue where the property that is the subject of the action is located when jurisdiction is predicated only on that section of the Judicial Code. However, if the stakeholder can use Rule 22, § 1332, and § 1367(a) to establish subject-matter jurisdiction, venue would be proper under the general venue statute, 28 U.S.C. § 1391(b)(2), and the stakeholder could sue in a district in which the property that is the subject of the action is situated, which would be impossible under § 1335 unless that district also happens to be the residence of one of the claimants. Thus, while § 1367 may have no net effect on subject-matter jurisdiction in interpleader actions, it might broaden the available venues in which interpleader actions can be brought.

Of course, today, whenever supplemental jurisdiction is examined in conjunction with the general grant of diversity jurisdiction in § 1332, one must take into account the possible effect of the Supreme Court's decision in the *Exxon Mobil* decision, discussed in Chapter 2(C)(4)*(e)(i)* & *(ii)* and in the preceding sections of this chapter examining supplemental jurisdiction in Rules 14, 19, and 20 joinder situations. It is possible that the Court might apply the "contamination" theory of *Exxon Mobil* to a Rule 22 action by a stakeholder against one diverse and one non-diverse claimant in which jurisdiction would be appropriate under § 1332 over the diverse claimant's claim and supplemental jurisdiction would be necessary over the non-diverse claimant's claim.[303] This might be true even though jurisdiction would also exist under § 1335. If the contamination theory applies to prevent supplemental jurisdiction in Rule 22 interpleader cases based on diversity, the general venue

---

303. Since diversity in rule interpleader actions under § 1332 requires complete diversity between the stakeholder on the one hand and all the claimants on the other, it is difficult to see why the contamination theory of *Exxon Mobil* would not apply.

provision, § 1391(b)(2), would not be available to the stakeholder unless the language of § 1391(b)(2) providing for venue in civil actions generally applies to the grant of jurisdiction in § 1335 as well as to the grant in § 1332, thus allowing the stakeholder to sue in the district where the property that is the subject of the action is located.

Illustration 8-42. *S*, a citizen of State *X*, possesses property located in the District of State *X*, where *S* resides. *C-1*, a citizen of State *Y*, claims the property, as does *C-2*, a citizen of State *X*. The property is worth $100,000. Under these circumstances, *S* can sue in a federal interpleader action under 28 U.S.C. § 1335, because diversity of citizenship exists between the claimants in the action. However, if *S* sues under § 1335, the action would have to be brought either in the district where *C-1* or the district where *C-2* resides, if §1397 is the exclusive venue provision applicable to § 1335 actions. If *S* brings a Rule 22 interpleader action, predicating jurisdiction on §§ 1332 and § 1367(a), with supplemental jurisdiction existing over *C-2's* claim, the action may be brought under 28 U.S.C. § 1391(b)(2) in the District of State *X* in which *S* resides.[304] However, this probably cannot be done after *Exxon Mobil.* Thus, the remaining possibility for the stakeholder is that § 1391(b)(2) may be interpreted to be applicable to interpleader actions under § 1335 as well as to such actions under § 1332. This would allow the stakeholder to bring the action in the district where the property is located as well as the district in which one of the claimants resides.[305]

(f) Rules Enabling Act Issues with Rule 22

Federal Rule 22 does not pose any serious issues of rule validity under the Rules Enabling Act. As with Rule 20, the ability to maintain federal interpleader when state law would forbid interpleader, or the inability to maintain interpleader under Rule 22 when state law would allow interpleader, involves no more than differences in procedural philosophy between the federal and state systems. These differences impose only tactical burdens and cannot be said to affect substantive rights seriously.[306] Furthermore, as in the case of other claim and party joinder rules discussed in this chapter and Chapter 7, if the plurality opinion in the *Shady Grove*

---

304. One federal court has held that "28 U.S.C. § 1367 does not apply to interpleader as the language of that statute refers only to 'Rule 14, 19, 20, or 24' " and "28 U.S.C. § 1367 may not be . . . used to limit the scope of Rule 22." *See* 6247 Atlas Corp. v. Marine Ins. Co., 155 F.R.D. 454, 465 n.7 (S.D.N.Y. 1994) (dictum; stakeholder was diverse from claimants and jurisdictional amount was satisfied). This statement is incorrect, because the omission of a reference to Rule 22 from § 1367(b) does not limit the scope of Rule 22 interpleader, but potentially expands it. The statement is, however, typical of the confusion that § 1367 has produced. In Mark E. Mitchell, Inc. v. Charleston Library Society, 114 F. Supp. 2d 259 (S.D.N.Y. 2000) (the consignor of a rare document sued the consignee of the document and the Library Society seeking an order directing the return of the document to the consignor. The consignee served an answer containing a counterclaim and a crossclaim for interpleader. The interpleader action was predicated on §§ 1335 & 2361 in order to obtain an injunction against an action pending in another district. However, none of the claimants resided in the district. The court, nevertheless, held that ancillary venue was proper over the interpleader claim.

305. *See also* Adam Hofmann, Comment, *Blurring Lines: How Supplemental Jurisdiction Unknowingly Gave the World Ancillary Personal Jurisdiction,* 38 U. SAN FRAN. L. REV. 809 (2004) (discussing the effect of the supplemental jurisdiction statute on crossclaims in statutory interpleader actions and arguing that the supplemental jurisdiction statute should not be interpreted to create such jurisdiction).

306. *See* section C(4)*(c) supra* (discussing Rules Enabling Act issues with Rule 20). Note also that a claimant who threatens a stakeholder with double liability in a federal action is a Rule 19(a)(2)(i) & (ii) party, and the stakeholder can be protected under that rule. *See* section C(3)*(b) supra* (discussing application of Rule 19).

case, discussed in Chapter 5,[307] someday becomes the view of the majority on the meaning of the substantive rights restriction of the Rules Enabling Act, Rule 22 would surely be valid in all cases. Undeniably, the rule is rationally classifiable as procedural.

(g) Interpleader "Stages"

Like state interpleader, federal interpleader is usually a two-stage procedure. In the first stage, the court determines whether the stakeholder has a right to force the claimants to litigate their claims in a single proceeding. Thus, for example, in the first stage of statutory interpleader, the court determines at the first stage whether either rule or statutory interpleader is appropriate, including whether subject-matter jurisdiction, venue, and personal jurisdiction are proper. In order to obtain statutory interpleader, the stakeholder must deposit the money or property that is the subject of the adverse claims into the court or post a bond that will insure that the stakeholder will comply with the judgment of the court.[308] During the first stage of interpleader, the court also determines whether this requirement has been satisfied and will not allow the action to proceed unless it has. Once the court has decided that interpleader is proper, it will enter an order enjoining the claimants from prosecuting any other action concerning the subject matter of the interpleader proceeding.[309] If the stakeholder is disinterested—*i.e.*, if the stakeholder is asserting no claim to the fund—the court will discharge the stakeholder.[310] If the court finds interpleader to be improper, it will dismiss the action.

In the second stage of interpleader, the claimants litigate their respective rights to the property. The court's initial order to the claimants may direct them to frame the issues for this second stage in their pleadings. The order also may make other provisions for the conduct of the second stage. Essentially, however, the

---

307. *See* Chapter 5(F)(6) *supra* ("The *Shady Grove* Decision").

308. *See* 28 U.S.C. § 1335(a)(2); *see also In re* Ambassador Group , Inc. Litig., 830 F. Supp. 147, 152 (E.D.N.Y. 1993) (to vest court with jurisdiction in a statutory interpleader action, plaintiff must deposit total amount sought by claimants, not what plaintiff views as its maximum liability). *See generally* David B. Levendusky, Annotation, *Availability of Interpleader to Insurance Company for Resolving Dispute as to Insurance Policy Under Federal Interpleader Acts (Presently 28 U.S.C.S. §§ 1335, 1397, 2361) and Rule 22 of Federal Rules of Civil Procedure*, 19 A.L.R. FED. 166 (1974).

309. In statutory interpleader actions, 28 U.S.C. § 2361 authorizes the court to enjoin the claimants from conducting proceedings in any state or federal court concerning the property that is the subject of the action. Section 2361 is an "expressly authorized exception" to the prohibition against enjoining state-court proceedings in 28 U.S.C. § 2283. However, § 2361 only applies in statutory interpleader cases, leaving the prohibition banning injunctions against injunctions against state proceedings intact in Rule 22 interpleader cases. It has been argued that injunctions against state proceedings should be available in Rule 22 interpleader cases, on the theory that such injunctions fit within another exception in § 2283 for orders "in aid of" the federal courts' "jurisdiction." *See* 7 CHARLES A. WRIGHT ET AL., FEDERAL PRACTICE AND PROCEDURE: CIVIL § 1717, at 661 (3d ed. 2001). However, given the fact that the "in aid of jurisdiction" exception would not allow an injunction against state proceedings in any other kind of parallel in personam state action, this seems questionable. *See generally* Donald L. Doernberg, *What's Wrong With This Picture?: Rule Interpleader, the Anti-Injunction Act, In Personam Jurisdiction, and M.C. Escher*, 67 U. COLO. L. REV. 551 (1996).

310. In Prudential Ins. Co. of America v. Hovis, 553 F.3d 258 (3d Cir. 2009), one of the claimants asserted a counterclaim against the insurance company stakeholder in the case and argued that the counterclaim made it improper to discharge the stakeholder from the interpleader action because the counterclaim created a possibility of independent liability to the claimant on the part of the stakeholder. The court agreed that when a counterclaim had such an effect, it was proper to keep the stakeholder in the second stage of interpleader to defendant against the counterclaim, but the court interpreted the counterclaim as simply the basis for the claimant's claim to the insurance policy and not as creating a possibility of independent liability.

second stage will proceed just as any other action in the absence of unusual circumstances. Thus, the action may be disposed of on summary judgment or after a trial before a judge or jury, whichever is appropriate. If one of the claimants asserts a counterclaim against the stakeholder for independent liability, that counterclaim, if permitted, may be adjudicated in the second stage. It may also be pushed to a third stage after the relative rights of the claimants to the stake have been determined. Generally, all of the Federal Rules of Civil Procedure governing pleading, claim joinder, and party joinder in ordinary cases apply to the second stage of interpleader.[311]

(h) Declaratory Judgment Actions as a Substitute for Interpleader

When interpleader is not available for some reason—for example, when it is confined by one or more of the traditional equity restrictions in a particular jurisdiction,[312] an action for a declaratory judgment can often be used as a substitute. When a person (the stakeholder) is in possession of money or property against which multiple adverse claims are asserted, a live controversy exists that the declaratory judgment remedy will serve a useful purpose in resolving.[313] Thus, a stakeholder faced with an inability to obtain interpleader for any reason should always consider the possibility of a declaratory judgment action against the claimants.

The declaratory judgment remedy is available in federal as well as state court. Therefore, it can also be used as a substitute for the remedies of statutory and rule interpleader discussed in the previous subsection. However, there will seldom be an advantage to substituting a federal declaratory judgment action for an interpleader action. Assuming, as seems probable, that the traditional equity restrictions on interpleader no longer exist under 28 U.S.C. § 1335 and Rule 22, federal interpleader will be as readily available, if not more so, than a declaratory judgment remedy. In a federal declaratory judgment action, the stakeholder, as plaintiff, will have to satisfy all requirements of federal subject-matter jurisdiction, venue, and personal jurisdiction, just as in any other action.[314]

In fact, certain features of the federal declaratory judgment procedure may make it unavailable in typical interpleader cases, depending on how the federal courts view the requirements of the remedy. State actions are often commenced by the claimants against the stakeholder before a federal interpleader action can be brought. In *Wilton v. Seven Falls Co.*,[315] the U.S. Supreme Court held in a non-interpleader case that federal declaratory judgment proceedings are discretionary and that such proceedings should be denied when they will not serve a useful purpose in resolving the dispute or controversy between the parties. One situation in which such a situation sometimes exists is when another action is pending

---

311. For a detailed discussion of the practice in federal interpleader actions, see 7 CHARLES A. WRIGHT ET AL., FEDERAL PRACTICE AND PROCEDURE: CIVIL §§ 1714-1718 (3d ed. 2001).

312. *See* subsection (a) *supra* ("History of Interpleader").

313. *See* Chapter 2(B)(2)*(c) supra* ("Determining Federal Question Jurisdiction in Declaratory Judgment Actions"); *see also* DAN B. DOBBS, LAW OF REMEDIES § 1.1, at 7 (2d student ed. 1993).

314. *See generally* Commercial Union Ins. Co. v. United States, 999 F.2d 581 (D.C. Cir. 1993).

315. 515 U.S. 277, 115 S. Ct. 2137, 132 L. Ed. 2d 214 (1995).

between the same parties that can resolve the entire controversy, even if the action is pending in state court. In *Wilton*, a parallel state proceeding existed, and the Supreme Court expressly declined to answer the question whether a federal court might properly dismiss a declaratory judgment action in the absence of such a proceeding. However, other federal courts have held that the existence of another action is only one of a number of factors to be considered in exercising discretion to hear or decline to hear a federal declaratory judgment action.[316]

The question is, how should these authorities be applied in interpleader situations? It is possible to reason that declaratory judgment actions brought as a substitute for interpleader should not be dismissed in preference to prior pending state actions, at least if the state actions exist in the form of multiple proceedings by the claimants. In such a case, the declaratory judgment action will arguably resolve in one proceeding what it will take multiple state actions to resolve and will thus serve a useful purpose in resolving the entire controversy that the state actions cannot serve. Nevertheless, at least one case has held that if a declaratory action is brought to determine that the stakeholder has no liability and interpleader is requested in the alternative, the district court may abstain from giving *both* declaratory and interpleader relief under the *Wilton* standard.[317]

It should also be noted that if one claimant sues the stakeholder for the money or property and leaves other claimants out of the action, the absent claimants are Rule 19(a)(1)(B)(i) & (ii) parties whose joinder is necessary in the action. The stakeholder may be able to obtain joinder of the absent claimants by counterclaim,[318] thus eliminating the Rule 19 problem. However, if not, the stakeholder can raise a Rule 19 objection and force the claimant-plaintiff to join the absent claimants in a court with proper subject-matter jurisdiction, venue, and personal jurisdiction. This, assumes, of course, that the absent claimants are parties without whose joinder the action may not proceed, and this, in turn, depends upon an analysis under Rule 19(b), as discussed above in section C(3)*(b)*. A recent decision by the U.S. Supreme Court in an interpleader action indicates that the claimants in the situation described may, indeed, have to be joined on pain of dismissal of the action if they are not.

In *Merrill Lynch, Pierce, Fenner and Smith, Inc. v. ENC Corp*,[319] a financial services firm brought an interpleader action to determine the ownership of a large fund established by the late Ferdinand E. Marcos, former president of the Philippines. The Republic of the Philippines, was made a defendant in this action, but successfully objected to its joinder on grounds of sovereign immunity. The Republic also insisted that it was an indispensable party to the action. (The Republic's view was that the money never belonged to Marcos, but to it, and did not, apparently, want an adjudication that would potentially give the money to some

---

316. *See* Aetna Cas. & Sur. Co. v. Ind-Com Elec. Co., 139 F.3d 419 (4th Cir. 1998) (district court did not abuse its discretion in declining to hear the action in spite of the fact that no state action was pending); *see also* Steven Plitt & Joshua D. Rogers, *Charting a Course for Federal Removal Through The Abstention Doctrine: A Titanic Experience in the Sargasso Sea of Jurisdictional Manipulation*, 56 DEPAUL L. REV. 107 (2006) (discussing defeat of federal removal through use of the discretion afforded in administering the declaratory judgment remedy).

317. *See* National Union Fire Ins. Co. v. Karp, 108 F.3d 17 (2d Cir. 1997).

318. *See* FED. R. CIV. P. 13(h), 22(a)(2).

319. 464 F.3d 885 (2006).

other claimant, a realistic fear, given that the district court awarded the fund to a class of human rights victims who had suffered under Marcos.) The Ninth Circuit Court of Appeals held that the Republic was a Rule 19(a) party, but not a party who had to be joined on pain of dismissal if it was not joined. Recall, from section (C)(3)*(b)* that in *Republic of the Phillippines v. Pimentel,*[320] the U.S. Supreme Court reversed the Ninth Circuit and held that the action had to be dismissed because there was no way in which to alleviate the prejudice that would accrue to the Republic. In addition, the Court held that the factor in Rule 19(b)(3), emphasizing whether a judgment in the claimant's absence would be "adequate," was also not satisfied in the case because the absentee would not be bound by the judgment in the interpleader action and thus the judgment would not satisfy the public interest in settling disputes in their entirety. The Court held that the stakeholder in the interpleader action would have an adequate remedy under Rule 19(b)(4) in any separate action by a claimant by moving to dismiss under Rule 19 in the absence of all of the parties who might sue it for the stake.

3. Intervention

Intervention is a procedure by which a person who is not a party to a pending action, but whose interests are affected by the action, may become a party. Intervention rules generally attempt to protect nonparties without unduly infringing upon the interests of the parties to the action.

(a) History of Intervention

Intervention was derived primarily from civil-law procedure. It was quite familiar in Roman law.[321] However, the common law restricted intervention because of a concern that it would interfere with the plaintiff's ability to control the action.[322] Nevertheless, some narrow procedures for intervention existed in early admiralty, common-law, and equity cases.[323]

Section 122 of the Field Code, as amended in 1851, provided a narrow right of intervention that generally corresponded to the pre-code equity practice.[324] In some code states, this Field Code provision was replaced by more lenient provisions extending the right of intervention to all sorts of civil actions in which a nonparty may have an interest in the subject matter of the suit or in the success or failure of either or both parties to the action.[325]

---

320. 553 U.S. 851, 128 S. Ct. 2180, 171 L. Ed. 2d 131 (2008).

321. *See* CHARLES E. CLARK, HANDBOOK OF THE LAW OF CODE PLEADING § 65, at 420 (2d ed. 1947). *But see* Peter A. Appel, *Intervention in Roman Law: A Case Study in the Hazards of Legal Scholarship,* 31 GA. J. INT'L & COMP. L. 33 (2002) (questioning whether, as traditionally asserted, intervention in Roman law was "extensive").

322. *See* 6 MOORE'S FEDERAL PRACTICE § 24App.100 (David R. Couillette et al. eds., 3d ed. 2012).

323. *See id.*

324.

> [W]hen, in an action for the recovery of real or personal property, a person, not a party to the action, but having an interest in the subject thereof, makes application to the court, to be made a party, it may order him to be brought in by the proper amendment.

Act of July 10, 1851, ch. 479, § 122, 1851 N.Y. Laws 876, 883.

325. *See, e.g.*, NEB. REV. STAT. §§ 25-328 to 25-330 (1995) (repealed and replaced 2003).

In the federal courts, intervention was governed by Equity Rule 37 and, in common-law actions, by the Conformity Acts. Rule 37 provided that "[a]nyone claiming an interest in the litigation may at any time be permitted to assert his right by intervention, but the intervention shall be in subordination to, and in recognition of, the propriety of the main proceeding."[326] This provision was replaced in 1938 by Federal Rule 24. Although the Advisory Committee Notes to the 1938 version of Rule 24 stated that it "amplifies and restates the present federal practice at law and in equity," Rule 24 made significant changes in federal practice. For one thing, Rule 24 distinguished intervention of right under Rule 24(a) from permissive intervention under Rule 24(b). This distinction was derived from English practice and had no basis in prior federal equity practice or code procedure. Furthermore, the provision in former Equity Rule 37 that intervention was to be "in subordination to, and in recognition of, the propriety of the main proceeding," was omitted in Rule 24.[327]

(b) Intervention Practice Under Rule 24

Federal Rule 24 exemplifies intervention practice in the federal courts and states that have adopted the Federal Rules model. An examination of Rule 24 will, therefore, provide a good illustration of modern intervention practice.

(i) Intervention as of Right

Federal Rule 24 has been amended several times since 1938. The most significant amendment occurred in 1966.[328] Original Rule 24(a) distinguished between persons whose interests were not represented adequately in the action and persons who might be affected adversely by a distribution of property in the action. This distinction was predicated on the two kinds of intervention statutes existing under the Codes.[329] The 1966 amendments to Rule 24(a) abolished this distinction. As the Advisory Committee noted, a nonparty's right to intervene should not have to depend on whether there is a fund to be distributed.[330] Rather, that right ought to depend upon more pragmatic considerations that the 1966 amendments sought to insure.

The 1938 version of Rule 24(a)(2) also required that a nonparty applying to intervene be in a situation such that the nonparty "is or may be bound by the judgment in the action." This language resulted in a Supreme Court holding that

---

326. 226 U.S. 627, 659 (1912).

327. *See generally* 7C CHARLES A. WRIGHT ET AL., FEDERAL PRACTICE AND PROCEDURE: CIVIL § 1903 (3d ed. 2007).

328. Before the 1966 amendment, Rule 24(a) read as follows:

> (a) Intervention of right. Upon timely application anyone shall be permitted to intervene in an action: (1) when a statute of the United States confers an unconditional right to intervene; or (2) when the representation of the applicant's interest by existing parties is or may be inadequate and the applicant is or may be bound by a judgment in the action; or (3) when the applicant is so situated as to be adversely affected by a distribution or other disposition of property in the custody of the court or an officer thereof.

308 U.S. at 690-91 (1938). Rule 24 was also restyled in 2007 as part of the general restyling of the Federal Rules.

329. *See* FED. R. CIV. P. 24 advisory committee's note to the 1938 version.

330. *See* FED. R. CIV. P. 24 advisory committee's note to the 1966 amendment.

intervention of right under Rule 24(a)(2) was possible only when the judgment in the action would *legally bind* the applicant for intervention.[331] Under this holding, it was technically impossible for a nonparty to intervene under Rule 24(a)(2). As the Advisory Committee observed, if a member of a class were represented inadequately in an action, that member could not be bound by the judgment in the action, but if the representation of the member's interest was adequate, intervention under Rule 24(a)(2) was impossible. The 1966 amendment to Rule 24(a) eliminated this requirement and replaced it with a test designed to make intervention depend upon the practical effect that the judgment in the action might have on the nonparty.

Today, upon timely motion,[332] Rule 24(a) provides for intervention of right in two situations. First, intervention of right is available when a federal statute confers an unconditional right to intervene.[333] Several situations fall within the first category described in Rule 24(a)(1).[334] However, the most important category of intervention of right cases is described in Rule 24(a)(2). Rule 24(a)(2) provides for intervention of right when the movant (1) claims an interest in the subject of the action and (2) is so situated that disposing of the action may, as a practical matter, impair or impede the movant's ability to protect its interest, unless existing parties adequately represent that interest.[335]

Federal Rule 24(a)(2) imposes three requirements on the would-be intervenor. First, the applicant must claim an interest relating to the property or transaction that is the subject of the action.[336] The key term here is "interest." Before the 1966 amendments, Rule 24(a) had been held to require a substantial, legally protectable interest in the action before intervention would be permitted as a matter of right.[337] Under new Rule 24(a)(2), this same requirement still exists. Thus, for example, the "interest" requirement is satisfied when a nonparty claims ownership of property that is the subject of the litigation or asserts a lien to the property, or when the nonparty would be bound by the judgment.[338]

---

331. *See* Sam Fox Publ'g Co. v. United States, 366 U.S. 683, 694, 81 S. Ct. 1309, 1315, 6 L. Ed. 2d 604, 612-13 (1961).

332. *See, e.g.*, Sierra Club v. Espy, 18 F.3d 1202 (5th Cir. 1994) (application for intervention timely even though action pending for eight years before application made; claims that affected applicants' interests not asserted until fourth amended complaint).

333. *See* FED. R. CIV. P. 24(a)(1).

334. *See, e.g.*, 28 U.S.C. § 2403 (intervention by United States or a state in actions involving constitutional questions); *see also* 7C CHARLES A. WRIGHT ET AL., FEDERAL PRACTICE AND PROCEDURE: CIVIL § 1906 (3d ed. 2007).

335. *See* FED. R. CIV. P. 24(a)(2).

336. *See* Smoke v. Norton, 252 F.3d 468 (D.C. Cir. 2001) (allowing intervention after judgment in an action in which intervenors had no reason to intervene prior to judgment; before judgment, government had been representing their interests, and only after government indicated it might not appeal the judgment did representation of intervenors' interests become inadequate; request for intervention, therefore, was also timely). *See generally* Eunice E. Eichelberger, Annotation, *What Is "Interest" Relating to Property or Transaction Which Is Subject of Action Sufficient to Satisfy That Requirement for Intervention as Matter of Right Under Rule 24(a)(2) of Federal Rules of Civil Procedure*, 73 A.L.R. FED. 448 (1985).

337. *See* 7C CHARLES A. WRIGHT ET AL., FEDERAL PRACTICE AND PROCEDURE: CIVIL § 1908 (3d ed. 2007).

338. *See id.* §§ 1905-1906, at 272-78; *see also* Jones v. Prince George's Cnty., 348 F.3d 1014 (D.C. Cir. 2003) (infant daughter of motorist who was shot and killed by police had concrete and cognizable interest in wrongful death action by personal representative of motorist's estate sufficient to give her Article III standing to intervene by representative in wrongful death action because favorable decision in action would remedy the emotional and financial support that she was deprived of by father's death, even though she did not have independent claim; however, intervention of right was not appropriate because her interests were adequately represented by personal representative of estate, even though there was disagreement about litigation tactics between infant and personal representative). *But see* Medical Liab. Mut. Ins. Co. v. Alan Curtis LLC, 485 F.3d 1006 (8th Cir. 2007) (plaintiff in negligence and wrongful death action sought to intervene under Rule 24(a)(2)

Illustration 8-43. *P* claims to own certain real property, which is in *D's* possession. *P* sues *D* for trespassing. *I* contends that *I* owns the property and seeks to intervene under Rule 24(a)(2) to resist *P's* claim. *I* also contends that *D* is a trespasser. Whether *P* owns the property depends on a question of law that will ultimately have to be resolved by an appellate court. *I* is claiming the kind of interest that is necessary for intervention under Rule 24(a).

* * * * *

However, several cases have gone further than the pre-1966 standard for determining the quality of interest necessary to satisfy the rule. These cases have focused on the policies underlying Rule 24(a)(2) intervention—to avoid multiple litigation over the same matter while simultaneously preventing a single lawsuit from becoming unnecessarily complex.[339] The cases have indicated that these policies can better be served by relaxing the kind of "interest" that is required to justify intervention and focusing instead on the second and third requirements of Rule 24(a)(2). These requirements are that the action practically affect the movant's interest and that the existing parties not adequately represent the applicant.

Illustration 8-44. In *Smuck v. Hobson*,[340] the parents of school children were allowed to intervene after judgment in a case when the board of education had decided not to appeal a desegregation order. The parents were perceived to have an interest in the ability of the school board to formulate effective educational policies. This interest would not have justified intervention before 1966, but it was enough to permit the parents to intervene for the limited purpose of attacking those portions of the desegregation order that imposed limitations on the school board's ability to formulate educational policies.

* * * * *

The second requirement of Rule 24(a)(2) is that the movant be so situated that disposition of the action, as a *practical matter*, might impair or impede the applicant's ability to protect the applicant's interests. This requirement abolishes the pre-1966 rule that the applicant must be legally bound by the judgment in order to intervene. Some decisions under this portion of the rule have gone so far as to indicate that the stare decisis effect of a case on a nonparty's interest may be sufficient to place the nonparty at a practical disadvantage in protecting the nonparty's interest.[341]

---

in action by insurance company seeking a declaratory judgment that it had no obligation to defend or indemnify nursing home operator that was defendant in plaintiff's lawsuit; held: plaintiff did not have sufficient interest under Rule 24(a)(2) to intervene; plaintiff had obtained no judgment against nursing home operator and her only interest in declaratory judgment action was to assure that defendant had sufficient resources to satisfy a judgment she hoped to obtain, an interest the court held too remote and indirect; nor was plaintiff a party to or intended beneficiary of contract between insurer and defendant; plaintiff's interest in litigating the statute of limitation applicable to one of her claims, which was raised in the declaratory judgment action, was not a legally protectable one, because she failed to show that the ruling in the insurer's favor would affect her in any material way apart from the ruling's effect on the insurer's overall liability).

339. *See, e.g.*, Smuck v. Hobson, 408 F.2d 175 (D.C. Cir. 1969); Nuesse v. Camp, 385 F.2d 694 (D.C. Cir. 1967).

340. 408 F.2d 175 (D.C. Cir. 1969).

341. *See* Atlantis Dev. Corp. v. United States, 379 F.2d 818, 828 (5th Cir. 1967); *Illustration 8-43, supra*; *see also* San Juan Cnty. v. United States, 503 F.3d 1163 (10th Cir. 2007) (court views with skepticism the commonplace statement that Rule 24(a)(2) intervention requires a "direct, substantial, and legally protectable interest," and states that the "applicant must have an interest that could be adversely affected by the litigation," but "practical judgment must be applied in determining whether the strength of the interest and the potential risk of injury to that interest justify intervention" rather than trying to "produce a rigid formula" that will result in a correct

The third requirement of Rule 24(a)(2) is that the applicant's interest not be adequately represented by existing parties. Clearly, if the nonparty's interest is not represented at all, no adequate representation is possible. In addition, if a party is on the same side of an issue as the nonparty, but is adverse or hostile to the nonparty, the nonparty's interests are not adequately represented. The best example of a case in which the nonparty's interest is adequately represented is a class action in which all the members of the class have exactly the same interests. Another typical "adequate representation" situation is a case in which the interests of the nonparty are represented by a formal representative, such as an executor or administrator.[342]

Illustration 8-45. Assume that an insurance company becomes subrogated to the rights of the insured party after paying a claim under an accident policy. The insurance company then sues the alleged tortfeasor. The insured's interest in recovering damages above the insurance coverage is not represented at all in the action.[343]

Illustration 8-46. On the facts of *Illustration 8-43*, *I's* interests are not adequately protected by *D* because *I* is claiming that *D* is a trespasser. Therefore, while both *I* and *D* have an interest in resisting *P's* claim, the adversity between *I* and *D* precludes the assumption that *D* will adequately protect *I's* interest.[344]

(ii) Permissive Intervention

Rule 24(b) provides for *permissive intervention* (*i.e.*, intervention in the discretion of the court) (1) when a person is given a conditional right to intervene by a federal statute (Rule 24(b)(1)(A)) or (2) when a nonparty has a claim or defense that shares with the main action a common question of law or fact (Rule 24(b)(1)(B)). In addition, (3) a federal or state officer or agency may be allowed to intervene when a party to the action has a claim or defense based on a statute or executive order administered by the officer or agency or is based on any regulation,

---

answer in every case; under this approach court held that an environmental organization could not intervene as a matter of right in an action by the county against the U.S. to quiet title, because although it possessed the proper interest, it failed to overcome the presumption that its interest was adequately protected by the United States).

342. *See* 7C CHARLES A. WRIGHT ET AL., FEDERAL PRACTICE AND PROCEDURE: CIVIL § 1909 (3d ed. 2007). *See generally* Eunice A. Eichelberger, Annotation, *When Is Interest of Proposed Intervenor Inadequately Represented by Existing Party so as to Satisfy that Requirement for Intervention as of Right Under Rule 24(a)(2) of Federal Rules of Civil Procedure*, 74 A.L.R. FED. 327 (1985).

343. *See* Glens Falls Ins. Co. v. Cook Bros., 23 F.R.D. 269 (S.D. Ind. 1959).

344. *See* Atlantis Dev. Corp. v. United States, 379 F.2d 818 (5th Cir. 1967); *see also* B. Fernandez & HNOS, Inc. v. Kellogg USA, Inc., 440 F.3d 541 (1st Cir. 2006) (cereal distributor was allowed to intervene as a matter of right in action by dealers against cereal manufacturer; fact that distributor and manufacturer were subsidiaries of same company did not mean that distributor's interests were adequately represented by manufacturer; underlying relief sought would have affected distributor, and distributor alleged that manufacturer was not a party to agreements that dealers' sought specific performance of, did no business in Puerto Rico, and had no involvement in underlying events); Mille Lacs Band of Chippewa Indians v. Minnesota, 989 F.2d 994 (8th Cir. 1993) (presumption exists that state adequately represents the interests of all its citizens; to overcome presumption, an intervenor must demonstrate an interest not shared by the general citizenry). *But see* San Juan Cnty. v. United States, 503 F.3d 1163 (10th Cir. 2007) (intervenor had proper interest, but failed to overcome presumption that United States would protect its interest).

order, requirement, or agreement issued or made under the statute or executive order (Rule 24(b)(2)).[345]

Several federal statutes confer a conditional right to intervene.[346] Like intervention of right, however, the most important category of permissive intervention cases falls outside the "statutory" or "state or federal official" provisions. Because Rule 24(b)(2) requires only that the intervenor's claim or defense share a common question of law or fact with the main action, it may appear that the intervention would be broadly available.[347] However, intervention under Rule 24(b) is discretionary with the court.[348] The court may deny intervention under Rule 24(b) even when the intervenor's claim and the principal action share a common question of law or fact, if the intervention would unduly delay adjudication of the case or otherwise prejudice the rights of the existing parties.[349]

(c) Subject-Matter Jurisdiction Problems Under Rule 24

As with many other federal party and claim joinder rules, some of the most complicated problems under Rule 24 concern subject-matter-jurisdiction limitations in federal cases. Some of these problems may have been alleviated in 1990 by the addition of 28 U.S.C. § 1367 to the Judicial Code.[350] As discussed in Chapter 2, § 1367 codifies and expands the doctrines of "ancillary" and "pendent" jurisdiction under the label "supplemental jurisdiction."[351] However, while § 1367 may have cured certain problems with the exercise of "ancillary jurisdiction" in intervention cases, it may also have created new difficulties of interpretation.[352]

Before 1966, it was generally held that if intervention was of right, ancillary jurisdiction was available to eliminate the need for independent jurisdictional grounds for intervention. On the other hand, if intervention was permissive, ancillary jurisdiction was not available, and the intervenor had to demonstrate

---

345. *See* Jessup v. Luther, 227 F.3d 993 (7th Cir. 2000) (newspaper sought to intervene to challenge the district court's decision to seal a settlement agreement between an employee of a state community college, on one side, and the college, its president, and the board of trustees on the other; district court denied permission to intervene under Rule 24(a) on the ground that the newspaper could not establish a direct and substantial interest in the subject matter of the litigation; court held Rule 24(b) intervention was improper because the newspaper was not asserting a claim or defense that had a question of law or fact in common with the lawsuit; court of appeals reversed, holding that Rule 24(b) intervention was proper because the newspaper was asserting a right of access to court proceedings and documents and this right established a question of law or fact in common between the parties' interest in confidentiality and the newspaper's and public's right to open access).

346. *See, e.g.*, 42 U.S.C. §§ 2000a-3(a), 2000-3-5(e) (public accommodations and unlawful employment practices provisions of the Civil Rights Act of 1964); *see also* 7C CHARLES A. WRIGHT ET AL., FEDERAL PRACTICE AND PROCEDURE: CIVIL § 1910 (3d ed. 2007).

347. *See* Solid Waste Agency v. United States Army Corps of Eng'rs, 101 F.3d 503 (7th Cir. 1996) (intervention of right denied because applicant's interest would be adequately protected by existing parties; case remanded for determination of whether permissive intervention appropriate because district court erroneously held that applicants lacked an interest sufficient to justify permissive intervention; Rule 24(b) does not require an "interest," only a common question).

348. *See* 7C CHARLES A. WRIGHT ET AL., FEDERAL PRACTICE AND PROCEDURE: CIVIL § 1913 (3d ed. 2007).

349. This requirement is imposed by the last sentence of Rule 24(b): "In exercising its discretion the court shall consider whether the intervention will unduly delay or prejudice the adjudication of the rights of the original parties." FED. R. CIV. P. 24(b).

350. *See* Chapter 2(E)(4) *supra* ("The Codification of Pendent and Ancillary Jurisdiction").

351. *See id.*

352. *See generally* Marilyn J. Ireland, *Supplemental Jurisdiction Over Claims in Intervention*, 23 N. MEX. L. REV. 57 (1993).

independent jurisdictional grounds before intervention would be permitted.[353] After 1966, the courts continued to hold that ancillary jurisdiction applied to Rule 24(a) intervention, but not to Rule 24(b) intervention.[354] Yet it is clear that the 1966 amendments broadened Rule 24(a), so that some cases that would have qualified for permissive intervention under Rule 24(b) before 1966 would qualify today for intervention as a matter of right under Rule 24(a).[355] Rule 82 states that the Federal Rules of Civil Procedure "shall not be construed to extend or limit the jurisdiction of the [federal] district courts or the venue of actions therein."[356] This provision led some commentators to raise a question about the application of the ancillary jurisdiction doctrine in Rule 24 cases: how could ancillary jurisdiction have been improper before the 1966 amendments over those claims that were appropriate only for permissive intervention under Rule 24(b), but be proper after 1966 over the same claims when they were moved into the intervention of right category?[357]

The answer to this question lies in the nature of ancillary jurisdiction. In determining whether ancillary jurisdiction was appropriate under Rule 24, the key questions should have been (1) whether the intervenor's claim and the principal claim were related sufficiently to be considered a part of the same "case or controversy" within Article III of the Constitution and (2) whether the other policies supporting the specific statutory grant of subject-matter jurisdiction applicable to the case would be served (or harmed) by allowing intervention.[358] Unfortunately, instead of directly asking these questions, the courts sought to decide the ancillary jurisdiction question on the basis of easy labels such as "intervention of right" and "permissive intervention." Had the courts instead focused directly on the bases of the ancillary jurisdiction doctrine, they would have understood that the statutory policies supporting grants of jurisdiction to the federal courts were the most important determinants of whether a case of intervention of right or permissive intervention is appropriate for the application of ancillary jurisdiction.[359] Under these policies, particularly in diversity actions,[360] ancillary jurisdiction was indeed inappropriate in permissive intervention cases. However, as discussed below, it

---

353. *See* 7C CHARLES A. WRIGHT ET AL., FEDERAL PRACTICE AND PROCEDURE: CIVIL § 1917 (3d ed. 2007).

354. *See id.*

355. *See id.*

356. FED. R. CIV. P. 82.

357. *See, e.g.*, 7C CHARLES A. WRIGHT ET AL., FEDERAL PRACTICE AND PROCEDURE: CIVIL § 1917 (3d ed. 2007).

358. *See* Chapter 2(E)(1)-(3) *supra* (discussing these requirements).

359. *But see* 7C CHARLES A. WRIGHT ET AL., FEDERAL PRACTICE AND PROCEDURE: CIVIL § 1917 (3d ed. 2007) (arguing that the pre-1966 test for ancillary jurisdiction should be applied under the amended rule).

360. Chapter 2(E)(3) *supra* ("The Statutory Basis of Pendent and Ancillary Jurisdiction") and section C(4) *supra* ("Permissive Joinder of Parties") discussed the Supreme Court's decision in *Finley v. United States*. *Finley* prohibited pendent party jurisdiction in federal question cases when the statutory grant of federal question jurisdiction being exercised did not affirmatively authorize jurisdiction over pendent parties. *Finley* involved the assertion of a federal question claim against one defendant and the joinder of another nondiverse defendant on a state claim. However, the Supreme Court's opinion in *Finley* was broad enough to encompass the assertion of a federal claim against a defendant by one plaintiff and the assertion of a state claim against the same defendant by a nondiverse plaintiff. *Finley* thus might have precluded intervention of nondiverse defendants who could not have been originally joined by a plaintiff who possessed only state claims against the intervenor. Likewise, *Finley* might have precluded intervention by nondiverse plaintiffs wishing to assert state claims against the defendant in a federal question action. However, the impact of *Finley* on intervention in federal question cases is not as clear as the impact of the *Kroger* decision, discussed below, on intervention in diversity actions. As discussed in Chapter 2(E)(3) and section C(4) *supra*, *Finley* has been rendered irrelevant by the enactment of 28 U.S.C. § 1367 in 1990.

should also have been held inappropriate in intervention of right cases under Rule 24(a)(2).

Illustration 8-47. *P*, a citizen of State *X*, *D*, a citizen of State *Y*, and *I*, a citizen of State *Y*, collide in their automobiles in State *Y*. *P* and *I* are injured. *P* sues *D* in the U.S. District Court for the District of State *Y*. *P* asserts a claim for $500,000 for personal injuries received in the accident. *I*, who also wants to assert a claim against *D* for personal injuries received in the accident, seeks to intervene in the action between *P* and *D*. Intervention is not proper as a matter of right under Rule 24(a)(2). *I* probably does not possess an interest "relating to" the transaction that is the subject of the action between *P* and *D*, even though *I's* claim also arises out of that action. Even if *I's* interest is sufficient under Rule 24(a)(2), however, *I* is not situated so that disposition of the action between *P* and *D* will impair or impede *I's* ability to protect the interest as a practical matter. *I* cannot be bound by the judgment between *P* and *D*, although *I* might be able to benefit from a judgment against *D* in the action.[361] Nevertheless, because there will be common questions of law and fact between *I's* claim and the main action, permissive intervention would be appropriate under Rule 24(b). However, ancillary jurisdiction over *I's* claim would not be appropriate. The close factual relationship between *I's* claim and the main action is sufficient to satisfy Article III of the Constitution.[362] However, under the policies of 28 U.S.C. § 1332 as interpreted in the *Kroger* case, discussed in section (C)(1)*(c)*, above, *I* is not a person in a defensive position who has been involuntarily haled into federal court, or someone whose rights would be irretreivably lost if they were not allowed access to federal court (here to assert a claim). Allowing *I* to intervene would pose an even greater danger of evading the policies of the diversity jurisdiction than the claim asserted in *Kroger* itself.

Illustration 8-48. On the facts of *Illustration 8-47*, assume that *I* is a citizen of State *X*. Assume further that *D* is asserting that *P* was contributorily negligent. *I* seeks to intervene because *I* anticipates a later suit by *P* against *I* and also wishes to assert that *P* was contributorily negligent. For the reasons given in *Illustration 8-47*, *I's* defense is not appropriate for intervention of right under Rule 24(a)(2). *I's* defense presents the kind of common questions of law and fact that would make permissive intervention proper under Rule 24(b). Although Article III of the Constitution would be satisfied by *I's* application for intervention, the statutory policies of 28 U.S.C. § 1332 would probably still not be satisfied here. In this situation, *I* is in a defensive position, but only potentially. *P* has not yet sued *I*. It is difficult to see how any of *I's* rights would be irretrievably lost by inability to intervene in the action. Therefore, under the *Kroger* decision, ancillary jurisdiction would not be appropriate over *I's* application for intervention.

* * * * *

In intervention-of-right cases, Federal Rule 24(a)(2) and Federal Rule 19(a)(1)(B)(i) overlap. A party seeking to intervene under Rule 24(a)(2) is, at least, a person whose joinder is needed for just adjudication under Rule 19(a), and the intervenor may be a person in whose absence the action would have to be dismissed

---

361. *See* Chapter 13(D)(1) *infra* ("Preclusion of Nonparties").

362. *See* Chapter 2(E)(2) *supra* ("The Constitutional Basis of Pendent and Ancillary Jurisdiction").

after evaluation under Rule 19(b). In either case, how should the ancillary jurisdiction doctrine be applied if the intervenor's joinder as an original matter would have destroyed federal subject-matter jurisdiction? Before 1990, the courts generally held that if the intervenor would have been an "indispensable party" under Rule 19(b), the doctrine of ancillary jurisdiction would not apply, even though joinder was being effected under Rule 24(a)(2) instead of under Rule 19. Thus, the action had to be dismissed. The purpose of this sensible "exception" to the general rule of ancillary jurisdiction was to prevent the evasion of federal subject-matter jurisdiction requirements through the use of Rule 24.[363] However, when the intervenor would not be an "indispensable party" under Rule 19(b), but only a party whose joinder was "necessary" for just adjudication under Rule 19(a), but who could be dispensed with, the courts permitted intervention under the doctrine of ancillary jurisdiction. The justification for this result was, apparently, that if it were impossible to use ancillary jurisdiction to permit Rule 19(a) parties to intervene, Rule 24(a)'s usefulness might be impaired.[364] However, it seems curious, especially in the face of Rule 82, that the desire to render a particular rule useful should result in an extension of federal jurisdiction to a claim or defense that could not otherwise be heard by the federal courts.[365] As stated above, a tighter focus on the policies supporting statutory grants of federal subject-matter jurisdiction by the courts would have revealed that Rule 24(a)(2) intervention should have been refused if joinder of the intervenor as an original matter would have made federal subject-matter jurisdiction improper.

After 1990, the problems of determining jurisdiction over applications for intervention will be governed by the codification of the doctrines of "ancillary" and "pendent" jurisdiction in 28 U.S.C. § 1367(a). Section 1367(a) authorizes "supplemental jurisdiction" over claims that are so related to claims over which the federal courts have original jurisdiction as to "form part of the same case or controversy under Article III of the United States Constitution."[366] As discussed in Chapter 2, it is possible both that an Article III case or controversy is broad enough to encompass factually unrelated federal and nonfederal claims and that § 1367(a) will be read as allowing such unrelated claims to be heard within the grant of

---

363. *See* 7C CHARLES A. WRIGHT ET AL., FEDERAL PRACTICE AND PROCEDURE: CIVIL § 1917 (3d ed. 2007); *cf. Illustration 8-33 supra*; Owen Equip. & Erection Co. v. Kroger, 437 U.S. 365, 376, 98 S. Ct. 2396, 2404, 57 L. Ed. 2d 274, 284 (1978) (discussed in subsection D(1)*(c) supra*).

364. *See* 7C CHARLES A. WRIGHT ET AL., FEDERAL PRACTICE AND PROCEDURE: CIVIL § 1917 (3d ed. 2007).

365. Furthermore, the Supreme Court's decision in Owen Equipment & Erection Co. v. Kroger, 437 U.S. 365, 98 S. Ct. 2396, 57 L. Ed. 2d 274 (1978) (discussed in section D(1)*(c) supra*), made it questionable whether the rationale articulated in the text was valid in all cases. In *Kroger*, the Court emphasized that ancillary jurisdiction "typically involves claims by a defending party haled into court against his will, or by another person whose rights might be irretrievably lost unless he could assert them in an ongoing action in a federal court." *Id.* at 376, 98 S. Ct. at 2404, 57 L. Ed. 2d at 284. One of the examples cited by the Supreme Court as an appropriate case for ancillary jurisdiction was a party's intervention to protect that party's interest in a fund or property controlled by federal litigation. *See id.* at 375-76 & n.18, 98 S. Ct. at 2403-04 & n.18, 57 L. Ed. 2d at 283-84 & n.18. Many intervention cases, under Rule 24(a)(2), may, in fact, be similar to this example, in that the intervenor would "irretrievably" lose rights unless permitted to intervene. However, it is doubtful that all intervention cases pose so serious a threat to the intervenor's interest under the practical standard enunciated in Rule 24(a)(2). After *Kroger*, therefore, it was arguable that the federal courts should have examined the facts of each intervention case under Rule 24(a)(2) with care to determine whether the congressional purposes supporting the statutory grant of diversity jurisdiction would be furthered or impaired by allowing intervention of a nondiverse Rule 19(a) party.

366. 28 U.S.C. § 1367(a).

supplemental jurisdiction to the federal courts.[367] If so, § 1367(a) standing alone[368] would textually authorize jurisdiction over all claims under both Rules 24(a) and (b). However, as also discussed in Chapter 2,[369] § 1367(a) should probably be read to limit supplemental jurisdiction to claims that arise out of the same transaction or occurrence as claims over which the federal courts have original jurisdiction. Under either interpretation of § 1367(a), the courts should focus on the newly prescribed test under the statute in all cases of Rule 24 intervention, rather than the old distinction between intervention of right and permissive intervention. Thus, under either interpretation of the statute, it is clear that at least some cases of permissive intervention—for example, the one discussed in *Illustration 8-48*—will fall within the scope of § 1367(a).[370] This analysis, however, focuses only on the necessary relationship between the intervenor's claim or defense and the principal action. It does not take into account other restrictions, such as the "contamination" theory of the U.S. Supreme Court's decision in the *Exxon Mobil* case, discussed in Chapter 2(C)(4)*(e)(i)* & *(ii)* and previous sections in conjunction with other multiple party joinder rules. *Exxon Mobil*'s application to intervention cases is examined below.

Section 1367(b) places special restrictions on the exercise of supplemental jurisdiction when the jurisdiction of the federal courts is based exclusively on diversity of citizenship between the parties.[371] These restrictions would operate to prohibit supplemental jurisdiction in certain kinds of cases, even if the test of § 1367(a) were met. As applied to intervention cases, § 1367(b) partly addresses one anomalous result that occurred under prior law, but it creates some additional problems of interpretation. Section 1367(b) partially solves the problem created by the overlap between Rule 24(a)(2) and Rule 19(a)(1)(B)(i). Section 1367(b) provides that in actions based solely on diversity jurisdiction, the district courts will not have supplemental jurisdiction over claims by plaintiffs against "persons made parties under Rule . . . 24" or over "claims by persons proposed to be joined as plaintiffs under Rule 19 . . . or seeking to intervene as plaintiffs under Rule 24."[372] The legislative history of § 1367(b) indicates that it was designed, at least in part, to deal with the overlap between Rules 19 and 24. The House Report stated as follows:

> Subsection (b) makes one small change in pre-*Finley* practice. Anomalously, under current practice, the same party might intervene as of right under Federal Rule of Civil Procedure

---

367. *See* Chapter 2(E)(5) *supra* ("The Scope of Supplemental Jurisdiction: Section 1367(a)").

368. As discussed further below, § 1367(b) addresses intervention problems specifically in diversity actions. Thus, the effect of § 1367(b) on those actions must be evaluated separately from the effect of § 1367(a) on the distinction between intervention of right and permissive intervention utilized to determine ancillary jurisdiction.

369. *See* Chapter 2(E)(5) *supra* ("The Scope of Supplemental Jurisdiction: Section 1367(a)").

370. In York Research Corp. v. Landgarten, No. 89 Civ. 5556(PNL), 1992 WL 373268, 1992 U.S. Dist. LEXIS 18321 (S.D.N.Y. Dec. 3, 1992), the court exercised supplemental jurisdiction over a permissive defendant intervenor. The court recognized that supplemental jurisdiction was ordinarily improper over applications for permissive intervention, but stated that failure to exercise jurisdiction would impair the intervenor's ability to pursue the claims, cause judicial inconvenience and expense to the parties, and risk inconsistent results. Because the action was commenced prior to the effective date of 28 U.S.C. § 1367, the court recognized that the statute was inapplicable, but stated that its analysis would not differ if it was applicable. However, the court's description of the intervenor's claim looks much like a description of an intervention of right claim under Rule 24(a)(2).

371. *See* 28 U.S.C. § 1367(b).

372. *Id.*; *see* Krueger v. Cartwright, 996 F.2d 928 (7th Cir. 1993) (holding it erroneous to allow intervention of a nondiverse plaintiff under § 1367(b)).

[24(a)][373] and take advantage of supplemental jurisdiction, but not come within supplemental jurisdiction if parties already in the action sought to effect the joinder under Rule 19. Subsection (b) would eliminate this anomaly, excluding Rule [24(a)] plaintiff-intervenors to the same extent as those sought to be joined as plaintiffs under Rule 19.

If this exclusion threatened unavoidable prejudice to the interests of the prospective intervenor if the action proceeded in its absence, the district court should be more inclined not merely to deny the intervention but to dismiss the whole action for refiling in state court under the criteria of Rule 19(b).[374]

The language and legislative history of 28 U.S.C. § 1367(b) explicitly address only the problem of claims asserted by intervening *plaintiffs*.[375] On the face of the statute, there is no prohibition against the exercise of supplemental jurisdiction over persons who intervene as defendants (but against whom no claim is asserted) under Rule 24(a)(2) and whose presence would destroy subject-matter jurisdiction if they had been joined originally in the action.[376] If it is indeed correct that nondiverse Rule 24(a)(2) defendants can intervene under § 1367, then Congress has only partially solved the problem of overlap between Rules 19(a)(1)(B)(i) and Rule 24(a)(2).

Recall from section C(3)*(c)*, however, that this same difficulty existed with the application of § 1367(b) to joinder under Rule 19—the statute seems only to preclude the plaintiff from asserting claims against persons joined as defendants under Rule 19, rather than precluding joinder of those parties altogether when their presence in the action originally would have destroyed subject-matter jurisdiction.[377] In section C(3)*(c)*, it was suggested that this anomaly could be avoided by interpreting the language of § 1367(a) and (b) to forbid joinder of the nondiverse

---

373. The House Report cited Federal Rule 23, but it is clear that the report should have cited Federal Rule 24. For one thing, Rule 23 (a) deals with class action prerequisites and does not speak of intervention. For another, the report cites an earlier edition of 7C CHARLES A. WRIGHT ET AL., FEDERAL PRACTICE AND PROCEDURE: CIVIL § 1917 (3d ed. 2007), which deals with the intervention problems discussed in the text.

374. H.R. REP. NO. 734, 101st Cong., 2d Sess. 29 (1990). It should be noted that the language recommended by the Federal Courts Study Committee only prohibited supplemental jurisdiction in diversity cases over claims asserted under Rule 24(b), although it prohibited claims asserted both by parties seeking to intervene as plaintiffs and by parties seeking to intervene as defendants. *See* 1 FEDERAL COURTS STUDY COMMITTEE WORKING PAPERS AND SUBCOMMITTEE REPORTS 567-68 (1990).

375. In Meredith v. Schreiner Transport, Inc., 814 F. Supp. 1001 (D. Kan. 1993), the court applied § 1367(b) to refuse jurisdiction over an intervenor's claim under Rule 24(a)(2), where the intervenor was asserting a lien against judgment proceeds. The jurisdictional amount requirement of 28 U.S.C. § 1332 was not satisfied by the intervenor's claim. In Atherton v. Casey, No. 92-1283, 1992 WL 167033, 1992 U.S. Dist. LEXIS 9976 (E.D. La. June 29, 1992), the applicant attempted to intervene as a defendant, but the court realigned the applicant as a plaintiff and held that diversity was destroyed. In TIG Insurance Co. v. Reliable Research Co., 334 F.3d 630 (7th Cir. 2003), an insurer brought suit against its insured, a title and escrow agent, seeking to rescind a policy for misrepresentation in the policy application. The title insurer intervened as a plaintiff, alleging jurisdictional facts that would make it of diverse citizenship with the defendant. The defendant countered with jurisdictional assertions that would make the intervenor and defendant co-citizens. The district court allowed intervention, but the court of appeals ordered the intervenor dismissed. The court held that § 1367(b) explicitly forbade intervention in cases of incomplete diversity and that the burden of establishing jurisdictional facts was on the party seeking to support federal jurisdiction, here the intervenor. Because the intervenor had not provided any factual basis for concluding that its version of the jurisdictional facts was true, it had not met its burden.

376. *See* Denis F. McLaughlin, *The Federal Supplemental Jurisdiction Statute—A Constitutional and Statutory Analysis*, 24 ARIZ. ST. L.J. 849, 958 (1992).

377. *See* subsection C(3)(c) *supra* ("Problems of Subject-Matter Jurisdiction, Venue, and Personal Jurisdiction Under Rule 19").

Rule 19 defendant altogether.[378] This same approach also seems to be the best solution in cases of Rule 24(a)(2) intervention. A party intervening as a defendant under Rule 24(a)(2) is, in fact, a Rule 19(a)(2)(i) party who should have been originally joined in the action. Intervention should not be permitted when the intervening defendant could not have been originally joined under 28 U.S.C. § 1332, such as when the citizenship of the intervenor is the same as that of the plaintiff.[379] Alternatively, if nondiverse defendants are permitted to intervene under § 1367(b), the plaintiff should only be precluded from asserting claims against the intervenor as long as the intervenor asserts no claims against the plaintiff.[380]

Illustration 8-49. On the facts of *Illustration 8-20*, assume that *C* applies to intervene in order to resist *P's* claim. *C* is both a Rule 24(a)(2) party and a Rule 19 (a)(1)(B)(i) party. For the same reasons that supplemental jurisdiction did not exist over *C* as a Rule 19(a)(2) party in *Illustration 8-20*, supplemental jurisdiction should not exist over *C* as an intervenor under Rule 24(a)(2).

* * * * *

Unfortunately, the case law does not support the arguments made above in the text. The trend in the courts of appeals is to consider that intervening non-diverse defendants do not offend § 1367(b), whether or not the intervenors are asserting claims against the plaintiff.[381]

It is not clear whether the Supreme Court's decision in the *Exxon Mobil* case (examined in Chapter 2(C)(4)*(e)(i)* & *(ii)*, and preceding sections involving the jurisdictional problems with other joinder rules) affects the analysis of intervening defendants under Rule 24(a)(2). Recall that in *Exxon Mobil*, the Court implied in dicta that in cases in which federal subject-matter jurisdiction is based on diversity of citizenship, a claim by or against a non-diverse party would not be within the supplemental jurisdiction of the federal courts, even if the claim were properly joined with a jurisdictionally sufficient claim on which diversity was complete. The

---

378. *See id.*

379. *But cf.* Range v. National R.R. Passenger Corp., 176 F.R.D. 85 (W.D.N.Y. 1997) (defendant allowed to intervene under Rule 24(a); however, intervenor's interests appeared to coincide with plaintiff's and court did not state whether intervenor was nondiverse from plaintiff or defendant). The same theoretical problem of the defendant against whom the plaintiff is not asserting a claim exists under Rule 24 and Rule 19. If the plaintiff really has no claim against a nondiverse applicant for intervention, § 1367(a), which provides only for supplemental jurisdiction over claims, would not seem to authorize subject-matter jurisdiction. If the plaintiff does have a claim against the intervenor (*e.g.*, for declaratory relief), then § 1367(b) would seem to disallow intervention. *See* section C(3)*(c) supra*. In Colonial Penn Insurance Co. v. American Centennial Ins. Co., No. 92 Civ. 3791 (RPP), 1992 WL 350838, 1992 U.S. Dist. LEXIS 17552 (S.D.N.Y. Nov. 17, 1992), the applicant sought to intervene as a plaintiff, but the court realigned the applicant as a defendant because the court stated that the applicant really wanted to assert a "defensive counterclaim." The plaintiff in the action was suing for a declaratory judgment to determine rights and obligations pursuant to reinsurance agreements. It seems clear that this claim for declaratory relief would be asserted against the intervenor and that any judgment on the declaratory claim would bind the intervenor. In addition, because the intervenor wanted to assert a counterclaim, that counterclaim would also satisfy § 1367(a). So viewed, however, the court exercised supplemental jurisdiction over the intervenor's claim, construing § 1367(b) as not prohibiting jurisdiction. This result is contrary to the result recommended in the text.

380. *See* section C(3)*(c) supra* ("Problems of Subject-Matter Jurisdiction, Venue, and Personal Jurisdiction Under Rule 19").

381. In Mattel, Inc. v. Bryant, 446 F.3d 1011 (9th Cir. 2006), the court held that § 1367(b) was not offended by the intervention of a non-indispensable Rule 24(a) intervenor because the policies of the diversity jurisdiction were not violated by the intervention. The court stated that "[n]either § 1332 nor § 1367 upset the long-established judge-made rule that the presence of a nondiverse and not indispensable defendant intervenor does not destroy complete diversity." *See also* Karsner v. Lothian, 532 F.3d 876 (D.C. Cir. 2008) (intervenor was not seeking to intervene as plaintiff, and thus jurisdiction existed over intervention); *In re* Olympic Mills Corp., 477 F.3d 1 (1st Cir. 2007) (intervention of dispensable, non-diverse intervenors of right as defendants does not destroy diversity).

jurisdictionally insufficient claim involving the non-diverse party "contaminates" the entire case, and prevents the operation of § 1367(a), making resort to § 1367(b) unnecessary. If the contamination theory is applied to the situation now under discussion, therefore, no supplemental jurisdiction would exist under § 1367(a) over the intervening defendant's claim, and the application of § 1367(b) to the claim would be unnecessary. Only when the jurisdictional deficiency is in the amount-in-controversy requirement of the diversity statute would supplemental jurisdiction exist over the jurisdictionally insufficient claim and the issue of the application of § 1367(b) thereby arise, just as discussed in conjunction with other joinder rules.

Doubt exists about the applicability of the contamination theory to Rule 24(a)(2) intervenors because of the Supreme Court's statement in *Owen Equipment* of the policies supporting the former doctrine of ancillary jurisdiction. Recall that *Owen* not only stated that ancillary jurisdiction is appropriate in cases in which a party asserting a claim has been placed in a defensive position, but also in cases in which someone's rights would be irretrievably lost if they were not allowed to resort to federal jurisdiction. This seems precisely to describe the situation of the Rule 24(a)(2) intervening defendant, who "is so situated that disposing of the action may as a practical matter impair or impede the [intervenor's] ability to protect its interest."[382] Because *Owen Equipment* is the case to which the federal courts look to determine the policies of the diversity jurisdiction, it is possible to reason that it trumps *Exxon Mobil* and makes the contamination theory inapplicable to any situation to which the policies of the former doctrine of ancillary jurisdiction are applicable. Whether this analysis is correct, however, is not clear. As indicated above, a non-diverse Rule 24(a)(2) intervenor is a Rule 19(a)(1)(B)(i) party who should have been joined in the first place. When analyzing the jurisdictional problems with Rule 19 joinder in section (C)(3)*(c)*, above, we saw that there is no reason that the contamination should not apply in Rule 19 joinder situations. Thus, whether the lower federal courts are correct to permit intervention of Rule 24(a)(2) defendants is problematic.

Nevertheless, in *Price v. Wolford*,[383] the Tenth Circuit Court of Appeals held that supplemental jurisdiction existed over the claim by a party intervening (and properly aligned) as a defendant because § 1367(b) did not apply to claims by intervening defendants against whom the plaintiff was not asserting a claim. Although the court cited *Exxon Mobil*, it did not discuss the case extensively and also did not consider the effect of the case's "contamination theory" on supplemental jurisdiction. One way to interpret cases such as *Price* might be this: even though the supplemental jurisdiction statute only authorizes jurisdiction over claims, the requirements of the statute are satisfied in cases like *Price* because the defendant is asserting a claim against the plaintiff, even though the plaintiff is not asserting a claim against the defendant. Furthermore, the *Exxon Mobil* contamination theory is arguably not applicable to claims asserted by defending parties, which should be considered counterclaims. Likewise, § 1367(b) does not apply to withdraw jurisdiction over counterclaims. The problem with this, of course, is that counter-

---

382. FED. R. CIV. P. 24(a)(2).
383. 608 F.3d 698 (10th Cir. 2010).

claims are technically considered to be claims against opposing parties, and opposing parties are persons who have previously asserted claims against the counterclaimant,[384] which does not fit the description of the plaintiff in the *Price* situaiton. On the whole, there seems to be no intellectually satisfying way to deal with these cases except to deny jurisdiction.

Whatever the case may be with regard to intervening Rule 24(a)(2) defendants, should the contamination theory of *Exxon Mobil* apply to persons attempting to intervene as plaintiffs under Rule 24(a)(2)? Plaintiff intervenors are Rule 24(a)(2) parties for the same reason as are defendant intervenors: unless they are allowed into the action, their ability to protect their interests may, as a practical matter, be impaired or impeded. This would also seem to fit the *Owen Equipment* statement of the policies of the ancillary jurisdiction. Note, however, if supplemental jurisdiction exists over such an intervening plaintiff's claim on this theory, jurisdiction would be withdrawn by § 1367(b) in any event, because, as discussed above, that section clearly takes away jurisdiction over claims asserted by intervening nondiverse plaintiffs.

One decision that may support the analysis in the preceding paragraph is *Griffin v. Lee*.[385] In *Griffin*, an action was brought in a Louisiana state court by a Mississippi citizen for fraud and breach of trust against multiple defendants, some of whom were citizens of Louisiana. The action was removed on the basis of diversity jurisdiction to the U.S. District Court for the Western District of Louisiana.[386] Subsequently, the plaintiff's attorney, a Louisiana citizen, withdrew from representation of the plaintiff and intervened under Rule 24(a) seeking attorney's fees of less than $75,000.01. The intervention was allowed under Rule 24(a)(2), and a judgment was ultimately rendered for the intervenor. On appeal by the plaintiff, the Fifth Circuit Court of Appeals raised the issue of subject-matter jurisdiction over the intervenor's claim and ultimately reversed. The court relied in part on *Exxon Mobil's* interpretation of the supplemental jurisdiction statute. However, the court did not make reference to the contamination theory of that case. Instead, it simply stated that "[i]t is clear that [the intervenor's] Petition satisfied the requirements of § 1367(a)."[387] The court then went on to hold that § 1367(b) withdrew the jurisdiction conferred by § 1367(a) because of the absence of both complete diversity between the intervening plaintiff and the defendants and the lack of the proper jurisdictional amount.[388] Although the result in *Griffin* is correct, the court's reasoning is suspect in its failure to consider whether the contamination theory destroyed the ability to obtain supplemental jurisdiction under § 1367(a), thus making § 1367(b) irrelevant.

---

384. *See* Chapter (2)(E)(6) *supra* ("Exceptions to the Scope of Supplemental Jurisdiction in Diversity Cases: Section 1367(b)").

385. 621 F.3d 380 (5th Cir. 2010).

386. Given the presence of Louisiana defendants in the action, it is not clear why removal was proper under the "resident defendant" restriction of 28 U.S.C. § 1441(b).

387. *Griffin*, 621 F.3d at 385.

388. *See id.* at 385-88. Note that the court aligned the intervenor as a platintiff with a claim against a co-plaintiff and a direct claim against the Trustee-defendant for a lien on the trust. *See id.* at 388. See also the discussion of alignment in intervention cases, below.

In *Aurora Loan Services, Inc. v. Craddieth*,[389] the Seventh Circuit Court of Appeals held that § 1367(b) did not destroy jurisdiction over the claim of a non-diverse intervenor on the plaintiff's side of the case. The court reasoned that § 1367(b) was designed to prevent parties from circumventing the requirements of the diversity jurisdiction by persons who, being of the same citizenship as the defendant, wait to sue until a diverse party with whose interests it is aligned sues the defendant and then joins the suit as an intervening plaintiff. In the case before the court, that was not what happened, because the intervening party had no claim at the commencement of the action. Instead, its claim arose after the action was commenced, when it turned out to be the high bidder in a mortgage foreclosure sale that the district court later refused to confirm. The court also relied on the rule that jurisdiction is determined as of commencement. It reasoned that if at the time of commencement there is a non-diverse indispensable party "lurking in the wings" who later tries to intervene, intervention will be prohibited. However, since the intervenor here had no claim at commencement, that was also not true.

Although the court's reasoning in *Aurora* is attractive, and the facts of the case before it are unlikely to recur often, the result is questionable in light of the Supreme Court's tendency to rely on odd perceptions of the plain language of § 1367. The language of § 1367(b) concerning plaintiff intervenors seems clear. It is questionable whether the Court that decided *Exxon Mobil* would approve of an interpretation of the statute that disregarded this language in preference to a purpose-based interpretation.

It is important to remember that the doctrine of realignment applies to intervening parties under Rule 24, just as it does to problems of Rule 19 joinder.[390] Thus, in determining whether § 1367 (a) or (b) will preclude supplemental jurisdiction over claims by persons seeking to intervene, the intervenors must first be properly aligned in the action. For example, in *Development Finance Corp. v. Alpha Housing & Health Care, Inc.*,[391] the intervening party in an action for breach of contract wished to challenge certain agreements between the plaintiffs and the defendant on the ground that they were ultra vires, a defense that could not be raised by the defendant under the applicable state law. The intervenor first moved to intervene as a defendant, but the district court denied the motion, and the intervenor did not appeal. The intervenor then sought to intervene as a plaintiff, but this motion was also denied by the district court. On appeal from the denial of the latter motion, the court of appeals considered whether the intervenor should be aligned as a plaintiff or defendant in order to determine whether § 1367(b) would preclude subject-matter jurisdiction over the intervenor's claims.[392] The court aligned the

---

389. 442 F.3d 1018 (7th Cir. 2006). The court in the *Griffin* case, discussed above, distinguished the *Aurora* case on the grounds that the intervenor in *Griffin* was not forced to intervene to protect its interest. This seems questionable. A better distinction would be based on the fact that the intervenor's claim in *Auroa* did not exist at commencement, as the court in the latter case reasoned.

390. *See* section C(2)*(c) supra* (discussing problems of subject-matter jurisdiction in Rule 19 cases, including problems of realignment); *see also* April N. Everette, United States Fidelity & Guaranty Co. v. A & S Manufacturing Co.: *Realignment of Parties in Diversity Jurisdiction Cases,* 74 N.C. L. REV. 1979 (1996).

391. 54 F.3d 156 (3d Cir. 1995).

392. Interestingly, in *Development Finance*, the court considered the applicability of § 1367(b) without first considering whether the intervenor's claim fit within § 1367(a). This failure to consider § 1367(a) first is a problem with the court's analysis because it was not obvious from the court's opinion what the relationship between the intervenor and the other parties in the action was, and as observed in Chapter 2(C)(4)*(e)(iii)*, some federal courts

intervenor as a defendant, treating the intervenor's application as raising counterclaims against the plaintiffs and a crossclaim against the defendant. Because the intervenor was a citizen of a different state than the plaintiffs, no problem of diversity jurisdiction was presented by the intervenor's counterclaims. (The intervenor was a co-citizen of the defendant.) In addition, because § 1367(b) does not exclude supplemental jurisdiction of crossclaims under Rule 13(g), the court held that supplemental jurisdiction existed over the crossclaims against the defendant under the "plain language" of the statute.[393]

Section 1367(b) applies not only to intervention under Rule 24(a), but also to intervention under Rule 24(b).[394] However, it would seem the contamination theory of *Exxon Mobil* ought to apply in full force as to nondiverse Rule 24(b) plaintiffs or defendants, thus rendering supplemental jurisdiction over their claims and defenses improper under § 1367(a), and thus rendering § 1367(b) irrelevant except in cases in which the jurisdictional deficiency is an inadequate amount-in-controversy. In addition, permissive intervenors, as either plaintiffs or defendants, cannot make use of the statement in *Owen Equipment*, examined above, of the ancillary jurisdiction policies. Permissive intervenors are only seeking intervention because of common questions of law or fact existing between their claims and defenses and those of the existing parties, not because in the absence of the ability to intervene their interests may be practically impaired or impeded. This raises further questions as to whether the "policies of diversity jurisdiction" would be satisfied by permissively intervening plaintiffs or defendants so as to prevent § 1367(b) from withdrawing supplemental jurisdiction, even if such jurisdiction is conferred by § 1367(a).

Assuming that § 1367(b) is relevant to permissive intervention, the analysis would proceed the same as in cases of Rule 24(a) intervention. As in the case of Rule 24(a)(2), when the Rule 24(b) intervenor seeks to enter the action on the plaintiff's side of the litigation, § 1367(b) specifically prohibits intervention when it would be inconsistent with the restrictions of 28 U.S.C. § 1332.[395] Thus, if a plaintiff intervenor under Rule 24(b) has a claim for less than $75,000.01, § 1367(b) prohibits the exercise of supplemental jurisdiction over the intervenor's claim. When the intervenor seeks to enter the action on the defendant's side of the case, the same result should follow, even though, as in the case of intervention under Rule 24(a)(2), the language of § 1367(b) does not literally prohibit supplemental jurisdiction unless the plaintiff is asserting a claim against the defendant.

The cases under Rule 24(b) generally agree that there is no reason to allow a party to intervene in the action under Rule 24(b) when original joinder of the party

---

have held that something more than a "loose factual relationship" between the freestanding and supplemental claims is necessary to satisfy the Article III case-or-controversy standard incorporated in § 1367(a).

393. *Cf.* American Honda Motor Co. v. Clair Int'l, Inc., No. C.A. 98-11254-MLW, 1999 WL 414323, 1999 U.S. Dist. LEXIS 9281 (D. Mass. Apr. 16, 1999) (party seeks to intervene to assert crossclaim; court concludes that intervenor should be realigned as a plaintiff and denies permission to intervene under § 1367(b), which prohibited intervention because intervenor was not diverse from defendant); *see also* Lennox Indus., Inc. v. Caicedo Yusti, 172 F.R.D. 617 (D.P.R. 1997) (Rule 24(a) intervenor realigned as a plaintiff and intervention denied under § 1367(b) because diversity did not exist between intervenor and defendant).

394. *See* 28 U.S.C. § 1367(b).

395. This result is produced by the language disallowing supplemental jurisdiction over claims by persons "seeking to intervene as plaintiffs under Rule 24." *See id.* Since there is no point in an intervening plaintiff coming into the action except to assert a claim, this language effectively prohibits intervention.

would have been prohibited by the restrictions of 28 U.S.C. § 1332.[396] Indeed, as with the similar case discussed under Rule 24(a)(2), intervention under Rule 24(b) in these circumstances would contravene the text of § 1367(b),[397] as well as the reasons that § 1367(b) was enacted.[398] Alternatively, however, if intervention of nondiverse Rule 24(b) defendants is permitted under § 1367, plaintiffs should only be prohibited from asserting claims against the intervenors as long as the intervenors do not directly assert claims against the plaintiffs, as argued in conjunction with Rule 24(a).[399]

In summary, the best interpretation of § 1367 is that supplemental jurisdiction should not be available to intervenors in any action in which jurisdiction is solely based on diversity of citizenship and there are defects of citizenship or jurisdictional amount present in the intervenor's motions to intervene. Supplemental jurisdiction should only be available over applications for intervention in federal question cases. Even in such cases, however, the text of § 1367(a) will constitute a barrier to intervention of defendants under Rule 24. Section 1367(a) only confers supplemental jurisdiction over claims. If a Rule 24 intervenor is not asserting a claim and if the plaintiff has no claim against the intervenor, § 1367(a) does not authorize supplemental jurisdiction.[400]

---

396. *See, e.g.,* Turner/Ozanne v. Hyman/Power, 111 F.3d 1312, 1319 (7th Cir. 1997) (after enactment of supplemental jurisdiction statute, course previously followed in cases of permissive intervention must continue to be followed); Betancourt-Torres v. Puerto Rico Elec. Power Auth., 164 F.R.D. 307 (D.P.R. 1996) (no supplemental jurisdiction over nondiverse plaintiffs seeking permissive intervention); Hallco Mfg. Co. v. Quaeck, 161 F.R.D. 98, 102 (D. Or. 1995) (same).

397. As with Rule 19 joinder and Rule 24(a)(2) joinder, discussed earlier in the text, the language of § 1367(b) prohibits "claims by plaintiffs against persons made parties under Rule . . . 24." This language literally would allow intervention if the requirements of § 1367(a) are satisfied, but would prohibit the plaintiff from asserting claims against, for example, a nondiverse intervenor once the intervenor is in the action (*i.e.*, "made a party"). Thus, this provision would allow a defendant-intervenor to assert defenses, or perhaps even claims, against the plaintiff, but the language of § 1367(b), read literally, would prevent the plaintiff from asserting claims against the intervenor. However, as noted in the text and notes, *supra*, and in the discussion of joinder of Rule 19 defendants in section C(3)*(c)* if the plaintiff is not asserting a claim against a defendant, § 1367(a) does not authorize supplemental jurisdiction over the intervenor in the first place. If the plaintiff is asserting a claim against the nondiverse intervenor, § 1367(b) prohibits intervention.

398. The House Report accompanying § 1367(b) states:

> In diversity-only actions the district courts may not hear plaintiffs' supplemental claims when exercising supplemental jurisdiction would encourage plaintiffs to evade the jurisdictional requirements of 28 U.S.C. § 1332 by the simple expedient of naming initially only those defendants whose joinder satisfies [§] 1332's requirements and later adding claims not within original federal jurisdiction against other defendants who have intervened or been joined on a supplemental basis.

H.R. REP. NO. 734, 101st Cong., 2d Sess. 29 (1990).

399. *See* section C(3)*(c) supra* ("Problems of Subject-Matter Jurisdiction, Venue, and Personal Jurisdiction Under Rule 19").

400. *See id.* The result in all the intervention cases differs from the result reached in cases of Rule 14 joinder of third-party defendants. In all cases in which intervention would violate the restrictions of 28 U.S.C. § 1332, the text recommends that intervention be prohibited. (The same was true, of course, of joinder under Rule 19.) However, in section D(1)*(c)*, *supra*, the text did not recommend that joinder of third-party defendants be disallowed under § 1367(b). Rather, it was suggested there that joinder be permitted, but the language of § 1367(b) be construed to limit the assertion of claims by the plaintiff against the third-party defendant only when the third-party defendant did not directly assert claims against the plaintiff. This construction was necessary in order to prevent unfair results from accruing to all the parties in the action—the defendant, the plaintiff, and the third-party defendant. *See* section D(1)(c) *supra* ("Problems of Subject-Matter Jurisdiction, Venue, and Personal Jurisdiction Under Rule 14"). However, in cases in which Rule 14 parties are joined, a claim is clearly being asserted against them that satisfies the requirements of § 1367(a). Such a situation may not exist in cases of intervening defendants under Rule 24. Furthermore, no parallel problems of unfairness exist in denying intervention to nondiverse Rule 24 defendants. No unfairness accrues to any of the persons already parties by disallowing intervention under either Rule 24(a)(2) or Rule 24(b). Likewise, no serious unfairness occurs to Rule 24(b) intervenors by disallowing intervention by them, as demonstrated in *Illustrations 8-47* and *8-48 supra.* Only persons seeking to intervene under 24(a)(2), whose interests might be adversely affected by the disposition of the action, could suffer harm of

In 2002, Congress enacted 28 U.S.C. § 1369, the Multiparty, Multiforum Trial Jurisdiction Act of 2002, to provide the district courts with subject-matter jurisdiction over certain multiparty mass accident cases based on minimal diversity of citizenship between the parties. This Act is discussed principally in Chapter 2(C)(3)*(e)*, above. As part of the Act, Congress provided special rights of intervention in 28 U.S.C. § 1369(d). Specifically, Congress provided that in any action in a district court that could have been brought "in whole or in part" under § 1369, any person with a claim arising from the accident that provides the basis of jurisdiction under the Act "shall be permitted to intervene as a party plaintiff in the action, even if that person could not have brought an action in a district court as an original matter."[401] In cases covered by this provision, the right to intervene will obviously be independent of the restrictions in § 1367(a) & (b), discussed above.

(d) Venue Problems Under Rule 24

Federal venue requirements have usually involved fewer problems under Rule 24 than subject-matter-jurisdiction limitations. Because venue is waivable, the courts have generally held that intervenors cannot complain that federal venue is improper as to them. By moving to intervene, the usual view is that an intervenor waives any venue objection they might have had as an original party.[402] Whether this is correct, however, may depend upon whether an intervenor is a Rule 24(a) or (b) intervenor. As discussed in earlier subsections, Rule 24(a)(2) intervenors are persons who should have been joined under Rule 19 in the first place and who are being allowed into the action because their interests might be irreparably affected by the action. As examined in conjunction with Rule 19, that rule explicitly preserves the right of Rule 19 parties to object to personal jurisdiction and venue. Furthermore, as discussed in the *Ross* case, examined in the next subsection, rules governing location of suit, such as personal jurisdiction and venue restrictions, often afford valuable protections against burdensome and inconvenient location of litigation to defending parties. These considerations may suggest that the traditional waiver rule governing intervenors is wrong. Further discussion of this possibility is postponed until the next subsection.

Can defending parties other than the intervenor object if intervention would render venue improper? It has been suggested that the answer should depend on whether ancillary jurisdiction—today, "supplemental jurisdiction"—exists over the case. Under this view, if supplemental jurisdiction exists, the ordinary venue requirements should be disregarded. If supplemental jurisdiction does not exist, venue objections raised by the original parties to the action should prevent intervention.[403] Even if the "supplemental jurisdiction" rule is followed, the

---

a serious nature by the denial of intervention. However, because these intervenors are also Rule 19(a)(2)(i) parties, the court is obligated either to protect them against that harm by taking appropriate steps under Rule 19(b), or to dismiss the action. *Cf.* H.R. REP. NO. 734, 101st Cong., 2d Sess. 29 (1990).

401. *See* 28 U.S.C. § 1369(d).

402. *See* 7C CHARLES A. WRIGHT ET AL., FEDERAL PRACTICE AND PROCEDURE: CIVIL § 1918 (3d ed. 2007).

403. *See id.* If the position of this text is adopted, supplemental jurisdiction would not extend to any case of intervention when the basis of jurisdiction is diversity of citizenship. Therefore, a venue standard keyed to supplemental jurisdiction could operate only in federal question cases.

question would remain whether to allow the original defendants to raise venue objections when subject-matter jurisdiction would be proper over them without resort to the doctrine of "ancillary" or "supplemental" jurisdiction, but the defendants are arguing that venue has been destroyed by the intervention. This situation might occur, for example, when complete diversity exists not only between the plaintiff and the original defendant, but also between the plaintiff and the intervenor, but the intervenor is a nonresident of the state and venue is proper over the original defendants based on their residence in the state.

In fact, however, there is no reason to allow the original defendants in an action to raise venue objections based on intervention in any case, whether subject-matter jurisdiction would exist if the intervenor is an originally joined party or the supplemental jurisdiction statute must be used to establish jurisdiction. As noted in section D(1)*(c)* and in Chapter 7(F)(4)*(b)*, above, the venue statutes are ordinarily applicable only to original claims in the action. This sensible rule should not be abandoned in intervention cases. Even though Rule 24(a)(2) intervenors will often be Rule 19(a) parties, as previously discussed,[404] Rule 19(a)(3) only preserves the right of the Rule 19 party to make venue objections, not the right of other parties to do so. Therefore, there is no reason to abandon the usual approach to venue because of a Rule 24(a) intervenor's status as a Rule 19 party, and if the Rule 24 intervenor is not a Rule 19 party (as in the case of Rule 24(b) intervenors), there is no arguable basis for allowing any venue objection to be made by the original defendants on the intervenor's behalf. As discussed in Chapter 4, even in actions not involving intervention, resident defendants cannot raise venue objections for nonresidents in cases where venue is based on the residence of the defendants in the state.[405] These cases are based on the reasoning that the defense of venue is personal to the party possessing it and can only be raised by that party.[406] There is no reason to reach a different result in intervention cases. If the existing defendants will be subjected to any kind of inconvenience due to the presence of the intervenor, they can move for a transfer of venue under 28 U.S.C. § 1404(a) or a dismissal on grounds of forum non conveniens, whichever is appropriate.[407] Lesser inconvenience can be dealt with, when appropriate, by conditioning the right to intervene in reasonable ways.[408]

(e) Personal Jurisdiction Problems Under Rule 24

As with venue objections, the courts have usually held that the intervenor waives any personal jurisdiction objections that the intervenor might otherwise have

---

404. *See* section C(3)*(c) supra* (discussing venue in Rule 19 cases).

405. *See* 28 U.S.C. § 1391(a)(1) & (b)(1). In cases in which venue is based on the occurrence of substantial events within the district or the presence of a substantial portion of the property that is the subject of the action within the district, it is difficult to envision cases in which intervention would arguably render venue improper that is otherwise proper under 28 U.S.C. § 1391(a)(2) or (b)(2). In addition, the fallback provisions in § 1391(a)(3) & (b)(3) make venue proper in a district in which "any defendant is subject to personal jurisdiction" or in which "any defendant may be found," respectively. Therefore, if one of the original defendants is subject to personal jurisdiction or found within the district, intervention would not even arguably make venue improper.

406. *See* Chapter 4(C)(2) *supra* (discussing venue based on defendants' residence).

407. *See* Chapter 4(D)(1)*(a)* & (2)*(a) supra* (discussing, respectively, forum non conveniens and transfer under § 1404(a)).

408. *See* 7C CHARLES A. WRIGHT ET AL., FEDERAL PRACTICE AND PROCEDURE: CIVIL § 1922 (3d ed. 2007) (discussing cases placing conditions on the right to intervene in both Rule 24(a) and 24(b) cases).

asserted in the principal action had the intervenor been originally joined as a defendant, though this result should not necessarily be true of other claims, such as permissive counterclaims, asserted against the intervenor by the original parties after intervention.[409] Although the usual result is to conclude that an intervenor has consented to personal jurisdiction, whether this should necessarily be so in all cases has recently been questioned by the Ninth Circuit Court of Appeals in *SEC v. Ross*.[410] In an unusual case, the Securities and Exchange Commission brought a civil enforcement action against a telecommunications company, its owners, and its sales and marketing partners for sale of unregistered securities, and the district court appointed a receiver for the company to manage it and preserve its assets for eventual distribution to the injured investors. After relief was granted against the sole owner of the company, the receiver made a motion to force the company's sales agents to disgorge their commissions on the sale of the unregistered securities, also requesting that the court act against the agents through summary proceedings. The SEC joined this motion, arguing that it was well settled that the district courts had the power to order disgorgement by non-parties. Subsequently, several of the agents moved to intervene under Rule 24(a)(2) while attempting also to preserve their jurisdictional objections. The district court permitted the intervention over the receiver's objections, and the agents answered, asserting several substantive defenses, as well as the defenses of lack of personal jurisdiction, improper venue, and "insufficient process." The district court held that the securities laws permitted nationwide service of process and that the agents' contacts with the United States were sufficient to support the exercise of personal jurisdiction over them under the Fifth Amendment. The court also held that venue was proper because the agents were scattered across the country and it was more efficient to try the case in one location.

The court of appeals reversed. The court held that while the district court had the power to exercise nationwide long-arm jurisdiction over the agents, the *ability* to exercise such jurisdiction was not *actual* exercise of jurisdiction. The receiver had neither served the agents with process, nor named them in the complaint, and had resisted at every stage their opportunity to participate as parties. Nor could the agents be considered only "nominal parties" whom it was not necessary to serve, or summary proceedings be used against them, because the receiver was alleging wrongdoing on their part and had not established jurisdiction over them based on the fact that the commissions were assets in the district.

Finally, the court held that the agents had not consented to personal jurisdiction by intervening. Although recognizing that courts usually hold that an intervenor consents to personal jurisdiction by intervening, the court refused to adopt a per se rule that this is always so. Where the intervening party objects in a timely and unambiguous fashion to the court's jurisdiction, this conclusion would not be drawn, even though the party, as in this case, has also asserted claims or defenses against the plaintiff. The court stated:

---

409. *See* Chapter 7(F)(4)*(b) supra* ("Supplemental (Ancillary) Venue and Personal Jurisdiction Over Counter-claims and Crossclaims").

410. 504 F.3d 1130 (9th Cir. 2007) (Bybee, J.).

> We do not see why an intervenor should be considered to have automatically consented to the jurisdiction of the court. The intervenor has consented to something, but it is not personal jurisdiction. Rather the *quid pro quo* for his intervention is that he consents to have the district court determine all issues in the case, including issues of jurisdiction, venue and service of process. . . . Intervention of right simply puts the intervenor into the position he would have been in had the plaintiff (or another party) properly named him to begin with.[411]

Although the Court's decision was contrary to the usual result in intervention cases, the opinion contains some important insights for future cases. Rule 24(a)(2) intervenors are also Rule 19(a)(1)(B)(i) parties who should have been joined in the first place. Given that the claim of a Rule 24(a)(2) (or Rule 19(a)(1)(B)(i)) party is that the action will have an adverse practical effect on its substantive interests, there is good reason to allow a party to intervene and insist that the court adjudicating the action be one that could exercise personal jurisdiction over it, and, as well, that the plaintiff has taken the proper steps to actually effectuate personal jurisdiction over the intervenor-defendant. Personal jurisdiction and venue[412] rules have an impact on a party's opportunity to litigate effectively in a particular location. Thus, there is no inherent reason why these objections should not be as proper a basis of intervention as substantive defenses.

What of personal jurisdiction over parties against whom claims are asserted by the intervenor? The principal parties to an action will seldom be able to raise effective jurisdictional objections when an intervenor asserts claims against them that are closely related to the original subject matter of the suit. It is conceivable, but unlikely, that a long-arm statute might extend to the original defendant based on actions the defendant has performed in the state, but not to the intervenor's closely related claim against the defendant. Certainly, if a statutory basis of jurisdiction exits, one would not expect minimum-contacts problems with the intervenor's claim when jurisdiction can be constitutionally asserted over a factually-related principal claim. However, the same may not be true of claims wholly unrelated to the main action joined under Rules 18(a) or 13(b). Both statutory and constitutional personal jurisdiction requirements might well exist and have to be satisfied independently over any such claims.[413]

---

411. *Id.* at 1150.

412. Given its ruling on the personal jurisdiction issue, the court found it unnecessary to decide the intervenor's venue objection.

413. *Cf.* 7C CHARLES A. WRIGHT ET AL., FEDERAL PRACTICE AND PROCEDURE: CIVIL § 1919 (3d ed. 2007). Again, however, this statement must be qualified in the same way it was in Chapter 7, in which the ability of a plaintiff to object to permissive counterclaims on jurisdictional grounds was discussed. The Supreme Court's decision in the *Burnham* case, discussed in Chapter 3(E)(2), may be interpreted to mean that commencement of an action in a particular location without more is sufficient to permit personal jurisdiction to be asserted over plaintiffs on claims arising outside the state. If so, when a defendant-intervenor asserts an unrelated claim against the plaintiff, the plaintiff would have no effective personal jurisdiction objection. A harder question is whether, if a plaintiff-intervenor joins an unrelated claim against the defendant under Rule 18, *Burnham* might be read to deprive the defendant of personal jurisdiction objections to the unrelated claim. Arguably, *Burnham* should not be read so broadly. When an intervenor comes into an action on the side of the plaintiff, the intervenor should be treated as an original party for purposes of assessing personal jurisdiction objections over claims asserted by the intervenor. If the intervenor could not have obtained personal jurisdiction over the defendant on a claim joined under Rule 18 if the intervenor had been an original plaintiff in the action, the defendant should not be deprived

(f) Rules Enabling Act Issues with Rule 24

Federal Rule 24 does not pose any serious Rules Enabling Act issues. The ability to intervene in a federal action when intervention is impossible under state law, or the inability to intervene under Rule 24 when state law would permit intervention, involves no more than differences in procedural philosophy between the federal and state systems. The differences impose nothing more than tactical burdens on parties and intervenors and do not significantly affect substantive rights. Furthermore, as with the other claim and party-joinder rules we have examined in Chapter 7 and this chapter, if the plurality's interpretation of the Rules Enabling Act in the *Shady Grove* case ultimately becomes the majority view of the Supreme Court, Rule 24 will be valid even if it conflicts with a state intervention rule supported by substantive policies, because there is no doubt that Rule 24 is a rule that is rationally classifiable as procedural.[414]

4. Class Actions

The class action procedure allows a suit to be brought by or against a party who is a representative of a large number of persons similarly situated to the representative, but who are not formally joined as parties in the action. Class actions are designed to avoid multiple litigation. In the absence of class actions, a large number of individual actions would often be necessary to settle existing claims. In addition, class actions provide for vindication of individual claims by representation when joinder of multiple parties or assertion of each claim singly is impractical.

(a) History of Class Actions

Nothing like the modern class action existed at common law. In common-law actions, rigid principles governed joinder of parties. The class action developed in equity as the bill of peace, which allowed an equity court to entertain an action by or against representatives of a group when the size of the group was so large as to make joinder of all its members impossible or impractical.[415] All members of the group had to share "a common *right*, a community of interest in the *subject-matter of the controversy*, or a common *title* from which all their separate claims and all the questions at issue arise."[416] The representatives also had to represent the interests of the absent members of the class adequately.[417]

---

of the personal jurisdiction objection merely because joinder has been achieved under Rule 24 rather than an alternative rule. *See* Chapter 7(C) *supra* ("Joinder of Claims by Plaintiffs under the Federal Rules").

414. *See* Chapter 5(F)(6) *supra* ("The *Shady Grove* Decision").

415. *See* ZECHARIAH CHAFEE, JR., SOME PROBLEMS OF EQUITY 149-50, 200-01 (1950); Thomas D. Rowe, Jr., *A Distant Mirror: The Bill of Peace in Early American Mass Torts and Its Implications for Modern Class Actions*, 39 ARIZ. L. REV. 711 (1997). The bill of peace is still available in some state courts. *See* Prestage Farms, Inc. v. Norman, 813 So. 2d 732 (Miss. 2002) (use of equitable bill of peace to join parties in nuisance action by several property owners against farmers and operator of hog farms).

416. 1 JOHN N. POMEROY, A TREATISE ON EQUITY JURISPRUDENCE § 268, at 596 (5th ed. 1941); *see also id.* at §§ 245-246, 269-269a.

417. *See* ZECHARIAH CHAFEE, JR., SOME PROBLEMS OF EQUITY 232 (1950).

These equity procedures for class suits were adopted by the codes. The Field Code provided that "when the question is one of a common or general interest of many persons, or when the parties are very numerous and it may be impracticable to bring them all before the court, one or more may sue or defend for the benefit of the whole."[418] This provision was duplicated widely and still exists in some states.[419]

In the federal system, the Federal Equity Rules and the Conformity Acts governed class action practice before 1938. The Federal Equity Rules of 1848 provided for class actions in Rule 48:

> Where the parties on either side are very numerous, and cannot, without manifest inconvenience and oppressive delays in the suit, be all brought before it, the court in its discretion may dispense with making all of them parties, and may proceed in the suit, having sufficient parties before it to represent all the adverse interests of the plaintiffs and the defendants in the suit properly before it. *But in such cases the decree shall be without prejudice to the rights and claims of all the absent parties.*[420]

The last sentence of this rule appeared to state that the judgment in a class action would not bind the members of the class—a rule contrary to the English practice[421] and one that would seriously impair the usefulness of the class action procedure. Cases both invoked and ignored this restriction.[422] Rule 38 of the Equity Rules of 1912 omitted the restriction: "When the question is one of common or general interest to many persons constituting a class so numerous as to make it impracticable to bring them all before the court, one or more may sue or defend for the whole."[423] However, questions continued about the binding effect of a judgment under Rule 38, apparently because of doubts about whether due process would be violated by a judgment that bound absent class members.[424]

When the Federal Rules of Civil Procedure were adopted in 1938, class actions were dealt with in Rule 23. The original rule was said to be "a substantial restatement of former Equity Rule 38"[425] and was applied to both law and equity cases.[426] Rule 23(a) divided class actions into three categories: "true" class actions

---

418. Act of Apr. 11, 1849, ch. 438, § 119, 1849 N.Y. Laws 613, 639.

419. *See, e.g.*, NEB. REV. STAT. § 25-319 (2008); *see generally* CHARLES E. CLARK, HANDBOOK OF THE LAW OF CODE PLEADING § 63 (2d ed. 1947).

420. 42 U.S. (1 How.) lvi (1848) (emphasis added).

421. *See* ZECHARIAH CHAFEE, JR., SOME PROBLEMS OF EQUITY 224-25 (1950).

422. *Compare* Smith v. Swormstedt, 57 U.S. (16 How.) 288, 303, 14 L. Ed. 942, 948-49 (1854) *with* Wabash R.R. Co. v. Adelbert College of W. Reserve Univ., 208 U.S. 609, 28 S. Ct. 425, 52 L. Ed. 642 (1908).

423. 226 U.S. 627, 659 (1912). This rule was influenced by the procedure in code class actions, discussed above.

424. *See* 7A CHARLES A. WRIGHT ET AL., FEDERAL PRACTICE AND PROCEDURE: CIVIL § 1751 (3d ed. 2005); *see* Christopher v. Brusselback, 302 U.S. 500, 58 S. Ct. 350, 82 L. Ed. 388 (1938); Supreme Tribe of Ben-Hur v. Cauble, 255 U.S. 356, 41 S. Ct. 338, 65 L. Ed. 673 (1921).

425. *See* FED. R. CIV. P. 23 advisory committee's note to the original rule.

426. Original Rule 23 read as follows:

> (a) Representation. If persons constituting a class are so numerous as to make it impracticable to bring them all before the court, such of them, one or more, as will fairly insure the adequate representation of all may, on behalf of all, sue or be sued, when the character of the right sought to be enforced for or against the class is
>
> (1) joint or common, or secondary in the sense that the owner of a primary right refuses to enforce that right and a member of the class thereby becomes entitled to enforce it;
>
> (2) several, and the object of the action is the adjudication of claims which do or may affect specific property involved in the action; or

(Rule 23(a)(1) actions); "hybrid" class actions (Rule 23(a)(2) actions); and "spurious" class actions (Rule 23(a)(3) actions).[427] Serious difficulties developed with this tripartite categorization. The "true" class action under Rule 23(a)(1) was one in which the right sought to be enforced was "joint," "common," or "secondary." A judgment in a "true" class action bound the absent members of the class.[428] However, as the Advisory Committee stated in 1966, "[i]n practice the terms 'joint,' 'common,' etc., which were used as the basis of the . . . classification proved obscure and uncertain."[429] The primary difficulty involved the inclusion of the term "common," which traditionally had not been used to govern joinder of parties.[430] It was difficult to distinguish between "common" rights, which made a class suit "true," and "several" rights, which made a class suit either "hybrid" or "spurious" under Rule 23(a)(2) and (3).[431]

All actions that were not "true" class actions had to be either "hybrid" or "spurious."[432] "Hybrid" class actions under Rule 23(a)(2) were actions in which the rights asserted by or against the class were "several" *and* in which the object of the action was the adjudication of claims pertaining to specific property in the action. The judgment in a "hybrid" class action bound the absent members of the class only with regard to their rights in the specific property that was the subject of the action.[433] A "spurious" class action resembled a "hybrid" action in that the rights asserted by or against the class in both were "several."[434] However, a "spurious" action did not adjudicate a claim affecting specific property. Instead, the "spurious" class action involved a common question of law or fact affecting the several rights *and* some common relief sought by or against the members of the class.[435] The judgment in a "spurious" class suit bound only those members of the class before the court, though courts sometimes held that class members could intervene after a favorable result in order to get the benefit of the judgment in a "spurious" class

---

(3) several, and there is a common question of law or fact affecting the several rights and a common relief is sought.

(b) Secondary Action by Shareholders. In an action brought to enforce a secondary right on the part of one or more shareholders in an association, incorporated or unincorporated, because the association refuses to enforce rights which may properly be asserted by it, the complaint shall be verified by oath and shall aver (1) that the plaintiff was a shareholder at the time of the transaction of which he complains or that his share thereafter devolved on him by operation of law and (2) that the action is not a collusive one to confer on a court of the United States jurisdiction of any action of which it would not otherwise have jurisdiction. The complaint shall also set forth with particularity the efforts of the plaintiff to secure from the managing directors or trustees and, if necessary, from the shareholders such action as he desires, and the reasons for his failure to obtain such action or the reasons for not making such effort.

(c) Dismissal or Compromise. A class action shall not be dismissed or compromised without the approval of the court. If the right sought to be enforced is one defined in paragraph (1) of subdivision (a) of this rule notice of the proposed dismissal or compromise shall be given to all members of the class in such manner as the court directs. If the right is one defined in paragraphs (2) or (3) of subdivision (a) notice shall be given only if the court requires it.

308 U.S. at 689-90 (1938).

427. *See* FED. R. CIV. P. 23 advisory committee's note to the 1966 Amendments.

428. *See id.*

429. *Id.*

430. *See* ZECHARIAH CHAFEE, JR., SOME PROBLEMS OF EQUITY 245-46, 255-57 (1950).

431. *See id.*; FED. R. CIV. P. 23 advisory committee's note to the 1966 Amendments.

432. *See* 7A CHARLES A. WRIGHT ET AL., FEDERAL PRACTICE AND PROCEDURE: CIVIL § 1752 (3d ed. 2005).

433. *See* FED. R. CIV. P. 23 advisory committee's note to the 1966 Amendments.

434. *See id.*

435. *See id.*

suit.[436] Obviously, the "spurious" class suit, in the absence of intervention by class members, was little more than a permissive joinder rule.[437]

The 1966 amendments to Rule 23 eliminated the three categories of class actions employed by the original rule. The structure of Rule 23 today requires a two-tiered analysis. First, an action must qualify generally for class action treatment under Rule 23(a). Second, the action must be found to fit within one of the three categories of class actions in Rule 23(b). Rule 23(c) and (d) govern various procedural matters, and Rule 23(e) states the requirements for settlement, dismissal, or compromise of a class action. Rule 23(f) confers discretion on the courts of appeals to permit appeals from orders granting or denying class certification. Rule 23(g) governs appointment and duties of class counsel. Finally, Rule 23(h) authorizes and regulates the award of attorney's fees in class actions. In addition, Rules 23.1 and 23.2 were added to the Federal Rules of Civil Procedure in 1966. Rule 23.1 governs derivative actions by shareholders, a particular kind of class action governed by Rule 23(b) before 1966. Rule 23.2 deals with actions brought by or against unincorporated associations. No specific provisions governed such actions prior to Rule 23.2. As a result, actions by or against associations had to qualify under one of the three categories of Rule 23(a) before 1966.

The criticisms of class and derivative actions since the 1966 amendments to Federal Rule 23 have been many and varied. These criticisms generally have focused on the ease with which in mass torts, securities, and some other kinds of litigation plaintiffs can bring "frivolous" actions that impose large defense costs on the party opposing the class. Thus, defendants are often inclined to settle class actions for substantial sums in order to avoid the greater litigational costs and the risks associated with a full defense of the action.[438] Numerous reforms to the class

---

436. *See id.*; York v. Guaranty Trust Co., 143 F.2d 503, 529 (2d Cir. 1944), *rev'd on other grounds*, 326 U.S. 99, 65 S. Ct. 1464, 89 L. Ed. 2079 (1945).

437. *See* 7A CHARLES A. WRIGHT ET AL., FEDERAL PRACTICE AND PROCEDURE: CIVIL § 1752 (3d ed. 2005). The Advisory Committee's Note to the 1966 Amendment to Rule 23 stated:

> The "spurious" action envisaged by original Rule 23 was in any event an anomaly because, although denominated a "class" action and pleaded as such, it was supposed not to adjudicate the rights or liabilities of any person not a party. It was believed to be an advantage of the "spurious" category that it would invite decisions that a member of the "class" could, like a member of the class in a "true" or "hybrid" action, intervene on an ancillary basis without being required to show an independent basis of Federal jurisdiction, and have the benefit of the date of the commencement of the action for purposes of the statute of limitations.

FED. R. CIV. P. 23 advisory committee's note to the 1966 Amendments.

438. *See, e.g.*, Janet Cooper Alexander, *Do the Merits Matter? A Study of Settlements in Securities Class Actions,* 43 STAN. L. REV. 497 (1991); John C. Anderson, Note, *Good "Brick" Walls Make Good Neighbors: Should A State Court Certify A Multistate or Nationwide Class of Indirect Purchasers?* 70 FORDHAM L. REV. 2019 (2002); John C. Coffee, Jr., *The Regulation of Entrepreneurial Litigation: Balancing Fairness and Efficiency in the Large Class Action,* 54 U. CHI. L. REV. 877 (1987); John C. Coffee, Jr., *Rethinking the Class Action: A Policy Primer on Reform,* 62 IND. L.J. 625 (1987); John C. Coffee, Jr., *Understanding the Plaintiff's Attorney: The Implications of Economic Theory for Private Enforcement of Law Through Class and Derivative Actions,* 86 COLUM. L. REV. 669 (1986); John C. Coffee, Jr., *The Unfaithful Champion: The Plaintiff as Monitor in Shareholder Litigation,* 48 LAW & CONTEMP. PROBS. 5 (Summer 1985); John C. Coffee, Jr., *Rescuing the Private Attorney General: Why the Model of the Lawyer as Bounty Hunter is Not Working,* 42 MD. L. REV. 215 (1983); Howard M. Downs, *Federal Class Actions: Diminished Protection for the Class and the Case for Reform,* 73 NEB. L. REV. 646 (1994); Howard M. Erichson, *Coattail Class Actions: Reflections on* Microsoft, *Tobacco, and the Mixing of Public and Private Lawyering in Mass Litigation*, 34 U.C. DAVIS L. REV. 1 (2000); Howard M. Erichson, *Mass Tort Litigation and Inquisitorial Justice,* 87 GEO. L.J. 1983 (1999); Owen M. Fiss, *The Political Theory of the Class Action,* 53 WASH. & LEE L. REV. 21 (1996); Elizabeth J. Goldstein, *Federal Rule of Civil Procedure 23: A Need for Technical Innovation,* 104 DICK. L. REV. 653 (2000); Geoffrey C. Hazard Jr., *Modeling Class Counsel,* 81 NEB. L. REV. 1397 (2003); Peter Margulies, *The New Class Action Jurisprudence and Public Interest Law*, 25 N.Y.U. REV. L. & SOC. CHANGE 487 (1999); Richard A. Nagareda, *The Preexistence Principle*

action procedure have been suggested, but few of these reforms have been implemented.[439]

In 1995, however, Congress responded to the criticisms of class actions in the securities area by enacting the Private Securities Litigation Reform Act of 1995.[440] The Act amends the Securities Act of 1933 and the Securities and Exchange Act of 1934 to impose special provisions governing class actions under those statutes. In general, the Act adds procedural provisions to the 1933 and 1934 Acts that are designed to discourage frivolous securities litigation. The Act contains (1) special certification requirements for securities class actions; (2) special notice requirements to the absent class members designed to allow other members to qualify as lead representative of the class; (3) restrictions on how frequently persons can serve as class representatives in securities actions; (4) proportionate per share restrictions on the amount that the class representative can recover; (5) reasonableness restrictions on the amount that attorneys can be paid keyed to the amount of damages and prejudgment interest paid to the class; (6) special regulation of class settlements, including specific statements that must be sent to the class concerning proposed settlements; and (7) regulations designed to assure that attorneys representing the class do not have a conflict of interest.[441] In addition, as noted in Chapter 6, above,[442] the Act alters the provisions of Federal Rule of Civil Procedure 11 as to class and non-class actions brought under the Securities Acts.[443]

---

and the Structure of the Class Action, 103 COLUM. L. REV. 149 (2003); Michael H. Pinkerton, Castano v. American Tobacco Company: *American's Nicotine Plaintiffs Have No Class,* 58 LA. L. REV. 647 (1998); George L. Priest, *Procedural Versus Substantive Controls of Mass Tort Class Actions,* 26 J. LEG. STUD. 521 (1997); Charles Silver, *"We're Scared To Death": Class Certification and Blackmail,* 78 N.Y.U. L. REV. 1357 (2003); Symposium, *Summing Up Procedural Justice: Exploring the Tension Between Collective Processes and Individual Rights in the Context of Settlement and Litigating Classes,* 30 U.C. DAVIS L. REV. 785 (1997); Symposium, *The Institute of Judicial Administration Research Conference on Class Actions,* 71 N.Y.U. L. REV. 1 (1996); Symposium, *National Mass Tort Conference,* 73 TEX. L. REV. 1523 (1995); Thomas Merton Woods, Note, *Wielding the Sledgehammer: Legislative Solutions for Class Action Jurisdictional Reform,* 75 N.Y.U. L. REV. 507 (2000); *see also* Note, *Risk-Preference Asymmetries in Class Action Litigation,* 119 HARV. L. REV. 587 (2005); Note, *When Should Courts Allow the Settlement of Duty-of-Loyalty Derivative Suits,* 109 HARV. L. REV. 1084 (1996). Professor David Shapiro has recently examined the class action in modern litigation and contrasted the "individual autonomy" model of class actions with the "entity" model, discussing the institutional obstacles created by these models that make it more difficult for the class action to reach its full potential. *See* David L. Shapiro, *Class Actions: The Class as Party and Client,* 73 NOTRE DAME L. REV. 913 (1998). For an article discussing whether class actions can be used to decide a defendant's entire liability for punitive damages arising from a defined course of conduct, see Joan Steinman, *Managing Punitive Damages: A Role for Mandatory "Limited Generosity" Classes and Anti-Suit Injunctions?* 36 WAKE FOREST L. REV. 1043 (2001). For an article that offers an interesting comparison, see Antonio Gidi, *Class Actions in Brazil—A Model for Civil Law Countries*, 51 AM. J. COMP. L. 311 (2003).

439. For example, one suggested reform is "judicial auctioning" of lawsuits as a means of more closely connecting the ownership and control of class actions and derivative litigation. The proceeds from the auction would be distributed among the plaintiff class. The winning bidder would be free to conduct the litigation in any manner the winner believes would be most appropriate. *See* Jonathan R. Macey & Geoffrey P. Miller, *The Plaintiffs' Attorney's Role in Class Action and Derivative Litigation: Economic Analysis and Recommendations for Reform,* 58 U. CHI. L. REV. 1 (1991); Randall S. Thomas & Robert G. Hansen, *Auctioning Class Action and Derivative Lawsuits: A Critical Analysis,* 87 NW. U. L. REV. 423 (1993); Jonathan R. Macey & Geoffrey P. Miller, *Auctioning Class Action and Derivative Law Suits: A Rejoinder,* 87 NW. U. L. REV. 458 (1993).

440. Pub. L. No. 104-67, 109 Stat. 737.

441. *See* Cohen v. United States Dist. Court, 586 F.3d 703 (9th Cir. 2009) (district court held not to have authority under the act to select lead counsel for the class action).

442. *See* Chapter 6(F)(3)*(c) supra* ("Sanctions and the 'Safe Harbor' Provision").

443. As discussed in Chapter 1(E)(5)*(b)*, *supra*, the Federal Rules of Civil Procedure are supposed to be "trans-substantive" in nature; *i.e.*, they are applicable to all civil actions, regardless of the substantive nature of the action. Obviously, reforms such as those found in the Securities Litigation Reform Act undermine this ideal.

Specific problems that have developed in class action practice under Rule 23 will be discussed in later subsections.

(b) Practice Under Rule 23

Federal Rule 23 governs class action practice in federal court and in states that have adopted the Federal Rules model. Therefore, an examination of practice under Rule 23 will provide a good illustration of modern class action practice in both federal and many state courts.

(i) Requirements for a Class Action

Rule 23(a) imposes four requirements for a valid class action. First, the class must be "so numerous that joinder of all members is impracticable."[444] Second, Rule 23(a)(2) requires that questions of law or fact common to the members of the class exist.[445] Third, Rule 23(a)(3) states that the claims or defenses of the representative parties must be typical of the claims or defenses of the class.[446] Fourth, Rule 23(a)(4) states that the representative parties must "fairly and adequately protect the interests of the class."[447]

---

444. *See* FED. R. CIV. P. 23(a)(1). There is no fixed number of persons that a class must contain to satisfy this "numerosity" requirement. *See, e.g.*, Kelley v. Norfolk & W. Ry. Co., 584 F.2d 34, 35 (4th Cir. 1978); Senter v. General Motors Corp., 532 F.2d 511, 523 n.24 (6th Cir. 1976); David v. Showtime/Movie Channel, Inc., 697 F. Supp. 752, 756 (S.D.N.Y. 1988). Obviously, however, the larger the class becomes, the more likely it is that joinder of all the class members will be deemed "impracticable."

445. "All that can be divined from the rule itself is that the use of the plural 'questions' suggests that more than one issue of law or fact must be common to members of the class." 7A CHARLES A. WRIGHT ET AL., FEDERAL PRACTICE AND PROCEDURE: CIVIL § 1763, at 217-18 (3d ed. 2005). Beyond this possible complication, the "common questions" requirement seems straightforward and easy to apply, just as it is in cases of permissive joinder under Rule 20. *See also* Thomas M. Byrne & Stacey A. McGavin, *Class Actions*, 61 MERCER L. REV. 1055 (2010) (discussing the commonality and typicality requirements in a RICO action in the Eleventh Circuit). *But see* Wal-Mart Stores, Inc. v. Dukes, 564 U.S. __, 131 S. Ct. 2541, 180 L. Ed. 2d 374 (2011) (rejecting class action status in a Title VII employment discrimination case for lack of commonality; Wal-Mart had permitted its managers to exercise great discretion in setting pay within a range as well as in making promotions; plaintiff's expert testified that some of these employment decisions were based upon a stereotypical view of gender roles; the expert, however, could not tell what percentage of the decisions were affected by that thinking; while recognizing that Rule 23(a) requires only a single question of law or fact in common to the class, the majority concluded that the claims by the class plaintiffs failed to raise any common questions of law or fact, *i.e.*, there was a common mode of exercising discretion that pervaded the entire company that tied the entire 1.5 million individual claims together).

446. Courts have taken varying approaches in determining whether this standard has been satisfied. Some courts pay little attention to the requirement, while others seem to view it as a requirement intended to buttress the adequacy of representation requirement of Rule 23(b)(4). Probably the best approach is to consider the requirement satisfied if the claims or defenses of the representative parties and the absent class members arise from a single occurrence or are based on the same legal or remedial theory. *See* Mersay v. First Republic Corp., 43 F.R.D. 465 (S.D.N.Y. 1968); Samuel-Bassett v. Kia Motors Corp., 34 A.3d 1 (Pa. 2011); 7A CHARLES A. WRIGHT ET AL., FEDERAL PRACTICE AND PROCEDURE: CIVIL § 1764 (3d ed. 2005).

447. Adequacy of representation is more critical under new Rule 23 than under the former rule because the judgment in all class actions under the new rule binds the absent members of the class. *See* FED. R. CIV. P. 23 advisory committee's note to the 1966 Amendments. Binding a party who has not had a day in court raises serious due process objections. One means of overcoming these objections is to insure that the interests of the absent members of the class are represented adequately in the action. *See* Hansberry v. Lee, 311 U.S. 32, 44-46, 61 S. Ct. 115, 119-20, 85 L. Ed. 22, 28-29 (1940). There is no fixed standard for determining when representation is adequate, and the determination must be made on a case-by-case basis. Relevant factors include the quality of the legal counsel employed by the representatives; the personal characteristics of the representatives, such as honesty; the extent of the representatives' interests in the action; and the extent to which the representatives' interests are adverse, antagonistic, or conflicting with the interests of members of the class. *See also* Wolfert *ex rel.* Estate of Wolfert v. Transamerica Home First, Inc., 439 F.3d 165 (2d Cir. 2006) (complaint in individual action dismissed on grounds of res judicata; plaintiff was adequately represented in prior California class action); Lee Anderson, *Preserving Adequacy of Representation When Dropping Claims in Class Actions,* 74 U.M.K.C. L. REV. 105

Illustration 8-50. *R* brings suit as the representative of all poor persons within the state against the state board of education. *R* alleges that the board is denying the members of the class its educational rights on the basis of economic status in violation of the Fourteenth Amendment. The class action is not proper. The designation of the class as "all poor persons within the state" is not adequate under Rule 23(a) because it is too vague.[448]

Illustration 8-51. *R*, a public school student, sued the local board of education. R sought an order to compel the board to desegregate the faculties of the public schools. *R* seeks to represent a class comprised of the local public school teachers and principals, whose constitutional rights are allegedly infringed by the segregated system maintained by the board. The class action is not proper under Rule 23(a), because *R* is not a member of the class *R* seeks to represent.[449]

Illustration 8-52. *P* sues *R*, the mayor of *City X*, as the representative of a defendant class comprised of the city council, which is comprised of the mayor and seven city council representatives. *P* seeks to have a city building desegregated. The class action is improper under Rule 23(a)(1), because the class is not so numerous that joinder of all of the class members is impracticable.[450]

Illustration 8-53. *R* sues as the representative of a class comprised of all persons who had been defrauded by *D*. *R* alleges that *D* defrauded some 3,000 persons over two years by making a variety of misrepresentations. The class action is improper under Rule 23(a)(2), because there are no questions of law or fact common to all the class members. The variety of misrepresentations prevents satisfaction of the common question requirement.[451]

Illustration 8-54. *R* sues as the representative of a class of 3,000 persons who were defrauded by *D* over a period of years. *R* purchased a replica of a work of art from *D*. *R* alleges that *D* failed to disclose that the replica of the work of art was made of brass rather than gold. *R* also alleges that *D* had a duty to disclose this information to potential purchasers. *R* alleges that the other class members were defrauded when *D* told them that replicas of the same work were made of gold, when they were really brass. A class action is not proper under Rule 23(a)(4), because the claim of the class representative, *R*, is not typical of the claims of the members of the class.

Illustration 8-55. *R* sues *D-1* and *D-2*. *R* brings the suit on *R's* own behalf and as representative of a class of persons who had signed loan contracts with

---

(2005); Marcel Kahan & Linda Silberman, *The Inadequate Search for "Adequacy" in Class Actions: A Critique of* Epstein v. MCA, Inc., 73 N.Y.U. L. REV. 765 (1998); Patrick Woolley, *Collateral Attack and the Role of Adequate Representation in Class Suits for Money Damages*, 58 KAN. L. REV. 917 (2010); Patrick Woolley, *The Availability of Collateral Attack for Inadequate Representation in Class Suits*, 79 TEX. L. REV. 383 (2000); *see generally* 7A CHARLES A. WRIGHT ET AL., FEDERAL PRACTICE AND PROCEDURE: CIVIL § 1766 (3d ed. 2005).; *cf.* Clark v. State Farm Mut. Auto. Ins. Co., 590 F.3d 1134 (10th Cir. 2009) (class action held moot when representative's claims satisfied by judgment prior to class certification). Requirements not spelled out in the rule are sometimes relevant to whether an action should be certified as a class action. *See, e.g.*, Tanya J. Monestier, *Transnational Class Actions and the Illusory Search for Res Judicata*, 86 TUL. L. REV. 1 (2011) (discussing the requirement sometimes imposed by the courts in transnational class actions that the home country of foreign class members would give a res judicata effect to the judgment in the class action so as to afford the defendant appropriate finality).

448. *See* Lopez Tijerina v. Henry, 48 F.R.D. 274 (D.N.M. 1969).

449. *See* Mapp v. Board of Educ., 319 F.2d 571 (6th Cir. 1963).

450. *See* Thaxton v. Vaughan, 321 F.2d 474 (4th Cir. 1963).

451. *See* Westlake v. Abrams, 98 F.R.D. 1 (N.D. Ga. 1981).

clauses that permitted the lender to confess judgment in a state court against the borrower without notice to the borrower. *D-1* and *D-2* are, respectively, the sheriff and clerk of the state court in question. *R* seeks an order restraining the defendants from entering or executing any judgments by confession. *R's* claim is that the practice is unconstitutional under the Due Process Clause of the Fourteenth Amendment because the class members did not knowingly waive their rights to a hearing when they signed the contracts in question. The class is comprised of about 2,000 persons, four percent of whom have incomes in excess of $50,000 per year and the rest of whom have incomes of less than $10,000 per year. *R's* income exceeds $50,000 per year. A class action is not proper under Rule 23(a)(4), because *R* is not a proper representative of members of the class making less than $10,000 per year. The members of the class, such as *R*, who have higher incomes are likely more educated. Thus, such members may be more capable of making an understanding and knowing waiver of their rights than those making lower incomes.[452]

(ii) Categories of Class Actions: Rule 23(b)(1)(A) (Risk of Inconsistent Adjudications) or Rule 23(b)(1)(B) (Impairment of Interests in the Absence of Class Action)

Once Rule 23(a) has been satisfied, the action must fit within one of the three categories of Rule 23(b) in order for the action to proceed as a class action. Rule 23(b)(1) allows an action to be maintained as a class action under two separate circumstances. Subsection (A) of Rule 23(b)(1) provides that the action may be maintained as a class action if prosecuting separate actions by or against individual members of the class would create a risk of " inconsistent or varying adjudications with respect to individual class members that would establish incompatible standards of conduct *for the party opposing the class. . . .*"[453] Thus, This subsection requires the court to estimate both whether multiple actions are likely to be brought against the party opposing the class and, if so, whether such actions would result in adjudications that would establish incompatible standards for the party opposing the class.[454]

Illustration 8-56. Assume that separate actions by individuals are commenced against a municipality concerning a bond issue. Some individuals want to invalidate the issue, others want to limit it, and still others want to enforce interest payments under the bonds. Under such circumstances, if one group of plaintiffs succeeded in invalidating the issue and another group succeeded in obtaining judgments ordering the payment of interest, the defendant municipality would be subject to incompatible standards with regard to the bond issue, and the action would be appropriate for class action treatment.[455]

Illustration 8-57. Assume that mass tort has occurred and the defendant might be sued by a number of injured plaintiffs, some of whom might recover

---

452. *See* Swarb v. Lennox, 314 F. Supp. 1091 (E.D. Pa. 1970), *aff'd on other grounds*, 405 U.S. 191, 92 S. Ct. 767, 31 L. Ed. 2d 138 (1972).

453. FED. R. CIV. P. 23(b)(1)(A) (emphasis added).

454. *See generally* 7AA CHARLES A. WRIGHT ET AL., FEDERAL PRACTICE AND PROCEDURE: CIVIL § 1773 (3d ed. 2005).

455. *See* FED. R. CIV. P. 23(b)(1)(A) advisory committee's note to the 1966 amendment.

judgments against the defendant and some of whom might lose their actions.[456] For the "incompatible standards of conduct" principle to be satisfied, the applicable substantive law must require or entitle the defendant to "pursue a uniform continuing course of conduct" with regard to the subject matter of the action.[457] The standard is thus forward looking and does not embrace circumstances like the mass tort situation, when the separate adjudications would not result in any inconsistent future obligations being imposed on the defendant. Traditionally, such an action would not be appropriate for class action treatment under Rule 23(b)(1)(A)[458]

* * * * *

Subsection (B) of Rule 23(b)(1) allows an action to be maintained as a class action when there is a risk of adjudications with respect to individual class members that, as a practical matter, would be dispositive of the interests of other members not parties to the individual adjudications or would substantially impair or impede their ability to protect their interests.[459] This standard obviously overlaps with the standard of compulsory joinder articulated in Rule 19(a)(1)(B)(i). Rule 23(b)(1)(B) thus offers an escape from the mandatory joinder requirement of Rule 19(a)(1)(B)(i) when the action can be qualified as a class action.

Illustration 8-58. Assume that some shareholders want to force a corporation to declare a dividend. Success in the action, practically speaking, would be dispositive of all other shareholders' interests and such an action would be appropriate for class treatment under Rule 23(b)(1)(B).[460]

(iii) Categories of Class Actions: Rule 23(b)(2) (Affecting an Entire Class by Acting or Refusing to Act)

Rule 23(b)(2) is the provision most often employed to justify class action treatment when declaratory or injunctive relief is sought. Rule 23(b)(2) permits a class action when the party opposing the class has acted or refused to act on grounds that apply generally to the class, so that final injunctive relief or corresponding declaratory relief is appropriate respecting the class as a whole.[461] The Advisory Committee explained that "[a]ction or inaction is directed to a class within the meaning of this subdivision even if it has taken effect or is threatened only as to one or a few members of the class, provided it is based on grounds which have general application to the class."[462]

Illustration 8-59. An example of such a case is a civil rights action in which the defendant is charged with unlawful discrimination against a class.[463]

---

456. *See, e.g.*, McDonnell-Douglas Corp. v. United States Dist. Court, 523 F.2d 1083 (9th Cir. 1975).

457. *See* 7AA CHARLES A. WRIGHT ET AL., FEDERAL PRACTICE AND PROCEDURE: CIVIL § 1773 (3d ed. 2005).

458. *But see* subsection *(vi) infra* (discussing contemporary problems administering Rule 13 class actions).

459. FED. R. CIV. P. 23(b)(1)(B).

460. *See* FED. R. CIV. P. 23(b)(1)(B) advisory committee's note to the 1966 amendment.

461. FED. R. CIV. P. 23(b)(2); *cf.* David E. Rigney, Annotation, *Permissibility of Action Against a Class of Defendants Under Rule 23(b)(2) of Federal Rules of Civil Procedure*, 85 A.L.R. FED. 263 (1987).

462. FED. R. CIV. P. 23(b)(2) advisory committee's note to the 1966 amendment.

463. *See id.*

(iv) Categories of Class Actions: Rule 23(b)(3) (Common Questions of Law or Fact)

Rule 23(b)(3) provides for maintenance of an action as a class action when the court finds that (1) the questions of law or fact common to class members predominate over any questions affecting only individual members and (2) a class action is superior to other available methods for fairly and efficiently adjudicating the controversy.[464] The Advisory Committee stated that the purposes of Rule 23(b)(3) were to achieve economies of time, effort, and expense as well as the promotion of uniformity of decision as to persons similarly situated without the sacrifice of procedural fairness or the production of other undesirable results.[465]

Illustration 8-60. Assume that a fraud has been perpetrated on numerous persons by similar misrepresentations. This situation would be appropriate for Rule 23(b)(3) treatment, even where separate assessments of the damages suffered by individuals in the class will be necessary.[466]

* * * * *

For an action to qualify under Rule 23(b)(3), the common questions of law or fact must be found to predominate over individual questions. Thus, *existence* of common questions alone is not enough unless they *predominate* over the individual questions.[467] The rule does not state any criteria for determining when common questions should be held to predominate.[468] The best approach is a pragmatic one:

---

464. *See* FED. R. CIV. P. 23(b)(3).

465. *See* FED. R. CIV. P. 23(b)(3) advisory committee's note to the 1966 amendment.

466. *See id.*

467. *See, e.g.*, Windham v. American Brands, Inc., 565 F.2d 59 (4th Cir. 1977), 7AA CHARLES A. WRIGHT ET AL., FEDERAL PRACTICE AND PROCEDURE: CIVIL § 1778 (3d ed. 2005); *see also* Wachtel *ex rel.* Jesse v. Guardian Life Ins. Co., 453 F.3d 179 (3d Cir. 2006) (class certification order must include a clear list of claims, issues and defenses to be given class treatment); *In re* Nassau County Strip Search Cases, 461 F.3d 219 (2d Cir. 2006) (district court may certify class action on a particular issue, such as liability, even though action as a whole action as a whole does not satisfy predominance requirement); *cf. In re* Wilborn, 609 F.3d 748 (5th Cir. 2010) (bankruptcy court had authority to certify debtors' class action, but questions of law or fact did not predominate).

468. *See* 7AA CHARLES A. WRIGHT ET AL., FEDERAL PRACTICE AND PROCEDURE: CIVIL § 1778 (3d ed. 1986). The need to apply the law of numerous states under the forum's conflict-of-laws rules has caused particular difficulty in satisfying the predominance requirement in both state and federal class actions. *See, e.g.*, Pilgrim v. Universal Health Card, LLC, 660 F.3d 943 (6th Cir. 2011) (laws of states where injuries occurred to class members would govern and those laws varied materially, thus defeating certification for lack of predominance); Sullivan v. DB Invs., Inc., 613 F.3d 134 (3d Cir. 2010) (certification improper because of the need to apply the laws of different states); *In re* Bridgestone/Firestone, Inc., 288 F.3d 1012 (7th Cir. 2002) (under applicable state conflict-of-laws principles, laws of states where SUV buyers and lessees resided rather than states in which manufacturers were headquartered applied to claims in class action and case was not manageable as either a nationwide class action or an action with classes certified for each of the 50 states); Compass Bank v. Snow, 823 So. 2d 667 (Ala. 2001) (need to apply the law of at least three states exacerbates the manageability problems in the case); General Motors Corp. v. Bryant, 374 Ark. 38, 285 S.W.3d 634 (2008) (Arkansas law does not require trial court to engage in a choice-of-law analysis before certifying a class action; Washington Mut. Bank v. Superior Court, 24 Cal. 4th 906, 15 P.3d 1071, 103 Cal. Rptr. 2d 320 (2001) (certification of nationwide class action without first determining effect of parties' choice-of-law agreements was erroneous); Sieglock v. Burlington N. Santa Fe Ry. Co., 2003 MT 355, 319 Mont. 8, 81 P.3d 495 (common question requirement defeated by fact that class had members from at least 24 states and court would have to apply substantive tort law from multiple jurisdictions); Ideal v. Burlington Res. Oil & Gas Co., 2010-NMSC-022, 148 N.M. 228, 233 P.3d 362 (New Mexico law correctly applied at certification stage; predominance requirement satisfied); Ferrell v. Allstate Ins. Co., 2008-NMSC-042, 144 N.M. 405, 188 P.3d 1156 (to defeat multi-state class certification on lack of predominance grounds, party opposing certification must demonstrate that laws of relevant states actually conflict, not that they might conflict); Masquat v. Daimler Chrysler Corp., 2008 OK 67, 195 P.3d 48 (under most significant relationship analysis of Oklahoma conflict-of-laws doctrine, Michigan law applied to breach of warranty claims by consumers against automobile manufacturer; therefore, predominance requirement satisfied as to these claims); Harvell v. Goodyear Tire & Rubber Co., 2006 OK 24, 164 P.3d 1028 (in nationwide consumer class action against national car repair company alleging that consumers were charged for shop supplies regardless of whether shop supplies were actually used, when the common questions represent an important aspect of the case and those questions can be resolved for the entire class in a single proceeding, they should be held to predominate even if a significant amount of time also will be spent on individual questions.[469] This approach is in accord with the purposes of Rule 23(b)(3) to achieve economies of time and to promote uniformity of decision as to similarly situated persons.[470]

In determining whether a Rule 23(b)(3) class action represents the superior available method for resolving the dispute, the court must compare the alternatives to the class action. Individual actions are the most likely available alternative to class treatment, and the liberal joinder of claims and parties under the 1966 amendments to the Federal Rules of Civil Procedure may make individual actions a viable alternative in some cases.[471] Rule 23(b)(3) enumerates four factors, which, *inter alia*, are to be taken into account in determining whether the class action is superior to the other available methods for the fair and efficient adjudication of the action: (1) the class members' interests in individually controlling the prosecution or defense of separate actions; (2) the extent and nature of any litigation concerning the controversy already begun by or against class members; (3) the desirability or undesirability of concentrating litigation of the claims in the particular forum; and (4) the likely difficulties in managing a class action.[472]

The first factor—the interest of individual class members in "controlling the prosecution or defense of separate actions"[473]—involves an estimation of the advantages of class action treatment compared with the advantages of individual actions. This factor often weighs in favor of class treatment when the damage

---

common question requirement for class actions was not satisfied for breach of contract claims because the law of 37 jurisdictions would have to be applied to those claims, and common issues of fact or law did not predominate on unjust enrichment claims because, in part, of state differences regarding misconduct and availability of adequate remedy at law); Citizens Ins. Co. of Am. v. Daccach, 217 S.W.3d 430 (Tex. 2007) (when ruling on motions for class certification, trial courts must conduct an extensive choice of law analysis before they can determine predominance, superiority, cohesiveness, and even manageability); National W. Life Ins. Co. v. Rowe, 164 S.W.3d 389 (Tex. 2005) (trial court erred in certifying class action by concluding that Texas law would apply to claims of all class members without examining whether laws in states in which class members resided would provide them with greater relief or whether those states have a particular interest in the claims being asserted); Compaq Computer Corp. v. Lapray, 135 S.W.3d 657 (Tex. 2004) (trial court may not postpone conflict-of-laws questions until after class certification; in the context of a nationwide class action, determination of the applicable substantive law is of paramount importance in determining whether variations in the applicable law would defeat the predominance requirement in a Rule 23(b)(3) action or the cohesiveness of a Rule 23(b)(2) action); State *ex rel.* Chemtall, Inc. v. Madden, 216 W. Va. 443, 607 S.E.2d 772 (2004) (lower court erred in not properly analyzing the conflict-of-laws question before certifying action for nationwide class treatment). For a discussion of how conflict-of-laws and other problems can affect the predominance requirement of Rule 23(b)(3), see Jeremy Bertsch, Note, *Missing the Mark: The Search for an Effective Class Certification Process,* 39 VAL. U. L. REV. 95 (2004); Jed J. Borghei, *Class Action Fairness: A Mature Solution to the 23(b)(3) Choice of Law Problem,* 95 GEO. L.J. 1645 (2007); Stephen R. Bough & Andrea G. Bough, *Conflict of Laws and Multi-State Class Actions: How Variations in State Law Affect the Predominance Requirement of Rule 23(b)(3),* 68 UMKC L. REV. 1 (1999); Allison M. Gruenwald, *Rethinking Place of Business as Choice of Law in Class Action Lawsuits,* 58 VAND. L. REV. 1925 (2005); Jon Romberg, *The Hybrid Class Action as Judicial Spork: Managing Individual Rights in a Stew of Common Wrong,* 39 J. MARSHALL L. REV. 231 (2006); Edward F. Sherman, *Consumer Class Actions: Who Are the Real Winners?* 56 MAINE L. REV. 223 (2004); Patrick Woolley, *Choice of Law and the Protection of Class Members in Class Suits Certified Under Federal Rule of Civil Procedure 23(b)(3),* 2004 MICH. ST. L. REV. 799; Genevieve G. York-Erwin, *The Choice of Law Problems in the Class Action Context,* 84 N.Y.U. L. REV. 1793 (2009).

469. *Cf.* 7AA CHARLES A. WRIGHT ET AL., FEDERAL PRACTICE AND PROCEDURE: CIVIL § 1778 (3d ed. 2005).

470. *See id.*

471. *See* FED. R. CIV. P. 23(b)(3) advisory committee's note to the 1966 amendment.

472. FED. R. CIV. P. 23(b)(3)(A)-(D).

473. FED. R. CIV. P. 23(b)(3)(A).

claims of individual class members are so small that separate prosecutions are impractical.[474]

The second factor listed in Rule 23(b)(3) is the pendency of any existing actions brought by or against individual class members.[475] The pendency of other actions concerning the same subject matter may destroy the ability to achieve economies of time and uniformity of result.[476] Furthermore, preexisting litigation may reveal that the interests of the individual members of the class in conducting separate lawsuits is so strong that it calls for denial of class action treatment.[477]

The third factor listed in Rule 23(b)(3) directs the court's attention to the advantages of concentrating the litigation in the particular forum.[478] This provision bears primarily on whether the location of witnesses, evidence, and other factors determining the geographical convenience of the lawsuit make it the proper place to settle the claims by or against the class.[479]

The fourth factor listed in Rule 23(b)(3) requires the court to consider the difficulties that are likely to be encountered in managing the action as a class action.[480] In considering this factor, the presence of numerous individual issues, the difficulties involved in providing notice to the absent class members under Rule 23(c)(2), and any other administrative difficulties must be balanced against the benefits of the class action.[481]

The Rule 23(b)(3) class action is the most controversial of the actions provided for in Rule 23. The class in Rule 23(b)(3) actions often will be more loosely knit than in Rule 23(b)(1) and (2) actions. As a consequence, serious due process questions exist about binding the absent members of the class in Rule 23(b)(3) actions. Thus, the problem of adequacy of representation is far more acute in Rule 23(b)(3) actions than in Rule 23(b)(1) and (2) actions.[482] In addition, to insure the due process validity of Rule 23(b)(3), Rule 23(c)(2)(B) provides for a mandatory notice to be given to the members of the class who can be notified through reasonable effort.[483] The notice must inform class members of the nature

---

474. *See* FED. R. CIV. P. 23(b)(3) advisory committee's note to the 1966 amendment.; *see also* Andrea Joy Parker, *Dare to Compare: Determining What "Other Available Methods" Can Be Considered Under Federal Rule 23(b)(3)'s Superiority Requirement*, 44 GA. L. REV. 581 (2010).

475. FED. R. CIV. P. 23(b)(3)(B).

476. *See* 7AA CHARLES A. WRIGHT ET AL., FEDERAL PRACTICE AND PROCEDURE: CIVIL § 1780 (3d ed. 2005).

477. *See* FED. R. CIV. P. 23(b)(3) advisory committee's note to the 1966 amendment.

478. FED. R. CIV. P. 23(b)(3)(C).

479. *See* 7AA CHARLES A. WRIGHT ET AL., FEDERAL PRACTICE AND PROCEDURE: CIVIL § 1780 (3d ed. 2005).

480. FED. R. CIV. P. 23(b)(3)(D).

481. *See generally* 7AA CHARLES A. WRIGHT ET AL., FEDERAL PRACTICE AND PROCEDURE: CIVIL § 1780 (3d ed. 2005).

482. *See id.* § 1786; *see also* subsection *(vi) infra* (discussing, *inter alia*, cases in which Rule 23(b)(3) overlaps with Rules 23(b)(1) and (2) and certification is sought under the latter sections to avoid the mandatory (c)(2)(B) notice).

483. *See* Benjamin Kaplan, *Continuing Work of the Civil Committee: 1966 Amendments of the Federal Rules of Civil Procedure (I)*, 81 HARV. L. REV. 356, 396 (1967); *see also* Jeannette Cox, Note, *Information Famine, Due Process, and the Revised Class Action Rule: When Should Courts Provide a Second Opportunity to Opt Out?* 80 NOTRE DAME L. REV. 377 (2004); *cf.* Wilkes *ex rel.* Mason v. Phoenix Home Life Mut. Ins. Co., 587 Pa. 590, 902 A.2d 366 (2006) (settlement of class action after notice to class that comported with due process was claim preclusive in second action by member of class); Citizens Ins. Co. of Am. v. Daccach, 217 S.W.3d 430 (Tex. 2007) (in certifying class action trial court erred in failing to consider effect of a judgment on abandoned claims, raising a risk of preclusion for absent class members; effective notice must be given to class members about the potential preclusive effect).

of the action, the definition of the certified class, and the claims, issues, and defenses involved in the class action. In addition, it must inform them that the court will exclude them from the class if they so request, that the judgment will bind them unless they request exclusion, and that if they do not request exclusion, they may enter an appearance through counsel.[484] The Supreme Court has held that this notice *must* be given to each individual member of the class who can be identified, contrary to the holdings of some lower courts that such notice was not required when the claims of the class members were so small that it was unlikely that any of them would opt out to pursue individual actions.[485] In the same case, the Court also held that the plaintiff must pay the cost of the notice in the action, even though the cost, as a practical matter, may result in termination of the suit.[486]

Although Rule 23(c)(1) directs the court to determine whether an action may be maintained as a class action "at an early practicable time," a determination that the action may be so maintained may be revised at a later stage.[487] Rule 23(c)(3) provides that the judgment in a Rule 23(b)(1) or (b)(2) class action must include and describe those whom the court finds to be members of the class. Rule 23(c)(3) additionally provides that in Rule 23(b)(3) actions, the judgment must "include and specify or describe" those to whom notice was directed, who have not opted out of the class, and whom the court finds are members of the class.[488]

(v) Court Management of Class Actions, Class Counsel, and Approval of Settlements

Rule 23(d) authorizes the court in a class action to make appropriate orders for the management of the class action. Such orders include but are not limited to notice to members of the class of various steps in the action, of the proposed extent of the judgment, of the opportunity of the members of the class to indicate whether they consider the representation fair and adequate or whether they want to intervene in the action.[489] In addition, Rule 23(g) requires the court to appoint class counsel for any certified class action after weighing various factors, such as counsel's experience, prior work on the case, resources, and knowledge.[490] Rule 23(h)

---

484. *See* FED. R. CIV. P. 23(c)(2)(B); *cf.* Cummings v. Connell, 402 F.3d 936 (9th Cir. 2005) (when nominal damages are awarded in a civil rights class action, every member of the class whose rights were violated is entitled to damages; although such an award is insignificant to individual class members, it may be significant to defendant who must pay the aggregate amount).

485. *See* Eisen v. Carlisle & Jacquelin, 417 U.S. 156, 94 S. Ct. 2140, 40 L. Ed. 2d 732 (1974); *cf.* Cummings v. Connell, 402 F.3d 936 (9th Cir. 2005) (when nominal damages are awarded in a civil rights class action, every member of the class whose rights were violated is entitled to damages; although such an award is insignificant to individual class members, it may be significant to defendant who must pay the aggregate amount).

486. *See id.*. *But see* Hunt v. Imperial Merchant Servs., Inc., 560 F.3d 1137 (9th Cir. 2009) (district court did not abuse discretion in ordering defendant to pay cost of class notice).

487. *See* FED. R. CIV. P. 23(c)(1)(A) & (C).

488. *See* FED. R. CIV. P. 23(c)(3).

489. *See* FED. R. CIV. P. 23(d)(1)(B)(i)-(iii); *see also* Nicholas Barnhorst, *How Many Kicks at the Cat?: Multiple Settlement Protests by Class Members Who Have Refused to Opt Out,* 38 TEXAS TECH L. REV. 107 (2005); Rima N. Daniels, *Monetary Damages in Mandatory Classes: When Should Opt-out Rights be Allowed?* 57 ALA. L. REV. 499 (2005); Alexandra D. Lahav, *The Law and Large Numbers: Preserving Adjudication in Complex Litigation,* 59 FLA. L. REV. 383 (2007); Alexandra Lahav, *Fundamental Principles for Class Action Governance,* 37 IND. L. REV. 65 (2003); Richard A. Nagareda, *Administering Adequacy in Class Representation,* 82 TEX. L. REV. 287 (2003).

490. *See* FED. R. CIV. P. 23(g)(1)(A)(i)-(iv);

provides procedures for awarding attorney's fees, including objections.[491] Finally, Rule 23(e) provides that a class action may not be dismissed or compromised without the approval of the court or notice to the class members.[492]

(vi) Contemporary Issues in the Administration of Rule 23

In recent years, several issues have arisen in the administration of Rule 23 that deserve comment. One issue concerns the application of Rule 23 to mass tort cases. In commenting on the 1966 revisions to Rule 23(b)(3), the Advisory Committee stated that

> [a] "mass accident" resulting in injuries to numerous persons is ordinarily not appropriate for a class action because of the likelihood that significant questions not only of damages but of liability and defenses of liability would be present, affecting the individuals in different ways. In these circumstances an action conducted nominally as a class action would degenerate in practice into multiple lawsuits separately tried.[493]

Despite this statement, the Advisory Committee seemed to concede that certain kinds of "mass tort" cases might be appropriate for class treatment.[494] In fact, federal courts have often certified mass tort cases as appropriate for class treatment under Rule 23(b)(3).[495] Nevertheless, such cases clearly present many kinds of management problems that make class certification difficult, and some federal courts of appeals have begun to scrutinize mass tort class certifications more closely than has been the case in the past.[496] These cases have not settled the question whether mass tort actions are appropriate for class treatment, and the debate over the issue is vigorous.[497] However, the problem of whether mass tort actions should be conducted in class action form is part of a larger concern about how complex

---

491. *See* FED. R. CIV. P. 23(h).

492. *See* FED. R. CIV. P. 23(e); Ayers v. Thompson, 358 F.3d 356 (5th Cir. 2004) (members of class dissatisfied with settlement did not have absolute right to opt out; action was not hybrid class action; the plaintiffs had sought only declaratory and injunctive relief throughout litigation and failed to show the existence of individual claims separate and distinct from those for class-wide relief).

493. FED. R. CIV. P. 23(b)(3) advisory committee's note to the 1966 amendment.

494. *See id.* (discussing fraud cases in which similar misrepresentations are made to the members of the class and damage claims arising out of concerted antitrust violations).

495. *See, e.g.*, AMERICAN LAW INSTITUTE, COMPLEX LITIGATION: STATUTORY RECOMMENDATIONS AND ANALYSIS WITH REPORTER'S STUDY 27-28 (1994). It may be that the "mass accident" example given by the Advisory Committee represents an especially difficult kind of "mass tort" insofar as class certification is concerned, while other kinds of mass torts present more tractable class certification problems.

496. *See, e.g.*, Castano v. American Tobacco Co., 84 F.3d 734 (5th Cir. 1996) (reversing certification of nicotine class action); *In re* American Med. Sys., Inc.,75 F.3d 1069 (6th Cir. 1996) (reversing certification of penile prostheses class action); *In re* Rhone-Poulenc Rorer, Inc., 51 F.3d 1293 (7th Cir. 1995) (reversing certification of class action brought against manufacturers of blood solids on behalf of hemophiliacs infected by the AIDS virus as a consequence of using the defendants' products); *see also* Byron G. Stier, *Resolving the Class Action Crisis: Mass Tort Litigation As Network,* 2005 UTAH L. REV. 863.

497. *See, e.g.*, John C. Coffee, Jr., *Class Wars: The Dilemma of the Mass Tort Class Action,* 95 COLUM. L. REV. 1343 (1995); Paul D. Carrington & Derek P. Apanovitch, *The Constitutional Limits of Judicial Rulemaking: The Illegitimacy of Mass-Tort Settlements Negotiated Under Federal Rule 23,* 39 ARIZ. L. REV. 461 (1997); Mary J. Davis, *Toward the Proper Role for Mass Tort Class Actions,* 77 ORE. L. REV. 157 (1998); Samuel Issacharoff, *Administering Damage Awards in Mass-Tort Litigation,* 10 REV. LITIG. 463 (1991); Barry F. McNeil & Beth L. Fanscal, *Mass Torts and Class Actions: Facing Increased Scrutiny,* 167 F.R.D. 483 (1996); Fred Misko, Jr. & Frank E. Goodrich, *Managing Complex Litigation: Class Actions and Mass Torts,* 48 BAY. L. REV. 1001 (1996); Richard A. Nagareda, *In the Aftermath of the Mass Tort Class Action,* 85 GEO. L.J. 295 (1996); Douglas G. Smith, *An Administrative Approach to the Resolution of Mass Torts?,* 2009U. ILL. L. REV. 895.

litigation of all sorts should be conducted.[498] Regardless of the merits of specific recommendations on this question, it seems likely that a comprehensive solution to the problem cannot be worked out by the courts on a case-by-case basis, but will have to be addressed by Congress and state legislatures.

A second question that has arisen under Rule 23 concerns the overlap between Rule 23(b)(1), (2) & (3) that sometimes allows class actions to be certified under multiple parts of the rule. Under such circumstances, the class representative has the obvious incentive to seek certification the action under Rule 23(b)(1) or (2), but not Rule 23(b)(3), because of the mandatory notice and opt-out provisions of subdivision (b)(3) of the rule. However, the mandatory notice and opt-out option required in Rule 23(b)(3) cases may be required as a matter of due process because the class in (b)(3) actions is more loosely knit than in (b)(1) or (b)(2) actions, which arguably requires the additional protection that notice will provide to the individual class members.[499] Thus, if an action is brought primarily for damages, but is certified under Rule 23(b)(1) or (2) because of other relief requested in the action, the question is whether the class must be given notice and an opportunity to opt out either under Rule 23 or as a matter of due process.

In *Ticor Title Insurance Co. v. Brown*,[500] the Supreme Court recognized this issue, but refused to decide it. In *Ticor*, an initial class action was settled under circumstances in which all money damage claims against the defendants were purportedly extinguished while injunctive relief and other nonmonetary relief was granted to the members of the class. The district court certified the class settlement under Rule 23(b)(1)(A) and (b)(2). The court rejected an objection by a member of the class that the action could not be certified under these provisions because the relief requested was primarily monetary in nature. Subsequently, a second class action was commenced on behalf of the class in another federal court, and the court granted summary judgment to the defendants on the ground, in part, that the

---

498. For a comprehensive set of recommendations concerning complex litigation generally, see AMERICAN LAW INSTITUTE, COMPLEX LITIGATION: STATUTORY RECOMMENDATIONS AND ANALYSIS WITH REPORTER'S STUDY (1994); *see also* John C. Coffee, Jr., *Litigation Governance: Taking Accountability Seriously*, 110 COLUM. L. REV. 288 (2010); Allan Kanner & Tibor Nagy, *Exploding the Blackmail Myth: A New Perspective on Class Action Settlements,* 57 BAY. L. REV. 681 (2005); Francis R. Kirkham, *Complex Civil Litigation—Have Good Intentions Gone Awry?* 70 F.R.D. 199 (1976); Francis R. Kirkham, *Problems of Complex Civil Litigation,* 83 F.R.D. 497 (1979); Jay Tidmarsh, *Unattainable Justice: The Form of Complex Litigation and the Limits of Judicial Power,* 60 GEO. WASH L. REV. 1683 (1992); Symposium, *Complexity and Aggregation in Choice of Law: An Introduction to the Landscape*, 14 ROGER WILLIAMS U. L. REV. 1 (2009).

499. As the Advisory Committee explained:

> In the degree that there is cohesiveness or unity in the class and the representation is effective, the need for notice to the class will tend toward a minimum. These indicators suggest that notice under subdivision (d)(2) may be particularly useful and advisable in certain class actions maintained under subdivision (b)(3), for example, to permit members of the class to object to the representation. Indeed, under subdivision (c)(2), notice must be ordered, and is not merely discretionary, to give the members in a subdivision (b)(3) class action an opportunity to secure exclusion from the class. This mandatory notice . . . is designed to fulfill requirements of due process to which the class action procedure is of course subject.

FED. R. CIV. P. 23(d)(2) advisory committee note to the 1966 amendment. In the 2003 amendments to Rule 23, the Rule 23(c)(2)(A) now specifically provides that even if the class is certified "under Rule 23(b)(1) or (2), the court may direct appropriate notice to the class." FED. R. CIV. P. 23(c)(2)(A). The Advisory Committee notes do point out that this authority "should be exercised with care" and that "[t]he court may decide not to direct notice after balancing the risk that notice costs may deter the pursuit of class relief against the benefits of notice." *Id.* advisory committee note to the 2003 amendment; *see also* Rhonda Wasserman, *The Curious Complications with Back-End Opt-Out Rights,* 49 WM. & MARY L. REV. 373 (2007) (discussing the problems with opt-out rights given to class members after the terms of the settlement are disclosed).

500. 511 U.S. 117, 114 S. Ct. 1359, 128 L. Ed. 2d 33 (1994).

plaintiffs were bound by the judgment in the prior class action. The court of appeals reversed, holding that it would violate due process to give a binding effect to the judgment in the original class action that involved money damage claims when the plaintiff bringing the second action had not been permitted to opt out in the first proceeding. The U.S. Supreme Court initially granted certiorari, but ultimately dismissed the writ as improvidently granted. A majority of the Court felt that the due process issue would be of no consequence if Rule 23 itself required notice and an opportunity to opt out of actions brought for damages. However, the Rule 23 issue could not be decided in the case because it was clearly res judicata, having been litigated and determined against the plaintiffs in the prior class action. Therefore, the Court reserved judgment on the question until an appropriate case in which the Rule 23 issue is open for decision.

Although Rule 23(b)(2) is specifically keyed to the propriety of declaratory or injunctive relief, Rule 23(b)(1) is not. Therefore, it would seem that the issue in *Ticor* ought not to depend upon whether the action is primarily for money damages, but on whether the class in the action is the "loosely knit" kind of class that was envisioned for (b)(3) cases or the more "tightly knit" kind of class that the drafters of Rule 23 envisioned as proper for (b)(1) actions.[501] If it is the former, the rule (and due process) should require notice and the opportunity to opt out of the class. If it is the latter, no such notice should be required, even if damages is the primary remedy sought. This conclusion, of course, assumes, as the Advisory Committee did, that adequacy of representation and the other protection of Rule 23(a) would suffice to protect the class in (b)(1) & (b)(2) actions without the need for notice. If this assumption is not true, due process may also require notice in the latter kinds of actions and the ability to opt out of the class.[502] Nevertheless, the Advisory Committee seems correct that the cohesiveness of the class will suffice in (b)(1) & (b)(2) actions to assure that due process is satisfied if the Rule 23(a) certification requirements are met.

---

501. *See* Jahn *ex rel.* Jahn v. ORCR, Inc., 92 P.3d 984 (Colo. 2004) (under state equivalent of Federal Rule 23, unnamed members of plaintiff class were not precluded from bringing subsequent action for damages because prior class action was certified under Rule 23(b)(2); minimal due process requires both notice and adequate representation to preclude class claims for monetary damages, whereas adequate representation alone will satisfy due process in class actions for injunctive relief); Compaq Computer Corp. v. Lapray, 135 S.W.3d 657 (Tex. 2004) (in considering certification of class suits for declaratory and injunctive relief based on party's refusal to act on grounds generally applicable to the class, trial courts must consider, and due process may require, individual notice to class members who seek monetary damages under any theory); *see also* Steven T.O. Cottreau, *The Due Process Right to Opt Out of Class Actions,* 73 N.Y.U. L. REV. 480 (1998); Patricia Anne Solomon, *Are Mandatory Class Actions Unconstitutional?*, 72 NOTRE DAME L. REV. 1627 (1997); *cf.* Lawrence J. Restieri, Jr., *The Class Action Dilemma: The Certification of Classes Seeking Equitable Relief and Monetary Damages After* Ticor Title Insurance Co. v. Brown, 63 FORDHAM L. REV. 1745 (1995) (arguing that it is not the presence of a damage claim that should preclude certification under Rule 23(b)(1) or (b)(2), but whether the class claim requires the court to issue a single decree, even if a damage remedy is part of the relief requested; under this standard, the author argues that the (b)(1) & (b)(2) certification in *Ticor* was improper because individual adjudications would not create inconsistent verdicts or different standards of conduct that the defendant would be unable to satisfy, and the class members did not have an ongoing relationship with one another that deprived the class of unity).

502. *See also* Maximilian A. Grant, *The Right Not to Sue: A First Amendment Rationale for Opting Out of Mandatory Class Actions,* 63 U. CHI. L. REV. 239 (1996) (arguing that a First Amendment right to opt out may be sounder than one based on the Due Process Clause because mandatory class actions compel association with, or financial or other support of, activities with which absent class members may disagree).

In *Wal-Mart Stores, Inc. v. Dukes*,[503] a case focusing primarily on the "commonality" requirement of Rule 23(a)(2),[504] the Supreme Court also had occasion to comment on the *Ticor* question. The Court held that it was improper for the lower federal courts to certify a class action under Rule 23(b)(2) when claims for monetary relief in the action were not "incidental" to the declaratory or injunctive relief requested.[505] Furthermore, the Court stated Rule 23(b)(2) applied only when a single injunction or declaratory judgment would provide relief to each member of the class.[506] The Court observed that the absence of a notice and opt-out provision in a class action predominately for money damages would violate due process.[507] While it did not hold due process would be violated by the absence of such a provision when monetary claims do not predominate, "the serious possibility that it might be so" provided a reason not to read Rule 23(b)(2) to include the monetary claims before it.[508] This required individualized determinations of each class member's damage claims, and, in turn, prevented the damage claims from being "incidental" to the request for declaratory and injunctive relief. The Court's decision will, therefore, seemingly eliminate the *Ticor* question whenever a class action requires individualized damage claims. Note, however, in light of the suggestion in the preceding paragraph, that such cases also may always involve "loosely knit" classes inappropriate for class action certification under Rule 23(b)(1) or 23(b)(2).

A final important issue concerns the legitimacy of and protection that is necessary in so-called "settlement" class actions. A settlement class action is one in which the representative parties (or, more accurately, their attorneys) arrive at a settlement with the defendant before the action is commenced. The representative party then commences the class action, and the parties ask the court to certify the class as the parties have defined it. The court reviews the settlement before certifying the action. If it finds the settlement fair, it will certify the action as a class action for settlement purposes only. Class counsel will then notify the members of the class simultaneously of the commencement of the suit, the class certification, and the settlement. The settlement class action is controversial because there are incentives for the representatives' attorneys[509] and the defendants to settle actions on terms that are not fair to all class members. In addition, many settlement class

---

503. 564 U.S. __, 131 S. Ct. 2541, 180 L. Ed. 2d 374 (2011) (involving a class action against Wal-Mart under Title VII of the Civil Rights Act of 1964 in which employees alleged sex discrimination in pay and promotions).

504. *See* section D(4)(b)(i) *supra* ("Requirements for a Class Action").

505. 564 U.S. at __, 131 S. Ct. at 2557, 180 L. Ed. 2d at 396.

506. *Id.*

507. *Id.* at __, 131 S. Ct. at 2559, 180 L. Ed. 2d at 397-98 (citing Phillips Petroleum Co. v. Shutts, 472 U.S. 797, 812, 105 S. Ct. 2965, 2974, 86 L. Ed. 2d 628, 642 (1985), which is discussed in section D(4)(d) *infra*).

508. *Id.* at __, 131 S. Ct. at 2559, 180 L. Ed. 2d at 398.

509. For an extensive argument that the problems of improper counsel behavior in the settlement class action context can be solved by suing the class counsel involved, see Susan P. Koniak & George M. Cohen, *Under Cloak of Settlement*, 82 VA. L. REV. 1051 (1996). One court has held that if the settlement of a class action results in a rift in the class, with some members objecting to the settlement, class counsel need not necessarily disqualify herself, but may continue to represent the class members who agree with the settlement. *See* Lazy Oil Co. v. Witco Corp., 166 F.3d 581 (3d Cir. 1999).

actions are also mass tort actions, which raise additional problems of whether the actions are proper under Rule 23.[510]

In 1996, the Advisory Committee proposed an amendment to Rule 23 that would have addressed some, but by no means all, of the problems with the settlement class action. The amendment was designed to resolve a conflict in the decisions resulting because some courts refused to certify a class action for settlement purposes unless the action could also be certified for trial.[511] Before this amendment could be adopted, it was rendered moot by the Supreme Court's decision in *Amchem Products, Inc. v. Windsor*.[512] In *Amchem*, the Court held that the adequate representation requirement of Rule 23(a)(4) and the predominance requirement of Rule 23(b)(3) were not satisfied by the settlement class action certified by the district court. The Court held that settlement is relevant to the propriety of class certification and that the question whether trial would produce intractable management problems is not a consideration when settlement-only certification is requested. However, the Court found the adequacy of representation and predominance problems overwhelming in the context of the case.[513]

Subsequently, in *Ortiz v. Fibreboard Corp.*,[514] the Court reversed a settlement class action under Rule 23(b)(1)(B). The Court held that in a (b)(1)(B) action involving a fund of money, there must be a demonstration that the fund in question is limited by more than the settlement agreement of the parties and has

---

510. *See, e.g.*, Roger C. Cramton, *Individualized Justice, Mass Torts, and "Settlement Class Actions": An Introduction*, 80 CORNELL L. REV. 811 (1995); John C. Coffee, Jr., *Class Wars: The Dilemma of the Mass Tort Class Action*, 95 COLUM. L. REV. 1343 (1995); James A. Henderson, Jr., Comment, *Settlement Class Actions and the Limits of Adjudication*, 80 CORNELL L. REV. 1014 (1995); Michael A. McCabe, Note, *Class Backwards: Does the Fairness, Adequacy and Reasonableness of a Negotiated Class Action Settlement Really Have Any Effect on Approval?:* General Motors v. Bloyed, 916 S.W.2d 949 (Tex. 1996), 28 TEXAS TECH L. REV. 159 (1997); Pamela M. Madas, *To Settlement Classes and Beyond: A Primer on Proposed Methods for Federalizing Mass Tort Litigation*, 28 SETON HALL L. REV. 540 (1997); Stephen E. Morrissey, Note, *State Settlement Class Actions that Release Exclusive Federal Claims: Developing a Framework for Multi-Jurisdictional Management of Shareholder Litigation*, 95 COLUM . L. REV. 1765 (1995); Richard A. Nagareda, *Turning From Tort to Administration*, 94 MICH. L. REV. 899 (1996); Martin H. Redish & Andrianna D. Kastanek, *Settlement Class Actions, the Case or Controversy Requirement, and the Nature of the Adjudicatory Process*, 73 U. CHI. L. REV. 545 (2006); William W. Schwarzer, *Structuring Multiclaim Litigation: Should Rule 23 Be Revised?* 94 MICH. L. REV. 1250 (1996); Jack B. Weinstein & Karen S. Schwartz, *Notes From the Cave: Some Problems of Judges in Dealing with Class Action Settlements*, 163 F.R.D. 369 (1995); Note, *Back to the Drawing Board: The Settlement Class Action and the Limits of Rule 23*, 109 HARV. L. REV. 828 (1996); *see also* Lazy Oil Co. v. Witco Corp., 166 F.3d 581 (3d Cir. 1999) (no per se disqualification of class counsel representing class required when class action settlement results in a rift in the class, with some members of the class objecting to the settlement and some members agreeing with the settlement); *In re* General Motors Corp. Pick-Up Truck Fuel Tank Prods. Liab. Litig., 55 F.3d 768 (3d Cir. 1995).

511. The proposed amendment would have added a new Rule 23(b)(4): "(4) the parties to a settlement request certification under subdivision (b)(3) for purposes of settlement even though the requirements of subdivision (b)(3) might not be met for trial." 167 F.R.D. 523, 529 (1996). The Advisory Committee recognized that there were both risks and benefits in the settlement class action and stated that the competing forces could be "reconciled by recognizing the legitimacy of settlement classes but increasing the protection afforded to class members." *Id.* at 564. However, the Committee stated that "[n]otice and the right to opt out provide the central means of protecting settlement class members under subdivision (b)(3)," but exhorted the courts to do a better job (a) in framing "clear and succinct" settlement notices that provide the information necessary to determine whether to object to the settlement and (b) to approach the definition of the class with care, so as not to define the class over broadly and thus, *e.g.*, include within it persons with conflicting interests. *See id.* Note, however, that the Advisory Committee did not write its exhortations into the text of the proposed amendment, which is, to say the least, a questionable way to proceed.

512. 521 U.S. 591, 117 S. Ct. 2231, 138 L. Ed. 2d 689 (1997).

513. For a suggestion that the Court's interpretation of Rule 23 in *Amchem*, to the extent that it allows certification of a settlement class that could not be certified as a litigation class, does not violate the Rules Enabling Act as currently interpreted, but that it might violate the Act under an expanded interpretation, see Note, *The Rules Enabling Act and the Limits of Rule 23*, 111 HARV. L. REV. 2294 (1998).

514. 527 U.S. 815, 119 S. Ct. 2295, 144 L. Ed. 2d 715 (1999).

been allocated to claimants within the class by a process that addresses any conflicting interests of the class members. The Court found that the certification of the class in *Ortiz* failed to demonstrate that the fund was limited except by the agreement of the parties, and the settlement also showed exclusions from the class and allocations of assets at odds with the concept of limited fund treatment and the structural protections of Rule 23(a) explained in *Amchem.*

Amchem and *Ortiz* do not formally preclude settlement class actions. However, taken together, the cases constitute a strong message from the Supreme Court that settlement class actions should receive closer scrutiny from the lower federal courts than they have been given in the past.[515] Nevertheless, it is questionable whether all the problems with settlement class actions can be solved on a case-by-case basis under existing Rule 23. Rather, the problems that have been identified to date with settlement class suits call for more vigorous treatment through the legislative or rulemaking processes.[516] One useful suggestion for reform is that class actions with preclusive effect should not be settled unless the court gives all class members the option to reject the settlement and exclude themselves from the class at the time of settlement.[517]

---

515. Mark C. Weber, *Thanks for Not Suing: The Prospects for State Court Class Action Litigation Over Tobacco Injuries*, 33 GA. L. REV. 979 (1999); Mark C. Weber, *Mass Jury Trials in Mass Tort Cases: Some Preliminary Issues*, 48 DE PAUL L. REV. 463 (1998); Thomas E. Willging, *Mass Torts Problems and Proposals: A Report to the Mass Torts Working Group*, 187 F.R.D. 328, 356-63 (1999) (discussing the limits of settlement class actions after *Amchem*); REPORT OF THE ADVISORY COMMITTEE ON CIVIL RULES AND THE WORKING GROUP ON MASS TORTS TO THE CHIEF JUSTICE OF THE UNITED STATES AND TO THE JUDICIAL CONFERENCE OF THE UNITED STATES, 187 F.R.D. 293 (1999). For a discussion of *Amchem* and *Ortiz* and an argument that class cohesion as a rationale for legitimizing representative litigation may be inferior to a normative principle based on protection and enhancement of client autonomy through various mechanisms, see John C. Coffee, Jr., *Class Action Accountability: Reconciling Exit, Voice, and Loyalty in Representative Litigation*, 100 COLUM. L. REV. 370 (2000). For a discussion of the problems involved when multiple class actions are brought on behalf of the same class, see Rhonda Wasserman, *Dueling Class Actions*, 80 B.U. L. REV. 461 (2000). For a discussion of recent proposals to expand federal diversity jurisdiction to include class actions in which only minimal diversity exists between plaintiffs and defendants, see John Conyers, Jr., *Class Action "Fairness"—A Bad Deal for the States and Consumers*, 40 HARV. J. LEGIS. 493 (2003).

516. For an empirical analysis of seventeen issues prevalent in class action litigation that pose potential challenges for the rulemaking process, see Thomas E. Willging et al., *An Empirical Analysis of Rule 23 to Address the Rulemaking Challenges,* 71 N.Y.U. L. REV. 74 (1996).

517. *See* Debra Lyn Bassett, *Constructing Class Action Reality,* 2006 B.Y.U. L. REV.1415; *see also* Kevin R. Bernier, Note, *The Inadequacy of the Broad Collateral Attack:* Stephenson v. Dow Chemical Company *and Its Effect on Class Action Settlements,* 84 B.U. L. REV. 1023 (2004); David R. Clay, Comment, *Federal Attraction for the Interstate Class Action: The Effect of* Devlin v. Scardelletti *and the Amendments to Federal Rule of Civil Procedure 23(e) on Class Action "Minimal Diversity" Concerns*, 52 EMORY L.J. 1877 (2003); Howard M. Erichson, *Beyond the Class Action: Lawyer Loyalty and Client Autonomy in Non-Class Collective Representation,* 2003 U. CHI. LEG. FORUM 519; Myriam Gilles, *Opting Out of Liability: The Forthcoming, Near-Total Demise of the Modern Class Action,* 104 MICH. L. REV. 373 (2005); Jeremy T. Grabill, *Multistate Class Actions Properly Frustrated by Choice-of-Law Complexities: The Role of Parallel Litigation in the Courts,* 80 TUL. L. REV. 299 (2005); Richard Marcus, *Reviving Judicial Gatekeeping of Aggregation: Scrutinizing the Merits on Class Certification*, 79 GEO. WASH. L. REV. 324 (2011); Katie Melnick, Note, *In Defense of the Class Action Lawsuit: An Examination of the Implicit Advantages and a Response to Common Criticisms,* 22 ST. JOHNS J. LEGAL COMMENTARY 755 (2008); Laura Offenbacher, Note, *The Multiparty, Multiforum Trial Jurisdiction Act: Opening the Door to Class Action Reform,* 23 REV. LITIG. 177 (2004); Bruce H. Kobayashi & Larry E. Ribstein, *Class Action Lawyers as Lawmakers,* 46 ARIZ. L. REV. 733 (2004); Martin H. Redish & Andrianna D. Kastanek, *Settlement Class Actions, the Case-or-Controversy Requirement, and the Nature of the Adjudicatory Process,* 73 U. CHI. L. REV. 545 (2006); David Rosenberg, *Adding a Second Opt-Out to Rule 23(b)(3) Class Actions: Cost Without Benefit,* 2003 U. CHI. LEGAL FORUM 19; Charles Silver, *"We're Scared to Death": Class Certification and Blackmail,* 78 N.Y.U. L. REV. 1357 (2003); Mark C. Weber, *A Consent-Based Approach to Class Action Settlement: Improving* Amchem Products, Inc. v. Windsor, 59 OHIO ST. L.J. 1155 (1998); Tobias Barrington Wolff, *Preclusion in Class Action Litigation,* 105 COLUM. L. REV. 717 (2005); Symposium, *Complex Litigation,* 37 AKRON L. REV. 589 (2004); ALI PRINCIPLES OF THE LAW OF AGGREGATE LITIGATION (2010).

In 2003, the Supreme Court promulgated amendments to Rule 23(c), (e), & (g) that addressed some of the issues discussed above. Amended Rule 23(c)(1)(A) now provides that when a person sues or is sued as the representative of a class, the court must determine by order whether to certify the action as a class action at an early practicable time. Rule 23(c)(1)(B) states that an order certifying a class action must define the class and the class claims, issues, and defenses, and must appoint class counsel. Rule 23(c)(2) provides that for any class certified under Rule 23(b)(1) or (2), the court may direct appropriate notification to the class, and further provides that for any class certified under Rule 23(b)(3), the court must direct the best notice practicable under the circumstances to class members, including individual notice to all members who can be identified through reasonable effort. The notice must "clearly and concisely state in plain, easily understood language: (i) the nature of the action; (ii) the definition of the class certified; (iii) the class claims, issues, or defenses; (iv) that a class member may enter an appearance through an attorney if the member so desires; (v) that the court will exclude from the class any member who requests exclusion; (vi) the time and manner for requesting exclusion; and (vii) the binding effect of a class judgment on members under Rule 23(c)(3)."

Rule 23(e) now provides that the claims, issues, or defenses of a certified class may be settled voluntarily, dismissed, or compromised only with the court's approval. Under Rule 23(e)(5), any class member may object to such a proposed settlement, voluntary dismissal, or compromise. Amended Rule 23(e)(1) also provides that the court must direct notice in a reasonable manner to all class members who would be bound by a proposed settlement, voluntary dismissal, or compromise. Under Rule 23(e)(2), the court may approve a settlement, voluntary dismissal, or compromise that would bind class members only after a hearing in which findings are made that the settlement, voluntary dismissal, or compromise is fair, reasonable, and adequate. Parties seeking approval of a settlement, voluntary dismissal, or compromise under Rule 23(e)(3) must file a statement identifying any agreement made in connection with the proposed settlement, dismissal, or compromise. Rule 23(e)(4) provides that in class actions certified under Rule 23(b)(3), the court may refuse to approve a settlement unless it affords a new opportunity to request exclusion to individual class members who had an earlier opportunity to request exclusion but did not do so.

Rule 23(g) contains extensive provisions governing the appointment of class counsel. Rule 23(g) is designed to guide the court in assessing proposed class counsel as part of the certification decision.

Rule 23(h) deals with awards of attorney's fees in class actions. Rule 23(h) recognizes that fee awards are an important influence on the way attorneys initiate, develop, and conclude class actions. Rule 23(h) applies to actions certified as class actions, including settlement class actions. This rule requires a motion for an award of attorney's fees, with notice of the motion to be served on all parties and, for motions by class counsel, directed to class members in a reasonable manner. Rule 23(h)(2) also provides for objections to the motion for attorney's fees by class members or parties from whom payment is sought. Rule 23(h)(3) provides that the court may hold a hearing and must find the facts and state its conclusions of law on the motion under Rule 52(a). The court is given discretion to refer issues related to the amount of the award to a special master or to a magistrate judge.

In recent years, litigants have attempted to avoid federal courts, which were perceived to be reluctant to certify actions for class treatment, by filing in state courts that were more hospitable to class certification. One federal court attempted to deal with this problem by enjoining certification of an action as a class action in state court after itself ordering decertification of an action as a nationwide class action in federal court.[518] Obviously, this solution will only work if a federal court first obtains jurisdiction of an action in which the plaintiff seeks class certification. If the action is instead commenced in state court and cannot be removed, the injunctive route to preclusion, whether desirable or undesirable, is unavailable.

More recently, however, Congress enacted the Class Action Fairness Act of 2005,[519] which is designed to broaden federal jurisdiction over nationwide class actions to prevent the perceived abuses that have occurred in some state courts in these actions. The provisions expanding the original and removal provisions of Title 28 in these cases are discussed in the next subsection. However, the Act also contains, in new 28 U.S.C. §§ 1711-1715, non-jurisdictional regulations of certain kinds of class actions.

Section 1712[520] is entitled "Coupon settlements." Section 1712(a) provides that if a proposed settlement in a class action provides an award of coupons to class members, the portion of the attorney's fee award that is attributable to the award of the coupons shall be based on the value to the class members of the coupons that are redeemed. This section is obviously designed to prevent class members from being left with relatively trivial recoveries in the form of coupons for a defendant's product while class attorneys collect large monetary fees. Section 1712(b) deals with other attorney's fee awards in coupon settlements. Section 1712(b)(1) provides that if a portion of the recovery of coupons in a proposed settlement is not used to determine the attorney's fee to be paid to class counsel, the fee award shall be based upon the amount of time that class counsel "reasonably expended" working on the action. Section 1712(b)(2) provides that fee awards under subsection (b) shall be subject to approval by the court and shall include a component for obtaining equitable relief, including injunctions. Section 1712(b) also states that nothing "in this subsection" shall be construed to prohibit application of a "lodestar with a multiplier method of determining attorney's fees." Section 1712(c) provides that if a proposed settlement provides both for an award of coupons and also provides for equitable relief, the portion of the attorney's fee to be paid to class counsel based on the coupon recovery shall be calculated under § 1712(a), and the portion of the fee not based on the coupon recovery shall be calculated in accord with § 1712(b). Section 1712(c) provides that in a class action involving a coupon award, the court may in its discretion upon motion of a party receive expert testimony from a witness qualified to provide information on the actual value to the class members of the

---

518. *See In re* Bridgestone/Firestone, Inc. Tires Prods. Liab. Litig., 333 F.3d 763 (7th Cir. 2003); *see also* Kara M. Moorcroft, Note, *The Path to Preclusion: Federal Injunctive Relief Against Nationwide Classes in State Court,* 54 DUKE L.J. 221 (2004).

519. Pub. L. No. 109-2, 119 Stat. 4 (2005) (codified as 28 U.S.C. §§ 1711-1715, 1332(d), 1453).

520. 28 U.S.C. § 1711 contains definitions.

coupons that are redeemed. Section 1712(e) provides that in cases in which a proposed coupon settlement is involved, the court may approve the proposed settlement only after a hearing and a written determination that it is fair, reasonable, and adequate for class members. In addition, § 1712(e) states that the court in its discretion may require that a proposed settlement agreement must provide for the distribution of a portion of the value of unclaimed coupons to one or more charitable or governmental organizations, as agreed to by the parties, and further provides that the distribution and redemption of any proceeds "under this subsection" shall not be used to calculate attorney's fees under this section.[521]

Section 1713 provides that the court may only approve of a proposed class settlement in which a class member is obligated to pay sums to class counsel that would result in a net loss to the class member after making a written finding that nonmonetary benefits to the class member substantially outweigh the monetary loss.[522] Section 1714 provides that the court may not approve a class settlement that provides for the payment of greater sums to some class members than to others based solely on the basis that the class members receiving the greater sums are located in closer geographic proximity to the court.[523]

Section 1715 contains provisions for notification to appropriate federal and state officials with regulatory responsibility with respect to the defendant in a class action.[524] Not more than ten days after a proposed settlement of a class action is filed in court, each defendant participating in the proposed settlement must serve upon the appropriate state and federal officials (1) a copy of the complaint and any materials filed with the complaint and any amended complaints, unless such materials are made electronically available on the internet in a manner that includes notice of how to access the materials electronically; (2) notice of any scheduled hearing in the class action; (3) any proposed or final notification to class members of (a) the members' right to request exclusion from the action, (b) if no right to exclusion exists, a statement that no such right exists, (c) a proposed settlement of a class action, (4) any proposed or final class action settlement; (5) any settlement or other agreement contemporaneously made between class counsel and counsel for the defendants; (6) any final judgment or notice of dismissal; (7) if feasible, the names of class members who reside in each state and the estimated proportionate share of the claims of such members to the entire settlement must be provided to that state's appropriate state official, and, if not feasible, a reasonable estimate of the number of class members in each state and the estimated proportionate share of the claims of such members to the entire settlement; and (8) any written judicial opinion relating to the materials described above.[525]

Section 1715(d) provides that an order giving final approval of a proposed settlement may not be issued earlier than 90 days after the later of the dates on which the appropriate federal and state institutions are served with the notice described above. Section 1715(e) provides that a class member may refuse to

---

521. *See* 28 U.S.C. § 1712(a)-(e).

522. *See id.* § 1713.

523. *See id.* § 1714.

524. *See id.* § 1715(b); *see also id.* § 1715(a)(1)-(2) (defining the "appropriate" federal and state officials).

525. *See id.* § 1715(b)(1)-(8); *see also id.* § 1715(c)(1)-(2) (stating how to provide the notice to federal depository and related institutions and state depository institutions).

comply with and may choose not to be bound by a settlement agreement or consent decree if the class member demonstrates that the notice described above has not been provided.[526] However, a class member may not refuse to comply if the notice was directed to the appropriate federal official and to either the state attorney general or the person that has primary regulatory, supervisory or licensing authority over the defendant.[527]

(c) Subject-Matter Jurisdiction Problems Under Rule 23

Like many other joinder devices, subject-matter jurisdiction problems are most acute in class actions based on diversity jurisdiction. The rule of complete diversity poses no serious problem because only the citizenship of the representative party is considered in determining whether diversity exists under 28 U.S.C. § 1332.[528] Therefore, the fact that some absent members of the class are citizens of the same state as the party opposing the class does not destroy diversity jurisdiction.

In contrast, jurisdictional amount problems can be serious under § 1332. The question is whether the claims of the class members may be aggregated in order to meet the amount-in-controversy requirement of the diversity statute. Recall that the general rule governing aggregation in non-class action party joinder cases is that several plaintiffs may aggregate their claims to meet the jurisdictional amount requirement only when they are suing to enforce a single title or right in which they have a common and undivided interest.[529] As applied to class actions before 1966, plaintiffs could aggregate their claims in "true" class actions, but not in "hybrid" or "spurious" class actions because in both of the latter actions the rights asserted were "several."[530]

There was hope that the 1966 amendments to Rule 23 would change the context in which the jurisdictional amount requirement operated and permit aggregation in all class actions. Because the judgment in all Rule 23 class actions would bind the absent members of the class after 1966, it was hoped that the amount

---

526. *See id.* § 1715(e)(1).

527. *Id.* § 1715(e)(2). Section 1715(e)(3) provides that the rights created by subsection (e) apply only to class members or persons acting on a class member's behalf and shall not be construed to limit any other rights affecting a class member's participation in a settlement. Section 1715(f) states that nothing in section 1715 shall be construed to expand the authority or or impose any obligations, duties, or responsibilities upon federal or state officials. *See also* Sue-Yun Ahn, *CAFA Choice-of-Law, and the Problem of Legal Maturity in Nationwide Class Actions,* 76 U. CIN. L. REV. 105 (2007); Allan Kanner & M. Ryan Casey, *Consumer Class Actions After CAFA,* 56 DRAKE L. REV. 303 (2008); Daniel R. Karon, *"How Do You Take Your Multi-State, Class-Action Litigation? One Lump or Two?" Infusing State Class-Action Jurisprudence into Federal Multi-State, Class-Certification Analyses in a "CAFA-Nated" World,* 46 SANTA CLARA L. REV. 567 (2006); Holly Kershell, *An Approach to Certification Issues in Multi-State Diversity Class Actions in Federal Court After the Class Action Fairness Act of 2005,* 40 U. SAN FRAN. L. REV. 769 (2006).

528. *See* Supreme Tribe of Ben-Hur v. Cauble, 255 U.S. 356, 41 S. Ct. 338, 65 L. Ed. 673 (1921); *In re* "Agent Orange" Prod. Liab. Litig., 818 F.2d 145, 162 (2d Cir. 1987); *In re* Cement Antitrust Litig., 688 F.2d 1297, 1309 (9th Cir. 1982), *aff'd sub nom.* Arizona v. United States Dist. Court, 459 U.S. 1191, 103 S. Ct. 1173, 75 L. Ed. 2d 425 (1983) (mem.). *But see* Sherman L. Cohn, *The New Federal Rules of Civil Procedure*, 54 GEO. L.J. 1204, 1219 (1966). One federal court has held that if a representative party adds other representative parties to the action who are not diverse to the defendant in order to defeat removal, the district court may not dismiss the added parties as long as it is clear that they are real parties in interest. *See* Garbie v. Chrysler Corp., 8 F. Supp. 2d 814 (N.D. Ill. 1998), *aff'd*, 211 F.3d 407 (7th Cir. 2000).

529. *See* Chapter 2(D)(3)*(b) supra* ("Aggregation of Claims with Multiple Parties: The 'Common and Undivided' Interest Test").

530. *See* 7A CHARLES A. WRIGHT ET AL., FEDERAL PRACTICE AND PROCEDURE: CIVIL § 1756 (3d ed. 2005).

in controversy could be satisfied by the aggregate amount claimed by or against the class.[531] Unfortunately, the Supreme Court has settled the rule to the contrary since 1966. In *Snyder v. Harris*,[532] the Court held that when the claims of the class members are all less than the jurisdictional amount, the claims can be aggregated only when the plaintiffs are attempting to enforce a single title or right in which they share a common and undivided interest. Subsequently, in *Zahn v. International Paper Co.*,[533] the Court held that when the claims of some members of the class meet the jurisdictional amount requirement and others do not, aggregation still is permitted only under the traditional test. Thus, each member of the class not possessing a claim in excess of $75,000 must be dismissed from the action unless the single-title-or-right test is satisfied.

The enactment of 28 U.S.C. § 1367 in 1990 should not have altered the results in *Snyder* and *Zahn*, but it has. Section 1367(b), which is designed to preserve the policies of the diversity jurisdiction, does not refer to Rule 23, as it does to other federal joinder rules. As discussed below, the Supreme Court in the *Exxon Mobil* decision examined in Chapter 2(C)(4)*(e)(i) & (ii)* and the preceding sections of this chapter dealing with other joinder rules, above, interpreted this omission to mean that § 1367(b) does not except class actions from the operation of § 1367(a).[534] This reading effectively overrules *Zahn*, because the claims of the absent members of a Rule 23 class usually, if not always, will be sufficiently related to the representative's claim to be within the supplemental jurisdiction conferred by § 1367(a). *Snyder*, however, remains good law, because for § 1367(a) to operate, there must be at least one claim in the action over which federal jurisdiction would exist if the claim were asserted by itself. In *Snyder,* none of the class members' claims exceeded $75,000 in amount.

Nevertheless, the Supreme Court's reading of the statute in *Exxon Mobil* is incorrect. The House Report accompanying § 1367(b) stated that "[t]he section is not intended to affect the jurisdictional requirements of 28 U.S.C. § 1332 in diversity-only class actions, as those requirements were interpreted prior to *Finley*."[535] Thus, despite the lack of reference to Rule 23 in § 1367(b), the legislative history of the statute supports retention of the *Snyder-Zahn* aggregation requirements. As previously discussed in Chapter 2 and earlier sections of this chapter, the Supreme Court was able to ignore this legislative history by pretending that § 1367 is clear and unambiguous, a patently preposterous proposition.

Justice Ginsburg's dissenting opinion in *Exxon Mobil* did argue that the "civil action" language at the beginning of § 1367(a) should be read to incorporate the complete diversity and aggregation rules of § 1332, thus avoiding the problem of § 1367(b). However, Justice Ginsburg did not discuss how this interpretation would affect the central purpose of the statute to overrule the *Finley* case (a question discussed in Chapter 2(C)(4)*(e)(ii)*, above). Justice Ginsburg stated that

---

531. *Cf. id.*

532. 394 U.S. 332, 89 S. Ct. 1053, 22 L. Ed. 2d 319 (1969).

533. 414 U.S. 291, 94 S. Ct. 505, 38 L. Ed. 2d 511 (1973).

534. *See* Denis F. McLaughlin, *The Federal Supplemental Jurisdiction Statute—A Constitutional and Statutory Analysis*, 24 ARIZ. ST. L.J. 849, 972 (1992).

535. H. REP. NO. 734, 101st Cong., 2d Sess. 29 (1990).

> [t]he Court is unanimous in reading § 1367(a) to permit pendent party jurisdiction in federal-question cases, and thus to overrule *Finley*. The basic jurisdictional grant, § 1331 . . . contain[s] no amount-in-controversy requirement. . . . Once there is a civil action presenting a qualifying claim arising under federal law, § 1331's sole requirement is met. District courts, we have held, may then adjudicate, additionally, state-law claims [that are factually related to the federal claims]. . . . Section 1367(a) enlarges that category to include not only state-law claims against the defendant named in the federal claim, but also "[state law] claims that involve the joinder or intervention of additional parties."[536]

The problem with this reasoning is that if the "civil action" language of § 1367(a) requires jurisdiction over the entire civil action filed by the plaintiff or plaintiffs in the case in diversity actions, it is difficult to see how the language does not require the same thing in federal question cases. There is no original jurisdiction under § 1331 over pendent parties against whom state claims only are asserted, and, therefore, under Justice Ginsburg's reasoning, the language providing for jurisdiction over claims that involve the joinder or intervention of additional parties would have nothing on which to operate. As a result, *Finley* would not be overruled.

Although *Exxon Mobil* has settled the application of § 1367 to class actions, the discussion in preceding sections of this chapter has demonstrated that the Court cannot have fully appreciated the implications of its decision in cases not before it. Specifically, the Court's "contamination theory" applied to other multiple party joinder rules renders § 1367(b) superfluous to diversity cases involving defects of citizenship and leaves it relevant only in cases involving defects in jurisdictional amount. Yet "all agree" that § 1367(b) was designed to apply to both kinds of problems (and that § 1367(a) was supposed to have a "claim specific" interpretation with regard to both diversity and amount-in-controversy problems). One can only hope that the Court will revisit the statute at a future date and eliminate the unintended consequences of the decision.

In 2005, Congress enacted the Class Action Fairness Act of 2005.[537] This Act has been discussed extensively in Chapter 2 at appropriate places and also in the preceding subsection. This subsection explores the effect of the Act on the jurisdictional problems discussed above.

As discussed in Chapter 2, the new Act confers original jurisdiction on the United States District Courts of class actions in which the amount in controversy exceeds $5,000,000, exclusive of interests and costs, and minimal diversity of citizenship exists.[538] In determining the amount in controversy, the new Act states that the claims of the individual class members may be aggregated to meet the $5,000,000 amount.[539] Removal of class actions is provided for without regard for the one-year limit on removal of diversity actions found in 28 U.S.C. § 1446[540] and

---

536. 545 U.S. at 587-88, 125 S. Ct. at 2637, 162 L. Ed. 2d at 539.
537. Pub. L. No. 109-2, 119 Stat. 4 (2005) (codified as 28 U.S.C. §§ 1711-1715, 1332(d), 1453).
538. *See* 28 U.S.C. § 1332(d)(2)(A)-(C).
539. *See id.* § 1332(d)(6).
540. *See* 28 U.S.C. § 1453(b).

is also allowed even if a defendant is a citizen of the state in which the action is brought, thus eliminating the restriction on removal by in-state defendants that exists in other kinds of diversity actions under 28 U.S.C. § 1441(b)(2).[541] Similarly, removal is also allowed by a single defendant, without the consent of the other defendants.[542]

These jurisdictional and removal provisions raise some interesting questions in light of the problems discussed earlier in this subsection. First, prior to the new Act, certain kinds of class actions would have met the traditional "common and undivided interest" test discussed above. That test was effectively abolished by the *Exxon Mobil* decision in class actions in which at least one of the representative parties has a claim in excess of $75,000. As a result, many more class actions below $5,000,000 in amount may now fall within the federal diversity jurisdiction. Those class actions in which aggregation would be permitted under the common-and-undivided-interest test will qualify for federal jurisdiction even if no member of the class has a claim in excess of $75,000, as long as the aggregate class recovery is in excess of that amount. Those class actions not qualifying under the common-and-undivided-interest test will nevertheless satisfy the amount requirement as long as at least one member of the class has a claim in excess of $75,000 and the other class members' claims are sufficiently related to satisfy the supplemental jurisdiction statute. Furthermore, class actions in which a recovery of $5,000,000 or more is sought will not be subject to the old "common and undivided interest" test, because the Class Action Fairness Act has eliminated that requirement for the actions to which it applies.

However, as discussed in Chapter 2, because the Class Action Fairness Act is a special provision now dealing specifically with class actions, it may produce some interpretive results not intended by Congress. Although it may be unlikely, an interpretive inference might be drawn by the courts that the Act is the exclusive provision governing federal jurisdiction in *all* class actions. This would mean that actions for amounts less than $5,000,000 that would qualify for subject-matter jurisdiction under the *Exxon Mobil* decision, or that would satisfy the common and undivided interest test, could no longer be brought in or removed to federal court by combining the provisions of 28 U.S.C. § 1332(a) (the general diversity statute) and 28 U.S.C. § 1441(a) & (b). Alternatively, it might be held that class actions for less than $5,000,000 are suitable for federal jurisdiction, but are subject to the other restrictions described in the new Act.

Closely related to these potential interpretive difficulties is the effect of new § 1453, governing removal of class actions. Removal under § 1453 is *not* keyed exclusively to the new class action original jurisdiction provisions of 28 U.S.C. § 1332(d), but is worded in such a manner as to apply to *all* class actions.[543] Thus, assume, contrary to the interpretive possibilities discussed in the preceding

---

541. *See id.*

542. *See id.; see also* United Steel Workers Int'l Union v. Shell Oil Co., 549 F.3d 1204 (9th Cir. 2008) (timely removal by one defendant under CAFA effectuated removal of entire action).

543. *See* 28 U.S.C. § 1453(b) (class action may be removed to a district court of the United States in accordance with § 1446 (except that the one-year limitation under § 1446(b) shall not apply), without regard to whether any defendant is a citizen of the state in which the action is brought, except that such action may be removed by any defendant without the consent of all defendants).

paragraph, that new § 1332(d) is not read to preclude subject-matter jurisdiction from being asserted under § 1332(a) in cases in which the amount sought is less than $5,000,000. Assume further a class action in state court in which original jurisdiction exists under § 1332(a), but in which the defendant is a citizen of the state in which the action is brought or only one of multiple defendants wishes to remove. Under the broad language of new § 1453(b), it is possible to conclude that removal of such a class action is now possible.

Finally, it should be noted that new § 1332(d) contains both permissive and mandatory "abstention" provisions. New § 1332(d)(3) provides:

> (3) A district court may, in the interests of justice and looking at the totality of the circumstances, decline to exercise jurisdiction under paragraph (2) [providing for original jurisdiction on the basis of minimal diversity] over a class action in which greater than one-third but less than two-thirds of the members of all proposed plaintiff classes in the aggregate and the primary defendants are citizens of the State in which the action was originally filed based on considerations of—
>
> > (A) whether the claims asserted involve matters of national or interstate interest;
> >
> > (B) whether the claims asserted will be governed by laws of the State in which the action was originally filed or by the laws of other States;
> >
> > (C) whether the class action has been pleaded in a manner that seeks to avoid Federal jurisdiction;
> >
> > (D) whether the action was brought in a forum with a distinct nexus with the class members, the alleged harm, or the defendants;
> >
> > (E) whether the number of citizens of the State in which the action was originally filed in all proposed plaintiff classes in the aggregate is substantially larger than the number of citizens from any other State, and the citizenship of the other members of the proposed class is dispersed among a substantial number of States; and
> >
> > (F) whether, during the 3-year period preceding the filing of that class action, 1 or more other class actions asserting the same or similar claims on behalf of the same or other persons have been filed.

Section 1332(d)(4), in contrast, provides for mandatory abstention in certain kinds of cases.[544] The subsection reads:

---

544. Section 1332(d)(4) is sometimes referred to as the "local controversy" exception to federal jurisdiction under the Act. In Evans v. Walter Industries, Inc., 449 F.3d 1159 (11th Cir. 2006), four defendants removed an Alabama state class action under CAFA, and the plaintiffs moved to remand on the basis of § 1332(d)(4)(A) on the basis that more than two-thirds of the plaintiff class were Alabama citizens and at least one Alabama defendant was from whom significant relief was sought within the meaning of the Act. The district court ordered the case remanded on this basis, but the court of appeals reversed, holding that the case did not fall within the "local controversy" exception. The court reasoned that Congress intended the exception to be a narrow one and that the burden of proof was on the plaintiffs to show that the case fell within the exception after defendants had demonstrated that the basic jurisdictional provisions of the Act had been satisfied. The court concluded that the plaintiffs had failed to satisfy their burden of showing that two-thirds of the plaintiff class were Alabama citizens

(4) A district court shall decline to exercise jurisdiction under paragraph (2) [the provision conferring original jurisdiction on the basis of minimal diversity]—

(A)(i) over a class action in which—

(I) greater than two-thirds of the members of all proposed plaintiff classes in the aggregate are citizens of the State in which the action was originally filed;

(II) at least 1 defendant is a defendant—

(aa) from whom significant relief is sought by members of the plaintiff class;

(bb) whose alleged conduct forms a significant basis of the claims asserted by the proposed plaintiff class; and

(cc) who is a citizen of the State in which the action was originally filed; and

(III) principal injuries resulting from the alleged conduct or any related conduct of each defendant were incurred in the State in which the action was originally filed; and

(ii) during the 3-year period preceding the filing of that class action, no other class action has been filed asserting the same or similar factual allegations against any of the defendants on behalf of the same or other persons;[545] or

(B) two-thirds or more of the members of all proposed plaintiff classes in the aggregate, and the primary defendants, are citizens of the State in which the action was originally filed.[546]

In addition to these unconscionably unwieldy abstention provisions, § 1332(d)(5) exempts from both the jurisdictional provisions and the abstention

---

and that the plaintiffs sought "significant relief" from an Alabama defendant. *See also* Morrison v. YTB Int'l, Inc., 649 F.3d 533 (7th Cir. 2011) (district court erred in dismissing out-of-state plaintiffs for lack of standing in class action under state consumer protection act and then dismissing under 28 U.S.C. § 1332(d)(4); plaintiffs proposed nationwide class and ability of out-of-state class members to recover was issue of choice-of-law, not standing); *cf.* Nevada v. Bank of Am. Corp., 672 F.3d 661 (9th Cir. 2012) (parens patriae enforcement suits filed by attorney general were not class actions under CAFA and suit did not qualify as a mass action). For an extensive discussion of the burden of proof on jurisdiction under CAFA, see Lonny Sheinkopf Hoffman, *Burdens of Jurisdictional Facts*, 59 UCLA PAC. BASIN L.J. 409 (2008).

545. *See, e.g.*, Williams v. Homeland Ins. Co., 657 F.3d 287 (5th Cir. 2011) (requirements that at least one defendant whose conduct formed significant basis for claims of class and that principal injuries resulting from the alleged conduct occurred in the state were satisfied so as to make local controversy exception applicable); Westerfeld v. Independent Processing, L.L.C., 621 F.3d 819 (8th Cir. 2010) (local controversy exception requires that an in-state defendant be a significant defendant—*i.e.* one from whom significant relief is sought; this requires consideration of all claims in the action); Coffey v. Freeport McMoran Copper & Gold, 581 F.3d 1240 (10th Cir. 2009) (district court did not clearly err in determining that activity of former operator was substantial activity that sufficed to establish operator's principal place of business in state as required to satisfy local controversy exception); Kaufman v. Allstate N.J. Ins. Co., 561 F.3d 144 (3d Cir. 2009) (significant defendant determination for purposes of local controversy exception requires consideration of only those defendants presently in the action, but requires local defendant's alleged conduct form a significant basis of all claims asserted); Davis v. HSBC Bank Nev. N.A., 557 F.3d 1026 (9th Cir. 2009) (because corporation did not have its principal place of business in California, it was not a California citizen and local controversy exception did not apply).

546. This is the so-called "home state" exception to the act. *In re* Sprint Nextel Corp., 593 F.3d 669 (7th Cir. 2010) (home state exception does not require court to consider other possible class actions; use of the plural language is meant to refer to the fact that there can be multiple classes in a single class action); *In re* Hannaford Bros. Customer Data Sec. Breach Litig., 564 F.3d 75 (1st Cir. 2009) (remand proper under home state exception when all class members and the only defendant were Florida citizens; home state exception does not require court to consider all previously filed class actions that fall within a core nucleus of operative facts such as to fall within the same Article III case or controversy).

provisions class actions in which (a) the primary defendants are states, state officials, or other governmental entities against whom the district court may be foreclosed from ordering relief; or (b) the number of members of all "proposed plaintiff classes" in the aggregate is less than 100.[547] The first exemption is obviously designed to accommodate concerns about actions that may be barred by the Eleventh Amendment from being heard in federal court. The purpose of the second exemption is unclear, as is the phrase "proposed plaintiff classes." It may be that the drafters of the statute meant to say "proposed plaintiff class members."

Class action reform is clearly desirable. However, the Class Action Fairness Act is undoubtedly a candidate for the worst drafted federal jurisdictional statute ever, and that is saying something.[548]

(d) Personal Jurisdiction Problems Under Rule 23

The most serious personal jurisdiction questions in class actions concern the ability of a court to assert jurisdiction over the absent members of the class. May a state or federal court sitting in a particular state enter a judgment that binds absent members of a plaintiffs' or defendants' class who do not have minimum contacts with the state? The earliest post-*International Shoe* case that offers support for jurisdiction over the absent members of the class is *Mullane v. Central Hanover Bank & Trust Co.*,[549] discussed in Chapter 3. However, the *Mullane* case may have involved a "jurisdiction by necessity" situation that may not exist in all class actions.[550] If New York had not had power to settle the accounts of the fund in *Mullane*, it seems certain that no other state would have the power to do so either. This peculiar situation may not be present in most Rule 23 actions. Particularly in Rule 23(b)(3) actions, when class members are scattered throughout the United States and members within each state might bring individual or class actions against a defendant, it is questionable whether the mere efficiency of bringing a single action to adjudicate the interests of the entire class will be permissible as against class members having no contacts with the forum state.

---

547. *See* 28 U.S.C. § 1332(d)(5).

548. The discussion in the text by no means exhausts the drafting problems with the statute. The statute, 28 U.S.C. § 1453(c)(1) states that a court of appeals may accept an appeal from a district court's grant or denial of a remand order if an application for an appeal is made "not less than 7 days after entry of the order." Literally read, this would permit appeals to be sought from 7 days to infinity. At least three courts of appeals have interpreted this provision to mean exactly the opposite of what it says—*i.e.,* that an application to appeal must be made not more than 7 days after entry of the order granting or denying remand. *See* Morgan v. Gay, 466 F.3d 276 (3d Cir. 2006); Amalgamated Transit Union Local 1309, AFL-CIO v. Laidlaw Transit Servs., Inc., 435 F.3d 1140 (9th Cir. 2006); Pritchett v. Office Depot, Inc., 420 F.3d 1090 (10th Cir. 2005). However, the Seventh Circuit has held that the actual language must be followed. *See* Spivey v. Vertrue, Inc., 528 F.3d 982 (7th Cir. 2008). The court observed that this did not give a limitless time within which to appeal, because in the absence of a specified deadline, Federal Rule of Appellate Procedure 4(a)'s time limit of 30 days would apply to provide a terminal date. *See also* Michael Isaac Miller, *The Class Action (Un)fairness Act of 2005: Could it Spell the End of the Multi-State Consumer Class Action?*, 36 PEPPERDINE L. REV. 879 (2009); Kristen L. Wenger, Note, *The Class Action Fairness Act of 2005: The Limits of its Text and the Need for Legislative Clarification, Not Judicial Interpretation*, 38 FLA. ST. U. L. REV. 679 (2011).

549. 339 U.S. 306, 70 S. Ct. 652, 94 L. Ed. 865 (1950).

550. *See* Chapter 3(I) *supra* ("Jurisdiction by Necessity") (discussing whether *Mullane* satisfies the conventional minimum contacts test or is a jurisdiction by necessity case).

The one Supreme Court decision bearing directly on this question is *Phillips Petroleum Co. v. Shutts*.[551] In *Phillips*, the Court sustained the constitutionality of a state court's assertion of jurisdiction to bind absent plaintiff class members who had no contacts with the state. However, the *Phillips* case involved a Rule 23(b)(3) class action, in which the absent members of the class received notice of the action and an opportunity to opt out of the class. The protection afforded to the absent class members by this procedure appeared to influence the Court's decision. Therefore, the *Phillips* case offers little support for the validity of jurisdictional assertions over absent class members when the notice and opt-out procedures are not available. The Court also emphasized the consequences to the absent class members in a plaintiffs' class action were not as serious as they might be in other types of actions, such as a defendants' class action. Thus, even the notice and opt-out provisions might not validate an assertion of jurisdiction to adjudicate a class action that posed the danger of more serious consequences to the class.[552]

(e) Venue Problems Under Rule 23

Before 1990, only the residence of the representative party was relevant for determining venue in class action cases.[553] Consequently, venue problems were no more substantial in class actions than in any other sort of action. However, now that residence of the plaintiff has been eliminated as a proper venue under 28 U.S.C. § 1391, venue has been accordingly narrowed in class actions, as in all other actions.[554] Residence of the representative party would only confer proper venue today in a "defendant's class action."

(f) Rule Validity Problems Under Rule 23

The issue of Rule 23's validity under the Rules Enabling Act when the rule conflicts with state laws that forbid class actions in particular circumstances was

---

551. 472 U.S. 797, 105 S. Ct. 2965, 86 L. Ed. 2d 628 (1985).

552. *See In re* Real Estate Title & Settlement Servs. Antitrust Litig., 869 F.2d 760 (3d Cir. 1989); *see also* Brown v. Ticor Title Ins. Co., 982 F.2d 386 (9th Cir. 1992) (minimal due process requirement in a class action wholly or predominantly for damages requires that members of plaintiff class be allowed to opt out of the class); Lamarque v. Fairbanks Capital Corp., 927 A.2d 753 (R.I. 2007) (a party seeking to avoid the binding effect of a prior judgment is entitled to collaterally attack the judgment on grounds of lack of personal jurisdiction; however, when an absent class member seeks to challenge the binding effect of a class action judgment on due process grounds, the scope of review is limited to a determination of whether appropriate procedures were adopted by the certifying court to insure that due process was afforded); *cf.* State v. Homeside Lending, Inc., 2003 VT 17, 175 Vt. 239, 826 A.2d 997 (where class action can impose monetary burdens on plaintiff class members that can exceed any benefits, a state court has personal jurisdiction only over those class members who have minimum contacts with the state); *see also* Carol Rice Andrews, *The Personal Jurisdiction Problem Overlooked in the National Debate About "Class Action Fairness,"* 58 S.M.U. L. REV. 1313 (2005); Debra Lyn Bassett, *U.S. Class Actions Go Global: Transnational Class Actions and Personal Jurisdiction,* 72 FORDHAM L. REV. 41 (2003); Elizabeth J. Cabraser, *The Manageable Nationwide Class: A Choice-of-Law Legacy of* Phillips Petroleum Co. v. Shutts, 74 U.M.K.C. L. REV. 543 (2006); Tanya J. Monestier, *Personal Jurisdiction Over Non-Resident Class Members: Have We Gone Down the Wrong Road?*, 45 TEX. INT'L L.J. 537 (2010); Linda S. Mullenix, *Gridlaw: The Enduring Legacy of* Phillips Petroleum Co. v. Shutts, 74 U.M.K.C. L. REV. 651 (2006); Richard A. Nagareda, *Bootstrapping in Choice of Law After the Class Action Fairness Act,* 74 U.M.K.C. L. REV. 661 (2006); R. D. Rees, Note, *Plaintiff Due Process Rights in Assertions of Personal Jurisdiction,* 78 N.Y.U. L. REV. 405 (2003).

553. *See, e.g.*, Appleton Elec. Co. v. Advance-United Expressways, 494 F.2d 126, 140 (7th Cir. 1974); *In re* Gap Stores Sec. Litig., 79 F.R.D. 283, 292 n.6 (N.D. Cal. 1978).

554. *See* Chapter 4(C)(1) *supra* ("Plaintiff's Residence as Proper Venue").

dealt with in the *Shady Grove* decision examined in Chapter 5.[555] As discussed there, a majority of five members of the Court interpreted Rule 23 as applicable to the case in federal court. The majority viewed Rule 23 as giving a right to a federal plaintiff to bring an action as a class action. This interpretation rejected the view of the Second Circuit Court of Appeals that the rule simply dealt with the question of the requirements to be met when a class action was otherwise permissible, while state law governed an antecedent question of when a class action would be permitted or forbidden in a particular class of cases. As observed in Chapter 5, this seemed, inconsistently, to be a return to the practice of broad interpretation of Federal Rules of Civil Procedure that had been rejected in the *Gasperini* and *Semtek* cases.[556]

With regard to the validity of Rule 23, the majority held that it did not abridge, enlarge, or modify substantive rights under the Rules Enabling Act. Here, however, the majority for upholding the rule's validity did not agree on how to interpret the Rules Enabling Act's substantive rights restriction. A plurality of the Court view it as irrelevant that a state procedural restriction might be supported by "substantive" policies. All that mattered to the plurality was whether a challenged Federal Rule itself met the *Sibbach* test of "really regulating procedure." If so, the fact that it conflicted with a state procedural rule that was enacted for substantive purposes would not render it invalid. Justice Steven's disagreed with this interpretation of the Act, however, as did the four dissenters. In Justice Steven's view, if a state procedural was enacted for substantive reasons (bound up with substantive rights) a Federal Rule of Civil Procedure that conflicts with it could not be validly applied in a particular case.[557] However, Justice Stevens' did not interpret the state law involved in the case as having been enacted for substantive purposes or as embodying substantive rights. Nevertheless, his method of interpreting the Enabling Act seems to coincide with that of the four dissenting justices. This means that there was a majority in favor of interpreting Federal Rules as invalid as applied when the rules conflict clearly enough with a state procedural rule that is clearly supported by policies that can be labeled as "substantive." This leaves other cases in which state laws that conflict with Rule 23 by restricting class actions uncertain.[558]

Beyond Rules Enabling Act problems with Rule 23, a serious separation-of-powers problem exists with new Rule 23(f). This problem is discussed elsewhere,[559] and will not be repeated here. As of this writing, there is only one court of appeals

---

555. *See* Chapter 5(E)(3) *supra* (examining the dissenters' opinion interpreting Rule 23 as not controlling the case before the Court); Chapter 5(F)(6) *supra* (discussing the majority holding that Rule 23 was applicable to the case and that Rule 23 was valid under the Enabling Act).

556. *See* Chapter 5(F)(6) *supra* ("The *Shady Grove* Decision").

557. For unexplained reasons, Justice Sotomayor failed to concur in this part of Justice Scalia's opinion; she also failed to concur in the part of Justice Scalia's opinion interpreting the Act. *See* Craig T. Cagney, *O Sonia, Where Art Thou?: Why Justice Sotomayor's Silent "Opinion" Should Serve as* Shady Grove's *Holding*, 80 FORDHAM L. REV. 189 (2011).

558. *Shady Grove* has excited substantial commentary and will doubtless continue to do so. The commentary available at the date of this writing is cited in Chapter 5 in conjunction with the discussion of the case there.

559. *See* Chapter 5(F)(7) *supra* ("Separation-of-Powers Restrictions on Judicial Rulemaking"); Chapter 12(B)(3)*(b)* *infra* ("Interlocutory Appeals").

decision interpreting Rule 23(f). In *Blair v. Equifax Check Services, Inc.*,[560] the Seventh Circuit indicated that appeals would be permitted under Rule 23(f) when (1) denial of class action treatment can be demonstrated to be questionable and would sound the death knell of the action; (2) granting of class action status is demonstrably questionable and would, in a large stakes suit, produce a risk of settlement or other disposition that would not reflect the merits of the action; or (3) an appeal would facilitate the development of class action law, whether or not the district judge's ruling can be demonstrated to be questionable. No issue concerning the validity of Rule 23(f) was discussed in *Blair*.[561]

(g) Shareholder Derivative Actions: Rule 23.1

Federal Rule 23.1 provides for a special type of class action known as a *shareholder derivative action*. A derivative action is brought by a stockholder of a corporation or a member of an unincorporated association. The action seeks to enforce a right of action belonging to the corporation or association that those in control of the corporation or association refuse to enforce. Prior to the Federal Rules, shareholder derivative actions in federal court were governed by Equity Rule 27 of the Equity Rules of 1912.[562] Original Rule 23(b) substantially duplicated Equity Rule 27.[563] Rule 23.1 was added to the Federal Rules of Civil Procedure in 1966 as a substitute for original Rule 23(b).

In addition to describing the basic nature of the derivative suit, Rule 23.1 imposes five requirements on the plaintiff.[564] First, the plaintiff must file a verified complaint alleging either that the plaintiff was a shareholder of the corporation or member of the association at the time of the transaction about which the plaintiff complains, or that the plaintiff's share or membership thereafter devolved on the plaintiff by operation of law. Second, the complaint also must allege that the action

---

560. 181 F.3d 832 (7th Cir. 1999).

561. *See also In re* Lorazepam & Clorazepate Antitrust Litig., 289 F.3d 98 (D.C. Cir. 2002) (denying interlocutory review of district court's decision to certify class action; test is whether (1) there is death-knell situation for either plaintiff or defendant that is independent of merits of underlying claims, coupled with class certification decision by district court that is questionable, taking into account district court's discretion over class certification; (2) certification decision presents unsettled and fundamental issue of law relating to class actions, important both to specific litigation and generally, that is likely to evade end-of-case review; and (3) district court's class certification decision is manifestly erroneous); *In re* Sumitomo Copper Litig., 262 F.3d 134 (2d Cir. 2001) (a party seeking Rule 23(f) review must demonstrate either (1) "the certification order will effectively terminate the litigation and there has been a substantial showing that the district court's decision is questionable" or (2) "the certification order implicates a legal question about which there is a compelling need for immediate resolution."); Newton v. Merrill Lynch, Pierce, Fenner & Smith, Inc., 259 F.3d 154 (3d Cir. 2001) (describing three categories when a grant of a Rule 23(f) petition would be appropriate: (1) cases in which accepting an appeal would end the effect of an imprudent class certification and thus is likely to be dispositive of the litigation; (2) cases involving an erroneous ruling; and (3) cases facilitating the development of the law on class certification); Lienhart v. Dryvit Sys., Inc., 255 F.3d 138 (4th Cir. 2001) (following the test in the *Prado-Steiman* case, below); Prado-Steiman *ex rel.* Prado v. Bush, 221 F.3d 1266 (11th Cir. 2000) (adopting a different five-factor test than the one in *Blair*, discussed in the principal text); Waste Mgmt. Holdings, Inc. v. Mowbray, 208 F.3d 288 (1st Cir. 2000) (adopting several variations on the Seventh Circuit's approach in *Blair*); Carey M. Erhard, Note, *A Discussion of the Interlocutory Review of Class Certification Orders Under Federal Rule of Civil Procedure 23(f)*, 51 DRAKE L. REV. 151 (2002); Charles R. Flores, *Appealing Class Action Certification Decisions Under Federal Rule of Civil Procedure 23(f)*, 4 SETON HALL CIRCUIT REV. 27 (2007); Michael E. Solimine & Christine Oliver Hines, *Deciding to Decide: Class Action Certification and Interlocutory Review by the United States Courts of Appeals Under Rule 23(f)*, 41 WM. & MARY L. REV. 1531 (2000).

562. *See* 226 U.S. 627, 656 (1912).

563. *See* 308 U.S. 645, 690 (1938).

564. *See* FED. R. CIV. P. 23.1.

is not a collusive one to confer jurisdiction on a federal court that it would not otherwise have. Third, the complaint must allege "with particularity" the plaintiff's efforts to obtain the action that the plaintiff desires by those in control of the corporation or association, or, if the plaintiff has made no such effort, why the plaintiff has not done so.[565] Fourth, Rule 23.1 states that the derivative action may not be maintained if it appears that the plaintiff is not an adequate representative of the interests of the other shareholders or members similarly situated.[566] Fifth, Rule 23.1 provides that a derivative action may not be dismissed or compromised without the court's permission and after notice to the absent shareholders and members.[567]

A corporation is a mandatory (indispensable) party to a shareholder derivative suit brought on behalf of the corporation, and this raises the question of how the corporation should be aligned for purposes of determining whether diversity jurisdiction exists.[568] Because the plaintiff is asserting a right belonging to the corporation, there is some logic in aligning the corporation as a plaintiff for the purpose of determining whether diversity exists. On the other hand, the corporation is often in the control of persons who are antagonistic to the plaintiff's interests. Frequently, this situation exists because officers or directors of the corporation are defendants in the suit. For this reason, it makes sense to refuse to align the corporation as a plaintiff for jurisdictional purposes, and, in fact, the Supreme Court has held that whenever a corporation opposes the litigation, it is to be aligned as a defendant.[569] Such an alignment will always be appropriate when the plaintiff makes a demand on the corporation to enforce its own rights under Rule 23.1 and the demand is refused.

As in class actions under Rule 23, the citizenship of the representative party is what counts in determining whether diversity jurisdiction exists. Therefore, like class actions, there are not the problems of incomplete diversity present that have been discussed in conjunction with the other joinder rules in this chapter. Similarly, the jurisdictional amount requirement in shareholder derivative actions is determined by the damage done to the corporation, rather than the plaintiff's individual financial stake in the action.[570] Therefore, the aggregation problems that exist with class actions under Rule 23 are not present under Rule 23.1. The result

---

565. *See, e.g.*, Wesley Kobylak, Annotation, *Application to Derivative Actions for Breach of Fiduciary Duty, Under § 36(b) of Investment Company Act of 1940 (15 U.S.C.S. § 80a-35(b)), of Requirement, Stated in Rule 23.1 of the Federal Rules of Civil Procedure, that Complaint in Derivative Actions Allege What Efforts Were Made by Shareholders to Obtain Desired Action or Reasons for Failure to Do So*, 65 A.L.R. FED. 542 (1983).

566. *See* David B. Levendusky, Annotation, *Requirement of Rule 23.1 of Federal Rules of Civil Procedure that Plaintiff in Shareholder Derivative Action "Fairly and Adequately Represent" Shareholders' Interests in Enforcing Corporation's Right*, 15 A.L.R. FED. 954 (1973).

567. *See* Annotation, *Notice to Shareholders and Court Approval of Dismissal or Compromise of Derivative Actions, Under Rule 23.1 of Federal Rules of Civil Procedure*, 26 A.L.R. FED. 465 (1976).

568. *See, e.g.*, City of Davenport v. Dows, 85 U.S. (18 Wall.) 626, 21 L. Ed. 938 (1874); Grosset v. Wenaas, 42 Cal. 4th 1100, 175 P.3d 1184, 72 Cal. Rptr. 3d 129 (2008) (corporation is an indispensable party to a shareholder derivative action; stockholder may not maintain an action in his individual capacity for a wrong done to the corporation and to bring a derivative action, shareholder must maintain continuous ownership of the stock from the occurrence of the transaction about which the stockholder complains and throughout the litigation).

569. *See* Smith v. Sperling, 354 U.S. 91, 77 S. Ct. 1112, 1 L. Ed. 2d 1205 (1957); Swanson v. Traer, 354 U.S. 114, 77 S. Ct. 1116, 1 L. Ed. 2d 1221 (1957). The U.S. Supreme Court has held that Rule 23.1 is not broad enough to govern the content of the demand requirement in shareholder derivative actions and that state law controls the content of the demand requirement in actions under the Investment Company Act of 1940. *See* Kamen v. Kemper Fin. Servs., Inc., 500 U.S. 90, 111 S. Ct. 1711, 114 L. Ed. 2d 152 (1991).

570. *See* 7C CHARLES A. WRIGHT ET AL., FEDERAL PRACTICE AND PROCEDURE: CIVIL § 1823 (3d ed. 2007).

of these rules is that the supplemental jurisdiction statute is irrelevant to shareholder derivative actions.

Two venue provisions are available in derivative actions, the ordinary venue provisions (§ 1391)[571] and a special venue provision (§ 1401), which states that "[a]ny civil action by a stockholder on behalf of his corporation may be prosecuted in any judicial district where the corporation might have sued the same defendants."[572] Thus, in a diversity action, the suit may be brought pursuant to § 1391 in a district where any defendant resides, if the other defendants reside in the same state; in a district where a substantial part of the events or omissions giving rise to the action occurred, or where a substantial part of the property that is the subject of the action is situated; or in a district where personal jurisdiction can be obtained over any defendant, if there is no other district in which the action may be brought.[573]

When the special venue provision of § 1401 is employed, a special service of process provision (28 U.S.C. § 1695) allows process to be served on the corporation in any district where the corporation is organized, licensed to do business, or doing business.[574] This provision is useful when the plaintiff sues the real defendants in their state of residence and the corporation has no contacts with that state.[575] When venue is based on § 1391, the ability to obtain jurisdiction over all defendants, including the corporate defendant, is governed by Rule 4, as in other cases.[576] However, it should be noted that § 1695 does not explicitly refer to § 1401, but is phrased so as to apply to all stockholder's derivative actions. Textually, therefore, this leaves open the possibility that § 1695 could be combined with § 1391 to broaden the scope of process available under the latter statute. Indeed, the language of § 1401 suggests that the general venue provisions of § 1391 are incorporated into the former provision, since a corporation could use them to sue a defendant.

(h) Actions by or Against Unincorporated Associations: Rule 23.2

Federal Rule 23.2 provides that an action brought by or against the members of an unincorporated association may be brought as a class action by naming as representative parties one or more members of the association who will adequately represent the interests of the association and its members. The provisions of Rule 23(d) and (e) also are made applicable to class suits by or against associations under Rule 23.2.[577]

The significance of Rule 23.2 can be understood by comparing the rule with the other methods by which an association may sue or be sued. These methods include suits against the association as an entity, when such an action is permitted

---

571. *See* 28 U.S.C. § 1391.

572. 28 U.S.C. § 1401.

573. Under the amendments to 28 U.S.C. § 1391(c), corporate defendants reside in any judicial district in which personal jurisdiction can be obtained over them at the time the action is commenced. *See* Chapter 4(C)(6) *supra* ("Residence of Corporations and Associations").

574. *See* 28 U.S.C. § 1695.

575. *See* 7C CHARLES A. WRIGHT ET AL., FEDERAL PRACTICE AND PROCEDURE: CIVIL § 1825 (3d ed. 2007).

576. *See id.*

577. *See* FED. R. CIV. P. 23.2.

or required under the law governing the association, and suits against the association by joining all of its members.[578] When suit is brought by or against an association as an entity or by joining all of its members, diversity jurisdiction must be determined by reference to the citizenship of all the members.[579] When suit is brought by or against the association as a class, diversity is determined by reference to the citizenship of the representative parties only.[580] As long as the damages in a Rule 23.2 action are measured either by the total damages to or against the association, the aggregation problems present in class actions should not be present. However, it is conceivable that state rules governing the binding effect on the individual members of associations and the ability to execute judgment against the private assets of those members may raise the same kinds of aggregation problems that were present in the general class action setting.[581] However, given the widespread practice of treating associations as entities under state law, this seems unlikely.

In *Denver & Rio Grande Western Railroad Co. v. Brotherhood of Railroad Trainmen*,[582] the Supreme Court held that unincorporated associations should be analogized to corporations for venue purposes. Extrapolating from this position to the existing provisions governing corporate venue gives the following results. Today, under new 28 U.S.C. § 1391(c)(2), if the association can be sued in its common name, it "shall be deemed to reside, if a defendant, in any judicial district in which [it] is subject to the court's personal jurisdiction . . . and, if a plaintiff, only in the judicial district in which it maintains its principal place of business."[583] Of course, if the association sues or is sued in class action form, as opposed to suing or being sued as an entity, venue will presumably be determined under 28 U.S.C. § 1391 as in class actions generally.

When all members of an association must be joined as defendants, service of process has to be made and personal jurisdiction obtained over each of them. When an association is sued as an entity, process must be served as prescribed in Federal Rule 4[584] and personal jurisdiction must exist over the entity.[585] When the

---

578. For a discussion of the methods of suit by and against associations and the consequences of each in terms of the binding effect of the judgment in the suit, see RESTATEMENT (SECOND) OF JUDGMENTS § 61 cmts. a, b (1982).

579. *See, e.g.*, Arbuthnot v. State Auto. Ins. Ass'n, 264 F.2d 260 (10th Cir. 1959); Lowry v. International Bhd. of Boilermakers of Am., 259 F.2d 568 (5th Cir. 1958).

580. *See* Supreme Tribe of Ben-Hur v. Cauble, 255 U.S. 356, 41 S. Ct. 338, 65 L. Ed. 673 (1921); Kerney v. Fort Griffin Fandangle Ass'n, Inc., 624 F.2d 717, 720 (5th Cir. 1980). It has been suggested that "the logic of treating [unincorporated associations] as a class indicates that the common claims of the individual members [usually] will be allowed to be aggregated to fulfill the . . . jurisdictional amount requirement." 7C CHARLES A. WRIGHT ET AL., FEDERAL PRACTICE AND PROCEDURE: CIVIL § 1861, at 246 (3d ed. 2007). If this suggestion is accepted, the aggregation problems experienced under Rule 23 will not exist under Rule 23.2. However, it is not clear that this view will prevail in the courts. *See* Air Line Dispatchers Ass'n v. California E. Airways, Inc., 127 F. Supp. 521 (N.D. Cal. 1954). Section 1367(b), discussed in conjunction with Rule 23 *supra* subsection *(c)*, makes no reference to Rule 23.2. Therefore, as in the case of Rule 23, § 1367(a) can be read to confer supplemental jurisdiction over the claims of members of the association, and § 1367(b)'s lack of reference to Rule 23.2 can be read as a refusal to exempt the claims from the jurisdiction conferred by § 1367(a). However, as in the case of Rule 23, this runs counter to the legislative history of the statute. Therefore, the best result would seem to be to read § 1367(b) as preserving whatever aggregation rules existed prior to its enactment.

581. *See* RESTATEMENT (SECOND) OF JUDGMENTS §§ 60, cmt. a, 61(2) (1982); Chapter 13(D)(1)*(iv)* (discussing the traditional and modern rules governing the effect of associational judgments on the members *infra*.

582. 387 U.S. 556, 87 S. Ct. 1746, 18 L. Ed. 2d 954 (1967).

583. *See* 28 U.S.C. § 1391(c)(2).

584. *See* FED. R. CIV. P. 4(h).

585. *See* FED. R. CIV. P. 4(k).

association is sued as a class, process need be served only on the named representatives and personal jurisdiction obtained over them.[586] This last conclusion, however, must be qualified by the same doubts previously raised regarding personal jurisdiction over absent class members under Rule 23.

---

586. *See generally* 7C CHARLES A. WRIGHT ET AL., FEDERAL PRACTICE AND PROCEDURE: CIVIL § 1861, at 243 (3d ed. 2007).

Chapter 9

DISCOVERY AND PRETRIAL CONFERENCES

SECTION A. DEVELOPMENT OF MODERN DISCOVERY

1. Discovery in Common-Law Actions

Common-law procedure relied heavily on the pleadings to narrow the dispute to a single issue. The pleadings also gave advance notice of each party's claims and defenses. In many instances, however, the pleadings became formalized statements of conclusions of law and fact.[1] Furthermore, by pleading the general issue, the defendant often could defer to trial the decision concerning the specific defense that the defendant would use.[2] As a result, the parties frequently had to guess what the opposing party's strategy and proof at trial would be.

Bills of particular satisfied part of the need to acquire information about the opposing party's claim.[3] In addition, through the procedure of *profert* and *oyer*, the parties could force the inspection of contracts under seal, deeds, bonds, and letters of administration when the opposing party's pleading relied upon them. However, a party could not use profert and oyer to inspect other writings, such as written agreements not under seal.[4] In real actions, a defendant could demand a *view* of the disputed land before pleading to determine the specific land the plaintiff sought to recover.[5] These forms of discovery provided only limited assistance to a party preparing for trial in a common-law court.

2. Discovery in Equity Actions

In contrast to the limited discovery in common-law actions, equity developed substantially broader discovery. Equity's discovery devices were principally interrogatories, production and inspection of documents, and depositions. These devices were the precursors of modern discovery practice.

A bill in equity contained, *inter alia*, a "stating" part, a "charging" part, and an "interrogating" part.[6] The stating part set forth the facts and circumstances on

---

1. *See* Chapter 6(A)(2) *supra* ("Stating the Plaintiff's Claim in the Declaration").
2. *See* Chapter 6(A)(3)*(f)* *supra* ("The General Issue").
3. *See* Chapter 6(A)(3)*(g)* *supra* ("Bills of Particulars").
4. Joseph H. Koffler & Alison Reppy, Handbook of Common Law Pleading § 52, § 184, at 368-69 (1969).
5. *Id.* § 185, at 370.
6. *See* Joseph Story, Equity Pleadings § 26, at 18 (9th ed. 1879) (dividing equity pleadings into nine parts).

which the plaintiff based the bill. The charging part detailed the plaintiff's evidence. The charging part allowed the plaintiff to anticipate the defendant's excuses or defenses as well as charge matters that disproved or avoided them. The interrogating part propounded questions to the defendant about prior statements or charges in the bill. In response to the bill, equity required the defendant to answer the plaintiff's allegations and interrogatories under oath.[7] Thus, every bill in equity was, in reality, a bill of discovery.[8]

When the plaintiff sought to discover documents dealing with the plaintiff's case that the defendant possessed or controlled, the plaintiff included a charge and interrogatories in the bill describing the documents. Like other charges and interrogatories in the bill, the defendant had to answer by either admitting or denying the possession or control of the documents. Once the possession or control was admitted and the plaintiff had adequately shown the documents' relevance to the plaintiff's case, the plaintiff could move for production and inspection.[9]

The Court of Chancery also granted discovery in aid of proceedings pending elsewhere. Equity courts permitted a party litigating in a common-law court to file a bill for the discovery of facts or documents. Before securing such a bill, the party had to demonstrate that the requested discovery was necessary to effectively defend or prosecute at trial. The party then could introduce the sworn answers to the interrogatories as admissions in the common-law trial. Thus, to a certain extent, a bill of discovery circumvented two traditional common-law rules: (1) the parties could not be compelled to testify at trial for or against each other; and (2) they were incompetent to do so even if they so desired.[10] Equity limited its intervention to the discovery of evidence needed to prove the discovering party's claim or defense at trial. Equity courts did not permit a party to discover what evidence the opposing party would use to prove the opposing party's case at trial.[11]

Equity courts also permitted bills to perpetuate testimony. A party could maintain such bills only when the party could not presently bring an action at law. The party had to demonstrate the necessity for preserving the evidence, such as the impending death or departure from the country of a material witness before the case could be investigated in a court of law. A party could also use a bill to perpetuate testimony of the sole witness to a matter because of the uncertainty of human life. The bill prayed for a subpoena to secure the testimony.[12] Furthermore, equity courts permitted bills to take testimony *de bene esse*. A party could use such a bill in aid of a *pending* common-law action when the witness was old, in ill health, or about to depart the country. A party could use the testimony obtained through bills to

---

7. *See id.* §§ 27, 31, 35-39.

8. *Id.* § 311, at 281.

9. *See* HENRY L. MCCLINTOCK, HANDBOOK OF THE PRINCIPLES OF EQUITY § 206, at 547-48 (2d ed. 1948).

10. *See* Robert Wyness Millar, *The Mechanism of Fact-Discovery: A Study in Comparative Civil Procedure IV*, 32 ILL. L. REV. 424, 440-41 (1937); HENRY L. MCCLINTOCK, HANDBOOK OF THE PRINCIPLES OF EQUITY § 206, at 547-48 (2d ed. 1948); *see also* Chapter 11(I)(1) *infra* ("Competency").

11. *See* JOSEPH STORY, EQUITY PLEADINGS §§ 311, 858 (9th ed. 1879); ROBERT W. MILLAR, CIVIL PROCEDURE OF THE TRIAL COURT IN HISTORICAL PERSPECTIVE 204 (1952).

12. *See* JOSEPH STORY, EQUITY PLEADINGS §§ 300-306 (9th ed. 1879).

perpetuate testimony or to examine witnesses *de bene esse* only if the witness, in fact, was unavailable.[13]

3. Reform in the United States

Court systems in the United States adopted, with minor variations, the general pattern of discovery developed by the English courts. The common-law courts in the United States permitted virtually no significant discovery. However, the parties could resort to equity courts for some assistance. Because the discovery process was cumbersome, slow, and expensive, several states initiated reforms. Some states permitted the incorporation of interrogatories in the complaint or the separate use of interrogatories in common-law actions without resort to an equity proceeding.[14] Several states also authorized their common-law courts to permit discovery of documents.[15]

The New York Field Code of 1848 permitted pretrial oral depositions.[16] Thus, oral examination of parties before trial replaced the chancery method of discovery by bill and answer.[17] If a party refused to attend and testify at the pretrial examination, the court could punish the party by contempt. The court could also reject the complaint, answer, or reply.[18] The Field Code also allowed either party to apply to the court to depose any witness who resided more than 100 miles from the place where the trial or hearing was to be held.[19] A party could use the deposition at trial if the witness was dead, did not reside within 100 miles of the place of trial, or was otherwise unable to attend.[20]

The state reforms of the nineteenth century, in effect, substituted statutory means of obtaining depositions and discovery for separate equity actions. Although the specific means varied from state to state and were not uniformly adopted, three principal devices emerged: (1) written interrogatories directed to adverse parties;

---

13. *See id.* §§ 307-310. Discovery permitted by equity was enforced principally through the use of the contempt power, supplemented by forfeiture of the recalcitrant party's property. Eventually, equity courts in England were empowered to enter a default judgment against a disobedient defendant as an alternative sanction. *Developments in the Law—Discovery*, 74 HARV. L. REV. 940, 947 (1961).

14. In 1831, for example, Virginia permitted either party to file "interrogatories addressed to the other, and for an order to answer the interrogatories when it had been made to appear 'by oath of the party filing the same or otherwise,' that they were material, pertinent, and such as the interrogated party could be bound to answer on a bill in chancery." ROBERT W. MILLAR, CIVIL PROCEDURE OF THE TRIAL COURT IN HISTORICAL PERSPECTIVE 205 (1952).

15. In 1828, for example, pursuant to a New York statute authorizing rules of court in accord with the "principles and practices of chancery courts in compelling discovery," either party could petition for the discovery and production of documents from the other to facilitate the drafting of a party's pleadings or to prepare for trial. *Id.* at 220-21.

16. Act of Apr. 12, 1848, ch. 379, §§ 345, 346, 354, 1848 N.Y. Laws 497, 559-60. The Field Code, *inter alia*, merged law and equity, simplified pleading, and liberalized traditional rules governing party and claim joinder. *See* Chapter 1(D)(9) *supra* ("The Field Code and the Reform of Procedure in the States"). In 1847, a statute permitted the parties to examine each other as witnesses at trial. The Field Code expanded on the statute by permitting such examinations to take place before trial by commission, before a judge of the court, or before a judge of the county court. FIRST REPORT OF THE COMMISSIONERS ON PRACTICE AND PLEADINGS 244-45 (1848).

17. ROBERT W. MILLAR, CIVIL PROCEDURE OF THE TRIAL COURT IN HISTORICAL PERSPECTIVE 206 (1952).

18. Such a rejection could result in a dismissal or a default judgment. *Id.* at 206-07.

19. The examination was held before the county judge, a justice of the peace, or a referee where the examination was to be conducted. *See* Act of Apr. 12, 1848, ch. 379, § 354, 1848 N.Y. Laws 497, 560.

20. *Id.* § 355, 1848 N.Y. Laws 497, 560. The court, however, could specially order the witness to attend in open court. After such an order was issued, the deposition could not be used. *See id.*

(2) depositions of parties; certain categories of witnesses related to the parties, such as their employees; and witnesses who might be unavailable at trial; and (3) production or inspection of documents in a party's possession or control.[21] Even though these devices had the potential for supporting a broad range of discovery, traditional equity restrictions on the use of the devices continued. These restrictions limited discovery to (1) facts pertaining to the case of the party seeking discovery and (2) facts or documents that would be admissible in evidence at trial.[22]

Discovery in federal courts in the United States also reflected the traditional patterns of discovery developed in England. Like traditional equity practice, the Judiciary Act of 1789[23] authorized the use of interrogatories, depositions, and discovery of documents. Parties at law or in equity could take depositions *de bene esse* without leave of court when a witness (1) was old or infirm, (2) lived more than 100 miles from the place of trial, (3) was bound on a sea voyage, (4) intended to leave the United States before trial, or (5) intended to go before trial to a place outside the district that was more than 100 miles from the place of trial. A deposition *in perpetuam rei memoriam* was available in equity to preserve testimony relevant to anticipated litigation.[24]

The Judiciary Act of 1789 did not provide for interrogation of a party at law. Equity courts rarely granted bills of discovery for this purpose because they considered the legal procedures provided at law to be adequate. Similarly, production of documents at law was unavailable before trial. Equity limited the production to documents that the parties could specify. In addition, the parties had to demonstrate the documents were relevant to their claim or defense and not solely to their opponent's claim or defense. When a nonparty gave a deposition, a subpoena duces tecum could force that nonparty to produce documents under the nonparty's control.[25]

The Conformity Act of 1872 did not make available the states' more liberal pretrial discovery devices to litigation at law in federal courts.[26] The courts regarded the specific federal provisions on witness testimony as impliedly excluding state discovery provisions.[27] Some changes in federal discovery practice occurred with the adoption of the Federal Equity Rules of 1912.[28] Under these rules, bills no longer contained charges and interrogatories. Instead, they consisted of a narrative statement and a prayer.[29] The Equity Rules provided for separate interrogatories to parties and document discovery.[30] However, the rules did not broaden the bases of

---

21. *See* ROBERT W. MILLAR, CIVIL PROCEDURE OF THE TRIAL COURT IN HISTORICAL PERSPECTIVE 211-28 (1952); Michael E. Wolfson, *Addressing the Adversarial Dilemma of Civil Discovery*, 36 CLEV. ST. L. REV. 17, 25-26 (1988).

22. *See* Michael E. Wolfson, *Addressing the Adversarial Dilemma of Civil Discovery*, 36 CLEV. ST. L. REV. 17, 25-26 (1988).

23. ch. 20, 1 Stat. 73.

24. *See id.* §§ 15, 30, 1 Stat. 73, 82, 88-90; *see also Developments in the Law—Discovery*, 74 HARV. L. REV. 940, 949 & n.54 (1961).

25. *Developments in the Law—Discovery*, 74 HARV. L. REV. 940, 949-50 (1961).

26. *Id.* at 950; *see* Chapter 1(D)(10) *supra* ("Early Procedure in the Federal Courts").

27. ROBERT W. MILLAR, CIVIL PROCEDURE OF THE TRIAL COURT IN HISTORICAL PERSPECTIVE 212 (1952).

28. These rules were influenced by reforms that had taken place in England. *Id.*

29. 226 U.S. 627, 655 (1912) (Rule 25).

30. *Id.* at 665-66 (Rule 58).

discovery, but "served only to streamline the cumbersome procedures on the equity side of the federal courts."[31]

4. Discovery Practice Under the Federal Rules of Civil Procedure

In 1938, the Federal Rules of Civil Procedure introduced a dramatic change in federal discovery practice. The basic philosophy of the rules was to insure that the parties could obtain disclosure of all relevant information in the possession of any person before trial, unless the information was privileged.[32] The Federal Rules provide five principal "instruments" of discovery: (1) depositions (both oral and upon written questions) of parties and witnesses; (2) interrogatories to parties; (3) production of documents and things (including entry upon property to inspect, copy, photograph, or conduct tests); (4) physical or mental examinations of parties or persons in the custody or under the "legal control" of parties; and (5) requests for admission of the genuineness of relevant documents or the truth of any matter within the general scope of discovery. The Federal Rules also provide a range of sanctions to punish unjustified failures to comply with discovery requests.[33]

The Federal Rules of Civil Procedure were amended in 1948 to correct uncertainties that experience with the discovery rules had disclosed. Minor amendments were also made in 1949, 1963, and 1966. In 1970, the discovery rules were rearranged and amended in several significant ways. Pursuant to this rearrangement, Federal Rule 26 governed the scope of discovery, Federal Rules 27 through 36 set forth the discovery devices, and Federal Rule 37 provided sanctions for the failure to make or cooperate in discovery. Minor changes were also made in 1972 and 1975.

In 1980 and 1983, amendments were again made in response to widespread criticism of "discovery abuse." The general problems were excessive discovery, withholding information, evasive or misleading responses, delay, harassment, misuse of interrogatories, and discovery requests disproportionate to the amount in controversy.[34] The 1980 and 1983 amendments provided, *inter alia*, for a conference before the court to establish a plan and schedule for discovery and to set

---

31. *Developments in the Law—Discovery*, 74 HARV. L. REV. 940, 950 (1961).

32. 8 CHARLES A. WRIGHT ET AL., FEDERAL PRACTICE AND PROCEDURE: CIVIL § 2001, at 18 (3d ed. 2010). In Hickman v. Taylor, 329 U.S. 495, 67 S. Ct. 385, 91 L. Ed. 451 (1947), the U.S. Supreme Court characterized the development of the pretrial deposition-discovery procedure as "one of the most significant innovations of the Federal Rules of Civil Procedure." The Court explained that the Federal Rules "restrict the pleadings to the task of general notice-giving and invest the deposition-discovery process with a vital role in the preparation for trial. The various instruments of discovery now serve (1) as a device, along with the pre-trial hearing under Rule 16, to narrow and clarify the basic issues between two parties, and (2) as a device for ascertaining the facts, or information as to the existence or whereabouts of facts, relative to those issues." The Court concluded that "civil trials in the federal courts no longer need to be carried on in the dark. The way is now clear, consistent with recognized privileges, for the parties to obtain the fullest possible knowledge of the issues and facts before trial." *Id.* at 500-01, 67 S. Ct. at 388-89, 91 L. Ed. at 457.

33. *See, e.g.*, Sun v. Board of Trustees, 473 F.3d 799, 811-12 (7th Cir. 2007) (default judgment was an unduly harsh sanction for defense counsel's discovery delays; court should have imposed increased monetary sanctions against defense attorneys who had caused discovery delays).

34. *See* Wayne D. Brazil, *Civil Discovery: Lawyer's Views of Its Effectiveness, Its Principal Problems and Abuses*, 1980 AM. B. FOUND. RES. J. 787, 824-25; *see also* Maurice Rosenberg & Warren R. King, *Curbing Discovery Abuse in Civil Litigation: Enough Is Enough*, 1981 B.Y.U. L. REV. 579.

possible limits on discovery by the parties.[35] These changes encouraged judges to take a "managerial approach" to discovery and other aspects of the litigation through frequent pretrial conferences.[36]

Despite these changes, concern over the cost of discovery and discovery abuse continued.[37] Influential studies proposed mandatory disclosure to alleviate abuses and hardball tactics at the discovery stage.[38] The Civil Justice Reform Act of 1990 required each federal district court to consider encouraging "cost-effective discovery" through (1) "voluntary exchange of information among litigants and their attorneys" and (2) "the use of cooperative discovery devices."[39] In 1991, the President's Council on Competitiveness recommended disclosure of "core information."[40] Also in 1991, the Advisory Committee on Civil Rules published for comment proposed amendments to the Federal Rules, including mandatory disclosures and other significant changes in discovery.[41]

The proposed rules evoked a strong negative reaction.[42] The principal criticisms focused on a predicted increase in discovery motions, the overproduction of marginally relevant information, and increased expense.[43] Critics also asserted that automatic disclosure would raise serious ethical concerns, undermine the adversary system, and invade the "work product" of lawyers.[44] After the public hearings in February 1992, the Advisory Committee abandoned the mandatory disclosure proposal.[45]

In April 1992, however, the Advisory Committee unexpectedly revived the proposal.[46] The final recommendation retained mandatory disclosure, but narrowed the disclosure requirement from information that "bears significantly on any claim or defense" to "discoverable information relevant to disputed facts alleged with

---

35. *See* section N *infra* ("Pretrial Conferences and Orders").

36. *See, e.g.*, Wayne D. Brazil, *Improving Judicial Controls Over the Pretrial Development of Civil Actions: Model Rules for Case Management and Sanctions*, 1981 AM. B. FOUND. RES. J. 873, 890-921.

37. *See, e.g.*, Harris & Associates, Inc., *Judges' Opinions on Procedural Issues: A Survey of State and Federal Trial Judges Who Spent at Least Half of Their Time on General Civil Cases*, 69 B.U. L. REV. 731, 735 (1989).

38. *See, e.g.*, William W. Schwarzer, *The Federal Rules, the Adversary Process and Discovery Reform*, 50 U. PITT. L. REV. 703 (1989); William W. Schwarzer, *Slaying the Monsters of Cost and Delay: Would Disclosure Be More Effective than Discovery?*, 74 JUDICATURE 178 (1991); *see also* Wayne D. Brazil, *The Adversary Character of Civil Discovery: A Critique and Proposals for Change*, 31 VAND. L. REV. 1295 (1978).

39. § 103, 104 Stat. 5089, 5091-92 (codified at 28 U.S.C. § 473(a)(4)).

40. PRESIDENT'S COUNCIL ON COMPETITIVENESS, AGENDA FOR CIVIL JUSTICE REFORM IN AMERICA 16-17 (1991) (recommending fifty specific changes in the current system of civil litigation, including such areas as discovery, voluntary dispute resolution, punitive damages, and attorney's fees).

41. Committee on Rules of Practice and Procedure of the Judicial Conference of the United States, Preliminary Draft of Proposed Amendments to the Federal Rules of Civil Procedure and Federal Rules of Evidence (Aug. 1991), *reprinted at* 112 S. Ct. 259 (1991).

42. *See, e.g.*, Carl Tobias, *Collision Course in Federal Civil Discovery*, 145 F.R.D. 139, 140 (1993) (original proposal "proved to be extremely controversial"); Randall Samborn, *U.S. Civil Procedure Revisited*, NAT'L L.J., May 4, 1992, at 1 (largely negative reaction to the proposed rules).

43. *See, e.g.*, Griffin B. Bell et al., *Automatic Disclosure in Discovery—The Rush to Reform*, 27 GA. L. REV. 1, 41-46 (1992).

44. *See, e.g.*, *id.* at 41, 46-48.

45. Randall Samborn, *U.S. Civil Procedure Revisited*, NAT'L L.J., May 4, 1992, at 1, 12 (reporting the decision to abandon the proposal); Carl Tobias, *Collision Course in Federal Civil Discovery*, 145 F.R.D. 139, 141 (1993) (by abandoning the proposal, the Advisory Committee would be able to capitalize on the experimentation taking place under the Civil Justice Reform Act); *see also* Carl Tobias, *In Defense of Experimentation with Automatic Disclosure*, 27 GA. L. REV. 665 (1993).

46. Carl Tobias, *Collision Course in Federal Civil Discovery*, 145 F.R.D. 139, 141-43 (1993). The Advisory Committee submitted its final recommendations on May 1, 1992. *Id.*

particularity in the pleadings."[47] In June 1992, the Standing Committee approved the proposed rules. In September 1992, the Judicial Conference forwarded the rules to the U.S. Supreme Court.[48] In April 1993, the Court promulgated the changes in the discovery rules as proposed and submitted them to Congress.[49] Three dissenting Justices described the amended rules as a "radical alteration" and "potentially disastrous."[50] Despite a vigorous effort in Congress to stop them, the changes took effect on December 1, 1993.[51] Because federal district courts had been experimenting with delay and cost reduction programs under the Civil Justice Reform Act, many districts chose to continue their own programs rather than to follow the new rules.[52]

Again, on September 15, 1999, the Judicial Conference recommended extensive amendments to discovery practice, effective December 1, 2000. Most of the changes were to the initial disclosures under Rule 26(a)(1). Under the 2000 amendments, individual districts were no longer permitted to opt out of the initial disclosure requirement; as a result, the courts now have uniform discovery practices. The scope of mandatory disclosures was narrowed to cover only documents that the disclosing party may use to *support* its positions (in contrast to the previous test of information relevant to "disputed facts alleged with particularity in the pleadings"). Information to be used solely for impeachment purposes was excluded from initial disclosures. Eight categories of proceedings were excluded from the initial disclosures (and a ninth was added in 2006). In addition, the 2000 amendments imposed a new dual standard for the scope of discovery by differentiating between party-controlled and court-ordered discovery.[53] In hindsight, the heated

---

47. *Id.*

48. *See id.* at 143; *see also* Ralph K. Winter, *In Defense of Discovery Reform*, 58 BROOKLYN L. REV. 263 (1992).

49. *See* Statement of Justice White, Amendments to the Federal Rules of Civil Procedure, Apr. 22, 1993, *reprinted in* 146 F.R.D. 501, 505-06 (1993).

50. *See* Dissenting Statement of Justice Scalia, joined by Justice Thomas and Justice Souter, *reprinted in* 146 F.R.D. at 507, 510-11 (1993) (pointing out the "nearly universal criticism from every conceivable sector of our judicial system, including judges, practitioners, litigants, academics, public interest groups, and national, state, and local bar and professional associations"); *see also* Memorandum to the Chief Justice of the United States and the Associate Justices of the Supreme Court: Comments on Proposed "Disclosure" Amendment to Federal Rule 26(a)(1), submitted by American Exchange Council, Association of Defense Trial Attorneys, Business Roundtable Lawyers Committee, Chamber of Commerce of the United States, Federation of Insurance and Corporate Counsel, Lawyers for Civil Justice, and Litigation Section of the District of Columbia Bar, Public Citizen Litigation Group (Feb. 10, 1993) (opposing amendments). The amended rules also contained controversial changes in Rule 11. *See* Chapter 6(F) *supra* ("Good Faith Pleading").

51. *See* Harrison Osborne, *Sweeping Changes for Federal Court Discovery*, LAW. WEEKLY, Dec. 6, 1993, at 1.

52. For example, on the day the new rules went into effect, the Judges of the Southern District of New York suspended the operation of the mandatory disclosure rule for purposes of further study. *See* David D. Siegel, *The Recent (Dec. 1, 1993) Changes in the Federal Rules of Civil Procedure: Background, the Question of Retroactivity, and a Word about Mandatory Disclosure*, 151 F.R.D. 147, 151-52 (1993) (describing the "opt out" possibilities under Rule 26(a)(1) concerning mandatory disclosure); *see also* Preliminary Draft of Proposed Amendments to the Federal Rules of Civil Procedure, 181 F.R.D. 18, 71 (1998) (describing widespread use of the opt-out provision).

53. *See* FED. R. CIV. P. 26 & advisory committee's note to the 2000 amendments. *See* Carl Tobias, *The 2000 Federal Civil Rules Revisions*, 38 SAN DIEGO L. REV. 875 (2001) (surveying the changes); Morgan Cloud, *The 2000 Amendments to the Federal Discovery Rules and the Future of Adversarial Pretrial Litigation*, 74 TEMPLE L. REV. 27 (2001) (surveying the changes and concluding that the amendments appear to be intended to move federal practice away from the traditional model of adversarial pretrial discovery conducted by largely autonomous attorneys and toward a model in which attorney autonomy is severely limited by formal rules and more active judicial management of pretrial litigation).

rhetoric and dire predictions accompanying these reforms appear to have been overstated in light of reports of actual disclosure and discovery practice.[54]

In 2006, the Federal Rules were again amended to recognize and deal with special discovery issues related to electronically stored information. Specifically, Rules 16, 26, 33, 34, 37, and 45 (and Form 52) were amended to incorporate appropriate references to "e-discovery" issues.[55] One significant (and the most controversial) change was the addition of Rule 26(b)(2)(B), which deals with electronically stored information that is "not reasonably accessible." Another was the addition of Rule 37(e), which provides a "safe harbor" for "good-faith" loss of such information.[56] In 2010, further changes were made to address issues concerning discovery regarding expert witnesses.[57]

The development of discovery in federal courts has had a substantial impact on state-court practice. Most states have adopted the periodic changes to the federal rules as well as the 1970 discovery rules in whole or large part.[58] The states have also been strongly influenced by the federal approach to "e-discovery."[59] However, the states have been much slower to embrace the mandatory disclosure discovery reforms.[60]

SECTION B. THE GENERAL SCOPE OF DISCOVERY UNDER THE FEDERAL RULES

Before the adoption of the Federal Rules, several restrictions limited the scope of discovery.[61] In sharp contrast, the 1970 reform of Federal Rule 26(b)(1) allowed the parties to discover any non-privileged matter "relevant to the subject matter involved in the pending action."[62] This standard established an exceedingly permissive scope for discovery. Clearly, under this standard, discovery was not limited to the "issues" raised by the pleadings. Federal Rule 26(b)(1) referred to the "subject matter" of the pending action, not merely the issues raised by the parties'

---

54. *See, e.g.*, Christopher C. Frost, Note, *The Sound and Fury or the Sound of Silence?: Evaluating the Pre-Amendment Predictions and Post-Amendment Effects of the Discovery Scope-Narrowing Language in the 2000 Amendments to Federal Rule of Civil Procedure 26(B)(1)*, 37 GA. L. REV. 1039, 1046 (2003) (stating, for example, "the veritable firestorm of satellite litigation and frustrated plaintiffs has thus far turned out to be a disappointing fizzle" and concluding that the discovery reforms have had "a modest effect on litigation as a whole").

55. These "e-discovery" amendments are discussed in the appropriate sections below. *See generally* Rachel K. Alexander, *E-Discovery Practice, Theory, and Precedent: Finding the Right Pond, Lure, and Lines Without Going on a Fishing Expedition*, 56 S.D. L. REV. 25 (2011); Ahunanya Anga, *Legal Research in an Electronic Age: Electronic Data Discovery, A Litigation Albatross of Gigantic Proportions*, 9 U. N.H. L. REV. 1 (2010).

56. *See* FED. R. CIV. P. 26(b)(2)(B) ("Special Limitations on Electronically Stored Information"), 37(e) ("Failure to Provide Electronically Stored Information").

57. *See* FED. R. CIV. P. 26(b)(2) & (b)(4)(B) & (C).

58. *See* Glen S. Koppel, *Reflections on the "Chimera" of a Uniform Code of State Civil Procedure: The Virtue of Vision in Procedural Reform*, 58 DEPAUL L. REV. 971 (2009) ("Until the mid- 1970s, state courts looked to the Federal Rules of Civil Procedure . . . as the gold standard" and replicated them a a nearly constant rate).

59. *See* Richard Marcus, *Confessions of a Federal "Bureaucrat": The Possibilities of Perfecting Procedural Reform*, 35 W. ST. U. L. REV. 103, 120 (2007).

60. *See* Glenn S. Koppel, *Toward a New Federalism in State Civil Justice: Developing a Uniform Code of State Civil Procedure Through a Collaborative Rule-Making Process*, 58 VAND. L. REV. 1167, 1214-45 (2005) (reviewing the growing procedural "disuniformity" and noting that only nine state jurisdictions had adopted mandatory disclosure).

61. *See* section A *supra* ("Development of Modern Discovery").

62. FED. R. CIV. P. 26(b)(1) (as amended in 1970).

claims or defenses. Nor was discovery limited to evidence that would be admissible at trial under the Federal Rules of Evidence.[63]

Illustration 9-1. Assume that *A* and *B* witnessed an auto accident that is the subject of litigation between *P* and *D*. At *A's* deposition, *P's* attorney asks *A*: "Who did *B* say was at fault in the accident?" Assume that *A* indicates that *B* said one or the other of the parties was at fault. *A's* answer would be hearsay and would likely be inadmissible at trial.[64] Nevertheless, *A's* answer is reasonably calculated to lead to the discovery of admissible evidence—the testimony of *B*.[65] Thus, this question would be within the permissible scope of discovery.

* * * * *

To protect against abuse of discovery under this broad relevance standard of Rule 26, the Rule also permitted the courts to limit discovery through *protective orders* (designed to prevent "annoyance, embarrassment, oppression, and undue burden or expense.")[66]

Under the 2000 amendments to the Federal Rules, the scope of discovery was reduced. The parties may now obtain discovery without the necessity of a court order "regarding any matter, not privileged, that is relevant to the *claim or defense of any party*."[67] The former standard of "*relevant to the subject matter* involved in the pending action" is still retained as the overall standard for the scope of discovery; however, under amended Rule 26(b)(1), such matters are now only discoverable by court order and only upon a showing of "good cause."[68]

Although amended Rule 26(b)(1) is clearly intended to tighten the scope of party-controlled discovery, the new standard ("relevant to the claim or defense of any party") is still very broad, and it should be sufficient to cover the typical discovery requests of the parties in the vast majority of cases. The rule continues to allow discovery of relevant information, even if it would "not be admissible at the trial, if the discovery appears reasonably calculated to lead to the discovery of admissible evidence."[69] The burden of making this showing is on the party seeking discovery. It can be met by articulating a plausible chain of inferences showing how discovery would lead to admissible evidence.[70]

---

63. *Id.* The 1970 version of Rule 26(b)(1) specifically stated that the information sought "need not be admissible at trial if the information sought appears reasonably calculated to lead to the discovery of admissible evidence." *Id.*

64. *See* Chapter 11(I)(3) *infra* ("Hearsay").

65. FED. R. CIV. P. 26(b)(1) (as amended in 1970).

66. *See* FED. R. CIV. P. 26(c) (restyled as Rule 26(c)(1)). Other provisions also limit discovery of certain materials prepared by or for a party or that party's representative in anticipation of litigation or for trial. *See* subsection 2 *infra* ("Attorney 'Work Product' and Trial-Preparation Materials").

67. FED. R. CIV. P. 26(b)(1) (emphasis added).

68. *Id.*

69. *See Illustration 9-1 supra.*

70. *Cf.* Oppenheimer Fund, Inc. v. Sanders, 437 U.S. 340, 98 S. Ct. 2380, 57 L. Ed. 2d 253 (1978) (the plaintiffs' request to require the defendants to compile a list of the names and addresses of the class members was not "relevant to the subject matter involved in the pending action" because the plaintiffs were not seeking information that bears on, or that reasonably could lead to other matters that could bear on, any issue that was or might be in the case); Food Lion, Inc. v. United Food & Commercial Workers Int'l Union, 103 F.3d 1007 (D.C. Cir. 1997) (in an abuse-of-process action, Food Lion sought discovery of documents from a nonparty that had served as a public relations firm to the defendant union; the documents sought related to "corporate campaigns" by other union clients of the public relations firm; discovery was denied on the ground that it was not reasonably likely to lead to the discovery of admissible evidence); Vardon Golf Co. v. BBMG Golf Ltd., 156 F.R.D. 641 (N.D. Ill. 1994) (burden not satisfied by plaintiff seeking information relating to defendant's settlement negotiations with

Interestingly, the Advisory Committee's Note to amended Rule 26(b)(1) failed to offer clear guidance as to the distinction between matters relevant to a "claim or defense" and those relevant only to the "subject matter" of the action.[71] The Advisory Committee Note did indicate, however, that certain matters "not directly pertinent to the incident in suit" could be, nevertheless, relevant to a claim or defense in a particular case. The Note explains that

> other incidents of the same type, or involving the same product, could be properly discoverable under the revised standard. Information about organizational arrangements or filing systems of a party could be discoverable if likely to yield or lead to the discovery of admissible information. Similarly, information that could be used to impeach a witness, although not otherwise relevant to the claims or defenses, might be properly discoverable.[72]

For those discovery requests falling outside the scope of the "claim or defense" standard, the Advisory Committee Note did not give specific guidance for assessing "good cause" sufficient to justify broader court-ordered discovery. The Advisory Committee Note simply indicated that "[t]he court may permit broader discovery in a particular case depending on the circumstances of the case, the nature of the claims and defenses, and the scope of the discovery requested."[73]

1. Privilege

Federal Rule 26(b)(1) provides for discovery of "nonprivileged matter[s]."[74] The usual view is that privilege rules apply to discovery in the same way they apply at trial.[75] The law of evidence determines whether a matter is privileged.[76] Except for privileges based on federal constitutional grounds, the extent to which particular jurisdictions recognize specific privileges varies. The holder of a privilege may waive the holder's objection to disclosure of the privileged matter. During discovery, such waiver may occur in several ways.[77]

---

third-party defendant; that information was inadmissible under Federal Rule of Evidence 408, which makes evidence relating to settlement negotiations inadmissible to prove the validity of a claim or its amount).

71. The Advisory Committee's Note concedes that the terms "cannot be defined with precision" and must be evaluated in each individual case "according to the reasonable needs of the action." FED. R. CIV. P. 26(b)(1) advisory committee's note to the 2000 amendment.

72. *Id.*; *see also* Anderson v. Hale, No. 00 C 2021, 2001 WL 641113, 2001 U.S. Dist. LEXIS 7538 (N.D. Ill. June 1, 2001) (allowing discovery of other incidents of the same type under amended Rule 26(b)(1)).

73. FED. R. CIV. P. 26(b)(1) advisory committee's note to the 2000 amendment.

74. FED. R. CIV. P. 26(b)(1).

75. 8 CHARLES A. WRIGHT ET AL., FEDERAL PRACTICE AND PROCEDURE: CIVIL § 2016, at 310-11 (3d ed. 2010).

76. Courts have recognized several privileges: doctor-patient, attorney-client, priest-penitent, journalist-confidential news source, psychotherapist-patient, government-informer, military or state secrets privilege, husband-wife, executive privilege, and a privilege against self-incrimination. Some of these privileges are based on constitutional grounds (*e.g.*, self-incrimination), some on statutory grounds (*e.g.*, journalist-confidential news source), and others on the common law (*e.g.*, attorney-client). *See* Chapter 11(I)(4) *infra* ("Privilege").

77. *See* Richard L. Marcus, *The Perils of Privilege: Waiver and the Litigator*, 84 MICH. L. REV. 1605 (1986); John T. Hundley, Annotation, *Waiver of Evidentiary Privilege by Inadvertent Disclosure—Federal Law*, 159 A.L.R. FED. 153 (2000).

Illustration 9-2. A party may have to produce otherwise "confidential" ("privileged") records if the party has answered interrogatories about matters contained in the records.[78] Similarly, if a party voluntarily answers (or permits another to answer) questions during a deposition about part of a privileged communication, that party waives the privilege for the entire communication.[79] Thus, a disclosure can result in a finding of "subject-matter waiver," which means that a producing party might have to make a further production of all privileged communications "on the same subject" as the previously disclosed documents.[80]

* * * * *

In order to preserve a claim of privilege, prudent parties have to conduct a pre-production privilege review. The burdens of such a review can result in very large costs, especially with electronically stored information. Electronic discovery may involve millions of documents, and the amount of information stored electronically continues to grow exponentially.[81] Obviously, a "record-by-record pre-production privilege review, on pain of subject matter waiver, would impose upon the parties costs of production that bear no proportionality to what is at stake in the litigation."[82] Keyword searches can be employed to narrow the universe of data, but tedious human review is still required.[83]

Parties also have attempted to minimize costs and delays by agreeing to "protocols" to minimize the risk of waiver. One approach has been to allow a "quick peek," in which the parties agree that requested materials will be provided for initial examination without waiving any privilege of protection. The requesting party then designates only the documents it wants produced through a Rule 34 request for production. That way, the responding party has to screen only those documents actually requested for formal production.[84] Another approach has been "claw back" agreements. Under those agreements, mistakes in production can be rectified if the producing party subsequently identifies the inadvertently produced documents. Such agreements usually provide for return of the documents under these circumstances. A party who has signed an agreement forgoes any argument that the disclosure by the other side has been a waiver.[85] Of course, one obvious limitation on "quick peek," "claw back," and other agreements is that they are voluntary.[86]

---

78. *See, e.g.*, Munzer v. Swedish Am. Line, 35 F. Supp. 493, 497 (S.D.N.Y. 1940) (hospital records).

79. *See, e.g.*, Daniels v. Hadley Mem. Hosp., 68 F.R.D. 583, 586-87 (D.D.C. 1975).

80. *See, e.g.*, *In re* Sealed Case, 877 F.2d 976 (D.C. Cir. 1989) (holding that inadvertent disclosure of documents during discovery resulted in an automatic "subject matter" waiver).

81. *See* George L. Paul & Jason R. Baron, *Information Inflation: Can the Legal System Adapt?* 13 RICH. J.L. & TECH. 10, ¶ 12 (2007) (pointing out, for example, that approximately 100 billion e-mails are sent daily and 30 billion e-mails are created or received by federal governmental agencies annually).

82. Hopson v. Mayor of Baltimore, 232 F.R.D. 228, 244 (D. Md. 2005).

83. Anonymous, *Down in the Data Mines: A Tale of Woe from the Basement of Legal Practice*, 94 ABA J., Dec. 2008, at 32.

84. *See* FED. R. CIV. P. 26(b)(5) advisory committee's note to the 2006 amendment.

85. *See id.*; *cf.* Prescient Partners, L.P. v. Fieldcrest Cannon, Inc., No. 96CIV.7590 (DAB)(JCF), 1997 WL 736726, 1997 U.S. Dist. LEXIS 18818 (S.D.N.Y. Nov. 26, 1997) (issuing a protective order enforcing a confidentiality agreement and finding no waiver from an inadvertent disclosure).

86. SHIRA A. SCHEINDLIN ET AL., ELECTRONIC DISCOVERY AND DIGITAL EVIDENCE: CASES AND MATERIALS 698 (2d ed. 2012). The authors aptly point out that "[w]here the discoverable electronic data on both sides is relatively equal, then all parties have an incentive to enter such an agreement. But where one side has most of the data—*e.g.*, an employment discrimination case brought by a fired employee, where all the e-mails are on the employer's server—then the party with few (if any) documents may not be inclined to limit the costs of the adversary's pre-production privilege review." *Id.* Nevertheless, there may still be some incentive to agree because

Two further developments help alleviate the risks and costs associated with e-discovery. First, as part of the 2006 "e-discovery" amendments to the Federal Rules, Rule 26(b)(5)(B) now permits privileged materials to be disclosed and then "recalled" or "clawed back" once the disclosing party realizes a claim for protection exists without the parties reaching a "claw back" agreement.[87] After receiving notice of a recall, a receiving party "must promptly return, sequester, or destroy the specified information and any copies it has."[88] In addition, that party "must not use or disclose the information until the claim is resolved," including "tak[ing] reasonable steps to retrieve the information if the party disclosed it before being notified."[89]

If the receiving party disagrees with the claim of privilege, that party can present the information to the court under seal for a determination of the claim of privilege. In the meantime, the producing party must preserve the information during the court's review of the assertion of privilege.[90] This change may be especially useful in keeping electronically stored information "moving along quickly since large amounts of data can be produced nearly instantaneously while still allowing time to review the data for protected information.[91] Rule 26(b)(5)(B) itself, however, does not address whether the privilege is preserved for information that was disclosed and then recalled.[92]

Second, Rule 502 of the Federal Rules of Evidence provides additional protections with regard to waiver.[93] If an "inadvertent" disclosure is made during the course of "a federal proceeding" or "to a federal office or agency," such disclosure does not operate as a waiver if "the holder of the privilege . . . took reasonable steps to prevent disclosure" and employed "reasonable steps to rectify the error, including (if applicable) following [Rule] 26(b)(5)(B)."[94] Rule 502(a) provides that if a waiver is found, that waiver applies only to the information

---

the party with little to produce may have "an interest in *expedited* discovery." Thus, "if there is no non-waiver agreement in effect, then the court is very likely to allow the party with custody of the data greater time to conduct a full pre-production privilege review." *Id.*

87. *See* FED. R. CIV. P. 26(b)(5)(B). The notification should be in writing and should be sufficiently detailed to allow the receiving parties to evaluate the claim of privilege. However, it is recognized that under some circumstances, a written notification will not be feasible, such as during a deposition. *See id.* advisory committee's note to the 2006 amendment. *See generally* Julie Cohen, Note, *Look Before You Leap: A Guide to the Law of Inadvertent Disclosure of Privileged Information in the Era of E-Discovery,* 93 IOWA L. REV. 627 (2008); Michael J. DiLernia, Note, *Federal Rule of Civil Procedure 26(b)(5)(B) and the Ethics of Inadvertent Disclosure,* 20 GEO J. LEGAL ETHICS 533 (2007); Kindall C. James, Comment, *Electronic Discovery: Substantially Increasing the Risk of Inadvertent Disclosure and the Costs of Privilege Review—Do the Proposed Amendments to the Federal Rules of Civil Procedure Help?,* 52 LOY. L. REV. 839 (2006).

88. FED. R. CIV. P. 26(b)(5)(B).

89. *Id.*

90. *Id.*

91. Andrew T. Schlosser, *How to Implement E-Discovery*, NEB. LAW., Mar. 2007, at 20, 22.

92. *See* FED. R. CIV. P. 26(b)(5)(B) advisory committee's note to the 2006 amendment.

93. Rule 502 was approved by the Judicial Conference and then enacted by both Houses of Congress. It took effect on September 19, 2008 when it was signed by the President. *See* Act of Sept. 19, 2008, Pub. L. No. 110-322, 122 Stat. 3537. *See generally* Julie Cohen, Note, *Look Before You Leap: A Guide to the Law of Inadvertent Disclosure of Privileged Information in the Era of E-Discovery*, 93 IOWA L. REV. 627 (2008) (discussing, *inter alia*, Rule 502 of the Federal Rules of Evidence as proposed).

94. FED. R. EVID. 502(b). The approach represents the "middle ground" among the conflicting approaches taken by the courts. On one end of the spectrum, some courts have held that the disclosure had to be intentional to be a waiver. On the other end, a few courts have held that any inadvertent disclosure constituted a waiver without regard to the efforts made to prevent such a disclosure. *See id.* advisory committee's note (part of the legislative history of Rule 502).

actually disclosed. It does not trigger a waiver of privilege for all otherwise protected communications and information involving the same "subject matter"—unless the information was selectively and unfairly disclosed to gain a tactical advantage.[95] Note, however, that Rule 502 applies only to attorney-client privilege and work product. It does not apply to other evidentiary privileges, such as doctor-patient or husband-wife privilege or other client "secrets."[96]

In order to make this rule effective, Rule 502(a) binds subsequent state court determinations on the scope of the waiver for inadvertent disclosures made at the federal level.[97] Furthermore, Rule 502(d) provides that if a federal court enters an order determining that a disclosure does not constitute a waiver, that order is enforceable against all persons and entities in any other federal or state proceeding.[98] For reasons similar to those supporting the tolling provisions of § 1367(d), these provisions in Rule 502(a) and (d) should be held to be constitutional exercises of congressional authority under Article III and the Necessary and Proper Clause.[99] With regard to disclosures initially made in a state proceeding, Rule 502(c) provides that admissibility of those disclosures in a subsequent federal proceeding will be determined by the law that is most protective against waiver.[100]

As noted above, parties have voluntarily entered into agreements to control the risks of waiver when privileged electronic data was disclosed during discovery. Such voluntary agreements on the effect of disclosure, however, generally only bind the parties to the agreement.[101] Thus, the parties to those agreements should be well motivated to have the agreements incorporated into a court order to bind non-parties to a finding of no waiver pursuant to Rule 502(d).[102]

If a party does decide to withhold "privileged" materials in response to a discovery request or from a required disclosure under Rule 26, the 1993 amendments require that party to notify other parties.[103] According to the Advisory Committee, "withhold[ing] materials without such notice is contrary to the rule, subjects the party to sanctions . . . and may be viewed as a waiver of the privilege or protection."[104] In addition to making the claim of privilege "expressly," the

---

95. *Id.* 502(a) & advisory committee's note (specifically rejecting the result in cases like *In re* Sealed Case, 877 F.2d 976 (D.C. Cir. 1989), which held that inadvertent disclosure constituted an authomatic subject-matter waiver).

96. *Id.* 502(g).

97. *Id.* 502(a) advisory committee's note ("to assure protection and predictability").

98. *Id.* 502(d) & advisory committee's note (noting that "the utility of a confidentiality order in reducing discovery costs [would be] substantially diminished if it provide[d] no protection outside the particular litigation in which the order [was] entered" and that "[p]arties are unlikely to be able to reduce the costs or pre-production review for privilege and work product if the consequence of disclosure is that the communications or information could be used by non-parties to the litigation").

99. *See* Chapter 2(D)(8) *supra* ("Tolling of Limitations for Dismissed Claims: Section 1367(d)").

100. FED. R. EVID. 502(c). The Advisory Committee explained that "[i]f . . . state law is more protective (such as [when it provides] that an inadvertent disclosure can never be a waiver), the holder of the privilege or protection may well have relied on that law when making the disclosure in the state proceeding [and] applying a more restrictive federal law of waiver could impair . . . state objective[s]." *Id.* advisory committee's note. However, "if . . . federal law is more protective, applying the state law of waiver to determine admissibility in federal court is likely to undermine the federal objective of limiting the costs of production." *Id.*

101. *Id.* 502(e).

102. *See id.* & advisory committee's note ("The rule makes clear that if parties want protection against non-parties from a finding of waiver by disclosure, the agreement must be made part of a court order.").

103. FED. R. CIV. P. 26(b)(5). Required disclosures under Rule 26 are discussed in section C *infra* ("Required Disclosures Under the Federal Rules").

104. FED. R. CIV. P. 26(b)(5) advisory committee's note to the 1993 amendment.

withholding party must "describe the nature of the documents, communications, or tangible things not produced or disclosed—and [do] so in a manner that, without revealing [the privileged] information itself. . . . will enable other parties to assess the claim."[105] In this way, the Advisory Committee envisioned that the need for an in camera judicial examination of the materials will be reduced.[106] In addition, before a party moves for an order compelling discovery, the 1993 amendments require that party to attempt in good faith to confer and resolve the matter without judicial intervention.[107]

2. Attorney "Work Product" and Trial-Preparation Materials

The broad scope of discovery authorized by the Federal Rules of Civil Procedure creates a special problem. To what extent may a party discover materials obtained or prepared in anticipation of litigation or in preparation for trial? On one hand, federal discovery clears the way, "consistent with recognized privileges, for the parties to obtain the fullest possible knowledge of the issues and the facts before trial."[108] On the other hand, such broad discovery may be disruptive of the adversary process. For example, litigants may decide to "sit back" and let their opponents investigate, analyze, and prepare the case. They then can attempt to take a "free ride" on their adversaries' efforts by obtaining through discovery the materials their adversaries gathered or prepared.[109]

In light of the conflicting decisions on the subject, the Advisory Committee in 1946 proposed an amendment to the Federal Rules of Civil Procedure to protect materials prepared in anticipation of litigation or trial.[110] The Advisory Committee submitted this proposed amendment to the U.S. Supreme Court after the Court had granted certiorari in a case involving the same subject. The Court did not adopt the proposed amendment, but instead attempted to resolve the matter by decision of the pending case, *Hickman v. Taylor*.[111]

---

105. FED. R. CIV. P. 26(b)(5)(A).

106. FED. R. CIV. P. 26(b)(5) advisory committee's note to the 1993 amendment.

107. *See* FED. R. CIV. P. 37(a)(1) (1993 amendment).

108. Hickman v. Taylor, 329 U.S. 495, 501, 67 S. Ct. 385, 389, 91 L. Ed. 451, 457 (1947) (footnote omitted).

109. *See* 8 CHARLES A. WRIGHT ET AL., FEDERAL PRACTICE AND PROCEDURE: CIVIL § 2021, at 473-74 (3d ed. 2010) (summarizing the disagreement among the courts concerning the permissible scope of discovery under these circumstances).

110. The Advisory Committee proposed that

> [t]he court shall not order the production or inspection of any writing obtained or prepared by the adverse party, his attorney, surety, indemnitor, or agent in anticipation of litigation or in preparation for trial unless satisfied that denial of production or inspection will unfairly prejudice the party seeking the production or inspection in preparing his claim or defense or will cause him undue hardship or injustice. The court shall not order the production or inspection of any part of the writing that reflects an attorney's mental impressions, conclusions, opinions, or legal theories, or, except as provided in Rule 35 [relating to court-ordered physical and mental examinations], the conclusions of an expert.

5 F.R.D. 433, 456-57 (1946).

111. 329 U.S. 495, 67 S. Ct. 385, 91 L. Ed. 451 (1947); *see* 8 CHARLES A. WRIGHT ET AL., FEDERAL PRACTICE AND PROCEDURE: CIVIL § 2021, at 478 (3d ed. 2010).

The principal issue in the *Hickman* case was whether the contents of witnesses' statements made to a party investigating an accident were discoverable under the Federal Rules. On February 7, 1943, the tug "John M. Taylor" sank while towing a car float. Five of the nine crewmen drowned, including the plaintiff's husband. Three days later, the owners of the tug retained Mr. Fortenbaugh, whose firm regularly had represented the owners for several years. The owners and their insurance carriers requested Mr. Fortenbaugh to defend on their behalf whatever litigation arose from the sinking of the tug. Pursuant to these general instructions, Mr. Fortenbaugh privately interviewed the four surviving members of the crew and took their written statements. These statements apparently were made shortly after a United States Steamboat Inspector's public hearing held on March 4th, at which the survivors had appeared and testified. The statements were signed on March 29th. Subsequently, Mr. Fortenbaugh interviewed other persons believed to have knowledge about the accident. In some instances, Mr. Fortenbaugh prepared memoranda reflecting what the witnesses told him.[112]

Approximately eight months after the witnesses' statements had been obtained, the wife of one of the deceased crewmen commenced an action under the Jones Act[113] against the owners of the tug and the owner of the car float to recover for her husband's death. One year later, the plaintiff served thirty-nine interrogatories. One of those interrogatories requested copies of any written statements made by crew members taken in conjunction with the accident. Also requested were any oral statements, which had to be "set forth in detail," including "the exact provisions of any such oral statements."[114] The defendants objected to this and other interrogatories. The defendants argued that the interrogatories called for privileged matter obtained in preparation for litigation and constituted an attempt to indirectly obtain counsel's private files.[115] The district court overruled the defendants' objection.[116] The owners of the tug and their attorney refused to comply with the district court's order. The district court then held them in contempt and ordered them imprisoned until they complied.[117] The Third Circuit Court of Appeals reversed. The U.S. Supreme Court affirmed the Third Circuit.[118]

Although the information was not privileged,[119] the Supreme Court recognized a "qualified" immunity from discovery.[120] *Written* statements "obtained or prepared by an adversary's counsel with an eye toward litigation" could be discovered when "relevant and non-privileged facts remain hidden in an attorney's file and [when] production of those facts is essential to the preparation of one's case."[121] In contrast, with respect to *oral* statements made by witnesses to the

---

112. Hickman v. Taylor, 4 F.R.D. 479, 480-81 (E.D. Pa. 1945).

113. 46 U.S.C. § 688.

114. Supplemental interrogatories requested copies of any other oral or written statements that had been obtained relating to the accident. *See Hickman*, 4 F.R.D. at 480.

115. *Hickman*, 329 U.S. at 498-99, 67 S. Ct. at 387-88, 91 L. Ed. at 455-56.

116. *Hickman*, 4 F.R.D. at 481-83.

117. *Hickman*, 329 U.S. at 500, 67 S. Ct. at 388, 91 L. Ed. at 456.

118. *Id.* at 500, 514, 67 S. Ct. at 388, 395, 91 L. Ed. at 456, 464.

119. The Supreme Court rejected the Third Circuit's view that the attorney-client privilege applied. *See id.* at 508, 67 S. Ct. at 392, 91 L. Ed. at 461.

120. *See id.* at 510-11, 67 S. Ct. at 393, 91 L. Ed. at 462.

121. *Id.* at 511, 67 S. Ct. at 394, 91 L. Ed. at 462-63.

investigating attorney (whether presently in the form of the attorney's mental impressions or memoranda), the Court held that no showing of necessity could be made to justify their production under the circumstances of the *Hickman* case. The Court reasoned that requiring lawyers to write out or repeat what witnesses have told them and to deliver those accounts to their adversaries would give rise to grave dangers of inaccuracy and untrustworthiness.[122]

The lower federal courts disagreed about how to apply the *Hickman* case.[123] A significant part of the 1970 revision of the Federal discovery rules was the addition of Rule 26(b)(3), which was designed to clarify discovery practice concerning work product. Rule 26(b)(3) applies to otherwise discoverable documents and other tangible things created for or by a party or that party's representative in anticipation of litigation or in preparation for trial. Such materials may be discovered only upon showing that (1) the party seeking them has a substantial need for the materials in order to prepare its case and (2) substantially equivalent information cannot be obtained from other sources without undue hardship.[124] It also provides that "[i]f the court orders discovery of those materials, it must protect against disclosure of the mental impressions, conclusions, opinions, or legal theories of a party's attorney or other representative concerning litigation."[125]

Rule 26(b)(3) also contains special provisions concerning the production of a party's or witness's own statement. Under the rule, any party or other person may obtain as a matter of right ("without [making] the required showing") a statement concerning the action or its subject matter that a party had previously

---

122. *Id.* at 512-13, 67 S. Ct. at 394, 91 L. Ed. at 463. The Court further noted that such testimony could not qualify as evidence, and using it for impeachment or corroborative purposes would harm the standards of the legal profession. The Court concluded that the denial of discovery would not hinder the plaintiff in the preparation of the plaintiff's case:

> Searching interrogatories directed to Fortenbaugh and the tug owners, production of written documents and statements upon a proper showing and direct interviews with the witnesses themselves all serve to reveal the facts in Fortenbaugh's possession to the fullest possible extent consistent with public policy. Petitioner's counsel frankly admits that he wants the oral statements only to help prepare himself to examine witnesses and to make sure that he has overlooked nothing. That is insufficient under the circumstances to permit him an exception to the policy underlying the privacy of Fortenbaugh's professional activities. If there should be a rare situation justifying production of these matters, petitioner's case is not of that type.

Id. at 513, 67 S. Ct. at 394-95, 91 L. Ed. at 463-64.

123. *See* Jeffrey F. Ghent, Annotation, *Development, Since* Hickman v. Taylor, *of Attorney's "Work Product" Doctrine*, 35 A.L.R.3D 412 (1971). Many of the Court's statements were dicta and the Court's policy of allowing discovery only on a substantial showing of necessity stimulated litigation about the scope and propriety of discovery in particular cases. Many states, otherwise adopting the scheme of federal discovery, adopted specific rules to resolve problems left open by *Hickman*. Often, such provisions were modeled on the 1946 amendment proposed by the Advisory Committee, but not promulgated by the Supreme Court. *See* 8 CHARLES A. WRIGHT ET AL., FEDERAL PRACTICE AND PROCEDURE: CIVIL § 2022, at 485-86 (3d ed. 2010).

124. Fed. R. Civ. P. 26(b)(3)(A).

125. FED. R. CIV. P. 26(b)(3)(B); *see also* Kevin M. Clermont, *Surveying Work Product*, 68 CORNELL L. REV. 755 (1983); Roger W. Kirst, *A Third Option: Regulating Discovery of Transaction Work Product Without Distorting the Attorney-Client Privilege*, 31 SETON HALL L. REV. 229 (2000); Warren H. Smith, Comment, *The Potential for Discovery of Opinion Work Product Under Rule 26(b)(3)*, 64 IOWA L. REV. 103 (1978); Note, *Protection of Opinion Work Product Under the Federal Rules of Civil Procedure*, 64 VA. L. REV. 333 (1978); John F. Wagner, Jr., Annotation, *Protection From Discovery of Attorney's Opinion Work Product Under Rule 26(b)(3), Federal Rules of Civil Procedure*, 84 A.L.R. FED. 779 (1987); Teresia B. Jovanovic, Annotation, *Fraud Exception to Work Product Privilege in Federal Courts*, 64 A.L.R. FED. 470 (1983); Russell J. Davis, Annotation, *Attorney's Work Product Privilege, Under Rule 26(b)(3) of Federal Rules of Civil Procedure, As Applicable to Documents Prepared in Anticipation of Terminated Litigation*, 41 A.L.R. FED. 123 (1979).

made. The rule defines a "previous statement" as one "signed or otherwise adopted or approved."[126] It may be a written statement or in the form of a stenographic, mechanical, electrical, or other recording, or a transcription of it, which recites substantially verbatim the person's oral statement.[127]

Rule 26(b)(4)(C), adopted in 2010, specifically protects attorney communications with any expert who is required to prepare a report,[128] regardless of the form of communications.[129] This blanket protection is subject to three exceptions. First, communications regarding the expert's compensation for study or testimony are not protected.[130] Second, communications that "identify facts or data that the party's attorney provided and that the expert considered in forming the opinions to be expressed" are not protected.[131] However, this exception applies only to the identification of facts, not to "communications about the potential relevance of the facts or data."[132] Third, communications that "identifying the assumptions that the party's attorney provided and that the expert relied on in forming the opinions to be expressed" are not protected.[133] This exception is limited to assumptions that counsel provides the expert, such as having the expert assume the truth of certain testimony (and only to the extent the expert actually relies on those assumptions). More general discussions between counsel and the expert concerning hypothetical possibilities are still protected.[134]

Rule 26(b)(5), discussed in the preceding section concerning claims of privilege, also applies to trial-preparation materials. After the 1993 amendments, the parties must notify other parties if they withhold trial-preparation material in response to a discovery request or from a required disclosure under Rule 26.[135] In addition, they must provide a sufficient description and explanation to enable other parties to assess whether the protection applies.[136] Furthermore, before a party moves for an order compelling discovery, the 1993 amendments require the party to attempt in good faith to confer and resolve the matter without court intervention.[137] Finally, Rule 26(b)(5)(B) now permits trial-preparation materials to be disclosed and then "recalled" or "clawed back" once the disclosing party realizes a claim for protection exists, and Federal Rule of Evidence 502 dealing with inadvertent disclosure also applies to trial-preparation materials.[138]

---

126. FED. R. CIV. P. 26(b)(3)(C).

127. *Id.*

128. As discussed in the next section, experts are required under Rule 26(a)(2)(B) to prepare a written report as part of the required disclosure process. *See* section C *infra* ("Required Disclosures Under the Federal Rules").

129. *See* FED. R. CIV. P. 26(b)(4)(C). Rule 26(b)(4)(B) also specifically protects drafts of any report or disclosure of an expert, whether or not they are required to prepare a report, regardless of the form in which the draft is recorded. It likewise protects any draft of a supplementation under Rule 26(e). *See* FED. R. CIV. P. 26(b)(4)(B) & advisory committee's note to the 2010 amendment.

130. FED. R. CIV. P. 26(b)(4)(C)(i).

131. FED. R. CIV. P. 26(b)(4)(C)(ii).

132. FED. R. CIV. P. 26(b)(4) advisory committee's note to the 2010 amendment.

133. FED. R. CIV. P. 26(b)(4)(C)(iii).

134. FED. R. CIV. P. 26(b)(4) advisory committee's note to the 2010 amendment.

135. FED. R. CIV. P. 26(b)(5)(A). Required disclosures under Rule 26 are discussed in section C *infra* ("Required Disclosures Under the Federal Rules").

136. *Id.*

137. *See* FED. R. CIV. P. 37(a)(1).

138. See the discussion of Rule 26(b)(5)(B) and Rule 502 in the preceding section *supra*.

SECTION C. REQUIRED DISCLOSURES UNDER THE FEDERAL RULES

The 1993 amendments to Federal Rule 26 imposed a duty of disclosure on the parties.[139] The disclosures take place in three phases: (1) early in the case, the parties must exchange basic information about potential witnesses, documentary evidence, damages, and insurance; (2) at an appropriate time during the discovery period, the parties must exchange information about expert witnesses and the details of their possible testimony; and (3) as the trial date approaches, the parties must identify the evidence they may offer at trial.[140]

1. Early Disclosures Concerning Potential Witnesses, Documentary Evidence, Damages, and Insurance

Rule 26(a)(1) requires all parties, without waiting for a discovery request, to provide information to other parties about (1) damages, (2) insurance, and (3) potential witnesses and documentary evidence. Unless the court directs or the parties stipulate otherwise,[141] or the action falls within one of the currently nine categories of exempt cases,[142] these disclosures are to take place at or within 14 days after the parties confer to prepare a discovery plan, which is required by Rule 26(f).[143] However, a party may object during the conference that initial disclosures are not appropriate in the circumstances of the action and state that objection in the Rule 26(f) discovery plan.[144] Thus, under the typical sequence envisioned by Rule 26(a) for early discovery events, (1) the court will schedule an initial scheduling conference; (2) the parties will then confer at least 21 days before the court's initial scheduling conference; (3) the parties then will make their mandatory disclosures;

---

139. *See* FED. R. CIV. P. 26(a) ("Required Disclosures"). *See generally* Leslie M. Kelleher, *The December 1993 Amendments to the Federal Rules of Civil Procedure—A Critical Analysis*, 12 TOURO L. REV. 7 (1995); Rogelio A. Lasso, *Gladiators Be Gone: The New Disclosure Rules Compel a Reexamination of the Adversary Process*, 36 B.C. L. REV. 479 (1995); Robert Matthew Lovein, *A Practitioner's Guide: Federal Rule of Civil Procedure 26(a)—Automatic Disclosure*, 47 SYRACUSE L. REV. 225 (1996); Linda S. Mullenix, *Adversarial Justice, Professional Responsibility, and the New Federal Discovery Rules*, 14 REV. LITIG. 13 (1994); Charles W. Sorenson, Jr., *Disclosure Under Federal Rule of Civil Procedure 26(a)—"Much Ado About Nothing,"* 46 HASTINGS L.J. 679 (1995); Lisa J. Trembly, *Mandatory Disclosure: A Historical Review of the Adoption of Rule 26 and an Examination of the Events that Have Transpired Since its Adoption*, 21 SETON H. LEGIS. J. 425 (1997).

140. *See* FED. R. CIV. P. 26(a) advisory committee's note to the 1993 amendment.

141. *See* FED. R. CIV. P. 26(a)(1)(A) (the parties may be prevented from so stipulating by court order).

142. Rule 26(a)(1)(B) exempts nine categories of cases from this disclosure requirement: (1) actions for review on an administrative record; (2) forfeiture actions in rem arising from federal statues; (3) habeas corpus petitions or similar challenges to criminal convictions or sentences; (4) pro se prisoner actions; (5) actions to enforce or quash an administrative summons or subpoena; (6) actions by the United States to recover benefit payments; (7) actions by the United States to collect on student loans guaranteed by the United States; (8) proceedings ancillary to proceedings in other courts; and (9) actions to enforce arbitration awards. *See* FED. R. CIV. P. 26(a)(1)(B).

143. FED. R. CIV. P. 26(a)(1)(C); *see* section D(1) *infra* ("The Parties' Discovery Planning Conference"); *see also* section N *infra* ("Pretrial Conferences and Orders").

144. *See* FED. R. CIV. P. 26(a)(1)(C). Disclosures are not required thereafter except as ordered by the court. *See* FED. R. CIV. P. 26(a)(1) advisory committee's note to the 2000 amendment. In ruling on the objection, the rule directs the court to determine what disclosures, if any, are to be made as well as to set the time for any such disclosures. *See* FED. R. CIV. P. 26(a)(1)(C).

and (4) the parties will then meet with the judge for the scheduling conference at which the timetable for the balance of the discovery will be established.[145]

Before these initial disclosures, Rule 26(g)(1) requires the parties to conduct a reasonable inquiry into the facts of the case.[146] The Advisory Committee's Notes to the 1993 Amendments indicate that this rule does not require "an exhaustive investigation."[147] According to the Advisory Committee, "reasonableness" depends on various factors, such as "the number and complexity of the issues; the location, nature, number, and availability of potentially relevant witnesses and documents; the extent of past working relationships between the attorney and the client, particularly in handling related or similar litigation; and . . . how long the party has to conduct an investigation, either before or after filing the case."[148]

Parties must make these initial disclosures even though (1) their investigation is incomplete or (2) another party has failed to make its disclosures or has made an inadequate disclosure.[149]

(a) Damages

Rule 26(a)(1)(A)(iii) requires parties to disclose how they calculated "each category of damages."[150] Although the rule technically refers only to "damages," courts should construe the rule to apply to restitutionary claims involving money.[151] In addition, Rule 26(a)(1)(A)(iii) functions as the equivalent of a standing request for production for documents.[152] The disclosing party must make available for inspection and copying "the documents or other evidentiary material, unless privileged or protected from disclosure, on which each computation is based, including materials bearing on the nature and extent of injuries suffered."[153] The Advisory Committee points out that parties must produce only documents that are "then reasonably available" to them. Furthermore, parties are not expected to provide calculations of damages dependent on information in the possession of other parties.[154]

Illustration 9-3. Assume that *P* sues *D* in federal court. *P's* complaint is similar to Federal Form 11. *P* alleges that on a certain date in a certain location, *D* "negligently drove a motor vehicle against plaintiff." *P* also alleges that "as a result,

---

145. Parties joined or first served after the required Rule 26(f) discovery conference must make the initial disclosures within 30 days after being joined or served, unless a different time is set by stipulation or court order. FED. R. CIV. P. 26(a)(1)(D).

146. *See* FED. R. CIV. P. 26(g)(1) (specifically requiring that disclosures must be signed and that the signature constitutes a certification "that to the best of the [signer's] knowledge, information, and belief, formed *after a reasonable inquiry,* [*the disclosure*] *is complete and correct as of the time it is made*") (emphasis added).

147. *See* FED. R. CIV. P. 26(a)(1) advisory committee's note to the 1993 amendment.

148. *Id.*

149. *See* FED. R. CIV. P. 26(a)(1)(E) & advisory committee's note to the 1993 amendment.

150. FED. R. CIV. P. 26(a)(1)(A)(iii).

151. Support for this conclusion is provided in the Advisory Committee's Note, which indicates that this provision applies to "a party claiming damages *or other monetary relief.*" FED. R. CIV. P. 26(a)(1) advisory committee's note to the 1993 amendment. The term "other monetary relief" could also extend to disclosure of other items, such as attorney's fees and costs.

152. FED. R. CIV. P. 26(a)(1) advisory committee's note to the 1993 amendment.

153. FED. R. CIV. P. 26(a)(1)(A)(iii). The inspection and copying would be carried out "as under Rule 34." *Id.*; *see* section H *infra* ("Production of Documents, Entries on Land, Testing, and Sampling").

154. FED. R. CIV. P. 26(a)(1) advisory committee's note to the 1993 amendment.

the plaintiff was physically injured, lost wages and income, suffered physical and mental pain, and incurred medical expenses of $100,000." Pursuant to Rule 26(a)(1)(A)(iii), *P* would have to include information concerning *P's* damages as part of *P's* initial disclosures. *P* would have to show how each category of damages (medical and hospital expenses, loss of wages, and pain and suffering) was calculated. *P* would also have to make available for inspection and copying the documents or other evidentiary material, not privileged or protected from disclosure, on which the calculation is based. Because these materials bear "on the nature and extent of injuries suffered," *P* would have to make available medical and hospital bills. *P's* required disclosures would also extend to evidence of loss of earning capacity. Furthermore, if *P* used a formula or some other system for calculating pain and suffering, that information would have to be disclosed.[155]

Illustration 9-4. Assume that *P Co.* sues *D Co.* in federal court for breach of warranty. *P's* complaint asserts that a product with components supplied by *D* is "defective" in some unspecified manner. In addition to seeking damages of $100,000, *P* also asserts a special damage claim for loss of profits of $500,000. Pursuant to Rule 26(a)(1)(C), *P* would have to include information about how *P* calculated damages as part of *P's* initial disclosures. For example, *P* might show that the difference between the contract price and market price for the machine was $100,000. With respect to *P's* special damage claim, *P* would be required to show how *P* calculated the lost profits. However, this calculation would only need to be a reasonable one under the circumstances. If expert testimony or an extensive study will be necessary to demonstrate proof of this loss, the continuing obligation to supplement or correct the initial disclosure would force the party to provide greater details as the information develops.

(b) Insurance

Federal Rule 26(a)(1)(A)(iv) requires the parties to disclose "any insurance agreement under which any insurance business may be liable to satisfy part or all of a possible judgment in the action or to indemnify or reimburse for payments made to satisfy the judgment" for purposes of inspection and copying.[156] The mandatory disclosure of insurance replaces Federal Rule 26(b)(2), which previously dealt with this matter.[157] According to the Advisory Committee, a principal purpose

---

155. *See* LARRY L. TEPLY, LEGAL NEGOTIATION IN A NUTSHELL 144-47 (2d ed. 2005) (discussing rules of thumb and formulas as methods for case evaluation).

156. FED. R. CIV. P. 26(a)(1)(A)(iv). The inspection and copying would be carried out "as under Rule 34." *Id.*; *see* section H *infra* ("Production of Documents, Entries on Land, Testing, and Sampling"). The obligation to disclose does not extend to applications for insurance nor does disclosure make the insurance agreement admissible in evidence. The prior rule covering insurance, Rule 26(b)(2), included specific statements to this effect. These statements were dropped from the new rule as "unnecessary." Their deletion does "not signify any change of law." *See* FED. R. CIV. P. 26(a)(1) advisory committee's note to the 1993 amendment.

157. When insurance would be provable at trial, there is no doubt that a party can discover the facts about insurance; but insurance is irrelevant at trial in determining whether a person acted negligently or otherwise wrongfully. *See* FED. R. EVID. 411. Indeed, the mention of insurance may result in a mistrial. The federal courts and states adopting rules similar to Federal Rule 26(b)(1) were divided sharply on whether disclosure of insurance coverage could be compelled through discovery. *See* Cook v. Welty, 253 F. Supp. 875, 876 (D.D.C. 1966). This division was resolved in 1970 for the federal courts. Federal Rule 26(b)(2) was added to the Federal Rules of Civil Procedure to permit discovery of the existence and contents of liability insurance agreements. This change had a

of these disclosures is "to accelerate the exchange of basic information about the case and to eliminate the paper work involved in requesting such information."[158]

Illustration 9-5. If the defendants in *Illustrations 9-3* or *9-4* have insurance agreements covering part or all of the potential judgment, they must disclose the existence of that insurance agreement and make it available for inspection and copying.

(c) Potential Witnesses and Documentary Evidence

Rule 26(a)(1)(A)(i) specifically requires the parties, without waiting for a request, to disclose "the name and, if known, the address and telephone number of each individual likely to have discoverable information—along with the subjects of that information—that the disclosing party may use to support its claims or defenses, unless the use would be solely for impeachment."[159] Similarly, Rule 26(a)(1)(A)(ii) requires the parties to disclose "a copy—or a description by category and location—of all documents, electronically stored information, and tangible things that the disclosing party has in its possession, custody, or control and [that the disclosing party] may use to support its claims or defenses, unless the use would be solely for impeachment."[160] Thus, these mandatory disclosures are limited to information favorable to the disclosing party. The word "use" in the rule covers any intended use at a pretrial conference, to support a motion, at trial, or during discovery, such as use of a document to question a witness during a deposition.[161] Under the 2000 amendments, Rule 5(d)(1) prohibits filing of disclosures under Rule 26(a)(1) until they are used in the proceeding or the court orders them filed.[162]

Illustration 9-6. In *Illustration 9-4*, *P* alleged that a product with components supplied by *D* was "defective" in some unspecified manner. Prior to the 2000 amendments, that allegation would not have imposed on *P* nor *D* the

---

marked influence on state practice even in those states that had not adopted the 1970 discovery amendments. *See, e.g.*, Walls v. Horbach, 189 Neb. 479, 203 N.W.2d 490 (1973) (allowing discovery, overruling a 1964 decision to the contrary); Cropp v. Woleslagel, 207 Kan. 627, 485 P.2d 1271 (1971) (insurance not discoverable, but the court may require disclosure at a pretrial conference).

158. *See* FED. R. CIV. P. 26(a) advisory committee's note to the 1993 amendment.

159. FED. R. CIV. P. 26(a)(1)(A)(i). Prior to the 2000 amendments, this provision required disclosure of such information when it was "relevant to disputed facts alleged with particularity in the pleadings." FED. R. CIV. P. 26(a)(1) advisory committee's notes to the 2000 amendment.

160. FED. R. CIV. P. 26(a)(1)(A)(ii). *See generally* Jeffrey W. Stempel & David F. Herr, *Applying Amended Rule 26(b)(1) in Litigation: The New Scope of Discovery*, 199 F.R.D. 396 (2001). Prior to the 2000 amendments, this provision required disclosure of such information when it was "relevant to disputed facts alleged with particularity in the pleadings." Under the 1993 amendments, the Advisory Committee had envisioned a common-sense, sliding scale approach: "[t]he greater the specificity and clarity of the allegations in the pleadings, the more complete should be the listing of potential witnesses and types of documentary evidence." FED. R. CIV. P. 26(a)(1) & advisory committee's note to the 1993 amendment. The Advisory Committee also envisioned that this rule would be construed and administered like all other rules: to secure the just, speedy, and inexpensive determination of the action. *Id.* (referring to the principles in Rule 1). Furthermore, the Advisory Committee assumed that the parties would clarify the issues as part of the required discovery planning meeting. *Id.* ("Although [disclosure requirements in the rule] by their terms refer to the factual disputes defined in the pleadings, the rule contemplates that these issues would be informally refined and clarified during the meeting of the parties [concerning the discovery plan] and that the disclosure obligations would be [accordingly] adjusted.").

161. *See* FED. R. CIV. P. 26(a)(1) advisory committee's note. "As case preparation continues, a party must supplement its disclosures when it determines that it may use a witness or document that it did not previously intend to use." *Id.*

162. *See* FED. R. CIV. P. 5(d)(1).

obligation in an initial disclosure to identify, for example, persons involved in or documents relating to the possible defective design, manufacture, or assembly of the product because it was not alleged with particularity.[163] After the 2000 amendments, *P* would, for example, have to disclose the individuals who are likely to have discoverable information that *P* may use to support *P's* claim that *D's* product was "defective" (unless they would be used solely for impeachment purposes). In doing so, *P* would have to identify the subjects of the discoverable information.

Illustration 9-7. Assume on the facts of *Illustration 9-3* that *D's* answer (1) admits *P's* allegations concerning jurisdiction, (2) denies *D's* negligence, (3) alleges *P's* contributory negligence, and (4) denies *P's* allegation of damages. On these facts, *D* would be required to disclose, for example, the names and, if known, the addresses and telephone numbers, of *W-1* and *W-2*, eyewitnesses to the accident, whom *D* plans to use to support the denial of *D's* negligence and *D's* affirmative defense of contributory negligence. In addition, *P* would have to disclose medical bills that *P* intends to use to support *P's* claim for damages for personal injuries. Note that no disclosures by either party would be necessary concerning jurisdiction because *D* did not dispute jurisdiction.

2. Disclosures and Discovery Concerning Experts

(a) Discovery Concerning Experts Prior to Required Disclosure Under the 1993 Amendments

Expert testimony is often used at trial. A party may use expert testimony when "scientific, technical, or other specialized knowledge will assist the trier of fact to understand the evidence or to determine a fact in issue."[164] In such circumstances, witnesses qualified as experts based upon their "knowledge, skill, experience, training, or education" may testify.[165]

Because the selection and use of experts was an integral part of an attorney's trial preparation, the early cases generally refused to allow discovery.[166] The proposed 1946 amendments to the Federal Rules of Civil Procedure on attorney work product included a provision creating an absolute immunity for conclusions of an expert.[167] The Supreme Court did not adopt the proposed 1946 amendments,

---

163. *Cf.* FED. R. CIV. P. 26(a)(1) advisory committee's note to the 1993 amendment.

164. FED. R. EVID. 702.

165. *Id.*

166. *See generally* Jack H. Friedenthal, *Discovery and Use of an Adverse Party's Expert Information*, 14 STAN. L. REV. 455 (1962).

167. "The Court shall not order the production or inspection of any part of [a] writing [obtained or prepared by the adverse party, his attorney, surety, indemnitor, or agent in anticipation of litigation or in preparation for trial] that reflects . . . , except as provided in Rule 35, the conclusions of an expert." 5 F.R.D. 433, 456-57 (1946). Federal Rule 35 permits court-ordered physical or mental examinations of a party (or of a person in the custody or under the legal control of a party) when that person's physical or mental condition is "in controversy." FED. R. CIV. P. 35(a)(1). Specifically, Rule 35(b) allows the party against whom the order was made to discover the medical report detailing the examining physician's findings. *See* FED R. CIV. P. 35(b)(1). Rule 35(b) further provides that after delivering the report, the party who moved for the examination is entitled to receive like reports of all earlier and later examinations of the same condition. *See* FED. R. CIV. P. 35(b)(3); *see* section I(2) *infra* ("The Physician's Report").

but instead attempted to deal with the general work-product issue by deciding the case of *Hickman v. Taylor*.[168] After *Hickman*, several courts continued to protect the reports and opinions of experts, but some courts took a liberal approach in allowing discovery. The 1970 amendments to the Federal Rules resolved the division among the lower federal courts.[169] The 1970 amendment recognized three categories of experts: (1) experts to be called at trial; (2) experts retained by counsel, but who will not be called at trial; and (3) experts who are consulted, but not retained.[170]

Under the 1970 amendment, a party could obtain, by written interrogatories and without any special showing, (1) the names of experts that any other party expects to call as witnesses at trial, (2) the subject on which they will testify, (3) the substance of the facts and opinions to which they are expected to testify, and (4) a summary of the grounds for each of their opinions.[171] The Advisory Committee's principal justification for permitting discovery of this information as a matter of course was to enable opposing counsel to prepare effectively for cross-examination of the expert. The Committee pointed out that lawyers, even with the help of their own experts, frequently could not anticipate the particular approach their adversary's expert would take or the data on which they would base their judgment.[172] Some courts required a substantial showing of need to obtain "further discovery,"[173] but most courts freely permitted further discovery from experts.[174]

Discovery was limited to those experts who were *expected* to testify. In answering an interrogatory under this subsection, parties did not need to disclose

---

168. *See* section B(2) *supra* ("Attorney 'Work Product' and Trial-Preparation Materials").

169. *See* FED. R. CIV. P. 26(b)(4) advisory committee's note to the 1970 amendment; *see also* Lori J. Henkel, Annotation, *Compelling Testimony of Opponent's Expert in State Court*, 66 A.L.R.4TH 213 (1988).

170. *See* FED. R. CIV. P. 26(b)(4) advisory committee's note to the 1970 amendment.

171. *Id.*; *see also* Thomas R. Trenkner, Annotation, *Pretrial Discovery of Facts Known and Opinions Held By Opponent's Experts Under Rule 26(b)(4) of Federal Rules of Civil Procedure*, 33 A.L.R. FED. 403 (1977). The effectiveness of using interrogatories to discover an expert's opinion was sharply criticized. As one commentator stated, the use of interrogatories is "a totally unsatisfactory method of providing preparation for cross-examination and rebuttal." Michael G. Graham, *Discovery of Experts Under Rule 26(b)(4) of the Federal Rules of Civil Procedure* (pt.2), 1977 U. ILL. L.F. 169, 172. The 1970 version of subdivision (A)(ii) of Federal Rule 26(b)(4) provided that "[u]pon motion, the court may order further discovery by other means," which presumably might include taking of the expert's deposition or the production of the expert's report. The court could restrict the scope of this further discovery. The court could also provide for payment of the expert's time spent in further discovery as well as a fair portion of the fee the opponent has paid to the expert.

172. FED. R. CIV. P. 26(b)(4) advisory committee's note to the 1970 amendment.

173. For example, in Wilson v. Resnick, 51 F.R.D. 510 (E.D. Pa. 1970), the court refused discovery of an expert physician's report concerning allegedly negligent medical treatment despite the plaintiff's claim that the summary of the opinions provided in the interrogatories was inadequate.

174. For example, in Herbst v. International Telephone & Telegraph Corp., 65 F.R.D. 528 (D. Conn. 1975), the court stated as follows:

> All but experts may be freely deposed before trial in keeping with the liberal spirit that pervades the federal rules. Once the traditional problem of allowing one party to obtain the benefit of another's expert cheaply has been solved, there is no reason to treat an expert differently than any other witness. Thus, the motion to compel oral depositions will be granted. If expenses have been incurred by the plaintiffs in obtaining these experts' opinions, and the parties are unable to agree upon an allocation of these costs, the issue may be submitted to the court on affidavits following the depositions. . . . The defendants shall, in addition, pay these experts a reasonable fee for the time spent in deposition.

Id. at 530-31. Professor Graham likewise concluded that "[i]n practice, full discovery is the rule, and practitioners use all available means of disclosure including both the discovery of expert's reports and depositions." Michael G. Graham, *Discovery of Experts Under Rule 26(b)(4)* (pt. 2), 1977 ILL. L.F. 169, 172. *See generally* Joseph M. McLaughlin, *Discoverability and Admissibility of Expert Testimony*, 63 NOTRE DAME L. REV. 760 (1988); Steven K. Sims, Note, *Treating Experts Like Ordinary Witnesses: Recent Trends in Discovery of Testifying Experts Under Federal Rule of Civil Procedure 26(b)(4)*, 66 WASH. U.L.Q. 787 (1988). The 1993 amendments conformed to this practice. *See* section C(2)*(b)(iii) infra* ("Further Discovery Concerning Experts").

the names of experts who *might* testify.[175] However, if a party decided to call an expert after the party had answered the interrogatory, the party was specifically required to supplement the response by identifying each person expected to be called as an expert witness at trial, the subject matter on which the person is expected to testify, and the substance of the person's testimony.[176] In contrast, courts rarely permitted discovery of facts known and opinions held by experts who had been "retained or specially employed by another party in anticipation of litigation or preparation for trial" but who were *not* expected to testify. Such discovery was allowed only as provided by Rule 35 (reports involving court-mandated examinations of physical or mental conditions in controversy) or upon a showing of exceptional circumstances under which it was impractical for the party seeking discovery to obtain facts or opinions on the same subject by other means.[177]

The 1970 amendments limited discovery to experts "retained or specially consulted." In contrast, discovery was entirely precluded with regard to expert who was informally consulted in preparation for trial, but who was not "retained" or "specially employed."[178] In order for this preclusion to apply, the expert information had to be acquired or developed either in anticipation of litigation or in preparation for trial. Thus, when an expert acquires information as "an actor or viewer with respect to transactions or occurrences that are part of the subject matter of the lawsuit," the expert will be treated as an ordinary witness.[179] Similarly, a litigant cannot avoid discovery merely because the litigant is an expert. For example, a doctor defending a malpractice action "should be subject to discovery with regard both to the facts [the doctor] knows and the opinions [the doctor] holds."[180]

(b) Required Disclosures and Discovery Concerning Experts After the 1993 Amendments

The 1993 amendments imposed a duty to disclose information concerning experts and their likely testimony at trial.[181] These requirements remain unchanged under the 2000 amendments, except that Rule 5(d) prohibits filing of disclosures

---

175. *See* 8A CHARLES A. WRIGHT ET AL., FEDERAL PRACTICE AND PROCEDURE: CIVIL § 2030, at 127 (3d ed. 2010).

176. FED. R. CIV. P. 26(e) advisory committee's notes to 1970 amendment.

177. *See* FED. R. CIV. P. 26(b)(4) advisory committee's notes to 1970 amendment.

178. *See id.*

179. *Id.*

180. 8A CHARLES A. WRIGHT ET AL., FEDERAL PRACTICE AND PROCEDURE: CIVIL § 2033, at 122-23 (3d ed. 2010). In Young v. United States, 181 F.R.D. 344 (W.D. Tex. 1997), a medical malpractice case, the plaintiff attempted to designate his treating physicians, who were Navy doctors employed by the defendant, as both fact and expert witnesses. The defendant objected on the grounds that treating physicians are not properly considered experts and that the *Code of Federal Regulations* prohibits such a designation. The court held that private litigants may not compel treating physicians to act as experts, but that a non-expert treating physician can be asked questions implicating his expertise only as long as they relate to his treatment. In addition, the court held that the government could not use the *Code of Federal Regulations* to create a privilege that would allow the defendant to prevent the testimony of the treating physician. On the latter question, the court held both that the *CFR* was not designed to create a privilege of the sort asserted and that Rule 45(c) adequately protected unretained experts from being called as expert witnesses against their will, in that the rule allows the court to quash or modify a subpoena for such a witness in its discretion.

181. FED. R. CIV. P. 26(a)(2) ("Disclosure of Expert Testimony").

under Rule 26(a)(2) until they are used in the proceeding or the court orders them filed.[182]

(i) Who Must Be Identified

Rule 26(a)(2)(A) requires that the parties disclose to other litigants "the identity of any witness [who may be] used at trial to present evidence under Rules 702, 703, or 705 of the Federal Rules of Evidence."[183] These Rules of Evidence govern testimony involving scientific, technical, and other specialized knowledge.[184]

(ii) Report Requirement

Rule 26(a)(2)(B) imposes a duty to prepare a written report on identified experts who (1) are retained or specially employed to provide expert testimony or (2) are the party's employees when they are regularly involved in giving expert testimony.[185] Thus, no written report is required for other experts, such as a treating physician called to testify at trial.[186] When a report is required, the report must provide a "complete statement of all opinions the witness will express" at trial and the "basis and reasons for them."[187] The report must also provide (1) "the facts or data considered by the witness in forming [the opinions];" (2) "any exhibits that will be used to summarize or support [the opinions];" (3) "the witness's qualifications, including a list of all publications authored in the previous 10 years;" (4) "a list of all other cases in which, during the previous 4 years, the witness testified as an expert at trial or by deposition;" and (5) "a statement of the compensation to be paid for the study and testimony in the case."[188]

As an incentive to the parties to make full disclosure, amended Rule 37(c)(1) provides an "automatic sanction."[189] A party may not use that information or expert testimony for the purpose of supplying evidence on a motion, at a hearing,

---

182. *See* FED. R. CIV. P. 5(d)(1).

183. FED. R. CIV. P. 26(a)(2)(A).

184. *See* FED. R. EVID. 702 ("Testimony by Experts") ("If scientific, technical, or other specialized knowledge will assist the trier of fact to understand the evidence or to determine a fact in issue, a witness qualified as an expert by knowledge, skill, experience, training, or education, may testify thereto in the form of an opinion or otherwise"), 703 ("Bases of Opinion Testimony by Experts"), 705 ("Disclosure of Facts or Data Underlying Expert Opinion").

185. FED. R. CIV. P. 26(a)(2)(B). This reporting requirement, however, can be waived for particular experts by local rule, court order, or written stipulation. *Id.* advisory committee's note to the 1993 amendment.

186. FED. R. CIV. P. 26(a)(2)(B) advisory committee's note to the 1993 amendment. Some courts followed the "plain meaning" of Rule 26(a)(2)(B) and exempted expert witnesses from the reporting requirements of the rule when the experts are either treating physicians or employees of a party; however, a larger number of courts interpreted the rule to require full disclosure by such witnesses. *See* Katherine A. Rocco, *Rule 26(a)(2)(B) of the Federal Rules of Civil Procedure: In the Interest of Full Disclosure,* 76 FORDHAM L. REV. 2227 (2008). In 2010, Rule 26(a)(2)(C) was added to make clear that such witnesses were exempted from the report requirement. Instead, a disclosure is required providing "a summary of the facts and opinions to which [such a] witness is expected to testify." FED. R. CIV. P. 26(a)(2)(C). This disclosure obligation does not include "facts unrelated to the expert opinions the witness will present." *Id.* advisory committee's note to the 2010 amendment.

187. FED. R. CIV. P. 26(a)(2)(B).

188. *Id.* Counsel can assist experts in preparing these reports. *Id.* advisory committee's note to the 1993 amendment ("Rule 26(a)(2)(B) does not preclude counsel from providing assistance to experts in preparing the reports, and, indeed, with experts such as automobile mechanics, this assistance may be needed").

189. FED. R. CIV. P. 37(c)(1) advisory committee's note to the 1993 amendment.

or at trial when a party has not properly disclosed—unless the failure was "substantially justified" or was "harmless."[190]

Rule 26(a)(2)(D) envisions that the court will prescribe a time for these disclosures in a pretrial scheduling order.[191] Ordinarily, the party with the burden of proof on an issue should be required to disclose its expert testimony before other parties are required to make their disclosures on the issue. In the absence of a specific time in a scheduling order or a stipulation by the parties, Rule 26(a)(2)(D) requires that these disclosures concerning experts be made by all parties at least 90 days before the trial date or the date by which the case is to be ready for trial.[192] However, the rule allows an additional 30 days after the disclosure has been made by another party if the expert testimony "is intended solely to contradict or rebut evidence on the same subject matter" that has been identified by another party's disclosure under this rule.[193] Rule 26(a)(2)(E) also specifically imposes a duty to supplement the disclosures concerning experts.[194]

(iii) Further Discovery Concerning Experts

Rule 26(b)(4) states that parties may depose persons who have been identified as experts whose opinions may be presented at trial.[195] Depositions of experts who must prepare a report can be taken only after the required report has been provided.[196] According to the Advisory Committee, these detailed reports may eliminate the need for further depositions or at least reduce their length.[197] Furthermore, the party taking such depositions will ordinarily have to bear the expert's fees involved in the deposition.[198] The disclosure rules continue the prior practice concerning depositions of experts who are specially retained or employed in anticipation of litigation or preparation for trial but who are not expected to testify.[199]

---

190. *See* FED. R. CIV. P. 37(c)(1).

191. *See* FED. R. CIV. P. 26(a)(2)(D).

192. *See* FED. R. CIV. P. 26(a)(2)(D)(i).

193. FED. R. CIV. P. 26(a)(2)(D)(ii) & advisory committee's note to the 1993 amendment.

194. FED. R. CIV. P. 26(a)(2)(E) (when required by Rule 26(e) governing supplementation generally).

195. FED. R. CIV. P. 26(b)(4)(A).

196. *Id.*

197. FED. R. CIV. P. 26(a)(2) & (b)(4) advisory committee's notes to the 1993 amendment.

198. *See* FED. R. CIV. P. 26(b)(4)(E). Rule 26(b)(4)(E) states that "[u]nless manifest injustice would result, the court must require the party seeking discovery [to] pay the expert a reasonable fee for time spent . . . ." *Id.* In M.T. McBrian, Inc. v. Liebert Corp., 173 F.R.D. 491 (N.D. Ill. 1997), the defendant took the deposition of the plaintiff's expert at the plaintiff's attorneys' offices in Chicago, to which the defendants' attorneys had to travel from St. Louis. The plaintiff sought an order to have the defendant pay the travel expenses of the expert in coming from Minnesota to Chicago for the deposition under this provision, which was previously designated as Rule 26(b)(4)(C). The court refused the order because the plaintiff wanted the deposition taken in Chicago, and in the absence of the plaintiff's request, the defendant could have as easily taken it in Minnesota where the expert lived and avoided the claimed travel expenses. The court also denied the plaintiff's request that the defendant reimburse the expert for time spent in preparing for the deposition as well as for time actually spent in giving the deposition. The court observed that this case was not a complex one in which the expert needed preparation time because it had been several months since he prepared his report. *Id.* at 492-94.

199. *See* FED. R. CIV. P. 26(b)(4)(D); section C(2)*(a) supra* ("Discovery Concerning Experts Under the Federal Rules Prior to the 1993 Amendments"); *see also* FED. R. CIV. P. 26(b)(4)(E) (continuing to provide that the party seeking discovery must ordinarily pay a reasonable fee for time spent in responding to this discovery as well as a fair portion of the fees and expenses reasonably incurred by the other party in obtaining facts and opinions from the expert).

3. Disclosures Identifying Particular Evidence that May Be Offered at Trial

The 1993 amendments also imposed a duty to disclose the specific evidence that the parties will offer at trial. These disclosures focus on information customarily needed in final preparation for trial.[200] These disclosures should be in writing, signed, served on the other parties, and filed with the court, unless the court orders otherwise.[201] The signature certifies that the disclosure is complete and correct.[202]

(a) Names of Witnesses

Rule 26(a)(3)(A) requires the parties to disclose the witnesses who may present substantive evidence at trial, whether in person or by deposition.[203] The rule does not require disclosure of evidence offered solely for "impeachment."[204] The parties must separately list the witnesses who are expected to be called as well as those who may be called if the need arises.[205] Witnesses expected to present testimony by deposition must also be designated. Furthermore, if the deposition of the witness is not taken stenographically, a transcript of the pertinent portions of the deposition must be provided to other parties at the time of the disclosure.[206]

As an incentive to provide full disclosure, revised Rule 37(c)(1) prohibits a party from calling any witness at trial who has not been properly disclosed, unless the party can demonstrate a substantial justification or show that the failure is harmless.[207] However, a party may call "an unlisted witness if the need for such testimony is based upon developments during trial that could not reasonably have been anticipated," such as an unexpected change of testimony by another witness.[208]

(b) Identification of Documents or Other Exhibits

Rule 26(a)(3)(A) requires the parties to disclose each document or exhibit, including summaries of other evidence, that may be offered as "substantive"

---

200. FED. R. CIV. P. 26(a)(3) ("Pretrial Disclosures") & advisory committee's note to the 1993 amendment. The parties must make these disclosures, without any request, pursuant to a scheduling order adopted by the court or by special order. In absence of such orders, the parties must make these disclosures at least 30 days before the commencement of the trial. FED. R. CIV. P. 26(a)(3)(B) & advisory committee's note to the 1993 amendment.

201. *See* FED. R. CIV. P. 26(a)(3)(A) & (4).

202. *See* FED. R. CIV. P. 26(g)(1)(A).

203. FED. R. CIV. P. 26(a)(3)(A)(i) & (ii).

204. *See* FED. R. CIV. P. 26(a)(3)(A); *see* Chapter 11(I)(6) *infra* ("Objection, Cross-Examination, and Impeachment").

205. FED. R. CIV. P. 26(a)(3)(A)(i) & (ii). In addition to the names of the witnesses, their addresses and telephone numbers must be listed if the party has not previously provided that information. FED. R. CIV. P. 26(a)(3)(A)(i). Listing a witness does not obligate a party to secure that person's attendance at trial. However, listing a witness should preclude the party from objecting if another party calls the witness to testify without previously listing the witness in a disclosure. *Id.* advisory committee's note to the 1993 amendment.

206. FED. R. CIV. P. 26(a)(3)(A)(ii). This disclosure allows other parties to verify the transcript which "is an obvious concern since counsel often utilize their own personnel to prepare transcripts from audio or video tapes." *Id.* advisory committee's notes to the 1993 amendment.

207. FED. R. CIV. P. 37(c)(1); *see* FED. R. CIV. P. 37(c)(1) advisory committee's note to the 1993 amendment (noting that the preclusion sanction does not apply to impeachment evidence).

208. FED. R. CIV. P. 26(a)(3)(A) advisory committee's note to the 1993 amendment.

evidence at trial.[209] Disclosure of evidence offered solely for "impeachment" purposes is not required.[210] In making the disclosures, the parties must separate (1) those documents and other exhibits that a party expects to offer from (2) those that the party may offer if the need arises.[211] To encourage full disclosure, revised Rule 37(c)(1) prohibits a party from offering any document or exhibit at trial that has not been properly disclosed. However, the court may permit a party to offer a non-disclosed document or exhibit if the party can demonstrate a substantial justification or that the failure is harmless.[212]

(c) Objecting to the Disclosures

After receiving these final disclosures, a party has 14 days to object to the matters disclosed. Specifically, a party must serve and file a list disclosing any objection to (1) the use of any designated deposition or (2) the admissibility of designated documents or exhibits.[213] Failure to object in this manner waives the objection "unless excused by the court for good cause."[214] This waiver provision does not apply to objections under Rule 402 (relevancy) or Rule 403 (exclusion of relevant evidence on grounds of prejudice, confusion, or waste of time) of the Federal Rules of Evidence.[215] However, listing a potential objection does not constitute making that objection.[216]

SECTION D. THE DISCOVERY PLANNING CONFERENCE, TIMING, SEQUENCE, PRIORITY, LIMITS, AND CERTIFICATION

1. The Parties' Discovery Planning Conference

The 1993 and 2000 amendments to Rule 26 require the parties to have an early conference for four purposes. The 2006 amendments to Rule 26 added two more. First, the parties are to discuss the nature and basis of their claims and defenses. Second, they are to discuss the possibility of a prompt settlement or resolution of the case. Third, they are to make or arrange for the required initial

---

209. *See* FED. R. CIV. P. 26(a)(3)(A)(iii).

210. *See* FED. R. CIV. P. 26(a)(3); *see also* FED. R. CIV. P. 37(c)(1) advisory committee's note to the 1993 amendment (noting that preclusion sanctions do not apply to impeachment evidence); Chapter 11(I)(6) *infra* ("Objections, Cross-Examination, and Impeachment").

211. *See* FED. R. CIV. P. 26(a)(3)(A)(iii). The Advisory Committee's notes indicate that each document or exhibit should be listed separately. However, the note also states that the rule "should permit voluminous items of a similar or standardized character to be described by meaningful categories." FED. R. CIV. P. 26(a)(3) advisory committee's note to the 1993 amendment.

212. FED. R. CIV. P. 37(c)(1) & advisory committee's note to the 1993 amendment (noting that the preclusion sanction does not apply to impeachment evidence).

213. FED. R. CIV. P. 26(a)(3)(B). A court may set an earlier time for disclosures of evidence and provide more time for disclosing potential objections. *Id.* advisory committee's note to the 1993 amendment.

214. FED. R. CIV. P. 26(a)(3)(B).

215. *Id.*; *see* Chapter 11(I) *infra* ("Evidence").

216. FED. R. CIV. P. 26(a)(3) advisory committee's note to the 1993 amendment. Thus, the court does not have to rule on the objection. Instead, the listing simply preserves a party's right to make the objection during trial. Nevertheless, the court may elect to treat the listing as a motion in limine and rule upon it prior to trial. *Id.*

disclosures. Fourth, they are to develop a proposed discovery plan in addition to the mandatory disclosures.[217] Fifth, they are to discuss issues relating to the disclosure or production of electronically stored information, including the sources of the data, the form in which it should be produced (in paper or electronic form, and, if electronic, how it will be made available), and the costs of that production.[218] Sixth, they are to discuss issues relating to claims of privilege or work product protection, including any procedures to be used in the event of the production of privileged information to the extent that they differ from the "recall" or "claw back" procedures set forth in Rule 26(b)(2)(B), discussed in section B, above.[219]

The responsibility for arranging and participating in this conference rests jointly upon the attorneys of record and all unrepresented parties who have appeared in the action.[220] They also share a joint responsibility for attempting in good faith to agree upon the proposed plan and to submit a written report outlining the plan within 14 days after the conference.[221] Failure to participate in good faith in framing the development and submission of a discovery plan may be sanctioned. After an opportunity to be heard, the court may require the party or the attorney to pay to any other party the reasonable expenses, including attorney's fees, caused by the failure.[222]

---

217. *See* FED. R. CIV. P. 26(f)(2). The forerunner of this type of conference was added by the 1980 amendments to the Federal Rules of Civil Procedure. Prior to a discovery conference, the Federal Rules envisioned that the parties had made a reasonable effort to reach agreement on four matters: (1) the issues as they then appear; (2) a proposed plan and schedule of discovery; (3) limitations that ought to be placed on discovery; and (4) any other matters governing discovery (that could be controlled by a court order). *See* FED. R. CIV. P. 26(f) (prior to the 1993 amendment). Each party and their respective attorneys were required to participate in good faith in formulating a discovery plan if such a plan was proposed by an attorney for any party. If an attorney had made a reasonable effort to reach agreement with the opposing attorneys on these matters but had not been able to do so, that party could move the court to conduct such a conference. *Id.* (prior to the 1993 amendment). The notice of the motion set forth the above matters. This notice was served on all parties and objections or additions to the matters raised by the motion had to be served not later than 10 days after service of the motion. After the conference, the court is required to "enter an order tentatively identifying the issues for discovery purposes, establishing a plan and schedule for discovery, [and] setting limitations on discovery, if any." *Id.* (prior to the 1993 amendment). The court could also allocate expenses and determine other matters necessary for the proper management of discovery. This discovery order could "be altered or amended whenever justice so require[d]." *Id.* (prior to the 1993 amendment). The 2000 amendments removed the requirement that the parties have a "meeting" before the discovery conference. Instead, the amended rule only requires that they have a "conference." However, the Rule 26(f) specifically authorizes the court to order the parties or attorneys to attend the conference in person. The time for the conference was changed from 14 days to at least 21 days before the Rule 16 pretrial scheduling conference, and the time for the report was changed from 10 days to no more than 14 days after the Rule 26(f) conference. The 2000 amendments also removed the authority to exempt cases by local rule from the discovery conference requirement. *See* FED. R. CIV. P. 26(f) advisory committee's note to the 2000 amendment. *See also* Jeffrey A. Parness, *Improving Judicial Settlement Conferences*, 39 U.C. DAVIS L. REV. 1891 (2006).

218. *See* FED. R. CIV. P 26(f)(3)(C) & the advisory committee's note to the 2006 amendment to Rule 26(f)(3).

219. *See* FED. R. CIV. P 26(f)(3)(D) & the advisory committee's note to the 2006 amendment to Rule 26(f)(4).

220. FED. R. CIV. P. 26(f)(2). The specific timing of this conference is discussed in section C(1) *supra* ("Early Disclosures Concerning Potential Witnesses, Documentary Evidence, Damages, and Insurance").

221. FED. R. CIV. P. 26(f)(2). However, if necessary to comply with an expedited schedule for Rule 16(b) conferences, the 2000 amendment to Rule 26(f) authorizes a court by local rule to require that the conference between the parties occur fewer than 21 days before the scheduling conference is held or a scheduling order is due under Rule 16(b) and to require a written report outlining the discovery plan be filed fewer than 14 days after the conference. It also permits a court by local rule to excuse the parties from submitting a written report and permit them to report orally on their discovery plan at the Rule 16(b) conference. *See* FED. R. CIV. P. 26(f) advisory committee's note to the 2000 amendment; *see also* Section N *infra* ("Pretrial Conferences and Orders").

222. FED. R. CIV. P. 37(f).

Illustration 9-8. Federal Form 52 illustrates the type of report that the parties are expected to file. First, the report, *inter alia*, should state who was present and where and when the conference took place. Second, the report should state when the parties exchanged or will exchange the initial disclosures required by Rule 26(a)(1) or an applicable local rule. Third, the report should propose a discovery plan that indicates items of disagreement. Fourth, the report should indicate any agreement regarding protections against inadvertent forfeiture or waiver of privilege or protection that the parties have reached. Fifth, the report should discuss other items relevant to processing the case, such as planned dates for completion of various aspects of the case.[223]

2. The Timing of Discovery

Unless authorized by a specific Federal Rule of Civil Procedure,[224] court order, or agreement of the parties, the 1993 amendments prohibit the parties from seeking discovery from any source before the parties have conferred to prepare a discovery plan.[225] This prohibition applies to formal discovery, not to informal interviews with witnesses and other informal means of gathering information.[226] Rule 30(b)(2)(A)(iii) allows early depositions of persons who are expected to leave the United States and thus be unavailable for examination in this country.[227] The court may also permit appropriate discovery in certain other circumstances, such as in conjunction with requests for preliminary injunctions or motions challenging personal jurisdiction.[228] The 2000 amendment to Rule 26(d) removed the prior authority to exempt cases by local rule from the moratorium on discovery before the Rule 26(f) conference.[229]

The Private Securities Litigation Reform Act of 1995 was enacted to reform securities class action litigation.[230] It provides that "all discovery and other proceedings shall be stayed during the pendency of any motion to dismiss, unless the court finds upon the motion of any party that particularized discovery is necessary to preserve evidence or to prevent undue prejudice to that party."[231] Furthermore, "[d]uring the pendency of any stay of discovery . . . , unless otherwise

---

223. *See* Federal Form 52 in the Appendix of Forms accompanying the Federal Rules of Civil Procedure.

224. *See* FED. R. CIV. P. 27(a) (depositions to perpetuate testimony before commencement of an action); FED. R. CIV. P. 30(a)(2)(A)(iii) (depositions of persons about to leave the country).

225. FED. R. CIV. P. 26(d)(1). This limitation does not apply to proceedings exempted from initial disclosure under Rule 26(a)(1)(B). The 2000 amendment to Rule 26(f) no longer requires the parties have a "meeting" before the discovery conference; instead, it only requires that they have a "conference."

226. FED. R. CIV. P. 26(d) advisory committee's note to the 1993 amendment.

227. *See* FED. R. CIV. P. 30(a)(2)(C) (requiring an appropriate certification in the notice).

228. FED. R. CIV. P. 26(d) advisory committee's note to the 1993 amendment (noting also that a local rule may exempt such situations).

229. *See* FED. R. CIV. P. 26(d) & the advisory committee's note to the 2000 amendment.

230. Pub. L. No. 104-67, 109 Stat. 737 (codified in scattered sections of 15 U.S.C.). In response to the concern that the cost of discovery resulting from "fishing expedition" lawsuits often forced innocent parties to settle frivolous securities litigation, Congress sought to limit "abusive" discovery in such cases.

231. *Id.* § 101(b)(3)(B), 109 Stat. 737, 747 (codified in 15 U.S.C. § 78u-4); *see* Powers v. Eichen, 961 F. Supp. 233 (S.D. Cal. 1997) (phrase "during the pendency of any motion to dismiss" in the Private Securities Litigation Reform Act includes the time period during which a court is considering a motion for reconsideration of a dismissal decision); *see also* Paul Tyrell & George de Verges, *A Chilling Effect: The Impact of the Motion to Dismiss Under the Private Securities Litigation Reform Act of 1995*, 173 F.R.D. 556 (1997).

ordered by the court, any party to the action with actual notice of the allegations contained in the complaint shall treat all documents, data compilations (including electronically recorded or stored data), and tangible objects that are in the custody or control of such person and that are relevant to the allegations, as if they were the subject of a continuing request for production of documents from an opposing party under the Federal Rules of Civil Procedure."[232]

3. Sequence and Priority of Discovery

Federal Rule 26(d) provides that "[u]nless, on motion, the court orders otherwise for the parties' and witnesses' convenience and in the interests of justice, . . .methods of discovery may be used in any sequence," with neither side gaining a priority of discovery.[233] This provision eliminated a "priority" rule that some courts had developed before 1970.[234]

4. Limits on Discovery

Rule 26(b)(2) provides that the court shall limit the frequency or extent of discovery if it finds one of the following. First, if the court finds that the discovery sought is unreasonably cumulative or duplicative, or can be obtained from some other source that is more convenient, less burdensome, or less expensive, the court is required to limit the discovery in an appropriate fashion. Second, if the court finds that the party seeking discovery has had ample opportunity to obtain the information sought by discovery in the action, the court must limit discovery. Third, if the burden or expense of the proposed discovery outweighs its likely benefit, the court must limit the discovery.[235]

---

232. Private Securities Litigation Reform Act of 1995, Pub. L. No. 104-67, § 101(b)(3)(C)(i), 109 Stat. 737, 747 (codified in 15 U.S.C. § 78u-4). Willful violations may be punished by the court through "appropriate sanctions." *Id.* § 101(b)(3)(C)(ii), 109 Stat. 737, 747 (codified in15 U.S.C. § 78u-4).

233. FED. R. CIV. P. 26(d)(2). The court has the inherent power to set priority and time periods of discovery. Such is often the case in complex litigation.

234. *See* 8A CHARLES A. WRIGHT ET AL., FEDERAL PRACTICE AND PROCEDURE: CIVIL §§ 2045-2046 (3d ed. 2010).

235. *See* FED. R. CIV. P. 26(b)(2) (renumbered in 1993 from 26(b)(1) to 26(b)(2)). This restriction was added in 1983 in "an attempt to address the problem of duplicative, redundant, and excessive discovery and reduce it." *Id.* advisory committee's note to the 1983 amendment previously numbered as Rule 26(b)(1). Prior to 1983, the last sentence of Federal Rule 26(a) provided that the frequency of the use of the discovery methods listed in Rule 26(a) was not limited unless the court otherwise ordered. In 1983, this sentence was eliminated and a new paragraph was added to Rule 26(b)(1) to deal with the frequency of discovery under the Federal Rules of Civil Procedure. *See* FED. R. CIV. P. 26 advisory committee's note to the 1983 amendment. The purpose of the amendments to Rule 26(a) and (b)(1) was to deal with problems of excessive discovery that had developed. The Advisory Committee stated that the grounds for limiting discovery listed in the amended rule reflected the existing practice of many federal courts. Nevertheless, because federal district judges on the whole had been reluctant to limit the use of discovery, amendments were considered appropriate in order to prevent redundant or disproportionate discovery. Although the design of the amendments is not "to deprive a party of discovery that is reasonably necessary to afford a fair opportunity to develop and prepare the case," the amendments reflect the reality that more judicial involvement in the discovery process is desirable. *See* FED. R. CIV. P. 26(b)(1) advisory committee's note to the 1983 amendment. *See generally* Randy L. Agnew, Comment, *Recent Changes in the Federal Rules of Civil Procedure: Prescriptions to Ease the Pain?* 15 TEX. TECH. L. REV. 887 (1984); Margaret L. Weissbrod, Note, *Sanctions Under Amended Rule 26—Scalpel or Meat-Ax? The 1983 Amendments to the Federal Rules of Civil Procedure*, 46 OHIO ST. L.J. 183 (1985).

In determining whether to limit discovery, the court must weigh (1) the needs of the case, (2) the amount in controversy, (3) the parties' resources, (4) the importance of the issues at stake in the litigation, and (5) the importance of the proposed discovery in resolving the issue.[236] Limitations on discovery may be raised by a motion for a protective order under Rule 26(c). In addition, the court may act on its own initiative to limit the frequency or extent of discovery after the court has provided reasonable notice to the parties.[237] The limitation of discovery may be accomplished in conjunction with a discovery conference under Rule 26(f) or some other pretrial conference authorized by the rules.[238]

The 1993 amendments also place presumptive limits on the frequency of certain types of discovery.[239] In absence of a stipulation by the parties in writing,[240] Rules 30(a)(2) and 31(a)(2) limit each side (the plaintiffs, the defendants, and third-party defendants) to a total of ten oral or written depositions.[241] The Advisory Committee expects the parties on each side of a multi-party case to confer and agree upon which depositions are "most needed." If the parties cannot agree, the court can be asked to resolve the dispute or to permit additional depositions.[242] The 1993 amendments also limit the number of written interrogatories to a total of twenty-five, counting all discrete subparts.[243]

To take additional depositions or to serve additional interrogatories, a party must obtain leave of court.[244] Leave of court is also required to depose a person more than once in the case.[245] Local rules or court orders may vary the numerical limitations on depositions and interrogatories.[246] In addition, local rules or court orders may limit the length of oral depositions under Rule 30. They also may limit

---

236. *See* FED. R. CIV. P. 26(b)(2). The 1993 revisions to this rule "provide the court with broader discretion to impose additional restriction on the scope and extent of discovery," thus enabling "the court to keep a tighter rein on the extent of discovery." *Id.* advisory committee's note to the 1993 amendment. It "also dispels any doubt as to the power of the court to impose limitations on the length of depositions under Rule 30 or the number of requests for admission under Rule 36." *Id.*

237. *See* FED. R. CIV. P. 26(b)(2).

238. *See* section N *infra* ("Pretrial Conferences and Orders").

239. FED. R. CIV. P. 26(b) advisory committee's note to the 1993 amendment.

240. Subject to court order or local rules, under the 1993 amendment to Rule 29, the parties can ordinarily modify the limitations on discovery without court approval. *See* FED. R. CIV. P. 29.

241. FED. R. CIV. P. 30(a)(2) & 31(a)(2). A deposition under Federal Rule 30(b)(6) naming as a deponent a public or private corporation, a partnership, an association, or government agency is to be treated as a single deposition even though the organization may designate more than one person to provide testimony. FED. R. CIV. P. 30(a)(2) advisory committee's note to the 1993 amendment.

242. FED. R. CIV. P. 30(a) advisory committee's note to the 1993 amendment.

243. FED. R. CIV. P. 33(a)(1).

244. FED. R. CIV. P. 30(a)(2), 31(a)(2), & 33(a)(1).

245. FED. R. CIV. P. 30(a)(2)(A)(ii) & 31(a)(2)(A)(ii). This requirement does not apply to a deposition that is temporarily recessed to gather additional materials or for the convenience of counsel or the deponent. The Advisory Committee points out that "[i]f significant travel costs would be incurred to resume the deposition, the parties should consider the feasibility of conducting the balance of the examination by telephonic means." FED. R. CIV. P. 30(a)(2) advisory committee's note to the 1993 amendment.

246. FED. R. CIV. P. 26(b)(2). The specific reference to local rules and orders was intended to provide the court with broader discretion to impose additional restrictions on the scope and extent of discovery. It also was intended to authorize courts that develop case tracking systems based on the complexity of cases to increase or decrease the presumptive limits allowed in particular types of cases. *Id.* advisory committee's note to the 1993 amendment.

the total number of requests for admissions under Rule 36.[247] However, in a deposition context, the court must allow additional time, if needed, for a fair examination of the deponent. The court must also allow additional time if the deponent or another party delays or otherwise impedes the examination.[248]

The 2000 amendment to Rule 30(d) established a presumption that no deposition should last more than one seven-hour day, absent an agreement among the parties or a court order.[249] The 2000 amendment also directed the courts to allow extra time when it is needed for a fair examination of the deponent or if the deponent or some other person or circumstance delays the examination.[250]

The 2006 amendments to the Federal Rules also established a special limitation on discovery for electronically stored information (such as e-mails, web pages, word processing files, and databases) from sources that a party identifies as "not reasonably accessible because of undue burden or cost."[251] Prior to the adoption of this specific rule (and others) to deal with "e-discovery," the courts had to deal with these "e-discovery" challenges in the context of the existing rules.[252]

Illustration 9-9. In *Zubulake v. UBS Warburg LLC* litigation,[253] which raised several "e-discovery" issues, a former female employee (Laura Zubulake) sued her former employer ("UBS"). She alleged violations of city, state, and federal

---

247. FED. R. CIV. P. 26(b)(2); *see also id.* advisory committee's note to the 1993 amendment (dispelling any doubt about a court's authority to impose such limitations). The Advisory Committee emphasizes that the parties should handle time limits on depositions by agreement. The Committee anticipates that limits on the length of depositions prescribed by local rules would be presumptive only, which could be modified by the court or the parties' agreement. This matter could be covered in the discovery plan and included in the court's scheduling order. FED. R. CIV. P. 30(d) advisory committee's note to the 1993 amendment.

248. FED. R. CIV. P. 30(d)(1).

249. *See* FED. R. CIV. P. 30(d) & the advisory committee's note to the 2000 amendment.

250. The 2000 Advisory Committee's Note outlines a variety of factors that the court should consider in extending the time limit—a deposition in which an interpreter is needed, a deposition covering a long series of events or voluminous documents, multi-party cases in which each party needs to examine the witness, and depositions involving expert witnesses. The court must also consider the general limitation whether the discovery is unnecessary or unreasonably duplicative or cumulative and whether the burden or expense of the proposed extension outweighs its likely benefit. *Id.*

251. *See* FED. R. CIV. P. 26(b)(2)(B). This provision, in effect, creates a so-called "two tiered system" that distinguishes between "accessible" and "not reasonably accessible" information. Under this provision, a party need not provide discovery of electronically stored information, even though relevant and otherwise discoverable, if the party identifies the "sources" of information "as not reasonably accessible due to undue burden or cost." The Advisory Committee Note gives several examples of such data, including back-up tapes intended for disaster recovery, legacy data from obsolete systems unintelligible on successor systems, and "deleted" data in fragmented form requiring a modern version of forensics to restore and retrieve. *See id.* advisory committee's note to the 2006 amendment.

252. It has also attracted widespread commentary. *See, e.g.*, Daniel B. Garrie et al., *Electronic Discovery and the Challenge Posed by the Sarbanes-Oxley Act*, 2005 UCLA J. L. & TECH. 2; Ronald J. Hedges, *A View from the Bench and the Trenches: A Critical Appraisal of Some of the Proposed Federal Rules of Civil Procedure*, 227 F.R.D. 123 (2005); Kindall C. James, Comment, *Electronic Discovery: Substantially Increasing the Risk of Inadvertent Disclosure and the Costs of Privilege Review—Do the Proposed Amendments to the Federal Rules Help?* 52 LOY. L. REV. 839 (2006); Jason Krause, *E-Discovery Gets Real*, 93 A.B.A. J. 44 (Feb. 2007); Henry S. Noyes, *Is E-Discovery So Different that It Requires New Discovery Rules? An Analysis of Proposed Amendments to the Federal Rules of Civil Procedure*, 71 TENN. L. REV. 585 (2004); Sarah A. L. Phillips, Comment, *Discoverability of Electronic Data Under the Proposed Federal Rules of Civil Procedure: How Effective Are Proposed Protections for "Not Reasonably Accessible" Data*, 83 N.C. L. REV. 984 (2005); Jessica Lynn Repa, Comment, *Adjudicating Beyond the Scope of Ordinary Business: Why the Inaccessibility Test in* Zubulake *Unduly Stifles Cost-Shifting During Electronic Discovery*, 54 AM. U. L. REV. 257 (2004); Bahar Shariati, Note, Zubulake v. UBS Warburg*: Evidence that the Federal Rules of Civil Procedure Provide the Means for Determining Cost Allocation in Electronic Discovery Disputes*? 49 VILL. L. REV. 393 (2004); Howard L. Speight & Lisa C. Kelly, *Electronic Discovery: Not Your Father's Discovery*, 37 ST. MARY'S L.J. 119 (2005).

253. *See* Zubulake v. UBS Warburg, LLC, 229 F.R.D. 422 (S.D.N.Y. 2004); Zubulake v. UBS Warburg, LLC, 220 F.R.D. 212 (S.D.N.Y. 2003); Zubulake v. UBS Warburg, LLC, 217 F.R.D. 309 (S.D.N.Y. 2003); Zubulake v. UBS Warburg, LLC, 216 F.R.D. 280 (S.D.N.Y. 2003).

law gender discrimination laws, coupled with retaliation claims. During discovery, a dispute arose concerning the former employee's request for production of e-mails that apparently only existed on UBS's "back-up" tapes. Those tapes had not been searched by UBS because UBS maintained that such a search would have been prohibitively costly (approximately $300,000). The former employee moved for an order compelling production of "archived" e-mails.[254]

In ruling on the motion, U.S. District Court Judge Scheindlin held that the employee was entitled to discovery of relevant e-mails that had been deleted and resided only on backup disks and that consideration of cost-shifting of discovery costs was proper. In doing so, the court developed a "three-step" analysis. First, the court must determine whether the data is an "accessible" medium. If the information is regarded as being "accessible," then the normal rules of discovery apply, which means that the responding party would generally bear the entire cost of production. Second, if the court finds that the data is not readily "accessible," the court should conduct a factual inquiry based on a small sample of the requested material. Third, based on the results of the sample, the court then should apply a "factor" test to determine whether a shift in the costs should be ordered.[255]

* * * * *

If the opposing party moves to compel discovery, Rule 26(2)(B), as added by the 2006 amendments, requires that the *responding* party "show that the information is not reasonably accessible because of undue delay or cost."[256] Even if this showing is made, the court may still order discovery, after considering the limitations of Rule 26(b)(2)(C) if the *requesting* party "shows good cause."[257] The court "may specify conditions for the discovery"[258] and, as stated in the Advisory Committee Note, in addition to limits on the amount and type of information to be produced, an order shifting all or part of the cost to the requesting party may be a possible condition.[259]

---

254. Zubulake v. UBS Warburg, LLC, 217 F.R.D. 309, 311-14 (S.D.N.Y. 2003).

255. *See id.* at 324. Those factors included (weighted in more or less the following order) (1) "[t]he extent to which the request is specifically tailored to discover relevant information"; (2) "[t]he availability of such information from other sources"; (3) "[t]he total cost of production, compared to the amount in controversy"; (4) "[t]he total coast of production, compared to the resources available to each party"; (5) "[t]he relative ability of each party to control costs and its incentive to do so"; (6) "[t]he importance of the issues at stake in the litigation"; and (7) "[t]he relative benefits to the parties of obtaining the information." *Id.* at 322.

256. FED. R. CIV. P. 26(b)(2)(B).

257. Rule 26(b)(2)(B) does not define what constitutes "good cause," leaving the issue to be decided on a case-by-case, fact-sensitive basis. The Advisory Committee noted several factors in determining "good cause":

> (1) the specificity of the discovery request; (2) the quantity of information available from other and more easily accessible sources; (3) the failure to produce relevant information that seems likely to have existed but is no longer available on more easily accessible sources; (4) the likelihood of finding relevant, responsive information that cannot be obtained from other, more easily accessible sources; (5) predictions as to the importance and usefulness of the further information; (6) the importance of the issues at stake in the litigation; and (7) the parties' resources.

FED. R. CIV. P. 26(b)(2)(B) advisory committee's note to the 2006 amendment. The factors for determining "good cause" noted by the Advisory Committee reflect factors similar to Judge Scheindlin's "seven-factor" cost-shifting test in *Zubulake* described in the preceding footnote Accordingly, pre-rule cases such as *Zubulake* discussed in *Illustration 9-9*, above, appear to remain relevant because they provide well-reasoned discussion of the propriety of "e-discovery" in terms of accessibility and cost allocation.

258. *See* FED. R. CIV. P. 26(b)(2)(B).

259. *See id.* advisory committee note to the 2006 amendment.

In addition, the 2006 amendments add a provision in Rule 45 containing identical procedures to Rule 26(b)(2)(B). The Rule 45 provisions are applicable when the discovery of electronically stored information is sought from a non-party through the service of a subpoena.[260]

5. Certification of Disclosures, Discovery Requests, Responses, and Objections

In 1983, subdivision (g) was added to Federal Rule 26. This subdivision imposed an affirmative duty to engage in pretrial discovery in a responsible manner.[261] The 1993 amendment extended the provisions of Rule 26(g) to apply to disclosures.[262] Rule 26(g) requires that all disclosures, requests for discovery, responses to discovery requests, and objections to discovery be signed by at least one attorney of record representing a party, or by the party when the party is not represented by an attorney.[263]

Rule 26(g) provides that the signature of an attorney or unrepresented party constitutes a certificate that the signer has read a discovery request, response, or objection, and that to the best of the signer's knowledge, information, and belief formed after a reasonable inquiry, it is: (1) consistent with the rules and warranted by existing law or a good faith argument for the extending, modifying, or reversing existing law; (2) not interposed for any improper purpose, such as to harass, delay, or needlessly increase the cost of litigation; and (3) neither unreasonably nor unduly burdensome or expensive, given the needs of the case, prior discovery in the case, the amount in controversy, and the importance of the issues at stake in the litigation.[264]

The signature on a disclosure "constitutes a certification that to the best of the signer's knowledge, information and belief, formed after a reasonable inquiry, the disclosure is complete and correct as of the time it is made."[265] An unsigned disclosure, request, response, or objection must be stricken unless it is promptly signed after the failure to sign is called to the attention of the party or attorney who is obligated to sign. Moreover, a party is not obligated to make any response to an unsigned discovery request, response, or objection.[266]

If the certification violates Rule 26(g) "without substantial justification," Federal Rule 26(g) requires the court to impose a sanction for the violation on the certifying person, or upon a party represented by an attorney who signed in violation of the rule, or both. The court may act after motion or on its own initiative

---

260. *See* FED. R. CIV. P. 45(d)(1)(D).
261. FED. R. CIV. P. 26(g) advisory committee's note to the 1983 amendment.
262. *Id.*
263. FED. R. CIV. P. 26(g)(1).
264. FED. R. CIV. P. 26(g)(2)(B)(i)-(iii); *cf.* FED. R. CIV. P. 11; Chapter 6(F) *supra* ("Good Faith Pleading").
265. FED. R. CIV. P. 26(g)(1).
266. FED. R. CIV. P. 26(g)(2).

in imposing the sanction.[267] However, the motion must include a certification that the moving party has in good faith conferred or attempted to confer with the person or party failing to make the disclosure or discovery.[268]

SECTION E. ORAL DEPOSITIONS

1. Commencing the Oral Deposition Process

(a) Notice of the Examination

A party commences the oral deposition process by giving "reasonable notice in writing to every other party to the action."[269] After the 1993 amendments, an oral deposition may be taken without leave of court after the parties have conferred to prepare a discovery plan.[270] However, leave of court to take a deposition must be obtained under certain limited circumstances, such as when the deponent is in prison.[271] The notice of the deposition must state "the time and place of the deposition and, if known, the deponent's name and address."[272] If the name is unknown, the notice must provide "a general description sufficient to identify the person or the particular class or group to which the person belongs."[273] The notice also must describe any documents or things the deponent will be required to produce at the deposition pursuant to a subpoena duces tecum.[274] If the "person" to be deposed is a corporation, partnership, association, governmental agency, or other organization, a party may simply name the organization and "describe with reasonable particularity the matters on which examination is requested."[275] Federal Rule 30(b)(6) then requires the named organization to "designate one or more officers, directors, or managing agents, or . . . other persons who consent to testify on its behalf . . . matters known or reasonably available to the organization."[276]

---

267. FED. R. CIV. P. 26(g)(3), 37(a). The sanction may include an order to pay the amount of the reasonable expenses incurred because of the violation, including a reasonable attorney's fee. *Id. See generally* Joel Slawotsky, *Rule 37 Discovery Sanctions—The Need for Supreme Court Ordered National Uniformity*, 104 DICK. L. REV. 471 (2000) (providing an overview and analysis of how the federal courts have invoked discovery sanctions and urging the Supreme Court to articulate objective criteria for sanction imposition so as to achieve national uniformity).

268. FED. R. CIV. P. 37(a)(3) & (4).

269. FED. R. CIV. P. 30(b)(1). Prior to the 1993 amendments, Federal Rule 30(a) provided that after commencement of an action, "any party may take the testimony of any person, including a party, by deposition upon oral examination." FED. R. CIV. P. 30(a) (prior to the 1993 amendments).

270. FED. R. CIV. P. 26(d)(2).

271. *See* FED. R. CIV. P. 30(a)(2). Leave of court is required if a party seeks to take a deposition before the parties have had their discovery planning conference. An exception is made when a party seeking to take a deposition certifies, with supporting facts, that the person to be examined is expected to leave the United States and will be unavailable for examination in this country unless that person is deposed before leaving. *See* FED. R. CIV. P. 30(a)(2)(A)(iii).

272. FED. R. CIV. P. 30(b)(1).

273. *Id.*

274. FED. R. CIV. P. 30(b)(2).

275. FED. R. CIV. P. 30(b)(6).

276. *Id.* This provision allows the organization to designate the particular matters on which each person will testify. *Id.* If it appears during the taking of the deposition that the person designated is unable to testify on the matters specified, the organization is under an immediate duty to designate a new person who will be able to provide that testimony. *See, e.g.*, Marker v. Union Fidelity Life Ins. Co., 125 F.R.D. 121, 126 (M.D.N.C. 1989). *See generally* Marlin M. Volz, *Depositions of Organizations: The Designation Procedure Under the Federal Rules*, 33 S.D. L. REV. 236 (1988).

Under the 1993 amendments, the party taking the deposition must also state the method by which the testimony will be recorded—sound, audiovisual, or stenographic means.[277] The party taking the deposition bears the cost of the selected method of recording. Any party may arrange for a transcription from the recording of a deposition not taken by stenographic means.[278] Furthermore, with prior notice to the deponent and other parties, any party may arrange for an additional method to record the deponent's testimony. That party bears the expense of making this additional record or transcript.[279]

(b) Subpoena to Compel Attendance

If the person to be deposed is a party, all that is necessary to take that party's deposition is the receipt of written notice of the taking of the deposition under Rule 30(b)(1).[280] When nonparties are involved, Rule 30(a)(1) specifically authorizes the use of a subpoena to compel attendance of witnesses at depositions.[281] Under the 1991 amendments to Rule 45(a), a subpoena for attendance at a deposition must issue from the district court for the district designated in the notice of deposition as the district where the deposition is to be taken.[282] The clerk in the district designated by the deposition notice issues a

---

277. FED. R. CIV. P. 30(b)(3)(A) (unless the court orders otherwise); *see* Riley v. Murdock, 156 F.R.D. 130 (E.D.N.C. 1994) (concluding that a video deposition "is a superior method of conveying to the fact finder the full message of the witness in a manner that assists the fact finder in assessing credibility"). *See generally* Henry H. Perritt, Jr., *Changing Litigation with Science and Technology: Video Depositions, Transcripts and Trials*, 43 EMORY L.J. 1071 (1994). Prior to the 1993 amendment, the parties could stipulate in writing or the court could order that the testimony at the deposition may be recorded by other means, such as a videotape. In such a case, the stipulation or order had to detail the "provisions to assure that the recorded testimony will be accurate and trustworthy." FED. R. CIV. P. 30(b)(4) (prior to the 1993 amendment); *see* John A. Glenn, Annotation, *Recording of Testimony at Deposition by Other Than Stenographic Means Under Rule 30(b)(4) of Federal Rules of Civil Procedure*, 16 A.L.R. FED. 969 (1973). These provisions included naming the person before whom the testimony would be taken and prescribing the manner of recording, preserving, and filing the deposition. If a party wanted a stenographic transcription of the testimony, that party could have one made at that party's own expense. FED. R. CIV. P. 30(b)(4) (prior to the 1993 amendment). The parties could also take a deposition by telephone if stipulated in writing or by court order upon motion. For purposes of service of the subpoena under former Rule 45(d) and other provisions of the Federal Rules of Civil Procedure, a deposition taken by telephone was taken in the district and at the place where the deponent was to answer the questions. *See* FED. R. CIV. P. 30(b)(7) (prior to the 1993 amendment).

278. FED. R. CIV. P. 30(b)(3)(B).

279. *Id.* (unless the court orders otherwise).

280. *See, e.g.*, Collins v. Wayland, 139 F.2d 677 (9th Cir. 1944); *see also* FED. R. CIV. P. 37(d) (providing sanctions for the failure of a party to appear for taking of that party's deposition after notice alone); Jeffrey S. Kinsler, *The Proper Location of Party-Depositions Under the Federal Rules of Civil Procedure*, 23 MEM. ST. U. L. REV. 763 (1993).

281. FED. R. CIV. P. 30(a)(1); *see also* Yousuf v. Samantar, 451 F.3d 248 (D.C. Cir. 2006) (United States is a "person" within the meaning of Rule 45 for purposes of a subpoena duces tecum issued in a case to which it is not a party). If a corporation or other organization is named in the subpoena and the designation procedure of Federal Rule 30(b)(6) is to be used, the subpoena must "advise a nonparty organization of its duty to make such a designation." FED. R. CIV. P. 30(b)(6). One advantage of using the notice of the taking of the deposition rather than a subpoena is that the party desiring to take the deposition probably has greater leeway in designating the place for taking it. Because a subpoena is not used, the restrictions set forth in Rule 45 do not apply. Nor is personal service required. It is sufficient to serve the notice on the party's attorney unless service on the party has been ordered previously. *See* FED. R. CIV. P. 5(a), (b). *See generally* M. Minnette Massey, *Depositions of Corporations: Problems and Solutions*, 1986 ARIZ. ST. L.J. 81.

282. FED. R. CIV. P. 45(a)(2). The 1991 amendments to Federal Rule 45 are discussed extensively in David D. Siegel, *Federal Subpoena Practice Under New Rule 45 of the Federal Rules of Civil Procedure*, 139 F.R.D. 197 (1992).

subpoena for attendance at a deposition.[283] As an officer of the court, an attorney "may also issue and sign a subpoena on behalf of (A) a court in which the attorney is authorized to practice; or (B) a court for a district in which a deposition or production is taken or production is to be made, if the attorney is authorized to practice in the court where the action is pending."[284]

After the subpoena has been issued, it must be served on the nonparty who will be deposed. Anyone (other than a party) who is at least 18 years old may serve the subpoena.[285] Rule 45(b)(1) provides that a subpoena shall be served by (1) delivering a copy of the subpoena to the person named (personal service) and (2) by tendering to that person the fees for one day's attendance and the mileage allowed by law.[286] Contrary to the procedure in many states, the witness and mileage fees must be tendered for the service to be valid.[287]

The subpoena may be served anywhere within the district of the court by which it was issued. It may also be served outside the district, provided service takes place within 100 miles of the place of the deposition specified in the subpoena. In addition, service may occur at any place within the state if authorized by a state statute or rule applicable to the state courts of general jurisdiction.[288]

---

283. FED. R. CIV. P. 45(a)(3). The clerk issues a signed, blank subpoena to the party requesting it. The party then must complete it before service. *Id.*

284. FED. R. CIV. P. 45(a)(3)(A) & (B); *see* Hay Group, Inc. v. E.B.S. Acquisition Corp., 360 F.3d 404 (3d Cir. 2004) (Rule 45 provides that subpoenas commanding attendance of a person issued separately from subpoenas for production or inspection must be issued by district court for district in which production or inspection is made; the rule does not prohibit issuance of subpoena duces tecum to non-party in arbitration proceeding for documentary evidence located outside the territory within which subpoena could be served on non-party; the rule applies only to subpoena duces tecum issued separate from subpoena commanding attendance, which could not be issued in arbitration proceeding, and term "production" in Rule 45 refers to delivery of documents and not their retrieval).

285. FED. R. CIV. P. 45(b)(1). When necessary, proof of service of the notice may be made by filing with the clerk "a copy of the notice" and "a statement of the date and manner of service and of the names of the persons served, certified by the person who made service." FED. R. CIV. P. 45(b)(3).

286. *See* FED. R. CIV. P. 45(b)(1). When the subpoena is issued on behalf of the United States or one of its agencies or officers, however, the fees and mileage do not need to be tendered. *Id.* With regard to "delivery" of the subpoena, *compare* Smith v. Midland Brake, Inc., 162 F.R.D. 683 (D. Kan. 1995) (service of a subpoena may not be accomplished by mail), Spencer Sav. Bank, SLA v. Excell Mortgage Co., C.A. No. 91-4909 (JCL), 1996 U.S. Dist. LEXIS 21125 (D.N.J. Feb. 15, 1996) (magistrate's authorization of Federal Express for service of a non-party subpoena held invalid where no signatures or receipts obtained from targets of subpoenas), *and* Agran v. City of New York, No. 95 Civ. 2170(JFK), 1997 WL 107452, 1997 U.S. Dist. LEXIS (S.D.N.Y. Mar. 10, 1997) (service by mail improper) *with* Doe v. Hersemann, 155 F.R.D. 630 (N.D. Ind. 1994) (service of a subpoena for a deposition can be accomplished by certified mail), King v. Crown Plastering Corp., 170 F.R.D. 355 (E.D.N.Y. 1997) (in-hand service not necessary; subpoenas served at place of residence and by mail), *and* Windsor v. Martindale, 175 F.R.D. 665 (D. Colo. 1997) (service by mail improper when attempted by plaintiff, but proper when by certified mail by United States Marshals); *see also* Khachikian v. BASF Corp., No. 91-CV-573, 1994 WL 86702, 1994 U.S. Dist. LEXIS 2881 (N.D.N.Y. Mar. 4, 1994) (delivery to attorney invalid); *cf.* Abbott v. Kidder, Peabody & Co., 1997 WL 337228, 1997 U.S. Dist. LEXIS 8500 (N.D. Ill. June 16, 1997) (process servers made repeated, but unsuccessful efforts to serve witness; service was finally made as witness was driving out of her driveway; she saw process servers, yelled "[g]o away," and honked her horn, but they placed subpoena and witness fee under her windshield wiper arm; service held proper; Rule 45 does not require in-hand service, but only service that "reasonably" insures actual receipt of the subpoena by the witness").

287. Under 28 U.S.C. § 1821, the witness fee is $40 per day; the mileage fee is based on the deponent's travel to the place of attendance and return to the deponent's residence. Mileage computations are calculated at the official rate for government employees and are based upon a uniform table of distances adopted by the Attorney General. These tables are available in the U.S. Marshals' offices.

288. FED. R. CIV. P. 45(b)(2).

Furthermore, if a federal statute authorizes such service, the court may, upon proper application, authorize service at any other place.[289]

Illustration 9-10. *P*, a citizen of State *X*, sues *D*, a citizen of State *Y*, for $100,000 in a U.S. District Court for the District of State *Y*. *P* wants to take the deposition of *W*, a citizen and resident of State *Z*, which is 500 miles from State *Y*. *P's* attorney is authorized to practice in the district court in State *Y*, but not in State *Z*. *P's* attorney issues a subpoena for *W* from the U.S. District Court for State *Z* (a single district state). The subpoena is properly served on *W* at *W's* home in State *Z*. It commands *W* to attend a deposition proceeding at a specific time and place in *W's* home town in State *Z*, and the proper witness and mileage fees were tendered to *W*. The subpoena is valid under Rule 45.[290] *P's* attorney was authorized to issue the subpoena because it pertained to an action pending in a court (the State *Y* district court) in which the attorney was authorized to practice. The subpoena was properly issued from the district court in State *Z*, where the deposition is to be taken. The subpoena was served on *W* within the district where the deposition is to be taken. Finally, the subpoena commands *W* to attend the deposition at a place within 100 miles of where *W* resides.

* * * * *

Both the notice to take the deposition and the subpoena must designate where the deposition will be held. On timely motion, the court by which the subpoena was issued may quash or modify the subpoena if it "requires the deponent who is not a party or officer of a party to travel to a place more than 100 miles from the place where that person resides, is employed, or regularly transacts business in person."[291]

Rule 45(a) permits a command to produce evidence or to permit inspection to be joined with a command to appear at a deposition.[292] Thus, in addition to commanding a person to attend and give testimony, a subpoena may command a person to produce and permit inspection and copying of designated documents, electronically stored information, or tangible things in that person's possession, custody, or of that person.[293] If a subpoena duces tecum is to be served, the designation of the materials to be produced must be attached to or included in the

---

289. *Id.*; *see also* Dynegy Midstream Servs., LP v. Trammochem, 451 F.3d 89 (2d Cir. 2006) (Rule 45 governs geographical area in which discovery subpoena may be served; because federal law did not authorize nationwide service of process in this case, court had no personal jurisdiction to enforce subpoena on defendant). A subpoena that is directed to a witness in a foreign country who is a national or resident of the United States is governed by 28 U.S.C. § 1783. *See also* section L *infra* ("Depositions in Foreign Countries").

290. For a detailed discussion of the complexities produced by the interaction of Rule 45(a)(2), (b)(2), and (c)(3)(A)(ii), see David D. Siegel, *Federal Subpoena Practice Under the New Rule 45 of the Federal Rules of Civil Procedure*, 139 F.R.D. 197 (1992). For example, on the facts of this illustration, suppose *W* moves to quash the subpoena on the ground that, while it was served on *W* within the district and designates *W's* hometown as the place where the deposition will be taken, *W* "regularly transacts business" at a place in State *Z* that is 200 miles from *W's* home town. *W* argues that Rule 45(c)(3)(A)(ii) requires the court to quash a subpoena whenever it requires a nonparty to travel to a place that is more than 100 miles from where the nonparty "resides, is employed *or* regularly transacts business in person." The alternative phrasing, *W* argues, means that a subpoena may not command attendance more than 100 miles from *any* of the listed locations. This interpretation is wrong, but it is nevertheless, supported by the language of the rule. *See id.* at 213.

291. FED. R. CIV. P. 45(c)(3)(A)(ii).

292. FED. R. CIV. P. 45(a)(1).

293. Fed. R. Civ. P. 45(a)(1)(A)(iii).

notice to other parties.[294] The subpoena may specify the form or forms in which electronically stored information is to be produced.[295]The subpoena may also require that person to permit inspection of premises.[296]

A command to produce evidence or to permit inspection may also be issued separately.[297] If it is issued separately, a subpoena for production or inspection is issued from the court for the district in which the production or inspection is to be made.[298] However, a person commanded to make separate production does not need to appear in person.[299]

(c) Duty to Avoid Imposing an Undue Burden and the Procedure for Objecting to the Subpoena

A party or an attorney who is responsible for issuing and serving a subpoena is required "to take reasonable steps to avoid imposing undue burden or expense on the person subject to the subpoena."[300] This protection is backed by the issuing court's authority to impose "an appropriate sanction," including lost earnings and a reasonable attorney's fees.[301] A person served with a subpoena compelling attendance at a deposition, production, or inspection may wish to object on a number of grounds.

Illustration 9-11. Examples of objections include the following: (1) the subpoena fails to allow a reasonable time for compliance;[302] (2) the subpoena was served by a party or a person under the age of eighteen;[303] (3) the fees were not tendered properly;[304] (4) the subpoena was left at the dwelling of the witness rather than personally served;[305] (5) service was made in a location not permitted by Rule 45;[306] (6) the place designated for the taking of the deposition is in a location not

---

294. FED. R. CIV. P. 30(b)(2).

295. FED. R. CIV. P. 45(1)(C).

296. FED. R. CIV. P. 45(a)(1)(A)(iii).

297. FED. R. CIV. P. 45(a)(1)(C).

298. FED. R. CIV. P. 45(a)(2). The subpoena for separate production and inspection may be issued by an attorney on behalf of a court in which the attorney is authorized to practice or a court for a district in which the production is compelled by the subpoena, if the production pertains to an action pending in a court in which the attorney is authorized to practice. FED. R. CIV. P. 45(a)(3).

299. FED. R. CIV. P. 45(c)(2)(A).

300. FED. R. CIV. P. 45(c)(1); *see* Goodyear Tire & Rubber Co. v. Kirk's Tire & Auto Servicenter, Inc., 211 F.R.D. 658 (D. Kan. 2003) (whether a subpoena imposes an undue burden on a witness is a case specific inquiry that turns on such factors as relevance, the need of the party for the documents, the breadth of the document request, the time period covered by it, the particularity with which the documents are described, and the burden imposed).

301. FED. R. CIV. P. 45(c)(1).

302. FED. R. CIV. P. 45(c)(3)(A)(i).

303. FED. R. CIV. P. 45(b)(1).

304. FED. R. CIV. P. 45(b)(1); *see* Klay v. All Defendants, 425 F.3d 977 (11th Cir. 2005) (Rule 45(c)(3)(B) requires that a license fee be paid to a party who has been compelled by subpoena to produce confidential data; under this requirement, the measure of compensation is the loss to the owner caused by the production of the material, not the gain to the party seeking the information; under this standard, because the AMA suffered no loss in the value of its property from compliance with the subpoena, the district court did not abuse its discretion in requiring the payment to the AMA of its production costs, but not the license fee for the data); Statutory Comm. of Unsecured Creditors v. Motorola, Inc., 218 F.R.D. 325 (D.D.C. 2003) (Rule 45(c)(3)(B)(ii) protects disclosure pursuant to a subpoena of an unretained expert's opinion or information resulting from the expert's study made not at the request of any party; the rule applies to prior expert opinions or pre-existing scholarship).

305. *See* FED. R. CIV. P. 45(b)(1).

306. *See* FED. R. CIV. P. 45(b)(2).

permitted by Rule 45;[307] (7) the person served is not an agent of the corporate deponent; (8) the time or place of the deposition is inconvenient or burdensome;[308] (9) the person does not have possession or control of the subpoenaed documents; and (10) the production of the subpoenaed documents may be too burdensome.[309]

* * * * *

A person who is commanded to produce and permit inspection and copying may serve a written objection on the party or attorney designated in the subpoena. This objection must be made before the earlier of either 14 days after the subpoena was served or the time specified for compliance.[310] If the objection relates to a claim of privilege or protected trial-preparation materials, the objecting party must expressly state that objection. To enable the demanding party to contest the claim, the objection must describe the nature of the documents, communications, or things for which protection is sought.[311] Failure to object expressly or to provide adequate information risks waiving the privilege. When such an objection is made, an order from the court issuing the subpoena must be obtained before such inspection or copying can occur. Upon notice to the person commanded to produce, the party serving the subpoena can move at any time for an order to compel production. If the court compels production, the court must protect any nonparty or officer of a party from significant expense resulting from the inspection and copying.[312] In addition, the 2006 Amendments add a provision in Rule 45 containing identical procedures to Rule 26(b)(2)(B). The Rule 45 provisions are applicable when the discovery of electronically stored information is sought from a non-party through the service of a subpoena.[313]

(d) Failure of a Nonparty to Obey a Subpoena or of a Party to Attend a Deposition After Proper Notice

Federal Rule 45(e) provides that the failure to obey a subpoena "without adequate excuse" may be a contempt of the court from which the subpoena was issued.[314] Rule 45(e) specifically provides that an adequate excuse for failure to obey exists when a person is served with a subpoena purporting to compel

---

307. *See* FED. R. CIV. P. 45(c)(3)(A)(ii).

308. *See* FED. R. CIV. P. 45(c)(3)(A)(iv).

309. *Id.*

310. FED. R. CIV. P. 45(c)(2)(B); *see* Concord Boat Corp. v. Brunswick Corp., 169 F.R.D. 44 (S.D.N.Y. 1996) (failure to object in writing within the time limits in Rule 45(c)(2)(B) normally results in waiver, but failure can be excused in unusual circumstances and for good cause).

311. FED. R. CIV. P. 45(d)(2). When a party objects to a subpoena on grounds of privilege, the party does not need to make the objection within the time limits specified in Rule 45(c)(2)(B); instead, Rule 45(d)(2) controls and allows a party claiming privilege to raise the objection at the time compliance with the subpoena is called for. *See* Tuite v. Henry, 98 F.3d 1411 (D.C. Cir. 1996).

312. FED. R. CIV. P. 45(c)(2)(B). The 1991 amendment to Rule 45 imposed a requirement on nonparties to produce the documents in the manner that are kept in the usual course of business. Otherwise, they must be organized and labeled corresponding with the categories in the subpoena. FED. R. CIV. P. 45(d)(1). This requirement parallels a similar duty imposed on parties. *See* section H(2) *infra* ("Responding to Production Requests").

313. *See* FED. R. CIV. P. 45(d)(1)(D).

314. FED. R. CIV. P. 45(e).

attendance or production at an improper location.[315] Other examples of "adequate excuse" may include the inability to comply because the deponent did not have the subpoenaed documents or was too ill to attend the deposition.[316]

Federal Rule 37(d) provides that if "a party or a party's officer, director, or managing agent—or a person designated under Rule 30(b)(6) [which requires a corporation or other organization to make such a designation to testify on behalf of a party] fails . . . to appear before the officer," the court may impose various sanctions for that failure.[317] These sanctions range from an order to pay reasonable expenses to an order striking out that party's pleadings.[318] Thus, parties may not remain completely silent even when they regard a notice to take the deposition as improper or objectionable.[319] The failure to act may not be "excused on the ground that the discovery sought was objectionable unless the party . . . has a pending motion for a protective order under Rule 26(c)."[320]

2. Taking the Deposition

(a) The Officer in Charge

Unless the parties have otherwise agreed, Federal Rule 30(b)(5) provides that a deposition must be conducted before an officer appointed or designated under Rule 28.[321] Federal Rule 28(a) designates the persons before whom depositions may be taken within the United States (*i.e.*, before an officer authorized to administer oaths by the federal law or the law of the place where the examination is held).[322] In addition, Rule 28(a) permits a deposition to be taken before a person appointed

---

315. *Id.* Otherwise, "adequate excuse" is undefined. FED. R. CIV. P. 45(e) advisory committee's note to the 1991 amendment. However, citing Walker v. City of Birmingham, 388 U.S. 307, 87 S. Ct. 1824, 18 L. Ed. 2d 1210 (1967), the Advisory Committee points out that a nonparty may "be guilty of contempt for refusing to obey a subpoena even though the subpoena manifestly overreaches the appropriate limits of the subpoena power." FED. R. CIV. P. 45(e) advisory committee's note to the 1991 amendment; *see* Chapter 6(G)(6)*(b) supra* ("Contempt"). At least when a nonparty has failed to obey the subpoena because it commanded attendance at an improper location, this should no longer be true. Rule 45(e) now explicitly provides for disobedience without fear of contempt when the subpoena commands attendance in violation of Rule 45(c)(3)(A), and the Advisory Committee's note seems to confirm that contempt is no longer permissible in this circumstance. *See* FED. R. CIV. P. 45(e) advisory committee's note to the 1991 amendment. More generally, it is arguable that the text of Rule 45(e) abolishes the *Walker* rule in any case in which an "adequate excuse" is found to exist. The *Walker* rule is discussed in Chapter 6(G)(6)*(b) supra* ("Contempt").

316. *See* 9A CHARLES A. WRIGHT & ARTHUR R. MILLER, FEDERAL PRACTICE AND PROCEDURE: CIVIL § 2465, at 532-34 (3d ed. 2008). Some authorities suggest that when service of a subpoena has been improper, the subpoena may be ignored. Under this view, the defense of want of jurisdiction may be raised at the subsequent contempt proceeding. *See, e.g.*, SHEPARD'S MANUAL OF FEDERAL PRACTICE § 7.09, at 506 (2d ed. 1979). On the other hand, Professors Wright and Miller suggest that the "better view is that [a] witness should not be permitted to disregard a subpoena that [the witness] has not challenged by a motion to quash." 9A CHARLES A. WRIGHT & ARTHUR R. MILLER, FEDERAL PRACTICE AND PROCEDURE: CIVIL § 2465, at 534-35 (3d ed. 2008).

317. FED. R. CIV. P. 37(d)(1).

318. *See* FED. R. CIV. P. 37(b), (d)(3).

319. FED. R. CIV. P. 37(d) advisory committee's note to 1970 amendment.

320. FED. R. CIV. P. 37(d)(2). Prior to the 1993 amendment establishing this rule, Rule 37(d) stated that "[t]he failure to act . . . may not be excused on the ground that the discovery is objectionable unless the party . . . has *applied* for a protective order." The 1993 amendment clarified that it is the *pendency* of the motion that may be urged as an excuse. "If the party's motion has been denied, the party cannot argue that [the party's] subsequent failure to comply would be justified." *Id.* advisory committee's note to the 1993 amendment to Rule 37(d).

321. FED. R. CIV. P. 30(b)(4).

322. FED. R. CIV. P. 28(a)(1)(A); *see also* section L *infra* ("Depositions in Foreign Countries").

by the court in which the action is pending.[323] Such an appointment would be necessary when the deposition is to be taken at an isolated place where there may be no one readily available to administer oaths and take testimony.[324] Federal Rule 29 also permits the parties to stipulate that depositions may be taken before any person, at any time or place, on any notice, and in any manner, unless otherwise directed by the court.[325]

(b) Beginning the Deposition

Pursuant to the 1993 amendments, the officer before whom the deposition is taken must begin by stating for the record: (1) the officer's name and business address; (2) the date, time, and place of the deposition; and (3) the deponent's name. The officer then administers the oath or affirmation and identifies all persons who are present.[326] The parties then proceed to examine and cross-examine the deponent.[327] The officer giving the oath or someone acting under the officer's direction records the testimony.[328] Rule 30(b)(5) specifically cautions that "[t]he deponent's and attorneys' appearance or demeanor of deponents must not be distorted through recording techniques."[329]

(c) Producing Documents and Things

Pursuant to Federal Rule 30(f)(2), documents and things produced during the deposition "must, on a party's request, be marked for identification and attached to the deposition," and they may be inspected or copied by any party.[330] Rule 30(f)(2) also provides, however, that a person producing materials at a deposition may instead "offer copies to be marked, attached to the deposition, and then used as originals—after giving all parties a fair opportunity to verify the copies by comparing them with the originals."[331] The person producing these items can also offer the originals to be marked for identification, after giving to each party an opportunity to inspect and copy them, in which event the materials may then be used in the same manner as if annexed to the deposition.[332] Rule 30(f)(2) permits

---

323. FED. R. CIV. P. 28(a)(1)(B).

324. 8A CHARLES A. WRIGHT ET AL., FEDERAL PROCEDURE AND PRACTICE: CIVIL § 2082, at 409-10 (3d ed. 2010).

325. FED. R. CIV. P. 29(a).

326. FED. R. CIV. P. 30(b)(5)(A). If the deposition is recorded by nonstenographic means, the officer must state these items at the beginning of each unit of recorded tape or other recording medium. FED. R. CIV. P. 30(b)(5)(B). Federal Rule 30(c) provides a party with the option not to participate in an oral examination, but instead to serve written questions in a sealed envelope on the party taking the deposition, who is required to transmit them to the officer before whom the testimony will be taken. At the deposition, the officer will ask the questions of the deponents. *See* FED. R. CIV. P. 30(c)(3).

327. *See* FED. R. CIV. P. 30(c)(1). If a deponent refuses to be sworn or to answer a question after being ordered to do so, the court in which the deposition is being taken may hold the deponent in contempt. FED. R. CIV. P. 37(b)(1).

328. *See* FED. R. CIV. P. 30(c)(1).

329. FED. R. CIV. P. 30(b)(5).

330. FED. R. CIV. P. 30(f)(2)(A).

331. *Id.*

332. *Id.*

any party to move for an order requiring that the original be annexed to the deposition, pending final disposition of the case.[333]

(d) Depositions Being Conducted in Bad Faith or in a Harassing Manner

If a deposition "is being conducted in bad faith or in a manner that unreasonably annoys, embarrasses, or oppresses the deponent or party," Federal Rule 30(d)(3) provides that a party or the deponent, at any time during the deposition, may seek court protection.[334] The court in which the action is pending or the court in the district where the deposition is being taken may order the officer conducting the examination to cease taking it. Alternatively, it may enter a protective order pursuant to Rule 26(c) limiting the scope or manner of the subsequent continuation of the deposition.[335]

(e) Rules of Evidence and Objections During the Examination

The examination and cross-examination of witnesses proceed as permitted at trial under the Federal Rules of Evidence. However, under the 1993 amendments, Rules 103 (dealing with offers of proof and timely objections) and 615 (exclusion of witnesses) do not apply.[336] During the course of the examination, objections may be made on a variety of grounds. The 1993 amendment to Rule 30 requires that any objection to evidence during a deposition "be stated concisely and in a non-argumentative and nonsuggestive manner."[337] This amendment reflects the Advisory Committee's concern that some "[d]epositions have been unduly prolonged, if not unfairly frustrated, by lengthy objections and colloquy, often suggesting how the deponent should respond."[338]

Illustration 9-12. For instance, a party may object because the matter may be privileged information outside the scope of discovery permitted by Rule 26(b); the form of the question may be objectionable (*e.g.*, the question is "leading"); the information is inadmissible (*e.g.*, hearsay); or the witness is incompetent or unqualified (*e.g.*, the witness is mentally incompetent or the witness is not an expert).

* * * * *

---

333. FED. R. CIV. P. 30(f)(2)(B).

334. FED. R. CIV. P. 30(d)(3)(A).

335. FED. R. CIV. P. 30(d)(3)(A) & (B); *see also* FED. R. CIV. P. 26(c); W.J. Dunn, Annotation, *Construction and Effect of Rules 30(b), (d), 31(d) of Federal Rules of Civil Procedure, and Similar State Statutes and Rules, Relating to Preventing, Limiting, or Terminating the Taking of Depositions*, 70 A.L.R.2D 685 (1960) (corresponding rules prior to the 1970 amendments).

336. FED. R. CIV. P. 30(c)(1). The exception in Rule 615 was designed to deal with the question whether other potential deponents could attend a deposition. According to the Advisory Committee, "[t]he revision provides that other witnesses are not automatically excluded from a deposition simply by the request of a party" invoking Rule 615. *Id.* advisory committee's note to the 1993 amendment to Rule 30(c). A court, however, can order exclusion under Rule 26(c)(5) as well as prevent the excluded witness from reading or otherwise being informed about the testimony given in the deposition. The revision applies only to potential deponents and does not attempt to deal with attendance by members of the public, the press, or other persons. *Id.*

337. FED. R. CIV. P. 30(c)(2).

338. *Id.* advisory committee's note to the 1993 amendment to Rule 30(c).

What happens when an objection is made? The answer depends on the nature of the objection. Previously, if the objection was that the matter asked is outside the scope of discovery, the objecting attorney would state the basis for the objection and direct the deponent not to answer the question. However, a 1993 amendment provides that an attorney may so instruct a deponent only to (1) preserve a privilege, (2) enforce a limitation on evidence directed by the court, or (3) present a motion seeking protection from a deposition being conducted in bad faith or in an unreasonably annoying, embarrassing, or oppressive manner.[339]

When an attorney directs a deponent not to answer, counsel asking the question should be sure that the record indicates that the deponent refused to answer. Often, however, this formal refusal to answer is unnecessary. Counsel frequently stipulate that if an attorney directs a witness not to answer a question, it will be deemed that the officer has directed the witness to answer, but the witness still refuses to answer.[340] When the deponent refuses to answer, the discovering party must seek an order compelling an answer.[341] If the application is for an order to a party, the party seeking the answer should apply to the court where the action is pending. If the application is for an order to a nonparty, the party seeking the answer should apply to the court in the district where the deposition is being taken.[342] In this way, the parties can obtain a judicial determination of the matter. The party seeking the answer has the option of completing or adjourning the examination before that party moves for such an order.[343] The party applying for the order must provide reasonable notice to other parties and all persons affected by the motion.[344] The court may award expenses pursuant to Federal Rule 37(a)(5)(A).[345] Ordinarily, a party should note other objections—for example, competency or hearsay—on the record and the deponent should answer the question.[346] If a party offers the deposition in evidence at the trial, the court will then rule on the objections.

(f) Effect of Failure to Object During the Examination

What happens if a party fails to object to the manner in which the deposition is taken or to the questions asked? The Federal Rules of Civil Procedure

---

339. FED. R. CIV. P. 30(c)(2); *cf.* Boyd v. University of Md. Med. Sys., 173 F.R.D. 143 (D. Md. 1997) (an attorney may not instruct a witness not to answer a question during a deposition unless to assert a privilege, but must deal with objectionable lines of questions either by seeking a protective order prior to the deposition or discontinuing the deposition and seeking such an order).

340. Guy O. Kornblum, *The Oral Civil Deposition: Preparation and Examination of Witnesses*, 17 PRAC. LAW., May, 1971, at 11, 15, 25-26.

341. *See* FED. R. CIV. P. 37(a).

342. FED. R. CIV. P. 37(a)(2) (as amended in 1993).

343. FED. R. CIV. P. 37(a)(3)(C).

344. FED. R. CIV. P. 37(a)(1).

345. Federal Rule 37(a)(5)(A) provides that if a motion to compel discovery is granted or the requested discovery is provided after the motion was filed, the court must require the party or deponent whose conduct necessitated the motion or the party's attorney advising the conduct to pay the reasonable expenses of the movant in making the motion, including reasonable attorney's fees. An opportunity to be heard must be given if it is shown that the motion was filed without the movant first making a good faith effort to obtain the discovery without court action, or that the deponent's refusal to answer was substantially justified, or that other circumstances make the award unjust. *See* FED. R. CIV. P. 37(a)(5)(A).

346. *See* FED. R. CIV. P. 30(c).

provide several answers, depending on the nature of the objection. The basic rule is that errors and irregularities occurring at the oral examination in "the manner of taking the deposition, the form of the question or answer, the oath or affirmation, or a party's conduct, or matters that might have been corrected at that time" are waived" if they are "not timely made during the deposition."[347] On the other hand, a party does not waive objections to competence, relevance, or materiality by not making them before or during the deposition, unless the ground of the objection might have been corrected at that time.[348]

In order to avoid the risk of waiver of objections, the parties frequently stipulate at the outset of the deposition that "all objections to questions propounded to the witness shall be reserved by each of the parties, save and except any objection to the form of the question."[349] However, this stipulation is both unnecessary and fraught with peril. While "form" of questions and answers are examples of objections which might be "corrected at the time" they do not comprise the entire class of such objections. Foundational objections also may corrected, especially if they relate to expert testimony.[350] More importantly, Rule 1101 of the Federal Rules of Evidence provides that "[t]he rule with respect to privileges applies at all stages of all actions, cases, and proceedings."[351] Unless a witness being deposed not only objects to questions calling for privileged information, but also refuses to answer short of a court order, the privilege will be deemed waived.[352] By stipulating that all objections except to form shall be reserved, the person being deposed may falsely assume that foundational and privilege objections may be asserted at trial. Rather than stipulating that the parties reserve all objections other than form, the parties should simply acknowledge that the deposition is being taken pursuant to the rules of civil procedure.

3. Review by the Witness, Changes, Signing, Certification, and Filing

If the deponent or a party wants the deponent to review the deposition prior to filing, the 1993 amendments require the deponent or the party to request the review before the deposition is completed. In response to that request, the deponent has 30 days to review the transcript or recording after being notified by the officer that it is available.[353] This change reflects an attempt by the Advisory Committee

---

347. FED. R. CIV. P. 32(d)(3)(B).

348. FED. R. CIV. P. 32(d)(3)(A).

349. Guy O. Kornblum, *The Oral Civil Deposition: Preparation and Examination of Witnesses*, 17 PRAC. LAW., May 1971, at 11, 15. The Advisory Committee likewise anticipates that the objections made during the depositions "should ordinarily be limited to those that under Rule 32(d)(3) might be waived if not made at that time." FED. R. CIV. P. 30(d)(1) advisory committee's note to the 1993 amendment.

350. *See* FED. R. EVID. 705.

351. FED. R. EVID. 1101(c).

352. *See, e.g.*, Daniels v. Hadley Mem. Hosp., 68 F.R.D. 583, 587 (D.D.C. 1975); Rosenfeld v. Ungar, 25 F.R.D. 340, 342 (S.D. Iowa 1960); Perrignon v. Bergen Brunswig Corp., 77 F.R.D. 455, 460-61 (N.D. Cal. 1978).

353. FED. R. CIV. P. 30(e)(1); *see* Innovative Mktg. & Tech., L.L.C. v. Norm Thompson Outfitters, Inc., 171 F.R.D. 203 (W.D. Tex. 1997) (interpreting Rule 30(e) to allow a deponent to make changes that clarify answers, correct misstatements, or correct responses that were incorrect because the deponent did not understand the question).

to reduce the problems sometimes encountered when depositions are recorded stenographically. Reporters often had difficulties obtaining signatures and return of the depositions from deponents.[354] If there are changes, the deponent is to sign a statement reciting any changes in form or substance.[355] The officer must then certify that the witness was sworn properly and that the deposition is a true record of the testimony given.[356] The certificate must also indicate whether any review was requested. If so, the changes that are made should be appended.[357]

Unless the court orders otherwise, the officer then seals the transcript securely in an envelope or package indorsed with the title of the action and marked "Deposition of ______."[358] The officer then promptly sends it to the attorney who arranged for the transcript or recording. The 2000 amendments to Rules 5(d) and 30(f) now prohibit the filing of depositions until they are used in the proceeding or the court orders filing.[359] The officer must also furnish copies of the transcript or other recording of the deposition to any party or the deponent upon payment of a reasonable fee.[360] After the deposition has been filed, prompt notice of its filing must be given to all other parties.[361]

Federal Rule 32(d)(4) provides that a party waives errors and irregularities in the manner in which the testimony is transcribed or the deposition is prepared, signed, certified, sealed, indorsed, filed, or otherwise dealt with by the officer if those errors or irregularities are not promptly raised after they become known or with reasonable diligence, could have been known.[362] The means for raising these defects is a motion to suppress the deposition.[363]

SECTION F. DEPOSITIONS UPON WRITTEN QUESTIONS

Another way in which a party may take a deposition is through the exchange of written questions. Prior to the 1993 amendments, any time after the commencement of an action, a party desiring to take such a deposition of any person, including a party, could serve a set of written questions upon every other

---

354. FED. R. CIV. P. 30(e) advisory committee's notes to the 1993 amendment.

355. FED. R. CIV. P. 30(e)(1). Prior to the 1993 amendment, if one of the parties requested that the deposition be transcribed, the deposition was submitted to the witness for examination. The witness or witnesses then read the transcript. The officer was then to note any changes in form or substance upon the deposition along with the reasons given by the witness for such changes. The witness and the parties could agree to waive this review. After the deposition had been reviewed, the witness signed the deposition, "unless the parties by stipulation waive the signing or the witness is ill or cannot be found or refuses to sign." *Id.* (prior to the 1993 amendment). If the deposition was not signed within 30 days of its submission to the witness, the officer signed it, stating for the record "the fact of the waiver or of the illness or absence of the witness or the fact of the refusal to sign together with the reason, if any, given therefor." *Id.*

356. FED. R. CIV. P. 30(f)(1). This certification must be in writing and must accompany the record of the deposition. *Id.*

357. FED. R. CIV. P. 30(e)(2).

358. FED. R. CIV. P. 30(f)(1).

359. *See* FED. R. CIV. P. 5(d)(1) & 30(f)(1).

360. FED. R. CIV. P. 30(f)(3).

361. FED. R. CIV. P. 30(f)(4).

362. FED. R. CIV. P. 32(d)(4).

363. *Id.*

party to the action along with a notice of the deposition.[364] After the 1993 amendments, a party may take a deposition upon written questions after the parties have met to prepare a discovery plan, subject to the presumptive limit of ten depositions per side.[365]

Like an oral deposition, the notice of a deposition upon written questions may use a general description to identify the proposed deponent of a corporation, partnership, association, or governmental agency pursuant to the provisions of Federal Rule 30(b)(6).[366] The 1993 amendments have shortened the total time for developing questions for cross-examination, redirect, and recross from 50 days to 28 days.[367] Within 14 days after the questions and notice have been served, a party may serve cross questions on all other parties. Within 7 days after the cross questions have been served, a party may serve redirect questions on all other parties. In turn, a party may serve recross questions within 7 days after being served with redirect questions.[368]

The person to be deposed may be compelled to attend the deposition by means of a subpoena.[369] After all questions have been exchanged, the party taking the deposition delivers a copy of the notice and copies of all questions to the officer designated in the notice. The officer then takes the testimony of the witness pursuant to the procedure for oral depositions prescribed by Federal Rule 30(c), (e), and (f) (oath, submission to witnesses, signing, certification, and filing).[370] After the deposition has been filed, notice of the filing must be given to all other parties.[371]

The same waiver rules described for oral depositions apply to errors and irregularities in the notice of the taking of the deposition, the qualifications of the officer, and the completion and return of the deposition upon written questions.[372] Objections to the form of the written questions submitted are waived unless such an objection is served in writing upon the party propounding them within the time allowed for serving the next succeeding cross or other questions and within 7 days after service of the last questions authorized.[373] Like oral depositions, objections to the competency of a witness or to the competency, relevance, or materiality of testimony are not waived by failure to make them before the taking of the deposition, unless the ground of the objection is one which might have been corrected if presented at that time.[374]

---

364. FED. R. CIV. P. 31(a) (prior to the 1993 amendment).

365. FED. R. CIV. P. 26(b)(2) & 31(a).

366. *See* FED. R. CIV. P. 30(b)(6), 31(4).

367. FED. R. CIV. P. 31(a)(5).

368. *Id.*

369. FED. R. CIV. P. 45(a)(1). Leave of court must be obtained to depose a person confined in prison or a person who has already been deposed in the action. FED. R. CIV. P. 31(a)(2)(B).

370. FED. R. CIV. P. 31(b); *see* section E(3) *supra* ("Review by the Witness, Changes, Signing, Certification, and Filing").

371. FED. R. CIV. P. 31(c). Note that the 2000 amendment to Rule 5(d)(1) prohibits the filing of depositions until they are used in the proceeding or the court orders filing. *See* FED. R. CIV. P. 5(d) & advisory committee's note to the 2000 amendment.

372. FED. R. CIV. P. 32(d)(1), (2), (4).

373. FED. R. CIV. P. 32(d)(3)(C).

374. FED. R. CIV. P. 32(d)(3)(A).

In practice, depositions upon written questions are rarely used.[375] The principal advantage of depositions upon written questions is that they usually cost less than oral depositions because counsel's attendance at them is unnecessary. The savings will be even greater when the deponent resides at a substantial distance.[376] Their principal disadvantage stems from their lack of flexibility: all direct, cross, redirect, and recross questions must be prepared before any of the deponent's answers are given.[377] Their effectiveness may also be hindered by the deponent's advance knowledge of the questions in certain instances.[378]

SECTION G. INTERROGATORIES TO PARTIES

1. Serving Interrogatories

Subject to the numerical limitations adopted by the 1993 amendments, Federal Rule 33 provides that any party may serve written interrogatories upon any other party.[379] Unlike depositions, which may be taken of any person, interrogatories cannot be served on nonparties.[380] Compared to depositions, interrogatories are simpler discovery devices. Interrogatories are merely questions directed to another party and thus do not involve complicated details that accompany arrangements for depositions, such as setting the time and place for the examination, obtaining a court reporter, ordering a transcription of the testimony, etc. As a result, interrogatories are ordinarily much less expensive than depositions.[381]

Interrogatories can be very useful for acquiring basic information and simple facts. Furthermore, with respect to corporate entities, interrogatories allow a party "to search the composite knowledge" of the corporate party because Federal Rule 33 requires it to answer on the basis of information "available" to it.[382] Thus, the person answering the interrogatories cannot avoid answering them by claiming

---

375. An early study found that depositions upon written questions were used in only two percent of the cases surveyed. In contrast, oral depositions were used in forty-nine percent of the cases. *See* WILLIAM A. GLASER, PRETRIAL DISCOVERY AND THE ADVERSARY SYSTEM 53 (1968).

376. *See* John R. Schmertz, Jr., *Written Depositions Under Federal and State Rules as Cost-Effective Discovery at Home and Abroad*, 16 VILL. L. REV. 7, 36, 42-43 (1970).

377. *See* 8A CHARLES A. WRIGHT ET AL., FEDERAL PRACTICE AND PROCEDURE: CIVIL § 2132, at 618-19 (3d ed. 2010). The authors suggest, however, that a deposition by telephone or other remote means might be a preferable alternative. *See id.* at 619; FED. R. CIV. P. 30(b)(4).

378. *See, e.g.*, Hamdi & Ibrahim Mango Co. v. Fire Ass'n, 20 F.R.D. 181 (S.D.N.Y. 1957) (deposition upon written questions need not be suppressed merely because counsel reviewed the questions with the deponent and supplied the deponent with a copy of them before the deposition took place).

379. FED. R. CIV. P. 33(a). Prior to the 1993 amendments, interrogatories could be served upon the plaintiff after the commencement of the action without leave of court. They could be served on any other party with or after service of the summons and complaint on that party. *Id.* (prior to the 1993 amendment); *see* section D(4) *supra* ("Limits on Discovery").

380. See FED. R. CIV. P. 33(a). *But see* Reed Dairy Farm v. Consumers Power Co., 227 Mich. App. 614, 576 N.W.2d 709 (1998) (provision in Michigan Civil Rules that was the equivalent of pre-1993 Rule 26(b)(4)(A)(iii), allowing the court, upon motion, to order further discovery "by other means," permitted interrogatories to nonparty experts under compelling circumstances); *cf.* FED. R. CIV. P. 26(b)(4)(B).

381. *See* 8B CHARLES A. WRIGHT ET AL., FEDERAL PRACTICE AND PROCEDURE: CIVIL § 2163, at 6-7 (3d ed. 2010).

382. *See* Donald P. Lay, *Plaintiff's Practical Use of Discovery Techniques*, 9 PRAC. LAW., Dec. 1963, at 43, 48; Iain D. Johnston & Robert G. Johnston, *Contention Interrogatories in Federal Court*, 148 F.R.D. 441 (1993).

ignorance when the information can be obtained from sources under the person's control, including employees or files.[383] On the other hand, interrogatories are not well suited to obtaining spontaneous statements because often the opposing attorney drafts the answers only after careful reflection.[384]

2. Answering Interrogatories

(a) Time for Response

The party served has 30 days after service of the interrogatories to serve a response, including objections.[385] The court may extend or shorten the time for response.[386] The parties may also agree in writing to a different time without leave of court, unless the agreement interferes with any time set for completion of discovery, for hearing of a motion, or for trial.[387] Note that the 2000 amendment to Rule 5(d) prohibits the filing of interrogatories and responses to them until they are used in the proceeding or the court orders filing.[388]

(b) Who Must Answer

Interrogatories are to be answered by the party served or, if the party is a public or private corporation or a partnership or association or governmental agency, by any officer or agent, who shall furnish such information available to the party.[389] When interrogatories are addressed to a corporate entity, the corporation is entitled to choose the officer or agent who will answer them.[390] Each interrogatory is to be answered separately and fully in writing under oath, and be signed by the person providing the answers.[391]

(c) Option to Produce Business Records

In some instances, the answer to an interrogatory may be determined by examining, auditing, compiling, abstracting, or summarizing a party's business

---

383. *See* 8B CHARLES A. WRIGHT ET AL., FEDERAL PRACTICE AND PROCEDURE: CIVIL § 2172, at 55, n.7 (3d ed. 2010) (citing cases).

384. *Id.* § 2163, at 7.

385. FED. R. CIV. P. 33(b)(2). Prior to the 1993 amendment, Rule 33 provided that a defendant could serve the answers or objections within 45 days after service of the summons and complaint. FED. R. CIV. P. 30(b) (prior to the 1993 amendment). The text of Rule 33 does not specifically address how outstanding interrogatories are to be handled upon removal from state to federal court. The Advisory Committee, however, indicates that the time to answer outstanding interrogatories should be measured from the date of the parties' discovery planning conference required by Rule 26(f). Furthermore, if the number of outstanding interrogatories exceeds the twenty-five permitted by Rule 33, the interrogating party has three alternatives: (1) the interrogating party can seek leave to allow the additional interrogatories; (2) the interrogating party can simply specify which twenty-five to be answered; or (3) the interrogating party can resubmit interrogatories that comply with the limits set by Rule 33. FED. R. CIV. P. 33(a) advisory committee's note to the 1993 amendment.

386. FED. R. CIV. P. 33(b)(2).

387. *Id.*; FED. R. CIV. P. 29(b).

388. *See* FED. R. CIV. P. 5(d)(1).

389. FED. R. CIV. P. 33(b)(1).

390. 8B CHARLES A. WRIGHT ET AL., FEDERAL PRACTICE AND PROCEDURE: CIVIL § 2172, at 57-58 (3d ed. 2010); *cf.* FED. R. CIV. P. 31 (deposition upon written questions must be answered by the person deposed).

391. FED. R. CIV. P. 33(a)(3) & (5).

records, including electronically stored information. In such a situation, Federal Rule 33(d) provides a responding party with an option to make the business records available to the party seeking the information instead of answering an interrogatory—provided that "the burden of deriving or ascertaining the answer will be substantially the same for either party."[392] If a party wants to produce business records for examination, the party should specify the records from which the answer may be derived or ascertained. Such a specification must be "in sufficient detail to enable the interrogating party to locate and identify them as readily as the responding party could."[393]

(d) Objections

A party may base proper objections on a variety of grounds. First, the interrogatory may seek information outside the scope of discovery, as defined by Rule 26(b). Second, the interrogatory may place an undue burden on the answering party. This burden may be a financial one arising from the cost of preparing the answers, or it may be in the form of inconvenience to the answering party. Third, the interrogatory may seek unnecessary or repetitious information. For instance, the information may have been covered by prior interrogatories (or, presumably after 1993, prior disclosures). Fourth, the interrogatory may be so broad that an effective response is impossible. Fifth, the interrogatory may constitute improper harassment. Sixth, the interrogatory may call for legal conclusions or matters of "pure" law.

With respect to the latter objection, Federal Rule 33(a)(2) states that "[a]n interrogatory is not objectionable merely because it asks for an opinion or contention that relates to fact or the application of law to fact . . . ."[394] This provision, adopted as part of the 1970 amendments, resolved a conflict among the courts about whether interrogatories may elicit opinions, contentions, and legal conclusions. The Advisory Committee explained:

> Rule 33 is amended to provide that an interrogatory is not objectionable merely because it calls for an opinion or contention that relates to fact or the application of law to fact. Efforts to draw sharp lines between facts and opinions have invariably been unsuccessful, and the clear trend of the cases is to permit "factual"

---

392. FED. R. CIV. P. 33(d). Rule 33 adopted this procedure from California practice as a means of relieving the answering party of a burdensome or expensive research into a party's own business records. *See* FED. R. CIV. P. 33(c) advisory committee's note to 1970 amendment to Rule 33(c) (as Federal Rule 33(d) was formerly designated). The 2006 "e-discovery" amendments make clear that "electronically stored information" are included within the term "business records" for purposes of Rule 33. *See* FED. R. CIV. P. 33(d) (2006 amendment).

393. FED. R. CIV. P. 33(d)(1); *cf.* J. Kraut, Annotation, *Propriety of Answer to Interrogatory Merely Referring to Other Documents or Sources of Information*, 96 A.L.R.2D 598 (1964). This provision was added in 1980 to prevent the answering party from directing the interrogating party to a mass of business records without specifying by category and location where the answer may be found. FED. R. CIV. P. 33(c) advisory committee's note to the 1980 amendment (as Federal Rule 33(d) was formerly designated).

394. FED. R. CIV. P. 33(a)(2) (formerly 33(b) and then later Rule 33(c)). Some interrogatories seek basic information and facts, such as the names of witnesses or the existence, location, and contents of documents. In contrast, "contention" interrogatories request an opposing party to (a) state what it contends; (b) state whether it makes a specified contention; (c) state all the facts upon which it bases a contention; (d) take a position, and explain or defend that position, with respect to how the law applies to facts; or (e) state the legal or theoretical basis for a contention. *See* B. Braun Med. Inc. v. Abbott Labs., 155 F.R.D. 525, 527 (E.D. Pa. 1994).

> opinions. As to requests for opinions or contentions that call for the application of law to fact, they can be most useful in narrowing and sharpening the issues, which is a major purpose of discovery. . . . [U]nder the new language interrogatories may not extend to issues of "pure law," *i.e.*, legal issues unrelated to the facts of the case.[395]

Before 1993, if a party objected to an interrogatory, Rule 33 provided that "the reasons for objection shall be stated in lieu of an answer."[396] The 1993 amendments changed this provision to require a specific statement of "*all* grounds for an objection."[397] The 2007 restyling amendments changed "all" back to "the," but the previous meaning should still prevail.[398] Furthermore, "[a]ny ground not stated in a timely objection is waived, unless the court, for good cause, excuses the failure."[399]

Illustration 9-13. Assume that *P* sends *D* an interrogatory requesting information concerning *D's* general pattern of consuming alcoholic beverages. *D* thinks that this interrogatory is intended solely to harass or embarrass *D*. *D* refuses to answer the interrogatory, but fails to state any reason for this objection. *D's* response is improper. Rule 33(b)(4) requires a specific statement of the grounds and "unstated . . . grounds for objection ordinarily are waived."[400]

Illustration 9-14. Assume, on the facts of *Illustration 9-13*, that *D* did object to the interrogatory and stated harassment as the reason. *D* has waived other grounds for objection, such as irrelevancy. In order to belatedly raise irrelevancy or other grounds as additional reasons for objection, *D* would have to convince the

---

395. FED. R. CIV. P. 33(b) advisory committee's note to 1970 amendment; *see* Ronald G. Baker, Comment, *Civil Procedure—Opinion Interrogatories After the 1970 Amendment to Federal Rule 33(b)*, 53 N.C. L. REV. 695 (1975). Because of notice pleadings, contention interrogatories are considered to be useful in helping an opposing party prepare for trial. With the presumptive limits on interrogatories in federal court, it is unlikely that contention interrogatories will be the source of a major abuse of the discovery process. Courts often defer answers to contention interrogatories until the end of the discovery period. *See, e.g.*, B. Braun Med. Inc. v. Abbott Labs., 155 F.R.D. 525, 527 (E.D. Pa. 1994). As the Advisory Committee stated,

> Since interrogatories involving mixed questions of law and fact may create disputes between the parties which are best resolved after much or all of the other discovery has been completed, the court is expressly authorized to defer an answer. Likewise, the court may delay determination until the pretrial conference, if it believes that the dispute is best resolved in the presence of the judge.

See FED. R. CIV. P. 33 advisory committee note to the 1970 amendment. This approach allows a party to complete the discovery process before a party has to finalize its position. Forcing a party to answer at an early point may later prejudice it. *Cf.* McCarthy v. Paine Webber Group, Inc., 168 F.R.D. 448 (D. Conn. 1996) (motion to compel answers to contention interrogatories denied as premature because of burden it would impose on plaintiffs while discovery is ongoing). However, sometimes, a court will not postpone the answers when they "serve to clarify the issues and narrow the scope of the dispute." *See* B. Braun Med. Inc. v. Abbott Labs., 155 F.R.D. 525, 528 (E.D. Pa. 1994) (refusing to defer the answers to the contention interrogatories dealing with "prior art" because the defendants were apparently familiar with the technology involved and thus should have been prepared to answer; the answers would help define exactly how the invention differed, or did not differ, from the prior art for the purpose of determining whether the plaintiff's combination produced a new or different patentable function; prior art was also directly relevant to defendants' "obviousness" defense, which would defeat the patentability of the plaintiff's product if it could be shown that the invention was "obvious" in light of the prior art).

396. FED. R. CIV. P. 33(a) (before 1993).

397. FED. R. CIV. P. 33(b)(4) (emphasis added) (prior to being restyled).

398. FED. R. CIV. P. 33(b)(4) & advisory committee's note to the 2007 amendments ("changes are intended to be stylistic only").

399. FED. R. CIV. P. 33(b)(4). Rule 26(g) also requires that a responding party indicate when information is being withheld under a claim of privilege or as trial-preparation materials. *See* section B(1) *supra* ("Privilege") & B(2) *supra* ("Attorney 'Work Product' and Trial-Preparation Materials").

400. FED. R. CIV. P. 33(b)(4) & advisory committee's note to the 1993 amendment.

court that good cause existed to excuse *D's* failure to raise these reasons in a timely manner.

* * * * *

The 1993 amendments require the responding party to "answer to the extent the interrogatory is not objectionable."[401] This change emphasizes the duty to provide full answers to the extent possible.[402] The attorney making the objections must sign them.[403]

Illustration 9-15. Assume that *P* sues *D* in federal court for violation of the federal antitrust laws. *D* manufactures aluminum siding. *P* sends *D* the following two interrogatories: (1) "State the name of all products manufactured from aluminum sheet"; and (2) "State the names of all manufacturers of aluminum sheet products in the United States, the locations of each manufacturer's facility, and the product or products produced at each of those facilities." Assume that these interrogatories are objectionable because of the overbreadth of the request. According to the Advisory Committee, if "an interrogatory seeking information concerning a lesser number of facilities or products would not have been objectionable, the interrogatory should be answered with respect to the latter, even if an objection is raised as to the balance of the facilities or products."[404] For example, if interrogatories referring only to aluminum siding and aluminum siding manufacturers would have been proper, *D* should answer as to them. Furthermore, even if *D* will need more time to answer some aspects of the questions, *D* must respond to those aspects of the questions that can be answered within the prescribed time.[405]

(e) Compelling an Answer

When a party has objected to an interrogatory or has otherwise failed to answer satisfactorily, the party submitting the interrogatory must apply for a court order to compel an answer.[406] However, before making the motion to compel a response, the 1993 amendments to the Federal Rules require the moving party to make a good faith attempt to confer and resolve the matter without court intervention.[407] Sanctions for an improper objection can be imposed.[408] Similarly, if the responding party has exercised the option to allow inspection of business records instead of answering, but the interrogating party believes that the burden on the requesting party to find the answers from the records is substantially greater than the party making the records available, the interrogating party may move for an order compelling a further answer under Rule 37(a).[409] If the court does not find the

---

401. FED. R. CIV. P. 33(b)(3).
402. FED. R. CIV. P. 33 advisory committee's note to the 1993 amendment to Rule 33(b)(1).
403. FED. R. CIV. P. 33(b)(5).
404. FED. R. CIV. P. 33 advisory committee's note to the 1993 amendment to Rule 33(b)(1).
405. *See id.*
406. *See* FED. R. CIV. P. 37(a).
407. *See* FED. R. CIV. P. 37(a)(1), (a)(2)(B) & 37(d).
408. *See* FED. R. CIV. P. 37(a)(5).
409. *See* 8B CHARLES A. WRIGHT ET AL., FEDERAL PRACTICE AND PROCEDURE: CIVIL § 2182, at 110 (3d ed. 2010).

burden to be substantially the same, the court still may refuse to order an unduly expensive or burdensome answer.[410]

(f) Correcting or Supplementing Responses

The 1993 amendments to Rule 26(e) require a party to correct or supplement in a timely manner a prior response to an interrogatory when the responding "party learns that in some material respect the . . . response is incomplete or incorrect."[411] Such a correction or supplementation is served as an amendment to the response.[412] However, an amendment is unnecessary if the additional or corrective information has otherwise been made known to the other parties during the discovery process or in writing.[413] In addition, under the 2000 amendments, a party must supplement its disclosures when the party determines that a witness or document may be used if the party previously had thought that the witness or document would not be used.[414]

SECTION H. PRODUCTION OF DOCUMENTS, ENTRIES ON LAND, TESTING, AND SAMPLING

1. Serving Production Requests on Parties

During litigation, a party frequently will want to inspect and copy various written documents, charts, photographs, drawings, graphs, records, or other data or data compilations in the control of another party. Similarly, a party may want to inspect, copy, test, or sample other tangible things in another party's control.[415] Subject to the limitations adopted by the 1993 amendments,[416] Federal Rule 34 allows a party to serve a request for production identifying and describing each item or category of items desired with reasonable particularity.[417] Similarly, as amended

---

410. *Id.* § 2178, at 100. In such a case, the court may require the interrogating party to reimburse the answering party for the expense of assembling the records and making them intelligible. *Id.*; *see also* 8A *id.* § 2038, at 184-85.

411. FED. R. CIV. P. 26(e)(2).

412. *See id.*

413. *Id.* For a discussion of the pre-1993 duties to supplement a response to an interrogatory, see William R. Slomanson, *Supplementation of Discovery Responses in Federal Civil Procedure*, 17 SAN DIEGO L. REV. 233 (1980).

414. *See* FED. R. CIV. P. 26(a)(1) advisory committee's note to the 2000 amendment.

415. *See* FED. R. CIV. P. 34(a).

416. *See* section D(4) *supra* ("Limits on Discovery").

417. FED. R. CIV. P. 34(a) & (b). Prior to the 1970 amendment of Federal Rule 34, a party was required to seek a court order for the production of documents and things for the purpose of inspection, copying, or photocopying. In making such a request, the party was required to show "good cause." The good cause requirement was eliminated in part because the 1970 amendments made special provision for the production of trial-preparation materials. Protective orders under Federal Rule 26(c) and the objection process provided by revised Federal Rule 34 were thought sufficient to handle claims of privacy, secrecy, undue burden, or undue expense. *See* FED. R. CIV. P. 34 advisory committee's note to the 1970 amendment.

in 1991, Rule 45 allows such evidence to be subpoenaed from a nonparty in conjunction with or independent of a deposition.[418]

In addition, a party may want to enter upon land or other property in the possession or control of another party to inspect, survey, photograph, test, or sample the property or a designated operation or object on the property.[419] The request must specify a reasonable time, place, and manner for the inspection or the performance of related acts, such as testing.[420] As amended in 1991, Rule 45 permits the issuance of a subpoena to compel the inspection of premises in the possession of a nonparty.[421]

The 2006 amendments update the provisions of Federal Rule 34(a) to specifically reflect the production of "electronically stored information" and modernize the description of the items that are included (*e.g.*, "sound recordings," "images," and "data").[422] In addition, the requesting party may specify the form or forms in which electronically stored information is to be produced.[423]

2. Responding to Production Requests

(a) Time for Response

The party receiving the request has 30 days after the service of the request to respond. The court may allow a shorter or longer time for response.[424] The parties may also agree in writing to a different time without leave of court.[425] Note that the 2000 amendment to Rule 5(d) prohibits the filing of production requests and responses to them until they are used in the proceeding or the court orders filing.[426]

---

418. FED. R. CIV. P. 45(a)(1)(A) & (D); *see* section E(1)*(b) supra* ("Subpoena to Compel Attendance"); *see generally* Thomas A. Cooper, Comment, *Jurisdictional, Procedural, and Economic Considerations for Non-Party Electronic Discovery*, 59 EMORY L.J. 1339 (2010).

419. FED. R. CIV. P. 34(a)(2). Federal Form 50 illustrates the proper format for a request for production of documents, production of objects, and entry on the property. *See* Federal Form 50 in the Appendix of Forms following the Federal Rules of Civil Procedure; *see also* Annotation, *Propriety of Discovery Order Permitting "Destructive Testing" of Chattel in Civil Case*, 11 A.L.R.4TH 1245 (1982).

420. FED. R. CIV. P. 34(b)(1).

421. FED. R. CIV. P. 45(a)(1); *see generally* Lucia Cucu, *The Requirement for Metadata Production Under* Williams v. Sprint/United Management Co.: *An Unnecessary Burden for Litigants Engaged in Electronic Discovery*, 93 CORNELL L. REV. 221 (2007); Vlad J. Kroll, *Default Production of Electronically Stored Information Under the Federal Rules of Civil Procedure: The Requirements of Rule 34(b)*, 59 HAST. L.J. 221 (2007); Richard L. Marcus, *A Modest Proposal: Recognizing (At Last) That the Federal Rules Do Not Declare That Discovery is Presumptively Public*, 81 CHI. KENT L. REV. 331 (2006); Richard L. Marcus, *E-Discovery & Beyond: Toward a Brave New World or 1984?* 25 REV. LIT. 633 (2006) (reprinted in 236 F.R.D. at 598); Andrew Moerke Mason, Recent Development, *Throwing Out the (Electronic) Trash: True Deletion Would Soothe E-Discovery Woes*, 7 MINN. J. L. SCI. TECH. 777 (2006).

422. *See* FED. R. CIV. P. 34(a).

423. *See* FED. R. CIV. P. 34(b)(1)(C).

424. *See* FED. R. CIV. P. 34(b)(2)(A); *cf.* Wolford v. JoEllen Smith Psychiatric Hosp., 96-2460 (La. 5/20/97) at *3-*4, 693 So. 2d 1164, 1166-67 (1997) (in a personal injury action, if the plaintiff requests production of any surveillance videotapes the defendant has taken of her, the defendant is entitled to depose the plaintiff about her physical injuries and activities during the time pictured in the videotapes before releasing the tapes). Prior to the 1993 amendments, a defendant had 45 days to respond after the service of the summons and complaint. *See* FED. R. CIV. P. 34(b) (prior to the 1993 amendment).

425. However, the agreement cannot interfere with any time set for completing discovery, for hearing of a motion, or for trial. *See* FED. R. CIV. P. 34(b)(2)(A); FED. R. CIV. P. 29.

426. *See* FED. R. CIV. P. 5(d)(1).

(b) Objections

Rule 34(b) provides that the response must state, with respect to each item or category, that inspection and related activities will be permitted as requested or that an objection is made. A party must state a specific reason for the objection. If the objection extends only to part of an item or category, the party must permit inspection of the remaining part.[427]

Illustration 9-16. Reasons for objection might include that the request is outside the scope of discovery authorized by Federal Rule 26(b); the item is not in a party's possession, custody, or control; the documents are not designated adequately; or the inspection may be unduly expensive or oppressive.

* * * * *

A 1980 amendment required that documents be produced as they are kept in the usual course of business or organized and labeled to correspond with the categories in the request. This amendment was designed to prevent parties from combining critical documents with others to obscure the critical documents' significance.[428] This provision also now specifically applies to the production of electronically stored information.[429] Furthermore, if a request does not specify a form for producing electronically stored information, Rule 34(b)(2)(E)(ii) requires a party to "produce it in a form or forms in which it is ordinarily maintained or in a reasonably usable form or forms."[430]

(c) Compelling Production

If a party refuses to produce requested documents or permit entry or testing, the party seeking discovery must seek an order compelling discovery pursuant to Federal Rule 37(a).[431] However, before making the motion to compel inspection, the 1993 amendments require the moving party to make a good faith attempt to confer and resolve the matter without court intervention.[432] The successful party may be entitled to receive payment of reasonable expenses in securing the order or opposing the motion unless the party's position was not "substantially justified" or other circumstances make the award of expenses unjust.[433]

Rule 37(e), originally adopted as Rule 37(f) as part of the 2006 "e-discovery" amendments before restyling, provides a "safe harbor" from sanctions

---

427. FED. R. CIV. P. 34(b). Rule 26(g) also requires that a responding party indicate when information is being withheld under a claim of privilege or as trial-preparation materials. *See* section B(1) *supra* ("Privilege") & B(2) *supra* ("Attorney 'Work Product' and Trial-Preparation Materials"); *see also In re* Ford Motor Co., 345 F.3d 1315 (11th Cir. 2003) (although Rule 34 allows requests to produce data compilations, but the rule does not grant unrestricted access to a party's database compilations; instead, it allows a requesting party to inspect and to copy the product).

428. FED. R. CIV. P. 34(b) advisory committee's note to the 1980 amendment. The 2006 amendments to Rule 34 also now provide that "if a request does not specify the form or forms for producing electronically stored information, [the] responding party must produce the information in a form or forms in which it is ordinarily maintained or in a form or forms that are reasonably useful." *See* FED. R. CIV. P. 34(b) (2006 amendment).

429. FED. R. CIV. P. 34(b)(2)(E)(i).

430. FED. R. CIV. P. 34(b)(2)(E)(ii).

431. FED. R. CIV. P. 37(a).

432. *See* FED. R. CIV. P. 37(a)(1).

433. FED. R. CIV. P. 37(a)(5).

resulting from "good-faith" loss of electronically stored information.[434] Recognizing that routine modification, overwriting, and deletion of information is an essential, and sometimes automatic feature of electronic information systems,[435] this rule provides that "[a]bsent exceptional circumstances, a court may not impose sanctions under these rules against a party for failing to provide electronically stored information lost as a result of the routine, good-faith operation of an electronic information system."[436] This "good-faith" standard is intended to prevent the intentional destruction of information by a party.[437]

(d) Correcting or Supplementing Responses

The 1993 amendments to Rule 26(e) require a party to correct or supplement a prior response to a request for production when the responding "party learns that the response is in some material respect incomplete or incorrect." Supplementation is accomplished by serving an amendment to the response.[438] However, an amendment is unnecessary if the additional or corrective information has otherwise been made known to the other parties during the discovery process or in writing.[439]

SECTION I. COMPULSORY PHYSICAL AND MENTAL EXAMINATIONS

1. Securing Physical or Mental Examinations

A party's physical or mental condition will often be at issue in a lawsuit.

Illustration 9-17. For example, did the defendant have defective eyesight? To what extent was the plaintiff injured as a result of a traffic accident?

* * * * *

One useful way of addressing the questions of physical and mental conditions is to force an individual to submit to an examination by a physician. Federal Rule 35 provides for such examinations in limited circumstances. Federal Rule 35 permits an order for a physical or mental examination of a party or of a person in the "custody" or the "legal control" of a party.[440] This rule requires that the condition examined must be "in controversy," and the party seeking the examination must show "good cause" for the order.[441] The order must specify (1)

---

434. *See* FED. R. CIV. P. 37(e) (adopted as Rule 37(f) in 2006).

435. *See id.* advisory committee's note to the 2006 amendment.

436. *See* FED. R. CIV. P. 37(e).

437. *See id.* advisory committee's note to the 2006 amendment.

438. FED. R. CIV. P. 26(e)(2).

439. *Id.* For a discussion of the pre-1993 duties to supplement a response to an interrogatory, see William R. Slomanson, *Supplementation of Discovery Responses in Federal Civil Procedure*, 17 SAN DIEGO L. REV. 233 (1980).

440. FED. R. CIV. P. 35(a)(1).

441. FED. R. CIV. P. 35(a)(2).

the time, place, manner, conditions, and scope of the examination and (2) the person(s) who will conduct it.[442]

The leading case construing the meaning of the "in controversy" and "good cause" requirements of Rule 35 is *Schlagenhauf v. Holder*.[443] In *Schlagenhauf*, a negligence action based on diversity of citizenship was brought in federal district court. The action sought damages for personal injuries suffered by passengers of a bus when the bus collided with the rear of a tractor-trailer. The named defendants were the owner of the bus, the bus driver (Schlagenhauf), the owner of the tractor, the driver of the tractor, and the owner of the trailer. Each defendant served an answer denying negligence. The bus owner crossclaimed against the owners of the tractor and trailer for damage to the bus. The bus owner alleged that the collision was due solely to their negligence in that the tractor-trailer was driven at an unreasonably low speed, had not remained in its lane, and was not equipped with proper rear lights. The owner of the tractor filed an answer to this crossclaim denying its negligence and asserting "[t]hat the negligence of the driver of the . . . bus proximately caused and contributed to . . . Greyhound's damages." It also alleged as part of its answer that the bus driver was "not mentally or physically capable of driving a bus at the time of the accident."[444]

The owners of the tractor and trailer then petitioned the district court for an order directing the bus driver to submit to both mental and physical examinations by one specialist in each of the following fields: (1) internal medicine, (2) ophthalmology, (3) neurology, and (4) psychiatry. The petition alleged that the mental and physical condition of the bus driver was "in controversy" on the ground that it had been raised by the tractor owner's answer to the bus company's cross-claim. The petitioning parties supported the petition with a brief of legal authorities and an affidavit by the tractor owner's attorney. The affidavit stated that the bus driver had seen red lights ten to fifteen seconds before the accident, that another witness had seen the rear lights of the trailer from a distance of three-quarters to one-half mile, and that the bus driver had been involved in a similar prior accident. While disposition of this petition was pending, the trailer owner filed its answer to the bus company's cross-claim and itself "crossclaimed" against the bus company and the bus driver for damage to its trailer. The answer asserted generally that the bus driver's negligence proximately caused the accident. The cross-claim additionally alleged that the bus company and the bus driver were negligent by permitting the bus to be operated when both the bus company and the bus driver knew that the bus driver's eyes and vision were impaired and deficient. The district court ordered the examinations on the basis of the tractor owner's petition and affidavit. The Court of Appeals denied mandamus.[445]

In vacating the judgment of the Court of Appeals and remanding the case for further consideration, the U.S. Supreme Court pointed out that the requirements of Federal Rule 35

---

442. *Id. See generally* Paula M. Becker, Note, *Court-Ordered Mental and Physical Examinations: A Survey of Federal Rule 35 and Illinois Rule 215*, 11 LOY. U. CHI. L.J. 725 (1980).

443. 379 U.S. 104, 85 S. Ct. 234, 13 L. Ed. 2d 152 (1964).

444. *Id.* at 106-07, 85 S. Ct. at 236-37, 13 L. Ed. 2d at 157.

445. *See id.* at 107-09 & n.3, 85 S. Ct. at 237 & n.3, 13 L. Ed. 2d at 157-58 & n.3.

> are not met by mere conclusionary allegations of the pleadings—nor by mere relevance to the case—but require an *affirmative showing* by the movant that each condition as to which the examination is sought is really and genuinely in controversy and that good cause exits for ordering each particular examination.[446]

According to the Court, the moving party's burden will sometimes be met by the pleadings alone, such as when the plaintiff's own mental or physical injuries are asserted by the plaintiff as the basis for recovery in a negligence action, or when the defendant's own mental or physical condition is asserted by the defendant as a defense to a claim.[447] The Court emphasized, however, that Schlagenhauf had not asserted his mental or physical condition as a defense. Reviewing the allegations in the pleadings and the affidavit, the Court concluded that the proper showing had not been made:

> Nothing in the pleadings or affidavit would afford a basis for a belief that Schlagenhauf was suffering from a mental or neurological illness warranting wide-ranging neurological examinations. Nor is there anything stated justifying the broad internal medicine examination.
>
> The only specific allegation made in support of the four examinations ordered was that the "eyes and vision" of Schlagenhauf were impaired. Considering this in conjunction with the affidavit, we would be hesitant to set aside a visual examination if it had been the only one ordered. However, as the case must be remanded to the District Court because of the other examinations ordered, it would be appropriate for the District Judge to reconsider also this order. . . .[448]

2. The Physician's Report

The party examined or against whom an order is entered is entitled to receive a copy of a detailed written report of the examining physician's findings, diagnoses, and conclusions along with all test results. If the discovering party delivers this report (and any like reports of earlier examinations of the same condition that the discovering party may have), the discovering party becomes entitled, upon request, to receive from the party against whom the order was made copies of reports of any examination, previously or thereafter made, of the same condition.[449] By requesting a copy of the examination or taking the deposition of the examiner, the party examined waives any doctor-patient privilege the party possesses with regard to other physicians who have examined the party for the same

---

446. *Id.* at 118, 85 S. Ct. at 243, 13 L. Ed. 2d at 164. The Court also noted that "[t]he ability of the movant to obtain the desired information by other means is also relevant." *Id.*

447. *Id.* at 119, 85 S. Ct. at 243, 13 L. Ed. 2d at 164.

448. *Id.* at 120-21, 85 S. Ct. at 244, 13 L. Ed. 2d at 165.

449. FED. R. CIV. P. 35(b)(1) (unless in the case of a report of an examination of a nonparty such as a person under a party's legal control, the party shows the inability to obtain it).

condition. The waiver applies in the action in which the examination is sought and in any other action involving the same controversy.[450]

3. Sanctions

The court may impose appropriate sanctions on a party who refuses to submit to an order providing for a physical or mental examination.[451] However, contempt of court is not available as a sanction.[452]

SECTION J. REQUESTS FOR ADMISSION

1. Requesting the Admissions

Subject to the limitations adopted by the 1993 amendments,[453] Federal Rule 36 permits a party to serve on any other party a request to admit (1) the truth of any matter within the scope of Federal Rule 26(b)(1) relating to facts, the application of law to fact, or opinions about either; or (2) the genuineness of any described documents.[454] Copies of the documents must be served with the request unless they have been furnished previously or made available for inspection and copying.[455]

2. Responding to the Request

If no response is made within 30 days, the matter is *admitted*.[456] The court, upon motion, may extend or shorten the time for response.[457] The parties may also agree in writing to a different time without leave of court, unless the agreement would interfere with any time set for completion of discovery, for hearing of a motion, or for trial.[458] If the party served with a request for admission intends to deny the request, Rule 36(a) requires that the denial be specific and provides that

---

450. *See* FED. R. CIV. P. 35(b)(3).

451. *See* FED. R. CIV. P. 37(b)(2).

452. FED. R. CIV. P. 37(b)(2)(B).

453. *See* section D(4) *supra* ("Limits on Discovery"). Specifically, requests for admissions may not be served until the parties have conferred under Rule 26(f) to arrange for automatic disclosure and develop a discovery plan. *See* FED. R. CIV. P. 26(d) & 36(a).

454. FED. R. CIV. P. 36(a)(1); *cf.* Russell G. Donaldson, Annotation, *Permissible Scope, Respecting Nature of Inquiry, of Demand for Admission Under Modern State Civil Rules of Procedure*, 42 A.L.R.4TH 489 (1985). Prior to the 1993 amendments, like interrogatories served under Federal Rule 33, requests for admission may be served upon the plaintiff after the commencement of the action without leave of court; they may be served on any other party with or after service of the summons and complaint on that party.

455. FED. R. CIV. P. 36(a)(2). Each matter should be set forth separately, as required by Rule 36(a)(2). *See* Federal Form 51 in the Appendix of Forms following the Federal Rules of Civil Procedure ("Request for Admission under Rule 36").

456. FED. R. CIV. P. 36(a)(3). Prior to the 1993 amendments, Rule 36(a) provided a defendant had 45 days to respond after the service of the summons and complaint before the matter was admitted. *Id.* (prior to the 1993 amendment).

457. FED. R. CIV. P. 36(a)(3); *see* Annotation, *Extension of Time for Serving Response to Request for Admissions Under Rule 36(a), as Amended, of Federal Rules of Civil Procedure*, 46 A.L.R. FED. 821 (1980).

458. FED. R. CIV. P. 29(b). Rule 5(d) prohibits filing of Rule 36 requests and responses until they are used in the proceeding or the court orders filing. *See* FED. R. CIV. P. 5(d)(1).

the denial must "fairly respond to the substance of the matter."[459] Furthermore, if "good faith requires that a party qualify an answer or deny only a part of the matter, the answer must specify the part admitted and qualify or deny the rest."[460]

What happens if a party cannot truthfully admit or deny the request? Rule 36(a) permits a party to so state, provided that party sets forth "in detail" the reasons. Lack of information and knowledge, however, is an acceptable reason only when the answering party "states that it has made reasonable inquiry and that the information it knows or can readily obtain is insufficient to enable it to admit or deny" the request.[461] The 1970 amendments added this provision to resolve a sharp split of authority concerning the extent to which an answering party had to seek out additional information before the answering party could base an answer on lack of information. The issue was resolved by establishing a duty to make a reasonable inquiry from readily obtainable sources.[462]

In addition to admitting or denying a request specifically or stating that the matter cannot be truthfully admitted or denied, a party may object to a request and thus refuse to answer. If an objection is made, Federal Rule 36(a) requires the party to state the reasons for the objection.[463] Such reasons include irrelevancy, privilege, or that the form of the request is so defective that an answer to it cannot be made.[464] The 1970 amendment to Rule 36(a) clarified that the answering party cannot object on the ground that the request relates to statements or opinions of fact or of the application of law to fact. An objection is still available when admissions of law unrelated to the facts of the case are requested.[465]

What happens when a party objects to a request or states that the party is unable to admit or deny the request? Currently, Federal Rule 36(a) provides that the party seeking the request "may move to determine the sufficiency of an answer or objection."[466] Thus, the party seeking the admissions has the option of seeking court intervention. This same procedure can be used to challenge answers that are not in conformity with the requirements of the rule, such as when a denial is not specific or when the inability to admit or deny the request has not been explained in detail.[467] If the court decides that an objection is unjustified, the court must order that an answer be served. If the court decides that an answer does not comply with the requirements of Federal Rule 36, the court "may order either that the matter is admitted or that an amended answer be served."[468] Instead of these orders, the court

---

459. FED. R. CIV. P. 36(a)(4).

460. *Id.*; *cf.* FED. R. CIV. P. 8(b) (similar requirements for responsive pleading).

461. FED. R. CIV. P. 36(a)(4).

462. *See* FED. R. CIV. P. 36(a) advisory committee note to the 1970 amendment; *see* J.P. Ludington, Annotation, *Party's Duty, Under Federal Rule of Civil Procedure 36(a) and Similar State Statutes and Rules, to Respond to Requests for Admission of Facts Not Within His Personal Knowledge*, 20 A.L.R.3D 756 (1968).

463. FED. R. CIV. P. 36(a)(5).

464. *See* 8B CHARLES A. WRIGHT ET AL., FEDERAL PRACTICE AND PROCEDURE § 2262, at 368-69 (3d ed. 2010).

465. *See* FED. R. CIV. P. 36(a)(1) & advisory committee's note to the 1970 amendment; *cf.* FED. R. CIV. P. 33(a)(2) (similar provision relating to interrogatories).

466. FED. R. CIV. P. 36(a)(6) & advisory committee's note to the 1970 amendment (noting the elimination of the requirement that the objecting party automatically move for a hearing on the objection); *cf.* Annotation, *Formal Sufficiency of Response to Request for Admissions Under State Discovery Rules*, 8 A.L.R.4TH 728 (1981).

467. FED. R. CIV. P. 36(a)(6).

468. *Id.*

may postpone ruling on the motion until a pretrial conference or another time before trial.[469]

Assume that a party denies the genuineness of a document or the truth of any matter as requested under Federal Rule 36 and that the requesting party proves the genuineness of the document or the truth of the matter at trial. The requesting party may then apply for a court order requiring the other party to pay that party's reasonable expenses incurred in making that proof, including reasonable attorney's fees. The court must so order unless (1) "the request was held objectionable pursuant to Rule 36(a)"; (2) "the admission sought was of no substantial importance"; (3) "the party failing to admit had a reasonable ground to believe that it might prevail on the matter"; or (4) "there was other good reason for the failure to admit."[470]

SECTION K. DISCOVERY BEFORE COMMENCING AN ACTION OR PENDING AN APPEAL

Special rules apply when a person wants to perpetuate testimony, inspect and copy documents or other things, or obtain a physical or mental examination of someone for use in a *future* action. To engage in such discovery, the person seeking it must file a verified petition in the name of the petitioner that meets the requirements of Rule 27(a).[471] The petition may be filed in any district where any one of the expected adverse parties resides.[472] Notice of when the petition will be heard, as well as the petition itself, must be served upon each person named in the petition pursuant to Federal Rule 4.[473]

If the petitioning party cannot make service on an expected adverse party after a diligent effort, the court may order service by other means. The court must also appoint an attorney to represent adverse parties not served pursuant to Rule 4.[474] Furthermore, if the court is "satisfied that perpetuating the testimony may prevent a failure or delay of justice, . . . the court may issue orders like those

---

469. *Id.*

470. FED. R. CIV. P. 37(c)(2).

471. FED. R. CIV. P. 27(a). The petition must demonstrate that (1) "the petitioner expects to be a party to an action cognizable in a United States court but cannot presently bring it or cause it to be brought"; (2) "the subject matter of the expected action and the petitioner's interest"; (3) the facts that the petitioner wants to establish by the proposed testimony and the reasons to perpetuate it" (4) "the names or a description of the persons whom the petitioner expects to be adverse parties and their addresses, so far as known"; and (5) "the name, address, and expected substance of the testimony of each deponent." *Id.* 27(a)(1); *see also* Elaine K. Zipp, Annotation, *Right to Perpetuation of Testimony Under Rule 27 of Federal Rules of Civil Procedure*, 60 A.L.R. FED. 924 (1982). A party seeking to perpetuate testimony need not show that the testimony is unique. *See In re* Bay Cnty. Middlegrounds Landfill Site, 171 F.3d 1044, 1047-48 (6th Cir. 1999) (testimony need not be unique, but only relevant). The courts are split whether Rule 27 can be used for the purpose of determining whether the plaintiff has a valid claim against the defendant. *Compare, e.g., In re* Ford, 170 F.R.D. 504 (M.D. Ala. 1997) (not available) *with In re* Alpha Indus., Inc., 159 F.R.D. 456 (S.D.N.Y. 1995) (inability to file because plaintiff did not know identity of defendant was sufficient to show that evidence was in danger of being lost).

472. FED. R. CIV. P. 27(a)(1).

473. FED. R. CIV. P. 27(a)(2).

474. *Id.*

authorized by [Federal] Rules 34 and 35."[475] Similarly, special rules apply to the perpetuation of testimony pending an appeal.[476]

SECTION L. DEPOSITIONS IN FOREIGN COUNTRIES

Rule 28(b) governs depositions taken in foreign countries.[477] Rule 28(b) was amended in 1993 "to make effective use of the Hague Convention on the Taking of Evidence Abroad in Civil or Commercial Matters."[478] As amended, the Federal Rules of Civil Procedure envision four methods for taking depositions in foreign countries: (1) according to any applicable treaty or convention; (2) by sending notice to the other parties of an intention to take a deposition before an officer who is authorized to administer oaths in the foreign country by either its law or the law of the United States; (3) by the court's commissioning of a person to give the oath and take the deposition in the foreign country; and (4) pursuant to a letter of request.[479] However, the party taking the deposition must ordinarily conform to an applicable treaty or convention if an effective deposition can be taken by such internationally approved means.[480]

SECTION M. USE OF DISCOVERY AT TRIAL

1. Rule 36 Admissions

Admissions under Federal Rule 36 are binding unless the court permits a party to withdraw or amend them. In the terms of Rule 36, the matter is "conclusively established."[481]

Illustration 9-18. Assume that a party has admitted the following request: "The defendant's barn is red." For purposes of the litigation, the fact that the barn is red is "conclusively established." It eliminates the issue and makes proof of the matter admitted unnecessary.

---

475. FED. R. CIV. P. 27(a)(3).

476. *See* FED. R. CIV. P. 27(b).

477. FED. R. CIV. P. 28(b).

478. *Id.* advisory committee's note to the 1993 amendment. The Hague Convention procedures are supplementary rather than mandatory replacement of the federal discovery rules. *See* Société Nationale Industrielle Aérocspatiale v. United States Dist. Court, 482 U.S. 522, 529-32, 107 S. Ct. 2542, 2548-50, 96 L. Ed. 2d 461, 474-77 (1987).

479. *See* FED. R. CIV. P. 28(b)(1). The 1993 amendment changed the reference from a "letter rogatory" to a "letter of request" because a letter of request is the primary method provided by the Hague Convention. A letter rogatory is "essentially a form of a letter of request." *Id.* advisory committee's note to the 1993 amendment. Letters rogatory are formal, written communications from a court in which an action is pending to a court or judge in a foreign country. Such letters request a foreign court to use its process to have the testimony of a witness within its jurisdiction taken before it. Ordinarily, letters rogatory are channeled through the U.S. State Department to the foreign country involved. Whether letters rogatory will be honored or not depends entirely on comity or applicable treaties. *See* 8A CHARLES A. WRIGHT ET AL., FEDERAL PRACTICE AND PROCEDURE: CIVIL § 2083, at 411-12 (3d ed. 2010).

480. FED. R. CIV. P. 28(b) advisory committee's note to the 1993 amendment. *See* Richard M. Dunn & Raquel M. Gonzalez, *The Thing About Non-U.S. Discovery for U.S. Litigation: It's Expensive and Complex*, 67 DEFENSE COUNS. J. 342 (2000) (while the Hague Convention has made it somewhat easier, complicated procedures, foreign policy considerations, and "blocking" statutes still pose significant problems).

481. FED. R. CIV. P. 36(b).

2. Answers to Interrogatories

In contrast to a Federal Rule 36 admission, an answer to a Federal Rule 33 interrogatory is not binding on the party.

Illustration 9-19. Assume the defendant responds to an interrogatory by stating that the defendant's barn is red. At trial, the defendant still may offer evidence that the barn is black. Obviously, the prior inconsistent answer weakens the defendant's case. The trier of fact in such an instance must weigh all of the evidence, including the inconsistent answer.[482]

3. Depositions

With respect to the use of testimony taken in a deposition, the Federal Rules of Civil Procedure show a clear preference for oral testimony of witnesses in open court.[483] Thus, the rules permit the parties to use depositions under limited circumstances at a hearing or trial. However, such use must be consistent with the Federal Rules of Evidence. An amendment to Rule 32 in 1993 added a special restriction when a party has taken a deposition of a person about to leave the country without leave of court. Such a deposition may not be used against a party who receives minimal notice but is unable to obtain a court ruling on a motion for a protective order seeking to delay or change the place of the deposition.[484]

Rule 32 of the Federal Rules of Civil Procedure prescribes three specific situations in which depositions may be used. First, any party may use any deposition to contradict or impeach the testimony of deponent as a witness.[485] Thus, the party would usually use such a deposition to show a prior inconsistent statement for impeachment purposes.

Illustration 9-20. *W*, an observer of an alleged drag race, testifies at a hearing or trial that *W* believes the vehicles were not drag racing. *W's* contrary statements in a prior deposition can be used to cast doubt on *W's* credibility.[486]

* * * * *

Second, an adverse party may use "for any purpose" the deposition of a party or anyone who at the time of taking the deposition was an officer, director, or managing agent, or a person designated under Federal Rule 30(b)(6) or 31(a)(4) to testify on behalf of a public or private corporation, partnership or association or governmental agency that is a party.[487] A party will frequently use such a deposition

---

482. *See, e.g.*, Freed v. Erie Lackawanna Ry. Co., 445 F.2d 619 (6th Cir. 1971).

483. *See* FED. R. CIV. P. 32(a)(4)(E).

484. FED. R. CIV. P. 32(a)(5); *see also* FED. R. CIV. P. 30(a)(2)(C).

485. FED. R. CIV. P. 32(a)(2).

486. The prior out-of-court statement of an ordinary witness can be used to impeach the testimony of the witness and is not consider hearsay for that purpose because of the theory of impeachment by prior inconsistent statement. Because of the effect of Federal Rule of Evidence 801(d)(1), such a statement would also be admissible as affirmative proof of the matters covered by the statement. Thus, in this situation, there would be some evidence before the jury that the parties were not drag racing based on *W's* testimony at the hearing or trial; there also would be some evidence before the jury that they were drag racing. *See* FED. R. EVID. 801(d)(1)(A); *see* Chapter 11(I)(6) *infra* ("Objections, Cross-Examination, and Impeachment").

487. FED. R. CIV. P. 32(a)(3).

at trial to prove something the deponent asserted in the deposition that is relevant to the action.

Illustration 9-21. If the defendant (*D*) admitted that *D* was drag racing in *D's* deposition, *P* could introduce *D's* statement in evidence to prove that the defendant was, in fact, drag racing. The plaintiff (*P*) could do so without regard to whether *D* was available to testify. Nor would *P* be limited to introducing the statement for impeachment purposes.[488]

* * * * *

Third, any party may use the deposition of a witness, whether or not a party, for any purpose if the witness has died or is unavailable due to another recognized cause.[489]

Illustration 9-22. Assume that *W*, a witness, stated in a deposition that *D's* car was drag racing. If *W* is unavailable, *P* may read the relevant portion of *W's* deposition at the hearing or trial to prove that *D*, in fact, was drag racing.

* * * * *

Unless the court otherwise directs, a party offering a deposition may offer it in a transcript or nontranscript form. If a party offers it in a nontranscript form, the offering party must provide the court with a transcript of the portions offered. Furthermore, on request of any party in a case tried before a jury, deposition testimony offered for purposes other than impeachment must be presented in transcript form, if available. The court may change this requirement if a party shows good cause.[490] If a party introduces part of the deposition into evidence, the adverse party may require the introduction of any other part which, in fairness, ought to be considered with the part introduced. In addition, any party may then offer any other part of the deposition in evidence.[491]

Illustration 9-23. Thus, in *Illustration 9-22*, *D* may require *P* to introduce the part of *W's* deposition admitting that *W* had consumed a twelve-pack of beer just before *W* observed the "race."

SECTION N. PRETRIAL CONFERENCES AND ORDERS

The original purposes of Federal Rule 16, governing pretrial conferences, were to improve the quality of justice in the federal courts by sharpening the preparation and presentation of cases, to eliminate trial surprise, and to improve and facilitate the settlement process. Rule 16 largely achieved these objectives. However, Rule 16 was not as successful in achieving effective and efficient case

---

488. *See* Chapter 11(I)(3)*(a) infra* ("Admissions of a Party Opponent").

489. FED. R. CIV. P. 32(a)(4). Rule 32(a)(4) permits the deposition to be used if the court finds (1) "that the witness is dead"; (2) that the witness is more than 100 miles from the place of trial or hearing or is out of the United States, unless it appears that the witness's absence was procured by the party offering the deposition"; (3) "that the witness cannot attend or testify because of age, illness, infirmity, or imprisonment"; (4) "that the party offering the deposition could not procure the witness's attendance by subpoena"; or (5) "on motion and notice, that exceptional circumstances make it desirable—in the interest of justice and with due regard to the importance of presenting live testimony in open court—to permit the deposition to be used." *Id.*; *see* Annotation, *Admissibility of Deposition, Under Rule 32(a)(3)(B) of Federal Rules of Civil Procedure, Where Court Finds That Witness Is More Than 100 Miles from Place of Trial or Hearing*, 71 A.L.R. FED. 382 (1985).

490. FED. R. CIV. P. 32(c).

491. FED. R. CIV. P. 32(a)(6).

management as it might have been. As a consequence, extensive amendments were made to the rule in 1983. The 1983 amendments involve the trial judge more actively in the management of the case. The primary focus of the rule shifted from trial preparation to case management, and it specifically recognized settlement as an appropriate goal.[492] Rule 16 was also amended in 1993, primarily to take into account the new disclosure provisions and to emphasize planning for efficient trial of cases.[493]

Rule 16(a) is entitled "Pretrial Conference; Objectives."[494] It gives the court discretion to order the attorneys for the parties and any unrepresented parties to appear for a pretrial conference. The list of purposes in Rule 16(a) includes specific references to the goals of management and control of the pretrial stages of the litigation, including settlement.[495] The provision for facilitating settlement is complemented by Rule 16(a)(1), which states that expediting the disposition of the action is a proper goal of the pretrial conference.[496] Finally, Rule 16(a)(4) includes improving the quality of the trial by "more thorough preparation" as a proper goal of the conference, a purpose implicit in the provisions of former Rule 16.[497] In short, the goals of the pretrial conference have been revised in such a way as to promote more effectively the objectives of the Federal Rules of Civil Procedure "to secure the just, speedy, and inexpensive determination of every action."[498]

1. Scheduling Orders

Federal Rule 16(b) is entitled "Scheduling" and contains the heart of the 1983 amendments to Rule 16. Rule 16(b)(1) provides that a scheduling order *must be entered* in every case that is not a part of a category of actions exempted by local

---

492. *See* FED. R. CIV. P. 16 advisory committee's note to the 1983 amendment. Criticisms of former Federal Rule 16 were severalfold. First, application of the rule sometimes resulted in overregulation of run-of-the-mill cases, which led to a burdensome series of mini-trials that wasted attorneys' time, especially when pretrial proceedings occurred long before trial. Second, because former Federal Rule 16 was discretionary and oriented toward a single conference late in the pretrial process, complex or protracted cases tended to be underadministered due to lack of judicial management at an early stage. Third, pretrial conferences often were seen as mere exchanges of legalistic contentions, without any real analysis of the particular case. Fourth, the result of a pretrial conference often was nothing more than a formal agreement on minutiae. Fifth, the pretrial conferences were unnecessary and time-consuming in the vast majority (over 90%) of cases that were settled before trial. Sixth, pretrial conferences often can be ceremonial and ritualistic, having little effect on the trial and being of minimal value, especially when the attorneys attending the sessions lack authority to make binding stipulations or are not the ones who will try the case. Seventh, when the order was issued far in advance of trial, the issues might not be formulated properly. Eighth, when cautious attorneys often tried to preserve in the order as many issues as possible, the order was unduly complicated and lacked proper focus. Ninth, when the judge who tried the case was not the one who issued the order, the judge sometimes had difficulty determining exactly what was agreed to at the conference. *See id.*

493. *See* FED. R. CIV. P. 16 advisory committee's note to the 1993 amendment.

494. *See* FED. R. CIV. P. 16(a).

495. *See* FED. R. CIV. P. 16(a)(2), (3), (5). Under former Rule 16, there was substantial disagreement whether promoting settlement was a proper purpose of the pretrial conference. *See* 6A CHARLES A. WRIGHT ET AL., FEDERAL PRACTICE AND PROCEDURE: CIVIL § 1522, at 303-04 (3d ed. 2010).

496. FED. R. CIV. P. 16(a)(1).

497. *See* FED. R. CIV. P. 16(a)(4).

498. FED. R. CIV. P. 1; *see also* Jeffrey A. Parness & Matthew R. Walker, *Thinking Outside the Civil Case Box: Reformulating Pretrial Conference Laws*, 50 U. KAN. L. REV. 347 (2002) (asserting that written pretrial conference laws for civil cases in both federal and state trial courts should be reformulated to encompass matters beyond presented claims and named parties so that unpresented claims and nonparty interests would also be handled with a view toward "just, speedy, and inexpensive" resolution).

rule from the scheduling-order requirement.[499] The order must be issued "as soon as practicable." The 1993 amendments increased the time for the initial scheduling order. As amended, the rule requires the order be entered (1) within 90 days after the date a defendant first appears or (2) within 120 days after service of the complaint on a defendant—whichever is earlier.[500] This increase in time was intended to alleviate problems in multi-defendant cases.[501] The district judge must enter the order unless a local rule authorizes a magistrate to do so.[502]

The scheduling order *must* limit the time to join parties and to amend the pleadings.[503] This requirement "assures that at some point both the parties and the pleadings will be fixed."[504] The order also must limit the time for filing motions and for completing discovery.[505] The Advisory Committee stated that the purpose of these requirements is to prevent delays in discovery and stalling through the use of motions.[506] Federal Rule 16(b) provides that a scheduling order *may* set dates for pretrial conferences and for trial.[507] The order may modify the timing of disclosures under Rules 26(a) and 26(e)(1) as well as the extent of the discovery permitted.[508] The order may also include "other appropriate matters."[509]

---

499. FED. R. CIV. P. 16(b)(1). A matter of importance under Rule 16(b) is what categories of cases will be exempted from the scheduling-order requirement by local rule. The Advisory Committee stated the reasons for this provision as follows:

> Although a mandatory scheduling order encourages the court to become involved in case management early in the litigation, it represents a degree of judicial involvement that is not warranted in many cases. Thus, subdivision (b) permits each district court to promulgate a local rule under Rule 83 exempting certain categories of cases in which the burdens of scheduling orders exceed the administrative efficiencies that would be gained. . . . Logical candidates for this treatment include social security disability matters, habeas corpus petitions, forfeitures, and reviews of certain administrative actions.

FED. R. CIV. P. 16(b) advisory committee's note to the 1983 amendment. Because the effectiveness of the scheduling-order requirement depends in part on how extensively the district courts exempt cases from the requirement, the nature and extent of the exemptions created by each district become critical. Also, because every case not exempted requires a scheduling order, the efficiency of the rule's operation will depend on how well the district courts provide exemptions by local rule for categories of cases not suitable for scheduling orders. Even in categories of cases exempted by local rule, scheduling orders can be issued under Rule 16. The only effect of an exemption is to remove the requirement that scheduling orders be issued in every case within the category.

500. FED. R. CIV. P. 16(b)(2) & advisory committee's note to the 1993 amendment. Prior to the 1993 amendment, the order had to be entered no later than 120 days after the date the complaint was filed.

501. FED. R. CIV. P. 16(b) advisory committee's note to the 1993 amendment.

502. FED. R. CIV. P. 16(b)(1). Federal Rule 16(b)(B) directs that, before entering the order, the judge or magistrate must consult with the attorneys for the parties by (1) a scheduling conference; (2) telephone; (3) mail; or (4) other suitable means. This provision makes it clear that the rule authorizes, but does not require, a scheduling conference. The Advisory Committee stated that the scheduling conference may be requested not only by the district judge or magistrate (where authorized by local rule), but by a party, provided a request is made within 120 days after the complaint is filed. *See* FED. R. CIV. P. 16(b) advisory committee's note to the 1983 amendment. The Advisory Committee's notes to the 1993 amendments indicate that the parties should submit to the court the report concerning their conference and discovery plan before the scheduling order is entered. FED. R. CIV. P. 16(b) advisory committee's note to the 1993 amendment. However, whether or not a scheduling conference is held, the scheduling order must be entered within the time period, "after some communication with the parties." FED. R. CIV. P. 16(b) advisory committee's note to the 1983 amendment.

503. *See* FED. R. CIV. P. 16(b)(3)(A).

504. FED. R. CIV. P. 16(b)(1) advisory committee's note to 1983 amendment.

505. *See* FED. R. CIV. P. 16(b)(3)(A).

506. *See* FED. R. CIV. P. 16(b) advisory committee's note to the 1983 amendment.

507. FED. R. CIV. P. 16(b)(3)(B)(v). The court is given discretion whether to include dates of pretrial conferences because such conferences may or may not be desirable in any given case. Complex cases may require multiple pretrial conferences and a more elaborate pretrial structure, but uncomplicated cases may require only one conference and little pretrial structure outside the matters mandated. *See* FED. R. CIV. P. 16(b) advisory committee's notes to the 1983 amendment.

508. FED. R. CIV. P. 16(b)(3)(B)(i) & (ii).

509. FED. R. CIV. P. 16(b)(3)(B)(vi).

Federal Rule 16(b) also provides that a schedule may not be modified except upon a showing of "good cause and with the judge's consent."[510] The "good cause" standard of Rule 16(b) is less stringent than the "manifest injustice" standard for modification of final pretrial orders under Rule 16(e).[511] "Good cause" exists if a schedule cannot be met "despite the diligence of the party seeking [an] extension [of time]."[512] It was feared that a more stringent standard would "encourage counsel to request the longest possible periods for completing pleading, joinder, and discovery."[513]

2. Subjects for Discussion at Pretrial Conferences

The amendments to Federal Rule 16(c) have continually expanded the matters that may be discussed at a pretrial conference if and when such a conference is held. The expansion continues Rule 16's emphasis on judicial management and control.[514]

As amended in 1983, Federal Rule 16(c) provides that the *formulation* as well as the simplification of issues may be discussed, and the court has the explicit authority to eliminate frivolous claims or defenses, without waiting for a formal motion for summary judgment.[515] Rule 16(c)(2)(B) directs the court to consider the necessity and desirability of amendments to the pleadings at a pretrial conference.[516] Rule 16(c)(2)(C) directs the court to the possibility of obtaining admissions of facts and documents that will avoid unnecessary proof. It also directs the court to consider and take action concerning stipulations regarding the authenticity of documents and to obtain advance rulings by the court on the admissibility of evidence.[517]

Federal Rule 16(c)(2)(D) gives the court explicit authority to avoid unnecessary proof, cumulative evidence, and restrictions on expert testimony. Rule 16(c)(2)(E) encourages the use of Rule 56 (summary judgment) to avoid or reduce the scope of the trial. Rule 16(c)(2)(F) focuses on the appropriateness of controlling and scheduling discovery and disclosures. Rule 16(c)(2)(G) deals with identification

---

510. FED. R. CIV. P. 16(b)(4).

511. *Compare* FED. R. CIV. P. 16(b)(4) *with* FED. R. CIV. P. 16(e); *see also* subsection 4 *infra* ("Pretrial Orders") discussing the provisions of Federal Rule 16(e).

512. *See* FED. R. CIV. P. 16(b) advisory committee's note to the 1983 amendment.

513. *Id.*

514. *See* FED. R. CIV. P. 16(c) advisory committee's note to the 1983 amendment. Rule 16(c)(1) provides that in any pretrial conference, at least one of the attorneys for each party must have the authority to enter into stipulations and to make admissions regarding all matters that the participants reasonably may anticipate being discussed. This provision was added in 1983 to meet the criticism that the pretrial conferences held under former Rule 16 often were ritualistic or ceremonial. The aim is to assure proper preconference preparation, not necessarily to compel stipulations or settlements that the attorneys consider unreasonable, or which concern matters that could not have been anticipated or that normally require prior consultation with the client. *See id.*; *cf.* Russell G. Donaldson, Annotation, *Authority of District Court, Under Rule 16 of Federal Rules of Civil Procedure, to Compel Parties to Agree on Pretrial Stipulations of Facts*, 40 A.L.R. FED. 859 (1978). The 1993 amendments added that the court could require a party or its representative be present or reasonably [be] available by telephone in order to consider possible settlement of the dispute. *See* FED. R. CIV. P. 16(c) advisory committee's note to the 1993 amendment.

515. *See* FED. R. CIV. P. 16(c)(2)(A).

516. *See* FED. R. CIV. P. 16(c)(2)(B).

517. *See* FED. R. CIV. P. 16(c)(2)(C).

of witnesses and documents, scheduling an exchange of pretrial briefs, and the dates for further conferences and trial. Rule 16(c)(2)(H) authorizes the court to consider the advisability of reference to a magistrate judge or master, whether or not the case is to be tried to a jury.[518]

Rule 16(c)(2)(I) authorizes the court to consider the possibility of settlement.[519] It also encourages the use of special procedures to assist in resolving the dispute when a statute or local rule authorizes such procedures.[520] Rule 16(c)(2)(J) explicitly authorizes consideration of and action upon the form and substance of the pretrial order.[521] Rule 16(c)(2)(K) authorizes the court to consider and act upon pending motions. This type of matter always has been within the purview of the pretrial conference under Rule 16. It is simply listed to encourage the court to consider it.[522] Rule 16(c)(2)(L) authorizes the court to consider and adopt special procedures for managing potentially difficult or protracted actions that may involve complex issues, multiple parties, difficult legal questions, or unusual proof problems. Like other subdivisions added in 1983, this subdivision encourages flexible, innovative, and vigorous case management in complex actions.[523]

The 1993 amendments added provisions calling attention to opportunities for structuring the trial. Rule 16(c)(2)(M) authorizes orders for separate trials pursuant to Rule 42.[524] Rule 16(c)(N) authorizes orders that direct a party to present evidence early in the trial on an issue which could be the basis for a judgment as a matter of law under Rule 50(a) or a judgment on partial findings under Rule 52(c).[525] Rule 16(c)(2)(O) supplements the power of the court to limit the extent of

---

518. *See* FED. R. CIV. P. 16(c)(2)(D)-(H).

519. *See* FED. R. CIV. P. 16(c)(2)(I). The Advisory Committee stated that it is not the Rule's intention to impose settlement on unwilling litigants. Rather, "it is believed that providing a neutral forum for discussing the subject [of settlement] might foster it." *See* FED. R. CIV. P. 16(c)(7) advisory committee's note to the 1983 amendment (now renumbered as 16(c)(9)). *See generally* Michael R. Hogan, *Judicial Settlement Conference: Empowering the Parties to Decide Through Negotiation*, 27 WILLAMETTE L. REV. 429 (1991); Jeffrey A. Parness & Tait J. Lundgren, *Nonparty Insurers in Federal Civil Actions: The Need for New Written Civil Procedure Laws,* 36 CREIGHTON L. REV. 191 (2003) (discussing, *inter alia,* compelling the attendance of nonparty insurers at settlement conferences); Leonard L. Riskin, *The Represented Client in a Settlement Conference: The Lesson of* G. Heileman Brewing Co. v. Joseph Oat Corp., 69 WASH. U. L.Q. 1059 (1991); Susan K. Antalovich, Note, Heileman Brewing Co., Inc. v. Joseph Oat Corporation*: Defining the Perimeters of Judicial Involvement in the Settlement Process*, 5 OHIO ST. J. ON DISP. RESOL. 115 (1989).

520. *See* FED. R. CIV. P. 16(c)(2)(I). This provision was added in 1983 to encourage innovative efforts by the litigants to explore "adjudicatory techniques outside the courthouse" to resolve the dispute. *Id.*; *see* Eric D. Green et al., *Settling Large Case Litigation: An Alternative Approach*, 11 LOY. L.A. L. REV. 493, 501-06 (1978) (six weeks of expedited, limited discovery and exchange of position papers and exhibits, followed by nonbinding "mini-trial" before top management executives of opposing companies and a mutually selected neutral adviser; management to meet after mini-trial and attempt to resolve dispute from new perspective gained at mini-trial; neutral adviser to submit written nonbinding opinion discussing strengths and weaknesses of parties' positions and predicting likely outcome of trial, in event management not able to resolve dispute in first meeting). *See* John F. Wagner, Jr., Annotation, *Validity and Effect of Local District Court Rules Providing for Use of Alternative Dispute Resolution Procedures as Pretrial Settlement Mechanisms*, 86 A.L.R. FED. 211 (1988); Chapter 1(E) *supra* ("Alternative Dispute Resolution").

521. *See* FED. R. CIV. P. 16(c)(2)(J). Although pretrial conferences obviously had permitted this type of action under former Rule 16, this subdivision was added in 1983 to encourage judges to consider the subject in order to provide better case management. *See* 6A CHARLES A. WRIGHT ET AL., FEDERAL PRACTICE AND PROCEDURE: CIVIL § 1525, at 357 (3d ed. 2010).

522. *See* FED. R. CIV. P. 16(c) advisory committee's note to the 1983 amendment.

523. *See id.*

524. See FED. R. CIV. P. 16(c)(2)(M).

525. *See* Chapter 11(H)(1) *infra* ("Involuntary Dismissals (Judgments on Partial Findings) and Directed Verdicts (Judgments as a Matter of Law)").

evidence offered at trial.[526] The underlying rationale of the Advisory Committee for these limits is to "provide the parties with a better opportunity to determine priorities and exercise selectivity in presenting evidence than when [such] limits are imposed during trial" pursuant to Rules 403 and 611(a) of the Federal Rules of Evidence. The Advisory Committee cautions, however, that "[a]ny such limits must be reasonable under the circumstances, and ordinarily the court should impose them only after receiving appropriate submissions from the parties" concerning expected testimony.[527]

Finally, Rule 16(c)(2)(P) authorizes the court to facilitate the just, speedy, and inexpensive disposition of the action in other ways.[528]

3. Final Pretrial Conference

Federal Rule 16(e) provides that the final pretrial conference must be held "as close to the start trial as is reasonable" under the circumstances.[529] At the conference, the participants must formulate a plan for trial, including a program to facilitate the admission of evidence. Unrepresented parties and at least one of the attorneys who will conduct the trial for each party *must* attend the conference. The exact timing of the final conference, if any, is left to the discretion of the court for purposes of flexibility.[530] Ten days to two weeks before trial is an "optimum" time.[531] The purpose of requiring the attendance of at least one attorney for each party who will try the case is to assure adequate structuring of the trial.[532]

4. Pretrial Orders

Federal Rule 16(d) requires that after *any* pretrial conference, an order must issue reciting the action taken at the conference. The order controls the subsequent course of the action unless a subsequent order modifies it.[533] However, Rule 16(e) provides that the order following a *final* pretrial conference may be modified "only to prevent manifest injustice."[534] Thus, a distinction is drawn between pretrial orders and orders following the final pretrial conference. The former may be modified without restriction at subsequent pretrial conferences (or otherwise). The latter may be modified only by meeting a stringent standard because allowing modification of that order without significant restriction would defeat its function to structure and control the course of the trial.[535]

Because the pretrial order controls the subsequent course of the litigation, admissions and stipulations embodied in the order will bind the parties and stand

---

526. *See* FED. R. CIV. P. 16(c)(2)(O).
527. *See* FED. R. CIV. P. 16(c) advisory committee's note to the 1993 amendment.
528. FED. R. CIV. P. 16(c)(2)(P).
529. FED. R. CIV. P. 16(e).
530. *Id.*
531. *See* FED. R. CIV. P. 16(d) advisory committee's note to the 1983 amendment.
532. *See id.*
533. *See* FED. R. CIV. P. 16(d).
534. *See* FED. R. CIV. P. 16(e).
535. *See* FED. R. CIV. P. 16(e) advisory committee's notes to 1983 amendment.

"as fully determined as if [the issues] had been adjudicated after the taking of testimony at trial."[536] Likewise, if issues are not preserved for trial in the pretrial order, even if the issues were disputed on the face of the pleadings, the trial court may refuse to allow evidence on the issues at trial or to give instructions on the issue.[537] Federal Rule 16, however, must be read in conjunction with other Federal Rules. Thus, if a party objects to evidence at trial on the grounds that it is beyond the scope of the pretrial order, the trial court may apply the standard in Rule 15(b) and allow amendment of the order if justice would be served.[538] Similarly, the formulation of an issue in the pretrial order does not preclude a court from granting a motion for summary judgment, if the court later determines that no genuine issue of fact exists.[539]

Federal Rule 16(d) does not state who is responsible for preparing the pretrial order. Some local rules make the plaintiff's attorney responsible; others allow the court to appoint any one of the attorneys to prepare the order; and still others leave it to the court.[540] Other suggested methods are (1) for the judge to dictate the order directly into the record at the conference or shortly thereafter, (2) to adopt the minutes of the conference as the pretrial order if minutes are prepared, (3) for counsel to meet within a specified time after the conference and draw up an order for submission to the court, or (4) for the court to submit an order to counsel for their objections.[541]

5. Sanctions

Rule 16(f) provides that sanctions may be imposed on a party or a party's attorney who fails to (1) obey a scheduling or pretrial order, (2) appear at a scheduling or pretrial conference, (3) be substantially prepared to participate in a scheduling or pretrial conference, or (4) participate in good faith in a scheduling or pretrial conference.[542] For any such failure, the judge, upon the judge's own initiative or a party's motion, may "issue just orders." Such orders may include (1) an order may refuse to allow the party to support or oppose designated claims or defenses, or prohibit the party from introducing designated matters in evidence;[543] (2) an order may strike out pleadings or parts thereof, or staying further proceedings until the court's orders are obeyed, or dismiss the action or proceeding or part

---

536. *See* 6A CHARLES A. WRIGHT ET AL., FEDERAL PRACTICE AND PROCEDURE: CIVIL § 1527, at 386 (3d ed. 2010).

537. *See, e.g.*, Youren v. Tintic Sch. Dist., 343 F.3d 1296 (10th Cir. 2003) (even though defendant pleaded statute-of-limitations defense in answer, defendant waived the defense by failing to preserve the issue in the pretrial order).

538. *See* 6A CHARLES A. WRIGHT ET AL., FEDERAL PRACTICE AND PROCEDURE: CIVIL § 1527.1, at 415-17 (3d ed. 2010).

539. *See, e.g.*, Irving Trust Co. v. United States, 221 F.2d 303 (2d Cir. 1955); *cf.* Security Abstract & Title Co. v. Smith Livestock, Inc., 2006 MT 265, 334 Mont. 172, 146 P.3d 732 (court may determine that party has waived its right to assert a legal theory or factual issue at trial when theory or issue is not specified in the pleadings or pretrial order, but pretrial order should be liberally construed to permit any issues at trial that are embraced within its language).

540. *See* FED. R. CIV. P. 16(e) advisory committee's note to the 1983 amendment.

541. *See* 5 BENDER'S FEDERAL PRACTICE FORMS 16-17 (2012).

542. FED. R. CIV. P. 16(f)(1).

543. *See* FED. R. CIV. P. 37(b)(2)(A)(ii).

thereof, or render a judgment by default against the party;[544] or (3) an order may treat as contempt of court the failure to obey a court order (unless the failure to obey is a failure to submit to a physical or mental examination).[545]

Federal Rule 16(f) also provides that in lieu of *or* in addition to any of the other sanctions imposed, the court *must* require the violating party, the party's attorney, or both to pay the reasonable expenses incurred because of any noncompliance with Federal Rule 16, including attorney's fees.[546] However, the court does not have to impose sanctions if it finds that the noncompliance was substantially justified or that other circumstances make an award of expenses unjust. The courts imposed sanctions for failure to comply with previous versions of Rule 16 even though Rule 16 did not mention sanctions. Therefore, the explicit provision for sanctions in Rule 16(f) simply confirmed existing practice. The expense/attorney's fees sanction is *mandated* unless a finding is made that the violation should be excused, thus emphasizing the propriety of imposing the costs of violation upon the violating party or that party's attorney, or both. However, the court may select whatever sanctions are appropriate to the circumstances of the case and will be reversed only for an abuse of discretion.[547]

---

544. *See* FED. R. CIV. P. 37(b)(2)(A)(iii)-(vi). *See generally* Jodi Golinsky, *The Second Circuit's Imposition of Litigation-Ending Sanctions for Failures to Comply With Discovery Orders: Should Rule 37(b)(2) Defaults and Dismissals be Determined by a Roll of the Dice?*, 62 BROOK. L. REV. 585 (1996).

545. *See* FED. R. CIV. P. 37(b)(2)(A)(viii).

546. FED. R. CIV. P. 16(f)(2).

547. *See* FED. R. CIV. P. 16(f) advisory committee's note to the 1983 amendment.

Chapter 10

DISPOSITION OF THE ACTION WITHOUT TRIAL

Modern procedural systems provide for disposition of actions without trial in several ways. For example, demurrers and motions to dismiss provide methods of challenging the legal sufficiency of an opposing party's pleading. If successful, such challenges can result in the entry of a judgment in the action.[1] Other formal devices can also be used to dispose of a case without a trial. They include (1) default judgments, (2) judgments on the pleadings, (3) summary judgments, (4) voluntary dismissals, and (5) involuntary dismissals. In addition, statutes or court rules often encourage settlements.[2] When effectuated, a settlement can be embodied in a formal judgment.[3]

SECTION A. DEFAULT JUDGMENT

In a common-law or equity case, the defendant had to appear before the court could adjudicate the action. Thus, the traditional systems developed many sanctions to compel the defendant to appear.[4] In contrast, if the defendant fails to appear or otherwise defend in modern systems, service of process on the defendant, without more, authorizes the court to enter a "default judgment." For example, failing to answer the complaint can result in a default judgment against the defendant.[5]

Rule 55 of the Federal Rules of Civil Procedure is an example of a typical default provision. Rule 55 has its roots in common-law and equity practice. At common law, if a defendant appeared but refused to answer or demur, or if the defendant had pleaded but refused to continue to plead until issue was joined, the court would enter a judgment against the defendant for want of a plea. This judgment was called a *judgment nil dicit*—literally, "he says nothing."[6] In equity, the equivalent of a judgment nil dicit was the *decree pro confesso*. The court entered this decree when the defendant did not answer the plaintiff's bill.[7] Before Federal Rule 55, decrees pro confesso could be entered under the Federal Equity Rules. Judgments nil dicit could be entered in accordance with state law under the

---

1. *See* Chapter 6(C)(3)*(a)* *supra* ("General Demurrers"); Chapter 6(C)(3)*(b)* *supra* ("Special Demurrers"); Chapter 6(D)(3)*(d)* *supra* ("Motions to Dismiss").

2. *See generally* Stephen McG. Bundy, *The Policy in Favor of Settlement in an Adversary System*, 44 HASTINGS L.J. 1 (1992) (surveying procedural innovations and discussing policy implications).

3. *See* section F *infra* ("Miscellaneous Methods of Disposing of an Action Without Trial").

4. *See* Chapter 3(K)(1) *supra* ("Service of Process in English and Early United States Practice").

5. *See* Chapter 6(D)(3)*(a)* *supra* ("Default").

6. *See* ANDREW B. MARTIN, CIVIL PROCEDURE AT COMMON LAW § 375, at 316 (1905).

7. *See* Thomson v. Wooster, 114 U.S. 104, 110-11, 5 S. Ct. 788, 791, 29 L. Ed. 105, 107 (1885).

Conformity Acts.[8] Rule 55 itself is based largely on Rules 16 and 17 of the Federal Equity Rules of 1912.[9]

Default under Federal Rule 55 involves a two-step process. First, Rule 55(a) allows the clerk to enter default in the record when a party against whom a judgment for affirmative relief is sought fails to plead or otherwise defend, provided that failure is made to appear by affidavit or otherwise. Second, the clerk or the court, depending on the circumstances, enters the default judgment.[10] Rule 55(b)(1) provides that the clerk, as opposed to the court, may enter a default judgment if three conditions are satisfied. First, the plaintiff's claim must be for a sum certain or for a sum that can be made certain by computation. Second, the defendant must have been defaulted for failure to appear. Finally, the defendant must not be an infant or incompetent person.[11] If any of these requirements is not satisfied, only the court can enter a judgment by default under Rule 55(b)(2), discussed below.

Illustration 10-1. *P* sues *D* in federal court. *D* moves to dismiss *P's* complaint for failure to state a claim upon which relief can be granted under Federal Rule 12(b)(6). The court overrules the motion. *D* then fails to answer within the time prescribed in Federal Rule 12(a). *P* files an affidavit making *D's* failure to answer known to the clerk. The clerk then enters *D's* default on the record. Under these circumstances, only the court can enter a default judgment against *D* under Rule 55(b). The motion to dismiss *P's* complaint constituted an appearance by *D*.[12] Once a defendant has appeared in an action, only the court can enter a default judgment under Rule 55(b)(2), discussed below.

Illustration 10-2. *P* sues *D* in federal court for an injunction. *D* fails to appear or otherwise defend the action. *P* files an affidavit making *D's* failure to appear known to the clerk. The clerk then enters the default on the record. Under these circumstances, only the court can enter a default judgment against *D* under Rule 55(b)(2). *P's* claim is for an injunction. Thus, it is not for a sum certain or a sum that can be made certain by computation. Even though *D* defaulted by failing to appear, only the court can enter judgment against *D*.

* * * * *

Under Rule 55(b)(2), the court is required to exercise discretion in determining whether to enter the judgment.[13] Rule 55(b)(2) states that if the party

---

8. FED. R. CIV. P. 55 advisory committee's note to the original rule; *see* Chapter 1(D)(10) *supra* ("Early Procedure in the Federal Courts").

9. 226 U.S. 649, 653 (1912).

10. FED. R. CIV. P. 55(a), (b).

11. FED. R. CIV. P. 55(b)(1).

12. *See* 10A CHARLES A. WRIGHT ET AL., FEDERAL PRACTICE AND PROCEDURE: CIVIL § 2686 (3d ed. 1998); *see also* State *ex rel.* White v. Brandt, 2008 SD 33, 748 N.W.2d 766 (not every exchange between the parties constitutes an appearance; to constitute an appearance, for purposes of default judgment provision, party must demonstrate to the opposing party a clear intent to defend against the lawsuit); Arbogast Family Trust v. River Crossings, L.L.C., 238 P.3d 1035, 2010 Utah 40 (a party must make a formal filing or submission to the district court in order to make an appearance under Rule 5(a) and require notice of default).

13. *See, e.g.*, Valley Hosp. Ass'n, Inc. v. Brauneis, 141 P.3d 726 (Alaska 2006) (trial court must exercise discretion in determining whether to enter default judgment; generally, if court determines that defendant is in default, allegations of the complaint, except those as to the amount of damages, will be taken as true; if the trial court determines that it is necessary for the plaintiff to present evidence before a default judgment will be entered, the plaintiff will not have to prove allegations by a preponderance of the evidence, but merely submit enough evidence to put the questioned allegation in controversy). In recent years some district courts have held hearings before entering a default judgment to determine whether they had personal jurisdiction over a non-appearing defendant. This practice is highly questionable, especially given the fact that, as observed in Chapter 3(B)(3), non-

against whom the default judgment is sought is a minor or incompetent person, no default judgment may be entered unless the person is represented by a general guardian, conservator, or other "like fiduciary" who has appeared in the action. In other cases, when the party against whom the default judgment is sought has appeared in the action, written notice of the application for judgment must be given to that party at least three days before the hearing of the application.[14] This procedure provides the party time to demonstrate why the court should not enter a default judgment. In addition, Rule 55(b)(2) authorizes, but does not require, the court to hear evidence to determine the truth of allegations made against the defaulting party, to establish the amount of damages,[15] or for other purposes.[16]

Rule 55(c) provides that even after a default has been entered in the record, the court may set the default aside for good cause. Similarly, if a default judgment has been entered, the court may set it aside under Rule 60(b) (governing relief from a judgment due to mistake, inadvertence, excusable neglect, newly discovered evidence, fraud, etc.).[17] Setting aside the entry of a default or a default judgment is

---

appearing defendants can challenge personal jurisdiction collaterally in another state when the plaintiff attempts to enforce a judgment against them there. It is clear that a finding in the judgment-rendering court that the court has personal jurisdiction over a non-appearing defendant is not issue preclusive in the judgment enforcing court. *See* Chapter 13(C)(1)(b), *infra*. The better practice is to recognize that there need be no affirmative finding of personal jurisdiction over a defaulting defendant. *See* Marcus Food Co. v. DiPanfilo, 671 F.3d 1159 (10th Cir. 2011) (not necessary for district court to make affirmative finding of personal jurisdiction over non-appearing defaulting defendant).

14. FED. R. CIV. P. 55(b)(2); *see* Town & Country Kids, Inc. v. Protected Venture Inv. Trust #1, Inc., 178 F.R.D. 453 (E.D. Va. 1998) (holding that a letter from defendants to plaintiff's counsel was not an appearance entitling the defendants to notice of a default judgment hearing under Rule 55(b)(2)).

15. *See* SEC v. Smyth, 420 F.3d 1225 (11th Cir. 2005) (when evidence essential to determining the amount of damages is not of record, an evidentiary hearing is ordinarily a prerequisite to entry of a default judgment).

16. FED. R. CIV. P. 55(b)(2); *see* Norfolk & W. Ry. Co. v. Central States Trucking Co., No. 97 C 3642, 1998 WL 26175, 1998 U.S. Dist. LEXIS 509 (N.D. Ill. Jan. 15, 1998) (holding that although there is no absolute right to a hearing on damages under Rule 55(b)(2), a hearing should be held unless the available evidence permits the court to establish damages without one, such as where the damages are liquidated or can be ascertained from definite figures contained in documentary evidence or detailed affidavits); *see also* Multiple Resort Ownership Plan, Inc. v. Design-Build-Manage, Inc., 2002 WY 67, 45 P.3d 647 (default under Wyoming equivalent of Rule 55 does not concede the amount demanded when the plaintiff seeks unliquidated damages and the burden is on the plaintiff to establish the amount of damages by affidavit or testimony).

17. FED. R. CIV. P. 55(c) & 60(b). In Robb v. Norfolk & Western Railway Co., 122 F.3d 354 (7th Cir. 1997), the plaintiff requested an extension of time from the defendant's attorney within which to file a brief in opposition to the defendant's motion for summary judgment. The defendant's attorney agreed, but the plaintiff did not seek an order of court for such an extension as required by local rule. As a result, the court granted summary judgment against the plaintiff for failure to respond to the motion. The plaintiff moved for relief under Rule 60(b), but the trial court denied it. The trial court felt bound by a Seventh Circuit precedent holding that attorney negligence could not constitute excusable neglect. The Seventh Circuit vacated the judgment and remanded the case. The Seventh Circuit relied on the Supreme Court's decision in Pioneer Investment Services Co. v. Brunswick Associates Ltd. Partnership, 507 U.S. 380, 113 S. Ct. 1489, 123 L. Ed.2d 74 (1993), a case which discussed excusable neglect in the bankruptcy context. The court held that based on *Pioneer*, attorney negligence can sometimes constitute excusable neglect. The court also indicated that the district court could, on remand, take into account that the plaintiff's attorney was one of the most conscientious in the bar in following deadlines in determining whether excusable neglect was present; *see also* Bramdt v. American Bankers Ins. Co., 653 F.3d 1108 (9th Cir. 2011) (when a defendant seeks relief from a default judgment on grounds of excusable neglect, the court applies the same three factors governing the setting aside of a default: (1) whether plaintiff will be prejudiced; (2) whether defendant has a meritorious defense; and (3) whether culpable conduct of defendant led to the default; a finding of culpable conduct will suffice to justify denial of relief, but the district court need not deny relief on the basis of such a finding and did not err in granting relief here); *cf.* African Methodist Episcopal Church, Inc. v. Ward, 185 F.3d 1201 (11th Cir. 1999) (district court erred in setting aside default and default judgment when parties, after being served, ignored process on advice of pastor of church and were defaulted as a result). *See generally* Adam Owen Glist, *Enforcing Courtesy: Default Judgments and the Civility Movement*, 69 FORDHAM L. REV. 757 (2000) (discussing the longstanding practice in which attorneys often provide other attorneys, as a matter of professional courtesy, with extra notice above what is required by the procedural rules before seeking a default judgment).

within the discretion of the court.[18] However, when the court has entered a default judgment, the court's discretion is confined by the requirements of Rule 60(b).[19] In determining whether good cause has been shown to set aside a default under Rule 55(c), the courts often rely on the factors listed in Rule 60(b).[20] Often, the courts require a party seeking to set aside the entry of a default or a default judgment to demonstrate that a meritorious defense exists to the opposing party's claim.[21]

SECTION B. JUDGMENT ON THE PLEADINGS

At common law, one party could challenge the legal sufficiency of the opposing party's pleading at any stage of the pleading process by a demurrer.[22] Even though the quest for the single issue under common-law pleading was ended and the number of pleadings were radically limited in code-pleading states, the demurrer continued to perform this function.[23] In the federal courts and many states, another device to test the legal sufficiency of a party's case after the close of the pleadings is a motion for judgment on the pleadings.[24]

Federal Rule 12(c) allows either party to move for judgment on the pleadings after the pleadings are closed "but early enough not to delay trial."[25] A motion for judgment on the pleadings allows a party to dispose of an action without trial when the pleadings demonstrate that the party is entitled to judgment as a matter of law. This motion performs basically the same function as a Rule 12(b)(6) defense when asserted by a defendant, but it performs that function after the close of all the pleadings. Furthermore, the motion allows a party asserting a claim to challenge the legal sufficiency of the defensive pleading of an opposing party. When a party moves for judgment on the pleadings, all of the well-pleaded facts in the opposing party's pleading are admitted for purposes of the motion, even if the moving party's own pleading has previously denied those factual allegations.[26]

---

18. *See, e.g.*, Inman v. American Home Furniture Placement, Inc., 120 F.3d 117 (8th Cir. 1997) (default judgment and refusal of relief under Rule 60(b) were not an abuse of discretion where defendant's attorney negligently failed to answer complaint, respond to discovery requests, and appear for a scheduled deposition because attorney was having "personal problems"). *But cf.* Argent v. Office of Pers. Mgmt., No. 96 CIV. 2516 (PKL), 1997 WL 278115, 1997 U.S. Dist. LEXIS 7216 (S.D.N.Y. May 22, 1997) (entry of default set aside, even though defendants did not present a meritorious defense, where default was the result of negligence rather than wilfulness and the plaintiff would not be prejudiced).

19. *See* FED. R. CIV. P. 55(c), 60(b); SEC v. Internet Solutions for Bus., Inc., 509 F.3d 1161 (9th Cir. 2007) (when a defendant moves to set aside a default judgment on grounds of absence of service of process but had actual notice of the action, the burden of proving absence of service is on the defendant); *see also* Chapter 12(F) *infra* ("Extraordinary Relief From a Judgment").

20. *See, e.g.*, Pretzel & Stouffer v. Imperial Adjusters, Inc., 28 F.3d 42 (7th Cir. 1994); *see also* 10A CHARLES A. WRIGHT ET AL., FEDERAL PRACTICE AND PROCEDURE: CIVIL § 2694, at 116-17 (3d ed. 1998).

21. *See, e.g.*, Park v. Tanaka, 75 Haw. 271, 859 P.2d 917 (1993); *cf.* J.L. Phillips & Assocs., Inc. v. E & H Plastic Corp., 217 Wis. 2d 348, 577 N.W.2d 13 (1998) (once a defaulted defendant presents a defense that would be legally sufficient, the court need not require the defendant to demonstrate a likelihood of success on that defense before relieving the defendant from a default judgment).

22. *See* Chapter 6(A) *supra* ("Common-Law Pleading").

23. *See, e.g.*, NEB. REV. STAT. §§ 25-806, 25-820 (1995) (repealed 2003).

24. *See* FED. R. CIV. P. 12(c).

25. *Id.*

26. *See, e.g.*, Ocello v. Koster, 354 S.W.3d 187 (Mo. 2011) (the well-pleaded facts of the opposing party's pleading are admitted for purposes of a motion for judgment on the pleadings, but the court will not "blindly" accept the legal conclusions drawn by the pleader from the facts).

Illustration 10-3. *P* alleges in a complaint against *D* that *D* was negligent. *D* denies the allegation of negligence in *D's* answer. If *D* moves for judgment on the pleadings, the court will assume that *D* was negligent for purposes of ruling on *D's* motion. In addition to assuming the truth of the opposing party's factual allegations for purposes of the motion, the court will draw all reasonable inferences from these facts in favor of the party opposing the motion. The party does not, however, admit conclusions of law, legally impossible facts, or matters that would be inadmissible at trial.[27]

Illustration 10-4. *P* sues *D*, alleging facts *X*, *Y*, and *Z* in the complaint. The complaint states a claim for relief. *D's* answer admits fact *X* but denies facts *Y* and *Z*. *P* moves for judgment on the pleadings. For purposes of ruling on the motion, the court will assume that fact *X* is true because *D's* answer admitted it. The court will assume that facts *Y* and *Z* are false because *D's* answer denied them. *P* will be able to obtain judgment on the pleadings under these circumstances only if fact *X* standing alone states a claim for relief against *D*.

Illustration 10-5. *P* sues *D*, alleging facts *X*, *Y*, and *Z* in the complaint. These facts state a claim for relief. *D's* answer admits facts *X*, *Y*, and *Z*. *D's* answer also alleges fact *Q* as an affirmative defense. *P* moves for judgment on the pleadings. Under these circumstances, the court will assume that facts *X*, *Y*, and *Z* are true because *D's* answer admitted them. In addition, the court will assume that fact *Q* is true because the court will assume that all well-pleaded factual allegations in the opposing party's pleading are true for purposes of ruling on a motion for judgment on the pleadings. *P* will be entitled to judgment on the pleadings only if affirmative defense *Q* is legally insufficient.

Illustration 10-6. On the facts of *Illustration 10-5*, assume that *P's* complaint does not state a claim for relief. However, *D* does not raise a Rule 12(b)(6) defense to the pleading. Instead, *D* admits the facts of the complaint and alleges an affirmative defense. *D's* affirmative defense is also legally insufficient. *P* moves for judgment on the pleadings. Under these circumstances, the court should grant judgment on the pleadings for *D*. Like a demurrer at common law, the motion for judgment on the pleadings "searches the record."[28] Thus, the court will return to the beginning of the pleadings, scrutinize each pleading for legal sufficiency, and rule against the party whose pleading is first legally insufficient. Here, that party is *P* because *P's* complaint does not state a claim for relief.[29]

Illustration 10-7. *P* sues *D*, alleging in the complaint facts *X*, *Y*, and *Z*. *D's* answer denies facts *X*, *Y*, and *Z*. *D's* answer also alleges affirmative defense *Q*. *D* moves for judgment on the pleadings. Under these circumstances, the court will assume that facts *X*, *Y*, and *Z* are true. The court will disregard the affirmative defense for purposes of ruling on the motion. *D* will be entitled to judgment on the pleadings only if facts *X*, *Y*, and *Z* do not state a claim upon which relief can be

---

27. *See* 5C CHARLES A. WRIGHT & ARTHUR R. MILLER, FEDERAL PRACTICE AND PROCEDURE: CIVIL § 1368, at 245 (3d ed. 2004). *See generally id.* at 243-54.

28. *See* Chapter 6(A)(4) *supra* ("Subsequent Pleading"); City Bank Farmers Trust Co. v. Hoey, 23 F. Supp. 831, 834 (S.D.N.Y. 1938), *aff'd*, 101 F.2d 9 (2d Cir. 1939).

29. *See* E.H. Schopler, Annotation, *Court's Power, on Motion for Judgment on the Pleadings, to Enter Judgment Against Movant*, 48 A.L.R.2D 1175 (1956).

granted. Thus, *D's* motion for judgment on the pleadings raises the same defense that *D* could have raised by a preanswer motion to dismiss under Federal Rule 12(b)(6) or a defense in the answer.

Illustration 10-8. *P* sues *D* in federal court, alleging in the complaint facts *X*, *Y*, and *Z*. *D's* answer denies facts *X*, *Y*, and *Z*. *D's* answer also alleges affirmative defenses *R* and *Q*. If *P* believes that affirmative defense *Q* is legally insufficient, the proper procedural action for *P* to take is a motion to strike the affirmative defense as insufficient under Federal Rule 12(f).[30] A motion for judgment on the pleadings would, technically, be improper because *P* is challenging only one of the defenses as legally insufficient. Under these circumstances, *P* is not entitled to judgment. *P* would only be entitled to judgment (and, therefore, to judgment on the pleadings) if (1) facts *X*, *Y*, and *Z* state a claim for relief; (2) *D* had admitted facts *X*, *Y*, and *Z*;[31] and (3) both affirmative defenses (*R* and *Q*) are legally insufficient.

* * * * *

Rule 12(d) provides that if a party supplements a motion for judgment on the pleadings with material outside the pleadings that the court does not exclude from consideration, the court must treat the motion as one for summary judgment. In that event, it should dispose of the motion pursuant to Rule 56.[32]

SECTION C. SUMMARY JUDGMENT

Summary judgment allows a party to demonstrate that material factual disputes in the pleadings are not authentic and that, once the apparent disputes are eliminated, the moving party is entitled to judgment as a matter of law. A motion for summary judgment thus resembles the Rule 12(b)(6) motion to dismiss for failure to state a claim upon which relief can be granted (in code-pleading states, the general demurrer) in that it challenges the legal sufficiency of the opposing party's case. However, a motion for summary judgment is unique. It allows this legal challenge to be raised in conjunction with a demonstration that actual disputes on the face of the pleadings are not real and that, as a result, no need exists for a trial.

The motion for summary judgment originated in English procedure, in which it was first applied only to narrow categories of cases.[33] By the time the Federal Rules of Civil Procedure were adopted in 1938, the English summary judgment procedure had been expanded to cover almost all cases.[34] Several

---

30. *But see* Moran v. Peralta Cmty. Coll. Dist., 825 F. Supp. 891, 893 (N.D. Cal. 1993) (partial judgments on the pleadings can be granted under Rule 12(c)).

31. When *D* denies facts *X*, *Y*, and *Z* in the answer, *P* cannot obtain judgment on the pleadings because for purposes of ruling on the motion made by *P*, *D's* denials must be accepted as representing the actual state of facts, *i.e.*, fact *X*, *Y*, and *Z* must be assumed to be false.

32. FED. R. CIV. P. 12(d); *see* section C *infra* ("Summary Judgment").

33. *See generally* John A. Bauman, *The Evolution of the Summary Judgment Procedure: An Essay Commemorating the Centennial Anniversary of Keating's Act*, 31 IND. L.J. 329 (1956); Charles E. Clark & Charles U. Samenow, *The Summary Judgment*, 38 YALE L.J. 423 (1929).

34. *See* FED. R. CIV. P. 56 advisory committee's note to the original rule.

American states also had adopted it.[35] In the Federal Rules, Rule 56 provides for summary judgment.[36] Many states have similar provisions.[37]

1. Summary Judgment Procedure

Rule 56(a) & (b)[38] provide that either party may move for a summary judgment at any time until the close of all discovery.[39] Under Rule 56(a), the party moving for summary judgment must identify each claim or defense or the part of each claim or defense on which summary judgment is sought. Rule 56(c) provides that a party asserting that a fact cannot be or is genuinely disputed must support the assertion by citing to particular parts of materials in the record and showing that the materials cited either do not establish the absence or presence of a genuine dispute or that an adverse party cannot produce admissible evidence to support the fact.[40]

Illustration 10-9. *P* sues *D* for $1,000,000 for personal injuries *P* allegedly received due to *D's* negligence in operating an automobile in violation of the speed limit. *D's* answer denies *D's* negligence and *P's* damages. *P* moves for summary judgment. *P* supports the motion with evidence demonstrating that *D* was convicted of speeding at the time of the accident. *P* has demonstrated *D's* negligence as a matter of law. However, the extent of *P's* damages is still in dispute. Thus, the court should grant partial summary judgment on the issue of liability. The only remaining issue for trial would be *P's* damages.

* * * * *

Because a motion for summary judgment is designed to pierce the allegations in the pleadings, materials outside the pleadings, like those mentioned in *Illustration 10-9*, normally accompany the motion in an attempt to demonstrate the absence of a genuine factual dispute. Rule 56(c) provides that the supporting materials for a motion for summary judgment include depositions, documents, electronically stored information, affidavits or declarations, stipulations (including those made for purposes of the motion only, admissions, interrogatory answers, or "other materials."[41] In addition, Rule 56(c)(3) provides that the court need not consider only the materials cited by the parties, but may consider other materials in

---

35. *See id.*

36. For a study of the operation of Rule 56, see William P. McLauchlan, *An Empirical Study of the Federal Summary Judgment Rule*, 6 J. LEGAL STUD. 427 (1977); *see also* Patricia M. Wald, *Summary Judgment at Sixty*, 76 TEX. L. REV. 1897 (1998).

37. *See, e.g.*, ILL. STAT. ANN. ch. 735, ¶ 5/2-1005 (Smith-Hurd 2003); MASS. R. CIV. P. 56; NEB. REV. STAT. §§ 25-1330 to 25-1336 (2008).

38. Rule 56 was revised in 2010 to "improve the procedures for presenting and deciding summary-judgment motions and to make the procedures more consistent with those already used in many courts." However, the "standard for granting summary judgment remains the same." *See* FED. R. CIV P. 56 advisory committee's note to the 2010 Amendment. The discussion that follows references the language and procedures in the amended rule. However, it must be kept in mind that summary judgment procedures in the states will, unless the states adopt the 2010 language of the new federal rule, be based on older versions of Rule 56. The discussion of the cases in subsection (2), below, is based on cases decided prior to the 2010 amendments. Because the standard for granting and denying summary judgment has not changed under the amendments, this case law should still be valid.

39. Successive motions for summary judgment are permissible in the court's discretion. *See, e.g.*, Hoffman v. Tonnemacher, 593 F.3d 908 (9th Cir. 2009) (district court did not abuse its discretion in allowing hospital to file successive motions for summary judgment).

40. *See* Fed. R. Civ. P. 56(c)(1)(A) & (B).

41. *See* FED. R. CIV. P. 56(c).

the record[42] Like judgment on the pleadings, a summary judgment can be granted for the party who did not move for summary judgment if the record shows that no genuine issue of fact exists and that the nonmoving party is entitled to judgment as a matter of law.[43] In addition, a court can order summary judgment on its own motion after identifying for the parties material facts that may not be genuinely in dispute.[44]

2. Applying the Summary Judgment Standard

Rule 56(a) provides that the court should grant summary judgment if the movant "shows that there is no genuine dispute as to any material fact and the movant is entitled to judgment as a matter of law."[45] Rule 56(e) provides that if a party fails to properly support an assertion of fact or fails to properly address another party's assertion of fact as required by Rule 56(c), the court may either given the party an opportunity to properly support or address the fact, may consider the fact undisputed for purposes of the motion, may grant summary judgment if the motion and supporting materials show that the movant is entitled to it, or issue any other appropriate order.[46]

Illustration 10-10. In *Adickes v. S.H. Kress & Co.*,[47] the plaintiff was a white school teacher. She was with six black students when they were refused service in the defendant's lunchroom. When they left defendant's store, they were arrested for vagrancy. She then commenced a federal civil rights action. She alleged that the defendant had conspired with a police officer in its store to deprive her of service and arrest her because she was a white accompanied by blacks. The defendant moved for summary judgment on the basis of the deposition of its store manager. The store manager maintained that no communication with the police about the plaintiff had occurred. The store manager also maintained that the plaintiff had been refused lunchroom service because the store manager was afraid there would be a riot in the store. The defendant also submitted affidavits by the chief of police and two arresting officers. These affidavits stated that the store manager had not asked that the plaintiff be arrested.

The plaintiff's own deposition admitted that she had no knowledge of any communication between the defendant's employees and the police. Instead, she relied on circumstantial evidence to support her claim of a conspiracy. Even though the plaintiff did not respond to the motion with materials that were acceptable under Rule 56,[48] the Supreme Court held that summary judgment against her was improper. The plaintiff was not obligated to submit materials under Rule 56 because the defendant had failed to meet its initial burden of demonstrating that no genuine issue of material fact existed in the case. The defendant had failed to meet its

42. *See* FED R.CIV. P. 56(c)(3).

43. Fed. R. Civ. P. 56(f)(1) now provides that the court may, after giving notice and a reasonable time to respond, "grant summary judgment for a nonmovant."

44. *See* FED. R. CIV. P. 56(f).

45. FED. R. CIV. P. 56(a).

46. FED. R. CIV. P. 56(e)(1)-(4).

47. 398 U.S. 144, 90 S. Ct. 1598, 26 L. Ed. 2d 142 (1970).

48. *See id.* at 159 & n.19, 90 S. Ct. at 1609 & n.19, 26 L. Ed. 2d at 155 & n.19.

burden because it did not "foreclose the possibility that there was a police [officer] in the Kress store while [plaintiff] was awaiting service, and that this police [officer] reached an understanding with some Kress employee that petitioner not be served."[49]

* * * * *

In ruling on a motion for summary judgment, a court is not supposed to try factual disputes.[50] Instead, the court's function is to determine when a "genuine" issue of material fact exists. However, Rule 56 provides no guidance concerning when a factual dispute should be considered "genuine." Courts applying the Rule 56 standard often employ catchy expressions to explain the genuineness standard.[51] Nevertheless, it is doubtful whether such explanations add much to the text of the rule. Furthermore, despite repeated statements to the contrary in their decisions, judges do make credibility determinations and weigh evidence in evaluating the genuineness and materiality of a factual dispute.[52] The best that can be said about the proper standard of judicial behavior under Rule 56 is that the judge should try to weed out those cases in which a trial will be useless. In doing so, the judge should take care not to deprive the party opposing the motion of the party's right to a trial—often by a jury—of legitimate factual disputes.

The "genuine issue" standard of Rule 56 is often equated with the standard for a judgment as a matter of law (directed verdict) under Federal Rule 50(a).[53] Under the Rule 50(a) standard, the judge is to direct a verdict when, under the governing law, reasonable minds cannot differ as to the result that must be reached on the existing evidence.[54] Thus, sometimes it is said that summary judgment should be granted when the state of the evidence is such that it would require a judgment as a matter of law (directed verdict) for the moving party.[55] This standard must be applied with an eye toward the burden of proof that would exist at trial on the moving and nonmoving parties.

Illustration 10-11. In *Anderson v. Liberty Lobby, Inc.*,[56] the plaintiffs commenced a diversity libel action against the defendants. The plaintiffs alleged that certain statements and illustrations in three magazine articles were false and derogatory. After discovery, the defendants moved for summary judgment. The defendants contended that the plaintiffs had to show actual malice under the applicable legal standard and that such malice was absent as a matter of law. The defendants' motion was accompanied by the affidavit of an employee of the

---

49. *Id.* at 157, 90 S. Ct. at 1608, 26 L. Ed. 2d at 154.

50. *See* 10A CHARLES A. WRIGHT ET AL., FEDERAL PRACTICE AND PROCEDURE: CIVIL § 2712, at 205-06 (3d ed. 1998).

51. *See id.* § 2725, at 424-37.

52. *See* the U.S. Supreme Court decisions discussed in *Illustrations 10-11* through *10-13 infra*; *see also* Michael Holley, *Making Credibility Determinations at Summary Judgment: How Judges Broaden Their Discretion While "Playing by the Rules,"* 20 WHITTIER L. REV. 865 (1999); *cf.* Suja A. Thomas, *Why Summary Judgment is Unconstitutional,* 93 VA. L. REV. 139 (2007).

53. *See* Chapter 11(H) *infra* ("Involuntary Dismissals, Directed Verdicts, Burden of Proof, and Presumptions").

54. *See* Anderson v. Liberty Lobby, Inc., 477 U.S. 242, 250-51, 106 S. Ct. 2505, 2511, 91 L. Ed. 2d 202, 213 (1986); Rojas v. Roman Catholic Diocese, 660 F.3d 98 (2d Cir. 2011) (district court properly made a limited assessment of the evidence that an employee had offered in opposition to summary judgment and concluded that no reasonable jury could believe it).

55. *See* 477 U.S. at 251, 106 S. Ct. at 2511, 91 L. Ed. 2d at 213.

56. *Id.* at 242, 106 S. Ct. 2505, 91 L. Ed. 2d 202 (1986).

defendants who had authored two of the articles in question. The affidavit detailed the quality of research and variety of sources used in the articles. Plaintiffs opposed the motion on the grounds that (1) numerous inaccuracies existed in the articles and (2) actual malice was present because several sources upon which the defendants had relied were patently unreliable. The district court granted the motion on the ground that the research and sources detailed by the defendants precluded a finding of actual malice. The court of appeals affirmed as to twenty-one and reversed as to nine of the allegedly libelous statements. In ruling on the summary judgment stage of the litigation, the court of appeals refused to apply the requirement that actual malice had to be proved by clear and convincing evidence.

The U.S. Supreme Court disagreed. The Supreme Court held that, in ruling on a motion for summary judgment, the judge must bear in mind the actual quantum and quality of proof necessary to succeed under the applicable burden of proof. As the dissenting justices pointed out, however, it is difficult to square the notion that the judge is to evaluate the evidence according to the burden of proof that would exist on the parties at trial with the notion that the judge is not to weigh the evidence on a motion for summary judgment, lest the judge encroach on the role of the jury.[57]

Illustration 10-12. In *Celotex Corp. v. Catrett*,[58] the plaintiff brought a wrongful death action. The plaintiff claimed that the death of her husband was the result of exposure to asbestos products manufactured by the defendant. The district court granted the defendant's motion for summary judgment because the plaintiff was unable to produce evidence that the decedent had been exposed to defendant's products. The court of appeals reversed on the ground that defendant's failure to support its motion with materials negating such exposure precluded summary judgment in the defendant's favor. The Supreme Court reversed. The Court held that it was unnecessary for a defending party to come forward with materials outside the pleadings to negate the opponent's claim.[59] Instead, the Court held that a party who bears the burden of proof on an element at trial must, after adequate

---

57. *See id.* at 257-58, 106 S. Ct. at 2515, 91 L. Ed. 2d at 217-18 (Brennan, J., dissenting); *id.* at 268-73, 106 S. Ct. at 2520-22, 91 L. Ed. 2d at 224-27 (Rehnquist, J., with whom Burger, C.J., joined, dissenting).

58. 477 U.S. 317, 106 S. Ct. 2548, 91 L. Ed. 2d 265 (1986); *see also* Brooke D. Coleman, *The Celotex Initial Burden Standard and an Opportunity to "Revivify" Rule 56*, 32 S. ILL. U. L.J. 295 (2008); David H. Simmons, *The* Celotex *Trilogy Revisited: How Misapplication of the Federal Summary Judgment Standard is Undermining the Seventh Amendment Right to a Jury Trial*, 1 FLA. A & M U. L. REV. 1 (2006); Adam N. Steinman, *The Irrepressible Myth of* Celotex: *Reconsidering Summary Judgment Burdens Twenty Years After the Trilogy*, 63 WASH. & LEE L. REV. 81 (2006).

59. *See* 477 U.S. at 323, 106 S. Ct. at 2553, 91 L. Ed. 2d at 274. The Court stated that

> the plain language of Rule 56[] mandates the entry of summary judgment, after adequate time for discovery and upon motion, against a party who fails to make a showing sufficient to establish the existence of an element essential to that party's case, and on which that party will bear the burden of proof at trial. In such a situation, there can be no "genuine issue as to any material fact," since a complete failure of proof concerning an essential element of the nonmoving party's case necessarily renders all other facts immaterial.

Id. at 322-23, 106 S. Ct. at 2552, 91 L. Ed. 2d at 272-73. In addition, the Court has stated that "[w]hen the nonmoving party bears the burden of proof at trial, summary judgment is warranted if the nonmovant fails to 'make a showing sufficient to establish the existence of an element essential to [its] case.'" Nebraska v. Wyoming, 507 U.S. 584, 589, 113 S. Ct. 1689, 1694, 123 L. Ed. 2d 317, 329 (1993) (citing *Celotex*); *see also* Cehic v. Mack Molding, Inc., 2006 VT 12, 179 Vt. 602, 895 A.2d 167 (when moving party does not have burden of proof at trial, it may satisfy its burden of production by showing that there is an absence of evidence in the record to support the nonmoving party's case).

time for discovery, be able to make a showing sufficient to establish the existence of the element.

* * * * *

It is commonly stated that on a motion for summary judgment, the evidence is viewed in the light most favorable to the nonmoving party and that the nonmoving party is given the benefit of all favorable inferences that can be drawn from it.[60] Nevertheless, some decisions seem to utilize the summary judgment procedure in a more vigorous fashion.[61]

Illustration 10-13. In *Matsushita Electric Industrial Co. v. Zenith Radio Corp.*,[62] the plaintiffs brought an antitrust action. The plaintiffs alleged that the defendants had conspired to raise, fix, and maintain artificially high prices for television sets in Japan and to fix artificially low prices for television sets in the United States. After several years of discovery, the defendants moved for summary judgment on all claims. The district court found that the admissible evidence submitted by the plaintiffs to defeat the motion did not raise a genuine issue of material fact and granted the motion. The court of appeals found summary judgment improper and reversed. The Supreme Court reversed. While paying lip service to the rule that the evidence is to be viewed in the light most favorable to the nonmoving party,[63] the Court stated that a plaintiff seeking recovery under the antitrust laws must present evidence that tends to show the inference of conspiracy is reasonable in light of the possible competing inferences of (1) independent action by the defendants and (2) collusive action that could not have harmed the plaintiffs.[64] After canvassing the nature of predatory pricing conspiracies and the defendants' behavior over the course of the alleged conspiracy involved in the action, the Court concluded that the defendants had no plausible motive to engage in the alleged conspiracy.[65] The Court's economic analysis of predatory pricing conspiracies may well have been correct.[66] Nevertheless, it is difficult to disagree

---

60. *See* 10A CHARLES A. WRIGHT ET AL., FEDERAL PRACTICE AND PROCEDURE: CIVIL § 2727, at 459 (3d ed. 1998).

61. For example, the *Anderson* decision discussed in *Illustration 10-11* seemed to involve the judge in the process of weighing evidence that is theoretically reserved for the jury after trial.

62. 475 U.S. 574, 106 S. Ct. 1348, 89 L. Ed. 2d 538 (1986).

63. *See id.* at 587, 106 S. Ct. at 1356, 89 L. Ed. 2d at 552-53.

64. *See id.* at 588, 106 S. Ct. at 1356-57, 89 L. Ed. 2d at 553.

65. The Court concluded that

> the absence of any plausible motive to engage in the conduct charged is highly relevant to whether a "genuine issue for trial" exists within the meaning of Rule 56(e). Lack of motive bears on the range of permissible conclusions that might be drawn from ambiguous evidence: if [defendants] had no rational economic motive to conspire, and if their conduct is consistent with other, equally plausible explanations, the conduct does not give rise to an inference of conspiracy.

Id. at 596-97, 106 S. Ct. at 1361, 89 L. Ed. 2d at 558-59.

66. *See generally* Daniel P. Collins, *Summary Judgment and Circumstantial Evidence*, 40 STAN. L. REV. 491 (1988); James F. Ponsoldt & Marc J. Lewyn, *Judicial Activism, Economic Theory and the Role of Summary Judgment in Sherman Act Conspiracy Cases: The Illogic of* Matsushita, 33 ANTITRUST BULL. 575 (1988). The U.S. Supreme Court has distinguished *Matsushita*, suggesting that the case does not represent a major expansion of the summary judgment power in antitrust cases. In Eastman Kodak Co. v. Image Technical Services, Inc., 504 U.S. 451, 112 S. Ct. 2072, 119 L. Ed. 2d 265 (1992), the Court stated that *Matsushita* did not "introduce a special burden on plaintiffs facing summary judgment in antitrust cases." Rather, *Matsushita* only held that the plaintiff's economic theory could not be "senseless," because a reasonable jury could not find in the plaintiff's favor on a senseless economic theory. *Id.* at 468, 112 S. Ct. at 2083, 119 L. Ed. 2d at 285. *See generally* William W. Schwarzer & Alan Hirsch, *Summary Judgment After* Eastman Kodak, 45 HASTINGS L.J. 1 (1993).

with the dissenting Justices, who stated that the majority was evaluating the persuasiveness of the plaintiffs' evidence, a task normally reserved for the jury.[67]

* * * * *

The decisions of the U.S. Supreme Court discussed in the above illustrations seem to encourage the use of the summary judgment motion more than in the past.[68] However, cases clearly exist in which summary judgment will still be inappropriate.

Illustration 10-14. *P*, an employee of *C*, was injured when a tank filled with asphalt materials *P* was heating exploded. The tank was supplied by *D* to *C*. *P* sued *D* for damages suffered in the accident. *D* moved for summary judgment against *P*. Under the applicable substantive law, *D* was not liable to *P* on a strict liability theory. Rather, *D* could only be held liable to *P* on a theory of negligence if *D* owed a duty of care to *P*. Under these circumstances, it would be inappropriate to grant summary judgment in *D's* favor. The question whether *D* owes a duty of care to *P* depends upon whether *D*, in performing services for *C*, should have recognized that the services were necessary for *P's* protection. If so, *D* would be obligated to exercise reasonable care in performing the services. Genuine issues of fact exist on this question because the resolution of the question depends upon the context in which the services were performed. In addition, the question of *D's* negligence—*i.e.*, whether *D* exercised reasonable care in performing the services—will usually also raise genuine issues of fact. Because questions of negligence involve the reasonableness of the party's conduct under the circumstances of the case, it is seldom possible to obtain summary judgment in negligence actions.[69]

SECTION D. VOLUNTARY DISMISSALS

At common law and equity, the courts allowed the plaintiff to dismiss a case voluntarily at any time prior to judgment. Such a voluntary dismissal was not "on the merits." Thus, a voluntary dismissal did not preclude the plaintiff from

---

67. *See* 475 U.S. at 598-607, 106 S. Ct. at 1362-66, 89 L. Ed. 2d at 560-65 (White, J., with whom Brennan, Blackmun, and Stevens joined, dissenting); *cf.* Poller v. CBS, Inc., 368 U.S. 464, 473, 82 S. Ct. 486, 491, 7 L. Ed. 2d 458, 464 (1962) ("We believe that summary procedures should be used sparingly in complex antitrust litigation where motive and intent play leading roles, the proof is largely in the hands of the alleged conspirators, and hostile witnesses thicken the plot").

68. *See* 10A CHARLES A. WRIGHT ET AL., FEDERAL PRACTICE AND PROCEDURE: CIVIL § 2727, at 468 (3d ed. 1998). *See generally* David Kessler, *Justices in the Jury Box: Video Evidence and Summary Judgment*, 31 HARV. J. L. & PUB. POLICY 423 (2008); Elizabeth M. Schneider, *The Dangers of Summary Judgment: Gender and Federal Civil Litigation*, 59 RUTGERS L. REV. 705 (2007); Paul W. Mollica, *Federal Summary Judgment at High Tide*, 84 MARQ. L. REV. 141 (2000) (describing "the emergence of summary judgment as the new fulcrum of federal civil dispute resolution" and extensively reviewing Supreme Court and lower court decisions); Marcy J. Levine, Comment, *Summary Judgment: The Majority View Undergoes a Complete Reversal in the 1986 Supreme Court*, 37 EMORY L.J. 171 (1988); Craig M. Reiser, *The Unconstitutional Application of Summary Judgment in Factually Intensive Inquiries*, 12 U. PA. J. CONST. L. 195 (2009); Robert K. Smith, Comment, *Federal Summary Judgment: The "New" Workhorse for an Overburdened Federal Court System*, 20 U.C. DAVIS L. REV. 955 (1987); Susan L. Watchman, Note, *Summary Judgment in Antitrust Cases—Is the Standard Changing?*, 20 ARIZ. ST. L.J. 591 (1988). *But see* Samuel Issacharoff & George Loewenstein, *Second Thoughts About Summary Judgment*, 100 YALE L.J. 73 (1990).

69. *See, e.g.*, Saddler v. Alaska Marine Lines, Inc., 856 P.2d 784 (Alaska 1993); *see also* Bomar v. Moser, 369 Ark. 123, 251 S.W.3d 234 (2007) (fraudulent concealment of facts will toll running of statute of limitations, but factual issues existed on fraudulent concealment issue that precluded summary judgment); 10A CHARLES A. WRIGHT ET AL., FEDERAL PRACTICE AND PROCEDURE: CIVIL § 2729 (3d ed. 1998).

recommencing an action on the same claim at a later time.[70] Under modern codes of civil procedure, voluntary dismissals are still available, but are usually restricted in various ways.[71]

Federal Rule 41(a) provides for voluntary dismissals.[72] The plaintiff may dismiss an action without the court's consent either (1) by filing a notice of dismissal at any time before service of an answer or motion for summary judgment, whichever occurs first, or (2) by filing a stipulation of dismissal signed by all parties who have appeared in the action.[73] A dismissal by either of these methods is without prejudice to the plaintiff's ability to recommence the action unless (1) stated to the contrary in the notice of dismissal or stipulation or (2) the plaintiff has previously dismissed the same action in any federal or state court.[74]

Illustration 10-15. *P* sues *D* in a state court. *P* then voluntarily dismisses the action without prejudice under a state rule that allows voluntary dismissals at any time before trial without penalty. Subsequently, *P* sues *D* in a U.S. District Court on the same claim in a diversity action. Before *D* answers, *P* dismisses this action under Rule 41(a)(1)(i) by filing a notice of dismissal. This second dismissal is with prejudice. Rule 41(a)(1)(B) provides that "a notice of dismissal operates as an adjudication upon the merits when filed by a plaintiff who has once dismissed in any court of the United States or of any state an action based on or including the same claim." Under the terms of Rule 41, the prior voluntary dismissal of the claim in state court caused the second dismissal of the claim in federal court to operate as an adjudication upon the merits. Thus, *P* may not bring another action against *D* on the same claim in a federal or state court.

Illustration 10-16. On the facts of *Illustration 10-15*, assume that the first dismissal had been in federal court under Rule 41(a)(1)(i) and the second dismissal had been in state court under a state rule that did not make the second dismissal an adjudication upon the merits. Under these circumstances, *P* could bring a third action against *D* on the claim in a state or federal court. Rule 41 cannot make the second dismissal an adjudication upon the merits unless the rule operates in the court system in which the second dismissal occurs. Thus, the law of the state in

---

70. *See* ROBERT W. MILLAR, CIVIL PROCEDURE OF THE TRIAL COURT IN HISTORICAL PERSPECTIVE 253-54 (1952).

71. *See e.g.*, NEB. REV. STAT. §§ 25-601 to 25-603 (2004); *see also* Michael E. Solimine & Amy E. Lippert, *Deregulating Voluntary Dismissals*, 36 U. MICH. J. L. REFORM 367 (2003) (arguing that to reduce the prejudice to defendants of voluntary dismissals, courts should automatically grant permission to plaintiffs to dismiss without prejudice as long as the plaintiffs pay the reasonable costs and attorneys' fees incurred by the defendant up to the time of dismissal). *See generally* ROBERT W. MILLAR, CIVIL PROCEDURE OF THE TRIAL COURT IN HISTORICAL PERSPECTIVE 256-58 (1952); Chapter 13(B)(2) *infra* ("Judgments 'on the Merits'").

72. FED. R. CIV. P. 41(a); *see also* Chapter 8(D)(4)*(b)(v) supra* (discussing dismissals of class actions).

73. FED. R. CIV. P. 41(a)(1)(A); *see In re* Bath & Kitchen Fixtures Antitrust Litig., 535 F.3d 161 (3d Cir. 2008) (Rule 12(b)(6) motion to dismiss for failure to state a claim upon which relief can be granted does not cut off the plaintiff's right to dismiss voluntarily under Rule 41(a)(1)(A)(i)); Finley Lines Joint Protective Bd. Unit 200 v. Norfolk S. Corp., 109 F.3d 993 (4th Cir. 1997) (the plaintiff's right to dismiss voluntarily is not automatically cut off when the defendant files and serves a motion to dismiss under Rule 12(b)(6), accompanied by affidavits).

74. FED. R. CIV. P. 41(a)(1). Rule 41(d) provides that if the plaintiff has previously dismissed an action and then commences an action in any court based on the same claim against the same defendant, the court may order the payment of costs of the action previously dismissed and may stay the proceedings in the action until the plaintiff has complied with that order. FED. R. CIV. P. 41(d). However, costs under these circumstances do not appear to include attorney's fees. *See* Edward X. Clinton, Jr., *Does Rule 41(d) Authorize an Award of Attorney's Fees*, 71 ST. JOHN'S L. REV. 81 (1997) (most reasonable conclusion is that Rule 41(d) does not authorize attorney's fees).

which the second dismissal occurred defines the effect of the judgment.[75] That law provides that the dismissal is without prejudice.[76]

* * * * *

Rule 41(a)(2) provides that unless one of the methods described in Rule 41(a)(1) is available, the plaintiff may obtain dismissal only by consent of court and under such terms and conditions as the court considers proper.[77] However, Rule 41(a)(2) also provides that an action may not be dismissed over the defendant's objection under certain circumstances. If the defendant has pleaded a counterclaim prior to the service of the plaintiff's motion to dismiss, the court may not dismiss the counterclaim unless the counterclaim can remain pending for independent adjudication. A dismissal under Rule 41(a)(2) is without prejudice, unless the court otherwise specifies in its order.[78]

SECTION E. INVOLUNTARY DISMISSALS

Rule 41(b) provides for involuntary dismissal on several grounds.[79] The first sentence of Rule 41(b) states that if the plaintiff fails to prosecute the action or to comply with "these rules or a court order," the defendant may move to dismiss the action or any claim asserted against the defendant.[80] The last sentence of Rule 41(b) states that unless the dismissal order states otherwise, a dismissal under Rule 41(b) and any other dismissal not provided for in Rule 41, with certain exceptions,

---

75. *See* Chapter 13(B)(2) *infra* ("Judgments 'on the Merits'").

76. In Nelson v. Napolitano, 657 F.3d 586 (7th Cir. 2011), the plaintiffs dismissed an action voluntarily without prejudice under Rule 41(a)(1) as a matter of right. They then made a motion to reinstate the action under Rule 60(b) after the statute of limitations had expired. The district court denied their motion, and the court of appeals held that this was not error. Although the court of appeals held that a voluntary dismissal as a matter of right did not terminate the jurisdiction of the district court to consider of reopening and setting aside the judgment of dismissal, it nevertheless held the district court did not abuse its discretion because the plaintiffs assumed that their right to reinstate the action was automatic and did not make a case for relief under Rule 60(b).

77. FED. R. CIV. P. 41(a)(2); *see* Wojtas v. Capital Guardian Trust Co., 477 F.3d 924 (7th Cir. 2007) (voluntary dismissal without prejudice to refiling in another jurisdiction is prejudicial to defendant when statute of limitations has run on plaintiff's claim); Versa Prods., Inc. v. Home Depot, USA, Inc., 387 F.3d 1325 (11th Cir. 2004) (after defendant requested and received transfer of case to another district, plaintiff moved for a voluntary dismissal without prejudice; court correctly conditioned dismissal on refiling in the transferee district to prevent defendant from having to relitigate the convenient forum issue); David J. Comeaux, Comment, *Avoiding Nonjudicious Nonsuits: Hearing the Defendant on Rule 41(a)(2) Motions*, 32 HOUS. L. REV. 159 (1995). *Compare* Ohlander v. Larson, 114 F.3d 1531 (10th Cir. 1997) (district court may not refuse permission to voluntarily dismiss an action on the grounds that the party seeking dismissal has engaged in contemptuous conduct) *with* Teck Gen. P'ship v. Crown Cent. Petroleum Corp., 28 F. Supp. 2d 989 (E.D. Va. 1998) (plaintiff violates a discovery scheduling order requiring the plaintiff to make disclosure of expert evidence before a certain date and is sanctioned by having stricken the evidence that was the subject of the order; plaintiff's motion for a voluntary dismissal to avoid the effect of the sanction should not be granted).

78. FED. R. CIV. P. 41(a)(2); *see* County of Santa Fe v. Public Serv. Co., 311 F.3d 1031 (10th Cir. 2002) (a voluntary dismissal with prejudice does not have to be granted by a court under circumstances in which the dismissal will prejudice the interests of intervenors). In Michigan Surgery Investment, L.L.C. v. Arman, 627 F.3d 572 (6th Cir. 2010), the plaintiffs moved for voluntary dismissal without prejudice, but the district court dismissed with prejudice. The court of appeals reversed, holding that before dismissing with prejudice, the district court was obligated to inform the plaintiffs that it intended to dismiss on the merits and give them an opportunity to withdraw their motion. In Thatcher v. Hanover Insurance Group, Inc., 659 F.3d 1212 (8th Cir. 2011), the defendants removed a class action under the Class Action Fairness Act discussed in Chapters 2 and 8 above. The plaintiff then moved under Rule 41(a)(2) to dismiss without prejudice, and the district court dismissed. The court of appeals reversed and held that the district court abused its discretion in granting the motion without first addressing whether it was an improper forum-shopping tactic.

79. Involuntary dismissal after presentation of the plaintiff's evidence in a trial to the court is discussed in Chapter 11(H) *infra* ("Involuntary Dismissals, Directed Verdicts, Burden of Proof, and Presumptions").

80. FED. R. CIV. P. 41(b).

operates as an adjudication on the merits.[81] The exceptions are dismissals for lack of jurisdiction, for improper venue, or for failure to join a party under Rule 19.[82]

In *Costello v. United States*,[83] the U.S. Supreme Court held that a failure to satisfy a precondition to suit would fit within the exception to Rule 41(b) for dismissals on grounds of lack of jurisdiction. After *Costello*, the question thus becomes, what may properly be considered a "precondition of suit"? The *Costello* interpretation of Rule 41(b) can be confined within reasonable boundaries if it is limited to dismissals that cannot be corrected through the liberal procedures available for the correction of error under the Federal Rules and modern systems of appellate review. *Costello* involved the failure to file an affidavit that was required before the action could be brought. Once the failure to file the affidavit had occurred, it could not be corrected by amendment, appeal, or any other available procedure. In contrast, a dismissal on Rule 12(b)(6) grounds for failure to state a claim upon which relief can be granted should not be considered a failure to satisfy a precondition to suit. The liberal notice pleading philosophy of the Federal Rules makes it easy for the plaintiff to state a claim for relief.[84] In addition, the liberal amendment policies of Rule 15 allow the plaintiff to correct any deficiency in stating the claim.[85] Furthermore, error committed by the trial court in concluding that the complaint did not state a claim can be readily corrected by appeal. Therefore, a failure to state a claim dismissal should not be considered a failure to satisfy a precondition of suit within the meaning of *Costello*.[86]

Illustration 10-17. *P* sues *D* in a federal diversity action on January 1. *P's* claim is based on a note that does not mature until December 1. The action is dismissed on the grounds that it is premature. A dismissal on prematurity grounds should fit within the *Costello* interpretation of the jurisdictional exception to Rule 41(b). Once the plaintiff makes the mistake of bringing the action prematurely, no procedural means exist under modern procedural systems, including the Federal Rules, to correct the error. The claim must simply mature. Therefore, the dismissal should be considered a dismissal for failure to satisfy a precondition of suit and, therefore, "without prejudice."

* * * * *

In *Semtek International, Inc. v. Lockheed Martin Corp.*,[87] the Supreme Court construed Rule 41(b) as inapplicable to a judgment of dismissal in a federal diversity action in California on the ground that the California statute of limitations

---

81. *Id.*; *see* Brereton v. Bountiful City Corp., 434 F.3d 1213 (10th Cir. 2006); Farmer v. Levenson, 79 Fed. App'x 918 (7th Cir. 2003) (holding that it was error to dismiss with prejudice for improper venue).

82. *See* FED. R. CIV. P. 41(b); *see also* FED. R. CIV. P. 41(c), (d).

83. 365 U.S. 265, 81 S. Ct. 534, 5 L. Ed. 2d 551 (1961).

84. Of course, today, this statement must be qualified somewhat by the *Twombly* and *Ashcroft* cases that have limited the ability to plead in a conclusory fashion in at least some cases. These cases are examined in Chapter 6(D)(2)(b) *supra* ("Notice Pleading").

85. *See* Chapter 6(D) *supra* ("Federal Rules Pleading") for a discussion of federal pleading and amendment practice; *see* Chapter 12(B) *infra* ("Appellate Review") for a discussion of the availability of appeal in federal court.

86. *Cf.* Betty K. Agencies, Ltd v. M/V Monada, 432 F.3d 1333 (11th Cir. 2005) (dismissal with prejudice was improper for failure of plaintiff to reply to defendant's counterclaim absent evidence that plaintiff acted willfully or contumaciously). *Costello* and the effect of Rule 12(b)(6) dismissals are discussed further in Chapter 13(B)(2) *infra* ("Judgments 'On the Merits'").

87. 531 U.S. 497, 121 S. Ct. 1021, 149 L. Ed. 2d 32 (2001). *Semtek* is discussed in Chapter 5 *supra* and in Chapter 13 *infra*.

barred the action. The Court construed Rule 41(b) as a rule governing the "internal procedure[] of the [judgment-]rendering court itself."[88] Thus, the Court held that Rule 41(b) did not preclude an action on the same claim in any court other than the one in which the judgment of dismissal was rendered.[89] Consequently, the effect of federal dismissals in state and other federal courts will be determined by common-law rules. Normally, the effect of dismissals in federal question cases will be determined by independent federal common-law rules of claim preclusion, while dismissals in diversity actions will be determined by the adoption of the law of the state in which the dismissal occurs, unless state law is incompatible with federal interests.[90]

Semtek casts doubt on the continuing accuracy of the above discussion of what the Supreme Court would hold in cases of Rule 12(b)(6) dismissals. If the Court adheres to the *Semtek* rationale in the case of a Rule 12(b)(6) dismissal that is allowed to become final by the plaintiff, the Court would hold that such a dismissal only precludes an action in the same federal court in which the judgment of dismissal is rendered. The judgment of dismissal would not have a claim preclusive effect in any other court, including, apparently, another federal court in a different district in the same state. In addition, as observed in Chapter 5, it is also possible that *Semtek* could have implications for the operations of claim preclusion under other Federal Rules of Civil Procedure, such as Rule 13(a) governing compulsory counterclaims.[91] However, as will be further explored in Chapter 13, *Semtek's* interpretation of Rule 41 is tortured. Consequently, it would not be surprising for the case to be confined to its facts, with the result that it would not be applied to any other Federal Rule, such as Rule 13(a), providing for preclusion in later actions.

Finally, note that *Semtek* did not discuss the possibility that *Costello*, discussed above, provides a basis for holding that a statute of limitations dismissal would fit within one of the exceptions of Rule 41(b).

SECTION F. MISCELLANEOUS METHODS OF DISPOSING OF AN ACTION WITHOUT TRIAL

1. Settlement: In General

Obviously, not all cases result in disposition by means of formal procedural devices. Many are settled out of court by the parties.[92] When the parties reach a settlement, they often embody their settlement in a consent judgment to protect against further litigation over the same claim. Consent judgments are both contracts

---

88. *See* 531 U.S. at 503, 121 S. Ct. at 1025, 149 L. Ed. 2d at 39-40.
89. *See id.*
90. *See id.* at 509, 121 S. Ct. at 1028-29, 149 L. Ed. 2d at 43.
91. *See* Chapter 5(F)(5) *supra* (discussing the implications of *Semtek* for other cases).
92. *See* Chapter 1(E) *supra* ("Alternative Dispute Resolution").

and judgments. The parties control the terms of a consent judgment to the same extent that they control the terms of any other contract.[93]

Some kinds of settlements may not be permissible under the prevailing rules of ethics and public policies of a state. So-called "Mary Carter agreements"[94] occur when a plaintiff sues multiple defendants and settles with one of the defendants, but the settling defendant remains in the action. For example, such an agreement might provide that if the plaintiff obtains a judgment against the nonsettling defendants that exceeds a particular amount, the settling defendant's money may be returned in whole or part. The settling defendant thus continues to exercise influence over the conduct of the action. In effect, the settling defendant combines with the plaintiff against the nonsettling defendants. These kinds of agreements have been criticized as unethical and a perversion of the adversary system.[95] Several courts have held them invalid.[96]

2. Settlement: Rule 68

(a) General Problems in Administering Rule 68

Modern procedural systems often contain rules designed to encourage settlement. For example, Federal Rule 68 provides a procedure whereby a defending party can make an offer to allow judgment to be taken against the party for a certain amount plus costs. If the offer is not accepted and the judgment that the offeree obtains is not more favorable than the unaccepted offer, the offeree must pay the costs incurred by the offeror after the making of the offer. The purpose of Rule 68 is obviously to encourage settlements. Comparable provisions often exist within the states.[97]

---

93. The primary difficulty with consent judgments is that because they do not involve actual litigation of issues of fact or law, they can have a claim preclusion effect, but not an issue preclusion effect. *See* Chapter 13 *infra* ("Finality in Litigation") for a complete discussion of the doctrines of claim and issue preclusion. However, the contractual nature of consent judgments means that if the parties intend for issue preclusion as well as claim preclusion to apply, the judgment can have both claim and issue preclusion effects. *See generally* 18A CHARLES A. WRIGHT ET AL., FEDERAL PRACTICE AND PROCEDURE: CIVIL § 4443, at 252-53 (2d ed. 2002); RESTATEMENT (SECOND) OF JUDGMENTS § 27 cmt. e (1982); *see also* Norfolk S. Corp. v. Chevron, U.S.A., Inc., 371 F.3d 1285 (11th Cir. 2004) (judgment of dismissal with prejudice based upon settlement agreement derives its force from agreement and consent of parties; judgment did not have res judicata effect because settlement agreement did not cover claims at issue).

94. The name is derived from Booth v. Mary Carter Paint Co., 202 So. 2d 8 (Fla. Dist. Ct. App. 1967).

95. *See* June F. Entman, *Mary Carter Agreements: An Assessment of Attempted Solutions*, 38 U. FLA. L. REV. 521 (1986); *see also* LARRY L. TEPLY, LEGAL NEGOTIATION IN A NUTSHELL 260-63 (2d ed. 2005); John E. Benedict, Note, *Its a Mistake to Tolerate the Mary Carter Agreement*, 87 COLUM. L. REV. 368 (1987); Warren Freedman, *The Expected Demise of "Mary Carter": She Never Was Well!*, 1975 INS. L.J. 602; David R. Miller, Comment, *Mary Carter Agreements: Unfair and Unnecessary*, 32 SW. L.J. 779 (1978).

96. *See, e.g.*, Dosdourian v. Carsten, 624 So. 2d 241 (Fla. 1993); Lum v. Stinnett, 87 Nev. 402, 488 P.2d 347 (1971); Elbaor v. Smith, 845 S.W.2d 240 (Tex. 1992); *see also* Christopher Carr, Note, *Sudden Death: The Supreme Court of Texas Kills Mary Carter*, 24 TEX. TECH. L. REV. 1227 (1993) (discussing the *Elbaor* case).

97. *See e.g.*, NEB. REV. STAT. §§ 25-901, 25-906 to 25-907 (2008); *see also* Jeffrey A. Parness, *Civil Claim Settlement Talks Involving Third Parties and Insurance Company Adjusters: When Should Lawyer Conduct Standards Apply?*, 77 ST. JOHN'S L. REV. 603 (2003).

The U.S. Supreme Court had interpreted Rule 68 in two significant decisions. First, in *Delta Air Lines, Inc. v. August*,[98] the U.S. Supreme Court held that Federal Rule 68 does not allow costs to be awarded against a plaintiff-offeree when the defendant obtains judgment in the case. Rather, the rule applies only to judgments obtained by plaintiffs in an amount less than the defendant offered. Second, in *Marek v. Chesny*,[99] a plaintiff in a civil rights action under 42 U.S.C. § 1983 recovered less than the amount offered by the defendant under Rule 68. The plaintiff moved for an award of attorney's fees under 42 U.S.C. § 1988. That section provides that a prevailing plaintiff in an action under 42 U.S.C. § 1983 may recover attorney's fees as part of the costs of the action. The U.S. Supreme Court held, however, that attorney's fees were to be included within the term "costs" in Rule 68 whenever such fees were properly awardable as costs under the applicable substantive statute. Thus, the plaintiff was not entitled to recover attorney's fees as costs under Rule 68 because the defendant had made a proper offer under the rule and the plaintiff had recovered less than the amount offered. Under *Marek*, once the defendant has made a proper Rule 68 offer, a prevailing plaintiff will only be able to recover attorney's fees as costs if the applicable substantive law classifies attorney's fees as "costs" *and* the plaintiff recovers more than the amount offered.[100]

---

98. 450 U.S. 346, 101 S. Ct. 1146, 67 L. Ed. 2d 287 (1981); *see also* Le v. University of Pa., 321 F.3d 403 (3d Cir. 2003) (an unapportioned offer of judgment made to multiple defendants under Rule 68 is not necessarily invalid where one defendant was contractually obligated to assume any financial responsibility that might result from the other's actions and thus the identity of the two defendants' pocketbooks was essentially the same); *cf.* Dearmore v. City of Garland, 519 F.3d 517 (5th Cir. 2008) (preliminary injunction based on an unambiguous indication of probable success on the merits makes an award of statutory attorneys' fees appropriate when the injunction causes the defendant to moot the action and prevents plaintiff from obtaining final relief on the merits). *But cf.* Biodiversity Conservation Alliance v. Stem, 519 F.3d 1226 (10th Cir. 2008) (preliminary injunction that does not provide relief on the merits does not make plaintiff a prevailing party for purposes of an award of statutory attorney's fees).

99. 473 U.S. 1, 105 S. Ct. 3012, 87 L. Ed. 2d 1 (1985).

100. *Id.* at 11, 105 S. Ct. at 3017-18, 87 L. Ed. 2d at 11; *see also* Thompson v. Southern Farm Bureau Cas. Ins. Co., 520 F.3d 902 (8th Cir. 2008) (under *Marek*, to be effective an offer of judgment may not exclude costs altogether, and an acceptance of the offer does not make a no costs offer valid); Berkla v. Corel Corp., 302 F.3d 909, 921-22 (9th Cir. 2002) (plaintiff's failure to accept settlement offer that was greater than amount actually recovered did not preclude recovery of costs because settlement offer did not comply with requirements of Rule 68); Shafer v. Kings Tire Serv., Inc., 215 W. Va. 169, 597 S.E.2d 302 (2004) (under state equivalent of Federal Rule 68, costs include attorney's fees when any statute applicable to the case defines costs as including attorney's fees); Daniel E. Burgoyne, Note, *Attorneys' Fees and the Conflict Between Rule 68 and the Clean Water Act's Citizen Suit Provision*, 33 B.C. ENVT'L AFF. L. REV. 627 (2006); Ian H. Fisher, *Federal Rule 68, A Defendant's Subtle Weapon: Its Use and Pitfalls*, 14 DE PAUL BUS. L.J. 89 (2001) (discussing strategic considerations in deciding the best situations in which to make an offer under Rule 68 and commenting upon its potential use to deprive a court of jurisdiction, particularly in the context of class actions); Danielle M. Shelton, *Rewriting Rule 68: Realizing the Benefits of the Federal Settlement Rule by Injecting Certainty Into Offers of Judgment*, 91 MINN. L. REV. 865 (2007); Georgia A. Staton, *Practitioner's Handy Guide to Rule 68 Offers of Judgment: Defense Counsel's Sword*, 67 DEF. COUNS. J. 366 (2000); Symposium, *Revitalizing FRCP 68: Can Offers of Judgment Provide Adequate Incentives for Fair, Early Settlement of Fee-Recovery Cases?*, 57 MERCER L. REV. 717 (2006). Rule 68 has received extensive attention from the Advisory Committee and the commentators. In August 1983, the Committee on Rules of Practice and Procedure of the Judicial Conference of the United States submitted to the bench and bar a preliminary draft of proposed amendments to the Federal Rules of Civil Procedure, including the draft of an amendment to Federal Rule 68. *See* 98 F.R.D. 361 (1983). In September 1984, the Committee submitted a substitute for this amendment. *See* 102 F.R.D. 432 (1984). Neither proposed amendment has ever been adopted by the Supreme Court. For a recent proposal to amend Rule 68 to allow plaintiffs to make formal offers of judgment and include attorney's fees as recoverable court costs, see Joshua P. Davis, *Toward a Jurisprudence of Trial and Settlement: Allocating Attorney's Fees by Amending Federal Rule of Civil Procedure 68*, 48 ALA. L. REV. 65 (1996). For a general analysis of the interpretation of Rule 68, as well as a critique of various proposals to reform the rule and another proposed amendment, see Lesley S. Bonney et al., *Rule 68: Awakening a Sleeping Giant*, 65 GEO. WASH. L. REV. 379 (1997) (proposing to amend Rule 68 would define costs as including attorney's fees, whether or not such fees are otherwise recoverable). For a criticism of the Committee's 1984 proposal (and implicitly other more recent proposals) on the ground that it exceeds the rulemaking authority of the Supreme

(b) Rules Enabling Act Problems in Administering Rule 68

With the increased interest in settlement, some states may adopt means of encouraging settlement in ways that potentially conflict with Federal Rule 68.[101] Given the way Rule 68 is currently configured, however, states may be able to avoid a direct confrontation between differing state and federal approaches. For example, a Wisconsin statute provides for double costs when the *plaintiff* obtains a favorable judgment after the defendant's refusal of the plaintiff's settlement demand. In *S.A. Healy Co. v. Milwaukee Metropolitan Sewerage District*,[102] the Seventh Circuit found no direct conflict between the Wisconsin statute and Rule 68 because Rule 68 deals only with settlement offers by defendants, not plaintiffs. Finding that, under *Erie*, the statute was "substantive," the court concluded that the statute had to be applied in diversity actions in federal court.[103] More serious conflicts may arise when the state provisions apply to defendants (in addition to plaintiffs) and shift attorney's fees.[104]

The Seventh Circuit was undoubtedly correct in holding that, if there is no conflict between Rule 68 and the state law, a federal diversity court should be required to apply the state law. However, it is not clear that the court's reasoning was entirely correct. As discussed in Chapter 5, the Supreme Court has consistently phrased the *Erie* policies in terms of forum shopping and discrimination against citizens of the forum state.[105] However, there would be no plaintiff forum shopping if the federal courts disregarded the kind of state settlement statute involved in *Healy*, because the state statute favored the plaintiff in the case. Furthermore, the defendant was the citizen of the forum in the case. A resident defendant cannot remove, and the defendant was the party who wanted the state statute disregarded. Thus, it is hard to see how there could be either forum shopping incentives for or discrimination against a citizen of the forum state on the actual facts. However, the Seventh Circuit stated correctly that disregard of the state statute would encourage

---

Court, see Stephen B. Burbank, *Proposals to Amend Rule 68—Time to Abandon Ship*, 19 U. MICH. J.L. REF. 425 (1986). *See generally* Peter Margulies, *After* Marek, *the Deluge: Harmonizing the Interaction Under Rule 68 of Statutes that Do and Do Not Classify Attorneys' Fees as 'Costs,'* 73 IOWA L. REV. 413 (1988); W.W. Schwarzer, *Fee Shifting Offers of Judgment—An Approach to Reducing the Cost of Litigation*, 76 JUDICATURE 147 (1993); Roy D. Simon, Jr., *Rule 68 at the Crossroads: The Relationship Between Offers of Judgment and Statutory Attorney's Fees*, 53 U. CIN. L. REV. 889 (1984); Roy D. Simon, Jr., *The Riddle of Rule 68*, 54 GEO. WASH. L. REV. 1 (1985); Victoria C. Choy, Note, *The Impact of Proposed Rule 68 on Civil Rights Litigation*, 84 COLUM. L. REV. 719 (1984); Thomas L. Cubbage III, Note, *Federal Rule 68 Offers of Judgment and Equitable Relief: Where Angels Fear to Tread*, 70 TEX. L. REV. 465 (1991); Jeffrey J. Rogers, Note, *Rule 68 and Equitable Relief—A Common Sense Solution*, 35 ARIZ. L. REV. 265 (1993); Note, *The Conflict Between Rule 68 and the Civil Rights Attorneys' Fees Statute: Reinterpreting the Rules Enabling Act*, 98 HARV. L. REV. 828 (1985). For a study indicating that Rule 68 could have a significant effect on litigation bargaining in civil rights actions if it is interpreted to include post-offer attorney's fees normally paid by plaintiff under 42 U.S.C. § 1988, see Thomas D. Rowe, Jr. & David A. Anderson, *One-Way Fee Shifting Statutes and Offer of Judgment Rules: An Experiment*, 36 JURIMETRICS J. 255 (1996). For a proposal to abolish Rule 68 and add settlement to Rule 11, see Bruce P. Merenstein, *More Proposals to Amend Rule 68: Time to Sink the Ship Once and For All*, 184 F.R.D. 145 (1999).

101. *See* Michael E. Solimine & Bryan Pacheco, *State Court Regulation of Offers of Judgment and Its Lessons for Federal Practice*, 13 OHIO ST. J. ON DISP. RESOL. 51 (1997).

102. 60 F.3d 305 (7th Cir. 1995).

103. *Id.* at 309-12.

104. *See, e.g.*, FLA. STAT. ANN. § 768.79 (West 2005); *see also* Jones v. United Space Alliance, L.L.C., 494 F.3d 1306 (11th Cir. 2007) (court avoids decision about whether Rule 68 "preempts" state offer-of-judgment statute by interpreting state statute as inapplicable under circumstances of case; however, court states that state statute is "substantive" for purposes of *Erie* doctrine).

105. *See* Chapter 5(E)(2), *Illustrations 5-11 & 5-13, supra.*

noncitizens to remove diversity actions in other cases.[106] As the Supreme Court indicated in the *Semtek* case, discussed in section E, above, the court was correct to view defendant forum shopping as within the *Erie* prohibition.[107]

Even if disregard of the state statute would not violate the *Erie* policies, however, the state statute ought not to be disregarded. As Chapter 5 also discussed, even when *Erie* is not violated, federal diversity courts should not disregard state law under circumstances that would undermine the policies supporting the diversity jurisdiction by driving non-citizen plaintiffs from the federal courts.[108] This will occur most obviously when a plaintiff would be deprived of a state rule of decision that would cause the plaintiff to lose an action in federal courts on the ultimate merits of the case that the plaintiff would win in state court. However, the state statute in *Healy* also gives the plaintiff substantial advantages. Under the state law, the plaintiff might be able to achieve settlements that would not occur in the absence of the law. Thus, the plaintiff might abandon a diversity action to obtain the benefit of the state settlement procedure if the federal courts were allowed to disregard the state law.[109]

A harder question is whether the Seventh Circuit was correct in concluding that Rule 68 was not broad enough to cover the case before the court because it only dealt with defendant's offers while the state statute included plaintiff's offers. As observed in Chapter 5, the Supreme Court has not applied a consistent methodology in interpreting Federal Rules of Civil Procedure to avoid conflicts with state law.[110] The Court's decisions in the *Gasperini* and *Semtek* cases could be interpreted to be a return to an interpretive methodology that is "more sensitive" to state interests.[111] If so, the approach taken to the interpretation of Rule 68 in *Healy* may be correct. However, the Court's later decision in the *Shady Grove* case, examined in Chapter 5, once again muddies the ability to forecast the method of Federal Rule interpretation that the Court will employ in the future.[112] Thus, there is sufficient doubt about this to inquire whether Rule 68 would be valid in a case of conflict between Rule 68 and the state law in *Healy*.[113]

Because there was no majority opinion on the meaning of the Rules Enabling Act's substantive rights restriction in the *Shady Grove* case,[114] the question of validity must still technically be determined by the standard articulated in the *Burlington Northern* case, discussed in Chapter 5.[115] Under this standard, a Federal Rule of Civil Procedure is valid if it does not impact on substantive rights

---

106. *See Healy*, 60 F.3d at 311.

107. *See also* Chapter 5(E)(2), *Illustration 5-13, supra*.

108. *See* Chapter 5(E)(2), *Illustration 5-12, supra*.

109. *See also* MRO Commc'ns, Inc. v. American Tel. & Tel. Co., 197 F.3d 1276 (9th Cir. 1999) (because defendant obtained judgment, Federal Rule 68 is inapplicable; state equivalent of Rule 68, which allows award of attorney's fees to defendant, must be applied to avoid violation of *Erie* policy).

110. *See* Chapter 5(F)(4) *supra* (discussing the holding in the *Burlington Northern* case that Federal Rule of Appellate Procedure 38, which governed frivolous appeals, applied to a nonfrivolous appeal).

111. *See* Chapter 5(F)(5) *supra* (discussing, *inter alia*, the *Gasperini* and *Semtek* cases).

112. *See* Chapter 5(E)-(F) *supra* (discussing, *inter alia*, the *Shady Grove* decision).

113. Also, as indicated in the text, above, other state settlement statutes may more directly conflict with Rule 68. *See* Cynthia L. Street, Comment, *Rule 68:* Erie *Go Again—Costs, Attorneys' Fees, and Plaintiffs' Offers—Substance or Procedure?*, 20 MISS. C. L. REV. 341 (2000).

114. *See* Chapter 5(F)(6) *supra* (discussing this point).

115. *See* Chapter 5(F)(4) *supra*.

more than incidentally and is reasonably necessary to the uniform scheme of procedure that it was the purpose of Congress to establish when it enacted the Rules Enabling Act. However, the Court has never described how to determine when a Federal Rule impacts on a state substantive right, when the impact is only incidental or more than incidental, or when a rule should be considered "reasonably necessary" to the uniform scheme of procedure that Congress wanted to establish under the Rules Enabling Act.

Arguably, a Federal Rule impacts on a state substantive right when (1) the policies supporting the state law with which the Federal Rule conflicts are substantive in the sense that they involve legislative judgments about matters other than efficiency and accuracy in the adjudicative process, or (2) when the operation of the Federal Rule would change the ultimate result of the litigation. Rule 68 would arguably have a "substantive" impact in both of these senses in a case like *Healy*. The Seventh Circuit described the Wisconsin rule as one that "imposes a sanction on defendants for turning down reasonable settlement demands"[116] and as a "rule [that] favors plaintiffs by giving them the option of putting the defendant to the unhappy choice of either settling on terms favorable to the plaintiff or running a substantial risk of increasing the amount of money to which the plaintiff will be entitled if the case is not settled but instead is tried and the plaintiff wins."[117] These are goals that transcend judicial efficiency and accuracy to favor one party in the litigation. Thus, they are rightly considered "substantive."[118] In addition, it seems clear that plaintiffs who have available the leverage of the state law will win favorable settlements on the "merits" more often than plaintiffs who do not. This potential effect on the ultimate result of cases is also appropriately classified as a substantive impact.

Assuming that Rule 68 would impact on a state substantive right within the meaning of the *Burlington Northern* case, it would seem that the impact ought to be classified as more than incidental. The application of Rule 68 to negate the ability of plaintiffs to make settlement offers would obliterate the operation of the state law in diversity actions. The only doubt about this is created by *Burlington Northern* itself, in which the Supreme Court construed Federal Rule of Appellate Procedure 38 as, in effect, an implied negation of any other authority to impose sanctions on defendants who took unsuccessful appeals. This effectively prohibited the operation of a state statute that provided for a 10% affirmance penalty against a defendant who took an unsuccessful appeal of a money judgment.[119] If the impact of a Federal Rule on the state law itself is all that counts in determining the rule's validity, then Rule 68 may have no more than the impact Rule 38 had in *Burlington Northern*. However, it is at least arguable that the operation of Rule 68 would have a more severe operation on the merits of cases than Rule 38, because Rule 68 would negate a state law that operates at the trial level of the litigation to give plaintiffs leverage.

---

116. *Healy*, 60 F.3d at 308.

117. *Id.* at 311.

118. The Seventh Circuit clearly considered the state law substantive, but it did so in the context of applying the general *Erie* doctrine rather than the Rules Enabling Act test of *Burlington Northern*. *See id.* at 311-12. Therefore, its classification of the rule, in and of itself, is not direct authority for the analysis in this text. However, the court's description of the purposes of the state law is instructive in applying the Rules Enabling Act test.

119. *See* Chapter 5(F)(4) *supra* (discussing *Burlington Northern*).

In contrast, Rule 38 only operated to negate a state law that would discourage defendants from taking appeals after a plaintiff had already won a verdict. This might cause plaintiffs to lose some cases in which defendants appeal a federal diversity judgment that they would not have appealed in state court, but, given the fact that the plaintiff has already won at one level, it seems that Rule 38 would affect the ultimate result on the merits far less often that the operation of Rule 68.

Assuming that Rule 68 has no more than an incidental impact on state substantive rights, the next question is whether Rule 68 is reasonably necessary to the operation of the uniform scheme of procedure that Congress intended to set up under the Rules Enabling Act. The question is a close one. Generally, it seems that rules like Rule 68, which are designed to encourage settlement, are important to the efficient operation of the federal courts. However, this is not the same as saying that the rule contributes to the operation of the rest of the Federal Rules of Civil Procedure in any significant way. Unlike Rule 15(c), which was discussed in Chapter 6,[120] Rule 68 does not interact with other provisions of the Federal Rules, such as the liberal "notice pleading" provisions, in a manner that contributes to their efficient operation. In fact, it is not clear that the removal of Rule 68 from the Federal Rules would in any way impair the operation of the rest of the rules. Therefore, to the extent that the Supreme Court means to measure the "reasonable necessity" of a Federal Rule by reference to its contribution to the operation of the general scheme of the rules, Rule 68 would not seem necessary. Of course, the Court has been cryptic in describing this part of the Rules Enabling Act validity test (as it has with other portions of the test). Thus, the Court appears to have in mind a broader test focusing on the efficient operation of the federal courts in general. If so, Rule 68 will probably meet this part of the *Burlington Northern* test, even assuming that the Court chooses to adhere to it in future cases, a matter that is at least doubtful after the *Shady Grove* decision and changes in the membership of the Court.

---

120. *See* Chapter 6(D)(5)*(d) supra* (discussing potential Rules Enabling Act problems with Rule 15(c)).

Chapter 11

TRIAL

SECTION A. THE TRIAL CALENDAR AND THE TRIAL DATE

Trial calendars are ordinarily divided into two types: (1) those for jury actions and (2) those for actions to be tried to the court without a jury.[1] Statutes, local rules of court, and local custom govern the manner in which cases are placed on the trial calendar and the order in which they will be heard. In some jurisdictions, the clerk will place the case on the appropriate trial calendar on the clerk's own initiative, typically after the pleadings have been closed. In many jurisdictions, however, one of the parties must request that the case be placed on the appropriate trial calendar. In that situation, the requesting party must give notice to the other parties.[2] Courts ordinarily hear cases in the same order that they are placed on the trial calendar.[3] The court sets a case for trial by entering an order fixing a certain date on or after which the court may call the case for trial.[4]

SECTION B. NATURE AND ORDER OF A TRIAL

1. Demanding a Jury Trial

For some types of cases, the state or federal constitution may guarantee a party the right to a jury trial. To exercise that right, a party must demand a jury trial. The following is a typical demand: "The plaintiff [or defendant] demands trial by jury of all issues in the above-entitled action." This demand may be filed separately or endorsed on the party's pleading.[5]

Illustration 11-1. Federal Rule 38 provides that a party may demand a trial by jury of any issue triable of right by a jury by serving upon the other parties a

---

1. *See* FED. R. CIV. P. 79(c). Courts maintain several types of calendars. *See* 9 CYCLOPEDIA OF FEDERAL PROCEDURE § 31.22, at 247-49 (3d rev. ed. 2011).

2. *See* 9 CYCLOPEDIA OF FEDERAL PROCEDURE § 31.22, at 246-47 (3d rev. ed. 2011).

3. Certain types of cases may be entitled to preferential treatment and thus advancement over others. *See* FED. R. CIV. P. 40. Preferential treatment also may be sought based upon the peculiar circumstances of a case. *See* 9 CYCLOPEDIA OF FEDERAL PROCEDURE § 31.23 (3d rev. ed. 2011).

4. The exact trial date is within the court's discretion and is often the subject of discussion at a pretrial conference. In setting the trial date, the judge will usually make an effort to select a date satisfactory to counsel as well as the court. Frequently, counsel will be required to estimate the time that the trial will take. Thus, prior to the conference, counsel should determine any potential conflicts that counsel may have and the times that clients and principal witnesses will be available for trial. *See* 4 AM. JUR. TRIALS 726 (1966).

5. FED. R. CIV. P. 38(b). Parties may limit their demands for a jury trial to specified issues: "Trial by jury in the above-entitled cause is demanded by the defendant [or plaintiff] of the following issues . . . ." In this situation, Federal Rule 38(c) provides that any other party may serve a demand for a jury trial of any or all other issues of fact in the action. *See* FED. R. CIV. P. 38(c).

written demand no later than 14 days after the service of the last pleading directed to the issue by filing the demand with the court.[6]

* * * * *

Provided all necessary pleadings have been served in an action removed from state court to federal court, a party entitled to trial by jury under Rule 38 may demand one within 14 days after the party files the notice of removal. The opposing party also has 14 days after receiving notice of removal to demand a jury trial.[7] If the party has demanded a jury trial prior to removal, however, the party does not need to make a new demand after removal.[8]

A demand for a jury trial cannot be withdrawn without the consent of *all* the parties.[9] Ordinarily, in both state and federal practice, a party who fails to demand a jury trial waives that right.[10] Jury trials may also be waived by contract.[11]

2. Selecting the Jury

In jury trials, the trial begins with selecting the jury from a panel of potential jurors called for jury duty. The particular qualifications for jury duty and the method of assembling lists of potential jurors vary from jurisdiction to jurisdiction.

Illustration 11-2. In federal courts, the names of prospective jurors may be drawn from voter registration lists or from lists of actual voters in the political subdivisions in the district. Federal law also provides that other sources of names must be used, when necessary, to yield a cross-section of the community that reflects the race, color, sex, religion, national origin, and economic status of the citizenry.[12]

---

6. FED. R. CIV. P. 38(b). Federal Rule 5(d) provides that "[a]ny paper after the complaint that is required to be served—together with a certificate of service—must be filed within a reasonable time after service." FED. R. CIV. P. 5(d)(1).

7. FED. R. CIV. P. 81(c)(3)(B).

8. *Id.* If applicable state law does not require the parties to make express demands to claim trial by jury, the parties need not make demands after removal unless the court orders them to do so within a specified time to obtain a jury trial. FED. R. CIV. P. 81(c)(3)(A).

9. FED. R. CIV. P. 38(d).

10. *See, e.g.*, FED. R. CIV. P. 38(d) & 39(b); CAL. CIV. PROC. CODE § 631(d) (West Supp. 2012); FLA. R. CIV. P. 1.430(d); *see also* Pacific Fisheries Corp. v. HIH Cas. & Gen. Ins., Ltd., 239 F.3d 1000 (9th Cir. 2001) (untimely request for jury trial must be denied unless some cause beyond mere inadvertence is shown). *See generally* ROBERT W. MILLAR, CIVIL PROCEDURE OF THE TRIAL COURT IN HISTORICAL PERSPECTIVE 260-63 (1952) ("Waiver of Jury Trial"); Joni Hersch, *Demand for a Jury Trial and the Selection of Cases for Trial,* 35 J. LEG. STUDIES 119 (2006). Judges often have the power to impanel an advisory jury when there is no right to trial by jury or when it has been waived. *See, e.g.,* FED. R. CIV. P. 39(c).

11. *See* Tracinda Corp. v. DaimlerChrysler AG, 502 F.3d 212 (3d Cir. 2007) (valid contractual jury trial waiver applicable to a corporation is equally valid to officers and directors and agents of corporation, even though they did not sign the contract); Jarod S. Gonzalez, *A Tale of Two Waivers: Waivers of the Jury Trial Defense Under the Federal Rules of Civil Procedure*, 87 NEB. L. REV. 675 (2009) (discussing the enforceability of pre-dispute contractual waivers and also whether the contractual waiver can itself be waived by failing to object to a jury trial demand made during the course of the litigation); Joel Andersen, Note, *The Indulgence of Reasonable Presumptions: Federal Court Contractual Civil Jury Trial Waivers,* 102 MICH. L. REV. 104 (2003).

12. *See* 28 U.S.C. §§ 1861-1863. A party may challenge the sufficiency of the entire selection process on constitutional or statutory grounds. This type of challenge is called a challenge to the array. *See id.* § 1867. The selection process has been amended in various ways, particularly in 1978. *See* Jury Selection Improvements Act of 1978, Pub. L. No. 95-572, 92 Stat. 2453. Note that even if state law absolutely disqualifies a particular category of persons from serving as jurors in a specific kind of case, it has been held that a federal court sitting with diversity jurisdiction is not compelled to follow that state law. *See* Nathan v. Boeing Co., 116 F.3d 422 (9th Cir. 1997)

(a) Challenges for Cause

When a court orders the selection of a jury panel,[13] summonses are issued for the required number of jurors. The prospective jurors are sworn to answer questions about their fitness to serve in a particular case. The manner of conducting this *voir dire examination* is generally within the court's discretion.[14] In federal courts, this examination is often conducted by the court alone.[15] In some jurisdictions, the parties' attorneys conduct the examination. In others, the attorneys and the court do so.[16] The purpose of the voir dire examination is to identify grounds justifying disqualification of a juror "for cause." The number of challenges for cause is not limited. The challenges may be exercised by the court or by the parties by making a timely objection.

Illustration 11-3. Grounds for challenging jurors *for cause* would include any bias or prejudice a juror might have, such as that produced by a juror's occupation or relationships with the parties or witnesses in the action.[17]

(b) Peremptory Challenges

In addition to challenges for cause, parties may make a limited number of *peremptory challenges*, which allow a party to exclude a particular juror without stating a reason. However, peremptory challenges are subject to constitutional restrictions—*e.g.*, restrictions that prohibit exclusion of jurors because of their race

---

(federal law, 28 U.S.C. § 1870, is broad enough to cover this case and thus governs this procedural question).

13. Prior to 1991, the Federal Rules assumed that all juries would consist of exactly twelve persons—or six persons if local district court rules allowed six. Alternative jurors were seated and heard all the evidence. However, they were excused if all of the regular jurors were able to deliberate. A 1991 amendment abolishes the use of alternate jurors. *See* FED. R. CIV. P. 47(b) advisory committee's note to the 1991 amendment. Under Federal Rule 48, the court now determines the exact size of the jury, depending on the particular case, but making certain that there are no more than twelve and no fewer than six jurors available to make the decision. All of the jurors seated participate in the verdict unless they are excused from service. *See* FED. R. CIV. P. 47(c) & 48(a) (allowing the court to excuse jurors from service during trial or deliberation for good cause). The Advisory Committee cautions that "it will ordinarily be prudent and necessary, in order to provide for sickness or disability among jurors, to seat more than six jurors." *See* FED. R. CIV. P. 48 advisory committee's note to the 1991 amendment; *cf.* Ballew v. Georgia, 435 U.S. 223, 98 S. Ct. 1029, 55 L. Ed. 2d 234 (1978) (criminal conviction by a jury of less than six persons violates due process). Federal Rule 48 provides that the verdict must be unanimous "[u]nless the parties stipulate otherwise." *See* FED. R. CIV. P. 48(b).

14. *See, e.g.*, FED. R. CIV. P. 47(a).

15. *See* 9 CYCLOPEDIA OF FEDERAL PROCEDURE § 31.52, at 333 (3d rev. ed. 2011).

16. *See* ROBERT W. MILLAR, CIVIL PROCEDURE OF THE TRIAL COURT IN HISTORICAL PERSPECTIVE 293-97 (1952); *see generally* Michael J. Ahlen, *Voir Dire: What Can I Ask and What Can I Say?*, 72 N.D. L. REV. 631 (1996).

17. *See, e.g.*, Caterpillar, Inc. v. Sturman Indus., Inc., 387 F.3d 1358 (Fed. Cir. 2004) (even a tiny financial interest in the outcome of litigation implies bias as a matter of law requiring exclusion of a potential juror); Poet v. Traverse City Osteopathic Hosp., 433 Mich. 228, 445 N.W.2d 115 (1989) (holding that the trial court abused its discretion in a medical malpractice action involving prenatal treatment and delivery by not sustaining challenge for cause of a registered nurse who (1) had special skill in reviewing quality-of-care issues in neonatal intensive care cases, (2) was in a close working relationship with the wife of the hospital vice president, (3) was acquainted with the vice-president himself (a witness in the case), and (4) had conceded that she had fairly strong personal feelings about damages). *See generally* William P. Barnette, *Ma, Ma, Where's My Pa? On Your Jury, Ha, Ha, Ha: A Constitutional Analysis of Implied Bias Challenges for Cause,* 84 U. DET. MERCY L. REV. 451 (2007) (discussing, *inter alia*, implied bias challenges in adjudication of class actions when jurors are related to member of class).

or sex.[18] The permitted number of such challenges varies according to the jurisdiction. In federal court, each party is allowed up to three challenges.[19] While the practice varies in state court, multiple defendants or plaintiffs in federal court may be treated as a single party for purposes of making challenges. The court, in its discretion, may allow additional peremptory challenges.[20]

3. Trial Procedure

After the jury has been impaneled (if there is going to be one), the party having the burden of proof on the principal issues, usually the plaintiff, makes an opening statement. Opening statements ordinarily explain the nature of the case and summarize the evidence that will be presented. The opposing party is often given the option to respond with an opening statement at this time, but frequently defers until just before presenting the opposing party's case.

After the opening statements, the party having the burden of proof (hereafter referred to as the plaintiff) then presents the *case in chief* by offering proof. After the plaintiff has presented evidence, the plaintiff *rests*. The opposing party (hereafter referred to as the defendant) then rebuts the plaintiff's initial evidence, offers additional evidence, and presents evidence on defenses and counterclaims. After the defendant has completed the defendant's case in chief, the plaintiff may offer *rebuttal* evidence to counter the defendant's evidence. Thereafter, the defendant may present *surrebuttal* evidence to answer the plaintiff's

---

18. In Batson v. Kentucky, 476 U.S. 79, 106 S. Ct. 1712, 90 L. Ed. 2d 69 (1986), the U.S. Supreme Court held that a prosecutor's use of peremptory challenges in a criminal trial to exclude jurors solely because of their race violates the Equal Protection Clause of the Constitution, at least when the defendant and the challenged jurors are of the same race. In 1991, the Supreme Court extended the *Batson* rule to civil jury trials to prohibit private, non-governmental parties from using peremptory challenges to exclude jurors on the basis of race. *See* Edmonson v. Leesville Concrete Co., 500 U.S. 614, 111 S. Ct. 2077, 114 L. Ed. 2d 660 (1991); *see also* J.E.B. v. Alabama *ex rel.* T.B., 511 U.S. 127, 114 S. Ct. 1419, 128 L. Ed. 2d 89 (1994) (extending *Batson* to peremptory jury strikes of all males from a jury in civil action by state to establish paternity and recover child support); Hurd v. Pittsburgh State Univ., 109 F.3d 1540 (10th Cir. 1997) (a party raising a *Batson* challenge to a peremptory challenge bears the burden of showing that a race-neutral, but factually mistaken, reason for the strike is pretextual); People v. Martin, 64 Cal. App. 4th 378, 75 Cal. Rptr. 2d 147 (1998) (holding it constitutional to strike a juror on the basis of religious beliefs that might produce bias); *see generally* Barbara Allen Babcock, *A Place in the Palladium: Women's Rights and Jury Service*, 61 U. CIN. L. REV. 1139 (1993) (asserting that peremptory strikes of women because of their gender should be prohibited); Cheryl G. Bader, Batson *Meets the First Amendment: Prohibiting Peremptory Challenges that Violate a Prospective Juror's Speech and Association Rights,* 24 HOFSTRA L. REV. 567 (1996); George P. Fletcher, *Political Correctness in Jury Selection*, 29 SUFFOLK U. L. REV. 1 (1995); Amy B. Gendleman, Comment, *The Equal Protection Clause, the Free Exercise Clause, and Religion-Based Peremptory Challenges,* 63 U. CHI. L. REV. 1639 (1996) (arguing that religion-based peremptory challenges are unconstitutional); Susan Hightower, Note, *Sex and the Peremptory Strike: An Empirical Analysis of* J.E.B. v. Alabama's *Five Years*, 52 STAN. L. REV. 895 (2000); Kenneth S. Klein & Theodore D. Klastorin, *Do Diverse Juries Aid or Impede Justice?* 1999 WIS. L. REV. 553; Lance Koonce, Note, J.E.B. v. Alabama *ex rel.* T.B. *and the Fate of the Peremptory Challenge*, 73 N.C. L. REV. 525 (1995); Nancy S. Marder, *Beyond Gender: Peremptory Challenges and the Roles of the Jury*, 73 TEX. L. REV. 1041 (1995); Edmund L. Quatmann, Jr., Note, J.E.B. v. Alabama *ex rel.* T.B.: *The Extension of the Equal Protection Clause to Gender-Based Peremptory Challenges—Is This the End?* 39 ST. LOUIS U. L.J. 1349 (1995); Andrew Weis, *Peremptory Challenges: The Last Barrier to Jury Service for People With Disabilities,* 33 WILLAMETTE L. REV. 1 (1997); Susan A. Winchurch, Note, J.E.B. v. Alabama *ex rel.* T.B.: *The Supreme Court Moves Closer to Elimination of the Peremptory Challenge*, 54 MD. L. REV. 261 (1995).

19. *See* 28 U.S.C. § 1870.

20. 9B CHARLES A. WRIGHT & ARTHUR R. MILLER, FEDERAL PRACTICE AND PROCEDURE: CIVIL § 2483, at 58-60 (3d ed. 2008). *But cf.* Morris B. Hoffman, *Preemptory Challenges Should Be Abolished: A Trial Judge's Perspective,* 64 U. CHI. L. REV. 809 (1997).

rebuttal. This process continues until each side rests. A reasonable limit may be placed on the time allowed for presenting evidence.[21]

Ordinarily, the witnesses testify orally in open court.[22] Witnesses may be compelled by subpoena to attend trial.[23] Examination of witnesses follows this pattern: (1) direct examination by the party who called the witness; (2) cross-examination by the opposing party (limited generally to the scope of the direct examination); (3) redirect examination (which is limited generally to matters raised by the cross-examination); (4) recross-examination (limited generally to matters raised by the redirect examination). This process continues until counsel have no further questions for the witness. After these presentations have concluded, *closing arguments* will be made. Usually, the plaintiff proceeds first, followed by the defendant's closing. Then the plaintiff is given the opportunity to make a brief conclusion.

When the case is tried to the court, the trial is completed after all the evidence has been presented and closing arguments have been made. In federal court, the judge will decide the case by entering *findings of fact* and *conclusions of law*.[24] When the case is tried to a jury, the court will *instruct* the jury on the law.[25] The court in some jurisdictions also may comment on the evidence or summarize the evidence. The jury then deliberates and returns its verdict.

SECTION C. TRIAL BY JURY IN ANGLO-AMERICAN LAW

1. Development of Jury Trials

Chapter 1 explained that the development of the forms of action was strongly influenced by the parties' desire to secure a more rational mode of trial—trial by jury.[26] However, in earlier times, the jury functioned differently than it does today. Unlike today's practice, jurors were chosen because of their knowledge about the facts and circumstances of the dispute. Jurors were drawn

---

21. *See* FED. R. CIV. P. 16(c)(2)(O) (matters for consideration at pretrial conference); Patrick E. Longan, *The Shot Clock Comes to Trial: Time Limits for Federal Civil Trials*, 35 ARIZ. L. REV. 663 (1993); *see also* Chapter 9(N) *supra* ("Pretrial Conferences and Orders").

22. *See* FED. R. CIV. P. 43(a).

23. *See* FED. R. CIV. P. 45(a)(2), (3). In 2002, Congress enacted 28 U.S.C. § 1369, the Multiparty, Multi-forum Trial Jurisdiction Act, to provide the district courts with subject-matter jurisdiction based on minimal diversity of citizenship between the parties of certain mass disaster cases. As part of the Act, Congress created new 28 U.S.C. § 1785, which provides that in actions under § 1369, "a subpoena for attendance at a hearing or trial may, if authorized by the court upon motion for good cause shown, and upon such terms and conditions as the court may impose, be served at any place within the United States, or anywhere outside the United States if otherwise permitted by law."

24. *See* FED. R. CIV. P. 52(a).

25. *See* section K of this chapter *infra* for a discussion of jury instructions.

26. *See* Chapter 1(D)(5) *supra* ("Modes of Trial Under the Writ System").

from the location where the matters giving rise to the dispute occurred, in the hope that they would be informed about these matters.[27]

Although early juries were required to decide issues of fact, the distinction between law and fact was not sharply defined. Indeed, certain kinds of factual issues were clearly issues of law. For example, when an English jury was asked to determine the custom of a particular place, the jury was being asked to determine the law because the custom and the law were the same.[28] Nevertheless, the modern division of functions between the judge and jury has long been established. The jury decides questions of fact and questions of application of law to fact. For example, a jury determines whether a person who causes an injury exercised the care that a reasonable person under similar circumstances would have exercised. In contrast, a judge decides "pure" questions of law.[29] To be sure, this division of function has been subject to some variation at the margins: at one time an issue might be classified as one of fact for the jury, while at another time it would be committed to the judge.[30] Nevertheless, the general law-fact division has long-standing roots.[31]

The right of trial by jury in Anglo-American law has often been depicted in glowing terms.[32] In recent times, however, this view of the jury has begun to disintegrate. Juries in civil cases have been criticized on the grounds that they are incompetent fact finders, that they unnecessarily extend the time required for trial, and that they are anachronistic.[33] As demonstrated in the following sections, the

---

27. *See* ROBERT W. MILLAR, CIVIL PROCEDURE OF THE TRIAL COURT IN HISTORICAL PERSPECTIVE 16, 20-23 (1952); Chapter 4(A) *supra* ("Transitory and Local Actions"); *see generally* Forum, *The Origins of the Jury*, 17 LAW & HIST. REV. 537 (1999) (discussing the origins of the jury in English law); Daniel D. Blinka, *Trial by Jury on the Eve of the Revolution: The Virginia Experience*, 71 UMKC L. REV. 529 (2003).

28. *Cf.* JAMES B. THAYER, A PRELIMINARY TREATISE ON EVIDENCE AT COMMON LAW 184 (1898).

29. *See, e.g.*, Fleming James, *Functions of Judge and Jury in Negligence Cases*, 58 YALE L.J. 667, 667-76 (1949).

30. *See* Stephen A. Weiner, *The Civil Jury Trial and the Fact-Law Distinction*, 54 CAL. L. REV. 1867, 1871-76, 1896-1902, 1910-18 (1966) (providing examples).

31. For a discussion of the history and difficulties with the law-fact distinction, see Ellen E. Sward, *The Seventh Amendment and the Alchemy of Fact and Law*, 33 SETON HALL L. REV. 573 (2003).

32. Blackstone described it as "the glory of the English law." 3 WILLIAM BLACKSTONE, COMMENTARIES ON THE LAWS OF ENGLAND *379 (Chitty ed. 1826). The U.S. Supreme Court has expansively praised the jury's ability to achieve just results:

> Twelve men of the average of the community, comprising men of education and men of little education, men of learning and men whose learning consists only in what they have themselves seen and heard, the merchant, the mechanic, the farmer, the laborer; these sit together, consult, apply their separate experience of the affairs of life to the facts proven, and draw a unanimous conclusion. This average judgment thus given it is the great effort of the law to obtain. It is assumed that twelve men know more of the common affairs of life than does one man, that they can draw wiser and safer conclusions from admitted facts thus occurring than can a single judge.

Railroad Co. v. Stout, 84 U.S. (17 Wall.) 657, 664, 21 L. Ed. 745, 749 (1874).

33. *See, e.g.*, JEROME FRANK, LAW AND THE MODERN MIND 180-81 (1930); Fleming James, Jr., *Trial by Jury and the New Federal Rules of Civil Procedure*, 45 YALE L.J. 1022, 1026 (1938); David W. Peck, *Do Juries Delay Justice?* 18 F.R.D. 455 (1956). *See generally* Kevin M. Clermont & Theodore Eisenberg, *Trial by Jury or Judge: Transcending Empiricism*, 77 CORNELL L. REV. 1124 (1992) (empirical study of federal trials of cases from 1979 through 1989 in which the parties had the right to a jury; finding that, *inter alia*, proportion of jury trials varied greatly depending on the category of case and that plaintiffs won considerably more often before judges than juries in products liability and medical malpractice trials); Theodore Eisenberg & Geoffrey P. Miller, *Do Juries Add Value? Evidence From an Empirical Study of Jury Trial Waiver Clauses in Large Corporate Contracts*, 4 J. EMPIRICAL LEG. STUD. 539 (2007). Several reforms in the jury system have been proposed, including raising the fees for parties who demand jury trials, streamlining jury trials with a variety of procedural reforms, restructuring the jury by altering its size or composition, constraining jury discretion in a variety of ways, such as by use of special verdict forms, and diverting juries to "non-jury forums." *See* Steven Landsman, *The Civil Jury in America*, 62 LAW & CONTEMP. PROBS. 285 (1999); Peter H. Shuck, *How to Respond to the Problems of the Civil Jury*, 77 JUDICATURE 236 (1994); Symposium: *The American Civil Jury: Illusion and Reality*, 48 DEPAUL L. REV. 197 (1998); *see also* Matthew P. Harrington, *The Law-Finding Function of the American Jury*, 1999 WIS. L. REV. 377.

"love-hate" relationship between American judges and lawyers and the civil jury is sometimes reflected in the modern decisions concerning jury trial issues.[34]

2. Methods of Controlling the Jury

With the development of juries in the judicial decision-making process, judges have searched for effective methods of controlling the jury.[35] The modern methods of jury control can be grouped into the following categories: (1) methods of control before trial; (2) methods of control during trial; and (3) methods of control after the verdict.

The methods of control before trial generally aim at keeping a case from the jury altogether. These methods include the devices such as (a) demurrers to the pleadings (or motions to dismiss);[36] (b) motions for judgments on the pleadings;[37] and (c) motions for summary judgment.[38]

The methods of control during trial include (a) admitting and excluding evidence; (b) directing verdicts against parties who fail to meet their burden of producing evidence (judgment as a matter of law in federal court); (c) instructing the jury; and (d) special verdicts and interrogatories,[39] discussed in later sections of this chapter.

The post-verdict methods of control include (a) the motion for judgment notwithstanding the verdict (judgment as a matter of law in federal court) and its common-law predecessors—motions in arrest of judgment or for judgment *non obstante verdicto*; and (b) the motion for new trial, discussed in Chapter 12.[40]

Ordinarily, post-verdict control of the jury exercised through the vehicle of a motion for new trial or other device cannot be based on testimony of jurors as to any matter or statement occurring during the course of the jury's deliberations, or to the effect of anything upon that or any other juror's mind or emotions as influencing the juror to assent to or dissent from the verdict or concerning the juror's mental processes in connection with the verdict.[41] Exceptions exist allowing

---

The viability of jury trial has also been caught up in criticism of the tort liability systems, which has resulted in large damage awards in cases considered to be of marginal, if any, merit by large segments of the public. As a result, it has been suggested that reforms such as "damage caps" would limit the jury's power to render excessive verdicts. Occasionally, it is suggested that such recommendations are beyond the power of Congress because of the limitations imposed by the Seventh Amendment. *See* Paul B. Weiss, *Reforming Tort Reform: Is There Substance to the Seventh Amendment?*, 38 CATH. U. L. REV. 737 (1989).

34. For example, courts have often gone to great lengths to prevent the adverse effects on the right to trial by jury that can potentially be produced by the merger of law and equity in modern procedural systems. *See* section E *infra* ("The Right to Trial by Jury in a Merged System: Operation of the Historical and Modern Federal Approaches"). On the other hand, courts have approved attempts to reduce the size of the civil jury from its historically established number (twelve) to a lesser number on the ground that such a reduction does not impair the basic right of jury trial, but merely regulates an "incident" of the right. *See* section F *infra* ("Right to Trial by Jury Versus Mere 'Incidents' of the Right").

35. In the past, various methods have been used to keep the jury within bounds. These methods have included the now defunct writ of attaint, the early use of fines to punish juries for judicial acts, the previously discussed law-fact distinction, demurrers to the evidence, and motions to arrest judgments. *See* JAMES B. THAYER, A PRELIMINARY TREATISE ON EVIDENCE AT COMMON LAW 137-81, 183-87, 234-38 (1898).

36. *See* Chapter 6(C)(3)*(b) supra* ("Demurrers") & Chapter 6(D)(3)*(d) supra* ("Motions to Dismiss").

37. *See* Chapter 10(B) *supra* ("Judgment on the Pleadings").

38. *See* Chapter 10(C) *supra* ("Summary Judgment").

39. *See, e.g.*, FED. R. CIV. P. 49.

40. *See* Chapter 12(A) *infra* ("Post-Trial Motions").

41. *See* FED. R. CIV. P. 60(b).

jurors to testify on the question whether extraneous prejudicial information was improperly brought to the jury's attention or whether any outside influence was improperly brought to bear upon any juror.[42]

It should also be noted that certain kinds of questions, such as questions of subject-matter jurisdiction, are reserved for decision by the trial judge. However, such questions can sometimes be intertwined with the merits of the plaintiff's claim. In such instances, the court must take care not to deprive the plaintiff of a right to a trial by jury on the merits through the guise of deciding an issue of subject-matter jurisdiction.[43]

3. The Basic Problems in Administering the Constitutional Right

In the United States, state and federal constitutions guarantee the right of jury trial in civil actions. The Seventh Amendment to the U.S. Constitution is typical of constitutional provisions concerning civil juries.[44] Like similar state constitutional provisions, the Seventh Amendment "preserves" the right to trial by jury. Thus, these provisions guarantee a trial by jury for those cases in which a jury trial would have been granted at the time the constitutional provision in question was adopted—1791 in the case of the Seventh Amendment.[45] In general, jury trials were allowed for cases denominated as "law" cases, or "common law" cases. They were not allowed in "equity" or "admiralty" cases.[46]

Jury trials in modern procedural systems pose three major problems. The first problem is determining whether a party has a right to a jury trial. Under the old dual system of law and equity courts, the court in which the action was brought determined the mode of trial. If the action was brought in a common-law court,

---

42. *See id.*; *see also, e.g.*, Stewart *ex. rel.* Stewart v. Rice, 47 P.3d 316 (Colo. 2002) (holding affidavits of jurors inadmissible to question the validity of a verdict under Colorado's equivalent of Rule 606(b)).

43. *Compare* Garcia v. Copenhaver, Bell & Assocs., 104 F.3d 1256 (11th Cir. 1997) *with* Scarfo v. Ginsburg, 175 F.3d 957 (11th Cir. 1999); *see also* Stefania A. Di Trolio, *Undermining and Unintwining: The Right To a Jury Trial and Rule 12(b)(1),* 33 SETON HALL L. REV. 1247 (2003) (discussing this problem).

44. The Seventh Amendment provides as follows:

> In suits at common law, where the value in controversy shall exceed twenty dollars, the right of trial by jury shall be preserved, and no fact tried by a jury shall be otherwise re-examined in any Court of the United States, than according to the rules of the common law.

U.S. CONST. amend. VII.

45. With regard to state constitutions, the date is usually when the relevant constitutional provision preserving the right came into existence. *See, e.g.*, State v. One 1981 Chevrolet Monte Carlo, 1999 ME 69, 728 A.2d 1259 (Maine Constitution guarantees a right to jury trial in all civil cases except when a case was decided without a jury under the common and statutory law that existed prior to the Maine Constitution of 1820; in rem civil forfeiture actions were ones in which right to jury trial existed); Housing Fin. & Dev. Corp. v. Ferguson, 91 Haw. 81, 979 P.2d 1107 (1999) (Seventh Amendment preserves right of jury trial that existed under English common law when Amendment was adopted in 1791, while state constitution preserves the right to jury trial that existed under the common law of the state at the time the Hawaii Constitution went into effect in 1959); DesMarais v. Desjardins, 664 A.2d 840 (Me. 1995) (plaintiff has right to jury trial unless it is affirmatively shown that a jury trial was unavailable in such a case in 1820).

46. *See* section D ("The Right to Trial by Jury in a Merged System: The Basic Approaches") & section E *infra* ("The Right to Trial by Jury in a Merged System: Operation of the Historical and Modern Federal Approaches"); *see also* Note, *The Twenty Dollars Clause,* 118 HARV. L. REV. 1665 (2005). *But see* Charles Wolfram, *The Constitutional History of the Seventh Amendment*, 57 MINN. L. REV. 730 (1973). Although jury trials are constitutionally guaranteed in only certain kinds of cases, it is universally considered to be a right that the parties may waive. *See* section B(1) *supra* ("Demanding a Jury Trial").

there would be a right of trial by jury (if the appropriate form of action was chosen). On the other hand, if the action was brought in an equity or admiralty court, no right of trial by jury existed. In modern merged systems, however, both legal and equitable matters can be litigated in the same court in a single action. In such cases, the question is how to determine whether the right to a trial by jury exists on issues of fact that are relevant to both the legal and equitable claims or remedies.

The second problem in modern systems is distinguishing between the "right" to a trial by jury and mere "incidents of the right." The distinction has recently become important in evaluating attempts to reduce the size of the jury from its historical number, twelve, to some lesser number. When a jurisdiction reduces jury size, the question arises whether the parties have been deprived of the "right" to trial by jury, or whether the basic right has been preserved while a mere "incident" of the right (the jury's size) has been modified.

The third problem in modern systems is whether jury trials are even feasible in certain kinds of complex cases. It has been claimed that there should be a "complex case" exception to the right to a jury trial, because a jury trial in complex cases deprives the parties of another basic right, the right to an opportunity to be heard in defense before life, liberty, or property can be taken from them—a right guaranteed by the due process clauses of the state and federal constitutions. The following sections explore these problems.

SECTION D. THE RIGHT TO TRIAL BY JURY IN A MERGED SYSTEM: THE BASIC APPROACHES

Section 208 of the Field Code of New York dealt with the problem of trial by jury in merged law and equity systems by providing that when "in an action for the recovery of money only, or of specific real or personal property, there shall be an issue of fact, it must be tried by a jury, unless a jury trial be waived. . . ."[47] Because equity courts had sometimes awarded "money only" or "specific real or personal property" in actions in which there was no right to a jury trial, this provision appeared to extend the right of trial by jury.[48] Indeed, the Commissioners stated that "[w]e propose an extension of the right of trial by jury to many cases, not within the constitutional provision."[49] Despite this expressed intention, the courts in other states adopting the Field Code provision generally construed it to be merely declaratory of the constitutional provision preserving jury trial rights in com-

---

47. Act of Apr. 12, 1848, ch. 379, § 208, 1848 N.Y. Laws 497, 536. Section 221 of the Field Code provided that a jury trial might be waived by failing to appear at the trial, by written consent in person or by attorney filed with the clerk, or by oral consent in open court. *See* Act of Apr. 12, 1848, ch. 379, § 221, 1848 N.Y. Laws 497, 538. These provisions were copied widely by other earlier codes and still exist in some states. *See* ROBERT W. MILLAR, CIVIL PROCEDURE OF THE TRIAL COURT IN HISTORICAL PERSPECTIVE 261 (1952); Fleming James, Jr., *Right to a Jury Trial in a Civil Action*, 72 YALE L.J. 655, 665-66 (1965); *cf.* NEB. REV. STAT. §§ 25-1104, 25-1126 (2008).

48. *See* Fleming James, Jr., *Right to a Jury Trial in a Civil Action,* 72 YALE L.J. 655, 666 (1965) (suggesting that this provision was unsatisfactory "because it specified the action as the unit to be dealt with rather than the component issues").

49. FIRST REPORT OF THE NEW YORK COMMISSIONERS ON PRACTICE AND PLEADINGS 185 (1848).

mon-law cases.[50] The result was that courts usually construed the Field Code provision to read like Federal Rule 38(a): "The right of trial by jury as declared by the Seventh Amendment to the Constitution—or as given by a federal statute—is preserved to the parties inviolate."[51]

The basic problem, then, is to determine how traditional constitutional provisions, exemplified by the Seventh Amendment, should be applied in a merged system. At least four different approaches to this problem have been taken, but only two are of major importance: (1) the "historical" or "analogical" approach and (2) the "modern federal" approach.[52] Many states follow the historical or analogical approach. A court using this approach "attempts to discern how the issues would have been tried before the merger of law and equity and to act accordingly."[53]

Illustration 11-4. If an action was triable exclusively by an equity court before the merger, there is no jury trial. For example, no jury would be required in a case seeking only the remedy of injunction. On the other hand, if the action was triable exclusively by a common-law court, the right of trial by jury would be preserved. For example, a jury trial would be allowed in a case seeking damages for personal injuries.[54]

* * * * *

The modern federal approach evolved under the leadership of the U.S. Supreme Court in cases determining jury trial rights under the Seventh Amendment and the Federal Rules of Civil Procedure. This approach originated in *Beacon Theatres, Inc. v. Westover*.[55] In *Beacon Theatres*, the plaintiff was the owner of a motion-picture theater. The plaintiff contracted with motion-picture distributors for the exclusive right to show the "first-run" of pictures in a designated area. The theater also had a "clearance" period during which no other theater in the area could exhibit the same pictures. The plaintiff sought a declaratory judgment against

---

50. *See* CHARLES E. CLARK, HANDBOOK OF THE LAW OF CODE PLEADING § 16, at 98-99 (1947); Fleming James, Jr., *Right to a Jury Trial in a Civil Action,* 72 YALE L.J. 655, 667 (1965); Note, *The Right to Jury Trial Under Merged Procedures,* 65 HARV. L. REV. 453, 454 (1952).

51. *See* FED. R. CIV. P. 38(a).

52. In addition to the "historical" and the "modern federal" approaches discussed in the text, one approach has been to identify the basic nature of the formulated issue. The federal courts used this approach until the U.S. Supreme Court decided Beacon Theatres, Inc. v. Westover, 359 U.S. 500, 79 S. Ct. 948, 3 L. Ed. 2d 988 (1959), discussed in the text *infra*. Under this approach, if the basic nature of the issue was legal, trial was to a jury, while if the basic nature of the issue was equitable, no jury trial right existed. To put it mildly, this test was unhelpful. The test gave no real guidance on how to determine whether the issue was "basically" legal or equitable, and often courts seemed to consider it as merely a version of the historical test, discussed in the text *infra*. *See* 9 CHARLES A. WRIGHT & ARTHUR R. MILLER, FEDERAL PRACTICE AND PROCEDURE: CIVIL § 2302 (3d ed. 2008). A second approach has been to give the court discretion whether to grant a trial by jury when a case contains factual disputes related to both legal and equitable matters in the case. *See id.* However, numerous difficulties exist with this approach as well. The use of discretion may result in the denial of jury trial rights in cases in which they historically have been guaranteed, it may result in extension of jury trial rights to cases in which they have never been given as a matter of right, and it certainly provides no guidance to courts and litigants as to the categories of cases in which jury trial is appropriate. *See* Fleming James, Jr., *Right to a Jury Trial in Civil Actions*, 72 YALE L.J. 655, 692-93 (1963).

53. *See* Aftercare of Clark Cnty. v. Justice Court, 120 Nev. 1, 82 P.3d 931 (2004) (Seventh Amendment guarantee of trial by jury does not apply to the states; consequently, most states look to the jury trial practice in their own territory or colony prior to statehood, in addition to the English practice, recognizing that the course of the common law may have been modified by territorial or colonial statute); *cf.* DAN B. DOBBS, LAW OF REMEDIES § 2.6(3), at 105-06 (2d student ed. 1993).

54. These examples are, of course, the simplest cases. More difficult issues concerning the historical method are discussed in section E of this chapter *infra*.

55. 359 U.S. 500, 79 S. Ct. 948, 3 L. Ed. 2d 988 (1959).

another motion-picture theater in the area. The plaintiff asserted that the distributors' grant of "clearance" between the plaintiff and the defendant was reasonable and did not violate the federal antitrust laws. The plaintiff also sought an injunction to prevent the defendant from instituting any action against the plaintiff and its distributors, pending outcome of the litigation arising out of these contracts.[56]

The defendant served an answer containing a counterclaim against the plaintiff and a crossclaim against a distributor who had intervened. The defendant asserted that substantial competition existed between the plaintiff's and the defendant's theaters and denied any threats of litigation. The defendant also asserted that the clearances were unreasonable and that a conspiracy between the plaintiff and its distributors to manipulate contracts and clearances violated the federal antitrust laws. The defendant sought to recover treble damages as a result of this alleged violation.[57]

The defendant demanded a jury trial of the factual issues involved pursuant to Federal Rule 38(b). The district court, however, rejected this demand, reasoning that the issues raised in the complaint, including the question of competition between the theaters, were "essentially equitable." The judge directed that these issues be tried to the court *before* a jury determined the validity of the defendant's antitrust counterclaim and crossclaim. The defendant petitioned the Ninth Circuit Court of Appeals for a writ of mandamus directing the district court judge to vacate this order. The Ninth Circuit denied the petition.[58]

On certiorari, the U.S. Supreme Court assumed that the complaint could be construed (1) to include a request for an injunction against threats of lawsuits and (2) to allege the kind of harassment by a multiplicity of lawsuits that traditionally would have justified equity to take jurisdiction of the case and settle it in one suit. Nonetheless, the Court held that under the Declaratory Judgment Act and the Federal Rules of Civil Procedure, neither of these assumptions could justify denying the defendant a trial by jury of all the issues in the antitrust controversy.[59] The Court recognized that irreparable harm and inadequacy of legal remedies have always been the basis of injunctive relief in the federal courts. The existence of inadequate remedies and irreparable harm, however, had to be "determined, not by precedents decided under discarded procedures, but in the light of the remedies now made available by the Declaratory Judgment Act and the Federal Rules."[60] This approach

---

56. *Id.* at 502-03, 79 S. Ct. at 952, 3 L. Ed. 2d at 992-93.

57. *Id.* at 503, 79 S. Ct. at 952, 3 L. Ed. 2d at 993.

58. *Id.* at 503-05, 79 S. Ct. at 952-53, 3 L. Ed. 2d at 993-94.

59. *Id.* at 506, 79 S. Ct. at 954, 3 L. Ed. 2d at 994-95.

60. *Id.* at 507, 79 S. Ct. at 955, 3 L. Ed. 2d at 995. The Court explained as follows:

> Since in the federal courts equity has always acted only when legal remedies were inadequate, the expansion of adequate legal remedies provided by the Declaratory Judgment Act and the Federal Rules necessarily affects the scope of equity. Thus, the justification for equity's deciding legal issues once it obtains jurisdiction, and refusing to dismiss a case, merely because subsequently a legal remedy becomes available, must be re-evaluated in the light of the liberal joinder provisions of the Federal Rules which allow legal and equitable causes to be brought and resolved in one civil action. Similarly the need for, and therefore, the availability of such equitable remedies as Bills of Peace, Qui Timet and Injunction must be reconsidered in view of the existence of the Declaratory Judgment Act [and] liberal joinder provision of the Rules. . . .
>
> If there should be cases [in which] the availability of declaratory judgment or joinder in one suit of legal and equitable causes would not in all respects protect the plaintiff seeking equitable relief from irreparable harm while affording a jury trial in the legal cause, the trial court will necessarily

is partly historical, in that it still asks whether an issue would have been triable historically at law or equity. However, because the merger of law and equity has made available in all actions a wide range of procedural advantages that previously were only available in equity, the "legal" remedy has became adequate in many situations in which it formerly would have been inadequate. Thus, the scope of "equity" has been narrowed accordingly. In effect, the *Beacon Theatres* approach results in a greater availability of jury trial than before the merger of law and equity.[61]

A troublesome feature of the *Beacon Theatres* opinion is the Court's conclusion that the Federal Rules of Civil Procedure and the Declaratory Judgment Act had increased the adequacy of *legal* remedies. However, there is no evidence that the Declaratory Judgment Act had such a purpose. Indeed, if the declaratory judgment is to be analogized to remedies prior to merger, it looks much more like an equitable remedy than a legal one.[62] Furthermore, the *Beacon Theatres* reasoning holds the potential for massive expansion of the jury trial right. Declaratory relief may be a potentially adequate alternative almost any time an injunction is requested. If so, the legal remedy will almost always be adequate, and the right to trial by jury will attach.[63]

SECTION E. THE RIGHT TO TRIAL BY JURY IN A MERGED SYSTEM: OPERATION OF THE HISTORICAL AND MODERN FEDERAL APPROACHES

The actual operation of the historical and modern federal approaches to jury trial rights can best be explored through comparison of the way these approaches operate in the following specific circumstances: (1) cases in which only legal or only equitable claims are presented; (2) cases in which, historically, an equity court had to act first; (3) cases in which, historically, a common-law court had to act first;

> have to use its discretion in deciding whether the legal or equitable cause should be tried first. Since the right to jury trial is a constitutional one, however, while no similar requirement protects trials by the court, that discretion is very narrowly limited and must, wherever possible, be exercised to preserve jury trial. . . . [O]nly under the most imperative circumstances, . . . can the right to a jury trial of legal issues be lost through a prior determination of equitable claims.

Id. at 509-11, 79 S. Ct. at 956-57, 3 L. Ed. 2d at 996-98 (footnotes omitted).

61. *See* 9 CHARLES A. WRIGHT & ARTHUR R. MILLER, FEDERAL PRACTICE AND PROCEDURE: CIVIL § 2302.1 (3d ed. 2008).

62. In dissent, Justices Stewart, Harlan, and Whitaker in *Beacon Theatres* asserted that the Declaratory Judgment Act "merely provided a new statutory remedy, neither legal nor equitable, but available in the areas of both equity and law." 359 U.S. at 515, 79 S. Ct. at 959, 3 L. Ed. 2d at 1000. In addition, the dissenting Justices emphasized that the inadequacy of legal remedy as a condition precedent to equity's assumption of jurisdiction was a principle traditionally used to limit the power of an equity court. The inadequacy doctrine, it was argued, should not be used a basis for any extension of the jury trial right, especially when the original claim was cognizable exclusively in equity. *Id.* at 519, 79 S. Ct. at 961, 3 L. Ed. 2d at 1002; *see also* Vatacs Group, Inc. v. Homeside Lending, Inc., 281 Ga. 50, 635 S.E.2d 758 (2006) (doctrine of latches is an equitable defense that is not applicable to declaratory judgment actions, which are actions at law).

63. *See* Fleming James, Jr., *Right to a Jury Trial in a Civil Action*, 72 YALE L.J. 655, 685-86 (1965). *See generally* John G. Gibbons, Comment, *From* Beacon Theatres *to* Dairy Queen *to* Ross*: The Seventh Amendment, the Federal Rules and a Receding Law-Equity Dichotomy*, 48 J. URBAN L. 459 (1971); Stanton D. Krauss, *The Original Understanding of the Seventh Amendment Right to Jury Trial,* 33 U. RICH. L. REV. 407 (1999); John C. McCoid, *Procedural Reform and the Right to Jury Trial: A Study of* Beacon Theatres, Inc. v. Westover, 116 U. PA. L. REV. 1 (1967); John M. Townsend, Comment, *The Right to Jury Trial in Declaratory Judgment Actions*, 3 CONN. L. REV. 564 (1971).

(4) cases in which the plaintiff could sue at either law or equity first; (5) cases in which the plaintiff asserts an equitable defense to a legal claim; (6) cases in which the plaintiff asserts a legal claim by means of a procedure available only in equity; and (7) cases in which a jury trial is sought in statutory or administrative proceedings.

1. Cases in Which Only Legal or Only Equitable Claims Are Presented

The simplest case, already referred to in *Illustration 11-4*, is an action in which the relief sought would have been either exclusively legal or exclusively equitable before the merger of law and equity—in other words, a case in which legal and equitable matters are not mixed. If a case was historically legal, a right of trial by jury exists. If a case was historically equitable, no such right exists.[64]

Illustration 11-5. A suit for an injunction in which no other relief is requested is purely equitable. Under both the historical and modern federal approaches, this type of case is resolved in the same way.[65]

* * * * *

This approach presents the real possibility that jury trial rights may be lost through issue preclusion.[66] If an action is brought on an equitable claim first, the judgment will ordinarily bind the losing party in a subsequent action on a legal claim. Thus, the party's right to a trial by jury in the second action may be lost. For example, in *Parklane Hosiery Co. v. Shore*,[67] the Securities and Exchange Commission sued to enjoin misleading statements being made by Parklane. The statements were found to be misleading and the injunction was granted. Shore had already sued Parklane in a class action to recover damages resulting from the misleading statements, but the SEC's action was adjudicated first. After the injunction had been granted, Shore moved for partial summary judgment on the ground that the doctrine of issue preclusion established that the statements were misleading for purposes of the damage action. Parklane argued that applying issue preclusion in the damage suit would deprive it of its Seventh Amendment right to a jury trial. Ultimately, however, the U.S. Supreme Court held that the doctrine of issue preclusion did apply and that its application did not deprive Parklane of its Seventh Amendment rights.[68]

In federal court, the *Parklane* situation will arise only if equitable and legal claims are properly separated. If, for some reason, the claims are improperly

---

64. *See, e.g., In re* Estate of Howard, 542 So. 2d 395 (Fla. Dist. Ct. App. 1989) (no right to jury trial in probate actions, which do not originate in common-law proceedings); *see also* DAN B. DOBBS, LAW OF REMEDIES § 2.6(3), at 105-06 (2d student ed. 1993).

65. *See* DAN B. DOBBS, LAW OF REMEDIES § 2.6(3), at 106 (2d student ed. 1993).

66. The doctrine of issue preclusion is discussed in Chapter 13(C) *infra* ("Issue Preclusion").

67. 439 U.S. 322, 99 S. Ct. 645, 58 L. Ed. 2d 552 (1979).

68. *Id.* at 333-37, 99 S. Ct. at 652-55, 58 L. Ed. 2d at 563-66; *accord* Nielson *ex rel.* Nielson v. Spanaway Gen. Med. Clinic, Inc., 135 Wash. 2d 255, 956 P.2d 312 (1998); Van Dissel v. Jersey Cent. Power & Light Co., 194 N.J. Super. 108, 476 A.2d 310 (1984). *Contra* Trapnell v. Sysco Food Servs., Inc., 850 S.W.2d 529 (Tex. Civ. App. 1992), *aff'd on other grounds*, 890 S.W.2d 796 (Tex. 1994). *See generally* David L. Shapiro & Daniel R. Coquillette, *The Fetish of Jury Trials in Civil Actions*, 85 HARV. L. REV. 442 (1971).

separated, the right to a trial by jury on the legal claim will not be lost. For example, in *Lytle v. Household Mfg., Inc.*,[69] the plaintiff joined legal and equitable claims against the defendant. The district court erroneously dismissed the legal claim. The court then adjudicated the equitable claim, without a jury, in favor of the defendant. The court of appeals affirmed. It held that the plaintiff could not litigate the legal claims, despite their erroneous dismissal. The district court's findings on the common issue of fact between the legal and equitable claims would bind the plaintiff if the case were remanded for a trial on the legal claim. The court of appeals rejected the plaintiff's assertion that this result violated the Seventh Amendment.

The U.S. Supreme Court remanded the case for a retrial before a jury on both the legal and equitable claims. The Court held that *Parklane* does not control when equitable claims are tried first solely because they are erroneously separated. Rather, *Beacon Theatres* and *Dairy Queen, Inc. v. Wood* (discussed in subsection 2*(b)*, below), required a trial by jury on the common issues of fact existing between the legal and equitable claims.[70]

2. Cases in Which the Plaintiff Asserts Both Legal and Equitable Claims

(a) The Historical Approach

(i) Cases in Which, Historically, the Equity Court Had to Act First

In certain actions, the plaintiff may raise some issues that historically were triable only in equity courts and some issues that historically were triable only in law courts. Before the merger of law and equity, a party sometimes had to resort first to an equity court to get any relief at all.

Illustration 11-6. If *P* and *D* entered into a contract which, because of a mutual mistake, did not embody their true agreement, one party might have to sue first in an equity court to obtain reformation of the contract in order to be able subsequently to obtain the legal relief to which that party was entitled under the contract. The equity suit might be required in either of two situations. First, assume that *P* sued *D* for damages at law. Assume also that the contract, as written, gave *P* a right to damages. *D* might contend, however, that a mistake had been made in framing the agreement. Once the mistake was rectified, *P* would not be entitled to

---

69. 494 U.S. 545, 110 S. Ct. 1331, 108 L. Ed. 2d 504 (1990).

70. If the plaintiff voluntarily separates the legal and equitable elements of a claim, the modern doctrine of claim preclusion would surely prevent a second action on the legal claim, *Lytle* notwithstanding. *See* Chapter 13(B) *infra* ("Claim Preclusion"). Similarly, if the plaintiff somehow possesses separate legal and equitable claims arising from the same facts, issue preclusion would surely bind the plaintiff if the claims are voluntarily separated and issues are adjudicated against the plaintiff in the equitable proceeding. *See* Chapter 13(C) *infra* ("Issue Preclusion"). Therefore, *Lytle* should only apply to erroneous separation of the claims by the court, rather than the voluntary action of a party. *Cf.* Aufderhar v. Data Dispatch, Inc., 452 N.W.2d 648 (Minn. 1990) (plaintiff who sought arbitration proceeding collaterally estopped in subsequent common-law damage action; right to trial by jury waived).

relief. Thus, *D* would sue *P* for reformation of the contract in equity. The equity court would enjoin the pending legal action until the question of mistake had been resolved. Second, assume that the party entitled to legal relief recognized at the outset that the parties' agreement was the product of mistake. Unless the agreement was reformed, the party would be unable to obtain legal relief. The party would sue in equity for reformation. If the mistake was found to exist, the equity court would order reformation of the contract. The court would also give the plaintiff the legal relief to which the plaintiff was entitled under the "clean up" doctrine.[71]

* * * * *

In either of the two situations described, no jury trial would take place on the equitable issue of mistake, which would, of necessity, be tried first. Under the historical approach, after the merger of law and equity, a jury trial should be denied. In this situation, courts using the historical approach conclude that equity had the real say. Even though a common-law court might be involved at some level, equity decided the determinative issue in the case first without a jury trial.[72]

(ii) Some Cases in Which, Historically, a Common-Law Court Had to Act First

Before the merger of law and equity, certain cases lent themselves to equitable relief, but an equity court would refuse to act until some issue had been first resolved by a law court.

Illustration 11-7. An example of such a suit would be an action for an injunction to prevent the defendant from trespassing on plaintiff's land but in which the plaintiff's title was disputed. Equity would not try the title to land.[73] Therefore, the title issue had to be resolved by a law court before the equity court would give relief. After the merger of law and equity, under the historical method of determining right to trial by jury, this type of case should be treated as one in which the legal issue predominates and a jury trial should be provided.[74]

---

71. *See* Fleming James, Jr., *Right to a Jury Trial in Civil Actions*, 72 YALE L.J. 655, 658-59, 670 (1963); *see also* Weinisch v. Sawyer, 123 N.J. 333, 587 A.2d 615 (1991) (no right to trial by jury in reformation action). The "clean up" doctrine is discussed in Chapter 7(A) *supra* ("Joinder of Claims by the Plaintiff at Common Law and in Equity") and *Illustration 7-6 supra*; *see also* Chapter 1(D)(6) *supra* ("Development of Equity Jurisdiction"); Taylor v. Highland Park Corp., 210 S.C. 254, 42 S.E.2d 335 (1947) (reformation, specific performance, and damages can be ordered in a single action).

72. *See* DAN B. DOBBS, THE LAW OF REMEDIES § 2.6(3), at 117 (2d student ed. 1993).

73. *See, e.g.*, Green v. Cowgill, 30 Del. Ch. 345, 61 A.2d 410 (1948); Nottingham v. Elliott, 209 Ga. 481, 74 S.E.2d 93 (1953); Moore v. McAllister, 216 Md. 497, 141 A.2d 176 (1958); St. Louis Smelting & Ref. Co. v. Hoban, 357 Mo. 436, 209 S.W.2d 119 (1948); Carelli v. Lyter, 430 Pa. 543, 244 A.2d 6 (1968); Frost v. Mischer, 463 S.W.2d 166 (Tex. 1971); Kertesz v. Falgiano, 140 W. Va. 469, 84 S.E.2d 744 (1954).

74. *See* Mobile Cnty. v. Knapp, 200 Ala. 114, 75 So. 881 (1917); *cf.* I.C. Gas Amcana, Inc. v. J.R. Hood, Inc., 1992 OK 119, 855 P.2d 597 (equitable quiet title claim no longer the primary issue after reassignment of rights from plaintiff to defendant, rendering defendant's counterclaim for damages predominant and requiring jury trial at request of plaintiff); Fleming James, Jr., *The Right to a Jury Trial in Civil Action*, 72 YALE L.J. 655, 663, 671, 673 (1963).

(iii) Cases in Which the Plaintiff Could Sue in Either Law or Equity First

In certain kinds of cases before merger of law and equity, the plaintiff could control whether a right of trial by jury existed.

Illustration 11-8. The plaintiff might want to sue the defendant for an injunction to prevent future trespasses on the plaintiff's land and also to obtain damages for past trespasses. If the plaintiff desired, the plaintiff could sue in an equity court for an injunction. The equity court would also award damages under the "clean-up" doctrine without a jury. On the other hand, the plaintiff could first bring suit for damages in a law court and obtain a jury trial. If successful, the plaintiff could then sue in equity for an injunction. The issues decided in the plaintiff's favor in the law action that were also pertinent to the equity suit would be res judicata.

* * * * *

After merger, under the historical approach, the plaintiff could decide to treat the case as one at "law," with a right to jury trial, or as one in "equity," without a jury, at the plaintiff's option.[75]

(b) The Modern Federal Approach

What would be the result in the above cases under the federal approach? Did the "clean-up" doctrine survive *Beacon Theatres*?[76] The U.S. Supreme Court answered this question in *Dairy Queen, Inc. v. Wood*.[77] In *Dairy Queen*, the plaintiff alleged that the defendant breached a trademark licensing agreement by failing to pay the agreed amount for the use of the plaintiff's trademark within a certain territory. The plaintiff further alleged that after it had cancelled the agreement for the material breach, the defendant continued the business. The plaintiff requested (1) temporary and permanent injunctions to restrain the defendant from any future use of or dealing in the franchise or trademark; (2) an accounting to determine the exact amount of money owed by the defendant and a judgment for that amount; and (3) an injunction pending the accounting to prevent the defendant from collecting any money from stores in the territory carrying the trademark.[78]

The defendant's answer raised several defenses, including (1) a denial of any breach of the contract, apparently because the contract allegedly had been orally modified to remove the required minimum annual payment; (2) laches and estoppel arising from the failure to raise the claim promptly; and (3) violations of the federal antitrust laws.[79] The federal district court granted a motion to strike the defendant's demand for a trial by jury in the action on alternative grounds. The court held that either (1) the action was "purely equitable" or (2) if not purely equitable, the legal

---

75. *See* Fleming James, Jr., *The Right to a Jury Trial in Civil Action*, 72 YALE L.J. 655, 672, 675 (1963).

76. The decision in *Beacon Theatres, Inc. v. Westover* is discussed in section D *supra* ("The Right to Trial by Jury in a Merged System: The Basic Approaches").

77. 369 U.S. 469, 82 S. Ct. 894, 8 L. Ed. 2d 44 (1962).

78. *Id.* at 473-75, 82 S. Ct. at 897-98, 8 L. Ed. 2d at 50.

79. *Id.* at 475-76, 82 S. Ct. at 898-99, 8 L. Ed. 2d at 49-50.

issues that were raised were "incidental" to the equitable issues. In either case, no right to trial by jury existed. The defendant then sought mandamus in the Court of Appeals for the Third Circuit to compel the district judge to vacate this order. After that court denied the request without opinion, the Supreme Court granted certiorari and reversed.[80]

The Court initially disposed of one of the grounds upon which the trial court acted in striking the demand for trial by jury—that the right may be lost as to legal issues when those issues are characterized as "incidental" to equitable issues. The Court reiterated the view taken in *Beacon Theatres*: when both legal and equitable issues are presented in a single case, the right to a jury trial of the legal issues can be lost through the prior determination of equitable claims only under the most imperative circumstances. The Court stated that this holding applied whether or not the trial judge chose to characterize the legal issues as "incidental" to the equitable issues. The sole question was whether the action contained "legal issues." In resolving this question, the Court emphasized that the complaint requested a money judgment.[81] The Court also rejected the plaintiff's contention that the money claim was purely equitable because it requested an equitable "accounting" rather than "damages." The Court stated:

> [T]he constitutional right to trial by jury cannot be made to depend upon the choice of words used in the pleadings. The necessary prerequisite to the right to maintain a suit for an equitable accounting [is] the absence of an adequate remedy at law. [To] maintain such a suit on a cause of action cognizable at law, as this one is, the plaintiff must be able to show that the "accounts between the parties" are of such a "complicated nature" that only a court of equity can satisfactorily unravel them. [In this case,] a jury, under proper instructions from the court, could readily determine the recovery, if any, to be had here, whether the theory finally settled upon is that of breach of contract, that of trademark infringement, or any combination of the two.[82]

The Court concluded that the district judge erred in refusing to grant defendant's demand for a jury trial on the factual issues related to the factual breach-of-contract issues. Because those issues were common with those upon which the plaintiff's claim to equitable relief was based, the legal claims involved in the action had to be determined before the court decided the outcome of the plaintiff's equitable claims.[83]

Thus, based on *Beacon Theatres* and *Dairy Queen*, a right to trial by jury would exist in all three of the situations discussed in subsections *(a)(i)-(iii)*, above. It is therefore immaterial under the federal approach whether equity had to act first,

---

80. *Id.* at 470, 82 S. Ct. at 896, 8 L. Ed. 2d at 47.

81. *Id.* at 472-73, 82 S. Ct. at 897, 8 L. Ed. 2d at 48.

82. *Id.* at 477-79, 82 S. Ct. at 900, 8 L. Ed. 2d at 51-52 (footnotes omitted) ("The legal remedy cannot be characterized as inadequate merely because the measure of damages may necessitate a look into petitioner's business records.").

83. *Id.* at 479-80, 82 S. Ct. at 900-01, 8 L. Ed. 2d at 52 (footnotes omitted).

a common-law court had to act first, or the plaintiff could control which court acted first.[84]

3. Cases in Which the Plaintiff Sues in Equity and the Defendant Asserts a Counterclaim for Legal Relief

Before the merger of law and equity, a plaintiff could sue in an equity court for an equitable remedy. In response, the defendant could assert a claim for legal relief against the plaintiff by cross-bill.[85] The defendant in such an action, however, did not have to assert the legal claim. Instead, the defendant could sue separately on the counterclaim in a law court. Thus, there could be (1) a single proceeding in equity without a jury or (2) two proceedings, one in equity without a jury and one at law, with a jury. When separate proceedings were maintained on the legal and equitable claims, the first proceeding to reach judgment would be res judicata in the other proceeding on the common issues.[86]

Courts following the historical approach after merger have arrived at different solutions in this situation. Some courts have held that no jury trial right exists when the defendant serves a legal counterclaim in an equitable action.[87] Other courts, following the federal approach in *Beacon Theatres*, have required a jury trial when the defendant asserts a compulsory "legal" counterclaim.[88] Finally, some courts have held that the judge has discretion whether to order a jury trial in this situation.[89]

4. Cases in Which the Defendant Asserts an Equitable Defense to a Legal Claim

At common law, the defendant could not interpose an equitable defense to a legal claim. For example, a defendant possessing a defense of fraud to a contract claim would have to sue in equity to obtain relief from the contract. The equity

---

84. Reception of the *Dairy Queen* approach in the states has been mixed. *See* DAN B. DOBBS, LAW OF REMEDIES § 2.6(4), at 120-21 (2d student ed. 1993); *see also* Fleet v. Sanguine, Ltd., 1993 OK 76, 854 P.2d 892 (when equitable and legal claims arise out of same transaction, the court may decide equity claims but legal issues must be decided by the jury); State v. Crees, 474 N.W.2d 282 (Iowa Ct. App. 1991) (trial court has discretion to try equitable and legal claims separately).

85. The converse was not possible: if the plaintiff sued at common law, the defendant could not counterclaim against the plaintiff for equitable relief. *See* Chapter 7(D) *supra* ("Joinder of Claims by Defendants at Common Law and in Equity").

86. *See* Fleming James, Jr., *Right to a Jury Trial in Civil Action*, 72 YALE L.J. 655, 681-83 (1963).

87. *See* DAN B. DOBBS, THE LAW OF REMEDIES § 2.6(4), at 122 (2d student ed. 1993); *cf.* Sargent Cnty. Bank v. Wentworth, 500 N.W.2d 862 (N.D. 1993) (legal counterclaim in equitable action really raised legal defenses to foreclosure action; therefore, no right to jury trial existed); Adolph Rub Trust v. Rub, 474 N.W.2d 73 (N.D. 1991) (same).

88. *See* DAN B. DOBBS, LAW OF REMEDIES § 2.6(4), at 122 (2d student ed. 1993); *see also* the discussion of *Beacon Theatres* in section D *supra* ("The Right to Trial by Jury in a Merged System: The Basic Approaches").

89. *See* DAN B. DOBBS, LAW OF REMEDIES § 2.6(4), at 122 (2d student ed. 1993). Such an order is particularly appropriate when the plaintiff sues for equitable relief on the basis of a ground that would be a defense in an action at law and the defendant interposes a legal counterclaim. *See* Fleming James, Jr., *Right to a Jury Trial in a Civil Action*, 72 YALE L.J. 655, 685 (1965).

court would enjoin the plaintiff at law from prosecuting the legal action until the equity suit had been tried. If the equitable "defense" was sustained, the entire suit would effectively be resolved. The equity court would dispose of any residual legal issues under the clean-up doctrine. If the equitable defense failed, the suit in equity would be dismissed and the parties would be left to their legal remedies.[90]

Under the historical approach in a merged system, the defendant simply pleads the equitable defense to the plaintiff's claim. The equitable issue is tried to the court first. If the equitable defense is valid, the entire case is resolved. Over time, however, some defenses that originally were recognized only in equity came to be recognized in law courts. These defenses had "worked over" into law.[91] When this situation occurred, equity regarded the remedy at law to be adequate and refused to act. Thus, before determining whether a jury trial is appropriate, a jurisdiction using the historical test must determine whether the defense in question had "worked over" prior to merger.[92]

Under the federal approach, the ability to raise "equitable defenses" under the Federal Rules of Civil Procedure renders the legal remedies adequate and requires a jury trial of all issues. This conclusion is the inevitable result of the Court's decisions in *Beacon Theatres* and *Dairy Queen*.

5. Cases in Which the Plaintiff Asserts a Legal Claim by Means of a Procedure Available Only in Equity

Before the merger of law and equity, certain procedures were available only in an equity court. For example, class actions were available only in an equity court.[93] When legal claims were asserted using these equitable procedures, no right of jury trial existed. Thus, under the historical test in a merged system, no right to jury trial would exist in such a case.[94]

The result in the federal courts today is dictated by the decision of *Ross v. Bernhard*.[95] In *Ross*, stockholders brought a derivative suit against the directors of a closed-end investment company and the corporation's brokers. The plaintiffs alleged that the defendant directors had converted assets of the corporation. The plaintiffs also alleged that the defendant brokers had violated the Investment Company Act of 1940 by extracting excessive fees from the corporation.[96] The plaintiffs demanded that the defendants "account for and pay to the Corporation for their profits and gains and its losses."[97]

---

90. *See* Fleming James, Jr., *Right to a Jury Trial in a Civil Action*, 72 YALE L.J. 655, 679 (1965).

91. *See id.* at 673, 679-80.

92. *See id.* at 679.

93. *See* Chapter 8(D)(4) *supra* ("Class Actions").

94. 9 CHARLES A. WRIGHT & ARTHUR R. MILLER, FEDERAL PRACTICE AND PROCEDURE: CIVIL § 2302.1 (3d ed. 2008).

95. 396 U.S. 531, 90 S. Ct. 733, 24 L. Ed. 2d 729 (1970).

96. *See* Investment Company Act of 1940, Pub. L. No. 76-686, tit. I, 54 Stat. 589 (codified as amended at 15 U.S.C. § 80a-1 to 80a-64).

97. *Ross*, 396 U.S. at 531-32, 90 S. Ct. at 734, 24 L. Ed. 2d at 732.

The plaintiffs requested a jury trial on the corporation's claim. The federal district court denied the defendants' motion to strike the jury trial demand. The Second Circuit, however, reversed. The Second Circuit held that a derivative action was entirely equitable in nature. Thus, a jury was not available to try any part of that action.[98] On certiorari, the U.S. Supreme Court reversed the Second Circuit.[99] The Court concluded that although the stockholders' standing to sue on behalf of the corporation was an equitable matter prior to merger, the underlying corporate "claim is, at least in part, a legal one."[100] The Court pointed out that had the law courts recognized the stockholders' right to sue, the basis for equitable relief would have disappeared. The Court indicated that the merger of law and equity under Federal Rules of Civil Procedure had the same effect. Thus, the Federal Rules of Civil Procedure removed the barrier to a jury trial of the corporate claim after there has been a nonjury adjudication of the stockholders' right to bring the derivative action. Because the case involved two claims, one equitable and one legal, the Court held that the Seventh Amendment required the corporation's claim to be tried by a jury.[101]

6. Right to a Jury Trial in Statutory and Administrative Proceedings

In the leading case of *Curtis v. Loether*,[102] the plaintiff commenced an action under § 812 of the Civil Rights Act of 1968. Section 812 authorized private plaintiffs to bring civil actions to redress fair housing violations. In *Curtis*, the plaintiff alleged that the defendants had refused to rent an apartment to her because of her race. The plaintiff initially sought only injunctive relief and punitive damages. Later, she amended her complaint to include a claim for compensatory damages. The Act provided that "[t]he court may grant as relief, as it deems appropriate, any permanent or temporary injunction, temporary restraining order,

---

98. Under premerger practice, the corporation's legal claim could have been disposed of by an equity court because the corporation refused to bring the action at law. Without equitable determination of standing, the stockholder could not sue. On this basis, the equity court remedied what would otherwise be irreparable injury.

99. *Id.* at 532, 90 S. Ct. at 735, 24 L. Ed. 2d at 733.

100. *Id.* at 542, 90 S. Ct. at 740, 24 L. Ed. 2d at 738. The Court stated that

> [t]he relief sought is money damages. There are allegations in the complaint of breach of fiduciary duty, but there are also allegations of ordinary breach of contract and gross negligence. The corporation, had it sued on its own behalf, would have been entitled to a jury's determination, at a minimum, of its damages against its broker under the brokerage contract and of its rights against its own directors because of their negligence.

Id.

101. *Id.* at 533-40, 90 S. Ct. at 735-39, 24 L. Ed. 2d at 733-37. In dissent, Justice Stewart, joined by Chief Justice Burger and Justice Harlan, asserted, *inter alia*, that the case differed from *Beacon Theatres* and *Dairy Queen* because those cases dealt with not only claims properly cognizable at law, but also claims triable in equity. In contrast, according to Justice Stewart, the shareholders' derivative suit had always been treated a single cause of action tried exclusively in equity. Thus, Justice Stewart rejected the Court's position that the proceeding to establish standing and the proceeding on the corporation's claim constituted two different elements of the action. *Id.* at 543-51, 90 S. Ct. at 740-45, 24 L. Ed. 2d at 739-43. Note, however, that if the corporation's *claim* is equitable, a trial by jury will not be required in a derivative action. *See* Kalish v. Franklin Advisers, Inc., 928 F.2d 590 (2d Cir. 1991).

102. 415 U.S. 189, 94 S. Ct. 1005, 39 L. Ed. 2d 260 (1974); *see also* Atlas Roofing Co. v. Occupational Safety & Health Review Comm'n, 430 U.S. 442, 97 S. Ct. 1261, 51 L. Ed. 2d 464 (1977); Pernell v. Southall Realty, 416 U.S. 363, 94 S. Ct. 1723, 40 L. Ed. 2d 198 (1974).

or other order, and may award to the plaintiff actual damages and not more than $1,000 punitive damages, together with court costs and reasonable attorney fees . . . ."[103]

The defendants demanded a jury trial. The trial court denied the jury trial request because the Civil Rights Act did not authorize a jury trial and the Seventh Amendment did not require one. The trial court dissolved a preliminary injunction after the plaintiff obtained other housing. At trial, the court found that the defendants had discriminated against the plaintiff because of her race. Although no actual damages were found, the court awarded $250 in punitive damages. The Seventh Circuit reversed on the jury trial issue. On certiorari, the U.S. Supreme Court affirmed the reversal.[104]

After reviewing several cases, the Court recognized that Congress had the "power to entrust enforcement of statutory rights to an administrative process or specialized court of equity free from the strictures of the Seventh Amendment."[105] The Court, however, stated that "when Congress provides for enforcement of statutory rights in an ordinary civil action in the district courts, where there is obviously no functional justification for denying the jury trial right, a jury trial must be available if the action involves rights and remedies of the sort typically enforced in an action at law."[106] With respect to damage actions under § 812, the Court stated that a § 812 damage action

> sounds basically in tort—the statute merely defines a new legal duty, and authorizes the courts to compensate a plaintiff for the injury caused by the defendant's wrongful breach. [Thus,] this cause of action is analogous to a number of tort actions recognized at common law [principally the common-law action against innkeepers who refused temporary lodging to a traveler without justification and dignitary torts]. More important, the relief sought here—actual and punitive damages—is the traditional form of relief offered in the courts of law.[107]

In *Tull v. United States*,[108] the federal government sought injunctive relief and civil penalties against a real estate developer for allegedly violating the Clean Water Act by dumping fill on protected wetlands. The Supreme Court held that the Seventh Amendment guaranteed a jury trial to determine the defendant's liability because the government's suit for civil penalties was most analogous to the eighteenth century common-law action of debt. Thus, a jury trial was guaranteed on the legal claim and all issues common between that claim and the injunctive relief sought.[109] On the other hand, because assessing civil penalties was not one of the fundamental "incidents" of a jury trial, the Court held that the Seventh Amendment

---

103. *Curtis*, 415 U.S. at 189-90, 94 S. Ct. at 1006, 39 L. Ed. 2d at 263-64.
104. *Id.* at 190-91, 94 S. Ct. at 1006-07, 39 L. Ed. 2d at 264-65.
105. *Id.* at 195, 94 S. Ct. at 1009, 39 L. Ed. 2d at 267.
106. *Id.*
107. *Id.* at 195-96, 94 S. Ct. at 1009, 39 L. Ed. 2d at 267.
108. 481 U.S. 412, 107 S. Ct. 1831, 95 L. Ed. 2d 365 (1987).
109. *Id.* at 417-25, 107 S. Ct. at 1835-39, 95 L. Ed. 2d at 372-78.

did not guarantee a jury determination of the amount of the statutory civil penalties.[110]

In *Feltner v. Columbia Pictures Television, Inc.*,[111] the plaintiff exercised his right to recover statutory damages under § 504 of the Copyright Act instead of actual damages. The district court denied the defendants' request for a jury trial and ultimately awarded plaintiff $8,800,000. The Supreme Court held that the Seventh Amendment guaranteed the defendants a right to jury trial under the circumstances. The Court found that before the Seventh Amendment, damage actions for copyright infringement were tried in courts of law before juries. *Tull* was distinguished on the grounds that there was no indication in that case that juries had historically determined the amount of civil penalties to be paid to the government and because an award of civil penalties could be viewed as analogous to sentencing in a criminal proceeding.[112]

In *City of Monterey v. Del Monte Dunes, Ltd.*,[113] the plaintiff sued under 42 U.S.C. § 1983 to obtain compensation from the city for a regulatory taking of property without compensation. The Supreme Court held that the Seventh Amendment right to jury trial applied on the issue of the plaintiff's regulatory takings claim. The Court reasoned that a suit for just compensation is, like ordinary money damages, a compensatory remedy that was legal in nature. Thus, because the plaintiff's suit sounded in tort and sought legal relief, it was an action at law to which the Seventh Amendment applied, even though there was no equivalent to § 1983 framed in specific terms for "vindicating constitutional rights" at the time the Seventh Amendment was ratified. The Seventh Amendment applies not only to common-law causes of action, but to statutory causes of action that are analogous to common-law causes of action that were ordinarily decided in English common-law courts in the late eighteenth century. The Court rejected the city's argument that it should focus on the nature of the underlying right, a "takings clause" claim, and deny the right to jury trial on the theory that the jury's role in estimating just compensation in condemnation proceedings was inconsistent and unclear at the time the Seventh Amendment was ratified. Among other things, the Court reasoned that condemnation proceedings were not properly analogous to § 1983 actions to redress uncompensated takings because liability is not an issue in condemnation proceedings, but it is in § 1983 actions.[114]

---

110. *Id.* at 425-27, 107 S. Ct. at 1839-40, 95 L. Ed. 2d at 378-79; *see also* Chauffeurs, Teamsters & Helpers Local No. 391 v. Terry, 494 U.S. 558, 110 S. Ct. 1339, 108 L. Ed. 2d 519 (1990) (employees seeking relief in the form of back pay for union's alleged breach of its duty of fair representation have a right to trial by jury); Granfinanciera, S.A. v. Nordberg, 492 U.S. 33, 109 S. Ct. 2782, 106 L. Ed. 2d 26 (1989). If a proceeding cannot be analogized to a proceeding at common law, no right of trial by jury will exist. *See* Vinson v. Hamilton, 854 P.2d 733 (Alaska 1993) (statutory forcible entry and detainer remedy analogized to equitable remedy); County of Sutter v. Davis, 234 Cal. App. 3d 319, 285 Cal. Rptr. 736 (1991) (paternity action; no right to jury trial in this kind of action at common law); Zora v. State Ethics Comm'n, 415 Mass. 640, 615 N.E.2d 180 (1993) (action to determine violations of conflict-of-interest law is sui generis and does not express claim recognized at common law entitling party to jury trial); Department of Revenue v. Jarvenpaa, 404 Mass. 177, 534 N.E.2d 286 (1989) (statutory claim by illegitimate child to establish support rights; no right of trial by jury existed because bastardy actions not tried to juries prior to 1780).

111. 523 U.S. 340, 118 S. Ct. 1279, 140 L. Ed. 2d 438 (1998).

112. *Id.* at 354-55, 118 S. Ct. at 1287-88, 140 L. Ed. 2d at 449-50.

113. 526 U.S. 687, 119 S. Ct. 1624, 143 L. Ed. 2d 882 (1999).

114. *Id.* at 708-22, 119 S. Ct. at 1638-44, 143 L. Ed. 2d at 904-13.

SECTION F. RIGHT TO TRIAL BY JURY VERSUS MERE "INCIDENTS" OF THE RIGHT

The Seventh Amendment and state constitutional provisions preserve the *right* to a jury trial but not mere "incidents" of the right. In the immediately preceding discussion of the *Tull* case, for example, the Court permitted the jury to determine liability, but refused to allow the jury to determine the amount of the civil penalty because the latter function was not a fundamental "incident" of a jury trial.[115]

How does one determine whether a historical practice is an essential part of the right to a jury trial or a mere incident of the right? The Supreme Court has principally explored this issue in the context of attempts to reduce the size of the jury. In *Colgrove v. Battin*,[116] the Court reviewed the validity of a local rule that provided that a jury for the trial of civil cases shall consist of six persons instead of the traditional twelve.[117] When the district court set this case for trial before a jury of only six, the plaintiff sought mandamus from the Court of Appeals for the Ninth Circuit to direct the judge to impanel a twelve-person jury. The plaintiff contended that the local rule violated the Seventh Amendment. The Court of Appeals found no merit in this contention, sustained the validity of the local rule, and denied the writ.[118]

On certiorari, the Supreme Court affirmed. The Court stated that the language of the Seventh Amendment is not directed to jury characteristics, such as size, but rather defines the kind of cases for which jury trial is preserved. From the Amendment's reference to "suits at common law," the Court concluded that the framers of the Seventh Amendment were concerned with preserving the right of trial by jury in civil cases in which the right existed at common law. However, the Court also concluded that the Seventh Amendment did not bind the courts to the exact procedural incidents or details of jury trial existing at the common law in 1791. The Court pointed out that new devices may be used to adapt the ancient institution to present needs and to make it an efficient instrument in the administration of justice. The Court rejected the notion that the reliability of the jury as a factfinder is a function of its size. The number twelve was not a substantive aspect of the right of trial by jury. Although it expressed no view as to whether any number

---

115. *See* Tull v. United States, 481 U.S. 412, 107 S. Ct. 1831, 95 L. Ed. 2d 365 (1987) (discussed in the preceding section); *cf.* Clark v. Container Corp. of Am., 589 So. 2d 184 (Ala. 1991) (statute providing that first $150,000 of future damages not be reduced to present value violates state constitutional right to trial by jury by removing from fact-finding function of jury the ability to determine amount of plaintiff's remedy for personal injuries).

116. 413 U.S. 149, 93 S. Ct. 2448, 37 L. Ed. 2d 522 (1973).

117. Prior to *Colgrove*, in Williams v. Florida, 399 U.S. 78, 90 S. Ct. 1893, 26 L. Ed. 2d 446 (1970), the Court sustained the constitutionality of a Florida statute providing for six-member juries in certain criminal cases. The constitutional challenge rejected in that case relied on the guarantees of jury trial secured the accused by Art. III, § 2, cl. 3, of the Constitution and by the Sixth Amendment. The Court expressly reserved, however, the question whether "additional references to the 'common law' that occur in the [S]eventh [A]mendment might support a different interpretation" with respect to jury trial in civil cases. *Id.* at 92 n.30, 90 S. Ct. at 1901 n.30, 26 L. Ed. 2d at 455-56 n.30.

118. *Colgrove*, 413 U.S. at 149-51, 93 S. Ct. at 2449-50, 37 L. Ed. 2d at 525.

less than six would suffice, the Court held that a jury of six satisfies the Seventh Amendment's guarantee of jury trial.[119]

SECTION G. THE RIGHT TO TRIAL BY JURY IN COMPLEX CASES

The U.S. Supreme Court stated three criteria to determine the "legal" nature of an issue for purposes of determining a right to a jury trial in a footnote in *Ross v. Bernhard*:[120] "first, the custom [prior to merger] with reference to such questions; second, the remedy sought; and third, the practical abilities and limitations of juries . . . ."[121] The third criterion suggested the Court might restrict the jury trial right in complex cases that are beyond the competence of a jury. To date, the Court has not recognized a "complexity exception."[122] However, several lower courts have considered arguments that such an exception should be recognized.

Illustration 11-9. In the *U.S. Financial Securities* case,[123] a federal district court, on its own motion, struck the demands for a jury trial because of the complexity of the issues, the massive amount of evidence, and the expected two-year duration of the trial.[124] On interlocutory appeal, the Ninth Circuit reversed. The court stated that "[w]e do not believe that *Ross* may be read as establishing a new test for determining when the Seventh Amendment applies."[125] The court maintained counsel had a duty to present the legal claims and supporting evidence in a comprehensible manner and concluded that "we do not believe any case is so overwhelmingly complex that it is beyond the abilities of a jury."[126]

Illustration 11-10. In the *Japanese Electronics* case,[127] the Third Circuit agreed with the Ninth Circuit that the Seventh Amendment guaranteed a right to trial by jury in complex cases. However, the Third Circuit concluded that the Due Process Clause of the Fifth Amendment prohibits a trial by jury of a suit that is too

---

119. *Id.* at 151-60, 93 S. Ct. at 2450-54, 37 L. Ed. 2d at 526-31; *see also* Cott v. Peppermint Twist Mgmt. Co., 253 Kan. 452, 856 P.2d 906 (1993) (Kansas statute providing for nonunanimous verdict of 10 of 12 jurors in civil action does not violate the Due Process Clause of the U.S. Constitution or the Kansas Constitution); *cf.* Jazzabi v. Allstate Ins. Co., 278 F.3d 979 (9th Cir. 2002) (jury must reject an affirmative defense unanimously before finding a defendant liable). For a reexamination of the empirical evidence on twelve and six member juries and an argument for return of the twelve member jury, see *Developments in the Law—The Civil Jury*, 110 HARV. L. REV. 1411, 1466-89 (1997); *see also* Shari Seidman Diamond et al., *Revisiting the Unanimity Requirement: The Behavior of the Non-Unanimous Civil Jury,* 100 NW. U. L. REV. 201 (2006).

120. 396 U.S. 531, 90 S. Ct. 733, 24 L. Ed. 2d 729 (1970) (involving a right to a jury trial in a derivative action). The *Ross v. Bernhard* decision is discussed in section E(5) *supra*.

121. *Id.* at 538 n.10, 90 S. Ct. at 738 n.10, 24 L. Ed. 2d at 736 n.10.

122. The third criterion listed in the *Ross* footnote was noticeably omitted from discussion in Tull v. United States, 481 U.S. 412, 417, 107 S. Ct. 1831, 1835, 95 L. Ed. 2d 365, 373 (1987), which was discussed in section E(6) *supra* ("Right to a Jury Trial in Statutory and Administrative Proceedings"). *See also* Rieff v. Evans, 672 N.W.2d 728 (Iowa 2003) (no complex case exception to jury trial right exists in Iowa); Catherine M. Sharkey, Book Review, *Punitive Damages: Should Juries Decide?,* 82 TEX. L. REV. 381 (2003) (reviewing CASS R. SUNSTEIN ET AL., PUNITIVE DAMAGES: HOW JURIES DECIDE (2002)).

123. *In re* United States Fin. Sec. Litig., 609 F.2d 411 (9th Cir. 1979).

124. *Id.* at 413, 416-17.

125. *Id.* at 424. The court added that "it is doubtful that the Supreme Court would attempt to make such a radical departure from its prior interpretation of a constitutional provision in a footnote." *Id.* at 425.

126. *Id.* at 432.

127. *In re* Japanese Elecs. Prods. Antitrust Litig., 631 F.2d 1069 (3d Cir. 1980), *aff'd in part and rev'd in part on other grounds following summary judgment*, 723 F.2d 238, 319 (3d Cir. 1983), *rev'd on other grounds*, 475 U.S. 574, 106 S. Ct. 1348, 89 L. Ed. 2d 538 (1986).

complex for a jury to decide it competently. Although the Third Circuit recognized that no specific precedent existed for finding a due process violation in the trial of any case to a jury, it maintained that

> [t]he primary value promoted by due process in factfinding procedures is "to minimize the risk of erroneous decisions." . . . A jury that cannot understand the evidence and the legal rules to be applied provides no reliable safeguard against erroneous decisions. . . . Unless the jury can understand the legal rules and evidence, we cannot realistically expect that the jury will rest its decision on them.[128]

In assessing whether a case is too complex for a jury to decide, the court stated that a federal district court should consider three factors:

> [F]irst, the overall size of the suit, the primary indicia of which are the estimated length of trial, the amount of evidence to be introduced and the number of issues that will require individual consideration; second, the conceptual difficulties in the legal issues and the factual predicates to the issues, which are likely to be reflected in the amount of expert testimony to be submitted and the probable length and detail of jury instructions; and third, the difficulty of segregating distinct aspects of the case, as indicated by the number of separately disputed issues related to single transactions or items of proof.[129]

SECTION H. INVOLUNTARY DISMISSALS, DIRECTED VERDICTS, BURDEN OF PROOF, AND PRESUMPTIONS

When a case goes to trial, the plaintiff ordinarily presents direct evidence first, followed by the defendant's direct evidence, the plaintiff's rebuttal evidence, the defendant's rebuttal evidence, and so forth until both sides rest.[130] The rules governing burden of proof and presumptions determine how much evidence the parties must produce and which parties must produce evidence. Involuntary dismissals (judgments on partial findings) and directed verdicts (judgments as a

---

128. 631 F.2d at 1084.

129. *Id.* at 1088-89. Although recognizing a "lack of precision in this standard," *id.* at 1089, the court opined that district judges would apply the standard "with a good faith concern for the general preservation of the right to jury trial." *Id.*; *see generally* Morris S. Arnold, *A Historical Inquiry into the Right to Trial by Jury in Complex Civil Litigation*, 128 U. PA. L. REV. 829 (1980); James S. Campbell & Nicolas LePoiderin, *Complex Cases and Jury Trials: A Reply to Professor Arnold*, 128 U. PA. L. REV. 965 (1980); Morris S. Arnold, *A Modest Replication to a Lengthy Discourse*, 128 U. PA. L. REV. 986 (1980); Laura G. Dooley, *National Juries for National Cases: Preserving Citizen Participation in Large-Scale Litigation*, 83 N.Y.U. L. REV. 411 (2008); Richard O. Lempert, *Civil Juries and Complex Cases: Let's Not Rush to Judgment*, 80 MICH. L. REV. 68 (1981); Frank M. Loo, *Rationale for an Exception to the Seventh Amendment Right to a Jury Trial:* In re Japanese Electronics Products Antitrust Litigation, 30 CLEV. ST. L. REV. 647 (1981); Joseph A. Miron, Jr., Note, *Constitutionality of a Complexity Exception to the Seventh Amendment*, 73 CHI.-KENT L. REV. 865 (1998); William W. Schwarzer, *Reforming Jury Trials*, 132 F.R.D. 575 (1991). For an examination of the jury's role in complex cases and a proposal that rulemakers adopt reforms which will help judges and attorneys empower juries to perform better in complex cases, see *Developments in the Law—The Civil Jury*, 110 HARV. L. REV. 1411, 1489-1513 (1997).

130. *See* section B(3) *supra* ("Trial Procedure").

matter of law) are the modern procedural means provided in the rules for taking advantage of failures to produce sufficient evidence.

1. Involuntary Dismissals (Judgments on Partial Findings) and Directed Verdicts (Judgments as a Matter of Law)

Historically, the earliest means of withdrawing a case from the jury during the course of a trial was a *demurrer to the evidence* at the close of the plaintiff's case. When the plaintiff had failed to introduce evidence to warrant a favorable verdict, even when the evidence was taken as true and construed as strongly as possible in the plaintiff's favor, a demurrer to the evidence would be sustained. In such circumstances, a judgment was entered in favor of the defendant and a later action on the same claim was barred. On the other hand, if the demurrer was overruled, a judgment was entered in favor of the plaintiff. In either event, the defendant was not allowed to offer evidence or argue that the plaintiff's evidence should not be believed, and the case was not submitted to the jury.[131]

Many American jurisdictions developed the practice of allowing the defendant to move for a *nonsuit*—a compulsory dismissal of the plaintiff's action for failure of proof when the plaintiff rested. If the court granted the motion, the court dismissed the action. However, the dismissal ordinarily did not bar a new action on the same claim.[132] If the court denied the motion, the defendant could then offer evidence. In some jurisdictions, this motion was called a *motion for involuntary dismissal*.

Another method of preventing a case from reaching the jury that developed in American jurisdictions was the motion for a *directed verdict*. When this motion is granted, the judgment has the same preclusive effect as a jury verdict. It thus bars a second action on the same claim. Traditionally, the defendant could make this motion at (1) the close of the plaintiff's case or (2) the close of all the evidence. The plaintiff could also move for a directed verdict at the close of the defendant's case.[133]

A 1991 amendment to Federal Rule 50(a) redesignates a motion for a directed verdict in federal court as a motion for *judgment as a matter of law*.[134] In contrast to prior practice, in which the motion could not be made before a party had rested its case-in-chief, this motion may now be made as soon as it is apparent that any party is unable to carry a burden of proof of any issue that is essential to that party's case.[135] The latest that such a motion may be made is just before the court

---

131. As Shipman pointed out, "[t]his step [was] taken only in cases in which it [was] very clear that the evidence ha[d] no tendency to prove the case; and naturally it [was] not often resorted to, for it is generally unsafe for a party to rest [the party's] case solely upon the test of what the evidence tends to prove." BENJAMIN J. SHIPMAN, HANDBOOK OF COMMON-LAW PLEADING §§ 328-329, at 526-27 (3d ed. 1923); *see generally* Charles H. King, Comment, *Trial Practice—Demurrer Upon Evidence as a Device for Taking a Case from the Jury*, 44 MICH. L. REV. 468 (1945).

132. *See* RESTATEMENT (FIRST) OF JUDGMENTS § 53 (1942).

133. *See* Fleming James, Jr., *Burden of Proof*, 47 VA. L. REV. 51, 56 (1961).

134. *See* FED. R. CIV. P. 50(a).

135. *See* FED. R. CIV. P. 50(a)(1) advisory committee's note to the 1991 amendment.

submits the case to the jury. The motion must specify the judgment sought and the law and the facts on which the moving party is entitled to the judgment.[136] One purpose of this requirement is to enable the responding party to correct any overlooked deficiencies in the proof.[137]

As revised in 1993, Rule 50(a)(1) specifies that a motion for judgment as a matter of law may be granted when "a reasonable jury would not have a legally sufficient evidentiary basis to find for the party on that issue" or "a claim or defense that, under the controlling law, can be maintained or defeated only with a favorable finding on that issue."[138] Before the 1991 amendment, Rule 50 had not stated a standard for granting the motion for a directed verdict. The Advisory Committee indicated that this reasonable jury standard had been "articulated in long standing case law" and "effect[ed] no change in the existing standard."[139] The U.S. Supreme Court, however, has not decided whether this standard can be validly applied in a diversity case when the state court would use a different standard.[140] The lower federal courts disagree on the answer to this question.[141] For example, some states follow the "scintilla rule." This rule requires that the judge deny the motion and submit the case to the jury if any evidence exists on which the jury could find in favor of the nonmoving party.[142] Applying a different standard under Federal Rule 50(a)(1) in a diversity action could affect how an issue is ultimately resolved in a "scintilla state," thus producing a conflict that would have to be resolved under the *Erie* doctrine.

It is unclear whether the Advisory Committee intended to establish a uniform "independent" federal standard for use in every case, or whether the Committee was simply leaving unresolved the question of the appropriate standard in diversity cases. In the *Gasperini* case, discussed in Chapter 5,[143] the Supreme

---

136. FED. R. CIV. P. 50(a)(2).

137. *Id.* advisory committee's note; *see also* Chapter 12 *infra* ("Post-Trail Motions, Appellate Review, and Extraordinary Relief from Judgments").

138. FED. R. CIV. P. 50(a)(1). The 1993 amendment corrected an ambiguity in the text of the 1991 revision of this rule. The 1993 "amendment makes clear that judgments as a matter of law in jury trials may be entered against both plaintiffs and defendants and with respect to issues or defenses that may not be wholly dispositive of a claim or defense." *Id.* advisory committee's note to the 1993 amendment.

139. FED. R. CIV. P. 50(a) advisory committee's note to the 1991 amendment.

140. *See* Mercer v. Theriot, 377 U.S. 152, 84 S. Ct. 1157, 12 L. Ed. 2d 206 (1964) (open question); Dick v. New York Life Ins. Co., 359 U.S. 437, 79 S. Ct. 921, 3 L. Ed. 2d 935 (1959) (same).

141. *Compare, e.g.*, Charleston Area Med. Ctr., Inc. v. Blue Cross & Blue Shield Mut., Inc., 6 F.3d 243, 247 (4th Cir. 1993) (sufficiency of evidence to create a jury question resolved on the basis of federal law) *with* Burke v. Deere & Co., 6 F.3d 497, 511 (8th Cir. 1993) (sufficiency of evidence is a matter of state law). Neither court discussed the possible significance of incorporating the test into a Federal Rule of Civil Procedure, which is governed by the standards of the Rules Enabling Act—as opposed to a test based on non-Federal Rule federal practice, which is governed by the Rules of Decision Act. *See* Chapter 5 *supra* ("Sources of Law"). *See generally* 9B CHARLES A. WRIGHT & ARTHUR R. MILLER, FEDERAL PRACTICE AND PROCEDURE: CIVIL § 2525 (3d ed. 2008) (citing cases).

142. *See, e.g.*, Barber v. Stephenson, 260 Ala. 151, 69 So. 2d 251 (1953). Furthermore, a state may make an issue always one for the jury. *See, e.g.*, Herron v. Southern Pac. Co., 283 U.S. 91, 51 S. Ct. 383, 75 L. Ed. 857 (1931) (pre-*Erie* case upholding federal judge's refusal in a diversity case to be bound by Arizona constitutional provision making the jury the sole arbiter of the issue of contributory negligence; the court directed a verdict for defendant when it appeared that the plaintiff was guilty of contributory negligence as a matter of law). In some instances, a state may make an issue one that will never be given to the jury. *Cf.* Byrd v. Blue Ridge Rural Elec. Coop., Inc., 356 U.S. 525, 78 S. Ct. 893, 2 L. Ed. 2d 953 (1958) (proper for a federal court in diversity case to refuse to follow South Carolina state court practice of having the court rather than the jury decide the affirmative defense of immunity concerning the status of an employee; factual issues are for the jury in federal court) (strong federal policy against allowing state rules to disrupt the judge-jury relationship in the federal courts).

143. *See* Chapter 5(F)(5) *supra* (discussing *Gasperini's* statement about rule interpretation).

Court seemed to signal that the federal courts should, in interpreting Federal Rules of Civil Procedure, turn back to a method that is more "sensitive" to state interests. If such a method were applied to Rule 50(a)(1), the courts would, of necessity, have to conclude that Rule 50(a)(1) does not incorporate an independent federal standard for determining a motion for a judgment as a matter of law, and thus there could be no conflict between Rule 50(a)(1) and state law.

However, a question would still be left under the Rules of Decision Act: can federal courts apply their own "common law" standard for determining whether the evidence is sufficient to go to the jury, or does *Erie* require that they follow the standard of the state in which they are sitting? *Gasperini* also seems relevant to this inquiry. Recall from Chapter 5 that in *Gasperini* the Court held that Federal Rule 59 was inapplicable to a question whether a new trial could be granted because a jury award on a state claim was excessive. The Court additionally held that *Erie* required that federal district courts follow the state standard for determining the excessiveness of jury awards to avoid forum shopping and inequitable administration of the laws.[144] The issue under Rule 50(a)(1) seems indistinguishable from that in *Gasperini* and would seem to call for the same result. If a more stringent federal standard for submitting a case to the jury were applied than would be applied in the forum state's courts, there would be no plaintiff forum shopping, because the more stringent standard would disadvantage plaintiffs. However, in cases involving nonresident defendants, the defendants would be encouraged to forum shop to obtain the more stringent federal standard, and this would also disadvantage a citizen of the forum state in violation of the *Erie* policies.[145] In addition, application of a more stringent federal standard would discourage noncitizen plaintiffs from invoking the diversity jurisdiction, which would illegitimately undermine the policies of the jurisdictional grant.[146]

If application of an independent federal standard to determine whether a case should be submitted to the jury violates the general *Erie* policies, it would be necessary to inquire whether sufficiently strong federal countervailing considerations are present to outweigh the outcome determinative effects. By analogy to *Byrd*, it might be argued that an independent standard is justifiable to avoid disrupting the judge-jury relationship in federal court.[147] However, granting a directed verdict or a motion for judgment as a matter of law is directly related to whether a party has satisfied the burden of proof applicable to the case. In diversity actions, the Supreme Court has uniformly held that state law controls the burden of

---

144. *See* Chapter 5(E)(3) *supra* (discussing the Rules of Decision Act holding of *Gasperini*). Furthermore, if the state standard is one that is "bound up" with state substantive rights, assuming that this is still a relevant inquiry under the Rules of Decision Act, the federal courts would be obligated to apply the standard without regard to the forum shopping and inequitable administration rationales. *See* Chapter 5(E)(2) *supra* (discussing the *Byrd* "bound up" category of cases); Chapter 5(E)(3) *supra* (suggesting that *Gasperini* may have discarded the "bound up" category of cases *sub silentio*).

145. *See* Chapter 5(E)(2), *Illustrations 5-11 & 5-13 supra* (advocating that defendant forum shopping be included in the *Erie* policies). Of course, if a less stringent standard were applied by federal courts, plaintiff forum shopping would be encouraged in violation of the Supreme Court's stated *Erie* policies, and discrimination against defendants who are citizens of the forum state would also occur.

146. *See* Chapter 5(E)(2), *Illustration 5-13 supra* (arguing that even if the *Erie* policies were inapplicable in the situation described, the policies of the diversity jurisdiction should dictate that the federal courts apply state law).

147. *See* Chapter 5(E)(2) *supra* (discussing this aspect of *Byrd*).

proof.[148] Given the burden-of-proof cases, therefore, it would seem unlikely that federal countervailing considerations of the *Byrd* variety could be found that would outweigh the outcome determinative violation that would occur by disregarding the state standard for submitting a case to the jury.

Assuming that Rule 50(a)(1) were held to incorporate an independent federal standard for determining whether a case should be submitted to a jury, there would be conflicts between the Rule and state law in some cases. Under these circumstances, it would be necessary to apply the standard for rule validity articulated in the *Burlington Northern* case discussed in Chapter 5.[149] This requires an inquiry into whether Rule 50(a)(1) would impact on a state substantive right, whether the impact would be "substantial" or only "incidental," and whether Rule 50(a)(1) would be reasonably necessary to the uniform scheme of procedure that it was the intent of Congress to establish under the Rules Enabling Act. Because the standard for submitting a case to the jury is closely linked to the burden of proof, it is possible to argue that an independent federal standard under Rule 50(a)(1) would impact on state substantive rights in cases in which the state standard is supported by policies transcending concerns of efficiency and judicial administration and aimed instead at "affecting the decision of the issue."[150] Under these circumstances, the substantive right upon which Rule 50(a)(1) would impact would be the "right" conferred by the state standard itself. However, even if the state standard is supported only by concerns of judicial administration and efficiency, it is arguable that Rule 50(a)(1) would impact on a state substantive right by producing an ultimate outcome on the merits of the case that would not occur under the state standard.

If either one of these impacts on substantive rights results, it would seem difficult to argue that the impact would only be "incidental" within the meaning of the *Burlington Northern* standard. Perhaps if the federal and state standards do not differ substantially in a particular case, the effect of the Rule 50(a)(1) standard might be classified as incidental. However, in all other cases, it would seem that the impact on substantive rights would be substantial and predictable, as the Federal Rule would either obliterate the policy of the state rule in all diversity cases in which it would otherwise be applicable or affect the outcome on the merits in such cases or both. Furthermore, even if Rule 50(a)(1) has only an incidental impact on state substantive rights, it is difficult to see how such a rule is reasonably necessary to the uniform operation of the Federal Rules scheme. If it is not necessary to the uniform operation of the Federal Rules to have uniform burden-of-proof rules in the first place, it is difficult to see how it is necessary to have an independent federal standard for determining whether a case should be submitted to the jury or not.

Because it appears that a strong case can be made that an independent federal standard incorporated in Rule 50(a)(1) would make the rule invalid under the Rules Enabling Act, the preferable result is to construe the rule as not

---

148. *See* Palmer v. Hoffman, 318 U.S. 109, 63 S. Ct. 477, 87 L. Ed. 645 (1943); Cities Serv. Oil Co. v. Dunlap, 308 U.S. 208, 60 S. Ct. 201, 84 L. Ed. 196 (1939).

149. *See* Chapter 5(F)(4) *supra* (discussing the *Burlington Northern* test).

150. *Cf.* RESTATEMENT (SECOND) OF CONFLICT OF LAWS § 133 (1971) (discussing burden-of-proof rules supported by such policies).

incorporating such a standard, as indicated above. This should produce the result that the standards of the forum state should be applied under the general *Erie* doctrine.

Former Federal Rule 41(b) provided for involuntary dismissals at the close of the *plaintiff's* case as a means of terminating a *nonjury* action on the merits when the plaintiff had failed to meet the burden of proof applicable to the plaintiff's claim.[151] Under amendments adopted in 1991, a motion to dismiss under former Rule 41 on the ground that a plaintiff's evidence is legally insufficient is now treated as a *motion for judgment on partial findings* as provided in a new Federal Rule 52(c). Rule 52(c) now authorizes the entry of judgment against the defendant as well as the plaintiff. As revised in 1993, Rule 52(c) specifies that after a party has been fully heard on an issue in a *nonjury* trial, the judge "may enter judgment against that party on a claim or defense that, under controlling law, can be maintained or defeated only with a favorable finding on that issue."[152] If the court renders such a judgment, it is required to make findings of facts and conclusions of law as provided in Federal Rule 52(a).[153] Because the judge is the trier of fact and thus decides factual issues, a motion for judgment on partial findings may be granted even though the judge would let the case go to the jury if there were one.[154]

2. Burden of Proof

To understand when a case should be prevented from reaching the jury through a directed verdict or a judgment as a matter of law, one must focus on the significance of the *burden of proof*. This term has two meanings: (1) the burden of persuasion; and (2) the burden of production.[155] In civil actions, the burden of persuasion is usually described as a requirement that there must be a *preponderance of evidence*, or that the *greater weight of the evidence* must exist in favor of the party having the burden of persuasion before that party is entitled to a verdict.[156] The burden of persuasion becomes relevant only at the end of the trial, when the trier of fact must decide the case.[157] If the trier of fact is a jury, the jury is told that the party having the burden of persuasion on each issue must have the issue decided

---

151. The basis of the defendant's motion for an involuntary dismissal is that "upon the facts and the law the plaintiff has shown no right to relief." FED. R. CIV. P. 41(b) (before 1991 amendment).

152. FED. R. CIV. P. 52(c). Like the 1993 amendment of Rule 50(a)(1), the 1993 amendment of the 1991 version of Rule 52(c) clarifies that the court may enter a judgment as a matter of law in a nonjury trial against both plaintiffs and defendants on issues or defenses that may not entirely dispose of a claim or defense. *Id.* advisory committee's note to the 1993 amendment.

153. *See* FED. R. CIV. P. 52(a), (c).

154. A judgment on partial findings differs from a summary judgment "in the nature of the evaluation made by the court." Summary judgment is based on facts established because of the absence of contrary evidence or because of presumptions which are, in effect, rulings on questions of law. On the other hand, a judgment on partial findings is made after all the evidence bearing on a crucial issue of fact has been heard. In order to be reversed on appeal, a judgment on partial findings must be found to be "clearly erroneous"; that stringent standard does not apply to summary judgment rulings. FED. R. CIV. P. 50(c) advisory committee's note; *see also* Chapter 12 *infra* ("Post-Trial Motions, Appellate Review, and Extraordinary Relief from Judgments").

155. *See* JAMES B. THAYER, A PRELIMINARY TREATISE ON EVIDENCE AT THE COMMON LAW 355 (1898); Fleming James, Jr., *Burden of Proof*, 47 VA. L. REV. 51, 51 (1961).

156. Fleming James, Jr., *Burdens of Proof*, 47 VA. L. REV. 51, 53 (1961).

157. *See* MCCORMICK ON EVIDENCE § 336 (Kenneth S. Broun et al., eds., 6th student ed. 2006).

against that person if the burden has not been satisfied.[158] Thus, because the burden of persuasion is only allocated at the end of the trial, it does not shift back and forth between the parties during the trial.

In contrast, the burden of production is the duty to produce evidence or to go forward with evidence. Unlike the burden of persuasion, the burden of production can shift back and forth between the parties during the trial.[159] The production burden begins at the outset of the trial. The plaintiff must introduce sufficient evidence on each of the propositions of fact that must be established as part of the plaintiff's case to justify a favorable verdict. The consequence of a failure to produce such evidence is loss of the case by means of a nonsuit, directed verdict, involuntary dismissal, or judgment as a matter of law.[160] Because the judge rules on these motions, the judge allocates the burden of production on each issue and determines whether the evidence is sufficient to meet the burden of production.[161]

Illustration 11-11. *P* sues *D* for libel, alleging that *D* sent a letter to *W* containing false statements about *P*. At trial, *P* calls *D* as a witness, but *D* denies ever sending the letter. *P* also calls *W* as a witness, but *W* denies ever receiving the letter. *P* has the burden of producing evidence that *D* sent the letter to *W*. On the state of the evidence described above, *P* would not satisfy the burden of production. To satisfy the burden of production, a party must ordinarily introduce some affirmative evidence that the fact in question has occurred. *P* has not done that. *D* and *W* denied the sending and receipt of the letter. *P* cannot ordinarily satisfy the burden of production by arguing that *D* and *W* are liars and the trier of fact should not believe their denials.[162]

* * * * *

Once a party has met the initial burden of going forward with the evidence on which the party has the production burden, the party escapes a nonsuit, directed verdict, involuntary dismissal, or judgment as a matter of law. At that point, the burden of production may or may not shift to the opposing party. If the party having the production burden simply offers enough evidence so that the trier of fact *may* infer the truth of the matter in question, but not so much that, without opposing evidence, the trier of fact will be *compelled* to infer the truth of the matter, the production burden will not shift.[163] Under these circumstances, even if the opposing

---

158. *See id.* Of course, if the trier of fact is a judge, the judge will simply decide the case in accord with the burden of persuasion.

159. *Id.*

160. *See* Fleming James, Jr., *Burdens of Proof*, 47 VA. L. REV. 51, 55-57 (1961); *see also* Smith v. Rapid Transit, Inc., 317 Mass. 469, 58 N.E.2d 754 (1945).

161. *See* Fleming James, Jr., *Burdens of Proof*, 47 VA. L. REV. 51, 56 (1961). The burden of production is "a device whereby the court determines whether, if the trial were stopped at any given point, it would send the case to the jury. If not, the court decides the case and the jury has no role to play. If the case is sent to the jury, the production burden drops out of the case and has no role to play. The jury will be concerned only with the persuasion burden." *Id.* at 57; *see also id.* at 58-63 (discussing the bases for allocating the burdens of proof); Edward W. Cleary, *Presuming and Pleading: An Essay on Juristic Immaturity*, 12 STAN. L. REV. 5, 5-16 (1959). For a discussion of burden of proof, shifting of the burden of going forward with evidence, and the standard for granting a motion for judgment notwithstanding the verdict in an employment discrimination case, see Reeves v. Sanderson Plumbing Prods., Inc., 530 U.S. 133, 120 S. Ct. 2097, 147 L. Ed. 2d 105 (2000).

162. *Cf.* Dyer v. MacDougall, 201 F.2d 265 (2d Cir. 1952).

163. *See generally* MCCORMICK ON EVIDENCE § 338 (Kenneth S. Broun et al., eds., 6th student ed. 2006).

party offers no evidence on the matter, the case will simply be submitted to the trier of fact and decided in accordance with the burden of persuasion.[164]

However, the party having the production burden may introduce enough evidence on the matter to compel the trier of fact to find for the party in the absence of any contrary evidence. Under these circumstances, if the opposing party fails to offer any evidence to controvert that proof, the initial proponent may be entitled to a directed verdict or judgment as a matter of law (in a jury trial)—if the proponent's evidence "leaves open no question of credibility, of evaluation of conduct, or of choice among competing inferences, about which reasonable minds might differ."[165] To prevent a directed verdict or judgment as a matter of law from being entered, the opponent must "offer evidence which either (a) presents a question for the jury, so that the production burden rests on neither party, or (b) is of such compelling force as to shift the production burden back again to the party who bore it at the outset . . . ."[166]

3. Presumptions

Parties may satisfy their respective burdens of production or persuasion in other ways than producing evidence on each issue at trial. As previously discussed, admissions made in the pleadings or during discovery may eliminate issues from trial. Furthermore, when no genuine dispute on an issue exists, partial summary judgment may eliminate it from trial.[167] In addition, a party seeking to establish a fact at trial may benefit from a *presumption*. A presumption is best defined as "a standardized practice, under which certain facts are held to call for uniform treatment with respect to their effect as proof of other facts."[168] Presumptions are either *rebuttable* or *conclusive*. However, it is generally agreed that a conclusive presumption is not a presumption in the true sense at all. Rather, a conclusive presumption, although cast in evidentiary language, is really a rule of substantive law.[169]

Illustration 11-12. *T* dies testate, leaving a life estate in land to *A*, the remainder to *A's* children. If *A* should die without issue, the land is to go to *B*. When *A* is 94 years old and after *A* has been surgically sterilized, *B* enters into a contract with *C* to sell *C* a fee simple title in the land, subject to *A's* life estate. When *C* later refuses to perform, *B* sues to compel performance. The court holds that *B* cannot convey marketable title due to a conclusive presumption that men and

---

164. *Cf.* Pan Am. World Airways, Inc. v. Port Auth., 995 F.2d 5 (2d Cir. 1993) (granting of Rule 50(a) motion by defendant for judgment as a matter of law was erroneous; plaintiff introduced sufficient evidence from which a jury could infer negligence by defendant).

165. *See* Fleming James, Jr., *Burdens of Proof*, 47 VA. L. REV. 51, 57 (1961).

166. *Id.*

167. *See* Chapter 10(C) *supra* ("Summary Judgment").

168. MCCORMICK ON EVIDENCE § 342 (Kenneth S. Broun et al., eds., 6th student ed. 2006; *see generally* Fleming James, Jr., *Burdens of Proof*, 47 VA. L. REV. 51, 63-70 (1961).

169. *See* MCCORMICK ON EVIDENCE § 342 (Kenneth S. Broun et al., eds., 6th student ed. 2006); *see also* Grisham v. Philip Morris U.S.A., Inc., 40 Cal. 4th 623, 151 P.3d 1151, 54 Cal. Rptr. 3d 735 (2007) (conclusive presumptions are not evidentiary rules so much as they are rules of substantive law).

women are capable of having children until they die.[170] This conclusive presumption is simply a substantive rule that disallows the sale of the property under the circumstances described to increase certainty and security of land titles.

* * * * *

True presumptions are always *rebuttable*.

Illustration 11-13. Assume that a person dies under unexplained circumstances. In general, courts recognize a rebuttable presumption against suicide as the cause of the death. This presumption can be overcome (rebutted) and disappears when either direct or circumstantial evidence is introduced showing suicide was the cause of death.[171]

SECTION I. EVIDENCE

The rules of evidence limit the parties' ability to prove the elements of their claim or defense. The rules are primarily designed to prevent the introduction of untrustworthy evidence and to assure the trial has reasonable boundaries. However, some rules of evidence, notably those conferring various evidentiary privileges, are designed to protect important values extraneous to the litigation at the expense of the search for truth.

The rules of evidence have evolved over centuries through the familiar common-law processes. Consequently, as with other common-law rules, evidence rules reflect the attitudes of common-law judges and lawyers at the time they were developed. From time to time there have been attempts to codify and reform the law of evidence. One such attempt is the enactment of the Federal Rules of Evidence.[172] The Federal Rules are typical of evidence rules generally. Therefore, they provide a good basis for a discussion of evidentiary problems.

Before examining particular evidence rules, one should understand certain concepts that operate in the general subject area of evidence. The first concept is *judicial notice*—a method of avoiding proof of certain kinds of facts at trial. When

---

170. *See, e.g.*, Walton v. Lee, 634 S.W.2d 159, 160-61 (Ky. 1982); Owings v. Owings, 247 S.W.2d 221 (Ky. 1952).

171. *See, e.g.*, Breckenridge v. Midlands Roofing Co., 222 Neb. 452, 455, 384 N.W.2d 298, 300 (1986). *Illustration 11-13* describes the "bursting bubble" theory of presumptions, which is the most widely accepted theory of the effect of presumptions in civil actions. *See* MCCORMICK ON EVIDENCE § 344 (Kenneth S. Broun et al., eds., 6th student ed. 2006). Under the bursting bubble theory, the effect of a presumption is to shift the production burden to the opposing party. Once the opposing party comes forward with evidence to rebut the presumption, it has no further value in the case. *See id.* Some courts give greater effect to presumptions. Especially when the presumptions are created for important policy reasons, courts sometimes place the burden of persuasion on the party opposing the presumption, as well as the production burden, or place a heavier-than-normal production burden on the opponent. *See id.*

172. The U.S. Supreme Court originally promulgated the Federal Rules of Evidence under 28 U.S.C. § 2072. However, because of objections that had been raised to the rules, particularly to the sections governing evidentiary privileges, Congress passed a statute suspending the operation of the rules unless Congress expressly approved them. *See* Act of Mar. 30, 1973, Pub. L. No. 93-12, 87 Stat. 9. After two years of study and changes in the rules, Congress enacted them into law. *See* Act of Jan. 2, 1975, Pub. L. No. 93-595, 88 Stat. 1926. Congress also supplied 28 U.S.C. § 2076, which, within certain limits, permitted the Supreme Court to amend the Federal Rules of Evidence. Section 2076 was repealed in 1988, and the power to prescribe rules of evidence was provided for in 28 U.S.C. §§ 2072-2074. *See generally* 21 CHARLES A. WRIGHT & KENNETH W. GRAHAM, JR., FEDERAL PRACTICE AND PROCEDURE: EVIDENCE § 5006 (2d ed. 2005). The Federal Rules of Evidence have since been adopted in a large number of states. *See* CHRISTOPHER B. MUELLER & LAIRD C. KIRKPATRICK, EVIDENCE xxix (4th ed. 2009) (indicating that 42 states had patterned their rules or codes on the federal model).

a fact is not subject to reasonable dispute because it is generally known to be true within the community or is subject to "demonstration" by resorting to readily available unimpeachable sources, the judge may take judicial notice of the fact. Judicial notice thus relieves the party who possesses the burden of proof from presenting evidence on undisputable facts. The purpose of judicial notice is obviously to save time and expense at trial when a fact is not reasonably controvertible.[173]

Illustration 11-14. Examples of judicially noticeable facts include historical facts (such as the date that the United States declared war on Japan in World War II), geographic facts (such as the location and name of the counties in the state in which the court is sitting), scientific and technological facts (such as that the speed of light is 186,282 miles per second or that the speed of sound is much slower than the speed of light), and commonly known facts in a community (such as there are no one way streets in a particular community).[174]

* * * * *

Second, several terms should be understood which relate to the different ways that evidence is categorized. All evidence is either *direct* or *circumstantial.* Direct evidence is evidence that tends to show the existence of a fact in issue without the intervention of any other fact.

Illustration 11-15. An example of direct evidence is eyewitness testimony on the occurrence of an event. Admissible direct evidence, such as the testimony of an eyewitness, usually presents no problems other than problems concerning the credibility of the witness—problems concerning whether the witness should be believed or not.

* * * * *

On the other hand, circumstantial evidence is evidence of a fact or circumstance from which the fact to be proved can be inferred.

Illustration 11-16. Suppose a party is trying to prove the color of the barn on April 1st. Testimony of an eyewitness who observed that the barn was red on April 1st would be direct evidence, but testimony by an eyewitness who observed that it was red on March 30th would be circumstantial evidence of its color on April 1st, because the trier of fact must infer that the barn remained red between March 30th and April 1st.

* * * * *

In addition to direct and circumstantial evidence, evidence is divided into *testimonial* and *real* evidence. Testimonial evidence is simply the testimony of a witness in open court. Real evidence is something produced for direct observation by the trier of fact, such as a photograph, a person's body, or a gun. Real evidence must be authenticated before it can be admitted.

Illustration 11-17. A document might be authenticated by the testimony of a person with personal knowledge that the document is what it is claimed to be.[175] The principal purposes of this requirement are to prevent fraud as well as to prevent

---

173. *See* FED. R. EVID. 201.

174. *See* MCCORMICK ON EVIDENCE §§ 329-330 (Kenneth S. Broun et al., eds., 6th student ed. 2006).

175. *See generally* FED. R. EVID. 901.

mistaken attribution of the document to someone who fortuitously happens to possess the same name as the real author of the document.[176]

* * * * *

Testimonial evidence is further divided into evidence of what the witness has observed or "knows" (often described as narrative testimony) and opinion evidence. Opinion evidence is most often encountered in expert testimony. When specialized knowledge will aid the trier of fact, a witness qualified as an expert may provide the specialized knowledge "in the form of an opinion or otherwise."[177] Nonexpert witnesses can also give opinion evidence, but a lay witness's opinion testimony is limited to those opinions or inferences which (1) are based rationally on the witness's perceptions and (2) are helpful in giving the trier of fact a clear understanding of that witness's testimony or of a fact in issue.[178] The distinction between opinion testimony and narrative testimony is only a matter of degree.

In evaluating evidence, a discrete division of functions exists between the judge and the jury. The judge determines preliminary questions of admissibility.

Illustration 11-18. In the first instance, the judge determines whether a witness is qualified as an expert or whether real evidence has been authenticated properly.[179] However, the weight to be given to the evidence is generally a matter for the jury. Thus, the question of whether an expert who is allowed to give an opinion should be believed is a jury decision.

* * * * *

An important qualification to this last rule exists. The judge can refuse to allow a case to go to the jury when a party has failed to satisfy that party's burden of producing evidence. As discussed in section H(2), above, this failure can occur when a party produces no evidence at all on an essential element of that party's case. However, the failure can also occur when the party produces evidence from which a reasonable person could not draw an inference of the truth of the fact to be proved. In such a situation, despite the rule that questions of weight and credibility are reserved for the jury, the judge is making a qualitative judgment about the state of the evidence that amounts to the same thing. Judges make similar determinations in connection with post-trial motions.[180] Likewise, a judge makes a related determination in ruling on a motion for summary judgment—that a factual dispute on the face of the pleadings is not *genuine*.[181]

---

176. McCormick on Evidence § 218 (Kenneth S. Broun et al., eds., 6th student ed. 2006).

177. Fed. R. Evid. 702. A particular problem exists when an expert wants to provide an opinion based on an "innovative" scientific or technical theory that is not generally accepted by those in the field. In Daubert v. Merrell Dow Pharmaceuticals, Inc., 509 U.S. 579, 113 S. Ct. 2786, 125 L. Ed. 2d 469 (1993), the Court held that scientific and technical evidence could be admitted only if the trial court found it to be relevant and to rest on a reliable foundation. Thus, the trial court should perform a "gatekeeper" function by excluding such expert testimony.

178. *See* Fed. R. Evid. 701.

179. *See* Fed. R. Evid. 104(a).

180. *See* Chapter 12(A) *infra* ("Post-Trial Motions").

181. *See* Chapter 10(C) *supra* ("Summary Judgment").

1. Competency

Traditionally, a witness has been allowed to testify only if the witness is *competent*. At common law, a witness could be incompetent for many reasons.[182] The most drastic ground of incompetence was embodied in the rule that parties and persons with a direct pecuniary or proprietary interest in the lawsuit could not testify. The party's self-interest in the outcome of the trial was thought to make the party's testimony on the party's own behalf unreliable. This rationale, however, did not explain why parties were given a privilege not to testify against themselves. The rule has been abolished both in this country and in England, but a vestige of the rule remains in some states in the form of *dead man's statutes*. These statutes disqualify a person from testifying concerning controversies over transactions or occurrences when another party to the transaction or occurrence has died. The fear is that "[t]he survivor could testify though the adverse party's lips would be sealed in death," a fear grounded in the theoretical unreliability of an interested party's testimony.[183] The general view today is that dead man's statutes impede justice. No solid reason exists why a survivor's testimony may not be tested by the same means[184] as all other testimony.

Today, under the Federal Rules of Evidence, "[e]very person is competent to be a witness except as otherwise provided in [the] rules."[185] The rules provide very few grounds of incompetence.[186] However, Rule 601 of the Federal Rules of Evidence also provides that "in civil actions and proceedings, with respect to an element of a claim or defense as to which state law supplies the rule of decision, the competency of a witness shall be determined in accordance with state law."[187]

2. Relevancy

To be admissible, all evidence must be *relevant*.[188] Rule 401 of the Federal Rules of Evidence defines relevant evidence as evidence having any tendency to make a fact of consequence more or less probable than it would be without the

---

182. At common law, the husband or wife of a party was incompetent to testify for or against the party in a civil or criminal case. When this rule continues to exist at all, it has been modified drastically. Spouses usually can testify for or against their husbands or wives in civil cases in most states. This rule of competence should be distinguished from the rule providing a privilege to prevent testimony about confidential communications between husband and wife, which still exists in some states. *See* MCCORMICK ON EVIDENCE §§ 66, 78-86 (Kenneth S. Broun et al., eds., 6th student ed. 2006). Other grounds of incompetence that still have broad support in most jurisdictions include the incompetence of a judge or juror to testify in the trial of a case in which the judge or juror is participating, *see* FED. R. EVID. 605, 606, incompetence on grounds of immaturity, and incompetence on grounds of mental capacity. *See* MCCORMICK ON EVIDENCE § 62 (Kenneth S. Broun et al., eds., 6th student ed. 2006). A ground of incompetence recognized at common law was the disqualification of a witness who had been convicted of a crime. This ground also has been abolished virtually everywhere, although conviction of crime can still be used for purposes of impeaching the credibility of a witness under certain circumstances. *See* FED. R. EVID. 609. A party who was unable to take a religious oath at common law also was disqualified from being a witness. This ground of incompetence has been abolished and probably is prohibited by the First and Fourteenth Amendments to the U.S. Constitution. *See* FED. R. EVID. 603, 610.

183. *See* MCCORMICK ON EVIDENCE § 65 (Kenneth S. Broun et al., eds., 6th student ed. 2006).

184. *See* subsection 6 *infra* ("Objections, Cross-Examination, and Impeachment").

185. FED. R. EVID. 601.

186. *See* FED. R. EVID. 605, 606.

187. FED. R. EVID. 601.

188. *See* FED. R. EVID. 401.

evidence.[189] This standard simply means that the evidence must have some tendency in logic, however slight, to prove or disprove a fact in issue. Rule 401 encompasses the traditional definition of both relevant and material evidence. Traditionally, evidence was immaterial if it had no bearing on any fact of consequence to the litigation, though it might have a great bearing on some inconsequential fact.

Illustration 11-19. If the fact of consequence is the color of the barn and a party attempts to introduce evidence proving the color of the house, the evidence is immaterial.

* * * * *

Irrelevant evidence, on the other hand, is evidence that is introduced to prove a fact of consequence to the action but has no logical tendency to do so. Obviously, relevance and materiality are closely related.

Illustration 11-20. The evidence described in *Illustration 11-19* bearing on the color of the barn may be described plausibly as either immaterial or irrelevant. To the extent that the party offers the evidence to prove the color of the house, the evidence is immaterial because the party is attempting to prove a fact of no consequence to the action. However, if the party offers evidence on the color of the house to prove the color of the barn, the evidence is irrelevant because it has no apparent logical bearing on the color of the barn.

* * * * *

Sometimes, however, evidence may be relevant only in connection with other evidence not yet offered. In such cases the apparently irrelevant evidence may be "connected up" later.[190]

Illustration 11-21. In the house example given in *Illustration 11-19*, for instance, the color of the house might be admitted conditioned on the subsequent introduction of evidence that the house and the barn were painted the same color.

* * * * *

Just because evidence is relevant does not mean that it is admissible. The Federal Rules of Evidence enumerate several categories of evidence which are inadmissible even if they are relevant. Relevant but inadmissible evidence includes the following: (1) evidence of character to prove that a person acted in conformity with that person's character on a particular occasion;[191] (2) evidence of subsequent remedial measures to prove negligence or culpable conduct;[192] (3) evidence of offers or acceptances of settlement of claims disputed as to validity or amount to prove liability for or invalidity of the claims;[193] (4) evidence of payments or offers to pay medical expenses to prove liability for an injury;[194] (5) evidence of certain pleas or statements made during criminal proceedings;[195] (6) evidence that a person

---

189. *See id.*
190. *See* FED. R. EVID. 104(b).
191. *See* FED. R. EVID. 404.
192. *See* FED. R. EVID. 407.
193. *See* FED. R. EVID. 408.
194. *See* FED. R. EVID. 409.
195. *See* FED. R. EVID. 410.

possessed liability insurance to prove negligence or wrongful conduct;[196] and (7) evidence of a sex offense victim's past sexual behavior, with certain exceptions.[197]

In addition, Rule 403 provides that the court may exclude otherwise relevant evidence if its probative value is substantially outweighed by the danger of unfair prejudice, confusion of the issues, misleading the jury, or by considerations of undue delay, waste of time, or needless presentation of cumulative evidence.[198]

3. Hearsay

Hearsay is a statement made out of court which is offered in court to prove the truth of the matter contained in the statement.[199]

Illustration 11-22. Suppose the color of the barn is at issue. If a witness takes the stand and testifies, based on personal knowledge, "The barn is red," there is no hearsay. However, if the witness takes the stand and states, "Farmer *X* told me that the barn was red," the testimony is objectionable as hearsay. The witness is attempting to relate an out-of-court statement (the statement of Farmer *X*) about the color of the barn, and the statement is being offered to prove the truth of the matter contained in the statement.

* * * * *

Hearsay is objectionable because the trier of fact cannot properly assess the credibility of the out-of-court declarant. The statement about the color of the barn in *Illustration 11-22* is objectionable because the trier of fact did not have the opportunity to observe Farmer *X* at the time Farmer *X* made the statement, nor was Farmer *X* subject to cross-examination at that time. Stated differently, hearsay statements are objectionable because the number of testimonial difficulties for the trier of fact doubles when hearsay is offered, but the means of dealing with the testimonial difficulties do not increase correspondingly.[200]

Illustration 11-23. When a witness testifies based on personal knowledge that the barn is red, the trier of fact can be said to be faced with four separate testimonial difficulties. First, the trier must determine whether problems of ambiguity exist. For example, when the witness uses the word "red," does the witness have in mind the same color as the trier of fact? Second, the trier must determine whether problems of insincerity exist. Does the witness really believe what is being communicated to the trier? Does the witness have any reason to lie about the color of the barn? Third, even if the trier of fact concludes that the witness believes what the witness is saying, the trier must determine whether problems of false memory exist. Is there reason to believe that the witness's memory about the color of the barn has faltered? Fourth, the trier must determine whether problems of inaccurate perception exist. Did the witness correctly perceive the color of the barn—for example, is the witness color blind? All of these testimonial difficulties

---

196. *See* FED. R. EVID. 411.
197. *See* FED. R. EVID. 412.
198. *See* FED. R. EVID. 403.
199. *See* FED. R. EVID. 801(c).
200. *See* Laurence H. Tribe, *Triangulating Hearsay*, 87 HARV. L. REV. 957 (1974).

can be considered by the trier of fact through the ordinary process of observing the witness's demeanor during cross-examination. When hearsay is involved, however, the number of testimonial difficulties doubles, because the witness is relating a statement made out of court about the color of the barn. The usual four testimonial difficulties discussed above are present with regard to the witness's testimony about the making of the statement, but in addition there exist four identical testimonial difficulties with the contents of the out-of-court statement. These latter difficulties cannot be explored in the same way that they are explored in the case of ordinary testimony. The trier of fact had no opportunity to observe the demeanor of the declarant at the time the declarant made the out-of-court statement, and the declarant, of course, was not subject to cross-examination about the statement at the time the declarant made it.[201]

* * * * *

It should not be assumed that all hearsay is inadmissible. In fact, numerous exceptions to the hearsay rule enormously complicate the operation of the rule. An exception to the hearsay rule is usually supported either by extraordinary guarantees of trustworthiness concerning a hearsay statement (produced by the absence of one or more of the testimonial difficulties described above), or by a special need for the hearsay statement in the trial of a case, or by both.

The exceptions to the hearsay rule in the Federal Rules of Evidence are found in Rules 803 and 804. Rule 803 contains twenty-four exceptions. Rule 804 contains five exceptions. In addition, Rule 801(d) defines hearsay as not including two kinds of statements that often were classified as exceptions to the hearsay rule at common law. An examination of a few of these exceptions will provide some indication of how the hearsay rule and its exceptions operate.

(a) Admissions of a Party Opponent

Rule 801(d)(2) provides the federal version of the traditional rule governing admissions of a party opponent. An out-of-court statement made by a party to the suit or that party's representative and offered by the party's opponent is defined as an admission by a party opponent.[202]

Illustration 11-24. *A* states to *B*, the tax assessor, "That's not my barn. It's not on my property. I don't own it." Later, *A* sues *C* for damages after *C* intentionally sets the barn on fire. *C* can offer the testimony of *B* about *A's* statement as evidence that *A* does not own the barn. The statement is admissible as an admission of a party opponent.

* * * * *

The Advisory Committee's Note to Rule 801(d)(2) states that "[a]dmissions by a party-opponent are excluded from the category of hearsay on the theory that their admissibility in evidence is the result of the adversary system rather than satisfaction of the conditions of the hearsay rule."[203] The Advisory Committee

---

201. *See generally id.*
202. *See* FED. R. EVID. 801(d)(2).
203. FED. R. EVID. 801(d)(2) advisory committee's note.

meant that there are not necessarily any special guarantees of trustworthiness, nor any special need to allow admissions into evidence. Rather, parties against whom admissions are offered should not be heard to complain that they had no opportunity to observe their own demeanor or cross-examine themselves.

(b) Present Sense Impressions and Excited Utterances

Rule 803 provides for a large number of exceptions to the hearsay rule that are available even though the declarant is available as a witness.[204] Two are found in Rule 803(1) and (2) under the heading of *present sense impressions* and *excited utterances*. At common law, both of these exceptions were sometimes lumped together under the label *res gestae*.[205] The exceptions are based upon special guarantees of trustworthiness that are thought to be inherent in these types of out-of-court declarations. A present sense impression is defined as a statement describing or explaining an event or condition made while the declarant is perceiving the event or condition or made immediately thereafter. The theory "is that substantial contemporaneity of event and statement negative the likelihood of deliberate or conscious misrepresentation."[206]

Illustration 11-25. In *Makuc v. American Honda Motor Co.*,[207] for example, a products liability action was brought in connection with a motorbike accident. The First Circuit Court of Appeals held that the district court properly admitted under Rule 803(1) the testimony of previous owners of the motorbike repeating statements made to them by a mechanic regarding the cost of repairs necessary to correct damage that had been done to the motorbike by the previous owners' grandsons. The mechanic's description or explanation of the condition of the motorbike at the time he had been engaged in examining it was regarded as a present sense impression.[208]

* * * * *

An excited utterance is defined as a statement relating to a startling event or condition made while the declarant was under the stress of excitement caused by the event or condition.[209] The theory "is simply that circumstances may produce a condition of excitement which temporarily stills the capacity of reflection and produces utterances free of conscious fabrication."[210]

Illustration 11-26. In *Hilyer v. Howat Concrete Co.*,[211] for example, a wrongful death action was brought when a construction worker was allegedly run over by the defendant's concrete mixer truck. A co-worker of the deceased construction worker told a police officer shortly after the accident that the decedent had moved in front of the truck without looking. The D.C. Circuit held that the district court properly admitted the police officer's testimony relating the statement.

---

204. *See* FED. R. EVID. 803.
205. *See* MCCORMICK ON EVIDENCE § 268 (Kenneth S. Broun et al., eds., 6th student ed. 2006).
206. FED. R. EVID. 803(1) & advisory committee's note.
207. 835 F.2d 389 (1st Cir. 1987).
208. *See id.* at 391-92.
209. FED. R. EVID. 803(2).
210. FED. R. EVID. 803(2) advisory committee's note.
211. 578 F.2d 422 (D.C. Cir. 1978).

The co-worker's statement was an excited utterance relating to a startling event or condition within the meaning of Rule 803(2).[212]

(c) Statements Against Interest

In contrast to Rule 803, Rule 804 provides certain exceptions to the hearsay rule that are available *only* if the declarant is unavailable as a witness.[213] One such exception is a statement against interest. A statement against interest is a statement that was contrary to the declarant's interest at the time it was made. Statements against interest are thought to possess an extra guarantee of trustworthiness because people do not usually make false statements contrary to their own interests. At common law, a statement against interest had to be against the declarant's pecuniary or proprietary interest to be admissible under the exception. Statements that tended to subject a person to civil or criminal liability did not qualify in all jurisdictions.

However, Rule 804(b)(3) defines a statement against interest to include statements against the declarant's pecuniary or proprietary interest, as well as statements that so tend "to subject the declarant to civil or criminal liability, or to render invalid a claim by the declarant against another, that a reasonable person in the declarant's position would not have made the statement unless [the declarant] believ[ed] it to be true."[214] Rule 804(b)(3) thus extends the exception to its logical limit.[215] Statements against interest are sometimes confused with admissions of a party opponent, but there are important differences between the two.

Illustration 11-27. Admissions of a party opponent do not have to be contrary to the party's interest at the time they are made, while statements against interest must be. The statement in *Illustration 11-24* by *A* to the tax assessor might not be against *A's* interest at the time it was made, if *A* was attempting to prevent the collector from assessing *A* taxes on the property. For that reason, if for no other, it could not qualify as a statement against interest, but it would qualify as an admission. In addition, for a statement against interest to be admissible, the declarant must be unavailable as a witness. The admissions rule contains no such requirement.[216]

(d) Dying Declarations

Traditionally, statements made by persons who were under the belief that their own death was imminent and who did, in fact, die were admissible in a

---

212. *See id.* at 424-25.

213. *See* FED. R. EVID. 804(a). The Advisory Committee explained the reason for the requirement of unavailability as follows:

> [H]earsay which admittedly is not equal in quality to testimony of the declarant on the stand may nevertheless be admitted if the declarant is unavailable and if his statement meets a specified standard. The rule expresses preferences: testimony given on the stand in person is preferred over hearsay, and hearsay, if of the specified quality, is preferred over complete loss of the evidence . . . .

FED. R. EVID. 803(2)(b) advisory committee's note.

214. *See* FED. R. EVID. 804(b)(3).

215. *See* FED. R. EVID. 804(b)(3) advisory committee's note (originally note to 804(b)(4)).

216. *Cf.* 5 JOHN H. WIGMORE, WIGMORE ON EVIDENCE § 1464 (J. Chadbourn rev. 1972); *see also* 4 *id.* § 1069.

criminal prosecution for homicide to prove the cause or circumstances of the person's impending death. Rule 804(b)(2) of the Federal Rules of Evidence extends the effect of this exception to civil actions. Rule 804(a) provides, in effect, that the declarant only need be unavailable as a witness on one of the grounds there listed, so that the declarant need not actually die for the exception to be available. The theory behind the "dying declarations" exception is that there is a strong likelihood that a person who believes death is imminent will tell the truth. Obviously, the basis of this theory is religious.[217]

Illustration 11-28. Assume that *A* was shot in the chest. Believing that death was imminent and that there was no hope of recovery, *A* tells *W* that *A* had been shot by *B*. *W's* testimony concerning *A's* statement is admissible in an action by *A* against *B* under Rule 804(b)(2).

(e) Hearsay Within Hearsay and Other Problems

There is the possibility of "hearsay within hearsay."[218] Furthermore, even if a hearsay statement falls within an exception, it may be challenged on other grounds.

Illustration 11-29. *C* may attempt to testify that *A* told *C* that *B* told *A* that the barn was red. Under these circumstances, *B's* statement is hearsay and so is *A's*, if they are offered to prove the color of the barn. For multiple hearsay statements to be admissible, each hearsay statement must fall within one of the exceptions to the hearsay rule.

Illustration 11-30. A hearsay declarant ordinarily must have personal knowledge about the matter contained in the statement and the statement must be relevant. If a hearsay statement is admitted, the credibility of the declarant can be attacked in the same way as the credibility of an ordinary witness.[219]

4. Privilege

Rules of privilege exclude otherwise relevant and admissible evidence to attain some socially beneficial goal unrelated to litigational efficiency. Numerous common-law, statutory, and constitutional privileges exist.[220] These rules of privilege are easily confused with rules of competency. However, important differences exist between competency and privilege rules. Rules of competency are designed to safeguard against unreliable evidence by excluding the testimony of persons who are incapable of giving an accurate or reliable account of the transactions or events. Rules of privilege are designed to exclude even reliable

---

217. *See* McCORMICK ON EVIDENCE §§ 309-315 (Kenneth S. Broun et al., eds., 6th student ed. 2006).

218. *See* FED. R. EVID. 805.

219. *See* FED. R. EVID. 806.

220. To list a few of the most important, there are privileges for (1) confidential communications between husband and wife, (2) confidential communications between attorney and client, (3) confidential information secured in the course of the physician-patient relationship, and (4) a privilege against self-incrimination. *See generally* McCORMICK ON EVIDENCE §§ 72, 76-77 (Kenneth S. Broun et al., eds., 6th student ed. 2006). Except to the extent that a privilege, such as the privilege against self-incrimination, is constitutionally based, a particular privilege may or may not exist in any given jurisdiction.

testimony to protect "interests and relationships which, rightly or wrongly, are regarded as of sufficient social importance to justify some sacrifice of availability of evidence relevant to the administration of justice."[221] In addition, rules of competency, if violated by a trial court, produce error which is reversible on appeal. If a claim of privilege is erroneously honored at trial, reversible error also is produced. However, if a claim of privilege is erroneously denied and privileged testimony is admitted into evidence, the purpose of privilege is destroyed and cannot be fulfilled by reversal of the trial court's judgment on appeal.

5. The Best Evidence Rule

Traditionally, in proving the terms of a writing, the courts have required that the original writing be produced unless the original is unavailable for some reason other than the fault of the proponent of the evidence.[222] The original writing is the "best evidence" of the content of the writing. In the Federal Rules of Evidence, the best evidence rule is embodied in Rules 1001-1004 and Rule 1007. By these rules, duplicates are admissible under certain circumstances.[223]

6. Objections, Cross-Examination, and Impeachment

To obtain the exclusion of inadmissible evidence, the party opposing the evidence must object as soon as the ground for objection becomes apparent. The objection also must reasonably specify the grounds for the objection, unless the ground for the objection is apparent from the context. If a party is unable reasonably to object before the objectionable evidence is admitted, an objection must be made promptly after the evidence comes in and the judge must be asked to instruct the jury to disregard the evidence.[224] Failure to abide by this "contemporaneous objection" rule gives the trier of fact discretion to weigh the evidence as it chooses and prevents the party opposing the evidence from complaining about its admission on appeal.

An important qualification of the contemporaneous objection rule is the so-called *plain error rule*. Even without an objection, a trial court judgment may be reversed when admitted evidence was so plainly inadmissible or so taints a trial that it is fundamentally biased.[225] This rule usually is applied to evidence that is constitutionally inadmissible in criminal proceedings and is rarely used in civil actions.[226] Of course, even evidence that is improperly admitted over objection must cause some harm to the opposing party to be the basis for a reversal on appeal.

If evidence is excluded after an objection, the party attempting to introduce the evidence may have to make an *offer of proof* to establish a record for a later

---

221. *Id.* § 72.
222. *See id.* § 230.
223. FED. R. EVID. 1001-1004, 1007.
224. *See* FED. R. EVID. 103(a)(1).
225. *See* FED. R. EVID. 103(d).
226. *See* MCCORMICK ON EVIDENCE § 52 (Kenneth S. Broun et al., eds., 6th student ed. 2006).

appeal.[227] An offer of proof is simply a statement of what the evidence would show had it been admitted. Such an offer should be made outside the hearing of the jury to prevent the jury from being prejudiced by the information. If the parties disagree about whether the evidence will show what its proponent claims, the evidence actually can be heard in the absence of the jury to make a record.

After a witness has testified, the opposing party may cross-examine and attempt to impeach the witness. In most jurisdictions, cross-examination of a witness is limited to the subjects covered in the direct examination and to matters affecting the credibility of the witness.[228] On cross-examination, however, the questioner is permitted to "lead" the witness, whereas such leading usually is not permitted on direct examination.[229] A *leading question* is simply one that suggests the answer to the witness.[230]

A witness may be *impeached* in a variety of ways. On cross-examination, the questioner may ask questions that demonstrate (1) biases, prejudices, or ambiguities in the witness's testimony; (2) the inability of the witness to observe what the witness claims to have seen; or (3) the inability to accurately remember the facts to which the witness has testified. The testimony of other witnesses giving their opinion of the original witness's character for truthfulness, or who can testify to the original witness's reputation for truthfulness in the community can be used to attack the witness's character.[231] Specific instances of the witness's conduct that bear on the original witness's truthfulness may be inquired into on cross-examination, though they may not be the subject of extrinsic evidence.[232] Evidence that a witness was convicted of a serious crime can be elicited, within certain limits, from the witness or established by public record during cross-examination.[233] Finally, a prior statement of a witness inconsistent with the witness's testimony on the stand can be introduced to impeach the witness.

Traditionally, a party was not permitted to impeach a witness that party had called to the stand. This rule left the party somewhat vulnerable when a witness gave testimony on direct examination that unexpectedly damaged the party. The federal courts and many states have abolished this rule.[234] Even when the rule remains in effect, however, a party can contradict a story told by a witness by calling other witnesses to testify to contrary facts.[235] *Impeachment by contradiction* also is open, of course, to the party opposing a witness's testimony.

Impeachment is simply a device aimed at getting the trier of fact to doubt a witness. When a witness has been impeached by one of the methods described above, the witness's testimony is not excluded from evidence. Since matters of weight and credibility are ordinarily for the trier of fact, whether impeachment is successful or unsuccessful depends upon the impression it makes on the trier.

---

227. *See* FED. R. EVID. 103(a)(2).
228. *See, e.g.*, FED. R. EVID. 611(b).
229. *See* FED. R. EVID. 611(c).
230. *See* MCCORMICK ON EVIDENCE § 6 (Kenneth S. Broun et al., eds., 6th student ed. 2006).
231. *See* FED. R. EVID. 608(a).
232. *See* FED. R. EVID. 608(b).
233. *See* FED. R. EVID. 609.
234. *See* FED. R. EVID. 607.
235. *See* MCCORMICK ON EVIDENCE § 38 (Kenneth S. Broun et al., eds., 6th student ed. 2006).

SECTION J. VARIANCES AND AMENDMENTS AT TRIAL

Evidence proving matters outside the pleadings and not directed to a proposition of consequence in the action could be objected to as "irrelevant." Such evidence produces a "variance" between the issues framed by the pleadings or pretrial order and the proof at trial. A variance at common law was fatal, even though the evidence may have disclosed a meritorious claim outside the pleadings. In 1833, a statute permitted judges at nisi prius (on circuit trying the case) to amend the pleadings at trial when a variance occurred.[236] Previously, such an amendment could not be made during trial because the judges on circuit were only authorized to try issues raised in the pleadings, not to alter the pleadings.[237]

When the codes were enacted, the drafters provided for liberal amendment of pleadings.[238] Under these general provisions governing amendments, the courts were vested with discretion to deal with variances by ruling on amendments to the pleadings after an objection had occurred. In guiding the courts in using their discretion, most codes directed the court to consider whether the variance was "material."[239] As noted in Chapter 6, however, some codes either explicitly or by interpretation prohibited amendments that "substantially changed the claim," and in those states the court's discretion to permit amendments to cure variances was significantly limited.[240]

Rule 15(b) of the Federal Rules of Civil Procedure provides that when an objection to evidence is made at trial on the grounds that the evidence is not within the issues made by the pleadings, the court may allow an amendment to the pleadings "when doing so will aid in presenting the merits and the objecting party fails to satisfy the court that the evidence would prejudice that party's action or defense on the merits."[241] Prejudice to the objecting party might take the form of surprise—that the party is not prepared to meet the unexpected evidence outside the

---

236. 3 & 4 Will. IV, ch. 42 (1833).

237. CHARLES E. CLARK, HANDBOOK OF THE LAW OF CODE PLEADING § 114, at 705 (2d ed. 1947).

238. Although there were minor differences in wording, most codes provided as follows:

> The court may, in furtherance of justice, and on such terms as may be proper, allow a party to amend any pleading or proceeding by adding or striking out the name of any party, or by correcting a mistake in the name of a party, or a mistake in any other respect; and may, upon like terms, enlarge the time for answer or demurrer. The court may likewise, in its discretion, after notice to the adverse party, allow, upon such terms as may be just, an amendment to any pleading or proceeding in other particulars. . . .

Id. § 115, at 710 (quoting CAL. CODE CIV. PROC. § 473 (Deering 1941)).

239. For example, the California Code of Civil Procedure provided as follows:

> No variance between the allegation in a pleading and the proof is to be deemed material, unless it has actually misled the adverse party to his prejudice in maintaining his action or defense upon the merits. Whenever it appears that a party has been so misled, the court may order the pleading to be amended upon such terms as may be just.
>
> Where the variance is not material, * * * the court may direct the fact to be found according to the evidence, or may order an immediate amendment, without costs.
>
> Where, however, the allegation of the claim or defense to which the proof is directed, is unproved, not in some particular or particulars only, but in its general scope and meaning, it is not to be deemed a case of variance, * * * but a failure of proof.

Id. § 120, at 739 (quoting CAL. CODE CIV. PROC. §§ 469-471 (Deering 1941)).

240. *Id.* § 115, at 711-12; *see* Chapter 6(C)(5) *supra* ("Amendments and Supplemental Pleadings").

241. FED. R. CIV. P. 15(b)(1).

pleadings. This ground for claiming prejudice is undercut, however, by the last sentence of Rule 15(b)(1): "The court may grant a continuance to enable the objecting party to meet the evidence."[242]

In the preceding discussion, it has been assumed that the opposing party objected to the evidence offered and the issue of variance was to be decided by the court's ruling on a subsequent amendment. What happens if the opposing party does not object to the evidence at the time it is offered? At common law, the doctrine of "aider by verdict" would cure variances in some cases. The basic rule presumed that after the verdict any fact necessary to sustain the verdict was sufficiently proved even if it was ill-pleaded. The common law, however, refused to allow aider by verdict when the declaration contained no averment at all, imperfect or otherwise, of the ultimate fact required to establish the pleader's case. Thus, it was said that "the verdict will supplement an incomplete pleading, but will not supply a total want of averment."[243]

If a party failed to object to evidence that varied from the pleadings in a code-pleading state, the matter might be deemed to have been *tried by consent*. If a matter were tried by consent, a party would be permitted in most code states to amend the pleadings to "conform" to the evidence so that they were consistent with the issues that were actually litigated at trial. Some codes, however, permitted such an amendment only when it did "not change substantially the claim or defense."[244]

Federal Rule 15(b) also envisions that issues may be tried by consent of the parties: "When an issue not raised by the pleadings is tried by the parties' express or implied consent, it must be treated in all respects as if raised in the pleadings."[245] Rule 15(b) directs the court to permit amendments of the pleadings so that they conform to the evidence, even after judgment.[246] Once a court determines that an issue has been tried by consent, the court cannot refuse the amendment. Furthermore, the issue tried by consent must be submitted by the court to the jury (if it is otherwise appropriate for it to do so) or the court in a nonjury trial must make a finding on the issue.[247]

SECTION K. JURY INSTRUCTIONS

At the close of a trial, the court instructs the jury. Instructions state the law that applies to the facts and issues in the case. They also explain the rules regulating

---

242. FED. R. CIV. P. 15(b)(1); *see* Robbins v. Jordan, 181 F.2d 793 (D.C. Cir. 1950). *But see* Moody v. FMC Corp., 995 F.2d 63 (5th Cir. 1993) (permission to amend at trial denied because of delay in requesting permission and prejudice to opposing party).

243. JOSEPH H. KOFFLER & ALISON REPPY, HANDBOOK OF COMMON LAW PLEADING § 299, at 556-57 (1969).

244. *See, e.g.*, NEB. REV. STAT. § 25-852 (2008); McCook Nat'l Bank v. Myers, 243 Neb. 853, 503 N.W.2d 200 (1993) (amendment cannot substantially change the claim or defense; prejudicial error occurs when amendment changes issues and affects quantum of proof as to any material fact); *see also* CHARLES E. CLARK, HANDBOOK OF THE LAW OF CODE PLEADING § 115, at 711 (2d ed. 1947); Chapter 6(C)(5) *supra* ("Amendments and Supplemental Pleadings").

245. FED. R. CIV. P. 15(b)(2).

246. *Id.*

247. 6A CHARLES A. WRIGHT ET AL., FEDERAL PRACTICE AND PROCEDURE: CIVIL § 1493, at 47-48 (3d ed. 2010).

how the jury should conduct its deliberations to arrive at a verdict.[248] If a party wants to request that a particular instruction or set of instructions be given, that request must be made at the close of the evidence or at an earlier time when the court reasonably so directs.[249] If no specific requests are made, the court must nevertheless charge the jury on all issues as the judge deems sufficient, provided the charge is correct, applicable, and not misleading—even though not all principles of law are not covered.[250] In many jurisdictions, however, each party is required by statute or rule to submit a proposed set of instructions. In federal court, the court is specifically required to inform counsel of its proposed action upon their requests prior to their arguments to the jury.[251] In federal court and in nearly all state courts, if counsel wants to object to the giving or the failure to give an instruction, that objection must be made before the jury retires to consider its verdict. Counsel must state the specific grounds of the objection.

SECTION L. VERDICTS AND FINDINGS BY THE COURT

The most common form of a verdict is the *general verdict*. In a general verdict, the jury simply finds either for the plaintiff and awards a certain dollar amount or finds for the defendant that the plaintiff shall take nothing. No explanation of the verdict is required.[252] In some state jurisdictions, however, *special verdicts*, rather than general verdicts, are routinely used.[253] A special verdict requires the jury to answer interrogatories submitted to it without concluding which party should prevail in the case. In the federal courts, special verdicts are authorized by Federal Rule 49(a), which gives the district judge discretion to require the jury to return a special verdict.[254]

Use of the general verdict accompanied by interrogatories has been described as a "middle course" between use of a general verdict form and use of a special verdict form.[255] The underlying rationale of this middle course is that the jury will be required "to give close attention to the more important issues and their

---

248. FED. R. CIV. P. 51. In 1987, Rule 51 was amended to give federal courts discretion to instruct the jury either before or after closing argument. In 2003, Rule 51 was again amended. The amended rule now regulates more explicitly the process of requesting jury instructions, the process whereby the court informs the parties of its proposed instructions and actions on requests for instructions, and the opportunity for the parties to object to the instructions. The amended rule also regulates the process of making objections and assigning error. *See id.*

249. *Id.*

250. *See* 9 CYCLOPEDIA OF FEDERAL PROCEDURE § 31.108, at 448 (3d rev. ed. 2011).

251. FED. R. CIV. P. 51.

252. A typical general verdict would be: "We, the jury in the above-entitled and numbered action, find in favor of plaintiff and against defendant, and assess plaintiff's damages at $_____ [or, find in favor of defendant and against plaintiff.]" *See* 23 AM. JUR. PLEADING AND PRACTICE FORMS §§ 376-394 (rev. ed. 2002).

253. *See, e.g.*, WIS. STAT. ANN. § 805.12(1) (West 1994) ("Unless it orders otherwise, the court shall direct the jury to return a special verdict"); *cf.* William V. Dorsaneo, III, *Broad-Form Submission of Jury Questions and the Standard of Review*, 46 SMU L. REV. 601 (1992) (discussing Texas practice).

254. *See* FED. R. CIV. P. 49(a); *see also* 9 BENDER'S FEDERAL PRACTICE FORMS 49:1 to 49:11 (2011). Rule 49(a) also provides that if, in submitting the special verdict and instructions to the jury, the court omits any issue of fact raised by the pleadings and evidence, each party waives the right to trial by jury of the omitted issue unless the party demands its submission to the jury before the jury retires. In the absence of such a demand by a party, the court may, in its discretion, make a finding on the omitted issue; but if it fails to do so, the court will be deemed to have made a finding in accord with the judgment on the special verdict. FED. R. CIV. P. 49(a).

255. *See* 9B CHARLES A. WRIGHT & ARTHUR R. MILLER, FEDERAL PRACTICE AND PROCEDURE: CIVIL § 2511 (3d ed. 2008).

answers serve to check the propriety of the general verdict."[256] When the general verdict and the answers to the interrogatories are harmonious, Rule 49(b) provides that an appropriate judgment must be entered on the verdict and answers pursuant to Rule 58.[257] When the answers are *consistent with each other*, but one or more answers are inconsistent with the general verdict, Rule 49(b) provides three options: (1) judgment may be entered under Rule 58 in accord with the answers; (2) the court may return the jury for further consideration of its answers and verdict; or (3) the court may order a new trial.[258] However, when the answers to the interrogatories are *inconsistent with each other* and one or more of the answers are inconsistent with the general verdict, Rule 49(b) directs the court either (1) to return the jury for further deliberation of the answers and verdict or (2) to order a new trial. Therefore, the court has no discretion to enter judgment under such circumstances.[259]

The equivalent of a jury verdict in actions tried to the court is findings of fact and conclusions of law by the judge. Some states permit the court to state its findings generally (*i.e.*, for the plaintiff or for the defendant), at least unless the parties request specific findings.[260] More typically, however, the trial court is required to make separate findings of fact and conclusions of law.

Illustration 11-31. Federal Rule 52(a) requires a federal court to "find the facts specially and state its conclusions of law separately [and] judgment must be entered under Rule 58."[261] Rule 52(a) also provides that "[t]he findings and conclusions may be stated on the record after the close of the evidence or may appear in an opinion or a memorandum of decision filed by the court."[262] Rule 52(a) further admonishes the reviewing courts that findings of fact must not be set aside unless clearly erroneous—with due regard to the trial judge's opportunity to judge the credibility of witnesses.[263]

SECTION M. JUDGMENT

The culmination of litigation at the trial court level is the *judgment*. A judgment is the decision of the court on the matters subject to litigation.[264] A judgment may be *final* or *interlocutory*, but this section limits the discussion to final judgments. As discussed in the next two chapters, the final judgment in a civil action has important effects on the ability to appeal and to pursue later litigation on the same subject matter. The entry of the final judgment also brings into play various devices for executing the judgment if it is not voluntarily paid or obeyed,

---

256. *Id.*

257. *See* FED. R. CIV. P. 49(b)(2).

258. *See* FED. R. CIV. P. 49(b)(3).

259. *See* FED. R. CIV. P. 49(b)(4); *see also* Toucet v. Maritime Overseas Corp., 991 F.2d 5 (1st Cir. 1993) (failure to object to inconsistency after verdict is read, but before jury is dismissed, waives objection).

260. *See, e.g.*, NEB. REV. STAT. § 25-1127 (2008).

261. FED. R. CIV. P. 52(a)(1).

262. *Id.*

263. FED. R. CIV. P. 52(a)(6); *See generally* Bryan L. Adamson, *Federal Rule of Civil Procedure 52(a) as an Ideological Weapon?*, 34 FLA. ST. U. L. REV. 1025 (2007).

264. For purposes of the Federal Rules, a judgment is defined to include "a decree or any order from which an appeal lies." FED. R. CIV. P. 54(a).

such as an execution sale of defendant's nonexempt assets to satisfy a money judgment in favor of the plaintiff.

A typical provision governing the entry of judgment is Rule 58 of the Federal Rules of Civil Procedure. Rule 58 provides that "upon a general verdict of a jury or a decision by the court that a party shall recover only a sum certain or costs or that all relief shall be denied, the clerk . . . shall forthwith prepare, sign, and enter the judgment without awaiting any direction from the court," unless the court otherwise orders. When the court grants other relief, or after the jury has returned a special verdict or a general verdict accompanied by interrogatories, the court "promptly" must approve the form of judgment.[265] After approval, the court "shall thereupon enter it."[266] Rule 58 also provides that a judgment must be set forth on a separate document. It is effective only when it is entered in the civil docket in accord with Federal Rule 79(a).[267]

When multiple claims or multiple parties are involved, Rule 54(b) allows the court to "direct the entry of a final judgment as to one or more, but fewer than all, claims or parties."[268] Such an entry of judgment, however, is conditioned on an express determination "that there is no just reason for delay."[269] When the court does not dispose of all the claims, the court may stay the enforcement of a judgment entered pursuant to Rule 54(b) until subsequent judgment or judgments are entered. The court may also prescribe appropriate conditions to secure the benefit of the stayed judgment.[270]

If a money judgment is not paid voluntarily, the defendant's assets can be seized on a writ of execution and sold to satisfy the judgment. Discovery devices available before trial also can be used at this stage of the litigation to locate nonexempt assets of the defendant.[271] Other kinds of judgments may order the defendant to deliver property to the plaintiff, or to do or cease doing other acts found unlawful by the court. The latter form of injunctive "judgments" or orders are enforced, if need be, through the use of contempt sanctions.[272]

Furthermore, as discussed in Chapter 1, the clerk may tax costs pursuant to Rule 54(d)(1).[273] In 1993, a revised procedure was established for presenting

---

265. FED. R. CIV. P. 58; *see* Forms 70 ("Judgment on a Jury Verdict") and 71 ("Judgment by the Court Without a Jury") in the Appendix of Forms following the Federal Rules of Civil Procedure. A judgment should not contain a recital of the pleadings, a master's report, or the record of prior proceedings. FED. R. CIV. P. 54(a).

266. FED. R. CIV. P. 58, 79(a).

267. *See* FED. R. CIV. P. 58(a).

268. FED. R. CIV. P. 54(b).

269. *Id.*

270. FED. R. CIV. P. 62(h).

271. *Cf.* FED. R. CIV. P. 69(a)(1).

272. *See* Chapter 6(G) *supra* ("Provisional Remedies"); *cf.* Callie v. Bowling, 123 Nev. 181, 160 P.3d 878 (2007) (when a judgment creditor seeks to collect on a judgment from a nonparty, the judgment creditor must commence an independent action as opposed to proceeding by a motion to amend the judgment to add the nonparty).

273. FED. R. CIV. P. 54(d)(1); *see* Chapter 1(C)(4)*(a) supra* ("Allocating the Direct Costs of Litigation"). Recoverable "costs" are usually prescribed by statute or court rule for each procedural system. *See, e.g.*, Little v. Mitsubishi Motors N. Am., Inc., 514 F.3d 699 (7th Cir. 2008) (costs of stenographically recording a videotaped deposition are taxable against the losing party); Sorbo v. United Parcel Serv., 432 F.3d 1169 (10th Cir. 2005) (case remanded because district court erroneously included as costs certain expenses not within scope of the costs statute).

claims for attorneys' fees and related nontaxable expenses.[274] Rule 54(d)(2) provides that such claims must be presented by motion. The motion must specify (1) the judgment, (2) the statute, rule, or other grounds entitling the moving party to the award, and (3) the amount or a fair estimate of the amount sought. Furthermore, if directed by the court, the motion must also disclose the terms of the fee agreement with the moving party's client.[275] Rule 54(d)(2) establishes a 14-day deadline for filing and serving motions for attorneys' fees after the court enters a final judgment, unless the court or a statute specifies otherwise.[276] The purpose of the time limit is to assure that opposing parties are informed of the claim before this time for appeal expires.[277] The rule also assures that the parties have an opportunity to make appropriate presentations concerning any issues regarding the fees or other nontaxable expenses—most likely through an evidentiary hearing. The rule explicitly authorizes the court to determine the liability for fees before receiving submissions bearing on the amount of the award.[278]

---

274. The purpose of this new procedure is "to harmonize and clarify procedures that had developed through case law and local rules." FED. R. CIV. P. 54(d) advisory committee's note to the 1993 amendment. The rule does not apply to fees awarded as sanctions under the Federal Rules nor to fees awarded under 28 U.S.C. § 1927. *Id.*

275. FED. R. CIV. P. 54(d)(2)(A) & (B).

276. FED. R. CIV. P. 54(d)(2)(B). The Advisory Committee pointed out that prior to the adoption of this provision, there was no general time limit on claims for attorneys' fees. *See* White v. New Hampshire Dep't of Employment Sec., 455 U.S. 445, 102 S. Ct. 1162, 71 L. Ed. 2d 325 (1982). However, some statutes establish specific deadlines. *See, e.g.*, Equal Access to Justice Act, 28 U.S.C. § 2412(d)(1)(B) (thirty-day filing period).

277. FED. R. CIV. P. 54(d) advisory committee's note to the 1993 amendment.

278. FED. R. CIV. P. 54(2)(C) & advisory committee's note to the 1993 amendment.

Chapter 12

POST-TRIAL MOTIONS, APPELLATE REVIEW, AND EXTRAORDINARY RELIEF FROM JUDGMENTS

SECTION A. POST-TRIAL MOTIONS

In early English practice, jury trials were often held away from the courts at Westminster.[1] When a verdict had been rendered during a "vacation" of the courts, judgment on the verdict was delayed until after the next term began. At the beginning of the term, the losing party could present motions designed to prevent entry of the judgment. These post-trial motions attempted to point out errors that appeared on the face of the record (which consisted of the process, pleadings, and verdict) or errors that had occurred during the trial.

Illustration 12-1. A defendant who had lost a trial could use a *motion in arrest of judgment* to raise a matter of law appearing on the face of the record, such as a defect in the pleadings. In effect, this motion was "a kind of [d]elayed [d]emurrer."[2] A plaintiff who lost at trial could raise substantive defects by moving for *judgment notwithstanding the verdict* (*judgment non obstante veredicto*). This motion was used primarily to test the legal sufficiency of a defense.[3] A motion for a new trial raised errors and irregularities that occurred during the trial.

* * * * *

In modern practice, after the trial has been completed and judgment has been entered, the parties are permitted to make the following post-trial motions: (1) a motion for judgment notwithstanding the verdict (now called a motion for judgment as a matter of law in federal court);[4] (2) a motion for a new trial; and (3) a motion to alter or amend the judgment. They are traditionally known in practice as *ten-day motions* because they traditionally had to be made "not later than 10 days after the entry of the judgment."[5] The 2009 amendments to the Federal Rules of Civil Procedure changed the time to 28 days after the entry of the judgment.[6]

---

1. *See* Chapter 4(A) *supra* ("Transitory and Local Actions").

2. JOSEPH H. KOFFLER & ALISON REPPY, HANDBOOK OF COMMON LAW PLEADING § 307, at 571 (1969). To obtain review, the defendant would obtain a "rule" directing the plaintiff to appear before the full court and to show cause why the judgment should not be arrested. If the court decided in the defendant's favor, the rule became absolute. If the court decided in the plaintiff's favor, the rule was discharged or refused. If the judgment was arrested, the plaintiff could commence the action again if the plaintiff believed success was possible.

3. As noted in Chapter 6, common-law pleading required the defendant to "confess" the plaintiff's right before it could be "avoided" by a defense. *See* Chapter 6(A)(3)*(e) supra* ("Pleas in Confession and Avoidance"). If the defense was insufficient, the plaintiff was entitled to a judgment because of the defendant's confession. JOSEPH H. KOFFLER & ALISON REPPY, HANDBOOK OF COMMON LAW PLEADING § 308, at 577 (1969).

4. *See* FED. R. CIV. P. 50(a) & advisory committee's note to the 1991 amendment.

5. *Cf.* FED. R. CIV. P. 50(b), 59(b) & (e) (prior to the 2009 amendment of these rules).

6. *See id.* (With current specific standards in federal courts).

As discussed in the following subsections, these motions differ in important ways from their common-law predecessors. In modern practice, post-trial motions are principally used for the following reasons: (1) to correct errors that occurred during the trial; (2) to challenge the sufficiency of the evidence on which the judgment rests; and (3) to rectify improper conduct by the parties, their attorneys, or the jury. Post-trial motions give the trial judge one last opportunity to correct these deficiencies before the complaining party is forced to seek an appeal.

1. Judgment Notwithstanding the Verdict (Judgment as a Matter of Law)

The modern judgment notwithstanding the verdict has its historical origin in the *judgment non obstante veredicto* (judgment n.o.v.). The common-law courts allowed plaintiffs to move for judgment in their favor, despite a jury verdict in favor of the defendant, when the defendant's plea was in proper form but failed to demonstrate any valid defense to the merits of the plaintiff's action. Defendants were later allowed to use this motion when the plaintiff's pleadings were insufficient to support a judgment in the plaintiff's favor.[7]

In the federal courts and states adopting the Federal Rules of Civil Procedure, the motion for judgment notwithstanding the verdict is governed by Rule 50(b). Before 1991, Federal Rule 50(b) provided that a party might move to have a jury verdict and judgment set aside and instead have judgment entered in the moving party's favor. A 1991 amendment to Federal Rule 50(b) redesignates this motion as a motion for *judgment as a matter of law* in federal court.[8] Pursuant to such a motion, the court will disregard a jury determination lacking a legally sufficient evidentiary basis. The court may then decide these issues as a matter of law and enter judgment when either (1) the jury has decided all other material issues based on legally sufficient evidence or (2) the court has decided all other material issues as a matter of law.[9]

A Rule 50 motion for judgment as a matter of law is determined by the same legal standard as a motion for summary judgment.[10] In federal practice, in order to make a *post-trial* motion for judgment as a matter of law, the same motion must have been made before the case was submitted to the jury.[11] This standard is also the same as the one used for a directed verdict (now also called a judgment as

---

7. *See* JOSEPH H. KOFFLER & ALISON REPPY, HANDBOOK OF COMMON LAW PLEADING § 308, at 577 (1969).

8. FED. R. CIV. P. 50(b). For further discussion of the standards applied in ruling on motions for directed verdicts (judgment as a matter of law), see Chapter 11(H)(1) *supra* ("Involuntary Dismissals (Judgments on Partial Findings) and Directed Verdicts (Judgments as a Matter of Law)").

9. FED. R. CIV. P. 50(b) advisory committee's note to 1991 amendment.

10. Reeves v. Sanderson Plumbing Prods., Inc., 530 U.S. 133, 150, 120 S. Ct. 2097, 2110, 147 L. Ed. 2d 105, 121 (2000).

11. FED. R. CIV. P. 50(b); *see* Chapter 11(H)(1) *supra* ("Involuntary Dismissals (Judgments on Partial Findings) and Directed Verdicts (Judgments as a Matter of Law)"); *see also* Wells v. State Farm Fire & Cas. Co., 993 F.2d 510 (5th Cir. 1993) (motion for judgment as a matter of law made by defendant at close of plaintiff's case denied; defendant and plaintiff then introduced additional evidence; defendant did not renew motion at close of plaintiff's rebuttal evidence, but waited until after jury returned verdict for plaintiff; failure to renew motion at the close of plaintiff's evidence waived right to plenary appellate review of sufficiency of the evidence).

a matter of law).[12] Chapter 11 addressed whether a motion for a judgment as a matter of law under Rule 50(a) before the verdict in a diversity action should be governed by an independent federal standard, either under Rule 50(a) or under a "federal common-law rule of procedure."[13] The issues are the same under Rule 50(b), and, therefore, the discussion of the Rules Enabling Act and Rules of Decision Act questions in Chapter 11 is also pertinent here.

Illustration 12-2. A judgment n.o.v. (or judgment as a matter of law) may be based on a variety of circumstances. Consider the following examples: (1) There was no evidence which, if believed, would authorize a verdict against the defendant; (2) there was no evidence to warrant the submission of the case to the jury; and (3) the verdict which the jury returned was based on speculation and conjecture.[14]

* * * * *

A motion for a new trial may be joined with a motion for judgment notwithstanding the verdict (or judgment as a matter of law).[15] Under Rule 50(c)(1), the court must rule on both motions. In this way, should an appellate court vacate or reverse the judgment as a matter of law, the appellate court will know whether the original judgment should be reinstated or a new trial should be ordered.[16]

In *Unitherm Food Systems, Inc. v. Swift-Eckrich, Inc.*,[17] the defendant moved for a judgment as a matter of law under Rule 50(a) before the case was submitted to the jury. The motion was denied, and the jury returned a verdict against the defendant. The defendant did not move under Rule 50(b) for a judgment as a matter of law after the verdict, but instead appealed. The court of appeals considered the defendant's claim that the evidence was insufficient to support the verdict on appeal and upheld the claim, ordering a new trial. The U.S. Supreme Court granted certiorari and reversed, holding it impermissible for the court of appeals to consider the insufficiency objection because the defendant did not renew its pre-verdict motion after verdict.

In an opinion by Justice Thomas, the Court was clearly influenced by the need for the trial judge to be able to exercise the maximum latitude under Rule 50 in determining insufficiency objections.[18] To accomplish this, the district court must be able to submit a case to the jury and then reconsider the insufficiency objection after verdict, because the verdict may resolve the issue for the court (if it is in favor of the moving party). The Court also indicated that determination of

---

12. FED. R. CIV. P. 50(a)(1) & advisory committee's note to the 1991 amendment; *see also* Chapter 11(H)(1) *supra* ("Involuntary Dismissals (Judgments on Partial Findings) and Directed Verdicts (Judgments as a Matter of Law)").

13. *See* Chapter 11(H)(1) *supra* ("Involuntary Dismissals (Judgments on Partial Findings) and Directed Verdicts (Judgments as a Matter of Law)").

14. Thus, a sharp distinction exists between the modern motion for judgment notwithstanding the verdict and its common-law predecessor. The modern motion "is actuated by the state of the evidence, instead of the state of the pleadings." ROBERT W. MILLAR, CIVIL PROCEDURE OF THE TRIAL COURT IN HISTORICAL PERSPECTIVE 330 (1952). The motion for judgment notwithstanding the verdict in modern practice is principally used as a device for controlling the jury. *See* Chapter 11(C)(2) *supra* ("Methods of Controlling the Jury"). Note that a court of appeals may direct the entry of judgment as a matter of law for the verdict loser upon determining that the verdict cannot be sustained due to error in the admission of evidence at trial and is not required to remand for a new trial determination. *See* Weisgram v. Marley Co., 528 U.S. 440, 120 S. Ct. 1011, 145 L. Ed. 2d 958 (2000).

15. *See* FED. R. CIV. P. 50(b).

16. *See* FED. R. CIV. P. 50(b) & (c)(1).

17. 546 U.S. 394, 126 S. Ct. 980, 163 L. Ed. 2d 974 (2006).

18. *See id.* at 405, 126 S. Ct. at 988, 163 L. Ed. 2d at 986.

whether a new trial should be granted or a judgment entered under Rule 50(b) calls for the judgment in the first instance of the judge who saw and heard the witnesses and has a feel for the case that no printed transcript could give the court of appeals.[19] The Rule 50(a) motion prior to verdict did not give the district judge the option to grant a new trial, and the district judge was "without power to do so under Rule 50(b) absent a post-verdict motion pursuant to that Rule."[20] The denial of the pre-verdict motion could not form the basis of respondent's appeal, because the denial of the motion was not error. It was simply an exercise of the district court's discretion to make an initial judgment under the rule about the sufficiency of the evidence, subject to later revision, if necessary, after the jury verdict. Later revision, however, requires a defendant to renew its objection after the verdict in order to give the district judge the maximum latitude in the exercise of its discretion.[21]

2. Motion for a New Trial

Federal Rule 59(a) exemplifies how the motion for new trial works in federal court and in states adopting the Federal Rules. Rule 59(a) permits a motion for a new jury trial to be granted on any grounds previously recognized in actions at law in federal court.[22] In the *Gasperini* case, discussed in Chapter 5, the Supreme Court held that Rule 59 did not incorporate an independent federal standard for granting new trials on the grounds that a jury verdict was excessive. Rather, the issue was governed by the general *Erie* standard under the Rules of Decision Act, which required the federal district court to follow state law on the issue to avoid the *Erie*-prohibited forum shopping and inequitable administration of the laws.[23] Rule 59(a) permits a motion for a new trial to be granted in a nonjury trial on any grounds previously recognized in suits in equity in federal courts.[24]

Illustration 12-3. The following are some examples of grounds on which a motion for new trial may be based: (1) The verdict is against the weight of the evidence;[25] (2) newly discovered evidence;[26] or (3) the jury verdict is excessive and appears to have been given under the influence of passion and prejudice.[27]

* * * * *

Furthermore, when the jury renders an unreasonably high verdict, judges have long had the power to condition the denial of the defendant's motion for a new trial on the plaintiff's consent to a *remittitur* (a reduction in the amount of the

---

19. *See id.* at 399-400, 126 S. Ct at 985-86, 163 L. Ed. 2d at 982-83.

20. *Id.* at 405, 126 S. Ct. at 988, 163 L. Ed. 2d at 986.

21. *See also* Nitco Holding Corp. v. Boujikian, 491 F.3d 1086 (9th Cir. 2007) (*Unitherm* precludes even "plain error review" of the sufficiency of the evidence when there is no post-verdict motion under Rule 50(b)).

22. FED. R. CIV. P. 59(a)(1)(A).

23. *See* Gasperini v. Center for Humanities, Inc., 518 U.S. 415, 116 S. Ct. 2211, 135 L. Ed. 2d 659 (1996); Chapter 5(E)(3) *supra* (discussing the Rules of Decision Act aspects of *Gasperini*) & 5(F)(5) *supra* (discussing the interpretation of Rule 59).

24. FED. R. CIV. P. 59(a)(1)(B).

25. *See* 11 CHARLES A. WRIGHT ET AL., FEDERAL PRACTICE AND PROCEDURE: CIVIL § 2806 (2d ed. 1995).

26. *See id.* § 2808.

27. *See* 11 BENDER'S FEDERAL PRACTICE FORMS 59-21 (2012) (Form 59:1).

verdict).[28] However, if the court of appeals orders a remittitur of damages on the ground that the evidence does not support such a large award, the Seventh Amendment requires that the plaintiff be allowed the option of a new trial on the damages issue, rather than forcing the plaintiff to accept a judgment for the lesser amount.[29]

Like a renewed motion for judgment as matter of law (judgment n.o.v.) in federal court, a motion for a new trial must be served not later than 28 days after the entry of the judgment.[30] This time limit may not be extended by the court or by stipulation of the parties.[31] Unlike a judgment as a matter of law (judgment n.o.v.), the court may order a new trial on its own.[32] When the motion for a new trial depends on factual grounds in federal court, the motion should be supported by affidavits filed at the same time as the motion.[33]

3. Motion to Alter or Amend the Judgment

Pursuant to Federal Rule 59(e), a party may move to have the court amend its judgment within 28 days after it has been entered.[34] Rule 59(e) does not specify the grounds that properly serve as the basis for the motion. In practice, it is used for a wide variety of matters. Typically, it is used "to correct manifest errors of law or fact upon which the judgment" is based. In addition, it may be used when there has been an intervening change in the controlling law or when newly discovered or previously unavailable evidence comes to light. It is also used "to prevent manifest injustice"[35] resulting from, for example, misconduct of counsel.[36] Still another use is to remedy the lack of complete diversity in limited circumstances.[37] Furthermore,

---

28. *See, e.g.*, Atlas Food Sys. & Servs., Inc. v. Crane Nat'l Vendors, Inc., 99 F.3d 587 (4th Cir 1996) (no abuse of discretion for district judge to order new trial after plaintiff refused remittitur of $3,000,000 punitive damage award to $1,000,000). Remittitur should not be used, however, when the verdict was the result of passion and prejudice because prejudice may have affected the determination of liability as well. Under such circumstances, a new trial should be ordered. *See* 11 CHARLES A. WRIGHT ET AL., FEDERAL PRACTICE AND PROCEDURE: CIVIL § 2815, at 165 (2d ed. 1995).

29. Hetzel v. Prince William Cnty., 523 U.S. 208, 118 S. Ct. 1210, 140 L. Ed. 2d 336 (1998). In addition, federal courts may not use *additur* to cure an inadequate verdict. Dimick v. Schiedt, 293 U.S. 474, 55 S. Ct. 296, 79 L. Ed. 603 (1935) (5-4 decision) (holding that additur in the federal courts violates the Seventh Amendment); *see also* Suja A. Thomas, *Re-Examining the Constitutionality of Remittitur Under the Seventh Amendment*, 64 OHIO ST. L.J. 731 (2003).

30. FED. R. CIV. P. 59(b).

31. *See* Ethel R. Alston, Annotation, *Motions for New Trial: Time Limitations Under Rule 59(b) of Federal Rules of Civil Procedure*, 45 A.L.R. FED. 104 (1979) (citing numerous cases in § 7).

32. FED. R. CIV. P. 59(d).

33. FED. R. CIV. P. 59(c); *see also* Crowe v. Bolduc, 365 F.3d 86 (1st Cir. 2004) (motion to alter or amend a judgment is the proper procedural vehicle with which to revise a judgment to include an initial award of prejudgment interest, whether mandatory or discretionary).

34. FED. R. CIV. P. 59(e).

35. Allstate Ins. Co. v. Herron, 634 F.3d 1101, 1111 (9 th Cir. 2011) (summarizing these basic grounds).

36. 11 WRIGHT ET AL., FEDERAL PRACTICE AND PROCEDURE: CIVIL §2810.1, at 127 (2d ed. 1995).

37. *See, e.g.*, C.L. Ritter Lumber Co. v. Consolidation Coal Co., 283 F.3d 226 (4th Cir. 2002) (diversity action in which some plaintiffs and some defendants were Texas citizens so that the district court could not exercise diversity jurisdiction over the case as it was originally pleaded, but none of the Texas plaintiffs asserted claims against any of the Texas defendants; the district court was not limited to dismissing the suit for lack of jurisdiction following judgment on a jury verdict for the plaintiffs; the court had the power to alter or amend the judgment by dividing the lawsuit into two cases pursuant to Rule 21 providing that the court could cure misjoinder of parties "at any stage of the action," to vacate the existing judgment, and to enter judgment in favor of the plaintiffs in each of the cases).

clerical mistakes "may be corrected by the court at any time [on] its own initiative or on the motion of any party."[38]

SECTION B. APPELLATE REVIEW

1. The Right to Appeal

Three fundamental rules govern the right to appeal. First, a prevailing party cannot appeal a judgment.[39] Second, a nonparty cannot appeal a judgment in an action between others. Third, a party cannot appeal a judgment entered against another party.[40] Several other closely related rules preclude parties from appealing based on their behavior in the action or in relation to the judgment.[41]

Illustration 12-4. *P's* truck was struck from the rear by a car driven by *D-1*. *P* commenced an action for personal injuries against a party designated as "*D*," and served *D-2*, *D-1's* father who lived at the same address as *D-1*. *D-2* served an answer denying that he was the driver of the automobile that hit *P* and asserting that *D-1*, his son, was the driver; *D-2* also filed a motion for summary judgment. The trial court granted *D-2's* motion for summary judgment and also granted a motion by *P* to amend her complaint to name *D-1* as the defendant and allowed this amendment to relate back to the filing of the complaint. An appeal was filed in which the notice of appeal and appellate brief were both in the name of "*D*." If *D-1* is the appellant, the appeal must be dismissed because *D-1* has not had a final, appealable order issued against him.[42] If *D-2* is the appellant, the appeal must also

---

38. FED. R. CIV. P. 60(a). However, after an appeal has been docketed, clerical mistakes may be corrected with leave of the appellate court. *Id.*

39. *See also* Fidel v. Farley, 534 F.3d 508 (6th Cir. 2008) (unnamed, nonintervening member of a Rule 23(b)(3) class may seek review of the approval of a settlement). *But cf.* Granite Mgmt. Corp. v. United States, 416 F.3d 1373 (Fed. Cir. 2005) (prevailing party must file a cross-appeal when acceptance of an argument that it makes on appeal (in response to appealing opposing party's case) would result in reversal or modification of judgment); Devlin v. Scardelletti, 536 U.S. 1, 122 S. Ct. 2005, 153 L. Ed. 2d 27 (2002) (nonnamed class member who objects to a proposed settlement at a fairness hearing is a "party" to the suit and may appeal denial of objection without intervening).

40. *See, e.g.*, Walker v. Kazi, 316 Ark. 616, 875 S.W.2d 47 (1994) (dismissing appeal because the appellant was the prevailing party and lacked standing to appeal for another party); *see also* Felzen v. Andreas, 134 F.3d 873 (7th Cir. 1998) (nonparties may not appeal from a decision of any kind in a class action), *aff'd by an equally divided court sub nom.* California Pub. Employees' Retirement Sys. v. Feltzan, 525 U.S. 315, 119 S. Ct. 720, 142 L. Ed. 2d 766 (1999); Valley Bank v. Ginsburg, 110 Nev. 440, 874 P.2d 729 (1994) (nonparty shareholders who had never intervened were not parties who had standing to appeal order approving settlement agreement). *But cf.* Rosenbaum v. MacAllister, 64 F.3d 1439 (10th Cir. 1995) (unnamed class member has standing to appeal award of attorney's fees to plaintiff's counsel without intervening). *See generally* 15A CHARLES A. WRIGHT ET AL., FEDERAL PRACTICE AND PROCEDURE: JURISDICTION AND RELATED MATTERS §§ 3902-3902.1 (2d ed. 1992).

41. For example, certain kinds of orders, such as orders voluntarily dismissing claims against the defendant, are not appealable, since they are not considered adverse to the plaintiff and do not have the effect of determining the case against the plaintiff. *See, e.g.*, American Water Dev., Inc. v. City of Alamosa, 874 P.2d 352, 374 (Colo. 1994). In addition, a party may not, pursuant to the doctrine of "invited error," ask the court to make a ruling in its favor and then complain on appeal about the ruling. *See, e.g.*, Security Pac. Hous. Servs., Inc. v. Friddle, 315 Ark. 178, 866 S.W.2d 375 (1993). A party may not accept the benefits of a judgment and then appeal from the judgment. *Cf.* Baker's Supermarkets, Inc. v. Feldman, 243 Neb. 684, 502 N.W.2d 428 (1993). Furthermore, a party who voluntarily complies with a judgment "acquiesces" in it and cannot appeal the judgment. *See, e.g.*, Varner v. Gulf Ins. Co., 254 Kan. 492, 866 P.2d 1044 (1994). For a thorough exploration of "standing to appeal," including the right of persons other than parties to appeal or defend an appeal in federal court, see Joan Steinman, *Shining a Light in a Dim Corner: Standing to Appeal and the Right to Defend a Judgment in the Federal Courts,* 38 GA. L. REV. 813 (2004).

42. *See* section B(3) *supra* (discussing the final judgment rule and its exceptions).

be dismissed. *D-2* is a prevailing party, and prevailing parties cannot appeal. If *D-2* is trying to appeal for *D-1*, *D-2* has no right to do so, because a party cannot appeal a judgment against another party.[43]

2. Jurisdiction on Appeal

The two basic functions of appellate courts are to (1) review the trial court record and (2) establish whether reversible error has occurred.[44] While the appeal is pending, the trial court has no jurisdiction.[45] The four specific methods of obtaining appellate "review" are discussed in the following subsections.

(a) Appeals as a Matter of Right

Statutory provisions generally determine which appeals are a matter of right and which appeals are within a court's discretion. The first level of appeal will ordinarily be an appeal as a matter of right.

Illustration 12-5. An appeal from the final decision of a federal district court to a federal court of appeals is a matter of right.[46]

(b) Discretionary Review

Review of some decisions is at the discretion of the appellate court. In such instances, a party ordinarily must first file a petition, which is usually called a petition for a writ of *certiorari*. In this petition, the party seeking review must persuade the court to hear the appeal. After a petition has been filed, the other party will ordinarily file an opposing brief. Today, virtually all of the cases heard by the U.S. Supreme Court are the result of discretionary review.[47] Several states with intermediate appellate courts also have systems for discretionary review in the highest courts of those states. These systems generally follow the same pattern used in the U.S. Supreme Court.

---

43. *See* Walker v. Kazi, 316 Ark. 616, 875 S.W.2d 47 (1994).

44. *See* DANIEL JOHN MEADOR & JORDANA SIMONE BERNSTEIN, APPELLATE COURTS IN THE UNITED STATES 55-58 (1994).

45. Miller v. United States, 114 F.2d 267, 269 (7th Cir. 1940).

46. *See* 28 U.S.C. § 1291. The Judiciary Act of 1789 established one federal district court in each state. The states were divided into three circuits. The district courts had only original jurisdiction. In contrast, the circuit courts had both original and appellate jurisdiction. The circuit courts were authorized to hear cases appealed from the district courts if the amount in controversy exceeded fifty dollars (in admiralty cases, three hundred dollars). As originally established, the U.S. Supreme Court had appellate jurisdiction over appeals from the circuit courts when the amount in controversy exceeded two thousand dollars. The Court also had appellate jurisdiction over judgments from the highest courts of the states when a federal question was presented. *See* ROBERT L. STERN, APPELLATE PRACTICE IN THE UNITED STATES § 1.3 (2d ed. 1988); 13 CHARLES A. WRIGHT ET AL., FEDERAL PRACTICE AND PROCEDURE: JURISDICTION AND RELATED MATTERS §§ 3503-3504 (3d ed. 2008). In 1891, the Evarts Act repealed the circuit courts' appellate jurisdiction and created the circuit courts of appeals (now called the U.S. Courts of Appeals). Act of Mar. 3, 1891, § 1, 26 Stat. 826, 826. Appellate jurisdiction of the state courts is likewise governed by statutory provisions.

47. *See* 28 U.S.C. § 1254 (decisions of federal courts of appeal reviewed by U.S. Supreme Court by writ of certiorari); 28 U.S.C. § 1257 (certain decisions of a highest state court reviewed by U.S. Supreme Court by writ of certiorari). For a long period, part of the appellate jurisdiction of the U.S. Supreme Court was of right. Although it was mandatory that the Court "hear" these appeals, full consideration of the case was often avoided by a summary dismissal of the case for "want of a substantial federal question."

(c) Certification

Another method of review is *certification*, which is a procedure whereby one court requests another court to review a question of law on which the requesting court needs guidance.

Illustration 12-6. A federal court of appeals may certify to the U.S. Supreme Court "any question of law in any civil or criminal case as to which instructions are desired."[48] Certification is one exception to the earlier statement that the litigants initiate appellate review. In this instance, a federal court of appeals certifies questions to the Supreme Court when it is in doubt and desires instructions. The Supreme Court has discretion in answering. The use of this procedure is rare. A few states also allow an intermediate appellate court to certify a question before a decision is reached.[49]

* * * * *

Certification of an interlocutory appeal by a federal district court judge under 28 U.S.C. § 1292(b) to a federal court of appeals is more common. Such appeals are permitted when the trial judge certifies (1) the matter "involves a controlling question of law as to which there is a substantial ground for difference of opinion and (2) an immediate appeal from the order may materially advance the ultimate termination of the litigation."[50] The federal court of appeals has discretion to hear the interlocutory appeal.[51] Although the process deviates in some ways, several states have similar methods of certification for review of interlocutory orders not otherwise appealable.[52]

Courts of *other* jurisdictions may certify questions to state supreme courts when a state has authorized this type of review. About half of the states permit certification from a federal court to their respective state supreme courts. A few states permit appellate courts of other states to do so also.[53] This method of determining state law is particularly useful for the federal courts as a means of fulfilling their obligation under the Rules of Decision Act, which requires federal courts to apply state substantive law in diversity cases.[54]

(d) Extraordinary Writs

A petition for an extraordinary writ technically commences an original action in the appellate court. Such a petition, however, often involves objections arising out of lower court proceedings. One of the principal extraordinary writs is *mandamus*, which is traditionally issued in response to abuses of judicial power.

---

48. 28 U.S.C. § 1254(2).

49. *See generally* EUGENE GRESSMAN ET AL., SUPREME COURT PRACTICE §§ 9.1-9.4 (9th ed. 2007).

50. 28 U.S.C. § 1292(b).

51. *See generally* MICHAEL E. TIGAR, FEDERAL APPEALS: JURISDICTION AND PRACTICE § 2.04 (3d ed. 1999); 16 CHARLES A. WRIGHT ET AL., FEDERAL PRACTICE AND PROCEDURE: JURISDICTION AND RELATED MATTERS §§ 3929-3931 (2d ed. 1996).

52. *See* ROBERT L. STERN, APPELLATE PRACTICE IN THE UNITED STATES § 4.5(a) & (b) (2d ed. 1988) (discussing similarities between § 1292 and state provisions as well as basic patterns of state deviations).

53. *See id.* § 1.3; *see also* UNIFORM CERTIFICATION OF QUESTIONS OF LAW ACT (1995), 12 U.L.A. 66 (West 2008).

54. *See* Chapter 5(H) *supra* ("Determination of State Law").

Illustration 12-7. When judges refuse to take a required action or take an action that they are not empowered to take, a writ of mandamus may be proper. For example, the Supreme Court has held that mandamus is appropriate when necessary to protect the Seventh Amendment right to a jury trial.[55]

* * * * *

Another extraordinary writ that may be used to "review" judicial proceedings is *prohibition*. Traditionally, a superior court issues this writ to prevent an inferior court from usurping matters not within its jurisdiction. This writ is directed to the judge of the inferior court and to the parties in the action. Still another extraordinary writ is *habeas corpus*, which today is primarily used to test the legality of a prisoner's detention.[56]

Note that mandamus, habeas corpus, and *quo warranto* (traditionally used to determine who has title to a public office) may be directed to public officers other than judges, and original jurisdiction over these actions may be vested in a trial court.[57] These writs are available only in exceptional circumstances, principally when other judicial remedies have failed or are considered inadequate.[58]

3. The Final Judgment Rule and Its Exceptions

(a) The Basic Rule

The common-law rule allowing an appeal only from a final judgment has been generally carried over into modern practice.[59]

Illustration 12-8. Section 1291 of Title 28 of the *United States Code* provides that "[t]he courts of appeals . . . shall have jurisdiction of appeals from all final decisions of the districts courts . . . except where a direct review may be had in the Supreme Court."[60]

* * * * *

---

55. *See* Dairy Queen, Inc. v. Wood, 369 U.S. 469, 472, 82 S. Ct. 894, 897, 8 L. Ed. 2d 44, 48 (1962); Beacon Theatres, Inc. v. Westover, 359 U.S. 500, 511, 79 S. Ct. 948, 957, 3 L. Ed. 2d 988, 998 (1959). *But see* First Nat'l Bank v. Warren, 796 F.2d 999 (7th Cir. 1986) (discussing U.S. Supreme Court decisions on mandamus in jury trial cases and indicating that mandamus is only available when a jury trial issue will not be reviewable on appeal from final judgment).

56. For an example of the use of habeas corpus, see *Illustration 1-4* in Chapter 1 *supra*. *See generally* EUGENE GRESSMAN ET AL., SUPREME COURT PRACTICE §§ 11.1-11.8 (9th ed. 2007).

57. *See, e.g.*, 28 U.S.C. § 1361 (jurisdiction is vested in federal district court for actions "in the nature of mandamus" to compel an officer or federal employee to "perform a duty owed to the plaintiff"). The power of federal courts to issue these extraordinary writs is based upon their inherent power and the "all writs" authority established by § 1651 of Title 28. Section 1651 provides that "[t]he Supreme Court and all courts established by Act of Congress may issue all writs necessary or appropriate in aid of their respective jurisdictions and agreeable to the usages and principles of law." 28 U.S.C. § 1651(a).

58. *See* 16 CHARLES A. WRIGHT ET AL., FEDERAL PRACTICE AND PROCEDURE: JURISDICTION AND RELATED MATTERS § 3932 (2d ed. 1996).

59. *See* Carleton M. Crick, *The Final Judgment as a Basis for Appeal,* 41 YALE L.J. 539, 543-52 (1932).

60. 28 U.S.C. § 1291. *See generally* Martin H. Redish, *The Pragmatic Approach to Appealability in the Federal Courts,* 75 COLUM. L. REV. 89 (1975). Congress has given the power to the Supreme Court to "define when a ruling of a district court is final for purposes of appeal under section 1291 of this title." 28 U.S.C. § 2072(c). Rulemaking power exercised under this provision may present separation of powers problems. These kinds of problems were discussed in Chapter 5(F)(6), *supra,* and will be discussed further in subsection *(b)*, *infra,* dealing with a similar grant of rulemaking power to expand jurisdiction over interlocutory appeals in 28 U.S.C. § 1292(e).

A "final judgment" is the order of the court[61] that is controlling and dispositive; it is one in which the trial court cannot reserve the ability to make further orders regarding the parties' rights or liabilities.[62]

Illustration 12-9. In the federal system, an order granting a new trial is not appealable because that order is not a "final judgment."[63]

* * * * *

The final judgment rule serves to unify all issues for appeal and to reduce delay.[64] In a multiple-claim or multiple-party action, Federal Rule 54(b) allows the trial court to "direct [the] entry of a final judgment as to one or more, but fewer than all, [of the] claims or parties only if the court expressly determines that there is no just reason for delay."[65]

(b) Interlocutory Appeals

An interlocutory appeal may be possible even when a final judgment has not been entered. In the federal system, § 1292(a)(1) of Title 28 allows, *inter alia*, appeals as a matter of right from orders of the district courts "granting, continuing, modifying, refusing or dissolving injunctions" or orders "refusing to dissolve or modify injunctions."[66]

---

61. Federal Rule 58 requires that "every judgment . . . be set out in a separate document." FED. R. CIV. P. 58(a). *See generally* Elaine A. Carlson & Karlene S. Dunn, *Navigating Procedural Minefields: Nuances in Determining Finality of Judgments, Plenary Power, and Appealability*, 41 S. TEX. L. REV. 953 (2000).

62. For example, in WMX Technologies, Inc. v. Miller, 104 F.3d 1133 (9th Cir. 1997), the district court dismissed three of the plaintiff's claims with prejudice and two claims without prejudice. The court gave the plaintiff leave to amend the latter two claims within thirty days. The plaintiff did not either amend or inform the court that it would not amend, but simply appealed. The appellate court dismissed the appeal because no final dismissal order had been entered. In National Distribution Agency v. Nationwide Mutual Insurance Co., 117 F.3d 432 (9th Cir. 1997), the district court dismissed the plaintiff's complaint with the qualification that "[t]he court may amend or amplify this order with a more specific statement of the grounds for its decision." The court of appeals held that this qualification made the order nonfinal and unappealable. The court of appeals also declined to treat the plaintiff's notice of appeals as an expression that the plaintiff would stand on his complaint rather than amend. *See also* Catlin v. United States, 324 U.S. 229, 233, 65 S. Ct. 631, 633, 89 L. Ed. 911, 916 (1945) (a final judgment is an order that "ends the litigation on the merits and leaves nothing for the court to do but execute the judgment"); Dubicz v. Commonwealth Edison Co., 377 F.3d 787 (7th Cir. 2004) (a district court's labeling of a decision as final is not conclusive on whether the decision is final for purposes of appeal; here, the district court dismissed three counts of the complaint without prejudice and three counts with prejudice; there was no indication that an attempt to amend the complaint would be futile); Kirchner v. Western Mont. Reg'l Cmty. Mental Health Ctr., 261 Mont. 227, 861 P.2d 927 (1993) (any decree that leaves matters undetermined is interlocutory in nature, not an appealable final judgment).

63. *See, e.g.*, Taylor v. Washington Terminal Co., 409 F.2d 145, 147 (D.C. Cir. 1969). If the new trial is granted as an alternative to the granting of a motion for judgment notwithstanding the verdict, then both rulings may be immediately appealed. *See* FED. R. CIV. P. 50(c).

64. *See* Note, *Appealability in the Federal Courts,* 75 HARV. L. REV. 351, 351-52 (1961).

65. FED. R. CIV. P. 54(b). In Ebrahimi v. City of Huntsville Board of Education, 114 F.3d 162 (11th Cir. 1997), the plaintiff sued fifteen defendants, alleging multiple civil rights claims against the defendants. The district court dismissed two of the claims and certified them as final under Rule 54(b). The Eleventh Circuit found the certification improper. The district court's conclusion was based on its determination that the dismissed claims should not have been brought by the plaintiff and thus no useful purpose would be served by postponing final disposition of them. However, the court of appeals viewed this as a commonplace reason for dismissal, and held that certification under these circumstances would produce piecemeal appeals. If the district court believed that appellate review of the dismissed claims prior to the trial of the other claims would avoid the necessity of a second trial if the dismissals were held erroneous, an interlocutory appeal under 28 U.S.C. § 1292 (discussed in the next subsection) would be more appropriate.

66. 28 U.S.C. § 1292(a)(1); *cf.* Petrello v. White, 533 F.3d 110 (2d Cir. 2008) (grant of partial summary judgment on specific performance claim did not direct defendants to perform specific acts or describe in detail what they were required to do; thus, order was not an appealable injunction). In Nutrasweet Co. v. Vit-Mar Enterprises, Inc., 112 F.3d 689 (3d Cir. 1997), the court held that a temporary restraining order entered with notice that was

Section 1292(b) provides another exception to the final judgment rule in the federal system. This section allows a district court to certify for appeal that (1) an order presents "controlling questions of law" on which a "substantial difference of opinion" exists and that (2) immediate review will "materially advance the ultimate termination of the litigation."[67] After such a certification is made, the party seeking review applies to the appropriate court of appeals for leave to appeal. The court of appeals may grant or deny the appeal in its discretion.[68]

Illustration 12-10. *P* sues *D* in U.S. District Court for personal injuries received in an automobile accident. *D* moves to dismiss the action on the ground that personal jurisdiction is improper under the "minimum contacts" test.[69] Assume that the district court denies the motion. However, at *D's* request, the court certifies that the order involves a controlling question of law as to which there is substantial ground for difference of opinion and that an immediate appeal from the order might materially advance the termination of the litigation. Personal jurisdiction issues are appropriate for certification under 28 U.S.C. § 1292(b),[70] as are subject-matter jurisdiction and venue issues.[71] However, in determining whether to accept the appeal, the court of appeals should make sure that the question is a truly difficult one. Otherwise, the final judgment rule of 28 U.S.C. § 1291 may be undermined by frequent interlocutory appeals on jurisdictional questions.

* * * * *

In 1992, Congress added subsection (e) to 28 U.S.C. § 1292, which authorized the Supreme Court to prescribe rules, in accordance with the Rules Enabling Act, to provide for interlocutory orders of the district courts to the courts of appeals that are not otherwise provided for in § 1292.[72] In 1998, the Supreme Court exercised this new power by creating subsection (f) to Rule 23 of the Federal Rules of Civil Procedure, which authorizes the courts of appeals, in their discretion, to permit an appeal from an order of a district court granting or denying class certification under Rule 23.[73] Rule 23(f) raises troubling separation-of-powers questions under the *Wayman* and *Sibbach* cases, discussed in Chapter 5.[74] The rule

---

continued beyond the period prescribed in Federal Rule 65(b) was the equivalent of a preliminary injunction and appealable under § 1292(a)(1). *See generally* Michael E. Solimine, *Revitalizing Interlocutory Appeals in the Federal Courts,* 58 GEO. WASH. L. REV. 1165 (1990).

67. 28 U.S.C. § 1292(b).

68. *See generally* Note, *Interlocutory Appeals in the Federal Courts Under 28 U.S.C. § 1292(b),* 88 HARV. L. REV. 607 (1975).

69. *See* Chapter 3(D) *supra* ("The Development of Modern Restrictions on State Court Jurisdiction: The Minimum Contacts Test").

70. *See, e.g.*, Donatelli v. National Hockey League, 893 F.2d 459 (1st Cir. 1990); Burchett v. Bardahl Oil Co., 470 F.2d 793 (10th Cir. 1972); *see also* Alexander & Alexander Servs., Inc. v. Lloyd's Syndicate 317, 925 F.2d 44 (2d Cir. 1991) (difficult interpretation of state long-arm statute).

71. *See* 16 CHARLES A. WRIGHT ET AL., FEDERAL PRACTICE AND PROCEDURE: JURISDICTION AND RELATED MATTERS § 3931, at 453-54 (2d ed. 1996).

72. *See* Pub. L. No. 102-572, § 101, 106 Stat. 4506, 4506.

73. *See* FED. R. CIV. P. 23(f); *see* Jenkins v. BellSouth Corp., 491 F.3d 1288 (11th Cir. 2007) (district courts lack authority to vacate and reenter orders granting or denying class certification after the specific deadline under Rule 23(f) has expired for seeking permission to appeal the order).

74. *See* Chapter 5(F)(6) *supra* (discussing potential separation-of-powers restrictions on judicial rule-making).

constitutes a clear expansion of (appellate) subject-matter jurisdiction,[75] which *Sibbach* suggested would be invalid.[76] In addition, in the words of *Wayman*, it cannot be said that appellate subject-matter jurisdiction is a matter "whose general superintendence" has traditionally been considered "properly within the judicial province" as a matter of rule making.[77] However, until the Supreme Court speaks, it cannot be determined with any certainty whether Rule 23(f) will be found to deal with what *Wayman* called an "important matter" beyond the legitimate province of judicial rule making, or one that merely concerns the "details" of procedure, which is within the rule making power. Perhaps the validity of Rule 23(f) will be saved by the fact that, in the Advisory Committee's language, "[t]he expansion of appeal opportunities effected by subdivision (f) is modest."[78] This, in the words of the Supreme Court in *Wayman*, may make the expansion of jurisdiction in Rule 23(f) a subject of "less interest" within the judicial rule making authority.[79]

(c) Extraordinary Writs

Another exception to the final judgment rule in the federal system is provided in 28 U.S.C. § 1651(a).[80] This provision allows the court of appeals to issue an extraordinary writ of mandamus, prohibition, or certiorari to review actions taken by the trial court. At one time, it appeared that mandamus might be available in either of two circumstances: (1) when an order may not be easily reparable on appeal; or (2) when mandamus is necessary to achieve supervisory control of the district court.[81] However, there is reason to believe that the supervisory use of mandamus has been limited in later cases to situations in which a district court repeatedly disregards the rules of procedure or other established rules of law.[82] If

---

75. Prior to Rule 23(f), § 1292(b) required that in all interlocutory appeals not covered by some other specific statutory provision the district court had to certify an issue for interlocutory appeal, and Rule 23(f) requires no such certification. In addition, § 1292(b) requires that an interlocutory order must involve a controlling question of law as to which there is substantial ground for difference of opinion and that an immediate appeal from the order have the potential to materially advance the ultimate termination of the litigation. Rule 23(f) contains no such requirement.

76. *See* Sibbach v. Wilson & Co., 312 U.S. 1, 10, 61 S. Ct. 422, 425, 85 L. Ed. 479, 483 (1941); Chapter 5(F)(6) *supra* (discussing the statement in *Sibbach* that "[t]here are other limitations on the authority to prescribe rules which might have been, but were not, mentioned in the [Rules Enabling Act]; for instance, the inability of a court, by rule, to extend or restrict the jurisdiction conferred by a statute").

77. *See* Wayman v. Southard, 23 U.S. (10 Wheat.) 1, 45, 6 L. Ed. 253, 263 (1825); Chapter 5(F)(6) *supra* (discussing potential separation of powers restrictions on judicial rule making, including the *Wayman* standard).

78. *See* advisory committee note to proposed amendment of Rule 23(f), 167 F.R.D. 565 (1996).

79. *See* Chapter 5(F)(6) *supra* (discussing *Wayman* and other potential separation of powers restrictions on judicial rule making authority); *see also* David L. Shapiro, *Federal Diversity Jurisdiction: A Survey and Proposal*, 91 HARV. L. REV. 317, 346-47 (1977) (arguing that properly circumscribed delegations of rule making power over subject-matter jurisdiction are constitutional). *But see* Bolin v. Sears, Roebuck & Co., 231 F.3d 970, 974 (5th Cir. 2000) (holding § 1292(e) to be a "permissible delegation of rulemaking authority with the judiciary's central mission"); Carey M. Erhard, Note, *A Discussion of the Interlocutory Review of Class Certification Orders Under Federal Rule of Civil Procedure 23(f)*, 51 DRAKE L. REV. 151, 179 (2002) (arguing that Rule 23(f) is constitutional and consistent with the Rules Enabling Act because it affects only the timing of appeals).

80. 28 U.S.C. § 1651(a).

81. *See* First Nat'l Bank v. Warren, 796 F.2d 999 (7th Cir. 1986) (Easterbrook, J.) (discussing these two strands of doctrine).

82. *See id.*; *see also* Will v. United States, 389 U.S. 90, 88 S. Ct. 269, 19 L. Ed. 2d 305 (1967).

so, the primary use of mandamus will be to obtain relief from orders that are not easily reparable on appeal.[83]

(d) Collateral Order Rule

The *collateral order* rule is a judicially created exception to the final judgment rule. The collateral order rule makes "final," for purposes of § 1291 (permitting appeals only from "final" judgments) certain orders which do not fully and finally determine the entire controversy between the parties. This rule originated in *Cohen v. Beneficial Industrial Loan Corp.*[84] In *Cohen*, the district court refused to order the plaintiff to post security for costs as required by a New Jersey statute governing stockholder derivative suits. The defendant sought immediate review of this question. In permitting the appeal, the U.S. Supreme Court recognized that there is a "small class" of decisions that "finally determine claims of right separable from, and collateral to, rights asserted in the action."[85] These rights are "too important to be denied review and too independent of the cause itself to require that appellate consideration be deferred until the whole case is adjudicated."[86]

---

83. *See generally* Amy Schmidt Jones, Note, *The Use of Mandamus to Vacate Mass Exposure Tort Class Certification Orders*, 72 N.Y.U. L. REV. 232 (1997); Elizabeth A. Snyder, Comment, *The Use of Extraordinary Writs for Interlocutory Appeals,* 44 TENN. L. REV. 137 (1976).

84. 337 U.S. 541, 69 S. Ct. 1221, 93 L. Ed. 1528 (1949).

85. *Id.* at 546, 69 S. Ct. at 1225-26, 93 L. Ed. at 1537.

86. *Id.*; *see also* Farmer v. Perrill, 275 F.3d 958 (10th Cir. 2001) (stating court of appeals had jurisdiction under the collateral order doctrine to review district court's ruling that the Federal Tort Claims Act did not bar *Bivens* claim by prisoner against corrections officers because the district court's ruling was conclusive, the ruling was separate from the merits of the prisoner's claim, and it was vitally important in that if unreversed, it would require corrections officials to proceed with discovery and trial, and the ruling was effectively unreviewable on appeal in the context of the officers' qualified immunity); Lloyd C. Anderson, *The Collateral Order Doctrine: A New "Serbonian Bog" and Four Proposals for Reform,* 46 DRAKE L. REV. 539 (1998); Comment, *Collateral Orders and Extraordinary Writs as Exceptions to the Finality Rule,* 51 NW. U. L. REV. 746 (1957). Most orders, however, are not considered to be collateral orders for purposes of appeal. *See, e.g.*, Cunningham v. Hamilton Cnty., 527 U.S. 198, 119 S. Ct. 1915, 144 L. Ed. 2d 184 (1999) (sanction imposed under Rule 37(a) against attorney no longer representing any party in case for failure to comply with discovery orders is not a collateral order; although the order was conclusive, appellate review of a sanctions order cannot remain entirely separate from the merits, it can be reviewed after final judgment, an immediate appeal would frustrate the purpose of Rule 37(a) sanctions, and no special considerations in favor of appeal existed just because the attorney was no longer participating in the case); Digital Equip. Corp. v. Desktop Direct, Inc., 511 U.S. 863, 114 S. Ct. 1992, 128 L. Ed. 2d 842 (1994) (holding that a refusal to enforce a settlement agreement claimed to shelter party from suit altogether not a basis for immediate appeal under collateral order doctrine); Stringfellow v. Concerned Neighbors in Action, 480 U.S. 370, 107 S. Ct. 1177, 94 L. Ed. 2d 389 (1987) (refusing to allow appeal in an intervention context); Young v. Prudential Ins. Co., 671 F.3d 1213, 1216 (11th Cir. 2012) (refusing to allow appeal from a partial summary judgment when the district court's order resolved some issues but left others undecided); Metabolic Res., Inc. v. Ferrell, 668 F.3d 1100, 1104 (9th Cir. 2012) (denial of motion to dismiss under anti-SLAPP (Strategic Lawsuit Against Public Participation) statute not immediately appealable under collateral order doctirne); Acoustic Sys., Inc. v. Wenger Corp., 207 F.3d 287 (5th Cir. 2000) (holding the denial of a summary judgment was not an appealable collateral order when it was based on a defense and not an immunity from suit).

In Will v. Hallock, 546 U.S. 345, 126 S. Ct. 952, 163 L. Ed.2d 836 (2006), the Supreme Court held that an order denying application of a judgment bar contained in the Federal Tort Claims Act is not an appealable collateral order. The judgment bar precludes actions against government employees after dismissal of actions under the Federal Tort Claims Act against the government. The Court distinguished the judgment bar from orders denying defenses based on the doctrine of qualified immunity, which do present collateral orders. The judgment bar was held not to involve the same sort of weighty public objectives as the immunity defenses. *See also* Doe v. Exxon Mobil Corp., 473 F.3d 345 (D.C. Cir. 2007) (district court's denial of defendant's motion to dismiss on political question grounds was not an immediately appealable collateral order); Goodman v. Harris Cnty., 443 F.3d 464 (5th Cir. 2006) (order directing that party must undergo a Rule 35 mental examination is not appealable under the collateral order doctrine; while the order resolved an issue separate from the merits, it was not sufficiently important to make denial of review improper); Newby v. Enron Corp., 443 F.3d 416 (5th Cir. 2006) (intervention order

(e) The Rejected "Death Knell" Doctrine

Several federal courts of appeals recognized another exception to the final judgment rule. This exception was known as the *death knell doctrine*, which allowed a party to appeal a non-final order when the order sounded the "death knell" of the action. Thus, this doctrine treated an order as "final" for purposes of 28 U.S.C. § 1291 (final judgment requirement) when the alternatives were either an appeal or an end to the lawsuit for all practical purposes. However, the U.S. Supreme Court rejected the death knell doctrine in *Coopers & Lybrand v. Livesay*.[87]

(f) Pendent Appellate Jurisdiction

In addition, some federal courts of appeals have recognized the doctrine of "pendent appellate jurisdiction" as a basis for reviewing orders that are not otherwise immediately reviewable when they are "closely related" to an order properly before the appellate court.[88] The courts of appeals have indicated that pendent appellate jurisdiction should be exercised "rarely" and only in "exceptional circumstances."[89] However, the Supreme Court has not yet indicated in what circumstance, if any, pendent appellate jurisdiction is appropriate.[90]

---

seeking discovery of protected discovery material is immediately appealable under collateral order doctrine because; order allowing intervention satisfied criteria for collateral order review because intervenor was not seeking to litigate claim, but to obtain access to confidential discovery material, intervention was independent of the underlying litigation and had no bearing on the merits of the litigation, and intervention order conclusively determined the intervention issue); Espinal-Dominguez v. Puerto Rico, 352 F.3d 490 (1st Cir. 2003) (appeal not allowable under collateral order doctrine because precluding immediate appellate review would not result in irreparable injury to Commonwealth on its contention that the 1991 Civil Rights Act failed validly to abrogate the states' Eleventh Amendment Immunity; question whether Commonwealth could be held liable for a certain kind of damages could adequately be reviewed following trial).

87. 437 U.S. 463, 98 S. Ct. 2454, 57 L. Ed. 2d 351 (1978) (involving a district court's determination that an action could not be maintained as a class action). *See generally* Kenneth A. Cohen, *"Not Dead But Only Sleeping": The Rejection of the Death Knell Doctrine and the Survival of Class Actions Denied Certification,* 59 B.U. L. REV. 257 (1979).

88. *See, e.g.*, Rendall-Speranza v. Nassim, 107 F.3d 913 (D.C. Cir. 1997) (a claim of immunity is rejected by the district court by denial of a motion to dismiss; at the same time the district court also denies a motion to dismiss on the basis of the statute of limitations; pendent appellate jurisdiction exists over the limitations issue when immunity ruling is immediately appealable); Freeman v. Complex Computing Co., 119 F.3d. 1044 (2d Cir. 1997) (where issues raised by appeal of an appealable order substantially overlap issues raised by nonappealable order, pendent appellate jurisdiction can be exercised over nonappealable order); National R.R. Passenger Corp. v. ExpressTrak, L.L.C., 330 F.3d 523 (D.C. Cir. 2003) (pendent appellate jurisdiction over an interlocutory order staying an action and ordering arbitration because the order was inextricably intertwined with an appealable order and review of the ruling was necessary to ensure meaningful review of an appealable decision); Meredith v. Oregon, 321 F.3d 807 (9th Cir. 2003) (indicating that when a district court refuses to abstain under doctrine of *Younger v. Harris* and issues a preliminary injunction, appellate court has pendent appellate jurisdiction to review the abstention decision in conjunction with the interlocutory appeal of the injunction); Huskey v. City of San Jose, 204 F.3d 893 (9th Cir. 2000) (holding pendent appellate jurisdiction proper over municipality's appeal of denial of its motion for summary judgment in a case in which an appeal properly was taken by individual defendants over denial of immunity claims). *But see* Jones v. InfoCure Corp., 310 F.3d 529 (7th Cir. 2002) (stating that when a preliminary injunction is denied and a case is transferred to another district, the transfer order is not necessarily reviewable on interlocutory appeal of the injunction under 28 U.S.C. § 1292(a)(1) under the doctrine of pendent appellate jurisdiction, since to allow review of the transfer order would be to open up an "end around" the restrictions on review of orders disposing of single claims and § 1404(a) transfer orders).

89. *See, e.g*, Natale v. Town of Ridgefield, 927 F.2d 101 (2d Cir. 1991) (holding pendent party appellate jurisdiction improper on the facts of the case).

90. *See* Swint v. Chambers Cnty. Comm'n, 514 U.S. 35, 50-51, 115 S. Ct. 1203, 1211, 131 L. Ed. 2d 60, 74 (1995) (refusing to "definitively or preemptively settle here whether or when it may be proper for a court of appeals with jurisdiction over one ruling, to review, conjunctively, related rulings that are not themselves independently appealable"). *See generally* Joan Steinman, *The Scope of Appellate Jurisdiction: Pendent Appellate*

SECTION C. APPELLATE PROCEDURE

A fundamental principle underlying appellate litigation is that at least one of the parties must ordinarily initiate appellate review of a trial court decision. Before the Federal Rules of Civil Procedure were adopted, initiating a federal appeal involved several complicated steps, each of which was considered to be jurisdictional. A failure to take any of the correct steps could result in a dismissal of the appeal. The Federal Rules simplified the appellate process by establishing just one jurisdictional step: the filing of a timely notice of appeal.[91]

To be timely, a party must file a notice of appeal with the district court within thirty days after the entry of the judgment or order from which the party appeals. The United States, its agencies, and its current or former employees sued in their individual capacity (arising out their duties preformed on behalf of the government) are allowed sixty days.[92] The time period for appeal is automatically extended while the court considers post-trial motions (*e.g.*, a motion for a new trial, a motion to alter or amend the judgment, etc.) and disposes of the last such remaining motion.[93] If a notice of appeal is filed while the court is considering such motions, the notice of appeal becomes effective when the order disposing of the last such motion is entered.[94]

A federal district court has limited power to extend the time for filing the notice of appeal. However, the court may do so only when a party has demonstrated good cause or excusable neglect.[95] A motion filed under Federal Rule 60(b) to reopen a judgment does not extend the time for filing a notice of appeal, unless it is filed no later than 28 days after the judgment is entered.[96]

Illustration 12-11. *P* sued *D* in U.S. District Court. After trial on the merits, the jury found in favor of *P* and awarded *P* seven million dollars in damages. The court then entered judgment in favor of *P*. *D* filed a notice of appeal with the district court within forty days after the court entered that judgment. *D's* notice of appeal is untimely because *D* was required to file the notice of appeal within thirty days after the judgment was entered. Assume instead that after judgment was entered, *D* believed that jury verdict was excessive and appeared to have been given under the influence of passion and prejudice. *D* moved for a new trial on this ground pursuant

---

Jurisdiction Before and After Swint, 49 HAST. L.J. 1337 (1998) (arguing that the existence and scope of pendent appellate jurisdiction do not lie exclusively with the legislature and rule makers, and that the prudent use of pendent appellate jurisdiction is more consistent with the purposes of § 1291 than would be rejection of the doctrine); 16 CHARLES A. WRIGHT ET AL., FEDERAL PRACTICE AND PROCEDURE: JURISDICTION AND RELATED MATTERS § 3937 (2d ed. 1996); Riyaz A. Kanji, *The Proper Scope of Pendent Appellate Jurisdiction in the Collateral Order Context,* 100 YALE L.J. 511 (1990).

91. *See* FED. R. APP. P. 3(a).

92. *See* FED. R. APP. P. 4(a)(1).

93. *See* FED. R. CIV. P. 4(a)(4)(A); *cf.* Marine Midland Bank v. Slyman, 995 F.2d 362 (2d Cir. 1993) (stipulation signed by parties was functional equivalent of Rule 59(e) motion to amend judgment and extended time for appeal).

94. *See* FED. R. APP. P. 4(a)(4)(B)(i).

95. *See* FED. R. APP. P. 4(a)(5); *see also* Bowles v. Russell, 551 U.S.205, 127 S. Ct. 2360, 168 L. Ed. 2d 1288 (2007) (time limits on taking an appeal are jurisdictional; "unique circumstances" doctrine, which created equitable exception to time limits, is overruled; this Court has no authority to create equitable exceptions to jurisdictional requirements).

96. FED. R. APP. P. 4(a)(4)(vi). The 28-day period is computed using the method set out in Federal Rule 6(a). *See* FED. R. CIV. P. 6(a) ("Computing Time").

to Rule 59 within 28 days after the entry of the judgment (as required by Federal Rule 59(b)). The time period for appeal is automatically extended while the court considers this post-trial motion. Assume that the court denies *D's* motion sixty days later. *D* then has up to thirty days to file a notice of appeal after the entry of the order disposing of *D's* motion for a new trial.

* * * * *

The basic procedure for review in the federal courts of appeals is stated in the Federal Rules of Appellate Procedure.[97] The federal courts of appeals have adopted additional rules governing practice in their respective courts.[98] In general, the notice of appeal must designate the following: (1) the judgment or some portion of the judgment that is being appealed; (2) the appealing party; and (3) the name of the court to which the appeal is taken.[99] Procedures for initiating appellate review vary in state courts, but they generally follow the same basic steps as appellate review in the federal courts. However, one important variation in a few states requires the parties to first file a *bill of exceptions* with the trial court in which their objections to a trial judge's rulings or jury instructions are stated for the record.[100]

The appellate review process ordinarily requires an appealing party to designate[101] the items to be included in the record on appeal, such as the pleadings, motions, orders, and transcripts.[102] The appellees are entitled to cross-designate other matters that they believe should be included in the record on appeal.[103] Typically, thirty to sixty days after the record has been filed, the appellant must then submit a brief.[104] After the appellee submits a brief, the appellant usually has the opportunity to file a reply brief. Oral arguments are then held in most cases.

SECTION D. SCOPE OF REVIEW

The scope of appellate review is generally limited to matters contained in the trial-court record. Thus, even if a question was presented to the trial court and was decided, that question will ordinarily not be subject to review unless the question is reflected in the record.[105] The scope of review is generally limited to

---

97. Appellate Rules 3 and 4 govern appeals as a matter of right; Rule 5 governs appeals by permission; Rule 7 governs bonds to cover costs; Rules 10 and 11 govern the record on appeal; Rule 12 governs the docketing of the appeal and filing of the record; Rules 28, 31, and 32 govern the preparation, serving, and filing of the briefs; and Rule 30 governs appendices to the briefs and appeals on original records.

98. *See* FED. R. APP. P. 474. Special rules apply for the review of interlocutory (non-final) decisions, such as preliminary injunctions.

99. FED. R. APP. P. 3(c).

100. *See* ROBERT L. STERN, APPELLATE PRACTICE IN THE UNITED STATES § 6.7(d)(4), at 162 (2d ed. 1988).

101. This designation process is important because appellate courts normally confine review to matters reflected in the record. *See* DANIEL JOHN MEADOR & JORDANA SIMONE BERNSTEIN, APPELLATE COURTS IN THE UNITED STATES 55 (1994). Thus, counsel should be sure that the record on appeal enables the court to fully and accurately comprehend the case and issues.

102. In federal courts of appeals, the Federal Rules of Appellate Procedure specify that the original papers and exhibits filed in the district court, a certified copy of the docket entries, and a transcript of the proceedings, if any, constitute the record on appeal. *See* FED. R. APP. P. 10(a).

103. *See* FED. R. APP. P. 10(b)(3)(B) (designation by appellee); *see also* FED. R. APP. P. 10(d) (agreed statement of the case on appeal in lieu of the record on appeal), 10(e) (correction or modification of the record on appeal).

104. *See, e.g.*, FED. R. APP. P. 31(a)(1) (40 days).

105. *See* DANIEL JOHN MEADOR & JORDANA SIMONE BERNSTEIN, APPELLATE COURTS IN THE UNITED STATES 55 (1994).

matters raised and preserved in the trial court.[106] In other words, alleged errors will be reviewed only if they were earlier presented to the trial court for decision. The delay and expense of an appeal cannot be justified when a matter could have been corrected had it been properly raised during trial. However, several exceptions exist.

Illustration 12-12. An appeal may be allowed when the error is so great as to render the lower court's judgment void even though the error was not raised until the appeal.[107]

* * * * *

Appellate review is usually limited to examining questions of law or determining whether substantial evidence supports the trial court's factual findings. If the trial was before a jury, the appeal is framed in terms of whether the jury might have reasonably found as it did in light of the evidence. The standard for appellate review in this context is similar to that used for a directed verdict.[108]

In a nonjury trial in federal court, the trial judge's factual findings will be set aside only if they are "clearly erroneous." Furthermore, "due regard" must be "given to the opportunity of the trial court to judge the credibility of the witnesses."[109] One question about the "clearly erroneous" standard is whether it should be applied to factual findings based entirely on documentary evidence. Most jurisdictions apparently apply the standard in this situation, although some courts take a contrary view.[110] A 1985 amendment of Rule 52(a) resolved this issue for the federal courts by adding the language "whether based on oral or documentary evidence, shall not be set aside unless clearly erroneous."[111]

A trial judge often makes several "discretionary" determinations.[112] In reviewing these rulings, appellate courts give the trial judge wide latitude. The appellate court will not reverse the trial court unless the appellate court finds that the trial court abused its discretion.[113]

---

106. *See* FED. R. CIV. P. 46.

107. Likewise, some courts will consider on appeal errors not presented to the trial court when they affect a party's fundamental rights or the public interest. *See* Allan D. Vestal, *Sua Sponte Consideration in Appellate Review,* 27 FORDHAM L. REV. 477 (1958).

108. *See* Chapter 11(H)(1) *supra* ("Involuntary Dismissals (Judgments on Partial Findings) and Directed Verdicts (Judgments as a Matter of Law").

109. FED. R. CIV. P. 52(a); *see also* United States v. United States Gypsum Co., 333 U.S. 364, 395, 68 S. Ct. 525, 542, 92 L. Ed. 746, 766 (1948) ("A finding is 'clearly erroneous' when although there is evidence to support it, the reviewing court on the entire evidence is left with the definite and firm conviction that a mistake has been committed").

110. *See* Charles Alan Wright, *The Doubtful Omniscience of Appellate Courts,* 41 MINN. L. REV. 751 (1957).

111. FED. R. CIV. P. 52(a); *see also* Steven Alan Childress, *Standards of Review Primer: Federal Civil Appeals,* 229 F.R.D. 267 (2005); Edward H. Cooper, *Civil Rule 50(a): Rationing and Rationalizing the Resources of Appellate Review,* 63 NOTRE DAME L. REV. 645 (1988); *cf.* Michael J. Hays, *Where Equity Meets Expertise, Re-thinking Appellate Review in Complex Litigation,* 41 U. MICH J. L. REFORM 421 (2008) (arguing for a revised scope of appellate review of party structure in complex cases).

112. For example, such rulings include the scope of discovery, severance or consolidation of issues for trial, the order in which the evidence is presented, whether the probative value of certain evidence is outweighed by its prejudicial effects, etc.

113. *See* Maurice Rosenberg, *Judicial Discretion of the Trial Court, Viewed from Above,* 22 SYRACUSE L. REV. 635 (1971).

SECTION E. HARMLESS ERROR

The two basic prerequisites for an appellate court to reverse a judgment are (1) error and (2) injury. Error is prejudicial only if the error affects (1) the outcome of the case and (2) a substantial right.[114] Errors that do not meet these prerequisites are considered to be "harmless."

Illustration 12-13. When the plaintiff has been granted all available relief, any error that the plaintiff complains of is harmless. Likewise, prejudicial error may be cured by later proceedings or by a judgment in favor of the complaining party.

* * * * *

In contrast, an error should not be considered to be harmless merely because the verdict finds support in the evidence. When review of the record leaves the appellate court uncertain as to the correctness of the jury findings or judgment, or uncertain whether the jury would have found as it did but for the error, reversal is appropriate. Furthermore, a demonstration of an infringement of a constitutional or statutory right may be the basis for reversal even when it is difficult to show specific injury resulting from that infringement. The cumulative effect of several minor errors, although harmless when independently considered, may also justify reversal when they are considered together.[115]

SECTION F. EXTRAORDINARY RELIEF FROM A JUDGMENT

Parties sometimes seek "extraordinary" relief from a judgment (1) when the time for ordinary post-verdict motions and appeal has expired and (2) when the effect of the judgment is questioned in a later action. Historically, the common-law courts could modify, reopen, or vacate a judgment during the term of the court in which it was rendered. The common-law writ of *error coram nobis*, which was addressed to the rendering court, was available both during and after expiration of the term. This writ was used to set aside a judgment for clerical errors in fact. It was not available for errors of judgment.[116] Another option available to a party to a common-law proceeding was to bring an independent suit in equity if a party had grounds for relief which could not have been pleaded in the action at law, such as fraud or mistake. Equity court decrees were challenged by a bill or petition to reopen the decree. Furthermore, a plea of invalidity could be asserted against a judgment set up by an adverse party in a subsequent action.[117]

---

114. *See* 28 U.S.C. § 2111 ("On the hearing of any appeal or writ of certiorari in any case, the court shall give judgment after an examination of the record without regard to errors or defects which do not affect the substantial rights of the parties"); *cf.* FED. R. CIV. P. 61 ("Unless justice so requires, no error in admitting or excluding evidence—or any other error by the court or a party—is ground for granting a new trial, for setting aside a verdict, or for vacating, modifying or other disturbing a judgment or order. At every stage of the proceeding, the court must disregard all errors and defects that do not affect any party's substantial rights."); FED. R. EVID. 103(a).

115. *See generally* 14 CYCLOPEDIA OF FEDERAL PROCEDURE §§ 68.50-68:54 (3d rev. ed. 2009).

116. *See* ROBERT W. MILLAR, CIVIL PROCEDURE OF THE TRIAL COURT IN HISTORICAL PERSPECTIVE 390-95 (1952).

117. *See id.* at 386, 396-401; 11 CHARLES A. WRIGHT ET AL., FEDERAL PRACTICE AND PROCEDURE: CIVIL § 2868 (2d ed. 1995).

Except for an independent suit in equity to set aside a judgment or the attempt to avoid the judgment in a subsequent action,[118] Federal Rule 60(b) supersedes all of these earlier devices for extraordinary relief from a judgment. Rule 60(b) authorizes post-judgment motions addressed to the judgment-rendering court on six grounds:

> (1) mistake, inadvertence, surprise, or excusable neglect;
> (2) newly discovered evidence that, with reasonable diligence, could not have been discovered in time to move for a new trial under Rule 59(b);
> (3) fraud (whether previously called intrinsic or extrinsic), misrepresentation, or other misconduct of an adverse party;
> (4) the judgment is void;
> (5) the judgment has been satisfied, released, or discharged; it is based on an earlier judgment that has been reversed or vacated; or applying it prospectively is no longer equitable; or
> (6) any other reason that justifies relief.[119]

Rule 60(c) requires that the motion "be made within a reasonable time—and for reasons (1), (2), (3) no more than a year after the judgment or order, or the date of the proceeding.[120]

In *Aguilar v. Felton,*[121] the Court had held that it was a violation of the Establishment Clause of the First Amendment for the New York School Board to send public school teachers into parochial schools to provide remedial education to disadvantaged children.[122] On remand, the district court issued a permanent injunction against the Board. Twelve years later, the Board moved under Rule 60(b)(5) for relief from the injunction on the grounds that intervening U.S. Supreme Court decisions had undermined the original decision upon which the injunction was based. The district court held that the Board had properly proceeded under Rule 60(b)(5), but the court denied the motion on the ground that the Supreme Court decision (*Aguilar v. Felton*) upon which the original injunction was based had not yet been formally overruled by the Court. The Court of Appeals for the Second Circuit affirmed for the same reasons. The U.S. Supreme Court granted certiorari

---

118. An independent action can be permitted only to prevent a "grave miscarriage of justice." *See* United States v. Beggerly, 524 U.S. 38, 47, 118 S. Ct. 1862, 1868, 141 L. Ed. 2d 32, 40 (1998) (not present in this case involving an independent action brought to vacate a consent decree entered in favor of the government in a previous quiet title action and to recover just compensation for the taking of the plaintiffs' property). Note that an independent basis of subject-matter jurisdiction need not exist when the suit brought in the same court as the original lawsuit. *Id.* at 45-46, 118 S. Ct. at 1867, 141 L. Ed. 2d at 39-40 ("ancillary jurisdiction" exists over the action).

119. FED. R. CIV. P. 60(b); *see* Flood v. Katz, 143 Idaho 454,147 P.3d 86 (2006) (district court erred in setting aside judgment for fraud under state equivalent of Rule 60(b); there is no fraud when the appellant did not investigate with due diligence).

120. FED. R. CIV. P. 60(b); *see also* Ariel Waldman, Comment, *Allocating the Burden of Proof in Rule 60(b)(4) Motions to Vacate a Default Judgment for Lack of Jurisdiction,* 68 U. CHI. L. REV. 521 (2001) (noting that Rule 60(b) is silent on the allocation of the burden of proof, that the courts are divided in their approaches; also noting that in over 90 percent of the reported cases in which courts have ruled on Rule 60(b)(4) motions to void a default judgment for lack of personal jurisdiction, the party bearing the burden of proof has lost; and arguing that courts should adopt a rule placing the burden on the movant, but that courts should condition the remedy to mitigate any resulting inequities).

121. 473 U.S. 402, 105 S. Ct. 3232, 87 L. Ed. 2d 290 (1985).

122. *Id.* at 409-14, 105 S. Ct. at 3236-39, 87 L. Ed. 2d at 297-301.

and reversed.[123] In *Agostini v. Felton,*[124] the Court held that Rule 60(b) was a proper vehicle with which to seek relief from the injunction, even though the Court recognized that the district court and court of appeals had correctly denied relief because *Aguilar* had not yet been overruled. The Court held that its intervening decisions had indeed undermined *Aguilar* and overruled the decision.[125]

The Court's prior decisions had established that Rule 60(b)(5) was a proper vehicle with which to obtain relief from an injunction where decisional law had changed to make legal what the injunction was designed to prevent. However, in *Agostini*, the Court noted that Rule 60(b)(5) was, on the facts of the case, also properly used to actually effect a change in the law rather than to recognize one that had already taken place. The Court emphasized that petitioners were seeking relief from an injunction that sought prospective relief and that intervening developments in the law by themselves rarely constitute the extraordinary circumstances required for relief under Rule 60(b) from judgments lacking any prospective component.[126]

Justice Ginsburg, joined by Justices Stevens, Souter, and Breyer, dissented, arguing, *inter alia,* that the Court erroneously used Rule 60(b) to effectuate a change in law rather than to recognize one that had already taken place. Justice Ginsburg expressed the opinion that the Court should have waited for a more appropriate case in which to overrule *Aguilar—i.e.,* one in which relief was not sought under Rule 60(b).[127]

---

123. *See* Agostini v. Felton, 521 U.S. 203, 117 S. Ct. 1997, 138 L. Ed. 2d 391 (1997).

124. *Id.*

125. *Id.* at 208-09, 117 S. Ct. at 2003, 138 L. Ed. 2d at 405.

126. *Id.* at 238-40, 117 S. Ct. at 2018, 138 L. Ed. 2d at 423-25.

127. *See id.* at 259-60, 117 S. Ct. at 2028, 138 L. Ed. 2d at 437 (Ginsburg, J., dissenting); *see also* Michael R. Tucci, *Putting the Cart Before the Horse:* Agostini v. Felton *Blurs the Line Between Res Judicata and Equitable Relief,* 49 CASE W. RES. L. REV. 407 (1999).

Chapter 13

FINALITY IN LITIGATION

SECTION A. INTRODUCTION

Rules of civil procedure attempt to secure the just, speedy, and inexpensive determination of civil actions.[1] To this end, procedural rules attempt to promote an accurate resolution of the merits of a dispute. Modern procedural rules thus aim to enhance the truth-finding capacity of the legal system. Obviously, this truth-finding objective of procedural rules must be qualified to some extent. For example, rules of evidentiary privilege protect socially beneficial interests that might be harmed by the introduction of entirely trustworthy evidence at trial.[2] Thus, the stronger societal policy of protecting privileged information qualifies the aim of securing the accurate determination of the action. The principle of finality in litigation also qualifies this truth-determining goal.

The principle of finality seeks to bring litigation over a particular matter to an end.[3] No matter how sophisticated a procedural system is or how many opportunities for the correction of error the system provides, it will never be possible to say with absolute certainty that the courts have accurately resolved a dispute. Consequently, both fairness and efficiency dictate that even if the courts sometimes err, litigation should be brought to a close after a reasonable opportunity to reach a correct result.[4] The principle of finality also reflects three other related policy interests: it "[1] relieve[s] parties of the cost and vexation of multiple lawsuits, [2] conserve[s] judicial resources, and [3] by preventing inconsistent decisions, encourage[s] reliance on adjudication."[5] In addition, preclusion rules also have important indirect effects on the settlement of disputes.[6] In the absence of

---

1. *See* FED. R. CIV. P. 1.

2. *See* Chapter 11(I)(4) *supra* ("Privilege").

3. *See, e.g.*, Stark v. Starr, 94 U.S. 477, 485, 24 L. Ed. 276, 278 (1877) ("[A party] is not at liberty to split up his demand[s] and prosecute by piecemeal, or present only a portion of the grounds upon which special relief is sought, and leave the rest to be presented in a second suit, if the first fails. There would be *no end of litigation* if such practice were permissible.") (emphasis added).

4. *See, e.g.*, Gardache v. City of New Orleans Police Dep't, 2007-2496 (La. 3/24/08); 977 So. 2d 891 (claim that a prior adjudication was incorrect because of an erroneous interpretation of law or because of reliance on a legal principle later overruled is immaterial to the principle of claim preclusion); Thompson v. State Dep't of Licensing, 138 Wash. 2d 783, 795, 982 P.2d 601, 608 (1999) (relieving a party from the issue preclusion effect of a judgment on the ground that it was incorrect as a matter of law would eviscerate the doctrine of issue preclusion).

5. Allen v. McCurry, 449 U.S. 90, 94, 101 S. Ct. 411, 415, 66 L. Ed. 2d 308, 313 (1980); *see also* Wilson v. Lucerne Canal & Power Co., 2007 WY 10, 150 P.3d 653 (general purpose of doctrines of claim and issue preclusion is to prevent piecemeal litigation, thereby preserving judicial resources); Edward W. Cleary, *Res Judicata Reexamined*, 57 YALE L.J. 339, 344-49 (1948) (principal justifications for the finality rule are (1) avoiding the danger of double recovery; (2) promoting the desirability of stable judicial determinations; (3) relieving defendants of the expense and vexation of repeated litigation; and (4) economizing judicial resources).

6. *See* Bruce L. Hay, *Some Settlement Effects of Preclusion*, 1993 U. ILL. L. REV. 21.

preclusion rules, the parties would be more likely to extract settlements unrelated to the merits of the dispute through threats of multiple litigation.[7]

The Anglo-American legal system groups the rules embodying the principle of finality under the label *res judicata*.[8] Res judicata literally means "a thing adjudicated."[9] It simply refers to the body of rules that limit a party's opportunity to litigate matters in a second action that were, or could have been, litigated in a prior action.[10] The nature of the procedural system substantially influences when a final judgment in an action will preclude litigation in another proceeding.[11] When a system narrowly confines the ability to plead a claim for relief, to join claims, to amend pleadings, and to correct trial errors by appeal, the rules of res judicata will be narrow in scope.[12] For example, the common-law system had restrictive pleading and joinder rules. Thus, it allowed more matters to be relitigated than modern procedural systems, which have more liberal pleading and joinder rules.[13]

Within the broad category of res judicata, finality rules are grouped under the labels *claim preclusion* and *issue preclusion*. Claim preclusion deals with the effect of a final judgment on the "cause of action" or "claim" involved in an action. Claim preclusion rules prevent a party from litigating in a subsequent action any matter that was a part of the same claim or cause of action adjudicated in a prior action.[14] These rules thus preclude from litigation any part of the claim that *might* have been litigated, even though the matter was *not actually* litigated in the action.[15] In contrast, issue preclusion rules prevent only issues *actually litigated* in an action from being relitigated in a subsequent proceeding.[16]

---

7. Professor Hay has suggested that although the prevailing view of finality rules is to regulate the litigation of disputes by preventing relitigation, the more important effect of such rules is to encourage the parties to settle their dispute for an amount close to the expected judicial valuation of the plaintiff's claim. *See id.* at 21-41.

8. *See* RESTATEMENT (SECOND) OF JUDGMENTS ch. 1, at 2 (1982) ("Introduction").

9. The less common spelling of the name of this doctrine is "res adjudicata." For a discussion of the historical origins of claim and issue preclusion as well as a discussion of the civil law on this subject, see Robert W. Millar, *The Historical Relation of Estoppel by Record to Res Judicata*, 35 ILL. L. REV. 41 (1940); Robert W. Millar, *The Premises of the Judgment as Res Judicata in Continental and Anglo-American Law* (pts. 1 & 2), 39 MICH. L. REV. 1, 238 (1940) (pointing out that res judicata entered English law from Roman law; in contrast, nothing in civil law corresponds to the principle of estoppel in English law, which was derived from Germanic law).

10. *See* RESTATEMENT (SECOND) OF JUDGMENTS ch. 1, at 1 (1982) ("Introduction").

11. *See generally id.* at 5-13.

12. *See id.* at 8-9.

13. *See id.* at 7; Ichtertz v. Orthopaedic Specialists, P.C., 273 Neb. 466, 750 N.W.2d 798 (2007) (claim preclusion bars relitigation of matters that might have been litigated in prior action); Marriage of Kolczak, 2004 MT 241, 322 Mont. 520, 97 P.3d 1091 (res judicata (claim preclusion) prevented husband from litigating whether he was required to provide health insurance to wife after termination of his employer-provided health insurance because husband had opportunity to litigate that matter in prior proceeding).

14. *See* RESTATEMENT (SECOND) OF JUDGMENTS ch. 1, at 6 (1982). Proceedings on appeal or remand from appeal do not constitute a separate action for purposes of the doctrine. *See* Knutsen v. Cegalis, 2009 Vt. 110, 989 A.2d 1010 (2009).

15. *See, e.g.*, Lawrence Cnty. v. Miller, 2010 SD 60, 786 N.W.2d 360 (preclusive effect of res judicata extends to an issue that was actually litigated on which could have been litigated); Hansuld v. Lariat Diesel Corp., 2010 WY 160, 245 P.3d 293 (2010) (res judicata (claim preclusion) applies to whole claims, whether litigated or not, whereas collateral estoppel (issue preclusion) applies to particular issues that have been contested and resolved).

16. *See id.*; *see also* Dickerson v. Dickerson, 247 Ga. App. 812, 545 S.E.2d 378 (2001) (collateral estoppel (issue preclusion) differs from res judicata (claim preclusion) in that the latter only applies when the causes of action in the first and second actions are the same); Somont Oil Co. v. A & G Drilling, Inc., 2008 MT 447, 348 Mont. 12, 199 P.3d 241 (claim preclusion applies to matters that could have been raised); State *ex rel.* McAmis Indus., Inc. v. M. Cutter Co., 161 Or. App. 631, 984 P.2d 909 (1999) (claim preclusion does not require that issues of fact or law actually be litigated; those requirements apply only to issue preclusion); Clay v. Weber, 2007 SD 45,

To avoid confusion, one point concerning terminology should be made about claim and issue preclusion. Some court opinions use the label "res judicata" to refer only to claim preclusion. These opinions label issue preclusion "collateral estoppel."[17] Other opinions use res judicata to include both claim and issue preclusion. These opinions describe specifically which of the two doctrines they are dealing with in a given case by using the labels "claim preclusion" or "issue preclusion."[18] Obviously, this varying use of terminology creates the potential for confusion. Fortunately, however, as courts recognize the confusion that can result when "res judicata" is used only to refer to claim preclusion, discussions of claim and issue preclusion are becoming more precise. Still, until usage becomes uniform, readers of judicial opinions must examine each case carefully to determine whether claim preclusion or issue preclusion is involved. In this chapter, the expression "res judicata" will be used, as it is in the *Restatement (Second) of Judgments*, to include both claim and issue preclusion. The expressions "claim preclusion" and "issue preclusion" will be used to describe the kind of res judicata rules involved.[19]

The rules of claim and issue preclusion do not prevent continued litigation over a matter in the original action in which a court has rendered judgment. For example, when a party appeals a judgment, res judicata rules do not operate because the appeal is simply a continuation at another level of the original litigation. The rules of res judicata come into play only after a judgment has become final and a second action is brought to litigate a matter that has been, or might have been, litigated in the first proceeding. Often, courts express this difference between the applicability of res judicata in original and subsequent proceedings in terms of *direct attack* versus *collateral attack*. It is often said that res judicata does not apply to "direct attacks" on judgments—attacks, such as appeals, designed to correct error in the original proceeding. Rather, res judicata applies only to "collateral attacks" on a judgment—attacks leveled at a judgment in a separate proceeding when the judgment in the original action is brought into issue in the separate (collateral) proceeding.[20]

---

733 N.W.2d 278 (judgment that bars a second action on the same claim extends not only to every matter offered and received to sustain or defeat the claim or demand, but also to all other admissible matters which might have been offered for the same purpose; if, however, the second action is on a different claim, the prior judgment precludes further consideration only of those issues which were actually litigated and determined).

17. *See* Kaspar Wire Works, Inc. v. Leco Eng'g & Mach., Inc., 575 F.2d 530, 535-36 (5th Cir. 1978). For an example of a case in which this confusion occurred at the trial level, see McCoy v. Cooke, 165 Mich. App. 662, 419 N.W.2d 44 (1988).

18. *See* Migra v. Warren City Sch. Dist. Bd. of Educ., 465 U.S. 75, 77 n.1, 104 S. Ct. 892, 894 n.1, 79 L. Ed. 2d 56, 59 n.1 (1984); *see also* Jarosz v. Palmer, 436 Mass. 526, 766 N.E.2d 482 (2002) (term "res judicata" includes both claim preclusion (also known as "merger" and "bar") and issue preclusion).

19. *See* RESTATEMENT (SECOND) OF JUDGMENTS ch. 3, at 131 (1982) ("Introductory Note"); Allan D. Vestal, *Res Judicata/Preclusion: Expansion*, 47 S. CAL. L. REV. 357, 359 (1974).

20. *But cf.* Arizona v. California, 460 U.S. 605, 618, 103 S. Ct. 1382, 1391, 75 L. Ed. 2d 318, 332 (1983) (a case within the original jurisdiction of the Supreme Court in which the Court had retained jurisdiction "to correct certain errors, to determine reserved questions, and if necessary, to make modifications in the decree"). The Court refused to "extrapolate" the discretionary doctrine of "law of the case," *see infra* section G, into its original jurisdiction "where jurisdiction to accommodate changed circumstances is often retained," because to do so "would weaken to an intolerable extent the finality of our decrees in original actions." 460 U.S. at 619, 103 S. Ct. at 1391, 75 L. Ed. 2d at 333 (footnote omitted). Rather, the Court applied the principles of res judicata, even though it recognized that those principles were not "strictly applicable" because they "do not apply if a party moves the rendering court in the same proceeding to correct or modify its judgment," as had been done in the case before the Court. *Id.* The same principles of finality underpinning the doctrine of res judicata were found to be strong in the case before the Court, which involved a prior determination of an issue concerning water rights in the Southwest,

By definition, the rules of res judicata apply only to *final* judgments.[21] The meaning of "final" for purposes of the res judicata rules is not precisely the same as finality for purposes of appellate review.[22] Compared to the requirement of finality for purposes of appellate review, finality for purposes of issue preclusion is treated somewhat less stringently. In a res judicata context, finality means any prior adjudication of an issue in another action that is sufficiently firm to be accorded conclusive effect.[23]

Illustration 13-1. *P* sues *D* for negligence. *D's* answer to the complaint denies negligence and pleads contributory negligence. The jurisdiction in which the action is filed permits "split" trials—a trial of liability followed by a separate trial

---

an adjudication that was calculated to provide assurance to the states and various private interests in the region of the amount of water they could anticipate receiving from the Colorado River system. *Id.* at 620, 103 S. Ct. at 1392, 75 L. Ed. 2d at 334; *see also* Orion Tire Corp. v. Goodyear Tire & Rubber Co., 268 F.3d 1133 (9th Cir. 2001) (in action number one, court entered summary judgment against plaintiff and plaintiff appealed; while appeal was pending, plaintiff commenced a duplicative action against the defendant in a U.S. District Court in another state; defendant defended on ground that judgment in action number one should have a claim preclusive effect, and court dismissed on this ground; defendant then contended in action number one on appeal that the appeal should be barred by the claim-preclusive effect of the judgment in action number two; the court held that defense to be invalid; an adverse judgment from which no appeal is taken is res judicata and bars any future action on the same claim; the direct appeal of a judgment that predates the judgment asserted to have a claim-preclusive effect is not a future action in this sense); State Dep't of Transp. v. Juliano, 801 So. 2d 101 (Fla. 2001) (when successive appeals are taken in the same case, res judicata is not involved because the same suit and not a new and different one is involved); Ohio Pyro, Inc. v. Ohio Dep't of Commerce Div., 2007 Ohio 5024, 115 Ohio St. 3d 375, 875 N.E.2d 550 (when a judgment is procured by fraud or issued without jurisdiction, it is void and subject to collateral attack; but in the absence of those deficiencies, it is not subject to collateral attack even if errors occurred in the resolution of the merits of the case); Mam v. State Dep't of Family Servs., 2004 WY 127, 99 P.3d 982 (doctrines of claim preclusion, issue preclusion, and judicial estoppel do not bar a motion for relief from judgment under Rule 60(b)).

21. *See* G. & C. Merriam Co. v. Saalfield, 241 U.S. 22, 28, 36 S. Ct. 477, 480, 60 L. Ed. 868, 872 (1916) ("familiar law that only a final judgment is res judicata").

22. *See* RESTATEMENT (SECOND) OF JUDGMENTS § 13 cmt. b (1982); Bay State HMO Mgmt., Inc. v. Tingley Sys., Inc., 181 F.3d 174, 178 (1st Cir. 1999) (finality for purposes of appeal does not mean final judgment has been rendered for purposes of claim preclusion; consolidated actions in which some "claims" dismissed and others remained for adjudication); Gonzalez v. Guilbot, 315 S.W.3d 533 (Tex. 2010) (judgment is final for purposes of claim or issue preclusion even while the case is on appeal); Lay v. Pettengill, 38 A.3d 1139 (Vt. 2011) (determination of probable cause issue in motion to dismiss in underlying criminal case against state trooper had issue preclusive effect in subsequent civil action by trooper for malicious prosecution); *see also* Grimmett v. S & W Auto Sales Co., 26 Kan. App. 2d 482, 487, 988 P.2d 755, 759 (1999) (res judicata intended to protect parties from cost and vexation of multiple suits on the same claim, while single appeal rule is designed to avoid piecemeal review of an action; because underlying purposes of the two doctrines are different, finality need not be defined the same way for both); Youren v. Tintic Sch. Dist., 2004 UT App. 33, 86 P.3d 771 (fact that a portion of the final judgment in a prior action is on appeal does not affect the finality of the judgment for purposes of res judicata); *cf.* Harvey Specialty & Supply, Inc. v. Anson Flowline Equip., Inc., 434 F.3d 320 (5th Cir. 2005) (action transferred under 28 U.S.C. § 1406 on the ground that forum selection clause made venue improper in the transferee district; after transfer, plaintiff voluntarily dismissed action and commenced new state action to litigate the validity of the forum selection clause; defendant attempted to reopen federal action to obtain injunction against plaintiff litigating issue in state court under "relitigation exception" to federal Anti-Injunction Act, 28 U.S.C. § 2283; order to transfer was not a final decision that precluded plaintiff from relitigating the validity of forum selection clause; therefore, defendant could not reopen federal action to obtain injunction); *But see* Rantz v. Kaufman, 109 P.3d 132 (Colo. 2005) (pending appeal prevents a prior judgment from being a final judgment for purposes of issue preclusion). *See generally* Seth Nesin, Note, *The Benefits of Applying Issue Preclusion to Interlocutory Judgments in Cases that Settle,* 76 N.Y.U. L. REV. 874 (2001); *see also* Chapter 12(B)(3) *supra* ("The Final Judgment Rule and Its Exceptions").

23. *See* RESTATEMENT (SECOND) OF JUDGMENTS § 13 cmt. a & g (1982); *see also* International Seafoods, Inc. v. Bissonette, 146 P.3d 561 (Alaska 2006) (denial of a petition for review does not constitute a determination of the issue in the case and is not a final judgment for purposes of res judicata); Spiker v. Spiker, 708 N.W.2d 347 (Iowa 2006) (to determine whether an order granting continuing relief, such as a child visitation order, is final for the purposes of having a preclusive effect, courts ask whether the issues in the two actions are materially different because of events that occurred in the period between the two actions, in which case preclusion is to be denied); Jarosz v. Palmer, 436 Mass. 526, 766 N.E.2d 482 (2002) (determination is considered final for purposes of issue preclusion when parties were fully heard, the judge's decision is supported by a reasoned opinion, and the earlier opinion was subject to review or was, in fact, reviewed).

on the issue of damages if liability is found. The jury finds *D* liable. Even if *D* cannot appeal this judgment under the rules of finality governing appeals in the jurisdiction, the verdict as to liability may be held conclusive as to the issues of *P's* and *D's* negligence in any separate action between them in which these issues arise.[24]

* * * * *

For a judgment to operate as res judicata, the judgment must be a valid judgment.[25] Mere error does not render a judgment invalid in the sense meant here. For a judgment to be invalid, the court must have rendered it without personal jurisdiction over the defendant or without subject-matter jurisdiction over the action.[26] Traditionally, absence of jurisdiction renders a judgment "void" and subject to collateral attack in a subsequent proceeding. In contrast, nonjurisdictional errors merely render a judgment "voidable" on direct attack. However, these statements should not be accepted uncritically. As discussed in section E, some judgments rendered without subject-matter or personal jurisdiction are immune from collateral attack. Furthermore, in some jurisdictions, violation of rules other than rules of subject-matter and personal jurisdiction may also render a judgment "void" and subject to collateral attack—for example, rules prohibiting the procurement of a judgment by fraud.[27]

SECTION B. CLAIM PRECLUSION

1. "Merger," "Bar," and the Rule Against Splitting a Claim

Traditionally, courts have expressed rules of claim preclusion in terms of *merger* and *bar*.[28] When a court has rendered a valid and final personal judgment in favor of the plaintiff, the plaintiff's claim or cause of action "merges" in the judgment. Thereafter, the plaintiff may not maintain an action on the original claim

---

24. *See* RESTATEMENT (SECOND) OF JUDGMENTS § 13 illus. 3 (1982); *see also id.* illus. 1 & 2; Fox v. Maulding, 112 F.3d 453 (10th Cir. 1997) (a judgment becomes final for purposes of claim preclusion under Oklahoma law after the time for appeal has expired and no appeal has been taken; judgment becomes final for purposes of issue preclusion as soon as a court has decided an issue of fact or law necessary to its judgment); Baltrusch v. Baltrusch, 2006 MT 51, 331 Mont. 281, 130 P.3d 1267 (court in prior action had not entered final judgment; therefore, final judgment requirement was not met for claim preclusion; however, there was sufficient finality for issue preclusion to apply to issues adjudicated in prior action). *But cf.* Mower v. Boyer, 811 S.W.2d 560 (Tex. 1991) (partial summary judgment not sufficiently firm and not subject to appeal; therefore, it had no issue preclusion effect).

25. *See* RESTATEMENT (SECOND) OF JUDGMENTS § 17 (1982).

26. *See id.* § 1; McGrew v. McGrew, 139 Idaho 551, 82 P.3d 833 (2003) (divorce judgment was void as to division of property and debts, but former wife was not entitled to seek relief from only part of judgment, but either had to accept division of property and debts in judgment or move to set division aside); Reiss v. Reiss, 118 S.W.3d 439 (Tex. 2003) (errors other than lack of jurisdiction merely render a judgment voidable so that it may be corrected through the ordinary appellate process or other proper proceedings, but do not subject the judgment to collateral attack); State *ex rel.* Richey v. Hill, 216 W. Va. 155, 603 S.E.2d 177 (2004) (an erroneous ruling of the court will not prevent the matter from being res judicata).

27. *See* section E *infra* ("Claim and Issue Preclusion on Questions of Subject-Matter and Personal Jurisdiction"); Nebraska Pub. Advocate v. Nebraska Pub. Serv. Comm'n, 279 Neb. 543, 779 N.W.2d 328 (2010) (when a judgment is attacked in a manner other than by a procedure in the original action to have it vacated, reversed, or modified by a proceeding in equity to prevent its enforcement, the attack is a "collateral attack."

28. *See, e.g.*, McCoy v. Cooke, 165 Mich. App. 662, 419 N.W.2d 44 (1988) (discussing merger, bar, and the distinction between claim and issue preclusion).

or cause of action.[29] The plaintiff may only execute the judgment against the defendant's property or bring a second action on the judgment itself.[30] Similarly, if the plaintiff brings an action on the judgment, the defendant cannot use any defenses that the defendant raised or could have raised in the initial action.[31] On the other hand, if the judgment in the first action is for the defendant, the operative concept is "bar" rather than merger. The rule is, simply, that "[a] valid and final personal judgment rendered in favor of the defendant bars another action by the plaintiff on the same claim."[32]

The rules of merger and bar are actually different components of a single rule: a party may not split a "claim" or "cause of action."[33] This rule obviously makes the "scope" of a claim or cause of action quite important. As noted in section A, above, the rigidity of the common-law system, particularly its limitations on joinder of causes of action,[34] produced a relatively narrow operation of the principle of finality. This narrow operation continued to be reflected in the traditional definitions of "cause of action" that evolved in the nineteenth century.[35] These definitions often conceptualized the scope of a cause of action in terms of the right being asserted by the plaintiff. Thus, it was common to speak of the plaintiff's "right of action" or "the right which is being enforced." Sometimes, the scope of a cause of action combined "the primary right" of the plaintiff with the "primary duty" of the defendant and the breach of that duty which infringed the plaintiff's

---

29. *See, e.g.*, C. Sys., Inc. v. McGee, 145 Idaho 559, 181 P.3d 485 (2008) (claim preclusion applies to successive actions based on same facts between same parties even though grounds asserted in second suit were different); Plunkett v. State, 869 A.2d 1185 (R.I. 2005) (plaintiff could have asserted a discrimination claim in the prior declaratory judgment action; two claims were transactionally related and no exceptions to claim preclusion existed; therefore, second action was precluded).

30. If the plaintiff is forced to bring a second action to enforce the judgment, as, for example, when the plaintiff must sue to enforce the judgment in another state, the judgment in the first action is not considered to be merged in any judgment the plaintiff obtains in the second proceeding. The plaintiff will be able to enforce either judgment by execution or otherwise. However, satisfaction of one judgment operates as satisfaction of the other. *See* RESTATEMENT (SECOND) OF JUDGMENTS § 18 cmt. j. (1982). When there are multiple parties that a plaintiff can potentially sue, the plaintiff will sometimes proceed successively against them. If the plaintiff loses the action against the first party, issue preclusion may prevent the second action if all of its prerequisites are satisfied and the doctrine of "mutuality," discussed in section C(3) *infra*, has been abolished. However, if the plaintiff wins the first action and recovers fully for the injury inflicted, and if the judgment is satisfied, the plaintiff cannot proceed against the second defendant in order to obtain a double recovery. *See* Brown v. Singleton, 337 S.C. 74, 522 S.E.2d 816 (1999).

31. *See* RESTATEMENT (SECOND) OF JUDGMENTS § 18 (1982); *see also* Harsh Int'l, Inc. v. Monfort Indus., Inc., 266 Neb. 82, 662 N.W.2d 574 (2003) (after settling lawsuit brought by employee for injuries incurred in the course of his employment, manufacturer of mixer that injured employee brought an action for indemnity against employer; held: manufacturer was precluded by res judicata from litigating that the employer's actions were the sole proximate cause of the employee's injuries, because that issue could have been litigated in the prior action; manufacturer attempted to join employer in prior action, but trial court in that action dismissed the third-party petition and manufacturer thereafter settled without appealing).

32. RESTATEMENT (SECOND) OF JUDGMENTS § 19 (1982).

33. *See* Kootenai Elec. Coop., Inc. v. Lamar Corp., 148 Idaho 116, 219 P.3d 440 (2009) (claim for indemnity precluded by claim preclusion where plaintiff had asserted claim as crossclaim against defendant in prior action and did not include the indemnity claim, which arose from the same facts); Coomer v. CSX Transp., Inc., 319 S.W.3d 366 (Ky. 2010) (rule against splitting claims is nothing more than that aspect of res judicata which requires the court to determine the scope of the prior claim); *cf.* City of New York v. Welsbach Elec. Corp., 9 N.Y.3d 124, 878 N.E.2d 966, 848 N.Y.S.2d 551 (2007) (res judicata (claim preclusion) only applies when a claim between the parties has been brought to a final conclusion; doctrine did not apply when parties were co-defendants in prior action, but did not assert claims against each other).

34. *See* Chapter 7(A) *supra* ("Joinder of Claims by the Plaintiff at Common Law and in Equity").

35. *See* RESTATEMENT (SECOND) OF JUDGMENTS § 24 cmt. a (1982).

right.[36] Another popular definition focused on whether "the evidence needed to sustain the second action would have sustained the first action."[37]

The modern tendency is to define "claim" or "cause of action" by reference to a factual grouping. A factual grouping includes all events comprising a single transaction or a series of connected transactions.[38] Sections 24 and 25 of the *Restatement (Second) of Judgments* describe the modern rules.[39] Section 24 states that when merger or bar extinguishes a plaintiff's claim, "the claim extinguished includes all rights of the plaintiff to remedies against the defendant with respect to all or any part of the transaction, or series of connected transactions, out of which the action arose."[40] Section 24 indicates that a pragmatic approach should be taken in determining "[w]hat factual grouping constitutes a 'transaction,' and what

---

36. *See id.* at 197; CHARLES E. CLARK, HANDBOOK OF THE LAW OF CODE PLEADING § 19, at 130-36 (2d ed. 1947).

37. RESTATEMENT (FIRST) OF JUDGMENTS § 61 (1942). The substantive problems with these definitions of the scope of a cause of action are described by the drafters of the *Restatement (Second) of Judgments*:

> "Claim," in the context of res judicata, has never been broader than the transaction to which it related. But in the days when civil procedure still bore the imprint of the forms of action and the division between law and equity, the courts were prone to associate claim with a single theory of recovery, so that, with respect to one transaction, a plaintiff might have as many claims as there were theories of the substantive law upon which he could seek relief against the defendant. Thus, defeated in an action based on one theory, the plaintiff might be able to maintain another action based on a different theory, even though both actions were grounded upon the defendant's identical act or connected acts forming a single life-situation. In those earlier days there was also some adherence to a view that associated claim with the assertion of a single primary right as accorded by the substantive law, so that, if it appeared that the defendant had invaded a number of primary rights conceived to be held by the plaintiff, the plaintiff had the same number of claims, even though they all sprang from a unitary occurrence. There was difficulty in knowing which rights were primary and what was their extent, but a primary right and the corresponding claim might turn out to be narrow. Thus it was held by some courts that a judgment for or against the plaintiff in an action for personal injuries did not preclude an action by him for property damage occasioned by the same negligent conduct on the part of the defendant—this deriving from the idea that the right to be free of bodily injury was distinct from the property right. Still another view of claim looked to sameness of evidence; a second action was precluded where the evidence to support it was the same as that needed to support the first. Sometimes this was made the sole test of identity of claim; sometimes it figured as a positive but not as a negative test; that is, in certain situations a second action might be precluded although the evidence material to it varied from that in the first action. Even so, claim was not coterminous with the transaction itself.

RESTATEMENT (SECOND) OF JUDGMENTS § 24 cmt. a (1982); *cf.* City of New York v. Welsbach Elec. Corp., 9 N.Y.3d 124, 878 N.E.2d 966, 848 N.Y.S.2d 551 (2007) (res judicata (claim preclusion) only applies when a claim between the parties has been brought to a final conclusion; doctrine did not apply when parties were co-defendants in prior action, but did not assert claims against each other).

38. *See* RESTATEMENT (SECOND) OF JUDGMENTS § 24 cmt. a (1982). As noted in section A *supra*, this modern trend is based upon the "ample procedural means" provided by modern systems for fully and fairly litigating all matters arising from a common factual basis in a single proceeding.

39. *Id.* § 24 ("Dimensions of 'Claim' for Purposes of Merger or Bar—General Rule Concerning 'Splitting'"), § 25 ("Exemplifications of General Rule Concerning Splitting"). *See generally* John F. Wagner, Jr., Annotation, *Proper Test to Determine Identity of Claims for Purposes of Claim Preclusion by Res Judicata Under Federal Law*, 82 A.L.R. FED. 829 (1987). A recurrent question involves the question whether a property damage claim and a personal injury claim resulting from a single tortious act give rise to one or two claims. Most, but not all, jurisdictions today hold that only one claim arises from such an event. However, some jurisdictions that recognize only one claim have a "subrogation exception." An insurer will sometimes require its insured to assign a claim for damage to the insured's automobile to the insurer before it will pay a collision insurance claim to its insured. When a property damage claim has been so assigned and litigated or settled, the insured can still maintain a claim for personal injuries under this exception. *See* Andrea G. Nadel, Annotation, *Simultaneous Injury to Person and Property as Giving Rise to Single Cause of Action—Modern Cases*, 24 A.L.R.4TH 646 (1983) (describing the prevailing views).

40. *See* RESTATEMENT (SECOND) OF JUDGMENTS § 24(1) (1982); *see also* Andrus v. Nicholson, 145 Idaho 774, 186 P.3d 630 (2008) (following rule of § 24); Bossian v. Anderson, 991 A.2d 1025 (R.I. 2010) (following transactional rule); Dakota Plains AG Ctr., LLC v. Smithey, 772 N.W.2d 170 (S.D. 2009) (a cause of action for purposes of res judicata is comprised of the facts that gave rise to or established the right the party seeks to enforce).

groupings constitute a 'series' for this purpose." Weight is to be given "to such considerations as whether the facts are related in time, space, origin, or motivation, whether they form a convenient trial unit, and whether their treatment as a unit conforms to the parties' expectations or business understanding or usage."[41] Section 25 states that this rule extinguishing the plaintiff's claim applies even if "the plaintiff is prepared in the second action (1) [t]o present evidence or grounds or theories of the case not presented in the first action, or (2) [t]o seek remedies or forms of relief not demanded in the first action."[42]

---

41. RESTATEMENT (SECOND) OF JUDGMENTS § 24(2) (1982); Pittston Co. v. United States, 199 F.3d 694 (4th Cir. 1999) (constitutional claims in second action would not have combined with calculation claim in prior action to form a convenient trial unit; therefore, same "cause of action" not involved in two actions); *see also* White v. State Dep't of Natural Res., 14 P.3d 956 (Alaska 2000) (under *Restatement (Second)* test, claim in the action was the same as claim in prior administrative proceeding and was barred); Weiss v. Weiss, 297 Conn. 446, 998 A.2d 766 (2010) (wife precluded by claim preclusion from litigating matter concerning marriage dissolution agreement that could have been litigated in prior divorce proceeding); Bowling v. Kentucky Dep't of Corrections, 301 S.W.3d 478 (Ky. 2010) (claim preclusion precluded inmate from challenging state's death penalty protocol on ground omitted from prior declaratory judgment action in which it could have been raised). Claim preclusion also operates to preclude the litigation of defenses in subsequent actions that should have been asserted to claims in a prior action. *See, e.g.*, Weaver v. Texas Capital Bank, 660 F.3d 900 (5th Cir. 2011) (defendant in first action attempted to litigate what should have been a defense in that action in a second action for a declaratory judgment; the court of appeals held that this was a defense that should have been litigated in the first action because it arose from the same transaction or occurrence as the claim in that first action).

42. *See* RESTATEMENT (SECOND) OF JUDGMENTS § 25 (1982). *See, e.g.*, Chiepalich v. Coale, 36 So. 3d 1 (Ala. 2009) (res judicata applies not only to exact legal theories presented in the prior legal action, but to all legal theories rising from the same nucleus of operative fact); Smith v. CSK Auto, Inc., 132 P.3d 818 (Alaska 2006) (preclusive effect of former judgment cannot be avoided by alleging the same facts under a new legal theory); Jayel Corp. v. Cochran, 366 Ark. 175, 234 S.W.3d 278 (2007) (when an action is based on the same events as a previous action, res judicata will apply even if the subsequent suit raises new legal issues and seeks additional remedies); AMEC Civil LLC v. Mitsubishi Int'l Corp., 940 A.2d 131 (D.C. 2007) (under Virginia law, a claim for legal fees based on a contract is part of the underlying contract provisions and ordinarily must be pursued in the first action or the claim will be extinguished by the judgment); Powder Basin Psychiatric Assocs., Inc. v. Ullrich, 129 Idaho 658, 931 P.2d 652 (1997) (first suit by employer against former employee for taking and wrongfully withholding office furniture settled and dismissed with prejudice; second action by employer against employee for wrongfully withholding $10,000 for services rendered while he was employed, but which belonged to employer, barred by claim preclusion); Woods v. Young, 732 N.W.2d 39 (Iowa 2007) (res judicata precludes a party from bringing a second action simply by alleging a new theory of recovery for the same wrong); Arnevik v. University of Minn. Bd. of Regents, 642 N.W.2d 315 (Iowa 2002) (employee of public university failed in respondeat superior-based indemnification action against public university after employee was involved in vehicle accident for which other driver recovered damages from employee; employee could not bring second contract-based indemnity action against same defendant because contract-based theory could have been pursued in first action); Portland Water Dist. v. Town of Standish, 2008 ME 23, 940 A.2d 1097 (if a claim is based on the same transaction, arises out of the same nucleus of operative facts, and seeks redress for essentially the same basic wrong as another claim, the claim is precluded even if the second action relies on a different legal theory); Kesterson v. State Farm Fire & Cas. Co., 242 S.W.3d 712 (Mo. 2008) (improper splitting of a claim occurs when a party sues on a claim which arises out of the same act, contract, or transaction as a previously litigated claim); North Country Envtl. Servs., Inc. v. Town of Bethlehem, 150 N.H. 606, 843 A.2d 949 (2004) (the term "cause of action" means the right to recover and refers to all theories on which relief could be claimed arising out of the same factual transaction); Lucas v. Porter, 2008 ND 160, 755 N.W.2d 88 (minority shareholder's prior action for involuntary dissolution of corporation under statute providing a broad range of remedies precluded subsequent claim that arose from the same set of facts centering on freezing minority shareholder out, even though the second action named individual majority shareholder and two closely held corporations and asserted different theories of recovery—breach of contract, breach of fiduciary duty, fraud, tortious inferences with contractual rights); Carlson v. Clark, 2009 VT 17, 970 A.2d 1269 (2009) (claim preclusion bars parties from litigating in second action not only matters previously litigated but also matters that could have been litigated); Faulkner v. Caledonia County Fair Ass'n, 2004 VT 123, 869 A.2d 103 (plaintiff won first action for damages against ride operator for head injuries; second action seeking damages for epilepsy allegedly caused by accident was precluded by claim preclusion because claim arose out of same transaction as claim in first action; application of claim preclusion was not so unfair as to violate constitutional right to a remedy at law). *But cf.* State *ex rel.* Coles v. Granville, 2007-Ohio-6057, 116 Ohio St.3d 231, 877 N.E.2d 968 (although in general res judicata bars all claims that were or might have been litigated in prior action, declaratory judgment, unlike other judgments, determines only what it actually decides and does not preclude other claims that might have been advanced).

Illustration 13-2. *P* sues *D* for breach of an oral contract for the sale of land. *D* asserts that the statute of frauds makes the contract unenforceable, and *D* wins. *P* then sues *D* for restitution to recover the money paid for the land. Under the modern rule, *P* may not sue for the restitutionary remedy in the second suit (assuming that *P* could have requested it in the first suit).[43] In contrast, under the traditional narrow view of a cause of action, courts would have permitted two separate suits because these two actions involved different "rights" and "wrongs."[44]

Illustration 13-3. *P* and *D* were involved in an automobile accident due to *D's* negligence. Immediately after the accident *D* jumped from the car, punched *P* in the nose, and falsely stated to a bystander that *P* was an alcoholic. *P* sues *D* for personal injuries received in the automobile accident and recovers a judgment. *P* then sues *D* for the assault and battery occurring immediately after the accident. *P* also sues *D* in a third action for slander. Under the modern rule, *P* may not maintain the second or third actions. The events on which *P's* injuries were based all arose out of the same transaction or series of connected transactions and are considered part of the same claim.[45] In contrast, a system that focused on a traditional definition of the scope of a "cause of action," such as the "primary right" of the plaintiff, may have permitted three separate actions under these circumstances.[46]

Illustration 13-4. *O* leases land to *L* for a two-year period. A dispute arises between *O* and *L* over the amount of land leased. As a result, *L* occupies a larger portion of the land than *L* leased. *O* contends that the fair rental value of this extra

---

43. *See* RESTATEMENT (SECOND) OF JUDGMENTS § 25 illus. 15 (1982); *see also* Silcox v. United Trucking Servs., Inc., 687 F.2d 848 (6th Cir. 1982); Plum Creek Dev. Co. v. City of Conway, 334 S.C. 30, 512 S.E.2d 106 (1999) (plaintiff sued for mandamus in first action and was precluded from suing for damages in second action where both actions based on same breach of contract); *cf.* Howard J. Alperin, Annotation, *Decree Allowing or Denying Specific Performance of Contract as Precluding, as a Matter of Res Judicata, Subsequent Action for Money Damages for Breach*, 38 A.L.R.3D 323 (1971).

44. *See* RESTATEMENT (FIRST) OF JUDGMENTS § 65 illus. 7 (1942); Smith v. Kirkpatrick, 305 N.Y. 66, 111 N.E.2d 209 (1953) (second action on a quantum meruit theory after the plaintiff had lost a prior action for the same sum on the ground that the oral contract was unenforceable because it did not comply with the statute of frauds). The *Smith* court stated:

> The two actions involve different "rights" and "wrongs." The requisite elements of proof and hence the evidence necessary to sustain recovery vary materially. The causes of action are different and distinct .... [T]he rights and interests established by the previous adjudication will not be impaired by a recovery, if that be the outcome, in quantum meruit.

Id. at 72, 111 N.E.2d at 211. The *Smith* case has now been overruled. *See* O'Brien v. City of Syracuse, 54 N.Y.2d 353, 429 N.E.2d 1158, 445 N.Y.S.2d 687 (1981). *See generally* Howard J. Alperin, Annotation, *Judgment in Action on Express Contract for Labor or Services as Precluding, as a Matter of Res Judicata, Subsequent Action on Implied Contract (Quantum Meruit) or Vice Versa*, 35 A.L.R.3D 874 (1971). For a discussion and critique of a New York statute providing that a judgment denying recovery in an action on a written agreement will not preclude a subsequent action for reformation of the agreement, *see* Bernard E. Gegan, *Claim Preclusion and Reformation of Contracts: New York CPLR 3002(d)*, 70 ST. JOHN'S L. REV. 539 (1996); *see also* Walter W. Heiser, *California's Unpredictable Res Judicata (Claim Preclusion) Doctrine*, 35 SAN DIEGO L. REV. 559 (1998) (discussing and critiquing the California "primary rights" doctrine).

45. *See* RESTATEMENT (SECOND) OF JUDGMENTS § 24 illus. 6 (1982); Hudson v. City of Chicago, 228 Ill. 2d 462, 889 N.E.2d 210 (2008) (plaintiff split claim when he voluntarily dismissed theory of willful and wanton misconduct in action, proceeded to adjudication on the merits of negligence theory, which was involuntarily dismissed, and then commenced second action on theory of willful and wanton misconduct).

46. *Cf.* RESTATEMENT (FIRST) OF JUDGMENTS § 62 cmt. f (1942) ("Where there are a number of successive acts which are substantially simultaneous ... [or which] are all substantially *of the same sort*, public convenience and fairness to the defendant may require that they be dealt with in one proceeding. Thus, where in a series of rapidly successive acts a person breaks into the house of another, beats him and takes his chattels, a judgment based upon a claim for any one of these harms is a bar to a subsequent action.") (emphasis added). Note that this comment uses a series of intentional torts rather than a series of causes of action based on different legal theories—*e.g.*, negligence, battery, and slander occurring in succession.

land is $1,000 per year. *L* refuses to pay the $1,000 due for either year. *O* sues *L* for the $1,000 owed for the first year, and *O* recovers. *O* then sues *L* for the $1,000 owed for the second year. Under the modern approach, the second action would not be permitted. The lease was a single transaction. Normally, a plaintiff would be expected to sue for the total amount due under that lease at one time. Alternatively, if the claim is not predicated on the lease, but on a restitutionary theory, the same would be true: the plaintiff would be expected to sue at the same time for all amounts due.[47]

Illustration 13-5. *P* pays state income taxes in Year 1 and Year 2. In Year 3, *P* sues the state for a refund of the Year 1 taxes and recovers. *P* then sues the state on the same factual and legal grounds for a refund of the Year 2 taxes. Under the modern transactional rule, these separate actions can be maintained. Each tax year represents a separate claim because of the parties' expectations and how tax years have been traditionally regarded.[48]

2. Judgments "On the Merits"

Traditionally, claim preclusion operated only when the court had rendered a final judgment *on the merits* of an action. Consequently, when the court dismissed a case for some reason not based upon the merits, the doctrine of bar generally did not preclude the plaintiff from bringing a second suit on the same claim or cause of action.[49] One important situation in which this rule operated was when the plaintiff's complaint was dismissed for legal insufficiency—for failure to state facts sufficient to constitute a cause of action (in code language) or failure to state a claim on which relief could be granted (Federal Rules). When such a dismissal occurred, the plaintiff could commence a new action in which the plaintiff cured the insufficiency in the complaint. Even though the plaintiff failed to take advantage of an opportunity to amend in the first action, the judgment in the first action would not be deemed "on the merits." Thus, the plaintiff could bring the second suit.[50]

---

47. *See* RESTATEMENT (SECOND) OF JUDGMENTS § 24(2) cmt. d, illus. 9 & reporter's note at 228 (1982); *cf.* Sutcliffe Storage & Warehouse Co. v. United States, 162 F.2d 849 (1st Cir. 1947).

48. *See* RESTATEMENT (SECOND) OF JUDGMENTS § 24(2) & illus. 9 (1982); Colvin v. Story Cnty. Bd. of Review, 653 N.W.2d 345 (Iowa 2002) (claim preclusion did not bar taxpayers' challenge to property tax assessment for 2002, even though they had already unsuccessfully challenged the 1999 assessment; taxes for separate years do not grow out of the same transaction).

49. *See* RESTATEMENT (FIRST) OF JUDGMENTS § 49 (1942); 4501 Northpoint LP v. Maricopa Cnty., 212 Ariz. 98, 128 P.3d 215 (2006) (judgment can be "on the merits" for purposes of claim preclusion even if it results from the parties' stipulation or certain pretrial rulings of the court rather than from a trial or hearing); Winkler v. Bethell, 362 Ark. 614, 210 S.W.3d 117 (2005) (res judicata bars subsequent litigation after summary judgment granted in favor of defendants in prior action; first suit resulted in final judgment on the merits and involved the same claims and parties); Dykes v. Sukup Mfg. Co., 781 N.W.2d 578 (Minn. 2010) (settlement agreement producing a dismissal with prejudice produces a final judgment on the merits); Travelers Ins. Co. v. Joachim, 315 S.W.3d 860 (Tex. 2010) (filing of nonsuit did not deprive trial court of jurisdiction to dismiss case with prejudice and although dismissal with prejudice was erroneous and voidable, dismissal was subject only to direct attack and not void; thus judgment was claim preclusive).

50. *See* RESTATEMENT (FIRST) OF JUDGMENTS § 50 cmt. c & e (1942); Touris v. Flathead Cnty., 2011 MT 165, 361 Mont. 172, 258 P.3d 1 (voluntary dismissal with prejudice in first action was final judgment on the merits for purposes of claim preclusion even though the first action was resolved without addressing the substance of the plaintiff's claims); Parker v. Martin, 905 A.2d 756 (D.C. 2006) (voluntary dismissal with prejudice produced judgment on the merits that precluded plaintiff from bringing second action against defendant even though first complaint incorrectly identified the property in issue an the second complaint correctly identified the property).

Illustration 13-6. *P* sued *D* for slander in a state court. *D* filed a demurrer on the ground that *P* did not allege special damages. The court ruled that the complaint failed to allege facts sufficient to constitute a cause of action for slander because an allegation of special damages was lacking, but the court granted *P* leave to amend. *P* did not amend, and a judgment was entered against *P*. *P* did not appeal. Instead, *P* filed a second action in the same court curing the pleading defect that caused the dismissal in the first action. Under the traditional rule reflected in the first *Restatement of Judgments*, the judgment in the first action would not be "on the merits," and the second suit would be permitted.[51]

* * * * *

Assume, however, that after a dismissal of the complaint for insufficiency, the plaintiff tried to bring a new action with a substantially unchanged complaint. The doctrine of *direct estoppel* would bar this new action.[52] Furthermore, when the plaintiff's complaint revealed on its face a defense to the action, the plaintiff was not permitted to bring a second suit, even if the plaintiff's second complaint did not disclose the defense. Similarly, when "an entire failure to state a cause of action" had occurred in the first action, a second action was precluded.[53]

Illustration 13-7. *P* sued *D* for violating *P's* right of privacy. Assume that the court sustained *D's* demurrer on the ground that the applicable law afforded no right of action for violation of *P's* privacy. Under the traditional rule, *P* could not commence a second action on the same claim against *D*, even if the highest court of the state recognized such a right of action between the first and second suit.[54]

* * * * *

The traditional "on the merits" rule is vulnerable to criticism today. Given the adequacy of modern procedures for (1) stating a claim or cause of action and (2) correcting pleading and other errors by amendment, no justification exists for restricting the scope of claim preclusion to judgments technically "on the merits." Although the plaintiff should always be afforded a reasonable opportunity to present the merits of the case, the rules of claim preclusion should apply when such an opportunity has been provided. Section 19 of the *Restatement (Second) of Judgments* now makes the general rule of bar applicable to a judgment for the defendant on demurrer or motion to dismiss granted due to the insufficiency of the plaintiff's complaint.[55] This rule of bar does not apply when the plaintiff's action

---

51. RESTATEMENT (FIRST) OF JUDGMENTS § 50 cmt. c (1942); Dellefratte v. Estate of Dellefratte, 941 A.2d 797 (R.I. 2007) (dismissal of plaintiff's complaint does not bar plaintiff from filing a new action based on a proper complaint at a later time).

52. *See* RESTATEMENT (FIRST) OF JUDGMENTS § 50 cmt. d (1942). Direct estoppel thus precludes a party from relitigating issues once litigated and determined against that party in cases in which a second action was based on the *same* claim or cause of action as the party's first action. In contrast, "collateral estoppel," which is discussed in section C *infra*, precluded a party from relitigating issues once litigated and determined against the party when the second action involved a *different* claim or cause of action than the first action (in which the issue was originally adjudicated). *See* Bachman v. Bachman, 997 S.W.2d 23 (Mo. Ct. App. 1999) (example of direct estoppel).

53. *See* RESTATEMENT (FIRST) OF JUDGMENTS § 50 cmt. c (1942).

54. *See id.*; Commonwealth v. Stephens, 451 Mass. 370, 885 N.E.2d 785 (2008) (direct estoppel involves a common issue that arises in a subsequent action on the same claim between the parties).

55. *See* RESTATEMENT (SECOND) OF JUDGMENTS § 19 cmt. d (1982); Farmer v. South Dakota Dep't of Rev., 2010 S.D. 35, 781 N.W.2d 655 (dismissal for failure to prosecute was on the merits and thus claim preclusive).

is dismissed "for lack of jurisdiction, for improper venue, or for nonjoinder or misjoinder of parties."[56]

Illustration 13-8. *P* sues *D* for personal injuries. The action is dismissed for improper venue. *P* may bring a second action in a court in which venue is proper.[57] On the other hand, assume that *P* commences a second action in the same court. *P* asserts the same claim and alleges that the judge erred in dismissing the first action for improper venue. The rules of issue preclusion (here direct estoppel) will preclude *P* from relitigating the venue issue.

Illustration 13-9. On the facts of *Illustration 13-6*, under the *Restatement (Second)*, *P* would be precluded from bringing the second action.[58] If the action had been brought in a federal court and the dismissal ordered pursuant to Federal Rule 12(b)(6) on the ground the complaint failed to state a claim upon which relief could be granted, Rule 41(b) appears to prescribe the same result—assuming the court did not specify otherwise in its order of dismissal. Rule 41(b) treats dismissals pursuant to Rule 41(b) and any other dismissal not otherwise provided for in Rule 41 as adjudications on the merits. Rule 41 makes an exception for dismissals based on lack of jurisdiction, improper venue, or failure to join a party under Rule 19.[59] However, the U.S. Supreme Court indicated in *Costello v. United States*,[60] that the word "jurisdiction" in Rule 41(b) includes a failure to satisfy a precondition of suit. The dismissal in *Costello* was not a Rule 12(b)(6) dismissal based on a failure to state a claim. Nevertheless, some federal courts have held that Rule 12(b)(6)

---

56. *See* RESTATEMENT (SECOND) OF JUDGMENTS § 20(1)(a) (1982); Brereton v. Bountiful City Corp., 434 F.3d 1213 (10th Cir. 2006) (dismissal for lack of standing should have been without prejudice); Dickens v. Associated Anesthesiologists, P.C., 709 N.W.2d 122 (Iowa 2006) (dismissal for lack of jurisdiction does not have claim preclusive effect, even if it is specified as with prejudice); Eicher v. Mid Am. Fin. Inv. Corp., 270 Neb. 370, 702 N.W.2d 792 (2005) (judgment of dismissal by a federal court for lack of standing is not a judgment on the merits); *cf.* Intera Corp. v. Henderson, 428 F.3d 605 (6th Cir. 2005) (specification of dismissal for lack of personal jurisdiction as with prejudice was clear error under Rule 41(b) and could be raised by a motion to alter or amend a judgment under Rule 59(e); denial of motion to alter or amend under these circumstances was reversible error); Farmer v. Levenson, 79 Fed. App'x 918 (7th Cir. 2003) (specification that a dismissal for improper venue was with prejudice was in error, even though made because of plaintiffs' continued failure to respond to motions to dismiss; although this action was not a collateral attack on the judgment, the result would be the same if it had been; RESTATEMENT (SECOND) OF JUDGMENTS § 20 cmt. d (1982) states (a) that a judgment may not have an effect contrary to that prescribed by a statute or rule and (b) even if no statute or rule exists, a dismissal on improper venue grounds is so clearly based on a threshold determination that a specification that the dismissal will be a bar should "ordinarily be of no effect").

57. *See* RESTATEMENT (SECOND) OF JUDGMENTS § 20 cmt. b, illus. 1 (1982). This result would follow under the *Restatement (Second)* even if the court erroneously specified the dismissal on venue grounds to be "with prejudice." Rule 41(b) explicitly states that venue dismissals are not on the merits, but even if a rule like Rule 41(b) did not exist, dismissal on venue grounds is so clearly a threshold determination that a "with prejudice" specification should be disregarded as an abuse of discretion. *See id.* § 20, cmt. d. Note that to do otherwise would be to force the plaintiff to appeal a possibly correct determination on the venue question merely in order to reverse the "with prejudice" designation, thus increasing appellate litigation unnecessarily. Such a consequence would run counter to the stated policies of the finality doctrine to hold down the level of litigation. *See also* Kulinski v. Medtronic Bio-Medicus, Inc., 112 F.3d 368 (8th Cir. 1997) (plaintiff files two federal actions, one on a federal claim and the second a diversity action on a state claim, arising from the same facts; the federal-claim action was dismissed for lack of subject-matter jurisdiction "with prejudice"; plea of res judicata in second action denied, the court holding that while the judgment could preclude relitigation of the subject-matter jurisdiction issue, it could not preclude the state claim because it was not "on the merits" despite the "with prejudice" specification).

58. *See* RESTATEMENT (SECOND) OF JUDGMENTS § 19 cmt. d, illus. 1 (1982).

59. FED. R. CIV. P. 41(b).

60. 365 U.S. 265, 81 S. Ct. 534, 5 L. Ed. 2d 551 (1961) (dismissal arising from a failure to file a good cause affidavit within the meaning of the "lack of jurisdiction" exception in Rule 41).

dismissals fit within the *Costello* rationale.[61] Given the ease of stating a claim for relief, the liberality of amendment under the Federal Rules, and the ability to reverse erroneous dismissals or refusals to allow amendments, however, the better result is that a Rule 12(b)(6) dismissal should be considered on the merits.[62]

However, this view may have to be qualified somewhat in the federal courts because of the Supreme Court's recent decision in the *Semtek* case, which was discussed in Chapters 5(E)(3) and 10(E), above, and will be discussed again in section F(2), below. In *Semtek*, the Court held that a dismissal in a diversity action on state statute of limitations grounds, although "on the merits" under Rule 41(b), would preclude a subsequent action only in the same court in which the dismissal occurred. By limiting the claim preclusive effect of the judgment to the dismissing court, the Court assured that a Rule 41(b) "on the merits" dismissal on limitations grounds would not preclude an action in another state. If the *Semtek* view of the effect of "on the merits" dismissals applies to Rule 12(b)(6) dismissals made "on the merits" by Rule 41(b), the preclusive effect of the judgment would also be limited to the dismissing court. This would be unfortunate, but it is only one of many problems created by the *Semtek* opinion.[63]

* * * * *

This rule of bar also does not apply when the judgment for the defendant "rests on the prematurity of the action or on the plaintiff's failure to satisfy a precondition to suit." Unless a second action is precluded by "operation of the substantive law," the judgment "does not bar another action by the plaintiff instituted after the claim has matured, or the precondition has been satisfied."[64]

---

61. *See, e.g.*, Nasser v. Isthmian Lines, 331 F.2d 124, 127 (2d Cir. 1964) (dictum) ("[T]he preclusive effect afforded dismissals by Rule 41(b) was intended to apply only to those situations in which a defendant must incur the inconvenience of preparing to meet the merits of the plaintiff's claims because there is no initial bar to the court's reaching the merits as there would be, for illustrative purposes, *if there were a defect in pleadings* or parties.") (emphasis added); Rambur v. Diehl Lumber Co., 144 Mont. 84, 93, 394 P.2d 745, 750 (1964) ("Rule 41(b) has no application to a motion to dismiss for failure to state a claim under Rule 12(b).").

62. *See, e.g.*, Glick v. Ballentine Produce, Inc., 397 F.2d 590, 592-93 (8th Cir. 1968) (The "distinction between a dismissal on the pleadings and a dismissal on the merits is irrelevant . . . because of Rule 41(b)." . . . [A] dismissal for failure to state a cause of action is a final judgment on the merits sufficient to raise the defense of res judicata in a subsequent action between the parties."); *see also* Hall v. Tower Land & Inv. Co., 512 F.2d 481 (5th Cir. 1975); *cf.* Schroeder v. Morton Grove Police Pension Bd., 219 Ill. App. 3d 697, 579 N.E.2d 997 (1991) (prior federal dismissal for failure to exhaust state remedies was not a judgment on the merits); Rinehart v. Locke, 454 F.2d 313, 315 (7th Cir. 1971); Velasquez v. Franz, 123 N.J. 498, 589 A.2d 143 (1991) (Rule 12(b)(6) dismissal on ground of lack of defendant's capacity to be sued is a judgment on the merits under Rule 41(b)); *cf.* Graziano v. Rhode Island State Lottery Comm'n, 810 A.2d 215 (R.I. 2002) (summary judgment in federal courts is a determination on the merits and is a final preclusive judgment); *cf.* Wolford v. Lasater, 1999-NMCA-024, 126 N.M. 614, 973 P.2d 866 (differing federal and state standards for summary judgment would not prevent the operation of claim preclusion).

63. With *Semtek*, compare Lambert v. Javed, 273 Va. 307, 641 S.E.2d 109 (2007) (dismissal with prejudice on statute-of-limitations ground produces claim preclusion); *see also* Hanneman v. Nygaard, 2010 N.D. 113, 784 N.W.2d 117 (2010) (when plaintiff failed to show up at hearing seeking domestic violence protection order against her boyfriend, court dismissed action for failure to prosecute; when plaintiff commenced second action based partly on allegations in first proceeding and partly on allegations in second proceeding, boyfriend invoked state equivalent of Rule 41(b) and argued claim preclusion; court refused to dismiss second proceeding, stating that claim and issue preclusion should be applied as "fairness and justice" require; court appeared to be influenced by fact that new allegations of abuse indicated a continuing abusive conduct).

64. RESTATEMENT (SECOND) OF JUDGMENTS § 20(2) (1982). The drafters did not consider the exceptions in § 20 to be rigid. They stated: "The rule of this [s]ubsection is not an inflexible one. In some instances, the doctrine of estoppel or laches could require the conclusion that it would be plainly unfair to subject the defendant to a second action." *Id.* cmt. n; *see also* State *ex rel.* Coles v. Granville, 2007-Ohio-6057, 116 Ohio St. 3d 231, 877 N.E.2d 968 (dismissal on grounds that one of the parties is not the real party in interest is not a judgment on the merits for purposes of res judicata); *cf.* Calomiris v. Calomiris, 3 A.3d 1186 (D.C. 2010) (action for attorneys' fees

Illustration 13-10. In consideration for the payment of $100 by *P*, *D* agrees to deliver certain goods to *P*. On January 1st, *P* sues *D*. *P* alleges that *D* failed to deliver the goods. At the trial, it appears the goods were to be delivered on June 1st. As a result, the court directs a verdict for *D* and enters a judgment on the verdict. If *D* fails to deliver the goods by June 1st, *P* may maintain a second action for breach of contract against *D*. The judgment in the first action was clearly based on the prematurity of the suit.[65]

* * * * *

Likewise, this rule of bar does not apply "when the plaintiff agrees to or elects a nonsuit (or voluntary dismissal) without prejudice or the court directs that the plaintiff be nonsuited (or that the action be otherwise dismissed) without prejudice."[66] Nor does it apply "[w]hen by statute or rule of court the judgment does not operate as a bar to another action on the same claim, or does not so operate unless the court specifies, and no such specification is made."[67] For example, Federal Rule 41(a) provides that a voluntary dismissal by the plaintiff or by stipulation of all the parties is without prejudice (unless it is otherwise stated in the notice of dismissal or the stipulation). Rule 41(a), however, makes a dismissal based on a notice of voluntary dismissal by the plaintiff "an adjudication upon the merits when [such a notice] is filed by a plaintiff who has once dismissed in any court of the United States or of any state an action based on or including the same claim."[68]

Illustration 13-11. *P* sues *D* in federal court. *P* subsequently files a notice of voluntary dismissal pursuant to Federal Rule 41(a). *P* may commence a new action in federal or state court. If the court then grants *P* another voluntary dismissal under a rule identical to Rule 41(a)(1), *P* would be thereafter precluded from commencing a new action on the same claim.[69]

3. General Exceptions

Section 26 of the *Restatement (Second)* recognizes six general exceptions to the rule against splitting a claim.[70] First, the rule against splitting does not apply

---

not precluded because claim would have been premature in prior action).

65. *See id.* RESTATEMENT (SECOND) OF JUDGMENTS § 20(2) illus. 5 (1982).

66. *Id.* § 20(1)(b).

67. *Id.* § 20(1)(c).

68. FED. R. CIV. P. 41(a)(1); Boeken v. Philip Morris USA, Inc., 48 Cal. 4th 788. 230 P.3d 342, 108 Cal. Rptr. 3d 806 (2010) (wife brought loss of consortium claim for her husband's lung cancer against cigarette manufacturer and dismissed it voluntarily with prejudice; subsequent action against manufacturer for wrongful death of husband was held precluded; the court stated that damages for anticipated premature death of spouse may be recovered in a loss of consortium action); *see also* FED. R. CIV. P. 41(b) (involuntary dismissals). *See generally* Chapter 10(D) *supra* ("Voluntary Dismissals") & 10(E) *supra* ("Involuntary Dismissals").

69. This "on the merits" rule in Rule 41(a) cases might also have to be qualified by the *Semtek* case discussed in *Illustration 13-9*, above. This would indeed be curious, however, since Rule 41(a) is specifically keyed to multiple dismissals, even in different courts, and seems to envision that a second dismissal will result in preclusion everywhere. Although extension of the *Semtek* rationale to Rule 41(a) "on the merits" dismissals would be unfortunate, it is not entirely clear how the Court would be able to avoid the consequences of its interpretation of Rule 41(b) in this situation.

70. RESTATEMENT (SECOND) OF JUDGMENTS § 26 (1982) ("Exceptions to the General Rule Concerning Splitting"). The exceptions recognized in § 26 deal with situations in which there has been "partial merger or bar"—with the plaintiff losing some of the freedom the plaintiff originally had to present the case. In contrast, the exceptions discussed at the end of the preceding subsection based on § 20 of the *Restatement (Second)* involve situations in which the general rule of bar does not apply at all. Furthermore, § 20 does not deal with situations in

when "[t]he parties have agreed in terms or in effect that the plaintiff may split [the plaintiff's] claim, or the defendant has acquiesced therein."[71]

Illustration 13-12. *P* and *D* are involved in an automobile accident. *P* files two actions in the same jurisdiction against *D*. One action is for personal injuries resulting from the accident. The other action is for property damage resulting from the accident. *D* could have objected in the second action on the ground that another action was pending concerning the same subject matter. However, *D* did not do so. Had *D* objected, *D* would have been entitled to have the second action consolidated with the first. After a judgment in *P's* favor in the personal injury action, *D* requests dismissal of the second action for property damage. *D* asserts that the judgment in the personal injury action is res judicata. The court should refuse to dismiss the second action because *D* has, in effect, consented to the splitting of the claim.[72] Res judicata is a defense that must be raised, or it is lost.[73]

* * * * *

Second, the general rule against splitting a claim does not apply when "[t]he court in the first action has expressly reserved the plaintiff's right to maintain the second action."[74]

Illustration 13-13. On the facts of *Illustration 13-2*, assume that the judgment in the defeated action for breach of contract had expressly reserved to the plaintiff the opportunity to commence a second action for restitution. A court would give effect to such a reservation under this exception.[75]

* * * * *

Third, the general rule against splitting a claim does not apply when "[t]he plaintiff was unable to rely on a certain theory of the case or to seek a certain remedy or form of relief in the first action" arising from either (1) "the limitations

---

which "policy reasons favoring the maintenance of the second action come to light only after the first action is completed." The latter situations are dealt with in § 26. *Id.* § 20 cmt. a.

71. *Id.* § 26(1)(a); *cf.* Collins v. D.R. Horton, Inc., 505 F.3d 874 (9th Cir. 2007) (judgment has potentially offensive nonmutual issue preclusion effect in subsequent arbitration proceeding, but arbitrators have broad discretion to determine whether preclusion is appropriate); Bennun v. Rutgers State Univ., 941 F.2d 154 (3d Cir. 1991) (prior action to compel arbitration did not preclude second action for employment discrimination when prior action was brought to enforce contractual right to arbitration); LaSalla v. Doctor's Assocs., Inc., 278 Conn. 578, 898 A.2d 803 (2006) (in the absence of a specific contractual provision governing claim preclusion, arbitrators are not required to apply claim preclusion based on prior arbitration proceedings, but are free to apply or reject claim preclusion to the extent they deem it appropriate because parties have bargained for their judgment).

72. *See* RESTATEMENT (SECOND) OF JUDGMENTS § 26(1)(a) cmt. a, illus. 1. (1982).

73. *See* FED. R. CIV. P. 8(c); *Ex parte* Beck, 988 So. 2d 950 (Ala. 2007) (res judicata waived if the defendant failed to raise it as an affirmative defense); McDonald v. Trihub, 173 P.3d 416 (Alaska 2007) (when party fails to assert the defense of collateral estoppel against an opposing party, the defense may be considered waived); Willis v. Crumbly, 368 Ark. 5, 242 S.W.3d 600 (2006) (res judicata is a defense and not a matter of subject-matter jurisdiction to be raised on a court's own motion); AMEC Civil LLC v. Mitsubishi Int'l Corp., 940 A.2d 131 (D.C. 2007) (under Virginia law, a party may waive the affirmative defense of res judicata by expressly or impliedly consenting to separate suits on a single cause of action); Rattigan v. Wile, 445 Mass. 850, 841 N.E.2d 680 (2006) (res judicata is an affirmative defense that must be raised in pleading to a preceding pleading; pretrial memorandum is not a pleading); Anderson v. LaVere, 895 So. 2d 828 (Miss. 2004) (burden of proving res judicata as a defense is on the defendant); Oklahoma Dep't of Pub. Safety v. McCrady, 2007 OK 39, 176 P.2d 1194 (issue preclusion is an affirmative defense that must be pleaded and proved). *But cf. In re* Marriage of Ginsberg, 750 N.W.2d 520 (Iowa 2008) (court need not decide whether claim preclusion can be raised sua sponte by court because court finds doctrine inapplicable).

74. RESTATEMENT (SECOND) OF JUDGMENTS § 26(1)(b) (1982); *see* In re General Rights of Gila River Sys., 212 Ariz. 64, 127 P.3d 882 (2006) (federal law of res judicata recognizes the right of parties or the court to limit the preclusive effect of a judgment); Norton v. Town of Long Island, 2005 ME 109, 883 A.2d 889 (claim preclusion does not apply when court in first action reserves the right of the party to maintain a second action).

75. *See* RESTATEMENT (SECOND) OF JUDGMENTS § 26(1)(b) cmt. b (1982).

on the subject matter jurisdiction of the courts or restrictions on their authority to entertain multiple theories" or (2) "demands for multiple remedies or forms of relief in a single action."[76] Under such circumstances, the plaintiff can rely on that theory or seek the unavailable remedy or form of relief in the second action.

Illustration 13-14. *P* suffers personal injuries resulting from *D's* negligence. Under the applicable substantive law, if *P* was *D's* employee at the time of the accident, *P's* sole remedy is under worker's compensation law. If *P* was not an employee, then *P* has only a common-law action for negligence. Assume that *P* files an action before the state worker's compensation commission, but loses because *P* is found not to have been *D's* employee. *P* is not precluded from maintaining a second action for common-law negligence because the workers' compensation and negligence remedies are mutually exclusive and each must be pursued in different forums.[77]

---

76. *Id.* § 26(1)(b); *see Ex parte* Sears, Roebuck & Co., 895 So. 2d 265 (Ala. 2004) (in prior federal court action, court refused to allow plaintiff to amend complaint to assert negligent installation claim; when it is unclear whether denial of leave to assert additional claims in first action rests on considerations of merits or on decision that those claims should be pursued in separate action, second action is not precluded by claim preclusion); Thornton v. Alpine Home Ctr., 2001 MT 310, 307 Mont. 529, 38 P.3d 855 (seller sued purchaser in small claims court and won; purchaser then sued seller in court of general jurisdiction; the court held that the purchaser's action was not precluded by res judicata because purchaser's claims could not have been asserted in small claims court); Parker v. Blauvelt Volunteer Fire Co., 93 N.Y.2d 343, 712 N.E.2d 647, 690 N.Y.S.2d 478 (1999) (claim preclusion is inapplicable when the plaintiff was unable to seek a certain remedy or form of relief in first action); Stewart Title Guar. Co. v. Tilden, 2008 WY 46, 181 P.3d 94 (claim preclusion did not prevent action for attorneys' fees that arbitrator did not have authority to award in first, arbitrated proceeding); *cf.* Ichtertz v. Orthopaedic Specialists, P.C., 273 Neb. 466, 730 N.W.2d 798 (2007) (res judicata does not apply when there has been an intervening change in facts or circumstances; allegations were that corporation failed to pay judgment against it, making individual liable for judgment; none of these "issues" were addressed in prior action, which, if proved, would constitute a change in circumstances). Importantly, when a party does not assert a state claim in a federal court arising from the same facts as a federal claim being considered in the action, the state claim will not be precluded if the federal court, in its discretion, "would clearly" have refused to exercise supplemental jurisdiction over the state claim. *See, e.g.*, Norton v. Town of Long Island, 2005 ME 109, 883 A.2d 889. *But cf.* Maher v. GSI Lumonics, Inc., 433 F.3d 123 (1st Cir. 2005) (action based on federal question jurisdiction with supplemental jurisdiction over state claim; federal claim dismissed on summary judgment and district court attempts to "transfer" state claim to state court; state court refuses transfer and dismisses without prejudice; plaintiff commences second action on state claim, and defendant removes to federal court on the basis of diversity and asserts claim preclusion; held; because diversity jurisdiction existed in federal action and was not asserted, federal judgment had claim preclusion effect!). Declaratory judgments are normally only preclusive on what they decide, not on matters left out that could have been decided. *See* State *ex rel.* Mora v. Wilkinson, 2005-Ohio-1509, 105 Ohio St. 3d 272, 824 N.E.2d 1000 (unlike other judgments, a declaratory judgment determines only what it actually decides and does not preclude other claims that might have been advanced); State *ex rel.* Shemo v. City of Mayfield Heights, 2002-Ohio-1627, 95 Ohio St. 3d 59, 765 N.E.2d 345 (a declaratory judgment is not res judicata on an issue or claim not determined by the judgment, even though it was known and existing at the time of the original action); Cupola Golf Course, Inc. v. Dooley, 2006 VT 25, 179 Vt. 427, 898 A.2d 134 (declaratory action determines only what it actually decides and does not have a claim preclusive effect on other contentions that might have been advanced); *cf.* Lincoln Loan Co. v. City of Portland, 340 Or. 613, 136 P.3d 1 (2006) (prior judgment barred plaintiff from bringing present declaratory judgment action on basis of claim preclusion). *But see* Chesterfield Village, Inc. v. City of Chesterfield, 64 S.W.3d 315 (Mo. 2002) (decision in landowner's first suit against city for declaratory and injunctive relief in zoning challenge had claim-preclusive effect in second action seeking damages; both suits were based on same facts and damages could have been sought in first action).

77. *See* RESTATEMENT (SECOND) OF JUDGMENTS § 26(1)(c) (1982); *see also id.* § 25 cmt. k, illus. 22; Matanuska Elec. Ass'n v. Chugach Elec. Ass'n, 152 P.3d 460 (Alaska 2007) (res judicata does not apply to extinguish a claim when the plaintiff is unable to annex all of its claims for relief or seek all desired remedies before the first tribunal); *In re* Dunkin Donuts S.P. Approval, 2008 Vt 139, 969 A.2d 683 (2008) (claim preclusion does not apply to administrative proceedings as an inflexible rule of law). *But cf.* Murray v. Alaska Airlines, Inc., 50 Cal.4th 860, 237 P.3d 565 (2010) (issue preclusion is applicable to final decisions of administrative agencies acting in a judicial capacity); Washington Metro. Area Transit Auth. v. D.C. Dep't of Employment Servs., 981 A.2d 1216 (D.C. 2009) (res judicata applicable to an administrative proceeding when agency is acting in a judicial capacity); George v. D.W. Zinser Co., 762 N.W.2d 865 (Iowa 2009) (agency determination is entitled to a preclusive effect when agency was acting in a judicial capacity and parties had a full and fair opportunity to litigate, but here no preclusion existed because agency proceeding was an investigation in which no such opportunity to litigate

Illustration 13-15. In contrast, assume that *P* sues *D* for negligently causing *P* personal injuries. Instead of suing in a court of general jurisdiction within the state, *P* brings suit in a court that has no jurisdiction to give judgments in excess of $500. At trial, the court assesses *P's* damages at $2,000 and enters judgment for *P* for $500. *P* cannot sue *D* in a second action in a court of general jurisdiction to recover the remainder of the $1,500. The exception does not apply to situations in which a court with broader jurisdiction is available. *P* has to choose the court with broader jurisdiction or *P* will lose the right to sue for the full amount.[78]

* * * * *

Fourth, the general rule against splitting a claim does not apply when "[t]he judgment in the first action was plainly inconsistent with the fair and equitable implementation of a statutory or constitutional scheme, or it is the sense of the scheme that the plaintiff should be permitted to split [the] claim."[79]

Illustration 13-16. A group of pupils and parents sue the Board of Education to enjoin a state tuition "voucher system." The plaintiffs allege that the law unconstitutionally promotes an establishment of religion. The court holds the law to be constitutional. The plaintiffs do not appeal because existing constitutional precedents do not justify an appeal. Subsequently, the U.S. Supreme Court holds a similar voucher system unconstitutional in another case. The same pupils and parents then commence a second action against the same defendants, asserting the same claim they asserted in the first action. According to the *Restatement (Second)*, this second suit can be maintained because "[i]n a matter of such public importance the policy of nationwide adherence to the authoritative constitutional interpretation overcomes the policies supporting the law of res judicata."[80]

* * * * *

---

existed); *In re* Fleet, 293 Kan. 768, 272 P.3d 583 (2012) (administrative agency was acting in judicial capacity when it made determination; therefore, the determination had claim and issue preclusive effects); Igal v. Brightstar Info. Tech. Group, Inc., 250 S.W.3d 78 (Tex. 2007) (final adjudication of worker's compensation tribunal dismissing employee's wage claim precluded subsequent action for breach of contract and declaratory judgment in Texas district court; in courts of law, claimant cannot ordinarily pursue a remedy to an unfavorable conclusion and then pursue the same remedy in a different proceeding; same rule applies when first proceeding is in worker's compensation tribunal, which acts in a judicial capacity when adjudicating employee's wage claim; to further the public policy of discouraging prolonged and piecemeal litigation, the orders of certain administrative agencies preclude the same claims from being relitigated in the court system); State *ex rel.* McGraw v. Johnson & Johnson, 226 W. Va. 677, 704 S.E.2d 677 (2010) (for issue or claim preclusion to apply based on "quasi judicial" administrative proceeding, the agency's adjudicatory authority and procedures must be substantially similar to those used in a court).

78. *See* Hindmarsh v. Mock, 138 Idaho 92, 57 P.3d 803 (2002) (motorist who brought action in small claims court for property damage arising out of automobile accident was precluded by doctrine of claim preclusion from asserting claim for personal injuries arising out of same accident in court of general jurisdiction); Molovinsky v. Monterey Coop., Inc., 689 A.2d 531 (D.C. App. 1997); Bagley v. Hughes A. Bagley, Inc., 465 N.W.2d 551 (Iowa Ct. App. 1990). *Compare* RESTATEMENT (SECOND) OF JUDGMENTS § 26(1)(c), cmt. c (1982) *with id.* § 24 cmt. g, illus. 13.

79. RESTATEMENT (SECOND) OF JUDGMENTS § 26(1)(d) (1982); *see* Carson v. Davidson, 248 Kan. 543, 808 P.2d 1377 (1991) (statute provided that no suit could be brought against an officer, director, or stockholder until a judgment had been obtained against the corporation; therefore, suit against corporation did not preclude action against stockholders).

80. *See* RESTATEMENT (SECOND) OF JUDGMENTS § 26(1)(d), cmt. e, illus. 6 (1982); G.C. Wallace, Inc. v. Eighth Judicial Dist. Court *ex rel.* County of Clark, 262 P.3d 1135 (Nev. 2011) (landlord who prevailed against tenant in summary eviction proceeding was not precluded by claim preclusion from suing tenant in second action for unpaid rent as damages; it was the sense of the statutory summary eviction scheme that landlord should be able to proceed under that scheme for eviction and seek damages in a later proceeding); *cf.* Berkson v. Lepome, 245 P.3d 560 (Nev. 2010) (statute that allowed plaintiff whose judgment was reversed on appeal to commence new action within one year precluded application of doctrine of res judicata but violated separation of powers doctrine).

Fifth, the general rule against splitting a claim does not apply when "for reasons of substantive policy in a case involving a continuing or recurrent wrong, the plaintiff is given an option to sue once for the total harm, both past and prospective, or to sue from time to time for the damages incurred to the date of suit, and chooses the latter course."[81]

Illustration 13-17. *P* and *D* enter into an employment contract. *D* commits a material breach. *D* requests that *P* allow the contract to continue. *P* agrees, but demands damages for the breach. *P* sues *D* for the breach and obtains a judgment. Subsequently, *P* sues *D* for a subsequent breach of the contract committed after the first action was commenced. This second action may be maintained. As a matter of substantive policy, a judgment in a breach action does not normally preclude *P* from maintaining a second action for later breaches occurring after commencement of the first action.[82] An argument can be made against this result in some cases—for example, when, although the first action has been commenced, it has not progressed so far that adding the claim for the second breach by supplemental pleading would be disruptive. The rule is different if the initial breach is accompanied by a repudiation, which gives rise to a claim for total breach.[83]

* * * * *

Sixth, the general rule against splitting a claim does not apply when "[i]t is clearly and convincingly shown that the policies favoring preclusion of a second action are overcome for an extraordinary reason."[84] Examples of such reasons include "the apparent invalidity of a continuing restraint or condition having a vital relation to personal liberty or the failure of the prior litigation to yield a coherent disposition of the controversy."[85]

Illustration 13-18. *P's* husband, *D*, deserts *P*. *P* sues *D* for separate maintenance and obtains a judgment. Subsequently, *P* sues *D* for a divorce on the same ground (desertion). *P* can maintain this second action. As a matter of policy, *P* should not be forced to demand the most drastic remedy against *D* in the first action. Nor would it be appropriate to deprive *P* of a divorce if *P* is now prepared to make the case for it.[86]

4. Counterclaims

(a) Application of Claim Preclusion Rules to Counterclaims

The rules of merger and bar generally apply to counterclaims interposed by the defendant in the plaintiff's action. If the defendant interposes a counterclaim in

---

81. RESTATEMENT (SECOND) OF JUDGMENTS § 26(1)(e) (1982); *cf.* Holt v. Regional Trustee Servs. Corp., 266 P.3d 602 (Nev. 2011) (denial of Foreclosure Mediation Program certificate did not preclude mortgagee from restarting the nonjudicial foreclosure process with a new notice of default).

82. RESTATEMENT (SECOND) OF JUDGMENTS § 26(1)(e) illus. 7 (1982).

83. *See* RESTATEMENT (SECOND) OF CONTRACTS § 236, cmt. b, § 250 (1979); *see* RESTATEMENT (SECOND) OF JUDGMENTS § 26(1)(e) cmt. g, illus. 7 (1982).

84. RESTATEMENT (SECOND) OF JUDGMENTS § 26(1)(f) (1982).

85. *Id.*; *cf.* Blethen v. West Virginia Dep't of Rev., 219 W. Va. 402, 633 S.E.2d 531 (2006) (res judicata does not prevent reexamination of the same question between the same parties when facts arise subsequent to the judgment that alter the rights of the litigants).

86. RESTATEMENT (SECOND) OF JUDGMENTS § 26(1)(f) cmt. i, illus. 8 (1982).

an action and the court renders a valid and final personal judgment against the defendant "on the counterclaim, the rules of bar are applicable to the judgment," subject to the exceptions in § 20 and § 26 of the *Restatement (Second)*, discussed above.[87] Likewise, if a defendant interposes a counterclaim and the court renders a judgment in the defendant's favor on the counterclaim, the counterclaim merges in the judgment.[88] Of course, if the defendant is unable to obtain a full recovery in the action because, for example, the court in which the action is brought can render judgments only up to a certain amount and the defendant is unable to remove the case to another court with broader power, merger does not operate.[89]

Illustration 13-19. *P*, a citizen of State *X*, sues *D*, also a citizen of State *X*, in a state court for breach of contract. *D* defends on the ground that the contract is illegal under state and federal antitrust laws. *D* also pleads a counterclaim under the state antitrust laws against *P*. The court enters judgment in the action for *D* on both *P's* contract claim and *D's* counterclaim. Subsequently, *D* sues *P* in federal court. *D* asserts a claim under the federal antitrust laws for additional relief obtainable only under those laws, a claim over which the federal courts have exclusive jurisdiction. *D* may maintain this second action because (1) *D* could not assert the federal claim as a counterclaim in state court because the federal courts have exclusive jurisdiction over the claim and (2) *D* did not have the option of choosing the forum in the first suit.[90]

(b) Jurisdictions with a Compulsory Counterclaim Rule

When the jurisdiction in question possesses a compulsory counterclaim rule, such as Federal Rule 13, and the counterclaim arises out of the same transaction or occurrence as the opposing party's[91] claim, the compulsory counterclaim rule bars the defendant from asserting an omitted claim in a subsequent proceeding.[92] If the counterclaim is factually unrelated to the opposing

---

87. RESTATEMENT (SECOND) OF JUDGMENTS § 23 (1982).

88. *See id.* § 21(1).

89. *See id.* § 21(2).

90. *Cf. id.* cmt. b, illus. 3. *But cf.* McDaneld v. Lynn Hickey Dodge, Inc., 1999 OK 30, 979 P.2d 252 (when a defendant is sued in a small claims court with a jurisdictional amount limit, the defendant is obligated to plead a compulsory counterclaim even if it exceeds the amount limit and seek removal to a court of general jurisdiction; otherwise the compulsory counterclaim rule will bar assertion of the claim in a separate action).

91. Tilzer v. Davis, Bethune & Jones, L.L.C., 288 Kan. 477, 204 P.3d 617 (2009) (by seeking to enforce attorney fees lien in a motion proceeding in the underlying action, the attorney was proceeding against the judgment itself and not against the former client; therefore, attorney was not an "opposing party" to the client so as to require client to assert malpractice claim under state compulsory counterclaim rule).

92. *See, e.g.*, Johnson v. First Carolina Fin. Corp., 200 Ga. App. 340, 408 S.E.2d 151 (1991); Jacobs v. Littleton, 241 Ga. App. 403, 525 S.E.2d 433 (1999) (a counterclaim asserted against a party to the prior action was compulsory as against the party because it bore a logical relationship to the party's claim against the plaintiff in the first action, but it was not compulsory as to the nonparty because the compulsory counterclaim rule does not operate against non-parties). Problems involved in determining when a counterclaim arises out of the same transaction or occurrence as an opposing party's claim were fully explored in Chapter 7(F)(2), *supra*. Again, the description of Rule 13 in the text may have to be qualified in federal court by the *Semtek* case discussed in *Illustration 13-9*, above. If the compulsory counterclaim rule is classified as a rule designed to regulate the internal procedures of the federal courts, as Rule 41(b) was classified in *Semtek*, it might also be held that assertion of such a counterclaim is only precluded in a subsequent action in the same federal court in which the counterclaim was originally omitted. This would be an unfortunate result, but it is only of many potential problems created by the Court's interpretation of Rule 41(b) in *Semtek*.

party's claim, the counterclaim is "permissive." Under such circumstances, the defendant can make it the subject of a subsequent action.[93]

(c) Jurisdictions Without a Compulsory Counterclaim Rule

When the jurisdiction does not possess a compulsory counterclaim rule, however, the situation becomes more complicated. When the defendant fails to interpose a factually unrelated counterclaim, the result should be the same as described above for permissive counterclaims under Federal Rule 13. On the other hand, if the counterclaim arises out of the same transaction or occurrence as the opposing party's claim, the result may be different. The rules of issue preclusion (discussed in the next section) may prevent the defendant from asserting the counterclaim in a subsequent action if the defendant loses the first action to the plaintiff. Even if the rules of issue preclusion do not prevent litigation of the counterclaim, however, the defendant may be prohibited from asserting the counterclaim in a subsequent action when the counterclaim will "so plainly operate to undermine the initial judgment that the principle of finality requires preclusion of such an action."[94]

Illustration 13-20. *P* commences an action against *D* to quiet title to Blackacre and obtains a judgment by default. *D* then brings an action against *P* to quiet title to the same property. *D* alleges that at the time of the first action *D* had acquired title by adverse possession. If successful, *D's* action will completely undermine the judgment obtained by *P*.[95] For this reason, *D* is precluded from bringing the action even in the absence of a compulsory counterclaim rule.[96]

* * * * *

Ordinarily, the fact that a defendant pleads matter in defense that also might be the subject of a counterclaim will not preclude the defendant from asserting the counterclaim in a subsequent action in the absence of (1) a compulsory counterclaim rule, (2) the operation of issue preclusion against the defendant, or (3) a relationship between the counterclaim and the plaintiff's claim which would nullify the judgment in the first action or impair rights established therein.[97] However, a caveat is in order. A few courts have held that asserting a defense, but not a

---

93. *See* RESTATEMENT (SECOND) OF JUDGMENTS §§ 22(1), 22(2)(a) (1982).

94. RESTATEMENT (SECOND) OF JUDGMENTS § 22 cmt. f (1982).

95. *See id.* illus. 10; *cf.* Lighthouse Landings, Inc. v. Connecticut Light & Power Co., 300 Conn. 325, 15 A.3d 601 (2011) (res judicata precluded tenant's claims of misrepresentation and unfair trade practices even though claims arose from facts occurring after action for termination of lease by landlord, because tenant's claims were all intended to support its single, underlying claim that landlord had improperly terminated lease); Gray v. Kelly, 161 N.H. 160, 13 A.3d 848 (2010) (default judgment in prior domestic violence action by wife resolved husband's rights to certain personal property and was therefore claim preclusive in husband's second action to recover propery). *But cf.* Setlock v. Setlock, 286 Ga. 384, 688 S.E.2d 346 (2010) (tenant who raised compulsory counterclaims in landlord's dispossessory action in magistrate court did not lose right to bring later quiet title action against landlord because magistrate court lacked jurisdiction over the counterclaims).

96. *See id.* § 22(2)(b); Wickenhauser v. Lehtinen, 2007 WI 82, 302 Wis. 2d 41, 734 N.W.2d 855 (second action was not barred by common-law compulsory counterclaim rule, because in first action party was successful on affirmative defense based on fraud, and second action was for damages based on same fraud); *cf.* Dakota Title & Escrow Co. v. World-Wide Steel Sys., Inc., 238 Neb. 519, 471 N.W.2d 430 (1991) (action for declaratory judgment was based on a defense that could have been raised in prior action against the declaratory judgment plaintiff; therefore, prior action was res judicata).

97. RESTATEMENT (SECOND) OF JUDGMENTS § 22 cmt. d (1982).

counterclaim, splits the defendant's cause of action when the facts constituting the defense and counterclaim are substantially the same.[98] Thus, the precedents in a particular state must be carefully examined to determine whether the decision to plead a defense also carries with it the duty to assert a closely related counterclaim.[99]

Illustration 13-21. *P* sues *D* for personal injuries arising out of an automobile accident. *P* alleges that *D's* negligence caused the accident. *D* wants to deny *D's* own negligence and assert *P's* contributory negligence in the action. However, *D* wants to omit a claim *D* possesses against *P* for personal injuries arising out of the same accident because *D* would prefer to assert that claim in a subsequent action. Assuming that the state in which the action is brought has no compulsory counterclaim rule and *D* fails to plead the counterclaim, *D* may encounter two obstacles: (1) the doctrine of issue preclusion might prevent *D* from asserting the claim in the second proceeding if *D* loses the first proceeding;[100] and (2) the rule in some jurisdictions that raising a defense, but not a counterclaim, based on the same facts may result in a splitting of the claim.

(d) Special Problems Involving Insureds and Their Insurers

In jurisdictions with compulsory counterclaim rules, the interests of insured defendants can conflict with their insurers.

Illustration 13-22. *P* and *D* are involved in an automobile accident. *P* sues *D* for personal injuries received in the accident. *P* alleges that *D's* negligence was the sole cause of the accident. *D's* insurer defends the action for *D* by denying *D's* negligence and asserting *P's* contributory negligence. After trial, the court enters judgment for *D*. Subsequently, *D* sues *P* for personal injuries received in the same accident. If the state has a compulsory counterclaim rule identical to Federal Rule 13(b), should *D* be allowed to assert the counterclaim? The insurance company may have little interest in pursuing such a counterclaim on behalf of its insured.[101] On the other hand, it is unfair to *P* to have to defend the second action when the matter could have been effectively handled in the first proceeding. Here, flexibility may be required to balance the competing interests.[102]

---

98. *See, e.g.*, Mitchell v. Federal Intermediate Credit Bank, 165 S.C. 457, 164 S.E. 136 (1932).

99. *Cf.* Fowler v. Vineyard, 261 Ga. 454, 405 S.E.2d 678 (1991) (bus driver asserted against codefendants crossclaims for indemnity and contribution which were later voluntarily dismissed with prejudice; dismissal precluded bus driver from asserting claims for personal injury against codefendants in later action).

100. *See* section C *infra* ("Issue Preclusion").

101. The stated obligation in the insurance contract is to "defend" against claims, not to assert them, Allen E. Smith, *The Miscegenetic Union of Liability Insurance and Tort Process in the Personal Injury Claims System*, 54 CORNELL L. REV. 645, 658 (1969), and the insurance company itself may not be compelled to interpose counterclaims on the insured's behalf. *See* Reynolds v. Hartford Accident & Idem. Co., 278 F. Supp. 331, 333-34 (S.D.N.Y. 1967) (to imply an obligation on the insurance carrier to bring affirmative claims on behalf of its insured would entail extra expenditures on the part of the carrier and would be manifestly unfair).

102. *Cf.* RESTATEMENT (SECOND) OF JUDGMENTS § 20 cmt. n (1982) (suggesting that the rule of that section is a flexible one). *Compare* Reynolds v. Hartford Accident & Indem. Co., 278 F. Supp. 331 (S.D.N.Y. 1967) (insureds should not be estopped because of a compulsory counterclaim rule from bringing a separate action for injuries suffered in the accident when attorneys retained by insurance carrier refused to assert counterclaims on behalf of the insureds) *and* Suchta v. Robinett, 596 P.2d 1380 (Wyo. 1979) (waiver or estoppel theory applied to compulsory counterclaim rule which, in effect, makes its application dependent upon the conduct of a litigant in failing to pursue the counterclaim) *with* Rothtrock v. Ohio Farmers Ins. Co., 233 Cal. App. 2d 616, 43 Cal. Rptr.

Illustration 13-23. *P* and *D* set out on a trip in *P's* automobile with *D* driving. Both *P* and *D* are injured in an accident. *P* sues *D* for personal injuries received in the accident. *P's* insurance company defends the action in accord with the requirements of a clause in *P's* insurance contract insuring persons who were driving *P's* automobile with *P's* permission. The insurance company notifies *D* to obtain a lawyer because the complaint requests damages in excess of the policy limits. *D* fails to do so. After the close of the pleadings, the insurer settles the action with *P*. A consent judgment is then entered in favor of *D*. Subsequently, *D* sues *P* for *D's* personal injuries received in the same accident. *D* alleges that *P* was negligent when *P* grabbed the steering wheel from *D*. Assuming that the state possesses a compulsory counterclaim rule identical to Federal Rule 13(a), should *D* be permitted to maintain this action? In *Dindo v. Whitney*,[103] the First Circuit Court of Appeals held on similar facts that a conscious failure to plead the counterclaim precluded the second action.[104] If the counterclaim had been raised in the suit, a serious conflict of interest would have resulted. In effect, the insurer would be on both sides of the suit. On the other hand, if the counterclaim had been pleaded, surely contributory negligence would also have been raised as a defense to the main claim and the counterclaim. In this situation, one of several things might then have occurred: (1) both parties might have been found negligent, in which case the insurance company would not be liable on either claim (in a jurisdiction in which contributory negligence is an absolute defense); (2) both parties might have been found not negligent, in which case, also, the insurance company would not be liable; or (3) one party might have been found negligent and the other not negligent, in which case the insurance company would be liable on *one claim* only. By failure to plead the counterclaim, if it can be asserted in a second action, the insurer could be held liable twice, once on the settlement and once in the second suit.

SECTION C. ISSUE PRECLUSION

1. The Basic Rule

A valid and final personal judgment can have a preclusive effect in two ways, either through claim preclusion or issue preclusion. Claim preclusion focuses on what a party ought to have litigated in the first action. Issue preclusion concerns only those issues that were actually litigated and determined in the first action.[105]

---

716 (1965) (insurer is liable to its own insured when the insurer knowingly authorized dismissal with prejudice of a municipal court action against its insured for damage to motorist's automobile by paying $250 to the motorist in settlement that as a result barred a pending superior court action by insured of a personal injury claim against the motorist).

103. 451 F.2d 1 (1st Cir. 1971).

104. *Id.* at 3.

105. One example of issue preclusion, described as "direct estoppel," was discussed in section B, *supra*. Direct estoppel results when an issue has actually been litigated and determined and a second action is brought on the same claim. *See* RESTATEMENT (SECOND) OF JUDGMENTS § 27 cmt. b (1982). Direct estoppel is distinguished from "collateral estoppel," in that collateral estoppel applies to issues actually litigated and determined in a first action when a second action is brought on a different claim as to which the earlier determined issues are also relevant. The rules governing when an issue will be precluded from relitigation are otherwise the same for both direct and collateral estoppel. *See id.* This section will deal primarily with issue preclusion in the collateral estoppel

Section 27 of the *Restatement (Second) of Judgments* states the basic rule of issue preclusion: "When an issue of fact or law is actually litigated and determined by a valid and final judgment, and the determination is essential to the judgment, the determination is conclusive in a subsequent action between the parties, whether on the same or a different claim."[106] Several discrete requirements appear within this rule.

(a) Identity of the Issue

For issue preclusion to apply, the issue litigated in the first and second actions must be the same.[107] This proposition seems straightforward enough, but the matter can become complicated. A party may in successive actions attempt to bring forward different grounds or evidence to support a conclusion the party wishes the trier of fact to reach. A total identity between the matters involved in the two actions may not exist. For example, the events in the suits may be separated in time or different rules of law may apply in the suits.[108] The *Restatement (Second)* does not articulate a fixed rule for resolving these scope-of-issue problems. Instead, the drafters suggest several factors that should be considered in determining whether

---

context.

106. *Id.* § 27. This rule can produce dramatic consequences. *See, e.g.*, State *ex rel.* West Va. Dep't of Health v. Cline, 185 W. Va. 318, 406 S.E.2d 749 (1991) (paternity issue precluded); *In re* Paternity of JRW, 814 P.2d 1256 (Wyo. 1991) (same); *see also* Jonathan Scott Baker, *The Use of Sentencing Findings as a Collateral Estoppel Weapon in Subsequent Civil Litigation*, 85 NOTRE DAME L. REV. 713 (2010).

107. *See, e.g.*, Unum Life Ins. Co. of Am. v. Wright, 897 So. 2d 1059 (Ala. 2004) (for doctrine of collateral estoppel or issue preclusion to apply, issue in prior action must have been identical to issue being litigated in present action, the issue must actually have been litigated in prior action, the resolution of the issue must have been necessary to the prior action, and the same parties must have been involved in both actions); Parson v. State Dep't of Rev., 189 P.3d 1032 (Alaska 2008) (issue preclusion not applicable unless issue identical); New Eng. Estates, LLC v. Town of Branford, 294 Conn. 817, 988 A.2d 299 (2010) (landowner's successive actions did not involve same issue; therefore, no preclusion); Pursue Energy Corp. v. Abernathy, 77 So. 3d 1094 (Miss. 2011) (issue in first action was whether oil company could recover expenses; issue in second action was whether oil company could recover expenses twice); Mayor v. Homebuilders Ass'n, 932 So. 2d 44 (Miss. 2006) (under doctrine of collateral estoppel, party is precluded from relitigating questions actually litigated and determined by and essential to the judgment in a prior action, even though a different cause of action is the subject of the present suit); Mansoldo v. State, 187 N.J. 50, 898 A.2d 1018 (2006) (collateral estoppel precludes a party from relitigating an issue if the issue was identical to the issue decided in the prior proceeding, was actually litigated in the prior proceeding, and the determination of the issue was essential to the judgment); City of New York v. Welsbach Elec. Corp., 9 N.Y.3d 124, 878 N.E.2d 966, 848 N.Y.S.2d 551 (2007) (collateral estoppel applies only if the issue in the second action is identical to an issue that was raised, necessarily decided, and material in the first action and the party to be bound had a full and fair opportunity to litigate the issue in the earlier action); Murphy v. Duquesne Univ. of Holy Ghost, 565 Pa. 571, 777 A.2d 418 (2001) (university law professor's prior action in federal court under the Age Discrimination in Employment Act precluded second state action for breach of his employment contract; first action necessarily included an examination of the university's termination proceedings to determine whether they were arbitrary and noncompliant with the university's handbook and the contract of employment).

108. *See* Guardianship of Jewel M., 2010 Me. 80, 2 A.3d 301 (issues in guardianship arose after prior proceeding and were not, therefore, precluded); Efstathiou v. Efstathiou, 2009 Me. 107, 982 A.2d 339 (issue preclusion not applicable in contempt proceeding on issue of contemnor's ability to pay judgment because circumstances may have changed since entry of judgment); *In re* M.N., 362 Mont. 186, 261 P.3d 1047 (2011) (mere fact that earlier and later petition to terminate parental rights alleged abuse and neglect did not mean that the issues in both actions were identical); *In re* Mastny Revocable Trust, 281 Neb. 188, 794 N.W.2d 700 (2011) (issue of whether notebooks established an asset of decedent's estate was not the same as whether they established an asset of her trust); Hebden v. Workmen's Comp. Appeal Bd., 534 Pa. 327, 632 A.2d 1302 (1993) (in first worker's compensation action worker was found to suffer irreversible condition; therefore, employer could not seek in second action to show worker was no longer suffering from disability, because in effect that was an attempt to relitigate an issue determined in prior action); Alden v. Alden, 2010 Vt. 3, 992 A.2d 298 (issue of how to distribute assets in trust termination action was not the same as issue of how to apportion damages in breach of fiduciary trust action against trustee); Peters v. Rivers Edge Mining, Inc., 224 W. Va. 160, 680 S.E.2d 791 (2009) (issues in prior arbitration action and current worker's compensation action were different; no preclusion).

the issues in the two proceedings are the same: (1) whether substantial overlap exists between the evidence or arguments made in the first and second actions; (2) whether the new evidence or argument involves the same rule of law as that involved in the first proceeding; (3) whether pre-trial preparation and discovery in the first action could reasonably be expected to have embraced the matters presented in the second proceeding; and (4) whether a close relationship exists between the claims in the two proceedings.[109] Two examples drawn from the *Restatement (Second)* demonstrate the difficulties that this "scope of the issue" inquiry poses.

Illustration 13-24. *P* sues *D* to recover an installment payment due under an oral contract between *P* and *D*. *D's* only defense is that the contract is unenforceable under the statute of frauds. After trial, the court enters judgment for *P* based on a specific finding that the oral contract is enforceable. *P* sues *D* in a subsequent action to recover a second installment that came due after the first action was brought. *D* may not raise the statute of frauds as a defense, even if *D* is prepared to assert arguments about the applicability of the statute that were not made in the first action. The scope of the issue is the same in the first and second actions. However, *D* may assert that the contract is not enforceable as a matter of law on any other ground.[110] For example, *D* could assert that the contract violated the state usury statutes.

Illustration 13-25. *P* sues *D* to recover for personal injuries received in an automobile accident. *P* alleges that *D* was negligent in driving at an excessive rate of speed. After trial, verdict and judgment are given for *D* on the ground that *D* was not negligent. Subsequently, *D* sues *P* for personal injuries received in the same accident. *D's* action is permitted because the state in question has no compulsory counterclaim rule. *P* is precluded from defending the second action on the ground that *D* was negligent in failing to keep a proper lookout. According to the *Restatement (Second)*, it is reasonable to require *P* to bring forward all evidence in support of *D's* alleged negligence in the first action.[111]

* * * * *

In *Illustration 13-25*, the drafters of the *Restatement (Second)* consider the issue to be *D's* negligence. However, in *Illustration 13-24*, the drafters considered the issue to be the "statute of frauds." Under the factors suggested by the *Restatement (Second)* for determining the scope of an issue, discussed above, the reasons for treating the scope of the issue differently between the two illustrations is clear. In *Illustration 13-25*, all four of the factors point toward defining the scope of the issue in the first action as "*D's* negligence."[112] In *Illustration 13-24*, however,

---

109. *See* RESTATEMENT (SECOND) OF JUDGMENTS § 27 cmt. c (1982).

110. *See id.* § 27 illus. 6.

111. *See id.* cmt. c, illus. 4.

112. That is, (1) substantial overlap exists between the evidence and arguments between the first and second actions (they both involve the same event and same legal theory); (2) the new evidence involves the same rule of law (negligence) as the one involved in the first proceeding; (3) pre-trial preparation and discovery in the first action could reasonably have been expected to have embraced the matters presented in the second proceeding (the different ways in which *D* might be negligent); and (4) a close relationship exists between the claims in the two proceedings (they both arose out of the same event).

only two of the factors point toward defining the scope of the issue as the same between the first and second actions.[113]

Nevertheless, the issue in *Illustration 13-24* can be stated at a different level of generality. For example, the issue can be characterized as the "enforceability of the contract." This characterization would preclude asserting any other grounds of unenforceability in an action to recover a second installment. Furthermore, it is difficult, as a matter of policy, to see why the defendant should not be required to bring forward all available grounds of unenforceability in the first action. The possible lack of a solidly grounded policy distinction between the two illustrations should lead the careful attorney to bring forward all available grounds that exist in support of an issue at the time of the first action.

(b) Actual Litigation Requirement

Issue preclusion applies only when an issue has actually been litigated and determined in the first action, not to issues which might have been litigated and determined but were not.[114] A party may choose not to raise an issue in a particular action for several reasons: (1) the amount in controversy may be small; (2) the

---

113. That is, pre-trial preparation and discovery in both actions might have been expected to reveal all bases upon which the contract was unenforceable and the claims in both actions are closely related because they both arise out of the same contract. *See also* Note, *Cross-Jurisdictional Forum Non Conveniens Preclusion,* 121 HARV. L. REV. 2178 (2008) (discussing identity of issue and other problems involved in determining the effect of a judgment of dismissal on grounds of forum non conveniens in one forum when suit is filed contrary to the dismissal in another forum).

114. *See, e.g.*, Urfirer v. Cornfeld, 408 F.3d 710 (11th Cir. 2005) (prior rulings by state court did not constitute issue preclusion on fraud and breach of fiduciary duty claims because rulings only reached the scope of a waiver and not whether the waiver was fraudulently obtained); McAlpine v. Pacarro, 262 P.3d 622(Alaska 2011) (separate actions for custody involved different claims; mother was precluded by issue preclusion from relitigating issues of domestic violence litigated in first action, but not issues of domestic violence that had not been litigated, even though non-litigated issues could have been litigated in prior action); Maness v. Daily, 184 P.3d 1 (Alaska 2008) (in prior federal sentencing hearing, issue of excessive force was held to be irrelevant; therefore, issue was not precluded in plaintiff's subsequent civil action against arresting officers because plaintiff did not have a full and fair opportunity to litigate issue); State Office of Child Support Enforcement v. Willis, 347 Ark. 6, 59 S.W.3d 438 (2001) (collateral estoppel requires actual litigation of an issue); Forsyth Cnty. v. Martin, 279 Ga. 215, 610 S.E.2d 512 (2005) (issue of ownership of dam was effectively litigated and determined in prior action ordering dam owners to repair dam because county was determined to be owner of dam for purposes of complying with order); Baird Oil Co. v. Idaho State Tax Comm'n, 144 Idaho 229, 159 P.3d 866 (2007) (issue of whether appellant was entitled to tax refund was litigated and determined against it in a prior action); Larson Mfg. Co. v. Thorson, 763 N.W.2d 842 (Iowa 2009) (issues in second action were not determined in prior action for purposes of issue preclusion); Allmerica Fin. Corp. v. Certain Underwriters at Lloyds, London, 449 Mass. 621, 871 N.E.2d 418 (2007) (agreement to settlement did not result in issue preclusion by binding defendant to facts in complaint because issue preclusion only applies when an issue of fact or law is litigated and determined by a valid and final and judgment); Abadir v. Dellinger, 227 W. Va. 388, 709 S.E.2d 743 (2011) (determination in prior action that employee's lawyer had apparent authority to enter into settlement on behalf of employee did not litigate issue of whether attorney had actual authority to settle action). *But see* First Union Nat'l Bank v. Penn Salem Marina, Inc., 190 N.J. 342, 921 A.2d 417 (2007) (default judgment in action on promissory note had issue preclusion effect that precluded use of higher per diem rate in foreclosure action than in action on note). *See also* Lamb v. Anderson, 126 P.3d 132 (Alaska 2005) (plea of no contest in criminal action collaterally estopped defendant from contesting the essential elements of the offense in a subsequent civil proceeding); Ammondson v. Northwestern Corp., 353 Mont. 28, 220 P.3d 1 (2009) (issue preclusion prevented party from asserting that claims were preempted by federal bankruptcy law when federal bankruptcy court had previously held that it lacked jurisdiction over party's attempt to terminate claims); *cf.* State v. Knight, 266 Conn. 658, 835 A.2d 47 (2003) (verdict of trial court that defendant was guilty of criminal possession of a firearm was not legally inconsistent with jury verdict that defendant was not guilty of carrying a pistol or revolver without a permit, given that each offense contained different elements); Augustine v. Arizant, Inc., 751 N.W.2d 95 (Minn. 2008) (by statute guilty plea in criminal action does not conclusively establish bad faith for purposes of subsequent action by criminal defendant to obtain reimbursement from corporation for indemnity for fines and costs of criminal defense).

forum may be inconvenient; (3) the timing of the litigation may be bad; or (4) many other factors may dictate that an issue not be litigated.[115] At the same time, insisting upon preclusion as to issues that might have been litigated could encourage litigation in the first action to the utmost extent to avoid preclusion. Such insistence might decrease economy of litigation by elevating the first action to such importance that it requires more judicial resources than two actions involving the same issue.[116]

An issue need not be disposed of after a full trial to meet the actual litigation requirement. For example, an issue may be litigated on a general demurrer or a motion to dismiss for failure to state a claim, on a motion for judgment on the pleadings, or on a motion for summary judgment.[117] On the other hand, an issue has not actually been litigated when judgment is entered for the plaintiff after the defendant has defaulted for failure to appear.[118] The issue must be actually raised, submitted for determination, and decided.[119]

---

115. *See* Cromwell v. County of Sac, 94 U.S. 351, 356, 24 L. Ed. 195, 199 (1877); RESTATEMENT (SECOND) OF JUDGMENTS § 27 cmt. e (1982) ("The interests of conserving judicial resources, of maintaining consistency, and of avoiding oppression or harassment of the adverse party are less compelling when an issue on which preclusion is sought has not actually been litigated before.").

116. RESTATEMENT (SECOND) OF JUDGMENTS § 27 cmt. e (1982).

117. *See id.* § 27 cmt. d; Albahary v. City of Bristol, 276 Conn. 426, 886 A.2d 802 (2005) (an issue is actually litigated if it is properly raised in the pleadings or otherwise, submitted for determination, and in fact determined; plaintiff's issue of inverse condemnation was decided against plaintiff in prior federal action); *In re* Goldstone, 445 Mass. 551, 839 N.E.2d 825 (2005) (summary judgments are entitled to preclusive effect when the parties were fully heard, the court's decision is supported by a reasoned opinion, and the opinion was subject to review or actually reviewed).

118. *See, e.g.*, Christian v. Sizemore, 185 W. Va. 409, 407 S.E.2d 715 (1991); *see also* Beebe v. Fountain Lake Sch. Dist., 365 Ark. 536, 231 S.W.3d 628 (2006) (issue preclusion did not apply because prior action was settled and nothing was litigated). The rule that a default judgment has no issue preclusion effect is not universally observed. For a discussion of the position of the *Restatement (Second)* and the contrary doctrine, see Jackson v. R.G. Whipple, Inc., 225 Conn. 705, 627 A.2d 374 (1993).

119. *See* RESTATEMENT (SECOND) OF JUDGMENTS § 27 cmt. d (1982); Truck Ins. Exch. v. Ashland Oil, Inc., 951 F.2d 787 (7th Cir. 1992) (issue of successor liability never litigated, even though that was the only basis for joining corporation in first action); Bradley Ventures, Inc. v. Farm Bureau Mut. Ins. Co., 371 Ark. 229, 264 S.W.3d 485 (2007) (guilty pleas do not produce issue preclusion because issue has not been actually litigated); Linder v. Missoula Cnty., 251 Mont. 292, 824 P.2d 1004 (1992) (consent judgment based on settlement agreement does not have issue preclusion effect unless parties intend it to have such an effect); *In re* T.C., 182 Vt. 467, 940 A.2d 706 (2007) (issue preclusion bars the subsequent relitigation of an issue that was actually litigated and decided in a prior case where that issue was necessary to the resolution of the dispute); *cf.* Estes v. Titus, 481 Mich. 573, 751 N.W.2d 493 (2008) (statutory issue was not barred by claim or issue preclusion by denial of prior motion to intervene on grounds of lack of jurisdiction; issue could not have been raised in motion and was not decided). *But cf.* Moore v. Peak Oilfield Serv. Co., 175 P.3d 1278 (Alaska 2008) (driver's plea of no contest to driving while intoxicated established as a matter of law that driver was negligent and reckless for purposes of third-party claim); Sun v. State, 830 P.2d 772 (Alaska 1992) (by statute, nolo contendere plea estops defendant from contesting issues in subsequent civil action); Morrison v. Morrison, 284 Ga. 112, 663 S.E.2d 714 (2008) (to be precluded issue must actually have been litigated and decided in a prior action *or* the issue necessarily had to be decided for the previous judgment to have been rendered); Bach v. Bagley, 148 Idaho 784, 229 P.3d 1146 (2010) (dismissal of complaint for failure to comply with Federal Rules did not preclude finding of issue preclusion because party had opportunity to amend and therefore a full and fair opportunity to litigate issue; also, party had full opportunity to litigate isssue in state court even though there was a default judgment, because a default judgment does not bar a finding of opportunity to litigate); Iowa Supreme Court Attorney Disciplinary Bd. v. Iversen, 723 N.W.2d 806 (Iowa 2006) (attorney was precluded from relitigating the issue of his criminal conduct in disciplinary proceedings by guilty plea in prior criminal action to charges of fraudulent practices); J.R. v. Malley, 62 So. 3d 902 (Miss. 2011) (guilty plea in criminal action sufficient to establish fault in tort as to two incidents that were the subject of the plea); Rennels v. Rennels, 257 P.3d 396 (Nev. 2011) (final judgment entered in a nonparental visitation matter has a preclusive effect whether it is rendered in a contested proceeding or by stipulation in order to prevent parties from relitigating the same issues); *In re* King, 170 Wash.2d 738, 246 P.3d 1232 (2011) (guilty plea in federal court to mail fraud conclusively established attorney's guilt at attorney disciplinary proceeding); David L. Shapiro, *Should a Guilty Plea Have Preclusive Effect?*, 70 IOWA L. REV. 27 (1984). For a criticism of California's application of the actual litigation requirement, see Walter W. Heiser, *California's Confusing Collateral Estoppel (Issue Preclusion) Doctrine*, 35 SAN DIEGO L. REV. 509 (1998).

Illustration 13-26. *P* sues *D* for personal injuries received in an automobile accident. *P* alleges that *D* was negligent. *D* admits negligence in the answer and asserts contributory negligence as a defense. After trial, the court enters judgment for *D* on the ground that *P* was contributorily negligent. Subsequently, *D* sues *P* for personal injuries received in the accident. *D's* action is permitted because the state has no compulsory counterclaim rule. *P* contends that the prior judgment establishes that *D* was negligent. As a result, *P* contends that *D's* suit is barred. However, the issue of *D's* negligence was not actually litigated in the prior action because *D* admitted it in *D's* pleading. Therefore, *P's* contention is not sound, and *D* can maintain the action.[120]

* * * * *

As observed in section B(2), above, to have a claim-preclusive effect, a judgment traditionally had to be "on the merits." However, even a judgment that is "without prejudice," or "not on the merits," can have an issue preclusion effect.[121] Unfortunately, a substantial number of courts, in stating the requirements for issue preclusion, include a boilerplate statement that a judgment must be "on the merits" for issue preclusion to operate.[122] Others correctly recognize that actions dismissed

---

120. *See* RESTATEMENT (SECOND) OF JUDGMENTS § 27 cmt. c (1982); *see also* Winnebago Indus., Inc. v. Haverly, 727 N.W.2d 567 (Iowa 2006) (employer's admission of liability in alternate-medical-care proceeding involving worker's compensation claimant's request for back surgery did not constitute actual litigation for purposes of issue preclusion); Mrozek v. Intra Fin. Corp., 2005 WI 73, 281 Wis. 2d 448, 699 N.W.2d 54 (guilty pleas in criminal action did not fulfill the actual litigation requirement for issue preclusion). *But see* Wilson v. MacDonald, 168 P.3d 887 (Alaska 2007) (party who pleaded no contest to charge of assault in criminal case was precluded from relitigating any element of the crime in plaintiff's subsequent civil action for assault and battery).

121. *See* section B(2), *Illustration 13-7* and accompanying text *supra* (discussing the doctrine of direct estoppel); Zeno v. United States, 451 Fed. App'x 268 (4th Cir. 2011) (prior dismissal in same court on questions of personal jurisdiction and venue were issue preclusive).

122. *See, e.g.* State v. Doherty, 167 P.3d 64 (Alaska 2007); Varilek v. City of Houston, 104 P.3d 849 (Alaska 2004); Natural Energy Res. Co. v. Upper Gunnison River Water Conservancy Dist., 142 P.3d 1265 (Colo. 2006); *In re* Water Rights, 139 P.3d 660 (Colo. 2006); K.H. v. R.H., 935 A.2d 328 (D.C. 2007); Kingman Park Civic Ass'n v. Williams, 924 A.2d 979 (D.C. 2007); Topps v. State, 865 So. 2d 1253 (Fla. 2004); Karan, Inc. v. Auto-Owners Ins. Co., 280 Ga. 545, 629 S.E.2d 260 (2006); Parker v. Parker, 277 Ga. 664, 594 S.E.2d 627 (2004) (issue preclusion precluded relitigation of issue previously decided against plaintiff in prior action); Bremer v. Weeks, 104 Haw. 43, 85 P.3d 150 (2004); Omerod v. Heirs of Kaheananui, 116 Haw. 239, 172 P.3d 983 (2007); Exotics Hawaii-Kona, Inc. v. E.I. Dupont De Nemours & Co., 104 Haw. 358, 90 P.3d 250 (2004); Navarro v. Yonkers, 144 Idaho 882,173 P.3d 1141 (2007); Ticor Title Co. v. Stanion, 144 Idaho 119, 157 P.3d 613 (2007); Schwan's Sales Enters., Inc. v. Idaho Transp. Dep't, 142 Idaho 826, 136 P.3d 297 (2006); *In re* City of Wichita, 277 Kan. 487, 86 P.3d 513 (2004); Kobrin v. Board of Registration in Med., 444 Mass. 837, 832 N.E.2d 628 (2005); Kubacki v. Molchan, 2007 MT 306, 340 Mont. 100, 172 P.3d 594; *In re* B.N.Y., 2006 MT 34, 331 Mont. 145, 130 P.3d 594; Lee v. USAA Cas. Ins. Co., 2004 MT 54, 320 Mont. 174,86 P.3d 562; Amanda C. *ex rel.* Richmond v. Case, 275 Neb. 757, 749 N.W.2d 429 (2008); Denny Wiekhorst Equip., Inc . v. Tri-State Outdoor Media Group, Inc., 269 Neb. 354, 693 N.W.2d 506 (2005); Sandoval v. Sandoval, 126 Nev. 15, 232 P.3d 422 (2010); Kahn v. Morse & Mowbray, 121 Nev. 464, 117 P.3d 227 (2005); State, Univ. Coll. Sys. v. Sutton, 120 Nev. 972, 103 P.3d 8 (2004); Olivieri v. Y.M.F. Carpet, Inc., 186 N.J. 511, 897 A.2d 1003 (2006); Gratech Co. v. Wold Eng'g, P.C., 2007 ND 46, 729 N.W.2d 326; Riemers v. Peters-Riemers, 2004 ND 153, 684 N.W.2d 619; Barackman v. Anderson, 338 Or. 365, 109 P.3d 370 (2005); Buckner v. Kennard, 2004 UT 78, 99 P.3d 842; *In re* Armitage, 2006 VT 113, 181 Vt. 241, 917 A.2d 437; *In re* Stormwater NPDES Petition, 2006 VT 91, 180 Vt. 261, 910 A.2d 824; State v. Eggleston, 164 Wash. 2d 61, 187 P.3d 233 (2008) (criminal case); *In re* Whitney, 155 Wash. 2d 451, 120 P.3d 550 (2005); Christensen v. Grant Cnty. Hosp. Dist. No. 1, 152 Wash. 2d 299, 96 P.3d 957 (2004); State Dep't of Revenue v. Exxon Mobil Corp., 2007 WY 112, 162 P.3d 515; Phillips v. Toner, 2006 WY 59, 133 P.3d 987; Aragon v. Aragon, 2005 WY 5, 104 P.3d 756; Pokorny v. Salas, 2003 WY 159, 81 P.3d 171; *cf.* Kennedy v. Lubar, 273 F.3d 1293 (10th Cir. 2001) (law of the case only applies to decisions on the merits). In Grynberg v. Questar Pipeline Co., 2003 UT 8, 70 P.3d 1, the court erroneously stated that issue preclusion requires a judgment on the merits and then further erroneously held that a partial summary judgment in a prior action was not a "final judgment on the merits" that would bring issue preclusion into play. In Stewart v. Bader, 154 N.H. 75, 907 A.2d 931 (2006), the court's phraseology indicated that it was not using the "on the merits" language in the traditional way. Rather than stating, as most courts do, that issue preclusion requires a judgment on the merits (or equivalent phraseology), the court stated that preclusion requires that "the first action must have resolved the *issue*

on procedural grounds can have a preclusive effect on the procedural issues actually litigated and determined in the action.[123] The cases stating that a judgment must be rendered "on the merits" before it may have an issue preclusion effect do not really seem to be using the "on the merits" phrase in its traditionally understood sense. Rather, they seem to be using the expression as a substitute for one of the other requirements for issue preclusion, such as the requirement that an issue must actually have been litigated and determined.[124] Thus, the courts seldom, if ever, reach incorrect results due to the misstatement of the issue preclusion requirements. Nevertheless, the courts sometimes give incorrect reasons for correct results,[125] and their incorrect statements of doctrine run the risk of confusing practitioners.

(c) Ability to Identify What Was Decided

The actual litigation requirement depends, of course, on the ability to identify what was decided. It must be possible in the second action to discern what issues were decided and how they were decided in the first proceeding.

---

finally on the merits." *Id.* at 80-81, 907 A.2d at 937.

123. *See, e.g.*, Pohlmann v. Bil-Jax, Inc., 176 F.3d 1110 (8th Cir. 1999) (issue of personal jurisdiction decided in a prior action precluded; dismissals without prejudice do not have a claim preclusion effect, but do have an issue preclusion effect on identical issues actually litigated and determined); Transaero, Inc. v. La Fuerza Aerea Boliviana, 162 F.3d 724 (2d Cir. 1998) (decision in prior action that party was improperly served has issue preclusion effect); Offshore Sportswear, Inc. v. Vuarnet Int'l, B.V., 114 F.3d 848 (9th Cir. 1997) (dismissal of U.S. District Court action under a forum selection clause; subsequent action commenced in state court and removed to federal court; held: prior dismissal, even though not on the merits, was preclusive on the issue of whether the action had to be litigated in Switzerland under the forum selection clause); *Ex parte* Ford Motor Credit Co., 772 So. 2d 437 (Ala. 2000) (issue preclusion applies to dismissal on grounds of forum non conveniens and precludes relitigation of the issue when the objective criteria and the underlying material facts were the same in the prior and subsequent actions; fact that dismissal was without prejudice did not mean that plaintiff could relitigate the forum non conveniens issue in the absence of a change in the material facts underlying the determination); Saudi v. Acomarit Mars. Servs., S.A., 114 Fed. App'x 449 (3d Cir. 2004) (prior judgment of dismissal for lack of personal jurisdiction was not claim preclusive because not on the merits; however, judgment did have an issue preclusion effect on whether jurisdiction could be asserted under Federal Rule 4(k)(2)); O'Marra v. MacKool, 361 Ark. 32, 204 S.W.3d 49 (2005) (describing the necessary elements of issue preclusion without mentioning an "on the merits" requirement); Hunter v. City of Des Moines Mun. Hous. Auth., 742 N.W.2d 578 (Iowa 2007) (describing the necessary elements of issue preclusion without mentioning an "on the merits" requirement); *cf.* Walker v. City of Huntsville, 62 So. 3d 474 (Ala. 2010) (discretionary dismissal by federal court of state claims over which court had supplemental jurisdiction did not preclude federal judgment from having issue preclusion effect in subsequent state action on claims based on federal judgment on § 1983 claims); Berthiaume v. McCormack, 153 N.H. 239, 891 A.2d 539 (2006) (prior motion to intervene determined right of plaintiffs in second action to litigate claim and was therefore preclusive in second proceeding); Cartesian Broad. Network, Inc. v. Robeco USA, 43 A.D.3d 311, 841 N.Y.S.2d 36 (2007) (dismissal for lack of jurisdiction was not on the merits, but adjudication precluded relitigation of issues actually decided); Oklahoma Dep't of Pub. Safety v. McCrady, 2007 OK 39, 176 P.3d 1194 (issue preclusion does not require a prior adjudication on the merits, but requires final determination of a material issue common to both actions).

124. In Stewart v. Hechtman, 254 Neb. 992, 581 N.W.2d 416 (1998), the Nebraska Supreme Court listed the "on the merits" requirement as one of the requirements of issue preclusion, but clearly seemed to mean only that the issue must actually have been decided by the court in the prior action. In the actual case, the court indicated that an issue of personal jurisdiction decided in a prior action was not precluded from relitigation because it was not identical with the issue in the second action. The clear implication of the court's opinion was that the issue would have been precluded if it had been identical, but this cannot be so if the judgment of dismissal in the prior action had to be on the merits in order to have an issue preclusion effect. *See also In re* Worker's Comp. Claim of Jacobs, 2009 Wy 118, 216 P.3d 1128 (stating that the prior action had not resulted in a judgment on the merits, but in discussion, clearly indicating that issue had not been decided at all); *cf.* Flaherty v. Lang, 199 F.3d 607 (2d Cir. 1999) (court states that refusal of permission to file supplemental complaint on an issue in prior action has issue preclusive effect because court's decision was "on the merits," but court clearly meant that the issue raised by the supplemental complaint was actually litigated and determined in the prior action).

125. *See* Shahan v. Shahan, 988 S.W.2d 529 (Mo. 1999) (stating, in part, that issue preclusion did not apply to determination of an issue in an action not decided on the merits, when real reason for denying preclusion was that determination of the issue did not support the judgment in the prior action); *see also* subsection *(d) infra*.

Illustration 13-27. *P* sues *D* for negligence. The record reveals that *D's* sole defense to the action is a denial of negligence. Thus, even after a general jury verdict, it is possible to determine what issue was decided.[126] However, assume that *D* denies negligence and asserts contributory negligence as a defense. If a jury delivers a general verdict in *D's* favor, there may be no way to tell upon what ground the judgment was based. The jury may have found *D* negligent and *P* contributorily negligent; or the jury may have found *D* not negligent and *P* not contributorily negligent; or the jury may have found *D* not negligent and the jury may never have reached the issue of *P's* contributory negligence. In such a case, the general verdict will not reveal the grounds for the decision and there can be no issue preclusion without resort to extrinsic evidence, as discussed below.[127]

* * * * *

Evidence extrinsic to the record in the first action may be introduced to show what issues were litigated and determined. For example, evidence contradicting the record is admissible. However, to be successful, this evidence must prove the extrinsic matter clearly and convincingly.[128] Courts will allow the subsequent testimony of a juror to demonstrate that the jury in a prior action was improperly

---

126. *See, e.g.,* Dowling v. Finley Assocs., Inc., 248 Conn. 364, 727 A.2d 1245 (1999) (general verdict will not support issue preclusion where there is no way to ascertain the basis of the jury's decision). Kret *ex rel.* Kret v. Brookdale Hosp. Med. Ctr., 93 A.D.2d 449, 462 N.Y.S.2d 896 (1983), *aff'd,* 61 N.Y.2d 861, 462 N.E.2d 147, 473 N.Y.S.2d 970 (1984). In *Kret,* the plaintiff first sued a physician for malpractice. The court submitted a number of interrogatories to the jury, some of which assumed that the physician had failed "to properly" monitor or check the patient's condition. Other interrogatories simply queried whether failure to perform certain actions was malpractice. The jury answered all the interrogatories in the negative. Judgment was entered in favor of the physician. In a second action, plaintiff sued the hospital. The court held that issue preclusion barred the action. In the court's view, the negative answers to the interrogatories in the first action inevitably meant that the patient did not suffer from the condition that allegedly caused the harm. Because of this conclusion, no recovery could be obtained from either the physician or the hospital. *See also* Kurtz & Perry, P.A. v. Emerson, 2010 ME 107, 8 A.3d 677 (to decide fee dispute, arbitration panel necessarily had to make factual findings as to whether client agreed to pay attorney fees to firm and whether the fees charged to her were reasonable and client had adequate opportunity and incentive to litigate).

127. *Cf.* Lee L. Saad Constr. Co. v. DPF Architects, P.C., 851 So. 2d 507 (Ala. 2002) (arbitrator did not explain rationale for his decisions and made no specific findings of fact; therefore, party seeking preclusion had not satisfied its burden of showing that issue had actually been decided in arbitration proceeding); Burlington Ditch Reservoir & Land Co. v. Metro Wastewater Reclamation Dist., 256 P.3d 645 (Colo. 2011) (court would not infer issue preclusion where issues were not identical and determinative and there was no evidence that parties litigated or court determined central issue in second action); Griffin v. Parker, 219 Conn. 363, 593 A.2d 124 (1991) (inconsistent jury verdict on state of mind in prior action makes it impossible to tell what was decided); Elwell v. Elwell, 947 A.2d 1136 (D.C. 2008) (when a prior judgment does not indicate clearly what issues were resolved, the result is that the opaque judgment fails to preclude relitigation); City of Johnson v. Christenson, 718 N.W.2d 290 (Iowa 2006) (in determining whether an issue has actually been decided in a prior action, an inference can be drawn that the issue was decided if it was necessary to support the judgment in the first action, and this inference can also satisfy the requirement that the issue be essential to the judgment in the prior action); Macomber v. MacQuinn-Tweedie, 2003 ME 121, 834 A.2d 131 (record in prior proceeding did not establish that court actually decided breach-of-contract issue; therefore, issue preclusion did not apply); Lee v. Musselshell Cnty., 2004 MT 64, 320 Mont. 294, 87 P.3d 423 (county's right of way interest in land was not precluded by judgment in prior quiet title action because evidence did not indicate that issue was adjudicated in prior action); State v. Eggleston, 164 Wash. 2d 61, 187 P.3d 233 (2008) (criminal case; collateral estoppel did not preclude state from litigating factual issue when jury in first case entered a general verdict of not guilty and that verdict could have been entered for a number of reasons); Doles v. State, 2007 WY 119, 163 P.3d 819 (acquittal of defendant on prior charges of delivery of drug paraphernalia and possession with intent to deliver drug paraphernalia did not result in issue preclusion that would prevent state from pursuing subsequent forfeiture action against items seized, because general verdict of jury did not reveal whether the jury determined that the seized items were not drug paraphernalia).

128. *See* RESTATEMENT (SECOND) OF JUDGMENTS § 77(2) (1982).

influenced or prejudiced.[129] Generally, judges are not allowed to testify to explain the basis for a prior judgment.[130] Nevertheless, courts have sometimes allowed judges to testify at a collateral proceeding when no other source exists to clarify the judgment.[131] Such testimony, however, can only clarify the judgment and not contradict it.[132] Nor can the judge's mental processes be questioned or cross-examined.[133] Thus, while extrinsic evidence may be admissible, only in compelling circumstances do most courts allow subsequent testimony by jurors or judges. Absent such testimony, determining what issues were decided in a prior action may sometimes be impossible.

(d) Supporting the Judgment in the First Action

Another basic rule also stems from the actual litigation requirement: an issue must support the judgment in the first action before the issue will be precluded in a later proceeding. The reason for this rule is that determinations not essential to the judgment "have the characteristics of dicta, and may not ordinarily be the subject of an appeal by the party against whom they were made."[134] Thus, no full and fair opportunity existed to litigate the finding before a tribunal that gave the issue full consideration in producing a decision.

Illustration 13-28. *P* sues *D* for negligence. *D* denies negligence and pleads contributory negligence as an affirmative defense. After a trial, the jury specifically finds *D* was negligent and *P* was contributorily negligent. The court enters a judgment for *D*. In a subsequent action, the finding of *D's* negligence is not precluded. The finding did not support the judgment in *D's* favor. The judgment in *D's* favor was supported only by the finding that *P* was contributorily negligent.

---

129. *See* FED. R. EVID. 606(b); *see also* Kazan v. Wolinski, 721 F.2d 911 (3d Cir. 1983) (holding the trial judge could consider a mid-deliberation jury note to ascertain the truth of the verdict, but the note could not be used in subsequent proceeding); Ohio-Sealy Mattress Mfg. Co. v. Kaplan, 90 F.R.D. 11 (N.D. Ill. 1980) (holding a juror's notes and affidavit were inadmissible to clarify the general verdict); *cf.* Katz v. Eli Lilly & Co., 84 F.R.D. 378 (E.D.N.Y. 1979) (holding that, where through permissible investigation apart from the compulsion of any court order a party demonstrates a factual basis for a belief that a judgment asserted against it as collateral estoppel was based on a compromise verdict, further inquiry into the facts by depositions of jurors shown to have information relevant to the issue is warranted).

130. *See, e.g.*, Grip-Pak, Inc. v. Illinois Tool Works, Inc., 694 F.2d 466 (7th Cir. 1982) (holding that the trial judge could not testify to explain verdict because the judgment should be the sole guide in interpreting the trial decision); Eaton v. Weaver Mfg. Co., 582 F.2d 1250 (10th Cir. 1978) (holding that the trial judge's subsequent remarks and the judge's letter to the attorneys in the case were not nunc pro tunc and were inadmissible because the record speaks for itself). Courts frequently cite the parol evidence rule as one justification for not allowing such testimony. *See* Timothy Travers, Annotation, *Judge as Witness in Cause Not on Trial Before Him*, 86 A.L.R.3D 633 (1978); *see also* Emerick v. Emerick, 28 Conn. App. 794, 613 A.2d 1351 (1992) (judge's testimony not allowed because the interpretation of the trial court judgment is limited to the express or implied intention within the written document).

131. *See, e.g.*, Woodward v. City of Waterbury, 113 Conn. 457, 155 A. 825 (1931).

132. *See, e.g.*, Schumert & Warfield v. Security Brewing Co., 199 F. 358 (E.D. La. 1912); *see also* Timothy Travers, Annotation, *Judge as Witness in Cause Not on Trial Before Him*, 86 A.L.R.3D 633 (1978).

133. *See* Gold v. Warden, 222 Conn. 312, 318-19, 610 A.2d 1153, 1156-57 (1992) (allowing testimony but limiting it to facts observed during trial); Brinkerhoff v. Home Trust & Sav. Bank, 109 Kan. 700, 708-09, 205 P. 779, 784 (1921) (a trial judge may testify to clarify the judgment but not about secret or unexpressed reasons for the decision); *cf.* United States v. Morgan, 313 U.S. 409, 61 S. Ct. 999, 85 L. Ed. 1429 (1941).

134. RESTATEMENT (SECOND) OF JUDGMENTS § 27 cmt. h (1982); *see* Dorrance v. Lee, 90 Haw. 143, 976 P.2d 904 (1999) (for issue preclusion to apply, the issue determined must be essential to the judgment in the first action); Jarosz v. Palmer, 436 Mass. 526, 766 N.E.2d 482 (2002) (issue determined in prior action was not essential to the plaintiff's claims and thus issue preclusion does not apply); Tyler v. Hannaford Bros., 161 N.H. 242, 13 A.3d 325 (2010) (compensation appeals board statement was akin to dicta and the judgment was not dependent on it.

The finding that *D* was negligent did not support the judgement because the finding was adverse to the party (*D*) who won the judgment. Preclusion does not apply because the winning party cannot ordinarily appeal a judgment. Thus, the winning party cannot correct any error that might have infected findings against the party.[135]

(e) Alternative Determinations

Traditionally, if a judgment were based upon the determination of two issues ("alternate determinations"), either of which standing alone would suffice to support the judgment, *both* issues were precluded from relitigation. The *Restatement (First) of Judgments* adopted this rule.[136]

Illustration 13-29. Assume in *Illustration 13-28* that the jury specifically had found that *D* was *not* negligent and that *P was* contributorily negligent. Under the traditional rule, both findings would be precluded from relitigation in a second action. Both findings are favorable to the winning party (*D*), and either finding alone would have supported the judgment. The first *Restatement* reasoned that "[i]t seems obvious that it should not be held that neither [finding] is material, and hence both should be held to be material."[137]

* * * * *

The *Restatement (Second) of Judgments* takes the opposite approach. If alternative determinations support the judgment in the first action, the judgment is not conclusive as to any of the determinations.[138] The *Restatement (Second)* reasons, first, that neither determination in the alternative may have been considered as carefully or as rigorously as if it were the only determination in support of the judgment. Second, "and of critical importance," the losing party may be dissuaded from appealing because of the likelihood that at least one of the determinations might be upheld. The judgment would thus be sustained against that party and the appeal would be rendered futile even if there was error in the other determination.[139] The reporters of the *Restatement (Second)* concede that the choice between the two approaches to preclusion is a close one. However, they are persuaded by the

---

135. *See* Bannister v. Commonwealth, 411 Mass. 130, 579 N.E.2d 163 (1991) (prior determination of liability made against defendant who obtained a favorable judgment in an action was not precluded in second suit). *cf.* Beechwood Restorative Care Ctr. v. Leeds, 436 F.3d 147 (2d Cir. 2006) (issue determined by administrative law judge in prior action not precluded because, although issue was "actually decided," the proponent of preclusion did not carry its burden of demonstrating that it was "necessary to support a valid and final judgment on the merits"); City of Johnston v. Christenson, 718 N.W.2d 290 (Iowa 2006) (in determining whether an issue was actually decided and essential to the judgment in a prior action, an inference can be drawn that it was if the issue was necessary to support the judgment and would have been essential to the judgment rendered).

136. RESTATEMENT (FIRST) OF JUDGMENTS § 68 cmt. n (1942).

137. *Id.*

138. RESTATEMENT (SECOND) OF JUDGMENTS § 27 cmt. i (1982). This situation should be compared to one in which two issues are decided that are both essential to the judgment. *See id.* cmt. g, illus. 12. In the later situation, both issues are precluded in a second action. For a discussion of the alternative determination problem, with emphasis on the conflict between federal courts of appeals on the problem, see Monica Renee Brownewell, Note, *Rethinking the Restatement View (Again!): Multiple Independent Holdings and the Doctrine of Issue Preclusion,* 37 VAL. U. L. REV. 879 (2003).

139. *See* RESTATEMENT (SECOND) OF JUDGMENTS § 27 cmt. i (1982).

reasoning of *Halpern v. Schwartz*,[140] which determined that preclusion should not apply to alternative determinations. If the judgment is appealed and the appellate court upholds one or both determinations, the *Restatement (Second)* reaches the opposite result. In such a case, the judgment is conclusive as to the determinations upheld.[141] The reason seems obvious: the party has not been deterred from appealing and has had a full and fair opportunity to litigate as to all issues.

In addition, the drafters of the *Restatement (Second)* were careful to distinguish the situation in which alternative determinations of two issues were involved from the situation "in which there are *alternative bases* for a determination that is essential to the judgment."[142] When alternative bases are involved, relitigation of the issues determined in the first action is precluded.[143]

Illustration 13-30. Assume that *P* brings an action to recover an installment of interest on a promissory note, the principal not yet being due. *D* defends on two grounds: (1) *D* was induced by fraud to execute the note and (2) *P* gave *D* a binding release of the obligation to pay interest. Findings in favor of *D* on both the fraud and release issues will not preclude *P* from relitigating the fraud issue if *D* raises that issue in a subsequent suit *for the principal of the note*. This situation is simply one of "alternative determinations," either of which standing alone would be sufficient to support the first judgment. On the other hand, the *Restatement (Second)* drafters state that in the above situation, if the second action is *for a second installment of interest*, the principal still not being due, the judgment in the first action is a complete defense to the second because the finding on the fraud and release issues were "alternative bases" for a determination essential to the judgment in the first action (*i.e.*, that no interest is due).[144]

* * * * *

The result in *Illustration 13-30* reflects the emphasis placed by the drafters on the availability of appeal as an important component of an adequate opportunity to be heard. When the second action is for the principal of the note, the fear of the *Restatement (Second)* drafters is that the plaintiff may have been deterred from

---

140. 426 F.2d 102 (2d Cir. 1970); *In re* Microsoft Corp. Antitrust Litig., 355 F.3d 322 (4th Cir. 2004) (trial court applied offensive collateral estoppel to preclude Microsoft from relitigating 350 factual findings made against it in prior proceeding that the district court found supported the judgment; this preclusion was error because some of the findings might have been alternative determinations); RESTATEMENT (SECOND) OF JUDGMENTS § 27, at 270 (1982) (reporter's note to cmt. i); *cf.* National Satellite Sports, Inc. v. Eliadis, Inc., 253 F.3d 900 (6th Cir. 2001) (refusing to decide whether alternative grounds for a judgment are each precluded or whether neither is precluded; holding, instead, that when one ground for the decision is clearly primary and the other only secondary, the secondary ground is not "necessary to the outcome" for purposes of issue preclusion and is, therefore, not precluded); Malloy v. Trombley, 50 N.Y.2d 46, 405 N.E.2d 213, 427 N.Y.S.2d 969 (1980). In *Malloy*, the New York Court of Appeals refused to adopt the flat rule of the *Restatement (Second)*. Instead, the court adopted a discretionary, case-by-case approach to determining whether alternative findings should be precluded. However, *Malloy* was a particularly strong case for nonpreclusion under the *Restatement (Second)*. In the first action, the issues of negligence and contributory negligence were both adjudicated against the plaintiff. In the second action, the plaintiff sued a different defendant. The finding of no negligence in the first action appeared unassailable, while the finding of contributory negligence appeared to have been thrown in by the trial judge in anticipation of an appeal. Thus, if the plaintiff had appealed, the appeal would likely have failed on the negligence issue. Furthermore, the issue of contributory negligence may well not have been considered as carefully by the trial judge as it would have if the finding of no negligence had not been so solid.

141. *See* RESTATEMENT (SECOND) OF JUDGMENTS § 27 cmt. o (1982).

142. *Id.* § 27 cmt. i (emphasis added).

143. *See id.*

144. *See id.* illus. 15 & 16.

appealing because one of the determinations could be upheld on appeal, even though the other one was erroneous. The result would be that the judgment would be affirmed. Thus, if the fraud determination happened to be the erroneous one, while the release determination was correct and, therefore, irreversible on appeal, the plaintiff would be deprived of an adequate opportunity to challenge the fraud determination on appeal. Consequently, the plaintiff should be allowed to relitigate the issue of fraud in the second action to recover the principal.

This rationale is not applicable when the second suit is for a second installment of interest. If either of the determinations in the first action is correct, the inevitable conclusion is that *no interest is due* because both the fraud and release determinations are relevant to a second suit for another installment of interest. Therefore, if either of the determinations is sound, a second suit for interest should not be permitted. If the plaintiff did not appeal because only one of the determinations was correct, logically no second action for the interest should be permitted. If the plaintiff did not appeal because both determinations were correct, the same is true. If both determinations were erroneous, and the plaintiff still did not appeal, the plaintiff cannot be heard to complain about preclusion produced by the plaintiff's own failure to resort to an appeal that would have been successful.

The impossibility of determining from the position of the second action which finding is solid and which erroneous, of course, creates the dilemma that makes this distinction necessary. Nevertheless, it is questionable whether the average lawyer or judge will appreciate the distinction. The drafters may well be "creating," rather than "restating," law that is too complex for ordinary practice.

2. Exceptions

Like claim preclusion, numerous exceptions to the basic rule of issue preclusion exit. The exceptions focus upon the ability of a party to have obtained a full and fair adjudication in the first action. The absence of a full and fair opportunity renders the principle of finality inapplicable because that principle is based upon the assumption that a party has had one adequate opportunity to present the merits of the party's case.[145]

(a) Inability to Obtain Review

Issue preclusion does not operate when a party is precluded as a matter of law from obtaining appellate review of a determination made in the first action. The inability to correct error in the judgment renders the opportunity to litigate less than adequate. This exception does not apply, however, when appellate review is available, but not sought by the losing party.[146]

---

145. *See* section A *supra* ("Introduction").

146. *See* RESTATEMENT (SECOND) OF JUDGMENTS § 28(1) cmt. a (1982); Askin v. District of Columbia, 728 A.2d 665 (D.C. 1999) (issue preclusion does not prevent a party from litigating issues when the party could not appeal from non-final and non-appealable orders); Glidden Co. v. Lumbermens Mut. Cas. Co., 2006-Ohio-6553, 112 Ohio St. 3d 470, 861 N.E.2d 109 (issues must have been determined by a final, appealable order for issue preclusion to prevent parties from relitigating those issues in a subsequent action); *cf.* Morris B. Chapman

Illustration 13-31. *P* sues *D* for negligence. *P* wins a verdict and judgment for $1,000. If there is a minimum jurisdictional amount in controversy of $2,000 on the state appellate court's jurisdiction, *D* would be precluded from obtaining a reversal of the judgment. Consequently, *D* would not be precluded from relitigating the determination in a subsequent proceeding.[147]

Illustration 13-32. *P* sues *D* for a declaratory judgment that a statute being enforced by *D* against *P* is unconstitutional. The trial court finds the statute constitutional as applied and enters judgment for *D*. *P* appeals, but the appeal is dismissed for mootness because *P* has ceased the activities prohibited by the statute. However, the judgment of the trial court is not vacated. Subsequently, *P* again undertakes the activities prohibited by the statute. *P* sues *D* again for a declaratory judgment that the statute is unconstitutional. The judgment in the first action does not preclude *P* from relitigating the constitutional issue because *P* was unable as a matter of law to obtain appellate review of the first determination.[148]

(b) Issues of Law

Another exception exists in some cases when the issue determined is one of law. Although issue preclusion applies to issues of law as well as to issues of fact, in some circumstances preclusion on an issue of law can operate unfairly. One such circumstance arises when the claims between the parties in the two actions are substantially unrelated. In this situation, it is thought unfair to bind the parties for all time by a rule of law announced in the first action.[149]

Illustration 13-33. *P* sues *City D* for personal injuries allegedly resulting from *D's* negligence. *D* defends on grounds of sovereign immunity, and this defense is sustained. Several years later, *P* sues *D* again for personal injuries inflicted in an unrelated accident occurring after the judgment in the first proceeding. Obviously, it would be unfair to prevent *P*, on the ground that the issue is res judicata, from arguing that the doctrine of sovereign immunity should be abolished, when *D's*

& Assocs., Ltd. v. Kitzman, 193 Ill. 2d 560, 739 N.E.2d 1263 (2000) (claim preclusion inapplicable to law firm that was not party to prior lawsuit or in privity with party; issue preclusion inapplicable to firm, which litigated fee issue because it was prevented as a matter of law from appealing adverse determination because it was not a party).

147. RESTATEMENT (SECOND) OF JUDGMENTS § 28(1) cmt. a (1982).

148. *Id.*; State Bldg. Venture v. O'Donnell, 239 Ill.2d 151, 940 N.E.2d 1122 (2010) (prior declaratory judgment action dismissed as moot; no issue preclusion effect).

149. *See* Bingaman v. Department of Treasury, 127 F.3d 1431 (Fed. Cir. 1997) (exception to issue preclusion for changes in the applicable legal context applicable to changes in the interpretation of a statutory standard by an administrative agency); Hackley v. Hackley, 426 Mich. 582, 395 N.W.2d 906 (1986) (issue of paternity is one of fact, not law). With the *Hackley* case, compare Dixon v. Pouncy, 979 P.2d 520 (Alaska 1999), in which the court allowed an attack on a paternity determination in a prior action under Alaska's equivalent of Federal Rule 60(b). The court held that Rule 60(b) attacks were "direct" rather than "collateral" attacks on judgments, so issue preclusion did not apply. Of course, one of the grounds for a Rule 60(b) attack must exist, and the dissenters argued that a Rule 60(b) attack was improper in the case because (1) it was foreseeable at the time of the initial proceeding that the party attacking the judgment was not the father and he actually contested the issue; and (2) Rule 60(b)(5) requires a change in either legal or factual conditions, which were not present because there was no change in law and the availability of a DNA test could not be considered a change in facts. *See also* Elysium Inst., Inc. v. County of Los Angeles, 232 Cal. App. 3d 408, 283 Cal. Rptr. 688 (1991) (county not prevented by issue preclusion from relitigating constitutionality of zoning ordinance pertaining to nudist camps when judgment in prior action arose out of different transaction and different ordinance).

other adversaries, who have not been parties to prior litigation, are free to argue that the rule should be overturned.[150]

* * * * *

For reasons similar to those given in the *Illustration 13-33*, it may be appropriate to allow relitigation in another situation involving a prior determination of issues of law. Sometimes even when the claims in two actions are substantially related, a new determination of an issue will be necessary to take account of an intervening change of law or to prevent an inequitable administration of the laws.[151]

Illustration 13-34. *State P* sues *D* to enjoin *D* from engaging in certain allegedly illegal business operations. *D* defends on the grounds that the business operations are legal. The court sustains this defense. Subsequently, *State P* sues *C*, a competitor of *D*, to enjoin *C* from engaging in the same kind of business. The highest court of the state holds that the business activities are illegal. The state should not be precluded from suing *D* again. To allow *D* to engage in activities from which *D's* competitors (and others) would be prohibited would be an inequitable administration of the laws as between persons similarly situated.[152]

(c) "Mediate Data" Versus "Ultimate Facts"

Traditionally, courts distinguished between the preclusive effect of a determination on matters of "ultimate fact" as opposed to "mediate data." An "ultimate fact" in an action is the logical conclusion that is drawn from the evidence produced. "Mediate data," or "evidentiary facts," are the steps leading to the "ultimate fact."

Illustration 13-35. In an action for personal injuries resulting from an automobile accident, the negligence of the defendant is an "ultimate fact." The evidence that the defendant was driving at an excessive speed is a "mediate datum."

* * * * *

A finding as to an "ultimate fact" could be used in a subsequent action to establish either an "ultimate fact" or a "mediate datum" in that proceeding, but a finding on a "mediate datum" could not be used at all in a subsequent proceeding.[153]

---

150. *See* RESTATEMENT (SECOND) OF JUDGMENTS § 28(2) cmt. b, illus. 2 (1982).

151. *See id.* cmt. c. At least one court has held that an exception exists to the doctrine of claim preclusion when there is an intervening change in the law that would validate a claim that has failed under prior law. *See* Statler v. Catalano, 293 Ill. App. 3d 483, 691 N.E.2d 384 (1997). Such a holding is clearly incorrect.

152. *See* RESTATEMENT (SECOND) OF JUDGMENTS § 28(2)(b) cmt. c, illus. 3 (1982). *But see* United States v. Stauffer Chem. Co., 464 U.S. 165, 104 S. Ct. 575, 78 L. Ed. 2d 388 (1984) (mutual defensive issue preclusion applicable against government on issue of law). In addition to the situations discussed in the text, preclusion on issues of law is often limited in successive litigation between the government and different parties for fear that binding the government by issue preclusion would thwart the development of important issues of law by freezing the issue as it was decided in the first case to proceed to judgment. *See* United States v. Mendoza, 464 U.S. 154, 104 S. Ct. 568, 78 L. Ed. 2d 379 (1984); Sikorsky Aircraft Corp. v. Commissioner of Revenue Servs., 297 Conn. 540, 1 A.3d 1033 (2010) (nonmutual issue preclusion may not be invoked against the government); Arcadia Unified Sch. Dist. v. State Dep't of Educ., 2 Cal. 4th 251, 825 P.2d 438, 5 Cal. Rptr. 2d 545 (1992). *See generally* A. Leo Levin & Susan M. Leeson, *Issue Preclusion Against the United States Government*, 70 IOWA L. REV. 113 (1984); Allan D. Vestal, *Relitigation by Federal Agencies: Conflict, Concurrence and Synthesis of Judicial Policies*, 55 N.C. L. REV. 123 (1977).

153. *See* RESTATEMENT (FIRST) OF JUDGMENTS § 68 cmt. p (1942); The Evergreens v. Nunan, 141 F.2d 927 (2d Cir. 1944). Commentators have criticized the *Evergreens* rule. *See, e.g.*, Maurice Rosenberg, *Collateral Estoppel in New York*, 44 ST. JOHN'S L. REV. 165, 182 (1969); Charles A. Heckman, *Collateral Estoppel as the Answer to Multiple Litigation Problems in Federal Tax Law: Another View of* Sunnen *and* The Evergreens, 19

The distinction between "ultimate facts" and "mediate data" was never entirely clear, and the rules really seemed to be directed at assuring that the issue in question was litigated in the first action with a full awareness of its implications for future proceedings. The modern approach, adopted by the *Restatement (Second)*,[154] directly asks whether it was sufficiently foreseeable at the time of the first action that the issue would arise in a subsequent proceeding.[155] If so, one can be relatively assured that the issue was litigated fully in the first proceeding. If not, relitigation of the issue is called for because an adequate opportunity to litigate the issue has not been afforded.[156]

(d) Differences in the Burden of Proof

Another exception to the rule of issue preclusion exists when the party against whom preclusion is sought had a heavier burden of persuasion on the issue in the first action than in the second action. An exception also exists when the adversary has a heavier burden than the party had in the first action.[157] The burden of persuasion has a potentially significant effect on the outcome of an action. When it shifts between two actions, the ordinary rules of issue preclusion should not apply.[158]

CASE W. RES. L. REV. 230 (1968).

154. *See* RESTATEMENT (SECOND) OF JUDGMENTS § 27 cmt. j (1982).

155. *See, e.g.*, Hyman v. Regenstein, 258 F.2d 502, 510-11 (5th Cir. 1958).

156. *See* RESTATEMENT (SECOND) OF JUDGMENTS § 27 cmt. j, § 28(5)(b) cmt. i (1982). The Nebraska Supreme Court, despite generally adhering to the scheme of the RESTATEMENT (SECOND), appears to have resurrected the ultimate-fact, mediate datum distinction. In Stevenson v. Wright, 273 Neb. 789, 733 N.W.2d 559 (2007), the court held that a prior judgment of conviction in a county court for careless, reckless, or negligent driving in violation of a local ordinance was not preclusive in a subsequent civil action. The court employed the "ultimate fact" rhetoric, *see* 273 Neb. at 796, 733 N.W.2d at 565, and stated that the criminal judgment was not preclusive of "liability" in the civil action because other issues, such as proximate cause and comparative negligence would be involved in the civil proceeding. Of course, this is beside the point. If an issue was necessarily involved and decided in the criminal proceeding to produce the judgment of conviction, it is irrelevant that other issues remain to be adjudicated in the civil action. In the absence of some other, legitimate exception to issue preclusion, the issues necessarily decided and also relevant to the civil action should be precluded from relitigation.

157. *See* RESTATEMENT (SECOND) OF JUDGMENTS § 28(4) (1982); State v. Wetzel, 2011 ND 218, 806 N.W.2d 193 (prior acquittal in criminal action in which burden of proof was beyond a reasonable doubt did not have issue preclusion effect in subsequent action to revoke probation in which burden was preponderance of the evidence).

158. *See, e.g.*, United States v. One Assortment of 89 Firearms, 465 U.S. 354, 104 S. Ct. 1099, 79 L. Ed. 2d 361 (1984). *Cf. In re* R.H., 2010 VT 95, 14 A.3d 267 (2010) (issue of abuse not precluded because determined under different standard in first proceeding). *But see* Office of Disciplinary Counsel v. Kiesewetter, 585 Pa. 477, 889 A.2d 47 (2005) (issue of fraud adjudicated against attorney in prior civil action was identical to issue of fraud in subsequent state disbarment proceeding; burden of proof on issue of fraud was the same, and burden of proof exception to issue preclusion was not applicable because burden of proof on fraud issue was the same, even though in bifurcated damages proceeding, burden of proof was only by a preponderance of the evidence on issue of damages); *cf.* State v. Oliver, 856 So. 2d 328 (Miss. 2003) (no issue preclusion when prior probation revocation proceeding in which criminal defendant was successful proceeded under more relaxed evidentiary and procedural rules and subsequent trial on indictment placed *heavier burden* of proof beyond a reasonable doubt on state!); New Jersey Div. of Youth & Fam. Servs. v. R.D., 207 N.J. 88, 23 A.3d 352 (2011) (unless parties are on notice that proceedings for the determination of abuse or neglect are to be conducted under higher "clear and convincing evidence" standard, such proceedings may not be given a preclusive effect in later proceedings). A criminal prosecution resulting in a judgment of conviction beyond a reasonable doubt can be used to establish facts essential to the conviction that arise in a later civil proceeding. *See, e.g.*, Doe v. Tobias, 715 N.E.2d 829 (Ind. 1999) (criminal conviction can be used in subsequent civil proceeding as offensive collateral estoppel). This is, of course, the opposite of the situation discussed in the text, because in the criminal proceeding the burden of proof is heavier on the state than it is on the plaintiff in the subsequent civil action. However, in addition, for the criminal conviction to be useful in an issue preclusion sense, the doctrine of mutuality of estoppel discussed in subsection 3, *infra*, must not exist in the judicial system in which the criminal judgment is rendered.

Illustration 13-36. *P* sues *D* for personal injuries resulting from an automobile accident. *P* alleges that *D* was negligent. In the state in which *P* brings the action, the plaintiff in a negligence suit is required to plead and prove the plaintiff's freedom from contributory negligence. After a trial, the court holds that *P* has failed to discharge that burden and finds *P* contributorily negligent. The court enters a judgment for *D* based on this finding. *D* then sues *P* for personal injuries received in the same accident. *D's* action is permitted because the state has no compulsory counterclaim rule. *D* contends that the judgment in the first action conclusively establishes *P's* negligence in the second. *D's* argument is not sound because *P* had a significantly heavier burden of proof in the first action than *P* will have in the second action.[159]

(e) Nature and Quality of the Procedures in the Original Action

Another exception to issue preclusion occurs when "differences [exist] in the quality or extensiveness of the procedures followed in the two courts or . . . factors [are present] relating to the allocation of jurisdiction between them."[160] Sometimes, the first action is brought in a court without subject-matter jurisdiction to consider claims presented in another court with broader jurisdiction. This factor alone should not prevent issue preclusion from operating. However, the determination in the first proceeding should not be binding in the second action when (1) the procedures available in the first court do not allow a full opportunity to litigate the issue in the action or (2) the legislative allocation of jurisdiction between the courts in the two actions is designed, for policy reasons, to prevent consideration of an issue "directly" by the first court.[161] This exception can operate as between (1) courts of the same state, (2) courts of different states, or (3) courts of a state and a federal court.[162]

Illustration 13-37. *P* sues *D* in a small claims court for property damage arising out of an automobile accident. The small claims court has a jurisdictional ceiling on its competence of $500 and operates informally without pleadings, counsel, or rules of evidence. The court finds that *D* was negligent and enters a judgment for *P*. Subsequently, *D* sues *P* in a state court of general jurisdiction for personal injuries received in the same accident. In the second action, the judgment in the small claims court does not establish conclusively that *D* was contributorily negligent. The quality and extensiveness of the procedures in the first court did not

---

159. *See* RESTATEMENT (SECOND) OF JUDGMENTS § 28(4) cmt. f, illus. 10 (1982).

160. *Id.* § 28(3); *cf.* Hackley v. Hackley, 426 Mich. 582, 395 N.W.2d 906 (1986) (successive actions in *same court*; change in rules of evidence between the two actions; rule existing in prior action did not prevent litigation of issue in question; therefore, issue preclusion operates).

161. *Cf.* Hurlbert v. Charles, 238 Ill. 2d 248, 938 N.E.2d 507 (2010) (although ordinary elements of issue preclusion satisfied, giving preclusive effect to results of statutory summary suspension hearing would render the legislative purpose behind the summary proceeding meaningless because it would encourage more extensive presentation of evidence in proceeding by state).

162. *See* RESTATEMENT (SECOND) OF JUDGMENTS § 28(3) cmt. d & e (1982); Town of Delafield v. Winkelman, 2004 WI 17, 269 Wis. 2d 109, 675 N.W.2d 470 (issue preclusion did not apply because procedures in previous certiorari review proceeding did not permit consideration of equitable arguments, whereas in enforcement action for injunctive relief court can consider all equitable issues); *see also* section F *infra* ("Complications Produced by the Federal System").

(arguably) give *D* a full and fair opportunity to litigate. This conclusion is based on issue preclusion, not on claim preclusion. It might be argued that if *D* could not counterclaim in action No. 1, *D* should not be precluded in action No. 2. However, this factor is relevant only to *claim* preclusion, *not* to issue preclusion. The doctrines must be analyzed separately. Even if claim preclusion does not apply, issue preclusion may.[163]

(f) Injustice in Particular Cases

Another exception to the rule of issue preclusion arises anytime the circumstances surrounding the first action did not afford "an adequate opportunity or incentive to obtain a full and fair adjudication in the initial action."[164] For example, a party may have had a physical or mental disability that impeded effective litigation. The jury's verdict in the first action may have resulted from a compromise. In addition, the amount in controversy in the first action may have been small in relation to the amount in the second action, resulting in a lack of incentive to litigate the issue vigorously in the first action.[165]

Illustration 13-38. *P* sues *D* for $50.00 in property damage resulting from an automobile accident. *P* alleges that *D* was negligent and *D* denies negligence. After a trial to the court, the court finds *D* negligent and enters judgment for *P*. Subsequently, *D* sues *P* for $10,000 in damages for personal injuries received in the same accident. *D's* action is permitted because the jurisdiction does not have a compulsory counterclaim rule. *P* contends that the judgment in the first action establishes *D's* negligence conclusively for purposes of the second action. *P's* argument is not sound. Because of the small amount involved in the first action, *D* did not have an adequate incentive to litigate fully the issue of *D's* negligence. This situation should be distinguished from *Illustration 13-37* in which it was specifically stated that the action had been brought in a small claims court. In this illustration, there is no indication that the court in the first action did not afford the quality or extensiveness of procedures holding preclusion applicable.[166] Therefore,

---

163. *See* RESTATEMENT (SECOND) OF JUDGMENTS § 28(3) cmt. d, illus. 7 (1982); *cf.* Board of Educ. v. Gray, 806 S.W.2d 400 (Ky. Ct. App. 1991) (procedures in prior unemployment compensation proceeding did not afford full and fair opportunity for defendant to litigate). In Henriksen v. Gleason, 263 Neb. 840, 643 N.W.2d 652 (2002), the court held that issue preclusion did not apply because the first action was in a small claims court and the second action was in a court of general jurisdiction. Thus, the quality and extensiveness of the procedures in the two actions differed substantively, and the exception in § 28(4) was applicable. Unfortunately, the court failed to observe that issue preclusion was not applicable under the basic rules of preclusion. The first action resulted in a default judgment for failure of the defendant to appear. Thus, no issues were actually litigated and determined in the action.

164. RESTATEMENT (SECOND) OF JUDGMENTS § 28(5)(c) (1982); *see* Mullins v. State, 294 S.W.3d 529 (Tenn. 2009) (although issue of doctor's negligence was actually litigated and determined in prior federal proceeding, personal representative of estate did not have full and fair opportunity to litigate issue in proceeding because of limits on her ability to recover damages against doctor in that proceeding).

165. *See* RESTATEMENT (SECOND) OF JUDGMENTS § 28(5)(c) cmt. j (1982).

166. *See id.* § 28(5)(c).

the lack of incentive to litigate in the first action is the only basis for avoiding preclusion.[167]

* * * * *

This general "injustice" exception can be criticized. The principle of finality supporting claim and issue preclusion aims at achieving a just and efficient legal order by preventing multiple litigation over the same basic matter. However, if exceptions become too numerous or too broad, the danger is great that this important objective will be undermined. Despite the value of an open-ended standard in preventing injustice in particular cases, such a standard may undermine the effectiveness of the entire doctrine of issue preclusion by encouraging widespread litigation over the preclusive effects of judgments in circumstances too numerous to foresee when the standard was originally adopted. Should this result, greater injustice than justice may flow from the exception.[168]

3. Nonmutual Preclusion

(a) The Mutuality of Estoppel Rule and Traditional Exceptions to the Rule

Traditionally, issue preclusion did not operate against a party to a first action when the party sued, or was sued by, someone not involved in the first action.[169] Under this *mutuality of estoppel* rule, all parties to an action had to be bound by the judgment for any to be bound.[170] Because a nonparty cannot ordinarily be bound by a judgment, the mutuality rule prevented a party to the prior action from being bound either. Today, many jurisdictions have abolished this rule.[171]

Illustration 13-39. Suppose a three-car collision occurred between *P-1*, *D*, and *P-2*. If *P-1* sued *D* and recovered based upon *D's* negligence, the finding against *D* would preclude relitigation of *D's* negligence in any subsequent action between *P-1* and *D*. However, if *P-2* sued *D*, issue preclusion would not operate

---

167. *See* Johnson v. Union Pac. R.R., 352 Ark. 534, 104 S.W.3d 745 (2003) (nonmutual offensive issue preclusion did not prevent railroad from raising defense where railroad did not have adequate incentive to litigate in first action; railroad withdrew its brief on cross-appeal of finding on issue because it was convinced that the appellate court would affirm on an alternative ground raised by plaintiff's direct appeal and thus railroad did not have adequate incentive to litigate cross-appeal; alternative holding); Hackley v. Hackley, 426 Mich. 582, 395 N.W.2d 906 (1986) (section 28(5)(c) does not create exception unless there is a compelling showing of unfairness in first action; showing not made in paternity action due to restrictive rule of evidence in first action, when the putative father had other means of litigating paternity issue).

168. *Compare* RESTATEMENT (SECOND) OF JUDGMENTS §§ 27-28 (1982) *with* RESTATEMENT (FIRST) OF JUDGMENTS §§ 68-71 (1942). In Faigin v. Kelly, 184 F.3d 67 (1st Cir. 1999), the court indicated substantial doubt whether a Rule 11 hearing in a prior action can ever provide a satisfactory basis for issue preclusion because of the way in which such hearings are circumscribed. In the prior action, the plaintiff had been sanctioned for failure to make an adequate factual investigation of the claim, and the court indicated that this did not mean that no objective facts actually existed to support the claim. However, as the court admitted, this really means the issues are not the same between the first and second actions, which provides an independent basis for refusing preclusion.

169. *See* RESTATEMENT (FIRST) OF JUDGMENTS § 93(b) (1942).

170. *See* Council of Co-Owners for Lakeshore Resort v. Glyneu, LLC, 367 Ark. 397, 240 S.W.3d 600 (2006) (nonparty to first action who was not in privity with party could not be bound issue preclusion).

171. But not all. *See, e.g.*, E.C. v. Katz, 731 So. 2d 1268 (Fla. 1999) (mutuality rule exists in Florida; identity of parties is required before issue preclusion can be used defensively against plaintiff in prior action); *cf.* O'Nesti v. DeBartolo Realty Corp., 2007-Ohio-1102, 113 Ohio St. 3d 59, 862 N.E.2d 803 (a stranger to the prior judgment, being not bound thereby, is not entitled to rely upon its effect under the claim of res judicata or collateral estoppel).

against *D*. Both parties to a proceeding had to be bound or neither was bound. *P-2* would not be bound by the judgment in the first action because *P-2* was not a party to that proceeding and had no opportunity to litigate the issues raised. As a result, under the mutuality of estoppel rule, *D* also could not be bound by the finding of negligence either, even though *D* had an adequate opportunity to litigate the issues in the first proceeding.[172]

* * * * *

Even when the rule of mutuality of estoppel generally prevailed, exceptions existed. One exception was recognized when an indemnitor-indemnitee relationship existed between the party to be bound and the nonparty.[173]

Illustration 13-40. Suppose an employee was driving the employer's car on the employer's business when the employee collided with *P*. Under the law applicable to the case, if the employee's negligence caused the accident, *P* is entitled to sue (1) the employer alone, (2) the employee alone, or (3) both of them together for *P's* injuries. If *P* sues the employer and recovers, the employer is entitled to be indemnified by the employee for the amount the employer had to pay to *P*. However, if *P* sued the employee first and the employee won, a difficulty was created. If *P* then could sue the employer and win, one of two unacceptable consequences would follow. If the employer could sue the employee for indemnity and recover, the employee would be deprived of the benefit of the judgment the employee won in the suit with *P*. On the other hand, if the employer was not permitted to recover from the employee, the employer would be deprived of the right of indemnity. To avoid this difficulty, an exception was created to the mutuality rule to allow an employer to plead the judgment in the employee's favor as res judicata in *P's* suit against the employer.[174] However, this exception did not exist if *P* sued the employer first and the employer won on the ground that there had been no negligence. Because the employer owed no duty of indemnity to the employee, the unacceptable consequences described above were not present when *P* sued the employee in a second suit. Thus, the mutuality of estoppel rule operated in full force, and *P* was not bound by the finding of no negligence.[175]

* * * * *

Another exception existed when the plaintiff in the initial action sued for a tort or a breach of contract and lost. If the court found no tort or breach and the plaintiff then sued a second defendant for inducing the tort or breach of contract that was the subject of the first suit, the second defendant could plead judgment in the first action as res judicata in the second proceeding. It was unacceptable to allow the second action to continue when the first proceeding had negated the existence of the tort or breach upon which the second action was based.[176]

---

172. RESTATEMENT (FIRST) OF JUDGMENTS § 93(b) cmt. d, illus. 7 (1942); *see, e.g.*, Dual & Assocs., Inc. v. Wells, 241 Va. 542, 403 S.E.2d 354 (1991).

173. *See* RESTATEMENT (FIRST) OF JUDGMENTS § 96 (1942).

174. *See id.* § 96 cmt. d, illus. 1.

175. *See id.* § 96 cmt. j, illus. 9. For an example of a case in which claim preclusion operated in favor of a nonparty, see Hundley v. J.F. Spann Timber, Inc., 962 So. 2d 187 (Ala. 2007) (if all tort claims against an agent are dismissed with prejudice, a subsequent tort action against the principal on the same facts will be precluded).

176. *See* RESTATEMENT (FIRST) OF JUDGMENTS § 99 (1942).

(b) Abolition of the Mutuality Rule

Direct challenge to the mutuality of estoppel rule first occurred in *Bernhard v. Bank of America National Trust & Savings Association.*[177] In *Bernhard* and many other cases abolishing the mutuality of estoppel rule, the judgment in the first action was used *defensively* in the second action against the person who was the plaintiff in the first suit.

Illustration 13-41. Suppose that in the first action *P* sues *D-1*, and *D-1* wins. In the second action, *P* sues *D-2*. Abolishing the doctrine of mutuality is easy in this case because the party being bound (*P*) picked the opponent, the time, and the court for suit in the first action. The judgment is simply being used to prevent *P* from trying again against a different adversary (*D-2*).[178]

* * * * *

However, more difficult cases exist.

Illustration 13-42. Suppose instead that *P* sues *D-1*, and *P* wins. If *D-1* then sues *D-2*, a case is presented in which, if mutuality of estoppel is abolished, the judgment in the first action would be used defensively in the second action against *D-1* (the defendant in the first action). Because *D-1* did not choose the opponent, the time, or the court for suit in the first action, it might be argued that the judgment should not bind *D-1*. On the other hand, the judgment still is being used only defensively to prevent the loser in the first action from affirmatively recovering in a second proceeding.

Illustration 13-43. When *P-1* sues *D-1*, *D-1* wins, and then *P-2* sues *P-1*, an even harder case is presented. The judgment would be used *offensively* if mutuality of estoppel has been abolished. However, the judgment would be used against the plaintiff in the first action (*P-1*), who picked the opponent, the time, and the place of suit. Nevertheless, if *P-1* knows issue preclusion can be used offensively against *P-1*, *P-1* may well be deterred from bringing the first suit. The doctrine of issue preclusion is supposed to cut down the amount of litigation, but not at the expense of discouraging persons from bringing what they believe are otherwise legitimate actions.

Illustration 13-44. The most difficult case of all in which to justify the abolition of the mutuality of estoppel rule is when issue preclusion is used offensively against a defendant in the initial action. Suppose that *P-1* sues *D*, and *P-1* wins. *P-2* then sues *D*. If mutuality of estoppel is abolished, the judgment will be used offensively against one who did not choose the opponent, the court, the time, nor the place of suit in the first action. This situation arises when a mass disaster occurs—for example, an airline crash, the collapse of a hotel walkway, or a fire. If the defendant loses the first suit and the mutuality rule has been abolished, enormous liability may result from the judgment. "The result is great disparity in litigating risks. [Thus,] it puts great pressure on a defendant who faces multiple

---

177. 19 Cal. 2d 807, 122 P.2d 892 (1942).

178. For a discussion of the application of these rules in a comparative negligence context, see David Polin, Annotation, *Comparative Negligence: Judgment Allocating Fault in Action Against Less Than All Potential Defendants as Precluding Subsequent Action Against Parties Not Sued in Original Action*, 4 A.L.R.5TH 753 (1992).

claimants to settle with each one rather than risk an adverse determination by going to trial."[179]

(c) Deciding when a Party Has Had a Full and Fair Opportunity to Litigate an Issue

Despite the problems involved with abolishing mutuality of estoppel, the modern tendency, exemplified by § 29 of the *Restatement (Second) of Judgments*, is to eliminate mutuality for all kinds of actions. The central focus is whether the party to be bound by the judgment had a full and fair opportunity to litigate in the first proceeding. Section 29 lists several factors that are used to make this determination. These factors operate in addition to the ordinary exceptions to issue preclusion applicable in subsequent litigation between the same parties.[180]

(i) Ordinary Exceptions Applicable

Recall that a factor listed by § 28 of the *Restatement (Second)* is whether an adequate incentive to litigate existed in the first action.

Illustration 13-45. *P-1* sues *D* in a small claims court for $100 in property damage arising from an automobile accident. After a trial, the court enters judgment for *P-1*, specifically finding that *D* was negligent. Subsequently, *P-2* sues *D* in a court of general jurisdiction in the state. *P-2* seeks $50,000 for personal injuries received in the same automobile accident. Even if the rule of mutuality has been abolished, *D* is not precluded from relitigating the issue of negligence by the judgment in *P-1 v. D*. Issue preclusion would not operate here even if the second action were between *P-1* and *D*. *D* did not have an adequate incentive to litigate in *P-1 v. D* because of the small amount involved in that action.[181]

(ii) Incompatibility with a Scheme of Remedies

According to § 29 of the *Restatement (Second)*, issue preclusion is inappropriate in subsequent litigation with a third party when "[t]reating [an] issue as conclusively determined [by a prior judgment] would be incompatible with [the] scheme of administering the remedies in the actions involved."[182]

---

179. FLEMING JAMES, JR. ET AL., CIVIL PROCEDURE § 11.25, at 718 (5th ed. 2001); Modiri v. 1342 Restaurant Group, Inc., 904 A.2d 391 (D.C. 2006) (under nonmutual offensive collateral estoppel, plaintiff seeks to preclude a defendant from relitigating the issues upon which the defendant previously litigated and lost against another plaintiff); District of Columbia v. Gould, 852 A.2d 50 (D.C. 2004) (offensive use of collateral estoppel allowed when a plaintiff seeks to estop a defendant from relitigating the issues that the defendant previously litigated and lost against another plaintiff); and Exotics Hawaii-Kona, Inc. v. E.I. Dupont De Nemours & Co., 104 Haw. 358, 90 P.3d 250 (2004) (non-mutual offensive issue preclusion is recognized under Hawaii law); *cf.* American Fam. Mut. Ins. Co. v. Savickas, 193 Ill. 2d 378, 739 N.E.2d 445 (2000) (criminal defendant could be bound by issue preclusion in subsequent suit by plaintiff who was stranger to the prior action).

180. *See* RESTATEMENT (SECOND) OF JUDGMENTS § 29 (1982). Recall that the exceptions to the rule of issue preclusion are found in § 28 of the *Restatement (Second)*; *see* subsection 2 for a discussion of exceptions to issue preclusion *supra*.

181. *See Illustration 13-38 supra*; RESTATEMENT (SECOND) OF JUDGMENTS § 28(5)(c) (1982).

182. *See* RESTATEMENT (SECOND) OF JUDGMENTS § 29(1) (1982).

Illustration 13-46. *P-1* sues *D Airline* for the wrongful death of *P-1's* spouse in a crash of one of *D's* airplanes. After trial, the court enters a judgment for *P-1* on the grounds that *D* was negligent and that *D's* negligence caused the fatal crash. Subsequently, *P-2* sues *D* for the wrongful death of *P-2's* spouse resulting from the same crash. The wrongful death statute applicable to the crash provides that a judgment rendered against a defendant in a mass disaster case shall have no preclusive effect in a subsequent action arising out of the same disaster. *D* may relitigate the issue of negligence in the action by *P-2*, notwithstanding the unfavorable judgment in *P-1's* action against *D*.[183]

(iii) Differences in Procedural Opportunities

Issue preclusion should not be applied if the issue determined in the first action would likely be decided differently in the second action because "the forum in the second action affords the party against whom preclusion is asserted procedural opportunities in the presentation and determination of the [case] that were not [present] in the first" action.[184]

Illustration 13-47. *P* sues *D-1* in a summary proceeding to recover on a note executed by *D-1* and cosigned by *D-2*. *D-1* defends on the ground of part payment of the note. Assume that *P* loses on this issue. In a subsequent action by *P* against *D-2*, the fact that *P* was compelled to litigate in a summary proceeding may be considered in determining whether *P* should be precluded on the issue of part payment.[185]

(iv) Inconsistency with Another Determination

In determining whether issue preclusion should be applied, it should be considered whether "the determination relied on . . . was itself inconsistent with another determination of the same issue" in an earlier action.[186] This factor affords some protection to the defendant in mass disaster litigation who successfully defends one or more actions with different plaintiffs before losing an action. However, the amount of protection afforded by the factor is questionable, given the strong incentive for the defendant to settle, rather than litigate, and the ability of

---

183. *See id.* § 29 cmt. c. *But cf.* Clayton Act § 5(a), 15 U.S.C. § 16(a) (Section 5(a) of the Clayton Act provides that judgments in government antitrust suits are prima facie evidence against the defendant in subsequent suits brought by private parties; however, a 1980 amendment to § 5(a) provides that nothing in this section "shall be construed to impose any limitation on the application of collateral estoppel"). This amendment legislatively overruled Illinois v. General Paving Co., 590 F.2d 680 (7th Cir. 1979) (holding that original § 5(a) permitted the court to give only prima facie, and not preclusive, effect to an earlier criminal conviction, even though the case was appropriate for preclusion under the doctrine of offensive collateral estoppel).

184. *See* RESTATEMENT (SECOND) OF JUDGMENTS § 29(2) (1982).

185. *See id.* cmt. d, illus. 1. *But see* Stewart v. Bader, 154 N.H. 75, 907 A.2d 931 (2006) (issue preclusion based on prior criminal trial of husband operated to preclude husband from relitigating issues of actual innocence in subsequent wrongful death action by wife's estate; husband's election not to testify at criminal trial did not deny him a full and fair opportunity to litigate). However, if the general exceptions in § 28(3) or § 28(5)(c) are inapplicable because *P* had a full and fair opportunity to litigate in the action with *D-1*, there is a strong argument that a "special exception" of this sort should not be recognized just because the second action is with a different party (*D-2*).

186. *See* RESTATEMENT (SECOND) OF JUDGMENTS § 29(4) (1982).

plaintiffs to select the most appealing case to try first among all the available actions.

Illustration 13-48. After the wreck of a passenger train, *P-1*, a passenger on the train, sues *D Railroad* for personal injuries. *P-1* alleges that *D's* negligence caused the accident. After a trial, verdict and judgment are given for *D* on the ground that it was not negligent. Subsequently, *P-2*, another passenger on the wrecked train, sues *D* for personal injuries alleging negligence. This time, verdict and judgment are given for *P-2* after a finding that *D* had been negligent. Subsequently, *P-3*, a third passenger on the train, sues *D* for personal injuries received in the accident. *P-3* contends that *D's* negligence is conclusively established by the judgment in *P-2 v. D*, the jurisdiction in question having abolished the mutuality rule. *P-3's* contention is unsound because of the inconsistent findings.[187] However, it may be fortuitous that *P-2* did not sue first and win, thus giving all others the benefit of issue preclusion. In addition, plaintiffs may sometimes cooperate to bring the action with the most sympathetic plaintiff to trial first. These considerations may indicate that the mutuality rule should be retained in mass disaster litigation.

(v) Ability to Join in the First Action

In determining whether issue preclusion should be applied, it is also relevant to determine whether the person seeking to invoke favorable preclusion or to avoid unfavorable preclusion could have joined the present adversary in the first action.[188] Professor Hay has argued that this rule has a sound economic underpinning.[189]

Illustration 13-49. *P* is injured in an accident while riding as a passenger in an automobile owned by *D-1* and driven by *D-2* during the course of *D-2's* employment by *D-1*. *P* sues *D-1* in an action for damages. *D-1* defends on the ground that *D-2* was not negligent. After trial, *D-1* wins, the court explicitly finding that *D-2* was not negligent. Subsequently, *P* sues *D-2* for damages based on the same event. *P* is precluded by the finding that *D-2* was not negligent. When "a

---

187. *See id.*; Hoppe v. G.D. Searle & Co., 779 F. Supp. 1425 (S.D.N.Y. 1991) (defendant had won sixteen of twenty prior suits reaching juries).

188. *See* RESTATEMENT (SECOND) OF JUDGMENTS § 29(3) (1982).

189. In absence of this restriction, no plaintiff (except those who have already sued and lost) can be excluded from the fruits of a prior action because the benefits of a favorable judgment under the nonmutuality rule are indivisible. This fact creates an incentive for plaintiffs to try to take a "free ride" on the efforts of others, particularly if effective collective action requires cost sharing by a large number of plaintiffs. The propensity to do so increases as the degree of dispersion of the benefits to noncontributing plaintiffs increases because it is less likely that the marginal gain from contributing will be worth the cost. Furthermore, "by suing separately from the group, the free rider gets two bites at the apple; if the group loses, [the free rider] is not bound by the adverse judgment." Bruce L. Hay, *Some Settlement Effects of Preclusion*, 1993 U. ILL. L. REV. 21, 49. Professor Hay gives the following illustration: "Suppose that claims have an expected judicial valuation of $100 if the plaintiffs sue separately, and $150 if they sue collectively; and assume that a plaintiff's litigation costs are the same whether [the plaintiff] sues alone or in a group. If nonmutual preclusion is available, [the plaintiff] gains little by joining. If others have already banded together, contributing has no point; most of the benefits of collective action probably will be realized whether or not [the plaintiff] contributes, and by holding back [the plaintiff] can get a second bite at the apple if the group loses." *Id.* nn.79-80 (also pointing out, however, that the conduct of prospective free riders is affected by their "place in line." If a plaintiff knows that the plaintiff's case will be tried before those of other plaintiffs, the plaintiff will be better off by contributing to a collective action because the chances of recovering alone are worse than the chances of recovering as a part of the group).

plaintiff brings a subsequent action involving the same issues against a person whom [the plaintiff] could appropriately have joined as a co-defendant in the first action, only strongly compelling circumstances justify withholding preclusion."[190]

(vi) Relationships Not Present in the Second Action and Compromise Verdicts

In determining whether issue preclusion should be applied, a court may consider whether relationships among the parties might have affected the results in the first action when those relationships are not present in the second action. An apparent compromise verdict or finding can also be taken into account.[191]

Illustration 13-50. A real estate developer advertises vacation lots for sale. A real estate broker and a retired schoolteacher each contract to buy a lot, but they both subsequently refuse to complete their contracts because the lots are not as advertised. Assume that the real estate developer sues the real estate broker for breach of contract. The broker successfully defends the action on the grounds that the broker reasonably relied on the advertising. Subsequently, the developer sues the schoolteacher for breach of contract. The finding in the action between the developer and the broker that the statements in the advertising were ones on which reliance might reasonably be placed is not binding on the developer in the action with the schoolteacher. The resolution of the issue may have resulted from the

---

190. *See* RESTATEMENT (SECOND) OF JUDGMENTS § 29(3) cmt. e (1982); *see also* Hunter v. City of Des Moines, 300 N.W.2d 121 (Iowa 1981) (defendant's motion to consolidate actions by different plaintiffs arising from same facts resisted by plaintiff in second action; issue preclusion denied when defendant loses the first action); Johnson v. Union Pac. R.R., 352 Ark. 534, 104 S.W.3d 745 (2003) (nonmutual offensive issue preclusion did not apply against railroad when plaintiff could easily have joined in first action against railroad in federal court; alternative holding). *Illustration 13-49* is basically illustration 4 of the *Restatement (Second)*, cited above. Yet, in the *Restatement (Second)'s* illustration, *P* would be bound by issue preclusion without the need to "weigh" the failure to join *D-2*. In *Hunter*, the plaintiff in the second action resisted consolidation of a separate action by a different plaintiff against the same defendant. It makes sense there to resort to a special exception to issue preclusion to prevent the plaintiff in the second action from obtaining the benefit of a judgment against the defendant in the first action. But how far should this approach extend? If the plaintiff in the second action simply did not join with the plaintiff in the first action, should this fact be given weight? To the drafters of the *Restatement (Second)*, the answer is apparently "yes." *See* RESTATEMENT (SECOND) OF JUDGMENTS § 29(3), illus. 4 (1982). However, if this factor is given substantial weight, it would prevent nonmutual offensive issue preclusion altogether in this and many other situations. Such a widespread application may have desirable economic effects:

> Desirable (from the plaintiffs' standpoint) collective action is therefore less likely to occur under nonmutuality. Because the rule converts favorable judgments into public goods, each plaintiff has an incentive to understate the value . . . of a favorable judgment and to decline to contribute to a collective effort at securing one. Suits will be brought individually even when the group as a whole would profit from a pooling of efforts. Precisely by making the benefits of a favorable judgment available to all, the rule reduces the likelihood that such a judgment will be rendered in the first place.
>
> . . . .
>
> The free-rider problem created by nonmutuality supports the principle, urged by the Second Restatement [in §29(3)] and adopted by the Supreme Court in the *Parklane Hosiery* case, that a plaintiff cannot take advantage of nonmutual preclusion if [the plaintiff] could have joined the earlier action. Though embraced mostly out of concern for fairness to the defendant, this restriction on nonmutual preclusion actually may benefit the plaintiffs as a group—particularly [when] sequential litigation enables the defendant to divide and conquer effectively. If effectively enforced, the restriction should give potential contributors the right incentives: they will join if and only if collective action increases the value of their claims. Without the restriction, these gains from cooperation are more likely to be lost, and the defendant will be better able to extract favorable settlements . . . .

Bruce L. Hay, *Some Settlement Effects of Preclusion*, 1993 U. ILL. L. REV. 21, 49-50 (footnotes omitted).

191. *See* RESTATEMENT (SECOND) OF JUDGMENTS § 29(5) (1982).

knowledge or comparative responsibility of the parties toward one another in the first proceeding.[192]

Illustration 13-51. *P-1* and *P-2* are killed in the wreck of *D's* car. *P-1's* personal representative sues *D* for $70,000 for wrongful death. At trial, the evidence of *D's* negligence is minimal, but the jury returns a verdict in *P-1's* favor for $35,000. Subsequently, *P-2's* representative sues *D* for $100,000 for wrongful death. Under these circumstances, the issue of *D's* negligence should not be deemed precluded by the judgment in *P-1's* representative *v. D*. It looks very much like the judgment in the first action was based on a compromise verdict. The evidence of negligence is weak, and the requested damages are divided in half.[193]

(vii) Inappropriate Foreclosure of the Opportunity to Review of Issues of Law

If "the issue determined in the prior action was one of law and treating it as conclusively determined would inappropriately foreclose opportunity for obtaining reconsideration of the legal rule on which it was based," issue preclusion should not operate.[194] However, the usefulness of this factor is highly questionable. There is an exception to issue preclusion even in successive actions between the same two parties when issues of law are involved and "the two actions are substantially unrelated or a new determination of the issue is warranted in order to take into account intervening changes in the applicable legal context or otherwise avoid inequitable administration of the law."[195] This exception would also be applicable in subsequent litigation between different parties and would be analytically prior to the application of a special exception for issues of law in nonmutual estoppel situations. However, it is difficult to think of a situation in which an issue of law would be precluded in litigation between the same two parties in spite of the ordinary exception for issues of law applicable to such cases, but would *not* be precluded in litigation between different parties because of the special exception for issues of law in those cases.

Illustration 13-52. *P* sued *D Bank* for damages, alleging that the bank breached a loan contract with *P* by charging a higher annual interest rate than permitted by a state statute, and alleging further that the bank's method of computing interest rates was illegal. The court granted summary judgment against *P* on the grounds that the rates charged by the bank were permissible under the statute and that the bank's method of computing interest was also lawful. Subsequently, *P* sued *C Bank* asserting claims against *C Bank* that are identical to the ones raised by *P* in the prior action against *D Bank*. Under these circumstances, issue preclusion would not apply even if *P's* action had been brought against *D*

---

192. *Id.* cmt. g, illus. 5.

193. *See id.* illus. 7.

194. *See* RESTATEMENT (SECOND) OF JUDGMENTS § 29(7) (1982).

195. *See id.* § 28(2); subsection 2*(b) supra* ("Issues of Law"); *see also* Johnson v. Union Pac. R.R., 352 Ark. 534, 104 S.W.3d 745 (2003) (nonmutual offensive issue preclusion did not apply against railroad because of appellate case intervening between first and second action that indicated issue of law decided in first action had been decided incorrectly).

Bank, if the claims in the two actions are unrelated. The reason is that it would be unfair to preclude *P* from arguing that the issues of law determined in the prior action were determined incorrectly, when all other customers of *D Bank* would be allowed to litigate that issue.[196] If issue preclusion would not operate in an action between the same two parties for this reason, it will also not operate in an action between different parties.[197] Therefore, even though there would also be a special exception in the situation described which would prevent issue preclusion from operating in a nonmutual defensive fashion against *P* in the suit against *C Bank*,[198] it would not be necessary to reach that exception in the case.[199]

(viii) Undesirable Effects on Subsequent Proceedings

A court may also consider whether treating an issue as conclusively determined by a prior action might complicate the determination of issues in the subsequent proceeding or prejudice the interests of a party to the second action.[200] If so, issue preclusion should not be applied.

Illustration 13-53. *P* is injured in a fight with an employee on the employer's business premises. The employee is tried in a criminal proceeding for assaulting *P*. The employee's defense is self-defense. The employee is convicted. *P* then joins the employee and the employer in an action to recover damages for the injuries *P* received in the assault. In *P's* action, the issue of employee's liability may be relitigated by both the employee and the employer, if it appears that precluding the employee would prejudice the employer's defense. Little will be gained by way of judicial economy in foreclosing the issue against the employee.

---

196. *See* subsection 2*(b)*, *Illustration 13-33*, *supra.*

197. The *Restatement (Second)* states that a person precluded from litigating with an opposing party is precluded from litigating with others unless one of the special exceptions to nonmutual preclusion found in § 29 is applicable. *See* RESTATEMENT (SECOND) OF JUDGMENTS § 29 (1982). Thus, the case should first be analyzed under the basic doctrine of issue preclusion applicable to successive actions between the same two parties and the exceptions to that doctrine *before* the special exceptions in § 29 are considered. This means that the exception in § 28(2) for issues of law in actions between the same parties must be applied to determine whether preclusion would exist before determining the applicability of the special exception for issues of law in nonmutual preclusion cases in § 29(7). *See also* Garcia v. General Motors Corp., 195 Ariz. 510, 990 P.2d 1069 (Ct. App. 1999). In *Garcia*, the plaintiffs were injured in a single-car accident in Idaho while riding in a General Motors van. One of the plaintiffs sued G.M. in the United States District Court in Idaho and recovered, the court, as required by Idaho law, excluding all evidence that the plaintiff was not wearing a seat belt to prove contributory negligence. Subsequently, other plaintiffs sued G.M. in Arizona state court to recover for their injuries suffered in the accident. G.M. again raised the seat belt defense, invoking Arizona law which permitted the introduction of such evidence to prove contributory negligence, and the plaintiffs argued that the Idaho federal court's ruling on the seat belt defense should have a preclusive effect in the Arizona action. The Arizona Court of Appeals held that issue preclusion did not apply. One reason given by the court was that if it reached a contrary result, one plaintiff in a multiple plaintiff case could bring suit in the forum most likely to make a favorable conflict-of-laws ruling and the other plaintiffs could then use that ruling against the defendant in subsequent actions in different jurisdictions. The court ultimately held that Arizona law applied and permitted evidence of seat belt nonuse.

198. *See* RESTATEMENT (SECOND) OF JUDGMENTS § 29(7) (1982), which would also prevent issue preclusion from operating in a successive action between different parties because it would inappropriately foreclose *P's* opportunity to obtain a reconsideration of the legal rules upon which the prior action was based.

199. In addition, as noted in section C(2)*(b)*, in footnote accompanying *Illustration 13-34, supra*, preclusion on issues of law is also sometimes limited in successive suits between the government and private parties in order not to thwart the development of important issues of law by freezing them as they were decided in the first case to proceed to judgment. As observed there, the policy of nonpreclusion applies with even more vigor in cases in which nonmutual preclusion is involved. *See also* Note, *Nonmutual Issue Preclusion Against States,* 109 HARV. L. REV. 792 (1997).

200. *See* RESTATEMENT (SECOND) OF JUDGMENTS § 29(6) (1982).

Much of the evidence that bears on the employee's liability will have to be introduced to determine the employer's liability.[201]

(ix) Other Compelling Circumstances

Finally, § 29(8) of the *Restatement (Second)* provides that issue preclusion should not apply if "other compelling circumstances" dictate that a party be able to relitigate an issue. Like the general exception to the rule of issue preclusion provided whenever a party has not had a full and fair opportunity to litigate,[202] this factor is subject to criticism on the ground that it could potentially undermine the entire doctrine of issue preclusion by encouraging litigation over the question of when "other compelling circumstances" are present.

SECTION D. PARTIES BOUND BY JUDGMENTS

1. Preclusion of Nonparties

As noted in the previous subsection, res judicata rules ordinarily do not operate *against* nonparties.[203] Due process generally requires that a party have an opportunity to be heard on a claim or issue before being bound by a judgment. However, exceptions exist to this rule. Certain representational relationships as well as certain substantive relationships between parties and nonparties to an action may result in the nonparties being bound by the judgment. These relationships can produce both claim and issue preclusion effects in appropriate cases.

---

201. *See id.* § 29(6) cmt. h, illus. 8; O'Connor v. O'Leary, 247 Cal. App. 2d 646, 56 Cal. Rptr. 1 (1967).

202. *See* section C(2)*(f)* ("Injustice in Particular Cases") and accompanying discussion of RESTATEMENT (SECOND) OF JUDGMENTS § 28(5)(c) *supra*; *see also* Vandenberg v. Superior Court, 21 Cal. 4th 815, 982 P.2d 229, 88 Cal. Rptr. 2d 366 (1999) (collateral estoppel will only apply when it comports with fairness and justice).

203. RESTATEMENT (SECOND) OF JUDGMENTS § 34(3) (1982); *see* Blockowicz v. Williams, 630 F.3d 563 (7th Cir. 2010) (host could not be compelled to remove defamatory material from website pursuant to permanant injunction issued in action to which they were not a party); Stewart Elliott, 239 P.3d 1236 (Alaska 2010) (determination in client's post-conviction proceedings that attorney provided deficient assistance of counsel in criminal action did not bind attorney, who was not a party to or in privity with a party to proceedings); Kahala Royal Corp. v. Goodsill Anderson Quinn & Stifel, 113 Haw. 251, 151 P.3d 732 (2007) (generally, one is not bound by a judgment in personam resulting from litigation in which he is not designated as a party or been made a party by service of process); Oregon Mut. Ins. Co. v. Farm Bureau Mut. Ins. Co., 148 Idaho 47, 218 P.3d 391 (2009) (default judgment had no preclusive effect against nonparties); Stoddard v. Hagadone Corp., 147 Idaho 186, 207 P.3d 162 (2009) (res judicata did not bar action by worker's compensation insurer against fund because fund was not a party to prior actio); *cf.* Channel v. Loyacono, 954 So. 2d 415 (Miss. 2007) (there was no identity between clients' tort cause of action against pharmaceutical company and malpractice and fraud action against law firm that represented clients and persuaded them to settle, firm was not a party to tort action and thus res judicata did not bar malpractice action despite the fact that it arose out of the same general facts as tort action); Osguthorpe v. Wolf Mountain Resorts, L.C., 2010 UT 29, 232 P.3d 999 (ski resorts were not parties to fee owner's prior action against business partner and were not bound by judgment deciding that agreement between fee owner and parties was a lease). *But see* Robert G. Bone, *Rethinking the "Day in Court" Ideal and Nonparty Preclusion*, 67 N.Y.U. L. REV. 193 (1992) (arguing for a broader definition of "participation"; preclusion should vary with the type of case).

(a) Representational Relations Binding Nonparties

One kind of exception exists when a person's interests are represented by another in an action.[204] For example, a nonparty may be bound by the judgment in a properly constituted class action.[205] Persons also are bound by the judgment in an action to a limited extent when, although they are not parties to the action, they control litigation brought by another or substantially participate in the control of a presentation made on their behalf. In this situation, nonparties are bound by the determination of the issues in the action they control, but not by the doctrine of claim preclusion. Although they have had a fair opportunity to litigate the issues by their control of the action, they, by definition, are not asserting a claim belonging to themselves in the action.[206]

---

204. See, e.g., Rucker v. Schmidt, 794 N.W.2d 114 (Minn. 2011) (attorney-client relationship did not alone establish that ex-husband and attorney were in privity in prior action where wife sued attorney in second action for fraud on the court after successfully recovering against husband); Taylor v. Taylor, 835 So. 2d 60 (Miss. 2003) (a minor represented by a next friend in the first action is bound by the judgment in the action); Simpson v. Chicago Pneumatic Tool Co., 2005 ND 55, 693 N.W.2d 612 (privity existed between defendant and its attorneys for purposes of invoking the doctrines of claim and issue preclusion against plaintiff's second action; second action was based on identical factual allegations that plaintiff had unsuccessfully litigated in prior action, and conduct of attorneys involved their response on behalf of discovery requests and orders in first action); Bower v. Harrah's Laughlin, Inc., 125 Nev. 470, 215 P.3d 709 (2009) (members of biker gangs did not adequately represent bystanders' interests in federal action in which jury returned verdict for casino as required for nonparty issue preclusion under federal law to bar bystanders' claims); Bowden v. Phillips Petroleum Co., 247 S.W.3d 690 (Tex. 2008) (class action suits are subject to the same preclusion rules as other procedural forms of litigation); *In re* Coday, 156 Wash. 2d 485, 130 P.3d 809 (2006) (where nominally different parties pursue claims as voters on behalf of the body politic generally, parties have sufficiently identical interests to produce issue preclusion, since their interests are represented in initial action); Beahm v. 7-Eleven, Inc., 223 W. Va. 269, 672 S.E.2d 598 (2008) (property owners were virtually represented in prior action and were therefore in privity with plaintiff in that action; application of res judicata to owners did not violate due process).

205. *See* Chapter 8(D)(4) *supra* ("Class Actions"); Barclay v. Waters, 357 Ark. 386. 182 S.W.3d 91 (2004) (issue preclusion prevented taxpayers from relitigating issue previously litigated and determined and that was necessary to the judgment in a prior class action encompassing the class to which the taxpayers belonged); Engle v. Liggett Group, Inc., 945 So. 2d 1246 (Fla. 2006) (prior action by state against cigarette companies and industry organizations seeking punitive damages did not assert interests of common concern to all state citizens as required to raise res judicata bar to subsequent private class action); Citizens Ins. Co. v. Daccach, 217 S.W.3d 430 (Tex. 2007) (basic rules of res judicata apply to class actions just as they do to any other form of litigation; thus res judicata can apply to preclude subsequent litigation of abandoned claims that cannot be litigated in class action suit, and application of res judicata to class action is not limited to claims that coult have been certified in the prior class action); Tobias Barrington Wolff, *Preclusion in Class Action Litigation,* 105 COLUM. L. REV. 717 (2005); Justin Vickers, *Res Judicata Claim Preclusion of Properly Filed Citizen Suits*, 104 NW. U. L. REV. 1623 (2010). *cf.* Becherer v. Merrill Lynch, Pierce, Fenner & Smith, 131 F.3d 580 (6th Cir. 1997) (holding members of plaintiff class who opted out of a settlement in a federal class action were not precluded from bringing a state-court action because they did not control the federal action, could not hold the plaintiffs in that action accountable for the result in the federal proceeding, and did not acquiesce to being represented in the federal action). Other similar examples include persons represented by a fiduciary, such as the trustee of an estate or an interest of which the persons are beneficiaries, or by an executor, administrator, guardian, or conservator. *See* RESTATEMENT (SECOND) OF JUDGMENTS § 41(1)(a), (c) (1982). Persons also may be bound by representation when they have given another the authority to represent them in an action. *See id.* § 41(1)(b). In addition, public officials or agencies are sometimes authorized to maintain or defend litigation on behalf of others who will be bound by the judgment in an action. In such cases, the authority of the official or agency may or may not preclude the represented individuals from enforcing their own interests. *See id.* § 41(1)(d) cmt. d; *see also* Fournier v. Illinois Cas. Co., 391 N.W.2d 258 (Iowa 1986) (administrator who sought to litigate defendant's obligations to her as administrator and individual in first action was bound by claim preclusion in second action brought in her individual capacity; discussing § 36). *See generally* Samuel Issacharoff & Richard A. Nagareda, *Class Settlements Under Attack*, 156 U. PA. L. REV. 1649 (2008) (discussing finality of class actions).

206. *See* RESTATEMENT (SECOND) OF JUDGMENTS § 39 cmt. b (1982); Harris v. Jackson, 192 S.W.3d 297 (Ky. 2006) (one who participates in litigation and actively assumes or manages its prosecution or defense is concluded by the judgment even though it is a nonparty to the action); Brigham Young Univ. v. Tremco Consultants, Inc., 2005 UT 19, 110 P.3d 678 (privity based on nonparty's control of litigation is applicable to issue preclusion, but not to claim preclusion; lower court did not identify issues to which nonparty should be bound or analyze whether the criteria for issue preclusion had been satisfied in the action; therefore, judgment reversed).

Illustration 13-54. Assume that *P* sues *D* for personal injuries received in an automobile accident. *D's* insurer defends the action on *D's* behalf. In this situation, a judgment favorable to *P* will preclude *D's* insurer from relitigating the issues determined against *D* in a subsequent action in which the company is a formal party. However, claim preclusion, even if otherwise appropriate, would not operate against the insurer.[207]

* * * * *

A person who agrees to be bound by the determination of issues in an action between others will be bound by the agreement.[208]

Illustration 13-55. On the facts of *Illustration 13-54*, *D's* insurer could agree to be bound by a judgment in an action against *D*, even when the insurer does not control the defense of that action.

* * * * *

A person who is a "nominal party" to an action also is bound by a judgment in most circumstances. Although an action must be brought in the name of the real party in interest and against the person from whom relief is sought, those parties may not be the persons who control the action. Nevertheless, the persons denominated as plaintiff or defendant usually will be bound by the judgment to the same extent as the persons who control the action, as long as they have put the person controlling the action in a position to denominate them as parties.[209] However, a person who lacks an interest in the action, even if denominated a party, will not be bound by the judgment if the opposing party knows of the nominal party's lack of interest.[210]

Illustration 13-56. Assume that an insurance company pays the loss of an insured party and becomes subrogated to the insured party's claim. The insurer may be permitted under the contract of insurance or the laws of a particular jurisdiction to bring suit on the claim in the name of the insured. In any such action, the insured will be bound by the judgment if the insured engages in conduct that would lead the opposing party to believe the insured owns the claim. This binding effect may result, for example, if the insured signs the complaint or participates in the action and gives no indication that the insured is not the owner of the claim.[211]

* * * * *

Numerous exceptions exist to the general rules of representation that are designed to ensure that a nonparty's interests will be adequately represented in an action before the nonparty is bound.[212]

---

207. *See* RESTATEMENT (SECOND) OF JUDGMENTS § 39 cmt. a, illus. 2 (1982).

208. *See id.* § 40.

209. *See id.* § 37 cmt. c, illus. 3.

210. *See id.* cmt. f, illus. 8.

211. *See id.* § 37 cmt. c, illus. 3; *see also* United Fire & Cas. Co. v. Shelly Funeral Home, Inc., 642 N.W.2d 648 (Iowa 2002) (issue preclusion prevents liability insurer from relitigating the insured's liability in a suit for a declaratory judgment on coverage because the insurer was so connected in interest with one party as to have had a full and fair opportunity to litigate the issue of the insured's negligent supervision of an employee).

212. These rules are summarized in § 42 of the *Restatement (Second) of Judgments*:

§ 42. Exceptions to the General Rule of Representation

(1) A person is not bound by a judgment for or against a party who purports to represent him if:

(a) Notice concerning the representation was required to be given to the represented person, or others who might act to protect his interest, and there was no substantial compliance with the requirement; or

(b) Substantive Relationships Binding Nonparties

A second category of cases in which a nonparty can be bound by a judgment in an action occurs when the applicable substantive law defines the nonparty's legal right in such a manner that a judgment for or against another person will conclude the nonparty's rights. These substantive relationships include (1) family; (2) contract; (3) property; (4) organizational affiliation; and (5) indemnitee and indemnitor.[213] Traditionally, when the substantive law regulates rights in a way that results in nonparties being bound by a judgment, it has been said that the nonparties were in "privity" with the parties in the action.[214] However, the reported decisions use the term "privity" to cover so many different situations that it has little descriptive value.[215] Therefore, in the discussion that follows, the term "privity" will be avoided.

(i) Family Relationships

An example of a situation in which family relationships will result in a judgment binding on a nonparty occurs when a person who is injured in an accident sues for injuries, and then dies from the injuries. A judgment in a personal injury action, whether favorable or unfavorable to the injured party, usually will prevent

---

(b) The subject matter of the action was not within the interests of the represented person that the party is responsible for protecting; or

(c) Before rendition of the judgment the party was divested of representative authority with respect to the matters as to which the judgment is subsequently invoked; or

(d) With respect to the representative of a class, there was such a substantial divergence of interest between him and the members of the class, or a group within the class, that he could not fairly represent them with respect to the matters as to which the judgment is subsequently invoked; or

(e) The representative failed to prosecute or defend the action with due diligence and reasonable prudence, and the opposing party was on notice of facts making that failure apparent.

(2) A person who has litigated on his own behalf in a previous action is not bound by or entitled to the benefits of a judgment in a subsequent action concerning the same claim that is brought or defended by a party representing him.

RESTATEMENT (SECOND) OF JUDGMENTS § 42 (1982).

213. *See id.* §§ 43-61 (preclusion as a result of a legal relationship).

214. *See, e.g.*, EEOC v. Pemco Aeroplex, Inc., 383 F.3d 1280 (11th Cir. 2004) (EEOC was not in privity with individual employees who lost prior action because (1) the employees did not act as virtual representatives of EEOC, (2) the EEOC did not effectively control the private litigation, and (3) the "equities of the case" weighed strongly against a finding of privity); State v. Hale, 978 P.2d 1276 (Alaska 1999) (no issue preclusion against person who was not a party to prior action or in privity with a party); Flaherty v. Muther, 2011 ME 32, 17 A.3d 640 (neighbors were not in privity with owners association for purposes of res judicata arising from prior settlement agreement relating to easement access to beach); Porter v. Coco, 154 N.H. 353, 910 A.2d 1187 (2006) (omission of landowner's predecessors in interest from previous quiet title action allowed landowners to attack judgment collaterally for lack of jurisdiction); State *ex rel.* Schachter v. Ohio Pub. Emps. Ret. Bd., 121 Ohio St. 3d 526, 905 N.E.2d 1210 (2009) (employee of county public defender office was in privity with director of office in director's prior action seeking service credit for office employees and thus employee's subsequent action for service credit was barred); Commercial Union Ins. Co. v. Pelchat, 727 A.2d 676 (R.I. 1999) (issue preclusion does not apply to a nonparty not in privity with a party to the prior action).

215. *See* Becherer v. Merrill Lynch, Pierce, Fenner & Smith, 43 F.3d 1054, 1069-70 (6th Cir. 1995); Huelsman v. Kansas Dep't of Revenue, 267 Kan. 456, 980 P.2d 1022 (1999) (whether a party is in privity with another for purposes of issue preclusion is a question of policy); *see also* Ear, Nose & Throat Group, P.C. v. Stanescu, 46 Conn. Supp. 14, 734 A.2d 152 (Super. Ct. 1999) (when liability of party is derivative of or predicated upon the liability of a primary party, the parties share the same legal right and privity exists; thus, if the primary party is not held liable, the other party is not liable either).

a wrongful death action by that person's beneficiaries after the injured party's death.[216]

(ii) Contractual Relationships

An example of a situation in which a contractual relationship will result in preclusion against a nonparty occurs when contract rights are assigned. Prior to an assignment, the assignor can sue to enforce the contract. After the assignment, the assignee can sue to enforce the contract. A judgment in favor of or against either the assignor or assignee will usually bind the other party.[217]

(iii) Property Relationships

The classic example of a situation in which a property relationship will result in a judgment binding on a nonparty is when a judgment is rendered against an owner of property which is later transferred. In such circumstances, the judgment binds the successors in ownership to the same extent that it bound the original owner.[218]

Illustration 13-57. Suppose the owner of Blackacre sues the owner of Whiteacre to establish an easement over Whiteacre by virtue of a conveyance by the owner. The court enters judgment for the owner of Whiteacre on the ground that the conveyance did not give the owner of Blackacre an easement. The owner of Blackacre thereafter conveys Blackacre to a third party. The judgment precludes the

---

216. *See* RESTATEMENT (SECOND) OF JUDGMENTS § 45-48 (1982) (legal relationships which result in preclusion in personal injury actions); Crowder v. American Eagle Airlines, Inc., 118 Fed. App'x 833 (5th Cir. 2004) (dismissal of decedent's personal injury suit precluded subsequent wrongful death action by surviving spouse and children when, even if survivors had a cause of action under statute when similar claim by decedent would be barred, issues of fact and liability common to actions were necessarily litigated and determined in favor of defendants); Brown v. Rahman, 231 Cal. App. 3d 1458, 282 Cal. Rptr. 815 (1991) (heirs of decedent in privity with decedent; heirs bound by determination on issue of negligence in favor of defendant in prior action); *cf.* Brown v. Pine Bluff Nursing Home, 359 Ark. 471, 199 S.W.3d 45 (2004) (wrongful death claim asserted by representative of estate was precluded by dismissal with prejudice of representative's previous negligence action based on same event).

217. *See* RESTATEMENT (SECOND) OF JUDGMENTS § 55 (1982); *see also* Buechel v. Bain, 97 N.Y.2d 295, 766 N.E.2d 914, 740 N.Y.S.2d 252 (2001) (attorneys were in privity with their former law partner for issue preclusion purposes and had a full and fair opportunity to litigate the validity of their fee arrangement in prior action brought by former partner). For other examples of the operation of res judicata based on contractual relationships, see C.C. Bjorklund, Annotation, *Judgment in Action Against Seller or Supplier of Product as Res Judicata in Action Against Manufacturer for Injury from Defective Product, or Vice Versa*, 34 A.L.R.3D 518 (1970).

218. *See* RESTATEMENT (SECOND) OF JUDGMENTS §§ 43-44 (1982); Argus Real Estate, Inc. v. E-470 Pub. Highway Auth., 109 P.3d 604 (Colo. 2005) (previous quiet title action involved the same claim as present action and plaintiff was in privity with plaintiff in prior action because it was successor in interest; claim for reformation asserted in second action could have been asserted in prior action); Kruckenberg v. Harvey, 2005 WI 43, 279 Wis. 2d 520, 694 N.W.2d 879 (landowner who was successor in interest to property was in privity with previous owner who was party to action that might involve the same claim because although the actions concerned separate activities by the defendant, they involved the same aggregate operative facts, namely the defendant's conduct in relation to the boundary line of the property; nevertheless, even if claim preclusion applied, exception to claim preclusion exists under RESTATEMENT (SECOND) OF JUDGMENTS § 26(1)(f) because the prior litigation did not yield a coherent disposition of the controversy since there was no litigation of the boundary line issue; issue preclusion did not apply for the same reason); Watkins v. Peacock, 145 Idaho 704, 184 P.3d 210 (2008) (prior action between plaintiff's predecessors in interest and defendant was preclusive as to existence of implied easement); Osborn v. Kilts, 2006 WY 142, 145 P.3d 1264 (identical parties requirement of res judicata is satisfied when either the parties are actually the same parties to the prior proceeding or they are in privity with those parties; owner of dominant estate precluded because he was successor in interest to prior litigant and thus in privity with that litigant).

third party from asserting an easement over Whiteacre on the same basis asserted in the prior litigation.[219]

(iv) Organizational Relationships

Membership in an organization can result in liability to a member of the organization who is not a party to an action. Such liability, however, varies with the characteristics of the organization and its treatment under applicable law. For example, a judgment against a corporation normally will not result in liability to a member of the corporation over and above the diminution in value of the member's share in the organization resulting from the judgment. However, such a judgment otherwise binds the members.[220]

Illustration 13-58. Suppose that *P Corp.* sues *D*, an officer of *P Corp.*, for allegedly breaching *D's* fiduciary duty to the corporation. The suit by the corporation will preclude a subsequent derivative action on the same claim by shareholders.[221]

* * * * *

There are exceptions to the rule against individual liability of corporate members.

Illustration 13-59. Under certain circumstances involving closely held corporations—ones owned by one or a few persons—shareholders can sometimes be held individually liable for the corporation's obligations.[222]

* * * * *

At common law, partnerships were treated as aggregations of individuals rather than entities. The result was that partners were treated as joint obligors and obligees in contract cases, and they all had to join or be joined in contract suits. Similarly, they were regarded as co-owners of partnership property who had to join or be joined in actions concerning the property. However, in tort actions, they were regarded as jointly and severally liable, so that one could be sued without joining the other.[223]

These common-law rules have been reshaped to a large extent by statute. As a result, the effect of a judgment on partners who are nonparties varies

---

219. *See* RESTATEMENT (SECOND) OF JUDGMENTS § 43 cmt. b & illus. 2 (1982); *see also* Kullick v. Skyline Homeowners Ass'n, 2003 MT 137, 316 Mont. 146, 69 P.3d 225 (claim of existing easement was barred by res judicata and collateral estoppel resulting from judgment against plaintiff's grantor in prior litigation with defendant).

220. *See* RESTATEMENT (SECOND) OF JUDGMENTS § 59 (1982); Bain v. Hofmann, 2010 VT 18, 993 A.2d 432 (Commissioner of Department of Corrections was in privity with operator of privately-owned out-of-state prison to which Commissioner had transferred inmate).

221. *See id.* § 59(2); Huck *ex rel.* Sea Air Shuttle Corp. v. Dawson, 106 F.3d 45 (3d Cir. 1997) (if corporation brings an action for injunctive relief and loses, a shareholder cannot bring an action for damages based on the same activity, but which accrued after the first action terminated). *But cf.* Deflon v. Sawyers, 2006-NMSC-025, 139 N.M. 637, 137 P.3d 577 (no privity relationship between corporation and corporate officers; corporation was sued in federal court for sexual harassment, while officers were sued in state court and theory of state suit could make officers liable on basis that corporation was not).

222. *See* RESTATEMENT (SECOND) OF JUDGMENTS § 59(3) (1982); *see also* Lane v. Montana Fourth Judicial Dist. Court, 2003 MT 130, 316 Mont. 55, 68 P.3d 819 (res judicata did not bar judgment creditor's alter ego claim against president of corporation based on prior judgment against corporation because although alter ego claim was raised in prior litigation, it was not decided in that litigation).

223. *See* RESTATEMENT (SECOND) OF JUDGMENTS § 60 cmt. a (1982).

considerably. If the applicable rules require all partners to join or be joined in an action, the action, of course, will result in a judgment binding on all of them individually. If the applicable rules allow one partner to sue or defend on behalf of all, the judgment will be binding on the absent partners to the extent of the partnership property, but no further, though the judgment may have evidentiary effect in a subsequent proceeding to establish the partners' individual liability.[224]

When the organization involved is an unincorporated association, the effect of a judgment will depend upon whether the association is given entity treatment by the applicable law. At common law, associations were not treated as entities, with the result that treatment of associations was substantially like that of partnerships, with one important exception. Partners were regarded as agents for other partners, but association members generally had to ratify the acts of other members for individual liability to result. Today, associations often are treated as entities. Thus, a judgment for or against the association has the same effect as a judgment for or against a corporation.[225]

If the association is not given entity treatment, a judgment in an action brought on behalf of the association by representative members will be binding on the members in accord with the rules of representation previously discussed. In suits against the association defended by representatives of the association, liability depends on the kind of suit involved. In property and contract cases, the underlying transaction upon which the action is based virtually always will have been ratified expressly or impliedly by the members, with corresponding individual member liability being the result. In tort cases, however, specific prior authorization of the tort is less likely, and subsequent ratification will require proof that each individual member participated in the wrongful act or approved the act later. Practically speaking, each member of the association to be held liable must be shown to have participated in the tort or to have approved of it for liability to attach, though this may be demonstrated in a suit brought against the association by naming a representative as a defendant. Furthermore, a judgment in favor of the injured party may not be enforced against association property unless all members are found liable. Because this situation is highly unlikely in a tort case, association property will be subject to the judgment only if the interests of liable members cannot be severed from those of nonliable members. Thus, enforcing a judgment against the association property is difficult or impossible.[226]

---

224. *See id.*; *see also* E.H. Schopler, Annotation, *Judgment for or Against Partner as Res Judicata in Favor of or Against Copartner Not a Party to the Judgment*, 11 A.L.R.2D 847 (1950).

225. *See* RESTATEMENT (SECOND) OF JUDGMENTS § 61(2) (1982).

226. *See id.* cmt. a; *see also* Pasko v. City of Milwaukee, 2002 WI 33, 252 Wis. 2d 1, 643 N.W.2d 72 (police officers association was not in privity with individual members and claim preclusion did not operate to preclude association from bringing action against city for mandamus to compel promotion of qualified officers to particular rank even though individual officers had previously commenced action against city for breach of collective bargaining agreement; interests of association and officers were not identical). For a discussion of the liability of members of an unincorporated association for torts committed by another member against a nonmember, see Ian Davis, Note, *Membership Has Its Privileges: Court Sets Forth the Liability of Individual Members of Unincorporated Associations for Torts Against Third Parties*: Juhl v. Airington, 39 TEX. SUP. CT. J. 830 (June 28, 1996), 28 TEX. TECH L. REV. 103 (1997).

(v) Indemnitee-Indemnitor Relationships

Finally, the relationship of indemnitor and indemnitee can result in a judgment binding on a nonparty. Assume that a person or entity such as an insurance company (the indemnitor) is obligated to indemnify another (the indemnitee) for the liability of the indemnitee to an injured party. If the injured party sues the indemnitee, the indemnitee can notify the indemnitor of the pendency of the action and call upon the indemnitor to defend the action. If the indemnitor does so, the indemnitor will be bound under the rule, discussed above, that parties who control an action are bound by the judgment in the action. However, even if the indemnitor does not defend the action, the indemnitor can be precluded from relitigating the issue of the indemnitee's liability to the injured person, though the indemnitor still may contest the obligation to indemnify.[227]

(c) Transformational Effects

One additional effect that a judgment may have on nonparties should be mentioned—what Professors James, Hazard, and Leubsdorf call the "transformational" effect of a judgment.[228] A judgment can transform relationships in ways that nonparties will be unable to contest.

Illustration 13-60. When a couple is validly divorced, nonparties ordinarily may not dispute the couple's marital status. This result is not derived from the operation of res judicata. Instead, the result reflects the change in the parties' relationship produced by the judgment.[229]

2. Preclusion Between Coparties

Traditionally, the rules of res judicata have applied only to determinations between persons in an adversary relationship.[230] The reason for this limitation is that, normally, only parties aligned on opposite sides of the litigation will have a full and fair opportunity to litigate matters determined in the action. Sometimes, however, coparties may find themselves in an adversary relationship on some issues while remaining aligned against a third party on other issues. This situation always occurs when there are cross-claims, third-party claims, or interpleader claims in the action;[231] but even when no such claims are present, coparties can find themselves in an adversary position.

Illustration 13-61. When a plaintiff sues two defendants in the alternative, each defendant may defend in part by pointing the finger at the other as the sole

---

227. The rules governing preclusion between the indemnitor and indemnitee are somewhat more complex than this simple statement indicates. The full scope of the rules is discussed in the RESTATEMENT (SECOND) OF JUDGMENTS §§ 57-58 (1982). For a complete description and discussion of the rules governing the binding effect of judgments on nonparties, *see id.* §§ 43-63.

228. *See* FLEMING JAMES, JR. ET AL., CIVIL PROCEDURE § 11.24 (5th ed. 2001).

229. *See id.* at 619.

230. *See* RESTATEMENT (SECOND) OF JUDGMENTS § 38 cmt. a (1982).

231. *See* Fowler v. Vineyard, 261 Ga. 454, 405 S.E.2d 678 (1991).

party responsible to the plaintiff. When such adversary relations arise, coparties have a sufficient opportunity and incentive to litigate the issues between them to bring into play the doctrine of issue preclusion.[232]

SECTION E. CLAIM AND ISSUE PRECLUSION ON QUESTIONS OF SUBJECT-MATTER AND PERSONAL JURISDICTION

As observed in section A, the rules of claim and issue preclusion only operate when a valid judgment—one rendered by a court with subject-matter and personal jurisdiction—has been rendered.[233] However, under certain circumstances, discussed below, a question of subject-matter or personal jurisdiction can be foreclosed by the judgment in a prior action.

Illustration 13-62. Assume that *P*, a citizen of State *X*, sues *D*, a citizen of State *Y*, in a state court of State *X*. If *D* perceives a deficiency in the State *X* court's personal or subject-matter jurisdiction, *D* ordinarily has two options. *D* may refuse to appear and defend the action, in which case a default judgment will be entered against *D*. In the typical course of events, *P* then will attempt to enforce the judgment against *D* in State *Y*, where *D* lives and owns assets that may be used to satisfy the judgment. Traditionally, *P* would have had to enforce the judgment by bringing an independent action on the judgment in a court of State *Y*.[234] When *P* brought this action, *D* would defend on the ground that the judgment was invalid because the judgment was rendered by a court without subject-matter or personal jurisdiction.[235]

* * * * *

However, the procedure described in *Illustration 13-62* entails substantial risks. If *D* is wrong about the jurisdictional objection, *D's* defense in State *Y* will fail. *D* will then be foreclosed from litigating the merits of *P's* claim against *D*. In

---

232. *See* RESTATEMENT (SECOND) OF JUDGMENTS § 38 cmt. a (1982); Buis v. Elliott, 142 S.W.3d 137 (Ky. 2004) (neither claim preclusion nor issue preclusion prevented assertion of claim by one co-defendant in prior action against other co-defendant in the action; default judgment had been rendered in prior action and refusal of court to relieve co-defendant seeking preclusion of the judgment was not on the merits as to crossclaims for indemnification, breach of contract, and unjust enrichment against other co-defendant; cross-claims are permissive and issues had not been litigated in prior action).

233. Traditionally, this rule has been expressed in terms of "void" versus "voidable" judgments. A judgment rendered without personal or subject-matter jurisdiction was considered "void" and subject to collateral attack in another proceeding. However, judgments infected with "mere" (*i.e.*, non-jurisdictional error) were merely "voidable" on direct attack of the judgment (as by appeal), but could not be attacked collaterally, *i.e.*, in a separate, subsequent action. *Cf. In re* Webber, 201 N.C. App. 212, 689 S.E.2d 468 (2009) (order requiring 180 days of involuntary commitment exceeded statutory 90-day maximum period for such commitment, but this did not make the order void and subject to collateral attack; trial court had jurisdiction when the order was issued).

234. However, forty-eight jurisdictions have adopted the Uniform Enforcement of Foreign Judgments Act, which provides a more streamlined procedure for enforcing judgments than the traditional common-law procedure. *See* UNIFORM ENFORCEMENT OF FOREIGN JUDGMENTS ACT (1964), 13 U.L.A. pt. I, at 155-56 (2002).

235. *See id.* §§ 1, 81; Patriot Commercial Leasing Co. v. Jerry Enis Motors, Inc., 928 So. 2d 856 (Miss. 2006) (Pennsylvania judgment subjected to successful collateral attack in Mississippi because service of process was defective under Pennsylvania law and this resulted in no personal jurisdiction being acquired over defendant); Brito v. Ryan, 151 N.H. 635, 864 A.2d 378 (2005) (when issue of personal jurisdiction has not been litigated in another state, a judgment rendered in that state may be challenged for lack of personal jurisdiction when enforcement is sought in the forum).; *cf.* Ronald R. Darbee, *Personal Jurisdiction as a Defense to the Enforcement of Foreign Arbitral Awards*, 41 MCGEORGE L. REV. 345 (2010).

other words, if *D's* jurisdictional objection is incorrect, the State *X* court will have entered a valid judgment against *D*. *D* will be precluded by res judicata from presenting defenses on the merits that *D* possessed against *P's* claim.[236] Therefore, if *D* has any doubt at all about the validity of the jurisdictional objection, and if *D* also possesses a potentially valid defense on the merits, *D* will not wish to default in the State *X* action.[237]

As noted in Chapter 3, every state now possesses a procedure that will allow *D* to raise jurisdictional objections without submitting to the jurisdiction of the State *X* court.[238] The procedures are either "special appearance" procedures, in which *D* appears only for the purposes of litigating the jurisdictional issue, or a motion procedure such as that described in Federal Rule 12, which accomplishes the same result. Thus, if in *Illustration 13-62,* above, *D* wishes to object to the jurisdiction of the State *X* court over *D*, *D* may employ one of these procedures to do so. If *D* does so and loses, however, the rules of issue preclusion will prevent *D* from relitigating the jurisdictional question in a subsequent proceeding to enforce the judgment against *D* in State *Y*.[239]

Thus, if *D* specially appears in the State *X* proceeding, objects to the court's personal jurisdiction, and wins, *D* has no problems. The action will be dismissed and *P* will have to sue *D* in a court with proper personal jurisdiction, such as a State *Y* court. If *D* loses, however, *D* must pursue whatever avenues State *X* provides for reversing the court's determination. For example, *D* may not lose on the jurisdictional objection at the trial level and then default in the expectation that *D* may relitigate the issue of jurisdiction in a later enforcement proceeding in State *Y*. If State *X* requires *D*, after losing on the jurisdictional objection, to litigate the merits of the action and then appeal on the jurisdictional issue (as well as any other errors *D* claims have been committed) after a final judgment has been rendered against *D*, that is what *D* must do. If *D* loses after both trial and appeal, *D* may attempt to obtain direct review of any federal constitutional question concerning the State *X*

---

236. *See* UNIFORM ENFORCEMENT OF FOREIGN JUDGMENTS ACT (1964), 13 U.L.A. pt. I, § 18(2) (2002).

237. In Dennis Garberg & Assocs., Inc. v. Pack-Tech Int'l Corp., 115 F.3d 767 (10th Cir. 1997), the court held that a district court should not enter a default judgment without first determining that it has personal jurisdiction. This holding may afford additional protection to nonresident defendants, but it should not be held to preclude relitigation of the jurisdictional question in a subsequent action to enforce the judgment. Under the ordinary rules of issue preclusion, the court's determination would not be binding because there has been no actual litigation of the issue. *See* section C(1)(*b*) *supra* (discussing the actual litigation requirement). Given the tradition under which subject-matter jurisdiction issues must be raised on a court's own motion while personal jurisdiction issues are not raised by the court, the decision seems questionable in any event. *See also* Legum v. Brown, 395 Md. 135, 909 A.2d 672 (2006) (properly authenticated copy of default judgment of another state is entitled to presumption of jurisdiction and burden is on party resisting judgment to demonstrate that court lacked personal or subject-matter jurisdiction).

238. *See* Chapter 3(B)(3) *supra* ("In Personam Jurisdiction: Consent, Appearance, and Waiver").

239. *See, e.g.*, Penkul v. Matarazzo, 2009 ME 113, 983 A.2d 375 (doctrine of issue preclusion precluded former wife's motion to enforce divorce judgment by contempt because trial court had previously denied motion to register judgment on grounds that it was rendered without personal jurisdiction over husband); Amerireach.com, LLC v.Walker, 290 Ga. 261, 719 S.E.2d 489 (2011) (a judgment is entitled to full faith and credit even as to questions of jurisdiction when the record discloses that those issues have been fully and fairly litigated in the action leading to the original judgment).

court's personal jurisdiction in the U.S. Supreme Court. If none of these avenues of relief succeeds, the judgment will bind *D*.[240]

The same result will occur if *D* actually litigates an issue of the State *X* court's subject-matter jurisdiction: issue preclusion will prevent *D* from relitigating the issue in a subsequent proceeding in State *Y*.[241] In addition, even if *D* litigates the merits of the State *X* action without raising a question of the court's subject-matter jurisdiction, *D* ordinarily will be precluded from raising subject-matter jurisdiction by way of collateral attack on the judgment. This result would obviously occur with regard to a personal jurisdiction objection because personal jurisdiction objections not raised in a timely fashion are waived.[242]

It might be thought that the rule on subject-matter jurisdiction should be different because subject-matter jurisdiction objections cannot be waived.[243] However, the rule that subject-matter jurisdiction objections cannot be waived is a rule that applies only to direct attacks on judgments. When a subject-matter jurisdiction objection exists but is not raised in a contested action, the objection is normally foreclosed from litigation on collateral attack by claim preclusion rules. Because subject-matter jurisdiction is ordinarily treated so seriously by the courts, however, some exceptions to this rule exist. Section 12 of the *Restatement (Second) of Judgments* describes these exceptions:

> When a court has rendered a judgment in a contested action, the judgment precludes the parties from litigating the question of the court's subject matter jurisdiction in subsequent litigation except if:

---

240. *See, e.g.*, Saudi v. Acomarit Mars. Servs., S.A., 114 Fed. App'x 449 (3d Cir. 2004) (prior dismissal for lack of personal jurisdiction was not claim preclusive because it was not on the merits; however, prior judgment did have issue preclusion effect on whether jurisdiction could be asserted under Federal Rule 4(k)(2)); Wall v. Stinson, 983 P.2d 736 (Alaska 1999) (Oregon judgment cannot be collaterally attacked in Alaska for lack of personal jurisdiction where defendant had vigorously litigated personal jurisdiction issue in Oregon and lost); Williams v. Williams, 997 S.W.2d 80 (Mo. Ct. App. 1999) (burden is on party challenging sister-state judgment to show it is not entitled to full faith and credit; finding by Oklahoma court that it had personal jurisdiction is binding when defendant litigated the issue in Oklahoma and did not show that the opportunity to litigate was inadequate); Schultz v. Doyle, 2000-0926 (La. 1/17/01), 776 So. 2d 1158 (judgment in another state entitled to full faith and credit when rendered after voluntary appearance of defendant, even though attorney allegedly withdrew special appearance to challenge jurisdiction without authority); Global Oceanic Enters., Inc. v. Hynum, 857 So. 2d 659 (Miss. 2003) (foreign judgment that court had personal jurisdiction was entitled to full faith and credit in creditor's action to enroll the judgment, even if the judgment creditor misrepresented judgment debtor's contacts with jurisdiction-asserting state to that state's courts, because judgment-rendering court had before it the judgment-debtor's defense of fraud and false statements, fraud was not extrinsic, issue of jurisdiction was completely litigated in judgment-rendering state, and judgment debtor did not appeal); Department of Human Servs. v. Shelnut, 772 So. 2d 1041 (Miss. 2000) (res judicata precluded defendant from contesting the issue of personal jurisdiction of a Canadian court when the defendant had contested jurisdiction in that court, lost, and failed to appeal); Gregoire v. Byrd, 338 S.C. 489, 527 S.E.2d 361 (Ct. App. 1999) (judgment debtor could not collaterally attack validity of another state's judgment on ground that court failed to fully and fairly litigate issue of personal jurisdiction over defendant because defendant litigated issue in foreign court). *But cf.* E. Howard St. Clair & Assocs., Inc. v. Northwest Carpets, Inc., 237 Ga. App. 537, 515 S.E.2d 660 (1999) (no presumption of jurisdiction when a foreign judgment is rendered by default and party seeking to domesticate the judgment bears the burden of negating the defense of lack of jurisdiction).

241. *See* RESTATEMENT (SECOND) OF JUDGMENTS § 12 cmt. c (1982).

242. *See* Chapter 6(D)(3)*(g)(ii) supra* ("Waiver"); *see also* Chapter 3(B)(3) *supra* ("In Personam Jurisdiction: Consent, Appearance, and Waiver").

243. *See* Chapter 2(A)(2) *supra* ("The 'No-Waiver, No-Consent' Rule") for a discussion of the rule that subject-matter jurisdiction objections cannot ordinarily be waived.

(1) The subject matter of the action was so plainly beyond the court's jurisdiction that its entertaining the action was a manifest abuse of authority; or

(2) Allowing the judgment to stand would substantially infringe the authority of another tribunal or agency of government; or

(3) The judgment was rendered by a court lacking capability to make an adequately informed determination of a question concerning its own jurisdiction and as a matter of procedural fairness the party seeking to avoid the judgment should have opportunity belatedly to attack the court's subject-matter jurisdiction.[244]

These rules are the normal ones governing collateral attack on grounds of lack of subject-matter or personal jurisdiction. There can be variation in the rules because of the combined effect of differences in local practice and 28 U.S.C. § 1738 (requiring the same effect to be given to judgments of other states that the judgments would be given in the rendering states).[245]

Illustration 13-63. If State *X* provides by its own domestic rules that subject-matter jurisdiction objections litigated and determined against a party can also be raised in subsequent proceedings in the courts of State *X*, then the objections can also be raised on collateral attack in a subsequent proceeding in State *Y*. Of course, State *X* would not be allowed to prescribe rules beyond its domestic competence. Thus, State *X* could not make default judgments immune from collateral attack in cases beyond its power under the U.S. Constitution. The State *Y* court would be entitled and, indeed, required to disregard such a rule and permit collateral attack. As to matters within the domestic competence of a state that are not limited by the Constitution, however, the rules can be varied.

* * * * *

The ordinary rules of issue preclusion also apply to questions of personal and subject-matter jurisdiction in the same way that they apply to "substantive" issues. Thus, the rules requiring a determination to support the judgment, and so forth, all apply to questions of personal and subject-matter jurisdiction.

Illustration 13-64. *P*, a citizen of State *X*, sues *D*, a citizen of State *Y*, in a state court in State *X*. *D* specially appears in accord with State *X* procedure to object to the State *X* court's personal jurisdiction under the Due Process Clause of the

---

244. RESTATEMENT (SECOND) OF JUDGMENTS § 12 (1982). *In re* Estate of LaRose, 2000 OK CIV APP 33, 1 P.3d 1018 (1999), was an Oklahoma guardianship proceeding in which the guardian presented a final account. The court held that a Michigan judgment was not entitled to full faith and credit in the Oklahoma proceeding because the Michigan court did not have jurisdiction over the guardianship assets and did not have jurisdiction to determine what charges could be made against the ward's estate. However, it appeared that the Michigan proceeding was a fully litigated one and that no one raised the jurisdictional issue in that proceeding. The court did not discuss whether this fact should have been held to foreclose litigation of the jurisdictional issue in Oklahoma; *see also* Lincoln Loan Co. v. City of Portland, 340 Or. 613, 136 P.3d 1 (2006) (plaintiff's argument that the court of appeals does not lawfully exist because a state constitutional provision establishing court is invalid should have been raised in prior proceeding; established claim-preclusion principles prevent the argument from being raised in subsequent action, because plaintiff has failed to show that the court of appeals review of judgment was so plainly beyond the court's jurisdiction that its entertaining the action was a manifest abuse of authority).

245. *Cf.* RESTATEMENT (SECOND) OF JUDGMENTS §§ 70, 82 (1982). Other complications in the enforcement of judgments produced by the federal system are discussed in section F *infra*.

Fourteenth Amendment and its subject-matter jurisdiction under State *X* law. The State *X* court holds that it has personal jurisdiction, but that it lacks subject-matter jurisdiction and dismisses the action. Subsequently, *P* sues *D* in a State *X* court of proper subject-matter jurisdiction. *D* specially appears and objects to personal jurisdiction. *D* is not precluded from relitigating the issue of personal jurisdiction by the judgment in the first action. The determination in that action that the court had personal jurisdiction over *D* did not support the judgment of dismissal in *D's* favor.[246]

SECTION F. COMPLICATIONS PRODUCED BY THE FEDERAL SYSTEM

In addition to the subject-matter and personal jurisdiction complications discussed in the preceding section, other problems exist because of (1) the existence of different rules among the fifty states defining the scope and effect of judgments, (2) different rules defining the scope and effect of federal and state-court judgments, and (3) differing approaches to the effect that should be given to the judgments of foreign nations. Each of these problems will be discussed in turn.

1. Enforcement of State Judgments

As noted in section E, above, and in Chapter 3, the U.S. Supreme Court's interpretation of 28 U.S.C. § 1738 requires the courts of each state to give the same effect to the valid judgments of other states as those judgments would receive in the state that rendered the judgments. The Full Faith and Credit Clause of the Constitution provides Congress with the authority to enact this statute: "Full faith and credit shall be given in each state to the public acts, records and judicial proceedings of every other state. And the Congress may by general laws prescribe the manner in which such acts, records and proceedings shall be proved, and the effect thereof."[247] The power to prescribe the effect that the judicial proceedings of one state should have in all others sustains the requirement in 28 U.S.C. § 1738 that the judgments of each state be given the same effect in the courts of other states as those judgments have in the states that render them.[248] In addition to prescribing the effect that state judgments must receive in the courts of other states, 28 U.S.C. § 1738 prescribes that federal courts shall give the same effect to state-court

---

246. *See* section C(1)*(d)*, *Illustration 13-28 supra*.

247. *U.S. Const.* art. IV, § 1; *see also* Brian M. Vines, *A Doctrine of Faith and Credit,* 94 VA. L. REV. 247 (2008).

248. *See* Chapter 3(A)(1) *supra* ("Personal Jurisdiction Restrictions Prior to the Adoption of the Fourteenth Amendment"). This, of course, means that if a state judgment is valid and res judicata where it is rendered, a court enforcing the judgment in another state must give it the same res judicata effect there and may not readjudicate the merits. *See, e.g.*, Pirtek, USA, L.L.C. v. Whitehead, 51 So. 3d 291 (Ala. 2010) (error for trial court to inquire into the merits after determining that Florida court had jurisdiction). This, in turn, means, however, that the judgment-enforcing court must be the body that determines the res judicata effect of the first judgment, even though that judgment is rendered in another state. *Cf.* Archer W. Contractors, Ltd. v. Benise-Dowling & Assocs., Inc., 33 So. 3d 1216 (Ala. 2009) (error for trial court to dismiss action without prejudice to action in any jurisdiction outside Alabama; Alabama courts do not have authority to direct other jurisdictions what effect to give to Alabama judgments).

judgments as those judgments would receive in the state where they were rendered.[249]

Section 1738 does not absolutely require that state and federal courts employ the same enforcement mechanisms that would be employed by the courts of the state that rendered a judgment. In *Baker ex rel. Thomas v. General Motors Corp.*,[250] the U.S. Supreme Court placed limits on the obligation of the states to enforce judgments of other states that would interfere with the operation of judicial proceedings in the judgment-enforcing state. In *Baker*, a Michigan court granted an injunction prohibiting a General Motors employee from testifying against G.M. as an expert witness. Subsequently, G.M. was sued by another party in a Missouri federal court in a wrongful death and products liability action, and the plaintiff sought to depose the employee and use him as a witness. G.M. resisted the employee's appearance on the basis of the Michigan injunction, but the federal district court allowed the employee to testify. Reversing the district court, the Eighth Circuit held that the Missouri court was obligated to give effect to the Michigan injunction. The U.S. Supreme Court reversed the Eighth Circuit and held that Michigan had no power to control courts and parties in other states by precluding them from determining which witnesses may testify.[251]

---

249. The statute actually states: "Such . . . judicial proceedings . . . shall have the same full faith and credit in every court within the United States and its Territories and Possessions as they have by law or usage in the courts of such State, Territory or Possession from which they are taken." 28 U.S.C. § 1738; *see also* Morris B. Chapman & Assocs., Ltd. v. Kitzman, 193 Ill. 2d 560, 739 N.E.2d 1263 (2000) (state courts must give same res judicata effect to sister state judgment as sister state would give to it); Rourke v. Amchem Prods., Inc., 384 Md. 329, 863 A.2d 926 (2004) (under both full-faith-and-credit analysis and common-law-collateral-estoppel analysis, Maryland does not have to give any greater preclusive effect to a Virginia judgment that it would receive in Virginia; because Virginia requires mutuality, it would not give preclusive effect of judgment in action between different parties; therefore, Maryland need not give judgment preclusive effect); Martin v. SAIF Corp., 2007 MT 234, 339 Mont. 167, 167 P.3d 916 (full faith and credit to judgment of another state generally requires that the judgment must receive at least the res judicata effect it would receive in the state which rendered it); Luna v. Dobson, 97 N.Y.2d 178, 763 N.E.2d 1146, 738 N.Y.S.2d 5 (2001) (judgment of state court should have same credit, validity, and effect in every other state as it has in the state where it was pronounced). *But see* Security Credit Leasing, Inc. v. D.J.'s, Inc., 140 N.C. App. 521, 537 S.E.2d 227 (2000) (stating incorrectly that the Full Faith and Credit Clause requires state courts to give other state judgments the same effect as would be given to domestic judgments of the judgment-enforcing state). *See also* Dennery v. Commonwealth Dep't of Transp., 791 A.2d 1279 (Pa. Commw. Ct. 2002) (full faith and credit did not bar the entry of licensee's driving-while-intoxicated conviction from another state in Pennsylvania license suspension proceeding, even though the driving under the influence order stated that the report of conviction shall not be evidential in any subsequent civil proceeding; in New Jersey, where driving under the influence conviction was entered, a license suspension is not a civil consequence of a conviction, but is part of the licensee's sentence for criminal conviction); JH v. RB, 796 A.2d 447 (R.I. 2002) (mother obtained judgment of divorce from husband in another state, the judgment stating that two children were born of the marriage, and mother also accepted benefits of judgment by obtaining child support payments from former husband under judgment; later mother commenced paternity action against defendant in Rhode Island; court held that summary judgment properly granted against mother; other state's divorce decree, including findings under decree, were entitled to full faith and credit; however, court confusingly and erroneously states at end of opinion that lower court was not obliged to consider doctrines of res judicata and collateral estoppel because it had held that the decree was entitled to full faith and credit; in fact, court did consider the res judicata effect of the divorce judgment under the law of the rendering state); *cf.* Starr v. George, 175 P.3d 50 (Alaska 2008) (judgment rendered without personal jurisdiction or adequate notice or opportunity to be heard will not be given full faith and credit in other states); Murray v. Ledbetter, 144 P.3d 492 (Alaska 2006) (although state judgment procured by fraud need not be enforced in another state, attorney's behavior leading to procurement of Idaho judgment was more akin to negligence than fraud; therefore, judgment would be enforced in Alaska).

250. 522 U.S. 222, 118 S. Ct. 657, 139 L. Ed. 2d 580 (1998).

251. *See also* National Union Fire Ins. Co. v. Greene, 195 Ariz. 105, 985 P.2d 590 (Ct. App. 1999) (full faith and credit does not make the laws of the judgment-rendering state applicable in enforcing judgments; enforcement is governed by the law of the state in which the judgment is domesticated); Brown v. Brown, 29 S.W.3d 491 (Tenn. Ct. App. 2000) (when judgment of another state is enrolled in Tennessee, it has the same effect and is subject to the same procedures, defenses, and proceedings for reopening, vacating, or staying as a judgment of a court of record in Tennessee and may be enforced or satisfied in a like manner, and thus the procedures for

The *Baker* holding appears to be a narrow one and does not create a broad exception to the general obligation of the states to give the same effect to judgments that the judgments would receive in the state that rendered them. The Court emphasized that it was not creating a "general exception to the full faith and credit command" and that its holding "surely does not permit a State court to refuse to honor a sister state judgment based on the forum's choice of law or policy preferences."[252] Rather, the Court's decision was based on "two critical counter principles to the near-automatic recognition of judgments."[253] The first was that the states need not "adopt the practices of other States regarding the time, manner, and mechanisms for enforcing judgments."[254] The second was that "[o]rders commanding action or inaction have been denied enforcement in a sister State when they purported to accomplish an official act within the exclusive province of that other State or interfered with litigation over which the ordering State had no authority."[255] Indeed, G.M. may simply have mistaken its remedy in the case. The Court itself recognized that the Michigan decree could operate against the employee to preclude him from volunteering his testimony.[256] Thus, G.M. might have sued the employee in a separate proceeding in Missouri to enforce the injunction against him.[257] In addition, it seems clear that G.M. could have enforced the injunction in Michigan by seeking a contempt citation against the employee there.[258]

Although *Baker* should eliminate any notion that there is a general public policy exception to the enforcement of state judgments under the implementing statute, it has not eliminated attempts by the state courts to create narrower public policy exceptions for particular situations. For example, in *Wamsley v. Nodak Mutual Insurance Co.*,[259] the Montana Supreme Court refused full faith and credit to a North Dakota judgment holding that North Dakota law applied to a "stacking"[260] issue under an insurance policy issued in North Dakota and a claim against that policy by the estate of deceased North Dakota citizens killed in a Montana accident. After the accident in Montana, there was extensive negotiation over whether the North Dakota policies could be stacked. After the Supreme Court of Montana held stacking permissible under Montana law, the insurance company initiated a declaratory judgment proceeding in North Dakota against the decedents'

---

vacating or reopening the judgment are those in the Tennessee Rules of Civil Procedure). *But cf.* Tel-Com Mgmt., Inc. v. Waveland Resort Inns, Inc., 782 So. 2d 149 (Miss. 2001) (judgment creditor brought an action in Mississippi to enforce a Louisiana judgment; the court held that the judgment was enforceable; in the process of doing so, the court considered an objection that the judgment violated the public policy of Mississippi; the court rejected the objection on the merits, but showed no awareness that it is impermissible to consider the public policy of the forum when asked to enforce another state's judgment).

252. *Baker*, 522 U.S. at 239, 118 S. Ct. at 667, 139 L. Ed. 2d at 596.

253. Patrick J. Borchers, *Conflict of Laws*, 49 SYRACUSE L. REV. 333, 336 (1999).

254. *Baker*, 522 U.S. at 235, 118 S. Ct. at 665, 139 L. Ed. 2d at 593.

255. *Id.*

256. *See id.* at 239, 118 S. Ct. at 667, 139 L. Ed. 2d at 595.

257. The Court itself indicated that it had "never placed equity decrees outside the full faith and credit domain." *See id.* at 234, 118 S. Ct. at 664, 139 L. Ed. 2d at 593. Coupled with its statement that the Michigan decree would have a preclusive effect against the employee, it appears that it could be enforced against the employee in Missouri.

258. *See* Patrick J. Borchers, *Conflict of Laws*, 49 SYRACUSE L. REV. 333, 337 (1999).

259. 2008 MT 56, 341 Mont. 467, 178 P.3d 102.

260. "Stacking" refers to the ability to add up the damage limits on insurance policies covering each automobile owned by an insured and insured by a company to obtain a total insurance award higher than could be obtained under the limits of the insured's automobile that was involved in the accident.

children, arguing that North Dakota law should be applied to determine the stacking question. Subsequently, the estate of the decedents initiated an action to recover under the policies in Montana. The North Dakota courts applied North Dakota law to the stacking question under the North Dakota choice-of-law system. This meant that no stacking would be allowed.[261]

Subsequently, the Montana trial court entered judgment under Montana law for the estate, holding that stacking was permissible. The Montana Supreme Court affirmed. The court first held (a) that the insurance company had waived the issue of personal jurisdiction over it in the Montana courts; (b) that the Montana trial court had not erred in exercising discretion not to dismiss under the "first filed rule" in deference to the North Dakota action; (c) and that the trial court correctly held that Montana conflict-of-laws doctrine, provided for the application of Montana law to the stacking issue.

Turning to the full faith and credit issue, the court held that res judicata criteria in Montana in the form of issue preclusion were satisfied because the children, who were the parties in North Dakota, were in privity with the estate, which was the party in Montana, and all other preclusion criteria were satisfied on the choice-of-law question. (Note that although it was technically error for the court to look to Montana preclusion law rather than North Dakota criteria, the error operated in favor of enforcement of the North Dakota judgment and would not thus conflict with the obligation to enforce that judgment, assuming that it was preclusive under North Dakota law.) The court also recognized that it would be inappropriate to refuse effect to the North Dakota judgment by invoking a general public policy exception. However, the court, relying in part on the Supreme Court's full faith and credit to judgments jurisprudence and in part on its public acts jurisprudence under the clause, held that a narrower exception applied. The court stated that the North Dakota proceeding was an improper attempt to interfere with "important interests" of Montana. Acknowledging that this exception would rarely be appropriate, the court stated:

> Here, the North Dakota declaratory judgment action was begun in an attempt to apply North Dakota law "through the back door" in Montana, and avoid a potentially adverse result here. As noted above, Nodak took advantage of the Estate's good graces by obtaining extensions to respond to its demands, all the while buying time to file a preemptive action in North Dakota. . . . It is evident that the declaratory judgment in North Dakota was brought for the purpose of preempting the District Court in Montana from exercising control over the judicial processes necessary to resolve this dispute. . . . [T]he North Dakota rulings simply constituted an "advisory opinion" on choice of law and stacking. The District Court in Montana was not bound by those rulings.
>
> We are troubled by Nodak's invocation of full faith and credit in an attempt to confer upon District Courts in North Dakota

---

261. *See* Nodak Mut. Ins. Co. v. Wamsley, 2004 ND 174, 687 N.W.2d 226.

> interlocutory control over District Courts in Montana. Nodak can point to no cases where full faith and credit has given one state the power to issue declaratory judgments aimed at exerting such control over *ongoing* litigation in a forum state. Permitting North Dakota's declaratory judgments to have preclusive effect over Montana courts in this case "would mean in effect that the courts of [North Dakota] can control what goes on in the courts of [Montana]." *Baker*, 522 U.S. at 236 n. 9 . . . .
>
> We emphasize that our decision here is not based upon the fact that anti-stacking statutes are contrary to public policy in Montana. We acknowledge there is no public policy exception to full faith and credit. We also recognize that this case presents a unique set of circumstances for which no clear rule in the full faith and credit jurisprudence has been established. *See Baker,* 522 U.S. at 245 . . . . Nonetheless, we conclude it would defeat the purpose of forging national unity to use full faith and credit to needlessly expand a single cause of action into multi-state litigation. If anything, such a use of the full faith and credit clause simply balkanizes the legal process, brings state courts into greater conflict, and diminishes respect for the type of state sovereignty the first Congress envisioned. For these reasons, we conclude the District Court did not err in declining to accord full faith and credit to the competing rulings issue by the North Dakota courts.[262]

The distinctions drawn by the Montana Supreme Court between the exception to the implementing statute that it recognized and a general public policy exception are not persuasive. In many cases involving parallel litigation in different states, it will often be possible to reason as the Montana court did—*i.e.,* that the sister-state court was engaging in an illegitimate attempt to undermine "important interests" of the forum. Thus, even if the exception were limited to cases in which a potential defendant has initiated declaratory judgment litigation in another state to obtain a choice-of-law advantage, it threatens to swallow most of the implementing statute's command. Furthermore, North Dakota had important interests in its own right in regulating the relationship of insurer and insured under a policy issued in North Dakota. The Montana court arguably gave North Dakota's contacts with the parties and the transaction, as well as its interests in applying its own law, inadequate consideration when it was assessing whether North Dakota's attempt to obtain application of its own law was an illegitimate attempt to obtain a "back door" choice-of-law advantage.

Apart from the *Baker* "exception" to § 1738, and creative policy exceptions such as the one created in *Wamsley*, the statute appears to operate more or less absolutely. Nevertheless, several important issues have arisen over the years concerning the application of § 1738 between different state courts and between state and federal courts. First, does § 1738 *ever* permit a state or federal court to

---

262. *Wamsley,* 2008 MT at ¶¶ 59-61, 341 Mont. at 485-86, 178 P.3d at 116.

give *less* effect to a state-court judgment than would be given to the judgment by the courts of the judgment-rendering state? Second, does § 1738 permit a state or federal court to give *more* effect to a state-court judgment than the judgment would be given by the judgment-rendering state? Third, does § 1738 require that federal (or state) courts give the same effect to a state-court judgment as the judgment would be given by the judgment-rendering state when the judgment determines federal issues?

(a) Giving Less Effect to State Judgments

As interpreted by the U.S. Supreme Court, § 1738 appears to be relatively absolute in its operation. Every state and federal court must give the same effect to judgments of other state courts rendered with jurisdiction as those judgments would receive in the state where they were rendered.[263] Thus, it appears that no *less* effect can ever be given to a state judgment than would be given to the judgment by the court that rendered the judgment. Nevertheless, commentators have expressed doubt whether the statute compels such a result.

> Collectively, [the] cases make it clear that full faith and credit embraces the central doctrines of res judicata. No other result could be tolerated in a federalistic society as mobile and litigious as ours. None of [the] decisions, however, compels the conclusion that full faith and credit incorporates every minute detail of res judicata doctrine. They simply do not address the compelling arguments that can be made for limiting full faith and credit to the rules that support the core values of finality, repose, and reliance, as well as some of the rules that facilitate control by the first court over its own procedure. . . . The essential point is that some aspects of modern preclusion doctrine should fall outside full faith and credit both because they are incidental to the central role of res judicata and because they may intrude on substantial interests of later courts.[264]

When should the policies implicit in § 1738 give way to the interests of "later courts"? Consider the following illustration, which will help indicate the

---

263. *See* Mills v. Duryee, 11 U.S. (7 Cranch) 481, 3 L. Ed. 411 (1813); D'Arcy v. Ketchum, 52 U.S. (11 How.) 165, 13 L. Ed. 648 (1851). These cases are discussed in Chapter 3(A)(1)*(d) supra* ("The 1790 Implementing Statute"). *See also, e.g.,* Holzemer v. Urbanski, 1999-Ohio-91, 86 Ohio St. 3d 129, 712 N.E.2d 713 (Ohio courts obligated to give same res judicata effect to probate proceeding in Michigan as that proceeding would have in Michigan). *But cf.* Sheldon R. Sharior, Annotation, *Res Judicata or Collateral Estoppel Effect, in State Where Real Property Is Located, of Foreign Decree Dealing with Such Property*, 32 A.L.R.3D 1330 (1970). Even if § 1738 requires that exactly the same effect be given to state judgments as they would receive in the states that rendered them, the judgment-enforcing state can still enact its own statute prescribing the procedures that must be used in authenticating and enforcing foreign judgments as long as the statute does not detract from the command of § 1738. *See, e.g.,* Conglis v. Radcliffe, 119 N.M. 287, 889 P.2d 1209 (1995).

264. 18B CHARLES A. WRIGHT ET AL., FEDERAL PRACTICE AND PROCEDURE: JURISDICTION AND RELATED MATTERS § 4467, at 35-36 (2d ed. 2002); *see also* Wilkes *ex rel.* Mason v. Phoenix Home Life Mut. Ins. Co., 587 Pa. 590, 902 A.2d 366 (2006) (discussing the possibility of applying Pennsylvania law to a New York judgment, but rejecting the possibility and applying New York law).

kinds of considerations that might operate to allow a court to give less effect to a state judgment than would be given to it in the judgment-rendering state.

Illustration 13-65. Suppose an airliner operated by *D Airways* crashes in State *X*. *D* is incorporated and has its principal place of business in State *X*. The survivors of one of the deceased passengers, who had resided in State *Y*, bring a wrongful death action in State *Y*. *D* is validly served with process by service on a managing agent in State *Y*, where the airline does a large amount of business. The action results in a verdict and judgment for the plaintiff for a substantial amount based on *D's* negligence. Under the rules of issue preclusion in State *Y*, the mutuality rule has been abolished. Thus, the judgment in the action described could be used to establish *D's* negligence in all subsequent actions by the survivors of deceased passengers in State *Y's* courts. Suppose, however, that a second wrongful death action is brought in State *X*, rather than State *Y*. Suppose further that State *X* has retained the mutuality rule in mass accident cases for the express purpose of protecting defendants with close connections to State *X* from ruinous liability based on a single judgment. The plaintiff in the State *X* action seeks to use the State *Y* judgment to establish the negligence of *D*. Does § 1738 compel State *X* to abandon its adherence to the mutuality rule and give the same nonmutual estoppel effect to the State *Y* judgment that it would receive in State *Y*? The answer ought to be "no." State *Y's* abandonment of mutuality is based upon its view that procedural efficiency and fairness will be best preserved, and litigation costs diminished, by nonmutual estoppel. These policies will be preserved substantially if State *Y* is able to enforce its rules of nonmutual preclusion in its own court system. Moreover, to require State *X* to apply nonmutual preclusion in its courts would be to force State *X* to give up a substantively based procedural rule designed to protect defendants with whom State *X* has a close connection in order to enforce a procedural rule of another state designed primarily to achieve litigational efficiency in that other state's courts. Based on the policies embodied in § 1738, State *X* should not be required to give the same effect to the State *Y* judgment that the judgment would receive in State *Y*.

* * * * *

As interpreted by the Supreme Court, § 1738 seems directed toward achieving nationwide finality and repose in dispute resolution by insisting that most res judicata questions be resolved by reference to the judgment-rendering state's law.[265] However, some state policies are remote from the core concerns of finality and repose that are embodied in the statute.[266] Consequently, when (1) it is possible to see, as in *Illustration 13-65*, that the judgment-rendering state's res judicata rules are based on narrow procedural policies applicable primarily or exclusively to litigation in the state's own courts and (2) these policies are opposed by important substantive concerns of the state where the second action is brought, § 1738 should not be read to require the second state to enforce the res judicata rules of the judgment-rendering state.

---

265. *See* 18B CHARLES A. WRIGHT ET AL., FEDERAL PRACTICE AND PROCEDURE: JURISDICTION AND RELATED MATTERS § 4467, at 637 (2d ed. 2002).

266. *See id.*

(b) Giving More Effect to State Judgments

Superficially, it may appear that if § 1738 *sometimes* permits the courts of a state to give less effect to judgments of other states than the judgments would receive where rendered, the statute should *always* permit a court to give *more* effect to a judgment than would be given in the judgment-rendering state. There is support for such a reading of the statute.[267] However, the wisdom of such a result is questionable.

Illustration 13-66. Assume again the basic facts of *Illustration 13-65* concerning an airline crash in State *X* and an initial action in State *Y*. Suppose, however, that State *Y* adheres to the mutuality rule for no good reason other than inertia, so far as it is possible to tell. Suppose further that State *X* has abandoned mutuality in all cases, even in mass accident cases. If a judgment is entered in favor of the plaintiff in the State *Y* action and a subsequent suit based on the same event is brought against the defendant by a different plaintiff in State *X*, should State *X* give nonmutual preclusive effect to the State *Y* judgment even though State *Y* would not do so? Section 1738 does not *require* State *X* to give more effect to State *Y* judgments than would State *Y*.[268] Moreover, it probably would be unwise for State *X* to do so. For one thing, the defendant may have relied on the judgment-rendering state's rule in either choosing to litigate rather than settle (because of the limited risks in other litigation that the mutuality rule of State *Y* afforded), or in litigating less vigorously than it would otherwise have done if nonmutual preclusion had been in effect. Even an examination of the first proceeding under the "full and fair opportunity to litigate" test of the *Restatement (Second) of Judgments* might not reveal the extent of the defendant's reliance after the fact.[269] Consequently, even in a case such as the one posed, when the judgment-rendering state retains the mutuality rule out of inertia, it seems that the policy of nationwide security of judgments supporting § 1738 is implicated sufficiently to require adherence to the judgment-rendering state's rule.[270]

* * * * *

The U.S. Supreme Court has not resolved the question whether a state can *ever* give greater effect to another state's judgments than would be given by the judgment-rendering state. However, the Court has concluded that in subsequent federal antitrust and civil rights actions, the federal courts may not generally give a greater claim preclusion effect to a state judgment than would be given to the

---

267. *See, e.g.*, Hart v. American Airlines, Inc., 61 Misc. 2d 41, 304 N.Y.S.2d 810 (Sup. Ct. 1969).

268. *See, e.g.*, New York *ex rel.* Halvey v. Halvey, 330 U.S. 610, 67 S. Ct. 903, 91 L. Ed. 1133 (1947); Meenach v. General Motors Corp., 891 S.W.2d 398 (Ky. 1995).

269. *Cf.* 18B CHARLES A. WRIGHT ET AL., FEDERAL PRACTICE AND PROCEDURE: JURISDICTION AND RELATED MATTERS § 4467, at 47-48 (2d ed. 2002). In addition,

> [a]ssertion of nonmutual preclusion in such circumstances would make it impossible for the first court to give effect to policies that may include broad freedom in selecting parties, freedom to litigate a particular case according to its own needs without concern about the impact on other cases, and acceptance of results that seem just between particular parties even though a new trial or directed verdict—or at least appeal—would be required if the stakes were greater.

18A *id.* § 4465.5, at 800.

270. The case, of course, would be made much stronger for this result if the judgment-rendering state retained the mutuality rule for substantive policy reasons, such as to protect defendants in whom the state has a legitimate interest from massive liability proceeding from a single judgment.

judgment by a state court.[271] These cases support a general interpretation of § 1738 that would forbid a greater effect from ever being given to a judgment than would be given the judgment in the judgment-rendering state.

(c) Giving Effect to State Judgments in Cases Applying Another State's Law or Federal Law

(i) Another State's Law

Section 1738 on its face does not provide for different effects to be given to state judgments depending upon the source of law being employed by the judgment-rendering court. Furthermore, it would be unwise to interpret § 1738 as permitting an exception to the "same effect" rule *merely* because the judgment-rendering state applied (or tried to apply) the substantive law of the judgment-enforcing state. Only when the judgment-rendering state's res judicata rules are based on procedural policies applicable exclusively in the courts of the judgment-rendering state, as in *Illustration 13-65*, should an exception be allowed.

Illustration 13-67. It does not matter that an Iowa court is applying (or attempting to apply) Mississippi law when it renders a judgment, nor that Mississippi's highest court would find that the Iowa court erred in determining the content of Mississippi law. The Iowa court's judgment must be given the same effect in Mississippi and all other states as it would be given in Iowa.[272]

(ii) Federal Law

Section 1738 does not provide for any exceptions for cases in which the state courts apply federal law in rendering a judgment. Nevertheless, questions exist in two areas about the extent to which state judgments should be given preclusive effect in subsequent federal actions. One area involves cases in which the first action is adjudicated in a state court and a second action is brought in federal court under a grant of exclusive jurisdiction to the federal courts. The basic question is whether a limited claim or issue preclusion effect should be given to the state judgment because of the policies underlying the grant of exclusive jurisdiction to the federal courts. The second area involves cases in which the first adjudication in the state courts is followed by a second proceeding in federal court under a federal civil rights act, such as 42 U.S.C. § 1983.[273] The question here is whether the policies supporting the various civil rights acts demand that a limited claim or issue preclusion effect be given to the state judgment.

Section 26(1)(c) of the *Restatement (Second) of Judgments* takes the position that if a plaintiff brings a state claim in state court and subsequently sues

---

271. *See* Marrese v. American Acad. of Orthopaedic Surgeons, 470 U.S. 373, 105 S. Ct. 1327, 84 L. Ed. 2d 274 (1985); *cf.* Migra v. Warren City Sch. Dist. Bd. of Educ., 465 U.S. 75, 104 S. Ct. 892, 79 L. Ed. 2d 56 (1984).

272. *See* Fauntleroy v. Lum, 210 U.S. 230, 28 S. Ct. 641, 52 L. Ed. 1039 (1908).

273. *Cf.* Joshua M. D. Segal, *Rebalancing Fairness and Efficiency: The Offensive Use of Collateral Estoppel In § 1983 Actions*, 89 B.U. L. REV. 1305 (2009).

on a federal claim in federal court over which the federal courts would have exclusive jurisdiction, there would be no claim-preclusion effect, even if the state and federal claims arose out of the same facts.

Illustration 13-68. Suppose that *P* commences an action in state court under the state antitrust laws and loses on the merits. *P* then commences an action in federal court against the same defendant under the federal antitrust laws, an action over which the federal courts have exclusive jurisdiction. Under the approach of the *Restatement (Second)*, even though both the state and federal actions are based on the same events, *P's* federal action is not precluded. The reason is simply that the state court had no subject-matter jurisdiction over the federal antitrust claim. Consequently, the *Restatement (Second)* provides that claim preclusion does not operate in this situation.[274]

* * * * *

In two decisions, the U.S. Supreme Court has cast substantial doubt about whether § 1738 will be interpreted in accord with the *Restatement (Second)'s* position. In *Marrese v. American Academy of Orthopaedic Surgeons*,[275] the Court held that the first inquiry in a case involving a state judgment must be whether state claim preclusion principles would prohibit a second action. Only if state law does prohibit a second action is it necessary to determine whether an exception should be created to § 1738 because a federal claim omitted from the state action was within the exclusive jurisdiction of the federal courts.[276] The Court also stated that once the question of an exception under § 1738 is presented, its answer depends "on the particular federal statute as well as the nature of the claim or issue involved in the subsequent federal action. Our previous decisions indicate that the primary consideration must be the intent of Congress."[277]

Subsequently, in *Matsushita Electric Industrial Co. v. Epstein*,[278] the Court was faced with a situation in which a state class action was brought in Delaware asserting state claims arising out of a tender offer made by Matsushita for the common stock of a Delaware Corporation. While the state action was pending, a federal class action was commenced in California under the federal securities laws based on the same facts, an action over which the federal courts had exclusive jurisdiction. The California district court refused to certify the action as a class action and dismissed the case. After the federal plaintiffs had appealed, the state class action in Delaware was settled. As part of the settlement, the class agreed to release all claims arising out of the tender offer, including the federal claims that were being asserted in the California action. Although the class members were given notice of the proposed settlement, they did not opt out of the class or object to the settlement in Delaware. After the settlement, Matsushita asserted that the Delaware judgment embodying the settlement had a claim preclusive effect on further prosecution of the California action. The Ninth Circuit Court of Appeals rejected Matsushita's argument on the grounds that the preclusive effect of the

---

274. RESTATEMENT (SECOND) OF JUDGMENTS § 26(1)(c) cmt. 1, illus. 2 (1982).
275. 470 U.S. 373, 105 S. Ct. 1327, 84 L. Ed. 2d 274 (1985).
276. *Id.* at 382-86, 105 S. Ct. at 1332-35, 84 L. Ed. 2d at 282-85.
277. *Id.* at 386, 105 S. Ct. at 1335, 84 L. Ed. 2d at 285.
278. 516 U.S. 367, 116 S. Ct. 873, 134 L. Ed. 2d 6 (1996).

Delaware judgment under § 1738 was limited to the state claims involved in the action.

The U.S. Supreme Court reversed. Following *Marrese*, the Court held that the first inquiry had to be whether Delaware would give a claim preclusive effect to the judgment that would include the federal claims. The Court indicated, as it had in *Marrese*, that examination of state law would not always give a clear answer to the preclusion question, because state courts will usually not have any occasion to pronounce upon the preclusive effect of a state judgment in a later action that can only be brought in federal court.[279] However, the Court stated that federal courts could obtain guidance from "general state law on the preclusive force of settlement judgments."[280] Examining Delaware law, the Court concluded that general Delaware preclusion principles as well as particular Delaware decisions speaking to the preclusive force of class-action settlements in federal court indicated that the state would give a preclusive effect to the judgment in question.[281]

The Court then turned to the question whether the exclusive grant of federal jurisdiction for federal securities claims should be interpreted to create an exception to § 1738. The Court held that for an exception to exist, there must be an irreconcilable conflict between the grant of exclusive jurisdiction and § 1738.[282] The Court found that the federal statutory grant of exclusive jurisdiction did not manifest any congressional intent either to create an exception to § 1738 or to prevent litigants in state court from releasing federal securities claims as part of a settlement within the jurisdiction of the state courts.[283] In addition, the Court found nothing in the legislative history of the grant of exclusive jurisdiction that would justify creating an exception to § 1738.[284] Other parts of the securities acts also suggested to the Court that Congress had contemplated dual litigation in state and federal court, but had, nevertheless, done nothing to "modify the background rule that where a state-court judgment precedes that of a federal court, the federal court must give full faith and credit to the state judgment."[285] Finally, the Court invoked its own prior decisions holding that state-court judgments could have an issue preclusion effect in subsequent federal actions and that parties can waive the right to have federal securities claims litigated in federal court by agreeing to arbitrate the claims.[286] Thus, the Court held that the Delaware judgment had to be given a preclusive effect on the federal claims by force of § 1738 and remanded for proceedings consistent with its opinion.[287]

---

279. *See id.* at 375, 116 S. Ct. at 878, 134 L. Ed. 2d at 18.

280. *See id.*

281. *See id.* at 376-78, 116 S. Ct. at 879-80, 134 L. Ed 2d at 18-20.

282. *See id.* at 381, 116 S. Ct. at 881, 134 L. Ed 2d at 21.

283. *See id.* at 381-82, 116 S. Ct. at 881-82, 134 L. Ed. 2d at 21-22.

284. *See id.* at 383, 116 S. Ct. at 882, 134 L. Ed. 2d at 23.

285. *Id.* at 383-84, 116 S. Ct. at 882, 134 L. Ed.2d at 23.

286. *See id.* at 384-85, 116 S. Ct. at 882-83, 134 L. Ed. 2d at 23-24.

287. On remand, the Ninth Circuit Court of Appeals held that the Supreme Court decision necessarily found that the Delaware judgment comported with due process and that the state court's determination of adequacy of representation under the Due Process Clause was not subject to broad collateral review. *See* Epstein v. MCA, Inc., 179 F.3d 641 (9th Cir. 1999); *see also* Dutch D. Chung, Note, *The Preclusive Effect of State Court Adjudication of Patent Issues and the Federal Courts' Choice of Preclusion Law*, 69 FORDHAM L. REV. 707 (2000). For a criticism of *Matsushita*, see Mollie A. Murphy, *The Intersystem Class Settlement: Of Comity, Consent, and Collusion*, 47 U. KAN. L. REV. 413 (1999). Of course, a state-court class settlement based on state law will normally

Taken together, *Marrese* and *Matsushita* are strong evidence that the *Restatement (Second)'s* position on preclusion of exclusive federal claims will not often prevail. In the absence of explicit statutory language or legislative history, which is seldom likely to exist,[288] the grant of exclusive jurisdiction is not likely to be read as creating an exception to § 1738.[289] The greatest difficulty that the federal courts will face in these cases is determining whether state claim preclusion principles would encompass federal claims that are omitted from a state action because they are within the exclusive jurisdiction of the federal courts. As *Matsushita* indicated, there will usually be no occasion for the state courts to pronounce upon such a question. However, in the event that the state courts have not explicitly addressed the question, *Matsushita* also indicated that federal courts can rely on general state preclusion principles to determine the question. Some federal courts have done this.[290]

Nevertheless, the question may not be easy to resolve on the basis of a state's general preclusion principles. For example, a state may follow the general position of the *Restatement (Second)* that claim preclusion does not occur when elements of a claim are omitted because they are not within the subject-matter jurisdiction of the court in which the action is brought. However, the state may also follow the rule that if a plaintiff has multiple courts in which to sue and picks a court with narrow subject-matter jurisdiction, the plaintiff should be precluded from later asserting claims arising out of the same facts that could have been joined if the action had been brought in a court of broader subject-matter jurisdiction.[291] Assuming that the plaintiff could have sued on both claims in federal court, joining the state claim within the federal court's supplemental jurisdiction,[292] should the state's general preclusion principles be interpreted to allow or forbid later assertion of the federal claim if the plaintiff chooses to litigate in state court instead? Suppose instead that the state has not indicated whether it would follow either of the above rules, but has indicated generally that it follows the *Restatement (Second)'s* approach to preclusion. Under these circumstances, should state law be interpreted as incorporating the rule, approved by the *Restatement (Second)*, that omission from a state action of a claim within the exclusive jurisdiction of the federal courts does not preclude later litigation of the claim in a federal action, even though *Marrese* and *Matsushita* indicate that the *Restatement's* position was not, in fact, a real

---

be given full faith and credit in federal court. *See* Gooch v. Life Investors Ins. Co. of Am., 672F.3d 402 (6th Cir. 2012).

288. *See* 18B CHARLES A. WRIGHT ET AL, FEDERAL PRACTICE AND PROCEDURE: JURISDICTION AND RELATED MATTERS § 4470.1, at 178-89 (2d ed. 2002).

289. *Cf.* Fox v. Maulding, 112 F.3d 453 (10th Cir. 1997) (parties argued that they should not be precluded from asserting their federal RICO claims by a state compulsory counterclaim rule, because at the time of the state action it was not clear that the state courts could adjudicate the claims, so they were omitted; court held that in the absence of clear authority that the state courts could not hear the claims, the parties at least had to try to assert them in the state court).

290. *See* Aquatherm Indus., Inc. v. Florida Power & Light Co., 84 F.3d 1388 (11th Cir. 1996) (Florida follows general rule that splitting of cause of action does not occur when suit is not brought in court that has jurisdiction over all of plaintiff's claims; therefore, claim within exclusive federal jurisdiction not precluded by state judgment); *see also* Gonzales v. Hernandez, 175 F.3d 1202 (10th Cir. 1999) (federal § 1983 action in which state law on the effect of a prior state judgment on vicarious liability was interpreted by relying on a prior state case following § 51(1) of the *Restatement (Second)*).

291. *See* section B(3), *Illustrations 13-14 & 13-15 supra.*

292. *See* Chapter 2(C)(4) *supra* ("Supplemental Jurisdiction").

restatement? These are not easy questions, and it does not seem likely that the answers given to them by federal courts will necessarily be the same as those that would be given by the state courts if they had an opportunity to answer the questions themselves.[293]

Issue preclusion poses similar problems in exclusive jurisdiction situations. However, as indicated above in the discussion of the *Matsushita* case, the Supreme Court has indicated that issue preclusion will be accepted in at least some cases where state courts adjudicate matters that later become relevant in federal actions within the exclusive jurisdiction of the federal courts.[294] However, the problems here are no easier to resolve than in the claim preclusion area.

Illustration 13-69. In a state suit for breach of contract, the defendant may assert that the contract is invalid under the federal antitrust laws. The state court has the authority to decide the federal antitrust issue raised as a defense, even though it would not have jurisdiction over the same issue if asserted as an affirmative claim by a plaintiff. If the state court decides against the defense and the state defendant then sues as a plaintiff in a federal antitrust action, the question is whether the exclusive grant of jurisdiction to federal courts over antitrust claims should be read to create an exception to § 1738 (assuming that the federal antitrust issue would be deemed res judicata in the state courts).

* * * * *

State courts also have authority to adjudicate factual issues that later may be relevant in actions within the exclusive jurisdiction of the federal courts.

Illustration 13-70. In a state action on a license agreement, the state court may determine that the agreement terminated as of a particular date. This determination also might be relevant in a later federal action for patent infringement within the exclusive jurisdiction of the federal courts. Again, the issue is whether the exclusive grant of jurisdiction to federal courts over patent infringement suits requires an exception to the ordinary rule of § 1738.

* * * * *

---

293. In fact, it seems that there is likely to be a good bit of confusion, at least for a time, about what it is proper for federal courts to do in these cases. For example, in RADS, P.C. v. Mercy Memorial Hospital, 3 F. Supp. 2d 772 (E.D. Mich. 1998), RADS had asserted state antitrust counterclaims against Mercy in an action in state court, and the state court had dismissed those counterclaims for failure to state a claim upon which relief could be granted. In a separate federal action asserting federal antitrust claims, but commenced before the state action, RADS had not asserted the state claims. The federal district court dismissed the federal action, holding that it was precluded by the dismissal of the state counterclaims. The court looked to state preclusion law and found that the subject matter of the state and federal actions was the same, the parties were the same, and the prior state judgment was on the merits. However, the state court did not have jurisdiction over the federal antitrust claims. The court may have been holding that the claims were split by the assertion of the state claims in state court, but compulsory counterclaim rules also have a preclusive effect in situations where no counterclaim is asserted at all by a defendant. Therefore, it would seem that a failure to assert the state counterclaims in the state action would also have to have a claim preclusive effect in the federal action. However, such an approach would mean that plaintiffs asserting federal claims within the exclusive jurisdiction of the federal courts would always have to join any related state claims that they possess if they are being sued in state court in a related matter. Otherwise, they may be met with a defense of res judicata on the federal claims by virtue of the operation of a state compulsory counterclaim rule. Thus, they would be forced to assert state claims that they do not wish to assert in the federal action in order to prevent preclusion on the federal claims. Such a result, to say the least, would violate the spirit of the doctrine of finality which aims to hold down the level of unnecessary litigation.

294. *See* Becher v. Contoure Labs., Inc., 279 U.S. 388, 49 S. Ct. 356, 73 L. Ed. 752 (1929) (issue preclusion in federal patent infringement action on issue of historical fact determined in prior state action).

Under the approach taken by § 28(3) of the *Restatement (Second) of Judgments*, "[t]he question in each . . . case would be resolved in the light of the legislative purpose in vesting exclusive jurisdiction in a particular court."[295] Issue preclusion seems to have been accepted most readily in cases in which the state courts have adjudicated issues of historical fact, mixed issues of fact and "legal evaluation," and application of state law to fact.[296]

When the state courts directly adjudicate issues of federal law, however, the proper result is less clear. As was true of the Supreme Court's approach to the problem of claim preclusion in the *Marrese* case, it is easy to state (as the *Restatement (Second)* does regarding issue preclusion) that the reasons for the exclusive grant of jurisdiction to the federal courts should be evaluated in each case and the determination made whether those purposes require an exception to the ordinary rule of preclusion under § 1738. It is quite another matter to find in the federal statutes granting exclusive jurisdiction to the federal courts or the legislative history of those statutes any concrete reasons why the state courts have been excluded from hearing certain kinds of cases.[297] As might be expected under such circumstances, the authorities are split on the correct result.[298] In addition, it seems likely that the first question in the issue preclusion area (as in the claim preclusion area) will be whether state preclusion rules would prohibit relitigation of issues of federal law in a later suit within exclusive federal jurisdiction. It will be no easier to find state precedent directly bearing on this question than it was to find state authority on preclusion of federal claims.

The argument was once made that federal civil rights laws, especially 42 U.S.C. § 1983, justify an exception to the ordinary preclusion rules that operate under § 1738. Basically, the argument was that the civil rights acts embody a congressional policy against final state-court adjudication in the situations to which they apply, thus requiring that the ordinary rules of claim and issue preclusion that the states would apply to their own judgments be superseded, § 1738 notwithstanding.

Although some questions remain in this area, the U.S. Supreme Court has thoroughly rejected this line of reasoning. In *Allen v. McCurry*,[299] the Court held that issue preclusion prevented the plaintiff from relitigating a federal constitutional issue in a federal civil rights action under § 1983 when that issue previously had been determined against him in a state criminal proceeding in which he was a defendant. In *Allen*, a criminal defendant had moved in his state trial to suppress evidence seized from him by the state police on the grounds that the search and seizure violated the Fourth and Fourteenth Amendments. The motion to suppress

---

295. RESTATEMENT (SECOND) OF JUDGMENTS § 28(3) cmt. e (1982).

296. *See id.*; Becher v. Contoure Labs., Inc., 279 U.S. 388, 49 S. Ct. 356, 73 L. Ed. 752 (1929); 18B CHARLES A. WRIGHT ET AL., FEDERAL PRACTICE AND PROCEDURE: JURISDICTION AND RELATED MATTERS § 4470.2, at 196-98 (2d ed. 2002), and authorities there cited.

297. *See* 18B CHARLES A. WRIGHT ET AL., FEDERAL PRACTICE AND PROCEDURE: JURISDICTION AND RELATED MATTERS § 4470.1, at 178-79 (2d ed. 2002).

298. *See id.* § 4470.2, at 196-205 & authorities there cited; RESTATEMENT (SECOND) OF JUDGMENTS § 28, reporter's note to subsection (3), at 288 (1982) and authorities there cited; *see also* Turnbow v. Pacific Mut. Life Ins. Co., 934 F.2d 1100 (9th Cir. 1991).

299. 449 U.S. 90, 101 S. Ct. 411, 66 L. Ed. 2d 308 (1980).

was denied, the defendant was convicted, and his conviction was upheld on appeal. Subsequently, the criminal defendant sued two of the police officers who conducted the search (and whom he had shot), as well as some other defendants, in a federal civil rights action under § 1983, seeking damages for the same unconstitutional search and seizure. The district court granted summary judgment on the grounds that issue preclusion prevented the plaintiff from relitigating the search and seizure question decided against him in the state courts. The Eighth Circuit reversed, holding that issue preclusion inapplicable in the particular case because an action under § 1983 was the only route to a federal forum for the plaintiff's constitutional claim. The Supreme Court granted certiorari and reversed.

The Court held that nothing in the language or legislative history of § 1983 demonstrated any intention to deny the binding effect to a state-court judgment that ordinarily would be required under § 1738. The Court stated that the history of § 1983 might support an exception to § 1738 when "state law did not provide for procedures for the litigation of constitutional claims, or [when] a state court failed to even acknowledge the existence of the constitutional principle on which a litigant based his claim."[300] However, such an exception

> would be essentially the same as the important general limit on rules of preclusion that already exists: collateral estoppel does not apply where the party against whom an earlier court decision is asserted did not have a full and fair opportunity to litigate the claim or issue decided by the first court.[301]

Subsequently, in *Migra v. Warren City School District Board of Education*,[302] the Court considered whether claim preclusion also applied when a state judgment was asserted as res judicata in a subsequent federal action under § 1983.[303] The Court reasoned that nothing in § 1983 would justify drawing a distinction between issue preclusion and claim preclusion. It rejected the argument that giving "state-court judgments full issue preclusive effect but not claim preclusive effect would enable litigants to bring their state claims in state court and their federal claims in federal court, thereby taking advantage of the relative expertise of both forums."[304] The Court stated § 1738 "embodies the view that it is more important to give full faith and credit to state-court judgments than to ensure

---

300. *Id.* at 101, 101 S. Ct. at 418, 66 L. Ed 2d at 317.

301. *Id.*

302. 465 U.S. 75, 104 S. Ct. 892, 79 L. Ed. 2d 56 (1984).

303. In *Migra*, the plaintiff first sued the Board of Education and three of its members who had voted not to renew her contract in state court, joining a breach of contract claim and a claim (against the individual Board members) for wrongful interference with her contract of employment. The state court found in plaintiff's favor on the breach of contract claim and ordered her reinstated to her position, awarding compensatory damages. Issues of conspiracy and individual Board member liability were dismissed without prejudice. Subsequently, the plaintiff commenced a federal action under § 1983, alleging that the Board's actions were designed to punish her for the exercise of her First Amendment rights, and that the actions deprived her of property without due process and of equal protection of the law. The district court granted summary judgment on grounds of res judicata, and the Sixth Circuit affirmed. The Supreme Court granted certiorari and ultimately vacated the judgment and remanded the case for further consideration of whether state res judicata rules would preclude the plaintiff's action.

304. *Id.* at 84-85, 104 S. Ct. at 898, 79 L. Ed. 2d at 64.

separate forums for federal and state claims."[305] The Court thus held that the state-court judgment in this litigation has the same claim preclusive effect in federal court that the judgment would have in the state courts.[306]

Subsequent decisions of the Court have expanded the reach of *Allen* to civil rights statutes other than § 1983. In *Kremer v. Chemical Construction Corp.*,[307] the Court held that the Title VII of the Civil Rights Act of 1964[308] does not create an exception to 28 U.S.C. § 1738.[309] On the central question involved in *Kremer*, the Court stated that an exception to § 1738 would not be recognized unless a later statute contained an express or implied partial repeal of the section. Title VII contained no express repeal. The Court found no implied repeal of § 1738 because no irreconcilable conflict existed between the two statutes. Furthermore, Title VII was not intended as a substitute for § 1738.[310]

In *San Remo Hotel, L.P. v. City & County of San Francisco,*[311] the Supreme Court continued its strict interpretation of § 1738 in an unusual case involving the federal doctrine of abstention. In *San Remo,* hotel owners brought a § 1983 action against the city to challenge the constitutionality of an ordinance on the ground that it effectuated a taking of property without due process. The Ninth Circuit Court of Appeals ordered the district court to abstain from decision while the plaintiffs sought compensation in state court. Abstention was ordered under the doctrine of *Railroad Commission v. Pullman Co.*,[312] because a decision of the state court might make the federal constitutional question unnecessary. Under *Pullman,* litigants forced into the state courts may reserve their federal constitutional issues for later decision by a federal court if the state proceeding does not make decision of those issues unnecessary.[313] The plaintiffs attempted to do so in the state proceeding in *San Remo.*

---

305. According to the Court, this view reflected "a variety of concerns, including notions of comity, the need to prevent vexatious litigation, and a desire to conserve judicial resources." The Court also pointed out that "[i]n the present litigation, petitioner does not claim that the state court would not have adjudicated her federal claims had she presented them in her original suit in state court. Alternatively, petitioner could have obtained a federal forum for her federal claim by litigating it first in a federal court. Section 1983, however, does not override state preclusion law and guarantee petitioner a right to proceed to judgment in state court on her state claims and then turn to federal court for adjudication of her federal claims." *Id.*

306. *Id.* Because it was unclear whether the district court had applied the Ohio law of preclusion, the court vacated the judgment of the Court of Appeals for further proceedings consistent with the Supreme Court's decision.

307. 456 U.S. 461, 102 S. Ct. 1883, 72 L. Ed. 2d 262 (1982).

308. 42 U.S.C. § 2000e to 2000e-17.

309. In *Kremer*, the plaintiff claimed that he had been discharged discriminatorily on grounds of national origin and religious faith. The plaintiff filed discrimination charges with the Equal Employment Opportunity Commission, which referred them to the New York State Division of Rights as required by Title VII. The state agency found against the plaintiff and he sought review of the administrative decision in the state's courts. This was his fatal mistake. The state courts upheld the agency determination, and the plaintiff brought a federal action under Title VII. The Supreme Court held that while state agency decisions are not given preclusive effect under § 1738, the state court proceedings reviewing the agency action were entitled to such effect under the section. Title VII requires that the EEOC defer action for sixty days while a state agency with jurisdiction over employment discrimination complaints has an opportunity to consider the discrimination charge. However, Title VII does not require the plaintiff to pursue state judicial review of the state agency's action. If the plaintiff does, however, § 1738 applies as it does to all other judicial action. *See Kremer,* 456 U.S. at 463-75, 102 S. Ct. at 1888-94, 72 L. Ed. 2d at 268-76.

310. *See id.* at 468-76, 102 S. Ct. at 1890-95, 72 L. Ed. 2d at 271-77.

311. 545 U.S. 323, 125 S. Ct. 2491,162 L. Ed. 2d 315 (2005).

312. 312 U.S. 496, 61 S. Ct. 643, 85 L. Ed. 971 (1941).

313. *See* England v. Louisiana Bd. of Med. Exam'rs, 375 U.S. 411, 84 S. Ct. 461, 11 L. Ed. 2d 440 (1964).

After the state court denied the plaintiffs' relief, they returned to federal court to litigate their federal constitutional questions. However, the plaintiffs' federal constitutional claims depended upon a number of issues that were identical to issues decided in the state court (because the state court had interpreted the relevant state takings law coextensively with federal law), and the district court held that relitigation of those issues was precluded by § 1738. The court of appeals affirmed, and the Supreme Court granted certiorari and affirmed the court of appeals. Because the plaintiffs had not simply reserved the federal constitutional question they sought to litigate in federal court, but had, in the state proceeding, broadened the litigation in state court in a manner that effectively asked that court to resolve the same federal issue they sought to reserve for federal court, they were not able to use the reservation procedure of the abstention doctrine to avoid the force of § 1738. Other issues litigated in state court had not been the subject of the abstention order and could not, therefore, be saved by a reservation of rights to litigate in federal court. In addition, the Supreme Court continued its refusal to allow federal courts to create exceptions to § 1738 when no subsequent federal statute contains an express or implied partial repeal of the provision and Congress had not clearly manifested its intent to depart from § 1738.[314]

Recall that in *Allen*, the Court indicated a state judgment would not be given preclusive effect in a subsequent federal action if a full and fair opportunity to litigate the federal issues had not been afforded by the state court. However, the Court did not indicate whether this "full and fair opportunity" exception was a federal or state standard. In other words, it was unclear from *Allen* whether the scope of the full and fair opportunity exception would be defined by state law, as are other questions under § 1738, or whether an independent federal standard would be utilized to measure the fairness of state procedures.[315] Later decisions have addressed this question. These decisions have resolved that the standard will be federal, but the scope of the federal standard is not yet clear.

In *Kremer*, discussed above, the Court seemed to state clearly that the federal standard would be the narrow one of whether the state procedures complied with the Due Process Clause of the Fourteenth Amendment:

> The State must, however, satisfy the applicable requirements of the Due Process Clause. A [s]tate may not grant preclusive effect in its own courts to a constitutionally infirm judgment, and other state and federal courts are not required to accord full faith and credit to such a judgment. Section 1738 does not suggest otherwise; other state and federal courts would still be providing a state court judgment with the "same" preclusive effect as the courts of the [s]tate from which the judgment emerged. In such a

---

314. *See also* Brother Records, Inc. v. Jardine, 432 F.3d 939 (9th Cir. 2005) (Full Faith and Credit Implementing Statute requires that federal court give preclusive effect to state-court decision holding that prior federal judgment did not bar subsequent state action, even if state court mistakenly rejected a claim of res judicata).

315. *See* 18B CHARLES A. WRIGHT ET AL., FEDERAL PRACTICE AND PROCEDURE: JURISDICTION AND RELATED MATTERS § 4471, at 245-46 (2d ed. 2002).

case, there could be no constitutionally recognizable preclusion at all.[316]

The apparent clarity of this statement was clouded by the Court's later decision in *Haring v. Prosise*.[317] In *Haring*, the Court, in an extended dictum, suggested that the exceptions to § 1738 may be broader than the due process exception articulated in *Kremer*.

> Title 28 U.S.C. § 1738 generally requires "federal courts to give preclusive effect to state-court judgments whenever the courts of the State from which the judgments emerged would do so" [citing *Allen v. McCurry*]. In federal actions, including § 1983 actions, a state-court judgment will not be given collateral estoppel effect, however, where "the party against whom an earlier court decision is asserted did not have a full and fair opportunity to litigate the claim or issue decided by the first court. . . ." Moreover, additional exceptions to collateral estoppel may be warranted in § 1983 actions in light of the "understanding of § 1983" that "the federal courts could step in where the state courts were unable to protect federal rights."[318]

2. Enforcement of Federal Judgments

The language of 28 U.S.C. § 1738 does not require state courts or other federal courts to give any particular effect to the prior judgments of federal courts. Nevertheless, it is settled that federal judgments must be given effect in other courts and that the effect to be given a federal judgment is a "federal question" reviewable by the Supreme Court on appeal from a state court.[319] The *Restatement (Second) of Judgments* flatly states this rule as follows: "Federal law determines the effects

---

316. *Kremer*, 456 U.S. at 482, 102 S. Ct. at 1898, 72 L. Ed. 2d at 281.

317. 462 U.S. 306, 103 S. Ct. 2368, 76 L. Ed. 2d 595 (1983). In *Haring*, a state criminal defendant pleaded guilty to manufacturing a controlled substance. No question of the legality of the search and seizure of the controlled substance that led to the defendant's arrest and conviction was raised in the state proceeding. Subsequently, however, the convicted person sued the police officers who conducted the search in a federal civil rights action under 42 U.S.C. § 1983, seeking damages on the grounds that the search was unconstitutional. The district court granted summary judgment on the grounds that the plaintiff's guilty plea barred the § 1983 claims. The guilty plea was held to be a waiver of the defendant's right to appeal the plea in a subsequent proceeding and an implied admission that the search was legal. The Fourth Circuit reversed and remanded for further proceedings, holding that the case should have been decided on the basis of 28 U.S.C. § 1738 and state preclusion principles. The Supreme Court granted certiorari and affirmed. The Court concluded that state principles of issue preclusion would not prevent the plaintiff from raising the constitutional claim in a later proceeding. This conclusion was all that was necessary to decide the case. *See id.* at 312-17, 103 S. Ct. at 2372-75, 76 L. Ed. 2d at 603-06.

318. *Id.* at 313-14, 103 S. Ct. at 2373, 76 L. Ed. 2d at 603-04 (footnotes omitted). *But see* Bar-Tec, Inc. v. Akrouche, 959 F. Supp. 793 (S.D. Ohio 1997) (state courts afforded plaintiffs due process, and, therefore, the exception to the doctrine of res judicata for the unwillingness or inability of state courts to protect federal rights is inapplicable). *See generally* 18B CHARLES A. WRIGHT ET AL., FEDERAL PRACTICE AND PROCEDURE: JURISDICTION AND RELATED MATTERS § 4471.2 (2d ed. 2002); David H. Bathe, Annotation, *Supreme Court's Views as to Res Judicata or Collateral Estoppel Effect of State Court Judgments on Federal Courts*, 72 L. Ed. 2d 911 (1983).

319. *See* 18B CHARLES A. WRIGHT ET AL., FEDERAL PRACTICE AND PROCEDURE: JURISDICTION AND RELATED MATTERS § 4468, at 70 (2d ed. 2002).

under the rules of res judicata of a judgment of a federal court."[320] The best explanation for *why* federal judgments are binding on state courts and other federal courts is that: (1) Article III of the Constitution limits the "judicial power" of the federal courts to cases and controversies; (2) proceedings that do not have at least the potential effect of precluding later relitigation of the same issues would fall outside the proper exercise of the judicial power; and (3) the Supremacy Clause of Article VI mandates that federal judgments be binding on state courts.[321]

When federal courts adjudicate questions of federal law, there is no controversy over the proposition that federal law also defines the res judicata effects of the judgment in subsequent actions in state or federal courts.[322] However, when state law provides the rule of decision, a question at one time existed about whether the law of the state where the federal court sits controlled the preclusive effect of the federal judgment.[323] It was argued that even in cases in which state law provides the rules of decision, the policies favoring determination by a court of its own judgments are so strong as to demand that federal law define the scope of federal diversity judgments.[324] This view was adopted by § 87 of the *Restatement (Second) of Judgments*, quoted above.

In *Semtek International, Inc. v. Lockheed Martin Corp.*,[325] discussed earlier in this chapter and in Chapters 5 and 10,[326] the Supreme Court resolved the question of what law governs the effect of a federal judgment in a diversity action. The Court held that federal law controls the scope of a federal diversity judgment, but that ordinarily federal law will adopt the res judicata law of the state in which the federal court is sitting to define the scope of the federal judgment. The Court

---

320. RESTATEMENT (SECOND) OF JUDGMENTS § 87 (1982); *see* Jean F. Rydstrom, Annotation, *Federal or State Law as Governing in Matters of Res Judicata and Collateral Estoppel in Federal Tort Claims Act Suit*, 49 A.L.R. FED. 326 (1980); Romualdo P. Eclavea, Annotation, *State or Federal Law as Governing Applicability of Doctrine of Res Judicata or Collateral Estoppel in Federal Court Action*, 19 A.L.R. FED. 709 (1974).

321. *See* CHARLES A. WRIGHT & MARY KAY KANE, THE LAW OF FEDERAL COURTS § 100A, at 738-39 (7th ed. 2011). *See generally* Stephen B. Burbank, *Federal Judgments Law: Sources of Authority and Sources of Rules*, 70 TEX. L. REV. 1551 (1992).

322. *See* CHARLES A. WRIGHT & MARY KAY KANE, THE LAW OF FEDERAL COURTS § 100A, at 739 (7th ed. 2011); *see also* Thacker v. City of Hyattsville, 135 Md. App. 268, 762 A.2d 172 (2000) (federal law determines the scope of a federal judgment in a federal question case); Insurance Co. v. HSBC Bank USA, 10 N.Y.3d 32, 882 N.E.2d 381, 852 N.Y.S.2d 812 (2008) (federal law determines the res judicata effect of a federal bankruptcy judgment); Pierson Sand & Gravel, Inc. v. Keeler Brass Co., 460 Mich. 372, 596 N.W.2d 153 (1999) (plaintiff brought an action in federal court on a federal claim, but did not join a state claim arising from the same transaction or occurrence; the federal court dismissed the federal claim on the merits, and the plaintiff brought a second action on the omitted state claim in state court; the state court may entertain the action if it believes that the federal court would have declined supplemental jurisdiction over the state claim after dismissing the federal claim; federal law governs the claim-preclusive effect of the federal judgment); Wong v. Cayetano, 111 Haw. 462, 143 P.3d 1 (2006) (under federal law, a plaintiff with a claim supported by both state and federal law may not bring separate actions on each ground; the first action will preclude the second if the court had jurisdiction to adjudicate both grounds; however, under federal law the scope of the litigation is framed by the complaint at the time it is filed; although later events giving rise to claims can be added by supplemental pleading, there is no requirement that the plaintiff do so).

323. *See* CHARLES A. WRIGHT & MARY KAY KANE, THE LAW OF FEDERAL COURTS § 100A, at 739 (7th ed. 2011).

324. *See* Kern v. Hettinger, 303 F.2d 333, 340 (2d Cir. 1962); CHARLES A. WRIGHT & MARY KAY KANE, THE LAW OF FEDERAL COURTS § 100A, at 739 (6th ed. 2011); *cf.* Stephanie Moser Goins, Comment, *Beware the Ides Of Marchington: The* Erie *Doctrine's Effect on Recognition and Enforcement of Tribal Court Judgments in Federal and State Courts,* 32 AM. IND. L. REV. 189 (2008).

325. 531 U.S. 497, 121 S. Ct. 1021, 149 L. Ed. 2d 32 (2001).

326. *See* section B, *Illustrations 13-9 & 13-11, supra*; section B(4)*(b) supra*; Chapter 5(E)(3) *supra*; Chapter 10(E) *supra*.

indicated that state law will not be used to define the scope of a federal diversity judgment when state law is "incompatible with federal interests,"[327] although the Court did not explain how to determine when such incompatibility would exist.

Semtek was extensively discussed and criticized in Chapters 5 and 10, and that discussion and criticism will not be repeated here. The decision will solve most of the problems that might have occurred if the federal courts had been authorized to apply an entirely independent common law of res judicata to define the scope of their judgments in diversity cases as they do in federal question cases. This is because the conflicts between state and federal common-law res judicata principles that would have occurred under an entirely independent federal approach will largely be eliminated by the *Semtek* decision. The as yet unanswered question about the Court's approach is how often litigants will choose to argue that state res judicata rules are incompatible with federal interests. If this occurs frequently, the *Semtek* approach will foment excessive litigation in an area in which clarity and stability ought to be paramount. In that eventuality, the Court will have to address the rule again.

Of greater concern is the Court's tortured interpretation of Rule 41(b) in *Semtek* and whether that approach will be extended to other Federal Rules of Civil Procedure that contain rules of claim preclusion. Recall that the Court interpreted Rule 41(b) as being designed to regulate the internal procedures of the federal courts, with the result that a judgment that is "on the merits" under that rule will not have a claim preclusive effect in any court but the federal court that rendered the judgment. If the Court applies this same approach to other Federal Rules of Civil Procedure, significant problems will result. In particular, as noted above, it is not clear whether the Court will distinguish Rule 41(a)(1)'s "second dismissal"[328] rule, or Rule 13(a)[329] dealing with compulsory counterclaims, from Rule 41(b). Nor is it clear whether the Court will hold that Rule 41(b)'s "on the merits" language will make a judgment of dismissal under Rule 12(b)(6) (for failure to state a claim upon which relief can be granted) preclusive in other courts or only, as in the case of the statute of limitations dismissal in *Semtek*, preclusive in another action in the judgment-rendering court itself.[330] One thing should be clear to state courts governed by rules identical to the Federal Rules of Civil Procedure: the mischief inherent in the Supreme Court's approach to the interpretation of Rule 41(b) makes the Court's approach unworthy of imitation. Furthermore, it is demonstrable that the concerns that the Court had in *Semtek* about the validity of Rule 41(b) under the Rules Enabling Act should not be extended to other rules. For example, Chapter 7

---

327. *See Semtek*, 531 U.S. at 509, 121 S. Ct. at 1028-29, 149 L. Ed. 2d at 43; Palmer & Cay, Inc. v. Marsh & McLennan Cos., 404 F.3d 1297 (11th Cir. 2005) (under *Semtek*, federal common law controls federal diversity judgment; federal common law adopts state law unless it is incompatible with federal interests; federal court should not have attempted to limit scope of declaratory judgment on non-competition agreement to Georgia when Georgia would not do so).

328. *See* section B, *Illustration 13-11, supra.*

329. *See* section B(4)*(b) supra.*

330. *See* section B, *Illustration 13-9, supra*; Anne Arundel Cnty. Bd. of Educ. v. Norville, 390 Md. 93, 887 A.2d 1029 (2005) (federal law controls the scope of a federal judgment; Rule 41(b) makes Rule 12(b)(6) dismissal in prior federal action claim preclusive in subsequent state action; no citation or discussion of *Semtek*). It would not be surprising to find other state and lower federal courts igoring *Semtek* in cases under other Federal Rules, i' as did the court in *Norville*.

examined the problems involved in the administration of compulsory counterclaims under Federal Rule 13.[331] Assume that Rule 13 would bar a defendant from asserting a compulsory counterclaim omitted from an initial action, but that under the applicable state law there exists no compulsory counterclaim rule. Under these circumstances, there is no legitimate problem of rule validity. In the first place, it is likely that an accurate analysis of whether Rule 13 conflicts with state law will produce the conclusion that no conflict exists. The state counterclaim rule is likely to be designed for operation only in the state's own courts, thus eliminating any real conflict with Rule 13.[332] Even if a conflict exists between Rule 13 and state law, however, there is no serious question of Rule validity involved. As discussed in Chapter 7, litigants can sometimes avoid any effect on their substantive rights that would be produced by noncompliance with a Federal Rule of Civil Procedure by adopting appropriate post-commencement behavior.[333] Thus, by pleading a compulsory counterclaim under Rule 13, a party can avoid the bar of the rule. Under these circumstances, there can be no serious contention that the operation of the Federal Rule substantially impacts on substantive rights.

The same is true of an interpretation of Rule 41(b) that would make dismissals under Rule 12(b)(6) "on the merits" and claim preclusive in all courts. Just as in the case of Rule 13(a), in most cases, conflicting state rules providing that dismissals on the pleadings are not claim preclusive are likely to be designed for application in state courts only, thus eliminating any conflict with Rule 41(b). Similarly, litigants can avoid the claim preclusive effect of federal a 12(b)(6) dismissal by availing themselves of the expansive procedural opportunities available in Federal Court for correcting defective pleadings. These include the right to amend and appeal in the action in which the dismissal takes place. These options, coupled with the ease of stating a claim under federal notice pleading standards, makes any effect that exists on state substantive rights by a claim preclusive dismissal "incidental."

The "second dismissal" principle of Rule 41(a)(1) is subject to a similar analysis. Any conflicting state rule is likely to be designed to control dismissals in state courts only. Furthermore, litigants in federal courts can avoid the claim preclusive effect of a second voluntary dismissal by not taking one. Thus, even if the Court's concerns about Rule 41(b)'s validity were realistic in the case of the dismissal on statute of limitations grounds involved in the *Semtek* case, they are not well founded in other situations in which the Federal Rules provide for a claim preclusive effect. The rules should therefore be interpreted to provide such a preclusive effect in all courts, not simply in the federal court in which the initial judgment was rendered.

---

331. *See* Chapter 7(F)(5) *supra* (discussing potential Rules Enabling Act problems with Rule 13).

332. *See* Chapter 5(F)(4) *supra* (discussing the desirability of determining whether the state's rule is limited to its own court system in order to avoid a conflict between applicable Federal Rules of Civil Procedure and state law).

333. *See* Chapter 7(F)(5) *supra* (discussing the Supreme Court's decision in the *Business Guides* case).

In *Taylor v. Sturgell,*[334] the Supreme Court granted certiorari to resolve a split among the courts of appeal about the permissibility and scope of the doctrine of "virtual representation." That doctrine, in diverse forms, had led some lower federal courts to hold non-parties to prior actions bound by the judgments in those actions on the grounds that they were "virtually represented" in the prior actions. The Court held that the established grounds for non-party preclusion reflected in the *Restatement (Second) of Judgments* were the exclusive grounds for binding non-parties. These are (i) a person who agrees to be bound by a judgment may be bound, even though the person is a non-party; (ii) non-parties may be bound because of the existence of certain substantive legal relations with parties, such as the relationship existing between successors in interest in property; (iii) a non-party, in certain instances, may be bound because the non-party's interests are represented in an action, as in a class action; (iv) in limited circumstances, a non-party may be bound when the non-party assumes control of an action; (v) a party bound by a judgment may not avoid the preclusive effect of a judgment by attempting to litigate anew through a proxy; and (vi) a statutory scheme may expressly foreclose successive litigation by non-parties.

The lower federal court had attempted to ground its virtual representation holding on the fact that the interests of the non-party in the case had been represented in the prior action. However, the Supreme Court held that the "representation" exception to the rule that non-parties may not be bound was inapplicable unless either special procedures were present to protect non-parties' interests in the prior action or that there was an understanding by the parties in the first action that it was brought in a representative capacity. Neither factor was present in the case. However, the Court did remand the action for a determination of whether the second action was a collusive attempt to relitigate the first proceeding through an agent or "proxy."

3. Enforcement of Foreign Judgments

Neither the full faith and credit clause nor 28 U.S.C. § 1738 applies to the judgments of foreign nations.[335] Consequently, the extent to which the judgment of a court of a foreign nation will be given effect in a state or federal court in the United States is governed by common-law rules. Chapter 3 discussed the variations in the rules governing the enforcement of foreign judgments. The traditional rule in the United States was announced by the Supreme Court in *Hilton v. Guyot.*[336] In *Hilton*, the Court held that the judgments of foreign courts rendered with jurisdiction would be given effect only to the extent that United States judgments

---

334. 580 U.S. 880, 128 S. Ct. 2161, 171 L. Ed. 2d 155 (2008); *see also* Beahm v. 7-Eleven, Inc., 223 W. Va. 269, 672 S.E.2d 598 (2008) (property owners were "virtually represented" in prior litigation and thus were in privity with plaintiffs in prior litigation; application of res judicata did not violate owners' due process rights); Victor Petrescu, *Crash and Burn:* Taylor v. Sturgell's *Radical Redefinition of the Virtual Representation Doctrine*, 64 U. MIAMI L. REV. 735 (2010).

335. *See, e.g.*, Aleem v. Aleem, 404 Md. 404, 947 A.2d 489 (2008) (Full Faith and Credit Clause does not apply to foreign nation judgments).

336. 159 U.S. 113, 16 S. Ct. 139, 40 L. Ed. 95 (1895).

would be given effect in the foreign courts. However, the English rule is that the judgments of foreign courts rendered with jurisdiction in the "international sense" are res judicata.[337] Today, most state courts give the same effect to foreign nation judgments as they give to sister-state judgments.[338] However, even though the reciprocity requirement has been widely rejected, it is still necessary for a foreign judgment to comply with the basic requirements of procedural fairness, which includes personal jurisdiction standards similar to those imposed by the Fourteenth Amendment on state courts.[339] In addition, American courts may refuse to enforce a foreign nation's judgment on the grounds that the judgment would violate the strong public policy of the enforcing court,[340] a ground of defense that is impermissible with judgments of sister states.[341]

The serious question today is what law should control the effect to be given a foreign judgment. The United States is not a party to any multilateral treaty providing for the recognition and enforcement of foreign nation judgments, which would effectively make the enforcement of foreign nation judgments a matter of federal law.[342] The prevailing view today is that state law governs the recognition

---

337. *See* Chapter 3(A)(1)*(a)* *supra* ("The Forms of Action in Suits on Foreign Judgments and the 'International' Rules of Jurisdiction").

338. *See* RESTATEMENT (THIRD) OF THE FOREIGN RELATIONS LAW OF THE UNITED STATES § 481 cmt. c & d (1987); Gabbanelli Accordions & Imports, L.L.C. v. Gabbanelli, 575 F.3d 693 (7th Cir. 2009) (American courts apply American doctrine of res judicata even to foreign judgment of nation that would not treat an American judgment the same way). For an excellent guide to enforcement of foreign judgments in the United States, see Robert E. Lutz, *Enforcement of Foreign Judgments, Part I: A Selected Bibliography of U.S. Enforcement of Judgments Rendered Abroad*, 27 INT'L LAW. 471 (1993). For a discussion of the treatment of U.S. judgments abroad, see Robert E. Lutz, *Enforcement of Foreign Judgments, Part II: A Selected Bibliography on Enforcement of U.S. Judgments in Foreign Countries*, 27 INT'L LAW. 1029 (1993).

339. *See* RESTATEMENT (THIRD) OF THE FOREIGN RELATIONS LAW OF THE UNITED STATES § 482(1) (1987); *see also* Monks Own, Ltd. v. Monastery of Christ, 2007-NMSC-054, 142 N.M. 549, 168 P.3d 121 (Canadian court had personal jurisdiction to render judgment enforceable under Uniform Money-Judgments Recognition Act because Canadian law granted personal jurisdiction to court and defendant had sufficient minimum contacts with Canada necessary to satisfy due process); Adams v. Adams, 2005 VT 4, 177 Vt. 448, 869 A.2d 124 (Honduran divorce decree was not valid under Honduran law and would not be recognized under the doctrine of comity in Vermont; Full Faith and Credit Clause does not apply to judgments obtained in a foreign country). In Society of Lloyd's v. Ashenden, 233 F.3d 473 (7th Cir. 2000), Lloyd's sought, in a diversity case, to use the Illinois Uniform Foreign Money Judgments Recognition Act to collect money judgments that it had obtained against the defendants. This was permissible under Rule 69(a). The defendants resisted on the grounds that under the Act, a foreign nation judgment is unenforceable if it is rendered under a system that does not provide impartial tribunals or procedures compatible with the requirements of due process of law. The judgments in question were rendered by the Queen's Bench Division of England's High Court. The Seventh Circuit held that any suggestion that the English system of courts does not provide impartial tribunals or *procedures* compatible with due process "borders on the risible." *see also* Thomas Kelly, Note, *An Unwise and Unmanageable Anachronism: Why the Time Has Come to Eliminate Systemic Inadequacy as a Basis for Nonrecognition of Foreign Judgments*, 42 GEO J. INT'L L. 555 (2011).

340. *See* RESTATEMENT (THIRD) OF THE FOREIGN RELATIONS LAW OF THE UNITED STATES § 483(2)(d) (1987); *see also* Diamond R. Fertilizer Co. v. Lake Packing P'ship, 743 So. 2d 547 (Fla. Ct. App. 1999) (judgment of foreign country does not effectuate a technical merger of the cause of action; whether merger occurs depends on comity); Department of Human Servs. v. Shelnut, 772 So. 2d 1041 (Miss. 2000) (enforcement of foreign nation judgment governed by state law and the principle of comity); Rains v. State, 98 Wash. App. 127, 989 P.2d 558 (1999) (Italian support order enforced as a matter of comity and given same effect as sister-state judgment).

341. *See* subsection 1 *supra* (discussing this rule).

342. The United States is a party to many bilateral treaties of Friendship, Commerce, and Navigation ("FCN"), and certain clauses in these treaties have been interpreted by some courts to impose an obligation to recognize and enforce the judgments of the other signatory to the treaty. *See* Choi v. Kim, 50 F.3d 244 (3d Cir. 1995) (interpreting the FCN between the U.S. and South Korea as imposing the obligation to treat Korean judgments as sister-state judgments, but applying New Jersey law to control the effect of the judgment in a diversity action); Vagenas v. Continental Gin Co., 988 F.2d 104 (11th Cir. 1993) (holding the FCN between the U.S. and Greece obligated the states to give the same treatment to a Greek national as would be given to a United States citizen in an action to enforce a judgment). *But cf.* Pollux Holding Ltd. v. Chase Manhattan Bank, 329 F.3d 64 (2d Cir. 2003) (Liberian corporations' decision to sue in the United States was not due the same degree of deference as a decision of a United States citizen to sue in his or her home state for forum non conveniens purposes,

and enforcement of foreign judgments in state courts and, under *Erie*, in federal diversity actions, though federal preclusion law governs in federal question cases.[343] It has been argued that the U.S. Supreme Court should create federal common-law rules to govern the effect of all foreign judgments, due to the difficulties of dealing with such judgments under the "potentially divergent law of fifty states and federal courts" and the fact that "recognition of foreign judgments at least touches concerns of foreign relations in which the national government has paramount interests."[344] However, given the difficulties of negotiating a general treaty on judgments with other countries, it is more plausible to argue that the creation of federal law in this area is beyond the legitimate prerogatives of the Court and should be left to the Executive and Congress.[345]

---

notwithstanding the fact that treaty between the United States and Liberia granted citizens of each country "freedom of access" to courts of the other country). *See generally* Edward A. Laing, *Equal Access/Non-Discrimination and Legitimate Discrimination in International Economic Law,* 14 WIS. INT'L L.J. 246 (1996); Herman Walker, Jr., *Modern Treaties of Friendship, Commerce and Navigation,* 42 MINN. L. REV. 805 (1958); Robert R. Wilson, *Access-to- Courts Provisions in United States Commercial Treaties,* 47 AM. J. INT'L L. 20 (1953). Currently, the United States has proposed a Hague Convention on Jurisdiction and Judgments in Civil and Commercial Matters. At this time the prospects for the treaty do not seem bright due to the concern by other nations with certain bases of personal jurisdiction used by United States' courts, as well as judgments for excessive and punitive damages rendered by our courts in certain torts cases. For a general discussion of the problems involved with negotiating the treaty, see Symposium, *Enforcing Judgments Abroad: The Global Challenge,* 24 BROOK. J. INT'L L. 1 (1998); *see also* Patrick J. Borchers, *Judgments Conventions and Minimum Contacts,* 61 ALBANY L. REV. 1161 (1998); Patrick J. Borchers, *Comparing Personal Jurisdiction in the United States and the European Community: Lessons for American Reform,* 40 AM. J. COMP. L. 121 (1992); Kevin M. Clermont, *Jurisdictional Salvation and the Hague Treaty,* 85 CORNELL L. REV. 89 (1999); Andrew L. Strauss, *Where America Ends and the International Order Begins: Interpreting the Jurisdictional Reach of the U.S. Constitution in Light of A Proposed Hague Convention on Jurisdiction and Satisfaction of Judgments,* 61 ALBANY L. REV. 1237 (1998). The American Law Institute has completed an international jurisdiction and judgments project to draft implementing legislation for the recognition and enforcement of foreign judgments, which would, if enacted, provide unilaterally for the recognition and enforcement of such judgments instate and federal court as a matter of federal law. *See* ALI RECOGNITION AND ENFORCEMENT OF FOREIGN JUDGMENTS: ANALYSIS AND PROPOSED FEDERAL STATUTE (2006). In Medellin v. Texas, 552 U.S. 491, 128 S. Ct. 1346, 170 L. Ed. 2d 190 (2008), the International Court of Justice ("ICJ") had held that the United States had violated Article 36(1)(b) of the Vienna Convention on Consular Relations by failing to inform 51 named Mexican nationals of their rights under the convention. The ICJ had found that the individuals in question were entitled to review and reconsideration of their sentences regardless of their failure to comply with generally applicable state riles governing challenges to criminal convictions. The Supreme Court held that the ICJ treaty was not a self-executing and was, therefore, not enforceable as domestic law in the absence of congressional implementing legislation, with the result that Texas was permitted to apply its rules governing abuse of the writ of habeas corpus to deny review to Medellin.

343. *See* RESTATEMENT (THIRD) OF THE FOREIGN RELATIONS LAW OF THE UNITED STATES § 481 cmt. a (1987) (state law controls); Southwest Livestock & Trucking Co. v. Ramon, 169 F.3d 317 (5th Cir. 1999) (*Erie* requires federal diversity courts to follow state law on the recognition of foreign country money judgments); Alfadda v. Fenn, 966 F. Supp. 1317 (S.D.N.Y. 1997) (federal preclusion law gives issue preclusion effect to French judgment in federal question case); Allstate Ins. Co. v. Administratia Asigurarilor de Stat, 962 F. Supp. 420 (S.D.N.Y. 1997) (New York law governs effect of foreign judgment in federal diversity action in New York); Russell J. Weintraub, *How Substantial Is Our Need For A Judgments-Recognition Convention and What Should We Bargain Away to Get It,* 24 BROOK. J. INT'L L. 167, 173-74, 177 (1998) (state law controls in state courts, state law controls in federal diversity and alienage cases, and federal law controls in federal question cases); *see also* Jerome A. Hoffman, *Recognition by Courts in the Eleventh Circuit of Judgments Rendered by Courts of Other Countries,* 29 CUMB. L. REV. 65 (1998-99).

344. 18B CHARLES A. WRIGHT ET AL, FEDERAL PRACTICE AND PROCEDURE: JURISDICTION AND RELATED MATTERS § 4473, at 403 (2d ed. 2002). Federal common law is discussed in Chapter 5(I) *supra*.

345. Thirty-one jurisdictions have adopted either the original or the revised versions of the Uniform Foreign Money-Judgments Recognition Act. *See* UNIFORM FOREIGN MONEY-JUDGMENTS RECOGNITION ACT (1962), 13 U.L.A. pt. II, at 39 (2002) (original version); *id.* at 18 (2012 Supp.) (revised version). Reciprocity is not required by either the original or revised version of the Act. *See id.* at 19 (2012 Supp.) (Prefatory Note to revised Act). However, Georgia, Massachusetts, and Texas added reciprocity requirements to their version of the original Act. *See id.* at 160-62 (original Act). *See* Manco Contracting Co. v. Bezdikian, 45 Cal. 4th 192, 195 P.3d 604, 85 Cal. Rptr. 3d 233 (2008) (deciding when a judgment from Qatar became final and what statute of limitations applied to its enforcement in California); Genujo Lok Beteiligungs GmbH v. Zorn, 2008 ME 50, 943 A.2d 573 (holding that German money judgments were rendered by a court system that provided procedures compatible with due

SECTION G. OTHER PRECLUSION DOCTRINES: STARE DECISIS, LAW OF THE CASE, AND JUDICIAL ESTOPPEL

Three doctrines should be distinguished from the principles of res judicata: stare decisis, the law of the case, and judicial estoppel.

1. Stare Decisis

Stare decisis is simply the doctrine that when a court has once established a principle of law as applicable to a certain state of facts, the court will follow that principle in all future cases in which the facts are substantially the same. Thus, even if the rules of issue preclusion do not preclude relitigation of an issue of law by a party, relitigation of the issue in a subsequent proceeding may prove futile because of the doctrine of stare decisis.

Stare decisis is based on policies of security and certainty. People rely upon principles of law declared by courts. As a consequence, departure from those principles should not be lightly regarded. Stare decisis, however, is a policy of discretion.[346] Courts can and often do depart from established principles when compelling reasons for doing so are present, and sometimes even when they are not.[347]

---

process, German court had personal jurisdiction over defendant, Maine court could recognize German judgments despite differences in Maine and German statutes regarding reciprocity, and debtor had no right to evidentiary hearing under Uniform Foreign Money-Judgments Recognition Act or Due Process Clause); Don Docksteader Motors, Ltd. v. Patal Enters., Ltd., 794 S.W.2d 760 (Tex. 1990) (Act permits enforcement of foreign nation judgment by registration under the Texas Uniform Enforcement of Foreign Judgments Act or by common-law action, just as in the case of state judgments); Matthew B. Berlin, Note & Comment, *The Hague Convention on Choice of Court Agreements: Creating an International Framework for Recognizing Foreign Judgments*, 3 B.Y.U. INT'L L. & MGMT. REV. 43 (2006); Gilles Cuniberti, *The Recognition of Foreign Judgments Lacking Reasons in Europe: Access to Justice, Foreign Court Avoidance, and Efficiency,* 57 INTL & COMP. L.Q. 25 (2008); Melinda Luthin, *U.S. Enforcement of Foreign Money Judgments and the Need for Reform,* 14 U.C. DAVIS J. INT'L L. & POL'Y 111 (2007); Charles W. Mondora, *The Public Policy Exception, "The Freedom of Speech, or of the Press," and the Uniform Foreign-Country Money Judgments Recognition Act,* 36 HOFSTRA L. REV. 1139 (2008); Vishali Singal, *Preserving Power Without Sacrificing Justice: Creating an Effective Reciprocity Regime for the Recognition and Enforcement of Foreign Judgments,* 59 HAST. L.J. 943 (2008). Certain kinds of judgments are also excluded from the act—judgments for taxes, fines or penalties and for matrimonial or family support, and the Act permits a public policy defense, as well as defenses based on a lack of procedural fairness in the judgment-rendering court. *See generally* Antonio F. Perez, *The International Recognition of Judgments: The Debate Between Private and Public Law Solutions,* 19 BERKELEY J. INT'L L. 44 (2001) (proposing a new multilateral agreement on recognition and enforcement of judgments as part of the World Trade Organization).

346. *See, e.g.,* Lowing v. Allstate Ins. Co., 176 Ariz. 101, 859 P.2d 724 (1993); Giampapa v. American Family Mut. Ins. Co., 64 P.3d 230 (Colo. 2003) (stare decisis binds the Supreme Court to a pre-existing rule unless the Court is clearly convinced that the rule was originally erroneous or is no longer sound due to changing conditions and more good than harm will come from departing from precedent); Hall v. Dillon Cos., 286 Kan. 777, 189 P.3d 508 (2008) (judicial devotion to the doctrine of stare decisis is indeed a justifiable concept, but it cannot be so strictly pursued that the court's view is opaqued and reality disregarded); It is important to note that the doctrine of stare decisis is only valuable in cases in which a court concludes that its prior decisions are wrong. If a prior decision is correct, the court should adhere to it for that reason alone. Thus, there must be something more than mere error in a prior decision to justify departing from it under principles of stare decisis. *See, e.g.,* State v. Gubitosi, 152 N.H. 673, 886 A.2d 1029 (2005) (decision of the Supreme Court to overrule a case should depend on some special reason over and above the belief that a prior case was wrongly decided).

347. Stare decisis can operate in cases in which claim and issue preclusion do not operate, or it can operate in addition to claim and issue preclusion. *See* State *ex rel.* Moore v. Molpus, 578 So. 2d 624 (Miss. 1991) (claim preclusion not operative; stare decisis and issue preclusion operative); *cf. In re* PCH Assocs., 949 F.2d 585 (2d Cir. 1991) (law of the case, claim preclusion, and issue preclusion all inoperative); Society of Separationists, Inc. v.

2. Law of the Case

The *law-of-the-case* doctrine precludes relitigation of issues of law at successive stages[348] of the same case.[349] This doctrine is designed to maintain consistency, to terminate litigation over particular matters, and to maintain the prestige of courts.[350] Like res judicata, however, the law of the case entails costs. When the doctrine is applied without regard to the correctness of the earlier determination, the values described above are attained at the expense of justice to the parties. This price is a much heavier one to pay within the confines of a single proceeding than it is between different proceedings. Perhaps for this reason, the doctrine is not applied rigidly and seems to be diminishing in importance.[351]

Herman, 939 F.2d 1207 (5th Cir. 1991) (stare decisis, claim preclusion, issue preclusion, and law of the case all inapplicable); *see also* Amy Coney Barrett, *Stare Decisis and Due Process*, 74 U. COLO. L. REV. 1011 (2003) (arguing that a too rigid doctrine of stare decisis can deny nonparties due process); Bradley Scott Shannon, *May Stare Decisis be Abrogated by Rule?*, 67 OHIO ST. L.J. 645 (2006); Max Minzner, *Saving Stare Decisis: Preclusion, Precedent, and Procedural Due Process*, 2010 B.Y.U. L. REV. 597.

348. *See* Harlow v. Children's Hosp., 432 F.3d 50 (1st Cir. 2005) (law of the case did not preclude U.S. District Court from reconsidering after removal an issue of personal jurisdiction decided adversely to defendant during state administrative proceeding in which issue was referred to Maine state court); Stichting Ter Behartiging Van De Belangen Van Oudaandeelhouders in Het Kapitaal Van Saybolt Int'l B.V. v. Schreiber, 407 F.3d 34 (2d Cir. 2005) (law of the case inapplicable to issue not squarely presented to district court or court of appeals on prior appeal, but mentioned only in passing); *cf.* Invention Submission Corp. v. Dudas, 413 F.3d 411 (4th Cir. 2005) (court of appeals mandate to dismiss case for lack of subject-matter jurisdiction did not permit district court to deviate from mandate and open case for further adjudication); Tien Fu Hsu v. County of Clark, 123 Nev. 625, 173 P.3d 724 (2007) (when supreme court of state makes an intervening decision that constitutes a change in controlling law, courts subject to previously decided law of the case may depart from it and apply the new rule of law); *In re* Estate of Siebrasse, 2006 SD 83, 722 N.W.2d 86 (question of law decided by Supreme Court on former appeal is law of the case); Allan D. Vestal, *Law of the Case: Single-Suit Preclusion*, 1967 UTAH L. REV. 1. These successive stages include when "(1) [a]n appellate court [rules] on a matter and then the same legal questions [is] raised in the trial court after the case has been remanded to that court for further proceedings"; "(2) [a]n appellate court [rules] on a matter and then the same legal question [is] raised in the same appellate court when the case is appealed a second time"; and "(3) [a] trial court [rules] on a matter and then the same legal question [is] raised a second time in the same trial court . . . before the same judge or before a different judge." *Id.* at 4. Successive stages of litigation also arise in transferred and consolidated cases as well as in multidistrict litigation. For an exhaustive treatment of law-of-the case issues in these latter contexts, see Joan Steinman, *Law of the Case: A Judicial Puzzle in Consolidated and Transferred Cases and in Multidistrict Litigation*, 135 U. PA. L. REV. 595 (1987).

349. The law-of-the-case doctrine "expresses the practice of the courts generally to refuse to reopen what has been decided, not a limit on their power." Messenger v. Anderson, 225 U.S. 436, 444, 32 S. Ct. 739, 740, 56 L. Ed. 1152, 1156 (1912); Riverwood Commercial Park, L.L.C. v. Standard Oil Co., 2007 ND 36, 729 N.W.2d 101 (if an appellate court has ruled on a legal issue and remanded the case to a lower court for further proceedings, the determination by the court of appeals is the law of the case and will not be differently determined on a subsequent appeal of the same case); Jundt v. Jurassic Res. Dev., N. Am. L.L.C., 2004 ND 65, 677 NW.2d 209 (finding after trial that ownership interest in limited liability company began on a certain date was law of the case in a second appeal in member's action to enforce his right to membership units; member did not raise in first appeal issue of when he should have received ownership interest); Gray's Disposal Co., Inc. v. Metropolitan Gov't, 318 S.W.3d 342 (2010) (not error to depart from prior ruling based on intervening U.S. Supreme Court case on point of law involved in case).

350. *See* Allan D. Vestal, *Law of the Case: Single-Suit Preclusion*, 1967 UTAH L. REV. 1, 1-4.

351. *See id.* at 30-31; *see also* Pacific Employers Ins. Co. v. Sav-a-Lot, 291 F.3d 392 (6th Cir. 2002) (after removal, law of the case does not prevent U.S. District Court from making a ruling under state law of relation back that was contrary to repeated rulings of the state trial court from which the action was removed; state court had made a clear mistake, had offered no rationale for its opinion, and later discovery in federal court had brought the factual picture into sharper focus; claim and issue preclusion also inapplicable because there had been no final judgment rendered in the state court; judicial estoppel also inapplicable because under Kentucky law, a party may be estopped from pleading limitations only when the party has induced inaction on the part of the plaintiff by false representations or fraudulent concealment, which did not occur here); Wilson v. Merrell Dow Pharm., Inc., 160 F.3d 625 (10th Cir. 1998) (law of the case does not preclude a new district judge from granting a motion for summary judgment previously denied twice by former judge when former judge would have had power to reconsider his rulings); Flibotte v. Pennsylvania Truck Lines, Inc., 131 F.3d 21 (1st Cir. 1997) (law of case does not require successor judge to deny a post-verdict motion for judgment as a matter of law when original judge had denied pre-verdict motion for judgment as a matter of law); Hanover Ins. Co. v. American Eng'g Co., 105 F.3d 306

3. Judicial Estoppel

Judicial estoppel is a doctrine that precludes a party from taking inconsistent positions in successive judicial proceedings. The policy supporting judicial estoppel is the protection of the integrity of the judicial processes. The integrity of the judicial process would be undermined if a party could take a position in litigation or administrative proceedings that produces a judgment or award in the party's favor and then take an inconsistent position in later litigation in an attempt to obtain a second favorable judgment.[352] The issue often seems to arise in disability cases in which a party contends in an initial proceeding that the party is disabled and obtains an award of disability benefits, but later commences a second action based on the premise that the party is not disabled. In these cases, the courts have invoked the doctrine of judicial estoppel to preclude the second action.[353] However, the judicial estoppel doctrine is not universal. Some courts have rejected it as inconsistent with modern pleading doctrine, which permits inconsistent and alternative pleading.[354] Others reject the doctrine because they feel it is an excessively costly interference with the truth-finding function of courts.[355]

(6th Cir. 1997) (court of appeals language erroneously describing state law was not law of the case, but dicta; even if language was law of the case, it falls within an exception to law of the case which permits departures from prior rulings when they are clearly erroneous and would cause manifest injustice). For an excellent treatment of law of the case issues in the context of transferred and consolidated cases, see Joan Steinman, *Law of the Case: A Judicial Puzzle in Consolidated and Transferred Cases and in Multidistrict Litigation*, 135 U. PA. L. REV. 595 (1987).

352. *See* 18B CHARLES A. WRIGHT ET AL, FEDERAL PRACTICE AND PROCEDURE: JURISDICTION AND RELATED MATTERS § 4477, at 553 (2d ed. 2002); Stichting Ter Behartiging Van De Belangen Van Oudaandeelhouders in Het Kapitaal Van Saybolt Int'l B.V. v. Schreiber, 407 F.3d 34 (2d Cir. 2005) (judicial estoppel inapplicable to issue that was inconsistent with that taken in later stage of same proceeding, but which was not adopted by the court); Alternative Sys. Concepts, Inc. v. Synopsys, Inc., 374 F.3d 23 (1st Cir. 2004) (manufacturer judicially estopped from claiming breach of an oral contract when it had successfully argued on a prior motion to dismiss that its claim was limited to claim for failure to negotiate in good faith); Montrose Med. Group Participating Sav. Plan v. Bulger, 243 F.3d 773 (3d Cir. 2001) (judicial estoppel does not apply to inconsistent positions taken in prior suit where suit was settled and the positions asserted were therefore never accepted by the district court); Smith v. U.S.R.V. Props., 141 Idaho 795, 118 P.3d 127 (2005) (judicial estoppel does not apply when party taking inconsistent position did not obtain advantage from position taken in prior action); Lofton Ridge, L.L.C. v. Norfolk S. Ry. Co., 268 Va. 377, 601 S.E.2d 648 (2004) (doctrine of judicial estoppel does not apply to a party who takes a position inconsistent with the position of another party unless the two parties have a derivative liability relationship; judicial estoppel does not require final judgment and may apply to prevent party from taking inconsistent positions in same action); *See generally* Eric A. Schreiber, *The Judiciary Says, You Can't Have it Both Ways: Judicial Estoppel—A Doctrine Precluding Inconsistent Positions,* 30 LOY. L.A. L. REV. 323 (1996).

353. *See, e.g.*, McConathy v. Dr. Pepper/Seven Up Corp., 131 F.3d 558 (5th Cir. 1998) (plaintiff estopped from suing her employer under the Americans with Disabilities Act because of statements she had made in an application for Social Security benefits to the effect that she did not see how she could hold any position even on a part time basis); Simon v. Safelite Glass Corp., 128 F.3d 68 (2d Cir. 1997) (plaintiff estopped from suing his employer under the Age Discrimination in Employment Act due to statements the plaintiff had made under penalty of perjury in an application for Social Security Benefits); Scarano v. Central R.R. Co., 203 F.2d 510 (3d Cir. 1953) (plaintiff precluded from suing his employer for reinstatement to his job because of judgment in prior action in which the plaintiff had obtained jury award for total and permanent disability).

354. *See, e.g.,* Konstantinidis v. Chen, 626 F.2d 933, 938 (D.C. Cir. 1980) (inconsistent with modern rules of pleading). It has been argued that this rationale is not a sound reason for rejecting judicial estoppel, because modern pleading only condones alternative and inconsistent pleading within a single case, while judicial estoppel is designed to prevent inconsistency between different judicial proceedings. *See* Ashley S. Deeks, Comment, *Raising the Cost of Lying: Rethinking* Erie *for Judicial Estoppel,* 64 U. CHI. L. REV. 873, 881 (1997).

355. *See* United States v. 49.01 Acres of Land, 802 F.2d 387, 390 (10th Cir. 1986); *see also* Longaberger Co. v. Kolt, 586 F.3d 459 (6th Cir. 2009) (judicial estoppel does not apply when inconsistent position is due to a change in the law).

The U.S. Supreme Court has recently discussed the use of judicial estoppel in cases arising under federal law. In *Cleveland v. Policy Management Systems Corp.*,[356] the Court held that a person who seeks and receives Social Security Disability Insurance (SSDI) benefits cannot automatically be precluded from pursuing a claim against her employer under the Americans with Disabilities Act (ADA). SSDI benefits are only available to people who are unable to engage in any substantial gainful activity by reason of a disability. The ADA prohibits covered employers from discriminating against disabled individuals who can perform the essential functions of their jobs, including those who can do so only with reasonable accommodations. Although it might seem that claims under the two acts will inevitably conflict, the Court held in *Cleveland* that this is not so, because there are situations in which a person may qualify for SSDI benefits and still remain capable of performing the essential functions of her job. Thus, the Court held that judicial estoppel could not be applied to prevent a claimant of SSDI benefits from asserting that she is a qualified individual under the ADA. However, the Court emphasized that its holding did not change the rules of judicial estoppel applicable to directly conflicting statements about purely factual matters. The Court also indicated that in order to avoid summary judgment, the plaintiff in the second action must explain any apparent discrepancies between her SSDI statements that she is totally disabled and her ADA claim that she can perform the essential functions of her job.[357]

The Court has not yet addressed whether the *Erie* doctrine requires federal diversity courts to follow state law on matters of judicial estoppel where it differs from the doctrine that the federal courts would apply in federal question cases.[358] It seems clear that if a federal diversity court either refuses to apply judicial estoppel when a state court would, or applies a less stringent judicial estoppel doctrine than the state courts, forum shopping will occur by plaintiffs in derogation of the *Erie* policies.[359] When the plaintiffs are noncitizens, this will cause the *Erie* prohibited "discrimination against citizens of the forum state."[360] On the other hand, if the federal court applies judicial estoppel when a state court would not, or applies a more stringent judicial estoppel doctrine than the state courts would apply, forum

---

356. 526 U.S. 795, 119 S. Ct. 1597, 143 L. Ed. 2d 966 (1999).

357. *See also* Link v. L.S.I., Inc., 2010 SD 103, 793 N.W.2d 44 (corporation not judicially estopped from arguing financial hardship as excuse for wanting to make installment payments on the basis of financial hardship after arguing financial hardship was irrelevant to its financial condition for purposes of another issue).

358. *See generally* Ashley S. Deeks, Comment, *Raising the Cost of Lying: Rethinking* Erie *for Judicial Estoppel*, 64 U. CHI. L. REV. 873 (1997) (concluding that federal diversity courts should apply the most aggressive version of judicial estoppel available to them). *But see* G-1 Holdings, Inc. v. Reliance Ins. Co., 586 F.3d 247 (3d Cir. 2009) (federal common law governs judicial estoppel).

359. *See* Ashley S. Deeks, Comment, *Raising the Cost of Lying: Rethinking* Erie *for Judicial Estoppel*, 64 U. CHI. L. REV. 873, 889 (1997); *cf.* Hall v. GE Plastic Pac. PTE Ltd., 327 F.3d 391 (5th Cir. 2003) (application of federal law of judicial estoppel in diversity action was not error for two reasons: (1) application of federal law is not outcome determinative because state law would "likely" require the same result; and (2) application of federal law of judicial estoppel is a federal procedural concern because second suit wound up in federal court by removal and thus it is the federal court that is in need of protection from manipulation).

360. *See* Chapter 5(E)(2), *Illustration 5-11 supra* (discussing the refinement of *Erie* by *Hanna v. Plumer* and the possibility that discrimination against noncitizens of the forum might also be included within the *Erie* prohibitions).

shopping by nonresident defendants will occur in some cases,[361] and in other cases in which resident defendants are involved, nonresident plaintiffs will be driven from federal court to obtain the benefit of the more lenient state rule, thus undermining the policies of the diversity jurisdiction.[362]

Because the policy supporting judicial estoppel is one of protecting the integrity of the judicial system,[363] it is arguable that this policy is a sufficiently strong "federal countervailing consideration" under the *Byrd* decision to justify federal disregard of state judicial estoppel doctrine in diversity cases.[364] However, as noted above, this would, at least in some cases, result in serious frustration of the policies of the diversity jurisdiction when federal courts applied an independent judicial estoppel doctrine that was more aggressive than the doctrine applied by the state courts. Because subject-matter jurisdiction policies are among the strongest policies applicable to litigation in the federal courts, it seems unjustified to elevate the policies of judicial estoppel above them. On balance, therefore, it seems more prudent to apply *Erie* straightforwardly to this issue and require federal diversity courts to duplicate state judicial estoppel doctrines.

On the other hand, the judicial integrity rationale is sufficiently persuasive to counsel state courts to adopt vigorous judicial estoppel doctrines as a matter of their own common law. If this is done, the problem in diversity actions will be eliminated, since both the state and federal courts (the latter by virtue of *Erie*) will apply judicial estoppel aggressively, thus assuring both judicial integrity and sound state-federal relationships.

* * * * *

---

361. *But see* Ashley S. Deeks, Comment, *Raising the Cost of Lying: Rethinking* Erie *for Judicial Estoppel,* 64 U. CHI. L. REV. 873, 887 (1997) (arguing that defendant forum shopping is irrelevant under *Hanna's* twin aims test). *Cf.* Chapter 5(E)(2), *Illustration 5-13 supra* (arguing that forum shopping by nonresident defendants should be included within the *Erie* prohibitions).

362. *See* Chapter 5(E)(2), *Illustration 5-12 supra* (discussing the problem of federal court application of rules that are more stringent than state rules from the plaintiff's point of view and how such a practice would undermine the policies of the diversity jurisdiction).

363. *See* Ashley S. Deeks, Comment, *Raising the Cost of Lying: Rethinking* Erie *for Judicial Estoppel,* 64 U. CHI. L. REV. 873, 888 (1997).

364. *See id.* at 891-96; Eastman v. Union Pacific R.R. Co., 493 F.3d 1151 (10th Cir. 2007) (citing *Erie* countervailing considerations doctrine in support of application of federal doctrine of judicial estoppel to pendent state claims; however, both proceedings were "federal question" cases, one an FELA case and one a bankruptcy proceeding); *cf.* Dallas Sales Co., Inc. v. Carlisle Silver Co., 134 S.W.3d 928 (Tex. Ct. App. 2004) (federal law of judicial estoppel applies in an action in which the prior judgment was in a federal bankruptcy court; primary purpose of judicial estoppel is to preserve judicial integrity; thus, it makes sense to apply the law applicable to the prior proceeding; court also reasons by analogy to U.S. Supreme Court decisions holding that federal law controls the res judicata effect of a prior federal judgment); Hall v. GE Plastic Pac. PTE Ltd., 327 F.3d 391 (5th Cir. 2003) (application of federal law of judicial estoppel is appropriate to allow federal court to protect itself from manipulation; this is a matter of federal procedure and is not a substantive concern). In state courts, "horizontal" conflict-of-laws problems similar to the *Erie* "vertical" choice of law problem may arise in determining whether to apply forum law or the law of another state on the issue of judicial estoppel. *But see* Middleton v. Caterpillar Indus., Inc., 979 So. 2d 53 (Ala. 2007) (judicial estoppel is treated as procedural for conflict-of-laws purposes and thus law of forum, here Alabama, applies; although party's failure to disclose claim against defendant in prior federal bankruptcy proceeding was an inconsistent position, party was not successful in bankruptcy proceeding and bankruptcy petition could and was amended after issue was raised in present proceeding; thus, party did not obtain unfair advantage or impose unfair detriment on defendant as is required for judicial estoppel to operate).

INDEX

References are to Pages.

‡